akespeare & G. B. Shaw & Shelley & Simonides of Ceos & Adam Smith & Sophocles & S
encer & Oswald Spengler & Edmund Spenser & Spinoza & Stendhal & Sterne & W. G. S
wift & Tacitus & R. H. Tawney & Tennyson & Tertullian &
e & Tolstoy & Toynbee & Turgot & Mark Twain & Vico &
Whitehead & Whitman & Wittgenstein & Wordsworth & Xenophon & W. B. Yeats & Ae
Ambrose & Anselm & Aquinas & Archimedes & Aristophanes & Aristotle & Arnold & Au
Jane Austen & Bacon & Bakunin & Simone de Beauvoir & Bede & Ruth Benedict & B
Bergson & Berkeley & Bernard of Clairvaux & Claude Bernard & Blake & Boethius &
Browne & Browning & Bunyan & Burke & Burns & Byron & Calhoun & Calvin & Carlyl
tes & Chaucer & Cicero & Clausewitz & Coke & Coleridge & Colette & Comte & Condo
greve & Copernicus & Croce & Dante & Darwin & Democritus & Descartes & Dewey &
Emily Dickinson & Isak Dinesen & Diogenes Laertius & Donne & Dostoevsky & Dryden
n & George Eliot & T. S. Eliot & Emerson & Engels & Epictetus & Epicurus & Euclid & E
Faraday & Fielding & FitzGerald & Fitzhugh & Fourier & Freud & Galen & Galileo & He
& Gibbon & Gilbert & Goethe & Gray & Grotius & Hamilton & Hammurabi & Hard
& Hawthorne & Hegel & Herder & Herodotus & Hesiod & Hippocrates & Hobbes & Hor
kins & Horace & Hume & Huxley & Huygens & William James & John Jay & Jefferso
f Salisbury & Samuel Johnson & Ben Jonson & Joyce & Juvenal & Kant & Keats & Kepl
aard & Susanne Langer & Laplace & Lavoisier & Leibniz & Lenin & Lincoln & Livy & Lo
ginus & Lucian & Lucretius & Luther & Machiavelli & Madison & Maimonides & Malthu
& Marcus Aurelius & Maritain & Marx & Margaret Mead & Melville & J. S. Mill & Mil
ère & Montaigne & Montesquieu & More & Newman & Newton & Nicomachus of Geras
he & Ovid & Pascal & C. S. Peirce & Planck & Plato & Pliny the Elder & Plotinus & Pluta
caré & Polybius & Pope & Proclus & Ptolemy & Quintilian & Rabelais & Raleigh & Ro
Ruskin & Bertrand Russell & Santayana & Sappho & Sartre & Schiller & Schopenhauer &
hakespeare & G. B. Shaw & Shelley & Simonides of Ceos & Adam Smith & Sophocles & S
encer & Oswald Spengler & Edmund Spenser & Spinoza & Stendhal & Sterne & W. G. S
wift & Tacitus & R. H. Tawney & Tennyson & Tertullian & Thoreau & Thucydides &
e & Tolstoy & Toynbee & Turgot & Mark Twain & Vico & Virgil & Voltaire & Washingto
Whitehead & Whitman & Wittgenstein & Wordsworth & Xenophon & W. B. Yeats & Ae
Ambrose & Anselm & Aquinas & Archimedes & Aristophanes & Aristotle & Arnold & Au
Jane Austen & Bacon & Bakunin & Simone de Beauvoir & Bede & Ruth Benedict & B
Bergson & Berkeley & Bernard of Clairvaux & Claude Bernard & Blake & Boethius &
Browne & Browning & Bunyan & Burke & Burns & Byron & Calhoun & Calvin & Carlyl
tes & Chaucer & Cicero & Clausewitz & Coke & Coleridge & Colette & Comte & Condo
greve & Copernicus & Croce & Dante & Darwin & Democritus & Descartes & Dewey &
Emily Dickinson & Isak Dinesen & Diogenes Laertius & Donne & Dostoevsky & Dryden
n & George Eliot & T. S. Eliot & Emerson & Engels & Epictetus & Epicurus & Euclid & E
Faraday & Fielding & FitzGerald & Fitzhugh & Fourier & Freud & Galen & Galileo & He
& Gibbon & Gilbert & Goethe & Gray & Grotius & Hamilton & Hammurabi & Hard
& Hawthorne & Hegel & Herder & Herodotus & Hesiod & Hippocrates & Hobbes & Hor
kins & Horace & Hume & Huxley & Huygens & William James & John Jay & Jefferso
f Salisbury & Samuel Johnson & Ben Jonson & Joyce & Juvenal & Kant & Keats & Kepl
aard & Susanne Langer & Laplace & Lavoisier & Leibniz & Lenin & Lincoln & Livy & Lo

Great Treasury
of Western Thought

GREAT TREASURY OF WESTERN THOUGHT

A Compendium of
Important Statements on Man and
His Institutions by the
Great Thinkers in Western History

EDITED BY

Mortimer J. Adler & Charles Van Doren

R. R. Bowker Company

NEW YORK & LONDON, 1977

Published by R. R. Bowker Company
1180 Avenue of the Americas, New York, N.Y. 10036

First Printing, July 1977
Second Printing, September 1977

Library of Congress Cataloging in Publication Data
Main entry under title:

Great treasury of Western thought.

  Includes indexes.
  1. Quotations, English.   I. Adler, Mortimer
Jerome, 1902–   II. Van Doren, Charles Lincoln,
1926–
PN6331.G675   080   77-154
ISBN 0-8352-0833-8

Copyright notices from publishers granting
permission to reprint material are listed in
the Acknowledgments section of this volume.

For
Elizabeth, John,
Douglas, and Philip

Contents

Preface

In the field of standard reference materials—dictionaries, encyclopedias, books of quotations, and the like—a mark of rare distinction belongs to those that not only perform their reference function efficiently but also serve another important purpose as well. By this criterion the great *Oxford English Dictionary* and the new Fifteenth Edition of *Encyclopaedia Britannica* stand out among all other works in the categories to which they belong. Because it is constructed on historical principles, the *Oxford English Dictionary* not only enables its user to look up the meaning, spelling, etymology, or pronunciation of a word, but also to descry the history of the word, amply documented by statements and examples that exhibit the growth and alteration of its significance. Because it is accompanied by a systematic outline of human knowledge that serves as a topical guide to its contents, the new *Encyclopaedia Britannica*—"Britannica 3"—not only enables its user to look up single items of information or obtain knowledge about a single subject, but also to pursue in a systematic fashion the sustained study of almost any field of subject matter.

The editors believe that *Great Treasury of Western Thought* will be recognized, in the category of books of quotations, as possessing the mark of rare distinction that makes the *Oxford English Dictionary* stand out among dictionaries and the new *Encyclopaedia Britannica* among encyclopedias. Its alphabetical Subject and Proper Name Index, containing upwards of 50,000 entries, enables it to serve as an efficient reference book, in which particular passages on particular subjects can be looked up. In addition, its carefully constructed Author Index allows the reader to discover whether favorite works or parts of works by particular authors have been mined for quotation, and where such quotations appear. At the same time, its organization, which consists of twenty chapters, each concerned with a set of related great ideas, totaling 127 sections, each prefaced by explanatory text, makes *Great Treasury of Western Thought* a book to be read for enjoyment and instruction as well as a reference book.

Great Treasury of Western Thought can be read with both enjoyment and profit primarily for two reasons. One has to do with its intellectual progenitor, as it were. The other has to do with the criteria employed by the editors in their choice of passages to be quoted.

When, just a quarter of a century ago, *Great Books of the Western World* was published, that collection of the most worthwhile books to be read both for pleasure and enlightenment was accompanied by an innovation that enabled the set to be used also as a reference work. The Syntopicon, or topical guide to passages in the great books wherein are discussed the fundamental ideas in the tradition of Western thought, allowed the user to look up the whole discussion of an idea or of one or more topics under it, as well as to be entertained or instructed by reading the great works contained in the set. The Syntopicon was hailed as a reference book in the sphere of ideas comparable to a dictionary in the sphere of words and an encyclopedia in the sphere of facts.

The publication of *Great Treasury of Western Thought* is a fitting and proper celebration of the twenty-fifth anniversary of the publication in 1952 of *Great Books of the Western World* and of its Syntopicon. Without the years of intellectual labor and the 400,000 man-hours of reading that produced the Syntopicon, the present work would probably not have been possible. In fact, without the Syntopicon in existence, both as a comprehensive chart of the great ideas in Western thought and as a systematic guide to their discussion in the great books, the present work might never have been conceived; and, even if it had been conceived, it could not have been produced with the thoroughness that the conception deserves.

This leads us to the second reason for this book's special character. Other books of quotations—among them are some notable works of recognized excellence—

consist mainly of short passages, often no more than a line or two. These passages are often well-known or familiar; they have been quoted again and again; they are memorable and should be remembered, but the individual who fails to remember them must have recourse to such books of quotations in order to recollect and quote them. The purpose behind the desire accurately to recall such memorable quotations is usually to enliven the style of a speech to be delivered or an essay to be written.

However, it is a striking and notable fact about *Great Treasury of Western Thought* that many if not most of the passages quoted in it are not either generally familiar or readily memorable. For one thing, the quoted passages are typically longer than those that appear in other books of quotations, running to more than 100 words on the average. For another thing, as many as three-quarters of the passages selected for quotation do not appear in other current books of quotations and may indeed never have appeared in such books, because the principle of selection that guided the editors was that each passage quoted should be a seminal statement about one of the great ideas in the tradition of Western thought. If the passage was either memorable or familiar, so much the better; the editors insisted that each passage had to be interesting and important in its own right; but they also demanded that it should be significant in relation to other passages on the same subject.

In a sense, then, the passages here assembled and quoted from the great books are precisely those to which reference is made in the Syntopicon; and *Great Treasury of Western Thought* is therefore a concrete realization of the Syntopicon and may satisfy those readers—not a few—who have regretted that the Syntopicon was "only" an index and did not contain within its pages the passages to which it referred. In another sense the passages from the great books that are gathered here are the very heart and soul of the Western tradition, that small part of it that will almost certainly survive any disaster, any holocaust, that can be imagined in the future. All of the great books, in their entirety, may not survive; many great works have already been lost in the vicissitudes of human history; but the essential things that the great books say, the irrecoverable insights that they offer us, are more likely to endure because they are collected here, "that he who runs may read."

Of course, not all of the passages referred to by the Syntopicon are quoted here; many such passages are inappropriate for a general audience (for example, technical discourses in science or philosophy), and others are too long. Nor, indeed, are the writers from whose works quotations were selected limited to those appearing in *Great Books of the Western World*. Almost twice as many other writers are included, and they are drawn not only from the literature of classical antiquity and the Middle Ages, but also from the literature of modern times. Consulting the Author Index (pp. 1431-1449) and examining the Contents on pp. vii-xi should enable anyone quickly to appraise the scope and the characteristics of the present work, which will distinguish it among all other books of quotations.

The possessor of *Great Treasury of Western Thought* may still wish to resort to those other books of quotations for the special purposes they serve—as aids to the memory or as stylistic aids. It is not the memory of the user that this work seeks to stimulate, but rather the user's intellect and imagination—the user's understanding and intuition of the greatest thought on the most important subjects. It is not the reader's style, either in speech or writing, but his mind, that *Great Treasury of Western Thought* aims to enliven, and enlighten as well in the process.

The editors of *Great Treasury of Western Thought* have been reading and teaching the great books, and other works quoted in this anthology, for many years—one of them for more than fifty years, the other for more than thirty. Nevertheless, they confess their own delight and fascination at being able—for the first time—to read in appropriate sequence (for the most part chronological) the passages that are here collected under each of the 127 subject headings that constitute the divisions of this book. They have found such reading to be both highly instructive and immensely enjoyable. They can think of nothing simpler and more truthful to say by way of recommending this book to those for whom they made it—as a work to read with pleasure, to dwell on, to learn from, as well as to refer to when that need arises. The more time that is spent with it, the more valuable it will become, for it is, literally, a compact treasury of the best thinking and deepest wisdom of the West. It reflects and epitomizes the intellectual tradition on which every cultivated person must build.

The editors wish to express their indebtedness to the many persons who worked on this book over a period of almost a quarter of a century. They especially wish to thank three friends without whose help the book could not have come to be: Marlys Allen, George Ducas, and Wayne Moquin.

MORTIMER J. ADLER
CHARLES VAN DOREN

Acknowledgments

The editors and publisher gratefully acknowledge the permissions granted by publishers to reprint copyrighted material in this volume. The copyright notices are listed below, arranged alphabetically by authors' names.

Aeschylus

"Agamemnon" and "Eumenides" (tr. by Richmond Lattimore) in *Orestia*, copyright © 1953 by University of Chicago; "Libation Bearers" (tr. by Richmond Lattimore), copyright © 1953 by University of Chicago; "Prometheus Bound" (tr. by David Grene), copyright © 1942 by University of Chicago; "Seven Against Thebes" (tr. by David Grene), copyright © 1956 by University of Chicago; "Suppliant Maidens" (tr. by Seth G. Benardett), copyright © 1956 by University of Chicago, all in *The Complete Greek Tragedies*, Vol. 1, David Grene and Richmond Lattimore, eds. Copyright © 1959 by University of Chicago. Reprinted by permission of David Grene, Richmond Lattimore, and the University of Chicago Press.

Ambrose, St.

"Letter to Simplicianus," in *Fathers of the Church*, tr. by Sister Mary Melchoir Beyenda. Copyright © 1954 by The Fathers of the Church. Reprinted by permission of The Catholic University of America.

Anselm, St.

Basic Writings, tr. by S. N. Deane. Copyright © 1903, 1962 by Open Court Publishing Co. Reprinted by permission of Open Court Publishing Co.

Aquinas, St. Thomas

On Kingship, tr. by Gerald B. Phelan. Copyright © 1949 by Mediaeval Studies of Toronto, Inc. Reprinted by permission of the Pontifical Institute of Mediaeval Studies.

Summa Contra Gentiles, Book 4, tr. by Charles J. O'Neil. Copyright © 1957 by Doubleday & Company. Reprinted by permission of Doubleday & Company, Inc.

"Summa Theologica," in *Basic Writings of St. Thomas Aquinas*, Vol. 1, ed. by Anton C. Pegis. Copyright © 1945 by Random House, Inc. Reprinted by permission of Benziger, Bruce and Glencoe, Inc.

Truth, Vol. 1, tr. by Robert W. Mulligan, Vol. 2, tr. by James V. McGlynn, Vol. 3, tr. by Robert W. Schmidt. Copyright © by Henry Regnery Co., published in 1952, 1953, 1954. Reprinted by permission of Henry Regnery Co.

Aristotle

"Categories," "Ethics," "Generation of Animals," "History of Animals," "Memory and Reminiscence," "Metaphysics," "On Generation and Corruption," "On Interpretation," "On the Gait of Animals," "On the Heavens," "On the Motion of Animals," "On the Sophistical Refutations," "On the Soul," "On Youth and Old Age," "On Life and Death," "On Breathing," "Parts of Animals," "Physics," "Poetics," "Politics," "Posterior Analytics," "Prophesying by Dreams," "Rhetoric," "Topics," all in *The Oxford Translation of Aristotle*, tr. and ed. by W. D. Ross. First Edition 1928. Reprinted by permission of the Oxford University Press, England.

Augustine, St.

Confessions, tr. by Francis J. Sheed. Copyright © 1943 by Sheed and Ward, Inc., New York. Reprinted by permission of Sheed and Ward, Inc.

Beauvoir, Simone de

The Second Sex, tr. and ed. by H. M. Parshley. Copyright © 1952 by Alfred A. Knopf, Inc. Reprinted by permission of Alfred A. Knopf, Inc., and Jonathan Cape Ltd.

Benedict, Ruth

Patterns of Culture. Copyright © 1934 by Ruth Benedict. Copyright © renewed 1962 by Ruth Valentine. Reprinted by permission of the publisher Houghton Mifflin Company and Routledge & Kegan Paul Ltd.

Bergson, Henri

Creative Evolution, tr. by Arthur Mitchell. Copyright © 1911 by Henry Holt and Company. Copyright © 1944 by Random House (Modern Library edition). Reprinted by permission of Holt, Rinehart and Winston, Inc., and Macmillan London and Basingstoke.

Creative Mind, tr. by Mabelle L. Anderson. Copyright © 1946 by the Philosophical Library. Reprinted by permission of the Philosophical Library, Inc.

Laughter, tr. by Cloudesley Brereton and Fred Rothwell. Copyright © by Macmillan and Co. Ltd., published in 1911. Reprinted by permission of Doubleday & Company, Inc.

Time and Free Will, tr. by F. L. Pogson. Published by George Allen & Unwin, London; the Macmillan Company, New York. Copyright © 1910. Reprinted by permission of Humanities Press, Inc., and George Allen & Unwin Ltd.

Two Sources of Morality and Religion, tr. by R. Ashley Audra and Cloudesley Brereton with the assistance of W. Horsfall Carter. Copyright © 1935 by Henry Holt and Company. Reprinted by permission of Holt, Rinehart and Winston, Inc., and Macmillan London and Basingstoke.

Bernard, Claude

An Introduction to the Study of Experimental Medicine, tr. by Henry C. Greene. Copyright © 1927 by Macmillan Co. Reprinted by permission of Thomas Y. Crowell Co., Inc.

Boethius, Anicius Manlius Severinus

The Consolation of Philosophy, tr. by W. V. Cooper. Published by Modern Library, New York. Copyright © 1943 by Random House, Inc. Reprinted by permission of Random House, Inc.

Boswell, James

London Journal. Copyright © 1950 by Yale University. Reprinted by permission of McGraw-Hill Book Company.

Chaucer, Geoffrey

Canterbury Tales, tr. by J. U. Nicolson. Copyright © 1934 by Covici, Friede, Inc. Copyright © renewed 1962 by Crown Publishers, Inc. Reprinted by permission of Crown Publishers, Inc.

Troilus and Cressida, English anew by George Philip Krapp. Copyright © 1932 and renewed 1960 by Elizabeth Knapp. Reprinted by permission of Random House, Inc.

Colette, Sidonie Gabrielle

The Break of Day, tr. by Enid McLeod. Copyright © 1961 by Martin Secker & Warburg, Ltd. Reprinted by permission of Farrar, Straus & Giroux, Inc.

Croce, Benedetto

History as the Story of Liberty, tr. by Sylvia Sprigge. Published in 1941 by W. W. Norton & Co. Reprinted by permission of W. W. Norton & Co., Inc., and George Allen & Unwin Ltd.

Descartes, René

The Philosophical Works of Descartes, tr. by Elizabeth S. Haldane and G. R. T. Ross. First Edition 1911, reprinted with corrections 1931. Reprinted by permission of the Cambridge University Press.

Dewey, John

Democracy and Education. Copyright © 1916 by Macmillan Company, renewed 1944 by John Dewey. Reprinted by permission of Macmillan Publishing Co., Inc.

Essays in Experimental Logic. Copyright © 1953 by Dover Publications. Reprinted by permission of Dover Publications.

Experience and Education. Copyright © 1938 by Kappa Delta Pi. Published by Macmillan Publishing Co., Inc., 1938, 1959. Reprinted by permission of Kappa Delta Pi. An Honor Society in Education.

Experience and Nature. Copyright © 1925 by Open Court Publishing Co. Reprinted by permission of the publisher.

Freedom and Culture. Copyright © 1939 by John Dewey. Reprinted by permission of G. P. Putnam's Sons.

Dewey, John, and Tufts, James H.

Dinesen, Isak [Karen Christence Dinesen, Baroness Blixen-Finecke]

Dostoevsky, Fyodor

Eckermann, Johann

Einstein, Albert

Eliot, Thomas Stearns

Euripides

Freud, Sigmund

"The Dynamics of Transference," paper XXVII, Vol. 2; "The Future Prospects of Psycho-Analytic Therapy," paper XXV, Vol. 2; "Instincts and Their Vicissitudes," paper VI, Vol. 4; "On Narcissism: An Introduction," paper III, Vol. 4; "The Sexual Enlightenment of Children," paper III, Vol. 2; "Thoughts for the Times on War and Death," paper XVII, Vol. 4, all in *Collected Papers*, Vols. 2 and 4, ed. by Ernest Jones, M.D., authorized translation under the supervision of Joan Riviere. Published by Basic Books, Inc., by arrangement with The Hogarth Press Ltd. and the Institute of Psycho-Analysis, London, copyright. Reprinted by permission of Basic Books, Inc.

The Ego and the Id, tr. by Joan Riviere. First published 1927 by The Hogarth Press Ltd. and the Institute of Psycho-Analysis. Reprinted by permission of The Hogarth Press Ltd.

A General Introduction to Psycho-Analysis, tr. by Joan Riviere. Copyright © 1920 by Edward L. Bernays, copyright © renewed 1948 by Joan Hoch, copyright © 1963 by Joan Riviere. Reprinted by permission of Liveright Publishing Corp. and George Allen & Unwin Ltd.

Group Psychology and the Analysis of the Ego, tr. by James Strachey. Copyright © 1922 by the International Psycho-Analytical Press. Reprinted by permission of W. W. Norton & Company, Inc., and The Hogarth Press Ltd.

The Interpretation of Dreams, tr. from the German and ed. by James Strachey. Published in the United States by Basic Books, Inc., by arrangement with George Allen & Unwin Ltd. and The Hogarth Press Ltd. Reprinted by permission of the publishers.

Moses and Monotheism, tr. by Katherine Jones. Copyright © 1939 by Alfred A. Knopf, Inc., and renewed 1967 by Ernest L. Freud. Reprinted by permission of Alfred A. Knopf, Inc., and The Hogarth Press Ltd.

New Introductory Lectures on Psycho-Analysis, tr. and ed. by James Strachey. Copyright © 1933 by Sigmund Freud, renewed 1961 by W. J. H. Sprott, 1964 by James Strachey. Reprinted by permission of W. W. Norton & Company, Inc., and The Hogarth Press Ltd.

The Origin and Development of Psycho-Analysis, tr. by Harry W. Chase. Published 1910 in *American Journal of Psychology*. Reprinted by permission of the University of Illinois Press.

Galileo Galilei

Dialogues Concerning Two New Sciences, tr. by Henry Crew and Alfonso De Salvio. First published 1914 by the Macmillan Company, reissued 1939 by the Editorial Board of Northwestern University Studies. Reprinted by permission of the Northwestern University Press.

Goethe, Johann Wolfgang von

Conversations with Eckermann. See Eckermann, Johann.

Faust, tr. by George Madison Priest. Copyright © 1941, 1969 by Alfred A. Knopf, Inc. Reprinted by permission of the publisher.

Hegel, Georg Wilhelm Friedrich

The Philosophy of Right, tr. by T. M. Knox. Published 1942 by Oxford University Press. Reprinted by permission of the publisher.

Homer

The Iliad, tr. by Richmond Lattimore. Copyright © 1951 by University of Chicago Press. Reprinted by permission of the University of Chicago Press and Richard Lattimore.

The Odyssey, tr. by Robert Fitzgerald. Copyright © 1961 by Robert Fitzgerald. Reprinted by permission of Doubleday & Company, Inc., and William Heinemann Ltd.

Hopkins, Gerard Manley

Poems of Gerard Manley Hopkins, ed. by W. H. Gardner. Copyright © 1948 by Oxford University Press. Reprinted by permission of the Oxford University Press.

James, William

"Letter to B. P. Blood," in *Letters of William James*, 2 vols. Published by Atlantic Monthly Press, copyright © 1920 by Henry James. Reprinted by permission of Alexander R. James.

Moral Equivalent of War, An Essay. First published by the Association for International Conciliation (Leaflet no. 27). Copyright © 1911 by Henry James. Reprinted by permission of Alexander R. James.

Pragmatism. Published by Longmans, Green & Co., copyright © 1907. Reprinted by permission of Alexander R. James.

Some Problems of Philosophy. Published by Longmans, Green & Co., copyright © 1911 by Henry James. Reprinted by permission of Alexander R. James.

Joyce, James

"The Dead," in *Dubliners*, Copyright © 1967 by the Estate of James Joyce. All rights reserved. Reprinted by permission of the Viking Press, Inc., and Jonathan Cape Ltd.

A Portrait of the Artist as a Young Man. Copyright © 1964 by the Estate of James Joyce. All rights reserved. Reprinted by permission of the Viking Press, Inc., and Jonathan Cape Ltd.

Ulysses. Copyright © 1914, 1918 by Margaret Caroline Anderson and renewed 1942, 1946 by Nora Joseph Hoyce. Reprinted by permission of Random House, Inc., and The Bodley Head Ltd.

Juvenal

The Satires, tr. by Rolfe Humphries. Copyright © 1958 by Indiana University Press. Reprinted by permission of the Indiana University Press.

Kierkegaard, Søren

Concluding Unscientific Postscript, tr. by David Swenson and Walter Lowrie. Copyright © 1941 by Princeton University Press; Princeton Paperback, 1968, for the American Scandinavian Foundation. Selection p. 275. Reprinted by permission of the Princeton University Press.

Fear and Trembling and *The Sickness Unto Death*, tr. with an Introduction and Notes by Walter Lowrie. Copyright © 1941, 1954 by Princeton University Press; Princeton Paperback, 1968. Selections pp. 130, 131 and 150, 151. Reprinted by permission of the Princeton University Press.

Philosophical Fragments, tr. by David Swenson. New Introduction and Commentary by Niels Thulstrup. Translation revised and commentary tr. by Howard V. Kong. Copyright © 1936, 1962 by Princeton University Press; Princeton Paperback, 1967. Selections pp. 47–96. Reprinted by permission of the Princeton University Press.

A Selection from the Journals of Søren Kierkegaard, tr. by Alexander Dru. Published 1938 by Oxford University Press. Reprinted by permission of the Oxford University Press, Oxford.

Langer, Susanne K.

Mind: An Essay on Human Feeling, Vol. 1. Copyright © 1967 by The Johns Hopkins University Press. Reprinted by permission of The Johns Hopkins University Press.

Leibniz, Gottfried Wilhelm

"Letters to Samuel Clarke," in *The Leibniz-Clarke Correspondence*, ed. by H. G. Alexander. Copyright © 1956 by Philosophical Library, Inc. All rights reserved. Reprinted by permission of Philosophical Library, Inc.

Theodicy, tr. by E. M. Huggard. Published 1952 by Yale University Press. Reprinted by permission of Routledge & Kegan Paul Ltd.

Lenin, Vladimir Ilich Ulyanov

State and Revolution. Copyright © 1932 and 1943 by International Publishers. Reprinted by permission of International Publishers Co., Inc.

Lucian

"The Fisher" and "Sale of Creeds," in *Works of Lucian of Samosata*, Vol. 1, tr. by H. W. Fowler and F. G. Fowler. Published 1905 by Oxford at the Clarendon Press. Reprinted by permission of the Oxford University Press.

Luther, Martin

"Commentary on Psalm 2," tr. by L. W. Spitz, Jr., and "Commentary on Psalm 110," tr. by H. Richard Klann, in *Luther's Works*, Vols. 12 and 13, ed. by Jaroslav Pelikan. Copyright © 1955 and © 1956 by Concordia Publishing House. Reprinted by permission of Concordia Publishing House.

"Table Talk," ed. and tr. by Theodore C. Tappert, in *Luther's Works*, Vol. 54. Copyright © 1967 by Fortress Press. Reprinted by permission of the Fortress Press.

"An Appeal to the Ruling Class of German Nationality as to the Amelioration of the State of Christendom," in *Reformation Writing of Martin Luther*, Vol. 1, tr. by Bertram Lee Woolf. Published 1952, all rights reserved. Reprinted by permission of Butterworth Press.

"The Babylonian Captivity of the Church," tr. by A. T. W. Steinhaueser, in *Three Treatises*. Copyright © 1943 by The Muhlenberg Press. Reprinted by permission of the Fortress Press.

Maimonides, Moses

The Preservation of Youth, tr. by Hirsch L. Gordon. Copyright © 1958 by the Philosophical Library, Inc. Reprinted by permission of the Philosophical Library, Inc.

Mann, Thomas

The Confessions of Felix Krull and *Confidence Man*, tr. by Denver Lindley. Copyright © 1955 by Alfred A. Knopf, Inc. Reprinted by permission of Alfred A. Knopf, Inc., and Martin Secker and Warburg Ltd.

Death in Venice, tr. by H. T. Lowe-Porter. Copyright © 1930 and renewed 1958 by Alfred A. Knopf, Inc. Reprinted by permission of Alfred A. Knopf, Inc., and Martin Secker and Warburg Ltd.

The Magic Mountain, tr. by H. T. Lowe-Porter. Copyright © 1927, 1955 by Alfred A. Knopf, Inc. Reprinted by permission of Alfred A. Knopf, Inc., and Martin Secker and Warburg Ltd.

Maritain, Jacques

Art and Scholasticism and *The Frontiers of Poetry*, tr. by Joseph W. Evans. Copyright © 1962 by Charles Scribner's Sons. Reprinted by permission of Charles Scribner's Sons and Garnstone Press Ltd.

Degrees of Knowledge, tr. by Gerald B. Phelan. Copyright © 1959 by Jacques Maritain. Published by Charles Scribner's Sons. Reprinted by permission of Charles Scribner's Sons and Garnstone Press, Ltd.

Freedom in the Modern World, tr. by Richard O'Sullivan. Copyright © 1936 by Charles Scribner's Sons. Reprinted by permission of Charles Scribner's Sons and Garnstone Press Ltd.

"Conquest of Freedom," in *Freedom, Its Meaning*, ed. by Ruth Nanda Anshen. Copyright © 1940 by Harcourt Brace and Company. Reprinted by permission of Harcourt Brace Jovanovich, Inc.

Introduction to Philosophy, tr. by E. Watkin. Published 1937 by Sheed and Ward, Inc., New York. Reprinted by permission of Sheed and Ward, Ltd. and Sheed and Ward, Inc.

The Rights of Man and *Natural Law*, tr. by Doris Anson. Copyright © 1943 by Charles Scribner's Sons. Reprinted by permission of Charles Scribner's Sons and Garnstone Press Ltd.

Scholasticism and Politics, ed. by Mortimer J. Adler. Published 1940 by Geoffrey Bles, the Centenary Press, London. Reprinted by permission of Geoffrey Bles, Ltd.

Theonas, tr. by Francis J. Sheed. Published 1933 by Sheed and Ward, Ltd. Reprinted by permission of Sheed and Ward, Ltd. and Sheed and Ward, Inc.

Marx, Karl

Contribution to the Critique of Hegel's Philosophy of Right, tr. by Annette Jolin and Joseph O'Malley. Published 1970 by Cambridge University Press. Reprinted by permission of the Cambridge University Press.

Critique of the Gotha Programme. Copyright © 1938 by International Publishers. Reprinted by permission of International Publishers Co., Inc.

Marx, Karl, and Friedrich Engels

The German Ideology, tr. by R. Pascal. Copyright © 1947 by International Publishers. Reprinted by permission of International Publishers Co., Inc.

Mead, Margaret

Coming of Age in Samoa. Copyright © 1928, 1955, 1961 by Margaret Mead. Reprinted by permission of William Morrow & Company, Inc.

Mill, John Stuart

Principles of Political Economy, Vols. 2 and 3 of *Collected Works of John Stuart Mill*. Copyright © 1965 by University of Toronto Press. Reprinted by permission of the University of Toronto Press.

Montaigne, Michel de

The Complete Essays of Montaigne, tr. and ed. by Donald M. Frame. Copyright © 1943 by Donald M. Frame, renewed 1971. Copyright © 1948, 1957, 1958 by Board of Trustees of the Leland Stanford Junior University. Reprinted by permission of the Stanford University Press.

Newman, John Henry

Apologia Pro Vita Sua. Copyright © 1947 by Longmans, Green and Company. Reprinted by permission of David McKay Company, Inc., and Longman Group Ltd.

An Essay on the Development of Christian Doctrine. Copyright © 1960 by Doubleday & Co., Inc. Reprinted by permission of Doubleday & Co.

Nietzsche, Friedrich

The Birth of Tragedy, tr. by Walter Kaufmann. Copyright © 1927 and renewed 1955 by Modern Library, Inc. Reprinted by permission of Random House, Inc.

"Beyond Good and Evil," in *The Complete Works of Friedrich Nietzsche*, Oscar Levy, general ed. (1909–1911). Copyright © 1964 by Russell & Russell, 1927, 1954 by Random House (Modern Library Edition). Reprinted by permission of Russell & Russell and George Allen & Unwin Ltd.

Twilight of the Idols and *The Anti-Christ*, tr. by R. J. Hollingdale (Penguin Classics 1968). Copyright © 1968 by R. J. Hollingdale. Reprinted by permission of Penguin Books Ltd.

Ovid [Publius Ovidius Naso]

The Art of Love, tr. by Rolfe Humphries. Copyright © 1957 by Indiana University Press. Reprinted by permission of the Indiana University Press.

Metamorphoses, tr. by Mary M. Innes (Penguin Classics 1955). Copyright © 1955 by Mary M. Innes. Reprinted by permission of Penguin Books Ltd.

Pascal, Blaise

Pensées, tr. by W. F. Trotter. An Everyman's Library Edition. Published in the United States by E. P. Dutton & Co., Inc., and reprinted with the permission of E. P. Dutton & Co., Inc., and J. M. Dent & Sons Ltd.

Planck, Max

The Universe in the Light of Modern Physics, tr. by W. H. Johnston. Published 1937 by George Allen & Unwin. Reprinted by permission of George Allen & Unwin Ltd.

Polybius

The Histories, 2 vols., tr. by Evelyn S. Shuckburgh. Copyright © 1962 by Indiana University Press. Reprinted by permission of the Indiana University Press.

Rousseau, Jean-Jacques

Confessions. An Everyman's Library Edition. Published in the United States by E. P. Dutton & Co., Inc. Reprinted by permission of E. P. Dutton & Co., Inc., and J. M. Dent & Sons Ltd.

Russell, Bertrand

Santayana, George

(London), renewed 1974 by Arnold J. Toynbee and Mrs. Dorothea Grace Somervell. Reprinted by permission of the Oxford University Press.

Voltaire, François-Marie Arouet de

"Candide," and "Micromegas," in *Candide, Zadig and Selected Stories*, tr. by Donald M. Frame. Copyright © 1961 by Donald M. Frame. Reprinted by permission of The New American Library, Inc.

Philosophical Dictionary, tr. with an Introduction and Glossary by Peter Gay; Preface by Andre Maurois. Copyright © 1962 by Basic Books Publishing Co., Inc. Reprinted by permission of Basic Books, Inc., New York.

Whitehead, Alfred North

Adventures of Ideas. Copyright © 1933 by Macmillan Publishing Co., Inc., renewed 1961 by Evelyn Whitehead. Reprinted by permission of Macmillan Publishing Co., Inc., and the Cambridge University Press.

Introduction to Mathematics. Published 1948 by Oxford University Press. Reprinted by permission of the Oxford University Press.

"The Aims of Education" and "The Place of Classics in Education," in *The Organization of Thought, Educational and Scientific*. Published 1917 by Williams & Norgate. Reprinted by permission of Ernest Benn Limited.

Process and Reality. Copyright © 1929 by Macmillan Publishing Co., Inc., renewed 1957 by Evelyn Whitehead. Reprinted by permission of Macmillan Publishing Co., Inc., and the Cambridge University Press.

Religion in the Making. Copyright © 1926 by Macmillan Publishing Co., Inc., renewed 1954 by Evelyn Whitehead. Reprinted by permission of Macmillan Publishing Co., Inc., and the Cambridge University Press.

Science and the Modern World. Copyright © 1925 by Macmillan Publishing Co., Inc., renewed 1953 by Evelyn Whitehead. Reprinted by permission of Macmillan Publishing Co., Inc., and the Cambridge University Press.

Wittgenstein, Ludwig

Tractatus-Logico-Philosophicus. Published 1921 by Harcourt Brace and Kegan Paul, Trench and Trubner & Co. Ltd. Reprinted by permission of the Humanities Press and Routledge & Kegan Paul Ltd.

Yeats, William Butler

"Among School Children," copyright © 1928 by Macmillan, renewed 1956 by Bertha Georgie Yeats; "Crazy Jane Talks with the Bishop," copyright © 1933 by Macmillan, renewed 1961 by Bertha Georgie Yeats; "Down by the Salley Gardens," copyright © 1906 by Macmillan, renewed 1934 by William Butler Yeats; "Easter 1916," copyright © 1924 by Macmillan, renewed 1952 by Bertha Georgie Yeats; "For Anne Gregory," copyright © 1933 by Macmillan, renewed 1961 by Bertha Georgie Yeats; "He Wishes for the Cloths of Heaven," copyright © 1906 by Macmillan, renewed 1934 by William Butler Yeats; "A Last Confession," copyright © 1933 by Macmillan, renewed 1961 by Bertha Georgie Yeats; "No Second Troy," copyright © 1912 by Macmillan, renewed 1940 by Bertha Georgie Yeats; "On Those that Hated 'The Playboy of the Western World,'" copyright © 1912 by Macmillan, renewed 1940 by Bertha Georgie Yeats; "A Prayer for Old Age," copyright © 1934 by Macmillan, renewed 1962 by Bertha Georgie Yeats; "Sailing to Byzantium," copyright © 1928 by Macmillan, renewed 1956 by Bertha Georgie Yeats; "The Second Coming," copyright © 1924 by Macmillan, renewed 1952 by Bertha Georgie Yeats; "To a Friend Whose Work Has Come to Nothing," copyright © 1916 by Macmillan, renewed 1944 by Bertha Georgie Yeats; "When You Are Old," copyright © 1906 by Macmillan, renewed 1934 by William Butler Yeats, all in *Collected Poems of W. B. Yeats*. Copyright © 1906, 1912, 1916, 1919, 1924, 1928, 1933, 1940, 1944, 1946, 1947, 1952, by the Macmillan Company. Copyright © 1934 by W. B. Yeats. Copyright © 1940 by Bertha Georgie Yeats. Reprinted by permission of Macmillan Publishing Co., Inc., New York; M. B. Yeats, Miss Ann Yeats and the Macmillan Co. of London and Basingstoke; and A. P. Watt & Son Ltd.

Chapter 1

MAN

Chapter 1 is divided into nine sections: 1.1 Man in the Universe: The Grandeur and Misery of Man; 1.2 The Human Condition; 1.3 The Ages of Man: Young and Old; 1.4 Self-Knowledge and Self-Love; 1.5 Honor, Reputation, and Fame or Glory; 1.6 Human Greatness: The Hero; 1.7 Woman and Man; 1.8 Life and Death: The Fear of Death; and 1.9 Suicide.

The consideration of man—of human nature, human life, and the human condition—begins in this opening chapter but it does not end here. It is inextricably connected with almost all of the subjects treated in the chapters that follow, where passages can be found that throw light on the nature, powers, and propensities of man. The consideration of man's place in the universe recurs in Chapter 20 on Religion and in Chapter 19 on Nature and the Cosmos; the discussion of the human condition recurs in Chapter 9 on Ethics, Chapter 10 on Politics, Chapter 11 on Economics, and Chapter 15 on History; the treatment of young and old and of women in relation to men will also be found in Chapter 2 on Family and in several sections of Chapter 3 on Love; certain as-

pects of man's concern with honor and reputation as well as fame and shame will also be found in Chapter 4 on Emotion, especially the sections dealing with desire, ambition, pride and humility, as well as in sections of Chapter 9 on Ethics dealing with virtue and vice; the consideration of great men and the heroic recurs in the section of Chapter 9 that treats courage and cowardice; and the discussion of the fear of death and of suicide recurs in other contexts in certain sections of Chapter 20 on Religion.

Of all the subjects to which chapters of this book are devoted, the subject of this opening chapter—the human species—is least in need of prefatory elucidation. In spite of all the different and often conflicting views of human nature, of man's relation to the rest of the universe, and of man's strengths and weaknesses, everyone has the same object in mind when using the word "man" in this general sense, and there is almost universal agreement about the range and significance of the questions that can be asked about it. In these respects, man comes near to being an ideal subject of controversy, for the differences of opinion can almost

1

always be brought into sharp focus. The passages assembled in this chapter indicate and often epitomize the main lines in the age-old and continuing controversy about man. The issues in that controversy are as multifarious as the sections of this chapter.

1.1 | *Man in the Universe*

THE GRANDEUR AND MISERY OF MAN

What man is and how he differs from everything else in the universe are questions that call for definitions and comparisons. Many of the texts presented in this section formulate definitions of man or state the respects in which man has certain unique properties or attributes that differentiate him from everything else. The latter are, of course, balanced by statements to the opposite effect—statements that point out the respects in which man is indistinguishable from other things except, perhaps, in the degree to which he possesses properties that are commonly shared by all.

However man is defined, and in whatever manner he is said to differ from or resemble other things, questions arise concerning his relation to them—especially his relation to other animals, to God or the gods, and to nature as a whole. The passages providing diverse and conflicting answers to such questions are plentiful. Because the relation of man to other animals, as well as the contrast between men and other animals, is of such central interest, quotations may not always mention animals in relation to men, or men in relation to animals, but they are almost always taken from contexts in which that is the subject of discussion.

Dominating the consideration of man's place in the universe, from antiquity on, is the view that man is at the apex of creation or at the center of the cosmos and that everything else is ordered to his good, subservient to his needs, and subject to his dominion. That view becomes less prevalent in modern times, and the reader will find a number of quotations in which it is rejected as an illusory conceit on man's part.

There are other quotations that tend to support the latter view by their emphasis on the weakness or puniness of man—how he is a plaything of the gods, a flitting shadow on the surface of the cosmos, a thing of the moment, here today and gone tomorrow. Some writers express cynical delight in depicting man as the most miserable of creatures, and enjoy deflating his ego by satirical barbs that puncture his self-esteem. These are, in turn, balanced by many quotations in the opposite vein—passages that put man on a pedestal, see him as having a tincture of the divine, or conceive his special grandeur in terms of the place he occupies in the cosmic scale, halfway between the beasts and the angels or on the borderline between the material and the spiritual worlds. Man is a connecting link between them.

1 And God said, Let us make man in our image,
after our likeness: and let them have dominion
over the fish of the sea, and over the fowl of the
air, and over the cattle, and over all the earth,
and over every creeping thing that creepeth upon
the earth.

So God created man in his own image, in the
image of God created he him; male and female
created he them.

And God blessed them, and God said unto
them, Be fruitful, and multiply, and replenish the
earth, and subdue it: and have dominion over the
fish of the sea, and over the fowl of the air, and
over every living thing that moveth upon the
earth.

Genesis 1:26–28

2 Then the Lord answered Job out of the whirlwind, and said,

Who is this that darkeneth counsel by words
without knowledge?

Gird up now thy loins like a man; for I will
demand of thee, and answer thou me.

Where wast thou when I laid the foundations of
the earth? declare, if thou hast understanding.

Who hath laid the measures thereof, if thou
knowest? or who hath stretched the line upon it?

Whereupon are the foundations thereof fastened? or who laid the corner stone thereof;

When the morning stars sang together, and all
the sons of God shouted for joy?

Or who shut up the sea with doors, when it
brake forth, as if it had issued out of the womb?

When I made the cloud the garment thereof,
and thick darkness a swaddlingband for it,

And brake up for it my decreed place, and set
bars and doors,

And said, Hitherto shalt thou come, but no further: and here shall thy proud waves be stayed?

Hast thou commanded the morning since thy
days; and caused the dayspring to know his place;

That it might take hold of the ends of the earth,
that the wicked might be shaken out of it?

It is turned as clay to the seal; and they stand
as a garment.

And from the wicked their light is withholden,
and the high arm shall be broken.

Hast thou entered into the springs of the sea? or
hast thou walked in the search of the depth?

Have the gates of death been opened unto thee?
or hast thou seen the doors of the shadow of
death?

Hast thou perceived the breadth of the earth?
declare if thou knowest it all.

Where is the way where light dwelleth? and as
for darkness, where is the place thereof,

That thou shouldest take it to the bound thereof, and that thou shouldest know the paths to the
house thereof?

Knowest thou it, because thou wast then born?
or because the number of thy days is great?

Hast thou entered into the treasures of the
snow? or hast thou seen the treasures of the hail,

Which I have reserved against the time of trouble, against the day of battle and war?

By what way is the light parted, which scattereth the east wind upon the earth?

Who hath divided a watercourse for the overflowing of waters, or a way for the lightning of
thunder;

To cause it to rain on the earth, where no man
is; on the wilderness, wherein there is no man;

To satisfy the desolate and waste ground; and
to cause the bud of the tender herb to spring
forth?

Hath the rain a father? or who hath begotten
the drops of dew?

Out of whose womb came the ice? and the
hoary frost of heaven, who hath gendered it?

The waters are hid as with a stone, and the face
of the deep is frozen.

Canst thou bind the sweet influences of Plêi-ă-
dēs, or loose the bands of Ō-rī-on?

Canst thou bring forth Măzz-ă-rŏth in his season? or canst thou guide Ärc-tū-rŭs with his sons?

Knowest thou the ordinances of heaven? canst
thou set the dominion thereof in the earth?

Canst thou lift up thy voice to the clouds, that
abundance of waters may cover thee?

Canst thou send lightnings, that they may go,
and say unto thee, Here we are?

Who hath put wisdom in the inward parts? or
who hath given understanding to the heart?

Who can number the clouds in wisdom? or who
can stay the bottles of heaven,

When the dust groweth into hardness, and the
clods cleave fast together?

Wilt thou hunt the prey for the lion? or fill the
appetite of the young lions,

When they couch in their dens, and abide in
the covert to lie in wait?

Who provideth for the raven his food? when his
young ones cry unto God, they wander for lack of
meat.

Knowest thou the time when the wild goats of
the rock bring forth? or canst thou mark when the
hinds do calve?

Canst thou number the months that they fulfil?
or knowest thou the time when they bring forth?

They bow themselves, they bring forth their
young ones, they cast out their sorrows.

Their young ones are in good liking, they grow
up with corn; they go forth, and return not unto
them.

Who hath sent out the wild ass free? or who
hath loosed the bands of the wild ass?

Whose house I have made the wilderness, and
the barren land his dwellings.

He scorneth the multitude of the city, neither regardeth he the crying of the driver.

The range of the mountains is his pasture, and he searcheth after every green thing.

Will the unicorn be willing to serve thee, or abide by thy crib?

Canst thou bind the unicorn with his band in the furrow? or will he harrow the valleys after thee?

Wilt thou trust him, because his strength is great? or wilt thou leave thy labour to him?

Wilt thou believe him, that he will bring home thy seed, and gather it into thy barn?

Gavest thou the goodly wings unto the peacocks? or wings and feathers unto the ostrich?

Which leaveth her eggs in the earth, and warmeth them in dust,

And forgetteth that the foot may crush them, or that the wild beast may break them.

She is hardened against her young ones, as though they were not her's: her labour is in vain without fear;

Because God hath deprived her of wisdom, neither hath he imparted to her understanding.

What time she lifteth up herself on high, she scorneth the horse and his rider.

Hast thou given the horse strength? hast thou clothed his neck with thunder?

Canst thou make him afraid as a grasshopper? the glory of his nostrils is terrible.

He paweth in the valley, and rejoiceth in his strength: he goeth on to meet the armed men.

He mocketh at fear, and is not affrighted; neither turneth he back from the sword.

The quiver rattleth against him, the glittering spear and the shield.

He swalloweth the ground with fierceness and rage: neither believeth he that it is the sound of the trumpet.

He saith among the trumpets, Ha, ha; and he smelleth the battle afar off, the thunder of the captains, and the shouting.

Doth the hawk fly by thy wisdom, and stretch her wings toward the south?

Doth the eagle mount up at thy command, and make her nest on high?

She dwelleth and abideth on the rock, upon the crag of the rock, and the strong place.

From thence she seeketh the prey, and her eyes behold afar off.

Her young ones also suck up blood: and where the slain are, there is she.

Moreover the Lord answered Job, and said,

Shall he that contendeth with the Almighty instruct him? he that reproveth God, let him answer it.

Then Job answered the Lord, and said,

Behold, I am vile.

Job 38–40:4

3 O Lord our Lord, how excellent is thy name in all the earth! who hast set thy glory above the heavens.

Out of the mouth of babes and sucklings hast thou ordained strength because of thine enemies, that thou mightest still the enemy and the avenger.

When I consider thy heavens, the work of thy fingers, the moon and the stars, which thou hast ordained;

What is man, that thou art mindful of him? and the son of man, that thou visitest him?

For thou hast made him a little lower than the angels, and hast crowned him with glory and honour.

Thou madest him to have dominion over the works of thy hands; thou hast put all things under his feet:

All sheep and oxen, yea, and the beasts of the field;

The fowl of the air, and the fish of the sea, and whatsoever passeth through the paths of the seas.

O Lord our Lord, how excellent is thy name in all the earth!

Psalm 8:1–9

4 As he [Zeus] watched the mourning horses the son
   of Kronos pitied them,
and stirred his head and spoke to his own spirit:
   'Poor wretches,
why then did we ever give you to the lord Peleus,
a mortal man, and you yourselves are immortal
   and ageless?
Only so that among unhappy men you also might
   be grieved?
Since among all creatures that breathe on earth
   and crawl on it
there is not anywhere a thing more dismal than
   man is.'

Homer, *Iliad,* XVII, 441

5 *Odysseus.* Of mortal creatures, all that breathe and
   move,
earth bears none frailer than mankind. What
   man
believes in woe to come, so long as valor
and tough knees are supplied him by the gods?
But when the gods in bliss bring miseries on,
then willy-nilly, blindly, he endures.
Our minds are as the days are, dark or bright,
blown over by the father of gods and men.

Homer, *Odyssey,* XVIII, 131

6 *Prometheus.* Hear what troubles there were among men, how I found them witless and gave them the use of their wits and made them masters of their minds. I will tell you this, not because I would blame men, but to explain the goodwill of my gift. For men at first had eyes but saw to no purpose; they had ears but did not hear. Like the shapes of dreams they dragged through their long lives and handled all things in bewilderment and confusion.

They did not know of building houses with bricks to face the sun; they did not know how to work in wood. They lived like swarming ants in holes in the ground, in the sunless caves of the earth. For them there was no secure token by which to tell winter nor the flowering spring nor the summer with its crops; all their doings were indeed without intelligent calculation until I showed them the rising of the stars, and the settings, hard to observe. And further I discovered to them numbering, pre-eminent among subtle devices, and the combining of letters as a means of remembering all things, the Muses' mother, skilled in craft. It was I who first yoked beasts for them in the yokes and made of those beasts the slaves of trace chain and pack saddle that they might be man's substitute in the hardest tasks; and I harnessed to the carriage, so that they loved the rein, horses, the crowning pride of the rich man's luxury. It was I and none other who discovered ships, the sail-driven wagons that the sea buffets. Such were the contrivances that I discovered for men.

Aeschylus, *Prometheus Bound,* 441

7 *Chorus.* Many the wonders but nothing walks
  stranger than man.
This thing crosses the sea in the winter's storm,
making his path through the roaring waves.
And she, the greatest of gods, the earth—
ageless she is, and unwearied—he wears her away
as the ploughs go up and down from year to year
and his mules turn up the soil.

Gay nations of birds he snares and leads,
wild beast tribes and the salty brood of the sea,
with the twisted mesh of his nets, this clever man.
He controls with craft the beasts of the open air,
walkers on hills. The horse with his shaggy mane
he holds and harnesses, yoked about the neck,
and the strong bull of the mountain.

Language, and thought like the wind
and the feelings that make the town,
he has taught himself, and shelter against the
  cold,
refuge from rain. He can always help himself.
He faces no future helpless. There's only death
that he cannot find an escape from. He has contrived
refuge from illnesses once beyond all cure.

Clever beyond all dreams
the inventive craft that he has
which may drive him one time or another to well
or ill.

Sophocles, *Antigone,* 332

8 *Chorus.* Ye men who are dimly existing below,
          who perish and fade as the leaf,
Pale, woebegone, shadowlike, spiritless folk,
          life feeble and wingless and brief,
Frail castings in clay, who are gone in a day,
          like a dream full of sorrow and sighing,

Come listen with care to the Birds of the air,
          the ageless, the deathless, who flying
In the joy and the freshness of Ether, are wont
          to muse upon wisdom undying.

Aristophanes, *Birds,* 685

9 *Timaeus.* Now, when all of them, both those who visibly appear in their revolutions as well as those other gods who are of a more retiring nature, had come into being, the creator of the universe addressed them in these words: "Gods, children of gods, who are my works, and of whom I am the artificer and father, my creations are indissoluble, if so I will. All that is bound may be undone, but only an evil being would wish to undo that which is harmonious and happy. Wherefore, since ye are but creatures, ye are not altogether immortal and indissoluble, but ye shall certainly not be dissolved, nor be liable to the fate of death, having in my will a greater and mightier bond than those with which ye were bound at the time of your birth. And now listen to my instructions:—Three tribes of mortal beings remain to be created—without them the universe will be incomplete, for it will not contain every kind of animal which it ought to contain, if it is to be perfect. On the other hand, if they were created by me and received life at my hands, they would be on an equality with the gods. In order then that they may be mortal, and that this universe may be truly universal, do ye, according to your natures, betake yourselves to the formation of animals, imitating the power which was shown by me in creating you. The part of them worthy of the name immortal, which is called divine and is the guiding principle of those who are willing to follow justice and you—of that divine part I will myself sow the seed, and having made a beginning, I will hand the work over to you. And do ye then interweave the mortal with the immortal, and make and beget living creatures, and give them food, and make them to grow, and receive them again in death."

Thus he spake, and once more into the cup in which he had previously mingled the soul of the universe he poured the remains of the elements, and mingled them in much the same manner; they were not, however, pure as before, but diluted to the second and third degree. And having made it he divided the whole mixture into souls equal in number to the stars, and assigned each soul to a star; and having there placed them as in a chariot, he showed them the nature of the universe, and declared to them the laws of destiny, according to which their first birth would be one and the same for all,—no one should suffer a disadvantage at his hands; they were to be sown in the instruments of time severally adapted to them, and to come forth the most religious of animals; and as human nature was of two kinds, the superior race would hereafter be called man.

Plato, *Timaeus,* 41A

10 Man, he [Protagoras] says, is the measure of all things, of the existence of things that are, and of the non-existence of things that are not.

Plato, *Theaetetus,* 152A

11 *Athenian Stranger.* Man . . . is a tame or civilized animal; nevertheless, he requires proper instruction and a fortunate nature, and then of all animals he becomes the most divine and most civilized; but if he be insufficiently or ill-educated he is the most savage of earthly creatures.

Plato, *Laws,* VI, 766A

12 Of the psychic powers . . . some kinds of living things . . . possess all, some less than all, others one only. Those we have mentioned are the nutritive, the appetitive, the sensory, the locomotive, and the power of thinking. Plants have none but the first, the nutritive, while another order of living things has this *plus* the sensory. If any order of living things has the sensory, it must also have the appetitive; for appetite is the genus of which desire, passion, and wish are the species; now all animals have one sense at least, viz. touch. . . . Certain kinds of animals possess in addition the power of locomotion, and still another order of animate beings, that is, man and possibly another order like man or superior to him, the power of thinking, that is, mind.

Aristotle, *On the Soul,* 414ª28

13 Taking the size of his body into account, man emits more sperm than any other animal.

Aristotle, *History of Animals,* 523ª15

14 In the great majority of animals there are traces of psychical qualities or attitudes, which qualities are more markedly differentiated in the case of human beings. For just as we pointed out resemblances in the physical organs, so in a number of animals we observe gentleness or fierceness, mildness or cross temper, courage, or timidity, fear or confidence, high spirit or low cunning, and, with regard to intelligence, something equivalent to sagacity. Some of these qualities in man, as compared with the corresponding qualities in animals, differ only quantitatively: that is to say, a man has more or less of this quality, and an animal has more or less of some other; other qualities in man are represented by analogous and not identical qualities: for instance, just as in man we find knowledge, wisdom, and sagacity, so in certain animals there exists some other natural potentiality akin to these. The truth of this statement will be the more clearly apprehended if we have regard to the phenomena of childhood: for in children may be observed the traces and seeds of what will one day be settled psychological habits, though psychologically a child hardly differs for the time being from an animal; so that one is quite justified in saying that, as regards man and animals, certain psychical qualities are identical with one another, whilst others resemble, and others are analogous to, each other.

Aristotle, *History of Animals,* 588ª17

15 Of all living beings with which we are acquainted man alone partakes of the divine, or at any rate partakes of it in a fuller measure than the rest.

Aristotle, *Parts of Animals,* 656ª8

16 That man alone is affected by tickling is due firstly to the delicacy of his skin, and secondly to his being the only animal that laughs.

Aristotle, *Parts of Animals,* 673ª7

17 Of all animals man alone stands erect, in accordance with his god-like nature and essence. For it is the function of the god-like to think and to be wise; and no easy task were this under the burden of a heavy body, pressing down from above and obstructing by its weight the motions of the intellect and of the general sense.

Aristotle, *Parts of Animals,* 686ª27

18 It is the opinion of Anaxagoras that the possession of . . . hands is the cause of man being of all animals the most intelligent. But it is more rational to suppose that his endowment with hands is the consequence rather than the cause of his superior intelligence. For the hands are instruments or organs, and the invariable plan of nature in distributing the organs is to give each to such animal as can make use of it; the invariable plan of nature in distributing the organs is to give each to such animal as can make use of it, as any prudent man would do. For it is a better plan to take a person who is already a flute-player and give him a flute, than to take one who possesses a flute and teach him the art of flute-playing. For nature adds that which is less to that which is greater and more important, and not that which is more valuable and greater to that which is less. Seeing then that such is the better course, and seeing also that of what is possible nature invariably brings about the best, we must conclude that man does not owe his superior intelligence to his hands, but his hands to his superior intelligence. For the most intelligent of animals is the one who would put the most organs to use; and the hand is not to be looked on as one organ but as many; for it is, as it were, an instrument for further instruments. This instrument, therefore,— the hand—of all instruments the most variously serviceable, has been given by nature to man, the animal of all animals the most capable of acquiring the most varied handicrafts.

Aristotle, *Parts of Animals,* 687ª8

19 No one would choose the whole world on condition of being alone, since man is a political creature and one whose nature is to live with others.

Aristotle, *Ethics*, 1169ᵇ18

20 That which is proper to each thing is by nature best and most pleasant for each thing; for man, therefore, the life according to reason is best and pleasantest, since reason more than anything else *is* man.

Aristotle, *Ethics*, 1178ᵃ5

21 While the whole life of the gods is blessed, and that of men too in so far as some likeness of such activity belongs to them, none of the other animals is happy, since they in no way share in contemplation.

Aristotle, *Ethics*, 1178ᵇ25

22 Man, when perfected, is the best of animals, but, when separated from law and justice, he is the worst of all; since armed injustice is the more dangerous, and he is equipped at birth with arms, meant to be used by intelligence and virtue, which he may use for the worst ends. Wherefore, if he have not virtue, he is the most unholy and the most savage of animals, and the most full of lust and gluttony.

Aristotle, *Politics*, 1253ᵃ31

23 If nature makes nothing incomplete, and nothing in vain, the inference must be that she has made all animals for the sake of man.

Aristotle, *Politics*, 1256ᵇ20

24 Imitation is natural to man from childhood, one of his advantages over the lower animals being this, that he is the most imitative creature in the world, and learns at first by imitation.

Aristotle, *Poetics*, 1448ᵇ6

25 The most evident difference between man and animal is this: the beast, in as much as it largely motivated by the senses and with little perception of the past or future, lives only for the present. But man, because he is endowed with reason by which he is able to perceive relationships, sees the causes of things, understands the reciprocal nature of cause and effect, makes analogies, easily surveys the whole course of his life, and makes the necessary preparations for its conduct.

Cicero, *De Officiis*, I, 4

26 In every inquiry about duty we must keep in mind the natural superiority of men over cattle and other animals. Animals deal only in sensual pleasure and are by instinct impelled to seek it. But the mind of man is nurtured by study and contemplation. He is always investigating or doing something. He is captivated by the pleasures of seeing and hearing.

Cicero, *De Officiis*, I, 30

27 Suppose he [a man] has a beautiful home and a handsome collection of servants, a lot of land under cultivation and a lot of money out at interest; not one of these things can be said to be in him— they are just things around him. Praise in him what can neither be given nor snatched away, what is peculiarly a man's. You ask what that is? It is his spirit, and the perfection of his reason in that spirit. For man is a rational animal. Man's ideal state is realized when he has fulfilled the purpose for which he was born.

Seneca, *Letters to Lucilius*, 41

28 And so it is written, The first man Adam was made a living soul; the last Adam was made a quickening spirit.

Howbeit that was not first which is spiritual, but that which is natural; and afterward that which is spiritual.

The first man is of the earth, earthy: the second man is the Lord from heaven.

As is the earthy, such are they also that are earthy: and as is the heavenly, such are they also that are heavenly.

And as we have borne the image of the earthy, we shall also bear the image of the heavenly.

I Corinthians, 15:45–49

29 Man is the only animal that knows nothing, and can learn nothing without being taught. He can neither speak nor walk nor eat, nor do anything at the prompting of nature, but only weep.

Pliny the Elder, *Natural History*, VII, 77

30 No beast is more savage than man when possessed with power answerable to his rage.

Plutarch, *Cicero*

31 God had need of irrational animals to make use of appearances, but of us to understand the use of appearances. It is therefore enough for them to eat and to drink, and to sleep and to copulate, and to do all the other things which they severally do. But for us, to whom He has given also the intellectual faculty, these things are not sufficient; for unless we act in a proper and orderly manner, and conformably to the nature and constitution of each thing, we shall never attain our true end. For where the constitutions of living beings are different, there also the acts and the ends are different. In those animals, then, whose constitution is adapted only to use, use alone is enough: but in an animal which has also the power of understanding the use, unless there be the due exercise

of the understanding, he will never attain his proper end. Well then God constitutes every animal, one to be eaten, another to serve for agriculture, another to supply cheese, and another for some like use; for which purposes what need is there to understand appearances and to be able to distinguish them? But God has introduced man to be a spectator of God and of His works; and not only a spectator of them, but an interpreter. For this reason it is shameful for man to begin and to end where irrational animals do, but rather he ought to begin where they begin, and to end where nature ends in us; and nature ends in contemplation and understanding.

Epictetus, *Discourses,* I, 6

32 If a thing is difficult to be accomplished by thyself, do not think that it is impossible for man: but if anything is possible for man and conformable to his nature, think that this can be attained by thyself too.

Marcus Aurelius, *Meditations,* VI, 19

33 If the gods have determined about me and about the things which must happen to me, they have determined well, for it is not easy even to imagine a deity without forethought; and as to doing me harm, why should they have any desire towards that? For what advantage would result to them from this or to the whole, which is the special object of their providence? But if they have not determined about me individually, they have certainly determined about the whole at least, and the things which happen by way of sequence in this general arrangement I ought to accept with pleasure and to be content with them. But if they determine about nothing—which it is wicked to believe, or if we do believe it, let us neither sacrifice nor pray nor swear by them nor do anything else which we do as if the gods were present and lived with us—but if however the gods determine about none of the things which concern us, I am able to determine about myself, and I can inquire about that which is useful; and that is useful to every man which is conformable to his own constitution and nature.

Marcus Aurelius, *Meditations,* VI, 44

34 Now in every living being the upper parts—head, face—are the most beautiful, the mid and lower members inferior. In the Universe the middle and lower members are human beings; above them, the Heavens and the Gods that dwell there; these Gods with the entire circling expanse of the heavens constitute the greater part of the Kosmos: the earth is but a central point, and may be considered as simply one among the stars. Yet human wrong-doing is made a matter of wonder; we are evidently asked to take humanity as the choice member of the Universe, nothing wiser existent! But humanity, in reality, is poised midway between gods and beasts, and inclines now to the one order, now to the other; some men grow like to the divine, others to the brute, the greater number stand neutral.

Plotinus, *Third Ennead,* II, 8

35 Man has come into existence, a living being but not a member of the noblest order; he occupies by choice an intermediate rank; still, in that place in which he exists, Providence does not allow him to be reduced to nothing; on the contrary he is ever being led upwards by all those varied devices which the Divine employs in its labour to increase the dominance of moral value. The human race, therefore, is not deprived by Providence of its rational being; it retains its share, though necessarily limited, in wisdom, intelligence, executive power and right doing, the right doing, at least, of individuals to each other—and even in wronging others people think they are doing right and only paying what is due.

Man is, therefore, a noble creation, as perfect as the scheme allows; a part, no doubt, in the fabric of the All, he yet holds a lot higher than that of all the other living things of earth.

Plotinus, *Third Ennead,* II, 9

36 How much human nature loves the knowledge of its existence, and how it shrinks from being deceived, will be sufficiently understood from this fact, that every man prefers to grieve in a sane mind, rather than to be glad in madness. And this grand and wonderful instinct belongs to men alone of all animals; for, though some of them have keener eyesight than ourselves for this world's light, they cannot attain to that spiritual light with which our mind is somehow irradiated, so that we can form right judgments of all things.

Augustine, *City of God,* XI, 27

37 God created only one single man, not, certainly, that he might be a solitary, bereft of all society, but that by this means the unity of society and the bond of concord might be more effectually commended to him, men being bound together not only by similarity of nature, but by family affection. And indeed He did not even create the woman that was to be given him as his wife, as he created the man, but created her out of the man, that the whole human race might derive from one man.

Augustine, *City of God,* XII, 21

38 Even in the body, though it dies like that of the beasts, and is in many ways weaker than theirs, what goodness of God, what providence of the great Creator, is apparent! The organs of sense and the rest of the members, are not they so placed, the appearance, and form, and stature of the body as a whole, is it not so fashioned as to indicate that it was made for the service of a rea-

sonable soul? Man has not been created stooping towards the earth, like the irrational animals; but his bodily form, erect and looking heavenwards, admonishes him to mind the things that are above.

Augustine, *City of God,* XXII, 24

39 The saying that man and animals have a like beginning in generation is true of the body, for all animals alike are made of earth. But it is not true of the soul. For the souls of brutes are produced by some power of the body, whereas the human soul is produced by God.

Aquinas, *Summa Theologica,* I, 75, 6

40 The modes of living are distinguished according to the degrees of living things. There are some living things in which there exists only vegetative power, as the plants. There are others in which with the vegetative there exists also the sensitive, but not the power of local movement; such are immovable animals, as shellfish. There are others which besides this have powers of local movement, as perfect animals, which require many things for their life, and consequently movement to seek necessaries of life from a distance. And there are some living things which with these have intellectual power—namely, men.

Aquinas, *Summa Theologica,* I, 78, 1

41 The human intellect . . . is the lowest in the order of intellects and the most removed from the perfection of the Divine intellect.

Aquinas, *Summa Theologica,* I, 79, 2

42 Other animals are so much lower than man that they cannot attain to the knowledge of truth, which reason seeks. But man attains, although imperfectly, to the knowledge of intelligible truth, which angels know. Therefore in the angels the power of knowledge is not of a different genus from that which is in the human reason, but is compared to it as the perfect to the imperfect.

Aquinas, *Summa Theologica,* I, 79, 8

43 Horns and claws, which are the weapons of some animals, and toughness of hide and quantity of hair or feathers, which are the clothing of animals, are signs of an abundance of the earthly element, which does not agree with the equability and softness of the human temperament. Therefore such things do not suit the nature of man. Instead of these, he has reason and hands whereby he can make himself arms and clothes, and other necessaries of life, of infinite variety. And so the hand is called by Aristotle "the organ of organs." Moreover this was more becoming to the rational nature, which is capable of conceiving an infinite number of things so as to make for itself an infinite number of instruments.

Aquinas, *Summa Theologica,* I, 91, 3

44 An upright stature was becoming to man for four reasons. First, because the senses are given to man, not only for the purpose of procuring the necessaries of life for which they are bestowed on other animals, but also for the purpose of knowledge. Hence, whereas the other animals take delight in the objects of the senses only as ordered to food and sex, man alone takes pleasure in the beauty of sensible objects for its own sake. Therefore, as the senses are situated chiefly in the face, other animals have the face turned to the ground, as it were for the purpose of seeking food and procuring a livelihood; but man has his face erect, in order that by the senses, and chiefly by sight, which is more subtle and penetrates further into the differences of things, he may freely survey the sensible objects around him, both heavenly and earthly, so as to gather intelligible truth from all things. Secondly, for the greater freedom of the acts of the interior powers; the brain, wherein these actions are, in a way, performed, not being low down, but lifted up above other parts of the body. Thirdly, because if man's stature were prone to the ground he would need to use his hands as fore-feet, and thus their utility for other purposes would cease. Fourthly, because if man's stature were prone to the ground and he used his hands as fore-feet, he would be obliged to take hold of his food with his mouth. Thus he would have a protruding mouth, with thick and hard lips, and also a hard tongue, so as to keep it from being hurt by exterior things, as we see in other animals. Moreover, such an attitude would quite hinder speech, which is reason's proper operation.

Nevertheless, though of erect nature, man is far above plants. For man's superior part, his head, is turned towards the superior part of the world, and his inferior part is turned towards the inferior world; and therefore he is perfectly disposed as to the general situation of his body. Plants have the superior part turned towards the lower world, since their roots correspond to the mouth, and their inferior parts towards the upper world. But brute animals have a middle disposition, for the superior part of the animal is that by which it takes food, and the inferior part that by which it rids itself of the surplus.

Aquinas, *Summa Theologica,* I, 91, 3

45 Man is as it were the horizon and boundary line of spiritual and corporeal nature, and intermediate, so to speak, between the two, sharing in both corporeal and spiritual perfections.

Aquinas, *Commentary on the Sentences of Peter Lombard,* III, Prologue

46 Man's basic capacity is to have a potentiality or power for being intellectual. And since this power can not be completely actualized in a single man or in any of the particular communities of men above mentioned, there must be a multitude in

mankind through whom this whole power can be actualized; just as there must be a multitude of created beings to manifest adequately the whole power of prime matter, otherwise there would have to be a power distinct from prime matter, which is impossible.

Dante, *De Monarchia*, I, 3

47 Because in the intellectual order of the universe the ascent and descent is by almost continuous steps, from the lowest form to the highest and from the highest to the lowest (as we see is the case in the sensible order), and between the angelic nature, which is an intellectual thing, and the human soul there is no intermediate step, but the one is, as it were, continuous with the other in the order of steps; and between the human soul and the most perfect soul of the brute animals there is also no intermediary, and we see many men so vile and of such base condition as scarce to seem other than beasts; in like manner we are to lay it down, and firmly to believe, that there be some so noble and of so lofty condition as to be scarce other than angels; otherwise the human species would not be continued in either direction, which may not be.

Dante, *Convivio*, III, 7

48 We have altogether a confounded, corrupt, and poisoned nature, both in body and soul; throughout the whole of man is nothing that is good.

Luther, *Table Talk*, H262

49 *Panurge*. Behold how nature,—having a fervent desire after its production of plants, trees, shrubs, herbs, sponges, and plant-animals, to eternize, and continue them unto all succession of ages—in their several kinds or sorts, at least, although the individuals perish—unruinable, and in an everlasting being,—hath most curiously armed and fenced their buds, sprouts, shoots, and seeds, wherein the above-mentioned perpetuity consisteth, by strengthening, covering, guarding, and fortifying them with an admirable industry, with husks, cases, scarfs and swads, hulls, cods, stones, films, cartels, shells, ears, rinds, barks, skins, ridges, and prickles, which serve them instead of strong, fair, and natural codpieces. As is manifestly apparent in pease, beans, fasels, pomegranates, peaches, cottons, gourds, pumpions, melons, corn, lemons, almonds, walnuts, filberts, and chestnuts; as likewise in all plants, slips or sets whatsoever, wherein it is plainly and evidently seen that the sperm and semence is more closely veiled, overshadowed, corroborated, and thoroughly harnessed, than any other part, portion, or parcel of the whole.

Nature, nevertheless, did not after that manner provide for the sempiternizing of the human race: but, on the contrary, created man naked, tender, and frail, without either offensive or defensive arms; and that in the estate of innocence, in the first age of all, which was the golden season; not as a plant, but living creature, born for peace, not war, and brought forth into the world with an unquestionable right and title to the plenary fruition and enjoyment of all fruits and vegetables, as also to a certain calm and gentle rule and dominion over all kinds of beasts, fowls, fishes, reptiles, and insects. Yet afterwards it happening in the time of the iron age, under the reign of Jupiter, when, to the multiplication of mischievous actions, wickedness and malice began to take root and footing within the then perverted hearts of men, that the earth began to bring forth nettles, thistles, thorns, briars, and such other stubborn and rebellious vegetables to the nature of man. Nor scarce was there any animal, which by a fatal disposition did not then revolt from him, and tacitly conspire, and covenant with one another, to serve him no longer, nor, in case of their ability to resist, to do him any manner of obedience, but rather, to the uttermost of their power, to annoy him with all the hurt and harm they could. The man, then, that he might maintain his primitive right and prerogative, and continue his sway and dominion over all, both vegetable and sensitive creatures; and knowing of a truth, that he could not be well accommodated, as he ought, without the servitude and subjection of several animals, bethought himself, that of necessity he must needs put on arms, and make provision of harness against wars and violence. By the holy Saint Babingoose, cried out Pantagruel, you are become, since the last rain, a great lifrelofre,—philosopher, I should say. Take notice, Sir, quoth Panurge, when Dame Nature had prompted him to his own arming, what part of the body it was, where, by her inspiration, he clapped on the first harness. It was forsooth by the double pluck of my little dog the ballock, and good Señor Don Priapos Stabostando,—which done, he was content, and sought no more.

Rabelais, *Gargantua and Pantagruel*, III, 8

50 Let us then consider for the moment man alone, without outside assistance, armed solely with his own weapons, and deprived of divine grace and knowledge, which is his whole honor, his strength, and the foundation of his being. Let us see how much presence he has in this fine array. Let him help me to understand, by the force of his reason, on what foundations he has built these great advantages that he thinks he has over other creatures. Who has persuaded him that that admirable motion of the celestial vault, the eternal light of those torches rolling so proudly above his head, the fearful movements of that infinite sea, were established and have lasted so many centuries for his convenience and his service? Is it possible to imagine anything so ridiculous as that this miserable and puny creature, who is not even master of

himself, exposed to the attacks of all things, should call himself master and emperor of the universe, the least part of which it is not in his power to know, much less to command? And this privilege that he attributes to himself of being the only one in this great edifice who has the capacity to recognize its beauty and its parts, the only one who can give thanks for it to the architect and keep an account of the receipts and expenses of the world: who has sealed him this privilege? Let him show us his letters patent for this great and splendid charge.

> Montaigne, *Essays,* II, 12,
> Apology for Raymond Sebond

51 Presumption is our natural and original malady. The most vulnerable and frail of all creatures is man, and at the same time the most arrogant. He feels and sees himself lodged here, amid the mire and dung of the world, nailed and riveted to the worst, the deadest, and the most stagnant part of the universe, on the lowest story of the house and the farthest from the vault of heaven, with the animals of the worst condition of the three; and in his imagination he goes planting himself above the circle of the moon, and bringing the sky down beneath his feet. It is by the vanity of this same imagination that he equals himself to God, attributes to himself divine characteristics, picks himself out and separates himself from the horde of other creatures, carves out their shares to his fellows and companions the animals, and distributes among them such portions of faculties and powers as he sees fit. How does he know, by the force of his intelligence, the secret internal stirrings of animals? By what comparison between them and us does he infer the stupidity that he attributes to them?

> Montaigne, *Essays,* II, 12,
> Apology for Raymond Sebond

52 When I play with my cat, who knows if I am not a pastime to her more than she is to me?

> Montaigne, *Essays,* II, 12,
> Apology for Raymond Sebond

53 Man must be constrained and forced into line inside the barriers of this order. The poor wretch is in no position really to step outside them; he is fettered and bound, he is subjected to the same obligation as the other creatures of his class, and in a very ordinary condition, without any real and essential prerogative or preeminence. That which he accords himself in his mind and in his fancy has neither body nor taste. And if it is true that he alone of all the animals has this freedom of imagination and this unruliness in thought that represents to him what is, what is not, what he wants, the false and the true, it is an advantage that is sold him very dear, and in which he has little cause to glory, for from it springs the principal source of the ills that oppress him: sin, disease, irresolution, confusion, despair.

> Montaigne, *Essays,* II, 12,
> Apology for Raymond Sebond

54 Movement belongs to the Earth as the home of the speculative creature. For it was not fitting that man, who was going to be the dweller in this world and its contemplator, should reside in one place of it as in a closed cubicle: in that way he would never have arrived at the measurement and contemplation of the so distant stars, unless he had been furnished with more than human gifts; or rather since he was furnished with the eyes which he now has and with the faculties of his mind, it was his office to move around in this very spacious edifice by means of the transportation of the Earth his home and to get to know the different stations, according as they are measurers—that is, to take a promenade—so that he could all the more correctly view and measure the single parts of his house.

> Kepler, *Epitome of Copernican
> Astronomy,* Bk. IV, II, 5

55 *Hamlet.* What a piece of work is a man! how noble in reason! how infinite in faculty! in form and moving how express and admirable! in action how like an angel! in apprehension how like a god! the beauty of the world! the paragon of animals! And yet, to me, what is this quintessence of dust?

> Shakespeare, *Hamlet,* II, ii, 315

56 *Isabella.*   Merciful Heaven,
Thou rather with thy sharp and sulphurous bolt
Split'st the unwedgeable and gnarled oak
Than the soft myrtle; but man, proud man,
Drest in a little brief authority,
Most ignorant of what he's most assured,
His glassy essence, like an angry ape,
Plays such fantastic tricks before high heaven
As make the angels weep.

> Shakespeare, *Measure for Measure,* II, ii, 114

57 *Lear.* Why, thou wert better in thy grave than to answer with thy uncovered body this extremity of the skies. Is man no more than this? Consider him well. Thou owest the worm no silk, the beast no hide, the sheep no wool, the cat no perfume. Ha! here's three on 's are sophisticated! Thou art the thing itself. Unaccommodated man is no more but such a poor, bare, forked animal as thou art. Off, off, you lendings! come, unbutton here. [*Tearing off his clothes.*]
Fool. Prithee, nuncle, be contented; 'tis a naughty night to swim in.

> Shakespeare, *Lear,* III, iv, 105

58 *Gloucester.* As flies to wanton boys, are we to the gods,

They kill us for their sport.

Shakespeare, *Lear,* IV, i, 38

59 *Trinculo.* What have we here? a man or a fish? Dead or alive? A fish; he smells like a fish; a very ancient and fish-like smell; a kind of not-of-the newest Poor-John. A strange fish! Were I in England now, as once I was, and had but this fish painted, not a holiday fool there but would give a piece of silver. There would this monster make a man; any strange beast there makes a man; when they will not give a doit to relieve a lame beggar, they will lay out ten to see a dead Indian. Legged like a man! and his fins like arms! Warm o' my troth! I do now let loose my opinion; hold it no longer. This is no fish, but an islander, that hath lately suffered by a thunderbolt.

Shakespeare, *Tempest,* II, ii, 25

60 *Miranda.*   O, wonder!
How many goodly creatures are there here!
How beauteous mankind is! O brave new world,
That has such people in 't!
    Prospero.   'Tis new to thee.

Shakespeare, *Tempest,* V, i, 182

61 I am a little world made cunningly
Of Elements, and an Angelike spright.

Donne, *Holy Sonnet V*

62 They that deny a God destroy man's nobility; for certainly man is of kin to the beasts by his body; and if he be not of kin to God by his spirit, he is a base and ignoble creature.

Bacon, *Of Atheism*

63 Man, if we look to final causes, may be regarded as the centre of the world; insomuch that if man were taken away from the world, the rest would seem to be all astray, without aim or purpose, to be like a besom without a binding, as the saying is, and to be leading to nothing. For the whole world works together in the service of man; and there is nothing from which he does not derive use and fruit. The revolutions and courses of the stars serve him both for distinction of the seasons and distribution of the quarters of the world. The appearances of the middle sky afford him prognostications of weather. The winds sail his ships and work his mills and engines. Plants and animals of all kinds are made to furnish him either with dwelling and shelter or clothing or food or medicine, or to lighten his labour, or to give him pleasure and comfort; insomuch that all things seem to be going about man's business and not their own.

Bacon, *Wisdom of the Ancients:* Prometheus

64 Man comes into the world naked and unarmed, as if Nature had destined him for a social creature, and ordained him to live under equitable laws and in peace; as if she had desired that he should be guided by reason rather than be driven by force; therefore did she endow him with understanding, and furnish him with hands, that he might himself contrive what was necessary to his clothing and protection.

William Harvey, *Animal Generation,* 56

65 Man is but a great mischievous baboon.

William Harvey, qu. by Aubrey, *Brief Lives*

66 As for the understanding or thought attributed by Montaigne and others to brutes, I cannot hold their opinion; not, however, because I am doubtful of the truth of what is commonly said, that men have absolute dominion over all the other animals; for while I allow that there are some which are stronger than we are, and I believe there may be some, also, which have natural cunning capable of deceiving the most sagacious men; yet I consider that they imitate or surpass us only in those of our actions which are not directed by thought.

Descartes, *Letter to the Marquis of Newcastle*

67 I know, indeed, that brutes do many things better than we do, but I am not surprised at it; for that, also, goes to prove that they act by force of nature and by springs, like a clock, which tells better what the hour is than our judgment can inform us.

Descartes, *Letter to the Marquis of Newcastle*

68 The principal argument, to my mind, which may convince us that the brutes are devoid of reason, is that, although among those of the same species, some are more perfect than others, as among men, which is particularly noticeable in horses and dogs, some of which have more capacity than others to retain what is taught them, and although all of them make us clearly understand their natural movements of anger, of fear, of hunger, and others of like kind, either by the voice or by other bodily motions, it has never yet been observed that any animal has arrived at such a degree of perfection as to make use of a true language; that is to say, as to be able to indicate to us by the voice, or by other signs, anything which could be referred to thought alone, rather than to a movement of mere nature; for the word is the sole sign and the only certain mark of the presence of thought hidden and wrapped up in the body; now all men, the most stupid and the most foolish, those even who are deprived of the organs of speech, make use of signs, whereas the brutes never do anything of the kind; which may be taken for the true distinction between man and brute.

Descartes, *Letter to Henry More (1649)*

69 It is yet not at all probable that all things have

been created for us in such a manner that God has had no other end in creating them. . . . Such a supposition would be certainly ridiculous and inept in reference to questions of Physics, for we cannot doubt that an infinitude of things exist, or did exist, though now they have ceased to exist, which have never been beheld or comprehended by man and which have never been of any use to him.

Descartes, *Principles of Philosophy,* III, 3

70 Nature tells me I am the Image of God, as well as Scripture: he that understands not thus much, hath not his introduction or first lesson, and is yet to begin the Alphabet of man.

Sir Thomas Browne,
Religio Medici, II, 11

71 For, in fact, what is man in nature? A Nothing in comparison with the Infinite, an All in comparison with the Nothing, a mean between nothing and everything. Since he is infinitely removed from comprehending the extremes, the end of things and their beginning are hopelessly hidden from him in an impenetrable secret; he is equally incapable of seeing the Nothing from which he was made, and the Infinite in which he is swallowed up.

What will he do then, but perceive the appearance of the middle of things, in an eternal despair of knowing either their beginning or their end. All things proceed from the Nothing, and are borne towards the Infinite. Who will follow these marvellous processes? The Author of these wonders understands them. None other can do so.

Pascal, *Pensées,* II, 72

72 Man is but a reed, the most feeble thing in nature; but he is a thinking reed. The entire universe need not arm itself to crush him. A vapour, a drop of water suffices to kill him. But, if the universe were to crush him, man would still be more noble than that which killed him, because he knows that he dies and the advantage which the universe has over him; the universe knows nothing of this.

Pascal, *Pensées,* VI, 347

73 The brutes do not admire each other. A horse does not admire his companion. Not that there is no rivalry between them in a race, but that is of no consequence; for, when in the stable, the heaviest and most ill-formed does not give up his oats to another, as men would have others do to them. Their virtue is satisfied with itself.

Pascal, *Pensées,* VI, 401

74 What a chimera, then, is man! What a novelty! What a monster, what a chaos, what a contradiction, what a prodigy! Judge of all things, imbecile worm of the earth; depositary of truth, a sink of uncertainty and error; the pride and refuse of the universe!

Pascal, *Pensées,* VII, 434

75 Let us make now Man in our image, Man
In our similitude, and let them rule
Over the Fish and Fowle of Sea and Aire,
Beast of the Field, and over all the Earth,
And every creeping thing that creeps the ground.
This said, he formd thee, *Adam,* thee O Man
Dust of the ground, and in thy nostrils breath'd
The breath of Life; in his own Image hee
Created thee, in the Image of God
Express, and thou becam'st a living Soul.
Male he created thee, but thy consort
Femal for Race; then bless'd Mankinde, and said,
Be fruitful, multiplie, and fill the Earth,
Subdue it, and throughout Dominion hold
Over Fish of the Sea, and Fowle of the Aire,
And every living thing that moves on the Earth.

Milton, *Paradise Lost,* VII, 519

76 The essence of man consists of certain modifications of the attributes of God; for the Being of substance does not pertain to the essence of man. It is therefore something which is in God, and which without God can neither be nor be conceived, or an affection or mode which expresses the nature of God in a certain and indeterminate manner.

Spinoza, *Ethics,* II, Prop. 10, Corol.

77 A proper regard, indeed, to one's own profit teaches us to unite in friendship with men, and not with brutes, nor with things whose nature is different from human nature. It teaches us, too, that the same right which they have over us we have over them. Indeed, since the right of any person is limited by his virtue or power, men possess a far greater right over brutes than brutes possess over men. I by no means deny that brutes feel, but I do deny that on this account it is unlawful for us to consult our own profit by using them for our own pleasure and treating them as is most convenient for us, inasmuch as they do not agree in nature with us, and their affects are different from our own.

Spinoza, *Ethics,* IV, Prop. 37, Schol. 1

78 All the different classes of beings whose union form the universe exist in the ideas of God only as so many ordinates of the same curve, the union of which does not allow the placing of others between them, because that would indicate disorder and imperfection. Men are connected with the animals, these with the plants, and these again with the fossils, which will be united in their turn with bodies which the senses and the imagination represent to us as perfectly dead and shapeless. Now since the law of continuity demands that when the essential determinations of a being approach those of another so that likewise accord-

ingly all the properties of the first must gradually approach those of the last, it is necessary that all the orders of natural beings form only one chain, in which the different classes, like so many links, connect so closely the one to the other, that it is impossible for the senses and the imagination to fix the precise point where any one begins or ends.

Leibniz, *Letter to an Unknown Person* (Oct. 16, 1707)

79 There are creatures in the world that have shapes like ours, but are hairy, and want language and reason. There are naturals amongst us that have perfectly our shape, but want reason, and some of them language too. There are creatures, as it is said . . . that, with language and reason and a shape in other things agreeing with ours, have hairy tails; others where the males have no beards, and others where the females have. If it be asked whether these be all *men* or no, all of human species? it is plain, the question refers only to the nominal essence: for those of them to whom the definition of the word man, or the complex idea signified by the name, agrees, are men, and the other not. But if the inquiry be made concerning the supposed real essence; and whether the internal constitution and frame of these several creatures be specifically different, it is wholly impossible for us to answer, no part of that going into our specific idea: only we have reason to think, that where the faculties or outward frame so much differs, the internal constitution is not exactly the same. But what difference in the real internal constitution makes a specific difference it is in vain to inquire; whilst our measures of species be, as they are, only our abstract ideas, which we know; and not that internal constitution, which makes no part of them. Shall the difference of hair only on the skin be a mark of a different internal specific constitution between a changeling and a drill, when they agree in shape, and want of reason and speech? And shall not the want of reason and speech be a sign to us of different real constitutions and species between a changeling and a reasonable man? And so of the rest, if we pretend that distinction of species or sorts is fixedly established by the real frame and secret constitutions of things.

Locke, *Concerning Human Understanding*, Bk. III, VI, 22

80 His Majesty [the King of Brobdignag] in another audience, was at the pains to recapitulate the sum of all I had spoken; compared the questions he made, with the answers I had given; then taking me into his hands, and stroaking me gently, delivered himself in these words, which I shall never forget, nor the manner he spoke them in. "My little friend Grildrig; you have made a most admirable panegyrick upon your country. You have clearly proved that ignorance, idleness, and vice, are the proper ingredients for qualifying a legislator. That laws are best explained, interpreted, and applied by those whose interest and abilities lie in perverting, confounding, and eluding them. I observe among you some lines of an institution, which in its orginal might have been tolerable; but these half erased, and the rest wholly blurred and blotted by corruptions. It doth not appear, from all you have said, how any one perfection is required towards the procurement of any one station among you; much less that men are ennobled on account of their virtue, that priests are advanced for their piety or learning, soldiers for their conduct or valour, judges for their integrity, senators for the love of their country, or counsellors for their wisdom. As for yourself (continued the king) who have spent the greatest part of your life in travelling, I am well disposed to hope you may hitherto have escaped many vices of your country. But, by what I have gathered from your own relation, and the answers I have with much pains wringed and extorted from you, I cannot but conclude the bulk of your natives, to be the most pernicious race of little odious vermin that nature ever suffered to crawl upon the surface of the earth."

Swift, *Gulliver's Travels*, II, 6

81 Know then thyself, presume not God to scan;
The proper study of Mankind is Man.
Plac'd on this isthmus of a middle state,
A being darkly wise, and rudely great:
With too much knowledge for the Sceptic side,
With too much weakness for the Stoic's pride,
He hangs between; in doubt to act, or rest,
In doubt to deem himself a God, or Beast;
In doubt his Mind or Body to prefer,
Born but to die, and reas'ning but to err;
Alike in ignorance, his reason such,
Whether he thinks too little, or too much:
Chaos of Thought and Passion, all confus'd;
Still by himself abus'd, or disabus'd;
Created half to rise, and half to fall;
Great lord of all things, yet a prey to all;
Sole judge of Truth, in endless Error hurl'd:
The glory, jest, and riddle of the world!

Pope, *Essay on Man*, Epistle II, 1

82 Brutes are deprived of the high advantages which we have; but they have some which we have not. They have not our hopes, but they are without our fears; they are subject like us to death, but without knowing it; even most of them are more attentive than we to self-preservation, and do not make so bad a use of their passions.

Man, as a physical being, is like other bodies governed by invariable laws. As an intelligent being, he incessantly transgresses the laws established by God, and changes those of his own instituting. He is left to his private direction, though a limited being, and subject, like all finite intelligences, to ignorance and error: even his imperfect knowledge he loses; and as a sensible creature, he is hurried away by a thousand impetuous passions. Such a being might every instant forget his Creator; God has therefore reminded him of his duty by the laws of religion. Such a being is liable every moment to forget himself; philosophy has provided against this by the laws of morality. Formed to live in society, he might forget his fellow-creatures; legislators have therefore by political and civil laws confined him to his duty.

Montesquieu, *Spirit of Laws*, I, 1

83 What a pitiful, what a sorry thing to have said that animals are machines bereft of understanding and feeling, which perform their operations always in the same way, which learn nothing, perfect nothing, etc.!

What! that bird which makes its nest in a semicircle when it is attaching it to a wall, which builds it in a quarter circle when it is in an angle, and in a circle upon a tree; that bird acts always in the same way? That hunting-dog which you have disciplined for three months, does it not know more at the end of this time than it knew before your lessons? Does the canary to which you teach a tune repeat it at once? do you not spend a considerable time in teaching it? have you not seen that it has made a mistake and that it corrects itself?

Is it because I speak to you, that you judge that I have feeling, memory, ideas? Well, I do not speak to you; you see me going home looking disconsolate, seeking a paper anxiously, opening the desk where I remember having shut it, finding it, reading it joyfully. You judge that I have experienced the feeling of distress and that of pleasure, that I have memory and understanding.

Bring the same judgment to bear on this dog which has lost its master, which has sought him on every road with sorrowful cries, which enters the house agitated, uneasy, which goes down the stairs, up the stairs, from room to room, which at last finds in his study the master it loves, and which shows him its joy by its cries of delight, by its leaps, by its caresses.

Voltaire, *Philosophical Dictionary:* Animals

84 Every animal has ideas, since it has senses; it even combines those ideas in a certain degree; and it is only in degree that man differs, in this respect, from the brute. Some philosophers have even maintained that there is a greater difference between one man and another than between some men and some beasts. It is not, therefore, so much the understanding that constitutes the specific difference between the man and the brute, as the human quality of free-agency. Nature lays her commands on every animal, and the brute obeys her voice. Man receives the same impulse, but

at the same time knows himself at liberty to acquiesce or resist: and it is particularly in his consciousness of this liberty that the spirituality of his soul is displayed. For physics may explain, in some measure, the mechanism of the senses and the formation of ideas; but in the power of willing or rather of choosing, and in the feeling of this power, nothing is to be found but acts which are purely spiritual and wholly inexplicable by the laws of mechanism.

Rousseau, *Origin of Inequality*, I

85 Oh, man! live your own life and you will no longer be wretched. Keep to your appointed place in the order of nature and nothing can tear you from it. Do not kick against the stern law of necessity. . . . Your freedom and your power extend as far and no further than your natural strength; anything more is but slavery, deceit, and trickery.

Rousseau, *Emile*, II

86 *Boswell.* "He [Harris] says plain things in a formal and abstract way, to be sure: but his method is good: for to have clear notions upon any subject, we must have recourse to analytick arrangement." *Johnson.* "Sir, it is what everybody does, whether they will or no. But sometimes things may be made darker by definition. I see a *cow,* I define her, *Animal quadrupes ruminans cornutum.* But a goat ruminates, and a cow may have no horns. *Cow* is plainer." *Boswell.* "I think Dr. Franklin's definition of *Man* a good one—'A tool-making animal.' " *Johnson.* "But many a man never made a tool; and suppose a man without arms, he could not make a tool."

Boswell, *Life of Johnson (Apr. 7, 1778)*

87 Nobody ever saw a dog make a fair and deliberate exchange of one bone for another with another dog. Nobody ever saw one animal by its gestures and natural cries signify to another, this is mine, that yours; I am willing to give this for that. When an animal wants to obtain something either of a man or of another animal, it has no other means of persuasion but to gain the favour of those whose service it requires. A puppy fawns upon its dam, and a spaniel endeavours by a thousand attractions to engage the attention of its master who is at dinner, when it wants to be fed by him. Man sometimes uses the same arts with his brethren, and when he has no other means of engaging them to act according to his inclinations, endeavours by every servile and fawning attention to obtain their good will.

Adam Smith, *Wealth of Nations*, I, 2

88 Man and generally any rational being *exists* as an end in himself, *not merely as a means* to be arbitrarily used by this or that will, but in all his actions, whether they concern himself or other rational

beings, must be always regarded at the same time as an end.

Kant, *Fundamental Principles of the Metaphysic of Morals*, II

89 Man is a being who, as belonging to the world of sense, has wants, and so far his reason has an office which it cannot refuse, namely, to attend to the interest of his sensible nature, and to form practical maxims, even with a view to the happiness of this life, and if possible even to that of a future. But he is not so completely an animal as to be indifferent to what reason says on its own account, and to use it merely as an instrument for the satisfaction of his wants as a sensible being. For the possession of reason would not raise his worth above that of the brutes, if it is to serve him only for the same purpose that instinct serves in them; it would in that case be only a particular method which nature had employed to equip man for the same ends for which it has qualified brutes, without qualifying him for any higher purpose.

Kant, *Critique of Practical Reason*, Pt. I, I, 2

90 If we go through the whole of nature, we do not find in it, as nature, any being capable of laying claim to the distinction of being the final end of creation. In fact it may even be proved *a priori* that what might do perhaps as an *ultimate end* for nature, endowing it with any conceivable qualities or properties we choose, could nevertheless in its character of a natural thing never be a final end.

Looking to the vegetable kingdom, we might at first be induced by the boundless fertility with which it spreads itself abroad upon almost every soil to think that it should be regarded as a mere product of the mechanism which nature displays in its formations in the mineral kingdom. But a more intimate knowledge of its indescribably wise organization precludes us from entertaining this view, and drives us to ask: For what purpose do these forms of life exist? Suppose we reply: For the animal kingdom, which is thus provided with the means of sustenance, so that it has been enabled to spread over the face of the earth in such a manifold variety of genera. The question again arises: For what purpose then do these herbivora exist? The answer would be something like this: For the carnivora, which are only able to live on what itself has animal life. At last we get down to the question: What is the end and purpose of these and all the preceding natural kingdoms? For man, we say, and the multifarious uses to which his intelligence teaches him to put all these forms of life. He is the ultimate end of creation here upon earth, because he is the one and only being upon it that is able to form a conception of ends and, from an aggregate of things purposively fashioned, to construct by the aid of his reason a system of ends.

Kant, *Critique of Teleological Judgement*, 82

91 There is a judgement which even the commonest understanding finds irresistible when it reflects upon the existence of the things in the world and the real existence of the world itself. It is the verdict that all the manifold forms of life, co-ordinated though they may be with the greatest art and concatenated with the utmost variety of final adaptations, and even the entire complex that embraces their numerous systems, incorrectly called *worlds*, would all exist for nothing, if man, or rational beings of some sort, were not to be found in their midst. Without man, in other words, the whole of creation would be a mere wilderness, a thing in vain, and have no final end.

Kant, *Critique of Teleological Judgement*, 86

92 If there is to be a *final end* at all, which reason must assign *a priori*, then it can only be *man*—or any rational being in the world—*subject to moral laws*. For—and this is the verdict of everyone—if the world only consisted of lifeless beings, or even consisted partly of living, but yet irrational beings, the existence of such a world would have no worth whatever, because there would exist in it no being with the least conception of what worth is.

Kant, *Critique of Teleological Judgement*, 87

93 *Mephistopheles.* Since you, O Lord, once more draw near
And ask how all is getting on, and you
Were ever well content to see me here,
You see me also midst your retinue.
Forgive, fine speeches I can never make,
Though all the circle look on me with scorn;
Pathos from me would make your sides with laughter shake,
Had you not laughter long ago forsworn.
Of suns and worlds I've naught to say worth mention.
How men torment them claims my whole attention.
Earth's little god retains his same old stamp and ways
And is as singular as on the first of days.
A little better would he live, poor wight,
Had you not given him that gleam of heavenly light.
He calls it Reason, only to pollute
Its use by being brutaler than any brute.
It seems to me, if you'll allow, Your Grace,
He's like a grasshopper, that long-legged race
That's made to fly and flying spring
And in the grass to sing the same old thing.
If in the grass he always were reposing!
But in each filthy heap he keeps on nosing.

Goethe, *Faust*, Prologue in Heaven, 271

94 If a man is not rising upwards to be an angel, depend upon it, he is sinking downwards to be a

devil. He cannot stop at the beast. The most savage of men are not beasts; they are worse, a great deal worse.

Coleridge, *Table Talk (Aug. 30, 1833)*

95 Oh, man! thou feeble tenant of an hour,
Debased by slavery, or corrupt by power,
Who knows thee well must quit thee with disgust,
Degraded mass of animated dust!
Thy love is lust, thy friendship all a cheat,
Thy smiles hypocrisy, thy words deceit!
By nature vile, ennobled but by name,
Each kindred brute might bid thee blush for
    shame.

Byron, *Inscription on the
Monument of a Newfoundland Dog*

96 The lower animals are the truly incomprehensible. A *man* cannot by imagination or conception enter into the nature of a *dog,* whatever resemblance he himself might have to it; it remains something altogether alien to him.

Hegel, *Philosophy of History,* Pt. I, III, 3

97 Man, finite when regarded *for himself,* is yet at the same time the image of God and a fountain of infinity *in himself.* He is the object of his own existence—has in himself an infinite value, an eternal destiny.

Hegel, *Philosophy of History,* Pt. III, III, 2

98 One might say with truth, Mankind are the devils of the earth, and the animals the souls they torment.

Schopenhauer, *Christian System*

99 Man is at bottom a wild and terrible animal. We know him only as what we call civilization has tamed and trained him; hence we are alarmed by the occasional breaking out of his true nature. But whenever the locks and chains of law and order are cast off, and anarchy comes in, he shows himself for what he really is.

Schopenhauer, *Parerga und Paralipomena,* II

100 A man is a god in ruin.

Emerson, *Nature,* VIII

101 Not in nature but in man is all the beauty and worth he sees. The world is very empty, and is indebted to this gilding, exalting soul for all its pride.

Emerson, *Spiritual Laws*

102 Man is the end of nature; nothing so easily organizes itself in every part of the universe as he; no moss, no lichen is so easily born; and he takes along with him and puts out from himself the whole apparatus of society and condition *extempore,* as an army encamps in a desert, and where all was just now blowing sand, creates a white city in an hour, a government, a market, a place for feasting, for conversation, and for love.

Emerson, *The Conservative*

103 Men may seem detestable as joint-stock companies and nations; knaves, fools, and murderers there may be; men may have mean and meagre faces; but man, in the ideal, is so noble and so sparkling, such a grand and glowing creature, that over any ignominious blemish in him all his fellows should run to throw their costliest robes. That immaculate manliness we feel within ourselves—so far within us, that it remains intact though all the outer character seem gone—bleeds with keenest anguish at the undraped spectacle of a valour-ruined man. Nor can piety itself, at such a shameful sight, completely stifle her upbraidings against the permitting stars. But this august dignity I treat of, is not the dignity of kings and robes, but that abounding dignity which has no robed investiture. Thou shalt see it shining in the arm that wields a pick or drives a spike; that democratic dignity which, on all hands, radiates without end from God Himself! The great God absolute! The centre and circumference of all democracy! His omnipresence, our divine equality!

Melville, *Moby Dick,* XXVI

104 There is no folly of the beasts of the earth which is not infinitely outdone by the madness of men.

Melville, *Moby Dick,* LXXXVII

105 Man's capacities have never been measured; nor are we to judge of what he can do by any precedents, so little has been tried.

Thoreau, *Walden:* Economy

106 We are conscious of an animal in us, which awakens in proportion as our higher nature slumbers. It is reptile and sensual, and perhaps cannot be wholly expelled; like the worms which, even in life and health, occupy our bodies. Possibly we may withdraw from it, but never change its nature. I fear that it may enjoy a certain health of its own; that we may be well, yet not pure. The other day I picked up the lower jaw of a hog, with white and sound teeth and tusks, which suggested that there was an animal health and vigor distinct from the spiritual. This creature succeeded by other means than temperance and purity. 'That in which men differ from brute beasts,' says Mencius, 'is a thing very inconsiderable; the common herd lose it very soon; superior men preserve it carefully.' Who knows what sort of life would result if we had attained to purity? If I knew so wise a man as could teach me purity I would go to seek him forthwith. 'A command over our passions, and over the external senses of the body, and good acts, are declared by the Ved to be indispensable in the mind's approximation to God.' Yet the spirit can for the time pervade and control every member and function of the body, and transmute

what in form is the grossest sensuality into purity and devotion. The generative energy, which, when we are loose, dissipates and makes us unclean, when we are continent invigorates and inspires us. Chastity is the flowering of man; and what are called Genius, Heroism, Holiness, and the like, are but various fruits which succeed it. Man flows at once to God when the channel of purity is open. By turns our purity inspires and our impurity casts us down. He is blessed who is assured that the animal is dying out in him day by day, and the divine being established. Perhaps there is none but has cause for shame on account of the inferior and brutish nature to which he is allied. I fear that we are such gods or demigods only as fauns and satyrs, the divine allied to beasts, the creatures of appetite, and that, to some extent, our very life is our disgrace.

Thoreau, *Walden:* Higher Laws

107 I think I could turn and live with animals, they're
    so placid and self-contain'd,
    I stand and look at them long and long.

They do not sweat and whine about their condition,
They do not lie awake in the dark and weep for
    their sins,
They do not make me sick discussing their duty to
    God,
Not one is dissatisfied, not one is demented with
    the mania of owning things,
Not one kneels to another, nor to his kind that
    lived thousands of years ago,
Not one is respectable or unhappy over the whole
    earth.

Whitman, *Song of Myself,* XXXII

108 Man in the rudest state in which he now exists is the most dominant animal that has ever appeared on this earth. He has spread more widely than any other highly organised form: and all others have yielded before him. He manifestly owes this immense superiority to his intellectual faculties, to his social habits, which lead him to aid and defend his fellows, and to his corporeal structure. The supreme importance of these characters has been proved by the final arbitrament of the battle for life. Through his powers of intellect, articulate language has been evolved; and on this his wonderful advancement has mainly depended. . . . He has invented and is able to use various weapons, tools, traps, etc., with which he defends himself, kills or catches prey, and otherwise obtains food. He has made rafts or canoes for fishing or crossing over to neighbouring fertile islands. He has discovered the art of making fire, by which hard and stringy roots can be rendered digestible, and poisonous roots or herbs innocuous. This discovery of fire, probably the greatest ever made by man, excepting language, dates from before the dawn of history. These several inventions, by which man in the rudest state has become so preeminent, are the direct results of the development of his powers of observation, memory, curiosity, imagination, and reason.

Darwin, *Descent of Man,* I, 2

109 Most of the more complex emotions are common to the higher animals and ourselves. Every one has seen how jealous a dog is of his master's affection, if lavished on any other creature; and I have observed the same fact with monkeys. This shews that animals not only love, but have desire to be loved. Animals manifestly feel emulation. They love approbation or praise; and a dog carrying a basket for his master exhibits in a high degree self-complacency or pride. There can, I think, be no doubt that a dog feels shame, as distinct from fear, and something very like modesty when begging too often for food. A great dog scorns the snarling of a little dog, and this may be called magnanimity. Several observers have stated that monkeys certainly dislike being laughed at; and they sometimes invent imaginary offences. . . . Dogs shew what may be fairly called a sense of humour, as distinct from mere play; if a bit of stick or other such object be thrown to one, he will often carry it away for a short distance; and then squatting down with it on the ground close before him, will wait until his master comes quite close to take it away. The dog will then seize it and rush away in triumph, repeating the same manœuvre, and evidently enjoying the practical joke.

Darwin, *Descent of Man,* I, 3

110 There can be no doubt that the difference between the mind of the lowest man and that of the highest animal is immense. An anthropomorphous ape, if he could take a dispassionate view of his own case, would admit that though he could form an artful plan to plunder a garden—though he could use stones for fighting or for breaking open nuts, yet that the thought of fashioning a stone into a tool was quite beyond his scope. Still less, as he would admit, could he follow out a train of metaphysical reasoning, or solve a mathematical problem, or reflect on God, or admire a grand natural scene. Some apes, however, would probably declare that they could and did admire the beauty of the coloured skin and fur of their partners in marriage. They would admit, that though they could make other apes understand by cries some of their perceptions and simpler wants, the notion of expressing definite ideas by definite sounds had never crossed their minds. They might insist that they were ready to aid their fellow-apes of the same troop in many ways, to risk their lives for them, and to take charge of their orphans; but they would be forced to acknowledge that disinterested love for all living creatures, the most noble attribute of man, was quite beyond their com-

prehension. Nevertheless the difference in mind between man and the higher animals, great as it is, certainly is one of degree and not of kind.

Darwin, *Descent of Man*, I, 4

111 The great break in the organic chain between man and his nearest allies, which cannot be bridged over by any extinct or living species, has often been advanced as a grave objection to the belief that man is descended from some lower form; but this objection will not appear of much weight to those who, from general reasons, believe in the general principle of evolution. Breaks often occur in all parts of the series, some being wide, sharp and defined, others less so in various degrees; as between the orang and its nearest allies—between the Tarsius and the other Lemuridæ—between the elephant, and in a more striking manner between the Ornithorhynchus or Echidna, and all other mammals. But these breaks depend merely on the number of related forms which have become extinct. At some future period, not very distant as measured by centuries, the civilised races of man will almost certainly exterminate, and replace, the savage races throughout the world. At the same time the anthropomorphous apes, as Professor Schaaffhausen has remarked, will no doubt be exterminated. The break between man and his nearest allies will then be wider, for it will intervene between man in a more civilised state, as we may hope, even than the Caucasian, and some ape as low as a baboon, instead of as now between the negro or Australian and the gorilla.

Darwin, *Descent of Man*, I, 6

112 Man may be excused for feeling some pride at having risen, though not through his own exertions, to the very summit of the organic scale; and the fact of his having thus risen, instead of having been aboriginally placed there, may give him hope for a still higher destiny in the distant future. But we are not here concerned with hopes or fears, only with the truth as far as our reason permits us to discover it; and I have given the evidence to the best of my ability. We must, however, acknowledge, as it seems to me, that man with all his noble qualities, with sympathy which feels for the most debased, with benevolence which extends not only to other men but to the humblest living creature, with his god-like intellect which has penetrated into the movements and constitution of the solar system—with all these exalted powers—Man still bears in his bodily frame the indelible stamp of his lowly origin.

Darwin, *Descent of Man*, III, 21

113 The question of questions for mankind—the problem which underlies all others, and is more deeply interesting than any other—is the ascertainment of the place which man occupies in nature and of his relations to the universe of things. Whence our race has come; what are the limits of our power over nature, and of nature's power over us; to what goal we are tending; are the problems which present themselves anew and with undiminished interest to every man born into the world.

T. H. Huxley, *Relations of Man to the Lower Animals*

114 Our reverence for the nobility of manhood will not be lessened by the knowledge that man is, in substance and in structure, one with the brutes; for, he alone possesses the marvellous endowment of intelligible and rational speech, whereby, in the secular period of his existence, he has slowly accumulated and organized the experience which is almost wholly lost with the cessation of every individual life in other animals; so that, now, he stands raised upon it as on a mountain top, far above the level of his humble fellows, and transfigured from his grosser nature by reflecting, here and there, a ray from the infinite source of truth.

T. H. Huxley, *Relations of Man to the Lower Animals*

115 Man is in the most literal sense of the word a *zoon politikon*, not only a social animal, but an animal which can develop into an individual only in society.

Marx, *Contribution to the Criticism of Political Economy*, Appendix, 1

116 Human nature is not a machine to be built after a model, and set to do exactly the work prescribed for it, but a tree, which requires to grow and develop itself on all sides, according to the tendency of the inward forces which make it a living thing.

Mill, *On Liberty*, III

117 O man, strange composite of Heaven and earth!
  Majesty dwarf'd to baseness! fragrant flower
  Running to poisonous seed! and seeming worth
    Cloaking corruption! weakness mastering
      power!

Newman, *The Dream of Gerontius*

118 A bee settling on a flower has stung a child. And the child is afraid of bees and declares that bees exist to sting people. A poet admires the bee sucking from the chalice of a flower and says it exists to suck the fragrance of flowers. A beekeeper, seeing the bee collect pollen from flowers and carry it to the hive, says that it exists to gather honey. Another beekeeper who has studied the life of the hive more closely says that the bee gathers pollen dust to feed the young bees and rear a queen, and that it exists to perpetuate its race. A botanist notices that the bee flying with the pollen of a male flower to a pistil fertilizes the latter, and sees in this the purpose of the bee's existence. Another, observing the migration of plants, notices that the

bee helps in this work, and may say that in this lies the purpose of the bee. But the ultimate purpose of the bee is not exhausted by the first, the second, or any of the processes the human mind can discern. The higher the human intellect rises in the discovery of these purposes, the more obvious it becomes that the ultimate purpose is beyond our comprehension.

All that is accessible to man is the relation of the life of the bee to other manifestations of life. And so it is with the purpose of historic characters and nations.

Tolstoy, *War and Peace,* I Epilogue, IV

119 To imagine a man perfectly free and not subject to the law of inevitability, we must imagine him all alone, *beyond space, beyond time,* and *free from dependence on cause.*

Tolstoy, *War and Peace,* II Epilogue, X

120 Man is the only animal that blushes. Or needs to.

Mark Twain, *Pudd'nhead Wilson's New Calendar,* XXVII

121 I'm quite sure that . . . I have no race prejudices, and I think I have no color prejudices nor creed prejudices. Indeed, I know it. I can stand any society. All I care to know is that a man is a human being—that is enough for me; he can't be any worse.

Mark Twain, *Concerning the Jews*

122 Man is absolutely not the crown of creation: every creature stands beside him at the same stage of perfection.

Nietzsche, *Antichrist,* XIV

123 Man is a rope stretched between the animal and the Superman—a rope over an abyss.

Nietzsche, *Thus Spake Zarathustra,* Prologue, 4

124 The earth, said he, hath a skin; and this skin hath diseases. One of these diseases, for example, is called "man."

Nietzsche, *Thus Spake Zarathustra,* II, 40

125 Man is born with a tendency to do more things than he has ready-made arrangements for in his nerve-centres. Most of the performances of other animals are automatic. But in him the number of them is so enormous, that most of them must be the fruit of painful study. If practice did not make perfect, nor habit economize the expense of nervous and muscular energy, he would therefore be in a sorry plight.

William James, *Psychology,* IV

126 The whole story of our dealings with the lower wild animals is the history of our taking advantage of the way in which they judge of everything by its mere label, as it were, so as to ensnare or kill

them. Nature, in them, has left matters in this rough way, and made them act *always* in the manner which would be *oftenest* right. There are more worms unattached to hooks than impaled upon them; therefore, on the whole, says Nature to her fishy children, bite at *every* worm and take your chances. But as her children get higher, and their lives more precious, she reduces the risks. Since what seems to be the same object may be now a genuine food and now a bait; since in gregarious species each individual may prove to be either the friend or the rival, according to the circumstances, of another; since any entirely unknown object may be fraught with weal or woe, *Nature implants contrary impulses to act on many classes of things,* and leaves it to slight alterations in the conditions of the individual case to decide which impulse shall carry the day. Thus, greediness and suspicion, curiosity and timidity, coyness and desire, bashfulness and vanity, sociability and pugnacity, seem to shoot over into each other as quickly, and to remain in as unstable equilibrium, in the higher birds and mammals as in man. They are all impulses, congenital, blind at first, and productive of motor reactions of a rigorously determinate sort. *Each one of them, then, is an instinct,* as instincts are commonly defined. *But they contradict each other—* "experience" in each particular opportunity of application usually deciding the issue. *The animal that exhibits them loses the "instinctive" demeanor and appears to lead a life of hesitation and choice, an intellectual life; not, however, because he has no instincts—rather because he has so many that they block each other's path.*

William James, *Psychology,* XXIV

127 In many respects man is the most ruthlessly ferocious of beasts. As with all gregarious animals, "two souls," as Faust says, "dwell within his breast," the one of sociability and helpfulness, the other of jealousy and antagonism to his mates. Though in a general way he cannot live without them, yet, as regards certain individuals, it often falls out that he cannot live with them either. Constrained to be a member of a tribe, he still has a right to decide, as far as in him lies, of which other members the tribe shall consist. Killing off a few obnoxious ones may often better the chances of those that remain. And killing off a neighboring tribe from whom no good thing comes, but only competition, may materially better the lot of the whole tribe. Hence the gory cradle, the *bellum omnium contra omnes,* in which our race was reared; hence the fickleness of human ties, the ease with which the foe of yesterday becomes the ally of to-day, the friend of to-day the enemy of to-morrow; hence the fact that we, the lineal representatives of the successful enactors of one scene of slaughter after another, must, whatever more pacific virtues we may also possess, still carry about with us, ready at any moment to burst into flame, the

smouldering and sinister traits of character by means of which they lived through so many massacres, harming others, but themselves unharmed.

William James, *Psychology*, XXIV

128 Man is simply the most formidable of all the beasts of prey, and, indeed, the only one that preys systematically on its own species.

William James, *Remarks at the Peace Banquet (Oct. 7, 1904)*

129 The rich are instinctively crying "Let us eat and drink; for tomorrow we die," and the poor, "How long, O Lord, how long?" But the pitiless reply still is that God helps those who help themselves. This does not mean that if Man cannot find the remedy no remedy will be found. The power that produced Man when the monkey was not up to the mark, can produce a higher creature than Man if Man does not come up to the mark. What it means is that if Man is to be saved, Man must save himself. There seems no compelling reason why he should be saved. He is by no means an ideal creature. At his present best many of his ways are so unpleasant that they are unmentionable in polite society, and so painful that they are compelled to pretend that pain is often a good. Nature holds no brief for the human experiment: it must stand or fall by its results. If Man will not serve, Nature will try another experiment.

Shaw, *Back to Methuselah*, Pref.

130 Man differs from the lower animals because he preserves his past experiences. What happened in the past is lived again in memory. About what goes on today hangs a cloud of thoughts concerning similar things undergone in bygone days. With the animals, an experience perishes as it happens, and each new doing or suffering stands alone. But man lives in a world where each occurrence is charged with echoes and reminiscences of what has gone before, where each event is a reminder of other things. Hence he lives not, like the beasts of the field, in a world of merely physical things but in a world of signs and symbols. A stone is not merely hard, a thing into which one bumps; but it is a monument of a deceased ancestor. A flame is not merely something which warms or burns, but is a symbol of the enduring life of the household, of the abiding source of cheer, nourishment and shelter to which man returns from his casual wanderings. Instead of being a quick fork of fire which may sting and hurt, it is the hearth at which one worships and for which one fights. And all this which marks the difference between bestiality and humanity, between culture and merely physical nature, is because man remembers, preserving and recording his experiences.

Dewey, *Reconstruction in Philosophy*, I

131 When a philosopher explains to us that it is reason, present in each of us, which constitutes the dignity of man . . . we must take care to know what we mean. That reason is the distinguishing mark of man no one will deny. That it is a thing of superior value, in the sense in which a fine work of art is indeed valuable, will also be granted. But we must explain how it is that its orders are absolute and why they are obeyed. Reason can only put forward reasons, which we are apparently always at liberty to counter with other reasons. Let us not then merely assert that reason, present in each of us, compels our respect and commands our obedience by virtue of its paramount value. We must add that there are, behind reason, the men who have made mankind divine, and who have thus stamped a divine character on reason, which is the essential attribute of man. It is these men who draw us towards an ideal society, while we yield to the pressure of the real one.

Bergson, *Two Sources of Morality and Religion*, I

132 What is meant here by saying that existence precedes essence? It means that, first of all, man exists, turns up, appears on the scene, and, only afterwards, defines himself. If man, as the existentialist conceives him, is indefinable, it is because at first he is nothing. Only afterward will he be something, and he himself will have made what he will be. Thus, there is no human nature, since there is no God to conceive it. Not only is man what he conceives himself to be, but he is also only what he wills himself to be after this thrust toward existence.

Sartre, *Existentialism*

1.2 | *The Human Condition*

This section contains many quotations that express general views of human life. The operative word here is "general." We have tried to exclude anything that does not comment on the state of man in general terms, that does not offer general recommendations or prescriptions for the conduct of life, or that does not deal generally with what might be called "the phenomenon of man."

The general descriptions of that phenomenon include portrayals of human nature in terms of its distinctive traits, discussions of the range of human abilities or capacities, comments on man's propensities and proclivities, and enumerations of human traits.

The quotations assembled here are not exclusively descriptive of man's condition.

Some evaluate it, varying from self-pity at one extreme to self-satisfaction at the other. Still another line of passages raises general questions about the difficulties of living like a human being; these are accompanied by quotations that offer counsel or guidance for facing up to the trials and tribulations of human life.

Some of the statements collected here might have been placed in the preceding section, dealing with the grandeur and misery of man, and some in Section 1.8 on LIFE AND DEATH: THE FEAR OF DEATH. They are here because the terms in which they are stated are identical with terms that are central to quotations that belong here and nowhere else.

---

1 Man that is born of a woman is of few days, and full of trouble.
　He cometh forth like a flower, and is cut down: he fleeth also as a shadow, and continueth not.
Job 14:1–2

2 Lord, make me to know mine end, and the measure of my days, what it is; that I may know how frail I am.
　Behold, thou hast made my days as an handbreadth; and mine age is as nothing before thee: verily every man at his best state is altogether vanity. Selah.
　Surely every man walketh in a vain shew: surely they are disquieted in vain: he heapeth up riches, and knoweth not who shall gather them. . . .
　When thou with rebukes dost correct man for iniquity, thou makest his beauty to consume away like a moth: surely every man is vanity.
Psalm 39:4–11

3 *Apollo.*　　　　　　　　　　Insignificant mortals, who are as leaves are, and now flourish and grow warm
with life, and feed on what the ground gives, but then again
fade away and are dead.
Homer, *Iliad*, XXI, 463

4 *Odysseus.* The cruel belly, can you hide its ache?
How many bitter days it brings! Long ships
with good stout planks athwart—would fighters rig them
to ride the barren sea, except for hunger?
Homer, *Odyssey*, XVII, 287

5 Oh! would that Nature had denied me birth
Midst this fifth race, this iron age of earth;
That long before within the grave I lay,
Or long hereafter could behold the day!
Corrupt the race, with toils and griefs oppress'd,
Nor day nor night can yield a pause of rest:
Still do the gods a weight of care bestow,
Though still some good is mingled with the woe.
Jove on this race of many-languaged man
Speeds the swift ruin, which but slow began;
For scarcely spring they to the light of day,
E'er age untimely strews their temples gray.
No fathers in the sons their features trace;
The sons reflect no more the father's face:
The most with kindness greets his guest no more;
And friends and brethren love not as of yore.
Reckless of Heaven's revenge, the sons behold
The hoary parents wax too swiftly old,
And impious point the keen dishonouring tongue,
With hard reproofs, and bitter mockeries hung;
Nor grateful in declining age repay
The nurturing fondness of their better day.

22

Now man's right hand is law; for spoil they wait,
And lay their mutual cities desolate.
Unhonour'd he, by whom his oath is fear'd,
Nor are the good beloved, the just revered.
With favour graced, the evil doer stands,
Nor curbs with shame nor equity his hands;
With crooked slanders wounds the virtuous man,
And stamps with perjury what hate began.
Lo! ill-rejoicing Envy, wing'd with lies,
Scattering calumnious rumours as she flies,
The steps of miserable men pursue,
With haggard aspect, blasting to the view:
Till those fair forms, in snowy raiment bright,
Quit the broad earth, and heavenward soar from
   sight:
Justice and Modesty, from mortals driven,
Rise to th' immortal family of heaven:
Dread sorrows to forsaken man remain;
No cure of ills; no remedy of pain.

Hesiod, *Works and Days*

6 *Cassandra.* Alas, poor men, their destiny. When all
   goes well
a shadow will overthrow it. If it be unkind
one stroke of a wet sponge wipes all the picture
   out;
and that is far the most unhappy thing of all.

Aeschylus, *Agamemnon*, 1327

7 *Amasis.* My wish for myself and for those whom I
love is to be now successful, and now to meet with
a check; thus passing through life amid alternate
good and ill, rather than with perpetual good fortune. For never yet did I hear tell of anyone succeeding in all his undertakings, who did not meet
with calamity at last, and come to utter ruin.

Herodotus, *History*, III, 40

8 When a child is born [to the Trausi] all its kindred
sit round about it in a circle and weep for the
woes it will have to undergo now that it is come
into the world, making mention of every ill that
falls to the lot of humankind; when, on the other
hand, a man has died, they bury him with laughter and rejoicings, and say that now he is free
from a host of sufferings, and enjoys the completest happiness.

Herodotus, *History*, V, 4

9 And now, as he looked and saw the whole Hellespont covered with the vessels of his fleet, and all
the shore and every plain about Abydos as full as
possible of men, Xerxes congratulated himself on
his good fortune; but after a little while he wept.
   Then Artabanus, the king's uncle (the same
who at the first so freely spake his mind to the
king, and advised him not to lead his army
against Greece), when he heard that Xerxes was
in tears, went to him, and said:—
   "How different, sire, is what thou art now
doing, from what thou didst a little while ago!

Then thou didst congratulate thyself; and now,
behold! thou weepest."
   "There came upon me," replied he, "a sudden
pity, when I thought of the shortness of man's life,
and considered that of all this host, so numerous
as it is, not one will be alive when a hundred years
are gone by."

Herodotus, *History*, VII, 45–46

10 *Chorus.* Not to be born surpasses thought and
   speech.
The second best is to have seen the light
And then to go back quickly whence we came.
The feathery follies of his youth once over,
What trouble is beyond the range of man?
What heavy burden will he not endure?
Jealousy, faction, quarreling, and battle—
The bloodiness of war, the grief of war.
And in the end he comes to strengthless age,
Abhorred by all men, without company,
Unfriended in that uttermost twilight
Where he must live with every bitter thing.

Sophocles, *Oedipus at Colonus*, 1224

11 *Orestes.* Alas,
we look for good on earth and cannot recognize it
when met, since all our human heritage runs
   mongrel.
At times I have seen descendants of the noblest
   family
grow worthless though the cowards had courageous sons;
inside the souls of wealthy men bleak famine lives
while minds of stature struggle trapped in starving
   bodies.
   How then can man distinguish man, what test
   can he use?
the test of wealth? that measure means poverty of
   mind;
of poverty? the pauper owns one thing, the sickness
of his condition, a compelling teacher of evil;
by nerve in war? yet who, when a spear is cast
   across
his face, will stand to witness his companion's
   courage?
We can only toss our judgments random on the
   wind.

Euripides, *Electra*, 367

12 Someone will say: Yes, Socrates, but cannot you
hold your tongue, and then you may go into a
foreign city, and no one will interfere with you?
Now I have great difficulty in making you [men of
Athens] understand my answer to this. For if I tell
you that to do as you say would be a disobedience
to the God, and therefore that I cannot hold my
tongue, you will not believe that I am serious; and
if I say again that daily to discourse about virtue,
and of those other things about which you hear
me examining myself and others, is the greatest

good of man, and that the unexamined life is not worth living, you are still less likely to believe me. Yet I say what is true, although a thing of which it is hard for me to persuade you.

Plato, *Apology,* 37B

13 *Socrates.* And now, I said, let me show in a figure how far our nature is enlightened or unenlightened:—Behold! human beings living in an underground den, which has a mouth open towards the light and reaching all along the den; here they have been from their childhood, and have their legs and necks chained so that they cannot move, and can only see before them, being prevented by the chains from turning round their heads. Above and behind them a fire is blazing at a distance, and between the fire and the prisoners there is a raised way; and you [Glaucon] will see, if you look, a low wall built along the way, like the screen which marionette players have in front of them, over which they show the puppets.

I see.

And do you see, I said, men passing along the wall carrying all sorts of vessels, and statues and figures of animals made of wood and stone and various materials, which appear over the wall? Some of them are talking, others silent.

You have shown me a strange image, and they are strange prisoners.

Like ourselves, I replied; and they see only their own shadows, the shadows of one another, which the fire throws on the opposite wall of the cave?

True, he said; how could they see anything but the shadows if they were never allowed to move their heads?

And of the objects which are being carried in like manner they would only see the shadows?

Yes, he said.

And if they were able to converse with one another, would they not suppose that they were naming what was actually before them?

Very true.

And suppose further that the prison had an echo which came from the other side, would they not be sure to fancy when one of the passers-by spoke that the voice which they heard came from the passing shadow?

No question, he replied.

To them, I said, the truth would be literally nothing but the shadows of the images.

That is certain.

And now look again, and see what will naturally follow if the prisoners are released and disabused of their error. At first, when any of them is liberated and compelled suddenly to stand up and turn his neck round and walk and look towards the light, he will suffer sharp pains; the glare will distress him, and he will be unable to see the realities of which in his former state he had seen the shadows; and then conceive some one saying to

him, that what he saw before was an illusion, but that now, when he is approaching nearer to being and his eye is turned towards more real existence, he has a clearer vision—what will be his reply? And you may further imagine that his instructor is pointing to the objects as they pass and requiring him to name them—will he not be perplexed? Will he not fancy that the shadows which he formerly saw are truer than the objects which are now shown to him?

Far truer.

And if he is compelled to look straight at the light, will he not have a pain in his eyes which will make him turn away to take refuge in the objects of vision which he can see, and which he will conceive to be in reality clearer than the things which are now being shown to him?

True, he said.

And suppose once more, that he is reluctantly dragged up a steep and rugged ascent, and held fast until he is forced into the presence of the sun himself, is he not likely to be pained and irritated? When he approaches the light his eyes will be dazzled, and he will not be able to see anything at all of what are now called realities.

Not all in a moment, he said.

He will require to grow accustomed to the sight of the upper world. And first he will see the shadows best, next the reflections of men and other objects in the water, and then the objects themselves; then he will gaze upon the light of the moon and the stars and the spangled heaven; and he will see the sky and the stars by night better than the sun or the light of the sun by day?

Certainly.

Last of all he will be able to see the sun, and not mere reflections of him in the water, but he will see him in his own proper place, and not in another; and he will contemplate him as he is.

Certainly.

He will then proceed to argue that this is he who gives the season and the years, and is the guardian of all that is in the visible world, and in a certain way the cause of all things which he and his fellows have been accustomed to behold?

Clearly, he said, he would first see the sun and then reason about him.

And when he remembered his old habitation, and the wisdom of the den and his fellow-prisoners, do you not suppose that he would felicitate himself on the change, and pity them?

Certainly, he would.

And if they were in the habit of conferring honours among themselves on those who were quickest to observe the passing shadows and to remark which of them went before, and which followed after, and which were together; and who were therefore best able to draw conclusions as to the future, do you think that he would care for such honours and glories, or envy the possessors of them? Would he not say with Homer,

Better to be the poor servant of a poor master,

and to endure anything, rather than think as they do and live after their manner?

Yes, he said, I think that he would rather suffer anything than entertain these false notions and live in this miserable manner.

Imagine once more, I said, such an one coming suddenly out of the sun to be replaced in his old situation; would he not be certain to have his eyes full of darkness?

To be sure, he said.

And if there were a contest, and he had to compete in measuring the shadows with the prisoners who had never moved out of the den, while his sight was still weak, and before his eyes had become steady (and the time which would be needed to acquire this new habit of sight might be very considerable), would he not be ridiculous? Men would say of him that up he went and down he came without his eyes; and that it was better not even to think of ascending; and if anyone tried to loose another and lead him up to the light, let them only catch the offender, and they would put him to death.

No question, he said.

This entire allegory, I said, you may now append, dear Glaucon, to the previous argument; the prison-house is the world of sight, the light of the fire is the sun, and you will not misapprehend me if you interpret the journey upwards to be the ascent of the soul into the intellectual world according to my poor belief, which, at your desire, I have expressed—whether rightly or wrongly God knows. But, whether true or false, my opinion is that in the world of knowledge the idea of good appears last of all, and is seen only with an effort; and, when seen, is also inferred to be the universal author of all things beautiful and right, parent of light and of the lord of light in this visible world, and the immediate source of reason and truth in the intellectual; and that this is the power upon which he who would act rationally either in public or private life must have his eye fixed.

I agree, he said, as far as I am able to understand you.

Moreover, I said, you must not wonder that those who attain to this beatific vision are unwilling to descend to human affairs; for their souls are ever hastening into the upper world where they desire to dwell; which desire of theirs is very natural, if our allegory may be trusted.

Plato, *Republic*, VII, 514A

14 It is sweet, when on the great sea the winds trouble its waters, to behold from land another's deep distress; not that it is a pleasure and delight that any should be afflicted, but because it is sweet to see from what evils you are yourself exempt. It is sweet also to look upon the mighty struggles of war arrayed along the plains without sharing yourself in the danger. But nothing is more welcome that to hold the lofty and serene positions well fortified by the learning of the wise, from which you may look down upon others and see them wandering all abroad and going astray in their search for the path of life, see the contest among them of intellect, the rivalry of birth, the striving night and day with surpassing effort to struggle up to the summit of power and be masters of the world.

O miserable minds of men! O blinded breasts! in what darkness of life and in how great dangers is passed this term of life whatever its duration!

Lucretius, *Nature of Things*, II

15 The man who is sick of home often issues forth from his large mansion, and as suddenly comes back to it, finding as he does that he is no better off abroad. He races to his country-house, driving his jennets in headlong haste, as if hurrying to bring help to a house on fire: he yawns the moment he has reached the door of his house, or sinks heavily into sleep and seeks forgetfulness, or even in haste goes back again to town. In this way each man flies from himself (but self from whom, as you may be sure is commonly the case, he cannot escape, clings to him in his own despite).

Lucretius, *Nature of Things*, III

16 O mortals, blind in fate, who never know
To bear high fortune, or endure the low!

Virgil, *Aeneid*, X

17 He [Aemilius Paulus] began to discourse of fortune and human affairs. "Is it meet," said he, "for him that knows he is but man, in his greatest prosperity to pride himself, and be exalted at the conquest of a city, nation, or kingdom, and not, rather, well to weigh this change of fortune, in which all warriors may see an example of their common frailty, and learn a lesson that there is nothing durable or constant? For what time can men select to think themselves secure, when that of victory itself forces us more than any to dread our own fortune? And a very little consideration on the law of things, and how all are hurried round, and each man's station changed, will introduce sadness in the midst of the greatest joy."

Plutarch, *Aemilius Paulus*

18 Nothing is more intractable than man when in felicity, nor anything more docile, when he has been reduced and humbled by fortune.

Plutarch, *Lucullus*

19 Good fortune will elevate even petty minds, and give them the appearance of a certain greatness and stateliness, as from their high place they look down upon the world; but the truly noble and resolved spirit raises itself, and becomes more conspicuous in times of disaster and ill fortune.

Plutarch, *Eumenes*

20 Know you not that in the course of a long time many and various kinds of things must happen; that a fever shall overpower one, a robber another, and a third a tyrant? Such is the condition of things around us, such are those who live with us in the world: cold and heat, and unsuitable ways of living, and journeys by land, and voyages by sea, and winds, and various circumstances which surround us, destroy one man, and banish another, and throw one upon an embassy and another into an army. Sit down, then, in a flutter at all these things, lamenting, unhappy, unfortunate, dependent on another, and dependent not on one or two, but on ten thousands upon ten thousands.

Epictetus, *Discourses*, III, 24

21 Of human life the time is a point, and the substance is in a flux, and the perception dull, and the composition of the whole body subject to putrefaction, and the soul a whirl, and fortune hard to divine, and fame a thing devoid of judgement. And, to say all in a word, everything which belongs to the body is a stream, and what belongs to the soul is a dream and vapour, and life is a warfare and a stranger's sojourn, and after-fame is oblivion.

Marcus Aurelius, *Meditations*, II, 17

22 To have contemplated human life for forty years is the same as to have contemplated it for ten thousand years. For what more wilt thou see?

Marcus Aurelius, *Meditations*, VII, 49

23 The art of life is more like the wrestler's art than the dancer's, in respect of this, that it should stand ready and firm to meet onsets which are sudden and unexpected.

Marcus Aurelius, *Meditations*, VII, 61

24 Murders, death in all its guises, the reduction and sacking of cities, all must be to us just such a spectacle as the changing scenes of a play; all is but the varied incident of a plot, costume on and off, acted grief and lament. For on earth, in all the succession of life, it is not the Soul within but the Shadow outside of the authentic man, that grieves and complains and acts out the plot on this world stage which men have dotted with stages of their own constructing. All this is the doing of man knowing no more than to live the lower and outer life.

Plotinus, *Third Ennead*, II, 15

25 Another of the king's chief men . . . presently added: "The present life of man, O king, seems to me, in comparison of that time which is unknown to us, like to the swift flight of a sparrow through the room wherein you sit at supper in winter, with your commanders and ministers, and a good fire in the midst, whilst the storms of rain and snow prevail abroad; the sparrow, I say, flying in at one door, and immediately out at another, whilst he is within, is safe from the wintry storm; but after a short space of fair weather, he immediately vanishes out of your sight, into the dark winter from which he had emerged. So this life of man appears for a short space, but of what went before, or what is to follow, we are utterly ignorant."

Bede, *Ecclesiastical History*, II, 13

26 O wretched lot of man, when he hath lost that for which he was made! O hard and terrible fate! Alas, what has he lost, and what has he found? What has departed, and what remains? He has lost the blessedness for which he was made, and has found the misery for which he was not made. That has departed without which nothing is happy, and that remains which, in itself, is only miserable. Man once did eat the bread of angels, for which he hungers now; he eateth now the bread of sorrows, of which he knew not then. Alas! for the mourning of all mankind, for the universal lamentation of the sons of Hades! He choked with satiety, we sigh with hunger. He abounded, we beg. He possessed in happiness, and miserably forsook his possession; we suffer want in unhappiness and feel a miserable longing, and alas! we remain empty.

Why did he not keep for us, when he could so easily, that whose lack we should feel so heavily? Why did he shut us away from the light, and cover us over with darkness? With what purpose did he rob us of life, and inflict death upon us? Wretches that we are, whence have we been driven out; whither are we driven on? Whence hurled? Whither consigned to ruin? From a native country into exile, from the vision of God into our present blindness, from the joy of immortality into the bitterness and horror of death. Miserable exchange of how great a good, for how great an evil! Heavy loss, heavy grief heavy all our fate!

Anselm of Canterbury, *Proslogium*, I

27 Man's nature may be looked at in two ways: first, in its integrity, as it was in our first parent before sin; secondly, as it is corrupted in us after the sin of our first parent. Now in both states human nature needs the help of God as First Mover to do or will any good whatsoever. . . . But in the state of integrity of nature, as regards the sufficiency of the operative power, man by his natural endowments could will and do the good proportionate to his nature, such as the good of acquired virtue, but not surpassing good, as the good of infused virtue. But in the state of corrupt nature, man falls short even of what he could do by his nature, so that he is unable to fulfil it by his own natural powers. Yet because human nature is not altogether corrupted by sin, so as to be shorn of every natural good, even in the state of corrupted na-

ture it can, by virtue of its natural endowments, work some particular good, as to build dwellings, plant vineyards, and the like; yet it cannot do all the good natural to it, so as to fall short in nothing, just as a sick man can of himself make some movements, yet he cannot be perfectly moved with the movements of one in health, unless by the help of medicine he be cured.

Aquinas, Summa Theologica, I–II, 109, 2

28 *Cacciaguida.* Thou shalt abandon everything beloved most dearly; this is the arrow which the bow of exile shall first shoot.
Thou shalt make trial of how salt doth taste another's bread, and how hard the path to descend and mount upon another's stair.

Dante, Paradiso, XVII, 55

29 He will be successful who directs his actions according to the spirit of the times, and . . . he whose actions do not accord with the times will not be successful. Because men are seen, in affairs that lead to the end which every man has before him, namely, glory and riches, to get there by various methods; one with caution, another with haste; one by force, another by skill; one by patience, another by its opposite; and each one succeeds in reaching the goal by a different method. One can also see of two cautious men the one attain his end, the other fail; and similarly, two men by different observances are equally successful, the one being cautious, the other impetuous; all this arises from nothing else than whether or not they conform in their methods to the spirit of the times.

Machiavelli, Prince, XXV

30 The world is like a drunken peasant. If you lift him into the saddle on one side, he will fall off on the other side. One can't help him, no matter how one tries. He wants to be the devil's.

Luther, Table Talk, 630

31 Those who accuse men of always gaping after future things, and teach us to lay hold of present goods and settle ourselves in them, since we have no grip on what is to come (indeed a good deal less than we have on what is past), put their finger on the commonest of human errors—if they dare to call an error something to which Nature herself leads us in serving the continuation of her work, and which, more zealous for our action than for our knowledge, she imprints in us like many other false notions. We are never at home, we are always beyond. Fear, desire, hope, project us toward the future and steal from us the feeling and consideration of what is, to busy us with what will be, even when we shall no longer be.

Montaigne, Essays, I, 3, Our
Feelings Reach Out

32 It is pleasanter to laugh than to weep, . . . because it is more disdainful, and condemns us more than the other; and it seems to me that we can never be despised as much as we deserve. Pity and commiseration are mingled with some esteem for the thing we pity; the things we laugh at we consider worthless. I do not think there is as much unhappiness in us as vanity, nor as much malice as stupidity. We are not so full of evil as of inanity; we are not as wretched as we are worthless.

Montaigne, Essays, I, 50, Of Democritus
and Heraclitus

33 We have as our share inconstancy, irresolution, uncertainty, grief, superstition, worry over things to come, even after our life, ambition, avarice, jealousy, envy, unruly, frantic, and untamable appetites, war, falsehood, disloyalty, detraction, and curiosity. Indeed we have strangely overpaid for this fine reason that we glory in, and this capacity to judge and know, if we have bought it at the price of this infinite number of passions to which we are incessantly a prey.

Montaigne, Essays, II, 12, Apology for
Raymond Sebond

34 Alas, poor man! You have enough necessary ills without increasing them by your invention, and you are miserable enough by nature without being so by art. You have real and essential deformities enough without forging imaginary ones.

Montaigne, Essays, III, 5, On Some Verses
of Virgil

35 We are great fools. "He has spent his life in idleness," we say; "I have done nothing today." What, have you not lived? That is not only the fundamental but the most illustrious of your occupations. "If I had been placed in a position to manage great affairs, I would have shown what I could do." Have you been able to think out and manage your own life? You have done the greatest task of all. To show and exploit her resources Nature has no need of fortune; she shows herself equally on all levels and behind a curtain as well as without one. To compose our character is our duty, not to compose books, and to win, not battles and provinces, but order and tranquility in our conduct. Our great and glorious masterpiece is to live appropriately. All other things, ruling, hoarding, building, are only little appendages and props, at most.

Montaigne, Essays, III, 13, Of Experience

36 What man that sees the ever-whirling wheele
Of Change, the which all mortall things doth
sway,
But that therby doth find, and plainly feele,
How Mutability in them doth play
Her cruell sports, to many mens decay?

Spenser, Faerie Queene, Bk. VII, VI, 1

37 Full little knowest thou that hast not tride,
What hell it is, in suing long to bide:
To loose good dayes, that might be better spent;
To wast long nights in pensive discontent;
To speed to day, to be put back to morrow;
To feed on hope, to pine with feare and sorrow;
To have thy Princes grace, yet want her Peeres;
To have thy asking, yet waite manie yeeres;
To fret thy soule with crosses and with cares;
To eate thy heart through comfortlesse dispaires;
To fawne, to crowche, to waite, to ride, to ronne,
To spend, to give, to want, to be undonne.
Unhappie wight, borne to desastrous end,
That doth his life in so long tendance spend!

> Spenser, *Complaints:* Mother
> Hubberds Tale, 895

38 *King Henry.* O God! methinks it were a happy life,
To be no better than a homely swain;
To sit upon a hill, as I do now,
To carve out dials quaintly, point by point,
Thereby to see the minutes how they run,
How many make the hour full complete;
How many hours bring about the day;
How many days will finish up the year;
How many years a mortal man may live.
When this is known, then to divide the times:
So many hours must I tend my flock;
So many hours must I take my rest;
So many hours must I contemplate;
So many hours must I sport myself;
So many days my ewes have been with young;
So many weeks ere the poor fools will ean;
So many years ere I shall shear the fleece:
So minutes, hours, days, months, and years,
Pass'd over to the end they were created,
Would bring white hairs unto a quiet grave.

> Shakespeare, *III Henry VI,* II, v, 21

39 *Puck.* Lord, what fools these mortals be!

> Shakespeare, *Midsummer-Night's
> Dream,* III, ii, 115

40 *Lewis.* There's nothing in this world can make me
joy:
Life is as tedious as a twice-told tale
Vexing the dull ear of a drowsy man.

> Shakespeare, *King John,* III, iv, 107

41 *Gratiano.* You look not well, Signior Antonio;
You have too much respect upon the world:
They lose it that do buy it with much care:
Believe me, you are marvellously changed.
  Antonio. I hold the world but as the world, Gra-
tiano;
A stage where every man must play a part,
And mine a sad one.

> Shakespeare, *Merchant of Venice,* I, i, 73

42 *Brutus.* There is a tide in the affairs of men
Which, taken at the flood, leads on to fortune;

Omitted, all the voyage of their life
Is bound in shallows and in miseries.
On such a full sea are we now afloat;
And we must take the current when it serves
Or lose our ventures.

> Shakespeare, *Julius Caesar,* IV, iii, 218

43 *Duke.* Thou seest we are not all alone unhappy:
This wide and universal theatre
Presents more woeful pageants than the scene
Wherein we play in.
  Jaques.   All the world's a stage,
And all the men and women merely players:
They have their exits and their entrances;
And one man in his time plays many parts.

> Shakespeare, *As You Like It,* II, vii, 136

44 *Macbeth.* To-morrow, and to-morrow, and to-mor-
row,
Creeps in this petty pace from day to day
To the last syllable of recorded time,
And all our yesterdays have lighted fools
The way to dusty death. Out, out, brief candle!
Life's but a walking shadow, a poor player
That struts and frets his hour upon the stage
And then is heard no more. It is a tale
Told by an idiot, full of sound and fury,
Signifying nothing.

> Shakespeare, *Macbeth,* V, v, 19

45 *3rd Fisherman.* Master, I marvel how the fishes live
in the sea.
  1st Fisherman. Why, as men do a-land; the great
ones eat up the little ones. I can compare our rich
misers to nothing so fitly as to a whale; a' plays
and tumbles, driving the poor fry before him, and
at last devours them all at a mouthful. Such
whales have I heard on o' the land, who never
leave gaping till they've swallowed the whole parish, church, steeple, bells, and all. . . .
  Pericles. [*Aside*] How from the finny subject of
the sea
These fishers tell the infirmities of men;
And from their watery empire recollect
All that may men approve or men detect!

> Shakespeare, *Pericles,* II, i, 30

46 *Prospero.* Our revels now are ended. These our
actors,
As I foretold you, were all spirits and
Are melted into air, into thin air,
And, like the baseless fabric of this vision,
The cloud-capp'd towers, the gorgeous palaces,
The solemn temples, that great globe itself,
Yea, all which it inherit, shall dissolve
And, like this insubstantial pageant faded,
Leave not a rack behind. We are such stuff
As dreams are made on, and our little life
Is rounded with a sleep.

> Shakespeare, *Tempest,* IV, i, 148

47 Like as the waves make towards the pebbled
    shore,
  So do our minutes hasten to their end;
  Each changing place with that which goes before,
  In sequent toil all forwards do contend.
  Nativity, once in the main of light,
  Crawls to maturity, wherewith being crown'd,
  Crooked eclipses 'gainst his glory fight,
  And Time that gave doth now his gift confound.
  Time doth transfix the flourish set on youth
  And delves the parallels in beauty's brow,
  Feeds on the rarities of nature's truth,
  And nothing stands but for his scythe to mow.
                Shakespeare, *Sonnet LX*

48 Ah, but says *Sancho*, your strolling Emperor's
Crowns and Sceptres are not of pure Gold, but
Tinsel and Copper. I grant it, said Don *Quixote;*
nor is it fit the Decorations of the Stage should be
real, but rather Imitations, and the Resemblance
of Realities, as the Plays themselves must be;
which, by the way, I wou'd have you love and
esteem, *Sancho*, and consequently those that write,
and also those that act 'em; for they are all instrumental to the Good of the Commonwealth, and
set before our Eyes those Looking-glasses that reflect a lively Representation of human Life; nothing being able to give us a more just Idea of Nature, and what we are or ought to be, than
Comedians and Comedies. Prithee tell me, Hast
thou never seen a Play acted, where Kings, Emperors, Prelates, Knights, Ladies, and other Characters, are introduced on the Stage? One acts a
Ruffian, another a Soldier; this Man a Cheat,
and that a Merchant; one plays a designing Fool,
and another a foolish Lover: But the Play done,
and the Actors undress'd, they are all equal, and
as they were before. All this I have seen, quoth
Sancho. Just such a Comedy, said Don *Quixote*, is
acted on the great Stage of the World, where some
play the Emperors, others the Prelates, and, in
short, all the Parts that can be brought into a
Dramatick Piece; till Death, which is the Catastrophe and End of the Action, strips the Actors of
all their Marks of Distinction, and levels their
Quality in the Grave. A rare Comparison, quoth
Sancho, though not so new, but that I have heard it
over and over. Just such another is that of a Game
at Chess, where while the Play lasts, every Piece
has its particular Office; but when the Game's
over, they are all mingl'd and huddled together,
and clapp'd into a Bag, just as when Life's ended
we are laid up in the Grave. Truly, *Sancho*, said
Don *Quixote*, thy Simplicity lessens, and thy Sense
improves every Day.
              Cervantes, *Don Quixote*, II, 12

49 If a man meditate much upon the universal frame
of nature, the earth with men upon it (the divineness of souls except) will not seem much other
than an anthill, whereas some ants carry corn,
and some carry their young, and some go empty,
and all to and fro a little heap of dust.
      Bacon, *Advancement of Learning*, Bk. I, VIII, 1

50 Whatsoever therefore is consequent to a time of
war, where every man is enemy to every man, the
same is consequent to the time wherein men live
without other security than what their own
strength and their own invention shall furnish
them withal. In such condition there is no place
for industry, because the fruit thereof is uncertain:
and consequently no culture of the earth; no navigation, nor use of the commodities that may be
imported by sea; no commodious building; no instruments of moving and removing such things as
require much force; no knowledge of the face of
the earth; no account of time; no arts; no letters;
no society; and which is worst of all, continual
fear, and danger of violent death; and the life of
man, solitary, poor, nasty, brutish, and short.
              Hobbes, *Leviathan*, I, 13

51 For the laws of nature, as *justice, equity, modesty, mer-*
cy, and, in sum, *doing to others as we would be done to*,
of themselves, without the terror of some power to
cause them to be observed, are contrary to our
natural passions, that carry us to partiality, pride,
revenge, and the like. And covenants, without the
sword, are but words and of no strength to secure
a man at all. Therefore, notwithstanding the laws
of nature (which every one hath then kept, when
he has the will to keep them, when he can do it
safely), if there be no power erected, or not great
enough for our security, every man will and may
lawfully rely on his own strength and art for caution against all other men. And in all places,
where men have lived by small families, to rob
and spoil one another has been a trade, and so far
from being reputed against the law of nature that
the greater spoils they gained, the greater was
their honour; and men observed no other laws
therein but the laws of honour; that is, to abstain
from cruelty, leaving to men their lives and instruments of husbandry. And as small families did
then; so now do cities and kingdoms, which are
but greater families (for their own security), enlarge their dominions upon all pretences of danger, and fear of invasion, or assistance that may be
given to invaders; endeavour as much as they can
to subdue or weaken their neighbours by open
force, and secret arts, for want of other caution,
justly; and are remembered for it in after ages
with honour.
              Hobbes, *Leviathan*, II, 17

52 For the World, I count it not an Inn, but an Hospital; and a place not to live, but to die in.
        Sir Thomas Browne, *Religio Medici*, II, 11

53 When I have occasionally set myself to consider
the different distractions of men, the pains and

perils to which they expose themselves at court or in war, whence arise so many quarrels, passions, bold and often bad ventures, etc., I have discovered that all the unhappiness of men arises from one single fact, that they cannot stay quietly in their own chamber. A man who has enough to live on, if he knew how to stay with pleasure at home, would not leave it to go to sea or to besiege a town. A commission in the army would not be bought so dearly, but that it is found insufferable not to budge from the town; and men only seek conversation and entering games, because they cannot remain with pleasure at home.

But, on further consideration, when, after finding the cause of all our ills, I have sought to discover the reason of it, I have found that there is one very real reason, namely, the natural poverty of our feeble and mortal condition, so miserable that nothing can comfort us when we think of it closely.

Pascal, *Pensées*, II, 139

54 Let us imagine a number of men in chains and all condemned to death, where some are killed each day in the sight of the others, and those who remain see their own fate in that of their fellows and wait their turn, looking at each other sorrowfully and without hope. It is an image of the condition of men.

Pascal, *Pensées*, III, 199

55 The last act is tragic, however happy all the rest of the play is; at the last a little earth is thrown upon our head, and that is the end forever.

Pascal, *Pensées*, III, 210

56 As I walked through the wilderness of this world, I lighted on a certain place where was a Den, and I laid me down in that place to sleep; and, as I slept, I dreamed a dream. I dreamed, and behold I saw a man clothed with rags, standing in a certain place, with his face from his own house, a book in his hand, and a great burden upon his back. . . . I looked and saw him open the book and read therein; and, as he read, he wept, and trembled; and not being able longer to contain, he brake out with a lamentable cry, saying, "What shall I do?" . . .

Now I saw, upon a time, when he was walking in the fields, that he was (as he was wont) reading in this book, and greatly distressed in his mind; and as he read, he burst out, as he had done before, crying, "What shall I do to be saved?"

Bunyan, *Pilgrim's Progress*, I

57 Behold the child, by Nature's kindly law,
Pleas'd with a rattle, tickled with a straw:
Some livelier play-thing gives his youth delight,
A little louder, but as empty quite:
Scarfs, garters, gold, amuse his riper stage;
And beads and pray'r-books are the toys of age:

Pleas'd with this bauble still, as that before;
'Till tir'd he sleeps, and Life's poor play is o'er!

Pope, *Essay on Man*, Epistle II, 275

58 It is universally acknowledged that there is a great uniformity among the actions of men, in all nations and ages, and that human nature remains still the same, in its principles and operations. The same motives always produce the same actions: The same events follow from the same causes. Ambition, avarice, self-love, vanity, friendship, generosity, public spirit: these passions, mixed in various degrees, and distributed through society, have been, from the beginning of the world, and still are, the source of all the actions and enterprises, which have ever been observed among mankind.

Hume, *Concerning Human Understanding*, VIII, 65

59 We are placed in this world, as in a great theatre, where the true springs and causes of every event are entirely concealed from us; nor have we either sufficient wisdom to foresee, or power to prevent, those ills with which we are continually threatened. We hang in perpetual suspense between life and death, health and sickness, plenty and want, which are distributed amongst the human species by secret and unknown causes, whose operation is oft unexpected, and always unaccountable.

Hume, *Natural History of Religion*, III

60 I live in a constant endeavour to fence against the infirmities of ill health, and other evils of life, by mirth; being firmly persuaded that every time a man smiles,—but much more so, when he laughs, it adds something to this Fragment of Life.

Sterne, *Tristram Shandy*, Dedication

61 What is the life of man! Is it not to shift from side to side?—from sorrow to sorrow?—to button up one cause of vexation—and unbutton another?

Sterne, *Tristram Shandy*, IV, 31

62 "Do you believe," said Candide, "that mankind have always been cutting one another's throats; that they were always liars, knaves, treacherous and ungrateful; always thieves, sharpers, highwaymen, lazy, envious and gluttons; always drunkards, misers, ambitious and blood-thirsty; always backbiters, debauchees, fanatics, hypocrites and fools?" "Do you not believe," said Martin, "that hawks have always preyed upon pigeons, when they could light upon them?"

Voltaire, *Candide*, XXI

63 "I [The Old Woman] want to know which is the worst;—to be ravished an hundred times by negro pirates, to run the gauntlet among the Bulgarians, to be whipped and hanged, to be dissected, to row in the galleys; in a word, to have suffered all the

miseries we have undergone, or to stay here, without doing anything?" "That is a great question," said Candide.

Voltaire, *Candide*, XXX

64 "Let us work," said Martin, "without disputing; it is the only way to render life supportable."

All their little society entered into this laudable design, according to their different abilities. Their little piece of ground produced a plentiful crop. Cunegonde was indeed very homely, but she became an excellent pastry cook. Paquetta worked at embroidery, and the old woman took care of the linen. There was no idle person in the company, not excepting even Girofflee; he made a very good carpenter, and became a very honest man.

As to Pangloss, he evidently had a lurking consciousness that his theory required unceasing exertions, and all his ingenuity, to sustain it. Yet he stuck to it to the last; his thinking and talking faculties could hardly be diverted from it for a moment. He seized every occasion to say to Candide, "All the events in this best of possible worlds are admirably connected. If a single link in the great chain were omitted, the harmony of the entire universe would be destroyed. If you had not been expelled from that beautiful castle, with those cruel kicks, for your love to Miss Cunegonde; if you had not been imprisoned by the inquisition; if you had not travelled over a great portion of America on foot; if you had not plunged your sword through the baron; if you had not lost all the sheep you brought from that fine country, Eldorado, together with the riches with which they were laden, you would not be here to-day, eating preserved citrons, and pistachio nuts."

"That's very well said, and may all be true," said Candide; "but let's cultivate our garden."

Voltaire, *Candide*, XXX

65 It needs twenty years to lead man from the plant state in which he is within his mother's womb, and the pure animal state which is the lot of his early childhood, to the state when the maturity of the reason begins to appear. It has needed thirty centuries to learn a little about his structure. It would need eternity to learn something about his soul. It takes an instant to kill him.

Voltaire, *Philosophical Dictionary:* General Reflection on Man

66 "They are surely happy," said the prince, "who have all these conveniencies, of which I envy none so much as the facility with which separated friends interchange their thoughts."

"The Europeans," answered Imlac, "are less unhappy than we, but they are not happy. Human life is everywhere a state in which much is to be endured, and little to be enjoyed."

Johnson, *Rasselas*, XI

67 *Johnson.* We would all be idle if we could.

Boswell, *Life of Johnson* (Apr. 3, 1776)

68 For though management and persuasion are always the easiest and the safest instruments of governments, as force and violence are the worst and the most dangerous, yet such, it seems, is the natural insolence of man that he almost always disdains to use the good instrument, except when he cannot or dare not use the bad one.

Adam Smith, *Wealth of Nations,* V, 1

69 There are two very natural propensities which we may distinguish in the most virtuous and liberal dispositions, the love of pleasure and the love of action. If the former is refined by art and learning, improved by the charms of social intercourse, and corrected by a just regard to economy, to health, and to reputation, it is productive of the greatest part of the happiness of private life. The love of action is a principle of a much stronger and more doubtful nature. It often leads to anger, to ambition, and to revenge; but when it is guided by the sense of propriety and benevolence, it becomes the parent of every virtue, and, if those virtues are accompanied with equal abilities, a family, a state, or an empire may be indebted for their safety and prosperity to the undaunted courage of a single man. To the love of pleasure we may therefore ascribe most of the agreeable, to the love of action we may attribute most of the useful and respectable, qualifications. The character in which both the one and the other should be united and harmonised would seem to constitute the most perfect idea of human nature.

Gibbon, *Decline and Fall of the Roman Empire,* XV

70 In the fall and the sack of great cities an historian is condemned to repeat the tale of uniform calamity: the same effects must be produced by the same passions; and when those passions may be indulged without control, small, alas! is the difference between civilised and savage man.

Gibbon, *Decline and Fall of the Roman Empire,* LXVIII

71 I think I may fairly make two postulata.

First, that food is necessary to the existence of man.

Secondly, that the passion between the sexes is necessary and will remain nearly in its present state.

These two laws, ever since we have had any knowledge of mankind, appear to have been fixed laws of our nature, and, as we have not hitherto seen any alteration in them, we have no right to conclude that they will ever cease to be what they now are without an immediate act of power in that Being who first arranged the system of the universe, and for the advantage of his creatures, still executes, according to fixed laws, all its various operations. . . .

Assuming then, my postulata as granted, I say that the power of population is indefinitely greater than the power in the earth to produce subsistence for man.

Population, when unchecked, increases in a geometrical ratio. Subsistence increases only in an arithmetical ratio. A slight acquaintance with numbers will show the immensity of the first power in comparison of the second.

By that law of our nature which makes food necessary to the life of man, the effects of these two unequal powers must be kept equal.

This implies a strong and constantly operating check on population from the difficulty of subsistence. This difficulty must fall somewhere and must necessarily be severely felt by a large portion of mankind.

Through the animal and vegetable kingdoms, nature has scattered the seeds of life abroad with the most profuse and liberal hand. She has been comparatively sparing in the room and the nourishment necessary to rear them. The germs of existence contained in this spot of earth, with ample food, and ample room to expand in, would fill millions of worlds in the course of a few thousand years. Necessity, that imperious all-pervading law of nature, restrains them within the prescribed bounds. The race of plants and the race of animals shrink under this great restrictive law. And the race of man cannot, by any efforts of reason, escape from it. Among plants and animals its effects are waste of seed, sickness, and premature death; among mankind, misery and vice. The former, misery, is an absolutely necessary consequence of it. Vice is a highly probable consequence, and we therefore see it abundantly prevail, but it ought not, perhaps, to be called an absolutely necessary consequence. The ordeal of virtue is to resist all temptation to evil.

This natural inequality of the two powers of population and or production in the earth and that great law of our nature which must constantly keep their effects equal form the great difficulty that to me appears insurmountable in the way to the perfectibility of society. All other arguments are of slight and subordinate consideration in comparison of this. I see no way by which man can escape from the weight of this law, which pervades all animated nature. No fancied equality, no agrarian regulations in their utmost extent, could remove the pressure of it even for a single century. And it appears, therefore, to be decisive against the possible existence of a society all the members of which should live in ease, happiness, and comparative leisure, and feel no anxiety about providing the means of subsistence for themselves and families.

Consequently, if the premises are just, the argument is conclusive against the perfectibility of the mass of mankind.

Malthus, *Population,* I

72 *Oswald.* Action is transitory—a step, a blow,
The motion of a muscle—this way or that—
'Tis done, and in the after-vacancy
We wonder at ourselves like men betrayed:
Suffering is permanent, obscure and dark,
And shares the nature of infinity.

Wordsworth, *The Borderers,* III, 405

73 *Mr. Bennet.* For what do we live, but to make sport for our neighbours, and laugh at them in our turn?

Jane Austen, *Pride and Prejudice,* LVII

74 *Demogorgon.* To suffer woes which Hope thinks infinite;
To forgive wrongs darker than death or night;
　To defy Power, which seems omnipotent;
To love, and bear; to hope till Hope creates
From its own wreck the thing it contemplates;
　Neither to change, nor falter, nor repent;
This, like thy glory, Titan, is to be
Good, great and joyous, beautiful and free;
This is alone Life, Joy, Empire, and Victory!

Shelley, *Prometheus Unbound,* IV, 570

75 Human life must be some kind of mistake.

Schopenhauer, *Vanity of Existence*

76 If we turn from contemplating the world as a whole, and, in particular, the generations of men as they live their little hour of mock-existence and then are swept away in rapid succession; if we turn from this, and look at life in its small details, as presented, say, in a comedy, how ridiculous it all seems! It is like a drop of water seen through a microscope, a single drop teeming with *infusoria;* or a speck of cheese full of mites invisible to the naked eye. How we laugh as they bustle about so eagerly, and struggle with one another in so tiny a space! And whether here, or in the little span of human life, this terrible activity produces a comic effect.

Schopenhauer, *Vanity of Existence*

77 Alas, poor devil! spectres are appointed to haunt him: one age he is hagridden, bewitched; the next, priestridden, befooled; in all ages, bedevilled. And now the Genius of Mechanism smothers him worse than any Nightmare did; till the Soul is nigh choked out of him, and only a kind of Digestive, Mechanic life remains.

Carlyle, *Sartor Resartus,* III, 3

78 Like a God-created, fire-breathing Spirit-host, we emerge from the Inane; haste stormfully across the astonished Earth; then plunge again into the Inane.

Carlyle, *Sartor Resartus,* III, 8

79 In the hour of death the only adequate consolation is that one has not evaded life, but has endured it. What a man shall accomplish or not accomplish, does not lie in his power to decide; he is not the One who will guide the world; he has only to obey. Everyone has, therefore, first and foremost (instead of asking which place is most comfortable for him, which connection is the most advantageous to him), to assure himself on the question of where Providence can use him, if it so pleases Providence. The point consists precisely in loving his neighbor, or, what is essentially the same thing, in living equally for every man. Every other point of view is a contentious one, however advantageous and comfortable and apparently significant this position may be. Providence cannot use one who has placed himself there, for he is plainly in rebellion against Providence. But he who duly took that overlooked, that despised and disdained place, without insisting on his earthly rights, without attaching himself to just one single man, essentially existing equally for all men, he will, even though he apparently achieves nothing, even if he becomes exposed to the derision of the poor, or to the ridicule of his superiors, or to both insult and ridicule, yet in the hour of death, he will confidently dare say to his soul: "I have done my best; whether I have accomplished anything, I do not know; whether I have helped anyone, I do not know; but that I have lived for them, that I do know, I know it from the fact that they insulted me. And this is my consolation, that I shall not have to take the secret with me to the grave, that I, in order to have good and undisturbed and comfortable days in life, have denied my kinship to other men, kinship with the poor, in order to live in aristocratic seclusion, or with the distinguished, in order to live in secret obscurity."

Kierkegaard, *Works of Love*, I, 2C

80 Life is a festival only to the wise. Seen from the nook and chimney-side of prudence, it wears a ragged and dangerous front.

Emerson, *Heroism*

81 Ring out a slowly dying cause,
    And ancient forms of party strife;
    Ring in the nobler modes of life,
With sweeter manners, purer laws.

Ring out the want, the care, the sin,
    The faithless coldness of the times;
    Ring out, ring out my mournful rhymes,
But ring the fuller minstrel in.

Ring out false pride in place and blood,
    The civic slander and the spite;
    Ring in the love of truth and right,
Ring in the common love of good.

Ring out old shapes of foul disease;
    Ring out the narrowing lust of gold;

Ring out the thousand wars of old,
Ring in the thousand years of peace.

Ring in the valiant man and free,
    The larger heart, the kindlier hand;
    Ring out the darkness of the land,
Ring in the Christ that is to be.

Tennyson, *In Memoriam*, CVI

82 There are certain queer times and occasions in this strange mixed affair we call life when a man takes this whole universe for a vast practical joke, though the wit thereof he but dimly discerns, and more than suspects that the joke is at nobody's expense but his own. However, nothing dispirits, and nothing seems worth while disputing. He bolts down all events, all creeds, and beliefs, and persuasions, all hard things visible and invisible, never mind how knobby; as an ostrich of potent digestion gobbles down bullets and gun flints. And as for small difficulties and worryings, prospects of sudden disaster, peril of life and limb; all these, and death itself, seem to him only sly, good-natured hits, and jolly punches in the side bestowed by the unseen and unaccountable old joker. That odd sort of wayward mood I am speaking of, comes over a man only in some time of extreme tribulation; it comes in the very midst of his earnestness, so that what just before might have seemed to him a thing most momentous, now seems but a part of the general joke.

Melville, *Moby Dick*, XLIX

83 Consider the subtleness of the sea; how its most dreaded creatures glide under water, unapparent for the most part, and treacherously hidden beneath the loveliest tints of azure. Consider also the devilish brilliance and beauty of many of its most remorseless tribes, as the dainty embellished shape of many species of sharks. Consider, once more, the universal cannibalism of the sea; all whose creatures prey upon each other, carrying on eternal war since the world began.

Consider all this; and then turn to this green, gentle, and most docile earth; consider them both, the sea and the land; and do you not find a strange analogy to something in yourself? For as this appalling ocean surrounds the verdant land, so in the soul of man there lies one insular Tahiti, full of peace and joy, but encompassed by all the horrors of the half-known life. God keep thee! Push not off from that isle, thou canst never return!

Melville, *Moby Dick*, LVIII

84 All men live enveloped in whale-lines. All are born with halters round their necks; but it is only when caught in the swift, sudden turn of death, that mortals realise the silent, subtle, everpresent perils of life.

Melville, *Moby Dick*, LX

85 Still we live meanly, like ants; though the fable tells us that we were long ago changed into men; like pygmies we fight with cranes; it is error upon error, and clout upon clout, and our best virtue has for its occasion a superfluous and evitable wretchedness. Our life is frittered away by detail. An honest man has hardly need to count more than his ten fingers, or in extreme cases he may add his ten toes, and lump the rest. Simplicity, simplicity, simplicity! I say, let your affairs be as two or three, and not a hundred or a thousand; instead of a million count half a dozen, and keep your accounts on your thumb-nail. In the midst of this chopping sea of civilized life, such are the clouds and storms and quicksands and thousand-and-one items to be allowed for, that a man has to live, if he would not founder and go to the bottom and not make his port at all, by dead reckoning, and he must be a great calculator indeed who succeeds. Simplify, simplify.

> Thoreau, *Walden:* Where I Lived, and What
> I Lived For

86 Why I left the woods? I do not think that I can tell. . . . Perhaps it is none of my business, even if it is yours. . . . There was a little stagnation, it may be. About two o'clock in the afternoon the world's axle creaked as if it needed greasing. . . . Perhaps if I lived there much longer, I might live there forever. One would think twice before he accepted heaven on such terms. A ticket to Heaven must include tickets to Limbo, Purgatory, and Hell.

> Thoreau, *Journal (1851)*

87 We are no other than a moving row
Of Magic Shadow-shapes that come and go
    Round with the Sun-illuminated Lantern held
In Midnight by the Master of the Show;

But helpless Pieces of the Game He plays
Upon this Checkerboard of Nights and Days;
    Hither and thither moves, and checks, and slays,
And one by one back in the Closet lays.

> FitzGerald, *Rubáiyát,* LXVIII-LXIX

88 Ah, Love! could you and I with Him conspire
To grasp this sorry Scheme of Things entire,
    Would not we shatter it to bits—and then
Remold it nearer to the Heart's Desire!

> FitzGerald, *Rubáiyát,* XCIX

89 It is a very plain and elementary truth, that the life, the fortune, and the happiness of every one of us, and, more or less, of those who are connected with us, do depend upon our knowing something of the rules of a game. . . . It is a game which has been played for untold ages, every man and woman of us being one of the two players in a game of his or her own. The chess-board is the world, the pieces are the phenomena of the universe, the rules of the game are what we call the laws of Nature. The player on the other side is hidden from us. We know that his play is always fair, just and patient. But also we know, to our cost, that he never overlooks a mistake, or makes the smallest allowance for ignorance. To the man who plays well, the highest stakes are paid, with that sort of overflowing generosity with which the strong shows delight in strength. And one who plays ill is checkmated—without haste, but without remorse.

> T. H. Huxley, *A Liberal Education*

90 There are three material things, not only useful, but essential to life. No one "knows how to live" till he has got them.

These are pure air, water, and earth.

There are three immaterial things, not only useful, but essential to life. No one knows how to live till he has got them also.

These are admiration, hope, and love.

Admiration—the power of discerning and taking delight in what is beautiful in visible form and lovely in human character; and, necessarily, striving to produce what is beautiful in form and to become what is lovely in character.

Hope—the recognition, by true foresight, of better things to be reached hereafter, whether by ourselves or others; necessarily issuing in the straightforward and undisappointable effort to advance, according to our proper power, the gaining of them.

Love—both of family and neighbour, faithful and satisfied.

> Ruskin, *An Idealist's Arraignment of the Age*

91 Ah, love, let us be true
To one another! for the world, which seems
To lie before us like a land of dreams,
So various, so beautiful, so new,
Hath really neither joy, nor love, nor light,
Nor certitude, nor peace, nor help for pain;
And we are here as on a darkling plain
Swept with confused alarms of struggle and flight,
Where ignorant armies clash by night.

> Arnold, *Dover Beach*

92 As a general rule, people, even the wicked, are much more naïve and simple-hearted than we suppose. And we ourselves are, too.

> Dostoevsky, *Brothers Karamazov,* Pt. I, I, 1

93 *Tom Sawyer.* There's plenty of boys that will come hankering and gruvvelling around when you've got an apple, and beg the core off you; but when *they've* got one, and you beg for the core and remind them how you give them a core one time, they make a mouth at you and say thank you 'most to death, but there ain't-a-going to *be* no core.

> Mark Twain, *Tom Sawyer Abroad,* I

94 Do not will anything beyond your power: there is a bad falseness in those who will beyond their power.

Especially when they will great things! For they awaken distrust in great things, these subtle false-coiners and stageplayers:—

—Until at last they are false towards themselves, squint-eyed, whited cankers, glossed over with strong words, parade virtues and brilliant false deeds.

Nietzsche, *Thus Spake Zarathustra*, IV, 73

95 If my reader can succeed in abstracting from all conceptual interpretation and lapse back into his immediate sensible life at this very moment, he will find it to be what someone has called a big blooming buzzing confusion, as free from contradiction in its 'much-at-onceness' as it is all alive and evidently there.

William James, *Some Problems of Philosophy*, IV

96 Who can decide offhand which is absolutely better, to live or to understand life? We must do both alternately, and a man can no more limit himself to either than a pair of scissors can cut with a single one of its blades.

William James, *Some Problems of Philosophy*, IV

97 Men are not gentle, friendly creatures wishing for love, who simply defend themselves if they are attacked, but . . . a powerful measure of desire for aggression has to be reckoned as part of their instinctual endowment. The result is that their neighbour is to them not only a possible helper or sexual object, but also a temptation to them to gratify their aggressiveness on him, to exploit his capacity for work without recompense, to use him sexually without his consent, to seize his posses-

sions, to humiliate him, to cause him pain, to torture and kill him. *Homo homini lupus;* who has the courage to dispute it in the face of all the evidence in his own life and in history?

Freud, *Civilization and Its Discontents*, V

98 Mankind likes to think in terms of extreme opposites. It is given to formulating its beliefs in terms of *Either-Ors*, between which it recognizes no intermediate possibilities. When forced to recognize that the extremes cannot be acted upon, it is still inclined to hold that they are all right in theory but that when it comes to practical matters circumstances compel us to compromise.

Dewey, *Experience and Education*, I

99 Happiness is the only sanction of life; where happiness fails, existence remains a mad and lamentable experiment.

Santayana, *Life of Reason*, I, 10

100 That life is worth living is the most necessary of assumptions and, were it not assumed, the most impossible of conclusions.

Santayana, *Life of Reason*, I, 10

101 Between the laughing and the weeping philosopher there is no opposition: *the same facts* that make one laugh make one weep. No whole-hearted man, no sane art, can be limited to either mood.

Santayana, *Persons and Places*, X

102 Nothing can be meaner than the anxiety to live on, to live on anyhow and in any shape; a spirit with any honour is not willing to live except in its own way, and a spirit with any wisdom is not over-eager to live at all.

Santayana, *Winds of Doctrine*, I

1.3 | *The Ages of Man*

YOUNG AND OLD

The quotations assembled here fall into two groups; on the one hand, statements about the general course of human life from birth to death—its various stages or periods and its developmental pattern; on the other hand, considerations of the differences between youth and age—the advantages and disadvantages of each, as well as the contrasts and conflicts between them.

Different writers enumerate and characterize the stages of human life differently, but they all appear to agree about the general pattern of human development—its cycle of growth and decline. Each of the main periods of human life has its defenders and its detractors—those who praise the innocence, exuberance, and joy of infancy and childhood and those who condemn the savagery and self-indulgence of the young; those who admire the full-bloom of human maturity, the calm of old age, the wisdom gained with years; and those who paint the opposite picture of crotchety and crabbed inflexibility in the aged, verging on the frailties and ineptitudes of the senile. A few quotations express the view that the best of human life lies in the middle years between youth and age.

Quotations on other aspects of the varying relationships between the young and the old will be found in Section 2.2 on PARENTS AND CHILDREN.

---

1 For all our days are passed away in thy wrath: we spend our years as a tale that is told.

The days of our years are three-score years and ten; and if by reason of strength they be fourscore years, yet is their strength labour and sorrow; for it is soon cut off, and we fly away.

Psalm 90:9–10

2 Rejoice, O young man, in thy youth; and let thy heart cheer thee in the days of thy youth, and walk in the ways of thine heart, and in the sight of thine eyes: but know thou, that for all these things God will bring thee into judgment.

Therefore remove sorrow from thy heart, and put away evil from thy flesh: for childhood and youth are vanity.

Ecclesiastes 11:9–10

3 Remember now thy Creator in the days of thy youth, while the evil days come not, nor the years draw nigh, when thou shalt say, I have no pleasure in them;

While the sun, or the light, or the moon, or the stars, be not darkened, nor the clouds return after the rain:

In the day when the keepers of the house shall tremble, and the strong men shall bow themselves, and the grinders cease because they are few, and those that look out of the windows be darkened.

And the doors shall be shut in the streets, when the sound of the grinding is low, and he shall rise up at the voice of the bird, and all the daughters of musick shall be brought low;

Also when they shall be afraid of that which is high, and fears shall be in the way, and the almond tree shall flourish, and the grasshopper shall be a burden, and desire shall fail: because man goeth to his long home, and the mourners go about the streets:

Or ever the silver cord be loosed, or the golden bowl be broken, or the pitcher be broken at the fountain, or the wheel broken at the cistern.

Then shall the dust return to the earth as it was: and the spirit shall return unto God who gave it.

Ecclesiastes 12:1–7

4 *Priam.*   For a young man all is decorous
   when he is cut down in battle and torn with the
      sharp bronze, and lies there
   dead, and though dead still all that shows about
      him is beautiful;
   but when an old man is dead and down, and the
      dogs mutilate
   the grey head and the grey beard and the parts
      that are secret,
   this, for all sad mortality, is the sight most pitiful.

Homer, *Iliad*, XXII, 71

5 *Penelope.* Men grow old soon in hardship.

Homer, *Odyssey*, XIX, 361

6 *Odysseus.*   "My strange one,
   must you again, and even now,
   urge me to talk? Here is a plodding tale;
   no charm in it, no relish in the telling.
   Teirêsias told me I must take an oar
   and trudge the mainland, going from town to
      town,
   until I discover men who have never known
   the salt blue sea, nor flavor of salt meat—
   strangers to painted prows, to watercraft
   and oars like wings, dipping across the water.
   The moment of revelation he foretold
   was this, for you may share the prophecy:
   some traveller falling in with me will say:
   'A winnowing fan, that on your shoulder, sir?'
   There I must plant my oar, on the very spot,
   with burnt offerings to Poseidon of the Waters:
   a ram, a bull, a great buck boar. Thereafter

when I come home again, I am to slay
full hekatombs to the gods who own broad
  heaven,
one by one.
         Then death will drift upon me
from seaward, mild as air, mild as your hand,
in my well-tended weariness of age,
contented folk around me on our island.
He said all this must come."

               Penélopê said:
"If by the gods' grace age at least is kind,
we have that promise—trials will end in peace."
           Homer, *Odyssey,* XXIII, 264

7 *Chorus.* Since the young vigor that urges
  inward to the heart
is frail as age, no warcraft yet perfect,
while beyond age, leaf
withered, man goes three footed
no stronger than a child is,
a dream that falters in daylight.
          Aeschylus, *Agamemnon,* 76

8 *Chorus.* Though he has watched a decent age pass
  by,
A man will sometimes still desire the world.
I swear I see no wisdom in that man.
The endless hours pile up a drift of pain
More unrelieved each day; and as for pleasure,
When he is sunken in excessive age,
You will not see his pleasure anywhere.
The last attendant is the same for all,
Old men and young alike, as in its season
Man's heritage of underworld appears:
There being then no epithalamion,
No music and no dance. Death is the finish.
      Sophocles, *Oedipus at Colonus,* 1211

9 *Chorus.* The feathery follies of his youth once over,
What trouble is beyond the range of man?
What heavy burden will he not endure?
Jealousy, faction, quarreling, and battle—
The bloodiness of war, the grief of war.
And in the end he comes to strengthless age,
Abhorred by all men, without company,
Unfriended in that uttermost twilight
Where he must live with every bitter thing.
      Sophocles, *Oedipus at Colonus,* 1230

10 *Deianira.* I see her youth is coming to full bloom
  while mine is fading. The eyes of men love to
  pluck
  the blossoms; from the faded flowers they turn
  away.
      Sophocles, *Women of Trachis,* 547

11 Growing bodies have the most innate heat; they
  therefore require the most food, for otherwise their
  bodies are wasted. In old persons the heat is feeble, and therefore they require little fuel, as it

were, to the flame, for it would be extinguished by
much. On this account, also, fevers in old persons
are not equally acute, because their bodies are
cold.

      Hippocrates, *Aphorisms,* I, 14

12 Old people, on the whole, have fewer complaints
  than young; but those chronic diseases which do
  befall them generally never leave them.
      Hippocrates, *Aphorisms,* II, 39

13 I [Socrates] replied: There is nothing which for
  my part I like better, Cephalus, than conversing
  with aged men; for I regard them as travellers
  who have gone a journey which I too may have to
  go, and of whom I ought to enquire, whether the
  way is smooth and easy, or rugged and difficult.
  And this is a question which I should like to ask of
  you who have arrived at that time which the poets
  call the "threshold of old age"—Is life harder towards the end, or what report do you give of it?
    I will tell you, Socrates, he said, what my own
  feeling is. Men of my age flock together; we are
  birds of a feather, as the old proverb says; and at
  our meetings the tale of my acquaintance commonly is—I cannot eat, I cannot drink; the pleasures of youth and love are fled away: there was a
  good time once, but now that is gone, and life is
  no longer life. Some complain of the slights which
  are put upon them by relations, and they will tell
  you sadly of how many evils their old age is the
  cause. But to me, Socrates, these complainers
  seem to blame that which is not really in fault.
  For if old age were the cause, I too being old, and
  every other old man, would have felt as they do.
  But this is not my own experience, nor that of
  others whom I have known. How well I remember
  the aged poet Sophocles, when in answer to the
  question, How does love suit with age, Sophocles—are you still the man you were? Peace, he
  replied; most gladly have I escaped the thing of
  which you speak; I feel as if I had escaped from a
  mad and furious master. His words have often occurred to my mind since, and they seem as good
  to me now as at the time when he uttered them.
  For certainly old age has a great sense of calm
  and freedom; when the passions relax their hold,
  then, as Sophocles says, we are freed from the
  grasp not of one mad master only, but of many.
  The truth is, Socrates, that these regrets, and also
  the complaints about relations, are to be attributed to the same cause, which is not old age, but
  men's characters and tempers; for he who is of a
  calm and happy nature will hardly feel the pressure of age, but to him who is of an opposite disposition youth and age are equally a burden.
      Plato, *Republic,* I, 328B

14 *Socrates.* In youth good men often appear to be
  simple, and are easily practised upon by the dis-

honest, because they have no examples of what evil is in their own souls.

Plato, *Republic*, III, 409A

15 *Athenian Stranger.* Where old men have no shame, there young men will most certainly be devoid of reverence. The best way of training the young is to train yourself at the same time; not to admonish them, but to be always carrying out your own admonitions in practice.

Plato, *Laws,* V, 729A

16 A young man is not a proper hearer of lectures on political science; for he is inexperienced in the actions that occur in life, but its discussions start from these and are about these; and further, since he tends to follow his passions, his study will be vain and unprofitable, because the end aimed at is not knowledge but action. And it makes no difference whether he is young in years or youthful in character; the defect does not depend on time, but on his living, and pursuing each successive object, as passion directs. For to such persons, as to the incontinent, knowledge brings no profit; but to those who desire and act in accordance with a rational principle knowledge about such matters will be of great benefit.

Aristotle, *Ethics,* 1095ª2

17 The friendship of young people seems to aim at pleasure; for they live under the guidance of emotion, and pursue above all what is pleasant to themselves and what is immediately before them. . . . This is why they quickly become friends and quickly cease to be so; their friendship changes with the object that is found pleasant, and such pleasure alters quickly. Young people are amorous too; for the greater part of the friendship of love depends on emotion and aims at pleasure; this is why they fall in love and quickly fall out of love, changing often within a single day. But these people do wish to spend their days and lives together; for it is thus that they attain the purpose of their friendship.

Aristotle, *Ethics,* 1156ª32

18 Young men have strong passions, and tend to gratify them indiscriminately. Of the bodily desires, it is the sexual by which they are most swayed and in which they show absence of self-control. They are changeable and fickle in their desires, which are violent while they last, but quickly over: their impulses are keen but not deep-rooted, and are like sick people's attacks of hunger and thirst. They are hot-tempered, and quick-tempered, and apt to give way to their anger; bad temper often gets the better of them, for owing to their love of honour they cannot bear being slighted, and are indignant if they imagine themselves unfairly treated. While they love honour, they love victory still more; for youth is eager for superiority over others, and victory is one form of this. They love both more than they love money, which indeed they love very little, not having yet learnt what it means to be without it. . . . They look at the good side rather than the bad, not having yet witnessed many instances of wickedness. They trust others readily, because they have not yet often been cheated. They are sanguine; nature warms their blood as though with excess of wine; and besides that, they have as yet met with few disappointments. Their lives are mainly spent not in memory but in expectation; for expectation refers to the future, memory to the past, and youth has a long future before it and a short past behind it: on the first day of one's life one has nothing at all to remember, and can only look forward. They are easily cheated, owing to the sanguine disposition just mentioned. Their hot tempers and hopeful dispositions make them more courageous than older men are; the hot temper prevents fear, and the hopeful disposition creates confidence; we cannot feel fear so long as we are feeling angry, and any expectation of good makes us confident. They are shy, accepting the rules of society in which they have been trained, and not yet believing in any other standard of honour. They have exalted notions, because they have not yet been humbled by life or learnt its necessary limitations; moreover, their hopeful disposition makes them think themselves equal to great things—and that means having exalted notions. They would always rather do noble deeds than useful ones: their lives are regulated more by moral feeling than by reasoning; and whereas reasoning leads us to choose what is useful, moral goodness leads us to choose what is noble. They are fonder of their friends, intimates, and companions than older men are, because they like spending their days in the company of others, and have not yet come to value either their friends or anything else by their usefulness to themselves. All their mistakes are in the direction of doing things excessively and vehemently. They disobey Chilon's precept by overdoing everything; they love too much and hate too much, and the same thing with everything else. They think they know everything, and are always quite sure about it; this, in fact, is why they overdo everything. If they do wrong to others, it is because they mean to insult them, not to do them actual harm. They are ready to pity others, because they think every one an honest man, or anyhow better than he is: they judge their neighbour by their own harmless natures, and so cannot think he deserves to be treated in that way. They are fond of fun and therefore witty, wit being well-bred insolence.

Aristotle, *Rhetoric,* 1389ª3

19 Elderly Men . . . have lived many years; they have often been taken in, and often made mistakes; and life on the whole is a bad business. The

result is that they are sure about nothing and *under-do* everything. They 'think', but they never 'know'; and because of their hesitation they always add a 'possibly' or a 'perhaps', putting everything this way and nothing positively. They are cynical; that is, they tend to put the worse construction on everything. Further, their experience makes them distrustful and therefore suspicious of evil. Consequently they neither love warmly nor hate bitterly, but . . . love as though they will some day hate and hate as though they will some day love. They are small-minded, because they have been humbled by life: their desires are set upon nothing more exalted or unusual than what will help them to keep alive. They are not generous, because money is one of the things they must have, and at the same time their experience has taught them how hard it is to get and how easy to lose. They are cowardly, and are always anticipating danger; unlike that of the young, who are warm-blooded, their temperament is chilly; old age has paved the way for cowardice; fear is, in fact, a form of chill. They love life; and all the more when their last day has come. . . . They are too fond of themselves; this is one form that small-mindedness takes. Because of this, they guide their lives too much by considerations of what is useful and too little by what is noble—for the useful is what is good for oneself, and the noble what is good absolutely. They are not shy, but shameless rather; caring less for what is noble than for what is useful, they feel contempt for what people may think of them. They lack confidence in the future; partly through experience—for most things go wrong, or anyhow turn out worse than one expects; and partly because of their cowardice. They live by memory rather than by hope; for what is left to them of life is but little as compared with the long past; and hope is of the future, memory of the past. This, again, is the cause of their loquacity; they are continually talking of the past, because they enjoy remembering it. Their fits of anger are sudden but feeble. Their sensual passions have either altogether gone or have lost their vigour: consequently they do not feel their passions much, and their actions are inspired less by what they do feel than by the love of gain. Hence men at this time of life are often supposed to have a self-controlled character; the fact is that their passions have slackened, and they are slaves to the love of gain. They guide their lives by reasoning more than by moral feeling; reasoning being directed to utility and moral feeling to moral goodness. If they wrong others, they mean to injure them, not to insult them. Old men may feel pity, as well as young men, but not for the same reason. Young men feel it out of kindness; old men out of weakness, imagining that anything that befalls any one else might easily happen to them. . . . Hence they are querulous, and not disposed to jesting or laughter—the love of laughter being the very opposite of querulousness.

Aristotle, *Rhetoric*, 1389ᵇ13

20 As for Men in their Prime, clearly we shall find that they have a character between that of the young and that of the old, free from the extremes of either. They have neither that excess of confidence which amounts to rashness, nor too much timidity, but the right amount of each. They neither trust everybody nor distrust everybody, but judge people correctly. Their lives will be guided not by the sole consideration either of what is noble or of what is useful, but by both; neither by parsimony nor by prodigality, but by what is fit and proper. So, too, in regard to anger and desire; they will be brave as well as temperate, and temperate as well as brave; these virtues are divided between the young and the old; the young are brave but intemperate, the old temperate but cowardly. To put it generally, all the valuable qualities that youth and age divide between them are united in the prime of life, while all their excesses or defects are replaced by moderation and fitness. The body is in its prime from thirty to five-and-thirty; the mind about forty-nine.

Aristotle, *Rhetoric*, 1390ᵃ28

21 *Cato.* The great affairs of life are not performed by physical strength, or activity, or nimbleness of body, but by deliberation, character, expression of opinion. Of these old age is not only not deprived, but, as a rule, has them in a greater degree.

Cicero, *Old Age,* VI

22 *Cato.* The course of life is fixed, and nature admits of its being run but in one way, and only once; and to each part of our life there is something specially seasonable; so that the feebleness of children, as well as the high spirit of youth, the soberness of maturer years, and the ripe wisdom of old age—all have a certain natural advantage which should be secured in its proper season.

Cicero, *Old Age,* X

23 *Cato.* The fact is that old age is respectable just as long as it asserts itself, maintains its proper rights, and is not enslaved to any one. For as I admire a young man who has something of the old man in him, so do I an old one who has something of a young man. The man who aims at this may possibly become old in body—in mind he never will.

Cicero, *Old Age,* XI

24 "Perhaps you may of Priam's fate enquire.
He, when he saw his regal town on fire,
His ruin'd palace, and his ent'ring foes,
On ev'ry side inevitable woes,
In arms, disus'd, invests his limbs, decay'd,
Like them, with age; a late and useless aid.
His feeble shoulders scarce the weight sustain;
Loaded, not arm'd, he creeps along with pain,
Despairing of success, ambitious to be slain!
Uncover'd but by heav'n, there stood in view
An altar; near the hearth a laurel grew,

Dodder'd with age, whose boughs encompass
round
The household gods, and shade the holy ground.
Here Hecuba, with all her helpless train
Of dames, for shelter sought, but sought in vain.
Driv'n like a flock of doves along the sky,
Their images they hug, and to their altars fly.
The Queen, when she beheld her trembling lord,
And hanging by his side a heavy sword,
'What rage,' she cried, 'has seiz'd my husband's
mind?
What arms are these, and to what use design'd?
These times want other aids! Were Hector here,
Ev'n Hector now in vain, like Priam, would ap-
pear.
With us, one common shelter thou shalt find,
Or in one common fate with us be join'd.'
She said, and with a last salute embrac'd
The poor old man, and by the laurel plac'd.

Virgil, *Aeneid,* II

25 We should cherish old age and enjoy it. It is full of
pleasure if you know how to use it. Fruit tastes
most delicious just when its season is ending. The
charms of youth are at their greatest at the time of
its passing. It is the final glass which pleases the
inveterate drinker, the one that sets the crowning
touch on his intoxication and sends him off into
oblivion. Every pleasure defers till its last its greatest delights. The time of life which offers the
greatest delight is the age that sees the downward
movement—not the steep decline—already begun; and in my opinion even the age that stands
on the brink has pleasures of its own—or else the
very fact of not experiencing the want of any pleasures takes their place. How nice it is to have outworn one's desires and left them behind!

Seneca, *Letters to Lucilius,* 12

26 At the same time came the disciples unto Jesus,
saying, Who is the greatest in the kingdom of
Heaven?

And Jesus called a little child unto him, and set
him in the midst of them,

And said, Verily I say unto you, Except ye be
converted, and become as little children, ye shall
not enter into the kingdom of heaven.

Whosoever therefore shall humble himself as
this little child, the same is greatest in the kingdom of heaven.

And whoso shall receive one such little child in
my name receiveth me.

But whoso shall offend one of these little ones
which believe in me, it were better fôr him that a
millstone were hanged about his neck, and that he
were drowned in the depth of the sea.

Matthew 18:1–6

27 Verily, verily, I say unto thee, When thou wast
young, thou girdest thyself, and walkedst whither
thou wouldest: but when thou shalt be old, thou
shalt stretch forth thy hands, and another shall
gird thee, and carry thee whither thou wouldest
not.

John 21:18

28 How are you desirous at the same time to live to
old age, and at the same time not to see the death
of any person whom you love?

Epictetus, *Discourses,* III, 24

29 The innocence of children is in the helplessness of
their bodies rather than any quality in their
minds. I have myself seen a small baby jealous; it
was too young to speak, but it was livid with anger
as it watched another infant at the breast.

There is nothing unusual in this. Mothers and
nurses will tell you that they have their own way
of curing these fits of jealousy. But at any rate it is
an odd kind of innocence when a baby cannot
bear that another—in great need, since upon that
one food his very life depends—should share the
milk that flows in such abundance. These childish
tempers are borne with lightly, not because they
are not faults, or only small faults; but because
they will pass with the years. This is clearly so: for
though we bear with them now, the same things
would not be tolerated in an older person.

Augustine, *Confessions,* I, 7

30 Lord, I do not remember living this age of my
infancy; I must take the word of others about it
and can only conjecture how I spent it—even if
with a fair amount of certainty—from watching
others now in the same stage. I am loth, indeed, to
count it as part of the life I live in this world. For
it is buried in the darkness of the forgotten as
completely as the period earlier still that I spent
in my mother's womb.

Augustine, *Confessions,* I, 7

31 Such is God's mercy towards the vessels of mercy
which He has prepared for glory that even the
first age of man, that is, infancy, which submits
without any resistance to the flesh, and which has
not yet understanding enough to undertake this
warfare, and therefore yields to almost every vicious pleasure (because though this age has the
power of speech, and may therefore seem to have
passed infancy, the mind is still too weak to comprehend the commandment), yet if either of these
ages has received the sacraments of the Mediator,
then, although the present life be immediately
brought to an end, the child having been translated from the power of darkness to the kingdom of
Christ, shall not only bè saved from eternal punishments, but shall not even suffer purgatorial torments after death. For spiritual regeneration of
itself suffices to prevent any evil consequences resulting after death from the connection with
death which carnal generation forms. But when
we reach that age which can now comprehend the
commandment, and submit to the dominion of
law, we must declare war upon vices and wage

this war keenly, lest we be landed in damnable sins. And if vices have not gathered strength, by habitual victory they are more easily overcome and subdued; but if they have been used to conquer and rule, it is only with difficulty and labour they are mastered.

Augustine, *City of God,* XXI, 16

32 Few indeed are they who are so happy as to have passed their youth without committing any damnable sins, either by dissolute or violent conduct, or by following some godless and unlawful opinions.

Augustine, *City of God,* XXI, 16

33 Youth is a cause of hope for three reasons. . . . And these three reasons may be gathered from the three conditions of the good which is the object of hope—namely, that it is future, arduous and possible. . . . For youth has much of the future before it, and little of the past; and therefore since memory is of the past, and hope of the future, it has little to remember and lives very much in hope. Again, youths, on account of the heat of their nature, are full of spirit, so that their heart expands, and it is owing to the heart being expanded that one tends to that which is arduous; therefore youths are spirited and hopeful. Likewise they who have not suffered defeat, nor had experience of obstacles to their efforts, are prone to count a thing possible to them. Therefore youths, through inexperience of obstacles and of their own shortcomings, easily count a thing possible, and consequently are of good hope.

Aquinas, *Summa Theologica,* I–II, 40, 6

34 Human life is divided into four ages. The first is called adolescence, that is, the 'increasing' of life. The second is called 'manhood,' that is to say, the age of achievement, which may give perfection, and in this sense it is itself called perfect, because none can give aught save what he hath. The third is called old age. The fourth is called decrepitude. . . .

As to the first, no one hesitates, but every sage agrees that it lasts up to the twenty-fifth year; and because up to that time our soul is chiefly intent on conferring growth and beauty on the body, whence many and great changes take place in the person, the rational part cannot come to perfect discretion; wherefore Reason lays down that before this age there are certain things a man may not do without a guardian of full age.

As for the second, which is truly the summit of our life, there is great diversity concerning the period to be taken; but passing over what philosophers and physicians have written about it, and having recourse to my own argumentation, I say that in the majority (on whom every judgment about a natural phenomenon may and should be based) this age lasts twenty years. And the argument which gives me this is that, if the apex of our

arch is at thirty-five, the age under discussion should have as long a period of descent as it has of ascent; and this rising and descending may be likened to the sustained height of the arch wherein but slight bending is to be discerned. We have it, then, that the prime of life is completed at the forty-fifth year.

And as adolescence lasts twenty-five years, mounting up to the prime of life, so the descent, that is, age, is a like period, succeeding to the prime of life; and so age ends at the seventieth year.

But inasmuch as adolescence (taking it as we have done above) does not begin at the beginning of life, but some eight months after, and inasmuch as our nature is eager to rise and hangs back from descending (because the natural heat is reduced and has small power, and the humid is thickened, not in quantity but in quality, and so is less easily evaporated and consumed) it comes to pass that beyond old age there remains perhaps to the amount of ten years of our life, or a little more or a little less. And this period is called decrepitude. Whence we have it of Plato—whom (both in the strength of his own nature, and because of the physiognomiscope which Socrates cast for him when first he saw him) we may believe to have had the most excellent nature—that he lived eighty-one years, as testifies Tully in that *Of Old Age.* And I believe that if Christ had not been crucified and had lived out the space which his life had power to cover according to its nature, he would have been changed at the eighty-first year from mortal body to eternal.

Dante, *Convivio,* IV, 24

35 *Pandar.* Remember time is wasting every hour
Some share of all the beauty now we see,
And thus, ere age shall all they charms devour,
Go love, for old, none will have aught of thee!
This saying may a lesson to you be,
'It might have been,' said Beauty, beauty past.

Chaucer, *Troilus and Cressida,* II, 57

36 For true it is, age has great advantage;
Experience and wisdom come with age;
Men may the old out-run, but not out-wit.

Chaucer, *Canterbury Tales:* Knight's Tale

37 But I am old; I will not play, for age;
Grass time is done, my fodder is rummage,
This white top advertises my old years,
My heart, too, is as mouldy as my hairs,
Unless I fare like medlar, all perverse.
For that fruit's never ripe until it's worse,
And falls among the refuse or in straw.
We ancient men, I fear, obey this law:
Until we're rotten we cannot be ripe;
We dance, indeed, the while the world will pipe.
Desire sticks in our nature like a nail
To have, if hoary head, a verdant tail,
As has the leek; for though our strength be gone,

Our wish is yet for folly till life's done.
For when we may not act, then will we speak;
Yet in our ashes is there fire to reek
    Four embers have we, which I shall confess:
Boasting and lying, anger, covetousness;
These four remaining sparks belong to eld.
Our ancient limbs may well be hard to wield,
But lust will never fail us, that is truth.
And yet I have had always a colt's tooth,
As many years as now are past and done
Since first my tap of life began to run.
For certainly, when I was born, I know
Death turned my tap of life and let it flow;
And ever since that day the tap has run
Till nearly empty now is all the tun.
The stream of life now drips upon the chime;
The silly tongue may well ring out the time
Of wretchedness that passed so long before;
For oldsters, save for dotage, there's no more.

       Chaucer, *Canterbury Tales:* Reeve's Prologue

38 But Lord Christ! When I do remember me
Upon my youth and on my jollity,
It tickles me about my heart's deep root.
To this day does my heart sing in salute
That I have had my world in my own time.
But age, alas! that poisons every prime,
Has taken away my beauty and my pith;
Let go, farewell, the devil go therewith!
The flour is gone, there is no more to tell,
The bran, as best I may, must I now sell;
But yet to be right merry I'll try.

       Chaucer, *Canterbury Tales:*
       Wife of Bath's Prologue

39 And though your time of green youth flower as
    yet,
Age creeps in always, silent as a stone;
Death threatens every age, nor will forget
For any state, and there escapes him none:
And just as surely as we know, each one,
That we shall die, uncertain are we all
What day it is when death shall on us fall.

       Chaucer, *Canterbury Tales:* Clerk's Tale

40 Young fellows are tempted by girls, men who are
thirty years old are tempted by gold, when they
are forty years old they are tempted by honor and
glory, and those who are sixty years old say to
themselves, 'What a pious man I have become!'

       Luther, *Table Talke,* 1601

41 Youth is impertinent. So we see lawyers who in
their first year are masters of all laws, in their
second year are Justinians, in their third year are
licentiates, in their fourth year give formal opinions, and in their fifth year finally become trembling students. This is the way a boy acts in a
bowling alley. First he expects to strike twelve
pins, then nine, then six, then three, and at last
he's satisified with one, and probably misses the
alley at that. It would be a good thing if young

people were wise and old people were strong, but
God has arranged things better.

       Luther, *Table Talk,* 4091

42 Gargantua, from three years upwards unto five,
was brought up and instructed in all convenient
discipline, by the commandment of his father;
and spent that time like the other little children of
the country, that is, in drinking, eating, and sleeping: in eating, sleeping, and drinking: and in
sleeping, drinking, and eating. Still he wallowed
and rolled himself up and down in the mire and
dirt: he blurred and sullied his nose with filth; he
blotted and smutched his face with any kind of
scurvy and stuff; he trod down his shoes in the
heel; at the flies he did often times yawn, and ran
very heartily after the butterflies, the empire
whereof belonged to his father.

       Rabelais, *Gargantua and Pantagruel,* I, 11

43 It is possible that in those who employ their time
well, knowledge and experience grow with living;
but vivacity, quickness, firmness, and other qualities much more our own, more important and
essential, wither and languish. . . . Sometimes it
is the body that first surrenders to age, sometimes,
too, it is the mind; and I have seen enough whose
brains were enfeebled before their stomach and
legs; and inasmuch as this is a malady hardly perceptible to the sufferer and obscure in its symptoms, it is all the more dangerous. For the time, I
complain of the laws, not that they leave us at
work too long, but that they set us to work too
late. It seems to me that considering the frailty of
our life and how many ordinary natural reefs it is
exposed to, we should not allot so great a part of it
to birth, idleness, and apprenticeship.

       Montaigne, *Essays,* I, 57, Of Age

44 This fault of not being able to recognize oneself
early and not feeling the impotence and extreme
alteration that age naturally brings to both body
and soul, and in my opinion equally, unless the
soul receives more than half of it, has ruined the
reputation of most of the world's great men.

       Montaigne, *Essays,* II, 8,
       Affection of Fathers

45 Old age puts more wrinkles in our minds than on
our faces; and we never, or rarely, see a soul that
in growing old does not come to smell sour and
musty. Man grows and dwindles in his entirety.

       Montaigne, *Essays,* III, 2, Of Repentance

46 The whiles some one did chaunt this lovely lay:—
Ah! see, who so fayre thing doest faine to see,
In springing flowre the image of thy day;
Ah! see the virgin rose, how sweetly shee
Doth first peepe foorth with bashful modestee,
That fairer seemes, the lesse ye see her may;
Lo! see soone after, how more bold and free
Her bared bosome she doth broad display;

Lo! see soone after, how she fades and falls away.

So passeth, in the passing of a day,
Of mortall life the leafe, the bud, the flowre,
Ne more doth florish after first decay,
That earst was sought to deck both bed and bowre
Of many a lady, and many a paramowre:
Gather therefore the rose, whilest yet is prime,
For soone comes age, that will her pride deflowre:
Gather the rose of love, whilest yet is time,
Whilest loving thou mayst loved be with equall
  crime.

  Spenser, *Faerie Queen*, Bk. II, XII, 74–75

47 *Chief Justice.* Do you set down your name in the
scroll of youth, that are written down old with all
the characters of age? Have you not a moist eye?
a dry hand? a yellow cheek? a white beard? a
decreasing leg? an increasing belly? is not your
voice broken? your wind short? your chin double?
your wit single? and every part about you blasted
with antiquity? and will you yet call yourself
young? Fie, fie, fie, Sir John!

Falstaff. My lord, I was born about three of the
clock in the afternoon, with a white head and
something a round belly. For my voice, I have lost
it with halloing and singing of anthems. To approve my youth further, I will not: the truth is, I
am only old in judgement and understanding;
and he that will caper with me for a thousand
marks, let him lend me the money, and have at
him!

  Shakespeare, *II Henry IV,* I, ii, 201

48 *Shallow.* O, Sir John, do you remember since we
lay all night in the windmill in Saint George's
field?

Falstaff. No more of that, good Master Shallow,
no more of that.

Shal. Ha! 'twas a merry night. And is Jane
Nightwork alive?

Fal. She lives, Master Shallow.

Shal. She never could away with me.

Fal. Never, never; she would always say she
could not abide Master Shallow.

Shal. By the mass, I could anger her to the
heart. She was then a bona-roba. Doth she hold
her own well?

Fal. Old, old, Master Shallow.

Shal. Nay, she must be old; she cannot choose
but be old; certain she's old; and had Robin
Nightwork by old Nightwork before I came to
Clement's Inn.

Silence. That's fifty five year ago.

Shal. Ha, cousin Silence, that thou hadst seen
that that this knight and I have seen! Ha, Sir
John, said I well?

Fal. We have heard the chimes at midnight,
Master Shallow.

Shal. That we have, that we have, that we have;
in faith, Sir John, we have: our watchword was
"Hem, boys!" Come, let's to dinner; come, let's to
dinner: Jesus, the days that we have seen! Come,
come.

  Shakespeare, *II Henry IV,* III, ii, 206

49 *Falstaff.* Lord, Lord, how subject we old men are
to this vice of lying!

  Shakespeare, *II Henry IV,* III, ii, 325

50 *King.* I know thee not, old man: fall to thy prayers;
How ill white hairs become a fool and jester!

  Shakespeare, *II Henry IV,* V, v, 51

51 *Jaques.*   All the world's a stage,
And all the men and women merely players:
They have their exits and their entrances;
And the man in his time plays many parts,
His acts being seven ages. At first the infant,
Mewling and puking in the nurse's arms.
And then the whining school-boy, with his satchel
And shining morning face, creeping like snail
Unwillingly to school. And then the lover,
Sighing like furnace, with a woeful ballad
Made to his mistress' eyebrow. Then a soldier,
Full of strange oaths and bearded like the pard,
Jealous in honour, sudden and quick in quarrel,
Seeking the bubble reputation
Even in the cannon's mouth. And then the justice,
In fair round belly with good capon lined,
With eyes severe and beard of formal cut,
Full of wise saws and modern instances;
And so he plays his part. The sixth age shifts
Into the lean and slipper'd pantaloon,
With spectacles on nose and pouch on side,
His youthful hose, well saved, a world too wide
For his shrunk shank; and his big manly voice,
Turning again toward childish treble, pipes
And whistles in his sound. Last scene of all,
That ends this strange eventful history,
Is second childishness and mere oblivion,
Sans teeth, sans eyes, sans taste, sans everything.

  Shakespeare, *As You Like It,* II, vii, 139

52 *Clown.* What is love? 'tis not hereafter;
Present mirth hath present laughter;
  What's to come is still unsure:
In delay there lies no plenty;
Then come kiss me, sweet and twenty,
  Youth's a stuff will not endure.

  Shakespeare, *Twelfth Night,* II, iii, 48

53 *Polonius.* What do you read, my lord?

Hamlet. Words, words, words.

Pol. What is the matter, my lord?

Ham. Between who?

Pol. I mean, the matter that you read, my lord.

Ham. Slanders, sir: for the satirical rogue says
here that old men have grey beards, that their
faces are wrinkled, their eyes purging thick amber
and plum-tree gum and that they have a plentiful

lack of wit, together with most weak hams.
>Shakespeare, *Hamlet,* II, ii, 193

54 *Hamlet.*   Rebellious hell,
If thou canst mutine in a matron's bones,
To flaming youth let virtue be as wax,
And melt in her own fire.
>Shakespeare, *Hamlet,* III, iv, 82

55 *Regan.*   O, sir, you are old;
Nature in you stands on the very verge
Of her confine. You should be ruled and led
By some discretion that discerns your state
Better than you yourself. Therefore, I pray you
That to our sister you do make return;
Say you have wrong'd her, sir.
   Lear.   Ask her forgiveness?
Do you but mark how this becomes the house:
"Dear daughter, I confess that I am old;
   Kneeling.
Age is unnecessary. On my knees I beg
That you'll vouchsafe me raiment, bed, and
   food."
   Reg. Good sir, no more; these are unsightly
   tricks.
>Shakespeare, *Lear,* II, iv, 148

56 *Macbeth.* I have lived long enough; my way of life
Is fall'n into the sear, the yellow leaf;
And that which should accompany old age,
As honour, love, obedience, troops of friends,
I must not look to have; but, in their stead,
Curses, not loud but deep, mouth-honour, breath,
Which the poor heart would fain deny, and dare
   not.
>Shakespeare, *Macbeth,* V, iii, 22

57 *Cleopatra.*   My salad days,
When I was green in judgement, cold in blood,
To say as I said then!
>Shakespeare, *Antony and Cleopatra,* I, v, 73

58 *Hermione.*   Come, I'll question you
Of my Lord's tricks and yours when you were
   boys.
You were pretty lordings then?
   Polixenes.   We were, fair Queen,
Two lads that thought there was no more behind
But such a day to-morrow as to-day,
And to be boy eternal.
   Her.   Was not my lord
The verier wag o' the two?
   Pol. We were as twinn'd lambs that did frisk i'
   the sun,
And bleat the one at the other. What we changed
Was innocence for innocence; we knew not
The doctrine of ill-doing, nor dream'd
That any did. Had we pursued that life,
And our weak spirits ne'er been higher rear'd
With stronger blood, we should have answer'd
   heaven

Boldly, "Not guilty."
>Shakespeare, *Winter's Tale,* I, ii, 60

59 Thou art thy mother's glass, and she in thee
Calls back the lovely April of her prime.
So thou through windows of thine age shalt see
Despite of wrinkles this thy golden time.
>Shakespeare, *Sonnet III*

60 When I consider every thing that grows
Holds in perfection but a little moment,
That this huge stage presenteth nought but shows
Whereon the stars in secret influence comment;
When I perceive that men as plants increase,
Cheered and check'd even by the self-same sky,
Vaunt in their youthful sap, at height decrease,
And wear their brave state out of memory;
Then the conceit of this inconstant stay
Sets you most rich in youth before my sight,
Where wasteful Time debateth with Decay,
To change your day of youth to sullied night.
>Shakespeare, *Sonnet XV*

61 That time of year thou mayst in me behold
When yellow leaves, or none, or few, do hang
Upon those boughs which shake against the cold,
Bare ruin'd choirs, where late the sweet birds
   sang.
In me thou see'st the twilight of such day
As after sunset fadeth in the west,
Which by and by black night doth take away,
Death's second self, that seals up all in rest.
In me thou see'st the glowing of such fire
That on the ashes of his youth doth lie,
As the death-bed whereon it must expire
Consumed with that which it was nourish'd by.
>Shakespeare, *Sonnet LXXIII*

62 To me, fair friend, you never can be old,
For as you were when first your eye I eyed,
Such seems your beauty still.
>Shakespeare, *Sonnet CIV*

63 When my love swears that she is made of truth
I do believe her, though I know she lies,
That she might think me some untutor'd youth,
Unlearned in the world's false subtleties.
Thus vainly thinking that she thinks me young,
Although she knows my days are past the best,
Simply I credit her false-speaking tongue:
On both sides thus is simple truth suppress'd.
But wherefore says she not she is unjust?
And wherefore say not I that I am old?
O, love's best habit is in seeming trust,
And age in love loves not to have years told.
>Shakespeare, *Sonnet CXXXVIII*

64 Crabbed age and youth cannot live together:
Youth is full of pleasance, age is full of care;
Youth like summer morn, age like winter
   weather;

Youth like summer brave, age like winter bare.
Youth is full of sport, age's breath is short;
Youth is nimble, age is lame;
Youth is hot and bold, age is weak and cold;
Youth is wild, and age is tame.
Age, I do abhor thee; youth, I do adore thee.

Shakespeare, *The Passionate Pilgrim*, XII

65 Come, my Celia, let us prove,
While we can, the sports of love;
Time will not be ours forever;
He at length our good will sever.

Jonson, *Come, My Celia*

66 Young men are fitter to invent than to judge; fitter for execution than for counsel; and fitter for new projects than for settled business. For the experience of age, in things that fall within the compass of it, directeth them; but in new things, abuseth them. The errors of young men are the ruin of business; but the errors of aged men amount but to this, that more might have been done, or sooner. Young men, in the conduct and manage of actions, embrace more than they can hold; stir more than they can quiet; fly to the end, without consideration of the means and degrees; pursue some few principles which they have chanced upon absurdly; care not to innovate, which draws unknown inconveniences; use extreme remedies at first; and, that which doubleth all errors, will not acknowledge or retract them; like an unready horse, that will neither stop nor turn. Men of age object too much, consult too long, adventure too little, repent too soon, and seldom drive business home to the full period, but content themselves with a mediocrity of success.

Bacon, *Of Youth and Age*

67 Alonso of Arragon was wont to say, in commendation of age, That age appeared to be best in four things: *Old wood best to burn; old wine to drink; old friends to trust; and old authors to read.*

Bacon, *Apophthegms*, LXXV

68 The proportion of the body to the extremities in children after their birth continues excessive until they begin to stand and run. Infants, therefore, resemble dwarfs in the beginning, and they creep about like quadrupeds, attempting progressive motion with the assistance of all their extremities; but they cannot stand erect until the length of the leg and thigh together exceeds the length of the rest of the body. And so it happens, that when they first attempt to walk, they move with the body prone, like the quadruped, and can scarcely rise so erect as the common dunghill foul.

William Harvey, *Animal Generation*, 56

69 Age doth not rectifie, but incurvate our natures, turning bad dispositions into worser habits, and (like diseases) brings on incurable vices; for every day as we grow weaker in age, we grow stronger in sin; and the number of our days doth make but our sins innumerable. The same vice committed at sixteen, is not the same, though it agree in all other circumstances, at forty, but swells and doubles from the circumstances of our ages, wherein, besides the constant and inexcusable habit of transgressing, the maturity of our judgement cuts off pretence unto excuse or pardon: every sin the oftner it is committed, the more it acquireth in the quality of evil; as it succeeds in time, so it proceeds in degrees of badness; for as they proceed they ever multiply, and like figures in Arithmetick, the last stands for more than all that went before it. And though I think no man can live well once, but he that could live twice, yet for my own part I would not live over my hours past, or begin again the thred of my days: not upon *Cicero's* ground, because I have lived them well, but for fear I should live them worse.

Sir Thomas Browne, *Religio Medici*, I, 42

70 Confound not the distinctions of thy Life which Nature hath divided: that is, Youth, Adolescence, Manhood, and old Age, nor in these divided Periods, wherein thou art in a manner Four, conceive thyself but One. Let every division be happy in its proper Virtues, nor one Vice run through all. Let each distinction have its salutary transition, and critically deliver thee from the imperfections of the former, so ordering the whole, that Prudence and Virtue may have the largest section. Do as a Child but when thou art a Child, and ride not on a Reed at twenty. He who hath not taken leave of the follies of his Youth, and in his maturer state scarce got out of that division, disproportionately divideth his Days, crowds up the latter part of his Life, and leaves too narrow a corner for the Age of Wisdom.

Sir Thomas Browne, *Christian Morals*, III, 8

71 How soon hath Time the suttle theef of youth,
Stoln on his wing my three and twentith yeer!
My hasting dayes flie on with full career,
But my late spring no bud or blossom shew'th.
Perhaps my semblance might deceive the truth,
That I to manhood am arriv'd so near,
And inward ripenes doth much less appear,
That som more timely-happy spirits indu'th.

Milton, *How soon hath Time
the suttle theef of youth*

72 This is old age; but then thou must outlive
Thy youth, thy strength, thy beauty, which will change
To withered weak & gray; thy Senses then
Obtuse, all taste of pleasure must forgoe,
To what thou hast, and for the Aire of youth
Hopeful and cheerful, in thy blood will reigne
A melancholly damp of cold and dry

To waigh thy spirits down, and last consume
The Balme of Life.

Milton, Paradise Lost, XI, 535

73   The childhood shews the man,
As morning shews the day.

Milton, Paradise Regained, IV, 220

74 *Dollabella.* Men are but children of a larger
growth;
Our appetites as apt to change as theirs,
And full as craving too, and full as vain.

Dryden, All for Love, IV, 43

75 *Mirabell.* An old woman's appetite is depraved like
that of a girl—'tis the greensickness of a second
childhood; and like the faint offer of a latter
spring, serves but to usher in the fall and withers
in an affected bloom.

Congreve, Way of the World, II, iv

76 He [the interpreter] gave me a particular account
of the Struldbruggs among them. He said they
commonly acted like mortals, until about thirty
years old, after which by degrees they grew melancholy and dejected, increasing in both until
they came to fourscore. This he learned from their
own confession; for otherwise, there not being
above two or three of that species born in an age,
they were too few to form a general observation
by. When they came to fourscore years, which is
reckoned the extremity of living in this country,
they had not only all the follies and infirmities of
other old men, but many more which arose from
the dreadful prospect of never dying. They were
not only opinionative, peevish, covetous, morose,
vain, talkative; but uncapable of friendship, and
dead to all natural affection, which never descended below their grand-children. Envy and
impotent desires, are their prevailing passions.
But those objects against which their envy seems
principally directed, are the vices of the younger
sort, and the deaths of the old. By reflecting on
the former, they find themselves cut off from all
possibility of pleasure; and whenever they see a
funeral, they lament and repine that others are
gone to a harbour of rest, to which they themselves never can hope to arrive. They have no remembrance of any thing but what they learned
and observed in their youth and middle age, and
even that is very imperfect: and for the truth or
particulars of any fact, it is safer to depend on
common traditions, than upon their best recollections. The least miserable among them, appear to
be those who turn to dotage, and entirely lose
their memories; these meet with more pity and
assistance, because they want many bad qualities
which abound in others.

If a Struldbrugg happen to marry one of his
own kind, the marriage is dissolved of course by
the courtesy of the kingdom, as soon as the younger of the two comes to be fourscore. For the law
thinks it a reasonable indulgence, that those who
are condemned without any fault of their own, to
a perpetual continuance in the world, should not
have their misery doubled by the load of a wife.

As soon as they have compleated the term of
eighty years, they are looked on as dead in law;
their heirs immediately succeed to their estates,
only a small pittance is reserved for their support,
and the poor ones are maintained at the publick
charge. After that period, they are held incapable
of any employment of trust or profit; they cannot
purchase lands, or take leases; neither are they
allowed to be witnesses in any cause, either civil
or criminal, not even for the decision of meers and
bounds.

At ninety they lose their teeth and hair; they
have at that age no distinction of taste, but eat
and drink what ever they can get, without relish
or appetite. The diseases they were subject to, still
continue without encreasing or diminishing. In
talking, they forget the common appellation of
things, and the names of persons, even of those
who are their nearest friends and relations. For
the same reason, they never can amuse themselves
with reading, because their memory will not serve
to carry them from the beginning of a sentence to
the end; and by this defect, they are deprived of
the only entertainment whereof they might otherwise be capable.

The language of this country being always
upon the flux, the Struldbruggs of one age, do not
understand those of another; neither are they able
after two hundred years, to hold any conversation
(farther than by a few general words) with their
neighbours the mortals; and thus they lye under
the disadvantage of living like foreigners in their
own country.

Swift, Gulliver's Travels, III, 10

77 They [the Yahoos] are prodigiously nimble from
their infancy; however, I once caught a young
male of three years old, and endeavoured by all
marks of tenderness to make it quiet; but the little
imp fell a squalling, and scratching, and biting
with such violence, that I was forced to let it go;
and it was high time, for a whole troop of old ones
came about us at the noise; but finding the cub
was safe, (for away it ran) and my sorrel nag
being by, they durst not venture near us. I observed the young animal's flesh to smell very rank,
and the stink was somewhat between a *weasel* and
a *fox,* but much more disagreeable. I forgot another circumstance, (and perhaps I might have the
readers pardon, if it were wholly omitted) that
while I held the odious vermin in my hands, it
voided its filthy excrements of a yellow liquid substance, all over my cloaths; but by good fortune
there was a small brook hard by, where I washed
myself as clean as I could; although I durst not
come into my master's presence, until I was sufficiently aired.

Swift, Gulliver's Travels, IV, 8

78 Invention is the Talent of Youth, and Judgment of Age; so that our Judgment grows harder to please, when we have fewer Things to offer it: This goes through the whole Commerce of Life. When we are old, our Friends find it difficult to please us, and are less concern'd whether we be pleas'd or no.

Swift, *Thoughts on Various Subjects*

79 No wise Man ever wished to be younger.

Swift, *Thoughts on Various Subjects*

80 Every Man desires to live long; but no Man would be old.

Swift, *Thoughts on Various Subjects*

81 Man has other enemies more formidable, against which he is not provided with such means of defence: these are the natural infirmities of infancy, old age, and illness of every kind, melancholy proofs of our weakness, of which the two first are common to all animals, and the last belongs chiefly to man in a state of society. With regard to infancy, it is observable that the mother, carrying her child always with her, can nurse it with much greater ease than the females of many other animals, which are forced to be perpetually going and coming, with great fatigue, one way to find subsistence, and another to suckle or feed their young. It is true that if the woman happens to perish, the infant is in great danger of perishing with her; but this risk is common to many other species of animals, whose young take a long time before they are able to provide for themselves. And if our infancy is longer than theirs, our lives are longer in proportion; so that all things are in this respect fairly equal; though there are other rules to be considered regarding the duration of the first period of life, and the number of young, which do not affect the present subject. In old age, when men are less active and perspire little, the need for food diminishes with the ability to provide it. As the savage state also protects them from gout and rheumatism, and old age is, of all ills, that which human aid can least alleviate, they cease to be, without others perceiving that they are no more, and almost without perceiving it themselves.

Rousseau, *Origin of Inequality*, I

82 Fix your eyes on nature, follow the path traced by her. She keeps children at work, she hardens them by all kinds of difficulties, she soon teaches them the meaning of pain and grief. They cut their teeth and are feverish, sharp colics bring on convulsions, they are choked by fits of coughing and tormented by worms, evil humours corrupt the blood, germs of various kinds ferment in it, causing dangerous eruptions. Sickness and danger play the chief part in infancy. One half of the children who are born die before their eighth year. The child who has overcome hardships has

gained strength, and as soon as he can use his life he holds it more securely.

This is nature's law; why contradict it? Do you not see that in your efforts to improve upon her handiwork you are destroying it; her cares are wasted? To do from without what she does within is according to you to increase the danger twofold. On the contrary, it is the way to avert it; experience shows that children delicately nurtured are more likely to die. Provided we do not overdo it, there is less risk in using their strength than in sparing it. Accustom them therefore to the hardships they will have to face; train them to endure extremes of temperature, climate, and condition, hunger, thirst, and weariness. Dip them in the waters of Styx. Before bodily habits become fixed you may teach what habits you will without any risk, but once habits are established any change is fraught with peril. A child will bear changes which a man cannot bear, the muscles of the one are soft and flexible, they take whatever direction you give them without any effort; the muscles of the grown man are harder and they only change their accustomed mode of action when subjected to violence. So we can make a child strong without risking his life or health, and even if there were some risk, it should not be taken into consideration. Since human life is full of dangers, can we do better than face them at a time when they can do the least harm?

Rousseau, *Emile*, I

83 The new-born infant cries, his early days are spent in crying. He is alternately petted and shaken by way of soothing him; sometimes he is threatened, sometimes beaten, to keep him quiet. We do what he wants or we make him do what we want, we submit to his whims or subject him to our own. There is no middle course; he must rule or obey.

Rousseau, *Emile*, I

84 Every old man complains of the growing depravity of the world, of the petulance and insolence of the rising generation. He recounts the decency and regularity of former times, and celebrates the discipline and sobriety of the age in which his youth was passed; a happy age which is now no more to be expected, since confusion has broken in upon the world, and thrown down all the boundaries of civility and reverence.

Johnson, *Rambler No. 50*

85 He that would pass the latter part of life with honour and decency, must, when he is young, consider that he shall one day be old; and remember, when he is old, that he has once been young.

Johnson, *Rambler No. 50*

86 To youth . . . it should be carefully inculcated, that to enter the road of life without caution or reserve, in expectation of general fidelity and jus-

tice, is to launch on the wide ocean without the instruments of steerage, and to hope that every wind will be prosperous and that every coast will afford a harbour.

Johnson, *Rambler No. 175*

87 Rasselas rose next day, and resolved to begin his experiments upon life. "Youth, cried he, is the time of gladness: I will join myself to the young men, whose only business is to gratify their desires, and whose time is all spent in a succession of enjoyments."

To such societies he was readily admitted, but a few days brought him back weary and disgusted. Their mirth was without images, their laughter without motive: their pleasures were gross and sensual, in which the mind had no part; their conduct was at once wild and mean; they laughed at order and at law, but the frown of power dejected, and the eye of wisdom abashed them.

Johnson, *Rasselas,* XVII

88 The old man trusts wholly to slow contrivance and gradual progression: the youth expects to force his way by genius, vigour, and precipitance. The old man pays regard to riches, and the youth reverences virtue. The old man defies prudence: the youth commits himself to magnanimity and chance. The young man, who intends no ill, believes that none is intended, and therefore acts with openness and candour: but his father, having suffered the injuries of fraud, is impelled to suspect, and too often allured to practice it. Age looks with anger on the temerity of youth, and youth with contempt on the scrupulosity of age.

Johnson, *Rasselas,* XXVI

89 There are few things that we so unwillingly give up, even in advanced age, as the supposition that we have still the power of ingratiating ourselves with the fair sex.

Johnson, *Miscellanies,* II

90 *Johnson.* Sir, I love the acquaintance of young people; because, in the first place, I don't like to think myself growing old. In the next place, young acquaintances must last longest, if they do last; and then, Sir, young men have more virtue than old men; they have more generous sentiments in every respect. I love the young dogs of this age: they have more wit and humour and knowledge of life than we had; but then the dogs are not so good scholars. Sir, in my early years I read very hard. It is a sad reflection, but a true one, that I knew almost as much at eighteen as I do now. My judgement, to be sure, was not so good; but I had all the facts. I remember very well, when I was at Oxford, an old gentleman said to me, 'Young man, ply your book diligently now, and acquire a stock of knowledge; for when years come upon you, you will find that poring upon books will be but an irksome task.'

Boswell, *Life of Johnson (July 21, 1763)*

91 *Goldsmith.* "I think, Mr. Johnson, you don't go near the theatres now. You give yourself no more concern about a new play, than if you had never had any thing to do with the stage." *Johnson.* "Why, Sir, our tastes greatly alter. The lad does not care for the child's rattle, and the old man does not care for the young man's whore." *Goldsmith.* "Nay, Sir, but your Muse was not a whore." *Johnson.* "Sir, I do not think she was. But as we advance in the journey of life, we drop some of the things which have pleased us; whether it be that we are fatigued and don't choose to carry so many things any farther, or that we find other things which we like better." *Boswell.* "But, Sir, why don't you give us something in some other way?" *Goldsmith.* "Ay, Sir, we have a claim upon you." *Johnson.* "No, Sir, I am not obliged to do any more. No man is obliged to do as much as he can do. A man is to have part of his life to himself. If a soldier has fought a good many campaigns, he is not to be blamed if he retires to ease and tranquillity. A physician, who has practised long in a great city, may be excused if he retires to a small town, and takes less practice. Now, Sir, the good I can do by my conversation bears the same proportion to the good I can do by my writings, that the practice of a physician, retired to a small town, does to his practice in a great city." *Boswell.* "But I wonder, Sir, you have not more pleasure in writing than in not writing." *Johnson.* "Sir, you *may* wonder."

Boswell, *Life of Johnson (1766)*

92 John Anderson, my jo, John,
    When we were first acquent;
Your locks were like the raven,
    Your bonnie brow was brent;
But now your brow is beld, John,
    Your locks are like the snow;
But blessings on your frosty pow,
    John Anderson, my jo.

Burns, *John Anderson, My Jo*

93 The constitution of New York, to avoid investigations that must for ever be vague and dangerous, has taken a particular age as the criterion of inability. No man can be a judge beyond sixty. I believe there are few at present who do not disapprove of this provision. There is no station, in relation to which it is less proper than to that of a judge. The deliberating and comparing faculties generally preserve their strength much beyond that period in men who survive it; and when, in addition to this circumstance, we consider how few there are who outlive the season of intellectual vigour, and how improbable it is that any consid-

erable portion of the bench, whether more or less numerous, should be in such a situation at the same time, we shall be ready to conclude that limitations of this sort have little to recommend them. In a republic, where fortunes are not affluent and pensions not expedient, the dismission of men from stations in which they have served their country long and usefully, on which they depend for subsistence, and from which it will be too late to resort to any other occupation for a livelihood, ought to have some better apology to humanity than is to be found in the imaginary danger of a superannuated bench.

Hamilton, *Federalist 79*

94 We are moved in the presence of childhood, but it is not because from the height of our strength and of our perfection we drop a look of pity on it; it is, on the contrary, because from the depths of our impotence, of which the feeling is inseparable from that of the real and determinate state to which we have arrived, we raise our eyes to the child's determinableness and pure innocence. The feeling we then experience is too evidently mingled with sadness for us to mistake its source. In the child all is disposition and destination; in us all is in the state of a completed, finished thing, and the completion always remains infinitely below the destination. It follows that the child is to us like a representation of the ideal; not, indeed, of the ideal as we have realized it, but such as our destination admitted; and, consequently, it is not at all the idea of its indigence, of its hindrances, that makes us experience emotion in the child's presence; it is, on the contrary, the idea of its pure and free force, of the integrity, the infinity of its being. This is the reason why, in the sight of every moral and sensible man, the child will always be a sacred thing; I mean an object which, by the grandeur of an idea, reduces to nothingness all grandeur realized by experience; an object which, in spite of all it may lose in the judgment of the understanding, regains largely the advantage before the judgment of reason.

Schiller, *Simple and Sentimental Poetry*

95 *Faust.* I'll feel, whatever my attire,
The pain of life, earth's narrow way.
I am too old to be content with play,
Too young to be without desire.
What can the world afford me now?
Thou shalt renounce! Renounce shalt thou!
That is the never-ending song
Which in the ears of all is ringing,
Which always, through our whole life long,
Hour after hour is hoarsely singing.

Goethe, *Faust* I, 1544

96 *Mephistopheles.* If, unadulterate, one says to youth
What does not please the callow brook—the truth!

And later after many a tide
They learn it painfully on their own hide,
Each fancies then it came from his own head;
"The Master was a fool!" is what is said.

Goethe, *Faust*, II, 2, 6744

97 *Bachelor of Arts.* This is youth's noblest message and most fit!
The world was not till I created it.
'Twas I that led the sun up from the sea;
The moon began its changeful course with me.
The day put on rich garments, me to meet;
The earth grew green and blossomed, me to greet.
At my behest in that primeval night
The stars unveiled their splendour to my sight.
Who, if not I, your own deliverance wrought
From fetters of Philistine, cramping thought?
I, as my spirit bids me, with delight
I follow onward mine own inner light.
Swift I proceed with mine own raptured mind,
Glory before me, darkness far behind.

Goethe, *Faust*, II, 2, 6793

98 —*A Simple* Child,
That lightly draws its breath,
And feels its life in every limb,
What should it know of death?

Wordsworth, *We Are Seven*

99 My heart leaps up when I behold
    A rainbow in the sky:
So was it when my life began;
So is it now I am a man;
So be it when I shall grow old,
    Or let me die!
The Child is father of the Man;
And I could wish my days to be
Bound each to each by natural piety.

Wordsworth, *My Heart Leaps Up
When I Behold*

100 There is a Flower, the lesser Celandine,
That shrinks, like many more, from cold and rain;
And, the first moment that the sun may shine,
Bright as the sun himself, 'tis out again!

When hailstones have been falling, swarm on swarm,
Or blasts the green field and the trees distrest,
Oft have I seen it muffled up from harm,
In close self-shelter, like a Thing at rest.

But lately, one rough day, this Flower I passed
And recognised it, though an altered form,
Now standing forth an offering to the blast,
And buffeted at will by rain and storm.

I stopped and said with inly-muttered voice,
"It doth not love the shower, nor seek the cold:
This neither is its courage nor its choice,
But its necessity in being old.

"The sunshine may not cheer it, nor the dew;
It cannot help itself in its decay;
Stiff in its members, withered, changed of hue."
And, in my spleen, I smiled that it was grey.

Wordsworth, *The Small Celandine*

101 There was a time when meadow, grove, and
stream,
The earth, and every common sight,
To me did seem
Apparelled in celestial light,
The glory and the freshness of a dream.
It is not now as it hath been of yore;—
Turn wheresoe'er I may,
By night or day,
The things which I have seen I now can see no
more.

Wordsworth, *Ode: Intimations of Immortality,* I

102 Our birth is but a sleep and a forgetting:
The Soul that rises with us, our life's Star,
Hath had elsewhere its setting,
And cometh from afar:
Not in entire forgetfulness,
And not in utter nakedness,
But trailing clouds of glory do we come
From God, who is our home:
Heaven lies about us in our infancy!
Shades of the prison-house begin to close
Upon the growing Boy,
But He beholds the light, and whence it flows,
He sees it in his joy;
The Youth, who daily farther from the east
Must travel, still is Nature's Priest,
And by the vision splendid
Is on his way attended;
At length the Man perceives it die away,
And fade into the light of common day.

Wordsworth, *Ode: Intimations of Immortality,* V

103 And O, ye Fountains, Meadows, Hills and
Groves,
Forebode not any severing of our loves!
Yet in my heart of hearts I feel your might;
I only have relinquished one delight
To live beneath your more habitual sway.
I love the Brooks which down their channels fret,
Even more than when I tripped lightly as they;
The innocent brightness of a new-born Day
Is lovely yet;
The Clouds that gather round the setting sun
Do take a sober colouring from an eye
That hath kept watch o'er man's mortality;
Another race hath been, and other palms are
won.
Thanks to the human heart by which we live,
Thanks to its tenderness, its joys, and fears,
To me the meanest flower that blows can give
Thoughts that do often lie too deep for tears.

Wordsworth, *Ode: Intimations
of Immortality,* XI

104 Bliss was it in that dawn to be alive,
But to be young was very Heaven!

Wordsworth, *The Prelude,* XI, 108

105 What is the worst of woes that wait on age?
What stamps the wrinkle deeper on the brow?
To view each loved one blotted from life's page,
And be alone on earth, as I am now.

Byron, *Childe Harold's
Pilgrimage,* II, 98

106 'Tis true, your budding Miss is very charming,
But shy and awkward at first coming out,
So much alarm'd that she is quite alarming,
All Giggle, Blush; half Pertness and half Pout;
And glancing at *Mamma,* for fear there's harm in
What you, she, it, or they, may be about,
The Nursery still lisps out in all they utter—
Besides, they always smell of bread and butter.

Byron, *Beppo,* XXXIX

107 Oh, talk not to me of a name great in story;
The days of our youth are the days of our glory;
And the myrtle and ivy of sweet two-and-twenty
Are worth all your laurels, though ever so plenty.

Byron, *Stanzas Written on the Road
Between Florence and Pisa*

108 Age generally makes men more tolerant; youth is
always discontented. The tolerance of age is the
result of the ripeness of a judgment which, not
merely as the result of indifferance, is satisfied
even with what is inferior, but, more deeply
taught by the grave experience of life, has been
led to perceive the substantial, solid worth of the
object in question. The insight then to which—in
contradistinction from those ideals—philosophy is
to lead us, is, that the real world is as it ought to
be, that the truly good, the universal divine reason, is not a mere abstraction, but a vital principle
capable of realizing itself.

Hegel, *Philosophy of History,*
Introduction, 3

109 Among the Greeks we feel ourselves immediately
at home, for we are in the region of spirit; and
though the origin of the nation, as also its philological peculiarities, may be traced farther—even
to India—the proper emergence, the true palin-
genesis of spirit must be looked for in Greece first.
At an earlier stage I compared the Greek world
with the period of adolescence; not, indeed, in *that*
sense, that youth bears within it a serious, antici-
pative destiny, and consequently by the very conditions of its culture urges towards an ulterior
aim—presenting thus an inherently incomplete
and immature form, and being then most defective when it would deem itself perfect—but in *that*
sense, that youth does not yet present the activity
of work, does not yet exert itself for a definite intelligent aim, but rather exhibits a concrete fresh-

ness of the soul's life. It appears in the sensuous, actual world, as incarnate spirit and spiritualized sense—in a unity which owed its origin to spirit. Greece presents to us the cheerful aspect of youthful freshness, or spiritual vitality. It is here first that advancing spirit makes *itself* the content of its volition and its knowledge; but in such a way that state, family, law, religion, are at the same time objects aimed at by individuality, while the latter *is* individuality only in virtue of those aims. The man, on the other hand, devotes his life to labor for an objective aim; which he pursues consistently, even at the cost of his individuality.

Hegel, *Philosophy of History*, II, Introduction

110 He who lives to see two or three generations is like a man who sits some time in the conjurer's booth at a fair, and witnesses the performance twice or thrice in succession. The tricks were meant to be seen only once; and when they are no longer a novelty and cease to deceive their effect is gone.

Schopenhauer, *Sufferings of the World*

111 A man's life begins with the illusion that a long, long time and a whole world lie before him, and he begins with the foolish conceit that he has plenty of time for all his many claims. The poet is the eloquent, inspired advocate of this foolish but beautiful conceit. But when in the infinite transformation a man discovers the eternal so near to life that there is not a single one of its claims, not a single one of its evasions, not a single one of its excuses, not a single one of its moments at a distance from what *he must do* at this very moment, this very second, this very instant: then he is in the way of becoming a Christian. The sign of childishness is to say: *"Me wants, me—me"*; the sign of youth is to say: *"I,"*—and *"I"*—and *"I"*; the sign of maturity and the introduction to the eternal is to will to understand that this "I" signifies nothing if it does not become the "thou" to whom eternity unceasingly speaks, and says: "Thou *shalt*, thou shalt, thou shalt." The youth wishes to be the only "I" in the whole world; maturity consists in understanding this "thou" for itself, even if it is not said to any other single man. Thou shalt, thou shalt love thy neighbor. O my hearer, it is not *you* to whom *I* speak; it is to me, to whom eternity says: "Thou shalt."

Kierkegaard, *Works of Love*, I, 2C

112 What pretty oracles nature yields us on this text in the face and behavior of children, babes, and even brutes! That divided and rebel mind, that distrust of a sentiment because our arithmetic has computed the strength and means opposed to our purpose, these have not. Their mind being whole, their eye is as yet unconquered; and when we look in their faces we are disconcerted. Infancy conforms to nobody; all conform to it; so that one babe commonly makes four or five out of the adults who prattle and play to it. So God has armed youth and puberty and manhood no less with its own piquancy and charm, and made it enviable and gracious and its claims not to be put by, if it will stand by itself. Do not think the youth has no force, because he cannot speak to you and me. Hark! in the next room his voice is sufficiently clear and emphatic. It seems he knows how to speak to his contemporaries. Bashful or bold then, he will know how to make us seniors very unnecessary.

Emerson, *Self-Reliance*

113 A boy is in the parlor what the pit is in the playhouse; independent, irresponsible, looking out from his corner on such people and facts as pass by, he tries and sentences them on their merits, in the swift, summary way of boys, as good, bad, interesting, silly, eloquent, troublesome. He cumbers himself never about consequences, about interests; he gives an independent, genuine verdict. You must court him; he does not court you. But the man is as it were clapped into jail by his consciousness. As soon as he has once acted or spoken with *éclat* he is a committed person, watched by the sympathy or the hatred of hundreds, whose affections must now enter into his account.

Emerson, *Self-Reliance*

114 It is time to be old,
To take in sail:
The gods of bounds,
Who sets to seas a shore,
Came to me in his fatal rounds,
And said: "No more!
No farther shoot
Thy broad ambitious branches, and thy root.
Fancy departs: no more invent;
Contract thy firmament
To compass of a tent."

Emerson, *Terminus*

115   My mariners,
Souls that have toil'd, and wrought, and thought with me,—
That ever with a frolic welcome took
The thunder and the sunshine, and opposed
Free hearts, free foreheads,—you and I are old;
Old age hath yet his honor and his toil.
Death closes all; but something ere the end,
Some work of noble note, may yet be done,
Not unbecoming men that strove with Gods.
The lights begin to twinkle from the rocks;
The long day wanes; the slow moon climbs; the deep
Moans round with many voices. Come, my friends.
'Tis not too late to seek a newer world.
Push off, and sitting well in order smite
The sounding furrows; for my purpose holds
To sail beyond the sunset, and the baths

Of all the western stars, until I die.
It may be that the gulfs will wash us down;
It may be we shall touch the Happy Isles,
And see the great Achilles, whom we knew.
Tho' much is taken, much abides; and tho'
We are not now that strength which in old days
Moved earth and heaven, that which we are, we
are,—
One equal temper of heroic hearts,
Made weak by time and fate, but strong in will
To strive, to seek, to find, and not to yield.

Tennyson, *Ulysses*

116 Practically, the old have no very important advice
to give the young, their own experience has been
so partial, and their lives have been such miserable failures, for private reasons, as they must believe; and it may be that they have some faith left
which belies that experience, and they are only
less young than they were. I have lived some thiry
years on this planet, and I have yet to hear the
first syllable of valuable or even earnest advice
from my seniors. They have told me nothing, and
probably cannot tell me anything to the purpose.
Here is life, an experiment to a great extent untried by me; but it does not avail me that they
have tried it.

Thoreau, *Walden:* Economy

117 The youth gets together his materials to build a
bridge to the moon, or perchance a palace or temple on the earth, and at length the middleaged
man concludes to build a wood-shed with them.

Thoreau, *Journal (July 14, 1852)*

118 How earthy old people become—mouldy as the
grave! Their wisdom smacks of the earth. There is
no foretaste of immortality in it. They remind me
of earthworms and mole crickets.

Thoreau, *Journal (Aug. 16, 1853)*

119 Old age, calm, expanded, broad with the haughty
breadth of the universe,
Old age, flowing free with the delicious near-by
freedom of death.

Whitman, *Song of the Open Road,* XII

120 Grow old along with me!
The best is yet to be,
The last of life, for which the first was made:
Our times are in his hand
Who saith, "A whole I planned,
Youth shows but half; trust God: see all, nor be
afraid!"

Browning, *Rabbi Ben Ezra*

121 He [Alyosha] was to some extent a youth of our
last epoch—that is, honest in nature, desiring the
truth, seeking for it and believing in it, and seeking to serve it at once with all the strength of his
soul, seeking for immediate action, and ready to
sacrifice everything, life itself, for it. Though these
young men unhappily fail to understand that the
sacrifice of life is, in many cases, the easiest of all
sacrifices, and that to sacrifice, for instance, five or
six years of their seething youth to hard and tedious study, if only to multiply tenfold their powers of serving the truth and the cause they have set
before them as their goal—such a sacrifice is utterly beyond the strength of many of them.

Dostoevsky, *Brothers Karamazov,* Pt. I, I, 5

122 Prince Vasíli seized Pierre's hand and said to
Anna Pávlovna: "Educate this bear for me! He
has been staying with me a whole month and this
is the first time I have seen him in society. Nothing is so necessary for a young man as the society
of clever women."

Tolstoy, *War and Peace,* I, 4

123 Natasha had not had a moment free since early
morning and had not once had time to think of
what lay before her.

In the damp chill air and crowded closeness of
the swaying carriage, she for the first time vividly
imagined what was in store for her there at the
ball, in those brightly lighted rooms—with music,
flowers, dances, the Emperor, and all the brilliant
young people of Petersburg. The prospect was so
splendid that she hardly believed it would come
true, so out of keeping was it with the chill darkness and closeness of the carriage. She understood
all that awaited her only when, after stepping
over the red baize at the entrace, she entered the
hall, took off her fur cloak, and, beside Sónya and
in front of her mother, mounted the brightly illuminated stairs between the flowers. Only then did
she remember how she must behave at a ball, and
tried to assume the majestic air she considered indispensable for a girl on such an occasion. But,
fortunately for her, she felt her eyes growing
misty, she saw nothing clearly, her pulse beat a
hundred to the minute, and the blood throbbed at
her heart. She could not assume that pose, which
would have made her ridiculous, and she moved
on almost fainting from excitement and trying
with all her might to conceal it. And this was the
very attitude that became her best.

Tolstoy, *War and Peace,* VI, 15

124 Consider well the proportions of things. It is better
to be a young June-bug than an old bird of paradise.

Mark Twain, *Pudd'nhead Wilson's
Calendar,* VIII

125 *The same space of time seems shorter as we grow older—*
that is, the days, the months, and the years do so;
whether the hours do so is doubtful, and the minutes and seconds to all appearance remain about
the same. . . . In youth we may have an absolutely new experience, subjective or objective, every

hour of the day. Apprehension is vivid, retentiveness strong, and our recollections of that time, like those of a time spent in rapid and interesting travel, are of something intricate, multitudinous, and long-drawn-out. But as each passing year converts some of this experience into automatic routine which we hardly note at all, the days and the weeks smooth themselves out in recollection to contentless units, and the years grow hollow and collapse.

William James, *Psychology,* XV

126 With the child, life is all play and fairy-tales and learning the external properties of "things"; with the youth, it is bodily exercises of a more systematic sort, novels of the real world, boon-fellowship and song, friendship and love, nature, travel and adventure, science and philosophy; with the man, ambition and policy, acquisitiveness, responsibility to others, and the selfish zest of the battle of life. If a boy grows up alone at the age of games and sports, and learns neither to play ball, nor row, nor sail, nor ride, nor skate, nor fish, nor shoot, probably he will be sedentary to the end of his days; and, though the best of opportunities be afforded him for learning these things later, it is a hundred to one but he will pass them by and shrink back from the effort of taking those necessary first steps the prospect of which, at an earlier age, would have filled him with eager delight. The sexual passion expires after a protracted reign; but it is well known that its peculiar manifestation in a given individual depend almost entirely on the habits he may form during the early period of its activity. Exposure to bad company then makes him a loose liver all his days; chastity kept at first makes the same easy later on.

William James, *Psychology,* XXIV

127 Men do not live long enough: they are, for all the purposes of high civilization, mere children when they die; and our Prime Ministers, though rated as mature, divide their time between the golf course and the Treasury Bench in parliament. Presumably, however, the same power that made this mistake can remedy it. If on opportunist grounds Man now fixes the term of his life at three score and ten years, he can equally fix it as three hundred, or three thousand, or even at the genuine Circumstantial Selection limit, which would be until a sooner-or-later-inevitable fatal accident makes an end of the individual. All that is necessary to make him extend his present span is that tremendous catastrophes such as the late war shall convince him of the necessity of at least outliving his taste for golf and cigars if the race is to be saved. This is not fantastic speculation: it is deductive biology, if there is such a science as biology. Here, then, is a stone that we have left unturned, and that may be worth turning. To make the suggestion more entertaining than it would be to most people in the form of a biological treatise, I have written Back to Methuselah as a contribution to the modern Bible.

Shaw, *Back to Methuselah,* Pref.

128 *Conrad.* We're not blaming you: you hadn't lived long enough. No more had we. Cant you see that three-score-and-ten, though it may be long enough for a very crude sort of village life, isnt long enough for a complicated civilization like ours? Flinders Petrie has counted nine attempts at civilization made by people exactly like us; and every one of them failed just as ours is failing. They failed because the citizens and statesmen died of old age or over-eating before they had grown out of schoolboy games and savage sports and cigars and champagne. The signs of the end are always the same: Democracy, Socialism, and Votes for Women. We shall go to smash within the lifetime of men now living unless we recognize that we must live longer.

Shaw, *Back to Methuselah,* II

129 *The Maiden.* Clothes are a nuisance. I think I shall do without them some day, as you ancients do.
The Ancient. Signs of maturity. Soon you will give up all these toys and games and sweets.
The Youth. What! And be as miserable as you?
The Ancient. Infant: one moment of the ecstasy of life as we live it would strike you dead.

Shaw, *Back to Methuselah,* V

130 Is there an infantile sexuality? you will ask. Is childhood not rather that period of life which is distinguished by the lack of the sexual impulse? No, gentlemen, it is not at all true that the sexual impulse enters into the child at puberty, as the devils in the gospel entered into the swine. The child has his sexual impulses and activities from the beginning, he brings them with him into the world, and from these the so-called normal sexuality of adults emerges by a significant development through manifold stages. It is not very difficult to observe the expressions of this childish sexual activity; it needs rather a certain art to overlook them or to fail to interpret them.

Freud, *Origin and Development of Psycho-Analysis,* IV

131 To be sure, if it is the purpose of educators to stifle the child's power of independent thought as early as possible, in order to produce that "good behaviour" which is so highly prized, they cannot do better than deceive children in sexual matters and intimidate them by religious means. The stronger characters will, it is true, withstand these influences; they will become rebels against the authority of their parents and later against every other form of authority. When children do not receive the explanations for which they turn to their elders, they go on tormenting themselves in secret with

the problem, and produce attempts at solution in which the truth they have guessed is mixed up in the most extraordinary way with grotesque inventions; or else they whisper confidences to each other which, because of the sense of guilt in the youthful inquirers, stamp everything sexual as horrible and disgusting.

Freud, *Sexual Enlightenment of Children*

132 This age of childhood, in which the sense of shame is unknown, seems a paradise when we look back upon it later, and paradise itself is nothing but the mass-phantasy of the childhood of the individual. This is why in paradise men are naked and unashamed, until the moment arrives when shame and fear awaken; expulsion follows, and sexual life and cultural development begin.

Freud, *Interpretation of Dreams*, V, D

133 If the infant could express itself, it would undoubtedly acknowledge that the act of sucking at its mother's breast is far and away the most important thing in life. It would not be wrong in this, for by this act it gratifies at the same moment the two greatest needs in life. Then we learn from psycho-analysis, not without astonishment, how much of the mental significance of this act is retained throughout life. Sucking for nourishment becomes the point of departure from which the whole sexual life develops, the unattainable prototype of every later sexual satisfaction, to which in times of need phantasy often enough reverts. The desire to suck includes within it the desire for the mother's breast, which is therefore the first *object* of sexual desire; I cannot convey to you any adequate idea of the importance of this first object in determining every later object adopted, of the profound influence it exerts, through transformation and substitution, upon the most distant fields of mental life.

Freud, *General Introduction to Psycho-Analysis*, XX

134 In the act of birth there is a real danger to life. We know what this means objectively; but what it means in a psychological sense we have no idea. The danger of birth has yet no mental content for the subject. One cannot possibly suppose that the foetus has any sort of knowledge that its life is in danger of being destroyed. It can only be aware of some vast upheaval in the economy of its narcissistic libido. Very large quantities of excitation crowd in upon it, giving rise to new sensations of unpleasure, and many organs acquire an increased cathexis, thus foreshadowing the object-cathexis which will soon set in.

Freud, *Inhibitions, Symptoms, and Anxiety*, VIII

135 God guard me from those thoughts men think
In the mind alone;
He that sings a lasting song
Thinks in a marrow-bone;

From all that makes a wise old man
That can be praised of all;
O what am I that I should not seem
For the song's sake a fool?

I pray—for fashion's word is out
And prayer comes round again—
That I may seem, though I die old,
A foolish, passionate man.

Yeats, *A Prayer for Old Age*

136 That is no country for old men. The young
In one another's arms, birds in the trees
—Those dying generations—at their song,
The salmon-falls, the mackerel-crowded seas,
Fish, flesh, or fowl, commend all summer long
Whatever is begotten, born, and dies.
Caught in that sensual music all neglect
Monuments of unaging intellect.

An aged man is but a paltry thing,
A tattered coat upon a stick, unless
Soul clap its hands and sing, and louder sing
For every tatter in its mortal dress,
Nor is there singing school but studying
Monuments of its own magnificence;
And therefore I have sailed the seas and come
To the holy city of Byzantium.

Yeats, *Sailing to Byzantium*

137 Old places and old persons in their turn, when spirit dwells in them, have an intrinsic vitality of which youth is incapable; precisely the balance and wisdom that comes from long perspectives and broad foundations.

Santayana, *My Host the World*, II

138 Never have I enjoyed youth so thoroughly as I have in my old age. . . . I have drunk the pleasure of life more pure, more joyful, than it ever was when mingled with all the hidden anxieties and little annoyances of actual living. Nothing is inherently and invincibly young except spirit. And spirit can enter a human being perhaps better in the quiet of old age and dwell there more undisturbed than in the turmoil of adventure.

Santayana, *My Host the World*, II

139 I at least have found that old age is the time for happiness, even for enjoying in retrospect the years of youth that were so distracted in their day; and I seem to detect a certain sardonic defiance, a sort of pride, in the whining old beggars that look so wretched as they stretch out a trembling hand for a penny. They are not dead yet; they can hold together in spite of everything; and they are not deceived about *you*, you well-dressed young per-

son. Your new shoes pinch you, and you are secretly racked by hopeless desires.

Santayana, *Persons and Places,* II

140 The young man who has not wept is a savage, and the old man who will not laugh is a fool.

Santayana, *Dialogues in Limbo,* III

1.4 | *Self-Knowledge and Self-Love*

The fact that man is a self-conscious or self-regarding animal underlies the two main themes treated in this section. One is the injunction first uttered by one of the seven wise men of ancient Greece—"Know thyself!" That commandment gets repeated in one form or another century after century, as a counsel of perfection or as the key to wisdom. Clearly, the task to be performed is not an easy one, since by implication it is one that few men discharge adequately.

Illusion and self-deception stand in the way of an honest, penetrating, and fearless self-appraisal. Though it would appear that we have access to the innermost core of our individual being, and that there is nothing in the world with which we are on more intimate terms than our own self, the self remains an elusive object of knowledge and understanding. Different reasons for this are given or suggested by different writers; and they also recommend different ways to overcome obstacles. For all these differences, the basic insights about the desirability and the difficulty of self-knowledge remain very much the same from Socrates and the Roman Stoics to Thoreau and Emerson, and to the psychoanalysts and existentialists in our own day.

According to many of the passages quoted in Chapter 3 on LOVE, the proper objects of love are God, other human beings, one's country, and such ideals as truth, beauty, and goodness. Yet one of the most famous of all statements about love—the Christian precepts of charity—commands us, first, to love God, and second, to love our neighbor as our self. And the same injunction is implied in Aristotle's conception of the ideal friend, the proper beloved, as an *alter ego*—another self. Self-love is in a sense the basis of true love of another.

Self-love, then, far from being castigated as a misdirection of the benevolent impulse, is conceived as inseparable from benevolence toward others. There are other terms for what is being discussed here—"self-esteem," "self-respect," "*amour propre*," and even "pride," when that term is used to signify a well-founded and well-deserved approval of one's self. Yet the fact that pride is also condemned as an overestimation of one's worth suggests that self-love can become so excessive or perverted that it excludes or subordinates all other loves. Whereas the passages dealing with the first theme in this section—self-knowledge—tend to be of the same tenor, the passages dealing with the second—self-love—are often ambivalent.

1 Let another man praise thee, and not thine own mouth; a stranger, and not thine own lips.

Proverbs 27:2

2 The gods help him who helps himself.

Euripides, *Fragment*

3 *Critias.* Self-knowledge would certainly be maintained by me to be the very essence of knowledge, and in this I agree with him who dedicated the inscription, "Know thyself!" at Delphi.

Plato, *Charmides,* 164B

4 *Socrates.* The wise or temperate man, and he only, will know himself.

Plato, *Charmides,* 167A

5 *Athenian Stranger.* The excessive love of self is in reality the source to each man of all offences. . . . Wherefore let every man avoid excess of self-love, and condescend to follow a better man than himself, not allowing any false shame to stand in the way.

Plato, *Laws,* V, 731B

6 Everyone has the obligation to ponder well his own specific traits of character. He must also regulate them adequately and not wonder whether someone else's traits might suit him better. The more definitely his own a man's character is, the better it fits him.

Cicero, *De Officiis,* I, 31

7 Every animal is attached to nothing so much as to its own interest. Whatever then appears to it an impediment to this interest, whether this be a brother, or a father, or a child, or beloved, or lover, it hates, spurns, curses: for its nature is to love nothing so much as its own interest; this is father, and brother and kinsman, and country, and God. . . .

If a man put in the same place his interest, sanctity, goodness, and country, and parents, and friends, all these are secured: but if he puts in one place his interest, in another his friends, and his country and his kinsmen and justice itself, all these give way being borne down by the weight of interest.

Epictetus, *Discourses,* II, 22

8 How much trouble he avoids who does not look to see what his neighbour says or does or thinks, but only to what he does himself, that it may be just and pure.

Marcus Aurelius, *Meditations,* IV, 18

9 Look within. Within is the fountain of good, and it will ever bubble up, if thou wilt ever dig.

Marcus Aurelius, *Meditations,* VII, 59

10 I have often wondered how it is that every man loves himself more than all the rest of men, but yet sets less value on his own opinion of himself than on the opinion of others.

Marcus Aurelius, *Meditations,* XII, 4

11 Withdraw into yourself and look. And if you do not find yourself beautiful yet, act as does the creator of a statue that is to be made beautiful: he cuts away here, he smoothes there, he makes this line lighter, this other purer, until a lovely face has grown upon his work. So do you also: cut away all that is excessive, straighten all that is crooked, bring light to all that is overcast, labour to make all one glow of beauty and never cease chiselling your statue, until there shall shine out on you from it the godlike splendour of virtue, until you shall see the perfect goodness surely established in the stainless shrine.

Plotinus, *First Ennead,* VI, 9

12 Man is a great deep, Lord. You number his very hairs and they are not lost in Your sight: but the hairs of his head are easier to number than his affections and the movements of his heart.

Augustine, *Confessions,* IV, 14

13 If I am deceived, I am. For he who is not, cannot be deceived; and if I am deceived, by this same token I am.

Augustine, *City of God,* XI, 26

14 For the most part, the human mind cannot attain to self-knowledge otherwise than by making trial of its powers through temptation, by some kind of experimental and not merely verbal self-interrogation.

Augustine, *City of God,* XVI, 32

15 It is a very ordinary and common thing amongst men to conceive, foresee, know, and presage the misfortune, bad luck, or disaster of another; but to have the understanding, providence, knowledge, and prediction of a man's own mishap, is very scarce, and rare to be found any where.

Rabelais, *Gargantua and Pantagruel,* III, 15

16 If, as we who study ourselves have learned to do, each man who hears a true statement immediately considered how it properly pertains to him, each man would find that it is not so much a good saying as a good whiplash to the ordinary stupidity of his judgment.

Montaigne, *Essays,* I, 23, Of Custom

17 This capacity for sifting truth, whatever it may amount to in me, and this free will not to enslave my belief easily, I owe principally to myself. For the firmest and most general ideas I have are those which, in a manner of speaking, were born with me. They are natural and all mine. I produced them crude and simple, with a conception

bold and strong, but a little confused and imperfect. Since then I have established and fortified them by the authority of others and the sound arguments of the ancients, with whom I found my judgment in agreement. These men have given me a firmer grip on my ideas and a more complete enjoyment and possession of them.

Montaigne, *Essays,* II, 17, Of Presumption

18 It is a rare life that remains well ordered even in private. Any man can play his part in the side show and represent a worthy man on the boards; but to be disciplined within, in his own bosom, where all is permissible, where all is concealed—that's the point.

Montaigne, *Essays,* III, 2, Of Repentance

19 It was a paradoxical command that was given us of old by that god at Delphi: "Look into yourself, know yourself, keep to yourself; bring back your mind and your will, which are spending themselves elsewhere, into themselves; you are running out, you are scattering yourself; concentrate yourself, resist yourself; you are being betrayed, dispersed, and stolen away from yourself. Do you not see that this world keeps its sight all concentrated inward and its eyes open to contemplate itself? It is always vanity for you, within and without; but it is less vanity when it is less extensive. Except for you, O man," said that god, "each thing studies itself first, and, according to its needs, has limits to its labors and desires. There is not a single thing as empty and needy as you, who embrace the universe: you are the investigator without knowledge, the magistrate without jurisdiction, and all in all, the fool of the farce."

Montaigne, *Essays,* III, 9, Of Vanity

20 It is an absolute perfection and virtually divine to know how to enjoy our being rightfully. We seek other conditions because we do not understand the use of our own, and go outside of ourselves because we do not know what it is like inside. Yet there is no use our mounting on stilts, for on stilts we must still walk on our own legs. And on the loftiest throne in the world we are still sitting only on our own rump.

Montaigne, *Essays,* III, 13, Of Experience

21 *Polonius.* This above all: to thine own self be true, And it must follow, as the night the day, Thou canst not then be false to any man.

Shakespeare, *Hamlet,* I, iii, 78

22 *Iago.* O villainous! I have looked upon the world for four times seven years; and since I could distinguish betwixt a benefit and an injury, I never found a man that knew how to love himself.

Shakespeare, *Othello,* I, iii, 312

23 It hath been well said that the arch-flatterer, with whom all the petty flatterers have intelligence, is a man's self.

Bacon, *Of Love*

24 For a long time I had remarked that it is sometimes requisite in common life to follow opinions which one knows to be most uncertain, exactly as though they were indisputable, as has been said above. But because in this case I wished to give myself entirely to the search after Truth, I thought that it was necessary for me to take an apparently opposite course, and to reject as absolutely false everything as to which I could imagine the least ground of doubt, in order to see if afterwards there remained anything in my belief that was entirely certain. Thus, because our senses sometimes deceive us, I wished to suppose that nothing is just as they cause us to imagine it to be; and because there are men who deceive themselves in their reasoning and fall into paralogisms, even concerning the simplest matters of geometry, and judging that I was as subject to error as was any other, I rejected as false all the reasons formerly accepted by me as demonstrations. And since all the same thoughts and conceptions which we have while awake may also come to us in sleep, without any of them being at that time true, I resolved to assume that everything that ever entered into my mind was no more true than the illusions of my dreams. But immediately afterwards I noticed that whilst I thus wished to think all things false, it was absolutely essential that the "I" who thought this should be somewhat, and remarking that this truth *"I think, therefore I am"* was so certain and so assured that all the most extravagant suppositions brought forward by the sceptics were incapable of shaking it, I came to the conclusion that I could receive it without scruple as the first principle of the Philosophy.

Descartes, *Discourse on Method,* IV

25 Whosoever looketh into himself and considereth what he doth when he does think, opine, reason, hope, fear, etc., and upon what grounds; he shall thereby read and know what are the thoughts and passions of all other men upon the like occasions. I say the similitude of passions, which are the same in all men,—desire, fear, hope, etc.; not the similitude of the objects of the passions, which are the things desired, feared, hoped, etc.: for these the constitution individual, and particular education, do so vary, and they are so easy to be kept from our knowledge, that the characters of man's heart, blotted and confounded as they are with dissembling, lying, counterfeiting, and erroneous doctrines, are legible only to him that searcheth hearts. And though by men's actions we do discover their design sometimes; yet to do it without

comparing them with our own, and distinguishing all circumstances by which the case may come to be altered, is to decipher without a key, and be for the most part deceived, by too much trust or by too much diffidence, as he that reads is himself a good or evil man.

Hobbes, *Leviathan,* Intro.

26 One must know oneself. If this does not serve to discover truth, it at least serves as a rule of life, and there is nothing better.

Pascal, *Pensées,* II, 66

27 Man is to himself the most wonderful object in nature; for he cannot conceive what the body is, still less what the mind is, and least of all how a body should be united to a mind. This is the consummation of his difficulties, and yet it is his very being.

Pascal, *Pensées,* II, 72

28 The nature of self-love and of this human Ego is to love self only and consider self only. But what will man do? He cannot prevent this object that he loves from being full of faults and wants. He wants to be great, and he sees himself small. He wants to be happy, and he sees himself miserable. He wants to be perfect, and he sees himself full of imperfections. He wants to be the object of love and esteem among men, and he sees that his faults merit only their hatred and contempt. This embarrassment in which he finds himself produces in him the most unrighteous and criminal passion that can be imagined; for he conceives a mortal enmity against that truth which reproves him and which convinces him of his faults. He would annihilate it, but, unable to destroy it in its essence, he destroys it as far as possible in his own knowledge and in that of others; that is to say, he devotes all his attention to hiding his faults both from others and from himself, and he cannot endure either that others should point them out to him, or that they should see them.

Truly it is an evil to be full of faults; but it is a still greater evil to be full of them and to be unwilling to recognise them, since that is to add the further fault of a voluntary illusion.

Pascal, *Pensées,* II, 100

29 If we do not know ourselves to be full of pride, ambition, lust, weakness, misery, and injustice, we are indeed blind. And if, knowing this, we do not desire deliverance, what can we say of a man . . .?

Pascal, *Pensées,* VII, 450

30 Since reason demands nothing which is opposed to nature, it demands, therefore, that every person should love himself, should seek his own profit,—what is truly profitable to him,—should desire everything that really leads man to greater perfec-

tion, and absolutely that every one should endeavour, as far as in him lies, to preserve his own being. This is all true as necessarily as that the whole is greater than its part.

Spinoza, *Ethics,* IV, Prop. 18, Schol.

31 We must consider what *person* stands for;—which, I think, is a thinking intelligent being, that has reason and reflection, and can consider itself as itself, the same thinking thing, in different times and places; which it does only by that consciousness which is inseparable from thinking, and, as it seems to me, essential to it: it being impossible for any one to perceive without *perceiving* that he does perceive. When we see, hear, smell, taste, feel, meditate, or will anything, we know that we do so. Thus it is always as to our present sensations and perceptions: and by this every one is to himself that which he calls *self.*

Locke, *Concerning Human Understanding,* Bk. II, XXVII, 9

32 Suppose I wholly lose the memory of some parts of my life, beyond a possibility of retrieving them, so that perhaps I shall never be conscious of them again; yet am I not the same person that did those actions, had those thoughts that I once was conscious of, though I have now forgot them? To which I answer, that we must here take notice what the word *I* is applied to; which, in this case, is the *man* only. And the same man being presumed to be the same person, I is easily here supposed to stand also for the same person. But if it be possible for the same man to have distinct incommunicable consciousness at different times, it is past doubt the same man would at different times make different persons; which, we see, is the sense of mankind in the solemnest declaration of their opinions, human laws not punishing the mad man for the sober man's actions, nor the sober man for what the mad man did,—thereby making them two persons: which is somewhat explained by our way of speaking in English when we say such an one is "not himself," or is "beside himself"; in which phrases it is insinuated, as if those who now, or at least first used them, thought that self was changed; the self-same person was no longer in that man.

Locke, *Concerning Human Understanding,* Bk. II, XXVII, 20

33 Self-esteem is the instrument of our conservation; it resembles the instrument of the perpetuity of the species: it is necessary, it is dear to us, it gives us pleasure, and it has to be hidden.

Voltaire, *Philosophical Dictionary:* Self-Esteem

34 Our first duties are to ourselves; our first feelings are centred on self; all our instincts are at first directed to our own preservation and our own welfare. Thus the first notion of justice springs not

from what we owe to others, but from what is due to us.

Rousseau, *Emile,* II

35 *Johnson.* A man should be careful never to tell tales of himself to his own disadvantage. People may be amused and laugh at the time, but they will be remembered, and brought out against him upon some subsequent occasion.

Boswell, *Life of Johnson (Mar. 14, 1776)*

36 *Johnson.* All censure of a man's self is oblique praise. It is in order to shew how much he can spare. It has all the invidiousness of self-praise, and all the reproach of falsehood.

Boswell, *Life of Johnson (Apr. 25, 1778)*

37 Man has almost constant occasion for the help of his brethren, and it is in vain for him to expect it from their benevolence only. He will be more likely to prevail if he can interest their self-love in his favour, and show them that it is for their own advantage to do for him what he requires of them. Whoever offers to another a bargain of any kind, proposes to do this. Give me that which I want, and you shall have this which you want, is the meaning of every such offer; and it is in this manner that we obtain from one another the far greater part of those good offices which we stand in need of. It is not from the benevolence of the butcher, the brewer, or the baker that we expect our dinner, but from their regard to their own interest. We address ourselves, not to their humanity but to their self-love, and never talk to them of our own necessities but of their advantages.

Adam Smith, *Wealth of Nations,* I, 2

38 It is absolutely impossible to make out by experience with complete certainty a single case in which the maxim of an action, however right in itself, rested simply on moral grounds and on the conception of duty. Sometimes it happens that with the sharpest self-examination we can find nothing beside the moral principle of duty which could have been powerful enough to move us to this or that action and to so great a sacrifice; yet we cannot from this infer with certainty that it was not really some secret impulse of self-love, under the false appearance of duty, that was the actual determining cause of the will. We like them to flatter ourselves by falsely taking credit for a more noble motive; whereas in fact we can never, even by the strictest examination, get completely behind the secret springs of action.

Kant, *Fundamental Principles of the Metaphysic of Morals,* II

39 Men often oppose a thing, merely because they have had no agency in planning it, or because it may have been planned by those whom they dislike. But if they have been consulted, and have happened to disapprove, opposition then becomes, in their estimation, an indispensable duty of self-love. They seem to think themselves bound in honour, and by all the motives of personal infallibility, to defeat the success of what has been resolved upon contrary to their sentiments. Men of upright, benevolent tempers have too many opportunities of remarking, with horror, to what desperate lengths this disposition is sometimes carried, and how often the great interests of society are sacrificed to the vanity, to the conceit, and to the obstinacy of individuals who have credit enough to make their passions and their caprices interesting to mankind.

Hamilton, *Federalist 70*

40 *Countess Tersky.* Every individual character is in the right that is in strict consistence with itself. Self-contradiction is the only wrong.

Schiller, *Wallenstein's Death,* I

41 Why is it that, in spite of all the mirrors in the world, no one really knows what he looks like?

Schopenhauer, *Further Psychological Observations*

42 Our Works are the mirror wherein the spirit first sees its natural lineaments. Hence, too, the folly of that impossible Precept, *Know thyself;* till it be translated into this partially possible one, *Know what thou canst work at.*

Carlyle, *Sartor Resartus,* II, 7

43 What I really lack is to be clear in my mind *what I am to do,* not what I am to know, except in so far as a certain understanding must precede every action. The thing is to understand myself, to see what God really wishes *me* to do; the thing is to find a truth which is true *for me,* to find *the idea for which I can live and die.* What would be the use of discovering so-called objective truth, of working through all the systems of philosophy and of being able, if required, to review them all and show up the inconsistencies within each system;—what good would it do me to be able to develop a theory of the state and combine all the details into a single whole, and so construct a world in which I did not live, but only held up to the view of others;—what good would it do me to be able to explain the meaning of Christianity if it had *no* deeper significance *for me and for my life;*—what good would it do me if truth stood before me, cold and naked, not caring whether I recognised her or not, and producing in me a shudder of fear rather than a trusting devotion? I certainly do not deny that I still recognise an *imperative of understanding* and that through it one can work upon men, *but it must be taken up into my life,* and *that is* what I now recognise as the most important thing. That is what my soul longs after, as the African desert

thirsts for water.

Kierkegaard, Journals (Aug. 1, 1835)

44 When a man has gone astray to the point of perdition and is about to sink, his last speech, the sign is: 'and yet something better in me is being lost'. It is like the bubbles rising to the surface from a drowning man; that is the sign—then he sinks. Just as self-isolation can be a man's downfall, because he will not reveal what is hidden, in the same way to pronounce those words spells destruction. For that declaration expresses the fact that he has become so objective to himself that he can talk of his own destruction as of something settled, which can now be of psychological interest to a third person. The hope that there was something better in him, which should have been used in silence to work for his salvation, that hope is made public and used as an ingredient in the funeral oration he pronounces upon himself.

Kierkegaard, Journals (1846)

45 To believe your own thought, to believe that what is true for you in your private heart is true for all men—that is genius. Speak your latent conviction, and it shall be the universal sense; for the inmost in due time becomes the outmost, and our first thought is rendered back to us by the trumpets of the Last Judgment. Familiar as the voice of the mind is to each, the highest merit we ascribe to Moses, Plato and Milton is that they set at naught books and traditions, and spoke not what men, but what *they* thought. A man should learn to detect and watch that gleam of light which flashes across his mind from within, more than the lustre of the firmament of bards and sages. Yet he dismisses without notice his thought, because it is his. In every work of genius we recognize our own rejected thoughts; they come back to us with a certain alienated majesty. Great works of art have no more affecting lesson for us than this. They teach us to abide by our spontaneous impression with good-humored inflexibility then most when the whole cry of voices is on the other side. Else to-morrow a stranger will say with masterly good sense precisely what we have thought and felt all the time, and we shall be forced to take with shame our own opinion from another.

Emerson, Self-Reliance

46 Trust thyself: every heart vibrates to that iron string.

Emerson, Self-Reliance

47 What I must do is all that concerns me, not what the people think. This rule, equally arduous in actual and in intellectual life, may serve for the whole distinction between greatness and meanness. It is the harder because you will always find those who think they know what is your duty better than you know it. It is easy in the world to live after the world's opinion; it is easy in solitude to live after our own; but the great man is he who in the midst of the crowd keeps with perfect sweetness the independence of solitude.

Emerson, Self-Reliance

48 The other terror that scares us from self-trust is our consistency; a reverence for our past act or word because the eyes of others have no other data for computing our orbit than our past acts, and we are loth to disappoint them.

But why should you keep your head over your shoulder? Why drag about this corpse of your memory, lest you contradict somewhat you have stated in this or that public place? Suppose you should contradict yourself; what then?

Emerson, Self-Reliance

49 Among those points of self-education which take up the form of mental discipline, there is one of great importance, and, moreover, difficult to deal with, because it involves an internal conflict, and equally touches our vanity and our ease. It consists in the tendency to deceive ourselves regarding all we wish for, and the necessity of resistance to these desires. It is impossible for any one who has not been constrained, by the course of his occupation and thoughts, to a habit of continual self-correction to be aware of the amount of error in relation to judgment arising from this tendency. The force of the temptation which urges us to seek for such evidence and appearances as are in favour of our desires, and to disregard those which oppose them, is wonderfully great. In this respect we are all, more or less, active promoters of error. In place of practising wholesome self-abnegation, we ever make the wish the father to the thought: we receive as friendly that which agrees with, we resist with dislike that which opposes us; whereas the very reverse is required by every dictate of common sense.

Faraday, Observations on Mental Education

50 I would rather sit on a pumpkin and have it all to myself than be crowded on a velvet cushion. I would rather ride on earth in an ox cart, with a free circulation, than go to heaven in the fancy car of an excursion train and breathe a *malaria* all the way.

Thoreau, Walden: Economy

51 I never dreamed of any enormity greater than I have committed. I never knew, and never shall know, a worse man than myself.

Thoreau, Walden: Economy

52 I only know myself as a human entity; the scene, so to speak, of thoughts and affections; and am sensible of a certain doubleness by which I can stand as remote from myself as from another. However intense my experience, I am conscious of

the presence and criticism of a part of me, which, as it were, is not a part of me, but spectator, sharing no experience, but taking note of it, and that is no more I than it is you.

Thoreau, *Walden:* Solitude

53 I celebrate myself, and sing myself.

Whitman, *Song of Myself,* I

54 Do I contradict myself?
Very well then I contradict myself,
(I am large, I contain multitudes.)

Whitman, *Song of Myself,* LI

55 It is not by wearing down into uniformity all that is individual in themselves, but by cultivating it, and calling it forth, within the limits imposed by the rights and interests of others, that human beings become a noble and beautiful object of contemplation; and as the works partake the character of those who do them, by the same process human life also becomes rich, diversified, and animating, furnishing more abundant aliment to high thoughts and elevating feelings, and strengthening the tie which binds every individual to the race, by making the race infinitely better worth belonging to.

Mill, *On Liberty,* III

56 Because the tyranny of opinion is such as to make eccentricity a reproach, it is desirable, in order to break through that tyranny, that people should be eccentric. Eccentricity has always abounded when and where strength of character has abounded; and the amount of eccentricity in a society has generally been proportional to the amount of genius, mental vigour, and moral courage it contained. That so few now dare to be eccentric marks the chief danger of the time.

Mill, *On Liberty,* III

57 We are all of us born in moral stupidity, taking the world as an udder to feed our supreme selves: Dorothea had early begun to emerge from that stupidity, but yet it had been easier to her to imagine how she would devote herself to Mr Casaubon, and become wise and strong in his strength and wisdom, than to conceive with that distinctness which is no longer reflection but feeling—an idea wrought back to the directness of sense, like the solidity of objects—that he had an equivalent centre of self, whence the lights and shadows must always fall with a certain difference.

George Eliot, *Middlemarch,* II, 21

58 An eminent philosopher among my friends, who can dignify even your ugly furniture by lifting it into the serene light of science, has shown me this pregnant little fact. Your pier-glass or extensive surface of polished steel made to be rubbed by a housemaid, will be minutely and multitudinously scratched in all directions; but place now against it a lighted candle as a centre of illumination, and lo! the scratches will seem to arrange themselves in a fine series of concentric circles round that little sun. It is demonstrable that the scratches are going everywhere impartially, and it is only your candle which produces the flattering illusion of a concentric arrangement, its light falling with an exclusive optical selection. These things are a parable. The scratches are events, and the candle is the egoism of any person now absent.

George Eliot, *Middlemarch,* III, 27

59 She [Mary Garth] sat to-night revolving, as she was wont, the scenes of the day, her lips often curling with amusement at the oddities to which her fancy added fresh drollery: people were so ridiculous with their illusions, carrying their fool's caps unawares, thinking their own lies opaque while everybody else's were transparent, making themselves exceptions to everything, as if when all the world looked yellow under a lamp they alone were rosy.

George Eliot, *Middlemarch,* III, 33

60 Consciousness is a source of self-cognition quite apart from and independent of reason. Through his reason man observes himself, but only through consciousness does he know himself.

Tolstoy, *War and Peace,* II Epilogue, VIII

61 We are unknown, we knowers, ourselves to ourselves: this has its own good reason. We have never searched for ourselves—how should it then come to pass, that we should ever *find* ourselves?

Nietzsche, *Genealogy of Morals,* Preface, 1

62 The most spiritual human beings, as the *strongest,* find their happiness where others would find their destruction: in the labyrinth, in severity towards themselves and others, in attempting; their joy lies in self-constraint: with them asceticism becomes nature, need, instinct.

Nietzsche, *Antichrist,* LVII

63 I am often confronted by the necessity of standing by one of my empirical selves and relinquishing the rest. Not that I would not, if I could, be both handsome and fat and well dressed, and a great athlete, and make a million a year, be a wit, a *bon-vivant,* and a lady-killer, as well as a philosopher; a philanthropist, statesman, warrior, and African explorer, as well as a "tone-poet" and saint. But the thing is simply impossible. The millionaire's work would run counter to the saint's; the *bon-vivant* and the philanthropist would trip each other up; the philosopher and the lady-killer could not well keep house in the same tenement of clay. Such different characters may conceivably at the outset of life be alike *possible* to a man. But to make any one of them actual, the rest

must more or less be suppressed. So the seeker of his truest, strongest, deepest self must review the list carefully, and pick out the one on which to stake his salvation. All other selves thereupon become unreal, but the fortunes of this self are real. Its failures are real failures, its triumphs real triumphs, carrying shame and gladness with them. . . . Our thought, incessantly deciding, among many things of a kind, which ones for it shall be realities, here chooses one of many possible selves or characters, and forthwith reckons it no shame to fail in any of those not adopted expressly as its own.

William James, *Psychology*, X

64 The consciousness of Self involves a stream of thought, each part of which as "I" can 1) remember those which went before, and know the things they knew; and 2) emphasize and care paramountly for certain ones among them as "me," and *appropriate to these* the rest. The nucleus of the *"me"* is always the bodily existence felt to be present at the time. Whatever remembered-past-feelings *resemble* this present feeling are deemed to belong to the same *me* with it. Whatever other things are perceived to be *associated* with this feeling are deemed to form part of that me's *experience,* and of them certain ones (which fluctuate more or less) are reckoned to be themselves *constituents* of the me in a larger sense,—such are the clothes, the material possessions, the friends, the honors and esteem which the person receives or may receive. This me is an empirical aggregate of things objectively known. The *I* which knows them cannot itself be an aggregate; neither for psychological purposes need it be considered to be an unchanging metaphysical entity like the Soul, or a principle like the pure Ego, viewed as "out of time." It is a *Thought,* at each moment different from that of the last moment, but *appropriative* of the latter, together with all that the latter called its own. All the experiential facts find their place in this description, unencumbered with any hypothesis save that of the existence of passing thoughts or states of mind. The same brain may subserve many conscious selves, either alternate or coexisting; but by what modifications in its action, or whether ultra-cerebral conditions may intervene, are questions which cannot now be answered.

William James, *Psychology*, X

65 The blindness in human beings . . . is the blindness with which we all are afflicted in regard to the feelings of creatures and people different from ourselves.

We are practical beings, each of us with limited functions and duties to perform. Each is bound to feel intensely the importance of his own duties and the significance of the situations that call these forth. But this feeling is in each of us a vital secret, for sympathy with which we vainly look to

others. The others are too much absorbed in their own vital secrets to take an interest in ours. Hence the stupidity and injustice of our opinions, so far as they deal with the significance of alien lives. Hence the falsity of our judgments, so far as they presume to decide in an absolute way on the value of other persons' conditions or ideals.

William James, *On a Certain Blindness in Human Beings*

66 A return from the over-estimation of the property of consciousness is the indispensable preliminary to any genuine insight into the course of psychic events . . . The unconscious must be accepted as the general basis of the psychic life. The unconscious is the larger circle which includes the smaller circle of the conscious; everything conscious has a preliminary unconscious stage, whereas the unconscious can stop at this stage, and yet claim to be considered a full psychic function. The unconscious is the true psychic reality; *in its inner nature it is just as much unknown to us as the reality of the external world, and it is just as imperfectly communicated to us by the data of consciousness as is the external world by the reports of our sense-organs.*

Freud, *Interpretation of Dreams*, VII, F

67 We must say that all the acts and manifestations which I notice in myself and do not know how to link up with the rest of my mental life must be judged as if they belonged to someone else and are to be explained by the mental life ascribed to that person. Further, experience shows that we understand very well how to interpret in others (i.e., how to fit into their mental context) those same acts which we refuse to acknowledge as mentally conditioned in ourselves. Some special hindrance evidently deflects our investigations from ourselves and interferes with our obtaining true knowledge of ourselves.

Freud, *The Unconscious*, I

68 Many good words get spoiled when the word self is prefixed to them: Words like pity, confidence, sacrifice, control, love. The reason is not far to seek. The word self infects them with a fixed introversion and isolation. It implies that the act of love or trust or control is turned back upon a self which already is in full existence and in whose behalf the act operates. Pity fulfils and creates a self when it is directed outward, opening the mind to new contacts and receptions. Pity for self withdraws the mind back into itself, rendering its subject unable to learn from the buffetings of fortune. Sacrifice may enlarge a self by bringing about surrender of acquired possessions to requirements of new growth. Self-sacrifice means a self-maiming which asks for compensatory pay in some later possession or indulgence. Confidence as an outgoing act is directness and courage in meeting the facts of life, trusting them to bring instruction and

support to a developing self. Confidence which terminates in the self means a smug complacency that renders a person obtuse to instruction by events. Control means a command of resources that enlarges the self; self-control denotes a self which is contracting, concentrating itself upon its own achievements, hugging them tight, and thereby estopping the growth that comes when the self is generously released; a self-conscious moral athleticism that ends in a disproportionate enlargement of some organ.

Dewey, *Human Nature and Conduct*, II, 5

69 "Never shall a young man,
Thrown into despair
By those great honey-colored
Ramparts at your ear,
Love you for yourself alone
And not your yellow hair."

"But I can get a hair-dye
And set such color there,
Brown, or black, or carrot,
That young men in despair
May love me for myself alone
And not my yellow hair."

"I heard an old religious man

But yesternight declare
That he had found a text to prove
That only God, my dear,
Could love you for yourself alone
And not your yellow hair."

Yeats, *For Anne Gregory*

70 The philosophies of Descartes and Kant' to the contrary, through the *I think* we reach our own self in the presence of others, and the others are just as real to us as our own self. Thus, the man who becomes aware of himself through the *cogito* also perceives all others, and he perceives them as the condition of his own existence. He realizes that he can not be anything (in the sense that we say that someone is witty or nasty or jealous) unless others recognize it as such. In order to get any truth about myself, I must have contact with another person. The other is indispensable to my own existence, as well as to my knowledge about myself. This being so, in discovering my inner being I discover the other person at the same time, like a freedom placed in front of me which thinks and wills only for or against me. Hence, let us at once announce the discovery of a world which we shall call inter-subjectivity; this is the world in which man decides what he is and what others are.

Sartre, *Existentialism*

1.5 | *Honor, Reputation, and Fame or Glory*

That the individual man should seek to know himself for what he really is and should esteem himself for his true worth make inevitable his desire to be known and esteemed by others according to his merits. Honor is the name that the ancients gave to the good that satisfies this natural desire; and they prized it highly among the goods that a virtuous man should seek—higher than wealth or sensual pleasure. The Greek and Roman writers quoted here stress the relation of honor to virtue or merit. They are, therefore, concerned with justice in the distribution or award of honors and with the

distinction between true honor and its counterfeits, the latter being undeserved.

Modern writers, in contrast, tend to substitute reputation for honor; though when they distinguish between a well-deserved reputation and one that is meretricious, they, too, are drawing a line that parallels the one that the ancients drew between honor and its counterfeits. Whether the term used is "honor" or "reputation," both ancient and modern writers also tend to agree that being well regarded or praised by others has little worth when those others are foolish or vicious, and so are not worthy enough to set store by their opinion. It is sometimes questioned whether one should care at all about the opinion of others; God alone is the judge of one's ultimate worth, and virtue is its own reward.

Three other terms were operative in the selection of the passages to be quoted here. One is shame, which is partly a synonym for dishonor or disgrace, and partly the name for the emotion or sentiment an individual experiences when he is aware of deficiencies in himself that stand in the way of his being justly honored. The other two terms are fame and glory, which are sometimes synonyms for reputation or at least for renown, but never synonyms for honor. Honor, properly conceived, or even a good reputation in the eyes of those whose judgment is worth heeding, cannot be pursued to the detriment of one's moral character; not so fame, for it belongs to the triad of things—money, fame, and power—that tempt men to those excesses of appetite which moralists condemn as lust and inordinate ambition. The price that one must pay for fame and glory is sometimes too high. Nevertheless, it is also recognized that fame and glory can be well deserved; and when not pursued they need not be gained at the expense of virtue.

These matters overlap the discussion of envy, and also of pride and humility, in Chapter 4 on EMOTION. They also have relation to the consideration of virtue and vice in Chapter 9 on ETHICS.

---

1 *Hektor.* I would feel deep shame
 before the Trojans, and the Trojan women with
   trailing garments,
 if like a coward I were to shrink aside from the
   fighting;
 and the spirit will not let me, since I have learned
   to be valiant
 and to fight always among the foremost ranks of
   the Trojans,
 winning for my own self great glory, and for my
   father.

   Homer, *Iliad*, VI, 441

2 *Achilles.* Fate is the same for the man who holds
   back, the same if he fights hard.
 We are all held in a single honour, the brave with
   the weaklings.
 A man dies still if he has done nothing, as one
   who has done much.

   Homer, *Iliad*, IX, 318

3 *Hektor.* Man, supposing you and I, escaping this
   battle,
 would be able to live on forever, ageless, immortal,
 so neither would I myself go on fighting in the
   foremost
 nor would I urge you into the fighting where men
   win glory.
 But now, seeing that the spirits of death stand
   close about us
 in their thousands, no man can turn aside nor
   escape them,

let us go on and win glory for ourselves, or yield it
   to others.

   Homer, *Iliad*, XII, 322

4 *Andromache.* Repute! repute! repute! how you've
   ballooned
 Thousands of good-for-nothings to celebrity!
 Men whose glory is come by honestly
 Have all my admiration. But impostors
 Deserve none: luck and humbug's all they are.

   Euripides, *Andromache*, 319

5 *Peleus.* When the public sets a war memorial up
 Do those who really sweated get the credit?
 Oh no! Some general wangles the prestige!—
 Who, brandishing his one spear among thousands,
 Did one man's work, but gets a world of praise.

   Euripides, *Andromache*, 694

6 It is only the love of honour that never grows old;
 and honour it is, not gain, as some would have it,
 that rejoices the heart of age and helplessness.

   Thucydides, *Peloponnesian War*, II, 44

7 *The Athenians.* In too many cases the very men that
 have their eyes perfectly open to what they are
 rushing into, let the thing called disgrace, by the
 mere influence of a seductive name, lead them on
 to a point at which they become so enslaved by
 the phrase as in fact to fall wilfully into hopeless
 disaster, and incur disgrace more disgraceful as
 the companion of error, than when it comes as the
 result of misfortune.

   Thucydides, *Peloponnesian War*, V, 111

8 *Phaedrus.* The principle which ought to be the guide of men who would nobly live—that principle, I say, neither kindred, nor honour, nor wealth, nor any other motive is able to implant so well as love. Of what am I speaking? Of the sense of honour and dishonour, without which neither states nor individuals ever do any good or great work.

Plato, *Symposium,* 178B

9 *Pausanias.* There is a dishonour in being overcome by the love of money, or of wealth, or of political power, whether a man is frightened into surrender by the loss of them, or, having experienced the benefits of money and political corruption, is unable to rise above the seductions of them. For none of these things are of a permanent or lasting nature; not to mention that no generous friendship ever sprang from them.

Plato, *Symposium,* 184A

10 *Diotima.* "Marvel not then at the love which all men have of their offspring; for that universal love and interest is for the sake of immortality."

I was astonished at her words, and said: "Is this really true, O thou wise Diotima?" And she answered with all the authority of an accomplished sophist: "Of that, Socrates, you may be assured;—think only of the ambition of men, and you will wonder at the senselessness of their ways, unless you consider how they are stirred by the love of an immortality of fame. They are ready to run all risks greater far than they would have run for their children, and to spend money and undergo any sort of toil, and even to die, for the sake of leaving behind them a name which shall be eternal."

Plato, *Symposium,* 208A

11 *Socrates.* He who at every age, as boy and youth and in mature life, has come out of the trial victorious and pure, shall be appointed a ruler and guardian of the State; he shall be honoured in life and death, and shall receive sepulture and other memorials of honour, the greatest that we have to give. But him who fails, we must reject. I am inclined to think that this is the sort of way in which our rulers and guardians should be chosen and appointed.

Plato, *Republic,* III, 413B

12 *Athenian Stranger.* A State which would be safe and happy, as far as the nature of man allows, must and ought to distribute honour and dishonour in the right way. And the right way is to place the goods of the soul first and highest in the scale, always assuming temperance to be the condition of them; and to assign the second place to the goods of the body; and the third place to money and property. And if any legislator or state departs from this rule by giving money the place of honour, or in any way preferring that which is really last, may we not say, that he or the state is doing an unholy and unpatriotic thing?

Plato, *Laws,* III, 697A

13 *Athenian Stranger.* Worthy of honour is he who does no injustice, and of more than twofold honour, if he not only does no injustice himself, but hinders others from doing any; the first may count as one man, the second is worth many men.

Plato, *Laws,* V, 730B

14 *Athenian Stranger.* The generality of cities are quite right in exhorting us to value a good reputation in the world, for there is no truth greater and more important than this—that he who is really good (I am speaking of the man who would be perfect) seeks for reputation with, but not without, the reality of goodness.

Plato, *Laws,* XII, 950A

15 With regard to honour and dishonour the mean is proper pride, the excess is known as a sort of 'empty vanity', and the deficiency is undue humility.

Aristotle, *Ethics,* 1107ᵇ21

16 It is chiefly with honours and dishonours, then, that the proud man is concerned; and at honours that are great and conferred by good men he will be moderately pleased, thinking that he is coming by his own or even less than his own; for there can be no honour that is worthy of perfect virtue, yet he will at any rate accept it since they have nothing greater to bestow on him; but honour from casual people and on trifling grounds he will utterly despise, since it is not this that he deserves, and dishonour too, since in his case it cannot be just. In the first place, then, as has been said, the proud man is concerned with honours; yet he will also bear himself with moderation towards wealth and power and all good or evil fortune, whatever may befall him, and will be neither over-joyed by good fortune nor over-pained by evil. For not even towards honour does he bear himself as if it were a very great thing. Power and wealth are desirable for the sake of honour (at least those who have them wish to get honour by means of them); and for him to whom even honour is a little thing the others must be so too.

Aristotle, *Ethics,* 1124ᵃ4

17 Shame should not be described as a virtue; for it is more like a feeling than a state of character. It is defined, at any rate, as a kind of fear of dishonour, and produces an effect similar to that produced by fear of danger; for people who feel disgraced blush, and those who fear death turn pale. Both, therefore, seem to be in a sense bodily conditions, which is thought to be characteristic of feeling rather than a state of character.

The feeling is not becoming to every age, but only to youth. For we think young people should be prone to the feeling of shame because they live by feeling and therefore commit many errors, but are restrained by shame; and we praise young people who are prone to this feeling, but an older person no one would praise for being prone to the sense of disgrace, since we think he should not do anything that need cause this sense. For the sense of disgrace is not even characteristic of a good man, since it is consequent on bad actions (for such actions should not be done; and if some actions are disgraceful in very truth and others only according to common opinion, this makes no difference; for neither class of actions should be done, so that no disgrace should be felt); and it is a mark of a bad man even to be such as to do any disgraceful action. To be so constituted as to feel disgraced if one does such an action, and for this reason to think oneself good, is absurd; for it is for voluntary actions that shame is felt, and the good man will never voluntarily do bad actions. But shame may be said to be conditionally a good thing; *if* a good man does such actions, he will feel disgraced; but the virtues are not subject to such a qualification. And if shamelessness—not to be ashamed of doing base actions—is bad, that does not make it good to be ashamed of doing such actions.

Aristotle, *Ethics,* 1128^{b}10

18 Those who desire honour from good men, and men who know, are aiming at confirming their own opinion of themselves; they delight in honour, therefore, because they believe in their own goodness on the strength of the judgement of those who speak about them.

Aristotle, *Ethics,* 1159^{a}22

19 Fame means being respected by everybody, or having some quality that is desired by all men, or by most, or by the good, or by the wise.

Aristotle, *Rhetoric,* 1361^{a}25

20 Since shame is a mental picture of disgrace, in which we shrink from the disgrace itself and not from its consequences, and we only care what opinion is held of us because of the people who form that opinion, it follows that the people before whom we feel shame are those whose opinion of us matters to us. Such persons are: those who admire us, those whom we admire, those by whom we wish to be admired, those with whom we are competing, and those whose opinion of us we respect. We admire those, and wish those to admire us, who possess any good thing that is highly esteemed; or from whom we are very anxious to get something that they are able to give us—as a lover feels. We compete with our equals. We respect, as true, the views of sensible people, such as our elders and those who have been well educated. And

we feel more shame about a thing if it is done openly, before all men's eyes. Hence the proverb, 'shame dwells in the eyes'. For this reason we feel most shame before those who will always be with us and those who notice what we do, since in both cases eyes are upon us.

Aristotle, *Rhetoric,* 1384^{a}23

21 Time as it goes round changes the seasons of things. That which was in esteem, falls at length into utter disrepute; and then another thing mounts up and issues out of its degraded state and every day is more and more coveted and blossoms forth high in honour when discovered and is in marvellous repute with men.

Lucretius, *Nature of Things,* V

22 No list of successes can bestow so much happiness as their diminution will cause annoyance.

Cicero, *Disputations,* I, 46

23 True fame has real substance and is precisely fashioned. It is not something ephemeral. It is, rather, the unanimous opinion of good men and the verdict of honest judges on an issue of outstanding merit. It is the echo of virtue's voice. Because fame is concerned with duties rightly done, good men do not disdain it. False fame, which tries to pass itself off as the true, is headstrong and thoughtless. It is compounded of faults and errors and seeks only public acclaim. By its counterfeit nature, it tarnishes the luster of real honor.

Cicero, *Disputations,* III, 2

24 Whom does false honour delight, or lying calumny terrify, except the vicious and sickly-minded?

Horace, *Epistles,* I, 16

25 What utter foolishness it is to be afraid that those who have a bad name can rob you of a good one.

Seneca, *Letters to Lucilius,* 91

26 A prophet is not without honour, save in his own country, and in his own house.

Matthew 13:57

27 Woe unto you, when all men shall speak well of you! for so did their fathers to the false prophets.

Luke 6:26

28 It is the fortune of all good men that their virtue rises in glory after their deaths, and that the envy which evil men conceive against them never outlives them long.

Plutarch, *Numa Pompilius*

29 It may be observed, in general, that when young men arrive early at fame and repute, if they are of a nature but slightly touched with emulation, this early attainment is apt to extinguish their thirst and satiate their small appetite; whereas the first

distinctions of more solid and weighty characters do but stimulate and quicken them and take them away like a wind in the pursuit of honour; they look upon these marks and testimonies to their virtue not as a recompense received for what they have already done, but as a pledge given by themselves of what they will perform hereafter, ashamed now to forsake or underlive the credit they have won, or, rather, not to exceed and obscure all that is gone before by the lustre of their following actions.

Plutarch, *Coriolanus*

30 He who least likes courting favour, ought also least to think of resenting neglect; to feel wounded at being refused a distinction can only arise from an overweening appetite to have it.

Plutarch, *Alcibiades and Coriolanus Compared*

31 There is something higher and greater in the admiration rendered by enemies to the virtue that had been their own obstacle, than in the grateful acknowledgments of friends. Since, in the one case, it is virtue alone that challenges itself the honour; while, in the other, it may be rather men's personal profit and advantage that is the real origin of what they do.

Plutarch, *Marcellus and Pelopidas Compared*

32 Lysander's father is said to have been Aristoclitus, who was not indeed of the royal family but yet of the stock of the Heraclidæ. He was brought up in poverty, and showed himself obedient and conformable, as ever any one did, to the customs of his country; of a manly spirit, also, and superior to all pleasures, excepting only that which their good actions bring to those who are honoured and successful; and it is accounted no base thing in Sparta for their young men to be overcome with this kind of pleasure. For they are desirous, from the very first, to have their youth susceptible to good and bad repute, to feel pain at disgrace, and exultation at being commended; and any one who is insensible and unaffected in these respects is thought poor-spirited and of no capacity for virtue.

Plutarch, *Lysander*

33 The man who is completely wise and virtuous has no need at all of glory, except so far as it disposes and eases his way to action by the greater trust that it procures him. A young man . . . may be permitted, while yet eager for distinction, to pride himself a little in his good deeds; for . . . his virtues, which are yet tender and, as it were, in the blade, cherished and supported by praises, grow stronger, and take the deeper root. But when this passion is exorbitant, it is dangerous in all men, and in those who govern a commonwealth, utterly destructive. For in the possession of large power and authority, it transports men to a degree of

madness; so that now they no more think what is good, glorious, but will have those actions only esteemed good that are glorious.

Plutarch, *Agis*

34 Returning to Rome with a great opinion of himself for these things, a ludicrous incident befell him, as he tells us himself. Meeting an eminent citizen in Campania, whom he accounted his friend, he asked him what the Romans said and thought of his actions, as if the whole city had been filled with the glory of what he had done. His friend asked him in reply, "Where is it you have been, Cicero?" This for the time utterly mortified and cast him down, to perceive that the report of his actions had sunk into the city of Rome as into an immense ocean, without any visible effect or result in reputation. And afterwards considering with himself that the glory he contended for was an infinite thing, and that there was no fixed end nor measure in its pursuit, he abated much of his ambitious thoughts. Nevertheless, he was always excessively pleased with his own praise, and continued to the very last to be passionately fond of glory; which often interfered with the prosecution of his wisest resolutions.

Plutarch, *Cicero*

35 An excessive display of outward honour would seem to be the most uncertain attestation of the real affection of a people for any king or potentate. Such shows lose their whole credit as tokens of affection . . . when we reflect that they may equally proceed from fear. The same decrees are voted upon the latter motive as upon the former. And therefore judicious men do not look so much to statues, paintings, or divine honours that are paid them, as to their own actions and conduct, judging hence whether they shall trust these as a genuine, or discredit them as a forced homage. As in fact nothing is less unusual than for a people, even while offering compliments, to be disgusted with those who accept them greedily, or arrogantly, or without respect to the free-will of the givers.

Plutarch, *Demetrius*

36 Be a good soldier, be good to your ward, be a
 person of honor.
If you are summoned to court, in a case uncertain
 and doubtful,
Even though Phalaris threatens and brings up his
 bull to suborn you,
Tell no lie, believe that the worst sin of all is preferring
Life to honor; don't lose, for life's sake, your reasons for living.
If a man is worthy of death, he is dead, though he
 banquets on oysters,
Though he bathes in a tub that reeks with the
 perfumes of Cosmos.

Juvenal, *Satire VIII*

37 Is anyone preferred before you at an entertainment, or in courtesies, or in confidential intercourse? If these things are good, you ought to rejoice that he has them; and if they are evil, do not be grieved that you have them not. And remember that you cannot be permitted to rival others in externals without using the same means to obtain them. For how can he who will not haunt the door of any man, will not attend him, will not praise him have an equal share with him who does these things? You are unjust, then, and unreasonable if you are unwilling to pay the price for which these things are sold, and would have them for nothing. For how much are lettuces sold? An obulus, for instance. If another, then, paying an obulus, takes the lettuces, and you, not paying it, go without them, do not imagine that he has gained any advantage over you. For as he has the lettuces, so you have the obulus which you did not give. So, in the present case, you have not been invited to such a person's entertainment because you have not paid him the price for which a supper is sold. It is sold for praise; it is sold for attendance. Give him, then, the value if it be for your advantage. But if you would at the same time not pay the one, and yet receive the other, you are unreasonable and foolish. Have you nothing, then, in place of the supper? Yes, indeed, you have—not to praise him whom you do not like to praise; not to bear the insolence of his lackeys.

Epictetus, *Encheiridion,* XXV

38 I [Tiberius] am mortal and limited to the functions of humanity, content if I can adequately fill the highest place; of this, I solemnly assure you [the Senators], and would have posterity remember it. They will more than sufficiently honour my memory by believing me to have been worthy of my ancestry, watchful over your interests, courageous in danger, fearless of enmity, when the State required it. These sentiments of your hearts are my temples, these my most glorious and abiding monuments. Those built of stone are despised as mere tombs, if the judgment of posterity passes into hatred. And therefore this is my prayer to our allies, our citizens, and to heaven itself; to the last, that, to my life's close, it grant me a tranquil mind, which can discern alike human and divine claims; to the first, that, when I die, they honour my career and the reputation of my name with praise and kindly remembrance.

Tacitus, *Annals,* IV, 38

39 The desire of glory is the last infirmity cast off even by the wise.

Tacitus, *Histories,* IV, 6

40 Perhaps the desire of the thing called fame will torment thee.—See how soon everything is forgotten, and look at the chaos of infinite time on each side of the present, and the emptiness of applause, and the changeableness and want of judgement in those who pretend to give praise, and the narrowness of the space within which it is circumscribed, and be quiet at last. For the whole earth is a point, and how small a nook in it is this thy dwelling, and how few are there in it, and what kind of people are they who will praise thee.

Marcus Aurelius, *Meditations,* IV, 3

41 Consider . . . the life lived by others in olden time, and the life of those who will live after thee, and the life now lived among barbarous nations, and how many know not even thy name, and how many will soon forget it, and how they who perhaps now are praising thee will very soon blame thee, and that neither a posthumous name is of any value, nor reputation, nor anything else.

Marcus Aurelius, *Meditations,* IX, 30

42 A man seeking the fame of eloquence—before a judge who is also a man, with a multitude of men standing about—inveighs against his adversary with inhuman hatred. Such a man will be most vigilantly on guard lest by a slip of the tongue he drop an 'h' and murder the word "human": yet worries not at all that by the fury of his mind he may murder a real human.

Augustine, *Confessions,* I, 18

43 Here, then, O God, is the memory still vivid in my mind. I would not have committed that theft alone: my pleasure in it was not what I stole but that I stole: yet I would not have enjoyed doing it, I would not have done it, alone. O friendship unfriendly, unanalysable attraction for the mind, greediness to do damage for the mere sport and jest of it, desire for another's loss with no gain to oneself or vengeance to be satisfied! Someone cries "Come on, let's do it"—and we would be ashamed to be ashamed!

Augustine, *Confessions,* II, 9

44 Love of praise tempts me even when I reprove it in myself, indeed in the very fact that I do reprove it: a man often glories the more vainly for his very contempt of vainglory: for which reason he does not really glory in his contempt of glory; in that he glories in it, he does not contemn it.

Augustine, *Confessions,* X, 38

45 Let the desire of glory be surpassed by the love of righteousness, so that, if there be seen anywhere "lying neglected things which are generally discredited," if they are good, if they are right, even the love of human praise may blush and yield to the love of truth. For so hostile is this vice to pious faith, if the love of glory be greater in the heart than the fear or love of God, that the Lord said, "How can ye believe, who look for glory from one another, and do not seek the glory which is from God alone?"

Augustine, *City of God,* V, 14

46 I do not see what it makes for the safety, good
morals, and certainly not for the dignity, of men,
that some have conquered and others have been
conquered, except that it yields them that most
insane pomp of human glory, in which "they have
received their reward" who burned with excessive
desire of it and carried on most eager wars.

Augustine, *City of God*, V, 17

47 Whosoever, without possessing that desire of glory
which makes one fear to displease those who judge
his conduct, desires domination and power, very
often seeks to obtain what he loves by most open
crimes. Therefore he who desires glory presses on
to obtain it either by the true way, or certainly by
deceit and artifice, wishing to appear good when
he is not. Therefore to him who possesses virtues it
is a great virtue to despise glory; for contempt of it
is seen by God, but is not manifest to human judgment.

Augustine, *City of God*, V, 19

48 Many men have got a great name from the false
opinions of the crowd. And what could be baser
than such a thing? For those who are falsely
praised, must blush to hear their praises. And if
they are justly won by merits, what can they add
to the pleasure of a wise man's conscience? For he
measures his happiness not by popular talk, but
by the truth of his conscience.

Boethius, *Consolation
of Philosophy*, III

49 It is impossible for happiness to consist in honour.
For honour is given to a man on account of some
excellence in him, and consequently it is a sign
and testimony of the excellence that is in the person honoured. Now a man's excellence is in proportion to his happiness, which is man's perfect
good; and to its parts, that is those goods by which
he has a certain share of happiness. And therefore
honour can result from happiness, but happiness
cannot principally consist therein.

Aquinas, *Summa Theologica*, I–II, 2, 2

50 Honour is not that reward of virtue, for which the
virtuous work, but they receive honour from men
by way of reward, as from those who have nothing
greater to offer. But virtue's true reward is happiness itself, for which the virtuous work, whereas if
they worked for honour, it would no longer be
virtue, but ambition.

Aquinas, *Summa Theologica*, I–II, 2, 2

51 O empty glory of human powers! How short the
time its green endures upon the top, if it be not
overtaken by rude ages!
Cimabue thought to hold the field in painting,
and now Giotto hath the cry, so that the fame
of the other is obscured.
Even so one Guido hath taken from the other the
glory of our tongue; and perchance one is born
who shall chase both from the nest.
Earthly fame is naught but a breath of wind,
which now cometh hence and now thence, and
changes name because it changes direction.
What greater fame shalt thou have, if thou strip
thee of thy flesh when old, than if thou hadst
died ere thou wert done with pap and chink,
before a thousand years are passed? which is
shorter space to eternity than the twinkling of
an eye to the circle which slowest is turned in
heaven.

Dante, *Purgatorio*, XI, 91

52 *Duke Theseus.* And gladder ought a friend be of his
death
When, in much honour, he yields up his breath,
Than when his name's grown feeble with old age;
For all forgotten, then, is his courage.
Hence it is best for all of noble name
To die when at the summit of their fame.

Chaucer, *Canterbury Tales:
Knight's Tale*

53 It is unnecessary for a prince to have all . . . good
qualities . . . but it is very necessary to appear to
have them. And I shall dare to say this also, that
to have them and always to observe them is injurious, and that to appear to have them is useful; to
appear merciful, faithful, humane, religious, upright, and to be so, but with a mind so framed
that should you require not to be so, you may be
able and know how to change to the opposite.

And you have to understand this, that a prince,
especially a new one, cannot observe all those
things for which men are esteemed, being often
forced, in order to maintain the state, to act contrary to faith, friendship, humanity, and religion.
Therefore it is necessary for him to have a mind
ready to turn itself accordingly as the winds and
variations of fortune force it, yet, as I have said
above, not to diverge from the good if he can
avoid doing so, but, if compelled, then to know
how to set about it.

For this reason a prince ought to take care that
he never lets anything slip from his lips that is not
replete with the above-named five qualities, that
he may appear to him who sees and hears him
altogether merciful, faithful, humane, upright,
and religious. There is nothing more necessary to
appear to have than this last quality, inasmuch as
men judge generally more by the eye than by the
hand, because it belongs to everybody to see you,
to few to come in touch with you. Every one sees
what you appear to be, few really know what you
are, and those few dare not oppose themselves to
the opinion of the many, who have the majesty of
the state to defend them; and in the actions of all
men, and especially of princes, which is not prudent to challenge, one judges by the result.

Machiavelli, *Prince*, XVIII

54 The role of true victory is in fighting, not in coming off safely; and the honor of valor consists in combating, not in beating.

Montaigne, *Essays,* I, 31, Of Cannibals

55 Of all the illusions in the world, the most universally received is the concern for reputation and glory, which we espouse even to the point of giving up riches, rest, life, and health, which are effectual and substantial goods, to follow that vain phantom and mere sound that has neither body nor substance. . . . And of the irrational humors of men, it seems that even the philosophers get rid of this one later and more reluctantly than any other.

Montaigne, *Essays,* I, 41, Not Communicating One's Glory

56 We lend our goods and our lives to the need of our friends; but to communicate one's honor and endow another with one's glory, that is hardly ever seen.

Montaigne, *Essays,* I, 41, Not Communicating One's Glory

57 God, who is himself all fullness and the acme of all perfection, cannot grow and increase within; but his name may grow and increase by the blessing and praise we give to his external works. Which praise, since we cannot incorporate it in him, inasmuch as he can have no accession of good, we attribute to his name, which is the part outside him that is nearest him. That is why it is to God alone that glory and honor belong. And there is nothing so remote from reason as for us to go in quest of it for ourselves; for since we are indigent and necessitous within, since our essence is imperfect and continually in need of betterment, it is this betterment that we should work for.

Montaigne, *Essays,* II, 16, Of Glory

58 We care more that people should speak of us than how they speak of us; and it is enough for us that our name should be current in men's mouths, no matter in what way it may be current. It seems that to be known is to have one's life and duration somehow in the keeping of others.

Montaigne, *Essays,* II, 16, Of Glory

59 It might perhaps be excusable for a painter or another artisan, or even for a rhetorician or a grammarian, to toil to acquire a name by his works; but the actions of virtue are too noble in themselves to seek any other reward than from their own worth, and especially to seek it in the vanity of human judgments.

Montaigne, *Essays,* II, 16, Of Glory

60 Those who judge and touch us inwardly make little account of the brilliance of our public acts, and see that these are only thin streams and jets of water spurting from a bottom otherwise muddy and thick; so likewise those who judge us by this brave outward appearance draw similar conclusions about our inner constitution, and cannot associate common faculties, just like their own, with these other faculties that astonish them and are so far beyond their scope.

Montaigne, *Essays,* III, 2, Of Repentance

61 Whatever it is, whether art or nature, that imprints in us this disposition to live with reference to others, it does us much more harm than good. We defraud ourselves of our own advantages to make appearances conform with public opinion. We do not care so much what we are in ourselves and in reality as what we are in the public mind. Even the joys of the mind, and wisdom, appear fruitless to us, if they are enjoyed by ourselves alone, if they do not shine forth to the sight and approbation of others.

Montaigne, *Essays,* III, 9, Of Vanity

62 *Joan La Pucelle.* Glory is like a circle in the water,
Which never ceaseth to enlarge itself
Till by broad spreading it disperse to nought.

Shakespeare, *I Henry VI,* I, ii, 133

63 *Mowbray.* The purest treasure mortal times afford
Is spotless reputation: that away,
Men are but gilded loam or painted clay.

Shakespeare, *Richard II,* I, i, 177

64 *Prince of Arragon.* O, that estates, degrees, and offices
Were not derived corruptly, and that clear honour
Were purchased by the merit of the wearer!
How many then should cover that stand bare!
How many be commanded that command!
How much low peasantry would then be glean'd
From the true seed of honour! and how much honour
Pick'd from the chaff and ruin of the times
To be new-varnish'd!

Shakespeare, *Merchant of Venice,* II, ix, 41

65 *Falstaff.* I would to God thou and I knew where a commodity of good names were to be bought.

Shakespeare, *I Henry IV,* I, ii, 91

66 *Hotspur.* By heaven, methinks it were an easy leap,
To pluck bright Honour from the pale-faced moon,
Or dive into the bottom of the deep,
Where fathom-line could never touch the ground,
And pluck up drowned Honour by the locks;
So he that doth redeem her thence might wear
Without corrival all her dignities.

Shakespeare, *I Henry IV,* I, iii, 201

67 *Falstaff.* Honour pricks me on. Yea, but how if honour prick me off when I come on? how then? Can honour set to a leg? no: or an arm? no: or take away the grief of a wound? no. Honour hath no skill in surgery, then? no. What is honour? a word. What is in that word honour? what is that honour? air. A trim reckoning! Who hath it? he that died o' Wednesday. Doth he feel it? no. Doth he hear it? no. 'Tis insensible, then? Yea, to the dead. But will it not live with the living? no. Why? detraction will not suffer it. Therefore I'll none of it. Honour is a mere scutcheon: and so ends my catechism.

Shakespeare, *I Henry IV,* V, i, 130

68 *Hamlet.* Oft it chances in particular men, That for some vicious mole of nature in them, As, in their birth—wherein they are not guilty, Since nature cannot choose his origin— By the o'ergrowth of some complexion, Oft breaking down the pales and forts of reason, Or by some habit that too much o'er-leavens The form of plausive manners, that these men, Carrying, I say, the stamp of one defect, Being nature's livery, or fortune's star— Their virtues else—be they as pure as grace, As infinite as man may undergo— Shall in the general censure take corruption From that particular fault: the dram of eale Doth all the noble substance of a doubt To his own scandal.

Shakespeare, *Hamlet,* I, iv, 23

69 *Hamlet.* Be thou as chaste as ice, as pure as snow, thou shalt not escape calumny.

Shakespeare, *Hamlet,* III, i, 139

70 *Ulysses.* Time hath, my lord, a wallet at his back, Wherein he puts alms for Oblivion, A great-sized monster of ingratitudes. Those scraps are good deeds past; which are devour'd As fast as they are made, forgot as soon As done. Perseverance, dear my lord, Keeps honour bright; to have done is to hang Quite out of fashion, like a rusty mail In monumental mockery. Take the instant way; For honour travels in a strait so narrow, Where one but goes abreast. Keep then the path; For Emulation hath a thousand sons That one by one pursue. If you give way, Or hedge aside from the direct forthright, Like to an enter'd tide, they all rush by And leave you hindmost; Or, like a gallant horse fall'n in first rank, Lie there for pavement to the abject rear, O'er-run and trampled on. Then what they do in present, Though less than yours in past, must o'ertop yours; For time is like a fashionable host

That slightly shakes his parting guest by the hand, And with his arms outstretch'd, as he would fly, Grasps in the comer. Welcome ever smiles, And farewell goes out sighing. O, let not virtue seek Remuneration for the thing it was; For beauty, wit, High birth, vigour of bone, desert in service, Love, friendship, charity, are subjects all To envious and calumniating Time. One touch of nature makes the whole world kin, That all with one consent praise new-born gawds, Though they are made and moulded of things past, And give to dust that is a little gilt More laud than gilt o'er-dusted. The present eye praises the present object.

Shakespeare, *Troilus and Cressida,* III, iii, 145

71 *Cassio.* Reputation, reputation, reputation! O, I have lost the immortal part of myself, and what remains is bestial. My reputation, Iago, my reputation!

Iago. As I am an honest man, I thought you had received some bodily wound; there is more sense in that than in reputation. Reputation is an idle and most false imposition; oft got without merit, and lost without deserving. You have lost no reputation at all, unless you repute yourself such a loser.

Shakespeare, *Othello,* II, iii, 262

72 *Iago.* Good name in man and woman, dear my lord, Is the immediate jewel of their souls. Who steals my purse steals trash; 'tis something, nothing; 'Twas mine, 'tis his, and has been slave to thousands; But he that filches from me my good name Robs me of that which not enriches him; And makes me poor indeed.

Shakespeare, *Othello,* III, iii, 155

73 *Lady Macbeth.* Yet do I fear thy nature; It is too full o' the milk of human kindness To catch the nearest way. Thou wouldst be great; Art not without ambition, but without The illness should attend it. What thou wouldst highly, That wouldst thou holily; wouldst not play false, And yet wouldst wrongly win.

Shakespeare, *Macbeth,* I, v, 17

74 *Volumnia.* I pray you, daughter, sing; or express yourself in a more comfortable sort. If my son were my husband, I should freelier rejoice in that absence wherein he won honour than in the embracements of his bed where he would show most love. When yet he was but tender-bodied and the only son of my womb, when youth with comeli-

ness plucked all gaze his way, when for a day of kings' entreaties a mother should not sell him an hour from her beholding, I, considering how honour would become such a person, that it was no better than picture-like to hang by the wall, if renown made it not stir, was pleased to let him seek danger where he was like to find fame. To a cruel war I sent him; from whence he returned, his brows bound with oak. I tell thee, daughter, I sprang not more in joy at first hearing he was a man-child than now in first seeing he had proved himself a man.

> Shakespeare, *Coriolanus*, I, iii, 1

75 *Wolsey.* Let's dry our eyes; and thus far hear me, Cromwell;
And, when I am forgotten, as I shall be,
And sleep in dull cold marble, where no mention
Of me more must be heard of, say, I taught thee,
Say, Wolsey, that once trod the ways of glory,
And sounded all the depths and shoals of honour,
Found thee a way, out of his wreck, to rise in;
A sure and safe one, though thy master miss'd it.
Mark but my fall, and that that ruin'd me.
Cromwell, I charge thee, fling away ambition.
By that sin fell the angels; how can man, then,
The image of his Maker, hope to win by it?
Love thyself last. Cherish those hearts that hate thee;
Corruption wins not more than honesty.
Still in thy right hand carry gentle peace.
To silence envious tongues. Be just, and fear not.
Let all the ends thou aim'st at be thy country's,
Thy God's, and truth's; then if thou fall'st, O Cromwell,
Thou fall'st a blessed martyr!

> Shakespeare, *Henry VIII*, III, ii, 431

76 *Griffith.* Men's evil manners live in brass; their virtues
We write in water.

> Shakespeare, *Henry VIII*, IV, ii, 46

77 I would have thee to know, that those Wounds that are given with the Instruments and Tools which a Man happens to have in his Hand, do not really disgrace the Person struck. We read it expresly in the Laws of Duels, *That if a Shoemaker strikes another Man with his Last which he held in his Hand, tho' it be of Wood, as a Cudgel is, yet the Party who was struck with it shall not be said to have been cudgell'd.* I tell thee this, that thou may'st not think we are in the least dishonour'd, tho' we have been horribly beaten in this Rencounter; for the Weapons which those Men us'd were but the Instruments of their Profession, and not one of 'em, as I very well remember, had either Tuck, or Sword, or Dagger. They gave me no Leisure, quoth *Sancho,* to examine things so narrowly; for I had no sooner laid my Hand on my Cutlass, but they cross'd my Shoulders with such a wooden Blessing, as settl'd me on the Ground without Sense or Motion, where you see me lie, and where I don't trouble my Head whether it be a Disgrace to be mawl'd with Cudgels or with Packstaves: Let 'em be what they will, I am only vex'd to feel them so heavy on my Shoulders, where I am afraid they are imprinted as deep as they are in my Mind. For all this, reply'd Don *Quixote,* I must inform thee, Friend *Sancho,* that there is no Remembrance which Time will not deface, nor no Pain to which Death will not put a Period. Thank you for nothing, quoth *Sancho!* What worse can befal us, than to have only Death to trust to? Were our Affliction to be cur'd with a Plaister or two, a Man might have some Patience; but, for ought I see, all the Salves in an Hospital won't set us on our best Legs again. Come, no more of this, cry'd Don *Quixote;* take Courage, and make a Virtue of Necessity; for 'tis what I am resolv'd to do.

> Cervantes, *Don Quixote*, I, 15

78 *Don Quixote.* I pray thee tell me now what does the Town say of me? What do the Neighbours, what do the People think of me? What say the Gentry, and the better Sort? How do the Knights discourse of my Valour, my high Feats of Arms, and my courteous Behaviour? What Thoughts do they entertain of my Design, to raise from the Grave of Oblivion the Order of Knight-Errantry, and restore it to the World? In short, tell me freely and sincerely whatever thou hast heard; neither enlarg'd with flattering Commendations, nor lessen'd by any Omission of my Dispraise; for 'tis the Duty of faithful Servants to lay Truth before their Masters in its honourable Nakedness. . . . Why then, quoth *Sancho,* first and foremost you are to know, that the common People take you for a downright Mad-man, and me for one that has not much Guts in his Brains.

> Cervantes, *Don Quixote*, II, 2

79 *Don Quixote.* There are two Paths to Dignity and Wealth; Arts and Arms. Arms I have chosen, and the Influence of the Planet *Mars* that presided at my Nativity, led me to that adventurous Road. So that all your Attempts to shake my Resolution are in vain: for in spite of all Mankind, I will pursue what Heaven has fated, Fortune ordain'd, what Reason requires, and (which is more) what my Inclination demands. I am sensible of the many Troubles and Dangers that attend the Prosecution of Knight-Errantry, but I also know what infinite Honours and Rewards are the Consequences of the Performance. The Path of Virtue is narrow, and the Way of Vice easy and open; but their Ends and Resting-places are very different. The latter is a broad Road indeed, and downhill all the way, but Death and Contempt are always met at the End of the Journey; whereas the former leads to Glory and Life, not a Life that soon must have an End, but an immortal Being.

> Cervantes, *Don Quixote*, II, 6

80 *Don Quixote.* I tell thee, *Sancho,* this Desire of Honour is a strange bewitching thing. What dost thou think made *Horatius,* arm'd at all Points, plunge headlong from the Bridge into the rapid *Tyber?* What prompted *Curtius* to leap into the profound flaming Gulph? What made *Mutius* burn his Hand? What forc'd *Caesar* over the *Rubicon,* spite of all the Omens that dissuaded his Passage? And to instance a more modern Example, what made the undaunted *Spaniards* sink their Ships, when under the most courteous *Cortez,* but that scorning the stale Honour of this so often conquer'd World, they sought a Maiden Glory in a new Scene of Victory? These and a Multiplicity of other great Actions, are owing to the immediate Thirst and Desire of Fame, which Mortals expect as the proper Price and immortal Recompence of their great Actions. But we that are Christian Catholick Knights-Errant must fix our Hopes upon a higher Reward, plac'd in the Eternal and Celestial Regions, where we may expect a permanent Honour and compleat Happiness; not like the Vanity of Fame, which at best is but the Shadow of great Actions, and must necessarily vanish, when destructive Time has eat away the Substance which it follow'd. So, my *Sancho,* since we expect a Christian Reward, we must suit our Actions to the Rules of Christianity. In Giants we must kill Pride and Arrogance: But our greatest Foes, and whom we must chiefly combat, are within. Envy we must overcome by Generosity and Nobleness of Soul; Anger, by a repos'd and easy Mind; Riot and Drowsiness, by Vigilance and Temperance; Lasciviousness, by our inviolable Fidelity to those who are Mistresses of our Thoughts; and Sloth, by our indefatigable Peregrinations through the Universe, to seek Occasions of Military, as well as Christian Honours. This, *Sancho,* is the Road to lasting Fame, and a good and honourable Renown.

Cervantes, *Don Quixote,* II, 8

81 When he [the Gentleman in Green] look'd on Don *Quixote,* he thought he had never beheld before such a strange appearance of a Man. He could not but admire at the Lankness of his Horse; he consider'd then the Long-back'd, Rawbon'd Thing that bestrid him; His wan, meagre Face, his Air, his Gravity, his Arms and Equipage; such a Figure, as perhaps had not been seen in that Country time our of mind. Don *Quixote* observed how intent the travelling Gentleman had been in surveying him, and reading his Desire in his Surprize, as he was the very Pink of Courtesy and fond of pleasing every one, without staying till he should question him, he thought fit to prevent him. Sir, said he, that you are surpriz'd at this Figure of mine, which appears so new and exotick, I do not wonder in the least; but your Admiration will cease when I have inform'd you, that I am one of those Knights who go in quest of Adventures. I have left my Country, Mortgaged

my Estate, quitted my Pleasures, and thrown myself into the Arms of Fortune. My design was to give a new Life to Knight-Errantry, that so long has been lost to the World; and thus, after infinite Toils and Hardships; sometimes stumbling, sometimes falling; casting myself headlong in one place, and rising again in another, I have compass'd a great part of my Desire, relieving Widows, protecting Damsels, assisting Marry'd Women and Orphans, the proper and natural Office of Knights-Errant; and so by many Valorous and Christian-like Atchievements, I have merited the Honour of the Press in almost all the Nations of the World. Thirty thousand Volumes of my History have been printed already, and thirty thousand Millions more are like to be printed, if Heaven prevent not. In short, to sum up all in one Word, know, I am Don *Quixote de la Mancha,* otherwise call'd, The Knight of the Woful Figure; I own it lessens the value of Praise to be the Publisher of its own self; yet 'tis what I am sometimes forc'd to, when there is none present to do me Justice. And now, good Sir, no longer let this Steed, this Lance, this Shield, this Armour, nor this Squire, nor the Paleness of my Looks, nor my exhausted Body, move your Admiration, since you know who I am, and the Profession I follow.

Cervantes, *Don Quixote,* II, 16

82 Ambition is like choler; which is an humour that maketh men active, earnest, full of alacrity, and stirring, if it be not stopped. But if it be stopped, and cannot have his way, it becometh adust, and thereby malign and venomous. So ambitious men, if they find the way open for their rising, and still get forward, they are rather busy than dangerous; but if they be checked in their desires, they become secretly discontent, and look upon men and matters with an evil eye.

Bacon, *Of Ambition*

83 Certainly, great persons had need to borrow other men's opinions, to think themselves happy; for if they judge by their own feeling, they cannot find it: but if they think with themselves what other men think of them, and that other men would fain be as they are, then they are happy as it were by report, when perhaps they find the contrary within.

Bacon, *Of Great Place*

84 Honour is, or should be, the place of virtue; and as in nature things move violently to their place, and calmly in their place; so virtue in ambition is violent, in authority settled and calm. All rising to great place is by a winding stair; and if there be factions, it is good to side a man's self whilst he is in the rising, and to balance himself when he is placed.

Bacon, *Of Great Place*

85 Fame is like a river, that beareth up things light

and swoln, and drowns things weighty and solid.

Bacon, *Of Praise*

86 A man is an ill husband of his honour, that entreth into any action, the failing wherein may disgrace him more than the carrying of it through can honour him.

Bacon, *Of Honour
and Reputation*

87 Although I do not care immoderately for glory, or, if I dare say so, although I even hate it, inasmuch as I judge it to be antagonistic to the repose which I esteem above all other things, at the same time I never tried to conceal my actions as though they were crimes, nor have I used many precautions against being known, partly because I should have thought it damaging to myself, and partly because it would have given me a sort of disquietude which would again have militated against the perfect repose of spirit which I seek. And forasmuch as having in this way always held myself in a condition of indifference as regards whether I was known or was not known, I have not yet been able to prevent myself from acquiring some sort of reputation, I thought that I should do my best at least to prevent myself from acquiring an evil reputation.

Descartes, *Discourse on Method,* VI

88 Grief for the discovery of some defect of ability is *shame,* or the passion that discovereth itself in blushing, and consisteth in the apprehension of something dishonourable; and in young men is a sign of the love of good reputation, and commendable: in old men it is a sign of the same; but because it comes too late, not commendable.

Hobbes, *Leviathan,* I, 6

89 Let a man, as most men do, rate themselves at the highest value they can, yet their true value is no more than it is esteemed by others.

Hobbes, *Leviathan,* I, 10

90 The manifestation of the value we set on one another is that which is commonly called *honouring* and *dishonouring.* To value a man at a high rate is to *honour* him; at a low rate is to *dishonour* him. But high and low, in this case, is to be understood by comparison to the rate that each man setteth on himself.

Hobbes, *Leviathan,* I, 10

91 We do not content ourselves with the life we have in ourselves and in our own being; we desire to live an imaginary life in the mind of others, and for this purpose we endeavour to shine. We labour unceasingly to adorn and preserve this imaginary existence and neglect the real. And if we possess calmness, or generosity, or truthfulness, we are eager to make it known, so as to attach these virtues

to that imaginary existence. We would rather separate them from ourselves to join them to it; and we would willingly be cowards in order to acquire the reputation of being brave. . . . We are so presumptuous that we would wish to be known by all the world, even by people who shall come after, when we shall be no more; and we are so vain that the esteem of five or six neighbours delights and contents us.

Pascal, *Pensées,* II, 147–148

92 Have you never seen people who, in order to complain of the little fuss you make about them, parade before you the example of great men who esteem them? In answer I reply to them, "Show me the merit whereby you have charmed these persons, and I also will esteem you."

Pascal, *Pensées,* V, 333

93 *Fame* is the spur that the clear spirit doth raise
(That last infirmity of Noble mind)
To scorn delights, and live laborious dayes;
But the fair Guerdon when we hope to find,
And think to burst out into sudden blaze,
Comes the blind *Fury* with th'abhorred shears,
And slits the thin spun life. But not the praise,
Phoebus repli'd, and touch'd my trembling ears;
Fame is no plant that grows on mortal soil,
Nor in the glistering foil
Set off to th'world, nor in broad rumour lies,
But lives and spreds aloft by those pure eyes,
And perfet witnes of all judging *Jove;*
As he pronounces lastly on each deed,
Of so much fame in Heav'n expect thy meed.

Milton, *Lycidas,* 70

94 I might relate of thousands, and thir names
Eternize here on Earth; but those elect
Angels contented with thir fame in Heav'n
Seek not the praise of men; the other sort
In might though wondrous and in Acts of Warr,
Nor of Renown less eager, yet by doome
Canceld from Heav'n and sacred memorie,
Nameless in dark oblivion let them dwell.
For strength from Truth divided and from Just,
Illaudable, naught merits but dispraise
And ignominie, yet to glorie aspires
Vain glorious, and through infamie seeks fame:
Therfore Eternal silence be thir doome.

Milton, *Paradise Lost,* VI, 373

95 O *Eve,* in evil hour thou didst give eare
To that false Worm, of whomsoever taught
To counterfet Mans voice, true in our Fall,
False in our promis'd Rising; since our Eyes
Op'nd we find indeed, and find we know
Both Good and Evil, Good lost, and Evil got,
Bad Fruit of Knowledge, if this be to know,
Which leaves us naked thus, of Honour void,
Of Innocence, of Faith, of Puritie,

Our wonted Ornaments now soild and staind,
And in our Faces evident the signes
Of foul concupiscence; whence evil store;
Even shame, the last of evils; of the first
Be sure then. How shall I behold the face
Henceforth of God or Angel, earst with joy
And rapture so oft beheld? those heav'nly shapes
Will dazle now this earthly, with thir blaze
Insufferable bright. O might I here
In solitude live savage, in some glade
Obscur'd, where highest Woods impenetrable
To Starr or Sun-light, spread thir umbrage broad,
And brown as Evening: Cover me ye Pines,
Ye Cedars, with innumerable boughs;
Hide me, where I may never see them more.
But let us now, as in bad plight, devise
What best may for the present serve to hide
The Parts of each from other, that seem most
To shame obnoxious, and unseemliest seen,
Some Tree whose broad smooth Leaves together
   sowd.
And girded on our loyns, may cover round
Those middle parts, that this new commer,
   Shame,
There sit not, and reproach us as unclean.
  So counsel'd hee, and both together went
Into the thickest Wood, there soon they chose
The Figtree. . . .
                         Those
They gatherd, broad as *Amazonian* Targe,
And with what skill they had, together sowd,
To gird thir waste, vain Covering if to hide
Thir guilt and dreaded shame; O how unlike
To that first naked Glorie.
            Milton, *Paradise Lost,* IX, 1067

96 What needs my *Shakespear* for his honour'd Bones,
   The labour of an age in piled Stones,
   Or that his hallow'd reliques should be hid
   Under a Star-ypointing *Pyramid?*
   Dear son of memory, great heir of Fame,
   What need'st thou such weak witnes of thy name?
   Thou in our wonder and astonishment
   Hast built thy self a live-long Monument. . . .
   And so Sepulcher'd in such pomp dost lie,
   That Kings for such a Tomb would wish to die.
              Milton, *On Shakespear*

97 The more a man imagines that he is praised by
   other men, the more is this joy strengthened; for
   the more a man imagines that he is praised by
   others, the more does he imagine that he affects
   others with joy accompanied by the idea of himself as a cause, and therefore he is affected with
   greater joy accompanied with the idea of himself.
        Spinoza, *Ethics,* III, Prop. 53, Corol.

98 What is called vainglory is self-satisfaction, nourished by nothing but the good opinion of the multitude, so that when that is withdrawn, the satisfaction, that is to say, the chief good which every

one loves, ceases. For this reason those who glory
in the good opinion of the multitude anxiously
and with daily care strive, labour, and struggle to
preserve their fame. For the multitude is changeable and fickle, so that fame, if it be not preserved, soon passes away. As every one, moreover,
is desirous to catch the praises of the people, one
person will readily destroy the fame of another;
and, consequently, as the object of contention is
what is commonly thought to be the highest good,
a great desire arises on the part of every one to
keep down his fellows by every possible means,
and he who at last comes off conqueror boasts
more because he has injured another person than
because he has profited himself. This glory of self-
satisfaction, therefore, is indeed vain, for it is really no glory.
        Spinoza, *Ethics,* IV, Prop. 58, Schol.

99 Shame, although it is not a virtue, is nevertheless
   good, in so far as it shows that a desire of living
   uprightly is present in the man who is possessed
   with shame, just as pain is called good in so far as
   it shows that the injured part has not yet putre-
   fied. A man, therefore, who is ashamed of what he
   has done, although he is sorrowful, is nevertheless
   more perfect than the shameless man who has no
   desire of living uprightly.
        Spinoza, *Ethics,* IV, Prop. 58, Schol.

100 Since nothing can be more natural than to encourage with esteem and reputation that wherein
   every one finds his advantage, and to blame and
   discountenance the contrary; it is no wonder that
   esteem and discredit, virtue and vice, should, in a
   great measure, everywhere correspond with the
   unchangeable rule of right and wrong, which the
   law of God hath established; there being nothing
   that so directly and visibly secures and advances
   the general good of mankind in this world, as obedience to the laws he has set them, and nothing
   that breeds such mischiefs and confusion, as the
   neglect of them. And therefore men, without renouncing all sense and reason, and their own interest, which they are so constantly true to, could
   not generally mistake, in placing their commendation and blame on that side that really deserved
   it not. Nay, even those men whose practice was
   otherwise, failed not to give their approbation
   right, few being depraved to that degree as not to
   condemn, at least in others, the faults they themselves were guilty of.
        Locke, *Concerning Human Understanding,*
                     Bk. II, XXVIII, 11

101 Ambition often puts Men upon doing the meanest
   Offices; so Climbing is performed in the same
   Posture with Creeping.
        Swift, *Thoughts on Various Subjects*

102 And now, having grasped his new-purchased
   sword in his hand, he [Tom Jones] was going to

issue forth, when the thought of what he was about to undertake laid suddenly hold of him, and he began to reflect that in a few minutes he might possibly deprive a human being of life, or might lose his own. "Very well," said he, "and in what cause do I venture my life? Why, in that of my honour. And who is this human being? A rascal who hath injured and insulted me without provocation. But is not revenge forbidden by Heaven? Yes, but it is enjoined by the world. Well, but shall I obey the world in opposition to the express commands of Heaven? Shall I incur the Divine displeasure rather than be called— ha—coward—scoundrel?—I'll think no more; I am resolved, and must fight him."

Fielding, *Tom Jones*, VII, 14

103 *Mrs. Fitzpatrick.* I made no doubt that his [Mr. Fitzpatrick's] designs were strictly honourable, as the phrase is; that is, to rob a lady of her fortune by way of marriage.

Fielding, *Tom Jones*, XI, 4

104 Honour sets all the parts of the body politic in motion, and by its very action connects them; thus each individual advances the public good, while he only thinks of promoting his own interest.

True it is that, philosophically speaking, it is a false honour which moves all the parts of the government; but even this false honour is as useful to the public as true honour could possible be to private persons.

Montesquieu, *Spirit of Laws*, III, 7

105 Honour . . . has its supreme laws, to which education is obliged to conform. The chief of these are that we are permitted to set a value upon our fortune, but are absolutely forbidden to set any upon our lives.

The second is that, when we are raised to a post or preferment, we should never do or permit anything which may seem to imply that we look upon ourselves as inferior to the rank we hold.

The third is that those things which honour forbids are more rigorously forbidden, when the laws do not concur in the prohibition; and those it commands are more strongly insisted upon, when they happen not to be commanded by law.

Montesquieu, *Spirit of Laws*, IV, 2

106 The savage lives within himself, while social man lives constantly outside himself, and only knows how to live in the opinion of others, so that he seems to receive the consciousness of his own existence merely from the judgment of others concerning him.

Rousseau, *Origin of Inequality*, II

107 Most men seem rather inclined to confess the want of virtue than of importance.

Johnson, *Rambler No. 13*

108 It is . . . of the utmost importance that those who have any intention of deviating from the beaten roads of life and acquiring a reputation superior to names hourly swept away by time among the refuse of fame should add to their reason and their spirit the power of persisting in their purposes, acquire the art of sapping what they cannot batter, and the habit of vanquishing obstinate resistance by obstinate attacks.

Johnson, *Rambler No. 43*

109 That praises are without reason lavished on the dead, and that the honours due only to excellence are paid to antiquity, is a complaint likely to be always continued by those who, being able to add nothing to truth, hope for eminence from the heresies of paradox; or those who, being forced by disappointment upon consolatory expedients, are willing to hope from posterity what the present age refuses, and flatter themselves that the regard which is yet denied by envy will be at last bestowed by time.

Johnson, *Preface to Shakespeare*

110 Honour makes a great part of the reward of all honourable professions. In point of pecuniary gain, all things considered, they are generally under-recompensed. . . . Disgrace has the contrary effect. The trade of a butcher is a brutal and an odious business; but it is in most places more profitable than the greater part of common trades. The most detestable of all employments, that of public executioner, is, in proportion to the quantity of work done, better paid than any common trade whatever.

Adam Smith, *Wealth of Nations*, I, 10

111 As long as mankind shall continue to bestow more liberal applause on their destroyers than on their benefactors, the thirst of military glory will ever be the vice of the most exalted characters.

Gibbon, *Decline and Fall of the Roman Empire*, I

112 Our estimate of personal merit is relative to the common faculties of mankind. The aspiring efforts of genius or virtue, either in active or speculative life, are measured not so much by their real elevation as by the height to which they ascend above the level of their age or country; and the same stature which in a people of giants would pass unnoticed, must appear conspicuous in a race of pigmies.

Gibbon, *Decline and Fall of the Roman Empire*, XLII

113 The road to eminence and power, from obscure condition, ought not to be made too easy, nor a thing too much of course. If rare merit be the rarest of all rare things, it ought to pass through some sort of probation. The temple of honour ought to be seated on an eminence. If it be opened through virtue, let it be remembered too, that virtue is never tried but by some difficulty and some struggle.

Burke, *Reflections on the Revolution in France*

114 Well is it known that ambition can creep as well as soar. The pride of no person in a flourishing condition is more justly to be dreaded than that of him who is mean and cringing under a doubtful and unprosperous fortune.

Burke, *Letters on a Regicide Peace,* III

115 *Respect* applies always to persons only—not to things. The latter may arouse inclination, and if they are animals (for example, horses, dogs, etc.), even *love* or *fear*, like the sea, a volcano, a beast of prey; but never *respect*. Something that comes nearer to this feeling is *admiration,* and this, as an affection, astonishment, can apply to things also, for example, lofty mountains, the magnitude, number, and distance of the heavenly bodies, the strength and swiftness of many animals, etc. But all this is not respect. A man also may be an object to me of love, fear, or admiration, even to astonishment, and yet not be an object of respect. His jocose humour, his courage and strength, his power from the rank he has amongst others, may inspire me with sentiments of this kind, but still inner respect for him is wanting. Fontenelle says, "I bow before a great man, but my mind does not bow." I would add, before an humble plain man, in whom I perceive uprightness of character in a higher degree than I am conscious of in myself, *my mind bows* whether I choose it or not, and though I bear my head never so high that he may not forget my superior rank. Why is this? Because his example exhibits to me a law that humbles my self-conceit when I compare it with my conduct. . . . *Respect* is a *tribute* which we cannot refuse to merit, whether we will or not; we may indeed outwardly withhold it, but we cannot help feeling it inwardly.

Kant, *Critique of Practical Reason,* Pt. I, I, 3

116 Men can never acquire respect by benevolence alone, though they may gain love, so that the greatest beneficence only procures them honour when it is regulated by worthiness.

Kant, *Critique of Practical Reason,* Pt. I, II, 2

117 If people insist that honor is dearer than life itself, what they really mean is that existence and well-being are as nothing compared with other people's opinions. Of course, this may be only an exaggerated way of stating the prosaic truth that reputation, that is, the opinion others have of us, in indispensable if we are to make any progress in the world.

Schopenhauer, *Position,* I

118 Nothing in life gives a man so much courage as the attainment or renewal of the conviction that other people regard him with favor; because it means that everyone joins to give him help and protection, which is an infinitely stronger bulwark against the ills of life than anything he can do himself.

Schopenhauer, *Position,* IV

119 The ultimate foundation of honor is the conviction that moral character is unalterable: a single bad action implies that future actions of the same kind will, under similar circumstances, also be bad.

Schopenhauer, *Position,* IV

120 Fame is something which must be won; honor, only something which must not be lost. The absence of fame is obscurity, which is only a negative; but loss of honor is shame, which is a positive quality.

Schopenhauer, *Position,* IV

121 Honor is concerned merely with such qualities as everyone may be expected to show under similar circumstances; fame only of those which cannot be required of any man. Honor is of qualities which everyone has a right to attribute to himself; fame only of those which should be left to others to attribute. Whilst our honor extends as far as people have knowledge of us; fame runs in advance, and makes us known wherever it finds its way. Everyone can make a claim to honor; very few to fame, as being attainable only in virtue of extraordinary achievements.

Schopenhauer, *Position,* V

122 Examine the man who lives in misery because he does not shine above other men; who goes about producing himself, pruriently anxious about his gifts and claims; struggling to force everybody, as it were begging everybody for God's sake, to acknowledge him a great man, and set him over the heads of men! Such a creature is among the wretchedest sights seen under this sun. A *great* man? A poor morbid prurient empty man; fitter for the ward of a hospital, than for a throne among men. I advise you to keep-out of his way. He cannot walk on quiet paths; unless you will look at him, wonder at him, write paragraphs about him, he cannot live. It is the *emptiness* of the man, not his greatness. Because there is nothing in himself, he hungers and thirsts that you would find something in him. In good truth, I believe no

great man, not so much as a genuine man who had health and real substance in him of whatever magnitude, was ever much tormented in this way.

Carlyle, *The Hero as King*

123 I trust a good deal to common fame, as we all must. If a man has good corn, or woods, or boards, or pigs to sell, or can make better chairs or knives, crucibles or church organs than anybody else, you will find a broad, hard-beaten road to his house, though it be in the woods.

Emerson, *Journal (Feb. 1855)*

124 The nature and strength of the feelings which we call regret, shame, repentance or remorse, depend apparently not only on the strength of the violated instinct, but partly on the strength of the temptation, and often still more on the judgment of our fellows. How far each man values the appreciation of others, depends on the strength of his innate or acquired feeling of sympathy; and on his own capacity for reasoning out the remote consequences of his acts. Another element is most important, although not necessary, the reverence or fear of the Gods, or Spirits believed in by each man: and this applies especially in cases of remorse.

Darwin, *Descent of Man*, I, 4

125 To do good unto others—to do unto others as ye would they should do unto you—is the foundation-stone of morality. It is, therefore, hardly possible to exaggerate the importance during rude times of the love of praise and the dread of blame. A man who was not impelled by any deep, instinctive feeling, to sacrifice his life for the good of others, yet was roused to such actions by a sense of glory, would by his example excite the same wish for glory in other men, and would strengthen by exercise the noble feeling of admiration.

Darwin, *Descent of Man*, I, 5

126 He [Mitya] felt unbearably awkward. All were clothed, while he was naked, and strange to say, when he was undressed he felt somehow guilty in their presence, and was almost ready to believe himself that he was inferior to them, and that now they had a perfect right to despise him.

"When all are undressed, one is somehow not ashamed, but when one's the only one undressed and everybody is looking, it's degrading," he kept repeating to himself, again and again. "It's like a dream; I've sometimes dreamed of being in such degrading positions."

Dostoevsky, *Brothers Karamazov*, Pt. III, IX, 6

127 *A man's Social Self* is the recognition which he gets from his mates. We are not only gregarious animals, liking to be in sight of our fellows, but we have an innate propensity to get ourselves noticed, and noticed favorably, by our kind. No more fiendish punishment could be devised, were such a thing physically possible, than that one should be turned loose in society and remain absolutely unnoticed by all the members thereof. If no one turned round when we entered, answered when we spoke, or minded what we did, but if every person we met "cut us dead," and acted as if we were non-existing things, a kind of rage and impotent despair would ere long well up in us, from which the cruellest bodily tortures would be a relief; for these would make us feel that, however bad might be our plight, we had not sunk to such a depth as to be unworthy of attention at all.

William James, *Psychology*, X

128 Hardly any of us have ethical energy enough for more than one really inflexible point of honor.

Shaw, *Doctor's Dilemma*, Pref.

129 *Tanner.* We live in an atmosphere of shame. We are ashamed of everything that is real about us; ashamed of ourselves, of our relatives, of our incomes, of our accents, of our opinions, of our experience, just as we are ashamed of our naked skins. . . . We are ashamed to walk, ashamed to ride in an omnibus, ashamed to hire a hansom instead of keeping a carriage, ashamed of keeping one horse instead of two and a groom-gardener instead of a coachman and footman. The more things a man is ashamed of, the more respectable he is.

Shaw, *Man and Superman*, I

130 The highest form of vanity is love of fame. It is a passion easy to deride but hard to understand, and in men who live at all by imagination almost impossible to eradicate. The good opinion of posterity can have no possible effect on our fortunes, and the practical value which reputation may temporarily have is quite absent in posthumous fame. The direct object of this passion—that a name should survive in men's mouths to which no adequate idea of its original can be attached—seems a thin and fantastic satisfaction, especially when we consider how little we should probably sympathise with the creatures that are to remember us. . . . Yet, beneath this desire for nominal longevity, apparently so inane, there may lurk an ideal ambition of which the ancients cannot have been unconscious when they set so high a value on fame. They often identified fame with immortality, a subject on which they had far more rational sentiments than have since prevailed.

Santayana, *Life of Reason*, II, 6

1.6 | *Human Greatness*

THE HERO

There is necessarily some overlapping and there is certainly a connection between matters covered in the preceding section and in this one. Great men are usually men who have won fame and glory for themselves; heroes are usually men who have been honored as such. What distinguishes the subjects of the two sections is the fact that here we are concerned with the attributes or characteristics that elevate a man above the commonplace, that make him outstanding among men, whether or not he is renowned and honored for his greatness. That a man has genius remains the case even if no tribute is paid by others to his extraordinary gifts.

The passages on greatness in men and women fall into two groups: on the one hand, statements about what human greatness consists in; on the other, examples of human greatness. There would be many more of the latter were it not for the fact that many of the examples have been quoted elsewhere: examples of greatness in women in Section 1.7; examples of great poets in Section 16.3; examples of great military commanders in Section 14.2, and so on.

In addition, there are quotations that discuss the phenomenon of human genius and that describe heroes and heroic deeds or achievements. The ancients magnify the hero and the heroic more than modern writers do. The controversy about the role of the great man in history is characteristically a modern one; and on this issue the reader will find the affirmations of Carlyle and Emerson opposed by the denials of Tolstoy.

---

1 *Artabanus.* Seest thou how God with his lightning smites always the bigger animals, and will not suffer them to wax insolent, while those of a lesser bulk chafe him not? How likewise his bolts fall ever on the highest houses and the tallest trees? So plainly does He love to bring down everything that exalts itself. Thus ofttimes a mighty host is discomfited by a few men, when God in his jealousy sends fear or storm from heaven, and they perish in a way unworthy of them. For God allows no one to have high thoughts but Himself.

Herodotus, *History*, VII, 10

2 Now there arose [at Thermopylae] a fierce struggle between the Persians and the Lacedæmonians over the body of Leonidas, in which the Greeks four times drove back the enemy, and at last by their great bravery succeeded in bearing off the body. This combat was scarcely ended when the Persians with Ephialtes approached; and the Greeks, informed that they drew nigh, made a change in the manner of their fighting. Drawing back into the narrowest part of the pass, and retreating even behind the cross wall, they posted themselves upon a hillock, where they stood all drawn up together in one close body, except only the Thebans. The hillock whereof I speak is at the entrance of the straits, where the stone lion stands which was set up in honour of Leonidas. Here they defended themselves to the last, such as still had swords using them, and the others resisting with their hands and teeth; till the barbarians, who in part had pulled down the wall and attacked them in front, in part had gone round and now encircled them upon every side, overwhelmed and buried the remnant which was left beneath showers of missile weapons. . . .

The slain were buried where they fell; and in their honour, nor less in honour of those who died before Leonidas sent the allies away, an inscription was set up, which said:—

Here did four thousand men from Pelops' land
Against three hundred myriads bravely stand.

This was in honour of all. Another was for the Spartans alone:—

Go, stranger, and to Lacedaemon tell
That here, obeying her behests, we fell.

Herodotus, *History,* VII, 225

3 *The Nurse.* Strange are the tempers of princes, and maybe because they seldom have to obey, and mostly lord it over others, change they their moods with difficulty. 'Tis better then to have been trained to live on equal terms. Be it mine to reach old age, not in proud pomp, but in security! . . . Greatness that doth o'erreach itself, brings no blessing to mortal men; but pays a penalty of greater ruin whenever fortune is wroth with a family.

Euripides, *Medea,* 119

4 *Medea.* Whoso is wise in his generation ought never to have his children taught to be too clever; for besides the reputation they get for idleness, they purchase bitter odium from the citizens. For if thou shouldst import new learning amongst dullards, thou will be thought a useless trifler, void of knowledge; while if thy fame in the city o'ertops that of the pretenders to cunning knowledge, thou wilt win their dislike.

Euripides, *Medea,* 294

5 *Pericles.* So died these men as became Athenians. You, their survivors, must determine to have as unfaltering a resolution in the field, though you may pray that it may have a happier issue. And not contented with ideas derived only from words of the advantages which are bound up with the defence of your country, though these would furnish a valuable text to a speaker even before an audience so alive to them as the present, you must yourselves realize the power of Athens, and feed your eyes upon her from day to day, till love of her fills your hearts; and then, when all her greatness shall break upon you, you must reflect that it was by courage, sense of duty, and a keen feeling of honour in action that men were enabled to win all this, and that no personal failure in an enterprise could make them consent to deprive their country of their valour, but they laid it at her feet as the most glorious contribution that they could offer. For this offering of their lives made in common by them all they each of them individually received that renown which never grows old, and for a sepulchre, not so much that in which their bones have been deposited, but that noblest of shrines wherein their glory is laid up to be eternally remembered upon every occasion on which deed or story shall call for its commemoration. For heroes have the whole earth for their tomb; and in lands far from their own, where the column with its epitaph declares it, there is enshrined in every breast a record unwritten with no tablet to preserve it, except that of the heart.

These take as your model and, judging happiness to be the fruit of freedom and freedom of valour, never decline the dangers of war. For it is not the miserable that would most justly be unsparing of their lives; these have nothing to hope for: it is rather they to whom continued life may bring reverses as yet unknown, and to whom a fall, if it came, would be most tremendous in its consequences. And surely, to a man of spirit, the degradation of cowardice must be immeasurably more grievous than the unfelt death which strikes him in the midst of his strength and patriotism!

Thucydides, *Peloponnesian War,* II, 43

6 *Alcibiades.* Many are the marvels which I might narrate in praise of Socrates; most of his ways might perhaps be paralleled in another man, but his absolute unlikeness to any human being that is or ever has been is perfectly astonishing. You may imagine Brasidas and others to have been like Achilles; or you may imagine Nestor and Antenor to have been like Pericles; and the same may be said of other famous men, but of this strange being you will never be able to find any likeness, however remote, either among men who now are or who ever have been—other than that which I have already suggested of Silenus and the satyrs; and they represent in a figure not only himself, but his words. For, although I forgot to mention this to you before, his words are like the images of Silenus which open; they are ridiculous when you first hear them; he clothes himself in language that is like the skin of the wanton satyr—for his talk is of pack-asses and smiths and cobblers and curriers, and he is always repeating the same things in the same words, so that any ignorant or inexperienced person might feel disposed to laugh at him; but he who opens the bust and sees what is within will find that they are the only words which have a meaning in them, and also the most divine, abounding in fair images of virtue, and of the widest comprehension, or rather extending to the whole duty of a good and honourable man.

Plato, *Symposium,* 221A

7 *Socrates.* When a man dies gloriously in war shall we not say, in the first place, that he is of the golden race?

Glaucon. To be sure.

Nay, have we not the authority of Hesiod for affirming that when they are dead

They are holy angels upon the earth, authors of good,
averters of evil, the guardians of speech-gifted men?

Yes; and we accept his authority.

We must learn of the god how we are to order the sepulture of divine and heroic personages, and what is to be their special distinction; and we must do as he bids?

By all means.

And in ages to come we will reverence them

and kneel before their sepulchres as at the graves of heroes. And not only they but any who are deemed pre-eminently good, whether they die from age, or in any other way, shall be admitted to the same honours.

Plato, *Republic,* V, 468B

8 It is possible to fail in many ways . . . while to succeed is possible only in one way (for which reason also one is easy and the other difficult—to miss the mark easy, to hit it difficult).

Aristotle, *Ethics,* 1106^b28

9 Is it to be expected that a farmer will busy himself sowing trees, no fruit of which his eyes will ever see, and a great man will not likewise sow the seeds of laws, institutions, and public policy?

Cicero, *Disputations,* I, 14

10 The altogether courageous and great spirit has, above all, two characteristics. First, he is indifferent to outward circumstances. Such a person is convinced that nothing but moral goodness and propriety are worth admiring and striving for. He knows he ought not be subject to any person, passion, or accident of fortune. His second characteristic is that when his soul has been disciplined in this way, he should do things that are not only great and highly useful, but also deeds that are arduous, laborious and fraught with danger to life and to those things that make life worthwhile.

Cicero, *De Officiis,* I, 20

11 Success comes to the ordinary individual, even to ordinary ability. But triumph over the disasters and fears of mortal life is only granted to great men. Certainly to be always content and to pass through life without a qualm is to be ignorant of half of nature. You may be a great man, but if Fortune gives you no chance to demonstrate your merit, how am I to know your greatness? If a man is to know himself, he must be tested. No one knows what he can accomplish except by trying. Some men have given themselves over voluntarily to sluggish Fortune and have looked for some chance to proclaim abroad their merit when it was about to sink into oblivion.

Seneca, *On Providence,* IV

12 *Aristotle.* No great genius has ever existed without some touch of madness.

Seneca, *On Tranquillity of Mind,* XVII

13 For what is a man profited, if he shall gain the whole world, and lose his own soul?

Matthew 16:26

14 In his journey [to Spain] as he was crossing the Alps, and passing by a small village of the barbarians with but few inhabitants, and those wretchedly poor, his companions asked the ques-

tion among themselves by way of mockery, if there were any canvassing for offices there, any contention which should be uppermost, or feuds of great men one against another. To which Cæsar made answer seriously, "For my part, I had rather be the first man among these fellows, than the second man in Rome."

Plutarch, *Caesar*

15 Cæsar was born to do great things, and had a passion after honour, and the many noble exploits he had done did not now serve as an inducement to him to sit still and reap the fruit of his past labours, but were incentives and encouragements to go on, and raised in him ideas of still greater actions, and a desire of new glory, as if the present were all spent. It was in fact a sort of emulous struggle with himself, as it had been with another, how he might outdo his past actions by his future.

Plutarch, *Caesar*

16 Cæsar was not of so slight or weak a temper as to suffer himself to be carried away by the indignation of the moment, into a civil war with his country, upon the sight of Antony and Cassius seeking refuge in his camp meanly dressed and in a hired carriage, without ever having thought of it or taken any such resolution long before. This was to him, who wanted a pretence of declaring war, a fair and plausible occasion; but the true motive that led him was the same that formerly led Alexander and Cyrus against all mankind, the unquenchable thirst of empire, and the distracted ambition of being the greatest man in the world, which was impracticable for him, unless Pompey were put down.

Plutarch, *Antony*

17 Nothing great . . . is produced suddenly, since not even the grape or the fig is. If you say to me now that you want a fig, I will answer to you that it requires time: let it flower first, then put forth fruit, and then ripen. Is, then, the fruit of a figtree not perfected suddenly and in one hour, and would you possess the fruit of a man's mind in so short a time and so easily? Do not expect it, even if I tell you.

Epictetus, *Discourses,* I, 15

18 Many have . . . perished, even good men, despising slow and safe success and hurrying on even at the cost of ruin to premature greatness.

Tacitus, *Annals,* III, 66

19 A wise man ought always to follow the paths beaten by great men, and to imitate those who have been supreme, so that if his ability does not equal theirs, at least it will savour of it. Let him act like the clever archers who, designing to hit the mark which yet appears too far distant, and knowing the limits to which the strength of their bow at-

tains, take aim much higher than the mark, not to
reach by their strength or arrow to so great a
height, but to be able with the aid of so high an
aim to hit the mark they wish to reach.

Machiavelli, Prince, VI

20 It was necessary . . . to Moses that he should find
the people of Israel in Egypt enslaved and oppressed by the Egyptians, in order that they
should be disposed to follow him so as to be delivered out of bondage. It was necessary that Romulus should not remain in Alba, and that he should
be abandoned at his birth, in order that he should
become King of Rome and founder of the fatherland. It was necessary that Cyrus should find
the Persians discontented with the government of
the Medes, and the Medes soft and effeminate
through their long peace. Theseus could not have
shown his ability had he not found the Athenians
dispersed. These opportunities, therefore, made
those men fortunate, and their high ability enabled them to recognize the opportunity whereby
their country was ennobled and made famous.

Machiavelli, Prince, VI

21 Without doubt princes become great when they
overcome the difficulties and obstacles by which
they are confronted, and therefore fortune, especially when she desires to make a new prince
great, who has a greater necessity to earn renown
than an hereditary one, causes enemies to arise
and form designs against him, in order that he
may have the opportunity of overcoming them,
and by them to mount higher, as by a ladder
which his enemies have raised.

Machiavelli, Prince, XX

22 *Pantagruel.* As a torch or candle, as long as it hath
life enough and is lighted, shines round about, disperses its light, delights those that are near it,
yields them its service and clearness, and never
causes any pain or displeasure; but as soon as it is
extinguished, its smoke and evaporation infect the
air, offend the by-standers, and are noisome to all:
so, as long as those noble and renowned souls inhabit their bodies, peace, profit, pleasure, and
honour never leave the places where they abide;
but as soon as they leave them, both the continent
and adjacent islands are annoyed with great commotions; in the air fogs, darkness, thunder, hail;
tremblings, pulsations, agitations of the earth;
storms and hurricanes at sea; together with sad
complaints amongst the people, broaching of religions, changes in governments, and ruins of commonwealths.

Rabelais, Gargantua and Pantagruel, IV, 26

23 Popular opinion is wrong: it is much easier to go
along the sides, where the outer edge serves as a
limit and a guide, than by the middle way, wide
and open, and to go by art than by nature; but it

is also much less noble and less commendable.
Greatness of soul is not so much pressing upward
and forward as knowing how to set oneself in order and circumscribe oneself. It regards as great
whatever is adequate, and shows its elevation by
liking moderate things better than eminent ones.
There is nothing so beautiful and legitimate as to
play the man well and properly, no knowledge so
hard to acquire as the knowledge of how to live
this life well and naturally; and the most barbarous of our maladies is to despise our being.

Montaigne, Essays, III, 13, Of Experience

24 *Thomalin.* And he that strives to touch the starres
Oft stombles at a strawe.

Spenser, Shepheardes Calendar (July)

25 *Marullus.* O you hard hearts, you cruel men of
Rome,
Knew you not Pompey? Many a time and oft
Have you climb'd up to walls and battlements,
To towers and windows, yea, to chimney-tops,
Your infants in your arms, and there have sat
The live-long day, with patient expectation,
To see great Pompey pass the streets of Rome:
And when you saw his chariot but appear,
Have you not made an universal shout,
That Tiber trembled underneath her banks
To hear the replication of your sounds
Made in her concave shores?
And do you now put on your best attire?
And do you now cull out a holiday?
And do you now strew flowers in his way
That comes in triumph over Pompey's blood?
Be gone!
Run to your houses, fall upon your knees,
Pray to the gods to intermit the plague
That needs must light on this ingratitude.

Shakespeare, Julius Caesar, I, i, 41

26 *Cassius.* I, as Æneas, our great ancestor,
Did from the flames of Troy upon his shoulder
The old Anchises bear, so from the waves of Tiber
Did I the tired Cæsar. And this man
Is now become a god, and Cassius is
A wretched creature and must bend his body,
If Cæsar carelessly but nod on him.

Shakespeare, Julius Caesar, I, ii, 112

27 *Cassius.* Why, man, he doth bestride the narrow
world
Like a Colossus, and we petty men
Walk under his huge legs and peep about
To find ourselves dishonourable graves. . . .
Brutus and Cæsar: what should be in that "Cæ-
sar"?
Why should that name be sounded more than
yours?
Write them together, yours is as fair a name;
Sound them, it doth become the mouth as well;
Weigh them, it is as heavy; conjure with 'em,

Brutus will start a spirit as soon as Cæsar.
Now, in the names of all the gods at once,
Upon what meat doth this our Cæsar feed
That he is grown so great? Age, thou art shamed!
Rome, thou hast lost the breed of noble bloods!
When went there by an age, since the great flood,
But it was famed with more than with one man?
When could they say till now, that talk'd of
  Rome,
That her wide walls encompass'd but one man?
Now is it Rome indeed and room enough,
When there is in it but one only man.
         Shakespeare, *Julius Caesar,* I, ii, 135

28 *Brutus.*   'Tis a common proof
That lowliness is young ambition's ladder,
Whereto the climber-upward turns his face;
But when he once attains the upmost round,
He then unto the ladder turns his back,
Looks in the clouds, scorning the base degrees
By which he did ascend.
         Shakespeare, *Julius Caesar,* II, i, 21

29 *Mark Antony.*   The noble Brutus
Hath told you Cæsar was ambitious:
If it were so, it was a grievous fault,
And grievously hath Cæsar answer'd it.
Here, under leave of Brutus and the rest—
For Brutus is an honourable man;
So are they all, all honourable men—
Come I to speak in Cæsar's funeral.
He was my friend, faithful and just to me:
But Brutus says he was ambitious;
And Brutus is an honourable man.
He hath brought many captives home to Rome,
Whose ransoms did the general coffers fill:
Did this in Cæsar seem ambitious?
When that the poor have cried, Cæsar hath wept:
Ambition should be made of sterner stuff:
Yet Brutus says he was ambitious;
And Brutus is an honourable man.
You all did see that on the Lupercal
I thrice presented him a kingly crown,
Which he did thrice refuse: was this ambition?
Yet Brutus says he was ambitious;
And, sure, he is an honourable man.
         Shakespeare, *Julius Caesar,* III, ii, 82

30 *Mark Antony.* This was the noblest Roman of them
  all:
All the conspirators save only he
Did that they did in envy of great Cæsar;
He only, in a general honest thought
And common good to all, made one of them.
His life was gentle, and the elements
So mix'd in him that Nature might stand up
And say to all the world, "This was a man!"
         Shakespeare, *Julius Caesar,* V, v, 68

31 *Olivia.* Be not afraid of greatness: some are born
  great, some achieve greatness, and some have

greatness thrust upon 'em.
         Shakespeare, *Twelfth Night,* II, v, 156

32 *Hamlet.*   Rightly to be great
Is not to stir without great argument,
But greatly to find quarrel in a straw
When honour's at the stake.
         Shakespeare, *Hamlet,* IV, iv, 53

33 *Cleopatra.* I dream'd there was an Emperor
  Antony. . . .
His legs bestrid the ocean; his rear'd arm
Crested the world; his voice was propertied
As all the tuned spheres, and that to friends;
But when he meant to quail and shake the orb,
He was as rattling thunder. For his bounty,
There was no winter in 't; an autumn 'twas
That grew the more by reaping. His delights
Were dolphin-like; they show'd his back above
The element they lived in. In his livery
Walk'd crowns and crownets; realms and islands
  were
As plates dropp'd from his pocket.
       Shakespeare, *Antony and Cleopatra,* V, ii, 75

34 *Wolsey.* I have touch'd the highest point of all my
  greatness;
And, from that full meridian of my glory,
I haste now to my setting. I shall fall
Like a bright exhalation in the evening,
And no man see me more.
         Shakespeare, *Henry VIII,* III, ii, 223

35 *Wolsey.* Farewell! a long farewell, to all my great-
  ness!
This is the state of man: to-day he puts forth
The tender leaves of hopes; to-morrow blossoms,
And bears his blushing honours thick upon him;
The third day comes a frost, a killing frost,
And, when he thinks, good easy man, full surely
His greatness is a-ripening, nips his root,
And then he falls, as I do. I have ventured,
Like little wanton boys that swim on bladders,
This many summers in a sea of glory,
But far beyond my depth. My high-blown pride
At length broke under me and now has left me,
Weary and old with service, to the mercy
Of a rude stream that must for ever hide me.
Vain pomp and glory of this world, I hate ye.
         Shakespeare, *Henry VIII,* III, ii, 352

36 It will, perhaps, be as well to distinguish three
species and degrees of ambition. First, that of men
who are anxious to enlarge their own power in
their country, which is a vulgar and degenerate
kind; next, that of men who strive to enlarge the
power and empire of their country over mankind,
which is more dignified but not less covetous; but
if one were to endeavor to renew and enlarge the
power and empire of mankind in general over the
universe, such ambition (if it may be so termed) is

both more sound and more noble than the other two.

Bacon, *Novum Organum*, I, 129

37 Men in great places are thrice servants: servants of the sovereign or state; servants of fame; and servants of business. So as they have no freedom, neither in their persons, nor in their actions, nor in their times. It is a strange desire, to seek power and to lose liberty; or to seek power over others and to lose power over a man's self.

Bacon, *Of Great Place*

38 If a true survey be taken of counsellors and statesmen, there may be found (though rarely) those which can make a small state great, and yet cannot fiddle: as, on the other side, there will be found a great many that can fiddle very cunningly, but yet are so far from being able to make a small state great, as their gift lieth the other way; to bring a great and flourishing estate to ruin and decay.

Bacon, *Of the True Greatness of Kingdoms and Estates*

39 The greatest baseness of man is the pursuit of glory. But it is also the greatest mark of his excellence; for whatever possessions he may have on earth, whatever health and essential comfort, he is not satisfied if he has not the esteem of men. He values human reason so highly that, whatever advantages he may have on earth, he is not content if he is not also ranked highly in the judgement of man. This is the finest position in the world. Nothing can turn him from that desire, which is the most indelible quality of man's heart.

And those who must despise men, and put them on a level with the brutes, yet wish to be admired and believed by men, and contradict themselves by their own feelings; their nature, which is stronger than all, convincing them of the greatness of man more forcibly than reason convinces them of their baseness.

Pascal, *Pensées*, VI, 404

40 All the glory of greatness has no lustre for people who are in search of understanding.

The greatness of clever men is invisible to kings, to the rich, to chiefs, and to all the worldly great. The greatness of wisdom, which is nothing if not of God, is invisible to the carnal-minded and to the clever. These are three orders differing in kind.

Great geniuses have their power, their glory, their greatness, their victory, their lustre, and have no need of worldly greatness, with which they are not in keeping. They are seen, not by the eye, but by the mind; this is sufficient.

The saints have their power, their glory, their victory, their lustre, and need no worldly or intellectual greatness, with which they have no affinity; for these neither add anything to them, nor take away anything from them. They are seen of God and the angels, and not of the body, nor of the curious mind. God is enough for them.

Archimedes, apart from his rank, would have the same veneration. He fought no battles for the eyes to feast upon; but he has given his discoveries to all men. Oh! how brilliant he was to the mind!

Pascal, *Pensées*, XII, 793

41 *Satan.* What matter where, if I be still the same,
And what I should be, all but less than hee
Whom Thunder hath made greater? Here at least
We shall be free; th' Almighty hath not built
Here for his envy, will not drive us hence:
Here we may reign secure, and in my choyce
To reign is worth ambition though in Hell:
Better to reign in Hell, then serve in Heav'n.

Milton, *Paradise Lost*, I, 256

42 One man, choosing a proper juncture, leaps into a gulf, thence proceeds a hero, and is called the saviour of his country: another achieves the same enterprise, but, unluckily timing it, has left the brand of madness fixed as a reproach upon his memory.

Swift, *Tale of a Tub*, IX

43 When a true Genius appears in the World, you may know him by this Sign, that the Dunces are all in confederacy against him.

Swift, *Thoughts on Various Subjects*

44 Who noble ends by noble means obtains,
Or failing, smiles in exile or in chains,
Like good Aurelius let him reign, or bleed
Like Socrates, that Man is great indeed.

Pope, *Essay on Man*, Epistle IV, 233

45 Through a fatality inseparable from human nature, moderation in great men is very rare: and as it is always much easier to push on force in the direction in which it moves than to stop its movement, so in the superior class of the people, it is less difficult, perhaps, to find men extremely virtuous, than extremely prudent.

Montesquieu, *Spirit of Laws*, XXVIII, 41

46 There have been men indeed splendidly wicked, whose endowments threw a brightness on their crimes, and whom scarce any villainy made perfectly detestable, because they never could be wholly divested of their excellencies; but such have been in all ages the great corrupters of the world, and their resemblance ought no more to be preserved, than the art of murdering without pain.

Johnson, *Rambler No. 4*

47 The errors and follies of a great genius are seldom without some radiations of understanding, by which meaner minds may be enlightened.

Johnson, *Rambler No. 29*

48 The wit, the hero, the philosopher, whom their tempers or their fortunes have hindered from intimate relations, die without any other effect than that of adding a new topic to the conversation of the day.

Johnson, *Rambler No. 78*

49 I said, I considered distinction of rank to be of so much importance in civilized society, that if I were asked on the same day to dine with the first Duke in England, and with the first man in Britain for genius, I should hesitate which to prefer. *Johnson.* "To be sure, if you were to dine only once, and it were never to be known where you dined, you would choose rather to dine with the first man for genius; but to gain most respect, you should dine with the first Duke in England. For nine people in ten that you meet with, would have a higher opinion of you for having dined with a Duke; and the great genius himself would receive you better, because you had been with the great Duke."

Boswell, *Life of Johnson*
(*July 20, 1763*)

50 True great genius is always accompanied with good sense.

Boswell, *London Journal*
(*Dec. 17, 1762*)

51 Every British name is effaced by the illustrious name of *Arthur,* the hereditary prince of the Silures, in South Wales, and the elective king or general of the nation. According to the most rational account, he defeated, in twelve successive battles, the Angles of the North and the Saxons of the West; but the declining age of the hero was embittered by popular ingratitude and domestic misfortunes. The events of his life are less interesting than the singular revolutions of his fame.

Gibbon, *Decline and Fall of the Roman Empire,* XXXVIII

52 The appellation of *great* has been often bestowed, and sometimes deserved, but *Charlemagne* is the only prince in whose favour the title has been indissolubly blended with the name.

Gibbon, *Decline and Fall of the Roman Empire,* XLIX

53 I want a hero: an uncommon want,
    When every year and month sends forth a new one,
Till, after cloying the gazettes with cant,
    The age discovers he is not the true one;
Of such as these I should not care to vaunt,
    I'll therefore take our ancient friend Don Juan—
We all have seen him, in the pantomime,
Sent to the devil somewhat ere his time.

Byron, *Don Juan,* I, 1

54 Once the state has been founded, there can no longer be any heroes. They come on the scene only in uncivilized conditions. Their aim is right, necessary, and political, and this they pursue as their own affair. The heroes who founded states, introduced marriage and agriculture, did not do this as their recognized right, and their conduct still has the appearance of being their particular will. But as the higher right of the Idea against nature, this heroic coercion is a rightful coercion. Mere goodness can achieve little against the power of nature.

Hegel, *Philosophy of Right,*
Additions, Par. 93

55 Cæsar was contending for the maintenance of his position, honor, and safety; and, since the power of his opponents included the sovereignty over the provinces of the Roman Empire, his victory secured for him the conquest of that entire empire; and he thus became, though leaving the form of the constitution, the autocrat of the state. That which secured for him the execution of a design, which in the first instance was of negative import, the autocracy of Rome, was, however, at the same time an independently necessary feature in the history of Rome and of the world. It was not, then, his private gain merely, but an unconscious impulse that occasioned the accomplishment of that for which the time was ripe. Such are all great historical men—whose own particular aims involve those large issues which are the will of the world-spirit. They may be called heroes, inasmuch as they have derived their purposes and their vocation, not from the calm, regular course of things, sanctioned by the existing order; but from a concealed fount—one which has not attained to phenomenal, present existence—from that inner spirit, still hidden beneath the surface, which, impinging on the outer world as on a shell, bursts it in pieces, because it is another kernel than that which belonged to the shell in question. They are men, therefore, who appear to draw the impulse of their life from themselves; and whose deeds have produced a condition of things and a complex of historical relations which appear to be only *their* interest, and *their* work.

Hegel, *Philosophy of History,*
Introduction, 3

56 World-historical men, the heroes of an epoch, must . . . be recognized as its clear-sighted ones; *their* deeds, *their* words are the best of that time. Great men have formed purposes to satisfy themselves, not others. Whatever prudent designs and counsels they might have learned from others would be the more limited and inconsistent features in their career; for it was they who best understood affairs; from whom *others* learned, and approved, or at least acquiesced in their policy. For that spirit which had taken this fresh step in

history is the inmost soul of all individuals; but in a state of unconsciousness which the great men in question aroused. Their fellows, therefore, follow these soul-leaders; for they feel the irresistible power of their own inner spirit thus embodied. If we go on to cast a look at the fate of these world-historical persons, whose vocation it was to be the agents of the world-spirit, we shall find it to have been no happy one. They attained no calm enjoyment; their whole life was labor and trouble; their whole nature was nought else but their master-passion. When their object is attained they fall off like empty hulls from the kernel. They die early, like Alexander; they are murdered, like Cæsar; transported to St. Helena, like Napoleon. This fearful consolation—that historical men have not enjoyed what is called happiness, and of which only private life (and this may be passed under very various external circumstances) is capable—this consolation those may draw from history, who stand in need of it; and it is craved by envy—vexed at what is great and transcendent—striving, therefore, to depreciate it, and to find some flaw in it. Thus in modern times it has been demonstrated *ad nauseam* that princes are generally unhappy on their thrones; in consideration of which the possession of a throne is tolerated, and men acquiesce in the fact that not themselves but the personages in question are its occupants. The free man, we may observe, is not envious, but gladly recognizes what is great and exalted, and rejoices that it exists.

It is in the light of those common elements which constitute the interest and therefore the passions of individuals, that these historical men are to be regarded. They are *great* men, because they willed and accomplished something great; not a mere fancy, a mere intention, but that which met the case and fell in with the needs of the age. . . .

A world-historical individual is not so unwise as to indulge a variety of wishes to divide his regards. He is devoted to the one aim, regardless of all else. It is even possible that such men may treat other great, even sacred interests, inconsiderately; conduct which is indeed obnoxious to moral reprehension. But so mighty a form must trample down many an innocent flower, crush to pieces many an object in its path.

Hegel, *Philosophy of History,* Introduction, 3

57 No difference of rank, position, or birth, is so great as the gulf that separates the countless millions who use their head only in the service of their belly, in other words, look upon it as an instrument of the will, and those very few and rare persons who have the courage to say: No! it is too good for that; my head shall be active only in its own service; it shall try to comprehend the wondrous and varied spectacle of this world, and then reproduce it in some form, whether as art or as literature, that may answer to my character as an individual.

Schopenhauer, *Genius*

58 Compared with the short span of time they live, men of great intellect are like huge buildings, standing on a small plot of ground. The size of the building cannot be seen by anyone, just in front of it; nor, for an analogous reason, can the greatness of a genius be estimated while he lives. But when a century has passed, the world recognizes it and wishes him back again.

Schopenhauer, *Reputation*

59 Every hero is a Samson. The strong man succumbs to the intrigues of the weak and the many; and if in the end he loses all patience he crushes both them and himself. Or he is like Gulliver at Liliput, overwhelmed by an enormous number of little men.

Schopenhauer, *A Few Parables*

60 It is natural for great minds—the true teachers of humanity—to care little about the constant company of others; just as little as the schoolmaster cares for joining in the gambols of the noisy crowd of boys which surround him. The mission of these great minds is to guide mankind over the sea of error to the haven of truth—to draw it forth from the dark abysses of a barbarous vulgarity up into the light of culture and refinement. Men of great intellect live in the world without really belonging to it; and so, from their earliest years, they feel that there is a perceptible difference between them and other people. But it is only gradually, with the lapse of years, that they come to a clear understanding of their position. Their intellectual isolation is then reinforced by actual seclusion in their manner of life; they let no one approach who is not in some degree emancipated from the prevailing vulgarity.

Schopenhauer, *Our Relation to Ourselves*

61 Faith is loyalty to some inspired Teacher, some spiritual Hero. And what therefore is loyalty proper, the life-breath of all society, but an effluence of Hero-worship, submissive admiration for the truly great? Society is founded on Hero-worship.

Carlyle, *The Hero as Divinity*

62 Show our critics a great man, a Luther for example, they begin to what they call 'account' for him; not to worship him, but take the dimensions of him,—and bring him out to be a little kind of man!

Carlyle, *The Hero as Divinity*

63 In all epochs of the world's history, we shall find the Great Man to have been the indispensable saviour of his epoch;—the lightning, without

which the fuel never would have burnt. The History of the World . . . was the Biography of Great Men.

Carlyle, *The Hero as Divinity*

64 To me . . . 'Hero-worship' becomes a fact inexpressibly precious; the most solacing fact one sees in the world at present. There is an everlasting hope in it for the management of the world. Had all traditions, arrangements, creeds, societies that men ever instituted, sunk away, this would remain. The certainty of Heroes being sent us; our faculty, our necessity, to reverence Heroes when sent: it shines like a polestar through smoke-clouds, dust-clouds, and all manner of down-rushing and conflagration.

Carlyle, *The Hero as King*

65 Every true man is a cause, a country, and an age; requires infinite spaces and numbers and time fully to accomplish his design; and posterity seem to follow his steps as a train of clients. A man Cæsar is born, and for ages after we have a Roman Empire. Christ is born, and millions of minds so grow and cleave to his genius that he is confounded with virtue and the possible of man. An institution is the lengthened shadow of one man.

Emerson, *Self-Reliance*

66 The hero is a mind of such balance that no disturbances can shake his will, but pleasantly and as it were merrily he advances to his own music, alike in frightful alarms and in the tipsy mirth of universal dissoluteness. There is somewhat not philosophical in heroism; there is somewhat not holy in it; it seems not to know that other souls are of one texture with it; it has pride; it is the extreme of individual nature. Nevertheless we must profoundly revere it. There is somewhat in great actions which does not allow us to go behind them. Heroism feels and never reasons, and therefore is always right; and although a different breeding, different religion and greater intellectual activity would have modified or even reversed the particular action, yet for the hero that thing he does is the highest deed, and is not open to the censure of philosophers or divines. It is the avowal of the unschooled man that he finds a quality in him that is negligent of expense, of health, of life, of danger, of hatred, of reproach, and knows that his will is higher and more excellent than all actual and all possible antagonists.

Emerson, *Heroism*

67 We have seen many counterfeits, but we are born believers in great men.

Emerson, *Character*

68 Hitch your wagon to a star. Let us not fag in paltry works which serve our pot and bag alone.

Emerson, *Civilization*

69 It will never make any difference to a hero what the laws are. His greatness will shine and accomplish itself unto the end, whether they second him or not. If he have earned his bread by drudgery, and in the narrow and crooked ways which were all an evil law had left him, he will make it at least honorable by his expenditure. Of the past he will take no heed; for its wrongs he will not hold himself responsible: he will say, All the meanness of my progenitors shall not bereave me of the power to make this hour and company fair and fortunate. Whatsoever streams of power and commodity flow to me, shall of me acquire healing virtue, and become fountains of safety. Cannot I too descend a Redeemer into nature? Whosoever hereafter shall name my name, shall not record a malefactor but a benefactor in the earth.

Emerson, *The Conservative*

70 Be a man's intellectual superiority what it will, it can never assume the practical, available supremacy over other men, without the aid of some sort of external arts and entrenchments, always, in themselves, more or less paltry and base. This it is, that for ever keeps God's true princes of the Empire from the world's hustings; and leaves the highest honours that this air can give, to those men who become famous more through their infinite inferiority to the choice hidden handful of the Divine Inert, than through their undoubted superiority over the dead level of the mass.

Melville, *Moby Dick*, XXXIII

71 The initiation of all wise or noble things comes and must come from individuals; generally at first from some one individual. The honour and glory of the average man is that he is capable of following that initiative; that he can respond internally to wise and noble things, and be led to them with his eyes open. I am not countenancing the sort of "hero-worship" which applauds the strong man of genius for forcibly seizing on the government of the world and making it do his bidding in spite of itself. All he can claim is, freedom to point out the way. The power of compelling others into it is not only inconsistent with the freedom and development of all the rest, but corrupting to the strong man himself. It does seem, however, that when the opinions of masses of merely average men are everywhere become or becoming the dominant power, the counterpoise and corrective to that tendency would be the more and more pronounced individuality of those who stand on the higher eminences of thought. It is in these circumstances most especially, that exceptional individuals, instead of being deterred, should be encouraged in acting differently from the mass. In other times there was no advantage in their doing so, unless they acted not only differently but better. In this age, the mere example of non-conformity,

the mere refusal to bend the knee to custom, is itself a service.

Mill, *On Liberty*, III

72 Great men are never the promoters of absolute and immutable truths. Each great man belongs to his time and can come only at his proper moment, in the sense that there is a necessary and ordered sequence in the appearance of scientific discoveries. Great men may be compared to torches shining at long intervals, to guide the advance of science. They light up their time, either by discovering unexpected and fertile phenomena which open up new paths and reveal unknown horizons, or by generalizing acquired scientific facts and disclosing truths which their predecessors had not perceived. If each great man makes the science which he vitalizes take a long step forward, he never presumes to fix its final boundaries, and he is necessarily destined to be outdistanced and left behind by the progress of successive generations. Great men have been compared to giants upon whose shoulders pygmies have climbed, who nevertheless see further than they. This simply means that science makes progress subsequently to the appearance of great men, and precisely because of their influence. The result is that their successors know many more scientific facts than the great men themselves had in their day. But a great man is, none the less, still a great man, that is to say,—a giant.

Claude Bernard, *Experimental Medicine*, I, 2

73 Man's mind cannot grasp the causes of events in their completeness, but the desire to find those causes is implanted in man's soul. And without considering the multiplicity and complexity of the conditions any one of which taken separately may seem to be the cause, he snatches at the first approximation to a cause that seems to him intelligible and says: "This is the cause!" In historical events (where the actions of men are the subject of observation) the first and most primitive approximation to present itself was the will of the gods and, after that, the will of those who stood in the most prominent position—the heroes of history. But we need only penetrate to the essence of any historic event—which lies in the activity of the general mass of men who take part in it—to be convinced that the will of the historic hero does not control the actions of the mass but is itself continually controlled.

Tolstoy, *War and Peace*, XIII, 1

74 When it is impossible to stretch the very elastic threads of historical ratiocination any farther, when actions are clearly contrary to all that humanity calls right or even just, the historians produce a saving conception of "greatness." "Greatness," it seems, excludes the standards of right and wrong. For the "great" man nothing is wrong, there is no atrocity for which a "great" man can be blamed.

"*C'est grand!*" say the historians, and there no longer exists either good or evil but only "*grand*" and "*not grand.*" *Grand* is good, not *grand* is bad. *Grand* is the characteristic, in their conception, of some special animals called "heroes." And Napoleon, escaping home in a warm fur coat and leaving to perish those who were not merely his comrades but were (in his opinion) men he had brought there, feels *que c'est grand*, and his soul is tranquil.

"*Du sublime* (he saw something sublime in himself) *au ridicule il n'y a qu'un pas*," said he. And the whole world for fifty years has been repeating: "*Sublime! Grand! Napoléon le Grand!*" *Du sublime au ridicule il n'y a qu'un pas.*

And it occurs to no one that to admit a greatness not commensurable with the standard of right and wrong is merely to admit one's own nothingness and immeasurable meanness.

For us with the standard of good and evil given us by Christ, no human actions are incommensurable. And there is no greatness where simplicity, goodness, and truth are absent.

Tolstoy, *War and Peace*, XIV, 18

75 To a lackey no man can be great, for a lackey has his own conception of greatness.

Tolstoy, *War and Peace*, XV, 5

76 I sought great human beings, I never found anything but the *apes* of their ideal.

Nietzsche, *Twilight of the Idols:* Maxims and Arrows

77 Great men, like great epochs, are explosive material in whom tremendous energy has been accumulated; their prerequisite has always been, historically and physiologically, that a protracted assembling, accumulating, economizing and preserving has preceded them—that there has been no explosion for a long time.

Nietzsche, *Twilight of the Idols:* Expeditions of an Untimely Man

78 Great human beings are necessary, the epoch in which they appear is accidental; that they almost always become master of their epoch is only because they are stronger, because they are older, because a longer assembling of force has preceded them.

Nietzsche, *Twilight of the Idols:* Expeditions of an Untimely Man

79 The genius—in his works, in his deeds—is necessarily a prodigal: his greatness lies in the fact that *he expends himself*.

Nietzsche, *Twilight of the Idols:* Expeditions of an Untimely Man

80 The huge world that girdles us about puts all sorts of questions to us, and tests us in all sorts of ways. Some of the tests we meet by actions that are easy, and some of the questions we answer in articulately formulated words. But the deepest question that is ever asked admits of no reply but the dumb turning of the will and tightening of our heartstrings as we say, "*Yes, I will even have it so!*" When a dreadful object is presented, or when life as a whole turns up its dark abysses to our view, then the worthless ones among us lose their hold on the situation altogether, and either escape from its difficulties by averting their attention, or if they cannot do that, collapse into yielding masses of plaintiveness and fear. The effort required for facing and consenting to such objects is beyond their power to make. But the heroic mind does differently. To it, too, the objects are sinister and dreadful, unwelcome, incompatible with wished-for things. But it can face them if necessary, without for that losing its hold upon the rest of life. The world thus finds in the heroic man its worthy match and mate; and the effort which he is able to put forth to hold himself erect and keep his heart unshaken is the direct measure of his worth and function in the game of human life. He can *stand* this Universe. He can meet it and keep up his faith in it in presence of those same features which lay his weaker brethren low. He can still find a zest in it, not by "ostrich-like forgetfulness," but by pure inward willingness to face the world with those deterrent objects there. And hereby he becomes one of the masters and the lords of life. He must be counted with henceforth; he forms a part of human destiny.

William James, *Psychology,* XXVI

81 In heroism, we feel, life's supreme mystery is hidden. We tolerate no one who has no capacity whatever for it in any direction. On the other hand, no matter what a man's frailties otherwise may be, if he be willing to risk death, and still more if he suffer it heroically, in the service he has chosen, the fact consecrates him forever. Inferior to ourselves in this or that way, if yet we cling to life, and he is able 'to fling it away like a flower' as caring nothing for it, we account him in the deepest way our born superior. Each of us in his own person feels that a high-hearted indifference to life would expiate all his shortcomings.

William James, *Varieties of Religious Experience,* XIV–XV

82 It is not . . . easy for mental giants who neither hate nor intend to injure their fellows to realize that nevertheless their fellows hate mental giants and would like to destroy them, not only enviously because the juxtaposition of a superior wounds their vanity, but quite humbly and honestly because it frightens them. Fear will drive men to any extreme; and the fear inspired by a superior being is a mystery which cannot be reasoned away.

Shaw, *Saint Joan,* Pref.

83 Men do not always take their great thinkers seriously, even when they profess most to admire them.

Freud, *Group Psychology and Analysis of the Ego,* IV

84 The first epic poet . . . invented the heroic myth. The hero was a man who by himself had slain the father—the father who still appeared in the myth as a totemistic monster. Just as the father had been the boy's first ideal, so in the hero who aspires to the father's place the poet now created the first ego ideal.

Freud, *Group Psychology and Analysis of the Ego,* XII

85 It is indeed too sad that in life it should be as it is in chess, when one false move may lose us the game, but with the difference that we can have no second game, no return-match. In the realm of fiction we discover that plurality of lives for which we crave. We die in the person of a given hero, yet we survive him, and are ready to die again with the next hero just as safely.

Freud, *Thoughts on War and Death,* II

1.7 | *Woman and Man*

Woman is the subject of this section: the quotations collected here are either statements about the characteristics of the female gender or statements about the relation of females to males. The reader, aware of the current movement for the liberation of women, must take cognizance of the fact that almost all the statements about women here quoted, including those that describe the extraordinary women of history and fiction, were written by men; and also the fact that almost all the statements that compare men and women are uncomplimentary to women or deprecatory of their endowments. What interpretation one puts upon these facts will depend on the position that the reader takes in the present controversy about the genders.

Among the ancient writers, two kinds of men (almost all of the authors being male) are represented. First, there are those who seem to have viewed women with more or less contempt, considering them as misbegotten males or as biological mistakes, or even relegating them to a quasi-human status, a little higher than the animals, perhaps, but not in the same class as men. Second, there are those who, not disputing the contention that women are essentially inferior to men, nevertheless give the impression of having tried harder to understand them, of having attempted to identify and evaluate the unique contributions of females to human society. Aeschylus, Sophocles, and Aristotle belong in the former group; Homer, Euripides, and Plato belong in the latter. Aristotle is practically unremitting in his contemptuous attitude toward the "weaker" sex. Plato, on the other hand, is almost unique in the ancient world in his view that women should share the same educational opportunities as men and that they should share in the rule of an ideal commonwealth. But it is nevertheless a misreading of Plato to hold, as some commentators do, that he considered men and women to be equals. The quotations from his works that are here assembled make that abundantly clear.

Among the more recent writers, Montaigne may be aligned with those who are adamant in their belief in woman's inferiority, while Shakespeare clearly belongs with those who see and appreciate the richness and human variety of the life and character of women. But it is not until the reader comes to the passages quoted from John Stuart Mill in the latter half of the nineteenth century that he finds a clear advocate for the social, economic, and political equality of women and men. After Mill there are others, of course; but the older views nevertheless continue to be expressed by writers right up to our own time. It is only recently that the tide has turned.

The one-sidedness of the quotations is strictly in function of the ages in which they were written. If this book were to be revised and brought up to date a hundred years from now, this obvious defect would most certainly be remedied.   It should be noted that women as mothers are treated in quotations appearing in Section 2.2 on PARENTS AND CHILDREN.

---

1 And the Lord God said, It is not good that the man should be alone; I will make him an help meet for him. . . .

And the Lord God caused a deep sleep to fall upon Adam, and he slept: and he took one of his ribs, and closed up the flesh instead thereof;

And the rib, which the Lord God had taken from man, made he a woman, and brought her unto the man.

And Adam said, This is now bone of my bones, and flesh of my flesh: she shall be called Woman, because she was taken out of Man.

Genesis 2:18–23

2 And she said unto him, How canst thou say, I love thee, when thine heart is not with me? thou hast mocked me these three times, and hast not told me wherein thy great strength lieth.

And it came to pass, when she pressed him daily with her words, and urged him, so that his soul was vexed unto death;

That he told her all his heart, and said unto her, There hath not come a razor upon mine head; for I have been a Nazarite unto God from my mother's womb: if I be shaven, then my strength will go from me, and I shall become weak, and be like any other man.

And when Delilah saw that he had told her all his heart, she sent and called for the lords of the Philistines, saying, Come up this once, for he hath shewed me all his heart. Then the lords of the Philistines came up unto her, and brought money in their hand.

And she made him sleep upon her knees; and she called for a man, and she caused him to shave off the seven locks of his head; and she began to afflict him, and his strength went from him.

And she said, The Philistines be upon thee, Samson. And he awoke out of his sleep, and said, I will go out as at other times before, and shake myself. And he wist not that the Lord was departed from him.

But the Philistines took him, and put out his eyes, and brought him down to Gaza, and bound him with fetters of brass; and he did grind in the prison house.

Judges 16:15–21

3 And when Jehu was come to Jezreel, Jezebel heard of it; and she painted her face, and tired her head, and looked out at a window.

And as Jehu entered in at the gate, she said, Had Zimri peace, who slew his master?

And he lifted up his face to the window, and said, Who is on my side? who? And there looked out to him two or three eunuchs.

And he said, Throw her down. So they threw her down: and some of her blood was sprinkled on the wall, and on the horses: and he trode her under foot.

And when he was come in, he did eat and drink, and said, Go, see now this cursed woman, and bury her: for she is a king's daughter.

And they went to bury her: but they found no more of her than the skull, and the feet, and the palms of her hands.

Wherefore they came again, and told him. And he said, This is the word of the Lord, which he spake by his servant Elijah the Tishbite, saying, In the portion of Jezreel shall dogs eat the flesh of Jezebel:

And the carcase of Jezebel shall be as dung upon the face of the field in the portion of Jezreel; so that they shall not say, This is Jezebel.

II Kings 9:30–37

4 It is better to dwell in a corner of the housetop, than with a brawling woman in a wide house.

Proverbs 21:9

5 Who can find a virtuous woman? for her price is far above rubies.

Proverbs 31:10

6 *Ghost of Agamemnon.* "There is no being more fell, more bestial than a wife in such an action, and what an action that one planned! The murder of her husband and her lord. Great god, I thought my children and my slaves at least would give me welcome. But that woman, plotting a thing so low, defiled herself and all her sex, all women yet to come, even those few who may be virtuous."

He paused then, and I [Odysseus] answered:

"Foul and dreadful. That was the way that Zeus who views the wide world vented his hatred on the sons of Atreus— intrigues of women, even from the start. Myriads died by Helen's fault, and Klytaimnéstra plotted against you half the world away."

And he at once said:

"Let it be a warning even to you. Indulge a woman never, and never tell her all you know. Some things a man may tell, some he should cover up."

Homer, *Odyssey*, XI, 425

7 Then said the Lady Kirkê: "So: all those trials are over. Listen with care to this, now, and a god will arm your mind. Square in your ship's path are Seirênês, crying beauty to bewitch men coasting by; woe to the innocent who hears that sound! He will not see his lady nor his children in joy, crowding about him, home from sea; the Seirênês will sing his mind away on their sweet meadow lolling. There are bones of dead men rotting in a pile beside them and flayed skins shrivel around the spot. Steer wide; keep well to seaward; plug your oarsmen's ears

with beeswax kneaded soft; none of the rest
should hear that song.
                        But if you wish to listen,
let the men tie you in the lugger, hand
and foot, back to the mast, lashed to the mast,
so you may hear those harpies' thrilling voices;
shout as you will, begging to be untied,
your crew must only twist more line around you
and keep their stroke up, till the singers fade."

                                Homer, *Odyssey,* XII, 36

8 *Penelope.*   Do not rage at me, Odysseus!
No one ever matched your caution! Think
what difficulty the gods gave: they denied us
life together in our prime and flowering years,
kept us from crossing into age together.
Forgive me, don't be angry. I could not
welcome you with love on sight! I armed myself
long ago against the frauds of men,
impostors who might come—and all those many
whose underhanded ways bring evil on!
Helen of Argos, daughter of Zeus and Leda,
would she have joined the stranger, lain with him,
if she had known her destiny? known the
    Akhaians
in arms would bring her back to her own country?
Surely a goddess moved her to adultery,
her blood unchilled by war and evil coming,
the years, the desolation; ours, too.
But here and now, what sign could be so clear
as this of our own bed?
No other man has ever laid eyes on it—
only my own slave, Aktoris, that my father
sent with me as a gift—she kept our door.
You make my stiff heart know that I am yours.

                                Homer, *Odyssey,* XXIII, 208

9 *Chorus.* It is like a woman indeed
to take the rapture before the fact has shown for
    true.

They believe too easily, are too quick to shift
from ground to ground; and swift indeed
the rumor voiced by a woman dies again.

                                Aeschylus, *Agamemnon,* 483

10 *Eteocles.* Neither in evils nor in fair good luck
may I share a dwelling with the tribe of women!
When she's triumphant, hers a confidence
past converse with another, when afraid
an evil greater both for home and city.

                                Aeschylus, *Seven Against Thebes,* 186

11 As for the carrying off of women, it is the deed,
they say, of a rogue: but to make a stir about such
as are carried off, argues a man a fool. Men of
sense care nothing for such women, since it is
plain that without their own consent they would
never be forced away.

                                Herodotus, *History,* I, 4

12 The two camps were then joined in one, the
Scythians living with the Amazons as their wives;
and the men were unable to learn the tongue of
the women, but the women soon caught up the
tongue of the men. When they could thus understand one another, The Scyths addressed the
Amazons in these words—"We have parents, and
properties, let us therefore give up this mode of
life, and return to our nation, and live with them.
You shall be our wives there no less than here,
and we promise you to have no others." But the
Amazons said—"We could not live with your
women—our customs are quite different from
theirs. To draw the bow, to hurl the javelin, to
bestride the horse, these are our arts—of womanly
employments we know nothing. Your women, on
the contrary, do none of these things; but stay at
home in their waggons, engaged in womanish
tasks, and never go out to hunt, or to do anything.
We should never agree together. But if you truly
wish to keep us as your wives, and would conduct
yourselves with strict justice towards us, go you
home to your parents, bid them give you your
inheritance, and then come back to us, and let us
and you live together by ourselves."

The youths approved of the advice, and followed it.

                                Herodotus, *History,* IV, 114–115

13 *Tecmessa.* He [Ajax] answered briefly in a well-
    worn phrase,
"Woman, a woman's decency is silence."

                                Sophocles, *Ajax,* 292

14 *Deianira.*   The young thing
grows in her own places; the heat of the sun-god
does not confound her, nor does the rain, nor any
    wind.
Pleasurably she enjoys an untroubled life
until the time she is no longer called a maiden
but woman, and takes her share of worry in the
    night,
fearful for her husband or for her children.

                                Sophocles, *Women of Trachis,* 144

15 *Medea.* Of all things that have life and sense we
women are the most hapless creatures; first must
we buy a husband at an exorbitant price, and o'er
ourselves a tyrant set which is an evil worse than
the first; and herein lies the most important issue,
whether our choice be good or bad. For divorce is
discreditable to women, nor can we disown our
lords. Next must the wife, coming as she does to
ways and customs new, since she hath not learnt
the lesson in her home, have a diviner's eye to see
how best to treat the partner of her life. If haply
we perform these tasks with thoroughness and
tact, and the husband live with us, without resenting the yoke, our life is a happy one; if not, 'twere
best to die. But when a man is vexed with what he
finds indoors, he goeth forth and rids his soul of its

disgust, betaking him to some friend or comrade of like age; whilst we must needs regard his single self. And yet they say we live secure at home, while they are at the wars, with their sorry reasoning, for I would gladly take my stand in battle array three times o'er, than once give birth.

Euripides, *Medea*, 230

16 Though a woman be timorous enough in all else, and as regards courage, a coward at the mere sight of steel, yet in the moment she finds her honour wronged, no heart is filled with deadlier thoughts than hers.

Euripides, *Medea*, 263

17 We women, though by nature little apt for virtuous deeds, are most expert to fashion any mischief.

Euripides, *Medea*, 408

18 *Jason.* You women have such strange ideas, that you think all is well so long as your married life runs smooth; but if some mischance occur to ruffle your love, all that was good and lovely erst you reckon as your foes. Yea, men should have begotten children from some other source, no female race existing; thus would no evil ever have fallen on mankind.

Euripides, *Medea*, 569

19 *Hippolytus.* Women! This coin which men find counterfeit!
Why, why, Lord Zeus, did you put them in the world,
in the light of the sun? If you were so determined
to breed the race of man, the source of it
should not have been women. Men might have dedicated
in your own temples images of gold,
silver, or weight of bronze, and thus have bought
the seed of progeny, . . . to each been given
his worth in sons according to the assessment
of his gift's value. So we might have lived
in houses free of the taint of women's presence.
But now, to bring this plague into our homes
we drain the fortunes of our homes. In this
we have a proof how great a curse is woman.
For the father who begets her, rears her up,
must add a dowry gift to pack her off
to another's house and thus be rid of the load.
And he again that takes the cursed creature
rejoices and enriches his heart's jewel
with dear adornment, beauty heaped on vileness.
With lovely clothes the poor wretch tricks her out
spending the wealth that underprops his house.
That husband has the easiest life whose wife
is a mere nothingness, a simple fool,
uselessly sitting by the fireside.
I hate a clever woman—God forbid
that I should ever have a wife at home
with more than woman's wits! Lust breeds mischief

in the clever ones. The limits of their minds
deny the stupid lecherous delights.
We should not suffer servants to approach them,
but give them as companions voiceless beasts,
dumb, . . . but with teeth, that they might not converse,
and hear another voice in answer.

Euripides, *Hippolytus*, 616

20 *Iphigenia.* A man's loss from his family is felt, while a woman's is of little moment.

Euripides, *Iphigenia in Tauris*, 1005

21 *Andromache.*   Nature tempers
The souls of women so they find a pleasure
In voicing their afflictions as they come.

Euripides, *Andromache*, 93

22 *Andromache.* They say one night of love suffices to dissolve
a woman's aversion to share the bed of any man.
I hate and loathe that woman who casts away the once
beloved, and takes another in her arms of love.
Even the young mare torn from her running mate and teamed
with another will not easily wear the yoke.

Euripides, *Trojan Women*, 665

23 *Lysistra.* I'll tell you now: 'tis meet ye all should know.
O ladies! sisters! if we really mean
To make the men make Peace, there's but one way,
We must abstain—
Myrrhina.   Well! tell us.
Ly.   Will ye do it?
My. Do it? ay, surely, though it cost our lives.
Ly. We must abstain—each—from the joys of Love.
How! what! why turn away? where are ye going?
What makes you pout your lips, and shake your heads?
What brings this falling tear, that changing colour?
Will ye, or will ye not? What mean ye, eh?
My. I'll never do it. Let the war go on.

Aristophanes, *Lysistrata*, 118

24 *Lysistra.* For if we women will but sit at home,
Powdered and trimmed, clad in our daintiest lawn,
Employing all our charms, and all our arts
To win men's love, and when we've won it, then
Repel them, firmly, till they end the war,
We'll soon get Peace again, be sure of that.

Aristophanes, *Lysistrata*, 149

25 *Pericles.* If I must say anything on the subject of female excellence to those of you who will now be in widowhood, it will be all comprised in this brief

exhortation. Great will be your glory in not falling short of your natural character; and greatest will be hers who is least talked of among the men, whether for good or for bad.

Thucydides, *Peloponnesian War,* II, 45

26 You are quite right, he [Glaucon] replied, in maintaining the general inferiority of the female sex: although many women are in many things superior to many men, yet on the whole what you say is true.

And if so, my friend, I [Socrates] said, there is no special faculty of administration in a state which a woman has because she is a woman, or which a man has by virtue of his sex, but the gifts of nature are alike diffused in both; all the pursuits of men are the pursuits of women also, but in all of them a woman is inferior to a man.

Plato, *Republic,* V, 455B

27 You agree then, I [Socrates] said, that men and women are to have a common way of life such as we have described—common education, common children; and they are to watch over the citizens in common whether abiding in the city or going out to war; they are to keep watch together, and to hunt together like dogs; and always and in all things, as far as they are able, women are to share with the men? And in so doing they will do what is best, and will not violate, but preserve the natural relation of the sexes.

Plato, *Republic,* V, 466B

28 Girls of this age [i.e., puberty] have much need of surveillance. For then in particular they feel a natural impulse to make usage of the sexual faculties that are developing in them; so that unless they guard against any further impulse beyond that inevitable one which their bodily development of itself supplies, even in the case of those who abstain altogether from passionate indulgence, they contract habits which are apt to continue into later life. For girls who give way to wantonness grow more and more wanton; and the same is true of boys, unless they be safeguarded from one temptation and another.

Aristotle, *History of Animals,* 581^b12

29 In all genera in which the distinction of male and female is found, Nature makes a similar differentiation in the mental characteristics of the two sexes. This differentiation is the most obvious in the case of human kind and in that of the larger animals and the viviparous quadrupeds. In the case of these latter the female is softer in character, is the sooner tamed, admits more readily of caressing, is more apt in the way of learning; as, for instance, in the Laconian breed of dogs the female is cleverer than the male. . . .

In all cases, excepting those of the bear and leopard, the female is less spirited than the male;

in regard to the two exceptional cases, the superiority in courage rests with the female. With all other animals the female is softer in disposition than the male, is more mischievous, less simple, more impulsive, and more attentive to the nurture of the young; the male, on the other hand, is more spirited than the female, more savage, more simple and less cunning. The traces of these differentiated characteristics are more or less visible everywhere, but they are especially visible where character is the more developed, and most of all in man.

The fact is, the nature of man is the most rounded off and complete, and consequently in man the qualities or capacities above referred to are found in their perfection. Hence woman is more compassionate than man, more easily moved to tears, at the same time is more jealous, more querulous, more apt to scold and to strike. She is, furthermore, more prone to despondency and less hopeful than the man, more void of shame or self-respect, more false of speech, more deceptive, and of more retentive memory. She is also more wakeful, more shrinking, more difficult to rouse to action, and requires a smaller quantity of nutriment.

As was previously stated, the male is more courageous than the female, and more sympathetic in the way of standing by to help. Even in the case of molluscs, when the cuttle-fish is struck with the trident the male stands by to help the female; but when the male is struck the female runs away.

Aristotle, *History of Animals,* 608^a22

30 As the first efficient or moving cause, to which belong the definition and the form, is better and more divine in its nature than the material on which it works, it is better that the superior principle whould be separated from the inferior. Therefore, wherever it is possible and so far as it is possible, the male is separated from the female. For the first principle of the movement, or efficient cause, whereby that which comes into being is male, is better and more divine than the material whereby it is female. The male, however, comes together and mingles with the female for the work of generation, because this is common to both.

Aristotle, *Generation of Animals,* 732^a3

31 The female is, as it were, a mutilated male.

Aristotle, *Generation of Animals,* 737^a28

32 Females are weaker and colder in nature, and we must look upon the female character as being a sort of natural deficiency.

Aristotle, *Generation of Animals,* 775^a15

33 What difference does it make whether women rule, or the rulers are ruled by women? The result is the same.

Aristotle, *Politics,* 1269^b33

34 *Mercury.* Woman's a various and a changeful
     thing.

Virgil, Aeneid, IV

35 Resistless thro' the war Camilla rode,
     In danger unappall'd, and pleas'd with blood.
     One side was bare for her exerted breast;
     One shoulder with her painted quiver press'd.
     Now from afar her fatal jav'lins play;
     Now with her ax's edge she hews her way:
     Diana's arms upon her shoulder sound;
     And when, too closely press'd, she quits the
        ground,
     From her bent bow she sends a backward wound.
     Her maids, in martial pomp, on either side,
     Larina, Tulla, fierce Tarpeia, ride:
     Italians all; in peace, their queen's delight;
     In war, the bold companions of the fight.
     So march'd the Tracian Amazons of old,
     When Thermodon with bloody billows roll'd:
     Such troops as these in shining arms were seen,
     When Theseus met in fight their maiden queen:
     Such to the field Penthisilea led,
     From the fierce virgin when the Grecians fled;
     With such, return'd triumphant from the war,
     Her maids with cries attend the lofty car;
     They clash with manly force their moony shields;
     With female shouts resound the Phrygian fields.

Virgil, Aeneid, XI

36 The angel Gabriel was sent from God unto a city
     of Galilee, named Nazareth,
     To a virgin espoused to a man whose name was
     Joseph, of the house of David; and the virgin's
     name was Mary.
     And the angel came in unto her, and said, Hail,
     thou that art highly favoured, the Lord is with
     thee: blessed art thou among women.
     And when she saw him, she was troubled at his
     saying, and cast in her mind what manner of salu-
     tation this should be.
     And the angel said unto her, Fear not, Mary:
     for thou hast found favour with God.
     And, behold, thou shalt conceive in thy womb,
     and bring forth a son, and shalt call his name
     Jesus.
     He shall be great, and shall be called the Son of
     the Highest: and the Lord God shall give unto
     him the throne of his father David:
     And he shall reign over the house of Jacob for
     ever; and of his kingdom there shall be no end.
     Then said Mary unto the angel, How shall this
     be, seeing I know not a man?
     And the angel answered and said unto her, The
     Holy Ghost shall come upon thee, and the power
     of the Highest shall overshadow thee: therefore
     also that holy thing which shall be born of thee
     shall be called the Son of God.
     And, behold, thy cousin Elisabeth, she hath
     also conceived a son in her old age: and this is the
     sixth month with her, who was called barren.

For with God nothing shall be impossible.
And Mary said, Behold the handmaid of the
Lord; be it unto me according to thy word. And
the angel departed from her.

Luke 1:26–38

37 And it came to pass, that, when Elisabeth heard
     the salutation of Mary, the babe leaped in her
     womb; and Elisabeth was filled with the Holy
     Ghost:
     And she spake out with a loud voice, and said,
     Blessed art thou among women, and blessed is the
     fruit of thy womb.
     And whence is this to me, that the mother of
     my Lord should come to me?
     For, lo, as soon as the voice of thy salutation
     sounded in mine ears, the babe leaped in my
     womb for joy.
     And blessed is she that believed: for there shall
     be a performance of those things which were told
     her from the Lord.
     And Mary said, My soul doth magnify the
     Lord,
     And my spirit hath rejoiced in God my Saviour.
     For he hath regarded the low estate of his
     handmaiden: for, behold, from henceforth all
     generations shall call me blessed.

Luke 1:41–48

38 Now it came to pass, as they went, that he entered
     into a certain village: and a certain woman
     named Martha received him into her house.
     And she had a sister called Mary, which also
     sat at Jesus' feet, and heard his word.
     But Martha was cumbered about much serving,
     and came to him, and said, Lord, dost thou not
     care that my sister hath left me to serve alone? bid
     her therefore that she help me.
     And Jesus answered and said unto her, Martha,
     Martha, thou art careful and troubled about
     many things:
     But one thing is needful: and Mary hath cho-
     sen that good part, which shall not be taken away
     from her.

Luke 10:38–42

39 The first day of the week cometh Mary Magda-
     lene early, when it was yet dark, unto the sepul-
     chre, and seeth the stone taken away from the
     sepulchre. . . .
     But Mary stood without at the sepulchre weep-
     ing: and as she wept, she stooped down, and
     looked into the sepulchre,
     And seeth two angels in white sitting, the one at
     the head, and the other at the feet, where the
     body of Jesus had lain.
     And they say unto her, Woman, why weepest
     thou? She saith unto them, Because they have
     taken away my Lord, and I know not where they
     have laid him.
     And when she had thus said, she turned herself

back, and saw Jesus standing, and knew not that it was Jesus.

Jesus saith unto her, Woman, why weepest thou? whom seekest thou? She, supposing him to be the gardener, saith unto him, Sir, if thou have borne him hence, tell me where thou hast laid him, and I will take him away.

Jesus saith unto her, Mary. She turned herself, and saith unto him, Răb-bō-nī; which is to say, Master.

John 20:1–16

40 For a man indeed ought not to cover his head, forasmuch as he is the image and glory of God: but the woman is the glory of the man.

For the man is not of the woman; but the woman of the man.

Neither was the man created for the woman; but the woman for the man.

I Corinthians 11:7–9

41 Doth not even nature itself teach you, that, if a man have long hair, it is a shame unto him?

But if a woman have long hair, it is a glory to her: for her hair is given her for a covering.

I Corinthians 11:14–15

42 Let your women keep silence in the churches: for it is not permitted unto them to speak; but they are commanded to be under obedience, as also saith the law.

And if they will learn anything, let them ask their husbands at home: for it is a shame for women to speak in the church.

I Corinthians 14:34–35

43 I will . . . that women adorn themselves in modest apparel, with shamefacedness and sobriety; not with broided hair, or gold, or pearls, or costly array;

But (which becometh women professing godliness) with good works.

Let the woman learn in silence with all subjection.

But I suffer not a woman to teach, nor to usurp authority over the man, but to be in silence.

For Adam was first formed, then Eve.

And Adam was not deceived, but the woman being deceived was in the transgression.

I Timothy 2:8–14

44 Likewise, ye wives, be in subjection to your own husbands; that, if any obey not the word, they also may without the word be won by the conversation of the wives;

While they behold your chaste conversation coupled with fear.

Whose adorning let it not be that outward adorning of plaiting the hair, and of wearing of gold, or of putting on of apparel;

But let it be the hidden man of the heart, in that which is not corruptible, even the ornament of a meek and quiet spirit, which is in the sight of God of great price.

For after this manner in the old time the holy women also, who trusted in God, adorned themselves, being in subjection unto their own husbands:

Even as Sara obeyed Abraham, calling him lord: whose daughters ye are, as long as ye do well, and are not afraid with any amazement.

Likewise, ye husbands, dwell with them according to knowledge, giving honour unto the wife, as unto the weaker vessel, and as being heirs together of the grace of life; that your prayers be not hindered.

I Peter 3:1–7

45 Women from fourteen years old are flattered by men with the title of mistresses. Therefore, perceiving that they are regarded only as qualified to give men pleasure, they begin to adorn themselves, and in that to place all their hopes. It is worth while, therefore, to try that they may perceive themselves honored only so far as they appear beautiful in their demeanor and modestly virtuous.

Epictetus, *Encheiridion,* XL

46 During this debate Severus Cæcina proposed that no magistrate who had obtained a province should be accompanied by his wife. He began by recounting at length how harmoniously he had lived with his wife, who had borne him six children, and how in his own home he had observed what he was proposing for the public, by having kept her in Italy, though he had himself served forty campaigns in various provinces. "With good reason," he said, "had it been formerly decided that women were not to be taken among our allies or into foreign countries. A train of women involves delays through luxury in peace and through panic in war, and converts a Roman army on the march into the likeness of a barbarian progress. Not only is the sex feeble and unequal to hardship, but, when it has liberty, it is spiteful, intriguing and greedy of power. They show themselves off among the soldiers and have the centurions at their beck. Lately a woman had presided at the drill of the cohorts and the evolutions of the legions. You should yourselves bear in mind that, whenever men are accused of extortion, most of the charges are directed against the wives. It is to these that the vilest of the provincials instantly attach themselves; it is they who undertake and settle business; two persons receive homage when they appear; there are two centres of government, and the women's orders are the more despotic and intemperate. Formerly they were restrained by the Oppian and other laws; now, loosed from every bond, they rule our houses, our tribunals, even our armies."

Tacitus, *Annals,* III, 33

47 Just as in the human soul there is one element which takes thought and dominates, another which is subjected to obedience, so woman has been created corporeally for man: for though she has indeed a nature like that of man in her mind and rational intelligence, yet by her bodily sex she is subjected to the sex of her husband, much as appetite, which is the source of action, must be subjected to reason.

Augustine, *Confessions,* XIII, 32

48 From the words, "Till we all come to a perfect man, to the measure of the age of the fullness of Christ," and from the words, "Conformed to the image of the Son of God," some conclude that women shall not rise women, but that all shall be men, because God made man only of earth and woman of the man. For my part, they seem to be wiser who make no doubt that both sexes shall rise. For there shall be no lust, which is now the cause of confusion. For before they sinned, the man and the woman were naked and were not ashamed. From those bodies, then, vice shall be withdrawn, while nature shall be preserved. And the sex of woman is not a vice, but nature. It shall then indeed be superior to carnal intercourse and child-bearing; nevertheless the female members shall remain adapted not to the old uses, but to a new beauty, which, so far from provoking lust, now extinct, shall excite praise to the wisdom and clemency of God, who both made what was not and delivered from corruption what He made.

Augustine, *City of God,* XXII, 17

49 It was necessary for woman to be made, as the Scripture says, as a helper to man; not, indeed, as a helpmate in other works, as some say, since man can be more efficiently helped by another man in other works, but as a helper in the work of generation.

Aquinas, *Summa Theologica,*
I, 92, 1

50 As regards the particular nature, woman is defective and misbegotten, for the active force in the male seed tends to the production of a perfect likeness in the masculine sex, while the production of woman comes from defect in the active force or from some material indisposition, or even from some external change, such as that of a south wind, which is moist, as the Philosopher observes. On the other hand, in relation to the universal nature, woman is not misbegotten, but is included in nature's intention as ordered to the work of generation. Now the universal intention of nature depends on God, Who is the universal Author of nature. Therefore, in producing nature, God formed not only the male but also the female.

Aquinas, *Summa Theologica,*
I, 92, 1

51 It was right for the woman to be made from a rib of man. First, to signify the social union of man and woman, for the woman should neither use authority over man, and so she was not made from his head; nor was it right for her to be subject to man's contempt as his slave, and so she was not made from his feet. Secondly, for the sacramental signification; for from the side of Christ sleeping on the Cross the Sacraments flowed— namely, blood and water—on which the Church was established.

Aquinas, *Summa Theologica,*
I, 92, 3

52 Already were mine eyes fixed on my Lady's countenance again, and my mind with them, from all other intent removed;
and she smiled not, but: "Were I to smile," she [Beatrice] began, "thou wouldst be such as was Semele, when she turned to ashes;
for my beauty, which, along the steps of the eternal palace kindleth more, as thou hast seen, the higher the ascent,
were it not tempered, so doth glow as that thy mortal power, at its flash, would be like foliage that the thunder shattereth.

Dante, *Paradiso,* XXI, 1

53 Nine times now, since my birth, the heaven of light had turned almost to the same point in its own gyration, when the glorious Lady of my mind, who was called Beatrice by many who knew not what to call her, first appeared before my eyes. She had already been in this life so long that in its course the starry heaven had moved toward the region of the East one of the twelve parts of a degree; so that at about the beginning of her ninth year she appeared to me, and I near the end of my ninth year saw her. She appeared to me clothed in a most noble color, a modest and becoming crimson, and she was girt and adorned in such wise as befitted her very youthful age. At that instant, I say truly that the spirit of life, which dwells in the most secret chamber of the heart, began to tremble with such violence that it appeared fearfully in the least pulses, and, trembling, said these words: *Ecce deus fortior me, qui veniens dominabitur mihi* [Behold a god stronger than I, who coming shall rule over me].

Dante, *Vita Nuova,* II

54 Ladies that have intelligence of Love,
I of my lady wish with you to speak;
Not that I can believe to end her praise,
But to discourse that I may ease my mind.
I say that when I think upon her worth,
So sweet doth Love make himself feel to me,
That if I then should lose not hardihood,
Speaking, I should enamour all mankind.
And I wish not so loftily to speak
As to become, through fear of failure, vile;
But of her gentle nature I will treat

In manner light compared with her desert.
Dante, Vita Nuova, XIX

55 Within her eyes my lady beareth Love,
    So that whom she regards is gentle made;
    All toward her turn, where'er her steps are
        stayed,
    And whom she greets, his heart doth trembling
        move;
So that with face cast down, all pale to view,
    For every fault of his he then doth sigh;
    Anger and pride away before her fly:—
    Assist me, dames, to pay her honor due.
Dante, Vita Nuova, XXI

56 After this sonnet, a wonderful vision appeared to
me, in which I saw things which made me resolve
to speak no more of this blessed one, until I could
more worthily treat of her. And to attain to this I
study to the utmost of my power, as she truly
knows. So that, if it shall please Him through
whom all things live, that my life be prolonged for
some years, I hope to say of her what was never
said of any woman [i.e., as it turned out, *The Divine Comedy*].
    And then may it please Him who is the Lord of
Grace, that my soul may go to behold the glory of
its lady, namely, of that blessed Beatrice, who in
glory looks upon the face of Him *qui est per omnia
saecula benedictus* [who is blessed forever].
Dante, Vita Nuova, XLIII

57 We women have, if I am not to lie,
In this love matter, a quaint fantasy;
Look out a thing we may not lightly have,
And after that we'll cry all day and crave.
Forbid a thing, and that thing covet we;
Press hard upon us, then we turn and flee.
Sparingly offer we our goods, when fair;
Great crowds at market make for dearer ware,
And what's too common brings but little price;
All this knows every woman who is wise.
Chaucer, Canterbury Tales: Wife
of Bath's Prologue

58 By God, if women had but written stories,
As have these clerks within their oratories,
They would have written of men more wickedness
Than all the race of Adam could redress.
Chaucer, Canterbury Tales: Wife
of Bath's Prologue

59 Command was given for silence in the hall,
And that the knight should tell before them all
What thing all worldly women love the best.
This knight did not stand dumb, as does a beast,
But to this question presently answered
With manly voice, so that the whole court heard:
"My liege lady, generally," said he,
"Women desire to have the sovereignty
As well upon their husband as their love,

And to have mastery their man above;
This thing you most desire, though me you kill
Do as you please, I am here at your will."
    In all the court there was no wife or maid
Or widow that denied the thing he said,
But all held, he was worthy to have life.
Chaucer, Canterbury Tales: Wife
of Bath's Tale

60 *The Friar.* There is, indeed, no serpent so cruel,
When man treads on his tail, nor half so fell,
As woman is when she is filled with ire;
Vengeance is then the whole of her desire.
Chaucer, Canterbury Tales: Summoner's Tale

61 "Eh! By God's mercy!" cried our host. Said he:
"Now such a wife I pray God keep from me!
Behold what tricks, and lo, what subtleties
In women are. For always busy as bees
Are they, us simple men thus to deceive,
And from the truth they turn aside and leave."
Chaucer, Canterbury Tales: Merchant's Tale,
Epilogue

62 *Merchant's Wife.* And well you know that women
    naturally
Desire six things, and even so do I.
For women all would have their husbands be
Hardy, and wise, and rich, and therewith free,
Obedient to the wife, and fresh in bed.
Chaucer, Canterbury Tales: Shipman's Tale

63 *Chanticleer.* For there is truth in *In principio
Mulier est hominis confusio*
(Madam, the meaning of this Latin is,
Woman is man's delight and all his bliss).
Chaucer, Canterbury Tales: Nun's Priest's Tale

64 But I'm a vulgar man, and thus say I,
There is no smallest difference, truly,
Between a wife who is of high degree,
If of her body she dishonest be,
And a poor unknown wench, other than this—
If it be true that both do what's amiss—
The gentlewoman, in her state above,
She shall be called his lady, in their love;
And since the other's but a poor woman,
She shall be called his wench or his leman.
And God knows very well, my own dear brother,
Men lay the one as low as lies the other.
Chaucer, Canterbury Tales: Manciple's Tale

65 Many good things may be perceived in a wife.
First, there is the Lord's blessing, namely, offspring. Then there is community of property.
These are some of the pre-eminently good things
that can overwhelm a man. Imagine what it
would be like without this sex. The home, cities,
economic life, and government would virtually
disappear. Men can't do without women. Even if
it were possible for men to beget and bear chil-

dren, they still couldn't do without women.

Luther, *Table Talk*, 1658

66 A woman that is neither fair nor good, to what use serves she? To make a nun of, said Gargantua. Yea, said the monk, to make shirts and smocks.

Rabelais, *Gargantua and Pantagruel*, I, 52

67 *Panurge.* Where there is no woman, I mean, the mother of a family, and wife in the union of a lawful wedlock, the crazy and diseased are in danger of being ill used, and of having much brabbling and strife about them: as by clear experience hath been made apparent in the persons of popes, legates, cardinals, bishops, abbots, priors, priests, and monks: but there, assure yourself, you shall not find me.

Rabelais, *Gargantua and Pantagruel*, III, 9

68 *Panurge.* The greater part of women, whatever it be that they see, do always represent unto their fancies, think and imagine, that it hath some relation to the sugared entering of the goodly ithyphallos, and graffing in the cleft of the overturned tree the quickset-imp of the pin of copulation. Whatever signs, shews, or gestures we shall make, or whatever our behaviour, carriage or demeanour shall happen to be in their view and presence, they will interpret the whole in reference to the act of androgynation, and the culbutizing exercise; by which means we shall be abusively disappointed of our designs, in regard that she will take all our signs for nothing else but tokens and representations of our desire to entice her unto the lists of a Cyprian combat, or catsenconny skirmish. Do you remember what happened at Rome two hundred and three-score years after the foundation thereof? A young Roman gentleman encountering by chance at the foot of Mount Celion with a beautiful Latin lady named Verona, who from her very cradle upwards had always been deaf and dumb, very civilly asked her, not without a chironomatic Italianising of his demand, with various jectigation of his fingers, and other gesticulations, as yet customary amongst the speakers of that country, What senators, in her descent from the top of the hill, she had met with going up thither. For you are to conceive, that he, knowing no more of her deafness than dumbness, was ignorant of both. She in the meantime, who neither heard nor understood so much as one word of what he said, straight imagined, by all that she could apprehend in the lively gesture of his manual signs, that what he then required of her was, what herself had a great mind to, even that which a young man doth naturally desire of a woman. Then was it, that by signs, which in all occurrences of venereal love are incomparably more attractive, valid and efficacious than words, she beckoned to him to come along with her to her house; which when he had done, she drew him aside to a privy room, and then made a most lively alluring sign unto him, to show that the game did please her. Whereupon, without any more advertisement, or so much as the uttering of one word on either side, they fell to, and bringuardised it lustily.

Rabelais, *Gargantua and Pantagruel*, III, 19

69 *Rondibilis.* The nature of women is set forth before our eyes, and represented to us by the moon in divers other things as well as in this, that they squat, skulk, constrain their own inclinations, and, with all the cunning they can, dissemble and play the hypocrite in the sight and presence of their husbands; who come no sooner to be out of the way, but that forthwith they take their advantage, pass the time merrily, desist from all labour, frolic it, gad abroad, lay aside their counterfeit garb, and openly declare and manifest the interior of their dispositions, even as the moon, when she is in conjunction with the sun, is neither seen in the heavens, nor on the earth, but in her opposition, when remotest from him shineth in her greatest fulness, and wholly appeareth in her brightest splendour whilst it is night. Thus women are but women.

When I say womankind, I speak of a sex so frail, so variable, so changeable, so fickle, inconstant, and imperfect, that, in my opinion, Nature, under favour nevertheless, of the prime honour and reverence which is due unto her, did in a manner mistake the road which she had traced formerly, and stray exceedingly from that excellence of providential judgment, by the which she had created and formed all other things, when she built, framed, and made up the woman. And having thought upon it a hundred and five times, I know not what else to determine therein, save only that in the devising, hammering, forging, and composing of the woman, she hath had a much tenderer regard, and by a great deal more respectful, heed to the delightful consortship, and sociable delectation of the man, than to the perfection and accomplishment of the individual womanishness or muliebrity. The divine philosopher Plato was doubtful in what rank of living creatures to place and collocate them, whether amongst the rational animals, by elevating them to an upper seat in the specifical classes of humanity; or with the irrational, by degrading them to a lower bench on the opposite side, of a brutal kind, and mere bestiality. For nature hath posited in a privy, secret and intestine place of their bodies, a sort of member, by some not impertinently termed an animal, which is not to be found in men. Therein sometimes are engendered certain humours, so saltish, brackish, clammy, sharp, nipping, tearing, prickling, and most eagerly tickling, that by their stinging acrimony, rending nitrosity, figging itch, wriggling mordancy, and smarting salsitude, (for the said member is altogether sinewy, and of a most quick and lively feeling,) their whole body is shaken and ebrangled their senses totally ravished and transported, the operations of their judgment and understanding utterly confounded, and all disordinate passions and perturbations of the mind throughly and absolutely allowed, admitted, and approved of; yea, in such sort, that if nature had not been so favourable unto them as to have sprinkled their forehead with a little tincture of bashfulness and modesty, you should see them in a so frantic mood run mad after lechery, and hie apace up and down with haste and lust, in quest of, and to fix some chamber-standard in their Paphian ground, that never did the Proëtides, Mimallonides, nor Lyæan Thyads deport themselves in the time of their Bacchanalian festivals more shamelessly, or with a so effronted and brazen-faced impudency; because this terrible animal is knit unto, and hath an union with all the chief and most principal parts of the body, as to anatomists is evident. Let it not here be thought strange that I should call it an animal, seeing therein I do no otherwise than follow and adhere to the doctrine of the academic and peripatetic philosophers. For if a proper motion be a certain mark and infallible token of the life and animation of the mover, as Aristotle writeth, and that any such thing as moveth of itself ought to be held animated, and of a living nature, then assuredly Plato with very good reason did give it the denomination of an animal, for that he perceived and observed in it the proper and self-stirring motions of suffocation, precipitation, corrugation, and of indignation, so extremely violent, that often-times by them is taken and removed from the woman all other sense and moving whatsoever, as if she were in a swounding lipothymy, benumbing syncope, epileptic, apoplectic palsy, and true resemblance of a pale-faced death.

Rabelais, *Gargantua and Pantagruel*, III, 32

70 What is the use of that art of virginal shame, that sedate coldness, that severe countenance, that profession of ignorance of things that they know better than we who instruct them in them, but to increase in us the desire to conquer, to overwhelm and subdue to our appetite all this ceremony and these obstacles? For there is not only pleasure but also glory in driving wild and seducing that soft sweetness and that childlike modesty, and in reducing a proud and commanding gravity to the mercy of our ardor.

Montaigne, *Essays*, II, 15, That Our Desire

71 If the wellborn ladies will take my advice, they will content themselves with displaying their own natural riches. They conceal and cover up their own beauties under foreign beauties. It is very simple-minded to put out your own light so as to shine by a borrowed light. They are buried and entombed under art. . . . The reason is that they

do not know themselves well enough. The world has nothing more beautiful; it is for them to do honor to the arts and to decorate decoration. What do they need but to live beloved and honored? They possess and know only too much for this; they need only arouse a little and rekindle the faculties that are in them. When I see them intent on rhetoric, astrology, logic, and similar drugs, so vain and useless for their needs, I begin to fear that the men who advise them to do this, do so as a means of gaining authority over them under this pretext. For what other excuse could I find for them? Enough that without our help they can adjust the charm of their eyes to gaiety, severity, or sweetness, season a "no" with harshness, uncertainty, or encouragement, and that they need no interpreter for the speeches we make in courting them. With this knowledge they hold the whip hand and master the schoolmasters and the school.

If, however, it vexes them to yield to us in any matter whatever, and if they want, out of curiosity, to have a share in book learning, poetry is an amusement suited to their needs; it is a wanton and subtle art, in fancy dress, wordy, all pleasure, all show, like themselves. They will also derive various benefits from history. In philosophy, from the part that is useful for life, they will take the lessons that will train them to judge our humors and characteristics, to defend themselves against our treacheries, to control the impetuosity of their own desires, to husband their freedom, to prolong the pleasures of life, and to bear humanly the inconstancy of a lover, the rudeness of a husband, and the annoyance of years and wrinkles; and things of that sort. That is the most I should assign to them in the matter of learning.

Montaigne, *Essays*, III, 3, Three Kinds of Association

72 Women are not wrong at all when they reject the rules of life that have been introduced into the world, inasmuch as it is the men who have made these without them. There is naturally strife and wrangling between them and us: the closest communion we have with them is still tumultuous and tempestuous.

Montaigne, *Essays*, III, 5, On Some Verses of Virgil

73 The most useful and honorable science and occupation for a woman is the science of housekeeping. I know some that are miserly, very few that are good managers. This is her ruling quality, which a man should seek out before any other, as the sole dowry on which the ruin or salvation of our households depends.

Montaigne, *Essays*, III, 9, Of Vanity

74 *Demetrius.* She is a woman, therefore may be woo'd;

She is a woman, therefore may be won.
Shakespeare, *Titus Andronicus,* II, i, 82

75 *Julia.*   Maids, in modesty, say "no" to that
Which they would have the profferer construe
"ay."
Shakespeare, *Two Gentlemen
of Verona,* I, ii, 55

76 *Romeo.* What lady is that, which doth enrich the
hand
Of yonder knight?
Servingman. I know not, sir.
Rom. O, she doth teach the torches to burn
bright!
It seems she hangs upon the cheek of night
Like a rich jewel in an Ethiope's ear;
Beauty too rich for use, for earth too dear!
So shows a snowy dove trooping with crows,
As yonder lady o'er her fellows shows.
The measure done, I'll watch her place of
stand,
And, touching hers, make blessed my rude
hand.
Did my heart love till now? forswear it, sight!
For I ne'er saw true beauty till this night.
Shakespeare, *Romeo and Juliet,* I, v, 43

77 *Portia.* You see me, Lord Bassanio, where I stand,
Such as I am: though for myself alone
I would not be ambitious in my wish,
To wish myself much better; yet, for you
I would be trebled twenty times myself;
A thousand times more fair, ten thousand times
More rich;
That only to stand high in your account,
I might in virtues, beauties, livings, friends,
Exceed account; but the full sum of me
Is sum of something, which, to term in gross,
Is an unlesson'd girl, unschool'd, unpractised;
Happy in this, she is not yet so old
But she may learn; happier than this,
She is not bred so dull but she can learn;
Happiest of all is that her gentle spirit
Commits itself to yours to be directed,
As from her lord, her governor, her king.
Shakespeare, *Merchant of Venice,* III, ii, 150

78 *Balthasar.* Sigh no more, ladies, sigh no more,
Men were deceivers ever,
One foot in sea and one on shore,
To one thing constant never:
Then sigh not so, but let them go,
And be you blithe and bonny,
Converting all your sounds of woe
Into Hey nonny, nonny.
Shakespeare, *Much Ado
About Nothing,* II, iii, 64

79 *Portia.* I grant I am a woman; but withal
A woman that Lord Brutus took to wife:

I grant I am a woman; but withal
A woman well-reputed, Cato's daughter.
Think you I am no stronger than my sex,
Being so father'd and so husbanded?
Tell me your counsels, I will not disclose 'em:
I have made strong proof of my constancy.
Giving myself a voluntary wound
Here, in the thigh: can I bear that with patience,
And not my husband's secrets?
Brutus.   O ye gods,
Render me worthy of this noble wife!
Shakespeare, *Julius Caesar,* II, i, 292

80 *Rosalind.* Do you not know I am a woman? when I
think, I must speak.
Shakespeare, *As You Like It,* III, ii, 263

81 It was a lover and his lass,
With a hey, and a ho, and a hey nonino,
That o'er the green corn-field did pass
In the spring time, the only pretty ring time,
When birds do sing, hey ding a ding, ding:
Sweet lovers love the spring.
Shakespeare, *As You Like It,* V, iii, 17

82 *Duke.*   Let still the woman take
An elder than herself: so wears she to him,
So sways she level in her husband's heart:
For, boy, however we do praise ourselves,
Our fancies are more giddy and unfirm,
More longing, wavering, sooner lost and worn,
Than women's are.
Viola.   I think it well, my lord.
Duke. Then let thy love be younger than thyself,
Or thy affection cannot hold the bent;
For women are as roses, whose fair flower
Being once display'd, doth fall that very hour.
Shakespeare, *Twelfth Night,* II, iv, 30

83 *Duke.* There is no woman's sides
Can bide the beating of so strong a passion
As love doth give my heart; no woman's heart
So big, to hold so much; they lack retention.
Alas, their love may be call'd appetite,
No motion of the liver, but the palate,
That suffer surfeit, cloyment, and revolt;
But mine is all as hungry as the sea,
And can digest as much: make no compare
Between that love a woman can bear me
And that I owe Olivia.
Viola.   Ay, but I know—
Duke. What dost thou know?
Vio. Too well what love women to men may
owe.
In faith, they are as true of heart as we.
My father had a daughter loved a man,
As it might be, perhaps, were I a woman,
I should your lordship
Duke.   And what's her history?
Vio. A blank, my lord. She never told her love,
But let concealment, like a worm i' the bud,

Feed on her damask cheek: she pined in thought,
And with a green and yellow melancholy
She sat like patience on a monument,
Smiling at grief. Was not this love indeed?

      Shakespeare, *Twelfth Night,* II, iv, 96

84 *Hamlet.*   Frailty, thy name is woman!

      Shakespeare, *Hamlet,* I, ii, 146

85 *Hamlet.* If thou wilt needs marry, marry a fool; for
wise men know well enough what monsters you
make of them.

      Shakespeare, *Hamlet,* III, i, 141

86 *Iago.* Come on, come on; you are pictures out of
    doors,
Bells in your parlours, wild-cats in your kitchens,
Saints in your injuries, devils being offended,
Players in your housewifery, and housewives in
    your beds.
  Desdemona. O, fie upon thee, slanderer!

      Shakespeare, *Othello,* II, i, 110

87 *Lear.* Behold yond simpering dame,
Whose face between her forks presages snow;
That minces virtue, and does shake the head
To hear of pleasure's name;
The fitchew, nor the soiled horse, goes to't
With a more riotous appetite.
Down from the waist they are Centaurs,
Though women all above;
But to the girdle do the gods inherit,
Beneath is all the fiends';
There's hell, there's darkness, there's the sulphu-
    rous pit,
Burning, scalding, stench, consumption; fie, fie,
fie! pah, pah! Give me an ounce of civet, good
apothecary, to sweeten my imagination.

      Shakespeare, *Lear,* IV, vi, 120

88 *Lear.* Cordelia, Cordelia! stay a little. Ha!
What is't thou say'st. Her voice was ever soft,
Gentle, and low, an excellent thing in woman.

      Shakespeare, *Lear,* V, iii, 271

89 *Enobarbus.* When she first met Mark Antony, she
    pursed up his heart, upon the river of Cyd-
    nus.
  Agrippa. There she appeared indeed; or my re-
  porter devised well for her.
  Eno. I will tell you.
The barge she sat in, like a burnish'd throne,
Burn'd on the water. The poop was beaten gold;
Purple the sails, and so perfumed that
The winds were love-sick with them; the oars
    were silver,
Which to the tune of flutes kept stroke, and made
The water which they beat to follow faster,
As amorous of their strokes. For her own person,
It beggar'd all description: she did lie
In her pavilion—cloth-of-gold of tissue—

O'er-picturing that Venus where we see
The fancy outwork nature. On each side her
Stood pretty dimpled boys, like smiling Cupids,
With divers-colour'd fans, whose wind did seem
To glow the delicate cheeks which they did cool,
And what they undid did.
  Agr.   O, rare for Antony!
  Eno. Her gentlewomen, like the Nereides,
So many mermaids, tended her i' the eyes,
And made their bends adornings. At the helm
A seeming mermaid steers; the silken tackle
Swell with the touches of those flower-soft hands,
That yarely frame the office. From the barge
A strange invisible perfume hits the sense
Of the adjacent wharfs. The city cast
Her people out upon her; and Antony,
Enthroned i' the market-place, did sit alone,
Whistling to the air; which, but for vacancy,
Had gone to gaze on Cleopatra too
And made a gap in nature.
  Agr.   Rare Egyptian!
  Eno. Upon her landing, Antony sent to her,
Invited her to supper. She replied,
It should be better he became her guest;
Which she entreated. Our courteous Antony,
Whom ne'er the word of "No" woman heard
    speak,
Being barber'd ten times o'er, goes to the feast,
And for his ordinary pays his heart
For what his eyes eat only.
  Agr.   Royal wench!
She made great Cæsar lay his sword to bed.
He plough'd her and she cropp'd.
  Eno.   I saw her once
Hop forty paces through the public street;
And having lost her breath, she spoke, and
    panted,
That she did make defect perfection,
And, breathless, power breathe forth.
  Mecaenas. Now Antony must leave her utterly.
  Eno. Never; he will not.
Age cannot wither her, nor custom stale
Her infinite variety. Other women cloy
The appetites they feed, but she makes hungry
Where most she satisfies; for vilest things
Become themselves in her, that the holy priests
Bless her when she is riggish.

      Shakespeare, *Antony and Cleopatra,* II, ii, 191

90 *Caesar.*   Women are not
In their best fortunes strong; but want will perjure
The ne'er-touch'd vestal.

      Shakespeare, *Antony and Cleopatra,* III, xii, 29

91 *Clown.* You must not think I am so simple but I
know the devil himself will not eat a woman. I
know that a woman is a dish for the gods, if the
devil dress her not. But, truly, these same whore-
son devils do the gods great harm in their women;

for in every ten that they make, the devils mar five.

Shakespeare, Antony and Cleopatra, V, ii, 273

92 *Posthumus.* Is there no way for men to be but
    women
Must be half-workers? We are all bastards;
And that most venerable man which I
Did call my father, was I know not where
When I was stamp'd; some coiner with his tools
Made me a counterfeit. Yet my mother seem'd
The Dian of that time; so doth my wife
The nonpareil of this. O, vengeance, vengeance!
Me of my lawful pleasure she restrain'd
And pray'd me oft forbearance; did it with
A pudency so rosy the sweet view on't
Might well have warm'd old Saturn; that I
    thought her
As chaste as unsunn'd snow. O, all the devils!
This yellow Iachimo, in an hour—was't not?—
Or less—at first?—perchance he spoke not, but,
Like a full-acorn'd boar, a German one,
Cried "O!" and mounted; found no opposition
But what he look'd for should oppose and she
Should from encounter guard. Could I find out
The woman's part in me! For there's no motion
That tends to vice in man, but I affirm
It is the woman's part: be it lying, note it,
The woman's; flattering, hers; deceiving, hers;
Lust and rank thoughts, hers, hers; revenges, hers;
Ambitions, covetings, change of prides, disdain,
Nice longing, slanders, mutability,
All faults that may be named, nay, that hell
    knows,
Why, hers, in part or all; but rather, all;
For even to vice
They are not constant, but are changing still
One vice, but of a minute old, for one
Not half so old as that. I'll write against them,
Detest them, curse them. Yet 'tis greater skill
In a true hate, to pray they have their will;
The very devils cannot plague them better.

Shakespeare, Cymbeline, II, v, 1

93 *Anne.*   By my troth and maidenhead,
I would not be a queen.
    Old Lady.   Beshrew me, I would,
And venture maidenhead for 't; and so would
    you,
For all this spice of your hypocrisy.
You, that have so fair parts of woman on you,
Have too a woman's heart; which ever yet
Affected eminence, wealth, sovereignty;
Which, to say sooth, are blessings; and which
    gifts,
Saving your mincing, the capacity
Of your soft cheveril conscience would receive,
If you might please to stretch it.

Shakespeare, Henry VIII, II, iii, 24

94 *Lothario.* You must remember, my Friend, that the Nature of Women is, at best, but weak and imperfect; and for that reason we should be so far from casting Rubs in its way, that we ought, with all imaginable Care, to remove every Appearance that might hinder its Course to that Perfection it wants, which is *Virtue*.

If you believe the Naturalists, the *Ermine* is a very white little Creature; when the Hunters have found its Haunts, they surround it almost with Dirt and Mire, towards which the *Ermine* being forc'd to fly, rather than sully its native White with Dirt, it suffers itself to be taken, preferring its Colour to its Liberty and Life. The virtuous Woman is our *Ermine*, whose Chastity is whiter than Snow; but to preserve its Colour unsully'd, you must observe just the contrary Method: The Addresses and Services of an importunate Lover, are the Mire into which you should never drive a Woman; for 'tis ten to one she will not be able to free herself and avoid it, being but too apt to stumble into it; and therefore That should be always remov'd, and only the Candour and Beauty of Virtue, and the Charms of a good Fame and Reputation plac'd before her. A good Woman is also not unlike a Mirrour of Crystal, which will infallibly be dimm'd and stain'd by breathing too much upon it: She must rather be us'd like the Reliques of Saints, ador'd but not touch'd; or like a Garden of curious tender Flowers, that may at a distance gratify the Eye, but are not permitted by the Master to be trampled on or touch'd by every Beholder.

Cervantes, Don Quixote, I, 33

95 Two of far nobler shape erect and tall,
Godlike erect, with native Honour clad
In naked Majestie seemd Lords of all,
And worthie seemd, for in thir looks Divine
The image of thir glorious Maker shon,
Truth, Wisdome, Sanctitude severe and pure,
Severe, but in true filial freedom plac't;
Whence true autoritie in men; though both
Not equal, as their sex not equal seemd;
For contemplation hee and valour formd,
For softness shee and sweet attractive Grace,
Hee for God only, shee for God in him:
His fair large Front and Eye sublime declar'd
Absolute rule; and Hyacinthin Locks
Round from his parted forelock manly hung
Clustring, but not beneath his shoulders broad:
Shee as a vail down to the slender waste
Her unadorned golden tresses wore
Disshevel'd, but in wanton ringlets wav'd
As the Vine curles her tendrils, which impli'd
Subjection, but requir'd with gentle sway,
And by her yeilded, by him best receivd,
Yeilded with coy submission, modest pride,
And sweet reluctant amorous delay.

Milton, Paradise Lost, IV, 288

96 So hand in hand they passd, the lovliest pair

That ever since in loves imbraces met,
Adam the goodliest man of men since born
His Sons, the fairest of her Daughters *Eve*.

Milton, *Paradise Lost*, IV, 321

97 To whom [Adam] thus *Eve* with perfet beauty
adornd.
My Author and Disposer, what thou bidst
Unargu'd I obey; so God ordains,
God is thy Law, thou mine: to know no more
Is womans happiest knowledge and her praise.
With thee conversing I forget all time,
All seasons and thir change, all please alike.

Milton, *Paradise Lost*, IV, 634

98 Who [God] stooping op'nd my left side, and took
From thence a Rib, with cordial spirits warme,
And Life-blood streaming fresh; wide was the
wound,
But suddenly with flesh fill'd up & heal'd:
The Rib he formd and fashond with his hands;
Under his forming hands a Creature grew,
Manlike, but different sex, so lovly faire,
That what seemd fair in all the World, seemd
now
Mean, or in her summd up, in her containd
And in her looks, which from that time infus'd
Sweetness into my heart, unfelt before,
And into all things from her Aire inspir'd
The spirit of love and amorous delight.

Milton, *Paradise Lost*, VIII, 465

99 *Adam.*   When I approach
Her loveliness, so absolute she seems
And in her self compleat, so well to know
Her own, that what she wills to do or say,
Seems wisest, vertuousest, discreetest, best;
All higher knowledge in her presence falls
Degraded, Wisdom in discourse with her
Looses discount'nanc't, and like folly shewes;
Authoritie and Reason on her waite,
As one intended first, not after made
Occasionally; and to consummate all,
Greatness of mind and nobleness thir seat
Build in her loveliest, and create an awe
About her, as a guard Angelic plac't.

Milton, *Paradise Lost*, VIII, 546

100 *Adam.*   Thus it shall befall
Him who to worth in Women overtrusting
Lets her Will rule; restraint she will not brook,
And left to her self, if evil thence ensue,
Shee first his weak indulgence will accuse.

Milton, *Paradise Lost*, IX, 1182

101 *Son of God.* Was shee thy God, that her thou didst
obey
Before his voice, or was shee made thy guide,
Superior, or but equal, that to her
Thou did'st resigne thy Manhood, and the Place
Wherein God set thee above her made of thee,
And for thee, whose perfection farr excell'd

Hers in all real dignitie: Adornd
She was indeed, and lovely to attract
Thy Love, not thy Subjection, and her Gifts
Were such as under Government well seem'd,
Unseemly to beare rule, which was thy part
And person, had'st thou known thy self aright.

Milton, *Paradise Lost*, X, 145

102 *Adam.*   O why did God,
Creator wise, that peopl'd highest Heav'n
With Spirits Masculine, create at last
This noveltie on Earth, this fair defect
Of Nature, and not fill the World at once
With Men as Angels without Feminine,
Or find some other way to generate
Mankind? this mischief had not then befall'n,
And more that shall befall, innumerable
Disturbances on Earth through Femal snares,
And straight conjunction with this Sex.

Milton, *Paradise Lost*, X, 888

103 *Chorus of Danites.*   Wisest Men
Have err'd, and by bad Women been deceiv'd;
And shall again.

Milton, *Samson Agonistes*, 210

104 *Dalila.* In argument with men a woman ever
Goes by the worse, whatever be her cause.

Milton, *Samson Agonistes*, 903

105 *Dorine.* A woman always has her revenge ready.

Molière, *Tartuffe*, II, ii

106 *Mirabell.* A fellow that lives in a windmill has not
a more whimsical dwelling than the heart of a
man that is lodged in a woman. There is no point
of the compass to which they cannot turn, and by
which they are not turned; and by one as well as
another, for motion, not method, is their occupation. To know this, and yet continue to be in love,
is to be made wise from the dictates of reason, and
yet persevere to play the fool by the force of instinct.

Congreve, *Way of the World*, II, vii

107 *Mrs. Marwood.* O, man, man! Woman, woman!
The devil's an ass: If I were a painter, I would
draw him like an idiot, a driveler with a bib and
bells. Man should have his head and horns, and
woman the rest of him. Poor simple fiend!

Congreve, *Way of the World*, III, vii

108 In the female nurseries, the young [Lilliputian]
girls of quality are educated much like the males,
only they are dressed by orderly servants of their
own sex, but always in the presence of a professor
or deputy, until they come to dress themselves,
which is at five years old. And if it be found, that
these nurses ever presume to entertain the girls
with frightful or foolish stories, or the common
follies practised by chamber-maids among us;

they are publickly whipped thrice about the city, imprisoned for a year, and banished for life to the most desolate parts of the country. Thus, the young ladies there are as much ashamed of being cowards and fools, as the men.

Swift, *Gulliver's Travels*, I, 6

109 Men, some to Business, some to Pleasure take;
But every Woman is at heart a Rake:
Men, some to Quiet, some to public Strife;
But every Lady would be Queen for life.

Pope, *Moral Essays*, Epistle II, 215

110 "I pity your country ignorance from my heart," cries the lady [Mrs. Western].—"Do you?" answered Western; "and I pity your town learning; I had rather be anything than a courtier, and a Presbyterian, and a Hanoverian too, as some people, I believe, are."—"If you mean me," answered she, "you know I am a woman, brother; and it signifies nothing what I am. Besides—"—"I do know you are a woman," cries the squire, "and it's well for thee that art one; if hadst been a man, I promise thee I had lent thee a flick long ago." —"Ay, there," said she, "in that flick lies all your fancied superiority. Your bodies, and not your brains, are stronger than ours. Believe me, it is well for you that you are able to beat us; or, such is the superiority of our understanding, we should make all of you what the brave, and wise, and witty, and polite are already—our slaves."

Fielding, *Tom Jones*, VI, 2

111 *Mrs. Fitzpatrick.* What is the reason, my dear, that we, who have understandings equal to the wisest and greatest of the other sex, so often make choice of the silliest fellows for companions and favourites? it raises my indignation to the highest pitch, to reflect on the numbers of women of sense who have been undone by fools.

Fielding, *Tom Jones*, XI, 4

112 *Of civil Laws contrary to the Law of Nature. . . .*
The law passed . . . which condemned every woman, who, having carried on a criminal commerce did not declare it to the king before she married him, violated the regard due to natural modesty. It is as unreasonable to oblige a woman to make this declaration, as to oblige a man not to attempt the defence of his own life.

Montesquieu, *Spirit of Laws*, XXVI, 3

113 There is nothing which I would recommend more earnestly to my female readers than the study of history as an occupation, of all others, the best suited both to their sex and education, much more instructive than their ordinary books of amusement, and more entertaining than those serious compositions which are usually to be found in their closets. Among other important truths which they may learn from history they may be informed of two particulars, the knowledge of which

may contribute very much to their quiet and repose: that our sex, as well as theirs, are far from being such perfect creatures as they are apt to imagine, and that Love is not the only passion which governs the male world, but is often overcome by avarice, ambition, vanity, and a thousand other passions.

Hume, *Of the Study of History*

114 All womankind, continued Trim . . . from the highest to the lowest, an' please your honour, love jokes; the difficulty is to know how they choose to have them cut; and there is no knowing that, but by trying, as we do with our artillery in the field, by raising or letting down their breeches, till we hit the mark.——
——I like the comparison, said my uncle Toby, better than the thing itself—
—Because your honour, quoth the corporal, loves glory, more than pleasure.

Sterne, *Tristram Shandy*, IX, 8

115 From the beginning of the world women have complained of the fickleness that is imputed to them in favour of the first new object which presents itself, and whose novelty is often its only merit. Many ladies (it must be confessed, despite the infinite respect we have for them) have treated men as they complain they have themselves been treated; and the story of Gioconda is much older than Ariosto.

Voltaire, *Philosophical Dictionary:*
New Novelties

116 I must not forget that precious half of the Republic, which makes the happiness of the other; and whose sweetness and prudence preserve its tranquillity and virtue. Amiable and virtuous daughters of Geneva, it will be always the lot of your sex to govern ours. Happy are we, so long as your chaste influence, solely exercised within the limits of conjugal union, is exerted only for the glory of the State and the happiness of the public. It was thus the female sex commanded at Sparta; and thus you deserve to command at Geneva. What man can be such a barbarian as to resist the voice of honour and reason, coming from the lips of an affectionate wife? Who would not despise the vanities of luxury, on beholding the simple and modest attire which, from the lustre it derives from you, seems the most favourable to beauty? It is your task to perpetuate, by your insinuating influence and your innocent and amiable rule, a respect for the laws of the State, and harmony among the citizens. It is yours to reunite divided families by happy marriages; and, above all things, to correct, by the persuasive sweetness of your lessons and the modest graces of your conversation, those extravagancies which our young people pick up in other countries, whence, instead of

many useful things by which they might profit, they bring home hardly anything, besides a puerile air and a ridiculous manner, acquired among loose women, but an admiration for I know not what so-called grandeur, and paltry recompenses for being slaves, which can never come near the real greatness of liberty. Continue, therefore, always to be what you are, the chaste guardians of our morals, and the sweet security for our peace, exerting on every occasion the privileges of the heart and of nature, in the interests of duty and virtue.

Rousseau, *Origin of Inequality,* Dedication

117 Next day, Sunday, July 31, I told him I had been that morning at a meeting of the people called Quakers, where I had heard a woman preach. *Johnson.* "Sir, a woman's preaching is like a dog's walking on his hinder legs. It is not done well; but you are surprized to find it done at all."

Boswell, *Life of Johnson (July 31, 1763)*

118 *Johnson.* Where there is no education, as in savage countries, men will have the upper hand of women. Bodily strength, no doubt, contributes to this; but it would be so, exclusive of that; for it is mind that always governs. When it comes to dry understanding, man has the better.

Boswell, *Life of Johnson (1776)*

119 He [Johnson] observed once, at Sir Joshua Reynolds's, that a beggar in the street will more readily ask alms from a *man,* though there should be no marks of wealth in his appearance, than from even a well-dressed *woman;* which he accounted for from the greater degree of carefulness as to money that is to be found in women; saying farther upon it, that the opportunities in general that they possess of improving their condition are much fewer than men have; and adding, as he looked round the company, which consisted of men only,—there is not one of us who does not think he might be richer if he would use his endeavour.

Boswell, *Life of Johnson (1780)*

120 In every age and country, the wiser, or at least the stronger, of the two sexes, has usurped the powers of the state, and confined the other to the cares and pleasures of domestic life. In hereditary monarchies, however, and especially in those of modern Europe, the gallant spirit of chivalry, and the law of succession, have accustomed us to allow a singular exception; and a woman is often acknowledged the absolute sovereign of a great kingdom, in which she would be deemed incapable of exercising the smallest employment, civil or military.

Gibbon, *Decline and Fall of the Roman Empire,* VI

121 The Germans treated their women with esteem and confidence, consulted them on every occasion of importance, and fondly believed that in their breasts resided a sanctity and wisdom more than human. Some of these interpreters of fate, such as Velleda, in the Batavian war, governed, in the name of the deity, the fiercest nations of Germany. The rest of the sex, without being adored as goddesses, were respected as the free and equal companions of soldiers; associated even by the marriage ceremony to a life of toil, of danger, and of glory. In their great invasions, the camps of the barbarians were filled with a multitude of women, who remained firm and undaunted amidst the sound of arms, the various forms of destruction, and the honourable wounds of their sons and husbands. Fainting armies of Germans have more than once been driven back upon the enemy by the generous despair of the women who dreaded death much less than servitude. If the day was irrecoverably lost, they well knew how to deliver themselves and their children, with their own hands, from an insulting victor. Heroines of such a cast may claim our admiration; but they were most assuredly neither lovely, nor very susceptible of love. Whilst they affected to emulate the stern virtues of *man,* they must have resigned that attractive softness in which principally consists the charm of *woman.* Conscious pride taught the German females to suppress every tender emotion that stood in competition with honour, and the first honour of the sex has ever been that of chastity. The sentiments and conduct of these high-spirited matrons may, at once, be considered as a cause, as an effect, and as a proof of the general character of the nation. Female courage, however it may be raised by fanaticism, or confirmed by habit, can be only a faint and imperfect imitation of the manly valour that distinguishes the age or country in which it may be found.

Gibbon, *Decline and Fall of the Roman Empire,* IX

122 There's nought but care on every han',
   In every hour that passes, O;
What signifies the life o' man,
   An' 'twere na for the lasses, O?
      Green grow the rashes, O!
      Green grow the rashes, O!
   The sweetest hours that e'er I spent,
   Were spent amang the lasses, O!

Burns, *Green Grow the Rashes*

123 With regard to the other sex, nature proposes to it simplicity of character as the supreme perfection to which it should reach. Accordingly, the love of pleasing in women strives after nothing so much as the appearance of simplicity; a sufficient proof, if it were the only one, that the greatest power of the sex reposes in this quality. But, as the principles that prevail in the education of women are

perpetually struggling with this character, it is as difficult for them in the moral order to reconcile this magnificent gift of nature with the advantages of a good education as it is difficult for men to preserve them unchanged in the intellectual order; and the woman who knows how to join a knowledge of the world to this sort of simplicity in manners is as deserving of respect as a scholar who joins to the strictness of scholastic rules the freedom and originality of thought.

Schiller, *Simple and Sentimental Poetry*

124 What is it men in women do require?
The lineaments of gratified desire.
What is it women do in men require?
The lineaments of gratified desire.

Blake, *Gnomic Verses, XVII, 4*

125 *Mephistopheles.* Girls have a great desire to know, it's true,
If one is sleek and pious, true to ancient isms.
They think: if there he knuckles, us he'll follow too.

Goethe, *Faust,* I, 3525

126 *Leader of the Chorus.* Impetuous and foolish, perfect woman-type!
Dependent on the moment, sport of every breeze
Of good and evil fortune, neither this nor that
Can ye with calmness bear.

Goethe, *Faust,* II, 3, 9127

127 In her first passion woman loves her lover,
In all the others all she loves is love,
Which grows a habit she can ne'er get over,
And fits her loosely—like an easy glove,
As you may find, whene'er you like to prove her:
One man alone at first her heart can move;
She then prefers him in the plural number,
Not finding that the additions much encumber.

Byron, *Don Juan,* III, 3

128 The roaring of the wind is my wife and the Stars through the window pane are my Children. The mighty abstract Idea I have of Beauty in all things stifles the more divided and minute domestic happiness—an amiable wife and sweet Children I contemplate as a part of that Beauty, but I must have a thousand of those beautiful particles to fill up my heart. I feel more and more every day, as my imagination strengthens, that I do not live in this world alone but in a thousand worlds—No sooner am I alone than shapes of epic greatness are stationed around me, and serve my Spirit the office which is equivalent to a King's bodyguard—then 'Tragedy with sceptred pall comes sweeping by.' According to my state of mind I am with Achilles shouting in the Trenches, or with Theocritus in the Vales of Sicily. Or I throw my whole being into Troilus, and repeating those lines, 'I wander like a lost Soul upon the stygian Banks staying for waftage,' I melt into the air with a voluptuousness so delicate that I am content to be alone. These things, combined with the opinion I have of the generality of women—who appear to me as children to whom I would rather give a sugar Plum than my time, form a barrier against Matrimony which I rejoice in.

Keats, *Letter to George and Georgiana Keats (c. Oct 25, 1818)*

129 It must be noticed in connexion with sex-relations that a girl in surrendering her body loses her honour. With a man, however, the case is otherwise, because he has a field for ethical activity outside the family. A girl is destined in essence for the marriage tie and for that only; it is therefore demanded of her that her love shall take the form of marriage and that the different moments in love shall attain their true rational relation to each other.

Hegel, *Philosophy of Right,* Additions, Par. 164

130 Women are capable of education, but they are not made for activities which demand a universal faculty such as the more advanced sciences, philosophy, and certain forms of artistic production. Women may have happy ideas, taste, and elegance, but they cannot attain to the ideal. The difference between men and women is like that between animals and plants. Men correspond to animals, while women correspond to plants because their development is more placid and the principle that underlies it is the rather vague unity of feeling. When women hold the helm of government, the state is at once in jeopardy, because women regulate their actions not by the demands of universality but by arbitrary inclinations and opinions. Women are educated—who knows how?— as it were by breathing in ideas, by living rather than by acquiring knowledge. The status of manhood, on the other hand, is attained only by the stress of thought and much technical exertion.

Hegel, *Philosophy of Right,* Additions, Par. 166

131 Women are directly fitted for acting as the nurses and teachers of our early childhood by the fact that they are themselves childish, frivolous and short-sighted; in a word, they are big children all their life long—a kind of intermediate stage between the child and the full-grown man, who is man in the strict sense of the word.

Schopenhauer, *Women*

132 The fundamental fault of the female character is that it has *no sense of justice.* This is mainly due to the fact . . . that women are defective in the powers of reasoning and deliberation; but it is also traceable to the position which Nature has assigned to them as the weaker sex. They are depen-

dent, not upon strength, but upon craft; and hence their instinctive capacity for cunning, and their ineradicable tendency to say what is not true. For as lions are provided with claws and teeth, and elephants and boars with tusks, bulls with horns, and cuttle fish with its clouds of inky fluid, so Nature has equipped woman, for her defense and protection, with the arts of dissimulation; and all the power which Nature has conferred upon man in the shape of physical strength and reason, has been bestowed upon women in this form. Hence, dissimulation is innate in woman, and almost as much a quality of the stupid as of the clever. It is as natural for them to make use of it on every occasion as it is for those animals to employ their means of defense when they are attacked; they have a feeling that in doing so they are only within their rights. Therefore a woman who is perfectly truthful and not given to dissimulation is perhaps an impossibility, and for this very reason they are so quick at seeing through dissimulation in others that it is not a wise thing to attempt it with them.

Schopenhauer, *Women*

133 The natural feeling between men is mere indifference, but between women it is actual enmity. The reason of this is that trade-jealousy—*odium figulinum*—which, in the case of men does not go beyond the confines of their own particular pursuit; but, with women, embraces the whole sex; since they have only one kind of business. Even when they meet in the street, women look at one another like Guelphs and Ghibellines.

Schopenhauer, *Women*

134 That woman is by nature meant to obey may be seen by the fact that every woman who is placed in the unnatural position of complete independence, immediately attaches herself to some man, by whom she allows herself to be guided and ruled. It is because she needs a lord and master. If she is young, it will be a lover; if she is old, a priest.

Schopenhauer, *Women*

135 As for myself, I do not hesitate to avow that although the women of the United States are confined within the narrow circle of domestic life, and their situation is in some respects one of extreme dependence, I have nowhere seen woman occupying a loftier position; and if I were asked, now that I am drawing to the close of this work, in which I have spoken of so many important things done by the Americans, to what the singular prosperity and growing strength of that people ought mainly to be attributed, I should reply: To the superiority of their women.

Tocqueville, *Democracy in America*, Vol. II, III, 12

136 *King.* Man is the hunter; woman is his game.
The sleek and shining creatures of the chase,
We hunt them for the beauty of their skins;
They love us for it, and we ride them down.

Tennyson, *The Princess*, V, 147

137 *King.* Man for the field and woman for the hearth;
Man for the sword, and for the needle she;
Man with the head, and woman with the heart;
Man to command, and woman to obey;
All else confusion.

Tennyson, *The Princess*, V, 437

138 It certainly at first appears a highly remarkable fact that the same female butterfly should have the power of producing at the same time three distinct female forms and a male; and that an hermaphrodite plant should produce from the same seed-capsule three distinct hermaphrodite forms, bearing three different kinds of females and three or even six different kinds of males. Nevertheless these cases are only exaggerations of the common fact that the female produces offspring of two sexes which sometimes differ from each other in a wonderful manner.

Darwin, *Origin of Species*, II

139 Man is more courageous, pugnacious and energetic than woman, and has a more inventive genius. His brain is absolutely larger, but whether or not proportionately to his larger body, has not, I believe, been fully ascertained. In woman the face is rounder; the jaws and the base of the skull smaller; the outlines of the body rounder, in parts more prominent; and her pelvis is broader than in man; but this latter character may perhaps be considered rather as a primary than a secondary sexual character. She comes to maturity at an earlier age than man.

Darwin, *Descent of Man*, III, 19

140 The chief distinction in the intellectual powers of the two sexes is shewn by man's attaining to a higher eminence, in whatever he takes up, than can woman—whether requiring deep thought, reason, or imagination, or merely the use of the senses and hands. If two lists were made of the most eminent men and women in poetry, painting, sculpture, music (inclusive both of composition and performance), history, science, and philosophy, with half-a-dozen names under each subject, the two lists would not bear comparison. We may also infer, from the law of the deviation from averages, so well illustrated by Mr. Galton, in his work on *Hereditary Genius,* that if men are capable of a decided pre-eminence over women in many subjects, the average of mental power in man must be above that of woman.

Darwin, *Descent of Man*, III, 19

141 To avoid enemies or to attack them with success, to capture wild animals, and to fashion weapons, requires the aid of the higher mental faculties, namely, observation, reason, invention, or imagination. These various faculties will thus have been continually put to the test and selected during manhood; they will, moreover, have been strengthened by use during this same period of life. Consequently in accordance with the principle often alluded to, we might expect that they would at least tend to be transmitted chiefly to the male offspring.

Darwin, *Descent of Man,* III, 19

142 It is, indeed, fortunate that the law of the equal transmission of characters to both sexes prevails with mammals; otherwise, it is probable that man would have become as superior in mental endowment to woman, as the peacock is in ornamental plumage to the peahen.

Darwin, *Descent of Man,* III, 19

143 With few insignificant exceptions, girls have been educated either to be drudges, or toys, beneath man; or a sort of angels above him; the highest ideal aimed at oscillating between Clärchen and Beatrice. The possibility that the ideal of womanhood lies neither in the fair saint, nor in the fair sinner; that the female type of character is neither better nor worse than the male, but only weaker; that women are meant neither to be men's guides nor their playthings, but their comrades, their fellows, and their equals, so far as Nature puts no bar to that equality, does not seem to have entered into the minds of those who have had the conduct of the education of girls.

If the present system of female education stands self-condemned, as inherently absurd; and if that which we have just indicated is the true position of woman, what is the first step towards a better state of things? We reply, emancipate girls. Recognise the fact that they share the senses, perceptions, feelings, reasoning powers, emotion, of boys, and that the mind of the average girl is less different from that of the average boy, than the mind of one boy is from that of another; so that whatever argument justifies a given education for all boys, justifies its application to girls as well. So far from imposing artificial restrictions upon the acquirement of knowledge by women, throw every facility in their way. . . . Let us have "sweet girl graduates" by all means. They will be none the less sweet for a little wisdom; and the "golden hair" will not curl less gracefully outside the head by reason of there being brains within. Nay, if obvious practical difficulties can be overcome, let those women who feel inclined to do so descend into the gladiatorial arena of life. . . . Let them, if they so please, become merchants, barristers, politicians. Let them have a fair field, but let them understand, as the necessary correlative, that they are to have no favour. Let Nature alone sit high above the lists, "rain influence and judge the prize."

T. H. Huxley, *Emancipation—Black and White*

144 Mankind have long since abandoned the only premises which will support the conclusion that women ought not to have votes. No one now holds that women should be in personal servitude; that they should have no thought, wish, or occupation, but to be the domestic drudges of husbands, fathers, or brothers. It is allowed to unmarried, and wants but little of being conceded to married women, to hold property, and have pecuniary and business interests, in the same manner as men. It is considered suitable and proper that women should think, and write, and be teachers. As soon as these things are admitted, the political disqualification has no principle to rest on. The whole mode of thought of the modern world is with increasing emphasis pronouncing against the claim of society to decide for individuals what they are and are not fit for, and what they shall and shall not be allowed to attempt. If the principles of modern politics and political economy are good for anything, it is for proving that these points can only be rightly judged of by the individuals themselves: and that, under complete freedom of choice, wherever there are real diversities of aptitude, the great number will apply themselves to the things for which they are on the average fittest, and the exceptional course will only be taken by the exceptions. Either the whole tendency of modern social improvements has been wrong, or it ought to be carried out to the total abolition of all exclusions and disabilities which close any honest employment to a human being.

Mill, *Representative Government,* VIII

145 All causes, social and natural, combine to make it unlikely that women should be collectively rebellious to the power of men. They are so far in a position different from all other subject classes, that their masters require something more from them than actual service. Men do not want solely the obedience of women, they want their sentiments. All men, except the most brutish, desire to have, in the woman most nearly connected with them, not a forced slave but a willing one, not a slave merely, but a favourite.

Mill, *Subjection of Women,* I

146 One thing we may be certain of—that what is contrary to women's nature to do, they never will be made to do by simply giving their nature free play. The anxiety of mankind to interfere in behalf of nature, for fear lest nature should not succeed in effecting its purpose, is an altogether unnecessary solicitude. What women by nature cannot do, it is quite superfluous to forbid them from doing. What they can do, but not so well as

the men who are their competitors, competition suffices to exclude them from; since nobody asks for protective duties and bounties in favour of women; it is only asked that the present bounties and protective duties in favour of men should be recalled. If women have a greater natural inclination for some things than for others, there is no need of laws or social inculcation to make the majority of them do the former in preference to the latter. Whatever women's services are most wanted for, the free play of competition will hold out the strongest inducements to them to undertake. And, as the words imply, they are most wanted for the things for which they are most fit; by the apportionment of which to them, the collective faculties of the two sexes can be applied on the whole with the greatest sum of valuable result.

Mill, *Subjection of Women,* I

147 The less fit a man is for the possession of power— the less likely to be allowed to exercise it over any person with that person's voluntary consent—the more does he hug himself in the consciousness of the power the law gives him, exact its legal rights to the utmost point which custom (the custom of men like himself) will tolerate, and take pleasure in using the power, merely to enliven the agreeable sense of possessing it. What is more; in the most naturally brutal and morally uneducated part of the lower classes, the legal slavery of the woman, and something in the merely physical subjection to their will as an instrument, causes them to feel a sort of disrespect and contempt towards their own wife which they do not feel towards any other woman, or any other human being, with whom they come in contact; and which makes her seem to them an appropriate subject for any kind of indignity. Let an acute observer of the signs of feeling, who has the requisite opportunities, judge for himself whether this is not the case: and if he finds that it is, let him not wonder at any amount of disgust and indignation that can be felt against institutions which lead naturally to this depraved state of the human mind.

Mill, *Subjection of Women,* II

148 The occupations of nine out of every ten men are special, those of nine out of every ten women general, embracing a multitude of details, each of which requires very little time. Women are in the constant practice of passing quickly from one manual, and still more from one mental operation to another, which therefore rarely costs them either effort or loss of time, while a man's occupation generally consists in working steadily for a long time at one thing, or one very limited class of things. But the situations are sometimes reversed, and with them the characters. Women are not found less efficient than men for the uniformity of factory work, or they would not so generally be

employed for it; and a man who has cultivated the habit of turning his hand to many things, far from being the slothful and lazy person described by Adam Smith, is usually remarkably lively and active. It is true, however, that change of occupation may be too frequent even for the most versatile. Incessant variety is even more fatiguing than perpetual sameness.

Mill, *Principles of Political Economy,*
Bk. I, VIII, 5

149 The same reasons which make it no longer necessary that the poor should depend on the rich, make it equally unnecessary that women should depend on men; and the least which justice requires is that law and custom should not enforce dependence (when the correlative protection has become superfluous) by ordaining that a woman, who does not happen to have a provision by inheritance, shall have scarcely any means open to her of gaining a livelihood, except as a wife and mother. Let women who prefer that occupation, adopt it; but that there should be no option, no other *carrière* possible for the great majority of women, except in the humbler departments of life, is a flagrant social injustice. The ideas and institutions by which the accident of sex is made the groundwork of an inequality of legal rights, and a forced dissimilarity of social functions, must ere long be recognised as the greatest hindrance to moral, social, and even intellectual improvement.

Mill, *Principles of Political Economy,*
Bk. IV, VII, 3

150 You may chisel a boy into shape, as you would a rock, or hammer him into it, if he be of a better kind, as you would a piece of bronze. But you cannot hammer a girl into anything. She grows as a flower does,—she will wither without sun; she will decay in her sheath, as a narcissus will, if you do not give her air enough; she may fall, and defile her head in dust, if you leave her without help at some moments of her life; but you cannot fetter her; she must take her own fair form and way, if she take any.

Ruskin, *Sesame and Lilies,* II, 78

151 The happiest women, like the happiest nations, have no history.

George Eliot, *The Mill on the Floss,* VI, 3

152 I should like to know what is the proper function of women, if it is not to make reasons for husbands to stay at home, and still stronger reasons for bachelors to go out.

George Eliot, *The Mill on the Floss,* VI, 6

153 She [Rosamond] spoke and wept with that gentleness which makes such words and tears omnipotent over a loving-hearted man. Lydgate drew his chair near to hers and pressed her delicate head

against his cheek with his powerful tender hand. He only caressed her; he did not say anything; for what was there to say? He could not promise to shield her from the dreaded wretchedness, for he could see no sure means of doing so. When he left her to go out again, he told himself that it was ten times harder for her than for him: he had a life away from home, and constant appeals to his activity on behalf of others. He wished to excuse everything in her if he could—but it was inevitable that in that excusing mood he should think of her as if she were an animal of another and feebler species. Nevertheless she had mastered him.

George Eliot, *Middlemarch,* VII, 65

154 *Mitya.* Try acknowledging you are in fault to a woman. Say, 'I am sorry, forgive me,' and a shower of reproaches will follow! Nothing will make her forgive you simply and directly, she'll humble you to the dust, bring forward things that have never happened, recall everything, forget nothing, add something of her own, and only then forgive you. And even the best, the best of them do it. She'll scrape up all the scrapings and load them on your head. They are ready to flay you alive, I tell you, every one of them, all these angels without whom we cannot live!

Dostoevsky, *Brothers Karamazov,*
Pt. IV, XI, 4

155 Vronsky followed the guard to the carriage, and at the door of the compartment he stopped short to make room for a lady who was getting out.

With the insight of a man of the world, from one glance at this lady's appearance Vronsky classified her as belonging to the best society. He begged pardon, and was getting into the carriage, but felt he must glance at her once more; not that she was very beautiful, not on account of the elegance and modest grace which were apparent in her whole figure, but because in the expression of her charming face, as she passed close by him, there was something peculiarly caressing and soft. As he looked round, she too turned her head. Her shining grey eyes, that looked dark from the thick lashes, rested with friendly attention on his face, as though she were recognising him, and then promptly turned away to the passing crowd, as though seeking someone. In that brief look Vronsky had time to notice the suppressed eagerness which played over her face, and flitted between the brilliant eyes and the faint smile that curved her red lips. It was as though her nature were so brimming over with something that against her will it showed itself now in the flash of her eyes, and now in her smile. Deliberately she shrouded the light in her eyes, but it shone against her will in the faintly perceptible smile.

Tolstoy, *Anna Karenina,* I, 18

156 We observe an identical difference between men as a whole and women as a whole. A young woman of twenty reacts with intuitive promptitude and security in all the usual circumstances in which she may be placed. Her likes and dislikes are formed; her opinions, to a great extent, the same that they will be through life. Her character is, in fact, finished in its essentials. How inferior to her is a boy of twenty in all these respects! His character is still gelatinous, uncertain what shape to assume, "trying it on" in every direction. Feeling his power, yet ignorant of the manner in which he shall express it, he is, when compared with his sister, a being of no definite contour. But this absence of prompt tendency in his brain to set into particular modes is the very condition which insures that it shall ultimately become so much more efficient than the woman's. The very lack of preappointed trains of thought is the ground on which general principles and heads of classification grow up; and the masculine brain deals with new and complex matter indirectly by means of these, in a manner which the feminine method of direct intuition, admirably and rapidly as it performs within its limits, can vainly hope to cope with.

William James, *Psychology,* XXII

157 *Pickering.* Excuse the straight question, Higgins. Are you a man of good character where women are concerned?

Higgins. [*moodily*] Have you ever met a man of good character where women are concerned?

Pick. Yes: very frequently.

Hig. [*dogmatically, lifting himself on his hands to the level of the piano, and sitting on it with a bounce*] Well, I haven't. I find that the moment I let a woman make friends with me, she becomes jealous, exacting, suspicious, and a damned nuisance. I find that the moment I let myself make friends with a woman, I become selfish and tyrannical. Women upset everything. When you let them into your life, you find that the woman is driving at one thing and you're driving at another.

Pick. At what, for example?

Hig. [*coming off the piano restlessly*] Oh, Lord knows! I suppose the woman wants to live her own life; and the man wants to live his; and each tries to drag the other on to the wrong track. One wants to go north and the other south; and the result is that both have to go east, though they both hate the east wind.

Shaw, *Pygmalion,* II

158 It is not necessary to wear trousers and smoke big cigars to live a man's life any more than it is necessary to wear petticoats to live a woman's. There are plenty of gowned and boticed women in ordinary civil life who manage their own affairs and other people's, including those of their menfolk, and are entirely masculine in their tastes and pursuits. There always were such women. . . . The

exemption of women from military service is founded, not on any natural inaptitude that men do not share, but on the fact that communities cannot reproduce themselves without plenty of women. Men are more largely dispensable, and are sacrificed accordingly.

Shaw, *Saint Joan*, Pref.

159 Man is no longer, like Don Juan, victor in the duel of sex. Whether he has ever really been may be doubted: at all events the enormous superiority of Woman's natural position in this matter is telling with greater and greater force.

Shaw, *Man and Superman*, Epistle Dedicatory

160 In Shakespear's plays the woman always takes the initiative. In his problem plays and his popular plays alike the love interest is the interest of seeing the woman hunt the man down. She may do it by charming him, like Rosalind, or by stratagem, like Mariana; but in every case the relation between the woman and the man is the same: she is the pursuer and contriver, he the pursued and disposed of. When she is baffled, like Ophelia, she goes mad and commits suicide; and the man goes straight from her funeral to a fencing match. No doubt Nature, with very young creatures, may save the woman the trouble of scheming: Prospero knows that he has only to throw Ferdinand and Miranda together and they will mate like a pair of doves. . . . But the mature cases all illustrate the Shakespearian law.

Shaw, *Man and Superman*, Epistle Dedicatory

161 We laugh at the haughty American nation because it makes the negro clean its boots and then proves the moral and physical inferiority of the negro by the fact that he is a shoeblack; but we ourselves throw the whole drudgery of creation on one sex, and then imply that no female of any womanliness or delicacy would initiate any effort in that direction. There are no limits to male hypocrisy in this matter.

Shaw, *Man and Superman*, Epistle Dedicatory

162 Home is the girl's prison and the woman's workhouse.

Shaw, *Man and Superman*, Maxims for Revolutionists

163 Complete object-love . . . is, properly speaking, characteristic of the man. It displays the marked sexual over-estimation which is doubtless derived from the original narcissism of the child, now transferred to the sexual object. This sexual over-estimation is the origin of the peculiar state of being in love, a state suggestive of a neurotic compulsion, which is thus traceable to an impoverishment of the ego in respect of libido in favour of the love-object. A different course is followed in the type most frequently met with in women,

which is probably the purest and truest feminine type. With the development of puberty, the maturing of the female sexual organs, which up till then have been in a condition of latency, seems to bring about an intensification of the original narcissism, and this is unfavourable to the development of a true object-love with its accompanying sexual over-estimation; there arises in the woman a certain self-sufficiency (especially when there is a ripening into beauty) which compensates her for the social restrictions upon her object-choice. Strictly speaking, such women love only themselves with an intensity comparable to that of the man's love for them. Nor does their need lie in the direction of loving, but of being loved; and that man finds favour with them who fulfils this condition. The importance of this type of woman for the erotic life of mankind must be recognized as very great. Such women have the greatest fascination for men, not only for aesthetic reasons, since as a rule they are the most beautiful, but also because of certain interesting psychological constellations.

Freud, *On Narcissism*, II

164 Throughout the ages, the problem of woman has puzzled people of every kind.

Freud, *New Introductory Lectures on Psycho-Analysis*, XXXIII

165 Male or female is the first differentiation that you make when you meet another human being, and you are used to making that distinction with absolute certainty. Anatomical science shares your certainty in one point, but not much more. . . . It points out to you that parts of the male sexual apparatus are also to be found in the body of the female, although in a rudimentary condition, and vice versa. Science sees in this phenomenon an indication of *bisexuality*, as though the individual were neither man nor woman, but both at the same time, only rather more the one than the other. It then expects you to make yourselves familiar with the idea that the proportions in which the masculine and the feminine mingle in an individual are subject to quite extraordinary variations. And even though, apart from very rare cases, only one kind of sexual product—ova or seminal cells—is present in any one individual, you will go wrong if you take this factor as being of decisive importance, and you must conclude that what constitutes masculinity or femininity is an unknown element which it is beyond the power of anatomy to grasp.

Freud, *New Introductory Lectures on Psycho-Analysis*, XXXIII

166 We must not overlook one particularly constant relation between femininity and instinctual life. The repression of their aggressiveness, which is imposed upon women by their constitutions and

by society, favours the development of strong masochistic impulses, which have the effect of binding erotically the destructive tendencies which have been turned inwards. Masochism is, then, as they say, truly feminine. But when, as so often happens, you meet with masochism in men, what else can you do but say that these men display obvious feminine traits of character?

You are now prepared for the conclusion that psychology cannot solve the riddle of femininity. The solution must, I think, come from somewhere else, and it cannot come until we have learned in general how the differentiation of living creatures into two sexes came about. We know nothing whatever about the matter.

Freud, *New Introductory Lectures
on Psycho-Analysis,* XXXIII

167 It must be admitted that women have but little sense of justice, and this is no doubt connected with the preponderance of envy in their mental life; for the demands of justice are a modification of envy; they lay down the conditions under which one is willing to part with it.

Freud, *New Introductory Lectures
on Psycho-Analysis,* XXXIII

168 Friends are generally of the same sex, for when men and women agree, it is only in their conclusions; their reasons are always different. So that while intellectual harmony between men and women is easily possible, its delightful and magic quality lies precisely in the fact that it does not arise from mutual understanding, but is a conspiracy of alien essences and a kissing, as it were, in the dark. As man's body differs from woman's in sex and strength, so his mind differs from hers in quality and function: they can co-operate but can never fuse. The human race, in its intellectual life, is organised like the bees: the masculine soul is a worker, sexually atrophied, and essentially dedicated to impersonal and universal arts; the feminine is a queen, infinitely fertile, omnipresent in its brooding industry, but passive and abounding in intuitions without method and passions without justice. Friendship with a woman is therefore apt to be more or less than friendship: less, because there is no intellectual parity; more, because (even when the relation remains wholly dispassionate, as in respect to old ladies) there is something mysterious and oracular about a woman's mind which inspires a certain instinctive deference and puts it out of the question to judge what she says by masculine standards. She has a kind of sibylline intuition and the right to be irrationally *à propos.* There is a gallantry of the mind which pervades all conversation with a lady, as there is a natural courtesy toward children and mystics; but such a habit of respectful concession, marking as it does an intellectual alienation as profound as that which separates us from the dumb animals, is radically incompatible with friendship.

Santayana, *Life of Reason,* II, 6

169 I do not intend, for the mere sake of correcting an inappropriate word, to enter upon a comparative study of the two sexes. Suffice it to say that woman is as intelligent as man, but that she is less capable of emotion, and that if there is any faculty or power of the soul which seems to attain less development in woman than in man, it is not intelligence, but sensibility. I mean of course sensibility in the depths, not agitation at the surface.

Bergson, *Two Sources of Morality
and Religion,* I

170 God of heaven theres nothing like nature the wild mountains then the sea and the waves rushing then the beautiful country with fields of oats and wheat and all kinds of things and all the fine cattle going about that would do your heart good to see rivers and lakes and flowers all sorts of shapes and smells and colours springing up even out of the ditches primroses and violets nature it is as for them saying theres no God I wouldn't give a snap of my two fingers for all their learning why dont they go and create something I often asked him atheists or whatever they call themselves go and wash the cobbles off themselves first and then go howling for the priest and they dying and why why because theyre afraid of hell on account of their bad conscience ah yes I know them well who was the first person in the universe before there was anybody that made it all who ah that they dont know neither do I so there you are they might as well try to stop the sun from rising tomorrow the sun shines for you he said the day we were lying among the rhododendrons on Howth head in the grey tweed suit and his straw hat the day I got him to propose to me yes first I gave him the bit of seedcake out of my mouth and it was leapyear like now yes 16 years ago my God after that long kiss I near lost my breath yes he said I was a flower of the mountain yes so we are flowers all a womans body yes that was one true thing he said in his life and the sun shines for you today yes that was why I liked him because I saw he understood or felt what a woman is and I knew I could always get round him and I gave him all the pleasure I could leading him on till he asked me to say yes and I wouldnt answer first only looked out over the sea and the sky I was thinking of so many things he didnt know of Mulvey and Mr Stanhope and Hester and father and old captain Groves and the sailors playing all birds fly and I say stoop and washing up dishes they called it on the pier and the sentry in front of the governors house with the thing round his white helmet poor devil half roasted and the Spanish girls laughing in their shawls and their tall combs and the auctions in the morning the Greeks and the jews and

the Arabs and the devil knows who else from all the ends of Europe and Duke street and the fowl market all clucking outside Larby Sharons and the poor donkeys slipping half asleep and the vague fellows in the cloaks asleep in the shade on the steps and the big wheels of the carts of the bulls and the old castle thousands of years old yes and those handsome Moors all in white and turbans like kings asking you to sit down in their little bit of a shop and Ronda with the old windows of the posadas glancing eyes a lattice hid for her lover to kiss the iron and the wineshops half open at night and the castanets and the night we missed the boat at Algeciras the watchman going about serene with his lamp and O that awful deepdown torrent O and the sea and the sea crimson sometimes like fire and the glorious sunsets and the figtrees in the Alameda gardens yes and all the queer little streets and pink and blue and yellow houses and the rosegardens and the jessamine and geraniums and cactuses and Gibraltar as a girl where I was a Flower of the mountain yes when I put the rose in my hair like the Andalusian girls used or shall I wear a red yes and how he kissed me under the Moorish wall and I thought well as well him as another and then I asked him with my eyes to ask again yes and then he asked me would I yes to say yes my mountain flower and first I put my arms around him yes and drew him down to me so he could feel my breasts all perfume yes and his heart was going like mad and yes I said yes I will Yes.

Joyce, *Ulysses*

1.8 | *Life and Death*

THE FEAR OF DEATH

It is often said that man alone among animals is conscious of the inevitability of dying, a fact that undoubtedly colors his attitude toward life, especially in advancing years. The passages assembled here revolve around that fundamental theme—the consciousness of death as inescapable, the attitudes of the living toward death, the fear of dying and the courage of those who, overcoming such fear, die well. Exemplifying the latter, there are quotations that describe famous death scenes in which the dying display admirable fortitude and calm. There are also passages that describe violent deaths—by murder or by catastrophe, such as plague or earthquake.

Another theme that runs through this chapter is man's contemplation of his mortality and his hopes for or visions of another life—a life after death. But serious discussion of the philosophical and theological problems of immortality—the survival of the soul after the death of the body, its reincarnation in another body, or the resurrection of its original body—involves subtleties and technicalities that preclude its being represented among the materials quoted here.

Still another theme is the one first enunciated by Socrates while awaiting his execution—that to study philosophy is to learn to die, or at least how to prepare for death. Montaigne affords us eloquent elaborations of this theme, and he is accompanied by others who, in one way or another, develop the point.

1 In the sweat of thy face shalt thou eat bread, till thou return unto the ground; for out of it wast thou taken: for dust thou art, and unto dust shalt thou return.

Genesis 3:19

2 I have set before you life and death, blessing and cursing: therefore choose life, that both thou and thy seed may live.

Deuteronomy 30:19

3 Then said his servants unto him, What thing is this that thou hast done? thou didst fast and weep for the child, while it was alive; but when the child was dead, thou didst rise and eat bread.

And he said, While the child was yet alive, I fasted and wept: for I said, Who can tell whether God will be gracious to me, that the child may live?

But now he is dead, wherefore should I fast? can I bring him back again? I shall go to him, but he shall not return to me.

II Samuel 12:21–23

4 The Lord gave, and the Lord hath taken away; blessed be the name of the Lord.

Job 1:21

5 Then in turn the shining son of Hippolochos [Glaukos] answered:
'High-hearted son of Tydeus, why ask of my generation?
As is the generation of leaves, so is that of humanity.
The wind scatters the leaves on the ground, but the live timber
burgeons with leaves again in the season of spring returning.
So one generation of men will grow while another dies.'

Homer, *Iliad,* VI, 144

6 *Achilleus.*   Of possessions
cattle and fat sheep are things to be had for the lifting,
and tripods can be won, and the tawny high heads of horses,
but a man's life cannot come back again, it cannot be lifted
nor captured again by force, once it has crossed the teeth's barrier.

Homer, *Iliad,* IX, 405

7 *Achilleus.* So, friend [Lykaon], you die also. Why all this clamour about it?
Patroklos also is dead, who was better by far than you are.
Do you not see what a man I am, how huge, how splendid
and born of a great father, and the mother who bore me immortal?

Yet even I have also my death and my strong destiny,
and there shall be a dawn or an afternoon or a noontime
when some man in the fighting will take the life from me also
either with a spearcast or an arrow flown from the bowstring.

Homer, *Iliad,* XXI, 106

8 *Odysseus.*   I bit my lip,
rising perplexed, with longing to embrace her [Odysseus' mother's ghost],
and tried three times, putting my arms around her,
but she went sifting through my hands, impalpable
as shadows are, and wavering like a dream.
Now this embittered all the pain I bore,
and I cried in the darkness:

'O my mother,
will you not stay, be still, here in my arms,
may we not, in this place of Death, as well,
hold one another, touch with love, and taste
salt tears' relief, the twinge of welling tears?
Or is this all hallucination, sent
against me by the iron queen, Perséphonê,
to make me groan again?'

My noble mother
answered quickly:

'O my child—alas,
most sorely tried of men—great Zeus's daughter,
Perséphonê, knits no illusion for you.
All mortals meet this judgment when they die.
No flesh and bone are here, none bound by sinew,
since the bright-hearted pyre consumed them down—
the white bones long exanimate—to ash;
dreamlike the soul flies, insubstantial.'

Homer, *Odyssey,* XI, 205

9 'But was there ever a man more blest by fortune than you, Akhilleus? Can there ever be?
We ranked you with immortals in your lifetime, we Argives did, and here your power is royal among the dead men's shades. Think, then, Akhilleus:
you need not be so pained by death.'

To this
he answered swiftly:
'Let me hear no smooth talk
of death from you, Odysseus, light of councils.
Better, I say, to break sod as a farm hand
for some poor country man, on iron rations,
than lord it over all the exhausted dead.'

Homer, *Odyssey,* XI, 483

10 *Apollo.* Zeus could undo shackles, such hurt can be made good,
and there is every kind of way to get out. But once

the dust has drained down all a man's blood, once
the man
has died, there is no raising of him up again.
This is a thing for which my father never made
curative spells. All other states, without effort
of hard breath, he can completely rearrange.

Aeschylus, *Eumenides*, 645

11 *Orestes*. No wise man I count him, who, when
death looms near, attempts to quell its terrors by
piteous laments, nor yet the man who bewails the
Death-god's arrival, when he has no hope of rescue; for he makes two evils out of one; he lets
himself be called a fool and all the same he dies;
he should let his fortune be.

Euripides, *Iphigenia in Tauris*, 484

12 *Hecuba*. You may go now, and hide the dead in his
poor tomb;
he has those flowers that are the right of the underworld.
I think it makes small difference to the dead, if
they
are buried in the tokens of luxury. All this
is an empty glorification left for those who live.

Euripides, *Trojan Women*, 1246

13 *Socrates*. Strange, indeed, would be my conduct, O
men of Athens, if I who, when I was ordered by
the generals whom you chose to command me at
Potidaea and Amphipolis and Delium, remained
where they placed me, like any other man, facing
death—if now, when, as I conceive and imagine,
God orders me to fulfil the philosopher's mission
of searching into myself and other men, I were to
desert my post through fear of death, or any other
fear; that would indeed be strange, and I might
justly be arraigned in court for denying the existence of the gods, if I disobeyed the oracle because
I was afraid of death, fancying that I was wise
when I was not wise. For the fear of death is indeed the pretence of wisdom, and not real wisdom, being a pretence of knowing the unknown;
and no one knows whether death, which men in
their fear apprehend to be the greatest evil, may
not be the greatest good.

Plato, *Apology*, 28B

14 *Socrates*. The difficulty . . . is not to avoid death,
but to avoid unrighteousness; for that runs faster
than death.

Plato, *Apology*, 39A

15 *Socrates*. There is a change and migration of the
soul from this world to another. Now if you suppose that there is no consciousness, but a sleep like
the sleep of him who is undisturbed even by
dreams, death will be an unspeakable gain. For if
a person were to select the night in which his sleep
was undisturbed even by dreams, and were to
compare with this the other days and nights of his
life, and then were to tell us how many days and
nights he had passed in the course of his life better
and more pleasantly than this one, I think that
any man, I will not say a private man, but even
the great king will not find many such days or
nights, when compared with the others. Now if
death be of such a nature, I say that to die is gain;
for eternity is then only a single night. But if
death is the journey to another place, and there,
as men say, all the dead abide, what good, O my
friends and judges, can be greater than this? If
indeed when the pilgrim arrives in the world below, he is delivered from the professors of justice
in this world, and finds the true judges who are
said to give judgment there, Minos and Rhadamanthus and Aecus and Triptolemus, and other
sons of God who were righteous in their own life,
that pilgrimage will be worth making. What
would not a man give if he might converse with
Orpheus and Musaeus and Hesiod and Homer?
Nay, if this be true, let me die again and again. I
myself, too, shall have a wonderful interest in
there meeting and conversing with Palamedes,
and Ajax the son of Telamon, and any other ancient hero who has suffered death through an unjust judgment; and there will be no small pleasure, as I think, in comparing my own sufferings
with theirs. Above all, I shall then be able to continue my search into true and false knowledge; as
in this world, so also in the next; and I shall find
out who is wise, and who pretends to be wise, and
is not. What would not a man give, O judges, to
be able to examine the leader of the great Trojan
expedition; or Odysseus or Sisyphus, or numberless others, men and women too! What infinite
delight would there be in conversing with them
and asking them questions! In another world they
do not put a man to death for asking questions:
assuredly not. For besides being happier than we
are, they will be immortal, if what is said is true.

Wherefore, O judges, be of good cheer about
death, and know of a certainty, that no evil can
happen to a good man, either in life or after
death.

Plato, *Apology*, 40B

16 *Socrates*. The hour of departure has arrived, and
we go our ways—I to die, and you to live. Which
is better God only knows.

Plato, *Apology*, 42B

17 *Socrates*. It has been proved to us by experience
that if we would have pure knowledge of anything
we must be quit of the body—the soul in herself
must behold things in themselves: and then we
shall attain the wisdom which we desire, and of
which we say that we are lovers; not while we live,
but after death; for if while in company with the
body, the soul cannot have pure knowledge, one
of two things follows—either knowledge is not to
be attained at all, or, if at all, after death. For

then, and not till then, the soul will be parted from the body and exist in herself alone. In this present life, I reckon that we make the nearest approach to knowledge when we have the least possible intercourse or communion with the body, and are not surfeited with the bodily nature, but keep ourselves pure until the hour when God himself is pleased to release us. And thus having got rid of the foolishness of the body we shall be pure and hold converse with the pure, and know of ourselves the clear light everywhere, which is no other than the light of truth. For the impure are not permitted to approach the pure. These are the sort of words, Simmias, which the true lovers of knowledge cannot help saying to one another, and thinking. You would agree; would you not?

Simmias. Undoubtedly, Socrates.

But, O my friend, if this be true, there is great reason to hope that, going whither I go, when I have come to the end of my journey, I shall attain that which has been the pursuit of my life. And therefore I go on my way rejoicing, and not I only, but every other man who believes that his mind has been made ready and that he is in a manner purified.

Certainly, replied Simmias.

And what is purification but the separation of the soul from the body, as I was saying before; the habit of the soul gathering and collecting herself into herself from all sides out of the body; the dwelling in her own place alone, as in another life, so also in this, as far as she can;—the release of the soul from the chains of the body?

Very true, he said.

And this separation and release of the soul from the body is termed death?

To be sure, he said.

And the true philosophers, and they only, are ever seeking to release the soul. Is not the separation and release of the soul from the body their especial study?

That is true.

And, as I was saying at first, there would be a ridiculous contradiction in men studying to live as nearly as they can in a state of death, and yet repining when it comes upon them.

Clearly.

And the true philosophers, Simmias, are always occupied in the practice of dying, wherefore also to them least of all men is death terrible.

Plato, *Phaedo,* 66B

18 Crito made a sign to the servant, who was standing by; and he went out, and having been absent for some time, returned with the jailer carrying the cup of poison. Socrates said: You, my good friend, who are experienced in these matters, shall give me directions how I am to proceed. The man answered: You have only to walk about until your legs are heavy, and then to lie down, and the poison will act. At the same time he handed the cup

to Socrates, who in the easiest and gentlest manner, without the least fear or change of colour or feature, looking at the man with all his eyes, Echecrates, as his manner was, took the cup and said: What do you say about making a libation out of this cup to any god? May I, or not? The man answered: We only prepare, Socrates, just so much as we deem enough. I understand, he said: but I may and must ask the gods to prosper my journey from this to the other world—even so—and so be it according to my prayer. Then raising the cup to his lips, quite readily and cheerfully he drank off the poison. And hitherto most of us had been able to control our sorrow; but now when we saw him drinking, and saw too that he had finished the draught, we could no longer forbear, and in spite of myself my own tears were flowing fast; so that I covered my face and wept, not for him, but at the thought of my own calamity in having to part from such a friend. Nor was I the first; for Crito, when he found himself unable to restrain his tears, had got up, and I followed; and at that moment, Apollodorus, who had been weeping all the time, broke out in a loud and passionate cry which made cowards of us all. Socrates alone retained his calmness: What is this strange outcry? he said. I sent away the women mainly in order that they might not misbehave in this way, for I have been told that a man should die in peace. Be quiet then, and have patience. When we heard his words we were ashamed, and refrained our tears; and he walked about until, as he said, his legs began to fail, and then he lay on his back, according to the directions, and the man who gave him the poison now and then looked at his feet and legs; and after a while he pressed his foot hard, and asked him if he could feel; and he said, No; and then his leg, and so upwards and upwards, and showed us that he was cold and stiff. And he felt them himself, and said: When the poison reaches the heart, that will be the end. He was beginning to grow cold about the groin, when he uncovered his face, for he had covered himself up, and said—they were his last words—he said: Crito, I owe a cock to Asclepius; will you remember to pay the debt? The debt shall be paid, said Crito; is there anything else? There was no answer to this question; but in a minute or two a movement was heard, and the attendants uncovered him; his eyes were set, and Crito closed his eyes and mouth.

Such was the end, Echecrates, of our friend; concerning whom I may truly say, that of all the men of his time whom I have known, he was the wisest and justest and best.

Plato, *Phaedo,* 117A

19 *Cephalus.* When a man thinks himself to be near death, fears and cares enter into his mind which he never had before; the tales of a world below and the punishment which is exacted there of

deeds done here were once a laughing matter to him, but now he is tormented with the thought that they may be true: either from the weakness of age, or because he is now drawing nearer to that other place, he has a clearer view of these things; suspicions and alarms crowd thickly upon him, and he begins to reflect and consider what wrongs he has done to others. And when he finds that the sum of his transgressions is great he will many a time like a child start up in his sleep for fear, and he is filled with dark forebodings. But to him who is conscious of no sin, sweet hope . . . is the kind nurse of his age.

Plato, *Republic,* I, 330B

20 As for his [Socrates'] claim that he was forewarned by "the deity" what he ought to do and what not to do, some may think that it must have been a delusion because he was condemned to death. But they should remember two facts. First, he had already reached such an age that, had he not died then, death must have come to him soon after. Secondly, he escaped the most irksome stage of life and the inevitable diminution of mental powers, and instead won glory by the moral strength revealed in the wonderful honesty and frankness and probity of his defence, and in the equanimity and manliness with which he bore the sentence of death.

Xenophon, *Memorabilia,* IV, 8

21 Now death is the most terrible of all things; for it is the end, and nothing is thought to be any longer either good or bad for the dead.

Aristotle, *Ethics,* 1115ª27

22 Death and wounds will be painful to the brave man and against his will, but he will face them because it is noble to do so or because it is base not to do so. And the more he is possessed of virtue in its entirety and the happier he is, the more he will be pained at the thought of death; for life is best worth living for such a man, and he is knowingly losing the greatest goods, and this is painful.

Aristotle, *Ethics,* 1117ᵇ7

23 Now life is defined in the case of animals by the power of perception, in that of man by the power of perception or thought; and a power is defined by reference to the corresponding activity, which is the essential thing; therefore life seems to be essentially the act of perceiving or thinking. And life is among the things that are good and pleasant in themselves.

Aristotle, *Ethics,* 1170ª16

24 Avarice . . . and blind lust of honours which constrain unhappy men to overstep the bounds of right and sometimes as partners and agents of crimes to strive night and day with surpassing effort to struggle up to the summit of power—these

sores of life are in no small measure fostered by the dread of death. For foul scorn and pinching want in every case are seen to be far removed from a life of pleasure and security and to be a loitering so to say before the gates of death. And while men driven on by an unreal dread wish to escape far away from these and keep them far from them, they amass wealth by civil bloodshed and greedily double their riches piling up murder on murder; cruelly triumph in the sad death of a brother and hate and fear the tables of kinsfolk. Often likewise from the same fear envy causes them to pine: they make moan that before their very eyes he is powerful, he attracts attention, who walks arrayed in gorgeous dignity, while they are wallowing in darkness and dirt. Some wear themselves to death for the sake of statues and a name. And often to such a degree through dread of death does hate of life and of the sight of daylight seize upon mortals, that they commit self-murder with a sorrowing heart, quite forgetting that this fear is the source of their cares, this fear which urges men to every sin, prompts this one to put all shame to rout, another to burst asunder the bonds of friendship, and in fine to overturn duty from its very base, since often ere now men have betrayed country and dear parents in seeking to shun the Acherusian quarters. For even as children are flurried and dread all things in the thick darkness, thus we in the daylight fear at times things not a whit more to be dreaded than what children shudder at in the dark and fancy sure to be. This terror therefore and darkness of mind must be dispelled not by the rays of the sun and glittering shafts of day, but by the aspect and law of nature.

Lucretius, *Nature of Things,* III

25 When the body has died, we must admit that the soul has perished, wrenched away throughout the body. To link forsooth a mortal thing with an everlasting and suppose that they can have sense in common and can be reciprocally acted upon, is sheer folly; for what can be conceived more incongruous, more discordant and inconsistent with itself, than a thing which is mortal, linked with an immortal and everlasting thing, trying in such union to weather furious storms.

Lucretius, *Nature of Things,* III

26 "Now no more shall thy house admit thee with glad welcome, nor a most virtuous wife and sweet children run to be the first to snatch kisses and touch thy heart with a silent joy. No more mayst thou be prosperous in thy doings, a safeguard to thine own. One disastrous day has taken from thee luckless man in luckless wise all the many prizes of life." This do men say; but add not thereto "and now no longer does any craving for these things beset thee withal." For if they could rightly perceive this in thought and follow up the

thought in words, they would release themselves from great distress and apprehension of mind. "Thou, even as now thou art, sunk in the sleep of death, shalt continue so to be all time to come, freed from all distressful pains; but we with a sorrow that would not be sated wept for thee, when close by thou didst turn to an ashen hue on thy appalling funeral pile, and no length of days shall pluck from our hearts our ever-during grief." This question therefore should be asked of this speaker, what there is in it so passing bitter, if it come in the end to sleep and rest, that any one should pine in never-ending sorrow.

Lucretius, *Nature of Things,* III

27 Once more what evil lust of life is this which constrains us with such force to be so mightily troubled in doubts and dangers? A sure term of life is fixed for mortals, and death cannot be shunned, but meet it we must. Moreover we are ever engaged, ever involved in the same pursuits, and no new pleasure is struck out by living on; but whilst what we crave is wanting, it seems to transcend all the rest; then, when it has been gotten, we crave something else, and ever does the same thirst of life possess us, as we gape for it open-mouthed. Quite doubtful it is what fortune the future will carry with it or what chance will bring us or what end is at hand. Nor by prolonging life do we take one tittle from the time past in death nor can we fret anything away, whereby we may haply be a less long time in the condition of the dead. Therefore you may complete as many generations as you please during your life; none the less however will that everlasting death await you; and for no less long a time will he be no more in being, who beginning with to-day has ended his life, than the man who has died many months and years ago.

Lucretius, *Nature of Things,* III

28 The philosopher's whole life is a preparation for death.

Cicero, *Disputations,* I, 30

29 Let us get rid of such old wives' tales as the one that tells us it is tragic to die before one's time. What "time" is that, I would like to know? Nature is the one who has granted us the loan of our lives, without setting any schedule for repayment. What has one to complain of if she calls in the loan when she will?

Cicero, *Disputations,* I, 39

30 What a poor dotard must he be who has not learnt in the course of so long a life that death is not a thing to be feared? Death, that is either to be totally disregarded, if it entirely extinguishes the soul, or is even to be desired, if it brings him where he is to exist forever. A third alternative, at any rate, cannot possibly be discovered. Why then should I be afraid if I am destined either not to be

miserable after death or even to be happy? After all, who is such a fool as to feel certain—however young he may be—that he will be alive in the evening? Nay, that time of life has many more chances of death than ours. Young men more easily contract diseases; their illnesses are more serious; their treatment has to be more severe. Accordingly, only a few arrive at old age. If that were not so, life would be conducted better and more wisely; for it is in old men that thought, reason, and prudence are to be found; and if there had been no old men, states would never have existed at all.

Cicero, *Old Age,* XIX

31 If I am wrong in thinking the human soul immortal, I am glad to be wrong; nor will I allow the mistake which gives me so much pleasure to be wrested from me as long as I live. But if when dead, as some insignificant philosophers think, I am to be without sensation, I am not afraid of dead philosophers deriding my errors. Again, if we are not to be immortal, it is nevertheless what a man must wish—to have his life end at its proper time. For nature puts a limit to living as to everything else. Now, old age is, as it were, the playing out of the drama, the full fatigue of which we should shun, especially when we also feel that we have had more than enough of it.

Cicero, *Old Age,* XXIII

32 Happy the man, who, studying nature's laws,
Through known effects can trace the secret cause—
His mind possessing in a quiet state,
Fearless of Fortune, and resigned to Fate!

Virgil, *Georgics,* II

33 In youth alone unhappy mortals live;
But ah! the mighty bliss is fugitive:
Discoloured sickness, anxious labours, come,
And age, and death's inexorable doom.

Virgil, *Georgics,* III

34 Ah! Postumus, Postumus, fast fly the years,
'And prayers to wrinkles and impending age
        Bring not delay; nor shalt assuage
        Death's stroke with pious tears;

No, not though on each day that comes to thee
With thrice a hundred bulls thou sought to gain
        Grim Pluto's pity, all were vain!
        Great Geryon he'll not free,

Or Tityos, from the gloomy stream, whose tide
Each child of earth must traverse shore to shore,
        Whether a crown on earth we bore,
        Or crofters lived and died.

Horace, *Odes,* II, 14

35 While you pray for life, study death. Fatted bulls fall from some slight wound, and creatures of

great stamina are downed by one blow from a man's hand. A tiny blade can sever the tendons of the neck; and when the head is severed the hulk of the body crumples in a heap. No secret corner of the body hides the soul. No knife can dig it out, nor any wound aimed at the vital parts; death is near at hand. For these death blows I have appointed no specific spot—anywhere you wish: the way is open. When breath departs the body, that moment we call dying is so brief we cannot be aware of it. Whether one is strangled or drowned, or the skull is fractured from a fall on the hard ground, or fire deprives us of air; whatever the case, the end comes quickly. Are you blushing for shame? For so long a time you are in fear of what is over so quickly.

Seneca, *On Providence,* VI

36 What is death? Either a transition or an end. I am not afraid of coming to an end, this being the same as never having begun, nor of transition, for I shall never be in confinement quite so cramped anywhere else as I am here.

Seneca, *Letters to Lucilius,* 65

37 As it is with a play, so it is with life—what matters is not how long the acting lasts, but how good it is. It is not important at what point you stop. Stop wherever you will—only make sure that you round it off with a good ending.

Seneca, *Letters to Lucilius,* 77

38 Then said Martha unto Jesus, Lord, if thou hadst been here, my brother had not died.

But I know, that even now, whatsoever thou wilt ask of God, God will give it thee.

Jesus saith unto her, Thy brother shall rise again.

Martha saith unto him, I know that he shall rise again in the resurrection at the last day.

Jesus said unto her, I am the resurrection, and the life: he that believeth in me, though he were dead, yet shall he live:

And whosoever liveth and believeth in me shall never die. Believest thou this?

She saith unto him, Yea, Lord: I believe that thou art the Christ, the Son of God, which should come into the world.

And when she had so said, she went her way, and called Mary her sister secretly, saying, The Master is come, and calleth for thee.

As soon as she heard that, she arose quickly, and came unto him.

Now Jesus was not yet come into the town, but was in that place where Martha met him.

The Jews then which were with her in the house, and comforted her, when they saw Mary, that she rose up hastily and went out, followed her, saying, She goeth unto the grave to weep there.

Then when Mary was come where Jesus was,

and saw him, she fell down at his feet, saying unto him, Lord, if thou hadst been here, my brother had not died.

When Jesus therefore saw her weeping, and the Jews also weeping which came with her, he groaned in the spirit, and was troubled,

And said, Where have ye laid him? They said unto him, Lord, come and see.

Jesus wept.

Then said the Jews, Behold how he loved him!

And some of them said, Could not this man, which opened the eyes of the blind, have caused that even this man should not have died?

Jesus therefore again groaning in himself cometh to the grave. It was a cave, and a stone lay upon it.

Jesus said, Take ye away the stone. Martha, the sister of him that was dead, saith unto him, Lord, by this time he stinketh: for he hath been dead four days.

Jesus saith unto her, Said I not unto thee, that, if thou wouldest believe, thou shouldest see the glory of God?

Then they took away the stone from the place where the dead was laid. And Jesus lifted up his eyes, and said, Father, I thank thee that thou hast heard me.

And I knew that thou hearest me always: but because of the people which stand by I said it, that they may believe that thou hast sent me.

And when he thus had spoken, he cried with a loud voice, Lazarus, come forth.

And he that was dead came forth, bound hand and foot with graveclothes: and his face was bound about with a napkin. Jesus saith unto them, Loose him, and let him go.

John 11:21–44

39 Verily, verily, I say unto you, Except a corn of wheat fall into the ground and die, it abideth alone: but if it die, it bringeth forth much fruit.

He that loveth his life shall lose it; and he that hateth his life in this world shall keep it unto life eternal.

John 12:24–25

40 For since by man came death, by man came also the resurrection of the dead.

For as in Adam all die, even so in Christ shall all be made alive.

But every man in his own order: Christ the firstfruits; afterward they that are the Christ's at his coming.

Then cometh the end, when he shall have delivered up the kingdom to God, even the Father; when he shall have put down all rule and all authority and power.

For he must reign, till he hath put all enemies under his feet.

The last enemy that shall be destroyed is death.

I Corinthians 15:21–26

41 All flesh is not the same flesh: but there is one kind of flesh of men, another flesh of beasts, another of fishes, and another of birds.

There are also celestial bodies, and bodies terrestrial: but the glory of the celestial is one, and the glory of the terrestrial is another.

There is one glory of the sun, and another glory of the moon, and another glory of the stars: for one star differeth from another star in glory.

So also is the resurrection of the dead. It is sown in corruption; it is raised in incorruption:

It is sown in dishonour; it is raised in glory: it is sown in weakness; it is raised in power:

It is sown a natural body; it is raised a spiritual body. There is a natural body, and there is a spiritual body. . . .

Now this I say, brethren, that flesh and blood cannot inherit the kingdom of God; neither doth corruption inherit incorruption. . . .

For this corruptible must put on incorruption, and this mortal must put on immortality.

So when this corruptible shall have put on incorruption, and this mortal shall have put on immortality, then shall be brought to pass the saying that is written, Death is swallowed up in victory.

O death, where is thy sting? O grave, where is thy victory?

I Corinthians 15:39–55

42 And I looked, and behold a pale horse: and his name that sat on him was Death, and Hell followed with him. And power was given unto them over the fourth part of the earth, to kill with sword, and with hunger, and with death, and with the beasts of the earth.

Revelation 6:8

43 The death of happy men is not . . . most grievous, but most blessed, since it secures their felicity, and puts it out of fortune's power. And that Spartan advised well, who, embracing Diagoras, that had himself been crowned in the Olympic Games, and saw his sons and grandchildren victors, said, "Die, Diagoras, for thou canst not be a god."

Plutarch, Pelopidas

44 One finds it also related by many that a soothsayer bade him prepare for some great danger on the Ides of March. When this day was come, Cæsar, as he went to the senate, met this soothsayer, and said to him by way of raillery, "The Ides of March are come," who answered him calmly, "Yes, they are come, but they are not past." The day before his assassination he supped with Marcus Lepidus; and as he was signing some letters according to his custom, as he reclined at table, there arose a question what sort of death was the best. At which he immediately, before any one could speak, said, "A sudden one."

Plutarch, Caesar

45 Throwing away then all things, hold to these only which are few; and besides bear in mind that every man lives only this present time, which is an indivisible point, and that all the rest of his life is either past or it is uncertain. Short then is the time which every man lives, and small the nook of the earth where he lives; and short too the longest posthumous fame, and even this only continued by a succession of poor human beings, who will very soon die, and who know not even themselves, much less him who died long ago.

Marcus Aurelius, Meditations, III, 10

46 Always observe how ephemeral and worthless human things are. . . . Pass then through this little space of time conformably to nature, and end thy journey in content, just as an olive falls off when it is ripe, blessing nature who produced it, and thanking the tree on which it grew.

Marcus Aurelius, Meditations, IV, 48

47 Soon, very soon, thou wilt be ashes, or a skeleton, and either a name or not even a name; but name is sound and echo. And the things which are much valued in life are empty and rotten and trifling, and like little dogs biting one another, and little children quarrelling, laughing, and then straightway weeping.

Marcus Aurelius, Meditations, V, 33

48 How can it be that the gods after having arranged all things well and benevolently for mankind, have overlooked this alone, that some men and very good men, and men who, as we may say, have had most communion with the divinity, and through pious acts and religious observances have been most intimate with the divinity, when they have once died should never exist again, but should be completely extinguished?

But if this is so, be assured that if it ought to have been otherwise, the gods would have done it. For if it were just, it would also be possible; and if it were according to nature, nature would have had it so. But because it is not so, if in fact it is not so, be thou convinced that it ought not to have been so.

Marcus Aurelius, Meditations, XII, 5

49 This devouring of Kind by Kind is necessary as the means to the transmutation of living things which could not keep form for ever even though no other killed them: what grievance is it that when they must go their despatch is so planned as to be serviceable to others?

Still more, what does it matter when they are devoured only to return in some new form? It comes to no more than the murder of one of the personages in a play; the actor alters his make-up and enters in a new rôle. The actor, of course, was not really killed; but if dying is but changing a body as the actor changes a costume, or even an exit from the body like the exit of the actor from the boards when he has no more to say or do, what is there so very dreadful in this transformation of living beings one into another?

Plotinus, *Third Ennead,* II, 15

50 Life in the Supreme is the native activity of Intellect; in virtue of that converse it brings forth gods, brings forth beauty, brings forth righteousness, brings forth all moral good; for of all these the soul is pregnant when it has been filled with God. This state is its first and its final, because from God it comes, its good lies There, and, once turned to God again, it is what it was. Life here, with the things of earth, is a sinking, a defeat, a failing of the wing.

Plotinus, *Sixth Ennead,* IX, 9

51 The soul in its nature loves God and longs to be at one with Him in the noble love of a daughter for a noble father; but coming to human birth and lured by the courtships of this sphere, she takes up with another love, a mortal, leaves her father and falls.

But one day coming to hate her shame, she puts away the evil of earth, once more seeks the father, and finds her peace.

Plotinus, *Sixth Ennead,* IX, 9

52 The soul lives by avoiding those things which if they are sought bring death. Refrain from the ugly savagery of pride, from the slothly pleasure of lust, from all that lyingly bears the name of science, that the wild beasts may be tamed, the cattle brought to subjection, and the serpents made harmless. For these animals are an allegory for the movements of the mind. The pomp of pride and the delight that is in lust and the poison of curiosity are the movements of a soul that is dead—not dead so that it has lost all movement, but dead by departing from the fountain of life so that it is taken up by the world that passes away and conformed to it. But Your word, O God, is a fountain of life everlasting and does not pass away.

Augustine, *Confessions,* XIII, 21

53 All these last offices and ceremonies that concern the dead, the careful funeral arrangements, and the equipment of the tomb, and the pomp of obsequies, are rather the solace of the living than the comfort of the dead.

Augustine, *City of God,* I, 12

54 The death . . . of the soul takes place when God forsakes it, as the death of the body when the soul forsakes it.

Augustine, *City of God,* XIII, 2

55 Of the first and bodily death, then, we may say that to the good it is good, and evil to the evil.

But, doubtless, the second, as it happens to none of the good, so it can be good for none.

Augustine, *City of God,* XIII, 2

56 As regards bodily death, that is, the separation of the soul from the body, it is good unto none while it is being endured by those whom we say are in the article of death. For the very violence with which body and soul are wrenched asunder, which in the living had been conjoined and closely intertwined, brings with it a harsh experience, jarring horridly on nature so long as it continues, till there comes a total loss of sensation, which arose from the very interpenetration of spirit and flesh. And all this anguish is sometimes forestalled by one stroke of the body or sudden flitting of the soul, the swiftness of which prevents it from being felt. But whatever that may be in the dying which with violently painful sensation robs of all sensation, yet, when it is piously and faithfully borne, it increases the merit of patience, but does not make the name of punishment inapplicable. Death, proceeding by ordinary generation from the first man, is the punishment of all who are born of him, yet, if it be endured for righteousness' sake, it becomes the glory of those who are born again; and though death be the award of sin, it sometimes secures that nothing be awarded to sin.

Augustine, *City of God,* XIII, 6

57 We enjoy some gratification when our good friends die; for though their death leaves us in sorrow, we have the consolatory assurance that they are beyond the ills by which in this life even the best of men are broken down or corrupted.

Augustine, *City of God,* XIX, 8

58 Now among all passions inflicted from without, death holds the first place, just as sexual concupiscences are chief among internal passions. Consequently, when a man conquers death and things directed to death, his is a most perfect victory.

Aquinas, *Summa Theologica,* III Suppl., 96, 6

59 *Ægëus.* "Just as there never died a man," quoth he,
"But he had lived on earth in some degree,
Just so there never lived a man," he said,
"In all this world, but must be sometime dead.
This world is but a thoroughfare of woe,
And we are pilgrims passing to and fro;
Death is the end of every worldly sore."

Chaucer, *Canterbury Tales:* Knight's Tale

60 I go to seek a great perhaps.

Rabelais, *Last Words* (ascribed to)

61 Man, that is born of a woman, hath but a short time to live, and is full of misery. He cometh up, and is cut down, like a flower; he fleeth as it were a shadow, and never continueth in one stay.

In the midst of life we are in death; of whom may we week for succour, but of thee, O Lord, who for our sins art justly displeased?

Book of Common Prayer

62 In everything else there may be sham: the fine reasonings of philosophy may be a mere pose in us; or else our trials, by not testing us to the quick, give us a chance to keep our face always composed. But in the last scene, between death and ourselves, there is no more pretending; we must talk plain French, we must show what there is that is good and clean at the bottom of the pot.

Montaigne, *Essays*, I, 19, That Our Happiness

63 There are gallant and fortunate deaths. I have seen death bring a wonderfully brilliant career, and that in its flower, to such a splendid end that in my opinion the dead man's ambitions and courageous designs had nothing so lofty about them as their interruption. He arrived where he aspired to without going there, more grandly and gloriously than he had desired or hoped. And by his fall he went beyond the power and the fame to which he had aspired by his career.

Montaigne, *Essays*, I, 19, That Our Happiness

64 It is uncertain where death awaits us; let us await it everywhere. Premeditation of death is premeditation of freedom. He who has learned how to die has unlearned how to be a slave. Knowing how to die frees us from all subjection and constraint. There is nothing evil in life for the man who has thoroughly grasped the fact that to be deprived of life is not an evil.

Montaigne, *Essays*, I, 20, That to Philosophize

65 What does it matter when it comes, since it is inevitable? To the man who told Socrates, "The thirty tyrants have condemned you to death," he replied: "And nature, them."

Montaigne, *Essays*, I, 20, That to Philosophize

66 Nature forces us to it. Go out of this world, she says, as you entered it. The same passage that you made from death to life, without feeling or fright, make it again from life to death. Your death is a part of the order of the universe; it is a part of the life of the world.

Montaigne, *Essays*, I, 20, That to Philosophize

67 Now I have often pondered how it happens that in wars the face of death, whether we see it in ourselves or in others, seems to us imcomparably less terrifying than in our houses—otherwise you would have an army of doctors and snivelers—

and, since death is always the same, why nevertheless there is much more assurance against it among villagers and humble folk than among others. I truly think it is those dreadful faces and trappings with which we surround it, that frighten us more than death itself: an entirely new way of living; the cries of mothers, wives, and children; the visits of people dazed and benumbed by grief; the presence of a number of pale and weeping servants; a darkened room; lighted candles; our bedside besieged by doctors and preachers; in short, everything horror and fright around us. There we are already shrouded and buried. Children fear even their friends when they see them masked, and so do we ours. We must strip the mask from things as well as from persons; when it is off, we shall find beneath only that same death which a valet or a mere chambermaid passed through not long ago without fear. Happy the death that leaves no leisure for preparing such ceremonies!

Montaigne, *Essays*, I, 20, That to Philosophize

68 It is not without reason that we are taught to study even our sleep for the resemblance it has with death. How easily we pass from waking to sleeping! With how little sense of loss we lose consciousness of the light and of ourselves! Perhaps the faculty of sleep, which deprives us of all action and all feeling, might seem useless and contrary to nature, were it not that thereby Nature teaches us that she has made us for dying and living alike, and from the start of life presents to us the eternal state that she reserves for us after we die, to accustom us to it and take away our fear of it.

Montaigne, *Essays*, II, 6, Of Practice

69 Life is full of fireworks; death, of love and courtesy.

Montaigne, *Essays*, II, 35, Of Three Good Women

70 *Gaunt.* O, but they say the tongues of dying men
Enforce attention like deep harmony:
Where words are scarce, they are seldom spent in vain,
For they breathe truth that breathe their words in pain.
He that no more must say is listen'd more
    Than they whom youth and ease have taught to glose;
More are men's ends mark'd than their lives before:
    The setting sun, and music at the close,
As the last taste of sweets, is sweetest last,
Writ in remembrance more than things long past.

Shakespeare, *Richard II,* II, i, 5

71 *Prince of Wales.* When that this body did contain a spirit,

A kingdom for it was too small a bound;
But now two paces of the vilest earth
Is room enough.

Shakespeare, *I Henry IV,* V, iv, 89

72 *Feeble.* By my troth, I care not; a man can die but
once: we owe God a death . . . and let it go which
way it will, he that dies this year is quit for the
next.

Shakespeare, *II Henry IV,* III, ii, 250

73 *Caesar.* Of all the wonders that I yet have heard,
It seems to me most strange that men should fear;
Seeing that death, a necessary end,
Will come when it will come.

Shakespeare, *Julius Caesar,* II, ii, 34

74 *Queen.* Good Hamlet, cast thy nighted colour off,
And let thine eye look like a friend on Denmark.
Do not for ever with thy vailed lids
Seek for thy noble father in the dust.
Thou know'st 'tis common; all that lives must die,
Passing through nature to eternity.
  Hamlet. Ay, madam, it is common.
  Queen.   If it be,
Why seems it so particular with thee?
  Ham. Seems, madam! nay, it is; I know not
"seems."
'Tis not alone my inky cloak, good mother,
Nor customary suits of solemn black,
Nor windy suspiration of forced breath,
No, nor the fruitful river in the eye,
Nor the dejected 'haviour of the visage,
Together with all forms, moods, shapes of grief,
That can denote me truly: these indeed seem,
For they are actions that a man might play:
But I have that within which passeth show;
These but the trappings and the suits of woe.

Shakespeare, *Hamlet,* I, ii, 68

75 *King.* Now, Hamlet, where's Polonius?
  Hamlet. At supper.
  King. At supper! where?
  Ham. Not where he eats, but where he is eaten.
A certain convocation of politic worms are e'en at
him. Your worm is your only emperor for diet. We
fat all creatures else to fat us, and we fat ourselves
for maggots. Your fat king and your lean beggar is
but variable service, two dishes, but to one table;
that's the end.
  King. Alas, alas!
  Ham. A man may fish with the worm that hath
eat of a king, and eat of the fish that hath fed of
that worm.
  King. What dost thou mean by this?
  Ham. Nothing but to show you how a king may
go a progress through the guts of a beggar.
  King. Where is Polonius?
  Ham. In heaven; send thither to see. If your
messenger find him not there, seek him i' the
other place yourself. But indeed, if you find him

not within this month, you shall nose him as you
go up the stairs into the lobby.
  King. Go seek him there.

[*To some Attendants.*
  Ham. He will stay till you come.

Shakespeare, *Hamlet,* IV, iii, 17

76 *Ophelia.* We must be patient; but I cannot choose
but weep, to think they should lay him i' the cold
ground.

Shakespeare, *Hamlet,* IV, v, 68

77 *Hamlet.* That skull had a tongue in it, and could
sing once. How the knave jowls it to the ground,
as if it were Cain's jaw-bone, that did the first
murder! It might be the pate of a politician,
which this ass now o'er-reaches; one that would
circumvent God, might it not?
  Horatio. It might, my lord.
  Ham. Or of a courtier; which could say "Good
morrow, sweet lord! How dost thou, good lord?"
This might be my Lord Such-a-one, that praised
my Lord Such-a-one's horse, when he meant to
beg it; might it not?
  Hor. Ay, my lord.
  Ham. Why, e'en so; and now my Lady Worm's;
chapless, and knocked about the mazzard with a
sexton's space. Here's fine revolution, an we had
the trick to see't. . . . There's another. Why may
not that be the skull of a lawyer? Where be his
quiddities now, his quillets, his cases, his tenures,
and his tricks? Why does he suffer this rude knave
now to knock him about the sconce with a dirty
shovel, and will not tell him of his action of battery? Hum! This fellow might be in's time a great
buyer of land, with his statutes, his recognizances,
his fines, his double vouchers, his recoveries. Is
this the fine of his fines, and the recovery of his
recoveries, to have his fine pate full of fine dirt?
Will his vouchers vouch him no more of his purchases, and double ones too, than the length and
breadth of a pair of indentures? The very conveyances of his lands will hardly lie in this box; and
must the inheritor himself have no more, ha?
  Hor. Not a jot more, my lord.

Shakespeare, *Hamlet,* V, i, 83

78 *Hamlet.* Alas, poor Yorick! I knew him, Horatio; a
fellow of infinite jest, of most excellent fancy. He
hath borne me on his back a thousand times; and
now, how abhorred in my imagination it is! my
gorge rises at it. Here hung those lips that I have
kissed I know not how oft. Where be your gibes
now? your gambols? your songs? your flashes of
merriment, that were wont to set the table on a
roar? Not one now, to mock your own grinning?
quite chap-fallen? Now get you to my lady's
chamber, and tell her, let her paint an inch thick,
to this favour she must come; make her laugh at
that.

Shakespeare, *Hamlet,* V, i, 202

79 *Hamlet.* To what base uses we may return, Horatio! Why may not imagination trace the noble dust of Alexander, till he find it stopping a bung-hole?

    Horatio. 'Twere to consider too curiously, to consider so.

    Ham. No, faith, not a jot; but to follow him thither with modesty enough, and likelihood to lead it; as thus: Alexander died, Alexander was buried, Alexander returneth into dust; the dust is earth; of earth we make loam; and why of that loam, whereto he was converted, might they not stop a beer-barrel?

                Shakespeare, *Hamlet*, V, i, 223

80 *Hamlet.* If it be now, 'tis not to come; if it be not to come, it will be now; if it be not now, yet it will come; the readiness is all. Since no man has aught of what he leaves, what is't to leave betimes?

                Shakespeare, *Hamlet*, V, ii, 231

81 *Duke.* Be absolute for death; either death or life
Shall thereby be the sweeter. Reason thus with
   life:
If I do lose thee, I do lose a thing
That none but fools would keep. A breath thou
   art,
Servile to all the skyey influences,
That dost this habitation, where thou keep'st,
Hourly afflict. Merely, thou art Death's fool;
For him thou labour'st by thy flight to shun
And yet runn'st toward him still. Thou art not
   noble;
For all the accommodations that thou bear'st
Are nursed by baseness. Thou'rt by no means
   valiant;
For thou dost fear the soft and tender fork
Of a poor worm. Thy best of rest is sleep,
And that thou oft provokest; yet grossly fear'st
Thy death, which is no more. Thou art not thy-
   self;
For thou exist'st on many a thousand grains
That issue out of dust. Happy thou art not;
For what thou hast not, still thou strivest to get,
And what thou hast, forget'st. Thou are not cer-
   tain;
For thy complexion shifts to strange effects,
After the moon. If thou art rich, thou'rt poor;
For, like an ass whose back with ingots bows,
Thou bear'st thy heavy riches but a journey,
And death unloads thee. Friend hast thou none;
For thine own bowels, which do call thee sire,
The mere effusion of thy proper loins,
Do curse the gout, serpigo, and the rheum,
For ending thee no sooner. Thou hast nor youth
   nor age,
But, as it were, an after-dinner's sleep,
Dreaming on both; for all thy blessed youth
Becomes as aged, and doth beg the alms
Of palsied eld; and when thou art old and rich,

Thou hast neither heat, affection, limb, nor
   beauty,
To make thy riches pleasant. What's yet in this
That bears the name of life? Yet in this life
Lie hid moe thousand deaths; yet death we fear,
That makes these odds all even.

        Shakespeare, *Measure for Measure*, III, i, 4

82 *Isabella.* The sense of death is most in apprehension;
And the poor beetle that we tread upon,
In corporal sufferance finds a pang as great
As when a giant dies.

      Shakespeare, *Measure for Measure*, III, i, 78

83 *Claudio.*   Death is a fearful thing.
    Isabella. And shamed life a hateful.
    Claud. Ay, but to die, and go we know not
   where;
To lie in cold obstruction and to rot;
This sensible warm motion to become
A kneaded clod; and the delighted spirit
To bathe in fiery floods, or to reside
In thrilling region of thick-ribbed ice;
To be imprison'd in the viewless winds,
And blown with restless violence round about
The pendent world; or to be worse than worst
Of those that lawless and incertain thought
Imagine howling; 'tis too horrible!
The weariest and most loathed wordly life
That age, ache, penury, and imprisonment
Can lay on nature is a paradise
To what we fear of death.
    Isab. Alas, alas!
       Shakespeare, *Measure for Measure*, III, i, 116

84 *Othello.* It is the cause, it is the cause, my soul—
Let me not name it to you, you chaste stars!—
It is the cause. Yet I'll not shed her blood;
Nor scar that whiter skin of hers than snow,
And smooth as monumental alabaster.
Yet she must die, else she'll betray more men.
Put out the light, and then put out the light.
If I quench thee, thou flaming minister,
I can again thy former light restore.
Should I repent me; but once put out thy light,
Thou cunning'st pattern of excelling nature,
I know not where is that Promethean heat
That can thy light relume. When I have pluck'd
   the rose,
I cannot give it vital growth again,
It must needs wither.

            Shakespeare, *Othello*, V, ii, 1

85 *Edgar.*   Men must endure
Their going hence, even as their coming hither;
Ripeness is all.

            Shakespeare, *Lear*, V, ii, 10

86 *Macbeth.* If it were done when 'tis done, then
   'twere well
It were done quickly. If the assassination

Could trammel up the consequence, and catch
With his surcease success; that but this blow
Might be the be-all and the end-all here,
But here, upon this bank and shoal of time,
We'd jump the life to come. But in these cases
We still have judgement here; that we but teach
Bloody instructions, which, being taught, return
To plague the inventor.

Shakespeare, *Macbeth,* I, vii, 1

87 *Macbeth.* There's one did laugh in's sleep, and one
    cried "Murder!"
That they did wake each other. I stood and heard
    them;
But they did say their prayers, and address'd them
Again to sleep.
    Lady Macbeth.   There are two lodged together.
    Macb. One cried "God bless us!" and "Amen"
    the other;
As they had seen me with these hangman's hands.
Listening their fear, I could not say "Amen,"
When they did say "God bless us!"
    Lady M.   Consider it not so deeply.
    Macb. But wherefore could not I pronounce
    "Amen"?
I had most need of blessing, and "Amen"
Stuck in my throat
    Lady M. These deeds must not be thought
After these ways; so, it will make us mad.
    Macb. Methought I heard a voice cry, "Sleep no
    more!
Macbeth does murder sleep," the innocent sleep,
Sleep that knits up the ravell'd sleave of care,
The death of each day's life, sore labour's bath,
Balm of hurt minds, great nature's second course,
Chief nourisher in life's feast—
    Lady M.   What do you mean?
    Macb. Still it cried, "Sleep no more!" to all the
    house;
"Glamis hath murder'd sleep, and therefore
    Cawdor
Shall sleep no more; Macbeth shall sleep no
    more."

Shakespeare, *Macbeth,* II, ii, 23

88 *Lady Macbeth.*   The sleeping and the dead
Are but as pictures; tis the eye of childhood
That fears a painted devil.

Shakespeare, *Macbeth,* II, ii, 53

89 *Macbeth.* Will all great Neptune's ocean wash this
    blood
Clean from my hand? No, this my hand will
    rather
The multitudinous seas incarnadine,
Making the green one red.

        Re-enter Lady Macbeth.

    Lady Macbeth. My hands are of your colour; but
    I shame

To wear a heart so white. [*Knocking within.*] I hear
    a knocking
At the south entry. Retire we to our chamber.
A little water clears us of this deed.

Shakespeare, *Macbeth,* II, ii, 60

90 *Macbeth.*   Better be with the dead,
Whom we, to gain our peace, have sent to peace,
Than on the torture of the mind to lie
In restless ectasy. Duncan is in his grave;
After life's fitful fever he sleeps well;
Treason has done his worst; nor steel, nor poison,
Malice domestic, foreign levy, nothing,
Can touch him further.

Shakespeare, *Macbeth,* III, ii, 19

91 *Cleopatra.* [*Antony dies.*] The crown o' the earth
    doth melt. My lord!
O, wither'd is the garland of the war,
The soldier's pole is fall'n; young boys and girls
Are level now with men; the odds is gone,
And there is nothing left remarkable
Beneath the visiting moon.

Shakespeare, *Antony and Cleopatra,* IV, xv, 63

92 *Guiderius.* Fear no more the heat o' the sun,
    Nor the furious winter's rages;
Thou thy worldly task hast done,
    Home art gone, and ta'en thy wages.
Golden lads and girls all must,
As chimney-sweepers, come to dust.

Shakespeare, *Cymbeline,* IV, ii, 258

93 *Stephano.* He that dies pays all debts.

Shakespeare, *Tempest,* III, ii, 140

94 No longer mourn for me when I am dead
Than you shall hear the surly sullen bell
Give warning to the world that I am fled
From this vile world, with vilest worms to dwell.

Shakespeare, *Sonnet LXXI*

95 Well! said Don *Quixote,* thou wilt never be silent
till thy Mouth's full of Clay; when thou'rt dead, I
hope I shall have some Rest. Faith and Troth now
Master, quoth *Sancho,* you did ill to talk of Death,
Heaven bless us, 'tis no Child's Play; you've e'en
spoil'd my Dinner; the very Thought of raw
Bones and lanthorn Jaws makes me sick. Death
eats up all Things, both the young Lamb and old
Sheep; and I have heard our Parson say, Death
values a Prince no more than a Clown; all's Fish
that comes to his Net; he throws at all, and sweeps
Stakes; he's no Mower that takes a Nap at Noon-
Day, but drives on, fair Weather or foul, and cuts
down the green Grass as well as the ripe Corn:
He's neither squeamish nor queesy-stomach'd, for
he swallows without chewing, and crams down all
things into his ungracious Maw; and tho' you can
see no Belly he has, he has a confounded Dropsy,
and thirsts after Men's Lives, which he guggles
down like Mother's Milk. Hold, hold, cry'd the

Knight, go no further, for thou art come to a very handsome Period; thou hast said as much of Death in thy home-spun Cant, as a good Preacher could have done: Thou hast got the Knack of Preaching, Man! I must get thee a Pulpit and Benefice, I think.

Cervantes, *Don Quixote,* II, 20

96 O eloquent, just, and mighty Death! whom none could advise, thou hast persuaded; what none hath dared, thou hast done; and whom all the world hath flattered, thou only hast cast out of the world and despised; thou hast drawn together all the far-stretched greatness, all the pride, cruelty, and ambition of man, and covered it all over with these two narrow words, *Hic jacet!*

Sir Walter Raleigh, *History of the World,* Bk. V, VI, 12

97 Wee can dye by it, if not live by love,
And if unfit for tombes and hearse
Our legend bee, it will be fit for verse;
And if no peece of Chronicle wee prove,
We'll build in sonnets pretty roomes;
As well a well wrought urne becomes
The greatest ashes, as halfe-acre tombes.

Donne, *The Canonization*

98 Death be not proud, though some have called thee
Mighty and dreadfull, for, thou art not soe,
For, those, whom thou think'st, thou dost over-throw,
Die not, poore death, nor yet canst thou kill mee.
From rest and sleepe, which but thy pictures bee,
Much pleasure, then from thee, much more must flow,
And soonest our best men with thee doe goe,
Rest of their bones, and soules deliverie.
Thou art slave to Fate, Chance, kings, and des-perate men,
And dost with poyson, warre, and sicknesse dwell,
And poppie, or charmes can make us sleepe as well,
And better than thy stroake; why swell'st thou then?
One short sleepe past, wee wake eternally,
And death shall be no more; death, thou shalt die.

Donne, *Holy Sonnet X*

99 Wouldst thou hear what man can say
In a little? Reader, stay.
Underneath this stone doth lie
As much beauty as could die;
Which in life did harbor give
To more virtue than doth live.
If at all she had a fault,
Leave it buried in this vault.
One name was Elizabeth;
Th' other, let it sleep with death:
Fitter, where it died, to tell,

Than that it lived at all. Farewell!

Jonson, *Epitaph on Elizabeth, L. H.*

100 Men fear death as children fear to go in the dark; and as that natural fear in children is increased with tales, so is the other. Certainly, the contem-plation of death, as the wages of sin and passage to another world, is holy and religious; but the fear of it, as a tribute due unto nature, is weak. Yet in religious meditations there is sometimes mixture of vanity and of superstition. . . . Groans and convulsions, and a discoloured face, and friends weeping, and blacks, and obsequies, and the like, show death terrible.

Bacon, *Of Death*

101 It is worthy the observing that there is no passion in the mind of man so weak but it mates and masters the fear of death; and therefore death is no such terrible enemy when a man hath so many attendants about him that can win the combat of him. Revenge triumphs over death; love slights it; honour aspireth to it; grief flieth to it; fear pre-occupateth it.

Bacon, *Of Death*

102 There is neither the word nor the thing of purga-tory, neither in this nor any other text; nor any-thing that can prove a necessity of a place for the soul without the body. . . . For God, that could give a life to a piece of clay, hath the same power to give life again to a dead man, and renew his inanimate and rotten carcass into a glorious, spiri-tual, and immortal body.

Hobbes, *Leviathan,* IV, 44

103 If the nearness of our last necessity brought a nearer conformity into it, there were a happiness in hoary hairs and no calamity in half senses. But the long habit of living indisposeth us for dying.

Sir Thomas Browne, *Urn-Burial,* V

104 To extend our memories by monuments whose death we daily pray for, and whose duration we cannot hope without injury to our expectations in the advent of the Last Day, were a contradiction to our beliefs. We whose generations are ordained in this setting part of time are providentially tak-en off from such imaginations, and, being necessi-tated to eye the remaining particle of futurity, are naturally constituted unto thoughts of the next world, and cannot excusably decline the consider-ation of that duration which maketh pyramids pillars of snow and all that's past a moment.

Sir Thomas Browne, *Urn-Burial,* V

105 The number of the dead long exceedeth all that shall live. The night of time far surpasseth the day, and who knows when was the equinox? Ev-ery hour adds unto that current arithmetic, which scarce stands one moment. And since death must

be the *Lucina* of life, and even pagans could doubt whether thus to live were to die; since our longest sun sets at right descensions and makes but winter arches, and therefore it cannot be long before we lie down in darkness and have our light in ashes; since the brother of death daily haunts us with dying mementos, and time, that grows old in itself, bids us hope no long duration, diuturnity is a dream and folly of expectation.

Sir Thomas Browne, *Urn-Burial,* V

106 To hold long subsistence seems but a scape in oblivion. But man is a noble animal, splendid in ashes and pompous in the grave, solemnizing nativities and deaths with equal lustre, nor omitting ceremonies of bravery in the infamy of his nature.

Sir Thomas Browne, *Urn-Burial,* V

107 To subsist in lasting monuments, to live in their productions, to exist in their names and predicament of chimaeras, was large satisfaction unto old expectations, and made one part of their Elysiums. But all this is nothing in the metaphysics of true belief. To live indeed is to be again ourselves, which being not only a hope, but an evidence, in noble believers, 'tis all one to lie in St. Innocent's churchyard as in the sands of Egypt; ready to be anything, in the ecstasy of being ever, and as content with six foot as the moles of Adrianus.

Sir Thomas Browne, *Urn-Burial,* V

108 As men are not able to fight against death, misery, ignorance, they have taken it into their heads, in order to be happy, not to think of them at all.

Despite these miseries, man wishes to be happy, and only wishes to be happy, and cannot wish not to be so. But how will he set about it? To be happy he would have to make himself immortal; but, not being able to do so, it has occurred to him to prevent himself from thinking of death.

Pascal, *Pensées,* II, 168–169

109 For it is not to be doubted that the duration of this life is but a moment; that the state of death is eternal, whatever may be its nature; and that thus all our actions and thoughts must take such different directions, according to the state of that eternity, that it is impossible to take one step with sense and judgement, unless we regulate our course by the truth of that point which ought to be our ultimate end.

There is nothing clearer than this; and thus, according to the principles of reason, the conduct of men is wholly unreasonable, if they do not take another course.

On this point, therefore, we condemn those who live without thought of the ultimate end of life, who let themselves be guided by their own inclinations and their own pleasures without reflection and without concern, and, as if they could annihilate eternity by turning away their thought from

it, think only of making themselves happy for the moment.

Yet this eternity exists, and death, which must open into it and threatens them every hour, must in a little time infallibly put them under the dreadful necessity of being either annihilated or unhappy for ever, without knowing which of these eternities is for ever prepared for them.

This is a doubt of terrible consequence. They are in peril of eternal woe and thereupon, as if the matter were not worth the trouble, they neglect to inquire whether this is one of those opinions which people receive with too credulous a facility, or one of those which, obscure in themselves, have a very firm, though hidden, foundation. Thus they know not whether there be truth or falsity in the matter, nor whether there be strength or weakness in the proofs. They have them before their eyes; they refuse to look at them; and in that ignorance they choose all that is necessary to fall into this misfortune if it exists, to await death to make trial of it, yet to be very content in this state, to make profession of it, and indeed to boast of it. Can we think seriously of the importance of this subject without being horrified at conduct so extravagant?

Pascal, *Pensées,* III, 195

110 We are fools to depend upon the society of our fellow-men. Wretched as we are, powerless as we are, they will not aid us; we shall die alone.

Pascal, *Pensées,* III, 211

111 *Eve.*   Dust I am, and shall to dust returne:
O welcom hour whenever! why delayes
His hand to execute what his Decree
Fixd on this day? why do I overlive,
Why am I mockt with death, and length'nd out
To deathless pain? how gladly would I meet
Mortalitie my sentence, and be Earth
Insensible, how glad would lay me down
As in my Mothers lap? there I should rest
And sleep secure.

Milton, *Paradise Lost,* X, 770

112 *Adam.*   Have I now seen Death? Is this the way
I must return to native dust? O sight
Of terrour, foul and ugly to behold,
Horrid to think, how horrible to feel!

Milton, *Paradise Lost,* XI, 462

113 *Michael.*   Many shapes
Of Death, and many are the wayes that lead
To his grim Cave, all dismal; yet to sense
More terrible at th' entrance then within.
Some, as thou saw'st, by violent stroke shall die,
By Fire, Flood, Famin, by Intemperance more
In Meats and Drinks, which on the Earth shal
     bring
Diseases dire.

Milton, *Paradise Lost,* XI, 467

114 *Manoa.* Come, come, no time for lamentation now,
Nor much more cause, *Samson* hath quit himself
Like *Samson,* and heroicly hath finish'd
A life Heroic, on his Enemies
Fully reveng'd, hath left them years of mourning,
And lamentation to the Sons of *Caphtor*
Through all *Philistian* bounds. To *Israel*
Honour hath left, and freedom, let but them
Find courage to lay hold on this occasion,
To himself and Fathers house eternal fame;
And which is best and happiest yet, all this
With God not parted from him, as was feard,
But favouring and assisting to the end.
Nothing is here for tears, nothing to wail
Or knock the breast, no weakness, no contempt,
Dispraise, or blame, nothing but well and fair,
And what may quiet us in a death so noble.

        Milton, *Samson Agonistes,* 1708

115 Beneath those rugged elms, that yew-tree's shade,
  Where heaves the turf in many a moldering
     heap,
Each in his narrow cell for ever laid,
  The rude Forefathers of the hamlet sleep.

The breezy call of incense-breathing Morn,
  The swallow twittering from the straw-built
     shed,
The cock's shrill clarion, or the echoing horn,
  No more shall rouse them from their lowly bed.

For them no more the blazing hearth shall burn,
  Or busy housewife ply her evening care:
No children run to lisp their sire's return,
  Or climb his knees the envied kiss to share.

      Gray, *Elegy Written in a Country Church-Yard*

116 If we were immortal we should all be miserable;
no doubt it is hard to die, but it is sweet to think
that we shall not live for ever, and that a better
life will put an end to the sorrows of this world. If
we had the offer of immortality here below, who
would accept the sorrowful gift?

          Rousseau, *Emile,* II

117 A frequent and attentive prospect of that moment
which must put a period to all our schemes and
deprive us of all our acquisitions, is indeed of the
utmost efficacy to the just and rational regulation
of our lives; nor would ever anything wicked, or
often anything absurd, be undertaken or prosecuted by him who should begin every day with a
serious reflection that he is born to die.

         Johnson, *Rambler No. 17*

118 When we were alone, I introduced the subject of
death, and endeavoured to maintain that the fear
of it might be got over. I told him that David
Hume said to me, he was no more uneasy to think
he should *not be* after this life, than that he *had not
been* before he began to exist. *Johnson.* "Sir, if he
really thinks so, his perceptions are disturbed; he

is mad: if he does not think so, he lies. He may tell
you, he holds his finger in the flame of a candle,
without feeling pain; would you believe him?
When he dies, he at least gives up all he has."
Boswell. "Foote, Sir, told me, that when he was
very ill he was not afraid to die." *Johnson.* "It is not
true, Sir. Hold a pistol to Foote's breast, or to
Hume's breast, and threaten to kill them, and
you'll see how they behave." *Boswell.* "But may we
not fortify our minds for the approach of death?"
Here I am sensible I was in the wrong, to bring
before his view what he ever looked upon with
horrour; for although when in a celestial frame, in
his *Vanity of Human Wishes,* he has supposed death
to be "kind Nature's signal for retreat," from this
state of being to "a happier seat," his thoughts
upon this aweful change were in general full of
dismal apprehensions. His mind resembled the
vast amphitheatre, the Colisæum at Rome. In the
centre stood his judgement, which, like a mighty
gladiator, combated those apprehensions that,
like the wild beasts of the *Arena,* were all around
in cells, ready to be let out upon him. After a
conflict, he drives them back into their dens; but
not killing them, they were still assailing him. To
my question, whether we might not fortify our
minds for the approach of death, he answered, in
a passion, "No, Sir, let it alone. It matters not how
a man dies, but how he lives. The act of dying is
not of importance, it lasts so short a time." He
added, (with an earnest look,) "A man knows it
must be so, and submits. It will do him no good to
whine."

      Boswell, *Life of Johnson (Oct. 26, 1769)*

119 It is plain that *the hope of a future life* arises from the
feeling, which exists in the breast of every man,
that the temporal is inadequate to meet and satisfy the demands of his nature.

      Kant, *Critique of Pure Reason,* Pref.
                    to 2nd Ed.

120 The average duration of human life will to a certain degree vary from healthy or unhealthy climates, from wholesome or unwholesome food,
from virtuous or vicious manners, and other causes, but it may be fairly doubted whether there is
really the smallest perceptible advance in the natural duration of human life since first we have
had any authentic history of man.

        Malthus, *Population,* IX

121 *Wagner.* Ah, God! how long is art!
And soon it is we die.
Oft when my critical pursuits I ply,
I truly grow uneasy both in head and heart.
How hard to gain the means whereby
A man mounts upward to the source!
And ere man's ended barely half the course,
Poor devil! I suppose he has to die.

         Goethe, *Faust,* I, 558

122 *Mephistopheles.* "Past"—'tis a stupid word.
　　Past—why?
　　Past and pure Naught, sheer Uniformity!
　　Of what avail's perpetual creation
　　If later swept off to annihilation?
　　"So it is past!" You see what that must mean?
　　It is the same as had it never been,
　　And yet whirls on as if it weren't destroyed.
　　I should prefer the Everlasting Void.
　　　　　　　　Goethe, *Faust,* II, 5, 11595

123 Peace, peace! he is not dead, he doth not sleep—
　　He hath awakened from the dream of life—
　　'Tis we, who, lost in stormy visions, keep
　　With phantoms an unprofitable strife,
　　And in mad trance strike with our spirit's knife
　　Invulnerable nothings. *We* decay
　　Like corpses in a charnel; fear and grief
　　Convulse us and consume us day by day,
　　And cold hopes swarm like worms within our liv-
　　　ing clay.

　　He has outsoared the shadow of our night;
　　Envy and calumny and hate and pain,
　　And that unrest which men miscall delight,
　　Can touch him not and torture not again;
　　From the contagion of the world's slow stain
　　He is secure, and now can never mourn
　　A heart grown cold, a head grown gray in vain;
　　Nor, when the spirit's self has ceased to burn,
　　With sparkless ashes loan an unlamented urn.
　　　　　　　　Shelley, *Adonais,* XXXIX–XL

124 'Whom the gods love die young,' was said of yore,
　　And many deaths do they escape by this:
　　The death of friends, and that which slays even
　　　more—
　　The death of friendship, love, youth, all that is,
　　Except mere breath; and since the silent shore
　　Awaits at last even those who longest miss
　　The old archer's shafts, perhaps the early grave
　　Which men weep over may be meant to save.
　　　　　　　　Byron, *Don Juan,* IV, 12

125 Darkling I listen; and, for many a time
　　I have been half in love with easeful Death,
　　Call'd him soft names in many a mused rhyme,
　　To take into the air my quiet breath;
　　Now more than ever seems it rich to die,
　　To cease upon the midnight with no pain,
　　　While thou art pouring forth thy soul abroad
　　　　In such an ecstasy!
　　Still wouldst thou sing, and I have ears in
　　　vain—
　　　To thy high requiem become a sod.
　　　　　　　　Keats, *Ode to a Nightingale*

126 'Vell, gov'ner, ve must all come to it, one day or
　　another.'
　　'So we must, Sammy,' said Mr. Weller the elder.
　　'There's a Providence in it all,' said Sam.

'O' course there is,' replied his father with a nod
of grave approval. 'Wot 'ud become of the undertakers vithout it, Sammy?'
　　　　　　　　Dickens, *Pickwick Papers,* LII

127 Sunset and evening star,
　　And one clear call for me!
　　And may there be no moaning of the bar,
　　When I put out to sea,

　　But such a tide as moving seems asleep,
　　Too full for sound and foam,
　　When that which drew from out the boundless
　　　deep
　　Turns again home.

　　Twilight and evening bell,
　　And after that the dark!
　　And may there be no sadness of farewell,
　　When I embark;

　　For tho' from out our bourne of Time and Place
　　The flood may bear me far,
　　I hope to see my Pilot face to face
　　When I have crost the bar.
　　　　　　　　Tennyson, *Crossing the Bar*

128 Methinks we have hugely mistaken this matter of
Life and Death. Methinks that what they call my
shadow here on earth is my true substance. Methinks that in looking at things spiritual, we are
too much like oysters observing the sun through
the water, and thinking that thick water the thin-
nest of air. Methinks my body is but the lees of my
better being. In fact take my body who will, take
it I say, it is not myself. And therefore three cheers
for Nantucket, and come a stove boat and stove
body when they will, for stave my soul, who can
do this?
　　　　　　　　Melville, *Moby Dick,* VII

129 The one visible quality in the aspect of the dead
which most appals the gazer, is the marble pallor
lingering there; as if indeed that pallor were
much like the badge of consternation in the other
world, as of mortal trepidation here. And from
that pallor of the dead, we borrow the expressive
hue of the shroud in which we wrap them.
　　　　　　　　Melville, *Moby Dick,* XLII

130 The life in us is like the water in the river. It may
rise this year higher than man has ever known it,
and flood the parched uplands; even this may be
the eventful year, which will drown out all our
muskrats. It was not always dry land where we
dwell. I see far inland the banks which the stream
anciently washed, before science began to record
its freshets. Every one has heard the story which
has gone the rounds of New England, of a strong
and beautiful bug which came out of the dry leaf
of an old table of apple-tree wood, which had
stood in a farmer's kitchen for sixty years, first in

Connecticut, and afterward in Massachusetts—from an egg deposited in the living tree many years earlier still, as appeared by counting the annual layers beyond it; which was heard gnawing out for several weeks, hatched perchance by the heat of an urn. Who does not feel his faith in a resurrection and immortality strengthened by hearing of this? Who knows what beautiful and winged life, whose egg has been buried for ages under many concentric layers of woodenness in the dead dry life of society, deposited at first in the alburnum of the green and living tree, which has been gradually converted into the semblance of its well-seasoned tomb—heard perchance gnawing out now for years by the astonished family of man, as they sat round the festive board—may unexpectedly come forth from amidst society's most trivial and handselled furniture, to enjoy its perfect summer life at last!

I do not say that John or Jonathan will realize all this; but such is the character of that morrow which mere lapse of time can never make to dawn. The light which puts out our eyes is darkness to us. Only that day dawns to which we are awake. There is more day to dawn. The sun is but a morning star.

Thoreau, *Walden:* Conclusion

131 Come lovely and soothing death,
Undulate round the world, serenely arriving,
   arriving,
In the day, in the night, to all, to each,
Sooner or later delicate death

Prais'd be the fathomless universe,
For life and joy, and for objects and knowledge
   curious,
And for love, sweet love—but praise! praise!
   praise!
For the sure-enwinding arms of cool-enfolding
   death.

Whitman, *When Lilacs Last in the Dooryard Bloom'd,* 135

132 *Ippolit Kirillovitch.* I imagine that he [Mitya] felt something like what criminals feel when they are being taken to the scaffold. They have another long, long street to pass down and at walking pace, past thousands of people. Then there will be a turning into another street and only at the end of that street the dread place of execution! I fancy that at the beginning of the journey the condemned man, sitting on his shameful cart, must feel that he has infinite life still before him. The houses recede, the cart moves on—oh, that's nothing, it's still far to the turning into the second street and he still looks boldly to right and to left at those thousands of callously curious people with their eyes fixed on him, and he still fancies that he is just such a man as they. But now the turning comes to the next street. Oh, that's nothing, noth-

ing, there's still a whole street before him, and however many houses have been passed, he will still think there are many left. And so to the very end, to the very scaffold.

Dostoevsky, *Brothers Karamazov,* Pt. IV, XII, 9

133 Whoever has lived long enough to find out what life is, knows how deep a dept of gratitude we owe to Adam, the first great benefactor of our race. He brought death into the world.

Mark Twain, *Pudd'nhead Wilson's Calendar,* III

134 Let us endeavour so to live that when we come to die even the undertaker will be sorry.

Mark Twain, *Pudd'nhead Wilson's Calendar,* VI

135 Why is it that we rejoice at a birth and grieve at a funeral? It is because we are not the person involved.

Mark Twain, *Pudd'nhead Wilson's Calendar,* IX

136 All say, 'How hard it is that we have to die'—a strange complaint to come from the mouths of people who have had to live.

Mark Twain, *Pudd'nhead Wilson's Calendar,* X

137 The reports of my death are greatly exaggerated.

Mark Twain, *Cable from London to the Associated Press (1897)*

138 Our own death is indeed unimaginable, and whenever we make the attempt to imagine it we can perceive that we really survive as spectators. Hence the psychoanalytic school could venture on the assertion that at bottom no one believes in his own death, or to put the same thing in another way, in the unconscious every one of us is convinced of his own immortality.

Freud, *Thoughts on War and Death,* II

139 Life is impoverished, it loses in interest, when the highest stake in the game of living, life itself, may not be risked. It becomes as flat, as superficial, as one of those American flirtations in which it is from the first understood that nothing is to happen, contrasted with a Continental love-affair in which both partners must constantly bear in mind the serious consequences.

Freud, *Thoughts on War and Death,* II

140 To endure life remains, when all is said, the first duty of all living beings. Illusion can have no value if it makes this more difficult for us.

We remember the old saying: If you desire peace, prepare for war.

It would be timely thus to paraphrase it: If you would endure life, be prepared for death.

Freud, *Thoughts on War and Death*, II

141 We perceive duration as a stream against which we cannot go. It is the foundation of our being, and, as we feel, the very substance of the world in which we live.

Bergson, *Creative Evolution*, I

142 Death is not an event of life. Death is not lived through.

If by eternity is understood not endless temporal duration but timelessness, then he lives eternally who lives in the present.

Our life is endless in the way that our visual field is without limit.

The temporal immortality of the human soul, that is to say, its eternal survival after death, is not only in no way guaranteed, but this assumption in the first place will not do for us what we always tried to make it do. Is a riddle solved by the fact that I survive for ever? Is this eternal life not as enigmatic as our present one? The solution of the riddle of life in space and time lies *outside* space and time.

Wittgenstein, *Tractatus Logico-Philosophicus,*
6.4311–6.4312

143 That the end of life should be death may sound sad: yet what other end can anything have? The end of an evening party is to go to bed; but its use is to gather congenial people together, that they may pass the time pleasantly. An invitation to the dance is not rendered ironical because the dance cannot last for ever; the youngest of us and the most vigorously wound up, after a few hours, has had enough of sinuous stepping and prancing. The transitoriness of things is essential to their physical being, and not at all sad in itself; it becomes sad by virtue of a sentimental illusion, which makes us imagine that they wish to endure, and that their end is always untimely; but in a healthy nature it is not so. What is truly sad is to have some impulse frustrated in the midst of its career, and robbed of its chosen object; and what is painful is to have an organ lacerated or destroyed when it is still vigorous, and not ready for its natural sleep and dissolution. We must not confuse the itch which our unsatisfied instincts continue to cause with the pleasure of satisfying and dismissing each of them in turn. Could they all be satisfied harmoniously we should be satisfied once for all and completely. Then doing and dying would coincide throughout and be a perfect pleasure.

Santayana, *A Long Way Round to Nirvana*

144 A few light taps upon the pane made him turn to the window. It had begun to snow again. He watched sleepily the flakes, silver and dark, falling obliquely against the lamplight. The time had come for him to set out on his journey westward. Yes, the newspapers were right; snow was general all over Ireland. It was falling on every part of the dark central plain, on the treeless hills, falling softly upon the Bog of Allen, and, farther westward, softly falling into the dark mutinous Shannon waves. It was falling, too, upon every part of the lonely churchyard on the hill where Michael Furey lay buried. It lay thickly drifted on the crooked crosses and headstones, on the spears of the little gate, on the barren thorns. His soul swooned slowly as he heard the snow falling faintly through the universe and faintly falling, like the descent of their last end, upon all the living and the dead.

Joyce, *The Dead*

1.9 | *Suicide*

Other animals, as for example the lemmings, may commit self-destruction *en masse*, and when they do so, they do so driven by instinct, but man alone deliberates about whether to take his own individual life, disputes the propriety or justification of such action, and actually commits the act with care and forethought.

The basic moral issue is one on which the pagan writers of antiquity, notably the Roman Stoics, and Christian theologians and philosophers take opposite sides. Suicide for the one is a dignified way out of life's insuperable difficulties; for the other, it is a grievous, mortal sin, resulting in eternal damnation. There is, in addition, a division of opinion among secular writers on whether deliberate suicide is an act of courage or cowardice or whether one has the right to take one's own life.

---

1 And the Philistines followed hard after Saul, and after his sons; and the Philistines slew Jonathan, and Ā-bĭn-ă-dăb, and Măl-<u>chi</u>-shû-ă, the sons of Saul.

And the battle went sore against Saul, and the archers hit him, and he was wounded of the archers.

Then said Saul to his armourbearer, Draw thy sword, and thrust me through therewith; lest these uncircumcised come and abuse me. But his armourbearer would not; for he was sore afraid. So Saul took a sword, and fell upon it.

And when his armourbearer saw that Saul was dead, he fell likewise on the sword, and died.

So Saul died, and his three sons, and all his house died together.

I Chronicles 10:2–6

2 When I say, My bed shall comfort me, my couch shall ease my complaint;

Then thou scarest me with dreams, and terrifiest me through visions:

So that my soul chooseth strangling, and death rather than my life.

I loathe it; I would not live alway: let me alone; for my days are vanity.

Job 7:13–16

3 *Socrates.* Any man who has the spirit of philosophy, will be willing to die; but he will not take his own life, for that is held to be unlawful. . . . The gods are our guardians, and . . . we men are a possession of theirs. . . . And if one of your own possessions, an ox or an ass, for example, took the liberty of putting himself out of the way when you had given no intimation of your wish that he should die, would you not be angry with him, and would you not punish him if you could? . . .

Then, if we look at the matter thus, there may be reason in saying that a man should wait, and not take his own life until God summons him.

Plato, *Phaedo,* 61B

4 Whether a man can treat himself unjustly or not, is evident from what has been said. For (*a*) one class of just acts are those acts in accordance with any virtue which are prescribed by the law; e.g. the law does not expressly permit suicide, and what it does not expressly permit it forbids. Again, when a man in violation of the law harms another (otherwise than in retaliation) voluntarily, he acts unjustly, and a voluntary agent is one who knows both the person he is affecting by his action and the instrument he is using; and he who through anger voluntarily stabs himself does this contrary to the right rule of life, and this the law does not allow; therefore he is acting unjustly. But towards whom? Surely towards the state, not towards himself. For he suffers voluntarily, but no one is voluntarily treated unjustly. This is also the reason why the state punishes; a certain loss of civil rights attaches to the man who destroys himself, on the ground that he is treating the state unjustly.

Aristotle, *Ethics,* 1138ª4

5 Then Juno, grieving that she [Dido] should sustain
A death so ling'ring, and so full of pain,
Sent Iris down, to free her from the strife
Of lab'ring nature, and dissolve her life.
For since she died, not doom'd by Heav'n's decree,
Or her own crime, but human casualty,
And rage of love, that plung'd her in despair,
The Sisters had not cut the topmost hair,
Which Proserpine and they can only know;
Nor made her sacred to the shades below.
Downward the various goddess took her flight,
And drew a thousand colors from the light;
Then stood above the dying lover's head,
And said: "I thus devote thee to the dead.
This off'ring to th' infernal gods I bear."
Thus while she spoke, she cut the fatal hair:
The struggling soul was loos'd, and life dissolv'd in air.

Virgil, *Aeneid,* IV

6 'Rehearse death.' To say this is to tell a person to rehearse his freedom. A person who has learned how to die has unlearned how to be a slave. He is above, or at any rate beyond the reach of, all political powers. What are prisons, warders, bars to him? He has an open door. There is but one chain holding us in fetters, and that is our love of life. There is no need to cast this love out altogether, but it does need to be lessened somewhat so that, in the event of circumstances ever demanding this, nothing may stand in the way of our being prepared to do at once what we must do at some time or other.

Seneca, *Letters to Lucilius,* 26

7 Then Judas, which had betrayed him, when he saw that he was condemned, repented himself, and brought again the thirty pieces of silver to the chief priests and elders,

Saying, I have sinned in that I have betrayed the innocent blood. And they said, What is that to us? see thou to that.

And he cast down the pieces of silver in the temple, and departed, and went and hanged himself.

And the chief priests took the silver pieces, and said, It is not lawful for to put them into the treasury, because it is the price of blood.

And they took counsel, and bought with them the potter's field, to bury strangers in.

Wherefore that field was called, The field of blood, unto this day.

Matthew 27:3–8

8 [Lycurgus] was now about that age in which life was still tolerable, and yet might be quitted without regret. Everything, moreover, about him was in a sufficiently prosperous condition. He therefore made an end of himself by a total abstinence from food, thinking it a statesman's duty to make his very death, if possible, an act of service to the state, and even in the end of his life to give some example of virtue and effect some useful purpose. He would, on the one hand, crown and consummate his own happiness by a death suitable to so honourable a life, and on the other hand, would secure to his countrymen the enjoyment of the advantages he had spent his life in obtaining for them, since they had solemnly sworn the maintenance of his institutions until his return.

Plutarch, Lycurgus

9 Chiefly being ashamed to sully the glory of his former great actions, and of his many victories and trophies, he [Themistocles] determined to put a conclusion to his life, agreeable to its previous course. He sacrificed to the gods, and invited his friends; and, having entertained them and shaken hands with them, drank bull's blood, as is the usual story; as others state, a poison producing instant death; and ended his days in the city of Magnesia, having lived sixty-five years, most of which he had spent in politics and in wars, in government and command. The king being informed of the cause and manner of his death, admired him more than ever, and continued to show kindness to his friends and relations.

Plutarch, Themistocles

10 Brutus, having to pass his army from Abydos to the continent on the other side, laid himself down one night, as he used to do, in his tent, and was not asleep, but thinking of his affairs, and what events he might expect. For he is related to have been the least inclined to sleep of all men who have commanded armies, and to have had the greatest natural capacity for continuing awake, and employing himself without need of rest. He thought he heard a noise at the door of his tent, and looking that way, by the light of his lamp,

which was almost out, saw a terrible figure, like that of a man, but of unusual stature and severe countenance. He was somewhat frightened at first, but seeing it neither did nor spoke anything to him, only stood silently by his bedside, he asked who it was. The spectre answered him, "Thy evil genius, Brutus, and thou shalt see me at Philippi." Brutus answered courageously, "Well, I shall see you," and immediately the appearance vanished.

When the time was come, he drew up his army near Philippi against Antony and Cæsar, and in the first battle won the day, routed the enemy, and plundered Cæsar's camp. The night before the second battle, the same phantom appeared to him again, but spoke not a word. He presently understood his destiny was at hand, and exposed himself to all the danger of the battle. Yet he did not die in the fight, but seeing his men defeated, got up to the top of a rock, and there presenting his sword to his naked breast, and assisted, as they say, by a friend, who helped him to give the thrust, met his death.

Plutarch, Caesar

11 Now the birds began to sing, and he again fell into a little slumber. At length Butas came back, and told him all was quiet in the port. Then Cato, laying himself down, as if he would sleep out the rest of the night, bade him shut the door after him. But as soon as Butas was gone out, he took his sword, and stabbed it into his breast; yet not being able to use his hand so well, on account of the swelling, he did not immediately die of the wound; but struggling, fell off the bed, and throwing down a little mathematical table that stood by, made such a noise that the servants, hearing it, cried out. And immediately his son and all his friends came into the chamber, where, seeing him lie weltering in his blood, a great part of his bowels out of his body, but himself still alive and able to look at them, they all stood in horror. The physician went to him, and would have put in his bowels, which were not pierced, and sewed up the wound; but Cato, recovering himself, and understanding the intention, thrust away the physician, plucked out his own bowels, and tearing open the wound, immediately expired.

In less time than one would think his own family could have known this accident, all the three hundred were at the door. And a little after, the people of Utica flocked thither, crying out with one voice he was their benefactor and their saviour, the only free and only undefeated man. . . .

Cæsar had been informed that Cato stayed at Utica, and did not seek to fly; that he had sent away the rest of the Romans, but himself, with his son and a few of his friends, continued there very unconcernedly, so that he could not imagine what might be his design. But having a great consideration for the man, he hastened thither with his army. When he heard of his death, it is related he said these words, "Cato, I grudge you your death, as you have grudged me the preservation of your life." And, indeed, if Cato would have suffered himself to owe his life to Cæsar, he would not so much have impaired his own honour, as augmented the other's glory.

Plutarch, *Cato the Younger*

12 Cicero's death excites our pity; for an old man to be miserably carried up and down by his servants, flying and hiding himself from that death which was, in the course of nature, so near at hand; and yet at last to be murdered. Demosthenes, though he seemed at first a little to supplicate, yet, by his preparing and keeping the poison by him, demands our admiration; and still more admirable was his using it. When the temple of the god no longer afforded him a sanctuary, he took refuge, as it were, at a mightier altar, freeing himself from from arms and soldiers, and laughing to scorn the cruelty of Antipater.

Plutarch, *Demosthenes and Cicero Compared*

13 When he understood she was alive, he eagerly gave order to the servants to take him up, and in their arms was carried to the door of the building. Cleopatra would not open the door, but, looking from a sort of window, she let down ropes and cords, to which Antony was fastened; and she and her two women, the only persons she had allowed to enter the monument, drew him up. Those that were present say that nothing was ever more sad than this spectacle, to see Antony, covered all over with blood and just expiring, thus drawn up, still holding up his hands to her, and lifting up his body with the little force he had left. As, indeed, it was no easy task for the women; and Cleopatra, with all her force, clinging to the rope, and straining with her head to the ground, with difficulty pulled him up, while those below encouraged her with their cries, and joined in all her efforts and anxiety.

When she had got him up, she laid him on the bed, tearing all her clothes, which she spread upon him; and, beating her breast with her hands, lacerating herself, and disfiguring her own face with the blood from his wounds, she called him her lord, her husband, her emperor, and seemed to have pretty nearly forgotten all her own evils, she was so intent upon his misfortunes. Antony, stopping her lamentations as well as he could, called for wine to drink, either that he was thirsty, or that he imagined that it might put him the sooner out of pain. When he had drunk, he advised her to bring her own affairs, so far as might be honourably done, to a safe conclusion, and that, among all the friends of Cæsar, she should rely on Proculeius; that she should not pity him in his last turn of fate, but rather rejoice for him in remembrance of his past happiness, who had been of all men the most illustrious and pow-

erful, and in the end had fallen not ignobly, a Roman by a Roman overcome.

Plutarch, *Antony*

14 Having made these lamentations, crowning the tomb with garlands and kissing it, she gave orders to prepare her a bath, and, coming out of the bath, she lay down and made a sumptuous meal. And a country fellow brought her a little basket, which the guards intercepting and asking what it was, the fellow put the leaves which lay uppermost aside, and showed them it was full of figs; and on their admiring the largeness and beauty of the figs, he laughed, and invited them to take some, which they refused, and, suspecting nothing, bade him carry them in. After her repast, Cleopatra sent to Cæsar a letter which she had written and sealed; and, putting everybody out of the monument but her two women, she shut the doors.

Cæsar, opening her letter, and finding pathetic prayers and entreaties that she might be buried in the same tomb with Antony, soon guessed what was doing. At first he was going himself in all haste, but, changing his mind, he sent others to see. The thing had been quickly done. The messengers came at full speed, and found the guards apprehensive of nothing; but on opening the doors they saw her stone-dead, lying upon a bed of gold, set out in all her royal ornaments. Iras, one of her women, lay dying at her feet, and Charmion, just ready to fall, scarce able to hold up her head, was adjusting her mistress's diadem. And when one that came in said angrily, "Was this well done of your lady, Charmion," "Extremely well," she answered, "and as became the descendant of so many kings;" and as she said this, she fell down dead by the bedside.

Plutarch, *Antony*

15 Take care that there be not among us any young men of such a mind that, when they have recognized their kinship to God, and that we are fettered by these bonds, the body, I mean, and its possessions, and whatever else on account of them is necessary to us for the economy and commerce of life, they should intend to throw off these things as if they were burdens painful and intolerable, and to depart to their kinsmen. . . . This is the labour that your teacher and instructor ought to be employed upon, if he really were what he should be. You should come to him and say, "Epictetus, we can no longer endure being bound to this poor body, and feeding it and giving it drink, and rest, and cleaning it, and for the sake of the body complying with the wishes of these and of those. Are not these things indifferent and nothing to us, and is not death no evil? And are we not in a manner kinsmen of God, and did we not come from Him? Allow us to depart to the place from which we came; allow us to be released at last

from these bonds by which we are bound and weighed down. Here there are robbers and thieves and courts of justice, and those who are named tyrants, and think that they have some power over us by means of the body and its possessions. Permit us to show them that they have no power over any man." And I on my part would say, "Friends, wait for God; when He shall give the signal and release you from this service, then go to Him; but for the present endure to dwell in this place where He has put you: short indeed is this time of your dwelling here, and easy to bear for those who are so disposed: for what tyrant or what thief, or what courts of justice, are formidable to those who have thus considered as things of no value the body and the possessions of the body? Wait then, do not depart without a reason."

Epictetus, *Discourses*, I, 9

16 When Claudius began to deliberate about the acquittal of Asiaticus, Vitellius, with tears in his eyes, spoke of his old friendship with the accused, and of their joint homage to the emperor's mother, Antonia. He then briefly reviewed the services of Asiaticus to the State, his recent campaign in the invasion of Britain, and everything else which seemed likely to win compassion, and suggested that he should be free to choose his death. Claudius's reply was in the same tone of mercy. Some friends urged on Asiaticus the quiet death of self-starvation, but he declined it with thanks. He took his usual exercise, then bathed and dined cheerfully, and saying that he had better have fallen by the craft of Tiberius or the fury of Caius Cæsar than by the treachery of a woman and the shameless mouth of Vitellius, he opened his veins, but not till he had inspected his funeral pyre, and directed its removal to another spot, lest the smoke should hurt the thick foliage of the trees. So complete was his calmness even to the last.

Tacitus, *Annals*, XI, 3

17 Seneca, quite unmoved, asked for tablets on which to inscribe his will, and, on the centurion's refusal, turned to his friends, protesting that as he was forbidden to requite them, he bequeathed to them the only, but still the noblest possession yet remaining to him, the pattern of his life, which, if they remembered, they would win a name for moral worth and steadfast friendship. At the same time he called them back from their tears to manly resolution, now with friendly talk, and now with the sterner language of rebuke. "Where," he asked again and again, "are your maxims of philosophy, or the preparation of so many years' study against evils to come? Who knew not Nero's cruelty? After a mother's and a brother's murder, nothing remains but to add the destruction of a guardian and a tutor."

Having spoken these and like words, meant, so to say, for all, he embraced his wife; then softening awhile from the stern resolution of the hour, he begged and implored her to spare herself the burden of perpetual sorrow, and, in the contemplation of a life virtuously spent, to endure a husband's loss with honourable consolations. She declared, in answer, that she too had decided to die, and claimed for herself the blow of the executioner. Thereupon Seneca, not to thwart her noble ambition, from an affection too which would not leave behind him for insult one whom he dearly loved, replied: "I have shown you ways of smoothing life; you prefer the glory of dying. I will not grudge you such a noble example. Let the fortitude of so courageous an end be alike in both of us, but let there be more in your decease to win fame."

Then by one and the same stroke they sundered with a dagger the arteries of their arms.

Tacitus, *Annals*, XV, 62–63

18 It happened at the time that the emperor was on his way to Campania and that Petronius, after going as far as Cumæ, was there detained. He bore no longer the suspense of fear or of hope. Yet he did not fling away life with precipitate haste, but having made an incision in his veins and then, according to his humour, bound them up, he again opened them, while he conversed with his friends, not in a serious strain or on topics that might win for him the glory of courage. And he listened to them as they repeated, not thoughts on the immortality of the soul or on the theories of philosophers, but light poetry and playful verses. To some of his slaves he gave liberal presents, a flogging to others. He dined, indulged himself in sleep, that death, though forced on him, might have a natural appearance. Even in his will he did not, as did many in their last moments, flatter Nero or Tigellinus or any other of the men in power. On the contrary, he described fully the prince's shameful excesses, with the names of his male and female companions and their novelties in debauchery, and sent the account under seal to Nero. Then he broke his signet-ring, that it might not be subsequently available for imperilling others.

Tacitus, *Annals*, XVI, 19

19 When thou hast assumed these names, good, modest, true, rational, a man of equanimity, and magnanimous, take care that thou dost not change these names; and if thou shouldst lose them, quickly return to them. . . . But if thou shalt perceive that thou fallest out of them and dost not maintain thy hold, go courageously into some nook where thou shalt maintain them, or even depart at once from life, not in passion, but with simplicity and freedom and modesty, after doing this one laudable thing at least in thy life, to have gone out of it thus.

Marcus Aurelius, *Meditations*, X, 8

20 In no passage of the holy canonical books there can be found either divine precept or permission to take away our own life, whether for the sake of entering on the enjoyment of immortality, or of shunning, or ridding ourselves of anything whatever. Nay, the law, rightly interpreted, even prohibits suicide, where it says, "Thou shalt not kill." . . . There is no limitation added nor any exception made in favour of any one, and least of all in favour of him on whom the command is laid! . . . The commandment is, "Thou shalt not kill man"; therefore neither another nor yourself, for he who kills himself still kills nothing else than man.

Augustine, *City of God,* I, 20

21 But this we affirm, this we maintain, this we every way pronounce to be right, that no man ought to inflict on himself voluntary death, for this is to escape the ills of time by plunging into those of eternity; that no man ought to do so on account of another man's sins, for this were to escape a guilt which could not pollute him, by incurring great guilt of his own; that no man ought to do so on account of his own past sins, for he has all the more need of this life that these sins may be healed by repentance; that no man should put an end to this life to obtain that better life we look for after death, for those who die by their own hand have no better life after death.

Augustine, *City of God,* I, 26

22 Parricide is more wicked than homicide, but suicide is the most wicked of all.

Augustine, *On Patience*

23 Nessus had not yet reached the other side, when we moved into a wood, which by no path was marked.

Not green the foliage, but of colour dusky; not smooth the branches, but gnarled and warped; apples none were there, but withered sticks with poison. . . .

Already I heard wailings uttered on every side, and saw no one to make them: wherefore I, all bewildered, stood still.

I think he thought that I was thinking so many voices came, amongst those stumps, from people who hid themselves on our account.

Therefore the Master said: "If thou breakest off any little shoot from one of these plants, the thoughts, which thou hast, will all become defective."

Then I stretched my hand a little forward, and plucked a branchlet from a great thorn; and the trunk of it cried, "Why dost thou rend me?"

And when it had grown dark with blood, it again began to cry: "Why dost thou tear me? hast thou no breath of pity?

Men we were, and now are turned to trees: truly thy hand should be more merciful, had we been souls of serpents."

As a green brand, that is burning at one end, at the other drops, and hisses with the wind which is escaping:

so from that broken splint, words and blood came forth together: whereat I let fall the top, and stood like one who is afraid. . . .

The Poet listened a while, and then said to me: "Since he is silent, lose not the hour; but speak, and ask him, if thou wouldst know more."

Whereat I to him: "Do thou ask him farther, respecting what thou thinkest will satisfy me; for I could not, such pity is upon my heart."

He therefore resumed: "So may the man do freely for thee what thy words entreat him, O imprisoned spirit, please thee

tell us farther, how the soul gets bound up in these knots; and tell us, if thou mayest, whether any ever frees itself from such members."

Then the trunk blew strongly, and soon that wind was changed into these words: "Briefly shall you be answered.

When the fierce spirit quits the body, from which it has torn itself, Minos sends it to the seventh gulf.

It falls into the wood, and no place is chosen for it; but wherever fortune flings it, there it sprouts, like grain of spelt;

shoots up to a sapling, and to a savage plant; the Harpies, feeding then upon its leaves, give pain, and to the pain an outlet.

Like the others, we shall go for our spoils, [but not to the end that any may be] clothe[d] with them again: for it is not just that a man have what he takes from himself.

Hither shall we drag them, and through the mournful wood our bodies shall be suspended, each on the thorny tree of its tormented shade."

Dante, *Inferno,* XIII, 1

24 And death is not the remedy for just one malady, but the remedy for all ills. It is a very sure haven, which is never to be feared, and often to be sought. It all comes to the same thing whether man gives himself his death or suffers it, whether he runs to meet his day or awaits it; wherever it comes from, it is still his; wherever the thread breaks, it is all there, that's the end of the skein.

The most voluntary death is the fairest.

Life depends on the will of others; death, on our own.

Montaigne, *Essays,* II, 3, Custom of Cea

25 Just as I do not violate the laws against thieves when I carry away my own money and cut my own purse, or those against firebugs when I burn my own wood, so I am not bound by the laws against murderers for having taken my own life.

Montaigne, *Essays,* II, 3, Custom of Cea

26 *Cassius.* Therein, ye gods, you make the weak most strong;

Therein, ye gods, you tyrants do defeat:
Nor stony tower, nor walls of beaten brass,
Nor airless dungeon, nor strong links of iron,
Can be retentive to the strength of spirit;
But life, being weary of these worldy bars,
Never lacks power to dismiss itself.

Shakespeare, Julius Caesar, I, iii, 91

27 *Hamlet.* To be, or not to be: that is the question.
Whether 'tis nobler in the mind to suffer
The slings and arrows of outrageous fortune,
Or to take arms against a sea of troubles,
And by opposing end them? To die; to sleep;
No more; and by a sleep to say we end
The heart-ache and the thousand natural shocks
That flesh is heir to, 'tis a consummation
Devoutly to be wish'd. To die, to sleep;
To sleep? perchance to dream. Ay, there's the
rub;
For in that sleep of death what dreams may come
When we have shuffled off this mortal coil,
Must give us pause. There's the respect
That makes calamity of so long life;
For who would bear the whips and scorns of time,
The oppressor's wrong, the proud man's
contumely,
The pangs of despised love, the law's delay,
The insolence of office and the spurns
That patient merit of the unworthy takes,
When he himself might his quietus make
With a bare bodkin? who would fardels bear,
To grunt and sweat under a weary life,
But that the dread of something after death,
The undiscover'd country from whose bourn
No traveller returns, puzzles the will
And makes us rather bear those ills we have
Than fly to others that we know not of?
Thus conscience does make cowards of us all;
And thus the native hue of resolution
Is sicklied o'er with the pale cast of thought,
And enterprises of great pitch and moment
With this regard their currents turn awry,
And lose the name of action.

Shakespeare, Hamlet, III, i, 56

28 *Cleopatra.* Then is it sin
To rush into the secret house of death,
Ere death dare come to us? How do you, women?
What, what! good cheer! Why, how now, Char-
mian!
My noble girls! Ah, women, women, look,
Our Lamp is spent, it's out! Good sirs, take heart.
We'll bury him; and then, what's brave, what's
noble,
Let's do it after the high Roman fashion,
And make death proud to take us. Come, away;
This case of that huge spirit now is cold.
Ah, women, women! come; we have no friend
But resolution and the briefest end.

Shakespeare, Antony and Cleopatra, IV, xv, 80

29 *Cleopatra.* Give me my robe, put on my crown; I
have
Immortal longings in me. Now no more
The juice of Egypt's grape shall moist this lip.
Yare, yare, good Iras; quick. Methinks I hear
Antony call; I see him rouse himself
To praise my noble act; I hear him mock
The luck of Cæsar, which the gods give men
To excuse their after wrath. Husband, I come:
Now to that name my courage prove my title!
I am fire and air; my other elements
I give to baser life. So; have you done?
Come then, and take the last warmth of my lips.
Farewell, kind Charmian; Iras, long farewell.
Kisses them. Iras falls and dies.
Have I the aspic in my lips? Dost fall?
If thou and nature can so gently part,
The stroke of death is as a lover's pinch,
Which hurts, and is desired. Dost thou lie still?
If thus thou vanishest, thou tell'st the world
It is not worth leave-taking.
Charmian. Dissolve, thick cloud, and rain; that I
may say,
The gods themselves do weep!
Cleo. This proves me base.
If she first meet the curled Antony,
He'll make demand of her, and spend that kiss
Which is my heaven to have. Come, thou mortal
wretch,
To an asp, which she applies to her breast.
With thy sharp teeth this knot intrinsicate
Of life at once untie. Poor venomous fool,
Be angry, and dispatch. O, couldst thou speak,
That I might hear thee call great Cæsar ass
Unpolicied!
Char. O eastern star!
Cleo. Peace, peace!
Dost thou not see my baby at my breast,
That sucks the nurse asleep?
Char. O, break! O, break!
Cleo. As sweet as balm, as soft as air, as gentle—
O Antony!—Nay, I will take thee too.
Applying another asp to her arm.
What should I stay— [*Dies.*]
Char. In this vile world? So, fare thee well.
Now boast thee, Death, in thy possession lies
A lass unparrallel'd. Downy windows, close;
And golden Phœbus never be beheld
Of eyes again so royal! Your crown's awry;
I'll mend it, and then play.
Enter the Guard, *rushing in.*
1st Guard. Where is the Queen?
Char. Speak softly, wake her not.
1st Guard. Cæsar hath sent—
Char. Too slow a messenger.
Applies an asp.
O, come apace, dispatch! I partly feel thee.
1st Guard. Approach, ho! All's not well; Cæsar's
beguiled.
2nd Guard. There's Dolabella sent from Cæsar;
call him.

1st Guard. What work is here! Charmian, is this well done?

Char. It is well done, and fitting for a princess
Descended of so many royal kings.
Ah, soldier!   [*Dies.*]

    Shakespeare, *Antony and Cleopatra,* V, ii, 283

30 *1st Guard.*   O Cæsar,
This Charmian lived but now; she stood and spake.
I found her trimming up the diadem
On her dead mistress; tremblingly she stood
And on the sudden dropp'd.
    Caesar.   ·   O noble weakness!
If they had swallow'd poison, 'twould appear
By external swelling; but she looks like sleep,
As she would catch another Antony
In her strong toil of grace.
    Dolabella.   Here, on her breast,
There is a vent of blood and something blown.
The like is on her arm.
    1st Guard. This is an aspic's trail; and these figleaves
Have slime upon them, such as the aspic leaves
Upon the caves of Nile.
    Caes.   Most probable
That so she died; for her physician tells me
She hath pursued conclusions infinite
Of easy ways to die. Take up her bed;
And bear her women from the monument.
She shall be buried by her Antony.
No grave upon the earth shall clip in it
A pair so famous.

    Shakespeare, *Antony and Cleopatra,* V, ii, 344

31 A man kills himself under compulsion by another when that other turns the right hand, with which the man had by chance laid hold of a sword, and compels him to direct the sword against his own heart; or the command of a tyrant may compel a man, as it did Seneca, to open his own veins, that is to say, he may desire to avoid a greater evil by a less. External and hidden causes also may so dispose his imagination and may so affect his body as to cause it to put on another nature contrary to that which it had at first, and one whose idea cannot exist in the mind; but a very little reflection will show that it is as impossible that a man, from the necessity of his nature, should endeavour not to exist, or to be changed into some other form, as it is that something should be begotten from nothing.

    Spinoza, *Ethics,* IV, Prop. 20, Schol.

32 We do not find in history that the Romans ever killed themselves without a cause; but the English are apt to commit suicide most unaccountably; they destroy themselves even in the bosom of happiness. This action among the Romans was the effect of education, being connected with their principles and customs; among the English it is the consequence of a distemper, being connected with the physical state of the machine, and independent of every other cause.

In all probability it is a defect of the filtration of the nervous juice: the machine, whose motive faculties are often unexerted, is weary of itself; the soul feels no pain, but a certain uneasiness in existing. Pain is a local sensation, which leads us to the desire of seeing an end of it; the burden of life, which prompts us to the desire of ceasing to exist, is an evil confined to no particular part.

    Montesquieu, *Spirit of Laws,* XIV, 12

33 That Suicide may often be consistent with interest and with our duty to ourselves, no one can question, who allows that age, sickness, or misfortune, may render life a burden, and make it worse even than annihilation. I believe that no man ever threw away life while it was worth keeping. For such is our natural horror of death, that small motives will never be able to reconcile us to it; and though perhaps the situation of man's health or fortune did not seem to require this remedy, we may at least be assured, that any one who, without apparent reason, has had recourse to it, was cursed with such an incurable depravity or gloominess of temper as must poison all enjoyment, and render him equally miserable as if he had been loaded with the most grievous misfortune. If Suicide be supposed a crime, it is only cowardice can impel us to it. If it be no crime, both prudence and courage should engage us to rid ourselves at once of existence when it becomes a burden. It is the only way that we can then be useful to society, by setting an example, which, if imitated, would preserve to every one his chance for happiness in life, and would effectually free him from all danger or misery.

    Hume, *On Suicide*

34 There are said to be occasions when a wise man kills himself, but generally speaking it is not an excess of reason that makes people take their own lives.

    Voltaire, *Letter to James Marriott*
    (Feb. 26, 1767)

35 We talked of the melancholy end of a gentleman who had destroyed himself. *Johnson.* "It was owing to imaginary difficulties in his affairs, which, had he talked with any friend, would soon have vanished." *Boswell.* "Do you think, Sir, that all who commit suicide are mad?" *Johnson.* "Sir, they are often not universally disordered in their intellects, but one passion presses so upon them, that they yield to it, and commit suicide, as a passionate man will stab another." He added, "I have often thought, that after a man has taken the resolution to kill himself, it is not courage in him to do any thing, however desperate, because he has nothing

to fear." *Goldsmith.* "I don't see that." *Johnson.* "Nay, but my dear Sir, why should not you see what every one else sees?" *Goldsmith.* "It is for fear of something that he has resolved to kill himself; and will not that timid disposition restrain him?" *Johnson.* "It does not signify that the fear of something made him resolve; it is upon the state of his mind, after the resolution is taken, that I argue. Suppose a man, either from fear, or pride, or conscience, or whatever motive, has resolved to kill himself; when once the resolution is taken, he has nothing to fear. He may then go and take the King of Prussia by the nose, at the head of his army. He cannot fear the rack, who is resolved to kill himself. When Eustace Budgel was walking down to the Thames, determined to drown himself, he might, if he pleased, without any apprehension of danger, have turned aside, and first set fire to St. James's palace."

Boswell, *Life of Johnson*
(*Apr. 21, 1773*)

36 The powers of this world have indeed lost their dominion over him who is resolved on death, and his arm can only be restrained by the religious apprehension of a future state. Suicides are enumerated by Virgil among the unfortunate, rather than the guilty, and the poetical fables of the infernal shades could not seriously influence the faith or practice of mankind. But the precepts of the Gospel or the church have at length imposed a pious servitude on the minds of Christians, and condemn them to expect, without a murmur, the last stroke of disease or the executioner.

Gibbon, *Decline and Fall of the Roman Empire*, XLIV

37 A man reduced to despair by a series of misfortunes feels wearied of life, but is still so far in possession of his reason that he can ask himself whether it would not be contrary to his duty to himself to take his own life. Now he inquires whether the maxim of his action could become a universal law of nature. His maxim is: "From self-love I adopt it as a principle to shorten my life when its longer duration is likely to bring more evil than satisfaction." It is asked then simply whether this principle founded on self-love can become a universal law of nature. Now we see at once that a system of nature of which it should be a law to destroy life by means of the very feeling whose special nature it is to impel to the improvement of life would contradict itself and, therefore, could not exist as a system of nature; hence that maxim cannot possibly exist as a universal law of nature and, consequently, would be wholly inconsistent with the supreme principle of all duty.

Kant, *Fundamental Principles of the Metaphysic of Morals*, II

38 He who contemplates suicide should ask himself whether his action can be consistent with the idea of humanity *as an end in itself.* If he destroys himself in order to escape from painful circumstance, he uses a person merely as *a mean* to maintain a tolerable condition up to the end of life. But a man is not a thing, that is to say, something which can be used merely as means, but must in all his actions be always considered as an end in himself. I cannot, therefore, dispose in any way of a man in my own person so as to mutilate him, to damage or kill him.

Kant, *Fundamental Principles of the Metaphysic of Morals*, II

39 Suicide is not abominable because God forbids it; God forbids it because it is abominable.

Kant, *Lecture (1775)*

40 Suicide may at a first glance be regarded as an act of courage, but only the false courage of tailors and servant girls. Or again it may be looked upon as a misfortune, since it is inward distraction which leads to it. But the fundamental question is: Have I a *right* to take my life? The answer will be that I, as *this* individual, am not master of my life, because life, as the comprehensive sum of my activity, is nothing external to personality, which itself is this immediate personality. Thus when a person is said to have a right over his life, the words are a contradiction, because they mean that a person has a right over himself. But he has no such right, since he does not stand over himself and he cannot pass judgement on himself. When Hercules destroyed himself by fire and when Brutus fell on his sword, this was the conduct of a hero against his personality. But as for an unqualified right to suicide, we must simply say that there is no such thing, even for heroes.

Hegel, *Philosophy of Right*, Additions, Par. 70

41 They tell us that suicide is the greatest piece of cowardice; that only a madman could be guilty of it; and other insipidities of the same kind; or else they make the nonsensical remark that suicide is *wrong;* when it is quite obvious that there is nothing in the world to which every man has a more unassailable title than to his own life and person.

Schopenhauer, *Suicide*

42 Suicide may also be regarded as an experiment—a question which man puts to Nature, trying to force her to an answer. The question is this: What change will death produce in a man's existence and in his insight into the nature of things? It is a clumsy experiment to make; for it involves the destruction of the very consciousness which puts the question and awaits the answer.

Schopenhauer, *Suicide*

43 I knew a young lady of the last "romantic" generation who after some years of an enigmatic passion for a gentleman, whom she might quite easily

have married at any moment, invented insuperable obstacles to their union, and ended by throwing herself one stormy night into a rather deep and rapid river from a high bank, almost a precipice, and so perished, entirely to satisfy her own caprice, and to be like Shakespeare's Ophelia. Indeed, if this precipice, a chosen and favourite spot of hers, had been less picturesque, if there had been a prosaic flat bank in its place, most likely the suicide would never have taken place. This is a fact, and probably there have been not a few similar instances in the last two or three generations.

Dostoevsky, Brothers Karamazov, Pt. I, I, 1

44 And all at once she thought of the man crushed by the train the day she had first met Vronsky, and she knew what she had to do. With a rapid, light step she went down the steps that led from the tank to the rails and stopped quite near the approaching train.

She looked at the lower part of the carriages, at the screws and chains, and the tall cast-iron wheel of the first carriage slowing moving up, and trying to measure the middle between the front and back wheels, and the very minute when that middle point would be opposite her.

"There," she said to herself, looking into the shadow of the carriage, at the sand and coal-dust which covered the sleepers—"there, in the very middle, and I will punish him and escape from everyone and from myself."

She tried to fling herself below the wheels of the first carriage as it reached her; but the red bag which she tried to drop out of her hand delayed her, and she was too late; she missed the moment. She had to wait for the next carriage. A feeling such as she had known when about to take the first plunge in bathing came upon her, and she crossed herself. That familiar gesture brought back into her soul a whole series of girlish and childish memories, and suddenly the darkness that had covered everything for her was torn apart, and life rose up before her for an instant with all its bright past joys. But she did not take her eyes from the wheels of the second carriage. And exactly at the moment when the space between the wheels came opposite her, she dropped the red bag, and drawing her head back into her shoulders, fell on her hands under the carriage, and lightly, as though she would rise again at once, dropped on to her knees. And at the same instant she was terror-stricken at what she was doing. "Where am I? What am I doing? What for?" She tried to get up, to drop backwards; but something huge and merciless struck her on the head and rolled her on her back. "Lord, forgive me all!" she said, feeling it impossible to struggle. A peasant muttering something was working at the iron above her. And the light by which she had read the book filled with troubles, falsehoods, sorrow, and evil, flared up more brightly than ever before, lighted up for her all that had been in darkness, flickered, began to grow dim, and was quenched for ever.

Tolstoy, Anna Karenina, VII, 31

45 The reasoning both of pessimist philosophy and of ordinary suicide is this: There is an animal self which is attracted to life, but the yearnings of this self can never be gratified. There is another self, a rational one, which has no longing for life, but merely critically contemplates all the false joy of life and the passions of the animal self and rejects them entirely.

If I yield to the first I see that my life is meaningless and that I am heading for misery, in which I am more and more involved. If I abandon myself to the second—the reasonable self—I no longer feel any attraction to life. I see that it is absurd and impossible to live for the one thing I want, that is, my personal happiness. It would be possible to live for reasonable consciousness, but it is not worth while and I do not want to. Serve that source from whence I came—God? Why? If God exists, he will find people to serve him without me. And why should I do it? One can contemplate this play of life as long as one does not find it dull, and when it is dull one can go away and kill oneself. And that is what I will do.

Tolstoy, On Life, XXII

46 The thought of suicide is a powerful comfort: it helps one through many a dreadful night.

Nietzsche, Beyond Good and Evil, IV, 157

47 The relatives of a suicide take it in ill part that he did not remain alive out of consideration for their reputation.

Nietzsche, Human, All-Too-Human, 322

48 All this about the impossibility of suicide is said on the supposition of *positive* motives. When possessed by the emotion of *fear,* however, we are in a *negative* state of mind; that is, our desire is limited to the mere banishing of something, without regard to what shall take its place. In this state of mind there can unquestionably be genuine thoughts, and genuine acts, of suicide, spiritual and social, as well as bodily. Anything, *anything,* at such times, so as to escape and not to be!

William James, Psychology, X

49 Fear of life in one form or other is the great thing to exorcise; but it isn't reason that will ever do it. Impulse without reason is enough, and reason without impulse is a poor makeshift. I take it that no man is educated who has never dallied with the thought of suicide.

William James, Letter to B. P. Blood
(June 28, 1896)

Chapter 2

FAMILY

Chapter 2 is divided into three sections: 2.1 THE INSTITUTION OF THE FAMILY, 2.2 PARENTS AND CHILDREN, and 2.3 MARRIAGE.

Certain of the passages quoted in this chapter could have been placed in two of the three sections, and some, perhaps, in all three. The institution of the family is inseparable from the marriage rite and all that it entails; the relation of husband and wife results from marriage and is fundamental to the institution of the family; the parental care and direction of children, as well as filial respect and obedience, are aspects of domestic government that take different forms in different types of familial institutions.

All of these points of coincidence or overlapping being acknowledged, it is, nevertheless, the case that the matters considered in the three sections are sufficiently distinct to justify a division of the texts accordingly.

However, the reader whose interest is in all of the many related aspects of the human family would do well to explore the materials of this chapter as a whole and to trace for himself the intricate pattern of insights and observations that are woven together in the fabric of our understanding of the one human institution with which every human being has had intimate experience.

There is probably no other subject treated in this book about which everyone has an opinion or judgment, and feelings, sentiments, or emotional attitudes, as well as wishes or desires, overt or covert, conscious or unconscious. There is probably no other subject on which there are comments from so wide a diversity of sources—from poets, novelists, dramatists, and historians; philosophers and theologians; moralists, economists, and political theorists; biologists, psychologists, and psychoanalysts.

2.1 | *The Institution of the Family*

One important relationship constitutive of most, if not all, families is that of siblings—brother and brother, sister and sister, brother and sister. It is a relationship that, as generalized under the notion of fraternity or brotherhood, is often set up as a model for those who are not bound to one another by any ties of consanguinity. On the other hand, as we are reminded by the opening text from *Genesis* about Cain and Abel, animosity and jealousy also tear at the hearts of those who are tied to one another by bonds of blood. Blood may be thicker than water, but it also has a lower boiling point.

Passages dealing with siblings, and their benevolence or malevolence, are assembled in this section, and are thus separated from the other two basic familial relationships (husband and wife, parents and children), which are treated in Sections 3 and 2 respectively.

Another, perhaps even more basic, theme in this section is the type of government that is regulative of family life. Who rules in the family—the husband alone, or both husband and wife; and who is ruled—the children alone or both wife and children? What power or authority is exercised in domestic government? What makes it legitimate? Is it absolute or limited and, if limited, what are its limits? Answers to questions of this sort usually involve comparisons of parental rule with despotic rule and constitutional government. Those interested in the passages that treat of such matters should, perhaps, look also at similar passages in Chapter 10 on POLITICS, especially Section 10.3 on GOVERNMENT: ITS NATURE, NECESSITY, AND FORMS, Section 10.4 on GOVERNMENT OF AND BY THE PEOPLE: REPUBLIC AND DEMOCRACY, and Section 10.6 on DESPOTISM AND TYRANNY. Doing so will help one to think about some of the most difficult problems of family life—the extent to which the domestic community can be organized as a democracy, and the safeguards that can be erected against tyrannical or despotic misrule.

---

1 And Adam knew Eve his wife; and she conceived, and bare Cain, and said, I have gotten a man from the Lord.

And she again bare his brother Abel. And Abel was a keeper of sheep, but Cain was a tiller of the ground.

And in process of time it came to pass, that Cain brought of the fruit of the ground an offering unto the Lord.

And Abel, he also brought of the firstlings of his flock and of the fat thereof. And the Lord had respect unto Abel and to his offering:

But unto Cain and to his offering he had not respect. And Cain was very wroth, and his countenance fell.

And the Lord said unto Cain, Why art thou wroth? and why is thy countenance fallen?

If thou doest well, shalt thou not be accepted? and if thou doest not well, sin lieth at the door.

And unto thee shall be his desire, and thou shalt rule over him.

And Cain talked with Abel his brother: and it came to pass, when they were in the field, that Cain rose up against Abel his brother, and slew him.

And the Lord said unto Cain, Where is Abel thy brother? And he said, I know not: Am I my brother's keeper?

Genesis 4:1–9

2 And the boys grew: and Esau was a cunning hunter, a man of the field; and Jacob was a plain man, dwelling in tents.

And Isaac loved Esau, because he did eat of his venison: but Rebekah loved Jacob.

And Jacob sod pottage: and Esau came from the field, and was faint:

And Esau said to Jacob, Feed me, I pray thee,

with that same red pottage; for I am faint: therefore was his name called Edom.

And Jacob said, Sell me this day thy birthright.

And Esau said, Behold, I am at the point to die: and what profit shall this birthright do to me?

And Jacob said, Swear to me this day; and he sware unto him: and he sold his birthright unto Jacob.

Then Jacob gave Esau bread and pottage of lentiles; and he did eat and drink, and rose up, and went his way: thus Esau despised his birthright.

Genesis 25:27–34

3 If a man have two wives, one beloved, and another hated, and they have born him children, both the beloved and the hated; and if the firstborn son be her's that was hated:

Then it shall be, when he maketh his sons to inherit that which he hath, that he may not make the son of the beloved firstborn before the son of the hated, which is indeed the firstborn:

But he shall acknowledge the son of the hated for the firstborn, by giving him a double portion of all that he hath: for he is the beginning of his strength; the right of the firstborn is his.

Deuteronomy 21:15–17

4 If brethren dwell together, and one of them die, and have no child, the wife of the dead shall not marry without unto a stranger: her husband's brother shall go in unto her, and take her to him to wife, and perform the duty of an husband's brother unto her.

And it shall be, that the firstborn which she beareth shall succeed in the name of his brother which is dead, that his name be not put out of Israel.

And if the man like not to take his brother's wife, then let his brother's wife go up to the gate unto the elders, and say, My husband's brother refuseth to raise up unto his brother a name in Israel, he will not perform the duty of my husband's brother.

Then the elders of his city shall call him, and speak unto him: and if he stand to it, and say, I like not to take her;

Then shall his brother's wife come unto him in the presence of the elders, and loose his shoe from off his foot, and spit in his face, and shall answer and say, So shall it be done unto that man that will not build up his brother's house.

Deuteronomy 24:5–9

5 *Odysseus.* And may the gods accomplish your desire:
a home, a husband, and harmonious
converse with him—the best thing in the world
being a strong house held in serenity
where man and wife agree. Woe to their enemies,

joy to their friends! But all this they know best.
Homer, Odyssey, VI, 179

6 *Odysseus.* Where shall a man find sweetness to surpass
his own home and his parents? In far lands
he shall not, though he find a house of gold.
Homer, Odyssey, IX, 34

7 *Teiresias.* I tell you, king, this man, this murderer
(whom you have long declared you are in search of,
indicting him in threatening proclamation
as murderer of Laius)—he is here.
In name he is a stranger among citizens
but soon he will be shown to be a citizen
true native Theban, and he'll have no joy
of the discovery: blindness for sight
and beggary for riches his exchange,
he shall go journeying to a foreign country
tapping his way before him with a stick.
He shall be proved father and brother both
to his own children in his house; to her
that gave him birth, a son and husband both;
a fellow sower in his father's bed
with that same father that he murdered.
Go within, reckon that out, and if you find me
mistaken, say I have no skill in prophecy.
Sophocles, Oedipus the King, 448

8 *Antigone.* O tomb, O marriage-chamber, hollowed out
house that will watch forever, where I go.
To my own people, who are mostly there;
Persephone has taken them to her.
Last of them all, ill-fated past the rest,
shall I descend, before my course is run.
Still when I get there I may hope to find
I come as a dear friend to my dear father,
to you, my mother, and my brother too.
All three of you have known my hand in death.
I washed your bodies, dressed them for the grave,
poured out the last libation at the tomb.
Last, Polyneices knows the price I pay
for doing final service to his corpse.
And yet the wise will know my choice was right.
Had I had children or their father dead,
I'd let them moulder. I should not have chosen
in such a case to cross the state's decree.
What is the law that lies behind these words?
One husband gone, I might have found another,
or a child from a new man in first child's place,
but with my parents hid away in death,
no brother, ever, could spring up for me.
Such was the law by which I honored you.
Sophocles, Antigone, 891

9 *Socrates.* Here, then, is one difficulty in our law about women, which we may say that we have now escaped; the wave has not swallowed us up alive for enacting that the guardians of either sex should have all their pursuits in common; to the

utility and also to the possibility of this arrangement the consistency of the argument with itself bears witness.

Glaucon. Yes, that was a mighty wave which you have escaped.

Yes, I said, but a greater is coming; you will not think much of this when you see the next.

Go on; let me see.

The law, I said, which is the sequel of this and of all that has preceded, is to the following effect—"that the wives of our guardians are to be common, and their children are to be common, and no parent is to know his own child, nor any child his parent."

Yes, he said, that is a much greater wave than the other; and the possibility as well as the utility of such a law are far more questionable.

I do not think, I said, that there can be any dispute about the very great utility of having wives and children in common; the possibility is quite another matter, and will be very much disputed.

I think that a good many doubts may be raised about both.

Plato, *Republic,* V, 457A

10 *Socrates.* How can marriages be made most beneficial?—that is a question which I put to you, because I see in your house dogs for hunting, and of the nobler sort of birds not a few. Now, I beseech you, do tell me, have you ever attended to their pairing and breeding?

Glaucon. In what particulars?

Why, in the first place, although they are all of a good sort, are not some better than others?

True.

And do you breed from them all indifferently, or do you take care to breed from the best only?

From the best.

And do you take the oldest or the youngest, or only those of ripe age?

I choose only those of ripe age.

And if care was not taken in the breeding, your dogs and birds would greatly deteriorate?

Certainly.

And the same of horses and animals in general?

Undoubtedly.

Good heavens! my dear friend, I said, what consummate skill will our rulers need if the same principle holds of the human species!

Certainly, the same principle holds.

Plato, *Republic,* V, 459A

11 Between man and wife friendship seems to exist by nature; for man is naturally inclined to form couples—even more than to form cities, inasmuch as the household is earlier and more necessary than the city, and reproduction is more common to man with the animals. With the other animals the union extends only to this point, but human beings live together not only for the sake of repro-

duction but also for the various purposes of life; for from the start the functions are divided, and those of man and woman are different; so they help each other by throwing their peculiar gifts into the common stock. It is for these reasons that both utility and pleasure seem to be found in this kind of friendship. But this friendship may be based also on virtue, if the parties are good; for each has its own virtue and they will delight in the fact. And children seem to be a bond of union (which is the reason why childless people part more easily); for children are a good common to both and what is common holds them together.

Aristotle, *Ethics,* 1162ª16

12 A husband and father . . . rules over wife and children, both free, but the rule differs, the rule over his children being a royal, over his wife a constitutional rule. For although there may be exceptions to the order of nature, the male is by nature fitter for command than the female.

Aristotle, *Politics,* 1259ª39

13 The citizens might conceivably have wives and children and property in common, as Socrates proposes in the *Republic* of Plato. Which is better, our present condition, or the proposed new order of society?

There are many difficulties in the community of women. And the principle on which Socrates rests the necessity of such an institution evidently is not established by his arguments. Further, as a means to the end which he ascribes to the state, the scheme, taken literally, is impracticable, and how we are to interpret it is nowhere precisely stated.

Aristotle, *Politics,* 1261ª4

14 Next after they had got themselves huts and skins and fire, and the woman united with the man passed with him into one domicile and the duties of wedlock were learnt by the two, and they saw an offspring born from them, then first mankind began to soften. For fire made their chilled bodies less able now to bear the frost beneath the canopy of heaven, and Venus impaired their strength and children with their caresses soon broke down the haughty temper of parents. Then too neighbours began to join in a league of friendship mutually desiring neither to do nor suffer harm; and asked for indulgence to children and womankind, when with cries and gestures they declared in stammering speech that meet it is for all to have mercy on the weak. And though harmony could not be established without exception, yet a very large portion observed their agreements with good faith, or else the race of man would then have been wholly cut off, nor could breeding have continued their generations to this day.

Lucretius, *Nature of Things,* V

15 *Aeneas.* Arm'd once again, my glitt'ring sword I
    wield,
  While th' other hand sustains my weighty shield,
  And forth I rush to seek th' abandon'd field.
  I went; but sad Creüsa stopp'd my way,
  And cross the threshold in my passage lay,
  Embrac'd my knees, and, when I would have
    gone,
  Shew'd me my feeble sire and tender son:
  'If death be your design, at least,' said she,
  'Take us along to share your destiny.
  If any farther hopes in arms remain,
  This place, these pledges of your love, maintain.
  To whom do you expose your father's life,
  Your son's, and mine, your now forgotten wife!'

  Virgil, *Aeneid,* II

16 There came then his brethren and his mother,
  and, standing without, sent unto him, calling him.
    And the multitude sat about him, and they said
  unto him, Behold, thy mother and thy brethren
  without seek for thee.
    And he answered them, saying, Who is my
  mother, or my brethren?
    And he looked round about on them which sat
  about him, and said, Behold my mother and my
  brethren!
    For whosoever shall do the will of God, the
  same is my brother, and my sister, and mother.

  Mark 3:31-35

17 Suppose ye that I am come to give peace on
  earth? I tell you, Nay; but rather division:
    For from henceforth there shall be five in one
  house divided, three against two, and two against
  three.
    The father shall be divided against the son, and
  the son against the father; the mother against the
  daughter, and the daughter against the mother;
  the mother in law against her daughter in law,
  and the daughter in law against her mother in
  law.

  Luke 12:51-53

18 Lycurgus was of a persuasion that children were
  not so much the property of their parents as of the
  whole commonwealth, and, therefore, would not
  have his citizens begot by the first-comers, but by
  the best men that could be found; the laws of
  other nations seemed to him very absurd and inconsistent, where people would be so solicitous for
  their dogs and horses as to exert interest and to
  pay money to procure fine breeding, and yet kept
  their wives shut up, to be made mothers only by
  themselves, who might be foolish, infirm, or diseased; as if it were not apparent that children of a
  bad breed would prove their bad qualities first
  upon those who kept and were rearing them, and
  well-born children, in like manner, their good
  qualities.

  Plutarch, *Lycurgus*

19 We are inquiring about ordinary marriages and
  those which are free from distractions, and making this inquiry we do not find the affair of marriage in this state of the world a thing which is
  especially suited to the Cynic.
    "How, then, shall a man maintain the existence
  of society?" In the name of God, are those men
  greater benefactors to society who introduce into
  the world to occupy their own places two or three
  grunting children, or those who superintend as far
  as they can all mankind, and see what they do,
  how they live, what they attend to, what they neglect contrary to their duty? Did they who left
  little children to the Thebans do them more good
  than Epaminondas who died childless? And did
  Priamus, who begat fifty worthless sons, or Danaus or Æolus contribute more to the community
  than Homer? then shall the duty of a general or
  the business of a writer exclude a man from marriage or the begetting of children, and such a man
  shall not be judged to have accepted the condition
  of childlessness for nothing; and shall not the royalty of a Cynic be considered an equivalent for
  the want of children? Do we not perceive his
  grandeur and do we not justly contemplate the
  character of Diogenes; and do we, instead of this,
  turn our eyes to the present Cynics, who are dogs
  that wait at tables and in no respect imitate the
  Cynics of old except perchance in breaking wind,
  but in nothing else? For such matters would not
  have moved us at all nor should we have wondered if a Cynic should not marry or beget children. Man, the Cynic is the father of all men; the
  men are his sons, the women are his daughters: he
  so carefully visits all, so well does he care for all.
  Do you think that it is from idle impertinence that
  he rebukes those whom he meets? He does it as a
  father, as a brother, and as the minister of the
  father of all, the minister of Zeus.

  Epictetus, *Discourses,* III, 22

20 They who care for the rest rule—the husband the
  wife, the parents the children, the masters the servants; and they who are cared for obey—the
  women their husbands, the children their parents,
  the servants their masters. But in the family of the
  just man who lives by faith . . . even those who
  rule serve those whom they seem to command; for
  they rule not from a love of power, but from a
  sense of the duty they owe to others—not because
  they are proud of authority, but because they love
  mercy.

  Augustine, *City of God,* XIX, 14

21 Now the saints of ancient times were, under the
  form of an earthly kingdom, foreshadowing and
  foretelling the kingdom of heaven. And on account of the necessity for a numerous offspring,
  the custom of one man having several wives was
  at that time blameless: and for the same reason it
  was not proper for one woman to have several

husbands, because a woman does not in that way become more fruitful, but, on the contrary, it is base harlotry to seek either gain or offspring by promiscuous intercourse. In regard to matters of this sort, whatever the holy men of those times did without lust, Scripture passes over without blame, although they did things which could not be done at the present time, except through lust.

Augustine, *Christian Doctrine,* III, 12

22 In comparing love to love we should compare one union with another. Accordingly we must say that friendship among blood relations is based upon their connection by natural origin, the friendship of fellow-citizens on their civic fellowship, and the friendship of those who are fighting side by side on the comradeship of battle. Therefore in matters pertaining to nature we should love our kindred most, in matters concerning relations between citizens, we should prefer our fellow-citizens, and on the battlefield our fellow-soldiers. . . .

If however we compare union with union, it is evident that the union arising from natural origin is prior to, and more stable than, all others, because it is something affecting the very substance, while other unions are something added above and may cease altogether. Therefore the friendship of kindred is more stable, while other friendships may be stronger in respect of that which is proper to each of them.

Aquinas, *Summa Theologica,* II-II, 26, 8

23 Although the father ranks above the mother, the mother has more to do with the offspring than the father has. Or we may say that woman was made chiefly in order to be man's helpmate in relation to the offspring, whereas the man was not made for this purpose. Wherefore the mother has a closer relation to the nature of marriage than the father has.

Aquinas, *Summa Theologica,* III Suppl., 44, 2

24 Love hates people to be attached to each other except by himself, and takes a laggard part in relations that are set up and maintained under another title, as marriage is. Connections and means have, with reason, as much weight in it as graces and beauty, or more. We do not marry for ourselves, whatever we say; we marry just as much or more for our posterity, for our family. The practice and benefit of marriage concerns our race very far beyond us. Therefore I like this fashion of arranging it rather by a third hand than by our own, and by the sense of others rather than by our own. How opposite is all this to the conventions of love!

Montaigne, *Essays,* III, 5, On Some Verses of Virgil

25 I was late in taking up the management of a household. Those whom nature had sent into the world before me relieved me of that burden for a long time. I had already contracted a different bent, more suitable to my disposition. At all events, from what I have seen of it, it is an occupation more bothersome than difficult: whoever is capable of anything else will very easily be capable of this.

Montaigne, *Essays,* III, 9, Of Vanity

26 *Don Quixote.* Another Thing makes me more uneasy: Suppose we have found out a King and a Princess, and I have fill'd the World with the Fame of my unparallel'd Atchievements, yet cannot I tell how to find out that I am of Royal Blood, though it were but second Cousin to an Emperor: For, 'tis not to be expected that the King will ever consent that I shall wed his Daughter 'till I have made this out by authentick Proofs, tho' my Service deserve it never so much; and thus for want of a Punctilio, I am in danger of losing what my Valour so justly merits. 'Tis true, indeed, I am a Gentleman, and of a noted ancient Family, and possess'd of an Estate of a hundred and twenty Crowns a Year; nay, perhaps the learned Historiographer who is to write the History of my Life, will so improve and beautify my Genealogy, that he will find me to be the fifth, or sixth at least, in Descent from a King; For, *Sancho,* there are two sorts of Originals in the World; some who sprung from mighty Kings and Princes, by little and little have been so lessen'd and obscur'd, that the Estates and Titles of the following Generations have dwindled to nothing, and ended in a Point like a Pyramid; others, who from mean and low Beginnings still rise and rise, till at last they are rais'd to the very Top of human Greatness: So vast the Difference is, that those who were Something are now Nothing, and those that were Nothing are now Something. And therefore who knows but that I may be one of those whose Original is so illustrious; which being handsomely made out, after due Examination, ought undoubtedly to satisfy the King, my Father-in-law. But even supposing he were still refractory, the Princess is to be so desperately in love with me, that she will marry me without his Consent, tho' I were a Son of the meanest Water-Carrier; and if her tender Honour scruples to bless me against her Father's Will, then it may not be amiss to put a pleasing Constraint upon her, by conveying her by Force out of the Reach of her Father, to whose Persecutions either Time or Death will be sure to put a Period.

Cervantes, *Don Quixote,* I, 21

27 He that hath wife and children hath given hostages to fortune; for they are impediments to great enterprises, either of virtue or mischief.

Bacon, *Of Marriage and Single Life*

28 Private bodies regular and lawful are those that are constituted without letters, or other written authority, saving the laws common to all other subjects. And because they be united in one person representative, they are held for regular; such as are all families, in which the father or master ordereth the whole family. For he obligeth his children, and servants, as far as the law permitteth, though not further, because none of them are bound to obedience in those actions which the law hath forbidden to be done. In all other actions, during the time they are under domestic government, they are subject to their fathers and masters, as to their immediate sovereigns.

Hobbes, *Leviathan*, II, 22

29 God, having made man such a creature that, in His own judgment, it was not good for him to be alone, put him under strong obligations of necessity, convenience, and inclination, to drive him into society, as well as fitted him with understanding and language to continue and enjoy it. The first society was between man and wife, which gave beginning to that between parents and children, to which, in time, that between master and servant came to be added. And though all these might, and commonly did, meet together, and make up but one family, wherein the master or mistress of it had some sort of rule proper to a family, each of these, or all together, came short of "political society," as we shall see if we consider the different ends, ties, and bounds of each of these.

Locke, *II Civil Government*, VII, 77

30 Paternal or parental power is nothing but that which parents have over their children to govern them, for the children's good, till they come to the use of reason, or a state of knowledge, wherein they may be supposed capable to understand that rule, whether it be the law of Nature or the municipal law of their country, they are to govern themselves by—capable, I say, to know it, as well as several others, who live as free men under that law. The affection and tenderness God hath planted in the breasts of parents towards their children makes it evident that this is not intended to be a severe arbitrary government, but only for the help, instruction, and preservation of their offspring. But happen as it will, there is, as I have proved, no reason why it should be thought to extend to life and death, at any time, over their children, more than over anybody else, or keep the child in subjection to the will of his parents when grown to a man and the perfect use of reason, any farther than as having received life and education from his parents obliges him to respect, honour, gratitude, assistance, and support, all his life, to both father and mother. And thus, it is true, the paternal is a natural government, but not at all extending itself to the ends and jurisdictions of that which is political. The power of the father doth not reach at all to the property of the child, which is only in his own disposing.

Locke, *II Civil Government*, XV, 170

31 *Witwoud.* Odso, brother, is it you? Your servant, brother.

Sir Wilfull. Your servant! Why, yours, sir. Your servant again—'sheart, and your friend and servant to that—and a—[*Puff.*]—and a flap-dragon for your service, sir: and a hare's foot, and a hare's scut for your service, sir; an you be so cold and so courtly!

Wit. No offense, I hope, brother.

Sir Wil. 'Sheart, sir, but there is, and much offense. A pox, is this your Inns o' Court breeding, not to know your friends and your relations, your elders and your betters?

Wit. Why, Brother Wilfull of Salop, you may be as short as a Shrewsbury cake, if you please. But I tell you 'tis not modish to know relations in town. You think you're in the country, where great lubberly brothers slabber and kiss one another when they meet, like a call of sergeants.—'Tis not the fashion here; 'tis not inded, dear brother.

Sir Wil. The fashion's a fool; and you're a fop, dear brother.

Congreve, *Way of the World*, III, xv

32 The first expansions of the human heart were the effects of a novel situation, which united husbands and wives, fathers and children, under one roof. The habit of living together soon gave rise to the finest feelings known to humanity, conjugal love and paternal affection. Every family became a little society, the more united because liberty and reciprocal attachment were the only bonds of its union. The sexes, whose manner of life had been hitherto the same, began now to adopt different ways of living. The women became more sedentary, and accustomed themselves to mind the hut and their children, while the men went abroad in search of their common subsistence. From living a softer life, both sexes also began to lose something of their strength and ferocity: but, if individuals became to some extent less able to encounter wild beasts separately, they found it, on the other hand, easier to assemble and resist in common.

Rousseau, *Origin of Inequality*, II

33 In the family, it is clear, for several reasons which lie in its very nature, that the father ought to command. In the first place, the authority ought not to be equally divided between father and mother; the government must be single, and in every division of opinion there must be one preponderant voice to decide. Secondly, however lightly we may regard the disadvantages peculiar to women, yet, as they necessarily occasion intervals of inaction, this is a sufficient reason for excluding them from this supreme authority: for when the balance is

perfectly even, a straw is enough to turn the scale. Besides, the husband ought to be able to superintend his wife's conduct, because it is of importance for him to be assured that the children, whom he is obliged to acknowledge and maintain, belong to no one but himself. Thirdly, children should be obedient to their father, at first of necessity, and afterwards from gratitude: after having had their wants satisfied by him during one half of their lives, they ought to consecrate the other half to providing for his. Fourthly, servants owe him their services in exchange for the provision he makes for them, though they may break off the bargain as soon as it ceases to suit them.

Rousseau, *Political Economy*

34 The most ancient of all societies, and the only one that is natural, is the family: and even so the children remain attached to the father only so long as they need him for their preservation. As soon as this need ceases, the natural bond is dissolved. The children, released from the obedience they owed to the father, and the father, released from the care he owed his children, return equally to independence. If they remain united, they continue so no longer naturally, but voluntarily; and the family itself is then maintained only by convention.

This common liberty results from the nature of man. His first law is to provide for his own preservation, his first cares are those which he owes to himself; and, as soon as he reaches years of discretion, he is the sole judge of the proper means of preserving himself, and consequently becomes his own master.

The family then may be called the first model of political societies: the ruler corresponds to the father, and the people to the children; and all, being born free and equal, alienate their liberty only for their own advantage. The whole difference is that, in the family, the love of the father for his children repays him for the care he takes of them, while, in the State, the pleasure of commanding takes the place of the love which the chief cannot have for the peoples under him.

Rousseau, *Social Contract*, I, 2

35 I talked of the little attachment which subsisted between near relations in London. "Sir, (said Johnson,) in a country so commercial as ours, where every man can do for himself, there is not so much occasion for that attachment. No man is thought the worse of here, whose brother was hanged."

Boswell, *Life of Johnson (Apr. 6, 1772)*

36 Poverty, though it no doubt discourages, does not always prevent marriage. It seems even to be favourable to generation. A half-starved Highland woman frequently bears more than twenty children, while a pampered fine lady is often incapa-

ble of bearing any, and is generally exhausted by two or three. Barrenness, so frequent among women of fashion, is very rare among those of inferior station. Luxury in the fair sex, while it inflames perhaps the passion for enjoyment, seems always to weaken, and frequently to destroy altogether, the powers of generation.

But poverty, though it does not prevent the generation, is extremely unfavourable to the rearing of children. The tender plant is produced, but in so cold a soil and so severe a climate, soon withers and dies. It is not uncommon, I have been frequently told, in the Highlands of Scotland for a mother who has borne twenty children not to have two alive.

Adam Smith, *Wealth of Nations*, I, 8

37 Laws frequently continue in force long after the circumstances which first gave occasion to them, and which could alone render them reasonable, are no more. In the present state of Europe, the proprietor of a single acre of land is as perfectly secure of his possession as the proprietor of a hundred thousand. The right of primogeniture, however, still continues to be respected, and as of all institutions it is the fittest to support the pride of family distinctions, it is still likely to endure for many centuries. In every other respect, nothing can be more contrary to the real interest of a numerous family than a right which, in order to enrich one, beggars all the rest of the children.

Adam Smith, *Wealth of Nations*, III, 2

38 Personal right of a real kind is the right to the *possession* of an external object as a thing, and to the *use* of it as a person. The mine and thine embraced under this right relate specially to the family and household; and the relations involved are those of free beings in reciprocal real interaction with each other. Through their relations and influence as persons upon one another, in accordance with the principle of external freedom as the *cause* of it, they form a society composed as a whole of members standing in community with each other as persons; and this constitutes the household. The mode in which this social status in acquired by individuals, and the functions which prevail within it, proceed neither by arbitrary individual action (*facto*), nor by mere contract (*pacto*), but by law (*lege*). And this law as being not only a right, but also as constituting possession in reference to a person, is a right rising above all *mere* real and personal right. It must, in fact, form the right of humanity in our own person; and, as such, it has as its consequence a natural permissive law, by the favour of which such acquisition becomes possible to us.

The acquisition that is founded upon this law is, as regards its objects, threefold. The man acquires a wife; the husband and wife acquire children, constituting a family; and the family acquire domestics. All these objects, while acquirable, are inalienable; and the right of possession in these objects is *the most strictly personal of all rights.*

Kant, *Science of Right*, 22-23

39 He heard it, but he heeded not—his eyes
Were with his heart and that was far away;
He reck'd not of the life he lost nor prize,
But where his rude hut by the Danube lay,
There were his young barbarians all at play,
There was their Dacian mother—he, their sire,
Butcher'd to make a Roman holiday.

Byron, *Childe Harold's Pilgrimage*, IV, 141

40 The family, as the immediate substantiality of mind, is specifically characterized by love, which is mind's feeling of its own unity. Hence in a family, one's frame of mind is to have self-consciousness of one's individuality within this unity as the absolute essence of oneself, with the result that one is in it not as an independent person but as a member.

Hegel, *Philosophy of Right*, 158

41 The ethical dissolution of the family consists in this, that once the children have been educated to freedom of personality, and have come of age, they become recognized as persons in the eyes of the law and as capable of holding free property of their own and founding families of their own, the sons as heads of new families, the daughters as wives. They now have their substantive destiny in the new family; the old family on the other hand falls into the background as merely their ultimate basis and origin, while *a fortiori* the clan is an abstraction, devoid of rights.

Hegel, *Philosophy of Right*, 177

42 The piety of the family relation should be respected in the highest degree by the state; by its means the state obtains as its members individuals who are already moral (for as mere *persons* they are not) and who in uniting to form a state bring with them that sound basis of a political edifice—the capacity of feeling one with a whole.

Hegel, *Philosophy of History*, Introduction, 3

43 Looking far enough back in the stream of time, and judging from the social habits of man as he now exists, the most probable view is that he aboriginally lived in small communities, each with a single wife, or if powerful with several, whom he jealously guarded against all other men. Or he may not have been a social animal, and yet have lived with several wives, like the gorilla; for all the natives "agree that but one adult male is seen in a band; when the young male grows up, a contest takes place for mastery, and the strongest, by killing and driving out the others, establishes himself as the head of the community." The younger males, being thus expelled and wandering about,

would, when at last successful in finding a partner, prevent too close interbreeding within the limits of the same family.

Darwin, *Descent of Man*, III, 20

44 However terrible and disgusting under the capitalist system the dissolution of the old family ties may appear, nevertheless, modern industry, by assigning as it does an important part in the process of production, outside the domestic sphere, to women, to young persons, and to children of both sexes, creates a new economic foundation for a higher form of the family and of the relations between the sexes. It is, of course, just as absurd to hold the Teutonic-Christian form of the family to be absolute and final as it would be to apply that character to the ancient Roman, the ancient Greek, or the Eastern forms which, moreover, taken together, form a series in historic development. Moreover, it is obvious that the fact of the collective working group being composed of individuals of both sexes and all ages, must necessarily, under suitable conditions, become a source of humane development; although in its spontaneously developed, brutal, capitalistic form, where the labourer exists for the process of production, and not the process of production for the labourer, that fact is a pestiferous source of corruption and slavery.

Marx, *Capital*, Vol. I, IV, 15

45 Abolition of the family! Even the most radical flare up at this infamous proposal of the Communists.

On what foundation is the present family, the bourgeois family, based? On capital, on private gain. In its completely developed form this family exists only among the bourgeoisie. But the state of things finds its complement in the practical absence of the family among the proletarians, and in public prostitution.

The bourgeois family will vanish as a matter of course when its complement vanishes, and both will vanish with the vanishing of capital.

Do you charge us with wanting to stop the exploitation of children by their parents? To this crime we plead guilty.

But, you will say, we destroy the most hallowed of relations when we replace home education by social.

And your education! Is not that also social, and determined by the social conditions under which you educate, by the intervention of society, direct or indirect, by means of schools, etc.? The Communists have not invented the intervention of society in education; they do but seek to alter the character of that intervention and to rescue education from the influence of the ruling class.

The bourgeois claptrap about the family and education, about the hallowed co-relation of parent and child, becomes all the more disgusting, the more, by the action of modern industry, all family ties among the proletarians are torn asunder and their children transformed into simple articles of commerce and instruments of labour.

Marx and Engels, *Communist Manifesto*, II

46 The duties of parents to their children are those which are indissolubly attached to the fact of causing the existence of a human being. The parent owes to society to endeavour to make the child a good and valuable member of it, and owes to the children to provide, so far as depends on him, such education, and such appliances and means, as will enable them to start with a fair chance of achieving by their own exertions a successful life. To this every child has a claim; and I cannot admit, that as a child he has a claim to more.

Mill, *Principles of Political Economy*,
Bk. II, II, 3

47 The family, justly constituted, would be the real school of the virtues of freedom. It is sure to be a sufficient one of everything else. It will always be a school of obedience for the children, of command for the parents. What is needed is, that it should be a school of sympathy in equality, of living together in love, without power on one side or obedience on the other. This it ought to be between the parents. It would then be an exercise of those virtues which each requires to fit them for all other association, and a model to the children of the feelings and conduct which their temporary training by means of obedience is designed to render habitual, and therefore natural, to them. The moral training of mankind will never be adapted to the conditions of the life for which all other human progress is a preparation, until they practise in the family the same moral rule which is adapted to the moral constitution of human society. Any sentiment of freedom which can exist in a man whose nearest and dearest intimacies are with those of whom he is absolute master, is not the genuine or Christian love of freedom, but, what the love of freedom generally was in the ancients and in the middle ages—an intense feeling of the dignity and importance of his own personality; making him disdain a yoke for himself, of which he has no abhorrence whatever in the abstract, but which he is abundantly ready to impose on others for his own interest or glorification.

Mill, *Subjection of Women*, II

48 The pleasure married people get from one another . . . is only the beginnings of marriage and not its whole significance, which lies in the family.

Tolstoy, *War and Peace*,
I Epilogue, X

49 Happy families are all alike; every unhappy family is unhappy in its own way.

Tolstoy, *Anna Karenina*, I, 1

50 In order to carry through any undertaking in family life, there must necessarily be either complete division between the husband and wife, or loving agreement. When the relations of a couple are vacillating and neither one thing nor the other, no sort of enterprise can be undertaken.

Many families remain for years in the same place, though both husband and wife are sick of it, simply because there is neither complete division nor agreement between them.

Tolstoy, *Anna Karenina*, VII, 23

51 Our immediate family is a part of ourselves. Our father and mother, our wife and babes, are bone of our bone and flesh of our flesh. When they die, a part of our very selves is gone. If they do anything wrong, it is our shame. If they are insulted, our anger flashes forth as readily as if we stood in their place. Our home comes next. Its scenes are part of our life; its aspects awaken the tenderest feelings of affection; and we do not easily forgive the stranger who, in visiting it, finds fault with its arrangements or treats it with contempt. All these different things are the objects of instinctive preferences coupled with the most important practical interests of life. We all have a blind impulse to watch over our body, to deck it with clothing of an ornamental sort, to cherish parents, wife and babes, and to find for ourselves a home of our own which we may live in and "improve."

William James, *Psychology*, X

52 We are told that sexual attraction is diverted from the members of the opposite sex in one family owing to their living together from early childhood; or that a biological tendency against in-breeding has a mental equivalent in the horror of incest! Whereby it is entirely overlooked that no such rigorous prohibitions in law and custom would be required if any trustworthy natural barriers against the temptation to incest existed. The opposite is the truth. The first choice of object in mankind is regularly an incestuous one, directed to the mother and sister of men, and the most stringent prohibitions are required to prevent this sustained infantile tendency from being carried into effect.

Freud, *General Introduction
to Psycho-Analysis*, XXI

53 The indestructible strength of the family as a natural group formation rests upon the fact that this necessary presupposition of the father's equal love can have a real application in the family.

Freud, *Group Psychology and Analysis
of the Ego*, X

54 The conditions of object-choice in women are often enough made unrecognizable by social consid-

erations. Where that choice is allowed to manifest itself freely, it often occurs according to the narcissistic ideal of the man whom the girl would have liked to be. If the girl has remained attached to her father, if, that is to say, she has remained in the Oedipus-complex, then she chooses according to a father-type. Since, when she turned from her mother to her father, the antagonistic part of her ambivalent feelings remained directed on to her mother, such a choice should ensure a happy marriage. But very often a factor emerges which in general imperils such solutions of the ambivalence-conflict. The antagonism which has been left behind may follow in the wake of the positive attachment, and extend to the new object. The husband, who had in the first instance inherited his position from the father, comes in the course of time to inherit the position of the mother as well. In this way it may easily occur that the second part of a woman's life is taken up with a struggle against her husband, just as the shorter earlier part was occupied with rebellion against her mother. After this reaction has been lived out, a second marriage may easily turn out far more satisfactorily.

Freud, *New Introductory Lectures on Psycho-Analysis,* XXXIII

55 Love is but a prelude to life, an overture in which the theme of the impending work is exquisitely hinted at, but which remains nevertheless only a symbol and a promise. What is to follow, if all goes well, begins presently to appear. Passion settles down into possession, courtship into partnership, pleasure into habit. A child, half mystery and half plaything, comes to show us what we have done and to make its consequences perpetual. We see that by indulging our inclinations we have woven about us a net from which we cannot escape: our choices, bearing fruit, begin to manifest our destiny. That life which once seemed to spread out infinitely before us is narrowed to one mortal career. We learn that in morals the infinite is a chimera, and that in accomplishing anything definite a man renounces everything else. He sails henceforth for one point of the compass.

Santayana, *Life of Reason,* II, 2

2.2 | *Parents and Children*

Some of the matters covered in Section 2.1 unavoidably spill over into this one, such as the authority of parents and the respect or obedience owed to them by their offspring. But there are, in addition, many new points of interest here, such as observations about the joys and pains of parenthood and of childhood, and insights into the complexities of the parent-child relationship. If every facet of the subject is not covered, or not covered with equal adequacy, it is at least possible to claim that this assemblage of passages represents a fair sampling of the wide diversity of opinions and attitudes across the centuries. Yet it is only recently—in the last hundred years or less—that our understanding of this human relationship has grown highly sophisticated and involves in-

sights that represent probing in depth, as the reader will discover for himself by comparing the observations of such moderns as Dostoevsky, Tolstoy, and Freud with the remarks of their predecessors.

Many of the passages quoted are not statements about the relation of parents and children, but rather examples or manifestations of that relationship. Like the catalogue of the ships in Homer's *Iliad,* the mere recital of the names of famous pairs or trios recorded in these passages has the effect of awakening our interest: David and Absalom, Thetis and Achilles, Priam and Hector, Odysseus and Telemachus, Clytemnestra and Orestes, Medea and her children, Hector and Astyanax, Socrates and his sons, Anchises and Aeneas, Gertrude and Hamlet,

Lear and Cordelia, Goneril, and Regan, Squire Western and Sophia, Rousseau and his father, Mill and his, Freud and his, Stephen Daedalus (i.e., James Joyce) and his.

---

1 Unto the woman he said, I will greatly multiply thy sorrow and thy conception; in sorrow thou shalt bring forth children.

Genesis 3:16

2 And Jephthah vowed a vow unto the Lord, and said, If thou shalt without fail deliver the children of Ammon into mine hands,

Then it shall be, that whatsoever cometh forth of the doors of my house to meet me, when I return in peace from the children of Ammon, shall surely be the Lord's, and I will offer it up for a burnt offering.

So Jephthah passed over unto the children of Ammon to fight against them; and the Lord delivered them into his hands. . . .

And Jephthah came to Mizpeh unto his house, and, behold, his daughter came out to meet him with timbrels and with dances: and she was his only child; beside her he had neither son nor daughter.

And it came to pass, when he saw her, that he rent his clothes, and said, Alas, my daughter! thou hast brought me very low, and thou art one of them that trouble me: for I have opened my mouth unto the Lord, and I cannot go back.

And she said unto him, My father, if thou hast opened thy mouth unto the Lord, do to me according to that which hath proceeded out of thy mouth; forasmuch as the Lord hath taken vengeance for thee of thine enemies, even of the children of Ammon.

And she said unto her father, Let this thing be done for me: let me alone two months, that I may go up and down upon the mountains, and bewail my virginity, I and my fellows.

And he said, Go. And he sent her away for two months: and she went with her companions, and bewailed her virginity upon the mountains.

And it came to pass at the end of two months, that she returned unto her father, who did with her according to his vow which he had vowed: and she knew no man.

Judges 11:30–39

3 And the king was much moved, and went up to the chamber over the gate, and wept: and as he went, thus he said, O my son Ăb-să-lom, my son, my son Ăb-să-lom! would God I had died for thee, O Ăb-să-lom, my son, my son!

II Samuel 18:33

4 Then came there two women, that were harlots, unto the king, and stood before him.

And the one woman said, O my lord, I and this woman dwell in one house; and I was delivered of a child with her in the house.

And it came to pass the third day after that I was delivered, that this woman was delivered also: and we were together; there was no stranger with us in the house, save we two in the house.

And this woman's child died in the night; because she overlaid it.

And she arose at midnight, and took my son from beside me, while thine handmaid slept, and laid it in her bosom, and laid her dead child in my bosom.

And when I rose in the morning to give my child suck, behold, it was dead: but when I had considered it in the morning, behold, it was not my son, which I did bear.

And the other woman said, Nay; but the living is my son, and the dead is thy son. And this said, No; but the dead is thy son, and the living is my son. Thus they spake before the king.

Then said the king, The one saith, This is my son that liveth, and thy son is the dead: and the other saith, Nay; but thy son is the dead, and my son is the living.

And the king said, Bring me a sword. And they brought a sword before the king.

And the king said, Divide the living child in two, and give half to the one, and half to the other.

Then spake the woman whose the living child was unto the king, for her bowels yearned upon her son, and she said, O my lord, give her the living child, and in no wise slay it. But the other said, Let it be neither mine nor thine, but divide it.

Then the king answered and said, Give her the living child, and in no wise slay it: she is the mother thereof.

I Kings 3:16–27

5 He that spareth his rod hateth his son: but he that loveth him chasteneth him betimes.

Proverbs 13:24

6 Train up a child in the way he should go: and when he is old, he will not depart from it.

Proverbs 22:6

7 But when the twelfth dawn after this day appeared, the gods who
live forever came back to Olympos all in a body and Zeus led them; nor did Thetis forget the entreaties

of her son, but she emerged from the sea's waves early

in the morning and went up to the tall sky and Olympos.

She found Kronos' broad-browed son apart from the others

sitting upon the highest peak of rugged Olympos.

She came and sat beside him with her left hand embracing

his knees, but took him underneath the chin with her right hand

and spoke in supplication to lord Zeus son of Kronos:

'Father Zeus, if ever before in word or action

I did you favour among the immortals, now grant what I ask for.

Now give honour to my son short-lived beyond all other

mortals. Since even now the lord of men Agamemnon

dishonours him, who has taken away his prize and keeps it.

Zeus of the counsels, lord of Olympos, now do him honour.

So long put strength into the Trojans, until the Achaians

give my son his rights, and his honour is increased among them.'

Homer, Iliad, I, 493

8 Then tall Hektor of the shining helm answered her. . . .

'I know this thing well in my heart, and my mind knows it:

there will come a day when sacred Ilion shall perish,

and Priam, and the people of Priam of the strong ash spear.

But it is not so much the pain to come of the Trojans

that troubles me, not even of Priam the king nor Hekabe,

not the thought of my brothers who in their numbers and valour

shall drop in the dust under the hands of men who hate them,

as troubles me the thought of you, when some bronze-armoured

Achaian leads you off, taking away your day of liberty,

in tears; and in Argos you must work at the loom of another,

and carry water from the spring Messeis or Hypereia,

all unwilling, but strong will be the necessity upon you;

and some day seeing you shedding tears a man will say of you:

"This is the wife of Hektor, who was ever the bravest fighter

of the Trojans, breakers of horses, in the days

when they fought about Ilion."

So will one speak of you; and for you it will be yet a fresh grief,

to be widowed of such a man who could fight off the day of your slavery.

But may I be dead and the piled earth hide me under before I

hear you crying and know by this that they drag you captive.'

So speaking glorious Hektor held out his arms to his baby,

who shrank back to his fair-girdled nurse's bosom

screaming, and frightened at the aspect of his own father,

terrified as he saw the bronze and the crest with its horse-hair,

nodding dreadfully, as he thought, from the peak of the helmet.

Then his beloved father laughed out, and his honoured mother,

and at once glorious Hektor lifted from his head the helmet

and laid it in all its shining upon the ground. Then taking

up his dear son he tossed him about in his arms, and kissed him,

and lifted his voice in prayer to Zeus and the other immortals:

'Zeus, and you other immortals, grant that this boy, who is my son,

may be as I am, pre-eminent among the Trojans,

great in strength, as am I, and rule strongly over Ilion;

and some day let them say of him: "He is better by far than his father",

as he comes in from the fighting; and let him kill his enemy

and bring home the blooded spoils, and delight the heart of his mother.'

So speaking he set his child again in the arms of his beloved

wife, who took him back again to her fragrant bosom

smiling in her tears.

Homer, Iliad, VI, 440

9 *Andromache.* The day

of bereavement leaves a child with no agemates to befriend him.

He bows his head before everyman, his cheeks are bewept, he

goes, needy, a boy among his father's companions,

and tugs at this man by the mantle, that man by the tunic,

and they pity him, and one gives him a tiny drink from a goblet,

enough to moisten his lips, not enough to moisten his palate.

But one whose parents are living beats him out of the banquet hitting him with his fists and in words also abuses him:

"Get out, you! Your father is not dining among us."

Homer, *Iliad*, XXII, 489

10 *Athena.* "But tell me this now, make it clear to me:
You must be, by your looks, Odysseus' boy?
The way your head is shaped, the fine eyes—yes,
how like him! We took meals like this together
many a time, before he sailed for Troy
with all the lords of Argos in the ships.
I have not seen him since, nor has he seen me."

And thoughtfully Telémakhos replied:

"Friend, let me put it in the plainest way.
My mother says I am his son; I know not
surely. Who has known his own engendering?
I wish at least I had some happy man
as father, growing old in his house—
but unknown death and silence are the fate
of him that, since you ask, they call my father."

Homer, *Odyssey*, I, 213

11 *Cilissa.*   A baby is like a beast, it does not think
but you have to nurse it, do you not, the way it wants.
For the child still in swaddling clothes can not tell us
if he is hungry or thirsty, if he needs to make water. Children's young insides are a law to themselves.

Aeschylus, *Libation Bearers*, 753

12 *Chorus.* Amongst mortals I do assert that they who are wholly without experience and have never had children far surpass in happiness those who are parents. The childless, because they have never proved whether children grow up to be a blessing or curse to men are removed from all share in many troubles; whilst those who have a sweet race of children growing up in their houses do wear away, as I perceive, their whole life through; first with the thought how they may train them up in virtue, next how they shall leave their sons the means to live; and after all this 'tis far from clear whether on good or bad children they bestow their toil. But one last crowning woe for every mortal man I now will name; suppose that they have found sufficient means to live, and seen their children grow to man's estate and walk in virtue's path, still if fortune so befall, comes Death and bears the children's bodies off to Hades. Can it be any profit to the gods to heap upon us mortal men beside our other woes this further grief for children lost, a grief surpassing all?

Euripides, *Medea*, 1090

13 *Medea.* My friends, I am resolved upon the deed; at once will I slay my children and then leave this land, without delaying long enough to hand them over to some more savage hand to butcher. Needs

must they die in any case; and since they must, I will slay them—I, the mother that bare them. O heart of mine, steel thyself! Why do I hesitate to do the awful deed that must be done? Come, take the sword, thou wretched hand of mine! Take it, and advance to the post whence starts the life of sorrow! Away with cowardice! Give not one thought to thy babes, how dear they are or how thou art their mother. This one brief day forget thy children dear, and after that lament; for though thou wilt slay them yet they were thy darlings still.

Euripides, *Medea*, 1236

14 *Andromache.* O darling child I loved too well for happiness,
your enemies will kill you and leave your mother forlorn.
Your own father's nobility, where others found protection, means your murder now. The memory of his valor comes ill-timed for you. O bridal bed,
O marriage rites that brought me home to Hector's house
a bride, you were unhappy in the end. I lived never thinking the baby I had was born for butchery
by Greeks, but for lordship over all Asia's pride of earth.
Poor child, are you crying too? Do you know what they
will do to you? Your fingers clutch my dress. What use,
to nestle like a young bird under the mother's wing?
Hector cannot come back, not burst from underground
to save you, that spear of glory caught in the quick hand,
nor Hector's kin, nor any strength of Phrygian arms.
Yours the sick leap head downward from the height, the fall
where none have pity, and the spirit smashed out in death.
O last and loveliest embrace of all, O child's sweet fragrant body. Vanity in the end. I nursed for nothing the swaddled baby at this mother's breast
in vain the wrack of the labor pains and the long sickness.
Now once again, and never after this, come close to your mother, lean against my breast and wind your arms
around my neck, and put your lips against my lips.

Euripides, *Trojan Women*, 740

15 *Iphis.* In grief I ask: Why cannot mortals be
Twice young, then reach old age a second time?
If anything goes wrong at home, we right it
By afterthoughts; but not so with a life.
If youth and age came twice, a double life

Would be our lot, and we could set things right
No matter what mistakes were made. When I saw others
With families, I became an adorer of children
And sorely longed for some to call my own.
If I had come to this experience
With children, and known what it is for a father to lose them,
Never would I have reached the point of woe
Where now I stand: to have started into life
A noble youth,˙ and then be robbed of him.
And now, in my wretchedness, what shall I do?
Return to my house, to see the emptiness
Of many rooms, and a hopeless round of living?
Or shall I go where Capaneus once dwelt?
What a delight that was, when I had this child!
But now she is no more—she who would draw
My cheek to her lips and clasp my head in her hands.
To an old father, nothing is more sweet
Than a daughter. Boys are more spirited, but their ways
Are not so tender.

Euripides, *Suppliant Women,* 1080

16 *Orestes.* I had two duties, two clear choices,
both of them conflicting.

My father begot me,
my mother gave me birth. She was the furrow
in which his seed was sown. But without the father,
there is no birth. That being so, I thought,
I ought to stand by him, the true agent
of my birth and being, rather than with her
who merely brought me up.

Euripides, *Orestes,* 552

17 *Orestes.*   Tell me, what would happen
if our women decided to adopt my mother's example,
killed their husbands and then came rushing home
to their children, exposing their breasts for pity?
Why, they could murder a man for any trifle,
on any pretext. But my "crime," as you call it,
has stopped that practice for good or kept it
from spreading.

I had every right to kill her.
I hated her, and I had every reason in the world
to hate.

Gods, my poor father away from home,
a soldier fighting in war in his country's service,
and what did she do? She took a lover
and betrayed his bed!

And when she was caught,
did she do the proper thing and put herself
to death?

Not my mother. No, she murdered him
to save herself.

I should not invoke the gods
when defending myself on a charge of murder,

but *in god's name, in the name of heaven,*
what was I supposed to do?

Shout hurrah
by keeping still?

Euripides, *Orestes,* 566

18 *Socrates.* When my sons are grown up, I would ask you, O my friends, to punish them; and I would have you trouble them, as I have troubled you, if they seem to care about riches, or anything, more than about virtue; or if they pretend to be something when they are really nothing,—then reprove them, as I have reproved you, for not caring about that for which they ought to care, and thinking that they are something when they are really nothing. And if you do this, both I and my sons will have received justice at your hands.

Plato, *Apology,* 41B

19 *Athenian Stranger.* All which a man has belongs to those who gave him birth and brought him up, and that he must do all that he can to minister to them, first, in his property, secondly, in his person, and thirdly, in his soul, in return for the endless care and travail which they bestowed upon him of old, in the days of his infancy, and which he is now to pay back to them when they are old and in the extremity of their need. And all his life long he ought never to utter, or to have uttered, an unbecoming word to them; for of light and fleeting words the penalty is most severe; Nemesis, the messenger of justice, is appointed to watch over all such matters. When they are angry and want to satisfy their feelings in word or deed, he should give way to them; for a father who thinks that he has been wronged by his son may be reasonably expected to be very angry. At their death, the most moderate funeral is best, neither exceeding the customary expense, nor yet falling short of the honour which has been usually shown by the former generation to their parents. And let a man not forget to pay the yearly tribute of respect to the dead, honouring them chiefly by omitting nothing that conduces to a perpetual remembrance of them, and giving a reasonable portion of his fortune to the dead. Doing this, and living after this manner, we shall receive our reward from the Gods and those who are above us [that is, the demons]; and we shall spend our days for the most part in good hope.

Plato, *Laws,* IV, 717A

20 *Athenian Stranger.* Of all animals the boy is the most unmanageable, inasmuch as he has the fountain of reason in him not yet regulated; he is the most insidious, sharp-witted, and insubordinate of animals. Wherefore he must be bound with many bridles; in the first place, when he gets away from mothers and nurses, he must be under the management of tutors on account of his childishness and foolishness; then, again, being a freeman, he

must be controlled by teachers, no matter what they teach, and by studies; but he is also a slave, and in that regard any freeman who comes in his way may punish him and his tutor and his instructor, if any of them does anything wrong; and he who comes across him and does not inflict upon him the punishment which he deserves, shall incur the greatest disgrace.

Plato, *Laws*, VII, 808B

21 In the matter of food we should help our parents before all others, since we owe our own nourishment to them, and it is more honourable to help in this respect the authors of our being even before ourselves; and honour too one should give to one's parents as one does to the gods, but not any and every honour; for that matter one should not give the same honour to one's father and one's mother.

Aristotle, *Ethics*, 1165ª21

22 Those are wrong who in their laws attempt to check the loud crying and screaming of children, for these contribute towards their growth, and, in a manner, exercise their bodies. Straining the voice has a strengthening effect similar to that produced by the retention of the breath in violent exertions.

Aristotle, *Politics*, 1336ª34

23 Begin, auspicious boy! to cast about
Thy infant eyes, and, with a smile, thy mother
single out.
Thy mother well deserves that short delight,
The nauseous qualms of ten long months and tra-
vail to requite.
Then smile! the frowning infant's doom is read,
No god shall crown the board, nor goddess bless
the bed.

Virgil, *Eclogues*, IV

24 *Coroebus.* Behold! Polites, one of Priam's sons,
Pursued by Pyrrhus, there for safety runs.
Thro' swords and foes, amaz'd and hurt, he flies
Thro' empty courts and open galleries.
Him Pyrrhus, urging with his lance, pursues,
And often reaches, and his thrusts renews.
The youth, transfix'd, with lamentable cries,
Expires before his wretched parent's eyes:
Whom gasping at his feet when Priam saw,
The fear of death gave place to nature's law;
And, shaking more with anger than with age,
'The gods,' said he, 'requite thy brutal rage!
As sure they will, barbarian, sure they must,
If there be gods in heav'n, and gods be just—
Who tak'st in wrongs an insolent delight;
With a son's death t' infect a father's sight.'

Virgil, *Aeneid*, II

25 *Aeneas.* Scarce had he said, when, on our left, we
hear
A peal of rattling thunder roll in air:

There shot a streaming lamp along the sky,
Which on the winged lightning seem'd to fly;
From o'er the roof the blaze began to move,
And, trailing, vanish'd in th' Idæan grove.
It swept a path in heav'n, and shone a guide,
Then in a steaming stench of sulphur died.
"The good old man with suppliant hands
implor'd
The gods' protection, and their star ador'd.
'Now, now,' said he, 'my son, no more delay!
I yield, I follow where Heav'n shews the way. . . .
'Haste, my dear father, ('tis no time to wait,)
And load my shoulders with a willing freight.
Whate'er befalls, your life shall be my care;
One death, or one deliv'rance, we will share.
My hand shall lead our little son; and you,
My faithful consort, shall our steps pursue."

Virgil, *Aeneid*, II

26 And lo a voice from heaven, saying, This is my beloved Son, in whom I am well pleased.

Matthew 3:17

27 Now his parents went to Jerusalem every year at the feast of the passover.

And when he was twelve years old, they went up to Jerusalem after the custom of the feast.

And when they had fulfilled the days, as they returned, the child Jesus tarried behind in Jerusalem; and Joseph and his mother knew not of it.

But they, supposing him to have been in the company, went a day's journey; and they sought him among their kinsfolk and acquaintance.

And when they found him not, they turned back again to Jerusalem, seeking him.

And it came to pass, that after three days they found him in the temple, sitting in the midst of the doctors, both hearing them, and asking them questions.

And all that heard him were astonished at his understanding and answers.

And when they saw him, they were amazed: and his mother said unto him, Son, why hast thou thus dealt with us? behold, thy father and I have sought thee sorrowing.

And he said unto them, How is it that ye sought me? wist ye not that I must be about my Father's business?

And they understood not the saying which he spake unto them.

And he went down with them, and came to Nazareth, and was subject unto them: but his mother kept all these sayings in her heart.

Luke 2:41–51

28 And he said, A certain man had two sons:

And the younger of them said to his father, Father, give me the portion of goods that falleth to me. And he divided unto them his living.

And not many days after the younger son gathered all together, and took his journey into a far country, and there wasted his substance with riotous living.

And when he had spent all, there arose a mighty famine in that land; and he began to be in want.

And he went and joined himself to a citizen of that country; and he sent him into his fields to feed swine.

And he would fain have filled his belly with the husks that the swine did eat: and no man gave unto him.

And when he came to himself, he said, How many hired servants of my father's have bread enough and to spare, and I perish with hunger!

I will arise and go to my father, and will say unto him, Father, I have sinned against heaven, and before thee,

And am no more worthy to be called thy son: make me as one of thy hired servants.

And he arose, and came to his father. But when he was yet a great way off, his father saw him, and had compassion, and ran, and fell on his neck, and kissed him.

And the son said unto him, Father, I have sinned against heaven, and in thy sight, and am no more worthy to be called thy son.

But the father said to his servants, Bring forth the best robe, and put it on him; and put a ring on his hand, and shoes on his feet:

And bring hither the fatted calf, and kill it; and let us eat, and be merry:

For this my son was dead, and is alive again; he was lost, and is found. And they began to be merry.

Now his elder son was in the field: and as he came and drew nigh to the house, he heard musick and dancing.

And he called one of the servants, and asked what these things meant.

And he said unto him, Thy brother is come; and thy father hath killed the fatted calf, because he hath received him safe and sound.

And he was angry, and would not go in: therefore came his father out, and intreated him.

And he answering said to his father, Lo, these many years do I serve thee, neither transgressed I at any time thy commandment: and yet thou never gavest me a kid, that I might make merry with my friends:

But as soon as this thy son was come, which hath devoured thy living with harlots, thou hast killed for him the fatted calf.

And he said unto him, Son, thou art ever with me, and all that I have is thine.

It was meet that we should make merry, and be glad: for this thy brother was dead, and is alive again; and was lost, and is found.

Luke 15:11–32

29 The sayings of Themistocles, who, when his son was making many demands of him by means of

his mother, said, "O woman, the Athenians govern the Greeks; I govern the Athenians, but you govern me, and your son governs you; so let him use his power sparingly, since, simple as he is, he can do more than all the Greeks together."

Plutarch, *Marcus Cato*

30 As soon as he [Cato] had a son born, though he had never such urgent business upon his hands, unless it were some public matter, he would be by when his wife washed it and dressed it in its swaddling clothes. For she herself suckled it; nay, she often, too, gave her breast to her servants' children, to produce, by suckling the same milk, a kind of natural love in them to her son. When he began to come to years of discretion, Cato himself would teach him to read, although he had a servant, a very good grammarian, called Chilo, who taught many others; but he thought not fit, as he himself said, to have his son reprimanded by a slave, or pulled, it may be, by the ears when found tardy in his lesson: nor would he have him owe to a servant the obligation of so great a thing as his learning; he himself, therefore (as we were saying), taught him his grammar, law, and his gymnastic exercises. Nor did he only show him, too, how to throw a dart, to fight in armour, and to ride, but to box also and to endure both heat and cold, and to swim over the most rapid and rough rivers. He says, likewise, that he wrote histories, in large characters, with his own hand, that so his son, without stirring out of the house, might learn to know about his countrymen and forefathers; nor did he less abstain from speaking anything obscene before his son, than if it had been in the presence of the sacred virgins, called vestals.

Plutarch, *Marcus Cato*

31 After the birth of our four sons you yearned for a daughter, and I seized the opportunity of giving her your dear name: I know that she was precious to you. Peculiar poignancy attaches to tenderness for children when their presence is altogether welcome and completely untainted by ill will and reproach. The child herself possessed a marvelous cheeriness of temper and gentleness, and her responsiveness to love and eagerness to please evoked not only pleasure but an appreciation of human goodness. She would invite her nurse to offer her breast not only to other infants but even to furnishings and toys in which she took delight. It was as if, out of humane sensibilities, she invited them to her own table, to share in the good things she had; what was most delightful to her she wished all who pleased her to enjoy.

I cannot see, my dear wife, why these and similar qualities which delighted us when she was alive should now distress and confound us when we bring them to mind. Rather do I fear lest we lose those memories along with our grief. . . . In general, nature avoids everything that causes distress. But in the case of our child, in the degree that she proved to us a thing most lovable to fondle and look at and hear, so the memory of her must abide with us and become part of us, and it will bring us a greater quantity and variety of joy than of sorrow.

Plutarch, *Consolation to His Wife*

32 So, shun damnable deeds. For this there's at least one good reason—
Lest our children repeat the crimes we have taught them. We all
Are easily led, too prone to imitate wicked behavior. . . .
To a child is due the greatest respect: in whatever
Nastiness you prepare, don't despise the years of your children,
But let your infant son dissuade you from being a sinner,
For if, in days to come, he earns the wrath of the censor,
Being a man like you not only in body and features,
But also the son of your ways, a walker in all of your footsteps,
Treading deeper in vice, you will—oh, of course!—be indignant,
Rail with bitter noise, and make a new will. That will teach him.
Yet what makes you assume the father's frown, and the father's
Freedom of speech and act, when you behave worse, as an old man,
Than he ever did, and the windy cupping-glass searches
Vainly around your head for brains that it cannot discover?

Juvenal, *Satire XIV*

33 Once a child is born, it is no longer in our power not to love it nor care about it.

Epictetus, *Discourses*, I, 23

34 Throw between yourself and your son a little estate, and you will know how soon he will wish to bury you and how soon you wish your son to die.

Epictetus, *Discourses*, II, 22

35 My mother [St. Monica] would not be satisfied but urged him [the bishop] with repeated entreaties and floods of tears to see me and discuss with me. He, losing patience, said: "Go your way; as sure as you live, it is impossible that the son of these tears should perish." In the conversations we had afterwards, she often said that she had accepted this answer as if it had sounded from heaven.

Augustine, *Confessions*, III, 12

36 What a gulf there is between the restraint of the marriage-covenant entered into for the sake of children and the mere bargain of a lustful love, where if children come they come unwanted— though when they are born, they compel our love.

Augustine, *Confessions*, IV, 2

37 Why I left the one country and went to the other, You Knew, O God, but You did not tell either me or my mother. She indeed was in dreadful grief at my going and followed me right to the seacoast. There she clung to me passionately, determined that I should either go back home with her or take her to Rome with me, but I deceived her with the pretence that I had a friend whom I did not want to leave until he had sailed off with a fair wind. Thus I lied to my mother, and such a mother.

Augustine, *Confessions*, V, 8

38 When the day was approaching on which she [St. Monica] was to depart this life—a day that You knew though we did not—it came about, as I believe by Your secret arrangement, that she and I stood alone leaning in a window, which looked inwards to the garden within the house where we were staying, at Ostia on the Tiber; for there we were away from everybody, resting for the sea-voyage from the weariness of our long journey by land. There we talked together, she and I alone, in deep joy; and *forgetting the things that were behind and looking forward to those that were before,* we were discussing in the presence of Truth, which You are, what the eternal life of the saints could be like, *which eye has not seen nor ear heard, nor has it entered into the heart of man.* But with the mouth of our heart we panted for the high waters of Your fountain, the fountain of the life which is with You: that being sprinkled from that fountain according to our capacity, we might in some sense meditate upon so great a matter.

And our conversation had brought us to this point, that any pleasure whatsoever of the bodily senses, in any brightness whatsoever of corporeal light, seemed to us not worth of comparison with the pleasure of that eternal Light, not worthy even of mention. Rising as our love flamed upward towards that Selfsame, we passed in review the various levels of bodily things, up to the heavens themselves, whence sun and moon and stars shine upon this earth. And higher still we soared, thinking in our minds and speaking and marvelling at Your works: and so we came to our own souls, and went beyond them to come at last to that region of richness unending, where You feed Israel forever with the food of truth.

Augustine, *Confessions*, IX, 10

39 When her [St. Monica's] illness was close to its end, meeting with expressions of endearment such services as I rendered, she called me a dutiful loving son, and said in the great affection of her love that she had never heard from my mouth any harsh or reproachful word addressed to herself.

But what possible comparison was there, O my God who made us, between the honour I showed her and the service she had rendered me?

Augustine, *Confessions*, IX, 12

40 A man's children are more lovable to him than his father. . . . First, because parents love their children as being part of themselves; but the father is not part of his son, so that the love of a father for his children, is more like a man's love for himself. Secondly, because parents know better that so and so is their child than vice versa. Thirdly, because children are nearer to their parents, as being part of them than their parents are to them to whom they stand in the relation of a principle. Fourthly, because parents have loved longer, for the father begins to love his child at once, while the child begins to love his father after a lapse of time; and the longer love lasts, the stronger it is.

Aquinas, *Summa Theologica*, II–II, 26, 9

41 Strictly speaking, . . . the father should be loved more than the mother. For father and mother are loved as principles of our natural origin. Now the father is principle in a more excellent way than the mother, because he is the active principle, while the mother is a passive and material principle. Consequently, strictly speaking, the father is to be loved more.

Aquinas, *Summa Theologica*, II–II, 26, 10

42 You fathers and you mothers fond, also,
If you have children, be it one or two,
Yours is the burden of their wise guidance
The while they are within your governance.
Beware that not from your own lax living,
Or by your negligence in chastening
They fall and perish; for I dare well say,
If that should chance you'll dearly have to pay.
Under a shepherd soft and negligent
Full many a sheep and lamb by wolf is rent.

Chaucer, *Canterbury Tales:* Physician's Tale

43 May not these fathers and mothers, think you, be sorrowful and heavy-hearted, when they see an unknown fellow, a vagabond stranger, a barbarous lout, a rude cur, rotten, fleshless, putrified, scraggy, boily, botchy, poor, a forlorn caitiff, and miserable sneak, by an open rapt, snatch away before their own eyes their so fair, delicate, neat, well-behavioured, richly provided for and healthful daughters, on whose breeding and education they had spared no cost nor charges, by bringing them up in an honest discipline to all the honourable and virtuous employments becoming one of their sex, descended of a noble parentage, hoping by those commendable and industrious means in an opportune and convenient time to bestow them on the worthy sons of their well-deserving neighbours and ancient friends, who had nourished, entertained, taught, instructed, and schooled their children with the same care and solicitude, to make them matches fit to attain to the felicity of a so happy marriage, that from them might issue an offspring and progeny no less heirs to the laudable endowments and exquisite qualifications of their parents, whom they every way resemble, than to their personal and real estates, moveables and inheritances? How doleful, trist, and plangorous would such a sight and pageantry prove unto them?

Rabelais, *Gargantua and Pantagruel*, III, 48

44 If there is any truly natural law, that is to say, any instinct that is seen universally and permanently imprinted in both the animals and ourselves (which is not beyond dispute), I may say that in my opinion, after the care every animal has for its own preservation and the avoidance of what is harmful, the affection that the begetter has for his begotten ranks second. And because Nature seems to have recommended it to us with a view to extending and advancing the successive parts of this machine of hers, it is no wonder if, turning backward, the affection of children for their fathers is not so great.

Montaigne, *Essays*, II, 8,
Affection of Fathers

45 A true and well-regulated affection should be born and increase with the knowledge children give us of themselves; and then, if they are worthy of it, the natural propensity going along with reason, we should cherish them with a truly paternal love; and we should likewise pass judgment on them if they are otherwise, always submitting to reason, notwithstanding the force of nature. It is very often the reverse; and most commonly we feel more excited over the stamping, the games, and the infantile tricks of our children than we do later over their grown-up actions, as if we had loved them for our pastime, like monkeys, not like men. And some supply toys very liberally for their childhood, who tighten up at the slightest expenditure they need when they are of age. Indeed it seems that the jealousy we feel at seeing them appear in the world and enjoy it when we are about to leave it makes us more stingy and tight with them; it vexes us that they are treading on our heels, as if to solicit us to leave. And if we had that to fear, then since in the nature of things they cannot in truth either be or live except at the expense of our being and our life, we should not have meddled with being fathers.

As for me, I think it is cruelty and injustice not to receive them into a share and association in our goods, and as companions in the understanding of our domestic affairs, when they are capable of it, and not to cut down and restrict our own comforts in order to provide for theirs, since we have begotten them to that end. It is an injustice that an old, broken, half-dead father should enjoy alone, in a corner of his hearth, possessions that would suffice for the advancement and maintenance of many children, and let them meanwhile, for lack of means, lose their best years without making progress in public service and the knowledge of men.

Montaigne, *Essays,* II, 8, Affection of Fathers

46 It is . . . wrong and foolish to prohibit children who have come of age from being familiar with their fathers, and to prefer to maintain an austere and disdainful gravity toward them, hoping thereby to keep them in fear and obedience. For that is a very futile farce, which makes fathers annoying to their children and, what is worse, ridiculous. They have in their hands youth and vigor, and consequently the wind and favor of the world behind them; and they receive with mockery these fierce and tyrannical looks from men who have no blood left in either heart or veins—real scarecrows in a hemp field. Even if I could make myself feared, I would much rather make myself loved.

Montaigne, *Essays,* II, 8, Affection of Fathers

47 My father loved to build up Montaigne, where he was born; and in all this administration of domestic affairs, I love to follow his example and his rules, and shall bind my successors to them as much as I can. If I could do better for him, I would. I glory in the fact that his will still operates and acts through me. God forbid that I should allow to fail in my hands any semblance of life that I could restore to so good a father. Whenever I have taken a hand in completing some old bit of wall and repairing some badly constructed building, it has certainly been out of regard more to his intentions than to my own satisfaction. And I blame my indolence that I have not gone further toward completing the things he began so handsomely in his house; all the more because I have a good chance of being the last of my race to possess it, and the last to put a hand to it.

Montaigne, *Essays,* III, 9, Of Vanity

48 *Launcelot.* It is a wise father that knows his own child.

Shakespeare, *Merchant of Venice,* II, ii, 80

49 *Ghost.* List, list, O, list!
If thou didst ever thy dear father love—
 Hamlet. O God!
 Ghost. Revenge his foul and most unnatural murder.
 Ham. Murder!
 Ghost. Murder most foul, as in the best it is;
But this most foul, strange, and unnatural.
 Ham. Haste me to know't, that I, with wings as swift

As meditation or the thoughts of love,
May sweep to my revenge.
 Ghost. I find thee apt;
And duller shouldst thou be than the fat weed
That roots itself in ease on Lethe wharf,
Wouldst thou not stir in this.

Shakespeare, *Hamlet,* I, v, 22

50 *Hamlet.* Now, mother, what's the matter?
 Queen. Hamlet, thou hast thy father much offended.
 Ham. Mother, you have my father much offended.
 Queen. Come, come, you answer with an idle tongue.
 Ham. Go, go, you question with a wicked tongue.
 Queen. Why, how now, Hamlet!
 Ham. What's the matter now?
 Queen. Have you forgot me?
 Ham. No, by the rood, not so:
You are the Queen, your husband's brother's wife;
And—would it were not so!—you are my mother.

Shakespeare, *Hamlet,* III, iv, 8

51 *Lear.* Give me the map there. Know that we have divided
In three our kingdom; and 'tis our fast intent
To shake all cares and business from our age;
Conferring them on younger strengths, while we
Unburthen'd crawl toward death. Our son of Cornwall,
And you, our no less loving son of Albany,
We have this hour a constant will to publish
Our daughters' several dowers, that future strife
May be prevented now. The Princes, France and Burgundy,
Great rivals in our youngest daughter's love,
Long in our court have made their amorous sojourn,
And here are to be answer'd. Tell me, my daughters—
Since now we will divest us, both of rule,
Interest of territory, cares of state—
Which of you shall we say doth love us most?

Shakespeare, *Lear,* I, i, 38

52 *Cordelia.* Unhappy that I am, I cannot heave
My heart into my mouth. I love your Majesty
According to my bond; nor more nor less.
 Lear. How, how, Cordelia! mend your speech a little,
Lest it may mar your fortunes.
 Cor. Good my lord,
You have begot me, bred me, loved me. I
Return those duties back as are right fit,
Obey you, love you, and most honour you.
Why have my sisters husbands, if they say
They love you all? Haply, when I shall wed,
That lord whose hand must take my plight shall carry

Half my love with him, half my care and duty.
Sure, I shall never marry like my sisters,
To love my father all.
    Lear. But goes thy heart with this?
    Cor.   Ay, good my lord.
    Lear. So young, and so untender?
    Cor. So young, my lord, and true.
    Lear. Let it be so; thy truth, then, be thy dower.

            Shakespeare, *Lear,* I, i, 93

53 *Lear.* Hear, Nature, hear; dear goddess, hear!
Suspend thy purpose, if thou didst intend
To make this creature fruitful!
Into her womb convey sterility!
Dry up in her the organs of increase;
And from her derogate body never spring
A babe to honour her! If she must teem,
Create her child of spleen; that it may live,
And be a thwart disnatured torment to her!
Let it stamp wrinkles in her brow of youth;
With cadent tears fret channels in her cheeks;
Turn all her mother's pains and benefits
To laughter and contempt; that she may feel
How sharper than a serpent's tooth it is
To have a thankless child! Away, away!

           Shakespeare, *Lear,* I, iv, 297

54 *Doctor.* Please you, draw near. Louder the music
    there!
    Cordelia. O my dear father! Restoration hang
Thy medicine on my lips; and let this kiss
Repair those violent harms that my two sisters
Have in thy reverence made!
    Kent.   Kind and dear Princess!
    Cor. Had you not been their father, these white
    flakes
Had challenged pity of them. Was this a face
To be opposed against the warring winds?
To stand against the deep dread-bolted thunder?
In the most terrible and nimble stroke
Of quick, cross lightning? to watch—poor per-
    du!—
With this thin helm? Mine enemy's dog,
Though he had bit me, should have stood that
    night
Against my fire; and wast thou fain, poor father,
To hovel thee with swine and rogues forlorn
In short and musty straw? Alack, alack!
'Tis wonder that thy life and wits at once
Had not concluded all. He wakes; speak to him.
    Doct. Madam, do you; 'tis fittest.
    Cor. How does my royal lord? How fares your
    Majesty?
    Lear. You do me wrong to take me out o' the
    grave.
Thou art a soul in bliss; but I am bound
Upon a wheel of fire, that mine own tears
Do scald like molten lead.
    Cor.   Sir, do you know me?
    Lear. You are a spirit, I know. When did you
    die?

    Cor. Still, still, far wide!
    Doct. He's scarce awake. Let him alone awhile.
    Lear. Where have I been? Where am I? Fair
    daylight?
I am mightily abused. I should e'en die with pity,
To see another thus. I know not what to say.
I will not swear these are my hands. Let's see;
I feel this pin prick. Would I were assured
Of my condition!
    Cor.   O, look upon me, sir,
And hold your hands in benediction o'er me.
No, sir, you must not kneel.
    Lear.   Pray, do not mock me.
I am a very foolish fond old man,
Fourscore and upward, not an hour more nor less;
And, to deal plainly,
I fear I am not in my perfect mind.
Methinks I should know you, and know this man;
Yet I am doubtful; for I am mainly ignorant
What place this is; and all the skill I have
Remembers not these garments; nor I know not
Where I did lodge last night. Do not laugh at me;
For, as I am a man, I think this lady
To be my child Cordelia.
    Cor.   And so I am, I am.
    Lear. Be your tears wet? yes, 'faith. I pray, weep
    not.
If you have poison for me, I will drink it.
I know you do not love me; for your sisters
Have, as I do remember, done me wrong.
You have some cause, they have not.
    Cor.   No cause, no cause.

           Shakespeare, *Lear,* IV, vii, 25

55 *Pericles.* A terrible childbed hast thou had, my
    dear;
No light, no fire; the unfriendly elements
Forgot thee utterly; nor have I time
To give thee hallow'd to thy grave, but straight
Must cast thee, scarcely coffin'd, in the ooze,
Where, for a monument upon thy bones,
And e'er-remaining lamps, the belching whale
And humming water must o'erwhelm thy corpse,
Lying with simple shells. O Lychorida,
Bid Nestor bring me spices, ink, and paper,
My casket and my jewels; and bid Nicander
Bring me the satin coffer. Lay the babe
Upon the pillow. Hie thee, whiles I say
A priestly farewell to her.

           Shakespeare, *Pericles,* III, i, 57

56 *Leontes.*   Looking on the lines
Of my boy's face, methoughts I did recoil
Twenty-three years, and saw myself unbreech'd,
In my green velvet coat, my dagger muzzled,
Lest it should bite its master, and so prove,
As ornaments oft do, too dangerous.
How like, methought, I then was to this kernel,
This squash, this gentleman.

         Shakespeare, *Winter's Tale,* I, ii, 153

57 Sir, reply'd Don *Quixote,* Children are the Flesh and Blood of their Parents, and, whether good or bad, are to be cherish'd as part of ourselves. 'Tis the Duty of a Father to train 'em up from their tenderest Years in the Paths of Vertue, in good Discipline and Christian Principles, that when they advance in Years they may become the Staff and Support of their Parents Age, and the Glory of their Posterity. But as for forcing them to this or that Study, 'tis a thing I don't so well approve. Persuasion is all, I think, that is proper in such a case; especially when they are so Fortunate as to be above studying for Bread, as having Parents that can provide for their future Subsistence, they ought in my Opinion to be indulged in the Pursuit of that Science to which their own Genius gives them the most Inclination.

Cervantes, *Don Quixote,* II, 16

58 Farewell, thou child of my right hand, and joy;
My sin was too much hope of thee, loved boy:
Seven years thou wert lent to me, and I thee pay,
Exacted by thy fate, on the just day.
O could I lose all father now! for why
Will man lament the state he should envy,
To have so soon 'scaped world's and flesh's rage,
And, if no other misery, yet age?
Rest in soft peace, and asked, say, "Here doth lie
Ben Jonson his best piece of poetry."

Jonson, *On My First Son*

59 The joys of parents are secret; and so are their griefs and fears. They cannot utter the one; nor they will not utter the other. Children sweeten labours; but they make misfortunes more bitter. They increase the cares of life; but they mitigate the remembrance of death. The perpetuity by generation is common to beasts; but memory, merit, and noble works are proper to men. And surely a man shall see the noblest works and foundations have proceeded from childless men; which have sought to express the images of their minds, where those of their bodies have failed. So the care of posterity is most in them that have no posterity. They that are the first raisers of their houses are most indulgent towards their children; beholding them as the continuance not only of their kind but of their work; and so both children and creatures.

Bacon, *Of Parents and Children*

60 There is also no need to distinguish as many kinds of love as there are diverse objects which we may love; for, to take an example, although the passions which an ambitious man has for glory, a miser for money, a drunkard for wine, a brutal man for a woman whom he desires to violate, a man of honour for his friend or mistress, and a good father for his children, may be very different, still, inasmuch as they participate in love, they are similar. But the four first only have love for the possession of the objects to which their passion relates, and do not have any for the objects themselves, for which they only have desire mingled with other particular passions. But the love which a good father has for his children is so pure that he desires to have nothing from them, and does not wish to possess them otherwise than he does, nor to be united with them more closely than he already is. For, considering them as replicas of himself, he seeks their good as his own, or even with greater care, because, in setting before himself that he or they form a whole of which he is not the best part, he often prefers their interests to his, and does not fear losing himself in order to save them.

Descartes, *Passions of the Soul,* LXXXII

61 Dominion is acquired two ways: by generation and by conquest. The right of dominion by generation is that which the parent hath over his children, and is called *paternal.* And is not so derived from the generation, as if therefore the parent had dominion over his child because he begat him, but from the child's consent, either express or by other sufficient arguments declared. For as to the generation, God hath ordained to man a helper, and there be always two that are equally parents: the dominion therefore over the child should belong equally to both, and he be equally subject to both, which is impossible; for no man can obey two masters. And whereas some have attributed the dominion to the man only, as being of the more excellent sex, they misreckon in it. For there is not always that difference of strength or prudence between the man and the woman as that the right can be determined without war. In Commonwealths this controversy is decided by the civil law: and for the most part, but not always, the sentence is in favour of the father, because for the most part Commonwealths have been erected by the fathers, not by the mothers of families. But the question lieth now in the state of mere nature where there are supposed no laws of matrimony, no laws for the education of children, but the law of nature and the natural inclination of the sexes, one to another, and to their children. . . .

If there be no contract, the dominion is in the mother. For in the condition of mere nature, where there are no matrimonial laws, it cannot be known who is the father unless it be declared by the mother; and therefore the right of dominion over the child dependeth on her will, and is consequently hers. Again, seeing the infant is first in the power of the mother, so as she may either nourish or expose it; if She nourish it, it oweth its life to the mother, and is therefore obliged to obey her rather than any other; and by consequence the dominion over it is hers. But if she expose it, and another find and nourish it, the dominion is in him that nourisheth it. For it ought to obey him by whom it is preserved, because preservation of life being the end for which one man becomes subject to another, every man is supposed to promise obedience to him in whose power it is to save or destroy him.

Hobbes, *Leviathan*, II, 20

62 And because the first instruction of children dependeth on the care of their parents, it is necessary that they should be obedient to them whilst they are under their tuition; and not only so, but that also afterwards, as gratitude requireth, they acknowledge the benefit of their education by external signs of honour. To which end they are to be taught that originally the father of every man was also his sovereign lord, with power over him of life and death; and that the fathers of families, when by instituting a Commonwealth they resigned that absolute power, yet it was never intended they should lose the honour due unto them for their education. For to relinquish such right was not necessary to the institution of sovereign power; nor would there be any reason why any man should desire to have children, or take the care to nourish and instruct them, if they were afterwards to have no other benefit from them than from other men. And this accordeth with the fifth Commandment.

Hobbes, *Leviathan*, II, 30

63 *Manoa.* His ransom, if my whole inheritance
May compass it, shall willingly be paid
And numberd down: much rather I shall chuse
To live the poorest in my Tribe, then richest,
And he in that calamitous prison left.
No, I am fixt not to part hence without him.
For his redemption all my Patrimony,
If need be, I am ready to forgo
And quit: not wanting him, I shall want nothing.
  Chorus. Fathers are wont to lay up for thir Sons,
Thou for thy Son art bent to lay out all;
Sons wont to nurse thir Parents in old age,
Thou in old age car'st how to nurse thy Son,
Made older then thy age through eye-sight lost.
  Man. It shall be my delight to tend his eyes.

Milton, *Samson Agonistes,* 1476

64 If parents carry it lovingly towards their children, mixing their mercies with loving rebukes, and their loving rebukes with fatherly and motherly compassions, they are more likely to save their children than by being churlish and severe towards them.

Bunyan, *Life and Death of Mr. Badman*

65 The power, then, that parents have over their children arises from that duty which is incumbent on them, to take care of their offspring during the imperfect state of childhood. To inform the mind, and govern the actions of their yet ignorant nonage, till reason shall take its place and ease them of that trouble, is what the children want, and the

parents are bound to. For God having given man an understanding to direct his actions, has allowed him a freedom of will and liberty of acting, as properly belonging thereunto within the bounds of that law he is under. But whilst he is in an estate wherein he has no understanding of his own to direct his will, he is not to have any will of his own to follow. He that understands for him must will for him too; he must prescribe to his will, and regulate his actions, but when he comes to the estate that made his father a free man, the son is a free man too.

Locke, *II Civil Government*, VI, 58

66 But though there be a time when a child comes to be as free from subjection to the will and command of his father as he himself is free from subjection to the will of anybody else, and they are both under no other restraint but that which is common to them both, whether it be the law of Nature or municipal law of their country, yet this freedom exempts not a son from that honour which he ought, by the law of God and Nature, to pay his parents, God having made the parents instruments in His great design of continuing the race of mankind and the occasions of life to their children. As He hath laid on them an obligation to nourish, preserve, and bring up their offspring, so He has laid on the children a perpetual obligation of honouring their parents, which, containing in it an inward esteem and reverence to be shown by all outward expressions, ties up the child from anything that may ever injure or affront, disturb or endanger the happiness or life of those from whom he received his, and engages him in all actions of defence, relief, assistance, and comfort of those by whose means he entered into being and has been made capable of any enjoyments of life. From this obligation no state, no freedom, can absolve children.

Locke, *II Civil Government*, VI, 66

67 Those . . . that intend ever to govern their children should begin it whilst they are very little, and look that they perfectly comply with the will of their parents. Would you have your son obedient to you when past a child, be sure then to establish the authority of a father as soon as he is capable of submission, and can understand in whose power he is. If you would have him stand in awe of you, imprint it in his infancy; and as he approaches more to a man, admit him nearer to your familiarity; so shall you have him your obedient subject (as is fit) whilst he is a child, and your affectionate friend when he is a man. For methinks they mightily misplace the treatment due to their children, who are indulgent and familiar when they are little, but severe to them, and keep them at a distance when they are grown up: for liberty and indulgence can do no good to children; their want of judgment makes them

stand in need of restraint and discipline; and on the contrary, imperiousness and severity is but an ill way of treating men who have reason of their own to guide them; unless you have a mind to make your children, when grown up, weary of you, and secretly to say within themselves, "When will you die, Father?"

Locke, *Some Thoughts Concerning Education,* 40

68 Their notions [the Lilliputians] relating to the duties of parents and children differ extremely from ours. For, since the conjunction of male and female is founded upon the great law of nature, in order to propagate and continue the species; the Lilliputians will needs have it, that men and women are joined together like other animals, by the motives of concupiscence; and that their tenderness towards their young, proceedeth from the like natural principle: for which reason they will never allow, that a child is under any obligation to his father for begetting him, or to his mother for bringing him into the world; which, considering the miseries of human life, was neither a benefit in itself, nor intended so by his parents, whose thoughts in their love-encounters were otherwise employed.

Swift, *Gulliver's Travels,* I, 6

69 "Pray, brother, have you not observed something very extraordinary in my niece lately?"—"No, not I," answered Western: "is anything the matter with the girl?" —"I think there is," replied she; "and something of much consequence too."— "Why, she doth not complain of anything," cries Western; "and she hath had the small-pox." — "Brother," returned she, "girls are liable to other distempers besides the small-pox, and sometimes possibly to much worse." Here Western interrupted her with much earnestness, and begged her, if anything ailed his daughter, to acquaint him immediately; adding, "she knew he loved her more than his own soul, and that he would send to the world's end for the best physician to her." "Nay, nay," answered she, smiling, "the distemper is not so terrible: but I believe, brother, you are convinced I know the world, and I promise you I was never more deceived in my life, if my niece be not most desperately in love."—"How! in love!" cries Western, in a passion; "in love, without acquainting me! I'll disinherit her; I'll turn her out of doors, stark naked, without a farthing. Is all my kindness vor 'ur, and vondness o'ur come to this, to fall in love without asking me leave?"— "But you will not," answered Mrs. Western, "turn this daughter, whom you love better than your own soul, out of doors, before you know whether you shall approve her choice. Suppose she should have fixed on the very person whom you yourself would wish, I hope you would not be angry then?" — "No, no," cries Western, "that would make a difference. If she marries the man I would ha' her,

she may love whom she pleases, I shan't trouble my head about that."

Fielding, *Tom Jones,* VI, 2

70 We now return to take leave of Mr. Jones and Sophia, who, within two days after their marriage, attended Mr. Western and Mr. Allworthy into the country. Western hath resigned his family seat, and the greater part of his estate, to his son-in-law, and hath retired to a lesser house of his in another part of the country, which is better for hunting. Indeed, he is often as a visitant with Mr. Jones, who, as well as his daughter, hath an infinite delight in doing everything in their power to please him. And this desire of theirs is attended with such success, that the old gentleman declares he was never happy in his life till now. He hath here a parlor and ante-chamber to himself, where he gets drunk with whom he pleases: and his daughter is still as ready as formerly to play to him whenever he desires it; for Jones hath assured her that, as next to pleasing her, one of his highest satisfactions is to contribute to the happiness of the old man; so, the great duty which she expresses and performs to her father, renders her almost equally dear to him with the love which she bestows on himself.

Sophia hath already produced him two fine children, a boy and a girl, of whom the old gentleman is so fond, that he spends much of his time in the nursery, where he declares the tattling of his little grand-daughter, who is above a year and a half old, is sweeter music than the finest cry of dogs in England.

Fielding, *Tom Jones,* XVIII, 13

71 Illicit conjunctions contribute but little to the propagation of the species. The father, who is under a natural obligation to nourish and educate his children, is not then fixed; and the mother, with whom the obligation remains, finds a thousand obstacles from shame, remorse, the constraint of her sex, and the rigour of laws; and besides, she generally wants the means.

Women who have submitted to public prostitution cannot have the convenience of educating their children: the trouble of education is incompatible with their station; and they are so corrupt that they can have no protection from the law.

It follows from all this that public continence is naturally connected with the propagation of the species.

Montesquieu, *Spirit of Laws,* XXIII, 2

72 I wish either my father or my mother, or indeed both of them, as they were in duty both equally bound to it, had minded what they were about when they begot me; had they duly considered how much depended upon what they were then doing; —that not only the production of a rational Being was concerned in it, but that possibly

the happy formation and temperature of his body, perhaps his genius and the very cast of his mind;—and, for aught they knew to the contrary, even the fortunes of his whole house might take their turn from the humours and dispositions which were then uppermost;— Had they duly weighed and considered all this, and proceeded accordingly,—I am verily persuaded I should have made a quite different figure in the world, from that in which the reader is likely to see me.

Sterne, *Tristram Shandy*, I, 1

73 Alack-o-day, replied the Corporal, brightening up his face—your honour knows I have neither wife or child—I can have no sorrows in this world.

Sterne, *Tristram Shandy*, IV, 4

74 I cannot recall to mind, without the sweetest emotions, the memory of that virtuous citizen, to whom I owe my being, and by whom I was often instructed, in my infancy, in the respect which is due to you. I see him still, living by the work of his hands, and feeding his soul on the sublimest truths. I see the works of Tacitus, Plutarch, and Grotius lying before him in the midst of the tools of his trade. At his side stands his dear son, receiving, alas with too little profit, the tender instructions of the best of fathers. But, if the follies of youth made me for a while forget his wise lessons, I have at length the happiness to be conscious that, whatever propensity one may have to vice, it is not easy for an education, with which love has mingled, to be entirely thrown away.

Rousseau, *Origin of Inequality*, Dedication

75 But is it not a thousand times more common and more dangerous for paternal rights openly to offend against humanity? How many talents have not been thrown away, and inclinations forced, by the unwise constraint of fathers? How many men, who would have distinguished themselves in a fitting estate, have died dishonoured and wretched in another for which they had no taste! How many happy, but unequal, marriages have been broken or disturbed, and how many chaste wives have been dishonoured, by an order of things continually in contradiction with that of nature! How many good and virtuous husbands and wives are reciprocally punished for having been ill-assorted! How many young and unhappy victims of their parents' avarice plunge into vice, or pass their melancholy days in tears, groaning in the indissoluble bonds which their hearts repudiate and gold alone has formed! Fortunate sometimes are those whose courage and virtue remove them from life before inhuman violence makes them spend it in crime or in despair. Forgive me, father and mother, whom I shall ever regret: my complaint embitters your griefs; but would they might be an eternal and terrible example to every one who dares,

in the name of nature, to violate her most sacred right.

Rousseau, *Origin of Inequality*, Appendix

76 I stated to him this case:—"Suppose a man has a daughter who he knows has been seduced, but her misfortune is concealed from the world? should he keep her in his house? Would he not, by doing so, be accessary to imposition? And, perhaps, a worthy, unsuspecting man might come and marry this woman, unless the father inform him of the truth." *Johnson.* "Sir, he is accessary to no imposition. His daughter is in his house; and if a man courts her, he takes his chance. If a friend, or, indeed, if any man asks his opinion whether he should marry her, he ought to advise him against it, without telling why, because his real opinion is then required. Or, if he has other daughters who know of her frailty, he ought not to keep her in his house. You are to consider the state of life is this; we are to judge of one another's characters as well as we can; and a man is not bound, in honesty or honour, to tell us the faults of his daughter or of himself. A man who has debauched his friend's daughter is not obliged to say to every body— 'Take care of me; don't let me into your houses without suspicion. I once debauched a friend's daughter. I may debauch yours.' "

Boswell, *Life of Johnson* (Apr. 5, 1776)

77 I said, I disliked the custom which some people had of bringing their children into company, because it in a manner forced us to pay foolish compliments to please their parents. *Johnson.* " You are right, Sir. We may be excused for not caring much about other people's children, for there are many who care very little about their own children. It may be observed, that men, who from being engaged in business, or from their course in life in whatever way, seldom see their children, do not care much about them. I myself should not have had much fondness for a child of my own." *Mrs. Thrale.* "Nay, Sir, how can you talk so?" *Johnson.* "At least, I never wished to have a child."

Boswell, *Life of Johnson* (Apr. 10, 1776)

78 I hesitate, from the apprehension of ridicule, when I approach the delicate subject of my early love. By this word I do not mean the polite attention, the gallantry, without hope or design, which has originated in the spirit of chivalry, and is interwoven with the texture of French manners. I understand by this passion the union of desire, friendship, and tenderness, which is inflamed by a single female, which prefers her to the rest of her sex, and which seeks her possession as the supreme or the sole happiness of our being. I need not blush at recollecting the object of my choice; and though my love was disappointed of success, I am rather proud that I was once capable of feeling such a pure and exalted sentiment. The personal attractions of Mademoiselle Susan Curchod were

embellished by the virtues and talents of the mind. Her fortune was humble, but her family was respectable. Her mother, a native of France, had preferred her religion to her country. The profession of her father did not extinguish the moderation and philosophy of his temper, and he lived content with a small salary and laborious duty in the obscure lot of minister of Crassy, in the mountains that separate the Pays de Vaud from the county of Burgundy. In the solitude of a sequestered village he bestowed a liberal, and even learned, education on his only daughter. She surpassed his hopes by her proficiency in the sciences and languages; and in her short visits to some relations at Lausanne, the wit, the beauty, and erudition of Mademoiselle Curchod were the theme of universal applause. The report of such a prodigy awakened my curiosity; I saw and loved. . . . At Crassy and Lausanne I indulged my dream of felicity: but on my return to England, I soon discovered that my father would not hear of this strange alliance, and that, without his consent, I was myself destitute and helpless. After a painful struggle I yielded to my fate; I sighed as a lover, I obeyed as a son; my wound was insensibly healed by time, absence, and the habits of a new life.

Gibbon, *Autobiography*

79 From the duty of man towards himself—that is, towards the humanity in his own person—there thus arises a personal right on the part of the members of the opposite sexes, as persons, to acquire one another really and reciprocally by marriage. In like manner, from the fact of *procreation* in the union thus constituted, there follows the duty of preserving and rearing *children* as the products of this union. Accordingly, children, as persons, have, at the same time, an original congenital right—distinguished from mere hereditary right—to be reared by the care of their parents till they are capable of maintaining themselves; and this provision becomes immediately theirs by law, without any particular juridical act being required to determine it.

For what is thus produced is a *person,* and it is impossible to think of a being endowed with personal freedom as produced merely by a physical process. And hence, *in the practical relation,* it is quite a correct and even a necessary idea to regard the act of generation as a process by which a person is brought without his consent into the world and placed in it by the responsible free will of others. This act, therefore, attaches an obligation to the parents to make their children—as far as their power goes—contented with the condition thus acquired. Hence parents cannot regard their child as, in a manner, a thing *of their own making;* for a being endowed with freedom cannot be so regarded. Nor, consequently, have they a right to destroy it as if it were their own property, or even to leave it to chance; because they have brought a

being into the world who becomes in fact a citizen of the world, and they have placed that being in a state which they cannot be left to treat with indifference, even according to the natural conceptions of right.

Kant, *Science of Right,* 28

80 *Mr. Bennet.* An unhappy alternative is before you, Elizabeth. From this day you must be a stranger to one of your parents. Your mother will never see you again if you do *not* marry Mr. Collins, and I will never see you again if you *do.*

Jane Austen, *Pride and Prejudice,* XX

81 Children have the right to maintenance and education at the expense of the family's common capital. The right of the parents to the service as service of their children is based upon and is restricted by the common task of looking after the family generally. Similarly, the right of the parents over the wishes of their children is determined by the object in view—discipline and education. The punishment of children does not aim at justice as such; the aim is more subjective and moral in character, i.e. to deter them from exercising a freedom still in the toils of nature and to lift the universal into their consciousness and will.

Children are potentially free and their life directly embodies nothing save potential freedom. Consequently they are not things and cannot be the property either of their parents or others. In respect of his relation to the family, the child's education has the positive aim of instilling ethical principles into him in the form of an immediate feeling for which differences are not yet explicit, so that thus equipped with the foundation of an ethical life, his heart may live its early years in love, trust, and obedience. In respect of the same relation, this education has the negative aim of raising children out of the instinctive, physical, level on which they are originally, to self-subsistence and freedom of personality and so to the level on which they have power to leave the natural unity of the family.

Hegel, *Philosophy of Right,* 174–175

82 The relation of love between husband and wife is in itself not objective, because even if their feeling is their substantial unity, still this unity has no objectivity. Such an objectivity parents first acquire in their children, in whom they can see objectified the entirety of their union. In the child, a mother loves its father and he its mother. Both have their love objectified for them in the child. While in their goods their unity is embodied only in an external thing, in their children it is embodied in a spiritual one in which the parents are loved and which they love.

Hegel, *Philosophy of Right,*
Additions, Par. 173

83 As a child, man must have lived with his parents encircled by their love and trust, and rationality must appear in him as his very own subjectivity. In the early years it is education by the mother especially which is important, since ethical principles must be implanted in the child in the form of feeling. It is noteworthy that on the whole children love their parents less than their parents love them. The reason for this is that they are gradually increasing in strength, and are learning to stand on their own feet, and so are leaving their parents behind them. The parents, on the other hand, possess in their children the objective embodiment of their union.

Hegel, *Philosophy of Right,*
Additions, Par. 175

84 When men live more for the remembrance of what has been than for the care of what is, and when they are more given to attend to what their ancestors thought than to think themselves, the father is the natural and necessary tie between the past and the present, the link by which the ends of these two chains are connected. In aristocracies, then, the father is not only the civil head of the family, but the organ of its traditions, the expounder of its customs, the arbiter of its manners. He is listened to with deference, he is addressed with respect, and the love that is felt for him is always tempered with fear.

When the condition of society becomes democratic and men adopt as their general principle that it is good and lawful to judge of all things for oneself, using former points of belief not as a rule of faith, but simply as a means of information, the power which the opinions of a father exercise over those of his sons diminishes as well as his legal power.

Perhaps the subdivision of estates that democracy brings about contributes more than anything else to change the relations existing between a father and his children. When the property of the father of a family is scanty, his son and himself constantly live in the same place and share the same occupations; habit and necessity bring them together and force them to hold constant communication. The inevitable consequence is a sort of familiar intimacy, which renders authority less absolute and which can ill be reconciled with the external forms of respect.

Now, in democratic countries the class of those who are possessed of small fortunes is precisely that which gives strength to the notions and a particular direction to the manners of the community. That class makes its opinions preponderate as universally as its will, and even those who are most inclined to resist its commands are carried away in the end by its example. I have known eager opponents of democracy who allowed their children to address them with perfect colloquial equality.

Thus at the same time that the power of aristocracy is declining, the austere, the conventional, and the legal part of parental authority vanishes and a species of equality prevails around the domestic hearth. I do not know, on the whole, whether society loses by the change, but I am inclined to believe that man individually is a gainer by it.

Tocqueville, *Democracy in America,*
Vol. II, III, 8

85 The eager fate which carried thee
Took the largest part of me:
For this losing is true dying;
This is lordly man's down-lying,
This his slow but sure reclining,
Star by star his world resigning.

O child of paradise,
Boy who made dear his father's home,
In whose deep eyes
Men read the welfare of the times to come,
I am too much bereft.

Emerson, *Threnody*

86 *Grieve not so, dear mother,* (the just-grown daughter speaks through her sobs,
The little sisters huddle around speechless and dismay'd,)
See, dearest mother, the letter says Pete will soon be better.

Alas poor boy, he will never be better, (not maybe needs to be better, that brave and simple soul,)
While they stand at home at the door he is dead already,
The only son is dead.

But the mother needs to be better,
She with thin form presently drest in black,
By day her meals untouch'd, then at night fitfully sleeping, often waking,
In the midnight waking, weeping, longing with one deep longing,
O that she might withdraw unnoticed, silent from life escape and withdraw,
To follow, to seek, to be with her dear dead son.

Whitman, *Come Up
From the Fields Father*

87 My father, in all his teaching, demanded of me not only the utmost that I could do, but much that I could by no possibility have done. What he was himself willing to undergo for the sake of my instruction, may be judged from the fact, that I went through the whole process of preparing my Greek lessons in the same room and at the same table at which he was writing: and as in those days Greek and English lexicons were not, and I could make no more use of a Greek and Latin lexicon than could be made without having yet

begun to learn Latin, I was forced to have recourse to him for the meaning of every word which I did not know. This incessant interruption, he, one of the most impatient of men, submitted to, and wrote under that interruption several volumes of his History and all else that he had to write during those years.

Mill, *Autobiography, I*

88 I remember the very place in Hyde Park where, in my fourteenth year, on the eve of leaving my father's house for a long absence, he told me that I should find, as I got acquainted with new people, that I had been taught many things which youths of my age did not commonly know; and that many persons would be disposed to talk to me of this, and to compliment me upon it. What other things he said on this topic I remember very imperfectly; but he wound up by saying, that whatever I knew more than others, could not be ascribed to any merit in me, but to the very unusual advantage which had fallen to my lot, of having a father who was able to teach me, and willing to give the necessary trouble and time; that it was no matter of praise to me, if I knew more than those who had not had a similar advantage, but the deepest disgrace to me if I did not.

Mill, *Autobiography, I*

89 I was sure you would be touched by the death of my poor little boy, to whom you have so often showed kindness. I imagine every one here thought he could not get through the winter, though they could give no special name to his complaint except to call it, with the doctors, "failure in vital power" following upon the slight shock given to him by his fall from a pony in Westmorland. But his mother and I had watched him through so many ebbings and flowings of his scanty stock of vital power that we had always hopes for him, and till I went into his room last Monday morning an hour before the end I did not really think he would die. The astonishing self-control which he had acquired in suffering was never shown more than in the last words he said to me, when his breath grew shorter and shorter, and from this, and the grieved face of the doctor as he entered the room, he knew, I am sure, that the end was come; and he turned to me, and—his mamma, who was always with him, and whom he adored, having gone into the next room for a moment—he whispered to me, in his poor labouring voice, "Don't let mamma come in." At his age that seems to me heroic self-control; and it was this patience and fortitude in him, joined to his great fragility and his exquisite turn for music, which interested so many people in him, and which brings us a sort of comfort now in all the kind and tender things that are said to us of him. But to Mrs. Arnold the loss of the occupation of her life—for so the care of him really was—will for some time to come be terrible.

Arnold, *Letter to Lady de Rothschild* *(Nov. 30, 1868)*

90 *Ivan.* "Who doesn't desire his father's death?" . . .

He turned suddenly to the audience. "My father has been murdered and they pretend they are horrified," he snarled, with furious contempt. "They keep up the sham with one another. Liars! They all desire the death of their fathers."

Dostoevsky, *Brothers Karamazov,* Pt. IV, XII, 5

91 "Well, madam," he [Prince Bolkonsky] began, stooping over the book close to his daughter and placing an arm on the back of the chair on which she sat, so that she felt herself surrounded on all sides by the acrid scent of old age and tobacco, which she had known so long. "Now, madam, these triangles are equal; please note that the angle *ABC* . . . "

The princess looked in a scared way at her father's eyes glittering close to her; the red patches on her face came and went, and it was plain that she understood nothing and was so frightened that her fear would prevent her understanding any of her father's further explanations, however clear they might be. Whether it was the teacher's fault or the pupil's, this same thing happened every day: the princess' eyes grew dim, she could not see and could not hear anything, but was only conscious of her stern father's withered face close to her, of his breath and the smell of him, and could think only of how to get away quickly to her own room to make out the problem in peace. The old man was beside himself: moved the chair on which he was sitting noisily backward and forward, made efforts to control himself and not become vehement, but almost always did become vehement, scolded, and sometimes flung the exercise book away.

The princess gave a wrong answer.

"Well now, isn't she a fool!" shouted the prince, pushing the book aside and turning sharply away; but rising immediately, he paced up and down, lightly touched his daughter's hair and sat down again.

He drew up his chair and continued to explain.

"This won't do, Princess; it won't do," said he, when Princess Mary, having taken and closed the exercise book with the next day's lesson, was about to leave: "Mathematics are most important, madam! I don't want to have you like our silly ladies. Get used to it and you'll like it," and he patted her cheek. "It will drive all the nonsense out of your head."

Tolstoy, *War and Peace,* I, 25

92 Nicholas' letter was read over hundreds of times, and those who were considered worthy to hear it

had to come to the countess, for she did not let it out of her hands. The tutors came, and the nurses, and Dmítri, and several acquaintances, and the countess reread the letter each time with fresh pleasure and each time discovered in it fresh proofs of Nikólenka's virtues. How strange, how extraordinary, how joyful it seemed, that her son, the scarcely perceptible motion of whose tiny limbs she had felt twenty years ago within her, that son about whom she used to have quarrels with the too-indulgent count, that son who had first learned to say "pear" and then "granny," that this son should now be away in a foreign land amid strange surroundings, a manly warrior doing some kind of man's work of his own, without help or guidance. The universal experience of ages, showing that children do grow imperceptibly from the cradle to manhood, did not exist for the countess. Her son's growth toward manhood, at each of its stages, had seemed as extra-ordinary to her as if there had never existed the millions of human beings who grew up in the same way. As twenty years before, it seemed impossible that the little creature who lived somewhere under her heart would ever cry, suck her breast, and begin to speak, so now she could not believe that that little creature could be this strong, brave man, this model son and officer that, judging by this letter, he now was.

Tolstoy, *War and Peace*, III, 6

93 Princess Mary, alarmed by her father's feverish and sleepless activity after his previous apathy, could not bring herself to leave him alone and for the first time in her life ventured to disobey him. She refused to go away and her father's fury broke over her in a terrible storm. He repeated every injustice he had ever inflicted on her. Trying to convict her, he told her she had worn him out, had caused his quarrel with his son, had harbored nasty suspicions of him, making it the object of her life to poison his existence, and he drove her from his study telling her that if she did not go away it was all the same to him. He declared that he did not wish to remember her existence and warned her not to dare to let him see her. The fact that he did not, as she had feared, order her to be carried away by force but only told her not to let him see her cheered Princess Mary. She knew it was a proof that in the depth of his soul he was glad she was remaining at home and had not gone away.

Tolstoy, *War and Peace*, X, 8

94 The passionate devotion of a mother—ill herself, perhaps—to a sick or dying child is perhaps the most simply beautiful moral spectacle that human life affords. Contemning every danger, triumphing over every difficulty, outlasting all fatigue, woman's love is here invincibly superior to any-

thing that man can show.

William James, *Psychology*, XXIV

95 It is unavoidable and quite normal that the child should make his parents the objects of his first object-choice. But his *libido* must not remain fixed on these first chosen objects, but must take them merely as a prototype and transfer from these to other persons in the time of definite object-choice. The breaking loose of the child from his parents is thus a problem impossible to escape if the social virtue of the young individual is not to be impaired. During the time that the repressive activity is making its choice among the partial sexual impulses and later, when the influence of the parents, which in the most essential way has furnished the material for these repressions, is lessened, great problems fall to the work of education, which at present certainly does not always solve them in the most intelligent and economic way.

Freud, *Origin and Development of Psycho-Analysis*, IV

96 For me . . . this book has an additional subjective significance, which I did not understand until after its completion. It reveals itself to me as a piece of my self-analysis, as my reaction to the death of my father, that is, to the most important event, the most poignant loss in a man's life.

Freud, *Interpretation of Dreams*, Pref. to 2nd (German) Ed.

97 If we look at the attitude of fond parents towards their children, we cannot but perceive it as a revival and reproduction of their own, long since abandoned narcissism. Their feeling, as is well known, is characterized by over-estimation, that sure indication of ·a narcissistic feature in object-choice which we have already appreciated. Thus they are impelled to ascribe to the child all manner of perfections which sober observation would not confirm, to gloss over and forget all his shortcomings—a tendency with which, indeed, the denial of childish sexuality is connected. Moreover, they are inclined to suspend in the child's favour the operation of all those cultural acquirements which their own narcissism has been forced to respect, and to renew in his person the claims for privileges which were long ago given up by themselves. The child shall have things better than his parents; he shall not be subject to the necessities which they have recognized as dominating life. Illness, death, renunciation of enjoyment, restrictions on his own will, are not to touch him; the laws of nature, like those of society, are to be abrogated in his favour; he is really to be the centre and heart of creation, "His Majesty the Baby," as once we fancied ourselves to be. He is to fulfil those dreams and wishes of his parents which they never carried out, to become a great man and a hero in his father's stead, or to marry a prince as a tardy compensation to the mother. At the weakest

point of all in the narcissistic position, the immortality of the ego, which is so relentlessly assailed by reality, security is achieved by fleeing to the child. Parental love, which is so touching and at bottom so childish, is nothing but parental narcissism born again and, transformed though it be into object-love, it reveals its former character infallibly.

Freud, *On Narcissism,* II

98 We find it far more offensive for love to be lacking between parents and children than between brothers and sisters. We have, so to speak, sanctified the former love while allowing the latter to remain profane. Yet everyday observation may show us how frequently the sentiments entertained towards each other by parents and grownup children fall short of the ideal set up by society, and how much hostility lies smouldering, ready to burst into flame if it were not stifled by considerations of filial or parental duty and by other, tender impulses. The motives for this hostility are well known, and we recognize a tendency for those of the same sex to become alienated, daughter from mother and father from son. The daughter sees in her mother the authority which imposes limits to her will, whose task it is to bring her to that renunciation of sexual freedom which society demands; in certain cases, too, the mother is still a rival, who objects to being set aside. The same thing is repeated still more blatantly between father and son. To the son the father is the embodiment of the social compulsion to which he so unwillingly submits, the person who stands in the way of his following his own will, of his early sexual pleasures and, when there is family property, of his enjoyment of it. When a throne is involved, this impatience for the death of the father may approach tragic intensity. The relation between father and daughter or mother and son would seem less liable to disaster; the latter relation furnishes the purest examples of unchanging tenderness, undisturbed by any egoistic consideration. . . .

The son, when quite a little child, already begins to develop a peculiar tenderness towards his mother, whom he looks upon as his own property, regarding his father in the light of a rival who disputes this sole possession of his; similarly the little daughter sees in her mother someone who disturbs her tender relation to her father and occupies a place which she feels she herself could very well fill. Observation shows us how far back these sentiments date, sentiments which we describe by the term *Oedipus complex,* because in the Oedipus myth the two extreme forms of the wishes arising from the situation of the son—the wish to kill the father and to marry the mother—are realized in an only slightly modified form. I do not assert that the Oedipus complex exhausts all the possible relations which may exist between par-

ents and children; these relations may well be a great deal more complicated. Again, this complex may be more or less strongly developed, or it may even become inverted, but it is a regular and very important factor in the mental life of the child; we are more in danger of underestimating than of overestimating its influence and that of the developments which may follow from it. Moreover, the parents themselves frequently stimulate the children to react with an Oedipus complex, for parents are often guided in their preferences by the difference in sex of their children, so that the father favours the daughter and the mother the son; or else, where conjugal love has grown cold, the child may be taken as a substitute for the love-object which has ceased to attract.

It cannot be said that the world has shown great gratitude to psycho-analytic research for the discovery of the Oedipus complex; on the contrary, the idea has excited the most violent opposition in grown-up people; and those who omitted to join in denying the existence of sentiments so universally reprehended and tabooed have later made up for this by proffering interpretations so wide of the mark as to rob the complex of its value. My own unchanged conviction is that there is nothing in it to deny or to gloss over. We ought to reconcile ourselves to facts in which the Greek myth itself saw the hand of inexorable destiny.

Freud, *General Introduction to Psycho-Analysis,* XIII

99 I have . . . described the relationship of a boy to his father and mother; things proceed in just the same way, with the necessary reversal, in little girls. The loving devotion to the father, the need to do away with the superfluous mother and to take her place, the early display of coquetry and the arts of later womanhood, make up a particularly charming picture in a little girl, and may cause us to forget its seriousness and the grave consequences which may later result from this situation.

Freud, *General Introduction to Psycho-Analysis,* XXI

100 From the time of puberty onward the human individual must devote himself to the great task of *freeing himself from the parents;* and only after this detachment is accomplished can he cease to be a child and so become a member of the social community. For a son, the task consists in releasing his libidinal desires from his mother, in order to employ them in the quest of an external love-object in reality; and in reconciling himself with his father if he has remained antagonistic to him, or in freeing himself from his domination if, in the reaction to the infantile revolt, he has lapsed into subservience to him. These tasks are laid down for every man; it is noteworthy how seldom they are carried through ideally, that is, how seldom they

are solved in a manner psychologically as well as socially satisfactory. In neurotics, however, this detachment from the parents is not accomplished at all; the son remains all his life in subjection to his father, and incapable of transferring his libido to a new sexual object. In the reversed relationship the daughter's fate may be the same. In this sense the Oedipus complex is justifiably regarded as the kernel of the neuroses.

Freud, *General Introduction to Psycho-Analysis,* XXI

101 The only thing that brings a mother undiluted satisfaction is her relation to a son; it is quite the most complete relationship between human beings, and the one that is the most free from ambivalence. The mother can transfer to her son all the ambition which she has had to suppress in herself, and she can hope to get from him the satisfaction of all that has remained to her of her masculinity complex. Even a marriage is not firmly assured until the woman has succeeded in making her husband into her child and in acting the part of a mother towards him.

Freud, *New Introductory Lectures on Psycho-Analysis,* XXXIII

102 A father, Stephen said, battling against hopelessness, is a necessary evil. . . . . Fatherhood, in the sense of conscious begetting, is unknown to man. It is a mystical estate, an apostolic succession, from only begetter to only begotten. On that mystery and not on the madonna which the cunning Italian intellect flung to the mob of Europe the church is founded and founded irremovably because founded, like the world, macro- and microcosm, upon the void. Upon incertitude, upon unlikelihood. *Amor matris,* subjective and objective genitive, may be the only true thing in life. Paternity may be a legal fiction. Who is the father of any son that any son should love him or he any son? . . .

They are sundered by a bodily shame so steadfast that the criminal annals of the world, stained with all other incests and bestialities hardly record its breach. Sons with mothers, sires with daughters, lesbic sisters, loves that dare not speak its name, nephews with grandmothers, jailbirds with keyholes, queens with prize bulls. The son unborn mars beauty: born, he brings pain, divides affection, increases care. He is a male: his growth is his father's decline, his youth his father's envy, his friend his father's enemy.

Joyce, *Ulysses*

2.3 | *Marriage*

This section, like its predecessor, contains many passages that reflect or manifest the relation of husband and wife rather than theorize or comment about it. Here, too, we can recite a moving list of famous pairs that the reader will recognize in passages quoted: Jacob and Rachel, Odysseus and Penelope, Oedipus and Jocasta, Alcibiades and Hipparete, Caesar and Pompeia, the Wife of Bath and all her husbands, Petruchio and Katherina, Benedick and Beatrice, Othello and Desdemona, Leontes and Hermione, Adam and Eve (in *Paradise Lost* as well as in *Genesis*), Mirabell and Millamant (in Congreve's *Way of the World*), Dr. and Mrs.

Samuel Johnson, J. S. Mill and Harriet Taylor, Pierre and Natasha (in *War and Peace*).

In addition to passages of the type just mentioned, there are, of course, many others that look at marriage from every point of view and express every variety of attitude toward it. The general impression one can hardly avoid getting is that of a great, blooming confusion, which may be the only one that an open-eyed appraisal affords. The reader who carefully explores the whole range of materials here assembled, and who compares later with earlier points of view, may also come away with the impression that our ancestors were more light-hearted about, or at least less plagued by, the inherent difficulties of the marriage bond than later generations for whom the bond is more easily dissolved by divorce.

The consideration of marriage cannot help touching on a number of related matters—not only divorce, but also conjugal love, or sex in marriage, and in incest, adultery, and cuckoldry. Relevant texts dealing with conjugal love, marital sex, and adultery will, also be found in Chapter 3 on LOVE, especially in Section 3.3 on SEXUAL LOVE.

---

1 Therefore shall a man leave his father and his mother, and shall cleave unto his wife: and they shall be one flesh.

Genesis 2:24

2 And Laban said unto Jacob, Because thou art my brother, shouldest thou therefore serve me for nought? tell me, what shall thy wages be?

And Laban had two daughters: the name of the elder was Leah, and the name of the younger was Rachel.

Leah was tender eyed; but Rachel was beautiful and well favoured.

And Jacob loved Rachel; and said, I will serve thee seven years for Rachel thy younger daughter.

And Laban said, It is better that I give her to thee, than that I should give her to another man: abide with me.

And Jacob served seven years for Rachel; and they seemed unto him but a few days, for the love he had to her.

Genesis 29:15–20

3 And Judah said unto Onan, Go in unto thy brother's wife, and marry her, and raise up seed to thy brother.

And Onan knew that the seed should not be his; and it came to pass, when he went in unto his brother's wife, that he spilled it on the ground, lest that he should give seed to his brother.

And the thing which he did displeased the Lord: wherefore he slew him also.

Genesis 38:8–10

4 The eye also of the adulterer waiteth for the twilight, saying, No eye shall see me: and disguiseth his face.

In the dark they dig through houses, which they had marked for themselves in the daytime: they know not the light.

For the morning is to them even as the shadow of death: if one know them, they are in the terrors of the shadow of death.

Job 24:15–17

5 A virtuous woman is a crown to her husband: but she that maketh ashamed is as rottenness in his bones.

Proverbs 12:4

6 House and riches are the inheritance of fathers: and a prudent wife is from the Lord.

Proverbs 19:14

7 Such is the way of an adulterous woman; she eateth, and wipeth her mouth, and saith, I have done no wickedness.

Proverbs 30:20

8 *Calypso.* "Son of Laërtês, versatile Odysseus, after these years with me, you still desire your old home? Even so, I wish you well. If you could see it all, before you go— all the adversity you face at sea— you would stay here, and guard this house, and be immortal—though you wanted her forever, that bride for whom you pine each day. Can I be less desirable than she is? Less interesting? Less beautiful? Can mortals compare with goddesses in grace and form?"

To this the strategist Odysseus answered:

"My lady goddess, here is no cause for anger. My quiet Penélopê—how well I know— would seem a shade before your majesty, death and old age being unknown to you, while she must die. Yet, it is true, each day I long for home, long for the sight of home."

Homer, *Odyssey*, V, 203

9 *Penelope.*   "Do not rage at me, Odysseus! No one ever matched your caution! Think what difficulty the gods gave: they denied us life together in our prime and flowering years, kept us from crossing into age together. Forgive me, don't be angry. I could not welcome you with love on sight! I armed myself long ago against the frauds of men, impostors who might come—and all those many whose underhanded ways bring evil on! Helen of Argos, daughter of Zeus and Leda, would she have joined the stranger, lain with him, if she had known her destiny? known the Akhaians

in arms would bring her back to her own country?
Surely a goddess moved her to adultery,
her blood unchilled by war and evil coming,
the years, the desolation; ours, too.
But here and now, what sign could be so clear
as this of our own bed?
No other man has ever laid eyes on it—
only my own slave, Aktoris, that my father
sent with me as a gift—she kept our door.
You make my stiff heart know that I am yours."

Now from his [Odysseus'] breast into his eyes the
    ache
of longing mounted, and he wept at last,
his dear wife, clear and faithful, in his arms,
longed for
        as the sunwarmed earth is longed for
          by a swimmer
spent in rough water where his ship went down
under Poseidon's blows, gale winds and tons of
    sea.
Few men can keep alive through a big surf
to crawl, clotted with brine, on kindly beaches
in joy, in joy, knowing the abyss behind:
and so she too rejoiced, her gaze upon her hus-
    band,
her white arms round him pressed as though for-
    ever.
The rose Dawn might have found them weeping
    still
had not grey-eyed Athena slowed the night
when night was most profound, and held the
    Dawn
under the Ocean of the East. That glossy team,
Firebright and Daybright, the Dawn's horses
that draw her heavenward for men—Athena
stayed their harnessing.

        Homer, *Odyssey*, XXIII, 208

10   So they [Odysseus and Penelope] came
into that bed so steadfast, loved of old,
opening glad arms to one another.
Telémakhos by now had hushed the dancing,
hushed the women. In the darkened hall
he and the cowherd and the swineherd slept.

The royal pair mingled in love again
and afterward lay revelling in stories:
hers of the siege her beauty stood at home
from arrogant suitors, crowding on her sight,
and how they fed their courtship on his cattle,
oxen and fat sheep, and drank up rivers
of wine out of the vats.
                Odysseus told
of what hard blows he had dealt out to others
and of what blows he had taken—all that story.
She could not close her eyes till all was told.

        Homer, *Odyssey*, XXIII, 295

11 Their [the Lycians'] customs are partly Cretan,
partly Carian. They have, however, one singular
custom in which they differ from every other nation in the world. They take the mother's and not
the father's name. Ask a Lycian who he is, and he
answers by giving his own name, that of his mother, and so on in the female line. Moreover, if a
free woman marry a man who is a slave, their
children are full citizens; but if a free man marry
a foreign woman, or live with a concubine, even
though he be the first person in the State, the
children forfeit all the rights of citizenship.

        Herodotus, *History*, I, 173

12 Once a year in each village the maidens of age to
marry were collected all together into one place;
while the men stood round them in a circle. Then
a herald called up the damsels one by one, and
offered them for sale. He began with the most
beautiful. When she was sold for no small sum of
money, he offered for sale the one who came next
to her in beauty. All of them were sold to be
wives. The richest of the Babylonians who wished
to wed bid against each other for the loveliest
maidens, while the humbler wife-seekers, who
were indifferent about beauty, took the more
homely damsels with marriage-portions. For the
custom was that when the herald had gone
through the whole number of the beautiful damsels, he should then call up the ugliest—a cripple,
if there chanced to be one—and offer her to the
men, asking who would agree to take her with the
smallest marriage-portion. And the man who offered to take the smallest sum had her assigned to
him. The marriage-portions were furnished by the
money paid for the beautiful damsels, and thus
the fairer maidens portioned out the uglier. No
one was allowed to give his daughter in marriage
to the man of his choice, nor might any one carry
away the damsel whom he had purchased without
finding bail really and truly to make her his wife;
if, however, it turned out that they did not agree,
the money might be paid back.

        Herodotus, *History*, I, 196

13 Their marriage-law [of the Amazons] lays it down
that no girl shall wed till she has killed a man in
battle. Sometimes it happens that a woman dies
unmarried at an advanced age, having never been
able in her whole lifetime to fulfil the condition.

        Herodotus, *History*, IV, 117

14 The Thracians who live above the Crestonæans
observe the following customs. Each man among
them has several wives; and no sooner does a man
die than a sharp contest ensues among the wives
upon the question which of them all the husband
loved most tenderly; the friends of each eagerly
plead on her behalf, and she to whom the honour
is adjudged, after receiving the praises both of
men and women, is slain over the grave by the
hand of her next of kin, and then buried with her
husband. The others are sorely grieved, for nothing is considered such a disgrace.

        Herodotus, *History*, V, 5

15 *Messenger.* When she came raging into the house she went
straight to her marriage bed, tearing her hair
with both her hands, and crying upon Laius
long dead—Do you remember, Laius,
that night long past which bred a child for us
to send you to your death and leave
a mother making children with her son?
And then she groaned and cursed the bed in which
she brought forth husband by her husband, children
by her own child, an infamous double bond.
How after that she died I do not know,—
for Oedipus distracted us from seeing.
He burst upon us shouting and we looked
to him as he paced frantically around,
begging us always: Give me a sword, I say,
to find this wife no wife, this mother's womb,
this field of double sowing whence I sprang
and where I sowed my children! As he raved
some god showed him the way—none of us there.
Bellowing terribly and led by some
invisible guide he rushed on the two doors,—
wrenching the hollow bolts out of their sockets,
he charged inside. There, there, we saw his wife
hanging, the twisted rope around her neck.
When he saw her, he cried out fearfully
and cut the dangling noose. Then, as she lay,
poor woman, on the ground, what happened after,
was terrible to see. He tore the brooches—
the gold chased brooches fastening her robe—
away from her and lifting them up high
dashed them on his own eyeballs, shrieking out
such things as: they will never see the crime
I have committed or had done upon me!

Sophocles, *Oedipus
the King*, 1241

16 *Athenian Stranger.* We will say to him who is born of good parents—O my son, you ought to make such a marriage as wise men would approve. Now they would advise you neither to avoid a poor marriage, nor specially to desire a rich one; but if other things are equal, always to honour inferiors, and with them to form connections;—this will be for the benefit of the city and of the families which are united; for the equable and symmetrical tends infinitely more to virtue than the unmixed. And he who is conscious of being too headstrong, and carried away more than is fitting in all his actions, ought to desire to become the relation of orderly parents; and he who is of the opposite temper ought to seek the opposite alliance. Let there be one word concerning all marriages:—Every man shall follow, not after the marriage which is most pleasing to himself, but after that which is most beneficial to the state. For somehow every one is by nature prone to that which is likest to himself, and in this way the whole city becomes unequal in property and in disposition; and hence there arise in most states the very results which we least desire to happen. Now, to add to the law an express provision, not only that the rich man shall not marry into the rich family, nor the powerful into the family of the powerful, but that the slower natures shall be compelled to enter into marriage with the quicker, and the quicker with the slower, may awaken anger as well as laughter in the minds of many; for there is a difficulty in perceiving that the city ought to be well mingled like a cup, in which the maddening wine is hot and fiery, but when chastened by a soberer God, receives a fair associate and becomes an excellent and temperate drink.

Plato, *Laws*, VI, 773A

17 *Athenian Stranger.* Drunkenness is always improper, except at the festivals of the God who gave wine; and peculiarly dangerous, when a man is engaged in the business of marriage; at such a crisis of their lives a bride and bridegroom ought to have all their wits about them.

Plato, *Laws*, VI, 775A

18 *Athenian Stranger.* The bride and bridegroom should consider that they are to produce for the state the best and fairest specimens of children which they can. Now all men who are associated in any action always succeed when they attend and give their mind to what they are doing, but when they do not give their mind or have no mind, they fail; wherefore let the bridegroom give his mind to the bride and to the begetting of children, and the bride in like manner give her mind to the bridegroom, and particularly at the time when their children are not yet born.

Plato, *Laws*, VI, 783B

19 The association of man and wife seems to be aristocratic; for the man rules in accordance with his worth, and in those matters in which a man should rule, but the matters that befit a woman he hands over to her. If the man rules in everything the relation passes over into oligarchy; for in doing so he is not acting in accordance with their respective worth, and not ruling in virtue of his superiority.

Aristotle, *Ethics*, 1160[b]33

20 Women should marry when they are about eighteen years of age, and men at seven and thirty; then they are in the prime of life, and the decline in the powers of both will coincide. Further, the children, if their birth takes place soon, as may reasonably be expected, will succeed in the beginning of their prime, when the fathers are already in the decline of life, and have nearly reached their term of three-score years and ten.

Aristotle, *Politics*, 1335[a]28

21 Ye have heard that it was said by them of old time, Thou shalt not commit adultery:

But I say unto you, That whosoever looketh on a woman to lust after her hath committed adultery with her already in his heart.

And if thy right eye offend thee, pluck it out, and cast it from thee: for it is profitable for thee that one of thy members should perish, and not that thy whole body should be cast into hell.

And if thy right hand offend thee, cut it off, and cast it from thee: for it is profitable for thee that one of thy members should perish, and not that thy whole body should be cast into hell.

It hath been said, Whosoever shall put away his wife, let him give her a writing of divorcement:

But I say unto you, That whosoever shall put away his wife, saving for the cause of fornication, causeth her to commit adultery: and whosoever shall marry her that is divorced committeth adultery.

Matthew 5:27–32

22 The Pharisees also came unto him, tempting him, and saying unto him, Is it lawful for a man to put away his wife for every cause?

And he answered and said unto them, Have ye not read, that he which made them at the beginning made them male and female,

And said, For this cause shall a man leave father and mother, and shall cleave to his wife: and they twain shall be one flesh?

Wherefore they are no more twain, but one flesh. What therefore God hath joined together, let not man put asunder.

They say unto him, Why did Moses then command to give a writing of divorcement, and to put her away?

He saith unto them, Moses because of the hardness of your hearts suffered you to put away your wives: but from the beginning it was not so.

And I say unto you, Whosoever shall put away his wife, except it be for fornication, and shall marry another, committeth adultery: and whoso marrieth her which is put away doth commit adultery.

His disciples say unto him, If the case of the man be so with his wife, it is not good to marry.

But he said unto them, All men cannot receive this saying, save they to whom it is given.

For there are some eunuchs, which were so born from their mother's womb: and there are some eunuchs, which were made eunuchs of men: and there be eunuchs, which have made themselves eunuchs for the kingdom of heaven's sake. He that is able to receive it, let him receive it.

Matthew 19:3–12

23 Now concerning the things whereof ye wrote unto me: It is good for a man not to touch a woman.

Nevertheless, to avoid fornication, let every man have his own wife, and let every woman have her own husband.

Let the husband render unto the wife due benevolence: and likewise also the wife unto her husband.

The wife hath not power of her own body, but the husband: and likewise also the husband hath not power of his own body, but the wife.

Defraud ye not one the other, except it be with consent for a time, that ye may give yourselves to fasting and prayer; and come together again, that Satan tempt you not for your incontinency.

But I speak this by permission, and not of commandment.

For I would that all men were even as I myself. But every man hath his proper gift of God, one after this manner, and another after that.

I say therefore to the unmarried and widows, It is good for them if they abide even as I.

But if they cannot contain, let them marry: for it is better to marry than to burn.

I Corinthians 7:1–9

24 Likewise, ye husbands, dwell with them according to knowledge, giving honour unto the wife, as unto the weaker vessel, and as being heirs together of the grace of life.

I Peter 3:7

25 With respect to wives and children, and that community which both, with a sound policy, appointed, to prevent all jealousy, their methods, however, were different. For when a Roman thought himself to have a sufficient number of children, in case his neighbour who had none should come and request his wife of him, he had a lawful power to give her up to him who desired her, either for a certain time, or for good. The Lacedæmonian husband, on the other hand, might allow the use of his wife to any other that desired to have children by her, and yet still keep her in his house, the original marriage obligation still subsisting as at first. Nay, many husbands, as we have said, would invite men whom they thought likely to procure them fine and good-looking children into their houses. What is the difference, then, between the two customs? Shall we say that the Lacedæmonian system is one of an extreme and entire unconcern about their wives, and would cause most people endless disquiet and annoyance with pangs and jealousies; the Roman course wears an air of a more delicate acquiescence, draws the veil of a new contract over the change, and concedes the general insupportableness of mere community?

Plutarch, *Lycurgus and Numa Compared*

26 Hipparete was a virtuous and dutiful wife, but, at last, growing impatient of the outrages done to her by her husband's continual entertaining of courtesans, as well strangers as Athenians, she departed from him and retired to her brother's house. Alcibiades seemed not at all concerned at

this, and lived on still in the same luxury; but the law requiring that she should deliver to the archon in person, and not by proxy, the instrument by which she claimed a divorce, when, in obedience to the law, she presented herself before him to perform this, Alcibiades came in, caught her up, and carried her home through the marketplace, no one daring to oppose him nor to take her from him. She continued with him till her death, which happened not long after, when Alcibiades had gone to Ephesus. Nor is this violence to be thought so very enormous or unmanly. For the law, in making her who desires to be divorced appear in public, seems to design to give her husband an opportunity of treating with her, and endeavouring to retain her.

Plutarch, *Alcibiades*

27 His first wife was Papiria, the daughter of Maso, who had formerly been consul. With her he lived a considerable time in wedlock, and then divorced her, though she had made him the father of noble children, being mother of the renowned Scipio and Fabius Maximus. The reason of this separation has not come to our knowledge; but there seems to be a truth conveyed in the account of another Roman's being divorced from his wife, which may be applicable here. This person being highly blamed by his friends, who demanded, "Was she not chaste? was she not fair? was she not fruitful?" holding out his shoe, asked them, whether it was not new and well made. "Yet," added he, "none of you can tell where it pinches me."

Plutarch, *Aemilius Paulus*

28 Cæsar at once dismissed Pompeia, but being summoned as a witness against Clodius, said he had nothing to charge him with. This looking like a paradox, the accuser asked him why he parted with his wife. Cæsar replied, "I wished my wife to be not so much as suspected." Some say that Cæsar spoke this as his real thought; others, that he did it to gratify the people, who were very earnest to save Clodius.

Plutarch, *Caesar*

29 When Philip was trying to force a woman against her will she said to him, "Let me go. All women are alike when the light is out." This is an excellent answer to adulterers and licentious men, but a married woman ought not be like any chance female when the light is out. It is when her body is invisible that her virtue and her sole devotion and affection for her husband should be evident.

Plutarch, *Marriage Counsel*

30 She who sleeps third in a big wide bed is certain to prosper.
Marry, and shut your mouth; the wages of silence are jewels!

After all this, do you think our sex deserves a verdict of *Guilty?*
That's like pardoning crows and laying all blame on the pigeons.

Juvenal, *Satire II*

31 A woman must not resist a husband in anger, by deed or even by word. . . . From the day they [hear] the matrimonial contract read to them they should regard it as an instrument by which they became servants; and from that time they should be mindful of their condition and not set themselves up against their masters.

Augustine, *Confessions,* IX, 9

32 A woman's sole purpose in marrying should be motherhood.

Augustine, *Contra Faustum,* XIX, 26

33 Adultery belongs not only to the sin of lust, but also to the sin of injustice, and in this respect may be brought under the head of covetousness . . . so that adultery is so much the more grievous than theft as a man loves his wife more than his chattels.

Aquinas, *Summa Theologica,* I–II, 73, 5

34 Matrimony did indeed exist under the Old Law, as a function of nature, but not as the sacrament of the union of Christ with the Church, for that union was not as yet brought about. Hence under the Old Law it was allowable to give a bill of divorce, which is contrary to the nature of a sacrament.

Aquinas, *Summa Theologica,* I–II, 102, 5

35 The marriage union is effected in the same way as the bond in material contracts. And since material contracts are not feasible unless the contracting parties express their will to one another in words, it follows that the consent which makes a marriage must also be expressed in words, so that the expression of words is to marriage what the outward washing is to Baptism.

Aquinas, *Summa Theologica,* III Suppl., 45, 2

36 In marriage there is a contract whereby one is bound to pay the other the marital debt: wherefore just as in other contracts, the bond is unfitting if a person bind himself to what he cannot give or do, so the marriage contract is unfitting, if it be made by one who cannot pay the marital debt. This impediment is called by the general name of impotence as regards coition, and can arise either from an intrinsic and natural cause, or from and extrinsic and accidental cause, for instance spell. . . . If it be due to a natural cause, this may happen in two ways. For either it is temporary, and can be remedied by medicine, or by the course of time, and then it does not void a marriage: or it is perpetual and then it voids marriage, so that the

party who labors under this impediment remains for ever without hope of marriage, while the other may *marry to whom she will . . . in the Lord.*

Aquinas, *Summa Theologica,* III Suppl., 58, 1

37 Our Lord permitted a man to put away his wife on account of fornication, in punishment of the unfaithful party and in favor of the faithful party, so that the latter is not bound to marital intercourse with the unfaithful one. There are however seven cases to be excepted in which it is not lawful to put away a wife who has committed fornication, when either the wife is not to be blamed, or both parties are equally blameworthy. The first is if the husband also has committed fornication; the second is if he has prostituted his wife; the third is if the wife, believing her husband dead on account of his long absence, has married again; the fourth is if another man has fraudulently impersonated her husband in the marriage-bed; the fifth is if she be overcome by force; the sixth is if he has been reconciled to her by having carnal intercourse with her after she has committed adultery; the seventh is if both having been married in the state of unbelief, the husband has given his wife a bill of divorce and she has married again; for then if both be converted the husband is bound to receive her back again.

Aquinas, *Summa Theologica,* III Suppl., 62, 1

38 The [marriage] debt may be demanded in two ways. First, explicitly, as when they ask one another by words; secondly, implicitly, when namely the husband knows by certain signs that the wife would wish him to pay the debt, but is silent through shame. And so even though she does not ask for the debt explicitly in words, the husband is bound to pay it, whenever his wife shows signs of wishing him to do so.

Aquinas, *Summa Theologica,* III Suppl., 64, 2

39 Since the wife has power of her husband's body, and *vice versa,* with regard to the act of procreation, the one is bound to pay the [marriage] debt to the other, at any season or hour, with due regard to the decorum required in such matters, for this must not be done at once openly.

Aquinas, *Summa Theologica,* III Suppl., 64, 9

40 "For then, the apostle says that I am free
To wed, in God's name, where it pleases me.
He says that to be wedded is no sin;
Better to marry than to burn within.
What care I though folk speak reproachfully
Of wicked Lamech and his bigamy?
I know well Abraham was holy man,
And Jacob, too, as far as know I can;
And each of them had spouses more than two;
And many another holy man also.
Or can you say that you have ever heard
That God has ever by His express word

Marriage forbidden? Pray you, now, tell me;
Or where commanded He virginity?
I read as well as you no doubt have read
The apostle when he speaks of maidenhead;
He said, commandment of the Lord he'd none.
Men may advise a woman to be one,
But such advice is not commandment, no;
He left the thing to our own judgment so.
For had Lord God commanded maidenhood,
He'd have condemned all marriage as not good;
And certainly, if there were no seed sown,
Virginity—where then should it be grown?
Paul dared not to forbid us, at the least,
A thing whereof his Master'd no behest.
The dart is set up for virginity;
Catch it who can; who runs best let us see.

"But this word is not meant for every wight,
But where God wills to give it, of His might.
I know well that the apostle was a maid;
Nevertheless, and though he wrote and said
He would that everyone were such as he,
All is not counsel to virginity;
And so to be a wife he gave me leave
Out of permission; there's no shame should grieve
In marrying me, if that my mate should die,
Without exception, too, of bigamy.
And though 'twere good no woman's flesh to touch,
He meant, in his own bed or on his couch;
For peril 'tis fire and tow to assemble;
You know what this example may resemble.
This is the sum: he held virginity
Nearer perfection than marriage for frailty.
And frailty's all, I say, save he and she
Would lead their lives throughout in chastity.

"I grant this well, I have no great envy
Though maidenhood's preferred to bigamy;
Let those who will be clean, body and ghost,
Of my condition I will make no boast.
For well you know, a lord in his household,
He has not every vessel all of gold;
Some are of wood and serve well all their days.
God calls folk unto Him in sundry ways,
And each one has from God a proper gift,
Some this, some that, as pleases Him to shift.

"Virginity is great perfection known,
And continence e'en with devotion shown.
But Christ, Who of perfection is the well,
Bade not each separate man he should go sell
All that he had and give it to the poor
And follow Him in such wise going before.
He spoke to those that would live perfectly;
And, masters, by your leave, such am not I.
I will devote the flower of all my age
To all the acts and harvests of marriage.

"Tell me also, to what purpose or end
The genitals were made, that I defend,
And for what benefit was man first wrought?
Trust you right well, they were not made for naught
Explain who will and argue up and down

That they were made for passing out, as known,
Of urine, and our two belongings small
Were just to tell a female from a male,
And for no other cause—ah, say you no?
Experience knows well it is not so;
And, so the clerics be not with me wroth,
I say now that they have been made for both,
That is to say, for duty and for ease
In getting, when we do not God displease.
Why should men otherwise in their books set
That man shall pay unto his wife his debt?
Now wherewith should he ever make payment,
Except he used his blessed instrument?
Then on a creature were devised these things
For urination and engenderings.
    "But I say not that every one is bound,
Who's fitted out and furnished as I've found,
To go and use it to beget an heir;
Then men would have for chastity no care.
Christ was a maid, and yet shaped like a man,
And many a saint, since this old world began,
Yet has lived ever in perfect chastity.
I bear no malice to virginity;
Let such be bread of purest white wheat-seed,
And let us wives be called but barley bread;
And yet with barley bread (if Mark you scan)
Jesus Our Lord refreshed full many a man.
In such condition as God places us
I'll persevere, I'm not fastidious.
In wifehood I will use my instrument
As freely as my Maker has it sent.
If I be niggardly, God give me sorrow!
My husband he shall have it, eve and morrow,
When he's pleased to come forth and pay his debt.
I'll not delay, a husband I will get
Who shall be both my debtor and my thrall
And have his tribulations therewithal
Upon his flesh, the while I am his wife.
I have the power during all my life
Over his own good body, and not he.
For thus the apostle told it unto me;
And bade our husbands that they love us well.
And all this pleases me wherof I tell."

Chaucer, *Canterbury Tales:* Wife of
Bath's Prologue

41 "Choose, now," said she, "one of these two things,
    aye,
To have me foul and old until I die,
And be to you a true and humble wife,
And never anger you in all my life;
Or else to have me young and very fair
And take your chance with those who will repair
Unto your house, and all because of me,
Or in some other place, as well may be.
Now choose which you like better and reply."

Chaucer, *Canterbury Tales:* Wife
of Bath's Tale

42 A merchant, dwelling once, at Saint-Denis,
Was rich, for which men held him wise, and he

Had got a wife of excellent beauty,
And very sociable and gay was she,
Which is a thing that causes more expense
Than all the good cheer and the deference
That men observe at festivals and dances;
Such salutations and masked countenances
Pass by as does a shadow on the wall;
But woe to him that must pay for it all.

Chaucer, *Canterbury Tales:* Shipman's Tale

43 A good wife, who is clean in deed and thought,
Should not be kept a prisoner, that's plain;
And certainly the labour is in vain
That guards a slut, for, sirs, it just won't be.
This hold I for an utter idiocy,
That men should lose their labour guarding
    wives;
So say these wise old writers in their lives.

Chaucer, *Canterbury Tales:* Manciple's Tale

44 In the choice of wives they carefully follow a custom which seemed to us foolish and absurd. Before marriage some responsible and honorable
woman, either a virgin or a widow, presents the
woman naked to her suitor and after that some
upright man presents the suitor naked to the
woman. We laughed at this and condemned it as
foolish. On the contrary they wonder at the stupidity of other people, who are exceedingly cautious in matters involving only a little money. For
example, men will refuse to buy a colt, unless they
take off its saddle and harness, which might conceal a sore. But in the choice of a mate, on which
one's happiness depends for the rest of one's life,
they act carelessly. They leave all but a hand's-
breadth of the woman's face covered with clothing
and judge her by it, so that in marrying a couple
runs a great risk of mutual dislike if later anything
in either's body should offend the other. Not all
men are so wise that they consider only a woman's
behavior. And even wise men think that physical
beauty in wives adds not a little to the virtues of
the mind. Certainly some deformity may lurk underneath clothing which will alienate a man from
his wife when it is too late to be separated from
her. If such a deformity is discovered after marriage, a man must bear his lot, so the Utopians
think care ought to be taken by law that no one
be deceived.

Thomas More, *Utopia,* II, 12

45 A preacher of the gospel, being regularly called,
ought, above all things, first, to purify himself before he teaches others. Is he able, with a good
conscience, to remain unmarried? let him so remain; but if he cannot abstain living chastely,
then let him take a wife; God has made that plaster for that sore.

Luther, *Table Talk,* H715

46 The preachers of Varennes, saith Panurge, detest and abhor the second marriages, as altogether foolish and dishonest. Foolish and dishonest? quoth Pantagruel. A plague take such preachers! Yea, but, quoth Panurge, the like mischief also befell the Friar Charmer, who in a full auditory making a sermon at Pareilly, and therein abominating the reiteration of marriage, and the entering again the bonds of a nuptial tie, did swear and heartily give himself to the swiftest devil in hell, if he had not rather choose, and would much more willingly undertake, the unmaidening or depucelating of a hundred virgins, than the simple drudgery of one widow.

Rabelais, *Gargantua and Pantagruel*, III, 6

47 *Panurge.* I will never be in the danger of being made a cuckold, for the defect hereof is *Causa sine qua non;* yea, the sole cause, as many think, of making husbands cuckolds. What makes poor scoundrel rogues to beg, I pray you? Is it not because they have not enough at home wherewith to fill their bellies and their pokes? What is it makes the wolves to leave the woods? Is it not the want of flesh meat? What maketh women whores? You understand me well enough.

Rabelais, *Gargantua and Pantagruel*, III, 14

48 I *N*. take thee *N*. to my wedded Wife [Husband], to have and to hold from this day forward, for better for worse, for richer for poorer, in sickness and in health, to love and to cherish, till death us do part, according to God's holy ordinance; and thereto I plight [give] thee my troth.

Book of Common Prayer

49 We have thought to tie the knot of our marriages more firmly by taking away all means of dissolving them; but the knot of will and affection has become loosened and undone as much as that of constraint has tightened. And on the contrary, what kept marriages in Rome so long in honor and security was everyone's freedom to break them off at will. They loved their wives the better because they might lose them; and, with full liberty of divorce, five hundred years and more passed before anyone took advantage of it.

Montaigne, *Essays*, II, 15, That Our Desire

50 A good marriage, if such there be, rejects the company and conditions of love. It tries to reproduce those of friendship. It is a sweet association in life, full of constancy, trust, and an infinite number of useful and solid services and mutual obligations. No woman who savors the taste of it . . . would want to have the place of a mistress or paramour to her husband. If she is lodged in his affection as a wife, she is lodged there much more honorably and securely. When he dances ardent and eager attention elsewhere, still let anyone ask him then on whom he would rather have some shame fall, on his wife or his mistress; whose misfortune would afflict him more; for whom he wishes more honor. These questions admit of no doubt in a sound marriage.

Montaigne, *Essays*, III, 5, On Some Verses of Virgil

51 Love and marriage are two intentions that go by separate and distinct roads. A woman may give herself to a man whom she would not at all want to have married; I do not mean because of the state of his fortune, but because of his personal qualities. Few men have married their mistresses who have not repented it.

Montaigne, *Essays*, III, 5, On Some Verses of Virgil

52 That man knew what it was all about, it seems to me, who said that a good marriage was one made between a blind wife and a deaf husband.

Montaigne, *Essays*, III, 5, On Some Verses of Virgil

53 *Katharina.* Fie, fie! unknit that threatening unkind
   brow,
And dart not scornful glances from those eyes,
To wound thy lord, thy king, thy governor:
It blots thy beauty as frosts do bite the meads,
Confounds thy fame as whirlwinds shake fair
   buds,
And in no sense is meet or amiable.
A woman moved is like a fountain troubled,
Muddy, ill-seeming, thick, bereft of beauty;
And while it is so, none so dry or thirsty
Will deign to sip or touch one drop of it.
Thy husband is thy lord, thy life, thy keeper,
Thy head, thy sovereign; one that cares for thee,
And for thy maintenance commits his body
To painful labour both by sea and land,
To watch the night in storms, the day in cold,
Whilst thou liest warm at home, secure and safe;
And craves no other tribute at thy hands
But love, fair looks, and true obedience;
Too little payment for so great a debt.
Such duty as the subject owes the prince
Even such a woman oweth to her husband;
And when she is froward, peevish, sullen, sour,
And not obedient to his honest will,
What is she but a foul contending rebel
And graceless traitor to her loving lord?
I am ashamed that women are so simple
To offer war where they should kneel for peace,
Or seek for rule, supremacy and sway,
When they are bound to serve, love, and obey.
Why are our bodies soft and weak and smooth,
Unapt to toil and trouble in the world,
But that our soft conditions and our hearts
Should well agree with our external parts?
Come, come, you froward and unable worms!
My mind hath been as big as one of yours,
My heart as great, my reason haply more,

To bandy word for word and frown for frown;
But now I see our lances are but straws,
Our strength as weak, our weakness past compare,
That seeming to be most which we indeed least
are.
Then vail your stomachs, for it is no boot,
And place your hands below your husband's foot:
In token of which duty, if he please,
My hand is ready; may it do him ease.

Shakespeare, *Taming of the Shrew*, V, ii, 136

54 *Leonato.* Well, niece, I hope to see you one day
fitted with a husband.

Beatrice. Not till God make men of some other
metal than earth. Would it not grieve a woman to
be overmastered with a piece of valiant dust? to
make an account of her life to a clod of wayward
marl? No, uncle, I'll none: Adam's sons are my
brethren; and, truly, I hold it a sin to match in
my kindred.

Leon. Daughter, remember what I told you: if
the Prince do solicit you in that kind, you know
your answer.

Beat. The fault will be in the music, cousin, if
you be not wooed in good time: if the Prince be
too important, tell him there is measure in everything and so dance out the answer. For, hear
me, Hero: wooing, wedding, and repenting, is as a
Scotch jig, a measure, and a cinque pace: the first
suit is hot and hasty, like a Scotch jig, and full as
fantastical; the wedding, mannerly-modest, as a
measure, full of state and ancientry; and then
comes repentance and, with his bad legs, falls into
the cinque pace faster and faster, till he sink into
his grave.

Leon. Cousin, you apprehend passing shrewdly.

Beat. I have a good eye, uncle; I can see a
church by daylight.

Shakespeare, *Much Ado
About Nothing*, II, i, 61

55 *Benedick.* The world must be peopled. When I said
I would die a bachelor, I did not think I should
live till I were married.

Shakespeare, *Much Ado
About Nothing*, II, iii, 251

56 *Jacques.* Will you be married, motley?

Touchstone. As the ox hath his bow, sir, the horse
his curb, and the falcon her bells, so man hath his
desires; and as pigeons bill, so wedlock would be
nibbling.

Shakespeare, *As You Like It*, III, iii, 79

57 *Rosalind.* Men are April when they woo, December when they wed: maids are May when they are
maids, but the sky changes when they are wives.

Shakespeare, *As You Like It*, IV, i, 147

58 *Touchstone.* God 'ild you, sir; I desire you of the
like. I press in here, sir, amongst the rest of the
country copulatives, to swear and to forswear; according as marriage binds and blood breaks: a
poor virgin, sir, an ill-favoured thing, sir, but
mine own; a poor humour of mine, sir, to take
that that no man else will: rich honesty dwells like
a miser, sir, in a poor house; as your pearl in your
foul oyster.

Shakespeare, *As You Like It*, V, iv, 56

59 *Slender.* I will marry her, sir, at your request; but if
there be no great love in the beginning, yet heav-
en may decrease it upon better acquaintance,
when we are married and have more occasion to
know one another. I hope, upon familiarity will
grow more contempt. But if you say, "Marry her,"
I will marry her; that I am freely dissolved, and
dissolutely.

Shakespeare, *Merry Wives
of Windsor*, I, i, 253

60 *Mistress Page.* Wives may be merry, and yet honest
too.

Shakespeare, *Merry Wives
of Windsor*, IV, ii, 108

61 *Clown.* He that ears my land spares my team and
gives me leave to in the crop; if I be his cuckold,
he's my drudge. He that comforts my wife is the
cherisher of my flesh and blood; he that cherishes
my flesh and blood loves my flesh and blood; he
that loves my flesh and blood is my friend; ergo,
he that kisses my wife is my friend.

Shakespeare, *All's Well That
Ends Well*, I, iii, 47

62 *Othello.*   O curse of marriage,
That we can call these delicate creatures ours
And not their appetites! I had rather be a toad,
And live upon the vapour of a dungeon,
Than keep a corner in the thing I love
For other's uses.

Shakespeare, *Othello*, III, iii, 268

63 *Desdemona.* I have heard it said so. O, these men,
   these men!
Dost thou in conscience think—tell me, Emilia—
That there be women do abuse their husbands
In such gross kind?

Emilia.   There be some such, no question.

Des. Wouldst thou do such a deed for all the
   world?

Emil. Why, would not you?

Des.   No, by this heavenly light!

Emil. Nor I neither by this heavenly light;
I might do't as well i' the dark.

Des. Wouldst thou do such a deed for all the
   world?

Emil. The world's a huge thing; it is a great
   price.
For a small vice.

Des.   In troth, I think thou wouldst not.

Emil. In troth, I think I should; and undo't when I had done. Marry, I would not do such a thing for a joint-ring, nor for measures of lawn, nor for gowns, petticoats, nor caps, nor any petty exhibition; but, for the whole world—why, who would not make her husband a cuckold to make him a monarch? I should venture purgatory for't.

Des. Beshrew me, if I would do such a wrong For the whole world.

Emil. Why, the wrong is but a wrong i' the world; and having the world for your labour, 'tis a wrong in your own world, and you might quickly make it right.

Des. I do not think there is any such woman.

Emil. Yes, a dozen; and as many to the vantage as would store the world they played for.
But I do think it is their husbands' faults
If wives do fall. Say that they slack their duties,
And pour our treasures into foreign laps,
Or else break out in peevish jealousies,
Throwing restraint upon us; or say they strike us,
Or scant our former having in despite;
Why, we have galls, and though we have some grace,
Yet have we some revenge. Let husbands know
Their wives have sense like them; they see and smell
And have their palates both for sweet and sour,
As husbands have. What is it that they do
When they change us for others? Is it sport?
I think it is. And doth affection breed it?
I think it doth. Is't frailty that thus errs?
It is so too. And have not we affections,
Desires for sport, and frailty, as men have?
Then let them use us well; else let them know,
The ills we do, their ills instruct us so.

Shakespeare, *Othello,* IV, iii, 60

64 *Leontes.*   There have been,
Or I am much deceived, cuckolds ere now;
And many a man there is, even at this present,
Now while I speak this, holds his wife by the arm,
That little thinks she has been sluiced in's absence
And his pond fish'd by his next neighbour, by
Sir Smile, his neighbour. Nay, there's comfort in't
Whiles other men have gates and those gates open'd,
As mine, against their will. Should all despair
That have revolted wives, the tenth of mankind
Would hang themselves. Physic for 't there is none;
It is a bawdy planet, that will strike
Where 'tis predominant; and 'tis powerful, think it,
From east, west, north and south. Be it concluded,
No barricado for a belly; know't;
It will let in and out the enemy
With bag and baggage. Many thousand on's
Have the disease, and feel't not.

Shakespeare, *Winter's Tale,* I, ii, 190

65 *Prospero.* Then, as my gift and thine own acquisition
Worthily purchased, take my daughter; but
If thou dost break her virgin-knot before
All sanctimonious ceremonies may
With full and holy rite be minister'd,
No sweet aspersion shall the heavens let fall
To make this contract grow; but barren hate,
Sour-eyed disdain, and discord shall bestrew
The union of your bed with weeds so loathly
That you shall hate it both. Therefore take heed,
As Hymen's lamps shall light you.

Ferdinand.   As I hope
For quiet days, fair issue, and long life,
With such love as 'tis now, the murkiest den,
The most opportune place, the strong'st suggestion;
Our worser genius can, shall never melt
Mine honour into lust, to take away
The edge of that day's celebration
When I shall think, or Phœbus' steeds are founder'd,
Or Night kept chain'd below.

Shakespeare, *Tempest,* IV, i, 13

66 Well, quoth *Sancho,* who had been silent, and list'-ning all the while, my Wife us'd to tell me, she would have every one marry with their Match. Like to like, quoth the Devil to the Collier, and every Sow to her own Trough, as t'other Saying is. . . . A Murrain seize those that will spoil a good Match between those that love one another! Nay, said Don *Quixote,* if Marriage should be always the Consequence of mutual Love, what would become of the Prerogative of Parents, and their Authority over their Children? If young Girls might always chuse their own Husbands, we should have the best Families intermarry with Coachmen and Grooms; and your Heiresses would throw themselves away upon the first wild young Fellows, whose promising Out-sides and Assurance makes 'em set up for Fortunes, though all their Stock consists in Impudence. For the Understanding which alone should distinguish and chuse in these Cases as in all others, is apt to be blinded or bias'd by Love and Affection; and Matrimony is so nice and critical a Point, that it requires not only our own cautious Management, but even the Direction of a superior Power to chuse right. Whoever undertakes a long Journey, if he be wise, makes it his Business to find out an agreeable Companion. How cautious then should He be, who is to take a Journey for Life, whose Fellow-Traveller must not part with him but at the Grave; his Companion at Bed and Board and Sharer of all the Pleasures and Fatigues of his Journey; as the Wife must be to the Husband! She is no such Sort of Ware, that a Man can be rid of when he pleases: When once that's purchas'd, no Exchange, no Sale, no Alienation can be made: She is an inseparable Accident to Man: Marriage is a Noose, which,

fasten'd about the Neck, runs the closer, and fits
more uneasy by our struggling to get loose: 'Tis a
Gordian Knot which none can unty, and being
twisted with our Thread of Life, nothing but the
Scythe of Death can cut it.

Cervantes, *Don Quixote*, II, 19

67 The Honourable Poor Man, said he [Don Quix-
ote], if the Poor can deserve that Epithet, when he
has a Beautiful Wife, is bless'd with a Jewel: He
that deprives him of her, robs him of his Honour,
and may be said to deprive him of his Life. The
Woman that is Beautiful, and keeps her Honesty
when her Husband is Poor, deserves to be
Crown'd with Laurel, as the Conquerors were of
Old. Beauty is a tempting Bait, that attracts the
Eyes of all Beholders, and the Princely Eagles,
and the most high-flown Birds stood to its pleasing
Lure. But when they find it in Necessity, then
Kites and Crows, and other ravenous Birds will
all be grappling with the alluring Prey. She that
can withstand these dangerous Attacks, well deserves to be the Crown of her Husband. However,
Sir, take this along with you, as the Opinion of a
Wise Man, whose Name I have forgot; he said,
there was but one good Woman in the World, and
his Advice was, that every Married Man should
think his own Wife was she, as being the only way
to live contented. For my own part, I need not
make the Application to myself, for I am not
Married, nor have I as yet any Thoughts that
way; but if I had, 'twould not be a Woman's Fortune, but her Character should recommend her;
for publick Reputation is the Life of a Lady's Vertue, and the outward Appearance of Modesty is in
one sense as good as the Reality; since a private
Sin is not so prejudicial in this World, as a publick
Indecency. If you bring a Woman honest to your
Bosom, 'tis easy keeping her so, and perhaps you
may improve her Vertues. If you take an unchaste
Partner to your Bed, 'tis hard mending her; for
the Extremes of Vice and Vertue are so great in a
Woman, and their Points so far asunder, that 'tis
very improbable, I won't say impossible, they
should ever be reconcil'd.

Cervantes, *Don Quixote*, II, 22

68 Grave natures, led by custom, and therefore constant, are commonly loving husbands; as was said
of Ulysses, *vetulam suam praetulit immortalitati* [he
preferred his aged wife to immortality]. Chaste
women are often proud and forward, as presuming upon the merit of their chastity. It is one of
the best bonds both of chastity and obedience in
the wife if she think her husband wise; which she
will never do if she find him jealous. Wives are
young men's mistresses; companions for middle
age; and old men's nurses. So as a man may have
a quarrel to marry when he will. But yet he was
reputed one of the wise men that made answer to
the question, when a man should marry?—"A

young man not yet, an elder man not at all." It is
often seen that bad husbands have very good
wives; whether it be that it raiseth the price of
their husband's kindness when it comes; or that
the wives take a pride in their patience. But this
never fails if the bad husbands were of their own
choosing, against their friends' consent; for then
they will be sure to make good their own folly.

Bacon, *Of Marriage and Single Life*

69 This said unanimous, and other Rites
Observing none, but adoration pure
Which God likes best, into thir inmost bower
Handed they went; and eas'd the putting off
These troublesom disguises which wee wear,
Strait side by side were laid, nor turned I weene
Adam from his fair Spouse, nor *Eve* the Rites
Mysterious of connubial Love refus'd:
Whatever Hypocrites austerely talk
Of puritie and place and innocence,
Defaming as impure what God declares
Pure, and commands to som, leaves free to all.
Our Maker bids increase, who bids abstain
But our Destroyer, foe to God and Man?
Haile wedded Love, mysterious Law, true sourse
Of human ofspring, sole proprietie,
In Paradise of all things common else.
By thee adulterous lust was driv'n from men
Among the bestial herds to raunge, by thee
Founded in Reason, Loyal, Just, and Pure,
Relations dear, and all the Charities
Of Father, Son, and Brother first were known.

Milton, *Paradise Lost*, IV, 736

70 *Adam.*   I now see
Bone of my Bone, Flesh of my Flesh, my Self
Before me; Woman is her Name, of Man
Extracted; for this cause he shall forgoe
Father and Mother, and to his Wife adhere;
And they shall be one Flesh, one Heart, one
  Soule.

Milton, *Paradise Lost*, VIII, 494

71 They looking back, all th' Eastern side beheld
Of Paradise, so late thir happie seat,
Wav'd over by that flaming Brand, the Gate
With dreadful Faces throng'd and fierie Armes:
Som natural tears they drop'd, but wip'd them
  soon;
The World was all before them, where to choose
Thir place of rest, and Providence thir guide:
They hand in hand with wandring steps and slow,
Through *Eden* took thir solitarie way.

Milton, *Paradise Lost*, XII, 641

72 If unchastity in a woman, whom St. Paul terms
the glory of man, be such a scandal and dishonour, then certainly in a man, who is both the image and glory of God, it must, though commonly
not so thought, be much more deflouring and dishonourable; in that he sins both against his own

body, which is the perfecter sex, and his own glory, which is in the woman; and, that which is worst, against the image and glory of God, which is in himself.

Milton, *Apology for Smectymnuus*

73 What thing more instituted to the solace and delight of man than marriage? And yet the misinterpreting of some scripture, directed mainly against the abusers of the law for divorce given by Moses, hath changed the blessing of matrimony not seldom into a familiar and coinhabiting mischief, at least into a drooping and disconsolate household captivity, without refuge or redemption—so ungoverned and so wild a race doth superstition run us from one extreme of abused liberty into the other of unmerciful restraint. For although God in the first ordaining of marriage taught us to what end he did it, in words expressly implying the apt and cheerful conversation of man with woman, to comfort and refresh him against the evil of solitary life, not mentioning the purpose of generation till afterwards, as being but a secondary end in dignity, though not in necessity: yet now, if any two be but once handed in the church, and have tasted in any sort the nuptial bed, let them find themselves never so mistaken in their dispositions through any error, concealment, or misadventure, that through their different tempers, thoughts and constitutions, they can neither be to one another a remedy against loneliness nor live in any union or contentment all their days; yet they shall, so they be but found suitably weaponed to the least possibility of sensual enjoyment, be made, spite of antipathy, to fadge together and combine as they may to their unspeakable wearisomeness and despair of all sociable delight in the ordinance which God established to that very end.

Milton, *Doctrine and Discipline of Divorce*, I, Pref.

74 With regard to marriage, it is plain that it is in accordance with reason, if the desire of connection is engendered not merely by external form, but by a love of begetting children and wisely educating them; and if, in addition, the love both of the husband and wife has for its cause not external form merely, but chiefly liberty of mind.

Spinoza, *Ethics*, IV, Appendix XX

75 The husband and wife, though they have but one common concern, yet having different understandings, will unavoidably sometimes have different wills too. It therefore being necessary that the last determination (that is, the rule) should be placed somewhere, it naturally falls to the man's share as the abler and the stronger. But this, reaching but to the things of their common interest and property, leaves the wife in the full and true possession of what by contract is her peculiar right, and at least gives the husband no more

power over her than she has over his life; the power of the husband being so far from that of an absolute monarch that the wife has, in many cases, a liberty to separate from him where natural right or their contract allows it, whether that contract be made by themselves in the state of Nature or by the customs or laws of the country they live in, and the children, upon such separation, fall to the father or mother's lot as such contract does determine.

Locke, *II Civil Government*, VII, 82

76 *Sharper.* Thus grief still treads upon the heels of pleasure;
Married in haste, we may repent at leisure.

Congreve, *The Old Bachelor*, V, iii

77 *Millamant.* Ah! I'll never marry, unless I am first made sure of my will and pleasure.

Mirabell. Would you have 'em both before marriage? Or will you be contented with the first now, and stay for the other till after grace?

Milla. Ah, don't be impertinent.—My dear liberty, shall I leave thee? My faithful solitude, my darling contemplation, must I bid you then adieu? Ay-h adieu—My morning thoughts, agreeable wakings, indolent slumbers, all ye *douceurs*, ye *sommeils du matin*, adieu.—I can't do't, 'tis more than impossible.—Positively, Mirabell, I'll lie abed in a morning as long as I please.

Mira. Then I'll get up in a morning as early as I please.

Milla. Ah, idle creature, get up when you will.—and d'ye hear? I won't be called names after I'm married; positively I won't be called names.

Mira. Names!

Milla. Aye, as wife, spouse, my dear, joy, jewel, love, sweetheart, and the rest of that nauseous cant, in which men and their wives are so fulsomely familiar—I shall never bear that.—Good Mirabell, don't let us be familiar or fond, nor kiss before folks, like my Lady Fadler and Sir Francis; nor go to Hyde Park together the first Sunday in a new chariot, to provoke eyes and whispers; and then never be seen there together again, as if we were proud of one another the first week, and ashamed of one another ever after. Let us never visit together, nor go to a play together, but let us be very strange and well bred; let us be as strange as if we had been married a great while; and as well bred as if we were not married at all.

Mira. Have you any more conditions to offer? Hitherto your demands are pretty reasonable.

Milla. Trifles—as liberty to pay and receive visits to and from whom I please; to write and receive letters, without interrogatories or wry faces on your part; to wear what I please; and choose conversation with regard only to my own taste; to have no obligation upon me to converse with wits that I don't like, because they are your acquaintance; or to be intimate with fools, because they may be your relations. Come to dinner when I please, dine in my dressing room when I'm out of humor, without giving a reason. To have my closet inviolate; to be sole empress of my tea table, which you must never presume to approach without first asking leave. And lastly, wherever I am, you shall always knock at the door before you come in. These articles subscribed, if I continue to endure you a little longer, I may by degrees dwindle into a wife.

Mira. Your bill of fare is something advanced in this latter account. Well, have I liberty to offer conditions—that when you are dwindled into a wife, I may not be beyond measure enlarged into a husband?

Milla. You have free leave, propose your utmost, speak and spare not.

Mira. I thank you. *Imprimis* then, I covenant that your acquaintance be general; that you admit no sworn confidante or intimate of your own sex; no she-friend to screen her affairs under your countenance and tempt you to make trial of a mutual secrecy. No decoy duck to wheedle you a fop—scrambling to the play in a mask—then bring you home in a pretended fright, when you think you shall be found out—and rail at me for missing the play, and disappointing the frolic which you had to pick me up and prove my constancy.

Milla. Detestable *imprimis!* I go to the play in a mask!

Mira. *Item,* I article, that you continue to like your own face as long as I shall; and while it passes current with me, that you endeavor not to new coin it. To which end, together with all vizards for the day, I prohibit all masks for the night, made of oiled-skins and I know not what—hog's bones, hare's gall, pig water, and the marrow of a roasted cat. In short, I forbid all commerce with the gentlewoman in what-d'ye-call-it court. *Item,* I shut my doors against all bawds with baskets, and pennyworths of muslin, china, fans, atlases, etc. *Item,* when you shall be breeding—

Milla. Ah! Name it not.

Mira. Which may be presumed, with a blessing on our endeavors—

Milla. Odious endeavors!

Mira. I denounce against all strait lacing, squeezing for a shape, till you mold my boy's head like a sugar loaf; and instead of a man-child, make me father to a crooked billet. Lastly, to the dominion of the tea table I submit.—But with proviso that you exceed not in your province; but restrain yourself to native and simple tea-table drinks, as tea, chocolate, and coffee. As likewise to genuine and authorized tea-table talk—such as mending of fashions, spoiling reputations, railing at absent friends, and so forth—but that on no account you encroach upon the men's prerogative, and presume to drink healths, or toast fellows; for prevention of which, I banish all foreign forces, all auxiliaries to the tea table, as orange brandy, all aniseed, cinnamon, citron and Barbados waters, together with ratafia and the most noble spirit of clary.—But for cowslip-wine, poppy water, and all dormitives, those I allow. These provisos admitted, in other things I may prove a tractable and complying husband.

Milla. O, horrid provisos! filthy strong waters! I toast fellows, odious men! I hate your odious provisos.

Mira. Then we're agreed. Shall I kiss your hand upon the contract?

Congreve, *Way of the World,* IV, v

78 Their [the Lilliputians'] maxim is, that among people of quality, a wife should be always a reasonable and agreeable companion, because she cannot always be young.

Swift, *Gulliver's Travels,* I, 6

79 This gentleman [Mr. Allworthy] had in his youth married a very worthy and beautiful woman, of whom he had been extremely fond: by her he had three children, all of whom died in their infancy. He had likewise had the misfortune of burying this beloved wife herself, about five years before the time in which this history chuses to set out. This loss, however great, he bore like a man of sense and constancy, though it must be confest he would often talk a little whimsically on this head; for he sometimes said he looked on himself as still married, and considered his wife as only gone a little before him, a journey which he should most certainly, sooner or later, take after her; and that he had not the least doubt of meeting her again in a place where he should never part with her more—sentiments for which his sense was arraigned by one part of his neighbours, his religion by a second, and his sincerity by a third.

Fielding, *Tom Jones,* I, 2

80 The squire, to whom that poor woman had been a faithful upper-servant all the time of their marriage, had returned that behaviour by making what the world calls a good husband. He very seldom swore at her (perhaps not above once a week) and never beat her: she had not the least occasion for jealousy, and was perfect mistress of her time; for she was never interrupted by her husband, who was engaged all the morning in his field exercises, and all the evening with bottle companions. She scarce indeed ever saw him but at meals; where she had the pleasure of carving those dishes which she had before attended at the dressing. From these meals she retired about five minutes after the other servants, having only stayed to drink "the king over the water." Such were, it seems, Mr. Western's orders; for it was a maxim with him, that women should come in with the first dish, and go out after the first glass.

Obedience to these orders was perhaps no difficult task; for the conversation (if it may be called so) was seldom such as could entertain a lady. It consisted chiefly of hallowing, singing, relations of sporting adventures, b—d—y, and abuse of women, and of the government.

Fielding, *Tom Jones*, VII, 4

81 "O my dear Sophy, you are a woman of sense; if you marry a man, as is most probable you will, of less capacity than yourself, make frequent trials of his temper before marriage, and see whether he can bear to submit to such a superiority.—Promise me, Sophy, you will take this advice; for you will hereafter find its importance." "It is very likely I shall never marry at all," answered Sophia; "I think, at least, I shall never marry a man in whose understanding I see any defects before marriage; and I promise you I would rather give up my own than see any such afterwards." "Give up your understanding!" replied Mrs. Fitzpatrick; "oh, fie, child! I will not believe so meanly of you. Everything else I might myself be brought to give up; but never this. Nature would not have allotted this superiority to the wife in so many instances, if she had intended we should all of us have surrendered it to the husband. This, indeed, men of sense never expect of us."

Fielding, *Tom Jones*, XI, 7

82 Young women who are conducted by marriage alone to liberty and pleasure, who have a mind which dares not think, a heart which dares not feel, eyes which dare not see, ears which dare not hear, who appear only to show themselves silly, condemned without intermission to trifles and precepts, have sufficient inducements to lead them on to marriage: it is the young men that want to be encouraged.

Montesquieu, *Spirit of Laws*, XXIII, 9

83 Of all the riddles of a married life, said my father, crossing the landing in order to set his back against the wall, whilst he propounded it to my uncle Toby—of all the puzzling riddles, said he, in a marriage state,—of which you may trust me, brother Toby, there are more asses' loads than all Job's stock of asses could have carried—there is not one that has more intricacies in it than this—that from the very moment the mistress of the house is brought to bed, every female in it, from my lady's gentlewoman down to the cinder-wench, becomes an inch taller for it; and give themselves more airs upon that single inch, than all the other inches put together.

I think rather, replied my uncle Toby, that 'tis we who sink an inch lower.——If I meet but a woman with child—I do it.

Sterne, *Tristram Shandy*, IV, 12

84 A senior magistrate of a French town had the misfortune to have a wife who was debauched by a priest before her marriage, and who since covered herself with disgrace by public scandals: he was so moderate as to leave her without noise. This man, about forty years old, vigorous and of agreeable appearance, needs a woman; he is too scrupulous to seek to seduce another man's wife, he fears intercourse with a public woman or with a widow who would serve him as concubine. In this disquieting and sad state, he addresses to his Church a plea of which the following is a précis:

My wife is criminal, and it is I who am punished. Another woman is necessary as a comfort to my life, to my virtue even; and the sect of which I am a member refuses her to me; it forbids me to marry an honest girl. The civil laws of to-day, unfortunately founded on canon law, deprive me of the rights of humanity. The Church reduces me to seeking either the pleasures it reproves, or the shameful compensations it condemns; it tries to force me to be criminal.

I cast my eyes over all the peoples of the earth; there is not a single one except the Roman Catholic people among whom divorce and a new marriage are not natural rights.

What upheaval of the rule has therefore made among the Catholics a virtue of undergoing adultery, and a duty of lacking a wife when one has been infamously outraged by one's own? . . .

That our priests, that our monks renounce wives, to that I consent; it is an outrage against population, it is a misfortune for them, but they merit this misfortune which they have made for themselves. They have been the victims of the popes who wanted to have in them slaves, soldiers without families and without fatherland, living solely for the Church: but I, magistrate, who serve the state all day, I need a wife in the evening; and the Church has not the right to deprive me of a benefit which God accords me. The apostles were married, Joseph was married, and I want to be. If I, Alsacian, am dependent on a priest who dwells at Rome, if this priest has the barbarous power to rob me of a wife, let him make a eunuch of me for the singing of *Misereres* in his chapel.

Voltaire, *Philosophical Dictionary:* Adultery

85 Johnson told me, with an amiable fondness, a little pleasing circumstance relative to this work. Mrs. Johnson, in whose judgement and taste he had great confidence, said to him, after a few numbers of *The Rambler* had come out, "I thought very well of you before; but I did not imagine you could have written any thing equal to this." Distant praise, from whatever quarter, is not so delightful as that of a wife whom a man loves and esteems.

Boswell, *Life of Johnson* (1750)

86 He [Johnson] talked of the heinousness of the crime of adultery, by which the peace of families

was destroyed. He said, "Confusion of progeny constitutes the essence of the crime; and therefore a woman who breaks her marriage vows is much more criminal than a man who does it. A man, to be sure, is criminal in the sight of *God:* but he does not do his wife a very material injury, if he does not insult her; if, for instance, from mere wantonness of appetite, he steals privately to her chambermaid. Sir, a wife ought not greatly to resent this. I would not receive home a daughter who had run away from her husband on that account. A wife should study to reclaim her husband by more attention to please him. Sir, a man will not, once in a hundred instances, leave his wife and go to a harlot, if his wife has not been negligent of pleasing."

Boswell, *Life of Johnson (1768)*

87 A gentleman who had been very unhappy in marriage, married immediately after his wife died: Johnson said, it was the triumph of hope over experience.

Boswell, *Life of Johnson (1770)*

88 A question was started, whether the state of marriage was natural to man. *Johnson.* "Sir, it is so far from being natural for a man and woman to live in a state of marriage, that we find all the motives which they have for remaining in that connection, and the restraints which civilized society imposes to prevent separation, are hardly sufficient to keep them together."

Boswell, *Life of Johnson (Mar. 31, 1772)*

89 On Friday, May 7, I breakfasted with him at Mr. Thrale's in the Borough. While we were alone, I endeavoured as well as I could to apologise for a lady who had been divorced from her husband by act of Parliament. I said, that he had used her very ill, had behaved brutally to her, and that she could not continue to live with him without having her delicacy contaminated; that all affection for him was thus destroyed; that the essence of conjugal union being gone, there remained only a cold form, a mere civil obligation; that she was in the prime of life, with qualities to produce happiness; that these ought not to be lost; and, that the gentleman on whose account she was divorced had gained her heart while thus unhappily situated. Seduced, perhaps, by the charms of the lady in question, I thus attempted to palliate what I was sensible could not be justified; for when I had finished my harangue, my venerable friend gave me a proper check: "My dear Sir, never accustom your mind to mingle virtue and vice. The woman's a whore, and there's an end on't."

Boswell, *Life of Johnson (May 7, 1773)*

90 *Boswell.* "Pray, Sir, do you not suppose that there are fifty women in the world, with any one of whom a man may be as happy, as with any one woman in particular?" *Johnson.* "Ay, Sir, fifty thousand." *Boswell.* "Then, Sir, you are not of opinion with some who imagine that certain men and certain women are made for each other; and that they cannot be happy if they miss their counterparts?" *Johnson.* "To be sure not, Sir. I believe marriages would in general be as happy, and often more so, if they were all made by the Lord Chancellor, upon a due consideration of characters and circumstances, without the parties having any choice in the matter."

Boswell, *Life of Johnson (Mar. 22, 1776)*

91 We then talked of marrying women of fortune; and I mentioned a common remark, that a man may be, upon the whole, richer by marrying a woman with a very small portion, because a woman of fortune will be proportionally expensive; whereas a woman who brings none will be very moderate in expenses. *Johnson.* "Depend upon it, Sir, this is not true. A woman of fortune being used to the handling of money, spends it judiciously: but a woman who gets the command of money for the first time upon her marriage, has such a gust in spending it, that she throws it away with great profusion."

Boswell, *Life of Johnson (Mar. 28, 1776)*

92 *Johnson.* "Between a man and his wife, a husband's infidelity is nothing. They are connected by children, by fortune, by serious considerations of community. Wise married women don't trouble themselves about the infidelity in their husbands." *Boswell.* "To be sure there is a great difference between the offence of infidelity in a man and that of his wife." *Johnson.* "The difference is boundless. The man imposes no bastards upon his wife."

Boswell, *Life of Johnson (Oct. 10, 1779)*

93 The domestic relations are founded on marriage, and marriage is founded upon the natural reciprocity or intercommunity . . . of the sexes. This natural union of the sexes proceeds according to the mere animal nature . . . , or according to the law. The latter is marriage . . . , which is the union of two persons of different sex for life-long reciprocal possession of their sexual faculties. The end of producing and educating children may be regarded as always the end of nature in implanting mutual desire and inclination in the sexes; but it is not necessary for the rightfulness of marriage that those who marry should set this before themselves as the end of their union, otherwise the marriage would be dissolved of itself when the production of children ceased.

Kant, *Science of Right*, 24

94 The relation of the married persons to each other is a relation of equality as regards the mutual possession of their persons, as well as of their goods.

Consequently marriage is only truly realized in monogamy; for in the relation of polygamy the person who is given away on the one side, gains only a part of the one to whom that person is given up, and therefore becomes a mere *res*. But in respect of their goods, they have severally the right to renounce the use of any part of them, although only by a special contract. . . . Hence the question may be raised as to whether it is not contrary to the equality of married persons when the law says in any way of the husband in relation to the wife, "he shall be thy master," so that he is represented as the one who commands, and she is the one who obeys. This, however, cannot be regarded as contrary to the natural equality of a human pair, if such legal supremacy is based only upon the natural superiority of the faculties of the husband compared with the wife, in the effectuation of the common interest of the household, and if the right to command is based merely upon this fact. For this right may thus be deduced from the very duty of unity and equality in relation to the *end* involved.

Kant, *Science of Right*, 26

95 It is a truth universally acknowledged, that a single man in possession of a good fortune, must be in want of a wife.

Jane Austen, *Pride and Prejudice*, I

96 'Tis pity learned virgins ever wed
   With persons of no sort of education,
   Or gentlemen, who, though well born and bred,
   Grow tired of scientific conversation:
   I don't choose to say much upon this head,
   I'm a plain man, and in a single station,
   But—Oh! ye lords of ladies intellectual,
   Inform us truly, have they not hen-peck'd you all?

Byron, *Don Juan*, I, 22

97 Think you, if Laura had been Petrarch's wife,
   He would have written sonnets all his life?

Byron, *Don Juan*, III, 8

98 Marriage results from the free surrender by both sexes of their personality—a personality in every possible way unique in each of the parties. Consequently, it ought not to be entered by two people identical in stock who are already acquainted and perfectly known to one another; for individuals in the same circle of relationship have no special personality of their own in contrast with that of others in the same circle. On the contrary, the parties should be drawn from separate families and their personalities should be different in origin. Since the very conception of marriage is that it is a freely undertaken ethical transaction, not a tie directly grounded in the physical organism and its desires, it follows that the marriage of blood-relations runs counter to this conception

and so also to genuine natural feeling.

Hegel, *Philosophy of Right*, 168

99 Familiarity, close acquaintance, the habit of common pursuits, should not precede marriage; they should come about for the first time within it. And their development has all the more value, the richer it is and the more facets it has.

Hegel, *Philosophy of Right*,
Additions, Par. 168

100 It is a much greater shock to modesty to go to bed with a man whom one has only seen twice, after half a dozen words mumbled in Latin by a priest, than to yield in spite of one's self to a man whom one has adored for two years.

Stendhal, *On Love*, I, 21

101 Among aristocratic nations birth and fortune frequently make two such different beings of man and woman that they can never be united to each other. Their passions draw them together, but the condition of society and the notions suggested by it prevent them from contracting a permanent and ostensible tie. The necessary consequence is a great number of transient and clandestine connections. Nature secretly avenges herself for the constraint imposed upon her by the laws of man.

This is not so much the case when the equality of conditions has swept away all the imaginary or the real barriers that separated man from woman. No girl then believes that she cannot become the wife of the man who loves her, and this renders all breaches of morality before marriage very uncommon; for, whatever be the credulity of the passions, a woman will hardly be able to persuade herself that she is beloved when her lover is perfectly free to marry her and does not.

Tocqueville, *Democracy in America*,
Vol. II, III, 11

102 *Mr. Weller.* Wen you're a married man, Samivel, you'll understand a good many things as you don't understand now; but vether it's worth while goin' through so much, to learn so little, as the charity-boy said ven he got to the end of the alphabet, is a matter o' taste.

Dickens, *Pickwick Papers*, XXVII

103 *Mr. Micawber.* Accidents will occur in the best-regulated families; and in families not regulated by that pervading influence which sanctifies while it enhances the —a—I would say, in short, by the influence of Woman, in the lofty character of Wife, they may be expected with confidence, and must be borne with philosophy.

Dickens, *David Copperfield*, XXVIII

104 Civilised men are largely attracted by the mental charms of women, by their wealth, and especially by their social position; for men rarely marry into a much lower rank. The men who succeed in ob-

taining the more beautiful women will not have a better chance of leaving a long line of descendants than other men with plainer wives, save the few who bequeath their fortunes according to primogeniture. With respect to the opposite form of selection, namely, of the more attractive men by the women, although in civilised nations women have free or almost free choice, which is not the case with barbarous races, yet their choice is largely influenced by the social position and wealth of the men; and the success of the latter in life depends much on their intellectual powers and energy, or on the fruits of these same powers in their forefathers.

Darwin, *Descent of Man,* III, 20

105 Man scans with scrupulous care the character and pedigree of his horses, cattle, and dogs before he matches them; but when he comes to his own marriage he rarely, or never, takes any such care. He is impelled by nearly the same motives as the lower animals, when they are left to their own free choice, though he is in so far superior to them that he highly values mental charms and virtues. On the other hand he is strongly attracted by mere wealth or rank. Yet he might by selection do something not only for the bodily constitution and frame of his offspring, but for their intellectual and moral qualities. Both sexes ought to refrain from marriage if they are in any marked degree inferior in body or mind; but such hopes are Utopian and will never be even partially realised until the laws of inheritance are thoroughly known. Everyone does good service, who aids towards this end.

Darwin, *Descent of Man,* III, 21

106 But you Communists would introduce community of women, screams the whole bourgeoisie in chorus.

The bourgeois sees in his wife a mere instrument of production. He hears that the instruments of production are to be exploited in common, and, naturally, can come to no other conclusion than that the lot of being common to all will likewise fall to the women.

He has not even a suspicion that the real point aimed at is to do away with the status of women as mere instruments of production.

For the rest, nothing is more ridiculous than the virtuous indignation of our bourgeois at the community of women which, they pretend, is to be openly and officially established by the Communists. The Communists have no need to introduce community of women; it has existed almost from time immemorial.

Our bourgeois, not content with having the wives and daughters of their proletarians at their disposal, not to speak of common prostitutes, take the greatest pleasure in seducing each other's wives.

Bourgeois marriage is in reality a system of wives in common and thus at the most what the Communists might possibly be reproached with is that they desire to introduce, in substitution for a hypocritically concealed, an openly legalized, community of women.

Marx and Engels, *Communist Manifesto,* II

107 What marriage may be in the case of two persons of cultivated faculties, identical in opinions and purposes, between whom there exists that best kind of equality, similarity of powers and capacities with reciprocal superiority in them—so that each can enjoy the luxury of looking up to the other, and can have alternately the pleasure of leading and of being led in the path of development—I will not attempt to describe. To those who can conceive it, there is no need; to those who cannot, it would appear the dream of an enthusiast. But I maintain, with the profoundest conviction, that this, and this only, is the ideal of marriage; and that all opinions, customs, and institutions which favour any other notion of it, or turn the conceptions and aspirations connected with it into any other direction, by whatever pretences they may be coloured, are relics of primitive barbarism. The moral regeneration of mankind will only really commence, when the most fundamental of the social relations is placed under the rule of equal justice, and when human beings learn to cultivate their strongest sympathy with an equal in rights and in cultivation.

Mill, *Subjection of Women,* IV

108 Natásha did not follow the golden rule advocated by clever folk, especially by the French, which says that a girl should not let herself go when she marries, should not neglect her accomplishments, should be even more careful of her appearance than when she was unmarried, and should fascinate her husband as much as she did before he became her husband. Natásha on the contrary had at once abandoned all her witchery, of which her singing had been an unusually powerful part. She gave it up just because it was so powerfully seductive. She took no pains with her manners or with delicacy of speech, or with her toilet, or to show herself to her husband in her most becoming attitudes, or to avoid inconveniencing him by being too exacting. She acted in contradiction to all those rules. She felt that the allurements instinct had formerly taught her to use would now be merely ridiculous in the eyes of her husband, to whom she had from the first moment given herself up entirely—that is, with her whole soul, leaving no corner of it hidden from him. She felt that her unity with her husband was not maintained by the poetic feelings that had attracted him to her, but by something else—indefinite but firm as the bond between her own body and soul.

Tolstoy, *War and Peace,* I Epilogue, X

109 If the purpose of dinner is to nourish the body, a man who eats two dinners at once may perhaps get more enjoyment but will not attain his purpose, for his stomach will not digest the two dinners. •

If the purpose of marriage is the family, the person who wishes to have many wives or husbands may perhaps obtain much pleasure, but in that case will not have a family.

If the purpose of food is nourishment and the purpose of marriage is the family, the whole question resolves itself into not eating more than one can digest, and not having more wives or husbands than are needed for the family—that is, one wife or one husband. Natásha needed a husband. A husband was given her and he gave her a family. And she not only saw no need of any other or better husband, but as all the powers of her soul were intent on serving that husband and family, she could not imagine and saw no interest in imagining how it would be if things were different.

Tolstoy, *War and Peace*, I Epilogue, X

110 Natásha and Pierre, left alone, also began to talk as only a husband and wife can talk, that is, with extraordinary clearness and rapidity, understanding and expressing each other's thoughts in ways contrary to all rules of logic, without premises, deductions, or conclusions, and in a quite peculiar way. Natásha was so used to this kind of talk with her husband that for her it was the surest sign of something being wrong between them if Pierre followed a line of logical reasoning. When he began proving anything, or talking argumentatively and calmly and she, led on by his example, began to do the same, she knew that they were on the verge of a quarrel.

Tolstoy, *War and Peace*, I Epilogue, XVI

111 Natásha would have had no doubt as to the greatness of Pierre's idea, but one thing disconcerted her. "Can a man so important and necessary to society be also my husband? How did this happen?" She wished to express this doubt to him. "Now who could decide whether he is really cleverer than all the others?" she asked herself, and passed in review all those whom Pierre most respected. Judging by what he had said there was no one he had respected so highly as Platón Karatáev.

"Do you know what I am thinking about?" she asked. "About Platón Karatáev. Would he have approved of you now, do you think?"

Pierre was not at all surprised at this question. He understood his wife's line of thought.

"Platón Karatáev?" he repeated, and pondered, evidently sincerely trying to imagine Karatáev's opinion on the subject. "He would not have understood . . . yet perhaps he would."

"I love you awfully!" Natásha suddenly said. "Awfully, awfully!"

"No, he would not have approved," said Pierre, after reflection. "What he would have approved of is our family life. He was always so anxious to find seemliness, happiness, and peace in everything, and I should have been proud to let him see us. There now—you talk of my absence, but you wouldn't believe what a special feeling I have for you after a separation. . . ."

"Yes, I should think . . ." Natásha began.

"No, it's not that. I never leave off loving you. And one couldn't love more, but this is something special. . . . Yes, of course—" he did not finish because their eyes meeting said the rest.

"What nonsense it is," Natásha suddenly exclaimed, "about honeymoons, and that the greatest happiness is at first! On the contrary, now is the best of all."

Tolstoy, *War and Peace*, I Epilogue, XVI

112 Even concubinage has been corrupted—by marriage.

Nietzsche, *Beyond Good and Evil*, IV, 123

113 Marriage is popular because it combines the maximum of temptation with the maximum of opportunity.

Shaw, *Man and Superman*, Maxims for Revolutionists

114 When two people are under the influence of the most violent, most insane, most delusive, and most transient of passions, they are required to swear that they will remain in that excited, abnormal, and exhausting condition continuously until death do them part.

Shaw, *Getting Married*, Pref.

115 *Liza.* Theres lots of women has to make their husbands drunk to make them fit to live with. You see, it's like this. If a man has a bit of a conscience, it always takes him when he's sober; and then it makes him low-spirited. A drop of booze just takes that off and makes him happy.

Shaw, *Pygmalion*, III

116 Owing to the subjection of women there has in most civilized communities been no genuine companionship between husbands and wives; their relation has been one of condescension on the one side and duty on the other. All the man's serious thoughts and purposes he has kept to himself, since robust thought might lead his wife to betray him. In most civilized communities women have been denied almost all experience of the world and of affairs. They have been kept artificially stupid and therefore uninteresting.

Russell, *Marriage and Morals*, III

117 It is . . . possible for a civilized man and woman to be happy in marriage, although if this is to be the case a number of conditions must be fulfilled. There must be a feeling of complete equality on both sides; there must be no interference with mutual freedom; there must be the most complete physical and mental intimacy; and there must be a certain similarity in regard to standards of values. (It is fatal, for example, if one values only money while the other values only good work.) Given all these conditions, I believe marriage to be the best and most important relation that can exist between two human beings. If it has not often been realized hitherto, that is chiefly because husband and wife have regarded themselves as each other's policeman. If marriage is to achieve its possibilities, husbands and wives must learn to understand that whatever the law may say, in their private lives they must be free.

Russell, *Marriage and Morals,* IX

118 We know the very widespread custom of breaking a vessel or a plate on the occasion of a rothal; everyone present possesses himself of a fragment in symbolic acceptance of the fact that he may no longer put forward any claim to the bride, presumably a custom which arose with monogamy.

Freud, *General Introduction to Psycho-Analysis,* XVII

Chapter 3

LOVE

This chapter is divided into six sections: 3.1 THE NATURE, KINDS, AND POWER OF LOVE, 3.2 HATE, 3.3 SEXUAL LOVE, 3.4 FRIENDSHIP, 3.5 CHARITY AND MERCY, and 3.6 LOVE OF COUNTRY: PATRIOTISM.

While many of the passages here quoted are so multifaceted in their significance that they could have been placed in two or more sections, the division of the texts holds up for the most part. We have placed first the passages that try to say what love is and what different types of love there are. That is immediately followed by quotations dealing with hate—the antithesis or, as some maintain, the correlate of love. Then come three sections each devoted to one of the principal kinds of love, and last a section dealing with a variant of one of these kinds.

The reader may wonder about the relation of this chapter to the one that precedes it. Conjugal love and the love between parents and children, treated in quotations included in the chapter on marriage, involve two of the types of love that are discussed here—sexual love and friendship. There are reasons for placing quotations of this sort in the chapter on FAMILY; however, the reader interested in these subjects can consult the index under appropriate terms to find the passages in Chapter 2 that might have been included in Sections 3.4 and 3.5 of this chapter.

There is also a problem about the relation of this chapter to the one that follows it. In the opinion of many, love is an emotion and might, therefore, have been covered in one of the several sections of Chapter 4. But this would have done violence to the opinion of those who maintain that love involves components that are not emotional or passional, and that certain types of love are the very antithesis of passion. In addition, the sheer quantity and variety of the quotations about love would have made it practically unfeasible to include them all without differentiation in a single section of Chapter 4.

3.1 | *The Nature, Kinds, and Power of Love*

As the title of the section indicates, the passages assembled here are of three sorts: they try to say what love is or what distinctively characterizes it; they try to distinguish the various kinds of love and to relate them to one another; and they express divers attitudes toward the power that love exerts over human beings.

Those who attempt to define what love is and what it is not cannot avoid facing questions about its relation to desire. Is the word "love" just a synonym for the word "desire"? Is desire only one of the components of love? Is the kind of desire that enters into love different from all the desires that are not transformed by love? Can there be love without desire? Different answers to such questions result in different conceptions of love and different classifications of the kinds of love. After reading the passages here that deal with these matters, the reader might find it useful to turn to the quotations dealing with desire in Section 4.4 of the chapter that follows.

The fact that English has only one word to cover what other languages use at least three words to name complicates the interpretation of passages that attempt to distinguish different types of love. The Greek triad of *eris, philia,* and *agape,* and the Latin triad of *amor, delictio,* and *caritas,* name three distinct types of love that can only be designated in English by such phrases as "erotic or sexual love," "friendly love" "divine love" or "the love of God and of one's self

and others as creatures of God." Though we do have single English words—"friendship" and "charity"—for the second and third types of love, our over-broad or over-narrow usage of them, together with a prevalent tendency to over-stress the sexual or erotic aspect of love, often obscures or distorts our understanding of the kinds of love and their relation to one another.

One consequence of these linguistic difficulties is the necessity of placing here not only passages that use the word "love" with maximum generality to cover every kind of love, but also passages that use the term in one or another more restricted sense without indicating the specific type of love that is intended. To have done otherwise would have required us to impose our interpretation upon the quotations. We felt that it was better to let the reader interpret them for himself, if he wishes, after he has explored the variety of loves that the quotations in later sections of this chapter discuss or exemplify.

The passages that express the attitudes writers have taken toward the force of love in human life range from admiration bordering on awe or reverence to complaints verging on fear or dread. Though in most of these quotations the word "love" is employed without any qualifying adjective, the reader, we think, will discover for himself that most of them are referring to sexual or erotic love, especially those that express qualms about the effects of love.

---

1 And Ruth said, Intreat me not to leave thee, or to return from following after thee: for whither thou goest, I will go; and where thou lodgest, I will lodge: thy people shall be my people, and thy God my God:

Where thou diest, will I die, and there will I be buried: the Lord do so to me, and more also, if ought but death part thee and me.

Ruth 1: 16–17

193

2 Set me as a seal upon thine heart, as a seal upon thine arm: for love is strong as death; jealousy is cruel as the grave: the coals thereof are coals of fire, which hath a most vehement flame.

Many waters cannot quench love, neither can the floods drown it: if a man would give all the substance of his house for love, it would utterly be contemned.

Song of Solomon 8:6–7

3 *Chorus.* Love unconquered in fight, love who falls on our havings.
You rest in the bloom of a girl's unwithered face.
You cross the sea, you are known in the wildest lairs.
Not the immortal gods can fly,
nor men of a day. Who has you within him is mad.

Sophocles, *Antigone,* 781

4 *Deianira.* How foolish one would be to climb into the ring
with Love and try to trade blows with him, like a boxer.
For he rules even the Gods as he pleases.

Sophocles, *Women of Trachis,* 441

5 *Chorus.* When in excess and past all limits Love doth come, he brings not glory or repute to man; but if the Cyprian queen in moderate might approach, no goddess is so full of charm as she.

Euripides, *Medea,* 627

6 *Chorus.* Cypris, you guide men's hearts
and the inflexible
hearts of the Gods and with you
comes Love with the flashing wings,
comes Love with the swiftest of wings.
Over the earth he flies
and the loud-echoing salt-sea.
He bewitches and maddens the heart
of the victim he swoops upon.
He bewitches the race of the mountain-hunting lions and beasts of the sea,
and all the creatures that earth feeds,
and the blazing sun sees—
and man, too—
over all you hold kingly power,
Love, you are only ruler
over all these.

Euripides, *Hippolytus,* 1268

7 *Socrates.* The soul of the lover will never forsake his beautiful one, whom he esteems above all; he has forgotten mother and brethren and companions, and he thinks nothing of the neglect and loss of his property; the rules and proprieties of life, on which he formerly prided himself, he now despises, and is ready to sleep like a servant, wherever he is allowed, as near as he can to his desired one, who is the object of his worship, and the physician who can alone assuage the greatness of his pain.

Plato, *Phaedrus,* 252A

8 *Pausanias.* Not every love, but only that which has a noble purpose, is noble and worthy of praise. The Love who is the offspring of the common Aphrodite is essentially common, and has no discrimination, being such as the meaner sort of men feel, and is apt to be of women as well as of youths, and is of the body rather than of the soul—the most foolish beings are the objects of this love which desires only to gain an end, but never thinks of accomplishing the end nobly, and therefore does good and evil quite indiscriminately. The goddess who is his mother is far younger than the other, and she was born of the union of the male and female, and partakes of both.

But the offspring of the heavenly Aphrodite is derived from a mother in whose birth the female has no part,—she is from the male only; this is that love which is of youths, and the goddess being older, there is nothing of wantonness in her. Those who are inspired by this love turn to the male, and delight in him who is the more valiant and intelligent nature; any one may recognise the pure enthusiasts in the very character of their attachments. For they love not boys, but intelligent beings whose reason is beginning to be developed, much about the time at which their beards begin to grow. And in choosing young men to be their companions, they mean to be faithful to them, and pass their whole life in company with them, not to take them in their inexperience, and deceive them, and play the fool with them, or run away from one to another of them. But the love of young boys should be forbidden by law, because their future is uncertain; they may turn out good or bad, either in body or soul, and much noble enthusiasm may be thrown away upon them.

Plato, *Symposium,* 181A

9 "What then is Love?" I [Socrates] asked; "Is he mortal?" "No." "What then?" "As in the former instance, he is neither mortal nor immortal, but in a mean between the two." "What is he, Diotima?" "He is a great spirit, and like all spirits he is intermediate between the divine and the mortal." "And what," I said, "is his power?" "He interprets," she [Diotima] replied, "between gods and men, conveying and taking across to the gods the prayers and sacrifices of men, and to men the commands and replies of the gods; he is the mediator who spans the chasm which divides them, and therefore in him all is bound together, and through him the arts of the prophet and the priest, their sacrifices and mysteries and charms, and all prophecy and incantation, find their way. For God mingles not with man; but through Love all the intercourse and converse of god with man,

whether awake or asleep, is carried on."

Plato, *Symposium*, 202B

10 "For love, Socrates, is not, as you imagine, the love of the beautiful only." "What then?" "The love of generation and of birth in beauty." "Yes," I said. "Yes, indeed," she [Diotima] replied. "But why of generation?" "Because to the mortal creature, generation is a sort of eternity and immortality," she replied; "and if, as has been already admitted, love is of the everlasting possession of the good, all men will necessarily desire immortality together with good: Wherefore love is of immortality."

All this she taught me at various times when she spoke of love. And I remember her once saying to me, "What is the cause, Socrates, of love, and the attendant desire? See you not how all animals, birds, as well as beasts, in their desire of procreation, are in agony when they take the infection of love, which begins with the desire of union; whereto is added the care of offspring, on whose behalf the weakest are ready to battle against the strongest even to the uttermost, and to die for them, and will let themselves be tormented with hunger or suffer anything in order to maintain their young. Man may be supposed to act thus from reason; but why should animals have these passionate feelings? Can you tell me why?" Again I replied that I did not know. She said to me: "And do you expect ever to become a master in the art of love, if you do not know this?" "But I have told you already, Diotima, that my ignorance is the reason why I come to you; for I am conscious that I want a teacher; tell me then the cause of this and of the other mysteries of love." "Marvel not," she said, "if you believe that love is of the immortal, as we have several times acknowledged; for here again, and on the same principle too, the mortal nature is seeking as far as is possible to be everlasting and immortal: and this is only to be attained by generation, because generation always leaves behind a new existence in the place of the old. Nay even in the life of the same individual there is succession and not absolute unity: a man is called the same, and yet in the short interval which elapses between youth and age, and in which every animal is said to have life and identity, he is undergoing a perpetual process of loss and reparation—hair, flesh, bones, blood, and the whole body are always changing. Which is true not only of the body, but also of the soul, whose habits, tempers, opinions, desires, pleasures, pains, fears, never remain the same in any one of us, but are always coming and going; and equally true of knowledge, and what is still more surprising to us mortals, not only do the sciences in general spring up and decay, so that in respect of them we are never the same; but each of them individually experiences a like change. For what is implied in the word 'recollection,' but the departure of knowledge, which is ever being forgotten, and is renewed and preserved by recollection, and appears to be the same although in reality new, according to that law of succession by which all mortal things are preserved, not absolutely the same, but by substitution, the old worn-out mortality leaving another new and similar existence behind—unlike the divine, which is always the same and not another? And in this way, Socrates, the mortal body, or mortal anything, partakes of immortality; but the immortal in another way. Marvel not then at the love which all men have of their offspring; for that universal love and interest is for the sake of immortality."

Plato, *Symposium*, 206B

11 The pleasure of the eye is the beginning of love. For no one loves if he has not first been delighted by the form of the beloved, but he who delights in the form of another does not, for all that, love him, but only does so when he also longs for him when absent and craves for his presence.

Aristotle, *Ethics*, 1167^{a}3

12 Those who have done a service to others feel friendship and love for those they have served even if these are not of any use to them and never will be. This is what happens with craftsmen too; every man loves his own handiwork better than he would be loved by it if it came alive; and this happens perhaps most of all with poets; for they have an excessive love for their own poems, doting on them as if they were their children. This is what the position of benefactors is like; for that which they have treated well is their handiwork, and therefore they love this more than the handiwork does its maker. The cause of this is that existence is to all men a thing to be chosen and loved, and that we exist by virtue of activity (that is, by living and acting), and that the handiwork *is* in a sense, the producer in activity; he loves his handiwork, therefore, because he loves existence. And this is rooted in the nature of things; for what he is in potentiality, his handiwork manifests in activity.

Aristotle, *Ethics*, 1167^{b}32

13 It is pleasant to be loved, for this . . . makes a man see himself as the possessor of goodness, a thing that every being that has a feeling for it desires to possess: to be loved means to be valued for one's own personal qualities.

Aristotle, *Rhetoric*, 1371^{a}18

14 Mother of the Aeneadae, darling of men and gods, increase-giving Venus, who beneath the gliding signs of heaven fillest with thy presence the ship-carrying sea, the corn-bearing lands, since through thee every kind of living things is conceived, rises up and beholds the light of the sun. Before thee, goddess, flee the winds, the clouds of heaven; before thee and thy advent; for

thee earth manifold in works puts forth sweet-smelling flowers; for thee the levels of the sea do laugh and heaven propitiated shines with out-spread light. For soon as the vernal aspect of day is disclosed, and the birth-favouring breeze of Favonius unbarred is blowing fresh, first the fowls of the air, O lady, show signs of thee and thy entering in, thoroughly smitten in heart by thy power. Next the wild herds bound over the glad pastures and swim the rapid rivers: in such wise each made prisoner by thy charms follows thee with desire, whither thou goest to lead it on. Yes, throughout seas and mountains and sweeping rivers and leafy homes of birds and grassy plains, striking fond love into the breasts of all thou constrainest them each after its kind to continue their races with desire. . . . Thou . . . art sole mistress of the nature of things and without thee nothing rises up into the divine borders of light, nothing grows to be glad or lovely.

Lucretius, *Nature of Things*, I

15 The passion we usually call love (and, heaven help me! I can come up with no other name for it) is so trivial that I can think of nothing to compare it with.

Cicero, *Disputations*, IV, 32

16 Love conquers all; and we must yield to Love.

Virgil, *Eclogues*, X

17 Not only man's imperial race, but they
That wing the liquid air, or swim the sea,
Or haunt the desert, rush into the flame:
For Love is lord of all, and is in all the same.
'Tis with this rage, the mother-lion stung,
Scours o'er the plain, regardless of her young:
Demanding rites of love, she sternly stalks,
And hunts her lover in his lonely walks.
'Tis then the shapeless bear his den forsakes;
In woods and fields, a wild destruction makes:
Boars with their tusks; to battle tigers move,
Enraged with hunger, more enraged with love.
Then woe to him, that, in the desert land
Of Libya, travels o'er the burning sand!
The stallion snuffs the well-known scent afar,
And snorts and trembles for the distant mare;
Nor bits nor bridles can his rage restrain,
And rugged rocks are interposed in vain:
He makes his way o'er mountains, and contemns
Unruly torrents, and unforded streams.
The bristled boar, who feels the pleasing wound,
New grinds his arming tusks, and digs the ground.
The sleepy lecher shuts his little eyes;
About his churning chaps the frothy bubbles rise:
He rubs his sides against a tree; prepares
And hardens both his shoulders for the wars.
What did the youth, when Love's unerring dart
Transfixed his liver and inflamed his heart?
Alone, by night, his watery way he took;
About him, and above the billows broke;

The sluices of the sky were open spread,
And rolling thunder rattled o'er his head;
The raging tempests called him back in vain,
And every boding omen of the main:
Nor could his kindred, nor the kindly force
Of weeping parents, change his fatal course;
No, not the dying maid, who must deplore
His floating carcase on the Sestian shore.

Virgil, *Georgics*, III

18 Now everyone recognizes that the emotional state for which we make this "Love" responsible rises in souls aspiring to be knit in the closest union with some beautiful object, and that this aspiration takes two forms, that of the good whose devotion is for beauty itself, and that other which seeks its consummation in some vile act. . . . It is sound, I think, to find the primal source of Love in a tendency of the Soul towards pure beauty, in a recognition, in a kinship, in an unreasoned consciousness of friendly relation.

Plotinus, *Third Ennead*, V, 1

19 Those that love beauty of person without carnal desire love for beauty's sake; those that have—for women, of course—the copulative love, have the further purpose of self-perpetuation: as long as they are led by these motives, both are on the right path, though the first have taken the nobler way.

Plotinus, *Third Ennead*, V, 1

20 A body tends by its weight towards the place proper to it—weight does not necessarily tend towards the lowest place but towards its proper place. Fire tends upwards, stone downwards. By their weight they are moved and seek their proper place. Oil poured over water is borne on the surface of the water, water poured over oil sinks below the oil: it is by their weight that they are moved and seek their proper place. Things out of their place are in motion: they come to their place and are at rest. My love is my weight: wherever I go my love is what brings me there.

Augustine, *Confessions*, XIII, 9

21 If we were beasts, we should love the fleshly and sensual life, and this would be our sufficient good; and when it was well with us in respect of it, we should seek nothing beyond. In like manner, if we were trees, we could not, indeed, in the strict sense of the word, love anything; nevertheless we should seem, as it were, to long for that by which we might become more abundantly and luxuriantly fruitful. If we were stones, or waves, or wind, or flame, or anything of that kind, we should want, indeed, both sensation and life, yet should possess a kind of attraction towards our own proper position and natural order. For the specific gravity of bodies is, as it were, their love, whether they are carried downwards by their weight, or upwards

by their levity. For the body is borne by its gravity, as the spirit by love, whithersoever it is borne. But we are men, created in the image of our Creator, Whose eternity is true, and Whose truth is eternal, Whose love is eternal and true.

Augustine, *City of God*, XI, 28

22 Two cities have been formed by two loves: the earthly by the love of self, even to the contempt of God: the heavenly by the love of God, even to the contempt of self. The former, in a word, glories in itself, the latter in the Lord. For the one seeks glory from men; but the greatest glory of the other is God, the witness of conscience.

Augustine, *City of God*, XIV, 28

23 Through Love the universe with constancy makes changes all without discord: earth's elements, though contrary, abide in treaty bound: Phœbus in his golden car leads up the glowing day; his sister rules the night that Hesperus brought: the greedy sea confines its waves in bounds, lest the earth's borders be changed by its beating on them: all these are firmly bound by Love, which rules both earth and sea, and has its empire in the heavens too. If Love should slacken this its hold, all mutual love would change to war; and these would strive to undo the scheme which now their glorious movements carry out with trust and with accord. By Love are peoples too kept bound together by a treaty which they may not break. Love binds with pure affection the sacred tie of wedlock, and speaks its bidding to all trusty friends. O happy race of mortals, if your hearts are ruled as is the universe, by Love!

Boethius, *Consolation of Philosophy*, II

24 The good we receive from God is twofold, the good of nature, and the good of grace. Now the fellowship of natural goods bestowed on us by God is the foundation of natural love, in virtue of which not only man, so long as his nature remains unimpaired, loves God above all things and more than himself, but also every single creature, each in its own way, that is, either by an intellectual, or by a rational, or by an animal, or at least by a natural love, as stones do, for instance, and other things bereft of knowledge, because each part naturally loves the common good of the whole more than its own particular good. This is evidenced by its operation, since the principal inclination of each part is towards common action conducive to the usefulness of the whole. It may also be seen in political virtues according to which sometimes the citizens suffer damage even to their own property and persons for the sake of the common good. And so much more is this realized with regard to the friendship of charity which is based on the fellowship of the gifts of grace. Therefore man ought, out of charity, to love God, Who is the common good of all, more than himself, since happiness is in God as in the universal and foun-

tain-head principle of all who are able to have a share of that happiness.

Aquinas, *Summa Theologica*, II–II, 26, 3

25 It is natural to a man to love his own work (thus it is to be observed that poets love their own poems); and the reason is that we love to be and to live, and these are made manifest especially in our action.

Aquinas, *Summa Theologica*, II–II, 26, 12

26 [Everything] hath its specific love, as, for example, the simple bodies have a love which has an innate affinity to their proper place; and that is why earth ever drops to the centre; but the love of fire is for the upper circumference, under the heaven of the moon, and therefore it ever riseth thereto.

Primary compound bodies, like the minerals, have a love for the place where their generation is ordained; and therein they grow, and thence draw vigour and power. Whence we see the magnet ever receive power from the direction of its generation.

Plants, which are the primary living things, have a more manifest love for certain places, according as their composition requires; and therefore we see certain plants almost always gather along watercourses, and certain on the ridges of mountains, and certain on slopes and at the foot of hills, the which, if we transplant them, either die altogether or live as if in gloom, like things parted from the place dear to them.

As for the brute animals, not only have they a more manifest love for their place, but we see that they love one another.

Men have their proper love for perfect and comely things. And because man (though his whole form be one sole substance) has in himself, by his nobility, something of the nature of each of these things, he may have all these loves, and has them all indeed. For in virtue of the nature of the simple body, which predominates in the subject, he naturally loves to descend; and therefore when he moves his body upward it is more toilsome. By the second nature, of a complex body, he loves the place and further the time of his generation, and therefore everyone is naturally of more efficient body at the place where he was generated, and at the time of his generation, than at any other. . . .

And by the third nature, to wit that of plants, man hath love for certain food, not in so far as it affects the sense but in so far as it is nutritious; and such food maketh the working of this nature most perfect; and other food does not so, but makes it imperfect. And therefore we see that some certain food shall make men fair of face and stout of limb, and of a lively colour; and certain other shall work the contrary of this. And in virtue of the fourth nature, that of animals, to wit the sensitive, man hath another love whereby he loveth according to sensible appearance, like to a beast; and this is the love in man which most needeth a ruler, because of its overmastering operation, especially in the delight of taste and touch. And by the fifth and last nature, that is to say the truly human or, rather say, the angelic, to wit the rational, man hath love to truth and to virtue; and from this love springeth the true and perfect friendship, drawn from nobility.

Dante, *Convivio*, III, 3

27 *Virgil.* Nor Creator, nor creature, my son, was ever without love, either natural or rational; and this thou knowest.

The natural is always without error; but the other may err through an evil object, or through too little or too much vigour.

While it is directed to the primal goods, and in the secondary, moderates itself, it cannot be the cause of sinful delight;

but when it is turned awry to evil, or speeds towards the good with more or less care than it ought, against the Creator his creature works.

Hence thou mayst understand that love must be the seed of every virtue in you, and of every deed that deserves punishment.

Now inasmuch as love can never turn its face from the weal of its subject, all things are safe from self-hatred;

and because no being can be conceived as existing alone in isolation from the Prime Being, every affection is cut off from hate of him.

It follows, if I judge well in my division, that the evil we love is our neighbour's, and this love arises in three ways in your clay.

There is he who through his neighbour's abasement hopes to excel, and solely for this desires that he be cast down from his greatness;

there is he who fears to lose power, favour, honour and fame because another is exalted, wherefore he groweth sad so that he loves the contrary;

and there is he who seems to be so shamed through being wronged, that he becomes greedy of vengeance, and such must needs seek another's hurt.

This threefold love down below is mourned for: now I desire that thou understand of the other, which hastes toward good in faulty degree.

Each one apprehends vaguely a good wherein the mind may find rest, and desires it; wherefore each one strives to attain thereto.

If lukewarm love draw you towards the vision of it or the gaining of it, this cornice, after due penitence, torments you for it.

Another good there is, which maketh not men happy; 'tis not happiness, 'tis not the good essence, the fruit and root of all good.

The love that abandons itself too much to this, is mourned for above us in three circles: but how it is distinguished in three divisions, I do not say, in order that thou search for it of thyself.

Dante, *Purgatorio*, XVII, 91

28 "Master, my vision is so quickened in thy light, that I discern clearly all that thy discourse imports or describes;

therefore I pray thee, sweet Father dear, that thou define love to me, to which thou dost reduce every good work and its opposite."

"Direct," said he [Virgil], "towards me the keen eyes of the understanding, and the error of the blind who make them guides shall be manifest to thee.

The mind which is created quick to love, is responsive to everything that is pleasing, soon as by pleasure it is awakened into activity.

Your apprehensive faculty draws an impression from a real object, and unfolds it within you, so that it makes the mind turn thereto.

And if, being turned, it inclines towards it, that inclination is love; that is nature, which through pleasure is bound anew within you.

Then, even as fire moves upward by reason of its form, whose nature it is to ascend, there where it endures longest in its material;

so the enamoured mind falls to desire, which is a spiritual movement, and never rests until the object of its love makes it rejoice.

Now may be apparent to thee, how deeply the truth is hidden from the folk who aver that every act of love is in itself a laudable thing,

because, forsooth, its material may seem always to be good; but not every imprint is good, albeit the wax may be good."

"Thy words and my attendant wit," I answered him, "have made love plain to me, but that has made me more teeming with doubt;

for if love is offered to us from without, and the soul walks with no other foot, it is no merit of hers whether she go straight or crooked."

And he to me: "So far as reason sees here, I can tell thee; from beyond that point, ever await Beatrice, for 'tis a matter of faith.

Every substantial form, which is distinct from matter and is in union with it, has a specific virtue contained within itself

which is not perceived save in operation, nor is manifested except by its effects, just as life in a plant by the green leaves.

Therefore man knows not whence the understanding of the first cognitions may come, nor the inclination to the prime objects of appetite,

which are in you, even as the instinct in bees to make honey; and this prime will admits no desert of praise or of blame.

Now in order that to this will every other may be related, innate with you is the virtue which giveth counsel, and ought to guard the threshold of assent.

This is the principle whence is derived the reason of desert in you, according as it garners and winnows good and evil loves.

Those who in their reasoning went to the founda-

tion, perceived this innate freedom, therefore
they left ethics to the world.
Wherefore suppose that every love which is kindled within you arise of necessity, the power to
arrest it is within you."

Dante, *Purgatorio*, XVIII, 10

29 So fared it with this rash and hardy knight [Troi-
lus],
Who was a king's son of most high degree,
For though he thought that nothing had the
might
To curb the heart of such a one as he,
Yet with a look, no longer was he free,
And he who stood but now in pride above
All men, at once was subject most to Love.

And now I bid you profit by this man,
Ye worthy folk, and wise and proud withal,
And scorn not Love, he who so lightly can
The freedom of rebellious hearts enthral;
For still the common fate on you must fall,
That love, at nature's very heart indwelling,
Shall bind all things by nature's might compel-
ling.

That this is true hath oftentimes been proved,
For well you know, and in wise books may read,
That men of greatest worth have deepest loved,
And none so powerful in word or deed,
But he the greater power of love must heed,
For all his fame or high nobility;
Thus hath it been and ever shall it be!

And fitting is it that it should be so,
For wisest men have most with love been pleased,
And those that dwelt in sorrow and in woe,
By love have often been consoled and eased,
And cruel wrath by love hath been appeased;
For love lends lustre to an honorable name,
And saves mankind from wickedness and shame.

Chaucer, *Troilus and Cressida*, I, 33–36

30 [Her] thought was this, "Alas, since I [Cressida]
am free,
Should I now love and risk my happy state
And maybe put in bonds my liberty?
What folly such a course to contemplate!
Am I not satisfied to see the fate
Of others, with their fear and joy and pain?
Who loveth not, no cause hath to complain.

"For lovers ever lead a stormy life,
And have done so since loving was begun,
For always some distrust and foolish strife
There is in love, some cloud across the sun.
Then nothing by us women can be done,
But weep in wretchedness and sit and think,
'This is our lot, the cup of woe to drink!'

"And slanderous tongues, they are so very quick
To do us harm, and men are so untrue,

And once they're satisfied, they soon grow sick
Of ancient love and look for something new!
But when all's done, then what can women do!
These men at first their love like mad will spend,
But sharp attacks oft weaken at the end.

"Full often it hath been exemplified,
The treason that to women men will show;
And that's the end, when such a love hath died,
For what becomes of it, when it doth go,
No living creature on this earth can know,
For then there's nothing left to love or spurn;
What once was naught, to nothing doth return.

"And if I love, how busy must I be
To guard against all idle people's chatter,
And fool them that they see no fault in me,
For true or not, to them it doesn't matter,
If but their lying tales amuse or flatter;
For who can stop the wagging of a tongue,
Or sound of bells the while that they are rung!"

Chaucer, *Troilus and Cressida*, II, 111–115

31 O happy light, of which the beams so clear
Illume the third expanse of heaven's air,
Loved of the sun, of Jove the daughter dear,
O Love's Delight, thou goodly one and fair,
In gentle hearts abiding everywhere,
Thou primal cause of joy and all salvation,
Exalted be thy name through all creation!

In heaven and hell, on earth and salty sea,
All creatures answer to thy might supernal,
For man, bird, beast, fish, herb and leafy tree,
Their seasons know from thy breath ever vernal.
God loves, and grants that love shall be eternal.
All creatures in the world through love exist,
And lacking love, lack all that may persist.

Mover of Jove to that so happy end,
Through which all earthly creatures live and be,
When mortal love upon him thou didst send,
For as thou wilt, the power lies with thee
Of ease in love or love's adversity,
And in a thousand forms is thy descent
On earth, in love to favor or prevent!

Fierce Mars for thee must subjugate his ire,
All hearts from thee receive their fates condign;
Yet ever when they feel thy sacred fire,
In dread of shame, their vices they resign,
And gentler grow, more brave and more benign;
And high or low, as each in his rank strives,
All owe to thee the joys of all their lives.

Houses and realms in greater unity,
And faith in friendship thou canst make to grow.
Thou understandest likings hard to see,
Which cause much wonder that they should be so,
As when in puzzlement, one seeks to know,
Why this loves that, why she by him is sought,
Why one and not the other fish is caught.

From thee comes law for all the universe,

And this I know, as all true lovers see,
That who opposeth, ever hath the worse.
Now, lady bright, in thy benignity,
Help me to honor those who honor thee,
And teach me, clerk of love, that I may tell
The joy of those who in thy service dwell.

Chaucer, *Troilus and Cressida*, III, 1–6

32 *Arcita.* Know you not well the ancient writer's saw
Of 'Who shall give a lover any law?'
Love is a greater law, aye by my pan,
Than man has ever given to earthly man.

Chaucer, *Canterbury Tales:*
Knight's Tale

33 *Proteus.* O, how this spring of love resembleth
The uncertain glory of an April day,
Which now shows all the beauty of the sun,
And by and by a cloud takes all away!

Shakespeare, *Two Gentlemen*
of Verona, I, iii, 84

34 *Biron.*   Love, first learned in a lady's eyes,
Lives not alone immured in the brain;
But, with the motion of all elements,
Courses as swift as thought in every power,
And gives to every power a double power,
Above their functions and their offices.
It adds a precious seeing to the eye;
A lover's eyes will gaze an eagle blind;
A lover's ear will hear the lowest sound,
When the suspicious head of theft is stopp'd:
Love's feeling is more soft and sensible
Than are the tender horns of cockled snails;
Love's tongue proves dainty Bacchus gross in
taste:
For valour, is not Love a Hercules,
Still climbing trees in the Hesperides?
Subtle as Sphinx; as sweet and musical
As bright Apollo's lute, strung with his hair;
And when Love speaks, the voice of all the gods
Make heaven drowsy with the harmony.
Never durst poet touch a pen to write
Until his ink were temper'd with Love's sighs;
O, then his lines would ravish savage ears
And plant in tyrants mild humility.

Shakespeare, *Love's Labour's Lost*, IV, iii, 327

35 *Juliet.* Dost thou love me? I know thou wilt say
"Ay,"
And I will take thy word: yet, if thou swear'st,
Thou mayst prove false; at lovers' perjuries,
They say, Jove laughs. O gentle Romeo,
If thou dost love, pronounce it faithfully:
Or if thou think'st I am too quickly won,
I'll frown and be perverse and say thee nay,
So thou wilt woo; but else, not for the world.
In truth, fair Montague, I am too fond,
And therefore thou mayst think my 'haviour
light:
But trust me, gentleman, I'll prove more true

Than those that have more cunning to be strange.

Shakespeare, *Romeo and Juliet*, II, ii, 90

36 *Lysander.* Ay me! for aught that I could ever read,
Could ever hear by tale or history,
The course of true love never did run smooth;
But, either it was different in blood—
Hermione. O cross! too high to be enthrall'd to
low.
Lys. Or else misgraffed in respect of years—
Her. O spite! too old to be engaged to young.
Lys. Or else it stood upon the choice of
friends—
Her. O hell! to choose love by another's eyes.
Lys. Or, if there were a sympathy in choice,
War, death, or sickness did lay siege to it,
Making it momentary as a sound,
Swift as a shadow, short as any dream;
Brief as the lightning in the collied night,
That, in a spleen, unfolds both heaven and earth,
And ere a man hath power to say "Behold!"
The jaws of darkness do devour it up:
So quick bright things come to confusion.

Shakespeare, *Midsummer-Night's*
Dream, I, i, 132

37 *Lorenzo.* The moon shines bright: in such a night
as this,
When the sweet wind did gently kiss the trees
And they did make no noise, in such a night
Troilus methinks mounted the Troyan walls
And sigh'd his soul toward the Grecian tents,
Where Cressid lay that night.
Jessica.   In such a night
Did Thisbe fearfully o'ertrip the dew
And saw the lion's shadow ere himself
And ran dismay'd away.
Lor.   In such a night
Stood Dido with a willow in her hand
Upon the wild sea banks, and waft her love
To come again to Carthage.
Jes.   In such a night
Medea gather'd the enchanted herbs
That did renew old Æson.
Lor.   In such a night
Did Jessica steal from the wealthy Jew,
And with an unthrift love did run from Venice
As far as Belmont.
Jes.   In such a night
Did young Lorenzo swear he loved her well,
Stealing her soul with many vows of faith
And ne'er a true one.
Lor.   In such a night
Did pretty Jessica, like a little shrew,
Slander her love, and he forgave it her.
Jes. I would out-night you, did no body come;
But, hark, I hear the footing of a man.

Shakespeare, *Merchant of Venice*, V, i, 1

38 *Benedick.* I do much wonder that one man, seeing
how much another man is a fool when he dedi-

cates his behaviours to love, will, after he hath laughed at such shallow follies in others, become the argument of his own scorn by falling in love: and such a man is Claudio. I have known when there was no music with him but the drum and the fife; and now had he rather hear the tabor and the pipe: I have known when he would have walked ten mile a-foot to see a good armour; and now will he lie ten nights awake, carving the fashion of a new doublet. He was wont to speak plain and to the purpose, like an honest man and a soldier; and now is he turned orthography; his words are a very fantastical banquet, just so many strange dishes. May I be so converted and see with these eyes? I cannot tell; I think not: I will not be sworn but love may transform me to an oyster; but I'll take my oath on it, till he have made an oyster of me, he shall never make me such a fool. One woman is fair, yet I am well; another is wise, yet I am well; another virtuous, yet I am well; but till all graces be in one woman, one woman shall not come in my grace. Rich she shall be, that's certain; wise, or I'll none; virtuous, or I'll never cheapen her; fair, or I'll never look on her; mild, or come not near me; noble, or not I for an angel; of good discourse, an excellent musician, and her hair shall be of what colour it please God.

Shakespeare, *Much Ado About Nothing*, II, iii, 7

39 *Rosalind.* Love is merely a madness, and, I tell you, deserves as well a dark house and a whip as madmen do: and the reason why they are not so punished and cured is that the lunacy is so ordinary that the whippers are in love too.

Shakespeare, *As You Like It*, III, ii, 420

40 *Rosalind.* Why, how now, Orlando! where have you been all this while? You a lover! An you serve me such another trick, never come in my sight more.

Orlando. My fair Rosalind, I come within an hour of my promise.

Ros. Break an hour's promise in love! He that will divide a minute into a thousand parts and break but a part of the thousandth part of a minute in the affairs of love, it may be said of him that Cupid hath clapped him o' the shoulder, but I'll warrant him heart-whole.

Shakespeare, *As You Like It*, IV, i, 38

41 *Rosalind.* The poor world is almost six thousand years old, and in all this time there was not any man died in his own person, *videlicet*, in a love-cause. Troilus had his brains dashed out with a Grecian club; yet he did what he could to die before, and he is one of the patterns of love. Leander, he would have lived many a fair year, though Hero had turned nun, if it had not been for a hot midsummer night; for, good youth, he went but forth to wash him in the Hellespont and being taken with the cramp was drowned: and the foolish chroniclers of that age found it was "Hero of Sestos." But these are all lies: men have died from time to time and worms have eaten them, but not for love.

Shakespeare, *As You Like It*, IV, i, 94

42 *Othello.* Most potent, grave, and reverend signiors,
My very noble and approved good masters,
That I have ta'en away this old man's daughter,
It is most true; true, I have married her:
The very head and front of my offending
Hath this extent, no more. Rude am I in my speech,
And little bless'd with the soft phrase of peace.
For since these arms of mine had seven years' pith,
Till now some nine moons wasted, they have used
Their dearest action in the tented field,
And little of this great world can I speak
More than pertains to feats of broil and battle,
And therefore little shall I grace my cause
In speaking for myself. Yet, by your gracious patience,
I will a round unvarnish'd tale deliver
Of my whole course of love; what drugs, what charms,
What conjuration, and what mighty magic,
For such proceeding I am charged withal,
I won his daughter. . . .
     Her father loved me; oft invited me;
Still question'd me the story of my life,
From year to year, the battles, sieges, fortunes,
That I have pass'd.
I ran it through, even from my boyish days,
To the very moment that he bade me tell it;
Wherein I spake of most disastrous chances,
Of moving accidents by flood and field,
Of hair-breadth scapes i' the imminent deadly breach,
Of being taken by the insolent foe
And sold to slavery, of my redemption thence
And portance in my travels' history;
Wherein of antres vast and deserts idle,
Rough quarries, rocks, and hills whose heads touch heaven,
It was my hint to speak—such was the process—
And of the Cannibals that each other eat,
The Anthropophagi and men whose heads
Do grow beneath their shoulders. This to hear
Would Desdemona seriously incline;
But still the house-affairs would draw her thence,
Which ever as she could with haste dispatch,
She'd come again, and with a greedy ear
Devour up my discourse; which I observing,
Took once a pliant hour, and found good means
To draw from her a prayer of earnest heart
That I would all my pilgrimage dilate,
Whereof by parcels she had something heard,
But not intentively. I did consent,

And often did beguile her of her tears
When I did speak of some distressful stroke
That my youth suffer'd. My story being done,
She gave me for my pains a world of sighs.
She swore, in faith, 'twas strange, 'twas passing
strange,
'Twas pitiful, 'twas wondrous pitiful.
She wish'd she had not heard it, yet she wish'd
That heaven had made her such a man. She
thank'd me,
And bade me, if I had a friend that loved her,
I should but teach him how to tell my story,
And that would woo her. Upon this hint I spake:
She loved me for the dangers I had pass'd,
And I loved her that she did pity them.
This only is the witchcraft I have used.
Here comes the lady; let her witness it.

Shakespeare, Othello, I, iii, 76

43 *Othello.* Excellent wretch! Perdition catch my soul,
But I do love thee! and when I love thee not,
Chaos is come again.

Shakespeare, Othello, III, iii, 90

44 *Othello.*   I pray you, in your letters,
When you shall these unlucky deeds relate,
Speak of me as I am; nothing extenuate,
Nor set down aught in malice. Then must you
speak
Of one that loved not wisely but too well;
Of one not easily jealous, but being wrought
Perplex'd in the extreme; of one whose hand,
Like the base Indian, threw a pearl away
Richer than all his tribe.

Shakespeare, Othello, V, ii, 340

45 *Cleopatra.* If it be love indeed, tell me how much.
Antony. There's beggary in the love than can be
reckon'd.
Cleo. I'll set a bourn how far to be beloved.
Ant. Then must thou needs find out new heav-
en, new earth.

Shakespeare, Antony and Cleopatra, I, i, 14

46 Not mine own fears, nor the prophetic soul
Of the wide world dreaming on things to come,
Can yet the lease of my true love control,
Supposed as forfeit to a confined doom.
The mortal moon hath her eclipse endured,
And the sad augurs mock their own presage;
Incertainties now crown themselves assured,
And peace proclaims olives of endless age.
Now with the drops of this most balmy time
My love looks fresh, and Death to me subscribes,
Since, spite of him, I'll live in this poor rhyme.

Shakespeare, Sonnet CVII

47 Let me not to the marriage of true minds
Admit impediments. Love is not love
Which alters when it alteration finds,
Or bends with the remover to remove.

O, no! it is an ever-fixed mark
That looks on tempests and is never shaken;
It is the star to every wandering bark,
Whose worth's unknown, although his height be
taken.
Love's not Time's fool, though rosy lips and
cheeks
Within his bending sickle's compass come;
Love alters not with his brief hours and weeks,
But bears it out even to the edge of doom.

Shakespeare, Sonnet CXVI

48 Reply'd Don *Quixote;* a Knight-Errant cannot be
without a Mistress; 'tis not more essential for the
Skies to have Stars; than 'tis to us to be in Love.
Insomuch, that I dare affirm, that no History ever
made mention of any Knight-Errant, that was not
a Lover; for were any Knight free from the Impulses of that generous Passion, he wou'd not be
allow'd to be a lawful Knight; but a mis-born In-
truder, and one who was not admitted within the
Pale of Knighthood at the Door, but leap'd the
Fence, and stole in like a Robber and a Thief.

Cervantes, Don Quixote, I, 13

49 *Don Quixote.* Dost thou not know, excommunicated
Traitor (for certainly Excommunication is the
least Punishment can fall upon thee, after such
Profanations of the peerless *Dulcinea's* Name) and
art thou not assur'd, vile Slave and ignominious
Vagabond, that I shou'd not have Strength suffi-
cient to kill a Flea, did not [Dulcinea] give
Strength to my Nerves, and infuse Vigour into my
Sinews? Speak, thou Villain with the Viper's
Tongue; Who do'st thou imagine has restor'd the
Queen to her Kingdom, cut off the Head of a
Giant, and made thee a Marquis (for I count all
this as done already) but the Power of *Dulcinea,*
who makes use of my Arm, as the Instrument of
her Act in me? She fights and overcomes in me;
and I live and breathe in her, holding Life and
Being from her.

Cervantes, Don Quixote, I, 30

50 Stand still, and I will read to thee
A lecture, love, in Love's philosophy.
These three hours that we have spent,
Walking here, two shadows went
Along with us, which we ourselves produced;
But, now the sun is just above our head,
We do those shadows tread,
And to brave clearness all things are reduced.
So whilst our infant loves did grow,
Disguises did, and shadows, flow
From us and our cares; but, now 'tis not so.

That love hath not attained the high'st degree,
Which is still diligent lest others see.

Except our loves at this noon stay,
We shall new shadows make the other way.
As the first were made to blind

Others, these which come behind
Will work upon ourselves, and blind our eyes.
If our loves faint, and westwardly decline,
   To me thou, falsely, thine,
And I to thee, mine actions shall disguise.
   The morning shadows wear away,
   But these grow longer all the day;
But oh, love's day is short, if love decay.

Love is a growing, or full constant light,
And his first minute after noon, is night.

      Donne, *A Lecture upon the Shadow*

51 Dull sublunary lovers' love
   (Whose soul is sense) cannot admit
  Absence, because it doth remove
  Those things which elemented it.

But we, by a love so much refined,
  That ourselves know not what it is,
Inter-assured of the mind,
  Care less, eyes, lips, and hands to miss.

Our two souls therefore, which are one,
  Though I must go, endure not yet
A breach, but an expansion,
  Like gold to airy thinness beat.

If they be two, they are two so
  As stiff twin compasses are two,
Thy soul the fixt foot, makes no show
  To move, but doth, if the other do.

And though it in the centre sit,
  Yet when the other far doth roam,
It leans, and hearkens after it,
  And grows erect, as that comes home.

Such wilt thou be to me, who must
  Like th' other foot, obliquely run;
Thy firmness makes my circle just,
  And makes me end, where I begun.

    Donne, *A Valediction: Forbidding Mourning*

52 The stage is more beholding to love than the life
of man. For as to the stage, love is ever matter of
comedies, and now and then of tragedies; but in
life it doth much mischief, sometimes like a siren,
sometimes like a fury.

      Bacon, *Of Love*

53 We may, it seems to me, find differences in love
according to the esteem which we bear to the object loved as compared with oneself: for when we
esteem the object of love less than ourselves, we
have only a simple affection for it; when we esteem it equally with ourselves, that is called
friendship; and when we esteem it more, the passion which we have may be called devotion.

    Descartes, *Passions of the Soul*, LXXXIII

54 The heart has its reasons, which reason does not
know. We feel it in a thousand things. I say that
the heart naturally loves the Universal Being, and

also itself naturally, according as it gives itself to
them; and it hardens itself against one or the
other at its will. You have rejected the one and
kept the other. Is it by reason that you love yourself?

      Pascal, *Pensées*, IV, 277

55 *Love* is joy with the accompanying idea of an external cause. This . . . explains with sufficient
clearness the essence of love; that which is given
by some authors, who define love to be the will of
the lover to unite himself to the beloved object,
expressing not the essence of love but one of its
properties, and in as much as these authors have
not seen with sufficient clearness what is the essence of love, they could not have a distinct conception of its properties, and consequently their
definition has by everybody been thought very obscure. I must observe, however, when I say that it
is a property in a lover to will a union with the
beloved object, that I do not understand by a will
a consent or deliberation or a free decree of the
mind . . . , nor even a desire of the lover to unite
himself with the beloved object when it is absent,
nor a desire to continue in its presence when it is
present, for love can be conceived without either
one or the other of these desires; but by will I
understand the satisfaction that the beloved object
produces in the lover by its presence, by virtue of
which the joy of the lover is strengthened, or at
any rate supported.

    Spinoza, *Ethics*, III, Prop. 59, Schol. 6

56 Any one reflecting upon the thought he has of the
delight which any present or absent thing is apt to
produce in him, has the idea we call *love*. For
when a man declares in autumn when he is eating
them, or in spring when there are none, that he
loves grapes, it is no more but that the taste of
grapes delights him: let an alteration of health or
constitution destroy the delight of their taste, and
he then can be said to love grapes no longer.

    Locke, *Concerning Human Understanding*,
                Bk. II, XX, 4

57 *Fainall*. For a passionate lover, methinks you are a
man somewhat too discerning in the failings of
your mistress.

  Mirabell. And for a discerning man, somewhat
too passionate a lover; for I like her with all her
faults, nay, like her for her faults. Her follies are
so natural, are so artful, that they become her,
and those affectations which in another woman
would be odious, serve but to make her more
agreeable. I'll tell thee, Fainall, she once used me
with that insolence that in revenge I took her to
pieces; sifted her, and separated her failings; I
studied 'em, and got 'em by rote. The catalogue
was so large that I was not without hopes, one day
or other, to hate her heartily: to which end I so
used myself to think of 'em that at length, con-

trary to my design and expectation, they gave me every hour less and less disturbance, till in a few days it became habitual to me to remember 'em without being displeased. They are now grown as familiar to me as my own frailties, and in all probability in a little time longer I shall like 'em as well.

Congreve, *Way of the World,* I, iii

58 *Mirabell.* Do you lock yourself up from me, to make my search more curious? Or is this pretty artifice contrived to signify that here the chase must end, and my pursuit be crowned, for you can fly no further?

Millamant. Vanity! No—I'll fly and be followed to the last moment. Though I am upon the very verge of matrimony, I expect you should solicit me as much as if I were wavering at the grate of a monastery, with one foot over the threshold. I'll be solicited to the very last, nay and afterwards.

Mira. What, after the last?

Milla. O, I should think I was poor and had nothing to bestow, if I were reduced to an inglorious ease; and freed from the agreeable fatigues of solicitation.

Mira. But do not you know that when favors are conferred upon instant and tedious solicitation, that they diminish in their value and that both the giver loses the grace, and the receiver lessens his pleasure?

Milla. It may be in things of common application, but never sure in love. O, I hate a lover that can dare to think he draws a moment's air, independent on the bounty of his mistress. There is not so impudent a thing in nature as the saucy look of an assured man, confident of success. The pedantic arrogance of a very husband has not so pragmatical an air.

Congreve, *Way of the World,* IV, v

59 To avoid, however, all contention, if possible, with these philosophers, if they will be called so; and to show our own disposition to accommodate matters peaceably between us, we shall here make them some concessions, which may possibly put an end to the dispute.

First, we will grant that many minds, and perhaps those of the philosophers, are entirely free from the least traces of such a passion.

Secondly, that what is commonly called love, namely, the desire of satisfying a voracious appetite with a certain quantity of delicate white human flesh, is by no means that passion for which I here contend. This is indeed more properly hunger; and as no glutton is ashamed to apply the word love to his appetite, and to say he LOVES such and such dishes; so may the lover of this kind, with equal propriety, say, he HUNGERS after such and such women.

Thirdly, I will grant, which I believe will be a most acceptable concession, that this love for

which I am an advocate, though it satisfies itself in a much more delicate manner, doth nevertheless seek its own satisfaction as much as the grossest of all our appetites.

And, lastly, that this love, when it operates towards one of a different sex, is very apt, towards its complete gratification, to call in the aid of that hunger which I have mentioned above; and which it is so far from abating, that it heightens all its delights to a degree scarce imaginable by those who have never been susceptible of any other emotions than what have proceeded from appetite alone.

In return to all these concessions, I desire of philosophers to grant, that there is in some (I believe in many) human breasts a kind and benevolent disposition, which is gratified by contributing to the happiness of others. That in this gratification alone, as in friendship, in parental and filial affection, as indeed in general philanthropy, there is a great and exquisite delight. That if we will not call such disposition love, we have no name for it. That though the pleasures arising from such pure love may be heightened and sweetened by the assistance of amorous desires, yet the former can subsist alone, nor are they destroyed by the intervention of the latter. Lastly, that esteem and gratitude are the proper motives to love, as youth and beauty are to desire, and, therefore, though such desire may naturally cease, when age or sickness overtakes its object; yet these can have no effect on love, nor ever shake or remove, from a good mind, that sensation or passion which hath gratitude and esteem for its basis.

Fielding, *Tom Jones,* VI, 1

60 Our connections with the fair sex are founded on the pleasure of enjoyment; on the happiness of loving and being loved; and likewise on the ambition of pleasing the ladies, because they are the best judges of some of those things which constitute personal merit. This general desire of pleasing produces gallantry, which is not love itself, but the delicate, the volatile, the perpetual simulation of love. According to the different circumstances of every country and age, love inclines more to one of those three things than to the other two.

Montesquieu, *Spirit of Laws,* XXVIII, 22

61 In general, it may be affirm'd, that there is no such passion in human minds, as the love of mankind, merely as such, independent of personal qualities, of services, or of relation to ourself. . . . We may affirm, that man in general, or human nature, is nothing but the object both of love and hatred, and requires some other cause, which by a double relation of impressions and ideas, may excite these passions.

Hume, *Treatise of Human Nature,* Bk. III, II 1

62 There are so many sorts of love that one does not know to whom to address oneself for a definition of it. The name of "love" is given boldly to a caprice lasting a few days, a sentiment without esteem, gallants' affectations, a frigid habit, a romantic fantasy, relish followed by prompt disrelish: people give this name to a thousand chimeras.

If philosophers want to probe to the bottom this barely philosophical matter, let them meditate on the banquet of Plato, in which Socrates, honourable lover of Alcibiades and Agathon, converses with them on the metaphysics of love.

Lucretius speaks of it more as a natural philosopher: Virgil follows in the steps of Lucretius; *amor omnibus idem.*

It is the stuff of nature broidered by nature. Do you want an idea of love? look at the sparrows in your garden; look at your pigeons; look at the bull which is brought to the heifer; look at this proud horse which two of your grooms lead to the quiet mare awaiting him; she draws aside her tail to welcome him; see how her eyes sparkle; hark to the neighing; watch the prancing, the curvetting, the ears pricked, the mouth opening with little convulsions, the swelling nostrils, the flaring breath, the manes rising and floating, the impetuous movement with which he hurls himself on the object which nature has destined for him; but be not jealous of him, and think of the advantages of the human species; in love they compensate for all those that nature has given to the animals—strength, beauty, nimbleness, speed. . . .

As men have received the gift of perfecting all that nature accords them, they have perfected love. Cleanliness, the care of oneself, by rendering the skin more delicate, increase the pleasure of contact; and attention to one's health renders the organs of voluptuousness more sensitive. All the other sentiments that enter into that of love, just like metals which amalgamate with gold: friendship, regard, come to help; the faculties of mind and body are still further chains.

Self-love above all tightens all these bonds. One applauds oneself for one's choice, and a crowd of illusions form the decoration of the building of which nature has laid the foundations.

That is what you have above the animals. But if you taste so many pleasures unknown to them, how many sorrows too of which the beasts have no idea! What is frightful for you is that over three-fourths of the earth nature has poisoned the pleasures of love and the sources of life with an appalling disease to which man alone is subject, and which infects in him the organs of generation alone.

Voltaire, *Philosophical Dictionary:* Love

63 To argue from her [Mrs. Johnson's] being much older than Johnson, or any other circumstances, that he could not really love her, is absurd; for love is not a subject of reasoning, but of feeling, and therefore there are no common principles upon which one can persuade another concerning it. Every man feels for himself, and knows how he is affected by particular qualities in the person he admires, the impressions of which are too minute and delicate to be substantiated in language.

Boswell, *Life of Johnson (1752)*

64 If our friend has been injured, we readily sympathise with his resentment, and grow angry with the very person with whom he is angry. If he has received a benefit, we readily enter into his gratitude, and have a very high sense of the merit of his benefactor. But if he is in love, though we may think his passion just as reasonable as any of the kind, yet we never think ourselves bound to conceive a passion of the same kind, and for the same person for whom he has conceived it. The passion appears to every body, but the man who feels it, entirely disproportioned to the value of the object; and love, though it is pardoned in a certain age because we know it is natural, is always laughed at, because we cannot enter into it.

Adam Smith, *Theory of Moral Sentiments*, I, 4

65 *Love* is a matter of *feeling*, not of will or volition, and I cannot love because I *will* to do so, still less because I *ought* (I cannot be necessitated to love); hence there is no such thing as a *duty to love*. Benevolence, however (*amor benevolentiae*), as a mode of action, may be subject to a law of duty. Disinterested benevolence is often called (though very improperly) *love;* even where the happiness of the other is not concerned, but the complete and free surrender of all one's own ends to the ends of another (even a superhuman) being, love is spoken of as being also our duty. But all duty is *necessitation* or constraint, although it may be self-constraint according to a law. But what is done from constraint is not done from love.

It is a duty *to do good* to other men according to our power, whether we love them or not, and this duty loses nothing of its weight, although we must make the sad remark that our species, alas! is not such as to be found particularly worthy of love when we know it more closely. *Hatred of men*, however, is always hateful: even though without any active hostility it consists only in complete aversion from mankind (the solitary misanthropy). For benevolence still remains a duty even towards the manhater, whom one cannot love, but to whom we can show kindness.

Kant, *Introduction to the Metaphysical Elements of Ethics*, XII

66 I went to the Garden of Love,
And saw what I never had seen:
A Chapel was built in the midst,
Where I used to play on the green.

And the gates of this chapel were shut,
And "Thou shalt not" writ over the door;
So I turned to the Garden of Love,
That so many sweet flowers bore;

And I saw it was fillèd with graves,
And tombstones where flowers should be;
And priests in black gowns were walking their
rounds,
And binding with briars my joys and desires.

Blake, *The Garden of Love*

67 "Love seeketh not Itself to please,
Nor for itself hath any care,
But for another gives its ease,
And builds a Heaven in Hell's despair."

So sung a little Clod of Clay
Trodden with the cattle's feet,
But a Pebble of the brook
Warbled out these metres meet:

"Love seeketh only Self to please,
To bind another to Its delight,
Joys in another's loss of ease,
And builds a Hell in Heaven's despite."

Blake, *The Clod and the Pebble*

68 No move towards the extinction of the passion between the sexes has taken place in the five or six
thousand years that the world has existed. Men in
the decline of life have in all ages declaimed
against a passion which they have ceased to feel,
but with as little reason as success. Those who
from coldness of constitutional temperament have
never felt what love is will surely be allowed to be
very incompetent judges with regard to the power
of this passion to contribute to the sum of pleasurable sensations in life. Those who have spent their
youth in criminal excesses and have prepared for
themselves, as the comforts of their age, corporal
debility and mental remorse, may well inveigh
against such pleasures as vain and futile, and unproductive of lasting satisfaction. But the pleasures of pure love will bear the contemplation of
the most improved reason, and the most exalted
virtue. Perhaps there is scarcely a man who has
once experienced the genuine delight of virtuous
love, however great his intellectual pleasures may
have been, that does not look back to the period
as the sunny spot in his whole life, where his imagination loves to bask, which he recollects and contemplates with the fondest regrets, and which he
would most wish to live over again.

Malthus, *Population,* XI

69 And if she met him, though she smiled no more,
    She look'd a sadness sweeter than her smile,
As if her heart had deeper thoughts in store
    She must not own, but cherish'd more the while
For that compression in its burning core;
    Even innocence itself has many a wile,

And will not dare to trust itself with truth,
And love is taught hypocrisy from youth.

Byron, *Don Juan,* I, 72

70 Love in a hut, with water and a crust,
Is—Love, forgive us!—cinders, ashes, dust;
Love in a palace is perhaps at last
More grievous torment than a hermit's fast.

Keats, *Lamia,* II, 1

71 Love means in general terms the consciousness of
my unity with another, so that I am not in selfish
isolation but win my self-consciousness only as the
renunciation of my independence and through
knowing myself as the unity of myself with another and of the other with me. Love, however, is
feeling, that is, ethical life in the form of something natural. In the state, feeling disappears;
there we are conscious of unity as law; there the
content must be rational and known to us. The
first moment in love is that I do not wish to be a
self-subsistent and independent person and that, if
I were, then I would feel defective and incomplete. The second moment is that I find myself in
another person, that I count for something in the
other, while the other in turn comes to count for
something in me. Love, therefore, is the most tremendous contradiction; the Understanding cannot resolve it since there is nothing more stubborn
than this point of self-consciousness which is ne-
gated and which nevertheless I ought to possess as
affirmative. Love is at once the propounding and
the resolving of this contradiction. As the resolving of it, love is unity of an ethical type.

Hegel, *Philosophy of Right,*
Additions, Par. 158

72 This is what goes on in the mind [in the birth of
love]:
    1. Admiration.
    2. One says to one's self: "How delightful to kiss
her, to be kissed in return," etc.
    3. Hope.
    One studies her perfections. It is at this moment
that a woman should surrender herself, to get the
greatest possible sensual pleasure. The eyes of
even the most modest women light up the moment hope is born; passion is so strong and pleasure is so acute that they betray themselves in the
most obvious manner.
    4. Love is born.
    To love is to derive pleasure from seeing, touch-
ing and feeling through all one's senses and as
closely as possible, a lovable person who loves us.
    5. The first crystallization begins.
    We take a joy in attributing a thousand perfec-
tions to a woman of whose love we are sure; we
analyze all our happiness with intense satisfaction. This reduces itself to giving ourselves an exaggerated idea of a magnificent possession which
has just fallen to us from Heaven in some way we

do not understand, and the continued possession of which is assured to us.

This is what you will find if you let a lover turn things over in his mind for twenty-four hours.

In the salt mines of Salzburg a bough stripped of its leaves by winter is thrown into the depths of the disused workings; two or three months later it is pulled out again, covered with brilliant crystals: even the tiniest twigs, no bigger than a timtit's claw, are spangled with a vast number of shimmering, glittering diamonds, so that the original bough is no longer recognizable.

I call crystallization that process of the mind which discovers fresh perfections in its beloved at every turn of events. . . .

This phenomenon which I have allowed myself to call *crystallization,* arises from the promptings of Nature which urge us to enjoy ourselves and drive the blood to our brains, from the feeling that our delight increases with the perfections of the beloved, and from the thought: "She is mine." The savage has no time to get beyond the first step. He grasps his pleasures, but his brain is concentrated on following the buck fleeing from him through the forest, and with whose flesh he must repair his own strength as quickly as possible, at the risk of falling beneath the hatchet of his enemy.

At the other extreme of civilization, I have no doubt that a sensitive woman arrives at the point of experiencing no sensual pleasure except with the man she loves. This is in direct opposition to the savage. But, amongst civilized communities woman has plenty of leisure, whilst the savage lives so close to essentials that he is obliged to treat his female as a beast of burden. If the females of many animals have an easier lot, it is only because the subsistence of the males is more assured.

But let us leave the forests and return to Paris. A passionate man sees nothing but perfection in the woman he loves; and yet his affections may still wander, for the spirit wearies of monotony, even in the case of the most perfect happiness.

So what happens to rivet his attention at this:
6. Doubt is born.

When his hopes have first of all been raised and then confirmed by ten or a dozen glances, or a whole series of other actions which may be compressed into a moment or spread over several days, the lover, recovering from his first amazement and growing used to his happiness, or perhaps merely guided by theory which, based always on his most frequent experiences, is really only correct in the case of light women, the lover, I say, demands more positive proofs of love and wants to advance the moment of his happiness.

If he takes too much for granted he will be met with indifference, coldness or even anger: in France there will be a suggestion of irony which seems to say: "You think you have made more progress than you really have." A woman behaves in this way either because she is recovering from a moment of intoxication and obeys the behests of modesty, which she is alarmed at having transgressed, or merely from prudence or coquettishness.

The lover begins to be less sure of the happiness which he has promised himself; he begins to criticize the reasons he gave himself for hoping.

He tries to fall back on the other pleasures of life. *He finds they no longer exist.* He is seized with a dread of appalling misery, and his attention becomes concentrated.

7. Second crystallization.

Now begins the second crystallization, producing as its diamonds various confirmations of the following idea:

"She loves me."

Every quarter of an hour, during the night following the birth of doubt, after a moment of terrible misery, the lover says to himself: "Yes, she loves me"; and crystallization sets to work to discover fresh charms; then gaunt-eyed doubt grips him again and pulls him up with a jerk. His heart misses a beat; he says to himself: "But does she love me?" Through all these harrowing and delicious alternations the poor lover feels acutely: "With her I would experience joys which she alone in the world could give me."

It is the clearness of this truth and the path he treads between an appalling abyss and the most perfect happiness, that make the second crystallization appear to be so very much more important than the first.

The lover hovers incessantly amongst these three ideas:

1. She is perfect in every way.
2. She loves me.
3. How can I get the strongest possible proof of her love for me?

The most heart-rending moment in love that is still young is when it finds that it has been wrong in its chain of reasoning and must destroy a whole agglomeration of crystals.

Even the fact of crystallization itself begins to appear doubtful.

Stendhal, *On Love,* I, 2

73 Man is not free to refuse to do the thing which gives him more pleasure than any other conceivable action.

Love is like a fever; it comes and goes without the will having any part in the process. That is one of the principal differences between sympathy-love and passion-love, and one can only congratulate one's self on the fine qualities of the person one loves as on a lucky chance.

Stendhal, *On Love,* I, 5

74 Give all to love;
Obey thy heart;
Friends, kindred, days,
Estate, good-fame,

Plans, credit and the Muse,—
Nothing refuse.

'Tis a brave master;
Let it have scope:
Follow it utterly,
Hope beyond hope:
High and more high
It dives into noon,
With wing unspent,
Untold intent;
But it is a god,
Knows its own path
And the outlets of the sky.

It was never for the mean;
It requireth courage stout.
Souls above doubt,
Valor unbending,
It will reward,—
They shall return
More than they were,
And ever ascending.

Leave all for love;
Yet, hear me, yet,
One word more thy heart behoved,
One pulse more of firm endeavor,—
Keep thee to-day,
To-morrow, forever,
Free as an Arab
Of thy beloved.

Cling with life to the maid;
But when the surprise,
First vague shadow of surmise
Flits across her bosom young,
Of a joy apart from thee,
Free be she, fancy-free;
Nor thou detain her vesture's hem,
Nor the palest rose she flung
From her summer diadem.

Though thou loved her as thyself,
As a self of purer clay,
Though her parting dims the day,
Stealing grace from all alive;
Heartily know,
When half-gods go,
The gods arrive.

Emerson, *Give All to Love*

75 I hold it true, whate'er befall;
  I feel it, when I sorrow most;
  'T is better to have loved and lost
Than never to have loved at all.

Tennyson, *In Memoriam*, XXVII

76 In the spring a livelier iris changes on the
  burnish'd dove;
  In the spring a young man's fancy lightly turns to
  thoughts of love.

Tennyson, *Locksley Hall*, 19

77 To love one maiden only, cleave to her,
And worship her by years of noble deeds,
Until they won her; for indeed I knew
Of no more subtle master under heaven
Than is the maiden passion for a maid,
Not only to keep down the base in man,
But teach high thought, and amiable words
And courtliness, and the desire of fame,
And love of truth, and all that makes a man.

Tennyson, *Guinevere*, 472

78 Young love-making—that gossamer web! Even
the points it clings to—the things whence its subtle interlacings are swung—are scarcely perceptible: momentary touches of finger-tips, meetings of
rays from blue and dark orbs, unfinished phrases,
lightest changes of cheek and lip, faintest tremors.
The web itself is made of spontaneous beliefs and
indefinable joys, yearnings of one life towards another, visions of completeness, indefinite trust.

George Eliot, *Middlemarch*, IV, 36

79 *Father Zossima.* Love in action is a harsh and
dreadful thing compared with love in dreams.
Love in dreams is greedy for immediate action,
rapidly performed and in the sight of all. Men
will even give their lives if only the ordeal does
not last long but is soon over, with all looking on
and applauding as though on the stage. But active
love is labour and fortitude, and for some people
too, perhaps, a complete science.

Dostoevsky, *Brothers Karamazov*, Pt. I, II, 4

80 She began to cry and a still greater sense of pity,
tenderness, and love welled up in Pierre. He felt
the tears trickle under his spectacles and hoped
they would not be noticed.

"We won't speak of it any more, my dear," said
Pierre, and his gentle, cordial tone suddenly
seemed very strange to Natásha.

"We won't speak of it, my dear—I'll tell him
everything; but one thing I beg of you, consider
me your friend and if you want help, advice, or
simply to open your heart to someone—not now,
but when your mind is clearer—think of me!" He
took her hand and kissed it. "I shall be happy if
it's in my power . . ."

Pierre grew confused.

"Don't speak to me like that. I am not worth
it!" exclaimed Natásha and turned to leave the
room, but Pierre held her hand.

He knew he had something more to say to her.
But when he said it he was amazed at his own
words.

"Stop, stop! You have your whole life before
you," said he to her.

"Before me? No! All is over for me," she replied
with shame and self-abasement.

"All over?" he repeated. "If I were not myself,
but the handsomest, cleverest, and best man in
the world, and were free, I would this moment ask

on my knees for your hand and your love!"

For the first time for many days Natásha wept tears of gratitude and tenderness, and glancing at Pierre she went out of the room.

Pierre too when she had gone almost ran into the anteroom, restraining tears of tenderness and joy that choked him, and without finding the sleeves of his fur cloak threw it on and got into his sleigh.

"Where to now, your excellency?" asked the coachman.

"Where to?" Pierre asked himself. "Where can I go now? Surely not to the Club or to pay calls?" All men seemed so pitiful, so poor, in comparison with this feeling of tenderness and love he experienced: in comparison with that softened, grateful, last look she had given him through her tears.

"Home!" said Pierre, and despite twenty-two degrees of frost Fahrenheit he threw open the bearskin cloak from his broad chest and inhaled the air with joy.

It was clear and frosty. Above the dirty, ill-lit streets, above the black roofs, stretched the dark starry sky. Only looking up at the sky did Pierre cease to feel how sordid and humiliating were all mundane things compared with the heights to which his soul had just been raised. At the entrance to the Arbát Square an immense expanse of dark starry sky presented itself to his eyes. Almost in the center of it, above the Prechístenka Boulevard, surrounded and sprinkled on all sides by stars but distinguished from them all by its nearness to the earth, its white light, and its long uplifted tail, shone the enormous and brilliant comet of 1812—the comet which was said to portend all kinds of woes and the end of the world. In Pierre, however, that comet with its long luminous tail aroused no feeling of fear. On the contrary he gazed joyfully, his eyes moist with tears, at this bright comet which, having traveled in its orbit with inconceivable velocity through immeasurable space, seemed suddenly—like an arrow piercing the earth—to remain fixed in a chosen spot, vigorously holding its tail erect, shining and displaying its white light amid countless other scintillating stars. It seemed to Pierre that this comet fully responded to what was passing in his own softened and uplifted soul, now blossoming into a new life.

Tolstoy, *War and Peace*, VIII, 22

81 "When loving with human love one may pass from love to hatred, but divine love cannot change. No, neither death nor anything else can destroy it. It is the very essence of the soul. Yet how many people have I hated in my life? And of them all, I loved and hated none as I did her." And . . . [Prince Andrew] vividly pictured to himself Natásha, not as he had done in the past with nothing but her charms which gave him delight, but for the first time picturing to himself her soul. And he understood her feelings, her sufferings, shame, and remorse. He now understood for the first time all the cruelty of his rejection of her, the cruelty of his rupture with her. "If only it were possible for me to see her once more! Just once, looking into those eyes to say . . ."

. . . And his attention was suddenly carried into another world, a world of reality and delirium in which something particular was happening. In that world some structure was still being erected and did not fall, something was still stretching out, and the candle with its red halo was still burning, and the same shirtlike sphinx lay near the door; but besides all this something creaked, there was a whiff of fresh air, and a new white sphinx appeared, standing at the door. And the sphinx had the pale face and shining eyes of the very Natásha of whom he had just been thinking.

"Oh, how oppressive this continual delirium is," thought Prince Andrew, trying to drive that face from his imagination. But the face remained before him with the force of reality and drew nearer. Prince Andrew wished to return to that former world of pure thought, but he could not, and delirium drew him back into its domain. The soft whispering voice continued its rhythmic murmur, something oppressed him and stretched out, and the strange face was before him. Prince Andrew collected all his strength in an effort to recover his senses, he moved a little, and suddenly there was a ringing in his ears, a dimness in his eyes, and like a man plunged into water he lost consciousness. When he came to himself, Natásha, that same living Natásha whom of all people he most longed to love with this new pure divine love that had been revealed to him, was kneeling before him. He realized that it was the real living Natásha, and he was not surprised but quietly happy. Natásha, motionless on her knees (she was unable to stir), with frightened eyes riveted on him, was restraining her sobs. Her face was pale and rigid. Only in the lower part of it something quivered.

Prince Andrew sighed with relief, smiled, and held out his hand.

"You?" he said. "How fortunate!"

With a rapid but careful movement Natásha drew nearer to him on her knees and, taking his hand carefully, bent her face over it and began kissing it, just touching it lightly with her lips.

"Forgive me!" she whispered, raising her head and glancing at him. "Forgive me!"

"I love you," said Prince Andrew.

"Forgive . . . !"

"Forgive what?" he asked.

"Forgive me for what I ha-ve do-ne!" faltered Natásha in a scarcely audible, broken whisper, and began kissing his hand more rapidly, just touching it with her lips.

"I love you more, better than before," said

Prince Andrew, lifting her face with his hand so as to look into her eyes.

Tolstoy, *War and Peace,* XI, 32

82 All men from their very earliest years know that besides the good of their animal personality there is another, a better, good in life, which is not only independent of the gratification of the appetites of the animal personality, but on the contrary the greater the renunciation of the welfare of the animal personality the greater this good becomes.

This feeling, solving all life's contradictions and giving the greatest good to man, is known to all. That feeling is *love.*

Life is the activity of animal personality subjected to the law of reason. Reason is the law to which, for his own good, man's animal personality must be subjected. Love is the only reasonable activity of man.

Tolstoy, *On Life,* XXII

83 Philosophy, when just escaping from its golden pupa-skin, mythology, proclaimed the great evolutionary agency of the universe to be Love. Or, since this pirate-lingo, English, is poor in such-like words, let us say Eros, the exuberance-love. Afterwards, Empedocles set up passionate-love and hate as the two co-ordinate powers of the universe. In some passages, kindness is the word. But certainly, in any sense in which it has an opposite, to be senior partner of that opposite, is the highest position that love can attain. Nevertheless, the ontological gospeller, in whose days those views were familiar topics, made the One Supreme Being, by whom all things have been made out of nothing, to be cherishing-love. What, then, can he say to hate? . . . [John's] statement that God is love seems aimed at that saying of Ecclesiastes that we cannot tell whether God bears us love or hatred. "Nay," says John, "we can tell, and very simply! We know and have trusted the love which God hath in us. God is love." There is no logic in this, unless it means that God loves all men. In the preceding paragraph, he had said, "God is light and in him is no darkness at all." We are to understand, then, that as darkness is merely the defect of light, so hatred and evil are mere imperfect stages of . . . love and loveliness. This concords with that utterance reported in John's Gospel: "God sent not the Son into the world to judge the world; but that the world should through him be saved. He that believeth on him is not judged: he that believeth not hath been judged already. . . . And this is the judgment, that the light is come into the world, and that men loved darkness rather than the light." That is to say, God visits no punishment on them; they punish themselves, by their natural affinity for the defective. Thus, the love that God is, is not a love of which hatred is the contrary; otherwise Satan would be a co-ordinate power; but it is a love which embraces ha-

tred as an imperfect stage of it, an Anteros—yea, even needs hatred and hatefulness as its object. For self-love is no love; so if God's self is love, that which he loves must be defect of love; just as a luminary can light up only that which otherwise would be dark.

C. S. Peirce, *Evolutionary Love*

84 Whatever is done from love always occurs beyond good and evil.

Nietzsche, *Beyond Good and Evil,* IV, 153

85 *Libido* is an expression taken from the theory of the emotions. We call by that name the energy (regarded as a quantitative magnitude, though not at present actually mensurable) of those instincts which have to do with all that may be comprised under the word *love.* The nucleus of what we mean by love naturally consists (and this is what is commonly called love, and what the poets sing of) in sexual love with sexual union as its aim. But we do not separate from this—what in any case has a share in the name *love*—on the one hand, self-love, and on the other, love for parents and children, friendship, and love for humanity in general, and also devotion to concrete objects and to abstract ideas. Our justification lies in the fact that psycho-analytic research has taught us that all these tendencies are an expression of the same instinctive activities; in relations between the sexes these instincts force their way towards sexual union, but in other circumstances they are diverted from this aim or are prevented from reaching it, though always preserving enough of their original nature to keep their identity recognizable (as in such features as the longing for proximity, and self-sacrifice).

We are of opinion, then, that language has carried out an entirely justifiable piece of unification in creating the word *love* with its numerous uses, and that we cannot do better than take it as the basis of our scientific discussions and expositions as well.

Freud, *Group Psychology and the Analysis of the Ego,* IV

86 In the development of mankind as a whole, just as in individuals, love alone acts as the civilizing factor in the sense that it brings a change from egoism to altruism. And this is true both of the sexual love for women, with all the obligations which it involves of sparing what women are fond of, and also of the desexualized, sublimated homosexual love for other men, which springs from work in common.

Freud, *Group Psychology and the Analysis of the Ego,* VI

87 A small minority are enabled . . . to find happiness along the path of love; but far-reaching mental transformations of the erotic function are nec-

essary before this is possible. These people make themselves independent of their object's acquiescence by transferring the main value from the fact of being loved to their own act of loving; they protect themselves against loss of it by attaching their love not to individual objects but to all men equally, and they avoid the uncertainties and disappointments of genital love by turning away from its sexual aim and modifying the instinct into an impulse with an *inhibited aim*. The state which they induce in themselves by this process—an unchangeable, undeviating, tender attitude—has little superficial likeness to the stormy vicissitudes of genital love, from which it is nevertheless derived.

Freud, *Civilization and Its Discontents,* IV

88 When a love-relationship is at its height, no room is left for any interest in the surrounding world; the pair of lovers are sufficient unto themselves, do not even need the child they have in common to make them happy. In no other case does Eros so plainly betray the core of his being, his aim of making one out of many.

Freud, *Civilization and Its Discontents,* V

89 An animal exhibits in its life-activity a multitude of acts of breathing, digesting, secreting, excreting, attack, defense, search for food, etc., a multitude of specific responses to specific stimulations of the environment. But mythology comes in and attributes them all to a nisus for self-preservation. Thence it is but a step to the idea that all conscious acts are prompted by self-love. This premiss is then elaborated in ingenious schemes, often amusing when animated by a cynical knowledge of the "world," tedious when of a would-be logical nature, to prove that every act of man including his apparent generosities is a variation played on the theme of self-interest.

Dewey, *Human Nature and Conduct,* II, 5

90 When you are old and gray and full of sleep,
And nodding by the fire, take down this book,
And slowly read, and dream of the soft look
Your eyes had once, and of their shadows deep;

How many loved your moments of glad grace,
And loved your beauty with love false or true,
But one man loved the pilgrim soul in you,
And loved the sorrows of your changing face;

And bending down beside the glowing bars,
Murmur, a little sadly, how Love fled
And paced upon the mountains overhead
And hid his face amid a crowd of stars.

Yeats, *When You Are Old*

91 Down by the salley gardens my love and I did
   meet;
   She passed the salley gardens with little snow-
   white feet.

She bid me take love easy, as the leaves grow on
   the tree;
But I, being young and foolish, with her would
   not agree.
In a field by the river my love and I did stand,
And on my leaning shoulder she laid her snow-
   white hand.
She bid me take life easy, as the grass grows on the
   weirs;
But I was young and foolish, and now am full of
   tears.

Yeats, *Down by the Salley Gardens*

92 Imagine a piece of music which expresses love. It is not love for any particular person. Another piece of music will express another love. Here we have two distinct emotional atmospheres, two different fragrances, and in both cases the quality of love will depend upon its essence and not upon its object. Nevertheless, it is hard to conceive a love which is, so to speak, at work, and yet applies to nothing. As a matter of fact, the mystics unanimously bear witness that God needs us, just as we need God. Why should He need us unless it be to love us? And it is to this very conclusion that the philosopher who holds to the mystical experience must come. Creation will appear to him as God undertaking to create creators, that He may have, besides Himself, beings worthy of His love.

We should hesitate to admit this if it were merely a question of humdrum dwellers on this corner of the universe called Earth. But, as we have said before, it is probable that life animates all the planets revolving round all the stars. It doubtless takes, by reason of the diversity of conditions in which it exists, the most varied forms, some very remote from what we imagine them to be; but its essence is everywhere the same, a slow accumulation of potential energy to be spent suddenly in free action. We might still hesitate to admit this, if we regarded as accidental the appearance amid the plants and animals that people the earth of a living creature such as man, capable of loving and making himself loved. But we have shown that this appearance, while not predetermined, was not accidental either. Though there were other lines of evolution running alongside the line which led to man, and though much is incomplete in man himself, we can say, while keeping closely to what experience shows, that it is man who accounts for the presence of life on our planet. Finally, we might well go on hesitating if we believed that the universe is essentially raw matter, and that life has been super-added to matter. We have shown, on the contrary, that matter and life, as we define them, are coexistent and interdependent. This being the case, there is nothing to prevent the philosopher from following to its logical conclusion the idea which mysticism suggests to him of a universe which is the mere visible and tangible aspect of love and of the need of loving, together with all the consequences entailed by this creative emotion: I mean the appearance of living creatures in which this emotion finds its complement; of an infinity of other beings without which they could not have appeared, and lastly of the unfathomable depths of material substance without which life would not have been possible.

Bergson, *Two Sources of Morality and Religion,* III

93 To be omnivorous is one pole of true love: to be exclusive is the other. A man whose heart, if I may say so, lies deeper, hidden under a thicker coat of mail, will have less play of fancy, and will be far from finding every charm charming, or every sort of beauty a stimulus to love. Yet he may not be less prone to the tender passion, and when once smitten may be so penetrated by an unimagined tenderness and joy, that he will declare himself incapable of ever loving again, and may actually be so. Having no rivals and in deeper soil, love can ripen better in such a constant spirit; it will not waste itself in a continual patter of little pleasures and illusions. But unless the passion of it is to die down, it must somehow assert its universality: what it loses in diversity it must gain in applicability. It must become a principle of action and an influence colouring everything that is dreamt of; otherwise it would have lost its dignity and sunk into a dead memory or a domestic bond.

True love, it used to be said, is love at first sight. Manners have much to do with such incidents, and the race which happens to set, at a given time, the fashion in literature makes its temperament public and exercises a sort of contagion over all men's fancies. If women are rarely seen and ordinarily not to be spoken to; if all imagination has to build upon is a furtive glance or casual motion, people fall in love at first sight. For they must fall in love somehow, and any stimulus is enough if none more powerful is forthcoming. When society, on the contrary, allows constant and easy intercourse between the sexes, a first impression, if not reinforced, will soon be hidden and obliterated by others. Acquaintance becomes necessary for love when it is necessary for memory. But what makes true love is not the information conveyed by acquaintance, not any circumstantial charms that may be therein discovered: it is still a deep and dumb instinctive affinity, an inexplicable emotion seizing the heart, an influence organising the world, like a luminous crystal, about one magic point. So that although love seldom springs up suddenly in these days into anything like a full-blown passion, it is sight, it is presence, that makes in time a conquest over the heart; for all virtues, sympathies, confidences will fail to move a man to tenderness and to worship, unless a poignant effluence from the object envelop him, so that he begins to walk, as it were, in a dream.

Santayana, *Life of Reason,* II, 1

94 If to create was love's impulse originally, to create is its effort still, after it has been chastened and has received some rational extension. The machinery which serves reproduction thus finds kindred but higher uses, as every organ does in a liberal life; and what Plato called a desire for birth in beauty may be sublimated even more, until it yearns for an ideal immortality in a transfigured world, a world made worthy of that love which its children have so often lavished on it in their dreams.

Santayana, *Life of Reason,* II, 1

3.2 | *Hate*

In almost all the traditional enumerations of the emotions, love and hate are joined together as contraries, along with such paired opposites as hope and desire, pleasure and pain, desire and aversion, and so on. If there are kinds of love that are either not emotional at all or involve bodily passion as just one, and perhaps even a minor, component, then it may be the case that there are also kinds of hate that are pure acts of will without passion or involve will as well as emotion. The reader should have this in mind as he discovers that there may be as many varieties of hate as there are of love. He should also explore related passages in Section 4.10 on Jealousy in the following chapter.

Where passages treat love and hate together, they are usually quoted here rather than under love. Also included here are passages from Freud that deal with instinctual aggressiveness, even though the word "hate" does not appear in them; in addition, of course, there are other passages from Freud in which his theory of love-hate ambivalence is set forth.

One of the major subjects covered in this section is misanthropy—hatred for mankind. The reader may wonder about the type of love that is its opposite. Is it friendship or charity or both? Comparing the texts with passages in Sections 3.4 and 3.5 may help him to arrive at an answer.

---

1 Terror drove them, and Fear, and Hate whose
    wrath is relentless,
  she the sister and companion of murderous Ares,
  she who is only a little thing at the first, but there-
    after
  grows until she strides on the earth with her head
    striking heaven.

Homer, *Iliad,* IV, 440

2 *Socrates.* I have said enough in answer to the charge of Meletus: any elaborate defence is unnecessary; but I know only too well how many are the enmities which I have incurred, and this is what will be my destruction if I am destroyed;—not Meletus, nor yet Anytus, but the envy and detraction of the world, which has been the death of many good men, and will probably be the death of many more; there is no danger of my being the last of them.

Plato, *Apology,* 28A

3 *Socrates.* Misanthropy arises out of the too great confidence of inexperience;—you trust a man and think him altogether true and sound and faithful, and then in a little while he turns out to be false and knavish; and then another and another, and when this has happened several times to a man, especially when it happens among those whom he deems to be his own most trusted and familiar friends, and he has often quarrelled with them, he at last hates all men, and believes that no one has any good in him at all. . . . Experience would have taught him the true state of the case, that few are the good and few the evil, and that the great majority are in the interval between them.

Plato, *Phaedo,* 89B

4 Enmity and Hatred should clearly be studied by reference to their opposites. Enmity may be produced by anger or spite or calumny. Now whereas anger arises from offences against oneself, enmity may arise even without that; we may hate people merely because of what we take to be their character. Anger is always concerned with individuals, . . . whereas hatred is directed also against classes: we all hate any thief and any informer. Moreover, anger can be cured by time; but hatred cannot. The one aims at giving pain to its object, the other at doing him harm; the angry man wants his victims to feel; the hater does not mind whether they feel or not. All painful things are felt; but the greatest evils, injustice and folly, are the least felt, since their presence causes no pain. And anger is accompanied by pain, hatred is not: the angry man feels pain, but the hater does not. Much may happen to make the angry man pity those who offend him, but the hater under no circumstances wishes to pity a man whom he has once hated: for the one would have the offenders suffer for what they have done; the other would have them cease to exist.

Aristotle, *Rhetoric,* 1382ª1

5 What I am most apprehensive about concerning you is this: because you are unaware of the real pathway to fame, you may think it is really glorious to have more power than anyone else and to lord it over your fellow citizens. If this is your opinion, you really are blind when it comes to knowing real fame. What really is glorious is to be a citizen held in high regard by all, deserving well of the republic, one who is praised, courted, and loved. But to be feared and hated is obnoxious. It is a proof of weakness and degeneracy.

Cicero, *Philippics,* I, 14

6 Injuries done to us by those of higher rank must be endured, and not only with composure, but with the appearance of good cheer. They will commit the same offense again if they are convinced they got away with it once. Those whose spirit has become overbearing because of good fortune have this serious fault: they hate those whom they have injured.

Seneca, *On Anger,* II, 33

7 He that saith he is in the light, and hateth his brother, is in darkness even until now.

  He that loveth his brother abideth in the light, and there is none occasion of stumbling in him.

But he that hateth his brother is in darkness, and walketh in darkness, and knoweth not whither he goeth, because that darkness hath blinded his eyes.

I John 2:9–11

8 For this is the message that ye heard from the beginning, that we should love one another.

Not as Cain, who was of that wicked one, and slew his brother. And wherefore slew he him? Because his own works were evil, and his brother's righteous.

Marvel not, my brethren, if the world hate you.

I John 3:11–13

9 If a man say, I love God, and hateth his brother, he is a liar: for he that loveth not his brother whom he hath seen, how can he love God whom he hath not seen?

I John 4:20

10 Benefits received are a delight to us as long as we think we can requite them; when that possibility is far exceeded, they are repaid with hatred instead of gratitude.

Tacitus, *Annals,* IV, 18

11 It is, indeed, human nature to hate the man whom you have injured.

Tacitus, *Agricola*

12 It is strange that we should not realise that no enemy could be more dangerous to us than the hatred with which we hate him, and that by our efforts against him we do less damage to our enemy than is wrought in our own heart.

Augustine, *Confessions,* I, 18

13 It is impossible for an effect to be stronger than its cause. Now every hatred arises from some love as its cause. . . . Therefore it is impossible absolutely for hatred to be stronger than love.

But furthermore, love must be stronger, absolutely speaking, than hatred. Because a thing is moved to the end more strongly than to the means. Now turning away from evil is ordered as a means to the gaining of good, as to amend. Therefore, absolutely speaking, the soul's movement in respect of good is stronger than its movement in respect of evil.

Nevertheless hatred sometimes seems to be stronger than love, for two reasons. First, because hatred is more keenly felt than love. . . . Secondly, because comparison is made between a hatred and a love which do not correspond to one another.

Aquinas, *Summa Theologica,* I–II, 29, 3

14 I saw two frozen in one hole so *closely,* that the one head was a cap to the other;

and as bread is chewed for hunger, so the upper-most put his teeth into the other there where the brain joins with the nape.

Not otherwise did Tydeus gnaw the temples of Menalippus for rage, than he the skull and the other parts.

"O thou! who by such brutal token shewest *thy* hate on him whom thou devourest, tell me why," I said; "on this condition,

that if thou with reason complainest of him, I, knowing who ye are and his offence, may yet repay thee in the world above, if that, wherewith I speak, be not dried up."

From the fell repast that sinner raised his mouth, wiping it upon the hair of the head he had laid waste behind.

Then he began: "Thou willest that I renew desperate grief, which wrings my heart, even at the very thought, before I tell thereof.

But if my words are to be a seed, that may bear fruit of infamy to the traitor whom I gnaw, thou shalt see me speak and weep at the same time.

I know not who thou mayest be, nor by what mode thou hast come down here; but, when I hear thee, in truth thou seemest to me a Florentine.

Thou hast to know that I was Count Ugolino, and this the Archbishop Ruggieri; now I will tell thee why I am such a neighbour *to him.*

That by the effect of his ill devices I, confiding in him, was taken and thereafter put to death, it is not necessary to say.

But that which thou canst not have learnt, that is, how cruel was my death, thou shalt hear—and know if he has offended me.

A narrow hole within the mew, which from me has the title of Famine, and in which others yet must be shut up,

had through its opening already shewn me several moons, when I slept the evil sleep that rent for me the curtain of the future.

This *man* seemed to me lord and master, chasing the wolf and his whelps, upon the mountain for which the Pisans cannot see Lucca.

With hounds meagre, keen, and dexterous, he had put in front of him Gualandi with Sismondi, and with Lanfranchi.

After short course, the father and his sons seemed to me weary; and methought I saw their flanks torn by the sharp teeth.

When I awoke before the dawn, I heard my sons [who were with me, weeping in their sleep, and] asking for bread.

Thou art right cruel, if thou dost not grieve already at the thought of what my heart foreboded; and if thou weepest not, at what are thou used to weep?

They were now awake, and the hour approaching at which our food used to be brought us, and each was anxious from his dream,

and below I heard the outlet of the horrible tower

locked up: whereat I looked into the faces of my
sons, without uttering a word.
I did not weep: so stony grew I within; they wept;
and my little Anselm said: 'Thou lookest so,
father, what ails thee?'
But I shed no tear, nor answered all that day, nor
the next night, till another sun came forth upon
the world.
When a small ray was sent into the doleful prison,
and I discerned in their four faces the aspect of
my own,
I bit *on* both my hands for grief. And they, thinking that I did it from desire of eating, of a sudden rose up,
and said: 'Father, it will give us much less pain, if
thou wilt eat of us: thou didst put upon us this
miserable flesh, and do thou strip it off.'
Then I calmed myself, in order not to make them
more unhappy; that day and the next we all
were mute. Ah, hard earth! why didst thou not
open?
When we had come to the fourth day, Gaddo
threw himself stretched out at my feet, saying:
'My father! why don't you help me?'
There he died; and even as thou seest me, saw I
the three fall one by one, between the fifth day
and the sixth: whence I betook me,
already blind, to groping over each, and for three
days called them, after they were dead; then
fasting had more power than grief.''
When he had spoken this, with eyes distorted he
seized the miserable skull again with his teeth,
which as a dog's were strong upon the bone.

                Dante, *Inferno,* XXXII, 124

15 The prince must consider . . . how to avoid those
things which will make him hated or contemptible; and as often as he shall have succeeded he
will have fulfilled his part, and he need not fear
any danger in other reproaches.

    It makes him hated above all things, as I have
said, to be rapacious, and to be a violator of the
property and women of his subjects, from both of
which he must abstain. And when neither their
property nor honour is touched, the majority of
men live content, and he has only to contend with
the ambition of a few, whom he can curb with
ease in many ways.

                Machiavelli, *Prince,* XIX

16 Hatred is acquired as much by good works as by
bad ones.

                Machiavelli, *Prince,* XIX

17 *Gloucester.* Now is the winter of our discontent
Made glorious summer by this sun of York;
And all the clouds that lour'd upon our house
In the deep bosom of the ocean buried.
Now are our brows bound with victorious
    wreaths;
Our bruised arms hung up for monuments;

Our stern alarums changed to merry meetings,
Our dreadful marches to delightful measures.
Grim-visaged War hath smooth'd his wrinkled
    front;
And now, instead of mounting barbed steeds
To fright the souls of fearful adversaries,
He capers nimbly in a lady's chamber
To the lascivious pleasing of a lute.
But I, that am not shaped for sportive tricks,
Nor made to court an amorous looking-glass;
I, that am rudely stamp'd, and want love's
    majesty
To strut before a wanton ambling nymph;
I, that am curtail'd of this fair proportion,
Cheated of feature by dissembling nature,
Deform'd, unfinish'd, sent before my time
Into this breathing world, scarce half made up,
And that so lamely and unfashionable
That dogs bark at me as I halt by them;
Why, I, in this weak piping time of peace,
Have no delight to pass away the time,
Unless to spy my shadow in the sun
And descant on mine own deformity:
And therefore, since I cannot prove a lover,
To entertain these fair well-spoken days,
I am determined to prove a villian
And hate the idle pleasures of these days.

        Shakespeare, *Richard III,* I, i, 1

18 *Lady Anne.* Poor key-cold figure of a holy king!
Pale ashes of the house of Lancaster!
Thou bloodless remnant of that royal blood!
Be it lawful that I invocate thy ghost,
To hear the lamentations of poor Anne,
Wife to thy Edward, to thy slaughter'd son,
Stabb'd by the selfsame hand [Richard's] that
    made these wounds!
Lo, in these windows that let forth thy life,
I pour the helpless balm of my poor eyes.
Cursed be the hand that made these fatal holes!
Cursed be the heart that had the heart to do it!
Cursed the blood that let this blood from hence!
More direful hap betide that hated wretch
That makes us wretched by the death of thee
Than I can wish to adders, spiders, toads,
Or any creeping venom'd thing that lives!
If ever he have child, abortive be it,
Prodigious, and untimely brought to light,
Whose ugly and unnatural aspect
May fright the hopeful mother at the view;
And that be heir to his unhappiness!
If ever he have wife, let her be made
As miserable by the death of him
As I am made by my poor lord and thee!

        Shakespeare, *Richard III,* I, ii, 5

19 *Shylock.* You'll ask me, why I rather choose to have
A weight of carrion flesh than to receive
Three thousand ducats: I'll not answer that:
But say it is my humour: is it answer'd?
What if my house be troubled with a rat

And I be pleased to give ten thousand ducats
To have it baned? What, are you answer'd yet?
Some men there are love not a gaping pig;
Some, that are mad if they behold a cat;
And others, when the bagpipe sings i' the nose,
Cannot contain their urine: for affection,
Mistress of passion, sways it to the mood
Of what it likes or loathes. Now, for your answer:
As there is no firm reason to be render'd,
Why he cannot abide a gaping pig;
Why he, a harmless necessary cat;
Why he, a woollen bag-pipe; but of force
Must yield to such inevitable shame
As to offend, himself being offended;
So can I give no reason, nor I will not,
More than a lodged hate and a certain loathing
I bear Antonio, that I follow thus
A losing suit against him. Are you answer'd?
   Bassannio. This is no answer, thou unfeeling man,
To excuse the current of thy cruelty.
   Shy. I am not bound to please thee with my answers.
   Bass. Do all men kill the things they do not love?
   Shy. Hates any man the thing he would not kill?
Shakespeare, *Merchant of Venice*, IV, i, 40

20 *Iago.* That Cassio loves her, I do well believe it;
That she loves him, 'tis apt and of great credit.
The Moor, howbeit that I endure him not,
Is of constant, loving, noble nature,
And I dare think he'll prove to Desdemona
A most dear husband. Now, I do love her too;
Not out of absolute lust, though peradventure
I stand accountant for as great a sin,
But partly led to diet my revenge,
For that I do suspect the lusty Moor
Hath leap'd into my seat; the thought whereof
Doth, like a poisonous mineral, gnaw my inwards;
And nothing can or shall content my soul
Till I am even'd with him, wife for wife,
Or failing so, yet that I put the Moor
At least into a jealousy so strong
That judgement cannot cure. Which thing to do,
If this poor trash of Venice, whom I trash
For his quick hunting, stand the putting on,
I'll have our Michael Cassio on the hip,
Abuse him to the Moor in the rank garb—
For I fear Cassio with my night-cap too—
Make the Moor thank me, love me, and reward me,
For making him egregiously an ass
And practising upon his peace and quiet
Even to madness.
Shakespeare, *Othello*, II, i, 295

21 *Timon.* Let me look back upon thee. O thou wall
That girdlest in those wolves, dive in the earth
And fence not Athens! Matrons, turn incontinent!
Obedience fail in children! slaves and fools,

Pluck the grave wrinkled Senate from the bench,
And minister in their steads! To general filths
Convert o' the instant, green virginity!
Do't in your parents' eyes! Bankrupts, hold fast;
Rather than render back, out with your knives
And cut your trusters' throats! Bound servants, steal!
Large-handed robbers your grave masters are,
And pill by law. Maid, to thy master's bed;
Thy mistress is o' the brothel! Son of sixteen,
Pluck the lined crutch from thy old limping sire,
With it beat out his brains! Piety, and fear,
Religion to the gods, peace, justice, truth,
Domestic awe, night-rest, and neighbourhood,
Instruction, manners, mysteries, and trades,
Degrees, observances, customs, and laws,
Decline to your confounding contraries,
And let confusion live! Plagues, incident to men,
Your potent and infectious fevers heap
On Athens, ripe for stroke! Thou cold sciatica,
Cripple our senators, that their limbs may halt
As lamely as their manners! Lust and liberty
Creep in the minds and marrows of our youth,
That 'gainst the stream of virtue they may strive,
And drown themselves in riot! Itches, blains,
Sow all the Athenian bosoms; and their crop
Be general leprosy! Breath infect breath,
That their society, as their friendship, may
Be merely poison! Nothing I'll bear from thee,
But nakedness, thou detestable town!
Take thou that too, with multiplying bans!
Timon will to the woods; where he shall find
The unkindest beast more kinder than mankind.
The gods confound—hear me, you good gods all—
The Athenians both within and out that wall!
And grant, as Timon grows, his hate may grow
To the whole race of mankind, high and low!
Amen.
Shakespeare, *Timon of Athens*, IV, i, 1

22 As for the passions, of hate, lust, ambition, and covetousness, what crimes they are apt to produce is so obvious to every man's experience and understanding as there needeth nothing to be said of them, saying that they are infirmities, so annexed to the nature, both of man and all other living creatures, as that their effects cannot be hindered but by extraordinary use of reason, or a constant severity in punishing them. For in those things men hate, they find a continual and unavoidable molestation; whereby either a man's patience must be everlasting, or he must be eased by removing the power of that which molesteth him: the former is difficult; the latter is many times impossible without some violation of the law.
Hobbes, *Leviathan*, II, 27

23 All men naturally hate one another. They employ lust as far as possible in the service of the public weal. But this is only a [*pretence*] and a false image

of love; for at bottom it is only hate.

Pascal, *Pensées,* VII, 451

24 *Love* is nothing but joy accompanied with the idea of an external cause, and *hatred* is nothing but sorrow with the accompanying idea of an external cause. We see too that he who loves a thing necessarily endeavours to keep it before him and to preserve it, and, on the other hand, he who hates a thing necessarily endeavours to remove and destroy it.

Spinoza, *Ethics,* III, Prop. 13, Schol.

25 Every one endeavours as much as possible to make others love what he loves, and to hate what he hates. And so we see that each person by nature desires that other persons should live according to his way of thinking; but if every one does this, then all are a hindrance to one another, and if every one wishes to be praised or beloved by the rest, then they all hate one another.

Spinoza, *Ethics,* III, Prop. 31, Corol.

26 No one can hate God. . . .

The idea of God which is in us is adequate and perfect, and therefore insofar as we contemplate God do we act, and consequently no sorrow can exist with the accompanying idea of God; that is to say, no one can hate God. . . .

Love to God cannot be turned into hatred. . . .

But some may object, that if we understand God to be the cause of all things, we do for that very reason consider Him to be the cause of sorrow. But I reply, that insofar as we understand the causes of sorrow, it ceases to be a passion, that is to say, it ceases to be sorrow; and therefore insofar as we understand God to be the cause of sorrow do we rejoice.

Spinoza, *Ethics,* V, Prop. 18

27 *Zara.* Heav'n has no Rage like Love to hatred turn'd,
Nor Hell a Fury like a Woman scorn'd.

Congreve, *The Mourning Bride,* III, ii

28 My wife and family received me with great surprize and joy, because they concluded me certainly dead; but I must freely confess, the sight of them filled me only with hatred, disgust and contempt; and the more, by reflecting on the near alliance I had to them. For, although since my unfortunate exile from the Houyhnhnm country, I had compelled my self to tolerate the sight of Yahoos, and to converse with Don Pedro de Mendez; yet my memory and imaginations were perpetually filled with the virtues and ideas of those exalted Houyhnhnms. And when I began to consider, that by copulating with one of the Yahoo-species, I had become a parent of more, it struck me with the utmost shame, confusion, and horror.

Swift, *Gulliver's Travels,* IV, 11

29 I have ever hated all nations, professions and communities, and all my love is toward individuals. . . . But principally I hate and detest that animal called man; although I heartily love John, Peter, Thomas, and so forth.

Swift, *Letter to Pope (Sept. 29, 1725)*

30 The body of Jonathan Swift, Doctor of Divinity, dean of this cathedral church, is buried here, where fierce indignation can no longer lacerate his heart. Go, passerby, and imitate if you can one who strove with all his strength to serve human liberty.

Swift, *Epitaph in St. Patrick's Cathedral, Dublin*

31 In this, we have said, he [Mr. Allworthy] did not agree with his wife; nor, indeed, in anything else: for though an affection placed on the understanding is, by many wise persons, thought more durable than that which is founded on beauty, yet it happened otherwise in the present case. Nay, the understandings of this couple were their principal bone of contention, and one great cause of many quarrels, which from time to time arose between them; and which at last ended, on the side of the lady, in a sovereign contempt for her husband; and on the husband's, in an utter abhorrence of his wife.

Fielding, *Tom Jones,* II, 7

32 One situation only of the married state is excluded from pleasure: and that is, a state of indifference: but as many of my readers, I hope, know what an exquisite delight there is in conveying pleasure to a beloved object, so some few, I am afraid, may have experienced the satisfaction of tormenting one we hate. It is, I apprehend, to come at this latter pleasure, that we see both sexes often give up that ease in marriage which they might otherwise possess, though their mate was never so disagreeable to them. Hence the wife often puts on fits of love and jealousy, nay, even denies herself any pleasure, to disturb and prevent those of her husband; and he again, in return, puts frequent restraints on himself, and stays at home in company which he dislikes, in order to confine his wife to what she equally detests. Hence, too, must flow those tears which a widow sometimes so plentifully sheds over the ashes of a husband with whom she led a life of constant disquiet and turbulency, and whom now she can never hope to torment any more.

Fielding, *Tom Jones,* II, 7

33 "If I was not as great philosopher as Socrates himself," returned Mrs. Western, "you would overcome my patience. What objection can you have to the young gentleman?"

"A very solid objection, in my opinion," says Sophia—"I hate him."

"Will you never learn a proper use of words?"

answered the aunt. "Indeed, child, you should consult Bailey's Dictionary. It is impossible you should hate a man from whom you have received no injury. By hatred, therefore, you mean no more than dislike, which is no sufficient objection against your marrying of him. I have known many couples, who have entirely disliked each other, lead very comfortable genteel lives. Believe me, child, I know these things better than you. You will allow me, I think, to have seen the world, in which I have not an acquaintance who would not rather be thought to dislike her husband than to like him. The contrary is such out-of-fashion romantic nonsense, that the very imagination of it is shocking."

Fielding, *Tom Jones,* VII, 3

34 *Johnson.* A man will please more upon the whole by negative qualities than by positive; by never offending, than by giving a great deal of delight. In the first place, men hate more steadily than they love; and if I have said something to hurt a man once, I shall not get the better of this, by saying many things to please him.

Boswell, *Life of Johnson (1777)*

35 *Ahab.* "All visible objects, man, are but as paste-board masks. But in each event—in the living act, the undoubted deed—there, some unknown but still reasoning thing puts forth the mouldings of its features from behind the unreasoning mask. If man will strike, strike through the mask! How can the prisoner reach outside except by thrusting through the wall? To me, the white whale is that wall, shoved near to me. Sometimes I think there's naught beyond. But 'tis enough. He tasks me; he heaps me; I see in him outrageous strength, with an inscrutable malice sinewing it. That inscrutable thing is chiefly what I hate; and be the white whale agent, or be the white whale principal, I will wreak that hate upon him. Talk not to me of blasphemy, man; I'd strike the sun if it insulted me."

Melville, *Moby Dick,* XXXVI

36 His three boats stove around him, and oars and men both, whirling in the eddies; one captain, seizing the line-knife from his broken prow, had dashed at the whale, as an Arkansas duellist at his foe, blindly seeking with a six-inch blade to reach the fathom-deep life of the whale. That captain was Ahab. And then it was, that suddenly sweeping his sickle-shaped lower jaw beneath him, Moby Dick had reaped away Ahab's leg, as a mower a blade of grass in the field. No turbaned Turk, no hired Venetian or Malay, could have smote him with more seeming malice. Small reason was there to doubt, then, that ever since that almost fatal encounter, Ahab had cherished a wild vindictiveness against the whale, all the more fell for that in his frantic morbidness he at last

came to identify with him, not only all his bodily woes, but all his intellectual and spiritual exasperations. The White Whale swam before him as the monomaniac incarnation of all those malicious agencies which some deep men feel eating in them, till they are left living on with half a heart and half a lung. That intangible malignity which has been from the beginning; to whose dominion even the modern Christians ascribe one-half of the worlds; which the ancient Ophites of the east reverenced in their statue devil;—Ahab did not fall down and worship it like them; but deliriously transferring its idea to the abhorred white whale, he pitted himself, all mutilated, against it. All that most maddens and torments; all that stirs up the lees of things; all truth with malice in it; all that cracks the sinews and cakes the brain; all the subtle demonisms of life and thought; all evil, to crazy Ahab, were visibly personified, and made practically assailable in Moby Dick. He piled upon the whale's white hump the sum of all the general rage and hate felt by his whole race from Adam down; and then, as if his chest had been a mortar, he burst his hot heart's shell upon it.

Melville, *Moby Dick,* XLI

37 Enmity or hatred seems also to be a highly persistent feeling, perhaps more so than any other that can be named. . . . Dogs are very apt to hate both strange men and strange dogs, especially if they live near at hand, but do not belong to the same family, tribe, or clan; this feeling would thus seem to be innate, and is certainly a most persistent one. It seems to be the complement and converse of the true social instinct. From what we hear of savages, it would appear that something of the same kind holds good with them. If this be so, it would be a small step in any one to transfer such feelings to any member of the same tribe if he had done him an injury and had become his enemy. Nor is it probable that the primitive conscience would reproach a man for injuring his enemy; rather it would reproach him, if he had not revenged himself. To do good in return for evil, to love your enemy, is a height of morality to which it may be doubted whether the social instincts would, by themselves, have ever led us. It is necessary that these instincts, together with sympathy, should have been highly cultivated and extended by the aid of reason, instruction, and the love or fear of God, before any such golden rule would ever be thought of and obeyed.

Darwin, *Descent of Man,* I, 4, fn. 27

38 *The hunting instinct* has [a] . . . remote origin in the evolution of the race. The hunting and the fighting instinct combine in many manifestations. They both support the emotion of anger; they combine in the fascination which stories of atrocity have for most minds; and the utterly blind excitement of giving the rein to our fury when our

blood is up (an excitement whose intensity is greater than that of any other human passion save one) is only explicable as an impulse aboriginal in character, and having more to do with immediate and overwhelming tendencies to muscular discharge than to any possible reminiscences of effects of experience, or association of ideas. I say this here, because the pleasure of disinterested cruelty has been thought a paradox, and writers have sought to show that it is no primitive attribute of our nature, but rather a resultant of the subtle combination of other less malignant elements of mind. This is a hopeless task. If evolution and the survival of the fittest be true at all, the destruction of prey and of human rivals *must* have been among the most important of man's primitive functions, the fighting and the chasing instincts *must* have become ingrained. Certain perceptions *must* immediately, and without the intervention of interferences and ideas, have prompted emotions and motor discharges; and both the latter must, from the nature of the case, have been very violent, and therefore, when unchecked, of an intensely pleasurable kind. It is just because human bloodthirstiness is such a primitive part of us that it is so hard to eradicate, especially where a fight or a hunt is promised as part of the fun.

William James, *Psychology,* XXIV

39 I will put the following case: Let there be a person near me whom I hate so strongly that I have a lively impulse to rejoice should anything happen to him. But the moral side of my nature does not give way to this impulse; I do not dare to express this sinister wish, and when something does happen to him which he does not deserve I suppress my satisfaction, and force myself to thoughts and expressions of regret. Everyone will at some time have found himself in such a position. But now let it happen that the hated person, through some transgression of his own, draws upon himself a well-deserved calamity; I shall now be allowed to give free rein to my satisfaction at his being visited by a just punishment, and I shall be expressing an opinion which coincides with that of other impartial persons. But I observe that my satisfaction proves to be more intense than that of others, for it has received reinforcement from another source—from my hatred, which was hitherto prevented by the inner censorship from furnishing the affect, but which, under the altered circumstances, is no longer prevented from doing so. This case generally occurs in social life when antipathetic persons or the adherents of an unpopular minority have been guilty of some offence. Their punishment is then usually commensurate not with their guilt, but with their guilt plus the ill-will against them that has hitherto not been put into effect.

Freud, *Interpretation of Dreams,* VI, H

40 It is noteworthy that in the use of the word *hate* no . . . intimate relation to sexual pleasure and the sexual function appears: on the contrary, the painful character of the relation seems to be the sole decisive feature. The ego hates, abhors, and pursues with intent to destroy all objects which are for it a source of painful feelings, without taking into account whether they mean to it frustration of sexual satisfaction or of gratification of the needs of self-preservation. Indeed, it may be asserted that the true prototypes of the hate-relation are derived not from sexual life, but from the struggle of the ego for self-preservation and self-maintenance.

Freud, *Instincts and Their Vicissitudes*

41 The relation of hate to objects is older than that of love. It is derived from the primal repudiation by the narcissistic ego of the external world whence flows the stream of stimuli. As an expression of the pain-reaction induced by objects, it remains in constant intimate relation with the instincts of self-preservation, so that sexual and ego-instincts readily develop an antithesis which repeats that of love and hate.

Freud, *Instincts and Their Vicissitudes*

42 Almost every intimate emotional relation between two people which lasts for some time—marriage, friendship, the relations between parents and children—leaves a sediment of feelings of aversion and hostility, which have first to be eliminated by repression. This is less disguised in the common wrangles between business partners or in the grumbles of a subordinate at his superior. The same thing happens when men come together in larger units. Every time two families become connected by a marriage, each of them thinks itself superior to or of better birth than the other. Of two neighbouring towns, each is the other's most jealous rival; every little canton looks down upon the others with contempt. Closely related races keep one another at arm's length; the South German cannot endure the North German, the Englishman casts every kind of aspersion upon the Scotchman, the Spaniard despises the Portuguese. We are no longer astonished that greater differences should lead to an almost insuperable repugnance, such as the Gallic people feel for the German, the Aryan for the Semite, and the white races for the coloured.

Freud, *Group Psychology and the Analysis of the Ego,* VI

43 In our unconscious we daily and hourly deport all who stand in our way, all who have offended or injured us. The expression: "Devil take him!" which so frequently comes to our lips in joking anger, and which really means "Death take him!" is in our unconscious an earnest, deliberate death-wish. Indeed, our unconscious will murder even

for trifles; like the ancient Athenian law of Draco, it knows no other punishment for crime than death; and this has a certain consistency, for every injury to our almighty and autocratic ego is at bottom a crime of *lèse-majesté*.

And so, if we are to be judged by the wishes in our unconscious, we are, like primitive man, simply a gang of murderers. It is well that all these wishes do not possess the potency which was attributed to them by primitive men; in the crossfire of mutual maledictions, mankind would long since have perished, the best and wisest of men and the lovliest and fairest of women with the rest.

Freud, *Thoughts on War and Death*, II

44 Men clearly do not find it easy to do without satisfaction of this tendency to aggression that is in them; when deprived of satisfaction of it they are ill at ease. There is an advantage, not to be undervalued, in the existence of smaller communities, through which the aggressive instinct can find an outlet in enmity towards those outside the group. It is always possible to unite considerable numbers of men in love towards one another, so long as there are still some remaining as objects for aggressive manifestations. . . . The Jewish people, scattered in all directions as they are, have in this way rendered services which deserve recognition to the development of culture in the countries where they settled; but unfortunately not all the massacres of Jews in the Middle Ages sufficed to procure peace and security for their Christian contemporaries.

Freud, *Civilization and Its Discontents*, V

3.3 | *Sexual Love*

The love that the Greeks called *eros* and the Romans *amor* is certainly always a love that involves intense bodily passions, persistent emotional drives, powerful, often disturbing, desires, and a mixture of sensual pleasures and pains that are usually inseparable from one another. This much is explicitly clear or plainly intimated in the passages that treat sexual or erotic love. But what may not be clear, and even perplexing, is the relation of sexuality itself to sexual love.

Are all sexual desires or acts impulses or embodiments of love—in men and other animals? Or does sexual behavior become a manifestation of love, or a kind of love, only when sexual desires and activities are somehow transformed by other sentiments and impulses, such as the sentiments and impulses that are involved in the kind of love called friendship? Such questions lead to still another. If there can be mere sexuality, i.e., sexual desire or performance, without love, can there also be love without sexual involvement of any kind? If the reader wishes to pursue such inquiries, he will find it useful to consider what is said about other kinds of love, as set forth in the next two sections.

Light on these matters may also come from a pivotal distinction that underlies many discussions of love and that is particularly germane to the consideration of sexual love—the distinction between acquisitive and benevolent impulses. Acquisitive desire aims at self-satisfaction or benefit to one's self, whereas the benevolent impulse tends in the opposite direction toward the good of another or benefit to the person beloved. The term "concupiscence" or "concupiscent" that occurs in certain of the quotations connotes acquisitive desire unaccompanied by any benevolent impulse. The answer to the question about the distinction between mere sexuality and sexual love may, therefore, turn on the answer to another question: Is concupiscence or purely acquisitive desire ever truly a form of love? The reader will find that the authors quoted do not agree on any single or simple answer to the question.

Wherever the truth of the matter lies, the fact that concupiscence enters into the consideration of sexual love impels us to include in this section texts that deal with lust in its myriad forms—not just sexual lust, but the lust for power, the lust for worldly goods, and so on. This, in turn, makes a certain amount of moralizing unavoidable; for, though love, especially sexual love, is either favored or feared, it is never condemned as immoral, as lust, sexual or otherwise, always is. If the moral problems that are raised interest the reader, he should turn to Chapter 9 on ETHICS, and especially to Section 9.10 on VIRTUE AND VICE and Section 9.12 on TEMPERANCE AND INTEMPERANCE.

The discussion of sexual love as well as lust also involves moral considerations of the sort connoted by such terms as "fornication" and "adultery" which are relevant to the treatment of marriage and conjugal love in the preceding chapter as well as here.

---

1 And it came to pass after these things, that his master's [Potiphar's] wife cast her eyes upon Joseph; and she said, Lie with me.

But he refused, and said unto his master's wife, Behold, my master wotteth not what is with me in the house, and he hath committed all that he hath to my hand;

There is none greater in this house than I; neither hath he kept back any thing from me but thee, because thou art his wife: how then can I do this great wickedness, and sin against God?

And it came to pass, as she spake to Joseph day by day, that he hearkened not unto her, to lie by her, or to be with her.

And it came to pass about this time, that Joseph went into the house to do his business; and there was none of the men of the house there within.

And she caught him by his garment, saying, Lie with me: and he left his garment in her hand, and fled, and got him out.

And it came to pass, when she saw that he had left his garment in her hand, and was fled forth,

That she called unto the men of her house, and spake unto them, saying, See, he hath brought in an Hebrew unto us to mock us; he came in unto me to lie with me, and I cried with a loud voice:

And it came to pass, when he heard that I lifted up my voice and cried, that he left his garment with me, and fled, and got him out.

And she laid up his garment by her, until his lord came home.

And she spake unto him, according to these words, saying, The Hebrew servant, which thou hast brought unto us, came in unto me to mock me:

And it came to pass, as I lifted up my voice and cried, that he left his garment with me, and fled out.

And it came to pass, when his master heard the words of his wife, which she spake unto him, saying, After this manner did thy servant to me; that his wrath was kindled.

And Joseph's master took him, and put him into the prison, a place where the king's prisoners were bound: and he was there in the prison.

Genesis 39:7–20

2 And it came to pass in an eveningtide, that David arose from off his bed, and walked upon the roof of the king's house: and from the roof he saw a woman washing herself: and the woman was very beautiful to look upon.

And David sent and enquired after the woman. And one said, Is not this Bath-sheba, the daughter of Ē-lī-ăm, the wife of Ū-rī-ăh the Hittite?

And David sent messengers, and took her; and she came in unto him, and he lay with her; for she was purified from her uncleanness: and she returned unto her house.

And the woman conceived, and sent and told David, and said, I am with child. . . . And it came to pass in the morning, that David wrote a letter to Joab, and sent it by the hand of Ū-rī-ăh.

And he wrote in the letter, saying, Set ye Ū-rī-ăh in the forefront of the hottest battle, and retire ye from him, that he may be smitten, and die.

And it came to pass, when Joab observed the city, that he assigned Ū-rī-ăh unto a place where he knew that valiant men were.

And the men of the city went out, and fought with Joab: and there fell some of the people of the servants of David: and Ū-rī-ăh the Hittite died also. . . . And when the wife of Ū-rī-ăh heard that Ū-rī-ăh her husband was dead, she mourned for her husband.

And when the mourning was past, David sent and fetched her to his house, and she became his wife, and bare him a son. But the thing that David had done displeased the Lord.

II Samuel 11:2–27

3 And Amnon said unto Tamar, Bring the meat into the chamber, that I may eat of thine hand. And Tamar took the cakes which she had made, and brought them into the chamber to Amnon her brother.

And when she had brought them unto him to eat, he took hold of her, and said unto her, Come lie with me, my sister.

And she answered him, Nay, my brother, do not force me; for no such thing ought to be done in Israel: do not thou this folly.

And I, whither shall I cause my shame to go? and as for thee, thou shalt be as one of the fools in Israel. Now therefore, I pray thee, speak unto the king; for he will not withhold me from thee. Howbeit he would not hearken unto her voice: but, being stronger than she, forced her, and lay with her.

Then Amnon hated her exceedingly; so that the hatred wherewith he hated her was greater than the love wherewith he had loved her. And Amnon said unto her, Arise, be gone.

And she said unto him, There is no cause: this evil in sending me away is greater than the other that thou didst unto me. But he would not hearken unto her.

Then he called his servant that ministered unto him, and said, Put now this woman out from me, and bolt the door after her.

And she had a garment of divers colours upon her: for with such robes were the king's daughters that were virgins apparelled. Then his servant brought her out, and bolted the door after her.

II Samuel 13:10–18

4 To keep thee from the evil woman, from the flattery of the tongue of a strange woman.

Lust not after her beauty in thine heart; neither let her take thee with her eyelids.

For by means of a whorish woman a man is brought to a piece of bread: and the adulteress will hunt for the precious life.

Can a man take fire in his bosom, and his clothes not be burned?

Can one go upon hot coals, and his feet not be burned?

So he that goeth in to his neighbour's wife; whosoever toucheth her shall not be innocent.

Proverbs 6:24–29

5 Now to his harp the blinded minstrel sang
of Arês' dalliance with Aphroditê:
how hidden in Hephaistos' house they played
at love together, and the gifts of Arês,
dishonoring Hephaistos' bed—and how
the word that wounds the heart came to the
    master
from Hêlios, who had seen the two embrace;

and when he learned it, Lord Hephaistos went
with baleful calculation to his forge.
There mightily he armed his anvil block
and hammered out a chain, whose tempered links
could not be sprung or bent; he meant that they
    should hold.
Those shackles fashioned, hot in wrath Hephais-
    tos
climbed to the bower and the bed of love,
pooled all his net of chain around the bed posts
and swung it from the rafters overhead—
light as a cobweb even gods in bliss
could not perceive, so wonderful his cunning.
Seeing his bed now made a snare, he feigned
a journey to the trim stronghold of Lemnos,
the dearest of earth's towns to him. And Arês?
Ah, golden Arês' watch had its reward
when he beheld the great smith leaving home.
How promptly to the famous door he came,
intent on pleasure with sweet Kythereia!
She, who had left her father's side but now,
sat in her chamber when her lover entered;
and tenderly he pressed her hand and said;

"Come and lie down, my darling, and be happy!
Hephaistos is no longer here, but gone
to see his grunting Sintian friends on Lemnos."

As she, too, thought repose would be most wel-
    come,
the pair went in to bed—into a shower
of clever chains, the netting of Hephaistos.
So trussed, they could not move apart, nor rise,
at last they knew there could be no escape,
they were to see the glorious cripple now—
for Hêlios had spied for him, and told him;
so he turned back, this side of Lemnos Isle,
sick at heart, making his way homeward.
Now in the doorway of the room he stood
while deadly rage took hold of him; his voice,
hoarse and terrible, reached all the gods:

"O Father Zeus, O gods in bliss forever,
here is indecorous entertainment for you,
Aphroditê, Zeus's daughter,
caught in the act, cheating me, her cripple,
with Arês—devastating Arês.
Cleanlimbed beauty is her joy, not these
bandylegs I came into the world with:
no one to blame but the two gods who bred me!
Come see this pair entwining here
in my own bed! How hot it makes me burn!
I think they may not care to lie much longer,
pressing on one another, passionate lovers;
they'll have enough of bed together soon.
And yet the chain that bagged them holds them
    down
till Father sends me back my wedding gifts—
all that I poured out for his damned pigeon,
so lovely, and so wanton."

             All the others
were crowding in, now, to the brazen house—

Poseidon who embraces earth, and Hermês
the runner, and Apollo, lord of Distance.
The goddesses stayed home for shame; but these
munificences ranged there in the doorway,
and irrepressible among them all
arose the laughter of the happy gods.
Gazing hard at Hephaistos' handiwork
the gods in turn remarked among themselves:

"No dash in adultery now."

              "The tortoise tags the hare—
Hephaistos catches Arês—and Arês outran the
wind."

"The lame god's craft has pinned him. Now shall
he
pay what is due from gods taken in cuckoldry."

They made these improving remarks to one another,
but Apollo leaned aside to say to Hermês:

"Son of Zeus, beneficent Wayfinder,
would you accept a coverlet of chain, if only
you lay by Aphroditê's golden side?"

To this the Wayfinder replied, shining:

"Would I not, though, Apollo of distances!
Wrap me in chains three times the weight of
these,
come goddesses and gods to see the fun;
only let me lie beside the pale-golden one!"

The gods gave way again to peals of laughter.
                Homer, *Odyssey,* VIII, 266

6 That man seems to me peer of gods, who sits in
thy presence, and hears close to him thy sweet
speech and lovely laughter; that indeed makes my
heart flutter in my bosom. For when I see thee but
a little, I have no utterance left, my tongue is broken down, and straightway a subtle fire has run
under my skin, with my eyes I have no sight, my
ears ring, sweat pours down, and a trembling
seizes all my body; I am paler than grass, and
seem in my madness little better than one dead.
       Sappho, *The Ode to Aphrodite* (fragment)

7 *The Nurse.* The chaste, they love not vice of their
   own will,
but yet they love it.
            Euripides, *Hippolytus,* 359

8 *Socrates.* In the friendship of the lover there is no
real kindness; he has an appetite and wants to
feed upon you. "Just as the wolf loves the lamb, so
the lover adores his beloved."
            Plato, *Phaedrus,* 241B

9 Aristophanes . . . had a mind to praise Love in
another way, unlike that either of Pausanias or
Eryximachus. Mankind, he said, judging by their

neglect of him, have never, as I think, at all understood the power of Love. For if they had understood him they would surely have built noble
temples and altars, and offered solemn sacrifices in
his honour; but this is not done, and most certainly ought to be done: since of all the gods he is the
best friend of men, the helper and the healer of
the ills which are the great impediment to the
happiness of the race. I will try to describe his
power to you [Eryximachus], and you shall teach
the rest of the world what I am teaching you. In
the first place, let me treat of the nature of man
and what has happened to it; for the original human nature was not like the present, but different.
The sexes were not two as they are now, but originally three in number; there was man, woman,
and the union of the two, having a name corresponding to this double nature, which had once a
real existence, but is now lost, and the word "Androgynous" is only preserved as a term of reproach. In the second place, the primeval man
was round, his back and sides forming a circle;
and he had four hands and four feet, one head
with two faces, looking opposite ways, set on a
round neck and precisely alike; also four ears, two
privy members, and the remainder to correspond.
He could walk upright as men now do, backwards
or forwards as he pleased, and he could also roll
over and over at a great pace, turning on his four
hands and four feet, eight in all, like tumblers
going over and over with their legs in the air; this
was when he wanted to run fast. Now the sexes
were three, and such as I have described them;
because the sun, moon, and earth are three; and
the man was originally the child of the sun, the
woman of the earth, and the man-woman of the
moon, which is made up of sun and earth, and
they were all round and moved round and round
like their parents. Terrible was their might and
strength, and the thoughts of their hearts were
great, and they made an attack upon the gods; of
them is told the tale of Otys and Ephialtes who, as
Homer says, dared to scale heaven, and would
have laid hands upon the gods. Doubt reigned in
the celestial councils. Should they kill them and
annihilate the race with thunderbolts, as they had
done the giants, then there would be an end of the
sacrifices and worship which men offered to them;
but, on the other hand, the gods could not suffer
their insolence to be unrestrained.

   At last, after a good deal of reflection, Zeus discovered a way. He said: "Methinks I have a plan
which will humble their pride and improve their
manners; men shall continue to exist, but I will
cut them in two and then they will be diminished
in strength and increased in numbers; this will
have the advantage of making them more profitable to us. They shall walk upright on two legs,
and if they continue insolent and will not be
quiet, I will split them again and they shall hop
about on a single leg." He spoke and cut men in

two, like a sorb-apple which is halved for pickling, or as you might divide an egg with a hair; and as he cut them one after another, he bade Apollo give the face and the half of the neck a turn in order that the man might contemplate the section of himself: he would thus learn a lesson of humility. Apollo was also bidden to heal their wounds and compose their forms. So he gave a turn to the face and pulled the skin from the sides all over that which in our language is called the belly, like the purses which draw in, and he made one mouth at the centre, which he fastened in a knot (the same which is called the navel); he also moulded the breast and took out most of the wrinkles, much as a shoemaker might smooth leather upon a last; he left a few, however, in the region of the belly and navel, as a memorial of the primeval state. After the division the two parts of man, each desiring his other half, came together, and throwing their arms about one another, entwined in mutual embraces, longing to grow into one, they were on the point of dying from hunger and self-neglect, because they did not like to do anything apart; and when one of the halves died and the other survived, the survivor sought another mate, man or woman as we call them,—being the sections of entire men or women,—and clung to that. They were being destroyed, when Zeus in pity of them invented a new plan: he turned the parts of generation round to the front, for this had not been always their position, and they sowed the seed no longer as hitherto like grasshoppers in the ground, but in one another; and after the transposition the male generated in the female in order that by the mutual embraces of man and woman they might breed, and the race might continue; or if man came to man they might be satisfied, and rest, and go their ways to the business of life: so ancient is the desire of one another which is implanted in us, reuniting our original nature, making one of two, and healing the state of man.

Each of us when separated, having one side only, like a flat fish, is but the indenture of a man, and he is always looking for his other half. Men who are a section of that double nature which was once called Androgynous are lovers of women; adulterers are generally of this breed, and also adulterous women who lust after men: the women who are a section of the woman do not care for men, but have female attachments; the female companions are of this sort. But they who are a section of the male follow the male, and while they are young, being slices of the original man, they hang about men and embrace them, and they are themselves the best of boys and youths, because they have the most manly nature. Some indeed assert that they are shameless, but this is not true; for they do not act thus from any want of shame, but because they are valiant and manly, and have a manly countenance, and they embrace that which is like them. And these when

they grow up become our statesmen, and these only, which is a great proof of the truth of what I am saying. When they reach manhood they are lovers of youth, and are not naturally inclined to marry or beget children,—if at all, they do so only in obedience to the law; but they are satisfied if they may be allowed to live with one another unwedded; and such a nature is prone to love and ready to return love, always embracing that which is akin to him. And when one of them meets with his other half, the actual half of himself, whether he be a lover of youth or a lover of another sort, the pair are lost in an amazement of love and friendship and intimacy, and will not be out of the other's sight, as I may say, even for a moment: these are the people who pass their whole lives together; yet they could not explain what they desire of one another. For the intense yearning which each of them has towards the other does not appear to be the desire of lover's intercourse, but of something else which the soul of either evidently desires and cannot tell, and of which she has only a dark and doubtful presentiment. Suppose Hephaestus, with his instruments, to come to the pair who are lying side by side and to say to them, "What do you people want of one another?" they would be unable to explain. And suppose further, that when he saw their perplexity he said: "Do you desire to be wholly one; always day and night to be in one another's company? for if this is what you desire, I am ready to melt you into one and let you grow together, so that being two you shall become one, and while you live live a common life as if you were a single man, and after your death in the world below still be one departed soul instead of two—I ask whether this is what you lovingly desire, and whether you are satisfied to attain this?"—there is not a man of them who when he heard the proposal would deny or would not acknowledge that this meeting and melting into one another, this becoming one instead of two, was the very expression of his ancient need. And the reason is that human nature was originally one and we were a whole, and the desire and pursuit of the whole is called love.

Plato, *Symposium,* 189A

10 Animals in general seem naturally disposed to this intercourse at about the same period of the year, and that is when winter is changing into summer. And this is the season of spring, in which almost all things that fly or walk or swim take to pairing. Some animals pair and breed in autumn also and in winter, as is the case with certain aquatic animals and certain birds. Man pairs and breeds at all seasons, as is the case also with domesticated animals, owing to the shelter and good feeding they enjoy: that is to say, with those whose period of gestation is also comparatively brief, as the sow and the bitch, and with those birds that breed

frequently. Many animals time the season of intercourse with a view to the right nurture subsequently of their young. In the human species, the male is more under sexual excitement in winter, and the female in summer.

Aristotle, *History of Animals,* 542ª20

11 Men in most cases continue to be sexually competent until they are sixty years old, and if that limit be overpassed then until seventy years; and men have been actually known to procreate children at seventy years of age. With many men and many women it so happens that they are unable to produce children to one another, while they are able to do so in union with other individuals. The same thing happens with regard to the production of male and female offspring; for sometimes men and women in union with one another produce male children or female, as the case may be, but children of the opposite sex when otherwise mated. And they are apt to change in this respect with advancing age: for sometimes a husband and wife while they are young produce female children and in later life male children; and in other cases the very contrary occurs. And just the same thing is true in regard to the generative faculty: for some while young are childless, but have children when they grow older; and some have children to begin with, and later on no more.

Aristotle, *History of Animals,* 585ᵇ6

12 As when in sleep a thirsty man seeks to drink and water is not given to quench the burning in his frame, but he seeks the idols of waters and toils in vain and thirsts as he drinks in the midst of the torrent stream, thus in love Venus mocks lovers with idols, nor can bodies satisfy them by all their gazing upon them nor can they with their hands rub aught off the soft limbs, wandering undecided over the whole body. At last when they have united and enjoy the flower of age, when the body now has a presage of delights and Venus is in the mood to sow the fields of woman, they greedily clasp each other's body and suck each other's lips and breathe in, pressing meanwhile teeth on each other's mouth; all in vain, since they can rub nothing off nor enter and pass each with his whole body into the other's body; for so sometimes they seem to will and strive to do: so greedily are they held in the chains of Venus, while their limbs melt overpowered by the might of the pleasure. At length when the gathered desire has gone forth, there ensues for a brief while a short pause in the burning passion; and then returns the same frenzy, then comes back the old madness, when they are at a loss to know what they really desire to get, and cannot find what device is to conquer that mischief; in such utter uncertainty they pine away by a hidden wound.

Lucretius, *Nature of Things,* IV

13 But anxious cares already seiz'd the queen:
She fed within her veins a flame unseen;
The hero's valor, acts, and birth inspire
Her soul with love, and fan the secret fire.
His words, his looks, imprinted in her heart,
Improve the passion, and increase the smart.

Virgil, *Aeneid,* IV

14 *Dido.* To this one error I might yield again;
For, since Sichæus was untimely slain,
This only man is able to subvert
The fix'd foundations of my stubborn heart.
And, to confess my frailty, to my shame,
Somewhat I find within, if not the same,
Too like the sparkles of my former flame.

Virgil, *Aeneid,* IV

15 What priestly rites, alas! what pious art,
What vows avail to cure a bleeding heart!
A gentle fire she feeds within her veins,
Where the soft god secure in silence reigns.
    Sick with desire, and seeking him she loves,
From street to street the raving Dido roves.
So when the watchful shepherd, from the blind,
Wounds with a random shaft the careless hind,
Distracted with her pain she flies the woods,
Bounds o'er the lawn, and seeks the silent floods,
With fruitless care; for still the fatal dart
Sticks in her side, and rankles in her heart.

Virgil, *Aeneid,* IV

16 The queen and prince, as love or fortune guides,
One common cavern in her bosom hides.
Then first the trembling earth the signal gave,
And flashing fires enlighten all the cave;
Hell from below, and Juno from above,
And howling nymphs, were conscious of their love
From this ill-omen'd hour in time arose
Debate and death, and all succeeding woes.
    The queen, whom sense of honor could not move,
No longer made a secret of her love,
But call'd it marriage, by that specious name
To veil the crime and sanctify the shame.

Virgil, *Aeneid,* IV

17 What I hate is the girl who gives with a feeling she has to,
    Dry in the bed, with her mind somewhere else, gathering wool.
Duty is all very well, but's let's not confuse it with pleasure;
    I do not want any girl doing her duty for me.
What I like to hear are the words of utter abandon,
    Words that say, "Not too soon!", words that say, "Wait just a while!"
Let me see my girl with eyes that confess her excitement;
    Let her, after she comes, want no more for a while.

What does youth know of delight? Some things
   ought not to be hurried;
   After some thirty-odd years, lovers begin to
   learn how.
Let the premature guzzle wine that is hardly fermented,
   I'll take wine from a jar mellowed in vintage
   with time.
Only the full-grown tree resists the heat of the
   sunlight,
   Meadows too recently sown offer the barefoot
   no joy.
Who wants Hermione, if Helen is his for the taking?
   Look for a woman, mature, not any slip of a
   girl.
Love is an art learned late, but if you are willing,
   and patient,
   Playing your part like a man, you will have
   fitting reward.

   Ovid, *Art of Love,* II, 685

18 What a girl ought to know is herself, adapting her
   method,
   Taking advantage of ways nature equips her to
   use.
Lie on your back, if your face and all of your
   features are pretty;
   If your posterior's cute, better be seen from behind.
Milanion used to bear Atalanta's legs on his
   shoulders;
   If you have beautiful legs, let them be lifted like
   hers.
Little girls do all right if they sit on top, riding
   horseback;
   Hector's Andromache knew she could not do
   this: too tall!
Press the couch with your knees and bend your
   neck backward a little,
   If your view, full-length, seems what a lover
   should crave.
If the breasts and thighs are youthful and lovely
   to look at,
   Let the man stand and the girl lie on a slant on
   the bed.
Let your hair come down, in the Laodamian fash-
   ion:
   If your belly is lined, better be seen from be-
   hind.
There are a thousand ways: a simple one, never
   too tiring,
   Is to lie on your back, turning a bit to the right.
My Muse can give you the truth, more truth than
   Apollo or Ammon;
   Take it from me, what I know took many les-
   sons to learn.
Let the woman feel the act of love to her marrow,
   Let the performance bring equal delight to the
   two.

Coax and flatter and tease, with inarticulate murmurs,
   Even with sexual words, in the excitement of
   play,
And if nature, alas! denies you the final sensation
   Cry out as if you had come, do your best to
   pretend.
Really, I pity the girl whose place, let us say, cannot give her
   Pleasure it gives to the man, pleasure she ought
   to enjoy.
So, if you have to pretend, be sure the pretense is
   effective,
   Do your best to convince, prove it by rolling
   your eyes,
Prove by your motions, your moans, your sighs,
   what a pleasure it gives you.
   Ah, what a shame! That part has its own intimate signs.

   Ovid, *Art of Love,* III, 771

19 Love not the world, neither the things that are in
   the world. If any man love the world, the love of
   the Father is not in him.
   For all that is in the world, the lust of the flesh,
   and the lust of the eyes, and the pride of life, is not
   of the Father, but is of the world.
   And the world passeth away, and the lust thereof: but he that doeth the will of God abideth for
   ever.

   I John 2:15–17

20 I came to Carthage, where a cauldron of illicit
   loves leapt and boiled about me. I was not yet in
   love, but I was in love with love, and from the
   very depth of my need hated myself for not more
   keenly feeling the need. I sought some object to
   love, since I was thus in love with loving; and I
   hated security and a life with no snares for my
   feet. For within I was hungry, all for the want of
   that spiritual food which is Thyself, my God; yet
   [though I was hungry for want of it] I did not
   hunger for it: I had no desire whatever for incorruptible food, not because I had it in abundance
   but the emptier I was, the more I hated the
   thought of it. Because of all this my soul was sick,
   and broke out in sores, whose itch I agonized to
   scratch with the rub of carnal things—carnal, yet
   if there were no soul in them, they would not be
   objects of love. My longing then was to love and
   to be loved, but most when I obtained the enjoyment of the body of the person who loved me.
   Thus I polluted the stream of friendship with
   the filth of unclean desire and sullied its limpidity
   with the hell of lust. And vile and unclean as I
   was, so great was my vanity that I was bent upon
   passing for clean and courtly. And I did fall in
   love, simply from wanting to. O my God, my
   Mercy, with how much bitterness didst Thou in
   Thy goodness sprinkle the delights of that time! I
   was loved, and our love came to the bond of con-

summation: I wore my chains with bliss but with torment too, for I was scourged with red hot rods of jealousy, with suspicions and fears and tempers and quarrels.

Augustine, *Confessions,* III, 1

21 I in my great worthlessness—for it was greater thus early—had begged You for chastity, saying "Grant me chastity and continence, but not yet." For I was afraid that You would hear my prayer too soon, and too soon would heal me from the disease of lust which I wanted satisfied rather than extinguished.

Augustine, *Confessions,* VIII, 7

22 Certainly, had not culpable disobedience been visited with penal disobedience, the marriage of Paradise should have been ignorant of this struggle and rebellion, this quarrel between will and lust, that the will may be satisfied and lust restrained, but those members, like all the rest, should have obeyed the will. The field of generation should have been sown by the organ created for this purpose, as the earth is sown by the hand. And whereas now, as we essay to investigate this subject more exactly, modesty hinders us and compels us to ask pardon of chaste ears, there would have been no cause to do so, but we could have discoursed freely, and without fear of seeming obscene, upon all those points which occur to one who meditates on the subject. There would not have been even words which could be called obscene, but all that might be said of these members would have been as pure as what is said of the other parts of the body. Whoever, then, comes to the perusal of these pages with unchaste mind, let him blame his disposition, not his nature; let him brand the actings of his own impurity, not the words which necessity forces us to use, and for which every pure and pious reader or hearer will very readily pardon me.

Augustine, *City of God,* XIV, 23

23 I define charity as a motion of the soul whose purpose is to enjoy God for His own sake and one's self and one's neighbor for the sake of God. Lust, on the other hand is a motion of the soul bent upon enjoying one's self, one's neighbor, and any creature without reference to God.

Augustine, *Christian Doctrine,* III, 10

24 Some of the earlier doctors, considering the nature of concupiscence as regards generation in our present state, concluded that in the state of innocence generation would not have been effected in the same way. Thus Gregory of Nyssa says that in Paradise the human race would have been multiplied by some other means, just as the angels were multiplied without coition by the operation of the Divine Power. He adds that God made man male and female before sin because He foreknew the mode of generation which would take place after sin, which He foresaw.

But this is unreasonable. For what is natural to man was neither acquired nor forfeited by sin. Now it is clear that generation by coition is natural to man by reason of his animal life, which he possessed even before sin . . . just as it is natural to other perfect animals, as the corporeal members make it clear. So we cannot allow that these members would have had a natural use, as other members had, before sin.

Aquinas, *Summa Theologica,* I, 98, 2

25 The virtue of chastity most of all makes man apt for contemplation, since sexual pleasures most of all weigh the mind down to sensible objects.

Aquinas, *Summa Theologica,* II–II, 180, 2

26 A remedy can be employed against concupiscence in two ways. First, on the part of concupiscence by repressing it in its root, and thus matrimony affords a remedy by the grace given therein. Secondly, on the part of its act, and this in two ways: first, by depriving the act to which concupiscence inclines of its outward shamefulness, and this is done by the marriage blessings which justify carnal concupiscence; secondly, by hindering the shameful act, which is done by the very nature of the act; because concupiscence, being satisfied by the conjugal act, does not incline so much to other wickedness.

Aquinas, *Summa Theologica,* III Suppl., 42, 3

27 No wise man should allow himself to lose a thing except for some compensation in the shape of an equal or better good. Wherefore for a thing that has a loss attached to it to be eligible, it needs to have some good connected with it, which by compensating for that loss makes that thing ordinate and right. Now there is a loss of reason incidental to the union of man and woman, both because the reason is carried away entirely on account of the vehemence of the pleasure, so that it is unable to understand anything at the same time . . . and again because of the tribulation of the flesh which such persons have to suffer from solicitude for temporal things. Consequently the choice of this union cannot be made ordinate except by certain compensation whereby that same union is righted; and these are the goods which excuse marriage and make it right.

Aquinas, *Summa Theologica,* III Suppl., 49, 1

28 Some say that whenever pleasure is the chief motive for the marriage act it is a mortal sin; that when it is an indirect motive it is a venial sin; and that when it spurns the pleasure altogether and is displeasing, it is wholly void of venial sin; so that it would be a mortal sin to seek pleasure in this act, a venial sin to take the pleasure when offered, but that perfection requires one to detest it. But

this is impossible since . . . the same judgment applies to pleasure as to action, because pleasure in a good action is good, and in an evil action, evil; wherefore, as the marriage act is not evil in itself, neither will it be always a mortal sin to seek pleasure therein. Consequently the right answer to this question is that if pleasure be sought in such a way as to exclude the honesty of marriage, so that, to wit, it is not as a wife but as a woman that a man treats his wife, and that he is ready to use her in the same way if she were not his wife, it is a mortal sin; wherefore such a man is said to be too ardent a lover of his wife, because his ardor carries him away from the goods of marriage. If, however, he seek pleasure within the bounds of marriage, so that it would not be sought in another than his wife, it is a venial sin.

Aquinas, *Summa Theologica*, III Suppl., 49, 6

29 Although old people have not sufficient calidity to procreate, they have sufficient to copulate. Wherefore they are allowed to marry, insofar as marriage is intended as a remedy, although it does not befit them as fulfilling an office of nature.

Aquinas, *Summa Theologica*, III Suppl., 58. 1

30 I came into a place void of all light, which bellows like the sea in tempest, when it is combated by warring winds.

The hellish storm, which never rests, leads the spirits with its sweep; whirling, and smiting it vexes them.

When they arrive before the ruin, there the shrieks, the moanings, and the lamentation; there they blaspheme the divine power.

I learnt that to such torment are doomed the carnal sinners, who subject reason to lust.

Dante, *Inferno*, V, 28

31 I began: "Poet [Virgil], willingly would I speak with those two that go together, and seem so light upon the wind."

And he to me: "Thou shalt see when they are nearer to us; and do thou then entreat them by that love, which leads them; and they will come."

Soon as the wind bends them to us, I raised my voice: "O wearied souls! come to speak with us, if none denies it."

As doves called by desire, with raised and steady wings come through the air to their loved nest, borne by their will:

so those spirits issued from the band where Dido is, coming to us through the malignant air; such was the force of my affectuous cry.

"O living creature, gracious and benign! that goest through the black air, visiting us who stained the earth with blood;

if the King of the Universe were our friend, we would pray him for thy peace; seeing that thou hast pity of our perverse misfortune.

Of that which it pleases thee to hear and to speak, we will hear and speak with you, whilst the wind, as now, is silent for us.

The town, where I was born, sits on the shore, where Po decends to rest with his attendant *streams*.

Love, which is quickly caught in gentle heart, took him with the fair body of which I was bereft; and the manner still afflicts me.

Love, which to no loved one permits excuse for loving, took me so strongly with delight in him, that, as thou seest, even now it leaves me not.

Love led us to one death; Caïna waits for him who quenched our life." These words from them were offered to us.

After I had heard those wounded souls, I bowed my face, and held it low until the Poet said to me: "What art thou thinking of?"

When I answered, I began: "Ah me! what sweet thoughts, what longing led them to the woful pass!"

Then I turned again to them; and I spoke, and began: "Francesca, thy torments make me weep with grief and pity.

But tell me: in the time of the sweet sighs, by what and how love granted you to know the dubious desires?"

And she to me: "*There is* no greater pain than to recall a happy time in wretchedness; and this thy teacher knows.

But if thou hast such desire to learn the first root of our love, I will do like one who weeps and tells.

One day, for pastime, we read of Lancelot, how love constrained him; we were alone, and without all suspicion.

Several times that reading urged our eyes to meet, and changed the colour of our faces; but one moment alone it was that overcame us.

When we read how the fond smile was kissed by such a lover, he, who shall never be divided from me,

kissed my mouth all trembling: the book, and he who wrote it, was a Galeotto; that day we read in it no farther."

Whilst the one spirit spake, the other wept so, that I fainted with pity, as if I have been dying; and fell, as a dead body falls.

Dante, *Inferno*, V, 73

32 And then he [Troilus] told him [Pandar] of his happy night,
And how at first he was afraid, and why,
And said, "I swear upon my honor bright
And by my faith in you and God on high,
I never knew what loving did imply;
For as my heart's desires rose in height,
The greater grew my love and my delight."

Chaucer, *Troilus and Cressida*, III, 236

33 Now, to speak of the first desire, that is, concupis-

cence, according to the law for our sexual parts, which were lawfully made and by rightful word of God; I say, for as much as man is not obedient to God, Who is his Lord, therefore is the flesh disobedient to Him, through concupiscence, which is also called the nourishing of and the reason for sin. Therefore all the while that a man has within himself the penalty of concupiscence, it is impossible but that he will be sometimes tempted and moved in his flesh to do sin. And this shall not fail so long as he lives; it may well grow feeble and remote by virtue of baptism and by the grace of God through penitence; but it shall never be fully quenched so that he shall never be moved within himself, unless he be cooled by sickness or by maleficence of sorcery or by opiates.

Chaucer, *Canterbury Tales:* Parson's Tale

34 This is the Devil's other hand, with five fingers to catch the people into his slavery. The first finger is the foolish interchange of glances between the foolish woman and the foolish man, which slays just as the basilisk slays folk by the venom of its sight; for the lust of the eyes follows the lust of the heart. The second finger is vile touching in wicked manner; and thereupon Solomon says that he who touches and handles a woman fares like the man that handles the scorpion which stings and suddenly slays by its poisoning; even as, if any man touch warm pitch, it defiles his fingers. The third is vile words, which are like fire, which immediately burns the heart. The fourth finger is kissing; and truly he were a great fool who would kiss the mouth of a burning oven or of a furnace. And the more fools they are who kiss in vileness; for that mouth is the mouth of Hell; and I speak specifically of these old dotard whoremongers, who will yet kiss though they cannot do anything, and so taste them. Certainly they are like dogs, for a dog, when he passes a rosebush, or other bushes, though he cannot piss, yet will he heave up his leg and make an appearance of pissing. And as for the opinion of many that a man cannot sin for any lechery he does with his wife, certainly that opinion is wrong. God knows, a man may slay himself with his own knife, and make himself drunk out of his own tun. Certainly, be it wife, be it child, or any worldly thing that a man loves more than he loves God, it is his idol, and he is an idolater. Man should love his wife with discretion, calmly and moderately; and then she is as it were his sister. The fifth finger of the Devil's hand is the stinking act of lechery. Truly, the five fingers of gluttony the Fiend thrusts into the belly of a man, and with his five fingers of lechery he grips him by the loins in order to throw him into the furnace of Hell; wherein he shall have the fire and the everlasting worms, and weeping and wailing, sharp hunger and thirst, and horror of devils that shall trample all over him, without respite and without end.

Chaucer, *Canterbury Tales:* Parson's Tale

35 Then said Pantagruel, How dost thou know that the privy parts of women are at such a cheap rate? For in this city there are many virtuous, honest, and chaste women besides the maids. *Et ubi prenus?* [And where will you find them?] said Panurge. I will give you my opinion of it, and that upon certain and assured knowledge. I do not brag, that I have bum-basted four hundred and seventeen, since I came into this city, though it be but nine days ago; but this very morning I met with a good fellow, who in a wallet, such as Æsop's was, carried two little girls, of two or three years old at the most, one before, and the other behind. He demanded alms of me, but I made him answer, that I had more cods than pence. Afterwards I asked him, Good man, these two girls, are they maids? Brother, said he, I have carried them thus these two years, and in regard of her that is before, whom I see continually, in my opinion she is a virgin; nevertheless, I will not put my finger in the fire for it; as for her that is behind, doubtless I can say nothing.

Rabelais, *Gargantua and Pantagruel*, II, 15

36 The woman who goes to bed with a man should put off her modesty with her skirt and put it on again with her petticoat.

Montaigne, *Essays*, I, 21, Power of the Imagination

37 Married people, whose time is all their own, should neither press their undertaking nor even attempt it if they are not ready; it is better to fail unbecomingly to handsel the nuptial couch, which is full of agitation and feverishness, and wait for some other more private and less tense opportunity, than to fall into perpetual misery for having been stunned and made desperate by a first refusal. Before taking possession, the patient should try himself out and offer himself, lightly, by sallies at different times, without priding himself and obstinately insisting on convincing himself definitively. Those who know that their members are naturally obedient, let them take care only to counteract the tricks of their fancies.

People are right to notice the unruly liberty of this member, obtruding so importunately when we have no use for it, and failing so importunately when we have the most use for it, and struggling for mastery so imperiously with our will, refusing with so much pride and obstinacy our solicitations, both mental and manual.

Montaigne, *Essays*, I, 21, Power of the Imagination

38 Truly it is also a fact worthy of consideration that the masters of the craft order as a remedy to amorous passions the entire and open sight of the body that we pursue; that to cool our love, we need only see freely what we love. . . . And although

this recipe may perhaps proceed from a somewhat cooled and delicate temperament, still it is a wonderful sign of our defectiveness that acquaintance and familiarity disgust us with one another. It is not so much modesty as artfulness and prudence that makes our ladies so circumspect in refusing us entry to their boudoirs before they are painted and dressed up for public display.

Montaigne, *Essays,* II, 12, Apology for Raymond Sebond

39 We eat and drink as the animals do, but these are not actions that hinder the operations of our mind. In these we keep our advantage over them. But this other puts every other thought beneath its yoke and by its imperious authority brutifies and bestializes all the theology and philosophy there is in Plato; and yet he does not complain of it. In everything else you can keep some decorum; all other operations come under the rules of decency. This one cannot even be imagined other than vicious or ridiculous. Just to see this, try to find a wise and discreet way of doing it. Alexander used to say that he knew himself to be mortal chiefly by this action and by sleep. Sleep suffocates and supresses the faculties of our mind; the sexual act likewise absorbs and dissipates them. Truly it is a mark not only of our original corruption but also of our inanity and deformity.

On the one hand Nature pushes us on to it, having attached to this desire the most noble, useful, and pleasant of all her operations; and on the other hand she lets us accuse and shun it as shameless and indecent, blush at it, and recommend abstinence. Are we not brutes to call brutish the operation that makes us?

The various nations in their religions have many conventions in common, such as sacrifices, lamps, burning incense, fasts, offerings, and, among other things, the condemnation of this action. All opinions come to this, besides the very widespread practice of cutting off the foreskin, which is a punishment of the act. Perhaps we are right to blame ourselves for making such a stupid production as man, to call the action shameful, and shameful the parts that are used for it.

Montaigne, *Essays,* III, 5, On Some Verses of Virgil

40 The truth is that it is contrary to the nature of love if it is not violent, and contrary to the nature of violence if it is constant. And those who are astonished at this and exclaim against it and seek out the causes of this malady in women as if it were unnatural and incredible, why don't they see how often they accept it in themselves without being appalled and calling it a miracle? It would perhaps be more strange to see any stability in it. It is not simply a bodily passion. If there is no end to avarice and ambition, neither is there any to lechery. It still lives after satiety; no constant satis-

faction or end can be prescribed to it, for it always goes beyond its possession.

Montaigne, *Essays,* III, 5, On Some Verses of Virgil

41 He who can await, the morning after, without dying of shame, the disdain of those fair eyes that have witnessed his limpness and impertinence, . . . has never felt the satisfaction and pride of having conquered them and put circles around them by the vigorous exercise of a busy and active night.

Montaigne, *Essays,* III, 5, On Some Verses of Virgil

42 Now this is a relationship that needs mutuality and reciprocity. The other pleasures that we receive may be acknowledged by recompenses of a different nature, but this one can be paid for only in the same kind of coin. In truth, in this delight the pleasure I give tickles my imagination more sweetly than that which I feel. Now there is no nobility in a man who can receive pleasure where he gives none; it is a mean soul that is willing to owe everything and takes pleasure in fostering relations with persons to whom he is a burden. There is neither beauty, nor grace, nor intimacy so exquisite that a gallant man should desire it at this price. If they can be kind to us only out of pity, I had much rather not live at all than live on alms.

Montaigne, *Essays,* III, 5, On Some Verses of Virgil

43 *Friar Laurence.* These violent delights have violent ends
And in their triumph die, like fire and powder,
Which as they kiss consume: the sweetest honey
Is loathsome in his own deliciousness
And in the taste confounds the appetite:
Therefore love moderately; long love doth so;
Too swift arrives as tardy as too slow.

Shakespeare, *Romeo and Juliet,* II, vi, 9

44 *Theseus.* Fair Hermia, question your desires;
Know of your youth, examine well your blood,
Whether, if you yield not to your father's choice,
You can endure the livery of a nun,
For aye to be in shady cloister mew'd,
To live a barren sister all your life,
Chanting faint hymns to the cold fruitless moon.
Thrice-blessed they that master so their blood
To undergo such maiden pilgrimage;
But earthlier happy is the rose distill'd
Than that which withering on the virgin thorn
Grows, lives, and dies in single blessedness.

Shakespeare, *Midsummer-Night's Dream,* I, i, 67

45 *Polonius.* I do know,
When the blood burns, how prodigal the soul

Lends the tongue vows: these blazes, daughter,
Giving more light than heat, extinct in both,
Even in their promise, as it is a-making,
You must not take for fire.

Shakespeare, Hamlet, I, iii, 115

46 *Queen.*   O Hamlet, speak no more.
Thou turn'st mine eyes into my very soul;
And there I see such black and grained spots
As will not leave their tinct.
   Hamlet.   Nay, but to live
In the rank sweat of an enseamed bed,
Stew'd in corruption, honeying and making love
Over the nasty sty—
   Queen.   O, speak to me no more;
These words, like daggers, enter in mine ears;
No more, sweet Hamlet!
   Ham.   A murderer and a villain;
A slave that is not twentieth part the tithe
Of your precedent lord; a vice of kings;
A cutpurse of the empire and the rule,
That from a shelf the precious diadem stole,
And put it in his pocket!
   Queen.   No more!

Shakespeare, Hamlet, III, iv, 88

47 *Fairies.* Fie on sinful fantasy!
   Fie on lust and luxury!
   Lust is but a bloody fire,
   Kindled with unchaste desire,
   Fed in heart, whose flames aspire
   As thoughts do blow them, higher and higher.
   Pinch him, fairies, mutually;
   Pinch him for his villainy;
Pinch him, and burn him, and turn him about,
Till candles and starlight and moonshine be out.

Shakespeare, Merry Wives
of Windsor, V, v, 97

48 *Cressida.* They say all lovers swear more performance than they are able and yet reserve an ability that they never perform, vowing more than the perfection of ten and discharging less than the tenth part of one.

Shakespeare, Troilus and Cressida, III, ii, 91

49 *Pandarus.* Go to, a bargain made. Seal it, seal it; I'll be the witness. Here I hold your hand, here my cousin's. If ever you prove false one to another, since I have taken such pains to bring you together, let all pitiful goers-between be called to the world's end after my name; call them all Pandars; let all constant men be Troiluses, all false women Cressids, and all brokers-between Pandars! say, amen.
   Troilus. Amen.
   Cressida. Amen.
   Pan. Amen. Whereupon I will show you a chamber with a bed; which bed, because it shall not speak of your pretty encounters, press it to death. Away!

And Cupid grant all tongue-tied maidens here
Bed, chamber, Pandar to provide this gear!

Shakespeare, Troilus and Cressida, III, ii, 204

50 *Iago.* Mark me with what violence she first loved the Moor, but for bragging and telling her fantastical lies; and will she love him still for prating? let not thy discreet heart think it. Her eye must be fed; and what delight shall she have to look on the devil? When the blood is made dull with the act of sport, there should be, again to inflame it and to give satiety a fresh appetite, loveliness in favour, sympathy in years, manners, and beauties; all which the Moor is defective in. Now, for want of these required conveniences, her delicate tenderness will find itself abused, begin to heave the gorge, disrelish and abhor the Moor; very nature will instruct her in it and compel her to some second choice.

Shakespeare, Othello, II, i, 224

51 *Fool.* Now a little fire in a wild field were like an old lecher's heart; a small spark, all the rest on 's body cold.

Shakespeare, Lear, III, iv, 116

52 *Gloucester.* The trick of that voice I do well remember.
Is't not the King?
   Lear.   Ay, every inch a king!
When I do stare, see how the subject quakes.
I pardon that man's life. What was thy cause?
Adultery?
Thou shalt not die. Die for adultery! No:
The wren goes to't, and the small gilded fly
Does lecher in my sight.
Let copulation thrive; for Gloucester's bastard son
Was kinder to his father than my daughters
Got 'tween the lawful sheets.
To't, luxury, pell-mell; for I lack soldiers.

Shakespeare, Lear, IV, vi, 108

53 *Philo.* Nay, but this dotage of our general's
O'erflows the measure. Those his goodly eyes,
That o'er the files and musters of the war
Have glow'd like plated Mars, now bend, now turn,
The office and devotion of their view
Upon a tawny front; his captain's heart,
Which in the scuffles of great fights hath burst
The buckles on his breast, reneges all temper,
And is become the bellows and the fan
To cool a gipsy's lust.

   Flourish. Enter Antony, Cleopatra, *her Ladies,
the Train, with Eunuchs fanning her.*

Look, where they come!
Take but good note, and you shall see in him
The triple pillar of the world transform'd
Into a strumpet's fool.

Shakespeare, Antony and Cleopatra, I, i, 1

54 *Prospero.* Look thou be true; do not give dalliance
   Too much the rein. The strongest oaths are straw
   To the fire i' the blood.

   Shakespeare, *Tempest*, IV, i, 51

55 The expense of spirit in a waste of shame
   Is lust in action; and till action, lust
   Is perjured, murderous, bloody, full of blame,
   Savage, extreme, rude, cruel, not to trust,
   Enjoy'd no sooner but despised straight,
   Past reason hunted, and no sooner had,
   Past reason hated, as a swallow'd bait
   On purpose laid to make the taker mad;
   Mad in pursuit, and in possession so;
   Had, having, and in quest to have, extreme;
   A bliss in proof, and proved, a very woe;
   Before, a joy proposed; behind, a dream.
      All this the world well knows; yet none knows
         well
      To shun the heaven that leads men to this hell.

   Shakespeare, *Sonnet CXXIX*

56 I could be content that we might procreate like
   trees, without conjunction, or that there were any
   way to perpetuate the World without this trivial
   and vulgar way of coition; it is the foolishest act a
   wise man commits in all his life; nor is there any
   thing that will more deject his cool'd imagination,
   when he shall consider what an odd and unworthy piece of folly he hath committed.

   Sir Thomas Browne,
   Religio Medici, II, 9

57 Lust has become natural to us and has made our
   second nature. Thus there are two natures in us—
   the one good, the other bad. Where is God?
   Where you are not, and the kingdom of God is
   within you.

   Pascal, *Pensées*, X, 660

58   When lust
   By unchaste looks, loose gestures, and foul talk,
   But most by leud and lavish act of sin,
   Lets in defilement to the inward parts,
   The soul grows clotted by contagion,
   Imbodies, and imbrutes, till she quite loose
   The divine property of her first being.

   Milton, *Comus*, 463

59 Nor those mysterious parts were then conceald,
   Then was not guiltie shame, dishonest shame
   Of natures works, honor dishonorable,
   Sin-bred, how have ye troubl'd all mankind
   With shews instead, meer shews of seeming pure,
   And banisht from mans life his happiest life,
   Simplicitie and spotless innocence.

   Milton, *Paradise Lost*, IV, 312

60 The love of a harlot, that is to say, the lust of
   sexual intercourse, which arises from mere external form, and absolutely all love which recognises
   any other cause than the freedom of the mind,
   easily passes into hatred, unless, which is worse, it
   becomes a species of delirium, and thereby discord
   is cherished rather than concord.

   Spinoza, *Ethics*, IV, Appendix XIX

61 He [Johnson] for a considerable time used to frequent the *Green Room,* and seemed to take delight
   in dissipating his gloom, by mixing in the sprightly chit-chat of the motley circle then to be found
   there. Mr. David Hume related to me from Mr.
   Garrick, that Johnson at last denied himself this
   amusement, from considerations of rigid virtue;
   saying, "I'll come no more behind your scenes,
   David; for the silk stockings and white bosoms of
   your actresses excite my amorous propensities."

   Boswell, *Life of Johnson* (1749)

62 *Boswell.* "So then, Sir, you would allow of no irregular intercourse whatever between the sexes?"
   Johnson. "To be sure I would not, Sir. I would punish it much more than it is done, and so restrain it.
   In all countries there has been fornication, as in
   all countries there has been theft; but there may
   be more or less of the one, as well as of the other,
   in proportion to the force of law. All men will
   naturally commit fornication, as all men will naturally steal. And, Sir, it is very absurd to argue, as
   has been often done, that prostitutes are necessary
   to prevent the violent effects of appetite from violating the decent order of life; nay, should be permitted, in order to preserve the chastity of our
   wives and daughters. Depend upon it, Sir, severe
   laws, steadily enforced, would be sufficient against
   those evils, and would promote marriage."

   Boswell, *Life of Johnson* (Apr. 5, 1776)

63 With the venerable proconsul [Gordianus], his
   son, who had accompanied him into Africa as his
   lieutenant, was likewise declared emperor. His
   manners were less pure, but his character was
   equally amiable with that of his father. Twenty-
   two acknowledge concubines, and a library of six-
   ty-two thousand volumes, attested the variety of
   his inclinations, and from the productions which
   he left behind him, it appears that the former as
   well as the latter were designed for use rather
   than ostentation.

   Gibbon, *Decline and Fall of the Roman
   Empire*, VII

64 Although the progress of civilisation has undoubtedly contributed to assuage the fiercer passions of
   human nature, it seems to have been less favourable to the virtue of chastity, whose most dangerous enemy is the softness of the mind. The refinements of life corrupt while they polish the
   intercourse of the sexes. The gross appetite of love
   becomes most dangerous when it is elevated, or
   rather, indeed, disguised by sentimental passion.

The elegance of dress, of motion, and of manners gives a lustre to beauty, and inflames the senses through the imagination. Luxurious entertainments, midnight dances, and licentious spectacles, present at once temptations and opportunity to female frailty.

Gibbon, *Decline and Fall of the Roman Empire*, IX

65 The laws of Constantine against rapes were dictated with very little indulgence for the most amiable weaknesses of human nature; since the description of that crime was applied not only to the brutal violence which compelled, but even to the gentle seduction which might persuade, an unmarried woman, under the age of twenty-five, to leave the house of her parents.

Gibbon, *Decline and Fall of the Roman Empire*, XIV

66 O Rose, thou art sick.
The invisible worm
That flies in the night
In the howling storm

Has found out thy bed
Of crimson joy,
And his dark secret love
Does thy life destroy.

Blake, *The Sick Rose*

67 *Mephistopheles.* What good is it to reap immediate pleasure?
The joy's not near so great, I say,
As if you first prepare the ground
With every sort of idle folly,
Knead and make ready your pretty dolly,
As many Romance tales expound.

Goethe, *Faust*, I, 2647

68   Julia's voice was lost, except in sighs,
Until too late for useful conversation;
The tears were gushing from her gentle eyes,
   I wish, indeed, they had not had occasion,
But who, alas! can love, and then be wise?
   Not that remorse did not oppose temptation;
A little still she strove, and much repented,
And whispering "I will ne'er consent"—consented.

Byron, *Don Juan*, I, 117

69 A wise woman should never give herself for the first time by appointment—it should be an unforeseen delight.

Stendhal, *On Love*, II, 60

70 If . . . one considers the important part which the sexual impulse in all its degrees and nuances plays not only on the stage and in novels, but also in the real world, where, next to the love of life, it shows itself the strongest and most powerful of motives, constantly lays claim to half the powers and thoughts of the younger portion of mankind, is the ultimate goal of almost all human effort, exerts an adverse influence on the most important events, interrupts the most serious occupations every hour, sometimes embarrasses for a while even the greatest minds, does not hesitate to intrude with its trash interfering with the negotiations of statesmen and the investigations of men of learning, knows how to slip its love letters and locks of hair even into ministerial portfolios and philosophical manuscripts, and no less devises daily the most entangled and the worst actions, destroys the most valuable relationships, breaks the firmest bonds, demands the sacrifice sometimes of life or health, sometimes of wealth, rank, and happiness, nay, robs those who are otherwise honest of all conscience, makes those who have hitherto been faithful, traitors; accordingly, on the whole, appears as a malevolent demon that strives to pervert, confuse, and overthrow everything;—then one will be forced to cry, Wherefore all this noise? Wherefore the straining and storming, the anxiety and want? It is merely a question of every Hans finding his Grethe. Why should such a trifle play so important a part, and constantly introduce disturbance and confusion into the well-regulated life of man? But to the earnest investigator the spirit of truth gradually reveals the answer. It is no trifle that is in question here; on the contrary, the importance of the matter is quite proportionate to the seriousness and ardour of the effort. The ultimate end of all love affairs, whether they are played in sock or cothurnus, is really more important than all other ends of human life, and is therefore quite worthy of the profound seriousness with which every one pursues it. That which is decided by it is nothing less than *the composition of the next generation.* The *dramatis personoe* who shall appear when we are withdrawn are here determined, both as regards their existence and their nature, by these frivolous love affairs.

Schopenhauer, *The World as Will and Idea*, Vol. III, 44

71 All love, however ethereally it may bear itself, is rooted in the sexual impulse alone, nay, it absolutely is only a more definitely determined, specialised, and indeed in the strictest sense individualised sexual impulse.

Schopenhauer, *The World as Will and Idea*, Vol. III, 44

72 With the great majority of animals . . . the taste for the beautiful is confined, as far as we can judge, to the attractions of the opposite sex.

Darwin, *Descent of Man*, I, 3

73 The law of battle for the possession of the female appears to prevail throughout the whole great class of mammals. Most naturalists will admit

that the greater size, strength, courage, and pugnacity of the male, his special weapons of offence, as well as his special means of defence, have been acquired or modified through that form of selection which I have called sexual. This does not depend on any superiority in the general struggle for life, but on certain individuals of one sex, generally the males, being successful in conquering other males, and leaving a larger number of offspring to inherit their superiority than do the less successful males.

Darwin, *Descent of Man*, II, 18

74 Of all the causes which have led to the differences in external appearance between the races of man, and to a certain extent between man and the lower animals, sexual selection has been the most efficient.

Darwin, *Descent of Man*, III, 20

75 *Ratikin*. There's something here, my dear boy [Alyosha], that you don't understand yet. A man will fall in love with some beauty, with a woman's body, or even with a part of a woman's body (a sensualist can understand that), and he'll abandon his own children for her, sell his father and mother, and his country, Russia, too. If he's honest, he'll steal; if he's humane, he'll murder; if he's faithful, he'll deceive. Pushkin, the poet of women's feet, sung of their feet in his verse. Others don't sing their praises, but they can't look at their feet without a thrill—and it's not only their feet. Contempt's no help here, brother, even if he did despise Grushenka. He does, but he can't tear himself away.

Dostoevsky, *Brothers Karamazov*, Pt. I, II, 7

76 Of the delights of *this* world man cares *most* for sexual intercourse. He will go any length for it—risk fortune, character, reputation, life itself. And what do you think he has done? In a thousand years you would never guess—*He has left it out of his heaven! Prayer takes its place.*

Mark Twain, *Notebook*

77 Christianity gave Eros poison to drink: he did not die of it but degenerated—into a vice.

Nietzsche, *Beyond Good and Evil*, IV, 168

78 What can be the aim of withholding from children, or let us say from young people, this information about the sexual life of human beings? Is it a fear of arousing interest in such matters prematurely, before it spontaneously stirs in them? Is it a hope of retarding by concealment of this kind the development of the sexual instinct in general, until such time as it can find its way into the only channels open to it in the civilized social order? Is it supposed that children would show no interest or understanding for the facts and riddles of sexual life if they were not prompted to do so by outside influence? Is it regarded as possible that the knowledge withheld from them will not reach them in other ways? Or is it genuinely and seriously intended that later on they should consider everything connected with sex as something despicable and abhorrent from which their parents and teachers wish to keep them apart as long as possible?

I am really at a loss to say which of these can be the motive for the customary concealment from children of everything connected with sex. I only know that these arguments are one and all equally foolish, and that I find it difficult to pay them the compliment of serious refutation.

Freud, *Sexual Enlightenment of Children*

79 Seriously, it is not so easy to define what the term *sexual* includes. Everything connected with the difference between the two sexes is perhaps the only way of hitting the mark; but you will find that too general and indefinite. If you take the sexual act itself as the central point, you will perhaps declare *sexual* to mean everything which is concerned with obtaining pleasurable gratification from the body (and particularly the sexual organs) of the opposite sex; in the narrowest sense, everything which is directed to the union of the genital organs and the performance of the sexual act. In doing so, however, you come very near to reckoning the sexual and the improper as identical, and childbirth would really have nothing to do with sex. If then you make the function of reproduction the kernel of sexuality you run the risk of excluding from it a whole host of things like masturbation, or even kissing, which are not directed towards reproduction, but which are nevertheless undoubtedly sexual. However, we have already found that attempts at definition always lead to difficulties; let us give up trying to do any better in this particular case.

Freud, *General Introduction to Psycho-Analysis*, XX

80 It is indeed one of the most important social tasks of education to restrain, confine, and subject to an individual control (itself identical with the demands of society) the sexual instinct when it breaks forth in the form of the reproductive function. In its own interests, accordingly, society would postpone the child's full development until it has attained a certain stage of intellectual maturity, since educability practically ceases with the full onset of the sexual instinct. Without this the instinct would break all bounds, and the laboriously erected structure of civilization would be swept away. Nor is the task of restraining it ever an easy one; success in this direction is often poor and, sometimes, only too great. At bottom society's motive is economic; since it has not means enough to support life for its members without work on their part, it must see to it that

the number of these members is restricted and their energies directed away from sexual activities on to their work—the eternal primordial struggle for existence, therefore, persisting to the present day.

Experience must have taught educators that the task of moulding the sexual will of the next generation can only be carried out by beginning to impose their influence very early, and intervening in the sexual life of children before puberty, instead of waiting till the storm bursts. Consequently almost all infantile sexual activities are forbidden or made disagreeable to the child; the ideal has been to make the child's life asexual, and in course of time it has come to this that it is really believed to be asexual, and is given out as such, even at the hands of science. In order, then, to avoid any contradiction with established beliefs and aims, the sexual activity of children is overlooked—no small achievement by the way—while science contents itself with otherwise explaining it away. The little child is supposed to be pure and innocent; he who says otherwise shall be condemned as a hardened blasphemer against humanity's tenderest and most sacred feelings.

The children alone take no part in this convention; they assert their animal nature naïvely enough and demonstrate persistently that they have yet to learn their *purity*. Strange to say, those who deny sexuality in children are the last to relax educative measures against it; they follow up with the greatest severity every manifestation of the *childish tricks* the existence of which they deny. Moreover, it is theoretically of great interest that the time of life which most flagrantly contradicts the prejudice about asexual childhood, the years of infancy up to five or six, is precisely the period which is veiled by oblivion in most people's memories; an oblivion which can only be dispelled completely by analysis but which even before this was sufficiently penetrable to allow some of the dreams of childhood to be retained.

> Freud, *General Introduction*
> *to Psycho-Analysis,* XX

81 A woman can be proud and stiff
When on love intent;
But Love has pitched his mansion in
The place of excrement;
For nothing can be sole or whole
That has not been rent.
> Yeats, *Crazy Jane Talks with the Bishop*

82 What lively lad most pleasured me
Of all that with me lay?
I answer that I gave my soul
And loved in misery,
But had great pleasure with a lad
That I loved bodily.

Flinging from his arms I laughed
To think his passion such
He fancied that I gave a soul
Did but our bodies touch,
And laughed upon his breast to think
Beast gave beast as much.

I gave what other women gave
That stepped out of their clothes,
But when this soul, its body off,
Naked to naked goes,
He it has found shall find therein
What none other knows,

And give his own and take his own
And rule in his own right;
And though it loved in misery
Close and cling so tight,
There's not a bird of day that dare
Extinguish that delight.
> Yeats, *A Last Confession*

3.4 | Friendship

Though friendship is exemplified and extolled in passages taken from the poets, biographers, and historians, the analysis of it is drawn mainly from the pages of philosophers, theologians, and essayists—especially Plato, Aristotle, and Cicero, Augustine and Aquinas, and Montaigne.

The most complete analysis is, perhaps, to be found in Aristotle's *Ethics*. He devotes two whole books of that work to the subject, from which there are many quotations here. His differentiation of the types of friendship sharply separates associations based on mutual pleasure or reciprocal utility from that relationship in which each of the persons is concerned with the good of the other. Only this, in his judgment, is true or genuine friendship; the others are counterfeits of it. True friendship, in other words, always involves the dominance of benevolent impulses, tending toward the benefit of the beloved, whereas the counterfeits of friendship spring primarily or purely from acquisitive desire—seeking something for one's self.

It is true friendship thus conceived that almost all the other writers have in mind when they discuss the subject or describe examples of it. It is also friendship thus conceived that is identified with a kind of love that is distinct from erotic or sexual love, whether between men and women or between persons of the same sex. How the love that is friendship is affected by the admixture of sexual love or by the absence of it is the obverse of a question raised earlier—how is sexual or erotic love affected by the admixture of friendship or the absence of it?

However these questions are answered, the reader will find that the difference between heterosexual and homosexual relationships enters into the consideration of the love that is friendship as well as into the consideration of sexual or erotic love. Can persons of the opposite sex be friends as readily and as enduringly as persons of the same gender? Are there fewer obstacles to genuine friendship among persons of the same sex?

---

1 Saul and Jonathan were lovely and pleasant in their lives, and in their death they were not divided: they were swifter than eagles, they were stronger than lions.

Ye daughters of Israel, weep over Saul, who clothed you in scarlet, with other delights, who put on ornaments of gold upon your apparel.

How are the mighty fallen in the midst of the battle! O Jonathan, thou wast slain in thine high places.

I am distressed for thee, my brother Jonathan: very pleasant hast thou been unto me: thy love to me was wonderful, passing the love of women.

II Samuel 1:23–26

2 Two are better than one; because they have a good reward for their labour.

For if they fall, the one will lift up his fellow: but woe to him that is alone when he falleth; for he hath not another to help him up.

Again, if two lie together, then they have heat: but how can one be warm alone?

And if one prevail against him, two shall withstand him; and a threefold cord is not quickly broken.

Ecclesiastes 4:9–12

3 *Diomedes.* When two go together, one of them at least looks forward
to see what is best; a man by himself, though he be careful,
still has less mind in him than two, and his wits have less weight.

Homer, *Iliad*, X, 224

4 *Darius.* There is nothing in all the world so pre-

cious as a friend who is at once wise and true.
Herodotus, History, V, 24

5 *Creon.*   To throw away
an honest friend is, as it were, to throw
your life away, which a man loves the best.
Sophocles, Oedipus the King, 611

6 *The Nurse.*   I have learned much
from my long life. The mixing bowl of friendship,
the love of one for the other, must be tempered.
Love must not touch the marrow of the soul.
Our affections must be breakable chains that we
can cast them off or tighten them.
Euripides, Hippolytus, 251

7 *Hecuba.*   Real friendship is shown in times of
    trouble;
prosperity is full of friends.
Euripides, Hecuba, 1227

8 *Menelaus.* Friends—and I mean real friends—re-
    serve nothing:
The property of one belongs to the other.
Euripides, Andromache, 376

9 *Pericles.* The doer of the favour is the firmer friend
of the two, in order by continued kindness to keep
the recipient in his debt; while the debtor feels less
keenly from the very consciousness that the return
he makes will be a payment, not a free gift.
Thucydides, Peloponnesian War, II, 40

10 *Socrates.* All people have their fancies; some desire
horses, and others dogs; and some are fond of
gold, and others of honour. Now, I have no violent desire of any of these things; but I have a
passion for friends; and I would rather have a
good friend than the best cock or quail in the
world: I would even go further, and say the best
horse or dog. Yea, by the dog of Egypt, I should
greatly prefer a real friend to all the gold of Darius, or even to Darius himself: I am such a lover
of friends as that. And when I see you and Lysis,
at your early age, so easily possessed of this treasure, and so soon, he of you, and you of him, I am
amazed and delighted, seeing that I myself, although I am now advanced in years, am so far
from having made a similar acquisition, that I do
not even know in what way a friend is acquired.
Plato, Lysis, 211B

11 Without friends no one would choose to live,
though he had all other goods; even rich men and
those in possession of office and of dominating
power are thought to need friends most of all; for
what is the use of such prosperity without the opportunity of beneficence, which is exercised chiefly and in its most laudable form towards friends?
Or how can prosperity be guarded and preserved
without friends? The greater it is, the more ex-

posed is it to risk. And in poverty and in other
misfortunes men think friends are the only refuge.
It helps the young, too, to keep from error; it aids
older people by ministering to their needs and
supplementing the activities that are failing from
weakness; those in the prime of life it stimulates to
noble actions . . . for with friends men are more
able both to think and to act.
Aristotle, Ethics, 1155^{a}5

12 There are therefore three kinds of friendship,
equal in number to the things that are lovable; for
with respect to each there is a mutual and recognized love, and those who love each other wish
well to each other in that respect in which they
love one another. Now those who love each other
for their utility do not love each other for themselves but in virtue of some good which they get
from each other. So too with those who love for
the sake of pleasure; it is not for their character
that men love ready-witted people, but because
they find them pleasant. Therefore those who love
for the sake of utility love for the sake of what is
good for *themselves,* and those who love for the sake
of pleasure do so for the sake of what is pleasant to
themselves, and not in so far as the other is the person loved but in so far as he is useful or pleasant.
And thus these friendships are only incidental; for
it is not as being the man he is that the loved
person is loved, but as providing some good or
pleasure. Such friendships, then, are easily dissolved, if the parties do not remain like themselves; for if the one party is no longer pleasant or
useful the other ceases to love him. . . .
    Perfect friendship is the friendship of men who
are good, and alike in virtue; for these wish well
alike to each other *qua* good, and they are good in
themselves. Now those who wish well to their
friends for their sake are most truly friends; for
they do this by reason of their own nature and not
incidentally; therefore their friendship lasts as
long as they are good—and goodness is an enduring thing. And each is good without qualification
and to his friend, for the good are both good without qualification and useful to each other. So too
they are pleasant; for the good are pleasant both
without qualification and to each other, since to
each his own activities and others like them are
pleasurable, and the actions of the good *are* the
same or like. And such a friendship is as might be
expected permanent, since there meet in it all the
qualities that friends should have. For all friendship is for the sake of good or of pleasure—good or
pleasure either in the abstract or such as will be
enjoyed by him who has the friendly feeling—and
is based on a certain resemblance; and to a friendship of good men all the qualities we have named
belong in virtue of the nature of the friends themselves; for in the case of this kind of friendship the
other qualities also are alike in both friends, and
that which is good without qualification is also

without qualification pleasant, and these are the most lovable qualities. Love and friendship therefore are found most and in their best form between such men.

But it is natural that such friendships should be infrequent; for such men are rare. Further, such friendship requires time and familiarity; as the proverb says, men cannot know each other till they have 'eaten salt together'; nor can they admit each other to friendship or be friends till each has been found lovable and been trusted by each. Those who quickly show the marks of friendship to each other wish to be friends, but are not friends unless they both are lovable and know the fact; for a wish for friendship may arise quickly, but friendship does not.

Aristotle, Ethics, 1156ᵃ7

13 Between sour and elderly people friendship arises less readily, inasmuch as they are less good-tempered and enjoy companionship less; for these are thought to be the greatest marks of friendship and most productive of it. This is why, while young men become friends quickly, old men do not; it is because men do not become friends with those in whom they do not delight; and similarly sour people do not quickly make friends either. But such men may bear goodwill to each other; for they wish one another well and aid one another in need; but they are hardly *friends* because they do not spend their days together nor delight in each other, and these are thought the greatest marks of friendship.

Aristotle, Ethics, 1158ᵃ1

14 There is another kind of friendship, viz. that which involves an inequality between the parties, for example that of father to son and in general of elder to younger, that of man to wife and in general that of ruler to subject. And these friendships differ also from each other; for it is not the same that exists between parents and children and between rulers and subjects, nor is even that of father to son the same as that of son to father, nor that of husband to wife the same as that of wife to husband. For the virtue and the function of each of these is different, and so are the reasons for which they love; the love and the friendship are therefore different also. Each party, then, neither gets the same from the other, nor ought to seek it; but when children render to parents what they ought to render to those who brought them into the world, and parents render what they should to their children, the friendship of such persons will be abiding and excellent. In all friendships implying inequality the love also should be proportional, that is, the better should be more loved than he loves, and so should the more useful, and similarly in each of the other cases; for when the love is in proportion to the merit of the parties, then in a sense arises equality, which is certainly held to be

characteristic of friendship.

Aristotle, Ethics, 1158ᵇ12

15 If, then, being is in itself desirable for the supremely happy man (since it is by its nature good and pleasant), and that of his friend is very much the same, a friend will be one of the things that are desirable. Now that which is desirable for him he must have, or he will be deficient in this respect. The man who is to be happy will therefore need virtuous friends.

Aristotle, Ethics, 1170ᵇ14

16 Friendship is a partnership, and as a man is to himself, so is he to his friend; now in his own case the consciousness of his being is desirable, and so therefore is the consciousness of his friend's being, and the activity of this consciousness is produced when they live together, so that it is natural that they aim at this. And whatever existence means for each class of men, whatever it is for whose sake they value life, in *that* they wish to occupy themselves with their friends; and so some drink together, others dice together, others join in athletic exercises and hunting, or in the study of philosophy, each class spending their days together in whatever they love most in life; for since they wish to live with their friends, they do and share in those things which give them the sense of living together. Thus the friendship of bad men turns out an evil thing (for because of their instability they unite in bad pursuits, and besides they become evil by becoming like each other), while the friendship of good men is good, being augmented by their companionship; and they are thought to become better too by their activities and by improving each other; for from each other they take the mould of the characteristics they approve—whence the saying 'noble deeds from noble men'.

Aristotle, Ethics, 1171ᵇ33

17 We may describe friendly feeling towards any one as wishing for him what you believe to be good things, not for your own sake but for his, and being inclined, so far as you can, to bring these things about. A friend is one who feels thus and excites these feelings in return: those who think they feel thus towards each other think themselves friends. This being assumed, it follows that your friend is the sort of man who shares your pleasure in what is good and your pain in what is unpleasant, for your sake and for no other reason. This pleasure and pain of his will be the token of his good wishes for you, since we all feel glad at getting what we wish for, and pained at getting what we do not. Those, then, are friends to whom the same things are good and evil.

Aristotle, Rhetoric, 1380ᵇ35

18 Kindness—under the influence of which a man is said to 'be kind'—may be defined as helpfulness

towards some one in need, not in return for anything, nor for the advantage of the helper himself, but for that of the person helped. Kindness is great if shown to one who is in great need, or who needs what is important and hard to get, or who needs it at an important and difficult crisis; or if the helper is the only, the first, or the chief person to give the help. Natural cravings constitute such needs; and in particular cravings, accompanied by pain, for what is not being attained. The appetites are cravings of this kind: sexual desire, for instance, and those which arise during bodily injuries and in dangers; for appetite is active both in danger and in pain. Hence those who stand by us in poverty or in banishment, even if they do not help us much, are yet really kind to us, because our need is great and the occasion pressing.

Aristotle, *Rhetoric,* 1385ª17

19 Now friendship may be thus defined: *a complete accord on all subjects human and divine, joined with mutual good will and affection.* And with the exception of wisdom, I am inclined to think nothing better than this has been given to man by the immortal gods. There are people who give the palm to riches or to good health, or to power and office, many even to sensual pleasures. This last is the ideal of brute beasts; and of the others we may say that they are frail and uncertain, and depend less on our own prudence than on the caprice of fortune. Then there are those who find the "chief good" in virtue. Well, that is a noble doctrine. But the very virtue they talk of is the parent and preserver of friendship, and without it friendship cannot possibly exist.

Cicero, *Friendship,* VI

20 *Laelius.* And great and numerous as are the blessings of friendship, this certainly is the sovereign one, that it gives us bright hopes for the future and forbids weakness and despair. In the face of a true friend a man sees as it were a second self. So that where his friend is he is; if his friend be rich, he is not poor; though he be weak, his friend's strength is his; and in his friend's life he enjoys a second life after his own is finished. This last is perhaps the most difficult to conceive. But such is the effect of the respect, the loving remembrance, and the regret of friends which follow us to the grave. While they take the sting out of death, they add a glory to the life of the survivors. Nay, if you eliminate from nature the tie of affection, there will be an end of house and city, nor will so much as the cultivation of the soil be left. If you don't see the virtue of friendship and harmony, you may learn it by observing the effects of quarrels and feuds. Was any family ever so well established, any state so firmly settled, as to be beyond the reach of utter destruction from animosities and factions? This may teach you the immense advantage of friendship.

Cicero, *Friendship,* VII

21 *Laelius.* True friendship is very difficult to find among those who engage in politics and the contest for office. Where can you find the man to prefer his friend's advancement to his own? And to say nothing of that, think how grievous and almost intolerable it is to most men to share political disaster. You will scarcely find any one who can bring himself to do that. And though what Ennius says is quite true—"the hour of need shows the friend indeed"—yet it is in these two ways that most people betray their untrustworthiness and inconstancy, by looking down on friends when they are themselves prosperous, or deserting them in their distress. A man, then, who has shown a firm, unshaken, and unvarying friendship in both these contingencies we must reckon as one of a class the rarest in the world, and all but superhuman.

Cicero, *Friendship,* XVII

22 Thinking of departed friends is to me something sweet and mellow. For when I had them with me it was with the feeling that I was going to lose them, and now that I have lost them I keep the feeling that I have them with me still.

Seneca, *Letters to Lucilius,* 63

23 Greater love hath no man than this, that a man lay down his life for his friends.

John 15:13

24 Did you never see little dogs caressing and playing with one another, so that you might say there is nothing more friendly? but, that you may know what friendship is, throw a bit of flesh among them, and you will learn.

Epictetus, *Discourses,* II, 22

25 During the period in which I first began to teach in the town of my birth, I had found a very dear friend, who was pursuing similar studies. He was about my own age, and was now coming, as I was, to the very flowering-time of young manhood. He had indeed grown up with me as a child and we had gone to school together and played together. Neither in those earlier days nor indeed in the later time of which I now speak was he a friend in the truest meaning of friendship: for there is no true friendship unless You weld it between souls that cleave together through that charity which is shed in our hearts by the Holy Ghost who is given to us.

Augustine, *Confessions,* IV, 4

26 All kinds of things rejoiced my soul in their [my friends'] company—to talk and laugh and do each other kindnesses; read pleasant books together, pass from lightest jesting to talk of the deepest things and back again; differ without rancour, as

a man might differ with himself, and when most rarely dissension arose find our normal agreement all the sweeter for it; teach each other or learn from each other; be impatient for the return of the absent, and welcome them with joy on their home-coming; these and such like things, proceeding from our hearts as we gave affection and received it back, and shown by face, by voice, by the eyes, and a thousand other pleasing ways, kindled a flame which fused our very souls and of many made us one. This is what men value in friends.

Augustine, *Confessions,* IV, 8–9

27 Is not the unfeigned confidence and mutual love of true and good friends our one solace in human society, filled as it is with misunderstandings and calamities? And yet the more friends we have, and the more widely they are scattered, the more numerous are our fears that some portion of the vast masses of the disasters of life may light upon them. For we are not only anxious lest they suffer from famine, war, disease, captivity, or the inconceivable horrors of slavery, but we are also affected with the much more painful dread that their friendship may be changed into perfidy, malice, and injustice. And when these contingencies actually occur—as they do the more frequently the more friends we have and the more widely they are scattered—and when they come to our knowledge, who but the man who has experienced it can tell with what pangs the heart is torn?

Augustine, *City of God,* XIX, 8

28 The happy man needs friends . . . not, indeed, to make use of them, since he suffices himself, nor to delight in them, since he possesses perfect delight in the operation of virtue, but for the purpose of a good operation, namely, that he may do good to them, that he may delight in seeing them do good, and again that he may be helped by them in his good work.

Aquinas, *Summa Theologica,* I–II, 4, 8

29 The movement of love has a twofold tendency: towards the good which a man wishes to someone, whether for himself or for another; and towards that to which he wishes some good. Accordingly, man has love of concupiscence towards the good that he wishes to another, and love of friendship towards him to whom he wishes good.

Aquinas, *Summa Theologica,* I–II, 26, 4

30 When our friends fall into sin, we ought not to deny them the benefits of friendship so long as there is hope of their mending their ways, and we ought to help them more readily to regain virtue than to recover money, had they lost it, since virtue is more akin than money to friendship. When, however, they fall into very great wickedness, and become incurable, we ought no longer to show

them friendliness.

Aquinas, *Summa Theologica,* II–II, 25, 6

31 Because the friendship of comrades originates through their own choice, love of this kind takes precedence of the love of kindred in matters where we are free to do as we choose, for instance in matters of action. Yet the friendship of kindred is more stable, since it is more natural, and preponderates over others in matters touching nature. Consequently we are more bound to them in the providing of necessaries.

Aquinas, *Summa Theologica,* II–II, 26, 8

32 *Pandar.* And I will gladly share with you your pain,
   If it turn out I can no comfort bring;
   For 'tis a friend's right, please let me explain,
   To share in woful as in joyful things.

Chaucer, *Troilus and Cressida,* I, 85

33 This perfect friendship I speak of is indivisible: each one gives himself so wholly to his friend that he has nothing left to distribute elsewhere; on the contrary, he is sorry that he is not double, triple, or quadruple, and that he has not several souls and several wills, to confer them all on this one object. Common friendships can be divided up: one may love in one man his beauty, in another his easygoing ways, in another his liberality, in one paternal love, in another brotherly love, and so forth; but this friendship that possesses the soul and rules it with absolute sovereignty cannot possibly be double. If two called for help at the same time, which one would you run to? If they demanded conflicting services of you, how would you arrange it? If one confided to your silence a thing that would be useful for the other to know, how would you extricate yourself? A single dominant friendship dissolves all other obligations. The secret I have sworn to reveal to no other man, I can impart without perjury to the one who is not another man: he is myself. It is a great enough miracle to be doubled, and those who talk of tripling themselves do not realize the loftiness of the thing: nothing is extreme that can be matched. And he who supposes that of two men I love one just as much as the other, and that they love each other and me just as much as I love them, multiplies into a fraternity the most singular and unified of all things, of which even a single one is the rarest thing in the world to find.

Montaigne, *Essays,* I, 28, Of Friendship

34 We need very strong ears to hear ourselves judged frankly; and because there are few who can endure frank criticism without being stung by it, those who venture to criticize us perform a remarkable act of friendship; for to undertake to wound and offend a man for his own good is to have a healthy love for him. I find it a rough task

to judge a man in whom the bad qualities exceed the good. Plato prescribes three qualities in a man who wants to examine another man's soul: knowledge, good will, boldness.

Montaigne, *Essays*, III, 13, Of Experience

35 *Amiens.* Blow, blow, thou winter wind,
Thou art not so unkind
　　As man's ingratitude;
Thy tooth is not so keen,
Because thou art not seen,
　　Although thy breath be rude. . . .
Freeze, freeze, thou bitter sky,
That dost not bite so nigh
　　As benefits forgot:
Though thou the waters warp,
Thy sting is not so sharp
　　As friend remember'd not.

Shakespeare, *As You Like It*, II, vii, 174

36 *Polonius.* Be thou familiar, but by no means vulgar.
Those friends thou hast, and their adoption tried,
Grapple them to thy soul with hoops of steel;
But do not dull thy palm with entertainment
Of each new-hatch'd, unfledged comrade.

Shakespeare, *Hamlet*, I, iii, 61

37 *Buckingham.* Heaven has an end in all; yet, you that hear me,
This from a dying man receive as certain:
Where you are liberal of your loves and counsels
Be sure you be not loose; for those you make friends
And give your hearts to, when they once perceive
The least rub in your fortunes, fall away
Like water from ye, never found again
But where they mean to sink ye.

Shakespeare, *Henry VIII*, II, i, 124

38 Well, *Sancho,* (said Don *Quixote* . . . turning to his 'Squire) did not I tell thee I should not want 'Squires; behold who offers me his Service, the most excellent Batchelor of Arts, *Sampson Carrasco,* the perpetual Darling of the Muses, and Glory of the *Salamanca-*Schools, sound and active of Body, patient of Labour, inur'd to Abstinence, silent in Misfortune, and in short, endow'd with all the Accomplishments that constitute a 'Squire. But forbid it Heav'n, that to indulge my private Inclinations I should presume to weaken the whole Body of Learning, by removing from it so substantial a Pillar, so vast a Repository of Sciences, and so eminent a Branch of the Liberal Arts. No, my Friend, remain thou another *Sampson* in thy Country, be the Honour of *Spain,* and the Delight of thy ancient Parents; I shall content myself with any 'Squire, since *Sancho* does not vouchsafe to go with me. I do, I do, (cry'd *Sancho,* relenting with Tears in his Eyes) I do vouchsafe; it shall never be said of *Sancho Pança,* no longer Pipe no longer Dance.

Cervantes, *Don Quixote,* II, 7

39 My Master, quoth the Squire of the Wood, is more stout than foolish, but more Knave than either. Mine is not like yours then, quoth *Sancho,* he has not one Grain of Knavery in him; he's as dull as an old crack'd Pitcher, hurts no Body, does all the Good he can to every Body; a Child may persuade him it is Night at Noon-Day, and he is so simple, that I can't help loving him, with all my Heart and Soul, and can't leave him, in spite of all his Follies.

Cervantes, *Don Quixote,* II, 13

40 It had been hard for him that spake it to have put more truth and untruth together in few words than in that speech, "Whosoever is delighted in solitude is either a wild beast or a god." For it is most true that a natural and secret hatred and aversation towards society in any man hath somewhat of the savage beast; but it is most untrue that it should have any character at all of the divine nature, except it proceed, not out of a pleasure in solitude, but out of a love and desire to sequester a man's self for a higher conversation, such as is found to have been falsely and feignedly in some of the heathen, as Epimenides the Candian, Numa the Roman, Empedocles the Sicilian, and Apollonius of Tyana, and truly and really in divers of the ancient hermits and holy fathers of the church. But little do men perceive what solitude is, and how far it extendeth. For a crowd is not company; and faces are but a gallery of pictures; and talk but a tinkling cymbal, where there is no love. The Latin adage meeteth with it a little: *Magna civitas, magna solitudo* [A great city is a great solitude]; because in a great town friends are scattered; so that there is not that fellowship, for the most part, which is in less neighbourhoods. But we may go further, and affirm most truly that it is a mere and miserable solitude to want true friends, without which the world is but a wilderness; and even in this sense also of solitude, whosoever in the frame of his nature and affections is unfit for friendship, he taketh it of the beast, and not from humanity.

Bacon, *Of Friendship*

41 We may have affection for a flower, a bird, a horse; but unless we have a very ill-regulated mind, we can have friendship for men alone. And they are so truly the object of this passion, that there is no man so imperfect that we cannot have for him a very perfect friendship, when we are loved by him, and when we have a truly noble and generous soul.

Descartes, *Passions of the Soul*, LXXXIII

42 Human life is thus only a perpetual illusion; men deceive and flatter each other. No one speaks of us in our presence as he does of us in our absence.

Human society is founded on mutual deceit; few friendships would endure if each knew what his friend said of him in his absence, although he then spoke in sincerity and without passion.

Man is, then, only disguise, falsehood, and hypocrisy, both in himself and in regard to others. He does not wish any one to tell him the truth; he avoids telling it to others, and all these dispositions, so removed from justice and reason, have a natural root in his heart. I set it down as a fact that if all men knew what each said of the other, there would not be four friends in the world.

Pascal, *Pensées*, II, 100–101

43 *Alceste.* The more we love our friends, the less we flatter them; it is by excusing nothing that pure love shows itself.

Molière, *Le Misanthrope*, II, v

44 In all distresses of our friends,
We first consult our private ends;
While nature, kindly bent to ease us,
Points out some circumstance to please us.

Swift, *On the Death of Dr. Swift*, 7

45 I hope my friends will pardon me when I declare, I know none of them without a fault; and I should be sorry if I could imagine I had any friend who could not see mine. Forgiveness of this kind we give and demand in turn. It is an exercise of friendship, and perhaps none of the least pleasant. And this forgiveness we must bestow, without desire of amendment. There is, perhaps, no surer mark of folly, than an attempt to correct the natural infirmities of those we love.

Fielding, *Tom Jones*, II, 7

46 The only way when friends quarrel is to see it out fairly in a friendly manner, as a man may call it, either with a fist, or sword, or pistol, according as they like, and then let it be all over; for my own part, d—n me if ever I love my friend better than when I am fighting with him! To bear malice is more like a Frenchman than an Englishman.

Fielding, *Tom Jones*, IX, 4

47 Friendship is the marriage of the soul; and this marriage is subject to divorce. It is a tacit contract between two sensitive and virtuous persons. I say "sensitive," because a monk, a recluse can be not wicked and live without knowing what friendship is. I say "virtuous," because the wicked have only accomplices; voluptuaries have companions in debauch, self-seekers have partners, politicians get partisans; the generality of idle men have attachments; princes have courtiers; virtuous men alone have friends.

Voltaire, *Philosophical Dictionary: Friendship*

48 [Johnson] was well acquainted with Mr. Henry Hervey, one of the branches of the noble family of that name, who had been quartered at Lichfield as an officer of the army, and had at this time a house in London, where Johnson was frequently entertained, and had an opportunity of meeting genteel company. Not very long before his death, he mentioned this, among other particulars of his life, which he was kindly communicating to me; and he described this early friend, "Harry Hervey," thus: "He was a vicious man, but very kind to me. If you call a dog *Hervey*, I shall love him."

Boswell, *Life of Johnson* (1737)

49 I have often thought, that as longevity is generally desired, and I believe, generally expected, it would be wise to be continually adding to the number of our friends, that the loss of some may be supplied by others. Friendship, "the wine of life," should like a well-stocked cellar, be thus continually renewed; and it is consolatory to think, that although we can seldom add what will equal the generous *first-growths* of our youth, yet friendship becomes insensibly old in much less time than is commonly imagined, and not many years are required to make it very mellow and pleasant. *Warmth* will, no doubt, make a considerable difference. Men of affectionate temper and bright fancy will coalesce a great deal sooner than those who are cold and dull.

The proposition which I have now endeavoured to illustrate was, at a subsequent period of his life, the opinion of Johnson himself. He said to Sir Joshua Reynolds, "If a man does not make new acquaintance as he advances through life, he will soon find himself left alone. A man, Sir, should keep his friendship *in constant repair*."

Boswell, *Life of Johnson* (1755)

50 A literary lady of large fortune was mentioned, as one who did good to many, but by no means "by stealth," and instead of "blushing to find it fame," acted evidently from vanity. *Johnson.* "I have seen no beings who do as much good from benevolence, as she does, from whatever motive. If there are such under the earth, or in the clouds, I wish they would come up, or come down. What Soame Jenyns says upon this subject is not to be minded; he is a wit. No, Sir; to act from pure benevolence is not possible for finite beings. Human benevolence is mingled with vanity, interest, or some other motive."

Boswell, *Life of Johnson* (Apr. 1776)

51 On Wednesday, May 19, I sat a part of the evening with him [Johnson], by ourselves. I observed, that the death of our friends might be a consolation against the fear of our own dissolution, because we might have more friends in the other world than in this. He perhaps felt this as a reflection upon his apprehension as to death; and said, with heat, "How can a man know *where* his departed friends are, or whether they will be his

friends in the other world? How many friendships have you known formed upon principles of virtue? Most friendships are formed by caprice or by chance, mere confederacies in vice or leagues in folly."

Boswell, *Life of Johnson* (May 19, 1784)

52 In civilised society [man] stands at all times in need of the cooperation and assistance of great multitudes, while his whole life is scarce sufficient to gain the friendship of a few persons.

Adam Smith, *Wealth of Nations,* I, 2

53 Love is an agreeable; resentment, a disagreeable, passion: and accordingly we are not half so anxious that our friends should adopt our friendships, as that they should enter into our resentments.

Adam Smith, *Theory of Moral Sentiments,* I, 1

54 They who would confine friendship to two persons, seem to confound the wise security of friendship with the jealousy and folly of love. The hasty, fond, and foolish intimacies of young people, founded commonly upon some slight similarity of character altogether unconnected with good conduct, upon a taste, perhaps, for the same studies, the same amusements, the same diversions, or upon their agreement in some singular principle or opinion not commonly adopted; those intimacies which a freak begins, and which a freak puts an end to, how agreeable soever they may appear while they last, can by no means deserve the sacred and venerable name of friendship.

Adam Smith, *Theory of Moral Sentiments,* I, 2

55 Friendship (in its perfection) is the union of two persons through equal mutual love and respect. One easily sees that it is an ideal in which a morally good will unites both parties in sympathy and shared well-being. If it does not also cause life's entire happiness, the acceptance of this ideal in such mutual sentiment includes the worthiness to be happy, so that friendship among men is our duty. It is easy to see that although aiming at friendship, as a maximum of good sentiment toward one another, is no ordinary duty but rather an honorable one proposed by reason, yet perfect friendship is a mere idea (but still a practically necessary one), unattainable in every attempt to realize it.

Kant, *Elements of Ethics,* 46

56 A friend in need—how much to be wished for (assuming that he is an active one, helpful at his own expense)! But it is also a great burden to feel oneself tied to the destiny of others and laden with alien responsibilities. Friendship, therefore, cannot be a bond aimed at mutual advantage, but must be purely moral; and the assistance which each may count on from the other in case of need must not be thought of as the end and determin-

ing ground of friendship (for thereby one person would partly lose the respect of the other), but only as the outward sign of their inner, heartfelt benevolence (without putting it to a test, which is always dangerous). Friendship is not based on advantage, for each friend is magnanimously concerned with sparing the other any burden, bearing any such burden entirely by himself, and, yes, even completely concealing it from the other; but each one, nevertheless, can always flatter himself with the idea that in case of need he could definitely count upon the other's help. But if one accepts a benefit from the other, then he can probably count on an equality in their love, but not in their respect; for he sees himself plainly as a step lower, inasmuch as he is obligated and yet not reciprocally able to obligate.

Kant, *Elements of Ethics,* 46

57 To stand in true relations with men in a false age is worth a fit of insanity, is it not? We can seldom go erect. Almost every man we meet requires some civility—requires to be humored; he has some fame, some talent, some whim of religion or philanthropy in his head that is not to be questioned, and which spoils all conversation with him. But a friend is a sane man who exercises not my ingenuity, but me. My friend gives me entertainment without requiring any stipulation on my part. A friend therefore is a sort of paradox in nature. I who alone am, I who see nothing in nature whose existence I can affirm with equal evidence to my own, behold now the semblance of my being, in all its height, variety and curiosity, reiterated in a foreign form; so that a friend may well be reckoned the masterpiece of nature.

Emerson, *Friendship*

58 "Wal'r, my boy," replied the captain, "in the Proverbs of Solomon you will find the following words, 'May we never want a friend in need, nor a bottle to give him!' When found, make a note of."

Dickens, *Dombey and Son,* I, 15

59 There is no place like a bed for confidential disclosures between friends. Man and wife, they say, there open the very bottom of their souls to each other; and some old couples often lie and chat over old times till nearly morning.

Melville, *Moby Dick,* X

60 I dream'd in a dream I saw a city invincible to the attacks of the whole of the rest of the earth, I dream'd that was the new city of Friends.

Whitman, *I Dream'd in a Dream*

61 *Father Zossima.* Until you have become really, in actual fact, a brother to everyone, brotherhood will not come to pass. No sort of scientific teaching, no kind of common interest, will ever teach

men to share property and privileges with equal consideration for all. Everyone will think his share too small and they will be always envying, complaining and attacking one another. You ask when it will come to pass; it will come to pass, but first we have to go through the period of isolation. . . . The isolation that prevails everywhere, above all in our age—it has not fully developed, it has not reached its limit yet. For everyone strives to keep his individuality as apart as possible, wishes to secure the greatest possible fullness of life for himself; but meantime all his efforts result not in attaining fullness of life but self-destruction, for instead of self-realisation he ends by arriving at complete solitude. All mankind in our age have split up into units, they all keep apart, each in his own groove; each one holds aloof, hides himself and hides what he has, from the rest, and he ends by being repelled by others and repelling them. He heaps up riches by himself and thinks, 'How strong I am now and how secure,' and in his madness he does not understand that the more he heaps up, the more he sinks into self-destructive impotence. For he is accustomed to rely upon himself alone and to cut himself off from the whole; he has trained himself not to believe in the help of others, in men and in humanity, and only trembles for fear he should lose his money and the privileges that he has won for himself. Everywhere in these days men have, in their mockery, ceased to understand that the true security is to be found in social solidarity rather than in isolated individual effort. But this terrible individualism must inevitably have an end, and all will suddenly understand how unnaturally they are separated from one another. It will be the spirit of the time, and people will marvel that they have sat so long in darkness without seeing the light. And then the sign of the Son of Man will be seen in the heavens. . . . But, until then, we must keep the banner flying. Sometimes even if he has to do it alone, and his conduct seems to be crazy, a man must set an example, and so draw men's souls out of their solitude, and spur them to some act of brotherly love, that the great idea may not die.

Dostoevsky, *Brothers Karamazov*, Pt. II, VI, 2

62 The holy passion of Friendship is of so sweet and steady and loyal and enduring a nature that it will last through a whole lifetime, if not asked to lend money.

Mark Twain, *Pudd'nhead Wilson's Calendar*, VIII

63 We have to conclude that all the feelings of sympathy, friendship, trust and so forth which we expend in life are genetically connected with sexuality and have developed out of purely sexual desires by an enfeebling of their sexual aim, however pure and non-sensual they may appear in the forms they take on to our conscious self-perception. To begin with we knew none but sexual objects; psycho-analysis shows us that those persons whom in real life we merely respect or are fond of may be sexual objects to us in our unconscious minds still.

Freud, *Dynamics of the Transference*

64 A friend's only gift is himself, and friendship is not friendship, it is not a form of free or liberal society, if it does not terminate in an ideal possession, in an object loved for its own sake. Such objects can be ideas only, not forces, for forces are subterranean and instrumental things, having only such value as they borrow from their ulterior effects and manifestations. To praise the utility of friendship, as the ancients so often did, and to regard it as a political institution justified, like victory or government, by its material results, is to lose one's moral bearings. The value of victory or good government is rather to be found in the fact that, among other things, it might render friendship possible. We are not to look now for what makes friendship useful, but for whatever may be found in friendship that may lend utility to life.

Santayana, *Life of Reason*, II, 6

65 Friendship may indeed come to exist without sensuous liking or comradeship to pave the way; but unless intellectual sympathy and moral appreciation are powerful enough to react on natural instinct and to produce in the end the personal affection which at first was wanting, friendship does not arise. Recognition given to a man's talent or virtue is not properly friendship. Friends must desire to live as much as possible together and to share their work, thoughts, and pleasures. Goodfellowship and sensuous affinity are indispensable to give spiritual communion a personal accent; otherwise men would be indifferent vehicles for such thoughts and powers as emanated from them, and attention would not be in any way arrested or refracted by the human medium through which it beheld the good.

Santayana, *Life of Reason*, II, 6

3.5 | Charity and Mercy

The main texts quoted in this section take their departure from the message of the Gospels that God is love and from the precepts of charity enunciated by Jesus Christ—that one should love God with all one's heart and all one's soul, and one's neighbor as one's self. The quotations from Christian theologians, apologists, and poets constitute an extended commentary on the love that is an obligation for those who follow the teachings of Christ. Augustine and Aquinas, particularly, show how fundamental and far-reaching the precepts of charity are, and explain why, of the three theological virtues—faith, hope, and charity—the greatest is charity.

One impulse of charity, too often allowed to obscure more important aspects of it, involves care or concern for the relief of the needy or suffering. We have, therefore, included passages that praise or recommend almsgiving. We have also included texts that extol mercy and recommend forgiveness to temper strict justice. These too reflect aspects of charity in the theological or religious sense, whether Jewish or Christian. But we have not included here passages that dwell on the benevolent impulses at the heart of friendship when pagan or later writers who treat such love approach it entirely from a secular and not a religious point of view.

---

1 Thou shalt love thy neighbour as thyself.

Leviticus 19:18

2 The Lord is merciful and gracious, slow to anger, and plenteous in mercy.

He will not always chide: neither will he keep his anger for ever.

He hath not dealt with us after our sins; nor rewarded us according to our iniquities.

For as the heaven is high above the earth, so great is his mercy toward them that fear him.

As far as the east is from the west, so far hath he removed our transgressions from us.

Like as a father pitieth his children, so the Lord pitieth them that fear him.

For he knoweth our frame; he remembereth that we are dust.

As for man, his days are as grass: as a flower of the field, so he flourisheth.

For the wind passeth over it, and it is gone; and the place thereof shall know it no more.

But the mercy of the Lord is from everlasting to everlasting upon them that fear him, and his righteousness unto children's children.

Psalm 103:8–17

3 If thine enemy be hungry, give him bread to eat; and if he be thirsty, give him water to drink:

For thou shalt heap coals of fire upon his head, and the Lord shall reward thee.

Proverbs 25:21–22

4 Take heed that ye do not your alms before men, to be seen of them: otherwise ye have no reward of your Father which is in heaven.

Therefore when thou doest thine alms, do not sound a trumpet before thee, as the hypocrites do in the synagogues and in the streets, that they may have glory of men. Verily I say unto you, They have their reward.

But when thou doest alms, let not thy left hand know what thy right hand doeth:

That thine alms may be in secret: and thy Father which seeth in secret himself shall reward thee openly.

Matthew 6:1–4

5 Therefore is the kingdom of heaven likened unto a certain king, which would take account of his servants.

And when he had begun to reckon, one was brought unto him, which owed him ten thousand talents.

But forasmuch as he had not to pay, his lord commanded him to be sold, and his wife, and children, and all that he had, and payment to be made.

The servant therefore fell down, and worshipped him, saying, Lord, have patience with me, and I will pay thee all.

Then the lord of that servant was moved with

compassion, and loosed him, and forgave him the debt.

But the same servant went out, and found one of his fellowservants, which owed him an hundred pence: and he laid hands on him, and took him by the throat, saying, Pay me that thou owest.

And his fellowservant fell down at his feet, and besought him, saying, Have patience with me, and I will pay thee all.

And he would not: but went and cast him into prison, till he should pay the debt.

So when his fellowservants saw what was done, they were very sorry, and came and told unto their lord all that was done.

Then his lord, after that he had called him, said unto him, O thou wicked servant, I forgave thee all that debt, because thou desiredst me:

Shouldest not thou also have had compassion on thy fellowservant, even as I had pity on thee?

And his lord was wroth, and delivered him to the tormentors, till he should pay all that was due unto him.

So likewise shall my heavenly Father do also unto you, if ye from your hearts forgive not every one his brother their trespasses.

Matthew 18:23–35

6 Then shall the King say unto them on his right hand, Come, ye blessed of my Father, inherit the kingdom prepared for you from the foundation of the world:

For I was an hungred, and ye gave me meat: I was thirsty, and ye gave me drink: I was a stranger, and ye took me in:

Naked, and ye clothed me: I was sick, and ye visited me: I was in prison, and ye came unto me.

Then shall the righteous answer him, saying, Lord, when saw we thee an hungred, and fed thee? or thirsty, and gave thee drink?

When saw we thee a stranger, and took thee in? or naked, and clothed thee?

Or when saw we thee sick, or in prison, and came unto thee?

And the King shall answer and say unto them, Verily I say unto you, Inasmuch as ye have done it unto one of the least of these my brethren, ye have done it unto me.

Matthew 25:34–40

7 And one of the scribes came, and having heard them reasoning together, and perceiving that he had answered them well, asked him, Which is the first commandment of all?

And Jesus answered him, The first of all the commandments is, Hear, O Israel; The Lord our God is one Lord:

And thou shalt love the Lord thy God with all thy heart, and with all thy soul, and with all thy mind, and with all thy strength: this is the first commandment.

And the second is like, namely this, Thou shalt love thy neighbour as thyself. There is none other commandment greater than these.

Mark 12:28–31

8 And, behold, a certain lawyer stood up, and tempted him, saying, Master, what shall I do to inherit eternal life?

He said unto him, What is written in the law? how readest thou?

And he answering said, Thou shalt love the Lord thy God with all thy heart, and with all thy soul, and with all thy strength, and with all thy mind; and thy neighbour as thyself.

And he said unto him, Thou hast answered right: this do, and thou shalt live.

But he, willing to justify himself, said unto Jesus, And who is my neighbour?

And Jesus answering said, A certain man went down from Jerusalem to Jericho, and fell among thieves, which stripped him of his raiment, and wounded him, and departed, leaving him half dead.

And by chance there came down a certain priest that way: and when he saw him, he passed by on the other side.

And likewise a Levite, when he was at the place, came and looked on him, and passed by on the other side.

But a certain Samaritan, as he journeyed, came where he was: and when he saw him, he had compassion on him,

And went to him, and bound up his wounds, pouring in oil and wine, and set him on his own beast, and brought him to an inn, and took care of him.

And on the morrow when he departed, he took out two pence, and gave them to the host, and said unto him, Take care of him; and whatsoever thou spendest more, when I come again, I will repay thee.

Which now of these three, thinkest thou, was neighbour unto him that fell among the thieves?

And he said, He that shewed mercy on him. Then said Jesus unto him, Go, and do thou likewise.

Luke 10:25–37

9 Jesus went unto the mount of Olives.

And early in the morning he came again into the temple, and all the people came unto him; and he sat down, and taught them.

And the scribes and Pharisees brought unto him a woman taken in adultery; and when they had set her in the midst,

They say unto him, Master, this woman was taken in adultery, in the very act.

Now Moses in the law commanded us, that such should be stoned: but what sayest thou?

This they said, tempting him, that they might have to accuse him. But Jesus stooped down, and with his finger wrote on the ground, as though he heard them not.

So when they continued asking him, he lifted up himself, and said unto them, He that is without sin among you, let him first cast a stone at her.

And again he stooped down, and wrote on the ground.

And they which heard it, being convicted by their own conscience, went out one by one, beginning at the eldest, even unto the last: and Jesus was left alone, and the woman standing in the midst.

When Jesus had lifted up himself, and saw none but the woman, he said unto her, Woman, where are those thine accusers? hath no man condemned thee?

She said, No man, Lord. And Jesus said unto her, Neither do I condemn thee: go, and sin no more.

John 8:1–11

10 It is more blessed to give than to receive.

Acts 20:35

11 Though I speak with the tongues of men and of angels, and have not charity, I am become as sounding brass, or a tinkling cymbal.

And though I have the gift of prophecy, and understand all mysteries, and all knowledge; and though I have all faith, so that I could remove mountains, and have not charity, I am nothing.

And though I bestow all my goods to feed the poor, and though I give my body to be burned, and have not charity, it profiteth me nothing.

Charity suffereth long, and is kind; charity envieth not; charity vaunteth not itself, is not puffed up,

Doth not behave itself unseemly, seeketh not her own, is not easily provoked, thinketh no evil;

Rejoiceth not in iniquity, but rejoiceth in the truth;

Beareth all things, believeth all things, hopeth all things, endureth all things.

Charity never faileth: but whether there be prophecies, they shall fail; whether there be tongues, they shall cease; whether there be knowledge, it shall vanish away.

For we know in part, and we prophesy in part.

But when that which is perfect is come, then that which is in part shall be done away.

When I was a child, I spake as a child, I understood as a child, I thought as a child: but when I became a man, I put away childish things.

For now we see through a glass, darkly; but then face to face: now I know in part; but then shall I know even as also I am known.

And now abideth faith, hope, charity, these three; but the greatest of these is charity.

I Corinthians 13:1–13

12 Charity shall cover the multitude of sins.

I Peter 4:8

13 Beloved, let us love one another: for love is of God; and every one that loveth is born of God, and knoweth God.

He that loveth not knoweth not God; for God is love.

I John 4:7–8

14 Kindness or humanity has a larger field than bare justice to exercise itself in; law and justice we cannot, in the nature of things, employ on others than men; but we may extend our goodness and charity even to irrational creatures; and such acts flow from a gentle nature, as water from an abundant spring. It is doubtless the part of a kind-natured man to keep even worn-out horses and dogs, and not only take care of them when they are foals and whelps, but also when they are grown old.

Plutarch, *Marcus Cato*

15 [The] divine Master inculcates two precepts—the love of God and the love of our neighbour—and as in these precepts a man finds three things he has to love—God, himself, and his neighbour—and that he who loves God loves himself thereby, it follows that he must endeavour to get his neighbour to love God, since he is ordered to love his neighbour as himself. He ought to make this endeavour in behalf of his wife, his children, his household, all within his reach, even as he would wish his neighbour to do the same for him if he needed it; and consequently he will be at peace, or in well-ordered concord, with all men, as far as in him lies.

Augustine, *City of God*, XIX, 14

16 We are commanded to love one another: but it is a question whether man is to be loved by man for his own sake, or for the sake of something else. If it is for his own sake, we enjoy him; if it is for the sake of something else, we use him. It seems to me, then, that he is to be loved for the sake of something else. For if a thing is to be loved for its own sake, then in the enjoyment of it consists a happy life, the hope of which at least, if not yet the reality, is our comfort in the present time. But a curse is pronounced on him who places his hope in man.

Augustine, *Christian Doctrine*, I, 22

17 But if they shall so love God with all their heart, and all their mind, and all their soul, that still all the heart, and all the mind, and all the soul shall not suffice for the worthiness of this love; doubtless they will so rejoice with all their heart, and all their mind, and all their soul, that all the heart, and all the mind, and all the soul shall not suffice for the fulness of their joy.

Anselm of Canterbury,
Proslogium, XXV

18 Charity signifies not only the love of God but also a certain friendship with Him; and this implies, besides love, a certain mutual return of love, together with mutual communion. . . . Now this fellowship of man with God, which consists in a certain familiar intercourse with Him, is begun here, in this life, by grace, but will be perfected in the future life, by glory; each of which things we hold by faith and hope. Therefore just as friendship with a person would be impossible if one disbelieved in, or despaired of, the possibility of his fellowship or familiar intercourse, so too, friendship with God, which is charity, is impossible without faith, so as to believe in this fellowship and intercourse with God, and to hope to attain to this fellowship. Therefore charity is altogether impossible without faith and hope.

Aquinas, *Summa Theologica*, I–II, 65, 5

19 Since good, in human acts, depends on their being regulated by the due rule, it is necessary that human virtue, which is a principle of good acts, consist in attaining the rule of human acts. Now the rule of human acts is twofold . . . , namely, human reason and God. Yet God is the first rule, by which even human reason must be regulated. Consequently the theological virtues which consist in attaining this first rule, since their object is God, are more excellent than the moral, or the intellectual virtues, which consist in attaining human reason: and it follows that among the theological virtues themselves, the first place belongs to that which attains God most.

Now that which is of itself always ranks before that which is by another. But faith and hope attain God indeed in so far as we derive from Him the knowledge of truth or the acquisition of good; but charity attains God Himself that it may rest in Him, but not that something may accrue to us from Him. Hence charity is more excellent than faith or hope, and, consequently, than all the other virtues, just as prudence, which by itself attains reason, is more excellent than the other moral virtues, which attain reason in so far as it appoints the mean in human operations of passions.

Aquinas, *Summa Theologica*, II–II, 23, 6

20 Charity . . . consists in man's loving God above all things, and subjecting himself to Him entirely, by referring all that is his to God. It is therefore of the very notion of charity that man should so love God as to wish to submit to Him in all things, and always to follow the rule of His commandments; for whatever is contrary to His commandments is manifestly contrary to charity, and therefore by its very nature is capable of destroying charity.

If indeed charity were an acquired habit dependent on the power of its subject, it would not necessarily be removed by one mortal sin, for act is directly contrary, not to habit but to act. Now the endurance of a habit in its subject does not require the endurance of its act, so that when a contrary act supervenes, the acquired habit is not at once done away. But charity, being an infused habit, depends on the action of God Who infuses it, Who stands in relation to the infusion and preservation of charity, as the sun does to the diffusion of light in the air. . . . Consequently, just as the light would cease at once in the air, were an obstacle placed to its being lit up by the sun, even so charity ceases at once to be in the soul through the placing of an obstacle to the outpouring of charity by God into the soul.

Now it is evident that through every mortal sin which is contrary to God's commandments, an obstacle is placed to the outpouring of charity, since from the very fact that a man chooses to prefer sin to God's friendship, which requires that we should follow His will, it follows that the habit of charity is lost at once through one mortal sin.

Aquinas, *Summa Theologica*, II–II, 24, 12

21 Love of one's enemies may be understood in three ways. First, as though we were to love our enemies as enemies; this is perverse, and contrary to charity, since it implies love of that which is evil in another.

Secondly love of one's enemies may mean that we love them as to their nature, but in a universal way, and in this sense charity requires that we should love our enemies, namely, that in loving God and our neighbour, we should not exclude our enemies from the love given to our neighbour in general.

Thirdly love of one's enemies may be considered as specially directed to them, namely, that we should have a special movement of love towards our enemies. Charity does not require this absolutely, because it does not require that we should have a special movement of love to every individual man, since this would be impossible. Nevertheless charity does require this, in respect of our being prepared in mind, namely that we should be ready to love our enemies individually, if the necessity were to occur.

That man should actually do so, and love his enemy for God's sake, without it being necessary for him to do so, belongs to the perfection of charity.

Aquinas, *Summa Theologica*, II–II, 25, 8

22 "I am more fasting from being satisfied," said I, "than if I had kept silent at first, and more perplexity I amass in my mind.

How can it be that a good when shared, shall make the greater number of possessors richer in it, than if it is possessed by a few?"

And he [Virgil] to me: "Because thou dost again fix thy mind merely on things of earth, thou drawest darkness from true light.

That infinite and ineffable Good, that is on high,

speedeth so to love as a ray of light comes to a
bright body.
As much of ardour as it finds, so much of itself
doth it give, so that how far soever love extends,
eternal goodness giveth increase upon it;
and the more people on high who comprehend
each other, the more there are to love well, and
the more love is there, and like a mirror one
giveth back to the other."

Dante, *Purgatorio*, XV, 58

23 Ye youth, so happy at the dawn of life,
In whom love springs as native to your days,
Estrange you from the world and its vain strife,
And let your hearts their eyes to him upraise
Who made you in his image! Give him praise,
And think this world is but a passing show,
Fading like blooms that all too briefly blow.

And love ye him who on the cross did buy
Our souls from timeless death to live for aye,
Who died and rose and reigns in heaven high!
Your deepest love his love will ne'er betray,
Your faith on him I bid you safely lay;
And since his love is best beyond compare,
Love of the world deny with all its care.

Chaucer, *Troilus and Cressida*, V, 263–264

24 The hearts of men, which fondly here admyre
Faire seeming shewes, and feed on vaine delight,
Transported with celestiall desyre
Of those faire formes, may lift themselves up hyer,
And learne to love with zealous humble dewty
Th' Eternall Fountaine of that heavenly Beauty.

Spenser, *Hymn of Heavenly Beautie*, 16

25 *Portia.* The quality of mercy is not strain'd,
It droppeth as the gentle rain from heaven
Upon the place beneath: it is twice blest;
It blesseth him that gives and him that takes:
'Tis mightiest in the mightiest: it becomes
The throned monarch better than his crown;
His sceptre shows the force of temporal power,
The attribute to awe and majesty,
Wherein doth sit the dread and fear of kings;
But mercy is above this sceptred sway;
It is enthroned in the hearts of kings,
It is an attribute to God himself;
And earthly power doth then show likest God's
When mercy seasons justice. Therefore, Jew,
Though justice be thy plea, consider this,
That, in the course of justice, none of us
Should see salvation: we do pray for mercy;
And that same prayer doth teach us all to render
The deeds of mercy.

Shakespeare, *Merchant of Venice*, IV, i, 184

26 *Isabella.*   Well, believe this,
No ceremony that to great ones 'longs,
Not the king's crown, nor the deputed sword,
The marshal's truncheon, nor the judge's robe,

Become them with one half so good a grace
As mercy does.

Shakespeare, *Measure for Measure*, II, ii, 58

27 *Angelo.* Your brother is a forfeit of the law.
And you but waste your words.
  Isabella.   Alas, alas!
Why, all the souls that were were forfeit once;
And He that might the vantage best have took
Found out the remedy. How would you be,
If He, which is the top of judgement, should
But judge you as you are? O, think on that;
And mercy then will breathe within your lips,
Like man new made.
  Ang.   Be you content, fair maid;
It is the law, not I, condemn your brother.
Were he my kinsman, brother, or my son,
It should be thus with him. He must die tomor-
row.
  Isab. To-morrow! O, that's sudden! Spare him,
spare him!
He's not prepared for death. Even for our kitchens
We kill the fowl of season. Shall we serve Heaven
With less respect than we do minister
To our gross selves?

Shakespeare, *Measure for Measure*, II, ii, 71

28 Cry'd Don *Quixote*, Is it for a Knight-Errant when
he meets with People laden with Chains, and under Oppression, to examine whether they are in
those Circumstances for their Crimes, or only
thro' Misfortune? We are only to relieve the Afflicted, to look on their Distress, and not on their
Crimes.

Cervantes, *Don Quixote*, I, 30

29 To forgive sin is not an act of injustice, though the
punishment have been threatened. Even amongst
men, though the promise of good bind the promis-
er; yet threats, that is to say, promises of evil, bind
them not; much less shall they bind God, who is
infinitely more merciful than men.

Hobbes, *Leviathan*, III, 38

30 The infinite distance between body and mind is a
symbol of the infinitely more infinite distance between mind and charity; for charity is supernatural.

Pascal, *Pensées*, XII, 793

31 He who lives according to the guidance of reason
strives as much as possible to repay the hatred,
anger, or contempt of others towards himself with
love or generosity.

All affects of hatred are evil, and, therefore, the
man who lives according to the guidance of reason will strive as much as possible to keep himself
from being agitated by the affects of hatred, and,
consequently, will strive to keep others from being
subject to the same affects. But hatred is increased
by reciprocal hatred, and, on the other hand, can
be extinguished by love, so that hatred passes into

love. Therefore he who lives according to the guidance of reason will strive to repay the hatred of another, etc., with love, that is to say, with generosity. . . .

He who wishes to avenge injuries by hating in return does indeed live miserably. But he who, on the contrary, strives to drive out hatred by love, fights joyfully and confidently, with equal ease resisting one man or a number of men, and needing scarcely any assistance from fortune. Those whom he conquers yield gladly, not from defect of strength, but from an increase of it.

Spinoza, *Ethics,* IV, Prop. 46

32 The intellectual love of the mind towards God is the very love with which He loves Himself, not in so far as He is infinite, but in so far as He can be manifested through the essence of the human mind, considered under the form of eternity; that is to say, the intellectual love of the mind towards God is part of the infinite love with which God loves Himself. . . .

Hence it follows that God, in so far as He loves Himself, loves men, and consequently that the love of God towards men and the intellectual love of the mind towards God are one and the same thing.

Spinoza, *Ethics,* V, Prop. 36, Corol.

33 "Those," he [Capt. Blifil] said, "came nearer to the Scripture meaning, who understood by it [charity] candour, or the forming of a benevolent opinion of our brethren, and passing a favourable judgment on their actions; a virtue much higher, and more extensive in its nature, than a pitiful distribution of alms, which, though we would never so much prejudice, or even ruin our families, could not reach many; whereas charity, in the other and truer sense, might be extended to all mankind."

Fielding, *Tom Jones,* II, 5

34 Thwackum was for doing justice, and leaving mercy to heaven.

Fielding, *Tom Jones,* III, 10

35 It is in endeavouring to instruct mankind that we are best able to practise that general virtue which comprehends the love of all.

Montesquieu, *Spirit of Laws,* Pref.

36 My uncle Toby had scarce a heart to retaliate upon a fly.

——Go—says he, one day at dinner, to an over-grown one which had buzzed about his nose, and tormented him cruelly all dinner-time,—and which after infinite attempts, he had caught at last, as it flew by him;—I'll not hurt thee, says my uncle Toby, rising from his chair, and going across the room, with the fly in his hand,—I'll not hurt a hair of thy head:—Go, says he, lifting up

the sash, and opening his hand as he spoke, to let it escape;—go, poor devil, get thee gone, why should I hurt thee?——This world surely is wide enough to hold both thee and me.

Sterne, *Tristram Shandy,* II, 12

37 "—She had since that, she told me, stray'd as far as Rome, and walk'd round St. Peter's once—and return'd back—that she found her way alone across the Apennines—had travell'd over all Lombardy without money,—and through the flinty roads of Savoy without shoes—how she had borne it, and how she had got supported, she could not tell—but God tempers the wind, said Maria, to the shorn lamb."

Sterne, *Sentimental Journey:* "Maria"

38 He who the Ox to wrath has mov'd
Shall never be by Woman lov'd.
The wanton Boy that kills the Fly
Shall feel the Spider's enmity.
He who torments the Chafer's sprite
Weaves a Bower in endless Night.
The Catterpiller on the Leaf
Repeats to thee thy Mother's grief.
Kill not the Moth nor Butterfly
For the Last Judgment draweth nigh.

Blake, *Auguries of Innocence,* 39

39 Give all thou canst; high Heaven rejects the lore
Of nicely-calculated less or more.

Wordsworth, *Ecclesiastical Sonnets,* III, 43

40 No love and no expression of love may, in the merely human and worldly sense, be deprived of a relationship to God. Love is a passionate emotion, but in this emotion, even before he enters into a relation with the object of his love, the man must first enter into a relationship with God, and thereby realize the claim that love is the fulfillment of the law. Love is a relation to another man or to other men, but it is by no means and dares by no means be a matrimonial, a friendly, a merely human agreement, however steadfast and tender the connection between man and man. Everyone individually before he in love enters into a relation with the beloved, with the friend, the loved ones, the contemporaries, has first to enter into a relation with God and with God's demands. As soon as one leaves out the God-relationship the questions at issue become merely human determinations of what they wish to understand by loving; what they will require of one another; and their mutual judgment because of this becomes the highest judgment. Not only the one who listens absolutely to the call of God will not belong to a woman, in order not to be delayed through wishing to please her; but also the one who in love belongs to a woman, will first and foremost belong to God; he will not seek first to please his wife, but will first endeavor to make his love pleasing unto

God. Hence it is not the wife who will teach her husband how he ought to love her, or the husband the wife, or the friend the friend, or the contemporary the contemporary, but it is God who will teach every individual how he ought to love, even if his love still only lays hold on the law referred to when the apostle says, "Love is the fulfillment of the law." This makes it quite natural that the one who has only a worldly, or a merely human conception about what love is, must come to regard that as self-love and unkindness which, understood in the Christian sense, is precisely love. When, on the other hand, the God-relationship determines what love is between man and man, then love is kept from pausing in any self-deception or illusion, while certainly the demand for self-abnegation and sacrifice is again made more infinite. The love which does not lead to God, the love which does not have this as its sole goal, to lead the lovers to love God, stops at the purely human judgment as to what love and what love's sacrifice and submission are; it stops and thereby escapes the possibility of the last and most terrifying horror of the collision: that in the love relationship there are infinite differences in the idea of what love is.

Kierkegaard, *Works of Love,* I, 3A

41 With malice toward none; with charity for all; with firmness in the right as God gives us to see the right, let us strive on to finish the work we are in; to bind up the nation's wounds; to care for him who shall have borne the battle, and for his widow, and his orphan—to do all which may achieve and cherish a just and a lasting peace, among ourselves and with all nations.

Lincoln, *Second Inaugural Address*

42 "I must make you one confession," Ivan began. "I could never understand how one can love one's neighbours. It's just one's neighbours, to my mind, that one can't love, though one might love those at a distance. I once read somewhere of John the Merciful, a saint, that when a hungry, frozen beggar came to him, he took him into his bed, held him in his arms, and began breathing into his mouth, which was putrid and loathsome from some awful disease. I am convinced that he did that from 'self-laceration,' from the self-laceration of falsity, for the sake of the charity imposed by duty, as a penance laid on him. For anyone to love a man, he must be hidden, for as soon as he shows his face, love is gone."

"Father Zossima has talked of that more than once," observed Alyosha; "he, too, said that the face of a man often hinders many people not practised in love, from loving him. But yet there's a great deal of love in mankind, and almost Christ-like love. I know that myself, Ivan."

Dostoevsky, *Brothers Karamazov,* Pt. II, V, 4

43 *Father Zossima.* And can it be a dream, that in the end man will find his joy only in deeds of light and mercy, and not in cruel pleasures as now, in gluttony, fornication, ostentation, boasting and envious rivalry of one with the other? I firmly believe that it is not and that the time is at hand. People laugh and ask: "When will that time come and does it look like coming?" I believe that with Christ's help we shall accomplish this great thing. And how many ideas there have been on earth in the history of man which were unthinkable ten years before they appeared! Yet when their destined hour had come, they came forth and spread over the whole earth. So it will be with us, and our people will shine forth in the world, and all men will say: "The stone which the builders rejected has become the cornerstone of the building."

Dostoevsky, *Brothers Karamazov,* Pt. II, VI, 3

44 Do not do unto others as you would that they should do unto you. Their tastes may not be the same.

Shaw, *Man and Superman,*
Maxims for Revolutionists

3.6 | *Love of Country*

PATRIOTISM

Unlike the diverse loves treated in the three preceding sections, patriotism, or love of one's country, is not a distinct type of love. It can probably be most closely aligned with the kind of love that is true friendship, the dominantly benevolent tendency which would impel a man to lay down his life for his friend. So, it is often said, the patriot too would, if necessary, lay down his life for his country.

For the most part, the writers here quoted praise patriotism as something desirable and even virtuous, while others raise doubts about its value or condemn an uncritical or blind patriotism. Dr. Johnson may have gone too far in that direction when he said that patriotism is the last refuge of a scoundrel, but that helps to preserve a balance against the other extreme which attaches no qualifications to its praise of patriotism.

---

1 Go tell the Spartans, thou who passest by,
  That here obedient to their laws we lie.
  Simonides, Epigram on Thermopylae

2 Had the Athenians, from fear of the approaching danger, quitted their country, or had they without quitting it submitted to the power of Xerxes, there would certainly have been no attempt to resist the Persians by sea; in which case the course of events by land would have been the following. Though the Peloponnesians might have carried ever so many breastworks across the Isthmus, yet their allies would have fallen off from the Lacedæmonians, not by voluntary desertion, but because town after town must have been taken by the fleet of the barbarians; and so the Lacedæmonians would at last have stood alone, and, standing alone, would have displayed prodigies of valour and died nobly. Either they would have done thus, or else, before it came to that extremity, seeing one Greek state after another embrace the cause of the Medes, they would have come to terms with King Xerxes—and thus, either way Greece would have been brought under Persia. For I cannot understand of what possible use the walls across the Isthmus could have been, if the king had had the mastery of the sea. If then a man should now say that the Athenians were the saviours of Greece, he would not exceed the truth. For they truly held the scales; and whichever side they espoused must have carried the day. They too it was who, when they had determined to maintain the freedom of Greece, roused up that portion of the Greek na-

tion which had not gone over to the Medes; and so, next to the gods, *they* repulsed the invader. Even the terrible oracles which reached them from Delphi, and struck fear into their hearts, failed to persuade them to fly from Greece. They had the courage to remain faithful to their land, and await the coming of the foe.
Herodotus, History, VII, 139

3 *Cassandra.* The Trojans have that glory which is loveliest:
  they died for their own country.
  Euripides, Trojan Women, 386

4 *Pericles.* There is justice in the claim that steadfastness in his country's battles should be as a cloak to cover a man's other imperfections; since the good action has blotted out the bad, and his merit as a citizen more than outweighed his demerits as an individual.
  Thucydides, Peloponnesian War, II, 42

5 *Pericles.* Your country has a right to your services in sustaining the glories of her position. These are a common source of pride to you all, and you cannot decline the burdens of empire and still expect to share its honours.
  Thucydides, Peloponnesian War, II, 63

6 *Alcibiades.* I hope that none of you will think any the worse of me if, after having hitherto passed as a lover of my country, I now actively join its worst enemies in attacking it, or will suspect what I say

as the fruit of an outlaw's enthusiasm. I am an outlaw from the iniquity of those who drove me forth, not, if you will be guided by me, from your service; my worst enemies are not you who only harmed your foes, but they who forced their friends to become enemies; and love of country is what I do not feel when I am wronged, but what I felt when secure in my rights as a citizen. Indeed I do not consider that I am now attacking a country that is still mine; I am rather trying to recover one that is mine no longer; and the true lover of his country is not he who consents to lose it unjustly rather than attack it, but he who longs for it so much that he will go all lengths to recover it.

Thucydides, *Peloponnesian War*, VI, 92

7 The good man should be a lover of self (for he will both himself profit by doing noble acts, and will benefit his fellows), but the wicked man should not; for he will hurt both himself and his neighbours, following as he does evil passions. For the wicked man, what he does clashes with what he ought to do, but what the good man ought to do he does; for reason in each of its possessors chooses what is best for itself, and the good man obeys his reason. It is true of the good man too that he does many acts for the sake of his friends and his country, and if necessary dies for them; for he will throw away both wealth and honours and in general the goods that are objects of competition, gaining for himself nobility; since he would prefer a short period of intense pleasure to a long one of mild enjoyment, a twelvemonth of noble life to many years of humdrum existence, and one great and noble action to many trivial ones. Now those who die for others doubtless attain this result; it is therefore a great prize that they choose for themselves.

Aristotle, *Ethics*, 1169ª12

8 Good 'tis and fine, for fatherland to die!
Death tracks him too who shirks; nor will He fail
To smite the coward loins that quail,
The coward limbs that fly!

Horace, *Odes*, III, 2

9 By what sweet charm I know not the native land draws all men nor allows them to forget her.

Ovid, *Epistulae Ex Ponto*, I, 3

10 [Sertorius] was a sincere lover of his country, and had a great desire to return home; but in his adverse fortune he showed undaunted courage, and behaved himself towards his enemies in a manner free from all dejection and mean-spiritedness; and when he was in his prosperity, and in the height of his victories, he sent word to Metellus and Pompey that he was ready to lay down his arms and live a private life if he were allowed to return home, declaring that he had rather live as the meanest citizen in Rome than, exiled from it, be

supreme commander of all other cities together.

Plutarch, *Sertorius*

11 A wise prince ought to adopt such a course that his citizens will always in every sort and kind of circumstance have need of the state and of him, and then he will always find them faithful.

Machiavelli, *Prince*, IX

12 Not because Socrates said it, but because it is really my feeling, and perhaps excessively so, I consider all men my compatriots, and embrace a Pole as I do a Frenchman, setting this national bond after the universal and common one. I am scarcely infatuated with the sweetness of my native air. Brand-new acquaintances that are wholly of my own choice seem to me to be well worth those other common chance acquaintances of the neighborhood. Friendships purely of our own acquisition usually surpass those to which community of climate or of blood binds us. Nature has put us into the world free and unfettered; we imprison ourselves in certain narrow districts, like the kings of Persia, who bound themselves never to drink any other water than that of the river Choaspes, stupidly gave up their right to use any other waters, and dried up all the rest of the world as far as they were concerned.

What Socrates did near the end of his life, in considering a sentence of exile against him worse than a sentence of death, I shall never, I think, be so broken or so strictly attached to my own country as to do. These divine lives have quite a few aspects that I embrace more by esteem than by affection. And there are also some so lofty and extraordinary that I cannot embrace them even by esteem, inasmuch as I cannot understand them. That was a very fastidious attitude for a man who considered the world his city.

Montaigne, *Essays*, III, 9, Of Vanity

13 *Gaunt.* This royal throne of kings, this scepter'd isle,
This earth of majesty, this seat of Mars,
This other Eden, demi-paradise,
This fortress built by Nature for herself
Against infection and the hand of war,
This happy breed of men, this little world,
This precious stone set in the silver sea,
Which serves it in the office of a wall
Or as a moat defensive to a house,
Against the envy of less happier lands,
This blessed plot, this earth, this realm, this England.

Shakespeare, *Richard II*, II, i, 40

14 There is an honour . . . which may be ranked amongst the greatest, which happeneth rarely; that is, of such as sacrifice themselves to death or danger for the good of their country.

Bacon, *Of Honour and Reputation*

15 What I distinguish by the name of *virtue,* in a republic, is the love of one's country, that is, the love of equality. It is not a moral, nor a Christian, but a political *virtue;* and it is the spring which sets the republican government in motion, as honour is the spring which gives motion to monarchy.

Montesquieu, *Spirit of Laws,* Advertisement

16 Do we wish men to be virtuous? Then let us begin by making them love their country: but how can they love it, if their country be nothing more to them than to strangers, and afford them nothing but what it can refuse nobody?

Rousseau, *Political Economy*

17 If children are brought up in common in the bosom of equality; if they are imbued with the laws of the State and the precepts of the general will; if they are taught to respect these above all things; if they are surrounded by examples and objects which constantly remind them of the tender mother who nourishes them, of the love she bears them, of the inestimable benefits they receive from her, and of the return they owe her; we cannot doubt that they will learn to cherish one another mutually as brothers, to will nothing contrary to the will of society, to substitute the actions of men and citizens for the futile and vain babbling of sophists, and to become in time defenders and fathers of the country of which they will have been so long the children.

Rousseau, *Political Economy*

18 As soon as any man says of the affairs of the State *What does it matter to me?* the State may be given up for lost.

Rousseau, *Social Contract,* III, 15

19 The [religion of the State] is good in that it unites the divine cult with love of the laws, and, making country the object of the citizens' adoration, teaches them that service done to the State is service done to its tutelary god. It is a form of theocracy, in which there can be no pontiff save the prince, and no priests save the magistrates. To die for one's country then becomes martyrdom; violation of its laws, impiety; and to subject one who is guilty to public execration is to condemn him to the anger of the gods: *Sacer estod.*

On the other hand, it is bad in that, being founded on lies and error, it deceives men, makes them credulous and superstitious, and drowns the true cult of the Divinity in empty ceremonial. It is bad, again, when it becomes tyrannous and exclusive, and makes a people bloodthirsty and intolerant, so that it breathes fire and slaughter, and regards as a sacred act the killing of every one who does not believe in its gods. The result is to place such a people in a natural state of war with all others, so that its security is deeply endangered.

Rousseau, *Social Contract,* IV, 8

20 Patriotism having become one of our topicks, Johnson suddenly uttered, in a strong determined tone, an apophthegm, at which many will start: "Patriotism is the last refuge of a scoundrel." But let it be considered, that he did not mean a real and generous love of our country, but that pretended patriotism which so many, in all ages and countries, have made a cloak for self-interest. I maintained, that certainly all patriots were not scoundrels. Being urged, (not by Johnson,) to name one exception, I mentioned an eminent person, whom we all greatly admired. *Johnson.* "Sir, I do not say that he is *not* honest; but we have no reason to conclude from his political conduct that he *is* honest. Were he to accept of a place from this ministry, he would lose that character of firmness which he has, and might be turned out of his place in a year."

Boswell, *Life of Johnson* (*Apr. 7, 1775*)

21 The more the operations of the national authority are intermingled in the ordinary exercise of government, the more the citizens are accustomed to meet with it in the common occurrences of their political life, the more it is familiarised to their sight and to their feelings, the further it enters into those objects which touch the most sensible chords and put in motion the most active springs of the human heart, the greater will be the probability that it will conciliate the respect and attachment of the community. Man is very much a creature of habit. A thing that rarely strikes his senses will generally have but little influence upon his mind. A government continually at a distance and out of sight can hardly be expected to interest the sensations of the people.

Hamilton, *Federalist 27*

22 Patriotism is often understood to mean only a readiness for exceptional sacrifices and actions. Essentially, however, it is the sentiment which, in the relationships of our daily life and under ordinary conditions, habitually recognizes that the community is one's substantive groundwork and end. It is out of this consciousness, which during life's daily round stands the test in all circumstances, that there subsequently also arises the readiness for extraordinary exertions. But since men would often rather be magnanimous than law-abiding, they readily persuade themselves that they possess this exceptional patriotism in order to be sparing in the expression of a genuine patriotic sentiment or to excuse their lack of it. If again this genuine patriotism is looked upon as that which may begin of itself and arise from subjective ideas and thoughts, it is being confused with opinion, because so regarded patriotism is deprived of its true ground, objective reality.

Hegel, *Philosophy of Right,* 268

23 Theirs not to make reply,
   Theirs not to reason why,
   Theirs but to do and die.
   Into the valley of Death
     Rode the six hundred.

   Tennyson, *The Charge of the Light Brigade*

24 It has been said of old, that in a despotism there is
   at most but one patriot, the despot himself; and
   the saying rests on a just appreciation of the effects of absolute subjection, even to a good and
   wise master.

   Mill, *Representative Government,* III

25 [The] feeling of nationality may have been generated by various causes. Sometimes it is the effect
   of identity of race and descent. Community of
   language, and community of religion, greatly contribute to it. Geographical limits are one of its
   causes. But the strongest of all is identity of political antecedents; the possession of a national history, and consequent community of recollections;
   collective pride and humiliation, pleasure and regret, connected with the same incidents in the
   past.

   Mill, *Representative Government,* XVI

26 It is natural for us who were not living in those
   days to imagine that when half Russia had been
   conquered and the inhabitants were fleeing to distant provinces, and one levy after another was
   being raised for the defense of the fatherland, all
   Russians from the greatest to the least were solely
   engaged in sacrificing themselves, saving their fatherland, or weeping over its downfall. The tales
   and descriptions of that time without exception
   speak only of the self-sacrifice, patriotic devotion,
   despair, grief, and the heroism of the Russians.
   But it was not really so. It appears so to us because
   we see only the general historic interest of that
   time and do not see all the personal human interests that people had. Yet in reality those personal
   interests of the moment so much transcend the
   general interests that they always prevent the
   public interest from being felt or even noticed.
   Most of the people at that time paid no attention
   to the general progress of events but were guided
   only by their private interests, and they were the
   very people whose activities at that period were
   most useful.

   Those who tried to understand the general
   course of events and to take part in it by self-
   sacrifice and heroism were the most useless members of society, they saw everything upside down,
   and all they did for the common good turned out
   to be useless and foolish.

   Tolstoy, *War and Peace,* XII, 4

Chapter 4
EMOTION

Chapter 4 is divided into eleven sections: 4.1 THE PASSIONS: THE RANGE OF THE EMOTIONS, 4.2 FEAR, 4.3 ANGER, 4.4 DESIRE, 4.5 HOPE AND DESPAIR, 4.6 JOY AND SORROW, 4.7 PLEASURE AND PAIN, 4.8 PITY AND ENVY, 4.9 GREED AND AVARICE, 4.10 JEALOUSY, and 4.11 PRIDE AND HUMILITY.

The section titles immediately tell the reader what to expect here. He is acquainted in his own experience with most of the feelings, dispositions, sentiments, moods, or states of mind and body that are named; those he has not experienced himself, he has met with in the behavior of others—in fact or fiction. Yet they are not all emotions or passions in the strict sense in which these terms have come to mean a state of feeling that arises from profound bodily changes, of relatively short duration, so intense that for a short time the individual is completely dominated by it. In fact, only fear and anger exemplify this very strict conception of emotion or passion involving widespread physiological changes that run a brief course during which they completely control and determine the individual's behavior. But we also use the words "fear" and "anger" to name much less violent upheavals—persistent feelings, moods, or sentiments that underlie and color an individual's attitudes or responses toward certain aspects of his environment. The same holds for desire, hope and despair, and joy and sorrow. All of these are emotions or passions in the sense just indicated—relatively persistent states of feeling, determinative of attitude or conduct, involving bodily changes that are milder than the violent seizures of fear and anger in their most intense occurrence.

In the discussion of these matters, "passion" is the older, "emotion" the newer term. In assembling the passages quoted in this chapter, we have treated them as synonymous. Still another traditional term that has similar meaning is "affect."

The study of emotion now falls within the province of psychology, and has for a century or more; but earlier than that the analysis and classification of the passions was mainly the work of moral and political philosophers, or even of those concerned with oratory. In fact, the first comprehensive account of the passions appears in Aristotle's *Rhetoric,* although the subject is also considered in his *Ethics* in connection with his analysis of such virtues as courage and temperance.

Section 4.1 sets the stage for all the sections to follow: its quotations, drawn from a wide variety of contexts, deal with emotion or passion in general, and with the enumeration and classification of specific passions or emotions, or even milder feelings or sentiments. It will be noted that, in such enumerations and classifications, some of the passions are paired opposites, such as joy and sorrow, or hope and despair, and some stand alone and do not have opposites, such as fear and anger. It will also be noted that different principles are employed in classifying the passions; sometimes they are divided into the irascible and the concupiscible; sometimes into the pleasant and the unpleasant; sometimes into the violent and the mild. In ordering the sections of this chapter, we have adopted still another principle.

We have put first, in Sections 4.2 through 4.7, emotions, passions, or feelings that, from the point of view of most moralists and of men generally, are in themselves neither good nor bad. Thus, for example, what we do about fear or anger, pleasure or pain, joy and sorrow, and desire—how we control such feelings or give into them—may be the subject of moral approval or disapproval, but not the feelings themselves. Nevertheless, hope and despair, included in this group, are not always treated merely as feelings without moral coloration; hope is also regarded as a theological virtue, and despair as its opposite—one of the mortal sins. This is also true of anger. Nevertheless, in the main, the subjects treated in Sections 4.2 through 4.7 are approached as phenomena to be examined rather than as dispositions to be praised or censured.

In contrast, the subjects treated in Sections 4.8 through 4.11 do, for the most part, elicit approbation or censure from those who discuss them. For example, such words as "envy," "greed," "avarice," and "jealousy," usually connote excessive or inordinate tendencies or dispositions—desire or other passions out of control. While this does not hold to the same extent for "pity," it, too, is frequently used in a pejorative sense. And while the terms "pride" and "humility" almost always connote attitudes or dispositions that are considered admirable or reprehensible, sometimes pride is condemned and humility praised, and sometimes the reverse.

One pair of feelings—love and hate, usually included in enumerations of the passions—are not given a special section in this chapter because Chapter 3 deals with them. However, an emotion closely connected with love and hate—jealousy—is treated here in Section 4.10.

A whole chapter might have been devoted to pleasure and pain, so extensive and so varied is the discussion of these subjects. While the main treatment of them will be found in Section 4.7, the reader will also find reference to them in other sections, for almost all the other passions or emotions are tinged with pleasure or pain, or at least with the affective tone of the pleasant or the unpleasant. They also appear, in connection with desire, under the guise of satisfaction and dissatisfaction. When our desires are satisfied, we are pleased; when they are unsatisfied, we are displeased or pained.

On the psychological plane, the matters treated in this chapter have a bearing on matters treated in Chapter 5 on MIND, especially Section 5.7 on WILL: FREE CHOICE, and even, to some extent, Section 5.6 on MADNESS. On the plane of moral philosophy, the connection is with subjects covered in Chapter 9 on ETHICS, especially Section 9.10 on

VIRTUE AND VICE, Section 9.11 on COURAGE AND COWARDICE, and Section 9.12 on TEMPERANCE AND INTEMPERANCE.

These remarks about the subject matter of Chapter 4 as a whole make it unnecessary to append forewords to each of its sections.

4.1 | *The Passions*

THE RANGE OF THE EMOTIONS

1 Since things that are found in the soul are of three kinds—passions, faculties, states of character, virtue must be one of these. By passions I mean appetite, anger, fear, confidence, envy, joy, friendly feeling, hatred, longing, emulation, pity, and in general the feelings that are accompanied by pleasure or pain; by faculties the things in virtue of which we are said to be capable of feeling these, for example, of becoming angry or being pained or feeling pity; by states of character the things in virtue of which we stand well or badly with reference to the passions, for example, with reference to anger we stand badly if we feel it violently or too weakly, and well if we feel it moderately; and similarly with reference to the other passions.

Now neither the virtues nor the vices are *passions,* because we are not called good or bad on the ground of our passions, but are so called on the ground of our virtues and our vices, and because we are neither praised nor blamed for our passions (for the man who feels fear or anger is not praised, nor is the man who simply feels anger blamed, but the man who feels it in a certain way), but for our virtues and our vices we *are* praised or blamed.

Aristotle, *Ethics,* 1105ᵇ19

2 The emotions are all those feelings that so change men as to affect their judgements, and that are also attended by pain or pleasure. Such are anger, pity, fear and the like, with their opposites.

Aristotle, *Rhetoric,* 1378ᵃ20

3 Now I assert that the mind and the soul are kept together in close union and make up a single nature, but that the directing principle which we call mind and understanding, is the head so to speak and reigns paramount in the whole body. It has a fixed seat in the middle region of the breast: here throb fear and apprehension, about these

spots dwell soothing joys; therefore here is the understanding or mind. All the rest of the soul disseminated through the whole body obeys and moves at the will and inclination of the mind. It by itself alone knows for itself, rejoices for itself, at times when the impression does not move either soul or body together with it. And as when some part of us, the head or the eye, suffers from an attack of pain, we do not feel the anguish at the same time over the whole body, thus the mind sometimes suffers pain by itself or is inspirited with joy, when all the rest of the soul throughout the limbs and frame is stirred by no novel sensation. But when the mind is excited by some more vehement apprehension, we see the whole soul feel in unison through all the limbs, sweats and paleness spread over the whole body, the tongue falter, the voice die away, a mist cover the eyes, the ears ring, the limbs sink under one; in short we often see men drop down from terror of mind; so that anybody may easily perceive from this that the soul is closely united with the mind, and, when it has been smitten by the influence of the mind, forthwith pushes and strikes the body.

Lucretius, *Nature of Things,* III

4 Every disturbance is the disruption of a mind either devoid of or contemptuous of reason, or disobedient to reason. Such a disruption is provoked in two ways, either by an idea of good or by an idea of evil. So we end up with four types of mental disruption. Two of them proceed from an idea of good. One of these is exultant pleasure, in other words, extreme joy brought on by the presence of some great good. The counterpart of this is an excessive longing for some great good. Such a longing is contrary to reason, and it may rightly be called desire or lust. These two instances, exultant pleasure and lust deriving from some idea of a good, both disrupt the soul. So do their two op-

posites, fear and distress, also cause such disruptions because of the idea of evil. Fear is the imagining of a threatened evil, and distress is occasioned by the presence of a serious evil. Distress is really the strong awareness of an evil real enough to cause genuine anguish. Thus the man who feels pain is convinced that he is meant to feel pain. With all our power we must strive to resist these disturbances, loosed as they are by folly coupled with a kind of evil spirit over the life of mankind, if we want to pass our days in peace and quiet.

Cicero, *Disputations*, III, 11

5 In our ethics, we do not so much inquire whether a pious soul is angry, as why he is angry; not whether he is sad, but what is the cause of his sadness; not whether he fears, but what he fears. For I am not aware that any right thinking person would find fault with anger at a wrongdoer which seeks his amendment, or with sadness which intends relief to the suffering, or with fear lest one in danger be destroyed. The Stoics, indeed, are accustomed to condemn compassion. But how much more honourable had it been in that Stoic we have been telling of had he been disturbed by compassion prompting him to relieve a fellow-creature than to be disturbed by the fear of shipwreck! . . . However, it may justly be asked, whether our subjection to these affections, even while we follow virtue, is a part of the infirmity of this life? For the holy angels feel no anger while they punish those whom the eternal law of God consigns to punishment, no fellow-feeling with misery while they relieve the miserable, no fear while they aid those who are in danger; and yet ordinary language ascribes to them also these mental emotions, because, though they have none of our weakness, their acts resemble the actions to which these emotions move us.

Augustine, *City of God*, IX, 5

6 The character of the human will is of moment; because, if it is wrong, these motions of the soul will be wrong, but if it is right, they will be not merely blameless, but even praiseworthy. For the will is in them all; yea, none of them is anything else than will. For what are desire and joy but a volition of consent to the things we wish? And what are fear and sadness but a volition of aversion from the things which we do not wish? But when consent takes the form of seeking to possess the things we wish, this is called desire; and when consent takes the form of enjoying the things we wish, this is called joy. In like manner, when we turn with aversion from that which we do not wish to happen, this volition is termed fear; and when we turn away from that which has happened against our will, this act of will is called sorrow. And generally in respect of all that we seek or shun, as a man's will is attracted or repelled, so it is changed and turned into these different affections.

Augustine, *City of God*, XIV, 6

7 The sensitive appetite is one generic power, and is called sensuality; but it is divided into two powers, which are species of the sensitive appetite—the irascible and the concupiscible. . . . Therefore . . . there must be two appetitive powers in the sensitive part—one through which the soul is inclined absolutely to seek what is suitable according to the senses, and to fly from what is hurtful, and this is called the concupiscible; and another by which an animal resists these attacks that hinder what is suitable and inflict harm, and this is called the irascible. . . .

Now these two are not to be reduced to one principle, for sometimes the soul busies itself with unpleasant things against the inclination of the concupiscible appetite in order that, following the impulse of the irascible appetite, it may fight against obstacles. Hence also the passions of the irascible appetite seem to go against the passions of the concupiscible appetite, since concupiscence, on being roused, diminishes anger, and anger being roused, diminishes concupiscence in many cases. This is clear also from the fact that the irascible is, as it were, the champion and defender of the concupiscible, when it rises up against what hinders the acquisition of the suitable things which the concupiscible desires, or against what inflicts harm, from which the concupiscible flies. And for this reason all the passions of the irascible appetite rise from the passions of the concupiscible appetite and terminate in them; for instance, anger rises from sadness, and having wrought vengeance, terminates in joy.

Aquinas, *Summa Theologica*, I, 81, 2

8 All the irascible passions imply movement towards something. Now this movement in the irascible part towards something may be due to two causes: one is the mere aptitude or proportion to the end, and this pertains to love or hatred; the other is the presence of good or evil, and this pertains to sadness or joy. . . .

Since then in the order of generation or sequence, proportion or aptitude to the end precedes the achievement of the end, it follows that, of all the irascible passions, anger is the last in the order of generation. And among the other passions of the irascible part which imply a movement arising from love of good or hatred of evil, those whose object is good, namely, hope and despair, must naturally precede those whose object is evil, namely, daring and fear. . . . In like manner fear, through being a movement from evil, precedes daring. . . .

And if we wish to know the order of all the passions in the way of generation, love and hatred are first; desire and aversion, second; hope and despair, third; fear and daring, fourth; anger, fifth; sixth and last, joy and sadness, which follow from all the passions . . . yet so that love precedes hatred; desire precedes aversion; hope precedes despair; fear precedes daring; and joy precedes sadness.

Aquinas, *Summa Theologica*, I–II, 25, 3

9 Joy relates to present good, sadness relates to present evil, hope regards future good, and fear, future evil. As to the other passions that concern good or evil, present or future, they all culminate in these four. For this reason have some said that these four are the principal passions, because they are general passions. And this is true, provided that by hope and fear we understand the common tendency of the appetite to desire or aversion for something.

Aquinas, *Summa Theologica*, I–II, 25, 4

10 All passions that allow themselves to be savored and digested are only mediocre.

Montaigne, *Essays*, I, 2, Of Sadness

11 Ambition can teach men valor, and temperance, and liberality, and even justice. Greed can implant in the heart of a shop apprentice, brought up in obscurity and idleness, the confidence to cast himself far from hearth and home, in a frail boat at the mercy of the waves and angry Neptune; it also teaches discretion and wisdom. Venus herself supplies resolution and boldness to boys still subject to discipline and the rod, and arms the tender hearts of virgins who are still in their mothers' laps. . . .

In view of this, a sound intellect will refuse to judge men simply by their outward actions; we must probe the inside and discover what springs set men in motion. But since this is an arduous and hazardous undertaking, I wish fewer people would meddle with it.

Montaigne, *Essays*, II, 1, Of the Inconsistency

12 *Hamlet.* O, what a rogue and peasant slave am I!
Is it not monstrous that this player here,
But in a fiction, in a dream of passion,
Could force his soul so to his own conceit
That from her working all his visage wann'd,
Tears in his eyes, distraction in's aspect,
A broken voice, and his whole function suiting
With forms to his conceit? and all for nothing!
For Hecuba!
What's Hecuba to him, or he to Hecuba,
That he should weep for her? What would he do,
Had he the motive and the cue for passion
That I have? He would drown the stage with tears
And cleave the general ear with horrid speech,
Make mad the guilty and appal the free,
Confound the ignorant, and amaze indeed
The very faculties of eyes and ears.
Yet I,
A dull and muddy-mettled rascal, peak,

Like John-a-dreams, unpregnant of my cause,
And can nothing; no, not for a king,
Upon whose property and most dear life
A damn'd defeat was made. Am I a coward?
Who calls me villain? breaks my pate across?
Plucks off my beard, and blows it in my face?
Tweaks me by the nose? gives me the lie i' the throat,
As deep as to the lungs? who does me this?
Ha!
'Swounds, I should take it: for it cannot be
But I am pigeon-liver'd and lack gall
To make oppression bitter, or ere this
I should have fatted all the region kites
With this slave's offal. Bloody, bawdy, villain!
Remorseless, treacherous, lecherous, kindless villain!
O, vengeance!
Why, what an ass am I! This is most brave,
That I, the son of a dear father murder'd
Prompted to my revenge by heaven and hell,
Must, like a whore, unpack my heart with words,
And fall a-cursing, like a very drab,
A scullion!
Fie upon't! foh!

Shakespeare, *Hamlet*, II, ii, 576

13 *Hamlet.*   Blest are those
Whose blood and judgement are so well commingled,
That they are not a pipe for fortune's finger
To sound what stop she please. Give me that man
That is not passion's slave, and I will wear him
In my heart's core, ay, in my heart of heart.

Shakespeare, *Hamlet*, III, ii, 73

14 I note . . . that we do not observe the existence of any subject which more immediately acts upon our soul than the body to which it is joined, and that we must consequently consider that what in the soul is a passion is in the body commonly speaking an action; so that there is no better means of arriving at a knowledge of our passions than to examine the difference which exists between soul and body in order to know to which of the two we must attribute each one of the functions which are within us.

Descartes, *Passions of the Soul*, II

15 The number of [passions] which are simple and primitive is not very large. For, in making a review of all those which I have enumerated, we may easily notice that there are but six which are such, that is, wonder, love, hatred, desire, joy and sadness; and that all the others are composed of some of these six, or are species of them.

Descartes, *Passions of the Soul*, LXIX

16 Whoever has lived in such a way that his conscience cannot reproach him for ever having failed to perform those things which he has judged

to be the best (which is what I here call following after virtue) receives from this a satisfaction which is so powerful in rendering him happy that the most violent efforts of the passions never have sufficient power to disturb the tranquillity of his soul.

Descartes, *Passions of the Soul,* CXLVIII

17 The soul may have pleasures of its own, but as to those which are common to it and the body, they depend entirely on the passions, so that the men whom they can most move are capable of partaking most of enjoyment in this life. It is true that such men may also find most bitterness when they do not know how to employ them well, or fortune is contrary to them. But the principal use of prudence of self-control is that it teaches us to be masters of our passions, and to so control and guide them that the evils which they cause are quite bearable, and that we even derive joy from them all.

Descartes, *Passions of the Soul,* CCXII

18 By knowing each man's ruling passion, we are sure of pleasing him; and yet each has his fancies, opposed to his true good, in the very idea which he has of the good. It is a singularly puzzling fact.

Pascal, *Pensées,* II, 106

19 There is internal war in man between reason and the passions.
If he had only reason without passions . . .
If he had only passions without reason . . .
But having both, he cannot be without strife, being unable to be at peace with the one without being at war with the other. Thus he is always divided against and opposed to himself.
This internal war of reason against the passions has made a division of those who would have peace into two sects. The first would renounce their passions and become gods; the others would renounce reason and become brute beasts. But neither can do so, and reason still remains, to condemn the vileness and injustice of the passions and to trouble the repose of those who abandon themselves to them; and the passions keep always alive in those who would renounce them.

Pascal, *Pensées,* VI, 412–413

20 The forms of speech by which the passions are expressed are partly the same and partly different from those by which we express our thoughts. And first generally all passions may be expressed *indicatively;* as, *I love, I fear, I joy, I deliberate, I will, I command:* but some of them have particular expressions by themselves, which nevertheless are not affirmations, unless it be when they serve to make other inferences besides that of the passion they proceed from. Deliberation is expressed *subjunctively;* which is a speech proper to signify suppositions, with their consequences; as, *If this be done, then this will follow;* and differs not from the language of reasoning, save that reasoning is in general words, but deliberation for the most part is of particulars. The language of desire, and aversion, is *imperative;* as, *Do this, forbear that;* which when the party is obliged to do, or forbear, is *command;* otherwise *prayer;* or else *counsel.* The language of vainglory, of indignation, pity and revengefulness, *optative:* but of the desire to know, there is a peculiar expression called *interrogative;* as, *What is it, when shall it, how is it done,* and *why so?* Other language of the passions I find none: for cursing, swearing, reviling, and the like do not signify as speech, but as the actions of a tongue accustomed.

Hobbes, *Leviathan,* I, 6

21 The mind is subject to passions in proportion to the number of inadequate ideas which it has, and . . . it acts in proportion to the number of adequate ideas which it has.

Spinoza, *Ethics,* III, Prop. 1, Corol.

22 Of joy, sorrow, and desire, and consequently of every effort which either, like vacillation of mind, is compounded of these, or, like love, hatred, hope, and fear, is derived from them, there are just as many kinds as there are kinds of objects by which we are affected.

Spinoza, *Ethics,* III, Prop. 56

23 *Envy* and *anger,* not being caused by pain and pleasure simply in themselves, but having in them some mixed considerations of ourselves and others, are not therefore to be found in all men, because those other parts, of valuing their merits, or intending revenge, is wanting in them. But all the rest [of the passions], terminating purely in pain and pleasure, are, I think, to be found in all men. For we love, desire, rejoice, and hope, only in respect of pleasure; we hate, fear, and grieve, only in respect of pain ultimately. In fine, all these passions are moved by things, only as they appear to be the causes of pleasure and pain, or to have pleasure or pain some way or other annexed to them.

Locke, *Concerning Human Understanding,*
Bk. II, XX, 14

24 Modes of Self-love the Passions we may call;
'Tis real good, or seeming, moves them all;
But since not every good we can divide,
And Reason bids us for our own provide;
Passions, tho' selfish, if their means be fair,
List under Reason, and deserve her care;
Those, that imparted, court a nobler aim,
Exalt their kind, and take some Virtue's name.

Pope, *Essay on Man,* Epistle II, 93

25 Strength of mind is Exercise, not Rest:
The rising tempest puts in act the soul,
Parts it may ravage, but preserves the whole.
On life's vast ocean diversely we sail,

Reason the card, but Passion is the gale.
Pope, *Essay on Man*, Epistle II, 104

26 On diff'rent senses diff'rent objects strike;
Hence diff'rent Passions more or less inflame,
As strong or weak, the organs of the frame;
And hence one master Passion in the breast,
Like Aaron's serpent, swallows up the rest.
    As Man, perhaps, the moment of his breath,
Receives the lurking principle of death;
The young disease, that must subdue at length,
Grows with his growth, and strengthens with his
    strength:
So, cast and mingled with his very frame,
The Mind's disease, its rulling Passion came.
Pope, *Essay on Man*, Epistle II, 128

27 Nothing can oppose or retard the impulse of passion, but a contrary impulse; and if this contrary
impulse ever arises from reason, that latter faculty
must have an original influence on the will, and
must be able to cause, as well as hinder any act of
volition. But if reason has no original influence,
'tis impossible it can withstand any principle,
which has such an efficacy, or ever keep the mind
in suspence a moment. Thus it appears, that the
principle, which opposes our passion, cannot be
the same with reason, and is only call'd so in an
improper sense. We speak not strictly and philosophically when we talk of the combat of passion
and of reason. Reason is, and ought only to be the
slave of the passions, and can never pretend to
any other office than to serve and obey them. As
this opinion may appear somewhat extraordinary,
it may not be improper to confirm it by some
other considerations.
Hume, *Treatise of Human Nature*,
Bk. II, III, 3

28 Reason is the discovery of truth or falshood. Truth
or falshood consists in an agreement or disagreement either to the *real* relations of ideas, or to
real existence and matter of fact. Whatever, therefore, is not susceptible of this agreement or disagreement, is incapable of being true or false, and
can never be an object of our reason. Now 'tis
evident our passions, volitions, and actions, are
not susceptible of any such agreement or disagreement; being original facts and realities, compleat in themselves, and implying no reference to
other passions, volitions, and actions. 'Tis impossible, therefore, they can be pronounced either true
or false, and be either contrary or conformable to
reason.
Hume, *Treatise of Human Nature*, Bk. III, I, 1

29 *Emotions* and *passions* are essentially distinct; the
former belong to *feeling* insofar as this coming before reflection makes it more difficult or even impossible. Hence emotion is called *hasty* (*animus
praeceps*). And reason declares through the notion

of virtue that a man should *collect* himself; but this
weakness in the life of one's understanding, joined
with the strength of a mental excitement, is only a
lack of virtue (*Untugend*), and as it were a weak and
childish thing, which may very well consist with
the best will, and has further this one good thing
in it, that this storm soon subsides. A propensity to
emotion (for example, *resentment*) is therefore not
so closely related to vice as passion is. *Passion*, on
the other hand, is the sensible *appetite* grown into a
permanent inclination (for example, *hatred* in contrast to *resentment*). The calmness with which one
indulges it leaves room for reflection and allows
the mind to frame principles thereon for itself;
and thus when the inclination falls upon what
contradicts the law, to brood on it, to allow it to
root itself deeply, and thereby to take up evil (as
of set purpose) into one's maxim; and this is then
specifically evil, that is, it is a true *vice*.
Kant, *Introduction to the Metaphysical
Elements of Ethics*, XVI

30 The lower animals, like man, manifestly feel pleasure and pain, happiness and misery. Happiness i
never better exhibited than by young anima'
such as puppies, kittens, lambs, &c., when playing
together, like our own children. Even insects play
together, as has been described by that excellent
observer, P. Huber, who saw ants chasing and
pretending to bite each other, like so many puppies.
    The fact that the lower animals are excited by
the same emotions as ourselves is so well established, that it will not be necessary to weary the
reader by many details. Terror acts in the same
manner on them as on us, causing the muscles to
tremble, the heart to palpitate, the sphincters to
be relaxed, and the hair to stand on end. Suspicion, the offspring of fear, is eminently characteristic of most wild animals. It is, I think, impossible
to read the account given by Sir E. Tennent, of
the behaviour of the female elephants, used as de-
coys, without admitting that they intentionally
practise deceit, and well know what they are
about. Courage and timidity are extremely variable qualities in the individuals of the same species,
as is plainly seen in our dogs. Some dogs and horses are ill-tempered, and easily turn sulky; others
are good-tempered; and these qualities are certainly inherited. Every one knows how liable animals are to furious rage, and how plainly they
shew it. Many, and probably true, anecdotes have
been published on the long-delayed and artful revenge of various animals. . . .
    The love of a dog for his master is notorious; as
an old writer quaintly says, "A dog is the only
thing on this earth that luvs you more than he
luvs himself."
    In the agony of death a dog has been known to
caress his master, and every one has heard of the
dog suffering under vivisection, who licked the

hand of the operator; this man, unless the operation was fully justified by an increase of our knowledge, or unless he had a heart of stone, must have felt remorse to the last hour of his life. . . .

Most of the more complex emotions are common to the higher animals and ourselves. Every one has seen how jealous a dog is of his master's affection, if lavished on any other creature; and I have observed the same fact with monkeys. This shews that animals not only love, but have desire to be loved. Animals manifestly feel emulation. They love approbation or praise; and a dog carrying a basket for his master exhibits in a high degree self-complacency or pride. There can, I think, be no doubt that a dog feels shame, as distinct from fear, and something very like modesty when begging too often for food. A great dog scorns the snarling of a little dog, and this may be called magnanimity. Several observers have stated that monkeys certainly dislike being laughed at; and they sometimes invent imaginary offences. In the Zoological Gardens I saw a baboon who always got into a furious rage when his keeper took out a letter or book and read it aloud to him; and his rage was so violent that, as I witnessed on one occasion, he bit his own leg till the blood flowed. Dogs shew what may be fairly called a sense of humour, as distinct from mere play; if a bit of stick or other such object be thrown to one, he will often carry it away for a short distance; and then squatting down with it on the ground close before him, will wait until his master comes quite close to take it away. The dog will then seize it and rush away in triumph, repeating the same manœuvre, and evidently enjoying the practical joke.

We will now turn to the more intellectual emotions and faculties, which are very important, as forming the basis for the development of the higher mental powers. Animals manifestly enjoy excitement, and suffer from ennui, as may be seen with dogs, and, according to Rengger, with monkeys. All animals feel *Wonder*, and many exhibit *Curiosity*. They sometimes suffer from this latter quality.

Darwin, *Descent of Man*, I, 3

31 In speaking of the instincts it has been impossible to keep them separate from the emotional excitements which go with them. Objects of rage, love, fear, etc., not only prompt a man to outward deeds, but provoke characteristic alterations in his attitude and visage, and affect his breathing, circulation, and other organic functions in specific ways. When the outward deeds are inhibited, these latter emotional expressions still remain, and we read the anger in the face, though the blow may not be struck, and the fear betrays itself in voice and color, though one may suppress all other sign. *Instinctive reactions and emotional expressions thus shade imperceptibly into each other. Every object that excites an instinct excites an emotion as well.* Emotions, however, fall short of instincts, in that the emotional reaction usually terminates in the subject's own body, whilst the instinctive reaction is apt to go farther and enter into practical relations with the exciting object.

William James, *Psychology*, XXV

32 Our natural way of thinking about these coarser emotions is that the mental perception of some fact excites the mental affection called the emotion, and that this latter state of mind gives rise to the bodily expression. My theory, on the contrary, is that *the bodily changes follow directly the perception of the exciting fact, and that our feeling of the same changes as they occur* IS *the emotion.* Common-sense says, we lose our fortune, are sorry and weep; we meet a bear, are frightened and run; we are insulted by a rival, are angry and strike. The hypothesis here to be defended says that this order of sequence is incorrect, that the one mental state is not immediately induced by the other, that the bodily manifestations must first be interposed between, and that the more rational statement is that we feel sorry because we cry, angry because we strike, afraid because we tremble, and not that we cry, strike, or tremble, because we are sorry, angry, or fearful, as the case may be. Without the bodily states following on the perception, the latter would be purely cognitive in form, pale, colorless, destitute of emotional warmth. We might then see the bear, and judge it best to run, receive the insult and deem it right to strike, but we should not actually *feel* afraid or angry.

William James, *Psychology*, XXV

33 If one should seek to name each particular [emotion] of which the human heart is the seat, it is plain that the limit to their number would lie in the introspective vocabulary of the seeker, each race of men having found names for some shade of feeling which other races have left undiscriminated. If then we should seek to break the emotions, thus enumerated, into groups, according to their affinities, it is again plain that all sorts of groupings would be possible, according as we chose this character or that as a basis, and that all groupings would be equally real and true. The only question would be, does this grouping or that suit our purpose best? The reader may then class the emotions as he will, as sad or joyous, sthenic or asthenic, natural or acquired, inspired by animate or inanimate things, formal or material, sensuous or ideal, direct or reflective, egoistic or non-egoistic, retrospective, prospective or immediate, organismally or environmentally initiated, or what more besides. All these are divisions which have been actually proposed. Each of them has its merits, and each one brings together some emotions which the others keep apart.

William James, *Psychology*, XXV

34 I think we shall gain a great deal by following the suggestion of a writer who, from personal motives, vainly insists that he has nothing to do with the rigours of pure science. I am speaking of Georg Groddeck, who is never tired of pointing out that the conduct through life of what we call our ego is essentially passive, and that, as he expresses it, we are "lived" by unknown and uncontrollable forces.

Freud, *Ego and Id,* II

35 The ego has the task of bringing the influence of the external world to bear upon the id and its tendencies, and endeavours to substitute the reality-principle for the pleasure-principle which reigns supreme in the id. In the ego, perception plays the part which in the id devolves upon in-stinct. The ego represents what we call reason and sanity, in contrast to the id which contains the passions. . . .

The functional importance of the ego is manifested in the fact that normally control over the approaches to motility devolves upon it. Thus in its relation to the id it is like a man on horseback, who has to hold in check the superior strength of the horse; with this difference, that the rider seeks to do so with his own strength while the ego uses borrowed forces. The illustration may be carried further. Often a rider, if he is not to be parted from his horse, is obliged to guide it where it wants to go; so in the same way the ego constantly carries into action the wishes of the id as if they were its own.

Freud, *Ego and Id,* II

4.2 | *Fear*

1 The Lord is my light and my salvation; whom shall I fear? the Lord is the strength of my life; of whom shall I be afraid?

Psalm 27:1

2 *Chorus.* There are times when fear is good.
It must keep its watchful place
at the heart's controls. There is advantage
in the wisdom won from pain.
Should the city, should the man
rear a heart that nowhere goes
in fear, how shall such a one
any more respect the right?

Aeschylus, *Eumenides,* 517

3 *Xerxes.* Fear not all things alike, nor count up every risk. For if in each matter that comes before us thou wilt look to all possible chances, never wilt thou achieve anything. Far better is it to have a stout heart always, and suffer one's share of evils, than to be ever fearing what may happen, and never incur a mischance.

Herodotus, *History,* VII, 50

4 *Peloponnesian Commanders.* A faint heart will make all art powerless in the face of danger. For fear takes away presence of mind, and without valour art is useless.

Thucydides, *Peloponnesian War,* II, 87

5 *Nicias.* I do not call animals or any other things which have no fear of dangers, because they are ignorant of them, courageous, but only fearless and senseless. Do you [Laches] imagine that I should call little children courageous, which fear no dangers because they know none? There is a difference, to my way of thinking, between fearlessness and courage.

Plato, *Laches,* 197A

6 *Socrates.* In my opinion the terrible and the hopeful are the things which do or do not create fear, and fear is not of the present, nor of the past, but is of future and expected evil.

Plato, *Laches,* 198A

7 Fear may be defined as a pain or disturbance due to a mental picture of some destructive or painful evil in the future. Of destructive or painful evils only; for there are some evils, for example, wickedness or stupidity, the prospect of which does not frighten us: I mean only such as amount to great pains or losses. And even these only if they appear not remote but so near as to be imminent: we do not fear things that are a very long way off: for instance, we all know we shall die, but we are not troubled thereby, because death is not close at hand. From this definition it will follow that fear is caused by whatever we feel has great power of destroying us, or of harming us in ways

that tend to cause us great pain.

Aristotle, *Rhetoric*, 1382ᵃ21

8 Of those we have wronged, and of our enemies or rivals, it is not the passionate and outspoken whom we have to fear, but the quiet, dissembling, unscrupulous; since we never know when they are upon us, we can never be sure they are at a safe distance.

Aristotle, *Rhetoric*, 1382ᵇ19

9 If fear is associated with the expectation that something destructive will happen to us, plainly nobody will be afraid who believes nothing can happen to him; we shall not fear things that we believe cannot happen to us, nor people who we believe cannot inflict them upon us; nor shall we be afraid at times when we think ourselves safe from them. It follows therefore that fear is felt by those who believe something to be likely to happen to them, at the hands of particular persons, in a particular form, and at a particular time. People do not believe this when they are, or think they are, in the midst of great prosperity, and are in consequence insolent, contemptuous, and reckless—the kind of character produced by wealth, physical strength, abundance of friends, power: nor yet when they feel they have experienced every kind of horror already and have grown callous about the future, like men who are being flogged and are already nearly dead—if they are to feel the anguish of uncertainty, there must be some faint expectation of escape.

Aristotle, *Rhetoric*, 1382ᵇ29

10 Even as children are flurried and dread all things in the thick darkness, thus we in the daylight fear at times things not a whit more to be dreaded than what children shudder at in the dark and fancy sure to be. This terror therefore and darkness of mind must be dispelled not by the rays of the sun and glittering shafts of day, but by the aspect and law of nature.

Lucretius, *Nature of Things*, VI

11 If one were successful in getting rid of all fear, then we would also be rid of that judicious manner of living that is most highly evidenced in those who fear the laws, magistrates, poverty, disgrace, and pain.

Cicero, *Disputations*, IV, 20

12 *Aeneas.* Mute and amaz'd, my hair with terror stood;
Fear shrunk my sinews, and congeal'd my blood.
Mann'd once again, another plant I try:
That other gush'd with the same sanguine dye.
Then, fearing guilt for some offense unknown,
With pray'rs and vows and Dryads I atone,
With all the sisters of the woods, and most
The God of Arms, who rules the Thracian coast,

That they, or he, these omens would avert,
Release our fears, and better signs impart.
Clear'd, as I thought, and fully fix'd at length
To learn the cause, I tugged with all my strength:
I bent my knees against the ground; once more
The violated myrtle ran with gore.
Scarce dare I tell the sequel: from the womb
Of wounded earth, and caverns of the tomb,
A groan, as of a troubled ghost, renew'd
My fright, and then these dreadful words ensued:
'Why dost thou thus my buried body rend?
O spare the corpse of thy unhappy friend!
Spare to pollute thy pious hands with blood:
The tears distil not from the wounded wood;
But ev'ry drop this living tree contains
Is kindred blood, and ran in Trojan veins.
O fly from this unhospitable shore,
Warn'd by my fate; for I am Polydore!
Here loads of lances, in my blood embrued,
Again shoot upward, by my blood renew'd.'
"My falt'ring tongue and shiv'ring limbs declare
My horror, and in bristles rose my hair.

Virgil, *Aeneid*, III

13 To be feared is to fear: no one has been able to strike terror into others and at the same time enjoy peace of mind himself.

Seneca, *Letters to Lucilius*, 105

14 There is no fear in love; but perfect love casteth out fear: because fear hath torment. He that feareth is not made perfect in love.

I John 4:18

15 It is irrational and poor-spirited not to seek conveniences for fear of losing them, for upon the same account we should not allow ourselves to like wealth, glory, or wisdom, since we may fear to be deprived of all these; nay, even virtue itself, than which there is no greater nor more desirable possession. . . . It is weakness that brings men, unarmed against fortune by reason, into these endless pains and terrors; and they indeed have not even the present enjoyment of what they dote upon, the possibility of the future loss causing them continual pangs, tremors, and distresses. We must not provide against the loss of wealth by poverty, or of friends by refusing all acquaintance, or of children by having none, but by morality and reason.

Plutarch, *Solon*

16 The strangeness of things often makes them seem formidable when they are not so; and . . . by our better acquaintance, even things which are really terrible lose much of their frightfulness.

Plutarch, *Caius Marius*

17 We are . . . in the condition of deer; when they flee from the huntsmen's feathers in fright, whith-

er do they turn and in what do they seek refuge as safe? They turn to the nets, and thus they perish by confounding things which are objects of fear with things that they ought not to fear. Thus we also act: in what cases do we fear? In things which are independent of the will. In what cases, on the contrary, do we behave with confidence, as if there were no danger? In things dependent on the will. To be deceived then, or to act rashly, or shamelessly or with base desire to seek something, does not concern us at all, if we only hit the mark in things which are independent of our will. But where there is death, or exile or pain or infamy, there we attempt to run away, there we are struck with terror. Therefore, as we may expect it to happen with those who err in the greatest matters, we convert natural confidence into audacity, desperation, rashness, shamelessness; and we convert natural caution and modesty into cowardice and meanness, which are full of fear and confusion. For if a man should transfer caution to those things in which the will may be exercised and the acts of the will, he will immediately, by willing to be cautious, have also the power of avoiding what he chooses: but if he transfer it to the things which are not in his power and will, and attempt to avoid the things which are in the power of others, he will of necessity fear, he will be unstable, he will be disturbed. For death or pain is not formidable, but the fear of pain or death.

Epictetus, *Discourses,* II, 1

18 In this abode of weakness, and in these wicked days, . . . anxiety has also its use, stimulating us to seek with keener longing for that security where peace is complete and unassailable.

Augustine, *City of God,* XIX, 10

19 Fear is twofold . . . one is filial fear, by which a son fears to offend his father or to be separated from him; the other is servile fear, by which one fears punishment. Now filial fear must increase when charity increases, even as an effect increases with the increase of its cause. For the more one loves a man, the more one fears to offend him and to be separated from him. On the other hand servile fear, as regards its servility, is entirely cast out when charity comes, although the fear of punishment remains as to its substance. . . . This fear decreases as charity increases, chiefly as regards its act, since the more a man loves God, the less he fears punishment; first, because he thinks less of his own good, to which punishment is opposed; secondly, because, the faster he clings, the more confident he is of the reward, and consequently, the less fearful of punishment.

Aquinas, *Summa Theologica,* II–II, 19, 10

20 [The prince] ought to be slow to believe and to act, nor should he himself show fear, but proceed in a temperate manner with prudence and hu-

manity, so that too much confidence may not make him incautious and too much distrust render him intolerable.

Upon this a question arises: whether it be better to be loved than feared or feared than loved? It may be answered that one should wish to be both, but, because it is difficult to unite them in one person, it is much safer to be feared than loved, when, of the two, either must be dispensed with. Because this is to be asserted in general of men, that they are ungrateful, fickle, false, cowardly, covetous, and as long as you succeed they are yours entirely; they will offer you their blood, property, life, and children, as is said above, when the need is far distant; but when it approaches they turn against you. And that prince who, relying entirely on their promises, has neglected other precautions, is ruined; because friendships that are obtained by payments, and not by greatness or nobility of mind, may indeed be earned, but they are not secured, and in time of need cannot be relied upon; and men have less scruple in offending one who is beloved than one who is feared, for love is preserved by the link of obligation which, owing to the baseness of men, is broken at every opportunity for their advantage; but fear preserves you by a dread of punishment which never fails.

Nevertheless a prince ought to inspire fear in such a way that, if he does not win love, he avoids hatred; because he can endure very well being feared whilst he is not hated, which will always be as long as he abstains from the property of his citizens and subjects and from their women.

Machiavelli, *Prince,* XVII

21 The thing I fear most is fear. . . . Those who have been well drubbed in some battle, and who are still all wounded and bloody—you can perfectly well bring them back to the charge the next day. But those who have conceived a healthy fear of the enemy—you would never get them to look him in the face. Those who are in pressing fear of losing their property, of being exiled, of being subjugated, live in constant anguish, losing even the capacity to drink, eat, and rest; whereas the poor, the exiles, and the slaves often live as joyfully as other men. And so many people who, unable to endure the pangs of fear, have hanged themselves, drowned themselves, or leaped to their death, have taught us well that fear is even more unwelcome and unbearable than death itself.

Montaigne, *Essays,* I, 18, Of Fear

22 Fear sometimes arises from want of judgment as well as from want of courage. All the dangers I have seen, I have seen with open eyes, with my sight free, sound, and entire; besides, it takes courage to be afraid.

Montaigne, *Essays,* III, 6, Of Coaches

23 He who fears he will suffer, already suffers from his fear.

Montaigne, *Essays*, III, 13, Of Experience

24 As to the significance of fear or terror, I do not see that it can ever be praiseworthy or useful; it likewise is not a special passion, but merely an excess of cowardice, astonishment and fear, which is always vicious, just as bravery is an excess of courage which is always good, provided that the end proposed is good; and because the principal cause of fear is surprise, there is nothing better for getting rid of it than to use premeditation and to prepare oneself for all eventualities, the fear of which may cause it.

Descartes, *Passions of the Soul*, CLXXVI

25 Being assured that there be causes of all things that have arrived hitherto, or shall arrive hereafter, it is impossible for a man, who continually endeavoureth to secure himself against the evil he fears, and procure the good he desireth, not to be in a perpetual solicitude of the time to come; so that every man, especially those that are overprovident, are in an estate like to that of Prometheus. For as Prometheus (which, interpreted, is *the prudent man*) was bound to the hill Caucasus, a place of large prospect, where an eagle, feeding on his liver, devoured in the day as much as was repaired in the night: so that man, which looks too far before him in the care of future time, hath his heart all the day long gnawed on by fear of death, poverty, or other calamity; and has no repose, nor pause of his anxiety, but in sleep.

Hobbes, *Leviathan*, I, 12

26 True fear comes from faith; false fear comes from doubt. True fear is joined to hope, because it is born of faith, and because men hope in the God in whom they believe. False fear is joined to despair, because men fear the God in whom they have no belief. The former fear to lose Him; the latter fear to find Him.

Pascal, *Pensées*, IV, 262

27 Fear was given us as a monitor to quicken our industry, and keep us upon our guard against the approaches of evil; and therefore to have no apprehension of mischief at hand, not to make a just estimate of the danger, but heedlessly to run into it, be the hazard what it will, without considering of what use or consequence it may be, is not the resolution of a rational creature, but brutish fury.

Locke, *Some Thoughts Concering Education*, 115

28 There is no passion so distressing as fear, which gives us great pain and makes us appear contemptible in our own eyes to the last degree.

Boswell, *London Journal (Nov. 18, 1762)*

29 Fear is in almost all cases a wretched instrument of government, and ought in particular never to be employed against any order of men who have the smallest pretensions to independency. To attempt to terrify them serves only to irritate their bad humour, and to confirm them in an opposition which more gentle usage perhaps might easily induce them either to soften, or to lay aside altogether.

Adam Smith, *Wealth of Nations*, V, 1

30 Fear has been the original parent of superstition, and every new calamity urges trembling mortals to deprecate the wrath of their invisible enemies.

Gibbon, *Decline and Fall of the Roman Empire*, XI

31 And now this spell was snapt: once more
I viewed the ocean green,
And looked far forth, yet little saw
Of what had else been seen—

Like one, that on a lonesome road
Doth walk in fear and dread,
And having once turned round walks on,
And turns no more his head;
Because he knows, a frightful fiend
Doth close behind him tread.

Coleridge, *The Rime of the Ancient Mariner*, 442

32 They [the Norsemen] understood in their heart that it was indispensable to be brave; that Odin would have no favour for them, but despise and thrust them out, if they were not brave. Consider too whether there is not something in this! It is an everlasting duty, valid in our day as in that, the duty of being brave. *Valour* is still *value*. The first duty for a man is still that of subduing *Fear*. We must get rid of Fear; we cannot act at all till then. A man's acts are slavish, not true but specious; his very thoughts are false, he thinks too as a slave and coward, till he have got Fear under his feet.

Carlyle, *The Hero as Divinity*

33 In civilized life . . . it has at last become possible for large numbers of people to pass from the cradle to the grave without ever having had a pang of genuine fear. Many of us need an attack of mental disease to teach us the meaning of the word. Hence the possibility of so much blindly optimistic philosophy and religion.

William James, *Psychology*, XXIV

34 *Napoleon.* There is only one universal passion: fear. Of all the thousand qualities a man may have, the only one you will find as certainly in the youngest drummer boy in my army as in me, is fear. It is fear that makes men fight: it is indifference that makes them run away: fear is the mainspring of war. Fear! I know fear well, better than you, bet-

ter than any woman. I once saw a regiment of good Swiss soldiers massacred by a mob in Paris because I was afraid to interfere: I felt myself a coward to the tips of my toes as I looked on at it. Seven months ago I revenged my shame by pounding that mob to death with cannon balls. Well, what of that? Has fear ever held a man back from anything he really wanted—or a woman either?

Shaw, *The Man of Destiny*

4.3 | *Anger*

1 He that is slow to anger is better than the mighty; and he that ruleth his spirit than he that taketh a city.

Proverbs 16:32

2 *Oedipus.* And as I journeyed I came to the place where, as you say, this king met with his death. Jocasta, I will tell you the whole truth.
When I was near the branching of the crossroads, going on foot, I was encountered by
a herald and a carriage with a man in it,
just as you tell me. He that led the way
and the old man himself wanted to thrust me
out of the road by force. I became angry
and struck the coachman who was pushing me.
When the old man saw this he watched his moment,
and as I passed he struck me from the carriage,
full on the head with his two pointed goad.
But he was paid in full and presently
my stick had struck him backwards from the car
and he rolled out of it. And then I killed them all.

Sophocles, *Oedipus the King,* 799

3 *Syracusan generals and Gylippus.* The fortune of our greatest enemies [the Athenians] having . . . betrayed itself, and their disorder being what I have described, let us engage in anger, convinced that, as between adversaries, nothing is more legitimate than to claim to sate the whole wrath of one's soul in punishing the aggressor, and nothing more sweet, as the proverb has it, than the vengeance upon an enemy, which it will now be ours to take. That enemies they are and mortal enemies you all know, since they came here to enslave our country, and if successful had in reserve for our men all that is most dreadful, and for our children and wives all that is most dishonourable.

Thucydides, *Peloponnesian War,* VII, 68

4 *Athenian Stranger.* Let this, then, be the law about abuse, which shall relate to all cases:—No one shall speak evil of another; and when a man disputes with another he shall teach and learn of the disputant and the company, but he shall abstain from evil-speaking; for out of the imprecations which men utter against one another, and the feminine habit of casting aspersions on one another, and using foul names, out of words light as air, in very deed the greatest enmities and hatreds spring up. For the speaker gratifies his anger, which is an ungracious element of his nature; and nursing up his wrath by the entertainment of evil thoughts, and exacerbating that part of his soul which was formerly civilized by education, he lives in a state of savageness and moroseness, and pays a bitter penalty for his anger. And in such cases almost all men take to saying something ridiculous about their opponent, and there is no man who is in the habit of laughing at another who does not miss virtue and earnestness altogether, or lose the better half of greatness.

Plato, *Laws,* XI, 934B

5 The man who is angry at the right things and with the right people, and, further, as he ought, when he ought, and as long as he ought, is praised. This will be the good-tempered man, then, since good temper is praised. For the good-tempered man tends to be unperturbed and not to be led by passion, but to be angry in the manner, at the things, and for the length of time, that the rule dictates.

Aristotle, *Ethics,* 1125^{b}32

6 Anger seems to listen to argument to some extent, but to mishear it, as do hasty servants who run out before they have heard the whole of what one says, and then muddle the order, or as dogs bark if there is but a knock at the door, before looking to see if it is a friend; so anger by reason of the warmth and hastiness of its nature, though it hears, does not hear an order, and springs to take

revenge. For argument or imagination informs us that we have been insulted or slighted, and anger, reasoning as it were that anything like this must be fought against, boils up straightway.

Aristotle, *Ethics*, 1149ᵃ25

7 Anger may be defined as an impulse, accompanied by pain, to a conspicuous revenge for a conspicuous slight directed without justification towards what concerns oneself or towards what concerns one's friends. If this is a proper definition of anger, it must always be felt towards some particular individual . . . and not 'man' in general. It must be felt because the other has done or intended to do something to him or one of his friends. It must always be attended by a certain pleasure—that which arises from the expectation of revenge. For since nobody aims at what he thinks he cannot attain, the angry man is aiming at what he can attain, and the belief that you will attain your aim is pleasant. . . . It is also attended by a certain pleasure because the thoughts dwell upon the act of vengeance, and the images then called up cause pleasure, like the images called up in dreams.

Aristotle, *Rhetoric*, 1378ᵃ31

8 Enmity is anger waiting for a chance for revenge.

Cicero, *Disputations*, IV, 9

9 She [Armata] flew to rage; for now the snake
     possess'd
Her vital parts, and poison'd all her breast;
She raves, she runs with a distracted pace,
And fills with horrid howls the public place.
And, as young striplings whip the top for sport,
On the smooth pavement of an empty court;
The wooden engine flies and whirls about,
Admir'd, with clamors, of the beardless rout;
They lash aloud; each other they provoke,
And lend their little souls at ev'ry stroke:
Thus fares the queen; and thus her fury blows
Amidst the crowd, and kindles as she goes.
Nor yet content, she strains her malice more,
And adds new ills to those contriv'd before:
She flies the town, and, mixing with a throng
Of madding matrons, bears the bride along,
Wand'ring thro' woods and wilds, and devious
     ways,
And with these arts the Trojan match delays.

Virgil, *Aeneid*, VII

10 Aghast he [Turnus] wak'd; and, starting from his
     bed,
Cold sweat, in clammy drops, his limbs o'erspread.
"Arms! arms!" he cries: "my sword and shield
     prepare!"
He breathes defiance, blood, and mortal war.
So, when with crackling flames a caldron fries,
The bubbling waters from the bottom rise:

Above the brims they force their fiery way;
Black vapors climb aloft, and cloud the day.

Virgil, *Aeneid*, VII

11 He who will not curb his passion, will wish that undone which his grief and resentment suggested, while he violently plies his revenge with unsated rancour. Rage is a short madness. Rule your passion, which commands, if it do not obey; do you restrain it with a bridle, and with fetters.

Horace, *Epistles*, I, 2

12 Hesitation is the best cure for anger. Seek this concession from anger right away, not to gain its pardon, but that it may evidence some discrimination. The first blows of anger are heavy, but if it waits, it will think again. Do not try to destroy it immediately. Attacked piecemeal, it will be entirely overcome.

Seneca, *On Anger*, II, 29

13 Marcius alone, himself, was neither stunned nor humiliated. In mien, carriage, and countenance he bore the appearance of entire composure, and, while all his friends were full of distress, seemed the only man that was not touched with his misfortune. Not that either reflection taught him, or gentleness of temper made it natural for him, to submit; he was wholly possessed, on the contrary, with a profound and deepseated fury, which passes with many for no pain at all. And pain, it is true, transmuted, so to say, by its own fiery heat into anger, loses every appearance of depression and feebleness; the angry man makes a show of energy, as the man in a high fever does of natural heat, while, in fact, all this action of soul is but mere diseased palpitation, distension, and inflamation.

Plutarch, *Coriolanus*

14 If any have offended against thee, consider first: What is my relation to men, and that we are made for one another. . . .
    Second, consider what kind of men they are . . . and particularly, under what compulsions in respect of opinions they are; and as to their acts, consider with what pride they do what they do.
    Third, that if men do rightly what they do, we ought not to be displeased; but if they do not right, it is plain that they do so involuntarily and in ignorance. . . .
    Fourth, consider that thou also doest many things wrong, and that thou art a man like others; and even if thou dost abstain from certain faults, still thou hast the disposition to commit them, though either through cowardice, or concern about reputation, or some such mean motive, thou dost abstain from such faults.
    Fifth, consider that thou dost not even understand whether men are doing wrong or not, for many things are done with a certain reference to

circumstances. And in short, a man must learn a great deal to enable him to pass a correct judgement on another man's acts.

Sixth, consider when thou art much vexed or grieved, that man's life is only a moment, and after a short time we are all laid out dead.

Seventh, that it is not men's acts which disturb us, for those acts have their foundation in men's ruling principles, but it is our own opinions which disturb us. . . .

Eighth, consider how much more pain is brought on us by the anger and vexation caused by such acts than by the acts themselves. . . .

Ninth, consider that a good disposition is invincible, if it be genuine, and not an affected smile and acting a part. For what will the most violent man do to thee, if thou continuest to be of a kind disposition towards him, and if, as opportunity offers, thou gently admonishest him and calmly correctest his errors at the very time when he is trying to do thee harm. . . .

Remember these nine rules, as if thou hadst received them as a gift from the Muses, and begin at last to be a man while thou lives.

Marcus Aurelius, *Meditations,* XI, 18

15 Anger does not arise except on account of some pain inflicted, and unless there be the desire and hope of revenge. . . . If the person who inflicted the injury excel very much, anger does not ensue, but only sorrow.

Aquinas, *Summa Theologica,* I–II, 46, 1

16 Unmerited contempt more than anything else is a provocative of anger. Consequently deficiency of littleness in the person with whom we are angry tends to increase our anger, insofar as it adds to the unmeritedness of being despised. For just as the higher a man's position is, the more undeservedly he is despised, so the lower it is the less reason he has for despising. Thus a nobleman is angry if he be insulted by a peasant; a wise man, if by a fool; a master, if by a servant.

Aquinas, *Summa Theologica,* I–II, 47, 4

17 We crossed the circle, to the other bank, near a fount, that boils and pours down through a cleft, which it has formed.
The water was darker far than perse; and we, accompanying the dusky waves, entered down by a strange path.
This dreary streamlet makes a Marsh, that is named Styx, when it has descended to the foot of the grey malignant shores.
And I, who stood intent on looking, saw muddy people in that bog, all naked and with a look of anger.
They were smiting each other, not with hands only, but with head, and with chest, and with feet; maiming one another with their teeth, piece by piece.

The kind Master said: "Son, now see the souls of those whom anger overcame; and also I would have thee to believe for certain,
that there are people underneath the water, who sob, and make it bubble at the surface; as thy eye may tell thee, whichever way it turns.
Fixed in the slime, they say: 'Sullen were we in the sweet air, that is gladdened by the Sun, carrying lazy smoke within our hearts;
now lie we sullen here in the black mire.' This hymn they gurgle in their throats, for they cannot speak it in full words."

Dante, *Inferno,* VII, 100

18 When I am angry I can write, pray, and preach well, for then my whole temperament is quickened, my understanding sharpened, and all mundane vexations and temptations depart.

Luther, *Table Talk,* H319

19 Aristotle says that anger sometimes serves as a weapon for virtue and valor. That is quite likely; yet those who deny it answer humorously that it is a weapon whose use is novel. For we move other weapons, this one moves us; our hand does not guide it, it guides our hand; it holds us, we do not hold it.

Montaigne, *Essays,* II, 31, Of Anger

20 *Norfolk.*   Stay, my lord,
And let your reason with your choler question
What 'tis you go about. To climb steep hills
Requires slow pace at first. Anger is like
A full hot horse, who being allow'd his way,
Self-mettle tires him.

Shakespeare, *Henry VIII,* I, i, 129

21 To seek to extinguish anger utterly is but a bravery of the Stoics.

Bacon, *Of Anger*

22 Anger is . . . a species of hatred or aversion which we have towards those who have done some evil to or have tried to injure not any chance person but more particularly ourselves. Thus it has the same content as indignation, and all the more so in that it is founded on an action which affects us, and for which we desire to avenge ourselves, for this desire almost always accompanies it; and it is directly opposed to gratitude, as indignation is to favour. But it is incomparably more violent than these three other passions, because the desire to repel harmful things and to revenge oneself, is the most persistent of all desires.

Descartes, *Passions of the Soul,* CXCIX

23 We can distinguish two kinds of anger: the one which is very hasty and manifests itself very much on the surface, but which yet has little effect and can be easily appeased; the other which does not

show itself so much to begin with, but which all the more powerfully gnaws the heart and has more dangerous effects. Those who have much goodness and much love are most subject to the first, for it does not proceed from a profound hatred, but from an instant aversion, which surprises them, because, being impelled to imagine that all things should go in the way which they judge to be best, so soon as it happens otherwise, they wonder and frequently are displeased, even although the matter does not affect them personally, because, having much affection, they interest themselves for those whom they love in the same way as for themselves. . . .

The other kind of anger in which hatred and sadness predominate, is not so apparent at first if it be not perhaps that it causes the face to grow pale; but its strength is little by little increased by the agitation of an ardent desire to avenge oneself excited in the blood, which, being mingled with the bile which is sent towards the heart from the lower part of the liver and spleen, excites there a very keen and ardent heat. And as it is the most generous souls who have most gratitude, it is those who have most pride, and who are most base and infirm, who most allow themselves to be carried away by this kind of anger; for the injuries appear so much the greater as pride causes us to esteem ourselves more, and likewise the more esteem the good things which they remove; which last we value so much the more, as our soul is the more feeble and base, because they depend on others.

Descartes, *Passions of the Soul*, CCI–CCII

24 *Betty.* They are gone, sir, in great anger.
Petulant. Enough, let 'em trundle. Anger helps complexion, saves paint.

Congreve, *Way of the World*, I, ix

25 I was angry with my friend:
I told my wrath, my wrath did end.
I was angry with my foe:
I told it not, my wrath did grow.

Blake, *A Poison Tree*

26 If you strike a child, take care that you strike it in anger, even at the risk of maiming it for life. A blow in cold blood neither can nor should be forgiven.

Shaw, *Man and Superman*, Maxims for Revolutionists

4.4 | *Desire*

1 *Socrates.* In every one of us there are two guiding and ruling principles which lead us whither they will; one is the natural desire of pleasure, the other is an acquired opinion which aspires after the best; and these two are sometimes in harmony and then again at war, and sometimes the one, sometimes the other conquers. When opinion by the help of reason leads us to the best, the conquering principle is called temperance; but when desire, which is devoid of reason, rules in us and drags us to pleasure, that power of misrule is called excess. Now excess has many names, and many members, and many forms, and any of these forms when very marked gives a name, neither honourable nor creditable, to the bearer of the name. The desire of eating, for example, which gets the better of the higher reason and the other desires, is called gluttony, and he who is possessed by it is called a glutton; the tyrannical desire of drink, which inclines the possessor of the desire to drink, has a name which is only too obvious, and there can be as little doubt by what name any other appetite of the same family would be called;—it will be the name of that which happens to be dominant. And now I think that you will perceive the drift of my discourse; but as every spoken word is in a manner plainer than the unspoken, I had better say further that the irrational desire which overcomes the tendency of opinion towards right, and is led away to the enjoyment of beauty, and especially of personal beauty, by the desires which are her own kin-

dred—that supreme desire, I say, which by leading conquers and by the force of passion is reinforced, from this very force, receiving a name, is called love.

Plato, Phaedrus, 237B

2 *Socrates.* Might a man be thirsty, and yet unwilling to drink?

Yes, he [Glaucon] said, it constantly happens.

And in such a case what is one to say? Would you not say that there was something in the soul bidding a man to drink, and something else forbidding him, which is other and stronger than the principle which bids him?

I should say so.

And the forbidding principle is derived from reason, and that which bids and attracts proceeds from passion and disease?

Clearly.

Then we may fairly assume that they are two, and that they differ from one another; the one with which a man reasons, we may call the rational principle of the soul, the other, with which he loves and hungers and thirsts and feels the flutterings of any other desire, may be termed the irrational or appetitive, the ally of sundry pleasures and satisfactions?

Yes, he said, we may fairly assume them to be different.

Then let us finally determine that there are two principles existing in the soul. And what of passion, or spirit? Is it a third, or akin to one of the preceding?

I should be inclined to say—akin to desire.

Well, I said, there is a story which I remember to have heard, and in which I put faith. The story is, that Leontius, the son of Aglaion, coming up one day from the Piraeus, under the north wall on the outside, observed some dead bodies lying on the ground at the place of execution. He felt a desire to see them, and also a dread and abhorrence of them; for a time he struggled and covered his eyes, but at length the desire got the better of him; and forcing them open, he ran up to the dead bodies, saying, Look, ye wretches, take your fill of the fair sight.

I have heard the story myself, he said.

The moral of the tale is, that anger at times goes to war with desire, as though they were two distinct things.

Yes; that is the meaning, he said.

And are there not many other cases in which we observe that when a man's desires violently prevail over his reason, he reviles himself, and is angry at the violence within him, and that in this struggle, which is like the struggle of factions in a State, his spirit is on the side of his reason—but for the passionate or spirited element to take part with the desires when reason decides that she should not be opposed, is a sort of thing which I believe that you never observed occurring in yourself, nor, as I should imagine, in any one else?

Plato, Republic, IV, 439A

3 *Athenian Stranger.* The class of men is small—they must have been rarely gifted by nature, and trained by education—who, when assailed by wants and desires, are able to hold out and observe moderation, and when they might make a great deal of money are sober in their wishes, and prefer a moderate to a large gain. But the mass of mankind are the very opposite: their desires are unbounded, and when they might gain in moderation they prefer gains without limit.

Plato, Laws, XI, 918B

4 These two at all events appear to be sources of movement: appetite and mind (if one may venture to regard imagination as a kind of thinking; for many men follow their imaginations contrary to knowledge, and in all animals other than man there is no thinking or calculation but only imagination).

Both of these then are capable of originating local movement, mind and appetite: (1) mind, that is, which calculates means to an end, i.e. mind practical (it differs from mind speculative in the character of its end); while (2) appetite is in every form of it relative to an end: for that which is the object of appetite is the stimulant of mind practical; and that which is last in the process of thinking is the beginning of the action. It follows that there is a justification for regarding these two as the sources of movement, i.e. appetite and practical thought; for the object of appetite starts a movement and as a result of that thought gives rise to movement, the object of appetite being to it a source of stimulation. So too when imagination originates movement, it necessarily involves appetite.

That which moves therefore is a single faculty and the faculty of appetite; for if there had been two sources of movement—mind and appetite—they would have produced movement in virtue of some common character. As it is, mind is never found producing movement without appetite (for wish is a form of appetite; and when movement is produced according to calculation it is also according to wish), but appetite can originate movement contrary to calculation, for desire is a form of appetite.

Aristotle, On the Soul, 433ª8

5 The primary objects of desire and of thought are the same. For the apparent good is the object of appetite, and the real good is the primary object of rational wish. But desire is consequent on opinion rather than opinion on desire; for the thinking is the starting-point.

Aristotle, Metaphysics, 1072ª27

6 The avarice of mankind is insatiable; at one time two obols was pay enough; but now, when this sum has become customary, men always want more and more without end; for it is of the nature of desire not to be satisfied, and most men live only for the gratification of it.

Aristotle, *Politics,* 1267ª42

7 That which *all* desire is good, as we have said; and so, the more a thing is desired, the better it is.

Aristotle, *Rhetoric,* 1365ª1

8 Whilst what we crave is wanting, it seems to transcend all the rest; then, when it has been gotten, we crave something else, and ever does the same thirst of life possess us, as we gape for it open-mouthed.

Lucretius, *Nature of Things,* III

9 To you everything appears small that you possess: to me all that I have appears great. Your desire is insatiable: mine is satisfied. To (children) who put their hand into a narrow-necked earthen vessel and bring out figs and nuts, this happens; if they fill the hand, they cannot take it out, and then they cry. Drop a few of them and you will draw things out. And do you part with your desires; do not desire many things and you will have what you want.

Epictetus, *Discourses,* III, 9

10 There is no profit from the things which are valued and eagerly sought to those who have obtained them; and to those who have not yet obtained them there is an imagination that when these things are come, all that is good will come with them; then, when they are come, the feverish feeling is the same, the tossing to and fro is the same, the satiety, the desire of things which are not present; for freedom is acquired not by the full possession of the things which are desired, but by removing the desire.

Epictetus, *Discourses,* IV, 1

11 Remember that you must behave as at a banquet. Is anything brought round to you? Put out your hand and take a moderate share. Does it pass by you? Do not stop it. Is it not yet come? Do not yearn in desire toward it, but wait till it reaches you. So with regard to children, wife, office, riches; and you will some time or other be worthy to feast with the gods. And if you do not so much as take the things which are set before you, but are able even to forego them, then you will not only be worthy to feast with the gods, but to rule with them also.

Epictetus, *Encheiridion,* XV

12 Theophrastus, in his comparison of bad acts—

such a comparison as one would make in accordance with the common notions of mankind—says, like a true philosopher, that the offences which are committed through desire are more blameable than those which are committed through anger. For he who is excited by anger seems to turn away from reason with a certain pain and unconscious contraction; but he who offends through desire, being overpowered by pleasure, seems to be in a manner more intemperate and more womanish in his offences. Rightly then, and in a way worthy of philosophy, he said that the offence which is committed with pleasure is more blameable than that which is committed with pain; and on the whole the one is more like a person who has been first wronged and through pain is compelled to be angry; but the other is moved by his own impulse to do wrong, being carried towards doing something by desire.

Marcus Aurelius, *Meditations,* II, 10

13 All things in their own way are inclined by appetite towards good, but in different ways. Some are inclined to good by their natural inclination, without knowledge, as plants and inanimate bodies. Such inclination towards good is called a natural appetite. Others, again, are inclined towards good, but with some knowledge: not that they know the aspect of goodness, but that they know some particular good; as the sense, which knows the sweet, the white, and so on. The inclination which follows this knowledge is called a sensitive appetite. Other things, again, have an inclination towards good, but with a knowledge whereby they know the aspect of good itself; this is proper to the intellect. This is most perfectly inclined towards good; not, indeed, as if it were merely guided by another towards good, like things devoid of knowledge, nor towards some particular good only, as things which have only sensitive knowledge, but as inclined towards good universal in itself. Such inclination is termed will.

Aquinas, *Summa Theologica,* I, 59, 1

14 Between two foods, distant and appetising in like measure, death by starvation would ensue ere a free man put either to his teeth.
So would a lamb stand still between two cravings of fierce wolves, in equipoise of dread; so would a dog stand still between two hinds.

Dante, *Paradiso,* IV, 1

15 Desires are either natural and necessary, like eating and drinking; or natural and not necessary, like intercourse with females; or neither natural nor necessary. Of this last type are nearly all those of men; they are all superfluous and artificial. For it is marvelous how little Nature needs to be content, how little she has left us to desire. The dressings of our cooking have nothing to do with her

ordaining. The Stoics say that a man could stay alive on one olive a day. The delicacy of our wines is no part of her teaching, nor the embellishments that we add to our amorous appetites. . . .

These extraneous desires, which ignorance of the good and a false opinion have insinuated into us, are in such great number that they drive out almost all the natural ones; neither more nor less than if there were such a great number of foreigners in a city that they put out the natural inhabitants, or extinguished their ancient authority and power, completely usurping it and taking possession of it.

Montaigne, *Essays,* II, 12,
Apology for Raymond Sebond

16 That passion which they say is produced by idleness in the hearts of young men, although it makes its way with leisure and a measured step, very evidently shows, to those who have tried to oppose its strength, the power of that conversion and alteration that our judgment suffers.

I attempted at one time to keep myself tensed to withstand it and beat it down: for I am so far from being one of those who invite vices, that I do not even follow them, unless they drag me away. I would feel it come to life, grow, and increase in spite of my resistance, and finally seize me, alive and watching, and possess me, to such an extent that, as from drunkenness, the picture of things began to seem to me other than usual. I would see the advantages of the object of my desire visibly expanding and growing, and increasing and swelling from the breath of my imagination; the difficulties of my undertaking growing easy and smooth, my reason and my conscience withdrawing. But, this fire having vanished all in an instant like a flash of lightning, I would see my soul regain another kind of sight, another state, and another judgment; the difficulties of the retreat would seem to me great and invincible, and the same things would appear in a light and aspect very different from that in which the heat of desire had presented them to me.

Montaigne, *Essays,* II, 12,
Apology for Raymond Sebond

17 It is an amusing conception to imagine a mind exactly balanced between two equal desires. For it is indubitable that it will never decide, since inclination and choice imply inequality in value; and if we were placed between the bottle and the ham with an equal appetite for drinking and for eating, there would doubtless be no solution but to die of thirst and of hunger.

Montaigne, *Essays,* II, 14, How Our Mind

18 *Salarino.* O, ten times faster Venus' pigeons fly
  To seal love's bonds new-made, than they are
    wont

To keep obliged faith unforfeited!
  Gratiano. That ever holds: who riseth from a
    feast
With that keen appetite that he sits down?
Where is the horse that doth untread again
His tedious measures with the unbated fire
That he did pace them first? All things that are,
Are with more spirit chased than enjoy'd.
How like a younker or a prodigal
The scarfed bark puts from her native bay,
Hugg'd and embraced by the strumpet wind!
How like the prodigal doth she return,
With over-weather'd ribs and ragged sails,
Lean, rent and beggar'd by the strumpet wind!

Shakespeare, *Merchant of Venice,* II, vi, 5

19 *Troilus.* This is the monstruosity in love, lady, that the will is infinite and the execution confined, that the desire is boundless and the act a slave to limit.

Shakespeare, *Troilus and Cressida,* III, ii, 87

20 The passion of desire is an agitation of the soul caused by the spirits which dispose it to wish for the future the things which it represents to itself as agreeable. Thus we do not only desire the presence of the absent good, but also the conservation of the present, and further, the absence of evil, both of that which we already have, and of that which we believe we might experience in time to come.

Descartes, *Passions of the Soul,* LXXXVI

21 That which men desire they are also said to love, and to hate those things for which they have aversion. So that desire and love are the same thing; save that by *desire,* we always signify the absence of the object; by *love,* most commonly the presence of the same. So also by *aversion,* we signify the absence; and by *hate,* the presence of the object.

Hobbes, *Leviathan,* I, 6

22 Continual success in obtaining those things which a man from time to time desireth, that is to say, continual prospering, is that men call *felicity;* I mean the felicity of this life. For there is no such thing as perpetual tranquillity of mind, while we live here; because life itself is but motion, and can never be without desire, nor without fear, no more than without sense.

Hobbes, *Leviathan,* I, 6

23 *Elmira.* The declaration is extremely gallant, but, to say the truth, it is a good deal surprising. Methinks you ought to have fortified your mind better, and to have reasoned a little upon a design of this nature. A devotee as you are, whom every one speaks of as——

  Tartuffe. Ah! being a devotee does not make me the less a man; and when one comes to view your celestial charms, the heart surrenders, and reasons no more. I know, that such language from me, seems somewhat strange; but, madam, after all, I am not an angel, and should you condemn the declaration I make, you must lay the blame upon your attractive charms.

       Molière, *Tartuffe*, III, iii

24 We do not desire a thing because we adjudge it to be good, but, on the contrary, we call it good because we desire it, and consequently everything to which we are averse we call evil. Each person, therefore, according to his affect judges or estimates what is good and what is evil, what is better and what is worse, and what is the best and what is the worst. Thus the covetous man thinks plenty of money to be the best thing and poverty the worst. The ambitious man desires nothing like glory, and on the other hand dreads nothing like shame. To the envious person, again, nothing is more pleasant than the misfortune of another, and nothing more disagreeable than the prosperity of another. And so each person according to his affect judges a thing to be good or evil, useful or useless.

     Spinoza, *Ethics*, III, Prop. 39, Schol.

25 *Desire* is the essence itself of man insofar as it is conceived as determined to any action by any one of his affections.

     Spinoza, *Ethics*, III, Prop. 59, Def. 1

26 That desire is a state of uneasiness, every one who reflects on himself will quickly find. Who is there that has not felt in desire what the wise man says of hope, (which is not much different from it), that it being "deferred makes the heart sick"; and that still proportionable to the greatness of the desire, which sometimes raises the uneasiness to that pitch, that it makes people cry out, "Give me children," give me the thing desired, "or I die." Life itself, and all its enjoyments, is a burden cannot be borne under the lasting and unremoved pressure of such an uneasiness.

      Locke, *Concerning Human
      Understanding*, Bk. II, XXI, 32

27 The Stoical Scheme of supplying our Wants, by lopping off our Desires, is like cutting off our Feet when we want Shoes.

     Swift, *Thoughts on Various Subjects*

28 Every desire is a viper in the bosom, who, while he was chill, was harmless; but when warmth gave him strength, exerted it in poison.

   Johnson, *Letter to James Boswell (Dec. 8, 1763)*

29 The desire of food is limited in every man by the narrow capacity of the human stomach; but the desire of the conveniences and ornaments of building, dress, equipage, and household furni-

ture, seems to have no limit or certain boundary.

     Adam Smith, *Wealth of Nations*, I, 11

30 The desire of a man for a woman is not directed at her because she is a human being, but because she is a woman. That she is a human being is of no concern to him.

     Kant, *Lecture at Königsberg (1775)*

31 Sooner murder an infant in its cradle than nurse unacted desires.

     Blake, *Marriage of Heaven and Hell*, 10

32 The evening arrived; the boys took their places. The master, in his cook's uniform, stationed himself at the copper; his pauper assistants ranged themselves behind him; the gruel was served out; and a long grace was said over the short commons. The gruel disappeared; the boys whispered each other, and winked at Oliver, while his next neighbors nudged him. Child as he was, he was desperate with hunger, and reckless with misery. He rose from the table; and advancing to the master, basin and spoon in hand, said: somewhat alarmed at his own temerity:

"Please, sir, I want some more."

The master was a fat, healthy man; but he turned very pale. He gazed in stupefied astonishment on the small rebel for some seconds, and then clung for support to the copper. The assistants were paralysed with wonder; the boys with fear.

"What!" said the master at length, in a faint voice.

"Please, sir," replied Oliver, "I want some more."

The master aimed a blow at Oliver's head with the ladle; pinioned him in his arms; and shrieked aloud for the beadle.

     Dickens, *Oliver Twist*, II

33 Ah, Love! could you and I with Him conspire
 To grasp this sorry Scheme of Things entire,
  Would not we shatter it to bits—and then
Remold it nearer to the Heart's Desire!

     FitzGerald, *Rubáiyát*, XCIX

34 *Mendoza.* There are two tragedies in life. One is to lose your heart's desire. The other is to gain it.

     Shaw, *Man and Superman*, IV

35 *Lady.* Havent you noticed that people always exaggerate the value of the things they havent got? The poor think they need nothing but riches to be quite happy and good. Everybody worships truth, purity, unselfishness, for the same reason: because they have no experience of them. Oh, if they only knew!

     Shaw, *The Man of Destiny*

4.5 | *Hope and Despair*

1 And Job spake, and said,
Let the day perish wherein I was born, and the night in which it was said, There is a man child conceived.

Let that day be darkness; let not God regard it from above, neither let the light shine upon it.

Let darkness and the shadow of death stain it; let a cloud dwell upon it; let the blackness of the day terrify it.

As for that night, let darkness seize upon it; let it not be joined unto the days of the year, let it not come into the number of the months.

Lo, let that night be solitary, let no joyful voice come therein.

· Let them curse it that curse the day, who are ready to raise up their mourning.

Let the stars of the twilight thereof be dark; let it look for light, but have none; neither let it see the dawning of the day:

Because it shut not up the doors of my mother's womb, nor hid sorrow from mine eyes.

Why died I not from the womb? why did I not give up the ghost when I came out of the belly?

Why did the knees prevent me? or why the breasts that I should suck?

For now should I have lain still and been quiet, I should have slept: then had I been at rest,

With kings and counsellors of the earth, which built desolate places for themselves;

Or with princes that had gold, who filled their houses with silver:

Or as an hidden untimely birth I had not been; as infants which never saw light.

Job 3:2–16

2 My days are swifter than a weaver's shuttle, and are spent without hope.

Job 7:6

3 My God, my God, why hast thou forsaken me? why art thou so far from helping me, and from the words of my roaring?

O my God, I cry in the daytime, but thou hearest not; and in the night season, and am not silent.

But thou art holy, O thou that inhabitest the praises of Israel.

Our fathers trusted in thee: they trusted, and thou didst deliver them.

They cried unto thee, and were delivered: they trusted in thee, and were not confounded.

But I am a worm, and no man; a reproach of men, and despised of the people.

Psalm 22:1–6

4 *Odysseus.* Then Sísyphos in torment I beheld being roustabout to a tremendous boulder.
Leaning with both arms braced and legs driving, he heaved it toward a height, and almost over, but then a Power spun him round and sent the cruel boulder bounding again to the plain.
Whereon the man bent down again to toil, dripping sweat, and the dust rose overhead.

Homer, *Odyssey*, XI, 594

5 *Athenians.* Hope, danger's comforter, may be indulged in by those who have abundant resources, if not without loss at all events without ruin; but its nature is to be extravagant, and those who go so far as to put their all upon the venture see it in its true colours only when they are ruined.

Thucydides, *Peloponnesian War*, V, 103

6 *Aeneas.* "Endure, and conquer! Jove will soon dispose
To future good our past and present woes.
With me, the rocks of Scylla you have tried;
Th' inhuman Cyclops and his den defied.
What greater ills hereafter can you bear?
Resume your courage and dismiss your care,
An hour will come, with pleasure to relate
Your sorrows past, as benefits of Fate.
Thro' various hazards and events, we move
To Latium and the realms foredoom'd by Jove.
Call'd to the seat (the promise of the skies)
Where Trojan kingdoms once again may rise,
Endure the hardships of your present state;
Live, and reserve yourselves for better fate."
These words he spoke, but spoke not from his heart;
His outward smiles conceal'd his inward smart.

Virgil, *Aeneid,* I

7 And he left them, and went out of the city into Bethany; and he lodged there.

Now in the morning as he returned into the city, he hungered.

And when he saw a fig tree in the way, he came to it, and found nothing thereon, but leaves only, and said unto it, Let no fruit grow on thee henceforward for ever. And presently the fig tree withered away.

And when the disciples saw it, they marvelled, saying, How soon is the fig tree withered away!

Matthew 21:17–20

8 And about the ninth hour Jesus cried with a loud voice, saying, Eli, Eli, lä-mä să-băch-thă-nī? that

is to say, My God, my God, why hast thou forsaken me?

Matthew 27:46

9 For we are saved by hope: but hope that is seen is not hope: for what a man seeth, why doth he yet hope for?

But if we hope for that we see not, then do we with patience wait for it. . . .

What shall we then say to these things? If God be for us, who can be against us?

He that spared not his own Son, but delivered him up for us all, how shall he not with him also freely give us all things? . . .

Who shall separate us from the love of Christ? shall tribulation, or distress, or persecution, or famine, or nakedness, or peril, or sword?

As it is written, For thy sake we are killed all the day long; we are accounted as sheep for the slaughter.

Nay, in all these things we are more than conquerors through him that loved us.

For I am persuaded, that neither death, nor life, nor angels, nor principalities, nor powers, nor things present, nor things to come,

Nor height, nor depth, nor any other creature, shall be able to separate us from the love of God, which is in Christ Jesus our Lord.

Romans 8:24–39

10 The species of a passion is taken from the object. Now, in the object of hope, we may note four conditions. First, that it is something good, since, properly speaking, hope regards only the good; in this respect, hope differs from fear, which regards evil. Secondly, that it is future, for hope does not regard that which is present and already possessed. In this respect, hope differs from joy which regards a present good. Thirdly, that it must be something arduous and difficult to obtain, for we do not speak of any one hoping for trifles, which are in one's power to have at any time; in this respect, hope differs from desire or cupidity, which regards the future good absolutely. Therefore it belongs to the concupiscible, while hope belongs to the irascible part. Fourthly, that this difficult thing is something possible to obtain, for one does not hope for that which one cannot get at all; and, in this respect, hope differs from despair. It is therefore evident that hope differs from desire, as the irascible passions differ from the concupiscible. For this reason, moreover, hope presupposes desire, just as all the irascible passions presuppose the passions of the concupiscible part.

Aquinas, *Summa Theologica*, I–II, 40, 1

11 Every mortal sin takes its principal malice and gravity from the fact of its turning away from God, for if it were possible to turn to a changeable good, even inordinately, without turning away from God, it would not be a mortal sin. Consequently a sin which, first and of its very nature, includes turning away from God, is most grievous among mortal sins.

Now unbelief, despair and hatred of God are opposed to the theological virtues; and among them, if we compare hatred of God and unbelief to despair, we shall find that, in themselves, that is, in respect of their proper species, they are more grievous. For unbelief is due to a man not believing God's own truth, while the hatred of God arises from man's will being opposed to God's goodness itself; but despair consists in a man ceasing to hope for a share of God's goodness. Hence it is clear that unbelief and hatred of God are against God as He is in Himself, while despair is against Him according as His good is shared in by us. Therefore strictly speaking it is a more grievous sin to disbelieve God's truth or to hate God than not to hope to receive glory from Him.

If, however, despair be compared to the other two sins from man's point of view, then despair is more dangerous, since hope withdraws us from evils and induces us to seek for good things, so that when hope is given up, men rush headlong into sin, and are drawn away from good works.

Aquinas, *Summa Theologica*, II–II, 20, 3

12 The good Master to me: "Thou askest not what spirits are these thou seest? I wish thee to know, before thou goest farther,

that they sinned not; and though they have merit, it suffices not: for they had not Baptism, which is the portal of the faith that thou believest;

and seeing they were before Christianity, they worshipped not God aright; and of these am I myself.

For such defects, *and* for no other fault, are we lost; and only in so far afflicted, that without hope we live in desire."

Great sadness took me at the heart on hearing this; because I knew men of much worth, who in that Limbo were suspense.

Dante, *Inferno*, IV, 31

13 "Hope," said I, "is a certain expectation of future glory, the product of divine grace and precedent merit."

Dante, *Paradiso*, XXV, 67

14 May heaven bring relief for all this sorrow!
There's ground for hope, for such is heaven's way;
For I have seen on many a misty morrow
Following oft a merry summer's day,
And after winter, comes along the May.
'Tis known, and vouched for by authorities,
That storms are presages of victories.

Chaucer, *Troilus and Cressida*, III, 152

15 Now enters despair, which is despair of the mercy of God, and comes sometimes of too extravagant

sorrows and sometimes of too great fear: for the victim imagines that he has done so much sin that it will avail him not to repent and forgo sin; because of which fear he abandons his heart to every kind of sin, as Saint Augustine says. This damnable sin, if it be indulged to the end, is called sinning in the Holy Ghost. This horrible sin is so dangerous that, as for him that is so desperate, there is no felony or sin that he hesitates to do; as was well showed by Judas. Certainly, then, above all other sins, this sin is most displeasing to Christ, and most hateful.

Chaucer, *Canterbury Tales:* Parson's Tale

16 Everything that is done in the world is done by hope. No husbandman would sow one grain of corn if he hoped not it would grow up and become seed; no bachelor would marry a wife if he hoped not to have children; no merchant or tradesman would set himself to work if he did not hope to reap benefit thereby.

Luther, *Table Talk,* H298

17 *Richmond.* True hope is swift and flies with swallow's wings;
Kings it makes gods and meaner creatures kings.

Shakespeare, *Richard III,* V, ii, 23

18 Hope is a disposition of the soul to persuade itself that what it desires will come to pass: and this is caused by a particular movement of the spirits, i.e. by that of joy and that of desire mingled together; and fear is another disposition of the soul which persuades it that the thing hoped for will not come to pass; and it must be observed that, although these two passions are contrary, we can nevertheless have them both at the same time, that is to say, when we represent to ourselves different reasons at the same time, some of which cause us to judge that the accomplishment of desire is easy, while the others make it seem difficult.

Descartes, *Passions of the Soul,* CLXV

19 When I see the blindness and the wretchedness of man, when I regard the whole silent universe and man without light, left to himself and, as it were, lost in this corner of the universe, without knowing who has put him there, what he has come to do, what will become of him at death, and incapable of all knowledge, I become terrified, like a man who should be carried in his sleep to a dreadful desert island and should awake without knowing where he is and without means of escape. And thereupon I wonder how people in a condition so wretched do not fall into despair.

Pascal, *Pensées,* XI, 693

20 *Elder Brother.* Where an equall poise of hope and fear

Does arbitrate th'event, my nature is
That I encline to hope, rather then fear,
And gladly banish squint suspicion.

Milton, *Comus,* 410

21 *Satan.* Me miserable! which way shall I flie
Infinite wrauth, and infinite despaire?
Which way I flie is Hell; my self am Hell;
And in the lowest deep a lower deep
Still threatning to devour me opens wide,
To which the Hell I suffer seems a Heav'n.

Milton, *Paradise Lost,* IV, 73

22 *Samson.*   Promise was that I
Should *Israel* from *Philistian* yoke deliver;
Ask for this great Deliverer now, and find him
Eyeless in *Gaza* at the Mill with slaves,
Himself in bonds under *Philistian* yoke.

Milton, *Samson Agonistes,* 38

23 *Samson.* O loss of sight, of thee I most complain!
Blind among enemies, O worse then chains,
Dungeon, or beggery, or decrepit age!
Light the prime work of God to me is extinct,
And all her various objects of delight
Annull'd, which might in part my grief have eas'd,
Inferiour to the vilest now become
Of man or worm; the vilest here excel me,
They creep, yet see, I dark in light expos'd
To daily fraud, contempt, abuse and wrong,
Within doors, or without, still as a fool,
In power of others, never in my own;
Scarce half I seem to live, dead more then half.
O dark, dark, dark, amid the blaze of noon,
Irrecoverably dark, total Eclipse
Without all hope of day!

Milton, *Samson Agonistes,* 67

24 *Despair* is sorrow arising from the idea of a past or future object from which cause for doubting is removed. Confidence, therefore, springs from hope and despair from fear, whenever the reason for doubting the issue is taken away; a case which occurs either because we imagine a thing past or future to be present and contemplate it as present, or because we imagine other things which exclude the existence of those which made us to doubt.

Spinoza, *Ethics,* III, Prop. 59, Def. 15

25 *Hope* is that pleasure in the mind, which every one finds in himself, upon the thought of a probable future enjoyment of a thing which is apt to delight him.

Locke, *Concerning Human Understanding,* Bk. II, XX, 9

26 *Despair* is the thought of the unattainableness of any good, which works differently in men's minds,

sometimes producing uneasiness or pain, sometimes rest and indolency.

Locke, Concerning Human
Understanding, Bk. II, XX, 11

27 Hope springs eternal in the human breast:
Man never Is, but always To be blest:
The soul, uneasy and confin'd from home,
Rests and expatiates in a life to come.

Pope, Essay on Man, Epistle I, 95

28 I have many years ago magnified in my own mind, and repeated to you, a ninth beatitude, added to the eighth in the Scripture: "Blessed is he who expects nothing, for he shall never be disappointed."

Pope, Letter to John Gay (Oct. 16, 1727)

29 It is necessary to hope, though hope should always be deluded; for hope itself is happiness, and its frustrations, however frequent, are yet less dreadful than its extinction.

Johnson, Idler No. 58

30 Hope is itself a species of happiness, and, perhaps, the chief happiness which this world affords: but, like all other pleasures immoderately enjoyed, the excesses of hope must be expiated by pain; and expectations improperly indulged, must end in disappointment. If it be asked, what is the improper expectation which it is dangerous to indulge, experience will quickly answer, that it is such expectation as is dictated not by reason, but by desire; expectation raised, not by the common occurrences of life, but by the wants of the expectant; an expectation that requires the common course of things to be changed, and the general rules of action to be broken.

Johnson, Letter (June 8, 1762)

31 *Faust.* Look up!—The peaks, gigantic and supernal,
Proclaim the hour most solemn now is nearing.
They early may enjoy the light eternal
That later to us here below is wended.
Now on the alpine meadows, sloping, vernal,
A clear and lavish glory has descended
And step by step fulfils its journey's ending.
The sun steps forth!—Alas, already blinded,
I turn away, the pain my vision rending.

Thus is it ever when a hope long yearning
Has made a wish its own, supreme, transcending,
And finds Fulfilment's portals outward turning;
From those eternal deeps bursts ever higher
Too great a flame, we stand, with wonder burning.
To kindle life's fair torch we did aspire
And seas of flame—and what a flame!—embrace us!

Is it Love? Is it Hate? that twine us with their fire,
In alternating joy and pain enlace us,
So that again toward earth we turn our gazing,
Baffled, to hide in youth's fond veils our faces.

Goethe, Faust, II, 1, 4695

32 Hopes, what are they?—Beads of morning
Strung on slender blades of grass;
Or a spider's web adorning
In a strait and treacherous pass.

Wordsworth, Inscription Supposed to be
Found in and Near a Hermit's Cell

33 The concept of the sickness unto death must be understood . . . in a peculiar sense. Literally it means a sickness the end and outcome of which is death. Thus one speaks of a mortal sickness as synonymous with a sickness unto death. In this sense despair cannot be called the sickness unto death. But in the Christian understanding of it death itself is a transition unto life. In view of this, there is from the Christian standpoint no earthly, bodily sickness unto death. For death is doubtless the last phase of the sickness, but death is not the last thing. If in the strictest sense we are to speak of a sickness unto death, it must be one in which the last thing is death, and death the last thing. And this precisely is despair.

Yet in another and still more definite sense despair is the sickness unto death. It is indeed very far from being true that, literally understood, one dies of this sickness, or that this sickness ends with bodily death. On the contrary, the torment of despair is precisely this, not to be able to die. So it has much in common with the situation of the moribund when he lies and struggles with death, and cannot die. So to be sick *unto* death is, not to be able to die—yet not as though there were hope of life; no, the hopelessness in this case is that even the last hope, death, is not available. When death is the greatest danger, one hopes for life; but when one becomes acquainted with an even more dreadful danger, one hopes for death. So when the danger is so great that death has become one's hope, despair is the disconsolateness of not being able to die.

It is in this last sense that despair is the sickness unto death, this agonizing contradiction, this sickness in the self, everlastingly to die, to die and yet not to die, to die the death. For dying means that it is all over, but dying the death means to live to experience death; and if for a single instant this experience is possible, it is tantamount to experiencing it forever. If one might die of despair as one dies of a sickness, then the eternal in him, the self, must be capable of dying in the same sense that the body dies of sickness. But this is an impossibility; the dying of despair transforms itself constantly into a living.

Kierkegaard, The Sickness Unto Death, I, I, C

34 *Ida.* Tears, idle tears, I know not what they mean,
Tears from the depth of some divine despair
Rise in the heart, and gather to the eyes,
In looking on the happy autumn-fields,
And thinking of the days that are no more. . . .

Dear as remember'd kisses after death,
And sweet as those by hopeless fancy feign'd
On lips that are for others; deep as love,
Deep as first love, and wild with all regret;
O Death in Life, the days that are no more!

Tennyson, *The Princess,* IV, 21

35 The mass of men lead lives of quiet desperation.
What is called resignation is confirmed desperation. From the desperate city you go into the desperate country, and have to console yourself with
the bravery of minks and muskrats. A stereotyped
but unconscious despair is concealed even under
what are called the games and amusements of
mankind. There is no play in them, for this comes
after work. But it is a characteristic of wisdom not
to do desperate things.

Thoreau, *Walden:* Economy

36 The Worldly Hope men set their Hearts upon
Turns Ashes—or it prospers; and anon,
   Like Snow upon the Desert's dusty Face,
Lighting a little hour or two—is gone.

FitzGerald, *Rubáiyát,* XVI

37 Not, I'll not, carrion comfort, Despair, not feast
   on thee;
Not untwist—slack they may be—these last
   strands of man

In me or, most weary, cry *I can no more.* I can;
Can something, hope, wish day come, not choose
   not to be.

G. M. Hopkins, *Carrion Comfort*

38 Zeus did not wish man, however much he might
be tormented by the other evils, to fling away his
life, but to go on letting himself be tormented
again and again. Therefore he gives man hope,—
in reality it is the worst of all evils, because it
prolongs the torments of man.

Nietzsche, *Human, All-Too-Human,* 71

39 As for despair, the term has a very simple meaning. It means that we shall confine ourselves to
reckoning only with what depends upon our will,
or on the ensemble of probabilities which make
our action possible. When we want something, we
always have to reckon with probabilities. I may be
counting on the arrival of a friend. The friend is
coming by rail or streetcar; this supposes that the
train will arrive on schedule, or that the streetcar
will not jump the track. I am left in the realm of
possibility; but possibilities are to be reckoned
with only to the point where my action comports
with the ensemble of these possibilities, and no
further. The moment the possibilities I am considering are not rigorously involved by my action, I
ought to disengage myself from them, because no
God, no scheme, can adapt the world and its possibilities to my will. When Descartes said, "Conquer yourself rather than the world," he meant
essentially the same thing.

Sartre, *Existentialism*

4.6 | *Joy and Sorrow*

1 And if ye take this also from me, and mischief
befall him, ye shall bring down my gray hairs
with sorrow to the grave.

Genesis 44:29

2 Weeping may endure for a night, but joy cometh
in the morning.

Psalm 30:5

3 It is better to go to the house of mourning, than to
go to the house of feasting: for that is the end of
all men; and the living will lay it to his heart.
   Sorrow is better than laughter: for by the sad-

ness of the countenance the heart is made better.
   The heart of the wise is in the house of mourning; but the heart of fools is in the house of mirth.
   It is better to hear the rebuke of the wise, than
for a man to hear the song of fools.
   For as the crackling of thorns under a pot, so is
the laughter of the fool: this also is vanity.

Ecclesiastes 7:2–6

4 *Achilleus.*   There is not
any advantage to be won from grim lamentation.
Such is the way the gods spun life for unfortunate
   mortals,

that we live in unhappiness, but the gods themselves have no sorrows.

Homer, *Iliad,* XXIV, 523

5 So spoke great Achilleus and went back into the
shelter
and sat down on the elaborate couch from which
he had risen,
against the inward wall, and now spoke his word
to Priam:
'Your son is given back to you, aged sir, as you
asked it.
He lies on a bier. When dawn shows you yourself
shall see him
as you take him away. Now you and I must remember our supper.
For even Niobe, she of the lovely tresses, remembered
to eat, whose twelve children were destroyed in
her palace,
six daughters, and six sons in the pride of their
youth, whom Apollo
killed with arrows from his silver bow, being an-
gered
with Niobe. . . .
But she remembered to eat when she was worn
out with weeping.'

Homer, *Iliad,* XXIV, 596

6 *Oedipus.* Who will be kind to Oedipus this evening
And give the wanderer charity?

Though he ask little and receive still less,
It is sufficient:
Suffering and time,
Vast time, have been instructors in contentment.

Sophocles, *Oedipus at Colonus,* 3

7 *Attendant.* There's nothing like the sight
Of an old enemy down on his luck.

Euripides, *Heracleidae,* 939

8 *Iphigenia.* The unfortunate, having once known
prosperity themselves, bear no kind feelings towards their luckier neighbours.

Euripides, *Iphigenia in Tauris,* 353

9 *Pericles.* Grief is felt not so much for the want of
what we have never known, as for the loss of that
to which we have been long accustomed.

Thucydides, *Peloponnesian War,* II, 44

10 It is difficult to convince a mourner that he
grieves by his own choice and because he thinks
he must.

Cicero, *Disputations,* III, 33

11 What first Æneas in this place beheld,
Reviv'd his courage, and his fear expell'd.

For while, expecting there the queen, he rais'd
His wond'ring eyes, and round the temple gaz'd,
Admir'd the fortune of the rising town,
The striving artists, and their arts' renown;
He saw, in order painted on the wall,
Whatever did unhappy Troy befall:
The wars that fame around the world had blown,
All to the life, and ev'ry leader known.
There Agamemnon, Priam here, he spies,
And fierce Achilles, who both kings defies.
He stopp'd, and weeping said: "O friend! ev'n
here
The monuments of Trojan woes appear!
Our known disasters fill ev'n foreign lands:
See there, where old unhappy Priam stands!
Ev'n the mute walls relate the warrior's fame,
And Trojan griefs the Tyrians' pity claim."

Virgil, *Aeneid,* I

12 No pleasure is unalloyed: some trouble ever intrudes upon our happiness.

Ovid, *Metamorphoses,* VII

13 So much more does joy without discretion transport and agitate the mind than either fear or sorrow.

Plutarch, *Aratus*

14 I must die. Must I then die lamenting? I must be
put in chains. Must I then also lament? I must go
into exile. Does any man then hinder me from
going with smiles and cheerfulness and contentment?

Epictetus, *Discourses,* I, 1

15 Imagine every man who is grieved at anything or
discontented to be like a pig which is sacrificed
and kicks and screams.

Marcus Aurelius, *Meditations,* X, 28

16 Every soul is wretched that is bound in affection
of mortal things: it is tormented to lose them, and
in their loss becomes aware of the wretchedness which in reality it had even before it lost
them.

Augustine, *Confessions,* IV, 6

17 Wherever the soul of man turns, unless towards
God, it cleaves to sorrow.

Augustine, *Confessions,* IV, 10

18 What is it in the soul . . . that makes it delight
more to have found or regained the things it loves
than if it had always had them? Creatures other
than man bear the same witness, and all things
are filled with testimonies acclaiming that it is so.
The victorious general has his triumph; but he
would not have been victorious if he had not
fought; and the greater danger there was in the
battle, the greater rejoicing in the triumph. The

storm tosses the sailors and threatens to wreck the ship; all are pale with the threat of death. But the sky grows clear, the sea calm, and now they are as wild with exultation as before with fear. A friend is sick and his pulse threatens danger; all who want him well feel as if they shared his sickness. He begins to recover, though he cannot yet walk as strongly as of old: and there is more joy than there was before, when he was still well and could walk properly.

Augustine, *Confessions*, VIII, 3

19 The pleasures of this life for which I should weep are in conflict with the sorrows of this life in which I should rejoice, and I know not on which side stands the victory. Woe is me, Lord, have pity on me! For I have likewise sorrows which are evil and these are in conflict with joys that are good, and I know not on which side stands the victory. Woe is me, Lord have mercy upon me! . . . Is not the life of man on earth a trial? Who would choose trouble and difficulty? Thou dost command us to endure them, not to love them. No one loves what he endures, though he may love to endure. For though he rejoices at his endurance, yet he would rather that there were nothing to endure. In adversity I desire prosperity, in prosperity I fear adversity. Yet what middle place is there between the two, where man's life may be other than trial? There is woe and woe again in the prosperity of this world, woe from the fear of adversity, woe from the corruption of joy! There is woe in the adversity of this world, and a second woe and a third, from the longing for prosperity, and because adversity itself is hard, and for fear that endurance may break! Is not man's life upon earth trial without intermission?

Augustine, *Confessions*, X, 28

20 Sadness may be considered in two ways: as existing actually, and as existing in the memory, and in both ways sadness can cause pleasure. Because sadness, as actually existing, causes pleasure, since it brings to mind that which is loved, the absence of which causes sadness; and yet the mere thought of it gives pleasure.—The recollection of sadness becomes a cause of pleasure on account of the subsequent deliverance, because absence of evil is looked upon as something good; hence according as a man thinks that he has been delivered from that which caused him sorrow and pain, so much reason has he to rejoice.

Aquinas, *Summa Theologica*, I–II, 32, 4

21 A hurtful thing hurts yet more if we keep it shut up, because the soul is more intent on it; but if it be allowed to escape, the soul's intention is dispersed as it were on outward things, so that the inward sorrow is lessened. This is why when men, burdened with sorrow, make outward show of their sorrow, by tears or groans or even by words,

their sorrow is assuaged.

Aquinas, *Summa Theologica*, I–II, 38, 2

22 Immoderate sorrow is a disease of the mind, but moderate sorrow is the mark of a well disposed soul according to the present state of life.

Aquinas, *Summa Theologica*, I–II, 59, 3

23 *Pandar.* For as all joys on earth are short and brief,
So time will bring for sorrow its relief.

Because if Fortune's wheel should cease to turn,
Then Fortune she at once no more would be;
And since in no fixed place she may sojourn,
It may chance, by mere mutability,
Such good luck she hath now in store for thee,
And such a boon to thee she soon will bring,
That for the joy of it, thy heart shall sing.

Chaucer, *Troilus and Cressida*, I, 121–122

24 *Pandar.* For that same ground that bears the useless weed,
Bears also wholesome herbs, and quite as oft;
And where the rough and stinging nettles breed,
Waxes the rose, so sweet and smooth and soft;
And next the valley, lifts the hill aloft,
And after night, then comes the glad tomorrow,
And so is joy the after end of sorrow.

Chaucer, *Troilus and Cressida*, I, 136

25 "O God," she cried, "these blessings temporal,
Which scholars falsely call felicity,
With bitterness are mingled and with gall!
God only knows what anguish then hath he
Who sees his empty joys before him flee!
For either joys arrive inopportune,
Or else they flit and vanish all too soon!

"O fickle fate! O worldly joy unstable!
Of men thou makest but a sport and play!
All know that they to hold their joy are able,
Or know it not—there is no other way.
Now if one knows it not, how may he say
That he of perfect joy perceives the spark,
If ignorance still leaves him in the dark?

"But if he knows that joy is transitory,
Since joy in every worldly thing must flee,
This troubling thought diminishes the glory
Of earthly joy, and so in such degree,
Imperfect must be his felicity;
If loss of joy he fears a jot or tittle,
This proves that earthly joy is worth but little.

"And so this problem I must thus decide,
That verily, for aught that I can see,
No perfect joy can in this world abide."

Chaucer, *Troilus and Cressida*, III, 117–120

26 O true it is, before they can be cured,
Whether of fever or other great disease,
The sick must drink, for all they have endured,
Full bitter drink, and for their better ease,

Must oft partake of things that do not please.
All this to Troilus may be applied,
Who after pain is glad and satisfied.

And sweetness now seemed more than ever sweet,
For all the bitterness that went before;
And now the time goes by on winged feet,
In joy so great, it never could be more,
Or better pay for all the griefs they bore.
And here I beg that lovers all will heed
This good example at their time of need!

Chaucer, *Troilus and Cressida*, III, 174–175

27 And to be glad they often her besought,
Which to her grief such mitigation brought
As for a splitting headache one might feel
If one were kindly rubbed upon the heel.

Chaucer, *Troilus and Cressida*, IV, 104

28 Good friends, my readers, who peruse this book,
Be not offended, whilst on it you look:
Denude yourselves of all deprav'd affection,
For it contains no badness nor infection:
'Tis true that it brings forth to you no birth
Of any value, but in point of mirth;
Thinking therefore how sorrow might your mind
Consume, I could no apter subject find;
One inch of joy surmounts of grief a span;
Because to laugh is proper to the man.

Rabelais, *Gargantua and Pantagruel*, I,
To the Readers

29 Metrodorus used to say that in sadness there is
some alloy of pleasure. I do not know whether he
meant something else, but for my part I indeed
imagine that there is design, consent, and pleasure
in feeding one's melancholy; I mean beyond the
ambition that can also be involved. There is some
shadow of daintiness and luxury that smiles on us
and flatters us in the very lap of melancholy.

Montaigne, *Essays*, II, 20, We Taste
Nothing Pure

30 *Richard.* I cannot weep; for all my body's moisture
Scarce serves to quench my furnace-burning
heart:
Nor can my tongue unload my heart's great
burthen;
For selfsame wind that I should speak withal
Is kindling coals that fires all my breast,
And burns me up with flames that tears would
quench.
To weep is to make less the depth of grief:
Tears then for babes; blows and revenge for me.

Shakespeare, *III Henry VI*, II, i, 84

31 *Pandulph.* You hold too heinous a respect of grief.
Constance. He talks to me that never had a son.
King Philip. You are as fond of grief as of your
child.
Const. Grief fills the room up of my absent child,

Lies in his bed, walks up and down with
Puts on his pretty looks, repeats his word
Remembers me of all his gracious parts,
Stuffs out his vacant garments with his for
Then, have I reason to be fond of grief?

Shakespeare, *King John*, III, iv, 90

32 *Claudio.* Silence is the perfectest herald of joy: I
were but little happy, if I could say how much.

Shakespeare, *Much Ado About
Nothing*, II, i, 317

33 *Benedick.* Every one can master a grief but he that
has it.

Shakespeare, *Much Ado About
Nothing*, III, ii, 29

34 *King.* 'Tis sweet and commendable in your nature,
Hamlet,
To give these mourning duties to your father:
But, you must know, your father lost a father;
That father lost, lost his, and the survivor bound
In filial obligation for some term
To do obsequious sorrow: but to persever
In obstinate condolement is a course
Of impious stubbornness; 'tis unmanly grief;
It shows a will most incorrect to heaven,
A heart unfortified, a mind impatient,
An understanding simple and unschool'd:
For what we know must be and is as common
As any the most vulgar thing to sense,
Why should we in our peevish opposition
Take it to heart? Fie! 'tis a fault to heaven,
A fault against the dead, a fault to nature,
To reason most absurd; whose common theme
Is death of fathers, and who still hath cried,
From the first corse till he that died-to-day,
"This must be so."

Shakespeare, *Hamlet*, I, ii, 87

35 *King.* When sorrows come, they come not single
spies,
But in battalions.

Shakespeare, *Hamlet*, IV, v, 78

36 *Ross.* Let not your ears despise my tongue for ever,
Which shall possess them with the heaviest sound
That ever yet they heard.
Macduff.   Hum! I guess at it.
Ross. Your castle is surprised; your wife and
babes
Savagely slaughter'd. To relate the manner
Were, on the quarry of these murder'd deer,
To add the death of you.
Malcolm.   Merciful heaven!
What, man! ne'er pull your hat upon your brows;
Give sorrow words. The grief that does not speak
Whispers the o'er-fraught heart and bids it break.
Macd. My children too?
Ross.   Wife, children, servants, all
That could be found.

Macd.   And I must be from thence!
My wife kill'd too?
   Ross.   I have said.
   Mal.   Be comforted.
Let's make us medicines of our great revenge
To cure this deadly grief.
   Macd. He has no children. All my pretty ones?
Did you say all? O hell-kite! All?
What, all my pretty chickens and their dam
At one fell swoop?
   Mal. Dispute it like a man.
   Macd.   I shall do so;
But I must also feel it as a man.
I cannot but remember such things were,
That were most precious to me.

                    Shakespeare, *Macbeth,* IV, iii, 201

37 However full of sadness a man may be, he is happy for the time, if you can prevail upon him to
enter into some amusement; and however happy
a man may be, he will soon be discontented and
wretched, if he be not diverted and occupied by
some passion or pursuit which prevents weariness
from overcoming him. Without amusement there
is no joy; with amusement there is no sadness.

                    Pascal, *Pensées,* II, 139

38 Hence loathed Melancholy
   Of *Cerberus,* and blackest midnight born,
   In *Stygian* Cave forlorn
      'Mongst horrid shapes, and shreiks, and sights
         unholy,
   Find out som uncouth cell,
      Where brooding darknes spreads his jealous
         wings,
   And the night-Raven sings;
      There under *Ebon* shades, and low-brow'd
         Rocks,
   As ragged as thy Locks,
      In dark *Cimmerian* desert ever dwell.
   But com thou Goddes fair and free,
   In heav'n ycleap'd *Euphrosyne,*
   And by men, heart-easing Mirth,
   Whom lovely *Venus* at a birth
   With two sister Graces more
   To Ivy-crowned *Bacchus* bore;
   Or whether (as som Sager sing)
   The frolick Wind that breathes the Spring,
   Zephir with *Aurora* playing,
   As he met her once a Maying,
   There on Beds of Violets blew,
   And fresh-blown Roses washt in dew,
   Fill'd her with thee a daughter fair,
   So bucksom, blith, and debonair.
   Haste thee nymph, and bring with thee
   Jest and youthful Jollity,
   Quips and Cranks, and wanton Wiles,
   Nods, and Becks, and Wreathed Smiles,
   Such as hang on *Hebe's* cheek,
   And love to live in dimple sleek;
   Sport that wrincled Care derides,

And Laughter holding both his sides.
Com, and trip it as ye go
On the light fantastick toe,
And in thy right hand lead with thee,
The Mountain Nymph, sweet Liberty;
And if I give thee honour due,
Mirth, admit me of thy crue
To live with her, and live with thee,
In unreproved pleasures free;
To hear the Lark begin his flight,
And singing startle the dull night,
From his watch-towre in the skies,
Till the dappled dawn doth rise;
Then to com in spight of sorrow,
And at my window bid good morrow,
Through the Sweet-Briar, or the Vine,
Or the twisted Eglantine.

                    Milton, *L'Allegro,* 1

39 Hence vain deluding joyes,
      The brood of folly without father bred,
   How little you bested,
      Or fill the fixed mind with all your toyes;
   Dwell in som idle brain,
      And fancies bond with gaudy shapes possess,
   As thick and numberless
      As the gay motes that people the Sun Beams,
   Or likest hovering dreams
      The fickle Pensioners of *Morpheus* train.
   But hail thou Goddes, sage and holy,
   Hail divinest Melancholy,
   Whose Saintly visage is too bright
   To hit the Sense of human sight;
   And therfore to our weaker view,
   Ore laid with black staid Wisdoms hue.
   Black, but such as in esteem,
   Prince *Memnons* sister might beseem,
   Or that Starr'd *Ethiope* Queen that strove
   To set her beauties praise above
   The Sea Nymphs, and their powers offended.
   Yet thou art higher far descended,
   Thee bright-hair'd *Vesta* long of yore,
   To solitary *Saturn* bore;
   His daughter she (in *Saturns* raign,
   Such mixture was not held a stain)
   Oft in glimmering Bowres, and glades
   He met her, and in secret shades
   Of woody *Ida's* inmost grove,
   While yet there was no fear of *Jove.*
   Com pensive Nun, devout and pure,
   Sober, stedfast, and demure,
   All in a robe of darkest grain,
   Flowing with majestick train,
   And sable stole of *Cipres* Lawn,
   Over thy decent shoulders drawn.
   Com, but keep thy wonted state,
   With eev'n step, and musing gate,
   And looks commercing with the skies,
   Thy rapt soul sitting in thine eyes:
   There held in holy passion still,
   Forget thy self to Marble, till

With a sad Leaden downward cast,
Thou fix them on the earth as fast.
And joyn with thee calm Peace, and Quiet,
Spare Fast, that oft with gods doth diet,
And hears the Muses in a ring,
Ay round about *Joves* Altar sing.
And adde to these retired Leasure,
That in trim Gardens takes his pleasure;
But first, and chiefest, with thee bring,
Him that yon soars on golden wing,
Guiding the fiery-wheeled throne,
The Cherub Contemplation,
And the mute Silence hist along,
'Less *Philomel* will daign a Song,
In her sweetest, saddest plight,
Smoothing the rugged brow of night,
While *Cynthia* checks her Dragon yoke,
Gently o're th'accustom'd Oke;
Sweet Bird that shunn'st the noise of folly,
Most musicall, most melancholy!

Milton, *Il Penseroso,* 1

40 Bring the rathe Primrose that forsaken dies.
The tufted Crow-toe, and pale Gessamine,
The white Pink, and the Pansie freakt with jeat,
The glowing Violet.
The Musk-rose, and the well attir'd Woodbine.
With Cowslips wan that hang the pensive hed,
And every flower that sad embroidery wears:
Bid *Amaranthus* all his beauty shed,
And Daffadillies fill their cups with tears,
To strew the Laureat Herse where *Lycid* lies. . . .
Look homeward Angel now, and melt with ruth.
And, O ye *Dolphins,* waft the haples youth.

Milton, *Lycidas,* 142

41 The desire which springs from joy, other things
being equal, is stronger than that which springs
from sorrow.

Spinoza, *Ethics,* IV, Prop. 18

42 *Joy* is a delight of the mind, from the consideration
of the present or assured approaching possession
of a good; and we are then possessed of any good,
when we have it so in our power that we can use
it when we please. Thus a man almost starved has
joy at the arrival of relief, even before he has the
pleasure of using it: and a father, in whom the
very well-being of his children causes delight, is
always, as long as his children are in such a state,
in the possession of that good; for he needs but to
reflect on it, to have that pleasure.

Sorrow is uneasiness in the mind, upon the
thought of a good lost, which might have been
enjoyed longer; or the sense of a present evil.

Locke, *Concerning Human Understanding,*
Bk. II, XX, 7–8

43 Remorse goes to sleep when our fortunes are prosperous, and makes itself felt more keenly in adversity.

Rousseau, *Confessions,* II

44 The subject of grief for the loss of relations and
friends being introduced, I observed that it was
strange to consider how soon it in general wears
away. Dr. Taylor mentioned a gentleman of the
neighbourhood as the only instance he had ever
known of a person who had endeavoured to *retain*
grief. He told Dr. Taylor, that after his Lady's
death, which affected him deeply, he *resolved* that
the grief, which he cherished with a kind of sacred
fondness, should be lasting; but that he found he
could not keep it long. *Johnson.* "All grief for what
cannot in the course of nature be helped, soon
wears away; in some sooner, indeed, in some later; but it never continues very long, unless where
there is madness. . . . If, indeed, the cause of our
grief is occasioned by our own misconduct, if grief
is mingled with remorse of conscience, it should be
lasting."

Boswell, *Life of Johnson (Sept. 14, 1777)*

45 Excess of sorrow laughs. Excess of joy weeps.

Blake, *Marriage of Heaven and Hell,* 8

46 A truth that's told with bad intent
Beats all the lies you can invent.
It is right it should be so;
Man was made for joy and woe;
And when this we rightly know,
Thro' the world we safely go.
Joy and woe are woven fine,
A clothing for the soul divine.

Blake, *Auguries of Innocence,* 53

47 On with the dance! let joy be unconfined;
No sleep till morn, when Youth and Pleasure
meet
To chase the glowing Hours with flying feet—
But hark!—that heavy sound breaks in once more
As if the clouds its echo would repeat.

Byron, *Childe Harold's Pilgrimage,* III, 22

48 *Joy* and *sorrow* are not ideas of the mind but affections of the will, and so they do not lie in the
domain of memory. We cannot recall our joys and
sorrows; by which I mean that we cannot renew
them. We can recall only the *ideas* that accompanied them; and, in particular, the things we were
led to say; and these form a gauge of our feelings
at the time. Hence our memory of joys and sorrows is always imperfect, and they become a matter of indifference to us as soon as they are over.
This explains the vanity of the attempt, which we
sometimes make, to revive the pleasures and the
pains of the past. Pleasure and pain are essentially
an affair of the will; and the will, as such, is not
possessed of memory, which is a function of the
intellect; and this in its turn gives out and takes in
nothing but thoughts and ideas, which are not
here in question.

It is a curious fact that in bad days we can very

vividly recall the good time that is now no more; but that in good days we have only a very cold and imperfect memory of the bad.

Schopenhauer, *Further Psychological Observations*

49 Such was the deck where now lay the Handsome Sailor. Through the rosetan of his complexion no pallor could have shown. It would have taken days of sequestration from the winds and the sun to have brought about the effacement of that. But the skeleton in the cheekbone at the point of its angle was just beginning delicately to be defined under the warm-tinted skin. In fervid hearts self-contained, some brief experiences devour our human tissue as secret fire in a ship's hold consumes cotton in the bale.

Melville, *Billy Budd*

50 "It is Rachel of old," said the elder [Father Zossima], "weeping for her children, and will not be comforted because they are not. Such is the lot set on earth for you mothers. Be not comforted. Consolation is not what you need. Weep and be not consoled, but weep. Only every time that you weep be sure to remember that your little son is one of the angels of God, that he looks down from there at you and sees you, and rejoices at your tears, and points at them to the Lord God; and a long while yet will you keep that great mother's grief. But it will turn in the end into quiet joy, and your bitter tears will be only tears of tender sorrow that purifies the heart and delivers it from sin."

Dostoevsky, *Brothers Karamazov*, Pt. I, II, 3

51 *Father Zossima.* This is not your place for the time. I bless you for great service in the world. Yours will be a long pilgrimage. And you will have to take a wife, too. You will have to bear *all* before you come back. There will be much to do. But I don't doubt of you, and so I send you forth. Christ is with you. Do not abandon Him and He will not abandon you. You will see great sorrow, and in

that sorrow you will be happy. This is my last message to you: in sorrow seek happiness.

Dostoevsky, *Brothers Karamazov*, Pt. I, II, 7

52 The spiritual haughtiness and nausea of every man who has suffered profoundly—it almost determines the order of rank *how* profoundly human beings can suffer—his shuddering certainty, which permeates and colors him through and through, that by virtue of his suffering he *knows* more than the cleverest and wisest could possibly know, and that he knows his way and has once been "at home" in many distant, terrifying worlds of which "*you* know nothing"—this spiritual and silent haughtiness of the sufferer, this pride of the elect of knowledge, of the "initiated," of the almost sacrificed, finds all kinds of disguises necessary to protect itself against contact with obtrusive and pitying hands and altogether against everything that is not its equal in suffering. Profound suffering makes noble; it separates.

Nietzsche, *Beyond Good and Evil*, IX, 270

53 The special kind of boredom from which modern urban populations suffer is intimately bound up with their separation from the life of Earth. It makes life hot and dusty and thirsty, like a pilgrimage in the desert. Among those who are rich enough to choose their way of life, the particular brand of unendurable boredom from which they suffer is due, paradoxical as this may seem, to their fear of boredom. In flying from the fructifying kind of boredom, they fall a prey to the other far worse kind. A happy life must be to a great extent a quiet life, for it is only in an atmosphere of quiet that true joy can live.

Russell, *The Conquest of Happiness*, I, 4

54 Too long a sacrifice
Can make a stone of the heart.
O when may it suffice?

Yeats, *Easter 1916*

4.7 | *Pleasure and Pain*

1 A man hath no better thing under the sun, than to eat, and to drink, and to be merry: for that shall abide with him of his labour the days of his life, which God giveth him under the sun.

Ecclesiastes 8:15

2 *Odysseus.* There is no boon in life more sweet, I say, than when a summer joy holds all the realm, and banqueters sit listening to a harper in a great hall, by rows of tables heaped with bread and roast meat, while a steward goes to dip up wine and brim your cups again. Here is the flower of life, it seems to me!

Homer, *Odyssey*, IX, 5

3 *Herald.* Who, except the gods, can live time through forever without any pain?

Aeschylus, *Agamemnon*, 553

4 *Chorus.* For sufferers it is sweet to know beforehand clearly the pain that still remains for them.

Aeschylus, *Prometheus Bound*, 698

5 *Phaedrus.* Bodily pleasures . . . almost always have previous pain as a condition of them, and therefore are rightly called slavish.

Plato, *Phaedrus*, 258B

6 *Socrates.* How singular is the thing called pleasure, and how curiously related to pain, which might be thought to be the opposite of it; for they are never present to a man at the same instant, and yet he who pursues either is generally compelled to take the other; their bodies are two, but they are joined by a single head.

Plato, *Phaedo*, 60A

7 *Glaucon.* Pleasure deprives a man of the use of his faculties quite as much as pain.

Plato, *Republic*, III, 402B

8 *Socrates.* He whose desires are drawn towards knowledge in every form will be absorbed in the pleasures of the soul, and will hardly feel bodily pleasure. . . . Such an one is sure to be temperate and the reverse of covetous; for the motives which make another man desirous of having and spending, have no place in his character.

Plato, *Republic*, VI, 485B

9 *Athenian Stranger.* The true life should neither seek for pleasures, nor, on the other hand, entirely avoid pains, but should embrace the middle state.

Plato, *Laws*, VII, 792B

10 Since no one nature or state either is or is thought the best for all, neither do all pursue the same pleasure; yet all pursue pleasure. And perhaps they actually pursue not the pleasure they think they pursue nor that which they would say they pursue, but the same pleasure; for all things have by nature something divine in them.

Aristotle, *Ethics*, 1153^{b}28

11 The pleasures of creatures different in kind differ in kind, and it is plausible to suppose that those of a single species do not differ. But they vary to no small extent, in the case of men at least; the same things delight some people and pain others, and are painful and odious to some, and pleasant to and liked by others. This happens, too, in the case of sweet things; the same things do not seem sweet to a man in a fever and a healthy man—nor hot to a weak man and one in good condition. The same happens in other cases. But in all such matters that which appears to the good man is thought to be really so. If this is correct, as it seems to be, and virtue and the good man as such are the measure of each thing, those also will be pleasures which appear so to him, and those things pleasant which he enjoys. If the things he finds tiresome seem pleasant to some one, that is nothing surprising; for men may be ruined and spoilt in many ways; but the things are not pleasant, but only pleasant to these people and to people in this condition. Those which are admittedly disgraceful plainly should not be said to be pleasures, except to a perverted taste; but of those that are thought to be good what kind of pleasure or what pleasure should be said to be that proper to man? Is it not plain from the corresponding activities? The pleasures follow these. Whether, then, the perfect and supremely happy man has one or more activities, the pleasures that perfect these will be said in the strict sense to be pleasures proper to man, and the rest will be so in a secondary and fractional way, as are the activities.

Aristotle, *Ethics*, 1176^{a}8

12 It is always the first sign of love, that besides enjoying some one's presence, we remember him when he is gone, and feel pain as well as pleasure, because he is there no longer. Similarly there is an element of pleasure even in mourning and lamentation for the departed. There is grief, indeed, at his loss, but pleasure in remembering him and as it were seeing him before us in his deeds and in his life.

Aristotle, *Rhetoric*, 1370^{b}22

13 We must consider that of desires some are natural, others vain, and of the natural some are necessary and others merely natural; and of the necessary some are necessary for happiness, others for the repose of the body, and others for very life. The right understanding of these facts enables us to refer all choice and avoidance to the health of the body and the soul's freedom from disturbance, since this is the aim of the life of blessedness. For it is to obtain this end that we always act, namely, to avoid pain and fear. And when this is once secured for us, all the tempest of the soul is dispersed, since the living creature has not to wander as though in search of something that is missing, and to look for some other thing by which he can fulfil the good of the soul and the good of the body. For it is then that we have need of pleasure, when we feel pain owing to the absence of pleasure; but when we do not feel pain, we no longer need pleasure. And for this cause we call pleasure the beginning and end of the blessed life. For we recognize pleasure as the first good innate in us, and from pleasure we begin every act of choice and avoidance, and to pleasure we return again, using the feeling as the standard by which we judge every good.

Epicurus, *Letter to Menoeceus*

14 O miserable minds of men! O blinded breasts! in what darkness of life and in how great dangers is passed this term of life whatever its duration! not choose to see that nature craves for herself no more than this, that pain hold aloof from the body, and she in mind enjoy a feeling of pleasure exempt from care and fear? Therefore we see that for the body's nature few things are needed at all, such and such only as take away pain.

Lucretius, *Nature of Things*, II

15 If someone maintains that pain is the greatest evil, what part can courage play in his philosophy? Courage is nothing less than indifference to hardship and pain.

Cicero, *De Officiis*, III, 33

16 The best thing we can say about pleasure is to admit that it may add some spice to life. But it certainly adds nothing really suitable.

Cicero, *De Officiis*, III, 33

17 Even when they're over, pleasures of a depraved nature are apt to carry feelings of dissatisfaction, in the same way as a criminal's anxiety doesn't end with the commission of the crime, even if it's undetected at the time. Such pleasures are insubstantial and unreliable; even if they don't do one any harm, they're fleeting in character. Look around for some enduring good instead.

Seneca, *Letters to Lucilius*, 27

18 The better pleasures gained in successful action and effort leave the baser appetites no time or place, and make active and heroic men forget them.

Plutarch, *Cimon and Lucullus Compared*

19 If you are dazzled by the semblance of any promised pleasure, guard yourself against being bewildered by it; but let the affair wait your leisure, and procure yourself some delay. Then bring to your mind both points of time—that in which you shall enjoy the pleasure, and that in which you will repent and reproach yourself, after you have enjoyed it—and set before you, in opposition to these, how you will rejoice and applaud yourself if you abstain. And even though it should appear to you a seasonable gratification, take heed that its enticements and allurements and seductions may not subdue you, but set in opposition to this how much better it is to be conscious of having gained so great a victory.

Epictetus, *Encheiridion*, XXXIV

20 The pleasure demanded for the Sage's life cannot be in the enjoyments of the licentious or in any gratifications of the body—there is no place for these, and they stifle happiness—nor in any violent emotions—what could so move the Sage?—it can be only such pleasure as there must be where Good is, pleasure that does not rise from movement and is not a thing of process, for all that is good is immediately present to the Sage and the Sage is present to himself: his pleasure, his contentment, stands, immovable.

Plotinus, *First Ennead*, IV, 12

21 In old age . . . [the Sage] will desire neither pains nor pleasures to hamper him; he will desire nothing of this world, pleasant or painful; his one desire will be to know nothing of the body. If he should meet with pain he will pit against it the powers he holds to meet it; but pleasure and health and ease of life will not mean any increase of happiness to him nor will their contraries destroy or lessen it.

Plotinus, *First Ennead*, IV, 14

22 Men procure the actual pleasures of human life by way of pain—I mean not only the pain that comes upon us unlooked for and beyond our will, but unpleasantness planned and willingly accepted. There is no pleasure in eating or drinking, unless the discomfort of hunger and thirst come before. Drunkards eat salty things to develop a thirst so great as to be painful, and pleasure arises when the liquor quenches the pain of the thirst. And it is the custom that promised brides do not give themselves at once lest the husband should hold the gift cheap unless delay had set him craving.

We see this in base and dishonourable pleasure, but also in the pleasure that is licit and permitted, and again in the purest and most honourable friendship. We have seen it in the case of him who had been dead and was brought back to life, who had been lost and was found. Universally the greater joy is heralded by greater pain.

Augustine, *Confessions,* VIII, 3

23 *Philosophy.* All pleasures have this way: those who enjoy them they drive on with stings. Pleasure, like the winged bee, scatters its honey sweet, then flies away, and with a clinging sting it strikes the hearts it touches.

Boethius, *Consolation of Philosophy,* III

24 Although the name of passion is more appropriate to those passions which have a corruptive and evil tendency, such as bodily ailments, and sadness and fear in the soul, yet some passions are ordered to something good. . . . And in this sense pleasure is called a passion.

Aquinas, *Summa Theologica,* I–II, 31, 1

25 We take pleasure both in those things which we desire naturally, when we get them, and in those things which we desire as a result of reason. But we do not speak of joy except when pleasure follows reason; and so we do not ascribe joy to irrational animals, but only pleasure.

Now whatever we desire naturally can also be the object of reasoned desire and pleasure, and consequently whatever can be the object of pleasure, can also be the object of joy in rational beings. And yet everything is not always the object of joy, since sometimes one feels a certain pleasure in the body without rejoicing in it according to reason. And accordingly pleasure extends to more things than does joy.

Aquinas, *Summa Theologica,* I–II, 31, 3

26 If . . . we compare intellectual pleasures with sensible pleasures according as we delight in the very actions, for instance in sensitive and in intellectual knowledge, without doubt intellectual pleasures are much greater than sensible pleasures. For man takes much more delight in knowing something, by understanding it, than in knowing something by perceiving it with his sense; both because intellectual knowledge is more perfect and because it is better known, since the intellect reflects on its own act more than sense does. Moreover intellectual knowledge is more loved; for there is no one who would not forfeit his bodily sight rather than his intellectual vision in the way beasts or fools are without the latter, as Augustine says in the *City of God.*

If, however, intellectual spiritual pleasures be compared with sensible bodily pleasures, then, in themselves and absolutely speaking, spiritual pleasures are greater. And this appears from the consideration of the three things needed for pleasure; namely, the good which is brought into con-

junction, that to which it is joined, and the union itself. For spiritual good is both greater and more loved than bodily good; a sign of this is that men abstain from even the greatest bodily pleasures, rather than suffer loss of honour which is an intellectual good. Likewise the intellectual part is much more noble and more knowing than the sensitive part. Also the conjunction is more intimate, more perfect and more firm. More intimate, because the senses stop at the outward accidents of a thing, while the intellect penetrates to the essence; for the object of the intellect is what a thing is. More perfect, because the conjunction of the sensible to the sense implies movement, which is an imperfect act; thus sensible pleasures are not wholly together at once, but some part of them is passing away, while some other part is looked forward to as yet to be realized, as is manifest in pleasures of the table and in sexual pleasures. But intelligible things are without movement; hence pleasures of this kind are realized all at once. They are more firm, because the objects of bodily pleasures are corruptible and soon pass away; but spiritual goods are incorruptible.

On the other hand, in relation to us, bodily pleasures are more vehement, for three reasons. First, because sensible things are more known to us than intelligible things. Secondly, because sensible pleasures, through being passions of the sensitive appetite, are accompanied by some alteration in the body; but this does not occur in spiritual pleasures unless by reason of a certain reaction of the superior appetite on the lower. Thirdly, because bodily pleasures are sought as remedies for bodily defects or troubles, from which various griefs arise. And so bodily pleasures, because they come after griefs of this kind, are felt the more, and consequently are more welcome than spiritual pleasures, which have no contrary griefs.

Aquinas, *Summa Theologica,* I–II, 31, 5

27 Doing good to another may give pleasure in three ways. First, in relation to the effect, which is the good conferred on another. In this respect, since through being united to others by love we look upon their good as being our own, we take pleasure in the good we do to others, especially to our friends, as in our own good. Secondly, in consideration of the end; as when a man, from doing good to another, hopes to get some good for himself, either from God or from man; for hope is a cause of pleasure. Thirdly, in consideration of the principle; and thus, doing good to another can give pleasure in respect of a three-fold principle. One is the power of doing good; and in this regard doing good to another becomes pleasant in so far as it arouses in man an imagination of abundant good existing in him, of which he is able to give others a share. Therefore men take pleasure in their children, and in their own works, as being

things on which they bestow a share of their own good. Another principle is a man's habitual inclination to do good, by reason of which doing good becomes connatural to him, for which reason the liberal man takes pleasure in giving to others. The third principle is the motive; for instance when a man is moved by one whom he loves to do good to someone. For whatever we do or suffer for a friend is pleasant, because love is the principle cause of pleasure.

Aquinas, *Summa Theologica*, I–II, 32, 6

28 Bodily pleasures hinder the use of reason in three ways. First, by distracting the reason . . . we attend much to that which pleases us. Now when the attention is firmly fixed on one thing, it is either weakened in respect of other things, or it is entirely withdrawn from them; and thus if the bodily pleasure be great, either it entirely hinders the use of reason, by concentrating the mind's attention on itself, or else it hinders it considerably. Secondly, by being contrary to reason. Because some pleasures, especially those that are in excess, are contrary to the order of reason, and in this sense the Philosopher says that bodily pleasures destroy the estimate of prudence, but not the speculative estimate, to which they are not opposed, for instance that the three angles of a triangle are together equal to two right angles. In the first sense, however, they hinder both estimates. Thirdly, by fettering the reason, in so far as bodily pleasure is followed by a certain alteration in the body, greater even than in the other passions, in proportion as the appetite is more vehemently affected towards a present than towards an absent thing. Now such bodily disturbances hinder the use of reason, as may be seen in the case of drunkards, in whom the use of reason is fettered or hindered.

Aquinas, *Summa Theologica*, I–II, 33, 3

29 Now the greatest good of everything is its last end. And the end . . . is twofold: namely, the thing itself, and the use of that thing; thus the miser's end is either money, or the possession of money. Accordingly, man's last end may be said to be either God Who is the Supreme Good absolutely; or the enjoyment of God, which denotes a certain pleasure in the last end. And in this sense a certain pleasure of man may be said to be the greatest among human goods.

Aquinas, *Summa Theologica*, I–II, 34, 3

30 Pain itself can be pleasurable accidentally in so far as it is accompanied by wonder, as in stage-plays; or in so far as it recalls a beloved object to one's memory, and makes one feel one's love for the thing, whose absence gives us pain. Consequently, since love is pleasant, both pain and whatever else results from love, in so far as they remind us of our love, are pleasant. And, for this

reason, we derive pleasure even from pains depicted on the stage, in so far as, in witnessing them, we perceive ourselves to conceive a certain love for those who are there represented.

Aquinas, *Summa Theologica*, I–II, 35, 3

31 The greatest of all pleasures consists in the contemplation of truth.

Aquinas, *Summa Theologica*, I–II, 38, 4

32 Every animal, as soon as it is born, whether rational or brute, loves itself and fears and flees those things which are counter to it, and hates them. . . .

I say, then, that from the beginning it loves itself, although without discrimination. Then it comes to distinguish the things which are most pleasant, and less and more detestable, and follows and flees in greater and less degree according as its consciousness distinguishes not only in other things which it loves secondarily, but just in itself which it loves primarily. And recognising in itself divers parts, it loves those in itself most which are most noble. And since the mind is a more noble part of man than the body, it loves that more; and thus, loving itself primarily and other things for its own sake, and loving the better part of itself better, it is clear that it loves the mind better than the body or aught else; which mind it ought by nature to love more than aught else. Wherefore if the mind always delights in the exercise of the thing it loves (which is the fruition of love), exercise in that thing which it loves most is the most delightful. The exercise of our mind then is most delightful to us; and that which is most delightful to us constitutes our felicity and our blessedness, beyond which there is no delight, nor any equal to it, as may be seen by whoso well considers the preceding argument.

Dante, *Convivio*, IV, 22

33 This should console us, that in the course of nature, if the pain is violent, it is short; if it is long, it is light. . . . You will not feel it very long, if you feel it too much; it will put an end to itself, or to you; both come to the same thing. If you cannot bear it, it will bear you off.

Montaigne, *Essays*, I, 14, That the Taste of Good

34 But to speak in good earnest, isn't man a miserable animal? Hardly is it in his power, by his natural condition, to taste a single pleasure pure and entire, and still he is at pains to curtail that pleasure by his reason.

Montaigne, *Essays*, I, 30, Of Moderation

35 If we got our headache before getting drunk, we should take care not to drink too much; but pleasure, to deceive us, walks ahead and hides her sequel from us.

Montaigne, *Essays*, I, 39, Of Solitude

36 When I imagine man besieged by desirable delights—let us put the case that all his members should be forever seized with a pleasure like that of generation at its most excessive point—I feel him sink under the weight of his delight, and I see him wholly incapable of supporting a pleasure so pure, so constant, and so universal. In truth, he flees it when he is in it, and naturally hastens to escape it, as from a place where he cannot stand firm, where he is afraid of sinking.

Montaigne, *Essays*, II, 20, We Taste Nothing Pure

37 Intemperance is the plague of sensual pleasure; and temperance is not its scourge, it is its seasoning.

Montaigne, *Essays*, III, 13, Of Experience

38 *Romeo.* He jests at scars that never felt a wound.
Shakespeare, *Romeo and Juliet*, II, ii, 1

39 *Juliet.*   Parting is such sweet sorrow.
Shakespeare, *Romeo and Juliet*, II, ii, 185

40 *Bolingbroke.* O, who can hold a fire in his hand
By thinking on the frosty Caucasus?
Or cloy the hungry edge of appetite
By bare imagination of a feast?
Or wallow naked in December snow
By thinking on fantastic summer's heat?
O, no! the apprehension of the good
Gives but the greater feeling to the worse:
Fell sorrow's tooth doth never rankle more
Than when he bites, but lanceth not the sore.
Shakespeare, *Richard II*, I, iii, 294

41 *Leonato.* There was never yet philosopher
That could endure the toothache patiently,
However they have writ the style of gods
And made a push at chance and sufferance.
Shakespeare, *Much Ado About Nothing*, V, i, 35

42 The pleasure and delight of knowledge and learning, it far surpasseth all other in nature. For, shall the pleasures of the affections so exceed the pleasure of the sense, as much as the obtaining of desire or victory exceedeth a song or a dinner? and must not of consequence the pleasures of the intellect or understanding exceed the pleasures of the affections? We see in all other pleasures there is satiety, and after they be used, their verdure departeth; which showeth well they be but deceits of pleasure, and not pleasures: and that it was the novelty which pleased, and not the quality.

Bacon, *Advancement of Learning*, Bk. I, VIII, 5

43 The deceiving of the senses is one of the pleasures of the senses.

Bacon, *Advancement of Learning*, Bk. II, X, 13

44 Pleasure . . . or delight is the appearance or sense of good; and molestation or displeasure, the appearance or sense of evil. And consequently all appetite, desire, and love is accompanied with some delight more or less; and all hatred and aversion with more or less displeasure and offence.

Of pleasures, or delights, some arise from the sense of an object present; and those may be called *pleasures of sense* (the word *sensual*, as it is used by those only that condemn them, having no place till there be laws). Of this kind are all onerations and exonerations of the body; as also all that is pleasant, in the sight, hearing, smell, taste, or touch. Others arise from the expectation that proceeds from foresight of the end or consequence of things, whether those things in the sense please or displease: and these are *pleasures of the mind* of him that draweth those consequences, and are generally called *joy*. In the like manner, displeasures are some in the sense, and called *pain;* others, in the expectation of consequences, and are called *grief*.

Hobbes, *Leviathan*, I, 6

45 The principles of pleasure are not firm and stable. They are different in all men, and they vary to such an extent in each individual that there is no man who differs more from another man than from himself at different times. A man has other pleasures than a woman has; a rich man and a poor man have different pleasures; a prince, a warrior, a merchant, a citizen, a peasant, the old, the young, the well, the sick, all vary in this respect; the slightest accidents change them.

Pascal, *Geometrical Demonstration*

46 *Raphael.*   Sense of pleasure we may well
Spare out of life perhaps, and not repine,
But live content, which is the calmest life:
But pain is perfet miserie, the worst
Of evils, and excessive, overturnes
All patience.

Milton, *Paradise Lost*, VI, 459

47 The pleasures of sense are really intellectual pleasures confusedly known. Music charms us, although its beauty consists only in the harmonies [*convenances*] of numbers and in the counting (of which we are unconscious but which nevertheless the soul does make) of the beats or vibrations of sounding bodies, which beats or vibrations come together at definite intervals. The pleasure which sight finds in good proportions is of the same nature; and the pleasures caused by the other senses will be found to amount to much the same thing, although we may not be able to explain it so distinctly.

Leibniz, *Principles of Nature and of Grace*, 17

48 Attention and repetition help much to the fixing

any ideas in the memory. But those which naturally at first make the deepest and most lasting impressions, are those which are accompanied with pleasure or pain. The great business of the senses being, to make us take notice of what hurts or advantages the body, it is wisely ordered by nature, as has been shown, that pain should accompany the reception of several ideas; which, supplying the place of consideration and reasoning in children, and acting quicker than consideration in grown men, makes both the old and young avoid painful objects with that haste which is necessary for their preservation; and in both settles in the memory a caution for the future.

Locke, *Concerning Human Understanding,*
Bk. II, X, 3

49 Amongst the simple ideas which we receive both from sensation and reflection, *pain* and *pleasure* are two very considerable ones. For as in the body there is sensation barely in itself, or accompanied with pain or pleasure, so the thought or perception of the mind is simply so, or else accompanied also with pleasure or pain, delight or trouble, call it how you please. These, like other simple ideas, cannot be described, nor their names defined; the way of knowing them is, as of the simple ideas of the senses, only by experience. For, to define them by the presence of good or evil, is no otherwise to make them known to us than by making us reflect on what we feel in ourselves, upon the several and various operations of good and evil upon our minds, as they are differently applied to or considered by us. . . .

Things then are good or evil, only in reference to pleasure or pain. . . . By pleasure and pain, I must be understood to mean of body or mind, as they are commonly distinguished; though in truth they are only different constitutions of the *mind,* sometimes occasioned by disorder in the body, sometimes by thoughts of the mind. . . .

Pleasure and pain and that which causes them,—good and evil, are the hinges on which our passions turn. And if we reflect on ourselves, and observe how these, under various considerations, operate in us; what modifications or tempers of mind, what internal sensations (if I may so call them) they produce in us we may thence form to ourselves the ideas of our passions.

Locke, *Concerning Human Understanding,*
Bk. II, XX, 1–3

50 Men may and should correct their palates, and give relish to what either has, or they suppose has none. The relish of the mind is as various as that of the body, and like that too may be altered; and it is a mistake to think that men cannot change the displeasingness or indifferency that is in actions into pleasure and desire, if they will do but what is in their power.

Locke, *Concerning Human Understanding,*
Bk. II, XXI, 71

51 The senses have not only that advantage over conscience, which things necessary must always have over things chosen, but they have likewise a kind of prescription in their favour. We feared pain much earlier than we apprehended guilt, and were delighted with the sensations of pleasure before we had capacities to be charmed with the beauty of rectitude.

Johnson, *Rambler No. 7*

52 The armies of pain send their arrows against us on every side, the choice is only between those which are more or less sharp, or tinged with poison of greater or less malignity; and the strongest armour which reason can supply will only blunt their points, but cannot repel them.

The great remedy which heaven has put in our hands is patience, by which, though we cannot lessen the torments of the body, we can in a great measure preserve the peace of the mind, and shall suffer only the natural and genuine force of an evil without heightening its acrimony or prolonging its effects.

Johnson, *Rambler No. 32*

53 *Johnson.* "When we talk of pleasure, we mean sensual pleasure. When a man says, he had pleasure with a woman, he does not mean conversation, but something of a very different nature. Philosophers tell you, that pleasure is *contrary* to happiness. Gross men prefer animal pleasure. So there are men who have preferred living among savages. Now what a wretch must he be, who is content with such conversation as can be had among savages! You may remember an officer at Fort Augustus, who had served in America, told us of a woman whom they were obliged to *bind,* in order to get her back from savage life." *Boswell.* "She must have been an animal, a beast." *Johnson.* "Sir, she was a speaking cat."

Boswell, *Life of Johnson*
(Apr. 7, 1778)

54 The universal communicability of a pleasure involves in its very concept that the pleasure is not one of enjoyment arising out of mere sensation, but must be one of reflection.

Kant, *Critique of Aesthetic Judgement,* 44

55 Epicurus was not wide of the mark when he said that at bottom all gratification is bodily sensation, and only misunderstood himself in ranking intellectual and even practical delight under the head of gratification.

Kant, *Critique of Aesthetic Judgement,* 54

56 The value of life for us, measured simply by *what we enjoy* (by the natural end of the sum of all our inclinations, that is by happiness), is easy to decide. It is less than nothing. For who would enter life afresh under the same conditions? Who would even do so according to a new, self-devised plan

(which should, however, follow the course of nature), if it also were merely directed to enjoyment?

Kant, *Critique of Teleological Judgement,* 83, fn. 1

57 The superiority of intellectual to sensual pleasures consists rather in their filling up more time, in their having a larger range, and in their being less liable to satiety, than in their being more real and essential.

Malthus, *Population,* XI

58 In the pursuit of every enjoyment, whether sensual or intellectual, reason, that faculty which enables us to calculate consequences, is the proper corrective and guide. It is probable, therefore, that improved reason will always tend to prevent the abuse of sensual pleasures, though it by no means follows that it will extinguish them.

Malthus, *Population,* XI

59 *Emma.* One half of the world cannot understand the pleasures of the other.

Jane Austen, *Emma,* IX

60 And the small ripple spilt upon the beach
   Scarcely o'erpass'd the cream of your champagne,
   When o'er the brim the sparkling bumpers reach,
   That spring-dew of the spirit! the heart's rain!
   Few things surpass old wine; and they may preach
   Who please,—the more because they preach in vain,—
   Let us have wine and women, mirth and laughter,
   Sermons and soda-water the day after.

   Man, being reasonable, must get drunk;
   The best of life is but intoxication:
   Glory, the grape, love, gold, in these are sunk
   The hopes of all men, and of every nation;
   Without their sap, how branchless were the trunk
   Of life's strange tree, so fruitful on occasion:
   But to return,—Get very drunk; and when
   You wake with headache, you shall see what then.

Byron, *Don Juan,* II, 178–179

61   You will find,
   Though sages may pour out their wisdom's treasure,
   There is no sterner moralist than Pleasure.

Byron, *Don Juan,* III, 65

62 To enjoy bodily warmth, some small part of you must be cold, for there is no quality in this world that is not what it is merely by contrast. Nothing exists in itself. If you flatter yourself that you are all over comfortable, and have been so a long time, then you cannot be said to be comfortable any more.

Melville, *Moby Dick,* XI

63 I discovered, though unconsciously and insensibly, that the pleasure of observing and reasoning was a much higher one than that of skill and sport.

Darwin, *Autobiography*

64 Men lose their high aspirations as they lose their intellectual tastes, because they have not time or opportunity for indulging them; and they addict themselves to inferior pleasures, not because they deliberately prefer them, but because they are either the only ones to which they have access, or the only ones which they are any longer capable of enjoying. It may be questioned whether any one who has remained equally susceptible to both classes of pleasures, ever knowingly and calmly preferred the lower; though many, in all ages, have broken down in an ineffectual attempt to combine both.

Mill, *Utilitarianism,* II

65 Now to decide whether this is really so; whether mankind do desire nothing for itself but that which is a pleasure to them, or of which the absence is a pain; we have evidently arrived at a question of fact and experience, dependent, like all similar questions, upon evidence. It can only be determined by practised self-consciousness and self-observation, assisted by observation of others. I believe that these sources of evidence, impartially consulted, will declare that desiring a thing and finding it pleasant, aversion to it and thinking of it as painful, are phenomena entirely inseparable, or rather two parts of the same phenomenon; in strictness of language, two different modes of naming the same psychological fact: that to think of an object as desirable (unless for the sake of its consequences), and to think of it as pleasant, are one and the same thing; and that to desire anything, except in proportion as the idea of it is pleasant, is a physical and metaphysical impossibility.

Mill, *Utilitarianism,* IV

66 It is at the same time indubitable that the replacement of the pleasure-principle by the reality-principle can account only for a small part, and that not the most intense, of painful experiences. Another and no less regular source of "pain" proceeds from the conflicts and dissociations in the psychic apparatus during the development of the ego towards a more highly co-ordinated organization. Nearly all the energy with which the apparatus is charged, comes from the inborn instincts, but not all of these are allowed to develop to the same stage. On the way, it over and again happens that particular instincts, or portions of them, prove irreconcilable in their aims or demands with others which can be welded into the comprehensive unity of the ego. They are, thereupon, split off from this unity by the process of repression, retained on lower stages of psychic devel-

opment, and for the time being cut off from all possibility of gratification. If they then succeed, as so easily happens with the repressed sex-impulses, in fighting their way through—along circuitous routes—to a direct or a substitutive gratification, this success, which might otherwise have brought pleasure, is experienced by the ego as "pain." In consequence of the old conflict which ended in repression, the pleasure-principle has been violated anew, just at the moment when certain impulses were at work on the achievement of fresh pleasure in pursuance of the principle. The details of the process by which repression changes a possibility of pleasure into a source of "pain" are not yet fully understood, or are not yet capable of clear presentation, but it is certain that all neurotic "pain" is of this kind, is pleasure which cannot be experienced as such.

Freud, *Beyond the Pleasure Principle,* I

67 The feeling of happiness produced by indulgence of a wild, untamed craving is incomparably more intense than is the satisfying of a curbed desire. The irresistibility of perverted impulses, perhaps the charm of forbidden things generally, may in this way be explained economically.

Freud, *Civilization and Its Discontents,* II

4.8 | *Pity and Envy*

1 Now Israel loved Joseph more than all his children, because he was the son of his old age: and he made him a coat of many colours.

And when his brethren saw that their father loved him more than all his brethren, they hated him, and could not speak peaceably unto him.

And Joseph dreamed a dream, and he told it his brethren: and they hated him yet the more.

And he said unto them, Hear, I pray you, this dream which I have dreamed:

For, behold, we were binding sheaves in the field, and, lo, my sheaf arose, and also stood upright; and, behold, your sheaves stood round about, and made obeisance to my sheaf.

And his brethren said to him, Shalt thou indeed reign over us? or shalt thou indeed have dominion over us? And they hated him yet the more for his dreams, and for his words.

And he dreamed yet another dream, and told it his brethren, and said, Behold, I have dreamed a dream more; and, behold, the sun and the moon and the eleven stars made obeisance to me.

And he told it to his father, and to his brethren: and his father rebuked him, and said unto him, What is this dream that thou hast dreamed? Shall I and thy mother and thy brethren indeed come to bow down ourselves to thee to the earth?

And his brethren envied him; but his father observed the saying. . . .

And when they saw him afar off, even before he came near unto them, they conspired against him to slay him.

And they said one to another, Behold, this dreamer cometh.

Come now therefore, and let us slay him, and cast him into some pit, and we will say, Some evil beast hath devoured him: and we shall see what will become of his dreams.

And Reuben heard it, and he delivered him out of their hands; and said, Let us not kill him.

And Reuben said unto them, Shed no blood, but cast him into this pit that is in the wilderness, and lay no hand upon him; that he might rid him out of their hands, to deliver him to his father again.

And it came to pass when Joseph was come unto his brethren, that they stript Joseph out of his coat, his coat of many colours that was on him;

And they took him, and cast him into a pit: and the pit was empty, there was no water in it.

And they sat down to eat bread: and they lifted up their eyes and looked, and, behold, a company of Ĭsh-méé-lītes came from Gĭl'-ĕ-ăd with their camels bearing spicery and balm and myrrh, going to carry it down to Egypt.

And Judah said unto his brethren, What profit is it if we slay our brother, and conceal his blood?

Come, and let us sell him to the Ĭsh-méé-lītes, and let not our hand be upon him; for he is our brother and our flesh. And his brethren were content.

Then there passed by Midianites merchantmen; and they drew and lifted up Joseph out of the pit, and sold Joseph to the Ĭsh-mêe-lītes for twenty pieces of silver: and they brought Joseph into Egypt.

Genesis 37:3–28

2 *Agamemnon.* In few men is it part of nature to respect
a friend's prosperity without begrudging him,
as envy's wicked poison settling to the heart
piles up the pain in one sick with unhappiness,
who, staggered under sufferings that are all his own,
winces again to the vision of a neighbor's bliss.

Aeschylus, *Agamemnon,* 832

3 *Periander.* How much better a thing it is to be envied than pitied.

Herodotus, *History,* III, 52

4 *Pericles.* Men can endure to hear others praised only so long as they can severally persuade themselves of their own ability to equal the actions recounted: when this point is passed, envy comes in and with it incredulity.

Thucydides, *Peloponnesian War,* II, 35

5 Pity may be defined as a feeling of pain caused by the sight of some evil, destructive or painful, which befalls one who does not deserve it, and which we might expect to befall ourselves or some friend of ours, and moreover to befall us soon. In order to feel pity, we must obviously be capable of supposing that some evil may happen to us or some friend of ours. . . . It is therefore not felt by those completely ruined, who suppose that no further evil can befall them, since the worst has befallen them already; nor by those who imagine themselves immensely fortunate—their feeling is rather presumptuous insolence, for when they think they possess all the good things of life, it is clear that the impossibility of evil befalling them will be included, this being one of the good things in question. Those who think evil *may* befall them are such as have already had it befall them and have safely escaped from it; elderly men, owing to their good sense and their experience; weak men, especially men inclined to cowardice; and also educated people, since these can take long views. Also those who have parents living, or children, or wives; for these are our own, and the evils mentioned above may easily befall them. And those who are neither moved by any courageous emotion such as anger or confidence (these emotions take no account of the future), nor by a disposition to presumptuous insolence (insolent men, too, take no account of the possibility that something evil will happen to them), nor yet by great fear (panic-stricken people do not feel pity, because they are taken up with what is happening to themselves); only those feel pity who are between these two extremes. In order to feel pity we must

also believe in the goodness of at least some people; if you think nobody good, you will believe that everybody deserves evil fortune. And, generally, we feel pity whenever we are in the condition of remembering that similar misfortunes have happened to us or ours, or expecting them to happen in future.

Aristotle, *Rhetoric,* 1385ᵇ13

6 Envy is pain at the sight of such good fortune as consists of the good things already mentioned; we feel it towards our equals; not with the idea of getting something for ourselves, but because the other people have it. We shall feel it if we have, or think we have, equals; and by 'equals' I mean equals in birth, relationship, age, disposition, distinction, or wealth. We feel envy also if we fall but a little short of having everything; which is why people in high place and prosperity feel it—they think every one else is taking what belongs to themselves. Also if we are exceptionally distinguished for some particular thing, and especially if that thing is wisdom or good fortune. Ambitious men are more envious than those who are not. So also those who profess wisdom; they are ambitious—to be thought wise. Indeed, generally, those who aim at a reputation for anything are envious on this particular point. And small-minded men are envious, for everything seems great to them.

Aristotle, *Rhetoric,* 1387ᵇ22

7 We envy those who are near us in time, place, age, or reputation. . . . Also our fellow-competitors, who are indeed the people just mentioned—we do not compete with men who lived a hundred centuries ago, or those not yet born, or the dead, or those who dwell near the Pillars of Hercules, or those whom, in our opinion or that of others, we take to be far below us or far above us. So too we compete with those who follow the same ends as ourselves: we compete with our rivals in sport or in love, and generally with those who are after the same things; and it is therefore these whom we are bound to envy beyond all others. . . . We also envy those whose possession of or success in a thing is a reproach to us: these are our neighbours and equals; for it is clear that it is our own fault we have missed the good thing in question; this annoys us, and excites envy in us. We also envy those who have what we ought to have, or have got what we did have once. Hence old men envy younger men, and those who have spent much envy those who have spent little on the same thing. And men who have not got a thing, or not got it yet, envy those who have got it quickly. We can also see what things and what persons give pleasure to envious people, and in what states of mind they feel it: the states of mind in which they feel pain are those under which they will feel pleasure in the contrary things. If therefore we

ourselves with whom the decision rests are put into an envious state of mind, and those for whom our pity, or the award of something desirable, is claimed are such as have been described, it is obvious that they will win no pity from us.

Aristotle, *Rhetoric,* 1388ª6

8 Emulation is pain caused by seeing the presence, in persons whose nature is like our own, of good things that are highly valued and are possible for ourselves to acquire; but it is felt not because others have these goods, but because we have not got them ourselves. It is therefore a good feeling felt by good persons, whereas envy is a bad feeling felt by bad persons.

Aristotle, *Rhetoric,* 1388ª30

9 The envious person wastes at the thriving condition of another: Sicilian tyrants never invented a greater torment than envy.

Horace, *Epistles,* I, 2

10 When you hear the name of someone who has become famous on account of a particular merit or achievement, you yap like puppies when they encounter strangers.

Seneca, *On the Happy Life,* XIX

11 Folly has habituated us to live with a view to others rather than to ourselves, and our nature holds so much envy and malice that our pleasure in our own advantages is not so great as our distress at others.

Plutarch, *Contentment*

12 When a man has done thee any wrong, immediately consider with what opinion about good or evil he has done wrong. For when thou hast seen this, thou wilt pity him, and wilt neither wonder nor be angry.

Marcus Aurelius, *Meditations,* VII, 26

13 The proud are without pity, because they despise others, and think them wicked, so that they account them as suffering deservedly whatever they suffer.

Aquinas, *Summa Theologica,* II–II, 30, 2

14 *Falcon.* That pity wells up soon in gentle heart,
Feeling its likeness in all pains that smart,
Is proved, and day by day, as men may see,
As well by deeds as by authority;
For gentle heart can spy out gentleness.

Chaucer, *Canterbury Tales: Squire's Tale*

15 He who asks for pity without reason is a man not to be pitied when there is reason. To be always lamenting for ourselves is the way never to be lamented; by continually putting on a pitiful act, we become pitiable to no one. He who acts dead when still alive is subject to be thought alive when

dying. I have seen it get some people's goat to be told that their color was good and their pulse even; I have seen them restrain their laughter because it betrayed their recovery, and hate health because it was not pitiable. What is more, they were not women.

Montaigne, *Essays,* III, 9, Of Vanity

16 *Caesar.* Let me have men about me that are fat;
Sleek-headed men and such as sleep o'nights:
Yond Cassius has a lean and hungry look;
He thinks too much: such men are dangerous;
    Antony. Fear him not, Cæsar; he's not dangerous;
He is a noble Roman and well given.
    Caes. Would he were fatter! But I fear him not:
Yet if my name were liable to fear,
I do not know the man I should avoid
So soon as that spare Cassius. He reads much;
He is a great observer and he looks
Quite through the deeds of men; he loves no plays,
As thou dost, Antony; he hears no music;
Seldom he smiles, and smiles in such a sort
As if he mock'd himself and scorn'd his spirit
That could be moved to smile at anything.
Such men as he be never at heart's ease
Whiles they behold a greater than themselves,
And therefore are they very dangerous.
I rather tell thee what is to be fear'd
Than what I fear; for always I am Cæsar.

Shakespeare, *Julius Caesar,* I, ii, 192

17 *Othello.* Ay, let her rot, and perish, and be damned to-night; for she shall not live. No, my heart is turned to stone; I strike it, and it hurts my hand. O, the world hath not a sweeter creature! She might lie by an emperor's side and command him tasks.
    Iago. Nay, that's not your way.
    Oth. Hang her! I do but say what she is: so delicate with her needle; an admirable musician: O! she will sing the savageness out of a bear. Of so high and plenteous wit and invention—
    Iago. She's the worse for all this.
    Oth. O, a thousand thousand times. And then, of so gentle a condition!
    Iago. Ay, too gentle.
    Oth. Nay, that's certain; but yet the pity of it, Iago! O Iago, the pity of it, Iago!

Shakespeare, *Othello,* IV, i, 191

18 *Macbeth.*   This Duncan
Hath borne his faculties so meek, hath been
So clear in his great office, that his virtues
Will plead like angels, trumpet-tongued, against
The deep damnation of his taking-off;
And pity, like a naked new-born babe,
Striding the blast, or heaven's cherubim, horsed
Upon the sightless couriers of the air,
Shall blow the horrid deed in every eye,

That tears shall drown the wind.
        Shakespeare, *Macbeth,* I, vii, 16

19 Envy keeps no holidays.
        Nothing but death can reconcile envy to virtue.
                Bacon, *Advancement of Learning,*
                        Bk. VI, III, 16

20 Deformed persons, and eunuchs, and old men,
and bastards, are envious. For he that cannot possibly mend his own case, will do what he can to
impair another's.

                Bacon, *Of Envy*

21 The consideration of the present good excites joy
in us, and that of evil, sadness, when it is a good or
an evil which is represented as belonging to us.
. . . But when it is represented to us as pertaining
to other men, we may esteem them either as worthy or unworthy of it; and when we esteem them
worthy, that does not excite in us any other passion but joy, inasmuch as it is some satisfaction to
us to see that things happen as they should. There
is only this difference, that the joy that comes
from what is good is serious, while what comes
from evil is accompanied by laughter and mockery. But if we esteem them unworthy of it, the
good excites envy and the evil pity, which are species of sadness.
        Descartes, *Passions of the Soul,* LXI–LXII

22 Pity is a species of sadness, mingled with love or
good-will towards those whom we see suffering
some evil of which we consider them undeserving.
It is thus contrary to envy by reason of its object,
and to scorn because it considers its objects in another way. . . . Those who feel themselves very
feeble and subject to the adversities of fortune appear to be more disposed to this passion than
others, because they represent the evil of others as
possibly occurring to themselves; and then they
are moved to pity more by the love that they bear
to themselves than by that which they bear to
others.
        Descartes, *Passions of the Soul,*
                CLXXXV-CLXXXVI

23 Pity is imagination or fiction of future calamity to
ourselves, proceeding from the sense of another
man's calamity. But when it lighteth on such as
we think have not deserved the same, the compassion is greater, because there then appeareth more
probability that the same may happen to us; for
the evil that happeneth to an innocent man may
happen to every man.
        Hobbes, *Human Nature,* IX

24 A man who lives according to the dictates of reason endeavours as much as possible to prevent
himself from being touched by pity.
        The man who has properly understood that ev-

erything follows from the necessity of the divine
nature, and comes to pass according to the eternal
laws and rules of nature, will in truth discover
nothing which is worthy of hatred, laughter, or
contempt, nor will he pity any one, but, so far as
human virtue is able, he will endeavour to *do well,*
as we say, and to *rejoice.* We must add also, that a
man who is easily touched by the affect of pity,
and is moved by the misery or tears of another,
often does something of which he afterward repents, both because from an affect we do nothing
which we certainly know to be good, and also because we are so easily deceived by false tears. But
this I say expressly of the man who lives according
to the guidance of reason. For he who is moved
neither by reason nor pity to be of any service to
others is properly called inhuman; for he seems to
be unlike a man.
        Spinoza, *Ethics,* IV, Prop. 50, Corol.; Schol.

25 It is a secret well known to great men, that, by
conferring an obligation, they do not always procure a friend, but are certain of creating many
enemies.

                Fielding, *Tom Jones,* I, 9

26 It is good proverb which says that "it is better to
be envious than to have pity." Let us be envious,
therefore, as hard as we can.
        Voltaire, *Philosophical Dictionary:* Envy

27 Most of the misery which the defamation of
blameless actions, or the obstruction of honest endeavours brings upon the world, is inflicted by
men that propose no advantage to themselves but
the satisfaction of poisoning the banquet which
they cannot taste, and blasting the harvest which
they have no right to reap.
                Johnson, *Rambler No. 183*

28 *Johnson.* Pity is not natural to man. Children are
always cruel. Savages are always cruel. Pity is acquired and improved by the cultivation of reason.
        Boswell, *Life of Johnson* (*July 20, 1763*)

29 *Johnson.* If a madman were to come into this room
with a stick in his hand, no doubt we should pity
the state of his mind; but our primary consideration would be to take care of ourselves. We
should knock him down first, and pity him afterwards.
        Boswell, *Life of Johnson* (*Apr. 3, 1776*)

30 Once, when midnight smote the air,
Eunuchs ran through Hell and met
On every crowded street to stare
Upon great Juan riding by:
Even like these to rail and sweat
Staring upon his sinewy thigh.
        Yeats, *On Those That Hated 'The
        Playboy of the Western World,'* 1907

31 True pity consists not so much in fearing suffering as in desiring it. The desire is a faint one and we should hardly wish to see it realized; yet we form it in spite of ourselves, as if Nature were committing some great injustice and it were necessary to get rid of all suspicion of complicity with her.

Bergson, *Time and Free Will,* I

4.9 | *Greed and Avarice*

1 He that loveth silver shall not be satisfied with silver; nor he that loveth abundance with increase: this is also vanity.

Ecclesiastes 5:10

2 He who will be covetous, will also be anxious: but he that lives in a state of anxiety, will never in my estimation be free.

Horace, *Epistles,* I, 16

3 And he said unto them, Take heed, and beware of covetousness: for a man's life consisteth not in the abundance of the things which he possesseth. . . .
Therefore I say unto you, Take no thought for your life, what ye shall eat; neither for the body, what ye shall put on.

The life is more than meat, and the body is more than raiment. . . .

Consider the lilies how they grow: they toil not, they spin not; and yet I say unto you, that Solomon in all his glory was not arrayed like one of these.

If then God so clothe the grass, which is to day in the field, and tomorrow is cast into the oven; how much more will he clothe you, O ye of little faith?

And seek not ye what ye shall eat, or what ye shall drink, neither be ye of doubtful mind.

For all these things do the nations of the world seek after: and your Father knoweth that ye have need of these things.

But rather seek ye the kingdom of God; and all these things shall be added unto you.

Fear not, little flock; for it is your Father's good pleasure to give you the kingdom.

Sell that ye have, and give alms; provide yourselves bags which wax not old, a treasure in the heavens that faileth not, where no thief approacheth, neither moth corrupteth.

For where your treasure is, there will your heart be also.

Luke 12:15–34

4 Here saw I too many more than elsewhere, both on the one side and on the other, with loud howlings, rolling weights by force of chests;

they smote against each other, and then each wheeled round just there, rolling aback, shouting "Why holdest thou?" and "Why throwest thou away?"

Thus they returned along the gloomy circle, on either hand, to the opposite point, [again] shouting [at each other] their reproachful measure.

Then every one, when he had reached it, turned through his half-circle towards the other joust.

And I, who felt my heart as it were stung, said: "My Master, now shew me what people these are; and whether all those tonsured on our left were of the clergy."

And he to me: "In their first life, all were so squint-eyed in mind, that they made no expenditure in it with moderation.

Most clearly do their voices bark out this, when they come to the two points of the circle, where contrary guilt divides them.

These were Priests, that have not hairy covering on their heads, and Popes and Cardinals, in whom avarice does its utmost."

And I: "Master, among this set, I surely ought to recognise some that were defiled by these evils."

And he to me: "Vain thoughts combinest thou: their undiscerning life, which made them sordid, now makes them *too* obscure for any recognition.

To all eternity they shall continue butting one another; these shall arise from their graves with closed fists; and these with hair shorn off.

Ill-giving, and ill-keeping, has deprived them of the bright world, and put them to this conflict; what a *conflict* it is, I adorn no words to tell."

Dante, *Inferno,* VII, 25

5 I stand up like a scholar in pulpit,
And when the ignorant people all do sit,

I preach, as you have heard me say before,
And tell a hundred false japes, less or more.
I am at pains, then, to stretch forth my neck,
And east and west upon the folk I beck,
As does a dove that's sitting on a barn.
With hands and swift tongue, then, do I so yarn
That it's a joy to see my busyness.
Of avarice and of all such wickedness
Is all my preaching, thus to make them free
With offered pence, the which pence come to me.
For my intent is only pence to win,
And not at all for punishment of sin.

> Chaucer, *Canterbury Tales:*
> Pardoner's Tale, Prologue

6 I preach no sermon, save for covetousness.
For that my theme is yet, and ever was,
'*Radix malorum est cupiditas.*'
Thus can I preach against that self-same vice
Which I indulge, and that is avarice.

> Chaucer, *Canterbury Tales:*
> Pardoner's Tale, Prologue

7 The wish to acquire is in truth very natural and common, and men always do so when they can, and for this they will be praised not blamed; but when they cannot do so, yet wish to do so by any means, then there is folly and blame.

> Machiavelli, *Prince,* III

8 *Shylock.* How now, Tubal! what news from Genoa? hast thou found my daughter?

Tubal. I often came where I did hear of her, but cannot find her.

Shy. Why, there, there, there, there! a diamond gone, cost me two thousand ducats in Frankfort! The curse never fell upon our nation till now; I never felt it till now: two thousand ducats in that; and other precious, precious jewels. I would my daughter were dead at my foot, and the jewels in her ear! would she were hearsed at my foot, and the ducats in her coffin! No news of them? Why, so: and I know not what's spent in the search: why, thou loss upon loss! the thief gone with so much, and so much to find the thief; and no satisfaction, no revenge: nor no ill luck stirring but what lights on my shoulders; no sighs but of my breathing; no tears but of my shedding.

Tub. Yes, other men have ill luck too: Antonio, as I heard in Genoa—

Shy. What, what, what? ill luck, ill luck?

Tub. Hath an argosy cast away, coming from Tripolis.

Shy. I thank God, I thank God. Is't true, is't true?

Tub. I spoke with some of the sailors that escaped the wreck.

Shy. I thank thee, good Tubal: good news, good news! ha, ha! where? in Genoa?

Tub. Your daughter spent in Genoa, as I heard, in one night fourscore ducats.

Shy. Thou stickest a dagger in me: I shall never see my gold again: fourscore ducats at a sitting! fourscore ducats!

Tub. There came divers of Antonio's creditors in my company to Venice, that swear he cannot choose but break.

Shy. I am very glad of it: I'll plague him; I'll torture him: I am glad of it.

Tub. One of them showed me a ring that he had of your daughter for a monkey.

Shy. Out upon her! Thou torturest me, Tubal: it was my turquoise; I had it of Leah when I was a bachelor: I would not have given it for a wilderness of monkeys.

> Shakespeare, *Merchant of Venice,* III, i, 85

9 *Brutus.* Let me tell you, Cassius, you yourself
Are much condemn'd to have an itching palm.

> Shakespeare, *Julius Caesar,* IV, iii, 9

10 It almost always happens that the man who grows rich changes his notions of poverty, states his wants by some new measure, and from flying the enemy that pursued him bends his endeavours to overtake those whom he sees before him. The power of gratifying his appetites increases their demands; a thousand wishes crowd in upon him, importunate to be satisfied, and vanity and ambition open prospects to desire, which still grow wider as they are more contemplated.

> Johnson, *Rambler No. 38*

11 Many there are who openly and almost professedly regulate all their conduct by their love of money, who have no reason for action or forbearance, for compliance or refusal, than that they hope to gain more by one than by the other. These are indeed the meanest and cruellest of human beings, a race with whom, as with some pestiferous animals, the whole creation seems to be at war, but who, however detested or scorned, long continue to add heap to heap, and when they have reduced one to beggary are still permitted to fasten on another.

> Johnson, *Rambler No. 175*

12 *Johnson.* No man was born a miser, because no man was born to possession. Every man is born *cupidus* —desirous of getting; but not *avarus*—desirous of keeping.

> Boswell, *Life of Johnson (Apr. 25, 1778)*

13 All for ourselves and nothing for other people, seems, in every age of the world, to have been the vile maxim of the masters of mankind.

> Adam Smith, *Wealth of Nations,* III, 4

14 Avarice is an insatiate and universal passion; since the enjoyment of almost every object that can afford pleasure to the different tastes and tem-

pers of mankind may be procured by the possession of wealth.

Gibbon, *Decline and Fall of the Roman Empire,* XXXI

15 Oh! But he was a tight-fisted hand at the grindstone, Scrooge! a squeezing, wrenching, grasping, scraping, clutching, covetous old sinner! Hard and sharp as flint, from which no steel had ever struck out generous fire; secret, and self-contained, and solitary as an oyster.

Dickens, *A Christmas Carol,* I

16 With the very earliest development of the circulation of commodities, there is also developed the necessity, and the passionate desire, to hold fast the product of the first metamorphosis. This product is the transformed shape of the commodity, or its gold chrysalis. Commodities are thus sold not for the purpose of buying others, but in order to replace their commodity form by their money form. From being the mere means of effecting the circulation of commodities, this change of form becomes the end and aim. The changed form of the commodity is thus prevented from functioning as its unconditionally alienable form, or as its merely transient money form. The money becomes petrified into a hoard, and the seller becomes a hoarder of money.

Marx, *Capital,* Vol. I, I, 3

17 With the possibility of holding and storing up exchange value in the shape of a particular commodity arises also the greed for gold. Along with the extension of circulation, increases the power of money, that absolutely social form of wealth ever ready for use. "Gold is a wonderful thing! Whoever possesses it is lord of all he wants. By means of gold one can even get souls into Paradise." (Columbus in his letter from Jamaica, 1503.) Since gold does not disclose what has been transformed into it, everything, commodity or not, is convertible into gold. Everything becomes saleable and buyable. Circulation becomes the great social retort into which everything is thrown, to come out again as crystallized gold. Not even are the bones of Saints, and still less are more delicate *res sacrosanctae extra commercium hominum* able to withstand this alchemy. Just as every qualitative difference between commodities is extinguished in money, so money, on its side, like the radical leveller that it is, does away with all distinctions. But money itself is a commodity, an external object, capable of becoming the private property of any individual. Thus social power becomes the private power of private persons. The ancients therefore denounced money as subversive of the economic and moral order of things. Modern society, which, soon after its birth, pulled Plutus by the hair of his head from the bowels of the earth, greets gold as its Holy Grail, as the glittering incarnation of the very principle of its own life.

Marx, *Capital,* Vol. I, I, 3

18 Capital has not invented surplus labour. Wherever a part of society possesses the monopoly of the means of production, the labourer, free or not free, must add to the working time necessary for his own maintenance an extra working time in order to produce the means of subsistence for the owners of the means of production, whether this proprietor be the Athenian [nobleman], Etruscan theocrat, [Roman citizen], Norman baron, American slave owner, Wallachian boyard, modern landlord or capitalist. It is, however, clear that in any given economic formation of society, where not the exchange value but the use-value of the product predominates, surplus labour will be limited by a given set of wants which may be greater or less, and that here no boundless thirst for surplus labour arises from the nature of the production itself. Hence, in antiquity overwork becomes horrible only when the object is to obtain exchange value in its specific independent money form; in the production of gold and silver. Compulsory working to death is here the recognized form of overwork. Only read Diodorus Siculus. Still, these are exceptions in antiquity. But as soon as people, whose production still moves within the lower forms of slave-labour, corvée-labour, etc., are drawn into the whirlpool of an international market dominated by the capitalistic mode of production, the sale of their products for export becoming their principal interest, the civilized horrors of overwork are grafted on the barbaric horrors of slavery, serfdom, etc. Hence, the negro labour in the Southern States of the American Union preserved something of a patriarchal character, so long as production was chiefly directed to immediate local consumption. But in proportion, as the export of cotton became of vital interest to these states, the overworking of the negro and sometimes the using up of his life in seven years' of labour became a factor in a calculated and calculating system. It was no longer a question of obtaining from him a certain quantity of useful products. It was now a question of production of surplus labour itself.

Marx, *Capital,* Vol. I, III, 10

19 It is self-evident that the labourer is nothing else, his whole life through, but labour power, that, therefore, all his disposable time is by nature and law labour time, to be devoted to the self-expansion of capital. Time for education, for intellectual development, for the fulfilling of social functions and for social intercourse, for the free play of his bodily and mental activity, even the rest time of Sunday (and that in a country of Sabbatarians!)—moonshine! But in its blind unrestrainable passion, its werewolf hunger for surplus labour, capital oversteps not only the moral, but even the

merely physical maximum bounds of the working day. It usurps the time for growth, development, and healthy maintenance of the body. It steals the time required for the consumption of fresh air and sunlight. It higgles over a meal time, incorporating it where possible with the process of production itself, so that food is given to the labourer as to a mere means of production, as coal is supplied to the boiler, grease and oil to the machinery. It reduces the sound sleep needed for the restoration, reparation, refreshment of the bodily powers to just so many hours of torpor as the revival of an organism, absolutely exhausted, renders essential. It is not the normal maintenance of the labour power which is to determine the limits of the working day; it is the greatest possible daily expenditure of labour power, no matter how diseased, compulsory, and painful it may be, which is to determine the limits of the labourers' period of repose. Capital cares nothing for the length of life of labour power. All that concerns it is simply and solely the maximum of labour power that can be rendered fluent in a working day. It attains this end by shortening the extent of the labourer's life, as a greedy farmer snatches increased produce from the soil by robbing it of its fertility.

Marx, *Capital,* Vol. I, III, 10

20 From its first day to this, sheer greed was the driving spirit of civilization; wealth and again wealth and once more wealth, wealth, not of society, but of the single scurvy individual—here was its one and final aim.

Engels, *Origin of the Family,* IX

4.10 | *Jealousy*

1 Jealousy is cruel as the grave: the coals thereof are coals of fire, which hath a most vehement flame.

Song of Solomon 8:6

2 With ambitious natures, otherwise not ill qualified for command, the feeling of jealousy of those near them in reputation continually stands in the way of the performance of noble actions; they make those their rivals in virtue, whom˙ they ought to use as their helpers to it.

Plutarch, *Lysander*

3 *Cressida.* "Another shame is this, that folk abuse
True love and say, 'Yea, jealousy is love!'
A bushel of venom such folk will excuse
If but a grain of love therein they shove.
But God knows this, who lives and reigns above,
If it be liker love or liker hate,
And by its name we should it designate.

"Some sorts of jealousy, I will confess,
Are more excusable than other kinds,
As when there's cause, or when folk long repress
Some harsh fantastic notion in their minds,
Which in expression no free outlet finds,
And on itself it thus doth grow and feed;
For such repression is a gentle deed.

"And some are filled with fury and despite
So full that it surpasses all restraint—
But, sweetheart, you are not in such plight,
Thank God, and all your grieving and your plaint,
I call it an illusive lover's taint
From love's excess, and from anxiety."

Chaucer, *Troilus and Cressida,* III, 147–149

4 Whatever justice there may be in jealousy, it still remains to be seen whether its agitation is really useful. Is there someone who thinks to shackle women by his ingenuity? . . . What occasion will not be enough for them in so knowing an age?

Curiosity is vicious in all things, but here it is pernicious. It is folly to want to be enlightened about a disease for which there is no medicine that does not make it worse and aggravate it; the shame of which is increased and made public principally by jealousy; revenge for which wounds our children more than it cures us. You dry up and die in quest of a proof so obscure.

Montaigne, *Essays,* III, 5, On Some Verses of Virgil

5 *Iago.*   O, beware, my lord, of jealousy;
It is the green-eyed monster which doth mock
The meat it feeds on. That cuckold lives in bliss
Who, certain of his fate, loves not his wronger;
But, O, what damned minutes tells he o'er
Who dotes, yet doubts, suspects, yet strongly loves!
  Othello. O misery!
  Iago. Poor and content is rich and rich enough,

But riches fineless is as poor as winter
To him that ever fears he shall be poor.
Good heaven, the souls of all my tribe defend
From jealousy!
    Oth.   Why, why is this?
Think'st thou I'd make a life of jealousy,
To follow still the changes of the moon
With fresh suspicions? No; to be once in doubt
Is once to be resolved. Exchange me for a goat,
When I shall turn the business of my soul
To such exsufflicate and blown surmises,
Matching thy inference. 'Tis not to make me jeal-
    ous
To say my wife is fair, feeds well, loves company,
Is free of speech, sings, plays, and dances well;
Where virtue is, these are more virtuous.
Nor from mine own weak merits will I draw
The smallest fear or doubt of her revolt;
For she had eyes, and chose me. No, Iago;
I'll see before I doubt; when I doubt, prove;
And on the proof, there is no more but this—
Away at once with love or jealousy!

                    Shakespeare, *Othello*, III, iii, 165

6 *Iago.*   Not poppy, nor mandragora,
Nor all the drowsy syrups of the world,
Shall ever medicine thee to that sweet sleep
Which thou owedst yesterday.
    Othello.   Ha! ha! false to me?
Iago. Why, how now, general! no more of that.
Oth. Avaunt! be gone! thou hast set me on the
    rack.
I swear 'tis better to be much abused
Than but to know 't a little.
    Iago.   How now, my lord!
Oth. What sense had I of her stol'n hours of lust?
I saw't not, thought it not, it harm'd not me.
I slept the next night well, was free and merry;
I found not Cassio's kisses on her lips.
He that is robb'd, not wanting what is stol'n,
Let him not know 't, and he's not robb'd at all.
    Iago. I am sorry to hear this.
    Oth. I had been happy, if the general camp,
Pioners and all, had tasted her sweet body,
So I had nothing known. O, now, for ever
Farewell the tranquil mind! farewell content!
Farewell the plumed troop, and the big wars,
That make ambition virtue! O, farewell!
Farewell the neighing steed, and the shrill trump,
The spirit-stirring drum, the ear-piercing fife,
The royal banner, and all quality,
Pride, pomp, and circumstance of glorious war!
And, O you mortal engines, whose rude throats
The immortal Jove's dread clamours counterfeit,
Farewell! Othello's occupation's gone!
    Iago. Is't possible, my lord?
    Oth. Villain, be sure thou prove my love a
    whore,
Be sure of it; give me the ocular proof;
Or, by the worth of man's eternal soul,
Thou hadst been better have been born a dog

Than answer my waked wrath!
    Iago.   Is't come to this?
    Oth. Make me to see't; or, at the least, so prove
    it
That the probation bear no hinge nor loop
To hang a doubt on; or woe upon thy life!
    Iago. My noble lord—
    Oth. If thou dost slander her and torture me,
Never pray more; abandon all remorse;
On horror's head horrors accumulate;
Do deeds to make heaven weep, all earth amazed;
For nothing canst thou to damnation add
Greater than that.

                    Shakespeare, *Othello*, III, iii, 330

7 *Desdemona.* Alas the day! I never gave him cause.
    Emilia. But jealous souls will not be answer'd so;
They are not ever jealous for the cause,
But jealous for they are jealous. 'Tis a monster
Begot upon itself, born on itself.

                    Shakespeare, *Othello*, III, iv, 158

8 *Leontes.*   Ha' not you seen, Camillo—
But that's past doubt, you have, or your eyeglass
Is thicker than a cuckold's horn—or heard—
For to a vision so apparent rumour
Cannot be mute—or thought—for cogitation
Resides not in that man that does not think—
My wife is slippery? If thou wilt confess,
Or else be impudently negative,
To have nor eyes nor ears nor thought, then say
My wife's a hobby-horse, deserves a name
As rank as any flax-wench that puts to
Before her troth-plight; say't and justify't.
    Camillo. I would not be a stander-by to hear
My sovereign mistress clouded so, without
My present vengeance taken. 'Shrew my heart,
You never spoke what did become you less
Than this; which to reiterate were sin
As deep as that, though true.
    Leon.   Is whispering nothing?
Is leaning cheek to cheek? is meeting noses?
Kissing with inside lip? stopping the career
Of laughter with a sigh?—a note infallible
Of breaking honesty—horsing foot on foot?
Skulking in corners? wishing clocks more swift?
Hours, minutes? noon, midnight? and all eyes
Blind with the pin and web but theirs, theirs only,
That would unseen be wicked? Is this nothing?
Why, then the world and all that's in't is nothing;
The covering sky is nothing; Bohemia nothing;
My wife is nothing; nor nothing have these noth-
    ings,
If this be nothing.
    Cam.   Good my lord, be cured
Of this diseased opinion, and betimes;
For 'tis most dangerous.
    Leon.   Say it be, 'tis true.
    Cam. No, no, my lord.
    Leon.   It is; you lie, you lie.

               Shakespeare, *Winter's Tale*, I, ii, 267

9 Jealousy is a species of fear which is related to the desire we have to preserve to ourselves the possession of some thing; and it does not so much proceed from the strength of the reasons that suggest the possibility of our losing that good, as from the high estimation in which we hold it, and which is the cause of our examining even the minutest subjects of suspicion, and taking them to be very considerable reasons for anxiety.

Descartes, *Passions of the Soul,* CLXVII

10 It is, indeed, very possible for jealous persons to kill the objects of their jealousy, but not to hate them.

Fielding, *Tom Jones,* VII, 4

11 It is hard to imagine what some jealous men can make up their mind to and overlook, and what they can forgive! The jealous are the readiest of all to forgive, and all women know it. The jealous man can forgive extraordinarily quickly (though, of course, after a violent scene), and he is able to forgive infidelity almost conclusively proved, the very kisses and embraces he has seen, if only he can somehow be convinced that it has all been "for the last time," and that his rival will vanish from that day forward, will depart to the ends of the earth, or that he himself will carry her away somewhere, where that dreaded rival will not get near her. Of course the reconciliation is only for an hour. For, even if the rival did disappear next day, he would invent another one and would be jealous of him. And one might wonder what there was in a love that had to be so watched over, what a love could be worth that needed such strenuous guarding. But that the jealous will never understand. And yet among them are men of noble hearts. It is remarkable, too, that those very men of noble hearts, standing hidden in some cupboard, listening and spying, never feel the stings of conscience at that moment, anyway, though they understand clearly enough with their "noble hearts" the shameful depths to which they have voluntarily sunk.

Dostoevsky, *Brothers Karamazov,*
Pt. III, VIII, 3

4.11 | *Pride and Humility*

1 Pride goeth before destruction, and an haughty spirit before a fall.

Proverbs 16:18

2 *Chorus.* The curse on great daring
shines clear; it wrings atonement
from those high hearts that drive to evil,
from houses blossoming to pride
and peril.

Aeschylus, *Agamemnon,* 374

3 *Creon.* These rigid spirits are the first to fall.
The strongest iron, hardened in the fire,
most often ends in scraps and shatterings.

Sophocles, *Antigone,* 473

4 *Athena.* The gods
Love men of steady sense and hate the proud.

Sophocles, *Ajax,* 132

5 *Messenger.* Wherever men forget their mere man's
nature,
Thinking a thought too high, they have no use
Of their huge bulk and boldness, but they fall

On most untoward disasters sent by Heaven.
Ajax, even when he first set out from home,
Proved himself foolish, when his father gave him
His good advice at parting. 'Child,' he said,
'Resolve to win, but always with God's help.'
But Ajax answered with a senseless boast:
'Father, with God's help even a worthless man
Could triumph. I propose, without that help,
To win my prize of fame.'

Sophocles, *Ajax,* 758

6 *Hecuba.* We boast, we are proud, we plume our confidence—
the rich man in his insolence of wealth,
the public man's conceit of office or success—
and we are nothing; our ambition, greatness,
pride,
all vanity.

Euripides, *Hecuba,* 623

7 *Electra.* There is no form of anguish with a name—
no suffering, no fate, no fall
inflicted by heaven, however terrible—

whose tortures human nature could not bear
or might not have to bear.

　　　　　　　I think of Tantalus,
born—or so they say—the son of Zeus himself
and blessed by birth and luck as few men are:
happy Tantalus. . . .
　　　　　I do not mock his fall,
and yet that same Tantalus now writhes and
　　trembles
in terror of the rock that overhangs his head,
though even as a man he sat as honored equal
at the table of the gods, but could not hold his
　　tongue,
being sick with pride.

　　　　　　　　　　　　Euripides, *Orestes*, 1

8 *Syracusan generals and Gylippus.* When men are once
checked in what they consider their special excellence, their whole opinion of themselves suffers
more than if they had not at first believed in their
superiority, the unexpected shock to their pride
causing them to give way more than their real
strength warrants.

　　　　　　Thucydides, *Peloponnesian War*, VII, 66

9 *Socrates.* The three kinds of vain conceit . . . the
vain conceit of beauty, of wisdom, and of wealth,
are ridiculous if they are weak, and detestable
when they are powerful.

　　　　　　　　　　Plato, *Philebus*, 49B

10 Pride seems even from its name to be concerned
with great things; what sort of great things, is the
first question we must try to answer. It makes no
difference whether we consider the state of character or the man characterized by it. Now the
man is thought to be proud who thinks himself
worthy of great things, being worthy of them; for
he who does so beyond his deserts is a fool, but no
virtuous man is foolish or silly. The proud man,
then, is the man we have described. For he who is
worthy of little and thinks himself worthy of little
is temperate, but not proud; for pride implies
greatness, as beauty implies a good-sized body,
and little people may be neat and well-propor-
tioned but cannot be beautiful. On the other
hand, he who thinks himself worthy of great
things, being unworthy of them, is vain; though
not every one who thinks himself worthy of more
than he really is worthy of is vain. The man who
thinks himself worthy of less than he is really worthy of is unduly humble, whether his deserts be
great or moderate, or his deserts be small but his
claims yet smaller. And the man whose deserts are
great would seem *most* unduly humble; for what
would he have done if they had been less? The
proud man, then, is an extreme in respect of the
greatness of his claims, but a mean in respect of
the rightness of them; for he claims what is in
accordance with his merits, while the others go to
excess or fall short.

If, then, he deserves and claims great things,

and above all the great things, he will be concerned with one thing in particular. Desert is relative to external goods; and the greatest of these,
we should say, is that which we render to the gods,
and which people of position most aim at, and
which is the prize appointed for the noblest deeds;
and this is honour; that is surely the greatest of
external goods. Honours and dishonours, therefore, are the objects with respect to which the
proud man is as he should be. And even apart
from argument it is with honour that proud men
appear to be concerned; for it is honour that they
chiefly claim, but in accordance with their deserts. The unduly humble man falls short both in
comparison with his own merits and in comparison with the proud man's claims. The vain man
goes to excess in comparison with his own merits,
but does not exceed the proud man's claims.

Now the proud man, since he deserves most,
must be good in the highest degree; for the better
man always deserves more, and the best man
most. Therefore the truly proud man must be
good. And greatness in every virtue would seem to
be characteristic of a proud man. And it would be
most unbecoming for a proud man to fly from
danger, swinging his arms by his sides, or to wrong
another; for to what end should he do disgraceful
acts, he to whom nothing is great? If we consider
him point by point we shall see the utter absurdity
of a proud man who is not good. Nor, again,
would he be worthy of honour if he were bad; for
honour is the prize of virtue, and it is to the good
that it is rendered. Pride, then, seems to be a sort
of crown of the virtues; for it makes them greater,
and it is not found without them. Therefore it is
hard to be truly proud; for it is impossible without
nobility and goodness of character.

　　　　　　　　　Aristotle, *Ethics*, 1123ª34

11 A slow step is thought proper to the proud man, a
deep voice, and a level utterance; for the man
who takes few things seriously is not likely to be
hurried, nor the man who thinks nothing great to
be excited, while a shrill voice and a rapid gait
are the results of hurry and excitement.

Such, then, is the proud man; the man who
falls short of him is unduly humble, and the man
who goes beyond him is vain. Now even these are
not thought to be bad (for they are not malicious),
but only mistaken. For the unduly humble man,
being worthy of good things, robs himself of what
he deserves, and seems to have something bad
about him from the fact that he does not think
himself worthy of good things, and seems also not
to know himself; else he would have desired the
things he was worthy of, since these were good.
. . . Vain people, on the other hand, are fools and
ignorant of themselves, and that manifestly; for,
not being worthy of them, they attempt honourable undertakings, and then are found out; and
they adorn themselves with clothing and outward

show and such things, and wish their strokes of good fortune to be made public, and speak about them as if they would be honoured for them.

Aristotle, *Ethics,* 1125ª13

12 We do not expect a vine to bear figs or an olive grapes, but when it comes to ourselves, if we do not possess the combined advantages of millionaire and scholar and general and philosopher, of the flatterer and the plain speaker, of the frugal and the extravagant, we calumniate ourselves and are irked with ourselves and despise ourselves as leading a drab and curtailed life.

Plutarch, *Contentment*

13 Consider what men are when they are eating, sleeping, generating, easing themselves and so forth. Then what kind of men they are when they are imperious and arrogant, or angry and scolding from their elevated place. But a short time ago to how many they were slaves and for what things; and after a little time consider in what a condition they will be.

Marcus Aurelius, *Meditations,* X, 19

14 The pride which is proud of its want of pride is the most intolerable of all.

Marcus Aurelius, *Meditations,* XII, 27

15 "Your might," said she [Cecilia], "is scarce a thing
   to dread;
   For power of every mortal man but is
   Like to a bladder full of wind, ywis.
   For with a needle's point, when it is blown,
   Prick it, and all the pride of it comes down."

Chaucer, *Canterbury Tales:* Second
Nun's Tale

16 I hold that a man should be cautious in making an estimate of himself, and equally conscientious in testifying about himself—whether he rates himself high or low makes no difference. If I seemed to myself good and wise or nearly so, I would shout it out at the top of my voice. To say less of yourself than is true is stupidity, not modesty. To pay yourself less than you are worth is cowardice and pusillanimity, according to Aristotle. No virtue is helped by falsehood, and truth is never subject to error. To say more of yourself than is true is not always presumption; it too is often stupidity. To be immoderately pleased with what you are, to fall therefore into an undiscerning self-love, is in my opinion the substance of this vice. The supreme remedy to cure it is to do just the opposite of what those people prescribe who, by prohibiting talking about oneself, even more strongly prohibit thinking about oneself. The pride lies in the thought; the tongue can have only a very slight share in it.

Montaigne, *Essays,* II, 6, Of Practice

17 *Ajax.* Why should a man be proud? How doth pride grow? I know not what pride is.

Agamemnon. Your mind is the clearer, Ajax, and your virtues the fairer. He that is proud eats up himself; pride is his own glass, his own trumpet, his own chronicle; and whatever praises itself but in the deed, devours the deed in the praise.

Ajax. I do hate a proud man, as I hate the engendering of toads.

Nestor. [*Aside.*] Yet he loves himself. Is't not strange?

Shakespeare, *Troilus and Cressida,* II, iii, 161

18 *Fool.* There was never yet fair woman but she made mouths in a glass.

Shakespeare, *Lear,* III, ii, 35

19 All those who form a good opinion of themselves for some other reason, whatever it may be, have not a true generosity, but merely a pride which is always very vicious, although it is all the more so, the more the cause for which we esteem ourselves is unjust. And the most unjust cause of all is when we are proud without any reason, that is to say, without our thinking so far as this goes that there is in us any merit for which we ought to be esteemed, simply taking the view that merit is not taken into consideration at all, and that as glory is regarded as nothing but usurpation, those who ascribe most of it to themselves really possess the greatest amount of it. This vice is so unreasonable and absurd, that I should scarcely have believed that there were men who could allow themselves to give way to it, if no one were ever unjustly praised; but flattery is everywhere so common that there is no man so defective that he does not often see himself esteemed for things that do not merit any praise, or even that merit blame; and this give occasion to the most ignorant and stupid to fall into this species of pride.

Descartes, *Passions of the Soul,* CLVII

20 The passion whose violence or continuance maketh madness is either great vainglory, which is commonly called *pride* and *self-conceit,* or great dejection of mind.

Pride subjecteth a man to anger, the excess whereof is the madness called *rage,* and *fury.* And thus it comes to pass that excessive desire of revenge, when it becomes habitual, hurteth the organs, and becomes rage: that excessive love, with jealousy, becomes also rage: excessive opinion of a man's own self, for devine inspiration, for wisdom, learning, form, and the like, becomes distraction and giddiness: the same, joined with envy, rage: vehement opinion of the truth of anything, contradicted by others, rage.

Hobbes, *Leviathan,* I, 8

21 I thank God, amongst those millions of Vices I do inherit and hold from *Adam,* I have escaped one,

and that a mortal enemy to Charity, the first and father-sin, not onely of man, but of the devil, Pride.

Sir Thomas Browne, Religio Medici, II, 8

22 Vanity is so anchored in the heart of man that a soldier, a soldier's servant, a cook, a porter brags and wishes to have his admirers. Even philosophers wish for them. Those who write against it want to have the glory of having written well; and those who read it desire the glory of having read it. I who write this have perhaps this desire, and perhaps those who will read it.

Pascal, Pensées, II, 150

23 He who will know fully the vanity of man has only to consider the causes and effects of love. The cause is a *je ne sais quoi,* and the effects are dreadful. This *je ne sais quoi,* so small an object that we cannot recognise it, agitates a whole country, princes, armies, the entire world.

Cleopatra's nose: had it been shorter, the whole aspect of the world would have been altered.

Pascal, Pensées, II, 162

24 *Contradiction.*—Pride counterbalancing all miseries. Man either hides his miseries, or, if he disclose them, glories in knowing them.

Pride counterbalances and takes away all miseries. Here is a strange monster and a very plain aberration. He is fallen from his place and is anxiously seeking it. This is what all men do. Let us see who will have found it.

Pascal, Pensées, VI, 405–406

25 When a man thinks too much of himself, this imagination is called *pride,* and is a kind of delirium, because he dreams with his eyes open, that he is able to do all those things to which he attains in imagination alone, regarding them therefore as realities, and rejoicing in them so long as he cannot imagine anything to exclude their existence and limit his power of action. Pride, therefore, is that joy which arises from a man's thinking too much of himself.

Spinoza, Ethics, III, Prop. 26, Schol.

26 Then I saw in my dream, that when they were got out of the wilderness, they presently saw a town before them, and the name of that town is Vanity; and at the town there is a fair kept, called Vanity Fair; it is kept all the year long; it beareth the name of Vanity Fair because the town where it is kept is lighter than vanity; and also because all that is there sold, or that cometh thither, is vanity. . . . This fair is no new-erected business, but a thing of ancient standing.

Bunyan, Pilgrim's Progress, I

27 Pride is a sin that sticks close to nature, and is one of the first follies wherein it shows itself to be pol-

luted. For even in childhood, even in little children, pride will first of all show itself; it is a hasty, an early appearance of the sin of the soul.

Bunyan, Life and Death of Mr. Badman

28 My reconcilement to the Yahoo-kind in general might not be so difficult, if they would be content with those vices and follies only which nature hath entitled them to. I am not in the least provoked at the sight of a lawyer, a pickpocket, a colonel, a fool, a lord, a gamester, a politician, a whoremonger, a physician, an evidence, a suborner, an attorney, a traytor, or the like: this is all according to the due course of things: but, when I behold a lump of deformity, and diseases both in body and mind, smitten with *pride,* it immediately breaks all the measures of my patience; neither shall I be ever able to comprehend how such an animal and such a vice could tally together. The wise and virtuous Houyhnhnms, who abound in all excellencies that can adorn a rational creature, have no name for this vice in their language, which hath no terms to express any thing that is evil, except those whereby they describe the detestable qualities of their Yahoos; among which they were not able to distinguish this of pride, for want of thoroughly understanding human nature, as it sheweth it self in other countries, where that animal presides. But I, who had more experience, could plainly observe some rudiments of it among the wild Yahoos.

But the Houyhnhnms, who live under the government of reason, are no more proud of the good qualities they possess, than I should be for not wanting a leg or an arm, which no man in his wits would boast of, although he must be miserable without them. I dwell the longer upon this subject from the desire I have to make the society of an English Yahoo by any means not insupportable; and therefore, I here intreat those who have any tincture of this absurd vice, that they will not presume to appear in my sight.

Swift, Gulliver's Travels, IV, 12

29 To be vain, is rather a Mark of Humility than Pride. Vain Men delight in telling what Honours have been done them, what great Company they have kept, and the like; by which they plainly confess, that these Honours were more than their Due, and such as their Friends would not believe if they had not been told: Whereas a Man truly proud, thinks the greatest Honours below his Merit, and consequently scorns to boast. I therefore deliver it as a Maxim, that whoever desires the Character of a proud Man, ought to conceal his Vanity.

Swift, Thoughts on Various Subjects

30 Of all the causes which conspire to blind
Man's erring judgement, and misguide the mind,
What the weak head with strongest bias rules,

Is pride, the never-failing vice of fools.

Pope, *Essay on Criticism*, II, 201

31 Vanity is as advantageous to a government as pride is dangerous. To be convinced of this we need only represent, on the one hand, the numberless benefits which result from vanity, as industry, the arts, fashions, politeness, and taste; on the other, the infinite evils which spring from the pride of certain nations, as laziness, poverty, a total neglect of everything—in fine, the destruction of the nations which have happened to fall under their government, as well as of their own. Laziness is the effect of pride; labour, a consequence of vanity.

Montesquieu, *Spirit of Laws*, XIX, 9

32 *Johnson.* He that stands to contemplate the crouds that fill the streets of a populous city, will see many passengers whose air and motion it will be difficult to behold without contempt and laughter; but if he examine what are the appearances that thus powerfully excite his risibility, he will find among them neither poverty nor disease, nor any involuntary or painful defect. The disposition to derision and insult, is awakened by the softness of foppery, the swell of insolence, the liveliness of levity, or the solemnity of grandeur; by the sprightly trip, the stately stalk, the formal strut, and the lofty mien; by gestures intended to catch the eye, and by looks elaborately formed as evidences of importance.

Boswell, *Life of Johnson (1750)*

33 *Johnson.* Scarce any man dies in publick, but with apparent resolution; from that desire of praise which never quits us.

Boswell, *Life of Johnson (Sept. 16, 1777)*

34 With the greater part of rich people, the chief enjoyment of riches consists in the parade of riches, which in their eye is never so complete as when they appear to possess those decisive marks of opulence which nobody can possess but themselves. In their eyes the merit of an object which is in any degree either useful or beautiful is greatly enhanced by its scarcity, or by the great labour which it requires to collect any considerable quantity of it, a labour which nobody can afford to pay but themselves. Such objects they are willing to purchase at a higher price than things much more beautiful and useful, but more common.

Adam Smith, *Wealth of Nations*, I, 11

35 The virtues are economists, but some of the vices are also. Thus, next to humility, I have noticed that pride is a pretty good husband. A good pride is, as I reckon it, worth from five hundred to fifteen hundred a year. Pride is handsome, economical; pride eradicates so many vices, letting none subsist but itself, that it seems as if it were a great gain to exchange vanity for pride. Pride can go without domestics, without fine clothes, can live in a house with two rooms, can eat potato, purslain, beans, lyed corn, can work on the soil, can travel afoot, can talk with poor men, or sit silent well contented in fine saloons. But vanity costs money, labor, horses, men, women, health and peace, and is still nothing at last; a long way leading nowhere. Only one drawback; proud people are intolerably selfish, and the vain are gentle and giving.

Emerson, *Wealth*

36 If one has no vanity in this life of ours, there is no sufficient reason for living.

Tolstoy, *The Kreutzer Sonata*, XXIII

Chapter 5

MIND

Chapter 5 is divided into seven sections: 5.1 INTELLIGENCE AND UNDERSTANDING, 5.2 THE SENSES AND SENSE PERCEPTION, 5.3 MEMORY, 5.4 IMAGINATION, 5.5 DREAMS, 5.6 MADNESS, and 5.7 WILL: FREE CHOICE.

We are employing the term "mind," as indeed it is often used, to cover a wide variety of human powers and functions. Understanding, sense perception, memory, and imagination all contribute in one way or another to the processes of thinking, problem-solving, learning, and knowing. In the sphere of human thought and in man's acquirement of knowledge, each not only makes a distinctive contribution, but all work together in an integrated fashion. Hence the reader should bear in mind that the contents of the first four sections are closely related and, to some extent, overlapping. He should also be aware that many points discussed in these sections recur, either explicitly or by implication, in Chapter 6 on KNOWLEDGE, especially Section 6.7 on REASONING, DEMONSTRATION, AND DISPUTATION.

The remaining three sections are included in this chapter each for a special reason. Dreaming involves memory and imagination and is a specifically mental phenomenon, even though it does not, in a strict sense, contribute to thought or knowledge, and involves emotions and desires as well as cognitive processes. As included here, madness covers all forms of mental disorder, not merely aberrations of thought or fancy. Though will, like emotion and desire, is not a cognitive power, it is usually distinguished from emotion and desire by its close relation to intellect or reason. This is especially true for those authors who affirm the will's freedom in its acts of choice. That is why the discussion of volition, and particularly of free will or free choice, is included here. Other discussions of freedom will be found in Chapter 13 on LIBERTY AND EQUALITY, and in Chapter 9 on ETHICS, Section 9.4 on MORAL FREEDOM. Some matters discussed in this chapter, are more fully considered in Chapter 4 on EMOTION, especially Section 4.1 on THE PASSIONS: THE RANGE OF THE EMOTIONS.

5.1 | Intelligence and Understanding

There are a large number of names for the human faculty, ability, or power that is the subject of this section. Sometimes it is simply called "mind," sometimes "intellect," sometimes "reason," sometimes "wit." The two names in the title of this section are also used. Each of these words has a somewhat different connotation; certain authors are at pains to distinguish reason from understanding, or intellect from intelligence; but all of these words have this common thread of meaning: they designate the power or ability by which men solve problems, make judgments, engage in reasoning or in deliberation, and make practical decisions.

Some modern writers use "mind" or "understanding" more broadly to include man's sensitive abilities as well—his powers of sense perception, memory, and imagination. However, since Sections 5.2, 5.3, and 5.4 are specifically devoted to the consideration of sense, memory, and imagination, we have restricted the materials included in this section to discussions of mind as the power of thought, judgment, insight, and reasoning. The reader will find related matters treated in Section 6.7 on REASONING, DEMONSTRATION, AND DISPUTATION.

The quotations collected here deal with questions about the relation of mind and body; about the immateriality or spirituality of mind or intellect; about the different acts of the intellect and how they are related; about the role of reason or intelligence in the sphere of action as well as in the sphere of thought; about wit, sagacity, and cunning as aspects of intelligence; and about human speech as indicative and expressive of the power and processes of human rationality. In this last connection, the reader is referred to related material in Section 7.1 on THE NATURE OF LANGUAGE.

---

1 For as he thinketh in his heart, so is he.
Proverbs 23:7

2 The earthy tabernacle weigheth down the mind that museth upon many things.
Wisdom of Solomon 9:15

3 *Socrates.* Tell me, then, are not the organs through which you perceive warm and hard and light and sweet, organs of the body?
Theaetetus. Of the body, certainly.
Soc. And you would admit that what you perceive through one faculty you cannot perceive through another; the objects of hearing, for example, cannot be perceived through sight, or the objects of sight through hearing?
Theaet. Of course not.
Soc. If you have any thought about both of them, this common perception cannot come to you, either through the one or the other organ?
Theaet. It cannot.
Soc. How about sounds and colours: in the first place you would admit that they both exist?
Theaet. Yes.
Soc. And that either of them is different from the other, and the same with itself?
Theaet. Certainly.
Soc. And that both are two and each of them one?
Theaet. Yes.
Soc. You can further observe whether they are like or unlike one another?
Theat. I dare say.
Soc. But through what do you perceive all this about them? for neither through hearing nor yet through seeing can you apprehend that which they have in common. Let me give you an illustration of the point at issue:—If there were any meaning in asking whether sounds and colours are saline or not, you would be able to tell me what faculty would consider the question. It would not be sight or hearing, but some other.
Theaet. Certainly; the faculty of taste.
Soc. Very good; and now tell me what is the

309

power which discerns, not only in sensible objects, but in all things, universal notions, such as those which are called being and not-being, and those others about which we were just asking—what organs will you assign for the perception of these notions?

Theaet. You are thinking of being and not-being, likeness and unlikeness, sameness and difference, and also of unity and other numbers which are applied to objects of sense; and you mean to ask, through what bodily organ the soul perceives odd and even numbers and other arithmetical conceptions.

Soc. You follow me excellently, Theaetetus; that is precisely what I am asking.

Theaet. Indeed, Socrates, I cannot answer; my only notion is, that these, unlike objects of sense, have no separate organ, but that the mind, by a power of her own, contemplates the universals in all things.

Plato, *Theaetetus*, 184B

4 Quick wit is a faculty of hitting upon the middle term instantaneously. It would be exemplified by a man who saw that the moon has her bright side always turned towards the sun, and quickly grasped the cause of this, namely that she borrows her light from him; or observed somebody in conversation with a man of wealth and divined that he was borrowing money, or that the friendship of these people sprang from a common enmity. In all these instances he has seen the major and minor terms and then grasped the causes, the middle terms.

Aristotle, *Posterior Analytics*, 89b10

5 If thinking is like perceiving, it must be either a process in which the soul is acted upon by what is capable of being thought, or a process different from but analogous to that. The thinking part of the soul must therefore be, while impassible, capable of receiving the form of an object; that is, must be potentially identical in character with its object without being the object. Mind must be related to what is thinkable, as sense is to what is sensible.

Therefore, since everything is a possible object of thought, mind in order, as Anaxagoras says, to dominate, that is, to know, must be pure from all admixture; for the copresence of what is alien to its nature is a hindrance and a block: it follows that it too, like the sensitive part, can have no nature of its own, other than that of having a certain capacity. Thus that in the soul which is called mind (by mind I mean that whereby the soul thinks and judges) is, before it thinks, not actually any real thing. For this reason it cannot reasonably be regarded as blended with the body: if so, it would acquire some quality, e.g. warmth or cold, or even have an organ like the sensitive faculty: as it is, it has none. It was a good idea to

call the soul 'the place of forms', though (1) this description holds only of the intellective soul, and (2) even this is the forms only potentially, not actually. . . .

Once the mind has become each set of its possible objects, as a man of science has, when this phrase is used of one who is actually a man of science (this happens when he is now able to exercise the power on his own initiative), its condition is still one of potentiality, but in a different sense from the potentiality which preceded the acquisition of knowledge by learning or discovery: the mind too is then able to think *itself.*

Aristotle, *On the Soul*, 429a13

6 Mind is in a sense potentially whatever is thinkable, though actually it is nothing until it has thought. What it thinks must be in it just as characters may be said to be on a writing-tablet on which as yet nothing actually stands written: this is exactly what happens with mind.

Mind is itself thinkable in exactly the same way as its objects are. For (*a*) in the case of objects which involve no matter, what thinks and what is thought are identical; for speculative knowledge and its object are identical. . . .

Since in every class of things, as in nature as a whole, we find two factors involved, (1) a matter which is potentially all the particulars included in the class, (2) a cause which is productive in the sense that it makes them all (the latter standing to the former, as e.g. an art to its material), these distinct elements must likewise be found within the soul.

And in fact mind as we have described it is what it is by virtue of becoming all things, while there is another which is what it is by virtue of making all things: this is a sort of positive state like light; for in a sense light makes potential colours into actual colours.

Mind in this sense of it is separable, impassible, unmixed, since it is in its essential nature activity (for always the active is superior to the passive factor, the originating force to the matter which it forms).

Actual knowledge is identical with its object: in the individual, potential knowledge is in time prior to actual knowledge, but in the universe as a whole it is not prior even in time. Mind is not at one time knowing and at another not. When mind is set free from its present conditions it appears as just what it is and nothing more: this alone is immortal and eternal (we do not, however, remember its former activity because, while mind in this sense is impassible, mind as passive is destructible), and without it nothing thinks.

Aristotle, *On the Soul*, 429b30

7 The nature of the mind and soul is bodily; for when it is seen to push the limbs, rouse the body from sleep, and alter the countenance and guide

and turn about the whole man, and when we see that none of these effects can take place without touch nor touch without body, must we not admit that the mind and the soul are of a bodily nature? . . .

I will now go on to explain in my verses of what kind of body the mind consists and out of what it is formed. First of all I say that it is extremely fine and formed of exceedingly minute bodies. That this is so you may, if you please to attend, clearly perceive from what follows: nothing that is seen takes place with a velocity equal to that of the mind when it starts some suggestion and actually sets it agoing; the mind therefore is stirred with greater rapidity than any of the things whose nature stands out visible to sight. But that which is so passing nimble, must consist of seeds exceedingly round and exceedingly minute, in order to be stirred and set in motion by a small moving power. . . . The following fact too likewise demonstrates how fine the texture is of which its nature is composed, and how small the room is in which it can be contained, could it only be collected into one mass: soon as the untroubled sleep of death has gotten hold of a man and the nature of the mind and soul has withdrawn, you can perceive then no diminution of the entire body either in appearance or weight: death makes all good save the vital sense and heat. Therefore the whole soul must consist of very small seeds and be inwoven through veins and flesh and sinews; inasmuch as, after it has all withdrawn from the whole body, the exterior contour of the limbs preserves itself entire and not a tittle of the weight is lost. Just in the same way when the flavour of wine is gone or when the delicious aroma of a perfume has been dispersed into the air or when the savour has left some body, yet the thing itself does not therefore look smaller.

Lucretius, *Nature of Things,* III

8 In so far as the mind is stronger than the body, so are the ills contracted by the mind more severe than those contracted by the body.

Cicero, *Philippics,* XI, 4

9 Which of you by taking thought can add one cubit unto his stature?

Matthew 6:27

10   But still, just for the sake of asking,
For the sake of something to give to the chapels, ritual entrails,
The consecrated meat of a little white pig, pray for one thing,
Pray for a healthy mind in a healthy body, a spirit
Unafraid of death, but reconciled to it, and able
To bear up, to endure whatever troubles afflict it,
Free from hate and desire, preferring Hercules' labors

To the cushions and loves and feasts of Sardanapallus.

Juvenal, *Satire X*

11 Indeed, for the power of seeing and hearing, and indeed for life itself, and for the things which contribute to support it, for the fruits which are dry, and for wine and oil give thanks to God: but remember that he has given you something else better than all these, I mean the power of using them, proving them and estimating the value of each. For what is that which gives information about each of these powers, what each of them is worth? Is it each faculty itself? Did you ever hear the faculty of vision saying anything about itself? or the faculty of hearing? or wheat, or barley, or a horse or a dog? No; but they are appointed as ministers and slaves to serve the faculty which has the power of making use of the appearances of things. And if you inquire what is the value of each thing, of whom do you inquire? who answers you? How then can any other faculty be more powerful than this, which uses the rest as ministers and itself proves each and pronounces about them? for which of them knows what itself is, and what is its own value? which of them knows when it ought to employ itself and when not? what faculty is it which opens and closes the eyes, and turns them away from objects to which it ought not to apply them and does apply them to other objects? No; but it is the faculty of the will.

Epictetus, *Discourses,* II, 23

12 It must necessarily be allowed that the principle of intellectual operation which we call the soul is a principle both incorporeal and subsistent. For it is clear that by means of the intellect man can know the natures of all corporeal things. Now whatever knows certain things cannot have any of them in its own nature because that which is in it naturally would impede the knowledge of anything else. Thus we observe that a sick man's tongue being vitiated by a feverish and bitter humour, cannot perceive anything sweet, and everything seems bitter to it. Therefore, if the intellectual principle contained the nature of any body it would be unable to know all bodies. Now every body has some determinate nature. Therefore it is impossible for the intellectual principle to be a body. It is likewise impossible for it to understand by means of a bodily organ, since the determinate nature of that bodily organ would prevent the knowledge of all bodies; as when a certain determinate colour is not only in the pupil of the eye, but also in a glass vase, the liquid in the vase seems to be of that same colour.

Therefore the intellectual principle which we call the mind or the intellect has an operation *per se* apart from the body. Now only that which subsists can have an operation *per se.* For nothing can operate except a being in act; hence a thing operates according as it is. For this reason we do not say that heat imparts heat, but that what is hot gives heat. We must conclude, therefore, that the human soul, which is called the intellect or the mind, is something incorporeal and subsistent.

Aquinas, *Summa Theologica*, I, 75, 2

13 The intellectual soul, because it can comprehend universals, has a power extending to the infinite; therefore it cannot be limited by nature either to certain fixed natural judgments, or to certain fixed means whether of defence or of clothing, as is the case with other animals, the souls of which have knowledge and power in regard to fixed particular things. Instead of all these, man has by nature his reason and his hands, which are the organs of organs, since by their means man can make for himself instruments of an infinite variety, and for any number of purposes.

Aquinas, *Summa Theologica*, I, 76, 5

14 To say that a thing is understood more by one than by another may be taken in two senses. First, so that the word more be taken as determining the act of understanding as regards the thing understood; and thus, one cannot understand the same thing more than another, because to understand it otherwise than as it is, either better or worse, would entail being deceived, and such a one would not understand it. . . . In another sense the word more can be taken as determining the act of understanding on the part of him who understands; and so one may understand the same thing better than someone else, through having a greater power of understanding, just as a man may see a thing better with his bodily sight, whose power is greater, and whose sight is more perfect. The same applies to the intellect in two ways. First, as regards the intellect itself, which is more perfect. For it is plain that the better the disposition of a body, the better the soul allotted to it, which clearly appears in things of different species. And the reason for this is that act and form are received into matter according to matter's capacity. Hence because some men have bodies of better disposition, their souls have a greater power of understanding. Thus it is said that we see that those who have delicate flesh are of apt mind. Secondly, this occurs in regard to the lower powers of which the intellect has need in its operation, for those in whom the imaginative, cogitative and remembering powers are of better disposition are better disposed to understand.

Aquinas, *Summa Theologica*, I, 85, 7

15 There are three classes of intellects: one which comprehends by itself; another which appreciates what others comprehend; and a third which neither comprehends by itself nor by the showing of others; the first is the most excellent, the second is good, the third is useless.

Machiavelli, *Prince*, XXII

16 Heavy thoughts bring on physical maladies; when the soul is oppressed, so is the body.

Luther, *Table Talk*, H645

17 Whenever . . . we meet with heathen writers, let us learn from that light of truth which is admirably displayed in their works, that the human mind, fallen as it is, and corrupted from its integrity, is yet invested and adorned by God with excellent talents.

Calvin, *Institutes of the Christian Religion*, II, 2

18 Meditation is a powerful and full study for anyone who knows how to examine and exercise himself vigorously: I would rather fashion my mind than furnish it. There is no occupation that is either weaker or stronger, according to the mind involved, than entertaining one's own thoughts. The greatest minds make it their profession, *to whom living is thinking* [Cicero]. Thus nature has favored it with this privilege, that there is nothing we can do so long, and no action to which we can devote ourselves more commonly and easily. It is the occupation of the gods, says Aristotle, from which springs their happiness and ours.

Montaigne, *Essays*, III, 3, Three Kinds of Association

19 *Hamlet.*   What is a man,
If his chief good and market of his time
Be but to sleep and feed? a beast, no more.
Sure, he that made us with such large discourse,
Looking before and after, gave us not
That capability and god-like reason
To fust in us unused.

Shakespeare, *Hamlet*, IV, iv, 33

20 *1st Gentleman.* But I much marvel that your lordship, having
Rich tire about you, should at these early hours
Shake off the golden slumber of repose.
'Tis most strange
Nature should be so conversant with pain,
Being thereto not compell'd.
   Cerimon.   I hold it ever
Virtue and cunning were endowments greater
Than nobleness and riches. Careless heirs
May the two latter darken and expend;
But immortality attends the former,
Making a man a god. 'Tis known, I ever
Have studied physic, through which secret art,
By turning o'er authorities, I have,
Together with my practice, made familiar
To me and to my aid the blest infusions

That dwell in vegetives, in metals, stones;
And I can speak of the disturbances
That nature works, and of her cures; which doth
    give me
A more content in course of true delight
Than to be thirsty after tottering honour,
Or tie my treasure up in silken bags,
To please the fool and Death.

Shakespeare, Pericles, III, ii, 21

21 The mind of man is far from the nature of a clear
and equal glass, wherein the beams of things
should reflect according to their true incidence;
nay, it is rather like an enchanted glass, full of
superstition and imposture, if it be not delivered
and reduced.

Bacon, Advancement of Learning,
Bk. II, XIV, 9

22 Our method, though difficult in its operation, is
easily explained. It consists in determining the degrees of certainty, whilst we, as it were, restore the
senses to their former rank, but generally reject
that operation of the mind which follows close
upon the senses, and open and establish a new
and certain course for the mind from the first actual perceptions of the senses themselves. This, no
doubt, was the view taken by those who have assigned so much to logic; showing clearly thereby
that they sought some support for the mind, and
suspected its natural and spontaneous mode of action. But this is now employed too late as a remedy, when all is clearly lost, and after the mind,
by the daily habit and intercourse of life, has
come prepossessed with corrupted doctrines, and
filled with the vainest idols. The art of logic,
therefore, being (as we have mentioned), too late
a precaution, and in no way remedying the matter, has tended more to confirm errors, than to
disclose truth. Our only remaining hope and salvation is to begin the whole labor of the mind
again.

Bacon, Novum Organum, Pref.

23 The human understanding, from its peculiar nature, easily supposes a greater degree of order and
equality in things than it really finds.

Bacon, Novum Organum, I, 45

24 The greatest and, perhaps, most radical distinction between different men's dispositions for philosophy and the sciences is this, that some are
more vigorous and active in observing the differences of things, others in observing their resemblances; for a steady and acute disposition can fix
its thoughts, and dwell upon and adhere to a
point, through all the refinements of differences,
but those that are sublime and discursive recognize and compare even the most delicate and general resemblances; each of them readily falls into
excess, by catching either at nice distinctions or
shadows of resemblance.

Bacon, Novum Organum, I, 55

25 Examining attentively that which I was, I saw
that I could conceive that I had no body, and that
there was no world nor place where I might be;
but yet that I could not for all that conceive that
I was not. On the contrary, I saw from the very
fact that I thought of doubting the truth of other
things, it very evidently and certainly followed
that I was; on the other hand if I had only ceased
from thinking, even if all the rest of what I had
ever imagined had really existed, I should have no
reason for thinking that I had existed. From that I
knew that I was a substance the whole essence or
nature of which is to think, and that for its existence there is no need of any place, nor does it
depend on any material thing; so that this "me,"
that is to say, the soul by which I am what I am,
is entirely distinct from body, and is even more
easy to know than is the latter; and even if body
were not, the soul would not cease to be what it is.

Descartes, Discourse on Method, IV

26 What of thinking? I find here that thought is an
attribute that belongs to me; it alone cannot be
separated from me. I am, I exist, that is certain.
But how often? Just when I think; for it might
possibly be the case if I ceased entirely to think,
that I should likewise cease altogether to exist. I
do not now admit anything which is not necessarily true: to speak accurately I am not more than a
thing which thinks, that is to say a mind or a soul,
or an understanding, or a reason, which are terms
whose significance was formerly unknown to me. I
am, however, a real thing and really exist; but
what thing? I have answered: a thing which
thinks.

Descartes, Meditations on First Philosophy, II

27 By virtues intellectual are always understood such
abilities of the mind as men praise, value, and
desire should be in themselves; and go commonly
under the name of a good wit; though the same
word, wit, be used also to distinguish one certain
ability from the rest.

    These virtues are of two sorts; natural and ac-
quired. By natural, I mean not that which a man
hath from his birth: for that is nothing else but
sense; wherein men differ so little one from another, and from brute beasts, as it is not to be reckoned amongst virtues. But I mean that wit which
is gotten by use only, and experience, without
method, culture, or instruction. This natural wit
consisteth principally in two things: celerity of imagining (that this, swift succession of one thought to

another); and *steady direction* to some approved end. On the contrary, a slow imagination maketh that defect or fault of the mind which is commonly called *dullness, stupidity,* and sometimes by other names that signify slowness of motion, or difficulty to be moved.

And this difference of quickness is caused by the difference of men's passions; that love and dislike, some one thing, some another: and therefore some men's thoughts run one way, some another, and are held to, and observe differently the things that pass through their imagination. And whereas in this succession of men's thoughts there is nothing to observe in the things they think on, but either in what they be like one another, or in what they be unlike, or what they serve for, or how they serve to such a purpose; those that observe their similitudes, in case they be such as are but rarely observed by others, are said to have a *good wit;* by which, in this occasion, is meant a *good fancy.* But they that observe their differences, and dissimilitudes, which is called *distinguishing,* and *discerning,* and *judging* between thing and thing, in case such discerning be not easy, are said to have a *good judgement:* and particularly in matter of conversation and business, wherein times, places, and persons are to be discerned, this virtue is called *discretion.*

Hobbes, *Leviathan,* I, 8

28 The secret thoughts of a man run over all things holy, prophane, clean, obscene, grave, and light, without shame, or blame; which verbal discourse cannot do, farther than the judgement shall approve of the time, place, and persons.

Hobbes, *Leviathan,* I, 8

29 There are then two kinds of intellect: the one able to penetrate acutely and deeply into the conclusions of given premises, and this is the precise intellect; the other able to comprehend a great number of premises without confusing them, and this is the mathematical intellect. The one has force and exactness, the other comprehension. Now the one quality can exist without the other; the intellect can be strong and narrow, and can also be comprehensive and weak.

Pascal, *Pensées,* I, 2

30 I can well conceive a man without hands, feet, head (for it is only experience which teaches us that the head is more necessary than feet). But I cannot conceive man without thought; he would be a stone or a brute.

Pascal, *Pensées,* VI, 339

31 All our dignity consists . . . in thought. By it we must elevate ourselves, and not by space and time which we cannot fill. Let us endeavour, then, to think well; this is the principle of morality.

Pascal, *Pensées,* VI, 347

32 *A thinking reed.*—It is not from space that I must seek my dignity, but from the government of my thought. I shall have no more if I possess worlds. By space the universe encompasses and swallows me up like an atom; by thought I comprehend the world.

Pascal, *Pensées,* VI, 348

33 *Satan.* The mind is its own place, and in it self Can make a Heav'n of Hell, a Hell of Heav'n.

Milton, *Paradise Lost,* I, 254

34 *Belial.*   For who would loose, Though full of pain, this intellectual being, Those thoughts that wander through Eternity, To perish rather, swallowd up and lost In the wide womb of uncreated night, Devoid of sense and motion?

Milton, *Paradise Lost,* II, 146

35 Man thinks.

Spinoza, *Ethics,* II, Axiom 2

36 The body cannot determine the mind to thought, neither can the mind determine the body to motion nor rest, nor to anything else, if there be anything else. . . . That is to say, that the mind and the body are one and the same thing, conceived at one time under the attribute of thought, and at another under that of extension. For this reason, the order or concatenation of things is one, whether nature be conceived under this or under that attribute, and consequently the order of the actions and passions of our body is coincident in nature with the order of the actions and passions of the mind. . . .

Although these things are so, and no ground for doubting remains, I scarcely believe, nevertheless, that, without a proof derived from experience, men will be induced calmly to weigh what has been said, so firmly are they persuaded that, solely at the bidding of the mind, the body moves or rests, and does a number of things which depend upon the will of the mind alone, and upon the power of thought.

Spinoza, *Ethics,* III, Prop. 2; Schol.

37 The more perfect a thing is, the more reality it possesses. . . .

Hence it follows that that part of the mind which abides, whether great or small, is more perfect than the other part. For the part of the mind which is eternal is the intellect, through which alone we are said to act, but that part which, as we have shown, perishes, is the imagination itself, through which alone we are said to suffer. Therefore that part which abides, whether great or small, is more perfect than the latter.

These are the things I proposed to prove concerning the mind, insofar as it is considered without relation to the existence of the body, and from these . . . it is evident that our mind, insofar as it understands, is an eternal mode of thought, which is determined by another eternal mode of thought, and this again by another, and so on *ad infinitum,* so that all taken together form the eternal and infinite intellect of God.

Spinoza, *Ethics,* V, Prop. 40

38 Dim as the borrow'd beams of moon and stars
To lonely, weary, wand'ring travelers,
Is Reason to the soul.

Dryden, *Religio Laici,* 1

39 Insofar as the concatenation of their perceptions is due to the principle of memory alone, men act like the lower animals, resembling the empirical physicians whose methods are those of mere practice without theory. Indeed, in three-fourths of our actions we are nothing but empirics. For instance, when we expect that there will be daylight to-morrow, we do so empirically, because it has always so happened until now. It is only the astronomer who thinks it on rational grounds.

But it is the knowledge of necessary and eternal truths that distinguishes us from the mere animals and gives us *Reason* and the sciences, raising us to the knowledge of ourselves and of God. And it is this in us that is called the rational soul or mind.

It is also through the knowledge of necessary truths, and through their abstract expression, that we rise to *acts of reflexion,* which make us think of what is called *I,* and observe that this or that is within us: and thus, thinking of ourselves, we think of being, of substance, of the simple and the compound, of the immaterial, and of God Himself, conceiving that what is limited in us is in Him without limits. And these acts of reflexion furnish the chief objects of our reasonings.

Leibniz, *Monadology,* 28–30

40 The other fountain from which experience furnisheth the understanding with ideas is,—the perception of the operations of our own mind within us, as it is employed about the ideas it has got;—which operations, when the soul comes to reflect on and consider, do furnish the understanding with another set of ideas, which could not be had from things without. And such are *perception, thinking, doubting, believing, reasoning, knowing, willing,* and all the different actings of our own minds;—which we being conscious of, and observing in ourselves, do from these receive into our understandings as distinct ideas as we do from bodies affecting our senses. This source of ideas every man has wholly in himself; and though it be not sense, as having

nothing to do with external objects, yet it is very like it, and might properly enough be called *internal sense.* But as I call the other SENSATION, so I call this REFLECTION, the ideas it affords being such only as the mind gets by reflecting on its own operations within itself. By reflection then, in the following part of this discourse, I would be understood to mean, that notice which the mind takes of its own operations, and the manner of them, by reason whereof there come to be ideas of these operations in the understanding. These two, I say, viz. external material things, as the objects of SENSATION, and the operations of our own minds within, as the objects of REFLECTION, are to me the only originals from whence all our ideas take their beginnings.

Locke, *Concerning Human
Understanding,* Bk. II, I, 4

41 Follow a child from its birth, and observe the alterations that time makes, and you shall find, as the mind by the senses comes more and more to be furnished with ideas, it comes to be more and more awake; thinks more, the more it has matter to think on. After some time it begins to know the objects which, being most familiar with it, have made lasting impressions. Thus it comes by degrees to know the persons it daily converses with, and distinguishes them from strangers; which are instances and effects of its coming to retain and distinguish the ideas the senses convey to it. And so we may observe how the mind, *by degrees,* improves in these; and *advances* to the exercise of those other faculties of enlarging, compounding, and abstracting its ideas, and of reasoning about them, and reflecting upon all these. . . .

In time the mind comes to reflect on its own operations about the ideas got by sensation, and thereby stores itself with a new set of ideas, which I call ideas of reflection. These are the impressions that are made on our senses by outward objects that are extrinsical to the mind; and its own operations, proceeding from powers intrinsical and proper to itself, which, when reflected on by itself, become also objects of its contemplation—are, as I have said, the original of all knowledge. Thus the first capacity of human intellect is,—that the mind is fitted to receive the impressions made on it; either through the senses by outward objects, or by its own operations when it reflects on them. This is the first step a man makes towards the discovery of anything, and the groundwork whereon to build all those notions which ever he shall have naturally in this world. All' those sublime thoughts which tower above the clouds, and reach as high as heaven itself, take their rise and footing here: in all that great extent wherein the mind wanders, in those remote specualtions it may seem to be elevated with, it stirs not one jot beyond those ideas which *sense* or *reflection* have offered for its contemplation.

Locke, *Concerning Human
Understanding*, Bk. II, I, 22–24

42 The power of perception is that which we call the *Understanding*. Perception, which we make the act of the understanding, is of three sorts:—1. The perception of ideas in our minds. 2. The perception of the signification of signs. 3. The perception of the connexion or repugnancy, agreement or disagreement, that there is between any of our ideas. All these are attributed to the understanding, or perceptive power, though it be the two latter only that use allows us to say we understand.

Locke, *Concerning Human
Understanding*, Bk. II, XXI, 5

43 The thoughts that come often unsought, and, as it were, drop into the mind, are the most valuable of any we have, and therefore should be secured, because they seldom return again.

Locke, *Letter to Samuel Bold (May 16, 1699)*

44 Some truths there are so near and obvious to the mind that a man need only open his eyes to see them. Such I take this important one to be, viz., that all the choir of heaven and furniture of the earth, in a word all those bodies which compose the mighty frame of the world, have not any subsistence without a mind, that their *being* is to be perceived or known; that consequently so long as they are not actually perceived by me, or do not exist in my mind or that of any other created spirit, they must either have no existence at all, or else subsist in the mind of some Eternal Spirit—it being perfectly unintelligible, and involving all the absurdity of abstraction, to attribute to any single part of them an existence independent of a spirit. To be convinced of which, the reader need only reflect, and try to separate in his own thoughts the *being* of a sensible thing from its *being perceived*.

Berkeley, *Principles of Human Knowledge*, 6

45 Far as Creation's ample range extends,
The scale of sensual, mental pow'rs ascends:
Mark how it mounts, to Man's imperial race,
From the green myriads in the peopled grass:
What modes of sight betwixt each wide extreme,
The mole's dim curtain, and the lynx's beam:
Of smell, the headlong lioness between,
And hound sagacious on the tainted green:
Of hearing, from the life that fills the flood,
To that which warbles thro' the vernal wood:
The spider's touch, how exquisitely fine!
Feels at each thread, and lives along the line:
In the nice bee, what sense so subtly true
From pois'nous herbs extracts the healing dew:
How Instinct varies in the grov'ling swine,
Compar'd, half-reas'ning elephant, with thine:
'Twixt that, and Reason, what a nice barrier;

For ever sep'rate, yet for ever near!
Remembrance and Reflection how ally'd;
What thin partitions Sense from Thought divide:
And Middle natures, how they long to join,
Yet never pass th' insuperable line!
Without this just gradation, could they be
Subjected these to those, or all to thee?
The pow'rs of all subdu'd by thee alone,
Is not thy Reason all these pow'rs in one?

Pope, *Essay on Man*, Epistle I, 207

46 Love, Hope, and Joy, fair pleasure's smiling train,
Hate, Fear, and Grief, the family of pain;
These mix'd with art, and to due bounds confin'd,
Make and maintain the balance of the mind.

Pope, *Essay on Man*, Epistle II, 117

47 We may divide all the perceptions of the mind into two classes or species, which are distinguished by their different degrees of force and vivacity. The less forcible and lively are commonly denominated *Thoughts* or *Ideas*. The other species want a name in our language, and in most others; I suppose, because it was not requisite for any, but philosophical purposes, to rank them under a general term or appellation. Let us, therefore, use a little freedom, and call them *Impressions;* employing that word in a sense somewhat different from the usual. By the term *impression,* then, I mean all our more lively perceptions, when we hear, or see, or feel, or love, or hate, or desire, or will. And impressions are distinguished from ideas, which are the less lively perceptions, of which we are conscious, when we reflect on any of those sensations or movements above mentioned.

Hume, *Concerning Human Understanding*, II, 12

48 Nothing, at first view, may seem more unbounded than the thought of man, which not only escapes all human power and authority, but is not even restrained within the limits of nature and reality. To form monsters, and join incongruous shapes and appearances, costs the imagination no more trouble than to conceive the most natural and familiar objects. And while the body is confined to one planet, along which it creeps with pain and difficulty; the thought can in an instant transport us into the most distant regions of the universe; or even beyond the universe, into the unbounded chaos, where nature is supposed to lie in total confusion. What never was seen, or heard of, may yet be conceived; nor is anything beyond the power of thought, except what implies an absolute contradiction.

But though our thought seems to possess this unbounded liberty, we shall find, upon a nearer examination, that it is really confined within very narrow limits, and that all this creative power of the mind amounts to no more than the faculty of compounding, transposing, augmenting, or diminishing the materials afforded us by the senses and experience. When we think of a golden mountain, we only join two consistent ideas, *gold,* and *mountain,* with which we were formerly acquainted. A virtuous horse we can conceive; because, from our own feeling, we can conceive virtue; and this we may unite to the figure and shape of a horse, which is an animal familiar to us. In short, all the materials of thinking are derived either from our outward or inward sentiment: the mixture and composition of these belongs alone to the mind and will. Or, to express myself in philosophical language, all our ideas or more feeble perceptions are copies of our impressions or more lively ones.

Hume, *Concerning Human Understanding,* II, 13

49 It is the nature of an hypothesis, when once a man has conceived it, that it assimilates every thing to itself, as proper nourishment; and, from the first moment of your begetting it, it generally grows the stronger by every thing you see, hear, read, or understand. This is of great use.

Sterne, *Tristram Shandy,* II, 19

50 A feeble body makes a feeble mind.

Rousseau, *Emile,* I

51 Such is the delight of mental superiority that none on whom nature or study have conferred it would purchase the gifts of fortune by its loss.

Johnson, *Rambler No. 150*

52 Reason never has an immediate relation to an object; it relates immediately to the understanding alone. It is only through the understanding that it can be employed in the field of experience. It does not *form* conceptions of objects, it merely *arranges* them and gives to them that unity which they are capable of possessing when the sphere of their application has been extended as widely as possible. Reason avails itself of the conception of the understanding for the sole purpose of producing totality in the different series. This totality the understanding does not concern itself with; its only occupation is the connection of experiences, by which *series* of conditions in accordance with conceptions are established. The object of reason is, therefore, the understanding and its proper destination. As the latter brings unity into the diversity of objects by means of its conceptions, so the former brings unity into the diversity of conceptions by means of ideas; as it sets the final aim of a collective unity to the operations of the understanding, which without this occupies itself with a distributive unity alone.

Kant, *Critique of Pure Reason,*
Transcendental Dialectic

53 Reason is not to be considered as an indefinitely extended plane, of the bounds of which we have only a general knowledge; it ought rather to be compared to a sphere, the radius of which may be found from the curvature of its surface—that is, the nature of *a priori* synthetical propositions—and, consequently, its circumference and extent. Beyond the sphere of experience there are no objects which it can cognize; nay, even questions regarding such supposititious objects relate only to the subjective principles of a complete determination of the relations which exist between the understanding-conceptions which lie within this sphere.

Kant, *Critique of Pure Reason,*
Transcendental Method

54 I should be inclined . . . to consider the world and this life as the mighty process of God, not for the trial, but for the creation and formation of mind, a process necessary to awaken inert, chaotic matter into spirit, to sublimate the dust of the earth into soul, to elicit an ethereal spark from the clod of clay.

Malthus, *Population,* XVIII

55 He gave man speech, and speech created thought,
Which is the measure of the universe;
And Science struck the thrones of earth and
   heaven,
Which shook, but fell not; and the harmonious
   mind
Poured itself forth in all-prophetic song;
And music lifted up the listening spirit
Until it walked, exempt from mortal care,
Godlike, o'er the clear billows of sweet sound.

Shelley, *Prometheus Unbound,* II, 72

56 What Exile from himself can flee?
   To zones, though more and more remote,
Still, still pursues, where-e'er I be,
   The blight of life—the demon Thought.

Byron, *Childe Harold's Pilgrimage,* I, To Inez

57 The history of mind is its own act. Mind is only what it does, and its act is to make itself the object of its own consciousness. In history its act is to gain consciousness of itself as mind, to apprehend itself in its interpretation of itself to itself. This apprehension is its being and its principle, and the completion of apprehension at one stage is at the same time the rejection of that stage and its transition to a higher. To use abstract phraseology, the mind apprehending this apprehension anew, or in other words returning to itself again out of its rejection of this lower stage of apprehension, is the mind of the stage higher than that on which it stood in its earlier apprehension.

The question of the perfectibility and *Education of the Human Race* arises here. Those who have maintained this perfectibility have divined something of the nature of mind, something of the fact that it is its nature to have self-knowledge as the law of its being, and, since it apprehends that which it is, to have a form higher than that which constituted its mere being. But to those who reject this doctrine, mind has remained an empty word, and history a superficial play of casual, so-called "merely human," strivings and passions. Even if, in connexion with history, they speak of Providence and the plan of Providence, and so express a faith in a higher power, their ideas remain empty because they expressly declare that for them the plan of Providence is inscrutable and incomprehensible.

Hegel, *Philosophy of Right*, 343

58 In the course of this work of the world mind, states, nations, and individuals arise animated by their particular determinate principle which has its interpretation and actuality in their constitutions and in the whole range of their life and condition. While their consciousness is limited to these and they are absorbed in their mundane interests, they are all the time the unconscious tools and organs of the world mind at work within them. The shapes which they take pass away, while the absolute mind prepares and works out its transition to its next higher stage.

Hegel, *Philosophy of Right*, 344

59 Will without freedom is an empty word, while freedom is actual only as will, as subject. . . . Mind is in principle thinking, and man is distinguished from beast in virtue of thinking. But it must not be imagined that man is half thought and half will, and that he keeps thought in one pocket and will in another, for this would be a foolish idea. The distinction between thought and will is only that between the theoretical attitude and the practical. These, however, are surely not two faculties; the will is rather a special way of thinking, thinking translating itself into existence, thinking as the urge to give itself existence.

Hegel, *Philosophy of Right*, Additions, Par. 4

60 When a hypothesis has once come to birth in the mind, or gained a footing there, it leads a life so far comparable with the life of an organism, as that it assimilates matter from the outer world only when it is like in kind with it and beneficial; and when, contrarily, such matter is not like in kind but hurtful, the hypothesis, equally with the organism, throws it off, or, if forced to take it, gets rid of it again entire.

Schopenhauer, *Some Forms of Literature*

61 Great intellectual gifts mean an activity pre-eminently nervous in its character, and consequently a very high degree of susceptibility to pain in every form.

Schopenhauer, *Personality*

62 Thought, true labour of any kind, highest virtue itself, is it not the daughter of Pain? Born as out of

the black whirlwind;—true *effort*, in fact, as a captive struggling to free himself: that is Thought.

Carlyle, *The Hero as Poet*

63 One should not think slightingly of the paradoxical; for the paradox is the source of the thinker's passion, and the thinker without a paradox is like a lover without feeling: a paltry mediocrity. But the highest pitch of every passion is always to will its own downfall; and so it is also the supreme passion of the Reason to seek a collision, though this collision must in one way or another prove its undoing. The supreme paradox of all thought is the attempt to discover something that thought cannot think.

Kierkegaard, *Philosophical Fragments*, III

64 How can we speak of the action of the mind under any divisions, as of its knowledge, of its ethics, of its works, and so forth, since it melts will into perception, knowledge into act? Each becomes the other. Itself alone is.

Emerson, *Intellect*

65 What is the hardest task in the world? To think.

Emerson, *Intellect*

66 There is one mind common to all individual men. Every man is an inlet to the same and to all of the same. He that is once admitted to the right of reason is made a freeman of the whole estate. What Plato has thought, he may think; what a saint has felt, he may feel; what at any time has befallen any man, he can understand. Who hath access to this universal mind is a party to all that is or can be done, for this is the only and sovereign agent.

Emerson, *History*

67 The brain is only one condition out of many on which intellectual manifestations depend; the others being, chiefly, the organs of the senses and the motor apparatuses, especially those which are concerned in prehension and in the production of articulate speech.

T. H. Huxley, *Relations of Man to the Lower Animals*

68 The spontaneous process which goes on within the mind itself is higher and choicer than that which is logical; for the latter, being scientific, is common property, and can be taken and made use of by minds who are personally strangers, in any true sense, both to the ideas in question and to their development.

Newman, *Essay on the Development of Christian Doctrine*, Pt. II, V, 4

69 The action of thinking may incidentally have other results; it may serve to amuse us, for example, and among *dilettanti* it is not rare to find those

who have so perverted thought to the purposes of pleasure that it seems to vex them to think that the questions upon which they delight to exercise it may ever get finally settled; and a positive discovery which takes a favorite subject out of the arena of literary debate is met with ill-concealed dislike.

C. S. Peirce, *How to Make Our Ideas Clear*

70 Consciousness . . . does not appear to itself chopped up in bits. Such words as "chain" or "train" do not describe it fitly as it presents itself in the first instance. It is nothing jointed; it flows. A "river" or a "stream" is the metaphor by which it is most naturally described. *In talking of it hereafter, let us call it the stream of thought, of consciousness, or of subjective life.*

William James, *Psychology,* IX

71 The mind is at every stage a theatre of simultaneous possibilities. Consciousness consists in the comparison of these with each other, the selection of some, and the suppression of the rest by the reinforcing and inhibiting agency of attention. The highest and most elaborated mental products are filtered from the data chosen by the faculty next beneath, out of the mass offered by the faculty below that, which mass in turn was sifted from a still larger amount of yet simpler material, and so on. The mind, in short, works on the data it receives very much as a sculptor works on his block of stone. In a sense the statue stood there from eternity. But there were a thousand different ones beside it, and the sculptor alone is to thank for having extricated this one from the rest. Just so the world of each of us, howsoever different our several views of it may be, all lay embedded in the primordial chaos of sensations, which gave the mere *matter* to the thought of all of us indifferently. We may, if we like, by our reasonings unwind things back to that black and jointless continuity of space and moving clouds of swarming atoms which science calls the only real world. But all the while the world *we* feel and live in will be that which our ancestors and we, by slowly cumulative strokes of choice, have extricated out of this, like sculptors, by simply rejecting certain portions of the given stuff. Other sculptors, other statues from the same stone! Other minds, other worlds from the same monotonous and inexpressive chaos! My world is but one in a million alike embedded, alike real to those who may abstract them. How different must be the worlds in the consciousness of ant, cuttle-fish, or crab!

William James, *Psychology,* IX

72 What happens in the brain after experience has done its utmost is what happens in every material mass which has been fashioned by an outward force,—in every pudding or mortar, for example, which I may make with my hands. The fashion-ing from without brings the elements into collocations which set new internal forces free to exert their effects in turn. And the random irradiations and resettlements of our ideas, which *supervene upon experience,* and constitute our free mental play, are due entirely to these secondary internal processes, which vary enormously from brain to brain, even though the brains be exposed to exactly the same "outer relations." The higher thought-processes owe their being to causes which correspond far more to the sourings and fermentations of dough, the setting of mortar, or the subsidence of sediments in mixtures, than to the manipulations by which these physical aggregates came to be compounded.

William James, *Psychology,* XXVIII

73 The causes of our mental structure are doubtless natural, and connected, like all our other peculiarities, with those of our nervous structure. Our interests, our tendencies of attention, our motor impulses, the æsthetic, moral, and theoretic combinations we delight in, the extent of our power of apprehending schemes of relation, just like the elementary relations themselves, time, space, difference and similarity and the elementary kinds of feeling, have all grown up in ways of which at present we can give no account. . . . And the more sincerely one seeks to trace the actual course of *psychogenesis,* the steps by which as a race we may have come by the peculiar mental attributes which we possess, the more clearly one perceives "the slowly gathering twilight close in utter night."

William James, *Psychology,* XXVIII

74 The man who listens to Reason is lost: Reason enslaves all whose minds are not strong enough to master her.

Shaw, *Man and Superman,*
Maxims for Revolutionists

75 Real life is, to most men, a long second-best, a perpetual compromise between the ideal and the possible; but the world of pure reason knows no compromise, no practical limitations, no barrier to the creative activity embodying in splendid edifices the passionate aspiration after the perfect from which all great work springs. Remote from human passions, remote even from the pitiful facts of Nature, the generations have gradually created an ordered cosmos, where pure thought can dwell as in its natural home, and where one, at least, of our nobler impulses can escape from the dreary exile of the actual world.

Russell, *Study of Mathematics*

76 The power of reason is thought small in these days, but I remain an unrepentant rationalist. Reason may be a small force, but is constant, and works always in one direction, while the forces of

unreason destroy one another in futile strife. Therefore every orgy of unreason in the end strengthens the friends of reason, and shows afresh that they are the only true friends of humanity.

Russell, *Sceptical Essays,* IX

77 Mental activity, which works its way from the memory-image to the production of identity of perception via the outer world, merely represents *a roundabout way to wish-fulfilment* made necessary by experience. Thinking is indeed nothing but a substitute for the hallucinatory wish; and if the dream is called a wish-fulfilment, this becomes something self-evident, since nothing but a wish can impel our psychic apparatus to activity. The dream, which fulfils its wishes by following the short regressive path, has thereby simply preserved for us a specimen of the *primary* method of operation of the psychic apparatus, which has been abandoned as inappropriate. What once prevailed in the waking state, when our psychic life was still young and inefficient, seems to have been banished into our nocturnal life; just as we still find in the nursery those discarded primitive weapons of adult humanity, the bow and arrow.

Freud, *Interpretation of Dreams,* VII, C

78 The first of these displeasing propositions of psycho-analysis is this: that mental processes are essentially unconscious, and that those which are conscious are merely isolated acts and parts of the whole psychic entity. Now I must ask you to remember that, on the contrary, we are accustomed to identify the mental with the conscious. Consciousness appears to us as positively the characteristic that defines mental life, and we regard psychology as the study of the content of consciousness. This even appears so evident that any contradiction of it seems obvious nonsense to us, and yet it is impossible for psycho-analysis to avoid this contradiction, or to accept the identity between the conscious and the psychic. The psycho-analytical definition of the mind is that it comprises processes of the nature of feeling, thinking, and wishing, and it maintains that there are such things as unconscious thinking and unconscious wishing. But in doing so psycho-analysis has forfeited at the outset the sympathy of the sober and scientifically minded, and incurred the suspicion of being a phantastic cult occupied with dark and unfathomable mysteries. You yourselves must find it difficult to understand why I should stigmatize an abstract proposition, such as "The psychic is the conscious," as a prejudice; nor can you guess yet what evolutionary process could have led to the denial of the unconscious, if it does indeed exist, nor what advantage could have been achieved by this denial. It seems like an empty wrangle over words to argue whether mental life is to be regarded as co-extensive with consciousness or whether it may be said to stretch beyond this limit, and yet I can assure you that the acceptance of unconscious mental processes represents a decisive step towards a new orientation in the world and in science.

Freud, *General Introduction to Psycho-Analysis,* I

79 Our best hope for the future is that the intellect— the scientific spirit, reason—should in time establish a dictatorship over the human mind. The very nature of reason is a guarantee that it would not fail to concede to human emotions, and to all that is determined by them, the position to which they are entitled. But the common pressure exercised by such a domination of reason would prove to be the strongest unifying force among men, and would prepare the way for further unifications. Whatever, like the ban laid upon thought by religion, opposes such a development is a danger for the future of mankind.

Freud, *New Introductory Lectures on Psycho-Analysis,* XXXV

80 *Demand for the solution of a perplexity is the steadying and guiding factor in the entire process of reflection.* Where there is no question of a problem to be solved or a difficulty to be surmounted, the course of suggestions flows on at random; we have the first type of thought described. If the stream of suggestions is controlled simply by their emotional congruity, their fitting agreeably into a single picture or story, we have the second type. But a question to be answered, an ambiguity to be resolved, sets up an end and holds the current of ideas to a definite channel. Every suggested conclusion is tested by its reference to this regulating end, by its pertinence to the problem in hand. This need of straightening out a perplexity also controls the kind of inquiry undertaken. A traveler whose end is the most beautiful path will look for other considerations and will test suggestions occurring to him on another principle than if he wishes to discover the way to a given city. *The problem fixes the end of thought* and *the end controls the process of thinking.*

Dewey, *How We Think,* Pt. I, I, 3

81 Thinking is stoppage of the immediate manifestation of impulse until that impulse has been brought into connection with other possible tendencies to action so that a more comprehensive and coherent plan of activity is formed. Some of the other tendencies to action lead to use of eye, ear, and hand to observe objective conditions; others result in recall of what has happened in the past. Thinking is thus a postponement of immediate action, while it effects internal control of impulse through a union of observation and memory, this union being the heart of reflection.

Dewey, *Experience and Education,* V

82 Reason is experimental intelligence, conceived af-

ter the pattern of science, and used in the creation of social arts; it has something to do. It liberates man from the bondage of the past, due to ignorance and accident hardened into custom. It projects a better future and assists man in its realization. And its operation is always subject to test in experience. The plans which are formed, the principles which man projects as guides of reconstructive action, are not dogmas. They are hypotheses to be worked out in practice, and to be rejected, corrected and expanded as they fail or succeed in giving our present experience the guidance it requires. We may call them programmes of action, but since they are to be used in making our future acts less blind, more directed, they are flexible. Intelligence is not something possessed once for all. It is in constant process of forming, and its retention requires constant alertness in observing consequences, an open-minded will to learn and courage in re-adjustment.

Dewey, *Reconstruction in Philosophy,* IV

83 If we could rid ourselves of all pride, if, to define our species, we kept strictly to what the historic and the prehistoric periods show us to be the constant characteristic of man and of intelligence, we should say not *Homo sapiens,* but *Homo faber.* In short, *intelligence, considered in what seems to be its original feature, is the faculty of manufacturing artificial objects, especially tools to make tools, and of indefinitely varying the manufacture.*

Bergson, *Creative Evolution,* II

84 Knowledge and action are . . . only two aspects of one and the same faculty. . . .

If instinct is, above all, the faculty of using an organized natural instrument, it must involve innate knowledge (potential or unconscious, it is true), both of this instrument and of the object to which it is applied. Instinct is therefore innate knowledge of a *thing.* But intelligence is the faculty of constructing unorganized—that is to say artificial—instruments. If, on its account, nature gives up endowing the living being with the instruments that may serve him, it is in order that the living being may be able to vary his construction according to circumstances. The essential function of intelligence is therefore to see the way out of a difficulty in any circumstances whatever, to find what is most suitable, what answers best the question asked. Hence it bears essentially on the relations between a given situation and the means of utilizing it. What is innate in intellect, therefore, is the tendency to establish relations, and this tendency implies the natural knowledge of certain very general relations, a kind of stuff that the activity of each particular intellect will cut up into more special relations. Where activity is directed toward manufacture, therefore, knowledge necessarily bears on relations. But this entirely *formal* knowledge of intelligence has an immense advan-

tage over the *material* knowledge of instinct. A form, just because it is empty, may be filled at will with any number of things in turn, even with those that are of no use. So that a formal knowledge is not limited to what is practically useful, although it is in view of practical utility that it has made its appearance in the world. An intelligent being bears within himself the means to transcend his own nature.

He transcends himself, however, less than he wishes, less also than he imagines himself to do. The purely formal character of intelligence deprives it of the ballast necessary to enable it to settle itself on the objects that are of the most powerful interest to speculation. Instinct, on the contrary, has the desired materiality, but it is incapable of going so far in quest of its object; it does not speculate. Here we reach the point that most concerns our present inquiry. The difference that we shall now proceed to denote between instinct and intelligence is what the whole of this analysis was meant to bring out. We formulate it thus: *There are things that intelligence alone is able to seek, but which, by itself, it will never find. These things instinct alone could find; but it will never seek them.*

Bergson, *Creative Evolution,* II

85 In the higher reaches of human nature, as much as in the lower, rationality depends on distinguishing the excellent; and that distinction can be made, in the last analysis, only by an irrational impulse. As life is a better form given to force, by which the universal flux is subdued to create and serve a somewhat permanent interest, so reason is a better form given to interest itself, by which it is fortified and propagated, and ultimately, perhaps, assured of satisfaction. The substance to which this form is given remains irrational; so that rationality, like all excellence, is something secondary and relative, requiring a natural being to possess or to impute it. When definite interests are recognised and the values of things are estimated by that standard, action at the same time veering in harmony with that estimation, then reason has been born and a moral world has arisen.

Santayana, *Life of Reason,* I, 1

86 Reason, as Hume said with profound truth, is an unintelligible instinct. It could not be otherwise if reason is to remain something transitive and existential; for transition is unintelligible, and yet is the deepest characteristic of existence. Philosophers, however, having perceived that the function of thought is to fix static terms and reveal eternal relations, have inadvertently transferred to the living act what is true only of its ideal object; and they have expected to find in the process, treated psychologically, that luminous deductive clearness which belongs to the ideal world it tends to reveal. The intelligible, however, lies at the periphery of experience, the surd at its core;

and intelligence is but one centrifugal ray darting from the slime to the stars. Thought must execute a metamorphosis; and while this is of course mysterious, it is one of those familiar mysteries, like motion and will, which are more natural than dialectical lucidity itself; for dialectic grows cogent by fulfilling intent, but intent or meaning is itself vital and inexplicable.

Santayana, *Life of Reason,* I, 3

5.2 | *The Senses and Sense Perception*

Whether mind, intellect, or the rational faculty is material or immaterial has long been debated and is still an issue in dispute. The reader will find indications of this controversy in Section 5.1. In contrast, he will find no disagreement here about the bodily or corporeal character of the senses.

From the very beginning of Western psychology, special sense-organs have been the recognized seats of man's power to see, hear, touch, taste, and smell. Modern anatomical and physiological investigations have discovered additional sense-organs and increased our knowledge of such organs as the eye and the ear. In consequence, the traditional enumeration of the five senses has been enlarged to include other modes of sensitivity. But while the study of the senses thus falls within the sphere of anatomy and physiology, the discussion of sensation and sense perception deals with questions that are psychological or philosophical in their basic terms.

For example, all the knowledge we have of the structure and functioning of the sense-organs does not fully explain how sensation takes place; nor does it help us to decide which of several competing theories of sense perception is the best account of that process. The reader will find these matters disputed in the quotations below. He will also find the consideration of such questions as the difference between sense-knowledge and intellectual knowledge, the relation of percepts to concepts, and the distinction between primary and secondary qualities; or between such things as size and motion which are perceptible by two or more senses and such things as color which is perceptible by the eye alone, or sound which is perceptible only by the ear.

Another problem that is discussed in a number of quotations is the problem of the trustworthiness and fallibility of the senses and of sense perception. Sensory deceptions, illusions, and hallucinations are often cited by the skeptic to support his case. On the other hand, it is said that the senses themselves make no mistakes; the errors attributed to the senses are errors of judgment, not of sense perception. For the discussion of related matters, the reader is referred to several sections in Chapter 6 on KNOWLEDGE, Section 6.2 on EXPERIENCE, Section 6.4 on ERROR, IGNORANCE, AND THE LIMITS OF HUMAN KNOWLEDGE, and Section 6.6 on DOUBT AND SKEPTICISM.

1 *Timaeus.* Sight in my opinion is the source of the greatest benefit to us, for had we never seen the stars, and the sun, and the heaven, none of the words which we have spoken about the universe would ever have been uttered. But now the sight of day and night, and the months and the revolutions of the years, have created number, and have given us a conception of time, and the power of enquiring about the nature of the universe; and from this source we have derived philosophy, than which no greater good ever was or will be given by the gods to mortal man. This is the greatest boon of sight: and of the lesser benefits why should I speak? even the ordinary man if he were deprived of them would bewail his loss, but in vain. Thus much let me say however: God invented and gave us sight to the end that we might behold the courses of intelligence in the heaven, and apply them to the courses of our own intelligence which are akin to them, the unperturbed to the perturbed; and that we, learning them and partaking of the natural truth of reason, might imitate the absolutely unerring courses of God and regulate our own vagaries. The same may be affirmed of speech and hearing: they have been given by the gods to the same end and for a like reason. For this is the principal end of speech, whereto it most contributes.

Plato, *Timaeus,* 47A

2 *Socrates.* The simple sensations which reach the soul through the body are given at birth to men and animals by nature, but their reflections on the being and use of them are slowly and hardly gained, if they are ever gained, by education and long experience.

Theaetetus. Assuredly.

Soc. And can a man attain truth who fails of attaining being?

Theaet. Impossible.

Soc. And can he who misses the truth of anything, have a knowledge of that thing?

Theaet. He cannot.

Soc. Then knowledge does not consist in impressions of sense, but in reasoning about them; in that only, and not in the mere impression, truth and being can be attained?

Theaet. Clearly.

Soc. And would you call the two processes by the same name, when there is so great a difference between them?

Theaet. That would certainly not be right.

Soc. And what name would you give to seeing, hearing, smelling, being cold and being hot?

Theaet. I should call all of them perceiving—what other name could be given to them?

Soc. Perception would be the collective name of them?

Theaet. Certainly.

Soc. Which, as we say, has no part in the attainment of truth any more than of being?

Theaet. Certainly not.

Soc. And therefore not in science or knowledge?

Theaet. No.

Soc. Then perception, Theaetetus, can never be the same as knowledge or science.

Plato, *Theaetetus,* 186A

3 Scientific knowledge is not possible through the act of perception. Even if perception as a faculty is of 'the such' and not merely of a 'this somewhat', yet one must at any rate actually perceive a 'this somewhat', and at a definite present place and time: but that which is commensurately universal and true in all cases one cannot perceive, since it is not 'this' and it is not 'now'; if it were, it would not be commensurately universal—the term we apply to what is always and everywhere. Seeing, therefore, that demonstrations are commensurately universal and universals imperceptible, we clearly cannot obtain scientific knowledge by the act of perception: nay, it is obvious that even if it were possible to perceive that a triangle has its angles equal to two right angles, we should still be looking for a demonstration—we should not (as some say) possess knowledge of it; for perception must be of a particular, whereas scientific knowledge involves the recognition of the commensurate universal. So if we were on the moon, and saw the earth shutting out the sun's light, we should not know the cause of the eclipse: we should perceive the present fact of the eclipse, but not the reasoned fact at all, since the act of perception is not of the commensurate universal. I do not, of course, deny that by watching the frequent recurrence of this event we might, after tracking the commensurate universal, possess a demonstration for the commensurate universal is elicited from the several groups of singulars.

The commensurate universal is precious because it makes clear the cause; so that in the case of facts like these which have a cause other than themselves universal knowledge is more precious than sense-perceptions and than intuition. (As regards primary truths there is of course a different account to be given.) Hence it is clear that knowledge of things demonstrable cannot be acquired by perception, unless the term perception is applied to the possession of scientific knowledge through demonstration. Nevertheless certain points do arise with regard to connexions to be proved which are referred for their explanation to a failure in sense-perception: there are cases when an act of vision would terminate our inquiry, not because in seeing we should be knowing, but because we should have elicited the universal from seeing; if, for example, we saw the pores in the glass and the light passing through, the reason of the kindling would be clear to us because we should at the same time see it in each instance and intuit that it must be so in all instances.

Aristotle, *Posterior Analytics,* 87b27

4 The following results applying to any and every sense may now be formulated.

(A) By a 'sense' is meant what has the power of receiving into itself the sensible forms of things without the matter. This must be conceived of as taking place in the way in which a piece of wax takes on the impress of a signet-ring without the iron or gold; we say that what produces the impression is a signet of bronze or gold, but its particular metallic constitution makes no difference: in a similar way the sense is affected by what is coloured or flavoured or sounding, but it is indifferent what in each case the *substance* is; what alone matters is what *quality* it has, i.e. in what *ratio* its constituents are combined.

(B) By 'an organ of sense' is meant that in which ultimately such a power is seated.

The sense and its organ are the same in fact, but their essence is not the same. What perceives is, of course, a spatial magnitude, but we must not admit that either the having the power to perceive or the sense itself is a magnitude; what they are is a certain ratio or power *in* a magnitude. This enables us to explain why objects of sense which possess one of two opposite sensible qualities in a degree largely in excess of the other opposite destroy the organs of sense; if the movement set up by an object is too strong for the organ, the equipoise of contrary qualities in the organ, which just *is* its sensory power, is disturbed; it is precisely as concord and tone are destroyed by too violently twanging the strings of a lyre. This explains also why plants cannot perceive, in spite of their having a portion of soul in them and obviously being affected by tangible objects themselves; for undoubtedly their temperature can be lowered or raised. The explanation is that they have no mean of contrary qualities, and so no principle in them capable of taking on the forms of sensible objects without their matter; in the case of plants the affection is an affection by form-and-matter together. The problem might be raised: Can what cannot smell be said to be affected by smells or what cannot see by colours, and so on? It might be said that a smell is just what can be smelt, and if it produces any effect it can only be so as to make something smell it, and it might be argued that what cannot smell cannot be affected by smells and further that what can smell can be affected by it only in so far as it has in it the power to smell (similarly with the proper objects of all the other senses). Indeed that this *is* so is made quite evident as follows. Light or darkness, sounds and smells leave *bodies* quite unaffected; what does affect bodies is not these but the bodies which are their vehicles, e.g. what splits the trunk of a tree is not the sound of the thunder but the air which accompanies thunder. Yes, but, it may be objected, bodies are affected by what is tangible and by flavours. If not, by what are things that are without soul affected, i.e. altered in quality? Must we not, then, admit that the objects of the other senses also may affect them? Is not the true account this, that all bodies *are* capable of being affected by smells and sounds, but that some on being acted upon, having no boundaries of their own, disintegrate, as in the instance of air, which does become odorous, showing that *some* effect is produced on it by what is odorous? But smelling is more than such an affection by what is odorous— *what* more? Is not the answer that, while the air owing to the momentary duration of the action upon it of what is odorous does itself become perceptible to the sense of smell, smelling is an *observing* of the result produced?

Aristotle, *On the Soul*, 424ᵃ16

5 Without touch there can be no other sense, and the organ of touch cannot consist of earth or of any other single element.

It is evident, therefore, that the loss of this one sense alone must bring about the death of an animal. For as on the one hand nothing which is not an animal can have this sense, so on the other it is the only one which is indispensably necessary to what is an animal. This explains, further, the following difference between the other senses and touch. In the case of all the others excess of intensity in the qualities which they apprehend, i.e. excess of intensity in colour, sound, and smell, destroys not the animal but only the organs of the sense (except incidentally, as when the sound is accompanied by an impact or shock, or where through the objects of sight or of smell certain other things are set in motion, which destroy by contact); flavour also destroys only in so far as it is at the same time tangible. But excess of intensity in tangible qualities, e.g. heat, cold, or hardness, destroys the animal itself. As in the case of every sensible quality excess destroys the organ, so here what is tangible destroys touch, which is the essential mark of life; for it has been shown that without touch it is impossible for an animal to be. That is why excess in intensity of tangible qualities destroys not merely the organ, but the animal itself, because this is the only sense which it must have.

All the other senses are necessary to animals, as we have said, not for their being, but for their well-being. Such, e.g. is sight, which, since it lives in air or water, or generally in what is pellucid, it must have in order to see, and taste because of what is pleasant or painful to it, in order that it may perceive these qualities in its nutriment and so may desire to be set in motion, and hearing that it may have communication made to it, and a tongue that it may communicate with its fellows.

Aristotle, *On the Soul*, 435ᵇ2

6 Since a particular figure felt by the hands in the dark is known to be the same which is seen in the

bright light of day, touch and sight must be excited by a quite similar cause. Well then if we handle a square thing and it excites our attention in the dark, in the daylight what square thing will be able to fall on our sight, except the image of that thing? Therefore the cause of seeing, it is plain, lies in images and no thing can be perceived without them.

Well the idols of things I speak of are borne along all round and are discharged and transmitted in all directions; but because we can see with the eyes alone, the consequence is that, to whatever point we turn our sight, there all the several things meet and strike it with their shape and colour. And the image gives the power to see and the means to distinguish how far each thing is distant from us; for as soon as ever it is discharged, it pushes before it and impels all the air which lies between it and the eyes; and thus that air all streams through our eyes and brushes so to say the pupils and so passes through. The consequence is that we see how far distant each thing is. And the greater the quantity of air which is driven on before it and the larger the current which brushes our eyes, the more distant each different thing is seen to be. You must know these processes go on with extreme rapidity, so that at one and the same moment we see what like a thing is and how far distant it is. And this must by no means be deemed strange herein that, while the idols which strike the eyes cannot be seen one at a time, the things themselves are seen. For thus when the wind too beats us with successive strokes and when piercing cold streams, we are not wont to feel each single particle of that wind and cold, but rather the whole result; and then we perceive blows take effect on our body just as if something or other were beating it and giving us a sensation of its body outside. Again when we thump a stone with a finger, we touch merely the outermost colour on the surface of the stone, and yet we do not feel that colour by our touch, but rather we feel the very hardness of the stone seated in its inmost depths.

Lucretius, *Nature of Things,* IV

7 You will find that from the senses first has proceeded the knowledge of the true and that the senses cannot be refuted. For that which is of itself to be able to refute things false by true things must from the nature of the case be proved to have the higher certainty. Well then what must fairly be accounted of higher certainty than sense? Shall reason founded on false sense be able to contradict them, wholly founded as it is on the senses? And if they are not true, then all reason as well is rendered false. Or shall the ears be able to take the eyes to task, or the touch the ears? Again shall the taste call in question this touch, or the nostrils refute or the eyes controvert it? Not so, I guess; for each apart has its own distinct office, each its own

power; and therefore we must perceive what is soft and cold or hot by one distinct faculty, by another perceive the different colours of things and thus see all objects which are conjoined with colour. Taste too has its faculty apart; smells spring from one source, sounds from another. It must follow therefore that any one sense cannot confute any other. No nor can any sense take itself to task, since equal credit must be assigned to it at all times. What therefore has at any time appeared true to each sense, is true. And if reason shall be unable to explain away the cause why things which close at hand were square, at a distance looked round, it yet is better, if you are at a loss for the reason, to state erroneously the causes of each shape, than to let slip from your grasp on any side things manifest and ruin the groundwork of belief and wrench up all the foundations on which rest life and existence. For not only would all reason give way, life itself would at once fall to the ground, unless you choose to trust the senses and shun precipices and all things else of this sort that are to be avoided, and to pursue the opposite things. All that host of words then be sure is quite unmeaning, which has been drawn out in array against the senses.

Lucretius, *Nature of Things,* IV

8 When therefore we force these voices forth from the depths of our body and discharge them straight out at the mouth, the pliant tongue deft fashioner of words gives them articulate utterance and the structure of the lips does its part in shaping them. Therefore when the distance is not long between the point from which each several voice has started and that at which it arrives, the very words too must be plainly heard and distinguished syllable by syllable; for each voice retains its structure and retains its shape. But if the space between be more than is suitable, the words must be huddled together in passing through much air and the voice be disorganised in its flight through the same. Therefore it is that you can hear a sound, yet cannot distinguish what the meaning of the words is: so huddled and hampered is the voice when it comes.

Lucretius, *Nature of Things,* IV

9 Now mark me, and I will duscuss the way in which the contact of smell affects the nostrils: and first there must be many things from which a varied flow of smells streams and rolls on; and we must suppose that they thus stream and discharge and disperse themselves among all things alike; but one smell fits itself better to one creature, another to another on account of their unlike shapes; and therefore bees are drawn on by the smell of honey through the air to a very great distance, and so are vultures by carcases.

Lucretius, *Nature of Things,* IV

10 All sense-perception can occur only through the medium of some bodily substance, since in the absence of body the soul is utterly absorbed in the Intellectual Sphere. Sense-perception being the gripping not of the Intellectual but of the sensible alone, the soul, if it is to form any relationship of knowledge, or of impression, with objects of sense, must be brought in some kind of contact with them by means of whatever may bridge the gap.

The knowledge, then, is realized by means of bodily organs.

Plotinus, *Fourth Ennead*, V, 1

11 Our fleshly sense is slow because it is fleshly sense: and that is the limit of its being. It can do what it was made to do; but it has no power to hold things transient as they run their course from their due beginning to their due end. For in Your word, by which they are created, they hear their law: "From this point: not beyond that."

Augustine, *Confessions*, IV, 10

12 Whatever things you perceive by fleshly sense you perceive only in part, not knowing the whole of which those things are but parts and yet they delight you so much. For if fleshly sense had been capable of grasping the whole—and had not for your punishment received part only of the whole as its just limit—you would wish that whatever exists in the present might pass on, that the whole might be perceived by you for your delight. What we speak, you hear by a bodily sense: and certainly you do not wish the same syllable to go on sounding but to pass away that other syllables may come and you may hear the whole speech. It is always so with all things that go to make up one whole: all that goes to make up the whole does not exist at one moment. If all could be perceived in one act of perception, it would obviously give more delight than any of the individual parts.

Augustine, *Confessions*, IV, 11

13 As far as regards the doctrine which treats of . . . rational philosophy, far be it from us to compare them [the Platonists] with those who attributed to the bodily senses the faculty of discriminating truth, and thought, that all we learn is to be measured by their untrustworthy and fallacious rules. . . . Such . . . were the Stoics, who ascribed to the bodily senses that expertness in disputation which they so ardently love, called by them dialectic, asserting that from the senses the mind conceives the notions of those things which they explicate by definition. And hence is developed the whole plan and connection of their learning and teaching. I often wonder, with respect to this, how they can say that none are beautiful but the wise; for by what bodily sense have they perceived that beauty, by what eyes of the flesh have they seen widsom's comeliness of form? Those, however, whom we justly rank before all others, have distin-

guished those things which are conceived by the mind from those which are perceived by the senses, neither taking away from the senses anything to which they are competent, nor attributing to them anything beyond their competency.

Augustine, *City of God*, VIII, 7

14 The intellectual soul . . . in the order of nature, holds the lowest place among intellectual substances; for it is not naturally gifted with the knowledge of truth, as the angels are, but has to gather knowledge from individual things by way of the senses. . . . But nature never fails in necessary things; therefore the intellectual soul had to be endowed not only with the power of understanding, but also with the power of feeling. Now the action of the senses is not performed without a corporeal instrument. Therefore the intellectual soul had to be united to a body which could be an adequate organ of sense.

Now all the other senses are based on the sense of touch. But the organ of touch has to be a medium between contraries, such as hot and cold, wet and dry, and the like, of which the sense of touch has the perception; thus it is in potency with regard to contraries, and is able to perceive them. Therefore the more the organ of touch is reduced to an even temperament, the more sensitive will be the touch. But the intellectual soul has the power of sense in all its completeness, because what belongs to the inferior nature pre-exists more perfectly in the superior. . . . Therefore the body to which the intellectual soul is united should be a mixed body, above all others reduced to the most even temperament. For this reason among animals man has the best sense of touch. And among men, those who have the best sense of touch have the best intellect. A sign of this is that we observe *those who are refined in body are well endowed in mind*, as stated in the book on the *Soul*.

Aquinas, *Summa Theologica*, I, 76, 5

15 The proper sense judges of the proper sensible by discerning it from other things which come under the same sense; for instance, by discerning white from black or green. But neither sight nor taste can discern white from sweet, because what discerns between two things must know both. Therefore the discerning judgment must be assigned to the common sense, to which, as to a common term, all apprehensions of the senses must be referred, and by which, again, all the intentions of the senses are perceived; as when someone sees that he sees. For this cannot be done by the proper sense, which only knows the form of the sensible by which it is changed, in which change the action of sight is completed, and from which change follows another in the common sense which perceives the act of vision.

Aquinas, *Summa Theologica*, I, 78, 4

16 Although the operation of the intellect has its origin in the senses, yet, in the thing apprehended through the senses, the intellect knows many things which the senses cannot perceive.

Aquinas, *Summa Theologica*, I, 78, 4

17 Our intellect's proper and proportionate object is the nature of a sensible thing. Now a perfect judgment concerning anything cannot be formed, unless all that pertains to that thing is known; especially if that which is the term and end of judgment is not known. . . . Now it is clear that a smith cannot judge perfectly of a knife unless he knows the work that must be done, and in like manner the natural philosopher cannot judge perfectly of natural things unless he knows sensible things. But in the present state of life whatever we understand we know by comparison to natural sensible things. Consequently it is not possible for our intellect to form a perfect judgment while the senses are suspended, through which sensible things are known to us.

Aquinas, *Summa Theologica*, I, 84, 8

18 This same deception that the senses convey to our understanding they receive in their turn. Our soul at times takes a like revenge; they compete in lying and deceiving each other. What we see and hear when stirred with anger, we do not hear as it is. . . . The object that we love seems to us more beautiful than it is . . . and uglier the one that we loathe. To a man vexed and ·afflicted the brightness of the day seems darkened and gloomy. Our senses are not only altered, but often completely stupefied by the passions of the soul. How many things we see which we do not notice if our mind is occupied elsewhere! . . . It seems as though the soul draws the powers of the senses inward and occupies them. Thus both the inside and the outside of man is full of weakness and falsehood.

Montaigne, *Essays,* II, 12, Apology for Raymond Sebond

19 To judge the appearances that we receive of objects, we would need a judicatory instrument; to verify this instrument, we need a demonstration; to verify the demonstration, an instrument: there we are in a circle.

Since the senses cannot decide our dispute, being themselves full of uncertainty, it must be reason that does so. No reason can be established without another reason: there we go retreating back to infinity.

Our conception is not itself applied to foreign objects, but is conceived through the mediation of the senses; and the senses do not comprehend the foreign object, but only their own impressions. And thus the conception and semblance we form is not of the object, but only of the impression and effect made on the sense; which impression and the object are different things. Wherefore whoever judges by appearances judges by something other than the object.

And for saying that the impressions of the senses convey to the soul the quality of the foreign objects by resemblance, how can the soul and understanding make sure of this resemblance, having of itself no communication with foreign objects? Just as a man who does not know Socrates, seeing his portrait, cannot say that it resembles him.

Now if anyone should want to judge by appearances anyway, to judge by all appearances is impossible, for they clash with one another by their contradictions and discrepancies, as we see by experience. Shall some selected appearances rule the others? We shall have to verify this selection by another selection, the second by a third; and thus it will never be finished. . . .

Finally, there is no existence that is constant, either of our being or of that of objects. And we, and our judgment, and all mortal things go on flowing and rolling unceasingly. Thus nothing certain can be established about one thing by another, both the judging and the judged being in continual change and motion.

Montaigne, *Essays,* II, 12, Apology for Raymond Sebond

20 The senses . . . are very sufficient to certify and report truth, though not always immediately, yet by comparison, by help of instrument, and by producing and urging such things as are too subtile for the sense to some effect comprehensible by the sense.

Bacon, *Advancement of Learning,* Bk. II, XIII, 4

21 Many experiences little by little destroyed all the faith which I had rested in my senses; for I from time to time observed that those towers which from afar appeared to me to be round, more closely observed seemed square, and that colossal statues raised on the summit of these towers, appeared as quite tiny statues when viewed from the bottom; and so in an infinitude of other cases I found error in judgments founded on the external senses. And not only in those founded on the external senses, but even in those founded on the internal as well; for is there anything more intimate or more internal than pain? And yet I have learned from some persons whose arms or legs have been cut off, that they sometimes seemed to feel pain in the part which had been amputated, which made me think that I could not be quite certain that it was a certain member which pained me, even although I felt pain in it. And to those grounds of doubt I have lately added two others, which are very general; the first is that I never have believed myself to feel anything in waking moments which I cannot also sometimes believe myself to feel when I sleep, and as I do not

think that these things which I seem to feel in sleep, proceed from objects outside of me, I do not see any reason why I should have this belief regarding objects which I seem to perceive while awake. The other was that being still ignorant, or rather supposing myself to be ignorant, of the author of my being, I saw nothing to prevent me from having been so constituted by nature that I might be deceived even in matters which seemed to me to be most certain. And as to the grounds on which I was formerly persuaded of the truth of sensible objects, I had not much trouble in replying to them. For since nature seemed to cause me to lean towards many things from which reason repelled me, I did not beleive that I should trust much to the teachings of nature. And although the ideas which I receive by the senses do not depend on my will, I did not think that one should for that reason conclude that they proceeded from things different from myself, since possibly some faculty might be discovered in me—though hitherto unknown to me—which produced them.

But now that I begin to know myself better, and to discover more clearly the author of my being, I do not in truth think that I should rashly admit all the matters which the senses seem to teach us, but, on the other hand, I do not think that I should doubt them all universally.

Descartes, *Meditations on First Philosophy*, VI

22 In order rightly to see what amount of certainty belongs to sense we must distinguish three grades as falling within it. To the first belongs the immediate affection of the bodily organ by external objects; and this can be nothing else than the motion of the particles of the sensory organs and the change of figure and position due to that motion. The second comprises the immediate mental result, due to the mind's union with the corporeal organ affected; such are the perceptions of pain, of pleasurable stimulation, of thirst, of hunger, of colours, of sound, savour, odour, cold, heat, and the like, which . . . arise from the union and, as it were, the intermixture of mind and body. Finally, the third contains all those judgments which, on the occasion of motions occurring in the corporeal organ, we have from our earliest years been accustomed to pass about things external to us.

For example, when I see a staff, it is not to be thought that *intentional species* fly off from it and reach the eye, by merely that rays of light reflected from the staff excite certain motions in the optic nerve and, but its mediation, in the brain as well. . . . It is in this cerebral motion, which is common to us and to the brutes, that the first grade of perception consists. But from this the second grade of perception results; and that merely extends to the perception of the colour or light reflected from the stick, and is due to the fact that the mind is so intimately conjoined with the brain

as to be affected by the motions arising in it. Nothing more than this should be assigned to sense, if we wish to distinguish it accurately from the intellect. For though my judgment that there is a staff situated without me, which judgment results from the sensation of colour by which I am affected, and likewise my reasoning from the extension of that colour, its boundaries, and its position relatively to the parts of my brain, to the size, the shape, and the distance of the said staff, are vulgarly assigned to sense, and are consequently here referred to the third grade of sensation, they clearly depend upon the understanding alone. . . . Magnitude, distance and figure can be perceived by reasoning alone, which deduces them one from another. . . .

From this it is clear that when we say that *the certitude obtainable by the understanding is much greater than that attaching to the senses* the meaning of those words is, that those judgments which when we are in full maturity new observations have led us to make, are surer than those we have formed in early infancy and apart from all reflection; and this is certainly true. For it is clear that here there is no question of the first or second grade of sense-perception, because in them no falsity can reside. When, therefore, it is alleged that refraction makes a staff appear broken in the water, it is the same as if it were said that it appears to us in the same way as it would to an infant who judged that it was broken, and as it does even to us who, owing to the prejudices to which we from our earliest years have grown accustomed, judge in the same way. . . . Hence, in this instance, it is the understanding solely which corrects the error of sense; and no case can ever be adduced in which error results from our trusting the operation of the mind more than sense.

Descartes, *Objections and Replies*, VI

23 There is no conception in a man's mind which hath not at first, totally or by parts, been begotten upon the organs of sense. The rest are derived from that original. . . .

The cause of sense is the external body, or object, which presseth the organ proper to each sense, either immediately, as in the taste and touch; or mediately, as in seeing, hearing, and smelling: which pressure, by the mediation of nerves and other strings and membranes of the body, continued inwards to the brain and heart, causeth there a resistance, or counter-pressure, or endeavour of the heart to deliver itself: which endeavour, because outward, seemeth to be some matter without. And this seeming, or fancy, is that which men call *sense;* and consisteth, as to the eye, in a light, or colour figured; to the ear, in a sound; to the nostril, in an odour; to the tongue and palate, in a savour; and to the rest of the body, in heat, cold, hardness, softness, and such other qualities as we discern by feeling. All which qualities called *sensible* are in the object that causeth them but so many several motions of the matter, by which it presseth our organs diversely. Neither in us that are pressed are they anything else but diverse motions (for motion produceth nothing but motion). But their appearance to us is fancy, the same waking that dreaming. And as pressing, rubbing, or striking the eye makes us fancy a light, and pressing the ear produceth a din; so do the bodies also we see, or hear, produce the same by their strong, though unobserved action. For if those colours and sounds were in the bodies or objects that cause them, they could not be severed from them, as by glasses and in echoes by reflection we see they are: where we know the thing we see is in one place; the appearance, in another. And though at some certain distance the real and very object seem invested with the fancy it begets in us; yet still the object is one thing, the image or fancy another. So that sense in all cases is nothing else but original fancy caused (as I have said) by the pressure that is, by the motion of external things upon our eyes, ears, and other organs, thereunto ordained.

Hobbes, *Leviathan,* I, 1

24 The homogeneal light and rays which appear red, or rather make objects appear so, I call rubrific or red-making; those which make objects appear yellow, green, blue, and violet, I call yellow-making, green-making, blue-making, violet-making, and so of the rest. And if at any time I speak of light and rays as coloured or endued with colours, I would be understood to speak not philosophically and properly, but grossly, and accordingly to such conceptions as vulgar people in seeing all these experiments would be apt to frame. For the rays, to speak properly, are not coloured. In them there is nothing else than a certain power and disposition to stir up a sensation of this or that colour. For as sound in a bell or musical string, or other sounding body, is nothing but a trembling motion, and in the air nothing but that motion propagated from the object, and in the sensorium 'tis a sense of that motion under the form of sound; so colours in the object are nothing but a disposition to reflect this or that sort of rays more copiously than the rest; in the rays they are nothing but their dispositions to propagate this or that motion into the sensorium, and in the sensorium they are sensations of those motions under the forms of colours.

Newton, *Optics,* I, 2

25 We might get to know the beauty of the universe in each soul, if we could unfold all that is enfolded in it and that is perceptibly developed only through time. But as each distinct perception of the soul includes an infinite number of confused perceptions, which involve the whole universe, the soul itself knows the things of which it has perception, only in so far as it has distinct and heightened [or unveiled] perceptions of them; and it has perfection in proportion to its distinct perceptions. Each soul knows the infinite, knows all, but confusedly; as when I walk on the sea-shore and hear the great noise the sea makes, I hear the particular sounds which come from the particular waves and which make up the total sound, but I do not discriminate them from one another. Our confused perceptions are the result of the impressions which the whole universe makes upon us.

Leibniz, *Principles of Nature and of Grace,* 13

26 The next thing to be considered is, how bodies produce ideas in us; and that is manifestly by impulse, the only way which we can conceive bodies to operate in.

If then external objects be not united to our minds when they produce ideas therein; and yet we perceive these *original* qualities in such of them as singly fall under our senses, it is evident that some motion must be thence continued by our nerves, or animal spirits, by some parts of our bodies, to the brains or the seat of sensation, there to produce in our minds the particular ideas we have of them. And since the extension, figure, number, and motion of bodies of an observable bigness, may be perceived at a distance by the sight, it is evident some singly imperceptible bodies must come from them to the eyes, and thereby convey to the brain some motion; which produces these ideas which we have of them in us.

After the same manner that the ideas of these original qualities are produced in us, we may conceive that the ideas of *secondary* qualities are also produced, viz. by the operation of insensible particles on our senses. For, it being manifest that there are bodies and good store of bodies, each whereof are so small, that we cannot by any of our senses discover either their bulk, figure, or motion,—as is evident in the particles of the air and water, and others extremely smaller than those; perhaps as much smaller than the particles of air and water, as the particles of air and water are smaller than peas or hail-stones;—let us suppose at present that the different motions and figures, bulk and number, of such particles, affecting the several organs of our senses, produce in us those different sensations which we have from the colours and smells of bodies; v.g. that a violet, by the impulse of such insensible particles of matter, of peculiar figures and bulks, and in different degrees and modifications of their motions, causes the ideas of the blue colour, and sweet scent of that flower to be produced in our minds. It being no more impossible to conceive that God should annex such ideas to such motions, with which they have no similitude, than that he should annex the idea of pain to the motion of a piece of steel dividing our flesh, with which that idea hath no resemblance.

What I have said concerning colours and smells may be understood also of tastes and sounds, and other the like sensible qualities; which, whatever reality we by mistake attribute to them, are in truth nothing in the objects themselves, but powers to produce various sensations in us; and depend on those primary qualities, viz. bulk, figure, texture, and motion of parts as I have said.

Locke, *Concerning Human Understanding,*
Bk. II, VIII, 11–14

27 It is for want of reflection that we are apt to think that our senses show us nothing but material things. Every act of sensation, when duly considered, gives us an equal view of both parts of nature, the corporeal and spiritual. For whilst I know, by seeing or hearing, etc., that there is some corporeal being without me, the object of that sensation, I do more certainly know, that there is some spiritual being within me that sees and hears. This, I must be convinced, cannot be the action of bare insensible matter; nor ever could be, without an immaterial thinking being.

Locke, *Concerning Human Understanding,*
Bk. II, XXIII, 15

28 I find I can excite ideas in my mind at pleasure, and vary and shift the scene as oft as I think fit. It is no more than willing, and straightway this or that idea arises in my fancy; and by the same power it is obliterated and makes way for another. This making and unmaking of ideas doth very properly denominate the mind active. Thus much is certain and grounded on experience; but when we think of unthinking agents or of exciting ideas exclusive of volition, we only amuse ourselves with words.

But, whatever power I may have over my own thoughts, I find the ideas actually perceived by Sense have not a like dependence on my will. When in broad daylight I open my eyes, it is not in my power to choose whether I shall see or no, or to determine what particular objects shall present themselves to my view; and so likewise as to the hearing and other senses; the ideas imprinted on them are not creatures of my will. There is therefore some *other* Will or Spirit that produces them.

Berkeley, *Principles of Human
Knowledge,* 28–29

29 The ideas imprinted on the Senses by the Author of nature are called *real things;* and those excited in the imagination being less regular, vivid, and constant, are more properly termed *ideas,* or *images of things,* which they copy and represent. But then our sensations, be they never so vivid and distinct, are nevertheless ideas, that is, they exist in the mind, or are perceived by it, as truly as the ideas

of its own framing. The ideas of Sense are allowed to have more reality in them, that is, to be more strong, orderly, and coherent than the creatures of the mind; but this is no argument that they exist without the mind. They are also less dependent on the spirit, or thinking substance which perceives them, in that they are excited by the will of another and more powerful spirit; yet still they are *ideas,* and certainly no idea, whether faint or strong, can exist otherwise than in a mind perceiving it. . . .

I do not argue against the existence of any one thing that we can apprehend either by sense or reflexion. That the things I see with my eyes and touch with my hands do exist, really exist, I make not the least question. The only thing whose existence we deny is that which *philosophers* call Matter or corporeal substance. And in doing of this there is no damage done to the rest of mankind, who, I dare say, will never miss it. . . . If the word *substance* be taken in the vulgar sense—for a combination of sensible qualities, such as extension, solidity, weight, and the like—this we cannot be accused of taking away: but if it be taken in a philosophic sense—for the support of accidents or qualities without the mind—then indeed I acknowledge that we take it away, if one may be said to take away that which never had any existence, not even in the imagination. . . . Since therefore the objects of sense exist only in the mind, and are withal thoughtless and inactive, I chose to mark them by the word *idea,* which implies those properties.

But, say what we can, some one perhaps may be apt to reply, he will still believe his senses, and never suffer any arguments, how plausible soever, to prevail over the certainty of them. Be it so; assert the evidence of sense as high as you please, we are willing to do the same. That what I see, hear, and feel doth exist, that is to say, is perceived by me, I no more doubt than I do of my own being. But I do not see how the testimony of sense can be alleged as a proof for the existence of anything which is not perceived by sense. We are not for having any man turn sceptic and disbelieve his senses; on the contrary, we give them all the stress and assurance imaginable. . . .

Secondly, it will be objected that there is a great difference betwixt real fire for instance, and the idea of fire, betwixt dreaming or imagining oneself burnt, and actually being so: if you suspect it to be only the idea of fire which you see, do but put your hand into it and you will be convinced with a witness. This and the like may be urged in opposition to our tenets. To all which the answer is evident from what hath been already said; and I shall only add in this place, that if real fire be very different from the idea of fire, so also is the real pain that it occasions very different from the idea of the same pain, and yet nobody will pretend that real pain either is, or can possibly be, in an unperceiving thing, or without the mind, any more than its idea.

Berkeley, *Principles of Human Knowledge,* 33–41

30 It seems evident, that men are carried, by a natural instinct or prepossession, to repose faith in their senses; and that, without any reasoning, or even almost before the use of reason, we always suppose an external universe, which depends not on our perception, but would exist, though we and every sensible creature were absent or annihilated. Even the animal creation are governed by a like opinion, and preserve this belief of external objects, in all their thoughts, designs, and actions.

It seems also evident, that, when men follow this blind and powerful instinct of nature, they always suppose the very images, presented by the senses, to be the external objects, and never entertain any suspicion, that the one are nothing but representations of the other. This very table which we see white, and which we feel hard, is believed to exist, independent of our perception, and to be something external to our mind, which perceives it. Our presence bestows not being on it: our absence does not annihilate it. It preserves its existence uniform and entire, independent of the situation of intelligent beings, who perceive or contemplate it.

But this universal and primary opinion of all men is soon destroyed by the slightest philosophy, which teaches us, that nothing can ever be present to the mind but an image or perception, and that the senses are only the inlets, through which these images are conveyed, without being able to produce any immediate intercourse between the mind and the object. The table, which we see, seems to diminish, as we remove farther from it: but the real table, which exists independent of us, suffers no alteration: it was, therefore, nothing but its image, which was present to the mind. These are the obvious dictates of reason; and no man, who reflects, ever doubted, that the existences, which we consider, when we say, *this house* and *that tree,* are nothing but perceptions in the mind, and fleeting copies or representations of other existences, which remain uniform and independent.

So far, then, are we necessitated by reasoning to contradict or depart from the primary instincts of nature, and to embrace a new system with regard to the evidence of our senses. But here philosophy finds herself extremely embarrassed, when she would justify this new system, and obviate the cavils and objections of the sceptics. She can no longer plead the infallible and irresistible instinct of nature: for that led us to a quite different system, which is acknowledged fallible and even erroneous. And to justify this pretended philosophical system, by a chain of clear and convincing argument, or even any appearance of argument, exceeds the power of all human capacity.

By what argument can it be proved, that the perceptions of the mind must be caused by external objects, entirely different from them, though resembling them (if that be possible) and could not arise either from the energy of the mind itself, or from the suggestion of some invisible and unknown spirit, or from some other cause still more unknown to us? It is acknowledged, that, in fact, many of these perceptions arise not from anything external, as in dreams, madness, and other diseases. And nothing can be more inexplicable than the manner, in which body should so operate upon mind as ever to convey an image of itself to a substance, supposed of so different, and even contrary a nature.

It is a question of fact, whether the perceptions of the senses be produced by external objects, resembling them: how shall this question be determined? By experience surely; as all other questions of a like nature. But here experience is, and must be entirely silent. The mind has never anything present to it but the perceptions, and cannot possibly reach any experience of their connexion with objects. The supposition of such a connexion is, therefore, without any foundation in reasoning.

Hume, *Concerning Human Understanding,* XII, 118–119

31 As we have no immediate experience of what other men feel, we can form no idea of the manner in which they are affected, but by conceiving what we ourselves should feel in the like situation. Though our brother is upon the rack, as long as we ourselves are at our ease, our senses will never inform us of what he suffers. They never did and never can carry us beyond our own person, and it is by the imagination only that we can form any conception of what are his sensations.

Adam Smith, *Theory of Moral Sentiments,* I, 1

32 In whatsoever mode, or by whatsoever means, our knowledge may relate to objects, it is at least quite clear that the only manner in which it immediately relates to them is by means of an intuition. To this as the indispensable groundwork, all thought points. But an intuition can take place only in so far as the object is given to us. This, again, is only possible, to man at least, on condition that the object affect the mind in a certain manner. The capacity for receiving representations (receptivity) through the mode in which we are affected by objects, is called *sensibility.* By means of sensibility, therefore, objects are given to us, and it alone furnishes us with intuitions; by the understanding they are *thought,* and from it arise conceptions. But all thought must directly, or indirectly, by means of certain signs, relate ultimately to intuitions; consequently, with us, to sensibility, because in no other way can an object be given to us.

The effect of an object upon the faculty of representation, so far as we are affected by the said object, is sensation. That sort of intuition which relates to an object by means of sensation is called an empirical intuition. The undetermined object of an empirical intuition is called *phenomenon.* That which in the phenomenon corresponds to the sensation, I term its *matter;* but that which effects that the content of the phenomenon can be arranged under certain relations, I call its *form.* But that in which our sensations are merely arranged, and by which they are susceptible of assuming a certain form, cannot be itself sensation. It is, then, the matter of all phenomena that is given to us *a posteriori;* the form must lie ready *a priori* for them in the mind, and consequently can be regarded separately from all sensation.

I call all representations *pure,* in the transcendental meaning of the word, wherein nothing is met with that belongs to sensation. And accordingly we find existing in the mind *a priori,* the pure form of sensuous intuitions in general, in which all the manifold content of the phenomenal world is arranged and viewed under certain relations. This pure form of sensibility I shall call *pure intuition.* Thus, if I take away from our representation of a body all that the understanding thinks as belonging to it, as substance, force, divisibility, etc., and also whatever belongs to sensation, as impenetrability, hardness, colour, etc.; yet there is still something left us from this empirical intuition, namely, extension and shape. These belong to pure intuition, which exists *a priori* in the mind, as a mere form of sensibility, and without any real object of the senses or any sensation.

Kant, *Critique of Pure Reason,*
Transcendental Aesthetic

33 In general, we receive impressions only in consequence of motion, and we might establish it as an axiom *that,* WITHOUT MOTION, THERE IS NO SENSATION. This general principle applies very accurately to the sensations of heat and cold: when we touch a cold body, the caloric which always tends to become *in equilibrio* in all bodies, passes from our hand into the body we touch, which gives us the feeling or sensation of cold. The direct contrary happens, when we touch a warm body, the caloric then passing from the body into our hand produces the sensation of heat. If the hand and the body touched be of the same temperature, or very nearly so, we receive no impression, either of heat or cold, because there is no motion or passage of caloric; and thus no sensation can take place without some correspondent motion to occasion it.

Lavoisier, *Elements of Chemistry,* I, 1

34 The eye—it cannot choose but see;
We cannot bid the ear be still;
Our bodies feel, where'er they be,
Against or with our will.

Wordsworth, *Expostulation and Reply*

35 O for a life of Sensations rather than of Thoughts!

Keats, *Letter to Benjamin Bailey*
(Nov. 22, 1817)

36 Only one absolute certainty is possible to man, namely, that at any given moment the feeling which he has exists.

T. H. Huxley, *Letter to J. G. T. Sinclair*
(July 21, 1890)

37 Are not the sensations we get from the same object, for example, always the same? Does not the same piano-key, struck with the same force, make us hear in the same way? Does not the same grass give us the same feeling of green, the same sky the same feeling of blue, and do we not get the same olfactory sensation no matter how many times we put our nose to the same flask of cologne? It seems a piece of metaphysical sophistry to suggest that we do not; and yet a close attention to the matter shows that *there is no proof that the same bodily sensation is ever got by us twice.*

What is got twice is the same OBJECT. We hear the same *note* over and over again; we see the same *quality* of green, or smell the same objective perfume, or experience the same *species* of pain. The realities, concrete and abstract, physical and ideal, whose permanent existence we believe in, seem to be constantly coming up again before our thought, and lead us, in our carelessness, to suppose that our "ideas" of them are the same ideas. When we come, some time later, to the chapter on Perception, we shall see how inveterate is our habit of not attending to sensations as subjective facts, but of simply using them as stepping-stones to pass over to the recognition of the realities whose presence they reveal. The grass out of the window now looks to me of the same green in the sun as in the shade, and yet a painter would have to paint one part of it dark brown, another part bright yellow, to give its real sensational effect. We take no heed, as a rule, of the different way in which the same things look and sound and smell at different distances and under different circumstances. The sameness of the *things* is what we are concerned to ascertain; and any sensations that assure us of that will probably be considered in a rough way to be the same with each other. This is what makes off-hand testimony about the subjective identity of different sensations well-nigh worthless as a proof of the fact. The entire history of Sensation is a commentary on our inability to tell whether two sensations received apart are exactly alike.

William James, *Psychology,* IX

38 Nature . . . is frugal in her operations, and will not be at the expense of a particular instinct to give us that knowledge which experience and habit will soon produce. Reproduced sights and contacts tied together with the present sensation

in the unity of a *thing* with a name, these are the complex objective stuff out of which my actually perceived table is made. Infants must go through a long education of the eye and ear before they can perceive the realities which adults perceive. *Every perception is an acquired perception.*

William James, *Psychology*, XIX

39 A sensation is rather like a client who has given his case to a lawyer and then has passively to listen in the courtroom to whatever account of his affairs, pleasant or unpleasant, the lawyer finds it most expedient to give.

William James, *Pragmatism*, VII

40 The state of becoming conscious is a special psychic act, different from and independent of the process of becoming fixed or represented, and consciousness appears to us as a sensory organ which perceives a content proceeding from another source.

Freud, *Interpretation of Dreams*, IV

5.3 | *Memory*

The two most famous metaphors that have been used to say what memory is—one, that it is the storehouse of ideas; the other, that it is decaying sense—may give us some grasp of the subject, but upon closer examination they are more misleading than instructive. Something must be experienced or learned before it can be remembered, and that which is remembered must somehow be retained between the time of acquisition and the time of recall or recollection; but after we have acknowledged these two points, we are left with many difficult questions about the objects of memory, about the kind of knowledge that memory is, about the difference between immediate memory and memory after a long interval of time, about the related processes of reminiscence, recollection, and recognition, about the gradual fading away of memories, and forgetfulness and forgetting.

The quotations collected here touch on all these matters as well as others, and represent the fascination of memory not only for psychologists and philosophers, but also for the poets and the historians, who are concerned with our sense of time and our knowledge of the past. That fascination is, perhaps, most eloquently expressed in the passages taken from Augustine's *Confessions*. The modern scientific and the psychoanalytical interest in the subject are represented here in the quotations from William James and Sigmund Freud.

1 Cebes added: Your favourite doctrine, Socrates, that knowledge is simply recollection, if true, also necessarily implies a previous time in which we have learned that which we now recollect. But this would be impossible unless our soul had been in some place before existing in the form of man; here then is another proof of the soul's immortality.

But tell me, Cebes, said Simmias, interposing, what arguments are urged in favour of this doctrine of recollection. I am not very sure at the moment that I remember them.

One excellent proof, said Cebes, is afforded by questions. If you put a question to a person in a right way, he will give a true answer of himself, but how could he do this unless there were knowledge and right reason already in him? And this is most clearly shown when he is taken to a diagram or to anything of that sort. . . .

And if we acquired this knowledge before we

were born, and were born having the use of it, then we also knew before we were born and at the instant of birth not only the equal or the greater or the less, but all other ideas; for we are not speaking only of equality, but of beauty, goodness, justice, holiness, and of all which we stamp with the name of essence in the dialectical process, both when we ask and when we answer questions. Of all this we may certainly affirm that we acquired the knowledge before birth?

We may.

But if, after having acquired, we have not forgotten what in each case we acquired, then we must always have come into life having knowledge, and shall always continue to know as long as life lasts—for knowing is the acquiring and retaining knowledge and not forgetting. Is not forgetting, Simmias, just the losing of knowledge?

Quite true, Socrates.

But if the knowledge which we acquired before birth was lost by us at birth, and if afterwards by the use of the senses we recovered what we previously knew, will not the process which we call learning be a recovering of the knowledge which is natural to us, and may not this be rightly termed recollection?

Very true.

So much is clear—that when we perceive something, either by the help of sight, or hearing, or some other sense, from that perception we are able to obtain a notion of some other thing like or unlike which is associated with it. but has been forgotten. Whence, as I was saying, one of two alternatives follows:—either we had this knowledge at birth, and continued to know through life; or, after birth, those who are said to learn only remember, and learning is simply recollection.

Plato, *Phaedo,*72B

2 *Socrates.* Tell me, then, whether I am right in saying that you may learn a thing which at one time you did not know?

Theaetetus. Certainly you may.

Soc. And another and another?

Theaet. Yes.

Soc. I would have you imagine, then, that there exists in the mind of man a block of wax, which is of different sizes in different men; harder, moister, and having more or less of purity in one than another, and in some of an intermediate quality.

Theaet. I see.

Soc. Let us say that this tablet is a gift of Memory, the mother of the Muses; and that when we wish to remember anything which we have seen, or heard, or thought in our own minds, we hold the wax to the perceptions and thoughts, and in that material receive the impression of them as from the seal of a ring; and that we remember and know what is imprinted as long as the image lasts; but when the image is effaced, or cannot be

taken, then we forget and do not know.

Plato, *Theaetetus,* 191A

3 Acts of recollection, as they occur in experience, are due to the fact that one movement has by nature another that succeeds it in regular order.

If this order be necessary, whenever a subject experiences the former of two movements thus connected, it will [invariably], experience the latter; if, however, the order be not necessary, but customary, only in the majority of cases will the subject experience the latter of the two movements. But it is a fact that there are some movements, by a single experience of which persons take the impress of custom more deeply than they do by experiencing others many times; hence upon seeing some things but once we remember them better than others which we may have seen frequently.

Whenever, therefore, we are recollecting, we are experiencing certain of the antecedent movements until finally we experience the one after which customarily comes that which we seek. This explains why we hunt up the series, having started in thought either from a present intuition or some other, and from something either similar, or contrary, to what we seek, or else from that which is contiguous with it. Such is the empirical ground of the process of recollection.

Aristotle, *Memory and Reminiscence,* 451ᵇ10

4 Many animals have memory, and are capable of instruction; but no other creature except man can recall the past at will.

Aristotle, *History of Animals,* 488ᵇ25

5 Men of fine genius are readily reminded of things, but those who receive with most pains and difficulty, remember best; every new thing they learn, being, as it were, burnt and branded in on their minds.

Plutarch, *Cato the Younger*

6 A memory has to do with something brought into ken from without, something learned or something experienced; the Memory-Principle, therefore, cannot belong to such beings as are immune from experience and from time.

No memory, therefore, can be ascribed to any divine being, or to the Authentic-Existent or the Intellectual-Principle: these are intangibly immune; time does not approach them; they possess eternity centred around Being; they know nothing of past and sequent; all is an unbroken state of identity, not receptive of change.

Plotinus, *Fourth Ennead,* III, 25

7 Memory, in point of fact, is impeded by the body: even as things are, addition often brings forgetfulness; with thinning and clearing away, memory will often revive. The soul is a stability; the shifting and fleeting thing which body is can be a

cause only of its forgetting not of its remembering—Lethe stream may be understood in this sense—and memory is a fact of the soul.

Plotinus, *Fourth Ennead,* III, 26

8 I shall mount beyond this power of my nature, still rising by degrees towards Him who made me. And so I come to the fields and vast palaces of memory, where are stored the innumerable images of material things brought to it by the senses. Further there is stored in the memory the thoughts we think, by adding to or taking from or otherwise modifying the things that sense has made contact with, and all other things that have been entrusted to and laid up in memory, save such as forgetfulness has swallowed in its grave. When I turn to memory, I ask it to bring forth what I want: and some things are produced immediately, some take longer as if they had to be brought out from some more secret place of storage; some pour out in a heap, and while we are actually wanting and looking for something quite different, they hurl themselves upon us in masses as though to say: "May it not be we that you want?" I brush them from the face of my memory with the hand of my heart, until at last the thing I want is brought to light as from some hidden place. Some things are produced just as they are required, easily and in right order; and things that come first give place to those that follow, and giving place are stored up again to be produced when I want them. This is what happens, when I say anything by heart.

In the memory all the various things are kept distinct and in their right categories, though each came into the memory by its own gate. For example, light and all the colors and shapes of bodies come in by the eyes, all the kinds of sound by the ears, all scents by the nostrils, all tastes by the mouth; and by a sense that belongs to the whole body comes in what is hard and what is soft, what is hot or cold, rough or smooth, heavy or light, whether outside the body or inside. All these things the vast recesses, the hidden and unsearchable caverns, of memory receive and store up, to be available and brought to light when need arises: yet all enter by their own various gates to be stored up in memory. Nor indeed do the things themselves enter: only the images of the things perceived by the senses are there for thought to remember them.

And even though we know by which senses they were brought in and laid up in the memory, who can tell how these images were formed? Even when I am in darkness and in silence, I can if I will produce colors in my memory, and distinguish black from white and any other colors if I choose; and sounds do not break in and disturb the image I am considering that came in through the eye, since the sounds themselves were already there and lie stored up apart. For I can summon

them too, if I like, and they are immediately present; and though my tongue is at rest and my throat silent I can sing as I will; nor do the images of the colors, although they are as truly present, interfere or interrupt when I call from the storehouse some other thing which came in by the ear. Similarly all other things that were brought in by the other senses and stored up in the memory can be called up at my pleasure: I distinguish the scent of lilies from the scent of violets, though at that instant I smell nothing; and I like honey better than wine, some smooth thing better than rough, though I am not tasting or handling but only remembering.

All this I do inside me, in the huge court of my memory. In my memory are sky and earth and sea, ready at hand along with all the things that I have ever been able to perceive in them and have not forgotten. And in my memory too I meet myself—I recall myself, what I have done, when and where and in what state of mind I was when I did it. In my memory are all the things I remember to have experienced myself or to have been told by others. From the same store I can weave into the past endless new likenesses of things either experienced by me or believed on the strength of things experienced; and from these again I can picture actions and events and hopes for the future; and upon them all I can meditate as if they were present. "I shall do this or that," I say to myself in the vast recess of my mind with its immeasurable store of images of things so great: and this or that follows. "O, if only this or that could be!" or again, "May God prevent this or that!" Such things I say within myself, and when I speak of them the images of all the things I mention are to hand from the same storehouse of memory, and if the images were not there I could not so much as speak of the things.

Great is this power of memory, exceedingly great, O my God, a spreading limitless room within me.

Augustine, *Confessions,* X, 8

9 Now when I hear that there are three kinds of questions: whether a thing is, what it is, of what sort it is: I do indeed retain the images of the sounds of which those words are composed, and I know that they passed through the air with a certain noise and now no longer are. But the things themselves which the sounds signified I could not come at by any bodily sense nor see them at all save by my mind; and what I stored in my memory was not their images but the truths themselves. But how they got into me, it is for them to tell if they can. For I run my mind over all the doorways of my body, but I cannot find any door by which they could have come in. For my eyes say: "If they were coloured, we reported them to you"; the nostrils say: "If they had any smell, they went in through us"; the sense of taste says: "Unless

there was any taste in them, there is no use in my being asked"; the sense of touch says: "If the thing is not a body, I did not handle it, and if I did not handle it, I did not report it to you." Very well then, whence and how did they get into my memory? I do not know. For when I first learned them I was not trusting some other man's mind, but recognized them in my own; and I saw them as true and committed them to my mind as if placing them where I could get at them again whenever I desired. Thus they must have been in my mind even before I learned them, though they were not in my memory. Then where were they, or how did it come that when I heard them spoken I recognized them and said: "It is so, it is true," unless they *were* in my memory already, but so far back, thrust away as it were in such remote recesses, that unless they had been drawn forth by some other man's teaching, I might perhaps never have managed to think of them at all?

Augustine, *Confessions*, X, 10

10 The memory also contains the innumerable principles and laws of numbers and dimensions; and none of these have been impressed upon it by any bodily sense, seeing that they have neither colour nor sound nor scent nor taste nor feel. I have heard the sounds of the words by which they are expressed when we discuss them, but the sounds are not the same as the truths themselves. For the sounds are of one kind in Greek, quite different in Latin, but the things themselves are neither Greek nor Latin nor of any other language. I have seen the lines drawn by architects, some of them as fine as a spider's web; but the truths are different, they are not the images of such things as the eye of my body has shown me. To know them is to recognize them interiorly without any concept of any kind of body whatsoever. With all my bodily senses I have perceived the numbers we use in counting; but the basic numbers *by* which we count are not the same as these, nor images of these; but really are. Let whoever does not see these truths laugh at me for talking thus: while he laughs at me I shall be sorry for him.

Augustine, *Confessions*, X, 12

11 Assuredly, Lord, I toil with this, toil within myself: I have become to myself a soil laborious and of heavy sweat. For I am not now considering the parts of the heavens, or measuring the distances of the stars, or seeking how the earth is held in space; it is I who remember, I, my mind. It is not remarkable if things that I am not are far from my knowledge: but what could be closer to me than myself? Yet the power of memory in me I do not understand, though without memory I could not even name myself.

Augustine, *Confessions*, X, 16

12 For memory sets before us, not what we choose, but what it pleases. Indeed there is nothing that imprints a thing so vividly on our memory as the desire to forget it: a good way to give our mind something to guard, and to impress it on her, is to solicit her to lose it.

Montaigne, *Essays*, II, 12, Apology for Raymond Sebond

13 If souls came from anything but a natural succession, and had been something else outside of the body, they would have a memory of their first existence, considering the natural faculties that are proper to them, of reflecting, reasoning, and remembering. . . .

For to value the condition of our souls as highly as we want to, we must presuppose them to be wholly knowing when they are in their natural simplicity and purity. Thus they would have been such, being free from the corporeal prison, as much before entering it as we hope they will be after they have gone out of it. And this knowledge they would have to remember still while in the body, as Plato said that what we learned was only a recollection of what we had known; a thing which each man by experience can maintain to be false. In the first place, because we recollect only precisely what we are taught, and if memory were doing its job purely, it would at least suggest to us some point beyond what we have learned. Second, what it knew when it was in its purity was a real knowledge, by its divine intelligence understanding things as they are, whereas here it is made to receive falsehood and vice, if it is instructed about them. In this it cannot use its power of reminiscence, this idea and conception never having lodged in it.

Montaigne, *Essays*, II, 12, Apology for Raymond Sebond

14 When to the sessions of sweet silent thought
I summon up remembrance of things past,
I sigh the lack of many a thing I sought,
And with old woes new wail my dear time's waste.
Then can I drown an eye, unused to flow,
For precious friends hid in death's dateless night,
And weep afresh love's long since cancell'd woe,
And moan the expense of many a vanish'd sight.

Shakespeare, *Sonnet XXX*

15 I make no more estimation of repeating a great number of names or words upon once hearing, or the pouring forth of a number of verses or rhymes *ex tempore*, or the making of a satirical simile of everything, or the turning of everything to a jest, or the falsifying or contradicting of everything by cavil, or the like (whereof in the faculties of the mind there is great copie, and such as by device and practice may be exalted to an extreme degree of wonder), than I do of the tricks of tumblers, funambuloes, baladines; the one being the same in the mind that the other is in the body, matters

of strangeness without worthiness.

Bacon, *Advancement of Learning,* Bk. II, XV, 2

16 Let the required nature be memory, or that which excites and assists memory. The constitutive instances are order or distribution, which manifestly assists memory; topics or common-places in artificial memory, which may be either places in their literal sense, as a gate, a corner, a window, and the like, or familiar persons and marks, or anything else (provided it be arranged in a determinate order), as animals, plants, and words, letters, characters, historical persons, and the like, of which, however, some are more convenient than others. All these common-places materially assist memory, and raise it far above its natural strength. Verse, too, is recollected and learnt more easily than prose. From this group of three instances—order, the common-places of artificial memory, and verses—is constituted one species of aid for the memory, which may be well termed a separation from infinity. For when a man strives to recollect or recall anything to memory, without a preconceived notion or perception of the object of his search, he inquires about, and labors, and turns from point to point, as if involved in infinity. But if he have any preconceived notion, this infinity is separated off, and the range of his memory is brought within closer limits. In the three instances given above, the preconceived notion is clear and determined. In the first, it must be something that agrees with order; in the second, an image which has some relation or agreement with the fixed common-places; in the third, words which fall into a verse: and thus infinity is divided off. Other instances will offer another species, namely, that whatever brings the intellect into contact with something that strikes the sense (the principal point of artificial memory), assists the memory. Others again offer another species, namely, whatever excites an impression by any powerful passion, as fear, wonder, shame, delight, assists the memory. Other instances will afford another species: thus those impressions remain most fixed in the memory which are taken from the mind when clear and least occupied by preceding or succeeding notions, such as the things we learn in childhood, or imagine before sleep, and the first time of any circumstance happening.

Bacon, *Novum Organum,* II, 26

17 The things perceived by sense remain in some animals; in others they do not remain. Those in whom they do not remain, however, have either no knowledge at all, or at least none beyond the simple perception of the things which do not remain; others, again, when they perceive, retain a certain something in their soul. Now, as there are many animals of this description, there is already a distinction between one animal and another; and to this extent, that in some there is reason

from the memory of things; and in others there is none. Memory, therefore, as is said, follows from sense; but from repeated recollection of the same thing springs experience (for repeated acts of memory constitute a single experience). . . .

Wherefore . . . there is no perfect knowledge which can be entitled ours, that is innate; none but what has been obtained from experience, or derived in some way from our senses; all knowledge, at all events, is examined by these, approved by them, and finally presents itself to us firmly grounded upon some preëxisting knowledge which we possessed: because without memory there is no experience, which is nothing else than reiterated memory; in like manner memory cannot exist without endurance of the things perceived, and the thing perceived cannot remain where it has never been.

William Harvey, *Animal Generation,* Intro.

18 Sometimes a man seeks what he hath lost; and from that place, and time, wherein he misses it, his mind runs back, from place to place, and time to time, to find where and when he had it; that is to say, to find some certain and limited time and place in which to begin a method of seeking. Again, from thence, his thoughts run over the same places and times to find what action or other occasion might make him lose it. This we call *remembrance,* or calling to mind.

Hobbes, *Leviathan,* I, 3

19 Time and Education begets experience; Experience begets Memory; Memory begets Judgment and Fancy: Judgment begets the strength and structure, and Fancy begets the ornaments of a Poem. The Ancients therefore fabled not absurdly, in making memory the mother of the Muses. For memory is the World (though not really, yet so as in a looking glass) in which the Judgment (the severer sister) busieth herself in a grave and rigid examination of all the parts of Nature, and in registring by Letters, their order, causes, uses, differences, and resemblances; Whereby the Fancy, when any work of Art is to be performed, findeth her materials at hand and prepared for use, and needs no more than a swift motion over them, that what she wants, and is there to be had, may not lye too long unspied. So that when she seemeth to fly from one Indies to the other, and from Heaven to Earth, and to penetrate into the hardest matter, and obscurest places, into the future and into her self, and all this in a point of time; the voyage is not very great, her self being all she seeks; and her wonderful celerity, consisteth not so much in motion, as in copious Imagery discreetly ordered, and perfectly registred in the memory.

Hobbes, *Answer to Sir Will. D'Avenant's Preface Before Gondibert*

20 But the iniquity of oblivion blindly scattereth her

poppy, and deals with the memory of men without distinction to merit of perpetuity. . . . Who knows whether the best of men be known, or whether there be not more remarkable persons forgot than any that stand remembered in the known account of time?

Sir Thomas Browne, *Urn-Burial*, V

21 Memory . . . is nothing else than a certain concatenation of ideas, involving the nature of things which are outside the human body, a concatenation which corresponds in the mind to the order and concatenation of the affections of the human body. I say, firstly, that it is a concatenation of those ideas only which involve the nature of things which are outside the human body, and not of those ideas which explain the nature of those things, for there are in truth ideas of the affections of the human body, which involve its nature as well as the nature of external bodies. I say, in the second place, that this concatenation takes place according to the order and concatenation of the affections of the human body, that I may distinguish it from the concatenation of ideas which takes place according to the order of the intellect, and enables the mind to perceive things through their first causes, and is the same in all men. Hence we can clearly understand how it is that the mind from the thought of one thing at once turns to the thought of another thing which is not in any way like the first. . . . In this manner each person will turn from one thought to another according to the manner in which the habit of each has arranged the images of things in the body. The soldier, for instance, if he sees the footsteps of a horse in the sand, will immediately turn from the thought of a horse to the thought of a horseman, and so to the thought of war. The countryman, on the other hand, from the thought of a horse will turn to the thought of his plough, his field, etc.; and thus each person will turn from one thought to this or that thought, according to the manner in which he has been accustomed to connect and bind together the images of things in his mind.

Spinoza, *Ethics*, II, Prop. 18, Schol.

22 Retention is the power to revive again in our minds those ideas which, after imprinting, have disappeared, or have been as it were laid aside out of sight. And thus we do, when we conceive heat or light, yellow or sweet,—the object being removed. This is *memory*, which is as it were the store-house of our ideas. For, the narrow mind of man not being capable of having many ideas under view and consideration at once, it was necessary to have a repository, to lay up those ideas which, at another time, it might have use of. But, our *ideas* being nothing but actual perceptions in the mind, which cease to be anything when there is no perception of them; this laying up of our

ideas in the repository of the memory signifies no more but this,—that the mind has a power in many cases to revive perceptions which it has once had, with this additional perception annexed to them, that *it has had them before*. And in this sense it is that our ideas are said to be in our memories, when indeed they are actually nowhere;—but only there is an ability in the mind when it will to revive them again, and as it were paint them anew on itself, though some with more, some with less difficulty; some more lively, and others more obscurely. And thus it is, by the assistance of this faculty, that we are said to have all those ideas in our understandings which, though we do not actually contemplate, yet we *can* bring in sight, and make appear again, and be the objects of our thoughts, without the help of those sensible qualities which first imprinted them there.

Locke, *Concerning Human Understanding*, Bk. II, X, 2

23 The memory of some men, it is true, is very tenacious, even to a miracle. But yet there seems to be a constant decay of all our ideas, even of those which are struck deepest, and in minds the most retentive; so that if they be not sometimes renewed, by repeated exercise of the senses, or reflection on those kinds of objects which at first occasioned them, the print wears out, and at last there remains nothing to be seen. Thus the ideas, as well as children, of our youth, often die before us: and our minds represent to us those tombs to which we are approaching; where, though the brass and marble remain, yet the inscriptions are effaced by time, and the imagery moulders away. The pictures drawn in our minds are laid in fading colours; and if not sometimes refreshed, vanish and disappear. How much the constitution of our bodies and the make of our animal spirits are concerned in this; and whether the temper of the brain makes this difference, that in some it retains the characters drawn on it like marble, in others like freestone, and in others little better than sand, I shall not here inquire; though it may seem probable that the constitution of the body does sometimes influence the memory, since we oftentimes find a disease quite strip the mind of all its ideas, and the flames of a fever in a few days calcine all those images to dust and confusion, which seemed to be as lasting as if graved in marble.

Locke, *Concerning Human Understanding*, Bk. II, X, 5

24 Music, when soft voices die,
Vibrates in the memory;
Odors, when sweet violets sicken,
Live within the sense they quicken.

Rose leaves, when the rose is dead,
Are heaped for the belovèd's bed;

And so thy thoughts, when thou art gone,
Love itself shall slumber on.

Shelley, *To—*

25 Blessed are the forgetful: for they get over their stupidities, too.

Nietzsche, *Beyond Good and Evil,* VII, 217

26 Try . . . to symbolize what goes on in a man who is racking his brains to remember a thought which occurred to him last week. The associates of the thought are there, many of them at least, but they refuse to awaken the thought itself. We cannot suppose that they do not irradiate *at all* into its brain-tract, because his mind quivers on the very edge of its recovery. Its actual rhythm sounds in his ears; the words seem on the imminent point of following, but fail. What it is that blocks the discharge and keeps the brain-excitement here from passing beyond the nascent into the vivid state cannot be guessed. But we see in the philosophy of desire and pleasure, that such nascent excitements, spontaneously tending to a crescendo, but inhibited or checked by other causes, may become potent mental stimuli and determinants of desire. All questioning, wonder, emotion of curiosity, must be referred to cerebral causes of some such form as this. The great difference between the effort to recall things forgotten and the search after the means to a given end, is that the latter have not, whilst the former have, already formed a part of our experience. . . .

The forgotten thing is felt by us as a gap in the midst of certain other things. If it is a thought, we possess a dim idea of where we were and what we were about when it occurred to us. We recollect the general subject to which it relates. But all these details refuse to shoot together into a solid whole, for the lack of the vivid traits of this missing thought, the relation whereof to each detail forms now the main interest of the latter. We keep running over the details in our mind, dissatisfied, craving something more. From each detail there radiate lines of association forming so many tentative guesses. Many of these are immediately seen to be irrelevant, are therefore void of interest, and lapse immediately from consciousness. Others are associated with the other details present, and with the missing thought as well. When *these* surge up, we have a peculiar feeling that we are "warm," as the children say when they play hide and seek; and such associates as these we clutch at and keep before the attention. Thus we recollect successively that when we had the thought in question we were at the dinner-table; then that our friend J. D. was there; then that the subject talked about was so and so; finally, that the thought came *à propos* of a certain anecdote, and then that it had something to do with a French quotation. Now all these added associations *arise independently of the will,* by the spontaneous process we know so well.

All that the will does is to emphasize and linger over those which seem pertinent, and ignore the rest. Through this hovering of the attention in the neighborhood of the desired object, the accumulation of associates becomes so great that the combined tensions of their neural processes break through the bar, and the nervous wave pours into the tract which has so long been awaiting its advent. And as the expectant, sub-conscious itching there, bursts into the fulness of vivid feeling, the mind finds an inexpressible relief.

William James, *Psychology,* XIV

27 The stream of thought flows on; but most of its segments fall into the bottomless abyss of oblivion. Of some, no memory survives the instant of their passage. Of others, it is confined to a few moments, hours, or days. Others, again, leave vestiges which are indestructible, and by means of which they may be recalled as long as life endures.

William James, *Psychology,* XVI

28 Memory proper, or secondary memory as it might be styled, is the knowledge of a former state of mind after it has already once dropped from consciousness; or rather *it is the knowledge of an event, or fact,* of which meantime we have not been thinking, *with the additional consciousness that we have thought or experienced it before.*

The first element which such a knowledge involves would seem to be the revival in the mind of an image or copy of the original event. And it is an assumption made by many writers that the revival of an image is all that is needed to constitute the memory of the original occurrence. But such a revival is obviously not a *memory,* whatever else it may be; it is simply a duplicate, a second event, having absolutely no connection with the first event except that it happens to resemble it. The clock strikes to-day; it struck yesterday; and may strike a million times ere it wears out. The rain pours through the gutter this week; it did so last week; and will do so *in soecula soeculorum.* But does the present clock-stroke become aware of the past ones, or the present stream recollect the past stream, because they repeat and resemble them? Assuredly not. . . . No memory is involved in the mere fact of recurrence. The successive editions of a feeling are so many independent events, each snug in its own skin. Yesterday's feeling is dead and buried; and the presence of to-day's is no reason why it should resuscitate. A farther condition is required before the present image can be held to stand for a *past original.*

That condition is that the fact imaged be *expressly referred to the past,* thought as *in the past.* But how can we think a thing as in the past, except by thinking of the past together with the thing, and of the relation of the two? And how can we think of the past? In the chapter on Time-perception we have seen that our intuitive or immediate consciousness of pastness hardly carries us more than a few seconds backward of the present instant of time. Remoter dates are conceived, not perceived; known symbolically by names, such as "last week," "1850"; or thought of by events which happened in them, as the year in which we attended such a school, or met with such a loss.—So that if we wish to think of a particular past epoch, we must think of a name or other symbol, or else of certain concrete events, associated therewithal. Both must be thought of, to think the past epoch adequately. And to "refer" any special fact to the past epoch is to think that fact *with* the names and events which characterize its date, to think it, in short, with a lot of contiguous associates.

But even this would not be memory. Memory requires more than mere dating of a fact in the past. It must be dated in *my* past. In other words, I must think that I directly experienced its occurrence. It must have that "warmth and intimacy" which . . . characteriz[es] all experiences "appropriated" by the thinker as his own.

William James, *Psychology,* XVI

29 In the practical use of our intellect, forgetting is as important a function as recollecting. . . .

This peculiar mixture of forgetting with our remembering is but one instance of our mind's selective activity. Selection is the very keel on which our mental ship is built. And in this case of memory its utility is obvious. If we remembered everything, we should on most occasions be as ill off as if we remembered nothing. It would take as long for us to recall a space of time as it took the original time to elapse, and we should never get ahead with our thinking. All recollected times undergo, accordingly, what M. Ribot calls foreshortening; and this foreshortening is due to the omission of an enormous number of the facts which filled them.

William James, *Psychology,* XVI

30 In human experience, the most compelling example of non-sensuous perception is our knowledge of our own immediate past. I am not referring to our memories of a day past, or of an hour past, or of a minute past. Such memories are blurred and confused by the intervening occasions of our personal existence. But our immediate past is constituted by that occasion, or by that group of fused occasions, which enters into experience devoid of any perceptible medium intervening between it and the present immediate fact. Roughly speaking, it is that portion of our past lying between a tenth of a second and half a second ago. It is gone, and yet it is here. It is our indubitable self, the foundation of our present existence. Yet the present occasion while claiming self-identity, while sharing the very nature of the byegone occasion in all its living activities, nevertheless is engaged in

modifying it, in adjusting it to *other* influences, in completing it with *other* values, in deflecting it to *other* purposes. The present moment is constituted by the influx of *the other* into that self-identity which is the continued life of the immediate past within the immediacy of the present.

Whitehead, *Adventures of Ideas,* XI, 12

31 Memory is the purest example of mirror knowledge. When I remember a piece of music or a friend's face, my state of mind resembles, though with a difference, what it was when I heard the music or saw the face. If I have sufficient skill, I can play the music or paint the face from memory, and then compare my playing or painting with the original, or rather with something which I have reason to believe closely similar to the original. But we trust our memory, up to a point, even if it does not pass this test. If our friend appears with a black eye, we say, "How did you get that injury?" not "I had forgotten that you had a black eye." The tests of memory, as we have already had occasion to notice, are only confirmations; a considerable degree of credibility attaches to a memory on its own account, particularly if it is vivid and recent.

A memory is accurate, not in proportion to the help it gives in handling present and future facts, but in proportion to its resemblance to a past fact. When Herbert Spencer, after fifty years, saw again the lady he had loved as a young man, whom he had imagined still young, it was the very accuracy of his memory which incapacitated him from handling the present fact. In regard to memory, the definition of "truth," and therefore of "knowledge," lies in the resemblance of present imagining to past sensible experience. Capacity for handling present and future facts may be confirmatory in certain circumstances, but can never *define* what we mean when we say that a certain memory is "knowledge."

Russell, *Human Knowledge,* VI, 1

32 When I had reached in my procedure with [my patients] a point at which they declared that they knew nothing more, I would assure them that they did know, that they must just tell it out, and I would venture the assertion that the memory which would emerge at the moment that I laid my hand on the patient's forehead would be the right one. In this way I succeeded, without hypnosis, in learning from the patient all that was necessary for a construction of the connection between the forgotten pathogenic scenes and the symptoms which they had left behind. This was a troublesome and in its length an exhausting proceeding, and did not lend itself to a finished technique. But I did not give it up without drawing definite conclusions from the data which I had gained. I had substantiated the fact that the forgotten memories were not lost. They were in the possession of the

patient, ready to emerge and form associations with his other mental content, but hindered from becoming conscious, and forced to remain in the unconscious by some sort of a force. The existence of this force could be assumed with certainty, for in attempting to drag up the unconscious memories into the consciousness of the patient, in opposition to this force, one got the sensation of his own personal effort striving to overcome it. One could get an idea of this force, which maintained the pathological situation, from the resistance of the patient.

It is on this idea of *resistance* that I based my theory of the psychic processes of hystericals. It had been found that in order to cure the patient it was necessary that this force should be overcome. Now with the mechanism of the cure as a starting point, quite a definite theory could be constructed. These same forces, which in the present situation as resistances opposed the emergence of the forgotten ideas into consciousness, must themselves have caused the forgetting, and repressed from consciousness the pathogenic experiences. I called this hypothetical process *repression* and considered that it was proved by the undeniable existence of resistance.

Freud, *Origin and Development of Psycho-Analysis*, II

33 It is quite true that the unconscious wishes are always active. They represent paths which are always practicable, whenever a quantum of excitation makes use of them. It is indeed an outstanding peculiarity of the unconscious processes that they are indestructible. Nothing can be brought to an end in the unconscious; nothing is past or forgotten. . . . Indeed, the fading of memories and the weak affect of impressions which are no longer recent, which we are apt to take as self-evident, and to explain as a primary effect of time on our psychic memory-residues, are in reality secondary changes brought about by laborious work.

Freud, *Interpretation of Dreams*, VII, D

34 The process of repression is not to be regarded as something which takes place once for all, the results of which are permanent, as when some living thing has been killed and from that time onward is dead; on the contrary, repression demands a constant expenditure of energy, and if this were discontinued the success of the repression would be jeopardized, so that a fresh act of repression would be necessary. We may imagine that what is repressed exercises a continuous straining in the direction of consciousness, so that the balance has to be kept by means of a steady counter-pressure. A constant expenditure of energy, therefore, is entailed in maintaining a repression, and economically its abrogation denotes a saving.

Freud, *Repression*

5.4 | *Imagination*

Imagination is the faculty of poetry and fiction—of imaginative literature in all its forms. The poets express their appreciation of its resources and of its gifts. Fancy and fantasy not only create realms that cannot be explored by sense; imagination also exercises a magic touch on sensible reality, reshaping and enlivening it in a variety of ways.

Imagination like memory is thought of by the philosophers and psychologists as a residue or by-product of sense and sense perception. Yet the products of imagination often go beyond the world of things perceived and remembered. The fictions or constructions of the imagination—such as mermaids, centaurs, unicorns, and golden mountains—may involve elements derived from sense perception, but they also represent compositions that have never been experienced. What mode of being, if any, is possessed by such objects of imagination? Or, for that matter, by the imaginary persons who are the characters in plays and novels?

The word "ideas" is used by some writers—Hume, for example—for the images that are derived from sense impressions. Other writers make a sharp distinction between images or phantasms—the products of imagination—and ideas or concepts which are the elements of thought and are attributed to the mind or intellect rather than to the imagination. When images and ideas or concepts are distinguished, problems arise concerning their inter-dependence. Can we conceive things that we cannot imagine? Is there a difference between the unimaginable and the inconceivable?

For the discussion of related matters, the reader is referred to Section 6.2 on EXPERIENCE, and to Section 16.3 on POETRY AND POETS; and also to Section 5.1 on INTELLIGENCE AND UNDERSTANDING.

---

1 Imagination is different from either perceiving or discursive thinking, though it is not found without sensation, or judgement without it. That this activity is not the same kind of thinking as judgement is obvious. For imagining lies within our own power whenever we wish (e.g. we can call up a picture, as in the practice of mnemonics by the use of mental images), but in forming opinions we are not free: we cannot escape the alternative of falsehood or truth. Further, when we think something to be fearful or threatening, emotion is immediately produced, and so too with what is encouraging; but when we merely imagine we remain as unaffected as persons who are looking at a painting of some dreadful or encouraging scene. Again within the field of judgement itself we find varieties—knowledge, opinion, prudence, and their opposites; of the differences between these I must speak elsewhere.

Thinking is different from perceiving and is held to be in part imagination, in part judgement: we must therefore first mark off the sphere of imagination and then speak of judgement. If then imagination is that in virtue of which an image arises for us, excluding metaphorical uses of the term, is it a single faculty or disposition relative to images, in virtue of which we discriminate and are either in error or not? The faculties in virtue of which we do this are sense, opinion, science, intelligence.

That imagination is not sense is clear from the following considerations: Sense is either a faculty or an activity, e.g. sight or seeing: imagination takes place in the absence of both, as e.g. in dreams. (2) Again, sense is always present, imagination not. If actual imagination and actual sensation were the same, imagination would be found in all the brutes: this is held not to be the case; e.g. it is not found in ants or bees or grubs. (3) Again, sensations are always true, imaginations are for the most part false. (4) Once more, even in ordinary speech, we do not, when sense functions precisely with regard to its object, say that we imagine it to be a man, but rather when there is some failure of accuracy in its exercise. And (5),

as we were saying before, visions appear to us even when our eyes are shut. Neither is imagination *any* of the things that are never in error: e.g. knowledge or intelligence; for imagination may be false.

It remains therefore to see if it is opinion, for opinion may be either true or false.

But opinion involves belief (for without belief in what we opine we cannot have an opinion), and in the brutes though we often find imagination we never find belief. Further, every opinion is accompanied by belief, belief by conviction, and conviction by discourse of reason: while there are some of the brutes in which we find imagination, without discourse of reason. It is clear then that imagination cannot, again, be (1) opinion *plus* sensation, or (2) opinion mediated by sensation, or (3) a blend of opinion and sensation; this is impossible both for these reasons and because the content of the supposed opinion cannot be different from that of the sensation (I mean that imagination must be the blending of the perception of white with the opinion that it is white: it could scarcely be a blend of the opinion that it is good with the perception that it is white): to imagine is therefore (on this view) identical with the thinking of exactly the same as what one in the strictest sense perceives. But what we imagine is sometimes false though our contemporaneous judgement about it is true; e.g. we imagine the sun to be a foot in diameter though we are convinced that it is larger than the inhabited part of the earth, and the following dilemma presents itself. Either (*a*) while the fact has not changed and the observer has neither forgotten nor lost belief in the true opinion which he had, that opinion has disappeared, or (*b*) if he retains it then his opinion is at once true and false. A true opinion, however, becomes false only when the fact alters without being noticed.

Imagination is therefore neither any one of the states enumerated, nor compounded out of them.

But since when one thing has been set in motion another thing may be moved by it, and imagination is held to be a movement and to be impossible without sensation, i.e. to occur in beings that are percipient and to have for its content what can be perceived, and since movement may be produced by actual sensation and that movement is necessarily similar in character to the sensation itself, this movement must be (1) necessarily (*a*) incapable of existing apart from sensation, (*b*) incapable of existing except when we perceive, (2) such that in virtue of its possession that in which it is found may present various phenomena both active and passive, and (3) such that it may be either true or false.

The reason of the last characteristic is as follows. Perception (1) of the special objects of sense is never in error or admits the least possible amount of falsehood. (2) That of the concomitance of the objects concomitant with the sensible qualities comes next: in this case certainly we may be deceived; for while the perception that there is white before us cannot be false, the perception that what is white is this or that may be false. (3) Third comes the perception of the universal attributes which accompany the concomitant objects to which the special sensibles attach (I mean e.g. of movement and magnitude); it is in respect of these that the greatest amount of sense-illusion is possible.

The motion which is due to the activity of sense in these three modes of its exercise will differ from the activity of sense; (1) the first kind of derived motion is free from error while the sensation is present; (2) and (3) the others may be erroneous whether it is present or absent, especially when the object of perception is far off. If then imagination presents no other features than those enumerated and is what we have described, then imagination must be a movement resulting from an actual exercise of a power of sense.

As sight is the most highly developed sense . . . imagination has been formed from light because it is not possible to see without light.

And because imaginations remain in the organs of sense and resemble sensations, animals in their actions are largely guided by them, some (i.e. the brutes) because of the non-existence in them of mind, others (i.e. men) because of the temporary eclipse in them of mind by feeling or disease or sleep.

About imagination, what it is and why it exists, let so much suffice.

Aristotle, *On the Soul*, 427^{b}14

2 And now that I have taught what the nature of the mind is and out of what things it is formed into one quickened being with the body, and how it is dissevered and returns into its first-beginnings, I will attempt to lay before you a truth which most nearly concerns these questions, the existence of things which we call idols of things: these, like films peeled off from the surface of things, fly to and fro through the air, and do likewise frighten our minds when they present themselves to us awake as well as in sleep, what time we behold strange shapes and idols of the light-bereaved, which have often startled us in appalling wise as we lay relaxed in sleep: this I will essay, that we may not haply believe that souls break loose from Acheron or that shades fly about among the living or that something of us is left behind after death, when the body and the nature of the mind destroyed together have taken their departure into their several first-beginnings.

Lucretius, *Nature of Things*, IV

3 In the present state of life in which the soul is united to a passible body, it is impossible for our intellect to understand anything actually except by turning to the phantasms. And of this there are two indications. First of all because the intellect, being a power that does not make use of a corporeal organ, would in no way be hindered in its act through the lesion of a corporeal organ if for its act there were not required the act of some power that does make use of a corporeal organ. Now sense, imagination and the other powers belonging to the sensitive part, make use of a corporeal organ. Therefore it is clear that for the intellect to understand actually, not only when it acquires fresh knowledge, but also when it uses knowledge already acquired, there is need for the act of the imagination and of the other powers. For when the act of the imagination is hindered by a lesion of the corporeal organ, for instance, in a case of frenzy, or when the act of the memory is hindered, as in the case of lethargy, we see that a man is hindered from actually understanding things of which he had a previous knowledge. Secondly, anyone can experience this of himself, that when he tries to understand something, he forms certain phantasms to serve him by way of examples, in which as it were he examines what he is striving to understand. It is for this reason that when we wish to make someone understand something, we lay examples before him, from which he can form phantasms for the purpose of understanding.

Now the reason of this is that the power of knowledge is proportioned to the thing known. Thus . . . the proper object of the human intellect, which is united to a body, is a quiddity or nature existing in corporeal matter, and through such natures of visible things it rises even to some knowledge of things invisible. Now it belongs to such a nature to exist in an individual, and this cannot be apart from corporeal matter. . . . And so the nature of a stone or any material thing cannot be known completely and truly, except according as it is known as existing in the individual. Now we apprehend the individual through the senses and the imagination. And, therefore, for the intellect to understand actually its proper object, it must of necessity turn to the phantasms in order to examine the universal nature existing in the individual.

Aquinas, *Summa Theologica*, I, 84, 7

4 O fantasy, that at times dost so snatch us out of ourselves that we are conscious of naught, even though a thousand trumpets sound about us, who moves thee, if the senses set naught before thee? A light moves thee which takes its form in heaven, of itself, or by a will that sendeth it down.

Dante, *Purgatorio*, XVII, 13

5 And I, who to the goal of all my longings was drawing nigh, even as was meet the ardour of the yearning quenched within me.
Bernard gave me the sign and smiled to me that I should look on high, but I already of myself was such as he would have me;
because my sight, becoming purged, now more and more was entering through the ray of the deep light which in itself is true.
Thenceforward was my vision mightier than our discourse, which faileth at such sight, and faileth memory at so great outrage.
As is he who dreaming seeth, and when the dream is gone the passion stamped remaineth, and naught else cometh to the mind again;
even such am I; for almost wholly faileth me my vision, yet doth the sweetness that was born of it still drop within my heart.
So doth the snow unstamp it to the sun, so to the wind on the light leaves was lost the Sibyl's wisdom.

Dante, *Paradiso*, XXXIII, 46

6 So it is with minds. Unless you keep them busy with some definite subject that will bridle and control them, they throw themselves in disorder hither and yon in the vague field of imagination. . . . And there is no mad or idle fancy that they do not bring forth in this agitation.

Montaigne, *Essays*, I, 8, Of Idleness

7 How many men have been made sick by the mere power of imagination?

Montaigne, *Essays*, II, 12, Apology for Raymond Sebond

8 *Holofernes.* This is a gift that I have, simple, simple; a foolish extravagant spirit, full of forms, figures, shapes, objects, ideas, apprehensions, motions, revolutions: these are begot in the ventricle of memory, nourished in the womb of *pia mater*, and delivered upon the mellowing of occasion.

Shakespeare, *Love's Labour's Lost*, IV, ii, 67

9 *Theseus.* Such tricks hath strong imagination,
That, if it would but apprehend some joy,
It comprehends some bringer of that joy;
Or in the night, imagining some fear,

How easy is a bush supposed a bear!

Shakespeare, *Midsummer-Night's Dream*, V, i, 18

10 Tell me where is fancy bred,
Or in the heart or in the head?
How begot, how nourished?
    Reply, reply.
It is engender'd in the eyes,
With gazing fed; and fancy dies
In the cradle where it lies.
    Let us all ring fancy's knell:
    I'll begin it—Ding, dong, bell.

Shakespeare, *Merchant of Venice*, III, ii, 63

11 *Chorus.* O for a Muse of fire, that would ascend
The brightest heaven of invention
A kingdom for a stage, princes to act
And monarchs to behold the swelling scene!
Then should the warlike Harry, like himself,
Assume the port of Mars; and at his heels,
Leash'd in like hounds, should famine, sword, and fire
Crouch for employment. But pardon, gentles all,
The flat unraised spirits that have dared
On this unworthy scaffold to bring forth
So great an object: can this cockpit hold
The vasty fields of France? or may we cram
Within this wooden O the very casques
That did affright the air at Agincourt?
O, pardon! since a crooked figure may
Attest in little place a million;
And let us, ciphers to this great accompt,
On your imaginary forces work.
Suppose within the girdle of these walls
Are now confined two mighty monarchies,
Whose high upreared and abutting fronts
The perilous narrow ocean parts asunder:
Piece out our imperfections with your thoughts;
Into a thousand parts divide one man,
And make imaginary puissance;
Think, when we talk of horses, that you see them
Printing their proud hoofs i' the receiving earth;
For 'tis your thoughts that now must deck our kings,
Carry them here and there; jumping o'er times,
Turning the accomplishment of many years
Into an hour-glass: for the which supply,
Admit me Chorus to this history.

Shakespeare, *Henry V*, Prologue

12 *Chorus.* Thus with imagined wing our swift scene flies
In motion of no less celerity
Than that of thought. Suppose that you have seen
The well-appointed king at Hampton pier
Embark his royalty; and his brave fleet
With silken streamers the young Phœbus fanning:
Play with your fancies, and in them behold
Upon the hempen tackle ship-boys climbing;
Hear the shrill whistle which doth order give
To sounds confused; behold the threaden sails,

Borne with the invisible and creeping wind,
Draw the huge bottoms through the furrow'd sea,
Breasting the lofty surge: O, do but think
You stand upon the rivage and behold
A city on the inconstant billows dancing;
For so appears this fleet majestical,
Holding due course to Harfleur. Follow, follow:
Grapple your minds to sternage of this navy,
And leave your England, as dead midnight still,
Guarded with grandsires, babies, and old women
Either past or not arrived to pith and puissance;
For who is he, whose chin is but enrich'd
With one appearing hair, that will not follow
These cull'd and choice-drawn cavaliers to
     France?
Work, work your thoughts, and therein see a
     siege;
Behold the ordnance on their carriages,
With fatal mouths gaping on girded Harfleur.
Suppose the ambassador from the French comes
     back;
Tells Harry that the King doth offer him
Katharine his daughter, and with her, to dowry,
Some petty and unprofitable dukedoms.
The offer likes not: and the nimble gunner
With linstock now the devilish cannon touches,
     Alarum, and chambers go off.
And down goes all before them. Still be kind,
And eke out our performance with your mind.

          Shakespeare, *Henry V,* III, Prologue

13 *Macbeth.*   Why do I yield to that suggestion
Whose horrid image doth unfix my hair
And make my seated heart knock at my ribs,
Against the use of nature? Present fears
Are less than horrible imaginings.

          Shakespeare, *Macbeth,* I, iii, 134

14 So, *Sancho,* as to the Use which I make of the Lady
Dulcinea, she is equal to the greatest Princesses in
the World. Pr'ythee tell me, Dost thou think the
Poets, who every one of 'em celebrate the Praises
of some Lady or other, had all real Mistresses? Or
that the *Amaryllis's,* the *Phyllis's,* the *Sylvia's,* the
Diana's, the *Galatea's,* the *Alida's,* and the like,
which you shall find in so many Poems, Romances, Songs and Ballads, upon ever Stage, and
even in every Barber's Shop, were Creatures of
Flesh and Blood, and Mistresses to those that did
and do celebrate 'em? No, no, never think it; for I
dare assure thee, the greatest Part of 'em were
nothing but the meer Imaginations of the Poets,
for a Ground-work to exercise their Wits upon,
and give to the World Occasion to look on the
Authors as Men of an amorous and gallant Disposition: And so 'tis sufficient for me to imagine,
that *Aldonza Lorenzo* is beautiful and chaste; as for
her Birth and Parentage, they concern me but little; for there's no need to make an Enquiry about
a Woman's Pedigree, as there is of us Men, when
some Badge of Honour is bestowed on us; and so

she's to me the greatest Princess in the World: For
thou ought'st to know, *Sancho,* if thou know'st it
not already, that there are but two things that
chiefly excite us to love a Woman, an attractive
Beauty, and unspotted Fame. Now these two Endowments are happily reconcil'd in *Dulcinea;* for as
for the one, she has not her Equal, and few can
vie with her in the other: But to cut off all Objections at once, I imagine, that All I say of her is
really so, without the least Addition or Diminution: I fancy her to be just such as I would have
her for Beauty and Quality. *Helen* cannot stand in
Competition with her; *Lucretia* cannot rival her;
and all the Heroines which Antiquity has to
boast, whether *Greeks, Romans* or *Barbarians,* are at
once out-done by her incomparable Perfections.
Therefore let the World say what it will; should
the Ignorant Vulgar foolishly censure me, I please
my self with the Assurances I have of the Approbation of Men of the strictest Morals, and the nic-
est Judgment.

          Cervantes, *Don Quixote,* I, 25

15 *Sancho.* Heaven defend me, said he to himself,
what a Heart of a Chicken have I! This now,
which to me is a sad Disaster, to my Master, Don
Quixote, would be a rare Adventure. He would
look upon these Caves and Dungeons as lovely
Gardens, and glorious Palaces, and hope to be led
out of these dark narrow Cells into some fine
Meadow; while I, luckless, helpless, heartless
Wretch that I am, every Step I take, expect to
sink into some deeper Pit than this, and go down
I don't know whither.

          Cervantes, *Don Quixote,* II, 55

16 That power by which we are properly said to
know things, is purely spiritual, and not less distinct from every part of the body than blood from
bone, or hand from eye. It is a single agency,
whether it receives impressions from the common
sense simultaneously with the fancy, or applies itself to those that are preserved in the memory, or
forms new ones. Often the imagination is so beset
by these impressions that it is unable at the same
time to receive ideas from the common sense, or to
transfer them to the motor mechanism in the way
befitting its purely corporeal character. In all
these operations this cognitive power is at one
time passive, at another active, and resembles now
the seal and now the wax. But the resemblance on
this occasion is only one of analogy, for among
corporeal things there is nothing wholly similar to
this faculty. It is one and the same agency which,
when applying itself along with the imagination
to the common sense, is said to see, touch, etc.; if
applying itself to the imagination alone in so far
as that is endowed with diverse impressions, it is
said to remember; if it turn to the imagination in
order to create fresh impressions, it is said to
imagine or conceive; finally if it act alone it is said

to understand. . . . Now it is the same faculty that in correspondence with those various functions is called either pure understanding, or imagination, or memory, or sense. It is properly called mind when it either forms new ideas in the fancy, or attends to those already formed. . . . But after having grasped these facts the attentive reader will gather what help is to be expected from each particular faculty, and discover how far human effort can avail to supplement the deficiencies of our mental powers.

Descartes, *Rules for Direction of the Mind*, XII

17 When a body is once in motion, it moveth (unless something else hinder it) eternally; and whatsoever hindreth it, cannot in an instant, but in time, and by degrees, quite extinguish it: and as we see in the water, though the wind cease, the waves give not over rolling for a long time after; so also it happeneth in that motion which is made in the internal parts of a man, then, when he sees, dreams, etc. For after the object is removed, or the eye shut, we still retain an image of the thing seen, though more obscure than when we see it. And this is it the Latins call *imagination*, from the image made in seeing. . . . Imagination, therefore, is nothing but *decaying sense;* and is found in men and many other living creatures, as well sleeping as waking.

The decay of sense in men waking is not the decay of the motion made in sense, but an obscuring of it, in such manner as the light of the sun obscureth the light of the stars; which stars do no less exercise their virtue by which they are visible in the day than in the night. . . . This *decaying sense*, when we would express the thing itself (I mean *fancy* itself), we call *imagination*, as I said before. But when we would express the *decay*, and signify that the sense is fading, old, and past, it is called *memory*. So that imagination and memory are but one thing, which for diverse considerations hath diverse names.

Hobbes, *Leviathan*, I, 2

18 It is that deceitful part in man, that mistress of error and falsity, the more deceptive that she is not always so; for she would be an infallible rule of truth, if she were an infallible rule of falsehood. But being most generally false, she gives no sign of her nature, impressing the same character on the true and the false.

I do not speak of fools, I speak of the wisest men; and it is among them that the imagination has the great gift of persuasion. Reason protests in vain; it cannot set a true value on things.

This arrogant power, the enemy of reason, who likes to rule and dominate it, has established in man a second nature to show how all-powerful she is. She makes men happy and sad, healthy and sick, rich and poor; she compels reason to believe, doubt, and deny; she blunts the senses, or quickens them; she has her fools and sages; and nothing vexes us more than to see that she fills her devotees with a satisfaction far more full and entire than does reason. Those who have a lively imagination are a great deal more pleased with themselves than the wise can reasonably be. They look down upon men with haughtiness; they argue with boldness and confidence, others with fear and diffidence; and this gaiety of countenance often gives them the advantage in the opinion of the hearers, such favour have the imaginary wise in the eyes of judges of like nature. Imagination cannot make fools wise; but she can make them happy, to the envy of reason which can only make its friends miserable; the one covers them with glory, the other with shame.

What but this faculty of imagination dispenses reputation, awards respect and veneration to persons, works, laws, and the great? How insufficient are all the riches of the earth without her consent!

Would you not say that this magistrate, whose venerable age commands the respect of a whole people, is governed by pure and lofty reason, and that he judges causes according to their true nature without considering those mere trifles which only affect the imagination of the weak? See him go to sermon, full of devout zeal, strengthening his reason with the ardour of his love. He is ready to listen with exemplary respect. Let the preacher appear, and let nature have given him a hoarse voice or a comical cast of countenance, or let his barber have given him a bad shave, or let by chance his dress be more dirtied than usual, then, however great the truths he announces, I wager our senator loses his gravity.

If the greatest philosopher in the world find himself upon a plank wider than actually necessary, but hanging over a precipice, his imagination will prevail, though his reason convince him of his safety. Many cannot bear the thought without a cold sweat. I will not state all its effects.

Pascal, *Pensées*, II, 82

19 Imagination has this peculiarity that it produces the greatest things with as little time and trouble as little things.

Pascal, *Concerning the Vacuum*

20 An imagination is an idea which indicates the present constitution of the human body rather than the nature of an external body, not indeed distinctly but confusedly, so that the mind is said to err. For example, when we look at the sun, we imagine his distance from us to be about 200 feet, and in this we are deceived so long as we remain in ignorance of the true distance. When this is known, the error is removed, but not the imagination, that is to say, the idea of the sun which manifests his nature in so far only as the body is affected by him; so that although we know his true distance, we nevertheless imagine him close to us.

For . . . it is not because we are ignorant of the sun's true distance that we imagine him to be so close to us, but because the mind conceives the magnitude of the sun just in so far as the body is affected by him. So when the rays of the sun falling upon a surface of water are reflected to our eyes, we imagine him to be in the water, although his true place is known to us. So with the other imaginations by which the mind is deceived; whether they indicate the natural constitution of the body or an increase or diminution in its power of action, they are not opposed to the truth, nor do they disappear with the presence of the truth. We know that when we groundlessly fear any evil, the fear vanishes when we hear correct intelligence; but we also know, on the other hand, that when we fear an evil which will actually come upon us, the fear vanishes when we hear false intelligence, so that the imaginations do not disappear with the presence of the truth, in so far as it is true, but because other imaginations arise which are stronger, and which exclude the present existence of the objects we imagine.

Spinoza, *Ethics*, IV, Prop. 1, Schol.

21 The composition of all poems is, or ought to be, of wit; and wit in the poet, or wit writing (if you will give me leave to use a school-distinction) is no other than the faculty of imagination in the writer, which like a nimble spaniel, beats over and ranges thro' the field of memory, till it springs the quarry it hunted after; or, without metaphor, which searches over all the memory for the species or ideas of those things which it designs to represent. Wit written is that which is well defin'd, the happy result of thought, or product of imagination.

Dryden, *Annus Mirabilis*, Pref.

22 True wit is Nature to advantage dressed,
What oft was thought, but ne'er so well expressed;
Something whose truth convinced at sight we find,
That gives us back the image of our mind.

Pope, *Essay on Criticism*, II, 297

23 It is evident that there is a principle of connexion between the different thoughts or ideas of the mind, and that, in their appearance to the memory or imagination, they introduce each other with a certain degree of method and regularity. In our more serious thinking or discourse this is so observable that any particular thought, which breaks in upon the regular tract or chain of ideas, is immediately remarked and rejected. And even in our wildest and most wandering reveries, nay in our very dreams, we shall find, if we reflect, that the imagination ran not altogether at adventures, but that there was still a connexion upheld among the different ideas, which succeeded each other. Were the loosest and freest conversation to

be transcribed, there would immediately be observed something which connected it in all its transitions. Or where this is wanting, the person who broke the thread of discourse might still inform you, that there had secretly revolved in his mind a succession of thought, which had gradually led him from the subject of conversation. Among different languages, even where we cannot suspect the least connexion or communication, it is found, that the words, expressive of ideas, the most compounded, do yet nearly correspond to each other: a certain proof that the simple ideas, comprehended in the compound ones, were bound together by some universal principle, which had an equal influence on all mankind.

Though it be too obvious to escape observation, that different ideas are connected together; I do not find that any philosopher has attempted to enumerate or class all the principles of association; a subject, however, that seems worthy of curiosity. To me, there appear to be only three principles of connexion among ideas, namely, *Resemblance, Contiguity* in time or place, and *Cause* or *Effect*.

Hume, *Concerning Human Understanding*, III, 18–19

24 Nothing is more free than the imagination of man; and though it cannot exceed that original stock of ideas furnished by the internal and external senses, it has unlimited power of mixing, compounding, separating, and dividing these ideas, in all the varieties of fiction and vision. It can feign a train of events, with all the appearance of reality, ascribe to them a particular time and place, conceive them as existent, and paint them out to itself with every circumstance, that belongs to any historical fact, which it believes with the greatest certainty.

Hume, *Concerning Human Understanding*, V, 39

25 The *imagination* of man is naturally sublime, delighted with whatever is remote and extraordinary, and running, without control, into the most distant parts of space and time in order to avoid the objects, which custom has rendered too familiar to it.

Hume, *Concerning Human Understanding*, XII, 130

26 The world of reality has its bounds, the world of imagination is boundless; as we cannot enlarge the one, let us restrict the other; for all the sufferings which really make us miserable arise from the difference between the real and the imaginary.

Rousseau, *Emile*, II

27 Our conversation to-day, I know not how, turned, (I think for the only time at any length, during

our long acquaintance,} upon the sensual intercourse between the sexes, the delight of which he [Johnson] ascribed chiefly to imagination. "Were it not for imagination, Sir, (said he,) a man would be as happy in the arms of a chambermaid as of a Duchess. But such is the adventitious charm of fancy, that we find men who have violated the best principles of society, and ruined their fame and their fortune, that they might possess a woman of rank."

Boswell, *Life of Johnson (May 9, 1778)*

28 In truth, it is not images of objects, but schemata, which lie at the foundation of our pure sensuous conceptions. No image could ever be adequate to our conception of a triangle in general. For the generalness of the conception it never could attain to, as this includes under itself all triangles, whether right-angled, acute-angled, etc., whilst the image would always be limited to a single part of this sphere. The schema of the triangle can exist nowhere else than in thought, and it indicates a rule of the synthesis of the imagination in regard to pure figures in space. Still less is an object of experience, or an image of the object, ever adequate to the empirical conception. On the contrary, the conception always relates immediately to the schema of the imagination, as a rule for the determination of our intuition, in conformity with a certain general conception. The conception of a dog indicates a rule, according to which my imagination can delineate the figure of a four-footed animal in general, without being limited to any particular individual form which experience presents to me, or indeed to any possible image that I can represent to myself *in concreto*. This schematism of our understanding in regard to phenomena and their mere form, is an art, hidden in the depths of the human soul, whose true modes of action we shall only with difficulty discover and unveil. Thus much only can we say: "The *image* is a product of the empirical faculty of the productive imagination—the *schema* of sensuous conceptions (of figures in space, for example) is a product, and, as it were, a monogram of the pure imagination *a priori*, whereby and according to which images first become possible, which, however, can be connected with the conception only mediately by means of the schema which they indicate, and are in themselves never fully adequate to it." On the other hand, the schema of a pure conception of the understanding is something that cannot be reduced into any image—it is nothing else than the pure synthesis expressed by the category, conformably to a rule of unity according to conceptions. It is a transcendental product of the imagination, a product which concerns the determination of the internal sense, according to conditions of its form (time) in respect to all representations, in so far as these representations must be conjoined *a priori* in one conception, conformably to the unity of apperception.

Kant, *Critique of Pure Reason,*
Transcendental Analytic

29 The imagination (as a productive faculty of cognition) is a powerful agent for creating, as it were, a second nature out of the material supplied to it by actual nature. It affords us entertainment where experience proves too commonplace; and we even use it to remodel experience, always following, no doubt, laws that are based on analogy, but still also following principles which have a higher seat in reason (and which are every whit as natural to us as those followed by the understanding in laying hold of empirical nature). By this means we get a sense of our freedom from the law of association (which attaches to the empirical employment of the imagination), with the result that the material can be borrowed by us from nature in accordance with that law, but be worked up by us into something else—namely, what surpasses nature.

Such representations of the imagination may be termed *ideas*. This is partly because they at least strain after something lying out beyond the confines of experience, and so seek to approximate to a presentation of rational concepts (i.e., intellectual ideas), thus giving to these concepts the semblance of an objective reality. But, on the other hand, there is this most important reason, that no concept can be wholly adequate to them as internal intuitions. The poet essays the task of interpreting to sense the rational ideas of invisible beings, the kingdom of the blessed, hell, eternity, creation, etc. Or, again, as to things of which examples occur in experience, e.g., death, envy, and all vices, as also love, fame, and the like, transgressing the limits of experience he attempts with the aid of an imagination which emulates the display of reason in its attainment of a maximum, to body them forth to sense with a completeness of which nature affords no parallel; and it is in fact precisely in the poetic art that the faculty of aesthetic ideas can show itself to full advantage. This faculty, however, regarded solely on its own account, is properly no more than a talent (of the imagination).

Kant, *Critique of Aesthetic Judgement*, 49

30 The IMAGINATION then, I consider either as primary, or secondary. The primary IMAGINATION I hold to be the living Power and prime Agent of all human Perception, and as a repetition in the finite mind of the eternal act of creation in the infinite I AM. The secondary Imagination I consider as an echo of the former, co-existing with the conscious will, yet still as identical with the primary in the *kind* of its agency, and differing only in *degree*, and in the *mode* of its operation. It dissolves, diffuses, dissipates, in order to re-create; or where this process is rendered impossible, yet still at all events it struggles to idealize and to unify. It is

essentially *vital*, even as all objects (*as* objects) are essentially fixed and dead.

FANCY, on the contrary, has no other counters to play with, but fixities and definites. The Fancy is indeed no other than a mode of Memory emancipated from the order of time and space; while it is blended with, and modified by that empirical phenomenon of the will, which we express by the word CHOICE. But equally with the ordinary memory the Fancy must receive all its materials ready made from the law of association.

Coleridge, *Biographia Literaria*, XIII

31 We want the creative faculty to imagine that which we know; we want the generous impulse to act that which we imagine; we want the poetry of life; our calculations have outrun conception; we have eaten more than we can digest. The cultivation of those sciences which have enlarged the limits of the empire of man over the external world has, for want of the poetical faculty, proportionally circumscribed those of the internal world; and man, having enslaved the elements, remains himself a slave.

Shelley, *Defence of Poetry*

32 Ever let the Fancy roam,
Pleasure never is at home:
At a touch sweet Pleasure melteth,
Like to bubbles when rain pelteth;
Then let winged Fancy wander
Through the thought still spread beyond her:
Open wide the mind's cage-door,
She'll dart forth, and cloudward soar. . . .

Oh, sweet Fancy! let her loose;
Every thing is spoilt by use;
Where's the cheek that doth not fade,
Too much gazed at? Where's the maid
Whose lip mature is ever new?
Where's the eye, however blue,
Doth not weary? Where's the face
One would meet in every place?
Where's the voice, however soft,
One would hear so very oft?
At a touch sweet Pleasure melteth
Like to bubbles when rain pelteth.
Let, then, winged Fancy find
Thee a mistress to thy mind:
Dulcet-eyed as Ceres' daughter
Ere the God of Torment taught her
How to frown and how to chide;
With a waist and with a side
White as Hebe's, when her zone
Slipt its golden clasp, and down
Fell her kirtle to her feet,
While she held the goblet sweet,
And Jove grew languid.—Break the mesh
Of the Fancy's silken leash;
Quickly break her prison-string,
And such joys as these she'll bring.—

Let the winged Fancy roam,
Pleasure never is at home.

Keats, *Fancy*

33 Adieu! the fancy cannot cheat so well
As she is famed to do, deceiving elf.

Keats, *Ode to a Nightingale*

34 I am certain of nothing but of the holiness of the Heart's affections, and the truth of Imagination. What the Imagination seizes as Beauty must be truth—whether it existed before or not,—for I have the same idea of all our passions as of Love: they are all, in their sublime, creative of essential Beauty. In a Word, you may know my favourite speculation by my first Book, and the little Song I sent in my last, which is a representation from the fancy of the probable mode of operating in these Matters. The Imagination may be compared to Adam's dream,—he awoke and found it truth.

Keats, *Letter to Benjamin Bailey*
(Nov. 22, 1817)

35 Fancy is a wilful, imagination a spontaneous act; fancy, a play as with dolls and puppets which we choose to call men and women; imagination, a perception and affirming of a real relation between a thought and some material fact. Fancy amuses; imagination expands and exalts us.

Emerson, *Poetry and Imagination*

36 There is a Catskill eagle in some souls that can alike dive down into the blackest gorges, and soar out of them again and become invisible in the sunny spaces. And even if he for ever flies within the gorge, that gorge is in the mountains; so that even in his lowest swoop the mountain eagle is still higher than other birds upon the plain, even though they soar.

Melville, *Moby Dick*, XCVI

37 What a faculty must that be which can paint the most barren landscape and humblest life in glorious colors! It is pure and invigorated senses reacting on a sound and strong imagination. Is not that the poet's case? The intellect of most men is barren. They neither fertilize nor are fertilized. It is the marriage of the soul with Nature that makes the intellect fruitful, that gives birth to imagination. When we were dead and dry as the highway, some sense which has been healthily fed will put us in relation with Nature, in sympathy with her; some grains of fertilizing pollen, floating in the air, fall on us, and suddenly the sky is all one rainbow, is full of music and fragrance and flavor. The man of intellect only, the prosaic man, is a barren, staminiferous flower; the poet is a fertile and perfect flower.

Thoreau, *Journal (Aug. 20, 1851)*

38 The *Imagination* is one of the highest prerogatives of man. By this faculty he unites former images

and ideas, independently of the will, and thus creates brilliant and novel results. A poet, as Jean Paul Richter remarks, "who must reflect whether he shall make a character say yes or no—to the devil with him; he is only a stupid corpse." Dreaming gives us the best notion of this power; as Jean Paul again says, "The dream is an involuntary art of poetry." The value of the products of our imagination depends of course on the number, accuracy, and clearness of our impressions, on our judgment and taste in selecting or rejecting the involuntary combinations, and to a certain extent on our power of voluntarily combining them. As dogs, cats, horses, and probably all the higher animals, even birds have vivid dreams, and this is shewn by their movements and the sounds uttered, we must admit that they possess some power of imagination. There must be something special, which causes dogs to howl in the night, and especially during moonlight, in that remarkable and melancholy manner called baying.

Darwin, *Descent of Man*, I, 3

39 *Sensations, once experienced, modify the nervous organism, so that copies of them arise again in the mind after the original outward stimulus is gone.* No mental copy, however, can arise in the mind, of any kind of sensation which has never been directly excited from without.

The blind may dream of sights, the deaf of sounds, for years after they have lost their vision or hearing; but the man *born* deaf can never be made to imagine what sound is like, nor can the man *born* blind ever have a mental vision. In Locke's words . . . "the mind can frame unto itself no one new simple idea." The originals of them all must have been given from without. Fantasy, or Imagination, are the names given to the faculty of reproducing copies of originals once felt. The imagination is called "reproductive" when the copies are literal; "productive" when elements from different originals are recombined so as to make new wholes.

After-images belong to sensation rather than to imagination; so that the most immediate phenomena of imagination would seem to be those tardier images . . . coercive hauntings of the mind by echoes of unusual experiences for hours after the latter have taken place. The phenomena ordinarily ascribed to imagination, however, are those mental pictures of possible sensible experiences, to which the ordinary processes of associative thought give rise.

When represented with surroundings concrete enough to constitute a *date,* these pictures, when they revive, form *recollections*. . . . When the mental pictures are of data freely combined, and reproducing no past combination exactly, we have acts of imagination properly so called.

William James, *Psychology*, XVIII

40 Renunciation of pleasure has always been very hard to man; he cannot accomplish it without some kind of compensation. Accordingly he has evolved for himself a mental activity in which all these relinquished sources of pleasure and abandoned paths of gratification are permitted to continue their existence, a form of existence in which they are free from the demands of reality and from what we call the exercise of *testing reality.* Every longing is soon transformed into the idea of its fulfilment; there is no doubt that dwelling upon a wish-fulfilment in phantasy brings satisfaction, although the knowledge that it is not reality remains thereby unobscured. In phantasy, therefore, man can continue to enjoy a freedom from the grip of the external world, one which he has long relinquished in actuality.

Freud, *General Introduction to Psycho-Analysis*, XXIII

41 In imagination, not in perception, lies the substance of experience, while knowledge and reason are but its chastened and ultimate form.

Santayana, *Life of Reason*, I, 2

5.5 | *Dreams*

Long before dreams and dreaming became the subject of psychological investigation and psychoanalytical theory, the occurrence and content of dreams were objects of wonder, fear, and speculation. The quotations drawn from the Old Testament and from the poets, historians, and biographers of antiquity bear witness to the influence of dreams and to the importance of the role played by soothsayers and prophets as interpreters of their content. Famous dreams and famous interpretations of dreams are here reported, along with discussions by the philosophers of antiquity concerning the art of divination through dreams. The ancients were not without their skeptical doubts about the supernatural origin of dreams or about their trustworthiness as forecasters of the future. Aristotle, for example, offers some purely naturalistic explanations of dreaming and dream content.

The modern treatment of dreams stresses the relation of dreaming to the powers of the imagination, and the reader is, therefore, advised to relate this section to the preceding one on the imagination. What is ordinarily called day-dreaming or fantasy is, of course, nothing but the imagination at work under more or less conscious control or with some directive purpose. In contrast, the dreams that take place during sleep, or in the process of awakening, manifest no such control or direction. It is precisely this fact that lies at the heart of Freud's unique contribution—his interpretation of dreams as an expression of the unconscious, revealing to the interpreter wishes, emotions, or tendencies of which the dreamer was himself unaware. The significance of dreams for the diagnosis and treatment of psychic disorders connects this section with the one that follows on madness.

---

1 And Jacob went out from Beersheba, and went toward Haran.

And he lighted upon a certain place, and tarried there all night, because the sun was set; and he took of the stones of that place, and put them for his pillows, and lay down in that place to sleep.

And he dreamed, and behold a ladder set up on the earth, and the top of it reached to heaven: and behold the angels of God ascending and descending on it.

And, behold, the Lord stood above it, and said, I am the Lord God of Abraham thy father, and the God of Isaac: the land whereon thou liest, to thee will I give it, and to thy seed;

And thy seed shall be as the dust of the earth, and thou shalt spread abroad to the west, and to the east, and to the north, and to the south: and in thee and in thy seed shall all the families of the earth be blessed.

And, behold, I am with thee, and will keep thee in all places whither thou goest, and will bring thee again into this land; for I will not leave thee, until I have done that which I have spoken to thee of.

And Jacob awaked out of his sleep, and he said, Surely the Lord is in this place; and I knew it not.

Genesis 28:10–16

2 Your old men shall dream dreams, your young men shall see visions.

Joel 2:28

3 *Penelope.* Two gates for ghostly dreams there are: one gateway
of honest horn, and one of ivory.
Issuing by the ivory gate are dreams
of glimmering illusion, fantasies,
but those that come through solid polished horn
may be borne out, if mortals only know them.

Homer, *Odyssey,* XIX, 562

351

4 *Chorus.* It is vain, to dream and to see splendors,
and the image slipping from the arms' embrace
escapes, not to return again,
on wings drifting down the ways of sleep.

Aeschylus, *Agamemnon,* 423

5 *Clytaemestra.* Eyes illuminate the sleeping brain,
but in the daylight man's future cannot be seen.

Aeschylus, *Eumenides,* 104

6 *Jocasta.* As to your mother's marriage bed,—don't
fear it.
Before this, in dreams too, as well as oracles,
many a man has lain with his own mother.

Sophocles, *Oedipus the King,* 980

7 *The Second Maiden.* Oh! to set foot, if only in a
dream, in my father's home and city, a luxury
sweet sleep affords, a pleasure shared by us with
wealth!

Euripides, *Iphigenia in Tauris,* 453

8 *Socrates.* Let me feast my mind with the dream as
day dreamers are in the habit of feasting themselves when they are walking alone; for before
they have discovered any means of effecting their
wishes—that is a matter which never troubles
them—they would rather not tire themselves by
thinking about possibilities; but assuming that
what they desire is already granted to them, they
proceed with their plan, and delight in detailing
what they mean to do when their wish has come
true—that is a way which they have of not doing
much good to a capacity which was never good
for much.

Plato, *Republic,* V, 457B

9 *Socrates.* When the reasoning and human and ruling power is asleep; then the wild beast within us,
gorged with meat or drink, starts up and having
shaken off sleep, goes forth to satisfy his desires;
and there is no conceivable folly or crime—not
excepting incest or any other unnatural union, or
parricide, or the eating of forbidden food—which
at such a time, when he has parted company with
all shame and sense, a man may not be ready to
commit.

Most true, he [Glaucon] said.

But when a man's pulse is healthy and temperate, and when before going to sleep he has awakened his rational powers, and fed them on noble
thoughts and enquiries, collecting himself in meditation; after having first indulged his appetites
neither too much nor too little, but just enough to
lay them to sleep, and prevent them and their
enjoyments and pains from interfering with the
higher principle—which he leaves in the solitude
of pure abstraction, free to contemplate and aspire to the knowledge of the unknown, whether in
past, present, or future: when again he has allayed the passionate element, if he has a quarrel
against anyone—I say, when, after pacifying the

two irrational principles, he rouses up the third,
which is reason, before he takes his rest, then, as
you know, he attains truth most nearly, and is
least likely to be the sport of fantastic and lawless
visions.

I quite agree.

In saying this I have been running into a digression; but the point which I desire to note is
that in all of us, even in good men, there is a
lawless wild-beast nature, which peers out in
sleep.

Plato, *Republic,* IX, 571B

10 It is not improbable that some of the presentations
which come before the mind in sleep may even be
causes of the actions cognate to each of them. For
as when we are about to act [in waking hours], or
are engaged in any course of action, or have already performed certain actions, we often find
ourselves concerned with these actions, or performing them, in a vivid dream; the cause whereof is that the dream-movement has had a way
paved for it from the original movements set up in
the daytime; exactly so, but conversely, it must
happen that the movements set up first in sleep
should also prove to be starting-points of actions
to be performed in the daytime, since the recurrence by day of the thought of these actions also
has had its way paved for it in the images before
the mind at night. Thus then it is quite conceivable that some dreams may be tokens and causes
[of future events].

Aristotle, *Prophesying by Dreams,* 463ª22

11 On the whole, forasmuch as certain of the lower
animals also dream, it may be concluded that
dreams are not sent by God, nor are they designed
for this purpose [to reveal the future]. They have a
divine aspect, however, for Nature [their cause] is
divinely planned, though not itself divine. A special proof [of their not being sent by God] is this:
the power of foreseeing the future and of having
vivid dreams is found in persons of inferior type,
which implies that God does not send their
dreams; but merely that all those whose physical
temperament is, as it were, garrulous and excitable, see sights of all descriptions; for, inasmuch as
they experience many movements of every kind,
they just chance to have visions resembling objective facts, their luck in these matters being merely
like that of persons who play at even and odd. For
the principle which is expressed in the gambler's
maxim: 'If you make many throws your luck must
change,' holds good in their case also.

Aristotle, *Prophesying by Dreams,* 463ᵇ11

12 Of all animals man is most given to dreaming.
Children and infants do not dream, but in most
cases dreaming comes on at the age of four or five
years. Instances have been known of full-grown
men and women that have never dreamed at all;
in exceptional cases of this kind, it has been observed that when a dream occurs in advanced life

it prognosticates either actual dissolution or a general break-up of the system.

Aristotle, *History of Animals*, 537ᵇ14

13 To whatever pursuit a man is closely tied down and strongly attached, on whatever subject we have previously much dwelt, the mind having been put to a more than usual strain in it, during sleep we for the most part fancy that we are engaged in the same; lawyers think they plead causes and draw up covenants of sale, generals that they fight and engage in battle, sailors that they wage and carry on war with the winds, we think we pursue our task and investigate the nature of things constantly and consign it when discovered to writings in our native tongue. So all other pursuits and arts are seen for the most part during sleep to occupy and mock the minds of men.

Lucretius, *Nature of Things*, IV

14 Two gates the silent house of Sleep adorn;
Of polish'd iv'ry this, that of transparent horn:
True visions thro' transparent horn arise;
Thro' polish'd iv'ry pass deluding lies.

Virgil, *Aeneid*, VI

15 Darius was by this time upon his march from Susa, very confident, not only in the number of his men, which amounted to six hundred thousand, but likewise in a dream, which the Persian soothsayers interpreted rather in flattery to him than according to the natural probability. He dreamed that he saw the Macedonian phalanx all on fire, and Alexander waiting on him, clad in the same dress which he himself had been used to wear when he was courier to the late king; after which, going into the temple of Belus, he vanished out of his sight. The dream would appear to have supernaturally signified to him the illustrious actions the Macedonians were to perform, and that as he, from a courier's place, had risen to the throne, so Alexander should come to be master of Asia, and not long surviving his conquests, conclude his life with glory.

Plutarch, *Alexander*

16 The senses are suspended in the sleeper through certain evaporations and the escape of certain exhalations, as we read in the book on *Sleep*. And, therefore, according to the disposition of such evaporation, the senses are more or less suspended. For when the motion of the vapors is considerable, not only are the senses suspended, but also the imagination, so that there are no phantasms; and this happens especially when a man falls asleep after eating and drinking copiously. If, however, the motion of the vapors be somewhat less, phantasms appear, but distorted and without order; thus it happens in a case of fever. And if the motion be still more attenuated, the phantasms will have a certain order; thus especially does it happen towards the end of sleep, in sober men and those who are gifted with a strong imagination. If the motion of the vapors is very slight,

not only does the imagination retain its freedom, but also the common sense is partly freed, so that sometimes while asleep a man may judge that what he sees is a dream, discerning, as it were, between things and their likenesses. Nevertheless, the common sense remains partly suspended, and therefore, although it discriminates some likenesses from the reality, yet is it always deceived in some particular. Therefore, while man is asleep, according as sense and imagination are free, so the judgment of his intellect is unfettered, though not entirely. Consequently, if a man syllogizes while asleep, when he wakes up he invariably recognizes a flaw in some respect.

Aquinas, *Summa Theologica*, I, 84, 8

17 *Pandar.* And all your dreams and other such like folly,
To deep oblivion let them be consigned;
For they arise but from your melancholy,
By which your health is being undermined.
A straw for all the meaning you can find
In dreams! They aren't worth a hill of beans,
For no one knows what dreaming really means.

Priests in the temples sometimes choose to say
That dreams come from the Gods as revelations;
But other times they speak another way,
And call them hellish false hallucinations!
And doctors say they come from complications,
Or fast or surfeit, or any other lie,
For who knows truly what they signify?

And others say that through impressions deep,
As when one has a purpose firm in mind,
There come these visions in one's sleep;
And others say that they in old books find,
That every season hath its special kind
Of dream, and all depends upon the moon;
But all such folk are crazy as a loon!

Dreams are the proper business of old wives,
Who draw their auguries from birds and fowls,
For which men often fear to lose their lives,
The raven's croak or mournful shriek of owls!
O why put trust in bestial shrieks and howls!
Alas, that noble man should be so brash
To implicate his mind in such like trash!

Chaucer, *Troilus and Cressida*, V, 52–55

18 Let us bend our course another way, and try a new sort of divination. Of what kind? asked Panurge. Of a good ancient and authentic fashion, answered Pantagruel; it is by dreams. For in dreaming, such circumstances and conditions being thereto adhibited, as are clearly enough described by Hippocrates . . . by Plato, Plotin, Iamblicus, Synesius, Aristotle, Xenophon, Galen, Plutarch, Artemidorus, Daldianus, Herophilus, Q. Calaber, Theocritus, Pliny, Athenæus, and others, the soul doth oftentimes foresee what is to come. How true this is, you may conceive by a very vulgar and familiar example; as when you see that at such a time as suckling babes, well nourished, fed

and fostered with good milk, sleep soundly and profoundly, the nurses in the interim get leave to sport themselves, and are licentiated to recreate their fancies at what range to them shall seem most fitting and expedient, their presence, sedulity, and attendance on the cradle being, during all that space, held unnecessary. Even just so, when our body is at rest, that the concoction is every where accomplished, and that, till it awake, it lacks for nothing, our soul delighteth to disport itself, and is well pleased in that folic to take a review of its native country, which is the heavens, where it receiveth a most notable participation of its first beginning, with an imbuement from its divine source, and in contemplation of that infinite and intellectual sphere, whereof the centre is every where, and the circumference in no place of the universal world, (to wit, God, according to the doctrine of Hermes Trismegistus,) to whom no new thing happeneth, whom nothing that is past escapeth, and unto whom all things are alike present; it remarketh not only what is *preterit* and gone, in the inferior course and agitation of sublunary matters, but withal taketh notice what is to come; then bringing a relation of those future events unto the body by the outward senses and exterior organs, it is divulged abroad unto the hearing of others. Whereupon the owner of that soul deserveth to be termed a vaticinator, or prophet. Nevertheless, the truth is, that the soul is seldom able to report those things in such sincerity as it hath seen them, by reason of the imperfection and frailty of the corporeal senses, which obstruct the effectuating of that office; even as the moon doth not communicate unto this earth of ours that light which she receiveth from the sun with so much splendour, heat, vigour, purity, and liveliness as it was given her. Hence it is requisite for the better reading, explaining, and unfolding of these somniatory vaticinations, and predictions, of that nature that a dexterous, learned, skilful, wise, industrious, expert, rational, and peremptory expounder or interpreter be pitched upon.

Rabelais, *Gargantua and Pantagruel*, III, 13

19 Those who have compared our life to a dream were perhaps more right than they thought. When we dream, our soul lives, acts, exercises all her faculties, neither more nor less than when she is awake; but if more loosely and obscurely, still surely not so much so that the difference is as between night and bright daylight; rather as between night and shade. There she sleeps, here she slumbers: more and less. It is always darkness, and Cimmerian darkness.

Sleeping we are awake, and waking asleep. I do not see so clearly in sleep; but my wakefulness I never find pure and cloudless enough. Moreover sleep in its depth sometimes puts dreams to sleep. But our wakefulness is never so awake as to purge and properly dissipate reveries, which are the

dreams of the waking, and worse than dreams.

Since our reason and our soul accept the fancies and opinions which arise in it while sleeping, and authorize the actions of our dreams with the same approbation as they do those of the day, why do we not consider the possibility that our thinking, our acting, may be another sort of dreaming, and our waking another kind of sleep?

Montaigne, *Essays*, II, 12, Apology for Raymond Sebond

20 I have no cause to complain of my imagination. I have had few thoughts in my life that have even interrupted the course of my sleep, unless they have been those of desire, which awakened me without afflicting me. I seldom dream, and then it is about fantastic things and chimeras usually produced by amusing thoughts, more ridiculous than sad. And I hold that it is true that dreams are faithful interpreters of our inclinations; but there is an art to sorting and understanding them. . . .

Plato says, moreover, that it is the function of wisdom to draw from them instructions for divining the future. I see nothing in that, except for the marvelous experiences related by Socrates, Xenophon, and Aristotle, personages of irreproachable authority.

Montaigne, *Essays*, III, 13, Of Experience

21 *Mercutio.* O, then, I see Queen Mab hath been with you.
She is the fairies' midwife, and she comes
In shape no bigger than an agate-stone
On the fore-finger of an alderman,
Drawn with a team of little atomies
Athwart men's noses as they lie asleep;
Her waggon-spokes made of long spinners' legs,
The cover of the wings of grasshoppers,
The traces of the smallest spider's web,
The collars of the moonshine's watery beams,
Her whip of cricket's bone, the lash of film,
Her waggoner a small grey-coated gnat,
Not half so big as a round little worm
Prick'd from the lazy finger of a maid;
Her chariot is an empty hazel-nut
Made by the joiner squirrel or old grub,
Time out o' mind the fairies' coachmakers.
And in this state she gallops night by night
Through lovers' brains, and then they dream of love;
O'er courtiers' knees, that dream on court'sies straight,
O'er lawyers' fingers, who straight dream on fees,
O'er ladies' lips, who straight on kisses dream,
Which oft the angry Mab with blisters plagues,
Because their breaths with sweetmeats tainted are:
Sometime she gallops o'er a courtier's nose,
And then dreams he of smelling out a suit;
And sometime comes she with a tithe-pig's tail
Tickling a parson's nose as a' lies asleep,

Then dreams he of another benefice:
Sometime she driveth o'er a soldier's neck,
And then dreams he of cutting foreign throats,
Of breaches, ambuscadoes, Spanish blades,
Of healths five-fathom deep; and then anon
Drums in his ear, at which he starts and wakes,
And being thus frighted swears a prayer or two
And sleeps again. This is that very Mab
That plats the manes of horses in the night,
And bakes the elf-locks in foul sluttish hairs,
Which once untangled much misfortune bodes:
This is the hag, when maids lie on their backs,
That presses them and learns them first to bear,
Making them women of good carriage:
This is she—
    Romeo. Peace, peace, Mercutio, peace!
Thou talk'st of nothing.
    Mer.   True, I talk of dreams,
Which are the children of an idle brain,
Begot of nothing but vain fantasy,
Which is as thin of substance as the air
And more inconstant than the wind, who wooes
Even now the frozen bosom of the north,
And, being anger'd, puffs away from thence,
Turning his face to the dew-dropping south.

> Shakespeare, *Romeo and Juliet,* I, iv, 54

22 *Brutus.* Between the acting of a dreadful thing
And the first motion, all the interim is
Like a phantasma or a hideous dream.

> Shakespeare, *Julius Caesar,* II, i, 62

23 *Hamlet.* O God, I could be bounded in a nutshell
and count myself a king of infinite space, were it
not that I have bad dreams.

> Shakespeare, *Hamlet,* II, ii, 260

24 The imaginations of them that sleep are those we
call *dreams.* And these also (as all other imaginations) have been before, either totally or by parcels, in the sense. And because in sense, the brain
and nerves, which are the necessary organs of
sense, are so benumbed in sleep as not easily to be
moved by the action of external objects, there can
happen in sleep no imagination, and therefore no
dream, but what proceeds from the agitation of
the inward parts of man's body; which inward
parts, for the connexion they have with the brain
and other organs, when they be distempered do
keep the same in motion; whereby the imaginations there formerly made, appear as if a man
were waking; saving that the organs of sense being
now benumbed, so as there is no new object which
can master and obscure them with a more vigorous impression, a dream must needs be more
clear, in this silence of sense, than are our waking
thoughts. . . .

And seeing dreams are caused by the distemper
of some of the inward parts of the body, diverse
distempers must needs cause different dreams.
And hence it is that lying cold breedeth dreams of
fear, and raiseth the thought and image of some
fearful object, the motion from the brain to the
inner parts, and from the inner parts to the brain
being reciprocal. . . . In sum, our dreams are the
reverse of our waking imaginations; the motion
when we are awake beginning at one end, and
when we dream, at another.

> Hobbes, *Leviathan,* I, 2

25 To say He hath spoken to him in a dream is no
more than to say he dreamed that God spake to
him; which is not of force to win belief from any
man that knows dreams are for the most part natural, and may proceed from former thoughts; and
such dreams as that, from self-conceit, and foolish
arrogance, and false opinion of a man's own goodliness, or other virtue, by which he thinks he hath
merited the favour of extraordinary revelation. To
say he hath seen a vision, or heard a voice, is to
say that he dreamed between sleeping and waking: for in such manner a man doth many times
naturally take his dream for a vision, as not having well observed his own slumbering.

> Hobbes, *Leviathan,* III, 32

26 Half our days we pass in the shadow of the earth,
and the brother of death exacteth a third part of
our lives. A good part of our sleeps is peered out
with visions, and phantastical objects wherin we
are confessedly deceived. The day supplyeth us
with truths, the night with fictions and falsehoods,
which uncomfortably divide the natural account
of our beings. And therefore having passed the
day in sober labours and rational enquiries of
truth, we are fain to betake ourselves unto such a
state of being, wherin the soberest heads have acted all the monstrosities of melancholy, and which
unto open eyes are no better than folly and madness.

> Sir Thomas Browne, *On Dreams*

27 If we dreamt the same thing every night, it would
affect us as much as the objects we see every day.
And if an artisan were sure to dream every night
for twelve hours' duration that he was a king, I
believe he would be almost as happy as a king,
who should dream every night for twelve hours on
end that he was an artisan.

If we were to dream every night that we were
pursued by enemies and harassed by these painful
phantoms, or that we passed every day in different occupations, as in making a voyage, we should
suffer almost as much as if it were real, and should
fear to sleep, as we fear to wake when we dread in
fact to enter on such mishaps. And, indeed, it
would cause pretty nearly the same discomforts as
the reality.

But since dreams are all different, and each single one is diversified, what is seen in them affects
us much less that what we see when awake, because of its continuity, which is not, however, so

continuous and level as not to change too; but it changes less abruptly, except rarely, as when we travel, and then we say, "It seems to me I am dreaming." For life is a dream a little less inconstant.

Pascal, *Pensées*, VI, 386

28 Methought I saw my late espoused Saint
    Brought to me like *Alcestis* from the grave,
    Whom *Joves* great Son to her glad Husband gave,
    Rescu'd from death by force though pale and faint.
Mine as whom washt from spot of child-bed taint,
    Purification in the old Law did save,
    And such, as yet once more I trust to have
    Full sight of her in Heaven without restraint,
Came vested all in white, pure as her mind:
    Her face was vail'd, yet to my fancied sight,
    Love, sweetness, goodness, in her person shin'd
So clear, as in no face with more delight.
    But O as to embrace me she enclin'd
    I wak'd, she fled, and day brought back my night.

Milton, *Methought I saw my late espoused Saint*

29 He [Johnson] related, that he had once in a dream a contest of wit with some other person, and that he was very much mortified by imagining that his opponent had the better of him. 'Now, (said he,) one may mark here the effect of sleep in weakening the power of reflection; for had not my judgement failed me, I should have seen, that the wit of this supposed antagonist, by whose superiority I felt myself depressed, was as much furnished by me, as that which I thought I had been uttering in my own character.'

Boswell, *Life of Johnson* (1780)

30 I would ask if dreams (from which our sleep is never free, although we rarely remember what we have dreamed), may not be a regulation of nature adapted to ends. For, when all the muscular forces of the body are relaxed, dreams serve the purpose of internally stimulating the vital organs by means of the imagination and the great activity which it exerts—an activity that in this state generally rises to psycho-physical agitation. This seems to be why imagination is usually more actively at work in the sleep of those who have gone to bed at night with a loaded stomach, just when this stimulation is most needed. Hence, I would suggest that without this internal stimulating force and fatiguing unrest that makes us complain of our dreams, which in fact, however, are probably curative, sleep, even in a sound state of health, would amount to a complete extinction of life.

Kant, *Critique of Teleological Judgement*, 67

31 *Her* lips were red, *her* looks were free,
    Her locks were yellow as gold:

Her skin was as white as leprosy,
The Night-mare LIFE-IN-DEATH was she,
Who thicks man's blood with cold.

Coleridge, *The Rime of the Ancient Mariner*, 190

32 Our life is twofold: Sleep hath its own world,
    A boundary between the things misnamed
    Death and existence: Sleep hath its own world,
    And a wide realm of wild reality.

Byron, *The Dream*, I

33 Was it a vision, or a waking dream?
    Fled is that music:—do I wake or sleep?

Keats, *Ode to a Nightingale*

34 When I was a child, I well remember a somewhat similar circumstance that befell me; whether it was a reality or a dream, I never could entirely settle. The circumstance was this. I had been cutting up some caper or other—I think it was trying to crawl up the chimney, as I had seen a little sweep do a few days previous; and my stepmother who, somehow or other, was all the time whipping me, or sending me to bed supperless,—my stepmother dragged me by the legs out of the chimney and packed me off to bed, though it was only two o'clock in the afternoon of the 21st June, the longest day in the year in our hemisphere. I felt dreadfully. But there was no help for it, so upstairs I went to my little room in the third floor, undressed myself as slowly as possible so as to kill time, and with a bitter sigh got between the sheets.

I lay there dismally calculating that sixteen entire hours must elapse before I could hope to get out of bed again. Sixteen hours in bed! the small of my back ached to think of it. And it was so light too; the sun shining in at the window, and a great rattling of coaches in the streets, and the sound of gay voices all over the house. I felt worse and worse—at last I got up, dressed, and softly going down in my stockinged feet, sought out my stepmother, and suddenly threw myself at her feet, beseeching her as a particular favour to give me a good slippering for my misbehaviour; anything indeed but condemning me to lie abed such an unendurable length of time. But she was the best and most conscientious of stepmothers, and back I had to go to my room. For several hours I lay there broad awake, feeling a great deal worse than I have ever done since, even from the greatest subsequent misfortunes. At last I must have fallen into a troubled nightmare of a doze; and slowly waking from it—half steeped in dreams—I opened my eyes, and the before sunlit room was now wrapped in outer darkness. Instantly I felt a shock running through all my frame; nothing was to be seen, and nothing was to be heard; but a supernatural hand seemed placed in mine. My arm hung over the counterpane, and the nameless, unimaginable, silent form or phantom, to which the hand belonged, seemed closely seated by my bedside. For what seemed ages piled on ages, I lay there, frozen with the most awful fears, not daring to drag away my hand; yet ever thinking that if I could but stir it one single inch, the horrid spell would be broken. I knew not how this consciousness at last glided away from me; but waking in the morning, I shudderingly remembered it all, and for days and weeks and months afterwards I lost myself in confounding attempts to explain the mystery. Nay, to this very hour, I often puzzle myself with it.

Melville, *Moby Dick*, IV

35 In a morbid condition of the brain, dreams often have a singular actuality, vividness, and extraordinary semblance of reality. At times monstrous images are created, but the setting and the whole picture are so truthlike and filled with details so delicate, so unexpectedly, but so artistically consistent, that the dreamer, were he an artist like Pushkin or Turgenev even, could never have invented them in the waking state. Such sick dreams always remain long in the memory and make a powerful impression on the overwrought and deranged nervous system.

Dostoevsky, *Crime and Punishment*, I, 5

36 The world of dreams is our real world whilst we are sleeping, because our attention then lapses from the sensible world. Conversely, when we wake the attention usually lapses from the dreamworld and that becomes unreal. But if a dream haunts us and compels our attention during the day it is very apt to remain figuring in our consciousness as a sort of sub-universe alongside of the waking world. Most people have probably had dreams which it is hard to imagine not to have been glimpses into an actually existing region of being, perhaps a corner of the "spiritual world." And dreams have accordingly in all ages been regarded as revelations, and have played a large part in furnishing forth mythologies and creating themes for faith to lay hold upon. The "larger universe" here, which helps us to believe both in the dream and in the waking reality which is its immediate reductive, is the *total* universe, of Nature *plus* the Supernatural. The dream holds true, namely, in one half of that universe; the waking perceptions in the other half.

William James, *Psychology*, XXI

37 In the dream life, the child, as it were, continues his existence in the man, with a retention of all his traits and wishes, including those which he was obliged to allow to fall into disuse in his later years. With irresistible might it will be impressed on you by what processes of development, of repression, sublimation, and reaction there arises out of the child, with its peculiar gifts and tenden-

cies, the so-called normal man, the bearer and partly the victim of our painfully acquired civilization.

Freud, *Origin and Development of Psycho-Analysis*, III

38 That all the material composing the content of a dream is somehow derived from experience, that it is reproduced or *remembered* in the dream—this at least may be accepted as an incontestable fact. Yet it would be wrong to assume that such a connection between the dream-content and reality will be easily obvious from a comparison between the two. On the contrary, the connection must be carefully sought, and in quite a number of cases it may for a long while elude discovery.

Freud, *Interpretation of Dreams*, I, B

39 The dream represents a certain state of affairs, such as I might wish to exist; *the content of the dream is thus the fulfilment of a wish; its motive is a wish.*

Freud, *Interpretation of Dreams*, II

40 The dream is not comparable to the irregular sounds of a musical instrument, which, instead of being played by the hand of a musician, is struck by some external force; the dream is not meaningless, not absurd, does not presuppose that one part of our store of ideas is dormant while another part begins to awake. It is a perfectly valid psychic phenomenon, actually a wish-fulfilment; it may be enrolled in the continuity of the intelligible psychic activities of the waking state; it is built up by a highly complicated intellectual activity.

Freud, *Interpretation of Dreams*, III

41 The dream often appears to have several meanings; not only may several wish-fulfilments be combined in it . . . but one meaning or one wish-fulfilment may conceal another, until in the lowest stratum one comes upon the fulfilment of a wish from the earliest period of childhood.

Freud, *Interpretation of Dreams*, V, B

42 In a certain sense, all dreams are *convenience-dreams;* they serve the purpose of continuing to sleep instead of waking. *The dream is the guardian of sleep, not its disturber. . . . The wish to sleep, to which the conscious ego has adjusted itself, and which . . . represents the ego's contribution to the dream, must thus always be taken into account as a motive of dream-formation, and every successful dream is a fulfilment of this wish.*

Freud, *Interpretation of Dreams*, V, C

43 It has been my experience—and to this I have found no exception—that every dream treats of oneself. Dreams are absolutely egoistic.

Freud, *Interpretation of Dreams*, VI, C

44 The inclusion of a certain content in *a dream within a dream* is, therefore, equivalent to the wish that

what has been characterized as a dream had never occurred. In other words: when a particular incident is represented by the dream-work in a dream, it signifies the strongest confirmation of the reality of this incident, the most emphatic *affirmation* of it. The dream-work utilizes the dream itself as a form of repudiation, and thereby confirms the theory that a dream is a wish-fulfilment.

Freud, *Interpretation of Dreams*, VI, C

45 The investigation of day-dreams might really have afforded the shortest and best approach to the understanding of nocturnal dreams.

Like dreams, they are wish-fulfilments; like dreams, they are largely based upon the impressions of childish experiences; like dreams, they obtain a certain indulgence from the censorship in respect of their creations. If we trace their formation, we become aware how the wish-motive which has been operative in their production has taken the material of which they are built, mixed it together, rearranged it, and fitted it together into a new whole. They bear very much the same relation to the childish memories to which they refer as many of the baroque palaces of Rome bear to the ancient ruins, whose hewn stones and columns have furnished the material for the structures built in the modern style.

Freud, *Interpretation of Dreams*, VI, I

46 Dreaming is on the whole an act of regression to the earliest relationships of the dreamer, a resuscitation of his childhood, of the impulses which were then dominant and the modes of expression which were then available. Behind this childhood of the individual we are then promised an insight into the phylogenetic childhood, into the evolution of the human race, of which the development of the individual is only an abridged repetition influenced by the fortuitous circumstances of life . . . and we are encouraged to expect, from the analysis of dreams, a knowledge of the archaic inheritance of man, a knowledge of psychical things in him that are innate. It would seem that dreams and neuroses have preserved for us more of the psychical antiquities than we suspected; so that psycho-analysis may claim a high rank among those sciences which endeavour to reconstruct the oldest and darkest phases of the beginnings of mankind.

Freud, *Interpretation of Dreams*, VII, B

47 And what of the value of dreams in regard to our knowledge of the future? That, of course, is quite out of the question. One would like to substitute the words: *in regard to our knowledge of the past.* For in every sense a dream has its origin in the past. The ancient belief that dreams reveal the future is not indeed entirely devoid of the truth. By representing a wish as fulfilled the dream certainly leads us into the future; but this future, which the dreamer accepts as his present, has been shaped in the likeness of the past by the indestructible wish.

Freud, *Interpretation of Dreams*, VII, F

48 Had I the heavens' embroidered cloths,
Enwrought with golden and silver light,
The blue and the dim and the dark cloths
Of night and light and the half-light,
I would spread the cloths under your feet:
But I, being poor, have only my dreams;
I have spread my dreams under your feet;
Tread softly because you tread on my dreams.

Yeats, *He Wishes for the Cloths of Heaven*

5.6 | *Madness*

Irrationality is peculiar to the so-called "rational animal." Though we sometimes refer to other animals as "mad," we do not do so in the sense in which human madness is understood as loss or disorder of mind. It is that sense of the term which runs through the quotations below, even when the word itself does not appear, but some other word—such as "frenzy," "lunacy," "melancholy," or "insanity"—takes its place. Only in quotations drawn from comparatively recent writers do such technical terms as "neurosis," "psychosis," or "hysteria" occur, together with the medical names for the symptoms or other manifestations of mental disease. The clinical picture of one mental disorder—epilepsy—was known to the ancients. Regarded popularly as "the sacred disease," it was treated in a scientific manner by Hippocrates.

The reader will find in the quotations from the poets, the historians, and the biographers a wide variety of examples of human madness, together with expressions of the awe or wonder that its manifestations inspire in those who behold it. There are, in addition, observations about the role of the emotions or passions in frenzy or lunacy, about the effect of madness on the rational processes and on the exercise of choice, and about the difference between the cogency of the insane and the lucidity of the sane. One special form of madness is often exemplified and commented on, and that is the madness of the lover—the divine madness.

The modern approach to mental disease, with its distinction between the symptoms of the illness and the disease process itself, and with its classification of neuroses and psychoses, is represented here in the quotations drawn from William James and Sigmund Freud.

---

1 *Orestes.* I go, an outcast wanderer from this land, and leave

behind, in life, in death, the name of what I did.
   Chorus. No, what you did was well done. Do not therefore bind
your mouth to foul speech. Keep no evil on your lips.
You liberated all the Argive city when
you lopped the heads of these two snakes with one clean stroke.
   Or. No!
Women who serve this house, they come like gorgons, they
wear robes of black, and they are wreathed in a tangle
of snakes. I can no longer stay.
   Ch. Orestes, dearest to your father of all men
what fancies whirl you? Hold, do not give way to fear.
   Or. These are no fancies of affliction. They are clear,
and real, and here; the bloodhounds of my mother's hate.
   Ch. It is the blood still wet upon your hands, that makes
this shaken turbulence be thrown upon your sense.
   Or. Ah, Lord Apollo, how they grow and multiply,
repulsive for the blood drops of their dripping eyes.
   Ch. There is one way to make you clean: let Loxias
touch you, and set you free from these disturbances.
   Or. You can not see them, but I see them. I am driven
from this place. I can stay here no longer.

         Aeschylus, *Libation Bearers,* 1042

2 Towards this tongue of land . . . the men to whom the business was assigned carried out a double bridge from Abydos; and while the Phœnicians constructed one line with cables of white flax, the Egyptians in the other used ropes made of papyrus. Now it is seven furlongs across from Abydos to the opposite coast. When, therefore, the channel had been bridged successfully, it happened that a great storm arising broke the whole work to pieces, and destroyed all that had been done.

So when Xerxes heard of it he was full of wrath, and straightway gave orders that the Hellespont should receive three hundred lashes, and that a pair of fetters should be cast into it. Nay, I have even heard it said that he bade the branders take their irons and therewith brand the Hellespont. It is certain that he commanded those who scourged the waters to utter, as they lashed them, these barbarian and wicked words: "Thou bitter water, thy lord lays on thee this punishment because thou hast wronged him without a cause, having suffered no evil at his hands. Verily King Xerxes will cross thee, whether thou wilt or no. Well dost thou deserve that no man should honour thee with sacrifice; for thou art of a truth a treacherous and unsavoury river." While the sea was thus punished by his orders, he likewise commanded that the overseers of the work should lose their heads.

         Herodotus, *History,* VII, 34–35

3 *Tecmessa.* In the depth of night, after the evening flares
Had all gone out, Ajax, with sword in hand,
Went slowly groping toward the door, intent
Upon some pointless errand. I objected,
And said, "Ajax, what are you doing? Why
Do you stir? No messenger has summoned you:

You have heard no trumpet. Why, the whole
   army now's asleep!"
He answered briefly in a well-worn phrase,
"Woman, a woman's decency is silence."
I heard, and said no more; he issued forth alone.
I don't know what horrors occurred outside,
But when he came back in, he brought with him
A mass of hobbled bulls and shepherd dogs
And woolly captives. He struck the heads off
   some;
Others' he severed with an upward cut;
And some, held fast in bonds, he kept abusing
With words and blows, as though they were hu-
   man beings—
And all the while he was vexing poor dumb
   beasts.
At length he darted out the door and spoke
Wild, rending words, directed toward some phan-
   tom,
Exulting with a harsh laugh how he'd paid them,
Odysseus and the sons of Atreus. Then
He sprang back in again, and somehow, slowly,
By painful stages came to his right mind.

                              Sophocles, *Ajax*, 285

4 *Messenger.* Offerings to Zeus were set before the
   hearth
to purify the house, for Heracles
had cast the body of the king outside.
There the children stood, in lovely cluster,
with Megara and the old man. In holy hush
the basket made the circle of the hearth.
And then, as Heracles reached out his hand
to take the torch and dip it in the water,
he stood stockstill. There he stood, not moving,
while the children stared. Suddenly he changed:
his eyes rolled and bulged from their sockets,
and the veins stood out, gorged with blood, and
   froth
began to trickle down his bearded chin.
Then he spoke, laughing like a maniac:
"Why hallow fire, Father, to cleanse the house
before I kill Eurystheus? Why double work,
when at one blow I might complete my task?
I'll go and fetch Eurystheus' head, add it
to that other corpse, then purify my hands.
Empty your water out! Drop those baskets!
Someone fetch my bow. Put weapons in my
   hands:
I march against Mycenae! Let me have
crowbars and picks: the Cyclopes built well,
cramping stone on stone with plumb and mallet,
but with my pick I'll rip them down again."
Then he fancied that his chariot stood there;
he made as though to leap its rails, and rode off,
prodding with his hand as though it held a goad.
   Whether to laugh or shudder, we could not tell.
We stared at one another. Then one man asked,
"Is the master playing, or is he . . . mad?"
Up and down, throughout the house, he drove,
and riding through the great hall, claimed it was
Nisus' city, though it was, in fact, his house.

He threw himself to the floor, and acted out
a feast. He tarried there a while, then said
he was approaching Isthmus' wooded valley.
He unstrapped his buckles and stripped himself
   bare,
and wrestled with no one; then called for silence
and crowned himself the victor of a match
that never was. Then raged against Eurystheus,
and said he'd come to Mycenae. His father
caught him by that muscled hand and said:
"What do you mean, my son? What is this journey
that you make? Or has the blood of those you've
   slain
made you mad?" He thought Eurystheus' father
had come, trembling, to supplicate his hand;
pushed him away, and set his bow and arrows
against his sons. He thought he was killing
Eurystheus' children. Trembling with terror,
they rushed here and there; one hid beneath
his mother's robes, one ran to the shadow
of a pillar, and the last crouched like a bird
below the altar. Their mother shrieked:
"You are their father! Will you kill your sons?"
And shouts broke from the old man and the
   slaves.
Around the pillar he pursued his son
in dreadful circles, then caught up with him
and pierced him to the heart. Backward he fell,
dying, and stained the flagstones with his blood.
His father shouted in triumph, exulting,
"Here is the first of Eurystheus' youngsters dead;
his death repays me for his father's hate."
He aimed his bow at the second, who crouched
below the altar's base, trying to hide.
The boy leaped first, fell at his father's knees
and held his hand up to his father's chin.
"Dearest Father," he cried, "do not murder me.
I am your own son, yours, not Eurystheus'!"
But he stared from stony gorgon eyes,
found his son too close to draw the bow,
and brought his club down on that golden head,
and smashed the skull, as though a blacksmith
smiting steel. Now that his second son lay dead,
he rushed to kill the single victim left.
But before he drew the bow, the mother
seized her child, ran within and locked the doors.
And, as though these were the Cyclopean walls,
he pried the panels up, ripped out the jambs,
and with one arrow brought down son and wife.
And then he rushed to kill his father too,
but look! a phantom came—or so it seemed to
   us—
Pallas, with plumed helm, brandishing a spear.
She hurled a rock; it struck him on the chest,
stopped short his murderous rage and knocked
   him
into sleep. He slumped to the floor and hit
his back against a pillar which had fallen there,
snapped in two pieces when the roof collapsed.
   Delivered from the fear that made us run,
we helped the old man lash him down with ropes

against the pillar, lest when he awakes
still greater grief be added to the rest.
He sleeps now, wretched man, no happy sleep,
killer of his wife and sons. I do not know
one man alive more miserable than this.

Euripides, Heracles, 922

5 *Messenger.* And now the stranger worked a miracle.
Reaching for the highest branch of a great fir,
he bent it down, down, down to the dark earth,
till it was curved the way a taut bow bends
or like a rim of wood when forced about the circle
of a wheel. Like that he forced that mountain fir
down to the ground. No mortal could have done
it.
Then he seated Pentheus at the highest tip
and with his hands let the trunk rise straightly up,
slowly and gently, lest it throw its rider.
And the tree rose, towering to heaven, with my
master
huddled at the top. And now the Maenads saw
him
more clearly than he saw them. But barely had
they seen,
when the stranger vanished and there came a
great voice
out of heaven—Dionysus', it must have been—
crying: "Women, I bring you the man who has
mocked
at you and me and at our holy mysteries.
Take vengeance upon him." And as he spoke
a flash of awful fire bound earth and heaven.
The high air hushed, and along the forest glen
the leaves hung still; you could hear no cry of
beasts.
The Bacchae heard that voice but missed its
words,
and leaping up, they stared, peering everywhere.
Again that voice. And now they knew his cry,
the clear command of god. And breaking loose
like startled doves, through grove and torrent,
over jagged rocks, they flew, their feet maddened
by the breath of god. And when they saw my master
perching in his tree, they climbed a great stone
that towered opposite his perch and showered him
with stones and javelins of fir, while the others
hurled their wands. And yet they missed their target,
poor Pentheus in his perch, barely out of reach
of their eager hands, treed, unable to escape.
Finally they splintered branches from the oaks
and with those bars of wood tried to lever up the
tree
by prying at the roots. But every effort failed.
Then Agave cried out: "Maenads, make a circle
about the trunk and grip it with your hands.
Unless we take this climbing beast, he will reveal
the secrets of the god." With that, thousands of
hands

tore the fir tree from the earth, and down, down
from his high perch fell Pentheus, tumbling
to the ground, sobbing and screaming as he fell,
for he knew his end was near. His own mother,
like a priestess with her victim, fell upon him
first. But snatching off his wig and snood
so she would recognize his face, he touched her
cheeks,
screaming, *"No, no, Mother! I am Pentheus,*
your own son, the child you bore to Echion!
Pity me, spare me, Mother! I have done a wrong,
but do not kill your own son for my offense."
But she was foaming at the mouth, and her crazed
eyes
rolling with frenzy. She was mad, stark mad,
possessed by Bacchus. Ignoring his cries of pity,
she seized his left arm at the wrist; then, planting
her foot upon his chest, she pulled, wrenching
away
the arm at the shoulder—not by her own strength,
for the god had put inhuman power in her hands.
Ino, meanwhile, on the other side, was scratching
off
his flesh. Then Autonoë and the whole horde
of Bacchae swarmed upon him. Shouts everywhere,
he screaming with what little breath was left,
they shrieking in triumph. One tore off an arm,
another a foot still warm in its shoe. His ribs
were clawed clean of flesh and every hand
was smeared with blood as they played ball with
scraps
of Pentheus' body.
The pitiful remains lie scattered,
one piece among the sharp rocks, others
lying lost among the leaves in the depths
of the forest. His mother, picking up his head,
impaled it on her wand. She seems to think it is
some mountain lion's head which she carries in
triumph
through the thick of Cithaeron. Leaving her sisters
at the Maenad dances, she is coming here, gloat-
ing
over her grisly prize. She calls upon Bacchus:
he is her "fellow-huntsman," "comrade of the
chase,
crowned with victory." But all the victory
she carries home is her own grief.

Euripides, Bacchae, 1063

6 *Socrates.* Of madness there were two kinds; one
produced by human infirmity, the other . . . a
divine release of the soul from the yoke of custom
and convention.
Phaedrus. True.
Soc. The divine madness was subdivided into
four kinds, prophetic, initiatory, poetic, erotic,
having four gods presiding over them; the first
was the inspiration of Apollo, the second that of

Dionysus, the third that of the Muses, the fourth that of Aphrodite and Eros. In the description of the last kind of madness, which was also said to be the best, we spoke of the affection of love in a figure, into which we introduced a tolerably credible and possibly true though partly erring myth, which was also a hymn in honour of Love, who is your lord and also mine, Phaedrus, and the guardian of fair children, and to him we sung the hymn in measured and solemn strain.

Plato, *Phaedrus,* 265A

7 A disaster followed, whether accidental or treacherously contrived by the emperor, is uncertain, as authors have given both accounts, worse, however, and more dreadful than any which have ever happened to this city by the violence of fire. It had its beginning in that part of the circus which adjoins the Palatine and Cælian hills, where, amid the shops containing inflammable wares, the conflagration both broke out and instantly became so fierce and so rapid from the wind that it seized in its grasp the entire length of the circus. For here there were no houses fenced in by solid masonry, or temples surrounded by walls, or any other obstacle to interpose delay. The blaze in its fury ran first through the level portions of the city, then rising to the hills, while it again devastated every place below them, it outstripped all preventive measures; so rapid was the mischief and so completely at its mercy the city, with those narrow winding passages and irregular streets, which characterised old Rome. . . . And no one dared to stop the mischief, because of incessant menaces from a number of persons who forbade the extinguishing of the flames, because again others openly hurled brands, and kept shouting that there was one who gave them authority, either seeking to plunder more freely, or obeying orders.

Nero at this time was at Antium, and did not return to Rome until the fire approached his house, which he had built to connect the palace with the gardens of Mæcenas. It could not, however, be stopped from devouring the palace, the house, and everything around it. However, to relieve the people, driven out homeless as they were, he threw open to them the Campus Martius and the public buildings of Agrippa, and even his own gardens, and raised temporary structures to receive the destitute multitude. Supplies of food were brought up from Ostia and the neighbouring towns, and the price of corn was reduced to three sesterces a peck. These acts, though popular, produced no effect, since a rumour had gone forth everywhere that, at the very time when the city was in flames, the emperor appeared on a private stage and sang of the destruction of Troy, comparing present misfortunes with the calamities of antiquity.

Tacitus, *Annals,* XV, 38–39

8 Every man prefers to grieve in a sane mind, rather than to be glad in madness.

Augustine, *City of God,* XI, 27

9 To suffer ecstasy means to be placed outside oneself. This happens as to the apprehensive power and as to the appetitive power. As to the apprehensive power, a man is said to be placed outside himself when he is placed outside the knowledge proper to him. This may be due to his being raised to a higher knowledge; thus, a man is said to suffer ecstasy because he is placed outside the connatural apprehension of his sense and reason, when he is raised up so as to comprehend things that surpass sense and reason. Or it may be due to his being cast down into a state of debasement; thus a man may be said to suffer ecstasy when he is overcome by violent passion or madness. As to the appetitive part, a man is said to suffer ecstasy when the appetite is borne towards something else, so that it goes forth out from itself, as it were.

The first of these ecstasies is caused by love by way of disposition, in so far, namely, as love makes the beloved to dwell in the lover's mind; and the more we give our mind to one thing, the less we think of others. The second ecstasy is caused by love directly; by love of friendship, absolutely, by love of concupiscence, not absolutely but in a relative sense. Because in love of concupiscence, the lover is taken out from himself, in a certain sense; in so far, namely, as not being satisfied with enjoying the good that he has, he seeks to enjoy something outside himself. But since he seeks to have this extrinsic good for himself, he does not go out from himself absolutely, and this affection remains finally within him. On the other hand, in the love of friendship, a man's affection goes out from itself absolutely, because he wishes and does good to his friend, as it were, caring and providing for him, for his sake.

Aquinas, *Summa Theologica,* I–II, 28, 3

10 Of what is the subtlest madness made, but the subtlest wisdom? As great enmities are born of great friendships, and mortal maladies of vigorous health, so are the greatest and wildest manias born of the rare and lively stirrings of our soul; it is only a half turn of the peg to pass from the one to the other. In the actions of the insane we see how neatly madness combines with the most vigorous operations of our soul. Who does not know how imperceptibly near is madness to the lusty flights of a free mind and the effects of supreme and extraordinary virtue?

Montaigne, *Essays,* II, 12, Apology for Raymond Sebond

11 Is there not some rashness in philosophy to consider that men produce their greatest deeds and those most closely approaching divinity when they are out of their minds and frenzied and mad? We

improve by the privation and deadening of our reason. The two natural ways to enter the cabinet of the gods and there foresee the course of destinies are madness and sleep. This is amusing to think about: by the dislocation that the passions bring about in our reason, we become virtuous; by the extirpation of reason that is brought about by madness or the semblance of death, we become prophets and soothsayers. I never was more willing to believe philosophy. It is a pure transport that the sacred truth inspired in the philosophical spirit, which wrests from it, against its intention, the admission that the tranquil state of our soul, the sedate state, the healthiest state that philosophy can acquire for her, is not her best state. Our waking is more asleep than sleep; our wisdom less wise than madness. Our dreams are worth more than our reasonings. The worst position we can take is in ourselves.

But does not philosophy think that we have enough sense to notice that the voice which makes the spirit when it is detached from man so clairvoyant, so great, so perfect, and while it is in man so earthly, ignorant, and shadowed, is a voice coming from the spirit which is a part of earthly, ignorant, and shadowed man, and for that reason a voice not to be trusted or believed?

Montaigne, *Essays*, II, 12, Apology for Raymond Sebond

12 *Malvolio.* I am not mad, Sir Topas: I say to you, this house is dark.

Clown. Madman, thou errest: I say, there is no darkness but ignorance; in which thou art more puzzled than the Egyptians in their fog.

Mal. I say, this house is as dark as ignorance, though ignorance were as dark as hell; and I say, there was never man thus abused.

Shakespeare, *Twelfth Night*, IV, ii, 44

13 *Polonius.* How now, Ophelia! What's the matter?

Ophelia. O, my lord, my lord, I have been so affrighted!

Pol. With what, i' the name of God?

Oph. My lord, as I was sewing in my closet, Lord Hamlet, with his doublet all unbraced; No hat upon his head; his stockings foul'd, Ungarter'd, and down-gyved to his ancle; Pale as his shirt; his knees knocking each other; And with a look so piteous in purport As if he had been loosed out of hell To speak of horrors—he comes before me.

Pol. Mad for thy love?

Oph.   My lord, I do not know; But truly, I do fear it.

Pol.   What said he?

Oph. He took me by the wrist and held me hard;

Then goes he to the length of all his arm;

And, with his other hand thus o'er his brow,

He falls to such perusal of my face

As he would draw it. Long stay'd he so;

At last, a little shaking of mine arm

And thrice his head thus waving up and down,

He raised a sigh so piteous and profound

As it did seem to shatter all his bulk

And end his being. That done, he lets me go;

And, with his head over his shoulder turn'd,

He seem'd to find his way without his eyes;

For out o'doors he went without their helps,

And, to the last, bended their light on me.

Pol. Come, go with me: I will go seek the King.

This is the very ecstasy of love,

Whose violent property fordoes itself

And leads the will to desperate undertakings

As oft as any passion under heaven

That does afflict our natures. I am sorry.

What, have you given him any hard words of late?

Oph. No, my good lord, but, as you did command,

I did repel his letters and denied

His access to me.

Pol.   That hath made him mad.

Shakespeare, *Hamlet*, II, i, 74

14 *Hamlet.* I am but mad north-north-west. When the wind is southerly I know a hawk from a handsaw.

Shakespeare, *Hamlet*, II, ii, 396

15 *Ophelia.* O, what a noble mind is here o'erthrown!

The courtier's, soldier's, scholar's, eye, tongue, sword,

The expectancy and rose of the fair state,

The glass of fashion and the mould of form,

The observed of all observers, quite, quite down!

And I, of ladies most deject and wretched,

That suck'd the honey of his music vows,

Now see that noble and most sovereign reason,

Like sweet bells jangled, out of tune and harsh;

That unmatch'd form and feature of blown youth

Blasted with ecstasy: O, woe is me,

To have seen what I have seen, see what I see!

Shakespeare, *Hamlet*, II, i, 158

16 *Queen.* To whom do you speak this?

Hamlet.   Do you see nothing there?

Queen. Nothing at all; yet all that is I see.

Ham. Nor did you nothing hear?

Queen.   No, nothing but ourselves.

Ham. Why, look you there! look, how it steals away!

My father, in his habit as he lived!

Look, where he goes, even now, out at the portal!

[*Exit* Ghost]

Queen. This is the very coinage of your brain.

This bodiless creation ecstasy

Is very cunning in.

Ham.   Ecstasy!

My pulse, as yours, doth temperately keep time,

And makes as healthful music. It is not madness

That I have utter'd. Bring me to the test,

And I the matter will re-word; which madness
Would gambol from. Mother, for love of grace,
Lay not that flattering unction to your soul,
That not your trespass, but my madness speaks.

> Shakespeare, *Hamlet*, III, iv, 131

17 *Laertes.* O heat, dry up my brains! tears seven
    times salt,
Burn out the sense and virtue of mine eye!
By heaven, thy madness shall be paid with
    weight,
Till our scale turn the beam. O rose of May!
Dear maid, kind sister, sweet Ophelia!
O heavens! is't possible, a young maid's wits
Should be as mortal as an old man's life?
Nature is fine in love, and where 'tis fine,
It sends some precious instance of itself
After the thing it loves.
    Ophelia. [*Sings*]
      "They bore him barefaced on the bier;
      Hey non nonny, nonny, hey nonny;
      And in his grave rain'd many a tear"—
Fare you well, my dove!
    Laer. Hadst thou thy wits, and didst persuade
    revenge,
It could not move thus.
    Oph. [*Sings*] "You must sing a-down a-down,
      An you call him a-down-a."
O, how the wheel becomes it! It is the false stew-
ard, that stole his master's daughter.
    Laer. This nothing's more than matter.
    Oph. There's rosemary, that's for remembrance,
pray, love, remember; and there is pansies, that's
for thoughts.
    Laer. A document in madness, thoughts and re-
membrance fitted.

> Shakespeare, *Hamlet*, IV, v, 155

18 *Lear.* You see me here, you gods, a poor old man,
As full of grief as age; wretched in both!
If it be you that stirs these daughters' hearts
Against their father, fool me not so much
To bear it tamely; touch me with noble anger,
And let not women's weapons, water-drops,
Stain my man's cheeks! No, you unnatural hags,
I will have such revenges on you both,
That all the world shall—I will do such things—
What they are, yet I know not; but they shall be
The terrors of the earth. You think I'll weep;
No, I'll not weep.
I have full cause of weeping; but this heart
Shall break into a hundred thousand flaws,
Or ere I'll weep. O Fool, I shall go mad!

> Shakespeare, *Lear*, II, iv, 275

19 *Lear.*   Pray, do not mock me.
I am a very foolish fond old man,
Fourscore and upward, not an hour more nor less;
And, to deal plainly,
I fear I am not in my perfect mind.

> Shakespeare, *Lear*, IV, vii, 60

20 *Doctor.* I have two nights watched with you, but
can perceive no truth in your report. When was it
she last walked?

    Gentlewoman. Since his Majesty went into the
field, I have seen her rise from her bed, throw her
nightgown upon her, unlock her closet, take forth
paper, fold it, write upon't, read it, afterwards seal
it, and again return to bed; yet all this while in a
most fast sleep.

    Doct. A great perturbation in nature, to receive
at once the benefit of sleep, and do the effects of
watching! In this slumbery agitation, besides her
walking and other actual performances, what, at
any time, have you heard her say?

    Gent. That, sir, which I will not report after her.

    Doct. You may to me; and 'tis most meet you
should.

    Gent. Neither to you nor any one; having no
witness to confirm my speech.

    Enter Lady Macbeth, *with a taper.*

Lo you, here she comes! This is her very guise;
and, upon my life, fast asleep. Observe her; stand
close.

    Doct. How came she by that light?

    Gent. Why, it stood by her. She has light by her
continually; 'tis her command.

    Doct. You see, her eyes are open.

    Gent. Ay, but their sense is shut.

    Doct. What is it she does now? Look, how she
rubs her hands.

    Gent. It is an accustomed action with her, to
seem thus washing her hands. I have known her
continue in this a quarter of an hour.

    Lady Macbeth. Yet here's a spot.

    Doct. Hark! she speaks. I will set down what
comes from her, to satisfy my remembrance the
more strongly.

    Lady M. Out, damned spot! out, I say! One;
two. Why, then 'tis time to do't. Hell is murky!
Fie, my lord, fie! a soldier, and afeard? What
need we fear who knows it, when none can call
our power to account? Yet who would have
thought the old man to have had so much blood
in him.

    Doct. Do you mark that?

    Lady M. The thane of Fife had a wife. Where is
she now? What, will these hands ne'er be clean?
No more o' that, my lord, no more o' that! You
mar all with this starting.

    Doct. Go to, go to; you have known what you
should not.

    Gent. She has spoke what she should not, I am
sure of that. Heaven knows what she has known.

    Lady M. Here's the smell of the blood still. All
the perfumes of Arabia will not sweeten this little
hand. Oh, oh, oh!

    Doct. What a sigh is there! The heart is sorely
charged.

    Gent. I would not have such a heart in my bo-
som for the dignity of the whole body.

Doct. Well, well, well—

Gent. Pray God it be, sir.

Doct. This disease is beyond my practice. Yet I have known those which have walked in their sleep who have died holily in their beds.

Lady M. Wash your hands, put on your night-gown; look not so pale. I tell you yet again, Banquo's buried; he cannot come out on's grave.

Doct. Even so?

Lady M. To bed, to bed! there's knocking at the gate. Come, come, come, come, give me your hand. What's done cannot be undone. To bed, to bed, to bed! [*Exit.*]

Doct. Will she go now to bed?

Gent. Directly.

Shakespeare, *Macbeth*, V, i, 1

21 *Macbeth.* How does your patient, doctor?

Doctor.   Not so sick, my lord.
As she is troubled with thick-coming fancies,
That keep her from her rest.

Macb.   Cure her of that.
Canst thou not minister to a mind diseased,
Pluck from the memory a rooted sorrow,
Raze out the written troubles of the brain,
And with some sweet oblivious antidote
Cleanse the stuff'd bosom of that perilous stuff
Which weighs upon the heart?

Doct.   Therein the patient
Must minister to himself.

Macb. Throw physic to the dogs; I'll none of it.

Shakespeare, *Macbeth*, V, iii, 37

22 Having thus lost his Understanding, he unluckily stumbled upon the oddest Fancy that ever enter'd into a Madman's Brain; for now he thought it convenient and necessary, as well for the Increase of his own Honour, as the Service of the Publick, to turn Knight-Errant, and roam through the whole World arm'd Cap-a-pee, and mounted on his Steed, in quest of Adventures; that thus imitating those Knight-Errants of whom he had read, and following their Course of Life, redressing all manner of Grievances, and exposing himself to Danger on all Occasions, at last, after a happy Conclusion of his Enterprizes, he might purchase everlasting Honour and Renown.

Cervantes, *Don Quixote*, I, 1

23 As they were thus discoursing, they discover'd some thirty or forty Wind-mills, that are in that Plain; and as soon as the Knight had spy'd them, Fortune, cry'd he, directs our Affairs better than we our selves could have wish'd: Look yonder, Friend *Sancho*, there are at least thirty outrageous Giants, whom I intend to encounter; and having depriv'd them of Life, we will begin to enrich our selves with their Spoils: For they are lawful Prize; and the Extirpation of that cursed Brood will be an acceptable Service to Heaven. What Giants, quoth *Sancho Pança?* Those whom thou see'st yonder, answer'd Don *Quixote*, with their long-extended Arms; some of that detested Race have Arms of so immense a Size, that sometimes they reach two Leagues in Length. Pray look better, Sir, quoth *Sancho;* those things yonder are no Giants, but Wind-mills, and the Arms you fancy, are their Sails, which being whirl'd about by the Wind, make the Mill go. 'Tis a Sign, cry'd Don *Quixote,* thou art but little acquainted with Adventures! I tell thee, they are Giants; and therefore if thou art afraid, go aside and say thy Prayers, for I am resolv'd to engage in a dreadful unequal Combat against them all. This said, he clapp'd Spurs to his Horse *Rozinante,* without giving Ear to his Squire *Sancho,* who bawl'd out to him, and assur'd him, that they were Wind-mills, and no Giants. But he was so fully possess'd with a strong Conceit of the contrary, that he did not so much as hear his Squire's Outcry, nor was he sensible of what they were, although he was already very near them: Far from that, Stand, Cowards, cry'd he as loud as he could; stand your Ground, ignoble Creatures, and fly not basely from a single Knight, who dares encounter you all. At the same Time the Wind rising, the Mill-Sails began to move, which, when Don *Quixote* spy'd, Base Miscreants, cry'd he, though you move more Arms than the Giant *Briareus,* you shall pay for your Arrogance. He most devoutly recommended himself to his Lady *Dulcinea,* imploring her Assistance in this perilous Adventure; and so covering himself with his Shield, and couching his Lance, he rush'd with *Rozinante's* utmost Speed upon the first Wind-mill he could come at, and running his Lance into the Sail, the Wind whirl'd it about with such Swiftness, that the Rapidity of the Motion presently broke the Lance into Shivers, and hurl'd away both Knight and Horse along with it, till down he fell rolling a good Way off in the Field. *Sancho Pança* ran as fast as his Ass could drive to help his Master, whom he found lying, and not able to stir, such a Blow he and *Rozinante* had receiv'd. Mercy o'me! cry'd *Sancho,* did not I give your Worship fair Warning? Did not I tell you they were Wind-mills, and that no Body could think otherwise, unless he had also Wind-mills in his Head? Peace, Friend *Sancho,* reply'd Don *Quixote:* There is nothing so subject to the Inconstancy of Fortune as War. I am verily perswaded, that cursed Necromancer *Freston,* who carry'd away my Study and my Books, has transform'd these Giants into Wind-mills, to deprive me of the Honour of the Victory; such is his inveterate Malice against me: But in the End, all his pernicious Wiles and Stratagems shall prove ineffectual against the prevailing Edge of my Sword. *Amen,* say I, reply'd *Sancho;* and so heaving him up again upon his Legs, once more the Knight mounted poor *Rozinate,* that was half Shoulder-slipp'd with his Fall.

Cervantes, *Don Quixote,* I, 8

24 Know then, my most faithful Squire, that *Amadis de Gaul* was one of the most accomplish'd Knights-Errant, nay, I should not have said, he was one of them, but the most perfect, the chief, and Prince of them all. And let not the *Belianises,* nor any others, pretend to stand in Competition with him for the Honour of Priority; for, to my Knowledge, should they attempt it, they would be egregiously in the wrong. I must also inform thee, that when a Painter studies to excel and grow famous in his Art, he takes care to imitate the best Originals; which Rule ought likewise to be observ'd in all other Arts and Sciences that serve for the Ornament of well-regulated Commonwealths. . . . Now, *Sancho,* I find that among the things which most display'd that Champion's Prudence and Fortitude, his Constancy and Love, and his other Heroick Virtues, none was more remarkable than his retiring from his disdainful *Oriana,* to do Penance on the *Poor Rock,* changing his Name into that of *Beltenebros,* or *The Lovely Obscure,* a Title certainly most significant, and adapted to the Life which he then intended to lead. So I am resolv'd to imitate him in this, the rather because I think it a more easy Task than it would be to copy his other Atchievements, such as cleaving the Bodies of Giants, cutting off the Heads of Dragons, killing dreadful Monsters, routing whole Armies, dispersing Navies, and breaking the Force of Magick Spells. And since these Mountainous Wilds offer me so fair an Opportunity, I see no Reason why I should neglect it, and therefore I'll lay hold on it now. Very well, quoth *Sancho;* but pray, Sir, what is it that you mean to do in this Fag-end of the World? Have I not already told thee, answer'd Don *Quixote,* that I intend to copy *Amadis* in his Madness, Despair, and Fury? Nay, at the same time I imitate the valiant *Orlando Furioso's* Extravagance, when he ran mad, after he had found the unhappy Tokens of the fair *Angelica's* dishonourable Commerce with *Medoro* at the Fountain; at which time, in his frantick Despair, he tore up Trees by the Roots, troubled the Waters of the clear Fountains, slew the Shepherds, destroy'd their Flocks, fir'd their Huts, demolish'd Houses, drove their Horses before him, and committed a hundred thousand other Extravagancies worthy to be recorded in the eternal Register of Fame. . . . Sir, quoth *Sancho,* I dare say the Knights who did these Penances had some Reason to be mad; but what need have You to be mad too? What Lady has sent you a packing, or so much as slighted you? When did you ever find that my Lady *Dulcinea del Toboso* did otherwise than she should do, with either *Moor* or *Christian?* Why, there's the Point, cry'd Don *Quixote;* in this consists the singular Perfection of my Undertaking: For, mark me, *Sancho,* for a Knight-Errant to run mad upon any just Occasion, is neither strange nor meritorious; no, the Rarity is to run mad without a Cause, without the least Constraint or Necessity.

Cervantes, *Don Quixote,* I, 25

25 At length he wak'd, and with a loud Voice, Blessed be the Almighty, cry'd he, for this great Benefit he has vouchsafed to do me! Infinite are his Mercies; they are greater, and more in Number than the Sins of Men. The Niece hearkening very attentively to these Words of her Uncle, and finding more Sense in them than there was in his usual Talk, at least since he had fallen ill; What do you say, Sir, said she, has any Thing extraordinary happen'd? What Mercies are these you mention? Mercies, answer'd he, that Heaven has this Moment vouchsafed to shew me, in spite of all my Iniquities. My Judgment is return'd clear and undisturb'd, and that Cloud of Ignorance is now remov'd, which the continual Reading of those damnable Books of Knight-Errantry had cast over my Understanding. Now I perceive their Nonsense and Impertinence, and am only sorry the Discovery happens so late, when I want Time to make Amends by those Studies that shou'd enlighten my Soul, and prepare me for Futurity. I find, Niece, my End approaches; but I wou'd have it such, that though my Life has got me the Character of a Mad-man, I may deserve a better at my Death. Dear Child, continu'd he, send for my honest Friend the Curate, the Batchelor *Carrasco,* and Master Nicholas the Barber, for I intend to make my Confession, and my Will. His Niece was sav'd the Trouble of sending, for presently they all three came in; which Don *Quixote* perceiving, My good Friends, said he, I have happy News to tell you; I am no longer Don *Quixote de la Mancha,* but *Alonso Quixano,* the same whom the World for his fair Behaviour has been formerly pleas'd to call *the Good.* I now declare my self an Enemy to *Amadis de Gaul,* and his whole Generation; all profane Stories of Knight-Errantry, all Romances I detest. I have a true Sense of the Danger of reading them, and of all my pass'd Follies, and through Heaven's Mercy, and my own Experience, I abhor them. His three Friends were not a little surprized to hear him talk at this rate, and concluded some new Frenzy had possess'd him. What now, said *Sampson* to him? What's all this to the Purpose, Signor Don *Quixote?* We have just had the News that the Lady *Dulcinea* is disinchanted; and now we are upon the point of turning Shepherds, to sing, and live like Princes, you are dwindl'd down to a Hermit.

Cervantes, *Don Quixote,* II, 74

26 If men were all to become even uniformly mad, they might agree tolerably well with each other.

Bacon, *Novum Organum,* I, 27

27 That madness is nothing else but too much appearing passion may be gathered out of the effects of wine, which are the same with those of the evil disposition of the organs. . . . For the effect of the wine does but remove dissimulation, and take from them the sight of the deformity of their passions. For, I believe, the most sober men, when

they walk alone without care and employment of
the mind, would be unwilling the vanity and extravagance of their thoughts at that time should
be publicly seen, which is a confession that passions unguided are for the most part mere madness.

Hobbes, *Leviathan,* I, 8

28 Men are so necessarily mad that not to be mad
would amount to another form of madness.

Pascal, *Pensées,* VI, 414

29 A daring pilot in extremity;
Pleas'd with the danger, when the waves went
high,
He sought the storms; but, for a calm unfit,
Would steer too nigh the sands, to boast his wit.
Great wits are sure to madness near allied,
And thin partitions do their bounds divide.

Dryden, *Absalom and
Achitophel,* 159

30 Madmen . . . do not appear to me to have lost
the faculty of reasoning, but having joined together some ideas very wrongly, they mistake them for
truths; and they err as men do that argue right
from wrong principles. For, by the violence of
their imaginations, having taken their fancies for
realities, they make right deductions from them.
Thus you shall find a distracted man fancying
himself a king, with a right inference require suitable attendance, respect, and obedience: others
who have thought themselves made of glass, have
used the caution necessary to preserve such brittle
bodies. Hence it comes to pass that a man who is
very sober, and of a right understanding in all
other things, may in one particular be as frantic
as any in Bedlam; if either by any sudden very
strong impression, or long fixing his fancy upon
one sort of thoughts, incoherent ideas have been
cemented together so powerfully, as to remain
united. But there are degrees of madness, as of
folly; the disorderly jumbling ideas together is in
some more, and some less. In short, herein seems
to lie the difference between idiots and madmen:
that madmen put wrong ideas together, and so
make wrong propositions, but argue and reason
right from them; but idiots make very few or no
propositions, and reason scarce at all.

Locke, *Concerning Human Understanding,*
Bk. II, XI, 13

31 The diseases of the mind do in almost every particular imitate those of the body. For which reason, we hope, that learned faculty, for whom we
have so profound a respect, will pardon us the
violent hands we have been necessitated to lay on
several words and phrases, which of right belong
to them, and without which our descriptions must
have been often unintelligible.

Now there is no one circumstance in which the
distempers of the mind bear a more exact analogy
to those which are called bodily, than that aptness
which both have to a relapse. This is plain in the
violent diseases of ambition and avarice. I have
known ambition, when cured at court by frequent
disappointments (which are the only physic for
it), to break out again in a contest for foreman of
the grand jury at an assizes; and have heard of a
man who had so far conquered avarice, as to give
away many a sixpence, that comforted himself, at
last, on his deathbed, by making a crafty and advantageous bargain concerning his ensuing funeral, with an undertaker who had married his only
child.

In the affair of love, which, out of strict conformity with the Stoic philosophy, we shall here
treat as a disease, this proneness to relapse is no
less conspicuous.

Fielding, *Tom Jones,* IV, 12

32 Johnson, upon the first violent attack of this disorder, strove to overcome it by forcible exertions. He
frequently walked to Birmingham and back
again, and tried many other expedients, but all in
vain. His expression concerning it to me was "I
did not then know how to manage it." His distress
became so intolerable, that he applied to Dr.
Swinfen, physician in Lichfield, his god-father,
and put into his hands a state of his case, written
in Latin. Dr. Swinfen was so much struck with the
extraordinary acuteness, research, and eloquence
of this paper, that in his zeal for his godson he
shewed it to several people. His daughter, Mrs.
Desmoulins, who was many years humanely supported in Dr. Johnson's house in London, told me,
that upon his discovering that Dr. Swinfen had
communicated his case, he was so much offended,
that he was never afterwards fully reconciled to
him. He indeed had good reason to be offended;
for though Dr. Swinfen's motive was good, he inconsiderately betrayed a matter deeply interesting
and of great delicacy, which had been entrusted
to him in confidence; and exposed a complaint of
his young friend and patient, which, in the superficial opinion of the generality of mankind, is attended with contempt and disgrace.

But let not little men triumph upon knowing
that Johnson was an HYPOCHONDRIACK, was subject
to what the learned, philosophical, and pious Dr.
Cheyne has so well treated under the title of "The
English Malady." Though he suffered severely
from it, he was not therefore degraded. The powers of his great mind might be troubled, and their
full exercise suspended at times; but the mind itself was ever entire. As a proof of this, it is only
necessary to consider, that, when he was at the
very worst, he composed that state of his own case,
which shewed an uncommon vigour, not only of
fancy and taste, but of judgement. I am aware
that he himself was too ready to call such a complaint by the name of *madness;* in conformity with
which notion, he has traced its gradations, with

exquisite nicety, in one of the chapters of his *Rasselas*. But there is surely a clear distinction between a disorder which affects only the imagination and spirits, while the judgement is sound, and a disorder by which the judgement itself is impaired. This distinction was made to me by the late Professor Gaubius of Leyden, physician to the Prince of Orange, in a conversation which I had with him several years ago, and he expanded it thus: "If (said he) a man tells me that he is grievously disturbed, for that he *imagines* he sees a ruffian coming against him with a drawn sword, though at the same time he is *conscious* it is a delusion, I pronounce him to have a disordered imagination; but if a man tells me that he *sees* this, and in consternation calls to me to look at it, I pronounce him to be *mad*."

Boswell, *Life of Johnson (1729)*

33 Dr. Johnson and I had a serious conversation by ourselves on melancholy and madness; which he was, I always thought, erroneously inclined to confound together. Melancholy, like "great wit," may be "near allied to madness"; but there is, in my opinion, a distinct separation between them. When he talked of madness, he was to be understood as speaking of those who were in any great degree disturbed, or as it is commonly expressed, "troubled in mind." Some of the ancient philosophers held, that all deviations from right reason were madness. . . .

Johnson said, "A madman loves to be with people whom he fears; not as a dog fears the lash; but of whom he stands in awe." I was struck with the justice of this observation. To be with those of whom a person, whose mind is wavering and dejected, stands in awe, represses and composes an uneasy tumult of spirits, and consoles him with the contemplation of something steady, and at least comparatively great.

He added, "Madmen are all sensual in the lower stages of the distemper. They are eager for gratifications to sooth their minds, and divert their attention from the misery which they suffer: but when they grow very ill, pleasure is too weak for them, and they seek for pain. Employment, Sir, and hardships, prevent melancholy. I suppose in all our army in America there was not one man who went mad."

Boswell, *Life of Johnson (Sept. 20, 1777)*

34 Who in the rainbow can draw the line where the violet tint ends and the orange tint begins? Distinctly we see the difference of the colors, but where exactly does the one first blendingly enter into the other? So with sanity and insanity.

Melville, *Billy Budd*

35 Human madness is oftentimes a cunning and most feline thing. When you think it fled, it may have

but become transfigured into still subtler form. Ahab's full lunacy subsided not, but deepeningly contracted; like the unabated Hudson, when that noble Northman flows narrowly, but unfathomably through the Highland gorge. But, as in his narrow-flowing monomania, not one jot of Ahab's broad madness had been left behind; so in that broad madness, not one jot of his great natural intellect had perished. That before living agent, now became the living instrument. If such a furious trope may stand, his special lunacy stormed his general sanity, and carried it, and turned all its concentrated cannon upon its own mad mark; so that far from having lost his strength, Ahab, to that one end, did now possess a thousand-fold more potency than ever he had sanely brought to bear upon any one reasonable object.

Melville, *Moby Dick, XLI*

36 Often, when forced from his hammock by exhausting and intolerably vivid dreams of the night, which, resuming his own intense thoughts through the day, carried them on amid a clashing of frenzies, and whirled them round and round in his blazing brain, till the very throbbing of his life-spot became insufferable anguish; and when, as was sometimes the case, these spiritual throes in him heaved his being up from its base, and a chasm seemed opening in him, from which forked flames and lightnings shot up, and accursed fiends beckoned him to leap down among them; when this hell in himself yawned beneath him, a wild cry would be heard through the ship; and with glaring eyes Ahab would burst from his stateroom, as though escaping from a bed that was on fire. Yet these, perhaps, instead of being the unsuppressable symptoms of some latent weakness, of fright at his own resolve, were but the plainest tokens of its intensity. For, at such times, Ahab, the scheming, unappeasedly steadfast hunter of the White Whale; this Ahab that had gone to his hammock, was not the agent that so caused him to burst from it in horror again. The latter was the eternal, living principle or soul in him; and in sleep, being for the time dissociated from the characterising mind, which at other times employed it for its outer vehicle or agent, it spontaneously sought escape from the scorching contiguity of the frantic thing, of which, for the time, it was no longer an integral. But as the mind does not exist unless leagued with the soul, therefore it must have been that, in Ahab's case, yielding up all his thoughts and fancies to his one supreme purpose; that purpose, by its own sheer inveteracy of will, forced itself against gods and devils into a kind of self-assumed, independent being of its own; nay, could grimly live and burn, while the common vitality to which it was conjoined, fled horror-stricken from the unbidden and unfeathered birth. Therefore, the tormented spirit that

glared out of bodily eyes, when what seemed
Ahab rushed from his room, was, for the time but
a vacated thing, a formless somnambulistic being,
a ray of living light, to be sure, but without an
object to colour, and therefore a blankness in itself. God help thee, old man, thy thoughts have
created a creature in thee; and he whose intense
thinking thus makes him a Prometheus; a vulture
feeds upon that heart for ever; that vulture the
very creature he creates.

Melville, Moby Dick, XLIV

37 Man's insanity is heaven's sense; and wandering
from all mortal reason, man comes at last to that
celestial thought, which, to reason, is absurd and
frantic; and weal or woe, feels then uncompro-
mised, indifferent as his God.

Melville, Moby Dick, XCIII

38 There is something both contemptible and frightful in the sort of evidence on which, of late years,
any person can be judicially declared unfit for the
management of his affairs; and after his death, his
disposal of his property can be set aside, if there is
enough of it to pay the expenses of litigation—
which are charged on the property itself. All the
minute details of his daily life are pried into, and
whatever is found which, seen through the medium of the perceiving and describing faculties of
the lowest of the low, bears an appearance unlike
absolute commonplace, is laid before the jury as
evidence of insanity, and often with success; the
jurors being little, if at all, less vulgar and ignorant than the witnesses; while the judges, with
that extraordinary want of knowledge of human
nature and life which continually astonishes us in
English lawyers, often help to mislead them.
These trials speak volumes as to the state of feeling and opinion among the vulgar with regard to
human liberty. So far from setting any value on
individuality—so far from respecting the right of
each individual to act, in things indifferent, as
seems good to his own judgment and inclinations,
judges and juries cannot even conceive that a person in a state of sanity can desire such freedom. In
former days, when it was proposed to burn atheists, charitable people used to suggest putting
them in a madhouse instead: it would be nothing
surprising now-a-days were we to see this done,
and the doers applauding themselves, because, instead of persecuting for religion, they had adopted
so humane and Christian a mode of treating these
unfortunates, not without a silent satisfaction at
their having thereby obtained their deserts.

Mill, On Liberty, III

39 His mind was not in a normal state. A healthy
man usually thinks of, feels, and remembers innumerable things simultaneously, but has the power
and will to select one sequence of thoughts or
events on which to fix his whole attention. A
healthy man can tear himself away from the
deepest reflections to say a civil word to someone
who comes in and can then return again to his
own thoughts. But Prince Andrew's mind was not
in a normal state in that respect. All the powers of
his mind were more active and clearer than ever,
but they acted apart from his will. Most diverse
thoughts and images occupied him simultaneously. At times his brain suddenly began to
work with a vigor, clearness, and depth it had
never reached when he was in health, but suddenly in the midst of its work it would turn to some
unexpected idea and he had not the strength to
turn it back again.

Tolstoy, War and Peace, XI, 32

40 Madness is rare in individuals—but in groups,
parties, nations, and ages it is the rule.

Nietzsche, Beyond Good and Evil, IV, 156

41 In the eyes of the general public, the symptoms
are the essence of a disease, and to them a cure
means the removal of the symptoms. In medicine,
however, we find it important to differentiate between symptoms and disease, and state that the
disappearance of the symptoms is by no means the
same as the cure of the disease. The only tangible
element of the disease that remains after the removal of the symptoms, however, is the capacity
to form new symptoms. Therefore for the moment
let us adopt the lay point of view and regard a
knowledge of the foundation of the symptoms as
equivalent to understanding the disease.

The symptoms—of course we are here dealing
with mental (or psychogenic) symptoms, and
mental disease—are activities which are detri-
mental, or at least useless, to life as a whole; the
person concerned frequently complains of them as
obnoxious to him or they involve distress and suffering for him. The principal injury they inflict
lies in the expense of mental energy they entail
and, besides this, in the energy needed to combat
them. Where the symptoms are extensively developed, these two kinds of effort may exact such a
price that the person suffers a very serious impoverishment in available mental energy, which
consequently disables him for all the important
tasks of life. This result depends principally upon
the amount of energy taken up in this way, therefore you will see that illness is essentially a practical conception. But if you look at the matter from
a theoretical point of view and ignore this question of degree you can very well say that we are
all ill, i.e., neurotic; for the conditions required for
symptom-formation are demonstrable also in normal persons.

Freud, General Introduction to
Psycho-Analysis, XXIII

42 If we throw a crystal to the ground, it breaks, but

it does not break haphazard; in accordance with the lines of cleavage it falls into fragments, whose limits were already determined by the structure of the crystal, although they were invisible. Psychotics are fissured and splintered structures such as these. We cannot deny them a measure of that awe with which madmen were regarded by the peoples of ancient times. They have turned away from external reality, but for that very reason they know more of internal psychic reality and can tell us much that would otherwise be inaccessible to us.

Freud, *New Introductory Lectures on Psycho-Analysis,* XXXI

43 Every actual animal is somewhat dull and somewhat mad. He will at times miss his signals and stare vacantly when he might well act, while at other times he will run off into convulsions and raise a dust in his own brain to no purpose. These imperfections are so human that we should hardly recognise ourselves if we could shake them off altogether. Not to retain any dulness would mean to possess untiring attention and universal interests, thus realising the boast about deeming nothing human alien to us; while to be absolutely without folly would involve perfect self-knowledge and self-control. The intelligent man known to history flourishes within a dullard and holds a lunatic in leash. He is encased in a protective shell of ignorance and insensibility which keeps him from being exhausted and confused by this too complicated world; but that integument blinds him at the same time to many of his nearest and highest interests. He is amused by the antics of the brute dreaming within his breast; he gloats on his passionate reveries, an amusement which sometimes costs him very dear. Thus the best human intelligence is still decidedly barbarous; it fights in heavy armour and keeps a fool at court.

Santayana, *Life of Reason,* I, 2

44 Philosophers have sometimes said that all ideas come from experience; they never could have been poets and must have forgotten that they were ever children. The great difficulty in education is to get experience out of ideas. Shame, conscience, and reason continually disallow and ignore what consciousness presents; and what are they but habit and latent instinct asserting themselves and forcing us to disregard our midsummer madness? Idiocy and lunacy are merely reversions to a condition in which present consciousness is in the ascendant and has escaped the control of unconscious forces. We speak of people being "out of their senses," when they have in fact fallen back into them; or of those who have "lost their mind," when they have lost merely that habitual control over consciousness which prevented it from flaring into all sorts of obsessions and agonies. Their bodies having become deranged, their minds, far from correcting that derangement, instantly share and betray it. A dream is always simmering below the conventional surface of speech and reflection. Even in the highest reaches and serenest meditations of science it sometimes breaks through. Even there we are seldom constant enough to conceive a truly natural world; somewhere passionate, fanciful, or magic elements will slip into the scheme and baffle rational ambition.

A body seriously out of equilibrium, either with itself or with its environment, perishes outright. Not so a mind. Madness and suffering can set themselves no limit; they lapse only when the corporeal frame that sustains them yields to circumstances and changes its habit. If they are unstable at all, it is because they ordinarily correspond to strains and conjunctions which a vigorous body overcomes, or which dissolve the body altogether. A pain not incidental to the play of practical instincts may easily be recurrent, and it might be perpetual if even the worst habits were not intermittent and the most useless agitations exhausting. Some respite will therefore ensue upon pain, but no magic cure. Madness, in like manner, if pronounced, is precarious, but when speculative enough to be harmless or not strong enough to be debilitating, it too may last for ever.

Santayana, *Life of Reason,* I, 2

5.7 | *Will*

FREE CHOICE

To the question, why a section on will occurs in a chapter on mind, the answer is that an overwhelming preponderance of the authors who discuss the subject conceive the will as a mental faculty closely associated with intellect or reason. In the mediaeval tradition, the will was referred to as the "intellectual" or "rational appetite." Other animals as well as man exhibit the phenomena of the passions; other animals manifest something akin to voluntary behavior; but in the predominant opinion only man exercises willpower and acts voluntarily through free choice, after deliberation and decision.

In addition to considering the nature of the will as a faculty, relating it to reason or intellect on the one hand, and to the passions or emotions on the other, and distinguishing between voluntary and involuntary behavior, the quotations below represent a fair sampling of the opposite voices in the great debate on the freedom of the will or man's freedom of choice. Ranged on the affirmative side, and advancing different arguments in support of their affirmation, are Lucretius, the Stoics, Aquinas, Descartes, Dr. Johnson, Locke, Kant, Hegel, Bergson, William James, and Sartre. On the opposite side are the denials of free choice by Hobbes, Spinoza, Hume, and Rousseau. Tolstoy straddles the fence. The moot question is whether, in the absence of free choice, there can be any basis for morality, for moral responsibility, and praise or blame. The opponents of free will claim there can be and Hume even goes so far as to maintain that, since a freely chosen act would be like a chance event, free will is incompatible with moral responsibility and praise or blame.

The introduction of an omnipotent and omniscient deity into the picture complicates the matter. The theologians, from Augustine to Luther and Calvin, attempt to reconcile free choice on man's part with predestination and providence. They are also concerned with the effect of original sin upon man's freedom of choice, as well as with the indispensability of such freedom as prerequisite to man's responsibility for sin. The reader will find related discussions in Section 20.13 on SIN AND TEMPTATION and in Section 20.14 on REDEMPTION AND SALVATION. For the treatment of other forms of freedom, the reader should turn to Section 9.4 on MORAL FREEDOM, to Section 12.3 on RIGHTS—NATURAL AND CIVIL, and to Section 13.1 on FREEDOM IN SOCIETY.

---

1 *Socrates.* When Er and the spirits arrived, their duty was to go at once to Lachesis; but first of all there came a prophet who arranged them in order; then he took from the knees of Lachesis lots and samples of lives, and having mounted a high pulpit, spoke as follows: "Hear the word of Lachesis, the daughter of Necessity. Mortal souls, behold a new cycle of life and mortality. Your genius will not be allotted to you, but you will choose your genius; and let him who draws the first lot have the first choice, and the life which he chooses shall be his destiny. Virtue is free, and as a man honours or dishonours her he will have more or less of her; the responsibility is with the chooser—

God is justified." When the Interpreter had thus spoken he scattered lots indifferently among them all, and each of them took up the lot which fell near him, all but Er himself (he was not allowed), and each as he took his lot perceived the number which he had obtained. Then the Interpreter placed on the ground before them the samples of lives; and there were many more lives than the souls present, and they were of all sorts. There were lives of every animal and of man in every condition. And there were tyrannies among them, some lasting out the tyrant's life, others which broke off in the middle and came to an end in poverty and exile and beggary; and there were lives of famous men, some who were famous for their form and beauty as well as for their strength and success in games, or, again, for their birth and the qualities of their ancestors; and some who were the reverse of famous for the opposite qualities. And of women likewise; there was not, however, any definite character in them, because the soul, when choosing a new life, must of necessity become different. But there was every other quality, and they all mingled with one another, and also with elements of wealth and poverty, and disease and health; and there were mean states also. And here, my dear Glaucon, is the supreme peril of our human state; and therefore the utmost care should be taken. Let each one of us leave every other kind of knowledge and seek and follow one thing only, if peradventure he may be able to learn and may find some one who will make him able to learn and discern between good and evil, and so to choose always and everywhere the better life as he has opportunity. He should consider the bearing of all these things which have been mentioned severally and collectively upon virtue; he should know what the effect of beauty is when combined with poverty or wealth in a particular soul, and what are the good and evil consequences of noble and humble birth, of private and public station, of strength and weakness, of cleverness and dullness, and of all the natural and acquired gifts of the soul, and the operation of them when conjoined; he will then look at the nature of the soul, and from the consideration of all these qualities he will be able to determine which is the better and which is the worse; and so he will choose, giving the name of evil to the life which will make his soul more unjust, and good to the life which will make his soul more just; all else he will disregard. For we have seen and know that this is the best choice both in life and after death. A man must take with him into the world below an adamantine faith in truth and right, that there too he may be undazzled by the desire of wealth or the other allurements of evil, lest, coming upon tyrannies and similar villainies, he do irremediable wrongs to others and suffer yet worse himself; but let him know how to choose the mean and avoid the extremes on either side, as far as possible, not only in this life but in all that which is to come. For this is the way of happiness.

And according to the report of the messenger from the other world this was what the prophet said at the time: "Even for the last comer, if he chooses wisely and will live diligently, there is appointed a happy and not undesirable existence. Let not him who chooses first be careless, and let not the last despair."

Plato, *Republic,* X, 617B

2 We deliberate about things that are in our power and can be done. . . . For nature, necessity, and chance are thought to be causes, and also reason and everything that depends on man. Now every class of men deliberates about the things that can be done by their own efforts. . . .

We deliberate not about ends but about means. For a doctor does not deliberate whether he shall heal, nor an orator whether he shall persuade, nor a statesman whether he shall produce law and order, nor does any one else deliberate about his end. They assume the end and consider how and by what means it is to be attained; and if it seems to be produced by several means they consider by which it is most easily and best produced, while if it is achieved by one only they consider how it will be achieved by this and by what means this will be achieved, till they come to the first cause, which in the order of discovery is last. . . .

The same thing is deliberated upon and is chosen, except that the object of choice is already determinate, since it is that which has been decided upon as a result of deliberation that is the object of choice. For every one ceases to inquire how he is to act when he has brought the moving principle back to himself and to the ruling part of himself; for this is what chooses. . . . The object of choice being one of the things in our own power which is desired after deliberation, choice will be deliberate desire of things in our own power; for when we have decided as a result of deliberation, we desire in accordance with our deliberation.

We may take it, then, that we have described choice in outline, and stated the nature of its objects and the fact that it is concerned with means.

Aristotle, *Ethics*, 1112ª30

3 Men make themselves responsible for being unjust or self-indulgent, in the one case by cheating and in the other by spending their time in drinking bouts and the like; for it is activities exercised on particular objects that make the corresponding character. This is plain from the case of people training for any contest or action; they practise the activity the whole time. Now not to know that it is from the exercise of activities on particular objects that states of character are produced is the mark of a thoroughly senseless person. Again, it is irrational to suppose that a man who acts unjustly does not wish to be unjust or a man who acts

self-indulgently to be self-indulgent. But if without being ignorant a man does the things which will make him unjust, he will be unjust voluntarily. Yet it does not follow that if he wishes he will cease to be unjust and will be just. For neither does the man who is ill become well on those terms. We may suppose a case in which he is ill voluntarily, through living incontinently and disobeying his doctors. In that case it was then open to him not to be ill, but not now, when he has thrown away his chance, just as when you have let a stone go it is too late to recover it; but yet it was in your power to throw it, since the moving principle was in you. So, too, to the unjust and to the self-indulgent man it was open at the beginning not to become men of this kind, and so they are unjust and self-indulgent voluntarily; but now that they have become so it is not possible for them not to be so.

Aristotle, *Ethics,* 1114ᵃ4

4 The origin of action—its efficient, not its final cause—is choice, and that of choice is desire and reasoning with a view to an end. This is why choice cannot exist either without reason and intellect or without a moral state; for good action and its opposite cannot exist without a combination of intellect and character. Intellect itself, however, moves nothing, but only the intellect which aims at an end and is practical; for this rules the productive intellect, as well, since every one who makes makes for an end, and that which is made is not an end in the unqualified sense (but only an end in a particular relation, and the end of a particular operation)—only that which is *done* is that; for good action is an end, and desire aims at this. Hence choice is either desiderative reason or ratiocinative desire, and such an origin of action is a man.

Aristotle, *Ethics,* 1139ᵃ31

5 There are things which are within our power, and there are things which are beyond our power. Within our power are opinion, aim, desire, aversion, and, in one word, whatever affairs are our own. Beyond our power are body, property, reputation, office, and, in one word, whatever are not properly our own affairs.

Now the things within our power are by nature free, unrestricted, unhindered; but those beyond our power are weak, dependent, restricted, alien. Remember, then, that if you attribute freedom to things by nature dependent and take what belongs to others for your own, you will be hindered, you will lament, you will be disturbed, you will find fault both with gods and men. But if you take for your own only that which is your own and view what belongs to others just as it really is, then no one will ever compel you, no one will restrict you; you will find fault with no one, you will accuse no one, you will do nothing against

your will; no one will hurt you, you will not have an enemy, nor will you suffer any harm.

Aiming, therefore, at such great things, remember that you must not allow yourself any inclination, however slight, toward the attainment of the others; but that you must entirely quit some of them, and for the present postpone the rest. But if you would have these, and possess power and wealth likewise, you may miss the latter in seeking the former; and you will certainly fail of that by which alone happiness and freedom are procured.

Epictetus, *Encheiridion,* I

6 You can be unconquerable if you enter into no combat in which it is not in your own power to conquer. When, therefore, you see anyone eminent in honors or power, or in high esteem on any other account, take heed not to be bewildered by appearances and to pronounce him happy; for if the essence of good consists in things within our own power, there will be no room for envy or emulation. But, for your part, do not desire to be a general, or a senator, or a consul, but to be free; and the only way to this is a disregard of things which lie not within our own power.

Epictetus, *Encheiridion,* XIX

7 What then do we mean when we speak of freedom in ourselves. . . .

My own reading is that, moving as we do amid adverse fortunes, compulsions, violent assaults of passion crushing the soul, feeling ourselves mastered by these experiences, playing slave to them, going where they lead, we have been brought by all this to doubt whether we are anything at all and dispose of ourselves in any particular.

This would indicate that we think of our free act as one which we execute of our own choice, in no servitude to chance or necessity or overmastering passion, nothing thwarting our will; the voluntary is conceived as an event amenable to will and occurring or not as our will dictates. Everything will be voluntary that is produced under no compulsion and with knowledge; our free act is what we are masters to perform.

Plotinus, *Sixth Ennead,* VIII, 1

8 So I set myself to examine an idea I had heard—namely that our free-will is the cause of our doing evil, and Your just judgment the cause of our suffering evil. I could not clearly discern this. I endeavoured to draw the eye of my mind from the pit, but I was again plunged into it; and as often as I tried, so often was I plunged back. But it raised me a little towards Your light that I now was as much aware that I had a will as that I had a life. And when I willed to do or not do anything, I was quite certain that it was myself and no other who willed, and I came to see that the cause of my sin lay there.

But what I did unwillingly, it still seemed to me

that I rather suffered than did, and I judged it to be not my fault but my punishment: though as I held You most just, I was quite ready to admit that I was being justly punished.

But I asked further: "Who made me? Was it not my God, who is not only Good but Goodness itself? What root reason is there for my willing evil and failing to will good, which would make it just for me to be punished? Who was it that set and ingrafted in me this root of bitterness, since I was wholly made by my most loving God? If the devil is the author, where does the devil come from? And if by his own perverse will he was turned from a good angel into a devil, what was the origin in him of the perverse will by which he became a devil, since by the all-good Creator he was made wholly angel?" By such thoughts I was cast down again and almost stifled; yet I was not brought down so far as the hell of that error, where no man confesses unto You, the error which holds rather that You suffer evil than that man does it.

Augustine, *Confessions*, VII, 3

9 Let . . . perplexing debatings and disputations of the philosophers go on as they may, we, in order that we may confess the most high and true God Himself, do confess His will, supreme power, and prescience. Neither let us be afraid lest, after all, we do not do by will that which we do by will, because He, Whose foreknowledge is infallible, foreknew that we would do it. It was this which Cicero was afraid of, and therefore opposed fore-knowledge. The Stoics also maintained that all things do not come to pass by necessity, although they contended that all things happen according to destiny. What is it, then, that Cicero feared in the prescience of future things? Doubtless it was this—that if all future things have been fore-known, they will happen in the order in which they have been foreknown; and if they come to pass in this order, there is a certain order of things foreknown by God; and if a certain order of things, then a certain order of causes, for nothing can happen which is not preceded by some efficient cause. But if there is a certain order of causes according to which everything happens which does happen, then by fate, says he, all things happen which do happen. But if this be so, then is there nothing in our own power, and there is no such thing as freedom of will.

Augustine, *City of God*, V, 9

10 There are some things which act not from any choice, but, as it were, moved and made to act by others; just as the arrow is directed to the target by the archer. Others act from some kind of choice, but not from free choice, such as irrational animals, for the sheep flies from the wolf by a kind of judgment whereby it considers it to be hurtful to itself; such a judgment is not a free one, but

implanted by nature. Only an agent endowed with an intellect can act with a judgment which is free in so far as it apprehends the common notion of good, from which it can judge this or the other thing to be good. Consequently, wherever there is intellect, there is free choice.

Aquinas, *Summa Theologica*, I, 59, 3

11 Man has free choice. Otherwise counsels, exhortations, commands, prohibitions, rewards and punishments would be in vain. . . .

Free choice is the cause of its own movement, because by his free choice man moves himself to act. But it does not of necessity belong to liberty that what is free should be the first cause of itself, as neither for one thing to be cause of another need it be the first cause. God, therefore, is the first cause, Who moves causes both natural and voluntary. And just as by moving natural causes He does not prevent their acts being natural, so by moving voluntary causes He does not deprive their actions of being voluntary, but rather is He the cause of this very thing in them; for He operates in each thing according to its own nature.

Aquinas, *Summa Theologica*, I, 83, 1

12 Man does not choose of necessity. And this is because that which is possible not to be, is not of necessity. Now the reason why it is possible not to choose, or to choose, may be gathered from a twofold power in man. For man can will and not will, act and not act; again, he can will this or that, and do this or that. The reason of this is seated in the very power of the reason. For the will can tend to whatever the reason can apprehend as good. Now the reason can apprehend as good, not only this, namely, to will or to act, but also this, namely, not to will or not to act. Again, in all particular goods, the reason can consider an aspect of some good and the lack of some good, which has the aspect of evil; and in this respect, it can apprehend any single one of such goods as to be chosen or to be avoided. The perfect good alone, which is Happiness, cannot be apprehended by the reason under the aspect of evil, or as lacking in any way. Consequently man wills Happiness of necessity, nor can he will not to be happy, or to be unhappy. Now since choice is not of the end, but of the means . . . it is not of the perfect good, which is Happiness, but of other particular goods. Therefore man chooses not of necessity but freely.

Aquinas, *Summa Theologica*, I–II, 13, 6

13 Commands and prohibitions should be imposed only upon one who can do or not do; otherwise they would be imposed in vain. But prohibitions and commands are divinely imposed upon man. It is therefore in man's power to do or not to do; and so he is endowed with free choice.

No one should be punished or rewarded for something which it is not in his power to do or not to do. But man is justly punished and rewarded by God for his deeds. Therefore man can do and not do; and so he is endowed with free choice.

Aquinas, *On Truth,* XXIV, 1

14 "The world is indeed so wholly desert of every virtue, even as thy words sound to me, and heavy and covered with sin;

but I pray that thou point the cause out to me, so that I may see it, and that I may show it to others; for one places it in the heavens and another here below."

A deep sigh, which grief compressed to "Alas!" he [Marco] first gave forth, and then began: "Brother, the world is blind, and verily thou comest from it.

Ye who are living refer every cause up to the heavens alone, even as if they swept all with them of necessity.

Were it thus, Freewill in you would be destroyed, and it were not just to have joy for good and mourning for evil.

The heavens set your impulses in motion; I say not all, but suppose I said it, a light is given you to know good and evil,

and Freewill, which, if it endure the strain in its first battlings with the heavens, at length gains the whole victory, if it be well nurtured.

Ye lie subject, in your freedom, to a greater power and to a better nature; and that creates in you mind which the heavens have not in their charge.

Therefore, if the world to-day goeth astray, in you is the cause, in you be it sought."

Dante, *Purgatorio,* XVI, 58

15 "Every substantial form, which is distinct from matter and is in union with it, has a specific virtue contained within itself

which is not perceived save in operation, nor is manifested except by its effects, just as life in a plant by the green leaves.

Therefore man knows not whence the understanding of the first cognitions may come, nor the inclination to the prime objects of appetite,

which are in you, even as the instinct in bees to make honey; and this prime will admits no desert of praise or of blame.

Now in order that to this will every other may be related, innate with you is the virtue which giveth counsel, and ought to guard the threshold of assent.

This is the principle whence is derived the reason of desert in you, according as it garners and winnows good and evil loves.

Those who in their reasoning went to the foundation, perceived this innate freedom, therefore they left ethics to the world.

Wherefore suppose that every love which is kindled within you arise of necessity, the power to arrest it is within you.

By the noble virtue Beatrice understands Freewill, and therefore, look that thou have this in mind, if she betake her to speak with thee thereof."

Dante, *Purgatorio,* XVIII, 49

16 The greatest gift God of his largess made at the creation, and the most conformed to his own excellence, and which he most prizeth,

was the will's liberty, wherewith creatures intelligent, both all and alone, were and are endowed.

Dante, *Paradiso,* V, 19

17 Mankind is at its best when it is most free. This will be clear if we grasp the principle of liberty. We must realize that the basic principle of our freedom is freedom to choose, which saying many have on their lips but few in their minds.

Dante, *De Monarchia,* I, 12

18 For if we believe it to be true that God foreknows and foreordains all things; that He can not be deceived or obstructed in His foreknowledge and predestination; and that nothing happens but at His will (which reason itself is compelled to grant), then on reason's own testimony, there can be no free will in man, or angel, or in any creature.

Luther, *Bondage of the Will*

19 *Hortensio.*   There's small choice in rotten apples.

Shakespeare, *Taming of the Shrew,* I, i, 138

20 *Cassius.* Men at some time are masters of their fates:

The fault, dear Brutus, is not in our stars, But in ourselves, that we are underlings.

Shakespeare, *Julius Caesar,* I, ii, 139

21 The faculty of will consists alone in our having the power of choosing to do a thing or choosing not to do it (that is, to affirm or deny, to pursue or to shun it), or rather it consists alone in the fact that in order to affirm or deny, pursue or shun those things placed before us by the understanding, we act so that we are unconscious that any outside force constrains us in doing so. For in order that I should be free it is not necessary that I should be indifferent as to the choice of one or the other of two contraries; but contrariwise the more I lean to the one—whether I recognise clearly that the reasons of the good and true are to be found in it, or whether God so disposes my inward thought—the more freely do I choose and embrace it. And undoubtedly both divine grace and natural knowledge, far from diminishing my liberty, rather increase it and strengthen it. Hence this indifference which I feel, when I am not swayed to one side rather than to the other by lack of reason, is the lowest grade of liberty, and rather evinces a lack or negation in knowledge than a perfection of

will: for if I always recognised clearly what was true and good, I should never have trouble in deliberating as to what judgment or choice I should make, and then I should be entirely free without ever being indifferent.

Descartes, *Meditations on First Philosophy,* IV

22 As to the freedom of the will, a very different account must be given of it as it exists in God and as it exists in us. For it is self-contradictory that the will of God should not have been from eternity indifferent to all that has come to pass or that ever will occur, because we can form no conception of anything good or true, of anything to be believed or to be performed or to be omitted, the idea of which existed in the divine understanding before God's will determined Him so to act as to bring it to pass. Nor do I here speak of priority of time; I mean that it was not even prior in order, or in nature, or in reasoned relation, as they say [in the schools], so that that idea of good impelled God to choose one thing rather than another. . . . Thus that supreme indifference in God is the supreme proof of his omnipotence. But as to man, since he finds the nature of all goodness and truth already determined by God, and his will cannot bear upon anything else, it is evident that he embraces the true and the good the more willingly and hence the more freely in proportion as he sees the true and the good the more clearly, and that he is never indifferent save when he does not know what is the more true or the better, or at least when he does not see clearly enough to prevent him from doubting about it. Thus the indifference which attaches to human liberty is very different from that which belongs to the divine. Neither does it here matter that the essences of things are said to be indivisible: for firstly no essence can belong in a univocal sense both to God and His creature; and finally indifference does not belong to the essence of human liberty, since we are free not only when our ignorance of the right renders us indifferent, but also, and chiefly, when a clear perception impels us to prosecute some definite course.

Descartes, *Objections and Replies,* VI

23 Liberty and necessity are consistent: as in the water that hath not only liberty, but a necessity of descending by the channel; so likewise in the actions which men voluntarily do, which, because they proceed from their will, proceed from liberty, and yet because every act of man's will and every desire and inclination proceedeth from some cause, and that from another cause, in a continual chain (whose first link is in the hand of God, the first of all causes), proceed from necessity. So that to him that could see the connexion of those causes, the necessity of all men's voluntary actions would appear manifest. And therefore God, that seeth and disposeth all things, seeth also that the liberty of man in doing what he will is accompanied with the necessity of doing that which God will, and no more, nor less. For though men may do many things which God does not command, nor is therefore author of them; yet they can have no passion, nor appetite to anything, of which appetite God's will is not the cause. And did not His will assure the necessity of man's will, and consequently of all that on man's will dependeth, the liberty of men would be a contradiction and impediment to the omnipotence and liberty of God. And this shall suffice, as to the matter in hand, of that natural liberty, which only is properly called liberty.

Hobbes, *Leviathan,* II, 21

24 It is not good to have too much liberty. It is not good to have all one wants.

Pascal, *Pensées,* VI, 379

25 Burden not the back of *Aries, Leo,* or *Taurus,* with thy faults; nor make *Saturn, Mars,* or *Venus,* guilty of thy Follies. Think not to fasten thy imperfections on the Stars, and so despairingly conceive thy self under a fatality of being evil. Calculate thy self within, seek not thy self in the Moon, but in thine own Orb or Microcosmical Circumference. Let celestial aspects admonish and advertise, not conclude and determine thy ways.

Sir Thomas Browne, *Christian Morals,* III, 7

26 *God.*   I made him [man] just and right,
Sufficient to have stood, though free to fall.
Such I created all th' Ethereal Powers
And Spirits, both them who stood & them who
    faild;
Freely they stood who stood, and fell who fell.
Not free, what proof could they have givn sincere
Of true allegiance, constant Faith or Love,
Where onely what they needs must do, appeard,
Not what they would? what praise could they re-
    ceive?
What pleasure I from such obedience paid,
When Will and Reason (Reason also is choice)
Useless and vain, of freedom both despoild,
Made passive both, had servd necessitie,
Not mee. They therefore as to right belongd,
So were created, nor can justly accuse
Thir maker, or thir making, or thir Fate;
As if Predestination over-rul'd
Thir will, dispos'd by absolute Decree
Or high foreknowledge; they themselves decreed
Thir own revolt, not I: if I foreknew,
Foreknowledge had no influence on their fault,
Which had no less prov'd certain unforeknown.

Milton, *Paradise Lost,* III, 98

27 I should say that human affairs would be much more happily conducted if it were equally in the power of men to be silent and to speak; but experience shows over and over again that there is nothing which men have less power over than the

tongue, and that there is nothing which they are less able to do than to govern their appetites, so that many persons believe that we do those things only with freedom which we seek indifferently; as the desire for such things can easily be lessened by the recollection of another thing which we frequently call to mind; it being impossible, on the other hand, to do those things with freedom which we seek with such ardour that the recollection of another thing is unable to mitigate it. But if, however, we had not found out that we do many things which we afterwards repent, and that when agitated by conflicting affects we see that which is better and follow that which is worse, nothing would hinder us from believing that we do everything with freedom. Thus the infant believes that it is by free will that it seeks the breast; the angry boy believes that by free will he wishes vengeance; the timid man thinks it is with free will he seeks flight; the drunkard believes that by a free command of his mind he speaks the things which when sober he wishes he had left unsaid. Thus the madman, the chatterer, the boy, and others of the same kind, all believe that they speak by a free command of the mind, whilst, in truth, they have no power to restrain the impulse which they have to speak, so that experience itself, no less than reason, clearly teaches that men believe themselves to be free simply because they are conscious of their own actions, knowing nothing of the causes by which they are determined: it teaches, too, that the decrees of the mind are nothing but the appetites themselves, which differ, therefore, according to the different temper of the body. For every man determines all things from his affect; those who are agitated by contrary affects do not know what they want, whilst those who are agitated by no affect are easily driven hither and thither. All this plainly shows that the decree of the mind, the appetite, and determination of the body are coincident in nature, or rather that they are one and the same thing, which, when it is considered under the attribute of thought and manifested by that, is called a decree, and when it is considered under the attribute of extension and is deduced from the laws of motion and rest, is called a determination.

Spinoza, *Ethics,* III, Prop. 2, Schol.

28 There being in us a great many uneasinesses, always soliciting and ready to determine the will, it is natural, as I have said, that the greatest and most pressing should determine the will to the next action; and so it does for the most part, but not always. For, the mind having in most cases, as is evident in experience, a power to suspend the execution and satisfaction of any of its desires; and so all, one after another; is at liberty to consider the objects of them, examine them on all sides, and weigh them with others. In this lies the liberty man has; and from the not using of it right comes all that variety of mistakes, errors, and faults which we run into in the conduct of our lives, and our endeavours after happiness; whilst we precipitate the determination of our wills, and engage too soon, before due examination. To prevent this, we have a power to suspend the prosecution of this or that desire; as every one daily may experiment in himself. This seems to me the source of all liberty; in this seems to consist that which is (as I think improperly) called free-will. For, during this suspension of any desire, before the will be determined to action, and the action (which follows that determination) done, we have opportunity to examine, view, and judge of the good or evil of what we are going to do; and when, upon due examination, we have judged, we have done our duty, all that we can, or ought to do, in pursuit of our happiness; and it is not a fault, but a perfection of our nature, to desire, will, and act according to the last result of a fair examination. . . . This is so far from being a restraint or diminution of freedom, that it is the very improvement and benefit of it; it is not an abridgment, it is the end and use of our liberty; and the further we are removed from such a determination, the nearer we are to misery and slavery.

Locke, *Concerning Human Understanding,*
Bk. II, XXI, 48–49

29 Philosophic liberty consists in the free exercise of the will; or at least, if we must speak agreeably to all systems, in an opinion that we have the free exercise of our will. Political liberty consists in security, or, at least, in the opinion that we enjoy security.

This security is never more dangerously attacked than in public or private accusations. It is, therefore, on the goodness of criminal laws that the liberty of the subject principally depends.

Montesquieu, *Spirit of Laws,* XII, 2

30 It will not require many words to prove, that all mankind have ever agreed in the doctrine of liberty as well as in that of necessity, and that the whole dispute, in this respect also, has been hitherto merely verbal. For what is meant by liberty, when applied to voluntary actions? We cannot surely mean that actions have so little connexion with motives, inclinations, and circumstances, that one does not follow with a certain degree of uniformity from the other, and that one affords no inference by which we can conclude the existence of the other. For these are plain and acknowledged matters of fact. By liberty, then, we can only mean a power of acting or not acting, according to the determinations of the will; that is, if we choose to remain at rest, we may; if we choose to move, we also may. Now this hypothetical liberty is universally allowed to belong to every one who is not a prisoner and in chains. Here, then, is no subject of dispute.

Whatever definition we may give of liberty, we should be careful to observe two requisite circumstances; first, that it be consistent with plain matter of fact; secondly, that it be consistent with itself. If we observe these circumstances, and render our definition intelligible, I am persuaded that all mankind will be found of one opinion with regard to it.

It is universally allowed that nothing exists without a cause of its existence, and that chance, when strictly examined, is a mere negative word, and means not any real power which has anywhere a being in nature. But it is pretended that some causes are necessary, some not necessary. Here then is the advantage of definitions. Let any one define a cause, without comprehending, as a part of the definition, a necessary connexion with its effect; and let him show distinctly the origin of the idea, expressed by the definition; and I shall readily give up the whole controversy. But if the foregoing explication of the matter be received, this must be absolutely impracticable. Had not objects a regular conjunction with each other, we should never have entertained any notion of cause and effect; and this regular conjunction produces that inference of the understanding, which is the only connexion, that we can have any comprehension of. Whoever attempts a definition of cause, exclusive of these circumstances, will be obliged either to employ unintelligible terms or such as are synonymous to the term which he endeavours to define. And if the definition above mentioned be admitted; liberty, when opposed to necessity, not to constraint, is the same thing with chance; which is universally allowed to have no existence.

Hume, *Concerning Human Understanding*, VIII, 73–74

31 What is the meaning of this phrase "to be free"? it means "to be able," or assuredly it has no sense. For the will "to be able " is as ridiculous at bottom as to say that the will is yellow or blue, round or square. To will is to wish, and to be free is to be able. Let us note step by step the chain of what passes in us, without obfuscating our minds by any terms of the schools or any antecedent principle.

It is proposed to you that you mount a horse, you must absolutely make a choice, for it is quite clear that you either will go or that you will no go. There is no middle way. It is therefore of absolute necessity that you wish yes or no. Up to there it is demonstrated that the will is not free. You wish to mount the horse; why? The reason, an ignoramus will say, is because I wish it. This answer is idiotic, nothing happens or can happen without a reason, a cause; there is one therefore for your wish: What is it? the agreeable idea of going on horseback which presents itself in your brain, the dominant idea, the determinant idea. But, you will say, can

I not resist an idea which dominates me? No, for what would be the cause of your resistance? None. By your will you can obey only an idea which will dominate you more.

Now you receive all your ideas; therefore you receive your wish, you wish therefore necessarily. The word "liberty" does not therefore belong in any way to your will.

You ask me how thought and wish are formed in us. I answer you that I have not the remotest idea. I do not know how ideas are made any more than how the world was made. All that is given to us is to grope for what passes in our incomprehensible machine.

The will, therefore, is not a faculty that one can call free. A free will is an expression absolutely void of sense, and what the scholastics have called will of indifference, that is to say willing without cause, is a chimera unworthy of being combated.

Where will be liberty then? in the power to do what one wills. I wish to leave my study, the door is open, I am free to leave it.

But, say you, if the door is closed, and I wish to stay at home, I stay there freely. Let us be explicit. You exercise then the power that you have of staying; you have this power, but you have not that of going out.

The liberty about which so many volumes have been written is, therefore, reduced to its accurate terms, only the power of acting.

In what sense then must one utter the phrase—"Man is free"? in the same sense that one utters the words, health, strength, happiness. Man is not always strong, always healthy, always happy.

A great passion, a great obstacle, deprive him of his liberty, his power of action.

The word "liberty," "free-will," is therefore an abstract word, a general word, like beauty, goodness, justice. These terms do not state that all men are always beautiful, good and just; similarly, they are not always free.

Voltaire, *Philosophical Dictionary: Free-Will*

32 Dr. Johnson shunned to-night any discussion of the perplexed question of fate and free will, which I attempted to agitate. "Sir, (said he,) we *know* our will is free, and *there's* an end on't."

Boswell, *Life of Johnson* (Oct. 10, 1769)

33 *Dr. Mayo.* (to Dr. Johnson,) "Pray, Sir, have you read *Edwards, of New England, on Grace!*" *Johnson.* "No, Sir." *Boswell.* "It puzzled me so much as to the freedom of the human will, by stating, with wonderful acute ingenuity, our being actuated by a series of motives which we cannot resist, that the only relief I had was to forget it." *Mayo.* "But he makes the proper distinction between moral and physical necessity." *Boswell.* "Alas, Sir, they come both to the same thing. You may be bound as hard by chains when covered by leather, as when

the iron appears. The argument for the moral necessity of human actions is always, I observe, fortified by supposing universal prescience to be one of the attributes of the Deity." *Johnson.* "You are surer that you are free, than you are of prescience; you are surer that you can lift up your finger or not as you please, than you are of any conclusion from a deduction of reasoning. But let us consider a little the objection from prescience. It is certain I am either to go home to-night or not; that does not prevent my freedom." *Boswell.* "That it is certain you are *either* to go home or not, does not prevent your freedom; because the liberty of choice between the two is compatible with that certainty. But if *one* of these events be certain *now*, you have no *future* power of volition. If it be certain you are to go home to-night, you *must* go home." *Johnson.* "If I am well acquainted with a man, I can judge with great probability how he will act in any case, without his being restrained by my judging. God may have this probability increased to certainty." *Boswell.* "When it is increased to *certainty*, freedom ceases, because that cannot be certainly foreknown, which is not certain at the time; but if it be certain at the time, it is a contradiction in terms to maintain that there can be afterwards any *contingency* dependent upon the exercise of will or any thing else." *Johnson.* "All theory is against the freedom of the will; all experience for it."—I did not push the subject any farther. I was glad to find him so mild in discussing a question of the most abstract nature, involved with theological tenets, which he generally would not suffer to be in any degree opposed.

Boswell, *Life of Johnson (Apr. 15, 1778)*

34 A free will and a will subject to moral laws are one and the same.

Kant, *Fundamental Principles of the Metaphysic of Morals,* III

35 If it were possible to have so profound an insight into a man's mental character as shown by internal as well as external actions as to know all its motives, even the smallest, and likewise all the external occasions that can influence them, we could calculate a man's conduct for the future with as great certainty as a lunar or solar eclipse; and nevertheless we may maintain that the man is free.

Kant, *Critique of Practical Reason,* Pt. I, I, 3

36 If we grant freedom to man, there is an end to the omniscience of God; for if the Divinity knows how I shall act, I must act so perforce.

Goethe, *Conversations with Eckermann (Oct. 12, 1825)*

37 The absolute goal, or, if you like, the absolute impulse, of free mind is to make its freedom its object, i.e. to make freedom objective as much in the

sense that freedom shall be the rational system of mind, as in the sense that this system shall be the world of immediate actuality. In making freedom its object, mind's purpose is to be explicitly, as Idea, what the will is implicitly. The definition of the concept of the will in abstraction from the Idea of the will is "the free will which wills the free will."

Hegel, *Philosophy of Right,* Introduction, 27

38 In . . . the will is rooted my ability to free myself from everything, abandon every aim, abstract from everything. Man alone can sacrifice everything, his life included; he can commit suicide. An animal cannot; it always remains merely negative, in an alien destiny to which it merely accustoms itself.

Hegel, *Philosophy of Right,* Additions, Par. 5

39 A will which resolves on nothing is no actual will; a characterless man never reaches a decision.

Hegel, *Philosophy of Right,* Additions, Par. 13

40 Every man, being what he is and placed in the circumstances which for the moment obtain, but which on their part also arise by strict necessity, can absolutely never do anything else than just what at that moment he does do. Accordingly, the whole course of a man's life, in all its incidents great and small, is as necessarily predetermined as the course of a clock.

Schopenhauer, *Free-Will and Fatalism*

41 Chance, freewill, and necessity—nowise incompatible—all interweavingly working together. The straight warp of necessity, not to be swerved from its ultimate course—its every alternating vibration, indeed, only tending to that; freewill still free to ply her shuttle between given threads; and chance, though restrained in its play within the right lines of necessity, and sideways in its motions modified by freewill, though thus prescribed to by both, chance by turns rules either, and has the last featuring blow at events.

Melville, *Moby Dick,* XLVII

42 We are conscious automata, endowed with free will in the only intelligible sense of that much-abused term—inasmuch as in many respects we are able to do as we like—but none the less parts of the great series of causes and effects which, in unbroken continuity, composes that which is, and has been, and shall be—the sum of existence.

T. H. Huxley, *Animal Automatism*

43 Correctly conceived, the doctrine called Philosophical Necessity is simply this: that, given the motives which are present to an individual's mind, and given likewise the character and disposition of the individual, the manner in which he will act might be unerringly inferred; that if we

knew the person thoroughly, and knew all the inducements which are acting upon him, we could foretell his conduct with as much certainty as we can predict any physical event. This proposition I take to be a mere interpretation of universal experience, a statement in words of what every one is internally convinced of. No one who believed that he knew thoroughly the circumstances of any case, and the characters of the different persons concerned, would hesitate to foretell how all of them would act. Whatever degree of doubt he may in fact feel arises from the uncertainty whether he really knows the circumstances, or the character of some one or other of the persons, with the degree of accuracy required; but by no means from thinking that if he did know these things, there could be any uncertainty what the conduct would be. Nor does this full assurance conflict in the smallest degree with what is called our feeling of freedom. We do not feel ourselves the less free because those to whom we are intimately known are well assured how we shall will to act in a particular case. We often, on the contrary, regard the doubt what our conduct will be as a mark of ignorance of our character, and sometimes even resent it as an imputation. The religious metaphysicians who have asserted the freedom of the will have always maintained it to be consistent with divine foreknowledge of our actions; and if with divine, then with any other foreknowledge. We may be free, and yet another may have reason to be perfectly certain what use we shall make of our freedom.

Mill, *System of Logic,* Bk. VI, II, 2

44 If history dealt only with external phenomena, the establishment of this simple and obvious law would suffice and we should have finished our argument. But the law of history relates to man. A particle of matter cannot tell us that it does not feel the law of attraction or repulsion and that that law is untrue, but man, who is the subject of history, says plainly: I am free and am therefore not subject to the law.

The presence of the problem of man's free will, though unexpressed, is felt at every step of history.

All seriously thinking historians have involuntarily encountered this question. All the contradictions and obscurities of history and the false path historical science has followed are due solely to the lack of a solution of that question.

If the will of every man were free, that is, if each man could act as he pleased, all history would be a series of disconnected incidents.

If in a thousand years even one man in a million could act freely, that is, as he chose, it is evident that one single free act of that man's in violation of the laws governing human action would destroy the possibility of the existence of any laws for the whole of humanity.

If there be a single law governing the actions of men, free will cannot exist, for then man's will is subject to that law.

In this contradiction lies the problem of free will, which from most ancient times has occupied the best human minds and from most ancient times has been presented in its whole tremendous significance.

The problem is that regarding man as a subject of observation from whatever point of view—theological, historical, ethical, or philosophic—we find a general law of necessity to which he (like all that exists) is subject. But regarding him from within ourselves as what we are conscious of, we feel ourselves to be free.

This consciousness is a source of self-cognition quite apart from and independent of reason. Through his reason man observes himself, but only through consciousness does he know himself.

Apart from consciousness of self no observation or application of reason is conceivable.

To understand, observe, and draw conclusions, man must first of all be conscious of himself as living. A man is only conscious of himself as a living being by the fact that he wills, that is, is conscious of his volition. But his will—which forms the essence of his life—man recognizes (and can but recognize) as free.

If, observing himself, man sees that his will is always directed by one and the same law (whether he observes the necessity of taking food, using his brain, or anything else) he cannot recognize this never-varying direction of his will otherwise than as a limitation of it. Were it not free it could not be limited. A man's will seems to him to be limited just because he is not conscious of it except as free.

You say: I am not free. But I have lifted my hand and let it fall. Everyone understands that this illogical reply is an irrefutable demonstration of freedom.

That reply is the expression of a consciousness that is not subject to reason.

If the consciousness of freedom were not a separate and independent source of self-consciousness it would be subject to reasoning and to experience, but in fact such subjection does not exist and is inconceivable.

A series of experiments and arguments proves to every man that he, as an object of observation, is subject to certain laws, and man submits to them and never resists the laws of gravity or impermeability once he has become acquainted with them. But the same series of experiments and arguments proves to him that the complete freedom of which he is conscious in himself is impossible, and that his every action depends on his organization, his character, and the motives acting upon him: yet man never submits to the deductions of these experiments and arguments. Having learned from experiment and argument that a stone falls downwards, a man indubitably believes this and always expects the law that he has learned to be fulfilled.

But learning just as certainly that his will is subject to laws, he does not and cannot believe this.

However often experiment and reasoning may show a man that under the same conditions and with the same character he will do the same thing as before, yet when under the same conditions and with the same character he approaches for the thousandth time the action that always ends in the same way, he feels as certainly convinced as before the experiment that he can act as he pleases. Every man, savage or sage, however incontestably reason and experiment may prove to him that it is impossible to imagine two different courses of action in precisely the same conditions, feels that without this irrational conception (which constitutes the essence of freedom) he cannot imagine life. He feels that however impossible it may be, it is so, for without this conception of freedom not only would he be unable to understand life, but he would be unable to live for a single moment.

He could not live, because all man's efforts, all his impulses to life, are only efforts to increase freedom. Wealth and poverty, fame and obscurity, power and subordination, strength and weakness, health and disease, culture and ignorance, work and leisure, repletion and hunger, virtue and vice, are only greater or lesser degrees of freedom.

A man having no freedom cannot be conceived of except as deprived of life.

If the conception of freedom appears to reason to be a senseless contradiction like the possibility of performing two actions at one and the same instant of time, or of an effect without a cause, that only proves that consciousness is not subject to reason.

This unshakable, irrefutable consciousness of freedom, uncontrolled by experiment or argument, recognized by all thinkers and felt by everyone without exception, this consciousness without which no conception of man is possible constitutes the other side of the question.

Man is the creation of an all-powerful, all-good, and all-seeing God. What is sin, the conception of which arises from the consciousness of man's freedom? That is a question for theology.

The actions of men are subject to general immutable laws expressed in statistics. What is man's responsibility to society, the conception of which results from the conception of freedom? That is a question for jurisprudence.

Man's actions proceed from his innate character and the motives acting upon him. What is conscience and the perception of right and wrong in actions that follows from the consciousness of freedom? That is a question for ethics.

Man in connection with the general life of humanity appears subject to laws which determine that life. But the same man apart from that connection appears to be free. How should the past life of nations and of humanity be regarded—as the result of the free, or as the result of the constrained, activity of man? That is a question for history.

Only in our self-confident day of the popularization of knowledge—thanks to that most powerful engine of ignorance, the diffusion of printed matter—has the question of the freedom of will been put on a level on which the question itself cannot exist. In our time the majority of so-called advanced people—that is, the crowd of ignoramuses—have taken the work of the naturalists who deal with one side of the question for a solution of the whole problem.

They say and write and print that the soul and freedom do not exist for the life of man is expressed by muscular movements and muscular movements are conditioned by the activity of the nerves; the soul and free will do not exist because at an unknown period of time we sprang from the apes. They say this, not at all suspecting that thousands of years ago that same law of necessity which with such ardor they are now trying to prove by physiology and comparative zoology was not merely acknowledged by all the religions and all the thinkers, but has never been denied. They do not see that the role of the natural sciences in this matter is merely to serve as an instrument for the illumination of one side of it. For the fact that, from the point of view of observation, reason and the will are merely secretions of the brain, and that man following the general law may have developed from lower animals at some unknown period of time, only explains from a fresh side the truth admitted thousands of years ago by all the religious and philosophic theories—that from the point of view of reason man is subject to the law of necessity; but it does not advance by a hair's breadth the solution of the question, which has another, opposite, side, based on the consciousness of freedom.

Tolstoy, *War and Peace*, II Epilogue, VIII

45 Man's free will differs from every other force in that man is directly conscious of it, but in the eyes of reason it in no way differs from any other force. The forces of gravitation, electricity, or chemical affinity are only distinguished from one another in that they are differently defined by reason. Just so the force of man's free will is distinguished by reason from the other forces of nature only by the definition reason gives it. Freedom, apart from necessity, that is, apart from the laws of reason that define it, differs in no way from gravitation, or heat, or the force that makes things grow; for reason, it is only a momentary undefinable sensation of life.

Tolstoy, *War and Peace*, II Epilogue, X

46 When scientific and moral postulates war thus with each other and objective proof is not to be had, the only course is voluntary choice, for scepticism itself, if systematic, is also voluntary choice. If, meanwhile, the will *be* undetermined, it would seem only fitting that the belief in its indetermination should be voluntarily chosen from amongst other possible beliefs. Freedom's first deed should be to affirm itself.

William James, *Psychology,* XXVI

47 Both free will and determinism have been inveighed against and called absurd, because each, in the eyes of its enemies, has seemed to prevent the 'imputability' of good or bad deeds to their authors. Queer antinomy this! Free will means novelty, the grafting on to the past of something not involved therein. If our acts were predetermined, if we merely transmitted the push of the whole past, the freewillists say, how could we be praised or blamed for anything? We should be 'agents' only, not 'principals,' and where then would be our precious imputability and responsibility?

But where would it be if we *had* free will? rejoin the determinists. If a 'free' act be sheer novelty, that comes not *from* me, the previous me, but *ex nihilo*, and simply tacks itself on to me, how can *I,* the previous I, be responsible? How can I have any permanent *character* that will stand still long enough for praise or blame to be awarded? The chaplet of my days tumbles into a cast of disconnected beads as soon as the thread of inner necessity is drawn out by the preposterous indeterminist doctrine. . . .

It may be good *ad hominem,* but otherwise it is pitiful. For I ask you, quite apart from other reasons, whether any man, woman or child, with a sense for realities, ought not to be ashamed to plead such principles as either dignity or imputability. Instinct and utility between them can safely be trusted to carry on the social business of punishment and praise. If a man does good acts we shall praise him, if he does bad acts we shall punish him—anyhow, and quite apart from theories as to whether the acts result from what was previous in him or are novelties in a strict sense. To make our human ethics revolve about the question of 'merit' is a piteous unreality—God alone can know our merits, if we have any. The real ground for supposing free will is indeed pragmatic, but it has nothing to do with this contemptible right to punish which has made such a noise in past discussions of the subject.

Free will pragmatically means *novelties in the world,* the right to expect that in its deepest elements as well as in its surface phenomena, the future may not identically repeat and imitate the past. That imitation *en masse* is there, who can deny? The general "uniformity of nature" is presupposed by every lesser law. But nature may be only approximately uniform; and persons in whom knowledge of the world's past has bred pessimism (or doubts as to the world's good character, which become certainties if that character be supposed eternally fixed) may naturally welcome free will as a *melioristic* doctrine. It holds up improvement as at least possible; whereas determinism assures us that our whole notion of possibility is born of human ignorance, and that necessity and impossibility between them rule the destinies of the world.

William James, *Pragmatism,* III

48 The existence of strict causality implies that the actions, the mental processes, and especially the will of every individual are completely determined at any given moment by the state of his mind, taken as a whole, in the previous moment, and by any influences acting upon him coming from the external world. We have no reason whatever for doubting the truth of this assertion. But the question of free will is not concerned with the question whether there is such a definite connection, but whether the person in question is aware of this connection. This, and this alone, determines whether a person can or cannot feel free. If a man were able to forecast his own future solely on the ground of causality, then and then only we would have to deny this consciousness of freedom of the will. Such a contingency is, however, impossible, since it contains a logical contradiction. Complete knowledge implies that the object apprehended is not altered by any events taking place in the knowing subject; and if subject and object are identical, this assumption does not apply. To put it more concretely, the knowledge of any motive or of any activity of will is an inner experience, from which a fresh motive may spring; consequently such an awareness increases the number of possible motives. But as soon as this is recognized, the recognition brings about a fresh act of awareness, which in its turn can generate yet another activity of the will. In this way the chain proceeds, without it ever being possible to reach a motive which is definitely decisive for any future action; in other words, to reach an awareness which is not in its turn the occasion of a fresh act of will. When we look back upon a finished action, which we can contemplate as a whole, the case is completely different. Here knowledge no longer influences will, and hence a strictly causal consideration of motives and will is possible, at least in theory.

If these considerations appear unintelligible—if it is thought that a mind could completely grasp the causes of its present state, provided it were intelligent enough—then such an argument is akin to saying that a giant who is big enough to look down on everybody else should be able to look down on himself as well. The fact is that no person, however clever, can derive the decisive motives of his own conscious actions from the causal law alone; he requires another law—the ethical law, for which the highest intelligence and the most subtle self-analysis are no adequate substitute.

Planck, *Universe in the Light of Modern Physics*, 6

49 To foresee future objective alternatives and to be able by deliberation to choose one of them and thereby weight its chances in the struggle for future existence, measures our freedom. It is assumed sometimes that if it can be shown that deliberation determines choice and deliberation is determined by character and conditions, there is no freedom. This is like saying that because a flower comes from root and stem it cannot bear fruit. The question is not what are the antecedents of deliberation and choice, but what are their consequences. What do they do that is distinctive? The answer is that they give us all the control of future possibilities which is open to us. And this control is the crux of our freedom. Without it, we are pushed from behind.

Dewey, *Human Nature and Conduct*, IV, 3

50 We are free when our acts spring from our whole personality, when they express it, when they have that indefinable resemblance to it which one sometimes finds between the artist and his work. It is no use asserting that we are then yielding to the all-powerful influence of our character. Our character is still ourselves; and because we are pleased to split the person into two parts so that by an effort of abstraction we may consider in turn the self which feels or thinks and the self which acts, it would be very strange to conclude that one of the two selves is coercing the other.

Bergson, *Time and Free Will*, III

51 Human free will does not exclude but presupposes the vast and complex dynamism of instincts, tendencies, psycho-physical dispositions, acquired habits, and hereditary traits, and it is at the top point where this dynamism emerges in the world of spirit that freedom of choice is exercised, to give or withhold decisive efficacy to the inclinations and urges of nature. It follows from this that freedom, as well as responsibility, is capable of a multiplicity of degrees of which the Author of being alone is judge. It does not follow from this that freedom does not exist—on the contrary! If it admits of degrees, then it exists.

Maritain, *The Conquest of Freedom*

52 It must be made clear that not only particular and partial goods, offered us by the finite world, but all the concrete goods which we may love and desire in this life, are thus the object of the will's free choice. Even the noblest good, even the divine good, is thus, and for the same reason, the object of the will's free choice.

Maritain, *Scholasticism and Politics*, V

53 Human-reality is free because it is not enough. It is free because it is perpetually wrenched away from itself and because it has been separated by a nothingness from what it is and from what it will be. It is free, finally, because its present being is itself a nothingness in the form of the "reflection-reflecting." Man is free because he is not himself but presence to himself. The being which is what it is can not be free. Freedom is precisely the nothingness which is made-to-be at the heart of man and which forces human-reality to make itself instead of to be. As we have seen, for human reality, to be is to choose oneself; nothing comes to it qer from the outside or from within which it can receive or accept.

Sartre, *Being and Nothingness*, Pt. IV, I, 1

Chapter 6

KNOWLEDGE

Chapter 6 is divided into seven sections: 6.1 THE CHARACTERISTICS AND CONDITIONS OF HUMAN KNOWLEDGE, 6.2 EXPERIENCE, 6.3 TRUTH, 6.4 ERROR, IGNORANCE, AND THE LIMITS OF HUMAN KNOWLEDGE, 6.5 OPINION, BELIEF, AND FAITH, 6.6 DOUBT AND SKEPTICISM, and 6.7 REASONING, DEMONSTRATION, AND DISPUTATION.

Man is pre-eminently a knowing animal. As one famous statement that comes down to us from antiquity puts it, "all men by nature desire to know." Knowing, feeling, and doing—these three, in separation and in combination, round out the whole orbit of human performance.

After the opening section of the chapter, in which the most general and persistent questions about knowledge are raised and discussed, the sections that follow deal with the contributions and values of experience, with truth as the good that is attained when we possess knowledge, with error as the contrary of truth and ignorance as the privation of knowledge, with opinion and belief as alternatives to knowledge, or even substitutes for it, with doubt and skepticism as checks against unwarranted assertions of knowledge, and with the ratiocinative process as that is involved in our effort to know, in the defence of our own opinions, and in the criticism of the opinions advanced by others.

The chapter most closely related to this one is, of course, Chapter 5 on MIND; but the reader will also find relevant passages in Chapter 17 on PHILOSOPHY, SCIENCE, AND MATHEMATICS, and some passages in Chapter 19 on NATURE AND THE COSMOS, particularly Section 19.3 on CAUSE and Section 19.4 on CHANCE.

6.1 | *The Characteristics and Conditions*
of Human Knowledge

On a number of points, the quotations collected here tend to be in substantial agreement: that knowledge, or the truth that is attained when we know, is the essential good of the mind; that it is both good in itself, to be loved for its own sake, and also good as a means to be used in action and production; that, while man aspires to know all that is knowable, human knowledge at its best is imperfect and limited; and that knowledge is a relation between a knower and an object known.

Other points made by some of the authors quoted are not concurred in or mentioned by others, such as the distinction between that which is more knowable in itself and that which is more knowable to us; the comparison between man's finite or limited knowledge and God's infinite knowledge; the difference between sensitive and intellectual knowledge; the difference between simple apprehensions which assert nothing and so are neither true nor false and judgments which, affirming or denying something, are capable of truth and falsity; the difference between knowledge by acquaintance (or knowledge *of*) and knowledge by description (or knowledge *about*); the difference between scientific and technical knowledge (or between know-that and know-how); and the difference between speculative and practical knowledge (or knowing what *is* the case and knowing what *ought* to be done or sought).

Beyond this, the reader will find that the quotations exhibit a pattern of manifold and intricate disagreements about the process of knowing itself—how we know whatever it is that we do know; about the precise nature of the relationship between knower and known; about the existential status of the object known; about the grades of human knowledge, either in terms of the character of the objects known or in terms of the degree of certainty or uncertainty with which something is known; about the distinction between knowledge and opinion; and about the limits of human knowledge. Some of these matters, merely hinted at in the passages quoted here, are more fully discussed in later sections of this chapter, especially Sections 6.4, 6.5, and 6.6.

---

1 The fear of the Lord is the beginning of knowledge: but fools despise wisdom and instruction.

Proverbs 1:7

2 *Persian soldier.* 'Tis the sorest of all human ills, to abound in knowledge and yet have no power over action.

Herodotus, *History,* IX, 16

3 *Socrates.* In questions of just and unjust, fair and foul, good and evil, which are the subjects of our present consultation, ought we to follow the opinion of the many and to fear them; or the opinion of the one man who has understanding? ought we not to fear and reverence him more than all the rest of the world: and if we desert him shall we not destroy and injure that principle in us which may be assumed to be improved by justice and deteriorated by injustice?

Plato, *Crito,* 47B

4 *Socrates.* What again shall we say of the actual acquirement of knowledge?—is the body, if invited to share in the enquiry, a hinderer or a helper? I mean to say, have sight and hearing any truth in them? Are they not, as the poets are always telling

us, inaccurate witnesses? and yet, if even they are inaccurate and indistinct, what is to be said of the other senses?—for you will allow that they are the best of them?

Certainly, he [Simmias] replied.

Then when does the soul attain truth?—for in attempting to consider anything in company with the body she is obviously deceived.

True.

Then must not true existence be revealed to her in thought, if at all?

Yes.

And thought is best when the mind is gathered into herself and none of these things trouble her— neither sounds nor sights nor pain nor any pleasure,—when she takes leave of the body, and has as little as possible to do with it, when she has no bodily sense or desire, but is aspiring after true being?

Certainly.

And in this the philosopher dishonours the body; his soul runs away from his body and desires to be alone and by herself?

That is true.

Well, but there is another thing, Simmias: Is there or is there not an absolute justice?

Assuredly there is.

And an absolute beauty and absolute good?

Of course.

But did you ever behold any of them with your eyes?

Certainly not.

Or did you ever reach them with any other bodily sense?—and I speak not of these alone, but of absolute greatness, and health, and strength, and of the essence or true nature of everything. Has the reality of them ever been perceived by you through the bodily organs? or rather, is not the nearest approach to the knowledge of their several natures made by him who so orders his intellectual vision as to have the most exact conception of the essence of each thing which he considers?

Certainly.

And he attains to the purest knowledge of them who goes to each with the mind alone, not introducing or intruding in the act of thought sight or any other sense together with reason, but with the very light of the mind in her own clearness searches into the very truth of each; he who has got rid, as far as he can, of eyes and ears and, so to speak, of the whole body, these being in his opinion distracting elements which when they infect the soul hinder her from acquiring truth and knowledge—who, if not he, is likely to attain to the knowledge of true being?

Plato, *Phaedo,* 65A

5 *Socrates.* You have to imagine . . . that there are two ruling powers, and that one of them is set over the intellectual world, the other over the visible. I do not say heaven, lest you should fancy that I am playing upon the name. May I suppose that you have this distinction of the visible and intelligible fixed in your mind?

Glaucon. I have.

Now take a line which has been cut into two unequal parts, and divide each of them again in the same proportion, and suppose the two main divisions to answer, one to the visible and the other to the intelligible, and then compare the subdivisions in respect of their clearness and want of clearness, and you will find that the first section in the sphere of the visible consists of images. And by images I mean, in the first place, shadows, and in the second place, reflections in water and in solid, smooth and polished bodies and the like: Do you understand?

Yes, I understand.

Imagine, now, the other section, of which this is only the resemblance, to include the animals which we see, and everything that grows or is made.

Very good.

Would you not admit that both the sections of this division have different degrees of truth, and that the copy is to the original as the sphere of opinion is to the sphere of knowledge?

Most undoubtedly.

Next proceed to consider the manner in which the sphere of the intellectual is to be divided.

In what manner?

Thus:—There are two subdivisions, in the lower of which the soul uses the figures given by the former division as images; the enquiry can only be hypothetical, and instead of going upwards to a principle descends to the other end; in the higher of the two, the soul passes out of hypotheses, and goes up to a principle which is above hypotheses, making no use of images as in the former case, but proceeding only in and through the ideas themselves.

I do not quite understand your meaning, he said.

Then I will try again; you will understand me better when I have made some preliminary remarks. You are aware that students of geometry, arithmetic, and the kindred sciences assume the odd and the even and the figures and three kinds of angles and the like in their several branches of science; these are their hypotheses, which they and every body are supposed to know, and therefore they do not deign to give any account of them either to themselves or others; but they begin with them, and go on until they arrive at last, and in a consistent manner, at their conclusion?

Yes, he said, I know.

And do you not know also that although they make use of the visible forms and reason about them, they are thinking not of these, but of the ideals which they resemble; not of the figures which they draw, but of the absolute square and the absolute diameter, and so on—the forms which they draw or make, and which have shadows and reflections in water of their own, are converted by them into images, but they are really seeking to behold the things themselves, which can only be seen with the eye of the mind?

That is true.

And of this kind I spoke as the intelligible, although in the search after it the soul is compelled to use hypotheses; not ascending to a first principle, because she is unable to rise above the region of hypothesis, but employing the objects of which the shadows below are resemblances in their turn as images, they having in relation to the shadows and reflections of them a greater distinctness, and therefore a higher value.

I understand, he said, that you are speaking of the province of geometry and the sister arts.

And when I speak of the other division of the intelligible, you will understand me to speak of that other sort of knowledge which reason herself attains by the power of dialectic, using the hypotheses not as first principles, but only as hypotheses—that is to say, as steps and points of departure into a world which is above hypotheses, in order that she may soar beyond them to the first principle of the whole; and clinging to this and then to that which depends on this, by successive steps she descends again without the aid of any sensible object, from ideas, through ideas, and in ideas she ends.

I understand you, he replied; not perfectly, for you seem to me to be describing a task which is really tremendous; but, at any rate, I understand you to say that knowledge and being, which the science of dialectic contemplates, are clearer than the notions of the arts, as they are termed, which proceed from hypotheses only: these are also contemplated by the understanding, and not by the senses: yet, because they start from hypotheses and do not ascend to a principle, those who contemplate them appear to you not to exercise the higher reason upon them, although when a first principle is added to them they are cognizable by the higher reason. And the habit which is concerned with geometry and the cognate sciences I suppose that you would term understanding and not reason, as being intermediate between opinion and reason.

You have quite conceived my meaning, I said; and now, corresponding to these four divisions, let there be four faculties in the soul—reason answering to the highest, understanding to the second, faith (or conviction) to the third, and perception of shadows to the last—and let there be a scale of them, and let us suppose that the several faculties have clearness in the same degree that their objects have truth.

Plato, *Republic*, VI, 509B

6 For everything that exists there are three instruments by which the knowledge of it is necessarily imparted; fourth, there is the knowledge itself, and, as fifth, we must count the thing itself which is known and truly exists. The first is the name, the second the definition, the third the image, and the fourth the knowledge. If you wish to learn what I mean, take these in the case of one instance, and so understand them in the case of all. A circle is a thing spoken of, and its name is that very word which we have just uttered. The second thing belonging to it is its definition, made up of names and verbal forms. For that which has the name "round," "annular," or "circle," might be defined as that which has the distance from its circumference to its centre everywhere equal. Third, comes that which is drawn and rubbed out again, or turned on a lathe and broken up—none of which things can happen to the circle itself—to which the other things mentioned have reference; for it is something of a different order from them. Fourth, comes knowledge, intelligence and right opinion about these things. Under this one head we must group everything which has its existence, not in words nor in bodily shapes, but in souls—from which it is clear that it is something different from the nature of the circle itself and from the three things mentioned before. Of these things intelligence comes closest in kinship and likeness to the fifth, and the others are farther distant.

The same applies to straight as well as to circular form, to colours, to the good, the beautiful, the just, to all bodies whether manufactured or coming into being in the course of nature, to fire, water, and all such things, to every living being, to character in souls, and to all things done and suffered. For in the case of all these no one, if he has not some how or other got hold of the four things first mentioned, can ever be completely a partaker of knowledge of the fifth. Further, on account of the weakness of language, these (i.e., the four) attempt to show what each thing is like, not less than what each thing is. For this reason no man of intelligence will venture to express his philosophical views in language, especially not in language that is unchangeable, which is true of that which is set down in written characters.

Plato, *Seventh Letter*

7 It does not appear to be true in all cases that correlatives come into existence simultaneously. The object of knowledge would appear to exist before knowledge itself, for it is usually the case that we acquire knowledge of objects already existing; it would be difficult, if not impossible, to find a branch of knowledge the beginning of the existence of which was contemporaneous with that of its object.

Again, while the object of knowledge, if it ceases to exist, cancels at the same time the knowledge which was its correlative, the converse of this is not true. It is true that if the object of knowledge does not exist there can be no knowledge: for there will no longer be anything to know. Yet it is equally true that, if the knowledge of a certain object does not exist, the object may nevertheless quite well exist. Thus, in the case of the squaring of the circle, if indeed that process is an object of knowledge, though it itself exists as an object of knowledge, yet the knowledge of it has not yet come into existence. Again, if all animals ceased to exist, there would be no knowledge, but there might yet be many objects of knowledge.

Aristotle, *Categories,* 7ᵇ21

8 Knowledge, as a genus, is explained by reference to something else, for we mean a knowledge *of something.* But particular branches of knowledge are not thus explained. The knowledge of grammar is not relative to anything external, nor is the knowledge of music, but these, if relative at all, are relative only in virtue of their genera; thus grammar is said to be the *knowledge* of something, not the grammar of something; similarly music is the *knowledge* of something, not the music of something.

Thus individual branches of knowledge are not relative. And it is because we possess these individual branches of knowledge that we are said to be such and such. It is these that we actually possess: we are called experts because we possess knowledge in some particular branch.

Aristotle, *Categories,* 11ᵃ24

9 There is a difference between what is prior and better known in the order of being and what is prior and better known to man. I mean that objects nearer to sense are prior and better known to man; objects without qualification prior and better known are those further from sense. Now the most universal causes are furthest from sense and particular causes are nearest to sense, and they are thus exactly opposed to one another.

Aristotle, *Posterior Analytics,* 71ᵇ34

10 It is hard to be sure whether one knows or not; for it is hard to be sure whether one's knowledge is based on the basic truths appropriate to each attribute—the differentia of true knowledge. We think we have scientific knowledge if we have reasoned from true and primary premisses. But that is not so: the conclusion must be homogeneous with the basic facts of the science.

Aristotle, *Posterior Analytics,* 76ᵃ26

11 In the case of all discoveries the results of previous labours that have been handed down from others have been advanced bit by bit by those who have taken them on, whereas the original discoveries generally make an advance that is small at first though much more useful than the development which later springs out of them. For it may be

that in everything, as the saying is, 'the first start is the main part': and for this reason also it is the most difficult; for in proportion as it is most potent in its influence, so it is smallest in its compass and therefore most difficult to see: whereas when this is once discovered, it is easier to add and develop the remainder in connexion with it.

Aristotle, *On Sophistical Refutations,* 183ᵇ17

12 When the objects of an inquiry, in any department, have principles, conditions, or elements, it is through acquaintance with these that knowledge, that is to say scientific knowledge, is attained. For we do not think that we know a thing until we are acquainted with its primary conditions or first principles, and have carried our analysis as far as its simplest elements. Plainly therefore in the science of Nature, as in other branches of study, our first task will be to try to determine what relates to its principles.

The natural way of doing this is to start from the things which are more knowable and obvious to us and proceed towards those which are clearer and more knowable by nature; for the same things are not 'knowable relatively to us' and 'knowable' without qualification. So in the present inquiry we must follow this method and advance from what is more obscure by nature, but clearer to us, towards what is more clear and more knowable by nature.

Aristotle, *Physics,* 184ᵃ10

13 All men by nature desire to know. An indication of this is the delight we take in our senses; for even apart from their usefulness they are loved for themselves; and above all others the sense of sight. For not only with a view to action, but even when we are not going to do anything, we prefer seeing (one might say) to everything else. The reason is that this, most of all the senses, makes us know and brings to light many differences between things.

Aristotle, *Metaphysics,* 980ᵃ1

14 For all men begin, as we said, by wondering that things are as they are, as they do about self-moving marionettes, or about the solstices or the incommensurability of the diagonal of a square with the side; for it seems wonderful to all who have not yet seen the reason, that there is a thing which cannot be measured even by the smallest unit. But we must end in the contrary and, according to the proverb, the better state, as is the case in these instances too when men learn the cause; for there is nothing which would surprise a geometer so much as if the diagonal turned out to be commensurable.

Aristotle, *Metaphysics,* 983ᵃ13

15 It is absurd to seek at the same time knowledge

and the way of attaining knowledge; and it is not easy to get even one of the two.

Aristotle, *Metaphysics*, 995ª13

16 Since men may know the same thing in many ways, we say that he who recognizes what a thing is by its being so and so knows more fully than he who recognizes it by its not being so and so, and in the former class itself one knows more fully than another, and he knows most fully who knows what a thing is, not he who knows its quantity or quality or what it can by nature do or have done to it.

Aristotle, *Metaphysics*, 996ᵇ14

17 That there is no science of the accidental is obvious; for all science is either of that which is always or of that which is for the most part. (For how else is one to learn or to teach another? The thing must be determined as occurring either always or for the most part, e.g. that honey-water is useful for a patient in a fever is true for the most part.) But that which is contrary to the usual law science will be unable to state, i.e. when the thing does *not* happen, e.g. 'on the day of new moon'; for even that which happens on the day of new moon happens then either always or for the most part; but the accidental is contrary to such laws.

Aristotle, *Metaphysics*, 1027ª19

18 What *scientific knowledge* is, if we are to speak exactly and not follow mere similarities, is plain from what follows. We all suppose that what we know is not even capable of being otherwise; of things capable of being otherwise we do not know, when they have passed outside our observation, whether they exist or not. Therefore the object of scientific knowledge is of necessity. Therefore it is eternal; for things that are of necessity in the unqualified sense are all eternal; and things that are eternal are ungenerated and imperishable. Again, every science is thought to be capable of being taught, and its object of being learned. And all teaching starts from what is already known, as we maintain in the *Analytics* also; for it proceeds sometimes through induction and sometimes by syllogism. Now induction is the starting-point which knowledge even of the universal presupposes, while syllogism proceeds, *from* universals. There are therefore starting-points from which syllogism proceeds, which are not reached by syllogism; it is therefore by induction that they are acquired. Scientific knowledge is, then, a state of capacity to demonstrate, and has the other limiting characteristics which we specify in the *Analytics*, for it is when a man believes in a certain way and the starting-points are known to him that he has scientific knowledge, since if they are not better known to him than the conclusion, he will have his knowledge only incidentally.

Aristotle, *Ethics*, 1139ᵇ19

19 The fact that men use the language that flows from knowledge proves nothing; for even men under the influence of these passions utter scientific proofs and verses of Empedocles, and those who have just begun to learn a science can string together its phrases, but do not yet know it; for it has to become part of themselves, and that takes time.

Aristotle, *Ethics*, 1147ª17

20 It is one thing . . . to remember, another to know. To remember is to safeguard something entrusted to your memory, whereas to know, by contrast, is actually to make each item your own, and not to be dependent on some original and be constantly looking to see what the master said.

Seneca, *Letters to Lucilius*, 33

21 Now as touching things offered unto idols, we know that we all have knowledge. Knowledge puffeth up, but charity edifieth.

And if any man think that he knoweth any thing, he knoweth nothing yet as he ought to know.

But if any man love God, the same is known of him.

I Corinthians 8:1–3

22 Knowledge, if it does not determine action, is dead to us.

Plotinus, *First Ennead*, II, 4

23 Yet, Lord God of truth, is any man pleasing to You for knowing such things? Surely a man is unhappy even if he knows all these things but does not know You; and that man is happy who knows You even though he knows nothing of them. and the man who knows both You and them is not the happier for them but only on account of You: if knowing You he glorifies You as You are and gives thanks and does not become vain in his thoughts. For just as he is better who knows he possesses a tree and gives thanks to You for the use it is to him, although he does not know how many cubits high it is or the width of its spread, than another man who can measure it and number its branches but neither possesses it nor knows and loves Him who created it; so it would be absurd to doubt that a true Christian— who in some sense possesses all this world of riches and who having nothing yet possesses all things by cleaving unto You whom all things serve—is better though he does not even know the circles of the Great Bear than one who can measure the heavens and number the stars and balance the elements, if in all this he neglects You who have *ordered all things in measure and number and weight.*

Augustine, *Confessions*, V, 4

24 The knowledge of the creature is, in comparison of the knowledge of the Creator, but a twilight;

and so it dawns and breaks into morning when the creature is drawn to the praise and love of the Creator; and night never falls when the Creator is not forsaken through love of the creature.

Augustine, *City of God*, XI, 7

25 Certain it is that, though philosophers disagree regarding the nature of things, and the mode of investigating truth, and of the good to which all our actions ought to tend, yet in these three great general questions all their intellectual energy is spent. And though there be a confusing diversity of opinion, every man striving to establish his own opinion in regard to each of these questions, yet no one of them all doubts that nature has some cause, science some method, life some end and aim. Then, again, there are three things which every artificer must possess if he is to effect anything—nature, education, practice. Nature is to be judged by capacity, education by knowledge, practice by its fruit.

Augustine, *City of God*, XI, 25

26 In ourselves beholding His image, let us, like that younger son of the gospel, come to ourselves, and arise and return to Him from Whom by our sin we had departed. There our being will have no death, our knowledge no error, our love no mishap.

Augustine, *City of God*, XI, 28

27 Owing to the liability of the human mind to fall into mistakes, this very pursuit of knowledge may be a snare to [man] unless he has a divine Master, whom he may obey without misgiving, and who may at the same time give him such help as to perserve his own freedom.

Augustine, *City of God*, XIX, 14

28 I think that it is well to warn studious and able young men, who fear God and are seeking for happiness of life, not to venture heedlessly upon the pursuit of the branches of learning that are in vogue beyond the pale of the Church of Christ, as if these could secure for them the happiness they seek; but soberly and carefully to discriminate among them. And if they find any of those which have been instituted by men varying by reason of the varying pleasure of their founders, and unknown by reason of erroneous conjectures, especially if they involve entering into fellowship with devils by means of leagues and covenants about signs, let these be utterly rejected and held in detestation. Let the young men also withdraw their attention from such institutions of men as are unnecessary and luxurious. But for the sake of the necessities of this life we must not neglect the arrangements of men that enable us to carry on intercourse with those around us. I think, however, there is nothing useful in the other branches of learning that are found among the heathen, ex-

cept information about objects, either past or present, that relate to the bodily senses, in which are included also the experiments and conclusions of the useful mechanical arts, except also the sciences of reasoning and of numbers. And in regard to all these we must hold by the maxim, "Not too much of anything"; especially in the case of those which, pertaining as they do to the senses, are subject to the relations of space and time.

Augustine, *Christian Doctrine*, II, 39

29 When the student of the Holy Scriptures . . . shall enter upon his investigations, let him constantly meditate upon that saying of the apostle's, "Knowledge puffeth up, but charity edifieth." For so he will feel that, whatever may be the riches he brings with him out of Egypt, yet unless he has kept the passover, he cannot be safe. Now Christ is our passover sacrificed for us. . . . Let them remember, then, that those who celebrated the passover at that time in type and shadow, when they were ordered to mark their door-posts with the blood of the lamb, used hyssop to mark them with. Now this is a meek and lowly herb, and yet nothing is stronger and more penetrating than its roots; that being rooted and grounded in love, we may be able to comprehend with all saints what is the breadth, and length, and depth, and height— that is, to comprehend the cross of our Lord, the breadth of which is indicated by the transverse wood on which the hands are stretched, its length by the part from the ground up to the cross-bar on which the whole body from the head downwards is fixed, its height by the part from the cross-bar to the top on which the head lies, and its depth by the part which is hidden, being fixed in the earth. And by this sign of the cross all Christian action is symbolized, viz., to do good works in Christ, to cling with constancy to Him, to hope for heaven, and not to desecrate the sacraments. And purified by this Christian action, we shall be able to know even "the love of Christ which passeth knowledge."

Augustine, *Christian Doctrine*, II, 41

30 The brevity of our life, the dullness of our senses, the torpor of our indifference, the futility of our occupation, suffer us to know but little: and that little is soon shaken and then torn from the mind by that traitor to learning, that hostile and faithless stepmother to memory, oblivion.

John of Salisbury, *Prologue to the Policraticus*

31 Our soul possesses two cognitive powers. One is the act of any corporeal organ, which naturally knows things existing in individual matter; hence sense knows only the singular. But there is another kind of cognitive power in the soul, called the intellect, and this is not the act of any corporeal organ. Therefore the intellect naturally knows na-

tures which have being only in individual matter; not however as they are in individual matter, but according as they are abstracted from it by the consideration of the intellect. Hence it follows that through the intellect we can understand things of this kind as universal, and this is beyond the power of sense. Now the angelic intellect naturally knows natures not existing in matter; but this is beyond the natural power of the intellect of our soul in the state of its present life, united as it is to the body.

Aquinas, *Summa Theologica*, I, 12, 4

32 Each thing is known insofar as its likeness is in the one who knows. Now this takes place in two ways. For since things which are like one and the same thing are like each other, the knowing power can be assimilated to any knowable object in two ways. In one way it is assimilated by the object itself, when it is directly informed by its likeness, and then the object is known in itself. In another way when informed by a species which resembles the object; and in this way the knowledge is not of the thing in itself, but of the thing in its likeness. For the knowledge of a man in himself differs from the knowledge of him in his image.

Aquinas, *Summa Theologica*, I, 12, 9

33 A thing is said to be comprehended when the end of the knowledge of it is attained, and this is accomplished when it is known as perfectly as it is knowable; as, for instance, a demonstrable proposition is comprehended when known by demonstration, but not, however, when it is known by some probable reason.

Aquinas, *Summa Theologica*, I, 14, 3

34 As the Philosopher [Aristotle] says, "one knowledge is preferable to another, either because it is about a higher object, or because it is more certain." Hence if the subject be equally good and sublime, that virtue will be the greater which possesses more certain knowledge. But a virtue which is less certain about a higher and better object, is preferable to that which is more certain about an object of inferior degree. Hence the Philosopher says that it is a great thing to be able to know something about celestial beings, though it be based on weak and probable reasoning; and again, that it is better to know a little about sublime things, than much about mean things. Accordingly wisdom, to which knowledge about God pertains, is beyond the reach of man, especially in this life, so as to be his possession, for this belongs to God alone; and yet this little knowledge about God which we can have through wisdom is preferable to all other knowledge.

Aquinas, *Summa Theologica*, I, 14, 5

35 Some knowledge is speculative only, some is practical only, and some is partly speculative and partly practical. In proof of this it must be observed that knowledge can be called speculative in three ways. First, on the part of the things known, which are not operable by the knower; such is the knowledge of man about natural or divine things. Secondly, as regards the manner of knowing—as, for instance, if a builder consider a house by defining and dividing, and considering what belongs to it in general, for this is to consider operable things in a speculative manner, and not as they are operable; for operable means the application of form to matter, and not the resolution of the composite into its universal formal principles. Thirdly, as regards the end; "for the practical intellect differs in its end from the speculative," as the Philosopher [Aristotle] says. For the practical intellect is ordered to the end of the operation, whereas the end of the speculative intellect is the consideration of truth. Hence if a builder should consider how a house can be made, not ordering this to the end of operation, but only to know (how to do it), this would be only a speculative consideration as regards the end, although it concerns an operable thing. Therefore knowledge which is speculative by reason of the thing itself known, is merely speculative. But that which is speculative either in its mode or as to its end is partly speculative and partly practical; and when it is ordered to an operative end it is simply practical.

Aquinas, *Summa Theologica*, I, 14, 16

36 The intellect knows principles naturally; and this knowledge in man causes the knowledge of conclusions, which are known by him not naturally, but by discovery, or by teaching.

Aquinas, *Summa Theologica*, I, 60, 2

37 Knowledge is loved not that any good may come to it but that it may be possessed.

Aquinas, *Summa Theologica*, I, 60, 3

38 The action of the intellect consists in this—that the notion of the thing understood is in the one who understands, while the act of the will consists in this—that the will is inclined to the thing itself as it is in itself. And therefore the Philosopher [Aristotle] says in the *Metaphysics* that good and evil, which are objects of the will, are in things, but truth and error, which are objects of the intellect, are in the mind. When, therefore, the thing in which there is good is nobler than the soul itself, in which is the idea understood, by comparison with such a thing the will is higher than the intellect. But when the thing which is good is less noble than the soul, then even in comparison with that thing the intellect is higher than the will. Therefore the love of God is better than the knowledge of God; but, on the contrary, the knowledge of corporeal things is better than the love of them. Absolutely, however, the intellect is

nobler than the will.

Aquinas, *Summa Theologica*, I, 82, 3

39 Material things known must exist in the knower not materially, but immaterially. The reason of this is because the act of knowledge extends to things outside the knower, for we also know the things that are outside us. Now by matter the form of a thing is determined to some one thing. Therefore it is clear that knowledge is in inverse ratio to materiality. And consequently things that are not receptive of forms save materially, have no power of knowledge whatever—such as plants, as the Philosopher [Aristotle] says. But the more immaterially a thing has the form of the thing known, the more perfect is its knowledge. Therefore the intellect which abstracts the species not only from matter, but also from the individuating conditions of matter, has more perfect knowledge than the senses, which receive the form of the thing known, without matter indeed, but subject to material conditions. Moreover, among the senses, sight has the most perfect knowledge because it is the least material . . . while among intellects the more perfect is the more immaterial.

Aquinas, *Summa Theologica*, I, 84, 2

40 Plato held that naturally man's intellect is filled with all intelligible species, but that, by being united to the body, it is hindered from the realization of its act. But this seems to be wrong. First, because, if the soul has a natural knowledge of all things, it seems impossible for the soul so far to forget this natural knowledge as not to know that it has it. For no man forgets what he knows naturally; that, for instance, every whole is larger than the part, and the like. And especially unreasonable does this seem if we suppose that it is natural to the soul to be united to the body . . . for it is unreasonable that the natural operation of a thing be totally hindered by that which belongs to it naturally. Secondly, the falseness of this opinion is clearly proved from the fact that if a sense be wanting, the knowledge of what is apprehended through that sense is wanting also; for instance, a man who is born blind can have no knowledge of colours. This would not be the case if the soul had innate species of all intelligible things. We must therefore conclude that the soul does not know corporeal things through innate species.

Aquinas, *Summa Theologica*, I, 84, 3

41 Good is the cause of love, as being its object. But good is not the object of the appetite, except as apprehended. And therefore love demands some apprehension of the good that is loved. . . . Accordingly knowledge is the cause of love for the same reason as good is, which can be loved only if known.

Aquinas, *Summa Theologica*, I–II, 27, 2

42 Something is required for the perfection of knowledge that is not requisite for the perfection of love. For knowledge pertains to the reason, whose function consists in distinguishing things which in reality are united, and in uniting together, after a fashion, things that are distinct, by comparing one with another. Consequently the perfection of knowledge requires that man should know one by one all that is in a thing, such as its parts, powers, and properties. On the other hand, love is in the appetitive power, which regards a thing as it is in itself; therefore it suffices, for the perfection of love, that a thing be loved according as it is apprehended in itself. Hence it is, therefore, that a thing is loved more than it is known, since it can be loved perfectly, even without being perfectly known. This is most evident in regard to the sciences, which some love through having a certain summary knowledge of them; for instance, they know that rhetoric is a science that enables man to persuade others, and this is what they love in rhetoric. The same applies to the love of God.

Aquinas, *Summa Theologica*, I–II, 27, 2

43 As saith the Philosopher [Aristotle] in the beginning of the First Philosophy, 'All men by nature desire to know'; the reason whereof may be, that each thing, impelled by its own natural foresight, inclines to its own perfection; wherefore, inasmuch as knowledge is the distinguishing perfection of our soul, wherein consists our distinguishing blessedness, all of us are naturally subject to the longing for it.

Dante, *Convivio*, I, 1

44 Before Noah's flood the world was highly learned, by reason men lived a long time, and so attained great experience and wisdom; now, ere we begin rightly to come to the true knowledge of a thing, we lie down and die. God will not have it that we should attain a higher knowledge of things.

Luther, *Table Talk*, H160

45 In truth, knowledge is a great and very useful quality; those who despise it give evidence enough of their stupidity. But yet I do not set its value at that extreme measure that some attribute to it, like Herillus the philosopher, who placed in it the sovereign good, and held that it was in its power to make us wise and content. That I do not believe, nor what others have said, that knowledge is the mother of all virtue, and that all vice is produced by ignorance. If that is true, it is subject to a long interpretation.

Montaigne, *Essays*, II, 12, Apology for Raymond Sebond

46 *Leontes.*   How blest am I
In my just censure, in my true opinion!
Alack, for lesser knowledge! how accursed
In being so blest! There may be in the cup

A spider steep'd, and one may drink, depart,
And yet partake no venom, for his knowledge
Is not infected; but if one present
The abhorr'd ingredient to his eye, make known
How he hath drunk, he cracks his gorge, his sides,
With violent hefts. I have drunk, and seen the
spider.

Shakespeare, *Winter's Tale*, II, i, 36

47 The contemplation of God's creatures and works
produceth (having regard to the works and creatures themselves) knowledge, but having regard to
God, no perfect knowledge, but wonder which is
broken knowledge.

Bacon, *Advancement of Learning*,
Bk. I, I, 3

48 The commandment of knowledge is yet higher
than the commandment over the will: for it is a
commandment over the reason, belief, and understanding of man, which is the highest part of the
mind, and giveth law to the will itself. For there is
no power on earth which setteth up a throne or
chair of estate in the spirits and souls of men, and
in their cogitations, imaginations, opinions, and
beliefs, but knowledge and learning.

Bacon, *Advancement of Learning*,
Bk. I, VIII, 3

49 Let this be a rule, that all partitions of knowledges
be accepted rather for lines and veins than for
sections and separations; and that the continuance and entireness of knowledge be preserved.
For the contrary hereof hath made particular sciences to become barren, shallow, and erroneous,
while they have not been nourished and maintained from the common fountain.

Bacon, *Advancement of Learning*,
Bk. II, IX, 1

50 Howbeit (if we will truly consider of it) more worthy it is to believe than to know as we now know.
For in knowledge man's mind suffereth from
sense; but in belief it suffereth from spirit, such
one as it holdeth for more authorized than itself,
and so suffereth from the worthier agent. Otherwise it is of the state of man glorified; for then
faith shall cease, and we shall know as we are
known.

Bacon, *Advancement of Learning*,
Bk. II, XXV, 2

51 The human understanding, when any proposition
has been once laid down (either from general admission and belief, or from the pleasure it affords),
forces everything else to add fresh support and
confirmation; and although most cogent and
abundant instances may exist to the contrary, yet
either does not observe or despises them, or gets
rid of and rejects them by some distinction, with
violent and injurious prejudice, rather than sacri-

fice the authority of its first conclusions.

Bacon, *Novum Organum*, I, 46

52 How much more exalted will that discovery be,
which leads to the easy discovery of everything
else! Yet (to speak the truth) in the same manner
as we are very thankful for light which enables us
to enter on our way, to practise arts, to read, to
distinguish each other, and yet sight is more excellent and beautiful than the various uses of light;
so is the contemplation of things as they are, free
from superstition or imposture, error or confusion,
much more dignified in itself than all the advantage to be derived from discoveries.

Bacon, *Novum Organum*, I, 129

53 Again, the meanness of my estate doth somewhat
move me: for though I cannot accuse myself that
I am either prodigal or slothful, yet my health is
not to spend, nor my course to get. Lastly, I confess that I have as vast contemplative ends, as I
have moderate civil ends: for I have taken all
knowledge to be my province; and if I could
purge it of two sorts of rovers, whereof the one
with frivolous disputations, confutations, and ver-
bosities, the other with blind experiments and auricular traditions and impostures, hath committed
so many spoils, I hope I should bring in industrious observations, grounded conclusions, and profitable inventions and discoveries; the best state of
that province.

Bacon, *Letter to Lord Burghley (1592)*

54 In the subjects we propose to investigate, our inquiries should be directed, not to what others have
thought, nor to what we ourselves conjecture, but
to what we can clearly and perspicuously behold
and with certainty deduce; for knowledge is not
won in any other way.

Descartes, *Rules for Direction
of the Mind*, III

55 Since we cannot be universal and know all that is
to be known of everything, we ought to know a
little about everything. For it is far better to know
something about everything than to know all
about one thing. This universality is the best. If
we can have both, still better; but if we must
choose, we ought to choose the former. And the
world feels this and does so; for the world is often
a good judge.

Pascal, *Pensées*, I, 37

56 Our intellect holds the same position in the world
of thought as our body occupies in the expanse of
nature.

Limited as we are in every way, this state which
holds the mean between two extremes is present in
all our impotence. Our senses perceive no extreme. Too much sound deafens us; too much
light dazzles us; too great distance or proximity

hinders our view. Too great length and too great brevity of discourse tend to obscurity; too much truth is paralysing (I know some who cannot understand that to take four from nothing leaves nothing). First principles are too self-evident for us; too much pleasure disagrees with us. Too many concords are annoying in music; too many benefits irritate us; we wish to have the wherewithal to overpay our debts. . . . We feel neither extreme heat nor extreme cold. Excessive qualities are prejudicial to us and not perceptible by the senses; we do not feel but suffer them. Extreme youth and extreme age hinder the mind, as also too much and too little education. In short, extremes are for us as though they were not, and we are not within their notice. They escape us, or we them.

This is our true state; this is what makes us incapable of certain knowledge and of absolute ignorance. We sail within a vast sphere, ever drifting in uncertainty, driven from end to end. When we think to attach ourselves to any point and to fasten to it, it wavers and leaves us; and if we follow it, it eludes our grasp, slips past us, and vanishes for ever. Nothing stays for us. This is our natural condition and yet most contrary to our inclination; we burn with desire to find solid ground and an ultimate sure foundation whereon to build a tower reaching to the Infinite. But our whole groundwork cracks, and the earth opens to abysses.

Let us, therefore, not look for certainty and stability. Our reason is always deceived by fickle shadows; nothing can fix the finite between the two Infinites, which both enclose and fly from it.

If this be well understood, I think that we shall remain at rest, each in the state wherein nature has placed him. As this sphere which has fallen to us as our lot is always distant from either extreme, what matters it that man should have a little more knowledge of the universe? If he has it, he but gets a little higher. Is he not always infinitely removed from the end, and is not the duration of our life equally removed from eternity, even if it lasts ten years longer?

In comparison with these Infinites, all finites are equal, and I see no reason for fixing our imagination on one more than on another. The only comparison which we make of ourselves to the finite is painful to us.

Pascal, *Pensées*, II, 72

57 We must not think to make a staple commodity of all the knowledge in the land, to mark and licence it like our broadcloth and our woolpacks.

Milton, *Areopagitica*

58 We boast our light; but if we look not wisely on the Sun itself, it smites us into darkness. Who can discern those planets that are oft combust, and those stars of brightest magnitude that rise and set

with the Sun, until the opposite motion of their orbs bring them to such a place in the firmament, where they may be seen evening or morning? The light which we have gained was given us, not to be ever staring on, but by it to discover onward things more remote from our knowledge.

Milton, *Areopagitica*

59 To be still searching what we know not by what we know, still closing up truth to truth as we find it (for all her body is homogeneal and proportional), this is the golden rule in theology as well as in arithmetic, and makes up the best harmony in a Church; not the forced and outward union of cold and neutral, and inwardly divided minds.

Milton, *Areopagitica*

60 A person who knows anything, by that very fact knows that he knows, and knows that he knows that he knows, and so *ad infinitum*.

Spinoza, *Ethics*, II, Prop. 21, Schol.

61 All efforts which we make through reason are nothing but efforts to understand, and the mind, in so far as it uses reason, adjudges nothing as profitable to itself excepting that which conduces to understanding.

Spinoza, *Ethics*, IV, Prop. 26

62 We do not know that anything is certainly good or evil excepting that which actually conduces to understanding, or which can prevent us from understanding.

Spinoza, *Ethics*, IV, Prop. 27

63 The highest good of the mind is the knowledge of God, and the highest virtue of the mind is to know God.

Spinoza, *Ethics*, IV, Prop. 28

64 *Faith.* There is . . . knowledge and knowledge. Knowledge that resteth in the bare speculation of things, and knowledge that is accompanied with the grace of faith and love, which puts a man upon doing even the will of God from the heart: the first of these will serve the Talker, but without the other the true Christian is not content.

Bunyan, *Pilgrim's Progress*, I

65 He that hawks at larks and sparrows has no less sport, though a much less considerable quarry, than he that flies at nobler game: and he is little acquainted with the subject of this treatise—the UNDERSTANDING—who does not know that, as it is the most elevated faculty of the soul, so it is employed with a greater and more constant delight than any of the other. Its searches after truth are a sort of hawking and hunting, wherein the very pursuit makes a great part of the pleasure. Every step the mind takes in its progress towards Knowl-

edge makes some discovery, which is not only new, but the best too, for the time at least.

For the understanding, like the eye, judging of objects only by its own sight, cannot but be pleased with what it discovers, having less regret for what has escaped it, because it is unknown. Thus he who has raised himself above the alms-basket, and, not content to live lazily on scraps of begged opinions, sets his own thoughts on work, to find and follow truth, will (whatever he lights on) not miss the hunter's satisfaction; every moment of his pursuit will reward his pains with some delight; and he will have reason to think his time not ill spent, even when he cannot much boast of any great acquisition.

Locke, *Concerning Human Understanding,*
Epistle to the Reader

66 Though the comprehension of our understandings comes exceeding short of the vast extent of things, yet we shall have cause enough to magnify the bountiful Author of our being, for that proportion and degree of knowledge he has bestowed on us, so far above all the rest of the inhabitants of this our mansion. Men have reason to be well satisfied with what God hath thought fit for them, since he hath given them . . . whatsoever is necessary for the conveniences of life and information of virtue; and has put within the reach of their discovery, the comfortable provision for this life, and the way that leads to a better. How short soever their knowledge may come of a universal or perfect comprehension of whatsoever is, it yet secures their great concernments, that they have light enough to lead them to the knowledge of their Maker, and the sight of their own duties. . . . It will be no excuse to an idle and untoward servant, who would not attend his business by candle light, to plead that he had not broad sunshine. The Candle that is set up in us shines bright enough for all our purposes. The discoveries we can make with this ought to satisfy us; and we shall then use our understandings right, when we entertain all objects in that way and proportion that they are suited to our faculties, and upon those grounds they are capable of being proposed to us; and not . peremptorily or intemperately require demonstration, and demand certainty, where probability only is to be had, and which is sufficient to govern all our concernments. If we will disbelieve everything, because we cannot certainly know all things, we shall do muchwhat as wisely as he who would not use his legs, but sit still and perish, because he had no wings to fly.

Locke, *Concerning Human Understanding,* Intro.

67 Since the mind, in all its thoughts and reasonings, hath no other immediate object but its own ideas, which it alone does or can contemplate, it is evident that our knowledge is only conversant about them. . . . *Knowledge* then seems to me to be nothing but *the perception of the connexion of and agreement,* or *disagreement and repugnancy of any of our ideas.* In this alone it consists. Where this perception is, there is knowledge, and where it is not, there, though we may fancy, guess, or believe, yet we always come short of knowledge.

Locke, *Concerning Human Understanding,*
Bk. IV, I, 1–2

68 The knowledge of our own being we have by intuition. The existence of a God, reason clearly makes known to us, as has been shown.

The knowledge of the existence of *any other thing* we can have only by *sensation:* for there being no necessary connexion of real existence with any *idea* a man hath in his memory; nor of any other existence but that of God with the existence of any particular man: no particular man can know the existence of any other being, but only when, by actual operating upon him, it makes itself perceived by him. For, the having the idea of anything in our mind, no more proves the existence of that thing, than the picture of a man evidences his being in the world, or the visions of a dream make thereby a true history.

Locke, *Concerning Human Understanding,*
Bk. IV, XI, 1

69 We should believe that God has dealt more bountifully with the sons of men than to give them a strong desire for that knowledge which he had placed quite out of their reach.

Berkeley, *Principles of Human Knowledge,*
Intro., 3

70 It is evident to any one who takes a survey of the *objects* of human knowledge, that they are either ideas actually imprinted on the senses; or else such as are perceived by attending to the passions and operations of the mind; or lastly, ideas formed by help of memory and imagination—either compounding, dividing, or barely representing those originally perceived in the aforesaid ways. By sight I have the ideas of light and colours, with their several degrees and variations. By touch I perceive hard and soft, heat and cold, motion and resistance, and of all these more and less either as to quantity or degree. Smelling furnishes me with odours; the palate with tastes; and hearing conveys sounds to the mind in all their variety of tone and composition. And as several of these are observed to accompany each other, they come to be marked by one name, and so to be reputed as one thing. Thus, for example a certain colour, taste, smell, figure and consistence having been observed to go together, are accounted one distinct thing, signified by the name *apple;* other collections of ideas constitute a stone, a tree, a book, and the like sensible things—which as they are pleasing or disagreeable excite the passions of love, hatred, joy, grief, and so forth.

But, besides all that endless variety of ideas or objects of knowledge, there is likewise something which knows or perceives them, and exercises divers operations, as willing, imagining, remembering, about them. This perceiving, active being is what I call *mind, spirit, soul,* or *myself*. By which words I do not denote any one of my ideas, but a thing entirely distinct from them, wherein, they exist, or, which is the same thing, whereby they are perceived—for the existence of an idea consists in being perceived.

That neither our thoughts, nor passions, nor ideas formed by the imagination, exist without the mind, is what everybody will allow. And it seems no less evident that the various sensations or ideas imprinted on the sense, however blended or combined together (that is, whatever objects they compose), cannot exist otherwise than in a mind perceiving them.—I think an intuitive knowledge may be obtained of this by any one that shall attend to what is meant by the term *exists,* when applied to sensible things. The table I write on I say exists, that is, I see and feel it; and if I were out of my study I should say it existed—meaning thereby that if I was in my study I might perceive it, or that some other spirit actually does perceive it. There was an odour, that is, it was smelt; there was a sound, that is, it was heard; a colour or figure, and it was perceived by sight or touch. This is all that I can understand by these and the like expressions. For as to what is said of the absolute existence of unthinking things without any relation to their being perceived, that seems perfectly unintelligible. Their *esse* is *percepi,* nor is it possible they should have any existence out of the minds or thinking things which perceive them.

It is indeed an opinion strangely prevailing amongst men, that houses, mountains, rivers, and in a word all sensible objects, have an existence, natural or real, distinct from their being perceived by the understanding. But, with how great an assurance and acquiescence soever this principle may be entertained in the world, yet whoever shall find in his heart to call it in question may, if I mistake not, perceive it to involve a manifest contradiction. For, what are the forementioned objects but the things we perceive by sense? and what do we perceive besides our own ideas or sensations? and is it not plainly repugnant that any one of these, or any combination of them, should exist unperceived?

Berkeley, *Principles of Human Knowledge,* 1–4

71 As several gentlemen in these times, by the wonderful force of genius only, without the least assistance of learning, perhaps without being well able to read, have made a considerable figure in the republic of letters; the modern critics, I am told, have lately begun to assert, that all kind of learning is entirely useless to a writer; and, indeed, no other than a kind of fetters on the natural sprightliness and activity of the imagination, which is thus weighed down, and prevented from soaring

to those high flights which otherwise it would be able to reach.

This doctrine, I am afraid, is at present carried much too far: for why should writing differ so much from all other arts? The nimbleness of a dancing-master is not at all prejudiced by being taught to move; nor doth any mechanic, I believe, exercise his tools the worse by having learnt to use them. For my own part, I cannot conceive that Homer or Virgil would have writ with more fire, if, instead of being masters of all the learning of their times, they had been as ignorant as most of the authors of the present age. Nor do I believe that all the imagination, fire, and judgment of Pitt, could have produced those orations that have made the senate of England, in these our times, a rival in eloquence to Greece and Rome, if he had not been so well read in the writings of Demosthenes and Cicero, as to have transferred their whole spirit into his speeches, and, with their spirit, their knowledge too.

I would not here be understood to insist on the same fund of learning in any of my brethren, as Cicero persuades us is necessary to the composition of an orator. On the contrary, very little reading is, I conceive, necessary to the poet, less to the critic, and the least of all to the politician. For the first, perhaps, Byshe's Art of Poetry, and a few of our modern poets, may suffice; for the second, a moderate heap of plays; and, for the last, an indifferent collection of political journals.

To say the truth, I require no more than that a man should have some little knowledge of the subject on which he treats, according to the old maxim of law, *Quam quisque norit artem in ea se exerceat.* With this alone a writer may sometimes do tolerably well; and, indeed, without this, all the other learning in the world will stand him in little stead.

For instance, let us suppose that Homer and Virgil, Aristotle and Cicero, Thucydides and Livy, could have met all together, and have clubbed their several talents to have composed a treatise on the art of dancing: I believe it will be readily agreed they could not have equalled the excellent treatise which Mr. Essex hath given us on that subject, entitled, The Rudiments of Genteel Education. And, indeed, should the excellent Mr. Broughton be prevailed on to set fist to paper, and to complete the above-said rudiments, by delivering down the true principles of athletics, I question whether the world will have any cause to lament, that none of the great writers, either antient or modern, have ever treated about that noble and useful art.

To avoid a multiplicity of examples in so plain a case, and to come at once to my point, I am apt to conceive, that one reason why many English writers have totally failed in describing the manners of upper life, may possibly be, that in reality they know nothing of it.

Fielding, *Tom Jones,* XIV, 1

72 Man is a reasonable being; and as such, receives from science his proper food and nourishment: But so narrow are the bounds of human understanding, that little satisfaction can be hoped for in this particular, either from the extent of security or his acquisitions. Man is a sociable, no less than a reasonable being: But neither can he always enjoy company agreeable and amusing, or preserve the proper relish for them. Man is also an active being; and from that disposition, as well as from the various necessities of human life, must submit to business and occupation: But the mind requires some relaxation, and cannot always support its bent to care and industry. It seems, then, that nature has pointed out a mixed kind of life as most suitable to the human race, and secretly admonished them to allow none of these biasses to *draw* too much, so as to incapacitate them for other occupations and entertainments. Indulge your passion for science, says she, but let your science be human, and such as may have a direct reference to action and society. Abstruse thought and profound researches I prohibit, and will severely punish, by the pensive melancholy which they introduce, by the endless uncertainty in which they involve you, and by the cold reception which your pretended discoveries shall meet with, when communicated.

Hume, *Concerning Human Understanding*, I, 4

73 The sweetest and most inoffensive path of life leads through the avenues of science and learning; and whoever can either remove any obstructions in this way, or open up any new prospect, ought so far to be esteemed a benefactor to mankind. And though these researches may appear painful and fatiguing, it is with some minds as with some bodies, which being endowed with vigorous and florid health, require severe exercise, and reap a pleasure from what, to the generality of mankind, may seem burdensome and laborious. Obscurity, indeed, is painful to the mind as well as to the eye; but to bring light from obscurity, by whatever labour, must needs be delightful and rejoicing.

Hume, *Concerning Human Understanding*, I, 6

74 What though these reasonings concerning human nature seem abstract, and of difficult comprehension? This affords no presumption of their falsehood. On the contrary, it seems impossible, that what has hitherto escaped so many wise and profound philosophers can be very obvious and easy. And whatever pains these researches may cost us, we may think ourselves sufficiently rewarded, not only in point of profit but of pleasure, if, by that means, we can make any addition to our stock of knowledge, in subjects of such unspeakable importance.

Hume, *Concerning Human Understanding*, I, 10

75 Whatever moralists may hold, the human understanding is greatly indebted to the passions, which, it is universally allowed, are also much indebted to the understanding. It is by the activity of the passions that our reason is improved; for we desire knowledge only because we wish to enjoy; and it is impossible to conceive any reason why a person who has neither fears nor desires should give himself the trouble of reasoning.

Rousseau, *Origin of Inequality*, I

76 Knowledge, for most of those who cultivate it, is only a kind of money. They value it greatly, but only in proportion as it is communicated; it is good only in commerce. Take from the learned the pleasure of being listened to, and knowledge would cease to be anything to them.

Rousseau, *La Nouvelle Héloïse*, XII

77 There are . . . many subjects of study which seem but remotely allied to useful knowledge and of little importance to happiness or virtue; nor is it easy to forbear some sallies of merriment or expressions of pity when we see a man wrinkled with attention and emaciated with solicitude in the investigation of questions of which, without visible inconvenience, the world may expire in ignorance.

Johnson, *Rambler No. 83*

78 Knowledge always desires increase: it is like fire, which must first be kindled by some external agent, but which will afterwards propagate itself.

Johnson, *Letter to William Drummond (Aug. 13, 1766)*

79 Deign on the passing world to turn thine eyes,
And pause awhile from letters, to be wise.

Johnson, *Vanity of Human Wishes*, 157

80 "Sir, (said he [Johnson]) a desire of knowledge is the natural feeling of mankind; and every human being, whose mind is not debauched, will be willing to give all that he has to get knowledge."

Boswell, *Life of Johnson (July 30, 1763)*

81 He [Johnson] observed, "All knowledge is of itself of some value. There is nothing so minute or inconsiderable, that I would not rather know it than not. In the same manner, all power, of whatever sort, is of itself desirable. A man would not submit to learn to hem a ruffle, of his wife, or his wife's maid; but if a mere wish could attain it, he would rather wish to be able to hem a ruffle."

Boswell, *Life of Johnson (Apr. 14, 1775)*

82 Mathematical science affords us a brilliant example, how far, independently of all experience, we may carry our *a priori* knowledge. It is true that the mathematician occupies himself with objects and cognitions only in so far as they can be repre-

sented by means of intuition. But this circumstance is easily overlooked, because the said intuition can itself be given *a priori,* and therefore is hardly to be distinguished from a mere pure conception. Deceived by such a proof of the power of reason, we can perceive no limits to the extension of our knowledge. The light dove cleaving in free flight the thin air, whose resistance it feels, might imagine that her movements would be far more free and rapid in airless space. Just in the same way did Plato, abandoning the world of sense because of the narrow limits it sets to the understanding, venture upon the wings of ideas beyond it, into the void space of pure intellect. He did not reflect that he made no real progress by all his efforts; for he met with no resistance which might serve him for a support, as it were, whereon to rest, and on which he might apply his powers, in order to let the intellect acquire momentum for its progress. It is, indeed, the common fate of human reason in speculation, to finish the imposing edifice of thought as rapidly as possible, and then for the first time to begin to examine whether the foundation is a solid one or no. Arrived at this point, all sorts of excuses are sought after, in order to console us for its want of stability, or rather, indeed, to enable us to dispense altogether with so late and dangerous an investigation.

Kant, *Critique of Pure Reason,*
Introduction, III

83 All our knowledge begins with sense, proceeds thence to understanding, and ends with reason, beyond which nothing higher can be discovered in the human mind for elaborating the matter of intuition and subjecting it to the highest unity of thought.

Kant, *Critique of Pure Reason,*
Transcendental Dialectic

84 It is a maxim universally admitted in geometry, and indeed in every branch of knowledge, that, in the progress of investigation, we should proceed from known facts to what is unknown. In early infancy, our ideas spring from our wants; the sensation of want excites the idea of the object by which it is to be gratified. In this manner, from a series of sensations, observations, and analyses, a successive train of ideas arises, so linked together that an attentive observer may trace back to a certain point the order and connection of the whole sum of human knowledge.

Lavoisier, *Elements of Chemistry,* Pref.

85 *Faust.* I've studied now Philosophy
And Jurisprudence, Medicine,
And even, alas! Theology
All through and through with ardour keen!
Here now I stand, poor fool, and see
I'm just as wise as formerly.
Am called a Master, even Doctor too,

And now I've nearly ten years through
Pulled my students by their noses to and fro
And up and down, across, about,
And see there's nothing we can know!
That all but burns my heart right out.

Goethe, *Faust,* I, 354

86 *Wagner.* But, ah, the world! the mind and heart of men!
Of these we each would fain know something just the same.
Faust. Yes, "know"! Men call it so, but then
Who dares to call the child by its right name?
The few who have some part of it descried,
Yet fools enough to guard not their full hearts, revealing
To riffraff both their insight and their feeling,
Men have of old burned at the stake and crucified.

Goethe, *Faust,* I, 586

87 *1st Destiny.*   Knowledge is not happiness, and science
But an exchange of ignorance for that
Which is another kind of ignorance.

Byron, *Manfred,* II, iv, 431

88 It is . . . the wish for rational insight, not the ambition to amass a mere heap of acquirements, that should be presupposed in every case as possessing the mind of the learner in the study of science.

Hegel, *Philosophy of History,*
Introduction, 3

89 Knowledge is the knowing that we can not know.
Emerson, *Montaigne; or, The Skeptic*

90 Knowledge comes, but wisdom lingers.
Tennyson, *Locksley Hall,* 141

91 Who loves not Knowledge? Who shall rail
Against her beauty? May she mix
With men and prosper! Who shall fix
Her pillars? Let her work prevail.
Tennyson, *In Memoriam,* CXIV

92 What is most of our boasted so-called knowledge but a conceit that we know something, which robs us of the advantage of our actual ignorance?
Thoreau, *Walking*

93 In science, as in life, learning and knowledge are distinct, and the study of things, and not of books, is the source of the latter.
T. H. Huxley, *A Lobster, or*
The Study of Zoölogy

94 The nature of our mind leads us to seek the essence or the *why* of things. Thus we aim beyond the goal that it is given us to reach; for experience

soon teaches us that we cannot get beyond the *how,* i.e., beyond the immediate cause or the necessary conditions of phenomena.

Claude Bernard, *Experimental Medicine,* II, 1

95 The nature or very essence of phenomena, whether vital or mineral, will always remain unknown. The essence of the simplest mineral phenomenon is as completely unknown to chemists and physicists to-day as is the essence of intellectual phenomena or of any other vital phenomenon to physiologists. That, moreover, is easy to apprehend; knowledge of the inmost nature or the absolute, in the simplest phenomenon, would demand knowledge of the whole universe; for every phenomenon of the universe is evidently a sort of radiation from that universe to whose harmony it contributes. In living bodies absolute truth would be still harder to attain; because, besides implying knowledge of the universe outside a living body, it would also demand complete knowledge of the òrganism which, as we have long been saying, is a little world (microcosm) in the great universe (macrocosm). Absolute knowledge could, therefore, leave nothing outside itself; and only on condition of knowing everything could man be granted its attainment. Man behaves as if he were destined to reach this absolute knowledge; and the incessant *why* which he puts to nature proves it. Indeed, this hope, constantly disappointed, constantly reborn, sustains and always will sustain successive generations in the passionate search for truth.

Claude Bernard, *Experimental Medicine,* II, 1

96 The communication of knowledge certainly is either a condition or the means of that sense of enlargement or enlightenment, of which at this day we hear so much in certain quarters: this cannot be denied; but next, it is equally plain, that such communication is not the whole of the process. The enlargement consists, not merely in the passive reception into the mind of a number of ideas hitherto unknown to it, but in the mind's energetic and simultaneous action upon and towards and among those new ideas, which are rushing in upon it. It is the action of a formative power, reducing to order and meaning the matter of our acquirements; it is a making the objects of our knowledge subjectively our own, or, to use a familiar word, it is a digestion of what we receive, into the substance of our previous state of thought; and without this no enlargement is said to follow. There is no enlargement, unless there be a comparison of ideas one with another, as they come before the mind, and a systematizing of them. We feel our minds to be growing and expanding *then,* when we not only learn, but refer what we learn to what we know already. It is not the mere addition to our knowledge that is the illumination; but the locomotion, the movement onwards, of that mental centre, to which both what we know, and what we are learning, the accumulating mass of our acquirements, gravitates. And therefore a truly great intellect, and recognized to be such by the common opinion of mankind, such as the intellect of Aristotle, or of St. Thomas, or of Newton, or of Goethe (I purposely take instances within and without the Catholic pale, when I would speak of the intellect as such), is one which takes a connected view of old and new, past and present, far and near, and which has an insight into the influence of all these one on another; without which there is no whole, and no centre. It possesses the knowledge, not only of things, but also of their mutual and true relations; knowledge, not merely considered as acquirement, but as philosophy.

Newman, *Idea of a University,*
Discourse VI

97 It is as easy by taking thought to add a cubit to one's stature, as it is to produce an idea acceptable to any of the Muses by merely straining for it, before it is ready to come. We haunt in vain the sacred well and throne of Mnemosyne; the deeper workings of the spirit take place in their own slow way, without our connivance. Let but their bugle sound, and we may then make our effort, sure of an oblation for the altar of whatsoever divinity its savor gratifies. Beside this inward process, there is the operation of the environment, which goes to break up habits destined to be broken up and so to render the mind lively. Everybody knows that the long continuance of a routine of habit make us lethargic, while a succession of surprises wonderfully brightens the ideas. Where there is a motion, where history is a-making, there is the focus of mental activity, and it has been said that the arts and sciences reside within the temple of Janus, waking when that is open, but slumbering when it is closed.

C. S. Peirce, *Evolutionary Love*

98 Better know nothing than half-know many things!
Nietzsche, *Thus Spake Zarathustra,* IV, 64

99 *The psychologist's attitude towards cognition . . . is a thorough-going dualism.* It supposes two elements, mind knowing and thing known, and treats them as irreducible. Neither gets out of itself or into the other, neither in any way *is* the other, neither *makes* the other. They just stand face to face in a common world, and one simply knows, or is known unto, its counterpart. This singular relation is not to be expressed in any lower terms, or translated into any more intelligible name. Some sort of *signal* must be given by the thing to the mind's brain, or the knowing will not occur—we find as a matter of fact that the mere *existence* of a thing outside the brain is not a sufficient cause for our knowing it: it must strike the brain in some way, as well as be there, to be known. But the brain being struck, the knowledge is constituted

by a new construction that occurs altogether *in* the mind. The thing remains the same whether known or not. And when once there, the knowledge may remain there, whatever becomes of the thing.

William James, *Psychology,* VIII

100 *There are two kinds of knowledge* broadly and practically distinguishable: we may call them respectively *knowledge of acquaintance* and *knowledge-about.* . . . I am acquainted with many people and things, which I know very little about, except their presence in the places where I have met them. I know the color blue when I see it, and the flavor of a pear when I taste it! I know an inch when I move my finger through it; a second of time, when I feel it pass; an effort of attention when I make it; a difference between two things when I notice it; but *about* the inner nature of these facts or what makes them what they are, I can say nothing at all. I cannot impart acquaintance with them to any one who has not already made it himself. I cannot *describe* them, make a blind man guess what blue is like, define to a child a syllogism, or tell a philosopher in just what respect distance is just what it is, and differs from other forms of relation. At most, I can say to my friends, Go to certain places and act in certain ways, and these objects will probably come. All the elementary natures of the world, its highest genera, the simple qualities of matter and mind, together with the kinds of relation that subsist between them, must either not be known at all, or known in this dumb way of acquaintance without *knowledge-about.* In minds able to speak at all there is, it is true, *some* knowledge about everything. Things can at least be classed, and the times of their appearance told. But in general, the less we analyze a thing, and the fewer of its relations we perceive, the less we know about it and the more our familiarity with it is of the acquaintance-type. The two kinds of knowledge are, therefore, as the human mind practically exerts them, relative terms. That is, the same thought of a thing may be called knowledge-about it in comparison with a simpler thought, or acquaintance with it in comparison with a thought of it that is more articulate and explicit still.

The grammatical sentence expresses this. Its "subject" stands for an object of acquaintance which, by the addition of the predicate, is to get something known about it. We may already know a good deal, when we hear the subject named—its name may have rich connotations. But, know we much or little then, we know more still when the sentence is done. We can relapse at will into a mere condition of acquaintance with an object by scattering our attention and staring at it in a vacuous trance-like way. We can ascend to knowledge *about* it by rallying our wits and proceeding to notice and analyze and think. What we are only acquainted with is only *present* to our minds; we *have* it, or the idea of it. But when we know about it, we do more than merely have it; we seem, as we think over its relations, to subject it to a sort of *treatment* and to *operate* upon it with our thought. The words *feeling* and *thought* give voice to the antithesis. Through feelings we become acquainted with things, but only by our thoughts do we know about them. Feelings are the germ and starting point of cognition, thoughts the developed tree. The minimum of grammatical subject, of objective presence, of reality known about, the mere beginning of knowledge, must be named by the word that says the least. Such a word is the interjection, as *lo! there! ecce! voilà!* or the article or demonstrative pronoun introducing the sentence, as *the, it, that.*

William James, *Psychology,* VIII

101 Common sense appears . . . as a perfectly definite stage in our understanding of things, a stage that satisfies in an extraordinarily successful way the purposes for which we think. 'Things' do exist, even when we do not see them. Their 'kinds' also exist. Their 'qualities' are what they act by, and are what we act on; and these also exist. These lamps shed their quality of light on every object in this room. We intercept *it* on its way whenever we hold up an opaque screen. It is the very sound that my lips emit that travels into your ears. It is the sensible heat of the fire that migrates into the water in which we boil an egg; and we can change the heat into coolness by dropping in a lump of ice. At this stage of philosophy all non-European men without exception have remained. It suffices for all the necessary practical ends of life; and, among our race even, it is only the highly sophisticated specimens, the minds debauched by learning, as Berkeley calls them, who have ever even suspected common sense of not being absolutely true.

But when we look back, and speculate as to how the common-sense categories may have achieved their wonderful supremacy, no reason appears why it may not have been by a process just like that by which the conceptions due to Democritus, Berkeley, or Darwin, achieved their similar triumphs in more recent times. In other words, they may have been successfully *discovered* by prehistoric geniuses whose names the night of antiquity has covered up; they may have been verified by the immediate facts of experience which they first fitted; and then from fact to fact and from man to man they may have *spread,* until all language rested on them and we are now incapable of thinking naturally in any other terms. Such a view would only follow the rule that has proved elsewhere so fertile, of assuming the vast and remote to conform to the laws of formation that we can observe at work in the small and near.

William James, *Pragmatism*, V

102 I maintain that the notion of 'mere knowledge' is a high abstraction which we should dismiss from our minds. Knowledge is always accompanied with accessories of emotion and purpose. Also we must remember that there are grades in the generality of ideas. Thus a general idea occurs in history in special forms determined by peculiar circumstances of race and of stage of civilization. The higher generalities rarely receive any accurate verbal expression.

Whitehead, *Adventures of Ideas*, I, 1

103 It is unconsciously assumed, as a premiss for a *reductio ad absurdum* of the analytic view, that, if A and B are immediate data, and A differs from B, then the fact that they differ must also be an immediate datum. It is difficult to say how this assumption arose, but I think it is to be connected with the confusion between "acquaintance" and "knowledge about." Acquaintance, which is what we derive from sense, does not, theoretically at least, imply even the smallest "knowledge about," i.e. it does not imply knowledge of any proposition concerning the object with which we are acquainted. It is a mistake to speak as if acquaintance had degrees: there is merely acquaintance and non-acquaintance. When we speak of becoming "better acquainted," as for instance with a person, what we must mean is, becoming acquainted with more parts of a certain whole; but the acquaintance with each part is either complete or non-existent. Thus it is a mistake to say that if we were perfectly acquainted with an object we should know all about it. "Knowledge about" is knowledge of propositions, which is not involved necessarily in acquaintance with the constituents of the propositions. To know that two shades of colour are different is knowledge about them; hence acquaintance with the two shades does not in any way necessitate the knowledge that they are different.

Russell, *Theory of Continuity*

104 From the point of view of knowledge, though not of logic, there is an important difference between positive and negative general propositions, namely that some general negative propositions seem to result from observation as directly as "This is not blue". . . . In *Through the Looking Glass,* the king says to Alice, "Who do you see coming along the road?" and she replies, "I see nobody coming," to which the king retorts, "What good eyes you must have! It's as much as I can do to see somebody by this light." The point, for us, is that "I see nobody" is *not* equivalent to "I do not see somebody." The latter statement is true if my eyes are shut, and affords no evidence that there is not somebody; but when I say, "I see nobody," I mean, "I see, but I do not see somebody," which is prima-facie evidence that there is not somebody. Such negative judgments are just as important as positive judgments in building up our empirical knowledge.

Russell, *Human Knowledge*, II, 10

105 Are there general *facts?* We may restate this question in the following form: Suppose I knew the truth or falsehood of every sentence not containing the word "all" or the word "some" or an equivalent of either of these words; what, then, should I not know? Would what I should not know be only something about my knowledge and belief, or would it be something that involves no reference to knowledge or belief? I am supposing that I can say, "Brown is here," "Jones is here," "Robinson is here," but not "Some men are here," still less "Exactly three men are here" or "Every man here is called 'Brown' or 'Jones' or 'Robinson.' " And I am supposing that though I know the truth or falsehood of every sentence of a certain sort, I do not know that my knowledge has this completeness. If I knew my list to be complete I could infer that there are three men here, but, as it is, I do not know that there are no others.

Russell, *Human Knowledge*, II, 10

106 It is clear that knowledge is a sub-class of true beliefs: every case of knowledge is a case of true belief, but not vice versa. It is very easy to give examples of true beliefs that are not knowledge. There is the man who looks at a clock which is not going, though he thinks it is, and who happens to look at it at the moment when it is right; this man acquires a true belief as to the time of day, but cannot be said to have knowledge. There is the man who believes, truly, that the last name of the Prime Minister in 1906 began with a B, but who believes this because he thinks that Balfour was Prime Minister then, whereas in fact it was Campbell Bannerman. There is the lucky optimist who, having bought a ticket for a lottery, has an unshakable conviction that he will win, and, being lucky, does win. Such instances can be multiplied indefinitely, and show that you cannot claim to have known merely because you turned out to be right.

What character in addition to truth must a belief have in order to count as knowledge? The plain man would say there must be sound evidence to support the belief. As a matter of common sense this is right in most of the cases in which doubt arises in practice, but if intended as a complete account of the matter it is very inadequate. "Evidence" consists, on the one hand, of certain matters of fact that are accepted as indubitable, and, on the other hand, of certain principles by means of which inferences are drawn from the matters of fact. It is obvious that this process is unsatisfactory unless we know the matters of fact and the principles of inference not merely by means of evidence, for otherwise we become involved in a vicious circle or an endless regress. We must therefore concentrate our attention on the matters of fact and the principles of inference. We may then say that what is known consists, first, of certain matters of fact and certain principles of inference, neither of which stands in need of extraneous evidence, and secondly, of all that can be ascertained by applying the principles of inference to the matters of fact. Traditionally, the matters of fact are those given in perception and memory, while the principles of inference are those of deductive and inductive logic.

There are various unsatisfactory features in this traditional doctrine, though I am not at all sure that, in the end, we can substitute anything very much better.

Russell, *Human Knowledge*, II, 11

107 It is difficult to define knowledge, difficult to decide whether we have any knowledge, and difficult, even if it is conceded that we sometimes have knowledge, to discover whether we can ever know that we have knowledge in this or that particular case.

Russell, *Analysis of Mind*, XIII

108 Knowing always has a *particular* purpose, and its solution must be a function of its conditions in connection with *additional* ones which are brought to bear. Every reflective knowledge, in other words, has a specific task which is set by a concrete and empirical situation, so that it can perform that task only by detecting and remaining faithful to the conditions in the situation in which the difficulty arises, while its purpose is a reorganization of its factors in order to get unity.

So far, however, there is no accomplished knowledge, but only knowledge coming to be—learning, in the classic Greek conception. Thinking gets no farther, as *thinking,* than a statement of elements constituting the difficulty at hand and a statement—a propounding, a proposition—of a method for resolving them. In fixing the framework of every reflective situation, this state of affairs also determines the further step which is needed if there is to be knowledge—knowledge in the eulogistic sense, as distinct from opinion, dogma, and guesswork, or from what casually passes current as knowledge. Overt action is demanded if the worth or validity of the reflective considerations is to be determined. Otherwise, we have, at most, only a hypothesis that the conditions of the difficulty are such and such, and that the way to go at them so as to get over or through them is thus and so. This way must be tried in action; it must be applied, physically, in the situation. By finding out what then happens, we test our intel-

lectual findings—our logical terms or projected metes and bounds. If the required reorganization is effected, they are confirmed, and reflection (on that topic) ceases; if not, there is frustration, and inquiry continues. That all knowledge, as issuing from reflection, is experimental (in the literal physical sense of experimental) is then a constituent proposition of this doctrine.

Upon this view, thinking, or knowledge-getting, is far from being the armchair thing it is often supposed to be. The reason it is not an armchair thing is that it is not an event going on exclusively within the cortex or the cortex and vocal organs. It involves the explorations by which relevant data are procured and the physical analyses by which they are refined and made precise; it comprises the readings by which information is got hold of, the words which are experimented with, and the calculations by which the significance of entertained conceptions or hypotheses is elaborated. Hands and feet, apparatus and appliances of all kinds are as much a part of it as changes in the brain. Since these physical operations (including the cerebral events) and equipments are a part of thinking, thinking is mental, not because of a peculiar stuff which enters into it or of peculiar non-natural activities which constitute it, but because of what physical acts and appliances *do:* the distinctive purpose for which they are employed and the distinctive results which they accomplish.

Dewey, *Essays in Experimental Logic*, Introduction, 2

109 Let me . . . call attention to an ambiguity in the term "knowledge." The statement that all knowledge involves reflection—or, more concretely, that it denotes an inference from evidence—gives offense to many; it seems a departure from fact as well as a wilful limitation of the word "knowledge." I have . . . endeavored to mitigate the obnoxiousness of the doctrine by referring to "knowledge which is intellectual or logical in character." Lest this expression be regarded as a futile evasion of a real issue, I shall now be more explicit.

It may well be admitted that there is a real sense in which knowledge (as distinct from thinking or inquiring with a guess attached) does not come into existence till thinking has terminated in the experimental act which fulfils the specifications set forth in thinking. But what is also true is that the object thus determined is an object of *knowledge* only because of the thinking which has preceded it and to which it sets a happy term. To run against a hard and painful stone is not of itself, I should say, an act of knowing; but if running into a hard and painful thing is an outcome predicted after inspection of data and elaboration of a hypothesis, then the hardness and the painful bruise which define the thing as a stone also constitute it emphatically an object of knowledge. In short, the object of knowledge in the strict sense is its objective; and this objective is not constituted till it is reached. Now this conclusion—as the word denotes—is thinking brought to a close, done with. If the reader does not find this statement satisfactory, he may, pending further discussion, at least recognize that the doctrine set forth has no difficulty in connecting knowledge with inference, and at the same time admitting that knowledge in the emphatic sense does not exist till inference has ceased. Seen from this point of view, so-called immediate knowledge or simple apprehension or acquaintance-knowledge represents a critical skill, a certainty of response which has accrued in consequence of reflection. A like sureness of footing apart from prior investigations and testings is found in instinct and habit. I do not deny that these may be better than knowing, but I see no reason for complicating an already too confused situation by giving them the name "knowledge" with its usual intellectual implications. From this point of view, the subject-matter of knowledge is precisely that which we do *not* think of, or mentally refer to in any way, being that which is taken as matter of course, but it is nevertheless knowledge in virtue of the inquiry which has led up to it.

Dewey, *Essays in Experimental Logic,* Intro., 2

110 Knowledge becomes relative, as soon as the intellect is made a kind of absolute.—We regard the human intellect, on the contrary, as relative to the needs of action. Postulate action, and the very form of the intellect can be deduced from it. This form is therefore neither irreducible nor inexplicable. And, precisely because it is not independent, knowledge cannot be said to depend on it: knowledge ceases to be a product of the intellect and becomes, in a certain sense, part and parcel of reality.

Bergson, *Creative Evolution,* II

111 In order to know an object, I must know not its external but all its internal qualities.

Wittgenstein, *Tractatus Logico-Philosophicus,* 2.01231

112 Only if there are objects can there be a fixed form of the world.

The fixed, the existent and the object are one.

The object is the fixed, the existent; the configuration is the changing, the variable.

The configuration of the objects forms the atomic fact.

In the atomic fact objects hang one in another, like the members of a chain.

In the atomic fact the objects are combined in a definite way.

The way in which objects hang together in the atomic fact is the structure of the atomic fact.

The form is the possibility of the structure.

The structure of the fact consists of the structures of the atomic facts.

The totality of existent atomic facts is the world.

The totality of existent atomic facts also determines which atomic facts do not exist.

The existence and non-existence of atomic facts is the reality.

(The existence of atomic facts we also call a positive fact, their non-existence a negative fact.)

Atomic facts are independent of one another.

From the existence or non-existence of an atomic fact we cannot infer the existence or non-existence of another.

The total reality is the world.

We make to ourselves pictures of facts.

The picture presents the facts in logical space, the existence and non-existence of atomic facts.

The picture is a model of reality.

To the objects correspond in the picture the elements of the picture.

The elements of the picture stand, in the picture, for the objects.

The picture consists in the fact that its elements are combined with one another in a definite way.

The picture is a fact.

That the elements of the picture are combined with one another in a definite way, represents that the things are so combined with one another.

This connexion of the elements of the picture is called its structure, and the possibility of this structure is called the form of representation of the picture.

The form of representation is the possibility that the things are combined with one another as are the elements of the picture.

Thus the picture is linked with reality; it reaches up to it.

It is like a scale applied to reality.

Wittgenstein, *Tractatus Logico-Philosophicus,* 2.026–2.1512

113 Knowledge is not eating, and we cannot expect to devour and possess *what we mean.* Knowledge is recognition of something absent; it is a salutation, not an embrace. It is an advance on sensation precisely because it is representative.

Santayana, *Life of Reason,* I, 3

114 Superstition, and sometimes philosophy, accepts imagination as a truer avenue to knowledge than is contact with things; but this is precisely what I endeavour to avoid by distinguishing matter, or the substance of dynamic things, from essence, or the direct datum, sensuous or intelligible, or intuition. Intuition represents the free life of the mind, the poetry native to it, which I am far from despising; but this is the subjective or ideal element in thought which we must discount if we are anxious to possess true knowledge.

Santayana, *Realms of Being,* Intro.

115 The enormous infusion of error that sense, passion, and language bring with them into human knowledge is therefore less misleading than might be supposed. Knowledge is not truth, but a view or expression of the truth; a glimpse of it secured by some animal with special organs under special circumstances. A lover of paradox might say that to be partly wrong is a condition of being partly right; or more soberly, that to be partial is, for knowledge, a condition of existing at all. To be partial and also to be relative: so that all the sensuous colour and local perspective proper to human views, and all the moral bias pervading them, far from rendering knowledge impossible, supply instruments for exploration, divers sensitive centres and divers inks, whereby in divers ways the facts may be recorded.

Santayana, *Realm of Truth,* VII

116 The love of knowledge belongs to the essence of spirit. Far from being, as Baconian pragmatism would have it, a love of power, it is a love of imagination; only that imagination needs to be fed by contact with external things and by widening vital rhythms. When the great explorers sailed in search of gold and of spices, imagination within them was dreaming of the wonders they might find, and of the splendours they might display at home after their return. The voyage too would be something glorious, to be described in fabulous books and woven into tapestries. This is a healthy love of knowledge, grounded on animal quests, but issuing in spiritual entertainment. Had the world turned out to be very small and handy, and the science of it as simple as it seemed to Descartes, spirit would have suffered no disappointment; there would have been more than matter enough for all the wit of man. Perhaps the environing blank would have positively helped to frame in the picture, and make it easier for a religion of the heart to understand and envelop existence.

There is a snare, however, in the very essence of knowledge in that it has to be a form of faith, and faith is something psychic rather than spiritual: an expectation and hope addressed to things not seen, because they would match potentialities in the soul. Actual belief (the expectation or affirmation in it) is a state of the spirit; but spirit could never fall into that state or maintain that assertiveness by a purely spiritual insight, since intuition is of the given and spirit is pure actuality. In knowledge, as distinguished from intuition, there is therefore a postulating element, an element of hunger unsatisfied; the datum hangs in the air, not being accepted for what it is, but taken as an index to a dynamic object that is perhaps nonexistent. This adventurous intent, this sense of the ulterior and potential, strains the spirit, spoils intuition, and opens the door to doubt, argument, error, and presumption. Faith belongs to earth and to purgatory: in heaven it would be a lapse into distraction.

Santayana, *Realm of Spirit,* VII

6.2 | *Experience*

Although it is a term that no one can avoid using, experience is seldom defined by those who use it. It would appear to be co-extensive with consciousness—the flow of experience from moment to moment being identical with what William James called "the stream of consciousness." It would appear to be impossible to be a sentient or conscious being and not to have experience at every waking moment and even when one's sleep is interrupted by dreams. To understand this much about experience is to recognize how much of what we know is somehow born of experience, and also to realize how special is the knowledge that some philosophers call transcendental because it is independent of and goes beyond experience.

A few of the writers quoted—namely, Aristotle, Hobbes, and Harvey—use the word "experience" in a more restricted sense. They point out that from repeated perceptions, memories are generated; and that from many memories, experience emerges. It is in this sense of the term that a man of experience about certain matters is said to have competence to judge about such matters, a competence comparable to, though perhaps inferior to, that of the artist or scientist with respect to the same matters. The latter, it is noted, have a knowledge based on experience that they can teach others, whereas the expertness of the man of experience is not similarly conveyable to others.

The value of experience is differently appraised in relation to different kinds of knowledge; it is of much less utility, or much less experience is needed, in mathematics, for example, than in ethics or politics. That is why, as some writers point out, young men with little experience can become experts in certain fields of learning, whereas in others we prefer to listen to older men and women whose counsel or wisdom reflects long and varied experience.

The human appetite for experience would appear to be as insatiable as the desire for knowledge. This craving for every variety of experience is celebrated by the poets, and especially by Goethe in his characterization of Faust's search for the uniquely satisfying experience in which he will gladly come to rest. For the poets, as the quotations indicate, experience is more likely to be valued for its own sake and not merely as a factor indispensable to the attainment of knowledge.

Two other points should be noted, especially for their bearing on the relationship between experience and knowledge. One is that experience, however indispensable it may be as a source of knowledge, is never by itself a form of knowledge. The other is a point to which Francis Bacon first called explicit attention; namely, that scientific method is a systematic effort to obtain and control experience by carefully planned observations. Philosophers may appeal to experiences that they have in common with other men; only scientists "manufacture" the special experiences they amass and interpret for their own purposes. The reader will find more detailed discussion of this point in Section 17.2.

---

1 A man that hath traveled knoweth many things; and he that hath much experience will declare wisdom. He that hath no experience knoweth little: but he that hath traveled is full of prudence. When I traveled, I saw many things; and I understand more than I can express.

Ecclesiasticus 34:9–11

2 Sing in me, Muse, and through me tell the story
of that man skilled in all ways of contending,
the wanderer, harried for years on end,
after he plundered the stronghold
on the proud height of Troy.
                    He saw the townlands
and learned the minds of many distant men,
and weathered many bitter nights and days
in his deep heart at sea, while he fought only
to save his life, to bring his shipmates home.

Homer, *Odyssey,* I, 1

3 On their road to Susa they presented themselves before Hydarnes. This Hydarnes was a Persian by birth, and had the command of all the nations that dwelt along the sea-coast of Asia. He accordingly showed them hospitality, and invited them to a banquet, where, as they feasted, he said to them: —

"Men of Lacedæmon, why will ye not consent to be friends with the king? Ye have but to look at me and my fortune to see that the king knows well how to honour merit. In like manner ye yourselves, were ye to make your submission to him, would receive at his hands, seeing that he deems you men of merit, some government in Greece."

"Hydarnes," they answered, "thou art a one-sided counsellor. Thou hast experience of half the matter; but the other half is beyond thy knowledge. A slave's life thou understandest; but, never having tasted liberty, thou canst not tell whether it be sweet or no. Ah! hadst thou known what freedom is, thou wouldst have bidden us fight for it, not with the spear only, but with the battle-axe."

So they answered Hydarnes.

Herodotus, *History,* VII, 135

4 *Socrates.* Well, then, if you and I, Callicles, were intending to set about some public business, and

were advising one another to undertake buildings, such as walls, docks or temples of the largest size, ought we not to examine ourselves, first, as to whether we know or do not know the art of building, and who taught us?—would not that be necessary, Callicles?

Callicles. True.

Soc. In the second place, we should have to consider whether we had ever constructed any private house, either of our own or for our friends, and whether this building of ours was a success or not; and if upon consideration we found that we had had good and eminent masters, and had been successful in constructing many fine buildings, not only with their assistance, but without them, by our own unaided skill—in that case prudence would not dissuade us from proceeding to the construction of public works. But if we had no master to show, and only a number of worthless buildings or none at all, then, surely, it would be ridiculous in us to attempt public works, or to advise one another to undertake them. Is not this true?

Cal. Certainly.

Soc. And does not the same hold in all other cases? If you and I were physicians, and were advising one another that we were competent to practise as state-physicians, should I not ask about you, and would you not ask about me, Well, but how about Socrates himself, has he good health? and was any one else ever known to be cured by him, whether slave or freeman? And I should make the same enquiries about you. And if we arrived at the conclusion that no one, whether citizen or stranger, man or woman, had ever been any the better for the medical skill of either of us, then, by Heaven, Callicles, what an absurdity to think that we or any human being should be so silly as to set up as state-physicians and advise others like ourselves to do the same, without having first practised in private, whether successfully or not, and acquired experience of the art! Is not this, as they say, to begin with the big jar when you are learning the potter's art; which is a foolish thing?

Plato, *Gorgias,* 514A

5 *Socrates.* Bear in mind the whole business of the midwives, and then you will see my meaning better:—No woman, as you are probably aware, who is still able to conceive and bear, attends other women, but only those who are past bearing.

Theaetetus. Yes, I know.

Soc. The reason of this is said to be that Artemis—the goddess of childbirth—is not a mother, and she honours those who are like herself; but she could not allow the barren to be midwives, because human nature cannot know the mystery of an art without experience; and therefore she assigned this office to those who are too old to bear.

Plato, *Theaetetus,* 149A

6 The animals other than man live by appearances and memories, and have but little of connected experience; but the human race lives also by art and reasonings. Now from memory experience is produced in men; for the several memories of the same thing produce finally the capacity for a single experience. And experience seems pretty much like science and art, but really science and art come to men *through* experience; for 'experience made art', as Polus says, 'but inexperience luck'.

Aristotle, *Metaphysics,* 980ᵇ25

7 With a view to action experience seems in no respect inferior to art, and men of experience succeed even better than those who have theory without experience. (The reason is that experience is knowledge of individuals, art of universals, and actions and productions are all concerned with the individual; for the physician does not cure *man,* except in an incidental way, but Callias or Socrates or some other called by some such individual name, who happens to be a man. If, then, a man has the theory without the experience, and recognizes the universal but does not know the individual included in this, he will often fail to cure; for it is the individual that is to be cured.) But yet we think that *knowledge* and *understanding* belong to art rather than to experience, and we suppose artists to be wiser than men of experience (which implies that Wisdom depends in all cases rather on knowledge); and this because the former know the cause, but the latter do not. For men of experience know that the thing is so, but do not know why, while the others know the 'why' and the cause. Hence we think also that the master-workers in each craft are more honourable and know in a truer sense and are wiser than the manual workers, because they know the causes of the things that are done (we think the manual workers are like certain lifeless things which act indeed, but act without knowing what they do, as fire burns,—but while the lifeless things perfor ı each of their functions by a natural tendency, the labourers perform them through habit); thus we view them as being wiser not in virtue of being able to act, but of having the theory for themselves and knowing the causes. And in general it is a sign of the man who knows and of the man who does not know, that the former can teach, and therefore we think art more truly knowledge than experience is; for artists can teach, and men of mere experience cannot.

Aristotle, *Metaphysics,* 981ª13

8 While young men become geometricians and mathematicians and wise in matters like these, it is thought that a young man of practical wisdom cannot be found. The cause is that such wisdom is concerned not only with universals but with par-

ticulars, which become familiar from experience, but a young man has no experience, for it is length of time that gives experience; indeed one might ask this question too, why a boy may become a mathematician, but not a philosopher or a physicist. It is because the objects of mathematics exist by abstraction, while the first principles of these other subjects come from experience, and because young men have no conviction about the latter but merely use the proper language, while the essence of mathematical objects is plain enough to them?

Aristotle, *Ethics,* 1142ª12

9 We ought to attend to the undemonstrated sayings and opinions of experienced and older people or of people of practical wisdom not less than to demonstrations; for because experience has given them an eye they see aright.

Aristotle, *Ethics,* 1143ᵇ11

10 Prove all things; hold fast that which is good.

I Thessalonians 5:21

11 Medicine, to produce health, has to examine disease, and music, to create harmony, must investigate discord; and the supreme arts of temperance, of justice, and of wisdom, as they are acts of judgment and selection, exercised not on good and just and expedient only, but also on wicked, unjust, and inexpedient objects, do not give their commendations to the mere innocence whose boast is its inexperience of evil, and whose truer name is, by their award, simpleness and ignorance of what all men who live aright should know. The ancient Spartans, at their festivals, used to force their Helots to swallow large quantities of raw wine, and then to expose them at the public tables, to let the young men see what it is to be drunk.

Plutarch, *Demetrius*

12 The object of hope is a future good, difficult but possible to obtain. Consequently a thing may be a cause of hope either because it makes something possible to a man or because it makes him think something possible. In the first way hope is caused by everything that increases a man's power; for instance riches, strength, and, among others, experience, for by experience man acquires the possibility of getting something easily, and the result of this is hope. Therefore Vegetius says: "No one fears to do that which he is sure of having learnt well."

In the second way, hope is caused by everything that makes man think that something is possible for him; and thus both teaching and persuasion may be a cause of hope. And in this way also experience is a cause of hope, in so far as it makes him consider something possible which before his experience he looked upon as impossible. However, in this way, experience can cause a lack of hope, because just as it makes a man think possible what he had previously thought impossible, so, conversely, experience makes a man consider as impossible that which hitherto he had thought possible. Accordingly experience causes hope in two ways, despair in one way; and for this reason we may say rather that it causes hope.

Aquinas, *Summa Theologica,* I–II, 40, 5

13 "I [Odysseus] departed from Circe, who beyond a
    year detained me there near Gaeta, ere Æneas
    thus had named it,
neither fondness for my son, nor reverence for my
    aged father, nor the due love that should have
    cheered Penelope,
could conquer in me the ardour that I had to gain
    experience of the world, and of human vice and
    worth;
I put forth on the deep open sea, with but one
    ship, and with that small company, which had
    not deserted me.
Both the shores I saw as far as Spain, far as Morocco; and *saw* Sardinia and the other isles
    which that sea bathes round.
I and my companions were old and tardy, when
    we came to that narrow pass, where Hercules
    assigned his landmarks
to hinder man from venturing farther; on the
    right hand, I left Seville; on the other, had already left Ceuta.
'O brothers!' I said, 'who through a hundred
    thousand dangers have reached the West, deny
    not, to this the brief vigil
of your senses that remains, experience of the unpeopled world behind the Sun.
Consider your origin: ye were not formed to live
    like brutes, but to follow virtue and knowledge.'
With this brief speech I made my companions so
    eager for the voyage, that I could hardly then
    have checked them;
and, turning the poop towards morning, we of our
    oars made wings for the foolish flight, always
    gaining on the left.
Night already saw the other pole, with all its stars;
    and ours so low, that it rose not from the ocean
    floor.
Five times the light beneath the Moon had been
    rekindled and quenched as oft, since we had
    entered on the arduous passage,
when there appeared to us a Mountain, dim with
    distance; and to me it seemed the highest I had
    ever seen.
We joyed, and soon our joy was turned to grief:
    for a tempest rose from the new land, and
    struck the forepart of our ship.
Three times it made her whirl round with all the
    waters; at the fourth, *made* the poop rise up and
    prow go down, as pleased Another, till the sea
    was closed above us."

Dante, *Inferno,* XXVI, 91

14 "Now listen, Troilus," replied his friend [Pandar],
"Perhaps I am a fool, yet it is so,
That folly oft can helpful counsel lend,
Whereby the wise the better way may know.
For I myself have seen a blind man go,
Where he would fall who sees both far and wide;
Sometimes a fool can be the safest guide.

"A whetstone is no carving instrument,
And yet it maketh sharp the carving tool;
And if you see my efforts wrongly spent,
Eschew that course and learn out of my school;
For thus the wise may profit by the fool,
And edge his wit, and grow more keen and wary,
For wisdom shines opposed to its contrary.

"For how might sweetness ever have been known
To him who never tasted bitterness?
Felicity exists for those alone
Who first have suffered sorrow and distress;
Thus white by black, honor by shame's excess,
More brightly shines by what the other seems,
As all men see and as the wise man deems.

"By opposites does one in wisdom grow,
And though I have in love vain effort made,
Then all the better I thereby should know
To guide thee on thy path when thou hast
    strayed.
Spurn not with scorn, therefore, my proffered aid,
For I desire nothing but to share
Thy grief, and make it easier to bear."

    Chaucer, *Troilus and Cressida,* I, 90–93

15 Those who strive to obtain the good graces of a
prince are accustomed to come before him with
such things as they hold most precious, or in
which they see him take most delight: whence one
often sees horses, arms, cloth of gold, precious
stones, and similar ornaments presented to
princes, worthy of their greatness.

   Desiring therefore to present myself to your
Magnificence [Lorenzo di Piero de' Medici] with
some testimony of my devotion towards you, I
have not found among my possessions anything
which I hold more dear than, or value so much as,
the knowledge of the actions of great men, acquired by long experience in contemporary affairs, and a continual study of antiquity; which,
having reflected upon it with great and prolonged
diligence, I now send, digested into a little volume, to your Magnificence.

   And although I may consider this work unworthy of your countenance, nevertheless I trust
much to your benignity that it may be acceptable,
seeing that it is not possible for me to make a
better gift than to offer you the opportunity of
understanding in the shortest time all that I have
learnt in so many years, and with so many troubles and dangers; which work I have not embellished with swelling or magnificent words, nor

stuffed with rounded periods, nor with any extrinsic allurements or adornments whatever, with
which so many are accustomed to load and embellish their works; for I have wished either that
no honour should be given it, or else that the truth
of the matter and the weightiness of the theme
shall make it acceptable.

    Machiavelli, *Prince,* Dedication

16 There is no desire more natural than the desire for
knowledge. We try all the ways that can lead us to
it. When reason fails us, we use experience . . .
which is a weaker and less dignified means. But
truth is so great a thing that we must not disdain
any medium that will lead us to it. Reason has so
many shapes that we know not which to lay hold
of; experience has no fewer. The inference that we
try to draw from the resemblance of events is uncertain, because they are always dissimilar: there
is no quality so universal in this aspect of things as
diversity and variety.

    Montaigne, *Essays,* III, 13, Of Experience

17 Whatever may be the fruit we can reap from experience, what we derive from foreign examples
will hardly be much use for our education, if we
make such little profit from the experience we
have of ourselves, which is more familiar to us,
and certainly sufficient to inform us of what we
need.

   I study myself more than any other subject.
That is my metaphysics, that is my physics.

    Montaigne, *Essays,* III, 13, Of Experience

18 *Antonio.* Tell me, Panthino, what sad talk was that
Wherewith my brother held you in the cloister?
    Panthino. 'Twas of his nephew Proteus, your son.
    Ant. Why, what of him?
    Pan.   He wonder'd that your lordship
Would suffer him to spend his youth at home,
While other men, of slender reputation,
Put forth their sons to seek preferment out:
Some to the wars, to try their fortune there;
Some to discover islands far away;
Some to the studious universities.
For any or for all these exercises
He said that Proteus your son was meet,
And did request me to importune you
To let him spend his time no more at home,
Which would be great impeachment to his age,
In having known no travel in his youth.
    Ant. Nor need'st thou much importune me to
        that
Whereon this month I have been hammering.
I have consider'd well his loss of time
And how he cannot be a perfect man,
Not being tried and tutor'd in the world:
Experience is by industry achieved
And perfected by the swift course of time.
Then tell me, whither were I best to send him?

    Shakespeare, *Two Gentlemen of Verona,* I, iii, 1

19 *Rosalind.* To have seen much and to have nothing, is to have rich eyes and poor hands. . . . I had rather have a fool to make me merry than experience to make me sad.

Shakespeare, *As You Like It,* IV, i, 23

20 Another error hath proceeded from too great a reverence, and a kind of adoration of the mind and understanding of man; by means whereof, men have withdrawn themselves too much from the contemplation of nature, and the observations of experience, and have tumbled up and down in their own reason and conceits. Upon these intellectualists, which are notwithstanding commonly taken for the most sublime and divine philosophers, Heraclitus gave a just censure, saying, "Men sought truth in their own little worlds, and not in the great and common world"; for they disdain to spell, and so by degrees to read in the volume of God's works: and contrariwise by continual meditation and agitation of wit do urge and, as it were, invocate their own spirits to divine and give oracles unto them, whereby they are deservedly deluded.

Bacon, *Advancement of Learning,* Bk. I, V, 6

21 The foundations of experience (our sole resource) have hitherto failed completely or have been very weak; nor has a store and collection of particular facts, capable of informing the mind or in any way satisfactory, been either sought after or amassed. On the contrary, learned, but idle and indolent, men have received some mere reports of experience, traditions as it were of dreams, as establishing or confirming their philosophy, and have not hesitated to allow them the weight of legitimate evidence. So that a system has been pursued in philosophy with regard to experience resembling that of a kingdom or state which would direct its councils and affairs according to the gossip of city and street politicians, instead of the letters and reports of ambassadors and messengers worthy of credit. Nothing is rightly inquired into, or verified, noted, weighed, or measured, in natural history; indefinite and vague observation produces fallacious and uncertain information. If this appear strange, or our complaint somewhat too unjust (because Aristotle himself, so distinguished a man and supported by the wealth of so great a king, has completed an accurate history of animals, to which others with greater diligence but less noise have made considerable additions, and others again have composed copious histories and notices of plants, metals, and fossils), it will arise from a want of sufficiently attending to and comprehending our present observations; for a natural history compiled on its own account, and one collected for the mind's information as a foundation for philosophy, are two different things. They differ in several respects,

but principally in this: the former contains only the varieties of natural species without the experiments of mechanical arts; for as in ordinary life every person's disposition, and the concealed feelings of the mind and passions are most drawn out when they are disturbed—so the secrets of nature betray themselves more readily when tormented by art than when left to their own course. We must begin, therefore, to entertain hopes of natural philosophy then only, when we have a better compilation of natural history, its real basis and support.

Bacon, *Novum Organum,* I, 98

22 As soon as age permitted me to emerge from the control of my tutors, I entirely quitted the study of letters. And resolving to seek no other science than that which could be found in myself, or at least in the great book of the world, I employed the rest of my youth in travel, in seeing courts and armies, in intercourse with men of diverse temperaments and conditions, in collecting varied experiences, in proving myself in the various predicaments in which I was placed by fortune, and under all circumstances bringing my mind to bear on the things which came before it, so that I might derive some profit from my experience. For it seemed to me that I might meet with much more truth in the reasonings that each man makes on the matters that specially concern him, and the issue of which would very soon punish him if he made a wrong judgment, than in the case of those made by a man of letters in his study touching speculations which lead to no result, and which bring about no other consequences to himself excepting that he will be all the more vain the more they are removed from common sense, since in this case it proves him to have employed so much the more ingenuity and skill in trying to make them seem probable. And I always had an excessive desire to learn to distinguish the true from the false, in order to see clearly in my actions and to walk with confidence in this life.

It is true that while I only considered the manners of other men I found in them nothing to give me settled convictions; and I remarked in them almost as much diversity as I had formerly seen in the opinions of philosophers. So much was this the case that the greatest profit which I derived from their study was that, in seeing many things which, although they seem to us very extravagant and ridiculous, were yet commonly received and approved by other great nations, I learned to believe nothing too certainly of which I had only been convinced by example and custom. Thus little by little I was delivered from many errors which might have obscured our natural vision and rendered us less capable of listening to Reason. But after I had employed several years in thus studying the book of the world and trying to acquire some experience, I one day formed the resolution of also making myself an object of study and of employing all the strength of my mind in choosing the road I should follow. This succeeded much better, it appeared to me, than if I had never departed either from my country or my books.

Descartes, *Discourse on Method,* I

23 As much experience is *prudence,* so is much science *sapience.* For though we usually have one name for them both; yet the Latins did always distinguish between *prudentia* and *sapientia;* ascribing the former to experience, the latter to science. But to make their difference appear more clearly, let us suppose one man endued with an excellent natural use and dexterity in handling his arms; and another to have added to that dexterity an acquired science of where he can offend, or be offended by his adversary, in every possible posture or guard: the ability of the former would be to the ability of the latter, as prudence to sapience; both useful, but the latter infallible. But they that, trusting only to the authority of books, follow the blind blindly, are like him that, trusting to the false rules of a master of fence, ventures presumptuously upon an adversary that either kills or disgraces him.

The signs of science are some certain and infallible; some, uncertain. Certain, when he that pretendeth the science of anything can teach the same; that is to say, demonstrate the truth thereof perspicuously to another: uncertain, when only some particular events answer to his pretence, and upon many occasions prove so as he says they must. Signs of prudence are all uncertain; because to observe by experience, and remember all circumstances that may alter the success, is impossible. But in any business, whereof a man has not infallible science to proceed by, to forsake his own natural judgment, and be guided by general sentences read in authors, and subject to many exceptions, is a sign of folly, and generally scorned by the name of pedantry.

Hobbes, *Leviathan,* I, 5

24 Two things instruct man about his whole nature; instinct and experience.

Pascal, *Pensées,* VI, 396

25 Let us then suppose the mind to be, as we say, white paper, void of all characters, without any ideas:—How comes it to be furnished? Whence comes it by that vast store which the busy and boundless fancy of man has painted on it with an almost endless variety? Whence has it all the *materials* of reason and knowledge? To this I answer, in one word, from EXPERIENCE. In that all our knowledge is founded; and from that it ultimately derives itself. Our observation employed either, about external sensible objects, or about the internal operations of our minds perceived and reflect-ed on by ourselves, is that which supplies our understandings with all the *materials* of thinking. These two are the fountains of knowledge, from whence all the ideas we have, or can naturally have, do spring.

Locke, *Concerning Human Understanding,*
Bk. II, I, 2

26 When it is asked, *What is the nature of all our reasonings concerning matter of fact?* the proper answer seems to be, that they are founded on the relation of cause and effect. When again it is asked, *What is the foundation of all our reasonings and conclusions concerning that relation?* it may be replied in one word, Experience. But if we still carry on our sifting humour, and ask, *What is the foundation of all conclusions from experience?* this implies a new question, which may be of more difficult solution and explication. . . . I say then, that, even after we have experience of the operations of cause and effect, our conclusions from that experience are *not* founded on reasoning, or any process of the understanding. . . .

All reasonings may be divided into two kinds, namely, demonstrative reasoning, or that concerning relations of ideas, and moral reasoning, or that concerning matter of fact and existence. That there are no demonstrative arguments in the case seems evident; since it implies no contradiction that the course of nature may change, and that an object, seemingly like those which we have experienced, may be attended with different or contrary effects. May I not clearly and distinctly conceive that a body, falling from the clouds, and which, in all other respects, resembles snow, has yet the taste of salt or feeling of fire? Is there any more intelligible proposition than to affirm, that all the trees will flourish in December and January, and decay in May and June? Now whatever is intelligible, and can be distinctly conceived, implies no contradiction, and can never be proved false by any demonstrative argument or abstract reasoning *a priori.*

If we be, therefore, engaged by arguments to put trust in past experience, and make it the standard of our future judgement, these arguments must be probable only, or such as regard matter of fact and real existence, according to the division above mentioned. But that there is no argument of this kind, must appear, if our explication of that species of reasoning be admitted as solid and satisfactory. We have said that all arguments concerning existence are founded on the relation of cause and effect; that our knowledge of that relation is derived entirely from experience; and that all our experimental conclusions proceed upon the supposition that the future will be conformable to the past. To endeavour, therefore, the proof of this last supposition by probable arguments, or arguments regarding existence, must be evidently going in a circle, and taking that for granted, which is the very point in question.

In reality, all arguments from experience are founded on the similarity which we discover among natural objects, and by which we are induced to expect effects similar to those which we have found to follow from such objects. And though none but a fool or madman will ever pretend to dispute the authority of experience, or to reject that great guide of human life, it may surely be allowed a philosopher to have so much curiosity at least as to examine the principle of human nature, which gives this mighty authority to experience, and makes us draw advantage from that similarity which nature has placed among different objects. From causes which appear *similar* we expect similar effects. This is the sum of all our experimental conclusions. Now it seems evident that, if this conclusion were formed by reason, it would be as perfect at first, and upon one instance, as after ever so long a course of experience. But the case is far otherwise. . . .

And it is certain we here advance a very intelligible proposition at least, if not a true one, when we assert that, after the constant conjunction of two objects—heat and flame, for instance, weight and solidity—we are determined by custom alone to expect the one from the appearance of the other. This hypothesis seems even the only one which explains the difficulty, why we draw, from a thousand instances, an inference which we are not able to draw from one instance, that is, in no respect, different from them. Reason is incapable of any such variation. The conclusions which it draws from considering one circle are the same which it would form upon surveying all the circles in the universe. But no man, having seen only one body move after being impelled by another, could infer that every other body will move after a like impulse. All inferences from experience, therefore, are effects of custom, not of reasoning.

Hume, *Concerning Human Understanding,*
IV, 28–V, 36

27 The general observations treasured up by a course of experience, give us the clue of human nature, and teach us to unravel all its intricacies. Pretexts and appearances no longer deceive us. Public declarations pass for the specious colouring of a cause. And though virtue and honour be allowed their proper weight and authority, that perfect disinterestedness, so often pretended to, is never expected in multitudes and parties; seldom in their leaders; and scarcely even in individuals of any rank or station. But were there no uniformity in human actions, and were every experiment which we could form of this kind irregular and anomalous, it were impossible to collect any general observations concerning mankind; and no experience, however accurately digested by reflection, would ever serve to any purpose. Why is the aged husbandman more skilful in his calling than

the young beginner but because there is a certain uniformity in the operation of the sun, rain, and earth towards the production of vegetables; and experience teaches the old practitioner the rules by which this operation is governed and directed.

Hume, *Concerning Human Understanding,*
VIII, 65

28 She [Mrs. Western] was, moreover, excellently well-skilled in the doctrine of amour, and knew better than anybody who and who were together; a knowledge which she the more easily attained, as her pursuit of it was never diverted by any affairs of her own; for either she had no inclinations, or they had never been solicited; which last is indeed very probable; for her masculine person, which was near six foot high, added to her manner and learning, possibly prevented the other sex from regarding her, notwithstanding her petticoats, in the light of a woman. However, as she had considered the matter scientifically, she perfectly well knew, though she had never practised them, all the arts which fine ladies use when they desire to give encouragement, or to conceal liking, with all the long appendage of smiles, ogles, glances, &c., as they are at present practised in the beau-monde. To sum the whole, no species of disguise or affectation had escaped her notice; but as to the plain simple workings of honest nature, as she had never seen any such, she could know but little of them.

Fielding, *Tom Jones,* VI, 2

29 Whose assistance shall I invoke to direct my pen?

First, Genius; thou gift of Heaven; without whose aid in vain we struggle against the stream of nature. . . . And thou, almost the constant attendant on true genius, Humanity, bring all thy tender sensations. . . . And thou, O Learning! (for without thy assistance nothing pure, nothing correct, can genius produce) do thou guide my pen. . . . Lastly, come Experience, long conversant with the wise, the good, the learned, and the polite. Nor with them only, but with every kind of character, from the minister at his levee, to the bailiff in his spunging-house; from the dutchess at her drum, to the landlady behind her bar. From thee only can the manners of mankind be known; to which the recluse pedant, however great his parts or extensive his learning may be, hath ever been a stranger.

Fielding, *Tom Jones,* XIII, 1

30 I mentioned Dr. Adam Smith's book on *The Wealth of Nations,* which was just published, and that Sir John Pringle had observed to me, that Dr. Smith, who had never been in trade, could not be expected to write well on that subject any more than a lawyer upon physick. *Johnson.* "He is mistaken, Sir: a man who has never been engaged in trade himself may undoubtedly write well upon

trade, and there is nothing which requires more to be illustrated by philosophy than trade does. As to mere wealth, that is to say, money, it is clear that one nation or one individual cannot increase its store but by making another poorer: but trade procures what is more valuable, the reciprocation of the peculiar advantages of different countries. A merchant seldom thinks but of his own particular trade. To write a good book upon it, a man must have extensive views. It is not necessary to have practised, to write well upon a subject." I mentioned law as a subject on which no man could write well without practice. *Johnson.* "Why, Sir, in England, where so much money is to be got by the practice of the law, most of our writers upon it have been in practice; though Blackstone had not been much in practice when he published his *Commentaries.* But upon the Continent, the great writers on law have not all been in practice: Grotius, indeed, was; but Puffendorf was not, Burlamaqui was not."

Boswell, *Life of Johnson (Mar. 16, 1776)*

31 It was a very remarkable circumstance about Johnson, whom shallow observers have supposed to have been ignorant of the world, that very few men had seen greater variety of characters; and none could observe them better, as was evident from the strong, yet nice portraits which he often drew.

Boswell, *Life of Johnson (Apr. 5, 1776)*

32 Under these melancholy circumstances [the invasion of the Germans], an inexperienced youth was appointed to save and to govern the provinces of Gaul, or rather, as he expresses it himself, to exhibit the vain image of Imperial greatness. The retired scholastic education of Julian, in which he had been more conversant with books than with arms, with the dead than with the living, left him in profound ignorance of the practical arts of war and government; and when he awkwardly repeated some military exercise which it was necessary for him to learn, he exclaimed with a sigh, "O Plato, Plato, what a task for a philosopher!"

Gibbon, *Decline and Fall of the Roman Empire,* XIX

33 The experience of past faults, which may sometimes correct the mature age of an individual, is seldom profitable to the successive generations of mankind. The nations of antiquity, careless of each other's safety, were separately vanquished and enslaved by the Romans. This awful lesson might have instructed the barbarians of the West to oppose, with timely counsels and confederate arms, the unbounded ambition of Justinian. Yet the same error was repeated, the same consequences were felt.

Gibbon, *Decline and Fall of the Roman Empire,* XLI

34 That all our knowledge begins with experience there can be no doubt. For how is it possible that the faculty of cognition should be awakened into exercise otherwise than by means of objects which affect our senses, and partly of themselves produce representations, partly rouse our powers of understanding into activity, to compare, to connect, or to separate these, and so to convert the raw material of our sensuous impressions into a knowledge of objects, which is called experience? In respect of time, therefore, no knowledge of ours is antecedent to experience, but begins with it.

But, though all our knowledge begins with experience, it by no means follows that all arises out of experience. For, on the contrary, it is quite possible that our empirical knowledge is a compound of that which we receive through impressions, and that which the faculty of cognition supplies from itself (sensuous impressions giving merely the *occasion*), an addition which we cannot distinguish from the original element given by sense, till long practice has made us attentive to, and skilful in separating it. It is, therefore, a question which requires close investigation, and not to be answered at first sight, whether there exists a knowledge altogether independent of experience, and even of all sensuous impressions? Knowledge of this kind is called *a priori,* in contradistinction to empirical knowledge, which has its sources *a posteriori,* that is, in experience.

But the expression, *"a priori,"* is not as yet definite enough adequately to indicate the whole meaning of the question above started. For, in speaking of knowledge which has its sources in experience, we are wont to say, that this or that may be known *a priori,* because we do not derive this knowledge immediately from experience, but from a general rule, which, however, we have itself borrowed from experience. Thus, if a man undermined his house, we say, "he might know *a priori* that it would have fallen;" that is, he needed not to have waited for the experience that it did actually fall. But still, *a priori,* he could not know even this much. For, that bodies are heavy, and, consequently, that they fall when their supports are taken away, must have been known to him previously, by means of experience.

By the term "knowledge *a priori,*" therefore, we shall in the sequel understand, not such as is independent of this or that kind of experience, but such as is absolutely so of *all* experience. Opposed to this is empirical knowledge, or that which is possible only *a posteriori,* that is, through experience. Knowledge *a priori* is that with which no empirical element is mixed up. For example, the proposition, "Every change has a cause," is a proposition *a priori,* but impure, because change is a conception which can only be derived from experience.

Kant, *Critique of Pure Reason,* Introduction, I

35 One impulse from a vernal wood
   May teach you more of man,
   Of moral evil and of good,
   Than all the sages can.

   Wordsworth, *The Tables Turned*

36 No facts are to me sacred; none are profane; I
   simply experiment, an endless seeker with no Past
   at my back.

   Emerson, *Circles*

37 The years teach much which the days never
   know.

   Emerson, *Experience*

38 I cannot rest from travel; I will drink
   Life to the lees. All times I have enjoy'd
   Greatly, have suffer'd greatly, both with those
   That love me, and alone; on shore, and when
   Thro' scudding drifts the rainy Hyades
   Vext the dim sea. I am become a name;
   For always roaming with a hungry heart
   Much have I seen and known,—cities of men
   And manners, climates, councils, governments,
   Myself not least, but honor'd of them all,—
   And drunk delight of battle with my peers,
   Far on the ringing plains of windy Troy.
   I am a part of all that I have met;
   Yet all experience is an arch wherethro'
   Gleams that untravell'd world whose margin
      fades
   For ever and for ever when I move.
   How dull it is to pause, to make an end,
   To rust unburnish'd, not to shine in use!
   As tho' to breathe were life! Life piled on life
   Were all too little, and of one to me
   Little remains; but every hour is saved
   From that eternal silence, something more,
   A bringer of new things; and vile it were
   For some three suns to store and hoard myself,
   And this gray spirit yearning in desire
   To follow knowledge like a sinking star,
   Beyond the utmost bound of human thought.

   Tennyson, *Ulysses*

39 All languages and literatures are full of general
   observations on life, both as to what it is, and how
   to conduct oneself in it; observations which everybody knows, which everybody repeats, or hears
   with acquiescence, which are received as truisms,
   yet of which most people first truly learn the
   meaning when experience, generally of a painful
   kind, has made it a reality to them. How often,
   when smarting under some unforeseen misfortune
   or disappointment, does a person call to mind
   some proverb or common saying, familiar to him
   all his life, the meaning of which, if he had ever
   before felt it as he does now, would have saved
   him from the calamity. There are indeed reasons
   for this, other than the absence of discussion;
   there are many truths of which the full meaning

cannot be realised until personal experience has
brought it home. But much more of the meaning
even of these would have been understood, and
what was understood would have been far more
deeply impressed on the mind, if the man had
been accustomed to hear it argued *pro* and *con* by
people who did understand it.

   Mill, *On Liberty*, II

40 Experience must be consulted in order to learn
   from it under what circumstances arguments from
   it will be valid. We have no ulterior test to which
   we subject experience in general; but we make
   experience its own test.

   Mill, *System of Logic*, Bk. III, IV, 2

41 Kutúzov looked round. He was listening to the
   general's report—which consisted chiefly of a criticism of the position at Tsárevo-Zaymíshche—as
   he had listened to Denísov, and seven years previously had listened to the discussion at the Auster-
   litz council of war. He evidently listened only because he had ears which, though there was a piece
   of tow in one of them, could not help hearing; but
   it was evident that nothing the general could say
   would surprise or even interest him, that he knew
   all that would be said beforehand, and heard it all
   only because he had to, as one has to listen to the
   chanting of a service of prayer. All that Denísov
   had said was clever and to the point. What the
   general was saying was even more clever and to
   the point, but it was evident that Kutúzov despised knowledge and cleverness, and knew
   of something else that would decide the matter—
   something independent of cleverness and knowledge. Prince Andrew watched the commander in
   chief's face attentively, and the only expression he
   could see there was one of boredom, curiosity as to
   the meaning of the feminine whispering behind
   the door, and a desire to observe propriety. It was
   evident that Kutúzov despised cleverness and
   learning and even the patriotic feeling shown by
   Denísov, but despised them not because of his own
   intellect, feelings, or knowledge— he did not try
   to display any of these—but because of something
   else. He despised them because of his old age and
   experience of life.

   Tolstoy, *War and Peace*, X, 15

42 Kutúzov like all old people did not sleep much at
   night. He often fell asleep unexpectedly in the
   daytime, but at night, lying on his bed without
   undressing, he generally remained awake thinking.
      So he lay now on his bed, supporting his large,
   heavy, scarred head on his plump hand, with his
   one eye open, meditating and peering into the
   darkness.
      Since Bennigsen, who corresponded with the
   Emperor and had more influence than anyone

else on the staff, had begun to avoid him, Kutúzov was more at ease as to the possibility of himself and his troops being obliged to take part in useless aggressive movements. The lesson of the Tarútino battle and of the day before it, which Kutúzov remembered with pain, must, he thought, have some effect on others too.

"They must understand that we can only lose by taking the offensive. Patience and time are my warriors, my champions," thought Kutúzov. He knew that an apple should not be plucked while it is green. It will fall of itself when ripe, but if picked unripe the apple is spoiled, the tree is harmed, and your teeth are set on edge. Like an experienced sportsman he knew that the beast was wounded, and wounded as only the whole strength of Russia could have wounded it, but whether it was mortally wounded or not was still an undecided question. Now by the fact of Lauriston and Barthélemi having been sent, and by the reports of the guerrillas, Kutúzov was almost sure that the wound was mortal. But he needed further proofs and it was necessary to wait.

"They want to run to see how they have wounded it. Wait and we shall see! Continual maneuvers, continual advances!" thought he. "What for? only to distinguish themselves! As if fighting were fun. They are like children from whom one can't get any sensible account of what has happened because they all want to show how well they can fight. But that's not what is needed now.

"And what ingenious maneuvers they all propose to me! It seems to them that when they have thought of two or three contingencies" (he remembered the general plan sent him from Petersburg) "they have foreseen everything. But the contingencies are endless."

Tolstoy, *War and Peace,* XIII, 17

43 If the realm of human knowledge were confined to abstract reasoning, then having subjected to criticism the explanation of "power" that juridical science gives us, humanity would conclude that power is merely a word and has no real existence. But to understand phenomena man has, besides abstract reasoning, experience by which he verifies his reflections. And experience tells us that power is not merely a word but an actually existing phenomenon.

Tolstoy, *War and Peace,* II Epilogue, V

44 We should be careful to get out of an experience only the wisdom that is in it—and stop there; lest we be like the cat that sits down on a hot stove-lid. She will never sit down on a hot stove-lid again—and that is well; but also she will never sit down on a cold one any more.

Mark Twain, *Pudd'nhead Wilson's New Calendar,* XI

45 *My experience is what I agree to attend to.* Only those

items which I *notice* shape my mind—without selective interest, experience is an utter chaos. Interest alone gives accent and emphasis, light and shade, background and foreground—intelligible perspective, in a word. It varies in every creature, but without it the consciousness of every creature would be a gray chaotic indiscriminateness, impossible for us even to conceive.

William James, *Psychology,* XI

46 In logic a concept is unalterable; but what are popularly called our "conceptions of things" alter by being used. The aim of "Science" is to attain conceptions so adequate and exact that we shall never need to change them. There is an everlasting struggle in every mind between the tendency to keep unchanged, and the tendency to renovate, its ideas. Our education is a ceaseless compromise between the conservative and the progressive factors. Every new experience must be disposed of under *some* old head. The great point is to find the head which has to be least altered to take it in. Certain Polynesian natives, seeing horses for the first time, called them pigs, that being the nearest head. My child of two played for a week with the first orange that was given him, calling it a "ball." He called the first whole eggs he saw "potatoes," having been accustomed to see his "eggs" broken into a glass, and his potatoes without the skin. A folding pocket-corkscrew he unhesitatingly called "bad-scissors." Hardly any one of us can make new heads easily when fresh experiences come. Most of us grow more and more enslaved to the stock conceptions with which we have once become familiar, and less and less capable of assimilating impressions in any but the old ways. Old-fogyism, in short, is the inevitable terminus to which life sweeps us on. Objects which violate our established habits of "apperception" are simply not taken account of at all; or, if on some occasion we are forced by dint of argument to admit their existence, twenty-four hours later the admission is as if it were not, and every trace of the unassimilable truth has vanished from our thought. Genius, in truth, means little more than the faculty of perceiving in an unhabitual way.

William James, *Psychology,* XIX

47 These are the most prominent of the tendencies which are worthy of being called instinctive in the human species. It will be observed that *no other mammal, not even the monkey, shows so large an array.* In a perfectly-rounded development, every one of these instincts would start a habit toward certain objects and inhibit a habit toward certain others. Usually this is the case; but, in the one-sided development of civilized life, it happens that the timely age goes by in a sort of starvation of objects, and the individual then grows up with gaps in his psychic constitution which future experiences can never fill. Compare the accomplished

gentleman with the poor artisan or tradesman of a city: during the adolescence of the former, objects appropriate to his growing interests, bodily and mental, were offered as fast as the interests awoke, and, as a consequence, he is armed and equipped at every angle to meet the world. Sport came to the rescue and completed his education where real things were lacking. He has tasted of the essence of every side of human life, being sailor, hunter, athlete, scholar, fighter, talker, dandy, man of affairs, etc., all in one. Over the city poor boy's youth no such golden opportunities were hung, and in his manhood no desires for most of them exist. Fortunate it is for him if gaps are the only anomalies his instinctive life presents; perversions are too often the fruit of his unnatural bringing up.

William James, *Psychology*, XXIV

48 Consciousness flickers; and even at its brightest, there is a small focal region of clear illumination, and a large penumbral region of experience which tells of intense experience in dim apprehension. The simplicity of clear consciousness is no measure of the complexity of complete experience. Also this character of our experience suggests that consciousness is the crown of experience, only occasionally attained, not its necessary base.

Whitehead, *Process and Reality*, III, 5

49 I feel that the concept of 'experience' has been very much over-emphasized, especially in the Idealist philosophy, but also in many forms of empiricism. I found, when I began to think about theory of knowledge, that none of the philosophers who emphasize 'experience' tells us what they mean by the word. They seem willing to accept it as an indefinable of which the significance should be obvious. They tend to think that only what is experienced can be known to exist and that it is meaningless to assert that some things exist although we do not know them to exist. I think that this sort of view gives much too much importance to knowledge, or at any rate to something analogous to knowledge. I think also that those who profess such views have not realized all their implications. Few philosophers seem to understand that one may know a proposition of the form 'All A is B' or 'There are A's' without knowing any single A individually. If you are on a pebbly beach you may be quite sure that there are pebbles on the beach that you have not seen or touched. Everybody, in fact, accepts innumerable propositions about things not experienced, but when people begin to philosophize they seem to think it necessary to make themselves artificially stupid. I will admit at once that there are difficulties in explaining how we acquire knowledge that transcends experience, but I think the view that we have no such knowledge is utterly untenable.

Russell, *My Philosophical Development*, XI

50 To place knowledge where it arises and operates in experience is to know that, as it arose because of the troubles of man, it is confirmed in reconstructing the conditions which occasioned those troubles. Genuine intellectual integrity is found in experimental knowing. Until this lesson is fully learned, it is not safe to dissociate knowledge from experiment nor experiment from experience.

Dewey, *Essays in Experimental Logic,*
Introduction, 7

51 Scientific principles and laws do not lie on the surface of nature. They are hidden, and must be wrested from nature by an active and elaborate technique of inquiry. Neither logical reasoning nor the passive accumulation of any number of observations—which the ancients called experience—suffices to lay hold of them. Active experimentation must force the apparent facts of nature into forms different to those in which they familiarly present themselves; and thus make them tell the truth about themselves, as torture may compel an unwilling witness to reveal what he has been concealing. Pure reasoning as a means of arriving at truth is like the spider who spins a web out of himself. The web is orderly and elaborate, but it is only a trap. The passive accumulation of experiences—the traditional empirical method—is like the ant who busily runs about and collects and piles up heaps of raw materials. True method, that which Bacon would usher in, is comparable to the operations of the bee who, like the ant, collects material from the external world, but unlike that industrious creature attacks and modifies the collected stuff in order to make it yield its hidden treasure.

Dewey, *Reconstruction in Philosophy*, II

52 We always live at the time we live and not at some other time, and only by extracting at each present time the full meaning of each present experience are we prepared for doing the same thing in the future. This is the only preparation which in the long run amounts to anything.

Dewey, *Experience and Education*, III

53 There is no discipline in the world so severe as the discipline of experience subjected to the tests of intelligent development and direction.

Dewey, *Experience and Education*, VIII

54 We should do well to remember that crude experience knows nothing of the distinction between subject and object. This distinction is a division in things, a contrast established between masses of images which show different characteristics in their modes of existence and relation. If this truth is overlooked, if subject and object are made conditions of experience instead of being, like body and mind, its contrasted parts, the revenge of fate

is quick and ironical; either subject or object must immediately collapse and evaporate altogether. All objects must become modifications of the subject or all subjects aspects or fragments of the object. . . . Reflection must . . . separate them, if knowledge (that is, ideas with eventual application and practical transcendence) is to exist at all. In other words, action must be adjusted to certain elements of experience and not to others, and those chiefly regarded must have a certain interpretation put upon them by trained apperception. The rest must be treated as moonshine and taken no account of except perhaps in idle and poetic revery. In this way crude experience grows reasonable and appearance becomes knowledge of reality.

Santayana, *Life of Reason,* I, 6

55 *April 26.* Mother is putting my new secondhand clothes in order. She prays now, she says, that I may learn in my own life and away from home and friends what the heart is and what it feels. Amen. So be it. Welcome, O life! I go to encounter for the millionth time the reality of experience and to forge in the smithy of my soul the uncreated conscience of my race.

Joyce, *Portrait of the Artist as a Young Man,* V

6.3 | *Truth*

Though it is not included among the passages here quoted, a memorable statement by Josiah Royce provides an apt introduction to the subject under consideration. "A liar," Professor Royce once said, "is a man who willfully misplaces his ontological predicates"—a man who, believing that something *is* the case, declares in speech that it is not the case; or believing that something is not the case, declares that it is. Accordingly, it is impossible to prevaricate in speech unless one thinks that one has the truth about the matter in question. When is anyone in that state of mind? Aristotle's answer to that question, in a famous passage quoted below, provides the basis for Royce's remark. We possess the truth mentally, he said, when we think that that which is, *is,* or that that which is not, is *not.* Falsity in the mind, like prevarication in speech, consists in thinking that which *is, is not,* or that which *is not, is.*

This classic definition of truth is acceptable only to those who affirm the existence of a reality independent of the knowing mind—a reality to which the mind can conform or fail to conform. In the absence of the possibility of a correspondence between the mind and an independent reality that it attempts to know, truth for the mind would have to consist in the internal coherence and consistency of its own thoughts. But even for those who hold that an independent reality provides the ultimate test of the mind's claim to possessing the truth, consistency—the avoidance of contradiction—is also of critical importance.

The question, *What is truth?,* to be answered by one or another definition of it, must never be confused with the question, *How can we tell whether a particular statement under consideration is true or false?* Answering the latter question, many of the philosophers quoted formulate different sets of criteria for discriminating between the true and the false; as, for example, William James and John Dewey in their promulgation of what came to be called "the pragmatic theory of truth," which, while it did not exclude the criterion of internal consistency, stressed the point that our best assurance of the truth of a statement comes from our finding that it works successfully when put into practice. "The true," said James, "is the expedient in the way of our thinking."

In addition to offering definitions of truth itself and enumerating the criteria for determining whether a particular statement is true or false, the passages here collected discuss the unity of Truth with a capital T as contrasted with the multiplicity of truths; the immutability of whatever is true in and of itself as against the mutability of the human mind's claims to knowing what is true and false; the difference between the truth of true statements about what is the case and the truth of true statements about what ought to be done or sought; the moral obligation to pursue and love the truth, and to be unswerving in one's adherence to it, a higher loyalty even than the one we owe to our friends; the necessity of complete freedom of expression and discussion for the cooperative pursuit of truth; and the acknowledgment of human fallibility in that pursuit.

The extent of that fallibility and the proneness of the human mind to error are discussed in Section 6.4 and points there made are further developed in Sections 6.5 and 6.6, where the questioning of human opinions and beliefs leads to skeptical doubts about the human mind's ability ever to get at the truth.

---

1 Truth lies at the bottom of a well.

> Democritus (qu. by Diogenes Laertius, *Lives of the Philosophers*)

2 *Socrates.* Protagoras . . . says that man is the measure of all things, and that things are to me as they appear to me, and that they are to you as they appear to you. Do you agree with him, or would you say that things have a permanent essence of their own?

Hermogenes. There have been times, Socrates, when I have been driven in my perplexity to take refuge with Protagoras; not that I agree with him at all. . . .

Soc. But if Protagoras is right, and the truth is that things are as they appear to any one, how can some of us be wise and some of us foolish?

Her. Impossible.

Soc. And if, on the other hand, wisdom and folly are really distinguishable, you will allow, I think, that the assertion of Protagoras can hardly be correct. For if what appears to each man is true to him, one man cannot in reality be wiser than another.

Her. He cannot.

Soc. Nor will you be disposed to say with Euthydemus, that all things equally belong to all men at the same moment and always; for neither on his view can there be some good and other bad, if virtue and vice are always equally to be attributed to all.

Her. There cannot.

Soc. But if neither is right, and things are not relative to individuals, and all things do not equally belong to all at the same moment and always, they must be supposed to have their own proper and permanent essence: they are not in relation to us, or influenced by us, fluctuating according to our fancy, but they are independent, and maintain to their own essence the relation prescribed by nature.

Her. I think, Socrates, that you have said the truth.

> Plato, *Cratylus,* 386A

3 Of the nature of the soul, though her true form be ever a theme of large and more than mortal discourse, let me speak briefly, and in a figure. And let the figure be composite—a pair of winged horses and a charioteer. Now the winged horses and the charioteers of the gods are all of them noble and of noble descent, but those of other races are mixed; the human charioteer drives his in a pair; and one of them is noble and of noble breed, and the other is ignoble and of ignoble breed; and the driving of them of necessity gives a great deal of trouble to him. I will endeavour to explain to you in what way the mortal differs from the immortal creature. The soul in her totality has the care of inanimate being everywhere, and traverses the whole heaven in divers forms appearing:—when perfect and fully winged she soars upward, and orders the whole world; whereas the imperfect soul, losing her wings and drooping in her flight at last settles on the solid ground—there, finding a home, she receives an earthly frame which appears to be self-moved, but is really moved by her power; and this composi-

tion of soul and body is called a living and mortal creature. For immortal no such union can be reasonably believed to be; although fancy, not having seen nor surely known the nature of God, may imagine an immortal creature having both a body and also a soul which are united throughout all time. Let that, however, be as God wills, and be spoken of acceptably to him. And now let us ask the reason why the soul loses her wings!

The wing is the corporeal element which is most akin to the divine, and which by nature tends to soar aloft and carry that which gravitates downwards into the upper region, which is the habitation of the gods. The divine is beauty, wisdom, goodness, and the like; and by these the wing of the soul is nourished, and grows apace; but when fed upon evil and foulness and the opposite of good, wastes and falls away. Zeus, the mighty lord, holding the reins of a winged chariot, leads the way in heaven, ordering all and taking care of all; and there follows him the array of gods and demigods, marshalled in eleven bands; Hestia alone abides at home in the house of heaven; of the rest they who are reckoned among the princely twelve march in their appointed order. They see many blessed sights in the inner heaven, and there are many ways to and fro, along which the blessed gods are passing, every one doing his own work; he may follow who will and can, for jealousy has no place in the celestial choir. But when they go to banquet and festival, then they move up the steep to the top of the vault of heaven. The chariots of the gods in even poise, obeying the rein, glide rapidly; but the others labour, for the vicious steed goes heavily, weighing down the charioteer to the earth when his steed has not been thoroughly trained:—and this is the hour of agony and extremest conflict for the soul. For the immortals, when they are at the end of their course, go forth and stand upon the outside of heaven, and the revolution of the spheres carries them round, and they behold the things beyond. But of the heaven which is above the heavens, what earthly poet ever did or ever will sing worthily? It is such as I will describe; for I must dare to speak the truth, when truth is my theme. There abides the very being with which true knowledge is concerned; the colourless, formless, intangible essence, visible only to mind, the pilot of the soul. The divine intelligence, being nurtured upon mind and pure knowledge, and the intelligence of every soul which is capable of receiving the food proper to it, rejoices at beholding reality, and once more gazing upon truth, is replenished and made glad, until the revolution of the worlds brings her round again to the same place. In the revolution she beholds justice, and temperance, and knowledge absolute, not in the form of generation or of relation, which men call existence, but knowledge absolute in existence absolute; and beholding the other true existences in like manner,

and feasting upon them, she passes down into the interior of the heavens and returns home; and there the charioteer putting up his horses at the stall, gives them ambrosia to eat and nectar to drink.

Such is the life of the gods; but of other souls, that which follows God best and is likest to him lifts the head of the charioteer into the outer world, and is carried round in the revolution, troubled indeed by the steeds, and with difficulty beholding true being; while another only rises and falls, and sees, and again fails to see by reason of the unruliness of the steeds. The rest of the souls are also longing after the upper world and they all follow, but not being strong enough they are carried round below the surface, plunging, treading on one another, each striving to be first; and there is confusion and perspiration and the extremity of effort; and many of them are lamed or have their wings broken through the ill-driving of the charioteers; and all of them after a fruitless toil, not having attained to the mysteries of true being, go away, and feed upon opinion. The reason why the souls exhibit this exceeding eagerness to behold the plain of truth is that pasturage is found there, which is suited to the highest part of the soul; and the wing on which the soul soars is nourished with this. And there is a law of Destiny, that the soul which attains any vision of truth in company with a god is preserved from harm until the next period, and if attaining always is always unharmed. But when she is unable to follow, and fails to behold the truth, and through some ill-hap sinks beneath the double load of forgetfulness and vice, and her wings fall from her and she drops to the ground, then the law ordains that this soul shall at her first birth pass, not into any other animal, but only into man; and the soul which has seen most of truth shall come to the birth as a philosopher, or artist, or some musical and loving nature; that which has seen truth in the second degree shall be some righteous king or warrior chief; the soul which is of the third class shall be a politician, or economist, or trader; the fourth shall be a lover of gymnastic toils, or a physician; the fifth shall lead the life of a prophet or hierophant; to the sixth the character of a poet or some other imitative artist will be assigned; to the seventh the life of an artisan or husbandman; to the eighth that of a sophist or demagogue; to the ninth that of a tyrant;—all these are states of probation, in which he who does righteously improves, and he who does unrighteously, deteriorates his lot.

Plato, *Phaedrus,* 246A

4 I cannot refute you, Socrates, said Agathon:—Let us assume that what you say is true.

Say rather, beloved Agathon, that you cannot refute the truth; for Socrates is easily refuted.

Plato, *Symposium,* 201B

5 *Socrates.* I would ask you to be thinking of the truth and not of Socrates: agree with me, if I seem to you to be speaking the truth; or if not, withstand me might and main, that I may not deceive you as well as myself in my enthusiasm, and like the bee, leave my sting in you before I die.

Plato, *Phaedo,* 91A

6 *Socrates.* I should not like to have my words repeated to the tragedians and the rest of the imitative tribe—but I do not mind saying to you, that all poetical imitations are ruinous to the understanding of the hearers, and that the knowledge of their true nature is the only antidote to them. . . . I have always from my earliest youth had an awe and love of Homer, which even now makes the words falter on my lips, for he is the great captain and teacher of the whole of that charming tragic company; but a man is not to be reverenced more than the truth.

Plato, *Republic,* X, 595A

7 *Athenian Stranger.* The greatest and highest truths have no outward image of themselves visible to man, which he who wishes to satisfy the soul of the enquirer can adapt to the eye of sense, and therefore we ought to train ourselves to give and accept a rational account of them; for immaterial things, which are the noblest and greatest, are shown only in thought and idea, and in no other way.

Plato, *Statesman,* 286A

8 As there are in the mind thoughts which do not involve truth or falsity, and also those which must be either true or false, so it is in speech. For truth and falsity imply combination and separation. Nouns and verbs, provided nothing is added, are like thoughts without combination or separation; 'man' and 'white', as isolated terms, are not yet either true or false.

Aristotle, *On Interpretation,* 16a10

9 The least initial deviation from the truth is multiplied later a thousandfold.

Aristotle, *On the Heavens,* 271b9

10 To give a satisfactory decision as to the truth it is necessary to be rather an arbitrator than a party to the dispute.

Aristotle, *On the Heavens,* 279b11

11 The investigation of the truth is in one way hard, in another easy. An indication of this is found in the fact that no one is able to attain the truth adequately, while, on the other hand, we do not collectively fail, but every one says something true about the nature of things, and while individually we contribute little or nothing to the truth, by the union of all a considerable amount is amassed. Therefore, since the truth seems to be like the pro-

verbial door, which no one can fail to hit, in this respect it must be easy, but the fact that we can have a whole truth and not the particular part we aim at shows the difficulty of it.

Perhaps, too, as difficulties are of two kinds, the cause of the present difficulty is not in the facts but in us. For as the eyes of bats to the blaze of day, so is the reason in our soul to the things which are by nature most evident of all.

Aristotle, *Metaphysics,* 993a30

12 It is right . . . that philosophy should be called knowledge of the truth. For the end of theoretical knowledge is truth, while that of practical knowledge is action (for even if they consider how things are, practical men do not study the eternal, but what is relative and in the present). Now we do not know a truth without its cause; and a thing has a quality in a higher degree than other things if in virtue of it the similar quality belongs to the other things as well (e.g. fire is the hottest of things; for it is the cause of the heat of all other things); so that that which causes derivative truths to be true is most true. Hence the principles of eternal things must be always most true (for they are not merely sometimes true, nor is there any cause of their being, but they themselves are the cause of the being of other things), so that as each thing is in respect of being, so is it in respect of truth.

Aristotle, *Metaphysics,* 993b19

13 Of one subject we must either affirm or deny any one predicate. This is clear, in the first place, if we define what the true and the false are. To say of what is that it is not, or of what is not that it is, is false, while to say of what is that it is, and of what is not that it is not, is true; so that he who says of anything that it is, or that it is not, will say either what is true or what is false; but neither what is nor what is not is said to be or not to be.

Aristotle, *Metaphysics,* 1011b24

14 It would perhaps be thought to be better, indeed to be our duty, for the sake of maintaining the truth even to destroy what touches us closely, especially as we are philosophers or lovers of wisdom; for, while both are dear, piety requires us to honour truth above our friends.

Aristotle, *Ethics,* 1096a13

15 The man who loves truth, and is truthful where nothing is at stake, will still more be truthful where something is at stake; he will avoid falsehood as something base, seeing that he avoided it even for its own sake; and such a man is worthy of praise. He inclines rather to understate the truth; for this seems in better taste because exaggerations are wearisome.

Aristotle, *Ethics,* 1127b3

16 The states by virtue of which the soul possesses truth by way of affirmation or denial are five in number, i.e. art, scientific knowledge, practical wisdom, philosophic wisdom, intuitive reason; we do not include judgement and opinion because in these we may be mistaken.

Aristotle, *Ethics*, 1139ᵇ16

17 Those who object that that at which all things aim is not necessarily good are, we may surmise, talking nonsense. For we say that that which every one thinks really is so; and the man who attacks this belief will hardly have anything more credible to maintain instead.

Aristotle, *Ethics*, 1172ᵇ35

18 Nature has instilled in our minds an insatiable desire to see truth.

Cicero, *Disputations*, I, 19

19 We don't believe a liar even when he tells the truth.

Cicero, *Divination*, II, 71

20 Then said Jesus to those Jews which believed on him, If ye continue in my word, then are ye my disciples indeed;

And ye shall know the truth, and the truth shall make you free.

John 8:31–32

21 Pilate therefore said unto him, Art thou a king then? Jesus answered, Thou sayest that I am a king. To this end was I born, and for this cause came I into the world, that I should bear witness unto the truth. Every one that is of the truth heareth my voice.

Pilate saith unto him, What is truth? And when he had said this, he went out again unto the Jews, and saith unto them, I find in him no fault at all.

John 18:37–38

22 Am I therefore become your enemy, because I tell you the truth?

Galatians 4:16

23 A liar ought to have a good memory.

Quintilian, *Institutio Oratoria*, IV, 2

24 Veritable truth is not accordance with an external; it is self-accordance; it affirms and is nothing other than itself and is nothing other; it is at once existence and self-affirmation.

Plotinus, *Fifth Ennead*, V, 2

25 And I looked upon other things, and I saw that they owed their being to You, and that all finite things are in You: but in a different manner, being in You not as in a place, but because You are and hold all things in the hand of Your truth, and all things are true inasmuch as they are: nor

is falsehood anything, save that something is thought to be which is not.

Augustine, *Confessions*, VII, 15

26 I have met many who wished to deceive, but not one who wished to be deceived.

Augustine, *Confessions*, X, 23

27 Why does truth call forth hatred? Why is Your servant treated as an enemy by those to whom he preaches the truth, if happiness is loved, which is simply joy in truth? Simply because truth is loved in such a way that those who love some other thing want it to be the truth, and, precisely because they do not wish to be deceived, are unwilling to be convinced that they are deceived. Thus they hate the truth for the sake of that other thing which they love because they take it for truth. They love truth when it enlightens them, they hate truth when it accuses them. Because they do not wish to be deceived and do wish to deceive, they love truth when it reveals itself, and hate it when it reveals them. Thus it shall reward them as they deserve: those who do not wish to be revealed by truth, truth will unmask against their will, but it will not reveal itself to them. Thus, thus, even thus, does the human mind, blind and inert, vile and ill-behaved, desire to keep itself concealed, yet desire that nothing should be concealed from itself. But the contrary happens to it—it cannot lie hidden from truth, but only truth from it. Even so, for all its worthlessness, the human mind would rather find its joy in truth than falsehood. So that it shall be happy if, with no other thing to distract, it shall one day come to rejoice in that sole Truth by which all things are true.

Augustine, *Confessions*, X, 23

28 Lying is wrong even to save chastity.

Augustine, *On Lying*, VII, 10

29 He who says that some lies are just, must be judged to say no other than that some sins are just, and therefore some things are just which are unjust: than which what can be more absurd?

Augustine, *To Consentius, Against Lying*, 18

30 "If any man makes search for truth with all his penetration, and would be led astray by no deceiving paths, let him turn upon himself the light of an inward gaze, let him bend by force the long-drawn wanderings of his thoughts into one circle; let him tell surely to his soul, that he has, thrust away within the treasures of his mind, all that he labours to acquire without. Then shall that truth, which now was hid in error's darkening cloud, shine forth more clear than Phœbus's self. For the body, though it brings material mass which breeds forgetfulness, has never driven forth all light from the mind. The seed of truth does surely cling with-

in, and can be roused as a spark by the fanning of philosophy. For if it is not so, how do ye men make answers true of your own instinct when teachers question you? Is it not that the quick spark of truth lies buried in the heart's low depths? And if the Muse of Plato sends through those depths the voice of truth, each man has not forgotten and is but reminding himself of what he learns."

When she [Philosophy] made an end, I said, "I agree very strongly with Plato; for this is the second time that you have reminded me of these thoughts. The first time I had lost them through the material influence of the body; the second, when overwhelmed by this weight of trouble."

Boethius, *Consolation of Philosophy*, III

31 As the good denotes that towards which the appetite tends, so the true denotes that towards which the intellect tends. Now there is this difference between the appetite and the intellect, or any knowledge whatsoever, that knowledge is according as the thing known is in the knower, whilst appetite is according as the desirer tends towards the thing desired. Thus the term of the appetite, namely good, is in the thing desirable, and the term of knowledge, namely true, is in the intellect itself.

Now as good exists in a thing so far as that thing is related to the appetite—and hence the aspect of goodness passes on from the desirable thing to the appetite, according as the appetite is called good if the thing desired is good, so, since the true is in the intellect in so far as it is conformed to the thing understood, the aspect of the true must pass from the intellect to the thing understood, so that also the thing understood is said to be true in so far as it has some relation to the intellect.

Now a thing understood may be in relation to an intellect either essentially or accidentally. It is related essentially to an intellect on which it depends as regards its being, but accidentally to an intellect by which it is knowable; even as we may say that a house is related essentially to the intellect of the architect, but accidentally to the intellect upon which it does not depend.

Now we do not judge of a thing by what is in it accidentally, but by what is in it essentially. Hence, everything is said to be true absolutely in so far as it is related to the intellect from which it depends; and thus it is that artificial things are said to be true as being related to our intellect. For a house is said to be true that expresses the likeness of the form in the architect's mind, and words are said to be true so far as they are the signs of truth in the intellect. In the same way natural things are said to be true in so far as they express the likeness of the species that are in the divine mind. For a stone is called true, because it expresses the nature proper to a stone, according

to the preconception in the divine intellect. Thus, then, truth is principally in the intellect, and secondarily in things according as they are related to the intellect as their principle.

Aquinas, *Summa Theologica*, I, 16, 1

32 Truth is found in the intellect according as it apprehends a thing as it is, and in things according as they have being conformable to an intellect. This is to the greatest degree found in God. For His being is not only conformed to His intellect, but it is the very act of His intellect, and His act of understanding is the measure and cause of every other being and of every other intellect, and He Himself is His own being and act of understanding. And so it follows not only that truth is in Him, but that He is truth itself, and the supreme and first truth.

Aquinas, *Summa Theologica*, I, 16, 5

33 Truth and good include one another; for truth is something good, otherwise it would not be desirable; and good is something true, otherwise it would not be intelligible. Therefore just as the object of the appetite may be something true, as having the aspect of good, for example, when some one desires to know the truth, so the object of the practical intellect is good directed to operation, and under the aspect of truth. For the practical intellect knows truth, just as the speculative, but it directs the known truth to operation.

Aquinas, *Summa Theologica*, I, 79, 11

34 No one envies another the knowledge of truth, which can be known entirely by many except perhaps one may envy another his superiority in the knowledge of it.

Aquinas, *Summa Theologica*, I–II, 28, 4

35 Being and truth in the universal cannot be the object of hatred because disagreement is the cause of hatred, and agreement is the cause of love, while being and truth are common to all things. But nothing hinders some particular being or some particular truth being an object of hatred, in so far as it is considered as something contrary and repugnant. . . .

Now it may happen in three ways that some particular truth is repugnant or contrary to the good we love. First, according as truth is in things as in its cause and origin. And thus man sometimes hates a particular truth when he wishes that what is true were not true. Secondly, according as truth is in man's knowledge, which hinders him from gaining the object loved; such is the case of those who wish not to know the truth of faith, that they may sin freely. . . . Thirdly, a particular truth is hated as something repugnant according as it is in the intellect of another man; as, for instance, when a man wishes to remain indolent in his sin, he hates that anyone should know the truth about his sin.

Aquinas, *Summa Theologica,* I–II, 29, 5

36 The greatest of all pleasures consists in the contemplation of truth. Now every pleasure assuages pain as stated above. Hence the contemplation of truth assuages pain or sorrow, and the more so the more perfectly one is a lover of wisdom.

Aquinas, *Summa Theologica,* I–II, 38, 4

37 A small error in the beginning is a great one in the end.

Aquinas, *Concerning Being and Essence,* Intro.

38 *True* expresses the correspondence of being to the knowing power, for all knowing is produced by an assimilation of the knower to the thing known, so that assimilation is said to be the cause of knowledge. Similarly, the sense of sight knows a color by being informed with a species of the color.

The first reference of being to the intellect, therefore, consists in its agreement with the intellect. This agreement is called "the conformity of thing and intellect." In this conformity is fulfilled the formal constituent of the true, and this is what *the true* adds to being, namely, the conformity or equation of thing and intellect. As we said, the knowledge of a thing is a consequence of this conformity; therefore, it is an effect of truth, even though the fact that the thing is a being is prior to its truth.

Aquinas, *On Truth,* I, 1

39 And the Friar: "I heard once at Bologna many of the Devil's vices told; amongst which, I heard that he is a liar and the father of lies."

Dante, *Inferno,* XXIII, 143

40 But first, I pray you, of your courtesy,
You'll not ascribe it to vulgarity
Though I speak plainly of this matter here,
Retailing you their words and means of cheer;
Nor though I use their very terms, nor lie.
For this thing do you know as well as I:
When one repeats a tale told by a man,
He must report, as nearly as he can,
Every least word, if he remember it,
However rude it be, or how unfit;
Or else he may be telling what's untrue,
Embellishing and fictionizing too.
He may not spare, although it were his brother;
He must as well say one word as another.
Christ spoke right broadly out, in holy writ,
And, you know well, there's nothing low in it.
And Plato says, to those able to read:
"The word should be the cousin to the deed."

Chaucer, *Canterbury Tales:* The Prologue

41 As thus: You know that each evangelist
Who tells the passion of Lord Jesus Christ
Says not in all things as his fellows do,

But nonetheless, each gospel is all true,
And all of them accord in their essence,
Howbeit there's in telling difference.
For some of them say more and some say less
When they His piteous passion would express;
I mean now Mark and Matthew, Luke and John;
Yet, without doubt, their meaning is all one.

Chaucer, *Canterbury Tales:* Prologue to
Melibeus

42 Superstition, idolatry, and hypocrisy have ample wages, but truth goes a begging.

Luther, *Table Talk,* H53

43 Anyone who does not feel sufficiently strong in memory should not meddle with lying. . . . Now liars either invent everything out of whole cloth, or else disguise and alter something fundamentally true. When they disguise and change a story, if you put them back onto it often enough they find it hard not to get tangled up. For since the thing as it is has become lodged first in the memory and has imprinted itself there by way of consciousness and knowledge, it is difficult for it not to present itself to the imagination, dislodging the falsehood, which cannot have so firm and secure a foothold. Likewise, the circumstances that were learned first, slipping into the mind every moment, tend to weaken the memory of the false or corrupted parts that have been added. In what liars invent completely, inasmuch as there is no contrary impression which clashes with the falsehood, they seem to have the less reason to fear making a mistake. Nevertheless even this, since it is an empty thing without a grip, is prone to escape any but a very strong memory.

Montaigne, *Essays,* I, 9, Of Liars

44 If falsehood, like truth, had only one face, we would be in better shape. For we would take as certain the opposite of what the liar said. But the reverse of truth has a hundred thousand shapes and a limitless field.

Montaigne, *Essays,* I, 9, Of Liars

45 How many arts there are that profess to consist of conjecture more than of knowledge, that do not decide on the true and the false and merely follow what seems to be! There are, they say, both a true and a false, and there is in us the means to seek it, but not to test it by a touchstone. We are much better if we let ourselves be led without inquisitiveness in the way of the world. A soul guaranteed against prejudice is marvelously advanced toward tranquility. People who judge and check their judges never submit to them as they ought. How much more docile and easily led, both by the laws of religion and by political laws, are the simple and incurious minds, than those minds that survey divine and human causes like pedagogues!

Montaigne, *Essays,* II, 12, Apology for
Raymond Sebond

46 If the human grip was capable and firm enough
to grasp the truth by our own means; these means
being common to all men, this truth would be
bandied from hand to hand, from one man to another; and at least there would be one thing in the
world, out of all there are, that would be believed
by all men with universal consent. But this fact,
that no proposition can be seen which is not debated and controverted among us, or which may
not be, well shows that our natural judgment does
not grasp very clearly what it grasps. For my
judgment cannot make my companion's judgment
accept it; which is a sign that I have grasped it by
some other means than by a natural power that is
in me and in all men.

> Montaigne, *Essays*, II, 12, Apology for
> Raymond Sebond

47 Truth is the first and fundamental part of virtue.
We must love it for itself. He who tells the truth
because he has some external obligation to do so
and because it serves him, and who does not fear
to tell a lie when it is not important to anybody, is
not sufficiently truthful.

> Montaigne, *Essays*, II, 17, Of Presumption

48 The way of truth is one and simple; that of private profit and the advantage of one's personal
business is double, uneven, and random.

> Montaigne, *Essays*, III, 1, The Useful and
> the Honorable

49 Truth itself does not have the privilege to be employed at any time and in any way; its use, noble
as it is, has its circumscriptions and limits. It often
happens, as the world goes, that people blurt it
out into a prince's ear not only fruitlessly, but
harmfully, and even unjustly. And no one will
make me believe that a righteous remonstrance
cannot be applied wrongfully, and that the interest of the substance must not often yield to the
interest of the form.

> Montaigne, *Essays*, III, 13, Of Experience

50 *Launcelot.* Truth will come to light; murder cannot
be hid long.

> Shakespeare, *Merchant of Venice*, II, ii, 82

51 *Hotspur.* I can teach thee, coz, to shame the devil
By telling truth: tell truth and shame the devil.

> Shakespeare, *I Henry IV*, III, i, 58

52 *Polonius.* See you now;
Your bait of falsehood takes this carp of truth:
And thus do we of wisdom and of reach,
With windlasses and with assays of bias,
By indirections find directions out.

> Shakespeare, *Hamlet*, II, i, 62

53 *Fool.* Truth's a dog must to kennel; he must be

whipped out, when Lady the brach may stand by
the fire and stink.

> Shakespeare, *Lear*, I, iv, 124

54 I thank thee for thy Good-will, dear *Sancho*,
reply'd Don *Quixote:* But I assure thee, that all
these seeming Extravagancies that I must run
through, are no Jests: Far from it, they must be all
perform'd seriously and solemnly; for otherwise
we should transgress the Laws of Chivalry, that
forbid us to tell Lyes upon the Pain of Degradation; now to pretend to do one Thing, and effect
another, is an Evasion, which I esteem to be as
bad as Lying. Therefore the Blows which I must
give my self on the Head, ought to be real, substantial, sound ones, without any Trick, or mental
Reservation; for which Reason I would have thee
leave me some Lint and Salve, since Fortune has
depriv'd us of the Sovereign Balsam which we
lost.

> Cervantes, *Don Quixote*, I, 25

55 With regard to authority, it is the greatest weakness to attribute infinite credit to particular authors, and to refuse his own prerogative to time,
the author of all authors, and, therefore, of all
authority. For truth is rightly named the daughter
of time, not of authority.

> Bacon, *Novum Organum*, I, 84

56 This same truth is a naked and open day-light,
that doth not shew the masques and mummeries
and triumphs of the world, half so stately and
daintily as candle-lights. Truth may perhaps
come to the price of a pearl, that sheweth best by
day; but it will not rise to the price of a diamond
or carbuncle, that sheweth best in varied lights. A
mixture of a lie doth ever add pleasure.

> Bacon, *Of Truth*

57 Howsoever these things are thus in men's depraved judgments and affections, yet truth, which
only doth judge itself, teacheth that the inquiry of
truth, which is the love-making or wooing of it,
the knowledge of truth, which is the presence of it,
and the belief of truth, which is the enjoying of it,
is the sovereign good of human nature.

> Bacon, *Of Truth*

58 It were far better never to think of investigating
truth at all, than to do so without a method. . . .
Moreover by a method I mean certain and simple
rules, such that, if a man observe them accurately,
he shall never assume what is false as true, and
will never spend his mental efforts to no purpose,
but will always gradually increase his knowledge
and so arrive at a true understanding of all that
does not surpass his powers.

> Descartes, *Rules for Direction
> of the Mind*, IV

59 Having but one truth to discover in respect to each matter, whoever succeeds in finding it knows in its regard as much as can be known.

Descartes, *Discourse on Method,* II

60 Having remarked that there was nothing at all in the statement *"I think, therefore I am"* which assures me of having thereby made a true assertion, excepting that I see very clearly that to think it is necessary to be, I came to the conclusion that I might assume, as a general rule, that the things which we conceive very clearly and distinctly are all true.

Descartes, *Discourse on Method,* IV

61 From the very fact that anyone girds himself up for an attack upon the truth, he makes himself less capable of perceiving the truth itself, since he withdraws his mind from the consideration of those reasons that tend to convince him of it, in order to discover others that have the opposite effect.

Descartes, *Objections and Replies,* II

62 When two names are joined together into a consequence, or affirmation, as thus, *A man is a living creature;* or thus, *If he be a man, he is a living creature;* if the latter name *living creature* signify all that the former name *man* signifieth, then the affirmation, or consequence, is *true;* otherwise *false.* For true and false are attributes of speech, not of things. And where speech is not, there is neither truth nor falsehood. Error there may be, as when we expect that which shall not be, or suspect what has not been; but in neither case can a man be charged with untruth.

Seeing then that truth consisteth in the right ordering of names in our affirmations, a man that seeketh precise truth had need to remember what every name he uses stands for, and to place it accordingly; or else he will find himself entangled in words, as a bird in lime twigs; the more he struggles, the more belimed.

Hobbes, *Leviathan,* I, 4

63 Every man is not a proper Champion for Truth, nor fit to take up the Gauntlet in the cause of Verity: Many, from the ignorance of these Maximes, and an inconsiderate Zeal unto Truth, have too rashly charged the Troops of Error, and remain as Trophies unto the enemies of Truth: A man may be in as just possession of Truth as of a City, and yet be forced to surrender; 'tis therefore far better to enjoy her with peace, than to hazzard her on a battle.

Sir Thomas Browne, *Religio Medici,* I, 6

64 It is a strange and tedious war when violence attempts to vanquish truth. All the efforts of violence cannot weaken truth, and only serve to give it fresh vigour. All the lights of truth cannot arrest

violence, and only serve to exasperate it. When force meets force, the weaker must succumb to the stronger; when argument is opposed to argument, the solid and the convincing triumphs over the empty and the false; but violence and verity can make no impression on each other. Let none suppose, however, that the two are, therefore, equal to each other; for there is this vast difference between them, that violence has only a certain course to run, limited by the appointment of Heaven, which overrules its effects to the glory of the truth which it assails; whereas verity endures forever and eventually triumphs over its enemies, being eternal and almighty as God himself.

Pascal, *Provincial Letters,* XII

65 We make an idol of truth itself; for truth apart from charity is not God, but His image and idol, which we must neither love nor worship; and still less must we love or worship its opposite, namely, falsehood.

Pascal, *Pensées,* VIII, 582

66 Truth is so obscure in these times, and falsehood so established, that, unless we love the truth, we cannot know it.

Pascal, *Pensées,* XIV, 864

67 Whatever the weight of antiquity, truth should always have the advantage, even when newly discovered, since it is always older than every opinion men have held about it, and only ignorance of its nature could imagine it began to be at the time it began to be known.

Pascal, *Preface to the Treatise on the Vacuum*

68 It is a disease natural to man to believe that he possesses the truth directly, and this is the reason he is always inclined to deny whatever he cannot understand. Whereas in fact he naturally knows nothing but error and should accept as true only those things whose contradictory appears to him to be false. Consequently, whenever a proposition is inconceivable, we must suspend our judgment and not deny it for that reason, but examine its contradictory; and if we find this manifestly false, we may boldly affirm the original statement, however incomprehensible it is.

Pascal, *Geometrical Demonstration*

69 I see indeed that truth is the same at Toulouse and at Paris.

Pascal, *Letter to Fermat (July 29, 1654)*

70 Thus while he spake, each passion dimm'd his [Satan's] face
Thrice chang'd with pale, ire, envie and despair,
Which marrd his borrow'd visage, and betraid
Him counterfet, if any eye beheld.
For heav'nly mindes from such distempers foule
Are ever cleer. Whereof hee soon aware,

Each perturbation smooth'd with outward calme,
Artificer of fraud; and was the first
That practisd falshood under saintly shew,
Deep malice to conceale, couch't with revenge.
Milton, Paradise Lost, IV, 114

71 Hard are the ways of truth, and rough to walk.
Milton, Paradise Regained, I, 478

72 And though all the winds of doctrine were let
loose to play upon the earth, so Truth be in the
field, we do injuriously, by licensing and prohibiting, to misdoubt her strength. Let her and Falsehood grapple; who ever knew Truth put to the
worse, in a free and open encounter?
Milton, Areopagitica

73 For who knows not that Truth is strong, next to
the Almighty? She needs no policies, nor stratagems, nor licensings to make her victorious; those
are the shifts and the defences that error uses
against her power. Give her but room, and do not
bind her when she sleeps, for then she speaks not
true.
Milton, Areopagitica

74 He who has a true idea knows at the same time
that he has a true idea, nor can he doubt the truth
of the thing. . . . For no one who has a true idea
is ignorant that a true idea involves the highest
certitude; to have a true idea signifying just this,
to know a thing perfectly or as well as possible. No
one, in fact, can doubt this, unless he supposes an
idea to be something dumb, like a picture on a
tablet, instead of being a mode of thought, that is
to say, intelligence itself. Moreover, I ask who can
know that he understands a thing unless he first of
all understands that thing? that is to say, who can
know that he is certain of anything unless he is
first of all certain of that thing? Then, again, what
can be clearer or more certain than a true idea as
the standard of truth? Just as light reveals both
itself and the darkness, so truth is the standard of
itself and of the false. I consider what has been
said to be a sufficient answer to the objection that
if a true idea is distinguished from a false idea
only in so far as it is said to agree with that of
which it is the idea, the true idea therefore has no
reality nor perfection above the false idea (since
they are distinguished by an external sign alone),
and consequently the man who has true ideas will
have no greater reality or perfection than he who
has false ideas only. I consider, too, that I have
already replied to those who inquire why men
have false ideas, and how a man can certainly
know that he has ideas which agree with those
things of which they are the ideas. For with regard to the difference between a true and a false
idea, it is evident . . . that the former is related to
the latter as being is to non-being. . . . With regard to . . . how a man can know that he has an

idea which agrees with that of which it is the
idea—I have shown almost more times than
enough that he knows it simply because he has an
idea which agrees with that of which it is the idea,
that is to say, because truth is its own standard.
We must remember, besides, that our mind, in so
far as it truly perceives things, is a part of the
infinite intellect of God, and therefore it must be
that the clear and distinct ideas of the mind are as
true as those of God.
Spinoza, Ethics, II, Prop. 43; Schol.

75 For Truth has such a face and such a mien,
As to be lov'd needs only to be seen.
Dryden, The Hind and the Panther, I, 33

76 There are . . . two kinds of *truths,* those of *reasoning*
and those of *fact.* Truths of reasoning are necessary and their opposite is impossible: truths of fact
are contingent and their opposite is possible.
When a truth is necessary, its reason can be found
by analysis, resolving it into more simple ideas
and truths, until we come to those which are primary.
Leibniz, Monadology, 33

77 The truth certainly would do well enough if she
were once left to shift for herself. She seldom has
received and, I fear, never will receive much assistance from the power of great men, to whom she is
but rarely known and more rarely welcome. She is
not taught by laws, nor has she any need of force
to procure her entrance into the minds of men.
Errors, indeed, prevail by the assistance of foreign
and borrowed succours. But if Truth makes not
her way into the understanding by her own light,
she will be but the weaker for any borrowed force
violence can add to her.
Locke, Letter Concerning Toleration

78 The imputation of Novelty is a terrible charge
amongst those who judge of men's heads, as they
do of their perukes, by the fashion, and can allow
none to be right but the received doctrines. Truth
scarce ever yet carried it by vote anywhere at its
first appearance: new opinions are always suspected, and usually opposed, without any other
reason but because they are not already common.
But truth, like gold, is not the less so for being
newly brought out of the mine. It is trial and examination must give it price, and not any antique
fashion; and though it be not yet current by the
public stamp, yet it may, for all that, be as old as
nature, and is certainly not the less genuine.
Locke, Concerning Human Understanding,
Dedication

79 Though, in compliance with the ordinary way of
speaking, I have shown in what sense and upon
what ground our ideas may be sometimes called
true or false; yet if we will look a little nearer into

the matter, in all cases where any idea is called true or false, it is from some *judgment* that the mind makes, or is supposed to make, that is true or false. For truth or falsehood, being never without some affirmation or negation, express or tacit, it is not to be found but where signs are joined or separated, according to the agreement or disagreement of the things they stand for. The signs we chiefly use are either ideas or words; wherewith we make either mental or verbal propositions. Truth lies in so joining or separating these representatives, as the things they stand for do in themselves agree or disagree; and falsehood in the contrary.

Locke, *Concerning Human Understanding,*
Bk. II, XXXII, 19

80 He that would seriously set upon the search of truth ought in the first place to prepare his mind with a love of it. For he that loves it not will not take much pains to get it; nor be much concerned when he misses it. There is nobody in the commonwealth of learning who does not profess himself a lover of truth: and there is not a rational creature that would not take it amiss to be thought otherwise of. And yet, for all this, one may truly say, that there are very few lovers of truth, for truth's sake, even amongst those who persuade themselves that they are so. How a man may know whether he be so in earnest, is worth inquiry: and I think there is one unerring mark of it, viz. The not entertaining any proposition with greater assurance than the proofs it is built upon will warrant. Whoever goes beyond this measure of assent, it is plain, receives not the truth in the love of it; loves not truth for truth's sake, but for some other bye-end.

Locke, *Concerning Human Understanding,*
Bk. IV, XIX, 1

81 He must surely be either very weak, or very little acquainted with the sciences, who shall reject a truth that is capable of demonstration, for no other reason but because it is newly known, and contrary to the prejudices of mankind.

Berkeley, *Principles of Human Knowledge,* Pref.

82 My master heard me with great appearances of uneasiness in his countenance; because *doubting* or *not believing,* are so little known in this country, that the inhabitants cannot tell how to behave themselves under such circumstances. And I remember in frequent discourses with my master concerning the nature of manhood, in other parts of the world, having occasion to talk of *lying* and *false representation,* it was with much difficulty that he comprehended what I meant; although he had otherwise a most acute judgment. For he argued thus; that the use of speech was to make us understand one another, and to receive information of facts; now if any one *said the thing which was not,* these ends were defeated; because I cannot prop-

erly be said to understand him; and I am so far from receiving information, that he leaves me worse than in ignorance; for I am led to believe a thing *black,* when it is *white;* and *short,* when it is *long.* And these were all the notions he had concerning that faculty of *lying,* so perfectly well understood, and so universally practised among human creatures.

Swift, *Gulliver's Travels,* IV, 4

83 He who tells a lie is not sensible of how great a task he undertakes; for he must be forced to invent twenty more to maintain that one.

Pope, *Thoughts on Various Subjects*

84 There are certain times when most people are in a disposition of being informed, and 'tis incredible what a vast good a little truth might do, spoken in such seasons.

Pope, *Letter to William Wycherley
(June 23, 1705)*

85 'Tis certain we cannot take pleasure in any discourse, where our judgment gives no assent to those images which are presented to our fancy. The conversation of those, who have acquir'd a habit of lying, tho' in affairs of no moment, never gives any satisfaction; and that because those ideas they present to us, not being attended with belief, make no impression upon the mind. Poets themselves, tho' liars by profession, always endeavour to give an air of truth to their fictions; and where that is totally neglected, their performances, however ingenious, will never be able to afford much pleasure. In short, we may observe, that even when ideas have no manner of influence on the will as passions, truth and reality are still requisite, in order to make them entertaining to the imagination.

Hume, *Treatise of Human Nature,* Bk. I, III, 10

86 Reason is the discovery of truth or falshood. Truth or falshood consists in an agreement or disagreement either to the *real* relations of ideas, or to *real* existence and matter of fact. Whatever, therefore, is not susceptible of this agreement or disagreement, is incapable of being true or false, and can never be an object of our reason.

Hume, *Treatise of Human Nature,* Bk. III, I, 1

87 Mr. Allworthy rightly observed, that there was a great difference between being guilty of a falsehood to excuse yourself, and to excuse another.

Fielding, *Tom Jones,* III, 5

88 The elegant Lord Shaftesbury somewhere objects to telling too much truth: by which it may be fairly inferred, that, in some cases, to lie is not only excusable, but commendable.

And surely there are no persons who may so

properly challenge a right to this commendable deviation from truth, as young women in the affair of love; for which they may plead precept, education, and above all, the sanction, nay, I may say the necessity of custom, by which they are restrained, not from submitting to the honest impulses of nature (for that would be a foolish prohibition), but from owning them.

Fielding, *Tom Jones,* XIII, 12

89 Humanly speaking, let us define truth, while waiting for a better definition, as—"a statement of the facts as they are."

Voltaire, *Philosophical Dictionary:* Truth

90 There are truths which are not for all men, nor for all occasions.

Voltaire, *Letter to Cardinal de Bernis* *(Apr. 23, 1761)*

91 Truth is a fruit which should not be plucked until it is quite ripe.

Voltaire, *Letter to Countess de Barcewitz* *(Dec. 24, 1761)*

92 Between falsehood and useless truth there is little difference. As gold which he cannot spend will make no man rich, so knowledge which he cannot apply will make no man wise.

Johnson, *Idler No. 84*

93 "Pilgrimage," said Imlac, "like many other acts of piety, may be reasonable or superstitious, according to the principles upon which it is performed. Long journeys in search of truth are not commanded. Truth, such as is necessary to the regulation of life, is always found where it is honestly sought."

Johnson, *Rasselas,* XI

94 *Goldsmith.* "There are people who tell a hundred political lies every day, and are not hurt by it. Surely, then, one may tell truth with safety." *Johnson.* "Why, Sir, in the first place, he who tells a hundred lies has disarmed the force of his lies. But besides; a man had rather have a hundred lies told of him, than one truth which he does not wish should be told." *Goldsmith.* "For my part, I'd tell truth, and shame the devil." *Johnson.* "Yes, Sir; but the devil will be angry. I wish to shame the devil as much as you do, but I should choose to be out of the reach of his claws." *Goldsmith.* "His claws can do you no harm, when you have the shield of truth."

Boswell, *Life of Johnson (Apr. 15, 1773)*

95 *Johnson.* Nobody has a right to put another under such a difficulty, that he must either hurt the person by telling the truth, or hurt himself by telling what is not true.

Boswell, *Life of Johnson (Apr. 25, 1778)*

96 We talked of the casuistical question, Whether it was allowable at any time to depart from *Truth?* *Johnson.* "The general rule is, that Truth should never be violated, because it is of the utmost importance to the comfort of life, that we should have a full security by mutual faith; and occasional inconveniences should be willingly suffered that we may preserve it. There must, however, be some exceptions. If, for instance, a murderer should ask you which way a man is gone, you may tell him what is not true, because you are under a previous obligation not to betray a man to a murderer. . . . But I deny the lawfulness of telling a lie to a sick man for fear of alarming him. You have no business with consequences; you are to tell the truth. Besides, you are not sure what effect your telling him that he is in danger may have. It may bring his distemper to a crisis, and that may cure him. Of all lying, I have the greatest abhorrence of this, because I believe it has been frequently practised on myself."

I cannot help thinking that there is much weight in the opinion of those who have held, that Truth, as an eternal and immutable principle, ought, upon no account whatever, to be violated, from supposed previous or superiour obligations, of which every man being to judge for himself, there is great danger that we too often, from partial motives, persuade ourselves that they exist; and probably whatever extraordinary instances may sometimes occur, where some evil may be prevented by violating this noble principle, it would be found that human happiness would, upon the whole, be more perfect were Truth universally preserved.

Boswell, *Life of Johnson (June 13, 1784)*

97 The protestant and philosophic readers of the present age will incline to believe that, in the account of his own conversion, Constantine attested a wilful falsehood by a solemn and deliberate perjury. They may not hesitate to pronounce that, in the choice of a religion, his mind was determined only by a sense of interest; and that . . . he used the altars of the church as a convenient footstool to the throne of the empire. A conclusion so harsh and so absolute is not, however, warranted by our knowledge of human nature, of Constantine, or of Christianity. In an age of religious fervour the most artful statesmen are observed to feel some part of the enthusiasm which they inspire; and the most orthodox saints assume the dangerous privilege of defending the cause of truth by the arms of deceit and falsehood. Personal interest is often the standard of our belief, as well as of our practice; and the same motives of temporal advantage which might influence the public conduct and professions of Constantine would insensibly dispose his mind to embrace a religion so propitious to his fame and fortunes. His vanity was gratified by the flattering assurance that *he* had

been chosen by Heaven to reign over the earth: success had justified his divine title to the throne, and that title was founded on the truth of the Christian revelation. As real virtue is sometimes excited by undeserved applause, the specious piety of Constantine, if at first it was only specious, might gradually, by the influence of praise, of habit, and of example, be matured into serious faith and fervent devotion.

Gibbon, *Decline and Fall of the Roman Empire,* XX

98 It is a humiliating consideration for human reason that it is incompetent to discover truth by means of pure speculation, but, on the contrary, stands in need of discipline to check its deviations from the straight path and to expose the illusions which it originates. But, on the other hand, this consideration ought to elevate and to give it confidence, for this discipline is exercised by itself alone, and it is subject to the censure of no other power. The bounds, moreover, which it is forced to set to its speculative exercise, form likewise a check upon the fallacious pretensions of opponents; and thus what remains of its possessions, after these exaggerated claims have been disallowed, is secure from attack or usurpation. The greatest, and perhaps the only, use of all philosophy of pure reason is, accordingly, of a purely negative character. It is not an organon for the extension, but a discipline for the determination, of the limits of its exercise; and without laying claim to the discovery of new truth, it has the modest merit of guarding against error.

Kant, *Critique of Pure Reason,* Transcendental Method

99 Truth can never be told so as to be understood, and not be believ'd.

Blake, *Marriage of Heaven and Hell,* 10

100 Veracity does not consist in saying, but in the intention of communicating, truth.

Coleridge, *Biographia Literaria,* IX

101 And, after all, what is a lie? 'T is but
The truth in masquerade; and I defy
Historians, heroes, lawyers, priests, to put
A fact without some leaven of a lie.

Byron, *Don Juan,* XI, 37

102 'Tis strange,—but true; for truth is always strange;
Stranger than fiction; if it could be told,
How much would novels gain by the exchange!
How differently the world would men behold!

Byron, *Don Juan,* XIV, 101

103 Truth is most beautiful undraped; and the impression it makes is deep in proportion as its expression has been simple. This is so partly because

it then takes unobstructed possession of the hearer's whole soul, and leaves him no by-thought to distract him; partly, also, because he feels that here he is not being corrupted or cheated by the arts of rhetoric, but that all the effect of what is said comes from the thing itself.

Schopenhauer, *Some Forms of Literature*

104 If you have reason to suspect that a person is telling you a lie, look as though you believed every word he said. This will give him courage to go on; he will become more vehement in his assertions, and in the end betray himself.

Schopenhauer, *Our Relation to Others*

105 The true must essentially be regarded as in conflict with this world; the world has never been so good, and will never become so good, that the majority will desire the truth, or have the true conception of it in such a way that its proclamation must consequently immediately gain the support of everyone. No, he who will proclaim some truth in truth, must prepare himself in some other way than by the help of such a foolish expectation; he must be willing essentially to relinquish the immediate.

Kierkegaard, *Works of Love,* II, 10

106 Truth is such a fly-away, such a sly-boots, so untransportable and unbarrelable a commodity, that it is as bad to catch as light.

Emerson, *Literary Ethics*

107 The soul is the perceiver and revealer of truth. We know truth when we see it, let sceptic and scoffer say what they choose. Foolish people ask you, when you have spoken what they do not wish to hear, 'How do you know it is truth, and not an error of your own?' We know truth when we see it, from opinion, as we know when we are awake that we are awake. . . . We are wiser than we know.

Emerson, *The Over-Soul*

108 God offers to every mind its choice between truth and repose. Take which you please—you can never have both.

Emerson, *Intellect*

109 "Jonah did the Almighty's bidding. And what was that, shipmates? To preach the truth to the face of Falsehood! That was it!

"This, shipmates, this is that other lesson; and woe to that pilot of the living God who slights it. Woe to him whom this world charms from Gospel duty! Woe to him who seeks to pour oil upon the waters when God has brewed them into a gale! Woe to him who seeks to please rather than to appal! Woe to him whose good name is more to him than goodness! Woe to him who, in this world, courts not dishonour! Woe to him who would not be true, even though to be false were salvation! Yea, woe to him who, as the great Pilot Paul has it, while preaching to others is himself a castaway!"

He dropped and fell away from himself for a moment; then lifting his face to them again, showed a deep joy in his eyes, as he cried out with a heavenly enthusiasm,—"but oh! shipmates! on the starboard hand of every woe, there is a sure delight; and higher the top of that delight, than the botton of the woe is deep. Is not the maintruck higher than the kelson is low? Delight is to him— a far, far upward, and inward delight—who against the proud gods and commodores of this earth, ever stands forth his own inexorable self. Delight is to him whose strong arms yet support him, when the ship of this base treacherous world has gone down beneath him. Delight is to him, who gives no quarter in the truth, and kill, burns, and destroys all sin though he pluck it out from under the robes of Senators and Judges. Delight,—top-gallant delight is to him, who acknowledges no law or lord, but the Lord his God, and is only a patriot to heaven. Delight is to him, whom all the waves of the billows of the seas of the boisterous mob can never shake from this sure Keel of the Ages. And eternal delight and deliciousness will be his, who coming to lay him down, can say with his final breath—O Father!— chiefly known to me by Thy rod—mortal or immortal, here I die. I have striven to be Thine, more than to be this world's, or mine own. Yet this is nothing; I leave eternity to Thee; for what is man that he should live out the lifetime of his God?"

Melville, *Moby Dick,* IX

110 The symmetry of form attainable in pure fiction cannot so readily be achieved in a narration essentially having less to do with fable than with fact. Truth uncompromisingly told will always have its ragged edges; hence the conclusion of such a narration is apt to be less finished than an architectural finial.

Melville, *Billy Budd*

111 The wildest dreams of wild men, even, are not the less true, though they may not recommend themselves to the sense which is most common among Englishmen and Americans to-day. It is not every truth that recommends itself to the common sense. Nature has a place for the wild clematis as well as for the cabbage. Some expressions of truth are reminiscent,—others merely *sensible,* as the phrase is,—others prophetic.

Thoreau, *Walking*

112 No face which we can give to a matter will stead us so well at last as the truth. This alone wears well. For the most part, we are not where we are, but in a false position. Through an infirmity of our natures, we suppose a case, and put ourselves into it, and hence are in two cases at the same time, and it is doubly difficult to get out. In sane moments we regard only the facts, the case that is. Say what you have to say, not what you ought. Any truth is better than make-believe.

Thoreau, *Walden:* Conclusion

113 If some great Power would agree to make me always think what is true and do what is right, on condition of being turned into a sort of clock and wound up every morning before I got out of bed, I should instantly close with the offer.

T. H. Huxley, *Descartes' "Discourse on Method"*

114 History warns us . . . that it is the customary fate of new truths to begin as heresies and to end as superstitions.

T. H. Huxley, *The Coming of Age of "The Origin of Species"*

115 Time, whose tooth gnaws away everything else, is powerless against truth.

T. H. Huxley, *Administrative Nihilism*

116 It is a piece of idle sentimentality that truth, merely as truth, has any inherent power denied to error of prevailing against the dungeon and the stake. Men are not more zealous for truth than they often are for error, and a sufficient application of legal or even of social penalties will generally succeed in stopping the propagation of either. The real advantage which truth has consists in this, that when an opinion is true, it may be extinguished once, twice, or many times, but in the course of ages there will generally be found persons to rediscover it, until some one of its reappearances falls on a time when from favourable circumstances it escapes persecution until it has made such head as to withstand all subsequent attempts to suppress it.

Mill, *On Liberty,* II

117 No one can be a great thinker who does not recognise, that as a thinker it is his first duty to follow his intellect to whatever conclusions it may lead. Truth gains more even by the errors of one who, with due study and preparation, thinks for himself, than by the true opinions of those who only hold them because they do not suffer themselves to think. Not that it is solely, or chiefly, to form great thinkers, that freedom of thinking is required. On the contrary, it is as much and even more indispensable to enable average human beings to attain the mental stature which they are capable of. There have been, and may again be, great individual thinkers in a general atmosphere of mental slavery. But there never has been, nor ever will be, in that atmosphere an intellectually active people. Where any people has made a tem-

porary approach to such a character, it has been because the dread of heterodox speculation was for a time suspended. Where there is a tacit convention that principles are not to be disputed; where the discussion of the greatest questions which can occupy humanity is considered to be closed, we cannot hope to find that generally high scale of mental activity which has made some periods of history so remarkable.

Mill, *On Liberty,* II

118 On every subject on which difference of opinion is possible, the truth depends on a balance to be struck between two sets of conflicting reasons.

Mill, *On Liberty,* II

119 Truth, in the great practical concerns of life, is so much a question of the reconciling and combining of opposites, that very few have minds sufficiently capacious and impartial to make the adjustment with an approach to correctness, and it has to be made by the rough process of a struggle between combatants fighting under hostile banners.

Mill, *On Liberty,* II

120 The essence of lying is in deception, not in words; a lie may be told by silence, by equivocation, by the accent on a syllable, by a glance of the eye attaching a peculiar significance to a sentence; and all these kinds of lies are worse and baser by many degrees than a lie plainly worded; so that no form of blinded conscience is so far sunk as that which comforts itself for having deceived, because the deception was by gesture or silence, instead of utterance; and, finally, according to Tennyson's deep and trenchant line, "A lie which is half a truth is ever the worst of lies."

Ruskin, *Modern Painters,* Pt. IX, 7

121 "I should never dare to say that I know the truth," said the Mason, whose words struck Pierre more and more by their precision and firmness. "No one can attain to truth by himself. Only by laying stone on stone with the cooperation of all, by the millions of generations from our forefather Adam to our own times, is that temple reared which is to be a worthy dwelling place of the Great God," he added, and closed his eyes.

Tolstoy, *War and Peace,* V, 2

122 If we would only stop lying, if we would only testify to the truth as we see it, it would turn out at once that there are hundreds, thousands, even millions of men just as we are, who see the truth as we do, are afraid as we are of seeming to be singular by confessing it, and are only waiting, again as we are, for some one to proclaim it.

Tolstoy, *The Kingdom of God Is Within You*

123 The person who confesses that there is such a thing as truth, which is distinguished from false-

hood simply by this, that if acted on it should, on full consideration, carry us to the point we aim at and not astray, and then, though convinced of this, dares not know the truth and seeks to avoid it, is in a sorry state of mind indeed.

C. S. Peirce, *Fixation of Belief*

124 Truths, on the average, have a greater tendency to get believed than falsities have. Were it otherwise, considering that there are myriads of false hypotheses to account for any given phenomenon, against one sole true one (or if you will have it so, against every true one), the first step toward genuine knowledge must have been next door to a miracle.

C. S. Peirce, *What Pragmatism Means*

125 You don't know about me without you have read a book by the name of *The Adventures of Tom Sawyer;* but that ain't no matter. That book was made by Mr. Mark Twain, and he told the truth, mainly. There was things which he stretched, but mainly he told the truth. That is nothing. I never seen anybody but lied one time or another.

Mark Twain, *Huckleberry Finn,* I

126 One of the most striking differences between a cat and a lie is that a cat has only nine lives.

Mark Twain, *Pudd'nhead Wilson's Calendar,* VII

127 When in doubt tell the truth.

Mark Twain, *Pudd'nhead Wilson's New Calendar,* II

128 The most common lie is the lie one tells to oneself; lying to others is relatively the exception.

Nietzsche, *Antichrist,* LV

129 Hands off: neither the whole of truth nor the whole of good is revealed to any single observer, although each observer gains a partial superiority of insight from the peculiar position in which he stands. Even prisons and sickrooms have their special revelations. It is enough to ask of each of us that he should be faithful to his own opportunities and make the most of his own blessings, without presuming to regulate the rest of the vast field.

William James, *On a Certain Blindness in Human Beings*

130 Our belief in truth itself, for instance, that there is a truth, and that our minds and it are made for each other—what is it but a passionate affirmation of desire, in which our social system backs us up? We want to have a truth; we want to believe that our experiments and studies and discussions must put us in a continually better and better position towards it; and on this line we agree to fight out our thinking lives. But if a Pyrrhonistic skeptic asks us *how we know* all this, can our logic find

a reply? No! certainly it cannot. It is just one volition against another—we willing to go in for life upon a trust or assumption which he, for his part, does not care to make.

William James, *The Will to Believe*

131 *The true is the name of whatever proves itself to be good in the way of belief, and good, too, for definite, assignable reasons.* Surely you must admit this, that if there were *no* good for life in true ideas, or if the knowledge of them were positively disadvantageous and false ideas the only useful ones, then the current notion that truth is divine and precious, and its pursuit a duty, could never have grown up or become a dogma. In a world like that, our duty would be to *shun* truth, rather. But in this world, just as certain foods are not only agreeable to our taste, but good for our teeth, our stomach, and our tissues; so certain ideas are not only agreeable to think about, or agreeable as supporting other ideas that we are fond of, but they are also helpful in life's practical struggles. If there be any life that it is really better we should lead, and if there be any idea which, if believed in, would help us to lead that life, then it would be really *better for us* to believe in that idea, *unless, indeed, belief in it incidentally clashed with other greater vital benefits.*

"What would be better for us to believe!" This sounds very like a definition of truth. It comes very near to saying "what we *ought* to believe": and in *that* definition none of you would find any oddity. Ought we ever not to believe what it is *better for us* to believe? And can we then keep the notion of what is better for us, and what is true for us, permanently apart?

Pragmatism says no, and I fully agree with her.

William James, *Pragmatism*, II

132 New truths thus are resultants of new experiences and of old truths combined and mutually modifying one another. And since this is the case in the changes of opinion of today, there is no reason to assume that it has not been so at all times. It follows that very ancient modes of thought may have survived through all the later changes in men's opinions. The most primitive ways of thinking may not yet be wholly expunged. Like our five fingers, our ear bones, our rudimentary caudal appendage, or our other 'vestigial' peculiarities, they may remain as indelible tokens of events in our race history. Our ancestors may at certain moments have struck into ways of thinking which they might conceivably not have found. But once they did so, and after the fact, the inheritance continues. When you begin a piece of music in a certain key, you must keep the key to the end. You may alter your house ad libitum, but the ground plan of the first architect persists—you can make great changes, but you cannot change a Gothic church into a Doric temple. You may rinse and rinse the bottle, but you can't get the taste of the medicine or whiskey that first filled it wholly out.

My thesis now is this, that *our fundamental ways of thinking about things are discoveries of exceedingly remote ancestors, which have been able to preserve themselves throughout the experience of all subsequent time.* They form one great stage of equilibrium in the human mind's development, the stage of *common sense.* Other stages have grafted themselves upon this stage, but have never succeeded in displacing it.

William James, *Pragmatism*, V

133 Pragmatism . . . asks its usual question. "Grant an idea or belief to be true," it says, "what concrete difference will its being true make in anyone's actual life? How will the truth be realized? What experiences will be different from those which would obtain if the belief were false? What, in short, is the truth's cash value in experiential terms?"

The moment pragmatism asks this question, it sees the answer: *True ideas are those that we can assimilate, validate, corroborate, and verify. False ideas are those that we cannot.* That is the practical difference it makes to us to have true ideas; that, therefore, is the meaning of truth, for it is all that truth is known as.

William James, *Pragmatism*, VI

134 *'The true,'* to put it very briefly, is only the expedient in the way of our thinking, just as 'the right' is only the expedient in the way of our behaving. Expedient in almost any fashion; and expedient in the long run and on the whole of course; for what meets expediently all the experience in sight won't necessarily meet all farther experiences equally satisfactorily. Experience, as we know, has ways of *boiling over,* and making us correct our present formulas.

The 'absolutely' true, meaning what no farther experience will ever alter, is that ideal vanishing point toward which we imagine that all our temporary truths will some day converge. It runs on all fours with the perfectly wise man, and with the absolutely complete experience; and, if these ideals are ever realized, they will all be realized together. Meanwhile we have to live today by what truth we can get today, and be ready tomorrow to call it falsehood. Ptolemaic astronomy, Euclidean space, Aristotelian logic, scholastic metaphysics, were expedient for centuries, but human experience has boiled over those limits, and we now call these things only relatively true, or true within those borders of experience. 'Absolutely' they are false; for we know that those limits were casual, and might have been transcended by past theorists just as they are by present thinkers.

William James, *Pragmatism*, VI

135 *The* Truth: what a perfect idol of the rationalistic mind! I read in an old letter—from a gifted friend who died too young—these words: "In everything,

in science, art, morals, and religion, there *must* be one system that is right and *every* other wrong." How characteristic of the enthusiasm of a certain stage of youth! At twenty-one we rise to such a challenge and expect to find the system. It never occurs to most of us even later that the question "what is *the* truth?" is no real question (being irrelative to all conditions) and that the whole notion of *the* truth is an abstraction from the fact of truths in the plural, a mere useful summarizing phrase like *the* Latin Language or *the* Law.

William James, *Pragmatism*, VII

136 The search for truth should be the goal of our activities; it is the sole end worthy of them. Doubtless we should first bend our efforts to assuage human suffering, but why? Not to suffer is a negative ideal more surely attained by the annihilation of the world. If we wish more and more to free man from material cares, it is that he may be able to employ the liberty obtained in the study and contemplation of truth.

But sometimes truth frightens us. And in fact we know that it is sometimes deceptive, that it is a phantom never showing itself for a moment except to ceaselessly flee, that it must be pursued further and ever further without ever being attained. Yet to work one must stop, as some Greek, Aristotle or another, has said. We also know how cruel the truth often is, and we wonder whether illusion is not more consoling, yea, even more bracing, for illusion it is which gives confidence. When it shall have vanished, will hope remain and shall we have the courage to achieve? Thus would not the horse harnessed to his treadmill refuse to go, were his eyes not bandaged? And then to seek truth it is necessary to be independent, wholly independent. If, on the contrary, we wish to act, to be strong, we should be united. This is why many of us fear truth; we consider it a cause of weakness. Yet truth should not be feared, for it alone is beautiful.

When I speak here of truth, assuredly I refer first to scientific truth; but I also mean moral truth, of which what we call justice is only one aspect. It may seem that I am misusing words, that I combine thus under the same name two things having nothing in common; that scientific truth, which is demonstrated, can in no way be likened to moral truth, which is felt. And yet I can not separate them, and whosoever loves the one can not help loving the other. To find the one, as well as to find the other, it is necessary to free the soul completely from prejudice and from passion; it is necessary to attain absolute sincerity. These two sorts of truth when discovered give the same joy; each when perceived beams with the same splendor, so that we must see it or close our eyes. Lastly, both attract us and flee from us; they are never fixed: when we think to have reached them, we find that we have still to advance, and he who

pursues them is condemned never to know repose. It must be added that those who fear the one will also fear the other; for they are the ones who in everything are concerned above all with consequences. In a word, I liken the two truths, because the same reasons make us love them and because the same reasons make us fear them.

Poincaré, *Value of Science*, Intro.

137 Truth telling is not compatible with the defence of the realm.

Shaw, *Heartbreak House*, Pref.

138 *Keegan.* My way of joking is to tell the truth. It's the funniest joke in the world.

Shaw, *John Bull's Other Island*, II

139 Truth is a qualification which applies to Appearance alone. Reality is just itself, and it is nonsense to ask whether it be true or false. Truth is the conformation of Appearance to Reality. This conformation may be more or less, also direct or indirect. Thus Truth is a generic quality with a variety of degrees and modes. In the Law-Courts, the wrong species of Truth may amount to perjury. For example, a portrait may be so faithful as to deceive the eye. Its very truthfulness then amounts to deception. A reflexion in a mirror is at once a truthful appearance and a deceptive appearance. The smile of a hypocrite is deceptive, and that of a philanthropist may be truthful. But both of them were truly smiling.

Whitehead, *Adventures of Ideas*, XVI, 2

140 Every belief which is not merely an impulse to action is in the nature of a picture, combined with a yes-feeling or a no-feeling; in the case of a yes-feeling it is "true" if there is a fact having to the picture the kind of similarity that a prototype has to an image; in the case of a no-feeling it is "true" if there is no such fact. A belief which is not true is called "false."

This is a definition of "truth" and "falsehood."

Russell, *Human Knowledge*, II, 11

141 The most mordant verities are heard at last, after the interests they injure and the emotions they rouse have exhausted their frenzy.

Freud, *Future of Psycho-Analytic Therapy*

142 The simplest explanation is not always the right one, truth is very often not simple.

Freud, *New Introductory Lectures on Psycho-Analysis*, XXX

143 The ordinary man knows only one *truth*—truth in the ordinary sense of the word. What may be meant by a higher, or a highest, truth, he cannot imagine. Truth seems to him as little capable of having degrees as death, and the necessary leap from the beautiful to the true is one that he can-

not make. Perhaps you will agree with me in thinking that he is right in this.

Freud, *New Introductory Lectures on Psycho-Analysis*, **XXXV**

144 For ordinary purposes, that is for practical purposes, the truth and the realness of things are synonymous. We are all children who say "really and truly." A reality which is taken in organic response so as to lead to subsequent reactions that are off the track and aside from the mark, while it is, existentially speaking, perfectly real, is not *good* reality. It lacks the hallmark of value. Since it is a certain *kind* of object which we want, one which will be as favorable as possible to a consistent and liberal or growing functioning, it is this kind, the *true* kind, which for us monopolizes the title of reality. Pragmatically, teleologically, this identification of truth and "reality" is sound and reasonable: rationalistically, it leads to the notion of the duplicate versions of reality, one absolute and static because exhausted; the other phenomenal and kept continually on the jump because otherwise its own inherent nothingness would lead to its total annihilation. Since it is only genuine or sincere things, things which are good for what they lay claim to in the way of consequences, which we want or are after, *morally* they alone are "real."

Dewey, *Practical Character of Reality*

145 To generalize the recognition that the true means the verified and means nothing else places upon men the responsibility for surrendering political and moral dogmas, and subjecting to the test of consequences their most cherished prejudices. Such a change involves a great change in the seat of authority and the methods of decision in society.

Dewey, *Reconstruction in Philosophy*, **VI**

146 An a priori true thought would be one whose possibility guaranteed its truth.

We could only know a priori that a thought is true if its truth was to be recognized from the thought itself (without an object of comparison).

Wittgenstein, *Tractatus Logico-Philosophicus*, 3.04–3.05

147 What is the function of philosophy? To disclose the absolute truth? But is it credible that the absolute truth should descend into the thoughts of a mortal creature, equipped with a few special senses and with a biassed intellect, a man lost amidst millions of his fellows and a prey to the epidemic delusions of the race? Possession of the absolute truth is not merely by accident beyond the range of particular minds; it is incompatible with being alive, because it excludes any particular station, organ, interest, or date of survey: the absolute truth is undiscoverable just because it is not a perspective. Perspectives are essential to animal apprehension; an observer, himself a part of the world he observes, must have a particular station in it; he cannot be equally near to everything, nor internal to anything but himself; of the rest he can only take views, abstracted according to his sensibility and foreshortened according to his interests. Those animals which I was supposing endowed with an adequate philosophy surely do not possess the absolute truth. They read nature in their private idioms. Their imagination, like the human, is doubtless incapable of coping with all things at once, or even with the whole of anything natural. Mind was not created for the sake of discovering the absolute truth. The absolute truth has its own intangible reality, and scorns to be known.

Santayana, *Realms of Being*, Pref.

148 Not the assertion as a psychological fact is true, but only that which it asserts: and the difference in quality and value between true ideas and false ideas, taken as states of mind, is a moral difference: the true ideas being safer and probably clearer and more humorous than the false, and marking a success on the mind's part in understanding the world, whereas false ideas would mark a failure.

Santayana, *Realm of Truth*, **V**

149 Truth is . . . not discoverable at all without some vital moral impulse prompting to survey it, and some rhetorical or grammatical faculty, synthesizing that survey and holding it up to attention in the form of a recognizable essence. Dramatic myth, however poetical it may be or merely analogous to the facts, in that at least it responds to the facts reflectively, has entered the arena of truth; it is more cognitive, more intelligent, and more useful than a mechanical record of those facts without any moral synthesis. I think it very doubtful whether, if religion and poetry should dry up altogether, mankind would be nearer the truth; or whether science would gain anything by correcting its philosophical pretensions, for instance the pretension to truth, in order to become merely the technology of the mechanical arts. Certainly nothing would be gained intellectually: and if we condemned intelligence, as well as imagination, to ticking like a clock, if not to total silence, we might outrage human nature too deeply, and provoke a violent reaction. It is more prudent for the critic of illusion to consider the truth that myth may possess rather than to attempt to escape from myth altogether.

Santayana, *Realm of Truth*, **VII**

150 The love of truth is often mentioned, the hatred of truth hardly ever, yet the latter is the commoner. People say they love the truth when they pursue it, and they pursue it when unknown: not therefore because of any felt affinity to it in their souls,

but probably because they need information for practical purposes, or to solve some conventional riddle. Where known, on the contrary, truth is almost always dismissed or disguised, because the aspect of it is hateful. And this apart from any devilish perversity in the natural man, or accidental vices that may fear the light. On the contrary, the cause is rather the natural man's innocence and courage in thinking himself the measure of all things. Life imposes selfish interests and subjective views on every inhabitant of earth: and in hugging these interests and these views the man hugs what he initially assumes to be the truth and the right. So that aversion from the real truth, a sort of antecedent hatred of it as contrary to presumption, is interwoven into the very fabric of thought.

Santayana, *Realm of Truth*, XII

151 There is no difficulty in understanding what is meant by the notion of *truth*. What is a true or truthful word? A word which expresses, as it really is, the speaker's thought; a word in conformity with that thought. What, then, is a true thought? A thought which represents, as it really is, the thing to which it refers; a thought in conformity

with that thing. We therefore conclude that *truth in the mind* consists in its *conformity with the thing*.

It is impossible to define truth otherwise without lying to ourselves, without falsifying the notion of truth of which in practice we make use, in the living exercise of our intelligence, each time that we think.

We may further remark that a thought false in all its constituents is an impossibility for, being in conformity with nothing whatsoever, it would be the zero of thought. If, for instance, I affirm that *stones have a soul,* this is undoubtedly a complete error. But it is true that stones exist, true also that certain beings have a soul; that is to say, all the constituents which compose this false thought are not false. Therefore error itself presupposes truth.

Maritain, *Introduction to Philosophy*, II, 4

152 All views are only probable, and a doctrine of probability which is not bound to a truth dissolves into thin air. In order to describe the probable, you must have a firm hold on the true. Therefore, before there can be any truth whatsoever, there must be an absolute truth.

Sartre, *Existentialism*

6.4 | *Error, Ignorance, and the Limits of Human Knowledge*

The mind that is in error about a certain matter and the mind that is ignorant of it are both in want of knowledge, but they do not stand in the same relation to the knowledge that they lack. To be in error is to claim to know what one does not know. It is, therefore, an unacknowledged ignorance of the matter in question, combined with a false presumption. In contrast, ignorance is simply a privation of knowledge unaccompanied by any pretension to know. Hence, from the point of view of the teacher, as Socrates suggests, ignorance is preferable to error, and especially an acknowledged igno-

rance—an explicit recognition that one does not know.

The passages collected here ring all the changes on these states of mind and point out their implications not only for teaching and learning, but also for the development of knowledge itself. On any point in question, there can be a multiplicity of errors all opposed to a single truth; and the sources or causes of error are also multitudinous. Writers such as Descartes and Bacon, who are concerned with rules for the proper conduct of the mind's efforts in seeking knowledge, therefore undertake to specify the pitfalls and stumbling blocks that must be avoided in order to steer clear of error.

Error, manifesting the fallibility of the human mind, and ignorance, betokening its failure to know, enter into the consideration of the question concerning the limits of human knowledge, discussed in a number of the quotations assembled here. What is the line that divides the unknown from the unknowable? Is the unknowable unknowable in itself or only to us because of the weakness of our intellects? Can the mind establish for itself the boundaries of attainable knowledge, and safeguard itself against the illusory pursuit of the unknowable beyond those borders? To questions of this sort, the writers quoted offer an interesting diversity of answers.

---

1 *Agamemnon.* Delusion is the elder daughter of Zeus,
    the accursed
who deludes all; her feet are delicate and they
    step not
on the firm earth, but she walks the air above
    men's heads
and leads them astray.

                Homer, *Iliad,* XIX, 91

2 *Teiresias.*   All men may err
but error once committed, he's no fool
nor yet unfortunate, who gives up his stiffness
and cures the trouble he has fallen in.
Stubbornness and stupidity are twins.

              Sophocles, *Antigone,* 1023

3 *Ajax.* Not knowing anything's the sweetest life—
Ignorance is an evil free from pain.

              Sophocles, *Ajax,* 554

4 *Diotima.* Herein is the evil of ignorance, that he who is neither good nor wise is nevertheless satisfied with himself: he has no desire for that of which he feels no want.

              Plato, *Symposium,* 204A

5 *Socrates.* Do you see, Meno, what advances he [the slave boy] has made in his power of recollection? He did not know at first, and he does not know now, what is the side of a figure of eight feet: but then he thought that he knew, and answered confidently as if he knew, and had no difficulty; now he has a difficulty, and neither knows nor fancies that he knows.

  Meno. True.

  Soc. Is he not better off in knowing his ignorance?

  Men. I think that he is.

  Soc. If we have made him doubt, and given him the "torpedo's shock," have we done him any harm?

  Men. I think not.

  Soc. We have certainly, as would seem, assisted him in some degree to the discovery of the truth; and now he will wish to remedy his ignorance, but then he would have been ready to tell all the world again and again that the double space should have a double side.

  Men. True.

  Soc. But do you suppose that he would ever have enquired into or learned what he fancied that he knew, though he was really ignorant of it, until he had fallen into perplexity under the idea that he did not know, and had desired to know?

  Men. I think not, Socrates.

  Soc. Then he was the better for the torpedo's touch?

  Men. I think so.

              Plato, *Meno,* 84A

6 *Socrates.* I am going to explain to you why I have such an evil name. When I heard the answer, I said to myself, What can the god mean? and what is the interpretation of his riddle? for I know that I have no wisdom, small or great. What then can he mean when he says that I am the wisest of men? And yet he is a god, and cannot lie; that would be against his nature. After long consideration, I thought of a method of trying the question. I reflected that if I could only find a man wiser than myself, then I might go to the god with a refutation in my hand. I should say to him, "Here is a man who is wiser than I am; but you said that I was the wisest." Accordingly I went to one who had the reputation of wisdom, and observed him—his name I need not mention; he was a politician whom I selected for examination—and the result was as follows: When I began to talk with him, I could not help thinking that he was not really wise, although he was thought wise by many, and still wiser by himself; and thereupon I tried to explain to him that he thought himself wise, but was not really wise; and the consequence was that he hated me, and his enmity was shared by several who were present and heard me. So I left him, saying to myself, as I went away: Well, although I do not suppose that either of us knows anything really beautiful and good, I am better off than he is,—for he knows nothing, and thinks that he knows; I neither know nor

think that I know. In this latter particular, then, I seem to have slightly the advantage of him. Then I went to another who had still higher pretensions to wisdom, and my conclusion was exactly the same. Whereupon I made another enemy of him, and of many others besides him.

Then I went to one man after another, being not unconscious of the enmity which I provoked, and I lamented and feared this: But necessity was laid upon me,—the word of God, I thought, ought to be considered first. And I said to myself, Go I must to all who appear to know, and find out the meaning of the oracle. And I swear to you, Athenians, by the dog I swear!—for I must tell you the truth—the result of my mission was just this: I found that the men most in repute were all but the most foolish; and that others less esteemed were really wiser and better. I will tell you the tale of my wanderings and of the "Herculean" labours, as I may call them, which I endured only to find at last the oracle irrefutable. After the politicians, I went to the poets; tragic, dithyrambic, and all sorts. And there, I said to myself, you will be instantly detected; now you will find out that you are more ignorant than they are. Accordingly, I took them some of the most elaborate passages in their own writings, and asked what was the meaning of them—thinking that they would teach me something. Will you believe me? I am almost ashamed to confess the truth, but I must say that there is hardly a person present who would not have talked better about their poetry than they did themselves. Then I knew that not by wisdom do poets write poetry, but by a sort of genius and inspiration; they are like diviners or soothsayers who also say many fine things, but do not understand the meaning of them. The poets appeared to me to be much in the same case; and I further observed that upon the strength of their poetry they believed themselves to be the wisest of men in other things in which they were not wise. So I departed, conceiving myself to be superior to them for the same reason that I was superior to the politicians.

At last I went to the artisans, for I was conscious that I knew nothing at all, as I may say, and I was sure that they knew many fine things; and here I was not mistaken, for they did know many things of which I was ignorant, and in this they certainly were wiser than I was. But I observed that even the good artisans fell into the same error as the poets;—because they were good workmen they thought that they also knew all sorts of high matters, and this defect in them overshadowed their wisdom; and therefore I asked myself on behalf of the oracle, whether I would like to be as I was, neither having their knowledge nor their ignorance, or like them in both; and I made answer to myself and to the oracle that I was better off as I was.

Plato, *Apology,* 21A

7 Ignorance—defined not as the negation of knowledge but as a positive state of mind—is error produced by inference.

Aristotle, *Posterior Analytics,* 79ᵇ23

8 The very limit of human blindness is to glory in being blind.

Augustine, *Confessions,* III, 3

9 It is clear that as regards its proper object the intellect is always true; and hence it is never deceived of itself, but whatever deception occurs must be ascribed to some lower power, such as the imagination or the like. Hence we see that when the natural power of judgment is free we are not deceived by such images, but only when it is not free, as is the case in sleep.

Aquinas, *Summa Theologica,* I, 94, 4

10 O Juvenal, how truly thou didst say,
The people never know for what they seek,
For what they want seems right in every way,
And clouds of error ever render weak
Their judgments, in what'er they do or speak.

Chaucer, *Troilus and Cressida,* IV, 29

11 O January, what might it now avail
Could your eyes see as far as ships can sail?
For it's as pleasant, blind, deceived to be
As be deceived while yet a man may see.
Lo, Argus, who was called the hundred-eyed,
No matter how he peered and watched and pried,
He was deceived; and God knows others too
Who think, and firmly, that it is not so.
Oblivion is peace; I say no more.

Chaucer, *Canterbury Tales:* Merchant's Tale

12 It may be said with some plausibility that there is an abecedarian ignorance that comes before knowledge, and another, doctoral ignorance that comes after knowledge: an ignorance that knowledge creates and engenders, just as it undoes and destroys the first.

Montaigne, *Essays,* I, 54, Of Vain Subtleties

13 Do you want a man to be healthy, do you want him disciplined and firmly and securely poised? Wrap him in darkness, idleness, and dullness. We must become like the animals in order to become wise, and be blinded in order to be guided.

Montaigne, *Essays,* II, 12,
Apology for Raymond Sebond

14 As by simplicity life becomes pleasanter, so also does it become better and more innocent, as I was starting to say a while back. The simple and ignorant, says Saint Paul, raise themselves to heaven, and take possession of it; and we, with all our learning, plunge ourselves into the infernal abyss.

Montaigne, *Essays,* II, 12,
Apology for Raymond Sebond

15 Many abuses are engendered in the world, or, to put it more boldly, all the abuses in the world are engendered, by our being taught to be afraid of professing our ignorance and our being bound to accept everything that we cannot refute.

Montaigne, *Essays,* III, 11, Of Cripples

16 Anyone who wants to be cured of ignorance must confess it. . . . Wonder is the foundation of all philosophy, inquiry its progress, ignorance its end. I'll go further: There is a certain strong and generous ignorance that concedes nothing to knowledge in honor and courage, an ignorance that requires no less knowledge to conceive it than does knowledge.

Montaigne, *Essays,* III, 11, Of Cripples

17 The human soul uses reason, sees many things, investigates many more; but, however well equipped, it gets light and the beginnings of knowledge from the outer senses, as from beyond a barrier—hence the very many ignorances and foolishnesses whereby our judgments and our life-actions are confused, so that few or none do rightly and duly order their acts.

William Gilbert, *On the Loadstone,* V, 12

18 *Messala.* O hateful error, melancholy's child,
Why dost thou show to the apt thoughts of men
The things that are not? O error, soon conceived,
Thou never comest unto a happy birth,
But kill'st the mother that engender'd thee!

Shakespeare, *Julius Caesar,* V, iii, 67

19 Four species of idols beset the human mind, to which (for distinction's sake) we have assigned names, calling the first idols of the tribe, the second idols of the den, the third idols of the market, the fourth idols of the theatre.

The formation of notions and axioms on the foundation of true induction is the only fitting remedy by which we can ward off and expel these idols. It is, however, of great service to point them out; for the doctrine of idols bears the same relation to the interpretation of nature as that of the confutation of sophisms does to common logic.

The idols of the tribe are inherent in human nature and the very tribe or race of man; for man's sense is falsely asserted to be the standard of things; on the contrary, all the perceptions both of the senses and the mind bear reference to man and not to the universe, and the human mind resembles those uneven mirrors which impart their own properties to different objects, from which rays are emitted and distort and disfigure them.

The idols of the den are those of each individual; for everybody (in addition to the errors common to the race of man) has his own individual den or cavern, which intercepts and corrupts the light of nature, either from his own peculiar and singular disposition, or from his education and intercourse with others, or from his reading, and the authority acquired by those whom he reverences and admires, or from the different impressions produced on the mind, as it happens to be preoccupied and predisposed, or equable and tranquil, and the like; so that the spirit of man (according to its several dispositions), is variable, confused, and, as it were, actuated by chance; and Heraclitus said well that men search for knowledge in lesser worlds, and not in the greater or common world.

There are also idols formed by the reciprocal intercourse and society of man with man, which we call idols of the market, from the commerce and association of men with each other; for men converse by means of language, but words are formed at the will of the generality, and there arises from a bad and unapt formation of words a wonderful obstruction to the mind. Nor can the definitions and explanations with which learned men are wont to guard and protect themselves in some instances afford a complete remedy; words still manifestly force the understanding, throw everything into confusion, and lead mankind into vain and innumerable controversies and fallacies.

Lastly, there are idols which have crept into men's minds from the various dogmas of peculiar systems of philosophy, and also from the perverted rules of demonstration, and these we denominate idols of the theatre: for we regard all the systems of philosophy hitherto received or imagined, as so many plays brought out and performed, creating fictitious and theatrical worlds.

Bacon, *Novum Organum,* I, 39–44

20 The power of will which I have received from God is not of itself the source of my errors—for it is very ample and very perfect of its kind—any more than is the power of understanding; for since I understand nothing but by the power which God has given me for understanding, there is no doubt that all that I understand, I understand as I ought, and it is not possible that I err in this. Whence then come my errors? They come from the sole fact that since the will is much wider in its range and compass than the understanding, I do not restrain it within the same bounds, but extend it also to things which I do not understand: and as the will is of itself indifferent to these, it easily falls into error and sin, and chooses the evil for the good, or the false for the true.

Descartes, *Meditations on First Philosophy,* IV

21 I . . . perceive that God could easily have created me so that I never should err, although I still remained free, and endowed with a limited knowledge, viz., by giving to my understanding a clear and distinct intelligence of all things as to which I should ever have to deliberate; or simply by His engraving deeply in my memory the resolution never to form a judgment on anything without

having a clear and distinct understanding of it, so that I could never forget it. And it is easy for me to understand that, in so far as I consider myself alone, and as if there were only myself in the world, I should have been much more perfect than I am, if God had created me so that I could never err. Nevertheless I cannot deny that in some sense it is a greater perfection in the whole universe that certain parts should not be exempt from error as others are than that all parts should be exactly similar. And I have no right to complain if God, having placed me in the world, has not called upon me to play a part that excels all others in distinction and perfection.

Descartes, *Meditations on First Philosophy,* IV

22 When a man reckons without the use of words, which may be done in particular things, as when upon the sight of any one thing, we conjecture what was likely to have preceded, or is likely to follow upon it; if that which he thought likely to follow follows not, or that which he thought likely to have preceded it hath not preceded it, this is called *error;* to which even the most prudent men are subject. But when we reason in words of general signification, and fall upon a general inference which is false; though it be commonly called *error,* it is indeed an *absurdity,* or senseless speech. For error is but a deception, in presuming that somewhat is past, or to come; of which, though it were not past, or not to come, yet there was no impossibility discoverable. But when we make a general assertion, unless it be a true one, the possibility of it is inconceivable. And words whereby we conceive nothing but the sound are those we call *absurd, insignificant,* and *nonsense.* And therefore if a man should talk to me of a *round quadrangle;* or *accidents of bread in cheese;* or *immaterial substances;* or of *a free subject; a free will;* or any *free* but free from being hindered by opposition; I should not say he were in an error, but that his words were without meaning; that is to say, absurd.

I have said before . . . that a man did excel all other animals in this faculty, that when he conceived anything whatsoever, he was apt to enquire the consequences of it, and what effects he could do with it. And now I add this other degree of the same excellence, that he can by words reduce the consequences he finds to general rules, called *theorems,* or *aphorisms;* that is, he can reason, or reckon, not only in number, but in all other things whereof one may be added unto or subtracted from another.

But this privilege is allayed by another; and that is by the privilege of absurdity, to which no living creature is subject, but men only. And of men, those are of all most subject to it that profess philosophy. For it is most true that Cicero saith of them somewhere; that there can be nothing so absurd but may be found in the books of philosophers. And the reason is manifest. For there is not one of them that begins his ratiocination from the definitions or explications of the names they are to use; which is a method that hath been used only in geometry, which conclusions have thereby been made indisputable.

Hobbes, *Leviathan,* I, 5

23 The chief malady of man is restless curiosity about things which he cannot understand; and it is not so bad for him to be in error as to be curious to no purpose.

Pascal, *Pensées,* I, 18

24 Man is only a subject full of error, natural and ineffaceable, without grace. Nothing shows him the truth. Everything deceives him. These two sources of truth, reason and the senses, besides being both wanting in sincerity, deceive each other in turn. The senses mislead the Reason with false appearances, and receive from Reason in their turn the same trickery which they apply to her; Reason has her revenge. The passions of the soul trouble the senses, and make false impressions upon them. They rival each other in falsehood and deception.

Pascal, *Pensées,* II, 83

25 *Satan.* One fatal Tree there stands of Knowledge call'd,
Forbidden them to taste: Knowledge forbidd'n?
Suspicious, reasonless. Why should thir Lord
Envie them that? can it be sin to know,
Can it be death? and do they onely stand
By Ignorance, is that thir happie state,
The proof of thir obedience and thir faith?

Milton, *Paradise Lost,* IV, 514

26 Many errors, of a truth, consist merely in the application of the wrong names to things. For if a man says that the lines which are drawn from the centre of the circle to the circumference are not equal, he understands by the circle, at all events for the time, something else than mathematicians understand by it. So when men make errors in calculation, the numbers which are in their minds are not those which are upon the paper. As far as their mind is concerned there is no error, although it seems as if there were, because we think that the numbers in their minds are those which are upon the paper. If we did not think so, we should not believe them to be in error. . . . This is the source from which so many controversies arise—that men either do not properly explain their own thoughts, or do not properly interpret those of other people; for, in truth, when they most contradict one another, they either think the same things or something different, so that those things which they suppose to be errors and absurdities in another person are not so.

Spinoza, *Ethics,* II, Prop. 47, Schol.

27 There is not so contemptible a plant or animal, that does not confound the most enlarged understanding. Though the familiar use of things about us take off our wonder, yet it cures not our ignorance.

Locke, *Concerning Human Understanding,*
Bk. III, VI, 9

28 Heav'n from all creatures hides the book of Fate,
All but the page prescrib'd, their present state;
From brutes what men, from men what spirits know:
Or who could suffer Being here below?
The lamb thy riot dooms to bleed to-day,
Had he thy Reason, would he skip and play?
Pleas'd to the last, he crops the flow'ry food,
And licks the hand just rais'd to shed his blood.
Oh blindness to the future! kindly giv'n,
That each may fill the circle mark'd by Heav'n;
Who sees with equal eye, as God of all,
A hero perish, or a sparrow fall,
Atoms or systems into ruin hurl'd,
And now a bubble burst, and now a world.

Pope, *Essay on Man,* Epistle I, 77

29 We may discover the reason why no philosopher, who is rational and modest, has ever pretended to assign the ultimate cause of any natural operation, or to show distinctly the action of that power, which produces any single effect in the universe. It is confessed, that the utmost effort of human reason is to reduce the principles, productive of natural phenomena, to a greater simplicity, and to resolve the many particular effects into a few general causes, by means of reasonings from analogy, experience, and observation. But as to the causes of these general causes, we should in vain attempt their discovery; nor shall we ever be able to satisfy ourselves, by any particular explication of them. These ultimate springs and principles are totally shut up from human curiosity and enquiry. Elasticity, gravity, cohesion of parts, communication of motion by impulse; these are probably the ultimate causes and principles which we shall ever discover in nature; and we may esteem ourselves sufficiently happy, if, by accurate enquiry and reasoning, we can trace up the particular phenomena to, or near to, these general principles.

Hume, *Concerning Human Understanding,* IV, 26

30 To each his suff'rings: all are men,
Condemn'd alike to groan;
The tender for another's pain,
Th' unfeeling for his own.
Yet ah! why should they know their fate?
Since sorrow never comes too late,
And happiness too swiftly flies.
Thought would destroy their paradise.
No more; where ignorance is bliss,
'Tis folly to be wise.

Gray, *Ode on a Distant Prospect of Eton College*

31 Now if you will venture to go along with me, and look down into the bottom of this matter, it will be found that the cause of obscurity and confusion, in the mind of a man, is threefold.

Dull organs, dear Sir, in the first place. Secondly, slight and transient impressions made by the objects, when the said organs are not dull. And thirdly, a memory like unto a sieve, not able to retain what it has received. . . .

Now you must understand that not one of these was the true cause of the confusion in my uncle Toby's discourse; and it is for that very reason I enlarge upon them so long, after the manner of great physiologists—to shew the world, what it did *not* arise from.

What it did arise from, I have hinted above, and a fertile source of obscurity it is,—and ever will be,—and that is the unsteady uses of words, which have perplexed the clearest and most exalted understandings.

Sterne, *Tristram Shandy,* II, 2

32 How is reason so precious a gift that we would not lose it for anything in the world? and how has this reason served only to make us the most unhappy of all beings?

Whence comes it that loving truth passionately, we are always betrayed to the most gross impostures?

Why is life still loved by this crowd of Indians deceived and enslaved by the bonzes, crushed by a Tartar's descendants, overburdened with work, groaning in want, assailed by disease, exposed to every scourge?

Whence comes evil, and why does evil exist?

O atoms of a day! O my companions in infinite littleness, born like me to suffer everything and to be ignorant of everything, are there enough madmen among you to believe that they know all these things? No, there are not; no, at the bottom of your hearts you feel your nonentity as I render justice to mine. But you are arrogant enough to want people to embrace your vain systems; unable to be tyrants over our bodies, you claim to be tyrants over our souls.

Voltaire, *Philosophical Dictionary:*
Ignorance

33 Ignorance is mere privation, by which nothing can be produced: it is a vacuity in which the soul sits motionless and torpid for want of attraction; and, without knowing why, we always rejoice when we learn, and grieve when we forget.

Johnson, *Rasselas,* XI

34 A lady once asked him [Johnson] how he came to define *Pastern* the *knee* of a horse: instead of making an elaborate defence, as she expected, he at once answered, "Ignorance, Madam, pure ignorance."

Boswell, *Life of Johnson* (1755)

35 *Johnson.* Mankind have a great aversion to intellectual labour; but even supposing knowledge to be easily attainable, more people would be content to be ignorant than would take even a little trouble to acquire it.

Boswell, *Life of Johnson (1763)*

36 Thus, Sir, I have disposed of this falsehood. But falsehood has a perennial spring.

Burke, *Speech on American Taxation (1774)*

37 The consciousness of ignorance—unless this ignorance is recognized to be absolutely necessary—ought, instead of forming the conclusion of my inquiries, to be the strongest motive to the pursuit of them. All ignorance is either ignorance of things or of the limits of knowledge. If my ignorance is accidental and not necessary, it must incite me, in the first case, to a *dogmatical* inquiry regarding the objects of which I am ignorant; in the second, to a *critical* investigation into the bounds of all possible knowledge. But that my ignorance is absolutely necessary and unavoidable, and that it consequently absolves from the duty of all further investigation, is a fact which cannot be made out upon empirical grounds—from *observation*—but upon critical grounds alone, that is, by a thoroughgoing *investigation* into the primary sources of cognition. It follows that the determination of the bounds of reason can be made only on *a priori* grounds; while the empirical limitation of reason, which is merely an indeterminate cognition of an ignorance that can never be completely removed, can take place only *a posteriori.* In other words, our empirical knowledge is limited by that which yet remains for us to know.

Kant, *Critique of Pure Reason,* Transcendental Method

38 It is . . . quite certain that we can never get a sufficient knowledge of organized beings and their inner possibility, much less get an explanation of them, by looking merely to mechanical principles of nature. Indeed, so certain is it, that we may confidently assert that it is absurd for men even to entertain any thought of so doing or to hope that maybe another Newton may some day arise, to make intelligible to us even the genesis of but a blade of grass from natural laws that no design has ordered. Such insight we must absolutely deny to mankind.

Kant, *Critique of Teleological Judgement, 75*

39 So numerous indeed and so powerful are the causes which serve to give a false bias to the judgment, that we, upon many occasions, see wise and good men on the wrong as well as on the right side of questions of the first magnitude to society. This circumstance, if duly attended to, would furnish a lesson of moderation to those who are ever so much persuaded of their being in the right in any controversy. And a further reason for caution, in this respect, might be drawn from the reflection that we are not always sure that those who advocate the truth are influenced by purer principles than their antagonists. Ambition, avarice, personal animosity, party opposition, and many other motives not more laudable than these, are apt to operate as well upon those who support as those who oppose the right side of a question.

Hamilton, *Federalist 1*

40 Though it cannot be pretended that the principles of moral and political knowledge have, in general, the same degree of certainty with those of the mathematics, yet they have much better claims in this respect than, to judge from the conduct of men in particular situations, we should be disposed to allow them. The obscurity is much oftener in the passions and prejudices of the reasoner than in the subject. Men, upon too many occasions, do not give their own understandings fair play; but, yielding to some untoward bias, they entangle themselves in words and confound themselves in subtleties.

Hamilton, *Federalist 31*

41 *Faust.* Oh, happy he who still hopes that he can Emerge from Error's boundless sea! What man knows not, is needed most by man, And what man knows, for that no use has he.

Goethe, *Faust,* I, 1064

42 That there should one Man die ignorant who had capacity for Knowledge, this I call a tragedy.

Carlyle, *Sartor Resartus,* III, 4

43 There are many things of which a wise man might wish to be ignorant.

Emerson, *Demonology*

44 So seemed it to me, as I stood at her helm, and for long hours silently guided the way of this fire-ship on the sea. Wrapped, for that interval, in darkness myself, I but the better saw the redness, the madness, the ghastliness of others. The continual sight of the fiend shapes before me, capering half in smoke and half in fire, these at last begat kindred visions in my soul, as soon as I began to yield to that unaccountable drowsiness which ever would come over me at a midnight helm.

But that night, in particular, a strange (and ever since inexplicable) thing occurred to me. Starting from a brief standing sleep, I was horribly conscious of something fatally wrong. The jawbone tiller smote my side, which leaned against it; in my ears was the low hum of sails, just beginning to shake in the wind; I thought my eyes were open; I was half conscious of putting my fingers to the lids and mechanically stretching them still further apart. But, spite of all this, I could see no compass before me to steer by; though it seemed but a minute since I had been watching the card, by the steady binnacle lamp illumining it. Nothing seemed before me but a jet gloom, now and then made ghastly by flashes of redness. Uppermost was the impression, that whatever swift, rushing thing I stood on was not so much bound to any haven ahead as rushing from all havens astern. A stark, bewildered feeling, as of death, came over me. Convulsively my hands grasped the tiller, but with the crazy conceit that the tiller was, somehow, in some enchanted way, inverted. My God! what is the matter with me? thought I. Lo! in my brief sleep I had turned myself about, and was fronting the ship's stern, with my back to her prow and the compass. In an instant I faced back, just in time to prevent the vessel from flying up into the wind, and very probably capsizing her. How glad and how grateful the relief from this unnatural hallucination of the night, and the fatal contingency of being brought by the lee!

Look not too long in the face of the fire, O man! Never dream with thy hand on the helm! Turn not thy back to the compass; accept the first hint of the hitching tiller; believe not the artificial fire, when its redness makes all things look ghastly. To-morrow, in the natural sun, the skies will be bright; those who glared like devils in the forking flames, the morn will show in far other, at least gentler, relief; the glorious, golden, glad sun, the only true lamp—all óthers but liars!

Melville, *Moby Dick,* XCVI

45 It has often and confidently been asserted, that man's origin can never be known: but ignorance more frequently begets confidence than does knowledge: it is those who know little, and not those who know much, who so positively assert that this or that problem will never be solved by science.

Darwin, *Descent of Man,* Intro.

46 So that while it is the summit of human wisdom to learn the limit of our faculties, it may be wise to recollect that we have no more right to make denials, than to put forth affirmatives, about what lies beyond that limit.

T. H. Huxley, *Hume,* Bishop Berkeley on the Metaphysics of Sensation

47 The fatal tendency of mankind to leave off thinking about a thing when it is no longer doubtful, is the cause of half their errors. A contemporary author has well spoken of "the deep slumber of a decided opinion."

But what! (it may be asked) Is the absence of unanimity an indispensable condition of true knowledge? Is it necessary that some part of mankind should persist in error to enable any to real-ise the truth? Does a belief cease to be real and vital as soon as it is generally received—and is a proposition never thoroughly understood and felt unless some doubt of it remains? As soon as mankind have unanimously accepted a truth, does the truth perish within them? The highest aim and best result of improved intelligence, it has hitherto been thought, is to unite mankind more and more in the acknowledgment of all important truths; and does the intelligence only last as long as it has not achieved its object? Do the fruits of conquest perish by the very completeness of the victory?

I affirm no such thing. As mankind improve, the number of doctrines which are no longer disputed or doubted will be constantly on the increase: and the well-being of mankind may almost be measured by the number and gravity of the truths which have reached the point of being uncontested. The cessation, on one question after another, of serious controversy, is one of the necessary incidents of the consolidation of opinion; a consolidation as salutary in the case of true opinions, as it is dangerous and noxious when the opinions are erroneous.

Mill, *On Liberty,* II

48 If you want to know whether you are thinking rightly, put your thoughts into words. In the very attempt to do this you will find yourselves, consciously or unconsciously, using logical forms. Logic compels us to throw our meaning into distinct propositions, and our reasonings into distinct steps. It makes us conscious of all the implied assumptions on which we are proceeding, and which, if not true, vitiate the entire process. It makes us aware what extent of doctrine we commit ourselves to by any course of reasoning, and obliges us to look the implied premises in the face, and make up our minds whether we can stand to them. It makes our opinions consistent with themselves and with one another, and forces us to think clearly, even when it cannot make us think correctly. It is true that error may be consistent and systematic as well as truth; but this is not the common case. It is no small advantage to see clearly the principles and consequences involved in our opinions, and which we must either accept, or else abandon those opinions. We are much nearer to finding truth when we search for it in broad daylight. Error, pursued rigorously to all that is implied in it, seldom fails to get detected by coming into collision with some known and admitted fact.

Mill, *Inaugural Address at St. Andrews*

49 Ignorance is not innocence but sin.

Browning, *The Inn Album,* V

50 Among all forms of mistake, prophecy is the most gratuitous.

George Eliot, *Middlemarch,* I, 10

51 Ignorance gives one a large range of probabilities.

George Eliot, *Daniel Deronda,* II, 13

52 *Father Zossima.* Of the pride of Satan what I think is this: it is hard for us on earth to comprehend it, and therefore it is so easy to fall into error and to share it, even imagining that we are doing something grand and fine. Indeed, many of the strongest feelings and movements of our nature we cannot comprehend on earth. Let not that be a stumbling-block, and think not that it may serve as a justification to you for anything. For the Eternal Judge asks of you what you can comprehend and not what you cannot. You will know that yourself hereafter, for you will behold all things truly then and will not dispute them. On earth, indeed, we are, as it were, astray, and if it were not for the precious image of Christ before us, we should be undone and altogether lost, as was the human race before the flood. Much on earth is hidden from us, but to make up for that we have been given a precious mystic sense of our living bond with the other world, with the higher heavenly world, and the roots of our thoughts and feelings are not here but in other worlds. That is why the philosophers say that we cannot apprehend the reality of things on earth.

Dostoevsky, *Brothers Karamazov,* Pt. II, VI, 3

53 I am thankful that the good God created us all ignorant. I am glad that when we change His plans in this regard we have to do it at our own risk.

Mark Twain, *Letter to the Alta California* [San Francisco] (May 28, 1867)

54 Philosophers can never hope finally to formulate . . . metaphysical first principles. Weakness of insight and deficiencies of language stand in the way inexorably. Words and phrases must be stretched towards a generality foreign to their ordinary usage; and however such elements of language be stabilized as technicalities, they remain metaphors mutely appealing for an imaginative leap.

There is no first principle which is in itself unknowable, not to be captured by a flash of insight. But, putting aside the difficulties of language, deficiency in imaginative penetration forbids progress in any form other than that of an asymptotic approach to a scheme of principles, only definable in terms of the ideal which they should satisfy.

Whitehead, *Process and Reality,* I, 1

55 Error is not only the absolute error of believing what is false, but also the quantitative error of believing more or less strongly than is warranted by the degree of credibility properly attaching to the proposition believed in relation to the believer's knowledge. A man who is quite convinced that a certain horse will win the Derby is

in error even if the horse does win.

Russell, *Human Knowledge,* V, 6

56 The proposition that symptoms vanish when their unconscious antecedents have been made conscious has been borne out by all subsequent research; although the most extraordinary and unexpected complications are met with in attempting to carry this proposition out in practice. Our therapy does its work by transforming something unconscious into something conscious, and only succeeds in its work in so far as it is able to effect this transformation.

Now for a rapid digression, lest you should run the risk of imagining that this therapeutic effect is achieved too easily. According to the conclusions we have reached so far, neurosis would be the result of a kind of ignorance, a not-knowing of mental processes which should be known. This would approach very closely to the well-known Socratic doctrine according to which even vice is the result of ignorance. Now it happens in analysis that an experienced practitioner can usually surmise very easily what those feelings are which have remained unconscious in each individual patient. It should not therefore be a matter of great difficulty to cure the patient by imparting his knowledge to him and so relieving his ignorance. At least, one side of the unconscious meaning of the symptom would be easily dealt with in this way, although it is true that the other side of it, the connection between the symptom and the previous experiences in the patient's life, can hardly be divined thus; for the analyst does not know what the experiences have been, he has to wait till the patient remembers them and tells him. But one might find a substitute even for this in many cases. One might ask for information about his past life from the friends and relations; they are often in a position to know what events have been of a traumatic nature, perhaps they can even relate some of which the patient is ignorant because they took place at some very early period of childhood. By a combination of these two means it would seem that the pathogenic ignorance of the patients might be overcome in a short time without much trouble.

If only it were so! But we have made discoveries that we were quite unprepared for at first. There is knowing and knowing; they are not always the same thing. There are various kinds of knowing, which psychologically are not by any means of equal value. . . . Knowing on the part of the physician is not the same thing as knowing on the part of the patient and does not have the same effect. When the physician conveys his knowledge to the patient by telling him what he knows, it has effect. No, it would be incorrect to say that. It does not have the effect of dispersing the symptoms; but it has a different one, it sets the analysis in motion, and the first result of this is often an energetic denial. The patient has learned something that he did not know before—the meaning of his symptom—and yet he knows it as little as ever. Thus we discover that there is more than one kind of ignorance. It requires a considerable degree of insight and understanding of psychological matters order to see in what the difference consists. But the proposition that symptoms vanish with the acquisition of knowledge of their meaning remains true, nevertheless. The necessary condition is that the knowledge must be founded upon an inner change in the patient which can only come about by a mental operation directed to that end.

Freud, *General Introduction to Psycho-Analysis*, XVIII

57 While the power of thought frees us from servile subjection to instinct, appetite, and routine, it also brings with it the occasion and possibility of error and mistake. In elevating us above the brute, it opens to us the possibility of failures to which the animal, limited to instinct, cannot sink.

Dewey, *How We Think*, Pt. I, II, 2

6.5 | *Opinion, Belief, and Faith*

The three subjects considered here all tend to bring the meaning of knowledge into sharper focus. Does the man who says "I know" signify a different state of mind from the man who says, of the same matter, "I opine," or "I think," or "I believe"? What is the difference? Are there some things of which we can only say "I think," "I opine," or "I believe," but not "I know"? Is faith a belief about things that we cannot know? These and similar questions are dealt with in the passages quoted below.

Employing the phrase "right opinion" to designate an opinion that happens to be true, Plato attempts to point out why it is better to have knowledge than right opinion even though both put the mind in possession of the truth. In a similar vein, Aristotle comments on the difference between knowing the truth of a theorem in geometry because one is able to demonstrate it and believing or opining that it is true on the authority of one's teacher. In subsequent elaborations of the same insight, knowledge and opinion or belief are differentiated by the distinction between that which the mind necessarily affirms and that to which it voluntarily gives its assent. If I cannot withhold my assent from the proposition that two plus two makes four, then I know it to be true; I do not opine or believe it. But if what is proposed is something that I can voluntarily accept or reject, then my affirmation or denial of the matter is an act of opinion or belief, not of knowledge. In geometry, for example, an axiom commands my assent, but I am free to accept or reject a postulate which asks me to take something for granted.

As the difference between knowledge, on the one hand, and opinion or belief, on the other, becomes clearer, the door to skepticism is opened by doubts concerning the extent of the area in which men can properly say that they know. This is countered by giving greater weight or credence to opinions and beliefs in proportion as they are well grounded in observed facts or supported by cogent reasons even though the facts and the reasons do not produce the certainty of self-evident or of demonstrated truths. Accordingly, the discussion of opinion and belief becomes involved with considerations of probability, and with efforts to ascertain the degree of probability that, for all practical purposes, is as good as certainty.

In common speech, the words "belief"

and "faith" are often used interchangeably, but the word "faith" has a special and distinct significance when it is employed by writers in the Judaeo-Christian tradition of Western thought. The passages quoted here reflecting that tradition set religious faith apart from the ordinary run of secular beliefs by confining it to the things that God has explicitly revealed to men in Sacred Scripture. Having such faith is thought to be a mark of divine grace. Men may exercise their own will to believe about other matters, but belief in the articles of religious faith is a gift that God himself bestows upon them. Because theology, or at least dogmatic theology, finds its first principles in the articles of religious faith and then attempts to explicate what is thus believed, some quotations dealing with theology are included here.

---

1 Thy word is a lamp unto my feet, and a light unto my path.

Psalm 119:105

2 And he said, Go, and tell this people, Hear ye indeed, but understand not; and see ye indeed, but perceive not.

Make the heart of this people fat, and make their ears heavy, and shut their eyes; lest they see with their eyes, and hear with their ears, and understand with their heart, and convert, and be healed.

Then said I, Lord, how long? And he answered, Until the cities be wasted without inhabitant, and the houses without man, and the land be utterly desolate,

And the Lord have removed men far away, and there be a great forsaking in the midst of the land.

Isaiah 6:9–12

3 *Socrates.* If a man knew the way to Larisa, or anywhere else, and went to the place and led others thither, would he not be a right and good guide?

Meno. Certainly.

Soc. And a person who had a right opinion about the way, but had never been and did not know, might be a good guide also, might he not?

Men. Certainly.

Soc. And while he has true opinion about that which the other knows, he will be just as good a guide if he thinks the truth, as he who knows the truth?

Men. Exactly.

Soc. Then true opinion is as good a guide to correct action as knowledge; and that was the point which we omitted in our speculation about the nature of virtue, when we said that knowledge only is the guide of right action; whereas there is also right opinion.

Men. True.

Soc. Then right opinion is not less useful than knowledge?

Men. The difference, Socrates, is only that he who has knowledge will always be right; but he who has right opinion will sometimes be right, and sometimes not.

Soc. What do you mean? Can he be wrong who has right opinion, so long as he has right opinion?

Men. I admit the cogency of your argument, and therefore, Socrates, I wonder that knowledge should be preferred to right opinion—or why they should ever differ.

Soc. And shall I explain this wonder to you?

Men. Do tell me.

Soc. You would not wonder if you had ever observed the images of Daedalus; but perhaps you have not got them in your country?

Men. What have they to do with the question?

Soc. Because they require to be fastened in order to keep them, and if they are not fastened they will play truant and run away.

Men. Well, what of that?

Soc. I mean to say that they are not very valuable possessions if they are at liberty, for they will walk off like runaway slaves; but when fastened, they are of great value, for they are really beautiful works of art. Now this is an illustration of the nature of true opinions: while they abide with us they are beautiful and fruitful, but they run away out of the human soul, and do not remain long, and therefore they are not of much value until they are fastened by the tie of the cause; and this fastening of them, friend Meno, is recollection, as you and I have agreed to call it. But when they are bound, in the first place, they have the nature of knowledge; and, in the second place, they are abiding. And this is why knowledge is more honourable and excellent than true opinion, because fastened by a chain.

Plato, Meno, 97A

4 *Socrates.* Seeing . . . that not only rhetoric works by persuasion, but that other arts do the same, as in the case of the painter, a question has arisen which is a very fair one: Of what persuasion is

rhetoric the artificer, and about what?—is not that a fair way of putting the question?

Gorgias. I think so.

Soc. Then, if you approve the question, Gorgias, what is the answer?

Gor. I answer, Socrates, that rhetoric is the art of persuasion in courts of law and other assemblies, as I was just now saying, and about the just and unjust.

Soc. And that, Gorgias, was what I was suspecting to be your notion; yet I would not have you wonder if by-and-by I am found repeating a seemingly plain question; for I ask not in order to confute you, but as I was saying that the argument may proceed consecutively, and that we may not get the habit of anticipating and suspecting the meaning of one another's words; I would have you develop your own views in your own way, whatever may be your hypothesis.

Gor. I think that you are quite right, Socrates.

Soc. Then let me raise another question; there is such a thing as "having learned"?

Gor. Yes.

Soc. And there is also "having believed"?

Gor. Yes.

Soc. And is the "having learned" the same as "having believed," and are learning and belief the same things?

Gor. In my judgment, Socrates, they are not the same.

Soc. And your judgment is right, as you may ascertain in this way:—If a person were to say to you, "Is there, Gorgias, a false belief as well as a true?"—you would reply, if I am not mistaken, that there is.

Gor. Yes.

Soc. Well, but is there a false knowledge as well as a true?

Gor. No.

Soc. No, indeed; and this again proves that knowledge and belief differ.

Gor. Very true.

Soc. And yet those who have learned as well as those who have believed are persuaded?

Gor. Just so.

Soc. Shall we then assume two sorts of persuasion,—one which is the source of belief without knowledge, as the other is of knowledge?

Gor. By all means.

Soc. And which sort of persuasion does rhetoric create in courts of law and other assemblies about the just and unjust, the sort of persuasion which gives belief without knowledge, or that which gives knowledge?

Gor. Clearly, Socrates, that which only gives belief.

Soc. Then rhetoric, as would appear, is the artificer of a persuasion which creates belief about the just and unjust, but gives no instruction about them?

Gor. True.

Plato, *Gorgias,* 454A

5 Things that are true and things that are better are, by their nature, practically always easier to prove and easier to believe in.

Aristotle, *Rhetoric,* 1355ª38

6 Jesus answered and said, I thank thee, O Father, Lord of heaven and earth, because thou hast hid these things from the wise and prudent, and hast revealed them unto babes.

Even so, Father: for so it seemed good in thy sight.

All things are delivered unto me of my Father: and no man knoweth the Son, but the Father; neither knoweth any man the Father, save the Son, and he to whomsoever the Son will reveal him.

Matthew 11:25–27

7 The disciples came, and said unto him, why speakest thou unto them in parables?

He answered and said unto them, Because it is given unto you to know the mysteries of the kingdom of heaven, but to them it is not given.

For whosoever hath, to him shall be given, and he shall have more abundance: but whosoever hath not, from him shall be taken away even that he hath.

Therefore speak I to them in parables: because they seeing see not; and hearing they hear not, neither do they understand.

And in them is fulfilled the prophecy of Ē-sāi'-ăs, which saith, By hearing ye shall hear, and shall not understand; and seeing ye shall see, and shall not perceive:

For this people's heart is waxed gross, and their ears are dull of hearing, and their eyes they have closed; lest at any time they should see with their eyes, and hear with their ears, and should understand with their heart, and should be converted, and I should heal them.

But blessed are your eyes, for they see: and your ears, for they hear.

For verily I say unto you, That many prophets and righteous men have desired to see those things which ye see, and have not seen them; and to hear those things which ye hear, and have not heard them.

Matthew 13:10–17

8 Verily I say unto you, If ye have faith as a grain of mustard seed, ye shall say unto this mountain, Remove hence to yonder place; and it shall remove; and nothing shall be impossible unto you.

Matthew 17:20

9 And straightway the father of the child cried out, and said with tears, Lord, I believe; help thou mine unbelief.

Mark 9:24

10 For verily I say unto you, That whosoever shall

say unto this mountain, Be thou removed, and be thou cast into the sea; and shall not doubt in his heart, but shall believe that those things which he saith shall come to pass; he shall have whatsoever he saith.

Therefore I say unto you, What things soever ye desire, when ye pray, believe that ye receive them, and ye shall have them.

Mark 11:23–24

11 Jesus saith unto him, Thomas, because thou hast seen me, thou hast believed: blessed are they that have not seen, and yet have believed.

John 20:29

12 Whosoever shall call upon the name of the Lord shall be saved.

How then shall they call on him in whom they have not believed? and how shall they believe in him of whom they have not heard? and how shall they hear without a preacher?

And how shall they preach, except they be sent? as it is written, How beautiful are the feet of them that preach the gospel of peace, and bring glad tidings of good things!

But they have not all obeyed the gospel. For E-sāi-̄as saith, Lord, who hath believed our report?

So then faith cometh by hearing, and hearing by the word of God.

Romans 10:13–17

13 O foolish Galatians, who hath bewitched you, that ye should not obey the truth, before whose eyes Jesus Christ hath been evidently set forth, crucified among you?

This only would I learn of you, Received ye the Spirit by the works of the law, or by the hearing of faith?

Are ye so foolish? having begun in the Spirit, are ye now made perfect by the flesh?

Have ye suffered so many things in vain? if it be yet in vain.

He therefore that ministereth to you the Spirit, and worketh miracles among you, doeth he it by the works of the law, or by the hearing of faith?

Even as Abraham believed God, and it was accounted to him for righteousness.

Know ye therefore that they which are of faith, the same are the children of Abraham.

And the scripture, foreseeing that God would justify the heathen through faith, preached before the gospel unto Abraham, saying, In thee shall all nations be blessed.

So then they which be of faith are blessed with faithful Abraham.

For as many as are of the works of the law are under the curse: for it is written, Cursed is every one that continueth not in all things which are written in the book of the law to do them.

But that no man is justified by the law in the sight of God, it is evident: for, The just shall live by faith.

Galatians 3:1–11

14 I have fought a good fight, I have finished my course, I have kept the faith.

II Timothy 4:7

15 Therefore we ought to give the more earnest heed to the things which we have heard, lest at any time we should let them slip.

For if the word spoken by angels was stedfast, and every transgression and disobedience received a just recompence of reward;

How shall we escape, if we neglect so great salvation; which at the first began to be spoken by the Lord, and was confirmed unto us by them that heard him;

God also bearing them witness, both with signs and wonders, and with divers miracles, and gifts of the Holy Ghost, according to his own will?

Hebrews 2:1–4

16 Now faith is the substance of things hoped for, the evidence of things not seen.

Hebrews 11:1

17 We have not followed cunningly devised fables, when we made known unto you the power and coming of our Lord Jesus Christ, but were eyewitnesses of his majesty.

For he received from God the Father honour and glory, when there came such a voice to him from the excellent glory, This is my beloved Son, in whom I am well pleased.

And this voice which came from heaven we heard, when we were with him in the holy mount.

We have also a more sure word of prophecy; whereunto ye do well that ye take heed, as unto a light that shineth in a dark place, until the day dawn, and the day star arise in your hearts.

II Peter 1:16–19

18 The Revelation of Jesus Christ, which God gave unto him, to shew unto his servants things which must shortly come to pass; and he sent and signified it by his angel unto his servant John:

Who bare record of the word of God, and of the testimony of Jesus Christ, and of all things that he saw.

Blessed is he that readeth, and they that hear the words of this prophecy, and keep those things which are written therein: for the time is at hand.

Revelation 1:1–3

19 I was glad also that the old scriptures of the Law and the Prophets were set before me now, no longer in that light in which they had formerly seemed absurd, when I criticised Your holy ones

for thinking this or that which in plain fact they did not think. And it was a joy to hear Ambrose who often repeated to his congregation, as if it were a rule he was most strongly urging upon them, the text: *the letter killeth, but the spirit giveth life.* And he would go on to draw aside the veil of mystery and lay open the spiritual meaning of things which taken literally would have seemed to teach falsehood.

Augustine, *Confessions,* VI, 4

20 I wanted to be as certain of things unseen as that seven and three make ten. For I had not reached the point of madness which denies that even this can be known; but I wanted to know other things as clearly as this, either such material things as were not present to my senses, or spiritual things which I did not know how to conceive save corporeally. By believing I might have been cured; for then the eye of my mind would have been clearer and so might in some way have been directed towards Your truth which abides for ever and knows no defect. But as usually happens, the man who has tried a bad doctor is afraid to trust even a good one, so it was with the health of my soul, which could not be healed save by believing, and refused to be healed that way for fear of believing falsehood. Thus I was resisting Your hands, for You first prepared for us the medicine of faith and then applied it to the diseases of the world and gave it such great power.

Augustine, *Confessions,* VI, 4

21 I continued my miserable complaining: "How long, how long shall I go on saying tomorrow and again tomorrow? Why not now, why not have an end to my uncleanness this very hour?"

Such things I said, weeping in the most bitter sorrow of my heart. And suddenly I heard a voice from some nearby house, a boy's voice or a girl's voice, I do not know: but it was a sort of sing-song, repeated again and again, "Take and read, take and read." I ceased weeping and immediately began to search my mind most carefully as to whether children were accustomed to chant these words in any kind of game, and I could not remember that I had ever heard any such thing. Damming back the flood of my tears I arose, interpreting the incident as quite certainly a divine command to open my book of Scripture and read the passage at which I should open. . . . So I was moved to return to the place where Alypius was sitting, for I had put down the Apostle's book there when I arose. I snatched it up, opened it and in silence read the passage upon which my eyes first fell: *Not in rioting and drunkenness, not in chambering and impurities, not in contention and envy, but put ye on the Lord Jesus Christ and make not provision for the flesh in its concupiscences.* [*Romans* xiii, 13.] I had no wish to read further, and no need. For in that instant, with the very ending of the sentence, it was as

though a light of utter confidence shone in all my heart, and all the darkness of uncertainty vanished away. . . .

Then we went in to my mother and told her, to her great joy. We related how it had come about: she was filled with triumphant exultation, and praised You who are mighty beyond what we ask or conceive: for she saw that You had given her more than with all her pitiful weeping she had ever asked. For You converted me to Yourself so that I no longer sought a wife nor any of this world's promises, but stood upon that same rule of faith in which You had shown me to her so many years before. Thus You changed her mourning into joy, a joy far richer than she had thought to wish, a joy much dearer and purer than she had thought to find in grandchildren of my flesh.

Augustine, *Confessions,* VIII, 12

22 This Mediator, having spoken what He judged sufficient first by the prophets, then by His own lips, and afterwards by the apostles, has besides produced the Scripture which is called canonical, which has paramount authority, and to which we yield assent in all matters of which we ought not to be ignorant, and yet cannot know of ourselves. For if we attain the knowledge of present objects by the testimony of our own senses, whether internal or external, then, regarding objects remote from our own senses, we need others to bring their testimony, since we cannot know them by our own, and we credit the persons to whom the objects have been or are sensibly present. Accordingly, as in the case of visible objects which we have not seen, we trust those who have (and likewise with all sensible objects), so in the case of things which are perceived by the mind and spirit, i.e., which are remote from our interior sense, it behoves us to trust those who have seen them set in that incorporeal light, or abidingly contemplate them.

Augustine, *City of God,* XI, 3

23 Men see Him just so far as they die to this world; and so far as they live to it they see Him not. But yet, although that light may begin to appear clearer, and not only more tolerable, but even more delightful, still it is only through a glass darkly that we are said to see, because we walk by faith, not by sight, while we continue to wander as strangers in this world, even though our conversation be in heaven.

Augustine, *Christian Doctrine,* II, 7

24 Just as poor as the store of gold and silver and garments which the people of Israel brought with them out of Egypt was in comparison with the riches which they afterwards attained at Jerusalem, and which reached their height in the reign of King Solomon, so poor is all the useful knowl-

edge which is gathered from the books of the heathen when compared with the knowledge of Holy Scripture. For whatever man may have learnt from other sources, if it is hurtful, it is there condemned; if it is useful, it is therein contained. And while every man may find there all that he has learnt of useful elsewhere, he will find there in much greater abundance things that are to be found nowhere else, but can be learnt only in the wonderful sublimity and wonderful simplicity of the Scriptures.

Augustine, *Christian Doctrine,* II, 42

25 What I understand I also believe, but I do not understand everything that I believe; for all which I understand I know, but I do not know all that I believe. But still I am not unmindful of the utility of believing many things which are not known. . . . And though the majority of things must remain unknown to me, yet I do know what is the utility of believing.

Augustine, *On the Teacher,* XI, 37

26 Although by the revelation of grace in this life we cannot know of God "what He is," and thus are united to Him as to one unknown, still we know Him more fully according as many and more excellent of His effects are demonstrated to us, and according as we attribute to Him some things known by divine revelation, to which natural reason cannot reach, as, for instance, that God is Three and One.

Aquinas, *Summa Theologica,* I, 12, 13

27 The light of faith makes us see what we believe. For just as, by the habits of the other virtues, man sees what is fitting to him in respect of that habit, so, by the habit of faith, the human mind is directed to assent to such things as are fitting to a right faith, and not to assent to others.

Aquinas, *Summa Theologica,* II–II, 1, 4

28 Unbelievers are in ignorance of things that are of faith, for neither do they see or know them in themselves, nor do they know them to be credible. The faithful, on the other hand, know them, not as by demonstration, but by the light of faith which makes them see that they ought to believe them.

Aquinas, *Summa Theologica,* II–II, 1, 5

29 Science and opinion about the same object can certainly be in different men, as we have stated above about science and faith. Yet it is possible for one and the same man to have science and faith about the same thing relatively, that is, in relation to the subject, but not in the same respect. For it is possible for the same person, about one and the same thing, to know one thing and to think another. And, in like manner, one may know by demonstration the unity of God, and believe that He is

a Trinity. On the other hand, in one and the same man, about the same thing, and in the same respect, science is incompatible with either opinion or faith, yet for different reasons. Because science is incompatible with opinion about the same thing absolutely, for the notion of science demands that what is known should be thought impossible to be otherwise, but the notion of opinion demands that the thing of which there is opinion may be thought possible to be otherwise. Yet that which is held by faith, on account of the certainty of faith, is also thought impossible to be otherwise; and the reason why science and faith cannot be about the same object and in the same respect is because the object of science is something seen, while the object of faith is the unseen, as stated above.

Aquinas, *Summa Theologica,* II–II, 1, 5

30 Whatever is in opposition to faith, whether it consist in a man's thoughts, or in outward persecution, increases the merit of faith, insofar as the will is shown to be more prompt and firm in believing, Hence the martyrs had more merit of faith, through not renouncing faith on account of persecution; and even the wise have greater merit of faith, through not renouncing their faith on account of the reasons brought forward by philosophers or heretics in opposition to faith.

Aquinas, *Summa Theologica,* II–II, 2, 10

31 Other things being equal sight is more certain than hearing. But if (the authority of) the person from whom we hear greatly surpasses that of the seer's sight, hearing is more certain than sight. Thus a man of little science is more certain about what he hears on the authority of an expert in science, than about what is apparent to him according to his own reason. And much more is a man certain about what he hears from God, Who cannot be deceived, than about what he sees with his own reason, which can be mistaken.

Aquinas, *Summa Theologica,* II–II, 4, 8

32 Faith is the substance of things hoped for, and argument of things which are not seen; and this I take to be its quiddity.

Dante, *Paradiso,* XXIV, 64

33 I believe in one God, sole and eternal, who moveth all the heaven, himself unmoved, with love and with desire.
And for such belief I have not only proofs physic and metaphysic, but it is given me likewise by the truth which hence doth rain
through Moses, through the Prophets and through the Psalms, through the Gospel and through you who wrote when the glowing Spirit had made you fosterers.
And I believe in three eternal Persons, and I believe them one Essence, so One and so Trine as to comport at once with *are* and *is.*

With the profound divine state whereof I speak,
my mind is stamped more times than once by
evangelic teaching.
This the beginning is; this is the spark which then
dilates into a living flame, and like a star in
heaven shineth in me.

> Dante, *Paradiso*, XXIV, 130

34 The principal lesson of theology is that Christ can
be known.

> Luther, *Table Talk*, 1353

35 Prior to faith and a knowledge of God, reason is
darkness, but in believers it's an excellent instrument. Just as all gifts and instruments of nature
are evil in godless men, so they are good in believers. Faith is now furthered by reason, speech, and
eloquence, whereas these were only impediments
prior to faith. Enlightened reason, taken captive
by faith, receives life from faith, for it is slain and
given life again.

> Luther, *Table Talk*, 2938b

36 Faith justifies not as a work, or as a quality, or as
knowledge, but as assent of the will and firm confidence in the mercy of God. For if faith were only
knowledge, then the devil would certainly be
saved because he possesses the greatest knowledge
of God and of all the works and wonders of God
from the creation of the world. Accordingly faith
must be understood otherwise than as knowledge.
In part, however, it is assent.

> Luther, *Table Talk*, 4655

37 Little children are saved only by faith without
any good works; therefore faith alone justifies. If
God's power be able to effect that in one, then he
is also able to accomplish it in all; for the power of
the child effects it not, but the power of faith;
neither is it done through the child's weakness or
disability; for then that weakness would be merit
of itself, or equivalent to merit. It is a mischievous
thing that we miserable, sinful wretches will upbraid God, and hit him in the teeth with our
works, and think thereby to be justified before
him; but God will not allow it.

> Luther, *Table Talk*, H304

38 Faith consists in a knowledge of God and of
Christ, not in reverence for the Church.

> Calvin, *Institutes of the Christian Religion*, III, 2

39 Faith is a knowledge of the benevolence of God
towards us, and a certain persuasion of his veracity.

> Calvin, *Institutes of the Christian Religion*, III, 2

40 The principal hinge on which faith turns is this—
that we must not consider the promises of mercy,
which the Lord offers, as true only to others, and

not to ourselves; but rather make them our own,
by embracing them in our hearts.

> Calvin, *Institutes of the Christian Religion*, III, 2

41 Perhaps it is not without reason that we attribute
facility in belief and conviction to simplicity and
ignorance; for it seems to me I once learned that
belief was a sort of impression made on our mind,
and that the softer and less resistant the mind, the
easier it was to imprint something on it. . . . The
more a mind is empty and without counterpoise,
the more easily it gives beneath the weight of the
first persuasive argument.

> Montaigne, *Essays*, I, 27, It Is Folly

42 Some make the world believe that they believe
what they do not believe. Others, in greater number, make themselves believe it, being unable to
penetrate what it means to believe.

> Montaigne, *Essays*, II, 12, Apology for
> Raymond Sebond

43 We must not give God chaff for wheat, as they
say. If we believed in him, I do not say by faith,
but with a simple belief; in fact (and I say it to
our great confusion), if we believed in him just as
in any other history, if we knew him like one of
our comrades, we would love him above all other
things, for the infinite goodness and beauty that
shines in him. At least he would march in the
same rank in our affection as riches, pleasures,
glory, and our friends.

> Montaigne, *Essays*, II, 12, Apology for
> Raymond Sebond

44 The participation that we have in the knowledge
of truth, whatever it may be, has not been acquired by our own powers. God has taught us that
clearly enough by the witnesses that he has chosen
from the common people, simple and ignorant, to
instruct us in his admirable secrets. Our faith is
not of our own acquiring, it is a pure present of
another's liberality. It is not by reasoning or by
our understanding that we have received our religion; it is by external authority and command.
The weakness of our judgment helps us more in
this than its strength, and our blindness more
than our clear-sightedness. It is by the mediation
of our ignorance more than of our knowledge that
we are learned with that divine learning.

> Montaigne, *Essays*, II, 12, Apology for
> Raymond Sebond

45 Reason does nothing but go astray in everything,
and especially when it meddles with divine things.
Who feels this more evidently than we? For even
though we have given it certain and infallible
principles, even though we light its steps with the
holy lamp of the truth which it has pleased God to
communicate to us, nevertheless we see daily how,
when it strays however little from the beaten path

and deviates or wanders from the way traced and trodden by the Church, immediately it is lost, it grows embarrassed and entangled, whirling round and floating in that vast, troubled, and undulating sea of human opinions, unbridled and aimless. As soon as it loses that great common highroad it breaks up and disperses onto a thousand different roads.

Montaigne, *Essays,* II, 12, Apology for Raymond Sebond

46 I do not at all hate opinions contrary to mine. I am so far from being vexed to see discord between my judgments and others', and from making myself incompatible with the society of men because they are of a different sentiment and party from mine, that on the contrary, since variety is the most general fashion that nature has followed, and more in minds than bodies, inasmuch ·as minds are of a substance suppler and susceptible, of more forms, I find it much rarer to see our humors and plans agree. And there were never in the world two opinions alike, any more than two hairs or two grains. Their most universal quality is diversity.

Montaigne, *Essays,* II, 37, Children and Fathers

47 I enter into discussion and argument with great freedom and ease, inasmuch as opinion finds in me a bad soil to penetrate and take deep roots in. No propositions astonish me, no belief offends me, whatever contrast it offers with my own. There is no fancy so frivolous and so extravagant that it does not seem to me quite suitable to the production of the human mind. We who deprive our judgment of the right to make decisions look mildly on opinions different from ours; and if we do not lend them our judgment, we easily lend them our ears. Where one scale of the balance is totally empty, I let the other vacillate under an old woman's dreams. And it seems to me excusable if I take rather the odd number than the even, Thursday rather than Friday; if I am happier to be twelfth or fourteenth than thirteenth at table; if I would rather see a hare skirting my path when I travel than crossing it, and rather give my left foot than my right to be booted first. All such idle fancies, which are in credit around us, deserve at least to be listened to. For me they outweigh only emptiness, but they do outweigh that. Popular and chance opinions count in weight for something, and not nothing, in nature. And he who does not let himself go that far may perhaps fall into the vice of obstinacy to avoid that of superstition.

Montaigne, *Essays,* III, 8, Of the Art of Discussion

48 I honoured our theology and aspired as much as anyone to reach to heaven, but having learned to

regard it as a most highly assured fact that the road is not less open to the most ignorant than to the most learned, and that the revealed truths which conduct thither are quite above our intelligence, I should not have dared to submit them to the feebleness of my reasonings; and I thought that, in order to undertake to examine them and succeed in so doing, it was necessary to have some extraordinary assistance from above and to be more than a mere man.

Descartes, *Discourse on Method,* I

49 Though the matters be obscure with which our faith is said to deal, nevertheless this is understood to hold only of the fact or matter of which it treats, and it is not meant that the formal reason on account of which we assent to matters of faith is obscure: for, on the other hand, this formal reason consists in a certain internal light, and it is when God supernaturally fills us with this illumination that we are confident that what is proposed for our belief has been revealed by Him, Himself, and that it is clearly impossible that He should lie: a fact more certain than any natural light and often indeed more evident than it on account of the light of grace.

Descartes, *Objections and Replies,* II

50 The Scripture was written to show unto men the kingdom of God, and to prepare their minds to become His obedient subjects, leaving the world, and the philosophy thereof, to the disputation of men for the exercising of their natural reason.

Hobbes, *Leviathan,* I, 8

51 Faith of supernatural law is not a fulfilling, but only an assenting to the same; and not a duty that we exhibit to God, but a gift which God freely giveth to whom He pleaseth; as also unbelief is not a breach of any of His laws, but a rejection of them all, except the laws natural.

Hobbes, *Leviathan,* II, 26

52 Disputing of God's nature is contrary to His honour, for it is supposed that in this natural kingdom of God, there is no other way to know anything but by natural reason; that is, from the principles of natural science; which are so far from teaching us anything of God's nature, as they cannot teach us our own nature, nor the nature of the smallest creature living. And therefore, when men out of the principles of natural reason dispute of the attributes of God, they but dishonour Him: for in the attributes which we give to God, we are not to consider the signification of philosophical truth, but the signification of pious intention to do Him the greatest honour we are able.

Hobbes, *Leviathan,* II, 31

53 Belief and unbelief never follow men's commands. Faith is a gift of God which man can neither give

nor take away by promise of rewards or menaces of torture.

Hobbes, *Leviathan*, III, 42

54 As for those wingy Mysteries in Divinity, and airy subtleties in Religion, which have unhing'd the brains of better heads, they never stretched the *Pia Mater* of mine. Methinks there be not impossibilities enough in Religion for an active faith; the deepest Mysteries ours contains have not only been illustrated, but maintained, by Syllogism and the rule of Reason. I love to lose my self in a mystery, to pursue my Reason to an *O altitudo!* 'Tis my solitary recreation to pose my apprehension with those involved Ænigma's and riddles of the Trinity, with Incarnation, and Resurrection. I can answer all the Objections of Satan and my rebellious reason with that odd resolution I learned of *Tertullian, Certum est quia impossibile est.* I desire to exercise my faith in the difficultest point; for to credit ordinary and visible objects is not faith, but perswasion. Some believe the better for seeing Christ's Sepulchre; and when they have seen the Red Sea, doubt not of the Miracle. Now contrarily, I bless my self and am thankful that I lived not in the days of Miracles, that I never saw Christ nor His Disciples; I would not have been one of those *Israelites* that pass'd the Red Sea, nor one of Christ's patients on whom he wrought his wonders; then had my faith been thrust upon me, nor should I enjoy that greater blessing pronounced to all that believe and saw not. 'Tis an easie and necessary belief, to credit what our eye and sense hath examined: I believe he was dead, and buried, and rose again; and desire to see him in his glory, rather than to contemplate him in his Cenotaphe or Sepulchre. Nor is this much to believe; as we have reason, we owe this faith unto History: they only had the advantage of a bold and noble Faith, who lived before his coming, who upon obscure prophesies and mystical Types could raise a belief, and expect apparent impossibilities.

Sir Thomas Browne, *Religio Medici,* I, 9

55 How shall the dead arise, is no question of my Faith; to believe only possibilities, is not Faith, but meer Philosophy.

Sir Thomas Browne, *Religio Medici,* I, 48

56 Faith indeed tells what the senses do not tell, but not the contrary of what they see. It is above them and not contrary tò them.

Pascal, *Pensées,* IV, 265

57 If we submit everything to reason, our religion will have no mysterious and supernatural element. If we offend the principles of reason, our religion will be absurd and ridiculous.

Pascal, *Pensées,* IV, 273

58 Instead of complaining that God had hidden Himself, you will give Him thanks for not having revealed so much of Himself; and you will also give Him thanks for not having revealed Himself to haughty sages, unworthy to know so holy a God.

Two kinds of persons know Him: those who have a humble heart, and who love lowliness, whatever kind of intellect they may have, high or low; and those who have sufficient understanding to see the truth, whatever opposition they may have to it.

Pascal, *Pensées,* IV, 288

59 The knowledge of God without that of man's misery causes pride. The knowledge of man's misery without that of God causes despair. The knowledge of Jesus Christ constitutes the middle course, because in Him we find both God and our misery.

Pascal, *Pensées,* VII, 527

60 We understand nothing of the works of God, if we do not take as a principle that He has willed to blind some and enlighten others.

Pascal, *Pensées,* VIII, 566

61 It is a wonderful thing, and worthy of particular attention, to see this Jewish people existing so many years in perpetual misery, it being necessary as a proof of Jesus Christ both that they should exist to prove Him and that they should be miserable because they crucified Him; and though to be miserable and to exist are contradictory, they nevertheless still exist in spite of their misery. They are visibly a people expressly created to serve as a witness to the Messiah (Isaiah 43.9; 44.8). They keep the books, and love them, and do not understand them. And all this was foretold; that God's judgments are entrusted to them, but as a sealed book.

Pascal, *Pensées,* IX, 640–641

62   What in me is dark
Illumine, what is low raise and support;
That to the highth of this great Argument
I may assert Eternal Providence,
And justifie the wayes of God to men.

Milton, *Paradise Lost,* I, 22

63   Thou Celestial light
Shine inward, and the mind through all her powers
Irradiate, there plant eyes, all mist from thence
Purge and disperse, that I may see and tell
Of things invisible to mortal sight.

Milton, *Paradise Lost,* III, 51

64 So spake the Seraph *Abdiel* faithful found,
Among the faithless, faithful only hee;
Among innumerable false, unmov'd,
Unshak'n, unseduc'd, unterrifi'd

His Loyaltie he kept, his Love, his Zeale;
Nor number, nor example with him wrought
To swerve from truth, or change his constant
    mind
Though single. From amidst them forth he passd,
Long way through hostile scorn, which he sus-
    teind
Superior, nor of violence fear'd aught;
And with retorted scorn his back he turn'd
On those proud Towrs to swift destruction
    doom'd.

                Milton, *Paradise Lost*, V, 893

65 Where there is much desire to learn, there of necessity will be much arguing, much writing, many
opinions; for opinion in good men is but knowledge in the making.

                Milton, *Areopagitica*

66 As in the whole course of my investigation I found
nothing taught expressly by Scripture, which does
not agree with our understanding, or which is repugnant thereto, and as I saw that the prophets
taught nothing, which is not very simple and easily to be grasped by all, and further, that they
clothed their teaching in the style, and confirmed
it with the reasons, which would most deeply
move the mind of the masses to devotion towards
God, I became thoroughly convinced, that the Bible leaves reason absolutely free, that it has nothing in common with philosophy, in fact, that Revelation and Philosophy stand on totally different
footings.

        Spinoza, *Theologico-Political Treatise*, Pref.

67 Scripture does not teach philosophy, but merely
obedience, and . . . all it contains has been
adapted to the understanding and established
opinions of the multitude. Those, therefore, who
wish to adapt it to philosophy, must needs ascribe
to the prophets many ideas which they never even
dreamed of, and give an extremely forced interpretation to their words: those on the other hand,
who would make reason and philosophy subservient to theology, will be forced to accept as Divine utterances the prejudices of the ancient Jews,
and to fill and confuse their mind therewith. In
short, one party will run wild with the aid of reason, and the other will run wild without the aid of
reason.

        Spinoza, *Theologico-Political Treatise*, XV

68 Faith is not built on disquisitions vain;
The things we must believe are few and plain.

              Dryden, *Religio Laici*, 431

69 Divine faith itself, when it is kindled in the soul, is
something more than an opinion, and depends
not upon the occasions or the motives that have
given it birth; it advances beyond the intellect,
and takes possession of the will and of the heart, to

make us act with zeal and joyfully as the law of
God commands. Then we have no further need to
think of reasons or to pause over the difficulties of
argument which the mind may anticipate.

              Leibniz, *Theodicy*, 29

70 Though everything said in the text be infallibly
true, yet the reader may be, nay, cannot choose
but be, very fallible in the understanding of it.
Nor is it to be wondered, that the will of God,
when clothed in words, should be liable to that
doubt and uncertainty which unavoidably attends
that sort of conveyance, when even his Son, whilst
clothed in flesh, was subject to all the frailties and
inconveniences of human nature, sin excepted.

      Locke, *Concerning Human Understanding*,
                    Bk. III, IX, 23

71 Though the common experience and the ordinary
course of things have justly a mighty influence on
the minds of men, to make them give or refuse
credit to anything proposed to their belief; yet
there is one case, wherein the strangeness of the
fact lessens not the assent to a fair testimony given
of it. For where such supernatural events are suitable to ends aimed at by Him who has the power
to change the course of nature, there, under such
circumstances, that may be the fitter to procure
belief, by how much the more they are beyond or
contrary to ordinary observation. This is the proper case of miracles, which, well attested, do not
only find credit themselves, but give it also to
other truths, which need such confirmation.

      Locke, *Concerning Human Understanding*,
                  Bk. IV, XVI, 13

72 Reason is natural revelation, whereby the eternal
Father of light and fountain of all knowledge,
communicates to mankind that portion of truth
which he has laid within the reach of their natural faculties: revelation is natural reason enlarged
by a new set of discoveries communicated by God
immediately; which reason vouches the truth of,
by the testimony and proofs it gives that they
come from God. So that he that takes away reason
to make way for revelation, puts out the light of
both, and does muchwhat the same as if he would
persuade a man to put out his eyes, the better to
receive the remote light of an invisible star by a
telescope.

      Locke, *Concerning Human Understanding*,
                  Bk. IV, XIX, 4

73 I believe that thousands of men would be orthodox enough in certain points, if divines had not
been too curious, or too narrow, in reducing orthodoxy within the compass of subtleties, niceties,
and distinctions, with little warrant from Scripture and less from reason or good policy.

            Swift, *Thoughts on Religion*

74 Lo! the poor Indian, whose untutor'd mind
　　Sees God in clouds, or hears him in the wind;
　　His soul proud Science never taught to stray
　　Far as the solar walk, or milky way;
　　Yet simple Nature to his hope has giv'n,
　　Behind the cloud-topt hill, an humbler heav'n;
　　Some safer world in depth of woods embrac'd,
　　Some happier island in the watry waste,
　　Where slaves once more their native land behold,
　　No fiends torment, no Christians thirst for gold!
　　To Be, contents his natural desire,
　　He asks no Angel's wing, no Seraph's fire;
　　But thinks, admitted to that equal sky,
　　His faithful dog shall bear him company.

　　　　　　　　Pope, *Essay on Man*, Epistle I, 99

75 For Modes of Faith, let graceless zealots fight;
　　His can't be wrong whose life is in the right.

　　　　　　　　Pope, *Essay on Man*, Epistle III, 305

76 When any opinion leads to absurdities, it is cer-
　　tainly false; but it is not certain that an opinion is
　　false, because it is of dangerous consequence.

　　　　　　　　Hume, *Concerning Human*
　　　　　　　　Understanding, VIII, 75

77 Upon the whole, we may conclude, that the
　　Christian religion not only was at first attended
　　with miracles, but even at this day cannot be be-
　　lieved by any reasonable person without one.
　　Mere reason is insufficient to convince us of its
　　veracity: And whoever is moved by faith to assent
　　to it, is conscious of a continued miracle in his
　　own person, which subverts all the principles of
　　his understanding, and gives him a determination
　　to believe what is most contrary to custom and
　　experience.

　　　　　　　　Hume, *Concerning Human*
　　　　　　　　Understanding, X, 101

78 The universal propensity to believe in an invisi-
　　ble, intelligent power, if not an original instinct,
　　being at least a general attendant of human na-
　　ture, may be considered as a kind of mark or
　　stamp, which the Divine workman has set upon
　　his work; and nothing surely can more dignify
　　mankind, than to be thus selected from all other
　　parts of the creation, and to bear the image or
　　impression of the universal Creator.

　　　　　　　　Hume, *Natural History of Religion*, XV

79 Mr. Murray praised the ancient philosophers for
　　the candour and good humour with which those
　　of different sects disputed with each other. *Johnson.*
　　"Sir, they disputed with good humour, because
　　they were not in earnest as to religion. Had the
　　ancients been serious in their belief, we should not
　　have had their Gods exhibited in the manner we
　　find them represented in the Poets. The people
　　would not have suffered it. They disputed with
　　good humour upon their fanciful theories, because

they were not interested in the truth of them:
when a man has nothing to lose, he may be in
good humour with his opponent. Accordingly you
see in Lucian, the Epicurean, who argues only
negatively, keeps his temper; the Stoick, who has
something positive to preserve, grows angry. Being
angry with one who controverts an opinion which
you value, is a necessary consequence of the uneasiness which you feel. Every man who attacks
my belief, diminishes in some degree my confidence in it, and therefore makes me uneasy; and I
am angry with him who makes me uneasy. Those
only who believed in revelation have been angry
at having their faith called in question; because
they only had something upon which they could
rest as matter of fact."

　　　　　　　　Boswell, *Life of Johnson (Apr. 3, 1776)*

80 The opinion of a learned Bishop of our acquain-
　　tance, as to there being merit in religious faith,
　　being mentioned;—*Johnson.* "Why, yes, Sir, the
　　most licentious man, were hell open before him,
　　would not take the most beautiful strumpet to his
　　arms. We must, as the Apostle says, live by faith,
　　not by sight."

　　　　　　　　Boswell, *Life of Johnson (June 3, 1781)*

81 Since . . . the most sublime efforts of philosophy
　　can extend no farther than feebly to point out the
　　desire, the hope, or, at most, the probability of a
　　future state, there is nothing, except a divine reve-
　　lation that can ascertain the existence and de-
　　scribe the condition of the invisible country which
　　is destined to receive the souls of men after their
　　separation from the body.

　　　　　　　　Gibbon, *Decline and Fall of the Roman*
　　　　　　　　Empire, XV

82 Personal interest is often the standard of our be-
　　lief, as well as of our practice.

　　　　　　　　Gibbon, *Decline and Fall of the Roman*
　　　　　　　　Empire, XX

83 The most sagacious of the Christian theologians,
　　the great Athanasius himself, has candidly con-
　　fessed that, whenever he forced his understanding
　　to meditate on the divinity of the *Logos*, his toil-
　　some and unavailing efforts recoiled on them-
　　selves; that the more he thought, the less he com-
　　prehended; and the more he wrote, the less
　　capable was he of expressing his thoughts. In ev-
　　ery step of the inquiry we are compelled to feel
　　and acknowledge the immeasurable disproportion
　　between the size of the object and the capacity of
　　the human mind. We may strive to abstract the
　　notions of time, of space, and of matter, which so
　　closely adhere to all the perceptions of our experi-
　　mental knowledge. But as soon as we presume to
　　reason of infinite substance, of spiritual genera-
　　tion, as often as we deduce any positive conclu-
　　sions from a negative idea, we are involved in

darkness, perplexity, and inevitable contradiction.

Gibbon, *Decline and Fall of the Roman Empire*, XXI

84 I maintain that all attempts of reason to establish a theology by the aid of speculation alone are fruitless, that the principles of reason as applied to nature do not conduct us to any theological truths, and, consequently, that a rational theology can have no existence, unless it is founded upon the laws of morality. For all synthetical principles of the understanding are valid only as immanent in experience; while the cognition of a Supreme Being necessitates their being employed transcendentally, and of this the understanding is quite incapable. If the empirical law of causality is to conduct us to a Supreme Being, this being must belong to the chain of empirical objects—in which case it would be, like all phenomena, itself conditioned. If the possibility of passing the limits of experience be admitted, by means of the dynamical law of the relation of an effect to its cause, what kind of conception shall we obtain by this procedure? Certainly not the conception of a Supreme Being, because experience never presents us with the greatest of all possible effects, and it is only an effect of this character that could witness to the existence of a corresponding cause. If, for the purpose of fully satisfying the requirements of Reason, we recognize her right to assert the existence of a perfect and absolutely necessary being, this can be admitted only from favour, and cannot be regarded as the result or irresistible demonstration. The physico-theological proof may add weight to others—if other proofs there are—by connecting speculation with experience; but in itself it rather prepares the mind for theological cognition, and gives it a right and natural direction, than establishes a sure foundation for theology.

Kant, *Critique of Pure Reason*, Transcendental Dialectic

85 Holding for true, or the subjective validity of a judgement in relation to conviction (which is, at the same time, objectively valid), has the three following degrees: opinion, belief, and knowledge. Opinion is a consciously insufficient judgement, subjectively as well as objectively. Belief is subjectively sufficient, but is recognized as being objectively insufficient. Knowledge is both subjectively and objectively sufficient. Subjective sufficiency is termed conviction (for myself); objective sufficiency is termed certainty (for all). I need not dwell longer on the explanation of such simple conceptions.

Kant, *Critique of Pure Reason*, Transcendental Method

86 When men exercise their reason coolly and freely on a variety of distinct questions, they inevitably fall into different opinions on some of them. When they are governed by a common passion, their opinions, if they are so to be called, will be the same.

Hamilton or Madison, *Federalist 50*

87 Public opinion . . . deserves to be as much respected as despised—despised for its concrete expression and for the concrete consciousness it expresses, respected for its essential basis, a basis which only glimmers more or less dimly in that concrete expression. But in itself it has no criterion of discrimination, nor has it the ability to extract the substantive element it contains and raise it to precise knowledge. Thus to be independent of public opinion is the first formal condition of achieving anything great or rational whether in life or in science. Great achievement is assured, however, of subsequent recognition and grateful acceptance by public opinion, which in due course will make it one of its own prejudices.

Hegel, *Philosophy of Right*, 318

88 Opinion is like a pendulum and obeys the same law. If it goes past the centre of gravity on one side, it must go a like distance on the other; and it is only after a certain time that it finds the true point at which it can remain at rest.

Schopenhauer, *Further Psychological Observations*

89 There is no other revelation than the thoughts of the wise, even though these thoughts, liable to error as is the lot of everything human, are often clothed in strange allegories and myths under the name of religion. So far, then, it is a matter of indifference whether a man lives and dies in reliance on his own or another's thoughts; for it is never more than human thought, human opinion, which he trusts. Still, instead of trusting what their own minds tell them, men have as a rule a weakness for trusting others who pretend to supernatural sources of knowledge. And in view of the enormous intellectual inequality between man and man, it is easy to see that the thoughts of one mind might appear as in some sense a revelation to another.

Schopenhauer, *Christian System*

90 Faith is the highest passion in a man. There are perhaps many in every generation who do not even reach it, but no one gets further.

Kierkegaard, *Fear and Trembling*, Epilogue

91 Mysticism has not the patience to wait for God's revelation.

Kierkegaard, *Journals (July 11, 1840)*

92 We are born believing. A man bears beliefs as a tree bears apples.

Emerson, *Worship*

93 The test of the true faith, certainly, should be its power to charm and command the soul, as the laws of nature control the activity of the hands—so commanding that we find pleasure and honor in obeying.

> Emerson, *Address to Harvard Divinity School*

94 Strong Son of God, immortal Love,
  Whom we, that have not seen thy face,
  By faith, and faith alone, embrace,
Believing where we cannot prove.

> Tennyson, *In Memoriam,* Pref.

95 *Ahab.* If the gods think to speak outright to man, they will honourably speak outright; not shake their heads, and give an old wife's darkling hint.

> Melville, *Moby Dick,* CXXXIII

96 It is remarkable that the highest intellectual mood which the world tolerates is the perception of the truth of the most ancient revelations, now in some respects out of date; but any direct revelation, any original thoughts, it hates like virtue. The fathers and the mothers of the town would rather hear the young man or young woman at their tables express reverence for some old statement of the truth than utter a direct revelation themselves. They don't want to have any prophets born into their families—damn them! So far as thinking is concerned, surely original thinking is the divinest thing. Rather we should reverently watch for the least motions, the least scintillations, of thought in this sluggish world, and men should run to and fro on the occasion more than at an earthquake. We check and repress the divinity that stirs within us, to fall down and worship the divinity that is dead without us. I go to see many a good man or good woman, so called, and utter freely that thought which alone it was given to me to utter; but there was a man who lived a long, long time ago, and his name was Moses, and another whose name was Christ, and if your thought does not, or does not appear to, coincide with what they said, the good man or the good woman has no ears to hear you. They think they love God! It is only his old clothes, of which they make scarecrows for the children. Where will they come nearer to God than in those very children?

> Thoreau, *Journal (Nov. 16, 1851)*

97 What we call rational grounds for our beliefs are often extremely irrational attempts to justify our instincts.

> T. H. Huxley, *On the Natural Inequality of Men,* fn. 1

98 There is the greatest difference between presuming an opinion to be true, because, with every opportunity for contesting it, it has not been refuted, and assuming its truth for the purpose of not permitting its refutation. Complete liberty of contra-dicting and disproving our opinion is the very condition which justifies us in assuming its truth for purposes of action; and on no other terms can a being with human faculties have any rational assurance of being right.

> Mill, *On Liberty,* II

99 The usefulness of an opinion is itself matter of opinion: as disputable, as open to discussion, and requiring discussion as much as the opinion itself. There is the same need of an infallible judge of opinions to decide an opinion to be noxious, as to decide it to be false, unless the opinion condemned has full opportunity of defending itself. And it will not do to say that the heretic may be allowed to maintain the utility or harmlessness of his opinion, though forbidden to maintain its truth. The truth of an opinion is part of its utility. If we would know whether or not it is desirable that a proposition should be believed, is it possible to exclude the consideration of whether or not it is true? In the opinion, not of bad men, but of the best men, no belief which is contrary to truth can be really useful: and can you prevent such men from urging that plea, when they are charged with culpability for denying some doctrine which they are told is useful, but which they believe to be false?

> Mill, *On Liberty,* II

100 Reason . . . is subservient to faith, as handling, examining, explaining, recording, cataloguing, defending the truths which faith, not reason, has gained for us, as providing an intellectual expression of supernatural facts, eliciting what is implicit, comparing, measuring, connecting each with each, and forming one and all into a theological system.

> Newman, *Essay on the Development of Christian Doctrine,* Pt. II, VII, 3

101 From the age of fifteen, dogma has been the fundamental principle of my religion: I know no other religion; I cannot enter into the idea of any other sort of religion; religion, as a mere sentiment, is to me a dream and a mockery.

> Newman, *Apologia Pro Vita Sua,* II

102 Ten thousand difficulties do not make one doubt.

> Newman, *Apologia Pro Vita Sua,* V

103 The Sea of Faith
Was once, too, at the full, and round earth's shore
Lay like the folds of a bright girdle furled.
But now I only hear
Its melancholy, long, withdrawing roar,
Retreating, to the breath
Of the night-wind, down the vast edges drear
And naked shingles of the world.

> Arnold, *Dover Beach*

104 That ancient deception which demands faith in what has no reasonable explanation, is already worn out and we can no longer return to it. . . . Man always understands everything through his reason and not through faith. It was once possible to deceive him by asserting that he knows only through faith and not through reason, but as soon as he knows two faiths and sees men who profess another faith in the same way that he professes his own, he is inevitably obliged to decide the matter by reason. . . . In our time the attempts made to infuse spirituality into man through faith apart from reason, are like attempts to feed a man otherwise than through his mouth.

Tolstoy, *On Life*, Appendix III

105 People today live without faith. On the one hand, the minority of wealthy, educated people, having freed themselves from the hypnotism of the Church, believe in nothing. They look upon all faiths as absurdities or as useful means of keeping the masses in bondage—no more. On the other hand, the vast majority, poor, uneducated, but for the most part truly sincere, remain under the hypnotism of the Church and therefore think they believe and have faith. But this is not really faith, for instead of throwing light on man's position in the world it only darkens it.

Tolstoy, *What Is Religion?*, VIII

106 Thought in action has for its only possible motive the attainment of thought at rest; and whatever does not refer to belief is no part of the thought itself.

And what, then, is belief? It is the demi-cadence which closes a musical phrase in the symphony of our intellectual life. We have seen that it has just three properties: First, it is something that we are aware of; second, it appeases the irritation of doubt; and, third, it involves the establishment in our nature of a rule of action, or, say for short, a *habit*. As it appeases the irritation of doubt, which is the motive for thinking, thought relaxes, and comes to rest for a moment when belief is reached. But, since belief is a rule for action, the application of which involves further doubt and further thought, at the same time that it is a stopping-place, it is also a new starting-place for thought. That is why I have permitted myself to call it thought at rest, although thought is essentially an action. The *final* upshot of thinking is the exercise of volition, and of this thought no longer forms a part; but belief is only a stadium of mental action, an effect upon our nature due to thought, which will influence future thinking.

C. S. Peirce, *How to Make Our Ideas Clear*

107 Whoever has theologian blood in his veins has a wrong and dishonest attitude towards all things from the very first. The pathos that develops out of this is called faith.

Nietzsche, *Antichrist*, IX

108 The 'will of God' (that is to say the conditions for preserving the power of the priest) has to be known—to this end a 'revelation' is required. In plain words: a great literary forgery becomes necessary, a 'sacred book' is discovered—it is made public with all hieratic pomp, with days of repentance and with lamentation over the long years of 'sinfulness'.

Nietzsche, *Antichrist*, XXVI

109 The logical reason of man operates in this field of divinity exactly as it has always operated in love, or in patriotism, or in politics, or in any other of the wider affairs of life, in which our passions or our mystical intuitions fix our beliefs beforehand. It finds arguments for our conviction, for indeed it *has* to find them. It amplifies and defines our faith, and dignifies it and lends it words and plausibility. It hardly ever engenders it; it cannot now secure it.

William James, *Varieties of Religious Experience*, XVIII

110 Our faith is faith in someone else's faith, and in the greatest matters this is most the case.

William James, *The Will to Believe*

111 So far as man stands for anything, and is productive or originative at all, his entire vital function may be said to have to deal with maybes. Not a victory is gained, not a deed of faithfulness or courage is done, except upon a maybe; not a service, not a sally of generosity, not a scientific exploration or experiment or textbook, that may not be a mistake. It is only by risking our persons from one hour to another that we live at all. And often enough our faith beforehand in an uncertified result *is the only thing that makes the result come true.* Suppose, for instance, that you are climbing a mountain, and have worked yourself into a position from which the only escape is by a terrible leap. Have faith that you can successfully make it, and your feet are nerved to its accomplishment. But mistrust yourself, and think of all the sweet things you have heard the scientists say of *maybes,* and you will hesitate so long that, at last, all unstrung and trembling, and launching yourself in a moment of despair, you roll in the abyss. In such a case (and it belongs to an enormous class), the part of wisdom as well as of courage is to *believe what is in the line of your needs,* for only by such belief is the need fulfilled. Refuse to believe, and you shall indeed be right, for you shall irretrievably perish. But believe, and again you shall be right, for you shall save yourself. You make one or the other of two possible universes true by your trust or mistrust,—both universes having been only *maybes,* in this particular, before you contributed your act.

William James, *Is Life Worth Living?*

112 These, then, are my last words to you: Be not afraid of life. Believe that life *is* worth living, and your belief will help create the fact. The 'scientific proof' that you are right may not be clear before the day of judgment (or some stage of being which that expression may serve to symbolize) is reached. But the faithful fighters of this hour, or the beings that then and there will represent them, may then turn to the faint-hearted, who here decline to go on, with words like those with which Henry IV greeted the tardy Crillon after a great victory had been gained: "Hang yourself, brave Crillon! we fought at Arques, and you were not there."

William James, *Is Life Worth Living?*

113 It is not disbelief that is dangerous in our society: it is belief.

Shaw, *Androcles and the Lion*, Pref.

114 William James accomplished a new advance in Pragmatism by his theory of the will to believe, or as he himself later called it, the right to believe. The discovery of the fundamental consequences of one or another belief has without fail a certain influence on that belief itself. If a man cherishes novelty, risk, opportunity and a variegated esthetic reality, he will certainly reject any belief in Monism, when he clearly perceives the import of this system. But if, from the very start, he is attracted by esthetic harmony, classic proportions, fixity even to the extent of absolute security, and logical coherence, it is quite natural that he should put faith in Monism. Thus William James took into account those motives of instinctive sympathy which play a greater rôle in our choice of a philosophic system than do formal reasonings; and he thought that we should be rendering a service to the cause of philosophical sincerity if we would openly recognize the motives which inspire us. He also maintained the thesis that the greater part of philosophic problems and especially those which touch on religious fields are of such a nature that they are not susceptible of decisive evidence one way or the other. Consequently he claimed the right of a man to choose his beliefs not only in the presence of proofs or conclusive facts, but also in the absence of all such proof. Above all when he is forced to choose between one meaning or another, or when by refusing to choose he has a right to assume the risks of faith, his refusal is itself equivalent to a choice. The theory of the will to believe gives rise to misunderstandings and even to ridicule; and therefore it is necessary to understand clearly in what way James used it. We are always obliged to act in any case; our actions and with them their consequences actually change according to the beliefs which we have chosen. Moreover it may be that, in order to discover the proofs which will ultimately be the intellectual justification of certain beliefs—the belief in freedom, for example, or the belief in God—it is necessary to begin to act in accordance with this belief.

Dewey, *Development of American Pragmatism*

115 Dogmas are at their best when nobody denies them, for then their falsehood sleeps, like that of an unconscious metaphor, and their moral function is discharged instinctively.

Santayana, *Life of Reason*, III, 5

6.6 | *Doubt and Skepticism*

It is not in the sphere of opinion or belief, but rather with respect to matters about which men claim to have knowledge, that doubt operates critically. Whatever is a matter of opinion or belief, even if appraised as highly probable, is subject to doubt. But when men claim to have certitude in their knowledge or possession of the truth, they hold what they affirm or deny to be beyond all reasonable doubt. It is such certitude that the skeptic challenges by his doubts.

As the passages collected here plainly show, skepticism is both an attitude of mind and a systematic method of dealing with the whole range of human opinions, beliefs, and claims to knowledge. In its ancient as well as in its modern forms, it sometimes goes to the extreme of universal doubt. We can have certainty about nothing, nor can we even validly assert that one proposition is more probable than another. One opinion is as good as another; all are equally true or false. The reader will find among the passages quoted, arguments against such extreme skepticism that take the form of reduction to absurdity: the skeptic cannot say that no statement is true without contradicting himself, for if his own statement is false, then at least some statements are true; and if his own statement is true, then it is false that no statements are true. Should the skeptic refuse to acknowledge the force of this argument, because he is willing to embrace self-contradiction, nothing remains to be said. Conversation between the extreme skeptic and his opponent must cease.

In other quotations the reader will find a more moderate skepticism recommended as a therapeutic method, seeking to sift the claims to knowledge and to winnow those that are valid from those that are without foundation. This is the method of beginning by doubting everything in order to come at last to the few things that one cannot doubt, and to discover from an examination of these the criteria of certitude. Moderate skepticism also takes the form of attenuating universal doubt by conceding moral or practical certitude to the beliefs one must embrace in order to carry on the conduct of one's life from day to day. The attempt to maintain a middle position between extreme skepticism, on the one hand, and extreme dogmatism, on the other, is sometimes described as being properly critical rather than skeptical. The reader will discern these nuances of method in quotations from Descartes, Hume, and Kant; but it is by reading the passages taken from Montaigne that he will become acquainted with skepticism as an attitude of mind that is both tolerant and uncompromising.

In still other passages, the reader will discover the range of reasons that are offered for the doubt or uncertainty that generates one or another form of skepticism: mistrust of the senses based on the illusions and hallucinations to which they are subject; mistrust of intellectual judgments based on the fallibility of the intellect and the errors to which it is prone; mistrust of even widely held opinions or firmly established beliefs based on the fact that contrary opinions and beliefs have also been regarded as acceptable or settled. It will be seen that the opponents of skepticism, certainly in its extreme form, do not dismiss such doubts as groundless, but rather try to confine them to the areas in which they are justified.

---

1 *Socrates.* What, according to you and your friend Gorgias, is the definition of virtue?

Meno. O Socrates, I used to be told, before I knew you, that you were always doubting yourself and making others doubt; and now you are casting your spells over me, and I am simply getting bewitched and enchanted, and am at my wits' end. And if I may venture to make a jest upon you, you seem to me both in your appearance and in your power over others to be very like the flat torpedo fish, who torpifies those who come near him and touch him, as you have now torpified me, I think. For my soul and my tongue are really torpid, and I do not know how to answer you; and though I have been delivered of an infinite variety of speeches about virtue before now, and to many persons—and very good ones they were, as I thought—at this moment I cannot even say what virtue is. And I think that you are very wise in not voyaging and going away from home, for if you did in other places as you do in Athens, you would be cast into prison as a magician.

Soc. You are a rogue, Meno, and had all but caught me.

Men. What do you mean, Socrates?

Soc. I can tell why you made a simile about me.

Men. Why?

Soc. In order that I might make another simile

about you. For I know that all pretty young gentlemen like to have pretty similes made about them—as well they may—but I shall not return the compliment. As to my being a torpedo, if the torpedo is torpid as well as the cause of torpidity in others, then indeed I am a torpedo, but not otherwise; for I perplex others, not because I am clear, but because I am utterly perplexed myself. And now I know not what virtue is, and you seem to be in the same case, although you did once perhaps know before you touched me.

Plato, *Meno*, 79B

2 *Socrates.* Tell me, Theodorus, do you suppose that you yourself, or any other follower of Protagoras, would contend that no one deems another ignorant or mistaken in his opinion?

Theodorus. The thing is incredible, Socrates.

Soc. And yet that absurdity is necessarily involved in the thesis which declares man to be the measure of all things.

Theod. How so?

Soc. Why, suppose that you determine in your own mind something to be true, and declare your opinion to me; let us assume, as he argues, that this is true to you. Now, if so, you must either say that the rest of us are not the judges of this opinion or judgment of yours, or that we judge you always to have a true opinion? But are there not thousands upon thousands who, whenever you form a judgment, take up arms against you and are of an opposite judgment and opinion, deeming that you judge falsely?

Theod. Yes, indeed, Socrates, thousands and tens of thousands, as Homer says, who give me a world of trouble.

Soc. Well, but are we to assert that what you think is true to you and false to the ten thousand others?

Theod. No other inference seems to be possible.

Soc. And how about Protagoras himself? If neither he nor the multitude thought, as indeed they do not think, that man is the measure of all things, must it not follow that the truth of which Protagoras wrote would be true to no one? But if you suppose that he himself thought this, and that the multitude does not agree with him, you must begin by allowing that in whatever proportion the many are more than one, in that proportion his truth is more untrue than true.

Theod. That would follow if the truth is supposed to vary with individual opinion.

Soc. And the best of the joke is, that he acknowledges the truth of their opinion who believe his own opinion to be false; for he admits that the opinions of all men are true.

Theod. Certainly.

Soc. And does he not allow that his own opinion is false, if he admits that the opinion of those who think him false is true?

Theod. Of course.

Soc. Whereas the other side do not admit that they speak falsely?

Theod. They do not.

Soc. And he, as may be inferred from his writings, agrees that this opinion is also true.

Theod. Clearly.

Soc. Then all mankind, beginning with Protagoras, will contend, or rather, I should say that he will allow, when he concedes that his adversary has a true opinion—Protagoras, I say, will himself allow that neither a dog nor any ordinary man is the measure of anything which he has not learned—am I not right?

Theod. Yes.

Soc. And the truth of Protagoras being doubted by all, will be true neither to himself nor to any one else?

Theod. I think, Socrates, that we are running my old friend too hard.

Plato, *Theaetetus*, 170B

3 All statements cannot be false nor all true, both because of many other difficulties which might be adduced as arising from this position, and because if all are false it will not be true to say even this, and if all are true it will not be false to say all are false.

Aristotle, *Metaphysics*, 1063^{b}30

4 If a man believe that nothing is known, he knows not whether this even can be known, since he admits he knows nothing. I will therefore decline to argue the case against him who places himself with head where his feet should be. And yet granting that he knows this, I would still put this question, since he has never yet seen any truth in things, whence he knows what knowing and not knowing severally are, and what it is that has produced the knowledge of the true and the false and what has proved the doubtful to differ from the certain.

Lucretius, *Nature of Things*, IV

5 But straightway Jesus spake unto them, saying, Be of good cheer; it is I; be not afraid.

And Peter answered him and said, Lord, if it be thou, bid me come unto thee on the water.

And he said, Come. And when Peter was come down out of the ship, he walked on the water, to go to Jesus.

But when he saw the wind boisterous, he was afraid; and beginning to sink, he cried, saying, Lord, save me.

And immediately Jesus stretched forth his hand, and caught him, and said unto him, O thou of little faith, wherefore didst thou doubt?

Matthew 14:27–31

6 But Thomas, one of the twelve, called Dĭd-ў̆-mŭs, was not with them when Jesus came.

The other disciples therefore said unto him, We

have seen the Lord. But he said unto them, Except I shall see in his hands the print of the nails, and put my finger into the print of the nails, and thrust my hand into his side, I will not believe.

John 20:24–25

7 *Zeus.* What have we left?

Hermes. There is Scepticism. Come along, Pyrrhias, and be put up. Quick's the word. The attendance is dwindling; there will be small competition. Well, who buys Lot 9?

Ninth Dealer. I. Tell me first, though, what do you know?

Scepticism. Nothing.

Ninth D. But how's that?

Sc. There does not appear to me to *be* anything.

Ninth D. Are not *we* something?

Sc. How do I know that?

Ninth D. And you yourself?

Sc. Of that I am still more doubtful.

Ninth D. Well, you *are* in a fix! And what have you got those scales for?

Sc. I use them to weigh arguments in, and get them evenly balanced. They must be absolutely equal—not a feather-weight to choose between them; then, and not till then, can I make uncertain which is right.

Ninth D. What else can you turn your hand to?

Sc. Anything; except catching a runaway.

Ninth D. And why not that?

Sc. Because, friend, everything eludes my grasp.

Ninth D. I believe you. A slow, lumpish fellow you seem to be. And what is the end of your knowledge?

Sc. Ignorance. Deafness. Blindness.

Ninth D. What! sight and hearing both gone?

Sc. And with them judgement and perception, and all, in short, that distinguishes man from a worm.

Ninth D. You are worth money!—What shall we say for him?

Her. Four pounds.

Ninth D. Here it is. Well, fellow; so you are mine?

Sc. I doubt it.

Ninth D. Nay, doubt it not! You are bought and paid for.

Sc. It is a difficult case. . . . I reserve my decision.

Ninth D. Now, come along with me, like a good slave.

Sc. But how am I to know whether what you say is true?

Ninth D. Ask the auctioneer. Ask my money. Ask the spectators.

Sc. Spectators? But can we be sure there are any?

Ninth D. Oh, I'll send you to the treadmill. That will convince you with a vengeance that I am your master.

Sc. Reserve your decision.

Ninth D. Too late. It is given.

Her. Stop that wrangling and go with your purchaser. Gentlemen, we hope to see you here again to-morrow, when we shall be offering some lots suitable for plain men, artisans, and shopkeepers.

Lucian, *Sale of Creeds*

8 For we are, and know that we are, and delight in our being, and our knowledge of it. Moreover, in these three things no true-seeming illusion disturbs us; for we do not come into contact with these by some bodily sense, as we perceive the things outside of us—colours, e.g., by seeing, sounds by hearing, smells by smelling, tastes by tasting, hard and soft objects by touching—of all which sensible objects it is the images resembling them but not themselves which we perceive in the mind and hold in the memory, and which excite us to desire the objects. But, without any delusive representation of images or phantasms, I am most certain that I am and that I know and delight in this. In respect of these truths, I am not at all afraid of the arguments of the Academicians, who say, "What if you are deceived?" For if I am deceived, I am. For he who is not, cannot be deceived; and if I am deceived, by this same token I am. And since I am if I am deceived, how am I deceived in believing that I am? for it is certain that I am if I am deceived. Since, therefore, I, the person deceived, should be, even if I were deceived, certainly I am not deceived in this knowledge that I am. And, consequently, neither am I deceived in knowing that I know. For, as I know that I am, so I know this also, that I know. And when I love these two things, I add to them a certain third thing, namely, my love, which is of equal moment. For neither am I deceived in this, that I love, since in those things which I love I am not deceived; though even if these were false, it would still be true that I loved false things. For how could I justly be blamed and prohibited from loving false things, if it were false that I loved them? But, since they are true and real, who doubts that when they are loved, the love of them is itself true and real?

Augustine, *City of God*, XI, 26

9 *Panurge.* By the flesh, blood, and body, I swear, reswear, forswear, abjure, and renounce: he evades and avoids, shifts and escapes me, and quite slips and winds himself out of my gripes and clutches.

At these words Gargantua arose, and said, Praised be the good God in all things, but especially for bringing the world into the height of refinedness beyond what it was when I first became acquainted therewith, that now the most learned and most prudent philosophers are not ashamed to be seen entering in at the porches and frontispieces of the schools of the Pyrrhonian, Aporrhetic, Sceptic, and Ephetic sects. Blessed be the holy name of God! Veritably, it is like henceforth to be found an enterprise of much more easy undertaking, to catch lions by the neck, horses by the mane, oxen by the horns, bulls by the muzzle, wolves by the tail, goats by the beard, and flying birds by the feet, than to entrap such philosophers in their words.

Rabelais, *Gargantua and Pantagruel,* III, 36

10 Ignorance that knows itself, that judges itself and condemns itself, is not complete ignorance: to be that, it must be ignorant of itself. So that the profession of the Pyrrhonians is to waver, doubt, and inquire, to be sure of nothing, to answer for nothing. Of the three functions of the soul, the imaginative, the appetitive, and the consenting, they accept the first two; the last they suspend and keep it ambiguous, without inclination or approbation, however slight, in one direction or the other.

Zeno pictured in a gesture his conception of this division of the faculties of the soul: the hand spread and open was appearance; the hand half shut and the fingers a little hooked, consent; the closed fist, comprehension; when with his left hand he closed his fist still tighter, knowledge.

Now this attitude of their judgment, straight and inflexible, taking all things in without adherence or consent, leads them to their Ataraxy, which is a peaceful and sedate condition of life, exempt from the agitations we receive through the impression of the opinion and knowledge we think we have of things. Whence are born fear, avarice, envy, immoderate desires, ambition, pride, superstition, love of novelty, rebellion, disobedience, obstinacy, and most bodily ills. Indeed, they free themselves thereby from jealousy on behalf of their doctrine. For they dispute in a very mild manner. They do not fear contradiction in their discussion. When they say that heavy things go down, they would be very sorry to have anyone take their word for it; and they seek to be contradicted, so as to create doubt and suspension of judgment, which is their goal. They advance their propositions only to combat those they think we believe in. . . .

Is it not an advantage to be freed from the necessity that curbs others? Is it not better to remain in suspense than to entangle yourself in the many errors that the human fancy has produced? Is it not better to suspend your conviction than to get mixed up in these seditious and quarrelsome divisions? . . .

The Pyrrhonians have kept themselves a wonderful advantage in combat, having rid themselves of the need to cover up. It does not matter to them that they are struck, provided they strike; and they do their work with everything. If they win, your proposition is lame; if you win, theirs is. If they lose, they confirm ignorance; if you lose, you confirm it. If they prove that nothing is known, well and good; if they do not know how to prove it, just as good.

Montaigne, *Essays,* II, 12, Apology for
Raymond Sebond

11 *Que sçais-je?* (What do I know?)
Montaigne (his motto)

12 *Hamlet.* Doubt thou the stars are fire;
    Doubt that the sun doth move;
Doubt truth to be a liar;
    But never doubt I love.
Shakespeare, *Hamlet,* II, ii, 116

13 *Othello.* Make me to see't; or, at the least, so prove
    it
That the probation bear no hinge nor loop
To hang a doubt on; or woe upon thy life!
    Iago. My noble lord—
    Oth. If thou dost slander her and torture me,
Never pray more; abandon all remorse;
On horror's head horrors accumulate;
Do deeds to make heaven weep, all earth amazed;
For nothing canst thou to damnation add
Greater than that.
Shakespeare, *Othello,* III, iii, 364

14 If a man will begin with certainties, he shall end in doubts; but if he will be content to begin with doubts, he shall end in certainties.
Bacon, *Advancement of Learning,* Bk. I, V, 8

15 The registering of doubts hath two excellent uses: the one, that it saveth philosophy from errors and falsehoods; when that which is not fully appearing is not collected into assertion, whereby error might draw error, but reserved in doubt: the other, that the entry of doubts are as so many suckers or sponges to draw use of knowledge; insomuch as that which, if doubts had not preceded, a man should never have advised, but passed it over without note, by the suggestion and solicitation of doubts is made to be attended and applied. But both these commodities do scarcely countervail an inconvenience, which will intrude itself if it be not debarred; which is, that when a doubt is once received, men labour rather how to keep it a doubt still, than how to solve it; and accordingly bend their wits. Of this we see the familiar example in lawyers and scholars, both which, if they have once admitted a doubt, it goeth ever after authorized for a doubt. But that use of wit and knowledge is to be allowed, which laboureth to make doubtful things certain, and not those which labour to make certain things doubtful. Therefore these kalendars of doubts I commend as excellent things; so that there be this caution used, that when they be thoroughly sifted and brought to resolution, they be from thenceforth omitted, decarded, and not continued to cherish and encour-

age men in doubting.

Bacon, *Advancement of Learning,*
Bk. II, VIII, 5

16 Our method and that of the sceptics agree in some respects at first setting out, but differ most widely, and are completely opposed to each other in their conclusion; for they roundly assert that nothing can be known; we, that but a small part of nature can be known, by the present method; their next step, however, is to destroy the authority of the senses and understanding, whilst we invent and supply them with assistance.

Bacon, *Novum Organum,* I, 37

17 I consider that I possess no senses; I imagine that body, figure, extension, movement and place are but the fictions of my mind. What, then, can be esteemed as true? Perhaps nothing at all, unless that there is nothing in the world that is certain.

But how can I know there is not something different from those things that I have just considered, of which one cannot have the slightest doubt? Is there not some God, or some other being by whatever name we call it, who puts these reflections into my mind? That is not necessary, for is it not possible that I am capable of producing them myself? I myself, am I not at least something? But I have already denied that I had senses and body. Yet I hesitate, for what follows from that? Am I so dependent on body and senses that I cannot exist without these? But I was persuaded that there was nothing in all the world, that there was no heaven, no earth, that there were no minds, nor any bodies: was I not then likewise persuaded that I did not exist? Not at all; of a surety I myself did exist since I persuaded myself of something [or merely because I thought of something]. But there is some deceiver or other, very powerful and very cunning, who ever employs his ingenuity in deceiving me. Then without doubt I exist also if he deceives me, and let him deceive me as much as he will, he can never cause me to be nothing so long as I think that I am something. So that after having reflected well and carefully examined all things, we must come to the definite conclusion that this proposition: I am, I exist, is necessarily true each time that I pronounce it, or that I mentally conceive it.

Descartes, *Meditations on First Philosophy,* II

18 After I have recognised that there is a God—because at the same time I have also recognised that all things depend upon Him, and that He is not a deceiver, and from that have inferred that what I perceive clearly and distinctly cannot fail to be true—although I no longer pay attention to the reasons for which I have judged this to be true, provided that I recollect having clearly and distinctly perceived it no contrary reason can be brought forward which could ever cause me to doubt of its truth; and thus I have a true and certain knowledge of it. And this same knowledge extends likewise to all other things which I recollect having formerly demonstrated, such as the truths of geometry and the like; for what can be alleged against them to cause me to place them in doubt?

Descartes, *Meditations on First Philosophy,* V

19 My statement that the entire testimony of the senses must be considered to be uncertain, nay, even false, is quite serious and so necessary for the comprehension of my meditations, that he who will not or cannot admit that, is unfit to urge any objection to them that merits a reply.

Descartes, *Objections and Replies,* V

20 What astonishes me most is to see that all the world is not astonished at its own weakness. Men act seriously, and each follows his own mode of life, not because it is in fact good to follow since it is the custom, but as if each man knew certainly where reason and justice are. They find themselves continually deceived, and, by a comical humility, think it is their own fault and not that of the art which they claim always to possess. But it is well there are so many such people in the world, who are not sceptics for the glory of scepticism, in order to show that man is quite capable of the most extravagant opinions, since he is capable of believing that he is not in a state of natural and inevitable weakness, but, on the contrary, of natural wisdom.

Nothing fortifies scepticism more than that there are some who are not sceptics; if all were so, they would be wrong.

Pascal, *Pensées,* VI, 374

21 As to what is said by Descartes, that we must doubt all things in which there is the least uncertainty, it would be preferable to express it by this better and more expressive precept: We ought to think what degree of acceptance or dissent everything merits; or more simply, We ought to inquire after the reasons of any dogma. Thus the Cartesian wranglings concerning doubt would cease.

Leibniz, *Animadversions on Descartes' Principles
of Philosophy*

22 If we will disbelieve everything, because we cannot certainly know all things, we shall do muchwhat as wisely as he who would not use his legs, but sit still and perish, because he had no wings to fly.

Locke, *Concerning Human Understanding,* Intro.

23 As for our own existence, we perceive it so plainly and so certainly, that it neither needs nor is capable of any proof. For nothing can be more evident to us than our own existence. I think, I reason, I feel pleasure and pain: can any of these be more

evident to me than my own existence? If I doubt of all other things, that very doubt makes me perceive my own existence, and will not suffer me to doubt of that. For if I know I feel pain, it is evident I have as certain perception of my own existence, as of the existence of the pain I feel: or if I know I doubt, I have as certain perception of the existence of the thing doubting, as of that thought which I call doubt. Experience then convinces us, that we have an intuitive knowledge of our own existence, and an internal infallible perception that we are. In every act of sensation, reasoning, or thinking, we are conscious to ourselves of our own being; and, in this matter, come not short of the highest degree of certainty.

Locke, *Concerning Human Understanding,*
Bk. IV, IX, 3

24 As these noble Houyhnhnms are endowed by nature with a general disposition to all virtues, and have no conceptions or ideas of what is evil in a rational creature, so their grand maxim is, to cultivate *reason,* and to be wholly governed by it. Neither is *reason* among them a point problematical as with us, where men can argue with plausibility on both sides of the question; but strikes you with immediate conviction; as it must needs do where it is not mingled, obscured, or discoloured by passion and interest. I remember it was with extreme difficulty that I could bring my master to understand the meaning of the word *opinion,* or how a point could be disputable; because *reason* taught us to affirm or deny, only where we are certain; and beyond our knowledge, we cannot do either. So that controversies, wranglings, disputes, and positiveness in false or dubious propositions, are evils unknown among the Houyhnhnms. In the like manner, when I used to explain to him our several systems of *natural philosophy,* he would laugh that a creature pretending to *reason,* should value it self upon the knowledge of other peoples conjectures, and in things, where that knowledge, if it were certain, could be of no use. Wherein he agreed entirely with the sentiments of Socrates, as Plato delivers them; which I mention as the highest honour I can do that prince of philosophers.

Swift, *Gulliver's Travels,* IV, 8

25 The Cartesian doubt . . . were it ever possible to be attained by any human creature (as it plainly is not) would be entirely incurable; and no reasoning could ever bring us to a state of assurance and conviction upon any subject.

Hume, *Concerning Human Understanding,*
XII, 116

26 The great subverter of Pyrrhonism or the excessive principles of scepticism is action, and employment, and the occupations of common life. These principles may flourish and triumph in the schools; where it is, indeed, difficult, if not impossible, to refute them. But as soon as they leave the shade, and by the presence of the real objects, which actuate our passions and sentiments, are put in opposition to the more powerful principles of our nature, they vanish like smoke, and leave the most determined sceptic in the same condition as other mortals.

The sceptic, therefore, had better keep within his proper sphere, and display those philosophical objections, which arise from more profound researches. Here he seems to have ample matter of triumph; while he justly insists, that all our evidence for any matter of fact, which lies beyond the testimony of sense or memory, is derived entirely from the relation of cause and effect; that we have no other idea of this relation than that of two objects, which have been frequently conjoined together; that we have no argument to convince us, that objects, which have, in our experience, been frequently conjoined, will likewise, in other instances, be conjoined in the same manner; and that nothing leads us to this inference but custom or a certain instinct of our nature; which it is indeed difficult to resist, but which, like other instincts, may be fallacious and deceitful. While the sceptic insists upon these topics, he shows his force, or rather, indeed, his own and our weakness; and seems, for the time at least, to destroy all assurance and conviction. These arguments might be displayed at greater length, if any durable good or benefit to society could ever be expected to result from them.

For here is the chief and most confounding objection to excessive scepticism, that no durable good can ever result from it; while it remains in its full force and vigour. We need only ask such a sceptic, What his meaning is? And what he proposes by all these curious researches? He is immediately at a loss, and knows not what to answer. A Copernican or Ptolemaic, who supports each his different system of astronomy, may hope to produce a conviction, which will remain constant and durable, with his audience. A Stoic or Epicurean displays principles, which may not be durable, but which have an effect on conduct and behaviour. But a Pyrrhonian cannot expect, that his philosophy will have any constant influence on the mind: or if it had, that its influence would be beneficial to society. On the contrary, he must acknowledge, if he will acknowledge anything, that all human life must perish, were his principles universally and steadily to prevail. All discourse, all action would immediately cease; and men remain in a total lethargy, till the necessities of nature, unsatisfied, put an end to their miserable existence. It is true; so fatal an event is very little to be dreaded. Nature is always too strong for principle. And though a Pyrrhonian may throw himself or others into a momentary amazement and confusion by his profound reasonings; the first and most trivial event in life will put to flight all his doubts and scruples, and leave him the same, in every point of action and speculation, with the philosophers of every other sect, or with those who never concerned themselves in any philosophical researches. When he awakes from his dream, he will be the first to join in the laugh against himself, and to confess, that all his objections are mere amusement, and can have no other tendency than to show the whimsical condition of mankind, who must act and reason and believe; though they are not able, by their most diligent enquiry, to satisfy themselves concerning the foundation of these operations, or to remove the objections, which may be raised against them.

Hume, *Concerning Human Understanding*, XII, 126–128

27 There is, indeed, a more mitigated scepticism or academical philosophy, which may be both durable and useful, and which may, in part, be the result of this Pyrrhonism, or excessive scepticism, when its undistinguished doubts are, in some measure, corrected by common sense and reflection. The greater part of mankind are naturally apt to be affirmative and dogmatical in their opinions; and while they see objects only on one side, and have no idea of any counterpoising argument, they throw themselves precipitately into the principles, to which they are inclined; nor have they any indulgence for those who entertain opposite sentiments. To hesitate or balance perplexes their understanding, checks their passion, and suspends their action. They are, therefore, impatient till they escape from a state, which to them is so uneasy: and they think, that they could never remove themselves far enough from it, by the violence of their affirmations and obstinacy of their belief. But could such dogmatical reasoners become sensible of the strange infirmities of human understanding, even in its most perfect state, and when most accurate and cautious in its determinations; such a reflection would naturally inspire them with more modesty and reserve, and diminish their fond opinion of themselves, and their prejudice against antagonists. The illiterate may reflect on the disposition of the learned, who, amidst all the advantages of study and reflection, are commonly still diffident in their determinations: and if any of the learned be inclined, from their natural temper, to haughtiness and obstinacy, a small tincture of Pyrrhonism might abate their pride, by showing them, that the few advantages, which they may have attained over their fellows, are but inconsiderable, if compared with the universal perplexity and confusion, which is inherent in human nature. In general, there is a degree of doubt, and caution, and modesty, which, in all kinds of scrutiny and decision, ought for ever to accompany a just reasoner.

Hume, *Concerning Human Understanding*, XII, 129

28 What danger can ever come from ingenious reasoning and inquiry? The worst speculative skeptic ever I knew was a much better man than the best superstitious devotee and bigot.

Hume, *Letter to Gilbert Elliot (Mar. 10, 1751)*

29 Doubt is not a pleasant condition, but certainty is an absurd one.

Voltaire, *Letter to Frederick the Great (Apr. 6, 1767)*

30 Talking of those who denied the truth of Christianity, he [Johnson] said, "It is always easy to be on the negative side. If a man were now to deny that there is salt upon the table, you could not reduce him to an absurdity. Come, let us try this a little further. I deny that Canada is taken, and I can support my denial by pretty good arguments. The French are a much more numerous people than we; and it is not likely that they would allow us to take it. 'But the ministry have assured us, in all the formality of *The Gazette,* that it is taken.'— Very true. But the ministry have put us to an enormous expence by the war in America, and it is their interest to persuade us that we have got something for our money.—'But the fact is confirmed by thousands of men who were at the taking of it.'—Ay, but these men have still more interest in deceiving us. They don't want that you should think the French have beat them, but that they have beat the French. Now suppose you should go over and find that it is really taken, that would only satisfy yourself; for when you come home we will not believe you. We will say, you have been bribed.—Yet, Sir, notwithstanding all these plausible objections, we have no doubt that Canada is really ours. Such is the weight of common testimony. How much stronger are the evidences of the Christian religion!"

Boswell, *Life of Johnson (July 14, 1763)*

31 *Johnson.* "Hume, and other sceptical innovators, are vain men, and will gratify themselves at any expence. Truth will not afford sufficient food to their vanity; so they have betaken themselves to errour. Truth, Sir, is a cow which will yield such people no more milk, and so they are gone to milk the bull. If I could have allowed myself to gratify my vanity at the expence of truth, what fame might I have acquired. Every thing which Hume has advanced against Christianity had passed through my mind long before he wrote. Always remember this, that after a system is well settled upon positive evidence, a few partial objections ought not to shake it. The human mind is so limited, that it cannot take in all the parts of a subject, so that there may be objections raised against any thing. There are objections against a *plenum,* and objections against a *vacuum;* yet one of them must certainly be true."

Boswell, *Life of Johnson (July 21, 1763)*

32 After we came out of the church, we stood talking for some time together of Bishop Berkeley's ingenious sophistry to prove the non-existence of matter, and that every thing in the universe is merely ideal. I observed, that though we are satisfied his doctrine is not true, it is impossible to refute it. I never shall forget the alacrity with which Johnson answered, striking his foot with mighty force against a large stone, till he rebounded from it, "I refute it *thus.*"

Boswell, *Life of Johnson (Aug. 6, 1763)*

33 When we apply reason to the objective synthesis of phenomena . . . reason establishes, with much plausibility, its principle of unconditioned unity; but it very soon falls into such contradictions that it is compelled, in relation to cosmology, to renounce its pretensions.

For here a new phenomenon of human reason meets us—a perfectly natural antithetic, which does not require to be sought for by subtle sophistry, but into which reason of itself unavoidably falls. It is thereby preserved, to be sure, from the slumber of a fancied conviction—which a merely one-sided illusion produces; but it is at the same time compelled, either, on the one hand, to abandon itself to a despairing scepticism, or, on the other, to assume a dogmatical confidence and obstinate persistence in certain assertions, without granting a fair hearing to the other side of the question. Either is the death of a sound philosophy, although the former might perhaps deserve the title of the euthanasia of pure reason.

Kant, *Critique of Pure Reason,* Transcendental Dialectic

34 The sceptical errors of this remarkably acute thinker [i.e., Hume] arose principally from a defect, which was common to him with the dogmatists, namely, that he had never made a systematic review of all the different kinds of *a priori* synthesis performed by the understanding. Had he done so, he would have found, to take one example among many, that the principle of permanence was of this character, and that it, as well as the principle of causality, anticipates experience. In this way he might have been able to describe the determinate limits of the *a priori* operations of understanding and reason. But he merely declared the understanding to be limited, instead of showing what its limits were; he created a general mistrust in the power of our faculties, without giving us any determinate knowledge of the bounds of our necessary and unavoidable ignorance; he examined and condemned some of the principles of the understanding, without investigating all its powers with the completeness necessary to criticism. He denies, with truth, certain powers to the understanding, but he goes further, and declares it to be utterly inadequate to the *a priori* extension of knowledge, although he has not fully examined all the powers which reside in the faculty; and thus the fate which always overtakes scepticism meets him too. That is to say, his own declarations are doubted, for his objections were based upon *facta,* which are contingent, and not upon principles, which can alone demonstrate the necessary invalidity of all dogmatical assertions.

Kant, *Critique of Pure Reason,* Transcendental Method

35 He who shall teach the Child to Doubt
The rotting Grave shall ne'er get out.
He who respects the Infant's faith
Triumphs over Hell & Death.

Blake, *Auguries of Innocence,* 87

36 *Mephistopheles.* I am the Spirit that denies!
And rightly too; for all that doth begin
Should rightly to destruction run;
'Twere better then that nothing were begun.

Goethe, *Faust,* I, 1338

37 *Dogmatist.* I'll not let screams lead me to war
With doubts and critic-cavils.
The Devil must be something, or
Else how could there be devils?
  Idealist. For once, as I see phantasy,
It is far too despotic.
In truth, if I be all I see,
Today I'm idiotic.
  Realist. This riot makes my torture sheer
And greatly irks me surely;
For the first time I'm standing here
On my feet insecurely.
  Supernaturalist. With much delight I join this crew
And share with them their revels;
For that there are good spirits too
I argue from these devils.
  Skeptic. They go to track the flamelets out
And think they're near the treasure.
Devil alliterates with Doubt,
So I am here with pleasure.

Goethe, *Faust,* I, 4343

38 The arrogant declamations current in our time against philosophy present the singular spectacle, on the one hand of deriving their justification from the superficiality to which that study has been degraded, and, on the other, of being themselves rooted in this element against which they turn so ungratefully. For by pronouncing the knowledge of truth a wild-goose chase, this self-styled philosophizing has reduced all thoughts and all topics to the same level, just as the despotism of the Roman Empire abolished the distinction between free men and slaves, virtue and vice, honour and dishonour, learning and ignorance. The result of this levelling process is that the concepts of what is true, the laws of ethics, likewise become nothing more than opinions and subjec-

tive convictions. The maxims of the worst of criminals, since they too are convictions, are put on the same level of value as those laws; and at the same time any object, however sorry, however accidental, any material however insipid, is put on the same level of value as what constitutes the interest of all thinking men and the bonds of the ethical world.

Hegel, *Philosophy of Right,* Pref.

39 The most dangerous form of scepticism is always that which least looks like it. The notion that pure thought is the positive truth for an existing individual, is sheer scepticism, for this positiveness is chimerical. It is a glorious thing to be able to explain the past, the whole of human history; but if the ability to understand the past is to be the summit of attainment for a living individual, this positiveness is scepticism, and a dangerous form of it, because of the deceptive quantity of things understood.

Kierkegaard, *Concluding Unscientific Postscript,* II, 3

40 I do not press the skepticism of the materialist. I know the quadruped opinion will not prevail. 'Tis of no importance what bats and oxen think. The first dangerous symptom I report is, the levity of intellect; as if it were fatal to earnestness to know much. Knowledge is the knowing that we can not know. The dull pray; the geniuses are light mockers. How respectable is earnestness on every platform! but intellect kills it.

Emerson, *Montaigne; or, The Skeptic*

41 I am the doubter and the doubt,
And I the hymn the Brahmin sings.

Emerson, *Brahma*

42 You say, but with no touch of scorn,
  Sweet-hearted, you, whose light-blue eyes
  Are tender over drowning flies,
You tell me, doubt is Devil-born.

I know not: one indeed I knew
  In many a subtle question versed,
  Who touch'd a jarring lyre at first,
But ever strove to make it true;

Perplext in faith, but pure in deeds,
  At last he beat his music out.
  There lives more faith in honest doubt,
Believe me, than in half the creeds.

He fought his doubts and gather'd strength,
  He would not make his judgment blind,
  He faced the spectres of the mind
And laid them; thus he came at length

To find a stronger faith his own,
  And Power was with him in the night,
  Which makes the darkness and the light,
And dwells not in the light alone,

But in the darkness and the cloud,
  As over Sinai's peaks of old,
  While Israel made their gods of gold,
Altho' the trumpet blew so loud.

Tennyson, *In Memoriam,* XCVI

43 Know ye, now, Bulkington? Glimpses do ye seem to see of that mortally intolerable truth; that all deep, earnest thinking is but the intrepid effort of the soul to keep the open independence of her sea; while the wildest winds of heaven and earth conspire to cast her on the treacherous, slavish shore?

But as in landlessness alone resides the highest truth, shoreless, indefinite as God—so, better is it to perish in that howling infinite, than be ingloriously dashed upon the lee, even if that were safety! For worm-like, then, oh! who would craven crawl to land! Terrors of the terrible! is all this agony so vain? Take heart, take heart, O Bulkington! Bear thee grimly, demigod! Up from the spray of thy ocean-perishing—straight up, leaps thy apotheosis!

Melville, *Moby Dick,* XXIII

44 Through all the thick mists of the dim doubts in my mind, divine intuitions now and then shoot, enkindling my fog with a heavenly ray. And for this I thank God; for all have doubts; many deny; but doubts or denials, few along with them, have intuitions. Doubts of all things earthly, and intuitions of some things heavenly; this combination makes neither believer nor infidel, but makes a man who regards them both with equal eye.

Melville, *Moby Dick,* LXXXV

45 Those who were more directly responsible for providing me with the knowledge essential to the right guidance of life (and who sincerely desired to do so), imagined they were discharging that most sacred duty by impressing upon my childish mind the necessity, on pain of reprobation in this world and damnation in the next, of accepting, in the strict and literal sense, every statement contained in the Protestant Bible. I was told to believe, and I did believe, that doubt about any of them was a sin, not less reprehensible than a moral delict. I suppose that, out of a thousand of my contemporaries, nine hundred, at least, had their minds systematically warped and poisoned, in the name of the God of truth, by like discipline.

T. H. Huxley, *Science and Christian Tradition,* Prologue

46 Why not, "The Way, the Truth, the Life?"

                              That way
Over the mountain, which who stands upon
Is apt to doubt if it be meant for a road;
While, if he views it from the waste itself,
Up goes the line there, plain from base to brow,
Not vague, mistakable! what's a break or two

Seen from the unbroken desert either side?
And then (to bring in fresh philosophy)
What if the breaks themselves should prove at last
The most consummate of contrivances
To train a man's eye, teach him what is faith?
And so we stumble at truth's very test!
All we have gained then by our unbelief
Is a life of doubt diversified by faith,
For one of faith diversified by doubt:
We called the chess-board white,—we call it
black.

Browning, *Bishop Blougram's Apology*

47 Philosophers of very diverse stripes propose that
philosophy shall take its start from one or another
state of mind in which no man, least of all a beginner in philosophy, actually is. One proposes
that you shall begin by doubting everything, and
says that there is only one thing that you cannot
doubt, as if doubting were "as easy as lying." Another proposes that we should begin by observing
"the first impressions of sense," forgetting that our
very percepts are the results of cognitive elaboration. But in truth, there is but one state of mind
from which you can "set out," namely, the very
state of mind in which you actually find yourself
at the time you do "set out"—a state in which you
are laden with an immense mass of cognition already formed, of which you cannot divest yourself
if you would; and who knows whether, if you
could, you would not have made all knowledge
impossible to yourself? Do you call it *doubting* to
write down on a piece of paper that you doubt? If
so, doubt has nothing to do with any serious business. But do not make believe; if pedantry has not
eaten all the reality out of you, recognize, as you
must, that there is much that you do not doubt, in
the least. Now that which you do not at all doubt,
you must and do regard as infallible, absolute
truth. . . .

Two things here are all-important to assure
oneself of and to remember. The first is that a
person is not absolutely an individual. His
thoughts are what he is "saying to himself," that
is, is saying to that other self that is just coming
into life in the flow of time. When one reasons, it
is that critical self that one is trying to persuade;
and all thought whatsoever is a sign, and is mostly
of the nature of language. The second thing to
remember is that the man's circle of society (however widely or narrowly this phrase may be understood), is a sort of loosely compacted person, in
some respects of higher rank than the person of an
individual organism. It is these two things alone
that render it possible for you—but only in the
abstract, and in a Pickwickian sense—to distinguish between absolute truth and what you do not
doubt.

C. S. Peirce, *What Pragmatism Means*

48 Our belief in truth itself . . . that there is a truth,
and that our minds and it are made for each
other,—what is it but a passionate affirmation of
desire, in which our social system backs us up? We
want to have a truth; we want to believe that our
experiments and studies and discussions must put
us in a continually better and better position towards it; and on this line we agree to fight out our
thinking lives. But if a pyrrhonistic sceptic asks us
how we know all this, can our logic find a reply?
No! certainly it cannot. It is just one volition
against another,—we willing to go in for life upon
a trust or assumption which he, for his part, does
not care to make.

William James, *Will to Believe*

49 Neither acquiescence in skepticism nor acquiescence in dogma is what education should produce.
What it should produce is a belief that knowledge
is attainable in a measure, though with difficulty;
that much of what passes for knowledge at any
given time is likely to be more or less mistaken,
but that the mistakes can be rectified by care and
industry. . . . Knowledge, like other good things,
is difficult, but not impossible; the dogmatist forgets the difficulty, the skeptic denies the possibility. Both are mistaken, and their errors, when
widespread, produce social disaster.

Russell, *Aims of Education*

50 I wish to propose for the reader's favourable consideration a doctrine which may, I fear, appear
wildly paradoxical and subversive. The doctrine
in question is this: that it is undesirable to believe
a proposition when there is no ground whatever
for supposing it true. I must, of course, admit that
if such an opinion became common it would completely transform our social life and our political
system; since both are at present faultless, this
must weigh against it. I am also aware (what is
more serious) that it would tend to diminish the
incomes of clairvoyants, bookmakers, bishops and
others who live on the irrational hopes of those
who have done nothing to deserve good fortune
here or hereafter. In spite of these grave arguments, I maintain that a case can be made out for
my paradox.

Russell, *Sceptical Essays*, I

51 If one regards oneself as a sceptic, it is well from
time to time to be sceptical about one's scepticism.

Freud, *New Introductory Lectures on
Psycho-Analysis*, XXX

52 The *Weltanschauung* to which I shall first refer is, as
it were, a counterpart of political anarchism, and
may perhaps have emanated from it. No doubt
there have been intellectual nihilists of this kind
before, but at the present day the theory of relativity of modern physics seems to have gone to
their heads. It is true that they start out from science, but they succeed in forcing it to cut the

ground from under its own feet, to commit suicide, as it were; they make it dispose of itself by getting it to refute its own premises. One often has an impression that this nihilism is only a temporary attitude, which will only be kept up until this task has been completed. When once science has been got rid of, some kind of mysticism, or, indeed, the old religious *Weltanschauung*, can spring up in the space that has been left vacant. According to this anarchistic doctrine, there is no such thing as truth, no assured knowledge of the external world. What we give out as scientific truth is only the product of our own needs and desires, as they are formulated under varying external conditions; that is to say, it is illusion once more. Ultimately we find only what we need to find, and see only what we desire to see. We can do nothing else. And since the criterion of truth, correspondence with an external world, disappears, it is absolutely immaterial what views we accept. All of them are equally true and false. And no one has a right to accuse any one else of error.

For a mind which is interested in epistemology, it would be tempting to enquire into the contrivances and sophistries by means of which the anarchists manage to elicit a final product of this kind from science. One would no doubt be brought up against situations like the one involved in the familiar example of the Cretan who says that all Cretans are liars. But I am not desirous, nor am I capable, of going deeper into this. I will merely remark that the anarchistic theory only retains its remarkable air of superiority so long as it is concerned with opinions about abstract things; it breaks down the moment it comes in contact with practical life. Now the behaviour of men is guided by their opinions and knowledge, and the same scientific spirit which speculates about the structure of the atom or the origin of man is concerned in the building of a bridge that will bear its load. If it were really a matter of indifference what we believed, if there were no knowledge which was distinguished from among our opinions by the fact that it corresponds with reality, then we might just as well build our bridges of cardboard as of stone, or inject a tenth of a gramme of morphia into a patient instead of a hundredth, or take tear-gas as a narcotic instead of ether. But the intellectual anarchists themselves would strongly repudiate such practical applications of their theory.

Freud, *New Introductory Lectures on Psycho-Analysis*, XXXV

53 For an answer which cannot be expressed the question too cannot be expressed.

The riddle does not exist.

If a question can be put at all, then it *can* also be answered.

Scepticism is *not* irrefutable, but palpably senseless, if it would doubt where a question cannot be asked.

For doubt can only exist where there is a question; a question only where there is an answer, and this only where something *can be said*.

We feel that even if *all possible* scientific questions be answered, the problems of life have still not been touched at all. Of course there is then no question left, and just this is the answer.

The solution of the problem of life is seen in the vanishing of this problem.

(Is not this the reason why men to whom after long doubting the sense of life became clear, could not then say wherein this sense consisted?)

Wittgenstein, *Tractatus Logico-Philosophicus*, 6.5–6.521

54 Scepticism is the chastity of the intellect, and it is shameful to surrender it too soon or to the first comer: there is nobility in preserving it coolly and proudly through a long youth, until at last, in the ripeness of instinct and discretion, it can be safely exchanged for fidelity and happiness.

Santayana, *Scepticism and Animal Faith*, IX

55 Was the being of truth . . . denied by the Sophists, or could they deny it? Yes, if we think only of the truth as proclaimed by particular opinions. All things *said* to be true might be false. Whatsoever depended on argument might be challenged by an opposed cleverer argument; whatsoever depended on usage, faith, or preference might be reversed by a contrary pose; so that every man remained free to think and do what he liked, and to deny all authority. This, though with a different moral tone and intention, was also the position of the Sceptics. They despised opinion, and collected contradictory arguments in order to liberate the mind from every pledge and the heart from every earthly bond. These indomitable doubters stood firm as rocks in their philosophy; and even the Sophists were sure of their wisdom and knowingness in playing their chosen parts in the world. For both schools, then, there was an *unspoken truth:* namely, that life was a treacherous predicament in which they found themselves without a reason, and that they were determined, whether nobly or nimbly, to make the best of it. Their moral philosophy left the cosmos problematical, while taking for granted abundant knowledge of human affairs and human character. If that age had had a turn for introspection and autobiography, it might have erected a doctrine of the march of experience. Trust in memory, in expectation, in the mutual communication of many minds might have issued in a system like modern psychologism: the view that all we see, say, and think is false, but that the only truth is that we see, say and think it. If nothing be real except experience, nothing can be true except biography. Society must then be conceived as carried on in a literary medium, with no regard to the natural basis of society. If the ancients never

hit upon such a system of biographical metaphysics, the reason doubtless was that they were too intelligent.

Santayana, *Realm of Truth,* XIII

56 As for the sceptics, who doubt, as least theoretically and in words, the reliability of our organs of knowledge, especially of the intellect or reason, it would obviously be waste of breath to attempt to demonstrate its reliability to them. For every demonstration rests on some previously admitted certainty, and it is their very profession to admit of none. To defend human knowledge against their attack it is sufficient (i) to show in what that knowledge consists and how it is attained; (ii) to refute the arguments they adduce; (iii) to make a *reductio ad absurdum.* When they say that they do not know whether any proposition is true, either they know that this proposition at any rate is true, in which case they obviously contradict themselves, or they do not know whether it is true, in which case they are either saying nothing whatever, or do not know what they say. The sole philosophy open to those who doubt the possibility of truth is absolute silence—even mental. That is to say, as Aristotle points out, such men must make themselves vegetables. No doubt reason often errs, especially in the highest matters, and, as Cicero said long ago, there is no nonsense in the world which has not found some philosopher to maintain it, so difficult is it to attain truth. But it is the error of cowards to mistake a difficulty for an impossibility.

Maritain, *Introduction to Philosophy,* II, 4

6.7 | *Reasoning, Demonstration, and Disputation*

The subjects treated in this section relate to subjects treated in earlier ones: reasoning is involved in the acquisition of knowledge, in the development of hypotheses or theories, and in the criticism of opinions or beliefs; demonstration or proof is regarded, in certain fields of learning (mathematics, for example), as a condition pre-requisite to the acceptance of a conclusion as valid knowledge; disputation or controversy arises when men attempt to resolve issues generated by conflicting theories, or conflicting opinions and beliefs. The reader will also find that the subjects treated here are relevant to the discussion of philosophy, science, and mathematics in Chapter 17; and to certain aspects of the consideration of mind in Chapter 5.

Some of the passages quoted undertake to formulate the logic of reasoning in rules that determine whether the reasoning is valid or invalid, such as Aristotle's rules of the syllogism; others describe reasoning in psychological rather than in logical terms, as a process by which the mind passes from one judgment to another. Different types of reasoning are distinguished, and fallacies in reasoning are noted. The difference between deduction and induction is considered in two ways: on the one hand, as a distinction between two kinds of reasoning; on the other hand, as a distinction between a ratiocinative process (deduction) and an intuitive leap (induction).

The contrast between that which the mind grasps discursively, through steps of reasoning or ratiocination, and that which it grasps intuitively, by immediate apprehension, is involved in a basic thesis concerning demonstration, advanced in certain of the passages quoted. Reasoning may be formally valid, in the sense that it does not violate any logical rules, while at the same time being materially false; i.e., reaching, from premises that are partly or wholly false, a conclusion that is false. When the term "demonstration" is applied, as it is by certain writers, to reasoning that is not only formally valid but also materially true (the establishment of a true conclusion from true premises), a question arises. Does this always require that the truth of the premises be demonstrated in turn? Or does demonstration presuppose the existence of indemonstrable propositions—axioms that cannot be demonstrated, yet the truth of which can still be known, intuitively and not by reasoning? Those who take a strict view of demonstration argue that it presupposes the indemonstrable.

At the opposite extreme from demonstration is the use of reasoning in what certain authors call the process of dialectic or disputation. On many issues reasonable men can take opposite sides, and when they do, they can marshall arguments for opposite conclusions. Those who draw a sharp line between the spheres of knowledge and opinion, or truth and probability, place demonstrative reasoning on one side of this line, and dialectical or disputatious reasoning on the other.

---

1 Come now, and let us reason together, saith the Lord.

Isaiah 1:18

2 *Wrong Logic.* Aye, say you so? why I have been half-burst; I do so long
To overthrow his arguments with arguments more strong.
I am the Lesser Logic? True: these Schoolmen call me so,
Simply because I was the first of all mankind to show
How old established rules and laws might contradicted be:
And this, as you may guess, is worth a thousand pounds to me,
To take the feebler cause, and yet to win the disputation.

Aristophanes, *Clouds,* 1031

3 *Socrates.* When a simple man who has no skill in dialectics believes an argument to be true which he afterwards imagines to be false, whether really false or not, and then another and another, he has no longer any faith left, and great disputers, as you know, come to think at last that they have grown to be the wisest of mankind; for they alone perceive the utter unsoundness and instability of all arguments, or indeed, of all things. . . . How melancholy, if there be such a thing as truth or certainty or possibility of knowledge—that a man should have lighted upon some argument or other which at first seemed true and then turned out to be false, and instead of blaming himself and his own want of wit, because he is annoyed, should at

last be too glad to transfer the blame from himself to arguments in general: and for ever afterwards should hate and revile them, and lose truth and the knowledge of realities.

Plato, *Phaedo,* 90A

4 *Socrates.* First principles, even if they appear certain, should be carefully considered; and when they are satisfactorily ascertained, then, with a sort of hesitating confidence in human reason, you may, I think, follow the course of the argument.

Plato, *Phaedo,* 107A

5 Verily, Glaucon, I [Socrates] said, glorious is the power of the art of contradiction!
Why do you say so?
Because I think that many a man falls into the practice against his will. When he thinks that he is reasoning he is really disputing, just because he cannot define and divide, and so know that of which he is speaking; and he will pursue a merely verbal opposition in the spirit of contention and not of fair discussion.

Plato, *Republic,* V, 454A

6 *Socrates.* That your feelings may not be moved to pity about our citizens who are now thirty years of age, every care must be taken in introducing them to dialectic.
Glaucon. Certainly.
There is a danger lest they should taste the dear delight too early; for youngsters, as you may have observed, when they first get the taste in their mouths, argue for amusement, and are always

contradicting and refuting others in imitation of those who refute them; like puppydogs, they rejoice in pulling and tearing at all who come near them.

Yes, he said, there is nothing which they like better.

And when they have made many conquests and received defeats at the hands of many, they violently and speedily get into a way of not believing anything which they believed before, and hence, not only they, but philosophy and all that relates to it is apt to have a bad name with the rest of the world.

Too true, he said.

But when a man begins to get older, he will no longer be guilty of such insanity; he will imitate the dialectician who is seeking for truth, and not the eristic, who is contradicting for the sake of amusement; and the greater moderation of his character will increase instead of diminishing the honour of the pursuit.

Plato, *Republic*, VII, 539A

7 What I now assert is that at all events we do know by demonstration. By demonstration I mean a syllogism productive of scientific knowledge, a syllogism, that is, the grasp of which is *eo ipso* such knowledge. Assuming then that my thesis as to the nature of scientific knowing is correct, the premisses of demonstrated knowledge must be true, primary, immediate, better known than and prior to the conclusion, which is further related to them as effect to cause. Unless these conditions are satisfied, the basic truths will not be 'appropriate' to the conclusion. Syllogism there may indeed be without these conditions, but such syllogism, not being productive of scientific knowledge, will not be demonstration. The premisses must be true: for that which is non-existent cannot be known—we cannot know, e.g. that the diagonal of a square is commensurate with its side. The premisses must be primary and indemonstrable; otherwise they will require demonstration in order to be known, since to have knowledge, if it be not accidental knowledge, of things which are demonstrable, means precisely to have a demonstration of them. The premisses must be the causes of the conclusion, better known than it, and prior to it; its causes, since we possess scientific knowledge of a thing only when we know its cause; prior, in order to be causes; antecedently known, this antecedent knowledge being not our mere understanding of the meaning, but knowledge of the fact as well. . . . In saying that the premisses of demonstrated knowledge must be primary, I mean that they must be the 'appropriate' basic truths, for I identify primary premiss and basic truth. A 'basic truth' in a demonstration is an immediate proposition. An immediate proposition is one which has no other proposition prior to it. . . . I call an immediate basic truth of syllogism a 'thesis' when,

though it is not susceptible of proof by the teacher, yet ignorance of it does not constitute a total bar to progress on the part of the pupil: one which the pupil must know if he is to learn anything whatever is an axiom. I call it an axiom because there are such truths and we give them the name of axioms *par excellence*. If a thesis assumes one part or the other of an enunciation, i.e. asserts either the existence or the non-existence of a subject, it is a hypothesis; if it does not so assert, it is a definition. Definition *is* a 'thesis' or a 'laying something down', since the arithmetician lays it down that to be a unit is to be quantitatively indivisible; but it is not a hypothesis, for to define what a unit is is not the same as to affirm its existence.

Now since the required ground of our knowledge—i.e. of our conviction—of a fact is the possession of such a syllogism as we call demonstration, and the ground of the syllogism is the facts constituting its premisses, we must not only know the primary premisses—some if not all of them—beforehand, but know them better than the conclusion.

Aristotle, *Posterior Analytics*, 71ᵇ16

8 Reasoning is an argument in which, certain things being laid down, something other than these necessarily comes about through them. (*a*) It is a 'demonstration', when the premisses from which the reasoning starts are true and primary, or are such that our knowledge of them has originally come through premisses which are primary and true: (*b*) reasoning, on the other hand, is 'dialectical', if it reasons from opinions that are generally accepted. Things are 'true' and 'primary' which are believed on the strength not of anything else but of themselves: for in regard to the first principles of science it is improper to ask any further for the why and wherefore of them; each of the first principles should command belief in and by itself. On the other hand, those opinions are 'generally accepted' which are accepted by every one or by the majority or by the philosophers—i.e. by all, or by the majority, or by the most notable and illustrious of them. Again (*c*), reasoning is 'contentious' if it starts from opinions that seem to be generally accepted, but are not really such, or again if it merely seems to reason from opinions that are or seem to be generally accepted. For not every opinion that seems to be generally accepted actually is generally accepted. For in none of the opinions which we call generally accepted is the illusion entirely on the surface, as happens in the case of the principles of contentious arguments; for the nature of the fallacy in these is obvious immediately, and as a rule even to persons with little power of comprehension. So then, of the contentious reasonings mentioned, the former really deserves to be called 'reasoning' as well, but the other should be called 'contentious reasoning', but not 'reasoning', since it appears to

reason, but does not really do so. Further (*d*), besides all the reasoning we have mentioned there are the mis-reasonings that start from the premisses peculiar to the special sciences, as happens (for example) in the case of geometry and her sister sciences. For this form of reasoning appears to differ from the reasonings mentioned above; the man who draws a false figure reasons from things that are neither true and primary, nor yet generally accepted. For he does not fall within the definition; he does not assume opinions that are received either by every one or by the majority or by philosophers—that is to say, by all, or by most, or by the most illustrious of them—but he conducts his reasoning upon assumptions which, though appropriate to the science in question, are not true; for he effects his mis-reasoning either by describing the semicircles wrongly or by drawing certain lines in a way in which they could not be drawn.

The foregoing must stand for an outline survey of the species of reasoning.

Aristotle, *Topics*, 100ª25

9 You should display your training in inductive reasoning against a young man, in deductive against an expert. You should try, moreover, to secure from those skilled in deduction their premisses, from inductive reasoners their parallel cases; for this is the thing in which they are respectively trained. In general, too, from your exercises in argumentation you should try to carry away either a syllogism on some subject or a refutation or a proposition or an objection, or whether some one put his question properly or improperly (whether it was yourself or some one else) and the point which made it the one or the other. For this is what gives one ability, and the whole object of training is to acquire ability, especially in regard to propositions and objections. For it is the skilled propounder and objector who is, speaking generally, a dialectician. . . .

Do not argue with every one, nor practise upon the man in the street; for there are some people with whom any argument is bound to degenerate. For against any one who is ready to try all means in order to seem not to be beaten, it is indeed fair to try all means of bringing about one's conclusion: but it is not good form. Wherefore the best rule is, not lightly to engage with casual acquaintances, or bad argument is sure to result. For you see how in practising together people cannot refrain from contentious argument.

It is best also to have ready-made arguments relating to those questions in which a very small stock will furnish us with arguments serviceable on a very large number of occasions. These are those that are universal, and those in regard to which it is rather difficult to produce points for ourselves from matters of everyday experience.

Aristotle, *Topics*, 164ª12

10 We must grasp the number of aims entertained by those who argue as competitors and rivals to the death. These are five in number, refutation, fallacy, paradox, solecism, and fifthly to reduce the opponent in the discussion to babbling—i.e. to constrain him to repeat himself a number of times; or it is to produce the appearance of each of these things without the reality. For they choose if possible plainly to refute the other party, or as the second best to show that he is committing some fallacy, or as a third best to lead him into paradox, or fourthly to reduce him to solecism, i.e. to make the answerer, in consequence of the argument, to use an ungrammatical expression; or, as a last resort, to make him repeat himself.

Aristotle, *On Sophistical Refutations*, 165ᵇ12

11 Precision is not to be sought for alike in all discussions, any more than in all the products of the crafts. Now fine and just actions, which political science investigates, admit of much variety and fluctuation of opinion, so that they may be thought to exist only by convention, and not by nature. And goods also give rise to a similar fluctuation because they bring harm to many people; for before now men have been undone by reason of their wealth, and others by reason of their courage. We must be content, then, in speaking of such subjects and with such premisses to indicate the truth roughly and in outline, and in speaking about things which are only for the most part true and with premisses of the same kind to reach conclusions that are no better. In the same spirit, therefore, should each type of statement be received; for it is the mark of an educated man to look for precision in each class of things just so far as the nature of the subject admits; it is evidently equally foolish to accept probable reasoning from a mathematician and to demand from a rhetorician scientific proofs.

Aristotle, *Ethics*, 1094ᵇ13

12 Scientific knowledge is judgement about things that are universal and necessary, and the conclusions of demonstration, and all scientific knowledge, follow from first principles (for scientific knowledge involves apprehension of a rational ground). This being so, the first principle from which what is scientifically known follows cannot be an object of scientific knowledge, of art, or of practical wisdom; for that which can be scientifically known can be demonstrated, and art and practical wisdom deal with things that are variable. Nor are these first principles the objects of philosophic wisdom, for it is a mark of the philosopher to have demonstration about some things. If, then, the states of mind by which we have truth and are never deceived about things invariable or even variable are scientific knowledge, practical wisdom, philosophic wisdom, and intuitive reason, and it cannot be any of the three (i.e. practical

wisdom, scientific knowledge, or philosophic wisdom), the remaining alternative is that it is intuitive reason that grasps the first principles.

Aristotle, *Ethics*, 1140ᵇ31

13 What things a man must learn in order to be able to apply the art of disputation, has been accurately shown by our philosophers; but with respect to the proper use of the things, we are entirely without practice. Only give to any of us, whom you please, an illiterate man to discuss with, and he cannot discover how to deal with the man. But when he has moved the man a little, if he answers beside the purpose, he does not know how to treat him, but he then either abuses or ridicules him, and says, "He is an illiterate man; it is not possible to do anything with him." Now a guide, when he has found a man out of the road leads him into the right way: he does not ridicule or abuse him and then leave him. Do you also show this illiterate man the truth, and you will see that he follows. But so long as you do not show him the truth, do not ridicule him, but rather feel your own incapacity.

How then did Socrates act? He used to compel his adversary in disputation to bear testimony to him, and he wanted no other witness. Therefore he could say, "I care not for other witnesses, but I am always satisfied with the evidence of my adversary, and I do not ask the opinion of others, but only the opinion of him who is disputing with me." For he used to make the conclusions drawn from natural notions so plain that every man saw the contradiction and withdrew from it.

Epictetus, *Discourses*, II, 12

14 When one of those who were present said, "Persuade me that logic is necessary," he replied: Do you wish me to prove this to you? The answer was, "Yes." Then I must use a demonstrative form of speech. This was granted. How then will you know if I am cheating you by argument? The man was silent. Do you see, said Epictetus, that you yourself are admitting that logic is necessary, if without it you cannot know so much as this, whether logic is necessary or not necessary?

Epictetus, *Discourses*, II, 25

15 There remain those branches of knowledge which pertain not to the bodily senses, but to the intellect, among which the science of reasoning and that of number are the chief. The science of reasoning is of very great service in searching into and unravelling all sorts of questions that come up in Scripture, only in the use of it we must guard against the love of wrangling and the childish vanity of entrapping an adversary. For there are many of what are called sophisms, inferences in reasoning that are false, and yet so close an imitation of the true, as to deceive not only dull people, but clever men too, when they are not on their guard. For example, one man lays before another with whom he is talking, the proposition, "What I am, you are not." The other assents, for the proposition is in part true, the one man being cunning and the other simple. Then the first speaker adds: "I am a man"; and when the other has given his assent to this also, the first draws his conclusion: "Then you are not a man." Now of this sort of ensnaring arguments, Scripture, as I judge, expresses detestation in that place where it is said, "There is one that showeth wisdom in words, and is hated"; although, indeed, a style of speech which is not intended to entrap, but only aims at verbal ornamentation more than is consistent with seriousness of purpose, is also called sophistical.

There are also valid processes of reasoning which lead to false conclusions, by following out to its logical consequences the error of the man with whom one is arguing; and these conclusions are sometimes drawn by a good and learned man, with the object of making the person from whose error these consequences result, feel ashamed of them, and of thus leading him to give up his error, when he finds that if he wishes to retain his old opinion, he must of necessity also hold other opinions which he condemns. For example, the apostle did not draw true conclusions when he said, "Then is Christ not risen," and again, "Then is our preaching vain, and your faith is also vain"; and further on drew other inferences which are all utterly false; for Christ has risen, the preaching of those who declared this fact was not in vain, nor was their faith in vain who had believed it. But all these false inferences followed legitimately from the opinion of those who said that there is no resurrection of the dead. These inferences, then, being repudiated as false, it follows that since they would be true if the dead rise not, there will be a resurrection of the dead. As, then, valid conclusions may be drawn not only from true but from false propositions, the laws of valid reasoning may easily be learnt in the schools, outside the pale of the Church. But the truth of propositions must be inquired into in the sacred books of the Church.

Augustine, *Christian Doctrine*, II, 31

16 Human intellects obtain their perfection in the knowledge of truth by a kind of movement and discursive intellectual operation; that is to say, as they advance from one known to another. But, if from the knowledge of a known principle they were straightway to perceive as known all its consequent conclusions, then discourse would have no place in them. Such is the condition of the angels, because in those things which they first know naturally, they at once behold all things whatsoever that can be known in them.

Aquinas, *Summa Theologica*, I, 58, 3

17 As in the intellect, when reasoning, the conclusion

is compared with the principle, so in the intellect composing and dividing, the predicate is compared with the subject. For if our intellect were to see at once the force of the conclusion in the principle, it would never understand by discursion and reasoning. In like manner, if the intellect in apprehending the quiddity of the subject were at once to have knowledge of all that can be attributed to, or removed from, the subject, it would never understand by composing and dividing, but only by understanding the essence. Thus it is evident that for the self-same reason our intellect understands by discursion, and by composing and dividing, namely, that in the first apprehension of anything newly apprehended it does not at once grasp all that is virtually contained in it. And this comes from the weakness of the intellectual light within us.

Aquinas, *Summa Theologica*, I, 58, 4

18 The discourse of reason always begins from an understanding and ends at an understanding, because we reason by proceeding from certain understood principles, and the discourse of reason is perfected when we come to understand what we did not know before. Hence the act of reasoning proceeds from something previously understood.

Aquinas, *Summa Theologica*, II–II, 8, 1

19 Axioms determined upon in argument can never assist in the discovery of new effects; for the subtilty of nature is vastly superior to that of argument.

Bacon, *Novum Organum*, I, 24

20 There are two ways by which we arrive at the knowledge of facts, viz. by experience and by deduction. We must further observe that while our inferences from experience are frequently fallacious, deduction, or the pure illation of one thing from another, though it may be passed over, if it is not seen through, cannot be erroneous when performed by an understanding that is in the least degree rational.

Descartes, *Rules for Direction of the Mind*, II

21 In reasoning we unite not names but the things signified by the names; and I marvel that the opposite can occur to anyone. For who doubts whether a Frenchman and a German are able to reason in exactly the same way about the same things, though they yet conceive the words in an entirely diverse way?

Descartes, *Objections and Replies*, III

22 All men by nature reason alike, and well, when they have good principles. For who is so stupid as both to mistake in geometry, and also to persist in it, when another detects his error to him?

By this it appears that reason is not, as sense and memory, born with us; nor gotten by experi-ence only, as prudence is; but attained by industry: first in apt imposing of names; and secondly by getting a good and orderly method in proceeding from the elements, which are names, to assertions made by connexion of one of them to another; and so to syllogisms, which are the connexions of one assertion to another, till we come to a knowledge of all the consequences of names appertaining to the subject in hand.

Hobbes, *Leviathan*, I, 5

23 Those who are accustomed to judge by feeling do not understand the process of reasoning, for they would understand at first sight and are not used to seek for principles. And others, on the contrary, who are accustomed to reason from principles, do not at all understand matters of feeling, seeking principles and being unable to see at a glance.

Pascal, *Pensées*, I, 3

24 When we wish to demonstrate a general theorem, we must give the rule as applied to a particular case; but if we wish to demonstrate a particular case, we must begin with the general rule. For we always find the thing obscure which we wish to prove and that clear which we use for the proof; for, when a thing is put forward to be proved, we first fill ourselves with the imagination that it is, therefore, obscure and, on the contrary, that what is to prove it is clear, and so we understand it easily.

Pascal, *Pensées*, I, 40

25 We must know where to doubt, where to feel certain, where to submit. He who does not do so understands not the force of reason. There are some who offend against these three rules, either by affirming everything as demonstrative, from want of knowing what demonstration is; or by doubting everything, from want of knowing where to submit; or by submitting in everything, from want of knowing where they must judge.

Pascal, *Pensées*, IV, 268

26 Permit me to remind you of a universal rule which is applicable to all the particular subjects in which our concern is with establishing truth. I do not doubt your acceptance of it since it is generally admitted by all who consider things with an open mind and since it constitutes the chief part of the method of the schools in dealing with the sciences and that used by seekers after what is really solid, filling and fully satisfying the mind. The rule is never to make a decisive judgment, affirming or denying a proposition, unless what one affirms or denies satisfies one of the two following conditions: either that of itself it appear so clearly and distinctly to sense or to reason, according as it is subject to one or the other, that the mind cannot doubt its certainty, and that is what we call a principle or axiom, as, for example, if

equals are added to equals, the results are equal; or that it be deduced as an infallible and necessary consequence from such principles or axioms, upon whose certainty entirely depends that of the consequences correctly drawn from them, as this proposition, the three angles of a triangle are equal to two right angles, "which not being self-evident," is evidently demonstrated as an infallible consequence of such axioms. Everything satisfying one of these two conditions is certain and true, and everything satisfying neither is considered doubtful and uncertain. We pass decisive judgment on things of the first kind and leave the rest undecided, calling them, according to their deserts, now a vision, now a caprice, occasionally a fancy, sometimes an idea, and at the most a happy thought; and since it is rash to affirm them, we incline rather to the negative, ready however to return to the affirmative if a convincing demonstration brings their truth to light.

Pascal, *Concerning the Vacuum*

27 The art which I call the art of persuading, and which is simply the management of perfect scientific proofs, consists of three essential parts: defining by clear definitions the terms to be used; laying down evident principles or axioms to prove the matter in question; always mentally substituting in the demonstration, in place of the things defined, their definitions.

The reason for this method is apparent, since it would be useless to put forward something capable of proof and to undertake its demonstration if we had not first clearly defined all unintelligible terms; and since likewise the demonstration must be preceded by the granting of the evident principles required for the demonstration, for if we do not make sure of the foundation, we can have no assurance of the building; and since finally while demonstrating we must mentally substitute the definition in place of the things defined, for otherwise we could be led astray by the different meanings encountered in the terms. It is easy to see that if we observe this method we are sure to convince, since, with all the terms so defined that they are understood and entirely free from ambiguity and with the principles granted, if in the demonstration we always substitute in thought the definitions in place of the things defined, the invincible force of the conclusions cannot fail of its full effect.

Pascal, *Geometrical Demonstration*

28 How vain . . . it is to expect demonstration and certainty in things not capable of it; and refuse assent to very rational propositions, and act contrary to very plain and clear truths, because they cannot be made out so evident, as to surmount every the least (I will not say reason, but) pretence of doubting. He that, in the ordinary affairs of life, would admit of nothing but direct plain demonstration, would be sure of nothing in this world, but of perishing quickly.

Locke, *Concerning Human Understanding,*
Bk. IV, XI, 10

29 As demonstration is the showing the agreement or disagreement of two ideas by the intervention of one or more proofs, which have a constant, immutable, and visible connexion one with another; so probability is nothing but the appearance of such an agreement or disagreement by the intervention of proofs, whose connexion is not constant and immutable, or at least is not perceived to be so, but is, or appears for the most part to be so, and is enough to induce the mind to judge the proposition to be true or false, rather than the contrary.

Locke, *Concerning Human Understanding,*
Bk. IV, XV, 1

30 If the use and end of right reasoning be to have right notions and a right judgment of things, to distinguish betwixt truth and falsehood, right and wrong, and to act accordingly, be sure not to let your son be bred up in the art and formality of disputing, either practicing it himself, or admiring it in others; unless instead of an able man, you desire to have him an insignificant wrangler, opiniator in discourse, and priding himself in contradicting others; or, which is worse, questioning everything, and thinking there is no such thing as truth to be sought, but only victory, in disputing. There cannot be anything so disingenuous, so misbecoming a gentleman or anyone who pretends to be a rational creature, as not to yield to plain reason and the conviction of clear arguments. Is there anything more consistent with civil conversation, and the end of all debate, than not to take an answer, though never so full and satisfactory, but still to go on with the dispute as long as equivocal sounds can furnish . . . a term to wrangle with on the one side, or a distinction on the other; whether pertinent or impertinent, sense or nonsense, agreeing with or contrary to what he had said before, it matters not. For this, in short, is the way and perfection of logical disputes, that the opponent never takes any answer, nor the respondent ever yields to any argument. This neither of them must do, whatever becomes of truth or knowledge, unless he will pass for a poor baffled wretch, and lie under the disgrace of not being able to maintain whatever he has once affirmed, which is the great aim and glory in disputing. Truth is to be found and supported by a mature and due consideration of things themselves, and not by artificial terms and ways of arguing: these lead not men so much into the discovery of truth as into a captious and fallacious use of doubtful words, which is the most useless and most offensive way of talking, and such as least suits a gentleman or a lover of truth of anything in the world.

Locke, *Some Thoughts Concerning
Education,* 189

31 Who reasons wisely is not therefore wise,
His pride in Reasoning not in Acting lies.

Pope, *Moral Essays,* Epistle I, 117

32 The gift of ratiocination and making syllogisms—
I mean in man—for in superior classes of beings,
such as angels and spirits—'tis all done, may it
please your worships, as they tell me, by Intuition;—and beings inferior, as your worships all
know—syllogize by their noses: though there is an
island swimming in the sea (though not altogether
at its ease) whose inhabitants, if my intelligence
deceives me not, are so wonderfully gifted, as to
syllogize after the same fashion, and oft-times to
make very well out too:——but that's neither
here nor there——

The gift of doing it as it should be, amongst us,
or—the great and principal act of ratiocination in
man, as logicians tell us, is the finding out the
agreement or disagreement of two ideas one with
another, by the intervention of a third (called the
medius terminus); just as a man, as Locke well observes, by a yard, finds two men's ninepin-alleys
to be of the same length, which could not be
brought together, to measure their equality, by
juxtaposition.

Had the same great reasoner looked on, as my
father illustrated his systems of noses, and observed my uncle Toby's deportment—what great
attention he gave to every word—and as oft as he
took his pipe from his mouth, with what wonderful seriousness he contemplated the length of it—
surveying it transversely as he held it betwixt his
finger and his thumb—then foreright—then this
way, and then that, in all its possible directions
and foreshortenings—he would have concluded
my uncle Toby had got hold of the *medius terminus,*
and was syllogizing and measuring with it the
truth of each hypothesis of long noses, in order, as
my father laid them before him. This, by the bye,
was more than my father wanted—his aim in all
the pains he was at in these philosophic lectures—
was to enable my uncle Toby not to discuss—but
comprehend—to hold the grains and scruples of
learning—not to weigh them.——My uncle
Toby, as you will read in the next chapter, did
neither the one nor the other.

Sterne, *Tristram Shandy,* III, 40

33 When one has had a good argument about spirit
and matter, one always finishes by not understanding each other. No philosopher has been
able with his own strength to lift this veil stretched
by nature over all the first principles of things.
Men argue, nature acts.

Voltaire, *Philosophical Dictionary:* Soul

34 One of the company took the other side. . . . This
appeared to me very satisfactory. Johnson did not
answer it; but talking for victory, and determined
to be master of the field, he had recourse to the
device which Goldsmith imputed to him in the
witty words of one of Cibber's comedies: "There is
no arguing with Johnson; for when his pistol misses fire, he knocks you down with the butt end of
it."

Boswell, *Life of Johnson (Oct. 26, 1769)*

35 Johnson having argued for some time with a per-
tinacious gentleman; his opponent, who had
talked in a very puzzling manner, happened to
say, "I don't understand you, Sir": upon which
Johnson observed, "Sir, I have found you an argument; but I am not obliged to find you an understanding."

Boswell, *Life of Johnson (June 1784)*

36 When reason employs conceptions alone, only one
proof of its thesis is possible, if any. When, therefore, the dogmatist advances with ten arguments
in favour of a proposition, we may be sure that
not one of them is conclusive. For if he possessed
one which proved the proposition he brings forward to demonstration—as must always be the
case with the propositions of pure reason—what
need is there for any more?

Kant, *Critique of Pure Reason,*
Transcendental Method

37 Myself when young did eagerly frequent
Doctor and Saint, and heard great argument
   About it and about; but evermore
Came out by the same door where in I went.

With them the seed of Wisdom did I sow,
And with mine own hand wrought to make it
      grow;
   And this was all the Harvest that I reaped—
"I came like Water, and like Wind I go."

FitzGerald, *Rubáiyát,* XXVII–XXVIII

38 When you cannot prove that people are wrong,
but only that they are absurd, the best course is to
let them alone.

T. H. Huxley, *On the Method of Zadig*

39 There is no greater mistake than the hasty conclusion that opinions are worthless because they are
badly argued.

T. H. Huxley, *Natural Rights and
Political Rights*

40 There are two forms of reasoning: first, the investigating or interrogative form used by men who do
not know and who wish to learn; secondly, the
demonstrating or affirmative form employed by
men who know or think they know, and who wish
to teach others.

Claude Bernard, *Experimental Medicine,* I, 2

41 Few persons care to study logic, because everybody conceives himself to be proficient enough in the art of reasoning already. But I observe that this satisfaction is limited to one's own ratiocination, and does not extend to that of other men.

We come to the full possession of our power of drawing inferences, the last of all our faculties; for it is not so much a natural gift as a long and difficult art.

C. S. Peirce, *Fixation of Belief*

42 The object of reasoning is to find out, from the consideration of what we already know, something else which we do not know. Consequently, reasoning is good if it be such as to give a true conclusion from true premisses, and not otherwise. Thus, the question of validity is purely one of fact and not of thinking. A being the facts stated in the premisses and B being that concluded, the question is, whether these facts are really so related that if A were B would generally be. If so, the inference is valid; if not, not. It is not in the least the question whether, when the premisses are accepted by the mind, we feel an impulse to accept the conclusion also. It is true that we do generally reason correctly by nature. But that is an accident; the true conclusion would remain true if we had no impulse to accept it; and the false one would remain false, though we could not resist the tendency to believe in it.

C. S. Peirce, *Fixation of Belief*

43 A friend of the writer gave as proof of the almost human intelligence of his dog that he took him one day down to his boat on the shore, but found the boat full of dirt and water. He remembered that the sponge was up at the house, a third of a mile distant; but, disliking to go back himself, he made various gestures of wiping out the boat and so forth, saying to his terrier, "Sponge, sponge; go fetch the sponge." But he had little expectation of a result, since the dog had never received the slightest training with the boat or the sponge. Nevertheless, off he trotted to the house, and, to his owner's great surprise and admiration, brought the sponge in his jaws. Sagacious as this was, it required nothing but ordinary contiguous association of ideas. The terrier was only exceptional in the minuteness of his spontaneous observation. Most terriers would have taken no interest in the boat-cleaning operation, nor noticed what the sponge was for. This terrier, in having picked those details out of the crude mass of his boat-experience distinctly enough to be reminded of them, was truly enough ahead of his peers on the line which leads to human reason. But his act was not yet an act of reasoning proper. It might fairly have been called so if, unable to find the sponge at the house, he had brought back a dipper or a mop instead. Such a substitution would have shown that, embedded in the very different appearances of these articles, he had been able to discriminate the identical partial attribute of capacity to take up water, and had reflected, "For the present purpose they are identical." This, which the dog did not do, any man but the very stupidest could not fail to do.

William James, *Psychology,* XXII

44 It is very desirable, in instruction, not merely to persuade the student of the accuracy of important theorems, but to persuade him in the way which itself has, of all possible ways, the most beauty. The true interest of a demonstration is not, as traditional modes of exposition suggest, concentrated wholly in the result; where this does occur, it must be viewed as a defect, to be remedied, if possible, by so generalizing the steps of the proof that each becomes important in and for itself. An argument which serves only to prove a conclusion is like a story subordinated to some moral which it is meant to teach: for aesthetic perfection no part of the whole should be merely a means.

Russell, *Study of Mathematics*

45 The proof of self-evident propositions may seem, to the uninitiated, a somewhat frivolous occupation. To this we might reply that it is often by no means self-evident that one obvious proposition follows from another obvious proposition; so that we are really discovering new truths when we prove what is evident by a method which is not evident. But a more interesting retort is, that since people have tried to prove obvious propositions, they have found that many of them are false. Self-evidence is often a mere will-o'-the-wisp, which is sure to lead us astray if we take it as our guide. For instance, nothing is plainer than that a whole always has more terms than a part, or that a number is increased by adding one to it. But these propositions are now known to be usually false. Most numbers are infinite, and if a number is infinite you may add ones to it as long as you like without disturbing it in the least. One of the merits of a proof is that it instils a certain doubt as to the result proved; and when what is obvious can be proved in some cases, but not in others, it becomes possible to suppose that in these other cases it is false.

Russell, *Mathematics and the Metaphysicians*

46 I have never been able to convince myself of the truth of the saying that "strife is the father of all things." I think the source of it was the philosophy of the Greek sophists and that it errs, as does the latter, through the overestimation of dialectics. It seems to me, on the contrary, that scientific controversy, so-called, is on the whole quite unfruitful, apart from the fact that it is almost always conducted in a highly personal manner.

Freud, *General Introduction to Psycho-Analysis,* XVI

47 Bacon's conviction of the quarrelsome, self-displaying character of the scholarship which had come down from antiquity was of course not so much due to Greek science itself as to the degenerate heritage of scholasticism in the fourteenth century, when philosophy had fallen into the hands of disputatious theologians, full of hair-splitting argumentativeness and quirks and tricks by which to win victory over somebody else.

But Bacon also brought his charge against the Aristotelian method itself. In its rigorous forms it aimed at demonstration, and in its milder forms at persuasion. But both demonstration and persuasion aim at conquest of mind rather than of nature. Moreover they both assume that some one is already in possession of a truth or a belief, and that the only problem is to convince some one else, or to teach. In contrast, his new method had an exceedingly slight opinion of the amount of truth already existent, and a lively sense of the extent and importance of truths still to be attained. It would be a logic of discovery, not a logic of argumentation, proof and persuasion. To Bacon, the old logic even at its best was a logic for teaching the already known, and teaching meant indoctrination, disciplining. It was an axiom of Aristotle that only that which was already known could be learned, that growth in knowledge consisted simply of bringing together a universal truth of reason and a particular truth of sense which had previously been noted separately. In any case, learning meant *growth* of knowledge, and growth belongs in the region of becoming, change, and hence is inferior to *possession* of knowledge in the syllogistic self-revolving manipulation of what was already known—demonstration.

In contrast with this point of view, Bacon eloquently proclaimed the superiority of discovery of new facts and truths to demonstration of the old. Now there is only one road to discovery, and that is penetrating inquiry into the secrets of nature.

Dewey, *Reconstruction in Philosophy,* II

48 Dialectic is the conscience of discourse and has the same function as morality elsewhere, namely, to endow the soul with integrity and to perfect it into a monument to its own radical impulse. But as virtue is a wider thing than morality, because it includes natural gifts and genial sympathies, or even heroic sacrifices, so wisdom is a wider thing than logic. To coherence in thought it adds docility to facts, and humility even of intellect, so that the integrity of its system becomes a human virtue, like the perfect use of a single language, without being an insult to the nature of things or a learned madness.

Santayana, *Realm of Essence,* VII

Chapter 7

LANGUAGE

Chapter 7 is divided into two sections: 7.1 THE NATURE OF LANGUAGE and 7.2 THE ARTS OF LANGUAGE.

The passages included in these two sections tend to overlap in certain respects, but the primary emphasis in the quotations assembled in Section 7.1 is on the characteristics of human speech, its elements and structure, whereas the primary emphasis in Section 7.2 is on how to put the power of speech to good use in a variety of ways.

Of all the subjects treated in this book, language, perhaps more than any other, is thought by many to have been a major field of speculation, analysis, and research only in the last hundred years or so. It is in that period that a variety of sciences bearing the name "linguistics" have been developed and that related disciplines such as philology, semantics, and semiotics have come into being or matured. Beginning less than a half century ago, a dominant school of Anglo-American thought emerged, calling itself "linguistic and analytic philosophy." Nevertheless, the reader will find that an interest in the nature and structure of language and in the arts of using it effectively begins with the Greeks and runs throughout the tradition of Western thought.

The matters covered in this chapter are related to questions touched on in other chapters, especially Chapter 1 on MAN, Chapter 5 on MIND, Chapter 6 on KNOWLEDGE, Chapter 8 on EDUCATION, Chapter 16 on ART AND AESTHETICS, and Chapter 17 on PHILOSOPHY, SCIENCE, AND MATHEMATICS.

7.1 | *The Nature of Language*

The passages assembled here deal with questions about the origin of language, the conventions of language, the diversity of languages, the power of words to perform the function of signs, and the relation of verbal signs to thought and knowledge, as well as to the objects of thought and knowledge.

Points are made about the manifold senses in which words can be used and their modes of ambiguity, about the distinction between words that name objects of thought or knowledge and words that play a role in sentences without naming anything, about the relation of spoken to written language, about the distinction between proper and common or general names, about the various uses to which language can be put, and about the conditions underlying its effective use for the purpose of communication.

That other animals communicate by sounds or gestures is acknowledged even by those writers who assert that man alone possesses a language in which questions can be asked and statements made in the service of inquiry and thought quite apart from the purposes of communication between individuals. Whether it is thought that the difference between man and other animals is one of kind or degree, it is universally agreed that the way in which the human species has developed and employed language is one of its most distinctive characteristics.

---

1 And out of the ground the Lord God formed every beast of the field, and every fowl of the air; and brought them unto Adam to see what he would call them: and whatsoever Adam called every living creature, that was the name thereof.

And Adam gave names to all cattle, and to the fowl of the air, and to every beast of the field.

Genesis 2:19–20

2 And the whole earth was of one language, and of one speech.

And it came to pass, as they journeyed from the east, that they found a plain in the land of Shi̅-när; and they dwelt there.

And they said one to another, Go to, let us make brick, and burn them thoroughly. And they had brick for stone, and slime had they for morter.

And they said, Go to, let us build us a city and a tower, whose top may reach unto heaven; and let us make us a name, lest we be scattered abroad upon the face of the whole earth.

And the Lord came down to see the city and the tower, which the children of men builded.

And the Lord said, Behold, the people is one, and they have all one language; and this they begin to do: and now nothing will be restrained from them, which they have imagined to do.

Go to, let us go down, and there confound their language, that they may not understand one another's speech.

So the Lord scattered them abroad from thence upon the face of all the earth: and they left off to build the city.

Therefore is the name of it called Babel; because the Lord did there confound the language of all the earth: and from thence did the Lord scatter them abroad upon the face of all the earth.

Genesis 11:1–9

3 *Socrates.* A name is an instrument of teaching and of distinguishing natures, as the shuttle is of distinguishing the threads of the web.

Plato, *Cratylus,* 388A

4 *Socrates.* I would recommend you . . . not to encourage yourself in this polemical and controversial temper, but to find out, in a friendly and congenial spirit, what we really mean when we say that all things are in motion, and that to every individual and state what appears, is. In this manner you will consider whether knowledge and sensation are the same or different, but you will not argue, as you were just now doing, from the customary use of names and words, which the vulgar pervert in all sorts of ways, causing infinite perplexity to one another.

Plato, *Theaetetus,* 168A

5 *Eleatic Stranger.* At present we are only agreed about the name, but of the thing to which we both apply the name possibly you have one notion and I another; whereas we ought always to come to an understanding about the thing itself in terms of a definition, and not merely about the name minus the definition.

Plato, *Sophist,* 218A

6 No man of intelligence will venture to express his philosophical views in language, especially not in language that is unchangeable, which is true of that which is set down in written characters.

Plato, *Seventh Letter*

7 Things are said to be named 'equivocally' when, though they have a common name, the definition corresponding with the name differs for each. Thus, a real man and a figure in a picture can both lay claim to the name 'animal'; yet these are equivocally so named, for, though they have a common name, the definition corresponding with the name differs for each. For should any one define in what sense each is an animal, his definition in the one case will be appropriate to that case only.

On the other hand, things are said to be named 'univocally' which have both the name and the definition answering to the name in common. A man and an ox are both 'animal', and these are univocally so named, inasmuch as not only the name, but also the definition, is the same in both cases: for if a man should state in what sense each is an animal, the statement in the one case would be identical with that in the other.

Things are said to be named 'derivatively', which derive their name from some other name, but differ from it in termination. Thus the grammarian derives his name from the word 'grammar', and the courageous man from the word 'courage'.

Aristotle, *Categories,* 1ª1

8 Spoken words are the symbols of mental experience and written words are the symbols of spoken words. Just as all men have not the same writing, so all men have not the same speech sounds, but the mental experiences, which these directly symbolize, are the same for all, as also are those things of which our experiences are the images.

Aristotle, *On Interpretation,* 16ª4

9 Nature . . . makes nothing in vain, and man is the only animal whom she has endowed with the gift of speech. And whereas mere voice is but an indication of pleasure or pain, and is therefore found in other animals (for their nature attains to the perception of pleasure and pain and the intimation of them to one another, and no further), the power of speech is intended to set forth the expedient and inexpedient, and therefore likewise the just and the unjust. And it is a characteristic of man that he alone has any sense of good and evil, of just and unjust, and the like, and the association of living beings who have this sense makes a family and a state.

Aristotle, *Politics,* 1253ª8

10 Why then should words challenge Eternity,
When greatest men, and greatest actions die?
Use may revive the obsoletest words,
And banish those that now are most in vogue;
Use is the judge, the law, and rule of speech.

Horace, *Ars Poetica*

11 I have . . . discovered by observation how I learned to speak. I did not learn by elders teaching me words in any systematic way, as I was soon after taught to read and write. But of my own motion . . . I strove with cries and various sounds and much moving of my limbs to utter the feelings of my heart—all this in order to get my own way. Now I did not always manage to express the right meanings to the right people. So I began to reflect. [I observed that] my elders would make some particular sound, and as they made it would point at or move towards some particular thing: and from this I came to realize that the thing was called by the sound they made when they wished to draw my attention to it. That they intended this was clear from the motions of their body, by a kind of natural language common to all races which consists in facial expressions, glances of the eye, gestures, and the tones by which the voice expresses the mind's state—for example whether things are to be sought, kept, thrown away, or avoided. So, as I heard the same words again and again properly used in different phrases, I came gradually to grasp what things they signified; and forcing my mouth to the same sounds, I began to use them to express my own wishes. Thus I learnt to convey what I meant to those about me.

Augustine, *Confessions,* I, 8

12 All instruction is either about things or about signs; but things are learnt by means of signs. I now use the word "thing" in a strict sense to signify that which is never employed as a sign of anything else: for example, wood, stone, cattle, and other things of that kind. Not, however, the wood which we read Moses cast into the bitter waters to make them sweet, nor the stone which Jacob used as a pillow, nor the ram which Abraham offered up instead of his son; for these, though they are things, are also signs of other things. There are signs of another kind, those which are never employed except as signs: for example, words. No one uses words except as signs of something else; and hence may be understood what I call signs: those things, to wit, which are used to indicate something else. Accordingly, every sign is also a thing; for what is not a thing is nothing at all.

Every thing, however, is not also a sign.

Augustine, *Christian Doctrine,* I, 2

13 When we speak, in order that what we have in our minds may enter through the ear into the mind of the hearer, the word which we have in our hearts becomes an outward sound and is called speech; and yet our thought does not lose itself in the sound, but remains complete in itself, and takes the form of speech without being modified in its own nature by the change.

Augustine, *Christian Doctrine,* I, 13

14 As when I was writing about things, I introduced the subject with a warning against attending to anything but what they are in themselves, even though they are signs of something else, so now, when I come in its turn to discuss the subject of signs, I lay down this direction, not to attend to what they are in themselves, but to the fact that they are signs, that is, to what they signify. For a sign is a thing which, over and above the impression it makes on the senses, causes something else to come into the mind as a consequence of itself: as when we see a footprint, we conclude that an animal whose footprint this is has passed by; and when we see smoke, we know that there is fire beneath; and when we hear the voice of a living man, we think of the feeling in his mind; and when the trumpet sounds, soldiers know that they are to advance or retreat, or do whatever else the state of the battle requires.

Now some signs are natural, others conventional. Natural signs are those which, apart from any intention or desire of using them as signs, do yet lead to the knowledge of something else, as, for example, smoke when it indicates fire. For it is not from any intention of making it a sign that it is so, but through attention to experience we come to know that fire is beneath, even when nothing but smoke can be seen. And the footprint of an animal passing by belongs to this class of signs. And the countenance of an angry or sorrowful man indicates the feeling in his mind, independently of his will: and in the same way every other emotion of the mind is betrayed by the tell-tale countenance, even though we do nothing with the intention of making it known. This class of signs, however, it is no part of my design to discuss at present. But as it comes under this division of the subject, I could not altogether pass it over. It will be enough to have noticed it thus far.

Conventional signs, on the other hand, are those which living beings mutually exchange for the purpose of showing, as well as they can, the feelings of their minds, or their perceptions, or their thoughts. Nor is there any reason for giving a sign except the desire of drawing forth and conveying into another's mind what the giver of the sign has in his own mind. We wish, then, to consider and discuss this class of signs so far as men are concerned with it, because even the signs which have been given us of God, and which are contained in the Holy Scriptures, were made known to us through men— those, namely, who wrote the Scriptures. The beasts, too, have certain signs among themselves by which they make known the desires in their mind. For when the poultry-cock has discovered food, he signals with his voice for the hen to run to him, and the dove by cooing calls his mate, or is called by her in turn; and many signs of the same kind are matters of common observation. Now whether these signs, like the expression or the cry of a man in grief, follow the movement of the mind instinctively and apart from any purpose, or whether they are really used with the purpose of signification, is another question, and does not pertain to the matter in hand. And this part of the subject I exclude from the scope of this work as not necessary to my present object.

Of the signs, then, by which men communicate their thoughts to one another, some relate to the sense of sight, some to that of hearing, a very few to the other senses. For, when we nod, we give no sign except to the eyes of the man to whom we wish by this sign to impart our desire. And some convey a great deal by the motion of the hands: and actors by movements of all their limbs give certain signs to the initiated, and, so to speak, address their conversation to the eyes: and the military standards and flags convey through the eyes the will of the commanders. And all these signs are as it were a kind of visible words. The signs that address themselves to the ear are, as I have said, more numerous, and for the most part consist of words. For though the bugle and the flute and the lyre frequently give not only a sweet but a significant sound, yet all these signs are very few in number compared with words. For among men words have obtained far and away the chief place as a means of indicating the thoughts of the mind. Our Lord, it is true, gave a sign through the odour of the ointment which was poured out upon His feet; and in the sacrament of His body and blood He signified His will through the sense of taste; and when by touching the hem of His garment the woman was made whole, the act was not wanting in significance. But the countless multitude of the signs through which men express their thoughts consist of words. For I have been able to put into words all those signs, the various classes of which I have briefly touched upon, but I could by no effort express words in terms of those signs.

Augustine, *Christian Doctrine,* II, 1–3

15 Because words pass away as soon as they strike upon the air, and last no longer than their sound, men have by means of letters formed signs of words. Thus the sounds of the voice are made visible to the eye, not of course as sounds, but by

means of certain signs.

Augustine, *Christian Doctrine,* II, 4

16 Since according to the Philosopher [Aristotle], words are signs of ideas, and ideas the similitude of things, it is evident that words relate to the meaning of things signified through the medium of the intellectual conception. It follows therefore that we can give a name to anything in as far as we can understand it. . . . Thus . . . the idea expressed by the name is the definition.

Aquinas, *Summa Theologica,* I, 13, 1

17 A name is communicable in two ways, properly, and by likeness. It is properly communicable in the sense that its whole signification can be given to many; by likeness it is communicable according to some part of the signification of the name. For instance this name "lion" is properly communicated to all things of the same nature as lion; by likeness it is communicable to those who participate in something lion-like, as for instance by courage, or strength, and those who thus participate are called lions metaphorically.

Aquinas, *Summa Theologica,* I, 13, 9

18 If man were by nature a solitary animal the passions of the soul by which he was conformed to things so as to have knowledge of them would be sufficient for him; but since he is by nature a political and social animal it was necessary that his conceptions be made known to others. This he does through vocal sound. Therefore there had to be significant vocal sounds in order that men might live together. Whence those who speak different languages find it difficult to live together in social unity.

Aquinas, *Commentary on Aristotle's*
"On Interpretation," I, 2

19 If man had only sensitive cognition, which is of the here and now, such significant vocal sounds as the other animals use to manifest their conceptions to each other would be sufficient for him to live with others. But man also has the advantage of intellectual cognition, which abstracts from the here and now, and as a consequence, is concerned with things distant in place and future in time as well as things present according to time and place. Hence the use of writing was necessary so that he might manifest his conceptions to those who are distant according to place and to those who will come in future time.

Aquinas, *Commentary on Aristotle's*
"On Interpretation," I, 2

20 Man alone amongst the animals speaks and has gestures and expression which we call rational, because he alone has reason in him. And if anyone should say in contradiction that certain birds talk, as seems to be the case with some, especially the magpie and the parrot, and that certain beasts have expression or gestures, as the ape and some others seem to have, I answer that it is not true that they speak, nor that they have gestures, because they have no reason, from which these things must needs proceed; nor have they the principle of these things within them, nor do they understand what it is; nor do they purpose to signify anything by them, but they merely reproduce what they see and hear. Wherefore, even as the image of bodies is reproduced by certain shining things (for instance, a mirror), and the corporeal image that the mirror displays is not real, so the semblance of reason, namely the expression and the speech which the brute beast reproduces or displays, is not real.

Dante, *Convivio,* III, 7

21 What we call the vernacular speech is that to which children are accustomed by those who are about them when they first begin to distinguish words; or to put it more shortly, we say that the vernacular speech is that which we acquire without any rule, by imitating our nurses. There further springs from this another secondary speech, which the Romans called grammar. And this secondary speech the Greeks also have, as well as others, but not all. Few, however, acquire the use of this speech, because we can only be guided and instructed in it by the expenditure of much time, and by assiduous study. Of these two kinds of speech also, the vernacular is the nobler, as well because it was the first employed by the human race, as because the whole world makes use of it, though it has been divided into forms differing in pronunciation and vocabulary. It is also the nobler as being natural to us, whereas the other is rather of an artificial kind.

Dante, *De Vulgari Eloquentia,* I, 1

22 In a certain bark of the dog the horse knows there is anger; at a certain other sound of his he is not frightened. Even in the beasts that have no voice, from the mutual services we see between them we easily infer some other means of communication; their motions converse and discuss. . . . Why not; just as well as our mutes dispute, argue, and tell stories by signs? I have seen some so supple and versed in this, that in truth they lacked nothing of perfection in being able to make themselves understood. Lovers grow angry, are reconciled, entreat, thank, make assignations, and in fine say everything, with their eyes. . . . What of the hands? We beg, we promise, call, dismiss, threaten, pray, entreat, deny, refuse, question, admire, count, confess, repent, fear, blush, doubt, instruct, command, incite, encourage, swear, testify, accuse, condemn, absolve, insult, despise, defy, vex, flatter, applaud, bless, humiliate, mock, reconcile, commend, exalt, entertain, rejoice, complain, grieve, mope, despair, wonder, exclaim, are silent, and what not, with a variation and multiplication

that vie with the tongue. With the head: we invite, send away, avow, disavow, give the lie, welcome, honor, venerate, disdain, demand, show out, cheer, lament, caress, scold, submit, brave, exhort, menace, assure, inquire. What of the eyebrows? What of the shoulders? There is no movement that does not speak both a language intelligible without instruction, and a public language; which means, seeing the variety and particular use of other languages, that this one must rather be judged the one proper to human nature.

Montaigne, *Essays*, II, 12,
Apology for Raymond Sebond

23 As for speech, it is certain that if it is not natural, it is not necessary. Nevertheless, I believe that a child who had been brought up in complete solitude, remote from all association (which would be a hard experiment to make), would have some sort of speech to express his ideas. And it is not credible that Nature has denied us this resource that she has given to many other animals: for what is it but speech, this faculty we see in them of complaining, rejoicing, calling to each other for help, inviting each other to love, as they do by the use of their voice? How could they not speak to one another? They certainly speak to us, and we to them. In how many ways do we not speak to our dogs? And they answer us. We talk to them in another language, with other names, than to birds, hogs, oxen, horses; and we change the idiom according to the species.

Montaigne, *Essays*, II, 12,
Apology for Raymond Sebond

24 *Juliet.* What's in a name? that which we call a rose
By any other name would smell as sweet.

Shakespeare, *Romeo and Juliet*, II, ii, 43

25 *Prospero.*   Abhorred slave,
Which any print of goodness wilt not take,
Being capable of all ill! I pitied thee,
Took pains to make thee speak, taught thee each
    hour
One thing or other. When thou didst not, savage,
Know thine own meaning, but wouldst gabble
    like
A thing most brutish, I endow'd thy purposes
With words that made them known. But thy vile
    race,
Though thou didst learn, had that in't which good
    natures
Could not abide to be with; therefore wast thou
Deservedly confined into this rock,
Who hadst deserved more than a prison.
    Caliban. You taught me language; and my prof-
    it on't
Is, I know how to curse. The red plague rid you
For learning me your language!

Shakespeare, *Tempest*, I, ii, 352

26 Custom is the most certain mistress of language, as the public stamp makes the current money. But we must not be too frequent with the mint, every day coining, nor fetch words from the extreme and utmost ages; since the chief virtue of a style is perspicuity, and nothing so vicious in it as to need an interpreter. Words borrowed of antiquity do lend a kind of majesty to style, and are not without their delight sometimes; for they have the authority of years, and out of their intermission do win themselves a kind of gracelike newness. But the eldest of the present, and newest of the past language, is the best. For what was the ancient language, which some men so dote upon, but the ancient custom? Yet when I name custom, I understand not the vulgar custom; for that were a precept no less dangerous to language than life, if we should speak or live after the manners of the vulgar: but that I call custom of speech, which is the consent of the learned; as custom of life, which is the consent of the good.

Jonson, *Discoveries:* Consuetudo

27 Men converse by means of language, but words are formed at the will of the generality, and there arises from a bad and unapt formation of words a wonderful obstruction to the mind.

Bacon, *Novum Organum*, I, 43

28 We may also recognise the difference that exists between men and brutes. For it is a very remarkable fact that there are none so depraved and stupid, without even excepting idiots, that they cannot arrange different words together, forming of them a statement by which they make known their thoughts; while, on the other hand, there is no other animal, however perfect and fortunately circumstanced it may be, which can do the same. It is not the want of organs that brings this to pass, for it is evident that magpies and parrots are able to utter words just like ourselves, and yet they cannot speak as we do, that is, so as to give evidence that they think of what they say. On the other hand, men who, being born deaf and dumb, are in the same degree, or even more than the brutes, destitute of the organs which serve the others for talking, are in the habit of themselves inventing certain signs by which they make themselves understood by those who, being usually in their company, have leisure to learn their language. And this does not merely show that the brutes have less reason than men, but that they have none at all, since it is clear that very little is required in order to be able to talk. And when we notice the inequality that exists between animals of the same species, as well as between men, and observe that some are more capable of receiving instruction than others, it is not credible that a monkey or a parrot, selected as the most perfect of its species, should not in these matters equal the stupidest child to be found, or at least a child

whose mind is clouded, unless in the case of the brute the soul were of an entirely different nature from ours. And we ought not to confound speech with natural movements which betray passions and may be imitated by machines as well as be manifested by animals; nor must we think, as did some of the ancients, that brutes talk, although we do not understand their language. For if this were true, since they have many organs which are allied to our own, they could communicate their thoughts to us just as easily as to those of their own race.

Descartes, *Discourse on Method,* V

29 The most noble and profitable invention of all other was that of *speech,* consisting of names or appellations, and their connexion; whereby men register their thoughts, recall them when they are past, and also declare them one to another for mutual utility and conversation; without which there had been amongst men neither Commonwealth, nor society, nor contract, nor peace, no more than amongst lions, bears, and wolves. The first author of speech was God himself, that instructed Adam how to name such creatures as He presented to his sight; for the Scripture goeth no further in this matter. But this was sufficient to direct him to add more names, as the experience and use of the creatures should give him occasion; and to join them in such manner by degrees as to make himself understood; and so by succession of time, so much language might be gotten as he had found use for.

Hobbes, *Leviathan,* I, 4

30 The manner how speech serveth to the remembrance of the consequence of causes and effects consisteth in the imposing of *names,* and the connexion of them.

Of names, some are *proper,* and singular to one only thing; as Peter, John, this man, this tree: and some are *common* to many things; as man, horse, tree; every of which, though but one name, is nevertheless the name of diverse particular things; in respect of all which together, it is called a *universal,* there being nothing in the world universal but names; for the things named are every one of them individual and singular.

Hobbes, *Leviathan,* I, 4

31 When a man, upon the hearing of any speech, hath those thoughts which the words of that speech, and their connexion, were ordained and constituted to signify, then he is said to understand it: *understanding* being nothing else but conception caused by speech. And therefore if speech be peculiar to man, as for ought I know it is, then is understanding peculiar to him also. And therefore of absurd and false affirmations, in case they be universal, there can be no understanding; though many think they understand then, when

they do but repeat the words softly, or con them in their mind.

Hobbes, *Leviathan,* I, 4

32 There are . . . those who go to the absurdity of explaining a word by the word itself. I know of some who have defined light in this way: "Light is a luminary motion of luminous bodies," as if we could understand the words *luminary* and *luminous* without understanding the word *light.*

We cannot undertake to define being without falling into this absurdity, for we cannot define any word without beginning with these words *it is,* and thus use the word defined in the definition.

It is sufficiently clear from this that there are words incapable of definition. And if nature had not made up for this defect by giving a like idea to all men, all our expressions would be confused; whereas we make use of them with the same assurance and the same certainty we should have if they had been explained in a perfectly unambiguous way, because nature itself has given us, without words, a clearer understanding of them than we gain through art with all our explanations.

Pascal, *Geometrical Demonstration*

33 The senses at first let in *particular* ideas, and furnish the yet empty cabinet, and the mind by degrees growing familiar with some of them, they are lodged in the memory, and names got to them. Afterwards, the mind proceeding further, abstracts them, and by degrees learns the use of general names. In this manner the mind comes to be furnished with ideas and language, the *materials* about which to exercise its discursive faculty. And the use of reason becomes daily more visible, as these materials that give it employment increase.

Locke, *Concerning Human Understanding,*
Bk. I, I, 15

34 Man . . . had by nature his organs so fashioned, as to be fit to frame articulate sounds, which we call words. But this was not enough to produce language; for parrots, and several other birds, will be taught to make articulate sounds distinct enough, which yet by no means are capable of language.

Besides articulate sounds, therefore, it was further necessary that he should be able to use these sounds as signs of internal conceptions; and to make them stand as marks for the ideas within his own mind, whereby they might be made known to others, and the thoughts of men's minds be conveyed from one to another.

But neither was this sufficient to make words so useful as they ought to be. It is not enough for the perfection of language, that sounds can be made signs of ideas, unless those signs can be so made use of as to comprehend several particular things: for the multiplication of words would have perplexed their use, had every particular thing need of a distinct name to be signified by. To remedy this inconvenience, language had yet a further improvement in the use of *general terms,* whereby one word was made to mark a multitude of particular existences: which advantageous use of sounds was obtained only by the difference of the ideas they were made signs of: those names becoming general, which are made to stand for *general ideas,* and those remaining particular, where the *ideas* they are used for are *particular.*

Besides these names which stand for ideas, there be other words which men make use of, not to signify any idea, but the want or absence of some ideas, simple or complex, or all ideas together; such as are *nihil* in Latin, and in English, *ignorance* and *barrenness.* All which negative or privative words cannot be said properly to belong to, or signify no ideas: for then they would be perfectly insignificant sounds; but they relate to positive ideas, and signify their absence.

Locke, *Concerning Human Understanding,*
Bk. III, I, 1–4

35 Because by familiar use from our cradles, we come to learn certain articulate sounds very perfectly, and have them readily on our tongues, and always at hand in our memories, but yet are not always careful to examine or settle their significations perfectly; it often happens that men, even when they would apply themselves to an attentive consideration, do set their thoughts more on words than things. Nay, because words are many of them learned before the ideas are known for which they stand: therefore some, not only children but men, speak several words no otherwise than parrots do, only because they have learned them, and have been accustomed to those sounds. But so far as words are of use and signification, so far is there a constant connexion between the sound and the idea, and a designation that the one stands for the other; without which application of them, they are nothing but so much insignificant noise.

Locke, *Concerning Human Understanding,*
Bk. III, II, 7

36 It is plain, by what has been said, that *general* and *universal* belong not to the real existence of things; but are the inventions and creatures of the understanding, made by it for its own use, and concern only signs, whether words or ideas. Words are general, as has been said, when used for signs of general ideas, and so are applicable indifferently to many particular things; and ideas are general when they are set up as the representatives of many particular things: but universality belongs not to things themselves, which are all of them particular in their existence, even those words and ideas which in their signification are general. When therefore we quit particulars, the generals that rest are only creatures of our own making;

their general nature being nothing but the capacity they are put into, by the understanding, of signifying or representing many particulars. For the signification they have is nothing but a relation that, by the mind of man, is added to them.

Locke, *Concerning Human Understanding,*
Bk. III, III, 11

37 Besides words which are names of ideas in the mind, there are a great many others that are made use of to signify the *connexion* that the mind gives to ideas, or to propositions, one with another. The mind, in communicating its thoughts to others, does not only need signs of the ideas it has then before it, but others also, to show or intimate some particular action of its own, at that time, relating to those ideas. This it does several ways; as *Is,* and *Is not,* are the general marks, of the mind, affirming or denying. But besides affirmation or negation, without which there is in words no truth or falsehood, the mind does, in declaring its sentiments to others, connect not only the parts of propositions, but whole sentences one to another, with their several relations and dependencies, to make a coherent discourse.

Locke, *Concerning Human Understanding,*
Bk. III, VII, 1

38 I leave it to be considered, whether it would not be well for mankind, whose concernment it is to know things as they are, and to do what they ought, and not to spend their lives in talking about them, or tossing words to and fro;—whether it would not be well, I say, that the use of words were made plain and direct; and that language, which was given us for the improvement of knowledge and bond of society, should not be employed to darken truth and unsettle people's rights; to raise mists, and render unintelligible both morality and religion? Or that at least, if this will happen, it should not be thought learning or knowledge to do so?

Locke, *Concerning Human Understanding,*
Bk. III, X, 13

39 There has been a late deservedly esteemed philosopher [Locke] who, no doubt, has given [the doctrine of abstraction] very much countenance, by seeming to think the having abstract general ideas is what puts the widest difference in point of understanding betwixt man and beast. . . . I readily agree with this learned author, that the faculties of brutes can by no means attain to abstraction. But then if this be made the distinguishing property of that sort of animals, I fear a great many of those that pass for men must be reckoned into their number. The reason that is here assigned why we have no grounds to think brutes have abstract general ideas is, that we observe in them no use of words or any other general signs; which is built on this supposition—that the making use of

words implies the having general ideas. From which it follows that men who use language are able to abstract or generalize their ideas. That this is the sense and arguing of the author will further appear by his answering the question he in another place puts: "Since all things that exist are only particulars, how come we by general terms?" His answer is: "Words become general by being made the signs of general ideas."—*Essay on Human Understanding,* III. iii. 6. But it seems that a word becomes general by being made the sign, not of an abstract general idea, but of several particular ideas, any one of which it indifferently suggests to the mind. For example, when it is said "the change of motion is proportional to the impressed force," or that "whatever has extension is divisible," these propositions are to be understood of motion and extension in general; and nevertheless it will not follow that they suggest to my thoughts an idea of motion without a body moved, or any determinate direction and velocity, or that I must conceive an abstract general idea of extension, which is neither line, surface, nor solid, neither great nor small, black, white, nor red, nor of any other determinate colour. It is only implied that whatever particular motion I consider, whether it be swift or slow, perpendicular, horizontal, or oblique, or in whatever object, the axiom concerning it holds equally true. As does the other of every particular extension, it matters not whether line, surface, or solid, whether of this or that magnitude or figure.

> Berkeley, *Principles of Human Knowledge,*
> Introduction, 11

40 Of late many have been very sensible of the absurd opinions and insignificant disputes which grow out of the abuse of words. And, in order to remedy these evils, they advise well, that we attend to the ideas signified, and draw off our attention from the words which signify them. But, how good soever this advice may be they have given others, it is plain they could not have a due regard to it themselves, so long as they thought the only immediate use of words was to signify ideas, and that the immediate signification of every general name was a determinate abstract idea.

But, these being known to be mistakes, a man may with greater ease prevent his being imposed on by words. He that knows he has no other than *particular* ideas, will not puzzle himself in vain to find out and conceive the *abstract* idea annexed to any name. And he that knows names do not always stand for ideas will spare himself the labour of looking for ideas where there are none to be had.

> Berkeley, *Principles of Human Knowledge,*
> Introduction, 23–24

41 We next went to the school of languages, where three professors sat in consultation upon improving that of their own country.

The first project was to shorten discourse by cutting polysyllables into one, and leaving out verbs and participles, because in reality all things imaginable are but nouns.

The other, was a scheme for entirely abolishing all words whatsoever: and this was urged as a great advantage in point of health as well as brevity. For, it is plain, that every word we speak is in some degree a diminution of our lungs by corrosion; and consequently contributes to the shortning of our lives. An expedient was therefore offered, that since words are only names for *things,* it would be more convenient for all men to carry about them, such *things* as were necessary to express the particular business they are to discourse on. And this invention would certainly have taken place, to the great ease as well as health of the subject, if the women in conjunction with the vulgar and illiterate had not threatned to raise a rebellion, unless they might be allowed the liberty to speak with their tongues, after the manner of their forefathers: such constant irreconcileable enemies to science are the common people. However, many of the most learned and wise adhere to the new scheme of expressing themselves by *things;* which hath only this inconvenience attending it; that if a man's business be very great, and of various kinds, he must be obliged in proportion to carry a greater bundle of *things* upon his back, unless he can afford one or two strong servants to attend him. I have often beheld two of those sages almost sinking under the weight of their packs, like pedlars among us; who, when they met in the streets would lay down their loads, open their sacks, and hold conversation for an hour together; then put up their implements, help each other to resume their burthens, and take their leave.

But, for short conversations, a man may carry implements in his pockets and under his arms, enough to supply him, and in his house he cannot be at a loss; therefore the room where company meet who practise this art, is full of all things ready at hand, requisite to furnish matter for this kind of artificial converse.

Another great advantage proposed by this invention, was, that it would serve as an universal language to be understood in all civilized nations, whose goods and utensils are generally of the same kind, or nearly resembling, so that their uses might easily be comprehended. And thus, embassadors would be qualified to treat with foreign princes or ministers of State, to whose tongues they were utter strangers.

> Swift, *Gulliver's Travels,* III, 5

42 This society hath a peculiar cant and jargon of their own, that no other mortal can understand, and wherein all their laws are written, which they take special care to multiply; whereby they have wholly confounded the very essence of truth and falshood, of right and wrong; so that it will take

thirty years to decide whether the field, left me by my ancestors for six generations, belong to me, or to a stranger three hundred miles off.

Swift, *Gulliver's Travels,* IV, 5

43 Jones now declared that they must certainly have lost their way; but this the guide insisted upon was impossible; a word which, in common conversation, is often used to signify not only improbable, but often what is really very likely, and, sometimes, what hath certainly happened; and hyperbolical violence like that which is so frequently offered to the words infinite and eternal; by the former of which it is usual to express a distance of half a yard, and by the latter, a duration of five minutes. And thus it is as usual to assert the impossibility of losing what is already actually lost. This was, in fact, the case at present.

Fielding, *Tom Jones,* XII, 11

44 Words do not constitute an overt act; they remain only in idea. When considered by themselves, they have generally no determinate signification; for this depends on the tone in which they are uttered. It often happens that in repeating the same words they have not the same meaning; this depends on their connection with other things, and sometimes more is signified by silence than by any expression whatever.

Montesquieu, *Spirit of Laws,* XII, 12

45 There is no such thing as abstract or general ideas, properly speaking; but . . . all general ideas are, in reality, particular ones, attached to a general term, which recalls, upon occasion, other particular ones, that resemble, in certain circumstances, the idea, present to the mind. Thus when the term Horse is pronounced, we immediately figure to ourselves the idea of a black or a white animal, of a particular size or figure: But as that term is also usually applied to animals of other colours, figures and sizes, these ideas, though not actually present to the imagination, are easily recalled; and our reasoning and conclusion proceed in the same way, as if they were actually present.

Hume, *Concerning Human Understanding,*
XII, 125, fn.

46 There is no complete language, no language which can express all our ideas and all our sensations; their shades are too numerous, too imperceptible. Nobody can make known the precise degree of sensation he experiences. One is obliged, for example, to designate by the general names of "love" and "hate" a thousand loves and a thousand hates all different from each other; it is the same with our pleasures and our pains. Thus all languages are, like us, imperfect.

Voltaire, *Philosophical Dictionary:*
Languages

47 The first [difficulty] which presents itself is to conceive how language can have become necessary; for as there was no communication among men and no need for any, we can neither conceive the necessity of this invention, nor the possibility of it, if it was not somehow indispensable. I might affirm, with many others, that languages arose in the domestic intercourse between parents and their children. But this expedient would not obviate the difficulty, and would besides involve the blunder made by those who, in reasoning on the state of nature, always import into it ideas gathered in a state of society. . . . For to say that the mother dictated to her child the words he was to use in asking her for one thing or another, is an explanation of how languages already formed are taught, but by no means explains how languages were originally formed.

We will suppose, however, that this first difficulty is obviated. Let us for a moment then take ourselves as being on this side of the vast space which must lie between a pure state of nature and that in which languages had become necessary, and, admitting their necessity, let us inquire how they could first be established. Here we have a new and worse difficulty to grapple with: for if men need speech to learn to think, they must have stood in much greater need of the art of thinking, to be able to invent that of speaking. And though we might conceive how the articulate sound of the voice came to be taken as the conventional interpreters of our ideas, it would still remain for us to inquire what could have been the interpreters of this convention for those ideas, which, answering to no sensible objects, could not be indicated either by gesture or voice; so that we can hardly form any tolerable conjectures about the origin of this art of communicating our thoughts and establishing a correspondence between minds.

Rousseau, *Origin of Inequality,* I

48 The first language of mankind, the most universal and vivid, in a word the only language man needed, before he had occasion to exert his eloquence to persuade assembled multitudes, was the simple cry of nature. But as this was excited only by a sort of instinct on urgent occasions, to implore assistance in case of danger, or relief in case of suffering, it could be of little use in the ordinary course of life, in which more moderate feelings prevail. When the ideas of men began to expand and multiply, and closer communication took place among them, they strove to invent more numerous signs and a more copious language. They multiplied the inflections of the voice, and added gestures, which are in their own nature more expressive, and depend less for their meaning on a prior determination. Visible and movable objects were therefore expressed by gestures, and audible ones by imitative sounds: but, as hardly anything can be indicated by gestures, ex-

cept objects actually present or easily described, and visible actions; as they are not universally useful—for darkness or the interposition of a material object destroys their efficacy—and as besides they rather request than secure our attention; men at length bethought themselves of substituting for them the articulate sounds of the voice, which, without bearing the same relation to any particular ideas, are better calculated to express them all, as conventional signs. Such an institution could only be made by common consent, and must have been effected in a manner not very easy for men whose gross organs had not been accustomed to any such exercise. It is also in itself still more difficult to conceive, since such a common agreement must have had motives, and speech seems to have been highly necessary to establish the use of it.

Rousseau, *Origin of Inequality*, I

49 General ideas cannot be introduced into the mind without the assistance of words, nor can the understanding seize them except by means of propositions. This is one of the reasons why animals cannot form such ideas, or ever acquire that capacity for self-improvement which depends on them. When a monkey goes from one nut to another, are we to conceive that he entertains any general idea of that kind of fruit, and compares its archetype with the two individual nuts? Assuredly he does not; but the sight of one of these nuts recalls to his memory the sensations which he received from the other, and his eyes, being modified after a certain manner, give information to the palate of the modification it is about to receive. Every general idea is purely intellectual; if the imagination meddles with it ever so little, the idea immediately becomes particular. If you endeavour to trace in your mind the image of a tree in general, you never attain to your end. In spite of all you can do, you will have to see it as great or little, bare or leafy, light or dark, and were you capable of seeing nothing in it but what is common to all trees, it would no longer be like a tree at all. Purely abstract beings are perceivable in the same manner, or are only conceivable by the help of language. The definition of a triangle alone gives you a true idea of it: the moment you imagine a triangle in your mind, it is some particular triangle and not another, and you cannot avoid giving it sensible lines and a coloured area. We must then make use of propositions and of language in order to form general ideas. For no sooner does the imagination cease to operate than the understanding proceeds only by the help of words. If then the first inventors of speech could give names only to ideas they already had, it follows that the first substantives could be nothing more than proper names.

Rousseau, *Origin of Inequality*, I

50 For myself, I am so aghast at the increasing difficulties which present themselves, and so well convinced of the almost demonstrable impossibility that languages should owe their original institution to merely human means, that I leave, to any one who will undertake it, the discussion of the difficult problem, which was most necessary, the existence of society to the invention of language, or the invention of language to the establishment of society.

Rousseau, *Origin of Inequality*, I

51 Talking of the origin of language; *Johnson.* "It must have come by inspiration. A thousand, nay, a million of children could not invent a language. While the organs are pliable, there is not understanding enough to form a language; by the time that there is understanding enough, the organs become stiff. We know that after a certain age we cannot learn to pronounce a new language. No foreigner, who comes to England when advanced in life, ever pronounces English tolerably well; at least such instances are very rare. When I maintain that language must have come by inspiration, I do not mean that inspiration is required for rhetorick, and all the beauties of language; for when once man has language, we can conceive that he may gradually form modifications of it. I mean only that inspiration seems to me to be necessary to give man the faculty of speech; to inform him that he may have speech; which I think he could no more find out without inspiration, than cows or hogs would think of such a faculty."

Boswell, *Life of Johnson* (Apr. 18, 1783)

52 So sensible were the Romans of the influence of language over national manners, that it was their most serious care to extend, with the progress of their arms, the use of the Latin tongue. The ancient dialects of Italy, the Sabine, the Etruscan, and the Venetian, sunk into oblivion; but in the provinces, the east was less docile than the west, to the voice of its victorious preceptors. This obvious difference marked the two portions of the empire with a distinction of colours, which, though it was in some degree concealed during the meridian splendour of prosperity, became gradually more visible as the shades of night descended upon the Roman world. The western countries were civilised by the same hands which subdued them. As soon as the barbarians were reconciled to obedience, their minds were opened to any new impressions of knowledge and politeness. The language of Virgil and Cicero, though with some inevitable mixture of corruption, was so universally adopted in Africa, Spain, Gaul, Britain, and Pannonia, that the faint traces of the Punic or Celtic idioms were preserved only in the mountains, or among the peasants. Education and study insensibly inspired the natives of those countries with the sentiments of Romans; and Italy gave fashions as well

as laws to her Latin provincials. They solicited with more ardour, and obtained with more facility, the freedom and honours of the state; supported the national dignity in letters and in arms; and, at length, in the person of Trajan, produced an emperor whom the Scipios would not have disowned for their countryman. The situation of the Greeks was very different from that of the Barbarians. The former had been since civilised and corrupted. They had too much taste to relinquish their language, and too much vanity to adopt any foreign institutions. Still preserving the prejudices after they had lost the virtues of their ancestors, they affected to despise the unpolished manners of the Roman conquerors, whilst they were compelled to respect their superior wisdom and power. Nor was the influence of the Grecian language and sentiments confined to the narrow limits of that once celebrated country. Their empire, by the progress of colonies and conquest, had been diffused from the Hadriatic to the Euphrates and the Nile. Asia was covered with Greek cities, and the long reign of the Macedonian kings had introduced a silent revolution into Syria and Egypt. In their pompous courts those princes united the elegance of Athens with the luxury of the East, and the example of the court was imitated, at an humble distance, by the higher ranks of their subjects. Such was the general division of the Roman empire into the Latin and Greek languages. To these we may add a third distinction for the body of the natives in Syria, and especially in Egypt. The use of their ancient dialects, by secluding them from the commerce of mankind, checked the improvements of those barbarians. The slothful effeminacy of the former, exposed them to the contempt; the sullen ferociousness of the latter, excited the aversion of the conquerors.

Gibbon, *Decline and Fall of the Roman Empire*, II

53 The use of letters is the principal circumstance that distinguishes a civilized people from a herd of savages incapable of knowledge or reflection. Without that artificial help, the human memory soon dissipates or corrupts the ideas intrusted to her charge; and the nobler faculties of the mind, no longer supplied with models or with materials, gradually forget their powers; the judgment becomes feeble and lethargic, the imagination languid or irregular. Fully to apprehend this important truth, let us attempt, in an improved society, to calculate the immense distance between the man of learning and the *illiterate* peasant. The former, by reading and reflection, multiplies his own experience, and lives in distant ages and remote countries; whilst the latter, rooted to a single spot, and confined to a few years of existence, surpasses, but very little, his fellow-labourer the ox in the exercise of his mental faculties. The same, and even a greater, difference will be found between

nations than between individuals; and we may safely pronounce that, without some species of writing, no people has ever preserved the faithful annals of their history, ever made any considerable progress in the abstract sciences, or ever possessed, in any tolerable degree of perfection, the useful and agreeable arts of life.

Gibbon, *Decline and Fall of the Roman Empire*, IX

54 Though the origin of most of our words is forgotten, each word was at first a stroke of genius, and obtained currency because for the moment it symbolized the world to the first speaker and to the hearer. The etymologist finds the deadest word to have been once a brilliant picture. Language is fossil poetry.

Emerson, *The Poet*

55 If we possessed a perfect pedigree of mankind, a genealogical arrangement of the races of man would afford the best classification of the various languages now spoken throughout the world; and if all extinct languages, and all intermediate and slowly changing dialects, were to be included, such an arrangement would be the only possible one. Yet it might be that some ancient languages had altered very little and had given rise to few new languages, whilst others had altered much owing to the spreading, isolation, and state of civilisation of the several co-descended races, and had thus given rise to many new dialects and languages. The various degrees of difference between the languages of the same stock, would have to be expressed by groups subordinate to groups; but the proper or even the only possible arrangement would still be genealogical; and this would be strictly natural, as it would connect together all languages, extinct and recent, by the closest affinities, and would give the filiation and origin of each tongue.

Darwin, *Origin of Species*, XIV

56 The habitual use of articulate language is . . . peculiar to man; but he uses, in common with lower animals, inarticulate cries to express his meaning, aided by gestures and the movements of the muscles of the face. This especially holds good with the more simple and vivid feelings, which are but little connected with our higher intelligence. Our cries of pain, fear, surprise, anger, together with their appropriate actions, and the murmur of a mother to her beloved child are more expressive than any words. That which distinguishes man from the lower animals is not the understanding of articulate sounds, for, as every one knows, dogs understand many words and sentences. In this respect they are at the same stage of development as infants, between the ages of ten and twelve months, who understand many words and short sentences, but cannot yet utter a single word. It is

not the mere articulation which is our distinguishing character, for parrots and other birds possess this power. Nor is it the mere capacity of connecting definite sounds with definite ideas; for it is certain that some parrots, which have been taught to speak, connect unerringly words with things, and persons with events. The lower animals differ from man solely in his almost infinitely larger power of associating together the most diversified sounds and ideas; and this obviously depends on the high development of his mental powers.

Darwin, *Descent of Man*, I, 3

57 Language is an art, like brewing or baking. . . . It certainly is not a true instinct, for every language has to be learnt.

Darwin, *Descent of Man*, I, 3

58 With respect to the origin of articulate language . . . I cannot doubt that language owes its origin to the imitation and modification of various natural sounds, the voices of other animals, and man's own instinctive cries, aided by signs and gestures.

Darwin, *Descent of Man*, I, 3

59 A great stride in the development of the intellect will have followed, as soon as the half-art and half-instinct of language came into use; for the continued use of language will have reacted on the brain and produced an inherited effect; and this again will have reacted on the improvement of language. As Mr. Chauncey Wright has well remarked, the largeness of the brain in man relatively to his body, compared with the lower animals, may be attributed in chief part to the early use of some simple form of language,—that wonderful engine which affixes signs to all sorts of objects and qualities, and excites trains of thought which would never arise from the mere impression of the senses, or if they did arise could not be followed out. The higher intellectual powers of man, such as those of ratiocination, abstraction, self-consciousness, etc., probably follow from the continued improvement and exercise of the other mental faculties.

Darwin, *Descent of Man*, III, 21

60 "Why, Huck, doan' de French people talk de same way we does?"

"No, Jim; you couldn't understand a word they said—not a single word."

"Well, now, I be ding-busted! How do dat come?"

"I don't know; but it's so. I got some of their jabber out of a book. S'pose a man was to come to you and say Polly-voo-franzy—what would you think?"

"I wouldn' think nuffn; I'd take en bust him over de head—dat is, ef he warn't white. I wouldn' 'low no nigger to call me dat."

"Shucks, it ain't calling you anything. It's only

saying, do you know how to talk French?"

"Well, den, why couldn't he say it?"

"Why, he *is* a-saying it. That's a Frenchman's *way* of saying it."

"Well, it's a blame' ridicklous way, en I doan' want to hear no mo' 'bout it. Dey ain' no sense in it."

"Looky here, Jim; does a cat talk like we do?"

"No, a cat don't."

"Well, does a cow?"

"No, a cow don't, nuther."

"Does a cat talk like a cow, or a cow talk like a cat?"

"No, dey don't."

"It's natural and right for 'em to talk different from each other, ain't it?"

"Course."

"And ain't it natural and right for a cat and a cow to talk different from *us?"*

"Why, mos' sholy it is."

"Well, then, why ain't it natural and right for a *Frenchman* to talk different from us? You answer me that."

"Is a cat a man, Huck?"

"No."

"Well, den, dey ain't no sense in a cat talkin' like a man. Is a cow a man?—er is a cow a cat?"

"No, she ain't either of them."

"Well, den, she ain' got no business to talk like either one er the yuther of 'em. Is a Frenchman a man?"

"Yes."

"Well, den! Dad blame it, why doan' he *talk* like a man? You answer me *dat!"*

I see it warn't no use wasting words—you can't learn a nigger to argue. So I quit.

Mark Twain, *Huckleberry Finn*, XIV

61 Language was originally made by men who were not psychologists, and most men to-day employ almost exclusively the vocabulary of outward things. The cardinal passions of our life, anger, love, fear, hate, hope, and the most comprehensive divisions of our intellectual activity, to remember, expect, think, know, dream, with the broadest genera of æsthetic feeling, joy, sorrow, pleasure, pain, are the only facts of a subjective order which this vocabulary deigns to note by special words. The elementary qualities of sensation, bright, loud, red, blue, hot, cold, are, it is true, susceptible of being used in both an objective and a subjective sense. They stand for outer qualities and for the feelings which these arouse. But the objective sense is the original sense; and still to-day we have to describe a large number of sensations by the name of the object from which they have most frequently been got. An orange color, an odor of violets, a cheesy taste, a thunderous sound, a fiery smart, etc., will recall what I mean. This absence of a special vocabulary for subjective facts hinders the study of all but the very coarsest

of them. Empiricist writers are very fond of emphasizing one great set of delusions which language inflicts on the mind. Whenever we have made a word, they say, to denote a certain group of phenomena, we are prone to suppose a substantive entity existing beyond the phenomena, of which the word shall be the name. But the *lack* of a word quite as often leads to the directly opposite error. We are then prone to suppose that no entity can be there; and so we come to overlook phenomena whose existence would be patent to us all, had we only grown up to hear it familiarly recognized in speech. It is hard to focus our attention on the nameless, and so there results a certain vacuousness in the descriptive parts of most psychologies.

But a worse defect than vacuousness comes from the dependence of psychology on common speech. Naming our thought by its own objects, we almost all of us assume that as the objects are, so the thought must be. The thought of several distinct things can only consist of several distinct bits of thought, or "ideas"; that of an abstract or universal object can only be an abstract or universal idea. As each object may come and go, be forgotten and then thought of again, it is held that the thought of it has a precisely similar independence, self-identity, and mobility. The thought of the object's recurrent identity is regarded as the identity of its recurrent thought; and the perceptions of multiplicity, of coexistence, of succession, are severally conceived to be brought about only through a multiplicity, a coexistence, a succession, of perceptions. The continuous flow of the mental stream is sacrificed, and in its place an atomism, a brickbat plan of construction, is preached for the existence of which no good introspective grounds can be brought forward, and out of which presently grow all sorts of paradoxes and contradictions, the heritage of woe of students of the mind.

These words are meant to impeach the entire English psychology derived from Locke and Hume, and the entire German psychology derived from Herbart, so far as they both treat "ideas" as separate subjective entities that come and go.

William James, *Psychology*, VII

62 The opinion so stoutly professed by many, that language is essential to thought, seems to have this much of truth in it, that all our inward images tend invincibly to attach themselves to something sensible, so as to gain in corporeity and life. Words serve this purpose, gestures serve it, stones, straws, chalk-marks, anything will do. As soon as any one of these things stands for the idea, the latter seems to be more real.

William James, *Psychology*, XXI

63 Language is a system of *signs,* different from the things signified, but able to suggest them. . . .

No doubt brutes have a number of such signs.

When a dog yelps in front of a door, and his master, understanding his desire, opens it, the dog may, after a certain number of repetitions, get to repeat in cold blood a yelp which was at first the involuntary interjectional expression of strong emotion. The same dog may be taught to "beg" for food, and afterwards come to do so deliberately when hungry. The dog also learns to understand the signs of men, and the word "rat" uttered to a terrier suggests exciting thoughts of the rat-hunt. If the dog had the varied impulse to vocal utterance which some other animals have, he would probably repeat the word "rat" whenever he spontaneously happened to think of a rat-hunt—he no doubt does have it as an auditory image, just as a parrot calls out different words spontaneously from its repertory, and having learned the name of a given dog will utter it on the sight of a different dog. In each of these separate cases the particular sign *may* be consciously noticed by the animal, as distinct from the particular thing signified, and will thus, so far as it goes, be a true manifestation of language. But when we come to man we find a great difference. *He has a deliberate intention to apply a sign to everything.* The linguistic impulse is with him generalized and systematic. For things hitherto unnoticed or unfelt, he *desires* a sign before he has one. Even though the dog should possess his "yelp" for this thing, his "beg" for that, and his auditory image "rat" for a third thing, the matter with him rests there. If a fourth thing interests him for which no sign happens already to have been learned, he remains tranquilly without it and goes no further. But the man *postulates* it, its absence irritates him, and he ends by inventing it. *This* GENERAL PURPOSE *constitutes, I take it, the peculiarity of human speech, and explains its prodigious development.*

How, then, does the general purpose arise? It arises as soon as the notion of a *sign as such,* apart from any particular import, is born; and this notion is born by dissociation from the outstanding portions of a number of concrete cases of signification. The "yelp," the "beg," the "rat," differ as to their several imports and natures. They agree only in so far as they have the same *use*—to *be signs,* to stand for something more important than themselves. The dog whom this similarity could strike would have grasped the sign *per se* as such, and would probably thereupon become a general sign-maker, or speaker in the human sense. But how can the similarity strike him? Not without the juxtaposition of the similars (in virtue of the law we have laid down, that in order to be segregated an experience must be repeated with varying concomitants)—not unless the "yelp" of the dog at the moment it occurs *recalls* to him his "beg," by the delicate bond of their subtle similarity of use—not till then can this thought flash through his mind: "Why, yelp and beg, in spite of all their unlikeness, are yet alike in this: that they are actions, signs, which lead to important boons. Other boons, *any* boons, may then be got by other signs!" This reflection made, the gulf is passed. Animals probably never make it, because the bond of similarity is not delicate enough. Each sign is drowned in *its* import, and never awakens other signs and other imports in juxtaposition. The rat-hunt idea is too absorbingly interesting in itself to be interrupted by anything so uncontiguous to it as the idea of the "beg for food," or of "the door-open yelp," nor in their turn do these awaken the rat-hunt idea.

In the human child, however, these ruptures of contiguous association are very soon made; far off cases of sign-using arise when we make a sign now; and soon language is launched. The child in each case makes the discovery for himself. No one can help him except by furnishing him with the conditions. But as he is constituted, the conditions will sooner or later shoot together into the result.

William James, *Psychology*, XXII

64 A language is not a universal mode of expressing all ideas whatsoever. It is a limited mode of expressing such ideas as have been frequently entertained, and urgently needed, by the group of human beings who developed that mode of speech. It is only during a comparatively short period of human history that there has existed any language with an adequate stock of general terms. Such general terms require a permanent literature to define them by their mode of employment.

The result is that the free handling of general ideas is a late acquirement. I am not maintaining that the brains of men were inadequate for the task. The point is that it took ages for them to develop first the appliances and then the habits which made generality of thought possible and prevalent. For ages, existing languages must have been ready for development. If men had been in contact with a superior race, either personally or by a survival of their literature, a process which requires scores or even hundreds of generations might have been antedated, so as to have been effected almost at once. Such, in fact, was the later history of the development of the races of Northern Europe. Again, a social system which encourages developments of thought can procure the advent. This is the way in which the result was first obtained. Society and language grew together.

Whitehead, *Religion in the Making*, I, 5

65 It is natural to think of the meaning of a word as something conventional. This, however, is only true with great limitations. A new word can be added to an existing language by a mere convention, as is done, for instance, with new scientific terms. But the basis of a language is not conventional, either from the point of view of the individual or from that of the community. A child learn-ing to speak is learning habits and associations which are just as much determined by the environment as the habit of expecting dogs to bark and cocks to crow. The community that speaks a language has learnt it, and modified it by processes almost all of which are not deliberate, but the results of causes operating according to more or less ascertainable laws. If we trace any Indo-European language back far enough, we arrive hypothetically (at any rate according to some authorities) at the stage when language consisted only of the roots out of which subsequent words have grown. How these roots acquired their meanings is not known, but a conventional origin is clearly just as mythical as the social contract by which Hobbes and Rousseau supposed civil government to have been established. We can hardly suppose a parliament of hitherto speechless elders meeting together and agreeing to call a cow a cow and a wolf a wolf. The association of words with their meanings must have grown up by some natural process, though at present the nature of the process is unknown.

Russell, *Analysis of Mind*, X

66 The essence of language lies, not in the use of this or that special means of communication, but in the employment of fixed associations (however these may have originated) in order that something now sensible—a spoken word, a picture, a gesture, or what not—may call up the "idea" of something else. Whenever this is done, what is now sensible may be called a "sign" or "symbol," and that of which it is intended to call up the "idea" may be called its "meaning." This is a rough outline of what constitutes "meaning."

Russell, *Analysis of Mind*, X

67 Language has two interconnected merits: first, that it is social, and second, that it supplies public expression for "thoughts" which would otherwise remain private. Without language, or some prelinguistic analogue, our knowledge of the environment is confined to what our own senses have shown us, together with such inferences as our congenital constitution may prompt; but by the help of speech we are able to know what others can relate, and to relate what is no longer sensibly present but only remembered. When we see or hear something which a companion is not seeing or hearing, we can often make him aware of it by the one word "look" or "listen," or even by gestures. But if half an hour ago we saw a fox, it is not possible to make another person aware of this fact without language. This depends upon the fact that the word "fox" applies equally to a fox seen or a fox remembered, so that our memories, which in themselves are private, are represented to others by uttered sounds, which are public. Without language, only that part of our life which consists of public sensations would be communicable,

and that only to those so situated as to be able to share the sensations in question.

Russell, *Human Knowledge*, II, 1

68 Language serves not only to express thoughts, but to make possible thoughts which could not exist without it. It is sometimes maintained that there can be no thought without language, but to this view I cannot assent: I hold that there can be thought, and even true and false belief, without language. But however that may, it cannot be denied that all fairly elaborate thoughts require words. I can know, in a sense, that I have five fingers without knowing the word "five," but I cannot know that the population of London is about eight millions unless I have acquired the language of arithmetic, nor can I have any thought at all closely corresponding to what is asserted in the sentence: "The ratio of the circumference of a circle to the diameter is approximately 3.14159." Language, once evolved, acquires a kind of autonomy: we can know, especially in mathematics, that a sentence asserts something true, although what it asserts is too complex to be apprehended even by the best minds.

Russell, *Human Knowledge*, II, 1

69 I think the elementary uses of a word may be distinguished as indicative, imperative, and interrogative. When a child sees his mother coming, he may say, "Mother"; this is the indicative use. When he wants her, he calls, "Mother!"; this is the imperative use. When she dresses up as a witch and he begins to pierce the disguise, he may say, "Mother?" This is the interrogative use. The indicative use must come first in the acquisition of language, since the association of word and object signified can only be created by the simultaneous presence of both. But the imperative use very quickly follows. This is relevant in considering what we mean by "thinking of" an object. It is obvious that the child who has just learned to call his mother has found verbal expression for a state in which he had often been previously, that this state was associated with his mother, and that it has now become associated with the word "Mother." Before language, his state was only partially communicable; an adult, hearing him cry, could know that he wanted something, but had to guess what it was. But the fact that the word "Mother!" expresses his state shows that even before the acquisition of language his state had a relation to his mother, namely, the relation called "thinking of." This relation is not created by language, but antedates it. What language does is to make it communicable.

Russell, *Human Knowledge*, II, 2

70 When one has familiarized oneself with the extensive employment of symbolism for the representation of sexual material in dreams, one naturally asks oneself whether many of these symbols have not a permanently established meaning, like the signs in shorthand; and one even thinks of attempting to compile a new dream-book on the lines of the cipher method. In this connection it should be noted that symbolism does not appertain especially to dreams, but rather to the unconscious imagination, and particularly to that of the people, and it is to be found in a more developed condition in folklore, myths, legends, idiomatic phrases, proverbs, and the current witticisms of a people than in dreams. We should have, therefore, to go far beyond the province of dream-interpretation in order fully to investigate the meaning of symbolism, and to discuss the numerous problems—for the most part still unsolved—which are associated with the concept of the symbol. We shall here confine ourselves to saying that representation by a symbol comes under the heading of the indirect representations, but that we are warned by all sorts of signs against indiscriminately closing symbolic representation with the other modes of indirect representation before we have clearly conceived its distinguishing characteristics. In a number of cases, the common quality shared by the symbol and the thing which it represents is obvious; in others, it is concealed; in these latter cases the choice of the symbol appears to be enigmatic. And these are the very cases that must be able to elucidate the ultimate meaning of the symbolic relation; they point to the fact that it is of a genetic nature. What is today symbolically connected was probably united, in primitive times, by conceptual and linguistic identity. The symbolic relationship seems to be a residue and reminder of a former identity. It may also be noted that in many cases the symbolic identity extends beyond the linguistic identity.

Freud, *Interpretation of Dreams*, VI, E

71 There is a specially close relation between true symbols and sexuality.

An important clue in this connection has recently been given to us in the view expressed by a philologist (H. Sperber, of Upsala, who works independently of psycho-analysis), that sexual needs have had the largest share in the origin and development of language. He says that the first sounds uttered were a means of communication, and of summoning the sexual partner, and that, in the later development, the elements of speech were used as an accompaniment to the different kinds of work carried on by primitive man. This work was performed by associated efforts, to the sound of rhythmically repeated utterances, the effect of which was to transfer a sexual interest to the work. Primitive man thus made his work agreeable, so to speak, by treating it as the equivalent of and substitute for sexual activities. The word uttered during the communal work had therefore two meanings, the one referring to the sexual act, the other to the labour which had come to be equivalent to it. In time the word was dissociated from its sexual significance and its application confined to the work. Generations later the same thing happened to a new word with a sexual signification, which was then applied to a new form of work. In this way a number of root-words arose which were all of sexual origin but had all lost their sexual meaning. If the statement here outlined be correct, a possibility at least of understanding dream-symbolism opens out before us. We should comprehend why it is that in dreams, which retain something of these primitive conditions, there is such an extraordinarily large number of sexual symbols; and why weapons and tools in general stand for the male, and materials and things worked on for the female. The symbolic relations would then be the survival of the old identity in words; things which once had the same name as the genitalia could now appear in dreams as symbolizing them.

> Freud, *General Introduction to Psycho-Analysis,* X

72 Things come and go; or we come and go, and either way things escape our notice. Our direct sensible relation to things is very limited. The suggestion of meanings by natural signs is limited to occasions of direct contact or vision. But a meaning fixed by a linguistic sign is conserved for future use. Even if the thing is not there to represent the meaning, the word may be produced so as to evoke the meaning. Since intellectual life depends on possession of a store of meanings, the impor-

tance of language as a tool of preserving meanings cannot be overstated. To be sure, the method of storage is not wholly aseptic; words often corrupt and modify the meanings they are supposed to keep intact, but liability to infection is a price paid by every living thing for the privilege of living.

> Dewey, *How We Think,* Pt. III, XIII, 1

73 As is often said, grammar expresses the unconscious logic of the popular mind. *The chief intellectual classifications that constitute the working capital of thought have been built up for us by our mother tongue.* Our very lack of explicit consciousness in using language that we are employing the intellectual systematizations of the race shows how thoroughly accustomed we have become to its logical distinctions and groupings.

> Dewey, *How We Think,* Pt. III, XIII, 1

74 Instruction always runs the risk of swamping the pupil's own vital, though narrow, experience under masses of communicated material. The instructor ceases and the teacher begins at the point where communicated matter stimulates into fuller and more significant life that which has entered by the strait and narrow gate of sense-perception and motor activity. Genuine communication involves contagion; its name should not be taken in vain by terming communication that which produces no community of thought and purpose between the child and the race of which he is the heir.

> Dewey, *How We Think,* Pt. III, XVI, 3

7.2 | *The Arts of Language*

Among the categories of art to which attention is called in the first section of Chapter 16 on Art and Aesthetics is the group of arts traditionally called "the seven liberal arts," divided into the trivium, or the three arts of grammar, logic, and rhetoric, and the quadrivium, or the four arts of arithmetic, geometry, music, and astronomy. The contemporary reader will immediately recognize the first three as arts of language; the reader

would probably understand the second four better if they were referred to as the mathematical arts of calculation and measurement.

Many of the passages quoted in this section recommend steps to be taken to make speech serve more effectively as an instrument of communication or of thought. They call attention to the fallacies or faults to be avoided by a careless or uncritical use of words. They propose remedies for the misuse and abuse of language.

Still other passages consider ways of making speech more effective as a means of persuasion, and touch on questions of style, both rhetorical and poetical. The fact that there are more passages that deal with rhetorical considerations than with the rules of grammar or logic is to be explained by the much more technical character of the latter, the treatment of which would be inappropriate in a book of this kind.

The liberal arts, especially the arts of language, are sometimes referred to as the arts of learning—the arts of teaching and being taught. It is not surprising, therefore, that certain matters covered in this section should be related to matters covered in Chapter 8 on EDUCATION, especially its third section, on teaching and learning. Since the liberal arts, especially logic, are involved in the process of inquiry and the formulation of knowledge, it is also the case that things touched on in this section are related to matters covered in Chapter 6 on KNOWLEDGE, Chapter 16 on ART AND AESTHETICS, and Chapter 17 on PHILOSOPHY, SCIENCE, AND MATHEMATICS.

---

1 *Hecuba.*   Why
do we make so much of knowledge, struggle so hard
to get some little skill not worth the effort?
But persuasion, the only art whose power
is absolute, worth any price we pay,
we totally neglect. And so we fail;
we lose our hopes.

> Euripides, *Hecuba*, 815

2 *Socrates.* I wish Protagoras either to ask or answer as he is inclined; but I would rather have done with poems and odes, if he does not object, and come back to the question about which I was asking you at first, Protagoras, and by your help make an end of that. The talk about the poets seems to me like a commonplace entertainment to which a vulgar company have recourse; who, because they are not able to converse or amuse one another, while they are drinking, with the sound of their own voices and conversation, by reason of their stupidity, raise the price of flute-girls in the market, hiring for a great sum the voice of a flute instead of their own breath, to be the medium of intercourse among them: but where the company are real gentlemen and men of education, you will see no flute-girls, nor dancing-girls, nor harp-girls; and they have no nonsense or games, but are contented with one another's conversation, of which their own voices are the medium, and which they carry on by turns and in an orderly manner, even though they are very liberal in their potations. And a company like this of ours, and men such as we profess to be, do not require the help of another's voice, or of the poets whom you cannot interrogate about the meaning of what they are saying; people who cite them declaring, some that the poet has one meaning, and others that he has another, and the point which is in dispute can never be decided. This sort of entertainment they decline, and prefer to talk with one another, and put one another to the proof in conversation. And these are the models which I desire that you and I should imitate. Leaving the poets, and keeping to ourselves, let us try the mettle of one another and make proof of the truth in conversation. If you have a mind to ask, I am ready to answer; or if you would rather, do you answer, and give me the opportunity of resuming and completing our unfinished argument.

> Plato, *Protagoras,* 347A

3 *Socrates.* The composers of speeches . . . always appear to me to be very extraordinary men . . . and their art is lofty and divine, and no wonder. For their art is a part of the great art of enchantment, and hardly, if at all, inferior to it: and whereas the art of the enchanter is a mode of charming snakes and spiders and scorpions, and other monsters and pests, this art of theirs acts upon dicasts and ecclesiasts and bodies of men, for the charming and pacifying of them.

> Plato, *Euthydemus,* 289B

4 *Socrates.* Every discourse ought to be a living creature, having a body of its own and a head and feet; there should be a middle, beginning, and end, adapted to one another and to the whole.

> Plato, *Phaedrus,* 264B

5 It is useful to have examined the number of meanings of a term both for clearness' sake (for a man is more likely to know what it is he asserts, if it has been made clear to him how many meanings it may have), and also with a view to ensuring that our reasonings shall be in accordance with the ac-

tual facts and not addressed merely to the term used. For as long as it is not clear in how many senses a term is used, it is possible that the answerer and the questioner are not directing their minds upon the same thing: whereas when once it has been made clear how many meanings there are, and also upon which of them the former directs his mind when he makes his assertion, the questioner would then look ridiculous if he failed to address his argument to this. It helps us also both to avoid being misled and to mislead by false reasoning: for if we know the number of meanings of a term, we shall certainly never be misled by false reasoning, but shall know if the questioner fails to address his argument to the same point; and when we ourselves put the questions we shall be able to mislead him, if our answerer happens not to know the number of meanings of our terms.

Aristotle, *Topics*, 108ª18

6 We ought to use our terms to mean the same things as most people mean by them, but when we ask what kind of things are or are not of such and such a kind, we should not here go with the multitude: e.g. it is right to call 'healthy' whatever tends to produce health, as do most men: but in saying whether the object before us tends to produce health or not, we should adopt the language no longer of the multitude but of the doctor.

Aristotle, *Topics*, 110ª17

7 It is impossible in a discussion to bring in the actual things discussed: we use their names as symbols instead of them; and therefore we suppose that what follows in the names, follows in the things as well, just as people who calculate suppose in regard to their counters. But the two cases (names and things) are not alike. For names are finite and so is the sum-total of formulae, while things are infinite in number. Inevitably, then, the same formulae, and a single name, have a number of meanings. Accordingly just as, in counting, those who are not clever in manipulating their counters are taken in by the experts, in the same way in arguments too those who are not well acquainted with the force of names misreason both in their own discussions and when they listen to others. For this reason, then, and for others to be mentioned later, there exists both reasoning and refutation that is apparent but not real.

Aristotle, *On Sophistical Refutations*, 165ª5

8 An incisive argument is one which produces the greatest perplexity: for this is the one with the sharpest fang.

Aristotle, *On Sophistical Refutations*, 182ᵇ32

9 Rhetorical study, in its strict sense, is concerned with the modes of persuasion. Persuasion is clearly a sort of demonstration, since we are most fully persuaded when we consider a thing to have been demonstrated.

Aristotle, *Rhetoric*, 1355ª3

10 It is absurd to hold that a man ought to be ashamed of being unable to defend himself with his limbs, but not of being unable to defend himself with speech and reason, when the use of rational speech is more distinctive of a human being than the use of his limbs. And if it be objected that one who uses such power of speech unjustly might do great harm, *that* is a charge which may be made in common against all good things except virtue, and above all against the things that are most useful, as strength, health, wealth, generalship. A man can confer the greatest of benefits by a right use of these, and inflict the greatest of injuries by using them wrongly.

It is clear, then, that rhetoric is not bound up with a single definite class of subjects, but is as universal as dialectic; it is clear, also, that it is useful. It is clear, further, that its function is not simply to succeed in persuading, but rather to discover the means of coming as near such success as the circumstances of each particular case allow. In this it resembles all other arts. For example, it is not the function of medicine simply to make a man quite healthy, but to put him as far as may be on the road to health; it is possible to give excellent treatment even to those who can never enjoy sound health. Furthermore, it is plain that it is the function of one and the same art to discern the real and the apparent means of persuasion, just as it is the function of dialectic to discern the real and the apparent syllogism. What makes a man a 'sophist' is not his faculty, but his moral purpose. In rhetoric, however, the term 'rhetorician' may describe either the speaker's knowledge of the art, or his moral purpose. In dialectic it is different: a man is a 'sophist' because he has a certain kind of moral purpose, a 'dialectician' in respect, not of his moral purpose, but of his faculty.

Aristotle, *Rhetoric*, 1355ª39

11 Rhetoric may be defined as the faculty of observing in any given case the available means of persuasion. This is not a function of any other art. Every other art can instruct or persuade about its own particular subject-matter; for instance, medicine about what is healthy and unhealthy, geometry about the properties of magnitudes, arithmetic about numbers, and the same is true of the other arts and sciences. But rhetoric we look upon as the power of observing the means of persuasion on almost any subject presented to us; and that is why we say that, in its technical character, it is not concerned with any special or definite class of subjects.

Aristotle, *Rhetoric*, 1355ᵇ26

12 Of the modes of persuasion furnished by the spo-

ken word there are three kinds. The first kind depends on the personal character of the speaker; the second on putting the audience into a certain frame of mind; the third on the proof, or apparent proof, provided by the words of the speech itself. Persuasion is achieved by the speaker's personal character when the speech is so spoken as to make us think him credible. We believe good men more fully and more readily than others. . . . This kind of persuasion, like the others, should be achieved by what the speaker says, not by what people think of his character before he begins to speak. . . . His character may almost be called the most effective means of persuasion he possesses. Secondly, persuasion may come through the hearers, when the speech stirs their emotions. Our judgements when we are pleased and friendly are not the same as when we are pained and hostile. . . . Thirdly, persuasion is effected through the speech itself when we have proved a truth or an apparent truth by means of the persuasive arguments suitable to the case in question.

Aristotle, *Rhetoric,* 1356ᵃ1

13 The duty of rhetoric is to deal with such matters as we deliberate upon without arts or systems to guide us, in the hearing of persons who cannot take in at a glance a complicated argument, or follow a long chain of reasoning. The subjects of our deliberation are such as seem to present us with alternative possibilities: about things that could not have been, and cannot now or in the future be, other than they are, nobody who takes them to be of this nature wastes his time in deliberation.

Aristotle, *Rhetoric,* 1356ᵇ40

14 There are three divisions of oratory—(1) political, (2) forensic, and (3) the ceremonial oratory of display.

Political speaking urges us either to do or not to do something: one of these two courses is always taken by private counsellors, as well as by men who address public assemblies. Forensic speaking either attacks or defends somebody: one or other of these two things must always be done by the parties in a case. The ceremonial oratory of display either praises or censures somebody. These three kinds of rhetoric refer to three different kinds of time. The political orator is concerned with the future: it is about things to be done hereafter that he advises, for or against. The party in a case at law is concerned with the past; one man accuses the other, and the other defends himself, with reference to things already done. The ceremonial orator is, properly speaking, concerned with the present, since all men praise or blame in view of the state of things existing at the time, though they often find it useful also to recall the past and to make guesses at the future.

Aristotle, *Rhetoric,* 1358ᵇ6

15 Since rhetoric exists to affect the giving of decisions—the hearers decide between one political speaker and another, and a legal verdict *is* a decision—the orator must not only try to make the argument of his speech demonstrative and worthy of belief; he must also make his own character look right and put his hearers, who are to decide, into the right frame of mind. Particularly in political oratory, but also in lawsuits, it adds much to an orator's influence that his own character should look right and that he should be thought to entertain the right feelings towards his hearers; and also that his hearers themselves should be in just the right frame of mind. That the orator's own character should look right is particularly important in political speaking: that the audience should be in the right frame of mind, in lawsuits. When people are feeling friendly and placable, they think one sort of thing; when they are feeling angry or hostile, they think either something totally different or the same thing with a different intensity: when they feel friendly to the man who comes before them for judgement, they regard him as having done little wrong, if any; when they feel hostile, they take the opposite view. Again, if they are eager for, and have good hopes of, a thing that will be pleasant if it happens, they think that it certainly will happen and be good for them: whereas if they are indifferent or annoyed, they do not think so.

There are three things which inspire confidence in the orator's own character—the three, namely, that induce us to believe a thing apart from any proof of it: good sense, good moral character, and goodwill. False statements and bad advice are due to one or more of the following three causes. Men either form a false opinion through want of good sense; or they form a true opinion, but because of their moral badness do not say what they really think; or finally, they are both sensible and upright, but not well disposed to their hearers, and may fail in consequence to recommend what they know to be the best course. These are the only possible cases. It follows that anyone who is thought to have all three of these good qualities will inspire trust in his audience. The way to make ourselves thought to be sensible and morally good must be gathered from the analysis of goodness already given: the way to establish your own goodness is the same as the way to establish that of others.

Aristotle, *Rhetoric,* 1377ᵇ21

16 The use of persuasive speech is to lead to decisions. (When we know a thing, and have decided about it, there is no further use in speaking about it.) This is so even if one is addressing a single person and urging him to do or not to do something, as when we scold a man for his conduct or try to change his views: the single person is as much your 'judge' as if he were one of many; we

may say, without qualification, that any one is your judge whom you have to persuade. Nor does it matter whether we are arguing against an actual opponent or against a mere proposition; in the latter case we still have to use speech and overthrow the opposing arguments, and we attack these as we should attack an actual opponent.

Aristotle, Rhetoric, 1391ᵇ8

17 Simplicity . . . makes the uneducated more effective than the educated when addressing popular audiences. . . . Educated men lay down broad general principles; uneducated men argue from common knowledge and draw obvious conclusions.

Aristotle, Rhetoric, 1395ᵇ27

18 The right thing in speaking really is that we should be satisfied not to annoy our hearers, without trying to delight them: we ought in fairness to fight our case with no help beyond the bare facts: nothing, therefore, should matter except the proof of those facts. Still, as has been already said, other things affect the result considerably, owing to the defects of our hearers. The arts of language cannot help having a small but real importance, whatever it is we have to expound to others: the way in which a thing is said does affect its intelligibility. Not, however, so much importance as people think. All such arts are fanciful and meant to charm the hearer. Nobody uses fine language when teaching geometry.

Aristotle, Rhetoric, 1404ᵃ3

19 Style to be good must be clear, as is proved by the fact that speech which fails to convey a plain meaning will fail to do just what speech has to do. It must also be appropriate, avoiding both meanness and undue elevation; poetical language is certainly free from meanness, but it is not appropriate to prose. Clearness is secured by using the words (nouns and verbs alike) that are current and ordinary. Freedom from meanness, and positive adornment too, are secured by using the other words mentioned in the *Art of Poetry*. Such variation from what is usual makes the language appear more stately. People do not feel towards strangers as they do towards their own countrymen, and the same thing is true of their feeling for language. It is therefore well to give to everyday speech an unfamiliar air: people like what strikes them, and are struck by what is out of the way. In verse such effects are common, and there they are fitting: the persons and things there spoken of are comparatively remote from ordinary life. In prose passages they are far less often fitting because the subject-matter is less exalted. Even in poetry, it is not quite appropriate that fine language should be used by a slave or a very young man, or about very trivial subjects: even in poetry the style, to be appropriate, must sometimes be toned down,

though at other times heightened. We can now see that a writer must disguise his art and give the impression of speaking naturally and not artificially. Naturalness is persuasive, artificiality is the contrary for our hearers are prejudiced and think we have some design against them, as if we were mixing their wines for them.

Aristotle, Rhetoric, 1404ᵇ2

20 Prose-writers must . . . pay specially careful attention to metaphor, because their other resources are scantier than those of poets. Metaphor, moreover, gives style clearness, charm, and distinction as nothing else can: and it is not a thing whose use can be taught by one man to another.

Aristotle, Rhetoric, 1405ᵃ5

21 The foundation of good style is correctness of language, which falls under five heads. (1) First, the proper use of connecting words, and the arrangement of them in the natural sequence which some of them require. . . . (2) The second lies in calling things by their own special names and not by vague general ones. (3) The third is to avoid ambiguities; unless, indeed, you definitely desire to be ambiguous, as those do who have nothing to say but are pretending to mean something. Such people are apt to put that sort of thing into verse. . . . (4) A fourth rule is to observe Protagoras' classification of nouns into male, female, and inanimate; for these distinctions also must be correctly given. . . . (5) A fifth rule is to express plurality, fewness, and unity by the correct wording. . . .

It is a general rule that a written composition should be easy to read and therefore easy to deliver. This cannot be so where there are many connecting words or clauses, or where punctuation is hard.

Aristotle, Rhetoric, 1407ᵃ19

22 An author can hold correct opinions and yet not be able to express them in polished style. To put one's thoughts on paper without being able to organize them or to express them clearly, or without being able to hold the reader with some kind of charm, means one is making an inexcusable misuse of both his leisure and his pen.

Cicero, Disputations, I, 3

23 Speech has a great deal to do with gaining propriety, and it has a double function. The first is oratory and the second is conversation. Oratory is the type of speech used in pleading court cases, addressing public assemblies, and in the Senate. Conversation finds its place in social gatherings, informal discussions, and in speaking with friends. It should also play a role in dinners. Rhetoricians lay down the rules for oratory, but there are no rules for conversation. I don't really know why there shouldn't be. Where there are students to

learn, teachers will be found. But there is no one who makes conversation a subject of study, while pupils surround rhetoricians everywhere. Yet the same rules that we apply to words and sentences in rhetoric would work equally well in conversation.

Cicero, *De Officiis*, I, 37

24 Conversation, in which the Socratics are the best models, ought to have the following qualities. It should be casual and not in the least dogmatic. It should be flavored with wit. The conversationalist should not hinder others from talking by monopolizing the conversation. In a general conversation he should be willing to let each person have his turn. He should pay attention, in the first place, to what the subject of the conversation is. If it is solemn, he should treat it seriously; if it is light, with humor. And above all, he should be careful lest his remarks give away some defect in his character. This is most likely to happen, when people, in jest or in earnest, delight in malicious and slanderous gossip behind someone's back, or set out to damage their reputations.

Cicero, *De Officiis*, I, 37

25 Neither can embellishments of language be found without arrangement and expression of thoughts, nor can thoughts be made to shine without the light of language.

Cicero, *De Oratore*, III, 6

26 Nobody ever admired an orator for merely speaking good Latin; if he speaks otherwise, they ridicule him; and not only do not think him an orator, but not even a man. Nor has any one ever extolled a speaker for merely speaking in such a manner that those who were present understood what he said; though every one has despised him who was not able to do so. Whom then do men regard with awe? What speaker do they behold with astonishment? At whom do they utter exclamations? Whom do they consider as a deity, if I may use the expression, amongst mortals? Him who speaks distinctly, explicitly, copiously, and luminously, both as to matter and words; who produces in his language a sort of rhythm and harmony; who speaks, as I call it, *gracefully*. Those also who treat their subject as the importance of things and persons requires, are to be commended for that peculiar kind of merit, which I term *aptitude and congruity.* . . . On my authority, therefore, deride and despise all those who imagine that from the precepts of such as are now called rhetoricians they have gained all the powers of oratory, and have not yet been able to understand what character they hold, or what they profess; for indeed, by an orator everything that relates to human life, since that is the field on which his abilities are displayed, and is the subject for his eloquence, should be examined, heard, read, dis-

cussed, handled, and considered; since eloquence is one of the most eminent virtues; and though all the virtues are in their nature equal and alike, yet one species is more beautiful and noble than another; as is this power, which, comprehending a knowledge of things, expresses the thoughts and purposes of the mind in such a manner, that it can impel the audience whithersoever it inclines its force; and, the greater is its influence, the more necessary it is that it should be united with probity and eminent judgment; for if we bestow the faculty of eloquence upon persons destitute of these virtues, we shall not make them orators, but give arms to madmen.

Cicero, *De Oratore*, III, 14

27 A speech, then, is to be made becoming in its kind, with a sort of complexion and substance of its own; for that it be weighty, agreeable, savoring of erudition and liberal knowledge, worthy of admiration, polished, having feeling and passion in it, as far as is required, are qualities not confined to particular members, but are apparent in the whole body; but that it be, as it were, strewed with flowers of language and thought, is a property which ought not to be equally diffused throughout the whole speech, but at such intervals, that, as in the arrangement of ornaments, there may be certain remarkable and luminous objects disposed here and there. Such a kind of eloquence, therefore, is to be chosen, as is most adapted to interest the audience, such as may not only delight, but delight without satiety.

Cicero, *De Oratore*, III, 25

28 As in most things, so in language, Nature herself has wonderfully contrived, that what carries in it the greatest utility, should have at the same time either the most dignity, or, as if often happens, the most beauty.

Cicero, *De Oratore*, III, 45

29 This orator of ours is so to be finished as to his style and thoughts in general, that, as those who study fencing and polite exercises, not only think it necessary to acquire a skill in parrying and striking, but also grace and elegance of motion, so he may use such words as are suited to elegant and graceful composition, and such thoughts as contribute to the impressiveness of language.

Cicero, *De Oratore*, III, 52

30 The best orator is the one whose address instructs, delights, and moves the minds of the hearers. The orator is obliged to instruct, while pleasure is a gratuity granted to the audience. But to stir the emotions is indispensable.

Cicero, *De Optimo Genere Oratorum*, I

31 The difference between the orator and the dialectician is as great as that between two rivers of an

opposite character. Streams that flow between high banks and at full flood have greater force than shallow brooks with water struggling against the opposition of pebbles.

Quintilian, *Institutio Oratoria,* XII, 2

32 As loose and incontinent livers are seldom fathers of many children, so loose and incontinent talkers seldom originate many sensible words.

Plutarch, *Lycurgus*

33 Rhetoric . . . is . . . the government of the souls of men, and . . . her chief business is to address the affections and passions, which are as it were the strings and keys to the soul, and require a skilful and careful touch to be played on as they should be.

Plutarch, *Pericles*

34 The most eloquent of public speakers [Demosthenes], in his oration against Midias, allows that Alcibiades, among other perfections, was a most accomplished orator. If, however, we give credit to Theophrastus, who of all philosophers was the most curious inquirer, and the greatest lover of history, we are to understand that Alcibiades had the highest capacity for inventing, for discerning what was the right thing to be said for any purpose, and on any occasion; but aiming not only at saying what was required, but also at saying it well, in respect, that is, of words and phrases, when these did not readily occur, he would often pause in the middle of his discourse for want of the apt word, and would be silent and stop till he could recollect himself, and had considered what to say.

Plutarch, *Alcibiades*

35 Extemporaneous speeches are deft and facile to abundance, but those who make them know neither where to begin nor where to stop.

Plutarch, *Education of Children*

36 This faculty of speaking and of ornamenting words, if there is indeed any such peculiar faculty, what else does it do, when there happens to be discourse about a thing, than to ornament the words and arrange them as hairdressers do the hair? But whether it is better to speak or to be silent, and better to speak in this way or that way, and whether this is becoming or not becoming, and the season for each and the use, what else tells us than the faculty of the will?

Epictetus, *Discourses,* II, 23

37 From Alexander the grammarian [I learned] to refrain from fault-finding, and not in a reproachful way to chide those who uttered any barbarous or solecistic or strange-sounding expression; but dexterously to introduce the very expression which ought to have been used, and in the way of

answer or giving confirmation, or joining in an inquiry about the thing itself, not about the word, or by some other fit suggestion.

Marcus Aurelius, *Meditations,* I, 10

38 The chief merit of language is clearness, and we know that nothing detracts so much from this as do unfamiliar terms; accordingly we employ those terms which the bulk of people are accustomed to use.

Galen, *Natural Faculties,* I, 1

39 We . . . are not to suppose that when certain rhetoricians pour ridicule upon that which they are quite incapable of refuting, without any attempt at argument, their words are really thereby constituted rhetoric. For rhetoric proceeds by persuasive reasoning; words without reasoning are buffoonery rather than rhetoric.

Galen, *Natural Faculties,* I, 16

40 A thing [is] not bound to be true because uttered eloquently, nor false because the utterance of the lips is ill-arranged; but . . . on the other hand a thing is not necessarily true because badly uttered, nor false because spoken magnificently. For it is with wisdom and folly as with wholesome and unwholesome food: just as either kind of food can be served equally well in rich dishes or simple, so plain or beautiful language may clothe either wisdom or folly indifferently.

Augustine, *Confessions,* V, 6

41 The art of rhetoric being available for the enforcing either of truth or falsehood, who will dare to say that truth in the person of its defenders is to take its stand unarmed against falsehood? For example, that those who are trying to persuade men of what is false are to know how to introduce their subject, so as to put the hearer into a friendly, or attentive, or teachable frame of mind, while the defenders of the truth shall be ignorant of that art? That the former are to tell their falsehoods briefly, clearly, and plausibly, while the latter shall tell the truth in such a way that it is tedious to listen to, hard to understand, and, in fine, not easy to believe it? That the former are to oppose the truth and defend falsehood with sophistical arguments, while the latter shall be unable either to defend what is true, or to refute what is false? That the former, while imbuing the minds of their hearers with erroneous opinions, are by their power of speech to awe, to melt, to enliven, and to rouse them, while the latter shall in defence of the truth be sluggish, and frigid, and somnolent? Who is such a fool as to think this wisdom? Since, then, the faculty of eloquence is available for both sides, and is of very great service in the enforcing either of wrong or right, why do not good men study to engage it on the side of truth, when bad men use it to obtain the triumph of wicked and worthless

causes, and to further injustice and error?

Augustine, *Christian Doctrine*, IV, 2

42 We must beware of the man who abounds in eloquent nonsense, and so much the more if the
hearer is pleased with what is not worth listening
to, and thinks that because the speaker is eloquent
what he says must be true. And this opinion is
held even by those who think that the art of rhetoric should be taught: for they confess that "though
wisdom without eloquence is of little service to
states, yet eloquence without wisdom is frequently
a positive injury, and is of service never."

Augustine, *Christian Doctrine*, IV, 5

43 *Let the language devoted to truth be plain and simple.*
Who speaks carefully unless he wants to speak affectedly?
[Seneca]. The elequence that diverts us to itself
harms its content.

As in dress it is pettiness to seek attention by
some peculiar and unusual fashion, so in language
the search for novel phrases and little-known
words comes from a childish and pedantic ambition. Would that I might use only those that are
used in the markets of Paris! Aristophanes the
grammarian did not know what he was talking
about when he criticized Epicurus for the simplicity of his words and the aim of his oratorical art,
which was simply lucidity of speech. The imitation of speech, because of its facility, may be
quickly picked up by a whole people; the imitation of judgment and invention does not come so
fast.

Montaigne, *Essays*, I, 26, Education
of Children

44 My language has no ease or polish; it is harsh and
disdainful, with a free and unruly disposition.
And I like it that way, if not by judgment, then by
inclination. But I am quite conscious that sometimes I let myself go too far, and that in the effort
to avoid art and affectation, I fall back into them
in another direction:

I strive to be concise,
And grow obscure.

HORACE

Plato says that length and brevity are properties which neither decrease nor increase the worth
of style.

Montaigne, *Essays*, II, 17,
Of Presumption

45 Handling and use by able minds give value to a
language, not so much by innovating as by filling
it out with more vigorous and varied services, by
stretching and bending it. They do not bring to it
new words, but they enrich their own, give more
weight and depth to their meaning and use; they
teach the language unaccustomed movements,
but prudently and shrewdly. And how little this

gift is given to all is seen in so many French writers of our time. They are bold and disdainful
enough not to follow the common road, but want
of invention and of discretion ruins them. There is
nothing to be seen in them but a wretched affectation of originality, cold and absurd disguises,
which instead of elevating the substance bring it
down. Provided they can strut gorgeously in their
novelty, they care nothing about effectiveness. To
seize a new word they abandon the ordinary one,
which is often stronger and more sinewy.

Montaigne, *Essays*, III, 5, On Some
Verses of Virgil

46 I do not avoid any [figures of speech] that are used
in the streets of France; those who would combat
usage with grammar make fools of themselves.

Montaigne, *Essays*, III, 5, On Some
Verses of Virgil

47 The most fruitful and natural exercise of our
mind, in my opinion, is discussion. I find it sweeter than any other action of our life; and that is the
reason why, if I were right now forced to choose, I
believe I would rather consent to lose my sight
than my hearing or speech. . . .

The study of books is a languishing and feeble
activity that gives no heat, whereas discussion
teaches and exercises us at the same time. If I
discuss with a strong mind and a stiff jouster, he
presses on my flanks, prods me right and left; his
ideas launch mine. Rivalry, glory, competition,
push me and lift me above myself. And unison is
an altogether boring quality in discussion.

As our mind is strengthened by communication
with vigorous and orderly minds, so it is impossible to say how much it loses and degenerates by
our continual association and frequentation with
mean and sickly minds. There is no contagion
that spreads like that one. I know by enough experience how much it is worth per yard. I love to
argue and discuss, but in a small group and for
my own sake. For to serve as a spectacle to the
great and make a competitive parade of one's wit
and chatter is an occupation that I find very unbecoming to a man of honor.

Montaigne, *Essays*, III, 8, Of the Art
of Discussion

48 Truly, *Sancho,* said Don *Quixote,* thy Simplicity
lessens, and thy Sense improves every Day. And
good Reason why, quoth *Sancho;* some of your
Worship's Wit must needs stick to me; for your
dry unkindly Land, with good dunging and tilling, will in time yield a good Crop. I mean, Sir,
that the Dung and Muck of your Conversation
being thrown on the barren Ground of my Wit,
together with the Time I ha' served your Worship,
and kept you Company; which is, as a body may
say, the Tillage; I must needs bring forth blessed
Fruit at last, so as not to shame my Master, but

keep in the Paths of good Manners, which you have beaten into my sodden Understanding,

Cervantes, *Don Quixote,* II, 12

49 In the next place, *Sancho,* said the Knight, do not overlard your common Discourse with that glut of Proverbs, which you mix in it continually; for though Proverbs are properly concise and pithy Sentences, yet as thou bring'st 'em in, in such a huddle, by the Head and Shoulders, thou makest 'em look like so many Absurdities. Alas! Sir, quoth *Sancho,* this is a Disease that Heaven alone can cure; for I've more Proverbs than will fill a Book; and when I talk, they crowd so thick and fast to my Mouth, that they quarrel which shall get out first; so that my Tongue is forc'd to let 'em out as fast, first come first serv'd, though nothing to my Purpose. But henceforwards I'll set a Watch on my Mouth, and let none fly out, but such as shall befit the Gravity of my Place. For in a rich Man's House the Cloth is soon laid; where there's Plenty the Guests can't be empty. A Blot's no Blot till 'tis hit. He's safe who stands under the Bells; you can't eat your Cake and have your Cake; and Store's no Sore.

Go on, go on, Friend, said Don *Quixote,* thread, tack, stitch on, heap Proverb on Proverb, out with 'em Man, spew them out! There's no body coming. My Mother whips me, and I whip the Gigg. I warn thee to forbear foisting in a Rope of Proverbs every where, and thou blunder'st out a whole Litany of old Saws, as much to the Purpose as *the last Year's Snow.* Observe me, *Sancho,* I condemn not the Use of Proverbs; but 'tis most certain, that such a Confusion and Hodge-podge of 'em, as thou throw'st out and dragg'st in by the Hair together, make Conversation fulsom and poor.

Cervantes, *Don Quixote,* II, 43

50 In all speech, words and sense are as the body and the soul. The sense is as the life and soul of language, without which all words are dead. Sense is wrought out of experience, the knowledge of human life and actions, or of the liberal arts. . . . Words are the people's, yet there is a choice of them to be made. . . . They are to be chose according to the persons we make speak, or the things we speak of. Some are of the camp, some of the council-board, some of the shop, some of the sheepcot, some of the pulpit, some of the bar, etc. And herein is seen their elegance and propriety, when we use them fitly and draw them forth to their just strength and nature by way of translation or metaphor.

Jonson, *Discoveries:* De Orationis Dignitate

51 Language most shows a man: Speak, that I may see thee.

Jonson, *Discoveries:* De Stilo

52 Speech that is uttered with labour and difficulty,

or speech that savoureth of the affectation of art and precepts, or speech that is framed after the imitation of some pattern of eloquence, though never so excellent; all this hath somewhat servile, and holding of the subject.

Bacon, *Advancement of Learning,* Bk. I, To the King, 2

53 Let us consider the false appearances that are imposed upon us by words, which are framed and applied according to the conceit and capacities of the vulgar sort: and although we think we govern our words, and prescribe it well . . . yet certain it is that words, as a Tartar's bow, do shoot back upon the understanding of the wisest, and mightily entangle and pervert the judgement. So as it is almost necessary, in all controversies and disputations, to imitate the wisdom of the mathematicians, in setting down in the very beginning the definitions of our words and terms, that others may know how we accept and understand them, and whether they concur with us or no. For it cometh to pass, for want of this, that we are sure to end there where we ought to have begun, which is, in questions and differences about words.

Bacon, *Advancement of Learning,* Bk. II, XIV, 11

54 Concerning speech and words, the consideration of them hath produced the science of grammar. For man still striveth to reintegrate himself in those benedictions, from which by his fault he hath been deprived. . . . So hath he sought to come forth of the . . . general curse which was the confusion of tongues by the art of grammar; whereof the use in a mother tongue is small, in a foreign tongue more; but most in such foreign tongues as have ceased to be vulgar tongues, and are turned only to learned tongues. The duty of it is of two natures: the one popular, which is for the speedy and perfect attaining languages, as well for intercourse of speech as for understanding of authors; the other philosophical, examining the power and nature of words, as they are the footsteps and prints of reason: which kind of analogy between words and reason is handled *sparism,* brokenly though not entirely; and therefore I cannot report it deficient, though I think it very worthy to be reduced into a science by itself.

Unto grammar also belongeth, as an appendix, the consideration of the accidents of words; which are measure, sound, and elevation or accent, and the sweetness and harshness of them; whence hath issued some curious observations in rhetoric, but chiefly poesy, as we consider it, in respect of the verse and not of the argument. Wherein though men in learned tongues do tie themselves to the ancient measures, yet in modern languages it seemeth to me as free to make new measures of verses as of dances: for a dance is a measured pace, as a verse is a measured speech. In these things the sense is better judge than the art.

Bacon, *Advancement of Learning,*
Bk. II, XVI, 4–5

55 The proofs and demonstrators of logic are toward all men indifferent and the same; but the proofs and persuasions of rhetoric ought to differ according to the auditors. . . . Which application, in perfection of idea, ought to extend so far, that if a man should speak of the same thing to several persons, he should speak to them all respectively and several ways.

Bacon, *Advancement of Learning,*
Bk. II, XVIII, 5

56 Men imagine that their reason governs words, whilst, in fact, words react upon the understanding; and this has rendered philosophy and the sciences sophistical and inactive. Words are generally formed in a popular sense, and define things by those broad lines which are most obvious to the vulgar mind; but when a more acute understanding, or more diligent observation is anxious to vary those lines, and to adapt them more accurately to nature, words oppose it. Hence the great and solemn disputes of learned men often terminate in controversies about words and names, in regard to which it would be better (imitating the caution of mathematicians) to proceed more advisedly in the first instance, and to bring such disputes to a regular issue by definitions. Such definitions, however, cannot remedy the evil in natural and material objects, because they consist themselves of words, and these words produce others; so that we must necessarily have recourse to particular instances, and their regular series and arrangement, as we shall mention when we come to the mode and scheme of determining notions and axioms.

The idols imposed upon the understanding by words are of two kinds. They are either the names of things which have no existence (for as some objects are from inattention left without a name, so names are formed by fanciful imaginations which are without an object), or they are the names of actual objects, but confused, badly defined, and hastily and irregularly abstracted from things. Fortune, the primum mobile, the planetary orbits, the element of fire, and the like fictions, which owe their birth to futile and false theories, are instances of the first kind. And this species of idols is removed with greater facility, because it can be exterminated by the constant refutation or the desuetude of the theories themselves. The others, which are created by vicious and unskilful abstraction, are intricate and deeply rooted. Take some word for instance, as moist, and let us examine how far the different significations of this word are consistent. It will be found that the word moist is nothing but a confused sign of different actions admitted of no settled and defined uniformity. For it means that which easily diffuses itself over another body; that which is indeterminable and cannot be brought to a consistency; that which yields easily in every direction; that which is easily divided and dispersed; that which is easily united and collected; that which easily flows and is put in motion; that which easily adheres to, and wets another body; that which is easily reduced to a liquid state though previously solid. When, therefore, you come to predicate or impose this name, in one sense flame is moist, in another air is not moist, in another fine powder is moist, in another glass is moist; so that it is quite clear that this notion is hastily abstracted from water only, and common ordinary liquors, without any due verification of it.

There are, however, different degrees of distortion and mistake in words. One of the least faulty classes is that of the names of substances, particularly of the less abstract and more defined species (those then of chalk and mud are good, of earth bad); words signifying actions are more faulty, as to generate, to corrupt, to change; but the most faulty are those denoting qualities (except the immediate objects of sense), as heavy, light, rare, dense. Yet in all of these there must be some notions a little better than others, in proportion as a greater or less number of things come before the senses.

Bacon, *Novum Organum,* I, 59–60

57 It is good, in discourse and speech of conversation, to vary and intermingle speech of the present occasion with arguments, tales with reasons, asking of questions with telling of opinions, and jest with earnest; for it is a dull thing to tire, and, as we say now, to jade, any thing too far.

Bacon, *Of Discourse*

58 Names have been conferred on things for the most part by the inexpert, and . . . for this reason they do not always fit the things with sufficient accuracy. . . . It is not our part to change them after custom has accepted them, but only to permit the emendation of their meanings, when we perceive that others do not understand them aright.

Descartes, *Objections and Replies,* V

59 Eloquence is power; because it is seeming prudence.

Hobbes, *Leviathan,* I, 10

60 Eloquence is an art of saying things in such a way (1) that those to whom we speak may listen to them without pain and with pleasure; (2) that they feel themselves interested, so that self-love leads them more willingly to reflection upon it.

It consists, then, in a correspondence which we seek to establish between the head and the heart of those to whom we speak, on the one hand, and, on the other, between the thoughts and the ex-

pressions which we employ. This assumes that we
have studied well the heart of man so as to know
all its powers and, then, to find the just proportions of the discourse which we wish to adapt to
them. We must put ourselves in the place of those
who are to hear us, and make trial on our own
heart of the turn which we give to our discourse in
order to see whether one is made for the other,
and whether we can assure ourselves that the
hearer will be, as it were, forced to surrender. We
ought to restrict ourselves, so far as possible, to the
simple and natural, and not to magnify that
which is little, or belittle that which is great. It is
not enough that a thing be beautiful; it must be
suitable to the subject, and there must be in it
nothing of excess or defect.

Pascal, Pensées, I, 16

61 *Eloquence.*—It requires the pleasant and the real;
but the pleasant must itself be drawn from the
true.

Pascal, Pensées, I, 25

62 There are some who speak well and write badly.
For the place and the audience warm them, and
draw from their minds more than they think of
without that warmth.

Pascal, Pensées, I, 47

63 When we find words repeated in a discourse and,
in trying to correct them, discover that they are so
appropriate that we would spoil the discourse, we
must leave them alone. This is the test; and our
attempt is the work of envy, which is blind, and
does not see that repetition is not in this place a
fault; for there is no general rule.

Pascal, Pensées, I, 48

64 The same meaning changes with the words which
express it. Meanings receive their dignity from
words instead of giving it to them.

Pascal, Pensées, I, 50

65 No matter what we wish to persuade of, we must
consider the person concerned, whose mind and
heart we must know, what principles he admits,
what things he loves, and then observe in the
thing in question what relations it has to these
admitted principles or to these objects of delight.
So that the art of persuasion consists as much in
knowing how to please as in knowing how to convince, so much more do men follow caprice than
reason.

Pascal, Geometrical Demonstration

66 It often happens that we imagine that we have in
our minds ideas of things, from supposing, wrongly, that we have already explained to ourselves the
terms of which we make use. And it is not true, as
some say, or at least it is very ambiguous, that we
cannot speak of anything, understanding fully

what we say, without having an idea of it. For
often we vaguely understand each of the terms, or
we remember that we have formerly understood
them; but as we content ourselves with this blind
thought and as we do not push far enough the
analysis of notions, it happens that unwittingly we
fall into the contradiction which the composite
idea may imply.

Leibniz, Thoughts on Knowledge, Truth
and Ideas

67 If we had some exact *language* (like the one called
Adamitic by some) or at least a kind of *truly philosophic writing,* in which the ideas were reduced to a
kind of *alphabet of human thought,* then all that follows rationally from what is given could be found
by a *kind of calculus,* just as arithmetical or geometrical problems are solved.

Such a language would amount to a *Cabala* of
mystical vocables or to the *arithmetic* of Pythagore-
an numbers or to the *Characteristic* language of
magi, that is, of the wise.

Leibniz, On the Universal Science:
Characteristic, XIV

68 To come back to the representations of ideas by
characters: I think that controversies will never
end nor silence be imposed upon the *sects,* unless
complicated reasonings can be reduced to simple
calculations, and words of vague and uncertain
meaning to determinate *characters.*

What must be achieved is in fact this: that every paralogism be recognized as an *error of calculation,* and that every *sophism,* when expressed in this
new kind of notation, appear as a *solecism or barbarism,* to be corrected easily by the laws of this philosophical grammar.

Once this is done, then when a controversy arises, disputation will no more be needed between
two philosophers than between two computers. It
will suffice that, pen in hand, they sit down to
their abacus and (calling in a friend, if they so
wish) say to each other: *let us calculate. . . .* Once
this true art of general analysis is established and
taken up by custom, men who understand it and
are experienced in it will under otherwise equal
conditions be as far superior to all others as the
literate is to the illiterate, the learned to the vulgar, the eminent geometrician to the apprentice,
and the outstanding algebraist to the common
calculator. Provided the required intelligence be
applied, anyone could with this reliable method
find out everything that can be obtained from the
available data, with the use of reason, even by the
greatest and most experienced mind. The only
difference remaining would be one of promptness,
which is more important in action than in meditation and invention. . . . If the invention of the
telescope and the microscope has brought so much
light into the sciences of nature, it will certainly
be understood how much can be achieved by this

new instrument (novum organon) by which the eye of the mind will be sharpened as much as is in the power of man.

Leibniz, *On the Universal Science:*
Characteristic, XIV

69 The natural languages are of very great value in reasoning, but full of innumerable equivocations and unable to function in a calculus: for if they were able to do this, errors in reasoning could be uncovered from the very form and construction of the words, namely, as solecisms and barbarisms. Hitherto only the arithmetical and the algebraic notations have offered this admirable advantage. For in these fields all reasoning consists in the use of characters, and a mental error and an error of calculation are identical.

Having pondered this matter more deeply, it became clear to me long ago that all human ideas can be resolved into a few as their primitives. If characters were assigned to these primitives, characters for derivative notions could be formed therefrom, and from these it would always be possible to discover the primitive notions which are necessary ingredients; in short, it would be possible to find correct definitions and values and, hence, also the properties which are demonstrably implied in the definitions. Once this is achieved, anyone who in his reasoning and writing is using characters of this kind, will either never fall into error or, if he does, he will always discover his errors himself by the simplest examinations, as anybody else will; and, moreover, he will find the truth which is implied in the available data. If these data should not be sufficient to find what he is searching for, he would see which experiments and notions would still be required, to approach truth as closely as the data permit, either through approximation or through determining the degree of greater probability. Sophisms and paralogisms would here be nothing other than what errors of calculation are in arithmetic and solecisms or barbarisms in speech.

This characteristic art, of which I conceived the idea, would contain the true organon of a general science of everything that is subject matter for human reasoning, but would be endowed throughout with the demonstrations of an evident calculus. It will therefore be necessary to present our characteristic art itself, that is, the art of using signs in a kind of rigorous calculus, as generally as possible.

Leibniz, *On the Universal Science:*
Characteristic, XV

70 The words whereby [the mind] . . . signifies what connexion it gives to the several affirmations and negations, that it unites in one continued reasoning or narration, are generally called *particles:* and it is in the right use of these that more particularly consists the clearness and beauty of a good style.

To think well, it is not enough that a man has ideas clear and distinct in his thoughts, nor that he observes the agreement or disagreement of some of them; but he must think in train, and observe the dependence of his thoughts and reasonings upon one another. And to express well such methodical and rational thoughts, he must have words to show what connexion, restriction, distinction, opposition, emphasis etc., he gives to each respective *part* of his discourse. To mistake in any of these, is to puzzle instead of informing his hearer: and therefore it is, that those words which are not truly by themselves the names of any ideas are of such constant and indispensable use in language, and do much contribute to men's well expressing themselves.

They show what relation the mind gives to its own thoughts. This part of grammar has been perhaps as much neglected as some others over-diligently cultivated. It is easy for men to write, one after another, of cases and genders, moods and tenses, gerunds and supines: in these and the like there has been great diligence used; and particles themselves, in some languages, have been, with great show of exactness, ranked into their several orders. But though *prepositions* and *conjunctions,* etc., are names well known in grammar, and the particles contained under them carefully ranked into their distinct subdivisions; yet he who would show the right use of particles, and what significancy and force they have, must take a little more pains, enter into his own thoughts, and observe nicely the several postures of his mind in discoursing.

They are all marks of some action or intimation of the mind. Neither is it enough, for the explaining of these words, to render them, as is usual in dictionaries, by words of another tongue which come nearest to their signification: for what is meant by them is commonly as hard to be understood in one as another language. They are all marks of some action or intimation of the mind; and therefore to understand them rightly, the several views, postures, stands, turns, limitations, and exceptions, and several other thoughts of the mind, for which we have either none or very deficient names, are diligently to be studied. Of these there is a great variety, much exceeding the number of particles that most languages have to express them by: and therefore it is not to be wondered that most of these particles have divers and sometimes almost opposite significations.

Locke, *Concerning Human Understanding,*
Bk. III, VII, 2–4

71 Since wit and fancy find easier entertainment in the world than dry truth and real knowledge, figurative speeches and allusion in language will hardly be admitted as an imperfection or abuse of it. I confess, in discourses where we seek rather pleasure and delight than information and improvement, such ornaments as are borrowed from

them can scarce pass for faults. But yet if we would speak of things as they are, we must allow that all the art of rhetoric, besides order and clearness; all the artificial and figurative application of words eloquence hath invented, are for nothing else but to insinuate wrong ideas, move the passions, and thereby mislead the judgment; and so indeed are perfect cheats: and therefore, however laudable or allowable oratory may render them in harangues and popular addresses, they are certainly, in all discourses that pretend to inform or instruct, wholly to be avoided; and where truth and knowledge are concerned, cannot but be thought a great fault, either of the language or person that makes use of them. What and how various they are, will be superfluous here to take notice; the books of rhetoric which abound in the world, will instruct those who want to be informed: only I cannot but observe how little the preservation and improvement of truth and knowledge is the care and concern of mankind; since the arts of fallacy are endowed and preferred. It is evident how much men love to deceive and be deceived, since rhetoric, that powerful instrument of error and deceit, has its established professors, is publicly taught, and has always been had in great reputation: and I doubt not but it will be thought great boldness, if not brutality, in me to have said thus much against it. Eloquence, like the fair sex, has too prevailing beauties in it to suffer itself ever to be spoken against. And it is in vain to find fault with those arts of deceiving, wherein men find pleasure to be deceived.

Locke, *Concerning Human Understanding,*
Bk. III, X, 34

72 It is not enough that men have ideas, determined ideas, for which they make these signs stand; but they must also take care to apply their words as near as may be to such ideas as common use has annexed them to. For words, especially of languages already framed, being no man's private possession, but the common measure of commerce and communication, it is not for any one at pleasure to change the stamp they are current in, nor alter the ideas they are affixed to; or at least, when there is a necessity to do so, he is bound to give notice of it. Men's intentions in speaking are, or at least should be, to be understood; which cannot be without frequent explanations, demands, and other the like incommodious interruptions, where men do not follow common use. Propriety of speech is that which gives our thoughts entrance into other men's minds with the greatest ease and advantage: and therefore deserves some part of our care and study, especially in the names of moral words. The proper signification and use of terms is best to be learned from those who in their writings and discourses appear to have had the clearest notions, and applied to them their terms with the exactest choice and fitness. This

way of using a man's words, according to the propriety of the language, though it have not always the good fortune to be understood; yet most commonly leaves the blame of it on him who is so unskilful in the language he speaks, as not to understand it when made use of as it ought to be.

Locke, *Concerning Human Understanding,*
Bk. III, XI, 11

73 In the ordinary affairs of life, any phrases may be retained, so long as they excite in us proper sentiments, or dispositions to act in such a manner as is necessary for our well-being, how false soever they may be if taken in a strict and speculative sense. Nay, this is unavoidable, since, propriety being regulated by custom, language is suited to the received opinions, which are not always the truest. Hence it is impossible, even in the most rigid, philosophic reasonings, so far to alter the bent and genius of the tongue we speak, as never to give a handle for cavillers to pretend difficulties and inconsistencies. But, a fair and ingenuous reader will collect the sense from the scope and tenor and connexion of a discourse, making allowances for those inaccurate modes of speech which use has made inevitable.

Berkeley, *Principles of Human Knowledge,* 52

74 ——And how did Garrick speak the soliloquy last night?——Oh, against all rule, my Lord,—most ungrammatically! betwixt the substantive and the adjective, which should agree together in number, case, and gender, he made a breach thus,—stopping, as if the point wanted settling;—and betwixt the nominative case, which your lordship knows should govern the verb, he suspended his voice in the epilogue a dozen times three seconds and three fifths by a stop-watch, my Lord, each time.——Admirable grammarian!——But in suspending his voice—was the sense suspended likewise? Did no expression of attitude or countenance fill up the chasm?—Was the eye silent? Did you narrowly look?——I looked only at the stop-watch, my Lord.——Excellent observer!

And what of this new book the whole world makes such a rout about?——Oh! 'tis out of all plumb, my Lord,——quite an irregular thing!—not one of the angles at the four corners was a right angle.——I had my rule and compasses, etc., my Lord, in my pocket.——Excellent critic!

——And for the epic poem your lordship bid me look at—upon taking the length, breadth, height, and depth of it, and trying them at home upon an exact scale of Bossu's—'tis out, my Lord, in every one of its dimensions.——Admirable connoisseur!

Sterne, *Tristram Shandy,* III, 12

75 Now before I venture to make use of the word Nose a second time—to avoid all confusion in what will be said upon it, in this interesting part

of my story, it may not be amiss to explain my own meaning, and define, with all possible exactness and precision, what I would willingly be understood to mean by the term: being of opinion, that 'tis owing to the negligence and perverseness of writers in despising this precaution, and to nothing else—that all the polemical writings in divinity are not as clear and demonstrative as those upon a Will o' the Wisp, or any other sound part of philosophy, and natural pursuit; in order to which, what have you to do, before you set out, unless you intend to go puzzling on to the day of judgment—but to give the world a good definition, and stand to it, of the main word you have most occasion for—changing it, Sir, as you would a guinea, into small coin?—which done—let the father of confusion puzzle you, if he can; or put a different idea either into your head, or your reader's head, if he knows how.

In books of strict morality and close reasoning, such as this I am engaged in—the neglect is inexcusable; and Heaven is witness, how the world has revenged itself upon me for leaving so many openings to equivocal strictures—and for depending so much as I have done, all along, upon the cleanliness of my readers' imaginations . . . therefore

I define a nose as follows—intreating only beforehand, and beseeching my readers, both male and female, of what age, complexion, and condition soever, for the love of God and their own souls, to guard against the temptations and suggestions of the devil, and suffer him by no art or wile to put any other ideas into their minds, than what I put into my definition—For by the word Nose, throughout all this long chapter of noses, and in every other part of my work, where the word Nose occurs—I declare, by that word I mean a nose, and nothing more, or less.

Sterne, *Tristram Shandy,* III, 31

76 Let it be considered how many ideas we owe to the use of speech; how far grammar exercises the understanding and facilitates its operations. Let us reflect on the inconceivable pains and the infinite space of time that the first invention of languages must have cost. To these reflections add what preceded, and then judge how many thousand ages must have elapsed in the successive development in the human mind of those operations of which it is capable.

Rousseau, *Origin of Inequality,* I

77 Wise men, if they try to speak their language to the common herd instead of its own, cannot possibly make themselves understood. There are a thousand kinds of ideas which it is impossible to translate into popular language. Conceptions that are too general and objects that are too remote are equally out of its range.

Rousseau, *Social Contract,* II, 7

78 At Mr. Thrale's, in the evening, he [Johnson] repeated his usual paradoxical declamation against action in publick speaking. "Action can have no effect upon reasonable minds. It may augment noise, but it never can enforce argument. If you speak to a dog, you use action; you hold up your hand thus, because he is a brute; and in proportion as men are removed from brutes, action will have the less influence upon them." *Mrs. Thrale.* "What then, Sir, becomes of Demosthenes's saying? 'Action, action, action!' " *Johnson.* "Demosthenes, Madam, spoke to an assembly of brutes; to a barbarous people."

I thought it extraordinary, that he should deny the power of rhetorical action upon human nature, when it is proved by innumerable facts in all stages of society. Reasonable beings are not solely reasonable. They have fancies which may be pleased, passions which may be roused.

Boswell, *Life of Johnson (Apr. 3, 1773)*

79 Johnson was at all times jealous of infractions upon the genuine English language, and prompt to repress colloquial barbarisms; such as, *pledging myself,* for *undertaking; line,* for *department,* or *branch,* as, the *civil line,* the *banking line.* He was particularly indignant against the almost universal use of the word *idea* in the sense of *notion* or *opinion,* when it is clear that *idea* can only signify something of which an image can be formed in the mind. We may have an *idea* or *image* of a mountain, a tree, a building; but we cannot surely have an *idea* or *image* of an *argument* or *proposition.* Yet we hear the sages of the law "delivering their *ideas* upon the question under consideration"; and the first speakers in parliament "entirely coinciding in the *idea* which has been ably stated by an honourable member";—or "reprobating an *idea* unconstitutional, and fraught with the most dangerous consequences to a great and free country." Johnson called this "modern cant."

Boswell, *Life of Johnson (Sept. 23, 1777)*

80 Talking of conversation, he [Johnson] said, "There must, in the first place, be knowledge, there must be materials; in the second place, there must be a command of words; in the third place, there must be imagination, to place things in such views as they are not commonly seen in; and in the fourth place, there must be presence of mind, and a resolution that is not to be overcome by failures: this last is an essential requisite; for want of it many people do not excel in conversation."

Boswell, *Life of Johnson (Mar. 21, 1783)*

81 The arts of persuasion, so diligently cultivated by the first Cæsars, were neglected by the military ignorance and Asiatic pride of their successors, and, if they condescended to harangue the soldiers, whom they feared, they treated with silent

disdain the senators, whom they despised.

Gibbon, *Decline and Fall of the
Roman Empire*, XXII

82 General logic . . . resolves the whole formal business of understanding and reason into its elements, and exhibits them as principles of all logical judging of our cognitions. This part of logic may, therefore, be called *analytic,* and is at least the negative test of truth, because all cognitions must first of all be estimated and tried according to these laws before we proceed to investigate them in respect of their content, in order to discover whether they contain positive truth in regard to their object. Because, however, the mere form of a cognition, accurately as it may accord with logical laws, is insufficient to supply us with material (objective) truth, no one, by means of logic alone, can venture to predicate anything of or decide concerning objects, unless he has obtained, independently of logic, well-grounded information about them, in order afterwards to examine, according to logical laws, into the use and connection, in a cohering whole, of that information, or, what is still better, merely to test it by them. Notwithstanding, there lies so seductive a charm in the possession of a specious art like this—an art which gives to all our cognitions the form of the understanding, although with respect to the content thereof we may be sadly deficient—that general logic, which is merely a canon of judgement, has been employed as an organon for the actual production, or rather for the semblance of production, of objective assertions, and has thus been grossly misapplied. Now general logic, in its assumed character of organon, is called *dialectic.*

Different as are the significations in which the ancients used this term for a science or an art, we may safely infer, from their actual employment of it, that with them it was nothing else than a logic of illusion—a sophistical art for giving ignorance, nay, even intentional sophistries, the colouring of truth, in which the thoroughness of procedure which logic requires was imitated, and their topic employed to cloak the empty pretensions. Now it may be taken as a safe and useful warning, that general logic, considered as an organon, must always be a logic of illusion, that is, be dialectical, for, as it teaches us nothing whatever respecting the content of our cognitions, but merely the formal conditions of their accordance with the understanding, which do not relate to and are quite indifferent in respect of objects, any attempt to employ it as an instrument (organon) in order to extend and enlarge the range of our knowledge must end in mere prating; any one being able to maintain or oppose, with some appearance of truth, any single assertion whatever.

Kant, *Critique of Pure Reason,*
Transcendental Logic, Intro.

83 Despite the great wealth of words which Europe-an languages possess, the thinker finds himself often at a loss for an expression exactly suited to his conception, for want of which he is unable to make himself intelligible either to others or to himself. To coin new words is a pretension to legislation in language which is seldom successful; and, before recourse is taken to so desperate an expedient, it is advisable to examine the dead and learned languages, with the hope and the probability that we may there meet with some adequate expression of the notion we have in our minds. In this case, even if the original meaning of the word has become somewhat uncertain, from carelessness or want of caution on the part of the authors of it, it is always better to adhere to and confirm its proper meaning—even although it may be doubtful whether it was formerly used in exactly this sense—than to make our labour vain by want of sufficient care to render ourselves intelligible.

For this reason, when it happens that there exists only a single word to express a certain conception, and this word, in its usual acceptation, is thoroughly adequate to the conception, the accurate distinction of which from related conceptions is of great importance, we ought not to employ the expression improvidently, or, for the sake of variety and elegance of style, use it as a synonym for other cognate words. It is our duty, on the contrary, carefully to preserve its peculiar signification, as otherwise it easily happens that when the attention of the reader is no longer particularly attracted to the expression, and it is lost amid the multitude of other words of very different import, the thought which it conveyed, and which it alone conveyed, is lost with it.

Kant, *Critique of Pure Reason,*
Transcendental Dialectic

84 That the strictest laws of honesty should be observed in the discussion of a purely speculative subject is the least requirement that can be made. If we could reckon with security even upon so little, the conflict of speculative reason regarding the important questions of God, immortality, and freedom, would have been either decided long ago, or would very soon be brought to a conclusion. But, in general, the uprightness of the defence stands in an inverse ratio to the goodness of the cause; and perhaps more honesty and fairness are shown by those who deny than by those who uphold these doctrines.

Kant, *Critique of Pure Reason,*
Transcendental Method

85 The arts of speech are *rhetoric* and *poetry*. Rhetoric is the art of transacting a serious business of the understanding as if it were a free play of the imagination; *poetry* that of conducting a free play of the imagination as if it were a serious business of the understanding.

Kant, *Critique of Aesthetic Judgement,* 51

86 The use of words is to express ideas. Perspicuity, therefore, requires not only that the ideas should be distinctly formed, but that they should be expressed by words distinctly and exclusively appropriate to them. But no language is so copious as to supply words and phrases for every complex idea, or so correct as not to include many equivocally denoting different ideas. Hence it must happen that however accurately objects may be discriminated in themselves, and however accurately the discrimination may be considered, the definition of them may be rendered inaccurate by the inaccuracy of the terms in which it is delivered. And this unavoidable inaccuracy must be greater or less, according to the complexity and novelty of the objects defined. When the Almighty himself condescends to address mankind in their own language, his meaning, luminous as it must be, is rendered dim and doubtful by the cloudy medium through which it is communicated.

Here, then, are three sources of vague and incorrect definitions: indistinctness of the object, imperfection of the organ of conception, inadequateness of the vehicle of ideas. Any one of these must produce a certain degree of obscurity.

Madison, *Federalist 37*

87 Grammar, in its extended and consistent form, is the work of thought, which makes its categories distinctly visible therein.

Hegel, *Philosophy of History,* Intro., 3

88 Consider for a moment what grammar is. It is the most elementary part of logic. It is the beginning of the analysis of the thinking process. The principles and rules of grammar are the means by which the forms of language are made to correspond with the universal forms of thought. The distinctions between the various parts of speech, between the cases of nouns, the moods and tenses of verbs, the functions of particles, are distinctions in thought, not merely in words. Single nouns and verbs express objects and events, many of which can be cognized by the senses: but the modes of putting nouns and verbs together express the relations of objects and events, which can be cognized only by the intellect; and each different mode corresponds to a different relation. The structure of every sentence is a lesson in logic.

Mill, *Inaugural Address at St. Andrews*

89 The things that words mean differ more than words do. There are different sorts of words, distinguished by the grammarians; and there are logical distinctions, which are connected to some extent, though not so closely as was formerly supposed, with the grammatical distinctions of parts of speech. It is easy, however, to be misled by grammar, particularly if all the languages we know belong to one family. In some languages, according to some authorities, the distinction of parts of speech does not exist; in many languages it is widely different from that to which we are accustomed in the Indo-European languages. These facts have to be borne in mind if we are to avoid giving metaphysical importance to mere accidents of our own speech.

Russell, *Analysis of Mind,* X

90 In psycho-analytic treatment nothing happens but an exchange of words between the patient and the physician. The patient talks, tells of his past experiences and present impressions, complains, and expresses his wishes and his emotions. The physician listens, attempts to direct the patient's thought-processes, reminds him, forces his attention in certain directions, gives him explanations and observes the reactions of understanding or denial thus evoked. The patient's unenlightened relatives—people of a kind to be impressed only by something visible and tangible, preferably by the sort of *action* that may be seen at a cinema—never omit to express their doubts of how "mere talk can possibly cure anybody." Their reasoning is of course as illogical as it is inconsistent. For they are the same people who are always convinced that the sufferings of neurotics are purely "in their own imagination." Words and magic were in the beginning one and the same thing, and even today words retain much of their magical power. By words one of us can give to another the greatest happiness or bring about utter despair; by words the teacher imparts his knowledge to the student; by words the orator sweeps his audience with him and determines its judgments and decisions. Words call forth emotions and are universally the means by which we influence our fellow-creatures. Therefore let us not despise the use of words in psycho-therapy.

Freud, *General Introduction to Psycho-Analysis,* I

91 Imagine that you had undertaken to replace a political leading article in a newspaper by a series of illustrations; you would have to abandon alphabetic characters in favour of hieroglyphics. The people and concrete objects mentioned in the article could be easily represented, perhaps even more satisfactorily, in pictorial form; but you would expect to meet with difficulties when you came to the portrayal of all the abstract words and all those parts of speech which indicate relations between the various thoughts, e.g., particles, conjunctions, and so forth. With the abstract words you would employ all manner of devices: for instance, you would try to render the text of the article into other words, more unfamiliar perhaps, but made up of parts more concrete and therefore more capable of such representation. This will remind you of the fact that most abstract words were originally concrete, their original significance having faded; and therefore you will fall

back on the original concrete meaning of these words wherever possible. So you will be glad that you can represent the *possessing* of an object as a literal, physical *sitting upon* it (possess = *potis + sedeo*). This is just how the dream-work proceeds. In such circumstances you can hardly demand great accuracy of representation, neither will you quarrel with the dream-work for replacing an element which is difficult to reduce to pictorial form, such as the idea of breaking marriage vows, by some other kind of breaking, e.g., that of an arm or leg. In this way you will to some extent succeed in overcoming the awkwardness of rendering alphabetic characters into hieroglyphs.

Freud, *General Introduction to Psycho-Analysis,* XI

92 The Chinese language, both spoken and written, nxceedingly ancient but is still used today by four hundred million people. Don't suppose that I understand it at all; I only obtained some information about it because I hoped to find in it analogies to the kinds of indefiniteness occurring in dreams; nor was I disappointed in my expectation, for Chinese is so full of uncertainties as positively to terrify one. As is well known, it consists of a number of syllabic sounds which are pronounced singly or doubled in combination. One of the chief dialects has about four hundred of these sounds, and since the vocabulary of this dialect is estimated at somewhere about four thousand words it is evident that every sound has an average of ten different meanings—some fewer, but some all the more. For this reason there are a whole series of devices to escape ambiguity, for the context alone will not show which of the ten possible meanings of the syllable the speaker wishes to convey to the hearer. Amongst these devices is the combining of two sounds into a single word and the use of four different "tones" in which these syllables may be spoken. For purposes of our comparison a still more interesting fact is that this language is practically without grammar: it is impossible to say of any of the one-syllable words whether it is a noun, a verb or an adjective; and, further there are no inflections to show gender, number, case, tense or mood. The language consists, as we may say, of the raw material only; just as our thought-language is resolved into its raw material by the dream-work omitting to express the relations in it. Wherever there is any uncertainty in Chinese the decision is left to the intelligence of the listener, who is guided by the context. I made a note of a Chinese saying which literally translated runs thus: "Little what see, much what wonderful." This is simple enough to understand. It may mean: "The less a man has seen, the more he finds to wonder at," or "There is much to wonder at for the man who has seen little." Naturally there is no occasion to choose between these two translations which differ only in grammatical construction. We are assured that in spite of these uncertainties the Chinese language is a quite exceptionally good medium of expression; so it is clear that indefiniteness does not necessarily lead to ambiguity.

Freud, *General Introduction to Psycho-Analysis,* XV

Chapter 8

EDUCATION

Chapter 8 is divided into three sections: 8.1 THE ENDS AND MEANS OF EDUCATION, 8.2 HABIT, and 8.3 THE ARTS OF TEACHING AND LEARNING.

Education, broadly conceived, covers much more than schooling, or the period in which the young are under tutelage. It embraces every activity by which an individual grows mentally, morally, and spiritually. Whatever contributes to the development of a human person or the fulfillment of his potentialities should be regarded as educative.

The development may be an improvement of the person's mind through acquired knowledge or skill; it may be an improvement of his character; it may be an improvement in the use of his body. For that improvement to be a stable and relatively permanent acquisition, and not a momentarily transient one, it must become habitual. That is why the subject of Section 8.2—habit and habit formation—is an important consideration in this chapter.

What is called formal or organized education, the kind that takes place in institutions of learning—schools at any level—usually involves teaching as well as learning, but even during the years of formal schooling, and certainly thereafter, there is much learning without teachers. This situation is reflected in an ambiguity in the word "learning." As a verb, the word connotes an activity of the pupil or student whereby he learns, usually under the guidance of an instructor. But as a noun, the word often refers to what has been or can be learned—and by extension to the whole range of things that men can know: the world of learning. Human beings who are at home in that world are ordinarily called learned, and they are usually conceived as no longer needing to be instructed, although even here there is an ambiguity, for the childlike innocence of the learned has often been noted and described.

Texts having to do with learning in the latter sense of the word will be found in Section 8.1, for in this sense of the word learning is the end, or an end, of education. Quotations having to do with learning in the former sense—where it refers to a process ordinarily undergone by students in schools—will be found in Section 8.3.

Education as a process of human improvement is intimately related to subjects treated in other chapters, especially Chapter 1 on Man, Chapter 5 on Mind, Chapter 6 on Knowledge, Chapter 7 on Language, Chapter 9 on Ethics, and Chapter 16 on Art and Aesthetics.

8.1 | *The Ends and Means of Education*

That the goal of education is the improvement of human beings can hardly be disputed; but that does not preclude wide differences of opinion about what constitutes such improvement and what factors or devices contribute to it. The quotations here assembled conceive the educative process differently according as they define in a different manner the end it should be designed to achieve and outline different programs for accomplishing it. Associated with these differences are differences in the way that the ideal of an educated man is portrayed.

Some of the passages quoted get down to the nuts and bolts of specific programs of instruction—the order of studies, the materials of learning, in short, the content of the curriculum. Some are concerned with the order of learning and with the stages or periods into which the whole process of education should be divided. Still others deal with the responsibility of the family and the state for the education of the young.

For the most part, the education of the young, under the tutelage of teachers, occupies the center of attention; but there are passages that concern themselves with education as the process of a lifetime, begun in school but not concluded there. Closely related to these are the biographical quotations in which men look back upon their early training and evaluate it in the light of what they have learned much later in life.

There are also quotations, for the most part written by very learned men, about the life of the scholar. It is interesting to note that many of these are uncomplimentary. The scholar or man of learning is often viewed as simple or vain, as hindered by the very weight of his learning from leading a normal, happy, successful life. Such animadversions are not universal, however, and there are texts that laud the scholar and recommend his way of life as the best of all.

---

1 *Socrates.* Indeed, Lysimachus, I should be very wrong in refusing to aid in the improvement of anybody. And if I had shown in this conversation that I had a knowledge which Nicias and Laches have not, then I admit that you would be right in inviting me to perform this duty; but as we are all in the same perplexity, why should one of us be preferred to another? I certainly think that no one should; and under these circumstances, let me offer you a piece of advice (and this need not go further than ourselves). I maintain, my friends, that every one of us should seek out the best teacher whom he can find, first for ourselves, who are greatly in need of one, and then for the youth, regardless of expense or anything. But I cannot advise that we remain as we are. And if any one laughs at us for going to school at our age, I would quote to them the authority of Homer, who says, that "Modesty is not good for a needy man." Let us, then, regardless of what may be said of us,

make the education of the youths our own education.

Plato, *Laches,* 200B

2 *Socrates.* Calculation and geometry and all the other elements of instruction, which are a preparation for dialectic, should be presented to the mind in childhood. . . .

That is a very rational notion, he [Glaucon] said.

Do you remember that the children, too, were to be taken to see the battle on horseback; and that if there were no danger they were to be brought close up and, like young hounds, have a taste of blood given them?

Yes, I remember.

The same practice may be followed, I said, in all these things—labours, lessons, dangers—and he who is most at home in all of them ought to be enrolled in a select number.

At what age?

At the age when the necessary gymnastics are over: the period whether of two or three years which passes in this sort of training is useless for any other purpose; for sleep and exercise are unpropitious to learning; and the trial of who is first in gymnastic exercises is one of the most important tests to which our youth are subjected.

Certainly, he replied.

After that time those who are selected from the class of twenty years old will be promoted to higher honour, and the sciences which they learned without any order in their early education will now be brought together, and they will be able to see the natural relationship of them to one another and to true being.

Yes, he said, that is the only kind of knowledge which takes lasting root.

Yes, I said; and the capacity for such knowledge is the great criterion of dialectical talent: the comprehensive mind is always the dialectical.

I agree with you, he said.

These, I said, are the points which you must consider; and those who have most of this comprehension, and who are more steadfast in their learning, and in their military and other appointed duties, when they have arrived at the age of thirty will have to be chosen by you out of the select class, and elevated to higher honour; and you will have to prove them by the help of dialectic, in order to learn which of them is able to give up the use of sight and the other senses, and in company with truth to attain absolute being. . . .

Suppose, I said, the study of philosophy to take the place of gymnastics and to be continued diligently and earnestly and exclusively for twice the number of years which were passed in bodily exercise—will that be enough?

Would you say six or four years? he asked.

Say five years, I replied; at the end of the time they must be sent down again into the den and compelled to hold any military or other office which young men are qualified to hold: in this way they will get their experience of life, and there will be an opportunity of trying whether, when they are drawn all manner of ways by temptation, they will stand firm or flinch.

And how long is this stage of their lives to last?

Fifteen years, I answered; and when they have reached fifty years of age, then let those who still survive and have distinguished themselves in every action of their lives and in every branch of knowledge come at last to their consummation; the time has now arrived at which they must raise the eye of the soul to the universal light which lightens all things, and behold the absolute good; for that is the pattern according to which they are to order the State and the lives of individuals, and the remainder of their own lives also; making philosophy their chief pursuit, but, when their turn comes, toiling also at politics and ruling for the public good, not as though they were performing some heroic action, but simply as a matter of duty; and when they have brought up in each generation others like themselves and left them in their place to be governors of the State, then they will depart to the Islands of the Blest and dwell there; and the city will give them public memorials and sacrifices and honour them, if the Pythian oracle consent, as demigods, but if not, as in any case blessed and divine.

You are a sculptor, Socrates, and have made statues of our governors faultless in beauty.

Yes, I said, Glaucon, and of our governesses too; for you must not suppose that what I have been saying applies to men only and not to women as far as their natures can go.

Plato, *Republic,* VII, 536B

3 *Athenian Stranger.* Any one who would be good at anything must practise that thing from his youth upwards, both in sport and earnest, in its several branches: for example, he who is to be a good builder, should play at building children's houses; he who is to be a good husbandman, at tilling the ground; and those who have the care of their education should provide them when young with mimic tools. They should learn beforehand the knowledge which they will afterwards require for their art. For example, the future carpenter should learn to measure or apply the line in play; and the future warrior should learn riding, or some other exercise, for amusement, and the teacher should endeavour to direct the children's inclinations and pleasures, by the help of amusements, to their final aim in life. The most important part of education is right training in the nursery. The soul of the child in his play should be guided to the love of that sort of excellence in which when he grows up to manhood he will have to be perfected. Do you agree with me thus far?

Cleinias. Certainly.

Ath. Then let us not leave the meaning of education ambiguous or ill-defined. At present, when we speak in terms of praise or blame about the bringing-up of each person, we call one man educated and another uneducated, although the uneducated man may be sometimes very well educated for the calling of a retail trader, or of a captain of a ship, and the like. For we are not speaking of education in this narrower sense, but of that other education in virtue from youth upwards, which makes a man eagerly pursue the ideal perfection of citizenship, and teaches him how rightly to rule and how to obey. This is the only education which, upon our view, deserves the name; that other sort of training, which aims at the acquisition of wealth or bodily strength, or mere cleverness apart from intelligence and justice, is mean and illiberal, and is not worthy to be called education at all. But let us not quarrel with one another about a word, provided that the proposition which has just been granted hold good: to wit, that those who are rightly educated generally become good men. Neither must we cast a slight upon education, which is the first and fairest thing that the best of men can ever have, and which, though liable to take a wrong direction, is capable of reformation. And this work of reformation is the great business of every man while he lives.

Plato, *Laws,* I, 643A

4 *Athenian Stranger.* I mean by education that training which is given by suitable habits to the first instincts of virtue in children;—when pleasure, and friendship, and pain, and hatred, are rightly implanted in souls not yet capable of understanding the nature of them, and who find them, after they have attained reason, to be in harmony with her. This harmony of the soul, taken as a whole, is virtue; but the particular training in respect of pleasure and pain, which leads you always to hate what you ought to hate, and love what you ought to love from the beginning of life to the end, may be separated off; and, in my view, will be rightly called education.

Plato, *Laws,* II, 653A

5 Every systematic science, the humblest and the noblest alike, seems to admit of two distinct kinds of proficiency; one of which may be properly called scientific knowledge of the subject, while the other is a kind of educational acquaintance with it. For an educated man should be able to form a fair off-hand judgement as to the goodness or badness of the method used by a professor in his exposition. To be educated is in fact to be able to do this; and even the man of universal education we deem to be such in virtue of his having this ability. It will, however, of course, be understood that we only ascribe universal education to one who in his own individual person is thus critical in all or nearly all branches of knowledge, and not to one who has a like ability merely in some special subject. For it is possible for a man to have this competence in some one branch of knowledge without having it in all.

Aristotle, *Parts of Animals,* 639ª1

6 Moral excellence is concerned with pleasures and pains; it is on account of the pleasure that we do bad things, and on account of the pain that we abstain from noble ones. Hence we ought to have been brought up in a particular way from our very youth, as Plato says, so as both to delight in and to be pained by the things that we ought; for this is the right education.

Aristotle, *Ethics,* 1104ᵇ9

7 The legislator should direct his attention above all to the education of youth; for the neglect of education does harm to the constitution. The citizen should be moulded to suit the form of government under which he lives. For each government has a peculiar character which originally formed and which continues to preserve it. The character of democracy creates democracy, and the character of oligarchy creates oligarchy; and always the better the character, the better the government. . . .

And since the whole city has one end, it is manifest that education should be one and the same for all, and that it should be public, and not private. . . . The training in things which are of common interest should be the same for all. Neither must we suppose that any one of the citizens belongs to himself, for they all belong to the state, and are each of them a part of the state, and the care of each part is inseparable from the care of the whole.

Aristotle, *Politics,* 1337ᵇ9

8 That education should be regulated by law and should be an affair of state is not to be denied, but what should be the character of this public education, and how young persons should be educated, are questions which remain to be considered. As things are, there is disagreement about the subjects. For mankind are by no means agreed about the things to be taught, whether we look to virtue or the best life. Neither is it clear whether education is more concerned with intellectual or with moral virtue. The existing practice is perplexing; no one knows on what principle we should proceed—should the useful in life, or should virtue, or should the higher knowledge, be the aim of our training; all three opinions have been entertained. Again, about the means there is no agreement; for different persons, starting with different ideas about the nature of virtue, naturally disagree about the practice of it.

Aristotle, *Politics,* 1337ª33

9 Nature herself . . . requires that we should be

able, not only to work well, but to use leisure well; for . . . the first principle of all action is leisure. Both are required, but leisure is better than occupation and is its end; and therefore the question must be asked, what ought we to do when at leisure? Clearly we ought not to be amusing ourselves, for then amusement would be the end of life. . . . It is clear then that there are branches of learning and education which we must study merely with a view to leisure spent in intellectual activity, and these are to be valued for their own sake; whereas those kinds of knowledge which are useful in business are to be deemed necessary, and exist for the sake of other things.

Aristotle, *Politics*, 1337ᵃ31

10 What greater or more beneficial service can I render the republic than to teach and train the youth, considering how far astray our young men have gone because of the prevailing moral looseness. The greatest effort will be needed to restore them and to point them in the right direction.

Cicero, *Divination*, II, 2

11 If you want a man to keep his head when the crisis comes you must give him some training before it comes.

Seneca, *Letters to Lucilius*, 18

12 Why 'liberal studies' are so called is obvious: it is because they are the ones considered worthy of a free man. But there is really only one liberal study that deserves the name—because it makes a person free—and that is the pursuit of wisdom. Its high ideals, its steadfastness and spirit make all other studies puerile and puny in comparison.

Seneca, *Letters to Lucilius*, 88

13 A father should, as soon as his son is born, conceive the greatest possible hopes for the child's future. He will thereby grow the more solicitous about his improvement from the very beginning. For it is an assertion without foundation that claims that "to very few people is granted the faculty of comprehending what is imparted to them, and that most, through dulness of understanding, lose their labour and their time." On the contrary, you will find that the greater number of men are both ready in apprehending and quick in learning, since such a faculty is natural to man. As birds are born to fly, horses to run, and wild beasts to show fierceness, so to us peculiarly belong activity and sagacity of understanding. Therefore the mind is considered to be a gift from heaven. Dull and unteachable persons are no more produced in the course of nature than are persons marked by deformity or monstrosity. Such are certainly few. A simple proof of this assertion is that among boys, most of them show good promise. And if it turns out that this promise never materializes, it is not usually for lack of latent

ability, but because care was never taken in nurturing it. You may respond that some surpass others in ability. I grant this to be true, in that some accomplish more and others less. But there is no one who does not gain by some studying.

Quintilian, *Institutio Oratoria*, I, 1

14 When a wise man like Numa had received the sovereignty over a new and docile people, was there anything that would better deserve his attention than the education of children, and the training up of the young, not to contrariety and discordance of character, but to the unity of the common model of virtue, to which from their cradle they should have been formed and moulded? One benefit among many that Lycurgus obtained by his course was the permanence which it secured to his laws. The obligation of oaths to preserve them would have availed but little, if he had not, by discipline and education, infused them into the children's characters, and imbued their whole early life with a love of his government.

Plutarch, *Lycurgus and Numa Compared*

15 Ingenious men have long observed a resemblance between the arts and the bodily senses. And they were first led to do so, I think, by noticing the way in which, both in the arts and with our senses, we examine opposites. Judgment once obtained, the use to which we put it differs in the two cases. Our senses are not meant to pick out black rather than white, to prefer sweet to bitter, or soft and yielding to hard and resisting objects; all they have to do is to receive impressions as they occur, and report to the understanding the impressions as received. The arts, on the other hand, which reason institutes expressly to choose and obtain some suitable, and to refuse and get rid of some unsuitable object, have their proper concern in the consideration of the former; though, in a casual and contingent way, they must also, for the very rejection of them, pay attention to the latter. . . .

In the same manner, it seems to me likely enough that we shall be all the more zealous and more emulous to read, observe, and imitate the better lives, if we are not left in ignorance of the blameworthy and the bad.

Plutarch, *Demetrius*

16 Socrates, the great sage of antiquity, used to say, and very aptly, that if such a thing were possible he would ascend to the loftiest height of the city and cry out: "Where, mankind are you heading? Upon the acquisition of money you bestow every zeal, but of your sons, to whom you will leave this money, you take little thought." For my part I should add that the procedure of such fathers is very like that of a man who would take thought for his shoe but neglect his foot. But many fathers reach such a pitch in their love of money as well as hatred of children that to avoid paying a larger

stipend they choose as teachers for their children men worth nothing at all, shopping for ignorance at bargain prices. On this point Aristippus very neatly and with great cleverness made a jesting remark to a father who had no sense and no brains. When the man asked him his price for educating his son, he replied "A thousand drachmas." "By Heracles," the man said, "what an exorbitant figure! I can buy a slave for a thousand." "Then you will have two slaves," Aristippus retorted, "your son and the fellow you buy."

Plutarch, *Education of Children*

17 Education is the learning how . . . to distinguish that of things some are in our power, but others are not; in our power are will and all acts which depend on the will; things not in our power are the body, the parts of the body, possessions, parents, brothers, children, country, and, generally, all with whom we live in society.

Epictetus, *Discourses,* I, 22

18 We must not believe the many, who say that free persons only ought to be educated, but we should rather believe the philosophers, who say that the educated only are free.

Epictetus, *Discourses,* II, 1

19 The carpenter does not come and say, "Hear me talk about the carpenter's art"; but having undertaken to build a house, he makes it, and proves that he knows the art. You also ought to do something of the kind; eat like a man, drink like a man, dress, marry, beget children, do the office of a citizen, endure abuse, bear with an unreasonable brother, bear with your father, bear with your son, neighbour, companion. Show us these things that we may see that you have in truth learned something from the philosophers.

Epictetus, *Discourses,* III, 21

20 My parents seemed to be amused at the torments inflicted upon me as a boy by my masters, though I was no less afraid of my punishments or zealous in my prayers to You for deliverance. But in spite of my terrors I still did wrong, by writing or reading or studying less than my set tasks. It was not, Lord, that I lacked mind or memory, for You had given me as much of these as my age required; but the one thing I revelled in was play; and for this I was punished by men who after all were doing exactly the same things themselves. But the idling of men is called business; the idling of boys, though exactly like, is punished by those same men: and no one pities either boys or men. Perhaps an unbiased observer would hold that I was rightly punished as a boy for playing with a ball: because this hindered my progress in studies— studies which would give me the opportunity as a man to play at things more degraded. And what difference was there between me and the master

who flogged me? For if on some trifling point he had the worst of the argument with some fellow-master, he was more torn with angry vanity than I when I was beaten in a game of ball.

Augustine, *Confessions,* I, 9

21 A clerk from Oxford was with us also,
Who'd turned to getting knowledge, long ago.
As meagre was his horse as is a rake,
Nor he himself too fat, I'll undertake,
But he looked hollow and went soberly.
Right threadbare was his overcoat; for he
Had got him yet no churchly benefice,
Nor was so worldly as to gain office.
For he would rather have at his bed's head
Some twenty books, all bound in black and red,
Of Aristotle and his philosophy
Than rich robes, fiddle, or gay psaltery.
Yet, and for all he was philosopher,
He had but little gold within his coffer;
But all that he might borrow from a friend
On books and learning he would swiftly spend,
And then he'd pray right busily for the souls
Of those who gave him wherewithal for schools.
Of study took he utmost care and heed.
Not one word spoke he more than was his need;
And that was said in fullest reverence
And short and quick and full of high good sense.
Pregnant of moral virtue was his speech;
And gladly would he learn and gladly teach.

Chaucer, *Canterbury Tales:* The Prologue

22 We can get along without burgomasters, princes, and noblemen, but we can't do without schools, for they must rule the world.

Luther, *Table Talk,* 5247

23 He put himself into such a road and way of studying that he lost not any one hour in the day, but employed all his time in learning, and honest knowledge. Gargantua awak'd, then about four o'clock in the morning. Whilst they were in rubbing of him, there was read unto him some chapter of the Holy Scripture aloud and clearly, with a pronunciation fit for the matter, and hereunto was appointed a young page born in Basché, named Anagnostes. According to the purpose and argument of that lesson, he oftentimes gave himself to worship, adore, pray, and send up his supplications to that good God, whose word did show his majesty and marvellous judgment. Then went he into the secret places to make excretion of his natural digestions. There his master repeated what had been read, expounding unto him the most obscure and difficult points. In returning, they considered the face of the sky, if it was such as they had observed it the night before, and into what signs the sun was entering, as also the moon for that day. This done, he was appareled, combed, curled, trimmed and perfumed, during which time they repeated to him the lessons of the

day before. He himself said them by heart, and upon them would ground some practical cases concerning the estate of man, which he would prosecute sometimes two or three hours, but ordinarily they ceased as soon as he was fully clothed. Then for three good hours he had a lecture read unto him. This done, they went forth, still conferring of the substance of the lecture, either unto a field near the university called the Brack, or unto the meadows where they played at the ball, the long-tennis, and at the pile trigone, most gallantly exercising their bodies, as formerly they had done their minds. All their play was but in liberty, for they left off when they pleased, and that was commonly when they did sweat over all their body, or were otherwise weary. Then were they very well wiped and rubbed, shifted their shirts, and walking soberly, went to see if dinner was ready. Whilst they stayed for that, they did clearly and eloquently pronounce some sentences that they had retained of the lecture. In the meantime Master Appetite came, and then very orderly sat they down at table. At the beginning of the meal, there was read some pleasant history of the warlike actions of former times, until he had taken a glass of wine. Then, if they thought good, they continued reading, or began to discourse merrily together; speaking first of the virtue, propriety, efficacy and nature of all that was served in at that table; of bread, of wine, of water, of salt, of fleshes, fishes, fruits, herbs, roots, and of their dressing. By means whereof, he learned in a little time all the passages competent for this, that were to be found in Pliny, Athenæus, Dioscorides, Julius Pollux, Galen, Porphyrius, Oppian, Polybius, Heliodorus, Aristotle, Ælian, and others. Whilst they talked of these things, many times, to be the more certain, they caused the very books to be brought to the table, and so well and perfectly did he in his memory retain the things above said, that in that time there was not a physician that knew half so much as he did. Afterwards they conferred of the lessons read in the morning, and, ending their repast with some conserve or marmalade of quinces, he picked his teeth with mastic tooth-pickers, washed his hands and eyes with fair fresh water, and gave thanks unto God in some fine canticks, made in praise of the divine bounty and munificence. This done, they brought in cards, not to play, but to learn a thousand pretty tricks, and new inventions, which were all grounded upon arithmetic. By this means he fell in love with that numerical science, and every day after dinner and supper he passed his time in it as pleasantly, as he was wont to do at cards and dice: so that at last he understood so well both the theory and practical part thereof, that Tunstal the Englishman, who had written very largely of that purpose, confessed that verily in comparison of him he had no skill at all. And not only in that, but in the other mathematical sciences, as geometry, astronomy, music,

etc. For in waiting on the concoction, and attending the digestion of his food, they made a thousand pretty instruments and geometrical figures, and did in some measure practice the astronomical canons.

After this they recreated themselves with singing musically, in four or five parts, or upon a set theme or ground at random, as it best pleased them. In matter of musical instruments, he learned to play upon the lute, the virginals, the harp, the Allman flute with nine holes, the violin, and the sackbut. This hour thus spent, and digestion finished, he did purge his body of natural excrements, then betook himself to his principal study for three hours together, or more, as well to repeat his matutinal lectures, as to proceed in the book wherein he was, as also to write handsomely, to draw and form the antique and Roman letters. This being done, they went out of their house, and with them a young gentleman of Touraine, named the Esquire Gymnast, who taught him the art of riding. Changing then his clothes, he rode a Naples courser, Dutch roussin, a Spanish gennet, a barbed or trapped steed, then a light fleet horse, unto whom he gave a hundred carieres, made him go the high saults, bounding in the air, free a ditch with a skip, leap over a stile or pale, turn short in a ring both to the right and left hand. There he broke not his lance; for it is the greatest foolery in the world to say, I have broken ten lances at tilts or in fight. A carpenter can do even as much. But it is a glorious and praiseworthy action, with one lance to break and overthrow ten enemies. Therefore with a sharp, stiff, strong, and well-steeled lance, would he usually force up a door, pierce a harness, beat down a tree, carry away the ring, lift up a cuirassier saddle, with the mail-coat and gauntlet. All this he did in complete arms from head to foot. As for the prancing flourishes, and smacking popisms, for the better cherishing of the horse, commonly used in riding, none did them better than he. The voltiger of Ferrara was but as an ape compared to him. He was singularly skilful in leaping nimbly from one horse to another without putting foot to ground, and these horses were called desultories. He could likewise from either side, with a lance in his hand, leap on horseback without stirrups, and rule the horse at his pleasure without a bridle, for such things are useful in military engagements. Another day he exercised the battle-axe, which he so dexterously wielded, both in the nimble, strong, and smooth management of that weapon, and that in all the feats practiceable by it, that he passed knight of arms in the field, and at all essays.

Then tossed he the pike, played with the two-handed sword, with the back sword, with the Spanish tuck, the dagger, poniard, armed, unarmed, with a buckler, with a cloak, with a target. Then would he hunt the hart, the roebuck, the bear, the fallow deer, the wild boar, the hare, the pheasant, the partridge and the bustard. He played at the balloon, and made it bound in the air, both with fist and foot. He wrestled, ran, jumped, not at three steps and a leap, called the hops, nor at *clochepied,* called the hare's leap, nor yet at the *Almanes;* for, said Gymnast, these jumps are for the wars altogether unprofitable, and of no use: but at one leap he would skip over a ditch, spring over a hedge, mount six paces upon a wall, ramp and grapple after this fashion up against a window, of the full height of a lance. He did swim in deep waters on his belly, on his back, sideways, with all his body, with his feet only, with one hand in the air, wherein he held a book, crossing thus the breadth of the River Seine, without wetting, and dragging along his cloak with his teeth, as did Julius Cæsar; then with the help of one hand he entered forcibly into a boat, from whence he cast himself again headlong into the water, sounded the depths, hollowed the rocks, and plunged into the pits and gulfs. Then turned he the boat about, governed it, led it swiftly or slowly with the stream and against the stream, stopped it in his course, guided it with one hand, and with the other laid hard about him with a huge great oar, hoisted the sail, hied up along the mast by the shrouds, ran upon the edge of the decks, set the compass in order, tackled the bowlines, and steered the helm. Coming out of the water, he ran furiously up against a hill, and with the same alacrity and swiftness ran down again. He climbed up trees like a cat, leaped from the one to the other like a squirrel. He did pull down the great boughs and branches, like another Milo; then with two sharp well-steeled daggers, and two tried bodkins, would be run up by the wall to the very top of a house like a rat; then suddenly come down from the top to the bottom with such an even composition of members, that by the fall he would catch no harm.

He did cast the dart, throw the bar, put the stone, practise the javelin, the boar spear or partisan, and the halbert. He broke the strongest bows in drawing, bended against his breast the greatest cross-bows of steel, took his aim by the eye with the hand-gun, and shot well, traversed and planted the cannon, shot at but-marks, at the papgay from below upwards, or to a height from above downwards, or to a descent; then before him sidewise, and behind him, like the Parthians. They tied a cable-rope to the top of a high tower, by one end whereof hanging near the ground he wrought himself with his hands to the very top; then upon the same tract came down so sturdily and firm that you could not on a plain meadow have run with more assurance. They set up a great pole fixed upon two trees. There would he hang by his hands, and with them alone, his feet touching at nothing, would go back and fore along the aforesaid rope with so great swiftness,

that hardly could one overtake him with running; and then, to exercise his breast and lungs, he would shout like all the devils in hell. I heard him once call Eudemon from St. Victor's gate to Montmartre. Stentor never had such a voice at the siege of Troy. Then for the strengthening of his nerves or sinews, they made him two great sows of lead, each of them weighing eight thousand and seven hundred quintals, which they called Alteres. Those he took up from the ground, in each hand one, then lifted them up over his head, and held them so without stirring three quarters of an hour or more, which was an inimitable force. He fought at barriers with the stoutest and most vigorous champions; and when it came to the cope, he stood so sturdily on his feet, that he abandoned himself unto the strongest, in case they could remove him from his place, as Milo was wont to do of old. In whose imitation likewise he held a pomegranate in his hand, to give it unto him that could take it from him. The time being thus bestowed, and himself rubbed, cleansed, wiped and refreshed with other clothes, he returned fair and softly; and passing through certain meadows, or other grassy places, beheld the trees and plants, comparing them with what is written of them in the books of the ancients, such as Theophrast, Dioscorides, Marinus, Pliny, Nicander, Macer, and Galen, and carried home to the house great handfuls of them, whereof a young page called Rizotomos had charge; together with little mattocks, pickaxes, grubbing hooks, cabbies, pruning knives, and other instruments requisite for herborising. Being come to their lodging, whilst supper was making ready, they repeated certain passages of that which had been read, and then sat down at table. Here remark, that his dinner was sober and thrifty, for he did then eat only to prevent the gnawings of his stomach, but his supper was copious and large; for he took then as much as was fit to maintain and nourish him; which indeed is the true diet prescribed by the art of good and sound physic, although a rabble of loggerheaded physicians, muzzled in the brabbling shop of sophisters, counsel the contrary. During that repast was continued the lesson read at dinner as long as they thought good: the rest was spent in good discourse, learned and profitable. After that they had given thanks, he set himself to sing vocally, and play upon harmonious instruments, or otherwise passed his time at some pretty sports, made with cards and dice, or in practising the feats of legerdemain with cups and balls. There they staid some nights in frolicking thus, and making themselves merry till it was time to go to bed; and on other nights they would go make visits unto learned men, or to such as had been travellers in strange and remote countries. When it was full night before they retired themselves, they went unto the most open place of the house to see the face of the sky, and there beheld the comets, if any were, as likewise the figures, situations, aspects, oppositions and conjunctions of both the fixed stars and planets.

Then with his master did he briefly recapitulate, after the manner of the Pythagoreans, that which he had read, seen, learned, done and understood in the whole course of that day.

Then prayed they unto God the Creator, in falling down before him, and strengthening their faith towards him, and glorifying him for his boundless bounty; and, giving thanks unto him for the time that was past, they recommended themselves to his divine clemency for the future. Which being done, they went to bed, and betook themselves to their repose and rest.

Rabelais, *Gargantua and Pantagruel,* I, 23

24 Since it is philosophy that teaches us to live, and since there is a lesson in it for childhood as well as for the other ages, why is it not imparted to children? . . . They teach us to live, when life is past. A hundred students have caught the syphilis before they came to Aristotle's lesson on temperance. . . . Our child is in much more of a hurry: he owes to education only the first fifteen or sixteen years of his life; the rest he owes to action. Let us use so short a time for the necessary teachings. The others are abuses: away with all those thorny subtleties of dialectics, by which our lives cannot be amended. Take the simple teachings of philosophy, know how to choose them and treat them at the right time; they are easier to understand than a tale of Boccaccio. A child is capable of that when he leaves his nurse, much more than of learning to read and write. Philosophy has lessons for the birth of men as well as for their decrepitude.

Montaigne, *Essays,* I, 26, Education of
Children

25 My late father, having made all the inquiries a man can make, among men of learning and understanding, about a superlative system of education, became aware of the drawbacks that were prevalent; and he was told that the long time we put into learning languages which cost the ancient Greeks and Romans nothing was the only reason we could not attain their greatness in soul and in knowledge. I do not think that that is the only reason. At all events, the expedient my father hit upon was this, that while I was nursing and before the first loosening of my tongue, he put me in the care of a German, who has since died a famous doctor in France, wholly ignorant of our language and very well versed in Latin. This man, whom he had sent for expressly, and who was very highly paid, had me constantly in his hands. There were also two others with him, less learned, to attend me and relieve him. These spoke to me in no other language than Latin. As for the rest of my father's household, it was an inviolable rule that neither my father himself, nor my mother, nor any valet or housemaid, should speak anything in my presence but such Latin words as each had learned in order to jabber with me.

It is wonderful how everyone profited from this. My father and mother learned enough Latin in this way to understand it, and acquired sufficient skill to use it when necessary, as did also the servants who were most attached to my service. Altogether, we Latinized ourselves so much that it overflowed all the way to our villages on every side, where there still remain several Latin names for artisans and tools that have taken root by usage. As for me, I was over six before I understood any more French or Perigordian than Arabic.

Montaigne, *Essays,* I, 26, Education of
Children

26 The ignorance that was naturally in us we have by long study confirmed and verified. To really learned men has happened what happens to ears of wheat: they rise high and lofty, heads erect and proud, as long as they are empty; but when they are full and swollen with grain in their ripeness, they begin to grow humble and lower their horns. Similarly, men who have tried everything and sounded everything, having found in that pile of knowledge and store of so many various things nothing solid and firm, and nothing but vanity, have renounced their presumption and recognized their natural condition.

Montaigne, *Essays,* II, 12,
Apology for Raymond Sebond

27 *Tranio. Mi perdonato,* gentle master mine,
I am in all affected as yourself;
Glad that you thus continue your resolve
To suck the sweets of sweet philosophy.
Only, good master, while we do admire
This virtue and this moral discipline,
Let's be no stoics nor no stocks, I pray;
Or so devote to Aristotle's checks
As Ovid be an outcast quite abjured:
Balk logic with acquaintance that you have
And practise rhetoric in your common talk;
Music and poesy use to quicken you;
The mathematics and the metaphysics,
Fall to them as you find your stomach serves you;
No profit grows where is no pleasure ta'en:
In brief, sir, study what you most affect.

Shakespeare, *Taming of the Shrew,* I, i, 25

28 *Biron.* Study is like the heaven's glorious sun
  That will not be deep-search'd with saucy
    looks:
Small have continual plodders ever won
  Save base authority from others' books.
These earthly godfathers of heaven's lights
  That give a name to every fixed star
Have no more profit of their shining nights

Than those that walk and wot not what they
are.
Too much to know is to know nought by fame;
And every godfather can give a name.

Shakespeare, *Love's Labour's Lost*, I, i, 84

29 Sir, said he, you seem to me to have frequented
the Schools; pray what Science has been your
particular Study? That of Knight-Errantry,
answer'd Don *Quixote*, which is as good as that of
Poetry, and somewhat better too. I don't know
what sort of a Science that is, said Don *Lorenzo*,
nor indeed did I ever hear of it before. 'Tis a Science answer'd Don *Quixote*, that includes in itself
all the other Sciences in the World, or at least the
greatest Part of them: Whoever professes it, ought
to be learned in the laws, and understand distributive and commutative Justice, in order to right
all Mankind. He ought to be a Divine, to give a
Reason of his Faith, and vindicate his Religion by
Dint of Argument. He ought to be skill'd in Physick, especially in the Botanick Part of it, that he
may know the Nature of Simples, and have recourse to those Herbs that can cure Wounds; for a
Knight-Errant must not expect to find Surgeons
in the Woods and Desarts. He must be an Astronomer, to understand the Motions of the Celestial
Orbs, and find out by the Stars the Hour of the
Night, and the Longitude and Latitude of the Climate on which Fortune throws him: and he ought
to be well instructed in all the other Parts of the
Mathematicks, that Science being of constant use
to a Professor of Arms, on many Accounts too
numerous to be related. I need not tell you, that
all the divine and moral Virtues must center in
his Mind. To descend to less material Qualifications; he must be able to swim like a Fish, know
how to shooe a Horse, mend a Saddle or Bridle:
and returning to higher Matters, he ought to be
inviolably devoted to Heaven and his Mistress,
Chaste in his Thoughts, Modest in Words, and
Liberal and Valiant in Deeds; Patient in Afflictions, Charitable to the Poor; and finally a Maintainer of Truth, though it cost him his Life to
defend it. These are the Endowments to constitute
a good Knight-Errant; and now, Sir, be you a
Judge, whether the Professors of Chivalry have an
easy Task to perform, and whether such a Science
may not stand in Competition with the most celebrated and best of those that are taught in Colleges?

Cervantes, *Don Quixote*, II, 18

30 Studies serve for delight, for ornament, and for
ability. Their chief use for delight is in privateness
and retiring; for ornament, is in discourse; and for
ability, in the judgment and disposition of business. For expert men can execute, and perhaps
judge of particulars, one by one; but the general
counsels, and the plots and marshalling of affairs,
come best from those that are learned. To spend

too much time in studies is sloth; to use them too
much for ornament is affectation; to make judgment wholly by their rules is the humour of a
scholar. They perfect nature, and are perfected by
experience: for natural abilities are like natural
plants, that need pruning by study; and studies
themselves do give forth directions too much at
large, except they be bounded in by experience.

Bacon, *Of Studies*

31 Crafty men contemn studies; simple men admire
them; and wise men use them: for they teach not
their own use; but that is a wisdom without them
and above them, won by observation.

Bacon, *Of Studies*

32 Histories make men wise; poets witty; the mathematics subtile; natural philosophy deep; moral
grave; logic and rhetoric able to contend. . . .
There is no stond or impediment in the wit, but
may be wrought out by fit studies: like as diseases
of the body may have appropriate exercises.

Bacon, *Of Studies*

33 The end of study should be to direct the mind
towards the enunciation of sound and correct
judgments on all matters that come before it.

Descartes, *Rules for Direction of the Mind*, I

34 The end . . . of learning is to repair the ruins of
our first parents by regaining to know God aright,
and out of that knowledge to love him, to imitate
him, to be like him, as we may the nearest by
possessing our souls of true virtue, which being
united to the heavenly grace of faith, makes up
the highest perfection.

Milton, *Of Education*

35 I call . . . a complete and generous education,
that which fits a man to perform justly, skilfully,
and magnanimously all the offices, both private
and public, of peace and war.

Milton, *Of Education*

36 There is nothing by which a person can better
show how much skill and talent he possesses than
by so educating men that at last they will live
under the direct authority of reason.

Spinoza, *Ethics*, IV, Appendix IX

37 Children when they come first into it, are surrounded with a world of new things, which, by a
constant solicitation of their senses, draw the mind
constantly to them; forward to take notice of new,
and apt to be delighted with the variety of changing objects. Thus the first years are usually employed and diverted in looking abroad. Men's
business in them is to acquaint themselves with
what is to be found without; and so growing up in
a constant attention to outward sensations, seldom
make any considerable reflection on what passes

within them, till they come to be of riper years; and some scarce ever at all.

Locke, *Concerning Human Understanding,* Bk. II, I, 8

38 A sound mind in a sound body is a short but full description of a happy state in this world. He that has these two has little more to wish for; and he that wants either of them will be but little the better for anything else. Men's happiness or misery is most part of their own making. He whose mind directs not wisely will never take the right way; and he whose body is crazy and feeble will never be able to advance in it. I confess there are some men's constitutions of body and mind so vigorous and well framed by nature that they need not much assistance from others; but by the strength of their natural genius they are from their cradles carried towards what is excellent; and by the privilege of their happy constitutions are able to do wonders. But examples of this kind are but few; and I think I may say that of all the men we meet with, nine parts of ten are what they are, good or evil, useful or not, by their education. 'Tis that which makes the great difference in mankind.

Locke, *Some Thoughts Concerning Education,* 1

39 'Tis virtue . . . which is the hard and valuable part to be aimed at in education, and not a forward pertness or any little arts of shifting. All other considerations and accomplishments should give way and be postponed to this. This is the solid and substantial good which tutors should not only read lectures and talk of, but the labor and art of education should furnish the mind with and fasten there, and never cease till the young man had a true relish of it, and placed his strength, his glory, and his pleasure in it.

The more this advances, the easier way will be made for other accomplishments in their turns. For he that is brought to submit to virtue will not be refractory, or restive, in anything that becomes him; and therefore I cannot but prefer breeding of a young gentleman at home in his father's sight, under a good governor, as much the best and safest way to this great and main end of education, when it can be had, and is ordered as it should be.

Locke, *Some Thoughts Concerning Education,* 70

40 He that at any rate procures his child a good mind, well-principled, tempered to virtue and usefulness, and adorned with civility and good breeding, makes a better purchase for him than if he laid out the money for an addition of more earth to his former acres. Spare it in toys and play-games, in silk and ribbons, laces, and other useless expenses, as much as you please; but be not sparing in so necessary a part as this. 'Tis not good husbandry to make his fortune rich, and his mind poor.

Locke, *Some Thoughts Concerning Education,* 90

41 From frequently reflecting upon the course and method of educating youth in this and a neighbouring kingdom, with the general success and consequence thereof, I am come to this determination, that education is always the worse in proportion to the wealth of and grandeur of the parents.

Swift, *Essay on Modern Education*

42 A little learning is a dangerous thing;
Drink deep, or taste not the Pierian spring.
There shallow draughts intoxicate the brain,
And drinking largely sobers us again.
Fired at first sight with what the Muse imparts,
In fearless youth we tempt the heights of arts,
While from the bounded level of our mind
Short views we take, nor see the lengths behind;
But more advanced, behold with strange surprise
New distant scenes of endless science rise!

Pope, *Essay on Criticism,* II, 215

43 The bookful blockhead, ignorantly read,
With loads of learnèd lumber in his head,
With his own tongue still edifies his ears,
And always list'ning to himself appears.

Pope, *Essay on Criticism,* III, 612

44 The mere philosopher is a character, which is commonly but little acceptable in the world, as being supposed to contribute nothing either to the advantage or pleasure of society; while he lives remote from communication with mankind, and is wrapped up in principles and notions equally remote from their comprehension. On the other hand, the mere ignorant is still more despised; nor is anything deemed a surer sign of an illiberal genius in an age and nation where the sciences flourish, than to be entirely destitute of all relish for those noble entertainments. The most perfect character is supposed to lie between those extremes; retaining an equal ability and taste for books, company, and business; preserving in conversation that discernment and delicacy which arise from polite letters; and in business, that probity and accuracy which are the natural result of a just philosophy.

Hume, *Concerning Human Understanding,* I, 4

45 Whatever propensity one may have to vice, it is not easy for an education, with which love has mingled, to be entirely thrown away.

Rousseau, *Origin of Inequality,* Dedication

46 From the first moment of life, men ought to begin learning to deserve to live; and, as at the instant of birth we partake of the rights of citizenship, that instant ought to be the beginning of the exercise of our duty. If there are laws for the age of maturity, there ought to be laws for infancy,

teaching obedience to others: and as the reason of each man is not left to be the sole arbiter of his duties, government ought the less indiscriminately to abandon to the intelligence and prejudices of fathers the education of their children, as that education is of still greater importance to the State than to the fathers: for, according to the course of nature, the death of the father often deprives him of the final fruits of education; but his country sooner or later perceives its effects. Families dissolve, but the State remains.

Rousseau, *Political Economy*

47 All that we lack at birth, all that we need when we come to man's estate, is the gift of education.

Rousseau, *Emile*, I

48 Education comes to us from nature, from men, or from things. The inner growth of our organs and faculties is the education of nature, the use we learn to make of this growth is the education of men, what we gain by our experience of our surroundings is the education of things.

Thus we are each taught by three masters. If their teaching conflicts, the scholar is ill-educated and will never be at peace with himself; if their teaching agrees, he goes straight to his goal, he lives at peace with himself, he is well-educated.

Rousseau, *Emile*, I

49 *Johnson*. While learning to read and write is a distinction, the few who have that distinction may be the less inclined to work; but when every body learns to read and write, it is no longer a distinction.

Boswell, *Life of Johnson* (Apr. 14, 1772)

50 He [Johnson] allowed very great influence to education. "I do not deny, Sir, but there is some original difference in minds; but it is nothing in comparison of what is formed by education. We may instance the science of *numbers*, which all minds are equally capable of attaining; yet we find a prodigious difference in the powers of different men, in that respect, after they are grown up, because their minds have been more or less exercised in it: and I think the same cause will explain the difference of excellence in other things, gradations admitting always some difference in the first principles."

Boswell, *Life of Johnson* (Mar. 16, 1776)

51 Though the common people cannot, in any civilised society, be so well instructed as people of some rank and fortune, the most essential parts of education, however, to read, write, and account, can be acquired at so early a period of life that the greater part even of those who are to be bred to the lowest occupations have time to acquire them before they can be employed in those occupations. For a very small expense the public can facilitate,

can encourage, and can even impose upon almost the whole body of the people the necessity of acquiring those most essential parts of education.

Adam Smith, *Wealth of Nations*, V, 1

52 A man without the proper use of the intellectual faculties of a man, is, if possible, more contemptible than even a coward, and seems to be mutilated and deformed in a still more essential part of the character of human nature. Though the state was to derive no advantage from the instruction of the inferior ranks of people, it would still deserve its attention that they should not be altogether uninstructed. The state, however, derives no inconsiderable advantage from their instruction. The more they are instructed the less liable they are to the delusions of enthusiasm and superstition, which, among ignorant nations, frequently occasion the most dreadful disorders. An instructed and intelligent people, besides, are always more decent and orderly than an ignorant and stupid one. They feel themselves, each individually, more respectable and more likely to obtain the respect of their lawful superiors, and they are therefore more disposed to respect those superiors. They are more disposed to examine, and more capable of seeing through, the interested complaints of faction and sedition, and they are, upon that account, less apt to be misled into any wanton or unnecessary opposition to the measures of government. In free countries, where the safety of government depends very much upon the favourable judgment which the people may form of its conduct, it must surely be of the highest importance that they should not be disposed to judge rashly or capriciously concerning it.

Adam Smith, *Wealth of Nations*, V, 1

53 Education is the art of making men ethical. It begins with pupils whose life is at the instinctive level and shows them the way to a second birth, the way to change their instinctive nature into a second, intellectual, nature, and makes this intellectual level habitual to them. At this point the clash between the natural and the subjective will disappears, the subject's internal struggle dies away. To this extent, habit is part of ethical life as it is of philosophic thought also, since such thought demands that mind be trained against capricious fancies, and that these be destroyed and overcome to leave the way clear for rational thinking. It is true that a man is killed by habit, i.e. if he has once come to feel completely at home in life, if he has become mentally and physically dull, and if the clash between subjective consciousness and mental activity has disappeared; for man is active only in so far as he has not attained his end and wills to develop his potentialities and vindicate himself in struggling to attain it. When this has been fully achieved, activity and vitality are at an end, and the result—loss of in-

terest in life—is mental or physical death.

Hegel, *Philosophy of Right,*
Additions, Par. 151

54 Man has to acquire for himself the position which he ought to attain; he is not already in possession of it by instinct. It is on this fact that the child's right to education is based. Peoples under patriarchal government are in the same position as children; they are fed from central stores and not regarded as self-subsistent and adults. The services which may be demanded from children should therefore have education as their sole end and be relevant thereto; they must not be ends in themselves, since a child in slavery is in the most unethical of all situations whatever. One of the chief factors in education is discipline, the purport of which is to break down the child's self-will and thereby eradicate his purely natural and sensuous self. We must not expect to achieve this by mere goodness, since it is just the immediate will which acts on immediate fancies and caprices, not on reasons and representative thinking. If we advance reasons to children, we leave it open to them to decide whether the reasons are weighty or not, and thus we make everything depend on their whim. So far as children are concerned, universality and the substance of things reside in their parents, and this implies that children must be obedient. If the feeling of subordination, producing the longing to grow up, is not fostered in children, they become forward and impertinent.

Hegel, *Philosophy of Right,*
Additions, Par. 174

55 A man sees a great many things when he looks at the world for himself, and he sees them from many sides; but this method of learning is not nearly so short or so quick as the method which employs abstract ideas and makes hasty generalizations about everything. Experience, therefore, will be a long time in correcting preconceived ideas, or perhaps never bring its task to an end; for wherever a man finds that the aspect of things seems to contradict the general ideas he has formed, he will begin by rejecting the evidence it offers as partial and one-sided; nay, he will shut his eyes to it altogether and deny that it stands in any contradiction at all with his preconceived notions, in order that he may thus preserve them uninjured. So it is that many a man carries about a burden of wrong notions all his life long—crotchets, whims, fancies, prejudices, which at last become fixed ideas. The fact is that he has never tried to form his fundamental ideas for himself out of his own experience of life, his own way of looking at the world, because he has taken over his ideas ready-made from other people; and this it is that makes him—as it makes how many others!—so shallow and superficial.

Schopenhauer, *Education*

56 No child under the age of fifteen should receive instruction in subjects which may possibly be the vehicle of serious error, such as philosophy, religion, or any other branch of knowledge where it is necessary to take large views; because wrong notions imbibed early can seldom be rooted out, and of all the intellectual faculties, judgment is the last to arrive at maturity. The child should give its attention either to subjects where no error is possible at all, such as mathematics, or to those in which there is no particular danger in making a mistake, such as languages, natural science, history and so on.

Schopenhauer, *Education*

57 If we think of it, all that a University, or final highest School can do for us, is still but what the first School began doing—teach us to *read.* We learn to *read,* in various languages, in various sciences; we learn the alphabet and letters of all manner of Books. But the place where we are to get knowledge, even theoretic knowledge, is the Books themselves! It depends on what we read, after all manner of Professors have done their best for us. The true University of these days is a Collection of Books.

Carlyle, *The Hero as Man of Letters*

58 Man is thus metamorphosed into a thing, into many things. The planter, who is Man sent out into the field to gather food, is seldom cheered by any idea of the true dignity of his ministry. He sees his bushel and his cart, and nothing beyond, and sinks into the farmer, instead of Man on the farm. The tradesman scarcely ever gives an ideal worth to his work, but is ridden by the routine of his craft, and the soul is subject to dollars. The priest becomes a form; the attorney a statutebook; the mechanic a machine; the sailor a rope of the ship.

In this distribution of functions the scholar is the delegated intellect. In the right state he is *Man Thinking.* In the degenerate state, when the victim of society, he tends to become a mere thinker, or still worse, the parrot of other men's thinking.

In this view of him, as Man Thinking, the theory of his office is contained. Him Nature solicits with all her placid, all her monitory pictures; him the past instructs; him the future invites.

Emerson, *The American Scholar*

59 Books are good only as far as a boy is ready for them. He sometimes gets ready very slowly. You send your child to the schoolmaster, but 't is the schoolboys who educate him. You send him to the Latin class, but much of his tuition comes, on his way to school, from the shop-windows. You like the strict rules and the long terms; and he finds his best leading in a by-way of his own, and refuses any companions but of his own choosing. He hates the grammar and *Gradus,* and loves guns,

fishing-rods, horses and boats. Well, the boy is right, and you are not fit to direct his bringing-up if your theory leaves out his gymnastic training. Archery, cricket, gun and fishing-rod, horse and boat, are all educators, liberalizers; and so are dancing, dress and the street talk; and provided only the boy has resources, and is of a noble and ingenuous strain, these will not serve him less than the books.

Emerson, *Culture*

60 One of the benefits of a college education is to show the boy its little avail.

Emerson, *Culture*

61 We are students of words: we are shut up in schools, and colleges, and recitation-rooms, for ten or fifteen years, and come out at last with a bag of wind, a memory of words, and do not know a thing.

Emerson, *New England Reformers*

62 At Mr. Wackford Squeers's Academy, Dotheboys Hall, at the delightful village of Dotheboys, near Greta Bridge in Yorkshire, Youth are boarded, clothed, booked, furnished with pocket-money, provided with all necessaries, instructed in all languages living and dead, mathematics, orthography, geometry, astronomy, trigonometry, the use of the globes, algebra, single stick (if required), writing, arithmetic, fortification, and every other branch of classical literature. Terms, twenty guineas per annum. No extras, no vacations, and diet unparalleled.

Dickens, *Nicholas Nickleby*, III

63 Perhaps many who watch over the interests of the community, and are anxious for its welfare, will conclude that the development of the judgment cannot properly be included in the general idea of education; that as the education proposed must, to a very large degree, be of *self,* it is so far incommunicable; that the master and the scholar merge into one, and both disappear; that the instructor is no wiser than the one to be instructed, and thus the usual relations of the two lose their power. Still, I believe that the judgment may be educated to a very large extent, and might refer to the fine arts, as giving proof in the affirmative; and though, as respects the community and its improvement in relation to common things, any useful education must be of *self,* I think that society, as a body, may act powerfully in the cause. Or it may still be objected that my experience is imperfect, is chiefly derived from exercise of the mind within the precincts of natural philosophy, and has not that generality of application which can make it of any value to society at large. I can only repeat my conviction, that society occupies itself now-a-days about physical matters, and judges them as common things. Failing in relation to

them, it is equally liable to carry such failures into other matters of life. The proof of deficient judgment in one department shows the habit of mind, and the general want, in relation to others. I am persuaded that all persons may find in natural things an admirable school for self-instruction, and a field for the necessary mental exercise; that they may easily apply their habits of thought, thus formed, to a social use; and that they ought to do this, as a duty to themselves and their generation.

Faraday, *Observations on Mental Education*

64 As for me, if, by any possibility, there be any as yet undiscovered prime thing in me; if I shall ever deserve any real repute in that small but high hushed world which I might not be unreasonably ambitious of; if hereafter I shall do anything that, upon the whole, a man might rather have done than to have left undone; if, at my death, my executors, or more properly my creditors, find any precious MSS. in my desk, then here I prospectively ascribe all the honour and the glory to whaling; for a whale ship was my Yale College and my Harvard.

Melville, *Moby Dick*, XXIV

65 The mode of founding a college is, commonly, to get up a subscription of dollars and cents, and then, following blindly the principles of a division of labor to its extreme—a principle which should never be followed but with circumspection—to call in a contractor who makes this a subject of speculation, and he employs Irishmen or other operatives actually to lay the foundations, while the students that are to be are said to be fitting themselves for it; and for these oversights successive generations have to pay. I think that it would be *better than this,* for the students, or those who desire to be benefited by it, even to lay the foundation themselves. The student who secures his coveted leisure and retirement by systematically shirking any labor necessary to man obtains leisure and an ignoble and unprofitable leisure, defrauding himself of the experience which alone can make leisure fruitful. 'But,' says one, 'you do not mean that the students should go to work with their hands instead of their heads?' I do not mean that exactly, but I mean something which he might think a good deal like that; I mean that they should not *play* life, or *study* it merely, while the community supports them at this expensive game, but earnestly *live* it from beginning to end. How could youths better learn to live than by at once trying the experiment of living? Methinks this would exercise their minds as much as mathematics. If I wished a boy to know something about the arts and sciences, for instance, I would not pursue the common course, which is merely to send him into the neighborhood of some professor, where anything is professed and practised but the art of life;—to survey the world through a telescope or a microscope,

and never with his natural eye; to study chemistry, and not learn how his bread is made, or mechanics, and not learn how it is earned; to discover new satellites to Neptune, and not detect the motes in his eyes, or to what vagabond he is a satellite himself; or to be devoured by the monsters that swarm all around him, while contemplating the monsters in a drop of vinegar. Which would have advanced the most at the end of a month—the boy who had made his own jackknife from the ore which he had dug and smelted, reading as much as would be necessary for this—or the boy who had attended the lectures on metallurgy at the Institute in the meanwhile, and had received a Rodgers penknife from his father? Which would be most likely to cut his fingers? . . . To my astonishment I was informed on leaving college that I had studied navigation!—why, if I had taken one turn down the harbor I should have known more about it. Even the *poor* student studies and is taught only *political* economy, while that economy of living which is synonymous with philosophy is not even sincerely professed in our colleges. The consequence is, that while he is reading Adam Smith, Ricardo, and Say, he runs his father in debt irretrievably.

Thoreau, *Walden:* Economy

66 Education is the instruction of the intellect in the laws of Nature, under which name I include not merely things and their forces, but men and their ways; and the fashioning of the affections and of the will into an earnest and loving desire to move in harmony with those laws.

T. H. Huxley, *A Liberal Education*

67 From the Factory system budded . . . the germ of the education of the future, an education that will, in the case of every child over a given age, combine productive labour with instruction and gymnastics, not only as one of the methods of adding to the efficiency of production, but as the only method of producing fully developed human beings.

Marx, *Capital,* Vol. I, IV, 15

68 When we turn to subjects infinitely more complicated, to morals, religion, politics, social relations, and the business of life, three-fourths of the arguments for every disputed opinion consist in dispelling the appearances which favour some opinion different from it. The greatest orator, save one, of antiquity, has left it on record that he always studied his adversary's case with as great, if not still greater, intensity than even his own. What Cicero practised as the means of forensic success requires to be imitated by all who study any subject in order to arrive at the truth. He who knows only his own side of the case, knows little of that. His reasons may be good, and no one may have been able to refute them. But if he is equally unable to refute the reasons on the opposite side; if he does not so much as know what they are, he has no ground for preferring either opinion. The rational position for him would be suspension of judgment, and unless he contents himself with that, he is either led by authority, or adopts, like the generality of the world, the side to which he feels most inclination. Nor is it enough that he should hear the arguments of adversaries from his own teachers, presented as they state them, and accompanied by what they offer as refutations. That is not the way to do justice to the arguments, or bring them into real contact with his own mind. He must be able to hear them from persons who actually believe them; who defend them in earnest, and do their very utmost for them. He must know them in their most plausible and persuasive form; he must feel the whole force of the difficulty which the true view of the subject has to encounter and dispose of; else he will never really possess himself of the portion of truth which meets and removes that difficulty.

Ninety-nine in a hundred of what are called educated men are in this condition; even of those who can argue fluently for their opinions. Their conclusion may be true, but it might be false for anything they know: they have never thrown themselves into the mental position of those who think differently from them, and considered what such persons may have to say; and consequently they do not, in any proper sense of the word, know the doctrine which they themselves profess. They do not know those parts of it which explain and justify the remainder; the considerations which show that a fact which seemingly conflicts with another is reconcilable with it, or that, of two apparently strong reasons, one and not the other ought to be preferred. All that part of the truth which turns the scale, and decides the judgment of a completely informed mind, they are strangers to; nor is it ever really known, but to those who have attended equally and impartially to both sides, and endeavoured to see the reasons of both in the strongest light. So essential is this discipline to a real understanding of moral and human subjects, that if opponents of all important truths do not exist, it is indispensable to imagine them, and supply them with the strongest arguments which the most skilful devil's advocate can conjure up.

Mill, *On Liberty,* II

69 A cultivated mind—I do not mean that of a philosopher, but any mind to which the fountains of knowledge have been opened, and which has been taught, in any tolerable degree, to exercise its faculties—finds sources of inexhaustible interest in all that surrounds it; in the objects of nature, the achievements of art, the imaginations of poetry, the incidents of history, the ways of mankind, past and present, and their prospects in the future. It is possible, indeed, to become indifferent to all this,

and that too without having exhausted a thousandth part of it; but only when one has had from the beginning no moral or human interest in these things, and has sought in them only the gratification of curiosity.

Now there is absolutely no reason in the nature of things why an amount of mental culture sufficient to give an intelligent interest in these objects of contemplation, should not be the inheritance of every one born in a civilised country.

Mill, *Utilitarianism,* II

70 It has often been said, and requires to be repeated still oftener, that books and discourses alone are not education; that life is a problem, not a theorem; that action can only be learned in action. A child learns to write its name only by a succession of trials; and is a man to be taught to use his mind and guide his conduct by mere precept? What can be learned in schools is important, but not all-important. The main branch of the education of human beings is their habitual employment, which must be either their individual vocation or some matter of general concern, in which they are called to take a part. The private money-getting occupation of almost everyone is more or less a mechanical routine; it brings but few of his faculties into action, while its exclusive pursuit tends to fasten his attention and interest exclusively upon himself, and upon his family as an appendage of himself—making him indifferent to the public, to the more generous objects and the nobler interests, and, in his inordinate regard for his personal comforts, selfish and cowardly. Balance these tendencies by contrary ones; give him something to do for the public, whether as a vestryman, a juryman, or an elector; and in that degree, his ideas and feelings are taken out of this narrow circle. He becomes acquainted with more varied business and a larger range of considerations. He is made to feel that besides the interests which separate him from his fellow citizens, he has interests which connect him with them; that not only the common weal is his weal but that it partly depends upon his exertions. Whatever might be the case in some other constitutions of society, the spirit of a commercial people will be, we are persuaded, essentially mean and slavish wherever public spirit is not cultivated by an extensive participation of the people in the business of government in detail: nor will the desideratum of a general diffusion of intelligence among either the middle or lower classes be realized, but by a corresponding dissemination of public functions, and a voice in public affairs.

Mill, *Review of Tocqueville's
"Democracy in America"*

71 Education . . . is one of the subjects which most essentially require to be considered by various minds, and from a variety of points of view. For, of all many-sided subjects, it is the one which has the greatest number of sides. Not only does it include whatever we do for ourselves, and whatever is done for us by others, for the express purpose of bringing us somewhat nearer to the perfection of our nature; it does more: in its largest acceptation, it comprehends even the indirect effects produced on character and on the human faculties, by things of which the direct purposes are quite different; by laws, by forms of government, by the industrial arts, by modes of social life; nay even by physical facts not dependent on human will; by climate, soil, and local position. Whatever helps to shape the human being; to make the individual what he is, or hinder him from being what he is not—is part of his education. And a very bad education it often is; requiring all that can be done by cultivated intelligence and will, to counteract its tendencies.

Mill, *Inaugural Address at St. Andrews*

72 Men are men before they are lawyers, or physicians, or merchants, or manufacturers; and if you make them capable and sensible men, they will make themselves capable and sensible lawyers or physicians. What professional men should carry away with them from an University, is not professional knowledge, but that which should direct the use of their professional knowledge, and bring the light of general culture to illuminate the technicalities of a special pursuit. Men may be competent lawyers without general education, but it depends on general education to make them philosophic lawyers—who demand, and are capable of apprehending, principles, instead of merely cramming their memory with details. And so of all other useful pursuits, mechanical included. Education makes a man a more intelligent shoemaker, if that be his occupation, but not by teaching him how to make shoes; it does so by the mental exercise it gives, and the habits it impresses.

Mill, *Inaugural Address at St. Andrews*

73 It has always seemed to me a great absurdity that history and geography should be taught in schools; except in elementary schools for the children of the labouring classes, whose subsequent access to books is limited. Who ever really learnt history and geography except by private reading? and what an utter failure a system of education must be, if it has not given the pupil a sufficient taste for reading to seek for himself those most attractive and easily intelligible of all kinds of knowledge? . . . Of the mere facts of history, as commonly accepted, what educated youth of any mental activity does not learn as much as is necessary, if he is simply turned loose into an historical library? What he needs on this, and on most other matters of common information, is not that he should be taught it in boyhood, but that abun-

dance of books should be accessible to him.
Mill, *Inaugural Address at St. Andrews*

74 Health is a good in itself, though nothing came of it, and is especially worth seeking and cherishing: yet, after all, the blessings which attend its presence are so great, while they are so close to it and so redound back upon it and encircle it, that we never think of it except as useful as well as good, and praise and prize it for what it does, as well as for what it is, though at the same time we cannot point out any definite and distinct work or production which it can be said to effect. And so as regards intellectual culture, I am far from denying utility in this large sense as the end of Education, when I lay it down, that the culture of the intellect is a good in itself and its own end; I do not exclude from the idea of intellectual culture what it cannot but be, from the very nature of things; I only deny that we must be able to point out, before we have any right to call it useful, some art, or business, or profession, or trade, or work, as resulting from it, and as its real and complete end. The parallel is exact: As the body may be sacrificed to some manual or other toil, whether moderate or oppressive, so may the intellect be devoted to some specific profession; and I do not call *this* the culture of the intellect. Again, as some member or organ of the body may be inordinately used and developed, so may memory, or imagination, or the reasoning faculty; and *this* again is not intellectual culture. On the other hand, as the body may be tended, cherished, and exercised with a simple view to its general health, so may the intellect also be generally exercised in order to its perfect state; and this *is* its cultivation.
Newman, *Idea of a University*, Discourse VII

75 Culture is indispensably necessary, and culture is *reading;* but reading with a purpose to guide it, and with system. He does a good work who does anything to help this: indeed, it is the one essential service now to be rendered to education.
Arnold, *Literature and Dogma*, Pref.

76 Soap and education are not as sudden as a massacre, but they are more deadly in the long run.
Mark Twain, *The Facts Concerning the Recent Resignation*

77 Education in the long run is an affair that works itself out between the individual student and his opportunities. Methods of which we talk so much, play but a minor part. Offer the opportunities, leave the student to his natural reaction on them, and he will work out his personal destiny, be it a high one or a low one.
William James, *Stanford's Ideal Destiny*

78 There are many paths to knowledge already discovered; and no enlightened man doubts that there are many more waiting to be discovered.

Indeed, all paths lead to knowledge; because even the vilest and stupidest action teaches us something about vileness and stupidity, and may accidentally teach us a good deal more.
Shaw, *Doctor's Dilemma*, Pref.

79 In truth, mankind cannot be saved from without, by schoolmasters or any other sort of masters: it can only be lamed and enslaved by them. It is said that if you wash a cat it will never again wash itself. This may or may not be true: what is certain is that if you teach a man anything he will never learn it; and if you cure him of a disease he will be unable to cure himself the next time it attacks him. Therefore, if you want to see a cat clean, you throw a bucket of mud over it, when it will immediately take extraordinary pains to lick the mud off, and finally be cleaner than it was before. In the same way doctors who are up-to-date (say .00005 per cent of all the registered practitioners, and 20 per cent of the unregistered ones), when they want to rid you of a disease or a symptom, inoculate you with that disease or give you a drug that produces that symptom, in order to provoke you to resist it as the mud provokes the cat to wash itself.
Shaw, *Back to Methuselah*, Pref.

80 Culture is activity of thought, and receptiveness to beauty and humane feeling. Scraps of information have nothing to do with it. A merely well-informed man is the most useless bore on God's earth. What we should aim at producing is men who possess both culture and expert knowledge in some special direction. Their expert knowledge will give them the ground to start from, and their culture will lead them as deep as philosophy and as high as art. We have to remember that the valuable intellectual development is self-development, and that it mostly takes place between the ages of sixteen and thirty. As to training, the most important part is given by mothers before the age of twelve.
Whitehead, *Aims of Education*

81 There is only one subject-matter for education, and that is Life in all its manifestations. Instead of this single unity, we offer children—Algebra, from which nothing follows; Geometry, from which nothing follows; Science, from which nothing follows; History, from which nothing follows; a Couple of Languages, never mastered; and lastly, most dreary of all, Literature, represented by plays of Shakespeare, with philological notes and short analyses of plot and character to be in substance committed to memory. Can such a list be said to represent Life, as it is known in the midst of the living of it? The best that can be said of it is, that it is a rapid table of contents which a deity might run over in his mind while he was thinking of creating a world, and had not yet determined

how to put it together.

Whitehead, *Aims of Education*

82 The merit of this study [of Roman history] in the education of youth is its concreteness, its inspiration to action, and the uniform greatness of persons, in their characters and their staging. Their aims were great, their virtues were great, and their vices were great. They had the saving merit of sinning with cart-ropes. Moral education is impossible apart from the habitual vision of greatness. If we are not great, it does not matter what we do or what is the issue. Now the sense of greatness is an immediate intuition and not the conclusion of an argument. It is permissible for youth in the agonies of religious conversion to entertain the feeling of being a worm and no man, so long as there remains the conviction of greatness sufficient to justify the eternal wrath of God. The sense of greatness is the groundwork of morals. We are at the threshold of a democratic age, and it remains to be determined whether the equality of man is to be realised on a high level or a low level. There was never a time in which it was more essential to hold before the young the vision of Rome: in itself a great drama, and with issues greater than itself.

Whitehead, *The Place of Classics in Education*

83 Education is, as a rule, the strongest force on the side of what exists and against fundamental change: threatened institutions, while they are still powerful, possess themselves of the educational machine, and instill a respect for their own excellence into the malleable minds of the young. Reformers retort by trying to oust their opponents from their position of vantage. The children themselves are not considered by either party; they are merely so much material, to be recruited into one army or the other. If the children themselves were considered, education would not aim at making them belong to this party or that, but at enabling them to choose intelligently between the parties; it would aim at making them able to think, not at making them think what their teachers think. Education as a political weapon could not exist if we respected the rights of children. If we respected the rights of children, we should educate them so as to give them the knowledge and the mental habits required for forming independent opinions; but education as a political institution endeavors to form habits and to circumscribe knowledge in such a way as to make one set of opinions inevitable.

Russell, *Education*

84 The joy of mental adventure is far commoner in the young than in grown men and women. Among children it is very common, and grows naturally out of the period of make-believe and fancy. It is rare in later life because everything is done to kill it during education.

Russell, *Education*

85 A community of men and women possessing vitality, courage, sensitiveness, and intelligence, in the highest degree that education can produce, would be very different from anything that has hitherto existed. Very few people would be unhappy. The main causes of unhappiness at present are: ill-health, poverty, and an unsatisfactory sex-life. All of these would become very rare. Good health could be almost universal, and even old age could be postponed. Poverty, since the industrial revolution, is only due to collective stupidity. Sensitiveness would make people wish to abolish it, intelligence would show them the way, and courage would lead them to adopt it. (A timid person would rather remain miserable than do anything unusual.) Most people's sex-life, at present, is more or less unsatisfactory. This is partly due to bad education, partly to persecution by the authorities and Mrs. Grundy. A generation of women brought up without irrational sex fears would soon make an end of this. Fear has been thought the only way to make women "virtuous," and they have been deliberately taught to be cowards, both physically and mentally. Women in whom love is cramped encourage brutality and hypocrisy in their husbands, and distort the instincts of their children. One generation of fearless women could transform the world, by bringing into it a generation of fearless children, not contorted into unnatural shapes, but straight and candid, generous, affectionate, and free. Their ardor would sweep away the cruelty and pain which we endure because we are lazy, cowardly, hard-hearted and stupid. It is education that gives us these bad qualities, and education that must give us the opposite virtues. Education is the key to the new world.

Russell, *Aims of Education*

86 The educability of a young person as a rule comes to an end when sexual desire breaks out in its final strength. Educators know this and act accordingly; but perhaps they will yet allow themselves to be influenced by the results of psycho-analysis so that they will transfer the main emphasis in education to the earliest years of childhood, from the suckling period onward. The little human being is frequently a finished product in his fourth or fifth year, and only gradually reveals in later years what lies buried in him.

Freud, *General Introduction to Psycho-Analysis*, XXII

87 We may reject knowledge of the past as the *end* of education and thereby only emphasize its importance as a *means*. When we do that we have a problem that is new in the story of education: How shall the young become acquainted with the

past in such a way that the acquaintance is a potent agent in appreciation of the living present?

Dewey, *Experience and Education,* I

88 Education as growth or maturity should be an ever-present process.

Dewey, *Experience and Education,* III

89 In its contrast with the ideas both of unfolding of latent powers from within, and of formation from without, whether by physical nature or by the cultural products of the past, the ideal of growth results in the conception that education is a constant reorganizing or reconstructing of experience. It has all the time an immediate end, and so far as activity is educative, it reaches that end—the direct transformation of the quality of experience. Infancy, youth, adult life—all stand on the same educative level in the sense that what is really *learned* at any and every stage of experience constitutes the value of that experience, and in the sense

that it is the chief business of life at every point to make living thus contribute to an enrichment of its own perceptible meaning.

We thus reach a technical definition of education: It is that reconstruction or reorganization of experience which adds to the meaning of experience, and which increases ability to direct the course of subsequent experience.

Dewey, *Democracy and Education,* VI

90 The only adequate training *for* occupations is training *through* occupations. The principle . . . that the educative process is its own end, and that the only sufficient preparation for later responsibilities comes by making the most of immediately present life, applies in full force to the vocational phases of education. The dominant vocation of all human beings at all times is living—intellectual and moral growth.

Dewey, *Democracy and Education,* XXIII

8.2 | *Habit*

The ancient saying that habit is a kind of second nature explains the significance of habit and habit-formation for the process of education. If men were born with their natures perfected, with no room for improvement, with no potentialities to be realized, they would not need and could not use education. Precisely because they are born with room for improvement, they can be and need to be educated, and this usually takes the form of giving them a "second nature"—a set of acquired habits that, once they are well established, operate as smoothly as their original nature.

Some of the passages quoted deal with the psychology of habit and habit-formation, and with the conditions under which habits are acquired, strengthened, weakened, and changed. Other passages present distinctions among kinds of habit, especially the differ-

ence between habits of mind (of thought and knowledge) and habits of character (of action and of emotion). This, of course, has a bearing on the distinction between intellectual and moral training—the effort, on the one hand, to form or inculcate good intellectual habits; and the effort, on the other hand, to instill good moral habits. The discussion here tends to move from the domain of psychology to that of ethics, for the qualification of habits as good and bad introduces the notions of virtue and vice.

Learning would be fruitless if what is learned were not retained. One aspect of such retention, especially when the learning is verbal, is discussed under the head of memory, in Section 5.3 of Chapter 5 on MIND. The other, and much broader, aspect is discussed here.

1 Those things which one has been accustomed to
for a long time, although worse than things which
one is not accustomed to, usually give less disturbance; but a change must sometimes be made to
things one is not accustomed to.

Hippocrates, *Aphorisms*, II, 50

2 *Socrates.* Is not the bodily habit spoiled by rest and
idleness, but preserved for a long time by motion
and exercise?

Theaetetus. True.

Soc. And what of the mental habit? Is not the
soul informed, and improved, and preserved by
study and attention, which are motions; but when
at rest, which in the soul only means want of attention and study, is uninformed, and speedily
forgets whatever she has learned?

Theaet. True.

Plato, *Theaetetus,* 153A

3 The effect which lectures produce on a hearer depends on his habits; for we demand the language
we are accustomed to, and that which is different
from this seems not in keeping but somewhat unintelligible and foreign because of its unwonted-
ness. For it is the customary that is intelligible.
The force of habit is shown by the laws, in which
the legendary and childish elements prevail over
our knowledge about them, owing to habit. Thus
some people do not listen to a speaker unless he
speaks mathematically, others unless he gives instances, while others expect him to cite a poet as
witness. And some want to have everything done
accurately, while others are annoyed by accuracy,
either because they cannot follow the connexion
of thought or because they regard it as pettifog-
gery. For accuracy has something of this character, so that as in trade so in argument some people
think it mean. Hence one must be already trained
to know how to take each sort of argument.

Aristotle, *Metaphysics*, 994b31

4 Virtue, then, being of two kinds, intellectual and
moral, intellectual virtue in the main owes both
its birth and its growth to teaching (for which reason it requires experience and time), while moral
virtue comes about as a result of habit, whence
also its name is one that is formed by a slight
variation from the word habit. From this it is also
plain that none of the moral virtues arises in us by
nature; for nothing that exists by nature can form
a habit contrary to its nature. For instance the
stone which by nature moves downwards cannot
be habituated to move upwards, not even if one
tries to train it by throwing it up ten thousand
times; nor can fire be habituated to move downwards, nor can anything else that by nature behaves in one way be trained to behave in another.
Neither by nature, then, nor contrary to nature
do the virtues arise in us; rather we are adapted

by nature to receive them, and are made perfect
by habit.

Again, of all the things that come to us by nature we first acquire the potentiality and later exhibit the activity (this is plain in the case of the
senses; for it was not by often seeing or often hearing that we got these senses, but on the contrary
we had them before we used them, and did not
come to have them by using them); but the virtues we get by first exercising them, as also happens in the case of the arts as well. For the things
we have to learn before we can do them, we learn
by doing them, for example, men become builders
by building and lyre-players by playing the lyre;
so too we become just by doing just acts, temperate by doing temperate acts, brave by doing brave
acts. . . .

Thus, in one word, states of character arise out
of like activities. This is why the activities we exhibit must be of a certain kind; it is because the
states of character correspond to the differences
between these. It makes no small difference, then,
whether we form habits of one kind or of another
from our very youth; it makes a very great difference, or rather *all* the difference.

Aristotle, *Ethics,* 1103a14

5 By abstaining from pleasures we become temperate, and it is when we have become so that we are
most able to abstain from them; and similarly too
in the case of courage; for by being habituated to
despise things that are terrible and to stand our
ground against them we become brave, and it is
when we have become so that we shall be most
able to stand our ground against them.

Aristotle, *Ethics,* 1104a33

6 Habit is a kind of second nature.

Cicero, *De Finibus,* V

7 Every habit and faculty is maintained and increased by the corresponding actions: the habit of
walking by walking, the habit of running by running. If you would be a good reader, read; if a
writer, write.

Epictetus, *Discourses,* II, 18

8 If you would make anything a habit, do it; if you
would not make it a habit, do not do it, but accustom yourself to do something else in place of it.

Epictetus, *Discourses,* II, 18

9 Some habits are infused by God into man, for two
reasons. The first reason is because there are some

habits by which man is well disposed to an end which exceeds the power of human nature, namely, the ultimate and perfect happiness of man. . . . And since habits must be in proportion with that to which man is disposed by them, therefore it is necessary that those habits, which dispose to this end, exceed the power of human nature. Hence such habits can never be in man except by Divine infusion, as is the case with all gratuitous virtues.

The other reason is, because God can produce the effects of second causes without these second causes. . . . Just as, therefore, sometimes, in order to show His power, He causes health without its natural cause, but which nature could have caused, so also, at times, for the manifestation of His power, He infuses into man even those habits which can be caused by a natural power.

Aquinas, *Summa Theologica*, I–II, 51, 4

10 A habit is like a second nature, and yet it falls short of it. And so it is that while the nature of a thing cannot in any way be taken away from a thing, a habit is removed, though with difficulty.

Aquinas, *Summa Theologica*, I–II, 53, 1

11 The destruction or diminution of a habit results through cessation from act, in so far, that is, as we cease from exercising an act which overcame the causes that destroyed or weakened that habit. For . . . habits are destroyed or diminished directly through some contrary agency. Consequently all habits that are gradually undermined by contrary agencies which need to be counteracted by acts proceeding from those habits are diminished or even destroyed altogether by long cessation from act, as is clearly seen in the case both of science and of virtue. For it is evident that a habit of moral virtue makes a man ready to choose the mean in deeds and passions. And when a man fails to make use of his virtuous habit in order to moderate his own passions or deeds, the necessary result is that many passions and deeds occur outside the mode of virtue, by reason of the inclination of the sensitive appetite and of other external agencies. Therefore virtue is destroyed or lessened through cessation from act.—The same applies to the intellectual habits, which render man ready to judge rightly of those things that are pictured by his imagination. Hence when man ceases to make use of his intellectual habits, strange fancies, sometimes in opposition to them, arise in his imagination, so that unless those fancies be, as it were, cut off or kept back by frequent use of his intellectual habits, man becomes less fit to judge rightly and sometimes is even wholly disposed to the contrary; and thus the intellectual habit is diminished or even wholly destroyed by cessation from act.

Aquinas, *Summa Theologica*, I–II, 53, 3

12 Virtue is a habit by which we work well.

Aquinas, *Summa Theologica*, I–II, 56, 3

13 Habit is a violent and treacherous schoolmistress. She establishes in us, little by little, stealthily, the foothold of her authority; but having by this mild and humble beginning settled and planted it with the help of time, she soon uncovers to us a furious and tyrannical face against which we no longer have the liberty of even raising our eyes. We see her at every turn forcing the rules of nature.

Montaigne, *Essays*, I, 23, Of Custom

14 I find that our greatest vices take shape from our tenderest childhood, and that our most important training is in the hands of nurses. It is a pastime for mothers to see a child wring the neck of a chicken or amuse itself by hurting a dog or a cat; and there are fathers stupid enough to take it as a good omen of a martial soul when they see a son unjustly striking a peasant or a lackey who is not defending himself, and as a charming prank when they see him trick his playmate by a bit of malicious dishonesty and deceit. Nevertheless these are the true seeds and roots of cruelty, tyranny, and treason; they sprout there, and afterward shoot up lustily, and flourish mightily in the hands of habit. And it is a very dangerous educational policy to excuse our children for these ugly inclinations on the grounds of their tender age and the triviality of the subject. In the first place, it is nature speaking, whose voice then is all the purer and stronger because it is more tenuous. Second, the ugliness of cheating does not depend on the difference between crown pieces and pins: it depends on itself. I find it much more just to come to this conclusion: "Why would he not cheat for crowns, since he cheats for pins?" than, as they do: "It is only for pins, he would never do it for crowns." Children must be carefully taught to hate vices for their own sake, and taught the natural deformity of vices, so that they will shun them not only in their actions but above all in their heart, so that the very thought of them may be odious, whatever mask they wear.

Montaigne, *Essays*, I, 23, Of Custom

15 Habituation puts to sleep the eye of our judgment.

Montaigne, *Essays*, I, 23, Of Custom

16 Habit is a second nature, and no less powerful. What my habit lacks, I hold that I lack. And I would almost as soon be deprived of life as have it reduced and cut down very far from the state in which I have lived it for so long.

Montaigne, *Essays*, III, 10, Of Husbanding
Your Will

17 *Hamlet.* Assume a virtue, if you have it not.
That monster, custom, who all sense doth eat,

Of habits devil, is angel yet in this,
That to the use of actions fair and good
He likewise gives a frock or livery,
That aptly is put on. Refrain to-night,
And that shall lend a kind of easiness
To the next abstinence; the next more easy;
For use almost can change the stamp of nature,
And either master the devil, or throw him out
With wondrous potency.

> Shakespeare, *Hamlet*, III, iv, 160

18 *Hamlet.* Has this fellow no feeling of his business, that he sings at grave-making?

Horatio. Custom hath made it in him a property of easiness.

Ham. 'Tis e'en so. The hand of little employment hath the daintier sense.

> Shakespeare, *Hamlet*, V, i, 73

19 Custom is most perfect when it beginneth in young years: this we call education; which is, in effect, but an early custom.

> Bacon, *Of Custom and Education*

20 Our senses, our appetites, and our passions, are our lawful and faithful guides in most things that relate solely to this life; and therefore, by the hourly necessity of consulting them, we gradually sink into an implicit submission and habitual confidence. Every act of compliance with their motions facilitates a second compliance, every new step towards depravity is made with less reluctance than the former, and thus the descent to life merely sensual is perpetually accelerated.

> Johnson, *Rambler No. 7*

21 Johnson observed, that the force of our early habits was so great, that though reason approved, nay, though our senses relished a different course, almost every man returned to them. I do not believe there is any observation upon human nature better founded than this; and, in many cases, it is a very painful truth; for where early habits have been mean and wretched, the joy and elevation resulting from better modes of life must be damped by the gloomy consciousness of being under an almost inevitable doom to sink back into a situation which we recollect with disgust. It surely may be prevented, by constant attention and unremitting exertion to establish contrary habits of superiour efficacy.

> Boswell, *Life of Johnson (Apr. 18, 1775)*

22 If habit is not a result of resolute and firm principles ever more and more purified, then, like any other mechanism of technically-practical reason, it is neither armed for all eventualities nor adequately secured against changes that may be brought about by new allurements.

> Kant, *Introduction to the Metaphysical Elements of Ethics*, II

23 The habitual practice of ethical living appears as a second nature which, put in the place of the initial, purely natural will, is the soul of custom permeating it through and through.

> Hegel, *Philosophy of Right*, 151

24 Habit is everything. Hence to be calm and unruffled is merely to anticipate a habit; and it is a great advantage not to need to form it.

> Schopenhauer, *Wisdom of Life: Aphorisms*

25 The force of character is cumulative. All the foregone days of virtue work their health into this.

> Emerson, *Self-Reliance*

26 That which is the result of habit affords no presumption of being intrinsically good.

> Mill, *Utilitarianism*, IV

27 Habit is habit, and not to be flung out of the window by any man, but coaxed downstairs a step at a time.

> Mark Twain, *Pudd'nhead Wilson's Calendar*, VI

28 Nothing so needs reforming as other people's habits.

> Mark Twain, *Pudd'nhead Wilson's Calendar*, XV

29 One will seldom go wrong if one attributes extreme actions to vanity, average ones to habit, and petty ones to fear.

> Nietzsche, *Human, All-Too-Human*, 74

30 Habit is . . . the enormous fly-wheel of society, its most precious conservative agent. It alone is what keeps us all within the bounds of ordinance, and saves the children of fortune from the envious uprisings of the poor. It alone prevents the hardest and most repulsive walks of life from being deserted by those brought up to tread them. It keeps the fisherman and the deck-hand at sea through the winter; it holds the miner in his darkness, and nails the countryman to his log-cabin and his lonely farm through all the months of snow; it protects us from invasion by the natives of the desert and the frozen zone. It dooms us all to fight out the battle of life upon the lines of our nurture or our early choice, and to make the best of a pursuit that disagrees, because there is no other for which we are fitted, and it is too late to begin again. It keeps different social strata from mixing. Already at the age of twenty-five you see the professional mannerism settling down on the young commercial traveller, on the young doctor, on the young minister, on the young counsellor-at-law. You see the little lines of cleavage running through the character, the tricks of thought, the prejudices, the ways of the "shop," in a word, from which the man can by-and-by no more es-

cape than his coat-sleeve can suddenly fall into a new set of folds. On the whole, it is best he should not escape. It is well for the world that in most of us, by the age of thirty, the character has set like plaster, and will never soften again.

William James, *Psychology,* IV

31 The physiological study of mental conditions is thus the most powerful ally of hortatory ethics. The hell to be endured hereafter, of which theology tells, is no worse than the hell we make for ourselves in this world by habitually fashioning our characters in the wrong way. Could the young but realize how soon they will become mere walking bundles of habits, they would give more heed to their conduct while in the plastic state. We are spinning our own fates, good or evil, and never to be undone. Every smallest stroke of virtue or of vice leaves its never so little scar. The drunken Rip Van Winkle, in Jefferson's play, excuses himself for every fresh dereliction by saying, "I won't count this time!" Well! he may not count it, and a kind Heaven may not count it; but it is being counted none the less. Down among his nerve-cells and fibres the molecules are counting it, registering and storing it up to be used against him when the next temptation comes. Nothing we ever do is, in strict scientific literalness, wiped out. Of course, this has its good side as well as its bad one. As we become permanent drunkards by so many separate drinks, so we become saints in the moral, and authorities and experts in the practical and scientific spheres, by so many separate acts and hours of work. Let no youth have any anxiety about the upshot of his education, whatever the line of it may be. If he keep faithfully busy each hour of the working-day, he may safely leave the final result to itself. He can with perfect certainty count on waking up some fine morning, to find himself one of the competent ones of his generation, in whatever pursuit he may have singled out. Silently, between all the details of his business, the *power of judging* in all that class of matter will have built itself up within him as a possession that will never pass away. Young people should know this truth in advance. The ignorance of it has probably engendered more discouragement and faint-heartedness in youths embarking on arduous careers than all other causes put together.

William James, *Psychology,* IV

32 We may say that an "instinctive" movement is a vital movement performed by an animal the first time that it finds itself in a novel situation; or, more correctly, one which it would perform if the situation were novel. . . .

On the other hand, a movement is "learnt," or embodies a "habit," if it is due to previous experience of similar situations, and is not what it would be if the animal had had no such experience.

Russell, *The Analysis of Mind,* II

33 The basic characteristic of habit is that every experience enacted and undergone modifies the one who acts and undergoes, while this modification affects, whether we wish it or not, the quality of subsequent experiences. For it is a somewhat different person who enters into them. The principle of habit so understood obviously goes deeper than the ordinary conception of *a* habit as a more or less fixed way of doing things, although it includes the latter as one of its special cases. It covers the formation of attitudes, attitudes that are emotional and intellectual; it covers our basic sensitivities and ways of meeting and responding to all the conditions which we meet in living.

Dewey, *Experience and Education,* III

34 It is a significant fact that in order to appreciate the peculiar place of habit in activity we have to betake ourselves to bad habits, foolish idling, gambling, addiction to liquor and drugs. When we think of such habits, the union of habit with desire and with propulsive power is forced upon us. When we think of habits in terms of walking, playing a musical instrument, typewriting, we are much given to thinking of habits as technical abilities existing apart from our likings and as lacking in urgent impulsion. We think of them as passive tools waiting to be called into action from without. A bad habit suggests an inherent tendency to action and also a hold, command over us. It makes us do things we are ashamed of, things which we tell ourselves we prefer not to do. It overrides our formal resolutions, our conscious decisions. When we are honest with ourselves we acknowledge that a habit has this power because it is so intimately a part of ourselves. It has a hold upon us because we are the habit.

Dewey, *Human Nature and Conduct,* I, 2

8.3 | *The Arts of Teaching and Learning*

The Greek sophists, we are told, were the first professional teachers, who performed their services for pay. In replying to his accusers at his trial, Socrates called attention to the fact that he never took money for the kind of teaching he did. Yet many of the passages quoted here and in other sections from the dialogues of Plato not only exhibit Socrates as an extraordinary teacher, but also expound his conception of teaching itself. Perhaps the most illuminating passage on the subject is the one in which Socrates compares himself to a midwife who does nothing more than help the mother give birth to offspring. So the teacher helps anyone wishing to learn give birth to ideas. The primary activity is in the learner, not the teacher, as it is in the mother, not the midwife.

There are other passages in which education and medicine, or teaching and healing, are compared. They are said to be alike in being arts that cooperate with living nature rather than make products by transforming inert matter. Human beings have a natural aptitude for acquiring knowledge and health without the help of teachers and physicians, though those who have skill in teaching or healing can facilitate the natural process.

One of the puzzling questions touched on by several of the writers quoted here is whether anything that one person can teach another must itself have been learned by someone without the aid of a teacher. From an affirmative answer spring controlling insights about the institutions, methods, and resources of education.

Another puzzling question is whether, or to what extent, coercion or punishment should be employed by the teacher in instructing his pupils. On the one hand, it is asserted that things learned under duress are not really learned, or at least not retained. On the other hand, it is pointed out that some kind of discipline must be maintained by the teacher if he is to do his job effectively.

Finally, on the side of learning itself, there is the fundamental distinction proposed by Aquinas—that between learning by instruction (i.e., with the aid of teachers) and learning by discovery (i.e., without the aid of teachers). But if, as other passages in this section suggest, the teacher is always only an instrumental, and never the principal, cause of learning, then perhaps all genuine learning is learning by discovery, involving intense activity on the part of the learner, whether such discovery is accomplished with the instrumentality of teachers or not.

---

1 Whoever is to acquire a competent knowledge of medicine, ought to be possessed of the following advantages: a natural disposition; instruction; a favorable position for the study; early tuition; love of labor; leisure. First of all, a natural talent is required; for, when Nature opposes, everything else is in vain; but when Nature leads the way to what is most excellent, instruction in the art takes place, which the student must try to appropriate to himself by reflection, becoming an early pupil in a place well adapted for instruction. He must also bring to the task a love of labor and perseverance, so that the instruction taking root may bring forth proper and abundant fruits.

Hippocrates, *The Law,* 2

2 Instruction . . . is like the culture of the productions of the earth. For our natural disposition is, as it were, the soil; the tenets of our teacher are, as it were, the seed; instruction in youth is like the

planting of the seed in the ground at the proper season; the place where the instruction is communicated is like the food imparted to vegetables by the atmosphere; diligent study is like the cultivation of the fields; and it is time which imparts strength to all things and brings them to maturity.

Hippocrates, *The Law,* 3

3 *Socrates.* We are enquiring, which of us is skilful or successful in the treatment of the soul, and which of us has had good teachers?

Laches. Well but, Socrates; did you never observe that some persons, who have had no teachers, are more skilful than those who have, in some things?

Soc. Yes, Laches, I have observed that; but you would not be very willing to trust them if they only professed to be masters of their art, unless they could show some proof of their skill or excellence in one or more works.

La. That is true.

Soc. And therefore, Laches and Nicias, as Lysimachus and Melesias, in their anxiety to improve the minds of their sons, have asked our advice about them, we too should tell them who our teachers were, if we say that we have had any, and prove them to be in the first place men of merit and experienced trainers of the minds of youth and also to have been really our teachers. Or if any of us says that he has no teacher, but that he has works of his own to show; then he should point out to them what Athenians or strangers, bond or free, he is generally acknowledged to have improved. But if he can show neither teachers nor works, then he should tell them to look out for others; and not run the risk of spoiling the children of friends, and thereby incurring the most formidable accusation which can be brought against any one by those nearest to him. As for myself, . . . I am the first to confess that I have never had a teacher of the art of virtue; although I have always from my earliest youth desired to have one. But I am too poor to give money to the Sophists, who are the only professors of moral improvement; and to this day I have never been able to discover the art myself, though I should not be surprised if Nicias or Laches may have discovered or learned it; for they are far wealthier than I am, and may therefore have learnt of others. And they are older too; so that they have had more time to make the discovery. And I really believe that they are able to educate a man; for unless they had been confident in their own knowledge, they would never have spoken thus decidedly of the pursuits which are advantageous or hurtful to a young man.

Plato, *Laches,* 185B

4 *Socrates.* Is not a Sophist, Hippocrates, one who deals wholesale or retail in the food of the soul? To me that appears to be his nature.

Hippocrates. And what, Socrates, is the food of the soul?

Surely, . . . knowledge is the food of the soul; and we must take care, my friend, that the Sophist does not deceive us when he praises what he sells, like the dealers wholesale or retail who sell the food of the body; for they praise indiscriminately all their goods, without knowing what are really beneficial or hurtful: neither do their customers know, with the exception of any trainer or physician who may happen to buy of them. In like manner those who carry about the wares of knowledge, and make the round of the cities, and sell or retail them to any customer who is in want of them, praise them all alike; though I should not wonder, O my friend, if many of them were really ignorant of their effect upon the soul; and their customers equally ignorant, unless he who buys of them happens to be a physician of the soul. If, therefore, you have understanding of what is good and evil, you may safely buy knowledge of Protagoras or of any one; but if not, then, O my friend, pause, and do not hazard your dearest interests at a game of chance. For there is far greater peril in buying knowledge than in buying meat and drink: the one you purchase of the wholesale or retail dealer, and carry them away in other vessels, and before you receive them into the body as food, you may deposit them at home and call in any experienced friend who knows what is good to be eaten or drunken, and what not, and how much, and when; and then the danger of purchasing them is not so great. But you cannot buy the wares of knowledge and carry them away in another vessel; when you have paid for them you must receive them into the soul and go your way, either greatly harmed or greatly benefited; and therefore we should deliberate and take counsel with our elders; for we are still young—too young to determine such a matter.

Plato, *Protagoras,* 313B

5 *Meno.* How will you enquire, Socrates, into that which you do not know? What will you put forth as the subject of enquiry? And if you find what you want, how will you ever know that this is the thing which you did not know?

Socrates. I know, Meno, what you mean; but just see what a tiresome dispute you are introducing. You argue that a man cannot enquire either about that which he knows, or about that which he does not know; for if he knows, he has no need to enquire; and if not, he cannot; for he does not know the very subject about which he is to enquire.

Men. Well, Socrates, and is not the argument sound?

Soc. I think not.

Men. Why not?

Soc. I will tell you why: I have heard from certain wise men and women who spoke of things divine that—

Men. What did they say?

Soc. They spoke of a glorious truth, as I conceive.

Men. What was it? and who were they?

Soc. Some of them were priests and priestesses, who had studied how they might be able to give a reason of their profession: there have been poets also, who spoke of these things by inspiration, like Pindar, and many others who were inspired. And they say . . . that the soul of man is immortal, and at one time has an end, which is termed dying, and at another time is born again, but is never destroyed. . . . The soul, then, as being immortal, and having been born again many times, and having seen all things that exist, whether in this world or in the world below, has knowledge of them all; and it is no wonder that she should be able to call to remembrance all that she ever knew about virtue, and about everything; for as all nature is akin, and the soul has learned all things, there is no difficulty in her eliciting or as men say learning, out of a single recollection all the rest, if a man is strenuous and does not faint; for all enquiry and all learning is but recollection. And therefore we ought not to listen to this sophistical argument about the impossibility of enquiry: for it will make us idle, and is sweet only to the sluggard; but the other saying will make us active and inquisitive.

Plato, *Meno,* 80B

6 *Socrates.* As little foundation is there for the report that I am a teacher, and take money; this accusation has no more truth in it than the other. Although, if a man were really able to instruct mankind, to receive money for giving instruction would, in my opinion, be an honour to him.

Plato, *Apology,* 19B

7 *Socrates.* The power and capacity of learning exists in the soul already; and . . . just as the eye was unable to turn from darkness to light without the whole body, so too the instrument of knowledge can only by the movement of the whole soul be turned from the world of becoming into that of being, and learn by degrees to endure the sight of being, and of the brightest and best of being, or in other words, of the good.

Plato, *Republic,* VII, 518B

8 *Socrates.* Such are the midwives, whose task is a very important one, but not so important as mine; for women do not bring into the world at one time real children, and at another time counterfeits which are with difficulty distinguished from them; if they did, then the discernment of the true and false birth would be the crowning achievement of the art of midwifery—you would think so?

Theaetetus. Indeed I should.

Soc. Well, my art of midwifery is in most respects like theirs; but differs, in that I attend men and not women, and I look after their souls when they are in labour, and not after their bodies: and the triumph of my art is in thoroughly examining whether the thought which the mind of the young man brings forth is a false idol or a noble and true birth. And like the midwives, I am barren, and the reproach which is often made against me, that I ask questions of others and have not the wit to answer them myself, is very just—the reason is, that the god compels me to be a midwife, but does not allow me to bring forth. And therefore I am not myself at all wise, nor have I anything to show which is the invention or birth of my own soul, but those who converse with me profit. Some of them appear dull enough at first, but afterwards, as our acquaintance ripens, if the god is gracious to them, they all make astonishing progress; and this in the opinion of others as well as in their own. It is quite clear that they never learned anything from me; the many fine discoveries to which they cling are of their own making. But to me and the god they owe their delivery. And the proof of my words is, that many of them in their ignorance, either in their self-conceit despising me, or falling under the influence of others, have gone away too soon; and have not only lost the children of whom I had previously delivered them by an ill bringing up, but have stifled whatever else they had in them by evil communications, being fonder of lies and shams than of the truth; and they have at last ended by seeing themselves, as others see them, to be great fools.

Plato, *Theaetetus,* 150A

9 I imagine there is nothing to prevent a man in one sense knowing what he is learning, in another not knowing it. The strange thing would be, not if in some sense he knew what he was learning, but if he were to know it in that precise sense and manner in which he was learning it.

Aristotle, *Posterior Analytics,* 71^{b}6

10 In general it is a sign of the man who knows and of the man who does not know, that the former can teach, and therefore we think art more truly knowledge than experience is; for artists can teach, and men of mere experience cannot.

Aristotle, *Metaphysics,* 981^{b}7

11 Learning proceeds for all in this way—through that which is less knowable by nature to that which is more knowable; and just as in conduct our task is to start from what is good for each and make what is without qualification good good for each, so it is our task to start from what is more knowable to oneself and make what is knowable by nature knowable to oneself. Now what is knowable and primary for particular sets of people is often knowable to a very small extent, and has little or nothing of reality. But yet one must start

from that which is barely knowable but knowable to oneself, and try to know what is knowable without qualification, passing, as has been said, by way of those very things which one does know.

Aristotle, *Metaphysics*, 1029^{b}4

12 The pleasures arising from thinking and learning will make us think and learn all the more.

Aristotle, *Ethics*, 1153^{a}22

13 The authority wielded by teachers is often a real hindrance to those who want to learn. Students fail to use their own judgment and rely on the opinions of their master to settle issues.

Cicero, *De Natura Deorum*, I, 5

14 Whosoever heareth these sayings of mine, and doeth them, I will liken him unto a wise man, which built his house upon a rock:

And the rain descended, and the floods came, and the winds blew, and beat upon that house; and it fell not: for it was founded upon a rock.

And every one that heareth these sayings of mine, and doeth them not, shall be likened unto a foolish man, which built his house upon the sand:

And the rain descended, and the floods came, and the winds blew, and beat upon that house; and it fell: and great was the fall of it.

And it came to pass, when Jesus had ended these sayings, the people were astonished at his doctrine:

For he taught them as one having authority, and not as the scribes.

Matthew 7:24–29

15 In education, it is most important to take care that the child does not come to despise working at lessons for which he has as yet developed no real appreciation. For then he will continue to dread them well beyond the years of childhood. Make his lessons an amusement for him. Question him on them and praise him for his work. Let him never be made to feel that he does not know a thing. Sometimes, if he is unwilling to learn, teach someone else first, and he may become envious. Let him be occasionally competitive and allow him to feel successful in his attainments. Appeal to his abilities by offering rewards that are attractive to him.

Quintilian, *Institutio Oratoria*, I, 1

16 Would that we ourselves did not corrupt the morals of our children. We enervate their very infancy with luxuries. That delicacy of education which we call fondness, weakens all their powers, both of body and mind. What luxury will he not covet in his manhood, who has crawled about on purple as a child. He cannot yet articulate his first words, when he can already distinguish scarlet and wants his purple finery. We prompt the palate of the child to develop fine tastes, before we teach him to speak. Our children grow up riding in sedan chairs. If they touch the ground, they cling to the hands of attendants who support them on each side. We are delighted if they utter something immodest. Expressions which would not even be tolerated from the effeminate youths of Alexandria, we hear from our own young people with a smile and a kiss. And this is hardly amazing, for we are the ones who have taught them. They have heard such language from ourselves. They see our mistresses and our male objects of affection. Every banquet hall rings with impure songs. Things that are shameful to talk about are on public display. From such practices spring habit, and out of habit character is formed. The unfortunate children learn these vices before they know that they are vices. Thus they are made effeminate and luxury-loving. They do not imbibe immorality from the schools; they carry it to school with them.

Quintilian, *Institutio Oratoria*, I, 2

17 There is nothing to prevent a "one pupil-one teacher" relationship from being put into practice in the classroom. But even if this situation cannot be developed in school, I still prefer the daylight of a good school to the dark solitude of a private education. Every eminent teacher delights in having a large number of pupils, and he thinks himself worthy of an even larger hearing than he gets. But inferior teachers are conscious of their lack of ability and do not hesitate to fasten themselves on single pupils if they can get them. But they amount to nothing more than pedant-babysitters.

Quintilian, *Institutio Oratoria*, I, 2

18 A good schoolmaster should not encumber himself with a greater number of pupils than he can adequately handle. We also feel it vitally important that the teacher be a real friend to his pupils, so that he will turn his task from a performance of duty into a labor of love.

Quintilian, *Institutio Oratoria*, I, 2

19 Narrow-necked vessels reject a great deal of any liquid that is poured over them, but are filled up with whatever is gradually poured into them. Likewise, it is for us to ascertain how much the minds of boys can receive at any one time. What is too much for their minds to grasp will not enter at all, because their minds are not sufficiently expanded to accept it. It is a real advantage for any boy to have classmates whom he may imitate, and eventually surpass. By this means he will gradually come to hope to reach higher excellence.

Quintilian, *Institutio Oratoria*, I, 2

20 I do not believe that boys should have to suffer corporal punishment, even though it has long been an accepted custom. First of all, it is a disgrace and a punishment fit for slaves, and (if you can imagine it being inflicted at a later age) an

affront. Secondly, if a boy's disposition is so abject that he cannot be corrected by reproof, he is only likely to be hardened, as a slave would be, by a whipping. And lastly, if the teacher really knows how to be a disciplinarian, there will not be the least need of any such chastisement. There currently seems to be so much negligence among teachers, that boys are not obliged to do what is right, yet they are punished whenever they have not done it. But consider, after you have coerced a boy with punishment, how will you treat him when he has become a young man to whom a threat of such punishment is meaningless, but whose studies are even more difficult? On top of all this, you realize that many unpleasant things often happen to boys as they are punished, things which they later recall with shame. Such shame depresses and enervates the mind, makes them shun other people, and feel constantly uneasy. Moreover, if there has been too little care taken in choosing teachers and tutors of reputable character, I am ashamed to mention how scandalously unworthy men may abuse their privilege of inflicting punishment, as well as what opportunities may be offered to others in the terrors of unhappy children.

Quintilian, *Institutio Oratoria*, I, 3

21 Looking upon the instruction and tuition of his youth to be of greater difficulty and importance than to be wholly trusted to the ordinary masters in music and poetry, and the common school subjects . . . he [Philip] sent for Aristotle, the most learned and most celebrated philosopher of his time, and rewarded him with a munificence proportionable to and becoming the care he took to instruct his son. For he repeopled his native city Stagira, which he had caused to be demolished a little before, and restored all the citizens, who were in exile or slavery, to their habitations.

As a place for the pursuit of their studies and exercise, he assigned the temple of the Nymphs, near Mieza, where, to this very day, they show you Aristotle's stone seats, and the shady walks which he was wont to frequent.

It would appear that Alexander received from him not only his doctrines of morals and of politics, but also something of those more abstruse and profound theories which these philosophers, by the very names they gave them, professed to reserve for oral communications to the initiated, and did not allow many to become acquainted with. . . .

Doubtless also it was to Aristotle that he owed the inclination he had, not to the theory only, but likewise to the practice of the art of medicine. For when any of his friends were sick, he would often prescribe them their course of diet, and medicines proper to their disease, as we may find in his epistles. He was naturally a great lover of all kinds of learning and reading; and Onesicritus informs us

that he constantly laid Homer's *Iliad* according to the copy corrected by Aristotle, called the casket copy, with his dagger under his pillow, declaring that he esteemed it a perfect portable treasure of all military virtue and knowledge. . . .

For a while he loved and cherished Aristotle no less, as he was wont to say himself, than if he had been his father, giving this reason for it, that as he had received life from the one, so the other had taught him to live well. But afterwards, upon some mistrust of him, yet not so great as to make him do him any hurt, his familiarity and friendly kindness to him abated so much of its former force and affectionateness, as to make it evident he was alienated from him. However, his violent thirst after and passion for learning, which were once implanted, still grew up with him, and never decayed.

Plutarch, *Alexander*

22 The teachers we select for our children must live lives immune to scandal, be irreproachable in conduct, and conversant with respectable society. The fountain and root of gentlemanliness is the acquisition of traditional education.

Plutarch, *Education of Children*

23 The memorizing aspect of learning contributes no small share not only to education but also to the practical conduct of life, for the memory of past deeds provides examples in taking good counsel for the future.

Plutarch, *Education of Children*

24 Each schoolboy, in turn, gets up, and, standing, delivers
What he's just read sitting down, in the most monotonous singsong.
This is the kind of rehash that kills unfortunate masters.

Juvenal, *Satire VII*

25 It is no easy task to keep your eye on the students, Watching the hands and the eyes of the impudent mischievous devils.
"That's your job," they say, and your pay, at the end of a twelve-month,
Equals a jockey's fee if he's ridden only one winner.

Juvenal, *Satire VII*

26 Not even wisdom perhaps is enough to enable a man to take care of youths: a man must have also a certain readiness and fitness for this purpose, and a certain quality of body, and above all things he must have God to advise him to occupy this office, as God advised Socrates to occupy the place of one who confutes error, Diogenes the office of royalty and reproof, and the office of teaching precepts.

Epictetus, *Discourses*, III, 21

27 He whose purpose is to know anything better than the multitude do must far surpass all others both as regards his nature and his early training. And when he reaches early adolescence he must become possessed with an ardent love for truth, like one inspired; neither day nor night may he cease to urge and strain himself in order to learn thoroughly all that has been said by the most illustrious of the Ancients. And when he has learnt this, then for a prolonged period he must test and prove it, observing what part of it is in agreement, and what in disagreement with obvious fact; thus he will choose this and turn away from that.

Galen, *Natural Faculties,* III, 10

28 I disliked learning and hated to be forced to it. But I *was* forced to it, so that good was done to me though it was not my doing. Short of being driven to it, I certainly would not have learned. But no one does well against his will, even if the thing he does is a good thing to do.

Augustine, *Confessions,* I, 12

29 The drudgery of learning a foreign language sprinkled bitterness over all the sweetness of the Greek tales. I did not know a word of the language: and I was driven with threats and savage punishments to learn. There had been a time of infancy when I knew no Latin either. Yet I learnt it without threat or punishment merely by keeping my eyes and ears open, amidst the flatterings of nurses and the jesting and pleased laughter of elders leading me on. I learnt it without the painful pressure of compulsion, by the sole pressure of my own desire to express what was in my mind, which would have been impossible unless I had learnt words: and I learnt them not through people teaching me but simply through people speaking: to whom I was striving to utter my own feelings. All this goes to prove that free curiosity is of more value in learning than harsh discipline.

Augustine, *Confessions,* I, 14

30 It is the duty . . . of the interpreter and teacher of Holy Scripture, the defender of the true faith and the opponent of error, both to teach what is right and to refute what is wrong, and in the performance of this task to conciliate the hostile, to rouse the careless, and to tell the ignorant both what is occurring at present and what is probable in the future. But once that his hearers are friendly, attentive, and ready to learn, whether he has found them so, or has himself made them so, the remaining objects are to be carried out in whatever way the case requires. If the hearers need teaching, the matter treated of must be made fully known by means of narrative. On the other hand, to clear up points that are doubtful requires reasoning and the exhibition of proofs. If, however, the hearers require to be roused rather than instructed, in order that they may be diligent to do what they already know, and to bring their feelings into harmony with the truths they admit, greater vigour of speech is needed. Here entreaties and reproaches, exhortations and upbraidings, and all the other means of rousing the emotions, are necessary.

Augustine, *Christian Doctrine,* IV, 4

31 To strive about words is not to be careful about the way to overcome error by truth, but to be anxious that your mode of expression should be preferred to that of another. The man who does not strive about words, whether he speak quietly, temperately, or vehemently, uses words with no other purpose than to make the truth plain, pleasing, and effective.

Augustine, *Christian Doctrine,* IV, 28

32 Do teachers profess that it is their thoughts which are perceived and grasped by the students, and not the sciences themselves which they convey through speaking? For who is so stupidly curious as to send his son to school in order that he may learn what the teacher thinks? But all those sciences which they profess to teach, and the science of virtue itself and wisdom, teachers explain through words. Then those who are called pupils consider within themselves whether what has been explained has been said truly; looking of course to that interior truth, according to the measure of which each is able. Thus they learn, and when the interior truth makes known to them that true things have been said, they applaud, but without knowing that instead of applauding teachers they are applauding learners, if indeed their teachers know what they are saying. But men are mistaken, so that they call those teachers who are not, merely because for the most part there is no delay between the time of speaking and the time of cognition. And since after the speaker has reminded them, the pupils quickly learn within, they think that they have been taught outwardly by him who prompts them.

Augustine, *On the Teacher,* XIV

33 Progress in knowledge occurs in two ways. First, on the part of the teacher, be he one or many, who makes progress in knowledge as time goes on. And this is the kind of progress that takes place in sciences devised by man. Secondly, on the part of the learner; thus the master, who has perfect knowledge of the art, does not deliver it all at once to his disciple from the very outset, for he would not be able to take it all in, but he condescends to the disciple's capacity and instructs him little by little.

Aquinas, *Summa Theologica,* II–II, 1, 7

34 Since there is a twofold way of acquiring knowledge—by discovery and by being taught—the way of discovery is the higher, and the way of

being taught is secondary.

Aquinas, *Summa Theologica*, III, 9, 4

35 Certain seeds of knowledge pre-exist in us, namely, the first concepts of understanding, which by the light of the agent intellect are immediately known through the species abstracted from sensible things. These are either complex, as axioms, or simple, as the notions of being, of the one, and so on, which the understanding grasps immediately. In these general principles, however, all the consequences are included as in certain seminal principles. When, therefore, the mind is led from these general notions to actual knowledge of the particular things, which it knew previously in general and, as it were, potentially, then one is said to acquire knowledge.

We must bear in mind, nevertheless, that in natural things something can pre-exist in potency in two ways. In one, it is in an active and completed potency, as when an intrinsic principle has sufficient power to flow into perfect act. Healing is an obvious example of this, for the sick person is restored to health by the natural power within him. The other appears in a passive potency, as happens when the internal principle does not have sufficient power to bring it into act. This is clear when air becomes fire, for this cannot result from any power existing in the air.

Therefore, when something pre-exists in active completed potency, the external agent acts only by helping the internal agent and providing it with the means by which it can enter into act. Thus, in healing the doctor assists nature, which is the principal agent, by strengthening nature and prescribing medicines, which nature uses as instruments for healing. On the other hand, when something pre-exists only in passive potency, then it is the external agent which is the principal cause of the transition from potency to act. Thus, fire makes actual fire of air, which is potentially fire.

Knowledge, therefore, pre-exists in the learner potentially, not, however, in the purely passive, but in the active, sense. Otherwise, man would not be able to acquire knowledge independently. Therefore, as there are two ways of being cured, that is, either through the activity of unaided nature or by nature with the aid of medicine, so also there are two ways of acquiring knowledge. In one way, natural reason by itself reaches knowledge of unknown things, and this way is called *discovery;* in the other way, when someone else aids the learner's natural reason, and this is called *learning by instruction.*

Aquinas, *On Truth*, XI, 1

36 We do not say that a teacher communicates knowledge to the pupil, as though the knowledge which is in the teacher is numerically the same as that which arises in the pupil. It is rather that the knowledge which arises in the pupil through teaching is similar to that which is in the teacher.

Aquinas, *On Truth*, XI, 1

37 A doctor heals in so far as he has health, not actually, but in the knowledge of his art. But the teacher teaches in so far as he has knowledge actually. Hence, he who does not have health actually can cause health in himself because he has health in the knowledge of his art. However, it is impossible for one actually to have knowledge and not to have it, in such a way that he could teach himself.

Aquinas, *On Truth*, XI, 2

38 *Pantagruel.* Nature, I am persuaded, did not without a cause frame our ears open, putting thereto no gate at all, nor shutting them up with any manner of inclosures, as she hath done upon the tongue, the eyes, and other such out-jetting parts of the body. The cause as I imagine, is, to the end that every day and every night, and that continually, we may be ready to hear, and by a perpetual hearing apt to learn. For, of all the senses, it is the fittest for the reception of the knowledge of arts, sciences, and disciplines.

Rabelais, *Gargantua and Pantagruel*, III, 16

39 Our tutors never stop bawling into our ears, as though they were pouring water into a funnel; and our task is only to repeat what has been told us. I should like the tutor to correct this practice, and right from the start, according to the capacity of the mind he has in hand, to begin putting it through its paces, making it taste things, choose them, and discern them by itself; sometimes clearing the way for him, sometimes letting him clear his own way. I don't want him to think and talk alone, I want him to listen to his pupil speaking in his turn. Socrates, and later Arcesilaus, first had their disciples speak, and then they spoke to them. . . . It is good that he should have his pupil trot before him, to judge the child's pace and how much he must stoop to match his strength. For lack of this proportion we spoil everything; and to be able to hit it right and to go along in it evenly is one of the hardest tasks that I know; it is the achievement of a lofty and very strong soul to know how to come down to a childish gait and guide it.

Montaigne, *Essays,* I, 26, Education of Children

40 Let the tutor make his charge pass everything through a sieve and lodge nothing in his head on mere authority and trust.

Montaigne, *Essays,* I, 26, Education of Children

41 To know by heart is not to know; it is to retain what we have given our memory to keep. What

we know rightly we dispose of, without looking at the model, without turning our eyes toward our book. Sad competence, a purely bookish competence!

Montaigne, *Essays,* I, 26, Education of Children

42 I condemn all violence in the education of a tender soul which is being trained for honor and liberty. There is a sort of servility about rigor and constraint; and I hold that what cannot be done by reason, and by wisdom and tact, is never done by force.

Montaigne, *Essays,* II, 8, Affection of Fathers

43 There is still more intelligence needed to teach others than to be taught.

Montaigne, *Essays,* II, 12, Apology for Raymond Sebond

44 The study of books is a languishing and feeble activity that gives no heat, whereas discussion teaches and exercises us at the same time.

Montaigne, *Essays,* III, 8, Of the Art of Discussion

45 As regards the academies, they are established in order to regulate the studies of the pupils and are concerned not to have the program of teaching change very often: in such places, because it is a question of the progress of the students, it frequently happens that the things which have to be chosen are not those which are most true but those which are most easy.

Kepler, *Epitome of Copernican Astronomy,* IV, To the Reader

46 *Portia.* It is a good divine that follows his own instructions: I can easier teach twenty what were good to be done, than be one of the twenty to follow mine own teaching.

Shakespeare, *Merchant of Venice,* I, ii, 15

47 Disciples do owe unto masters only a temporary belief and a suspension of their own judgement till they be fully instructed, and not an absolute resignation or perpetual captivity.

Bacon, *Advancement of Learning,* Bk. I, IV, 12

48 There is no defect in the faculties intellectual, but seemeth to have a proper cure contained in some studies: as, for example, if a child be bird-witted, that is, hath not the faculty of attention, the mathematics giveth a remedy thereunto; for in them, if the wit be caught away but a moment, one is new to begin. And as sciences have a propriety towards faculties for cure and help, so faculties or powers have a sympathy towards sciences for excellency or speedy profiting: and therefore it is an inquiry of great wisdom, what kinds of wits

and natures are most apt and proper for what sciences.

Bacon, *Advancement of Learning,* Bk. II, XIX, 2

49 Practise all things chiefly at two several times, the one when the mind is best disposed, the other when it is worst disposed; that by the one you may gain a great step, by the other you may work out the knots and stonds of the mind, and make the middle times the more easy and pleasant.

Bacon, *Advancement of Learning,* Bk. II, XXII, 10

50 But all animals which along with memory have the faculty of hearing are susceptible of education. Other creatures, again, live possessed of fancy and memory, but they have little store of experience; the human kind, however, have both art and reasoning. Now experience comes to man through memory; for many memories of the same thing have the force of a single experience: so that experience appears to be almost identical with certain kinds of art and science; and, indeed, men acquire both art and science by experience: for experience, as Polus rightly remarks, begets art, inexperience is waited on by accident.

By this he plainly tells us that no one can truly be entitled discreet or well-informed, who does not of his own experience, *i.e.,* from repeated memory, frequent perception by sense, and diligent observation, know that a thing is so in fact. Without these, indeed, we only imagine or believe, and such knowledge is rather to be accounted as belonging to others than to us. The method of investigating truth commonly pursued at this time, therefore, is to be held as erroneous and almost foolish, in which so many inquire what others have said, and omit to ask whether the things themselves be actually so or not; and single universal conclusions being deduced from several premises, and analogies being thence shaped out, we have frequently mere verisimilitudes handed down to us instead of positive truths.

William Harvey, *Animal Generation,* Intro.

51 When we wish to correct with advantage and to show another that he errs, we must notice from what side he views the matter, for on that side it is usually true, and admit that truth to him, but reveal to him the side on which it is false. He is satisfied with that, for he sees that he was not mistaken and that he only failed to see all sides. Now, no one is offended at not seeing everything; but one does not like to be mistaken, and that perhaps arises from the fact that man naturally cannot see everything, and that naturally he cannot err in the side he looks at, since the perceptions of our senses are always true.

Pascal, *Pensées,* I, 9

52 People are generally better persuaded by the reasons which they have themselves discovered than by those which have come into the mind of others.

Pascal, *Pensées,* I, 10

53 Discerning minds know how much difference there is between two similar remarks, depending upon the place and accompanying circumstances. Will anyone really believe that two persons who have read and learned by heart the same book know it equally well, if one understands it in such a way that he knows all its principles, the force of its conclusions, the replies to the objections that can be made, and the entire organization of the work, whereas in the other the book is dead words and seeds which, though the same as those that produced such fertile trees, have remained dry and unfruitful in the sterile mind which received them in vain?

Pascal, *Geometrical Demonstration*

54 The usual lazy and short way by chastisement and the rod, which is the only instrument of government that tutors generally know or ever think of, is the most unfit of any to be used in education.

Locke, *Some Thoughts Concerning Education,* 47

55 *Esteem* and *disgrace* are, of all others, the most powerful incentives to the mind, when once it is brought to relish them,. If you can once get into children a love of credit, and an apprehension of shame and disgrace, you have put into 'em the true principle, which will constantly work and incline them to the right.

Locke, *Some Thoughts Concerning Education,* 56

56 Children are not to be taught by rules which will be always slipping out of their memories. What you think necessary for them to do, settle in them by an indispensable practice, as often as the occasion returns; and if it be possible, make occasions. This will beget habits in them which being once established, operate of themselves easily and naturally, without the assistance of the memory.

Locke, *Some Thoughts Concerning Education,* 66

57 God has stamped certain characters upon men's minds, which like their shapes, may perhaps be a little mended, but can hardly be totally altered and transformed into the contrary. He therefore that is about children should well study their natures and aptitudes, and see by often trials what turn they easily take, and what becomes them; observe what their native stock is, how it may be improved, and what it is fit for: he should consider what they want, whether they be capable of having it wrought into them by industry, and incorporated there by practice; and whether it be worth while to endeavor it. For in many cases, all that we can do, or should aim at, is to make the best of what nature has given, to prevent the vices and faults to which such a constitution is most inclined, and give it all the advantages it is capable of. Everyone's natural genius should be carried as far as it could; but to attempt the putting another upon him will be but labor in vain; and what is so plastered on will at best sit but untowardly, and have always hanging to it the ungracefulness of constraint and affectation.

Locke, *Some Thoughts Concerning Education,* 66

58 Of all the ways whereby children are to be instructed, and their manners formed, the plainest, easiest, and most efficacious, is to set before their eyes the examples of those things you would have them do or avoid; which, when they are pointed out to them, in the practice of persons within their knowledge, with some reflections on their beauty and unbecomingness, are of more force to draw or deter their imitation than any discourses which can be made to them. Virtues and vices can by no words be so plainly set before their understandings as the actions of other men will show them, when you direct their observation, and bid them view this or that good or bad quality in their practice. And the beauty or uncomeliness of many things, in good and ill breeding, will be better learnt and make deeper impressions on them, in the examples of others, than from any rules or instructions can be given about them.

Locke, *Some Thoughts Concerning Education,* 82

59 As the father's example must teach the child respect for his tutor, so the tutor's example must lead the child into those actions he would have him do. His practice must by no means cross his precepts, unless he intend to set him wrong. It will be to no purpose for the tutor to talk of the restraint of the passions whilst any of his own are let loose; and he will in vain endeavor to reform any vice or indecency in his pupil which he allows in himself.

Locke, *Some Thoughts Concerning Education,* 89

60 In all the whole business of education, there is nothing like to be less hearkened to, or harder to be well observed, than what I am now going to say; and that is, that children should, from their first beginning to talk, have some discreet, sober, nay, wise person about them, whose care it should be to fashion them aright, and keep them from all ill, especially the infection of bad company. I think this province requires great sobriety, temperance, tenderness, diligence, and discretion; qualities hardly to be found united in persons that are to be had for ordinary salaries, nor easily to be found anywhere.

Locke, *Some Thoughts Concerning Education,* 90

61 The great skill of a teacher is to get and keep the attention of his scholar; whilst he has that, he is sure to advance as fast as the learner's abilities

will carry him; and without that, all his bustle and pother will be to little or no purpose. To attain this, he should make the child comprehend, as much as may be, the usefulness of what he teaches him, and let him see, by what he has learned, that he can do something which he could not do before; something which gives him some power and real advantage above others who are ignorant of it. To this he should add sweetness in all his instructions, and by a certain tenderness in his whole carriage make the child sensible that he loves him and designs nothing but his good, the only way to beget love in the child, which will make him hearken to his lessons, and relish what he teaches him.

Locke, *Some Thoughts Concerning Education,* 167

62 There are a thousand unnoticed openings, continued my father, which let a penetrating eye at once into a man's soul; and I maintain it, added he, that a man of sense does not lay down his hat in coming into a room,—or take it up in going out of it, but something escapes, which discovers him.

It is for these reasons, continued my father, that the governor I make choice of shall neither lisp, or squint, or wink, or talk loud, or look fierce, or foolish;—or bite his lips, or grind his teeth, or speak through his nose, or pick it, or blow it with his fingers.——

He shall neither walk fast,—or slow, or fold his arms,—for that is laziness;—or hang them down,—for that is folly; or hide them in his pocket, for that is nonsense.—

He shall neither strike, or pinch, or tickle,—or bite, or cut his nails, or hawk, or spit, or snift, or drum with his feet or fingers in company;—nor (according to Erasmus) shall he speak to any one in making water,—nor shall he point to carrion or excrement.——Now this is all nonsense again, quoth my uncle Toby to himself.——

I will have him, continued my father, cheerful, faceté, jovial; at the same time, prudent, attentive to business, vigilant, acute, argute, inventive, quick in resolving doubts and speculative questions;—he shall be wise, and judicious, and learned:—And why not humble, and moderate, and gentle-tempered, and good? said Yorick:—And why not, cried my uncle Toby, free, and generous, and bountiful, and brave?——He shall, my dear Toby, replied my father, getting up and shaking him by his hand.

Sterne, *Tristram Shandy,* VI, 5

63 Contrary to the received opinion, a child's tutor should be young, as young indeed as a man may well be who is also wise. Were it possible, he should become a child himself, that he may be the companion of his pupil and win his confidence by sharing his games.

Rousseau, *Emile,* I

64 It is very strange that ever since people began to think about education they should have hit upon no other way of guiding children than emulation, jealousy, envy, vanity, greediness, base cowardice, all the most dangerous passions, passions ever ready to ferment, ever prepared to corrupt the soul even before the body is full-grown. With every piece of precocious instruction which you try to force into their minds you plant a vice in the depths of their hearts; foolish teachers think they are doing wonders when they are making their scholars wicked in order to teach them what goodness is, and then they tell us seriously, "Such is man." Yes, such is man, as you have made him.

Rousseau, *Emile,* II

65 In the country of the blind the one-eyed are kings; I passed for a good master, since all the rest were bad.

Rousseau, *Confessions,* V

66 Johnson, upon all occasions, expressed his approbation of enforcing instructions by means of the rod. "I would rather (said he) have the rod to be the general terrour to all, to make them learn, than tell a child, if you do thus, or thus, you will be more esteemed than your brothers or sisters. The rod produces an effect which terminates in itself. A child is afraid of being whipped, and gets his task, and there's an end on't; whereas, by exciting emulation and comparisons of superiority, you lay the foundation of lasting mischief; you make brothers and sisters hate each other."

Boswell, *Life of Johnson* (1719)

67 *Johnson.* "In my early years I read very hard. It is a sad reflection, but a true one, that I knew almost as much at eighteen as I do now. My judgement, to be sure, was not so good; but I had all the facts. I remember very well, when I was at Oxford, an old gentleman said to me, 'Young man, ply your book diligently now, and acquire a stock of knowledge; for when years come upon you, you will find that poring upon books will be but an irksome task.' "

Boswell, *Life of Johnson* (July 21, 1763)

68 We talked of the education of children; and I asked him what he thought was best to teach them first. *Johnson.* "Sir, it is no matter what you teach them first, any more than what leg you shall put into your breeches first. Sir, you may stand disputing which is best to put in first, but in the mean time your breech is bare. Sir, while you are considering which of two things you should teach your child first, another boy has learnt them both."

Boswell, *Life of Johnson* (July 26, 1763)

69 *Johnson.* The government of a schoolmaster is somewhat of the nature of military government;

that is to say, it must be arbitrary, it must be exercised by the will of one man, according to particular circumstances. You must shew some learning upon this occasion. You must shew, that a schoolmaster has a prescriptive right to beat; and that an action of assault and battery cannot be admitted against him, unless there is some great excess, some barbarity. This man has maimed none of his boys. They are all left with the full exercise of their corporeal faculties. In our schools in England, many boys have been maimed; yet I never heard of an action against a schoolmaster on that account. Puffendorf, I think, maintains the right of a schoolmaster to beat his scholars.

Boswell, *Life of Johnson* (Mar. 23, 1772)

70 On Saturday, April 11, he [Johnson] appointed me to come to him in the evening, when he should be at leisure to give me some assistance for the defence of Hastie, the schoolmaster of Campbelltown, for whom I was to appear in the House of Lords. When I came, I found him unwilling to exert himself. I pressed him to write down his thoughts upon the subject. He said, "There's no occasion for my writing. I'll talk to you." He was, however, at last prevailed on to dictate to me, while I wrote as follows:

"The charge is, that he has used immoderate and cruel correction. Correction, in itself, is not cruel; children, being not reasonable, can be governed only by fear. To impress this fear, is therefore one of the first duties of those who have the care of children. It is the duty of a parent; and has never been thought inconsistent with parental tenderness. It is the duty of a master, who is in his highest exaltation when he is *loco parentis*. Yet, as good things become evil by excess, correction, by being immoderate, may become cruel. But when is correction immoderate? When it is more frequent or more severe than is required *ad monendum et docendum*, for reformation and instruction. No severity is cruel which obstinacy makes necessary; for the greatest cruelty would be to desist, and leave the scholar too careless for instruction, and too much hardened for reproof. Locke, in his treatise of Education, mentions a mother, with applause, who whipped an infant eight times before she had subdued it; for had she stopped at the seventh act of correction, her daughter, says he, would have been ruined. The degrees of obstinacy in young minds are very different; as different must be the degrees of persevering severity. A stubborn scholar must be corrected till he is subdued. The discipline of a school is military. There must be either unbounded licence or absolute authority. The master, who punishes, not only consults the future happiness of him who is the immediate subject of correction; but he propagates obedience through the whole school; and establishes regularity by exemplary justice. The victorious obstinacy of a single boy would make his future endeavours of reformation or instruction totally ineffectual. Obstinacy, therefore, must never be victorious. Yet, it is well known, that there sometimes occurs a sullen and hardy resolution, that laughs at all common punishment, and bids defiance to all common degrees of pain. Correction must be proportioned to occasions. The flexible will be reformed by gentle discipline, and the refractory must be subdued by harsher methods. The degrees of scholastick, as of military punishment, no stated rules can ascertain. It must be enforced till it overpowers temptation; till stubbornness becomes flexible, and perverseness regular."

Boswell, *Life of Johnson* (Apr. 11, 1772)

71 *Johnson.* A child should not be discouraged from reading any thing that he takes a liking to, from a notion that it is above his reach. If that be the case, the child will soon find it out and desist; if not, he of course gains the instruction; which is so much the more likely to come, from the inclination with which he takes up the study.

Boswell, *Life of Johnson* (1780)

72 It has been considered as of so much importance that a proper number of young people should be educated for certain professions, that sometimes the public and sometimes the piety of private founders have established many pensions, scholarships, exhibitions, bursaries, etc., for this purpose, which draw many more people into those trades than could otherwise pretend to follow them. In all Christian countries, I believe, the education of the greater part of churchmen is paid for in this manner. Very few of them are educated altogether at their own expense. The long, tedious, and expensive education, therefore, of those who are, will not always procure them a suitable reward, the church being crowded with people who, in order to get employment, are willing to accept of a much smaller recompense than what such an education would otherwise have entitled them to. . . .

[The greater part of] that unprosperous race of men commonly called men of letters are pretty much in the situation which lawyers and physicians probably would be in upon the foregoing supposition. In every part of Europe the greater part of them have been educated for the church, but have been hindered by different reasons from entering into holy orders. They have generally, therefore, been educated at the public expense, and their numbers are everywhere so great as commonly to reduce the price of their labour to a very paltry recompense.

Before the invention of the art of printing, the only employment by which a man of letters could make anything by his talents was that of a public or private teacher, or by communicating to other people the curious and useful knowledge which he had acquired himself: and this is still surely a more honourable, a more useful, and in general even a more profitable employment than that other of writing for a bookseller, to which the art of printing has given occasion. The time and study, the genius, knowledge, and application requisite to qualify an eminent teacher of the sciences, are at least equal to what is necessary for the greatest practitioners in law and physic. But the usual reward of the eminent teacher bears no proportion to that of the lawyer or physician; because the trade of the one is crowded with indigent people who have been brought up to it at the public expense; whereas those of the other two are encumbered with very few who have not been educated at their own. . . .

This inequality is upon the whole, perhaps, rather advantageous than hurtful to the public. It may somewhat degrade the profession of a public teacher; but the cheapness of literary education is surely an advantage which greatly overbalances this trifling inconveniency.

Adam Smith, *Wealth of Nations,* I, 10

73 In . . . [some] universities the teacher is prohibited from receiving any honorary or fee from his pupils, and his salary constitutes the whole of the revenue which he derives from his office. His interest is, in this case, set as directly in opposition to his duty as it is possible to set it. It is the interest of every man to live as much at his ease as he can; and if his emoluments are to be precisely the same, whether he does or does not perform some very laborious duty, it is certainly his interest, at least as interest is vulgarly understood, either to neglect it altogether, or, if he is subject to some authority which will not suffer him to do this, to perform it in as careless and slovenly a manner as that authority will permit. If he is naturally active and a lover of labour, it is his interest to employ that activity in any way from which he can derive some advantage, rather than in the performance of his duty, from which he can derive none.

If the authority to which he is subject resides in the body corporate, the college, or university, of which he himself is a member, and which the greater part of the other members are, like himself, persons who either are or ought to be teachers, they are likely to make a common cause, to be all very indulgent to one another, and every man to consent that his neighbour may neglect his duty, provided he himself is allowed to neglect his own. In the university of Oxford, the greater part of the public professors have, for these many years, given up altogether even the pretence of teaching.

Adam Smith, *Wealth of Nations,* V, 1

74 No discipline is ever requisite to force attendance upon lectures which are really worth the attending, as is well known wherever any such lectures are given. Force and restraint may, no doubt, be in some degree requisite in order to oblige children, or very young boys, to attend to those parts of education which it is thought necessary for them to acquire during that early period of life; but after twelve or thirteen years of age, provided the master does his duty, force or restraint can scarce ever be necessary to carry on any part of education. Such is the generosity of the greater part of young men, that, so far from being disposed to neglect or despise the instructions of their master, provided he shows some serious intention of being of use to them, they are generally inclined to pardon a great deal of incorrectness in the performance of his duty, and sometimes even to conceal from the public a good deal of gross negligence.

Adam Smith, *Wealth of Nations,* V, 1

75 In England it becomes every day more and more the custom to send young people to travel in foreign countries immediately upon their leaving school, and without sending them to any university. Our young people, it is said, generally return home much improved by their travels. A young man who goes abroad at seventeen or eighteen, and returns home at one and twenty, returns three or four years older than he was when he went abroad; and at that age it is very difficult not to improve a good deal in three or four years. In the course of his travels he generally acquires some knowledge of one or two foreign languages; a knowledge, however, which is seldom sufficient to enable him either to speak or write them with propriety. In other respects he commonly returns home more conceited, more unprincipled, more dissipated, and more incapable of any serious application either to study or to business than he could well have become in so short a time had he lived at home. By travelling so very young, by spending in the most frivolous dissipation the most precious years of his life, at a distance from the inspection and control of his parents and relations, every useful habit which the earlier parts of his education might have had some tendency to form in him, instead of being riveted and confirmed, is almost necessarily either weakened or effaced. Nothing but the discredit into which the universities are allowing themselves to fall could ever have brought into repute so very absurd a practice as that of travelling at this early period of life. By sending his son abroad, a father delivers himself at least for some time, from so disagreeable an object as that of a son unemployed, neglected, and going to ruin before his eyes.

Adam Smith, *Wealth of Nations,* V, 1

76 The power of instruction is seldom of much efficacy, except in those happy dispositions where it is almost superfluous.

Gibbon, *Decline and Fall of the Roman Empire,* IV

77 Although education may furnish, and, as it were, engraft upon a limited understanding rules borrowed from other minds, yet the power of employing these rules correctly must belong to the pupil himself; and no rule which we can prescribe to him with this purpose is, in the absence or deficiency of this gift of nature, secure from misuse. A physician therefore, a judge or a statesman, may have in his head many admirable pathological, juridical, or political rules, in a degree that may enable him to be a profound teacher in his particular science, and yet in the application of these rules he may very possibly blunder—either because he is wanting in natural judgement (though not in understanding) and, whilst he can comprehend the general *in abstracto,* cannot distinguish whether a particular case *in concreto* ought to rank under the former; or because his faculty of judgement has not been sufficiently exercised by examples and real practice. Indeed, the grand and only use of examples, is to sharpen the judgement. For as regards the correctness and precision of the insight of the understanding, examples are commonly injurious rather than otherwise, because, as *casus in terminis,* they seldom adequately fulfil the conditions of the rule. Besides, they often weaken the power of our understanding to apprehend rules or laws in their universality, independently of particular circumstances of experience; and hence, accustom us to employ them more as formulae than as principles. Examples are thus the go-cart of the judgement, which he who is naturally deficient in that faculty cannot afford to dispense with.

Kant, *Critique of Pure Reason,* Transcendental Analytic

78 It is not to the history of the science, or of the human mind, that we are to attend in an elementary treatise: our only aim ought to be ease and perspicuity and with the utmost care to keep everything out of view which might draw aside the attention of the student; it is a road which we should be continually rendering more smooth, and from which we should endeavour to remove every obstacle which can occasion delay.

Lavoisier, *Elements of Chemistry,* Pref.

79 Instead of developing the child's own faculties of discernment, and teaching it to judge and think for itself, the teacher uses all his energies to stuff its head full of the ready-made thoughts of other people.

Schopenhauer, *Education*

80 The fatal tendency to be satisfied with words instead of trying to understand things—to learn phrases by heart, so that they may prove a refuge in time of need—exists, as a rule, even in children; and the tendency lasts on into manhood, making the knowledge of many learned persons to consist in mere verbiage.

Schopenhauer, *Education*

81 The memory should be specially taxed in youth, since it is then that it is strongest and most tenacious. But in choosing the things that should be committed to memory the utmost care and forethought must be exercised; as lessons well learnt in youth are never forgotten.

Schopenhauer, *Education*

82 The Socratic dialectics, so magnificently exemplified in the dialogues of Plato, were a contrivance . . . [for making the difficulties of a question present to the learner's consciousness]. They were essentially a negative discussion of the great question of philosophy and life, directed with consummate skill to the purpose of convincing any one who had merely adopted the common-places of received opinion that he did not understand the subject—that he as yet attached no definite meaning to the doctrines he professed; in order that, becoming aware of his ignorance, he might be put in the way to obtain a stable belief, resting on a clear apprehension both of the meaning of doctrines and of their evidence. The school disputations of the Middle Ages had a somewhat similar object. They were intended to make sure that the pupil understood his own opinion, and (by necessary correlation) the opinion opposed to it, and could enforce the grounds of the one and confute those of the other.

Mill, *On Liberty,* II

83 It is but a poor education that associates ignorance with ignorance, and leaves them, if they care for knowledge, to grope their way to it without help, and to do without it if they do not. What is wanted is, the means of making ignorance aware of itself, and able to profit by knowledge; accustoming minds which know only routine to act upon, and feel the value of, principles: teaching them to compare different modes of action, and learn, by the use of their reason, to distinguish the best. When we desire to have a good school, we do not eliminate the teacher. The old remark, "as the schoolmaster is, so will be the school," is as true of the indirect schooling of grown people by public business as of the schooling of youth in academies and colleges.

Mill, *Representative Government,* XV

84 A pupil from whom nothing is ever demanded which he cannot do, never does all he can.

Mill, *Autobiography,* I

85 I do not believe that boys can be induced to apply themselves with vigour, and what is so much more difficult, perseverance, to dry and irksome studies,

by the sole force of persuasion and soft words. Much must be done, and much must be learnt, by children, for which rigid discipline and known liability to punishment are indispensable as means. It is, no doubt, a very laudable effort, in modern teaching, to render as much as possible of what the young are required to learn easy and interesting to them. But when this principle is pushed to the length of not requiring them to learn anything *but* what has been made easy and interesting, one of the chief objects of education is sacrificed. I rejoice in the decline of the old brutal and tyrannical system of teaching, which, however, did succeed in enforcing habits of application; but the new, as it seems to me, is training up a race of men who will be incapable of doing anything which is disagreeable to them. I do not, then, believe that fear, as an element in education, can be dispensed with; but I am sure that it ought not to be the main element; and when it predominates so much as to preclude love and confidence on the part of the child to those who should be the unreservedly trusted advisers of after-years, and perhaps to seal up the fountains of frank and spontaneous communicativeness in the child's nature, it is an evil for which a large abatement must be made from the benefits, moral and intellectual, which may flow from any other part of the education.

Mill, *Autobiography,* II

86 There is a need for educators who are themselves educated; superior, noble spirits, who prove themselves every moment by what they say and by what they do not say: cultures grown ripe and sweet—and *not* the learned boors which grammar school and university offer youth today as 'higher nurses.'

Nietzsche, *Twilight of the Idols: What the Germans Lack*

87 Things learned thus in a few hours, on one occasion, for one purpose, cannot possibly have formed many associations with other things in the mind. Their brain-processes are led into by few paths, and are relatively little liable to be awakened again. Speedy oblivion is the almost inevitable fate of all that is committed to memory in this simple way. Whereas, on the contrary, the same materials taken in gradually, day after day, recurring in different contexts, considered in various relations, associated with other external incidents, and repeatedly reflected on, grow into such a system, form such connections with the rest of the mind's fabric, lie open to so many paths of approach, that they remain permanent possessions. This is the *intellectual* reason why habits of continuous application should be enforced in educational establishments. Of course there is no moral turpitude in cramming. If it led to the desired end of secure learning it would be infinitely the best

method of study. But it does not; and students themselves should understand the reason why.

William James, *Psychology,* XVI

88 As the art of reading (after a certain stage in one's education) is the art of skipping, so the art of being wise is the art of knowing what to overlook. The first effect on the mind of growing cultivated is that processes once multiple get to be performed by a single act. Lazarus has called this the progressive "condensation" of thought. But in the psychological sense it is less a condensation than a loss, a genuine dropping out and throwing overboard of conscious content. Steps really sink from sight. An advanced thinker sees the relations of his topics in such masses and so instantaneously that when he comes to explain to younger minds it is often hard to say which grows the more perplexed, he or the pupil. In every university there are admirable investigators who are notoriously bad lecturers. The reason is that they never spontaneously see the subject in the minute articulate way in which the student needs to have it offered to his slow reception. They grope for the links, but the links do not come. Bowditch, who translated and annotated Laplace's *Mécanique céleste,* said that whenever his author prefaced a proposition by the words "it is evident," he knew that many hours of hard study lay before him.

William James, *Psychology,* XXII

89 In all pedagogy the great thing is to strike the iron while hot, and to seize the wave of the pupil's interest in each successive subject before its ebb has come, so that knowledge may be got and a habit of skill acquired—a headway of interest, in short, secured, on which afterward the individual may float. There is a happy moment for fixing skill in drawing, for making boys collectors in natural history, and presently dissectors and botanists; then for initiating them into the harmonies of mechanics and the wonders of physical and chemical law. Later, introspective psychology and the metaphysical and religious mysteries take their turn; and, last of all, the drama of human affairs and worldly wisdom in the widest sense of the term. In each of us a saturation-point is soon reached in all these things; the impetus of our purely intellectual zeal expires, and unless the topic be one associated with some urgent personal need that keeps our wits constantly whetted about it, we settle into an equilibrium, and live on what we learned when our interest was fresh and instinctive, without adding to the store. Outside of their own business, the ideas gained by men before they are twenty-five are practically the only ideas they shall have in their lives. They *cannot* get anything new. Disinterested curiosity is past, the mental grooves and channels set, the power of assimilation gone. If by chance we ever do learn anything about some entirely new topic we are

afflicted with a strange sense of insecurity, and we fear to advance a resolute opinion. But with things learned in the plastic days of instinctive curiosity we never lose entirely our sense of being at home. There remains a kinship, a sentiment of intimate acquaintance, which, even when we know we have failed to keep abreast of the subject, flatters us with a sense of power over it, and makes us feel not altogether out of the pale.

William James, *Psychology*, XXIV

90 He who can, does. He who cannot, teaches.

Shaw, *Man and Superman*, Maxims for Revolutionists

91 The result of teaching small parts of a large number of subjects is the passive reception of disconnected ideas, not illumined with any spark of vitality. Let the main ideas which are introduced into a child's education be few and important, and let them be thrown into every combination possible.

Whitehead, *Aims of Education*

92 The mind is never passive; it is a perpetual activity, delicate, receptive, responsive to stimulus. You cannot postpone its life until you have sharpened it. Whatever interest attaches to your subject-matter must be evoked here and now; whatever powers you are strengthening in the pupil, must be exercised here and now; whatever possibilities of mental life your teaching should impart, must be exhibited here and now. That is the golden rule of education, and a very difficult rule to follow.

Whitehead, *Aims of Education*

93 A man who is to educate really well, and is to make the young grow and develop into their full stature, must be filled through and through with the spirit of reverence. It is reverence towards others that is lacking in those who advocate machine-made cast-iron systems. . . . Reverence requires imagination and vital warmth; it requires most imagination in respect of those who have least actual achievement or power. The child is weak and superficially foolish, the teacher is strong, and in an everyday sense wiser than the child. The teacher without reverence, or the bureaucrat without reverence, easily despises the child for these outward inferiorities.

Russell, *Education*

94 What makes obedience seem necessary in schools is the large classes and overworked teachers demanded by a false economy. Those who have no experience of teaching are incapable of imagining the expense of spirit entailed by any really living instruction. They think that teachers can reasonably be expected to work as many hours as bank clerks.

Russell, *Education*

95 A teacher ought to have only as much teaching as can be done, on most days, with actual pleasure in the work, and with an awareness of the pupil's mental needs. The result would be a relation of friendliness instead of hostility between teacher and pupil, a realization on the part of most pupils that education serves to develop their own lives and is not merely an outside imposition, interfering with play and demanding many hours of sitting still.

Russell, *Education*

96 Passive acceptance of the teacher's wisdom is easy to most boys and girls. It involves no effort of independent thought, and seems rational because the teacher knows more than his pupils; it is moreover the way to win the favor of the teacher unless he is a very exceptional man. Yet the habit of passive acceptance is a disastrous one in later life. It causes men to seek a leader, and to accept as a leader whoever is established in that position.

Russell, *Education*

97 Let us get a clear idea of what the primary business of education is. The child has to learn to control its instincts. To grant it complete freedom, so that it obeys all its impulses without any restriction, is impossible. It would be a very instructive experiment for child-psychologists, but it would make life impossible for the parents and would do serious damage to the children themselves, as would be seen partly at the time, and partly during subsequent years. The function of education, therefore, is to inhibit, forbid, and suppress, and it has at all times carried out this function to admiration. But we have learnt from analysis that it is this very suppression of instincts that involves the danger of neurotic illness. You will remember that we have gone into the question of how this comes about in some detail. Education has therefore to steer its way between the Scylla of giving the instincts free play and the Charybdis of frustrating them. Unless the problem is altogether insoluble, an optimum of education must be discovered, which will do the most good and the least harm. It is a matter of finding out how much one may forbid, at which times, and by what methods. And then it must further be considered that the children have very different constitutional dispositions, so that the same educational procedure cannot possibly be equally good for all children. A moment's consideration will show us that, so far, education has fulfilled its function very badly, and has done children serious injury. If we can find an optimum of education which will carry out its task ideally, then we may hope to abolish one of the factors in the aetiology of neurotic illness, viz., the influence of accidental infantile traumas. The other factor, the power of a refractory instinctual constitution, can never be got rid of by education. When, therefore, one comes to think of the diffi-

cult tasks with which the educator is confronted; when one reflects that he has to recognize the characteristic constitution of each child, to guess from small indications what is going on in its un-formed mind, to give him the right amount of love and at the same time to preserve an effective de-gree of authority, then one cannot help saying to oneself that the only adequate preparation for the profession of educator is a good grounding in psy-cho-analysis. The best thing would be for him to be analysed himself, for, after all, without person-al experience one cannot get a grasp of analysis. The analysis of teachers and educators seems to be a more practicable prophylactic measure than the analysis of children themselves; and there are not such great obstacles against putting it into prac-tice.

Freud, *New Introductory Lectures on Psycho-Analysis,* XXXIV

98 No one would question that a child in a slum tenement has a different experience from that of a child in a cultured home; that the country lad has a different kind of experience from the city boy, or a boy on the seashore one different from the lad who is brought up on inland prairies. . . . A pri-mary responsibility of educators is that they not only be aware of the general principle of the shap-ing of actual experience by environing conditions, but that they also recognize in the concrete what surroundings are conducive to having experiences that lead to growth. Above all, they should know how to utilize the surroundings, physical and so-cial, that exist so as to extract from them all that they have to contribute to building up experiences that are worthwhile.

Traditional education did not have to face this problem; it could systematically dodge this re-sponsibility. The school environment of desks, blackboards, a small school yard, was supposed to suffice. There was no demand that the teacher should become intimately acquainted with the conditions of the local community, physical, his-torical, economic, occupational, etc., in order to utilize them as educational resources. A system of education based upon the necessary connection of education with experience must, on the contrary, if faithful to its principle, take these things con-stantly into account. This tax upon the educator is another reason why progressive education is more difficult to carry on than was ever the traditional system.

Dewey, *Experience and Education,* III

99 Almost everyone has had occasion to look back upon his school days and wonder what has be-come of the knowledge he was supposed to have amassed during his years of schooling, and why it is that the technical skills he acquired have to be learned over again in changed form in order to stand him in good stead. Indeed, he is lucky who does not find that in order to make progress, in order to go ahead intellectually, he does not have to unlearn much of what he learned in school. These questions cannot be disposed of by saying that the subjects were not actually learned, for they were learned at least sufficiently to enable a pupil to pass examinations in them. One trouble is that the subject-matter in question was learned in isolation; it was put, as it were, in a water-tight compartment. When the question is asked, then, what has become of it, where has it gone to, the right answer is that it is still there in the special compartment in which it was originally stowed away. If exactly the same conditions recurred as those under which it was acquired, it would also recur and be available. But it was segregated when it was acquired and hence is so disconnected from the rest of experience that it is not available under the actual conditions of life. It is contrary to the laws of experience that learning of this kind, no matter how thoroughly engrained at the time, should give genuine preparation.

Dewey, *Experience and Education,* III

100 The principle that development of experience comes about through interaction means that edu-cation is essentially a social process. This quality is realized in the degree in which individuals form a community group. It is absurd to exclude the teacher from membership in the group. As the most mature member of the group he has a pecu-liar responsibility for the conduct of the interac-tions and intercommunications which are the very life of the group as a community. That children are individuals whose freedom should be re-spected while the more mature person should have no freedom as an individual is an idea too absurd to require refutation. The tendency to ex-clude the teacher from a positive and leading share in the direction of the activities of the com-munity of which he is a member is another in-stance of reaction from one extreme to another. When pupils were a class rather than a social group, the teacher necessarily acted largely from the outside, not as a director of processes of ex-change in which all had a share. When education is based upon experience and educative experi-ence is seen to be a social process, the situation changes radically. The teacher loses the position of external boss or dictator but takes on that of leader of group activities.

Dewey, *Experience and Education,* IV

101 That teaching is an art and the true teacher an artist is a familiar saying. Now the teacher's own claim to rank as an artist is measured by his abili-ty to foster the attitude of the artist in those who study with him, whether they be youth or little children. Some succeed in arousing enthusiasm, in communicating large ideas, in evoking energy. So far, well; but the final test is whether the stimulus

thus given to wider aims succeeds in transforming itself into power, that is to say, into the attention to detail that ensures mastery over means of execution. If not, the zeal flags, the interest dies out, the ideal becomes a clouded memory. Other teachers succeed in training facility, skill, mastery of the technique of subjects. Again it is well—so far. But unless enlargement of mental vision, power of increased discrimination of final values, a sense for ideas—for principles—accompanies this training, forms of skill ready to be put indifferently to any end be the result. Such modes of technical skill may display themselves, according to circumstances, as cleverness in serving self-interest, as docility in carrying out the purposes of others, or as unimaginative plodding in ruts. To nurture inspiring aim and executive means into harmony with each other is at once the difficulty and the reward of the teacher.

Dewey, *How We Think,* Pt. III, XVI, 2

Chapter 9

ETHICS

Chapter 9 is divided into fifteen sections: 9.1 MORAL PHILOSOPHY AND MORALITY, 9.2 CUSTOM, 9.3 MORAL LAW, 9.4 MORAL FREEDOM, 9.5 CONSCIENCE, 9.6 GOOD AND EVIL, 9.7 RIGHT AND WRONG, 9.8 HAPPINESS, 9.9 DUTY: MORAL OBLIGATION, 9.10 VIRTUE AND VICE, 9.11 COURAGE AND COWARDICE, 9.12 TEMPERANCE AND INTEMPERANCE, 9.13 PRUDENCE, 9.14 HONESTY, and 9.15 WISDOM AND FOLLY.

An ancient tradition divided philosophy into two principal domains: one called "speculative" or "theoretical" because it was concerned with the nature of things, with the order and structure of the cosmos, and with being and becoming; the other called "practical" because it was concerned with action, both on the part of the individual and on the part of society, and, in the sphere of human action, with what ought to be sought or ought to be done, not with what exists or occurs. Practical philosophy was divided into two main branches, either called "ethics" and "politics," or "moral philosophy" and "political philosophy." This chapter is devoted to the persistent themes or topics that have been discussed

from antiquity to the present day by those concerned with moral or ethical questions.

The opening two sections deal with questions about the character, scope, and method of ethics or moral philosophy as a discipline, and questions about the relation of morality to custom. The next two sections consider subjects that are treated in other contexts, such as law and freedom; but here, in Sections 9.3 and 9.4, the treatment is specifically directed to law and freedom in their moral aspects. Conscience, which is involved in the application of the moral law and in the exercise of moral freedom, is treated in Section 9.5.

Next come the four pivotal issues in moral philosophy, posed by divergent answers to questions about good and evil (Section 9.6), right and wrong (Section 9.7), happiness (Section 9.8), and duty or moral obligation (Section 9.9). These four sections, the reader will find, contain quotations that often deal with two or more of the concepts involved in these issues; the discussion of happiness, for example, employs the notions of good and evil; and the discussion of duty or moral obligation cannot avoid considerations of right and wrong; and there is a cross fire between passages that emphasize happiness and the good and those that stress duty and the right.

The chapter concludes with six sections that begin with the consideration of virtue and vice (Section 9.10) and then take up particular virtues and vices, such as courage and cowardice (Section 9.11), temperance and intemperance (Section 9.12), prudence (Section 9.13), honesty (Section 9.14), and wisdom and folly (Section 9.15). The reader may query the absence of justice and injustice from this list. In order to avoid unnecessary duplication, this virtue and vice, together with the consideration of what is just and unjust in human conduct, are treated in Section 9.7 along with right and wrong. Justice and right are also treated in other contexts in Chapter 12 on LAW AND JUSTICE. For the consideration of matters closely related to the subjects of this chapter, the reader is referred to Chapter 20 on RELIGION.

9.1 | *Moral Philosophy and Morality*

The reader will find that some writers use the word "ethics" to name the discipline that other writers call "moral philosophy." Under whichever name it goes, the subject matter and problems being considered are substantially the same. However, among those who use "ethics" as the name for it, some will speak of the discipline as "the science of ethics" but their doing so does not mean that they differ from those who regard ethics and politics as branches of moral, practical, or normative philosophy. They are not using the word "science," as it is used in Section 17.2 on SCIENCE AND SCIENTIFIC METHOD, to signify a sphere of knowledge or inquiry that differs in method and subject matter from philosophy, as that is discussed in Section 17.1 on PHILOSOPHY AND PHILOSOPHERS.

The statement made above that moral philosophy or ethics is a practical and normative discipline means that its principles and conclusions are concerned with human action or conduct, with its ends and means, and that, with regard to human conduct and its ends and means, the basic propositions of moral philosophy or ethics prescribe what ought to be sought and what ought to be done. They do not simply describe how men do in fact behave, or what goals they seek and how they seek them.

However, some of the passages quoted below deal with morals and morality in a descriptive manner, reporting what general rules of conduct prevail in a particular society or culture and discussing the difference between the *mores*—the established canons of behavior—that exist at one time and another, or in one place and another. The relativity of the *mores* or customary morality is more fully treated in Section 9.2 on CUSTOM. Other problems touched on here, such as the relation between knowing what it is right to do and doing it, or the degree of precision with which moral problems can be solved, are commented on in subsequent sections of this chapter. For the consideration of politics as a related branch of moral phi-losophy, the reader is referred to Section 10.2 on THE REALM OF POLITICS.

---

1 The whole account of matters of conduct must be given in outline and not precisely . . . the accounts we demand must be in accordance with the subject-matter; matters concerned with conduct and questions of what is good for us have no fixity, any more than matters of health. The general account being of this nature, the account of particular cases is yet more lacking in exactness; for they do not fall under any art or precept but the agents themselves must in each case consider what is appropriate to the occasion.

Aristotle, *Ethics,* 1104ª2

2 Everything morally right derives from one of four sources: it concerns either full perception or intelligent development of what is true; or the preservation of organized society, where every man is rendered his due and all obligations are faithfully discharged; or the greatness and strength of a noble, invincible spirit; or order and moderation in everything said and done, whereby there is temperance and self-control.

Cicero, *De Officiis,* I, 5

3 In theory, there is nothing which draws us away from following what is taught; but in the matters of life, many are the things which distract us.

Epictetus, *Discourses,* I, 26

4 It is not by running hither and thither outside of itself that the soul understands morality and right conduct: it learns them of its own nature, in its contact with itself, in its intellectual grasp of itself, seeing deeply impressed upon it the images of its primal state.

Plotinus, *Fourth Ennead,* VII, 10

5 The moral precepts, distinct from the ceremonial and judicial precepts, are about things pertaining of their very nature to good morals. Now since human morals depend on their relation to reason, which is the proper principle of human acts, those morals are called good which accord with reason, and those are called bad which are discordant from reason. And as every judgment of speculative reason proceeds from the natural knowledge of first principles, so every judgment of practical reason proceeds from principles known naturally . . . from which principles one may proceed in various ways to judge of various matters. For some matters connected with human actions are so evident that after very little consideration one is able at once to approve or disapprove of them by means of these general first principles. But some matters cannot be the subject of judgment without much consideration of the various circumstances, which all are not able to do carefully, but only those who are wise, just as it is not possible for all to consider the particular conclusions of sciences, but only for those who are versed in philosophy. And lastly there are some matters of which man cannot judge unless he be helped by Divine instruction, such as the articles of faith.

It is therefore evident that since the moral precepts are about matters which concern good morals, and since good morals are those which are in accord with reason, and since also every judgment of human reason must be derived in some way from natural reason, it follows, of necessity, that all of the moral precepts belong to the law of nature.

Aquinas, *Summa Theologica,* I–II, 100, 1

6 Moral philosophy is nothing else but the science of what is good and evil in the conversation and society of mankind. *Good* and *evil* are names that signify our appetites and aversions, which in different tempers, customs, and doctrines of men are different: and diverse men differ not only in their judgement on the senses of what is pleasant and unpleasant to the taste, smell, hearing, touch, and sight; but also of what is conformable or disagreeable to reason in the actions of common life. Nay, the same man, in diverse times, differs from himself; and one time praiseth, that is, calleth good, what another time he dispraiseth, and calleth evil: from whence arise disputes, controversies, and at last war. And therefore so long as a man is in the condition of mere nature, which is a condition of war, private appetite is the measure of good and evil: and consequently all men agree on this, that peace is good, and therefore also the way or means of peace, which (as I have shown before) are *justice, gratitude, modesty, equity, mercy,* and the rest of the laws of nature, are good; that is to say, moral virtues; and their contrary vices, evil. Now the science of virtue and vice is moral philosophy; and therefore the true doctrine of the laws of nature is the true moral philosophy. But the writers of moral philosophy, though they acknowledge the same virtues and vices; yet, not seeing wherein consisted their goodness, nor that they come to be praised as the means of peaceable, sociable, and comfortable living, place them in a mediocrity of passions: as if not the cause, but the degree of daring, made fortitude; or not the cause, but the quantity of a gift, made liberality.

Hobbes, *Leviathan,* I, 15

7 Physical science will not console me for the igno-

rance of morality in the time of affliction. But the science of ethics will always console me for the ignorance of the physical sciences.

Pascal, *Pensées,* II, 67

8 The best thing . . . we can do, so long as we lack a perfect knowledge of our affects, is to conceive a right rule of life, or sure maxims of life—to commit these latter to memory, and constantly to apply them to the particular cases which frequently meet us in life, so that our imagination may be widely affected by them, and they may always be ready to hand.

Spinoza, *Ethics,* V, Prop. 10, Schol.

9 If natural philosophy in all its parts, by pursuing this method, shall at length be perfected, the bounds of moral philosophy will be also enlarged. For so far as we can know by natural philosophy what is the First Cause, what power He has over us, and what benefits we receive from Him, so far our duty towards Him, as well as that towards one another, will appear to us by the light of Nature. And no doubt, if the worship of false gods had not blinded the heathen, their moral philosophy would have gone farther than to the four cardinal virtues; and instead of teaching the transmigration of souls, and to worship the Sun and Moon, and dead heroes, they would have taught us to worship our true Author and Benefactor, as their ancestors did under the government of Noah and his sons before they corrupted themselves.

Newton, *Optics,* III, 1

10 A good life, in which consist not the least part of religion and true piety, concerns also the civil government; and in it lies the safety both of men's souls and of the commonwealth. Moral actions belong, therefore, to the jurisdiction both of the outward and inward court; both of the civil and domestic governor; I mean both of the magistrate and conscience. Here, therefore, is great danger, lest one of these jurisdictions intrench upon the other, and discord arise between the keeper of the public peace and the overseers of souls.

Locke, *Letter Concerning Toleration*

11 Confident I am, that, if men would in the same method, and with the same indifferency, search after moral as they do mathematical truths, they would find them have a stronger connexion one with another, and a more necessary consequence from our clear and distinct ideas, and to come nearer perfect demonstration than is commonly imagined. But much of this is not to be expected, whilst the desire of esteem, riches, or power makes men espouse the well-endowed opinions in fashion, and then seek arguments either to make good their beauty, or varnish over and cover their deformity. Nothing being so beautiful to the eye as truth is to the mind; nothing so deformed and

irreconcilable to the understanding as a lie.

Locke, *Concerning Human Understanding,*
Bk. IV, III, 20

12 The merit of delivering true general precepts in ethics is indeed very small. Whoever recommends any moral virtues, really does no more than is implied in the terms themselves. That people who invented the word charity, and used it in a good sense, inculcated more clearly, and much more efficaciously, the precept, Be charitable, than any pretended legislator or prophet who should insert such a maxim in his writings.

Hume, *Of the Standard of Taste*

13 The end of all moral speculations is to teach us our duty; and, by proper representations of the deformity of vice, and beauty of virtue, beget correspondent habits, and engage us to avoid the one, and embrace the other. But is this ever to be expected from inferences and conclusions of the understanding, which of themselves have no hold of the affections, or set in motion the active powers of men? They discover truths: But where the truths which they discover are indifferent, and beget no desire or aversion, they can have no influence on conduct and behaviour. What is honourable, what is fair, what is becoming, what is noble, what is generous, takes possession of the heart, and animates us to embrace and maintain it. What is intelligible, what is evident, what is probable, what is true, procures only the cool assent of the understanding; and gratifying a speculative curiosity, puts an end to our researches.

Hume, *Concerning Principles of Morals,* I

14 If morality had naturally no influence on human passions and actions, 'twere in vain to take such pains to inculcate it; and nothing wou'd be more fruitless than that multitude of rules and precepts, with which all moralists abound. Philosophy is commonly divided into *speculative* and *practical;* and as morality is always comprehended under the latter division, 'tis supposed to influence our passions and actions, and to go beyond the calm and indolent judgments of the understanding. And this is confirm'd by common experience, which informs us, that men are often govern'd by their duties, and are deter'd from some actions by the opinion of injustice, and impell'd to others by that of obligation.

Since morals, therefore, have an influence on the actions and affections, it follows, that they cannot be deriv'd from reason; and that because reason alone, as we have already prov'd, can never have any such influence. Morals excite passions, and produce or prevent actions. Reason of itself is utterly impotent in this particular. The rules of morality, therefore, are not conclusions of our reason.

Hume, *Treatise of Human Nature,* Bk. III, I, 1

15 It is then certain that compassion is a natural feeling, which, by moderating the violence of love of self in each individual, contributes to the preservation of the whole species. It is this compassion that hurries us without reflection to the relief of those who are in distress: it is this which in a state of nature supplies the place of laws, morals and virtues, with the advantage that none are tempted to disobey its gentle voice: it is this which will always prevent a sturdy savage from robbing a weak child or a feeble old man of the sustenance they may have with pain and difficulty acquired, if he sees a possibility of providing for himself by other means: it is this which, instead of inculcating that sublime maxim of rational justice, *Do to others as you would have them do unto you,* inspires all men with that other maxim of natural goodness, much less perfect indeed, but perhaps more useful; *Do good to yourself with as little evil as possible to others.* In a word, it is rather in this natural feeling than in any subtle arguments that we must look for the cause of that repugnance, which every man would experience in doing evil, even independently of the maxims of education. Although it might belong to Socrates and other minds of the like craft to acquire virtue by reason, the human race would long since have ceased to be, had its preservation depended only on the reasonings of the individuals composing it.

Rousseau, *Origin of Inequality,* I

16 "I have found," said the prince at his return to Imlac, "a man who can teach all that is necessary to be known; who, from the unshaken throne of rational fortitude, looks down on the scenes of life changing beneath him. He speaks, and attention watches his lips. He reasons, and conviction closes his periods. This man shall be my future guide; I will learn his doctrines, and imitate his life."

"Be not too hasty," said Imlac, "to trust or to admire the teachers of morality: they discourse like angels, but they live like men."

Johnson, *Rasselas,* XVIII

17 In every civilised society, in every society where the distinction of ranks has once been completely established, there have been always two different schemes or systems of morality current at the same time; of which the one may be called the strict or austere; the other the liberal, or, if you will, the loose system. The former is generally admired and revered by the common people: the latter is commonly more esteemed and adopted by what are called people of fashion. The degree of disapprobation with which we ought to mark the vices of levity, the vices which are apt to arise from great prosperity, and from the excess of gaiety and good humour, seems to constitute the principal distinction between those two opposite schemes or systems. In the liberal or loose system, luxury, wanton and even disorderly mirth, the pursuit of pleasure to some degree of intemperance, the breach of chastity, at least in one of the two sexes, etc., provided they are not accompanied with gross indecency, and do not lead to falsehood or injustice, are generally treated with a good deal of indulgence, and are easily either excused or pardoned altogether. In the austere system, on the contrary, those excesses are regarded with the utmost abhorrence and detestation. The vices of levity are always ruinous to the common people, and a single week's thoughtlessness and dissipation is often sufficient to undo a poor workman for ever, and to drive him through despair upon committing the most enormous crimes. The wiser and better sort of the common people, therefore, have always the utmost abhorrence and detestation of such excesses, which their experience tells them are so immediately fatal to people of their condition. The disorder and extravagance of several years, on the contrary, will not always ruin a man of fashion, and people of that rank are very apt to consider the power of indulging in some degree of excess as one of the advantages of their fortune, and the liberty of doing so without censure or reproach as one of the privileges which belong to their station. In people of their own station, therefore, they regard such excesses with but a small degree of disapprobation, and censure them either very slightly or not at all.

Adam Smith, *Wealth of Nations,* V, 1

18 A censor may maintain, he can never restore, the morals of a state. It is impossible for such a magistrate to exert his authority with benefit, or even with effect, unless he is supported by a quick sense of honour and virtue in the minds of the people, by a decent reverence for the public opinion, and by a train of useful prejudices combating on the side of national manners. In a period when these principles are annihilated, the censorial jurisdiction must either sink into empty pageantry, or be converted into a partial instrument of vexatious oppression.

Gibbon, *Decline and Fall of the Roman Empire,* X

19 We do not need science and philosophy to know what we should do to be honest and good, yea, even wise and virtuous. Indeed we might well have conjectured beforehand that the knowledge of what every man is bound to do, and therefore also to know, would be within the reach of every man, even the commonest.

Kant, *Fundamental Principles of the Metaphysic of Morals,* I

20 Morality, and humanity as capable of it, is that which alone has dignity. Skill and diligence in labour have a market value; wit, lively imagination, and humour, have fancy value; on the other hand, fidelity to promises, benevolence from prin-

ciple (not from instinct), have an intrinsic worth. Neither nature nor art contains anything which in default of these it could put in their place, for their worth consists not in the effects which spring from them, not in the use and advantage which they secure, but in the disposition of mind, that is, the maxims of the will which are ready to manifest themselves in such actions, even though they should not have the desired effect. These actions also need no recommendation from any subjective taste or sentiment, that they may be looked on with immediate favour and satisfaction: they need no immediate propension or feeling for them; they exhibit the will that performs them as an object of an immediate respect, and nothing but reason is required to *impose* them on the will; not to *flatter* it into them, which, in the case of duties, would be a contradiction. This estimation therefore shows that the worth of such a disposition is dignity, and places it infinitely above all value, with which it cannot for a moment be brought into comparison or competition without as it were violating its sanctity.

Kant, *Fundamental Principles of the Metaphysic of Morals*, II

21 Morality is not properly the doctrine how we should *make* ourselves happy, but how we should become *worthy* of happiness.

Kant, *Critique of Practical Reason*, Pt. I, II, 2

22 Morality . . . must have the more power over the human heart the more purely it is exhibited. Whence it follows that, if the law of morality and the image of holiness and virtue are to exercise any influence at all on our souls, they can do so only so far as they are laid to heart in their purity as motives, unmixed with any view to prosperity, for it is in suffering that they display themselves most nobly.

Kant, *Critique of Practical Reason*, II, Methodology of Pure Practical Reason

23 The supreme principle of ethics (the doctrine of virtue) is: "Act on a maxim, the *ends* of which are such as it might be a universal law for everyone to have." On this principle a man is an end to himself as well as others, and it is not enough that he is not permitted to use either himself or others merely as means (which would imply that he might be indifferent to them), but it is in itself a duty of every man to make mankind in general his end.

The principle of ethics being a categorical imperative does not admit of proof, but it admits of a justification from principles of pure practical reason. Whatever in relation to mankind, to oneself, and others, *can* be an end, that *is* an end for pure practical reason: for this is a faculty of assigning ends in general; and to be indifferent to them, that is, to take no interest in them, is a contradic-

tion; since in that case it would not determine the maxims of actions (which always involve an end), and consequently would cease to be practical reasons. Pure reason, however, cannot command any ends *a priori,* except so far as it declares the same to be also a duty, which duty is then called a *duty of virtue.*

Kant, *Introduction to the Metaphysical Elements of Ethics*, IX

24 No free communities ever existed without morals, and . . . morals are the work of woman.

Tocqueville, *Democracy in America*, Vol. II, III, 9

25 A moral being is one who is capable of comparing his past and future actions or motives, and of approving or disapproving of them. We have no reason to suppose that any of the lower animals have this capacity; therefore, when a Newfoundland dog drags a child out of the water, or a monkey faces danger to rescue its comrade, or takes charge of an orphan monkey, we do not call its conduct moral. But in the case of man, who alone can with certainty be ranked as a moral being, actions of a certain class are called moral, whether performed deliberately, after a struggle with opposing motives, or impulsively through instinct, or from the effects of slowly-gained habit.

Darwin, *Descent of Man*, I, 4

26 It was assumed formerly by philosophers of the derivative school of morals that the foundation of morality lay in a form of Selfishness; but more recently the "Greatest happiness principle" has been brought prominently forward. It is, however, more correct to speak of the latter principle as the standard, and not as the motive of conduct. Nevertheless, all the authors whose works I have consulted, with a few exceptions, write as if there must be a distinct motive for every action, and that this must be associated with some pleasure or displeasure. But man seems often to act impulsively, that is from instinct or long habit, without any consciousness of pleasure, in the same manner as does probably a bee or ant, when it blindly follows its instincts. Under circumstances of extreme peril, as during a fire, when a man endeavours to save a fellow-creature without a moment's hesitation, he can hardly feel pleasure; and still less has he time to reflect on the dissatisfaction which he might subsequently experience if he did not make the attempt. Should he afterwards reflect over his own conduct, he would feel that there lies within him an impulsive power widely different from a search after pleasure or happiness; and this seems to be the deeply planted social instinct.

Darwin, *Descent of Man*, I, 4

27 It must not be forgotten that although a high standard of morality gives but a slight or no ad-

vantage to each individual man and his children over the other men of the same tribe, yet that an increase in the number of well-endowed men and an advancement in the standard of morality will certainly give an immense advantage to one tribe over another. A tribe including many members who, from possessing in a high degree the spirit of patriotism, fidelity, obedience, courage, and sympathy, were always ready to aid one another, and to sacrifice themselves for the common good, would be victorious over most other tribes; and this would be natural selection. At all times throughout the world tribes have supplanted other tribes; and as morality is one important element in their success, the standard of morality and the number of well-endowed men will thus everywhere tend to rise and increase.

Darwin, *Descent of Man*, I, 5

28 I regard utility as the ultimate appeal on all ethical questions; but it must be utility in the largest sense, grounded on the permanent interests of a man as a progressive being. Those interests, I contend, authorise the subjection of individual spontaneity to external control, only in respect to those actions of each, which concern the interest of other people. If any one does an act hurtful to others, there is a *prima facie* case for punishing him, by law, or, where legal penalties are not safely applicable, by general disapprobation. There are also many positive acts for the benefit of others, which he may rightfully be compelled to perform; such as to give evidence in a court of justice; to bear his fair share in the common defence, or in any other joint work necessary to the interest of the society of which he enjoys the protection; and to perform certain acts of individual beneficence, such as saving a fellow creature's life, or interposing to protect the defenceless against ill-usage, things which whenever it is obviously a man's duty to do, he may rightfully be made responsible to society for not doing. A person may cause evil to others not only by his actions but by his inaction, and in either case he is justly accountable to them for the injury. The latter case, it is true, requires a much more cautious exercise of compulsion than the former. To make any one answerable for doing evil to others is the rule; to make him answerable for not preventing evil is, comparatively speaking, the exception. Yet there are many cases clear enough and grave enough to justify that exception. In all things which regard the external relations of the individual, he is *de jure* amenable to those whose interests are concerned, and, if need be, to society as their protector. There are often good reasons for not holding him to the responsibility; but these reasons must arise from the special expediencies of the case: either because it is a kind of case in which he is on the whole likely to act better, when left to his own discretion, than when controlled in any way in which society

have it in their power to control him; or because the attempt to exercise control would produce other evils, greater than those which it would prevent. When such reasons as these preclude the enforcement of responsibility, the conscience of the agent himself should step into the vacant judgment seat, and protect those interests of others which have no external protection; judging himself all the more rigidly, because the case does not admit of his being made accountable to the judgment of his fellow creatures.

Mill, *On Liberty*, I

29 The creed which accepts as the foundation of morals, Utility, or the Greatest Happiness Principle, holds that actions are right in proportion as they tend to promote happiness, wrong as they tend to produce the reverse of happiness. By happiness is intended pleasure, and the absence of pain; by unhappiness, pain, and the privation of pleasure. To give a clear view of the moral standard set up by the theory, much more requires to be said; in particular, what things it includes in the ideas of pain and pleasure; and to what extent this is left an open question. But these supplementary explanations do not affect the theory of life on which this theory of morality is grounded—namely, that pleasure, and freedom from pain, are the only things desirable as ends; and that all desirable things (which are as numerous in the utilitarian as in any other scheme) are desirable either for the pleasure inherent in themselves, or as means to the promotion of pleasure and the prevention of pain.

Mill, *Utilitarianism*, II

30 It is the business of ethics to tell us what are our duties, or by what test we may know them; but no system of ethics requires that the sole motive of all we do shall be a feeling of duty; on the contrary, ninety-nine hundredths of all our actions are done from other motives, and rightly so done, if the rule of duty does not condemn them.

Mill, *Utilitarianism*, II

31 Knowledge is one thing, virtue is another; good sense is not conscience, refinement is not humility, nor is largeness and justness of view faith. Philosophy, however enlightened, however profound, gives no command over the passions, no influential motives, no vivifying principles.

Newman, *Idea of a University*, Discourse V

32 Then he [Satan] said: "The difference between man and me? The difference between a mortal and an immortal? between a cloud and a spirit?" He picked up a wood-louse that was creeping along a piece of bark: "What is the difference between Cæsar and this?"

I said, "One cannot compare things which by their nature and by the interval between them are not comparable."

"You have answered your own question," he said. "I will expand it. Man is made of dirt—I saw him made. I am not made of dirt. Man is a museum of diseases, a home of impurities; he comes today and is gone tomorrow; he begins as dirt and departs as stench; I am of the aristocracy of the Imperishables. And man has the *Moral Sense.* You understand? He has the *Moral Sense.* That would seem to be difference enough between us, all by itself."

Mark Twain, *Mysterious Stranger,* III

33 There was a question which we wanted to ask Father Peter, and finally we went there the second evening, a little diffidently, after drawing straws, and I asked it as casually as I could, though it did not sound as casual as I wanted, because I didn't know how:

"What is the Moral Sense, sir?"

He looked down, surprised, over his great spectacles, and said, "Why, it is the faculty which enables us to distinguish good from evil."

It threw some light but not a glare, and I was a little disappointed, also to some degree embarrassed. He was waiting for me to go on, so, in default of anything else to say, I asked, "Is it valuable?"

"Valuable? Heavens! lad, it is the one thing that lifts man above the beasts that perish and makes him heir to immortality!"

Mark Twain, *Mysterious Stranger,* IV

34 I said it was a brutal thing.

"No, it was a human thing [said Satan]. You should not insult the brutes by such a misuse of that word; they have not deserved it," and he went on talking like that. "It is like your paltry race—always lying, always claiming virtues which it hasn't got, always denying them to the higher animals, which alone possess them. No brute ever does a cruel thing—that is the monopoly of those with the Moral Sense. When a brute inflicts pain he does it innocently; it is not wrong; for him there is no such thing as wrong. And he does not inflict pain for the pleasure of inflicting it—only man does that. Inspired by that mongrel Moral Sense of his! A sense whose function is to distinguish between right and wrong, with liberty to choose which of them he will do. Now what advantage can he get out of that? He is always choosing, and in nine cases out of ten he prefers the wrong. There shouldn't be any wrong; and without the Moral Sense there couldn't be any. And yet he is such an unreasoning creature that he is not able to perceive that the Moral Sense degrades him to the bottom layer of animated beings and is a shameful possession."

Mark Twain, *Mysterious Stranger,* V

35 To be ashamed of one's immorality—that is a step

on the staircase at whose end one is also ashamed of one's morality.

Nietzsche, *Beyond Good and Evil,* IV, 95

36 All naturalism in morality, that is all *healthy* morality, is dominated by an instinct of life—some commandment of life is fulfilled through a certain canon of 'shall' and 'shall not', some hindrance and hostile element on life's road is thereby removed. *Anti-natural* morality, that is virtually every morality that has hitherto been taught, reverenced and preached, turns on the contrary precisely *against* the instincts of life—it is a now secret, now loud and impudent *condemnation* of these instincts. By saying 'God sees into the heart' it denies the deepest and the highest desires of life and takes God for the *enemy of life.*

Nietzsche, *Twilight of the Idols:*
Morality as Anti-Nature

37 An act has no ethical quality whatever unless it be chosen out of several all equally possible. To sustain the arguments for the good course and keep them ever before us, to stifle our longing for more flowery ways, to keep the foot unflinchingly on the arduous path, these are characteristic ethical energies. But more than these; for these but deal with the means of compassing interests already felt by the man to be supreme. The ethical energy *par excellence* has to go farther and choose which *interest* out of several, equally coercive, shall become supreme. The issue here is of the utmost pregnancy, for it decides a man's entire career. When he debates, Shall I commit this crime? choose that profession? accept that office, or marry this fortune?—his choice really lies between one of several equally possible future characters. What he shall *become* is fixed by the conduct of this moment. . . . The problem with the man is less what act he shall now choose to do, than what being he shall now resolve to become.

William James, *Psychology,* IX

38 It is obvious . . . that the whole idea of good and bad has some connection with *desire. Prima facie,* anything that we all desire is "good," and anything that we all dread is "bad." If we all agreed in our desires, the matter could be left there, but unfortunately our desires conflict. If I say "what I want is good," my neighbour will say "No, what *I* want." Ethics is an attempt—though not, I think, a successful one—to escape from this subjectivity.

Russell, *Religion and Science,* IX

39 The ideally virtuous man, if we had got rid of asceticism, would be the man who permits the enjoyment of all good things whenever there is no evil consequence to outweigh the enjoyment.

Russell, *The Conquest of Happiness,* I, 7

40 Morals must be a growing science if it is to be a

science at all, not merely because all truth has not yet been appropriated by the mind of man, but because life is a moving affair in which old moral truth ceases to apply.

Dewey, *Human Nature and Conduct,* III, 7

41 There is a peculiar inconsistency in the current idea that morals *ought* to be social. The introduction of the moral "ought" into the idea contains an implicit assertion that morals depend upon something apart from social relations. Morals *are* social. The question of ought, should be, is a question of better and worse *in* social affairs.

Dewey, *Human Nature and Conduct,* IV, 4

42 Morality comprises two different parts, one of which follows from the original structure of human society, while the other finds its explanation in the principle which explains this structure. In the former, obligation stands for the pressure exerted by the elements of society on one another in order to maintain the shape of the whole; a pressure whose effect is prefigured in each of us by a system of habits which, so to speak, go to meet it: this mechanism, of which each separate part is a habit, but whose whole is comparable to an instinct, has been prepared by nature. In the second, there is still obligation, if you will, but that obligation is the force of an aspiration or an impetus, of the very impetus which culminated in the human species, in social life, in a system of habits which bears a resemblance more or less to instinct: the primitive impetus here comes into play directly, and no longer through the medium of the mechanisms it had set up, and at which it had provisionally halted. In short, to sum up what has gone before, we should say that nature, setting down the human species along the line of evolution, intended it to be sociable, in the same way as it did the communities of ants and bees; but since intelligence was there, the maintenance of social life had to be entrusted to an all but intelligent mechanism: intelligent in that each piece could be remodelled by human intelligence, yet instinctive in that man could not, without ceasing to be a man, reject all the pieces together and cease to accept a mechanism of preservation. Instinct gave place temporarily to a system of habits, each one of which became contingent, their convergence towards the preservation of society being alone necessary, and this necessity bringing back instinct with it. The necessity of the whole, felt behind the contingency of the parts, is what we call moral obligation in general—it being understood that the parts are contingent in the eyes of society only; to the individual, into whom society inculcates its habits, the part is as necessary as the whole.

Bergson, *Two Sources of Morality*
and Religion, I

43 A mock feeling and a true feeling are almost indistinguishable; to decide that I love my mother and will remain with her, or to remain with her by putting on an act, amount somewhat to the same thing. In other words, the feeling is formed by the acts one performs; so, I cannot refer to it in order to act upon it. Which means that I can neither seek within myself the true condition which will impel me to act, nor apply to a system of ethics for concepts which will permit me to act. . . . No general ethics can show you what is to be done; there are no omens in the world.

Sartre, *Existentialism*

9.2 | *Custom*

The line between conduct that conforms to moral rules and conduct that exemplifies customary manners is often shadowy. The word "mores," which signifies the established customs of a society or culture, has an obvious etymological connection with the word "morals." A certain brand of skepticism about the universality of moral principles derives from the tendency of sociologists and cultural anthropologists to identify what they call the "value system" of a community, and hence its morality, with its *mores*—its customary patterns of conduct, its customary standards of approbation, its customary taboos or prohibitions. Since the *mores* differ from community to community and, in a given community, from one time to another, the conclusion is easily—but, perhaps, illicitly—reached that morality is relative to the institutions of a particular society and varies with the time and place. Quotations taking the opposite point of view, in defense of universal moral truths, will be found in Section 9.1 on MORAL PHILOSOPHY AND MORALITY and in Section 9.3 on the MORAL LAW.

The quotations collected here discuss custom as a conservative force in society, relate social customs to the stable habits of society's members, call attention to and comment on the wide diversity of customs, assess the authority that attaches to or derives from social conventions, and discuss the causes and effects of change in customs. The consideration of established customs as having the force of law occurs both here and in Section 12.1 on LAW AND LAWYERS. The effect of custom on standards of taste in the sphere of art and on the prevalence of certain opinions in the sphere of thought is touched on here, but it is also discussed in Section 16.7 on CRITICISM AND THE STANDARDS OF TASTE and in Section 6.5 on OPINION, BELIEF, AND FAITH.

---

1 If one were to offer men to choose out of all the customs in the world such as seemed to them the best, they would examine the whole number, and end by preferring their own; so convinced are they that their own usages far surpass those of all others.

Herodotus, *History*, III, 38

2 *Callicles*. Convention and nature are generally at variance with one another.

Plato, *Gorgias*, 482B

3 *Athenian Stranger*. All the matters which we are now describing are commonly called by the general name of unwritten customs, and what are termed the laws of our ancestors are all of similar nature. And the reflection which lately arose in our minds, that we can neither call these things laws, nor yet leave them unmentioned, is justified; for they are the bonds of the whole state, and come in between the written laws which are or are hereafter to be laid down; they are just ancestral customs of great antiquity, which, if they are rightly ordered and made habitual, shield and preserve the previously existing written law; but if they depart from right and fall into disorder, then they are like the props of builders which slip away out of their place and cause a universal ruin—one part drags another down, and the fair superstructure falls because the old foundations are undermined. Reflecting upon this, Cleinias, you ought to bind together the new state in every possible way, omitting nothing, whether great or small, of what are called laws or manners or pursuits, for by these means a city is bound together, and all these things are only lasting when they depend upon one another; and, therefore, we must not wonder if we find that many apparently trifling customs or usages come pouring in and lengthening out our laws.

Plato, *Laws*, VII, 793A

4 If you are at Rome live in the Roman style; if you are elsewhere live as they live elsewhere.

Ambrose, qu. by Taylor, *Ductor Dubitantium*, I, 1

5 Ignorant men who apply the tests of their human minds, and measure all the conduct of the human race by the measure of their own custom . . . are like a man handling armour and not knowing what piece is meant for what part of the body and so putting a greave on his head and a helmet on his feet and complaining that they do not fit.

Augustine, *Confessions*, III, 7

6 Actions which are against the customs of human societies are to be avoided according to the variety of such customs; so that that which is agreed upon by the custom, or decreed by the law, of state or people, is not to be violated at the mere pleasure whether of citizen or alien. For every part is defective that is not in harmony with the whole.

But when God orders something against the custom or covenant of a state, though it never had been done it must be done; and if it was . . . allowed to lapse, it must be restored; and if it was not a law before, it must be made a law now.

Augustine, *Confessions*, III, 8

7 When men unacquainted with other modes of life than their own meet with the record of such actions, unless they are restrained by authority, they look upon them as sins, and do not consider that their own customs either in regard to marriage, or feasts, or dress, or the other necessities and adorn-

ments of human life, appear sinful to the people of other nations and other times. And, distracted by this endless variety of customs, some . . . have thought that there was no such thing as absolute right, but that every nation took its own custom for right; and that, since every nation has a different custom, and right must remain unchangeable, it becomes manifest that there is no such thing as right at all. Such men did not perceive, to take only one example, that the precept, "Whatsoever ye would that men should do to you, do ye even so to them," cannot be altered by any diversity of national customs. And this precept, when it is referred to the love of God, destroys all vices; when to the love of one's neighbour, puts an end to all crimes.

Augustine, *Christian Doctrine*, III, 14

8 When a thing is done again and again, it seems to proceed from a deliberate judgment of reason. Accordingly, custom has the force of a law, abolishes law, and is the interpreter of law.

Aquinas, *Summa Theologica*, I–II, 97, 3

9 And what all philosophy cannot implant in the head of the wisest men, does not custom by her sole ordinance teach the crudest common herd?

Montaigne, *Essays*, I, 23, Of Custom

10 The principal effect of the power of custom is to seize and ensnare us in such a way that it is hardly within our power to get ourselves back out of its grip and return into ourselves to reflect and reason about its ordinances. In truth, because we drink them with our milk from birth, and because the face of the world presents itself in this aspect to our first view, it seems that we are born on condition of following this course. And the common notions that we find in credit around us and infused into our soul by our fathers' seed, these seem to be the universal and natural ones. Whence it comes to pass that what is off the hinges of custom, people believe to be off the hinges of reason: God knows how unreasonably, most of the time.

Montaigne, *Essays*, I, 23, Of Custom

11 Each man calls barbarism whatever is not his own practice; for indeed it seems we have no other test of truth and reason than the example and pattern of the opinions and customs of the country we live in.

Montaigne, *Essays*, I, 31, Of Cannibals

12 We are nothing but ceremony; ceremony carries us away, and we leave the substance of things; we hang on to the branches and abandon the trunk and body.

Montaigne, *Essays*, II, 17, Of Presumption

13 True is, that whilome that good poet sayd,

The gentle minde by gentle deeds is knowne:
For a man by nothing is so well bewrayd
As by his manners, in which plaine is showne
Of what degree and what race he is growne.

Spenser, *Faerie Queene*, Bk. VI, III, 1

14 *King Henry.* Nice customs curtsy to great kings.

Shakespeare, *Henry V*, V, ii, 291

15 *Corin.* Those that are good manners at the court are as ridiculous in the country as the behaviour of the country is most mockable at the court.

Shakespeare, *As You Like It*, III, ii, 46

16 *Polonius.* Costly thy habit as thy purse can buy,
But not express'd in fancy; rich, not gaudy;
For the apparel oft proclaims the man.

Shakespeare, *Hamlet*, I, iii, 70

17 Where a man will plead a title of prescription of custom, he shall say that such custom hath been used from time whereof the memory of man runneth not to the contrary, that is as much as to say, no man then alive hath heard any proof to the contrary.

Sir Edward Coke, *Commentary Upon Littleton*, 170

18 Men's thoughts are much according to their inclination; their discourse and speeches according to their learning and infused opinions; but their deeds are after as they have been accustomed. And therefore as Machiavel well noteth (though in an evil-favoured instance,) there is no trusting to the force of nature nor to the bravery of words, except it be corroborate by custom.

Bacon, *Of Custom and Education*

19 I . . . recognised in the course of my travels that all those whose sentiments are very contrary to ours are yet not necessarily barbarians or savages, but may be possessed of reason in as great or even a greater degree than ourselves. I also considered how very different the self-same man, identical in mind and spirit, may become, according as he is brought up from childhood amongst the French or Germans, or has passed his whole life amongst Chinese or cannibals. I likewise noticed how even in the fashions of one's clothing the same thing that pleased us ten years ago, and which will perhaps please us once again before ten years are passed, seems at the present time extravagant and ridiculous. I thus concluded that it is much more custom and example that persuade us than any certain knowledge, and yet in spite of this the voice of the majority does not afford a proof of any value in truths a little difficult to discover, because such truths are much more likely to have been discovered by one man than by a nation.

Descartes, *Discourse on Method*, II

20 For we must not misunderstand ourselves; we are as much automatic as intellectual; and hence it comes that the instrument by which conviction is attained is not demonstrated alone. How few things are demonstrated! Proofs only convince the mind. Custom is the source of our strongest and most believed proofs. It bends the automaton, which persuades the mind without its thinking about the matter.

Pascal, *Pensées,* IV, 252

21 Montaigne is wrong. Custom should be followed only because it is custom, and not because it is reasonable or just. But people follow it for this sole reason, that they think it just. Otherwise they would follow it no longer, although it were the custom; for they will only submit to reason or justice. Custom without this would pass for tyranny; but the sovereignty of reason and justice is no more tyrannical than that of desire. They are principles natural to man.

It would, therefore, be right to obey laws and customs, because they are laws; but we should know that there is neither truth nor justice to introduce into them, that we know nothing of these, and so must follow what is accepted. By this means we would never depart from them. But people cannot accept this doctrine; and, as they believe that truth can be found, and that it exists in law and custom, they believe them and take their antiquity as a proof of their truth, and not simply of their authority apart from truth. Thus they obey laws, but they are liable to revolt when these are proved to be valueless; and this can be shown of all, looked at from a certain aspect.

Pascal, *Pensées,* V, 325

22 Ideas that in themselves are not all of kin, come to be so united in some men's minds, that it is very hard to separate them; they always keep in company, and the one no sooner at any time comes into the understanding, but its associate appears with it; and if they are more than two which are thus united, the whole gang, always inseparable, show themselves together.

This strong combination of ideas, not allied by nature, the mind makes in itself either voluntarily or by chance; and hence it comes in different men to be very different, according to their different inclinations, education, interests, etc. *Custom* settles habits of thinking in the understanding, as well as of determining in the will, and of motions in the body: all which seems to be but trains of motions in the animal spirits, which, once set a going, continue in the same steps they have used to; which, by often treading, are worn into a smooth path, and the motion in it becomes easy, and as it were natural.

Locke, *Concerning Human Understanding,*
Bk. II, XXXIII, 5–6

23 How many men have no other ground for their tenets, than the supposed honesty, or learning, or number of those of the same profession? As if honest or bookish men could not err; or truth were to be established by the vote of the multitude: yet this with most men serves the turn. The tenet has had the attestation of reverend antiquity; it comes to me with the passport of former ages, and therefore I am secure in the reception I give it: other men have been and are of the same opinion, (for that is all is said,) and therefore it is reasonable for me to embrace it. A man may more justifiably throw up cross and pile for his opinions, than take them up by such measures. All men are liable to error, and most men are in many points, by passion or interest, under temptation to it. If we could but see the secret motives that influenced the men of name and learning in the world, and the leaders of parties, we should not always find that it was the embracing of truth for its own sake, that made them espouse the doctrines they owned and maintained. This at least is certain, there is not an opinion so absurd, which a man may not receive upon this ground. There is no error to be named, which has not had its professors: and a man shall never want crooked paths to walk in, if he thinks that he is in the right way, wherever he has the footsteps of others to follow.

Locke, *Concerning Human Understanding,*
Bk. IV, XX, 17

24 Custom . . . is the great guide of human life. It is that principle alone which renders our experience useful to us, and makes us expect, for the future, a similar train of events with those which have appeared in the past. Without the influence of custom, we should be entirely ignorant of every matter of fact beyond what is immediately present to the memory and senses. We should never know how to adjust means to ends, or to employ our natural powers in the production of any effect. There would be an end at once of all action, as well as of the chief part of speculation.

Hume, *Concerning Human Understanding,* V, 36

25 Since no man has a natural authority over his fellow, and force creates no right, we must conclude that conventions form the basis of all legitimate authority among men.

Rousseau, *Social Contract,* I, 4

26 Most peoples, like most men, are docile only in youth; as they grow old they become incorrigible. When once customs have become established and prejudices inveterate, it is dangerous and useless to attempt their reformation; the people, like the foolish and cowardly patients who rave at sight of the doctor, can no longer bear that any one should lay hands on its faults to remedy them.

Rousseau, *Social Contract,* II, 8

27 [The] most important [law] of all . . . is not graven on tablets of marble or brass, but on the
hearts of the citizens. This forms the real constitution of the State, takes on every day new powers,
when other laws decay or die out, restores them or
takes their place, keeps a people in the ways in
which it was meant to go, and insensibly replaces
authority by the force of habit. I am speaking of
morality, of custom, above all of public opinion; a
power unknown to political thinkers, on which
none the less success in everything else depends.
With this the great legislator concerns himself in
secret, though he seems to confine himself to particular regulations; for these are only the arc of
the arch, while manners and morals, slower to
arise, form in the end its immovable keystone.

Rousseau, *Social Contract,* II, 12

28 The great art of living easy and happy in society
is to study proper behaviour, and even with our
most intimate friends to observe politeness; otherwise we will insensibly treat each other with a
degree of rudeness, and each will find himself despised in some measure by the other.

Boswell, *London Journal (Dec. 1, 1762)*

29 Johnson's profound reverence for the Hierarchy
made him expect from bishops the highest degree
of decorum; he was offended even at their going
to taverns; "A bishop (said he,) has nothing to do
at a tippling-house. It is not indeed immoral in
him to go to a tavern; neither would it be immoral in him to whip a top in Grosvenor-square. But,
if he did, I hope the boys would fall upon him,
and apply the whip to *him.* There are gradations
in conduct; there is morality,—decency,—propriety. None of these should be violated by a bishop. A bishop should not go to a house where he
may meet a young fellow leading out a wench."

Boswell, *Life of Johnson (March 1781)*

30 Mere *customary life* (the watch wound up and going
on of itself) is that which brings on natural death.
Custom is activity without opposition, for which
there remains only a formal duration; in which
the fulness and zest that originally characterized
the aim of life are out of the question—a merely
external sensuous existence which has ceased to
throw itself enthusiastically into its object. Thus
perish individuals, thus perish peoples by a natural death; and though the latter may continue in
being, it is an existence without intellect or vitality; having no need of its institutions, because the
need for them is satisfied—a political nullity and
tedium. In order that a truly universal interest
may arise, the spirit of a people must advance to
the adoption of some new purpose; but whence
can this new purpose originate? It would be a
higher, more comprehensive conception of itself, a
transcending of its principle, but this very act

would involve a principle of a new order, a new
national spirit.

Hegel, *Philosophy of History,* Introduction, 3

31 No way of thinking or doing, however ancient,
can be trusted without proof. What everybody
echoes or in silence passes by as true today may
turn out to be falsehood tomorrow, mere smoke of
opinion, which some had trusted for a cloud that
would sprinkle fertilizing rain on their fields.
What old people say you cannot do, you try and
find that you can. Old deeds for old people, and
new deeds for new.

Thoreau, *Walden:* Economy

32 Nobody denies that people should be so taught
and trained in youth as to know and benefit by
the ascertained results of human experience. But
it is the privilege and proper condition of a human being, arrived at the maturity of his faculties,
to use and interpret experience in his own way. It
is for him to find out what part of recorded experience is properly applicable to his own circumstances and character. The traditions and customs
of other people are, to a certain extent, evidence
of what their experience has taught *them;* presumptive evidence, and as such, have a claim to
his deference: but, in the first place, their experience may be too narrow; or they may not have
interpreted it rightly. Secondly, their interpretation of experience may be correct, but unsuitable
to him. Customs are made for customary circumstances and customary characters; and his circumstances or his character may be uncustomary.
Thirdly, though the customs be both good as customs, and suitable to him, yet to conform to custom, merely *as* custom, does not educate or develop in him any of the qualities which are the
distinctive endowment of a human being. The human faculties of perception, judgment, discrimi-
native feeling, mental activity, and even moral
preference, are exercised only in making a choice.
He who does anything because it is the custom
makes no choice. He gains no practice either in
discerning or in desiring what is best. The mental
and moral, like the muscular powers, are improved only by being used. The faculties are
called into no exercise by doing a thing merely
because others do it, no more than by believing a
thing only because others believe it. If the grounds
of an opinion are not conclusive to the person's
own reason, his reason cannot be strengthened,
but is likely to be weakened, by his adopting it:
and if the inducements to an act are not such as
are consentaneous to his own feelings and character (where affection, or the rights of others, are not
concerned) it is so much done towards rendering
his feelings and character inert and torpid, instead of active and energetic.

Mill, *On Liberty,* III

33 It is important to give the freest scope possible to

uncustomary things, in order that it may in time appear which of these are fit to be converted into customs.

Mill, *On Liberty*, III

34 A man's *fame,* good or bad, and his *honor* or dishonor, are names for one of his social selves. The particular social self of a man called his honor is usually the result of one of those splittings of which we have spoken. It is his image in the eyes of his own "set," which exalts or condemns him as he conforms or not to certain requirements that may not be made of one in another walk of life. Thus a layman may abandon a city infected with cholera; but a priest or a doctor would think such an act incompatible with his honor. A soldier's honor requires him to fight or to die under circumstances where another man can apologize or run away with no stain upon his social self. A judge, a statesman, are in like manner debarred by the honor of their cloth from entering into pecuniary relations perfectly honorable to persons in private life. Nothing is commoner than to hear people discriminate between their different selves of this sort: "As a man I pity you, but as an official I must show you no mercy; as a politician I regard him as an ally, but as a moralist I loathe him"; etc., etc. What may be called "club-opinion" is one of the very strongest forces in life. The thief must not steal from other thieves; the gambler may pay his gambling-debts, though he pay no other debts in the world. The code of honor of fashionable society has throughout history been full of permissions as well as of vetoes, the only reason for following either of which is that so we best serve one of our social selves. You must not lie in general, but you may lie as much as you please if asked about your relations with a lady; you must accept a challenge from an equal, but if challenged by an inferior you may laugh him to scorn: these are examples of what is meant.

William James, *Psychology*, X

35 In general, parents and similar authorities follow the dictates of their own super-egos in the upbringing of children. Whatever terms their ego may be on with their super-ego, in the education of the child they are severe and exacting. They have forgotten the difficulties of their own childhood, and are glad to be able to identify themselves fully at last with their own parents, who in their day subjected them to such severe restraints. The result is that the super-ego of the child is not really built up on the model of the parents, but on that of the parents' super-ego; it takes over the same content, it becomes the vehicle of tradition and of all the age-long values which have been handed down in this way from generation to generation.

Freud, *New Introductory Lectures on Psycho-Analysis*, XXXI

36 The girl thought for a time of what he had said. "I suppose," she then said, "that even in your country you have parties, balls and *conversazione?*"

"Yes," he said, "we have those."

"Then you will know," she went on slowly, "that the part of a guest is different from that of a host or hostess, and that people do not want or expect the same things in the two different capacities?"

"I think you are right," said Augustus.

"Now God," she said, "when he created Adam and Eve . . . arranged it so that man takes, in these matters, the part of a guest, and woman that of a hostess. Therefore man takes love lightly, for the honor and dignity of his house is not involved therein. And you can also, surely, be a guest to many people to whom you would never want to be a host. Now, tell me, Count, what does a guest want?"

"I believe," said Augustus when he had thought for a moment, "that if we do, as I think we ought to here, leave out the crude guest, who comes to be regaled, takes what he wants and goes away, a guest wants first of all to be diverted, to get out of his daily monotony or worry. Secondly the decent guest wants to shine, to expand himself and impress his own personality upon his surroundings. And thirdly, perhaps, he wants to find some justification for his existence altogether. But since you put it so charmingly, Signora, please tell me now: What does a hostess want?"

"The hostess," said the young lady, "wants to be thanked."

Isak Dinesen, *The Roads Around Pisa*, IV

37 The life-history of the individual is first and foremost an accommodation to the patterns and standards traditionally handed down in his community. From the moment of his birth the customs into which he is born shape his experience and behaviour. By the time he can talk, he is the little creature of his culture, and by the time he is grown and able to take part in its activities, its habits are his habits, its beliefs his beliefs, its impossibilities his impossibilities. Every child that is born into his group will share them with him, and no child born into one on the opposite side of the globe can ever achieve the thousandth part. There is no social problem it is more incumbent upon us to understand than this of the rôle of custom. Until we are intelligent as to its laws and varieties, the main complicating facts of human life must remain unintelligible.

Benedict, *Patterns of Culture*, I

38 Custom did not challenge the attention of social theorists because it was the very stuff of their own thinking: it was the lens without which they could not see at all.

Benedict, *Patterns of Culture*, I

9.3 | *Moral Law*

When the word "law" is used to signify a rule of conduct that individuals may obey or violate, or a prescribed course of behavior to which they may or may not conform, such expressions as "natural law" and "law of nature" are interchangeable with "moral law." To characterize a law as natural or as moral is, negatively at least, to say the same thing; namely, that it represents a rule of conduct which is *not* made by a political ruler or ruling body and is *not* enforced by the state. On the positive side, the reader will find that whereas some authors regard the moral law as based on the needs or tendencies of human nature (and so they think of it as natural in that sense), other authors regard it as emanating from the dictates of reason (and so they think of it as a law of reason rather than as a law of nature).

For the discussion of rules of conduct that are man-made and state-enforced, the reader is referred to Section 12.1 on LAW AND LAWYERS. Quotations both here and in that section consider the relation of positive law or the law of the state to the natural moral law

or the law of reason. Another body of law is mentioned here—the law of God or the divine law, which to the extent that it lays down rules of conduct as contrasted with prescribing religious rituals or ceremonies consists of rules that are often identical in substance with the prescriptions of the natural moral law. The law that, according to the Old Testament, God gave to Moses includes, in addition to many ceremonial precepts, the Ten Commandments, at least six of which prescribe virtuous conduct or prohibit iniquitous or unrighteous acts.

The reader will find the moral law epitomized in the golden rule and in the categorical imperative; he will find some quotations that indicate the connection between the natural law and natural rights, and some that derive moral duties or obligations from the basic oughts and ought-nots of the moral law. For the discussion of these matters in other contexts, the reader is referred to Section 12.3 on RIGHTS—NATURAL AND CIVIL, Section 9.9 on DUTY: MORAL OBLIGATION, and Section 20.8 on WORSHIP AND SERVICE.

---

1 And God spake all these words, saying,

I am the Lord thy God, which have brought thee out of the land of Egypt, out of the house of bondage.

Thou shalt have no other gods before me.

Thou shalt not make unto thee any graven image, or any likeness of any thing that is in heaven above, or that is in the earth beneath, or that is in the water under the earth:

Thou shalt not bow down thyself to them, nor serve them: for I the Lord thy God am a jealous God, visiting the iniquity of the fathers upon the children unto the third and fourth generation of them that hate me;

And shewing mercy unto thousands of them that love me, and keep my commandments.

Thou shalt not take the name of the Lord thy

God in vain; for the Lord will not hold him guiltless that taketh his name in vain.

Remember the sabbath day, to keep it holy.

Six days shalt thou labour, and do all thy work:

But the seventh day is the sabbath of the Lord thy God: in it thou shalt not do any work, thou, nor thy son, nor thy daughter, thy manservant, nor thy maidservant, nor thy cattle, nor thy stranger that is within thy gates:

For in six days the Lord made heaven and earth, the sea, and all that in them is, and rested the seventh day: wherefore the Lord blessed the sabbath day, and hallowed it.

Honour thy father and thy mother: that thy days may be long upon the land which the Lord thy God giveth thee.

Thou shalt not kill.

Thou shalt not commit adultery.

Thou shalt not steal.

Thou shalt not bear false witness against thy neighbour.

Thou shalt not covet thy neighbour's house, thou shalt not covet thy neighbour's wife, nor his manservant, nor his maidservant, nor his ox, nor his ass, nor any thing that is thy neighbour's.

Exodus 20:1–17

2 *Hecuba.*   The gods are strong, and over them there stands some absolute, some moral order or principle of law more final still.
Upon this moral law the world depends;
through it the gods exist; by it we live,
defining good and evil.

Euripides, *Hecuba,* 799

3 *Athenian Stranger.* Dealings between man and man require to be suitably regulated. The principle of them is very simple: Thou shalt not, if thou canst help, touch that which is mine, or remove the least thing which belongs to me without my consent; and may I be of a sound mind, and do to others as I would that they should do to me.

Plato, *Laws,* XI, 913A

4 If by nature one man desires to promote the welfare of another man, whoever he may be, only because he is a fellow human being; then it follows that in accordance with that same nature, there are some interests all men have in common. If this is true, we are all subject to the same law of nature. And if this is true, the law of nature forbids us to wrong our neighbor.

Cicero, *De Officiis,* III, 6

5 We possess no living image of true law or of genuine justice. The barest outline is all that we have. Would that we could be true to even this; for it is drawn from the models that nature and truth afford.

Cicero, *De Officiis,* III, 17

6 When the Gentiles, which have not the law, do by nature the things contained in the law, these, having not the law, are a law unto themselves:

Which shew the work of the law written in their hearts, their conscience also bearing witness, and their thoughts the mean while accusing or else excusing one another.

Romans 2:14–15

7 Do not look around thee to discover other men's ruling principles, but look straight to this, to what nature leads thee, both the universal nature through the things which happen to thee, and thy own nature through the acts which must be done by thee. But every being ought to do that which is according to its constitution; and all other things

have been constituted for the sake of rational beings, just as among irrational things the inferior for the sake of the superior, but the rational for the sake of one another.

The prime principle then in man's constitution is the social. And the second is not to yield to the persuasions of the body, for it is the peculiar office of the rational and intelligent motion to circumscribe itself, and never to be overpowered either by the motion of the senses or of the appetites, for both are animal; but the intelligent motion claims superiority and does not permit itself to be overpowered by the others. And with good reason, for it is formed by nature to use all of them. The third thing in the rational constitution is freedom from error and from deception. Let then the ruling principle holding fast to these things go straight on, and it has what is its own.

Marcus Aurelius, *Meditations,* VII, 55

8 Your law, O Lord, punishes theft; and this law is so written in the hearts of men that not even the breaking of it blots it out.

Augustine, *Confessions,* II, 4

9 Those sins which are against nature, like those of the men of Sodom, are in all times and places to be detested and punished. Even if all nations committed such sins, they should all alike be held guilty by God's law which did not make men so that they should use each other thus.

Augustine, *Confessions,* III, 8

10 All those things to which man has a natural inclination are naturally apprehended by reason as being good, and consequently as objects of pursuit, and their contraries as evil, and objects of avoidance. Therefore the order of the precepts of the natural law is according to the order of natural inclinations.

Aquinas, *Summa Theologica,*
I–II, 94, 2

11 There is in man an inclination to good, according to the nature of his reason, which nature is proper to him; thus man has a natural inclination to know the truth about God, and to live in society. And in this respect, whatever pertains to this inclination belongs to the natural law; for instance, to shun ignorance, to avoid offending those among whom one has to live, and other such things regarding the above inclination.

Aquinas, *Summa Theologica,*
I–II, 94, 2

12 A thing is said to belong to the natural law in two ways. First, because nature inclines there; for example, that one should not do harm to another. Secondly, because nature did not bring in the contrary; thus we might say that for man to be

naked is of the natural law, because nature did not give him clothes, but art invented them. In this sense, "the possession of all things in common, and uniform freedom" are said to be of the natural law, because, that is, the distinction of possessions and slavery were not brought in by nature, but devised by human reason for the benefit of human life. Accordingly the law of nature was not changed in this respect, except by addition.

Aquinas, *Summa Theologica,*
I–II, 94, 5

13 As to . . . common principles, the natural law, in its universal character, can in no way be blotted out from men's hearts. But it is blotted out in the case of a particular action, in so far as reason is hindered from applying the common principle to a particular point of practice, on account of concupiscence or some other passion. . . . But as to the other, that is, the secondary precepts, the natural law can be blotted out from the human heart, either by evil persuasions, just as in speculative matters errors occur in respect of necessary conclusions; or by vicious customs and corrupt habits, as among some men, theft, and even unnatural vices.

Aquinas, *Summa Theologica,*
I–II, 94, 6

14 The goodness of the human will depends on the eternal law much more than on human reason. And when human reason fails we must have recourse to the Eternal Reason.

Aquinas, *Summa Theologica,*
I–II, 19, 4

15 Natural law is a practical first principle in the sphere of morality; it forbids evil and commands good. Positive law is a decision that takes circumstances into account and conforms with natural law on credible grounds. The basis of natural law is God, who has created this light, but the basis of positive law is civil authority.

Luther, *Table Talk,* 3911

16 The moral law . . . with which I shall begin, being comprised in two leading articles, of which one simply commands us to worship God with pure faith and piety, and the other enjoins us to embrace men with sincere love,—this law, I say, is the true and eternal rule of righteousness, prescribed to men of all ages and nations, who wish to conform their lives to the will of God. For this is his eternal and immutable will, that he himself be worshipped by us all, and that we mutually love one another.

Calvin, *Institutes of the
Christian Religion,* IV, 20

17 Whatsoever men are to take knowledge of for law, not upon other men's words, but every one from his own reason, must be such as is agreeable to the reason of all men; which no law can be, but the law of nature. The laws of nature therefore need not any publishing nor proclamation; as being contained in this one sentence, approved by all the world, *Do not that to another which thou thinkest unreasonable to be done by another to thyself.*

Hobbes, *Leviathan,* II, 26

18 That part of the Scripture which was first law was the Ten Commandments, written in two tables of stone and delivered by God Himself to Moses, and by Moses made known to the people. Before that time there was no written law of God, who, as yet having not chosen any people to be His peculiar kingdom, had given no law to men, but the law of nature, that is to say, the precepts of natural reason, written in every man's own heart.

Hobbes, *Leviathan,* III, 42

19 To act absolutely in conformity with virtue is nothing but acting according to the laws of our own proper nature. But only in so far as we understand do we act. Therefore, to act in conformity with virtue is nothing but acting, living, and preserving our being as reason directs, and doing so from the ground of seeking our own profit.

Spinoza, *Ethics,* IV, Prop. 24,
Demonst.

20 The state of Nature has a law of Nature to govern it, which obliges every one, and reason, which is that law, teaches all mankind who will but consult it, that being all equal and independent, no one ought to harm another in his life, health, liberty or possessions; for men being all the workmanship of one omnipotent and infinitely wise Maker; all the servants of one sovereign Master, sent into the world by His order and about His business; they are His property, whose workmanship they are made to last during His, not one another's pleasure. And, being furnished with like faculties, sharing all in one community of Nature, there cannot be supposed any such subordination among us that may authorise us to destroy one another, as if we were made for one another's uses, as the inferior ranks of creatures are for ours. Every one as he is bound to preserve himself, and not to quit his station wilfully, so by the like reason, when his own preservation comes not in competition, ought he as much as he can to preserve the rest of mankind, and not unless it be to do justice on an offender, take away or impair the life, or what tends to the preservation of the life, the liberty, health, limb, or goods of another.

Locke, *II Civil Government,* II, 6

21 I think *there cannot any one moral rule be proposed whereof a man may not justly demand a reason:* which

would be perfectly ridiculous and absurd if they were innate; or so much as self-evident, which every innate principle must needs be, and not need any proof to ascertain its truth, nor want any reason to gain it approbation. He would be thought void of common sense who asked on the one side, or on the other side went to give a reason *why* "it is impossible for the same thing to be and not to be." It carries its own light and evidence with it, and needs no other proof: he that understands the terms assents to it for its own sake or else nothing will ever be able to prevail with him to do it. But should that most unshaken rule of morality and foundation of all social virtue, "That one should do as he would be done unto," be proposed to one who never heard of it before, but yet is of capacity to understand its meaning; might he not without any absurdity ask a reason why? And were not he that proposed it bound to make out the truth and reasonableness of it to him? Which plainly shows it not to be innate; for if it were it could neither want nor receive any proof; but must needs (at least as soon as heard and understood) be received and assented to as an unquestionable truth, which a man can by no means doubt of. So that the truth of all these moral rules plainly depends upon some other antecedent to them, and from which they must be *deduced;* which could not be if either they were innate or so much as self-evident.

Locke, *Concerning Human Understanding,* Bk. I, II, 4

22 That God has given a rule whereby men should govern themselves, I think there is nobody so brutish as to deny. He has a right to do it; we are his creatures: he has goodness and wisdom to direct our actions to that which is best: and he has power to enforce it by rewards and punishments of infinite weight and duration in another life; for nobody can take us out of his hands. This is the only true touchstone of moral rectitude; and, by comparing them to this law, it is that men judge of the most considerable moral good or evil of their actions; that is, whether, as duties or sins, they are like to procure them happiness or misery from the hands of the Almighty.

Locke, *Concerning Human Understanding,* Bk. II, XXVIII, 8

23 The mind of man is so formed by nature that, upon the appearance of certain characters, dispositions, and actions, it immediately feels the sentiment of approbation or blame; nor are there any emotions more essential to its frame and constitution. The characters which engage our approbation are chiefly such as contribute to the peace and security of human society; as the characters which excite blame are chiefly such as tend to public detriment and disturbance: Whence it may reasonably be presumed, that the moral senti-

ments arise, either mediately or immediately, from a reflection of these opposite interests.

Hume, *Concerning Human Understanding,* VIII, 80

24 I assume that there are pure moral laws which determine, entirely *a priori* (without regard to empirical motives, that is, to happiness), the conduct of a rational being, or in other words, the use which it makes of its freedom, and that these laws are *absolutely* imperative (not merely hypothetically, on the supposition of other empirical ends), and therefore in all respects necessary. I am warranted in assuming this, not only by the arguments of the most enlightened moralists, but by the moral judgement of every man who will make the attempt to form a distinct conception of such a law.

Kant, *Critique of Pure Reason,* Transcendental Method

25 I call the world *a moral world,* in so far as it may be in accordance with all the ethical laws—which, by virtue of the *freedom* of reasonable beings, it *can* be, and according to the necessary laws of *morality* it *ought to be.* But this world must be conceived only as an intelligible world, inasmuch as abstraction is therein made of all conditions (ends), and even of all impediments to morality (the weakness or pravity of human nature). So far, then, it is a mere idea—though still a practical idea—which may have, and ought to have, an influence on the world of sense, so as to bring it as far as possible into conformity with itself. The idea of a moral world has, therefore, objective reality, not as referring to an object of intelligible intuition—for of such an object we can form no conception whatever—but to the world of sense—conceived, however, as an object of pure reason in its practical use—and to a *corpus mysticum* of rational beings in it, in so far as the *liberum arbitrium* of the individual is placed, under and by virtue of moral laws, in complete systematic unity both with itself and with the freedom of all others.

Kant, *Critique of Pure Reason,* Transcendental Method

26 Not only are moral laws with their principles essentially distinguished from every other kind of practical knowledge in which there is anything empirical, but all moral philosophy rests wholly on its pure part. When applied to man, it does not borrow the least thing from the knowledge of man himself (anthropology), but gives laws *a priori* to him as a rational being. No doubt these laws require a judgement sharpened by experience, in order on the one hand to distinguish in what cases they are applicable, and on the other to procure for them access to the will of the man and effectual influence on conduct; since man is acted on by

so many inclinations that, though capable of the idea of a practical pure reason, he is not so easily able to make it effective *in concreto* in his life.

Kant, *Fundamental Principles of the Metaphysic of Morals,* Pref.

27 The moral worth of an action does not lie in the effect expected from it, nor in any principle of action which requires to borrow its motive from this expected effect. For all these effects—agreeableness of one's condition and even the promotion of the happiness of others—could have been also brought about by other causes, so that for this there would have been no need of the will of a rational being; whereas it is in this alone that the supreme and unconditional good can be found. The pre-eminent good which we call moral can therefore consist in nothing else than *the conception of law* in itself, *which certainly is only possible in a rational being,* in so far as this conception, and not the expected effect, determines the will. This is a good which is already present in the person who acts accordingly, and we have not to wait for it to appear first in the result.

Kant, *Fundamental Principles of the Metaphysic of Morals,* I

28 There is . . . but one categorical imperative, namely, this: *Act only on that maxim whereby thou canst at the same time will that it should become a universal law.*

Kant, *Fundamental Principles of the Metaphysic of Morals,* II

29 We are indeed legislative members of a moral kingdom rendered possible by freedom, and presented to us by reason as an object of respect; but yet we are subjects in it, not the sovereign, and to mistake our inferior position as creatures, and presumptuously to reject the authority of the moral law, is already to revolt from it in spirit, even though the letter of it is fulfilled.

Kant, *Critique of Practical Reason,* Pt. I, I, 3

30 That in the order of ends, man (and with him every rational being) is an end in himself, that is, that he can never be used merely as a means by any (not even by God) without being at the same time an end also himself, that therefore humanity in our person must be holy to ourselves, this follows now of itself because he is the subject of the moral law, in other words, of that which is holy in itself, and on account of which and in agreement with which alone can anything be termed holy. For this moral law is founded on the autonomy of his will, as a free will which by its universal laws must necessarily be able to agree with that to which it is to submit itself.

Kant, *Critique of Practical Reason,* Pt. I, II, 2

31 Two things fill the mind with ever new and increasing admiration and awe, the oftener and the more steadily we reflect on them: the starry heavens above and the moral law within.

Kant, *Critique of Practical Reason,* II, Conclusion

32 Imagine a man at the moment when his mind is disposed to moral feeling! If, amid beautiful natural surroundings, he is in calm and serene enjoyment of his existence, he feels within him a need—a need of being grateful for it to some one. Or, at another time, in the same frame of mind, he may find himself in the stress of duties which he can only perform and will perform by submitting to a voluntary sacrifice; then he feels within him a need—a need of having, in so doing, carried out some command and obeyed a Supreme Lord. Or he may in some thoughtless manner have diverged from the path of duty, though not so as to have made himself answerable to man; yet words of stern self-reproach will then fall upon an inward ear, and he will seem to hear the voice of a judge to whom he has to render account. In a word, he needs a moral intelligence; because he exists for an end, and this end demands a Being that has formed both him and the world with that end in view. It is waste of labour to go burrowing behind these feelings for motives; for they are immediately connected with the purest moral sentiment: *gratitude, obedience,* and *humiliation*—that is, submission before a deserved chastisement—being special modes of a mental disposition towards duty. . . . It may be that such a disposition of the mind is but a rare occurrence, or, again, does not last long, but rather is fleeting and of no permanent effect, or, it may be, passes away without the mind bestowing a single thought upon the object so shadowed forth, and without troubling to reduce it to clear conceptions. Yet the source of this disposition is unmistakable. It is the original moral bent of our nature, as a subjective principle, that will not let us be satisfied, in our review of the world, with the finality which it derives through natural causes, but leads us to introduce into it an underlying supreme Cause governing nature according to moral laws.

Kant, *Critique of Teleological Judgement,* 86

33 *The Lord.* A good man, though his striving be obscure,
Remains aware that there is one right way.

Goethe, *Faust,* Prologue in Heaven, 328

34 The sentiment of virtue is a reverence and delight in the presence of certain divine laws. It perceives that this homely game of life we play, covers, under what seem foolish details, principles that astonish. The child amidst his baubles is learning

the action of light, motion, gravity, muscular force; and in the game of human life, love, fear, justice, appetite, man, and God, interact. These laws refuse to be adequately stated. They will not be written out on paper, or spoken by the tongue. They elude our persevering thought; yet we read them hourly in each other's faces, in each other's actions, in our own remorse. The moral traits which are all globed into every virtuous act and thought—in speech we must sever, and describe or suggest by painful enumeration of many particulars. Yet, as this sentiment is the essence of all religion, let me guide your eye to the precise objects of the sentiment. . . .

The intuition of the moral sentiment is an insight of the perfection of the laws of the soul. These laws execute themselves. They are out of time, out of space, and not subject to circumstance. Thus in the soul of man there is a justice whose retributions are instant and entire. He who does a good deed is instantly ennobled. He who does a mean deed is by the action itself contracted. He who puts off impurity, thereby puts on purity. If a man is at heart just, then in so far is he God.

Emerson, *Address to Harvard Divinity School*

35 If, as is my own belief, the moral feelings are not innate, but acquired, they are not for that reason the less natural. It is natural to man to speak, to reason, to build cities, to cultivate the ground, though these are acquired faculties. The moral feelings are not indeed a part of our nature, in the sense of being in any perceptible degree present in all of us; but this, unhappily, is a fact admitted by those who believe the most strenuously in their transcendental origin. Like the other acquired capacities above referred to, the moral faculty, if not a part of our nature, is a natural outgrowth from it; capable, like them, in a certain small degree, of springing up spontaneously; and susceptible of being brought by cultivation to a high degree of development. Unhappily it is also susceptible, by a sufficient use of the external sanctions and of the force of early impressions, of being cultivated in almost any direction: so that there is hardly anything so absurd or so mischievous that it may not,

by means of these influences, be made to act on the human mind with all the authority of conscience.

Mill, *Utilitarianism*, III

36 Since man is endowed with intelligence and determines his own ends, it is up to him to put himself in tune with the ends necessarily demanded by his nature. This means that there is, by very virtue of human nature, an order or a disposition which human reason can discover and according to which the human will must act in order to attune itself to the necessary ends of the human being. The unwritten law, or natural law, is nothing more than that.

Maritain, *Rights of Man and Natural Law*, II

37 Natural law is not a written law. Men know it with greater or less difficulty, and in different degrees, running the risk of error here as elsewhere. The only practical knowledge all men have naturally and infallibly in common is that we must do good and avoid evil. This is the preamble and the principle of natural law; it is not the law itself. Natural law is the ensemble of things to do and not to do which follow therefrom in *necessary* fashion, and *from the simple fact that man is man*, nothing else being taken into account. That every sort of error and deviation is possible in the determination of these things merely proves that our sight is weak and that innumerable accidents can corrupt our judgment. Montaigne maliciously remarked that, among certain peoples, incest and thievery were considered virtuous acts. Pascal was scandalized by this. We are scandalized by the fact that cruelty, denunciation of parents, the lie for the service of the party, the murder of old or sick people should be considered virtuous actions by young people educated according to Nazi methods. All this proves nothing against natural law, any more than a mistake in addition proves anything against arithmetic, or the mistakes of certain primitive peoples, for whom the stars were holes in the tent which covered the world, prove anything against astronomy.

Maritain, *Rights of Man and Natural Law*, II

9.4 | *Moral Freedom*

The image of the man deprived of freedom as one in chains or behind bars, or as one coerced or intimidated into acting contrary to his own wishes, typifies the kind of liberty that is discussed in Section 13.1 on FREEDOM IN SOCIETY, but not here. The man in prison and the slave in chains, the poor man lacking the means of satisfying his desires and the oppressed subjects of a tyrant, all these can enjoy the kind of inner or moral freedom that is discussed here. It is neither freedom of choice (which is treated in Section 5.7) nor freedom to do as one wills, but rather the freedom that consists in being able to will as one ought. It is sometimes described, negatively, as freedom from the passions, subjection to which Spinoza characterizes as "human bondage." It is also described as a liberty that derives from having the willpower to do one's duty or to act in conformity with the moral law.

As the reader will find in the quotations below, moral freedom takes many forms, varying remarkably as one passes from the discussion of it by Plato and the Roman Stoics in antiquity, to what is said on the subject by Spinoza, Rousseau, Kant, and Hegel, or by Freud and Dewey. However, what is common to them all is the fact that a man's possession of moral freedom does not in any way depend on the outer circumstances of his life or upon his inherited nature, but upon his acquirement of virtue, or wisdom or a certain type of moral character, or even, as in the case of Freud, a certain type of psychological adjustment. The other element that is common to moral liberty in all its forms is the moral law or the moral ideal to which a man can conform only by mastering the intransigent, recalcitrant, or antagonistic factors in his own make-up. That is why the morally free man is said to have achieved self-mastery. The reader is, therefore, referred to Section 9.3 on MORAL LAW for materials relevant to moral freedom.

---

1 If a man were born so divinely gifted that he could naturally apprehend the truth, he would have no need of laws to rule over him; for there is no law or order which is above knowledge, nor can mind, without impiety, be deemed the subject or slave of any man, but rather the lord of all. I speak of mind, true and free, and in harmony with nature. But then there is no such mind anywhere, or at least not much; and therefore we must choose law and order, which are second best.

Plato, *Laws*, IX, 875B

2 The most learned men have told us that only the wise man is free. What is freedom but the ability to live as one will? The man who lives as he wills is none other than the one who strives for the right, who does his duty, who plans his life with forethought, and who obeys the laws because he knows it is good for him, and not out of fear. Everything he says, does, or thinks is spontaneous and free. His tasks and conduct begin and end in himself, because nothing has so much influence over him as his own counsel and decision. Even the supreme power of fortune is submissive to him. The wise poet has reminded us that fortune is moulded for each man by the manner of his life. Only the wise man does nothing against his will, or with regret and by compulsion. Though this truth deserves to be discussed at greater length, it is nevertheless proverbial that no one is free except the wise. Evil men are nothing but slaves.

Cicero, *Paradoxes of the Stoics*, V

3 To conclude that the condition of slavery involves a person's whole being, is an error. The better part of the man is exempt. The slave-master has at his disposition only the body of the slave; but the mind is its own master. It is free and unchained; it is not even the prisoner of the body. It can use its own powers, follow its own great aims,

572

and escape into infinity to keep company with the stars.

Seneca, *On Benefits,* III, 20

4 Behold the wretched and dismal slavery of him who is in thrall to pleasures and pains, those utterly capricious and tyrannical masters. We, however, must escape to freedom. But this is only possible if we are indifferent to Fortune. Then we shall attain that one overriding blessing—the serenity and exhaltation of a firmly anchored mind. For when error is banished, we shall have the great and satisfying joy that comes from the discovery of truth, plus a kind disposition and cheerfulness of mind. The source of our pleasure in these things will not derive from their being good, but that they emerge from a good that is one's own.

Seneca, *On the Happy Life,* IV

5 So far as I am concerned that body is nothing more or less than a fetter on my freedom. I place it squarely in the path of fortune, letting her expend her onslaught on it, not allowing any blow to get through it to my actual self. For that body is all that is vulnerable about me: within this dwelling so liable to injury there lives a spirit that is free. Never shall that flesh compel me to feel fear, never shall it drive me to any pretence unworthy of a good man; never shall I tell a lie out of consideration for this petty body. I shall dissolve our partnership when this seems the proper course, and even now while we are bound one to the other the partnership will not be on equal terms: the soul will assume undivided authority. Refusal to be influenced by one's body assures one's freedom.

Seneca, *Letters to Lucilius,* 65

6 Then said Jesus to those Jews which believed on him, If ye continue in my word, then are ye my disciples indeed;

And ye shall know the truth, and the truth shall make you free.

John 8:31–32

7 We ourselves also were sometimes foolish, disobedient, deceived, serving divers lusts and pleasures, living in malice and envy, hateful, and hating one another.

But after that the kindness and love of God our Saviour toward man appeared,

Not by works of righteousness which we have done, but according to his mercy he saved us.

Titus 3:3–5

8 No one . . . who lives in error is free. Do you wish to live in fear? Do you wish to live in sorrow? Do you wish to live in perturbation? "By no means." No one . . . who is in a state of fear or sorrow or perturbation is free; but whoever is delivered from sorrows and fears and perturbations, he is at the same time also delivered from servitude.

Epictetus, *Discourses,* II, 1

9 He is free who lives as he wishes to live; who is neither subject to compulsion nor to hindrance, nor to force; whose movements to action are not impeded, whose desires attain their purpose, and who does not fall into that which he would avoid. Who, then, chooses to live in error? No man. Who chooses to live deceived, liable to mistake, unjust, unrestrained, discontented, mean? No man. Not one then of the bad lives as he wishes; nor is he, then, free. And who chooses to live in sorrow, fear, envy, pity, desiring and failing in his desires, attempting to avoid something and falling into it? Not one. Do we then find any of the bad free from sorrow, free from fear, who does not fall into that which he would avoid, and does not obtain that which he wishes? Not one; nor then do we find any bad man free.

Epictetus, *Discourses,* IV, 1

10 The man who is not under restraint is free, to whom things are exactly in that state in which he wishes them to be; but he who can be restrained or compelled or hindered, or thrown into any circumstances against his will, is a slave. But who is free from restraint? He who desires nothing that belongs to others. And what are the things which belong to others? Those which are not in our power either to have or not to have, or to have of a certain kind or in a certain manner. Therefore the body belongs to another, the parts of the body belong to another, possession belongs to another. If, then, you are attached to any of these things as your own, you will pay the penalty which it is proper for him to pay who desires what belongs to another. This road leads to freedom, that is the only way of escaping from slavery, to be able to say at last with all your soul

Lead me, O Zeus, and thou O destiny,
The way that I am bid by you to go.

Epictetus, *Discourses,* IV, 1

11 Being naturally noble, magnanimous and free, man sees that of the things which surround him some are free from hindrance and in his power, and the other things are subject to hindrance and in the power of others; that the things which are free from hindrance are in the power of the will; and those which are subject to hindrance are the things which are not in the power of the will. And, for this reason, if he thinks that his good and his interest be in these things only which are free from hindrance and in his own power, he will be free, prosperous, happy, free from harm, magnanimous, pious, thankful to God for all things; in no matter finding fault with any of the things which have not been put in his power, nor blaming any of them. But if he thinks that his good and his interest are in externals and in things which are not in the power of his will, he must of necessity be hindered, be impeded, be a slave to those

who have the power over things which he admires and fears; and he must of necessity be impious because he thinks that he is harmed by God, and he must be unjust because he always claims more than belongs to him; and he must of necessity be abject and mean.

Epictetus, *Discourses,* IV, 7

12 Do what thou hast in hand with perfect and simple dignity, and feeling of affection, and freedom, and justice; and . . . give thyself relief from all other thoughts. And thou wilt give thyself relief, if thou doest every act of thy life as if it were the last, laying aside all carelessness and passionate aversion from the commands of reason, and all hypocrisy, and self-love, and discontent with the portion which has been given to thee. Thou seest how few the things are, the which if a man lays hold of, he is able to live a life which flows in quiet, and is like the existence of the gods; for the gods on their part will require nothing more from him who observes these things.

Marcus Aurelius, *Meditations,* II, 5

13 Let the part of thy soul which leads and governs be undisturbed by the movements in the flesh, whether of pleasure or of pain; and let it not unite with them, but let it circumscribe itself and limit those affects to their parts. But when these affects rise up to the mind by virtue of that other sympathy that naturally exists in a body which is all one, then thou must not strive to resist the sensation, for it is natural: but let not the ruling part of itself add to the sensation the opinion that it is either good or bad.

Marcus Aurelius, *Meditations,* V, 26

14 It is in thy power to live free from all compulsion in the greatest tranquillity of mind, even if all the world cry out against thee as much as they choose, and even if wild beasts tear in pieces the members of this kneaded matter which has grown around thee. For what hinders the mind in the midst of all this from maintaining itself in tranquillity and in a just judgement of all surrounding things and in a ready use of the objects which are presented to it, so that the judgement may say to the thing which falls under its observation: This thou art in substance (reality), though in men's opinion thou mayest appear to be of a different kind; and the use shall say to that which falls under the hand: Thou art the thing that I was seeking; for to me that which presents itself is always a material for virtue both rational and political, and in a word, for the exercise of art, which belongs to man or God.

Marcus Aurelius, *Meditations,* VII, 68

15 Remember that to change thy opinion and to follow him who corrects thy error is as consistent with freedom as it is to persist in thy error.

Marcus Aurelius, *Meditations,* VIII, 16

16 Soul becomes free when it moves, through Intellectual-Principle, towards The Good; what it does in that spirit is its free act; Intellectual-Principle is free in its own right. That principle of Good is the sole object of desire and the source of self-disposal to the rest, to soul when it fully attains, to Intellectual-Principle by connate possession.

Plotinus, *Sixth Ennead,* VIII, 7

17 The wise man is always free; he is always held in honor; he is always master of the laws. The law is not made for the just but for the unjust. The just man is a law unto himself and he does not need to summon the law from afar, for he carries it enclosed in his heart. . . .

The wise man is free, since one who does as he wishes is free. Not every wish is good, but the wise man wishes only that which is good; he hates evil for he chooses what is good. Because he chooses what is good he is master of his choice and because he chooses his work is free. Then, because he does what he wishes the free man is wise. The wise man does well everything that he does. One who does all things well does all things rightly. But one who does all things rightly does everything without offense, without blame, without loss and disturbance within himself. And one who does nearly everything without giving offense acts blamelessly and acts without disturbance to himself, without loss. He does not act unwisely but wisely in all things. One who acts with wisdom has nothing to fear, for fear lies in sin. Where there is no fear there is liberty; where there is liberty there is the power of doing what one wishes. Therefore, only the wise man is free.

Ambrose, *Letter to Simplicianus (Benedictine 37)*

18 I was bound not with the iron of another's chains, but by my own iron will. The enemy held my will; and of it he made a chain and bound me. Because my will was perverse it changed to lust, and lust yielded to became habit, and habit not resisted became necessity. These were like links hanging one on another—which is why I have called it a chain— and their hard bondage held me bound hand and foot. The new will which I now began to have, by which I willed to worship You freely and to enjoy You, O God, the only certain Joy, was not yet strong enough to overcome that earlier will rooted deep through the years. My two wills, one old, one new, one carnal, one spiritual, were in conflict and in their conflict wasted my soul.

Augustine, *Confessions,* VIII, 5

19 To the just all the evils imposed on them by unjust rulers are not the punishment of crime, but the test of virtue. Therefore the good man, although he is a slave, is free; but the bad man, even if he

reigns, is a slave, and that not of one man, but, what is far more grievous, of as many masters as he has vices.

Augustine, *City of God*, IV, 3

20 The good will . . . is the work of God; for God created him with it. But the first evil will, which preceded all man's evil acts, was rather a kind of falling away from the work of God to its own works than any positive work. And therefore the acts resulting were evil, not having God, but the will itself for their end; so that the will or the man himself, so far as his will is bad, was as it were the evil tree bringing forth evil fruit. Moreover, the bad will, though it be not in harmony with, but opposed to nature, inasmuch as it is a vice or blemish, yet it is true of it as of all vice, that it cannot exist except in a nature, and only in a nature created out of nothing, and not in that which the Creator has begotten of Himself, as He begot the Word, by Whom all things were made. For though God formed man of the dust of the earth, yet the earth itself, and every earthly material, is absolutely created out of nothing; and man's soul, too, God created out of nothing, and joined to the body, when He made man. But evils are so thoroughly overcome by good that, though they are permitted to exist for the sake of demonstrating how the most righteous foresight of God can make a good use even of them, yet good can exist without evil, as in the true and supreme God Himself, and as in every invisible and visible celestial creature that exists above this murky atmosphere; but evil cannot exist without good, because the natures in which evil exists, in so far as they are natures, are good. And evil is removed, not by removing any nature, or part of a nature, which had been introduced by the evil, but by healing and correcting that which had been vitiated and depraved. The will, therefore, is then truly free, when it is not the slave of vices and sins. Such was it given us by God; and this being lost by its own fault, can only be restored by Him Who was able at first to give it. And therefore the truth says, "If the Son shall make you free, ye shall be free indeed"; which is equivalent to saying, "If the Son shall save you, ye shall be saved indeed." For He is our Liberator, inasmuch as He is our Saviour.

Augustine, *City of God*, XIV, 11

21 As, after the resurrection, the body, having become wholly subject to the spirit, will live in perfect peace to all eternity; even in this life we must make it an object to have the carnal habit changed for the better, so that its inordinate affections may not war against the soul. And until this shall take place, "the flesh lusteth against the spirit, and the spirit against the flesh"; the spirit struggling, not in hatred, but for the mastery, because it desires that what it loves should be subject to the higher principle; and the flesh struggling, not in hatred, but because of the bondage of habit which it has derived from its parent stock, and which has grown in upon it by a law of nature till it has become inveterate. The spirit, then, in subduing the flesh, is working as it were to destroy the ill-founded peace of an evil habit, and to bring about the real peace which springs out of a good habit.

Augustine, *Christian Doctrine*, I, 24

22 Our sensual appetite, where the passions reside, is not entirely subject to reason; hence at times our passions forestall and hinder reason's judgment, at other times they follow after reason's judgment, accordingly as the sensual appetite obeys reason to some extent. But in the state of innocence the inferior appetite was wholly subject to reason, so that in that state the passions of the soul existed only as consequent upon the judgment of reason.

Aquinas, *Summa Theologica*, I, 95, 2

23 Perfection of moral virtue does not wholly take away the passions, but regulates them.

Aquinas, *Summa Theologica*, I, 95, 2

24 In spiritual things there is a twofold servitude and a twofold freedom: for there is the servitude of sin and the servitude of justice; and there is likewise a twofold freedom, from sin, and from justice. . . .

Now the servitude of sin or justice consists in being inclined to evil by a habit of sin, or inclined to good by a habit of justice: and in like manner freedom from sin is not to be overcome by the inclination to sin, and freedom from justice is not to be held back from evil for the love of justice. Nevertheless, since man, by his natural reason, is inclined to justice, while sin is contrary to natural reason, it follows that freedom from sin is true freedom which is united to the servitude of justice, since they both incline man to that which is becoming to him. In like manner true servitude is the servitude of sin, which is connected with freedom from justice, because man is thereby hindered from attaining that which is proper to him.

Aquinas, *Summa Theologica*, II–II, 183, 4

25 It must be observed that so far as men are concerned, in order that any one attain to a state of freedom or servitude there is required first of all an obligation or a release. For the mere fact of serving someone does not make a man a slave, since even the free serve. . . . Nor again does the mere fact of ceasing to serve make a man free, as in the case of a runaway slave. But properly speaking a man is a slave if he be bound to serve, and a man is free if he be released from service. Secondly, it is required that the above obligation be imposed with a certain solemnity, even as a certain solemnity is observed in other matters which among men obtain a settlement in perpetu-

ity. Accordingly, properly speaking, one is said to be in the state of perfection not through having the act of perfect love, but through binding himself in perpetuity and with a certain solemnity to those things that pertain to perfection.

Aquinas, *Summa Theologica,* II–II, 184, 4

26 One must bear in mind that the sons of God are driven not as slaves, but as free men. For, since he is free who is for his own sake, we do that freely which we do of our very selves. But this is what we do of our will, but what we do against our will we do not freely but as slaves: be the violence absolute, as when "the whole principle is extrinsic, with the sufferer contributing nothing"—for instance, a man is pushed into motion; or be the violence mixed with the voluntary—for instance, when one wishes to do or to suffer what is less contrary to his will to avoid what is more contrary to it. But the Holy Spirit so inclines us to act that He makes us act voluntarily, in that He makes us lovers of God. Therefore, the sons of God are impelled by the Holy Spirit freely out of love, not slavishly out of fear.

Aquinas, *Summa Contra Gentiles,* IV, 22

27 *Marco.* From his hands who fondly loves her ere she is in being, there issues, after the fashion of a little child that sports, now weeping, now laughing,

the simple, tender soul, who knoweth naught save that, sprung from a joyous maker, willingly she turneth to that which delights her.

First she tastes the savour of a trifling good; there she is beguiled and runneth after it, if guide or curb turn not her love aside.

Wherefore 'twas needful to put law as a curb, needful to have a ruler who might discern at least the tower of the true city.

Laws there are, but who putteth his hand to them? None; because the shepherd that leads may chew the cud, but hath not the hoofs divided.

Wherefore the people, that see their guide aiming only at that good whereof he is greedy, feed on that and ask no further.

Clearly canst thou see that evil leadership is the cause which hath made the world sinful, and not nature that may be corrupted within you.

Dante, *Purgatorio,* XVI, 85

28 And he [Virgil] to me: "So far as reason sees here, I can tell thee; from beyond that point, ever await Beatrice, for 'tis a matter of faith.

Every substantial form, which is distinct from matter and is in union with it, has a specific virtue contained within itself

which is not perceived save in operation, nor is manifested except by its effects, just as life in a plant by the green leaves.

Therefore man knows not whence the under-

standing of the first cognitions may come, nor the inclination to the prime objects of appetite, which are in you, even as the instinct in bees to make honey; and this prime will admits no desert of praise or of blame.

Now in order that to this will every other may be related, innate with you is the virtue which giveth counsel, and ought to guard the threshold of assent.

This is the principle whence is derived the reason of desert in you, according as it garners and winnows good and evil loves.

Those who in their reasoning went to the foundation, perceived this innate freedom, therefore they left ethics to the world.

Wherefore suppose that every love which is kindled within you arise of necessity, the power to arrest it is within you.

Dante, *Purgatorio,* XVIII, 46

29 A Christian man has no need of any work or of any law in order to be saved, since through faith he is free from every law and does all that he does out of pure liberty and freely, seeking neither benefit nor salvation, since he already abounds in all things and is saved through the grace of God because of his faith, and now seeks only to please God.

Luther, *Freedom of a Christian*

30 All their [the Thelemites] life was spent not in laws, statutes, or rules, but according to their own free will and pleasure. They rose out of their beds when they thought good: they did eat, drink, labour, sleep, when they had a mind to it, and were disposed for it. None did awake them, none did offer to constrain them to eat, drink, nor to do any other thing; for so had Gargantua established it. In all their rule, and strictest tie of their order, there was but this one clause to be observed.

DO WHAT THOU WILT.

Because men that are free, well-born, well-bred, and conversant in honest companies, have naturally an instinct and spur that prompteth them unto virtuous actions, and withdraws them from vice, which is called honour. Those same men, when by base subjection and constraint they are brought under and kept down, turn aside from that noble disposition, by which they formerly were inclined to virtue, to shake off and break that bond of servitude, wherein they are so tyrannously enslaved; for it is agreeable with the nature of man to long after things forbidden, and to desire what is denied us.

By this liberty they entered into a very laudable emulation, to do all of them what they saw did please one.

Rabelais, *Gargantua and Pantagruel,* I, 57

31 The children of God are liberated by regeneration

from the servitude of sin; not that they have already obtained the full possession of liberty, and experience no more trouble from the flesh, but there remains in them a perpetual cause of contention to exercise them; and not only to exercise them, but also to make them better acquainted with their own infirmity. And on this subject all sound writers are agreed—that there still remains in a regenerate man a fountain of evil, continually producing irregular desires, which allure and stimulate him to the commission of sin.

Calvin, *Institutes of the Christian Religion,* III, 3

32 Since it has pleased God to give us some capacity for reason, so that we should not be, like the animals, slavishly subjected to the common laws, but should apply ourselves to them by judgment and voluntary liberty, we must indeed yield a little to the simple authority of Nature, but not let ourselves be carried away tyrannically by her: reason alone must guide our inclinations.

Montaigne, *Essays,* II, 8, Affection of
Fathers

33 True freedom is to have power over oneself for everything.

Montaigne, *Essays,* III, 12, Of Physiognomy

34 *Hamlet.*   Blest are those
Whose blood and judgement are so well commingled,
That they are not a pipe for fortune's finger
To sound what stop she please. Give me that man
That is not passion's slave, and I will wear him
In my heart's core, ay, in my heart of heart.

Shakespeare, *Hamlet,* III, ii, 73

35 The impotence of man to govern or restrain the affects I call bondage, for a man who is under their control is not his own master, but is mastered by fortune, in whose power he is, so that he is often forced to follow the worse, although he sees the better before him.

Spinoza, *Ethics,* IV, Preface

36 It will easily be seen in what consists the difference between a man who is led by affect or opinion alone and one who is led by reason. The former, whether he wills it or not, does those things of which he is entirely ignorant, but the latter does the will of no one but himself, and does those things only which he knows are of greatest importance in life, and which he therefore desires above all things. I call the former, therefore, a slave, and the latter free.

Spinoza, *Ethics,* IV, Prop. 66, Schol.

37 We may say that we are immune from bondage in so far as we act with a distinct knowledge, but that we are the slaves of passion in so far as our perceptions are confused. In this sense we have

not all the freedom of spirit that were to be desired, and we may say with St. Augustine that being subject to sin we have the freedom of a slave. Yet a slave, slave as he is, nevertheless has freedom to choose according to the state wherein he is, although more often than not he is under the stern necessity of choosing between two evils, because a superior force prevents him from attaining the goods whereto he aspires. That which in a slave is effected by bonds and constraint in us is effected by passions, whose violence is sweet, but none the less pernicious. In truth we will only that which pleases us: but unhappily what pleases us now is often a real evil, which would displease us if we had the eyes of the understanding open. Nevertheless that evil state of the slave, which is also our own, does not prevent us, any more than him, from making a free choice of that which pleases us most, in the state to which we are reduced, in proportion to our present strength and knowledge.

Leibniz, *Theodicy,* 289

38 If through defects that may happen out of the ordinary course of Nature, any one comes not to such a degree of reason wherein he might be supposed capable of knowing the law, and so living within the rules of it, he is never capable of being a free man, he is never let loose to the disposure of his own will; because he knows no bounds to it, has not understanding, its proper guide, but is continued under the tuition and government of others all the time his own understanding is incapable of that charge.

Locke, *II Civil Government,* VI, 60

39 A man on the rack is not at liberty to lay by the idea of pain, and divert himself with other contemplations: and sometimes a boisterous passion hurries our thoughts, as a hurricane does our bodies, without leaving us the liberty of thinking on other things, which we would rather choose. But as soon as the mind regains the power to stop or continue, begin or forbear, any of these motions of the body without, or thoughts within, according as it thinks fit to prefer either to the other, we then consider the man as a *free agent* again.

Locke, *Concerning Human
Understanding,* Bk. II, XXI, 12

40 Without liberty, the understanding would be to no purpose: and without understanding, liberty (if it could be) would signify nothing. If a man sees what would do him good or harm, what would make him happy or miserable, without being able to move himself one step towards or from it, what is he the better for seeing? And he that is at liberty to ramble in perfect darkness, what is his liberty better than if he were driven up and down as a bubble by the force of the wind? The being acted by a blind impulse from without, or from within,

is little odds. The first, therefore, and great use of liberty is to hinder blind precipitancy; the principal exercise of freedom is to stand still, open the eyes, look about, and take a view of the consequence of what we are going to do, as much as the weight of the matter requires.

Locke, *Concerning Human Understanding,* Bk. II, XXI, 69

41 When a man gives himself up to the government of a ruling passion,—or, in other words, when his Hobby-Horse grows headstrong,—farewell cool reason and fair discretion!

Sterne, *Tristram Shandy,* II, 5

42 Moral liberty . . . alone makes [man] truly master of himself; for the mere impulse of appetite is slavery, while obedience to a law which we prescribe to ourselves is liberty.

Rousseau, *Social Contract,* I, 8

43 In vain do we seek freedom under the power of the laws. The laws! Where is there any law? Where is there any respect for law? Under the name of law you have everywhere seen the rule of self-interest and human passion. But the eternal laws of nature and of order exist. For the wise man they take the place of positive law; they are written in the depths of his heart by conscience and reason; let him obey these laws and be free; for there is no slave but the evil-doer, for he always does evil against his will. Liberty is not to be found in any form of government, she is in the heart of the free man, he bears her with him everywhere.

Rousseau, *Emile,* V

44 It is . . . the moral law, of which we become directly conscious (as soon as we trace for ourselves maxims of the will), that *first* presents itself to us, and leads directly to the concept of freedom, inasmuch as reason presents it as a principle of determination not to be outweighed by any sensible conditions, nay, wholly independent of them.

Kant, *Critique of Practical Reason,* Pt. I, I, 1

45 Freedom and the consciousness of it as a faculty of following the moral law with unyielding resolution is *independence of inclinations,* at least as motives determining (though not as *affecting*) our desire, and so far as I am conscious of this freedom in following my moral maxims, it is the only source of an unaltered contentment which is necessarily connected with it and rests on no special feeling.

Kant, *Critique of Practical Reason,* Pt. I, II, 2

46 Virtue . . . in so far as it is based on internal freedom, contains a positive command for man, namely, that he should bring all his powers and inclinations under his rule (that of reason); and this is a positive precept of command over himself which is additional to the prohibition, namely, that he should not allow himself to be governed by his feelings and inclinations (the duty of *apathy*); since, unless reason takes the reins of government into its own hands, the feelings and inclinations play the master over the man.

Kant, *Introduction to the Metaphysical Elements of Ethics,* XVI

47 The laws of freedom, as distinguished from the laws of nature, are *moral* laws. So far as they refer only to external actions and their lawfulness, they are called *juridical*; but if they also require that, as laws, they shall themselves be the determining principles of our actions, they are *ethical.* The agreement of an action with juridical laws is its *legality;* the agreement of an action with ethical laws is its *morality.* The freedom to which the former laws refer, can only be freedom in external practice; but the freedom to which the latter laws refer is freedom in the internal as well as the external exercise of the activity of the will in so far as it is determined by laws of reason. So, in theoretical philosophy, it is said that only the objects of the external senses are in space, but all the objects both of internal and external sense are in time; because the representations of both, as being representations, so far belong all to the internal sense. In like manner, whether freedom is viewed in reference to the external or the internal action of the will, its laws, as pure practical laws of reason for the free activity of the will generally, must at the same time be inner principles for its determination, although they may not always be considered in this relation.

Kant, *General Introduction to the Metaphysic of Morals,* I

48 I am free . . . when my existence depends upon myself. This self-contained existence of spirit is none other than self-consciousness, consciousness of one's own being. Two things must be distinguished in consciousness; first, the fact *that I know;* secondly, *what I know.* In *self* consciousness these are merged in one; for spirit *knows itself.* It involves an appreciation of its own nature, as also an energy enabling it to realize itself; to make itself *actually* that which it is *potentially.*

Hegel, *Philosophy of History,* Introduction, 3

49 The slave is doomed to worship Time and Fate and Death, because they are greater than anything he finds in himself, and because all his thoughts are of things which they devour. But, great as they are, to think of them greatly, to feel their passionless splendor, is greater still. And such thought makes us free men; we no longer bow before the inevitable in Oriental subjection, but we absorb it, and make it a part of ourselves.

To abandon the struggle for private happiness, to expel all eagerness of temporary desire, to burn with passion for eternal things—this is emancipation, and this is the free man's worship.

Russell, *A Free Man's Worship*

50 Anyone who has successfully undergone the training of learning and recognizing the truth about himself is henceforth strengthened against the dangers of immorality, even if his standard of morality should in some respect deviate from the common one.

Freud, *General Introduction to Psycho-Analysis,* XXVII

51 One might compare the relation of the ego to the id with that between a rider and his horse. The horse provides the locomotive energy, and the rider has the prerogative of determining the goal and of guiding the movements of his powerful mount towards it. But all too often in the relations between the ego and the id we find a picture of the less ideal situation in which the rider is obliged to guide his horse in the direction in which it itself wants to go.

Freud, *New Introductory Lectures on Psycho-Analysis,* XXXI

52 If we state the moral law . . . as the injunction to each self on every occasion to identify the self with a new growth that is possible, then obedience to law is one with moral freedom.

Dewey, *Ethics,* Pt. II, XV, 5

53 The office of the moral law is that of a pedagogue, to protect and educate us in the use of freedom. At the end of this period of instruction, we are enfranchised from every servitude, even from the servitude of law, since Love made us one in spirit with the wisdom that is the source of Law.

Maritain, *Freedom in the Modern World*

9.5 | *Conscience*

According to its etymology, the word "conscience," deriving as it does from *conscire,* should have almost the same meaning as "conscious," indicating awareness or knowledge. But that is not the meaning of the word as it has come to be used in discourse about moral problems. In that context, it is used either to signify a sense of right and wrong, whether innate or acquired; or to signify the inner voice that determines the judgment an individual makes concerning what he should or should not do, or approve of, in a particular case.

Conscience does not displace but rather applies the principles or rules of the moral law, which is discussed in Section 9.3. Such principles or rules are universal or general formulations applicable to a wide variety of individual cases, some of which clearly fall under the rule and some of which involve aspects that might make them exceptions to the rule. Conscience is needed to make the judgment that considers the principle or rule in relation to this or that particular case, deciding either that the case calls for conformity to the rule or that the case justifies dispensation from it.

One quotation that the reader might expect to find here—Hamlet's statement that "conscience doth make cowards of us all"—has been placed elsewhere because, when it is read in the context of the whole "To be or not to be" speech, the meaning is clearly that it is a certain kind of knowledge, not the moral conscience, that causes us to become overtimid or overcautious when contemplating suicide.

Among the quotations assembled below, the reader will find some that discuss freedom of conscience and the right of private judgment in moral matters. These should be read in connection with related passages that have been placed in Section 13.2 on FREEDOM OF THOUGHT AND EXPRESSION: CENSORSHIP. The reader will also find, in quotations taken from Freud, the discussion of psychological phenomena that are related to conscience—remorse and a sense of guilt. Other passages from Freud on the sense of guilt with be found in Section 12.4 on CRIME AND PUNISHMENT. In Freud's theory of the matter, the reader will learn, the repressive strictures of the superego represent the voice of conscience.

---

1 The best audience for the practice of virtue is the approval of one's own conscience.

Cicero, *Disputations,* II, 26

2 Where there is a bad conscience, some circumstance or other may provide one with impunity, but never with freedom from anxiety.

Seneca, *Letters to Lucilius,* 105

3 There is nothing so preoccupied, so distracted, so rent and torn by so many and such varied passions as an evil mind. For when it cherishes some dark design, it is tormented with hope, care and anguish of spirit, and even when it has accomplished its criminal purpose, it is racked by anxiety, remorse and the fear of all manner of punishments.

Quintilian, *Institutio Oratoria,* XII, 1

4 Conscience is said to witness, to bind, or stir up, and also to accuse, torment, or rebuke. And all these follow the application of knowledge or science to what we do, which application is made in three ways. One way in so far as we recognize that we have done or not done something: *Thy conscience knoweth that thou hast often spoken evil of others,* and according to this, conscience is said to witness. In another way, so far as through the conscience we judge that something should be done or not done, and in this sense, conscience is said to stir up or to bind. In the third way, so far as by conscience we judge that something done is well done or ill done, and in this sense conscience is said to excuse, accuse, or torment. Now, it is clear that all these things follow the actual application of knowledge to what we do.

Aquinas, *Summa Theologica,* I, 79, 13

5 The laws of conscience, which we say are born of nature, are born of custom. Each man, holding in inward veneration the opinions and the behavior approved and accepted around him, cannot break loose from them without remorse, or apply himself to them without self-satisfaction.

Montaigne, *Essays,* I, 23, Of Custom

6 *King Richard.* Conscience is but a word that cowards use,

Devised at first to keep the strong in awe:
Our strong arms be our conscience, swords our law.

Shakespeare, *Richard III,* V, iii, 309

7 *Macbeth.*   Better be with the dead,
Whom we, to gain our peace, have sent to peace,
Than on the torture of the mind to lie
In restless ecstasy.

Shakespeare, *Macbeth,* III, ii, 19

8 Another doctrine repugnant to civil society is that whatsoever a man does against his conscience is sin; and it dependeth on the presumption of making himself judge of good and evil. For a man's conscience and his judgement is the same thing; and as the judgement, so also the conscience may be erroneous. Therefore, though he that is subject to no civil law sinneth in all he does against his conscience, because he has no other rule to follow but his own reason, yet it is not so with him that lives in a Commonwealth, because the law is the public conscience by which he hath already undertaken to be guided.

Hobbes, *Leviathan,* II, 29

9 *God.* And I will place within them as a guide
My Umpire *Conscience,* whom if they will hear,
Light after light well us'd they shall attain,
And to the end persisting, safe arrive.

Milton, *Paradise Lost,* III, 194

10 *Adam.* O Conscience, into what Abyss of fears
And horrors hast thou driv'n me; out of which
I find no way, from deep to deeper plung'd!

Milton, *Paradise Lost,* X, 842

11 A good conscience is never lawless in the worst regulated state, and will provide those laws for itself, which the neglect of legislators hath forgotten to supply.

Fielding, *Tom Jones,* XVII, 3

12 Surely if there is any thing in this life which a man may depend upon, and to the knowledge of which he is capable of arriving upon the most in-

disputable evidence, it must be this very thing,—
whether he has a good conscience or no.

Sterne, *Tristram Shandy,* II, 17

13 Whenever a man talks loudly against religion, always suspect that it is not his reason, but his passions, which have got the better of his creed. A
bad life and a good belief are disagreeable and
troublesome neighbours, and where they separate,
depend upon it, 'tis for no other cause but quietness' sake.

Sterne, *Tristram Shandy,* II, 17

14 I need only consult myself with regard to what I
wish to do; what I feel to be right is right, what I
feel to be wrong is wrong; conscience is the best
casuist; and it is only when we haggle with conscience that we have recourse to the subtleties of
argument.

Rousseau, *Emile,* IV

15 There is . . . at the bottom of our hearts an innate principle of justice and virtue, by which, in
spite of our maxims, we judge our own actions or
those of others to be good or evil; and it is this
principle that I call conscience.

Rousseau, *Emile,* IV

16 *Johnson.* Conscience is nothing more than a conviction felt by ourselves of something to be done,
or something to be avoided; and in questions of
simple unperplexed morality, conscience is very
often a guide that may be trusted. But before conscience can determine, the state of the question is
supposed to be completely known. In questions of
law, or of fact, conscience is very often confounded with opinion. No man's conscience can tell him
the right of another man; they must be known by
rational investigation or historical enquiry. Opinion, which he that holds it may call his conscience, may teach some men that religion would
be promoted, and quiet preserved, by granting to
the people universally the choice of their ministers. But it is a conscience very ill informed that
violates the rights of one man, for the convenience
of another.

Boswell, *Life of Johnson (May 1, 1773)*

17 Conscience is not a thing to be acquired, and it is
not a duty to acquire it; but every man, as a moral being, has it originally within him. To be
bound to have a conscience would be as much as
to say to be under a duty to recognize duties. For
conscience is practical reason which, in every case
of law, holds before a man his duty for acquittal
or condemnation; consequently it does not refer to
an object, but only to the subject (affecting the
moral feeling by its own act); so that it is an inevitable fact, not an obligation and duty. When,
therefore, it is said, "This man *has* no conscience,"

what is meant is that he pays no heed to its dictates. For if he really had none, he would not take
credit to himself for anything done according to
duty, nor reproach himself with violation of duty,
and therefore he would be unable even to conceive the duty of having a conscience.

I pass by the manifold subdivisions of conscience, and only observe what follows from what
has just been said, namely, that there is no such
thing as an *erring* conscience. No doubt it is possible sometimes to err in the objective judgement
whether something is a duty or not; but I cannot
err in the subjective whether I have compared it
with my practical (here judicially acting) reason
for the purpose of that judgement: for if I erred I
would not have exercised practical judgement at
all, and in that case there is neither truth nor
error. *Unconscientiousness* is not want of conscience,
but the propensity not to heed its judgement. But
when a man is conscious of having acted according to his conscience, then, as far as regards guilt
or innocence, nothing more can be required of
him, only he is bound to enlighten his *understanding*
as to what is duty or not; but when it comes or has
come to action, then conscience speaks involuntarily and inevitably. To act conscientiously can,
therefore, not be a duty, since otherwise it would
be necessary to have a second conscience, in order
to be conscious of the act of the first.

The duty here is only to cultivate our conscience, to quicken our attention to the voice of
the internal judge, and to use all means to secure
obedience to it, and is thus our indirect duty.

Kant, *Introduction to the Metaphysical
Elements of Ethics,* XII

18 Conscience is an instinct to pass judgment upon
ourselves in accordance with moral laws. It is not
a mere faculty, but an instinct; and its judgment
is not logical, but judicial. We have the faculty to
judge ourselves logically in terms of laws of morality; we can make such use as we please of this
faculty. But conscience has the power to summon
us against our will before the judgment-seat to be
judged on account of the righteousness or unrighteousness of our actions. It is thus an instinct and
not merely a faculty of judgment, and it is an
instinct to judge, not in the logical, but in the
judicial sense.

Kant, *Lectures on Ethics,* Conscience

19 He who has no immediate loathing for what is
morally wicked, and finds no pleasure in what is
morally good, has no moral feeling, and such a
man has no conscience. He who goes in fear of
being prosecuted for a wicked deed, does not reproach himself on the score of the wickedness of
his misdemeanour, but on the score of the painful
consequences which await him; such a one has no
conscience, but only a semblance of it. But he who
has a sense of the wickedness of the deed itself, be

the consequences what they may, has a conscience.

Kant, *Lectures on Ethics,* Conscience

20 Conscience is the representative within us of the divine judgment-seat: it weighs our dispositions and actions in the scales of a law which is holy and pure; we cannot deceive it, and, lastly, we cannot escape it because, like the divine omnipresence, it is always with us.

Kant, *Lectures on Ethics,* Conscience

21 We may speak in a very lofty strain about duty, and talk of the kind is uplifting and broadens human sympathies, but if it never comes to anything specific it ends in being wearisome. Mind demands particularity and is entitled to it. But conscience is this deepest inward solitude with oneself where everything external and every restriction has disappeared—this complete withdrawal into oneself. As conscience, man is no longer shackled by the aims of particularity, and consequently in attaining that position he has risen to higher ground, the ground of the modern world, which for the first time has reached this consciousness, reached this sinking into oneself. The more sensuous consciousness of earlier epochs had something external and given confronting it, either religion or law. But conscience knows itself as thinking and knows that what alone has obligatory force for me is this that I think.

When we speak of conscience, it may easily be thought that, in virtue of its form, which is abstract inwardness, conscience is at this point without more ado true conscience. But true conscience determines itself to will what is absolutely good and obligatory and is this self-determination.

Hegel, *Philosophy of Right,* Additions,
Pars. 136–137

22 A man could not have anything upon his conscience if God did not exist, for the relationship between the individual and God, the God-relationship, is the conscience, and that is why it is so terrible to have even the least thing upon one's conscience, because one is immediately conscious of the infinite weight of God.

Kierkegaard, *Works of Love,* I, 3B

23 The conscience really does not, and ought not to monopolize the whole of our lives, any more than the heart or the head. It is as liable to disease as any other part. I have seen some whose consciences, owing undoubtedly to former indulgence, had grown to be as irritable as spoilt children, and at length gave them no peace.

Thoreau, *The Christian Fable*

24 I fully subscribe to the judgment of those writers who maintain that of all the differences between man and the lower animals, the moral sense or conscience is by far the most important. . . . It is summed up in that short but imperious word *ought,* so full of high significance. It is the most noble of all the attributes of man, leading him without a moment's hesitation to risk his life for that of a fellow-creature; or after due deliberation, impelled simply by the deep feeling of right or duty, to sacrifice it in some great cause.

Darwin, *Descent of Man,* I, 4

25 The moral sense follows, firstly, from the enduring and ever-present nature of the social instincts; secondly, from man's appreciation of the approbation and disapprobation of his fellows; and thirdly, from the high activity of his mental faculties, with past impressions extremely vivid; and in these latter respects he differs from the lower animals. Owing to this condition of mind, man cannot avoid looking both backwards and forwards, and comparing past impressions. Hence after some temporary desire or passion has mastered his social instincts, he reflects and compares the now weakened impression of such past impulses with the ever-present social instincts; and he then feels that sense of dissatisfaction which all unsatisfied instincts leave behind them, he therefore resolves to act differently for the future,—and this is conscience.

Darwin, *Descent of Man,* III, 21

26 It is not because men's desires are strong that they act ill; it is because their consciences are weak. There is no natural connection between strong impulses and a weak conscience. The natural connection is the other way. To say that one person's desires and feelings are stronger and more various than those of another, is merely to say that he has more of the raw material of human nature, and is therefore capable, perhaps of more evil, but certainly of more good. Strong impulses are but another name for energy. Energy may be turned to bad uses; but more good may always be made of an energetic nature, than of an indolent and impassive one. Those who have most natural feeling are always those whose cultivated feelings may be made the strongest. The same strong susceptibilities which make the personal impulses vivid and powerful, are also the source from whence are generated the most passionate love of virtue, and the sternest self-control. It is through the cultivation of these that society both does its duty and protects its interests: not by rejecting the stuff of which heroes are made, because it knows not how to make them.

Mill, *On Liberty,* III

27 The internal sanction of duty, whatever our standard of duty may be, is one and the same—a feeling in our own mind; a pain, more or less intense, attendant on violation of duty, which in properly cultivated moral natures rises, in the more serious cases, into shrinking from it as an impossibility.

This feeling, when disinterested, and connecting itself with the pure idea of duty, and not with some particular form of it, or with any of the merely accessory circumstances, is the essence of Conscience.

Mill, *Utilitarianism,* III

28 I regard the bad conscience as the serious illness which man was bound to contract under the stress of the most radical change which he has ever experienced—that change, when he found himself finally imprisoned within the pale of society and of peace.

Nietzsche, *Genealogy of Morals,* II, 16

29 What means does civilization make use of to hold in check the aggressiveness that opposes it, to make it harmless, perhaps to get rid of it? Some of these measures we have already come to know, though not yet the one that is apparently the most important. We can study it in the evolution of the individual. What happens in him to render his craving for aggression innocuous? Something very curious, that we should never have guessed and that yet seems simple enough. The aggressiveness is introjected, *internalized;* in fact, it is sent back

where it came from, ie., directed against the ego. It is there taken over by a part of the ego that distinguishes itself from the rest as a super-ego, and now, in the form of *conscience,* exercises the same propensity to harsh aggressiveness against the ego that the ego would have liked to enjoy against others. The tension between the strict super-ego and the subordinate ego we call the *sense of guilt;* it manifests itself as the need for punishment. Civilization, therefore, obtains the mastery over the dangerous love of aggression in individuals by enfeebling and disarming it and setting up an institution within their minds to keep watch over it, like a garrison in a conquered city.

Freud, *Civilization and Its Discontents,* VII

30 This increased sensitivity of morals in consequence of ill-luck has been illustrated by Mark Twain in a delicious little story: *The First Melon I ever Stole.* This melon, as it happened, was unripe. I heard Mark Twain tell the story himself in one of his lectures. After he had given out the title, he stopped and asked himself in a doubtful way: "Was it the first?" This was the whole story.

Freud, *Civilization and Its Discontents,* VII

9.6 | *Good and Evil*

The terms good and evil are used in other contexts than those of ethical or moral discourse. According to *Genesis,* God surveying his creation judged it to be good, very good. Similar judgments are made by human artists, expressing their estimation of the excellence or perfection of the work produced. In this meaning of the word, beauty, excellence, or perfection represents a goodness inherent in the very being of the thing judged good, without regard to its bearing on human conduct or its value for human life. Such goodness is sometimes called "ontological," in contradistinction to the moral goodness of the things that are good for man or good in his behavior. It is in this ontological sense that a mouse is said to be more

good than a pearl, though a pearl is more valuable to man.

As the reader will find in the quotations below, the human good or the good for man is sometimes discussed in the singular and sometimes spoken of as a class of goods. The reader will find passages that consider "the Good," or that assert that the only morally good thing in the whole world is a good will. On the other hand, the reader will find enumerations of the variety of goods, discussions of the order of goods and of the relation of one good to another, and different classifications of goods, such as the threefold division of them into external goods, goods of the body, and goods of the soul.

One distinction that is made by the ancients has great importance for later discussion. It is the distinction between the real and the apparent good. While acknowledging that men always regard as good that which they in fact desire, Socrates calls attention to the fact that they can be mistaken in their judgment, for what they desire may in fact not be good for them or to their advantage. It is generally admitted that the notion of the good and the notion of the desirable are correlative, but the question remains whether we call something good because we desire it; or ought to desire it, whether we do or not, because it is in fact good for us; or both. Fundamental differences in the approach to moral philosophy emerge from different answers to this question.

The quotations below touch on many other points: whether pleasure is the only good or just one of the goods; the goodness of God and the problem of the existence of evil in the world that He created; our knowledge of good and evil and the diremption between knowing what is good and seeking it; the inherent or natural goodness of man and the sources or origin of his propensities for evil. Other discussions of the theological aspects of this subject will be found in Section 20.5 on GOD and in Section 20.13 on SIN AND TEMPTATION. Psychological aspects of it are treated in Section 4.4 on DESIRE and Section 4.7 on PLEASURE AND PAIN; and also in Section 5.7 on WILL: FREE CHOICE. The reader is also referred to Section 16.6 on BEAUTY AND THE BEAUTIFUL for the relation of goodness to beauty; and to Section 11.2 on WEALTH AND POVERTY for the economic discussion of value and for the consideration of economic goods. In this chapter, Section 9.7 on RIGHT AND WRONG, Section 9.8 on HAPPINESS, and Section 9.10 on VIRTUE AND VICE deal with matters closely related to themes treated here.

---

1 And God saw every thing that he had made, and, behold, it was very good.

Genesis 1:31

2 So I returned, and considered all the oppressions that are done under the sun: and behold the tears of such as were oppressed, and they had no comforter; and on the side of their oppressors there was power; but they had no comforter.

Wherefore I praised the dead which are already dead more than the living which are yet alive.

Yea, better is he than both they, which hath not yet been, who hath not seen the evil work that is done under the sun.

Ecclesiastes 4:1–3

3 For all this I considered in my heart even to declare all this, that the righteous, and the wise, and their works, are in the hand of God: no man knoweth either love or hatred by all that is before them.

All things come alike to all: there is one event to the righteous, and to the wicked; to the good and to the clean, and to the unclean; to him that sacrificeth, and to him that sacrificeth not: as is the good, so is the sinner; and he that sweareth, as he that feareth an oath.

This is an evil among all things that are done under the sun, that there is one event unto all: yea, also the heart of the sons of men is full of evil, and madness is in their heart while they live, and after that they go to the dead.

Ecclesiastes 9:1–3

4 *Philoctetes.* The Gods . . . find their pleasure in turning back from Death the rogues and tricksters, but the just and good they are always sending out of the world.

Sophocles, *Philoctetes,* 447

5 *Hecuba.*   Goodness can be taught,
and any man who knows what goodness is
knows evil too, because he judges
from the good.

Euripides, *Hecuba,* 600

6 *Chorus Leader.* I hate all evil men who plot injustice,
Then trick it out with subterfuge. I would
Prefer as friend a good man ignorant
Than one more clever who is evil too.

Euripides, *Ion,* 832

7 *Socrates.* The good are like one another, and friends to one another; and . . . the bad, as is often said of them, are never at unity with one another or with themselves; for they are passionate and restless, and anything which is at variance and enmity with itself is not likely to be in union or harmony with any other thing.

Plato, *Lysis,* 214B

8 *Socrates.* No man voluntarily pursues evil, or that which he thinks to be evil. To prefer evil to good is not in human nature; and when a man is compelled to choose one of two evils, no one will choose the greater when he may have the less.

Plato, *Protagoras,* 358B

9 *Meno.* Well then, Socrates, virtue, as I take it, is when he, who desires the honourable, is able to provide it for himself; so the poet says, and I say too—

Virtue is the desire of things honourable and the power of attaining them.

Socrates. And does he who desires the honourable also desire the good?

Men. Certainly.

Soc. Then are there some who desire the evil and others who desire the good? Do not all men, my dear sir, desire good?

Men. I think not.

Soc. There are some who desire evil?

Men. Yes.

Soc. Do you mean that they think the evils which they desire, to be good; or do they know that they are evil and yet desire them?

Men. Both, I think.

Soc. And do you really imagine, Meno, that a man knows evils to be evils and desires them notwithstanding?

Men. Certainly I do.

Soc. And desire is of possession?

Men. Yes, of possession.

Soc. And does he think that the evils will do good to him who possesses them, or does he know that they will do him harm?

Men. There are some who think that the evils will do them good, and others who know that they will do them harm.

Soc. And, in your opinion, do those who think that they will do them good know that they are evils?

Men. Certainly not.

Soc. Is it not obvious that those who are ignorant of their nature do not desire them; but they desire what they suppose to be goods although they are really evils; and if they are mistaken and suppose the evils to be good they really desire goods?

Men. Yes, in that case.

Soc. Well, and do those who, as you say, desire evils, and think that evils are hurtful to the possessor of them, know that they will be hurt by them?

Men. They must know it.

Soc. And must they not suppose that those who are hurt are miserable in proportion to the hurt which is inflicted upon them?

Men. How can it be otherwise?

Soc. But are not the miserable ill-fated?

Men. Yes, indeed.

Soc. And does any one desire to be miserable and ill-fated?

Men. I should say not, Socrates.

Soc. But if there is no one who desires to be miserable, there is no one, Meno, who desires evil; for what is misery but the desire and possession of evil?

Men. That appears to be the truth, Socrates, and I admit that nobody desires evil.

Soc. And yet, were you not saying just now that virtue is the desire and power of attaining good?

Men. Yes, I did say so.

Soc. But if this be affirmed, then the desire of good is common to all, and one man is no better than another in that respect?

Men. True.

Soc. And if one man is not better than another in desiring good, he must be better in the power of attaining it?

Men. Exactly.

Soc. Then, according to your definition, virtue would appear to be the power of attaining good?

Men. I entirely approve, Socrates, of the manner in which you now view this matter.

Soc. Then let us see whether what you say is true from another point of view; for very likely you may be right.

Plato, *Meno,* 77A

10 *Socrates.* God, if he be good, is not the author of all things, as the many assert, but he is the cause of a few things only, and not of most things that occur to men. For few are the goods of human life, and many are the evils, and the good is to be attributed to God alone; of the evils the causes are to be sought elsewhere, and not in him. . . . That God being good is the author of evil to any one is to be strenuously denied, and not to be said or sung or heard in verse or prose by any one whether old or young in any well-ordered commonwealth.

Plato, *Republic,* II, 379B

11 *Socrates.* No one can deny that all percipient beings desire and hunt after good, and are eager to catch and have the good about them, and care not for the attainment of anything which is not accompanied by good.

Protarchus. That is undeniable.

Soc. Now let us part off the life of pleasure from the life of wisdom, and pass them in review.

Pro. How do you mean?

Soc. Let there be no wisdom in the life of pleasure, nor any pleasure in the life of wisdom, for if either of them is the chief good, it cannot be supposed to want anything, but if either is shown to want anything, then it cannot really be the chief good.

Pro. Impossible.

Soc. And will you help us to test these two lives?

Pro. Certainly.

Soc. Then answer.

Pro. Ask.

Soc. Would you choose, Protarchus, to live all your life long in the enjoyment of the greatest pleasures?

Pro. Certainly I should.

Soc. Would you consider that there was still anything wanting to you if you had perfect pleasure?

Pro. Certainly not.

Soc. Reflect; would you not want wisdom and intelligence and forethought, and similar qualities? would you not at any rate want sight?

Pro. Why should I? Having pleasure I should have all things.

Soc. Living thus, you would always throughout your life enjoy the greatest pleasures?

Pro. I should.

Soc. But if you had neither mind, nor memory, nor knowledge, nor true opinion, you would in the first place be utterly ignorant of whether you were pleased or not, because you would be entirely devoid of intelligence.

Pro. Certainly.

Soc. And similarly, if you had no memory you would not recollect that you had ever been pleased, nor would the slightest recollection of the pleasure which you feel at any moment remain with you; and if you had no true opinion you would not think that you were pleased when you were; and if you had no power of calculation you would not be able to calculate on future pleasure, and your life would be the life, not of a man, but of an oyster or *pulmo marinus.* Could this be otherwise?

Pro. No.

Soc. But is such a life eligible?

Pro. I cannot answer you, Socrates; the argument has taken away from me the power of speech.

Soc. We must keep up our spirits;—let us now take the life of mind and examine it in turn.

Pro. And what is this life of mind?

Soc. I want to know whether any one of us would consent to live, having wisdom and mind and knowledge and memory of all things, but having no sense of pleasure or pain, and wholly unaffected by these and the like feelings?

Pro. Neither life, Socrates, appears eligible to me, or is likely, as I should imagine, to be chosen by any one else.

Soc. What would you say, Protarchus, to both of these in one, or to one that was made out of the union of the two?

Pro. Out of the union, that is, of pleasure with mind and wisdom?

Soc. Yes, that is the life which I mean.

Pro. There can be no difference of opinion; not some but all would surely choose this third rather than either of the other two, and in addition to them.

Soc. But do you see the consequence?

Pro. To be sure I do. The consequence is, that two out of the three lives which have been proposed are neither sufficient nor eligible for man or for animal.

Plato, *Philebus,* 20B

12 *Athenian Stranger.* Goods are of two kinds: there are human and there are divine goods, and the human hang upon the divine; and the state which attains the greater, at the same time acquires the less, or, not having the greater, has neither. Of the lesser goods the first is health, the second beauty, the third strength, including swiftness in running and bodily agility generally, and the fourth is wealth. . . . Wisdom is chief and leader of the divine class of goods, and next follows temperance; and from the union of these two with courage springs justice, and fourth in the scale of virtue is courage.

Plato, *Laws,* I, 631A

13 *Athenian Stranger.* The goods of which the many speak are not really good: first in the catalogue is placed health, beauty next, wealth third; and then innumerable others, as for example to have a keen eye or a quick ear, and in general to have all the senses perfect; or, again, to be a tyrant and do as you like; and the final consummation of happiness is to have acquired all these things, and when you have acquired them to become at once immortal. . . . While to the just and holy all these things are the best of possessions, to the unjust they are all, including even health, the greatest of evils.

Plato, *Laws,* II, 661A

14 Let us . . . state, in view of the fact that all knowledge and every pursuit aims at some good, what it is that we say political science aims at and what is the highest of all goods achievable by action. Verbally there is very general agreement; for both the general run of men and people of superior refinement say that it is happiness, and identify living well and doing well with being happy; but with regard to what happiness is they differ, and the many do not give the same account as the wise. For the former think it is some plain and obvious thing, like pleasure, wealth, or honour; they differ, however, from one another—and often even the same man identifies it with different things, with health when he is ill, with wealth

when he is poor; but, conscious of their ignorance, they admire those who proclaim some great ideal that is above their comprehension. . . .

To judge from the lives that men lead, most men, and men of the most vulgar type, seem (not without some ground) to identify the good, or happiness, with pleasure; which is the reason why they love the life of enjoyment. For there are, we may say, three prominent types of life—that just mentioned, the political, and thirdly the contemplative life. Now the mass of mankind are evidently quite slavish in their tastes, preferring a life suitable to beasts. . . . A consideration of the prominent types of life shows that people of superior refinement and of active disposition identify happiness with honour; for this is, roughly speaking, the end of the political life. But it seems too superficial to be what we are looking for, since it is thought to depend on those who bestow honour rather than on him who receives it, but the good we divine to be something proper to a man and not easily taken from him. . . .

The life of money-making is one undertaken under compulsion, and wealth is evidently not the good we are seeking; for it is merely useful and for the sake of something else. And so one might rather take the aforenamed objects to be ends; for they are loved for themselves. But it is evident that not even these are ends; yet many arguments have been thrown away in support of them.

Aristotle, *Ethics*, 1095ª13

15 Goods have been divided into three classes, and some are described as external, others as relating to soul or to body; we call those that relate to soul most properly and truly goods, and psychical actions and activities we class as relating to soul. Therefore our account must be sound, at least according to this view, which is an old one and agreed on by philosophers. It is correct also in that we identify the end with certain actions and activities; for thus it falls among goods of the soul and not among external goods. Another belief which harmonizes with our account is that the happy man lives well and does well; for we have practically defined happiness as a sort of good life and good action. The characteristics that are looked for in happiness seem also, all of them, to belong to what we have defined happiness as being. For some identify happiness with virtue, some with practical wisdom, others with a kind of philosophic wisdom, others with these, or one of these, accompanied by pleasure or not without pleasure; while others include also external prosperity. Now some of these views have been held by many men and men of old, others by a few eminent persons; and it is not probable that either of these should be entirely mistaken, but rather that they should be right in at least some one respect or even in most respects.

With those who identify happiness with virtue or some one virtue our account is in harmony; for to virtue belongs virtuous activity. But it makes, perhaps, no small difference whether we place the chief good in possession or in use, in state of mind or in activity. For the state of mind may exist without producing any good result, as in a man who is asleep or in some other way quite inactive, but the activity cannot; for one who has the activity will of necessity be acting, and acting well and as in the Olympic Games it is not the most beautiful and the strongest that are crowned but those who compete. . . . So those who act win, and rightly win, the noble and good things in life.

Aristotle, *Ethics*, 1098ᵇ13

16 It is harder to fight with pleasure than with anger, to use Heraclitus' phrase, but both art and virtue are always concerned with what is harder; for even the good is better when it is harder.

Aristotle, *Ethics*, 1105ª8

17 It is no easy task to be good. For in everything it is no easy task to find the middle, e.g. to find the middle of a circle is not for every one but for him who knows; so, too, any one can get angry—that is easy—or give or spend money; but to do this to the right person, to the right extent, at the right time, with the right motive, and in the right way, *that* is not for every one, nor is it easy; wherefore goodness is both rare and laudable and noble.

Aristotle, *Ethics*, 1109ª24

18 Those who say that the good is the object of wish must admit in consequence that that which the man who does not choose aright wishes for is not an object of wish (for if it is to be so, it must also be good; but it was, if it so happened, bad); while those who say the apparent good is the object of wish must admit that there is no natural object of wish, but only what seems good to each man. Now different things appear good to different people, and, if it so happens, even contrary things.

If these consequences are unpleasing, are we to say that absolutely and in truth the good is the object of wish, but for each person the apparent good; that that which is in truth an object of wish is an object of wish to the good man, while any chance thing may be so to the bad man, as in the case of bodies also the things that are in truth wholesome are wholesome for bodies which are in good condition, while for those that are diseased other things are wholesome—or bitter or sweet or hot or heavy, and so on; since the good man judges each class of things rightly, and in each the truth appears to him? For each state of character has its own ideas of the noble and the pleasant, and perhaps the good man differs from others most by seeing the truth in each class of things, being as it were the norm and measure of them. In most things the error seems to be due to pleasure; for it appears a good when it is not. We therefore choose the pleasant as a good, and avoid pain as an evil.

Aristotle, Ethics, 1113ª17

19 Evil destroys even itself, and if it is complete becomes unbearable.

Aristotle, Ethics, 1126ª12

20 Those who have done many terrible deeds and are hated for their wickedness even shrink from life and destroy themselves. And wicked men seek for people with whom to spend their days, and shun themselves; for they remember many a grevious deed, and anticipate others like them, when they are by themselves, but when they are with others they forget. And having nothing lovable in them they have no feeling of love to themselves. Therefore also such men do not rejoice or grieve with themselves; for their soul is rent by faction, and one element in it by reason of its wickedness grieves when it abstains from certain acts, while the other part is pleased, and one draws them this way and the other that, as if they were pulling them in pieces. If a man cannot at the same time be pained and pleased, at all events after a short time he is pained *because* he was pleased, and he could have wished that these things had not been pleasant to him; for bad men are laden with repentance.

Therefore the bad man does not seem to be amicably disposed even to himself, because there is nothing in him to love; so that if to be thus is the height of wretchedness, we should strain every nerve to avoid wickedness and should endeavour to be good; for so and only so can one be either friendly to oneself or a friend to another.

Aristotle, Ethics, 1166ᵇ12

21 Some think that we are made good by nature, others by habituation, others by teaching. Nature's part evidently does not depend on us, but as a result of some divine causes is present in those who are truly fortunate; while argument and teaching, we may suspect, are not powerful with all men, but the soul of the student must first have been cultivated by means of habits for noble joy and noble hatred, like earth which is to nourish the seed. For he who lives as passion directs will not hear argument that dissuades him, nor understand it if he does; and how can we persuade one in such a state to change his ways? And in general passion seems to yield not to argument but to force. The character, then, must somehow be there already with a kinship to virtue, loving what is noble and hating what is base.

Aristotle, Ethics, 1179ᵇ20

22 Ignorance of good and evil is the most upsetting factor of human life. Because of mistaken ideas on these two matters, we are frequently deprived of

our greatest pleasures, and our minds are overcome with anxiety.

Cicero, De Finibus, I, 13

23 Here [in Happy Groves] patriots live, who, for their country's good,
In fighting fields, were prodigal of blood:
Priests of unblemish'd lives here make abode
And poets worthy their inspiring god;
And searching wits, of more mechanic parts,
Who grac'd their age with new-invented arts:
Those who to worth their bounty did extend,
And those who knew that bounty to commend.
The heads of these with holy fillets bound,
And all their temples were with garlands crown'd.

Virgil, Aeneid, VI

24 The most part of us desire what is evil through our strangeness to and ignorance of good.

Plutarch, Artaxerxes

25 What a man applies himself to earnestly, that he naturally loves. Do men then apply themselves earnestly to the things which are bad? By no means. Well, do they apply themselves to things which in no way concern themselves? Not to these either. It remains, then, that they employ themselves earnestly only about things which are good; and if they are earnestly employed about things, they love such things also.

Epictetus, Discourses, II, 22

26 The business of the wise and good man is to use appearances conformably to nature: and as it is the nature of every soul to assent to the truth, to dissent from the false, and to remain in suspense as to that which is uncertain; so it is its nature to be moved toward the desire of the good, and to aversion from the evil; and with respect to that which is neither good nor bad it feels indifferent. For as the money-changer is not allowed to reject Cæsar's coin, nor the seller of herbs, but if you show the coin, whether he chooses or not, he must give up what is sold for the coin; so it is also in the matter of the soul. When the good appears, it immediately attracts to itself; the evil repels from itself. But the soul will never reject the manifest appearance of the good, any more than persons will reject Cæsar's coin.

Epictetus, Discourses, III, 3

27 Seek not the good in things external; seek it in yourselves: if you do not, you will not find it.

Epictetus, Discourses, III, 24

28 As a mark is not set up for the sake of missing the aim, so neither does the nature of evil exist in the world.

Epictetus, Encheiridion, XXVII

29 Nothing is evil which is according to nature.

Marcus Aurelius, Meditations, II, 17

30 It is a ridiculous thing for a man not to fly from his own badness, which is indeed possible, but to fly from other men's badness, which is impossible.

Marcus Aurelius, *Meditations*, VII, 71

31 No longer talk at all about the kind of man that a good man ought to be, but be such.

Marcus Aurelius, *Meditations*, X, 16

32 Health and freedom from pain; which of these has any great charm? As long as we possess them, we set no store upon them. Anything which, present, has no charm and adds nothing to happiness, which when lacking is desired because of the presence of an annoying opposite, may reasonably be called a necessity but not a Good.

Plotinus, *First Ennead*, IV, 6

33 As necessarily as there is Something after the First, so necessarily there is a Last: this Last is Matter, the thing which has no residue of good in it: here is the necessity of Evil.

Plotinus, *First Ennead*, VIII, 7

34 The light streaming from the Soul is dulled, is weakened, as it mixes with Matter which offers Birth to the Soul, providing the means by which it enters into generation, impossible to it if no recipient were at hand.

This is the fall of the Soul, this entry into Matter: thence its weakness: not all the faculties of its being retain free play, for Matter hinders their manifestation; it encroaches upon the Soul's territory and, as it were, crushes the Soul back; and it turns to evil all that it has stolen, until the Soul finds strength to advance again.

Thus the cause, at once, of the weakness of Soul and of all its evil is Matter.

Plotinus, *First Ennead*, VIII, 11

35 Each several thing must be a separate thing; there must be acts and thoughts that are our own; the good and evil done by each human being must be his own; and it is quite certain that we must not lay any vileness to the charge of the All.

Plotinus, *Third Ennead*, I, 4

36 This Universe is good not when the individual is a stone, but when everyone throws in his own voice towards a total harmony, singing out a life—thin, harsh, imperfect, though it be.

Plotinus, *Third Ennead*, II, 17

37 If we do not possess good, we cannot bestow it; nor can we ever purvey any good thing to one that has no power of receiving good.

Plotinus, *Fourth Ennead*, IV, 45

38 To the lowest of things the good is its immediate higher; each step represents the good to what stands lower so long as the movement does not tend awry but advances continuously towards the superior: thus there is a halt at the Ultimate, beyond which no ascent is possible: that is, the First Good, the authentic, the supremely sovereign, the source of good to the rest of things.

Matter would have Forming-Idea for its good, since, were it conscious, it would welcome that; body would look to soul, without which it could not be or endure; soul must look to virtue; still higher stands Intellectual-Principle; above that again is the principle we call the Primal. Each of these progressive priors must have act upon those minors to which they are, respectively, the good: some will confer order and place, others life, others wisdom and the good life.

Plotinus, *Sixth Ennead*, VII, 25

39 It was by Your gift that I desired what You gave and no more, by Your gift that those who suckled me willed to give me what You had given them: for it was by the love implanted in them by You that they gave so willingly that milk which by Your gift flowed in the breasts. It was a good for them that I received good from them, though I received it not *from* them but only through them: since all good things are from You, O God.

Augustine, *Confessions*, I, 6

40 In goodness of will is our peace.

Augustine, *Confessions*, XIII, 9

41 Though good and bad men suffer alike, we must not suppose that there is no difference between the men themselves, because there is no difference in what they both suffer. For even in the likeness of the sufferings, there remains an unlikeness in the sufferers; and though exposed to the same anguish, virtue and vice are not the same thing. For as the same fire causes gold to glow brightly, and chaff to smoke; and under the same flail the straw is beaten small, while the grain is cleansed; and as the lees are not mixed with the oil, though squeezed out of the vat by the same pressure, so the same violence of affliction proves, purges, clarifies the good, but damns, ruins, exterminates the wicked.

Augustine, *City of God*, I, 8

42 According to the utility each man finds in a thing, there are various standards of value, so that it comes to pass that we prefer some things that have no sensation to some sentient beings. And so strong is this preference, that, had we the power, we would abolish the latter from nature altogether, whether in ignorance of the place they hold in nature, or, though, we know it, sacrificing them to our own convenience. Who, for example, would not rather have bread in his house than mice, gold than fleas? But there is little to wonder at in this, seeing that even when valued by men themselves (whose nature is certainly of the highest dignity),

more is often given for a horse than for a slave, for a jewel than for a maid. Thus the reason of one contemplating nature prompts very different judgments from those dictated by the necessity of the needy, or the desire of the voluptuous; for the former considers what value a thing in itself has in the scale of creation, while necessity considers how it meets its need.

Augustine, *City of God*, XI, 16

43 God, the author of natures, not of vices, created man upright; but man, being of his own will corrupted and justly condemned, begot corrupted and condemned children. For we all were in that one man, since we all were that one man, who fell into sin by the woman who was made from him before the sin. . . . And thus, from the bad use of free will, there originated the whole train of evil, which, with its concatenation of miseries, convoys the human race from its depraved origin, as from a corrupt root, on to the destruction of the second death, which has no end, those only being excepted who are freed by the grace of God.

Augustine, *City of God*, XIII, 14

44 The possession of goodness is by no means diminished by being shared with a partner either permanent or temporarily assumed; on the contrary, the possession of goodness is increased in proportion to the concord and charity of each of those who share it. In short, he who is unwilling to share this possession cannot have it; and he who is most willing to admit others to a share of it will have the greatest abundance to himself.

Augustine, *City of God*, XV, 5

45 Life eternal is the supreme good, death eternal the supreme evil.

Augustine, *City of God*, XIX, 4

46 He [God] judged it better to bring good out of evil, than not to permit any evil to exist.

Augustine, *Enchiridion*, XXVII

47 Good and being are really the same, and differ only according to reason, which is clear from the following argument. The essence of good consists in this, that it is in some way desirable. Hence the Philosopher [Aristotle] says "The good is what all desire." Now it is clear that a thing is desirable only in so far as it is perfect; for all desire their own perfection. But everything is perfect so far as it is in act. Therefore it is clear that a thing is good so far as it is being; for it is being is the actuality of all things. . . . Hence it is clear that good and being are the same really. But good presents the aspect of desirableness, which being does not present.

Aquinas, *Summa Theologica*, I, 5, 1

48 Non-being is desirable not of itself, but only acci-

dentally—that is, in so far as the removal of an evil, which can only be removed by non-being, is desirable. Now the removal of an evil cannot be desirable except so far as this evil deprives a thing of some being. Therefore being is desirable of itself, and non-being only accidentally, in so far as one seeks some being of which one cannot bear to be deprived; thus even non-being can be spoken of as relatively good.

Aquinas, *Summa Theologica*, I, 5, 2

49 No being can be spoken of as evil, in so far as it is being, but only so far as it lacks being. Thus a man is said to be evil because he lacks the being of virtue; and an eye is said to be evil because it lacks the power to see well.

Aquinas, *Summa Theologica*, I, 5, 3

50 He who has a will is said to be good, so far as he has a good will, because it is by our will that we employ whatever powers we may have. Hence a man is said to be good, not by his good understanding, but by his good will. Now the will relates to the end as to its proper object. Thus the saying, "we are because God is good" has reference to the final cause.

Aquinas, *Summa Theologica*, I, 5, 4

51 The evil which consists in the defect of action is always caused by the defect of the agent. But in God there is no defect, but the highest perfection. . . . Hence, the evil which consists in defect of action, or which is caused by defect of the agent, is not reduced to God as to its cause.

But the evil which consists in the corruption of some things is reduced to God as the cause. And this appears as regards both natural things and voluntary things. For . . . some agent, in so far as it produces by its power a form to which follows corruption and defect, causes by its power that corruption and defect. But it is manifest that the form which God chiefly intends in things created is the good of the order of the universe. Now, the order of the universe requires . . . that there should be some things that can, and do sometimes, fail. And thus God, by causing in things the good of the order of the universe, consequently and as it were by accident, causes the corruptions of things. . . . But when we read that *God hath not made death*, the sense is that God does not will death for its own sake. Nevertheless the order of justice belongs to the order of the universe, and this requires that penalty should be dealt out to sinners. And so God is the author of the evil which is penalty, but not of the evil which is fault, by reason of what is said above.

Aquinas, *Summa Theologica*, I, 49, 2

52 It appears . . . that there is no one first principle of evil, as there is one first principle of good.

First, indeed, because the first principle of good

is essentially good. . . . But nothing can be essentially bad. For . . . every being, as such, is good, and . . . evil can exist only in good as in its subject.

Secondly, because the first principle of good is the highest and perfect good which contains beforehand in itself all goodness. . . . But there cannot be a supreme evil, because . . . although evil always lessens good, yet it never wholly consumes it; and thus, since good always remains, nothing can be wholly and perfectly bad. Therefore, the Philosopher [Aristotle] says that "if the wholly evil could be, it would destroy itself," because all good being destroyed (which it need be for something to be wholly evil), evil itself would be taken away, since its subject is good.

Aquinas, *Summa Theologica*, I, 49, 3

53 Evil can only have an accidental cause. . . . Hence reduction to any *per se* cause of evil is impossible. And to say that evil is in the greater number is simply false. For things which are generated and corrupted, in which alone can there be natural evil, are the smaller part of the whole universe. And again, in every species the defect of nature is in the smaller number. In man alone does evil appear as in the greater number, because the good of man as regards the senses is not the good of man as man—that is, in regard to reason, and more men follow the senses than the reason.

Aquinas, *Summa Theologica*, I, 49, 3

54 As being is the first thing that falls under the apprehension absolutely, so good is the first thing that falls under the apprehension of the practical reason, which is directed to action; for every agent acts for an end, which has the aspect of good. Consequently the first principle in the practical reason is one founded on the notion of good, namely, that the good is what all desire. Hence this is the first precept of law, that good is to be pursued and done, and evil is to be avoided. All other precepts of the natural law are based upon this, so that whatever the practical reason naturally apprehends as man's good belongs to the precepts of the natural law as something to be done or avoided.

Aquinas, *Summa Theologica*, I–II, 94, 2

55 Generally it may be stated that what people consider to be good is really bad and most of the things that are considered to be bad are really good.

Maimonides, *Preservation of Youth*, III

56 Men, says an old Greek maxim, are tormented by the opinions they have of things, not by the things themselves. There would be a great point gained for the relief of our wretched human lot if someone could prove this statement true in every case. For if evils have no entry into us but by our judg-

ment, it seems to be in our power to disdain them or turn them to good use. If things give themselves up to our mercy, why shall we not dispose of them and arrange them to our advantage? If what we call evil and torment is neither evil nor torment in itself, if it is merely our fancy that gives it this quality, it is in us to change it. And having the choice, if no one forces us, we are strangely insane to tense ourselves for the course that is more painful to us, and to give sicknesses, poverty, and slights a bitter and unpleasant taste if we can give them a good one and if, fortune furnishing merely the material, it is for us to give it form. But let us see whether this can be maintained: that what we call evil is not evil in itself—or at least, whatever it is, that it depends on us to give it a different savor and a different complexion; for all this comes to the same thing.

Montaigne, *Essays*, I, 14,
That the Taste of Good

57 Confidence in the goodness of others is no slight testimony to one's own goodness.

Montaigne, *Essays*, I, 14,
That the Taste of Good

58 *Antonio.* An evil soul producing holy witness
Is like a villain with a smiling cheek,
A goodly apple rotten at the heart:
O, what a goodly outside falsehood hath!

Shakespeare, *Merchant of Venice*, I, iii, 100

59 *Falstaff.* If sack and sugar be a fault, God help the wicked! if to be old and merry be a sin, then many an old host that I know is damned: if to be fat be to be hated, then Pharaoh's lean kine are to be loved.

Shakespeare, *I Henry IV*, II, iv, 516

60 *King Henry.* There is some soul of goodness in things evil,
Would men observingly distil it out.
For our bad neighbour makes us early stirrers,
Which is both healthful and good husbandry:
Besides, they are our outward consciences,
And preachers to us all, admonishing
That we should dress us fairly for our end.
Thus may we gather honey from the weed,
And make a moral of the devil himself.

Shakespeare, *Henry V*, IV, i, 4

61 *Hamlet.*   One may smile, and smile, and be a villain.

Shakespeare, *Hamlet*, I, v, 108

62 *Hamlet.* There is nothing either good or bad, but thinking makes it so.

Shakespeare, *Hamlet*, II, ii, 255

63 *Pandarus.* O world! world! world! thus is the poor agent despised! O traitors and bawds, how ear-

nestly are you set a-work, and how ill requited! why should our endeavour be so loved and the performance so loathed?

Shakespeare, *Troilus and Cressida,* V, x, 36

64 *Gloucester.* Here, take this purse, thou whom the
    heavens' plagues
Have humbled to all strokes. That I am wretched
Makes thee the happier. Heavens, deal so still!
Let the superfluous and lust-dieted man,
That slaves your ordinance, that will not see
Because he doth not feel, feel your power quickly;
So distribution should undo excess,
And each man have enough.

Shakespeare, *Lear,* IV, i, 67

65 *Albany.* Wisdom and goodness to the vile seem
    vile;
Filths savour but themselves.

Shakespeare, *Lear,* IV, ii, 38

66 *Lady Macduff.*   Whither should I fly?
I have done no harm. But I remember now
I am in this earthly world; where to do harm
Is often laudable, to do good sometime
Accounted dangerous folly. Why then, alas,
Do I put up that womanly defence,
To say I have done no harm?

Shakespeare, *Macbeth,* IV, ii, 73

67 *Antony.* But when we in our viciousness grow
    hard—
O misery on't!—the wise gods seel our eyes;
In our own filth drop our clear judgements; make
    us
Adore our errors; laugh at's, while we strut
To our confusion.

Shakespeare, *Antony and
Cleopatra,* II, xiii, 111

68 No more be grieved at that which thou hast done:
Roses have thorns, and silver fountains mud;
Clouds and eclipses stain both moon and sun,
And loathsome canker lives in sweetest bud.

Shakespeare, *Sonnet XXXV*

69   Sweetest things turn sourest by their deeds;
Lilies that fester smell far worse than weeds.

Shakespeare, *Sonnet XCIV*

70 We are much beholden to Machiavel and others, that write what men do, and not what they ought to do. For it is not possible to join serpentine wisdom with the columbine innocency, except men know exactly all the conditions of the serpent; his baseness and going upon his belly, his volubility and lubricity, his envy and sting, and the rest; that is, all forms and natures of evil. For without this, virtue lieth open and unfenced. Nay, an honest man can do no good upon those that are wicked, to reclaim them, without the help of the knowledge of evil. For men of corrupted minds presuppose that honesty groweth out of simplicity of manners, and believing of preachers, schoolmasters, and men's exterior language. So as, except you can make them perceive that you know the utmost reaches of their own corrupt opinions, they despise all morality.

Bacon, *Advancement of Learning,*
Bk. II, XXI, 9

71 Whatsoever is the object of any man's appetite or desire, that is it which he for his part calleth *good;* and the object of his hate and aversion, *evil;* and of his contempt, *vile* and *inconsiderable.* For these words of *good, evil,* and *contemptible* are ever used with relation to the person that useth them: there being nothing simply and absolutely so; nor any common rule of good and evil to be taken from the nature of the objects themselves; but from the person of the man, where there is no Commonwealth; or, in a Commonwealth, from the person that representeth it; or from an arbitrator or judge, whom men disagreeing shall by consent set up and make his sentence the rule thereof.

Hobbes, *Leviathan,* I, 6

72 Evil is easy, and has infinite forms; good is almost unique. But a certain kind of evil is as difficult to find as what we call good; and often on this account such particular evil gets passed off as good. An extraordinary greatness of soul is needed in order to attain to it as well as to good.

Pascal, *Pensées,* VI, 408

73 Men never do evil so completely and cheerfully as when they do it from religious conviction.

Pascal, *Pensées,* XIV, 895

74 Nothing is more common than good things; the only question is how to discern them; it is certain that all of them are natural and within our reach and even known by every one. But we do not know how to distinguish them. This is universal. It is not in things extraordinary and strange that excellence of any kind is found. We reach up for it, and we are further away; more often than not we must stoop. The best books are those whose readers think they could have written them. Nature, which alone is good, is familiar and common throughout.

Pascal, *Geometrical Demonstration*

75 To measure life, learn thou betimes, and know
    Toward solid good what leads the nearest way;
    For other things mild Heav'n a time ordains,
And disapproves that care, though wise in show,
    That with superfluous burden loads the day,
    And when God sends a cheerful hour, refrains.

Milton, *Cyriack, whose Grandsire on the
Royal Bench*

76 *Satan.* To do ought good never will be our task,
But ever to do ill our sole delight.
Milton, *Paradise Lost,* I, 159

77   Whence,
But from the Author of all ill could Spring
So deep a malice, to confound the race
Of mankind in one root, and Earth with Hell
To mingle and involve, done all to spite
The great Creatour?
Milton, *Paradise Lost,* II, 380

78 Such Pleasure took the Serpent to behold
This Flourie Plat, the sweet recess of *Eve*
Thus earlie, thus alone; her Heav'nly forme
Angelic, but more soft, and Feminine,
Her graceful Innocence, her every Aire
Of gesture or lest action overawd
His Malice, and with rapine sweet bereav'd
His fierceness of the fierce intent it brought:
That space the Evil one abstracted stood
From his own evil, and for the time remaind
Stupidly good, of enmitie disarm'd
Of guile, of hate, of envie, of revenge;
But the hot Hell that alwayes in him burnes,
Though in mid Heav'n, soon ended his delight,
And tortures him now more, the more he sees
Of pleasure not for him ordain'd: then soon
Fierce hate he recollects, and all his thoughts
Of mischief, gratulating, thus excites.
Milton, *Paradise Lost,* IX, 455

79   Good unknown, sure is not had, or had
And yet unknown, is as not had at all.
Milton, *Paradise Lost,* IX, 756

80 *Samson.*   Weakness is thy excuse,
And I believe it, weakness to resist
Philistian gold: if weakness may excuse,
What Murtherer, what Traytor, Parricide,
Incestuous, Sacrilegious, but may plead it?
All wickedness is weakness: that plea therefore
With God or Man will gain thee no remission.
Milton, *Samson Agonistes,* 829

81 Good and evil we know in the field of this world
grow up together almost inseparably; and the
knowledge of good is so involved and interwoven
with the knowledge of evil, and in so many cunning resemblances hardly to be discerned, that
those confused seeds which were imposed upon
Psyche as an incessant labour to cull out, and sort
asunder, were not more intermixed. It was from
out the rind of one apple tasted, that the knowledge of good and evil, as two twins cleaving together, leaped forth into the world. And perhaps
this is that doom which Adam fell into of knowing
good and evil, that is to say of knowing good by
evil. As therefore the state of man now is; what
wisdom can there be to choose, what continence
to forbear without the knowledge of evil? He that

can apprehend and consider vice with all her
baits and seeming pleasures, and yet abstain, and
yet distinguish, and yet prefer that which is truly
better, he is the true wayfaring Christian.
Milton, *Areopagitica*

82 If all things have followed from the necessity of
the most perfect nature of God, how is it that so
many imperfections have arisen in nature—corruption, for instance, of things till they stink; deformity, exciting disgust; confusion, evil, crime,
etc.? But, as I have just observed, all this is easily
answered. For the perfection of things is to be
judged by their nature and power alone; nor are
they more or less perfect because they delight or
offend the human senses, or because they are beneficial or prejudicial to human nature.
Spinoza, *Ethics,* I, Appendix

83 With regard to good and evil, these terms indicate
nothing positive in things considered in themselves, nor are they anything else than modes of
thought, or notions which we form from the comparison of one thing with another. For one and
the same thing may at the same time be both good
and evil or indifferent. Music, for example, is
good to a melancholy person, bad to one mourning, while to a deaf man it is neither good nor
bad. But although things are so, we must retain
these words. For since we desire to form for ourselves an idea of man upon which we may look as
a model of human nature, it will be of service to
us to retain these expressions in the sense I have
mentioned. By *good,* therefore, I understand . . .
everything which we are certain is a means by
which we may approach nearer and nearer to the
model of human nature we set before us. By *evil,*
on the contrary, I understand everything which
we are certain hinders us from reaching that model. Again, I shall call men more or less perfect or
imperfect in so far as they approach more or less
nearly to this same model. For it is to be carefully
observed, that when I say that an individual passes from a less to a greater perfection and *vice versa,*
I do not understand that from one essence or form
he is changed into another (for a horse, for instance, would be as much destroyed if it were
changed into a man as if it were changed into an
insect), but rather we conceive that his power of
action, in so far as it is understood by his own
nature, is increased or diminished. Finally, by
perfection generally, I understand . . . . reality;
that is to say, the essence of any object in so far as
it exists and acts in a certain manner, no regard
being paid to its duration. For no individual thing
can be said to be more perfect because for a longer time it has persevered in existence.
Spinoza, *Ethics,* IV, Preface

84 Things then are good or evil, only in reference to
pleasure or pain. That we call *good,* which is apt to

cause or increase pleasure, or diminish pain in us; or else to procure or preserve us the possession of any other good or absence of any evil. And, on the contrary, we name that *evil* which is apt to produce or increase any pain, or diminish any pleasure in us: or else to procure us any evil, or deprive us of any good.

Locke, *Concerning Human Understanding*, Bk. II, XX, 2

85 As for the mixture of pain or uneasiness which is in the world, pursuant to the general laws of nature, and the actions of finite, imperfect spirits, this, in the state we are in at present, is indispensably necessary to our well-being. But our prospects are too narrow. We take, for instance, the idea of some one particular pain into our thoughts, and account it *evil;* whereas, if we enlarge our view, so as to comprehend the various ends, connexions, and dependencies of things, on what occasions and in what proportions we are affected with pain and pleasure, the nature of human freedom, and the design with which we are put into the world; we shall be forced to acknowledge that those particular things which, considered in themselves, appear to be evil, have the nature of good, when considered as linked with the whole system of beings.

Berkeley, *Principles of Human Knowledge*, 153

86 Absolute good and evil are unknown to us. In this life they are blended together; we never enjoy any perfectly pure feeling, nor do we remain for more than a moment in the same state. The feelings of our minds, like the changes in our bodies, are in a continual flux. Good and ill are common to all, but in varying proportions. The happiest is he who suffers least; the most miserable is he who enjoys least. Ever more sorrow than joy—this is the lot of all of us. Man's happiness in this world is but a negative state; it must be reckoned by the fewness of his ills.

Rousseau, *Emile*, II

87 "The causes of good and evil," answered Imlac, "are so various and uncertain, so often entangled with each other, so diversified by various relations, and so much subject to accidents which cannot be foreseen, that he who would fix his condition upon incontestable reasons of preference, must live and die inquiring and deliberating."

Johnson, *Rasselas*, XVI

88 *Johnson.* If possibility of evil be to exclude good, no good ever can be done. If nothing is to be attempted in which there is danger, we must all sink into hopeless inactivity. The evils that may be feared from this practice arise not from any defect in the institution, but from the infirmities of human nature. Power, in whatever hands it is

placed, will be sometimes improperly exerted; yet courts of law must judge, though they will sometimes judge amiss. A father must instruct his children, though he himself may often want instruction. A minister must censure sinners, though his censure may be sometimes erroneous by want of judgement, and sometimes unjust by want of honesty.

Boswell, *Life of Johnson* (1776)

89 Nothing can possibly be conceived in the world, or even out of it, which can be called good, without qualification, except a good will. Intelligence, wit, judgement, and the other *talents* of the mind, however they may be named, or courage, resolution, perserverance, as qualities of temperament, are undoubtedly good and desirable in many respects; but these gifts of nature may also become extremely bad and mischievous if the will which is to make use of them, and which, therefore, constitutes what is called *character,* is not good.

Kant, *Fundamental Principles of the Metaphysic of Morals*, I

90 A good will is good not because of what it performs or effects, not by its aptness for the attainment of some proposed end, but simply by virtue of the volition; that is, it is good in itself, and considered by itself is to be esteemed much higher than all that can be brought about by it in favour of any inclination, nay even of the sum total of all inclinations.

Kant, *Fundamental Principles of the Metaphysic of Morals*, I

91 The only objects of practical reason are therefore those of *good* and *evil*. For by the former is meant an object necessarily desired according to a principle of reason; by the latter one necessarily shunned, also according to a principle of reason.

Kant, *Critique of Practical Reason*, Pt. I, I, 2

92 What we call *good* must be an object of desire in the judgement of every rational man, and *evil* an object of aversion in the eyes of everyone.

Kant, *Critique of Practical Reason*, Pt. I, I, 2

93 The evils visited upon us, now by nature, now by the truculent egoism of man, evoke the energies of the soul, and give it strength and courage to submit to no such force, and at the same time quicken in us a sense that in the depths of our nature there is an aptitude for higher ends.

Kant, *Critique of Teleological Judgement*, 83

94 Without Contraries is no progression. Attraction and Repulsion, Reason and Energy, Love and Hate, are necessary to Human existence.

From these contraries spring what the religious call Good & Evil. Good is the passive that obeys Reason. Evil is the active springing from Energy. Good is Heaven. Evil is Hell.

Blake, *Marriage of Heaven and Hell,* 3

95 *The voice of the Devil.* All Bibles or sacred codes have been the causes of the following Errors:

1. That Man has two real existing principles; Viz: a Body & a Soul.

2. That Energy, calld Evil, is alone from the Body, & that Reason, calld Good, is alone from the Soul.

3. That God will torment Man in Eternity for following his Energies. But the following Contraries to these are True:

1. Man has no Body distinct from his Soul; for that calld Body is a portion of Soul discernd by the five Senses, the chief inlets of Soul in this age.

2. Energy is the only life, and is from the Body; and Reason is the bound or outward circumference of Energy.

3. Energy is Eternal Delight.

Blake, *Marriage of Heaven and Hell,* 4

96 It seems highly probable that moral evil is absolutely necessary to the production of moral excellence. A being with only good placed in view may be justly said to be impelled by a blind necessity. The pursuit of good in this case can be no indication of virtuous propensities. It might be said, perhaps, that Infinite Wisdom cannot want such an indication as outward action, but would foreknow with certainty whether the being would choose good or evil. This might be a plausible argument against a state of trial, but will not hold against the supposition that mind in this world is in a state of formation. Upon this idea, the being that has seen moral evil and has felt disapprobation and disgust at it is essentially different from the being that has seen only good. They are pieces of clay that have received distinct impressions: they must, therefore, necessarily be in different shapes; or, even if we allow them both to have the same lovely form of virtue, it must be acknowledged that one has undergone the further process necessary to give firmness and durability to its substance, while the other is still exposed to injury, and liable to be broken by every accidental impulse. An ardent love and admiration of virtue seems to imply the existence of something opposite to it, and it seems highly probable that the same beauty of form and substance, the same perfection of character could not be generated without the impressions of disapprobation which arise from the spectacle of moral evil.

Malthus, *Population,* XIX

97 Evil exists in the world not to create despair but activity. We are not patiently to submit to it, but to exert ourselves to avoid it. It is not only the interest but the duty of every individual to use his utmost efforts to remove evil from himself and from as large a circle as he can influence, and the more he exercises himself in this duty, the more wisely he directs his efforts, and the more successful these efforts are, the more he will probably improve and exalt his own mind, and the more completely does he appear to fulfill the will of his Creator.

Malthus, *Population,* XIX

98 The Christian doctrine that man is by nature evil is loftier than the other which takes him to be by nature good. This doctrine is to be understood as follows in accordance with the philosophical exegesis of it: As mind, man is a free substance which is in the position of not allowing itself to be determined by natural impulse. When man's condition is immediate and mentally undeveloped, he is in a situation in which he ought not to be and from which he must free himself. This is the meaning of the doctrine of original sin without which Christianity would not be the religion of freedom.

Hegel, *Philosophy of Right,*
Additions, Par. 18

99 It is only man who is good, and he is good only because he can also be evil. Good and evil are inseparable, and their inseparability is rooted in the fact that the concept becomes an object to itself, and as object it *eo ipso* acquires the character of difference. The evil will wills something opposed to the universality of the will, while the good will acts in accordance with its true concept.

Hegel, *Philosophy of Right,*
Additions, Par. 139

100 Individuals, to the extent of their freedom, are responsible for the depravation and enfeeblement of morals and religion. This is the seal of the absolute and sublime destiny of man—that he knows what is good and what is evil; that his destiny *is* his very ability to will either good or evil—in one word, that he is the subject of moral imputation, imputation not only of evil, but of good; and not only concerning this or that particular matter, and all that happens *ab extra,* but *also* the good and evil attaching to his individual freedom. The brute alone is simply innocent.

Hegel, *Philosophy of History,*
Introduction, 3

101 This is a deep truth, that evil lies in consciousness: for the brutes are neither evil nor good; the merely natural man quite as little.

Hegel, *Philosophy of History,*
Pt. III, III, 2

102 In a list of definitions included in the authentic translation of Plato, a list attributed to him, oc-

curs this: "Natural Depravity: a depravity according to nature," a definition which, though savoring of Calvinism, by no means involves Calvin's dogma as to total mankind. Evidently its intent makes it applicable but to individuals. Not many are the examples of this depravity which the gallows and jail supply. At any rate, for notable instances, since these have no vulgar alloy of the brute in them, but invariably are dominated by intellectuality, one must go elsewhere. Civilization, especially if of the austerer sort, is auspicious to it. It folds itself in the mantle of respectability. It has its certain negative virtues serving as silent auxiliaries. It never allows wine to get within its guard. It is not going too far to say that it is without vices or small sins. There is a phenomenal pride in it that excludes them. It is never mercenary or avaricious. In short, the depravity here meant partakes nothing of the sordid or sensual. It is serious, but free from acerbity. Though no flatterer of mankind it never speaks ill of it.

But the thing which in eminent instances signalizes so exceptional a nature is this: Though the man's even temper and discreet bearing would seem to intimate a mind peculiarly subject to the law of reason, not the less in heart he would seem to riot in complete exemption from that law, having apparently little to do with reason further than to employ it as an ambidexter implement for effecting the irrational. That is to say: Toward the accomplishment of an aim which in wantonness of atrocity would seem to partake of the insane, he will direct a cool judgment sagacious and sound. These men are madmen, and of the most dangerous sort, for their lunacy is not continuous, but occasional, evoked by some special object; it is protectively secretive, which is as much as to say it is self-contained, so that when, moreover, most active it is to the average mind not distinguishable from sanity, and for the reason above suggested: that whatever its aims may be—and the aim is never declared—the method and the outward proceeding are always perfectly rational.

Now something such a one was Claggart, in whom was the mania of an evil nature, not engendered by vicious training or corrupting books or licentious living, but born with him and innate, in short "a depravity according to nature."

Melville, *Billy Budd*

103 Men have a singular desire to be good without being good for anything, because, perchance, they think vaguely that so it will be good for them in the end.

Thoreau, *The Christian Fable*

104 Men say, practically, Begin where you are and such as you are, without aiming mainly to become of more worth, and with kindness aforethought go about doing good. If I were to preach at all in this strain, I should say rather, Set about being good.

As if the sun should stop when he has kindled his fires up to the splendor of a moon or a star of the sixth magnitude, and go about like a Robin Goodfellow, peeping in at every cottage window, inspiring lunatics, and tainting meats, and making darkness visible, instead of steadily increasing his genial heat and beneficence till he is of such brightness that no mortal can look him in the face, and then, and in the meanwhile too, going about the world in his own orbit, doing it good, or rather, as a truer philosophy has discovered, the world going about him getting good. . . .

There is no odor so bad as that which arises from goodness tainted. It is human, it is divine, carrion. If I knew for a certainty that a man was coming to my house with the conscious design of doing me good, I should run for my life, as from that dry and parching wind of the African deserts called the simoom, which fills the mouth and nose and ears and eyes with dust till you are suffocated, for fear that I should get some of his good done to me—some of its virus mingled with my blood. No—in this case I would rather suffer evil the natural way.

Thoreau, *Walden:* Economy

105 It is a misapprehension of the utilitarian mode of thought, to conceive it as implying that people should fix their minds upon so wide a generality as the world, or society at large. The great majority of good actions are intended not for the benefit of the world, but for that of individuals, of which the good of the world is made up; and the thoughts of the most virtuous man need not on these occasions travel beyond the particular persons concerned, except so far as is necessary to assure himself that in benefiting them he is not violating the rights, that is, the legitimate and authorised expectations, of any one else.

Mill, *Utilitarianism*, II

106 Absolute fiends are as rare as angels, perhaps rarer: ferocious savages, with occasional touches of humanity, are however very frequent: and in the wide interval which separates these from any worthy representatives of the human species, how many are the forms and gradations of animalism and selfishness, often under an outward varnish of civilisation and even cultivation, living at peace with the law, maintaining a creditable appearance to all who are not under their power, yet sufficient often to make the lives of all who are so, a torment and a burthen to them!

Mill, *Subjection of Women*, II

107 Good is not only good, but reproductive of good; this is one of its attributes; nothing is excellent, beautiful, perfect, desirable for its own sake, but it overflows, and spreads the likeness of itself all around it. Good is prolific; it is not only good to the eye, but to the taste; it not only attracts us, but

it communicates itself: it excites first our admiration and love, then our desire and our gratitude, and that, in proportion to its intenseness and fulness in particular instances. A great good will impart great good.

Newman, *Idea of a University,*
Discourse VII

108 "I can's say what I should have done about that, Godfrey. I should never have married anybody else. But I wasn't worth doing wrong for—nothing is in this world. Nothing is as good as it seems beforehand—not even our marrying wasn't, you see." There was a faint sad smile on Nancy's face as she said the last words.

George Eliot, *Silas Marner,* XVIII

109 What is good?—All that heightens the feeling of power, the will to power, power itself in man.
What is bad?—All that proceeds from weakness.

Nietzsche, *Antichrist,* II

110 All Goods are disguised by the vulgarity of their concomitants, in this work-a-day world; but woe to him who can only recognize them when he thinks them in their pure and abstract form!

William James, *Psychology,* IV

111 I find myself willing to take the universe to be really dangerous and adventurous, without therefore backing out and crying "no play." I am willing to think that the prodigal son attitude, open to us as it is in many vicissitudes, is not the right and final attitude toward the whole of life. I am willing that there should be real losses and real losers, and no total preservation of all that is. I can believe in the ideal as an ultimate, not as an origin, and as an extract, not the whole. When the cup is poured off, the dregs are left behind for ever, but the possibility of what is poured off is sweet enough to accept. . . .

Those puritans who answered "yes" to the question: Are you willing to be damned for God's glory? were in this objective and magnanimous condition of mind. The way of escape from evil on this system is *not* by getting it *'aufgehoben'* ["compensated"], or preserved in the whole as an element essential but 'overcome.' *It is by dropping it out altogether, throwing it overboard and getting beyond it, helping to make a universe that shall forget its very place and name.*

It is then perfectly possible to accept sincerely a drastic kind of a universe from which the element of 'seriousness' is not to be expelled. Whoso does so is, it seems to me, a genuine pragmatist. He is willing to live on a scheme of uncertified possibilities which he trusts; willing to pay with his own person, if need be, for the realization of the ideals which he frames.

William James, *Pragmatism,* VIII

112 The method of averting one's attention from evil, and living simply in the light of good is splendid as long as it will work. It will work with many persons; it will work far more generally than most of us are ready to suppose; and within the sphere of its successful operation there is nothing to be said against it as a religious solution. But it breaks down impotently as soon as melancholy comes; and even though one be quite free from melancholy one's self, there is no doubt that healthy-mindedness is inadequate as a philosophical doctrine, because the evil facts which it refuses positively to account for are a genuine portion of reality; and they may after all be the best key to life's significance, and possibly the only openers of our eyes to the deepest levels of truth.

William James, *Varieties of Religious Experience,* VI-VII

113 If a man cannot look evil in the face without illusion, he will never know what it really is, or combat it effectually.

Shaw, *Major Barbara,* Pref.

114 The common character of all evil is that its realization in fact involves that there is some concurrent realization of a purpose towards elimination. The purpose is to secure the avoidance of evil. The fact of the instability of evil is the moral order in the world.

Evil, triumphant in its enjoyment, is so far good in itself; but beyond itself it is evil in its character of a destructive agent among things greater than itself. In the summation of the more complete fact it has secured a descent towards nothingness, in contrast to the creativeness of what can without qualification be termed good. Evil is positive and destructive; what is good is positive and creative. . . .

Thus evil promotes its own elimination by destruction, or degradation, or by elevation. But in its own nature it is unstable. It must be noted that the state of degradation to which evil leads, when accomplished, is not in itself evil, except by comparison with what might have been. A hog is not an evil beast, but when a man is degraded to the level of a hog, with the accompanying atrophy of finer elements, he is no more evil than a hog. The evil of the final degradation lies in the comparison of what is with what might have been. During the process of degradation the comparison is an evil for the man himself, and at its final stage it remains an evil for others. . . .

The contrast in the world between evil and good is the contrast between the turbulence of evil and the "peace which passeth all understanding." There is a self-preservation inherent in that which is good in itself. Its destruction may come from without but not from within. Good people of narrow sympathies are apt to be unfeeling and unprogressive, enjoying their egotistical goodness.

Their case, on a higher level, is analogous to that of the man completely degraded to a hog. They have reached a state of stable goodness, so far as their own interior life is concerned. This type of moral correctitude is, on a larger view, so like evil that the distinction is trivial.

Whitehead, *Religion in the Making*, III, 4

115 I will say nothing of how you may appear in your own eyes, but have you met with so much good-will in your superiors and rivals, so much chivalry in your enemies and so little envy amongst your acquaintances, that you feel it incumbent on you to protest against the idea of the part played by egoistic baseness in human nature? Do you not know how uncontrolled and unreliable the average human being is in all that concerns sexual life? Or are you ignorant of the fact that all the excesses and aberrations of which we dream at night are crimes actually committed every day by men who are wide awake? What does psychoanalysis do in this connection but confirm the old saying of Plato that the good are those who content themselves with dreaming of what others, the wicked, actually do?

And now look away from individuals to the great war still devastating Europe: think of the colossal brutality, cruelty and mendacity which is now allowed to spread itself over the civilized world. Do you really believe that a handful of unprincipled place-hunters and corrupters of men would have succeeded in letting loose all this latent evil, if the millions of their followers were not also guilty? Will you venture, even in these circumstances, to break a lance for the exclusion of evil from the mental constitution of humanity?

You will accuse me of taking a one-sided view of war, and tell me that it has also called out all that is finest and most noble in mankind, heroism, self-sacrifice, and public spirit. That is true; but do not now commit the injustice, from which psycho-analysis has so often suffered, of reproaching it that it denies one thing because it affirms another. It is no part of our intention to deny the nobility in human nature, nor have we ever done anything to disparage its value. On the contrary, I show you not only the evil wishes which are censored but also the censorship which suppresses them and makes them unrecognizable. We dwell upon the evil in human beings with the greater emphasis only because others deny it, thereby making the mental life of mankind not indeed better, but incomprehensible. If we give up the one-sided ethical valuation then, we are sure to find the truer formula for the relation of evil to good in human nature.

Freud, *General Introduction to Psycho-Analysis*, IX

116 In reality, there is no such thing as *eradicating* evil

tendencies. . . . The inmost essence of human nature consists of elemental instincts, which are common to all men and aim at the satisfaction of certain primal needs. These instincts in themselves are neither good nor evil. We but classify them and their manifestations in that fashion, according as they meet the needs and demands of the human community. It is admitted that all those instincts which society condemns as evil—let us take as representatives the selfish and the cruel—are of this primitive type.

These primitive instincts undergo a lengthy process of development before they are allowed to become active in the adult being. They are inhibited, directed towards other aims and departments, become commingled, alter their objects, and are to some extent turned back upon their possessor. Reaction-formations against certain instincts take the deceptive form of a change in content, as though egoism had changed into altruism, or cruelty into pity. . . .

It is not until all these *vicissitudes to which instincts are subject* have been surmounted that what we call the character of a human being is formed, and this, as we know, can only very inadequately be classified as *good* or *bad*. A human being is seldom altogether good or bad; he is usually *good* in one relation and *bad* in another, or *good* in certain external circumstances and in others decidedly *bad*. It is interesting to learn that the existence of strong *bad* impulses in infancy is often the actual condition for an unmistakable inclination towards *good* in the adult person. Those who as children have been the most pronounced egoists may well become the most helpful and self-sacrificing members of the community; most of our sentimentalists, friends of humanity, champions of animals, have been evolved from little sadists and animal-tormentors.

Freud, *Thoughts on War and Death*, I

117 Good consists in the meaning that is experienced to belong to an activity when conflict and entanglement of various incompatible impulses and habits terminate in a unified orderly release in action. This human good, being a fulfilment conditioned upon thought, differs from the pleasures which an animal nature—of course we also remain animals so far as we do not think—hits upon accidentally. Moreover there is a genuine difference between a false good, a spurious satisfaction, and a "true" good, and there is an empirical test for discovering the difference.

Dewey, *Human Nature and Conduct*, III, 5

118 It would take a good deal of time to become a misanthrope if we confined ourselves to the observation of others. It is when we detect our own weaknesses that we come to pity or despise mankind. The human nature from which we then turn away is the human nature we have discovered in

the depths of our own being. The evil is so well screened, the secret so universally kept, that in this case each individual is the dupe of all: however severely we may profess to judge other men, at bottom we think them better than ourselves. On this happy illusion much of our social life is grounded.

Bergson, Two Sources of Morality and Religion, I

9.7 | *Right and Wrong*

In ethics or moral philosophy, there is a fundamental division between two types of problems: on the one hand, the problem of what is good or evil for the individual man considered without reference to other men or to the community in which he lives; on the other hand, the problem of what is right or wrong in the behavior of one individual as it affects the lives of others or the welfare of the community. Unfortunately, this does not give us a rigid rule for using the words "good" and "right" in a nonoverlapping way; for it is often said in ordinary discourse that what is really good for the individual is right for him to seek, and that the individual who acts rightly toward others is a good man or one whose conduct is good. Nevertheless, the words "right" and "wrong" are most frequently applied to acts that affect others or the community. Wrongdoing injures others; conduct is said to be rightful or righteous if it benefits others or at least avoids injuring them.

Because the words "right" and "wrong" are usually employed with this connotation, they are often interchangeable with another pair of terms—"just" and "unjust." We have, therefore, placed here quotations that discuss justice and injustice in the conduct of one individual toward others or toward the community, and along with them discussions of the just and unjust man, justice as a moral virtue and injustice as a vice, and considerations of the question of whether it is better to do injustice or to suffer it, to wrong others or be wronged by them. The reader will find that the treatment of Justice and Injustice in Section 12.2 deals mainly with social, political, and economic justice, not justice as a moral virtue or as a quality of human acts. The placement here of quotations dealing with justice as a virtue also explains why the enumeration of the virtues in the titles of Sections 9.11 through 9.15 omits justice and injustice.

Other closely related terms appear in the quotations below, such as righteousness, wickedness, benevolence, and iniquity. Since it is thought that to wrong another involves the violation or transgression of one's rights, the reader should consult the discussion of Rights—Natural and Civil in Section 12.3. Since it is also thought that wrongdoing involves the violation of the moral law and that it is one's basic moral obligation or duty to act righteously or in conformity with the moral law, the reader should consult Section 9.3 on Moral Law, Section 9.9 on Duty: Moral Obligation, and Section 20.13 on Sin and Temptation.

1 And David said to Saul, Wherefore hearest thou men's words, saying, Behold, David seeketh thy hurt?

Behold, this day thine eyes have seen how that the Lord had delivered thee to day into mine hand in the cave: and some bade me kill thee: but mine eye spared thee; and I said, I will not put forth mine hand against my lord; for he is the Lord's anointed.

Moreover, my father, see, yea, see the skirt of thy robe in my hand: for in that I cut off the skirt of thy robe, and killed thee not, know thou and see that there is neither evil nor transgression in mine hand, and I have not sinned against thee; yet thou huntest my soul to take it.

The Lord judge between me and thee, and the Lord avenge me of thee: but mine hand shall not be upon thee.

As saith the proverb of the ancients, Wickedness proceedeth from the wicked: but mine hand shall not be upon thee.

After whom is the king of Israel come out? after whom dost thou pursue? after a dead dog, after a flea.

The Lord therefore be judge, and judge between me and thee, and see, and plead my cause, and deliver me out of thine hand.

And it came to pass, when David had made an end of speaking these words unto Saul, that Saul said, Is this thy voice, my son David? And Saul lifted up his voice, and wept.

And he said to David, Thou art more righteous than I: for thou hast rewarded me good, whereas I have rewarded thee evil.

And thou hast shewed this day how that thou hast dealt well with me: forasmuch as when the Lord had delivered me into thine hand, thou killedst me not.

For if a man find his enemy, will he let him go well away? wherefore the Lord reward thee good for that thou hast done unto me this day.

I Samuel 24:9–19

2 How should man be just with God?

If he will contend with him, he cannot answer him one of a thousand.

He is wise in heart, and mighty in strength: who hath hardened himself against him, and hath prospered?

Which removeth the mountains, and they know not: which overturneth them in his anger.

Which shaketh the earth out of her place, and the pillars thereof tremble.

Which commandeth the sun, and it riseth not; and sealeth up the stars.

Which alone spreadeth out the heavens, and treadeth upon the waves of the sea.

Which maketh Ărc-tū́-rŭs, Ō-rī́-ǫn, and Plḗí-ă-dḗs, and the chambers of the south.

Which doeth great things past finding out; yea, and wonders without number.

Lo, he goeth by me, and I see him not: he passeth on also, but I perceive him not.

Behold, he taketh away, who can hinder him? who will say unto him, What doest thou?

If God will not withdraw his anger, the proud helpers do stoop under him.

How much less shall I answer him, and choose out my words to reason with him?

Whom, though I were righteous, yet would I not answer, but I would make supplication to my judge.

If I had called, and he had answered me; yet would I not believe that he had hearkened unto my voice.

For he breaketh me with a tempest, and multiplieth my wounds without cause.

He will not suffer me to take my breath, but filleth me with bitterness.

If I speak of strength, lo, he is strong: and if of judgment, who shall set me a time to plead?

If I justify myself, mine own mouth shall condemn me: if I say, I am perfect, it shall also prove me perverse.

Though I were perfect, yet would I not know my soul: I would despise my life.

This is one thing, therefore I said it, He destroyeth the perfect and the wicked.

If the scourge slay suddenly, he will laugh at the trial of the innocent.

The earth is given into the hand of the wicked: he covereth the faces of the judges thereof; if not, where, and who is he?

Job 9:2–24

3 Blessed is the man that walketh not in the counsel of the ungodly, nor standeth in the way of sinners, nor sitteth in the seat of the scornful.

But his delight is in the law of the Lord; and in his law doth he meditate day and night.

And he shall be like a tree planted by the rivers of water, that bringeth forth his fruit in his season; his leaf also shall not wither; and whatsoever he doeth shall prosper.

The ungodly are not so: but are like the chaff which the wind driveth away.

Therefore the ungodly shall not stand in the judgment, nor sinners in the congregation of the righteous.

For the Lord knoweth the way of the righteous: but the way of the ungodly shall perish.

Psalm 1:1–6

4 Withhold not good from them to whom it is due, when it is in the power of thine hand to do it.

Say not unto thy neighbour, Go, and come again, and to morrow I will give; when thou hast it by thee.

Devise not evil against thy neighbour, seeing he dwelleth securely by thee.

Strive not with a man without cause, if he have done thee no harm.

Envy thou not the oppressor, and choose none of his ways.

For the froward is abomination to the Lord: but his secret is with the righteous.

The curse of the Lord is in the house of the wicked: but he blesseth the habitation of the just.

Proverbs 3:27–33

5 Execute true judgment, and shew mercy and compassions every man to his brother:

And oppress not the widow, nor the fatherless, the stranger, nor the poor; and let none of you imagine evil against his brother in your heart.

Zechariah 7:9–10

6 *Chorus.* The man who does right, free-willed, without constraint
shall not lose happiness
nor be wiped out with all his generation.
But the transgressor, I tell you, the bold man
who brings in confusion of goods unrightly won,
at long last and perforce, when ship toils
under tempest must strike his sail
in the wreck of his rigging.

Aeschylus, *Eumenides,* 550

7 *Chorus.* God will not punish the man
Who makes return for an injury:
Deceivers may be deceived.

Sophocles, *Oedipus at Colonus,* 228

8 *Athenians at the Congress of the Peloponnesian Confederacy.* Men's indignation, it seems, is more excited by legal wrong than by violent wrong; the first looks like being cheated by an equal, the second like being compelled by a superior.

Thucydides, *Peloponnesian War,* I, 77

9 *Glaucon.* Now that those who practise justice do so involuntarily and because they have not the power to be unjust will best appear if we imagine something of this kind: having given both to the just and the unjust power to do what they will, let us watch and see whither desire will lead them; then we shall discover in the very act the just and unjust man to be proceeding along the same road, following their interest, which all natures deem to be their good, and are only diverted into the path of justice by the force of law. The liberty which we are supposing may be most completely given to them in the form of such a power as is said to have been possessed by Gyges the ancestor of Croesus the Lydian. According to the tradition, Gyges was a shepherd in the service of the king of Lydia; there was a great storm, and an earthquake made an opening in the earth at the place where he was feeding his flock. Amazed at the sight, he descended into the opening, where, among other marvels, he beheld a hollow brazen horse, having doors, at which he stooping and looking in saw a dead body of stature, as appeared to him, more

than human, and having nothing on but a gold ring; this he took from the finger of the dead and reascended. Now the shepherds met together, according to custom, that they might send their monthly report about the flocks to the king; into their assembly he came having the ring on his finger, and as he was sitting among them he chanced to turn the collet of the ring inside his hand, when instantly he became invisible to the rest of the company and they began to speak of him as if he were no longer present. He was astonished at this, and again touching the ring he turned the collet outwards and reappeared; he made several trials of the ring, and always with the same result—when he turned the collet inwards he became invisible, when outwards he reappeared. Whereupon he contrived to be chosen one of the messengers who were sent to the court; where as soon as he arrived he seduced the queen, and with her help conspired against the king and slew him, and took the kingdom. Suppose now that there were two such magic rings, and the just put on one of them and the unjust the other; no man can be imagined to be of such an iron nature that he would stand fast in justice. No man would keep his hands off what was not his own when he could safely take what he liked out of the market, or go into houses and lie with any one at his pleasure, or kill or release from prison whom he would, and in all respects be like a God among men. Then the actions of the just would be as the actions of the unjust; they would both come at last to the same point. And this we may truly affirm to be a great proof that a man is just, not willingly or because he thinks that justice is any good to him individually, but of necessity, for wherever any one thinks that he can safely be unjust, there he is unjust. For all men believe in their hearts that injustice is far more profitable to the individual than justice, and he who argues as I have been supposing, will say that they are right. If you could imagine any one obtaining this power of becoming invisible, and never doing any wrong or touching what was another's, he would be thought by the lookers-on to be a most wretched idiot, although they would praise him to one another's faces, and keep up appearances with one another from a fear that they too might suffer injustice. Enough of this.

Now, if we are to form a real judgment of the life of the just and unjust, we must isolate them; there is no other way; and how is the isolation to be effected? I answer: Let the unjust man be entirely unjust, and the just man entirely just; nothing is to be taken away from either of them, and both are to be perfectly furnished for the work of their respective lives. First, let the unjust be like other distinguished masters of craft; like the skilful pilot or physician, who knows intuitively his own powers and keeps within their limits, and who, if he fails at any point, is able to recover himself. So let the unjust make his unjust attempts in the right way, and lie hidden if he means to be great in his injustice (he who is found out is nobody): for the highest reach of injustice is, to be deemed just when you are not. Therefore I say that in the perfectly unjust man we must assume the most perfect injustice; there is to be no deduction, but we must allow him, while doing the most unjust acts, to have acquired the greatest reputation for justice. If he have taken a false step he must be able to recover himself; he must be one who can speak with effect, if any of his deeds come to light, and who can force his way where force is required by his courage and strength, and command of money and friends. And at his side let us place the just man in his nobleness and simplicity, wishing, as Aeschylus says, to be and not to seem good. There must be no seeming, for if he seem to be just he will be honoured and rewarded, and then we shall not know whether he is just for the sake of justice or for the sake of honours and rewards; therefore, let him be clothed in justice only, and have no other covering; and he must be imagined in a state of life the opposite of the former. Let him be the best of men, and let him be thought the worst; then he will have been put to the proof; and we shall see whether he will be affected by the fear of infamy and its consequences. And let him continue thus to the hour of death; being just and seeming to be unjust. When both have reached the utttermost extreme, the one of justice and the other of injustice, let judgment be given which of them is the happier of the two.

Socrates. Heavens! my dear Glaucon . . . how energetically you polish them up for the decision, first one and then the other, as if they were two statues.

I do my best, he said. And now that we know what they are like there is no difficulty in tracing out the sort of life which awaits either of them. This I will proceed to describe; but as you may think the description a little too coarse, I ask you to suppose, Socrates, that the words which follow are not mine. Let me put them into the mouths of the eulogists of injustice: They will tell you that the just man who is thought unjust will be scourged, racked, bound—will have his eyes burnt out; and, at last, after suffering every kind of evil, he will be impaled: Then he will understand that he ought to seem only, and not to be, just.

Plato, *Republic*, II, 359A

10 *Socrates.* And surely . . . we have explained again and again how and by virtue of what quality a man will be just.

Adeimantus. That is very certain.

And is justice dimmer in the individual, and is her form different, or is she the same which we found her to be in the State?

There is no difference in my opinion, he said.

Because, if any doubt is still lingering in our minds, a few commonplace instances will satisfy us of the truth of what I am saying.

What sort of instances do you mean?

If the case is put to us, must we not admit that the just State, or the man who is trained in the principles of such a State, will be less likely than the unjust to make away with a deposit of gold or silver? Would any one deny this?

No one. . . .

Will the just man or citizen ever be guilty of sacrilege or theft, or treachery either to his friends or to his country?

Never.

Neither will he ever break faith where there have been oaths or agreements?

Impossible.

No one will be less likely to commit adultery, or to dishonour his father and mother, or to fail in his religious duties?

No one.

And the reason is that each part of him is doing its own business, whether in ruling or being ruled?

Exactly so.

Are you satisfied then that the quality which makes such men and such states is justice, or do you hope to discover some other?

Not I, indeed.

Then our dream has been realized; and the suspicion which we entertained at the beginning of our work of construction, that some divine power must have conducted us to a primary form of justice, has now been verified?

Yes, certainly.

And the division of labour which required the carpenter and the shoemaker and the rest of the citizens to be doing each his own business, and not another's, was a shadow of justice, and for that reason it was of use?

Clearly.

But in reality justice was such as we were describing, being concerned however, not with the outward man, but with the inward, which is the true self and concernment of man: for the just man does not permit the several elements within him to interfere with one another, or any of them to do the work of others,—he sets in order his own inner life, and is his own master and his own law, and at peace with himself; and when he has bound together the three principles within him, which may be compared to the higher, lower, and middle notes of the scale, and the intermediate intervals—when he has bound all these together, and is no longer many, but has become one entirely temperate and perfectly adjusted nature, then he proceeds to act, if he has to act, whether in a matter of property, or in the treatment of the body, or in some affair of politics or private business; always thinking and calling that which preserves and co-operates with this harmonious condition, just and good action, and the knowledge which presides over it, wisdom, and that which at any time impairs this condition, he will call unjust action, and the opinion which presides over it ignorance.

You have said the exact truth, Socrates.

Very good; and if we were to affirm that we had discovered the just man and the just State, and the nature of justice in each of them, we should not be telling a falsehood?

Most certainly not.

Plato, *Republic*, IV, 442B

11 *Athenian Stranger.* And now I can define to you clearly, and without ambiguity, what I mean by the just and unjust, according to my notion of them:—When anger and fear, and pleasure and pain, and jealousies and desires, tyrannize over the soul, whether they do any harm or not—I call all this injustice. But when the opinion of the best, in whatever part of human nature states or individuals may suppose that to dwell, has dominion in the soul and orders the life of every man, even if it be sometimes mistaken, yet what is done in accordance therewith, and the principle in individuals which obeys this rule, and is best for the whole life of man, is to be called just; although the hurt done by mistake is thought by many to be involuntary injustice.

Plato, *Laws*, IX, 863B

12 The one thing which is wholly right and noble is to strive for that which is most honourable for a man's self and for his country, and to face the consequences whatever they may be.

Plato, *Seventh Letter*

13 It is only between what *is* right and what *seems* right from habit, that some people are mad enough to see no difference.

Aristotle, *On Generation and Corruption*, 325ª22

14 There being three objects of choice and three of avoidance, the noble, the advantageous, the pleasant, and their contraries, the base, the injurious, the painful, about all of these the good man tends to go right and the bad man to go wrong, and especially about pleasure.

Aristotle, *Ethics*, 1104ᵇ31

15 Not every action nor every passion admits of a mean; for some have names that already imply badness, e.g. spite, shamelessness, envy, and in the case of actions adultery, theft, murder; for all of these and suchlike things imply by their names that they are themselves bad, and not the excesses or deficiencies of them. It is not possible, then, ever to be right with regard to them; one must always be wrong. Nor does goodness or badness with regard to such things depend on committing adultery with the right woman, at the right time, and in the right way, but simply to do any of

them is to go wrong. It would be equally absurd, then, to expect that in unjust, cowardly, and voluptuous action there should be a mean, an excess, and a deficiency; for at that rate there would be a mean of excess and of deficiency, an excess of excess, and a deficiency of deficiency. But as there is no excess and deficiency of temperance and courage because what is intermediate is in a sense an extreme, so too of the actions we have mentioned there is no mean nor any excess and deficiency, but however they are done they are wrong.

Aristotle, *Ethics*, 1107ª9

16 Justice, alone of the virtues, is thought to be 'another's good', because it is related to our neighbour; for it does what is advantageous to another, either a ruler or a copartner. Now the worst man is he who exercises his wickedness both towards himself and towards his friends, and the best man is not he who exercises his virtue towards himself but he who exercises it towards another; for this is a difficult task. Justice in this sense, then, is not part of virtue but virtue entire, nor is the contrary injustice a part of vice but vice entire.

Aristotle, *Ethics*, 1130ª3

17 It is a good precept that tells us not to do a thing if there is doubt whether it is right or wrong. Righteousness shines with its own brilliance. But doubt is a sign that we are possibly considering a wrong.

Cicero, *De Officiis*, I, 9

18 While wrong may be committed by force or by treachery, both ways are bestial. Treachery belongs to the fox and force to the lion. Both are utterly unworthy of a man. But treachery is the more contemptible.

Cicero, *De Officiis*, I, 13

19 The man that's just and resolute of mood
No craze of people's perverse vote can shake,
   Nor frown of threat'ning monarch make
      To quit a purposed good.

Horace, *Odes*, III, 3

20 It is a mark of a good way of life that, among other things, it satisfies and abides; bad behaviour, constantly changing, not for the better, simply into different forms, has none of this stability.

Seneca, *Letters to Lucilius*, 47

21 Enter ye in at the strait gate: for wide is the gate, and broad is the way, that leadeth to destruction, and many there be which go in thereat:

Because strait is the gate, and narrow is the way, which leadeth unto life, and few there be that find it.

Matthew 7:13–14

22 Even so every good tree bringeth forth good fruit;

but a corrupt tree bringeth forth evil fruit.

A good tree cannot bring forth evil fruit, neither can a corrupt tree bring forth good fruit.

Every tree that bringeth not forth good fruit is hewn down, and cast into the fire.

Wherefore by their fruits ye shall know them.

Matthew 7:17–20

23 Dearly beloved, avenge not yourselves, but rather give place unto wrath: for it is written, Vengeance is mine; I will repay, saith the Lord.

Therefore if thine enemy hunger, feed him; if he thirst, give him drink: for in so doing thou shalt heap coals of fire on his head.

Romans 12:19–20

24 Who can hesitate to number among the faults an affectation which makes one ashamed to do what is right?

Quintilian, *Institutio Oratoria*, XII, 5

25 Courage and wisdom are, indeed, rarities amongst men, but of all that is good, a just man it would seem is the most scarce.

Plutarch, *Flamininus*

26 In his ordinary language he [Agesilaus] was always observed to be a great maintainer of justice, and would commend it as the chief of virtues, saying, that valour without justice was useless, and if all the world were just, there would be no need of valour.

Plutarch, *Agesilaus*

27 A good man does nothing for the sake of appearance, but for the sake of doing right.

Epictetus, *Discourses*, III, 24

28 I who have seen the nature of the good that it is beautiful, and of the bad that it is ugly, and the nature of him who does wrong, that it is akin to me, not only of the same blood or seed, but that it participates in the same intelligence and the same portion of the divinity, I can neither be injured by any of them, for no one can fix on me what is ugly, nor can I be angry with my kinsman, nor hate him. For we are made for co-operation, like feet, like hands, like eyelids, like the rows of the upper and lower teeth. To act against one another then is contrary to nature; and it is acting against one another to be vexed and to turn away.

Marcus Aurelius, *Meditations*, II, 1

29 One thing here is worth a great deal, to pass thy life in truth and justice, with a benevolent disposition even to liars and unjust men.

Marcus Aurelius, *Meditations*, VI, 47

30 Generally, wickedness does no harm at all to the universe; and particularly, the wickedness of one man does no harm to another. It is only harmful to him who has it in his power to be released from it, as soon as he shall choose.

Marcus Aurelius, *Meditations*, VIII, 55

31 It is owing to the various conditions of men that certain acts are virtuous for some, as being proportionate and fitting to them, while they are vicious for others, as being not proportioned to them.

Aquinas, *Summa Theologica*, I–II, 94, 3

32 To his neighbours a man behaves himself well both in particular and in general. In particular, as to those to whom he is indebted by paying his debts, and in this sense is to be taken the commandment about honouring one's parents. In general, as to all men by doing harm to none, either by deed, or by word, or by thought. By deed harm is done to one's neighbour sometimes in his person, that is, to his personal existence, and this is forbidden by the words, *Thou shalt not kill;* sometimes in a person united to him as to the propagation of offspring, and this is prohibited by the words, *Thou shalt not commit adultery;* sometimes in his possessions, which are directed to both of these, and with regard to this it is said, *Thou shalt not steal.* Harm done by word is forbidden when it is said, *Thou shalt not bear false witness against thy neighbour;* harm done by thought is forbidden in the words, *Thou shalt not covet.*

Aquinas, *Summa Theologica*, I–II, 100, 5

33 If we speak of legal justice, it is evident that it stands foremost among all the moral virtues, for as much as the common good transcends the individual good of one person. In this sense the Philosopher [Aristotle] declares that *the most excellent of the virtues would seem to be justice, and more glorious than either the evening or the morning star.* But, even if we speak of particular justice, it excels the other moral virtues for two reasons. The first reason may be taken from the subject, because justice is in the more excellent part of the soul, viz. the rational appetite or will, whereas the other moral virtues are in the sensitive appetite, whereunto appertain the passions which are the matter of the other moral virtues. The second reason is taken from the object, because the other virtues are commendable in respect of the sole good of the virtuous person himself, whereas justice is praiseworthy in respect of the virtuous person being well disposed towards another, so that justice is somewhat the good of another person.

Aquinas, *Summa Theologica*, II–II, 58, 12

34 Every excellence proper to a thing is to be loved in that thing; as in masculinity to be well bearded, and in femininity to be well smooth of beard over all the face. As in a setter, good scent, and in a boarhound, good speed. And the more proper is the excellence the better is it to be loved; where-

fore, though every virtue is to be loved in man,
that is most to be loved in him which is most human; and that is justice, which abides only in the
rational or intellectual part, to wit in the will.
This is so much to be loved that . . . they who are
its foes, as are robbers and plunderers, love it; and
therefore we see that its contrary, to wit injustice,
is most hated; as treachery, ingratitude, forgery,
theft, rapine, cheating and their likes.

Dante, *Convivio,* I, 12

35 Enough is opened to thee now the labyrinth
  which hid from thee the living justice of which
  thou hast made question so incessantly;
for thou didst say: 'A man is born upon the bank
  of Indus and there is none to tell of Christ, nor
  none to read, nor none to write;
and all his volitions and his deeds are good so far
  as human reason seeth, sinless in life or in discourse.
He dieth unbaptised and without faith; where is
  that justice which condemneth him? where is
  his fault, in that he not believes?'
Now who art thou who wouldst sit upon the seat
  to judge at a thousand miles away with the
  short sight that carries but a span?
Truly to him who goeth subtly to work with me,
  were not the Scripture over you, there were
  marvellous ground for questioning.
O animals of earth, minds gross! the primal Will,
  good in itself, never departed from its own self
  which is the highest good.
All is just which doth harmonise with it; no created good draweth it to itself, but it by raying
  forth giveth rise to it.

Dante, *Paradiso,* XIX, 67

36 There are lawful vices, as there are many either
  good or excusable actions that are unlawful.

Montaigne, *Essays,* III, 1, The
Useful and the Honorable

37 *The King.* What stronger breastplate than a heart
    untainted!
  Thrice is he arm'd that hath his quarrel just,
  And he but naked, though lock'd up in steel,
  Whose conscience with injustice is corrupted.

Shakespeare, *II Henry VI,* III, ii, 232

38 *Lear.* O, ho, are you there with me? No eyes in
    your head, nor no money in your purse? Your
    eyes are in a heavy case, your purse in a light. Yet
    you see how this world goes.
  Gloucester. I see it feelingly.
  Lear. What, art mad? A man may see how this
    world goes with no eyes. Look with thine ears: see
    how yond justice rails upon yond simple thief.
    Hark, in thine ear: change places; and, handy-
    dandy, which is the justice, which is the thief?
    Thou hast seen a farmer's dog bark at a beggar?
  Glou. Ay, sir.

Lear. And the creature run from the cur?
There thou mightst behold the great image of authority: a dog's obeyed in office.
Thou rascal beadle, hold thy bloody hand!
Why dost thou lash that whore? Strip thine own
  back;
Thou hotly lust'st to use her in that kind
For which thou whipp'st her. The usurer hangs
  the cozener.
Through tatter'd clothes small vices do appear;
Robes and furr'd gowns hide all. Plate sin with
  gold,
And the strong lance of justice hurtless breaks;
Arm it in rags, a pigmy's straw does pierce it.
None does offend, none, I say, none; I'll able 'em.
Take that of me, my friend, who have the power
To seal the accuser's lips. Get thee glass eyes;
And, like a scurvy politician, seem
To see the things thou dost not.

Shakespeare, *Lear,* IV, vi, 148

39 The names of *just* and *unjust,* when they are attributed to men, signify one thing, and when they are
attributed to actions, another. When they are attributed to men, they signify conformity, or inconformity of manners, to reason. But when they are
attributed to actions, they signify the conformity,
or inconformity to reason, not of manners, or
manner of life, but of particular actions. A just
man therefore is he that taketh all the care he can
that his actions may be all just; and an unjust
man is he that neglecteth it. And such men are
more often in our language styled by the names of
righteous and *unrighteous* than *just* and *unjust,* though
the meaning be the same. Therefore a righteous
man does not lose that title by one or a few unjust
actions that proceed from sudden passion, or mistake of things or persons, nor does an unrighteous
man lose his character for such actions as he does,
or forbears to do, for fear: because his will is not
framed by the justice, but by the apparent benefit
of what he is to do. That which gives to human
actions the relish of justice is a certain nobleness
or gallantness of courage, rarely found, by which
a man scorns to be beholding for the contentment
of his life to fraud, or breach of promise. This
justice of the manners is that which is meant
where justice is called a *virtue;* and injustice, a *vice.*

But the justice of actions denominates men, not
just, but *guiltless:* and the injustice of the same
(which is also called injury) gives them but the
name of *guilty.*

Hobbes, *Leviathan,* I, 15

40 Wrong-doing cannot be conceived of, but under
dominion—that is, where, by the general right of
the whole dominion, it is decided what is good
and what evil, and where no one does anything
rightfully, save what he does in accordance with
the general decree or consent. For that . . . is
wrong-doing, which cannot lawfully be commit-

ted, or is by law forbidden. But obedience is the constant will to execute that, which by law is good, and by the general decree ought to be done.

Yet we are accustomed to call that also wrong, which is done against the sentence of sound reason, and to give the name of obedience to the constant will to moderate the appetite according to the dictate of reason: a manner of speech which I should quite approve, did human liberty consist in the licence of appetite, and slavery in the dominion of reason. But as human liberty is the greater, the more man can be guided by reason, and moderate his appetite, we cannot without great impropriety call a rational life obedience, and give the name of wrong-doing to that which is, in fact, a weakness of the mind, not a licence of the mind directed against itself, and for which a man may be called a slave, rather than free.

Spinoza, *Political Treatise,* II, 19–20

41 We find in history a thousand examples of pusillanimous or ambitious rulers, who were ruined by their slackness or their pride; not one who suffered for having been strictly just. But we ought not to confound negligence with moderation, or clemency with weakness. To be just, it is necessary to be severe; to permit vice, when one has the right and the power to suppress it, is to be oneself vicious.

Rousseau, *Political Economy*

42 Right . . . comprehends the whole of the conditions under which the voluntary actions of any one person can be harmonized in reality with the voluntary actions of every other person, according to a universal law of freedom.

Kant, *Introduction to the Science of Right,* B

43 The dictum of equity may be put thus: "The strictest right is the greatest wrong."

Kant, *Introduction to the Science of Right,* F

44 "Do wrong to no one." This formula may be rendered so as to mean: "Do no wrong to any one, even if thou shouldst be under the necessity, in observing this duty, to cease from all connection with others and to avoid all society."

Kant, *Division of the Science of Right,* A

45 It is not enough to do what is right, but we should practise it solely on the ground of its being right.

Kant, *Critique of Aesthetic Judgement,* 53

46 Life as the sum of ends has a right against abstract right. If for example it is only by stealing bread that the wolf can be kept from the door, the action is of course an encroachment on someone's property, but it would be wrong to treat this action as an ordinary theft. To refuse to allow a man in jeopardy of his life to take such steps for self-pres-

ervation would be to stigmatize him as without rights, and since he would be deprived of his life, his freedom would be annulled altogether. Many diverse details have a bearing on the preservation of life, and when we have our eyes on the future we have to engage ourselves in these details. But the only thing that is necessary is to live *now,* the future is not absolute but ever exposed to accident. Hence it is only the necessity of the immediate present which can justify a wrong action, because not to do the action would in turn be to commit an offence, indeed the most wrong of all offences, namely the complete destruction of the embodiment of freedom.

Hegel, *Philosophy of Right,* Additions, Par. 127

47 Act singly, and what you have already done singly will justify you now. Greatness appeals to the future. If I can be firm enough to-day to do right and scorn eyes, I must have done so much right before as to defend me now. Be it how it will, do right now.

Emerson, *Self-Reliance*

48 The only freedom I care about is the freedom to do right; the freedom to do wrong I am ready to part with on the cheapest terms to any one who will take it of me.

T. H. Huxley, *Descartes' "Discourse on Method"*

49 Speaking in a general way, a person is understood to deserve good if he does right, evil if he does wrong; and in a more particular sense, to deserve good from those to whom he does or has done good, and evil from those to whom he does or has done evil. The precept of returning good for evil has never been regarded as a case of the fulfilment of justice, but as one in which the claims of justice are waived, in obedience to other considerations.

Mill, *Utilitarianism,* V

50 We do not call anything wrong, unless we mean to imply that a person ought to be punished in some way or other for doing it; if not by law, by the opinion of his fellowcreatures; if not by opinion, by the reproaches of his own conscience. This seems the real turning point of the distinction between morality and simple expediency.

Mill, *Utilitarianism,* V

51 *Prince Andrew.* It is not given to man to know what is right and what is wrong. Men always did and always will err, and in nothing more than in what they consider right and wrong.

Tolstoy, *War and Peace,* V, 11

52 Thou art indeed just, Lord, if I contend
With thee; but, sir, so what I plead is just.
Why do sinners' ways prosper? and why must

Disappointment all I endeavour end?
    Wert thou my enemy, O thou my friend,
How wouldst thou worse, I wonder, than thou
    dost
Defeat, thwart me? Oh, the sots and thralls of lust
Do in spare hours more thrive than I that spend,
Sir, life upon thy cause. See, banks and brakes
Now, leavèd how thick! lacèd they are again
With fretty chervil, look, and fresh wind shakes
Them; birds build—but not I build; no, but
    strain,
Time's eunuch, and not breed one work that
    wakes.

Mine, O thou lord of life, send my roots rain.
    G. M. Hopkins, *Thou Art Indeed Just, Lord*

53 To talk of intrinsic right and intrinsic wrong is
absolutely nonsensical; intrinsically, an injury, an
oppression, an exploitation, an annihilation can
be nothing wrong, inasmuch as life is *essentially*
(that is, in its cardinal functions) something which
functions by injuring, oppressing, exploiting, and
annihilating, and is absolutely inconceivable
without such a character.

    Nietzsche, *Genealogy of Morals*, II, 11

9.8 | *Happiness*

In the discussion of this pivotal notion, concerning which there appear to be many disagreements, several points that have seldom if ever been disputed stand out. One is the fact that the word "happiness" is generally used to name something that is desired for its own sake, not as a means to some end beyond itself. Another is the fact that happiness is not one good among others, which a man might possess and still desire many other goods; it is rather the complete good, or summation of goods. The reader will find this conception of happiness expressed in Augustine's "Happy is he who has all that he desires, provided that he desire nothing amiss," and in the statement by Boethius that happiness consists in the possession in aggregate of all good things.

The understanding of these two points is profoundly affected by a fundamental difference among the writers quoted here in their use of the word "happiness." Some of them use it in an exclusively ethical sense to denote the quality of a whole human life. When it is thus used, happiness is not something that can be experienced at a particular time, or enjoyed at one time and not at another. Other writers—and most people generally—use the term to denote a psychological state, a feeling of contentment, joy, or satisfaction, which can be experienced at one time and not at another.

Writers who use the word in such totally different senses may appear to disagree with one another in what they say about happiness, but, in view of their equivocal use of the term, they will be only in apparent, not real disagreement. Thus, for example, Kant, who uses the term "happiness" to name a feeling of contentment that results from the satisfaction of whatever desires a person may happen to have, whether or not one's desires are themselves morally sound, may reach the ethical conclusion that persons who obey the moral law do not seek happiness but rather seek to deserve it. That conclusion does not really disagree with the ethical principle enunciated by Aristotle, Augustine, and others that people should seek happiness conceived as a whole life made good by the possession of all the goods that a virtuous person ought to desire.

The reader will find that in most of the quotations from the poets and the historians as well as from the philosophers, the word "happiness" is used mainly or exclusively in the psychological sense in which we tend to use it in daily life when we say that we feel happy or miserable. For other quotations that use "joy" and "sorrow" as synonyms for "happiness" and "misery," the reader is referred to Chapter 4 on EMOTION, Section 4.6 on JOY AND SORROW; and for the relation of happiness to pleasure and pain, the reader is referred to Section 4.7 in that chapter.

To avoid misunderstanding certain of the quotations below from philosophers and theologians, the reader must keep the other meaning of happiness clearly in mind, the meaning in which it is not a feeling or emotion, but the ultimate goal that is achieved by a morally virtuous life. In this connection, the reader is referred to Section 9.10 on VIRTUE AND VICE; and is also advised that theologians often use such terms as "beatitude" or "blessedness" interchangeably with "happiness." The other term that appears in discussions of happiness—the term *summum bonum* or supreme good—the reader will find in Section 9.6 on GOOD AND EVIL; and will find the conception of eternal happiness, the beatitude of the blessed in heaven, treated in Section 20.14 on REDEMPTION AND SALVATION and in Section 20.15 on HEAVEN AND HELL.

---

1 *Agamemnon.*   Call that man only blest who has in sweet tranquillity brought his life to close.

Aeschylus, *Agamemnon,* 928

2 *Solon.* Oh! Crœsus . . . thou askedst a question concerning the condition of man, of one who knows that the power above us is full of jealousy, and fond of troubling our lot. A long life gives one to witness much, and experience much oneself, that one would not choose. Seventy years I regard as the limit of the life of man. In these seventy years are contained, without reckoning intercalary months, twenty-five thousand and two hundred days. Add an intercalary month to every other year, that the seasons may come round at the right time, and there will be, besides the seventy years, thirty-five such months, making an addition of one thousand and fifty days. The whole number of the days contained in the seventy years will thus be twenty-six thousand two hundred and fifty, whereof not one but will produce events unlike the rest. Hence man is wholly accident. For thyself, oh! Crœsus, I see that thou art wonderfully rich, and art the lord of many nations; but with respect to that whereon thou questionest me, I have no answer to give, until I hear that thou hast closed thy life happily. For assuredly he who possesses great store of riches is no nearer happiness than he who has what suffices for his daily needs, unless it so hap that luck attend upon him, and so he continue in the enjoyment of all his good things to the end of life. For many of the wealthiest men have been unfavoured of fortune, and many whose means were moderate have had excellent luck. Men of the former class excel those of the latter but in two respects; these last excel the former in many. The wealthy man is better able to content his desires, and to bear up against a sudden buffet of calamity. The other has less ability to withstand these evils (from which, however, his good luck keeps him clear), but he enjoys all these following blessings: he is whole of limb, a stranger to disease, free from misfortune, happy in his children, and comely to look upon. If, in addition to all this, he end his life well, he is of a truth the man of whom thou art in search, the man who may rightly be termed happy. Call him, however, until he die, not happy but fortunate. Scarcely, indeed, can any man unite all these advantages: as there is no country which contains within it all that it needs, but each, while it possesses some things, lacks others, and the best country is that which contains the most; so no single human being is complete in every respect—something is always lacking. He who unites the greatest number of advantages, and retaining them to the day of his death, then dies peaceably, that man alone, sire, is, in my judgment, entitled to bear the name of 'happy.' But in every matter it behoves us to mark well the end: for oftentimes God gives men a gleam of happiness, and then plunges them into ruin.

Herodotus, *History,* I, 32

3 *Chorus.* What man, what man on earth wins more of happiness than a seeming and after that turning away?

Sophocles, *Oedipus the King,* 1190

4 *Chorus.*   Count no mortal happy till
he has passed the final limit of his life secure from
  pain.

Sophocles, *Oedipus the King,* 1529

5 *1st Semichorus.* Happy the man who cries *Evohé!*
stretched out full length and making merry,
for whom the wine keeps flowing,
whose arms are open to his friend!
Lucky man, upon whose bed there blows
the soft bloom of a lovely girl
with gleaming hair, sweet with oil!
who cries: "Who'll open me the door?"

Euripides, *Cyclops,* 495

6 *Chorus.* Excess of happiness—it drives
men's minds awry; in its train
comes on corrupted power.
No man foresees the final stretch of time.
Evil lures him, justice races by,
until he wrecks at last the somber car
   that holds his happiness.

Euripides, *Heracles,* 774

7 *Maiden.* If a man is born and bred in hardships, he
fainteth not under them; but happiness is subject
to change, and to be afflicted after prosperous
days is a grievous lot for mortals.

Euripides, *Iphigenia in Tauris,* 1119

8 If a person had wealth and all the goods of which
we were just now speaking, and did not use them,
would he be happy because he possessed them?

No indeed, Socrates.

Then, I said, a man who would be happy must
not only have the good things, but he must also
use them; there is no advantage in merely having
them?

True.

Well, Cleinias, but if you have the use as well as
the possession of good things, is that sufficient to
confer happiness?

Yes, in my opinion.

And may a person use them either rightly or
wrongly?

He must use them rightly.

That is quite true, I said. And the wrong use of
a thing is far worse than the non-use; for the one
is an evil, and the other is neither a good nor an
evil. You admit that?

He assented.

Now in the working and use of wood, is not that
which gives the right use simply the knowledge of
the carpenter?

Nothing else, he said.

And surely, in the manufacture of vessels,
knowledge is that which gives the right way of
making them?

He agreed.

And in the use of the goods of which we spoke
at first—wealth and health and beauty, is not
knowledge that which directs us to the right use of
them, and regulates our practice about them?

He assented.

Then in every possession and every use of a
thing, knowledge is that which gives a man not
only good-fortune but success?

He again assented.

And tell me, I said, O tell me, what do possessions profit a man, if he have neither good sense
nor wisdom? Would a man be better off, having
and doing many things without wisdom, or a few
things with wisdom? Look at the matter thus: If
he did fewer things would he not make fewer mistakes? if he made fewer mistakes would he not
have fewer misfortunes? and if he had fewer misfortunes would he not be less miserable?

Certainly, he said.

And who would do least—a poor man or a rich
man?

A poor man.

A weak man or a strong man?

A weak man.

A noble man or a mean man?

A mean man.

And a coward would do less than a courageous
and temperate man?

Yes.

And an indolent man less than an active man?

He assented.

And a slow man less than a quick; and one who
had dull perceptions of seeing and hearing less
than one who had keen ones?

All this was mutually allowed by us.

Then, I said, Cleinias, the sum of the matter
appears to be that the goods of which we spoke
before are not to be regarded as goods in themselves, but the degree of good and evil in them
depends on whether they are or are not under the
guidance of knowledge: under the guidance of ignorance, they are greater evils than their opposites, inasmuch as they are more able to minister
to the evil principle which rules them; and when
under the guidance of wisdom and prudence, they
are greater goods: but in themselves they are
nothing?

That, he replied, is obvious.

What then is the result of what has been said?
Is not this the result—that other things are indifferent, and that wisdom is the only good, and ignorance the only evil?

He assented.

Let us consider a further point, I said: Seeing
that all men desire happiness, and happiness, as
has been shown, is gained by a use, and a right
use, of the things of life, and the right use of them,
and good fortune in the use of them, is given by
knowledge,—the inference is that everybody
ought by all means to try and make himself as
wise as he can?

Plato, *Euthydemus,* 280B

9 *Socrates.* Should we not offer up a prayer first of all to the local deities?

Phaedrus. By all means.

Soc. Beloved Pan, and all ye other gods who haunt this place, give me beauty in the inward soul; and may the outward and inward man be at one. May I reckon the wise to be the wealthy, and may I have such a quantity of gold as a temperate man and he only can bear and carry. —Anything more? The prayer, I think, is enough for me.

Phaedr. Ask the same for me, for friends should have all things in common.

Plato, *Phaedrus,* 279B

10 We call that which is in itself worthy of pursuit more final than that which is worthy of pursuit for the sake of something else, and that which is never desirable for the sake of something else more final than the things that are desirable both in themselves and for the sake of that other thing, and therefore we call final without qualification that which is always desirable in itself and never for the sake of something else.

Now such a thing happiness, above all else, is held to be; for this we choose always for itself and never for the sake of something else, but honour, pleasure, reason, and every virtue we choose indeed for themselves (for if nothing resulted from them we should still choose each of them), but we choose them also for the sake of happiness, judging that by means of them we shall be happy. Happiness, on the other hand, no one chooses for the sake of these, nor, in general, for anything other than itself.

Aristotle, *Ethics,* 1097a30

11 The final good is thought to be self-sufficient. Now by self-sufficient we do not mean that which is sufficient for a man by himself, for one who lives a solitary life, but also for parents, children, wife, and in general for his friends and fellow citizens, since man is born for citizenship. But some limit must be set to this; for if we extend our requirement to ancestors and descendants and friends' friends we are in for an infinite series. Let us examine this question, however, on another occasion; the self-sufficient we now define as that which when isolated makes life desirable and lacking in nothing; and such we think happiness to be; and further we think it most desirable of all things, without being counted as one good thing among others—if it were so counted it would clearly be made more desirable by the addition of even the least of goods; for that which is added becomes an excess of goods, and of goods the greater is always more desirable. Happiness, then, is something final and self-sufficient, and is the end of action.

Aristotle, *Ethics,* 1097b8

12 To say that happiness is the chief good seems a platitude, and a clearer account of what it is is still desired. This might perhaps be given, if we could first ascertain the function of man. For just as for a flute-player, a sculptor, or an artist, and, in general, for all things that have a function or activity, the good and the 'well' is thought to reside in the function, so would it seem to be for man, if he has a function. Have the carpenter, then, and the tanner certain functions or activities, and has man none? Is he born without a function? Or as eye, hand, foot, and in general each of the parts evidently has a function, may one lay it down that man similarly has a function apart from all these? What then can this be? Life seems to be common even to plants, but we are seeking what is peculiar to man. Let us exclude, therefore, the life of nutrition and growth. Next there would be a life of perception, but *it* also seems to be common even to the horse, the ox, and every animal. There remains, then, an active life of the element that has a rational principle; of this, one part has such a principle in the sense of being obedient to one, the other in the sense of possessing one and exercising thought. And, as 'life of the rational element' also has two meanings, we must state that life in the sense of activity is what we mean; for this seems to be the more proper sense of the term. Now if the function of man is an activity of soul which follows or implies a rational principle, and if we say 'so-and-so' and 'a good so-and-so' have a function which is the same in kind, e.g. a lyre-player and a good lyre-player, and so without qualification in all cases, eminence in respect of goodness being added to the name of the function (for the function of a lyre-player is to play the lyre, and that of a good lyre-player is to do so well): if this is the case, [and we state the function of man to be a certain kind of life, and this to be an activity or actions of the soul implying a rational principle, and the function of a good man to be the good and noble performance of these, and if any action is well performed when it is performed in accordance with the appropriate excellence: if this is the case,] human good turns out to be activity of soul in accordance with virtue, and if there are more than one virtue, in accordance with the best and most complete.

But we must add 'in a complete life'. For one swallow does not make a summer, nor does one day; and so too one day, or a short time, does not make a man blessed and happy.

Aristotle, *Ethics,* 1097b22

13 Must no one at all, then, be called happy while he lives; must we, as Solon says, see the end? Even if we are to lay down this doctrine, is it also the case that a man *is* happy when he is *dead?* Or is not this quite absurd, especially for us who say that happiness is an activity? But if we do not call the dead man happy, and if Solon does not mean this, but

that one can then safely *call* a man blessed as being at last beyond evils and misfortunes, this also affords matter for discussion; for both evil and good are thought to exist for a dead man, as much as for one who is alive but not aware of them; for example, honours and dishonours and the good or bad fortunes of children and in general of descendants. And this also presents a problem; for though a man has lived happily up to old age and has had a death worthy of his life, many reverses may befall his descendants—some of them may be good and attain the life they deserve, while with others the opposite may be the case; and clearly too the degrees of relationship between them and their ancestors may vary indefinitely. It would be odd, then, if the dead man were to share in these changes and become at one time happy, at another wretched; while it would also be odd if the fortunes of the descendants did not for *some* time have *some* effect on the happiness of their ancestors.

But we must return to our first difficulty; for perhaps by a consideration of it our present problem might be solved. Now if we must see the end and only then call a man happy, not as being happy but as having been so before, surely this is a paradox, that when he is happy the attribute that belongs to him is not to be truly predicated of him because we do not wish to call living men happy, on account of the changes that may befall them, and because we have assumed happiness to be something permanent and by no means easily changed, while a single man may suffer many turns of fortune's wheel. For clearly if we were to keep pace with his fortunes, we should often call the same man happy and again wretched, making the happy man out to be a 'chameleon and insecurely based'. Or is this keeping pace with his fortunes quite wrong? Success or failure in life does not depend on these, but human life, as we said, needs these as mere additions, while virtuous activities or their opposites are what constitute happiness or the reverse. . . . The attribute in question, then, will belong to the happy man, and he will be happy throughout his life; for always, or by preference to everything else, he will be engaged in virtuous action and contemplation, and he will bear the chances of life most nobly and altogether decorously, if he is 'truly good' and 'foursquare beyond reproach'.

Now many events happen by chance, and events differing in importance; small pieces of good fortune or of its opposite clearly do not weigh down the scales of life one way or the other, but a multitude of great events if they turn out well will make life happier (for not only are they themselves such as to add beauty to life, but the way a man deals with them may be noble and good), while if they turn out ill they crush and maim happiness; for they both bring pain with them and hinder many activities. Yet even in

these nobility shines through, when a man bears with resignation many great misfortunes, not through insensibility to pain but through nobility and greatness of soul.

If activities are, as we said, what gives life its character, no happy man can become miserable; for he will never do the acts that are hateful and mean. For the man who is truly good and wise, we think, bears all the chances of life becomingly and always makes the best of circumstances, as a good general makes the best military use of the army at his command and a good shoemaker makes the best shoes out of the hides that are given him; and so with all other craftsmen. And if this is the case, the happy man can never become miserable; though he will not reach *blessedness,* if he meet with fortunes like those of Priam.

Nor, again, is he many-coloured and changeable; for neither will he be moved from his happy state easily or by any ordinary misadventures, but only by many great ones, nor, if he has had many great misadventures, will he recover his happiness in a short time, but if at all, only in a long and complete one in which he has attained many splendid successes.

Why then should we not say that he is happy who is active in accordance with complete virtue and is sufficiently equipped with external goods, not for some chance period but throughout a complete life? Or must we add 'and who is destined to live thus and die as befits his life'? Certainly the future is obscure to us, while happiness, we claim, is an end and something in every way final. If so, we shall call happy those among living men in whom these conditions are, and are to be, fulfilled—but happy *men.*

Aristotle, *Ethics,* 1100ª10

14 If happiness is activity in accordance with virtue, it is reasonable that it should be in accordance with the highest virtue; and this will be that of the best thing in us. Whether it be reason or something else that is this element which is thought to be our natural ruler and guide and to take thought of things noble and divine, whether it be itself also divine or only the most divine element in us, the activity of this in accordance with its proper virtue will be perfect happiness. That this activity is contemplative we have already said.

Now this would seem to be in agreement both with what we said before and with the truth. For, firstly, this activity is the best (since not only is reason the best thing in us, but the objects of reason are the best of knowable objects); and secondly, it is the most continuous, since we can contemplate truth more continuously than we can *do* anything. And we think happiness has pleasure mingled with it, but the activity of philosophic wisdom is admittedly the pleasantest of virtuous activities; at all events the pursuit of it is thought to offer pleasures marvellous for their purity and their enduringness, and it is to be expected that those who know will pass their time more pleasantly than those who inquire. And the self-sufficiency that is spoken of must belong most to the contemplative activity. For while a philosopher, as well as a just man or one possessing any other virtue, needs the necessaries of life, when they are sufficiently equipped with things of that sort the just man needs people towards whom and with whom he shall act justly, and the temperate man, the brave man, and each of the others is in the same case, but the philosopher, even when by himself, can contemplate truth, and the better the wiser he is; he can perhaps do so better if he has fellow-workers, but still he is the most self-sufficient. And this activity alone would seem to be loved for its own sake; for nothing arises from it apart from the contemplating, while from practical activities we gain more or less apart from the action. And happiness is thought to depend on leisure; for we are busy that we may have leisure, and make war that we may live in peace. Now the activity of the practical virtues is exhibited in political or military affairs, but the actions concerned with these seem to be unleisurely. Warlike actions are completely so (for no one chooses to be at war, or provokes war, for the sake of being at war; any one would seem absolutely murderous if he were to make enemies of his friends in order to bring about battle and slaughter); but the action of the statesman is also unleisurely, and—apart from the political action itself—aims at despotic power and honours, or at all events happiness, for him and his fellow citizens—a happiness different from political action, and evidently sought as being different. So if among virtuous actions political and military actions are distinguished by nobility and greatness, and these are unleisurely and aim at an end and are not desirable for their own sake, but the activity of reason, which is contemplative, seems both to be superior in serious worth and to aim at no end beyond itself, and to have its pleasure proper to itself (and this augments the activity), and the self-sufficiency, leisureliness, unweariedness (so far as this is possible for man), and all the other attributes ascribed to the supremely happy man are evidently those connected with this activity, it follows that this will be the complete happiness of man, if it be allowed a complete term of life (for none of the attributes of happiness in *in*complete).

But such a life would be too high for man; for it is not in so far as he is man that he will live so, but in so far as something divine is present in him; and by so much as this is superior to our composite nature is its activity superior to that which is the exercise of the other kind of virtue. If reason is divine, then, in comparison with man, the life according to it is divine in comparison with human life. But we must not follow those who advise us, being men, to think of human things, and, being

mortal, of mortal things, but must, so far as we can, make ourselves immortal, and strain every nerve to live in accordance with the best thing in us; for even if it be small in bulk, much more does it in power and worth surpass everything. This would seem, too, to be each man himself, since it is the authoritative and better part of him. It would be strange, then, if he were to choose not the life of his self but that of something else. And what we said before will apply now; that which is proper to each thing is by nature best and most pleasant for each thing; for man, therefore, the life according to reason is best and pleasantest, since reason more than anything else *is* man. This life therefore is also the happiest.

Aristotle, *Ethics,* 1177ª12

15 Certainly no one will dispute the propriety of that partition of goods which separates them into three classes, viz. external goods, goods of the body, and goods of the soul, or deny that the happy man must have all three. For no one would maintain that he is happy who has not in him a particle of courage or temperance or justice or prudence, who is afraid of every insect which flutters past him, and will commit any crime, however great, in order to gratify his lust of meat or drink, who will sacrifice his dearest friend for the sake of half-a-farthing, and is as feeble and false in mind as a child or a madman. These propositions are almost universally acknowledged as soon as they are uttered, but men differ about the degree or relative superiority of this or that good. Some think that a very moderate amount of virtue is enough, but set no limit to their desires of wealth, property, power, reputation, and the like. To whom we reply by an appeal to facts, which easily prove that mankind do not acquire or preserve virtue by the help of external goods, but external goods by the help of virtue, and that happiness, whether consisting in pleasure or virtue, or both, is more often found with those who are most highly cultivated in their mind and in their character, and have only a moderate share of external goods, than among those who possess external goods to a useless extent but are deficient in higher qualities; and this is not only matter of experience, but, if reflected upon, will easily appear to be in accordance with reason. For, whereas external goods have a limit, like any other instrument, and all things useful are of such a nature that where there is too much of them they must either do harm, or at any rate be of no use, to their possessors, every good of the soul, the greater it is, is also of greater use, if the epithet useful as well as noble is appropriate to such subjects. No proof is required to show that the best state of one thing in relation to another corresponds in degree of excellence to the interval between the natures of which we say that these very states are states: so that, if the soul is more noble than our possessions or our bodies, both ab-

solutely and in relation to us, it must be admitted that the best state of either has a similar ratio to the other. Again, it is for the sake of the soul that goods external and goods of the body are eligible at all, and all wise men ought to choose them for the sake of the soul, and not the soul for the sake of them.

Let us acknowledge then that each one has just so much of happiness as he has of virtue and wisdom, and of virtuous and wise action. God is a witness to us of this truth, for he is happy and blessed, not by reason of any external good, but in himself and by reason of his own nature. And herein of necessity lies the difference between good fortune and happiness; for external goods come of themselves, and chance is the author of them, but no one is just or temperate by or through chance. In like manner, and by a similar train of argument, the happy state may be shown to be that which is best and which acts rightly; and rightly it cannot act without doing right actions, and neither individual nor state can do right actions without virtue and wisdom. Thus the courage, justice, and wisdom of a state have the same form and nature as the qualities which give the individual who possesses them the name of just, wise, or temperate.

Aristotle, *Politics*, 1323ᵃ24

16 Because no evil, foolish, or lazy man can enjoy well-being, it follows that the good, courageous, and wise man cannot live miserably. Nor can anyone whose virtue and character merit praise fail to lead a praiseworthy life. Such a life is not something to be shunned. Yet it would be shunned if it were miserable. Hence, whatever is praiseworthy must also be considered happy, prosperous, and desirable.

Cicero, *Paradoxes of the Stoics*, II

17 Happy the man, who, studying nature's laws,
Through known effects can trace the secret
    cause—
His mind possessing in a quiet state,
Fearless of Fortune, and resigned to Fate!
And happy too is he, who decks the bowers
Of sylvans, and adores the rural powers—
Whose mind, unmoved, the bribes of courts can
    see,
Their glittering baits, and purple slavery—
Nor hopes the people's praise, nor fears their
    frown,
Nor, when contending kindred tear the crown,
Will set up one, or pull another down.
  Without concern he hears, but hears from far,
Of tumults, and descents, and distant war;
Nor with a superstitious fear is awed,
For what befalls at home, or what abroad.
Nor his own peace disturbs with pity for the poor.
Nor envies he the rich their happy store,
He feeds on fruits, which, of their own accord,

The willing ground and laden trees afford.
From his loved home no lucre him can draw;
The senate's mad decrees he never saw;
Nor heard, at bawling bars, corrupted law.

Virgil, *Georgics,* II

18 The wealthy man thou could'st not rightly choose
As the supremely happy; rightlier goes
  The name to him, who wisely knows
    The gifts of Heaven to use;

Knows too to face reverse without a sigh,
Nor death before dishonour fears to take;
  Ready for dear companions' sake,
    Or native land, to die.

Horace, *Odes,* IV, 9

19 And seeing the multitudes, he went up into a mountain: and when he was set, his disciples came unto him:

And he opened his mouth, and taught them, saying,

Blessed are the poor in spirit: for their's is the kingdom of heaven.

Blessed are they that mourn: for they shall be comforted.

Blessed are the meek: for they shall inherit the earth.

Blessed are they which do hunger and thirst after righteousness: for they shall be filled.

Blessed are the merciful: for they shall obtain mercy.

Blessed are the pure in heart: for they shall see God.

Blessed are the peacemakers: for they shall be called the children of God.

Blessed are they which are persecuted for righteousness' sake: for their's is the kingdom of heaven.

Blessed are ye, when men shall revile you, and persecute you, and shall say all manner of evil against you falsely, for my sake.

Rejoice, and be exceeding glad: for great is your reward in heaven: for so persecuted they the prophets which were before you.

Matthew 5:1–12

20 It seems the province of some god to lessen that happiness which is too great and inordinate, and so to mingle the affairs of human life that no one should be entirely free and exempt from calamities. . . . Those should think themselves truly blessed to whom fortune has given an equal share of good and evil.

Plutarch, *Aemilius Paulus*

21 For him that would attain to true happiness, which for the most part is placed in the qualities and disposition of the mind, it is . . . of no other disadvantage to be of a mean, obscure country,

than to be born of a small or plain-looking woman.

Plutarch, *Demosthenes*

22 If we crave for the goal that is worthy and fitting for man, namely, happiness of life—and this is accomplished by philosophy alone and by nothing else, and philosophy, as I said, means for us desire for wisdom, and wisdom the science of the truth in things, and of things some are properly so called, others merely share the name—it is reasonable and most necessary to distinguish and systematize the accidental qualities of things.

Nicomachus, *Arithmetic*, I, 2

23 Good and evil . . . are not what vulgar opinion accounts them; many who seem to be struggling with adversity are happy; many, amid great affluence, are utterly miserable, if only the first bear their hard lot with patience, and the latter make a foolish use of their prosperity.

Tacitus, *Annals*, VI, 22

24 If thou workest at that which is before thee, following right reason seriously, vigorously, calmly, without allowing anything else to distract thee, but keeping thy divine part pure, as if thou shouldst be bound to give it back immediately; if thou holdest to this, expecting nothing, fearing nothing, but satisfied with thy present activity according to nature, and with heroic truth in every word and sound which thou utterest, thou wilt live happy. And there is no man who is able to prevent this.

Marcus Aurelius, *Meditations*, III, 12

25 To put Happiness in actions is to put it in things that are outside virtue and outside the Soul; for the Soul's expression is not in action but in wisdom, in a contemplative operation within itself; and this, this alone, is Happiness.

Plotinus, *First Ennead*, V, 10

26 We [cannot] ask to be happy when our actions have not earned us happiness; the good, only, are happy; divine beings are happy only because they are good.

Plotinus, *Third Ennead*, II, 4

27 Not I alone, or a handful of men besides, but surely all men whatsoever want to be happy. And unless we knew the thing with certain knowledge, we could not will it with so certain a will. Yet notice this: If two men were asked whether they want to go with the army, it might happen that one of them would say Yes, and the other No: but if they were asked whether they wanted to be happy, each would instantly and without hesitation say Yes—and the one would have no reason for wanting to go with the army nor the other for not wanting to go, save to be happy. May it be that one gets joy from this, one from that? All agree that they desire happiness, just as they would agree, if they were asked, that they desire joy: and indeed they think joy and happiness are the same thing. One man may get it one way, another another, yet all alike are striving to attain this one thing, namely that they may be joyful. It is something that no one can say that he has had no experience of, which is why he finds it in his memory and recognizes it when he hears the word *happiness*.

Augustine, *Confessions*, X, 21

28 *Philosophy.* The trouble of the many and various aims of mortal men bring them much care, and herein they go forward by different paths but strive to reach one end, which is happiness. And that good is that, to which if any man attain, he can desire nothing further. It is that highest of all good things, and it embraces in itself all good things: if any good is lacking, it cannot be the highest good, since then there is left outside it something which can be desired. Wherefore happiness is a state which is made perfect by the union of all good things. This end all men seek to reach, as I said, though by different paths. For there is implanted by nature in the minds of men a desire for the true good; but error leads them astray towards false goods by wrong paths.

Boethius, *Consolation of Philosophy*, III

29 It is impossible for any created good to constitute man's happiness. For happiness is the perfect good, which quiets the appetite altogether since it would not be the last end if something yet remained to be desired. Now the object of the will, that is, of man's appetite, is the universal good, just as the object of the intellect is the universal true. Hence it is evident that nothing can quiet man's will except the universal good. This is to be found not in any creature, but in God alone, because every creature has goodness by participation. Therefore God alone can satisfy the will of man.

Aquinas, *Summa Theologica*, I–II, 2, 8

30 Final and perfect happiness can consist in nothing else than the vision of the Divine Essence. To make this clear, two points must be observed. First, that man is not perfectly happy, so long as something remains for him to desire and seek; secondly, that the perfection of any power is determined by the nature of its object. Now "the object of the intellect is what a thing is, that is, the essence of a thing," according to the book on the *Soul*. Therefore the intellect attains perfection in so far as it knows the essence of a thing. If therefore an intellect know the essence of some effect in which it is not possible to know the essence of the cause, that is, to know of the cause "what it is," that intellect cannot be said to reach that cause absolutely, although it may be able to gather from

the effect the knowledge that the cause is. Consequently, when man knows an effect, and knows that it has a cause, there naturally remains in man the desire to know about that cause, "what it is." And this desire is one of wonder, and causes inquiry, as is stated in the beginning of [Aristotle's] *Metaphysics.* For instance, if a man, knowing the eclipse of the sun, consider that it must be due to some cause, and know not what that cause is, he wonders about it, and from wondering proceeds to inquire. Nor does this inquiry cease until he arrive at a knowledge of the essence of the cause.

If therefore the human intellect, knowing the essence of some created effect, knows no more of God than that He is, the perfection of that intellect does not yet reach absolutely the First Cause, but there remains in it the natural desire to seek the cause. And so it is not yet perfectly happy. Consequently, for perfect happiness the intellect needs to reach the very Essence of the First Cause. And thus it will have its perfection through union with God as with that object in which alone man's happiness consists.

Aquinas, *Summa Theologica,* I–II, 3, 8

31 A certain participation of Happiness can be had in this life, but perfect and true Happiness cannot be had in this life. . . . Since happiness is a perfect and sufficient good, it excludes every evil, and fulfils every desire. But in this life every evil cannot be excluded. For this present life is subject to many unavoidable evils: to ignorance on the part of the intellect, to disordered affection on the part of the appetite, and to many penalties on the part of the body. . . . Likewise neither can the desire for good be satiated in this life. For man naturally desires the good which he has to be abiding. Now the goods of the present life pass away, since life itself passes away, which we naturally desire to have, and would wish to hold abidingly, for man naturally shrinks from death. Therefore it is impossible to have true Happiness in this life.

Aquinas, *Summa Theologica,* I–II, 5, 3

32 This definition of Happiness given by some,— Happy is the man that has all he desires, or, whose every wish is fulfilled, is a good and adequate definition if it be understood in a certain way, but an inadequate definition if understood in another. For if we understand it absolutely of all that man desires by his natural appetite, thus it is true that he who has all that he desires, is happy, since nothing satisfies man's natural desire except the perfect good which is Happiness. But if we understand it of those things that man desires according to the apprehension of the reason, in this way it does not pertain to Happiness to have certain things that man desires; rather does it belong to unhappiness, in so far as the possession of such things hinders man from having all that he desires

naturally; just as reason also sometimes accepts as true things that are a hindrance to the knowledge of truth. And it was through taking this into consideration that Augustine added so as to include perfect Happiness,—that "he desires nothing amiss," although the first part suffices if rightly understood, that is to say, that "happy is he who has all he desires."

Aquinas, *Summa Theologica,* I–II, 5, 8

33 [The] beatitudes are most suitably enumerated. To make this evident it must be observed that happiness has been held to consist in one of three things: for some have ascribed it to a sensual life, some to an active life, and some to a contemplative life. Now these three kinds of happiness stand in different relations to future Happiness, by hoping for which we are said to be happy. Because sensual happiness, being false and contrary to reason, is an obstacle to future Happiness, while happiness of the active life is a disposition to future Happiness, and contemplative happiness, if perfect, is the very essence of future Happiness, and, if imperfect, is a beginning of it.

And so Our Lord, in the first place, indicated certain beatitudes as removing the obstacle of sensual happiness. For a life of pleasure consists of two things. First, in the affluence of external goods whether riches or honours. Man is withdrawn from these by a virtue, so that he uses them in moderation; and by a gift, in a more excellent way, so that he despises them altogether. Hence the first beatitude is: *Blessed are the poor in spirit,* which may refer either to the contempt of riches, or to the contempt of honours, which results from humility. Secondly, the sensual life consists in following the bent of one's passions, whether irascible or concupiscible. Man is withdrawn from following the irascible passions by a virtue, so that they are kept within the bounds appointed by the ruling of reason; and by a gift, in a more excellent manner, so that man, according to God's will, is altogether undisturbed by them. Hence the second beatitude is: *Blessed are the meek.* Man is withdrawn from following the concupiscible passions by a virtue so that man uses these passions in moderation; and by a gift, so that, if necessary, he casts them aside altogether; nay more, so that if need be, he makes a deliberate choice of sorrow. Hence the third beatitude is: *Blessed are they that mourn.*

Active life consists chiefly in man's relations with his neighbour, either by way of duty or by way of spontaneous benefit. To the former we are disposed by a virtue, so that we do not refuse to do our duty to our neighbour, which pertains to justice; and by a gift, so that we do the same much more heartily, by accomplishing works of justice with an ardent desire, even as a hungry and thirsty man eats and drinks with eager appetite. Hence the fourth beatitude is: *Blessed are they that*

hunger and thirst after justice. With regard to spontaneous favours we are perfected by a virtue, so that
we give where reason dictates we should give, for
example to our friends or others united to us,
which pertains to the virtue of liberality; and by a
gift, so that, through reverence for God, we consider only the needs of those on whom we bestow
our gratuitous bounty. Hence it is written: *When
thou makest a dinner or supper, call not thy friends, nor thy
brethren,* etc. . . . *but* . . . *call the poor, the maimed,*
etc.; which, properly is to have mercy. Hence the
fifth beatitude is: *Blessed are the merciful.*

Those things which concern the contemplative
life are either final Happiness itself, or some beginning of it, and so they are included in the beatitudes not as merits, but as rewards. Yet the effects
of the active life, which dispose man for the contemplative life, are included in the beatitudes as
merits. Now the effect of the active life as regards
those virtues and gifts by which man is perfected
in himself is the cleansing of man's heart, so that
it is not defiled by the passions. Hence the sixth
beatitude is: *Blessed are the clean of heart.* But as
regards the virtues and gifts by which man is perfected in relation to his neighbour, the effect of
the active life is peace . . . *The work of justice shall
be peace.* Hence the seventh beatitude is: *Blessed are
the peacemakers.*

Aquinas, *Summa Theologica,* I–II, 69, 3

34 And she [Francesca] to me: "*There is* no greater
pain than to recall a happy time in wretchedness;
and this thy teacher knows."

Dante, *Inferno,* V, 121

35 *Pandar.* Of fickle fortune's sharp adversities,
The very worst misfortune of them all,
Is this, to know and lose all joy and ease,
And have but bitter memories to recall.

Chaucer, *Troilus and Cressida,* III, 233

36 We should have wife, children, goods, and above
all health, if we can; but we must not bind ourselves to them so strongly that our happiness depends on them. We must reserve a back shop all
our own, entirely free, in which to establish our
real liberty and our principal retreat and solitude.
Here our ordinary conversation must be between
us and ourselves, and so private that no outside
association or communication can find a place;
here we must talk and laugh as if without wife,
without children, without possessions, without retinue and servants, so that, when the time comes to
lose them, it will be nothing new to us to do without them. We have a soul that can be turned upon
itself; it can keep itself company; it has the means
to attack and the means to defend, the means to
receive and the means to give: let us not fear that
in this solitude we shall stagnate in tedious idleness.

Montaigne, *Essays,* I, 39, Of Solitude

37 The goods of fortune, even such as they really are,
still need taste to enjoy them. It is the enjoying,
not the possessing, that makes us happy.

Montaigne, *Essays,* I, 42, Of the Inequality

38 Even if I should not follow the straight road because of its straightness, I would follow it because
I have found by experience that when all is said
and done it is generally the happiest and the most
useful.

Montaigne, *Essays,* II, 16, Of Glory

39 *Orlando.* O, how bitter a thing it is to look into
happiness through another man's eyes!

Shakespeare, *As You Like It,* V, ii, 47

40 *Edgar.* Yet better thus, and known to be
contemn'd,
Than still contemn'd and flatter'd. To be worst,
The lowest and most dejected thing of fortune,
Stands still in esperance, lives not in fear.
The lamentable change is from the best;
The worst returns to laughter.

Shakespeare, *Lear,* IV, i, 1

41 *Edgar.* And worse I may be yet; the worst is not
So long as we can say, "This is the worst."

Shakespeare, *Lear,* IV, i, 29

42 *Trinculo.* Misery acquaints a man with strange
bed-fellows.

Shakespeare, *Tempest,* II, ii, 42

43 It seems to me right to pause for a while in order
to contemplate God Himself, to ponder at leisure
His marvellous attributes, to consider, and admire, and adore, the beauty of this light so resplendent, at least as far as the strength of my
mind, which is in some measure dazzled by the
sight, will allow me to do so. For just as faith
teaches us that the supreme felicity of the other
life consists only in this contemplation of the Divine Majesty, so we continue to learn by experience that a similar meditation, though incomparably less perfect, causes us to enjoy the greatest
satisfaction of which we are capable in this life.

Descartes, *Meditations on First Philosophy,* III

44 The felicity of this life consisteth not in the repose
of a mind satisfied. For there is no such *finis ultimus*
(utmost aim) nor *summum bonum* (greatest good) as
is spoken of in the books of the old moral philosophers. Nor can a man any more live whose desires
are at an end than he whose senses and imaginations are at a stand. Felicity is a continual progress of the desire from one object to another, the
attaining of the former being still but the way to
the latter. The cause whereof is that the object of
man's desire is not to enjoy once only, and for one
instant of time, but to assure forever the way of his
future desire. And therefore the voluntary actions

and inclinations of all men tend not only to the procuring, but also to the assuring of a contented life, and differ only in the way, which ariseth partly from the diversity of passions in diverse men, and partly from the difference of the knowledge or opinion each one has of the causes which produce the effect desired.

Hobbes, *Leviathan*, I, 11

45 In vain we admire the Lustre of any thing seen: that which is truly glorious is invisible. *Paradise* was but a part of the Earth, lost not only to our Fruition but our Knowledge. And if, according to old Dictates, no Man can be said to be happy before Death, the happiness of this Life goes for nothing before it be over, and while we think ourselves happy we do but usurp that Name. Certainly true Beatitude groweth not on Earth, nor hath this World in it the Expectations we have of it. He Swims in Oyl, and can hardly avoid sinking, who hath such light Foundations to support him. 'Tis therefore happy that we have two Worlds to hold on. To enjoy true happiness we must travel into a very far Countrey, and even out of our selves; for the Pearl we seek for is not to be found in the *Indian*, but in the *Empyrean* Ocean.

Sir Thomas Browne, *Christian Morals*, III, 11

46 Live happy in the *Elizium* of a virtuously composed Mind, and let Intellectual Contents exceed the Delights wherein mere Pleasurists place their Paradise. Bear not too slack reins upon Pleasure, nor let complexion or contagion betray thee unto the exorbitancy of Delight. Make Pleasure thy Recreation or intermissive Relaxation, not thy *Diana*, Life and Profession. Voluptuousness is as insatiable as Covetousness. Tranquillity is better than Jollity, and to appease pain than to invent pleasure. Our hard entrance into the world, our miserable going out of it, our sicknesses, disturbances, and sad Rencounters in it, do clamorously tell us we come not into the World to run a Race of Delight, but to perform the sober Acts and serious purposes of Man; which to omit were foully to miscarry in the advantage of humanity, to play away an uniterable Life, and to have lived in vain.

Sir Thomas Browne, *Christian Morals*, III, 23

47 If our condition were truly happy, we would not need diversion from thinking of it in order to make ourselves happy.

Pascal, *Pensées*, II, 165

48 Solomon and Job have best known and best spoken of the misery of man; the former the most fortunate, and the latter the most unfortunate of men; the former knowing the vanity of pleasures from experience, the latter the reality of evils.

Pascal, *Pensées*, II, 174

49 All men seek happiness. This is without exception. Whatever different means they employ, they all tend to this end. The cause of some going to war, and of others avoiding it, is the same desire in both, attended with different views. The will never takes the least step but to this object. This is the motive of every action of every man, even of those who hang themselves.

And yet, after such a great number of years, no one without faith has reached the point to which all continually look. All complain, princes and subjects, noblemen and commoners, old and young, strong and weak, learned and ignorant, healthy and sick, of all countries, all times, all ages, and all conditions.

A trial so long, so continuous, and so uniform, should certainly convince us of our inability to reach the good by our own efforts. But example teaches us little. No resemblance is ever so perfect that there is not some slight difference; and hence we expect that our hope will not be deceived on this occasion as before. And thus, while the present never satisfies us, experience dupes us and, from misfortune to misfortune, leads us to death, their eternal crown.

What is it, then, that this desire and this inability proclaim to us, but that there was once in man a true happiness of which there now remain to him only the mark and empty trace, which he in vain tries to fill from all his surroundings, seeking from things absent the help he does not obtain in things present? But these are all inadequate, because the infinite abyss can only be filled by an infinite and immutable object, that is to say, only by God Himself.

Pascal, *Pensées*, VII, 425

50 It is . . . most profitable to us in life to make perfect the intellect or reason as far as possible, and in this one thing consists the highest happiness or blessedness of man; for blessedness is nothing but the peace of mind which springs from the intuitive knowledge of God, and to perfect the intellect is nothing but to understand God, together with the attributes and actions of God, which flow from the necessity of His nature. The final aim, therefore, of a man who is guided by reason, that is to say, the chief desire by which he strives to govern all his other desires, is that by which he is led adequately to conceive himself and all things which can be conceived by his intelligence.

Spinoza, *Ethics*, IV, Appendix IV

51 Blessedness consists in love towards God, which arises from the third kind of knowledge, and this love, therefore, must be related to the mind in so far as it acts. Blessedness, therefore, is virtue itself, which was the first thing to be proved. Again, the more the mind delights in this divine love or blessedness, the more it understands, that is to say, the greater is the power it has over its affects, and

t suffers from affects which are evil.
, it is because the mind delights in this
*v*e or blessedness that it possesses the
restraining the lusts; and because the
man to restrain the affects is in the intellect alone, no one, therefore, delights in blessedness because he has restrained his affects, but, on the contrary, the power of restraining his lusts springs from blessedness itself.

Spinoza, *Ethics*, V, Prop. 42, Demonst.

52 I have finished everything I wished to explain concerning the power of the mind over the affects and concerning its liberty. From what has been said we see what is the strength of the wise man, and how much he surpasses the ignorant who is driven forward by lust alone. For the ignorant man is not only agitated by external causes in many ways, and never enjoys true peace of soul, but lives also ignorant, as it were, both of God and of things, and as soon as he ceases to suffer ceases also to be. On the other hand, the wise man, in so far as he is considered as such, is scarcely ever moved in his mind, but, being conscious by a certain eternal necessity of himself, of God, and of things, never ceases to be, and always enjoys true peace of soul. If the way which, as I have shown, leads hither seem very difficult, it can nevertheless be found. It must indeed be difficult since it is so seldom discovered; for if salvation lay ready to hand and could be discovered without great labour, how could it be possible that it should be neglected almost by everybody? But all noble things are as difficult as they are rare.

Spinoza, *Ethics*, V, Prop. 42, Scholium

53 The love of God enables us to enjoy a foretaste of future felicity. And although this love is disinterested, it constitutes by itself our greatest good and interest, even though we may not seek these in it and though we may consider only the pleasure it gives without regard to the advantage it brings; for it gives us perfect confidence in the goodness of our Author and Master, which produces real tranquillity of mind, not as in the case of the Stoics, who forcibly school themselves to patience, but through a present content which also assures to us a future happiness. And besides the present pleasure it affords, nothing can be of more advantage for the future than this love of God, for it fulfils our expectations also and leads us in the way of supreme happiness, because in virtue of the perfect order that is established in the universe, everything is done as well as possible both for the general good and also for the greatest individual good of those who believe in it and who are satisfied with the Divine government. And this belief and satisfaction must inevitably be the characteristic of those who have learned to love the Source of all good. It is true that supreme felicity (by whatever *beatific vision,* or knowledge of God, it may be accompanied) can never be complete, because God, being infinite, cannot be entirely known. Thus our happiness will never consist (and it is right that it should not consist) in complete enjoyment, which would leave nothing more to be desired and would make our mind [*esprit*] stupid; but it must consist in a perpetual progress to new pleasures and new perfections.

Leibniz, *Principles of Nature and of Grace,* 18

54 As . . . the highest perfection of intellectual nature lies in a careful and constant pursuit of true and solid happiness; so the care of ourselves, that we mistake not imaginary for real happiness, is the necessary foundation of our liberty. The stronger ties we have to an unalterable pursuit of happiness in general, which is our greatest good, and which, as such, our desires always follow, the more are we free from any necessary determination of our will to any particular action, and from a necessary compliance with our desire, set upon any particular, and then appearing preferable good, till we have duly examined whether it has a tendency to, or be inconsistent with, our real happiness: and therefore, till we are as much informed upon this inquiry as the weight of the matter, and the nature of the case demands, we are, by the necessity of preferring and pursuing true happiness as our greatest good, obliged to suspend the satisfaction of our desires in particular cases.

Locke, *Concerning Human Understanding,*
Bk. II, XXI, 52

55 Happy the man whose wish and care
 A few paternal acres bound,
Content to breathe his native air,
   In his own ground.

Whose herds with milk, whose fields with bread,
 Whose flocks supply him with attire,
Whose trees in summer yield him shade,
   In winter fire.

Blest, who can unconcernedly find
 Hours, days, and years slide soft away,
In health of body, peace of mind,
   Quiet by day,

Sound sleep by night; study and ease,
 Together mixed; sweet recreation;
And innocence, which most does please
   With meditation.

Thus let me live, unseen, unknown;
 Thus unlamented let me die;
Steal from the world, and not a stone
   Tell where I lie.

Pope, *Ode on Solitude*

56 "Mankind," said he [Jacques], "must have somewhat corrupted their nature; for they were not born wolves, and yet they have become wolves;

God has given them neither cannon of twenty-four pounds, nor bayonets; and yet they have made cannon and bayonets to destroy one another, I might throw into the account bankrupts; and the law which seizes on the effects of bankrupts only to bilk the creditors." "All this was indispensable," replied the one-eyed doctor, "and private misfortunes constitute the general good; so that the more private misfortunes there are, the whole is better."

Voltaire, *Candide,* IV

57 "If you want nothing [said Imlac], how are you unhappy?"

"That I want nothing," said the prince, "or that I know not what I want, is the cause of my complaint; if I had any known want, I should have a certain wish; that wish would excite endeavor, and I should not then repine to see the sun move so slowly towards the western mountain, or lament when the day breaks, and sleep will no longer hide me from myself. When I see the kids and the lambs chasing one another, I fancy that I should be happy if I had something to pursue. But, possessing all that I can want, I find one day and one hour exactly like another, except that the latter is still more tedious than the former. Let your experience inform me how the day may now seem as short as in my childhood, while nature was yet fresh and every moment showed me what I never had observed before. I have already enjoyed too much; give me something to desire."

The old man was surprised at this new species of affliction and knew not what to reply, yet was unwilling to be silent. "Sir," said he, "if you had seen the miseries of the world you would know how to value your present state." "Now," said the prince, "you have given me something to desire. I shall long to see the miseries of the world, since the sight of them is necessary to happiness."

Johnson, *Rasselas,* III

58 I mentioned Hume's notion, that all who are happy are equally happy; a little miss with a new gown at a dancing school ball, a general at the head of a victorious army, and an orator, after having made an eloquent speech in a great assembly. *Johnson.* "Sir, that all who are happy, are equally happy, is not true. A peasant and a philosopher may be equally *satisfied,* but not equally *happy.* Happiness consists in the multiplicity of agreeable consciousness. A peasant has not capacity for having equal happiness with a philosopher."

Boswell, *Life of Johnson (Feb. 1766)*

59 He [Johnson] asserted that *the present* was never a happy state to any human being; but that, as every part of life, of which we are conscious, was at some point of time a period yet to come, in which felicity was expected, there was some happiness produced by hope. Being pressed upon this subject, and asked if he really was of opinion, that though, in general, happiness was very rare in human life, a man was not sometimes happy in the moment that was present, he answered, "Never, but when he is drunk."

Boswell, *Life of Johnson (Apr. 10, 1775)*

60 Happiness alone is, in the view of reason, far from being the complete good. Reason does not approve of it (however much inclination may desire it), except as united with desert. On the other hand, morality alone, and with it, mere *desert,* is likewise far from being the complete good. To make it complete, he who conducts himself in a manner not unworthy of happiness, must be able to hope for the possession of happiness. Even reason, unbiased by private ends, or interested considerations, cannot judge otherwise, if it puts itself in the place of a being whose business it is to dispense all happiness to others.

Kant, *Critique of Pure Reason,*
Transcendental Method

61 The notion of happiness is so indefinite that although every man wishes to attain it, yet he never can say definitely and consistently what it is that he really wishes and wills. The reason of this is that all the elements which belong to the notion of happiness are altogether empirical, i.e., they must be borrowed from experience, and nevertheless the idea of happiness requires an absolute whole, a maximum of welfare in my present and all future circumstances. Now it is impossible that the most clear-sighted and at the same time most powerful being (supposed finite) should frame to himself a definite conception of what he really wills in this. Does he will riches, how much anxiety, envy, and snares might he not thereby draw upon his shoulders? Does he will knowledge and discernment, perhaps it might prove to be only an eye so much the sharper to show him so much the more fearfully the evils that are now concealed from him, and that cannot be avoided, or to impose more wants on his desires, which already give him concern enough. Would he have long life? who guarantees to him that it would not be a long misery? would he at least have health? how often has uneasiness of the body restrained from excesses into which perfect health would have allowed one to fall? and so on. In short, he is unable, on any principle, to determine with certainty what would make him truly happy; because to do so he would need to be omniscient. We cannot therefore act on any definite principles to secure happiness, but only on empirical counsels, e.g. of regimen, frugality, courtesy, reserve, etc., which experience teaches do, on the average, most promote well-being. Hence it follows that the imperatives of prudence do not, strictly speaking, command at all, that is, they cannot present actions objectively

as practically *necessary;* that they are rather to be regarded as counsels than precepts of reason, that the problem to determine certainly and universally what action would promote the happiness of a rational being is completely insoluble, and consequently no imperative respecting it is possible which should, in the strict sense, command to do what makes happy; because happiness is not an ideal of reason but of imagination, resting solely on empirical grounds, and it is vain to expect that these should define an action by which one could attain the totality of a series of consequences which is really endless.

Kant, *Fundamental Principles of the Metaphysic of Morals,* II

62 Pure practical reason does not require that we should *renounce* all claim to happiness, but only that the moment duty is in question we should take *no account* of happiness. It may even in certain respects be a duty to provide for happiness; partly, because (including skill, wealth, riches) it contains means for the fulfilment of our duty; partly, because the absence of it (e.g., poverty) implies temptations to transgress our duty. But it can never be an immediate duty to promote our happiness, still less can it be the principle of all duty. Now, as all determining principles of the will, except the law of pure practical reason alone (the moral law), are all empirical and, therefore, as such, belong to the principle of happiness, they must all be kept apart from the supreme principle of morality and never be incorporated with it as a condition; since this would be to destroy all moral worth just as much as any empirical admixture with geometrical principles would destroy the certainty of mathematical evidence, which in Plato's opinion is the most excellent thing in mathematics, even surpassing their utility.

Kant, *Critique of Practical Reason,* Pt. I, I, 3

63 The conception of the *summum* itself contains an ambiguity which might occasion needless disputes if we did not attend to it. The *summum* may mean either the supreme or the perfect. The former is that condition which is itself unconditioned, i.e., is not subordinate to any other; the second is that whole which is not a part of a greater whole of the same kind. It has been shown in the Analytic that *virtue* (as worthiness to be happy) is the *supreme condition* of all that can appear to us desirable, and consequently of all our pursuit of happiness, and is therefore the *supreme* good. But it does not follow that it is the whole and perfect good as the object of the desires of rational finite beings; for this requires happiness also, and that not merely in the partial eyes of the person who makes himself an end, but even in the judgement of an impartial reason, which regards persons in general as ends in themselves. For to need happiness, to deserve it,

and yet at the same time not to participate in it, cannot be consistent with the perfect volition of a rational being possessed at the same time of all power, if, for the sake of experiment, we conceive such a being. Now inasmuch as virtue and happiness together constitute the possession of the *summum bonum* in a person, and the distribution of happiness in exact proportion to morality (which is the worth of the person, and his worthiness to be happy) constitutes the *summum bonum* of a possible world; hence this *summum bonum* expresses the whole, the perfect good, in which, however, virtue as the condition is always the supreme good, since it has no condition above it; whereas happiness, while it is pleasant to the possessor of it, is not of itself absolutely and in all respects good, but always presupposes morally right behaviour as its condition.

Kant, *Critique of Practical Reason,* Pt. I, II, 2

64 *Faust.* If ever I lay me on a bed of sloth in peace,
That instant let for me existence cease!
If ever with lying flattery you can rule me
So that contented with myself I stay,
If with enjoyment you can fool me,
Be that for me the final day!
That bet I offer!
  Mephistopheles. Done!
  Faust. Another hand-clasp! There!
If to the moment I shall ever say:
"Ah, linger on, thou art so fair!"
Then may you fetters on me lay,
Then will I perish, then and there!
Then may the death-bell toll, recalling
Then from your service you are free;
The clock may stop, the pointer falling.
And time itself be past for me!
  Meph. Consider well, we'll not forget it.

Goethe, *Faust,* I, 1692

65 *Mephistopheles.* To you no goal is set, nor measure.
If you should like to nibble everything,
To snatch up something on the wing,
May all agree with you that gives you pleasure!
Fall to, I say, and don't be coy.
  Faust. You hear indeed, I do not speak of joy.
Life's wildering whirl be mine, its painfulest enjoyment,
Enamoured hate, and quickening annoyment.
My bosom, of all thirst for knowledge cured,
Shall close itself henceforth against no woe;
Whatever to all mankind is assured,
I, in my inmost being, will enjoy and know,
Seize with my soul the highest and most deep;
Men's weal and woe upon my bosom heap;
And thus this self of mine to all their selves expanded,
Like them I too at last be stranded.

Goethe, *Faust,* I, 1760

66 *Faust.*   Spirit sublime, thou gav'st me, gav'st
      me all
   For which I prayed. Thou hast not turned in vain
   Thy countenance to me in fire and flame.
   Thou gav'st me glorious nature as a royal realm,
   The power to feel and to enjoy her. Not
   Amazed, cold visits only thou allow'st;
   Thou grantest me to look in her deep breast
   Even as in the bosom of a friend.
   Thou leadest past a series of the living
   Before me, teaching me to know my brothers
   In silent covert and in air and water.
   And when the storm roars screeching through the
      forest,
   When giant fir tree plunges, sweeping down
   And crushing neighbouring branches, neighbour-
      ing trunks,
   And at its fall the hills, dull, hollow, thunder:
   Then leadest thou me to the cavern safe,
   Show'st me myself, and my own heart becomes
   Aware of deep mysterious miracles.
   And when before my gaze the stainless moon
   Soothing ascends on high: from rocky walls
   And from damp covert float and soar about me
   The silvery forms of a departed world
   And temper contemplation's austere joy.
      Oh, that for man naught perfect ever is,
   I now do feel. Together with this rapture
   That brings me near and nearer to the gods,
   Thou gav'st the comrade whom I now no more
   Can do without, though, cold and insolent,
   He lowers me in my own sight, transforms
   With but a word, a breath, thy gifts to nothing.
   Within my breast he fans with busy zeal
   A savage fire for that fair, lovely form.
   Thus from desire I reel on to enjoyment
   And in enjoyment languish for desire.

      Goethe, *Faust*, I, 3217

67 Serene will be our days and bright,
   And happy will our nature be,
   When love is an unerring light,
   And joy its own security.

      Wordsworth, *Ode to Duty*

68   It is a flaw
   In happiness, to see beyond our bourn.—
   It forces us in summer skies to mourn,
   It spoils the singing of the Nightingale.

      Keats, *Epistle to John Hamilton Reynolds*, 82

69 I have reminded the reader that every state of
   welfare, every feeling of satisfaction, is negative in
   its character; that is to say, it consists in freedom
   from pain, which is the positive element of existence. It follows, therefore, that the happiness of
   any given life is to be measured, not by its joys
   and pleasures, but by the extent to which it has
   been free from suffering—from positive evil. If this
   is the true standpoint, the lower animals appear
   to enjoy a happier destiny than man. Let us examine the matter a little more closely.

However varied the forms that human happiness and misery may take, leading a man to seek
the one and shun the other, the material basis of it
all is bodily pleasure or bodily pain. This basis is
very restricted: it is simply health, food, protection from wet and cold, the satisfaction of the sexual instinct; or else the absence of these things.
Consequently, as far as real physical pleasure is
concerned, the man is not better off than the
brute, except in so far as the higher possibilities of
his nervous system make him more sensitive to
every kind of pleasure, but also, it must be remembered, to every kind of pain. But then compared with the brute, how much stronger are the
passions aroused in him! what an immeasurable
difference there is in the depth and vehemence of
his emotions!—and yet, in the one case, as in the
other, all to produce the same result in the end:
namely, health, food, clothing, and so on.

The chief source of all this passion is that
thought for what is absent and future, which, with
man, exercises such a powerful influence upon all
he does. It is this that is the real origin of his cares,
his hopes, his fears—emotions which affect him
much more deeply than could ever be the case
with those present joys and sufferings to which the
brute is confined. In his powers of reflection,
memory and foresight, man possesses, as it were, a
machine for condensing and storing up his pleasures and his sorrows. But the brute has nothing of
the kind; whenever it is in pain, it is as though it
were suffering for the first time, even though the
same thing should have previously happened to it
times out of number. It has no power of summing
up its feelings. Hence its careless and placid temper: how much it is to be envied! But in man
reflection comes in, with all the emotions to which
it gives rise; and taking up the same elements of
pleasure and pain which are common to him and
the brute, it develops his susceptibility to happiness and misery to such a degree that, at one moment the man is brought in an instant to a state of
delight that may even prove fatal, at another to
the depths of despair and suicide.

      Schopenhauer, *Sufferings of the World*

70 In a world where all is unstable, and nought can
   endure, but is swept onwards at once in the hurrying whirlpool of change; where a man, if he is to
   keep erect at all, must always be advancing and
   moving, like an acrobat on a rope—in such a
   world, happiness is inconceivable. How can it
   dwell where, as Plato says, *continual Becoming and
   never Being* is the sole form of existence? In the first
   place, a man never is happy, but spends his whole
   life in striving after something which he thinks
   will make him so; he seldom attains his goal, and
   when he does, it is only to be disappointed; he is
   mostly shipwrecked in the end, and comes into
   harbour with masts and rigging gone. And then, it

is all one whether he has been happy or miserable; for his life was never anything more than a present moment always vanishing; and now it is over.

Schopenhauer, *Vanity of Existence*

71 A Book of Verses underneath the Bough,
A Jug of Wine, a Loaf of Bread—and Thou
   Beside me singing in the Wilderness—
Oh, Wilderness were Paradise enow!

FitzGerald, *Rubáiyát,* XII

72 When . . . it is . . . positively asserted to be impossible that human life should be happy, the assertion, if not something like a verbal quibble, is at least an exaggeration. If by happiness be meant a continuity of highly pleasurable excitement, it is evident enough that this is impossible. A state of exalted pleasure lasts only moments, or in some cases, and with some intermissions, hours or days, and is the occasional brilliant flash of enjoyment, not its permanent and steady flame. Of this the philosophers who have taught that happiness is the end of life were as fully aware as those who taunt them. The happiness which they meant was not a life of rapture; but moments of such, in an existence made up of few and transitory pains, many and various pleasures, with a decided predominance of the active over the passive, and having as the foundation of the whole, not to expect more from life than it is capable of bestowing. A life thus composed, to those who have been fortunate enough to obtain it, has always appeared worthy of the name of happiness. And such an existence is even now the lot of many, during some considerable portion of their lives. The present wretched education, and wretched social arrangements, are the only real hindrance to its being attainable by almost all.

Mill, *Utilitarianism,* II

73 The only proof capable of being given that an object is visible, is that people actually see it. The only proof that a sound is audible, is that people hear it: and so of the other sources of our experience. In like manner, I apprehend, the sole evidence it is possible to produce that anything is desirable, is that people do actually desire it. If the end which the utilitarian doctrine proposes to itself were not, in theory and in practice, acknowledged to be an end, nothing could ever convince any person that it was so. No reason can be given why the general happiness is desirable, except that each person, so far as he believes it to be attainable, desires his own happiness. This, however, being a fact, we have not only all the proof which the case admits of, but all which it is possible to require, that happiness is a good: that each person's happiness is a good to that person, and the general happiness, therefore, a good to the ag-

gregate of all persons. Happiness has made out its title as *one* of the ends of conduct, and consequently one of the criteria of morality.

Mill, *Utilitarianism,* IV

74 *Grand Inquisitor.* But the flock will come together again and will submit once more, and then it will be once for all. Then we shall give them the quiet humble happiness of weak creatures such as they are by nature. Oh, we shall persuade them at last not to be proud, for Thou didst lift them up and thereby taught them to be proud. We shall show them that they are weak, that they are only pitiful children, but that childlike happiness is the sweetest of all. They will become timid and will look to us and huddle close to us in fear, as chicks to the hen. They will marvel at us and will be awestricken before us, and will be proud at our being so powerful and clever that we have been able to subdue such a turbulent flock of thousands of millions. They will tremble impotently before our wrath, their minds will grow fearful, they will be quick to shed tears like women and children, but they will be just as ready at a sign from us to pass to laughter and rejoicing, to happy mirth and childish song. Yes, we shall set them to work, but in their leisure hours we shall make their life like a child's game, with children's songs and innocent dance. Oh, we shall allow them even sin, they are weak and helpless, and they will love us like children because we allow them to sin. We shall tell them that every sin will be expiated, if it is done with our permission, that we allow them to sin because we love them, and the punishment for these sins we take upon ourselves. And we shall take it upon ourselves, and they will adore us as their saviours who have taken on themselves their sins before God. And they will have no secrets from us. We shall allow or forbid them to live with their wives and mistresses, to have or not to have children—according to whether they have been obedient or disobedient—and they will submit to us gladly and cheerfully. The most painful secrets of their conscience, all, all they will bring to us, and we shall have an answer for all. And they will be glad to believe our answer, for it will save them from the great anxiety and terrible agony they endure at present in making a free decision for themselves. And all will be happy, all the millions of creatures except the hundred thousand who rule over them. For only we, we who guard the mystery, shall be unhappy. There will be thousands of millions of happy babes, and a hundred thousand sufferers who have taken upon themselves the curse of the knowledge of good and evil. Peacefully they will die, peacefully they will expire in Thy name, and beyond the grave they will find nothing but death. But we shall keep the secret, and for their happiness we shall allure them with the reward of heaven and eternity. Though if

there were anything in the other world, it certainly would not be for such as they.

Dostoevsky, *Brothers Karamazov,*
Pt. II, V, 5

75 My God, a moment of bliss. Why, isn't that enough for a whole lifetime?

Dostoevsky, *White Nights*

76 While imprisoned in the shed Pierre had learned not with his intellect but with his whole being, by life itself, that man is created for happiness, that happiness is within him, in the satisfaction of simple human needs, and that all unhappiness arises not from privation but from superfluity. And now during these last three weeks of the march he had learned still another new, consolatory truth—that nothing in this world is terrible. He had learned that as there is no condition in which man can be happy and entirely free, so there is no condition in which he need be unhappy and lack freedom. He learned that suffering and freedom have their limits and that those limits are very near together; that the person in a bed of roses with one crumpled petal suffered as keenly as he now, sleeping on the bare damp earth with one side growing chilled while the other was warming; and that when he had put on tight dancing shoes he had suffered just as he did now when he walked with bare feet that were covered with sores—his footgear having long since fallen to pieces. He discovered that when he had married his wife—of his own free will as it had seemed to him—he had been no more free than now when they locked him up at night in a stable. Of all that he himself subsequently termed his sufferings, but which at the time he scarcely felt, the worst was the state of his bare, raw, and scab-covered feet. (The horseflesh was appetizing and nourishing, the saltpeter flavor of the gunpowder they used instead of salt was even pleasant; there was no great cold, it was always warm walking in the daytime, and at night there were the campfires; the lice that devoured him warmed his body.) The one thing that was at first hard to bear was his feet.

After the second day's march Pierre, having examined his feet by the campfire, thought it would be impossible to walk on them; but when everybody got up he went along, limping, and, when he had warmed up, walked without feeling the pain, though at night his feet were more terrible to look at than before. However, he did not look at them now, but thought of other things.

Only now did Pierre realize the full strength of life in man and the saving power he has of transferring his attention from one thing to another, which is like the safety valve of a boiler that allows superfluous steam to blow off when the pressure exceeds a certain limit.

He did not see and did not hear how they shot the prisoners who lagged behind, though more than a hundred perished in that way. He did not think of Karatáev who grew weaker every day and evidently would soon have to share that fate. Still less did Pierre think about himself. The harder his position became and the more terrible the future, the more independent of that position in which he found himself were the joyful and comforting thoughts, memories, and imaginings that came to him.

Tolstoy, *War and Peace,* XIV, 12

77 For the mediocre it is happiness to be mediocre.

Nietzsche, *Antichrist,* LVII

78 *Morell.* An honest man feels that he must pay Heaven for every hour of happiness with a good spell of hard unselfish work to make others happy. We have no more right to consume happiness without producing it than to consume wealth without producing it.

Shaw, *Candida,* I

79 *Octavius.* Oh, Jack, you talk of saving me from my highest happiness.

Tanner. Yes, a lifetime of happiness. If it were only the first half hour's happiness, Tavy, I would buy it for you with my last penny. But a lifetime of happiness! No man alive could bear it: it would be hell on earth.

Shaw, *Man and Superman,* I

80 Men who are unhappy, like men who sleep badly, are always proud of the fact. Perhaps their pride is like that of the fox who had lost his tail; if so, the way to cure it is to point out to them how they can grow a new tail. Very few men, I believe, will deliberately choose unhappiness if they see a way of being happy. I do not deny that such men exist, but they are not sufficiently numerous to be important.

Russell, *Conquest of Happiness,* I, 1

81 Happiness is fundamental in morals only because happiness is not something to be sought for, but is something now attained, even in the midst of pain and trouble, whenever recognition of our ties with nature and with fellow-men releases and informs our action.

Dewey, *Human Nature and Conduct,* III, 9

9.9 | *Duty*

MORAL OBLIGATION

Not all the authors who acknowledge that man is bound by duty or moral obligation to act or to refrain from acting in certain ways explicitly employ the words "duty" or "obligation" in their ethical treatises or moral discourse. Some writers who assert that there are certain things that a person ought or ought not to do if one is going to act rightly, or certain things that one ought or ought not to desire if one is going to seek real, not merely apparent goods, make these points in the context of discussing virtue and vice rather than duty or obligation.

The reader is, therefore, referred to Section 9.10 on VIRTUE AND VICE for statements about what ought or ought not to be done or sought, which imply the existence of duties or obligations even though they are not so denominated. In the ancient world, the Roman writers rather than the Greeks stress duties and enumerate or classify them; in the modern world, the same thing is true of the German moralists, such as Kant and Hegel, as contrasted with such English writers as Locke, Hume, and J. S. Mill.

Closely connected with this difference in emphasis is the importance accorded to law—civil, moral, and divine—in the consideration of right and wrong in human conduct. Those who lay great stress on law and obedience to it also tend to conceive acting rightly as doing one's duty or fulfilling one's obligation; and they also differentiate duties as legal or civil, moral, and religious according to the kind of law that one is under obligation to obey. Because of their concern with the divine law and the natural moral law as well as with eternal salvation or beatitude, Christian moralists and theologians conceive right conduct in terms of duty as well as in terms of virtue and happiness. For the relation of duty to law, the reader is referred to Section 9.3 on MORAL LAW and Section 12.1 on LAW AND LAWYERS.

---

1 Fear God, and keep his commandments: for this is the whole duty of man.

Ecclesiastes 12:13

2 What doth the Lord require of thee, but to do justly, and to love mercy, and to walk humbly with thy God?

Micah 6:8

3 *Hector.*   You [Rhesus] owe us much. You have spurned it
and to your friends in distress come with late relief.
Yet here are others, who are not our kin by blood,
who came long ago, and some of them have fallen and lie
buried in their mounds, who greatly kept faith with our city,

while others, in their armor, by their chariot teams,
have stood whatever cold winds or thirsty heat the god
sends, and still do endure it, without
sleeping, as you did, snug beneath the covers.

Euripides, *Rhesus*, 411

4 No aspect of life, public or private, in business or in the home, in personal matters or in dealing with others, is without its moral duty. To discharge such duty fulfills all that is morally right. To neglect it is inherently morally wrong.

Cicero, *De Officiis*, I, 2

5 We are not born for our own sake. Our country claims a share of our lives, and our friends claim a share.

Cicero, *De Officiis*, I, 7

6 If any set of priorities were established to decide where we owe most of our moral duty, country and parents would be listed first. It is they that have laid us under the heaviest obligations. Next in line would be our children and the rest of the family, because they look to us alone for support and do not have any other protection. Lastly we must list our kinsmen. We live with them on good terms and their lot is pretty much cast with ours.

Cicero, *De Officiis*, I, 17

7 We are obligated to respect, defend, and maintain the common bonds of union and fellowship that exist among all members of the human race.

Cicero, *De Officiis*, I, 41

8 Arriving there, he [Mercury] found the Trojan prince
New ramparts raising for the town's defense.
A purple scarf, with gold embroider'd o'er,
(Queen Dido's gift,) about his waist he wore;
A sword, with glitt'ring gems diversified,
For ornament, not use, hung idly by his side.
Then thus, with winged words, the god began,
Resuming his own shape: "Degenerate man,
Thou woman's property, what mak'st thou here,
These foreign walls and Tyrian tow'rs to rear,
Forgetful of thy own? All-pow'rful Jove,
Who sways the world below and heav'n above,
Has sent me down with this severe command:
What means thy ling'ring in the Libyan land?
If glory cannot move a mind so mean,
Nor future praise from flitting pleasure wean,
Regard the fortunes of thy rising heir:
The promis'd crown let young Ascanius wear,
To whom th' Ausonian scepter, and the state
Of Rome's imperial name is ow'd by fate."

Virgil, *Aeneid*, IV

9 Remember that you are an actor in a drama of such sort as the Author chooses—if short, then in a short one; if long, then in a long one. If it be his pleasure that you should enact a poor man, or a cripple, or a ruler, or a private citizen, see that you act it well. For this is your business—to act well the given part, but to choose it belongs to another.

Epictetus, *Encheiridion*, XVII

10 I do my duty: other things trouble me not; for they are either things without life, or things without reason, or things that have rambled and know not the way.

Marcus Aurelius, *Meditations*, VI, 22

11 It is thy duty to order thy life well in every single act; and if every act does its duty, as far as is possible, be content; and no one is able to hinder thee so that each act shall not do its duty.—But something external will stand in the way.—Noth-ing will stand in the way of thy acting justly and soberly and considerately.—But perhaps some other active power will be hindered.—Well, but by acquiescing in the hindrance and by being content to transfer thy efforts to that which is allowed, another opportunity of action is immediately put before thee in place of that which was hindered, and one which will adapt itself to this ordering of which we are speaking.

Marcus Aurelius, *Meditations*, VIII, 32

12 No man has a right to lead such a life of contemplation as to forget in his own ease the service due to his neighbour; nor has any man a right to be so immersed in active life as to neglect the contemplation of God.

Augustine, *City of God*, XIX, 19

13 Since you cannot do good to all, you are to pay special regard to those who, by the accidents of time, or place, or circumstance, are brought into closer connection with you.

Augustine, *Christian Doctrine*, I, 28

14 A precept implies the notion of duty. But it is easy for a man, especially for a believer, to understand that, of necessity, he owes certain duties to God and to his neighbour. But that in matters which regard himself and not another, man has of necessity certain duties to himself, is not so evident; for, at first glance, it seems that everyone is free in matters that concern himself. And therefore the precepts which prohibit disorders of a man with regard to himself reach the people through the instruction of men who are versed in such matters.

Aquinas, *Summa Theologica*, I–II, 100, 5

15 It is our duty to hate, in the sinner, his being a sinner, and to love in him, his being a man capable of bliss. And this is to love him truly, out of charity, for God's sake.

Aquinas, *Summa Theologica*, II–II, 25, 6

16 We cannot be bound beyond our powers and means. For this reason—that we have no power to effect and accomplish, that there is nothing really in our power but will—all man's rules of duty are necessarily founded and established in our will.

Montaigne, *Essays*, I, 7,
That Intention Is Judge

17 The knowledge of his duty should not be left to each man's judgment; it should be prescribed to him, not left to the choice of his reason. Otherwise, judging by the imbecility and infinite variety of our reasons and opinions, we would finally forge for ourselves duties that would set us to eating one another.

Montaigne, *Essays*, II, 12,
Apology for Raymond Sebond

18 Those who evade the common duties and that infinite number of thorny and many-faceted rules that bind a man of precise probity in civil life, achieve, in my opinion, a fine saving, whatever point of especial rigor they may impose on themselves. It is in a sense dying to escape the trouble of living well. They may have some other prize; but the prize of difficulty it has never seemed to me they had, nor do I think there is anything more arduous than keeping oneself straight amid the waves and rush of the world, loyally responding to and satisfying every part of one's charge.

Montaigne, *Essays*, II, 33,
The Story of Spurina

19 Human wisdom has never yet come up to the duties that she has prescribed for herself; and if she ever did come up to them, she would prescribe herself others beyond, to which she would ever aim and aspire, so hostile to consistency is our condition.

Montaigne, *Essays*, III, 9, Of Vanity

20 *Orlando.* O good old man, how well in thee appears
The constant service of the antique world,
When service sweat for duty, not for meed!
Thou art not for the fashion of these times,
Where none will sweat but for promotion,
And having that, do choke their service up
Even with the having.

Shakespeare, *As You Like It*, II, iii, 56

21 Duty is subdivided into two parts: the common duty of every man, as a man or member of a state; the other, the respective or special duty of every man, in his profession, vocation, and place.

Bacon, *Advancement of Learning*,
Bk. II, XXI, 7

22 When our passion leads us to do something, we forget our duty; for example, we like a book and read it, when we ought to be doing something else. Now, to remind ourselves of our duty, we must set ourselves a task we dislike; we then plead that we have something else to do and by this means remember our duty.

Pascal, *Pensées*, II, 104

23 The whole future is doubtless determined; but since we know not what it is, nor what is foreseen or resolved, we must do our duty, according to the reason that God has given us and according to the rules that he has prescribed for us; and thereafter we must have a quiet mind, and leave to God himself the care for the outcome. For he will never fail to do that which shall be the best, not only in general but also in particular, for those who have true confidence in him, that is, a confidence composed of true piety, a lively faith and fervent char-

ity, by virtue of which we will, as far as in us lies, neglect nothing appertaining to our duty and his service. It is true that we cannot 'render service' to him, for he has need of nothing: but it is 'serving him', in our parlance, when we strive to carry out his presumptive will, co-operating in the good as it is known to us, wherever we can contribute thereto. For we must always presume that God is prompted towards the good we know, until the event shows us that he had stronger reasons, although perhaps unknown to us, which have made him subordinate this good that we sought to some other greater good of his own designing, which he has not failed or will not fail to effect.

Leibniz, *Theodicy*, 58

24 The more laws are multiplied, the more they are despised, and all the new officials appointed to supervise them are only so many more people to break them, and either to share the plunder with their predecessors, or to plunder apart on their own. The reward of virtue soon becomes that of robbery; the vilest of men rise to the greatest credit; the greater they are the more despicable they become; their infamy appears even in their dignities, and their very honours dishonour them. If they buy the influence of the leaders or the protection of women, it is only that they may sell justice, duty, and the State in their turn: in the meantime, the people, feeling that its vices are not the first cause of its misfortunes, murmurs and complains that all its misfortunes come solely from those whom it pays to protect it from such things.

It is under these circumstances that the voice of duty no longer speaks in men's hearts, and their rulers are obliged to substitute the cry of terror, or the lure of an apparent interest, of which they subsequently trick their creatures.

Rousseau, *Political Economy*

25 I have drawn the great moral lesson, perhaps the only one of any practical value, to avoid those situations of life which bring our duties into conflict with our interests, and which show us our own advantage in the misfortunes of others; for it is certain that, in such situations, however sincere our love of virtue, we must, sooner or later, inevitably grow weak without perceiving it, and become unjust and wicked in act, without having ceased to be just and good in our hearts.

Rousseau, *Confessions*, II

26 Is not a patron . . . one who looks with unconcern on a man struggling for life in the water, and, when he has reached ground, encumbers him with help? The notice which you [the Earl of Chesterfield] have been pleased to take of my labors, had it been early, had been kind; but it has been delayed till I am indifferent, and cannot enjoy it; till I am solitary, and cannot impart it; till

I am known, and do not want it. I hope it is no very cynical asperity not to confess obligations where no benefit has been received, or to be unwilling that the public should consider me as owing that to a patron which Providence has enabled me to do for myself.

Johnson, *Letter to the Earl of Chesterfield
(Feb. 7, 1755)*

27 *Johnson.* It is our first duty to serve society, and, after we have done that, we may attend wholly to the salvation of our own souls.

Boswell, *Life of Johnson (Feb. 1766)*

28 *Johnson.* "Sir, you must consider that we have perfect and imperfect obligations. Perfect obligations, which are generally not to do something, are clear and positive; as, 'thou shalt not kill.' But charity, for instance, is not definable by limits. It is a duty to give to the poor; but no man can say how much another should give to the poor, or when a man has given too little to save his soul. In the same manner it is a duty to instruct the ignorant, and of consequence to convert infidels to Christianity; but no man in the common course of things is obliged to carry this to such a degree as to incur the danger of martyrdom, as no man is obliged to strip himself to the shirt in order to give charity."

Boswell, *Life of Johnson (May 7, 1773)*

29 The discipline of colleges and universities is in general contrived, not for the benefit of the students, but for the interest, or more properly speaking, for the ease of the masters. Its object is, in all cases, to maintain the authority of the master, and whether he neglects or performs his duty, to oblige the students in all cases to behave to him as if he performed it with the greatest diligence and ability. It seems to presume perfect wisdom and virtue in the one order, and the greatest weakness and folly in the other. Where the masters, however, really perform their duty, there are no examples, I believe, that the greater part of the students ever neglect theirs.

Adam Smith, *Wealth of Nations,* V, 1

30 A private citizen may feel his interest repugnant to his duty; but it must be from a deficiency of sense or courage that an absolute monarch can separate his happiness from his glory, or his glory from the public welfare.

Gibbon, *Decline and Fall of the
Roman Empire,* XLVIII

31 If adversity and hopeless sorrow have completely taken away the relish for life; if the unfortunate one, strong in mind, indignant at his fate rather than desponding or dejected, wishes for death, and yet preserves his life without loving it—not from inclination or fear, but from duty—then his maxim has a moral worth.

Kant, *Fundamental Principles of the
Metaphysic of Morals,* I

32 The necessity of acting from *pure* respect for the practical law is what constitutes duty, to which every other motive must give place, because it is the condition of a will being good *in itself,* and the worth of such a will is above everything.

Kant, *Fundamental Principles of the
Metaphysic of Morals,* I

33 A command to like to do a thing is in itself contradictory, because if we already know of ourselves what we are bound to do, and if further we are conscious of liking to do it, a command would be quite needless; and if we do it not willingly, but only out of respect for the law, a command that makes this respect the motive of our maxim would directly counteract the disposition commanded. That law of all laws, therefore, like all the moral precepts of the Gospel, exhibits the moral disposition in all its perfection, in which, viewed as an ideal of holiness, it is not attainable by any creature, but yet is the pattern which we should strive to approach, and in an uninterrupted but infinite progress become like to. In fact, if a rational creature could ever reach this point, that he thoroughly *likes* to do all moral laws, this would mean that there does not exist in him even the possibility of a desire that would tempt him to deviate from them; for to overcome such a desire always costs the subject some sacrifice and therefore requires self-compulsion, that is, inward constraint to something that one does not quite like to do; and no creature can ever reach this stage of moral disposition. For, being a creature, and therefore always dependent with respect to what he requires for complete satisfaction, he can never be quite free from desires and inclinations, and as these rest on physical causes, they can never of themselves coincide with the moral law, the sources of which are quite different; and therefore they make it necessary to found the mental disposition of one's maxims on moral obligation, not on ready inclination, but on respect, which *demands* obedience to the law, even though one may not like it; not on love, which apprehends no inward reluctance of the will towards the law. Nevertheless, this latter, namely, love to the law (which would then cease to be a *command,* and then morality, which would have passed subjectively into holiness, would cease to be *virtue*) must be the constant though unattainable goal of his endeavours.

Kant, *Critique of Practical Reason,* Pt. I, I, 3

34 *Duty!* Thou sublime and mighty name that dost embrace nothing charming or insinuating, but requirest submission, and yet seekest not to move the will by threatening aught that would arouse natural aversion or terror, but merely holdest forth a law which of itself finds entrance into the

mind, and yet gains reluctant reverence (though not always obedience), a law before which all inclinations are dumb, even though they secretly counter-work it; what origin is there worthy of thee, and where is to be found the root of thy noble descent which proudly rejects all kindred with the inclinations; a root to be derived from which is the indispensable condition of the only worth which men can give themselves?

Kant, *Critique of Practical Reason*, Pt. I, I, 3

35 The majesty of duty has nothing to do with enjoyment of life; it has its special law and its special tribunal, and though the two should be never so well shaken together to be given well mixed, like medicine, to the sick soul, yet they will soon separate of themselves; and if they do not, the former will not act; and although physical life might gain somewhat in force, the moral life would fade away irrecoverably.

Kant, *Critique of Practical Reason*, Pt. I, I, 3

36 Stern Daughter of the Voice of God!
O Duty! if that name thou love
Who art a light to guide, a rod
To check the erring, and reprove;
Thou, who art victory and law
When empty terrors overawe;
From vain temptations dost set free;
And calm'st the weary strife of frail humanity!

Wordsworth, *Ode to Duty*

37 In duty the individual finds his liberation; first, liberation from dependence on mere natural impulse and from the depression which as a particular subject he cannot escape in his moral reflections on what ought to be and what might be; secondly, liberation from the indeterminate subjectivity which, never reaching reality or the objective determinacy of action, remains self-enclosed and devoid of actuality. In duty the individual acquires his substantive freedom.

Hegel, *Philosophy of Right*, 149

38 I have my own stern claims and perfect circle. It denies the name of duty to many offices that are called duties.

Emerson, *Self-Reliance*

39 *Captain Vere.* But your scruples: do they move as in a dusk? Challenge them. Make them advance and declare themselves. Come now; do they import something like this: If, mindless of palliating circumstances, we are bound to regard the death of the master-at-arms as the prisoner's deed, then does that deed constitute a capital crime whereof the penalty is a mortal one? But in natural justice is nothing but the prisoner's overt act to be considered? How can we adjudge to summary and shameful death a fellow creature innocent before God, and whom we feel to be so?—Does that state

it aright? You sign sad assent. Well, I too feel that, the full force of that. It is Nature. But do these buttons that we wear attest that our allegiance is to Nature? No, to the King. Though the ocean, which is inviolate Nature primeval, though this be the element where we move and have our being as sailors, yet as the King's officers lies our duty in a sphere correspondingly natural? So little is that true, that in receiving our commissions we in the most important regards ceased to be natural free agents. When war is declared are we the commissioned fighters previously consulted? We fight at command. If our judgments approve the war, that is but coincidence. So in other particulars. So now. For suppose condemnation to follow these present proceedings. Would it be so much we ourselves that would condemn as it would be martial law operating through us? For that law and the rigor of it, we are not responsible. Our vowed responsibility is in this: That however pitilessly that law may operate in any instances, we nevertheless adhere to it and administer it.

Melville, *Billy Budd*

40 Action from principle, the perception and the performance of right, changes things and relations; it is essentially revolutionary, and does not consist wholly with anything which was. It not only divides states and churches, it divides families; ay, it divides the *individual,* separating the diabolical in him from the divine.

Thoreau, *Civil Disobedience*

41 Man prompted by his conscience, will through long habit acquire such perfect self-command, that his desires and passions will at last yield instantly and without a struggle to his social sympathies and instincts, including his feeling for the judgment of his fellows. The still hungry, or the still revengeful man will not think of stealing food, or of wreaking his vengeance. It is possible, or as we shall hereafter see, even probable, that the habit of self-command may, like other habits, be inherited. Thus at last man comes to feel, through acquired and perhaps inherited habit, that it is best for him to obey his more persistent impulses. The imperious word *ought* seems merely to imply the consciousness of the existence of a rule of conduct, however it may have originated.

Darwin, *Descent of Man*, I, 4

42 What are called duties to ourselves are not socially obligatory, unless circumstances render them at the same time duties to others. The term duty to oneself, when it means anything more than prudence, means self-respect or self-development, and for none of these is any one accountable to his fellow creatures, because for none of them is it for the good of mankind that he be held accountable to them.

Mill, *On Liberty*, IV

43 It is a part of the notion of Duty in every one of its forms, that a person may rightfully be compelled to fulfil it. Duty is a thing which may be *exacted* from a person, as one exacts a debt. Unless we think that it may be exacted from him, we do not call it his duty. Reasons of prudence, or the interest of other people, may militate against actually exacting it; but the person himself, it is clearly understood, would not be entitled to complain.

Mill, *Utilitarianism*, V

44 The feeling of "ought," of personal obligation (to take up again the train of our inquiry), has had, as we saw, its origin in the oldest and most original personal relationship that there is, the relationship between buyer and seller, creditor and ower: here it was that individual confronted individual, and that individual *matched himself against* individual. There has not yet been found a grade of civilisation so low, as not to manifest some trace of this relationship.

Nietzsche, *Genealogy of Morals*, II, 8

45 Each one of us should devise *his own* virtue, *his own* categorical imperative. A people perishes if it mistakes *its own* duty for the concept of duty in general.

Nietzsche, *Antichrist*, XI

46 When an exceptional human being handles the mediocre more gently than he does himself or his equals, this is not mere politeness of the heart—it is simply his *duty*.

Nietzsche, *Antichrist*, LVII

47 *Centurion.* [*sulkily*] I do my duty. That is enough for me.

Apollodorus. Majesty: when a stupid man is doing something he is ashamed of, he always declares that it is his duty.

Shaw, *Caesar and Cleopatra*, III

48 *Napoleon.* The English are a race apart. No Englishman is too low to have scruples: no Englishman is high enough to be free from their tyranny. But every Englishman is born with a certain miraculous power that makes him master of the world. When he wants a thing, he never tells himself that he wants it. He waits patiently until there comes into his mind, no one knows how, a burning conviction that it is his moral and religious duty to conquer those who possess the thing he wants. Then he becomes irresistible. Like the aristocrat, he does what pleases him and grabs what he covets: like the shopkeeper, he pursues his purpose with the industry and steadfastness that come from strong religious conviction and deep sense of moral responsibility. He is never at a loss for an effective moral attitude. As the great champion of freedom and national independence, he conquers and annexes half the world, and calls it Colonization. When he wants a new market for his adulterated Manchester goods, he sends a missionary to teach the natives the Gospel of Peace. The natives kill the missionary: he flies to arms in defence of Christianity; fights for it; conquers for it; and takes the market as a reward from heaven. In defence of his island shores, he puts a chaplain on board his ship; nails a flag with a cross on it to his top-gallant mast; and sails to the ends of the earth, sinking, burning, and destroying all who dispute the empire of the seas with him. He boasts that a slave is free the moment his foot touches British soil; and he sells the children of his poor at six years of age to work under the lash in his factories for sixteen hours a day. He makes two revolutions, and then declares war on our one in the name of law and order. There is nothing so bad or so good that you will not find Englishmen doing it; but you will never find an Englishman in the wrong. He does everything on principle. He fights you on patriotic principles; he robs you on business principles; he enslaves you on imperial principles; he bullies you on manly principles; he supports his king on loyal principles and cuts off his king's head on republican principles. His watchword is always Duty; and he never forgets that the nation which lets its duty get on the opposite side to its interest is lost.

Shaw, *The Man of Destiny*

49 A sense of duty is useful in work, but offensive in personal relations.

Russell, *Conquest of Happiness*, II, 10

9.10 | Virtue and Vice

The main contributions to the theory of virtue and vice come down to us from the ancient Greeks. The Roman moralists borrowed from the Greeks and translated the basic terms into Latin, including the names of the particular virtues and vices. The Christian theologians also borrowed from the Greeks, but they contributed elaborations of their own and added to the list of virtues the three—faith, hope, and charity—which are specifically theological rather than moral virtues. Modern secular writers have placed much less emphasis on virtue and vice in their discussion of moral problems and in their consideration of what is good and bad or right and wrong; and when they have used the terms, their use has seldom reflected the main points in the analysis of virtue and vice given to us by the Greeks.

The reader will find in the quotations from Plato, Aristotle, and other Greek writers an analysis that includes a conception of virtue and vice as habits or habitual dispositions, respectively good and bad; an elaborate classification of particular virtues or aspects of virtue; a division of the virtues into moral and intellectual virtues; an indication of which among all the virtues are cardinal or pivotal in the pursuit of happiness; a consideration of the way in which virtue is acquired, involving a dispute over the question whether virtue (more specifically, moral virtue) can be taught; an examination of the development of good or bad moral character in terms of virtue and vice; an assertion of the indispensability of moral virtue for the achievement of happiness; and—most difficult and subtle of all—apparently opposite views on the question whether there are many particular virtues, some of which a person may possess and some of which a person may lack, or only many different aspects of virtue, all of which a person must possess in order to be genuinely virtuous.

On all of these points in the theory of virtue and vice, other relevant discussions will be found in Section 8.2 on Habit, Section 9.6 on Good and Evil, Section 9.7 on Right and Wrong, Section 9.8 on Happiness, and Section 9.9 on Duty: Moral Obligation. The treatment of particular virtues or of particular aspects of virtue, both moral and intellectual, will be found in Section 9.11 on Courage and Cowardice, Section 9.12 on Temperance and Intemperance, Section 9.13 on Prudence, Section 9.14 on Honesty, and Section 9.15 on Wisdom and Folly. Though not explicitly mentioned in the title of Section 9.7, justice and injustice are treated there.

In addition, since moral virtue is discussed as involving reason's control over the emotions or its moderation of the passions, the reader is referred to Chapter 4 on Emotion. In that chapter the reader will find, in Sections 4.8 through 4.11, the treatment of such subjects as pity, envy, greed, avarice, jealousy, pride, and humility, which are often regarded as vices or sins.

The quotations below include the presentations by the poets, biographers, historians, and essayists of outstanding examples of human virtue and vice. They also include considerations of the advantages and disadvantages of virtue in the arena of politics, as well as what is involved in being a virtuous ruler and a virtuous citizen. For other discussions of these matters, the reader is referred to Section 10.2 on The Realm of Politics and Section 10.5 on Citizenship.

Finally, the reader's attention must be called to a highly restricted use of the word "virtue" that has come to the fore in modern literature—the use in which it is identified with chastity, sexual purity, or conformity to the sexual *mores* of the tribe. The reader will thus find passages in which that is all that is meant when men or women—and, regrettably, mainly women—are called virtuous.

---

1 *Penelope.* The hard man and his cruelties will be cursed behind his back, and mocked in death. But one whose heart and ways are kind—of him strangers will bear report to the wide world, and distant men will praise him.

Homer, Odyssey, XIX, 330

2 *Phaedra.*   Our lives are worse than the mind's quality
would warrant. There are many who know virtue.
We know the good, we apprehend it clearly.
But we can't bring it to achievement. Some
are betrayed by their own laziness, and others
value some other pleasure above virtue.

Euripides, Hippolytus, 377

3 *Chorus.* Many are the natures of men,
Various their manners of living,
Yet a straight path is always the right one;
And lessons deeply taught
Lead man to paths of righteousness;
Reverence, I say, is wisdom
And by its grace transfigures—
So that we seek virtue
With a right judgment.
From all of this springs honor
Bringing ageless glory into
Man's life. Oh, a mighty quest
Is the hunting out of virtue—
Which for womankind
Must be a love in quietness,
But, for men, infinite are the ways
To order and augment
The state.

Euripides, Iphigenia in Aulis, 558

4 *Nicias.* Every man is good in that in which he is wise, and bad in that in which he is unwise.

Plato, Laches, 194B

5 *Protagoras.* No one would instruct, no one would rebuke, or be angry with those whose calamities they suppose to be due to nature or chance; they do not try to punish or to prevent them from being what they are; they do but pity them. Who is so foolish as to chastise or instruct the ugly, or the diminutive, or the feeble? And for this reason. Because he knows that good and evil of this kind is the work of nature and of chance; whereas if a man is wanting in those good qualities which are attained by study and exercise and teaching, and has only the contrary evil qualities, other men are angry with him, and punish and reprove him —of these evil qualities one is impiety, another injustice, and they may be described generally as the very opposite of political virtue. In such cases any man will be angry with another, and reprimand him—clearly because he thinks that by study and learning, the virtue in which the other is deficient may be acquired.

Plato, Protagoras, 323B

6 Then, I [Socrates] said, these, Hippias and Prodicus, are our premises; and I would beg Protagoras to explain to us how he can be right in what he said at first. I do not mean in what he said quite at first, for his first statement, as you may remember, was that whereas there were five parts of virtue none of them was like any other of them; each of them had a separate function. To this, however, I am not referring, but to the assertion which he afterwards made that of the five virtues four were nearly akin to each other, but that the fifth, which was courage, differed greatly from the others. And of this he gave me the following proof. He said: You will find, Socrates, that some of the most impious, and unrighteous, and intemperate, and ignorant of men are among the most courageous; which proves that courage is very different from the other parts of virtue. I was surprised at his saying this at the time, and I am still more surprised now that I have discussed the matter with you. So I asked him whether by the brave he meant the confident. Yes, he replied, and the impetuous or goers. (You may remember, Protagoras, that this was your answer.)

He [Protagoras] assented.

Well then, I said, tell us against what are the courageous ready to go—against the same dangers as the cowards?

No, he answered.

Then against something different?

Yes, he said.

Then do cowards go where there is safety, and the courageous where there is danger?

Yes, Socrates, so men say.

Very true, I said. But I want to know against what do you say that the courageous are ready to go—against dangers, believing them to be dangers, or not against dangers?

No, said he; the former case has been proved by you in the previous argument to be impossible.

That, again, I replied, is quite true. And if this has been rightly proven, then no one goes to meet what he thinks to be dangers, since the want of self-control, which makes men rush into dangers, has been shown to be ignorance.

He assented.

And yet the courageous man and the coward alike go to meet that about which they are confident; so that, in this point of view, the cowardly and the courageous go to meet the same things.

And yet, Socrates, said Protagoras, that to which the coward goes is the opposite of that to which the courageous goes; the one, for example, is ready to go to battle, and the other is not ready.

And is going to battle honourable or disgraceful? I said.

Honourable, he replied.

And if honourable, then already admitted by us to be good; for all honourable actions we have admitted to be good.

That is true; and to that opinion I shall always adhere.

True, I said. But which of the two are they who, as you say, are unwilling to go to war, which is a good and honourable thing?

The cowards, he replied.

And what is good and honourable, I said, is also pleasant?

It has certainly been acknowledged to be so, he replied.

And do the cowards knowingly refuse to go to the nobler, and pleasanter, and better?

The admission of that, he replied, would belie our former admissions.

But does not the courageous man also go to meet the better, and pleasanter, and nobler?

That must be admitted.

And the courageous man has no base fear or base confidence?

True, he replied.

And if not base, then honourable?

He admitted this.

And if honourable, then good?

Yes.

But the fear and confidence of the coward or foolhardy or madman, on the contrary, are base?

He assented.

And these base fears and confidences originate in ignorance and uninstructedness?

True, he said.

Then, as to the motive from which the cowards act, do you call it cowardice or courage?

I should say cowardice, he replied.

And have they not been shown to be cowards through their ignorance of dangers?

Assuredly, he said.

And because of that ignorance they are cowards?

He assented.

And the reason why they are cowards is admitted by you to be cowardice?

He again assented.

Then the ignorance of what is and is not dangerous is cowardice?

He nodded assent.

But surely courage, I said, is opposed to cowardice?

Yes.

Then the wisdom which knows what are and are not dangers is opposed to the ignorance of them?

To that again he nodded assent.

And the ignorance of them is cowardice?

To that he very reluctantly nodded assent.

And the knowledge of that which is and is not dangerous is courage, and is opposed to the ignorance of these things?

At this point he would no longer nod assent, but was silent.

And why, I said, do you neither assent nor dissent, Protagoras?

Finish the argument by yourself, he said.

I only want to ask one more question, I said. I want to know whether you still think that there are men who are most ignorant and yet most courageous?

You seem to have a great ambition to make me answer, Socrates, and therefore I will gratify you, and say, that this appears to me to be impossible consistently with the argument.

My only object, I said, in continuing the discussion, has been the desire to ascertain the nature and relations of virtue; for if this were clear, I am very sure that the other controversy which has been carried on at great length by both of us—you affirming and I denying that virtue can be taught—would also become clear. The result of our discussion appears to me to be singular. For if the argument had a human voice, that voice would be heard laughing at us and saying: "Protagoras and Socrates, you are strange beings; there are you, Socrates, who were saying that virtue cannot be taught, contradicting yourself now by your attempt to prove that all things are knowledge, including justice, and temperance, and courage,—which tends to show that virtue can certainly be taught; for if virtue were other than knowledge, as Protagoras attempted to prove, then clearly virtue cannot be taught; but if virtue is entirely knowledge, as you are seeking to show, then I cannot but suppose that virtue is capable of being taught. Protagoras, on the other hand, who started by saying that it might be taught, is now eager to prove it to be anything rather than knowledge; and if this is true, it must be quite incapable of being taught." Now I, Protagoras, perceiving this terrible confusion of our ideas, have a great desire that they should be cleared up. And I should like to carry on the discussion until we ascertain what virtue is, and whether capable of being taught or not.

Plato, *Protagoras*, 359A

7 *Socrates.* Seeing then that men become good and useful to states, not only because they have knowledge, but because they have right opinion, and

that neither knowledge nor right opinion is given to man by nature or acquired by him—(do you imagine either of them to be given by nature?

Meno. Not I.)

Soc. Then if they are not given by nature, neither are the good by nature good?

Men. Certainly not.

Soc. And nature being excluded, then came the question whether virtue is acquired by teaching?

Men. Yes.

Soc. If virtue was wisdom [or knowledge], then, as we thought, it was taught?

Men. Yes.

Soc. And if it was taught it was wisdom?

Men. Certainly.

Soc. And if there were teachers, it might be taught; and if there were no teachers, not?

Men. True.

Soc. But surely we acknowledge that there were no teachers of virtue?

Men. Yes.

Soc. Then we acknowledged that it was not taught, and was not wisdom?

Men. Certainly.

Soc. And yet we admitted that it was a good?

Men. Yes.

Soc. And the right guide is useful and good?

Men. Certainly.

Soc. And the only right guides are knowledge and true opinion—these are the guides of man; for things which happen by chance are not under the guidance of man: but the guides of man are true opinion and knowledge.

Men. I think so too.

Soc. But if virtue is not taught, neither is virtue knowledge.

Men. Clearly not.

Soc. Then of two good and useful things, one, which is knowledge, has been set aside, and cannot be supposed to be our guide in political life.

Men. I think not.

Soc. And therefore not by any wisdom, and not because they were wise, did Themistocles and those others of whom Anytus spoke govern states. This was the reason why they were unable to make others like themselves—because their virtue was not grounded on knowledge.

Men. That is probably true, Socrates.

Soc. But if not by knowledge, the only alternative which remains is that statesmen must have guided states by right opinion, which is in politics what divination is in religion; for diviners and also prophets say many things truly, but they know not what they say.

Men. So I believe.

Soc. And may we not, Meno, truly call those men "divine" who, having no understanding, yet succeed in many a grand deed and word?

Men. Certainly.

Soc. Then we shall also be right in calling divine those whom we were just now speaking of as diviners and prophets, including the whole tribe of poets. Yes, and statesmen above all may be said to be divine and illumined, being inspired and possessed of God, in which condition they say many grand things, not knowing what they say.

Men. Yes.

Soc. And the women too, Meno, call good men divine—do they not? and the Spartans, when they praise a good man, say "that he is a divine man."

Men. And I think, Socrates, that they are right; although very likely our friend Anytus may take offence at the word.

Soc. I do not care; as for Anytus, there will be another opportunity of talking with him. To sum up our enquiry—the result seems to be, if we are at all right in our view, that virtue is neither natural nor acquired, but an instinct given by God to the virtuous. Nor is the instinct accompanied by reason, unless there may be supposed to be among statesmen some one who is capable of educating statesmen. And if there be such an one, he may be said to be among the living what Homer says that Tiresias was among the dead, "he alone has understanding; but the rest are flitting shades"; and he and his virtue in like manner will be a reality among shadows.

Men. That is excellent, Socrates.

Soc. Then, Meno, the conclusion is that virtue comes to the virtuous by the gift of God. But we shall never know the certain truth until, before asking how virtue is given, we enquire into the actual nature of virtue.

Plato, *Meno,* 98B

8 *Socrates.* Daily to discourse about virtue . . . is the greatest good of man, and . . . the unexamined life is not worth living.

Plato, *Apology,* 38A

9 *Socrates.* Virtue is one, but . . . the forms of vice are innumerable.

Plato, *Republic,* IV, 445B

10 Virtue is free, and as a man honours or dishonours her he will have more or less of her; the responsibility is with the chooser.

Plato, *Republic,* X, 617B

11 Some of the virtues are intellectual and others moral, philosophic wisdom and understanding and practical wisdom being intellectual, liberality and temperance moral. For in speaking about a man's character we do not say that he is wise or has understanding but that he is good-tempered or temperate; yet we praise the wise man also with respect to his state of mind; and of states of mind we call those which merit praise virtues.

Aristotle, *Ethics,* 1103ª4

12 The question might be asked, what we mean by saying that we must become just by doing just

acts, and temperate by doing temperate acts; for if men do just and temperate acts, they are already just and temperate, exactly as, if they do what is in accordance with the laws of grammar and of music, they are grammarians and musicians.

Or is this not true even of the arts? It is possible to do something that is in accordance with the laws of grammar, either by chance or at the suggestion of another. A man will be a grammarian, then, only when he has both done something grammatical and done it grammatically; and this means doing it in accordance with the grammatical knowledge in himself.

Again, the case of the arts and that of the virtues are not similar; for the products of the arts have their goodness in themselves, so that it is enough that they should have a certain character, but if the acts that are in accordance with the virtues have themselves a certain character it does not follow that they are done justly or temperately. The agent also must be in a certain condition when he does them; in the first place he must have knowledge, secondly he must choose the acts, and choose them for their own sakes, and thirdly his action must proceed from a firm and unchangeable character. These are not reckoned in as conditions of the possession of the arts, except the bare knowledge; but as a condition of the possession of the virtues knowledge has little or no weight, while the other conditions count not for a little but for everything, i.e. the very conditions which result from often doing just and temperate acts.

Actions, then, are called just and temperate when they are such as the just or the temperate man would do; but it is not the man who does these that is just and temperate, but the man who also does them *as* just and temperate men do them. It is well said, then, that it is by doing just acts that the just man is produced, and by doing temperate acts the temperate man; without doing these no one would have even a prospect of becoming good.

Aristotle, *Ethics,* 1105ª17

13 Virtue . . . is a state of character concerned with choice, lying in a mean, i.e. the mean relative to us, this being determined by a rational principle, and by that principle by which the man of practical wisdom would determine it. Now it is a mean between two vices, that which depends on excess and that which depends on defect; and again it is a mean because the vices respectively fall short of or exceed what is right in both passions and actions, while virtue both finds and chooses that which is intermediate. Hence in respect of its substance and the definition which states its essence virtue is a mean, with regard to what is best and right an extreme.

Aristotle, *Ethics,* 1106ᵇ36

14 There are three kinds of disposition . . . two of them vices, involving excess and deficiency respectively, and one a virtue, viz. the mean, and all are in a sense opposed to all; for the extreme states are contrary both to the intermediate state and to each other, and the intermediate to the extremes; as the equal is greater relatively to the less, less relatively to the greater, so the middle states are excessive relatively to the deficiencies, deficient relatively to the excesses, both in passions and in actions. For the brave man appears rash relatively to the coward, and cowardly relatively to the rash man; and similarly the temperate man appears self-indulgent relatively to the insensible man, insensible relatively to the self-indulgent, and the liberal man prodigal relatively to the mean man, mean relatively to the prodigal. Hence also the people at the extremes push the intermediate man each over to the other, and the brave man is called rash by the coward, cowardly by the rash man, and correspondingly in the other cases.

Aristotle, *Ethics,* 1108ᵇ11

15 With regard to the virtues in general we have stated their genus in outline, viz. that they are means and that they are states of character, and that they tend, and by their own nature, to the doing of the acts by which they are produced, and that they are in our power and voluntary, and act as the right rule prescribes. But actions and states of character are not voluntary in the same way; for we are masters of our actions from the beginning right to the end, if we know the particular facts, but though we control the beginning of our states of character the gradual progress is not obvious any more than it is in illnesses; because it was in our power, however, to act in this way or not in this way, therefore the states are voluntary.

Aristotle, *Ethics,* 1114ᵇ26

16 We said . . . that it [happiness] is not a disposition; for if it were it might belong to some one who was asleep throughout his life, living the life of a plant, or, again, to some one who was suffering the greatest misfortunes. If these implications are unacceptable, and we must rather class happiness as an activity, as we have said before, and if some activities are necessary, and desirable for the sake of something else, while others are so in themselves, evidently happiness must be placed among those desirable in themselves, not among those desirable for the sake of something else; for happiness does not lack anything, but is self-sufficient. Now those activities are desirable in themselves from which nothing is sought beyond the activity. And of this nature virtuous actions are thought to be; for to do noble and good deeds is a thing desirable for its own sake.

Pleasant amusements also are thought to be of this nature; we choose them not for the sake of other things; for we are injured rather than benefited by them, since we are led to neglect our bodies and our property. But most of the people who are deemed happy take refuge in such pastimes, which is the reason why those who are ready-witted at them are highly esteemed at the courts of tyrants; they make themselves pleasant companions in the tyrants' favourite pursuits, and that is the sort of man they want. Now these things are thought to be of the nature of happiness because people in despotic positions spend their leisure in them, but perhaps such people prove nothing; for virtue and reason, from which good activities flow, do not depend on despotic position; nor, if these people, who have never tasted pure and generous pleasure, take refuge in the bodily pleasures, should these for that reason be thought more desirable; for boys, too, think the things that are valued among themselves are the best. It is to be expected, then, that, as different things seem valuable to boys and to men, so they should to bad men and to good. Now . . . those things are both valuable and pleasant which are such to the good man; and to each man the activity in accordance with his own disposition is most desirable, and, therefore, to the good man that which is in accordance with virtue. Happiness, therefore, does not lie in amusement; it would, indeed, be strange if the end were amusement, and one were to take trouble and suffer hardship all one's life in order to amuse oneself. For, in a word, everything that we choose we choose for the sake of something else—except happiness, which is an end. Now to exert oneself and work for the sake of amusement seems silly and utterly childish. But to amuse oneself in order that one may exert oneself, as Anacharsis puts it, seems right; for amusement is a sort of relaxation, and we need relaxation because we cannot work continuously. Relaxation, then, is not an end; for it is taken for the sake of activity.

The happy life is thought to be virtuous; now a virtuous life requires exertion, and does not consist in amusement. And we say that serious things are better than laughable things and those connected with amusement, and that the activity of the better of any two things—whether it be two elements of our being or two men—is the more serious; but the activity of the better is *ipso facto* superior and more of the nature of happiness. And any chance person—even a slave—can enjoy the bodily pleasures no less than the best man; but no one assigns to a slave a share in happiness—unless he assigns to him also a share in human life. For happiness does not lie in such occupations, but, . . . in virtuous activities.

Aristotle, *Ethics*, 1176ª33

17 The forms of Virtue are justice, courage, temperance, magnificence, magnanimity, liberality, gentleness, prudence, wisdom. If virtue is a faculty of beneficence, the highest kinds of it must be those which are most useful to others, and for this reason men honour most the just and the courageous, since courage is useful to others in war, justice both in war and in peace. Next comes liberality; liberal people let their money go instead of fighting for it, whereas other people care more for money than for anything else. Justice is the virtue through which everybody enjoys his own possessions in accordance with the law; its opposite is injustice, through which men enjoy the possessions of others in defiance of the law. Courage is the virtue that disposes men to do noble deeds in situations of danger, in accordance with the law and in obedience to its commands; cowardice is the opposite. Temperance is the virtue that disposes us to obey the law where physical pleasures are concerned; incontinence is the opposite. Liberality disposes us to spend money for others' good; illiberality is the opposite. Magnanimity is the virtue that disposes us to do good to others on a large scale; [its opposite is meanness of spirit]. Magnificence is a virtue productive of greatness in matters involving the spending of money. The opposites of these two are smallness of spirit and meanness respectively. Prudence is that virtue of the understanding which enables men to come to wise decisions about the relation to happiness of the goods and evils that have been previously mentioned.

Aristotle, *Rhetoric*, 1366ª39

18 *Laelius.* If we wish to avoid anxiety we must avoid virtue itself, which necessarily involves some anxious thoughts in showing its loathing and abhorrence for the qualities which are opposite to itself—as kindness for ill nature, self-control for licentiousness, courage for cowardice. Thus you may notice that it is the just who are most pained at injustice, the brave at cowardly actions, the temperate at depravity. It is then characteristic of a rightly ordered mind to be pleased at what is good and grieved at the reverse.

Cicero, *Friendship*, XIII

19 Anyone who separates the supreme good from virtue and measures it only in terms of self-interest—if he is always consistent and never over-ruled by his better nature—could find no value in friendship, justice, or generosity. No one can be brave who considers pain the supreme evil. Nor could anyone be temperate who regards pleasure as the highest good.

Cicero, *De Officiis*, I, 2

20 It is virtue, to fly vice; and the highest wisdom to have lived free from folly.

Horace, *Epistles*, I, 1

21 Nature does not give a man virtue: the process of becoming a good man is an art.

Seneca, *Letters to Lucilius*, 90

22 All vices are at odds with nature, all abandon the proper order of things.

Seneca, Letters to Lucilius, 122

23 A man must cast virtue out from his heart if he is to admit anger, because vices and virtues do not mix well together. One can no more be angry and kind at the same time than he can be sick and well.

Seneca, On Anger, II, 12

24 Vice quickly creeps in; virtue is difficult to find; she requires ruler and guide. But vice can be acquired even without a tutor.

Seneca, Quaestiones Naturales, III, 30

25 Either make the tree good, and his fruit good; or else make the tree corrupt, and his fruit corrupt: for the tree is known by his fruit.

Matthew 12:33

26 Whatsoever things are true, whatsoever things are honest, whatsoever things are just, whatsoever things are pure, whatsoever things are lovely, whatsoever things are of good report; if there be any virtue, and if there be any praise, think on these things.

Philippians 4:8

27 Vice, the opposite of virtue, shows us more clearly what virtue is. Justice becomes more obvious when we have injustice to compare it to. Many such things are proved by their contraries.

Quintilian, Institutio Oratoria, XII, 1

28 Real excellence . . . is most recognised when most openly looked into; and in really good men, nothing which meets the eyes of external observers so truly deserves their admiration, as their daily common life does that of their nearer friends.

Plutarch, Pericles

29 The most glorious exploits do not always furnish us with the clearest discoveries of virtue or vice in men; sometimes a matter of less moment, an expression or a jest, informs us better of their characters and inclinations, than the most famous sieges, the greatest armaments, or the bloodiest battles whatsoever.

Plutarch, Alexander

30 The true love of virtue is in all men produced by the love and respect they bear to him that teaches it; and those who praise good men, yet do not love them, may respect their reputation, but do not really admire, and will never imitate their virtue.

Plutarch, Cato the Younger

31 There is . . . a method very exact and necessary for all discussion of the nature of the universe which very clearly and indisputably presents to us the fact that that which is fair and limited, and which subjects itself to knowledge, is naturally prior to the unlimited, incomprehensible, and ugly, and furthermore that the parts and varieties of the infinite and unlimited are given shape and boundaries by the former, and through it attain to their fitting order and sequence, and like objects brought beneath some seal or measure, all gain a share of likeness to it and similarity of name when they fall under its influence. For thus it is reasonable that the rational part of the soul will be the agent which puts in order the irrational part, and passion and appetite, which find their places in the two forms of inequality, will be regulated by the reasoning faculty as though by a kind of equality and sameness. And from this equalizing process there will properly result for us the so-called ethical virtues, sobriety, courage, gentleness, self-control, fortitude, and the like.

Nicomachus, Arithmetic, I, 23

32 Modest actions preserve the modest man, and immodest actions destroy him: and actions of fidelity preserve the faithful man, and the contrary actions destroy him. And on the other hand contrary actions strengthen contrary characters: shamelessness strengthens the shameless man, faithlessness the faithless man, abusive words the abusive man, anger the man of an angry temper, and unequal receiving and giving make the avaricious man more avaricious.

For this reason philosophers admonish us not to be satisfied with learning only, but also to add study, and then practice.

Epictetus, Discourses, II, 9

33 If thou findest in human life anything better than justice, truth, temperance, fortitude, and, in a word, anything better than thy own mind's self-satisfaction in the things which it enables thee to do according to right reason, and in the condition that is assigned to thee without thy own choice; if, I say, thou seest anything better than this, turn to it with all thy soul, and enjoy that which thou hast found to be the best. . . . If thou findest everything else smaller and of less value than this, give place to nothing else, for if thou dost once diverge and incline to it, thou wilt no longer without distraction be able to give the preference to that good thing which is thy proper possession and thy own; for it is not right that anything of any other kind, such as praise from the many, or power, or enjoyment of pleasure, should come into competition with that which is rationally and politically or practically good.

Marcus Aurelius, Meditations, III, 6

34 When thou wishest to delight thyself, think of the virtues of those who live with thee; for instance, the activity of one, and the modesty of another, and the liberality of a third, and some other good

quality of a fourth. For nothing delights so much as the examples of the virtues, when they are exhibited in the morals of those who live with us and present themselves in abundance, as far as is possible. Wherefore we must keep them before us.

Marcus Aurelius, *Meditations,* VI, 48

35 The perfection of moral character consists in this, in passing every day as the last, and in being neither violently excited nor torpid nor playing the hypocrite.

Marcus Aurelius, *Meditations,* VII, 69

36 For most or even all forms of evil serve the Universe—much as the poisonous snake has its use—though in most cases their function is unknown. Vice itself has many useful sides: it brings about much that is beautiful, in artistic creations for example, and it stirs us to thoughtful living, not allowing us to drowse in security.

Plotinus, *Second Ennead,* III, 18

37 Nothing is utterly condemnable save vice.

Augustine, *Confessions,* II, 3

38 No one without true piety—that is, true worship of the true God—can have true virtue.

Augustine, *City of God,* V, 19

39 In Scripture they are called God's enemies who oppose His rule, not by nature, but by vice; having no power to hurt Him, but only themselves. For they are His enemies, not through their power to hurt, but by their will to oppose Him. For God is unchangeable, and wholly proof against injury. Therefore the vice which makes those who are called His enemies resist Him, is an evil not to God, but to themselves. And to them it is an evil, solely because it corrupts the good of their nature. It is not nature, therefore, but vice, which is contrary to God. For that which is evil is contrary to the good. And who will deny that God is the supreme good? Vice, therefore, is contrary to God, as evil to good. Further, the nature it vitiates is a good, and therefore to this good also it is contrary. But while it is contrary to God only as evil to good, it is contrary to the nature it vitiates, both as evil and as hurtful. For to God no evils are hurtful; but only to natures mutable and corruptible, though, by the testimony of the vices themselves, originally good. For were they not good, vices could not hurt them. For how do they hurt them but by depriving them of integrity, beauty, welfare, virtue, and, in short, whatever natural good vice is wont to diminish or destroy? But if there be no good to take away, then no injury can be done, and consequently there can be no vice. For it is impossible that there should be a harmless vice. Whence we gather, that though vice cannot injure the unchangeable good, it can injure nothing but good; because it does not exist where it does not injure.

Augustine, *City of God,* XII, 3

40 If the Creator is truly loved, that is, if He Himself is loved and not another thing in His stead, He cannot be evilly loved; for love itself is to be ordinately loved, because we do well to love that which, when we love it, makes us live well and virtuously. So that it seems to me that it is a brief but true definition of virtue to say, it is the order of love.

Augustine, *City of God,* XV, 22

41 Though the soul may seem to rule the body admirably, and the reason the vices, if the soul and reason do not themselves obey God, as God has commanded them to serve Him, they have no proper authority over the body and the vices. For what kind of mistress of the body and the vices can that mind be which is ignorant of the true God, and which, instead of being subject to His authority, is prostituted to the corrupting influences of the most vicious demons? It is for this reason that the virtues which it seems to itself to possess, and by which it restrains the body and the vices that it may obtain and keep what it desires, are rather vices than virtues so long as there is no reference to God in the matter.

Augustine, *City of God,* XIX, 25

42 Man is judged to be good or bad chiefly according to the pleasure of the human will; for that man is good and virtuous who takes pleasure in the works of virtue, and that man evil who takes pleasure in evil works.

Aquinas, *Summa Theologica,* I–II, 34, 4

43 One can make bad use of a virtue taken as an object, for instance, by having evil thoughts about a virtue, that is, by hating it, or by being proud of it; but one cannot make bad use of virtue as principle of action, so that an act of virtue be evil.

Aquinas, *Summa Theologica,* I–II, 55, 4

44 Human virtue is a habit perfecting man in view of his doing good deeds. Now, in man there are but two principles of human actions, namely, the intellect or reason and the appetite; for these are the two principles of movement in man as stated in [Aristotle's] book on the *Soul.* Consequently every human virtue must be a perfection of one of these principles. Accordingly if it perfects man's speculative or practical intellect in order that his deed may be good, it will be an intellectual virtue, but if it perfects his appetite, it will be a moral virtue. It follows therefore that every human virtue is either intellectual or moral.

Aquinas, *Summa Theologica,* I–II, 58, 3

45 Moral virtue can be without some of the intellectual virtues, namely, wisdom, science, and art, but

not without understanding and prudence. Moral virtue cannot be without prudence, because moral virtue is a habit of choosing, that is, making us choose well. Now in order that a choice be good, two things are required. First, that the intention be directed to a due end; and this is done by moral virtue, which inclines the appetitive power to the good that is in accord with reason, which is a due end. Secondly, that man take rightly those things which have reference to the end, and he cannot do this unless his reason counsel, judge and command rightly, which is the function of prudence and the virtues joined to it.

Aquinas, *Summa Theologica*, I–II, 58, 4

46 Things may be numbered either in respect of their formal principles, or according to their subjects, and in either way we find that there are four cardinal virtues.

For the formal principle of the virtue of which we speak now is the good of reason, which good can be considered in two ways. First, as consisting in the consideration itself of reason; and thus we have one principal virtue, called Prudence.—Secondly, according as the reason puts its order into something else: either into operations, and then we have Justice; or into passions, and then there must be two virtues. For the need of putting the order of reason into the passions is due to their going against reason, and this occurs in two ways. First, by the passions inciting to something against reason, and then the passions need a curb, which we call Temperance. Secondly, by the passions withdrawing us from following the dictate of reason, for instance, through fear of danger or toil, and then man needs to be strengthened for that which reason dictates, lest he turn back; and to this end there is Fortitude.

Aquinas, *Summa Theologica*, I–II, 61, 2

47 Virtues are understood differently by various writers. For some take them as signifying certain general conditions of the human soul, to be found in all the virtues, so that, namely, prudence is merely a certain rectitude of discernment in any actions or matters whatever; justice, a certain rectitude of the soul by which man does what he ought in any matters; temperance, a disposition of the soul moderating any passions or operations, so as to keep them within bounds; and fortitude, a disposition by which the soul is strengthened for that which is in accord with reason, against any assaults of the passions, or the toil involved by any operations. To distinguish these four virtues in this way does not imply that justice, temperance and fortitude are distinct virtuous habits. For it pertains to every moral virtue, from the fact that it is a habit, that it should be accompanied by a certain firmness so as not to be moved by its contrary, and this, we have said, belongs to fortitude. Moreover, since it is a virtue, it is directed to good

which involves the notion of right and due, and this, we have said, belongs to justice. Again, owing to the fact that it is a moral virtue partaking of reason, it observes the mode of reason in all things, and does not exceed its bounds, which has been stated to belong to temperance. It is only in the point of having discernment which we ascribed to prudence, that there seems to be a distinction from the other three, since discernment belongs essentially to reason; but the other three imply a certain participation of reason by way of a kind of application (of reason) to passions or operations. According to the above explanation, then, prudence would be distinct from the other three virtues but these would not be distinct from one another; for it is evident that one and the same virtue is both habit, and virtue, and moral virtue.

Others, however, with better reason, take these four virtues, according as they have their special determinate matter, each its own matter, in which special praise is given to that general condition from which the virtue's name is taken. . . . In this way it is clear that the aforesaid virtues are distinct habits, differentiated in respect of their diverse objects.

Aquinas, *Summa Theologica*, I–II, 61, 4

48 Speaking absolutely, the intellectual virtues, which perfect the reason, are more excellent than the moral virtues, which perfect the appetite.

But if we consider virtue in its relation to act, then moral virtue, which perfects the appetite, whose function it is to move the other powers to act . . . is more excellent. And since virtue is called so from its being a principle of action, for it is the perfection of a power, it follows again that the nature of virtue agrees more with moral than with intellectual virtue.

Aquinas, *Summa Theologica*, I–II, 66, 3

49 Men who are well disposed are led willingly to virtue by being admonished better than by coercion; but men who are evilly disposed are not led to virtue unless they are compelled.

Aquinas, *Summa Theologica*, I–II, 95, 1

50 Virtue is praised because of the will, not because of the ability: and therefore if a man fall short of equality which is the mean of justice, through lack of ability, his virtue deserves no less praise, provided there be no failing on the part of his will.

Aquinas, *Summa Theologica*, II–II, 81, 6

51 *Cressida.* In everything there should be moderation,
For though one might forbid all drunkenness,
One could not say that men through all creation
Should never drink—'twere folly, nothing less.

Chaucer, *Troilus and Cressida*, II, 103

52 That servant and that nurse unto the vices
Which men do call in English Idleness,
Portress at Pleasure's gate, by all advices
We should avoid, and by her foe express,
That is to say, by lawful busyness,
We ought to live with resolute intent,
Lest by the Fiend through sloth we should be rent.

For he, that with his thousand cords and sly
Continually awaits us all to trap,
When he a man in idleness may spy
He easily the hidden snare will snap,
And till the man has met the foul mishap,
He's not aware the Fiend has him in hand;
We ought to work and idleness withstand.

And though men never dreaded they must die,
Yet men see well, by reason, idleness
Is nothing more than rotten sluggardry,
Whereof comes never good one may possess;
And see sloth hold her in a leash, no less,
Only to sleep and eat and always drink
And to absorb all gain of others' swink.

Chaucer, *Canterbury Tales:*
Second Nun's Prologue

53 A man who wishes to act entirely up to his professions of virtue soon meets with what destroys him among so much that is evil.

Hence it is necessary for a prince wishing to hold his own to know how to do wrong, and to make use of it or not according to necessity. . . . He need not make himself uneasy at incurring a reproach for those vices without which the state can only be saved with difficulty, for if everything is considered carefully, it will be found that something which looks like virtue, if followed, would be his ruin; whilst something else, which looks like vice, yet followed brings him security and prosperity.

Machiavelli, *Prince,* XV

54 As if our touch were infectious, we by our handling corrupt things that of themselves are beautiful and good. We can grasp virtue in such a way that it will become vicious, if we embrace it with too sharp and violent a desire. Those who say that there is never any excess in virtue, inasmuch as it is no longer virtue if there is excess in it, are playing with words.

Montaigne, *Essays,* I, 30, Of Moderation

55 It seems to me that virtue is something other and nobler than the inclinations toward goodness that are born in us. Souls naturally regulated and well-born follow the same path, and show the same countenance in their actions, as virtuous ones. But virtue means something greater and more active than letting oneself, by a happy disposition, be led gently and peacefully in the footsteps of reason. He who through a natural mildness and easygoingness should despise injuries received would do a very fine and praiseworthy thing; but he who, outraged and stung to the quick by an injury, should arm himself with the arms of reason against this furious appetite for vengeance, and after a great conflict should finally master it, would without doubt do much more. The former would do well, and the other virtuously; one action might be called goodness, the other virtue. For it seems that the name of virtue presupposes difficulty and contrast, and that it cannot be exercised without opposition. Perhaps this is why we call God good, strong, liberal, and just, but we do not call him virtuous: his operations are wholly natural and effortless.

Montaigne, *Essays,* II, 11, Of Cruelty

56 Virtue refuses facility for her companion; and . . . the easy, gentle, and sloping path that guides the footsteps of a good natural disposition is not the path of true virtue. It demands a rough and thorny road; it wants to have either external difficulties to struggle with . . . by means of which fortune takes pleasure in breaking up the unwaveringness of a man's career; or internal difficulties created by the disordered appetites and imperfections of our nature.

Montaigne, *Essays,* II, 11, Of Cruelty

57 When I confess myself religiously to myself, I find that the best goodness I have has some tincture of vice.

Montaigne, *Essays,* II, 20,
We Taste Nothing Pure

58 The acknowledgment of virtue carries no less weight in the mouth of the man who hates it, inasmuch as truth wrests it from him by force, and if he will not receive it within, at least he covers himself with it as an ornament.

Montaigne, *Essays,* III, 1,
Of the Useful and the Honorable

59 There is no vice truly a vice which is not offensive, and which a sound judgment does not condemn; for its ugliness and painfulness is so apparent that perhaps the people are right who say it is chiefly produced by stupidity and ignorance. So hard it is to imagine anyone knowing it without hating it.

Montaigne, *Essays,* III, 2, Of Repentance

60 *Portia.* How far that little candle throws his beams!
So shines a good deed in a naughty world.

Shakespeare, *Merchant of Venice,* V, i, 90

61 *Clown.* Any thing that's mended is but patched: virtue that transgresses is but patched with sin; and sin that amends is but patched with virtue.

Shakespeare, *Twelfth Night,* I, v, 52

62 *Sir Toby.* Dost thou think, because thou art virtu-

ous, there shall be no more cakes and ale?
Shakespeare, *Twelfth Night,* II, iii, 123

63 *Laertes.* Fear it, Ophelia, fear it, my dear sister,
And keep you in the rear of your affection,
Out of the shot and danger of desire.
The chariest maid is prodigal enough,
If she unmask her beauty to the moon:
Virtue itself 'scapes not calumnious strokes:
The canker galls the infants of the spring,
Too oft before their buttons be disclosed,
And in the morn and liquid dew of youth
Contagious blastments are most imminent.
Be wary then; best safety lies in fear:
Youth to itself rebels, though none else near.
　Ophelia. I shall the effect of this good lesson
　　keep,
As watchman to my heart. But, good my brother,
Do not, as some ungracious pastors do,
Show me the steep and thorny way to heaven;
Whiles, like a puff'd and reckless libertine,
Himself the primrose path of dalliance treads,
And recks not his own rede.
Shakespeare, *Hamlet,* I, iii, 33

64 *1st Lord.* Our virtues would be proud, if our faults
whipped them not; and our crimes would despair,
if they were not cherished by our virtues.
Shakespeare, *All's Well That
Ends Well,* IV, iii, 82

65 *Duke.* Heaven doth with us as we with torches do,
Not light them for themselves; for if our virtues
Did not go forth of us, 'twere all alike
As if we had them not. Spirits are not finely
　touch'd
But to fine issues, nor Nature never lends
The smallest scruple of her excellence
But, like a thrifty goddess, she determines
Herself the glory of a creditor,
Both thanks and use.
Shakespeare, *Measure for Measure,* I, i, 33

66 *Iago.* Virtue! a fig! 'tis in ourselves that we are
thus or thus. Our bodies are our gardens, to the
which our wills are gardeners; so that if we will
plant nettles, or sow lettuce, set hyssop and weed
up thyme, supply it with one gender of herbs, or
distract it with many, either to have it sterile with
idleness or manured with industry, why, the power and corrigible authority of this lies in our wills.
If the balance of our lives had not one scale of
reason to poise another of sensuality, the blood
and baseness of our natures would conduct us to
most preposterous conclusions; but we have reason to cool our raging motions, our carnal stings,
our unbitted lusts; whereof I take this that you
call love to be a sect or scion.
Shakespeare, *Othello,* I, iii, 322

67 *Edgar.* The gods are just, and of our pleasant vices

Make instruments to plague us.
Shakespeare, *Lear,* V, iii, 170

68 *Griffith.*　　　　　　Noble madam,
Men's evil manners live in brass; their virtues
We write in water.
Shakespeare, *Henry VIII,* IV, ii, 45

69 'Tis better to be vile than vile esteem'd,
When not to be receives reproach of being,
And the just pleasure lost, which is so deem'd
Not by our feeling but by others' seeing.
Shakespeare, *Sonnet CXXI*

70 I am a Knight, and a Knight will I die, if so it
please Omnipotence. Some chuse the high Road
of haughty Ambition; others the low Ways of base
servile Flattery; a Third sort take the crooked
Path of deceitful Hypocrisy; and a few, very few,
that of true Religion. I for my own Part, guided
by my Stars, follow the narrow Track of Knight-
Errantry; and for the Exercise of it, I despise
Riches, but not Honour. I have redress'd Grievances, and righted the Injur'd, chastis'd the Insolent, vanquish'd Giants, and trod Elves and Hob-
goblins under my Feet! I am in Love, but no more
than the Profession of Knight-Errantry obliges me
to be; yet I am none of this Age's vicious Lovers,
but a chaste Platonick. My Intentions are all directed to vertuous Ends, and to do no Man
Wrong, but Good to all the World. And now let
your Graces judge, most excellent Duke and
Dutchess, whether a Person who makes it his only
Study to practise all this, deserves to be upbraided
for a Fool.
Cervantes, *Don Quixote,* II, 32

71 Men abandoned to vice do not so much corrupt
manners, as those that are half good and half evil.
Bacon, *Advancement of Learning,* Bk. I, VI, 9

72 The arts which flourish in times while virtue is in
growth, are military; and while virtue is in state,
are liberal; and while virtue is in declination, are
voluptuary.
Bacon, *Advancement of Learning,* Bk. II, X, 13

73 Virtue is like precious odours, most fragrant when
they are incensed or crushed; for prosperity doth
best discover vice, but adversity doth best discover
virtue.
Bacon, *Of Adversity*

74 Virtue is like a rich stone, best plain set; and surely virtue is best in a body that is comely, though
not of delicate features; and that hath rather dignity of presence, than beauty of aspect.
Bacon, *Of Beauty*

75 We do not believe ourselves to be exactly sharing
in the vices of the vulgar when we see that we are

sharing in those of great men; and yet we do not observe that in these matters they are ordinary men.

Pascal, *Pensées*, II, 103

76 The strength of a man's virtue must not be measured by his efforts, but by his ordinary life.

Pascal, *Pensées*, VI, 352

77 When we would pursue virtues to their extremes on either side, vices present themselves, which insinuate themselves insensibly there, in their insensible journey towards the infinitely little; and vices present themselves in a crowd towards the infinitely great, so that we lose ourselves in them and no longer see virtues. We find fault with perfection itself.

Pascal, *Pensées*, VI, 357

78 We do not sustain ourselves in virtue by our own strength, but by the balancing of two opposed vices, just as we remain upright amidst two contrary gales. Remove one of the vices, and we fall into the other.

Pascal, *Pensées*, VI, 359

79 *Attendant Spirit.* Before the starry threshold of *Joves* Court
My mansion is, where those immortal shapes
Of bright aëreal Spirits live insphear'd
In Regions milde of calm and serene Ayr,
Above the smoak and stirr of this dim spot,
Which men call Earth, and with low-thoughted care
Confin'd, and pester'd in this pin-fold here,
Strive to keep up a frail, and Feaverish being
Unmindfull of the crown that Vertue gives
After this mortal change, to her true Servants
Amongst the enthron'd gods on Sainted seats.
Yet som there be that by due steps aspire
To lay their just hands on that Golden Key
That ope's the Palace of Eternity:
To such my errand is, and but for such,
I would not soil these pure Ambrosial weeds,
With the rank vapours of this Sin-worn mould.

Milton, *Comus*, 1

80 *Elder Brother.* Som say no evil thing that walks by night
In fog, or fire, by lake, or moorish fen,
Blew meager Hag, or stubborn unlaid ghost,
That breaks his magick chains at *curfeu* time,
No goblin, or swart faëry of the mine,
Hath hurtfull power o're true virginity.
Do ye beleeve me yet, or shall I call
Antiquity from the old Schools of Greece
To testifie the arms of Chastity?
Hence had the huntress *Dian* her dred bow
Fair silver-shafted Queen for ever chaste,
Wherwith she tam'd the brinded lioness
And spotted mountain pard, but set at nought

The frivolous bolt of *Cupid,* gods and men
Fear'd her stern frown, and she was queen oth' Woods.
What was that snaky-headed *Gorgon* sheild
That wise *Minerva* wore, unconquer'd Virgin,
Wherwith she freez'd her foes to congeal'd stone?
But rigid looks of Chast austerity,
And noble grace that dash't brute violence
With sudden adoration, and blank aw.
So dear to Heav'n is Saintly chastity,
That when a soul is found sincerely so,
A thousand liveried Angels lacky her,
Driving far off each thing of sin and guilt,
And in cleer dream, and solemn vision
Tell her of things that no gross ear can hear,
Till oft convers with heav'nly habitants
Begin to cast a beam on th'outward shape,
The unpolluted temple of the mind,
And turns it by degrees to the souls essence,
Till all be made immortal.

Milton, *Comus*, 432

81 *Elder Brother.*   This I hold firm,
Vertue may be assail'd, but never hurt,
Surpriz'd by unjust force, but not enthrall'd,
Yea even that which mischief meant most harm,
Shall in the happy trial prove most glory.
But evil on it self shall back recoyl,
And mix no more with goodness, when at last
Gather'd like scum, and setl'd to it self
It shall be in eternal restless change
Self-fed, and self-consum'd, if this fail,
The pillar'd firmament is rott'nness,
And earths base built on stubble.

Milton, *Comus*, 588

82 I cannot praise a fugitive and cloistered virtue, unexercised and unbreathed, that never sallies out and sees her adversary, but slinks out of the race, where that immortal garland is to be run for, not without dust and heat. Assuredly we bring not innocence into the world, we bring impurity much rather; that which purifies us is trial, and trial is by what is contrary. That virtue therefore which is but a youngling in the contemplation of evil, and knows not the utmost that vice promises to her followers, and rejects it, is but a blank virtue, not a pure; her whiteness is but an excremental whiteness.

Milton, *Areopagitica*

83 *Philinte.* If everyone were clothed with integrity, if every heart were just, frank, kindly, the other virtues would be well-nigh useless, since their chief purpose is to make us bear with patience the injustice of our fellows.

Molière, *Le Misanthrope*, IV, i

84 By virtue and power, I understand the same thing; that is to say, virtue, in so far as it is related to man, is the essence itself or nature of the man

in so far as it has the power of affecting certain things which can be understood through the laws of its nature alone.

Spinoza, *Ethics,* IV, Definition 8

85 The more each person strives and is able to seek his own profit, that is to say, to preserve his being, the more virtue does he possess; on the other hand, in so far as each person neglects his own profit, that is to say, neglects to preserve his own being, is he impotent.

Spinoza, *Ethics,* IV, Prop. 20

86 There is no single thing in nature which is more profitable to man than a man who lives according to the guidance of reason. For that is most profitable to man which most agrees with his own nature, that is to say, man. . . . But a man acts absolutely from the laws of his own nature when he lives according to the guidance of reason, and so far only does he always necessarily agree with the nature of another man; therefore there is no single thing more profitable to man than man.
. . .

When each man seeks most that which is profitable to himself, then are men most profitable to one another; for the more each man seeks his own profit and endeavours to preserve himself, the more virtue does he possess, or, in other words, the more power does he possess to act according to the laws of his own nature, that is to say, to live according to the guidance of reason. But men most agree in nature when they live according to the guidance of reason, therefore . . . men will be most profitable to one another when each man seeks most what is profitable to himself.

Spinoza, *Ethics,* IV, Prop. 35, Corols. 1–2

87 Though that passes for vice in one country which is counted a virtue, or at least not vice, in another, yet everywhere virtue and praise, vice and blame, go together. Virtue is everywhere, that which is thought praiseworthy; and nothing else but that which has the allowance of public esteem is called virtue.

Locke, *Concerning Human Understanding,*
Bk. II, XXVIII, 11

88 Virtue is harder to be got than a knowledge of the world.

Locke, *Some Thoughts Concerning Education,* 70

89 [Lemuel Gulliver lists the negative blessings of living among the Houyhnhnms] I did not feel the treachery or inconstancy of a friend, nor the injuries of a secret or open enemy. I had no occasion of bribing, flattering or pimping, to procure the favour of any great man, or of his minion. I wanted no fence against fraud or oppression: here was neither physician to destroy my body, nor lawyer to ruin my fortune: no informer to watch my words and actions, or forge accusations against me for hire: here were no gibers, censurers, backbiters, pickpockets, highwaymen, house-breakers, attorneys, bawds, buffoons, gamesters, politicians, wits, spleneticks, tedious talkers, controvertists, ravishers, murderers, robbers, virtuosoes; no leaders or followers of party and faction; no encouragers to vice, by seducement or examples: no dungeon, axes, gibbets, whipping-posts, or pillories: no cheating shop-keepers or mechanicks: no pride, vanity or affectation: no fops, bullies, drunkards, strolling whores, or poxes: no ranting, lewd expensive wives: no stupid, proud pedants: no importunate, over-bearing, quarrelsome, noisy, roaring, empty, conceited, swearing companions: no scoundrels raised from the dust upon the merit of their vices; or nobility thrown into it, on account of their virtues: no lords, fiddlers, judges, or dancing-màsters.

Swift, *Gulliver's Travels,* IV, 10

90 As fruits ungrateful to the planter's care
On savage stocks inserted learn to bear;
The surest Virtues thus from Passions shoot,
Wild Nature's vigor working at the root.
What crops of wit and honesty appear
From spleen, from obstinacy, hate, or fear!
See anger, zeal and fortitude supply;
Ev'n av'rice, prudence; sloth, philosophy;
Lust, thro' some certain strainers well refin'd,
Is gentle love, and charms all womankind:
Envy, to which th'ignoble mind's a slave,
Is emulation in the learn'd or brave:
Nor Virtue, male or female, can we name,
But what will grow on Pride, or grow on Shame.

Pope, *Essay on Man,* Epistle II, 181

91 Vice is a monster of so frightful mien,
As, to be hated, needs but to be seen;
Yet seen too oft, familiar with her face,
We first endure, then pity, then embrace.

Pope, *Essay on Man,* Epistle II, 217

92 Virtuous and vicious ev'ry Man must be,
Few in th'extreme, but all in the degree.

Pope, *Essay on Man,* Epistle II, 231

93 This gentleman [Mr. Square the philosopher] and Mr. Thwackum scarce ever met without a disputation; for their tenets were indeed diametrically opposite to each other. Square held human nature to be the perfection of all virtue, and that vice was a deviation from our nature, in the same manner as deformity of body is. Thwackum, on the contrary, maintained that the human mind, since the fall, was nothing but a sink of iniquity, till purified and redeemed by grace. In one point only they agreed, which was, in all their discourses on morality never to mention the word goodness. The favourite phrase of the former, was the natural beauty of virtue; that of the latter, was the

divine power of grace. The former measured all actions by the unalterable rule of right, and the eternal fitness of things; the latter decided all matters by authority; but in doing this, he always used the scriptures and their commentators, as the lawyer doth his Coke upon Lyttleton, where the comment is of equal authority with the text.

Fielding, *Tom Jones*, III, 3

94 The foibles and vices of men, in whom there is great mixture of good, become more glaring objects from the virtues which contrast them and shew their deformity; and when we find such vices attended with their evil consequence to our favourite characters, we are not only taught to shun them for our own sake, but to hate them for the mischiefs they have already brought on those we love.

Fielding, *Tom Jones*, X, 1

95 There are a set of religious, or rather moral writers, who teach that virtue is the certain road to happiness, and vice to misery, in this world. A very wholesome and comfortable doctrine, and to which we have but one objection, namely, that it is not true.

Fielding, *Tom Jones*, XV, 1

96 The human mind feels such an exquisite pleasure in the exercise of power; even those who are lovers of virtue are so excessively fond of themselves that there is no man so happy as not still to have reason to mistrust his honest intentions; and, indeed, our actions depend on so many things that it is infinitely easier to do good, than to do it well.

Montesquieu, *Spirit of Laws*, XXVIII, 41

97 In the present order of things, virtue is attended with more peace of mind than vice, and meets with a more favourable reception from the world.

Hume, *Concerning Human Understanding*, XI, 108

98 Whatever may be the consequence of such a miraculous transformation of mankind as would endow them with every species of virtue, and free them from every species of vice, this concerns not the magistrate, who aims only at possibilities. He cannot cure every vice by substituting a virtue in its place. Very often he can only cure one vice by another; and in that case, he ought to prefer what is least pernicious to society.

Hume, *Of Refinement in the Arts*

99 What is virtue? Beneficence towards the fellow-creature. Can I call virtue things other than those which do me good? I am needy, you are generous. I am in danger, you help me. I am deceived, you tell me the truth. I am neglected, you console me. I am ignorant, you teach me. Without difficulty I shall call you virtuous. But what will become of

the cardinal and divine virtues? Some of them will remain in the schools.

Voltaire, *Philosophical Dictionary:* Virtue

100 The most depraved of men always pay some sort of homage to public faith; and even robbers, who are the enemies of virtue in the great society, pay some respect to the shadow of it in their secret caves.

Rousseau, *Political Economy*

101 The noblest virtues are negative, they are also the most difficult, for they make little show, and do not even make room for that pleasure so dear to the heart of man, the thought that some one is pleased with us. If there be a man who does no harm to his neighbours, what good must he have accomplished! What a bold heart, what a strong character it needs! It is not in talking about this maxim, but in trying to practise it, that we discover both its greatness and its difficulty.

Rousseau, *Emile*, II

102 Virtue presented singly to the imagination or the reason is so well recommended by its own graces and so strongly supported by arguments, that a good man wonders how any can be bad.

Johnson, *Rambler No. 175*

103 Neither our virtues nor vices are all our own. If there were no cowardice there would be little insolence. Pride cannot rise to any great degree but by the concurrence of blandishment or the sufferance of tameness.

Johnson, *Rambler No. 180*

104 Those who labor in the earth are the chosen people of God, if ever He had a chosen people, whose breasts He has made His peculiar deposit for substantial and genuine virtue. It is the focus in which he keeps alive that sacred fire, which otherwise might escape from the face of the earth. Corruption of morals in the mass of cultivators is a phenomenon of which no age nor nation has furnished an example. It is the mark set on those, who, not looking up to heaven, to their own soil and industry, as does the husbandman, for their subsistence, depend for it on casualties and caprice of customers. Dependence begets subservience and venality, suffocates the germ of virtue, and prepares fit tools for the designs of ambition. This, the natural progress and consequence of the arts, has sometimes perhaps been retarded by accidental circumstances; but, generally speaking, the proportion which the aggregate of the other classes of citizens bears in any State to that of its husbandmen, is the proportion of its unsound to its healthy parts, and is a good enough barometer whereby to measure its degree of corruption.

Jefferson, *Notes on Virginia*, XIX

105 It is always easy, as well as agreeable, for the inferior ranks of mankind to claim a merit from the contempt of that pomp and pleasure which fortune has placed beyond their reach. The virtue of the primitive Christians, like that of the first Romans, was very frequently guarded by poverty and ignorance.

Gibbon, *Decline and Fall of the Roman Empire*, XV

106 We may learn from the example of Cato that a character of pure and inflexible virtue is the most apt to be misled by prejudice, to be heated by enthusiasm, and to confound private enmities with public justice.

Gibbon, *Decline and Fall of the Roman Empire*, XXXIX

107 There are very few of those virtues which are not capable of being imitated, and even outdone in many of their most striking effects, by the worst of vices.

Burke, *Speech on Economical Reform (Feb. 11, 1780)*

108 When the thinking man has conquered the temptations to vice, and is conscious of having done his (often hard) duty, he finds himself in a state of peace and satisfaction which may well be called *happiness*, in which virtue is her own reward.

Kant, *Preface to the Metaphysical Elements of Ethics*

109 Virtue signifies a moral strength of will. But this does not exhaust the notion; for such strength might also belong to a *holy* (super-human) being, in whom no opposing impulse counteracts the law of his rational will; who therefore willingly does everything in accordance with the law. Virtue then is the moral strength of a *man's* will in his obedience to *duty;* and this is a moral *necessitation* by his own law giving reason, inasmuch as this constitutes itself a power *executing* the law. It is not itself a duty, nor is it a duty to possess it (otherwise we should be in duty bound to have a duty), but it commands, and accompanies its command with a moral constraint (one possible by laws of internal freedom). But since this should be irresistible, strength is requisite, and the degree of this strength can be estimated only by the magnitude of the hindrances which man creates for himself, by his inclinations. Vices, the brood of unlawful dispositions, are the monsters that he has to combat; wherefore this moral strength as *fortitude* constitutes the greatest and only true martial glory of man; it is also called the true *wisdom,* namely, the practical, because it makes the *ultimate end* of the existence of man on earth its own end. Its possession alone makes man free, healthy, rich, a king, etc., nor can either chance or fate deprive him of

this, since he possesses himself, and the virtuous cannot lose his virtue.

Kant, *Introduction to the Metaphysical Elements of Ethics,* XIV

110　That best portion of a good man's life,
His little, nameless, unremembered, acts
Of kindness and of love.

Wordsworth, *Tintern Abbey*, 33

111 The principle of self-interest rightly understood is not a lofty one, but it is clear and sure. It does not aim at mighty objects, but it attains without excessive exertion all those at which it aims. As it lies within the reach of all capacities, everyone can without difficulty learn and retain it. By its admirable conformity to human weaknesses it easily obtains great dominion; nor is that dominion precarious, since the principle checks one personal interest by another, and uses, to direct the passions, the very same instrument that excites them.

The principle of self-interest rightly understood produces no great acts of self-sacrifice, but it suggests daily small acts of self-denial. By itself it cannot suffice to make a man virtuous; but it disciplines a number of persons in habits of regularity, temperance, moderation, foresight, self-command; and if it does not lead men straight to virtue by the will, it gradually draws them in that direction by their habits. If the principle of interest rightly understood were to sway the whole moral world, extraordinary virtues would doubtless be more rare; but I think that gross depravity would then also be less common. The principle of interest rightly understood perhaps prevents men from rising far above the level of mankind, but a great number of other men, who were falling far below it, are caught and restrained by it. Observe some few individuals, they are lowered by it; survey mankind, they are raised.

Tocqueville, *Democracy in America,* Vol. II, II, 8

112 Virtues are, in the popular estimate, rather the exception than the rule. There is the man *and* his virtues. Men do what is called a good action, as some piece of courage or charity, much as they would pay a fine in expiation of daily non-appearance on parade. Their works are done as an apology or extenuation of their living in the world—as invalids and the insane pay a high board. Their virtues are penances.

Emerson, *Self-Reliance*

113 My strength is as the strength of ten,
Because my heart is pure.

Tennyson, *Sir Galahad*

114 You who govern public affairs, what need have

you to employ punishments? Love virtue, and the people will be virtuous. The virtues of a superior man are like the wind; the virtues of a common man are like the grass; the grass, when the wind passes over it, bends.

> Thoreau, *Walden:* The Village

115 Our whole life is startlingly moral. There is never an instant's truce between virtue and vice. Goodness is the only investment that never fails.

> Thoreau, *Walden:* Higher Laws

116 The first element of good government . . . being the virtue and intelligence of the human beings composing the community, the most important point of excellence which any form of government can possess is to promote the virtue and intelligence of the people themselves.

> Mill, *Representative Government,* II

117 Bulstrode shrank from a direct lie with an intensity disproportionate to the number of his more indirect misdeeds. But many of these misdeeds were like the subtle muscular movements which are not taken account of in the consciousness, though they bring about the end that we fix our mind on and desire. And it is only what we are vividly conscious of that we can vividly imagine to be seen by Omniscience.

> George Eliot, *Middlemarch,* VII, 68

118 It seems not to be true that there is a power in the universe, which watches over the well-being of every individual with parental care and brings all his concerns to a happy ending. On the contrary, the destinies of man are incompatible with a universal principle of benevolence or with—what is to some degree contradictory—a universal principle of justice. Earthquakes, floods, and fires do not differentiate between the good and devout man, and the sinner and unbeliever. And, even if we leave inanimate nature out of account and consider the destinies of individual men in so far as they depend on their relations with others of their own kind, it is by no means the rule that virtue is rewarded and wickedness punished, but it happens often enough that the violent, the crafty, and the unprincipled seize the desirable goods of the earth for themselves, while the pious go empty away. Dark, unfeeling, and unloving powers determine human destiny; the system of rewards and punishments, which, according to religion, governs the world, seems to have no existence.

> Freud, *New Introductory Lectures on Psycho-Analysis,* XXXV

9.11 | *Courage and Cowardice*

Of all the virtues, the one most frequently extolled by the poets is courage. Many of the memorable characters of the great epics and tragedies of antiquity, of the plays of Shakespeare, and of modern fiction are depicted as lionhearted men, men who have the fortitude to withstand the onslaughts of misfortune, or the valor to attempt what the timid or craven would never dare. The historians and the biographers, too, give us portraits of bold and daring leaders, of men whose strength of character enables them to remain steady on their course, overcoming what appear to be insuperable obstacles. Courage is the stuff out of which heroes are made and the heroic temper is moulded. Relevant, therefore, to the consideration of courage are quotations that will be found in Section 1.6 on HUMAN GREATNESS: THE HERO.

The reader will have noted the vocabulary of epithets applicable to this virtue and its associated vice: for courageous, brave, bold, daring, valorous, fearless; for cowardly, timid, craven, pusillanimous, effeminate. The name given the virtue itself is frequently fortitude rather than courage, the one word in its etymology implying strength—strength of moral character, not of physique; the other suggesting robustness of spirit.

The analysis given by the philosophers instructs us that courage is not fearlessness. He who, by reason of a certain inborn temperamental disposition, lacks fear is not a courageous man and will never become one. Rather it is he who, suffering the impulses of fear or the disinclination to suffer pain, overcomes them for the sake of a good deed to be done or a right objective to be gained. Furthermore, the courageous man is not one who appears to act courageously or even does so in one circumstance or two, but rather the man who has the firmly established habitual disposition to suffer pains and overcome fears for a good purpose. When the threatening pains are bodily and the fears recoil from bodily attack that may cause death or injury, the virtue is often called "physical courage," to distinguish it from the moral fortitude exhibited by the man who risks disapprobation, contumely, or even dishonor for a good cause. However, in both cases, the strength lies in the man's moral character, not in his physique.

Cowardice is not the only vice that philosophers have opposed to courage. If the coward is one who gives in too readily to his fears, fears the wrong things, or fails to overcome his fears when he ought to, the foolhardy man at the other extreme is one who dismisses his fears too readily, and lacks sufficient respect for the dangers involved. In between these two extremes, the courageous man is seen as one who exercises a reasonable or prudent judgment concerning how to manage his fears, how to moderate or control them. Hence some of the writers about courage introduce the notion of prudence or of sound judgment into their discussion. For the consideration of this related virtue, the reader is referred to Section 9.13 on PRUDENCE; and for treatment of the emotion that is chiefly involved in courage and cowardice, the reader is referred to Section 4.2 on FEAR.

---

1 If thou faint in the day of adversity, thy strength is small.

> *Proverbs* 24:10

2 *Idomeneus.* The skin of the coward changes colour one way and another,
and the heart inside him has no control to make him sit steady,
but he shifts his weight from one foot to another, then settles firmly
on both feet, and the heart inside his chest pounds violent
as he thinks of the death spirits, and his teeth chatter together:
but the brave man's skin will not change colour, nor is he too much
frightened, once he has taken his place in the hidden position,
but his prayer is to close as soon as may be in bitter division.

> Homer, *Iliad,* XIII, 279

3 *Artabanus.* It is best for men, when they take counsel, to be timorous, and imagine all possible calamities, but when the time for action comes, then to deal boldly.

> Herodotus, *History,* VII, 49

4 *Pericles.* The palm of courage will surely be adjudged most justly to those, who best know the difference between hardship and pleasure and yet are never tempted to shrink from danger.

> Thucydides, *Peloponnesian War,* II, 40

5 *Pericles.* They whose minds are least sensitive to calamity, and whose hands are most quick to meet it, are the greatest men and the greatest communities.

> Thucydides, *Peloponnesian War,* II, 64

6 *Socrates.* Is not courage, Simmias, a quality which is specially characteristic of the philosopher?
Simmias. Certainly.
There is temperance again, which even by the vulgar is supposed to consist in the control and regulation of the passions, and in the sense of superiority to them—is not temperance a virtue belonging to those only who despise the body, and who pass their lives in philosophy?
Most assuredly.
For the courage and temperance of other men, if you will consider them, are really a contradiction.
How so?

Well, he said, you are aware that death is regarded by men in general as a great evil.

Very true, he said.

And do not courageous men face death because they are afraid of yet greater evils?

That is quite true.

Then all but the philosophers are courageous only from fear, and because they are afraid; and yet that a man should be courageous from fear, and because he is a coward, is surely a strange thing.

Plato, *Phaedo,* 68A

7 With what sort of terrible things . . . is the brave man concerned? Surely with the greatest; for no one is more likely than he to stand his ground against what is awe-inspiring. Now death is the most terrible of all things; for it is the end, and nothing is thought to be any longer either good or bad for the dead. But the brave man would not seem to be concerned even with death in *all* circumstances, e.g. at sea or in disease. In what circumstances, then? Surely in the noblest. Now such deaths are those in battle; for these take place in the greatest and noblest danger. . . . Properly, then, he will be called brave who is fearless in face of a noble death, and of all emergencies that involve death; and the emergencies of war are in the highest degree of this kind.

Aristotle, *Ethics,* 1115^{a}24

8 What is terrible is not the same for all men; but we say there are things terrible even beyond human strength. These, then, are terrible to every one—at least to every sensible man; but the terrible things that are *not* beyond human strength differ in magnitude and degree, and so too do the things that inspire confidence. Now the brave man is as dauntless as man may be. Therefore, while he will fear even the things that are not beyond human strength, he will face them as he ought and as the rule directs, for honour's sake; for this is the end of virtue. But it is possible to fear these more, or less, and again to fear things that are not terrible as if they were. Of the faults that are committed one consists in fearing what one should not, another in fearing as we should not, another in fearing when we should not, and so on; and so too with respect to the things that inspire confidence. The man, then, who faces and who fears the right things and from the right motive, in the right way and at the right time, and who feels confidence under the corresponding conditions, is brave; for the brave man feels and acts according to the merits of the case and in whatever way the rule directs.

Aristotle, *Ethics,* 1115^{b}7

9 Of those who go to excess he who exceeds in fearlessness has no name . . . but he would be a sort of madman or insensible person if he feared nothing, neither earthquakes nor the waves, as they say the Celts do not; while the man who exceeds in confidence about what really is terrible is rash. The rash man, however, is also thought to be boastful and only a pretender to courage; at all events, as the brave man *is* with regard to what is terrible, so the rash man wishes to *appear;* and so he imitates him in situations where he can. Hence also most of them are a mixture of rashness and cowardice; for, while in these situations they display confidence, they do not hold their ground against what is really terrible. The man who exceeds in fear is a coward; for he fears both what he ought not and as he ought not, and all the similar characterizations attach to him. He is lacking also in confidence; but he is more conspicuous for his excess of fear in painful situations. The coward . . . is a despairing sort of person; for he fears everything. The brave man, on the other hand, has the opposite disposition; for confidence is the mark of a hopeful disposition. The coward, the rash man, and the brave man, then, are concerned with the same objects but are differently disposed towards them; for the first two exceed and fall short, while the third holds the middle, which is the right, position; and rash men are precipitate, and wish for dangers beforehand but draw back when they are in them, while brave men are keen in the moment of action, but quiet beforehand.

As we have said, then, courage is a mean with respect to things that inspire confidence or fear.

Aristotle, *Ethics,* 1115^{b}24

10 Experience with regard to particular facts is . . . thought to be courage; this is indeed the reason why Socrates thought courage was knowledge. Other people exhibit this quality in other dangers, and professional soldiers exhibit it in the dangers of war; for there seem to be many empty alarms in war, of which these have had the most comprehensive experience; therefore they seem brave, because the others do not know the nature of the facts. Again, their experience makes them most capable in attack and in defence, since they can use their arms and have the kind that are likely to be best both for attack and for defence; therefore they fight like armed men against unarmed or like trained athletes against amateurs; for in such contests too it is not the bravest men that fight best, but those who are strongest and have their bodies in the best condition. Professional soldiers turn cowards, however, when the danger puts too great a strain on them and they are inferior in numbers and equipment; for they are the first to fly, while citizen-forces die at their posts, as in fact happened at the temple of Hermes. For to the latter flight is disgraceful and death is preferable to safety on those terms; while the former from the very beginning faced the danger on the assumption that they were stronger, and when they know the

facts they fly, fearing death more than disgrace; but the brave man is not that sort of person.

Aristotle, *Ethics*, 1116^b3

11 Though courage is concerned with feelings of confidence and of fear, it is not concerned with both alike, but more with the things that inspire fear; for he who is undisturbed in face of these and bears himself as he should towards these is more truly brave than the man who does so towards the things that inspire confidence. It is for facing what is painful, then . . . that men are called brave. Hence also courage involves pain, and is justly praised; for it is harder to face what is painful than to abstain from what is pleasant.

Aristotle, *Ethics*, 1117^a29

12 It is generally agreed by the learned and the untaught alike that men who are brave, high-spirited, patient, and superior to human vicissitudes, will endure pain with patience. Nor would anyone disagree that a man who so suffers merits praise. When such endurance is both expected of brave men and praised when it is found, is it not ignoble to shy away from the onset of pain or be unable to bear it? But perhaps, even if all right-minded states are called virtuous, the term may not cover all virtues. All may have received the name from the one single virtue that was considered as outshining all the others, because the word "virtue" comes from the word for man. And man's special virtue is courage. Of courage there are two principle types, the scorn of death and the scorn of pain.

Cicero, *Disputations*, II, 18

13 *Turnus.* Fortune befriends the bold.

Virgil, *Aeneid*, X

14 Then with a close embrace he [Aeneas] strain'd his son,
And, kissing thro' his helmet, thus begun:
"My son, from my example learn the war,
In camps to suffer, and in fields to dare;
But happier chance than mine attend thy care!
This day my hand thy tender age shall shield,
And crown with honors of the conquer'd field:
Thou, when thy riper years shall send thee forth
To toils of war, be mindful of my worth;
Assert thy birthright, and in arms be known,
For Hector's nephew, and Æneas' son."

Virgil, *Aeneid*, XII

15 It is truly very commendable to abhor and shun the doing any base action; but to stand in fear of every kind of censure or disrepute may argue a gentle and openhearted, but not an heroic temper.

Plutarch, *Aemilius Paulus and Timoleon Compared*

16 Cato Major, hearing some commend one that was rash, and inconsiderately daring in a battle, said, There is a difference between a man's prizing valour at a great rate, and valuing life at little.

Plutarch, *Pelopidas*

17 To do a wrong thing is base, and to do well where there is no danger, common; the good man's characteristic is to do so where there is danger.

Plutarch, *Caius Marius*

18 The ancients, I think, did not imagine bravery to be plain fearlessness, but a cautious fear of blame and disgrace.

Plutarch, *Cleomenes*

19 Be like the promontory against which the waves continually break, but it stands firm and tames the fury of the water around it.

Unhappy am I, because this has happened to me.—Not so, but happy am I, though this has happened to me, because I continue free from pain, neither crushed by the present nor fearing the future. For such a thing as this might have happened to every man; but every man would not have continued free from pain on such an occasion. Why then is that rather a misfortune than this a good fortune? And dost thou in all cases call that a man's misfortune, which is not a deviation from man's nature? And does a thing seem to thee to be a deviation from man's nature, when it is not contrary to the will of man's nature? Well, thou knowest the will of nature. Will then this which has happened prevent thee from being just, magnanimous, temperate, prudent, secure against inconsiderate opinions and falsehood; will it prevent thee from having modesty, freedom, and everything else, by the presence of which man's nature obtains all that is its own? Remember too on every occasion which leads thee to vexation to apply this principle: not that this is a misfortune, but that to bear it nobly is good fortune.

Marcus Aurelius, *Meditations*, IV, 49

20 Here sighs, plaints, and deep wailings resounded through the starless air: it made me weep at first.
Strange tongues, horrible outcries, words of pain, tones of anger, voices deep and hoarse, and sounds of hands amongst them,
made a tumult, which turns itself unceasing in that air for ever dyed, as sand when [it eddies in a whirlwind].
And I, my head begirt with horror, said: "Master, what is this that I hear? and who are these that seem so overcome with pain?"
And he to me: "This miserable mode the dreary souls of those sustain, who lived without blame, and without praise.

They are mixed with the caitiff choir of the angels, who were not rebellious, nor were faithful
to God; but were for themselves.

Heaven chased them forth to keep its beauty from
impair; and the deep Hell receives them not,
for the wicked would have some glory over
them."

And I: "Master what is so grievous to them, that
makes them lament thus bitterly?" He answered: "I will tell it to thee very briefly.

These have no hope of death; and their blind life
is so mean, that they are envious of every other
lot.

Report of them the world permits not to exist;
Mercy and [Justice] disdains them: let us not
speak of them; but look, and pass."

And I, who looked, saw an ensign, which whirling
ran so quickly that it seemed to scorn all pause;

and behind it came so long a train of people, that
I should never have believed death had undone
so many.

After I had recognised some amongst them, I [saw
and knew] the shadow of him who from cowardice made the great refusal.

Forthwith I understood and felt assured, that this
was the crew of caitiffs, hateful to God and to
his enemies.

> Dante, *Inferno*, III, 22

21 *Pandar.* Remember, too, it is no idle boast
That fortune helps the brave in his emprise,
But from the coward wretch she ever flies.
> Chaucer, *Troilus and Cressida*, IV, 86

22 The precepts of resoluteness and constancy do not
state that we must not protect ourselves as much
as it lies in our power from the evils and troubles
that threaten us; nor consequently that we should
not fear being taken by surprise. On the contrary,
all honorable means of safeguarding ourselves
from evils are not only permitted but laudable.
And constancy's part is played principally in
bearing troubles patiently where there is no remedy.
> Montaigne, *Essays*, I, 12, Of Constancy

23 Valor has its limits like the other virtues, and
these limits once transgressed, we find ourselves
on the path of vice; so that we may pass through
valor to temerity, obstinacy, and madness, unless
we know its limits well—and they are truly hard
to discern near the borderlines.
> Montaigne, *Essays*, I, 15, One Is Punished

24 The worth and value of a man is in his heart and
his will; there lies his real honor. Valor is the
strength, not of legs and arms, but of heart and
soul; it consists not in the worth of our horse or
our weapons, but in our own. . . . He who relaxes
none of his assurance, no matter how great the
danger of imminent death; who, giving up his

soul, still looks firmly and scornfully at his enemy—he is beaten not by us, but by fortune; he is
killed, not conquered.
> Montaigne, *Essays*, I, 31, Of Cannibals

25 Cowardice is the mother of cruelty.
> Montaigne, *Essays*, II, 27,
> Cowardice, Mother of Cruelty

26 *Hotspur.* Out of this nettle, danger, we pluck this
flower, safety.
> Shakespeare, *I Henry IV*, II, iii, 10

27 *Falstaff.* To die, is to be a counterfeit; for he is but
the counterfeit of a man who hath not the life of a
man: but to counterfeit dying, when a man thereby liveth, is to be no counterfeit, but the true and
perfect image of life indeed. The better part of
valour is discretion.
> Shakespeare, *I Henry IV*, V, iv, 116

28 *Benedick.* In a false quarrel there is no true valour.
> Shakespeare, *Much Ado About
> Nothing*, V, i, 120

29 *Caesar.* Cowards die many times before their
deaths;
The valiant never taste of death but once.
> Shakespeare, *Julius Caesar*, II, ii, 32

30 *King.*   That we would do,
We should do when we would; for this "would"
changes
And hath abatements and delays as many
As there are tongues, are hands, are accidents;
And then this "should" is like a spendthrift sigh,
That hurts by easing.
> Shakespeare, *Hamlet*, IV, vii, 119

31 *Nestor.*   The sea being smooth,
How many shallow bauble boats dare sail
Upon her patient breast, making their way
With those of nobler bulk!
But let the ruffian Boreas once enrage
The gentle Thetis, and anon behold
The strong-ribb'd bark through liquid mountains
cut,
Bounding between the two moist elements,
Like Perseus' horse; where's then the saucy boat
Whose weak untimber'd sides but even now
Co-rivall'd greatness? Either to harbour fled,
Or made a toast for Neptune. Even so
Doth valour's show and valour's worth divide
In storms of fortune; for in her ray and brightness
The herd hath more annoyance by the breese
Than by the tiger; but when the splitting wind
Makes flexible the knees of knotted oaks,
And flies fled under shade, why, then the thing of
courage
As roused with rage, with rage doth sympathize,
And with an accent tuned in selfsame key

Retorts to chiding fortune.

Shakespeare, *Troilus and Cressida*, I, iii, 34

32 *Troilus.*   Manhood and honour
Should have hare-hearts, would they but fat their
     thoughts
With this cramm'd reason, Reason and respect
Make livers pale and lustihood deject.

Shakespeare, *Troilus and Cressida*, II, ii, 47

33 *Lucio.*   Our doubts are traitors
And make us lose the good we oft might win
By fearing to attempt.

Shakespeare, *Measure for Measure*, I, iv, 77

34 *Kent.*   None of these rogues and cowards
But Ajax is their fool.

Shakespeare, *Lear*, II, ii, 132

35 *Lady Macbeth.*   Art thou afeard
To be the same in thine own act and valour
As thou art in desire? Wouldst thou have that
Which thou esteem'st the ornament of life,
And live a coward in thine own esteem,
Letting "I dare not" wait upon "I would,"
Like the poor cat i' the adage?

Shakespeare, *Macbeth*, I, vii, 39

36 *Lady Macbeth.*   I have given suck, and know
How tender 'tis to love the babe that milks me;
I would, while it was smiling in my face,
Have pluck'd my nipple from his boneless gums
And dash'd the brains out, had I so sworn as you
Have done to this.
     Macbeth.   If we should fail?
     Lady M.   We fail!
But screw your courage to the sticking-place,
And we'll not fail.

Shakespeare, *Macbeth*, I, vii, 54

37 After they had gone a pretty way under a pleasing
Covert of Chestnut-Trees, they came into a
Meadow adjoining to certain Rocks, from whose
Top there was a great Fall of Waters. At the Foot
of those Rocks they discover'd certain old ill-
contriv'd Buildings, that rather look'd like Ruins
than inhabited Houses; and they perceiv'd that
the terrifying Noise of the Blows, which yet continued, issu'd out of that Place. When they came
nearer, even patient *Rozinante* himself started at
the dreadful Sound; but being hearten'd and
pacify'd by his Master, he was at last prevail'd
with to draw nearer and nearer with wary Steps;
the Knight recommending himself all the way
most devoutly to his *Dulcinea,* and now and then
also to Heaven, in short Ejaculations. As for *Sancho,* he stuck close to his Master, peeping all the
way through *Rozinante's* Legs, to see if he could
perceive what he dreaded to find out. When a
little farther, at the doubling of the Point of a
Rock, they plainly discover'd (kind Reader, do

not take it amiss) Six huge Fulling-Mill Hammers, which interchangeably thumping several
Pieces of Cloth, made the terrible Noise that
caus'd all Don *Quixote's* Anxieties and *Sancho's*
Tribulation that Night.

Don *Quixote* was struck dumb at this unexpected
Sight, and was ready to drop from his Horse with
Shame and Confusion. *Sancho* star'd upon him,
and saw him down his Head, with a desponding
dejected Countenance, like a Man quite dispirited
with this cursed Disappointment. At the same
Time he look'd upon *Sancho,* and seeing by his
Eyes, and his Cheeks swell'd with Laughter, that
he was ready to burst, he could not forbear laugh-
ing himself in spight of all his Vexation; so that
Sancho seeing his Master begin, immediately gave
a Loose to his Mirth, and broke out into such a
Fit of Laughing, that he was forc'd to hold his
Sides with both his Knuckles, for fear of bursting
his aking Paunch. Four times he ceas'd, and four
times renew'd his obstreperous Laughing; which
Sauciness Don *Quixote* began to resent with great
Indignation; and the more when *Sancho,* in a jeer-
ing Tone, presum'd to ridicule him with his own
Words, repeating part of the vain Speech he made
when first they heard the Noise; *Know,* Sancho, *I
was born in this Iron Age to restore the Age of Gold. I am
the Man for whom Heaven has reserv'd the most dangerous and glorious Adventures,* &c. Thus he went on, till
his Master, dreadfully inrag'd at his Insolence, hit
him two such Blows on the Shoulders with his
Lance, that had they fallen upon his Head they
had sav'd Don *Quixote* the trouble of paying him
his Wages, whatever he must have done to his
Heirs. Thereupon *Sancho,* finding his Jest turn'd to
Earnest, begg'd Pardon with all Submission: Mercy, good your Worship, cry'd he, spare my Bones I
beseech you! I meant no harm, I did but joke a
little. And because You joke, I do not, cry'd Don
Quixote. Come hither, good Mr Jester, you who
pretend to rally, tell me, had this been a dangerous Adventure, as well as it proves only a false
Alarm, have I not shewn Resolution enough to
undertake and finish it? Am I, who am a Knight,
bound to know the Meaning of every Mechanick
Noise, and distinguish between Sound and
Sound? Besides, it might happen, as really it is,
that I had never seen a Fulling-Mill before, tho'
thou, like a base Scoundrel as thou art, wert born
and brought up among such mean Implements of
Drudgery. But let the six Fulling-Hammers be
transform'd into so many Giants, and then set
them at me one by one, or all together; and if I do
not lay 'em at my Feet with their Heels upwards,
then I'll give thee Leave to exercise thy ill-bred
Railery as much as thou pleasest.

Cervantes, *Don Quixote,* I, 20

38 The Keeper observing the Posture Don *Quixote*
had put himself in, and that it was not possible for
him to prevent letting out the Lions, without in-

curring the Resentment of the desperate Knight, set the Door of the foremast Cage wide open; where, as I have said, the Male Lion lay, who appeared of a monstrous Bigness, and of a hideous frightful Aspect. The first thing he did was to roll and turn himself round in his Cage; in the next Place he stretch'd out one of his Paws, put forth his Claws, and rouz'd himself. After that he gap'd and yawn'd for a good while, and shew'd his dreadful Fangs, and then thrust out half a Yard of Broad Tongue, and with it lick'd the Dust out of his Eyes and Face. Having done this, he thrust his Head quite out of the Cage, and star'd about with his Eyes that look'd like two live Coals of Fire; a Sight and Motion, enough to have struck Terror into Temerity itself. But Don *Quixote* only regarded it with Attention, wishing his grim Adversary would leap out of his Hold, and come within his reach, that he might exercise his Valour, and cut the Monster piece-meal. To his Height of Extravagance had his Folly transported him; but the generous Lion, more gentle than arrogant, taking no notice of his Vapouring and Bravadoos, after he had look'd about him a while, turn'd his Tail, and having shew'd Don *Quixote* his Posteriors, very contentedly lay down again in his Apartment. Don *Quixote* seeing this, commanded the Keeper to rouze him with his Pole, and force him out whether he would or no. Not I, indeed, Sir, answer'd the Keeper; I dare not do it for my Life; for if I provoke him, I'm sure to be the first he'll tear to Pieces. Let me advise you, Sir, to be satisfy'd with your Day's Work. 'Tis as much as the bravest He that wears a Head can pretend to do. Then pray go no farther, I beseech you: The Door stands open, the Lion is at his Choice, whether he will come out or no. You have waited for him, you see he does not care to look you in the Face, and since he did not come out at the first, I dare engage he will not stir out this Day. You have shewn enough the Greatness of your Courage. No man is obliged to do more than challenge his Enemy, and wait for him in the Field. If he comes not, that's his own Fault, and the Scandal is his, as the Honour the Challenger's. 'Tis true, reply'd Don *Quixote*. Come, shut the Cage-Door, Honest Friend, and give me a Certificate under thy Hand in the amplest Form thou can'st devise, of what thou hast seen me perform; how thou did'st open the Cage for the Lion; how I expected his coming, and he did not come out. How, upon his not coming out then, I stay'd his own Time, and instead of meeting me, he turned Tail and lay down. I am oblig'd to do no more. So, Inchantments avant; and Heaven prosper Truth, Justice, and Knight-Errantry! Shut the Door, as I bid thee, while I make Signs to those that ran away from us, and get 'em to come back, that they may have an Account of this Exploit from thy own Mouth.

Cervantes, *Don Quixote,* II, 17

39 Every Knight has his particular Employment. Let the Courtier wait on the Ladies; let him with splendid Equipage adorn his Prince's Court, and with a magnificent Table support poor Gentlemen. Let him give Birth to Feasts and Tournaments, and shew his Grandeur, Liberality, and Munificence, and especially his Piety; in all these things he fulfils the Duties of his Station. But as for the Knight-Errant, let him search into all the Corners of the World, enter into the most intricate Labyrinths, and every Hour be ready to attempt Impossibility itself. Let him in desolate Wilds baffle the Rigor of the Weather, the scorching Heat of the Sun's fiercest Beams, and the Inclemency of Winds and Snow: Let Lions never fright him, Dragons daunt him, not evil Spirits deter him. To go in Quest of these, to meet, to dare, to conflict, and to overcome 'em all, is his principal and proper Office. Since then my Stars have decreed me to be one of those Adventurous Knights, I think my self obliged to attempt every thing that seems to come within the Verge of my Profession. This, Sir, engag'd me to encounter those Lions just now, judging it to be my immediate Business, tho' I was sensible of the extreme Rashness of the Undertaking. For well I know, that Valour is a Virtue situate between the two vicious Extremes of Cowardice and Temerity. But certainly 'tis not so ill for a Valiant Man to rise to a Degree of Rashness, as 'tis to fall short and border upon Cowardice. For as 'tis easier for a Prodigal to become Liberal, than a Miser; so 'tis easier for the hardy and rash Person to be reduced to true Bravery, than for the Coward ever to rise to that Virtue: And therefore in thus attempting Adventures, believe me, Signor Don *Diego,* 'tis better to exceed the Bounds a little, and over-do, rather than underdo the thing; because it sounds better in People's Ears to hear it said, how that such a Knight is Rash and Hardy, than such a Knight is Dastardly and Timorous.

Cervantes, *Don Quixote,* II, 17

40 *Courage* (by which I mean the contempt of wounds and violent death) inclineth men to private revenges, and sometimes to endeavour the unsettling of the public peace: and *timorousness* many times disposeth to the desertion of the public defence. Both these, they say, cannot stand together in the same person.

Hobbes, *Leviathan,* IV, Review and Conclusion

41 *Satan.*   What though the field be lost?
All is not lost; the unconquerable Will,
And study of revenge, immortal hate,
And courage never to submit or yield.

Milton, *Paradise Lost,* I, 105

42 *Raphael.* Servant of God, well done, well hast thou fought

The better fight, who single hast maintaind
Against revolted multitudes the Cause
Of Truth, in word mightier then they in Armes;
And for the testimonie of Truth hast born
Universal reproach, far worse to beare
Then violence.

> Milton, *Paradise Lost*, VI, 29

43 *Raphael.*   No thought of flight,
None of retreat, no unbecoming deed
That argu'd fear; each on himself reli'd,
As onely in his arm the moment lay
Of victorie.

> Milton, *Paradise Lost*, VI, 236

44 Flight at the proper time, just as well as fighting,
is to be reckoned, therefore, as showing strength of
mind in a man who is free; that is to say, a free
man chooses flight by the same strength or presence of mind as that by which he chooses battle.

> Spinoza, *Ethics*, IV, Prop. 69, Corol.

45 None but the brave deserves the fair.

> Dryden, *Alexander's Feast*, 15

46 Fortitude is the guard and support of the other
virtues; and without courage a man will scarce
keep steady to his duty, and fill up the character
of a truly worthy man.

> Locke, *Some Thoughts*
> *Concerning Education*, 115

47 'Tis unwise to punish Cowards with Ignominy; for
if they had regarded that, they would not have
been Cowards: Death is their proper Punishment,
because they fear it most.

> Swift, *Thoughts on Various Subjects*

48 We have already observed that great heat enervates the strength and courage of men, and that in
cold climates they have a certain vigour of body
and mind, which renders them patient and intrepid, and qualifies them for arduous enterprises.
This remark holds good, not only between different nations, but even in the different parts of the
same country. In the north of China people are
more courageous than those in the south; and
those in the south of Korea have less bravery than
those in the north.

We ought not, then, to be astonished that the
effeminacy of the people in hot climates has almost always rendered them slaves; and that the
bravery of those in cold climates has enabled
them to maintain their liberties. This is an effect
which springs from a natural cause.

This has also been found true in America; the
despotic empires of Mexico and Peru were near
the Line, and almost all the little free nations
were, and are still, near the Poles.

> Montesquieu, *Spirit of Laws*, XVII, 2

49 In a military nation, cowardice supposes other
vices; it is an argument of a person's having devi-
ated from the principles of his education, of his
being insensible of honour, and of having refused
to be directed by those maxims which govern
other men; it shows that he neither fears their
contempt, nor sets any value upon their esteem.
Men of any tolerable extraction seldom want
either the dexterity requisite to co-operate with
strength, or the strength necessary to concur with
courage; for as they set a value upon honour, they
are practised in matters without which this honour cannot be obtained. Beside, in a military nation, where strength, courage and prowess are esteemed, crimes really odious are those which arise
from fraud, artifice, and cunning, that is, from
cowardice.

> Montesquieu, *Spirit of Laws*, XXVIII, 17

50 *Johnson.* Courage is a quality so necessary for
maintaining virtue, that it is always respected,
even when it is associated with vice.

> Boswell, *Life of Johnson (June 11, 1784)*

51 A coward, a man incapable either of defending or
of revenging himself, evidently wants one of the
most essential parts of the character of a man. He
is as much mutilated and deformed in his mind as
another is in his body, who is either deprived of
some of its most essential members, or has lost the
use of them. He is evidently the more wretched
and miserable of the two; because happiness and
misery, which reside altogether in the mind, must
necessarily depend more upon the healthful or
unhealthful, the mutilated or entire state of the
mind, than upon that of the body. Even though
the martial spirit of the people were of no use
towards the defence of the society, yet to prevent
that sort of mental mutilation, deformity, and
wretchedness, which cowardice necessarily involves in it, from spreading themselves through
the great body of the people, would still deserve
the most serious attention of government, in the
same manner as it would deserve its most serious
attention to prevent a leprosy or any other loathsome and offensive disease, though neither mortal
nor dangerous, from spreading itself among them,
though perhaps no other public good might result
from such attention besides the prevention of so
great a public evil.

> Adam Smith, *Wealth of Nations*, V, 1

52 Female courage, however it may be raised by fanaticism, or confirmed by habit, can be only a
faint and imperfect imitation of the manly valour
that distinguishes the age or country in which it
may be found.

> Gibbon, *Decline and Fall*
> *of the Roman Empire*, IX

53 Experience has proved the distinction of active

and passive courage; the fanatic who endures without a groan the torture of the rack or the stake, would tremble and fly before the face of an armed enemy.

Gibbon, *Decline and Fall of the Roman Empire*, XLVII

54 The weak in courage is strong in cunning.

Blake, *Marriage of Heaven and Hell*, 9

55 The intrinsic worth of courage as a disposition of mind is to be found in the genuine, absolute, final end, the sovereignty of the state. The work of courage is to actualize this final end, and the means to this end is the sacrifice of personal actuality. This form of experience thus contains the harshness of extreme contradictions: a self-sacrifice which yet is the real existence of one's freedom; the maximum self-subsistence of individuality, yet only as a cog playing its part in the mechanism of an external organization; absolute obedience, renunciation of personal opinions and reasonings, in fact complete *absence* of mind, coupled with the most intense and comprehensive *presence* of mind and decision in the moment of acting; the most hostile and so most personal action against individuals, coupled with an attitude of complete indifference or even liking towards them as individuals.

Hegel, *Philosophy of Right*, 328

56 To risk one's life is better than merely fearing death, but is still purely negative and so indeterminate and without value in itself. It is the positive aspect, the end and content, which first gives significance to this spiritedness. Robbers and murderers bent on crime as their end, adventurers pursuing ends planned to suit their own whims, etc., these too have spirit enough to risk their lives.

The principle of the modern world—thought and the universal—has given courage a higher form, because its display now seems to be more mechanical, the act not of this particular person, but of a member of a whole. Moreover, it seems to be turned not against single persons, but against a hostile group, and hence personal bravery appears impersonal. It is for this reason that thought has invented the gun, and the invention of this weapon, which has changed the purely personal form of bravery into a more abstract one, is no accident.

Hegel, *Philosophy of Right*, 328

57 Personal courage is really a very subordinate virtue,—merely the distinguishing mark of a subaltern,—a virtue, indeed, in which we are surpassed by the lower animals; or else you would not hear people say, *as brave as a lion*.

Schopenhauer, *Position*, IV

58 An utterly fearless man is a far more dangerous comrade than a coward.

Melville, *Moby Dick*, XXVI

59 Few men's courage is proof against protracted meditation unrelieved by action.

Melville, *Moby Dick*, XLVI

60 I am less affected by their heroism who stood up for half an hour in the front line at Buena Vista, than by the steady and cheerful valor of the men who inhabit the snowplow for their winter quarters; who have not merely the three-o'-clock-in-the-morning courage, which Bonaparte thought was the rarest, but whose courage does not go to rest so early, who go to sleep only when the storm sleeps or the sinews of their iron steed are frozen.

Thoreau, *Walden:* Sounds

61 It is . . . impossible to decide in many cases whether certain social instincts have been acquired through natural selection, or are the indirect result of other instincts and faculties, such as sympathy, reason, experience, and a tendency to imitation; or again, whether they are simply the result of long-continued habit. So remarkable an instinct as the placing sentinels to warn the community of danger, can hardly have been the indirect result of any of these faculties; it must, therefore, have been directly acquired. On the other hand, the habit followed by the males of some social animals of defending the community, and of attacking their enemies or their prey in concert, may perhaps have originated from mutual sympathy; but courage, and in most cases strength, must have been previously acquired, probably through natural selection.

Darwin, *Descent of Man*, I, 4

62 *Dólokhov.* If you are going to fight a duel, and you make a will and write affectionate letters to your parents, and if you think you may be killed, you are a fool and are lost for certain. But go with the firm intention of killing your man as quickly and surely as possible, and then all will be right. . . . Everyone fears a bear . . . but when you see one your fear's all gone, and your only thought is not to let him get away!

Tolstoy, *War and Peace*, IV, 4

63 At the approach of danger there are always two voices that speak with equal power in the human soul: one very reasonably tells a man to consider the nature of the danger and the means of escaping it; the other, still more reasonably, says that it is too depressing and painful to think of the danger, since it is not in man's power to foresee everything and avert the general course of events, and it is therefore better to disregard what is painful till it comes, and to think about what is pleasant.

Tolstoy, *War and Peace*, X, 17

64 Courage is resistance to fear, mastery of fear—not absence of fear. Except a creature be part coward it is not a compliment to say it is brave; it is merely a loose misapplication of the word. Consider the flea!—incomparably the bravest of all the creatures of God, if ignorance of fear were courage. Whether you are asleep or awake he will attack you, caring nothing for the fact that in bulk and strength you are to him as are the massed armies of the earth to a sucking child; he lives both day and night and all days and nights in the very lap of peril and the immediate presence of death, and yet is no more afraid than is the man who walks the streets of a city that was threatened by an earthquake ten centuries before. When we speak of Clive, Nelson, and Putnam as men who 'didn't know what fear was', we ought always to add the flea—and put him at the head of the procession.

Mark Twain, *Pudd'nhead Wilson's Calendar,* XII

65 There are several good protections against temptations, but the surest is cowardice.

Mark Twain, *Pudd'nhead Wilson's New Calendar,* XXXVI

66 Now all the truth is out,
Be secret and take defeat
From any brazen throat,
For how can you compete,
Being honor bred, with one
Who, were it proved he lies
Were neither shamed in his own
Nor in his neighbors' eyes?
Bred to a harder thing
Than Triumph, turn away
And like a laughing string

Whereon mad fingers play
Amid a place of stone,
Be secret and exult,
Because of all things known
That is most difficult.

Yeats, *To a Friend Whose Work Has Come to Nothing*

67 If people throw up to us our works of fiction in which we write about people who are soft, weak, cowardly, and sometimes even downright bad, it's not because these people are soft, weak, cowardly, or bad; because if we were to say, as Zola did, that they are that way because of heredity, the workings of environment, society, because of biological or psychological determinism, people would be reassured. They would say, "Well, that's what we're like, no one can do anything about it." But when the existentialist writes about a coward, he says that this coward is responsible for his cowardice. He's not like that because he has a cowardly heart or lung or brain; he's not like that on account of his physiological makeup; but he's like that because he has made himself a coward by his acts. There's no such thing as a cowardly constitution; there are nervous constitutions; there is poor blood, as the common people say, or strong constitutions. But the man whose blood is poor is not a coward on that account, for what makes cowardice is the act of renouncing or yielding. A constitution is not an act; the coward is defined on the basis of the acts he performs. People feel, in a vague sort of way, that this coward we're talking about is guilty of being a coward, and the thought frightens them. What people would like is that a coward or a hero be born that way.

Sartre, *Existentialism*

9.12 | *Temperance and Intemperance*

The quality of moderation that is sometimes identified with virtue itself is more often identified with one particular virtue or one aspect of virtue—temperance. When the latter is the case, the moderation involved represents a control over the desires or appetites. The maxim of temperance "Nothing overmuch" calls not for total abstinence, but rather an avoidance of excess.

In the case of courage, as the reader will find in Section 9.11, the obvious examples of fortitude exhibit the overcoming of excessive fear of physical pain or injury. Here the obvious examples of temperance exhibit the overcoming of cravings for bodily pleasures, expecially the pleasures of food, drink, and sex. The intemperate characters portrayed by the poets or reported by the biographers and historians are epitomes of gluttony, inebriation, and lust. The reader will also find in Section 9.11 on COURAGE AND COWARDICE that the poets and historians tend to give us portrayals of courage rather than cowardice, for brave men are the heroes of history and fiction. Here, however, the poets and historians more frequently dwell on the exploits and depravities of the intemperate; the person of temperate character or of moderate desires seldom attracts attention or dominates the scene.

Temperance and intemperance are seldom if ever attributed to a single act. The temperate person is one who is disposed by habit to restrain the appetites and keep them within the bounds of reason in order to prevent them from distracting from the pursuit of objectives worthier than the gratification of desires. The intemperate person is one who habitually indulges himself without rein, preferring the pleasures of the moment to the achievement of goals that require the exercise of restraint here and now. Because the intemperate person manifests great self-indulgence, this person is sometimes described as being childish in character, on the supposition that an excess that is natural in the very young should be corrected by the development of temperance with maturity.

Since temperance and intemperance are for the most part concerned with the moderation or indulgence of desires and with a reasonable or prudent enjoyment of pleasures, the reader is referred, for relevant materials, to Section 4.4 on DESIRE, Section 4.7 on PLEASURE AND PAIN, and Section 9.13 on PRUDENCE.

---

1 Neither repletion, nor fasting, nor anything else, is good when more than natural.

Hippocrates, *Aphorisms,* II, 4

2 *Socrates.* Every man is his own ruler; but perhaps you think that there is no necessity for him to rule himself; he is only required to rule others?

Callicles. What do you mean by his "ruling over himself"?

Soc. A simple thing enough; just what is commonly said, that a man should be temperate and master of himself, and ruler of his own pleasures and passions.

Cal. What innocence! you mean those fools—the temperate?

Soc. Certainly—any one may know that to be my meaning.

Cal. Quite so, Socrates; and they are really fools, for how can a man be happy who is the servant of anything? On the contrary, I plainly assert, that he who would truly live ought to allow his desires to wax to the uttermost, and not to chastise them; but when they have grown to their greatest he should have courage and intelligence to minister to them and to satisfy all his longings. And this I affirm to be natural justice and nobility. To this however the many cannot attain; and

they blame the strong man because they are ashamed of their own weakness, which they desire to conceal, and hence they say that intemperance is base. As I have remarked already, they enslave the nobler natures, and being unable to satisfy their pleasures, they praise temperance and justice out of their own cowardice. For if a man had been originally the son of a king, or had a nature capable of acquiring an empire or a tyranny or sovereignty, what could be more truly base or evil than temperance—to a man like him, I say, who might freely be enjoying every good, and has no one to stand in his way, and yet has admitted custom and reason and the opinion of other men to be lords over him?—must not he be in a miserable plight whom the reputation of justice and temperance hinders from giving more to his friends than to his enemies, even though he be a ruler in his city? Nay, Socrates, for you profess to be a votary of the truth, and the truth is this: that luxury and intemperance and licence, if they be provided with means, are virtue and happiness—all the rest is a mere bauble, agreements contrary to nature, foolish talk of men, nothing worth.

Soc. There is a noble freedom, Callicles, in your way of approaching the argument; for what you say is what the rest of the world think, but do not like to say. And I must beg of you to persevere, that the true rule of human life may become manifest. Tell me, then:—you say, do you not, that in the rightly-developed man the passions ought not to be controlled, but that we should let them grow to the utmost and somehow or other satisfy them, and that this is virtue?

Cal. Yes; I do.

Soc. Then those who want nothing are not truly said to be happy?

Cal. No indeed, for then stones and dead men would be the happiest of all.

Soc. But surely life according to your view is an awful thing. . . . I would fain prove to you that you should change your mind, and, instead of the intemperate and insatiate life, choose that which is orderly and sufficient and has a due provision for daily needs. Do I make any impression on you, and are you coming over to the opinion that the orderly are happier than the intemperate? Or do I fail to persuade you, and, however many tales I rehearse to you, do you continue of the same opinion still?

Cal. The latter, Socrates, is more like the truth.

Plato, *Gorgias*, 491B

3 *Socrates.* Listen to me, then, while I recapitulate the argument:—Is the pleasant the same as the good? Not the same. Callicles and I are agreed about that. And is the pleasant to be pursued for the sake of the good? or the good for the sake of the pleasant? The pleasant is to be pursued for the sake of the good. And that is pleasant at the presence of which we are pleased, and that is good at the presence of which we are good? To be sure. And we are good, and all good things whatever are good when some virtue is present in us or them? That, Callicles, is my conviction. But the virtue of each thing, whether body or soul, instrument or creature, when given to them in the best way comes to them not by chance but as the result of the order and truth and art which are imparted to them: Am I not right? I maintain that I am. And is not the virtue of each thing dependent on order or arrangement? Yes, I say. And that which makes a thing good is the proper order inhering in each thing? Such is my view. And is not the soul which has an order of her own better than that which has no order? Certainly. And the soul which has order is orderly? Of course. And that which is orderly is temperate? Assuredly. And the temperate soul is good? No other answer can I give, Callicles dear; have you any?

Callicles. Go on, my good fellow.

Soc. Then I shall proceed to add, that if the temperate soul is the good soul, the soul which is in the opposite condition, that is, the foolish and intemperate, is the bad soul. Very true.

And will not the temperate man do what is proper, both in relation to the gods and to men;— for he would not be temperate if he did not? Cer-tainly he will do what is proper. In his relation to other men he will do what is just; and in his relation to the gods he will do what is holy; and he who does what is just and holy must be just and holy? Very true. And must he not be courageous? for the duty of a temperate man is not to follow or to avoid what he ought not, but what he ought, whether things or men or pleasures or pains, and patiently to endure when he ought; and therefore, Callicles, the temperate man, being, as we have described, also just and courageous and holy, cannot be other than a perfectly good man, nor can the good man do otherwise than well and perfectly whatever he does; and he who does well must of necessity be happy and blessed, and the evil man who does evil, miserable: now this latter is he whom you were applauding—the intemperate who is the opposite of the temperate. Such is my position, and these things I affirm to be true. And if they are true, then I further affirm that he who desires to be happy must pursue and practise temperance and run away from intemperance as fast as his legs will carry him: he had better order his life so as not to need punishment; but if either he or any of his friends, whether private individual or city, are in need of punishment, then justice must be done and he must suffer punishment, if he would be happy. This appears to me to be the aim which a man ought to have, and towards which he ought to direct all the energies both of himself and of the state, acting so that he may have temperance and justice present with him and be happy, not suffering his lusts to be unrestrained, and in the never-ending desire to satisfy them leading a robber's life. Such a one is the friend neither of God nor man, for he is incapable of communion, and he who is incapable of communion is also incapable of friendship. And philosophers tell us, Callicles, that communion and friendship and orderliness and temperance and justice bind together heaven and earth and gods and men, and that this universe is therefore called Cosmos or order, not disorder or misrule, my friend.

Plato, *Gorgias*, 506B

4 *Protarchus.* The temperate are restrained by the wise man's aphorism of "Never too much," which is their rule, but excess of pleasure possessing the minds of fools and wantons becomes madness and makes them shout with delight.

Plato, *Philebus*, 45B

5 *Athenian Stranger.* He who knows the temperate life will describe it as in all things gentle, having gentle pains and gentle pleasures, and placid desires and loves not insane; whereas the intemperate life is impetuous in all things, and has violent pains and pleasures, and vehement and stinging desires, and loves utterly insane; and in the temperate life the pleasures exceed the pains, but in the intem-

perate life the pains exceed the pleasures in greatness and number and frequency. Hence one of the two lives is naturally and necessarily more pleasant and the other more painful, and he who would live pleasantly cannot possibly choose to live intemperately. And if this is true, the inference clearly is that no man is voluntarily intemperate; but that the whole multitude of men lack temperance in their lives, either from ignorance, or from want of self-control, or both.

Plato, *Laws,* V, 733B

6 I came to Italy and Sicily on my first visit. My first impressions on arrival were those of strong disapproval—disapproval of the kind of life which was there called the life of happiness, stuffed full as it was with the banquets of the Italian Greeks and Syracusans, who ate to repletion twice every day, and were never without a partner for the night; and disapproval of the habits which this manner of life produces. For with these habits formed early in life, no man under heaven could possibly attain to wisdom—human nature is not capable of such an extraordinary combination. Temperance also is out of the question for such a man; and the same applies to virtue generally. No city could remain in a state of tranquillity under any laws whatsoever, when men think it right to squander all their property in extravagant excesses, and consider it a duty to be idle in everything else except eating and drinking and the laborious prosecution of debauchery.

Plato, *Seventh Letter*

7 Temperance and self-indulgence . . . are concerned with the kind of pleasures that the other animals share in, which therefore appear slavish and brutish; these are touch and taste. But even of taste they appear to make little or no use; for the business of taste is the discriminating of flavours, which is done by winetasters and people who season dishes; but they hardly take pleasure in making these discriminations, or at least self-indulgent people do not, but in the actual enjoyment, which in all cases comes through touch, both in the case of food and in that of drink and in that of sexual intercourse. This is why a certain gourmand prayed that his throat might become longer than a crane's, implying that it was the contact that he took pleasure in. Thus the sense with which self-indulgence is connected is the most widely shared of the senses; and self-indulgence would seem to be justly a matter of reproach, because it attaches to us not as men but as animals. To delight in such things, then, and to love them above all others, is brutish.

Aristotle, *Ethics,* 1118ª24

8 The temperate man . . . neither enjoys the things that the self-indulgent man enjoys most—but rather dislikes them—nor in general the things that he should not, nor anything of this sort to excess, nor does he feel pain or craving when they are absent, or does so only to a moderate degree, and not more than he should, nor when he should not, and so on; but the things that, being pleasant, make for health or for good condition, he will desire moderately and as he should, and also other pleasant things if they are not hindrances to these ends, or contrary to what is noble, or beyond his means. For he who neglects these conditions loves such pleasures more than they are worth, but the temperate man is not that sort of person, but the sort of person that the right rule prescribes.

Aristotle, *Ethics,* 1119ª11

9 All our disorders result from intemperance. It is the revolt from all common sense and right reason. It is so completely foreign to reason that such lust of the soul cannot be curbed. Just as temperance allays the cravings and makes them obey reason, thus keeping the mind well balanced; so the enemy, intemperance, utterly disrupts the normal condition of the mind. Hence one is beset with anxiety, fears, and all other disorders.

Cicero, *Disputations,* IV, 9

10 The appetites must be made subject to the control of reason, and not allowed to run ahead of it or to lag behind because of indolence or listlessness. Everyone should enjoy a quiet soul and be free from every type of passion. Then will strength of character and self-control shine through in all their brilliance. But when appetites are unleashed to run wild, either in desire or aversion, and are not reined in by reason, they exceed all restraint and measure. They throw off obedience and leave it behind. They refuse to obey the rule of reason to which they ought to be subject by the law of nature. Both the mind and the body can be well put in disarray by the appetites.

Cicero, *De Officiis,* I, 29

11 There is a mean in things; finally, there are certain boundaries, on either side of which moral rectitude cannot exist.

Horace, *Satires,* I, 1

12 Safer thou'lt sail life's voyage, if thou steer
Neither right out to sea, nor yet, when rise
The threat'ning tempests, hug the shore too near,
    Unwisely wise.

What man soe'er the golden mean doth choose,
Prudent will shun the hovel's foul decay;
But with like sense, a palace will refuse
    And vain display.

Horace, *Odes,* II, 10

13 Drunkenness inflames and lays bare every vice, removing the reserve that acts as a check on impulses to wrong behaviour. For people abstain

from forbidden things far more often through feelings of inhibition when it comes to doing what is wrong than through any will to good.

Seneca, *Letters to Lucilius*, 83

14 To want to know more than is sufficient is a form of intemperance.

Seneca, *Letters to Lucilius*, 88

15 In the constitution of the rational animal I see no virtue which is opposed to justice; but I see a virtue which is opposed to love of pleasure, and that is temperance.

Marcus Aurelius, *Meditations*, VIII, 39

16 I strive daily against greediness in eating and drinking. For this is not the kind of thing I can resolve once and for all to cut off and touch no more, as I could with fornication. For the reins of the throat are to be held somewhere between too lightly and too tightly.

Augustine, *Confessions*, X, 31

17 Nature inclines everything to whatever is becoming to it. Wherefore man naturally desires pleasures that are becoming to him. Since, however, man as such is a rational being, it follows that those pleasures are becoming to man which are in accordance with reason. From such pleasures temperance does not withdraw him, but from those which are contrary to reason. Wherefore it is clear that temperance is not contrary to the inclination of human nature, but is in accord with it.

Aquinas, *Summa Theologica*, II–II, 141, 1

18 Temperance is about desires and pleasures in the same way as fortitude is about fear and daring. Now fortitude is about fear and daring with respect to the greatest evils whereby nature itself is dissolved; and such are dangers of death. Wherefore in like manner temperance must needs be about desires for the greatest pleasures. And since pleasure results from a natural operation, it is so much the greater according as it results from a more natural operation. Now to animals the most natural operations are those which preserve the nature of the individual by means of meat and drink, and the nature of the species by the union of the sexes. Hence temperance is properly about pleasures of meat and drink and sexual pleasures. Now these pleasures result from the sense of touch. Wherefore it follows that temperance is about pleasures of touch.

Aquinas, *Summa Theologica*, II–II, 141, 4

19 Sins of intemperance are said to be childish. For the sin of intemperance is one of unchecked concupiscence, which is likened to a child in three ways. First, as regards that which they both desire, for like a child concupiscence desires something disgraceful. This is because in human affairs a thing is beautiful according as it harmonizes with reason. . . . Now a child does not attend to the order of reason; and in like manner *concupiscence does not listen to reason.* . . . Secondly, they are alike as to the result. For a child, if left to his own will, becomes more self-willed: hence it is written: *A horse not broken becometh stubborn, and a child left to himself will become headstrong.* So, too, concupiscence, if indulged, gathers strength: wherefore Augustine says: *Lust served became a custom, and custom not resisted became necessity.* Thirdly, as to the remedy which is applied to both. For a child is corrected by being restrained; hence it is written: *Withhold not correction from a child . . . Thou shalt beat him with a rod, and deliver his soul from Hell.* In like manner by resisting concupiscence we moderate it according to the demands of virtue. Augustine indicates this when he says that if the mind be lifted up to spiritual things, and remain fixed *thereon, the impulse of custom,* i.e. carnal concupiscence, *is broken, and being suppressed is gradually weakened: for it was stronger when we followed it, and though not wholly destroyed, it is certainly less strong when we curb it.* Hence the Philosopher [Aristotle] says that *as a child ought to live according to the direction of his tutor, so ought the concupiscible to accord with reason.*

Aquinas, *Summa Theologica*, II–II, 142, 2

20 I discern new torments, and new tormented *souls,* whithersoever I move, and turn, and gaze.

I am in the Third Circle, *that* of the eternal, accursed, cold, and heavy rain; its [law] and quality is never new.

Large hail, and turbid water, and snow, [pour down] through the darksome air; the ground, on which it falls, emits a putrid smell.

Cerberus, a monster fierce and strange, with three throats, barks dog-like over those that are immersed in it.

His eyes are red, his beard [greasy] and black, his belly wide, and clawed his hands; he clutches the spirits, flays, and piecemeal rends them.

The rain makes them howl like dogs; with one side they screen the other; they often turn themselves, the impious wretches.

When Cerberus, the great Worm, perceived us, he opened his mouths and shewed his tusks: no limb of him kept still.

My Guide, spreading his palms, took up earth; and, with full fists, cast it into his ravening gullets.

As the dog, that barking craves, and grows quiet when he bites his food, for he strains and battles only to devour it:

so did those squalid visages of Cerberus the Demon, who thunders on the spirits so, that they would fain be deaf.

We passed over the shadows whom the heavy rain subdues; and placed our soles upon their emptiness, which seems a body.

They all were lying on the ground save one, who

sat up forthwith when he saw us pass before him.

"O thou, who through this Hell art led," he said to me, "recognise me if thou mayest; thou wast made before I was unmade."

And I to him: "The anguish which thou hast, perhaps withdraws thee from my memory, so that it seems not as if I ever saw thee.

But tell me who art thou, that art put in such a doleful place, and in such punishment; that, though other may be greater, none is so displeasing."

And he to me: "Thy city, which is so full of envy that the sack already overflows, contained me in the clear life.

You, citizens, called me Ciacco: for the baneful crime of Gluttony, as thou seest, I languish in the rain;

and I, wretched spirit, am not alone, since all these for like crime are in like punishment"; and more he said not.

Dante, *Inferno,* VI, 4

21 O gluttony, full of all wickedness,
O first cause of confusion to us all,
Beginning of damnation and our fall,
Till Christ redeemed us with His blood again!
Behold how dearly, to be brief and plain,
Was purchased this accursed villainy;
Corrupt was all this world with gluttony!
    Adam our father, and his wife also,
From Paradise to labour and to woe
Were driven for that vice, no doubt; indeed
The while that Adam fasted, as I read,
He was in Paradise; but then when he
Ate of the fruit forbidden of the tree,
Anon he was cast out to woe and pain
O gluttony, of you we may complain!

Chaucer, *Canterbury Tales:* Pardoner's Tale

22 Drink until misfortune overtakes you! People like you won't reach old age, for the best part of mankind perishes from too much drink.

Luther, *Table Talk,* 3468

23 *Grangousier and his neighbors.* Which was first, thirst or drinking? Thirst, for who in the time of innocence would have drunk without being athirst? Nay, sir, it was drinking; for *privatio praesupponit habitum.* I am learned, you see: *Foecundi calices quem non fecere disertum?* We poor innocents drink but too much without thirst. Not I truly, who am a sinner, for I never drink without thirst, either present or future. To prevent it, as you know, I drink for the thirst to come. I drink eternally. This is to me an eternity of drinking, and drinking of eternity. Let us sing, let us drink, and tune up our roundlays. Where is my funnel? What, it seems I do not drink but by an attorney? Do you wet yourselves to dry, or do you dry to wet you? Pish, I understand not the rhetoric (theoric I should say), but I

help myself somewhat by the practice. Beast, enough! I sup, I wet, I humect, I moisten my gullet, I drink, and all for fear of dying. Drink always and you shall never die. If I drink not, I am a ground dry, gravelled and spent. I am stark dead without drink, and my soul ready to fly into some marsh amongst frogs: the soul never dwells in a dry place, drought kills it. O you butlers, creators of new forms, make me of no drinker a drinker, perenity and everlastingness of sprinkling, and bedewing me through these my parched and sinewy bowels. He drinks in vain, that feels not the pleasure of it.

Rabelais, *Gargantua and Pantagruel,* I, 5

24 *Grangousier.* I have a remedy against thirst, quite contrary to that which is good against the biting of a mad dog. Keep running after a dog, and he will never bite you; drink always before the thirst, and it will never come upon you.

Rabelais, *Gargantua and Pantagruel,* I, 5

25 Is it still temperance and frugality to avoid expenses and pleasures whose use and knowledge are imperceptible to us? An easy way to reform and a cheap one!

Montaigne, *Essays,* I, 3, Our Feelings Reach Out

26 Virtue's tool is moderation, not strength.

Montaigne, *Essays,* I, 26, Education of Children

27 Enough for the sage to curb and moderate his inclinations; for to do away with them is not in him.

Montaigne, *Essays,* II, 2, Of Drunkenness

28 It is perhaps easier to do without the whole sex than to behave rightly in every respect in association with our wives; and a man may live more carefree in poverty than in justly dispensed abundance. Enjoyment conducted according to reason is more arduous than abstinence. Moderation is a virtue that gives more trouble than suffering does.

Montaigne, *Essays,* II, 33, The Story of Spurina

29 *Salisbury.* To guard a title that was rich before,
To gild refined gold, to paint the lily,
To throw a perfume on the violet,
To smooth the ice, or add another hue
Unto the rainbow, or with taper-light
To seek the beauteous eye of heaven to garnish,
Is wasteful and ridiculous excess.

Shakespeare, *King John,* IV, ii, 10

30 *Nerissa.* They are as sick that surfeit with too much as they that starve with nothing. It is no mean happiness therefore, to be seated in the mean: superfluity comes sooner by white hairs,

but competency lives longer.

Shakespeare, *Merchant of Venice*, I, ii, 5

31 *Falstaff.* Now, Hal, what time of day is it, lad?

Prince of Wales. Thou art so fat-witted, with drinking of old sack and unbuttoning thee after supper and sleeping upon benches after noon, that thou hast forgotten to demand that truly which thou wouldst truly know. What a devil hast thou to do with the time of the day? Unless hours were cups of sack and minutes capons and clocks the tongues of bawds and dials the signs of leaping-houses and the blessed sun himself a fair hot wench in flame-coloured taffeta, I see no reason why thou shouldst be so superfluous to demand the time of the day.

Shakespeare, *I Henry IV*, I, ii, 1

32 *Worcestor.* Hear you, cousin; a word.

Hotspur. All studies here I solemnly defy,
Save how to gall and pinch this Bolingbroke:
And that same sword-and-buckler Prince of
Wales,
But that I think his father loves him not
And would be glad he met with some mischance,
I would have him poison'd with a pot of ale.

Wor. Farewell, kinsman: I'll talk to you
When you are better temper'd to attend.

Northumberland. Why, what a wasp-stung and
impatient fool
Art thou to break into this woman's mood,
Tying thine ear to no tongue but thine own!

Hot. Why, look you, I am whipp'd and scourged
with rods,
Nettled and stung with pismires, when I hear
Of this vile politician, Bolingbroke.
In Richard's time—what do you call the place?—
A plague upon it, it is in Gloucestershire;
'Twas where the madcap duke his uncle kept,
His uncle York; where I first bow'd my knee
Unto this king of smiles, this Bolingbroke—
'Sblood!—
When you and he came back from Ravenspurgh.

North. At Berkley castle.

Hot. You say true:
Why, what a candy deal of courtesy
This fawning greyhound then did proffer me!
Look, "When his infant fortune came to age,"
And "gentle Harry Percy," and "kind cousin";
O, the devil take such cozeners! God forgive me!
Good uncle, tell your tale; I have done.

Wor. Nay, if you have not, to it again;
We will stay your leisure.

Hot.   I have done, i' faith.

Shakespeare, *I Henry IV*, I, iii, 227

33 *Rosalind.* Why then, can one desire too much of a good thing?

Shakespeare, *As You Like It*, IV, i, 123

34 *Lucio.* Why, how now, Claudio! whence comes this restraint?

Claudio. From too much liberty, my Lucio,
liberty.
As surfeit is the father of much fast,
So every scope by the immoderate use
Turns to restraint. Our natures do pursue,
Like rats that ravin down their proper bane,
A thirsty evil; and when we drink we die.

Shakespeare, *Measure for Measure*, I, ii, 128

35 *Cassio.* I remember a mass of things, but nothing distinctly; a quarrel, but nothing wherefore. O God, that men should put an enemy in their mouths to steal away their brains! that we should, with joy, pleasance, revel, and applause, transform ourselves into beasts!

Shakespeare, *Othello*, II, iii, 289

36 *Iago.* Come, come, good wine is a good familiar creature, if it be well used; exclaim no more against it.

Shakespeare, *Othello*, II, iii, 312

37 *Porter.* Drink, sir, is a great provoker of three things.

Macduff. What three things does drink especially provoke?

Port. Marry, sir, nose-painting, sleep, and urine. Lechery, sir, it provokes, and unprovokes; it provokes the desire but it takes away the performance; therefore, much drink may be said to be an equivocator with lechery: it makes him, and it mars him; it sets him on, and it takes him off; it persuades him, and disheartens him; makes him stand to, and not stand to; in conclusion, equivocates him in a sleep, and, giving him the lie, leaves him.

Shakespeare, *Macbeth*, II, iii, 29

38 *Macduff.*   Boundless intemperance
In nature is a tyranny; it hath been
The untimely emptying of the happy throne
And fall of many kings.

Shakespeare, *Macbeth*, IV, iii, 67

39 There is, said *Michael*, if thou well observe
The rule of not too much, by temperance taught
In what thou eatst and drinkst, seeking from
thence
Due nourishment, not gluttonous delight.

Milton, *Paradise Lost*, XI, 527

40 Blessedness is not the reward of virtue, but is virtue itself; nor do we delight in blessedness because we restrain our lusts; but, on the contrary, because we delight in it, therefore are we able to restrain them.

Spinoza, *Ethics*, V, Prop. 42

41 To say truth, nothing is more erroneous than the common observation, that men who are ill-natured and quarrelsome when they are drunk, are

very worthy persons when they are sober: for drink, in reality, doth not reverse nature, or create passions in men which did not exist in them before. It takes away the guard of reason, and consequently forces us to produce those symptoms, which many, when sober, have art enough to conceal. It heightens and inflames our passions (generally indeed that passion which is uppermost in our mind), so that the angry temper, the amorous, the generous, the good-humoured, the avaricious, and all other dispositions of men, are in their cups heightened and exposed.

Fielding, *Tom Jones,* V, 9

42 *Johnson.* To temperance, every day is bright; and every hour is propitious to diligence.

Boswell, *Life of Johnson (1758)*

43 Moderation in the affections and passions, self-control, and calm deliberation are not only good in many respects, but even seem to constitute part of the intrinsic worth of the person; but they are far from deserving to be called good without qualification, although they have been so unconditionally praised by the ancients. For without the principles of a good will, they may become extremely bad, and the coolness of a villain not only makes him far more dangerous, but also directly makes him more abominable in our eyes than he would have been without it.

Kant, *Fundamental Principles of the Metaphysic of Morals,* I

44 The road of excess leads to the palace of wisdom.

Blake, *Marriage of Heaven and Hell,* 7

45 *Faust.* Fear not! This league with you I shall not break!
The aim and goal of all my energy
Is to fulfil the promise I now make.
I've puffed myself too high, I see;
Only within your ranks do I deserve to be.
The Mighty Spirit spurned me with a scoff,
And Nature turns herself away from me.
The thread of thought is broken off,
To me all learning's long been nauseous.
In depths of sensuality
Let us our glowing passions still!
In magic's veils impervious
Prepared at once be every marvel's thrill!
Come, let us plunge into Time's rushing dance,
Into the roll of Circumstance!
There may then pain and joyance,
Successes and annoyance,

Alternately follow as they can,
Only restlessly active is a man!

Goethe, *Faust,* I, 1741

46 Every excess causes a defect; every defect an excess. Every sweet hath its sour; every evil its good. Every faculty which is a receiver of pleasure has an equal penalty put on its abuse. It is to answer for its moderation with its life.

Emerson, *Compensation*

47 He who distinguishes the true savor of his food can never be a glutton; he who does not cannot be otherwise. A puritan may go to his brown-bread crust with as gross an appetite as ever an alderman to his turtle.

Thoreau, *Walden:* Higher Laws

48 All sensuality is one, though it takes many forms; all purity is one. It is the same whether a man eat, or drink, or cohabit, or sleep sensually. They are but one appetite, and we only need to see a person do any one of these things to know how great a sensualist he is. The impure can neither stand nor sit with purity. When the reptile is attacked at one mouth of his burrow, he shows himself at another. If you would be chaste, you must be temperate. What is chastity? How shall a man know if he is chaste? He shall not know it. We have heard of this virtue, but we know not what it is. We speak conformably to the rumor which we have heard. From exertion come wisdom and purity; from sloth ignorance and sensuality. In the student sensuality is a sluggish habit of mind. An unclean person is universally a slothful one, one who sits by a stove, whom the sun shines on prostrate, who reposes without being fatigued. If you would avoid uncleanness, and all the sins, work earnestly, though it be at cleaning a stable.

Thoreau, *Walden:* Higher Laws

49 A person who shows rashness, obstinacy, self-conceit—who cannot live within moderate means—who cannot restrain himself from hurtful indulgences—who pursues animal pleasures at the expense of those of feeling and intellect—must expect to be lowered in the opinion of others, and to have a less share of their favourable sentiments; but of this he has no right to complain, unless he has merited their favour by special excellence in his social relations, and has thus established a title to their good offices, which is not affected by his demerits towards himself.

Mill, *On Liberty,* IV

9.13 | *Prudence*

Whereas courage and temperance, as virtues, are traits of character, the virtue of prudence is a quality of mind. That is why it is sometimes called an "intellectual virtue," along with science, art, and wisdom. But it also differs from these other intellectual virtues in that it is not concerned with knowledge, or understanding, or even with know-how or skill in making things, but with action. Another name for prudence, the reader will find in the quotations below, is "practical wisdom"—wisdom in the choice of means to achieve the goals of life. Hence of all the intellectual virtues, prudence or practical wisdom is the one most integrally related to the moral virtues of courage, temperance, and justice. The reader will find the treatment of speculative or philosophical wisdom in Section 9.15 on WISDOM AND FOLLY.

As certain quotations below expressly indicate, the crucial question is whether it is possible to be wise (i.e., practically wise or prudent) without being good (i.e., morally virtuous), or good without being wise. If the answer to that question affirms the inseparability of prudence and moral virtue, then, as another quotation points out, cleverness in the choice of means to achieve morally reprehensible ends—for example, the cunning of the thief—is not genuine prudence, but a counterfeit of it.

The prudent man, we are told, is one who has the habitual disposition to take counsel or advice and then to weigh the advantages and disadvantages in a process of deliberation before coming to a decision about what ought to be done in the particular case under consideration. The prudent man is a man of sound judgment, not about things in general, nor about the principles or rules of morality, but about the circumstances of particular cases in which decisions have to be made for or against particular courses of action. Lack of prudence manifests itself in the making of rash or impetuous decisions, on the one hand, or in prolonged indecision, on the other.

---

1 Themistocles was a man who exhibited the most indubitable signs of genius; indeed, in this particular he has a claim on our admiration quite extraordinary and unparalleled. By his own native capacity, alike unformed and unsupplemented by study, he was at once the best judge in those sudden crises which admit of little or of no deliberation, and the best prophet of the future, even to its most distant possibilities. An able theoretical expositor of all that came within the sphere of his practice, he was not without the power of passing an adequate judgment in matters in which he had no experience. He could also excellently divine the good and evil which lay hid in the unseen future. In fine, whether we consider the extent of his natural powers, or the slightness of his application, this extraordinary man must be allowed to have surpassed all others in the faculty of intuitively meeting an emergency.

Thucydides, *Peloponnesian War*, I, 138

2 *Socrates.* Let us consider the goods of the soul: they are temperance, justice, courage, quickness of apprehension, memory, magnanimity, and the like?

Meno. Surely.

Soc. And such of these as are not knowledge, but of another sort, are sometimes profitable and sometimes hurtful; as, for example, courage wanting prudence, which is only a sort of confidence? When a man has no sense he is harmed by courage, but when he has sense he is profited?

Men. True.

Soc. And the same may be said of temperance and quickness of apprehension; whatever things are learned or done with sense are profitable, but when done without sense they are hurtful?

Men. Very true.

Soc. And in general, all that the soul attempts or endures, when under the guidance of wisdom, ends in happiness; but when she is under the guidance of folly, in the opposite?

Men. That appears to be true.

Soc. If then virtue is a quality of the soul, and is admitted to be profitable, it must be wisdom or prudence, since none of the things of the soul are either profitable or hurtful in themselves, but they are all made profitable or hurtful by the addition of wisdom or of folly; and therefore if virtue is profitable, virtue must be a sort of wisdom or prudence?

Men. I quite agree.

Soc. And the other goods, such as wealth and the like, of which we were just now saying that they are sometimes good and sometimes evil, do not they also become profitable or hurtful, accordingly as the soul guides and uses them rightly or wrongly; just as the things of the soul herself are benefited when under the guidance of wisdom and harmed by folly?

Men. True.

Soc. And the wise soul guides them rightly, and the foolish soul wrongly.

Men. Yes.

Soc. And is not this universally true of human nature? All other things hang upon the soul, and the things of the soul herself hang upon wisdom, if they are to be good; and so wisdom is inferred to be that which profits—and virtue, as we say, is profitable?

Men. Certainly.

Soc. And thus we arrive at the conclusion that virtue is either wholly or partly wisdom?

Men. I think that what you are saying, Socrates, is very true.

Plato, *Meno,* 88A

3 Regarding *practical wisdom* we shall get at the truth by considering who are the persons we credit with it. Now it is thought to be the mark of a man of practical wisdom to be able to deliberate well about what is good and expedient for himself, not in some particular respect . . . but about what sorts of thing conduce to the good life in general. This is shown by the fact that we credit men with practical wisdom in some particular respect when they have calculated well with a view to some good end which is one of those that are not the object of any art. It follows that in the general sense also the man who is capable of deliberating has practical wisdom. Now no one deliberates about things that are invariable, nor about things that it is impossible for him to do. Therefore, since scientific knowledge involves demonstration, but there is no demonstration of things whose first principles are variable (for all such things might actually be otherwise), and since it is impossible to deliberate about things that are of necessity, prac-

tical wisdom cannot be scientific knowledge nor art; not science because that which can be done is capable of being otherwise, not art because action and making are different kinds of thing. The remaining alternative, then, is that it is a true and reasoned state of capacity to act with regard to the things that are good or bad for man. For while making has an end other than itself, action cannot; for good action itself is its end. It is for this reason that we think Pericles and men like him have practical wisdom, viz. because they can see what is good for themselves and what is good for men in general; we consider that those can do this who are good at managing households or states. (This is why we call temperance by this name; we imply that it preserves one's practical wisdom. Now what it preserves is a judgement of the kind we have described. For it is not any and every judgment that pleasant and painful objects destroy and pervert, e.g. the judgement that the triangle has or has not its angles equal to two right angles, but only judgements about what is to be done. For the originating causes of the things that are done consist in the end at which they are aimed; but the man who has been ruined by pleasure or pain forthwith fails to see any such originating cause—to see that for the sake of this or because of this he ought to choose and do whatever he chooses and does; for vice is destructive of the originating cause of action.) Practical wisdom, then, must be a reasoned and true state of capacity to act with regard to human goods. But further, while there is such a thing as excellence in art, there is no such thing as excellence in practical wisdom; and in art he who errs willingly is preferable, but in practical wisdom, as in the virtues, he is the reverse. Plainly, then, practical wisdom is a virtue and not an art. There being two parts of the soul that can follow a course of reasoning, it must be the virtue of one of the two, i.e. of that part which forms opinions; for opinion is about the variable and so is practical wisdom. But yet it is not only a reasoned state; this is shown by the fact that a state of that sort may be forgotten but practical wisdom cannot.

Aristotle, *Ethics,* 1140ᵃ24

4 Practical wisdom . . . is concerned with things human and things about which it is possible to deliberate; for we say this is above all the work of the man of practical wisdom, to deliberate well, but no one deliberates about things invariable, nor about things which have not an end, and that a good that can be brought about by action. The man who is without qualification good at deliberating is the man who is capable of aiming in accordance with calculation at the best for man of things attainable by action. Nor is practical wisdom concerned with universals only—it must also recognize the particulars; for it is practical, and practice is concerned with particulars. This is why

some who do not know, and especially those who have experience, are more practical than others who know.

Aristotle, *Ethics,* 1141ᵇ7

5 Understanding, also, and goodness of understanding, in virtue of which men are said to be men of understanding or of good understanding, are neither entirely the same as opinion or scientific knowledge (for at that rate all men would have been men of understanding), nor are they one of the particular sciences, such as medicine, the science of things connected with health, or geometry, the science of spatial magnitudes. For understanding is neither about things that are always and are unchangeable, nor about any and every one of the things that come into being, but about things which may become subjects of questioning and deliberation. Hence it is about the same objects as practical wisdom; but understanding and practical wisdom are not the same. For practical wisdom issues commands, since its end is what ought to be done or not to be done; but understanding only judges. (Understanding is identical with goodness of understanding, men of understanding with men of good understanding.) Now understanding is neither the having nor the acquiring of practical wisdom; but as learning is called understanding when it means the exercise of the faculty of knowledge, so 'understanding' is applicable to the exercise of the faculty of opinion for the purpose of judging of what some one else says about matters with which practical wisdom is concerned—and of judging soundly; for 'well' and 'soundly' are the same thing. And from this has come the use of the name 'understanding' in virtue of which men are said to be 'of good understanding', viz. from the application of the word to the grasping of scientific truth; for we often call such grasping understanding.

What is called judgement, in virtue of which men are said to 'be sympathetic judges' and to 'have judgement', is the right discrimination of the equitable. This is shown by the fact that we say the equitable man is above all others a man of sympathetic judgement, and identify equity with sympathetic judgement about certain facts. And sympathetic judgement is judgement which discriminates what is equitable and does so correctly; and correct judgement is that which judges what is true.

Now all the states we have considered converge, as might be expected, to the same point; for when we speak of judgement and understanding and practical wisdom and intuitive reason we credit the same people with possessing judgement and having reached years of reason and with having practical wisdom and understanding. For all these faculties deal with ultimates, i.e. with particulars; and being a man of understanding and of good or sympathetic judgement consists in being able to judge about the things with which practical wisdom is concerned; for the equities are common to all good men in relation to other men.

Aristotle, *Ethics,* 1142ᵇ34

6 As in the part of us which forms opinions there are two types, cleverness and practical wisdom, so too in the moral part there are two types, natural virtue and virtue in the strict sense, and of these the latter involves practical wisdom. This is why some say that all the virtues are forms of practical wisdom, and why Socrates in one respect was on the right track while in another he went astray; in thinking that all the virtues were forms of practical wisdom he was wrong, but in saying they implied practical wisdom he was right. This is confirmed by the fact that even now all men, when they define virtue, after naming the state of character and its objects add 'that (state) which is in accordance with the right rule'; now the right rule is that which is in accordance with practical wisdom. All men, then, seem somehow to divine that this kind of state is virtue, viz. that which is in accordance with practical wisdom. But we must go a little further. For it is not merely the state in accordance with the right rule, but the state that implies the *presence* of the right rule, that is virtue; and practical wisdom is a right rule about such matters. Socrates, then, thought the virtues were rules or rational principles (for he thought they were, all of them, forms of scientific knowledge), while we think they *involve* a rational principle.

It is clear, then, from what has been said, that it is not possible to be good in the strict sense without practical wisdom, nor practically wise without moral virtue. But in this way we may also refute the dialectical argument whereby it might be contended that the virtues exist in separation from each other; the same man, it might be said, is not best equipped by nature for all the virtues, so that he will have already acquired one when he has not yet acquired another. This is possible in respect of the natural virtues, but not in respect of those in respect of which a man is called without qualification good; for with the presence of the one quality, practical wisdom, will be given all the virtues. And it is plain that, even if it were of no practical value, we should have needed it because it is the virtue of the part of us in question; plain too that the choice will not be right without practical wisdom any more than without virtue; for the one determines the end and the other makes us do the things that lead to the end.

Aristotle, *Ethics,* 1144ᵇ14

7 The beginning and the greatest good is prudence. Wherefore prudence is a more precious thing even than philosophy; for from prudence are sprung all the other virtues, and it teaches us that it is not possible to live pleasantly without living prudently and honourably and justly, nor, again, to live a

life of prudence, honour, and justice without living pleasantly. For the virtues are by nature
bound up with the pleasant life, and the pleasant
life is inseparable from them.

Epicurus, *Letter to Menoeceus*

8 Then the father [Phoebus] rubbed his son's [Phae-
thon's] face with a divine ointment, to enable him
to endure the searing flames. On his head he
placed his own rays, and, sighing deeply from his
troubled heart—for he foresaw the grief that was
in store for him—he said: 'At least obey your
father's instructions, my son, if you can. Use the
goad sparingly, and hold in the reins with all your
strength. The horses set a fast pace of their own
accord: the difficulty is to check their keenness.
And do not try to drive straight across the five
zones of heaven—there is a track that slants in a
broad curve, confined within the boundaries of
three zones, which avoids the Southern Pole, and
also the North with its chilling winds. Travel by
this road, where you will see clear marks of
wheels. To allow earth and heaven to share equally in your warmth, do not go too low, nor yet force
your way into the upper air: if you drive too high,
you will set the dome of heaven on fire, and if you
are too low you will scorch the earth. The middle
way is safest. Nor must you swerve to the right,
towards the coiling Serpent, nor to the left, where
the low-lying Altar shines. Hold your course between them both.'

Ovid, *Metamorphoses*, II

9 What shall I say of that virtue which is called
prudence? Is not all its vigilance spent in the discernment of good from evil things, so that no mistake may be admitted about what we should desire and what avoid? And thus it is itself a proof
that we are in the midst of evils, or that evils are
in us; for it teaches us that it is an evil to consent
to sin, and a good to refuse this consent.

Augustine, *City of God*, XIX, 4

10 It is requisite for prudence, which is right reason
about things to be done, that man be well disposed with regard to the ends, and this depends
on the rectitude of his appetite. Therefore, for
prudence there is need of a moral virtue, which
rectifies the appetite. On the other hand, the good
of things made by art is not the good of man's
appetite, but the good of those artificial things
themselves, and therefore art does not presuppose
rectitude of the appetite. The consequence is that
more praise is given to a craftsman who is at fault
willingly, than to one who is unwillingly; but it is
more contrary to prudence to sin willingly than
unwillingly, since rectitude of the will is essential
to prudence, but not to art. Accordingly it is evident that prudence is a virtue distinct from art.

Aquinas, *Summa Theologica*, I–II, 57, 4

11 Prudence is of good counsel about matters regarding man's entire life, and the end of human life.
But in some arts there is counsel about matters
concerning the ends proper to those arts. Hence
some men, in so far as they are good counsellors in
matters of warfare, or government, are said to be
prudent officers or rulers, but not prudent absolutely; only those are prudent absolutely who give
good counsel about all the concerns of life.

Aquinas, *Summa Theologica*, I–II, 57, 4

12 Prudence is the principal of all the virtues absolutely.

Aquinas, *Summa Theologica*, I–II, 61, 2

13 No moral virtue can be without prudence, for the
reason that it is proper to moral virtue to make a
right choice, since it is an elective habit. Now
right choice requires not only the inclination to a
due end, which inclination is the direct outcome
of moral virtue, but also the right choice of means,
which choice is made by prudence, that counsels,
judges, and commands in those things that are
directed to the end. In like manner one cannot
have prudence unless one has the moral virtues,
since prudence is right reason about things to be
done, and the starting-point of reason is the end of
the thing to be done, to which end man is rightly
disposed by moral virtue. Hence, just as we cannot have speculative science unless we have the
understanding of the principles, so neither can we
have prudence without the moral virtues.

Aquinas, *Summa Theologica*, I–II, 65, 1

14 Prudence has no business with supreme matters
which are the object of wisdom, but its command
covers things ordered to wisdom, namely, how
men are to obtain wisdom. Therefore prudence,
or political science, is, in this way, the servant of
wisdom, for it leads to wisdom, preparing the way
for her, as the porter for the king.

Aquinas, *Summa Theologica*, I–II, 66, 5

15 Prudence considers the means of acquiring happiness, but wisdom considers the very object of happiness.

Aquinas, *Summa Theologica*, I–II, 66, 5

16 Prudence is threefold. There is a false prudence,
which takes its name from its likeness to true prudence. For since a prudent man is one who disposes well of the things that have to be done for a
good end, whoever disposes well of such things as
are fitting for an evil end, has false prudence, in so
far as that which he takes for an end, is good, not
in truth but in appearance. Thus a man is called
a good robber, and in this way we may speak of *a
prudent robber*, by way of similarity, because he devises fitting ways of committing robbery. This is
the prudence of which the Apostle says: *The prudence of the flesh is death*, because, to wit, it places its
ultimate end in the pleasures of the flesh.

The second prudence is indeed true prudence,

because it devises fitting ways of obtaining a good end; and yet it is imperfect, from a twofold source. First, because the good which it takes for an end, is not the common end of all human life, but of some particular affair; thus when a man devises fitting ways of conducting business or of sailing a ship, he is called a prudent business-man, or a prudent sailor:—secondly, because he fails in the chief act of prudence, as when a man takes counsel aright, and forms a good judgment, even about things concerning life as a whole, but fails to make an effective command.

The third prudence is both true and perfect, for it takes counsel, judges and commands aright in respect of the good end of man's whole life: and this alone is prudence simply so-called, and cannot be in sinners, whereas the first prudence is in sinners alone, while imperfect prudence is common to good and wicked men, especially that which is imperfect through being directed to a particular end, since that which is imperfect on account of a failing in the chief act, is only in the wicked.

Aquinas, *Summa Theologica,* II–II, 47, 13

17 For any man who hath a house to found,
Runs not at once the labor to begin
With reckless hand, but first will look around,
And send his heart's line outward from within,
To see how best of all his end to win.

Chaucer, *Troilus and Cressida,* I, 153

18 The virtue assigned to the affairs of the world is a virtue with many bends, angles, and elbows, so as to join and adapt itself to human weakness; mixed and artificial, not straight, clean, constant, or purely innocent. . . . He who walks in the crowd must step aside, keep his elbows in, step back or advance, even leave the straight way, according to what he encounters. He must live not so much according to himself as according to others, not according to what he proposes to himself but according to what others propose to him, according to the time, according to the men, according to the business.

Montaigne, *Essays,* III, 9, Of Vanity

19 *Fool.* Mark it, nuncle:
"Have more than thou showest,
Speak less than thou knowest,
Lend less than thou owest,
Ride more than thou goest,
Learn more than thou trowest,
Set less than thou throwest,
Leave thy drink and thy whore,
And keep in-a-door,
And thou shalt have more
Than two tens to a score."
Kent. This is nothing, fool.

Shakespeare, *Lear,* I, iv, 130

20 *Apemantus.* Immortal gods, I crave no pelf;
I pray for no man but myself.
Grant I may never prove so fond,
To trust man on his oath or bond;
Or a harlot, for her weeping;
Or a dog, that seems a-sleeping;
Or a keeper with my freedom;
Or my friends, if I should need 'em.
Amen.

Shakespeare, *Timon of Athens,* I, ii, 63

21 There is no great concurrence between learning and wisdom. For of the three wisdoms which we have set down to pertain to civil life, for wisdom of behaviour, it is by learned men for the most part despised, as an inferior to virtue and an enemy to meditation; for wisdom of government, they acquit themselves well when they are called to it, but that happeneth to few; but for the wisdom of business, wherein man's life is most conversant, there be no books of it, except some few scattered advertisements, that have no proportion to the magnitude of this subject. For if books were written of this as the other, I doubt not but learned men with mean experience, would far excel men of long experience without learning, and outshoot them in their own bow.

Bacon, *Advancement of Learning,*
Bk. II, XXIII, 4

22 Prudence is a *presumption* of the future, contracted from the experience of time past: so there is a presumption of things past taken from other things, not future, but past also. For he that hath seen by what courses and degrees a flourishing state hath first come into civil war, and then to ruin; upon the sight of the ruins of any other state will guess the like war and the like courses have been there also. But this conjecture has the same uncertainty almost with the conjecture of the future, both being grounded only upon experience.

Hobbes, *Leviathan,* I, 3

23 When the thoughts of a man that has a design in hand, running over a multitude of things, observes how they conduce to that design, or what design they may conduce unto; if his observations be such as are not easy, or usual, this wit of his is called *prudence,* and dependeth on much experience, and memory of the like things and their consequences heretofore.

Hobbes, *Leviathan,* I, 8

24 A man that doth his business by the help of many and prudent counsellors, with every one consulting apart in his proper element, does it best; as he that useth able seconds at tennis play, placed in their proper stations. He does next best that useth his own judgement only; as he that has no second at all. But he that is carried up and down to his business in a framed counsel, which cannot move

but by the plurality of consenting opinions, the execution whereof is commonly, out of envy or interest, retarded by the part dissenting, does it worst of all, and like one that is carried to the ball, though by good players, yet in a wheelbarrow, or other frame, heavy of itself, and retarded also by the inconcurrent judgements and endeavours of them that drive it; and so much the more, as they be more that set their hands to it; and most of all, when there is one or more amongst them that desire to have him lose. And though it be true that many eyes see more than one, yet it is not to be understood of many counsellors, but then only when the final resolution is in one man.

Hobbes, *Leviathan*, II, 25

25 Nothing more unqualifies a Man to act with Prudence, than a Misfortune that is attended with Shame and Guilt.

Swift, *Thoughts on Various Subjects*

26 Prudence and circumspection are necessary even to the best of men. They are indeed, as it were, a guard to Virtue, without which she can never be safe. It is not enough that your designs, nay, that your actions, are intrinsically good; you must take care they shall appear so. If your inside be never so beautiful, you must preserve a fair outside also.

Fielding, *Tom Jones*, III, 7

27 Where prudence is made too much of, not enough is made of fortune; opportunity is let slip, and deliberation results in the loss of its object.

Rousseau, *Social Contract*, III, 2

28 Prudence! Prudence which is ever bidding us look forward into the future, a future which in many cases we shall never reach; here is the real source of all our troubles! How mad it is for so short-lived a creature as man to look forward into a future to which he rarely attains, while he neglects the present which is his? this madness is all the more

fatal since it increases with years, and the old, always timid, prudent, and miserly, prefer to do without necessaries to-day that they may have luxuries at a hundred.

Rousseau, *Emile*, II

29 If we could always be prudent, we should rarely need to be virtuous.

Rousseau, *Confessions*, II

30 The principle of *private happiness* . . . is . . . most objectionable, not merely because it is false, and experience contradicts the supposition that prosperity is always proportioned to good conduct, nor yet merely because it contributes nothing to the establishment of morality—since it is quite a different thing to make a prosperous man and a good man, or to make one prudent and sharp-sighted for his own interests and to make him virtuous—but because the springs it provides for morality are such as rather undermine it and destroy its sublimity, since they put the motives to virtue and to vice in the same class and only teach us to make a better calculation, the specific difference between virtue and vice being entirely extinguished.

Kant, *Fundamental Principles of the Metaphysic of Morals*, II

31 Prudence reproaches; conscience accuses. If a man has acted unwisely and reproaches himself for his imprudence no longer than is necessary for him to learn his lesson, he is observing a rule of prudence and it must be accounted to him for honour, for it is a sign of strength of character. But the accusation of conscience cannot be so readily dismissed, neither should it be.

Kant, *Lectures on Ethics*, Conscience

32 Prudence is a rich, ugly old maid courted by Incapacity.

Blake, *Marriage of Heaven and Hell*, 7

9.14 | *Honesty*

A wide diversity of moral traits are treated here under the heading of honesty. As the quotations indicate, the word has been applied to truthfulness of statement, to fairness in dealing with others, to keeping one's promises, to trustworthiness, to repaying one's debts, and to a general rectitude of intention and action. Such things as lying, deceiving, cheating, bearing false witness, stealing, and defrauding are—obviously—instances of dishonesty.

It would appear, at first glance, as if "honesty" were another name for justice, since the examples given above of honest and dishonest actions are also examples of just and unjust conduct. However, there are some unjust actions—for example, murdering another man or enslaving him—that would not be called dishonest. Honesty seems to be confined to that area of conduct in which truthfulness or fairness in dealing with others is called for as a matter of justice. For the treatment of justice as a moral virtue, the reader is referred to Section 9.7 on RIGHT AND WRONG. The reader will also find some quotations concerned with truthfulness and lying in Section 6.3 on TRUTH.

All of us know and most of us repeat the oft-quoted maxim "Honesty is the best policy," thinking it to be morally sound. But, according to Kant, it is the maxim of a dishonest man—one who refrains from dishonesty only because it is expedient, not because it is just to do so. The maxim about honesty, Kant suggests, should be "Honesty is better than all policy."

---

1 Thou shalt not raise a false report: put not thine hand with the wicked to be an unrighteous witness.

Exodus 23:1

2 Keep thee far from a false matter; and the innocent and righteous slay thou not: for I will not justify the wicked.

Exodus 23:7

3 If a soul sin, and commit a trespass against the Lord, and lie unto his neighbour in that which was delivered him to keep, or in fellowship, or in a think taken away by violence, or hath deceived his neighbour;

Or have found that which was lost, and lieth concerning it, and sweareth falsely; in any of all these that a man doeth, sinning therein:

Then it shall be, because he hath sinned, and is guilty, that he shall restore that which he took violently away, or the thing which he hath deceitfully gotten, or that which was delivered him to keep, or the lost thing which he found,

Or all that about which he hath sworn falsely; he shall even restore it in the principal, and shall add the fifth part more thereto, and give it unto him to whom it appertaineth, in the day of his trespass offering.

And he shall bring his trespass offering unto the Lord, a ram without blemish out of the flock, with thy estimation, for a trespass offering, unto the priest:

And the priest shall make an atonement for him before the Lord: and it shall be forgiven him for any thing of all that he hath done in trespassing therein.

Leviticus 6:2–7

4 Who shall ascend into the hill of the Lord? or who shall stand in his holy place?

He that hath clean hands, and a pure heart; who hath not lifted up his soul unto vanity, nor sworn deceitfully.

Psalms 24:3–4

5 A false balance is abomination to the Lord: but a just weight is his delight.

Proverbs 11:1

6 *Odysseus.* Take it to heart, and pass the word along:
fair dealing brings more profit in the end.

Homer, *Odyssey,* XXII, 374

7 *Darius.* Whether men lie, or say true, it is with one

668

and the same object. Men lie, because they think to gain by deceiving others; and speak the truth, because they expect to get something by their true speaking, and to be trusted afterwards in more important matters. Thus, though their conduct is so opposite, the end of both is alike.

Herodotus, *History*, III, 72

8 *Creon.* Time is the only test of honest men,
one day is space enough to know a rogue.

Sophocles, *Oedipus the King*, 614

9 *Envoys of the Mitylenians.* There can never be any solid friendship between individuals, or union between communities that is worth the name, unless the parties be persuaded of each other's honesty.

Thucydides, *Peloponnesian War*, III, 10

10 He who claims more than he has with no ulterior object is a contemptible sort of fellow (otherwise he would not have delighted in falsehood), but seems futile rather than bad; but if he does it for an object, he who does it for the sake of reputation or honour is (for a boaster) not very much to be blamed, but he who does it for money, or the things that lead to money, is an uglier character (it is not the capacity that makes the boaster, but the purpose; for it is in virtue of his state of character and by being a man of a certain kind that he is a boaster); as one man is a liar because he enjoys the lie itself, and another because he desires reputation or gain. Now those who boast for the sake of reputation claim such qualities as win praise or congratulation, but those whose object is gain claim qualities which are of value to one's neighbours and one's lack of which is not easily detected, e.g. the powers of a seer, a sage, or a physician. For this reason it is such things as these that most people claim and boast about; for in them the above-mentioned qualities are found.

Mock-modest people, who understate things, seem more attractive in character; for they are thought to speak not for gain but to avoid parade; and here too it is qualities which bring reputation that they disclaim, as Socrates used to do. Those who disclaim trifling and obvious qualities are called humbugs and are more contemptible; and sometimes this seems to be boastfulness, like the Spartan dress; for both excess and great deficiency are boastful. But those who use understatement with moderation and understate about matters that do not very much force themselves on our notice seem attractive. And it is the boaster that seems to be opposed to the truthful man; for he is the worse character.

Aristotle, *Ethics*, 1127ᵇ9

11 No type of injustice is more glaring than that of the hypocrite who, in the very instant of being most false, makes the pretence of appearing virtuous.

Cicero, *De Officiis*, I, 13

12 Let your communication be, Yea, yea; Nay, nay: for whatsoever is more than these cometh of evil.

Matthew 5:37

13 A certain man named Ăn-ă-nī-ăs, with Sapphira his wife, sold a possession,

And kept back part of the price, his wife also being privy to it, and brought a certain part, and laid it at the apostles' feet.

But Peter said, Ăn-ă-nī-ăs, why hath Satan filled thine heart to lie to the Holy Ghost, and to keep back part of the price of the land?

Whiles it remained, was it not thine own? and after it was sold, was it not in thine own power? why has thou conceived this thing in thine heart? thou hast not lied unto men, but unto God.

And Ăn-ă-nī-ăs hearing these words fell down, and gave up the ghost: and great fear came on all them that heard these things.

And the young men arose, wound him up, and carried him out, and buried him.

And it was about the space of three hours after, when his wife, not knowing what was done, came in.

And Peter answered unto her, Tell me whether ye sold the land for so much? And she said, Yea, for so much.

Then Peter said unto her, How is it that ye have agreed together to tempt the Spirit of the Lord? behold, the feet of them which have buried thy husband are at the door, and shall carry thee out.

Then fell she down straightway at his feet, and yielded up the ghost: and the young men came in, and found her dead, and, carrying her forth, buried her by her husband.

Acts 5:1–10

14 *Solon.* Men keep their promises when neither side can get anything by the breaking of them.

Plutarch, *Solon*

15   If you want to be Somebody, these days,
Have the nerve to commit an act that rates jailing or exile:
Probity merits praise—and has to starve on the highways.

Juvenal, *Satire I*

16 Never value anything as profitable to thyself which shall compel thee to break thy promise, to lose thy self-respect, to hate any man, to suspect, to curse, to act the hypocrite, to desire anything which needs walls and curtains.

Marcus Aurelius, *Meditations*, III, 7

17 External conduct has the character of honesty, in so far as it reflects internal rectitude. For this rea-

son honesty consists radically in the internal choice, but its expression lies in the external conduct.

Aquinas, *Summa Theologica,* II–II, 145, 1

18 Because fraud is a vice peculiar to man, it more displeases God.

Dante, *Inferno,* XI, 25

19 Anyone who does not feel sufficiently strong in memory should not meddle with lying.

Montaigne, *Essays,* I, 9, Of Liars

20 In truth lying is an accursed vice. We are men, and hold together, only by our word. If we recognized the horror and the gravity of lying, we would persecute it with fire more justly than other crimes. I find that people ordinarily fool around chastising harmless faults in children very inappropriately, and torment them for thoughtless actions that leave neither imprint nor consequences. Only lying, and a little below it obstinacy, seem to me to be the actions whose birth and progress one should combat insistently. They grow with the child. And once the tongue has been put on this wrong track, it cannot be called back without amazing difficulty.

Montaigne, *Essays,* I, 9, Of Liars

21 Lying is an ugly vice, which an ancient paints in most shameful colors when he says that it is giving evidence of contempt for God, and at the same time of fear of men. It is not possible to represent more vividly the horror, the vileness, and the profligacy of it. For what can you imagine uglier than being a coward toward men and bold toward God? Since mutual understanding is brought about solely by way of words, he who breaks his word betrays human society. It is the only instrument by means of which our wills and thoughts communicate, it is the interpreter of our soul. If it fails us, we have no more hold on each other, no more knowledge of each other. If it deceives us, it breaks up all our relations and dissolves all the bonds of our society.

Montaigne, *Essays,* II, 18, Of Giving the Lie

22 There are rules both false and lax in philosophy. The example that is proposed to us for making private utility prevail over our pledged word does not receive enough weight from the circumstance that they introduce into it. Robbers have seized you; they have set you free again after extracting from you an oath to pay a certain sum. People are wrong to say that an honest man will be quit of his word without paying, once he is out of their hands. Nothing of the sort. What fear has once made me will, I am bound still to will when without fear. And even if it has forced only my tongue without my will, I am still bound to make good

my word to the last penny. As for me, when my tongue has sometimes thoughtlessly run ahead of my thoughts, I have scrupled to disavow it for all that. Otherwise we shall come by degrees to overthrow all the rights that a third person obtains from our promises and oaths. . . . In this alone does private interest have the right to excuse us for failing our promise, if we have promised something wicked and unjust in itself; for the rights of virtue must prevail over the rights of our obligation.

Montaigne, *Essays,* III, 1, The Useful and the Honorable

23 *Falstaff.* Lord, Lord, how this world is given to lying!

Shakespeare, *I Henry IV,* V, iv, 148

24 *Verges.* I thank God I am as honest as any man living that is an old man and no honester than I.

Shakespeare, *Much Ado About Nothing,* III, v, 15

25 *Nym.* You'll pay me the eight shillings I won of you at betting?

Pistol. Base is the slave that pays.

Shakespeare, *Henry V,* II, i, 99

26 *King Henry.* A good leg will fall; a straight back will stoop; a black beard will turn white; a curled pate will grow bald; a fair face will wither; a full eye will wax hollow: but a good heart . . . is the sun and the moon; or rather the sun and not the moon; for it shines bright and never changes, but keeps his course truly.

Shakespeare, *Henry V,* V, ii, 168

27 *Touchstone.* Honesty coupled to beauty is to have honey a sauce to sugar.

Shakespeare, *As You Like It,* III, iii, 30

28 *Hamlet.* To be honest, as this world goes, is to be one man picked out of ten thousand.

Shakespeare, *Hamlet,* II, ii, 178

29 *Iago.* The Moor is of a free and open nature
That thinks men honest that but seem to be so,
And will as tenderly be led by the nose
As asses are.

Shakespeare, *Othello,* I, iii, 405

30 *Cornwall.*   This is some fellow,
Who, having been praised for bluntness, doth affect
A saucy roughness, and constrains the garb
Quite from his nature. He cannot flatter, he,
An honest mind and plain, he must speak truth!
An they will take it, so; if not, he's plain.
These kind of knaves I know, which in this plainness

Harbour more craft and more corrupter ends
Than twenty silly ducking observants
That stretch their duties nicely.
Shakespeare, Lear, II, ii, 102

31 *Duncan.*   There's no art
To find the mind's construction in the face.
He was a gentleman on whom I built
An absolute trust.
Shakespeare, Macbeth, I, iv, 12

32 *Menenius.* His nature is too noble for the world.
He would not flatter Neptune for his trident,
Or Jove for's power to thunder. His heart's his
mouth.
What his breast forges, that his tongue must vent;
And, being angry, does forget that ever
He heard the name of death.
Shakespeare, Coriolanus, III, i, 255

33 *Autolycus.* Ha, ha! what a fool Honesty is! and
Trust, his sworn brother, a very simple gentle-
man!
Shakespeare, Winter's Tale, IV, iv, 605

34 *Autolycus.* Though I am not naturally honest, I am
so sometimes by chance.
Shakespeare, Winter's Tale, IV, iv, 731

35 It will be acknowledged, even by those that practise it not, that clear and round dealing is the
honour of man's nature; and that mixture of falsehood is like allay in coin of gold and silver; which
may make the metal work the better, but it
embaseth it.
Bacon, Of Truth

36 Winding and crooked courses are the goings of the
serpent; which goeth basely upon the belly, and
not upon the feet. There is no vice that doth so
cover a man with shame as to be found false and
perfidious.
Bacon, Of Truth

37 He who counterfeiteth, acts a part; and is as it
were out of himself: which, if long, proves so irksome, that Men are glad to pull of their Vizards,
and resume themselves again; no practice being
able to naturalize such unnaturals, or make a
Man rest content not to be himself. And therefore
since Sincerity is thy Temper, let veracity be thy
Virtue in Words, Manners, and Actions.
Sir Thomas Browne, Christian Morals, III, 20

38 To tell the truth is useful to those to whom it is
spoken, but disadvantageous to those who tell it,
because it makes them disliked.
Pascal, Pensées, II, 100

39 Although people may have no interest in what
they are saying, we must not absolutely conclude

from this that they are not lying; for there are
some people who lie for the mere sake of lying.
Pascal, Pensées, II, 108

40   On th' other side up rose
Belial, in act more graceful and humane;
A fairer person lost not Heav'n; he seemd
For dignity compos'd and high exploit:
But all was false and hollow; though his Tongue
Dropt Manna, and could make the worse appear
The better reason, to perplex and dash
Maturest Counsels: for his thoughts were low;
To vice industrious, but to Nobler deeds
Timorous and slothful: yet he pleas'd the eare.
Milton, Paradise Lost, II, 108

41 Lying is so ready and cheap a cover for any miscarriage, and so much in fashion among all sorts
of people, that a child can hardly avoid observing
the use is made of it on all occasions, and so can
scarce be kept without great care from getting
into it. But it is so ill a quality, and the mother of
so many ill ones that spawn from it and take shelter under it, that a child should be brought up in
the greatest abhorrence of it imaginable.
Locke, Some Thoughts Concerning
Education, 131

42 *Scandal.* He that first cries out stop Thief, is often
he that has stol'n the Treasure.
Congreve, Love for Love, III, iv

43 Honesty hath no fence against superior cunning.
Swift, Gulliver's Travels, I, 6

44 As universal a Practice as Lying is, and as easy a
one as it seems, I do not remember to have heard
three good Lyes in all my Conversation, even
from those who were most celebrated in that Faculty.
Swift, Thoughts on Various Subjects

45 A Wit's a feather, and a Chief a rod;
An honest Man's the noblest work of God.
Pope, Essay on Man, Epistle IV, 247

46 Sometimes, in his wild way of talking, he [Yorick]
would say, that Gravity was an errant scoundrel,
and he would add,—of the most dangerous kind
too,—because a sly one; and that he verily believed, more honest, well-meaning people were
bubbled out of their goods and money by it in one
twelve-month, than by pocket-picking and shop-
lifting in seven. In the naked temper which a merry heart discovered, he would say there was no
danger,—but to itself:—whereas the very essence
of gravity was design, and consequently deceit;—
'twas a taught trick to gain credit of the world for
more sense and knowledge than a man was worth;
and that, with all its pretensions,—it was no better, but often worse, than what a French wit had

long ago defined it,—viz. "A mysterious carriage of the body to cover the defects of the mind";—which definition of gravity, Yorick, with great imprudence, would say, deserved to be wrote in letters of gold.

Sterne, *Tristram Shandy,* I, 11

47 It is impossible to see the long scrolls in which every contract is included, with all their appendages of seals and attestation, without wondering at the depravity of those beings who must be restrained from violation of promise by such formal and public evidences, and precluded from equivocation and subterfuge by such punctilious minuteness.

Johnson, *Rambler No. 131*

48 *Johnson.* Why, Sir, if the fellow does not think as he speaks, he is lying; and I see not what honour he can propose to himself from having the character of a lyar. But if he does really think that there is no distinction between virtue and vice, why, Sir, when he leaves our houses let us count our spoons.

Boswell, *Life of Johnson (July 1763)*

49 I asked him whether, as a moralist, he did not think that the practice of the law, in some degree, hurt the nice feeling of honesty. *Johnson.* "Why no, Sir, if you act properly. You are not to deceive your clients with false representations of your opinion: you are not to tell lies to a judge." *Boswell.* "But what do you think of supporting a cause which you know to be bad?" *Johnson.* "Sir, you do not know it to be good or bad till the Judge determines it. I have said that you are to state facts fairly; so that your thinking, or what you call knowing, a cause to be bad, must be from reasoning, must be from your supposing your arguments to be weak and inconclusive. But, Sir, that is not enough. An argument which does not convince yourself, may convince the Judge to whom you urge it: and if it does convince him, why, then, Sir, you are wrong, and he is right. It is his business to judge; and you are not to be confident in your own opinion that a cause is bad, but to say all you can for your client, and then hear the Judge's opinion." *Boswell.* "But, Sir, does not affecting a warmth when you have no warmth, and appearing to be clearly of one opinion when you are in reality of another opinion, does not such dissimulation impair one's honesty? Is there not some danger that a lawyer may put on the same mask in common life, in the intercourse with his friends?" *Johnson.* "Why no, Sir. Everybody knows you are paid for affecting warmth for your client; and it is, therefore, properly no dissimulation: the moment you come from the bar you resume your usual behaviour. Sir, a man will no more carry the artifice of the bar into the common intercourse of society, than a man who is paid for tumbling upon his hands will continue to tumble upon his hands when he should walk on his feet."

Boswell, *Life of Johnson (1768)*

50 *Johnson.* It must be considered, that a man who only does what every one of the society to which he belongs would do, is not a dishonest man.

Boswell, *Life of Johnson (April 6, 1772)*

51 While we were at breakfast, Johnson gave a very earnest recommendation of what he himself practised with the utmost conscientiousness: I mean a strict attention to truth, even in the most minute particulars. "Accustom your children (said he,) constantly to this; if a thing happened at one window, and they, when relating it, say that it happened at another, do not let it pass, but instantly check them; you do not know where deviation from truth will end." *Boswell.* "It may come to the door: and when once an account is at all varied in one circumstance, it may by degrees be varied so as to be totally different from what really happened." Our lively hostess, whose fancy was impatient of the rein, fidgeted at this, and ventured to say, "Nay, this is too much. If Mr. Johnson should forbid me to drink tea, I would comply, as I should feel the restraint only twice a day; but little variations in narrative must happen a thousand times a day, if one is not perpetually watching." *Johnson.* "Well, Madam, and you *ought* to be perpetually watching. It is more from carelessness about truth than from intentional lying, that there is so much falsehood in the world."

In his review of Dr. Warton's *Essay on the Writings and Genius of Pope,* Johnson has given the following salutary caution upon this subject:

"Nothing but experience could evince the frequency of false information, or enable any man to conceive that so many groundless reports should be propagated, as every man of eminence may hear of himself. Some men relate what they think, as what they know; some men of confused memories and habitual inaccuracy, ascribe to one man what belongs to another; and some talk on, without thought or care. A few men are sufficient to broach falsehoods, which are afterwards innocently diffused by successive relaters."

Had he lived to read what Sir John Hawkins and Mrs. Piozzi have related concerning himself, how much would he have found his observation illustrated. He was indeed so much impressed with the prevalence of falsehood, voluntary or unintentional, that I never knew any person who upon hearing an extraordinary circumstance told, discovered more of the *incredulus odi.* He would say, with a significant look and decisive tone, "It is not so. Do not tell this again." He inculcated upon all his friends the importance of perpetual vigilance against the slightest degrees of falsehood; the effect of which, as Sir Joshua Reynolds observed to me, has been, that all who were of his *school* are distinguished for a love of truth and accuracy, which they would not have possessed in the same degree, if they had not been acquainted with Johnson.

Boswell, *Life of Johnson (March 31, 1778)*

52 We talked of the casuistical question, Whether it was allowable at any time to depart from *Truth?* *Johnson.* "The general rule is, that Truth should never be violated, because it is of the utmost importance to the comfort of life, that we should have a full security by mutual faith; and occasional inconveniences should be willingly suffered that we may preserve it. There must, however, be some exceptions. If, for instance, a murderer should ask you which way a man is gone, you may tell him what is not true, because you are under a previous obligation not to betray a man to a murderer."

Boswell, *Life of Johnson (June 13, 1784)*

53 The honest man, though e'er sae poor,
    Is king o' men for a' that!

Burns, *A Man's a Man for a' That*

54 [A man] finds himself forced by necessity to borrow money. He knows that he will not be able to repay it, but sees also that nothing will be lent to him unless he promises stoutly to repay it in a definite time. He desires to make this promise, but he has still so much conscience as to ask himself: "Is it not unlawful and inconsistent with duty to get out of a difficulty in this way?" Suppose however that he resolves to do so: then the maxim of his action would be expressed thus: "When I think myself in want of money, I will borrow money and promise to repay it, although I know that I never can do so." Now this principle of self-love or of one's own advantage may perhaps be consistent with my whole future welfare; but the question now is, "Is it right?" I change then the suggestion of self-love into a universal law, and state the question thus: "How would it be if my maxim were a universal law?" Then I see at once that it could never hold as a universal law of nature, but would necessarily contradict itself. For supposing it to be a universal law that everyone when he thinks himself in a difficulty should be able to promise whatever he pleases, with the purpose of not keeping his promise, the promise itself would become impossible, as well as the end that one might have in view in it, since no one would consider that anything was promised to him, but would ridicule all such statements as vain pretences.

Kant, *Fundamental Principles of the Metaphysic of Morals,* II

55 He who is thinking of making a lying promise to others will see at once that he would be using another man *merely as a mean,* without the latter containing at the same time the end in himself. For he whom I propose by such a promise to use

for my own purposes cannot possibly assent to my mode of acting towards him and, therefore, cannot himself contain the end of this action.

Kant, *Fundamental Principles of the Metaphysic of Morals,* II

56 Though this proposition, *"honesty is the best policy,"* announces a theory, too frequently, alas! contradicted by experience; yet no objection will ever overthrow this: honesty is better than all policy, and is even an essential condition of it.

Kant, *Perpetual Peace,* Appendix, 1

57 In this kingdom of illusions we grope eagerly for stays and foundations. There is none but a strict and faithful dealing at home and a severe barring out of all duplicity or illusion there. Whatever games are played with us, we must play no games with ourselves, but deal in our privacy with the last honesty and truth. I look upon the simple and childish virtues of veracity and honesty as the root of all that is sublime in character. Speak as you think, be what you are, pay your debts of all kinds. I prefer to be owned as sound and solvent, and my word as good as my bond, and to be what cannot be skipped, or dissipated, or undermined, to all the *éclat* in the universe. This reality is the foundation of friendship, religion, poetry, and art. At the top or at the bottom of all illusions, I set the cheat which still leads us to work and live for appearances; in spite of our conviction, in all sane hours, that it is what we really are that avails, with friends, with strangers, and with fate or fortune.

Emerson, *Illusions*

58 Absolutely speaking, Do unto others as you would that they should do unto you is by no means a golden rule, but the best of current silver. An honest man would have but little occasion for it. It is golden not to have any rule at all in such a case.

Thoreau, *The Christian Fable*

59 Speaking truth is like writing fair, and comes only by practice; it is less a matter of will than of habit, and I doubt if any occasion can be trivial which permits the practice and formation of such a habit. To speak and act truth with constancy and precision is nearly as difficult, and perhaps as meritorious, as to speak it under intimidation or penalty; and it is a strange thought how many men there are, as I trust, who would hold to it at the cost of fortune or life, for one who would hold to it at the cost of a little daily trouble. And seeing that of all sin there is, perhaps, no one more flatly opposite to the Almighty, no one more "wanting the good of virtue and of being," than this of lying, it is surely a strange insolence to fall into the foulness of it on light or on no temptation, and surely becoming an honourable man to resolve, that, whatever semblances or fallacies the neces-

sary course of his life may impel him to bear or to believe, none shall disturb the serenity of his voluntary actions, nor diminish the reality of his chosen delights.

Ruskin, *Seven Lamps of Architecture*, II, 1

60 *Father Zossima*. The man who lies to himself and listens to his own lie comes to such a pass that he cannot distinguish the truth within him, or around him, and so loses all respect for himself and for others. And having no respect he ceases to love, and in order to occupy and distract himself without love he gives way to passions and coarse pleasures, and sinks to bestiality in his vices, all

from continual lying to other men and to himself. The man who lies to himself can be more easily offended than anyone. You know it is sometimes very pleasant to take offence, isn't it? A man may know that nobody has insulted him, but that he has invented the insult for himself, has lied and exaggerated to make it picturesque, has caught at a word and made a mountain out of a molehill— he knows that himself, yet he will be the first to take offence, and will revel in his resentment till he feels great pleasure in it, and so pass to genuine vindictiveness.

Dostoevsky, *Brothers Karamazov*, Pt. I, II, 2

9.15 | *Wisdom and Folly*

Of all the qualities of mind or character that are called virtues, excellences, or perfections, wisdom is, perhaps, the one most universally admired, as it is also, perhaps, the one that is generally thought most difficult to achieve. Socrates is famous for his unwillingness to accept the oracle's judgment of himself as the wisest man in Greece, declaring that only God is wise and that men show some semblance of wisdom only if they realize how little they know. According to Socrates, the philosopher must not be thought of as a wise man, but rather as a lover of or seeker after wisdom.

Some of the quotations below define philosophical or speculative wisdom as the highest form of attainable knowledge, consisting in an understanding of first principles or ultimate causes. The greatest praise that has been given to philosophy is accorded to it by those who identify it with wisdom. For other quotations that express this view or quotations questioning it, the reader is re-

ferred to Section 17.1 on PHILOSOPHY AND PHILOSOPHERS.

Wisdom and folly are often thought of by the poets and the historians, as in books of the Old and the New Testament, not as consisting in profound knowledge and abysmal ignorance; rather the wise man is one who knows how to manage all the affairs of life well, while the fool stumbles and blunders and goes astray. This treatment of wisdom overlaps the discussion of prudence or practical wisdom, which the reader will find in Section 9.13. It also touches on the same fundamental question that is raised there— whether or not it is possible to be a wise man without being a man of good moral character.

The quotations below include not only the praise of wisdom, but also the praise of folly, especially the kinds of folly that, upon examination, emerge as wisdom in disguise. They give us examples of fools who speak wisely about matters concerning which pretenders to wisdom fall into folly. They distinguish true wisdom from the counterfeit of wisdom that is exemplified in the cunning of the Serpent. And they place the beginning of wisdom in wonder or in the fear of the Lord.

---

1 In Gibeon the Lord appeared to Solomon in a dream by night: and God said, Ask what I shall give thee.

And Solomon said, Thou hast shewed unto thy servant David my father great mercy, according as he walked before thee in truth, and in righteousness, and in uprightness of heart with thee; and thou hast kept for him this great kindness, that thou hast given him a son to sit on his throne, as it is this day.

And now, O Lord my God, thou hast made thy servant king instead of David my father: and I am but a little child: I know not how to go out or come in.

And thy servant is in the midst of thy people which thou hast chosen, a great people, that cannot be numbered nor counted for multitude.

Give therefore thy servant an understanding heart to judge thy people, that I may discern between good and bad: for who is able to judge this thy so great a people?

And the speech pleased the Lord, that Solomon had asked this thing.

And God said unto him, Because thou hast asked this thing, and hast not asked for thyself long life; neither hast asked riches for thyself, nor hast asked the life of thine enemies; but hast asked for thyself understanding to discern judgment;

Behold, I have done according to thy words: lo, I have given thee a wise and an understanding heart; so that there was none like thee before thee, neither after thee shall any arise like unto thee.

And I have also given thee that which thou hast not asked, both riches, and honour: so that there shall not be any among the kings like unto thee all thy days.

I Kings 3:5–13

2 The price of wisdom is above rubies.

Job 28:18

3 The fear of the Lord is the beginning of wisdom.

Psalms 111:10

4 A reproof entereth more into a wise man than an hundred stripes into a fool.

Proverbs 17:10

5 Speak not in the ears of a fool: for he will despise the wisdom of thy words.

Proverbs 23:9

6 Answer a fool according to his folly, lest he be wise in his own conceit.

Proverbs 26:5

7 I gave my heart to know wisdom, and to know madness and folly: I perceived that this also is vexation of spirit.

For in much wisdom is much grief: and he that increaseth knowledge increaseth sorrow.

Ecclesiastes 1:17–18

8 I saw that wisdom excelleth folly, as far as light excelleth darkness.

The wise man's eyes are in his head; but the fool walketh in darkness: and I myself perceived also that one event happeneth to them all.

Then said I in my heart, As it happeneth to the fool, so it happeneth even to me; and why was I then more wise? Then I said in my heart, that this also is vanity.

For there is no remembrance of the wise more than of the fool forever; seeing that which now is in the days to come shall all be forgotten. And how dieth the wise man? as the fool.

Ecclesiastes 2:13–16

9 Wisdom is better than strength: nevertheless the poor man's wisdom is despised, and his words are not heard.

Ecclesiastes 9:16

10 *Chorus.* Zeus, who guided men to think,
who has laid it down that wisdom
comes alone through suffering.

Aeschylus, *Agamemnon*, 176

11 *Oceanos.* It is a profitable thing, if one is wise, to seem foolish.

Aeschylus, *Prometheus Bound*, 386

12 *Haemon.* A man, though wise, should never be ashamed
of learning more, and must unbend his mind.

Sophocles, *Antigone*, 710

13 They amongst men who pretend to wisdom and expend deep thought on words do incur a serious charge of folly.

Euripides, *Medea*, 1225

14 *Theseus.* What fools men are! You work and work for nothing,

you teach ten thousand tasks to one another,
invent, discover everything. One thing only
you do not know: one thing you never hunt for—
a way to teach fools wisdom.

Euripides, *Hippolytus,* 916

15 *Chorus.* A tongue without reins,
defiance, unwisdom—
their end is disaster.
But the life of quiet good,
the wisdom that accepts—
these abide unshaken,
preserving, sustaining
the houses of men.
Far in the air of heaven,
the sons of heaven live.
But they watch the lives of men.
And what passes for wisdom is not;
unwise are those who aspire,
who outrange the limits of man.
Briefly, we live. Briefly,
then die. Wherefore, I say,
he who hunts a glory, he who tracks
some boundless, superhuman dream,
may lose his harvest here and now
and garner death. Such men are mad,
their counsels evil.

Euripides, *Bacchae,* 387

16 *Socrates.* If you are wise, all men will be your
friends and kindred, for you will be useful and
good; but if you are not wise, neither father, nor
mother, nor kindred; nor any one else, will be
your friends.

Plato, *Lysis,* 210B

17 *Socrates.* God only is wise; and . . . the wisdom of
men is worth little or nothing. . . . He . . . is the
wisest, who, like Socrates, knows that his wisdom
is in truth worth nothing.

Plato, *Apology,* 23A

18 *Socrates.* First among the virtues found in the State,
wisdom comes into view, and in this I detect a
certain peculiarity.

Glaucon. What is that?

The State which we have been describing is
said to be wise as being good in counsel?

Very true.

And good counsel is clearly a kind of knowledge, for not by ignorance, but by knowledge, do
men counsel well?

Clearly.

And the kinds of knowledge in a State are
many and diverse?

Of course.

There is the knowledge of the carpenter; but is
that the sort of knowledge which gives a city the
title of wise and good in counsel?

Certainly not; that would only give a city the
reputation of skill in carpentering.

Then a city is not to be called wise because
possessing a knowledge which counsels for the best
about wooden implements?

Certainly not.

Nor by reason of a knowledge which advises
about brazen pots, I said, nor as possessing any
other similar knowledge?

Not by reason of any of them, he said.

Nor yet by reason of knowledge which cultivates the earth; that would give the city the name
of agricultural?

Yes.

Well, I said, and is there any knowledge in our
recently-founded State among any of the citizens
which advises, not about any particular thing in
the State, but about the whole, and considers how
a State can best deal with itself and with other
States?

There certainly is.

And what is this knowledge, and among whom
is it found? I asked.

It is the knowledge of the guardians, he replied,
and is found among those whom we were just now
describing as perfect guardians.

And what is the name which the city derives
from the possession of this sort of knowledge?

The name of good in counsel and truly wise.

And will there be in our city more of these true
guardians or more smiths?

The smiths, he replied, will be far more numerous.

Will not the guardians be the smallest of all the
classes who receive a name from the profession of
some kind of knowledge?

Much the smallest.

And so by reason of the smallest part or class,
and of the knowledge which resides in this presiding and ruling part of itself, the whole State, being
thus constituted according to nature, will be wise;
and this, which has the only knowledge worthy to
be called wisdom, has been ordained by nature to
be of all classes the least.

Plato, *Republic,* IV, 428A

19 *Socrates.* God is never in any way unrighteous—he
is perfect righteousness; and he of us who is the
most righteous is most like him. . . . To know this
is true wisdom and virtue, and ignorance of this is
manifest folly and vice. All other kinds of wisdom
or cleverness, which seem only, such as the wisdom of politicians, or the wisdom of the arts, are
coarse and vulgar.

Plato, *Theaetetus,* 176A

20 *Socrates.* And of all the virtues, is not wisdom the
one which the mass of mankind are always claiming, and which most arouses in them a spirit of
contention and lying conceit of wisdom?

Protarchus. Certainly.

Soc. And may not all this be truly called an evil condition?

Pro. Very evil.

Plato, *Philebus,* 49A

21 All men suppose what is called Wisdom to deal with the first causes and the principles of things; so that . . . the man of experience is thought to be wiser than the possessors of any sense-perception whatever, the artist wiser than the men of experience, the master-worker than the mechanic, and the theoretical kinds of knowledge to be more of the nature of Wisdom than the productive. Clearly then Wisdom is knowledge about certain principles and causes.

Aristotle, *Metaphysics,* 981b28

22 We must inquire of what kind are the causes and the principles, the knowledge of which is Wisdom. If one were to take the notions we have about the wise man, this might perhaps make the answer more evident. We suppose first, then, that the wise man knows all things, as far as possible, although he has not knowledge of each of them in detail; secondly, that he who can learn things that are difficult, and not easy for man to know, is wise (sense-perception is common to all, and therefore easy and no mark of Wisdom); again, that he who is more exact and more capable of teaching the causes is wiser, in every branch of knowledge; and that of the sciences, also, that which is desirable on its own account and for the sake of knowing it is more of the nature of Wisdom than that which is desirable on account of its results, and the superior science is more of the nature of Wisdom than the ancillary; for the wise man must not be ordered but must order, and he must not obey another, but the less wise must obey *him.*

Aristotle, *Metaphysics,* 982a5

23 *Wisdom* (1) in the arts we ascribe to their most finished exponents, e.g. to Phidias as a sculptor and to Polyclitus as a maker of portrait-statues, and here we mean nothing by wisdom except excellence in art; but (2) we think that some people are wise in general, not in some particular field or in any other limited respect. . . . Therefore wisdom must plainly be the most finished of the forms of knowledge. It follows that the wise man must not only know what follows from the first principles, but must also possess truth about the first principles. Therefore wisdom must be intuitive reason combined with scientific knowledge—scientific knowledge of the highest objects which has received as it were its proper completion. Of the highest objects, we say; for it would be strange to think that the art of politics, or practical wisdom, is the best knowledge, since man is not the best thing in the world.

Aristotle, *Ethics,* 1141a9

24 It is evident . . . that philosophic wisdom and the art of politics cannot be the same; for if the state of mind concerned with a man's own interests is to be called philosophic wisdom, there will be many philosophic wisdoms; there will not be one concerned with the good of all animals (any more than there is one art of medicine for all existing things), but a different philosophic wisdom about the good of each species.

But if the argument be that man is the best of the animals, this makes no difference; for there are other things much more divine in their nature even than man, e.g., most conspicuously, the bodies of which the heavens are framed. From what has been said it is plain, then, that philosophic wisdom is scientific knowledge, combined with intuitive reason, of the things that are highest by nature.

Aristotle, *Ethics,* 1141a28

25 Fools admire and like all things the more which they perceive to be concealed under involved language, and determine things to be true which can prettily tickle the ears and are varnished over with finely sounding phrase.

Lucretius, *Nature of Things,* I

26 Because law ought to reform vice and promote virtue, the guiding principles of life can be inferred from it. Wisdom is the mother of all good things, and philosophy has taken its name from the Greek expression that means "love of wisdom." Of all the gifts of the gods to the human race, philosophy is the richest, most bountiful, and most exalted. Besides all its other wisdom, philosophy has informed us that the most difficult thing in the world is to know ourselves. This adage is so decisive for us that credit for it is given not to some person, but to the god at Delphi. The man who knows himself will acknowledge that he has a divine spark within him. He will regard his own nature as a consecrated reflection of God. Therefore what he does and thinks will be worthy of this great gift of the gods. When he has examined and tried himself, he will understand how nobly equipped by nature he entered into life. He will realize how various are the ways for attaining wisdom. At first his mind contained only vague concepts, but these were later illuminated by the help of wisdom. He learns how to be a good man and consequently a happy man.

Cicero, *Laws,* I, 22

27 Think, while there's time, how soon Death's pyre may blaze;
And some brief folly mix with prudent ways:
    At the fit hour 'tis sweet to unbend.

Horace, *Odes,* IV, 12

28 Only the wise man is content with what is his. All foolishness suffers the burden of dissatisfaction with itself.

Seneca, *Letters to Lucilius,* 9

29 Let no man deceive himself. If any man among you seemeth to be wise in this world, let him become a fool, that he may be wise.

For the wisdom of this world is foolishness with God. For it is written, He taketh the wise in their own craftiness.

I Corinthians 3:18–19

30 For ye suffer fools gladly, seeing ye yourselves are wise.

II Corinthians 11:19

31 [Cato] used to assert . . . that wise men profited more by fools, than fools by wise men; for that wise men avoided the faults of fools, but that fools would not imitate the good examples of wise men.

Plutarch, *Marcus Cato*

32 All that comes to be, work of nature or of craft, some wisdom has made: everywhere a wisdom presides at a making.

No doubt the wisdom of the artist may be the guide of the work; it is sufficient explanation of the wisdom exhibited in the arts; but the artist himself goes back, after all, to that wisdom in Nature which is embodied in himself; and this is not a wisdom built up of theorems but one totality, not a wisdom consisting of manifold detail co-ordinated into a unity but rather a unity working out into detail.

Plotinus, *Fifth Ennead*, VIII, 5

33 Wisdom insinuates itself into holy souls, and makes them the friends of God and His prophets, and noiselessly informs them of His works.

Augustine, *City of God*, XI, 4

34 We were ensnared by the wisdom of the serpent: we are set free by the foolishness of God. Moreover, just as the former was called wisdom, but was in reality the folly of those who despised God, so the latter is called foolishness, but is true wisdom in those who overcome the devil.

Augustine, *Christian Doctrine*, I, 14

35 If wisdom in the knowledge of the created world is lovely, how lovely is the wisdom which has created all things from nothing!

Anselm of Canterbury, *Proslogium*, XXIV

36 Whatever is divided and multiplied in creatures exists in God simply and unitedly. Now man has different kinds of knowledge, according to the different objects of His knowledge. He has *intelligence* as regards the knowledge of principles; he has *science* as regards knowledge of conclusions; he has *wisdom*, according as he knows the highest cause; he has *counsel* or *prudence*, according as he knows what is to be done. But God knows all these by one simple act of knowledge . . . Hence the simple knowledge of God can be named by all these names; in such a way, however, that there must

be removed from each of them, so far as they enter into the divine predication, everything that savors of imperfection; and everything that expresses perfection is to be retained in them. Hence it is said, *With Him is wisdom and strength, He hath counsel and understanding.*

Aquinas, *Summa Theologica*, I, 14, 1

37 Wisdom is a kind of science in so far as it has that which is common to all the sciences, namely, to demonstrate conclusions from principles. But since it has something proper to itself above the other sciences, in so far, that is, as it judges of them all, not only as to their conclusions, but also as to their first principles, therefore it is a more perfect virtue than science.

Aquinas, *Summa Theologica*, I–II, 57, 2

38 Since the word knowledge implies certitude of judgment . . . if this certitude of the judgment is derived from the highest cause, the knowledge has a special name, which is wisdom. For a wise man in any branch of knowledge is one who knows the highest cause of that kind of knowledge, and is able to judge of all matters by that cause; and a wise man absolutely, is one who knows the cause which is absolutely highest, namely God. Hence the knowledge of Divine things is called wisdom, while the knowledge of human things is called knowledge, this being the common name denoting certitude of judgment, and appropriated to the judgment which is formed through second causes. Accordingly, if we take knowledge in this way, it is a distinct gift from the gift of wisdom, so that the gift of knowledge is only about human or created things.

Aquinas, *Summa Theologica*, II–II, 9, 2

39 Since wisdom is the knowledge of Divine things . . . it is considered by us in one way, and in another way by philosophers. For, seeing that our life is ordered to the enjoyment of God, and is directed to this according to a participation of the Divine Nature, conferred on us through grace, wisdom, as we look at it, is considered not only as making us know God, as it is with the philosophers, but also as directing human conduct; since this is directed not only by the human law, but also by the Divine law. . . .

Accordingly the beginning of wisdom as to its essence consists in the first principles of wisdom, which are the articles of faith, and in this sense faith is said to be the beginning of wisdom. But as regards the effect, the beginning of wisdom is the point where wisdom begins to work, and in this way fear is the beginning of wisdom, yet servile fear in one way, and filial fear, in another. For servile fear is like a principle disposing a man to wisdom from without, in so far as he refrains from sin through fear of punishment, and is thus fashioned for the effect of wisdom. . . . On the other hand, chaste or filial fear is the beginning of wisdom, as being the first effect of wisdom. For since the regulation of human conduct by the Divine law belongs to wisdom, in order to make a beginning, man must first of all fear God and submit himself to Him; thus the result will be that in all things he will be ruled by God.

Aquinas, *Summa Theologica*, II–II, 19, 7

40 Wisdom denotes a certain rectitude of judgment according to the Eternal Law. Now rectitude of judgment is twofold: first, on account of perfect use of reason, secondly, on account of a certain connaturality with the matter about which one has to judge in a given instance. Thus, about matters of chastity, a man after inquiring with his reason forms a right judgment if he has learnt the science of morals, while he who has the habit of chastity judges rightly of such matters by a kind of connaturality.

Accordingly it pertains to the wisdom that is an intellectual virtue to pronounce right judgment about Divine things after reason has made its inquiry, but it pertains to wisdom as a gift of the Holy Ghost to judge rightly about them on account of a certain connaturality with them. . . . Now this sympathy or connaturality for Divine things is the result of charity, which unites us to God: *He who is joined to the Lord, is one spirit.* Consequently wisdom which is a gift, has its cause in the will, which cause is charity, but it has its essence in the intellect, whose act is to judge rightly.

Aquinas, *Summa Theologica*, II–II, 45, 2

41 Folly is fittingly opposed to wisdom. For *sapiens* (wise) as Isidore says "is so named from *sapor* (savour), because just as the taste is quick to distinguish between savours of meats, so is a wise man in discerning things and causes." Therefore it is manifest that folly is opposed to wisdom as its contrary, while fatuity is opposed to it as a pure negation, for the fatuous man lacks the sense of judgment; the fool has the sense, though dulled, and the wise man has the sense acute and penetrating.

Aquinas, *Summa Theologica*, II–II, 46, 1

42 It is part of folly that a man should have a distaste for God and His gifts.

Aquinas, *Summa Theologica*, II–II, 46, 3

43 [Pantagruel] took all things in good part, and interpreted every action to the best sense. He never vexed nor disquieted himself with the least pretence of dislike to anything, because he knew that he must have most grossly abandoned the divine mansion of reason, if he had permitted his mind to be never so little grieved, afflicted, or altered at any occasion whatsoever. For all the goods that the heaven covereth, and that the earth containeth, in all their dimensions of height, depth, breath, and length, are not of so much worth, as that we should for them disturb or disorder our

affections, trouble or perplex our senses or spirits.

Rabelais, *Gargantua and Pantagruel*, III, 2

44 *Pantagruel.* As he who narrowly takes heed to what concerns the dexterous management of his private affairs, domestic businesses, and those adoes which are confined within the strait-laced compass of one family,—who is attentive, vigilant, and active in the economic rule of his own house,—whose frugal spirit never strays from home,—who loseth no occasion whereby he may purchase to himself more riches, and build up new heaps of treasure on his former wealth,—and who knows warily how to prevent the inconveniences of poverty, is called a worldly wise man, though perhaps in the second judgment of the intelligences which are above, he be esteemed a fool,—so, on the contrary is he most like, even in the thoughts of celestial spirits, to be not only sage, but to presage events to come by divine inspiration, who laying quite aside those cares which are conducible to his body, or his fortunes, and, as it were departing from himself, rids all his senses of terrene affections, and clears his fancies of those plodding studies which harbour in the minds of thriving men. All which neglects of sublunary things are vulgarly imputed folly.

Rabelais, *Gargantua and Pantagruel*, III, 37

45 It seems to me that all peculiar and out-of-the-way fashions come rather from folly and ambitious affectation than from true reason, and that the wise man should withdraw his soul within, out of the crowd, and keep it in freedom and power to judge things freely; but as for externals, he should wholly follow the accepted fashions and forms. Society in general can do without our thoughts; but the rest—our actions, our work, our fortunes, and our very life—we must lend and abandon to its service and to the common opinions, just as the great and good Socrates refused to save his life by disobedience to the magistrate, even to a very unjust and very iniquitous magistrate. For it is the rule of rules, and the universal law of laws, that each man should observe those of the place he is in.

Montaigne, *Essays*, I, 23, Of Custom

46 Stupidity and wisdom meet at the same point of feeling and of resolving to endure human accidents. The wise curb and control the evil; the others are not aware of it. The latter are, so to speak, on this side of accidents, the former beyond them; for the wise man, after having well weighed and considered their qualities and measured and judged them for what they are, springs above them by the power of a vigorous courage. He disdains them and tramples them underfoot, having a strong and solid soul, against which the arrows of fortune, when they come to strike, must necessarily bounce off and be blunted, meeting a body

on which they can make no impression. The ordinary and middle condition of men lodges between these two extremes; which is that of those who perceive evils, feel them, and cannot endure them.

Montaigne, *Essays,* I, 54, Of Vain Subtleties

47 What does truth preach to us, when she exhorts us to flee worldly philosophy, when she so often inculcates in us that our wisdom is but folly before God; that of all vanities the vainest is man; that the man who is presumptuous of his knowledge does not yet know what knowledge is; and that man, who is nothing, if he thinks he is something, seduces and deceives himself? These statements of the Holy Spirit express so clearly and so vividly what I wish to maintain, that no other proof would be needed against men who would surrender with all submission and obedience to its authority. But these men insist on being whipped to their own cost and will not allow us to combat their reason except by itself.

Montaigne, *Essays,* II, 12, Apology for Raymond Sebond

48 The wisest man that ever was, when they asked him what he knew, answered that he knew this much, that he knew nothing. He was verifying what they say, that the greatest part of what we know is the least of those parts that we do not know; that is to say that the very thing we think we know is a part, and a very small part, of our ignorance.

Montaigne, *Essays,* II, 12, Apology for Raymond Sebond

49 Anyone who has once been very foolish will never at any other time be very wise.

Montaigne, *Essays,* III, 6, Of Coaches

50 *Gratiano.* There are a sort of men whose visages
Do cream and mantle like a standing pond,
And do a wilful stillness entertain,
With purpose to be dress'd in an opinion
Of wisdom, gravity, profound conceit,
As who should say, "I am Sir Oracle,
And when I ope my lips let no dog bark!"
O my Antonio, I do know of these
That therefore only are reputed wise
For saying nothing, when, I am very sure,
If they should speak, would almost damn those
    ears
Which, hearing them, would call their brothers
    fools.

Shakespeare, *Merchant of Venice,* I, i, 88

51 *Portia.* If to do were as easy as to know what were good to do, chapels had been churches and poor men's cottages princes' palaces.

Shakespeare, *Merchant of Venice,* I, ii, 13

52 *Dogberry.* I am a wise fellow, and, which is more,

an officer, and, which is more, a householder, and, which is more, as pretty a piece of flesh as any is in Messina, and one that knows the law, go to; and a rich fellow enough, go to; and a fellow that hath had losses, and one that hath two gowns and everything handsome about him.

Shakespeare, *Much Ado About Nothing,* IV, ii, 82

53 *Celia.* Always the dulness of the fool is the whetstone of the wits.

Shakespeare, *As You Like It,* I, ii, 58

54 *Jaques.*   O noble fool!
A worthy fool! Motley's the only wear.

Shakespeare, *As You Like It,* II, vii, 33

55 *Jaques.* Invest me in my motley; give me leave
To speak my mind, and I will through and
    through
Cleanse the foul body of the infected world,
If they will patiently receive my medicine.

Shakespeare, *As You Like It,* II, vii, 58

56 *Touchstone.* The fool doth think he is wise, but the wise man knows himself to be a fool.

Shakespeare, *As You Like It,* V, i, 34

57 *Viola.* This fellow is wise enough to play the fool;
And to do that well craves a kind of wit.

Shakespeare, *Twelfth Night,* III, i, 66

58 *Lear.* Dost thou call me fool, boy?
    Fool. All thy other titles thou hast given away;
that thou wast born with.
    Kent. This is not altogether fool, my Lord.

Shakespeare, *Lear,* I, iv, 162

59 *Fool.* Prithee, nuncle, keep a schoolmaster that can teach thy Fool to lie. I would fain learn to lie.
    Lear. An you lie, sirrah, we'll have you whipped.
    Fool. I marvel what kin thou and thy daughters are. They'll have me whipped for speaking true, thou'lt have me whipped for lying; and sometimes I am whipped for holding my peace. I had rather be any kind o' thing than a Fool; and yet I would not be thee, nuncle; thou hast pared thy wit o' both sides, and left nothing i' the middle.

Shakespeare, *Lear,* I, iv, 195

60 *Fool.* If thou wert my fool, nuncle, I'd have thee beaten for being old before thy time.
    Lear. How's that?
    Fool. Thou shouldst not have been old till thou hadst been wise.

Shakespeare, *Lear,* I, v, 44

61 *Kent.* Why, fool?
    Fool. We'll set thee to school to an ant, to teach

thee there's no labouring i' the winter. All that
follow their noses are led by their eyes but blind
men; and there's not a nose among twenty but
can smell him that's stinking. Let go thy hold
when a great wheel runs down a hill, lest it break
thy neck with following it; but the great one that
goes up the hill, let him draw thee after. When a
wise man gives thee better counsel, give me mine
again. I would have none but knaves follow it,
since a fool gives it.

Shakespeare, *Lear,* II, iv, 67

62 *Fool.* He's mad that trusts in the tameness of a
wolf, a horse's health, a boy's love, or a whore's
oath.

Shakespeare, *Lear,* III, vi, 19

63 They that have power to hurt and will do none,
That do not do the thing they most do show,
Who, moving others, are themselves as stone,
Unmoved, cold, and to temptation slow,
They rightly do inherit heaven's graces
And husband nature's riches from expense;
They are the lords and owners of their faces,
Others but stewards of their excellence.

Shakespeare, *Sonnet XCIV*

64 Oh! Sir [Batchelor], reply'd Don *Antonio,* what
have you to answer for, in robbing the World of
the most diverting Folly, that ever was expos'd
among Mankind?

Cervantes, *Don Quixote,* II, 65

65 Silence is the virtue of a fool.

Bacon, *Advancement of Learning,*
Bk. VI, III, 31

66 There is in human nature generally more of the
fool than of the wise; and therefore those faculties
by which the foolish part of men's minds is taken
are most potent.

Bacon, *Of Boldness*

67 The folly of one man is the fortune of another. For
no man prospers so suddenly as by others' errors.

Bacon, *Of Fortune*

68 The sciences taken all together are identical with
human wisdom.

Descartes, *Rules for Direction
of the Mind,* I

69 I cannot justifie that contemptible Proverb, *That
fools only are Fortunate;* or that insolent Paradox,
That a wise man is out of the reach of Fortune. . . . 'Tis,
I confess, the common fate of men of singular gifts
of mind to be destitute of those of Fortune, which
doth not any way deject the Spirit of wiser judgments, who throughly understand the justice of
this proceeding; and being inrich'd with higher
donatives, cast a more careless eye on these vulgar

parts of felicity.

Sir Thomas Browne, *Religio Medici,* I, 18

70 Let Providence provide for Fools: 'tis not partiality, but equity in God, who deals with us but as
our natural Parents; those that are able of Body
and Mind, he leaves to their deserts; to those of
weaker merits he imparts a larger portion, and
pieces out the defect of one, by the access of the
other.

Sir Thomas Browne, *Religio Medici,* I, 18

71 The world is a good judge of things, for it is in
natural ignorance, which is man's true state. The
sciences have two extremes which meet. The first
is the pure natural ignorance in which all men
find themselves at birth. The other extreme is that
reached by great intellects, who, having run
through all that men can know, find they know
nothing, and come back again to that same ignorance from which they set out; but this is a
learned ignorance which is conscious of itself.
Those between the two, who have departed from
natural ignorance and not been able to reach the
other, have some smattering of this vain knowledge and pretend to be wise. These trouble the
world and are bad judges of everything. The people and the wise constitute the world; these despise it, and are despised. They judge badly of
everything, and the world judges rightly of them.

Pascal, *Pensées,* V, 327

72 *Adam.*   Apte the Mind or Fancie is to roave
Uncheckt, and of her roaving is no end;
Till warn'd, or by experience taught, she learn
That not to know at large of things remote
From use, obscure and suttle, but to know
That which before us lies in daily life,
Is the prime Wisdom, what is more, is fume,
Or emptiness, or fond impertinence.

Milton, *Paradise Lost,* VIII, 188

73 *Samson.* What is strength without a double share
Of wisdom, vast, unwieldy, burdensom,
Proudly secure, yet liable to fall
By weakest suttleties, not made to rule,
But to subserve where wisdom bears command.

Milton, *Samson Agonistes,* 53

74 *God.*   He who receives
Light from above, from the fountain of light,
No other doctrine needs, though granted true;
But these are false, or little else but dreams,
Conjectures, fancies, built on nothing firm.
The first and wisest of them all profess'd
To know this only, that he nothing knew;
The next to fabling fell and smooth conceits,
A third sort doubted all things, though plain
sence;
Others in vertue plac'd felicity,
But vertue joyn'd with riches and long life,

In corporal pleasure he, and careless ease,
The Stoic last in Philosophic pride,
By him call'd vertue; and his vertuous man,
Wise, perfect in himself, and all possessing
Equal to God, oft shames not to prefer,
As fearing God nor man, contemning all
Wealth, pleasure, pain or torment, death and life,
Which when he lists, he leaves, or boasts he can,
For all his tedious talk is but vain boast,
Or subtle shifts conviction to evade.
Alas what can they teach, and not mislead;
Ignorant of themselves, of God much more,
And how the world began, and how man fell
Degraded by himself, on grace depending?
Much of the Soul they talk, but all awrie,
And in themselves seek vertue, and to themselves
All glory arrogate, to God give none,
Rather accuse him under usual names,
Fortune and Fate, as one regardless quite
Of mortal things. Who therefore seeks in these
True wisdom, finds her not, or by delusion
Far worse, her false resemblance only meets,
An empty cloud.

Milton, *Paradise Regained,* IV, 288

75 No God and no human being, except an envious
one, is delighted by my impotence or my trouble,
or esteems as any virtue in us tears, sighs, fears,
and other things of this kind, which are signs of
mental impotence; on the contrary, the greater
the joy with which we are affected, the greater the
perfection to which we pass thereby, that is to say,
the more do we necessarily partake of the divine
nature. To make use of things, therefore, and to
delight in them as much as possible (provided we
do not disgust ourselves with them, which is not
delighting in them), is the part of a wise man. It is
the part of a wise man, I say, to refresh and invig-
orate himself with moderate and pleasant eating
and drinking, with sweet scents and the beauty of
green plants, with ornament, with music, with
sports, with the theatre, and with all things of this
kind which one man can enjoy without hurting
another. For the human body is composed of a
great number of parts of diverse nature, which
constantly need new and varied nourishment, in
order that the whole of the body may be equally
fit for everything which can follow from its nature, and consequently that the mind may be
equally fit to understand many things at once.
This mode of living best of all agrees both with
our principles and with common practice; therefore this mode of living is the best of all, and is to
be universally commended.

Spinoza, *Ethics,* IV, Prop. 45, Schol.

76 The ignorant man is not only agitated by external
causes in many ways, and never enjoys true peace
of soul, but lives also ignorant, as it were, both of
God and of things, and as soon as he ceases to
suffer ceases also to be. On the other hand, the
wise man, in so far as he is considered as such, is
scarcely ever moved in his mind, but, being conscious by a certain eternal necessity of himself, of
God, and of things, never ceases to be, and always
enjoys true peace of soul. If the way which, as I
have shown, leads hither seem very difficult, it
can nevertheless be found. It must indeed be difficult since it is so seldom discovered.

Spinoza, *Ethics,* V, Prop. 42, Schol.

77 The latter Part of a wise man's Life is taken up in
curing the Follies, Prejudices, and false Opinions
he had contracted in the former.

Swift, *Thoughts on Various Subjects*

78 The learn'd is happy nature to explore,
The fool is happy that he knows no more.

Pope, *Essay on Man,* Epistle II, 263

79 No place so sacred from such fops is barred,
Nor is Paul's church more safe than Paul's
churchyard:
Nay, fly to Altars; there they'll talk you dead:
For Fools rush in where Angels fear to tread.
Distrustful sense with modest caution speaks,
It still looks home, and short excursions makes;
But rattling nonsense in full volleys breaks,
And never shocked, and never turned aside,
Bursts out, resistless, with a thund'ring tide.

Pope, *Essay on Criticism,* III, 622

80 [Johnson's] superiority over other learned men
consisted chiefly in what may be called the art of
thinking, the art of using his mind; a certain continual power of seizing the useful substance of all
that he knew, and exhibiting it in a clear and
forcible manner; so that knowledge, which we often see to be no better than lumber in men of dull
understanding, was, in him, true, evident, and actual wisdom.

Boswell, *Life of Johnson (1784)*

81 The greybeard, old Wisdom, may boast of his
treasures,—
Give me with gay Folly to live;
I grant him calm-blooded, time-settled pleasures,
But Folly has raptures to give.

Burns, *Written on a Window of the "Globe
Tavern," Dumfries*

82 The hours of folly are measur'd by the clock; but
of wisdom, no clock can measure.

Blake, *Marriage of Heaven and Hell,* 7

83 If the fool would persist in his folly he would become wise.

Blake, *Marriage of Heaven and Hell,* 7

84 *Faust.* Through the world I have but flown.
Whatever I craved, I seized it by the hair,
Whatever sufficed not, I let fare.

Whatever escaped, I let it go.
I've but desired and but achieved, each hour,
And then again have wished, and so with power
Stormed through my life; at first with power and
   greatness;
But now life moves with cautious, wise sedateness.
Well do I know the sphere of earth and men.
The view beyond is barred to mortal ken;
A fool! who thither turns his blinking eyes
And dreams he'll find his like above the skies.
Let him stand fast and look around on earth;
Not mute is this world to a man of worth.
Why need he range through all eternity?
Here he can seize all that he knows to be.
Thus let him wander down his earthly day;
When spirits spook, let him pursue his way;
Let him find pain and bliss as on he stride,
He! every moment still unsatisfied.

> Goethe, *Faust*, II, 5, 11433

85 *Faust.* Yes, to this thought I hold unswerving,
To wisdom's final fruit, profoundly true:
Of freedom and of life he only is deserving
Who every day must conquer them anew.
Thus here, by danger girt, the active day
Of childhood, manhood, age will pass away.
Aye! such a throng I fain would see,
Stand on free soil among a people free.
Then might I say, that moment seeing:
"Ah, linger on, thou art so fair!"
The traces of my earthly being
Can perish not in æons—they are there!
That lofty moment I now feel in this:
I now enjoy the highest moment's bliss.

> Goethe, *Faust*, II, 5, 11573

86 Wisdom is oft-times nearer when we stoop
Than when we soar.

> Wordsworth, *The Excursion*, III, 231

87 Wisdom attempts nothing enormous and disproportioned to its powers, nothing which it cannot perform or nearly perform.

> Emerson, *The Conservative*

88 The wise through excess of wisdom is made a fool.

> Emerson, *Experience*

89 It is a characteristic of wisdom not to do desperate things.

> Thoreau, *Walden:* Economy

90 Wisdom is of the soul, is not susceptible of proof, is its own proof,

Applies to all stages and objects and qualities and is content,
Is the certainty of the reality and immortality of things, and the excellence of things;
Something there is in the float of the sight of things that provokes it out of the soul.

> Whitman, *Song of the Open Road*, VI

91 The only medicine for suffering, crime, and all the other woes of mankind, is wisdom. Teach a man to read and write, and you have put into his hands the great keys of the wisdom box. But it is quite another matter whether he ever opens the box or not.

> T. H. Huxley, *A Liberal Education*

92 There is a limit to human knowledge, and both sacred and profane writers witness that overwisdom is folly.

> Newman, *Essay on the Development of Christian Doctrine*, Pt. II, V, 6

93 *Pierre.* All we can know is that we know nothing. And that's the height of human wisdom.

> Tolstoy, *War and Peace*, V, 1

94 *The Mason.* The highest wisdom is not founded on reason alone, not on those worldly sciences of physics, history, chemistry, and the like, into which intellectual knowledge is divided. The highest wisdom is one. The highest wisdom has but one science—the science of the whole—the science explaining the whole creation and man's place in it. To receive that science it is necessary to purify and renew one's inner self, and so before one can know, it is necessary to believe and to perfect one's self. And to attain this end, we have the light called conscience that God has implanted in our souls.

> Tolstoy, *War and Peace*, V, 2

95 The king says. . . . Hain't we got all the fools in town on our side? And ain't that a big enough majority in any town?

> Mark Twain, *Huckleberry Finn*, XXVI

96 Behold, the fool saith, 'Put not all thine eggs in the one basket'—which is but a manner of saying, 'Scatter your money and your attention;' but the wise man saith, 'Put all your eggs in the one basket and—WATCH THAT BASKET.'

> Mark Twain, *Pudd'nhead Wilson's Calendar*, XV

Chapter 10

POLITICS

Chapter 10 is divided into nine sections: 10.1 Society and the State, 10.2 The Realm of Politics, 10.3 Government: Its Nature, Necessity, and Forms, 10.4 Government of and by the People: Republic and Democracy, 10.5 Citizenship, 10.6 Despotism and Tyranny, 10.7 Slavery, 10.8 Classes and Class Conflict, and 10.9 Revolution.

For the most part, the term "politics" is used here to cover the range of questions or issues that have been discussed in political philosophy or political theory, though the quotations often go afield to touch on related topics in the wider domain of social thought. The opening section, for example, is concerned with human association in all its forms—with different types of societies or communities, not just civil society, the political community, or state; and Section 10.2 not only includes passages that discuss politics as a discipline or branch of practical philosophy, but also passages that offer counsel or guidance to the statesman or politician and try to formulate the rules of statecraft or the policies to adopt for success in the struggle for power. Similarly, Sections

10.7, 10.8, and 10.9, in dealing with slavery, class conflict, and revolution, introduce economic and sociological considerations in addition to the more narrowly political ones.

The central sections in this chapter are devoted to the problems of government, especially the government of the political community or state. Section 10.3 prepares the way for the sections to follow by assembling quotations concerning the nature of government, its necessity, and the various forms it takes or can take. Section 10.4 deals with constitutional government or a government of laws, as contrasted with absolute or unlimited government, which is treated in Section 10.6 under the head of despotism and tyranny. Since citizenship, in a strict sense, comes into existence only with the creation of republics and the question of who shall be admitted to citizenship is mainly raised in connection with democracy, Section 10.5, Citizenship, follows directly after the section in which republics and democracies are discussed. Similarly, since slavery or subjection is the condition of those who are governed tyrannically or despotically, Section 10.7, SLAVERY, follows directly after the section in which despotism and tyranny are discussed. The last two sections of the chapter are also closely related to one another; for, as the reader will find, one of the main points made in both Sections 10.8 and 10.9 is that class conflict breeds revolution.

Four other chapters deal with subjects and problems that either fall within the domain of politics or are closely related to it. They are Chapter 11 on ECONOMICS, Chapter 12 on LAW AND JUSTICE, Chapter 13 on LIBERTY AND EQUALITY, and Chapter 14 on WAR AND PEACE. The reader is advised to consult these chapters for matters that are not fully treated here, or for the discussion of matters that throw light on what is treated here.

10.1 | *Society and the State*

Man, it is said, is both a social and a political animal. Of these two ascriptions, "social" has the broader connotation. Like other animals, man is gregarious rather than solitary. His gregariousness is manifested in various forms of human association: the family is one of these; the tribe or village, another; and a third is the state. It is only in virtue of this last form of association that man is called a "political" animal; and among gregarious or social animals, man alone is political.

The political community or civil society may be a city-state or a nation-state, and it might, at some future date, even be a world-state. In any of these embodiments, the state differs in a number of respects from all other forms of society, among which the most distinctive, perhaps, is that it may include within its domain other societies, such as families or tribes, but while it remains an independent or autonomous state, it is itself included in no larger community.

The reader will find that ancient and modern writers offer different characterizations of the state, as well as different accounts of its nature and origin. However, careful reading will discover that, although the moderns employ the fiction of a social contract as the original constitution of the state, there is underlying agreement that the state is both natural and conventional—natural in the sense that man is by nature political and needs the state for the perfection of human life, and conventional in the sense that the state comes into existence through human institutions, intelligently devised and voluntarily adopted.

The foregoing considerations affect the answers given to such questions as whether man is made for the state or the state for man; whether man is a part of the state and subordinate to it as an organic part is subordinate to the body of which it is a member; whether the end that the state serves is the happiness of its constituent beings; whether the state can exist without law or government; and whether, as contrasted with the state of nature and the state of war, civil society is identical with civil peace. The reader will find that these questions are also discussed in other contexts—in Section 9.8

on HAPPINESS; in Section 10.3 on GOVERN-
MENT: ITS NATURE, NECESSITY, AND FORMS; in
Section 12.1 on LAW AND LAWYERS; in Section
14.3 on THE CONDITIONS OF PEACE.

1 *Socrates.* Mankind at first lived dispersed, and there were no cities. But the consequence was that they were destroyed by the wild beasts, for they were utterly weak in comparison of them, and their art was only sufficient to provide them with the means of life, and did not enable them to carry on war against the animals: food they had, but not as yet the art of government, of which the art of war is a part. After a while the desire of self-preservation gathered them into cities; but when they were gathered together, having no art of government, they evil intreated one another, and were again in process of dispersion and destruction. Zeus feared that the entire race would be exterminated, and so he sent Hermes to them, bearing reverence and justice to be the ordering principles of cities and the bonds of friendship and conciliation.

Plato, *Protagoras,* 322A

2 *Socrates.* A State . . . arises, as I conceive, out of the needs of mankind; no one is self-sufficing, but all of us have many wants. Can any other origin of a State be imagined?

Adeimantus. There can be no other.

Then as we have many wants, and many persons are needed to supply them, one takes a helper for one purpose and another for another; and when these partners and helpers are gathered together in one habitation the body of inhabitants is termed a State.

True, he said.

And they exchange with one another, and one gives, and another receives, under the idea that the exchange will be for their good.

Very true.

Then, I said, let us begin and create in idea a State; and yet the true creator is necessity, who is the mother of our invention.

Plato, *Republic,* II, 369A

3 *Socrates.* Can there be any greater evil than discord and distraction and plurality where unity ought to reign? or any greater good than the bond of unity?

Glaucon. There cannot.

And there is unity where there is community of pleasures and pains—where all the citizens are glad or grieved on the same occasions of joy and sorrow?

No doubt.

Yes; and where there is no common but only private feeling a State is disorganized—when you have one half of the world triumphing and the other plunged in grief at the same events happening to the city or the citizens?

Certainly.

Such differences commonly originate in a disagreement about the use of the terms "mine" and "not mine," "his" and "not his."

Exactly so.

And is not that the best-ordered State in which the greatest number of persons apply the terms "mine" and "not mine" in the same way to the same thing?

Quite true.

Or that again which most nearly approaches to the condition of the individual—as in the body, when but a finger of one of us is hurt, the whole frame, drawn towards the soul as a centre and forming one kingdom under the ruling power therein, feels the hurt and sympathizes all together with the part affected, and we say that the man has a pain in his finger; and the same expression is used about any other part of the body, which has a sensation of pain at suffering or of pleasure at the alleviation of suffering.

Very true, he replied; and I agree with you that in the best-ordered State there is the nearest approach to this common feeling which you describe.

Then when any one of the citizens experiences any good or evil, the whole State will make his case their own, and will either rejoice or sorrow with him?

Yes, he said, that is what will happen in a well-ordered State.

Plato, *Republic,* V, 462A

4 Man is a political creature and one whose nature is to live with others.

Aristotle, *Ethics,* 1169^{b}18

5 Every state is a community of some kind, and every community is established with a view to some good; for mankind always act in order to obtain that which they think good. But, if all communities aim at some good, the state or political community, which is the highest of all, and which embraces all the rest, aims at good in a greater degree than any other, and at the highest good.

Aristotle, *Politics,* 1252^{a}1

6 When several villages are united in a single complete community, large enough to be nearly or quite self-sufficing, the state comes into existence, originating in the bare needs of life, and continuing in existence for the sake of a good life. And therefore, if the earlier forms of society are natural, so is the state, for it is the end of them, and the

nature of a thing is its end. For what each thing is when fully developed, we call its nature, whether we are speaking of a man, a horse, or a family. Besides, the final cause and end of a thing is the best, and to be self-sufficing is the end and the best.

Hence it is evident that the state is a creation of nature, and that man is by nature a political animal. And he who by nature and not by mere accident is without a state, is either a bad man or above humanity. . . .

Further, the state is by nature clearly prior to the family and to the individual, since the whole is of necessity prior to the part; for example, if the whole body be destroyed, there will be no foot or hand, except in an equivocal sense, as we might speak of a stone hand; for when destroyed the hand will be no better than that. But things are defined by their working and power; and we ought not to say that they are the same when they no longer have their proper quality, but only that they have the same name. The proof that the state is a creation of nature and prior to the individual is that the individual, when isolated, is not self-sufficing; and therefore he is like a part in relation to the whole. But he who is unable to live in society, or who has no need because he is sufficent for himself, must be either a beast or a god: he is no part of a state. A social instinct is implanted in all men by nature, and yet he who first founded the state was the greatest of benefactors.

Aristotle, Politics, 1252ᵇ28

7 As a means to the end which he [Plato] ascribes to the state, the scheme, taken literally, is impracticable, and how we are to interpret it is nowhere precisely stated. I am speaking of the premiss from which the argument of Socrates proceeds, 'that the greater the unity of the state the better'. Is it not obvious that a state may at length attain such a degree of unity as to be no longer a state?—since the nature of a state is to be a plurality.

Aristotle, Politics, 1261ᵃ13

8 A state exists for the sake of a good life, and not for the sake of life only: if life only were the object, slaves and brute animals might form a state, but they cannot, for they have no share in happiness or in a life of free choice. Nor does a state exist for the sake of alliance and security from injustice, nor yet for the sake of exchange and mutual intercourse. . . . Virtue must be the care of a state which is truly so called, and not merely enjoys the name: for without this end the community becomes a mere alliance which differs only in place from alliances of which the members live apart; and law is only a convention, 'a surety to one another of justice', as the sophist Lycophron says, and has no real power to make the citizens good and just. . . . It is clear then that a state is

not a mere society, having a common place, established for the prevention of mutual crime and for the sake of exchange. These are conditions without which a state cannot exist; but all of them together do not constitute a state, which is a community of families and aggregation of families in well-being, for the sake of a perfect and self-sufficing life. Such a community can only be established among those who live in the same place and intermarry. Hence arise in cities family connexions, brotherhoods, common sacrifices, amusements which draw men together. But these are created by friendship, for the will to live together is friendship. The end of the state is the good life, and these are the means towards it. And the state is the union of families and villages in a perfect and self-sufficing life, by which we mean a happy and honourable life.

Our conclusion, then, is that political society exists for the sake of noble actions, and not of mere companionship. Hence they who contribute most to such a society have a greater share in it than those who have the same or a greater freedom or nobility of birth but are inferior to them in political virtue; or than those who exceed them in wealth but are surpassed by them in virtue.

Aristotle, Politics, 1280ᵃ32

9 A state . . . only begins to exist when it has attained a population sufficient for a good life in the political community: it may indeed, if it somewhat exceed this number, be a greater state. But . . . there must be a limit. What should be the limit will be easily ascertained by experience. For both governors and governed have duties to perform; the special functions of a governor are to command and to judge. But if the citizens of a state are to judge and to distribute offices according to merit, then they must know each other's characters; where they do not possess this knowledge, both the election to offices and the decision of lawsuits will go wrong. When the population is very large they are manifestly settled at haphazard, which clearly ought not to be. . . . Clearly then the best limit of the population of a state is the largest number which suffices for the purposes of life, and can be taken in at a single view.

Aristotle, Politics, 1326ᵇ8

10 States require property, but property, even though living beings are included in it, is no part of a state; for a state is not a community of living beings only, but a community of equals, aiming at the best life possible. Now, whereas happiness is the highest good, being a realization and perfect practice of virtue, which some can attain, while others have little or none of it, the various qualities of men are clearly the reason why there are various kinds of states and many forms of government; for different men seek after happiness in different ways and by different means, and so

make for themselves different modes of life and forms of government.

Aristotle, *Politics,* 1328ª35

11 Let us . . . enumerate the functions of a state, and we shall easily elicit what we want:

First, there must be food; secondly, arts, for life requires many instruments; thirdly, there must be arms, for the members of a community have need of them, and in their own hands, too, in order to maintain authority both against disobedient subjects and against external assailants; fourthly, there must be a certain amount of revenue, both for internal needs, and for the purposes of war; fifthly, or rather first, there must be a care of religion, which is commonly called worship; sixthly, and most necessary of all, there must be a power of deciding what is for the public interest, and what is just in men's dealings with one another.

These are the services which every state may be said to need. For a state is not a mere aggregate of persons, but a union of them sufficing for the purposes of life; and if any of these things be wanting, it is as we maintain impossible that the community can be absolutely self-suffing. A state then should be framed with a view to the fulfilment of these functions. There must be husbandmen to procure food, and artisans, and a warlike and a wealthy class, and priests, and judges to decide what it necessary and expedient.

Aristotle, *Politics,* 1328ᵇ4

12 The principles of fellowship and society that nature has established among men must be traced back to their origins. The first principle subsists among all members of the human race. It is that connecting link of reason and speech by which the several processes of teaching, learning, communicating, discussing, and debating associate men together and unite them in a kind of brotherhood. In no other particular are we more distinct from the animals. We may grant them courage (for example, horses and lions). But we do not credit them with justice, equity, and goodness, because they are not endowed with reason or speech.

Cicero, *De Officiis,* I, 16

13 As a foot is no longer a foot if it is detached from the body, so you are no longer a man if you are separated from other men. For what is a man? A part of a state, of that first which consists of Gods and of men; then of that which is called next to it, which is a small image of the universal state.

Epictetus, *Discourses,* II, 5

14 If we . . . say that a people is an assemblage of reasonable beings bound together by a common agreement as to the objects of their love, then, in order to discover the character of any people, we have only to observe what they love. Yet whatever it loves, if only it is an assemblage of reasonable

beings and not of beasts, and is bound together by an agreement as to the objects of love, it is reasonably called a people; and it will be a superior people in proportion as it is bound together by higher interests, inferior in proportion as it is bound together by lower.

Augustine, *City of God,* XIX, 24

15 The light of reason is placed by nature in every man, to guide him in his acts towards his end. Wherefore, if man were intended to live alone, as many animals do, he would require no other guide to his end. Each man would be a king unto himself, under God, the highest King, inasmuch as he would direct himself in his acts by the light of reason given him from on high. Yet it is natural for man, more than for any other animal, to be a social and political animal, to live in a group.

Aquinas, *On Kingship,* I, 1

16 The preservation of states is a thing that probably surpasses our understanding.

Montaigne, *Essays,* III, 9, Of Vanity

17 *Archbishop of Canterbury.* Therefore doth heaven divide
The state of man in divers functions,
Setting endeavour in continual motion;
To which is fixed, as an aim or butt,
Obedience: for so work the honey-bees,
Creatures that by a rule in nature teach
The act of order to a peopled kingdom.
They have a king and officers of sorts;
Where some, like magistrates, correct at home,
Others, like merchants, venture trade abroad,
Others, like soldiers, armed in their stings,
Make boot upon the summer's velvet buds,
Which pillage they with merry march bring home
To the tent-royal of their emperor;
Who, busied in his majesty, surveys
The singing masons building roofs of gold,
The civil citizens kneading up the honey,
The poor mechanic porters crowding in
Their heavy burdens at his narrow gate,
The sad-eyed justice, with his surly hum,
Delivering o'er to executors pale
The lazy yawning drone.

Shakespeare, *Henry V,* I, ii, 183

18 *Ulysses.* The providence that's in a watchful state
Knows almost every grain of Plutus' gold,
Finds bottom in the uncomprehensive deeps,
Keeps place with thought and almost, like the gods,
Does thoughts unveil in their dumb cradles.
There is a mystery—with whom relation
Durst never meddle—in the soul of state;
Which hath an operation more divine
Than breath or pen can give expressure to.

Shakespeare, *Troilus and Cressida,* III, iii, 196

19 In the youth of a state, arms do flourish: in the middle age of a state, learning; and then both of them together for a time: in the declining age of a state, mechanical arts and merchandize.

Bacon, *Of Vicissitude of Things*

20 A state is a perfect body of free men, united together in order to enjoy common rights and advantages.

Grotius, *Rights of War and Peace,* Bk. I, I, 14

21 Nature (the art whereby God hath made and governs the world) is by the art of man, as in many other things, so in this also imitated, that it can make an artificial animal. For seeing life is but a motion of limbs, the beginning whereof is in some principal part within, why may we not say that all automata (engines that move themselves by springs and wheels as doth a watch) have an artificial life? For what is the heart, but a spring; and the nerves, but so many strings; and the joints, but so many wheels, giving motion to the whole body, such as was intended by the Artificer? Art goes yet further, imitating that rational and most excellent work of Nature, *man.* For by art is created that great LEVIATHAN called a COMMONWEALTH, or STATE, which is but an artificial man, though of greater stature and strength than the natural, for whose protection and defence it was intended; and in which the sovereignty is an artificial soul, as giving life and motion to the whole body; the magistrates and other officers of judicature and execution, artificial joints; reward and punishment (by which fastened to the seat of the sovereignty, every joint and member is moved to perform his duty) are the nerves, that do the same in the body natural; the wealth and riches of all the particular members are the strength; the people's safety its business; counsellors, by whom all things needful for it to know are suggested unto it, are the memory; equity and laws, an artificial reason and will; concord, health; sedition, sickness; and civil war, death. Lastly, the pacts and covenants, by which the parts of this body politic were at first made, set together, and united, resemble that *fiat,* or the *Let us make man,* pronounced by God, in the Creation.

Hobbes, *Leviathan,* Intro.

22 The final cause, end, or design of men (who naturally love liberty, and dominion over others) in the introduction of that restraint upon themselves, in which we see them live in Commonwealths, is the foresight of their own preservation, and of a more contented life thereby; that is to say, of getting themselves out from that miserable condition of war which is necessarily consequent . . . to the natural passions of men when there is no visible power to keep them in awe, and tie them by fear of punishment to the performance of their covenants.

Hobbes, *Leviathan,* II, 17

23 Irrational creatures cannot distinguish between injury and damage; and therefore as long as they be at ease, they are not offended with their fellows: whereas man is then most troublesome when he is most at ease; for then it is that he loves to show his wisdom, and control the actions of them that govern the Commonwealth. . . .

The agreement of [irrational] creatures is natural; that of men is by covenant only, which is artificial: and therefore it is no wonder if there be somewhat else required, besides covenant, to make their agreement constant and lasting; which is a common power to keep them in awe and to direct their actions to the common benefit.

The only way to erect such a common power, as may be able to defend them from the invasion of foreigners, and the injuries of one another, and thereby to secure them in such sort as that by their own industry and by the fruits of the earth they may nourish themselves and live contentedly, is to confer all their power and strength upon one man, or upon one assembly of men, that may reduce all their wills, by plurality of voices, unto one will: which is as much as to say, to appoint one man, or assembly of men, to bear their person; and everyone to own and acknowledge himself to be author of whatsoever he that so beareth their person shall act, or cause to be acted, in those things which concern the common peace and safety; and therein to submit their wills, every one to his will, and their judgements to his judgement. This is more than consent, or concord; it is a real unity of them all in one and the same person, made by covenant of every man with every man, in such manner as if every man should say to every man: *I authorise and give up my right of governing myself to this man, or to this assembly of men, on this condition; that thou give up thy right to him, and authorise all his actions in like manner.* This done, the multitude so united in one person is called a COMMONWEALTH. . . . This is the generation of that great LEVIATHAN, or rather, to speak more reverently, of that mortal god to which we owe, under the immortal God, our peace and defence.

Hobbes, *Leviathan,* II, 17

24 Though nothing can be immortal which mortals make; yet, if men had the use of reason they pretend to, their Commonwealths might be secured, at least, from perishing by internal diseases. For by the nature of their institution, they are designed to live as long as mankind, or as the laws of nature, or as justice itself, which gives them life. Therefore when they come to be dissolved, not by external violence, but intestine disorder, the fault is not in men as they are the *matter,* but as they are the *makers* and orderers of them.

Hobbes, *Leviathan,* II, 29

25 It is by the highest right of nature that each person exists, and consequently it is by the highest

right of nature that each person does those things which follow from the necessity of his nature; and therefore it is by the highest right of nature that each person judges what is good and what is evil, consults his own advantage as he thinks best, avenges himself, and endeavours to preserve what he loves and to destroy what he hates. If men lived according to the guidance of reason, every one would enjoy this right without injuring any one else. But because men are subject to affects which far surpass human power or virtue, they are often drawn in different directions and are contrary to one another, although they need one another's help.

In order, then, that men may be able to live in harmony and be a help to one another, it is necessary for them to cede their natural right, and beget confidence one in the other that they will do nothing by which one can injure the other. . . . By this law, therefore, can society be strengthened, if only it claims for itself the right which every individual possesses of avenging himself and deciding what is good and what is evil, and provided, therefore, that it possess the power of prescribing a common rule of life, of promulgating laws and supporting them, not by reason, which cannot restrain the affects, but by penalties.

This society, firmly established by law and with a power of self-preservation, is called a *State,* and those who are protected by its right are called *Citizens.* We can now easily see that in the natural state there is nothing which by universal consent is good or evil, since every one in a natural state consults only his own profit; deciding according to his own way of thinking what is good and what is evil with reference only to his own profit, and is not bound by any law to obey any one but himself. Hence in a natural state sin cannot be conceived, but only in a civil state, where it is decided by universal consent what is good and what is evil, and where every one is bound to obey the State. *Sin,* therefore, is nothing but disobedience, which is punished by the law of the State alone; obedience, on the other hand, being regarded as a *merit* in a citizen, because on account of it he is considered worthy to enjoy the privileges of the State. Again, in a natural state no one by common consent is the owner of anything, nor is there anything in nature which can be said to be the rightful property of this and not of that man, but all things belong to all, so that in a natural state it is impossible to conceive a desire of rendering to each man his own or taking from another that which is his; that is to say, in a natural state there is nothing which can be called just or unjust, but only in a civil state, in which it is decided by universal consent what is one person's and what is another's. Justice and injustice, therefore, sin and merit, are external notions, and not attributes, which manifest the nature of the mind.

Spinoza, *Ethics,* IV, Prop. 37, Schol. 2

26 If all the members of a state wish to disregard the law, by that very fact they dissolve the state and destroy the commonwealth.

Spinoza, *Theologico-Political Treatise,* III

27 The commonwealth seems to me to be a society of men constituted only for the procuring, preserving, and advancing their own civil interests.

Civil interests I call life, liberty, health, and indolency of body; and the possession of outward things, such as money, lands, houses, furniture, and the like.

Locke, *Letter Concerning Toleration*

28 The political society is instituted for no other end, but only to secure every man's possession of the things of this life. The care of each man's soul and of the things of heaven, which neither does belong to the commonwealth nor can be subjected to it, is left entirely to every man's self.

Locke, *Letter Concerning Toleration*

29 Man being born . . . with a title to perfect freedom and an uncontrolled enjoyment of all the rights and privileges of the law of Nature, equally with any other man, or number of men in the world, hath by nature a power not only to preserve his property—that is, his life, liberty, and estate, against the injuries and attempts of other men, but to judge of and punish the breaches of that law in others, as he is persuaded the offence deserves, even with death itself, in crimes where the heinousness of the fact, in his opinion, requires it. But because no political society can be, nor subsist, without having in itself the power to preserve the property, and in order thereunto punish the offences of all those of that society, there, and there only, is political society where every one of the members hath quitted this natural power, resigned it up into the hands of the community in all cases that exclude him not from appealing for protection to the law established by it. . . . Wherever, therefore, any number of men so unite into one society as to quit every one his executive power of the law of Nature, and to resign it to the public, there and there only is a political or civil society.

Locke, *II Civil Government,* VII, 87–89

30 Mankind, notwithstanding all the privileges of the state of Nature, being but in an ill condition while they remain in it are quickly driven into society. Hence it comes to pass, that we seldom find any number of men live any time together in this state. The inconveniencies that they are therein exposed to by the irregular and uncertain exercise of the power every man has of punishing the transgressions of others, make them take sanctuary under the established laws of government, and therein seek the preservation of their property. It is this makes them so willingly give up every one

his single power of punishing to be exercised by such alone as shall be appointed to it amongst them, and by such rules as the community, or those authorised by them to that purpose, shall agree on. And in this we have the original right and rise of both the legislative and executive power as well as of the governments and societies themselves.

For in the state of Nature to omit the liberty he has of innocent delights, a man has two powers. The first is to do whatsoever he thinks fit for the preservation of himself and others within the permission of the law of Nature; by which law, common to them all, he and all the rest of mankind are one community, make up one society distinct from all other creatures, and were it not for the corruption and viciousness of degenerate men, there would be no need of any other, no necessity that men should separate from this great and natural community, and associate into lesser combinations. The other power a man has in the state of Nature is the power to punish the crimes committed against that law. Both these he gives up when he joins in a private, if I may so call it, or particular political society, and incorporates into any commonwealth separate from the rest of mankind.

The first power—viz., of doing whatsoever he thought fit for the preservation of himself and the rest of mankind, he gives up to be regulated by laws made by the society, so far forth as the preservation of himself and the rest of that society shall require; which laws of the society in many things confine the liberty he had by the law of Nature.

Secondly, the power of punishing he wholly gives up, and engages his natural force, which he might before employ in the execution of the law of Nature, by his own single authority, as he thought fit, to assist the executive power of the society as the law thereof shall require. For being now in a new state, wherein he is to enjoy many conveniencies from the labour, assistance, and society of others in the same community, as well as protection from its whole strength, he is to part also with as much of his natural liberty, in providing for himself, as the good, prosperity, and safety of the society shall require, which is not only necessary but just, since the other members of the society do the like.

Locke, *II Civil Government*, IX, 127–130

31 In the state of nature . . . all men are born equal, but they cannot continue in this equality. Society makes them lose it, and they recover it only by the protection of the laws.

Montesquieu, *Spirit of Laws*, VIII, 3

32 I suppose men to have reached the point at which the obstacles in the way of their preservation in the state of nature show their power of resistance to be greater than the resources at the disposal of each individual for his maintenance in that state. That primitive condition can then subsist no longer; and the human race would perish unless it changed its manner of existence.

But, as men cannot engender new forces, but only unite and direct existing ones, they have no other means of preserving themselves than the formation, by aggregation, of a sum of forces great enough to overcome the resistance. These they have to bring into play by means of a single motive power, and cause to act in concert.

This sum of forces can arise only where several persons come together: but, as the force and liberty of each man are the chief instruments of his self-preservation, how can he pledge them without harming his own interests, and neglecting the care he owes to himself? This difficulty, in its bearing on my present subject, may be stated in the following terms:

"The problem is to find a form of association which will defend and protect with the whole common force the person and goods of each associate, and in which each, while uniting himself with all, may still obey himself alone, and remain as free as before." This is the fundamental problem of which the *Social Contract* provides the solution.

The clauses of this contract are so determined by the nature of the act that the slightest modification would make them vain and ineffective; so that, although they have perhaps never been formally set forth, they are everywhere the same and everywhere tacitly admitted and recognised, until, on the violation of the social compact, each regains his original rights and resumes his natural liberty, while losing the conventional liberty in favour of which he renounced it.

These clauses, properly understood, may be reduced to one—the total alienation of each associate, together with all his rights, to the whole community; for, in the first place, as each gives himself absolutely, the conditions are the same for all; and, this being so, no one has any interest in making them burdensome to others.

Moreover, the alienation being without reserve, the union is as perfect as it can be, and no associate has anything more to demand: for, if the individuals retained certain rights, as there would be no common superior to decide between them and the public, each, being on one point his own judge, would ask to be so on all; the state of nature would thus continue, and the association would necessarily become inoperative or tyrannical.

Finally, each man, in giving himself to all, gives himself to nobody; and as there is no associate over whom he does not acquire the same right as he yields others over himself, he gains an equivalent for everything he loses, and an increase of force for the preservation of what he has.

Rousseau, *Social Contract*, I, 6

33 The passage from the state of nature to the civil state produces a very remarkable change in man, by substituting justice for instinct in his conduct, and giving his actions the morality they had formerly lacked. Then only, when the voice of duty takes the place of physical impulses and right of appetite, does man, who so far had considered only himself, find that he is forced to act on different principles, and to consult his reason before listening to his inclinations. Although, in this state, he deprives himself of some advantages which he got from nature, he gains in return others so great, his faculties are so stimulated and developed, his ideas so extended, his feelings so ennobled, and his whole soul so uplifted, that, did not the abuses of this new condition often degrade him below that which he left, he would be bound to bless continually the happy moment which took him from it for ever, and, instead of a stupid and unimaginative animal, made him an intelligent being and a man.

Rousseau, *Social Contract,* I, 8

34 The social compact sets up among the citizens an equality of such a kind, that they all bind themselves to observe the same conditions and should therefore all enjoy the same rights. Thus, from the very nature of the compact, every act of Sovereignty, that is, every authentic act of the general will, binds or favours all the citizens equally; so that the Sovereign recognises only the body of the nation, and draws no distinctions between those of whom it is made up. What, then, strictly speaking, is an act of Sovereignty? It is not a convention between a superior and an inferior, but a convention between the body and each of its members. It is legitimate, because based on the social contract, and equitable, because common to all; useful, because it can have no other object than the general good, and stable, because guaranteed by the public force and the supreme power. So long as the subjects have to submit only to conventions of this sort, they obey no-one but their own will; and to ask how far the respective rights of the Sovereign and the citizens extend, is to ask up to what point the latter can enter into undertakings with themselves, each with all, and all with each.

Rousseau, *Social Contract,* II, 4

35 What is the end of political association? The preservation and prosperity of its members. And what is the surest mark of their preservation and prosperity? Their numbers and population. Seek then nowhere else this mark that is in dispute. The rest being equal, the government under which, without external aids, without naturalisation or colonies, the citizens increase and multiply most, is beyond question the best.

Rousseau, *Social Contract,* III, 9

36 The opposite of the state of nature is the *civil* state

as the condition of a society standing under a distributive justice. In the state of nature, there may even be juridicial forms of society—such as marriage, parental authority, the household, and such like. For none of these, however, does any law *a priori* lay it down as an incumbent obligation: "Thou *shalt* enter into this state." But it may be said of the *juridical* state that: "All men who *may* even involuntarily come into relations of right with one another *ought* to enter into this state."

The natural or non-juridical social state may be viewed as the sphere of private right, and the civil state may be specially regarded as the sphere of public right. The latter state contains no more and no other duties of men towards each other than what may be conceived in connection with the former state; the matter of private right is, in short, the very same in both. The laws of the civil state, therefore, only turn upon the juridical form of the coexistence of men under a common constitution; and, in this respect, these laws must necessarily be regarded and conceived as public laws.

Kant, *Science of Right,* 41

37 Before a legal state of society can be publicly established, individual men, nations, and states, can never be safe against violence from each other; and this is evident from the consideration that every one of his own will naturally does *what seems good and right in his own eyes,* entirely independent of the opinion of others. Hence, unless the institution of right is to be renounced, the first thing incumbent on men is to accept the principle that it is necessary to leave the state of nature, in which every one follows his own inclinations, and to form a union of all those who cannot avoid coming into reciprocal communication, and thus subject themselves in common to the external restraint of public compulsory laws. Men thus enter into a civil union, in which every one has it determined by law what shall be recognized as his; and this is secured to him by a competent external power distinct from his own individuality. Such is the primary obligation, on the part of all men, to enter into the relations of a civil state of society.

Kant, *Science of Right,* 44

38 The state is the actuality of the ethical Idea. It is ethical mind *qua* the substantial will manifest and revealed to itself, knowing and thinking itself, accomplishing what it knows and in so far as it knows it. The state exists immediately in custom, mediately in individual self-consciousness, knowledge, and activity, while self-consciousness in virtue of its sentiment towards the state finds in the state, as its essence and the end and product of its activity, its substantive freedom. . . .

The state is absolutely rational inasmuch as it is the actuality of the substantial will which it possesses in the particular self-consciousness once that consciousness has been raised to consciousness of its universality. This substantial unity is an absolute unmoved end in itself, in which freedom comes into its supreme right. On the other hand this final end has supreme right against the individual, whose supreme duty is to be a member of the state.

If the state is confused with civil society, and if its specific end is laid down as the security and protection of property and personal freedom, then the interest of the individuals as such becomes the ultimate end of their association, and it follows that membership of the state is something optional. But the state's relation to the individual is quite different from this. Since the state is mind objectified, it is only as one of its members that the individual himself has objectivity, genuine individuality, and an ethical life.

Hegel, *Philosophy of Right*, 257–258

39 A nation does not begin by being a state. The transition from a family, a horde, a clan, a multitude, etc., to political conditions is the realization of the Idea in the form of that nation. Without this form, a nation, as an ethical substance—which is what it is implicitly, lacks the objectivity of possessing in its own eyes and in the eyes of others, a universal and universally valid embodiment in laws, that is, in determinate thoughts, and as a result it fails to secure recognition from others. So long as it lacks objective law and an explicitly established rational constitution, its autonomy is formal only and is not sovereignty. . . .

It is the absolute right of the Idea to step into existence in clear-cut laws and objective institutions, beginning with marriage and agriculture, . . . whether this right be actualized in the form of divine legislation and favour, or in the form of force and wrong. This right is the right of heroes to found states.

Hegel, *Philosophy of Right*, 349–350

40 The rational end of man is life in the state, and if there is no state there, reason at once demands that one be founded. Permission to enter a state or leave it must be given by the state; this then is not a matter which depends on an individual's arbitrary will and therefore the state does not rest on contract, for contract presupposes arbitrariness. It is false to maintain that the foundation of the state is something at the option of all its members. It is nearer the truth to say that it is absolutely necessary for every individual to be a citizen.

Hegel, *Philosophy of Right*, Additions, Par. 75

41 When we walk the streets at night in safety, it does not strike us that this might be otherwise. This habit of feeling safe has become second nature, and we do not reflect on just how this is due solely to the working of special institutions. Commonplace thinking often has the impression that force holds the state together, but in fact its only bond is the fundamental sense of order which everybody possesses.

Hegel, *Philosophy of Right*, Additions, Par. 268

42 We should desire to have in the state nothing except what is an expression of rationality. The state is the world which mind has made for itself; its march, therefore, is on lines that are fixed and absolute. How often we talk of the wisdom of God in nature! But we are not to assume for that reason that the physical world of nature is a loftier thing than the world of mind. As high as mind stands above nature, so high does the state stand above physical life. Man must therefore venerate the state as a secular deity, and observe that if it is difficult to comprehend nature, it is infinitely harder to understand the state.

Hegel, *Philosophy of Right*, Additions, Par. 272

43 The state of nature is . . . predominantly that of injustice and violence, of untamed natural impulses, of inhuman deeds and feelings. Limitation is certainly produced by society and the state, but it is a limitation of the mere brute emotions and rude instincts; as also, in a more advanced stage of culture, of the premeditated self-will of caprice and passion. This kind of constraint is part of the instrumentality by which only, the consciousness of freedom and the desire for its attainment, in its true—that is, rational and ideal form—can be obtained. . . . Society and the state are the very conditions in which freedom is realized.

Hegel, *Philosophy of History*, Introduction, 3

44 In dealing with the State we ought to remember that its institutions are not aboriginal, though they existed before we were born; that they are not superior to the citizen; that every one of them was once the act of a single man; every law and usage was a man's expedient to meet a particular case; that they all are imitable, all alterable; we may make as good, we may make better.

Emerson, *Politics*

45 The power of love, as the basis of a State, has never been tried.

Emerson, *Politics*

46 The highest conceivable form of human society is that in which the desire to do what is best for the whole, dominates and limits the action of every member of that society.

T. H. Huxley, *Science and Christian Tradition*, Prologue

47 The proletariat seizes the state power, and transforms the means of production in the first instance into state property. But in doing this, it puts an end to itself as the proletariat, it puts an end to all

class differences and class antagonisms, it puts an end also to the state as the state. Former society, moving in class antagonisms, had need of the state, that is, an organisation of the exploiting class at each period for the maintenance of its external conditions of production; that is, therefore, for the forcible holding down of the exploited class in the conditions of oppression (slavery, villeinage or serfdom, wage labour) determined by the existing mode of production. The state was the official representative of society as a whole, its embodiment in a visible corporation; but it was this only in so far as it was the state of that class which itself, in its epoch, represented society as a whole; in ancient times, the state of the slave-owning citizens; in the Middle Ages, of the feudal nobility; in our epoch, of the bourgeoisie. When ultimately it becomes really representative of society as a whole, it makes itself superfluous. As soon as there is no longer any class of society to be held in subjection; as soon as, along with class domination and the struggle for individual existence based on the former anarchy of production, the collisions and excesses arising from these have also been abolished, there is nothing more to be repressed which would make a special repressive force, a state, necessary. The first act in which the state really comes forward as the representative of society as a whole—the taking possession of the means of production in the name of society—is at the same time its last independent act as a state. The interference of the state power in social relations becomes superfluous in one sphere after another, and then ceases of itself. The government of persons is replaced by the administration of things and the direction of the processes of production. The state is not "abolished," *it withers away.*

Engels, *Anti-Dühring,* III, 2

48 Though society is not founded on a contract, and though no good purpose is answered by inventing a contract in order to deduce social obligations from it, every one who receives the protection of society owes a return for the benefit, and the fact of living in society renders it indispensable that each should be bound to observe a certain line of conduct towards the rest.

Mill, *On Liberty,* IV

49 I used the word "State": my meaning is self-evident, namely, a herd of blonde beasts of prey, a race of conquerors and masters, which with all its warlike organisation and all its organising power pounces with its terrible claws on a population, in numbers possibly tremendously superior, but as

yet formless, as yet nomad. Such is the origin of the "State." That fantastic theory that makes it begin with a contract is, I think, disposed of. He who can command, he who is a master by "nature," he who comes on the scene forceful in deed and gesture—what has he to do with contracts? Such beings defy calculation, they come like fate, without cause, reason, notice, excuse, they are there like the lightning is there, too terrible, too sudden, too convincing, too "different," to be personally even hated. Their work is an instinctive creating and impressing of forms, they are the most involuntary, unconscious artists that there are:—their appearance produces instantaneously a scheme of sovereignty which is *live,* in which the functions are partitioned and apportioned, in which above all no part is received or finds a place, until pregnant with a "meaning" in regard to the whole.

Nietzsche, *Genealogy of Morals,* II, 17

50 The truth is that the social order is fixed by laws of nature precisely analogous to those of the physical order. The most that man can do is by ignorance and self-conceit to mar the operation of social laws. The evils of society are to a great extent the result of the dogmatism and self-interest of statesmen, philosophers, and ecclesiastics who in past time have done just what the socialists now want to do. Instead of studying the natural laws of the social order, they assumed that they could organize society as they chose; they made up their minds what kind of a society they wanted to make; and they planned their little measures for the ends they had resolved upon. It will take centuries of scientific study of the facts of nature to eliminate from human society the mischievous institutions and traditions which the said statesmen, philosophers, and ecclesiastics have introduced into it.

W. G. Sumner, *Socialism*

51 The teaching of Marx and Engels regarding the inevitability of a violent revolution refers to the bourgeois state. It *cannot* be replaced by the proletarian state (the dictatorship of the proletariat) through "withering away," but, as a general rule, only through a violent revolution. . . .

The replacement of the bourgeois by the proletarian state is impossible without a violent revolution. The abolition of the proletarian state, i.e. of all states, is only possible through "withering away."

Lenin, *State and Revolution,* I, 4

10.2 | *The Realm of Politics*

The word "politics" is frequently used to designate a sphere of action in which men engage, vying with one another for power or position, scheming or planning to achieve certain objectives either in concert with their fellows or through control or domination of them. But the word is also used to name a learned discipline, a department of human thought or inquiry, an art or science. In the latter meaning, "politics" is short for political philosophy, political theory, political science, or the art of politics. The quotations collected here are concerned with the realm of politics in both senses of the term.

Those dealing with politics as a learned discipline or a department of thought and inquiry offer different answers to the question whether politics is a science or an art; and if a science, what type of science, appealing to what sort of principles, and offering what kind of evidence or arguments for its conclusions. Similar questions are asked about ethics or moral philosophy, as the reader will see by turning to Section 9.1; and by putting together quotations in that section and in this one, the reader will be reminded of some of the views that have been held about the relation of ethics and politics to one another. The main point at issue is whether politics is a normative discipline, one concerned with standards of justice, with such goods as liberty and equality, with what ought to be the ends and means of political action, not merely with what has been or can be done. Considerations relevant to this issue will be found in Section 11.1 on PROPERTY, Section 11.2 on WEALTH AND POVERTY, Section 12.2 on JUSTICE AND INJUSTICE, Section 13.1 on FREEDOM IN SOCIETY, and Section 13.3 on EQUALITY.

The quotations dealing with politics as a sphere of action tend to concentrate on the maxims, rules, or policies that the individual should put into practice if the individual wishes to succeed in attaining one's objectives, whatever they may be, good or bad. How far the person should be restrained by moral scruples, to what extent the person should let one's striving for success justify the employment of any means that promise to achieve it, what compromises with honesty the person must make—these and similar questions run through or lie behind the advice offered by such men of practical experience as Machiavelli and Francis Bacon, as well as by such philosophers as Plato and Aristotle. Outstanding examples of political sagacity and political ineptitude, of genuine statesmanship and of successful chicanery, are provided by the historians and the poets.

The favorable and unfavorable connotations that are often attached to the terms "statesman" and "politician" derive from different evaluations placed on political virtue, skill, or technique. Antipolitical writers, such as Thoreau, tend to regard the realm of politics as one from which virtue, honesty, and conscience are totally excluded.

---

1 *Menelaus.*   As with sailing, so with politics: make your cloth too taut, and your ship will dip and keel, but slacken off and trim your sails, and things head up again. The gods, you know, resent being importuned too much; in the same way the people dislike being pushed or hustled. Too much zeal offends where indirection works.

Euripides, *Orestes,* 706

2 *Praxagora.* Ye are to blame for this, Athenian people,

Ye draw your wages from the public purse,
Yet each man seeks his private gain alone.
So the State reels, like any Aesimus.
Still, if ye trust me, ye shall yet be saved.
I move that now the womankind be asked
To rule the State. In our own homes, ye know,
They are the managers and rule the house.

1st Woman. O good, good, good! speak on, speak
on, dear man!

Aristophanes, *Ecclesiazusae,* 205

3 *Cleon.* Ordinary men usually manage public affairs better than their more gifted fellows. The latter are always wanting to appear wiser than the laws, and to overrule every proposition brought forward, thinking that they cannot show their wit in more important matters, and by such behaviour too often ruin their country; while those who mistrust their own cleverness are content to be less learned than the laws, and less able to pick holes in the speech of a good speaker; and being fair judges rather than rival athletes, generally conduct affairs successfully.

Thucydides, *Peloponnesian War,* III, 37

4 *Socrates.* Do I understand you, . . . and is your meaning that you teach the art of politics, and that you promise to make men good citizens?

Protagoras. That, Socrates, is exactly the profession which I make.

Then, I said, you do indeed possess a noble art, if there is no mistake about this; for I will freely confess to you, Protagoras, that I have a doubt whether this art is capable of being taught, and yet I know not how to disbelieve your assertion. And I ought to tell you why I am of opinion that this art cannot be taught or communicated by man to man. I say that the Athenians are an understanding people, and indeed they are esteemed to be such by the other Hellenes. Now I observe that when we are met together in the assembly, and the matter in hand relates to building, the builders are summoned as advisers; when the question is one of shipbuilding, then the shipwrights; and the like of other arts which they think capable of being taught and learned. And if some person offers to give them advice who is not supposed by them to have any skill in the art, even though he be good-looking, and rich, and noble, they will not listen to him, but laugh and hoot at him, until either he is clamoured down and retires of himself; or if he persist, he is dragged away or put out by the constables at the command of the prytanes. This is their way of behaving about professors of the arts. But when the question is an affair of state, then everybody is free to have a say—carpenter, tinker, cobbler, sailor, passenger; rich and poor, high and low—any one who likes gets up, and no one reproaches him, as in the former case, with not having learned, and having no teacher, and yet giving advice; evidently because they are under the impression that this sort of knowledge cannot be taught. And not only is this true of the state, but of individuals; the best and wisest of our citizens are unable to impart their political wisdom to others: as for example, Pericles, the father of these young men, who gave them excellent instruction in all that could be learned from masters, in his own department of politics neither taught them, nor gave them teachers; but they were allowed to wander at their own free will in a sort of hope that they would light upon virtue of their own accord.

Plato, *Protagoras,* 319A

5 *Socrates.* Some one may wonder why I go about in private giving advice and busying myself with the concerns of others, but do not venture to come forward in public and advise the state. I will tell you why. . . . I am certain, O men of Athens, that if I had engaged in politics, I should have perished long ago, and done no good either to you or to myself. And do not be offended at my telling you the truth: for the truth is, that no man who goes to war with you or any other multitude, honestly striving against the many lawless and unrighteous deeds which are done in a state, will save his life; he who will fight for the right, if he would live even for a brief space, must have a private station and not a public one.

Plato, *Apology,* 31B

6 *Socrates.* Good men do not wish to be openly demanding payment for governing and so to get the name of hirelings, nor by secretly helping themselves out of the public revenues to get the name of thieves. And not being ambitious they do not care about honour. Wherefore necessity must be laid upon them, and they must be induced to serve from the fear of punishment. And this, as I imagine, is the reason why the forwardness to take office, instead of waiting to be compelled, has been deemed dishonourable. Now the worst part of the punishment is that he who refuses to rule is liable to be ruled by one who is worse than himself. And the fear of this, as I conceive, induces the good to take office, not because they would, but because they cannot help—not under the idea that they are going to have any benefit or enjoyment themselves, but as a necessity, and because they are not able to commit the task of ruling to any one who is better than themselves, or indeed as good. For there is reason to think that if a city were composed entirely of good men, then to avoid office would be as much an object of contention as to obtain office is at present; then we should have plain proof that the true ruler is not meant by nature to regard his own interest, but that of his subjects; and every one who knew this would choose rather to receive a benefit from another than to have the trouble of conferring one.

Plato, *Republic,* I, 347A

7 *Eleatic Stranger.* Then the true and natural art of statesmanship will never allow any State to be formed by a combination of good and bad men, if this can be avoided; but will begin by testing human natures in play, and after testing them, will entrust them to proper teachers who are the ministers of her purposes—she will herself give orders, and maintain authority; just as the art of weaving continually gives orders and maintains authority over the carders and all the others who prepare the material for the work, commanding the subsidiary arts to execute the works which she deems necessary for making the web.

Young Socrates. Quite true.

Str. In like manner, the royal science appears to me to be the mistress of all lawful educators and instructors, and having this queenly power, will not permit them to train men in what will produce characters unsuited to the political constitution which she desires to create, but only in what will produce such as are suitable. Those which have no share of manliness and temperance, or any other virtuous inclination, and, from the necessity of an evil nature, are violently carried away to godlessness and insolence and injustice, she gets rid of by death and exile, and punishes them with the greatest of disgraces.

Y. Soc. That is commonly said.

Str. But those who are wallowing in ignorance and baseness she bows under the yoke of slavery.

Y. Soc. Quite right.

Str. The rest of the citizens, out of whom, if they have education, something noble may be made, and who are capable of being united by the Statesman, the kingly art blends and weaves together; taking on the one hand those whose natures tend rather to courage, which is the stronger element and may be regarded as the warp, and on the other hand those which incline to order and gentleness, and which are represented in the figure as spun thick and soft, after the manner of the woof—these, which are naturally opposed, she seeks to bind and weave together. . . . This then we declare to be the completion of the web of political action, which is created by a direct intertexture of the brave and temperate natures, whenever the royal science has drawn the two minds into communion with one another by unanimity and friendship, and having perfected the noblest and best of all the webs which political life admits, and enfolding therein all other inhabitants of cities, whether slaves or freemen, binds them in one fabric and governs and presides over them, and, in so far as to be happy is vouchsafed to a city, in no particular fails to secure their happiness.

Plato, *Statesman,* 308B

8 *Athenian Stranger.* There is a difficulty in apprehending that the true art of politics is concerned, not with private but with public good (for public good binds together states, but private only distracts them); and that both the public and private good as well of individuals as of states is greater when the state and not the individual is first considered. In the second place, although a person knows in the abstract that this is true, yet if he be possessed of absolute and irresponsible power, he will never remain firm in his principles or persist in regarding the public good as primary in the state, and the private good as secondary. Human nature will be always drawing him into avarice and selfishness, avoiding pain and pursuing pleasure without any reason, and will bring these to the front, obscuring the juster and better; and so working darkness in his soul will at last fill with evils both him and the whole city.

Plato, *Laws,* IX, 875A

9 Every art and every inquiry, and similarly every action and pursuit, is thought to aim at some good; and for this reason the good has rightly been declared to be that at which all things aim. . . .

If . . . there is some end of the things we do, which we desire for its own sake (everything else being desired for the sake of this), and if we do not choose everything for the sake of something else (for at that rate the process would go on to infinity, so that our desire would be empty and vain), clearly this must be the good and the chief good. Will not the knowledge of it, then, have a great influence on life? Shall we not, like archers who have a mark to aim at, be more likely to hit upon what is right? If so, we must try, in outline at least, to determine what it is, and of which of the sciences or capacities it is the object. It would seem to belong to the most authoritative art and that which is most truly the master art. And politics appears to be of this nature; for it is this that ordains which of the sciences should be studied in a state, and which each class of citizens should learn and up to what point they should learn them; and we see even the most highly esteemed of capacities to fall under this, for example, strategy, economics, rhetoric; now, since politics uses the rest of the sciences, and since, again, it legislates as to what we are to do and what we are to abstain from, the end of this science must include those of the others, so that this end must be the good for man. For even if the end is the same for a single man and for a state, that of the state seems at all events something greater and more complete whether to attain or to preserve; though it is worthwhile to attain the end merely for one man, it is finer and more godlike to attain it for a nation or for city-states.

Aristotle, *Ethics,* 1094^{a}1

10 Political science does not make men, but takes them from nature and uses them.

Aristotle, *Politics,* 1258^{a}21

11 It is obvious that government too is the subject of a single science, which has to consider what government is best and of what sort it must be, to be most in accordance with our aspirations, if there were no external impediment, and also what kind of government is adapted to particular states. For the best is often unattainable, and therefore the true legislator and statesman ought to be acquainted, not only with (1) that which is best in the abstract, but also with (2) that which is best relatively to circumstances. We should be able further to say how a state may be constituted under any given conditions (3); both how it is originally formed and, when formed, how it may be longest preserved; the supposed state being so far from having the best constitution that it is unprovided even with the conditions necessary for the best; neither is it the best under the circumstances, but of an inferior type.

He ought, moreover, to know (4) the form of government which is best suited to states in general; for political writers, although they have excellent ideas, are often unpractical. We should consider, not only what form of government is best, but also what is possible and what is easily attainable by all.

Aristotle, Politics, 1288ᵇ21

12 Above all every state should be so administered and so regulated by law that its magistrates cannot possibly make money. . . . For the people do not take any great offence at being kept out of the government—indeed they are rather pleased than otherwise at having leisure for their private business—but what irritates them is to think that their rulers are stealing the public money; then they are doubly annoyed; for they lose both honour and profit. If office brought no profit, then and then only could democracy and aristocracy be combined; for both notables and people might have their wishes gratified. All would be able to hold office, which is the aim of democracy, and the notables would be magistrates, which is the aim of aristocracy. And this result may be accomplished when there is no possibility of making money out of the offices; for the poor will not want to have them when there is nothing to be gained from them—they would rather be attending to their own concerns; and the rich, who do not want money from the public treasury, will be able to take them; and so the poor will keep to their work and grow rich, and the notables will not be governed by the lower class.

Aristotle, Politics, 1308ᵇ31

13 Let us now address those who, while they agree that the life of virtue is the most eligible, differ about the manner of practising it. For some renounce political power, and think that the life of the freeman is different from the life of the statesman and the best of all; but others think the life of the statesman best. The argument of the latter is that he who does nothing cannot do well, and that virtuous activity is identical with happiness. To both we say: 'you are partly right and partly wrong.' The first class are right in affirming that the life of the freeman is better than the life of the despot; for there is nothing grand or noble in having the use of a slave, in so far as he is a slave; or in issuing commands about necessary things. But it is an error to suppose that every sort of rule is despotic like that of a master over slaves, for there is as great a difference between the rule over freemen and the rule over slaves as there is between slavery by nature and freedom by nature, about which I have said enough at the commencement of this treatise. And it is equally a mistake to place inactivity above action, for happiness is activity, and the actions of the just and wise are the realization of much that is noble.

But perhaps some one, accepting these premisses, may still maintain that supreme power is the best of all things, because the possessors of it are able to perform the greatest number of noble actions. If so, the man who is able to rule, instead of giving up anything to his neighbour, ought rather to take away his power; and the father should make no account of his son, nor the son of his father, nor friend of friend; they should not bestow a thought on one another in comparison with this higher object, for the best is the most eligible and 'doing well' is the best. There might be some truth in such a view if we assume that robbers and plunderers attain the chief good. But this can never be; their hypothesis is false. For the actions of a ruler cannot really be honourable, unless he is as much superior to other men as a husband is to a wife, or a father to his children, or a master to his slaves. And therefore he who violates the law can never recover by any success, however great, what he has already lost in departing from virtue. For equals the honourable and the just consist in sharing alike, as is just and equal. But that the unequal should be given to equals, and the unlike to those who are like, is contrary to nature, and nothing which is contrary to nature is good. If, therefore, there is any one superior in virtue and in the power of performing the best actions, him we ought to follow and obey, but he must have the capacity for action as well as virtue.

Aristotle, Politics, 1325ᵃ16

14 Far better it is to obey in peace and quiet than to wish to rule with power supreme and be the master of kingdoms.

Lucretius, Nature of Things, V

15 People who have a natural ability for administering public affairs should not hesitate to run for public office and take part in directing the government. In no other way can a government be run or greatness of spirit be demonstrated. States-

men no less than philosophers (perhaps more so) should embody that quality of nobility and an indifference toward outward circumstances that I refer to so often. They also need a peaceful spirit and freedom from care, if they are to be rid of worries and lead a life of constancy. This is easier for philosophers to do, because their lives are less exposed to the exigencies of fortune. They also have fewer wants, so if misfortune does befall them, the blow is not so calamitous. With good reason, therefore, are stronger emotions aroused in those who deal in public affairs than in those who live in quietude. Greater too is the ambition of the former to succeed. So much more, then, do they require greatness of spirit and freedom from wearying cares.

Cicero, *De Officiis,* I, 21

16 The magistrate ought definitely to bear in mind that he represents the state. It is his duty to uphold its honor and dignity, to enforce its laws, to dispense to everyone his constitutional rights, and to remember that all this has been committed to him as a sacred trust.

Cicero, *De Officiis,* I, 34

17 They [the chief priests] send unto him certain of the Pharisees and of the Hĕrō̄-dĭ-ăns, to catch him in his words.

And when they were come, they say unto him, Master, we know that thou art true, and carest for no man: for thou regardest not the person of men, but teachest the way of God in truth: Is it lawful to give tribute to Cæsar, or not?

Shall we give, or shall we not give? But he, knowing their hypocrisy, said unto them, Why tempt ye me? bring me a penny, that I may see it.

And they brought it. And he saith unto them, Whose is this image and superscription? And they said unto him, Cæsar's.

And Jesus answering said unto them, Render to Cæsar the things that are Cæsar's, and to God the things that are God's. And they marvelled at him.

Mark 12:13–17

18 A ruler's first aim is to maintain his office, which is done no less by avoiding what is unfit than by observing what is suitable. Whoever is either too remiss or too strict is no more a king or a governor, but either a demagogue or a despot, and so becomes either odious or contemptible to his subjects. . . . The one seems to be the fault of easiness and good-nature, the other of pride and severity.

Plutarch, *Romulus and Theseus Compared*

19 People do not obey, unless rulers know how to command; obedience is a lesson taught by commanders. A true leader himself creates the obedience of his own followers; as it is the last attainment in the art of riding to make a horse gentle and tractable, so is it of the science of government,

to inspire men with a willingness to obey.

Plutarch, *Lycurgus*

20 The conduct of a wise politician is ever suited to the present posture of affairs; often by foregoing a part he saves the whole, and by yielding in a small matter secures a greater.

Plutarch, *Poplicola and Solon Compared*

21 *Fabius.* It is no inglorious thing to have fear for the safety of our country, but to be turned from one's course by men's opinions, by blame, and by misrepresentation, shows a man unfit to hold an office such as this, which, by such conduct, he makes the slave of those whose errors it is his business to control.

Plutarch, *Fabius*

22 If the motions of rulers be constantly opposite and cross to the tempers and inclinations of the people, they will be resented as arbitrary and harsh; as, on the other side, too much deference, or encouragement, as too often it has been, to popular faults and errors, is full of danger and ruinous consequences.

Plutarch, *Phocion*

23 Ambitious men, whose minds, doting on glory, which is a mere image of virtue, produce nothing that is genuine or uniform, but only, as might be expected of such a conjunction, misshapen and unnatural actions. . . .

For this is indeed the true condition of men in public life, who, to gain the vain title of being the people's leaders and governors, are content to make themselves the slaves and followers of all the people's humours and caprices. For as the lookout men at the ship's prow, though they see what is ahead before the men at the helm, yet constantly look back to the pilots there, and obey the orders they give; so these men, steered, as I may say, by popular applause, though they bear the name of governors, are in reality the mere underlings of the multitude.

Plutarch, *Agis*

24 Fear and force . . . are not . . . the adamantine chains which secure . . . power, but the love, zeal, and affection inspired by clemency and justice, which, though they seem more pliant than the stiff and hard bonds of severity, are nevertheless the strongest and most durable ties to sustain a lasting government.

Plutarch, *Dion*

25 Take care that thou art not made into a Cæsar, that thou art not dyed with this dye; for such things happen. Keep thyself then simple, good, pure, serious, free from affectation, a friend of justice, a worshipper of the gods, kind, affectionate, strenuous in all proper acts. Strive to continue to

be such as philosophy wished to make thee. Reverence the gods, and help men. Short is life. There is only one fruit of this terrene life, a pious disposition and social acts. Do everything as a disciple of Antoninus. Remember his constancy in every act which was conformable to reason, and his evenness in all things, and his piety, and the serenity of his countenance, and his sweetness, and his disregard of empty fame, and his efforts to understand things; and how he would never let anything pass without having first most carefully examined it and clearly understood it; and how he bore with those who blamed him unjustly without blaming them in return; how he did nothing in a hurry; and how he listened not to calumnies, and how exact an examiner of manners and actions he was; and not given to reproach people, nor timid, nor suspicious, nor sophist; and with how little he was satisfied, such as lodging, bed, dress, food, servants; and how laborious and patient; and how he was able on account of his sparing diet to hold out to the evening, not even requiring to relieve himself by any evacuations except at the usual hour; and his firmness and uniformity in his friendships; and how he tolerated freedom of speech in those who opposed his opinions; and the pleasure that he had when any man showed him anything better; and how religious he was without superstition. Imitate all this that thou mayest have as good a conscience, when thy last hour comes, as he had.

Marcus Aurelius, *Meditations,* VI, 30

26 Mastership has a twofold meaning. First, as opposed to slavery, in which sense a master means one to whom another is subject as a slave. In another sense mastership is referred in a general sense to any kind of subject, and in this sense even he who has the office of governing and directing free men can be called a master. In the state of innocence man could have been a master of men, not in the former but in the latter sense.

Aquinas, *Summa Theologica,* I, 96, 4

27 If . . . a multitude of free men is ordered by the ruler towards the common good of the multitude, that rulership will be right and just, as is suitable to free men. If, on the other hand, a rulership aims, not at the common good of the multitude, but at the private good of the ruler, it will be an unjust and perverted rulership.

Aquinas, *On Kingship,* I, 1

28 He who is the cause of another becoming powerful is ruined; because that predominancy has been brought about either by astuteness or else by force, and both are distrusted by him who has been raised to power.

Machiavelli, *Prince,* III

29 In seizing a state, the usurper ought to examine closely into all those injuries which it is necessary for him to inflict, and to do them all at one stroke so as not to have to repeat them daily; and thus by not unsettling men he will be able to reassure them, and win them to himself by benefits. He who does otherwise, either from timidity or evil advice, is always compelled to keep the knife in his hand; neither can he rely on his subjects, nor can they attach themselves to him, owing to their continued and repeated wrongs.

Machiavelli, *Prince,* VIII

30 A prince who does not understand the art of war . . . cannot be respected by his soldiers, nor can he rely on them. He ought never, therefore, to have out of his thoughts this subject of war, and in peace he should addict himself more to its exercise than in war; this he can do in two ways, the one by action, the other by study.

Machiavelli, *Prince,* XIV

31 It would be well to be reputed liberal. Nevertheless, liberality exercised in a way that does not bring you the reputation for it, injures you; for if one exercises it honestly and as it should be exercised, it may not become known, and you will not avoid the reproach of its opposite. Therefore, any one wishing to maintain among men the name of liberal is obliged to avoid no attribute of magnificence; so that a prince thus inclined will consume in such acts all his property, and will be compelled in the end, if he wish to maintain the name of liberal, to unduly weigh down his people, and tax them, and do everything he can to get money. This will soon make him odious to his subjects, and becoming poor he will be little valued by any one; thus, with his liberality, having offended many and rewarded few, he is affected by the very first trouble and imperilled by whatever may be the first danger; recognizing this himself, and wishing to draw back from it, he runs at once into the reproach of being miserly.

Therefore, a prince, not being able to exercise this virtue of liberality in such a way that it is recognized, except to his cost, if he is wise he ought not to fear the reputation of being mean, for in time he will come to be more considered than if liberal, seeing that with his economy his revenues are enough, that he can defend himself against all attacks, and is able to engage in enterprises without burdening his people; thus it comes to pass that he exercises liberality towards all from whom he does not take, who are numberless, and meanness towards those to whom he does not give, who are few.

Machiavelli, *Prince,* XVI

32 A prince ought to inspire fear in such a way that, if he does not win love, he avoids hatred; because he can endure very well being feared whilst he is not hated, which will always be as long as he ab-

stains from the property of his citizens and subjects and from their women. But when it is necessary for him to proceed against the life of someone, he must do it on proper justification and for manifest cause, but above all things he must keep his hands off the property of others, because men more quickly forget the death of their father than the loss of their patrimony.

Machiavelli, *Prince,* XVII

33 Everyone admits how praiseworthy it is in a prince to keep faith, and to live with integrity and not with craft. Nevertheless our experience has been that those princes who have done great things have held good faith of little account, and have known how to circumvent the intellect of men by craft, and in the end have overcome those who have relied on their word. . . . A prince, therefore, being compelled knowingly to adopt the beast, ought to choose the fox and the lion; because the lion cannot defend himself against snares and the fox cannot defend himself against wolves. Therefore, it is necessary to be a fox to discover the snares and a lion to terrify the wolves. Those who rely simply on the lion do not understand what they are about. Therefore a wise lord cannot, nor ought he to, keep faith when such observance may be turned against him, and when the reasons that caused him to pledge it exist no longer. If men were entirely good this precept would not hold, but because they are bad, and will not keep faith with you, you too are not bound to observe it with them. Nor will there ever be wanting to a prince legitimate reasons to excuse this nonobservance. Of this endless modern examples could be given, showing how many treaties and engagements have been made void and of no effect through the faithlessness of princes; and he who has known best how to employ the fox has succeeded best.

But it is necessary to know well how to disguise this characteristic, and to be a great pretender and dissembler; and men are so simple, and so subject to present necessities, that he who seeks to deceive will always find someone who will allow himself to be deceived. One recent example I cannot pass over in silence. Alexander VI did nothing else but deceive men, nor ever thought of doing otherwise, and he always found victims; for there never was a man who had greater power in asserting, or who with greater oaths would affirm a thing, yet would observe it less; nevertheless his deceits always succeeded according to his wishes, because he well understood this side of mankind.

Therefore it is unnecessary for a prince to have all the good qualities I have enumerated, but it is very necessary to appear to have them. And I shall dare to say this also, that to have them and always to observe them is injurious, and that to appear to have them is useful; to appear merciful, faithful, humane, religious, upright, and to be so,

but with a mind so framed that should you require not to be so, you may be able and know how to change to the opposite.

Machiavelli, *Prince,* XVIII

34 The prince who has more to fear from the people than from foreigners ought to build fortresses, but he who has more to fear from foreigners than from the people ought to leave them alone. . . . For this reason the best possible fortress is—not to be hated by the people, because, although you may hold the fortresses, yet they will not save you if the people hate you, for there will never be wanting foreigners to assist a people who have taken arms against you.

Machiavelli, *Prince,* XX

35 The choice of servants is of no little importance to a prince, and they are good or not according to the discrimination of the prince. And the first opinion which one forms of a prince, and of his understanding, is by observing the men he has around him; and when they are capable and faithful he may always be considered wise, because he has known how to recognize the capable and to keep them faithful. But when they are otherwise one cannot form a good opinion of him, for the prime error which he made was in choosing them.

Machiavelli, *Prince,* XXII

36 A prince . . . ought always to take counsel, but only when he wishes and not when others wish; he ought rather to discourage every one from offering advice unless he asks it; but, however, he ought to be a constant inquirer, and afterwards a patient listener concerning the things of which he inquired; also, on learning that any one, on any consideration, has not told him the truth, he should let his anger be felt.

Machiavelli, *Prince,* XXIII

37 If there are some who think that a prince who conveys an impression of his wisdom is not so through his own ability, but through the good advisers that he has around him, beyond doubt they are deceived, because this is an axiom which never fails: that a prince who is not wise himself will never take good advice, unless by chance he has yielded his affairs entirely to one person who happens to be a very prudent man. In this case indeed he may be well governed, but it would not be for long, because such a governor would in a short time take away his state from him.

But if a prince who is not experienced should take counsel from more than one he will never get united counsels, nor will he know how to unite them. Each of the counsellors will think of his own interests, and the prince will not know how to control them or to see through them. And they are not to be found otherwise, because men will always prove untrue to you unless they are kept honest by constraint. Therefore it must be inferred that good counsels, whencesoever they come, are born of the wisdom of the prince, and not the wisdom of the prince from good counsels.

Machiavelli, *Prince,* XXIII

38 Government consists mainly in so keeping your subjects that they shall be neither able nor disposed to injure you; and this is done by depriving them of all means of injuring you, or by bestowing such benefits upon them that it would not be reasonable for them to desire any change of fortune.

Machiavelli, *Discourses,* II, 23

39 We owe subjection and obedience equally to all kings, for that concerns their office; but we do not owe esteem, any more than affection, except to their virtue. Let us make this concession to the political order: to suffer them patiently if they are unworthy, to conceal their vices, to abet them by commending their indifferent actions if their authority needs our support. But, our dealings over, it is not right to deny to justice and to our liberty the expression of our true feelings, and especially to deny good subjects the glory of having reverently and faithfully served a master whose imperfections were so well known to them, and thus to deprive posterity of such a useful example.

Montaigne, *Essays,* I, 3, Our Feelings Reach Out

40 Truly it is no small thing to have to rule others, since in ruling ourselves so many difficulties occur. As for commanding, which seems to be so sweet: considering the imbecility of human judgment and the difficulty of choice in new and doubtful things, I am strongly of this opinion, that it is much easier and pleasanter to follow than to guide, and that it is a great rest for the mind to have only to hold to a mapped-out path and to be answerable only for oneself.

Montaigne, *Essays,* I, 42, Of the Inequality

41 It may be said, on the one hand, that to give factions a loose rein to entertain their own opinions is to scatter and sow division; it is almost lending a hand to augment it, there being no barrier or coercion of the laws to check or hinder its course. But on the other hand, one could also say that to give factions a loose rein to entertain their own opinions is to soften and relax them through facility and ease, and to dull the point, which is sharpened by rarity, novelty, and difficulty. And yet I prefer to think, for the reputation of our kings' piety, that having been unable to do what they would, they have pretended to will what they could.

Montaigne, *Essays,* II, 19, Of Freedom of Conscience

42 Liberality itself is not in its proper light in the hands of a sovereign; private people have more right to exercise it. For, to be precise about it, a king has nothing that is properly his own; he owes his very self to others.

The authority to judge is not given for the sake of the judge, but for the sake of the person judged. A superior is never appointed for his own benefit, but for the benefit of the inferior, and a doctor for the sick, not for himself. All authority, like all art, has its end outside of itself. . . .

Wherefore the tutors of young princes who make it a point to impress on them this virtue of liberality and preach to them not to know how to refuse anything, and to think nothing so well spent as what they give away (a lesson that I have seen in great favor in my time), either look more to their own profit than to their master's, or do not well understand to whom they speak. It is all too easy to impress liberality on a man who has the means to practice it all he wants at the expense of others. And since its value is reckoned not by the measure of the gift, but by the measure of the giver's means, it amounts to nothing in such powerful hands. They find themselves prodigal before they are liberal. Therefore liberality is little to be commended compared with other royal virtues, and it is the only one, as the tyrant Dionysius said, that goes with tyranny itself.

Montaigne, *Essays,* III, 6, Of Coaches

43 *King Henry.* Ah, what a life were this! how sweet! how lovely!
Gives not the hawthorn-bush a sweeter shade
To shepherds looking on their silly sheep
Than doth a rich embroider'd canopy
To kings that fear their subjects' treachery?
O, yes it doth; a thousand-fold it doth.
And to conclude, the shepherd's homely curds,
His cold thin drink out of his leather bottle,
His wonted sleep under a fresh tree's shade,
All which secure and sweetly he enjoys,
Is far beyond a prince's delicates,
His viands sparkling in a golden cup,
His body couched in a curious bed,
When care, mistrust, and treason waits on him.

Shakespeare, *III Henry VI,* II, v, 41

44 *Ulysses.*   O, when degree is shaked,
Which is the ladder to all high designs,
The enterprise is sick! How could communities,
Degrees in schools and brotherhoods in cities,
Peaceful commerce from dividable shores,
The primogenitive and due of birth,
Prerogative of age, crowns, sceptres, laurels,
But by degree, stand in authentic place?
Take but degree away, untune that string,
And, hark, what discord follows! Each thing meets
In mere oppugnancy. The bounded waters
Should lift their bosoms higher than the shores

And make a sop of all this solid globe.
Strength should be lord of imbecility,
And the rude son should strike his father dead.
Force should be right; or rather, right and wrong,
Between whose endless jar justice resides,
Should lose their names, and so should justice too.
Then everything includes itself in power,
Power into will, will into appetite;
And appetite, an universal wolf,
So doubly seconded with will and power,
Must make perforce an universal prey,
And last eat up himself. Great Agamemnon,
This chaos, when degree is suffocate,
Follows the choking.
And this neglection of degree it is
That by a pace goes backward, with a purpose
It hath to climb. The general's disdain'd
By him one step below, he by the next,
That next by him beneath; so every step,
Exampled by the first pace that is sick
Of his superior, grows to an envious fever
Of pale and bloodless emulation.

> Shakespeare, *Troilus and Cressida,* I, iii, 101

45 *1st Officer.* Come, come, they are almost here. How many stand for consulships?

2nd Officer. Three, they say; but 'tis thought of every one Coriolanus will carry it.

1st Off. That's a brave fellow; but he's vengeance proud, and loves not the common people.

2nd Off. Faith, there have been many great men that have flattered the people, who ne'er loved them; and there be many that they have loved, they know not wherefore; so that, if they love they know not why, they hate upon no better a ground; therefore, for Coriolanus neither to care whether they love or hate him manifests the true knowledge he has in their disposition.

> Shakespeare, *Coriolanus,* II, ii, 1

46 Well then, quoth *Sancho,* let me have this Island, and I'll do my best to be such a Governor, that, in spite of Rogues, I shan't want a small Nook in Heaven one Day or other. 'Tis not out of Covetousness neither, that I'd leave my little Cott, and set up for somebody, but meerly to know what Kind of Thing it is to be a Governor. Oh! *Sancho,* said the Duke, when once you've had a Taste of it, you'll never leave licking your Fingers, 'tis so sweet and bewitching a Thing to command and be obey'd. I am confident, when your Master comes to be an Emperor (as he cannot fail to be, according to the Course of his Affairs) he will never by any Consideration be persuaded to Abdicate; his only Grief will be, that he was one no sooner.

Troth, Sir, reply'd *Sancho,* I am of your Mind; 'tis a dainty Thing to command, though 'twere but a Flock of Sheep. Oh! *Sancho,* cry'd the Duke, let me live and die with thee; for thou hast an Insight into every Thing. I hope thou'lt prove as good a Governor as thy Wisdom bespeaks thee. But no more at this Time,—to Morrow, without further Delay, you set forward to your Island, and shall be furnish'd this Afternoon with Equipage and Dress answerable to your Post, and all other Necessaries for your Journey.

Let 'em dress me as they will, quoth *Sancho,* I shall be the same *Sancho Pança* still.

> Cervantes, *Don Quixote,* II, 42

47 Being come to himself, he [Sancho] ask'd what 'twas a Clock? They answer'd, 'twas now break of Day. He said nothing, but, without any Words, began to put on his Clothes. While this was doing, and he continu'd seriously silent, all the Eyes of the Company were fix'd upon him, wondring what could be the meaning of his being in such haste to put on his Clothes. At last he made an End of dressing himself, and creeping along softly, (for he was too much bruis'd to go along very fast) he got to the Stable, follow'd by all the Company, and coming to *Dapple,* he embrac'd the quiet Animal, gave him a loving Kiss on the Forehead, and, with Tears in his Eyes, Come hither, said he, my Friend, thou faithful Companion, and Fellow-sharer in my Travels and Miseries; when thee and I consorted together, and all my Cares were but to mend thy Furniture, and feed thy little Carcase, then happy were my Days, my Months, and Years. But since I forsook Thee, and clamber'd up the Towers of Ambition and Pride, a thousand Woes, a thousand Torments, and four thousand Tribulations have haunted and worry'd my Soul. While he was talking thus, he fitted on his Pack-Saddle, no Body offering to say any thing to him. This done, with a great deal of Difficulty he mounted his Ass, and then addressing himself to the Steward, the Secretary, the Gentleman-waiter, and Doctor *Pedro Rezio,* and many others that stood by; Make Way, Gentlemen, said he, and let me return to my former Liberty. Let me go that I may seek my old Course of Life, and rise again from that Death that buries me here alive. I was not born to be a Governor, nor to defend Islands nor Cities from Enemies that break in upon 'em. I know better what belongs to Ploughing, Delving, Pruning and Planting of Vineyards, than how to make Laws, and defend Countries and Kingdoms. St *Peter* is very well at *Rome:* Which is as much as to say, let every one stick to the Calling he was born to. A Spade does better in My Hand than a Governor's Truncheon; and I had rather fill my Belly with a Mess of plain Porridge, than lie at the Mercy of a Coxcombly Physick-monger that starves me to Death. I had rather solace my self under the Shade of an Oak in Summer, and wrap my Corps up in a double Sheep-skin in the Winter at my Liberty, than lay me down with the Slavery of a Government in fine Holland Sheets, and case my Hide in Furs and richest Sables. Heaven be with you, Gentlefolks, and pray tell

my Lord Duke from me, that naked I was born, and naked I am at present. I have neither won nor lost, which is as much as to say, Without a Penny I came to this Government, and without a Penny I leave it, quite contrary to what other Governors of Islands use to do, when they leave 'em. Clear the Way then, I beseech you, and let me pass.

Cervantes, *Don Quixote*, II, 53

48 The wisdom of a lawmaker consisteth not only in a platform of justice, but in the application thereof; taking into consideration by what means laws may be made certain, and what are the causes and remedies of the doubtfulness and incertainty of law; by what means laws may be made apt and easy to be executed, and what are the impediments and remedies in the execution of laws; what influence laws touching private right of *meum* and *tuum* have into the public state, and how they may be made apt and agreeable; how laws are to be penned and delivered, whether in texts or in acts, brief or large, with preambles, or without; how they are to be pruned and reformed from time to time, and what is the best means to keep them from being too vast in volumes, or too full of multiplicity and crossness; how they are to be expounded, when upon causes emergent and judicially discussed, and when upon responses and conferences touching general points or questions; how they are to be pressed, rigorously or tenderly; how they are to be mitigated by equity and good conscience, and whether discretion and strict law are to be mingled in the same courts, or kept apart in several courts; again, how the practice, profession, and erudition of law is to be censured and governed; and many other points touching the administration, and (as I may term it) animation of laws.

Bacon, *Advancement of Learning*, Bk. II, XXIII, 49

49 The great advantages of simulation and dissimulation are three. First, to lay asleep opposition, and to surprise. For where a man's intentions are published, it is an alarum to call up all that are against them. The second is, to reserve to a man's self a fair retreat. For if a man engage himself by a manifest declaration, he must go through, or take a fall. The third is, the better to discover the mind of another. For to him that opens himself men will hardly shew themselves adverse; but will (fair) let him go on, and turn their freedom of speech to freedom of thought. And therefore it is a good shrewd proverb of the Spaniard, *Tell a lie and find a troth;* as if there were no way of discovery but by simulation. There be also three disadvantages, to set it even. The first, that simulation and dissimulation commonly carry with them a shew of fearfulness, which in any business doth spoil the feathers of round flying up to the mark. The sec-

ond, that it puzzleth and perplexeth the conceits of many that perhaps would otherwise co-operate with him, and makes a man walk almost alone to his own ends. The third and greatest is, that it depriveth a man of one of the most principal instruments for action, which is trust and belief. The best composition and temperature is to have openness in fame and opinion; secrecy in habit; dissimulation in seasonable use; and a power to feign, if there be no remedy.

Bacon, *Of Simulation and Dissimulation*

50 All rising to great place is by a winding stair; and if there be factions, it is good to side a man's self whilst he is in the rising, and to balance himself when he is placed. Use the memory of thy predecessor fairly and tenderly; for if thou dost not, it is a debt will sure be paid when thou art gone. If thou have colleagues, respect them, and rather call them when they look not for it, than exclude them when they have reason to look to be called. Be not too sensible or too remembering of thy place in conversation and private answers to suitors; but let it rather be said, *When he sits in place he is another man.*

Bacon, *Of Great Place*

51 Above all things, good policy is to be used, that the treasure and moneys in a state be not gathered into few hands. For otherwise a state may have a great stock, and yet starve. And money is like muck, not good except it be spread. This is done chiefly by suppressing, or at the least keeping a strait hand upon the devouring trades of usury, engrossing, great pasturages, and the like.

Bacon, *Of Seditions and Troubles*

52 To give moderate liberty for griefs and discontentments to evaporate (so it be without too great insolency or bravery) is a safe way. For he that turneth the humours back, and maketh the wound bleed inwards, endangereth malign ulcers and pernicious impostumations.

Bacon, *Of Seditions and Troubles*

53 Let princes, against all events, not be without some great person, one or rather more, of military valour, near unto them, for the repressing of seditions in their beginnings. For without that, there useth to be more trepidation in court upon the first breaking out of troubles than were fit. . . . But let such military persons be assured, and well reputed of, rather than factious and popular; holding also good correspondence with the other great men in the state; or else the remedy is worse than the disease.

Bacon, *Of Seditions and Troubles*

54 The wisest princes need not think it any diminution to their greatness, or derogation to their sufficiency, to rely upon counsel. God himself is not

without, but hath made it one of the great names of his blessed Son; *The Counsellor.*

Bacon, *Of Counsel*

55 A king, when he presides in counsel, let him beware how he opens his own inclination too much in that which he propoundeth; for else counsellors will but take the wind of him, and instead of giving free counsel, sing him a song of *placebo.*

Bacon, *Of Counsel*

56 He that is to govern a whole nation must read in himself, not this or that particular man; but mankind.

Hobbes, *Leviathan,* Intro.

57 The power of a man, to take it universally, is his present means to obtain some future apparent good. . . . The greatest of human powers is that which is compounded of the powers of most men, united by consent, in one person, natural or civil, that has the use of all their powers depending on his will; such as is the power of a Commonwealth: or depending on the wills of each particular; such as is the power of a faction, or of diverse factions leagued. Therefore to have servants is power; to have friends is power: for they are strengths united.

Hobbes, *Leviathan,* I, 10

58 If the essential rights of sovereignty . . . be taken away, the Commonwealth is thereby dissolved, and every man returneth into the condition and calamity of a war with every other man, which is the greatest evil that can happen in this life; it is the office of the sovereign to maintain those rights entire, and consequently against his duty, first, to transfer to another or to lay from himself any of them. For he that deserteth the means deserteth the ends; and he deserteth the means that, being the sovereign, acknowledgeth himself subject to the civil laws, and renounceth the power of supreme judicature; or of making war or peace by his own authority; or of judging of the necessities of the Commonwealth; or of levying money and soldiers when and as much as in his own conscience he shall judge necessary; or of making officers and ministers both of war and peace; or of appointing teachers, and examining what doctrines are conformable or contrary to the defence, peace, and good of the people.

Hobbes, *Leviathan,* II, 30

59 He that is minded to obey all the commonwealth's orders, whether through fear of its power or through love of quiet, certainly consults after his own heart his own safety and interest.

Spinoza, *Political Treatise,* III, 3

60 It is easy to understand to what end the legislative power ought to be directed and by what measures regulated; and that is the temporal good and outward prosperity of the society; which is the sole reason of men's entering into society, and the only thing they seek and aim at in it. And it is also evident what liberty remains to men in reference to their eternal salvation, and that is that every one should do what he in his conscience is persuaded to be acceptable to the Almighty, on whose good pleasure and acceptance depends their eternal happiness. For obedience is due, in the first place, to God and, afterwards to the laws.

But some may ask: "What if the magistrate should enjoin anything by his authority that appears unlawful to the conscience of a private person?" I answer that, if government be faithfully administered and the counsels of the magistrates be indeed directed to the public good, this will seldom happen. But if, perhaps, it do so fall out, I say, that such a private person is to abstain from the action that he judges unlawful, and he is to undergo the punishment which it is not unlawful for him to bear. For the private judgement of any person concerning a law enacted in political matters, for the public good, does not take away the obligation of that law, nor deserve a dispensation. But if the law, indeed, be concerning things that lie not within the verge of the magistrate's authority (as, for example, that the people, or any party amongst them, should be compelled to embrace a strange religion, and join in the worship and ceremonies of another Church), men are not in these cases obliged by that law, against their consciences. For the political society is instituted for no other end, but only to secure every man's possession of the things of this life. The care of each man's soul and of the things of heaven, which neither does belong to the commonwealth nor can be subjected to it, is left entirely to every man's self.

Locke, *Letter Concerning Toleration*

61 I think it may not be amiss to set down what I take to be political power. That the power of a magistrate over a subject may be distinguished from that of a father over his children, a master over his servant, a husband over his wife, and a lord over his slave. All which distinct powers happening sometimes together in the same man, if he be considered under these different relations, it may help us to distinguish these powers one from another, and show the difference betwixt a ruler of a commonwealth, a father of a family, and a captain of a galley.

Political power, then, I take to be a right of making laws, with penalties of death, and consequently all less penalties for the regulating and preserving of property, and of employing the force of the community in the execution of such laws, and in the defence of the commonwealth from foreign injury, and all this only for the public good.

Locke, *II Civil Government,* I, 2–3

62 But these two powers, political and paternal, are so perfectly distinct and separate, and built upon so different foundations. and given to so different ends, that every subject that is a father has as much a paternal power over his children as the prince has over his. And every prince that has parents owes them as much filial duty and obedience as the meanest of his subjects do to theirs, and can therefore contain not any part or degree of that kind of dominion which a prince or magistrate has over his subject.

Locke, *II Civil Government*, VI, 71

63 Since a rational creature cannot be supposed, when free, to put himself into subjection to another for his own harm . . . prerogative can be nothing but the people's permitting their rulers to do several things of their own free choice where the law was silent, and sometimes too against the direct letter of the law, for the public good and their acquiescing in it when so done. For as a good prince, who is mindful of the trust put into his hands and careful of the good of his people, cannot have too much prerogative—that is, power to do good, so a weak and ill prince, who would claim that power his predecessors exercised, without the direction of the law, as a prerogative belonging to him by right of his office, which he may exercise at his pleasure to make or promote an interest distinct from that of the public, gives the people an occasion to claim their right and limit that power, which, whilst it was exercised for their good, they were content should be tacitly allowed.

Locke, *II Civil Government*, XIV, 164

64 In chusing persons for all employments, they [the Lilliputians] have more regard to good morals than to great abilities: for, since government is necessary to mankind, they believe that the common size of human understandings, is fitted to some station or other; and that Providence never intended to make the management of publick affairs a mystery, to be comprehended only by a few persons of sublime genius, of which there seldom are three born in an age: but, they suppose truth, justice, temperance, and the like, to be in every man's power; the practice of which virtues, assisted by experience and a good intention, would qualify any man for the service of his country, except where a course of study is required. But they thought the want of moral virtues was so far from being supplied by superior endowments of the mind, that employments could never be put into such dangerous hands as those of persons so qualified; and at least, that the mistakes committed by ignorance in a virtuous disposition, would never be of such fatal consequence to the publick weal, as the practices of a man whose inclinations led him to be corrupt, and had great abilities to manage, to multiply, and defend his corruptions.

Swift, *Gulliver's Travels*, I, 6

65 The king [of Brobdingnag] was struck with horror at the description I had given of those terrible engines, and the proposal I had made [to show him how to make gun powder and cannon]. He was amazed how so impotent and grovelling an insect as I (these were his expressions) could entertain such inhuman ideas, and in so familiar a manner as to appear wholly unmoved at all the scenes of blood and desolation, which I had painted as the common effects of those destructive machines; whereof he said, some evil genius, enemy to mankind, must have been the first contriver. As for himself, he protested, that although few things delighted him so much as new discoveries in art or in nature; yet he would rather lose half his kingdom, than be privy to such a secret; which he commanded me, as I valued my life, never to mention any more.

A strange effect of *narrow principles* and *short views!* that a prince possessed of every quality which procures veneration, love and esteem; of strong parts, great wisdom and profound learning; endued with admirable talents for government, and almost adored by his subjects; should from a *nice unnecessary scruple*, whereof in Europe we can have no conception, let slip an opportunity put into his hands, that would have made him absolute master of the lives, the liberties, and the fortunes of his people.

Swift, *Gulliver's Travels*, II, 7

66 I take this defect among them [the Brobdingnagians] to have risen from their ignorance; by not having hitherto reduced *politicks* into a *science*, as the more acute wits of Europe have done. For, I remember very well, in a discourse one day with the king, when I happened to say, there were several thousand books among us, written upon the *art of government*, it gave him (directly contrary to my intention) a very mean opinion of our understandings. He professed both to abominate and despise all *mystery, refinement*, and *intrigue*, either in a prince or a minister. He could not tell what I meant by *secrets of State*, where an enemy or some rival nation were not in the case. He confined the knowledge of governing within very *narrow bounds;* to common sense and reason, to justice and lenity, to the speedy determination of civil and criminal causes; with some other obvious topicks which are not worth considering. And, he gave it for his opinion, that whoever could make two ears of corn, or two blades of grass to grow upon a spot of ground where only one grew before, would deserve better of mankind, and do more essential service to his country, than the whole race of politicians put together.

Swift, *Gulliver's Travels*, II, 7

67 Politicks, as the Word is commonly understood, are nothing but Corruptions, and consequently of no Use to a good King, or a good Ministry, for

which Reason Courts are so over-run with Politicks.

Swift, *Thoughts on Various Subjects*

68 So many are the advantages which monarchs gain by clemency, so greatly does it raise their fame, and endear them to their subjects, that it is generally happy for them to have an opportunity of displaying it.

Montesquieu, *Spirit of Laws*, VI, 21

69 Constant experience shows us that every man invested with power is apt to abuse it, and to carry his authority as far as it will go. . . . To prevent this abuse, it is necessary from the very nature of things that power should be a check to power.

Montesquieu, *Spirit of Laws*, XI, 4

70 The manners of a prince contribute as much as the laws themselves to liberty; like these he may transform men into brutes, and brutes into men. If he prefers free and generous spirits, he will have subjects; if he likes base, dastardly souls, he will have slaves. Would he know the great art of ruling, let him call honour and virtue to attend his person; and let him encourage personal merit. He may even sometimes cast an eye on talents and abilities. Let him not be afraid of those rivals who are called men of merit; he is their equal when once he loves them. Let him gain the hearts of his people, without subduing their spirits. Let him render himself popular; he ought to be pleased with the affections of the lowest of his subjects, for they too are men. The common people require so very little condescension, that it is fit they should be humoured; the infinite distance between the sovereign and them will surely prevent them from giving him any uneasiness. Let him be exorable to supplication, and resolute against demands; let him be sensible, in fine, that his people have his refusals, while his courtiers enjoy his favours.

Montesquieu, *Spirit of Laws*, XII, 27

71 Politics is a smooth file, which cuts gradually, and attains its end by a slow progression.

Montesquieu, *Spirit of Laws*, XIV, 13

72 The only precaution necessary for the father of a family is to guard himself against depravity, and prevent his natural inclinations from being corrupted; whereas it is these themselves which corrupt the Magistrate. In order to act aright, the first has only to consult his heart; the other becomes a traitor the moment he listens to his. Even his own reason should be suspect to him, nor should he follow any rule other than the public reason, which is the law. Thus nature has made a multitude of good fathers of families; but it is doubtful whether, from the very beginning of the world, human wisdom has made ten men capable of governing their peers.

Rousseau, *Political Economy*

73 The most pressing interest of the ruler, and even his most indispensable duty . . . is to watch over the observation of the laws of which he is the minister, and on which his whole authority is founded. At the same time, if he exacts the observance of them from others, he is the more strongly bound to observe them himself, since he enjoys all their favour. For his example is of such force, that even if the people were willing to permit him to release himself from the yoke of the law, he ought to be cautious in availing himself of so dangerous a prerogative, which others might soon claim to usurp in their turn, and often use to his prejudice. At bottom, as all social engagements are mutual in nature, it is impossible for any one to set himself above the law, without renouncing its advantages.

Rousseau, *Political Economy*

74 A fool, if he be obeyed, may punish crimes as well as another: but the true statesman is he who knows how to prevent them.

Rousseau, *Political Economy*

75 That government which confines itself to mere obedience will find difficulty in getting itself obeyed. If it is good to know how to deal with men as they are, it is much better to make them what there is need that they should be. The most absolute authority is that which penetrates into a man's inmost being, and concerns itself no less with his will than with his actions. It is certain that all peoples become in the long run what the government makes them; warriors, citizens, men, when it so pleases: or merely populace and rabble, when it chooses to make them so. Hence every prince who despises his subjects, dishonours himself, in confessing that he does not know how to make them worthy of respect. Make men, therefore, if you would command men: if you would have them obedient to the laws, make them love the laws, and then they will need only to know what is their duty to do it.

Rousseau, *Political Economy*

76 A careful and well-intentioned government, vigilant incessantly to maintain or restore patriotism and morality among the people, provides beforehand against the evils which sooner or later result from the indifference of the citizens to the fate of the Republic, keeping within narrow bounds that personal interest which so isolates the individual that the State is enfeebled by his power, and has nothing to hope from his good-will. Wherever men love their country, respect the laws, and live simply, little remains to be done in order to make them happy; and in public administration, where chance has less influence than in the lot of individuals, wisdom is so nearly allied to happiness,

that the two objects are confounded.

Rousseau, *Political Economy*

77 It is not enough to have citizens and to protect them, it is also necessary to consider their subsistence. Provision for the public wants is an obvious inference from the general will, and the third essential duty of government. This duty is not, we should feel, to fill the granaries of individuals and thereby to grant them a dispensation from labour, but to keep plenty so within their reach that labour is always necessary and never useless for its acquisition.

Rousseau, *Political Economy*

78 We know for ourselves that we must put up with a bad government when it is there; the question is how to find a good one.

Rousseau, *Social Contract*, III, 6

79 You say with pride, "My people are my subjects." Granted, but what are you? The subject of your ministers. And your ministers, what are they? The subjects of their clerks, their mistresses, the servants of their servants. Grasp all, usurp all, and then pour out your silver with both hands; set up your batteries, raise the gallows and the wheel; make laws, issue proclamations, multiply your spies, your soldiers, your hangmen, your prisons, and your chains. Poor little men, what good does it do you? You will be no better served, you will be none the less robbed and deceived, you will be no nearer absolute power. You will say continually, "It is our will," and you will continually do the will of others.

Rousseau, *Emile*, II

80 *Dr. Johnson.* Let us . . . now consider what the people would really gain by a general abolition of the right of patronage. What is most to be desired by such a change is, that the country should be supplied with better ministers. But why should we suppose that the parish will make a wiser choice than the patron? . . . It may be urged, that though the parish might not choose better ministers, they would at least choose ministers whom they like better, and who would therefore officiate with greater efficacy. That ignorance and perverseness should always obtain what they like, was never considered as the end of government; of which it is the great and standing benefit, that the wise see for the simple, and the regular act for the capricious. But that this argument supposes the people capable of judging, and resolute to act according to their best judgements, though this be sufficiently absurd, it is not all its absurdity. It supposes not only wisdom, but unanimity in those, who upon no other occasions are unanimous or wise.

Boswell, *Life of Johnson (May 1, 1773)*

81 Like the modesty affected by Augustus, the state maintained by Diocletian was a theatrical representation; but it must be confessed that, of the two comedies, the former was of a much more liberal and manly character than the latter. It was the aim of the one to disguise, and the object of the other to display, the unbounded power which the emperors possessed over the Roman world.

Ostentation was the first principle of the new system instituted by Diocletian. The second was division. He divided the empire, the provinces, and every branch of the civil as well as military administration. He multiplied the wheels of the machine of government, and rendered its operations less rapid but more secure. Whatever advantages and whatever defects might attend these innovations, they must be ascribed in a very great degree to the first inventor.

Gibbon, *Decline and Fall of the Roman Empire*, XIII

82 Julian recollected with terror the observation of his master Plato, that the government of our flocks and herds is always committed to beings of a superior species; and that the conduct of nations requires and deserves the celestial powers of the Gods or of the Genii. From this principle he justly concluded that the man who presumes to reign should aspire to the perfection of the divine nature; that he should purify his soul from her mortal and terrestrial part; that he should extinguish his appetites, enlighten his understanding, regulate his passions, and subdue the wild beast which, according to the lively metaphor of Aristotle, seldom fails to ascend the throne of a despot. The throne of Julian, which the death of Constantius fixed on an independent basis, was the seat of reason, of virtue, and perhaps of vanity. He despised the honours, renounced the pleasures, and discharged with incessant diligence the duties of his exalted station: and there were few among his subjects who would have consented to relieve him from the weight of the diadem, had they been obliged to submit their time and their actions to the rigorous laws which their philosophic emperor imposed on himself.

Gibbon, *Decline and Fall of the Roman Empire*, XXII

83 To secure any degree of sobriety in the propositions made by the leaders in any public assembly, they ought to respect, in some degree perhaps to fear, those whom they conduct. To be led any otherwise than blindly, the followers must be qualified, if not for actors, at least for judges; they must also be judges of natural weight and authority. Nothing can secure a steady and moderate conduct in such assemblies, but that the body of them should be respectably composed, in point of condition in life, of permanent property, of education, and of such habits as enlarge and liberalize

the understanding.

Burke, *Reflections on the Revolution in France*

84 All persons possessing any portion of power ought to be strongly and awfully impressed with an idea that they act in trust: and that they are to account for their conduct in that trust to the one great Master, Author, and Founder of society.

Burke, *Reflections on the Revolution in France*

85 Magnanimity in politics is not seldom the truest wisdom; and a great empire and little minds go ill together.

Burke, *Speech on Conciliation with the Colonies (Mar. 22, 1775)*

86 True politics can never take a step, without having previously rendered homage to morality; united with this, it is no longer a difficult or complicated art; morality cuts the knot which politics is incapable of untying, whenever they are in opposition to each other. The rights of man ought to be religiously respected, should sovereigns in rendering it make the greatest sacrifices. One cannot compromise here between right and utility; politics must bend the knee before morality; but by this means it may also expect insensibly to attain to an eminence, where it will shine with an immortal glory.

Kant, *Perpetual Peace,* Appendix, 1

87 In politics, as in religion, it is equally absurd to aim at making proselytes by fire and sword. Heresies in either can rarely be cured by persecution.

Hamilton, *Federalist 1*

88 The science of politics . . . like most other sciences, has received great improvement. The efficacy of various principles is now well understood, which were either not known at all, or imperfectly known to the ancients. The regular distribution of power into distinct departments; the introduction of legislative balances and checks; the institution of courts composed of judges holding their offices during good behaviour; the representation of the people in the legislature by deputies of their own election: these are wholly new discoveries, or have made their principal progress towards perfection in modern times. They are means, and powerful means, by which the excellences of republican government may be retained and its imperfections lessened or avoided. To this catalogue of circumstances that tend to the amelioration of popular systems of civil government, I shall venture, however novel it may appear to some, to add one more, on a principle which has been made the foundation of an objection to the new Constitution; I mean the *enlargement* of the *orbit* within which such systems are to revolve, either in respect to the dimensions of a single State, or to the

consolidation of several smaller States into one great Confederacy.

Hamilton, *Federalist 9*

89 Experience has instructed us that no skill in the science of government has yet been able to discriminate and define, with sufficient certainty, its three great provinces—the legislative, executive, and judiciary; or even the privileges and powers of the different legislative branches. Questions daily occur in the course of practice which prove the obscurity which reigns in these subjects, and which puzzle the greatest adepts in political science.

Madison, *Federalist 37*

90 There is nothing so apt to agitate the passions of mankind as personal considerations, whether they relate to ourselves or to others, who are to be the objects of our choice or preference. Hence, in every exercise of the power of appointing to offices by an assembly of men, we must expect to see a full display of all the private and party likings and dislikes, partialities and antipathies, attachments and animosities, which are felt by those who compose the assembly. The choice which may at any time happen to be made under such circumstances will of course be the result either of a victory gained by one party over the other or of a compromise between the parties. In either case, the intrinsic merit of the candidate will be too often out of sight. In the first, the qualifications best adapted to uniting the sufrages of the party will be more considered than those which fit the person for the station. In the last, the coalition will commonly turn upon some interested equivalent: "Give us the man we wish for this office, and you shall have the one you wish for that." This will be the usual condition of the bargain. And it will rarely happen that the advancement of the public service will be the primary object either of party victories or of party negotiations.

Hamilton, *Federalist 76*

91 The three ends which a statesman ought to propose to himself in the government of a nation, are — 1. Security to possessors; 2. Facility to acquirers; and 3. Hope to all.

Coleridge, *Table-Talk (June 25, 1831)*

92 Only that will which obeys law is free; for it obeys itself—it is independent and so free. When the state or our country constitutes a community of existence; when the subjective will of man submits to laws—the contradiction between liberty and necessity vanishes.

Hegel, *Philosophy of History,* Introduction, 3

93 Men are not corrupted by the exercise of power or debased by the habit of obedience, but by the exercise of a power which they believe to be illegitimate, and by obedience to a rule which they con-

sider to be usurped and oppressive.

Tocqueville, *Democracy in America,* Intro.

94 Government has come to be a trade, and is managed solely on commercial principles. A man plunges into politics to make his fortune, and only cares that the world shall last his days.

Emerson, *Letter to Thomas Carlyle*
(Oct. 7, 1835)

95 Head winds are far more prevalent than winds from astern. . . . For the most part the commodore on the quarterdeck gets his atmosphere at secondhand from the sailors on the forecastle. He thinks he breathes it first; but not so. In much the same way do the commonalty lead their leaders in many other things, at the same time that the leaders little suspect it.

Melville, *Moby Dick,* I

96 Unjust laws exist: shall we be content to obey them, or shall we endeavor to amend them, and obey them until we have succeeded, or shall we transgress them at once? Men generally, under such a government as this, think that they ought to wait until they have persuaded the majority to alter them. They think that, if they should resist, the remedy would be worse than the evil. But it is the fault of the government itself that the remedy *is* worse than the evil. *It* makes it worse.

Thoreau, *Civil Disobedience*

97 The government does not concern me much, and I shall bestow the fewest possible thoughts on it. It is not many moments that I live under a government, even in this world. If a man is thought-free, fancy-free, imagination-free, that which *is not* never for a long time appearing *to be* to him, unwise rulers or reformers cannot fatally interrupt him.

Thoreau, *Civil Disobedience*

98 Politics is, as it were, the gizzard of society, full of grit and gravel, and the two political parties are its two opposite halves—sometimes split into quarters, it may be, which grind on each other. Not only individuals, but states, have thus a confirmed dyspepsia.

Thoreau, *Life Without Principle*

99 I do not allow myself to suppose that either the convention or the League have concluded to decide that I am either the greatest or best man in America, but rather they have concluded that it is not best to swap horses while crossing the river, and have further concluded that I am not so poor a horse that they might not make a botch of it in trying to swap.

Lincoln, *Speech to the National Union League*
Delegation (June 9, 1864)

100 While, in the morality of the best Pagan nations, duty to the State holds even a disproportionate place, infringing on the just liberty of the individual; in purely Christian ethics, that grand department of duty is scarcely noticed or acknowledged. It is in the Koran, not the New Testament, that we read the maxim—"A ruler who appoints any man to an office, when there is in his dominions another man better qualified for it, sins against God and against the State." What little recognition the idea of obligation to the public obtains in modern morality is derived from Greek and Roman sources, not from Christian; as, even in the morality of private life, whatever exists of magnanimity, highmindedness, personal dignity, even the sense of honour, is derived from the purely human, not the religious part of our education, and never could have grown out of a standard of ethics in which the only worth, professedly recognised, is that of obedience.

Mill, *On Liberty,* II

101 To determine the point at which evils, so formidable to human freedom and advancement, begin, or rather at which they begin to predominate over the benefits attending the collective application of the force of society, under its recognised chiefs, for the removal of the obstacles which stand in the way of its well-being; to secure as much of the advantages of centralised power and intelligence as can be had without turning into governmental channels too great a proportion of the general activity—is one of the most difficult and complicated questions in the art of government. It is, in a great measure, a question of detail, in which many and various considerations must be kept in view, and no absolute rule can be laid down. But I believe that the practical principle in which safety resides, the ideal to be kept in view, the standard by which to test all arrangements intended for overcoming the difficulty, may be conveyed in these words: the greatest dissemination of power consistent with efficiency; but the greatest possible centralisation of information, and diffusion of it from the centre.

Mill, *On Liberty,* V

102 The power in society which has any tendency to convert itself into political power is not power quiescent, power merely passive, but active power; in other words, power actually exerted; that is to say, a very small portion of all the power in existence. Politically speaking, a great part of all power consists in will. How is it possible, then, to compute the elements of political power, while we omit from the computation anything which acts on the will? To think that because those who wield the power in society wield in the end that of government, therefore it is of no use to attempt to influence the constitution of the government by acting on opinion, is to forget that opinion is itself one of the greatest active social forces. One person

with a belief is a social power equal to ninety-nine who have only interests. They who can succeed in creating a general persuasion that a certain form of government, or social fact of any kind, deserves to be preferred, have made nearly the most important step which can possibly be taken towards ranging the powers of society on its side.

Mill, *Representative Government,* I

103 In quiet and untroubled times it seems to every administrator that it is only by his efforts that the whole population under his rule is kept going, and in this consciousness of being indispensable every administrator finds the chief reward of his labor and efforts. While the sea of history remains calm the ruler-administrator in his frail bark, holding on with a boat hook to the ship of the people and himself moving, naturally imagines that his efforts move the ship he is holding on to. But as soon as a storm arises and the sea begins to heave and the ship to move, such a delusion is no longer possible. The ship moves independently with its own enormous motion, the boat hook no longer reaches the moving vessel, and suddenly the administrator, instead of appearing a ruler and a source of power, becomes an insignificant, useless, feeble man.

Tolstoy, *War and Peace,* XI, 25

104 Politics is largely governed by sententious platitudes which are devoid of truth.

Russell, *Unpopular Essays,* VII

10.3 | *Government*

ITS NATURE, NECESSITY, AND FORMS

The distinction made by certain writers between a state of nature and a civil society or commonwealth (discussed in quotations in Section 10.1) turns on the absence or presence of government and its institutions, mainly the enactment and enforcement of laws and the adjudication of disputes by judicial tribunals or courts. The absence of government is anarchy. It would, therefore, appear to be the case that the presence of government is essential or indispensable to the existence of the state or commonwealth, and to the civil peace that is identical with civil society.

That is the view which predominates in the passages assembled here. The opposing view, advanced by the proponents of anarchy, is not well represented, though some indications of it will be found in quotations from Thoreau and Emerson. For other indications of it, and for considerations relevant to this fundamental issue about government, the reader should turn to Section 13.1 on FREEDOM IN SOCIETY and Section 14.3 on THE CONDITIONS OF PEACE.

A large number of quotations name and classify diverse forms of government. In an early instance of this type of discussion reported by Herodotus, the principal differentiation is made in terms of whether government is by the one, the few, or the many; and it is in such terms that Plato and Aristotle, and others after them, distinguish such forms of government as monarchy, aristocracy, and democracy, or propose a mixed regimine that combines government by the one, the few, and the many. When a further criterion is introduced—whether government is for the private benefit of the ruler of for the public good of the ruled—differentiation is made between good and bad government by the one (monarchy vs. tyranny), good and bad government by the few (aristocracy vs. oligarchy), and good and bad government by the many (polity vs. democracy).

Some political philosophers, including those already mentioned, dismiss the foregoing classification of the forms of government as superficial, and propose instead the basic distinction between a government of laws and a government of men—between constitutional or republican government, on the one hand, and absolute or despotic government, on the other. When this is made the pivotal distinction, such terms as monarchy, tyranny, aristocracy, oligarchy, and democracy take on different meanings, as the reader will see by examining the passages below with this in mind. Thus, for example, an absolute monarchy may be benevolent or tyrannical; a constitutional government may be aristocratic, oligarchical, or democratic according to the qualifications it sets up for citizenship and public office; and most republics would appear to have the characteristics of the mixed regime, involving the one, the few, and the many in different functions or departments of government. On all these matters, the reader will find additional quotations in subsequent sections of this chapter, especially Sections 10.4, 10.5, and 10.6.

Other matters treated here include the division of the branches or functions of government into the legislative, the judicial, and the executive; questions concerning the primacy of the legislative and the prerogatives of the executive; and the issue concerning the limitations, if any, that should be imposed upon the authority and power of government. One bit of wisdom on this moot question is expressed in Abraham Lincoln's memorable statement that government should do for the people whatever they cannot do for themselves.

---

1 The conspirators met together to consult about the situation of affairs. At this meeting speeches were made, to which many of the Greeks give no credence, but they were made nevertheless. Otanes recommended that the management of public affairs should be entrusted to the whole nation. "To me," he said, "it seems advisable, that we should no longer have a single man to rule over us—the rule of one is neither good nor pleasant. Ye cannot have forgotten to what lengths Cambyses went in his haughty tyranny, and the haughtiness of the Magi ye have yourselves experienced. How indeed is it possible that monarchy should be a well-adjusted thing, when it allows a man to do as he likes without being answerable? Such licence is enough to stir strange and unwonted thoughts in the heart of the worthiest of men. Give a person this power, and straightway his manifold good things puff him up with pride, while envy is so natural to human kind that it cannot but arise in him. But pride and envy together include all wickedness—both of them leading on to deeds of savage violence. True it is that kings, possessing as they do all that heart can desire, ought to be void of envy; but the contrary is seen in their conduct towards the citizens. They are jealous of the most virtuous among their subjects, and wish their death; while they take delight in the meanest and basest, being ever ready to listen to the tales of slanderers. A king, besides, is beyond all other men inconsistent with himself. Pay him court in moderation, and he is angry because you do not show him more profound respect—show him profound respect, and he is offended again, because (as he says) you fawn on him. But the worst of all is, that he sets aside the laws of the land, puts men to death without trial, and subjects women to violence. The rule of the many, on the other hand, has, in the first place, the fairest of names, to wit, *isonomy;* and further it is free from all those outrages which a king is wont to commit. There, places are given by lot, the magistrate is answerable for what he does, and measures rest with the commonalty. I vote, therefore, that we do away with monarchy, and raise the people to power. For the people are all in all."

Such were the sentiments of Otanes. Megabyzus spoke next, and advised the setting up of an oligarchy:—"In all that Otanes has said to persuade you to put down monarchy," he observed, "I fully concur; but his recommendation that we should call the people to power seems to me not the best advice. For there is nothing so void of understanding, nothing so full of wantonness, as the unwieldy rabble. It were folly not to be borne, for men, while seeking to escape the wantonness of a tyrant, to give themselves up to the wantonness of a rude unbridled mob. The tyrant, in all his doings, at least knows what is he about, but a mob is altogether devoid of knowledge; for how should there be any knowledge in a rabble, untaught, and with no natural sense of what is right and fit? It rushes wildly into state affairs with all the fury of a stream swollen in the winter, and confuses everything. Let the enemies of the Persians be ruled by democracies; but let us choose out from the citizens a certain number of the worthiest, and put the government into their hands. For thus both we ourselves shall be among the governors, and power being entrusted to the best men, it is likely that the best counsels will prevail in the state."

This was the advice which Megabyzus gave, and after him Darius came forward, and spoke as follows:—"All that Megabyzus said against democracy was well said, I think; but about oligarchy he did not speak advisedly; for take these three forms of government—democracy, oligarchy, and monarchy—and let them each be at their best, I maintain that monarchy far surpasses the other two. What government can possibly be better than that of the very best man in the whole state? The counsels of such a man are like himself, and so he governs the mass of the people to their heart's content; while at the same time his measures against evil-doers are kept more secret than in other states. Contrariwise, in oligarchies, where men vie with each other in the service of the commonwealth, fierce enmities are apt to arise between man and man, each wishing to be leader, and to carry his own measures; whence violent quarrels come, which lead to open strife, often ending in bloodshed. Then monarchy is sure to follow; and this too shows how far that rule surpasses all others. Again, in a democracy, it is impossible but that there will be malpractices: these malpractices, however, do not lead to enmities, but to close friendships, which are formed among those engaged in them, who must hold well together to carry on their villainies. And so things go on until a man stands forth as champion of the commonalty, and puts down the evil-doers. Straightway the author of so great a service is admired by all, and from being admired soon comes to be appointed king; so that here too it is plain that monarchy is the best government. Lastly, to sum up all in a word, whence, I ask, was it that we got the freedom which we enjoy?—did democracy give it us, or oligarchy, or a monarch? As a single man recovered our freedom for us, my sentence is that we keep to the rule of one. Even apart from this, we ought not to change the laws of our forefathers when they work fairly; for to do so is not well."

Such were the three opinions brought forward

at this meeting; the four other Persians voted in favour of the last. Otanes, who wished to give his countrymen a democracy, when he found the decision against him, arose a second time, and spoke thus before the assembly:—"Brother conspirators, it is plain that the king who is to be chosen will be one of ourselves, whether we make the choice by casting lots for the prize, or by letting the people decide which of us they will have to rule over them, in or any other way. Now, as I have neither a mind to rule nor to be ruled, I shall not enter the lists with you in this matter. I withdraw, however, on one condition—none of you shall claim to exercise rule over me or my seed for ever." The six agreed to these terms, and Otanes withdrew and stood aloof from the contest. And still to this day the family of Otanes continues to be the only free family in Persia; those who belong to it submit to the rule of the king only so far as they themselves choose; they are bound, however, to observe the laws of the land like the other Persians.

Herodotus, *History,* III, 80–83

2 *Eleatic Stranger.* Monarchy divides into royalty and tyranny; the rule of the few into aristocracy, which has an auspicious name, and oligarchy; and democracy or the rule of the many, which before was one, must now be divided.

Young Socrates. On what principle of division?

Str. On the same principle as before, although the name is now discovered to have a twofold meaning. For the distinction of ruling with law or without law, applies to this as well as to the rest.

Y. Soc. Yes.

Str. The division made no difference when we were looking for the perfect State, as we showed before. But now that this has been separated off, and, as we said, the others alone are left for us, the principle of law and the absence of law will bisect them all.

Y. Soc. That would seem to follow, from what has been said.

Str. Then monarchy, when bound by good prescriptions or laws, is the best of all the six, and when lawless is the most bitter and oppressive to the subject.

Y. Soc. True.

Str. The government of the few, which is intermediate between that of the one and many, is also intermediate in good and evil; but the government of the many is in every respect weak and unable to do either any great good or any great evil, when compared with the others, because the offices are too minutely subdivided and too many hold them. And this therefore is the worst of all lawful governments, and the best of all lawless ones. If they are all without the restraints of law, democracy is the form in which to live is best; if they are well ordered, then this is the last which you should choose, as royalty, the first form, is the best, with the exception of the seventh, for that excels them all, and is among States what God is among men.

Plato, *Statesman*, 302B

3 The distinction which is made between the king and the statesman is as follows: When the government is personal, the ruler is a king; when, according to the rules of the political science, the citizens rule and are ruled in turn, then he is called a statesman.

Aristotle, *Politics*, 1252a13

4 The rule of a master is not a constitutional rule, and . . . all the different kinds of rule are not, as some affirm, the same with each other. For there is one rule exercised over subjects who are by nature free, another over subjects who are by nature slaves. The rule of a household is a monarchy, for every house is under one head: whereas constitutional rule is a government of freemen and equals.

Aristotle, *Politics*, 1255b16

5 The words constitution and government have the same meaning, and the government, which is the supreme authority in states, must be in the hands of one, or of a few, or of the many. The true forms of government, therefore, are those in which the one, or the few, or the many, govern with a view to the common interest; but governments which rule with a view to the private interest, whether of the one, or of the few, or of the many, are perversions. For the members of a state, if they are truly citizens, ought to participate in its advantages. Of forms of government in which one rules, we call that which regards the common interests, kingship or royalty; that in which more than one, but not many, rule, aristocracy; and it is so called, either because the rulers are the best men, or because they have at heart the best interests of the state and of the citizens. But when the citizens at large administer the state for the common interest, the government is called by the generic name,—a constitution. And there is a reason for this use of language. One man or a few may excel in virtue; but as the number increases it becomes more difficult for them to attain perfection in every kind of virtue, though they may in military virtue, for this is found in the masses. Hence in a constitutional government the fighting-men have the supreme power, and those who possess arms are the citizens.

Of the above-mentioned forms, the perversions are as follows:—of royalty, tyranny; of aristocracy, oligarchy; of constitutional government, democracy. For tyranny is a kind of monarchy which has in view the interest of the monarch only; oligarchy has in view the interest of the wealthy; democracy, of the needy: none of them the common good of all.

Aristotle, *Politics*, 1279a25

6 If we call the rule of many men, who are all of them good, aristocracy, and the rule of one man royalty, then aristocracy will be better for states than royalty, whether the government is supported by force or not, provided only that a number of men equal in virtue can be found.

Aristotle, *Politics*, 1286b4

7 Democracies are safer and more permanent than oligarchies, because they have a middle class which is more numerous and has a greater share in the government; for when there is no middle class, and the poor greatly exceed in number, troubles arise, and the state soon comes to an end. . . .

These considerations will help us to understand why most governments are either democratical or oligarchical. The reason is that the middle class is seldom numerous in them, and whichever party, whether the rich or the common people, transgresses the mean and predominates, draws the constitution its own way, and thus arises either oligarchy or democracy. There is another reason—the poor and the rich quarrel with one another, and whichever side gets the better, instead of establishing a just or popular government, regards political supremacy as the prize of victory, and the one party sets up a democracy and the other an oligarchy.

Aristotle, *Politics*, 1296a14

8 All constitutions have three elements, concerning which the good lawgiver has to regard what is expedient for each constitution. When they are well-ordered, the constitution is well-ordered, and as they differ from one another, constitutions differ. There is one element which deliberates about public affairs; secondly that concerned with the magistracies—the questions being, what they should be, over what they should exercise authority, and what should be the mode of electing to them; and thirdly that which has judicial power.

Aristotle, *Politics*, 1297b37

9 The forms of government are four—democracy, oligarchy, aristocracy, monarchy. The supreme right to judge and decide always rests, therefore, with either a part or the whole of one or other of these governing powers.

A Democracy is a form of government under which the citizens distribute the offices of state among themselves by lot, whereas under oligarchy there is a property qualification, under aristocracy one of education. By education I mean that education which is laid down by the law; for it is those who have been loyal to the national institutions that hold office under an aristocracy. These are bound to be looked upon as 'the best men', and it is from this fact that this form of government has derived its name ('the rule of the best'). Monarchy, as the word implies, is the constitution in which one man has authority over all. There are two forms of monarchy: kingship, which is limited by prescribed conditions, and 'tyranny', which is not limited by anything.

Aristotle, *Rhetoric,* 1365ᵇ29

10 The end of democracy is freedom; of oligarchy, wealth; of aristocracy, the maintenance of education and national institutions; of tyranny, the protection of the tyrant.

Aristotle, *Rhetoric,* 1366ᵃ4

11 Sovereignty in a state is thrown like a ball from kings to tyrants, from tyrants to aristocrats (or to the people at large), and finally to an oligarchy or to another tyrant. No single type of government lasts very long. This being the case, I regard monarchy as the best of the three basic types of government. But a moderate, mixed type of government, combining all three elements, is even better. There should be a monarchical element in the state. The leading citizens ought also to have some power. And the people themselves should have some say in running the affairs of the nation. This kind of constitution promotes a high degree of equality—something free men cannot do without for long. Such a constitution also provides stability. The three basic forms of government too easily degenerate into their corresponding perversions: monarchy into despotism, aristocracy into an oligarchy, and democracy into mob rule or anarchy. These forms often change to new types, but a mixed constitution does not unless grievous errors are made in governing. There appears no reason to change the form of government, if all the citizens have a feeling of security. Nor does this form have an opposite perversion into which it can easily slide.

Cicero, *Republic,* I, 44

12 All nations and cities are ruled by the people, the nobility, or by one man. A constitution, formed by selection out of these elements . . . is easy to commend but not to produce; or, if it is produced, it cannot be lasting.

Tacitus, *Annals,* IV, 33

13 Two points are to be observed concerning the right ordering of rulers in a state or nation. One is that all should take some share in the government, for this form of constitution ensures peace among the people, commends itself to all, and is guarded by all. . . . The other point is to be observed in respect of the kinds of government, or the different ways in which the constitutions are established. . . . The best form of government is in a state or kingdom, where one is given the power to preside over all, while under him are others having governing powers; and yet a government of this kind is shared by all, both because all are eligible to govern, and because the rulers are cho-

sen by all. For this is the best form of polity, being partly kingdom, since there is one at the head of all; partly aristocracy, in so far as a number of persons are set in authority; partly democracy, that is, government by the people, in so far as the rulers can be chosen from the people, and the people have the right to choose their rulers.

Aquinas, *Summa Theologica,* I–II, 105, 1

14 If an unjust government is carried on by one man alone, who seeks his own benefit from his rule and not the good of the multitude subject to him, such a ruler is called a *tyrant*—a word derived from *strength*—because he oppresses by might instead of ruling by justice. Thus among the ancients all powerful men were called tyrants. If an unjust government is carried on, not by one but by several, and if they be few, it is called an *oligarchy,* that is, the rule of a few. This occurs when a few, who differ from the tyrant only by the fact that they are more than one, oppress the people by means of their wealth. If, finally, the bad government is carried on by the multitude, it is called a *democracy,* i.e. control by the populace, which comes about when the plebeian people by force of numbers oppress the rich. In this way the whole people will be as one tyrant.

Aquinas, *On Kingship,* I, 1

15 All those who have written upon civil institutions demonstrate (and history is full of examples to support them) that whoever desires to found a state and give it laws, must start with assuming that all men are bad and ever ready to display their vicious nature, whenever they may find occasion for it. If their evil disposition remains concealed for a time, it must be attributed to some unknown reason; and we must assume that it lacked occasion to show itself; but time, which has been said to be the father of all truth, does not fail to bring it to light.

Machiavelli, *Discourses,* I, 3

16 Not in theory, but in truth, the best and most excellent government for each nation is the one under which it has preserved its existence. Its form and essential fitness depend on habit. We are prone to be discontented with the present state of things. But I maintain, nevertheless, that to wish for the government of a few in a democratic state, or another type of government in a monarchy, is foolish and wrong.

Montaigne, *Essays,* III, 9, Of Vanity

17 *Gonzalo.* I' the commonwealth I would by contraries
Execute all things; for no kind of traffic
Would I admit; no name of magistrate;
Letters should not be known; riches, poverty,
And use of service, none; contract, succession,
Bourn, bound of land, tilth, vineyard, none;

No use of metal, corn, or wine, or oil;
No occupation; all men idle, all;
And women too, but innocent and pure;
No sovereignty—
   Sebastian.   Yet he would be king on't.
   Antonio. The latter end of his commonwealth
forgets the beginning.
   Gon. All things in common nature should pro-
      duce
Without sweat or endeavor. Treason, felony,
Sword, pike, knife, gun, or need of any engine,
Would I not have; but nature should bring forth,
Of it own kind, all foison, all abundance,
To feed my innocent people.
   Seb. No marrying 'mong his subjects?
   Ant. None, man; all idle. Whores and knaves.
   Gon. I would with such perfection govern, sir,
To excel the golden age.
                  Shakespeare, *Tempest*, II, i, 144

18 When any of the four pillars of government are
mainly shaken or weakened (which are religion,
justice, counsel, and treasure), men had need to
pray for fair weather.
           Bacon, *Of Seditions and Troubles*

19 It is not in the power of man to devise any form of
government free from imperfections and dangers.
      Grotius, *Rights of War and Peace*, Bk. I, III, 8

20 Desire of knowledge, and arts of peace, inclineth
men to obey a common power: for such desire
containeth a desire of leisure, and consequently
protection from some other power than their own.
             Hobbes, *Leviathan*, I, 11

21 The power to coin money, to dispose of the estate
and persons of infant heirs, to have pre-emption
in markets, and all other statute prerogatives may
be transferred by the sovereign, and yet the power
to protect his subjects be retained. But if he transfer the militia, he retains the judicature in vain,
for want of execution of the laws; or if he grant
away the power of raising money, the militia is in
vain; or if he give away the government of doctrines, men will be frighted into rebellion with the
fear of spirits. And so if we consider any one of the
said rights, we shall presently see that the holding
of all the rest will produce no effect in the conservation of peace and justice, the end for which all
Commonwealths are instituted. And this division
is it whereof it is said, *a kingdom divided in itself
cannot stand:* for unless this division precede, division into opposite armies can never happen.
            Hobbes, *Leviathan*, II, 18

22 The difference of Commonwealths consisteth in
the difference of the sovereign, or the person representative of all and every one of the multitude.
And because the sovereignty is either in one man,
or in an assembly of more than one; and into that
assembly either every man hath right to enter, or
not every one, but certain men distinguished from
the rest; it is manifest there can be but three kinds
of Commonwealth. For the representative must
needs be one man, or more; and if more, then it is
the assembly of all, or but of a part. When the
representative is one man, then is the Commonwealth a monarchy; when an assembly of all that
will come together, then it is a democracy, or popular Commonwealth; when an assembly of a
part only, then it is called an aristocracy. Other
kind of Commonwealth there can be none: for
either one, or more, or all, must have the sovereign power (which I have shown to be indivisible)
entire.

   There be other names of government in the histories and books of policy; as tyranny and oligarchy; but they are not the names of other forms
of government, but of the same forms misliked.
For they that are discontented under monarchy
call it tyranny; and they that are displeased with
aristocracy call it oligarchy: so also, they which
find themselves grieved under a democracy call it
anarchy, which signifies want of government; and
yet I think no man believes that want of government is any new kind of government: nor by the
same reason ought they to believe that the government is of one kind when they like it, and another
when they mislike it or are oppressed by the governors.
            Hobbes, *Leviathan*, II, 19

23 The sovereign power, whether placed in one man,
as in monarchy, or in one assembly of men, as in
popular and aristocratical Commonwealths, is as
great as possibly men can be imagined to make it.
And though of so unlimited a power, men may
fancy many evil consequences, yet the consequences of the want of it, which is perpetual war
of every man against his neighbour, are much
worse.
            Hobbes, *Leviathan*, II, 20

24 *Temporal* and *spiritual* government are but two
words brought into the world to make men see
double and mistake their lawful sovereign. It is
true that the bodies of the faithful, after the resurrection, shall be not only spiritual, but eternal;
but in this life they are gross and corruptible.
There is therefore no other government in this
life, neither of state nor religion, but temporal;
nor teaching of any doctrine lawful to any subject
which the governor both of the state and of the
religion forbiddeth to be taught. And that governor must be *one;* or else there must needs follow
faction and civil war in the Commonwealth between the Church and State; between spiritualists
and temporalists; between the sword of justice
and the shield of faith; and, which is more, in
every Christian man's own breast between the
Christian and the man.
            Hobbes, *Leviathan*, III, 39

25 We have defined an aristocratic dominion as that which is held not by one man, but by certain persons chosen out of the multitude, whom we shall henceforth call patricians. I say expressly, "that which is held by certain persons chosen." For the chief difference between this and a democracy is, that the right of governing depends in an aristocracy on election only, but in a democracy for the most part on some right either congenital or acquired by fortune. . . . And therefore, although in any dominion the entire multitude be received into the number of the patricians, provided that right of theirs is not inherited, and does not descend by some law to others, the dominion will for all that be quite an aristocracy, because none are received into the number of the patricians save by express election. . . . We must observe a very great difference, which exists between the dominion which is conferred on one man and that which is conferred on a sufficiently large council. For, in the first place, the power of one man is . . . very inadequate to support the entire dominion; but this no one, without manifest absurdity, can affirm of a sufficiently large council. For, in declaring the council to be sufficiently large, one at the same time denies, that it is inadequate to support the dominion. A king, therefore, is altogether in need of counsellors, but a council like this is not so in the least. In the second place, kings are mortal, but councils are everlasting. And so the power of the dominion which has once been transferred to a large enough council never reverts to the multitude. . . . Thirdly, a king's dominion is often on sufferance, whether from his minority, sickness, or old age, or from other causes; but the power of a council of this kind, on the contrary, remains always one and the same. In the fourth place, one man's will is very fluctuating and inconstant; and, therefore, in a monarchy, all law is, indeed, the explicit will of the king . . . but not every will of the king ought to be law; but this cannot be said of the will of a sufficiently numerous council. For since the council itself, as we have just shown, needs no counsellors, its every explicit will ought to be law. And hence we conclude, that the dominion conferred upon a large enough council is absolute, or approaches nearest to the absolute. For if there be any absolute dominion, it is, in fact, that which is held by an entire multitude.

Spinoza, *Political Treatise*, VIII, 1–3

26 I easily grant that civil government is the proper remedy for the inconveniences of the state of Nature, which must certainly be great where men may be judges in their own case, since it is easy to be imagined that he who was so unjust as to do his brother an injury will scarce be so just as to condemn himself for it.

Locke, *II Civil Government*, II, 13

27 The great and chief end . . . of men uniting into commonwealths, and putting themselves under government, is the preservation of their property.

Locke, *II Civil Government*, IX, 124

28 In the state of Nature there are many things wanting. Firstly, there wants an established, settled, known law, received and allowed by common consent to be the standard of right and wrong, and the common measure to decide all controversies between them. For though the law of Nature be plain and intelligible to all rational creatures, yet men, being biased by their interest, as well as ignorant for want of study of it, are not apt to allow of it as a law binding to them in the application of it to their particular cases.

Secondly, in the state of Nature there wants a known and indifferent judge, with authority to determine all differences according to the established law. For every one in that state being both judge and executioner of the law of Nature, men being partial to themselves, passion and revenge is very apt to carry them too far, and with too much heat in their own cases, as well as negligence and unconcernedness, make them too remiss in other men's.

Thirdly, in the state of Nature there often wants power to back and support the sentence when right, and to give it due execution. They who by any injustice offended will seldom fail where they are able by force to make good their injustice. Such resistance many times makes the punishment dangerous, and frequently destructive to those who attempt it.

Locke, *II Civil Government*, IX, 124–126

29 The legislative cannot transfer the power of making laws to any other hands, for it being but a delegated power from the people, they who have it cannot pass it over to others. The people alone can appoint the form of the commonwealth, which is by constituting the legislative, and appointing in whose hands that shall be. And when the people have said, "We will submit, and be governed by laws made by such men, and in such forms," nobody else can say other men shall make laws for them; nor can they be bound by any laws but such as are enacted by those whom they have chosen and authorised to make laws for them.

Locke, *II Civil Government*, XI, 141

30 In well-ordered commonwealths, where the good of the whole is so considered as it ought, the legislative power is put into the hands of divers persons who, duly assembled, have by themselves, or jointly with others, a power to make laws, which when they have done, being separated again, they are themselves subject to the laws they have made; which is a new and near tie upon them to take care that they make them for the public good.

Locke, *II Civil Government*, XII, 143

31 Where the laws cannot be executed it is all one as

if there were no laws, and a government without laws is, I suppose, a mystery in politics inconceivable to human capacity, and inconsistent with human society.

Locke, *II Civil Government*, XIX, 219

32 A government is like everything else: to preserve it we must love it.

Montesquieu, *Spirit of Laws*, IV, 5

33 Republics end with luxury; monarchies with poverty.

Montesquieu, *Spirit of Laws*, VII, 4

34 In all governments, there is a perpetual intestine struggle, open or secret, between Authority and Liberty; and neither of them can ever absolutely prevail in the contest.

Hume, *Of the Origin of Government*

35 The legislative power belongs to the people, and can belong to it alone. It may, on the other hand, readily be seen, from the principles laid down above, that the executive power cannot belong to the generality as legislature or Sovereign, because it consists wholly of particular acts which fall outside the competency of the law, and consequently of the Sovereign, whose acts must always be laws.

The public force therefore needs an agent of its own to bind it together and set it to work under the direction of the general will, to serve as a means of communication between the State and the Sovereign, and to do for the collective person more or less what the union of soul and body does for man. Here we have what is, in the State, the basis of government, often wrongly confused with the Sovereign, whose minister it is.

What then is government? An intermediate body set up between the subjects and the Sovereign, to secure their mutual correspondence, charged with the execution of the laws and the maintenance of liberty, both civil and political.

Rousseau, *Social Contract*, III, 1

36 It is not good for him who makes the laws to execute them.

Rousseau, *Social Contract*, III, 4

37 A people that would always govern well would not need to be governed.

Rousseau, *Social Contract*, III, 4

38 Law being purely the declaration of the general will, it is clear that, in the exercise of the legislative power, the people cannot be represented; but in that of the executive power, which is only the force that is applied to give the law effect, it both can and should be represented.

Rousseau, *Social Contract*, III, 15

39 *Johnson.* I would not give half a guinea to live under one form of government rather than another. It is of no moment to the happiness of an individual.

Boswell, *Life of Johnson*
(*March 31, 1772*)

40 Talking of different governments,—*Johnson.* "The more contracted that power is, the more easily it is destroyed. A country governed by a despot is an inverted cone. Government there cannot be so firm, as when it rests upon a broad basis gradually contracted, as the government of Great Britain, which is founded on the parliament, then is in the privy council, then in the King." *Boswell.* "Power, when contracted into the person of a despot, may be easily destroyed, as the prince may be cut off. So Caligula wished that the people of Rome had but one neck, that he might cut them off at a blow." *Oglethorpe.* "It was of the Senate he wished that. The Senate by its usurpation controuled both the Emperour and the people. And don't you think that we see too much of that in our own Parliament?"

Boswell, *Life of Johnson*
(*Apr. 14, 1778*)

41 When the judicial is united to the executive power, it is scarce possible that justice should not frequently be sacrificed to what is vulgarly called politics. The persons entrusted with the great interests of the state may, even without any corrupt views, sometimes imagine it necessary to sacrifice to those interests the rights of a private man. But upon the impartial administration of justice depends the liberty of every individual, the sense which he has of his own security. In order to make every individual feel himself perfectly secure in the possession of every right which belongs to him, it is not only necessary that the judicial should be separated from the executive power, but that it should be rendered as much as possible independent of that power. The judge should not be liable to be removed from his office according to the caprice of that power. The regular payment of his salary should not depend upon the good-will or even upon the good economy of that power.

Adam Smith, *Wealth of Nations*, V, 1

42 Sometimes it is said that man cannot be trusted with the government of himself. Can he, then, be trusted with the government of others? Or have we found angels in the forms of kings to govern him? Let history answer this question.

Jefferson, *First Inaugural Address*

43 A wise and frugal government, which shall restrain men from injuring one another, which shall leave them otherwise free to regulate their own pursuits of industry and improvement, and shall not take from the mouth of labor the bread it has

earned: this is the sum of good government.

Jefferson, *First Inaugural Address*

44 The two Antonines . . . governed the Roman world forty-two years, with the same invariable spirit of wisdom and virtue. Although Pius had two sons, he preferred the welfare of Rome to the interest of his family, gave his daughter Faustina in marriage to young Marcus, obtained from the senate the tribunitian and proconsular powers, and with a noble disdain, or rather ignorance of jealousy, associated him to all the labours of government. Marcus [Aurelius], on the other hand, revered the character of his benefactor, loved him as a parent, obeyed him as his sovereign, and, after he was no more, regulated his own administration by the example and maxims of his predecessor. Their united reigns are possibly the only period of history in which the happiness of a great people was the sole object of government.

Gibbon, *Decline and Fall
of the Roman Empire*, III

45 Administration of justice and of the finances [are] the two objects which, in a state of peace, comprehend almost all the respective duties of the sovereign and of the people; of the former, to protect the citizens who are obedient to the laws; of the latter, to contribute the share of their property which is required for the expenses of the state.

Gibbon, *Decline and Fall
of the Roman Empire*, XVII

46 The three powers in the state as regards their relations to each other, are . . . *coordinate* with one another as so many moral persons, and the one is thus the complement of the other in the way of completing the constitution of the state; they are likewise *subordinate* to one another, so that the one cannot at the same time usurp the function of the other by whose side it moves, each having its own principle and maintaining its authority in a particular person, but under the condition of the will of a superior; and further, by the *union* of both these relations, they assign distributively to every subject in the state his own rights.

Considered as to their respective dignity, the three powers may be thus described. The will of the sovereign legislator, in respect of what constitutes the external mine and thine, is to be regarded as irreprehensible; the executive function of the supreme ruler is to be regarded as irresistible; and the judicial sentence of the supreme judge is to be regarded as irreversible, being beyond appeal.

Kant, *Science of Right*, 48

47 The idea of a national government involves in it, not only an authority over the individual citizens, but an indefinite supremacy over all persons and things, so far as they are objects of lawful government. Among a people consolidated into one nation, this supremacy is completely vested in the national legislature.

Madison, *Federalist 39*

48 In a government where numerous and extensive prerogatives are placed in the hands of an hereditary monarch, the executive department is very justly regarded as the source of danger, and watched with all the jealousy which a zeal for liberty ought to inspire. In a democracy, where a multitude of people exercise in person the legislative functions, and are continually exposed, by their incapacity for regular deliberation and concerted measures, to the ambitious intrigues of their executive magistrates, tyranny may well be apprehended, on some favourable emergency, to start up in the same quarter. But in a representative republic, where the executive magistracy is carefully limited, both in the extent and the duration of its power; and where the legislative power is exercised by an assembly which is inspired, by a supposed influence over the people, with an intrepid confidence in its own strength; which is sufficiently numerous to feel all the passions which actuate a multitude, yet not so numerous as to be incapable of pursuing the objects of its passions, by means which reason prescribes; it is against the enterprising ambition of this department that the people ought to indulge all their jealousy and exhaust all their precautions.

Madison, *Federalist 48*

49 What is government itself but the greatest of all reflections on human nature? If men were angels, no government would be necessary.

Hamilton or Madison, *Federalist 51*

50 A good government implies two things: first, fidelity to the object of government, which is the happiness of the people; secondly, a knowledge of the means by which that object can be best attained. Some governments are deficient in both these qualities; most governments are deficient in the first.

Hamilton or Madison, *Federalist 62*

51 No government, any more than an individual, will long be respected without being truly respectable; nor be truly respectable without possessing a certain portion of order and stability.

Hamilton or Madison, *Federalist 62*

52 The state as a political entity is . . . cleft into three substantive divisions:

(*a*) the power to determine and establish the universal—the Legislature;

(*b*) the power to subsume single cases and the spheres of particularity under the universal—the Executive;

(*c*) the power of subjectivity, as the will with the power of ultimate decision—the Crown. In the crown, the different powers are bound into an individual unity which is thus at once the apex and basis of the whole, i.e. of constitutional monarchy.

Hegel, *Philosophy of Right,* 273

53 A distinction must be made when aristocracies and democracies accuse each other of facilitating corruption. In aristocratic governments, those who are placed at the head of affairs are rich men, who are desirous only of power. In democracies, statesmen are poor and have their fortunes to make. The consequence is that in aristocratic states the rulers are rarely accessible to corruption and have little craving for money, while the reverse is the case in democratic nations.

But in aristocracies, as those who wish to attain the head of affairs possess considerable wealth, and as the number of persons by whose assistance they may rise is comparatively small, the government is, if I may so speak, put up at auction. In democracies, on the contrary, those who are covetous of power are seldom wealthy, and the number of those who confer power is extremely great. Perhaps in democracies the number of men who might be bought is not smaller, but buyers are rarely to be found; and, besides, it would be necessary to buy so many persons at once that the attempt would be useless.

Tocqueville, *Democracy in America,* I, 13

54 Aristocracies are infinitely more expert in the science of legislation than democracies ever can be. They are possessed of a self-control that protects them from the errors of temporary excitement; and they form far-reaching designs, which they know how to mature till a favorable opportunity arrives. Aristocratic government proceeds with the dexterity of art; it understands how to make the collective force of all its laws converge at the same time to a given point. Such is not the case with democracies, whose laws are almost always ineffective or inopportune. The means of democracy are therefore more imperfect than those of aristocracy, and the measures that it unwittingly adopts are frequently opposed to its own cause; but the object it has in view is more useful.

Tocqueville, *Democracy in America,* I, 14

55 The less government we have the better—the fewer laws, and the less confided power. The antidote to this abuse of formal government is the influence of private character, the growth of the Individual; the appearance of the principal to supersede the proxy; the appearance of the wise man; of whom the existing government is, it must be owned, but a shabby imitation.

Emerson, *Politics*

56 The only government that I recognize—and it matters not how few are at the head of it, or how small its army—is that power that establishes justice in the land, never that which establishes injustice. What shall we think of a government to which all the truly brave and just men in the land are enemies, standing between it and those whom it oppresses?

Thoreau, *Plea for Captain John Brown*

57 I heartily accept the motto, "That government is best which governs least"; and I should like to see it acted up to more rapidly and systematically. Carried out, it finally amounts to this, which also I believe, "That government is best which governs not at all"; and when men are prepared for it, that will be the kind of government which they will have. Government is at best but an expedient; but most governments are usually, and all governments are sometimes, inexpedient.

Thoreau, *Civil Disobedience*

58 I went to the store the other day to buy a bolt for our front door, for, as I told the storekeeper, the Governor was coming here. 'Aye,' said he, 'and the Legislature too.' 'Then I will take two bolts,' said I. He said that there had been a steady demand for bolts and locks of late, for our protectors were coming.

Thoreau, *Journal (Sept. 8, 1859)*

59 The legitimate object of government is to do for a community of people whatever they need to have done, but cannot do at all, or cannot so well do for themselves in their separate and individual capacities. In all that the people can individually do as well for themselves, government ought not to interfere.

Lincoln, *Fragment on Government
(July 1, 1854)*

60 The . . . most cogent reason for restricting the interference of government is the great evil of adding unnecessarily to its power. Every function superadded to those already exercised by the government causes its influence over hopes and fears to be more widely diffused, and converts, more and more, the active and ambitious part of the public into hangers-on of the government, or of some party which aims at becoming the government. If the roads, the railways, the banks, the insurance offices, the great joint-stock companies, the universities, and the public charities, were all of them branches of the government; if, in addition, the municipal corporations and local boards, with all that now devolves on them, became departments of the central administration; if the employees of all these different enterprises were appointed and paid by the government, and looked to the government for every rise in life; not all the freedom of the press and popular constitu-

tion of the legislature would make this or any other country free otherwise than in name. And the evil would be greater, the more efficiently and scientifically the administrative machinery was constructed—the more skilful the arrangements for obtaining the best qualified hands and heads with which to work it.

Mill, *On Liberty,* V

61 The proper functions of a government are not a fixed thing, but different in different states of society; much more extensive in a backward than in an advanced state.

Mill, *Representative Government,* II

62 The interest of the monarch, or the interest of the aristocracy, either collective or that of its individual members, is promoted, or they themselves think that it will be promoted, by conduct opposed to that which the general interest of the community requires. The interest, for example, of the government is to tax heavily: that of the community is to be as little taxed as the necessary expenses of good government permit. The interest of the king, and of the governing aristocracy, is to possess, and exercise, unlimited power over the people; to enforce, on their part, complete conformity to the will and preferences of the rulers. The interest of the people is to have as little control exercised over them in any respect as is consistent with attaining the legitimate ends of government. The interest, or apparent and supposed interest, of the king or aristocracy is to permit no censure of themselves, at least in any form which they may consider either to threaten their power, or seriously to interfere with their free agency. The interest of the people is that there should be full liberty of censure on every public officer, and on every public act or measure. The interest of a ruling class, whether in an aristocracy or an aristocratic monarchy, is to assume to themselves an endless variety of unjust privileges, sometimes benefiting their pockets at the expense of the people, sometimes merely tending to exalt them above others, or, what is the same thing in different words, to degrade others below themselves. If the people are disaffected, which under such a government they are very likely to be, it is the interest of the king or aristocracy to keep them at a low level of intelligence and education, foment dissensions among them, and even prevent them from being too well off, lest they should "wax fat, and kick"; agreeably to the maxim of Cardinal Richelieu in his celebrated *Testament Politique.* All these things are for the interest of a king or aristocracy, in a purely selfish point of view, unless a sufficiently strong counter-interest is created by the fear of provoking resistance. All these evils have been, and many of them still are, produced by the sinister interests of kings and aristocracies, where their power is sufficient to raise them above the opinion of the rest of the community; nor is it rational to expect, as a consequence of such a position, any other conduct.

Mill, *Representative Government,* VI

63 Where the sentiment of nationality exists in any force, there is a *prima facie* case for uniting all the members of the nationality under the same government, and a government to themselves apart. This is merely saying that the question of government ought to be decided by the governed. One hardly knows what any division of the human race should be free to do if not to determine with which of the various collective bodies of human beings they choose to associate themselves.

Mill, *Representative Government,* XVI

64 It is already a common, and is rapidly tending to become the universal, condition of the more backward populations, to be either held in direct subjection by the more advanced, or to be under their complete political ascendancy; there are in this age of the world few more important problems than how to organise this rule, so as to make it a good instead of an evil to the subject people; providing them with the best attainable present government, and with the conditions most favourable to future permanent improvement. But the mode of fitting the government for this purpose is by no means so well understood as the conditions of good government in a people capable of governing themselves. We may even say that it is not understood at all.

Mill, *Representative Government,* XVIII

65 The government of a people by itself has a meaning and a reality; but such a thing as government of one people by another does not and cannot exist. One people may keep another as a warren or preserve for its own use, a place to make money in, a human cattle farm to be worked for the profit of its own inhabitants. But if the good of the governed is the proper business of a government, it is utterly impossible that a people should directly attend to it. The utmost they can do is to give some of their best men a commission to look after it; to whom the opinion of their own country can neither be much of a guide in the performance of their duty, nor a competent judge of the mode in which it has been performed.

Mill, *Representative Government,* XVIII

66 The ends of government are as comprehensive as those of the social union. They consist of all the good, and all the immunity from evil, which the

existence of government can be made either directly or indirectly to bestow.

Mill, *Principles of Political Economy,*
Bk. V, II, 2

67 Government neither subsists nor arises because it is good or useful, but solely because it is inevitable.

Santayana, *Life of Reason,* II, 3

10.4 | *Government of and by the People*

REPUBLIC AND DEMOCRACY

The kind of government being discussed in this section has been variously characterized as constitutional government, duly constituted government, limited and responsible government, a government of laws, lawful government, *de jure* government (or government by right rather than by might), government with the consent of the governed, and government based on the sovereignty of the people. While most of the authors quoted here are advocates or defenders of such government, usually regarding it as the only just or the only legitimate form of rule, they differ among themselves about the provisions that constitutional government should make for popular participation either through citizenship and suffrage or through election to public office.

The issue debated here can be expressed in the questions: Which portion or portions of the total population of the state shall be regarded as "the people" in the strict political sense of "qualified participants" in affairs of state? Which shall be treated as wards of the state, to be ruled for their own good, rather than as members of the ruling class? To understand these questions, it is necessary to understand the constitution that sets up a republic as an arrangement of offices, each given a certain limited authority to be exercised by men only in virtue of

their being officeholders, selected or elected from the body of men who are admitted to citizenship. Hence the qualifications for citizenship and for the other offices of government become the critical consideration in differentiating one constitution from another. Section 10.5 on CITIZENSHIP contains quotations relevant to this point.

The opponents of democracy argue for republics in which suffrage is restricted, the most frequent insistence being that the citizens should be men of property, although race, gender, education, and religion have also been defended as disqualifying criteria. The reader will also find a rejection of democracy that is based on the identification of it with direct participation on the part of the citizens, as in the republics of ancient Greece. The writers of *The Federalist* argue against direct democracy and for republican government, understood by them as consisting in government not directly by the people, but by their representatives.

The proponents of democracy differ among themselves on how far they would extend suffrage. In the ancient world, the advocates of democracy as against oligarchy proposed that, among men born free, suffrage and public office should be open to poor and rich alike; but they had no qualms about excluding slaves, for example. As late as the eighteenth century, such writers as Locke, Rousseau, and Kant combined their advocacy of constitutional government with an acceptance of disfranchised classes in the population. The reader will find that J. S. Mill, writing in the middle of the nineteenth century, is the first among political theorists to argue for universal suffrage, including the enfranchisement of women.

One other basic issue appears in this sec-tion—justification of rule by the majority. It is enlightened by Rousseau's insight that unanimity is required for the establishment of majority rule. Allowing the majority to prevail does not preclude misrule by the ma-jority or repression of minorities. This raises the difficult question of what safeguards can be set up to prevent misrule by the majority without at the same time nullifying majority rule itself.

---

1 *Theseus.*   One moment, stranger.
   Your start was wrong, seeking a master here.
   This city is free, and ruled by no one man.
   The people reign, in annual succession.
   They do not yield the power to the rich;
   The poor man has an equal share in it.
      Herald. That one point gives the better of the
         game
   To me. The town I come from is controlled
   By one man, not a mob. And there is no one
   To puff it up with words, for private gain,
   Swaying it this way, that way. Such a man
   First flatters it with wealth of favors; then
   He does it harm, but covers up his blunders
   By blaming other men, and goes scot-free.
   The people is no right judge of arguments;
   Then how can it give right guidance to a city?
   A poor man, working hard, could not attend
   To public matters, even if ignorance
   Were not his birthright. When a wretch, a noth-
         ing,
   Obtains respect and power from the people
   By talk, his betters sicken at the sight.
                  Euripides, *Suppliant Women,* 403

2 *Athenagoras.* It will be said, perhaps, that democra-cy is neither wise nor equitable, but that the hold-ers of property are also the best fitted to rule. I say, on the contrary, first, that the word *demos,* or people, includes the whole state, oligarchy only a part; next, that if the best guardians of property are the rich, and the best counsellors the wise, none can hear and decide so well as the many; and that all these talents, severally and collec-tively, have their just place in a democracy.
                  Thucydides, *Peloponnesian War,* VI, 39

3 *Socrates.* Democracy comes into being after the poor have conquered their opponents, slaugh-tering some and banishing some, while to the re-mainder they give an equal share of freedom and power; and this is the form of government in which the magistrates are commonly elected by lot.

Adeimantus. Yes . . . that is the nature of democ-racy, whether the revolution has been effected by arms, or whether fear has caused the opposite par-ty to withdraw.

And now what is their manner of life, and what sort of a government have they? for as the govern-ment is, such will be the man.

Clearly, he said.

In the first place, are they not free; and is not the city full of freedom and frankness—a man may say and do what he likes?

'Tis said so, he replied.

And where freedom is, the individual is clearly able to order for himself his own life as he pleases?

Clearly.

Then in this kind of State there will be the greatest variety of human natures?

There will.

This, then, seems likely to be the fairest of States, being like an embroidered robe which is spangled with every sort of flower. And just as women and children think a variety of colours to be of all things most charming, so there are many men to whom this State, which is spangled with the manners and characters of mankind, will ap-pear to be the fairest of States.

Yes.

Yes, my good Sir, and there will be no better in which to look for a government.

Why?

Because of the liberty which reigns there—they have a complete assortment of constitutions; and he who has a mind to establish a State, as we have been doing, must go to a democracy as he would to a bazaar at which they sell them, and pick out the one that suits him; then, when he has made his choice, he may found his State.

He will be sure to have patterns enough.

And there being no necessity, I said, for you to govern in this State, even if you have the capacity, or to be governed, unless you like, or go to war when the rest go to war, or to be at peace when others are at peace, unless you are so disposed—

there being no necessity also, because some law forbids you to hold office or be a dicast, that you should not hold office or be a dicast, if you have a fancy—is not this a way of life which for the moment is supremely delightful?

For the moment, yes.

And is not their humanity to the condemned in some cases quite charming? Have you not observed how, in a democracy, many persons, although they have been sentenced to death or exile, just stay where they are and walk about the world—the gentleman parades like a hero, and nobody sees or cares?

Yes, he replied, many and many a one.

See too, I said, the forgiving spirit of democracy, and the "don't care" about trifles, and the disregard which she shows of all the fine principles which we solemnly laid down at the foundation of the city—as when we said that, except in the case of some rarely gifted nature, there never will be a good man who has not from his childhood been used to play amid things of beauty and make of them a joy and a study—how grandly does she trample all these fine notions of ours under her feet, never giving a thought to the pursuits which make a statesman, and promoting to honour any one who professes to be the people's friend.

Yes, she is of a noble spirit.

These and other kindred characteristics are proper to democracy, which is a charming form of government, full of variety and disorder, and dispensing a sort of equality to equals and unequals alike.

We know her well.

Plato, *Republic*, VIII, 557A

4 *Socrates.* Democracy has her own good, of which the insatiable desire brings her to dissolution?

Adeimantus. What good?

Freedom, I replied; which, as they tell you in a democracy, is the glory of the State—and that therefore in a democracy alone will the freeman of nature deign to dwell.

Yes; the saying is in everybody's mouth.

I was going to observe, that the insatiable desire of this and the neglect of other things introduces the change in democracy, which occasions a demand for tyranny.

How so?

When a democracy which is thirsting for freedom has evil cup-bearers presiding over the feast, and has drunk too deeply of the strong wine of freedom, then, unless her rulers are very amenable and give a plentiful draught, she calls them to account and punishes them, and says that they are cursed oligarchs.

Yes, he replied, a very common occurrence.

Yes, I said; and loyal citizens are insultingly termed by her slaves who hug their chains and men of naught; she would have subjects who are like rulers, and rulers who are like subjects: these are men after her own heart, whom she praises

and honours both in private and public. Now, in such a State, can liberty have any limit?

Certainly not.

By degrees the anarchy finds a way into private houses, and ends by getting among the animals and infecting them.

How do you mean?

I mean that the father grows accustomed to descend to the level of his sons and to fear them, and the son is on a level with his father, he having no respect or reverence for either of his parents; and this is his freedom, and the metic is equal with the citizen and the citizen with the metic, and the stranger is quite as good as either.

Yes, he said, that is the way.

And these are not the only evils, I said—there are several lesser ones: In such a state of society the master fears and flatters his scholars, and the scholars despise their masters and tutors; young and old are all alike; and the young man is on a level with the old, and is ready to compete with him in word or deed; and old men condescend to the young and are full of pleasantry and gaiety; they are loth to be thought morose and authoritative, and therefore they adopt the manners of the young.

Quite true, he said.

The last extreme of popular liberty is when the slave bought with money, whether male or female, is just as free as his or her purchaser; nor must I forget to tell of the liberty and equality of the two sexes in relation to each other.

Why not, as Aeschylus says, utter the word which rises to our lips?

That is what I am doing, I replied; and I must add that no one who does not know would believe, how much greater is the liberty which the animals who are under the dominion of man have in a democracy than in any other State: for truly, the she-dogs, as the proverb says, are as good as their she-mistresses, and the horses and asses have a way of marching along with all the rights and dignities of freemen; and they will run at any body who comes in their way if he does not leave the road clear for them: and all things are just ready to burst with liberty.

When I take a country walk, he said, I often experience what you describe. You and I have dreamed the same thing.

And above all, I said, and as the result of all, see how sensitive the citizens become; they chafe impatiently at the least touch of authority and at length, as you know, they cease to care even for the laws, written or unwritten; they will have no one over them.

Yes, he said, I know it too well.

Such, my friend, I said, is the fair and glorious beginning out of which springs tyranny.

Plato, *Republic*, VIII, 562A

5 *Athenian Stranger.* The state in which the law is above the rulers, and the rulers are the inferiors of

the law, has salvation, and every blessing which the Gods can confer.

Plato, *Laws,* IV, 715B

6 If the people are not utterly degraded, although individually they may be worse judges than those who have special knowledge—as a body they are as good or better.

Aristotle, *Politics,* 1282ª15

7 As a feast to which all the guests contribute is better than a banquet furnished by a single man, so a multitude is a better judge of many things than any individual.

Again, the many are more incorruptible than the few. . . . The individual is liable to be overcome by anger or by some other passion, and then his judgement is necessarily perverted; but it is hardly to be supposed that a great number of persons would all get into a passion and go wrong at the same moment.

Aristotle, *Politics,* 1286ª28

8 It must not be assumed, as some are fond of saying, that democracy is simply that form of government in which the greater number are sovereign, for in oligarchies, and indeed in every government, the majority rules; nor again is oligarchy that form of government in which a few are sovereign. . . . We should rather say that democracy is the form of government in which the free are rulers, and oligarchy in which the rich; it is only an accident that the free are the many and the rich are the few. Otherwise a government in which the offices were given according to stature . . . or according to beauty, would be an oligarchy; for the number of tall or good-looking men is small. And yet oligarchy and democracy are not sufficiently distinguished merely by these two characteristics of wealth and freedom. Both of them contain many other elements, and therefore we must carry our analysis further, and say that the government is not a democracy in which the freemen, being few in number, rule over the many who are not free. . . . Neither is it a democracy when the rich have the government because they exceed in number. . . . But the form of government is a democracy when the free, who are also poor and the majority, govern, and an oligarchy when the rich and the noble govern, they being at the same time few in number.

Aristotle, *Politics,* 1290ª30

9 Of forms of democracy first comes that which is said to be based strictly on equality. In such a democracy the law says that it is just for the poor to have no more advantage than the rich; and that neither should be masters, but both equal. For if liberty and equality . . . are chiefly to be found in democracy, they will be best attained when all persons alike share in the government to the utmost. And since the people are the majority, and the opinion of the majority is decisive, such a government must necessarily be a democracy. Here then is one sort of democracy. There is another, in which the magistrates are elected according to a certain property qualification, but a low one; he who has the required amount of property has a share in the government, but he who loses his property loses his rights. Another kind is that in which all the citizens who are under no disqualification share in the government, but still the law is supreme. In another, everybody, if he be only a citizen, is admitted to the government, but the law is supreme as before. A fifth form of democracy, in other respects the same, is that in which, not the law, but the multitude, have the supreme power, and supersede the law by their decrees. This is a state of affairs brought about by the demagogues.

Aristotle, *Politics,* 1291ᵇ30

10 There are various ways in which all may share in the government; they may deliberate, not all in one body, but by turns, as in the constitution of Telecles the Milesian. There are other constitutions in which the boards of magistrates meet and deliberate, but come into office by turns, and are elected out of the tribes and the very smallest divisions of the state, until every one has obtained office in his turn. The citizens, on the other hand, are assembled only for the purposes of legislation, and to consult about the constitution, and to hear the edicts of the magistrates. In another variety of democracy the citizens form one assembly, but meet only to elect magistrates, to pass laws, to advise about war and peace, and to make scrutinies. Other matters are referred severally to special magistrates, who are elected by vote or by lot out of all the citizens. Or again, the citizens meet about election to offices and about scrutinies, and deliberate concerning war or alliances while other matters are administered by the magistrates, who, as far as is possible, are elected by vote. I am speaking of those magistracies in which special knowledge is required. A fourth form of democracy is when all the citizens meet to deliberate about everything, and the magistrates decide nothing, but only make the preliminary inquiries; and that is the way in which the last and worst form of democracy, corresponding, as we maintain, to the close family oligarchy and to tyranny, is at present administered. All these modes are democratical.

Aristotle, *Politics,* 1298ª11

11 In democracies of the more extreme type there has arisen a false idea of freedom which is contradictory to the true interests of the state. For two principles are characteristic of democracy, the government of the majority and freedom. Men think that what is just is equal; and that equality is the supremacy of the popular will; and that

freedom means the doing what a man likes. In such democracies every one lives as he pleases. . . . But this is all wrong; men should not think it slavery to live according to the rule of the constitution; for it is their salvation.

Aristotle, *Politics*, 1310ª24

12 The voice of the people has something divine; else how could so many agree in one thing?

Marvel not if the vulgar speak truer than the great, for they speak safer.

Bacon, *Advancement of Learning,*
Bk. VI, III, 9

13 There never was any government so purely popular, as not to require the exclusion of the poor, of strangers, women, and minors from the public councils.

Grotius, *Rights of War and Peace,*
Bk. I, III, 8

14 A democracy, in effect, is no more than an aristocracy of orators, interrupted sometimes with the temporary monarchy of one orator.

Hobbes, *Elements of Law*, Pt. II, II, 5

15 The majority is the best way, because it is visible and has strength to make itself obeyed. Yet it is the opinion of the least able.

Pascal, *Pensées*, XIV, 878

16 To make the people fittest to choose, and the chosen fittest to govern, will be to mend our corrupt and faulty education, to teach the people faith, not without virtue, temperance, modesty, sobriety, parsimony, justice; not to admire wealth or honor; to hate turbulence and ambition; to place every one his private welfare and happiness in the public peace, liberty, and safety.

Milton, *Ready and Easy Way*

17 Political power is that power which every man having in the state of Nature has given up into the hands of the society, and therein to the governors whom the society hath set over itself, with this express or tacit trust, that it shall be employed for their good and the preservation of their property. Now this power, which every man has in the state of Nature, and which he parts with to the society in all such cases where the society can secure him, is to use such means for the preserving of his own property as he thinks good and Nature allows him; and to punish the breach of the law of Nature in others so as (according to the best of his reason) may most conduce to the preservation of himself and the rest of mankind; so that the end and measure of this power, when in every man's hands, in the state of Nature, being the preservation of all of his society—that is, all mankind in general—it can have no other end or measure, when in the hands of the magistrate, but to pre-

serve the members of that society in their lives, liberties, and possessions, and so cannot be an absolute, arbitrary power over their lives and fortunes, which are as much as possible to be preserved; but a power to make laws, and annex such penalties to them as may tend to the preservation of the whole, by cutting off those parts, and those only, which are so corrupt that they threaten the sound and healthy, without which no severity is lawful. And this power has its original only from compact and agreement and the mutual consent of those who make up the community.

Locke, *II Civil Government*, XV, 171

18 Perhaps it will be said that the people being ignorant and always discontented, to lay the foundation of government in the unsteady opinion and uncertain humour of the people, is to expose it to certain ruin; and no government will be able long to subsist if the people may set up a new legislative whenever they take offence at the old one. To this I answer, quite the contrary. People are not so easily got out of their old forms as some are apt to suggest. They are hardly to be prevailed with to amend the acknowledged faults in the frame they have been accustomed to. And if there be any original defects, or adventitious ones introduced by time or corruption, it is not an easy thing to get them changed, even when all the world sees there is an opportunity for it.

Locke, *II Civil Government*, XIX, 223

19 The people, in whom the supreme power resides, ought to have the management of everything within their reach: that which exceeds their abilities must be conducted by their ministers.

But they cannot properly be said to have their ministers, without the power of nominating them: it is, therefore, a fundamental maxim in this government, that the people should choose their ministers—that is, their magistrates.

Montesquieu, *Spirit of Laws*, II, 2

20 The people are extremely well qualified for choosing those whom they are to entrust with part of their authority. They have only to be determined by things to which they cannot be strangers, and by facts that are obvious to sense. They can tell when a person has fought many battles, and been crowned with success; they are, therefore, capable of electing a general. They can tell when a judge is assiduous in his office, gives general satisfaction, and has never been charged with bribery: this is sufficient for choosing a prætor. They are struck with the magnificence or riches of a fellow-citizen; no more is requisite for electing an edile. These are facts of which they can have better information in a public forum than a monarch in his palace. But are they capable of conducting an intricate affair, of seizing and improving the opportunity and critical moment of action? No;

this surpasses their abilities.
Montesquieu, *Spirit of Laws,* II, 2

21 In republican governments, men are all equal; equal they are also in despotic governments: in the former, because they are everything; in the latter, because they are nothing.
Montesquieu, *Spirit of Laws,* VI, 2

22 The principle of democracy is corrupted not only when the spirit of equality is extinct, but likewise when they fall into a spirit of extreme equality, and when each citizen would fain be upon a level with those whom he has chosen to command him. Then the people, incapable of bearing the very power they have delegated, want to manage everything themselves, to debate for the senate, to execute for the magistrate, and to decide for the judges.
Montesquieu, *Spirit of Laws,* VIII, 2

23 The great advantage of representatives is their capacity of discussing public affairs. For this the people collectively are extremely unfit, which is one of the chief inconveniences of a democracy.
Montesquieu, *Spirit of Laws,* XI, 6

24 Ordinarily there is no comparison between the crimes of the great who are always ambitious, and the crimes of the people who always want, and can want only liberty and equality. These two sentiments, Liberty and Equality, do not lead direct to calumny, rapine, assassination, poisoning, the devastation of one's neighbours' lands, etc.; but ambitious might and the mania for power plunge into all these crimes whatever be the time, whatever be the place.

Popular government is in itself, therefore, less iniquitous, less abominable than despotic power.

The great vice of democracy is certainly not tyranny and cruelty: there have been mountain-dwelling republicans, savage, ferocious; but it is not the republican spirit that made them so, it is nature.

The real vice of a civilized republic is in the Turkish fable of the dragon with many heads and the dragon with many tails. The many heads hurt each other, and the many tails obey a single head which wants to devour everything.

Democracy seems suitable only to a very little country, and further it must be happily situated. Small though it be, it will make many mistakes, because it will be composed of men. Discord will reign there as in a monastery; but there will be no St. Bartholomew, no Irish massacres, no Sicilian vespers, no inquisition, no condemnation to the galleys for having taken some water from the sea without paying for it, unless one supposes this republic composed of devils in a corner of hell.

One questions every day whether a republican government is preferable to a king's government?

The dispute ends always by agreeing that to govern men is very difficult.
Voltaire, *Philosophical Dictionary:* Democracy

25 The general will is always right and tends to the public advantage; but it does not follow that the deliberations of the people are always equally correct. Our will is always for our own good, but we do not always see what that is; the people is never corrupted, but it is often deceived, and on such occasions only does it seem to will what is bad.
Rousseau, *Social Contract,* II, 3

26 I . . . give the name "Republic" to every State that is governed by laws, no matter what the form of its administration may be: for only in such a case does the public interest govern, and the *res publica* rank as a *reality.* Every legitimate government is republican.
Rousseau, *Social Contract,* II, 6

27 If we take the term in the strict sense, there never has been a real democracy, and there never will be. It is against the natural order for the many to govern and the few to be governed.
Rousseau, *Social Contract,* III, 4

28 There is no government so subject to civil wars and intestine agitations as democratic or popular government, because there is none which has so strong and continual a tendency to change to another form, or which demands more vigilance and courage for its maintenance as it is.
Rousseau, *Social Contract,* III, 4

29 Were there a people of gods, their government would be democratic. So perfect a government is not for men.
Rousseau, *Social Contract,* III, 4

30 There is but one law which, from its nature, needs unanimous consent. This is the social compact; for civil association is the most voluntary of all acts. Every man being born free and his own master, no one, under any pretext whatsoever, can make any man subject without his consent. To decide that the son of a slave is born a slave is to decide that he is not born a man.

If then there are opponents when the social compact is made, their opposition does not invalidate the contract, but merely prevents them from being included in it. They are foreigners among citizens. When the State is instituted, residence constitutes consent; to dwell within its territory is to submit to the Sovereign.

Apart from this primitive contract, the vote of the majority always binds all the rest. This follows from the contract itself. But it is asked how a man can be both free and forced to conform to wills that are not his own. How are the opponents at once free and subject to laws they have not agreed to?

I retort that the question is wrongly put. The citizen gives his consent to all the laws, including those which are passed in spite of his opposition, and even those which punish him when he dares to break any of them. The constant will of all the members of the State is the general will; by virtue of it they are citizens and free. When in the popular assembly a law is proposed, what the people is asked is not exactly whether it approves or rejects the proposal, but whether it is in conformity with the general will, which is their will. Each man, in giving his vote, states his opinion on that point; and the general will is found by counting votes. When therefore the opinion that is contrary to my own prevails, this proves neither more nor less than that I was mistaken, and that what I thought to be the general will was not so. If my particular opinion had carried the day I should have achieved the opposite of what was my will; and it is in that case that I should not have been free.

This presupposes, indeed, that all the qualities of the general will still reside in the majority: when they cease to do so, whatever side a man may take, liberty is no longer possible.

Rousseau, *Social Contract*, IV, 2

31 The basis of our political systems is the right of the people to make and to alter their constitutions of government. But the constitution which at any time exists, till changed by an explicit and authentic act of the whole people, is sacredly obligatory upon all. The very idea of the power and the right of the people to establish government presupposes the duty of every individual to obey the established government.

Washington, *Farewell Address*

32 In every government on earth is some trace of human weakness, some germ of corruption and degeneracy, which cunning will discover, and wickedness insensibly open, cultivate and improve. Every government degenerates when trusted to the rulers of the people alone. The people themselves therefore are its only safe depositories. And to render even them safe, their minds must be improved to a certain degree. This indeed is not all that is necessary, though it be essentially necessary. An amendment of our constitution must here come in aid of the public education. The influence over government must be shared among all the people. If every individual which composes their mass participates of the ultimate authority, the government will be safe; because the corrupting the whole mass will exceed any private resources of wealth; and public ones cannot be provided but by levies on the people. In this case every man would have to pay his own price.

Jefferson, *Notes on Virginia*, XIV

33 I am persuaded myself that the good sense of the people will always be found to be the best army. They may be led astray for a moment, but will soon correct themselves.

The people are the only censors of their governors; and even their errors will tend to keep these to the true principles of their institution. To punish these errors too severely would be to suppress the only safeguard of the public liberty.

Jefferson, *Letter to Edward Carrington*
(Jan. 16, 1787)

34 All . . . will bear in mind this sacred principle, that though the will of the majority is in all cases to prevail, that will to be rightful must be reasonable; that the minority possess their equal rights, which equal law must protect, and to violate would be oppression.

Jefferson, *First Inaugural Address*

35 There is a natural aristocracy among men. The grounds of this are virtue and talents. Formerly, bodily powers gave place among the *aristoi*. But since the invention of gunpowder has armed the weak as well as the strong with missile death, bodily strength, like beauty, good humor, politeness, and other accomplishments, has become but an auxiliary ground of distinction.

There is also an artificial aristocracy, founded on wealth and birth, without either virtue or talents; for with these it would belong to the first class. The natural aristocracy I consider as the most precious gift of nature, for the instruction, the trusts, and government of society. And, indeed, it would have been inconsistent in Creation to have formed man for the social state and not to have provided virtue and wisdom enough to manage the concerns of the society. May we not even say that that form of government is the best which provides the most effectually for a pure selection of these natural *aristoi* into the offices of government? The artificial aristocracy is a mischievous ingredient in government, and provision should be made to prevent its ascendancy.

Jefferson, *Letter to John Adams*
(Oct. 28, 1813)

36 To deliver an opinion, is the right of all men; that of constituents is a weighty and respectable opinion, which a representative ought always to rejoice to hear; and which he ought always most seriously to consider. But authoritative instructions; mandates issued, which the member is bound blindly and implicitly to obey, to vote, and to argue for, though contrary to the clearest conviction of his judgment and conscience,—these are things utterly unknown to the laws of this land, and which arise from a fundamental mistake of the whole order and tenor of our constitution.

Parliament is not a congress of ambassadors

from different and hostile interests; which interests each must maintain, as an agent and advocate, against other agents and advocates; but parliament is a deliberative assembly of one nation, with one interest, that of the whole; where, not local purposes, not local prejudices, ought to guide, but the general good, resulting from the general reason of the whole. You choose a member indeed; but when you have chosen him, he is not member for Bristol, but he is a member of parliament. If the local constituent should have an interest, or should form an hasty opinion, evidently opposite to the real good of the rest of the community, the member for that place ought to be as far, as any other, from any endeavour to give it effect.

Burke, *Speech at Bristol (Nov. 3, 1774)*

37 Where popular authority is absolute and unrestrained, the people . . . are, themselves, in a great measure, their own instruments. . . . They are less under responsibility to one of the greatest controlling powers on earth, the sense of fame and estimation. . . . Their own approbation of their own acts has to them the appearance of a public judgment in their favour. A perfect democracy is therefore the most shameless thing in the world. As it is the most shameless, it is also the most fearless. No man apprehends in his person that he can be made subject to punishment.

Burke, *Reflections on the Revolution in France*

38 A democracy . . . is the most complex of all the forms of the state, for it has to begin by uniting the will of all so as to form a people; and then it has to appoint a sovereign over this common union, which sovereign is no other than the united will itself.

Kant, *Science of Right,* 51

39 The problem of a constitution is solvable even to a nation of devils (I shall be forgiven what is offensive in the expression) if this people is but endowed with understanding.

Kant, *Perpetual Peace,* Supplement I

40 After an unequivocal experience of the inefficiency of the subsisting federal government, you are called upon to deliberate on a new Constitution for the United States of America. The subject speaks its own importance; comprehending in its consequences nothing less than the existence of the Union, the safety and welfare of the parts of which it is composed, the fate of an empire in many respects the most interesting in the world. It has been frequently remarked that it seems to have been reserved to the people of this country, by their conduct and example, to decide the important question, whether societies of men are really capable or not of establishing good govern-

ment from reflection and choice, or whether they are forever destined to depend for their political constitutions on accident and force. If there be any truth in the remark, the crisis at which we are arrived may with propriety be regarded as the era in which that decision is to be made; and a wrong election of the part we shall act may, in this view, deserve to be considered as the general misfortune of mankind.

Hamilton, *Federalist 1*

41 It is not a new observation that the people of any country (if, like the Americans, intelligent and well-informed) seldom adopt and steadily persevere for many years in an erroneous opinion respecting their interests.

Jay, *Federalist 3*

42 A pure democracy, by which I mean a society consisting of a small number of citizens, who assemble and administer the government in person, can admit of no cure for the mischiefs of faction. A common passion or interest will, in almost every case, be felt by a majority of the whole; a communication and concert result from the form of government itself; and there is nothing to check the inducements to sacrifice the weaker party or an obnoxious individual. Hence it is that such democracies have ever been spectacles of turbulence and contention; have ever been found incompatible with personal security or the rights of property; and have in general been as short in their lives as they have been violent in their deaths. Theoretic politicians, who have patronised this species of government, have erroneously supposed that by reducing mankind to a perfect equality in their political rights, they would, at the same time, be perfectly equalised and assimilated in their possessions, their opinions, and their passions.

A republic, by which I mean a government in which the scheme of representation takes place, opens a different prospect, and promises the cure for which we are seeking. Let us examine the points in which it varies from pure democracy, and we shall comprehend both the nature of the cure and the efficacy which it must derive from the Union.

The two great points of difference between a democracy and a republic are: first, the delegation of the government, in the latter, to a small number of citizens elected by the rest; secondly, the greater number of citizens, and greater sphere of country, over which the latter may be extended.

The effect of the first difference is, on the one hand, to refine and enlarge the public views, by passing them through the medium of a chosen body of citizens, whose wisdom may best discern the true interest of their country, and whose patriotism and love of justice will be least likely to sacrifice it to temporary or partial considerations.

Under such a regulation, it may well happen that the public voice, pronounced by the representatives of the people, will be more consonant to the public good than if pronounced by the people themselves, convened for the purpose. On the other hand, the effect may be inverted. Men of factious tempers, of local prejudices, or of sinister designs, may, by intrigue, by corruption, or by other means, first obtain the suffrages, and then betray the interests, of the people. The question resulting is, whether small or extensive republics are more favourable to the election of proper guardians of the public weal; and it is clearly decided in favour of the latter by two obvious considerations:

In the first place, it is to be remarked that, however small the republic may be, the representatives must be raised to a certain number, in order to guard against the cabals of a few; and that, however large it may be, they must be limited to a certain number, in order to guard against the confusion of a multitude. Hence the number of representatives in the two cases not being in proportion to that of the two constituents, and being proportionally greater in the small republic, it follows that, if the proportion of fit characters be not less in the large than in the small republic, the former will present a greater option, and consequently a greater probability of a fit choice.

In the next place, as each representative will be chosen by a greater number of citizens in the large than in the small republic, it will be more difficult for unworthy candidates to practise with success the vicious arts by which elections are too often carried; and the suffrages of the people being more free, will be more likely to centre in men who possess the most attractive merit and the most diffusive and established character.

Madison, *Federalist 10*

43 In a democracy the people meet and exercise the government in person; in a republic, they assemble and administer it by their representatives and agents. A democracy, consequently, will be confined to a small spot. A republic may be extended over a large region.

Madison, *Federalist 14*

44 As the natural limit of a democracy is that distance from the central point which will just permit the most remote citizens to assemble as often as their public functions demand, and will include no greater number than can join in those functions; so the natural limit of a republic is that distance from the centre which will barely allow the representatives to meet as often as may be necessary for the administration of public affairs.

Madison, *Federalist 14*

45 It is said to be necessary that all classes of citizens should have some of their own number in the rep-

resentative body, in order that their feelings and interests may be the better understood and attended to. But we have seen that this will never happen under any arrangement that leaves the votes of the people free. Where this is the case, the representative body, with too few exceptions to have any influence on the spirit of the government, will be composed of landholders, merchants, and men of the learned professions.

Hamilton, *Federalist 35*

46 Nothing can be more fallacious than to found our political calculations on arithmetical principles. Sixty or seventy men may be more properly trusted with a given degree of power than six or seven. But it does not follow that six or seven hundred would be proportionably a better depositary. And if we carry on the supposition to six or seven thousand, the whole reasoning ought to be reversed. The truth is, that in all cases a certain number at least seems to be necessary to secure the benefits of free consultation and discussion, and to guard against too easy a combination for improper purposes; as, on the other hand, the number ought at most to be kept within a certain limit, in order to avoid the confusion and intemperance of a multitude. In all very numerous assemblies, of whatever character composed, passion never fails to wrest the sceptre from reason. Had every Athenian citizen been a Socrates, every Athenian assembly would still have been a mob.

Hamilton or Madison, *Federalist 55*

47 The aim of every political constitution is, or ought to be, first to obtain for rulers men who possess most wisdom to discern, and most virtue to pursue, the common good of the society; and in the next place, to take the most effectual precautions for keeping them virtuous whilst they continue to hold their public trust. The elective mode of obtaining rulers is the characteristic policy of republican government. The means relied on in this form of government for preventing their degeneracy are numerous and various. The most effectual one is such a limitation of the term of appointments as will maintain a proper responsibility to the people.

Hamilton or Madison, *Federalist 57*

48 It is a misfortune incident to republican government, though in a less degree than to other governments, that those who administer it may forget their obligations to their constituents, and prove unfaithful to their important trust. In this point of view, a senate, as a second branch of the legislative assembly, distinct from, and dividing the power with, a first, must be in all cases a salutary check on the government. It doubles the security to the people, by requiring the concurrence of two distinct bodies in schemes of usurpation or perfidy, where the ambition or corruption of one

would otherwise be sufficient. This is a precaution founded on such clear principles, and now so well understood in the United States, that it would be more than superfluous to enlarge on it. I will barely remark, that as the improbability of sinister combinations will be in proportion to the dissimilarity in the genius of the two bodies, it must be politic to distinguish them from each other by every circumstance which will consist with a due harmony in all proper measures, and with the genuine principles of republican government.

> Hamilton or Madison, *Federalist 62*

49 It is a just observation that the people commonly *intend* the PUBLIC GOOD. This often applies to their very errors. But their good sense would despise the adulator who should pretend that they always *reason right* about the *means* of promoting it. They know from experience that they sometimes err; and the wonder is that they so seldom err as they do, beset, as they continually are, by the wiles of parasites and sycophants, by the snares of the ambitious, the avaricious, the desperate, by the artifices of men who possess their confidence more than they deserve it, and of those who seek to possess rather than to deserve it.

> Hamilton, *Federalist 71*

50 A constitution is not just something manufactured; it is the work of centuries, it is the Idea, the consciousness of rationality so far as that consciousness is developed in a particular nation. No constitution, therefore, is just the creation of its subjects.

> Hegel, *Philosophy of Right*, Additions,
> Par. 274

51 Public opinion is the unorganized way in which a people's opinions and wishes are made known. What is actually made authoritative in the state must operate in an organized manner as the parts of the constitution do. But at all times public opinion has been a great power and it is particularly so in our day when the principle of subjective freedom has such importance and significance. What is to be authoritative nowadays derives its authority, not at all from force, only to a small extent from habit and custom, really from insight and argument.

> Hegel, *Philosophy of Right*, Additions,
> Par. 316

52 To those for whom the word "democracy" is synonymous with disturbance, anarchy, spoliation, and murder, I have attempted to show that democracy may be reconciled with respect for property, with deference for rights, with safety to freedom, with reverence for religion; that, if democratic government fosters less than another some of the finer possibilities of the human spirit, it has its great and noble aspects; and that perhaps, af-

ter all, it is the will of God to bestow a lesser grade of happiness upon all men than to grant a greater share of it to a smaller number and to bring a few to the verge of perfection. I have undertaken to demonstrate to them that, whatever their opinion on this point may be, it is too late to deliberate; that society is advancing and dragging them along with it toward equality of conditions; that the sole remaining alternative lies between evils henceforth irresistible; that the question is not whether aristocracy or democracy can be maintained but whether we are to live under a democratic society, devoid indeed of poetry and greatness, but at least orderly and moral, or under a democratic society, lawless and depraved, abandoned to the frenzy of revolution or subjected to a yoke heavier than any of those which have crushed mankind since the fall of the Roman Empire.

> Tocqueville, *Letter to Eugene Stoffels*
> *(Feb. 21, 1835)*

53 I confess that in America I saw more than America; I sought there the image of democracy itself, with its inclinations, its character, its prejudices, and its passions, in order to learn what we have to fear or to hope from its progress.

> Tocqueville, *Democracy in America*, Intro.

54 Democracy not only lacks that soundness of judgment which is necessary to select men really deserving of their confidence, but often have not the desire or the inclination to find them out. It cannot be denied that democratic institutions strongly tend to promote the feeling of envy in the human heart; not so much because they afford to everyone the means of rising to the same level with others as because those means perpetually disappoint the persons who employ them. Democratic institutions awaken and foster a passion for equality which they can never entirely satisfy.

> Tocqueville, *Democracy in America*, I, 13

55 A democracy can obtain truth only as the result of experience; and many nations may perish while they are awaiting the consequences of their errors.

> Tocqueville, *Democracy in America*, I, 13

56 Governments usually perish from impotence or from tyranny. In the former case, their power escapes from them; it is wrested from their grasp in the latter. Many observers who have witnessed the anarchy of democratic states have imagined that the government of those states was naturally weak and impotent. The truth is that when war is once begun between parties, the government loses its control over society. But I do not think that a democratic power is naturally without force or resources; say, rather, that it is almost always by the abuse of its force and the misemployment of its resources that it becomes a failure. Anarchy is al-

most always produced by its tyranny or its mistakes, but not by its want of strength.

It is important not to confuse stability with force, or the greatness of a thing with its duration. In democratic republics the power that directs society is not stable, for it often changes hands and assumes a new direction. But whichever way it turns, its force is almost irresistible. The governments of the American republics appear to me to be as much centralized as those of the absolute monarchies of Europe, and more energetic than they are. I do not, therefore, imagine that they will perish from weakness.

If ever the free institutions of America are destroyed, that event may be attributed to the omnipotence of the majority, which may at some future time urge the minorities to desperation and oblige them to have recourse to physical force. Anarchy will then be the result, but it will have been brought about by despotism.

Tocqueville, *Democracy in America*, I, 15

57 I think . . . that the species of oppression by which democratic nations are menaced is unlike anything that ever before existed in the world; our contemporaries will find no prototype of it in their memories. I seek in vain for an expression that will accurately convey the whole of the idea I have formed of it; the old words *despotism* and *tyranny* are inappropriate: the thing itself is new, and since I cannot name, I must attempt to define it.

I seek to trace the novel features under which despotism may appear in the world. The first thing that strikes the observation is an innumerable multitude of men, all equal and alike, incessantly endeavoring to procure the petty and paltry pleasures with which they glut their lives. Each of them, living apart, is as a stranger to the fate of all the rest; his children and his private friends constitute to him the whole of mankind. As for the rest of his fellow citizens, he is close to them, but he does not see them; he touches them, but he does not feel them; he exists only in himself and for himself alone; and if his kindred still remain to him, he may be said at any rate to have lost his country.

Above this race of men stands an immense and tutelary power, which takes upon itself alone to secure their gratifications and to watch over their fate. That power is absolute, minute, regular, provident, and mild. It would be like the authority of a parent if, like that authority, its object was to prepare men for manhood; but it seeks, on the contrary, to keep them in perpetual childhood: it is well content that the people should rejoice, provided they think of nothing but rejoicing. For their happiness such a government willingly labors, but it chooses to be the sole agent and the only arbiter of that happiness; it provides for their security, foresees and supplies their necessities, facilitates their pleasures, manages their principal concerns, directs their industry, regulates the descent of property, and subdivides their inheritances: what remains, but to spare them all the care of thinking and all the trouble of living?

Thus it every day renders the exercise of the free agency of man less useful and less frequent; it circumscribes the will within a narrower range and gradually robs a man of all the uses of himself. The principle of equality has prepared men for these things; it has predisposed men to endure them and often to look on them as benefits.

Tocqueville, *Democracy in America*,
Vol. II, IV, 6

58 We may naturally believe that it is not the singular prosperity of the few, but the greater well-being of all that is most pleasing in the sight of the Creator and Preserver of men. What appears to me to be man's decline is, to His eye, advancement; what afflicts me is acceptable to Him. A state of equality is perhaps less elevated, but it is more just: and its justice constitutes its greatness and its beauty. I would strive, then, to raise myself to this point of the divine contemplation and thence to view and to judge the concerns of men.

Tocqueville, *Democracy in America*,
Vol. II, IV, 8

59 There are two different modes in which the sense of the community may be taken: one, simply by the right of suffrage, unaided; the other, by the right through a proper organism. Each collects the sense of the majority. But one regards numbers only and considers the whole community as a unit, having but one common interest throughout, and collects the sense of the greater number of the whole as that of the community. The other, on the contrary, regards interests as well as numbers—considering the community as made up of different and conflicting interests as far as the action of the government is concerned—and takes the sense of each, through its majority or appropriate organ, and the united sense of all as the sense of the entire community. The former of these I shall call the numerical or absolute majority; and the latter, the concurrent or constitutional majority. I call it the constitutional majority, because it is an essential element in every constitutional government—be its form what it may. So great is the difference, politically speaking, between the two majorities that they cannot be confounded without leading to great and fatal errors; and yet the distinction between them has been so entirely overlooked that, when the term *majority* is used in political discussions, it is applied exclusively to designate the numerical—as if there were no other. Until this distinction is recognized, and better understood, there will continue to be great liability to error in properly constructing constitutional governments, especially of the popular form, and of preserving them when properly con-

structed. Until then, the latter will have a strong tendency to slide, first, into the government of the numerical majority and, finally, into absolute government of some other form.

J. C. Calhoun, *Disquisition on Government*

60 The practical reason why, when the power is once in the hands of the people, a majority are permitted, and for a long period continue, to rule is not because they are most likely to be in the right, nor because this seems fairest to the minority, but because they are physically the strongest. But a government in which the majority rule in all cases cannot be based on justice, even as far as men understand it. Can there not be a government in which majorities do not virtually decide right and wrong, but conscience?—in which majorities decide only those questions to which the rule of expediency is applicable? Must the citizen ever for a moment, or in the least degree, resign his conscience to the legislator? Why has every man a conscience, then? I think that we should be men first, and subjects afterward. It is not desirable to cultivate a respect for the law, so much as for the right. The only obligation which I have a right to assume is to do at any time what I think right.

Thoreau, *Civil Disobedience*

61 The authority of government, even such as I am willing to submit to—for I will cheerfully obey those who know and can do better than I, and in many things even those who neither know nor can do so well—is still an impure one: to be strictly just, it must have the sanction and consent of the governed. It can have no pure right over my person and property but what I concede to it. The progress from an absolute to a limited monarchy, from a limited monarchy to a democracy, is a progress toward a true respect for the individual. Even the Chinese philosopher was wise enough to regard the individual as the basis of the empire. Is a democracy, such as we know it, the last improvement possible in government? Is it not possible to take a step further toward recognizing and organizing the rights of man? There will never be a really free and enlightened state until the state comes to recognize the individual as a higher and independent power, from which all its own power and authority are derived, and treats him accordingly. I please myself with imagining a state at last which can afford to be just to all men, and to treat the individual with respect as a neighbor; which even would not think it inconsistent with its own repose if a few were to live aloof from it, not meddling with it, nor embraced by it, who fulfilled all the duties of neighbors and fellow men. A state which bore this kind of fruit, and suffered it to drop off as fast as it ripened, would prepare the way for a still more perfect and glorious state, which also I have imagined, but not yet anywhere seen.

Thoreau, *Civil Disobedience*

62 No man is good enough to govern another man without that other's consent. I say this is the leading principle—the sheet anchor of American republicanism.

Lincoln, *Speech at Peoria, Ill.*
(Oct. 16, 1854)

63 Plainly, the central idea of secession is the essence of anarchy. A majority, held in restraint by constitutional checks, and limitations, and always changing easily with deliberate changes of popular opinions and sentiments, is the only true sovereign of a free people. Whoever rejects it does, of necessity, fly to anarchy or to despotism. Unanimity is impossible; the rule of a minority, as a permanent arrangement, is wholly inadmissible; so that, rejecting the majority principle, anarchy, or despotism in some form, is all that is left.

Lincoln, *First Inaugural Address*

64 Fourscore and seven years ago our fathers brought forth on this continent a new nation conceived in liberty and dedicated to the proposition that all men are created equal. Now we are engaged in a great civil war testing whether that nation, or any nation so conceived and so dedicated, can long endure. We are met on a great battlefield of that war. We have come to dedicate a portion of that field as a final resting place for those who here gave their lives that that nation might live. It is altogether fitting and proper that we should do this. But, in a larger sense, we cannot dedicate, we cannot consecrate, we cannot hallow this ground. The brave men, living and dead, who struggled here have consecrated it far above our poor power to add or detract. The world will little note nor long remember what we say here, but it can never forget what they did here. It is for us the living rather to be dedicated here to the unfinished work which they who fought here have thus far so nobly advanced. It is rather for us to be here dedicated to the great task remaining before us—that from these honored dead we take increased devotion to that cause for which they gave the last full measure of devotion—that we here highly resolve that these dead shall not have died in vain, that this nation under God shall have a new birth of freedom, and that government of the people, by the people, for the people, shall not perish from the earth.

Lincoln, *Gettysburg Address*

65 At present individuals are lost in the crowd. In politics it is almost a triviality to say that public opinion now rules the world. The only power deserving the name is that of masses, and of governments while they make themselves the organ of the tendencies and instincts of masses. This is as true in the moral and social relations of private life as in public transactions. Those whose opin-

ions go by the name of public opinion are not always the same sort of public: in America they are the whole white population; in England, chiefly the middle class. But they are always a mass, that is to say, collective mediocrity. And what is a still greater novelty, the mass do not now take their opinions from dignitaries in Church or State, from ostensible leaders, or from books. Their thinking is done for them by men much like themselves, addressing them or speaking in their name, on the spur of the moment, through the newspapers.

Mill, *On Liberty,* III

66 No government by a democracy or a numerous aristocracy, either in its political acts or in the opinions, qualities, and tone of mind which it fosters, ever did or could rise above mediocrity, except in so far as the sovereign Many have let themselves be guided (which in their best times they always have done) by the counsels and influence of a more highly gifted and instructed One or Few.

Mill, *On Liberty,* III

67 One of the greatest dangers . . . of democracy, as of all other forms of government, lies in the sinister interest of the holders of power: it is the danger of class legislation; of government intended for (whether really effecting it or not) the immediate benefit of the dominant class, to the lasting detriment of the whole. And one of the most important questions demanding consideration, in determining the best constitution of a representative government, is how to provide efficacious securities against this evil.

If we consider as a class, politically speaking, any number of persons who have the same sinister interest—that is, whose direct and apparent interest points towards the same description of bad measures; the desirable object would be that no class, and no combination of classes likely to combine, should be able to exercise a preponderant influence in the government.

Mill, *Representative Government,* VI

68 All trust in constitutions is grounded on the assurance they may afford, not that the depositaries of power will not, but that they cannot, misemploy it. Democracy is not the ideally best form of government unless this weak side of it can be strengthened; unless it can be so organised that no class, not even the most numerous, shall be able to reduce all but itself to political insignificance, and direct the course of legislation and administration by its exclusive class interest. The problem is, to find the means of preventing this abuse, without sacrificing the characteristic advantages of popular government.

Mill, *Representative Government,* VIII

69 Among the foremost benefits of free government is that education of the intelligence and of the sentiments which is carried down to the very lowest ranks of the people when they are called to take a part in acts which directly affect the great interests of their country.

Mill, *Representative Government,* VIII

70 Whoever, in an otherwise popular government, has no vote, and no prospect of obtaining it, will either be a permanent malcontent, or will feel as one whom the general affairs of society do not concern; for whom they are to be managed by others; who "has no business with the laws except to obey them," nor with public interests and concerns except as a looker-on. What he will know or care about them from this position may partly be measured by what an average woman of the middle class knows and cares about politics, compared with her husband or brothers.

Independently of all these considerations, it is a personal injustice to withhold from any one, unless for the prevention of greater evils, the ordinary privilege of having his voice reckoned in the disposal of affairs in which he has the same interest as other people. If he is compelled to pay, if he may be compelled to fight, if he is required implicitly to obey, he should be legally entitled to be told what for; to have his consent asked, and his opinion counted at its worth, though not at more than its worth. There ought to be no pariahs in a full-grown and civilised nation; no persons disqualified, except through their own default. Every one is degraded, whether aware of it or not, when other people, without consulting him, take upon themselves unlimited power to regulate his destiny. And even in a much more improved state than the human mind has ever yet reached, it is not in nature that they who are thus disposed of should meet with as fair play as those who have a voice. Rulers and ruling classes are under a necessity of considering the interests and wishes of those who have the suffrage; but of those who are excluded, it is in their option whether they will do so or not, and, however honestly disposed, they are in general too fully occupied with things which they *must* attend to, to have much room in their thoughts for anything which they can with impunity disregard. No arrangement of the suffrage, therefore, can be permanently satisfactory in which any person or class is peremptorily excluded; in which the electoral privilege is not open to all persons of full age who desire to obtain it.

Mill, *Representative Government,* VIII

71 All human beings have the same interest in good government; the welfare of all is alike affected by it, and they have equal need of a voice in it to secure their share of its benefits. If there be any difference, women require it more than men, since, being physically weaker, they are more de-

pendent on law and society for protection.

Mill, *Representative Government,* VIII

72 The majority of the male sex are, and will be all their lives, nothing else than labourers in corn-fields or manufactories; but this does not render the suffrage less desirable for them, nor their claim to it less irresistible, when not likely to make a bad use of it. Nobody pretends to think that woman would make a bad use of the suffrage. The worst that is said is that they would vote as mere dependents, at the bidding of their male relations. If it be so, so let it be. If they think for themselves, great good will be done, and if they do not, no harm. It is a benefit to human beings to take off their fetters, even if they do not desire to walk.

Mill, *Representative Government,* VIII

73 I have said that the new and more democratic force which is now superseding our old middle-class Liberalism cannot yet be rightly judged. It has its main tendencies still to form. We hear promises of its giving us administrative reform, law reform, reform of education, and I know not what; but those promises come rather from its ad-vocates, wishing to make a good plea for it and to justify it for superseding middle-class Liberalism, than from clear tendencies which it has itself yet developed. But meanwhile it has plenty of well-intentioned friends against whom culture may with advantage continue to uphold steadily its ideal of human perfection; that this is *an inward spiritual activity, having for its characters increased sweet-ness, increased light, increased life, increased sympathy.* Mr. Bright, who has a foot in both worlds, the world of middle-class Liberalism and the world of democracy, but who brings most of his ideas from the world of middle-class Liberalism in which he was bred, always inclines to inculcate that faith in machinery to which, as we have seen, Englishmen are so prone, and which has been the bane of mid-dle-class Liberalism. . . . It is the same fashion of teaching a man to value himself not on what he *is,* not on his progress in sweetness and light, but on the number of the railroads he has constructed, or the bigness of the tabernacle he has built. Only the middle classes are told they have done it all with their energy, self-reliance, and capital, and the democracy are told they have done it all with their hands and sinews. But teaching the democ-racy to put its trust in achievements of this kind is merely training them to be Philistines to take the place of the Philistines whom they are supersed-ing; and they too, like the middle class, will be encouraged to sit down at the banquet of the fu-ture without having on a wedding garment, and nothing excellent can then come from them. Those who know their besetting faults, those who have watched them and listened to them, or those who will read the instructive account recently giv-en of them by one of themselves, the *Journeyman*

Engineer, will agree that the idea which culture sets before us of perfection—an increased spiritual activity, having for its characters increased sweet-ness, increased light, increased life, increased sym-pathy—is an idea which the new democracy needs far more than the idea of the blessedness of the franchise, or the wonderfulness of its own in-dustrial performances.

Arnold, *Culture and Anarchy,* I

74 Democracy substitutes election by the incompe-tent many for appointment by the corrupt few.

Shaw, *Man and Superman,* Maxims
for Revolutionists

75 The question I would raise concerns why we pre-fer democratic and humane arrangements to those which are autocratic and harsh. And by "why," I mean the *reason* for preferring them, not just the *causes* which lead us to the preference. One *cause* may be that we have been taught not only in the schools but by the press, the pulpit, the platform, and our laws and law-making bodies that democracy is the best of all social institutions. We may have so assimilated this idea from our surroundings that it has become an habitual part of our mental and moral make-up. But similar causes have led other persons in different sur-roundings to widely varying conclusions—to pre-fer fascism, for example. The cause for our prefer-ence is not the same thing as the reason why we *should* prefer it.

It is not my purpose here to go in detail into the reason. But I would ask a single question: Can we find any reason that does not ultimately come down to the belief that democratic social arrange-ments promote a better quality of human experi-ence, one which is more widely accessible and en-joyed, than do non-democratic and anti-demo-cratic forms of social life?

Dewey, *Experience and Education,* III

76 No estimate of the effects of culture upon the ele-ments that now make up freedom begins to be adequate that does not take into account the mor-al and religious splits that are found in our very make-up as persons. The problem of creation of genuine democracy cannot be successfully dealt with in theory or in practice save as we create intellectual and moral integration out of present disordered conditions. Splits, divisions, between attitudes emotionally and congenially attuned to the past and habits that are forced into existence because of the necessity of dealing with present conditions are a chief cause of continued profes-sion of devotion to democracy by those who do not think nor act day by day in accord with the moral demands of the profession. The consequence is a further weakening of the environing conditions upon which genuine democracy occurs, whether the division is found in business men, in clergy-men, in educators or in politicians. The serious

threat to our democracy is not the existence of foreign totalitarian states. It is the existence within our own personal attitudes and within our own institutions of conditions similar to those which have given a victory to external authority, disci-pline, uniformity and dependence upon The Leader in foreign countries. The battlefield is also accordingly here—within ourselves and our institutions.

Dewey, *Freedom and Culture*, II

10.5 | *Citizenship*

Constitutional government and citizenship come into existence simultaneously; until the advent of republics, men either lived in subjection to despots or in enslavement by tyrants. The citizen is a politically free man, as the subject and the slave are not; being a constituent of government, having suffrage and access to public office, having a voice in government either directly or by representation, and being self-governing; as a member of the ruling class, the citizen is both ruler and ruled. Whether all adult human beings should be admitted to citizenship, as a matter of justice or natural right, is the central question in the dispute about democracy. The reader will find much that is relevant to this issue in Section 10.4 on GOVERNMENT OF AND BY THE PEOPLE: REPUBLIC AND DEMOCRACY.

That issue is, of course, apparent in this section also. In addition, there is discussion of the office of citizenship itself, its privileges and duties; enumerations of the characteristics desirable in a citizen; attempts to define the ideal of a good citizen and to distinguish what is involved in being a good citizen and in being a good man. The last point poses the problem that confronts a virtuous man who happens to be a citizen in a bad society.

1 *Ion.* I pray my mother is Athenian,
So that through her I may have rights of speech.
For when a stranger comes into a city
Of pure blood, though in name a citizen,
His mouth remains a slave: he has no right
Of speech.

Euripides, *Ion*, 671

2 *Eleatic Stranger.* No citizen should do anything contrary to the laws, and any infringement of them should be punished with death and the most extreme penalties.

Plato, *Statesman*, 297B

3 *Athenian Stranger.* There is something over and above law which lies in a region between admonition and law, and has several times occurred to us in the course of discussion; for example, in the education of very young children there were things, as we maintain, which are not to be de-fined, and to regard them as matters of positive law is a great absurdity. Now, our laws and the whole constitution of our state having been thus delineated, the praise of the virtuous citizen is not complete when he is described as the person who serves the laws best and obeys them most, but the higher form of praise is that which describes him as the good citizen who passes through life unde-filed and is obedient to the words of the legislator, both when he is giving laws and when he assigns praise and blame. This is the truest word that can be spoken in praise of a citizen; and the true legislator ought not only to write his laws, but also to interweave with them all such things as seem to him honourable and dishonourable. And the perfect citizen ought to seek to strengthen these no less than the principles of law which are sanctioned by punishments.

Plato, *Laws*, VII, 822B

4 The principle of compensation . . . is the salvation of states. Even among freemen and equals this is a principle which must be maintained, for they cannot all rule together, but must change at the end of a year or some other period of time or in some order of succession. The result is that upon this plan they all govern; just as if shoemakers and carpenters were to exchange their occupations, and the same persons did not always continue shoemakers and carpenters. And since it is better that this should be so in politics as well, it is clear that while there should be continuance of the same persons in power where this is possible, yet where this is not possible by reason of the natural equality of the citizens, and at the same time it is just that all should share in the government (whether to govern be a good thing or a bad), an approximation to this is that equals should in turn retire from office and should, apart from official position, be treated alike. Thus the one party rule and the others are ruled in turn, as if they were no longer the same persons.

Aristotle, *Politics*, 1261ª30

5 A state is composite, like any other whole made up of many parts;—these are the citizens, who compose it. It is evident, therefore, that we must begin by asking, Who is the citizen, and what is the meaning of the term? For here . . . there may be a difference of opinion. He who is a citizen in a democracy will often not be a citizen in an oligarchy. Leaving out of consideration those who have been made citizens, or who have obtained the name of citizen in any other accidental manner, we may say, first, that a citizen is not a citizen because he lives in a certain place, for resident aliens and slaves share in the place; nor is he a citizen who has no legal right except that of suing and being sued; for this right may be enjoyed under the provisions of a treaty. . . . The citizen whom we are seeking to define is a citizen in the strictest sense, against whom no such exception can be taken, and his special characteristic is that he shares in the administration of justice, and in offices. Now of offices some are discontinuous, and the same persons are not allowed to hold them twice, or can only hold them after a fixed interval; others have no limit of time,—for example, the office of dicast of ecclesiast. It may, indeed, be argued that these are not magistrates at all, and that their functions give them no share in the government. But surely it is ridiculous to say that those who have the supreme power do not govern. Let us not dwell further upon this, which is a purely verbal question; what we want is a common term including both dicast and ecclesiast. Let us, for the sake of distinction, call it 'indefinite office', and we will assume that those who share in such office are citizens. This is the most comprehensive definition of a citizen, and best suits all those who are generally so called. . . .

The citizen . . . of necessity differs under each form of government; and our definition is best adapted to the citizen of a democracy; but not necessarily to other states. For in some states the people are not acknowledged, nor have they any regular assembly, but only extraordinary ones; and suits are distributed by sections among the magistrates. At Lacedaemon, for instance, the Ephors determine suits about contracts, which they distribute among themselves, while the elders are judges of homicide, and other causes are decided by other magistrates. . . . We may, indeed, modify our definition of the citizen so as to include these states. In them it is the holder of a definite, not of an indefinite office, who legislates and judges, and to some or all such holders of definite offices is reserved the right of deliberating or judging about some things or about all things. The conception of the citizen now begins to clear up.

He who has the power to take part in the deliberative or judicial administration of any state is said by us to be a citizen of that state; and, speaking generally, a state is a body of citizens sufficing for the purposes of life.

Aristotle, *Politics*, 1274ᵇ38

6 There is a rule . . . which is exercised over freemen and equals by birth—a constitutional rule, which the ruler must learn by obeying, as he would learn the duties of general of cavalry by being under the orders of a general of cavalry, or the duties of a general of infantry by being under the orders of a general of infantry, and by having had the command of a regiment and of a company. It has been well said that 'he who has never learned to obey cannot be a good commander'. The two are not the same, but the good citizen ought to be capable of both; he should know how to govern like a freeman, and how to obey like a freeman—these are the virtues of a citizen. And, although the temperance and justice of a ruler are distinct from those of a subject, the virtue of a good man will include both; for the virtue of the good man who is free and also a subject, for example, his justice, will not be one but will comprise distinct kinds, the one qualifying him to rule, the other to obey.

Aristotle, *Politics*, 1277ᵇ8

7 In the perfect state the good man is absolutely the same as the good citizen; whereas in other states the good citizen is only good relatively to his own form of government.

Aristotle, *Politics*, 1293ᵇ4

8 First among the materials required by the statesman is population: he will consider what should be the number and character of the citizens, and then what should be the size and character of the country. Most persons think that a state in order

to be happy ought to be large; but even if they are right, they have no idea what is a large and what a small state. For they judge of the size of the city by the number of the inhabitants; whereas they ought to regard, not their number, but their power. A city too, like an individual, has a work to do; and that city which is best adapted to the fulfilment of its work is to be deemed greatest, in the same sense of the word great in which Hippocrates might be called greater, not as a man, but as a physician, than some one else who was taller. And even if we reckon greatness by numbers, we ought not to include everybody, for there must always be in cities a multitude of slaves and sojourners and foreigners; but we should include those only who are members of the state, and who form an essential part of it. The number of the latter is a proof of the greatness of a city; but a city which produces numerous artisans and comparatively few soldiers cannot be great, for a great city is not to be confounded with a populous one.

Aristotle, Politics, 1326ᵃ5

9 Since we are here speaking of the best form of government, i.e. that under which the state will be most happy (and happiness, as has been already said, cannot exist without virtue), it clearly follows that in the state which is best governed and possesses men who are just absolutely, and not merely relatively to the principle of the constitution, the citizens must not lead the life of mechanics or tradesmen, for such a life is ignoble and inimical to virtue. Neither must they be husbandmen, since leisure is necessary both for the development of virtue and the performance of political duties.

Again, there is in a state a class of warriors, and another of councillors, who advise about the expedient and determine matters of law, and these seem in an especial manner parts of a state. Now, should these two classes be distinguished, or are both functions to be assigned to the same persons? Here again there is no difficulty in seeing that both functions will in one way belong to the same, in another, to different persons. To different persons in so far as these employments are suited to different primes of life, for the one requires wisdom and the other strength. But on the other hand, since it is an impossible thing that those who are able to use or to resist force should be willing to remain always in subjection, from this point of view the persons are the same; for those who carry arms can always determine the fate of the constitution. It remains therefore that both functions should be entrusted by the ideal constitution to the same persons, not, however, at the same time, but in the order prescribed by nature, who has given to young men strength and to older men wisdom. Such a distribution of duties will be expedient and also just, and is founded upon a principle of conformity to merit. Besides, the ruling class should be the owners of property, for

they are citizens, and the citizens of a state should be in good circumstances; whereas mechanics or any other class which is not a producer of virtue have no share in the state. This follows from our first principle, for happiness cannot exist without virtue, and a city is not to be termed happy in regard to a portion of the citizens, but in regard to them all. And clearly property should be in their hands, since the husbandmen will of necessity be slaves or barbarian Perioeci.

Aristotle, Politics, 1328ᵇ33

10 Never in reply to the question, to what country you belong, say that you are an Athenian or a Corinthian, but that you are a citizen of the world. For why do you say that you are an Athenian, and why do you not say that you belong to the small nook only into which your poor body was cast at birth? Is it not plain that you call yourself an Athenian or Corinthian from the place which has a greater authority and comprises not only that small nook itself and all your family, but even the whole country from which the stock of your progenitors is derived down to you? He then who has observed with intelligence the administration of the world, and has learned that the greatest and supreme and the most comprehensive community is that which is composed of men and God, and that from God have descended the seeds not only to my father and grandfather, but to all beings which are generated on the earth and are produced . . . why should not such a man call himself a citizen of the world?

Epictetus, Discourses, I, 9

11 What . . . does the character of a citizen promise? To hold nothing as profitable to himself; to deliberate about nothing as if he were detached from the community, but to act as the hand or foot would do, if they had reason and understood the constitution of nature, for they would never put themselves in motion nor desire anything otherwise than with reference to the whole.

Epictetus, Discourses, II, 10

12 In the consulship of Aulus Vitellius and Lucius Vipstanus the question of filling up the Senate was discussed, and the chief men of Gallia Comata, as it was called, who had long possessed the rights of allies and of Roman citizens, sought the privilege of obtaining public offices at Rome. There was much talk of every kind on the subject, and it was argued before the emperor with vehement opposition. "Italy," it was asserted, "is not so feeble as to be unable to furnish its own capital with a senate. Once our native-born citizens sufficed for peoples of our own kin, and we are by no means dissatisfied with the Rome of the past. To this day we cite examples, which under our old customs the Roman character exhibited as to valour and renown. Is it a small thing that Veneti

and Insubres have already burst into the Senate-house, unless a mob of foreigners, a troop of captives, so to say, is now forced upon us? What distinctions will be left for the remnants of our noble houses, or for any impoverished senators from Latium? Every place will be crowded with these millionaires, whose ancestors of the second and third generations at the head of hostile tribes destroyed our armies with fire and sword, and actually besieged the divine Julius at Alesia. These are recent memories. What if there were to rise up the remembrance of those who fell in Rome's citadel and at her altar by the hands of these same barbarians! Let them enjoy indeed the title of citizens, but let them not vulgarise the distinctions of the Senate and the honours of office."

These and like arguments failed to impress the emperor. He at once addressed himself to answer them, and thus harangued the assembled Senate. "My ancestors, the most ancient of whom was made at once a citizen and a noble of Rome, encourage me to govern by the same policy of transferring to this city all conspicuous merit, wherever found. And indeed I know, as facts, that the Julii came from Alba, the Coruncanii from Camerium, the Porcii from Tusculum, and not to inquire too minutely into the past, that new members have been brought into the Senate from Etruria and Lucania and the whole of Italy, that Italy itself was at last extended to the Alps, to the end that not only single persons but entire countries and tribes might be united under our name. We had unshaken peace at home; we prospered in all our foreign relations, in the days when Italy beyond the Po was admitted to share our citizenship, and when, enrolling in our ranks the most vigorous of the provincials, under colour of settling our legions throughout the world, we recruited our exhausted empire. Are we sorry that the Balbi came to us from Spain, and other men not less illustrious from Narbon Gaul? Their descendants are still among us, and do not yield to us in patriotism.

"What was the ruin of Sparta and Athens, but this, that mighty as they were in war, they spurned from them as aliens those whom they had conquered? Our founder Romulus, on the other hand, was so wise that he fought as enemies and then hailed as fellow-citizens several nations on the very same day. Strangers have reigned over us. That freedmen's sons should be intrusted with public offices is not, as many wrongly think, a sudden innovation, but was a common practice in the old commonwealth. But, it will be said, we have fought with the Senones. I suppose then that the Volsci and Æqui never stood in array against us. Our city was taken by the Gauls. Well, we also gave hostages to the Etruscans, and passed under the yoke of the Samnites. On the whole, if you review all our wars, never has one been finished in a shorter time than that with the Gauls. Thence-

forth they have preserved an unbroken and loyal peace. United as they now are with us by manners, education, and intermarriage, let them bring us their gold and their wealth rather than enjoy it in isolation. Everything, Senators, which we now hold to be of the highest antiquity, was once new. Plebeian magistrates came after patrician; Latin magistrates after plebeian; magistrates of other Italian peoples after Latin. This practice too will establish itself, and what we are this day justifying by precedents, will be itself a precedent."

Tacitus, *Annals,* XI, 23–24

13 My nature is rational and social; and my city and country, so far as I am Antoninus, is Rome, but so far as I am a man, it is the world.

Marcus Aurelius, *Meditations,* VI, 44

14 The life of a citizen is happy, who continues a course of action which is advantageous to his fellow-citizens, and is content with whatever the state may assign to him.

Marcus Aurelius, *Meditations,* X, 6

15 As the Philosopher [Aristotle] says, a man is said to be a citizen in two ways: first, absolutely; secondly, in a restricted sense. A man is a citizen absolutely if he has all the rights of citizenship, for instance, the right of debating or voting in the popular assembly. On the other hand, any man may be called citizen in a restricted sense only, if he dwells within the state—even common people or children or old men, who are not fit to enjoy power in matters pertaining to the common good.

Aquinas, *Summa Theologica,* I–II, 105, 3

16 Men are not born fit for citizenship, but must be made so.

Spinoza, *Political Treatise,* V, 2

17 Submitting to the laws of any country, living quietly and enjoying privileges and protection under them, makes not a man a member of that society; it is only a local protection and homage due to and from all those who, not being in a state of war, come within the territories belonging to any government, to all parts whereof the force of its law extends. But this no more makes a man a member of that society, a perpetual subject of that commonwealth, than it would make a man a subject to another in whose family he found it convenient to abide for some time, though, whilst he continued in it, he were obliged to comply with the laws and submit to the government he found there. And thus we see that foreigners, by living all their lives under another government, and enjoying the privileges and protection of it, though they are bound, even in conscience, to submit to its administration as far forth as any denizen, yet do not thereby come to be subjects or members of that commonwealth. Nothing can make any man

so but his actually entering into it by positive engagement and express promise and compact.

Locke, *II Civil Government*, VIII, 122

18 There can be no patriotism without liberty, no liberty without virtue, no virtue without citizens; create citizens, and you have everything you need; without them, you will have nothing but debased slaves, from the rulers of the State downwards. To form citizens is not the work of a day; and in order to have men it is necessary to educate them when they are children.

Rousseau, *Political Economy*

19 Most people mistake a town for a city, and a townsman for a citizen. They do not know that houses make a town, but citizens a city. The same mistake long ago cost the Carthaginians dear. I have never read of the title of citizens being given to the subjects of any prince, not even the ancient Macedonians or the English of to-day, though they are nearer liberty than any one else. The French alone everywhere familiarly adopt the name of citizens, because, as can be seen from their dictionaries, they have no idea of its meaning; otherwise they would be guilty in usurping it, of the crime of *lèse-majesté:* among them, the name expresses a virtue, and not a right. When Bodin spoke of our citizens and townsmen, he fell into a bad blunder in taking the one class for the other. M. d'Alembert has avoided the error, and, in his article on Geneva, has clearly distinguished the four orders of men (or even five, counting mere foreigners) who dwell in our town, of which two only compose the Republic. No other French writer, to my knowledge, has understood the real meaning of the word citizen.

Rousseau, *Social Contract*, I, 6, fn.

20 Suppose the State is composed of ten thousand citizens. The Sovereign can only be considered collectively and as a body; but each member, as being a subject, is regarded as an individual: thus the Sovereign is to the subject as ten thousand to one, i.e., each member of the State has as his share only a ten-thousandth part of the sovereign authority, although he is wholly under its control. If the people numbers a hundred thousand, the condition of the subject undergoes no change, and each equally is under the whole authority of the laws, while his vote, being reduced to a hundred-thousandth part, has ten times less influence in drawing them up. The subject therefore remaining always a unit, the relation between him and the Sovereign increases with the number of the citizens. From this it follows that, the larger the State, the less the liberty.

Rousseau, *Social Contract*, III, 1

21 As soon as public service ceases to be the chief business of the citizens, and they would rather serve with their money than with their persons, the State is not far from its fall. When it is necessary to march out to war, they pay troops and stay at home: when it is necessary to meet in council, they name deputies and stay at home. By reason of idleness and money, they end by having soldiers to enslave their country and representatives to sell it. . . .

The better the constitution of a State is, the more do public affairs encroach on private in the minds of the citizens. Private affairs are even of much less importance, because the aggregate of the common happiness furnishes a greater proportion of that of each individual, so that there is less for him to seek in particular cares. In a well-ordered city every man flies to the assemblies: under a bad government no one cares to stir a step to get to them, because no one is interested in what happens there, because it is foreseen that the general will will not prevail, and lastly because domestic cares are all-absorbing. Good laws lead to the making of better ones; bad ones bring about worse. As soon as any man says of the affairs of the State *What does it matter to me?* the State may be given up for lost.

Rousseau, *Social Contract*, III, 15

22 It was a maxim of ancient jurisprudence, that as a slave had not any country of his own, he acquired with his liberty an admission into the political society of which his patron was a member. The consequences of this maxim would have prostituted the privileges of the Roman city to a mean and promiscuous multitude. Some seasonable exceptions were therefore provided; and the honourable distinction was confined to such slaves only, as for just causes, and with the approbation of the magistrate, should receive a solemn and legal manumission. Even these chosen freed-men obtained no more than the private rights of citizens, and were rigorously excluded from civil or military honours. Whatever might be the merit or fortune of their sons, *they* likewise were esteemed unworthy of a seat in the senate; nor were the traces of a servile origin allowed to be completely obliterated till the third or fourth generation.

Gibbon, *Decline and Fall of the Roman Empire*, II

23 The members of a civil society . . . united for the purpose of legislation, and thereby constituting a state, are called its *citizens;* and there are three juridical attributes that inseparably belong to them by right. These are:—1. constitutional freedom, as the right of every citizen to have to obey no other law than that to which he has given his consent or approval; 2. civil equality, as the right of the citizen to recognise no one as a superior among the people in relation to himself, except in so far as such a one is as subject to *his* moral power to impose obligations, as that other has power to

impose obligations upon him; and 3. political independence, as the right to owe his existence and continuance in society not to the arbitrary will of another, but to his own rights and powers as a member of the commonwealth, and, consequently, the possession of a civil personality, which cannot be represented by any other than himself.

Kant, *Science of Right,* 46

24 The capability of voting by possession of the suffrage properly constitutes the political qualification of a citizen as a member of the state. But this, again, presupposes the independence or self-sufficiency of the individual citizen among the people, as one who is not a mere incidental part of the commonwealth, but a member of it acting of his own will in community with others. The last of the three qualities involved necessarily constitutes the distinction between *active* and *passive* citizenship although the latter conception appears to stand in contradiction to the definition of a citizen as such. The following examples may serve to remove this difficulty. The apprentice of a merchant or tradesman, a servant who is not in the employ of the state, a minor, all women, and, generally, every one who is compelled to maintain himself not according to his own industry, but as it is arranged by others (the state excepted), are without civil personality, and their existence is only, as it were, incidentally included in the state. The woodcutter whom I employ on my estate; the smith in India who carries his hammer, anvil, and bellows into the houses where he is engaged to work in iron, as distinguished from the European carpenter or smith, who can offer the independent products of his labour as wares for public sale; the resident tutor as distinguished from the schoolmaster; the ploughman as distinguished from the farmer and such like, illustrate the distinction in question. In all these cases, the former members of the contrast are distinguished from the latter by being mere subsidiaries of the commonwealth and not active independent members of it, because they are of necessity commanded and protected by others, and consequently possess no political self-sufficiency in themselves. Such dependence on the will of others and the consequent inequality are, however, not inconsistent with the freedom and equality of the individuals *as men* helping to constitute the people. Much rather is it the case that it is only under such conditions that a people can become a state and enter into a civil constitution. But all are not equally qualified to exercise the right of suffrage under the constitution, and to be full citizens of the state, and not mere passive subjects under its protection. For, although they are entitled to demand to be treated by all the other citizens according to laws of natural freedom and equality, as *passive* parts of the state, it does not follow that they ought themselves to have the right to deal with the state as active members of it, to reorganize it, or to take action by way of introducing certain laws. All they have a right in their circumstances to claim may be no more than that whatever be the mode in which the positive laws are enacted, these laws must not be contrary to the natural laws that demand the freedom of all the people and the equality that is conformable thereto; and it must therefore be made possible for them to raise themselves from this passive condition in the state to the condition of active citizenship.

Kant, *Science of Right,* 46

25 I think that we should be men first, and subjects afterward.

Thoreau, *Civil Disobedience*

26 It is a great discouragement to an individual, and a still greater one to a class, to be left out of the constitution; to be reduced to plead from outside the door to the arbiters of their destiny, not taken into consultation within. The maximum of the invigorating effect of freedom upon the character is only obtained when the person acted on either is, or is looking forward to becoming, a citizen as fully privileged as any other.

Mill, *Representative Government,* III

27 If a noble and civilised democracy is to subsist, the common citizen must be something of a saint and something of a hero. We see therefore how justly flattering and profound, and at the same time how ominous, was Montesquieu's saying that the principle of democracy is virtue.

Santayana, *Life of Reason,* II, 5

10.6 | *Despotism and Tyranny*

Until fairly recently in the tradition of Western politics, monarchies, kingships, or autocracies have been the rule, and republics the exception. A single man seated on a throne and holding the sceptre of sovereignty has been the prevalent image of the ruler. In fact, for many centuries the words "prince" or "king" and "sovereign" were interchangeable. Our English word "king" carries the meaning that once attached to the Greek word *tyrannis* as well as to the Latin word *rex*. The tyrant was a monarch with absolute power; and the word "despot" derives from a Greek word that designates the rule of a master over his slaves.

With the beginnings of political philosophy in the writings of Plato and Aristotle, these terms take on the meanings they have for us today. A tyrant is a ruler who exploits for his own interests the subjects in his power; tyranny is the archetype of misrule, whether the power of government is in the hands of the one, the few, or the many. An elite can also misrule in a manner that deserves the appellation "tyrannical"; and since the beginnings of popular government and extensions of the franchise in the nineteenth century, there has been much concern about "the tyranny of the majority."

The reader will find relevant materials on this in Section 10.4.

Despotism, as contrasted with tyranny, is sometimes qualified by the term "benevolent." Both despotism and tyranny signify absolute power—government without the consent of the governed and with no participation on their part. But when such absolute power is exercised with some regard for the rights and welfare of the ruled, in a quasi-paternalistic manner, the despot is said to be benevolent.

The reader will find the authors quoted here in opposition on many points, some defending absolute monarchy as the ideal form of government or, as in the case of Hobbes, the only legitimate form of government; and some, like Locke and Rousseau, saying that absolute monarchy is not a form of civil government at all and has no legitimacy. The reader will also find a discussion of the question whether benevolent despotism is ever justified by the uncivilized or politically immature condition of the people over whom and for whose benefit it is exercised. For the condition of those subject to tyrannical or despotic rule and for their response to it, the reader should turn to Section 10.7 on SLAVERY and Section 10.9 on REVOLUTION.

---

1 As a roaring lion, and a ranging bear; so is a wicked ruler over the poor people.

    The prince that wanteth understanding is also a great oppressor: but he that hateth covetousness shall prolong his days.

                    Proverbs 28:15–16

2 Her princes in the midst thereof are like wolves ravening the prey, to shed blood, and to destroy souls, to get dishonest gain.

                    Ezekiel 22:27

3 *Nestor.*   Nor . . . think to match your strength with

the king, since never equal with the rest is the portion of honour
of the sceptred king to whom Zeus gives magnificence. Even
though you are the stronger man, and the mother who bore you was immortal,
yet is this man greater who is lord over more than you rule.

                    Homer, *Iliad,* I, 277

4 *Chorus.* Death is a softer thing by far than tyranny.
                Aeschylus, *Agamemnon,* 1365

5 Pisistratus, at a time when there was civil conten-

tion in Attica between the party of the Sea-coast headed by Megacles the son of Alcmæon, and that of the Plain headed by Lycurgus, one of the Aristolaïds, formed the project of making himself tyrant, and with this view created a third party. Gathering together a band of partisans, and giving himself out for the protector of the Highlanders, he contrived the following stratagem. He wounded himself and his mules, and then drove his chariot into the market-place, professing to have just escaped an attack of his enemies, who had attempted his life as he was on his way into the country. He besought the people to assign him a guard to protect his person, reminding them of the glory which he had gained when he led the attack upon the Megarians, and took the town of Nisæa, at the same time performing many other exploits. The Athenians, deceived by his story, appointed him a band of citizens to serve as a guard, who were to carry clubs instead of spears, and to accompany him wherever he went. Thus strengthened, Pisistratus broke into revolt and seized the citadel. In this way he acquired the sovereignty of Athens, which he continued to hold without disturbing the previously existing offices or altering any of the laws. He administered the state according to the established usages, and his arrangements were wise and salutary.

Herodotus, *History*, I, 59

6 *Theseus.* Naught is more hostile to a city than a despot; where he is, there are in the first place no laws common to all, but one man is tyrant, in whose keeping and in his alone the law resides, and in that case equality is at an end.

Euripides, *Suppliants*, 429

7 Wherever there were tyrants, their habit of providing simply for themselves, of looking solely to their personal comfort and family aggrandizement, made safety the great aim of their policy, and prevented anything great proceeding from them; though they would each have their affairs with their immediate neighbours.

Thucydides, *Peloponnesian War*, I, 17

8 *Polus.* Then you would not wish to be a tyrant?
   Socrates. Not if you mean by tyranny what I mean.
   Pol. I mean . . . the power of doing whatever seems good to you in a state, killing, banishing, doing in all things as you like.

Plato, *Gorgias*, 469B

9 *Socrates.* How then does a protector begin to change into a tyrant? Clearly when he does what the man is said to do in the tale of the Arcadian temple of Lycaean Zeus.
   Adeimantus. What tale?
   The tale is that he who has tasted the entrails of

a single human victim minced up with the entrails of other victims is destined to become a wolf. Did you never hear it?
   O yes.
   And the protector of the people is like him; having a mob entirely at his disposal, he is not restrained from shedding the blood of kinsmen; by the favourite method of false accusation he brings them into court and murders them, making the life of man to disappear, and with unholy tongue and lips tasting the blood of his fellow citizen; some he kills and others he banishes, at the same time hinting at the abolition of debts and partition of lands: and after this, what will be his destiny? Must he not either perish at the hands of his enemies, or from being a man become a wolf—that is, a tyrant?
   Inevitably.
   This, I said, is he who begins to make a party against the rich?
   The same.
   After a while he is driven out, but comes back, in spite of his enemies, a tyrant full grown.

Plato, *Republic*, VIII, 565B

10 [Socrates said] He who is the real tyrant, whatever men may think, is the real slave, and is obliged to practise the greatest adulation and servility, and to be the flatterer of the vilest of mankind. He has desires which he is utterly unable to satisfy, and has more wants than any one, and is truly poor, if you know how to inspect the whole soul of him: all his life long he is beset with fear and is full of convulsions, and distractions, even as the State which he resembles: and surely the resemblance holds?
   Very true, he [Adeimantus] said.
   Moreover, as we were saying before, he grows worse from having power: he becomes and is of necessity more jealous, more faithless, more unjust, more friendless, more impious, than he was at first; he is the purveyor and cherisher of every sort of vice, and the consequence is that he is supremely miserable, and that he makes everybody else as miserable as himself.
   No man of any sense will dispute your words.
   Come then, I said, and as the general umpire in theatrical contests proclaims the result, do you also decide who in your opinion is first in the scale of happiness, and who second, and in what order the others follow: there are five of them in all—they are the royal, timocratical, oligarchical, democratical, tyrannical.
   The decision will be easily given, he replied; they shall be choruses coming on the stage, and I must judge them in the order in which they enter, by the criterion of virtue and vice, happiness and misery.
   Need we hire a herald, or shall I announce, that the son of Ariston [the best] has decided that the best and justest is also the happiest, and that

this is he who is the most royal man and king over himself; and that the worst and most unjust man is also the most miserable, and that this is he who being the greatest tyrant of himself is also the greatest tyrant of his State?

Make the proclamation yourself, he said.

And shall I add, "whether seen or unseen by gods and men"?

Let the words be added.

Plato, *Republic,* IX, 579B

11 A man is not a king unless he is sufficient to himself and excels his subjects in all good things; and such a man needs nothing further; therefore he will not look to his own interests but to those of his subjects; for a king who is not like that would be a mere titular king. Now tyranny is the very contrary of this; the tyrant pursues his own good. And it is clearer in the case of tyranny that it is the worst deviation-form; but it is the contrary of the best that is worst. Monarchy passes over into tyranny; for tyranny is the evil form of one-man rule and the bad king becomes a tyrant.

Aristotle, *Ethics,* 1160b3

12 The appointment of a king is the resource of the better classes against the people, and he is elected by them out of their own number, because either he himself or his family excel in virtue and virtuous actions; whereas a tyrant is chosen from the people to be their protector against the notables, and in order to prevent them from being injured. History shows that almost all tyrants have been demagogues who gained the favour of the people by their accusation of the notables. At any rate this was the manner in which the tyrannies arose in the days when cities had increased in power. Others which were older originated in the ambition of kings wanting to overstep the limits of their hereditary power and become despots. Others again grew out of the class which were chosen to be chief magistrates; for in ancient times the people who elected them gave the magistrates, whether civil or religious, a long tenure. Others arose out of the custom which oligarchies had of making some individual supreme over the highest offices. In any of these ways an ambitious man had no difficulty, if he desired, in creating a tyranny, since he had the power in his hands already, either as king or as one of the officers of state.

Aristotle, *Politics,* 1310b8

13 Kingly rule is little affected by external causes, and is therefore lasting; it is generally destroyed from within. And there are two ways in which the destruction may come about; when the members of the royal family quarrel among themselves, and when the kings attempt to administer the state too much after the fashion of a tyranny, and to extend their authority contrary to the law. Royalties do not now come into existence; where such forms of government arise, they are rather monarchies or tyrannies. For the rule of a king is over voluntary subjects, and he is supreme in all important matters; but in our own day men are more upon an equality, and no one is so immeasurably superior to others as to represent adequately the greatness and dignity of the office. Hence mankind will not, if they can help, endure it, and any one who obtains power by force or fraud is at once thought to be a tyrant. In hereditary monarchies a further cause of destruction is the fact that kings often fall into contempt, and, although possessing not tyrannical power, but only royal dignity, are apt to outrage others. Their overthrow is then readily effected; for there is an end to the king when his subjects do not want to have him, but the tyrant lasts, whether they like him or not.

Aristotle, *Politics,* 1312b39

14 As to tyrannies, they are preserved in two most opposite ways. One of them is the old traditional method in which most tyrants administer their government. Of such arts Periander of Corinth is said to have been the great master, and many similar devices may be gathered from the Persians in the administration of their government. There are firstly the prescriptions mentioned some distance back, for the preservation of a tyranny, in so far as this is possible; viz. that the tyrant should lop off those who are too high; he must put to death men of spirit; he must not allow common meals, clubs, education, and the like; he must be upon his guard against anything which is likely to inspire either courage or confidence among his subjects; he must prohibit literary assemblies or other meetings for discussion, and he must take every means to prevent people from knowing one another (for acquaintance begets mutual confidence). Further, he must compel all persons staying in the city to appear in public and live at his gates; then he will know what they are doing: if they are always kept under, they will learn to be humble. In short, he should practise these and the like Persian and barbaric arts, which all have the same object. A tyrant should also endeavour to know what each of his subjects says or does, and should employ spies, like the 'female detectives' at Syracuse, and the eavesdroppers whom Hiero was in the habit of sending to any place of resort or meeting; for the fear of informers prevents people from speaking their minds, and if they do, they are more easily found out. Another art of the tyrant is to sow quarrels among the citizens; friends should be embroiled with friends, the people with the notables, and the rich with one another. Also he should impoverish his subjects; he thus provides against the maintenance of a guard by the citizens, and the people, having to keep hard at work, are prevented from conspiring. The Pyramids of Egypt afford an example of this policy; also the offerings of the family of Cypselus, and the build-

ing of the temple of Olympian Zeus by the Peisistratidae, and the great Polycratean monuments at Samos; all these works were alike intended to occupy the people and keep them poor. Another practice of tyrants is to multiply taxes, after the manner of Dionysius at Syracuse, who contrived that within five years his subjects should bring into the treasury their whole property. The tyrant is also fond of making war in order that his subjects may have something to do and be always in want of a leader. And whereas the power of a king is preserved by his friends, the characteristic of a tyrant is to distrust his friends, because he knows that all men want to overthrow him, and they above all have the power.

Aristotle, *Politics*, 1313ª34

15 By the standard of popular opinion, I cannot imagine what greater boon could fall to a man than to be a king. But when I begin to consider the question from the point of view of the standard of truth, then I can think of nothing more disadvantageous than to have risen to such a height by means of injustice. For can it be regarded as an advantage to anyone to be confronted with all sorts of reasons for worry, anxiety, and fear day in and day out, and to live a life beset from all sides with plots and perils?

Cicero, *De Officiis*, III, 21

16 A kingdom is the best form of government of the people, so long as it is not corrupt. But since the power granted to a king is so great, it easily degenerates into tyranny, unless he to whom this power is given be a very virtuous man; for "it is only the virtuous man that conducts himself well in the midst of prosperity," as [Aristotle] observes.

Aquinas, *Summa Theologica*, I–II, 105, 1

17 A tyrannical government is not just, because it is directed, not to the common good, but to the private good of the ruler. . . . Consequently there is no sedition in disturbing a government of this kind, unless indeed the tyrant's rule be disturbed so inordinately that his subjects suffer greater harm from the consequent disturbance than from the tyrant's government. Indeed it is the tyrant rather that is guilty of sedition, since he encourages discord and sedition among his subjects, that he may lord over them more securely.

Aquinas, *Summa Theologica*, II–II, 42, 2

18 The government of tyrants . . . cannot last long because it is hateful to the multitude, and what is against the wishes of the multitude cannot be long preserved.

Aquinas, *On Kingship*, I, 10

19 Between a tyrant or usurping chief
And any outlawed man or errant thief,
It's just the same, there is no difference.

One told to Alexander this sentence:
That, since the tyrant is of greater might,
By force of numbers, to slay men outright
And burn down house and home even as a plane,
Lo! for that he's a captain, that's certain;
And since the outlaw has small company
And may not do so great a harm as he,
Nor bring a nation into such great grief,
Why, he's called but an outlaw or a thief.

Chaucer, *Canterbury Tales:* Manciple's Tale

20 He who obtains sovereignty by the assistance of the nobles maintains himself with more difficulty than he who comes to it by the aid of the people, because the former finds himself with many around him who consider themselves his equals, and because of this he can neither rule nor manage them to his liking. But he who reaches sovereignty by popular favour finds himself alone, and has none around him, or few, who are not prepared to obey him. Besides this, one cannot by fair dealing, and without injury to others, satisfy the nobles, but you can satisfy the people, for their object is more righteous than that of the nobles, the latter wishing to oppress, whilst the former only desire not to be oppressed.

Machiavelli, *Prince*, IX

21 *Richmond.* More than I have said, loving countrymen,
The leisure and enforcement of the time
Forbids to dwell upon: yet remember this,
God and our good cause fight upon our side;
The prayers of holy saints and wronged souls,
Like high-rear'd bulwarks, stand before our faces;
Richard except, those whom we fight against
Had rather have us win than him they follow:
For what is he they follow? truly, gentlemen,
A bloody tyrant and a homicide;
One raised in blood, and one in blood establish'd;
One that made means to come by what he hath,
And slaughter'd those that were the means to help him;
A base foul stone, made precious by the foil
Of England's chair, where he is falsely set;
One that hath ever been God's enemy:
Then, if you fight against God's enemy,
God will in justice ward you as his soldiers;
If you do sweat to put a tyrant down,
You sleep in peace, the tyrant being slain.

Shakespeare, *Richard III*, V, iii, 237

22 *King Richard.* For God's sake, let us sit upon the ground
And tell sad stories of the death of kings:
How some have been deposed; some slain in war;
Some haunted by the ghosts they have deposed;
Some poison'd by their wives; some sleeping kill'd;
All murder'd: for within the hollow crown
That rounds the mortal temples of a king

Keeps Death his court and there the antic sits,
Scoffing his state and grinning at his pomp,
Allowing him a breath, a little scene,
To monarchize, be fear'd, and kill with looks,
Infusing him with self and vain conceit,
As if this flesh which walls about our life
Were brass impregnable, and humour'd thus
Comes at the last and with a little pin
Bores through his castle wall, and farewell king!

> Shakespeare, *Richard II*, III, ii, 155

23 *Pandulph.* A sceptre snatch'd with an unruly hand
Must be as boisterously maintain'd as gain'd;
And he that stands upon a slippery place
Makes nice of no vile hold to stay him up.

> Shakespeare, *King John*, III, iv, 135

24 *King Henry.*   What infinite heart's-ease
Must kings neglect, that private men enjoy!
And what have kings, that privates have not too,
Save ceremony, save general ceremony?
And what art thou, thou idol Ceremony?
What kind of god art thou, that suffer'st more
Of mortal griefs than do thy worshippers?
What are thy rents? what are thy comings in?
O Ceremony, show me but thy worth!
What is thy soul of adoration?
Art thou aught else but place, degree, and form,
Creating awe and fear in other men?
Wherein thou art less happy being fear'd
Than they in fearing.
What drink'st thou oft, instead of homage sweet,
But poison'd flattery? O, be sick, great greatness,
And bid thy Ceremony give thee cure!
Think'st thou the fiery fever will go out
With titles blown from adulation?
Will it give place to flexure and low bending?
Canst thou, when thou command'st the beggar's
    knee,
Command the health of it? No, thou proud
    dream,
That play'st so subtly with a king's repose;
I am a king that find thee, and I know
'Tis not the balm, the sceptre, and the ball,
The sword, the mace, the crown imperial,
The intertissued robe of gold and pearl,
The farced title running 'fore the King,
The throne he sits on, nor the tide of pomp
That beats upon the high shore of this world,
No, not all these, thrice-gorgeous Ceremony,
Not all these, laid in bed majestical,
Can sleep so soundly as the wretched slave,
Who with a body fill'd and vacant mind
Gets him to rest, cramm'd with distressful bread;
Never sees horrid night, the child of hell,
But, like a lackey, from the rise to set
Sweats in the eye of Phœbus and all night
Sleeps in Elysium; next day after dawn,
Doth rise and help Hyperion to his horse,
And follows so the ever-running year,
With profitable labour, to his grave:

And, but for ceremony, such a wretch,
Winding up days with toil and nights with sleep,
Had the fore-hand and vantage of a king.
The slave, a member of the country's peace,
Enjoys it; but in gross brain little wots
What watch the King keeps to maintain the
    peace,
Whose hours the peasant best advantages.

> Shakespeare, *Henry V*, IV, i, 253

25 *Brutus.* As Cæsar loved me, I weep for him; as he
was fortunate, I rejoice at it; as he was valiant, I
honour him: but, as he was ambitious, I slew him.
There is tears for his love; joy for his fortune; honour for his valour; and death for his ambition.

> Shakespeare, *Julius Caesar*, III, ii, 25

26 *Menteith.*   What does the tyrant?
   Caithness. Great Dunsinane he strongly fortifies.
Some say he's mad; others that lesser hate him
Do call it valiant fury; but, for certain,
He cannot buckle his distemper'd cause
Within the belt of rule.
   Angus.   Now does he feel
His secret murders sticking on his hands;
Now minutely revolts upbraid his faith-breach;
Those he commands move only in command,
Nothing in love; now does he feel his title
Hang loose about him, like a giant's robe
Upon a dwarfish thief.

> Shakespeare, *Macbeth*, V, ii, 11

27 *Macduff.*   Turn, hell-hound, turn!
   Macbeth. Of all men else I have avoided thee.
But get thee back; my soul is too much charged
With blood of thine already.
   Macd.   I have no words;
My voice is in my sword. Thou bloodier villain
Than terms can give thee out!
   They fight.
   Macb.   Thou losest labour.
As easy mayst thou the intrenchant air
With thy keen sword impress as make me bleed.
Let fall thy blade on vulnerable crests;
I bear a charmed life, which must not yield
To one of woman born.
   Macd.   Despair thy charm;
And let the angel whom thou still hast served
Tell thee, Macduff was from his mother's womb
Untimely ripp'd.
   Macb. Accursed be that tongue that tells me so,
For it hath cow'd my better part of man!
And be these juggling fiends no more believed
That palter with us in a double sense;
That keep the word of promise to our ear,
And break it to our hope. I'll not fight with thee.
   Macd. Then yield thee, coward,
And live to be the show and gaze o' the time!
We'll have thee, as our rarer monsters are,
Painted upon a pole, and underwrit,
"Here may you see the tyrant."

Macb.   I will not yield,
To kiss the ground before young Malcolm's feet
And to be baited with the rabble's curse.
Though Birnam wood be come to Dunsinane,
And thou opposed, being of no woman born,
Yet I will try the last. Before my body
I throw my warlike shield. Lay on, Macduff,
And damn'd be him that first cries, "Hold,
   enough!"

Shakespeare, *Macbeth*, V, viii, 4

28 *Pericles.* 'Tis time to fear when tyrants seem to kiss.

Shakespeare, *Pericles*, I, ii, 79

29 *Wolsey.*   O, how wretched
Is that poor man that hangs on princes' favours!
There is, betwixt that smile we would aspire to,
That sweet aspect of princes, and their ruin,
More pangs and fears than wars or women have;
And when he falls, he falls like Lucifer,
Never to hope again.

Shakespeare, *Henry VIII*, III, ii, 366

30 It is a miserable state of mind to have few things
to desire and many things to fear; and yet that
commonly is the case of kings.

Bacon, *Of Empire*

31 Princes are like to heavenly bodies, which cause
good or evil times; and which have much veneration, but no rest.

Bacon, *Of Empire*

32 I put for a general inclination of all mankind a
perpetual and restless desire of power after power,
that ceaseth only in death. And the cause of this is
not always that a man hopes for a more intensive
delight than he has already attained to, or that he
cannot be content with a moderate power, but
because he cannot assure the power and means to
live well, which he hath present, without the acquisition of more. And from hence it is that kings,
whose power is greatest, turn their endeavours to
the assuring it at home by laws, or abroad by
wars: and when that is done, there succeedeth a
new desire; in some, of fame from new conquest;
in others, of ease and sensual pleasure; in others,
of admiration, or being flattered for excellence in
some art or other ability of the mind.

Hobbes, *Leviathan*, I, 11

33 In a body politic, if the representative be one
man, whatsoever he does in the person of the body
which is not warranted in his letters, nor by the
laws, is his own act, and not the act of the body,
nor of any other member thereof besides himself:
because further than his letters or the laws limit,
he representeth no man's person, but his own. But
what he does according to these is the act of every
one: for of the act of the sovereign every one is
author, because he is their representative unlimited; and the act of him that recedes not from the
letters of the sovereign is the act of the sovereign,
and therefore every member of the body is author
of it.

Hobbes, *Leviathan*, II, 22

34 The name of tyranny signifieth nothing more nor
less than the name of sovereignty, be it in one or
many men, saving that they that use the former
word are understood to be angry with them they
call *tyrants;* I think the toleration of a professed
hatred of tyranny is a toleration of hatred to
Commonwealth in general, and another evil seed,
not differing much from the former.

Hobbes, *Leviathan*, IV, Review
and Conclusion

35 Tyranny consists in the desire of universal power
beyond its scope.

There are different assemblies of the strong, the
fair, the sensible, the pious, in which each man
rules at home, not elsewhere. And sometimes they
meet, and the strong and the fair foolishly fight as
to who shall be master, for their mastery is of different kinds. They do not understand one another, and their fault is the desire to rule everywhere.
Nothing can effect this, not even might, which is
of no use in the kingdom of the wise, and is only
mistress of external actions. So these expressions
are false and tyrannical: "I am fair, therefore I
must be feared. I am strong, therefore I must be
loved. I am . . ."

Tyranny is the wish to have in one way what
can only be had in another. We render different
duties to different merits; the duty of love to the
pleasant; the duty of fear to the strong; duty of
belief to the learned.

We must render these duties; it is unjust to refuse them, and unjust to ask others. And so it is
false and tyrannical to say, "He is not strong,
therefore I will not esteem him; he is not able,
therefore I will not fear him."

Pascal, *Pensées*, V, 332

36 *Michael.* Reason in man obscur'd, or not obeyd,
Immediately inordinate desires
And upstart Passions catch the Government
From Reason, and to servitude reduce
Man till then free. Therefore since hee permits
Within himself unworthie Powers to reign
Over free Reason, God in Judgement just
Subjects him from without to violent Lords;
Who oft as undeservedly enthrall
His outward freedom: Tyrannie must be,
Though to the Tyrant thereby no excuse.

Milton, *Paradise Lost*, XII, 86

37 That people must needs be mad or strangely infatuated that build the chief hope of their common happiness or safety on a single person; who,
if he happen to be good, can do no more than

another man; if to be bad, hath in his hands to do more evil without check than millions of other men.

Milton, *Ready and Easy Way*

38 It is lawful, and hath been held so through all ages, for any, who have the power, to call to account a tyrant or wicked king, and after due conviction, to depose and put him to death.

Milton, *Tenure of Kings and Magistrates*

39 To say kings are accountable to none but God, is the overturning of all law and government. For if they may refuse to give account, then all covenants made with them at coronation, all oaths are in vain, and mere mockeries, all laws which they swear to keep, made to no purpose: for if the king fear not God (as how many of them do not?) we hold then our lives and estates by the tenure of his mere grace and mercy, as from a god, not a mortal magistrate—a position that none but court parasites or men besotted would maintain.

Milton, *Tenure of Kings and Magistrates*

40 They are much mistaken, who suppose that one man *can* by himself hold the supreme right of a commonwealth. For the only limit of right . . . is power. But the power of one man is very inadequate to support so great a load. And hence it arises, that the man, whom the multitude has chosen king, looks out for himself generals, or counsellors, or friends, to whom he entrusts his own and the common welfare; so that the dominion, which is thought to be a perfect monarchy, is in actual working an aristocracy, not, indeed, an open but a hidden one, and therefore the worst of all.

Spinoza, *Political Treatise*, VI, 5

41 It is evident that absolute monarchy, which by some men is counted for the only government in the world, is indeed inconsistent with civil society, and so can be no form of civil government at all. For the end of civil society being to avoid and remedy those inconveniencies of the state of Nature which necessarily follow from every man's being judge in his own case, by setting up a known authority to which every one of that society may appeal upon any injury received, or controversy that may arise, and which every one of the society ought to obey. Wherever any persons are who have not such an authority to appeal to, and decide any difference between them there, those persons are still in the state of Nature. And so is every absolute prince in respect of those who are under his dominion.

Locke, *II Civil Government*, VII, 90

42 As usurpation is the exercise of power which another hath a right to, so tyranny is the exercise of power beyond right, which nobody can have a right to; and this is making use of the power any one has in his hands, not for the good of those who are under it, but for his own private, separate advantage. When the governor, however entitled, makes not the law, but his will, the rule, and his commands and actions are not directed to the preservation of the properties of his people, but the satisfaction of his own ambition, revenge, covetousness, or any other irregular passion. . . .

It is a mistake to think this fault is proper only to monarchies. Other forms of government are liable to it as well as that; for wherever the power that is put in any hands for the government of the people and the preservation of their properties is applied to other ends, and made use of to impoverish, harass, or subdue them to the arbitrary and irregular commands of those that have it, there it presently becomes tyranny, whether those that thus use it are one or many. . . .

Wherever law ends, tyranny begins.

Locke, *II Civil Government*, XVIII, 199–202

43 *Jones.* I know but of one solid objection to absolute monarchy. The only defect in which excellent constitution seems to be, the difficulty of finding any man adequate to the office of an absolute monarch: for this indispensably require three qualities very difficult, as it appears from history, to be found in princely natures: first, a sufficient quantity of moderation in the prince, to be contented with all the power which is possible for him to have. 2ndly, Enough of wisdom to know his own happiness. And, 3rdly, Goodness sufficient to support the happiness of others, when not only compatible with, but instrumental to his own.

Now if an absolute monarch, with all these great and rare qualifications, should be allowed capable of conferring the greatest good on society; it must be surely granted, on the contrary, that absolute power, vested in the hands of one who is deficient in them all, is likely to be attended with no less a degree of evil.

In short, our own religion furnishes us with adequate ideas of the blessing, as well as curse, which may attend absolute power. The pictures of heaven and of hell will place a very lively image of both before our eyes; for though the prince of the latter can have no power, but what he originally derives from the omnipotent Sovereign in the former, yet it plainly appears from Scripture, that absolute power in his infernal dominions is granted to their diabolical ruler. This is indeed the only absolute power which can by Scripture be derived from heaven. If, therefore, the several tyrannies upon earth can prove any title to a Divine authority, it must be derived from this original grant to the prince of darkness; and these subordinate deputations must consequently come immediately from him whose stamp they so expressly bear.

To conclude, as the examples of all ages show us that mankind in general desire power only to do harm, and, when they obtain it, use it for no other purpose; it is not consonant with even the least degree of prudence to hazard an alteration, where our hopes are poorly kept in countenance by only two or three exceptions out of a thousand instances to alarm our fears. In this case it will be much wiser to submit to a few inconveniences arising from the dispassionate deafness of laws, than to remedy them by applying to the passionate open ears of a tyrant.

Fielding, *Tom Jones*, XII, 12

44 It is not enough to have intermediate powers in a monarchy; there must be also a depositary of the laws. This depositary can only be the judges of the supreme courts of justice, who promulgate the new laws, and revive the obsolete. The natural ignorance of the nobility, their indolence and contempt of civil government, require that there should be a body invested with the power of reviving and executing the laws, which would be otherwise buried in oblivion. The prince's council is not a proper depositary. They are naturally the depositary of the momentary will of the prince, and not of the fundamental laws. Besides, the prince's council is continually changing; it is neither permanent nor numerous; neither has it a sufficient share of the confidence of the people; consequently it is capable of setting them right in difficult conjunctures, or of reducing them to proper obedience.

Despotic governments, where there are no fundamental laws, have no such kind of depositary. Hence it is that religion has generally so much influence in those countries, because it forms a kind of permanent depositary; and if this cannot be said of religion, it may of the customs that are respected instead of laws.

Montesquieu, *Spirit of Laws*, II, 4

45 Honour is far from being the principle of despotic government: mankind being here all upon a level, no one person can prefer himself to another; and as on the other hand they are all slaves, they can give themselves no sort of preference.

Montesquieu, *Spirit of Laws*, III, 8

46 As virtue is necessary in a republic, and in a monarchy honour, so fear is necessary in a despotic government: with regard to virtue, there is no occasion for it, and honour would be extremely dangerous.

Here the immense power of the prince devolves entirely upon those whom he is pleased to entrust with the administration. Persons capable of setting a value upon themselves would be likely to create disturbances. Fear must therefore depress their spirits, and extinguish even the least sense of ambition.

Montesquieu, *Spirit of Laws* III, 9

47 Luxury is . . . absolutely necessary in monarchies; as it is also in despotic states. In the former, it is the use of liberty; in the latter, it is the abuse of servitude. A slave appointed by his master to tyrannise over other wretches of the same condition, uncertain of enjoying tomorrow the blessings of to-day, has no other felicity than that of glutting the pride, the passions, and voluptuousness of the present moment.

Montesquieu, *Spirit of Laws*, VII, 4

48 In despotic governments women do not introduce, but are themselves an object of, luxury. They must be in a state of the most rigorous servitude. Every one follows the spirit of the government, and adopts in his own family the customs he sees elsewhere established. As the laws are very severe and executed on the spot, they are afraid lest the liberty of women should expose them to danger. Their quarrels, indiscretions, repugnancies, jealousies, piques, and that art, in fine, which little souls have of interesting great ones, would be attended there with fatal consequences.

Montesquieu, *Spirit of Laws*, VII, 9

49 There are two sorts of tyranny: one real, which arises from oppression; the other is seated in opinion, and is sure to be felt whenever those who govern establish things shocking to the existing ideas of a nation.

Montesquieu, *Spirit of Laws*, XIX, 3

50 One gives the name of tyrant to the sovereign who knows no laws but those of this caprice, who takes his subjects' property, and who afterwards enrols them to go to take the property of his neighbours. There are none of these tyrants in Europe.

One distinguishes between the tyranny of one man and that of many. The tyranny of many would be that of a body which invaded the rights of other bodies, and which exercised despotism in favour of the laws corrupted by it. Nor are there any tyrants of this sort in Europe.

Under which tyranny would you like to live? Under neither; but if I had to choose, I should detest the tyranny of one man less than that of many. A despot always has his good moments; an assembly of despots never. If a tyrant does me an injustice, I can disarm him through his mistress, his confessor or his page; but a company of grave tyrants is inaccessible to all seductions. When it is not unjust, it is at the least hard, and never does it bestow favours.

Voltaire, *Philosophical Dictionary:* Tyranny

51 The strongest is never strong enough to be always the master, unless he transforms strength into right, and obedience into duty. Hence the right of the strongest, which, though to all seeming meant ironically, is really laid down as a fundamental principle. But are we never to have an explana-

tion of this phrase? Force is a physical power, and I fail to see what moral effect it can have. To yield to force is an act of necessity, not of will—at the most, an act of prudence. In what sense can it be a duty?

Suppose for a moment that this so-called "right" exists. I maintain that the sole result is a mass of inexplicable nonsense. For, if force creates right, the effect changes with the cause: every force that is greater than the first succeeds to its right. As soon as it is possible to disobey with impunity, disobedience is legitimate; and, the strongest being always in the right, the only thing that matters is to act so as to become the strongest. But what kind of right is that which perishes when force fails? If we must obey perforce, there is no need to obey because we ought; and if we are not forced to obey, we are under no obligation to do so. Clearly, the word "right" adds nothing to force: in this connection, it means absolutely nothing.

Obey the powers that be. If this means yield to force, it is a good precept, but superfluous: I can answer for its never being violated. All power comes from God, I admit; but so does all sickness: does that mean that we are forbidden to call in the doctor? A brigand surprises me at the edge of a wood: must I not merely surrender my purse on compulsion; but, even if I could withhold it, am I in conscience bound to give it up? For certainly the pistol he holds is also a power.

Let us then admit that force does not create right, and that we are obliged to obey only legitimate powers.

Rousseau, *Social Contract*, I, 3

52 A people, says Grotius, can give itself to a king. Then, according to Grotius, a people is a people before it gives itself. The gift is itself a civil act, and implies public deliberation. It would be better, before examining the act by which a people gives itself to a king, to examine that by which it has become a people; for this act, being necessarily prior to the other, is the true foundation of society.

Rousseau, *Social Contract*, I, 5

53 Kings desire to be absolute, and men are always crying out to them from afar that the best means of being so is to get themselves loved by their people. This precept is all very well, and even in some respects very true. Unfortunately, it will always be derided at court. The power which comes of a people's love is no doubt the greatest; but it is precarious and conditional, and princes will never rest content with it. The best kings desire to be in a position to be wicked, if they please, without forfeiting their mastery: political sermonisers may tell them to their hearts' content that, the people's strength being their own, their first interest is that the people should be prosperous, numerous and

formidable; they are well aware that this is untrue. Their first personal interest is that the people should be weak, wretched, and unable to resist them. I admit that, provided the subjects remained always in submission, the prince's interest would indeed be that it should be powerful, in order that its power, being his own, might make him formidable to his neighbours; but, this interest being merely secondary and subordinate, and strength being incompatible with submission, princes naturally give the preference always to the principle that is more to their immediate advantage.

Rousseau, *Social Contract*, III, 6

54 For a monarchical State to have a chance of being well governed, its population and extent must be proportionate to the abilities of its governor. It is easier to conquer than to rule.

Rousseau, *Social Contract*, III, 6

55 If, according to Plato, the "king by nature" is such a rarity, how often will nature and fortune conspire to give him a crown? And, if royal education necessarily corrupts those who receive it, what is to be hoped from a series of men brought up to reign? It is, then, wanton self-deception to confuse royal government with government by a good king. To see such government as it is in itself, we must consider it as it is under princes who are incompetent or wicked: for either they will come to the throne wicked or incompetent, or the throne will make them so.

Rousseau, *Social Contract*, III, 6

56 Instead of governing subjects to make them happy, despotism makes them wretched in order to govern them.

Rousseau, *Social Contract*, III, 8

57 *Johnson*. If a sovereign oppresses his people to a great degree, they will rise and cut off his head. There is a remedy in human nature against tyranny, that will keep us safe under every form of government.

Boswell, *Life of Johnson (Mar. 31, 1772)*

58 *Johnson*. "Why, Sir, absolute princes seldom do any harm. But they who are governed by them are governed by chance. There is no security for good government." *Cambridge*. "There have been many sad victims to absolute government." *Johnson*. "So, Sir, have there been to popular factions." *Boswell*. "The question is, which is worst, one wild beast or many?"

Boswell, *Life of Johnson (April 18, 1775)*

59 There is not a crowned head in Europe whose talents or merit would entitle him to be elected a vestryman by the people of any parish in America.

Jefferson, *Letter to Washington (May 2, 1788)*

60 I have sworn upon the altar of God, eternal hostility against every form of tyranny over the mind of man.

> Jefferson, *Letter to Benjamin Rush*
> *(Sept. 23, 1800)*

61 The obvious definition of a monarchy seems to be that of a state, in which a single person, by whatsoever name he may be distinguished, is entrusted with the execution of the laws, the management of the revenue, and the command of the army. But, unless public liberty is protected by intrepid and vigilant guardians, the authority of so formidable a magistrate will soon degenerate into despotism. The influence of the clergy, in an age of superstition, might be usefully employed to assert the rights of mankind; but so intimate is the connection between the throne and the altar, that the banner of the church has very seldom been seen on the side of the people. A martial nobility and stubborn commons, possessed of arms, tenacious of property, and collected into constitutional assemblies, form the only balance capable of preserving a free constitution against enterprises of an aspiring prince.

> Gibbon, *Decline and Fall*
> *of the Roman Empire,* III

62 Of the various forms of government which have prevailed in the world, an hereditary monarchy seems to present the fairest scope for ridicule. Is it possible to relate, without an indignant smile, that, on the father's decease, the property of a nation, like that of a drove of oxen, descends to his infant son, as yet unknown to mankind and to himself; and that the bravest warriors and the wisest statesmen, relinquishing their natural right to empire, approach the royal cradle with bended knees and protestations of inviolable fidelity? Satire and declamation may paint these obvious topics in the most dazzling colours, but our more serious thoughts will respect a useful prejudice, that establishes a rule of succession, independent of the passions of mankind; and we shall cheerfully acquiesce in any expedient which deprives the multitude of the dangerous, and indeed the ideal, power of giving themselves a master.

> Gibbon, *Decline and Fall*
> *of the Roman Empire,* VII

63 The generality of princes, if they were stripped of their purple and cast naked into the world, would immediately sink to the lowest rank of society, without a hope of emerging from their obscurity.

> Gibbon, *Decline and Fall*
> *of the Roman Empire,* XXII

64 Kings will be tyrants from policy, when subjects are rebels from principle.

> Burke, *Reflections on the Revolution in France*

65 Tyrants seldom want pretexts.

> Burke, *Letter to a Member of the National*
> *Assembly*

66 The accumulation of all powers, legislative, executive, and judiciary, in the same hands, whether of one, a few, or many, and whether hereditary, self-appointed, or elective, may justly be pronounced the very definition of tyranny.

> Madison, *Federalist 47*

67 *Salemenes.* Think'st thou there is no tyranny but that
Of blood and chains? The despotism of vice,
The weakness and the wickedness of luxury,
The negligence, the apathy, the evils
Of sensual sloth—produce ten thousand tyrants,
Whose delegated cruelty surpasses
The worst acts of one energetic master,
However harsh and hard in his own bearing.

> Byron, *Sardanapalus,* I, ii, 113

68 Strip your Louis Quatorze of his king-gear, and there *is* left nothing but a poor forked raddish with a head fantastically carved.

> Carlyle, *The Hero*
> *as Man of Letters*

69 God said, I am tired of kings,
I suffer them no more;
Up to my ear the morning brings
The outrage of the poor.

> Emerson, *Boston Hymn*

70 Even despotism does not produce its worst effects, so long as individuality exists under it; and whatever crushes individuality is despotism, by whatever name it may be called, and whether it professes to be enforcing the will of God or the injunctions of men.

> Mill, *On Liberty,* III

71 A people may prefer a free government, but if, from indolence, or carelessness, or cowardice, or want of public spirit, they are unequal to the exertions necessary for preserving it; if they will not fight for it when it is directly attacked; if they can be deluded by the artifices used to cheat them out of it; if by momentary discouragement, or temporary panic, or a fit of enthusiasm for an individual, they can be induced to lay their liberties at the feet even of a great man, or trust him with powers which enable him to subvert their institutions; in all these cases they are more or less unfit for liberty: and though it may be for their good to have had it even for a short time, they are unlikely long to enjoy it. Again, a people may be unwilling or unable to fulfil the duties which a particular form of government requires of them. A rude people, though in some degree alive to the benefits of civ-

ilised society, may be unable to practise the forbearance which it demands: their passions may be too violent, or their personal pride too exacting, to forego private conflict, and leave to the laws the avenging of their real or supposed wrongs. In such a case, a civilised government, to be really advantageous to them, will require to be in a considerable degree despotic: to be one over which they do not themselves exercise control, and which imposes a great amount of forcible restraint upon their actions.

Mill, *Representative Government,* I

72 A people in a state of savage independence, in which every one lives for himself, exempt, unless by fits, from any external control, is practically incapable of making any progress in civilisation until it has learnt to obey. The indispensable virtue, therefore, in a government which establishes itself over a people of this sort is, that it make itself obeyed. To enable it to do this, the constitution of the government must be nearly, or quite, despotic. A constitution in any degree popular, dependent on the voluntary surrender by the different members of the community of their individual freedom of action, would fail to enforce the first lesson which the pupils, in this stage of their progress, require. Accordingly, the civilisation of such tribes, when not the result of juxtaposition with others already civilised, is almost always the work of an absolute ruler.

Mill, *Representative Government,* II

73 I am far from condemning, in cases of extreme exigency, the assumption of absolute power in the form of a temporary dictatorship. Free nations have, in times of old, conferred such power by their own choice, as a necessary medicine for diseases of the body politic which could not be got rid of by less violent means. But its acceptance, even for a time strictly limited, can only be excused, if . . . the dictator employs the whole power he assumes in removing the obstacles which debar the nation from the enjoyment of freedom. A good despotism is an altogether false ideal, which practically (except as a means to some temporary purpose) becomes the most senseless and dangerous of chimeras. Evil for evil, a good despotism, in a country at all advanced in civilisation, is more noxious than a bad one; for it is far more relaxing and enervating to the thoughts, feelings, and ener-

gies of the people.

Mill, *Representative Government,* III

74 There are, as we have already seen, conditions of society in which a vigorous despotism is in itself the best mode of government for training the people in what is specifically wanting to render them capable of a higher civilisation. There are others, in which the mere fact of despotism has indeed no beneficial effect, the lessons which it teaches having already been only too completely learnt; but in which, there being no spring of spontaneous improvement in the people themselves, their almost only hope of making any steps in advance depends on the chances of a good despot. Under a native despotism, a good despot is a rare and transitory accident: but when the dominion they are under is that of a more civilised people, that people ought to be able to supply it constantly. The ruling country ought to be able to do for its subjects all that could be done by a succession of absolute monarchs, guaranteed by irresistible force against the precariousness of tenure attendant on barbarous despotisms, and qualified by their genius to anticipate all that experience has taught to the more advanced nation. Such is the ideal rule of a free people over a barbarous or semi-barbarous one. We need not expect to see that ideal realised; but unless some approach to it is, the rulers are guilty of a dereliction of the highest moral trust which can devolve upon a nation: and if they do not even aim at it, they are selfish usurpers, on a par in criminality with any of those whose ambition and rapacity have sported from age to age with the destiny of masses of mankind.

Mill, *Representative Government,* XVIII

75 By and by, when they was asleep and snoring, Jim says:

"Don't it s'prise you de way dem kings carries on, Huck?"

"No," I say, "it don't."

"Why don't it, Huck?"

"Well, it don't, because it's in the breed. I reckon they're all alike."

"But, Huck, dese kings o' ourn is reglar rapscallions; dat's jist what dey is; dey's reglar rapscallions."

"Well, that's what I'm a-saying; all kings is mostly rapscallions, as fur as I can make out."

Mark Twain, *Huckleberry Finn,* XXIII

10.7 | *Slavery*

The meaning of slavery can be summed up by the negation of liberty, equality, property, and rights. Slavery is a deprivation of freedom, the subordination of one man to another as inferior to superior, the condition of being completely propertyless because one's whole being is the property of another, and a status totally devoid of rights. The reader will, therefore, find that the discussion of slavery in this section involves notions treated elsewhere: in Section 11.1 on PROPERTY, in Section 12.3 on RIGHTS—NATURAL AND CIVIL, in Section 13.1 on FREEDOM IN SOCIETY, and in Section 13.3 on EQUALITY. The reader will also find relevant materials in Section 10.6 on DESPOTISM AND TYRANNY.

The passages quoted here define slavery; distinguish different types of slavery; contrast the economic roles of the slave and the artisan, the feudal serf, the peasant, and the proletariat; discuss the policies of masters in the treatment of their slaves; and regard the institution of slavery as one of the consequences of sin. The crucial question, however, concerns the justice of slavery.

One justification of slavery maintains that, as a matter of fact, some men are by nature slaves and, therefore, should be ruled for the benefit of those who are by nature free. Another justification applies only to those who are taken prisoners in a just war and, having forfeited their lives, can therefore be justly enslaved. Still another turns on regarding slaves as something less than human and, therefore, without human rights.

The condemnation of slavery as intrinsically unjust and a clear violation of man's natural rights to life, liberty, and the pursuit of happiness rests on the affirmation of human equality, the equality of men as men overshadowing their inequalities in all other respects. Rousseau's comment on Aristotle's doctrine of natural slavery calls attention to the central question of fact: Are those who appear to be slavish by nature merely men who have been born into slavery and have had their characters conditioned by their treatment as slaves? If, in fact, no men are by nature slaves, then Aristotle must be counted among those who condemn the enslavement of men as being contrary to nature and, therefore, unjust.

---

1 Of the children of the strangers that do sojourn among you, of them shall ye buy, and of their families that are with you, which they begat in your land; and they shall be your possession.
Leviticus 25:45

2 *Eumaios.* Zeus who views the wide world takes away
half the manhood of a man, that day
he goes into captivity and slavery.
Homer, *Odyssey,* XVII, 321

3 *Servant.* He is a poor thing who does not feel as his masters do,
grieve in their grief, be happy in their happiness.
I, though I wear the name of lackey, yet aspire
to be counted in the number of the generous

slaves, for I do not have the name of liberty
but have the heart. Better this, than for a single man
to have the double evil of an evil spirit
and to be named by those about him as a slave.
Euripides, *Helen,* 726

4 *Callicles.* The suffering of injustice is not the part of a man, but of a slave, who indeed had better die than live; since when he is wronged and trampled upon, he is unable to help himself, or any other about whom he cares.
Plato, *Gorgias,* 483A

5 *Athenian Stranger.* The right treatment of slaves is to behave properly to them, and to do to them, if possible, even more justice than to those who are

our equals; for he who naturally and genuinely reverences justice, and hates injustice, is discovered in his dealings with any class of men to whom he can easily be unjust. And he who in regard to the natures and actions of his slaves is undefiled by impiety and injustice, will best sow the seeds of virtue in them; and this may be truly said of every master, and tyrant, and to every other having authority in relation to his inferiors.

Plato, *Laws*, VI, 777B

6 Now instruments are of various sorts; some are living, others lifeless; in the rudder, the pilot of a ship has a lifeless, in the look-out man, a living instrument; for in the arts the servant is a kind of instrument. Thus, too, a possession is an instrument for maintaining life. And so, in the arrangement of the family, a slave is a living possession, and property a number of such instruments; and the servant is himself an instrument which takes precedence of all other instruments. For if every instrument could accomplish its own work, obeying or anticipating the will of others . . . if . . . the shuttle would weave and the plectrum touch the lyre without a hand to guide them, chief workmen would not want servants, nor masters slaves.

Aristotle, *Politics*, 1253ᵇ27

7 The master is only the master of the slave; he does not belong to him, whereas the slave is not only the slave of his master, but wholly belongs to him. Hence we see what is the nature and office of a slave; he who is by nature not his own but another's man, is by nature a slave; and he may be said to be another's man who, being a human being, is also a possession. And a possession may be defined as an instrument of action, separable from the possessor.

But is there any one thus intended by nature to be a slave, and for whom such a condition is expedient and right, or rather is not all slavery a violation of nature? There is no difficulty in answering this question, on grounds both of reason and of fact. For that some should rule and others be ruled is a thing not only necessary, but expedient; from the hour of their birth, some are marked out for subjection, others for rule.

Aristotle, *Politics*, 1254ᵃ12

8 We may firstly observe in living creatures both a despotical and a constitutional rule; for the soul rules the body with a despotical rule, whereas the intellect rules the appetites with a constitutional and royal rule. And it is clear that the rule of the soul over the body, and of the mind and the rational element over the passionate, is natural and expedient; whereas the equality of the two or the rule of the inferior is always hurtful. The same holds good of animals in relation to men; for tame animals have a better nature than wild, and all

tame animals are better off when they are ruled by man; for then they are preserved. Again, the male is by nature superior, and the female inferior; and the one rules, and the other is ruled; this principle, of necessity, extends to all mankind. Where then there is such a difference as that between soul and body, or between men and animals (as in the case of those whose business is to use their body, and who can do nothing better), the lower sort are by nature slaves, and it is better for them as for all inferiors that they should be under the rule of a master. For he who can be, and therefore is, another's, and he who participates in rational principle enough to apprehend, but not to have, such a principle, is a slave by nature. Whereas the lower animals cannot even apprehend a principle; they obey their instincts. And indeed the use made of slaves and of tame animals is not very different; for both with their bodies minister to the needs of life. Nature would like to distinguish between the bodies of freemen and slaves, making the one strong for servile labour, the other upright, and although useless for such services, useful for political life in the arts both of war and peace. But the opposite often happens—that some have the souls and others have the bodies of freemen. And doubtless if men differed from one another in the mere forms of their bodies as much as the statues of the Gods do from men, all would acknowledge that the inferior class should be slaves of the superior. And if this is true of the body, how much more just that a similar distinction should exist in the soul? but the beauty of the body is seen, whereas the beauty of the soul is not seen. It is clear, then, that some men are by nature free, and others slaves, and that for these latter slavery is both expedient and right.

Aristotle, *Politics*, 1254ᵇ2

9 What difference does it make how many masters a man has? Slavery is only one, and yet the person who refuses to let the thought of it affect him is a free man no matter how great the swarm of masters around him.

Seneca, *Letters to Lucilius*, 28

10 'They're slaves,' people say. No. They're human beings. 'They're slaves.' But they share the same roof as ourselves. 'They're slaves.' No, they're friends, humble friends. 'They're slaves.' Strictly speaking they're our fellow-slaves, if you once reflect that fortune has as much power over us as over them.

Seneca, *Letters to Lucilius*, 47

11 How about reflecting that the person you call your slave traces his origin back to the same stock as yourself, has the same good sky above him, breathes as you do, lives as you do, dies as you do? It is as easy for you to see in him a free-born man

as for him to see a slave in you.

Seneca, Letters to Lucilius, 47

12 Effort is free once it is towards a fully recognised good; the involuntary is, precisely, motion away from a good and towards the enforced, towards something not recognised as a good; servitude lies in being powerless to move towards one's good, being debarred from the preferred path in a menial obedience. Hence the shame of slavedom is incurred not when one is held from the hurtful but when the personal good must be yielded in favour of another's.

Plotinus, Sixth Ennead, VIII, 4

13 He did not intend that His rational creature, who was made in His image, should have dominion over anything but the irrational creation—not man over man, but man over the beasts. And hence the righteous men in primitive times were made shepherds of cattle rather than kings of men, God intending thus to teach us what the relative position of the creatures is, and what the desert of sin; for it is with justice, we believe, that the condition of slavery is the result of sin. And this is why we do not find the word "slave" in any part of Scripture until righteous Noah branded the sin of his son with this name. It is a name, therefore, introduced by sin and not by nature. The origin of the Latin word for slave is supposed to be found in the circumstance that those who by the law of war were liable to be killed were sometimes preserved by their victors, and were hence called servants. And these circumstances could never have arisen save through sin. For even when we wage a just war, our adversaries must be sinning; and every victory, even though gained by wicked men, is a result of the first judgment of God, who humbles the vanquished either for the sake of removing or of punishing their sins. Witness that man of God, Daniel, who, when he was in captivity, confessed to God his own sins and the sins of his people, and declares with pious grief that these were the cause of the captivity. The prime cause, then, of slavery is sin, which brings man under the dominion of his fellow—that which does not happen save by the judgment of God, with Whom is no unrighteousness, and Who knows how to award fit punishments to every variety of offence. But our Master in heaven says, "Every one who doeth sin is the servant of sin." And thus there are many wicked masters who have religious men as their slaves, and who are yet themselves in bondage; "for of whom a man is overcome, of the same is he brought in bondage." And beyond question it is a happier thing to be the slave of a man than of a lust; for even this very lust of ruling, to mention no others, lays waste men's hearts with the most ruthless dominion. Moreover, when men are subjected to one another in a peaceful order, the lowly position does as much good to the servant as the proud position does harm to the master. But by nature, as God first created us, no one is the slave either of man or of sin. This servitude is, however, penal, and is appointed by that law which enjoins the preservation of the natural order and forbids its disturbance; for if nothing had been done in violation of that law, there would have been nothing to restrain by penal servitude. And therefore the apostle admonishes slaves to be subject to their masters, and to serve them heartily and with good-will, so that, if they cannot be freed by their masters, they may themselves make their slavery in some sort free, by serving not in crafty fear, but in faithful love, until all unrighteousness pass away, and all principality and every human power be brought to nothing, and God be all in all.

Augustine, City of God, XIX, 15

14 Subjection is twofold. One is servile, by virtue of which a superior makes use of a subject for his own benefit, and this kind of subjection began after sin. There is another kind of subjection, which is called economic or civil, whereby the superior makes use of his subjects for their own benefit and good; and this kind of subjection existed even before sin.

Aquinas, Summa Theologica, I, 92, 1

15 A slave differs from a free man in that the latter "has the disposal of himself," as is stated in the beginning of [Aristotle's] Metaphysics, but a slave is ordered to another. So that one man is master of another as his slave when he refers the one whose master he is, to his own—namely, the master's, use. And since every man's proper good is desirable to himself, and consequently it is a grievous matter to anyone to yield to another what ought to be one's own, therefore such dominion implies of necessity a pain inflicted on the subject. And therefore in the state of innocence such a mastership could not have existed between man and man.

Aquinas, Summa Theologica, I, 96, 4

16 The master of the servant is master also of all he hath, and may exact the use thereof; that is to say, of his goods, of his labour, of his servants, and of his children, as often as he shall think fit. For he holdeth his life of his master by the covenant of obedience; that is, of owning and authorising whatsoever the master shall do. And in case the master, if he refuse, kill him, or cast him into bonds, or otherwise punish him for his disobedience, he is himself the author of the same, and cannot accuse him of injury.

Hobbes, Leviathan, II, 20

17 Freedom from absolute, arbitrary power is so necessary to, and closely joined with, a man's preservation, that he cannot part with it but by what

forfeits his preservation and life together. For a man, not having the power of his own life, cannot by compact or his own consent enslave himself to any one, nor put himself under the absolute, arbitrary power of another to take away his life when he pleases. Nobody can give more power than he has himself, and he that cannot take away his own life cannot give another power over it. . . .

The perfect condition of slavery . . . is nothing else but the state of war continued between a lawful conqueror and a captive, for if once compact enter between them, and make an agreement for a limited power on the one side, and obedience on the other, the state of war and slavery ceases as long as the compact endures; for, as has been said, no man can by agreement pass over to another that which he hath not in himself—a power over his own life.

Locke, *II Civil Government*, IV, 22–23

18 There is another sort of servant which by a peculiar name we call slaves, who being captives taken in a just war are, by the right of Nature, subjected to the absolute dominion and arbitrary power of their masters. These men having, as I say, forfeited their lives and, with it, their liberties, and lost their estates, and being in the state of slavery, not capable of any property, cannot in that state be considered as any part of civil society, the chief end whereof is the preservation of property.

Locke, *II Civil Government*, VII, 85

19 Slavery, properly so called, is the establishment of a right which gives to one man such a power over another as renders him absolute master of his life and fortune. The state of slavery is in its own nature bad. It is neither useful to the master nor to the slave; not to the slave, because he can do nothing through a motive of virtue; nor to the master, because by having an unlimited authority over his slaves he insensibly accustoms himself to the want of all moral virtues, and thence becomes fierce, hasty, severe, choleric, voluptuous, and cruel.

Montesquieu, *Spirit of Laws*, XV, 1

20 Were I to vindicate our right to make slaves of the negroes, these should be my arguments:

The Europeans, having extirpated the Americans, were obliged to make slaves of the Africans, for clearing such vast tracts of land.

Sugar would be too dear if the plants which produce it were cultivated by any other than slaves.

These creatures are all over black, and with such a flat nose that they can scarcely be pitied.

It is hardly to be believed that God, who is a wise Being, should place a soul, especially a good soul, in such a black ugly body.

It is so natural to look upon colour as the criterion of human nature, that the Asiatics, among whom eunuchs are employed, always deprive the blacks of their resemblance to us by a more opprobrious distinction.

The colour of the skin may be determined by that of the hair, which, among the Egyptians, the best philosophers in the world, was of such importance that they put to death all the red-haired men who fell into their hands.

The negroes prefer a glass necklace to that gold which polite nations so highly value. Can there be a greater proof of their wanting common sense?

It is impossible for us to suppose these creatures to be men, because, allowing them to be men, a suspicion would follow that we ourselves are not Christians.

Weak minds exaggerate too much the wrong done to the Africans. For were the case as they state it, would the European powers, who make so many needless conventions among themselves, have failed to enter into a general one, in behalf of humanity and compassion?

Montesquieu, *Spirit of Laws*, XV, 5

21 In moderate governments it is a point of the highest importance that there should not be a great number of slaves. The political liberty of those states adds to the value of civil liberty; and he who is deprived of the latter is also bereft of the former. He sees the happiness of a society, of which he is not so much as a member; he sees the security of others fenced by laws, himself without any protection. He perceives that his master has a soul, capable of enlarging itself: while his own labours under a continual depression. Nothing more assimilates a man to a beast than living among freedmen, himself a slave. Such people as these are natural enemies of society; and their number must be dangerous.

Montesquieu, *Spirit of Laws*, XV, 12

22 Man is born free; and everywhere he is in chains. One thinks himself the master of others, and still remains a greater slave than they.

Rousseau, *Social Contract*, I, 2

23 Aristotle . . . had said that men are by no means equal naturally, but that some are born for slavery, and others for dominion.

Aristotle was right; but he took the effect for the cause. Nothing can be more certain than that every man born in slavery is born for slavery. Slaves lose everything in their chains, even the desire of escaping from them: they love their servitude, as the comrades of Ulysses loved their brutish condition. If then there are slaves by nature, it is because there have been slaves against nature. Force made the first slaves, and their cowardice perpetuated the condition.

Rousseau, *Social Contract*, I, 2

24 The right of conquest has no foundation other

than the right of the strongest. If war does not give the conqueror the right to massacre the conquered peoples, the right to enslave them cannot be based upon a right which does not exist. No one has a right to kill an enemy except when he cannot make him a slave, and the right to enslave him cannot therefore be derived from the right to kill him. It is accordingly an unfair exchange to make him buy at the price of his liberty his life, over which the victor holds no right. Is it not clear that there is a vicious circle in founding the right of life and death on the right of slavery, and the right of slavery on the right of life and death?

Rousseau, *Social Contract,* I, 4

25 Is liberty maintained only by the help of slavery? It may be so. Extremes meet. Everything that is not in the course of nature has its disadvantages, civil society most of all. There are some unhappy circumstances in which we can only keep our liberty at others' expense, and where the citizen can be perfectly free only when the slave is most a slave. Such was the case with Sparta. As for you, modern peoples, you have no slaves, but you are slaves yourselves; you pay for their liberty with your own. It is in vain that you boast of this preference; I find in it more cowardice than humanity.

I do not mean by all this that it is necessary to have slaves, or that the right of slavery is legitimate: I am merely giving the reasons why modern peoples, believing themselves to be free, have representatives, while ancient peoples had none. In any case, the moment a people allows itself to be represented, it is no longer free: it no longer exists.

Rousseau, *Social Contract,* III, 15

26 After supper I accompanied him [Johnson] to his apartment, and at my request he dictated to me an argument in favour of the negro who was then claiming his liberty, in an action in the Court of Session in Scotland. He had always been very zealous against slavery in every form, in which I, with all deference, thought that he discovered "a zeal without knowledge." Upon one occasion, when in company with some very grave men at Oxford, his toast was, "Here's to the next insurrection of the negroes in the West Indies." His violent prejudice against our West Indian and American settlers appeared whenever there was an opportunity. Towards the conclusion of his *Taxation no Tyranny,* he says, "how is it that we hear the loudest *yelps* for liberty among the drivers of negroes?" . . .

The argument dictated by Dr. Johnson was as follows:—

"It must be agreed that in most ages many countries have had part of their inhabitants in a state of slavery; yet it may be doubted whether slavery can ever be supposed the natural condition of man. It is impossible not to conceive that men in their original state were equal; and very difficult to imagine how one would be subjected to another but by violent compulsion. An individual may, indeed, forfeit his liberty by a crime; but he cannot by that crime forfeit the liberty of his children. What is true of a criminal seems true likewise of a captive. A man may accept life from a conquering enemy on condition of perpetual servitude; but it is very doubtful whether he can entail that servitude on his descendants; for no man can stipulate without commission for another. The condition which he himself accepts, his son or grandson perhaps would have rejected. If we should admit, what perhaps may with more reason be denied, that there are certain relations between man and man which may make slavery necessary and just, yet it can never be proved that he who is now suing for his freedom ever stood in any of those relations. He is certainly subject by no law, but that of violence, to his present master; who pretends no claim to his obedience, but that he bought him from a merchant of slaves, whose right to sell him never was examined. . . . The sum of the argument is this:—No man is by nature the property of another: The defendant is, therefore, by nature free: The rights of nature must be some way forfeited before they can be justly taken away: That the defendant has by any act forfeited the rights of nature we require to be proved; and if no proof of such forfeiture can be given, we doubt not but the justice of the court will declare him free."

I record Dr. Johnson's argument fairly upon this particular case; where, perhaps, he was in the right. But I beg leave to enter my most solemn protest against his general doctrine with respect to the *Slave Trade.* For I will resolutely say—that his unfavourable notion of it was owing to prejudice, and imperfect or false information. The wild and dangerous attempt which has for some time been persisted in to obtain an act of our Legislature, to abolish so very important and necessary a branch of commercial interest, must have been crushed at once, had not the insignificance of the zealots who vainly took the lead in it, made the vast body of Planters, Merchants, and others, whose immense properties are involved in that trade, reasonably enough suppose that there could be no danger. The encouragement which the attempt has received excites my wonder and indignation: and though some men of superiour abilities have supported it; whether from a love of temporary popularity, when prosperous; or a love of general mischief, when desperate, my opinion is unshaken. To abolish a *status,* which in all ages GOD has sanctioned, and man has continued, would not only be *robbery* to an innumerable class of our fellow-subjects; but it would be extreme cruelty to the African Savages, a portion of whom it saves from massacre, or intolerable bondage in their own country, and introduces into a much happier state of life; especially now when their passage to the West Indies and their treatment there is humanely regulated. To abolish that trade would be to —*shut the gates of mercy on mankind.*

Boswell, *Life of Johnson (Sept. 23, 1777)*

27 There must doubtless be an unhappy influence on the manners of our people produced by the existence of slavery among us. The whole commerce between master and slave is a perpetual exercise of the most boisterous passions, the most unremitting despotism on the one part, and degrading submissions on the other. Our children see this, and learn to imitate it; for man is an imitative animal. This quality is the germ of all education in him. From his cradle to his grave he is learning to do what he sees others do. If a parent could find no motive either in his philanthropy or his self-love, for restraining the intemperance of passion towards his slave, it should always be a sufficient one that his child is present. But generally it is not sufficient. The parent storms, the child looks on, catches the lineaments of wrath, puts on the same airs in the circle of smaller slaves, gives a loose to the worst of passions, and thus nursed, educated, and daily exercised in tyranny, cannot but be stamped by it with odious peculiarities. The man must be a prodigy who can retain his manners and morals undepraved by such circumstances. And with what execration should the statesman be loaded, who, permitting one half the citizens thus to trample on the rights of the other, transforms those into despots, and these into enemies, destroys the morals of the one part, and the *amor patriae* of the other. For if a slave can have a country in this world, it must be any other in preference to that in which he is born to live and labor for another; in which he must lock up the faculties of his nature, contribute as far as depends on his individual endeavors to the evanishment of the human race, or entail his own miserable condition on the endless generations proceeding from him. With the morals of the people, their industry also is destroyed. For in a warm climate, no man will labor for himself who can make another labor for him. This is so true, that of the proprietors of slaves a very small proportion indeed are ever seen to labor. And can the liberties of a nation be thought secure when we have removed their only firm basis, a conviction in the minds of the people that these liberties are of the gift of God? That they are not to be violated but with his wrath? Indeed I tremble for my country when I reflect that God is just; that his justice cannot sleep forever; that considering numbers, nature and natural means only, a revolution of the wheel of fortune, an exchange of situation is among possible events; that it may become probable by supernatural interference! The Almighty has no attribute which can take side with us in such a contest.

Jefferson, *Notes on Virginia*, XVIII

28 In the free states of antiquity the domestic slaves were exposed to the wanton rigour of despotism. The perfect settlement of the Roman empire was preceded by ages of violence and rapine. The slaves consisted, for the most part, of barbarian captives, taken in thousands by the chance of war, purchased at a vile price, accustomed to a life of independence, and impatient to break and to revenge their fetters. Against such internal enemies, whose desperate insurrections had more than once reduced the republic to the brink of destruction, the most severe regulations, and the most cruel treatment, seemed almost justified by the great law of self-preservation. But when the principal nations of Europe, Asia, and Africa, were united under the laws of one sovereign, the source of foreign supplies flowed with much less abundance, and the Romans were reduced to the milder but more tedious method of propagation. In their numerous families, and particularly in their country estates, they encouraged the marriage of their slaves. The sentiments of nature, the habits of education, and the possession of a dependent species of property, contributed to alleviate the hardships of servitude. The existence of a slave became an object of greater value, and though his happiness still depended on the temper and circumstances of the master, the humanity of the latter, instead of being restrained by fear, was encouraged by the sense of his own interest. The progress of manners was accelerated by the virtue or policy of the emperors; and by the edicts of Hadrian and the Antonines, the protection of the laws was extended to the most abject part of mankind. The jurisdiction of life and death over the slaves, a power long exercised and often abused, was taken out of private hands, and reserved to the magistrates alone. The subterraneous prisons were abolished; and, upon a just complaint of intolerable treatment, the injured slave obtained either his deliverance, or a less cruel master.

Gibbon, *Decline and Fall of the Roman Empire*, II

29 No individual in the state can indeed be entirely without dignity; for he has at least that of being a citizen, except when he has lost his civil status by a crime. As a criminal he is still maintained in life, but he is made the mere instrument of the will of another, whether it be the state or a particular citizen. In the latter position, in which he could only be placed by a juridical judgement, he would practically become a *slave,* and would belong as property to another, who would be not merely his master but his owner. Such an owner would be entitled to exchange or alienate him as a thing, to use him at will except for shameful purposes, and to *dispose of his powers,* but not of his life and members. No one can bind himself to such a condition of dependence, as he would thereby cease to be a person, and it is only as a person that

he can make a contract.

Kant, *Science of Right,* 49

30 Even if by committing a crime [a person] has *personally* become subjected to another, this subject-condition does not become *hereditary;* for he has only brought it upon himself by his own wrong-doing. Neither can one who has been begotten by a slave be claimed as property on the ground of the cost of his rearing, because such rearing is an absolute duty naturally incumbent upon parents; and in case the parents are slaves, it devolves upon their masters or owners, who, in undertaking the possession of such subjects, have also made themselves responsible for the performance of their duties.

Kant, *Science of Right,* 49

31 Let the case of the slaves be considered, as it is in truth, a peculiar one. Let the compromising expedient of the Constitution be mutually adopted, which regards them as inhabitants, but as debased by servitude below the equal level of free inhabitants; which regards the slave as divested of two-fifths of the man.

Hamilton or Madison, *Federalist 54*

32 To adhere to man's absolute freedom—one aspect of the matter—is *eo ipso* to condemn slavery. Yet if a man is a slave, his own will is responsible for his slavery, just as it is its will which is responsible if a people is subjugated. Hence the wrong of slavery lies at the door not simply of enslavers or conquerors but of the slaves and the conquered themselves. Slavery occurs in man's transition from the state of nature to genuinely ethical conditions; it occurs in a world where a wrong is still right. At that stage wrong has validity and so is necessarily in place.

Hegel, *Philosophy of Right,* Additions,
Par. 57

33 Mr. [Henry] Clay said to me: "In our Southern states there are a great many districts where white people cannot get acclimatized and where the blacks live and prosper. I imagine that in time the black population of the South, as it becomes free, will concentrate in that portion of the American territory, and the white population, on the other hand, will gradually move out. In that way a population will be formed entirely descended from the Africans, which will be able to have its own nationality and to enjoy its own laws. I can see no other solution to the great question of slavery. I do not think that the blacks will ever mingle sufficiently completely with the white to form a single people with them. The introduction of this foreign race is anyhow the one great plague of America."

Tocqueville, *Journey to America*
(Sept. 18, 1831)

34 Interview with Mr. [John Quincy] Adams (the former President). . . .

Do you look on slavery as a great plague for the United States?

Yes, certainly. That is the root of almost all the troubles of the present and fears for the future.

Do the Southerners realize that state of affairs?

Yes, at the bottom of their hearts. But it is a truth that they will not admit, although they are clearly preoccupied about it. Slavery has altered the whole state of society in the South. There the whites form a class to themselves which has all the ideas, all the passions, all the prejudices of an aristocracy. But do not be mistaken; nowhere is equality between the whites so complete as in the South. Here we have great equality before the law, but it simply does not affect our ways of life. There are upper classes and working classes. Every white man in the South is an equally privileged being whose destiny it is to make the Negroes work without working himself. You cannot conceive how far the idea that work is shameful has entered into the spirit of the Americans of the South. Any undertaking in which the Negroes cannot serve in a subordinate role is sure not to succeed in that part of the Union. All those who trade in a large way in Charleston and the towns have come from New England.

I remember a Southern congressman who was dining with me in Washington, and who could not conceal his surprise at seeing white servants serving us at table. He said to Mrs. Adams: "I feel that it is degrading the human race to have white men for servants. When one of them comes to change my plate, I am always tempted to offer him my place at table." From the idleness in which the whites in the South live spring great differences in their character. They devote themselves to bodily exercises, to hunting and races. They are strongly built, brave, and very honorable; they are more touchy about "points of honor" than people anywhere else; duels are frequent.

Do you think that actually it is impossible to do without Negroes in the South?

I am convinced to the contrary. Europeans cultivate the land in Greece and in Sicily; why should they not do so in Virginia or the Carolinas? It is not hotter there.

Is the number of slaves increasing?

It is diminishing in all the provinces to the east of the Delaware because there wheat and tobacco are grown, and for those crops Negroes are more hindrance than help. So they are sent from there to the provinces where cotton and sugar are grown; in those provinces their numbers increase. In the states of the West where they have been introduced, their numbers remain small.

Tocqueville, *Journey to America (Oct. 1, 1831)*

35 I hold that, in the present state of civilization,

where two races of different origin and distinguished by color and other physical differences, as well as intellectual, are brought together, the relation now existing in the slaveholding states between the two is, instead of an evil, a good—a positive good. I feel myself called upon to speak freely upon the subject, where the honor and interests of those I represent are involved. I hold, then, that there never has yet existed a wealthy and civilized society in which one portion of the community did not, in point of fact, live on the labor of the other. Broad and general as is this assertion, it is fully borne out by history.

J. C. Calhoun, *Speech on the Reception of Abolitionist Petitions (Feb. 1837)*

36 If you put a chain around the neck of a slave, the other end fastens itself around your own.

Emerson, *Compensation*

37 What of it, if some old hunks of a sea-captain orders me to get a broom and sweep down the decks? What does that indignity amount to, weighed, I mean, in the scales of the New Testament? Who is not a slave? Tell me that. Well, then, however the old sea-captains may order me about—however they may thump and punch me about, I have the satisfaction of knowing that it is all right: that everybody else is one way or other served in much the same way—either in a physical or metaphysical point of view, that is; and so the universal thump is passed round, and all hands should rub each other's shoulder-blades, and be content.

Melville, *Moby Dick*, I

38 Although volume upon volume is written to prove slavery a very good thing, we never hear of the man who wishes to take the good of it, by being a slave himself.

Lincoln, *Fragment on Slavery (July 1, 1854)*

39 If A can prove, however conclusively, that he may of right enslave B, why may not B snatch the same argument and prove equally that he may enslave A?

You say A is white, and B is black. It is color, then; the lighter having the right to enslave the darker? Take care. By this rule, you are to be slave to the first man you meet with a fairer skin than your own.

You do not mean color exactly? You mean the whites are intellectually the superiors of the blacks, and therefore have the right to enslave them? Take care again. By this rule, you are to be slave to the first man you meet with an intellect superior to your own.

But, say you, it is a question of interest; and if you can make it your interest, you have the right to enslave another. Very well. And if he can make

it his interest, he has the right to enslave you.

Lincoln, *Fragment on Slavery (July 1, 1854)*

40 If we shall suppose that American slavery is one of those offenses which, in the providence of God, must needs come, but which, having continued through His appointed time, He now wills to remove, and that He gives to both North and South this terrible war as the woe due to those by whom the offense came, shall we discern therein any departure from those divine attributes which the believers in a living God always ascribe to Him? Fondly do we hope—fervently do we pray—that this mighty scourge of war may speedily pass away. Yet, if God wills that it continue, until all the wealth piled by the bondman's two hundred and fifty years of unrequited toil shall be sunk, and until every drop of blood drawn with the lash shall be paid by another drawn with the sword, as was said three thousand years ago, so still it must be said "the judgments of the Lord are true and righteous altogether."

Lincoln, *Second Inaugural Address*

41 In slave labour, even that part of the working day in which the slave is only replacing the value of his own means of existence, in which, therefore, in fact, he works for himself alone, appears as labour for his master. All the slave's labour appears as unpaid labour.

Marx, *Capital*, Vol. I, VI, 19

42 In this and most other civilised countries . . . an engagement by which a person should sell himself, or allow himself to be sold, as a slave, would be null and void; neither enforced by law nor by opinion. The ground for thus limiting his power of voluntarily disposing of his own lot in life, is apparent, and is very clearly seen in this extreme case. The reason for not interfering, unless for the sake of others, with a person's voluntary acts, is consideration for his liberty. His voluntary choice is evidence that what he so chooses is desirable, or at least endurable, to him, and his good is on the whole best provided for by allowing him to take his own means of pursuing it. But by selling himself for a slave, he abdicates his liberty; he foregoes any future use of it beyond that single act. He therefore defeats, in his own case, the very purpose which is the justification of allowing him to dispose of himself. He is no longer free; but is thenceforth in a position which has no longer the presumption in its favour, that would be afforded by his voluntarily remaining in it. The principle of freedom cannot require that he should be free not to be free. It is not freedom to be allowed to alienate his freedom.

Mill, *On Liberty*, V

43 All mankind is divided, as it was at all times and is still, into slaves and freemen; for whoever has

not two-thirds of his day for himself is a slave, be he otherwise whatever he likes, statesman, merchant, official, or scholar.

Nietzsche, *Human, All-Too-Human,* 283

44 In the relation of master to slave the master does not make a point of the need that he has for the other; he has in his grasp the power of satisfying this need through his own action; whereas the slave, in his dependent condition, his hope and fear, is quite conscious of the need he has for his master. Even if the need is at bottom equally urgent for both, it always works in favor of the oppressor and against the oppressed.

Simone de Beauvoir, *The Second Sex,* Intro.

10.8 | *Classes and Class Conflict*

The notion of the class struggle or class conflict was not invented by Karl Marx, though it is often attributed to him, as is also the conception of a classless society. The reader will find a passage from the *Republic* in which Plato declares that there are two cities, not one, the city of the rich and the city of the poor; and they are forever in conflict with one another. The reader will also find a statement by Aristotle setting forth his conception of the ideal polity as one that approximates classlessness through the overwhelming preponderance of a middle class, neither rich nor poor.

Toynbee's observation that war and class are the twin evils that have plagued all historic civilizations and brought their downfall is corroborated by much that is said in the quotations gathered below. Among the class divisions mentioned, the two that have exerted the greatest divisiveness upon society are, first, the chasm that separates the haves from the have-nots, the rich from the poor, the propertied class from the unpropertied; and the second, the one that sets a ruling class apart from a subject class, those with political power and privileges and those excluded from active participation in political life.

The acceptance of class divisions and class conflict is not confined to the ancients. The reader will find it in quotations drawn from Montesquieu, Rousseau, and even from Thomas Jefferson, who, in proposing an educational system for Virginia, thought of the children as divided into those who were destined for labor and those who were destined for leisure and learning. The reader will also find a quotation from the tenth *Federalist* paper, in which Madison argues that since factions and factional conflict cannot be eliminated from society, the best we can hope to do is to find ways of remedying or attenuating their baneful effects.

A class-structured society promotes and preserves inequalities of treatment, status, and opportunity. Hence those who advocate a universal equality of conditions favor the ideal of a classless society. For other relevant discussion, the reader is referred to Section 11.2 on Wealth and Poverty, Section 13.3 on Equality, Section 10.4 on Government of and by the People: Republic and Democracy, and Section 10.9 on Revolution.

1 *Theseus.* The classes of citizens are three. The rich
Are useless, always lusting after more.
Those who have not, and live in want, are a men-
ace,
Ridden with envy and fooled by demagogues;
Their malice stings the owners. Of the three,
The middle part saves cities: it guards the order
A community establishes.

Euripides, *Suppliant Women,* 238

2 Any city, however small, is in fact divided into
two, one the city of the poor, the other of the rich;
these are at war with one another; and in either
there are many smaller divisions, and you would
be altogether beside the mark if you treated them
all as a single State.

Plato, *Republic,* IV, 422B

3 The city of Hippodamus was composed of 10,000
citizens divided into three parts,—one of artisans,
one of husbandmen, and a third of armed defenders of the state. He also divided the land into three
parts, one sacred, one public, the third private:—
the first was set apart to maintain the customary
worship of the gods, the second was to support the
warriors, the third was the property of the husbandmen.

Aristotle, *Politics,* 1267ᵇ30

4 States . . . are composed, not of one, but of many
elements. One element is the food-producing
class, who are called husbandmen; a second, the
class of mechanics who practise the arts without
which a city cannot exist;—of these arts some are
absolutely necessary, others contribute to luxury
or to the grace of life. The third class is that of
traders, and by traders I mean those who are engaged in buying and selling, whether in commerce or in retail trade. A fourth class is that of
the serfs or labourers. The warriors make up the
fifth class, and they are as necessary as any of the
others, if the country is not to be the slave of every
invader.

Aristotle, *Politics,* 1290ᵇ38

5 All claim to possess political ability, and think
that they are quite competent to fill most offices.
But the same persons cannot be rich and poor at
the same time. For this reason the rich and the
poor are regarded in an especial sense as parts of a
state. Again, because the rich are generally few in
number, while the poor are many, they appear to
be antagonistic, and as the one or the other prevails they form the government. Hence arises the
common opinion that there are two kinds of government—democracy and oligarchy.

Aristotle, *Politics,* 1291ᵇ5

6 The best political community is formed by citizens of the middle class, and . . . those states are
likely to be well-administered, in which the middle class is large, and stronger if possible than
both the other classes, or at any rate than either
singly; for the addition of the middle class turns
the scale, and prevents either of the extremes from
being dominant. Great then is the good fortune of
a state in which the citizens have a moderate and
sufficient property; for where some possess much,
and the others nothing, there may arise an extreme democracy, or a pure oligarchy; or a tyranny may grow out of either extreme,—either out of
the most rampant democracy, or out of an oligarchy; but it is not so likely to arise out of the
middle constitutions and those akin to them.

Aristotle, *Politics,* 1295ᵇ35

7 Every kingdom divided against itself is brought to
desolation; and every city or house divided
against itself shall not stand.

Matthew 12:25

8 Of all his measures the most commended was his
distribution of the people by their trades into
companies or guilds; for as the city consisted, or
rather did not consist of, but was divided into, two
different tribes, the diversity between which could
not be effaced and in the meantime prevented all
unity and caused perpetual tumult and ill-blood,
reflecting how hard substances that do not readily
mix when in the lump may, by being beaten into
powder, in that minute form be combined, he
[Numa Pompilius] resolved to divide the whole
population into a number of small divisions, and
thus hoped, by introducing other distinctions, to
obliterate the original and great distinction,
which would be lost among the smaller. So, distinguishing the whole people by the several arts and
trades, he formed the companies of musicians,
goldsmiths, carpenters, dyers, shoemakers, skin-
ners, braziers, and potters; and all other handicraftsmen he composed and reduced into a single
company, appointing every one their proper
courts, councils, and religious observances. In this
manner all factious distinctions began, for the first
time, to pass out of use, no person any longer
being either thought of or spoken of under the
notion of a Sabine or a Roman, a Romulian or a
Tatian; and the new division became a source of
general harmony and intermixture.

Plutarch, *Numa Pompilius*

9 The Athenians, now the Cylonian sedition was
over and the polluted gone into banishment, fell
into their old quarrels about the government,
there being as many different parties as there
were diversities in the country. The Hill quarter
favoured democracy, the Plain, oligarchy, and
those that lived by the Seaside stood for a mixed
sort of government, and so hindered either of the
other parties from prevailing. And the disparity of
fortune between the rich and the poor, at that
time, also reached its height; so that the city
seemed to be in a truly dangerous condition, and

no other means for freeing it from disturbances and settling it to be possible but a despotic power. All the people were indebted to the rich; and either they tilled their land for their creditors, paying them a sixth part of the increase, and were, therefore, called Hectemorii and Thetes, or else they engaged their body for the debt, and might be seized, and either sent into slavery at home, or sold to strangers; some (for no law forbade it) were forced to sell their children, or fly their country to avoid the cruelty of their creditors; but the most part and the bravest of them began to combine together and encourage one another to stand to it, to choose a leader, to liberate the condemned debtors, divide the land, and change the government.

Plutarch, *Solon*

10 *Don Quixote*. All the Lineages and Descents of Mankind, are reduceable to these four Heads: First, Of those, who from a very small and obscure Beginning, have rais'd themselves to a spreading and prodigious Magnitude. Secondly, Of those who deriving their Greatness from a noble Spring, still preserve the Dignity and Character of their original Splendor. A Third, Are those who, though they had large Foundations, have ended in a Point like a Pyramid, which by little and little dwindle as it were into nothing, or next to nothing, in comparison of its Basis. Others there are (and those are the Bulk of Mankind) who have neither had a good Beginning, nor a rational Continuance, and whose Ending shall therefore be obscure; such are the common People, the *Plebeian* Race. The *Ottoman* Family is an Instance of the first Sort, having deriv'd their present Greatness from the poor Beginning of a base-born Shepherd. Of the second Sort, there are many Princes who being born such, enjoy their Dominions by Inheritance, and leave them to their Successors without Addition or Dimunution. Of the third Sort, there is an infinite Number of Examples; for all the *Pharaohs* and *Ptolomies* of *Egypt*, your *Caesars* of *Rome*, and all the Swarm (if I may use that Word) of Princes, Monarchs, Lords, *Medes, Assyrians, Persians, Greeks* and *Barbarians*: All these Families and Empires have ended in a Point, as well as those who gave rise to 'em: for it were impossible at this Day to find any of their Descendants, or if we cou'd find 'em, it would be in a poor groveling Condition. As for the Vulgar, I say nothing of 'em, more than that they are thrown in as Cyphers to increase the Number of Mankind, without deserving any other Praise.

Cervantes, *Don Quixote*, II, 6

11 There are four classes of men who pay the debts of the state: the proprietors of the land, those engaged in trade, the labourers and artificers, and, in fine, the annuitants either of the state or of private people. Of these four classes the last, in a case of necessity one would imagine, ought least to be spared, because it is a class entirely passive, while the state is supported by the active vigour of the other three. But as it cannot be higher taxed, without destroying the public confidence, of which the state in general and these three classes in particular have the utmost need; as a breach in the public faith cannot be made on a certain number of subjects without seeming to be made on all; as the class of creditors is always the most exposed to the projects of ministers, and always in their eye, and under their immediate inspection, the state is obliged to give them a singular protection, that the part which is indebted may never have the least advantage over that which is the creditor.

Montesquieu, *Spirit of Laws*, XXII, 18

12 Every political society is composed of other smaller societies of different kinds, each of which has its interests and its rules of conduct: but those societies which everybody perceives, because they have an external and authorised form, are not the only ones that actually exist in the State: all individuals who are united by a common interest compose as many others, either transitory or permanent, whose influence is none the less real because it is less apparent, and the proper observation of whose various relations is the true knowledge of public morals and manners. The influence of all these tacit or formal associations causes, by the influence of their will, as many different modifications of the public will. The will of these particular societies has always two relations; for the members of the association, it is a general will; for the great society, it is a particular will; and it is often right with regard to the first object, and wrong as to the second. An individual may be a devout priest, a brave soldier, or a zealous senator, and yet a bad citizen. A particular resolution may be advantageous to the smaller community, but pernicious to the greater. It is true that particular societies being always subordinate to the general society in preference to others, the duty of a citizen takes precedence of that of a senator, and a man's duty, of that of a citizen: but unhappily personal interest is always found in inverse ratio to duty, and increases in proportion as the association grows narrower, and the engagement less sacred; which irrefragably proves that the most general will is always the most just also, and that the voice of the people is in fact the voice of God.

Rousseau, *Political Economy*

13 It is on the middle classes alone that the whole force of the law is exerted; they are equally powerless against the treasures of the rich and the penury of the poor. The first mocks them, the second escapes them. The one breaks the meshes, the other passes through them.

Rousseau, *Political Economy*

14 Are not all the advantages of society for the rich and powerful? Are not all lucrative posts in their hands? Are not all privileges and exemptions reserved for them alone? Is not the public authority always on their side? If a man of eminence robs his creditors, or is guilty of other knaveries, is he not always assured of impunity? Are not the assaults, acts of violence, assassinations, and even murders committed by the great, matters that are hushed up in a few months, and of which nothing more is thought? But if a great man himself is robbed or insulted, the whole police force is immediately in motion, and woe even to innocent persons who chance to be suspected. If he has to pass through any dangerous road, the country is up in arms to escort him. If the axle-tree of his chaise breaks, everybody flies to his assistance. If there is a noise at his door, he speaks but a word, and all is silent. If he is incommoded by the crowd, he waves his hand and every one makes way. If his coach is met on the road by a wagon, his servants are ready to beat the driver's brains out, and fifty honest pedestrians going quietly about their business had better be knocked on the head than an idle jackanapes be delayed in his coach. Yet all this respect costs him not a farthing: it is the rich man's right, and not what he buys with his wealth. How different is the case of the poor man! the more humanity owes him, the more society denies him. Every door is shut against him, even when he has a right to its being opened: and if ever he obtains justice, it is with much greater difficulty than others obtain favours. If the militia is to be raised or the highway to be mended, he is always given the preference; he always bears the burden which his richer neighbour has influence enough to get exempted from. On the least accident that happens to him, everybody avoids him: if his cart be overturned in the road, so far is he from receiving any assistance, that he is lucky if he does not get horse-whipped by the impudent lackeys of some young Duke; in a word, all gratuitous assistance is denied to the poor when they need it, just because they cannot pay for it. I look upon any poor man as totally undone, if he has the misfortune to have an honest heart, a fine daughter, and a powerful neighbour.

Rousseau, *Political Economy*

15 I mentioned that old Mr. Sheridan complained of the ingratitude of Mr. Wedderburne and General Fraser, who had been much obliged to him when they were young Scotchmen entering upon life in England. *Johnson.* "Why, Sir, a man is very apt to complain of the ingratitude of those who have risen far above him. A man when he gets into a higher sphere, into other habits of life, cannot keep up all his former connections. Then, Sir, those who knew him formerly upon a level with themselves, may think that they ought still to be treated as on a level, which cannot be; and an acquaintance in a former situation may bring out things which it would be very disagreeable to have mentioned before higher company, though, perhaps, every body knows of them." He placed this subject in a new light to me, and shewed that a man who has risen in the world, must not be condemned too harshly for being distant to former acquaintance, even though he may have been much obliged to them. It is, no doubt, to be wished that a proper degree of attention should be shewn by great men to their early friends. But if either from obtuse insensibility to difference of situation, or presumptuous forwardness, which will not submit even to an exterior observance of it, the dignity of high place cannot be preserved, when they are admitted into the company of those raised above the state in which they once were, encroachment must be repelled, and the kinder feelings sacrificed.

Boswell, *Life of Johnson (Mar. 28, 1776)*

16 Men may live together in society with some tolerable degree of security, though there is no civil magistrate to protect them from the injustice of those passions. But avarice and ambition in the rich, in the poor the hatred of labour and the love of present ease and enjoyment, are the passions which prompt to invade property, passions much more steady in their operation, and much more universal in their influence.

Adam Smith, *Wealth of Nations*, V, 1

17 Civil government, so far as it is instituted for the security of property, is in reality instituted for the defence of the rich against the poor, or of those who have some property against those who have none at all.

Adam Smith, *Wealth of Nations*, V, 1

18 At the discharging of the pupils from the elementary schools, the two classes separate—those destined for labor will engage in the business of agriculture or enter into apprenticeships to such handicraft art as may be their choice; their companions, destined to the pursuits of science, will proceed to the college, which will consist first of general schools and second of professional schools. The general schools will constitute the second grade of education.

The learned class may still be subdivided into two sections; first, those who are destined for learned professions, as a means of livelihood; and second, the wealthy, who, possessing independent fortunes, may aspire to share in conducting the affairs of the nation or to live with usefulness and respect in the private ranks of life. Both of these sections will require instruction in all the higher branches of science; the wealthy to qualify them for either public or private life; the professional section will need those branches especially which are the basis of their future profession, and a general knowledge of the others as auxiliary to that and necessary to their standing and associating with the scientific class.

Jefferson, *Letter to Peter Carr*
(*Sept. 7, 1814*)

19 Most of the crimes which disturb the internal peace of society are produced by the restraints which the necessary, but unequal, laws of property have imposed on the appetites of mankind, by confining to a few the possession of those objects that are coveted by many. Of all our passions and appetites, the love of power is of the most imperious and unsociable nature, since the pride of one man requires the submission of the multitude. In the tumult of civil discord, the laws of society lose their force, and their place is seldom supplied by those of humanity. The ardour of contention, the pride of victory, the despair of success, the memory of past injuries, and the fear of future dangers, all contribute to inflame the mind, and to silence the voice of pity. From such motives almost every page of history has been stained with civil blood.

Gibbon, *Decline and Fall
of the Roman Empire,* IV

20 When Cæsar subdued the Gauls, that great nation was already divided into three orders of men; the clergy, the nobility, and the common people. The first governed by superstition, the second by arms, but the third and last was not of any weight or account in their public councils. It was very natural for the plebeians, oppressed by debt or apprehensive of injuries, to implore the protection of some powerful chief, who acquired over their persons and property the same absolute rights as, among the Greeks and Romans, a master exercised over his slaves. The greatest part of the nation was gradually reduced in a state of servitude; compelled to perpetual labour on the estates of the Gallic nobles, and confined to the soil, either by the real weight of fetters, or by the no less cruel and forcible restraints of the laws. During the long series of troubles which agitated Gaul, from the reign of Gallienus to that of Diocletian, the condition of those servile peasants was peculiarly miserable; and they experienced at once the complicated tyranny of their masters, of the barbarians, of the soldiers, and of the officers of the revenue.

Their patience was at last provoked into despair. On every side they rose in multitudes, armed with rustic weapons, and with irresistible fury. The ploughman became a foot soldier, the shepherd mounted on horseback, the deserted villages and open towns were abandoned to the flames, and the ravages of the peasants equalled those of the fiercest barbarians. They asserted the natural rights of men, but they asserted those rights with the most savage cruelty. The Gallic nobles, justly dreading their revenge, either took refuge in the fortified cities, or fled from the wild

scene of anarchy. The peasants reigned without control; and two of their most daring leaders had the folly and rashness to assume the Imperial ornaments. Their power soon expired at the approach of the legions. The strength of union and discipline obtained an easy victory over a licentious and divided multitude. A severe retaliation was inflicted on the peasants who were found in arms: the affrighted remnant returned to their respective habitations, and their unsuccessful effort for freedom served only to confirm their slavery. So strong and uniform is the current of popular passions, that we might almost venture, from very scanty materials, to relate the particulars of this war; but we are not disposed to believe that the principal leaders, Ælianus and Amandus, were Christians, or to insinuate that the rebellion, as it happened in the time of Luther, was occasioned by the abuse of those benevolent principles of Christianity which inculcate the natural freedom of mankind.

Gibbon, *Decline and Fall
of the Roman Empire,* XIII

21 Such is the constitution of civil society, that, whilst a few persons are distinguished by riches, by honours, and by knowledge, the body of the people is condemned to obscurity, ignorance, and poverty.

Gibbon, *Decline and Fall
of the Roman Empire,* XV

22 Those who contend for a simple democracy, or a pure republic, actuated by the sense of the majority and operating within narrow limits, assume or suppose a case which is altogether fictitious. They found their reasoning on the idea that the people composing the society enjoy not only an equality of political rights but that they have all precisely the same interests and the same feelings in every respect. Were this in reality the case, their reasoning would be conclusive. The interest of the majority would be that of the minority, also; the decisions could only turn on mere opinion concerning the good of the whole, of which the major voice would be the safest criterion; and within a small sphere, this voice could be most easily collected and the public affairs most accurately managed.

We know, however, that no society ever did, or can, consist of so homogeneous a mass of citizens. In the savage state, indeed, an approach is made toward it, but in that state little or no government is necessary. In all civilized societies distinctions are various and unavoidable. A distinction of property results from that very protection which a free government gives to unequal faculties of acquiring it. There will be rich and poor; creditors and debtors; a landed interest, a monied interest, a mercantile interest, a manufacturing interest. These classes may again be subdivided according to the different productions of different situations and soils, and according to different branches of commerce and of manufactures. In addition to these natural distinctions, artificial ones will be founded on accidental differences in political, religious, or other opinions, or an attachment to the persons of leading individuals. However erroneous or ridiculous these grounds of dissension and faction may appear to the enlightened statesman or the benevolent philosopher, the bulk of mankind, who are neither statesmen nor philosophers, will continue to view them in a different light.

Madison, Letter to Jefferson (Oct. 24, 1787)

23 By a faction, I understand a number of citizens, whether amounting to a majority or minority of the whole, who are united and actuated by some common impulse of passion, or of interest, adverse to the rights of other citizens, or to the permanent and aggregate interests of the community.

There are two methods of curing the mischiefs of faction: the one, by removing its causes; the other, by controlling its effects.

There are again two methods of removing the causes of faction: the one, by destroying the liberty which is essential to its existence; the other, by giving to every citizen the same opinions, the same passions, and the same interests. . . .

The second expedient is as impracticable as the first would be unwise. As long as the reason of man continues fallible, and he is at liberty to exercise it, different opinions will be formed. As long as the connection subsists between his reason and his self-love, his opinions and his passions will have a reciprocal influence on each other; and the former will be objects to which the latter will attach themselves. The diversity in the faculties of men, from which the rights of property originate, is not less an insuperable obstacle to a uniformity of interests. The protection of these faculties is the first object of government. From the protection of different and unequal faculties of acquiring property, the possession of different degrees and kinds of property immediately results; and from the influence of these on the sentiments and views of the respective proprietors, ensues a division of the society into different interests and parties.

The latent causes of faction are thus sown in the nature of man; and we see them everywhere brought into different degrees of activity, according to the different circumstances of civil society. A zeal for different opinions concerning religion, concerning government, and many other points, as well of speculation as of practice; an attachment of different leaders ambitiously contending for pre-eminence and power; or to persons of other descriptions whose fortunes have been interesting to the human passions, have, in turn, divided mankind into parties, inflamed them with mutual animosity, and rendered them much more disposed to vex and oppress each other than to cooperate for their common good. So strong is this propensity of mankind to fall into mutual animosities, that where no substantial occasion presents itself, the most frivolous and fanciful distinctions have been sufficient to kindle their unfriendly passions and excite their most violent conflicts. But the most common and durable source of factions has been the various and unequal distribution of property. Those who hold and those who are without property have ever formed distinct interests in society. Those who are creditors, and those who are debtors, fall under a like discrimination. A landed interest, a manufacturing interest, a mercantile interest, a moneyed interest, with many lesser interests, grow up of necessity in civilised nations, and divide them into different classes, actuated by different sentiments and views. The regulation of these various and interfering interests forms the principal task of modern legislation, and involves the spirit of party and faction in the necessary and ordinary operations of the government. . . .

It is in vain to say that enlightened statesmen will be able to adjust these clashing interests, and render them all subservient to the public good. Enlightened statesmen will not always be at the helm. Nor, in many cases, can such an adjustment be made at all without taking into view indirect and remote considerations, which will rarely prevail over the immediate interest which one party may find in disregarding the rights of another or the good of the whole.

The inference to which we are brought is, that the *causes* of faction cannot be removed, and that relief is only to be sought in the means of controlling its *effects*.

Madison, Federalist 10

24 It is of great importance in a republic not only to guard the society against the oppression of its rulers, but to guard one part of the society against the injustice of the other part. Different interests necessarily exist in different classes of citizens. If a majority be united by a common interest, the rights of the minority will be insecure. There are but two methods of providing against this evil: the one by creating a will in the community independent of the majority—that is, of the society itself; the other, by comprehending in the society so many separate descriptions of citizens as will render an unjust combination of a majority of the whole very improbable, if not impracticable.

Hamilton or Madison, Federalist 51

25 It appears that a society constituted according to the most beautiful form that imagination can conceive, with benevolence for its moving principle, instead of self-love, and with every evil disposition in all its members corrected by reason and not force, would, from the inevitable laws of nature, and not from any original depravity of man, in a

very short period degenerate into a society constructed upon a plan not essentially different from that which prevails in every known state at present; I mean a society divided into a class of proprietors, and a class of laborers, and with self-love the main spring of the great machine.

Malthus, *Population*, X

26 The ways and means of sharing in the capital of society are left to each man's particular choice, but the subdivision of civil society into different general branches is a necessity. The family is the first precondition of the state, but class divisions are the second. The importance of the latter is due to the fact that although private persons are self-seeking, they are compelled to direct their attention to others. Here then is the root which connects self-seeking to the universal, i.e. to the state, whose care it must be that this tie is a hard and fast one.

In our day agriculture is conducted on methods devised by reflective thinking, i.e. like a factory. This has given it a character like that of industry and contrary to its natural one. Still, the agricultural class will always retain a mode of life which is patriarchal and the substantial frame of mind proper to such a life. The member of this class accepts unreflectively what is given him and takes what he gets, thanking God for it and living in faith and confidence that this goodness will continue. What comes to him suffices him; once it is consumed, more comes again. This is the simple attitude of mind not concentrated on the struggle for riches. It may be described as the attitude of the old nobility which just ate what there was. So far as this class is concerned, nature does the major part, while individual effort is secondary. In the business class, however, it is intelligence which is the essential thing, and natural products can be treated only as raw materials.

In the business class, the individual is thrown back on himself, and this feeling of self-hood is most intimately connected with the demand for law and order. The sense of freedom and order has therefore arisen above all in towns. The agricultural class, on the other hand, has little occasion to think of itself; what it obtains is the gift of a stranger, of nature. Its feeling of dependence is fundamental to it, and with this feeling there is readily associated a willingness to submit to whatever may befall it at other men's hands. The agricultural class is thus more inclined to subservience, the business class to freedom.

When we say that a man must be a "somebody," we mean that he should belong to some specific social class, since to be a somebody means to have substantive being. A man with no class is a mere private person and his universality is not actualized. On the other hand, the individual in his particularity may take himself as the universal and presume that by entering a class he is surrendering himself to an indignity. This is the false idea that in attaining a determinacy necessary to it, a thing is restricting and surrendering itself.

Hegel, *Philosophy of Right*,
Additions, Pars. 201–207

27 The middle class, to which civil servants belong, is politically conscious and the one in which education is most prominent. For this reason it is also the pillar of the state so far as honesty and intelligence are concerned. A state without a middle class must therefore remain on a low level.

Hegel, *Philosophy of Right*,
Additions, Par. 297

28 On the whole, the class of landed property owners is divided into an educated section and a section of farmers. But over against both of these sorts of people there stands the business class, which is dependent on needs and concentrated on their satisfaction, and the civil servant class, which is essentially dependent on the state. The security and stability of the agricultural class may be still further increased by the institution of primogeniture, though this institution is desirable only from the point of view of politics, since it entails a sacrifice for the political end of giving the eldest son a life of independence.

Hegel, *Philosophy of Right*,
Additions, Par. 306

29 "It's always best on these occasions to do what the mob do."

"But suppose there are two mobs?" suggested Mr. Snodgrass.

"Shout with the largest," replied Mr. Pickwick.

Dickens, *Pickwick Papers*, XIII

30 The *Manifesto* being our joint production, I consider myself bound to state that the fundamental proposition which forms its nucleus belongs to Marx. That proposition is: That in every historical epoch the prevailing mode of economic production and exchange, and the social organization necessarily following from it, form the basis upon which is built up, and from which alone can be explained, the political and intellectual history of that epoch; that, consequently, the whole history of mankind (since the dissolution of primitive tribal society, holding land in common ownership) has been a history of class struggles, contests between exploiting and exploited, ruling and oppressed classes; that the history of these class struggles forms a series of evolutions in which, nowadays, a stage has been reached where the exploited and oppressed class—the proletariat—cannot attain its emancipation from the sway of the exploiting and ruling class—the bourgeoisie—without at the same time, and once and for all, emancipating society at large from all exploita-

tion, oppression, class distinctions and class struggles.

This proposition, which in my opinion is destined to do for history what Darwin's theory has done for biology, we, both of us, had been gradually approaching for some years before 1845. How far I had independently progressed towards it is best shown by my *Condition of the Working Class in England.* But when I again met Marx at Brussels in the spring of 1845, he had it already worked out, and put it before me in terms almost as clear as those in which I have stated it here.

Engels, *Communist Manifesto,* Pref.

31 The history of all hitherto existing society is the history of class struggles.

Marx and Engels, *Communist Manifesto,* I

32 The bourgeoisie has played a most revolutionary role in history.

The bourgeoisie, wherever it has got the upper hand, has put an end to all feudal, patriarchal, idyllic relations. It has pitilessly torn asunder the motley feudal ties that bound man to his "natural superiors," and has left no other bond between man and man than naked self-interest, than callous "cash payment." It has drowned the most heavenly ecstasies of religious fervour, of chivalrous enthusiasm, of philistine sentimentalism, in the icy water of egotistical calculation. It has resolved personal worth into exchange value, and in place of the numberlesss indefeasible chartered freedoms has set up that single, unconscionable freedom—Free Trade. In one word, for exploitation, veiled by religious and political illusions, it has substituted naked, shameless, direct, brutal exploitation.

Marx and Engels, *Communist Manifesto,* I

33 The essential condition for the existence and sway of the bourgeois class is the formation and augmentation of capital; the condition for capital is wage labour. Wage labour rests exclusively on competition between the labourers. The advance of industry, whose involuntary promoter is the bourgeoisie, replaces the isolation of the labourers, due to competition, by their revolutionary combination, due to association. The development of modern industry, therefore, cuts from under its feet the very foundation on which the bourgeoisie produces and appropriates products. What the bourgeoisie, therefore, produces above all are its own grave-diggers. Its fall and the victory of the proletariat are equally inevitable.

Marx and Engels, *Communist Manifesto,* I

34 Political power, properly so called, is merely the organized power of one class for oppressing another. If the proletariat during its contest with the bourgeoisie is compelled by the force of circumstances to organize itself as a class; if by means of

a revolution it makes itself the ruling class and, as such, sweeps away by force the old conditions of production, then it will, along with these conditions, have swept away the conditions for the existence of class antagonisms and of classes generally, and will thereby have abolished its own supremacy as a class.

In place of the old bourgeois society, with its classes and class antagonisms, we shall have an association in which the free development of each is the condition for the free development of all.

Marx and Engels, *Communist Manifesto,* II

35 The reason why, in any tolerable constituted society, justice and the general interest mostly in the end carry their point, is that the separate and selfish interests of mankind are almost always divided; some are interested in what is wrong, but some, also, have their private interest on the side of what is right: and those who are governed by higher considerations, though too few and weak to prevail against the whole of the others, usually after sufficient discussion and agitation become strong enough to turn the balance in favour of the body of private interests which is on the same side with them. The representative system ought to be so constituted as to maintain this state of things: it ought not to allow any of the various sectional interests to be so powerful as to be capable of prevailing against truth and justice and the other sectional interests combined.

Mill, *Representative Government,* VI

36 I . . . contend for the principle of plural voting. I do not propose the plurality as a thing in itself undesirable, which, like the exclusion of part of the community from the suffrage, may be temporarily tolerated while necessary to prevent greater evils. I do not look upon equal voting as among the things which are good in themselves, provided they can be guarded against inconveniences. I look upon it as only relatively good; less objectionable than inequality of privilege grounded on irrelevant or adventitious circumstances, but in principle wrong, because recognising a wrong standard, and exercising a bad influence on the voter's mind. It is not useful, but hurtful, that the constitution of the country should declare ignorance to be entitled to as much political power as knowledge. The national institutions should place all things that they are concerned with before the mind of the citizen in the light in which it is for his good that he should regard them: and as it is for his good that he should think that every one is entitled to some influence, but the better and wiser to more than others, it is important that this conviction should be professed by the State, and embodied in the national institutions.

Mill, *Representative Government,* VIII

37 *Napoleon.* There are three sorts of people in the

world: the low people, the middle people, and the high people. The low people and the high people are alike in one thing: they have no scruples, no morality. The low are beneath morality, the high above it. I am not afraid of either of them; for the low are unscrupulous without knowledge, so that they make an idol of me; whilst the high are unscrupulous without purpose, so that they go down before my will. Look you: I shall go over all the mobs and all the courts of Europe as a plough goes over a field. It is the middle people who are dangerous: they have both knowledge and purpose. But they, too, have their weak point. They are full of scruples: chained hand and foot by their morality and respectability.

Shaw, *The Man of Destiny*

38 War and Class have been with us ever since the first civilizations emerged above the level of primitive human life some five or six thousand years ago, and they have always been serious complaints. Of the twenty or so civilizations known to modern Western historians, all except our own appear to be dead or moribund, and, when we diagnose each case, *in extremis* or *post mortem*, we invariably find that the cause of death has been either War or Class or some combination of the two.

Toynbee, *Civilization on Trial*, II

10.9 | *Revolution*

As indicated in passages drawn from the historians of antiquity and from the ancient political philosophers, revolution and civil strife were regarded as a regular part of normal political life. The conception of a society so constituted that it might be exempt from revolutionary action, either by force or by fraud, was projected as an almost utopian idea. Insofar as injustice, class conflicts, and an inequality of conditions abound in the very imperfect societies that exist, revolution is always and everywhere brewing.

Some of the writers quoted here attempt to distinguish different types of revolution, to specify the causes productive of revolution, and to consider what those in power can do to prevent themselves from being overthrown. Others among the authors represented concern themselves mainly with the defense of rebellion or revolution as a drastic remedy that is justified when relief from oppression or injustice cannot be achieved in any other way. They suggest that it is the tyrant who is the rebel, the lawless one, rather than his mistreated subjects. When they speak of a "right of revolution" or a "right of rebellion," they are, in effect, asserting that revolutions are justifiable under certain circumstances. They are opposed in this conviction by others who deny that resistance to established authority can ever be justified.

The discussion of revolution in this section is for the most part concerned with political upheavals or insurrections. For related matters, the reader is referred to other sections in this chapter on POLITICS, especially Section 10.6 on DESPOTISM AND TYRANNY and Section 10.8 on CLASSES AND CLASS CONFLICT; and to Section 12.3 on RIGHTS—NATURAL AND CIVIL and Section 14.1 on WARFARE AND THE STATE OF WAR. However, certain passages from Karl Marx included here touch on revolutions that affect the economic organization of society; and in this connection the reader is referred to Section 11.1 on PROPERTY, Section 11.2 on WEALTH AND POVERTY, and Section 11.3 on LABOR.

1 The sufferings [in the Hellenic countries] which revolution entailed . . . were many and terrible, such as have occurred and always will occur, as long as the nature of mankind remains the same. . . . Words had to change their ordinary meaning and to take that which was now given them. Reckless audacity came to be considered the courage of a loyal ally; prudent hesitation, specious cowardice; moderation was held to be a cloak for unmanliness; ability to see all sides of a question, inaptness to act on any. Frantic violence became the attribute of manliness; cautious plotting, a justifiable means of self-defence. The advocate of extreme measures was always trustworthy; his opponent a man to be suspected. To succeed in a plot was to have a shrewd head, to divine a plot a still shrewder; but to try to provide against having to do either was to break up your party and to be afraid of your adversaries. In fine, to forestall an intending criminal, or to suggest the idea of a crime where it was wanting, was equally commended, until even blood became a weaker tie than party, from the superior readiness of those united by the latter to dare everything without reserve; for such associations had not in view the blessings derivable from established institutions but were formed by ambition for their overthrow; and the confidence of their members in each other rested less on any religious sanction than upon complicity in crime. The fair proposals of an adversary were met with jealous precautions by the stronger of the two, and not with a generous confidence. Revenge also was held of more account than self-preservation. Oaths of reconciliation, being only proffered on either side to meet an immediate difficulty, only held good so long as no other weapon was at hand; but when opportunity offered, he who first ventured to seize it and to take his enemy off his guard, thought this perfidious vengeance sweeter than an open one, since, considerations of safety apart, success by treachery won him the palm of superior intelligence.

Thucydides, *Peloponnesian War*, III, 82

2 If [a man's country] should appear to him to be following a policy which is not a good one, he should say so, provided that his words are not likely either to fall on deaf ears or to lead to the loss of his own life. But force against his native land he should not use in order to bring about a change of constitution, when it is not possible for the best constitution to be introduced without driving men into exile or putting them to death; he should keep quiet and offer up prayers for his own welfare and for that of his country.

Plato, *Seventh Letter*

3 Inferiors revolt in order that they may be equal, and equals that they may be superior. Such is the state of mind which creates revolutions.

Aristotle, *Politics*, 1302a29

4 Revolutions are effected in two ways, by force and by fraud. Force may be applied either at the time of making the revolution or afterwards. Fraud, again, is of two kinds; for sometimes the citizens are deceived into acquiescing in a change of government, and afterwards they are held in subjection against their will. . . . In other cases the people are persuaded at first, and afterwards, by a repetition of the persuasion, their goodwill and allegiance are retained.

Aristotle, *Politics*, 1304b7

5 Among ourselves the sons of the ruling class in an oligarchy live in luxury, but the sons of the poor are hardened by exercise and toil, and hence they are both more inclined and better able to make a revolution.

Aristotle, *Politics*, 1310a22

6 If to provide itself with a king belongs to the right of a given multitude, it is not unjust that the king be deposed or have his power restricted by that same multitude if, becoming a tyrant, he abuses the royal power. It must not be thought that such a multitude is acting unfaithfully in deposing the tyrant, even though it had previously subjected itself to him in perpetuity, because he himself has deserved that the covenant with his subjects should not be kept, since, in ruling the multitude, he did not act faithfully as the office of a king demands.

Aquinas, *On Kingship*, I, 6

7 Men change their rulers willingly, hoping to better themselves, and this hope induces them to take up arms against him who rules: wherein they are deceived, because they afterwards find by experience they have gone from bad to worse.

Machiavelli, *Prince*, III

8 He who becomes master of a city accustomed to freedom and does not destroy it, may expect to be destroyed by it, for in rebellion it has always the watchword of liberty and its ancient privileges as a rallying point, which neither time nor benefits will ever cause it to forget. And what ever you may do or provide against, they never forget that name or their privileges unless they are disunited or dispersed, but at every chance they immediately rally to them.

Machiavelli, *Prince*, V

9 It ought to be remembered that there is nothing more difficult to take in hand, more perilous to conduct, or more uncertain in its success, than to take the lead in the introduction of a new order of things. Because the innovator has for enemies all those who have done well under the old conditions, and lukewarm defenders in those who may do well under the new. This coolness arises partly from fear of the opponents, who have the laws on

their side, and partly from the incredulity of men, who do not readily believe in new things until they have had a long experience of them. Thus it happens that whenever those who are hostile have the opportunity to attack they do it like partisans, whilst the others defend lukewarmly, in such wise that the prince is endangered along with them.

It is necessary, therefore, if we desire to discuss this matter thoroughly, to inquire whether these innovators can rely on themselves or have to depend on others: that is to say, whether, to consummate their enterprise, have they to use prayers or can they use force? In the first instance they always succeed badly, and never compass anything; but when they can rely on themselves and use force, then they are rarely endangered. Hence it is that all armed prophets have conquered, and the unarmed ones have been destroyed. Besides the reasons mentioned, the nature of the people is variable, and whilst it is easy to persuade them, it is difficult to fix them in that persuasion. And thus it is necessary to take such measures that, when they believe no longer, it may be possible to make them believe by force.

Machiavelli, *Prince,* VI

10 A prince ought to have two fears, one from within, on account of his subjects, the other from without, on account of external powers. From the latter he is defended by being well armed and having good allies, and if he is well armed he will have good friends, and affairs will always remain quiet within when they are quiet without, unless they should have been already disturbed by conspiracy; and even should affairs outside be disturbed, if he has carried out his preparations and has lived as I have said, as long as he does not despair, he will resist every attack. . . .

But concerning his subjects, when affairs outside are disturbed he has only to fear that they will conspire secretly, from which a prince can easily secure himself by avoiding being hated and despised, and by keeping the people satisfied with him, which it is most necessary for him to accomplish. . . . And one of the most efficacious remedies that a prince can have against conspiracies is not to be hated and despised by the people, for he who conspires against a prince always expects to please them by his removal; but when the conspirator can only look forward to offending them, he will not have the courage to take such a course, for the difficulties that confront a conspirator are infinite. . . . On the side of the conspirator, there is nothing but fear, jealousy, prospect of punishment to terrify him; but on the side of the prince there is the majesty of the principality, the laws, the protection of friends and the state to defend him; so that, adding to all these things the popular goodwill, it is impossible that any one should be so rash as to conspire. For whereas in general

the conspirator has to fear before the execution of his plot, in this case he has also to fear the sequel to the crime; because on account of it he has the people for an enemy, and thus cannot hope for any escape. . . .

For this reason I consider that a prince ought to reckon conspiracies of little account when his people hold him in esteem; but when it is hostile to him, and bears hatred towards him, he ought to fear everything and everybody. And well-ordered states and wise princes have taken every care not to drive the nobles to desperation, and to keep the people satisfied and contented, for this is one of the most important objects a prince can have.

Machiavelli, *Prince,* XIX

11 Those who give the first shock to a state are apt to be the first ones swallowed up in its ruin. The fruits of the trouble rarely go to the one who has stirred it up; he beats and disturbs the water for other fishermen.

Montaigne, *Essays,* I, 23,
Of Custom

12 It takes a lot of self-love and presumption to have such esteem for one's own opinions that to establish them one must overthrow the public peace and introduce so many inevitable evils, and such a horrible corruption of morals, as civil wars and political changes bring with them in a matter of such weight—and introduce them into one's own country. Isn't it bad management to encourage so many certain and known vices in order to combat contested and debatable errors? Is there any worse kind of vices than those which attack our conscience and our understanding of one another?

Montaigne, *Essays,* I, 23,
Of Custom

13 *Menenius.* There was a time when all the body's members
　Rebell'd against the belly, thus accused it:
　That only like a gulf it did remain
　I' the midst o' the body, idle and unactive,
　Still cupboarding the viand, never bearing
　Like labour with the rest, where the other instruments
　Did see and hear, devise, instruct, walk, feel,
　And mutually participate, did minister
　Unto the appetite and affection common
　Of the whole body. The belly answer'd—
　　1st Citizen. Well, sir, what answer made the belly?
　　Men. Sir, I shall tell you. With a kind of smile,
　Which ne'er came from the lungs, but even thus—
　For, look you, I may make the belly smile
　As well as speak—it tauntingly replied
　To the discontented members, the mutinous parts
　That envied his receipt; even so most fitly
　As you malign our senators for that
　They are not such as you.

1st Cit.   Your belly's answer? What?
The kingly-crowned head, the vigilant eye,
The counsellor heart, the arm our soldier,
Our steed the leg, the tongue our trumpeter,
With other muniments and petty helps
In this our fabric, if that they—
   Men.   What then?
'Fore me, this fellow speaks: What then? what
   then
   1st Cit. Should by the cormorant belly be
   restrain'd,
Who is the sink o' the body—
   Men.   Well, what then?
   1st Cit. The former agents, if they did complain,
What could the belly answer?
   Men.   I will tell you;
If you'll bestow a small—of what you have little—
Patience awhile, you'll hear the belly's answer—
   1st Cit. Ye're long about it.
   Men.   Note me this, good friend;
Your most grave belly was deliberate,
Not rash like his accusers, and thus answer'd:
"True is it, my incorporate friends," quoth he,
"That I receive the general food at first,
Which you do live upon; and fit it is,
Because I am the store-house and the shop
Of the whole body. But, if you do remember,
I send it through the rivers of your blood,
Even to the court, the heart, to the seat o' the
   brain;
And, through the cranks and offices of man,
The strongest nerves and small inferior veins
From me receive that natural competency
Whereby they live: and though that all at once,
You, my good friends"—this says the belly, mark
   me—
   1st Cit. Ay, sir; well, well.
   Men.   "Though all at once cannot
See what I do deliver out to each,
Yet I can make my audit up, that all
From me do back receive the flour of all,
And leave me but the bran." What say you to't?
   1st Cit. It was an answer. How apply you this?
   Men. The senators of Rome are this good belly,
And you the mutinous members; for examine
Their counsels and their cares, digest things right-
   ly
Touching the weal o' the common, you shall find
No public benefit which you receive
But it proceeds or comes from them to you
And no way from yourselves. What do you think,
You, the great toe of this assembly?
   1st Cit. I the great toe! Why the great toe?
   Men. For that, being one o' the lowest, basest,
   poorest,
Of this most wise rebellion, thou go'st foremost;
Thou rascal, that art worst in blood to run,
Lead'st first to win some vantage.

                 Shakespeare, *Coriolanus*, I, i, 99

14 In civil matters even a change for the better is
suspected on account of the commotion it occasions, for civil government is supported by authority, unanimity, fame, and public opinion, and not
by demonstration.

                 Bacon, *Novum Organum*, I, 90

15 Shepherds of people had need know the kalendars
of tempests in state; which are commonly greatest
when things grow to equality; as natural tempests
are greatest about the *Æquinoctia*. And as there are
certain hollow blasts of wind and secret swellings
of seas before a tempest, so are there in states. . . .
Libels and licentious discourses against the state,
when they are frequent and open; and in like sort,
false news, often running up and down, to the disadvantage of the state, and hastily embraced; are
amongst the signs of troubles.

               Bacon, *Of Seditions and Troubles*

16 The causes and motives of seditions are: innovation in religion; taxes; alteration of laws and customs; breaking of privileges; general oppression;
advancement of unworthy persons; strangers;
dearths; disbanded soldiers; factions grown desperate; and whatsoever, in offending people, join-
eth and knitteth them in a common cause.

               Bacon, *Of Seditions and Troubles*

17 The infliction of what evil soever on an innocent
man that is not a subject, if it be for the benefit of
the Commonwealth, and without violation of any
former covenant, is no breach of the law of nature. For all men that are not subjects are either
enemies, or else they have ceased from being so by
some precedent covenants. But against enemies,
whom the Commonwealth judgeth capable to do
them hurt, it is lawful by the original right of nature to make war; wherein the sword judgeth not,
nor doth the victor make distinction of nocent and
innocent as to the time past, nor has other respect
of mercy than as it conduceth to the good of his
own people. And upon this ground it is that also
in subjects who deliberately deny the authority of
the Commonwealth established, the vengeance is
lawfully extended, not only to the fathers, but also
to the third and fourth generation not yet in
being, and consequently innocent of the fact for
which they are afflicted: because the nature of
this offence consisteth in the renouncing of subjection, which is a relapse into the condition of war
commonly called *rebellion;* and they that so offend,
suffer not as subjects, but as enemies. For rebellion
is but war renewed.

               Hobbes, *Leviathan*, II, 28

18 The art of opposition and of revolution is to unsettle established customs, sounding them even to
their source, to point out their want of authority
and justice. We must, it is said, get back to the
natural and fundamental laws of the State, which

an unjust custom has abolished. It is a game certain to result in the loss of all; nothing will be just on the balance. Yet people readily lend their ear to such arguments. They shake off the yoke as soon as they recognise it; and the great profit by their ruin and by that of these curious investigators of accepted customs. But from a contrary mistake men sometimes think they can justly do everything which is not without an example. That is why the wisest of legislators said that it was necessary to deceive men for their own good. . . . We must not see the fact of usurpation; law was once introduced without reason, and has become reasonable. We must make it regarded as authoritative, eternal, and conceal its origin, if we do not wish that it should soon come to an end.

Pascal, *Pensées*, V, 294

19 A civil state, which has not done away with the causes of seditions, where war is a perpetual object of fear, and where, lastly, the laws are often broken, differs but little from the mere state of nature, in which everyone lives after his own mind at the great risk of his life.

Spinoza, *Political Treatise*, V, 2

20 The inhabitants of any country, who are descended and derive a title to their estates from those who are subdued, and had a government forced upon them, against their free consents, retain a right to the possession of their ancestors, though they consent not freely to the government, whose hard conditions were, by force, imposed on the possessors of that country. For the first conqueror never having had a title to the land of that country, the people, who are the descendants of, or claim under those who were forced to submit to the yoke of a government by constraint, have always a right to shake it off, and free themselves from the usurpation or tyranny the sword hath brought in upon them, till their rulers put them under such a frame of government as they willingly and of choice consent to (which they can never be supposed to do, till either they are put in a full state of liberty to choose their government and governors, or at least till they have such standing laws to which they have, by themselves or their representatives, given their free consent, and also till they are allowed their due property, which is so to be proprietors of what they have that nobody can take away any part of it without their own consent, without which, men under any government are not in the state of free men, but are direct slaves under the force of war).

Locke, *II Civil Government*, XVI, 192

21 Whensoever . . . the legislative shall transgress this fundamental rule of society, and either by ambition, fear, folly, or corruption, endeavour to grasp themselves, or put into the hands of any other, an absolute power over the lives, liberties, and estates of the people, by this breach of trust they forfeit the power the people had put into their hands for quite contrary ends, and it devolves to the people, who have a right to resume their original liberty, and by the establishment of a new legislative (such as they shall think fit), provide for their own safety and security, which is the end for which they are in society.

Locke, *II Civil Government*, XIX, 222

22 Revolutions happen not upon every little mismanagement in public affairs. Great mistakes in the ruling part, many wrong and inconvenient laws, and all the slips of human frailty will be borne by the people without mutiny or murmur. But if a long train of abuses, prevarications, and artifices, all tending the same way, make the design visible to the people, and they cannot but feel what they lie under, and see whither they are going, it is not to be wondered that they should then rouse themselves, and endeavour to put the rule into such hands which may secure to them the ends for which government was at first erected, and without which, ancient names and specious forms are so far from being better, that they are much worse than the state of Nature or pure anarchy; the inconveniencies being all as great and as near, but the remedy farther off and more difficult.

Locke, *II Civil Government*, XIX, 225

23 The popular insurrection that ends in the death or deposition of a Sultan is as lawful an act as those by which he disposed, the day before, of the lives and fortunes of his subjects. As he was maintained by force alone, it is force alone that overthrows him. Thus everything takes place according to the natural order; and, whatever may be the result of such frequent and precipitate revolutions, no one man has reason to complain of the injustice of another, but only of his own ill-fortune or indiscretion.

Rousseau, *Origin of Inequality*, II

24 When, in the course of human events, it becomes necessary for one people to dissolve the political bands which have connected them with another, and to assume, among the powers of the earth, the separate and equal station to which the laws of nature and of nature's God entitle them, a decent respect to the opinions of mankind requires that they should declare the causes which impel them to the separation.

Jefferson, *Declaration of Independence*

25 Prudence, indeed, will dictate that governments long established should not be changed for light and transient causes; and, accordingly, all experience hath shown, that mankind are more disposed

to suffer, while evils are sufferable, than to right themselves by abolishing the forms to which they are accustomed. But, when a long train of abuses and usurpations, pursuing invariably the same object, evinces a design to reduce them under absolute despotism, it is their right, it is their duty, to throw off such government, and to provide new guards for their future security.

Jefferson, *Declaration of Independence*

26 I hold it that a little rebellion now and then is a good thing, and as necessary in the political world as storms in the physical. Unsuccessful rebellions, indeed, generally establish the encroachments on the rights of the people which have produced them. An observation of this truth should render honest republican governors so mild in their punishment of rebellions as not to discourage them too much. It is a medicine necessary for the sound health of government.

Jefferson, *Letter to James Madison*
(Jan. 30, 1787)

27 General rebellions and revolts of an whole people never were encouraged, now or at any time. They are always provoked.

Burke, *Letter to the Sheriffs of Bristol*
(Apr. 3, 1777)

28 Resistance on the part of the people to the supreme legislative power of the state is in no case legitimate; for it is only by submission to the universal legislative will, that a condition of law and order is possible. Hence there is no right of sedition, and still less of rebellion, belonging to the people.

Kant, *Science of Right*, 49

29 It is the duty of the people to bear any abuse of the supreme power, even then though it should be considered to be unbearable. And the reason is that any resistance of the highest legislative authority can never but be contrary to the law, and must even be regarded as tending to destroy the whole legal constitution.

Kant, *Science of Right*, 49

30 When on the success of a revolution a new constitution has been founded, the unlawfulness of its beginning and of its institution cannot release the subjects from the obligation of adapting themselves, as good citizens, to the new order of things; and they are not entitled to refuse honourably to obey the authority that has thus attained the power in the state.

Kant, *Science of Right*, 49

31 Why is the experiment of an extended republic to be rejected, merely because it may comprise what is new? Is it not the glory of the people of America, that, whilst they have paid a decent regard to the opinions of former times and other nations, they have not suffered a blind veneration for antiquity, for custom, or for names, to overrule the suggestions of their own good sense, the knowledge of their own situation, and the lessons of their own experience? To this manly spirit, posterity will be indebted for the possession, and the world for the example, of the numerous innovations displayed on the American theatre, in favour of private rights and public happiness. Had no important step been taken by the leaders of the Revolution for which a precedent could not be discovered, no government established of which an exact model did not present itself, the people of the United States might, at this moment, have been numbered among the melancholy victims of misguided councils, must at best have been labouring under the weight of some of those forms which have crushed the liberties of the rest of mankind. Happily for America, happily, we trust, for the whole human race, they pursued a new and more noble course. They accomplished a revolution which has no parallel in the annals of human society. They reared the fabrics of governments which have no model on the face of the globe.

Madison, *Federalist 14*

32 If the representatives of the people betray their constituents, there is then no resource left but in the exertion of that original right of self-defence which is paramount to all positive forms of government, and which against the usurpations of the national rulers, may be exerted with infinitely better prospect of success than against those of the rulers of an individual State. In a single State, if the persons intrusted with supreme power become usurpers, the different parcels, subdivisions, or districts of which it consists, having no distinct government in each, can take no regular measures for defence. The citizens must rush tumultuously to arms, without concert, without system, without resource; except in their courage and despair. The usurpers, clothed with the forms of legal authority, can too often crush the opposition in embryo. The smaller the extent of the territory, the more difficult will it be for the people to form a regular or systematic plan of opposition, and the more easy will it be to defeat their early efforts. Intelligence can be more speedily obtained of their preparations and movements, and the military force in the possession of the usurpers can be more rapidly directed against the part where the opposition has begun. In this situation there must be a peculiar coincidence of circumstances to insure success to the popular resistance.

Hamilton, *Federalist 28*

33 The political condition of France . . . [before the French Revolution] presents nothing but a con-

fused mass of privileges altogether contravening thought and reason—an utterly irrational state of things, and one with which the greatest corruption of morals, of spirit was associated—an empire characterized by destitution of right, and which, when its real state begins to be recognized, becomes shameless destitution of right. The fearfully heavy burdens that pressed upon the people, the embarrassment of the government to procure for the court the means of supporting luxury and extravagance, gave the first impulse to discontent. The new spirit began to agitate men's minds: oppression drove men to investigation. It was perceived that the sums extorted from the people were not expended in furthering the objects of the state, but were lavished in the most unreasonable fashion. The entire political system appeared one mass of injustice. The change was necessarily violent, because the work of transformation was not undertaken by the government.

Hegel, *Philosophy of History,* Pt. IV, III, 3

34 Amid the ruins which surround me shall I dare to say that revolutions are not what I most fear for coming generations? If men continue to shut themselves more closely within the narrow circle of domestic interests and to live on that kind of excitement, it is to be apprehended that they may ultimately become inaccessible to those great and powerful public emotions which perturb nations, but which develop them and recruit them. When property becomes so fluctuating and the love of property so restless and so ardent, I cannot but fear that men may arrive at such a state as to regard every new theory as a peril, every innovation as an irksome toil, every social improvement as a stepping-stone to revolution, and so refuse to move altogether for fear of being moved too far. I dread, and I confess it, lest they should at last so entirely give way to a cowardly love of present enjoyment as to lose sight of the interests of their future selves and those of their descendants and prefer to glide along the easy current of life rather than to make, when it is necessary, a strong and sudden effort to a higher purpose.

It is believed by some that modern society will be always changing its aspect; for myself, I fear that it will ultimately be too invariably fixed in the same institutions, the same prejudices, the same manners, so that mankind will be stopped and circumscribed; that the mind will swing backwards and forwards forever without begetting fresh ideas; that man will waste his strength in bootless and solitary trifling, and, though in continual motion, that humanity will cease to advance.

Tocqueville, *Democracy in America,* Vol. II, III, 21

35 If there is any period one would desire to be born in, is it not the age of Revolution; when the old and the new stand side by side and admit of being compared; when the energies of all men are searched by fear and by hope; when the historic glories of the old can be compensated by the rich possibilities of the new era? This time, like all times, is a very good one, if we but know what to do with it.

Emerson, *The American Scholar*

36 By the rude bridge that arched the flood,
  Their flag to April's breeze unfurled,
Here once the embattled farmers stood
  And fired the shot heard round the world.

Emerson, *Concord Hymn*

37 All men recognize the right of revolution; that is, the right to refuse allegiance to, and to resist, the government, when its tyranny or its inefficiency are great and unendurable.

Thoreau, *Civil Disobedience*

38 Any people anywhere, being inclined and having the power, have the *right* to rise up, and shake off the existing government, and form a new one that suits them better. This is a most valuable,—a most sacred right—a right, which we hope and believe, is to liberate the world. Nor is this right confined to cases in which the whole people of an existing government, may choose to exercise it. Any portion of such people that *can, may* revolutionize, and make their *own,* of so much of the territory as they inhabit. More than this, a *majority* of any portion of such people may revolutionize, putting down a *minority,* intermingled with, or near about them, who may oppose their movement.

Lincoln, *Speech on the Mexican War
(Jan. 12, 1848)*

39 This country, with its institutions, belongs to the people who inhabit it. Whenever they shall grow weary of the existing government, they can exercise their constitutional right of amending it or their revolutionary right to dismember or overthrow it.

Lincoln, *First Inaugural Address*

40 Let the ruling classes tremble at a Communist revolution. The proletarians have nothing to lose but their chains. They have a world to win.
  Workingmen of all countries, unite!

Marx and Engels, *Communist Manifesto,* IV

41 *Pierre.* Every violent reform deserves censure, for it quite fails to remedy evil while men remain what they are, and also because wisdom needs no violence.

Tolstoy, *War and Peace,* VI, 7

42 All who achieve real distinction in life begin as revolutionists. The most distinguished persons be-

come more revolutionary as they grow older, though they are commonly supposed to become more conservative owing to their loss of faith in conventional methods of reform.

Shaw, *Man and Superman,*
Revolutionist's Handbook, Preface

43 Even if for every hundred correct things we did we committed ten thousand mistakes, our revolution would still be—and it will be in the judgment of history—great and invincible; for this is the first time that not a minority, not the rich alone, not the educated alone, but the real masses, the overwhelming majority of the working people are themselves building a new life and are by their own experience solving the most difficult problems of socialist organisation.

Lenin, *Letter to American Workers*
(Aug. 20, 1918)

Chapter 11

ECONOMICS

Chapter 11 is divided into six sections: 11.1 PROPERTY, 11.2 WEALTH AND POVERTY, 11.3 LABOR, 11.4 MONEY, 11.5 TRADE, COMMERCE, AND INDUSTRY, and 11.6 TAXATION.

It is not surprising that, among the great writers, the economists Adam Smith and Karl Marx should be the two most frequently represented in this chapter. However, many others, among them notably Plato, Aristotle, Locke, Rousseau, and J. S. Mill, contribute insights and observations that broaden and deepen the consideration of economic matters, especially in relation to the pursuit of happiness, virtue and vice, justice and rights, and law and government.

In its Greek origin, economics was conceived as the science or art of household management, concerned largely with the acquisition by the family of its supply of consumable goods and with the husbanding of its resources. The labor power involved in the domestic production of wealth was largely that of the household's slaves. Though production by independent artisans existed, and though retail trade within the community and commerce between cities

flourished, these were not thought to be subjects of concern to economics.

In the eighteenth century, the science became transformed into the much broader study of national wealth and, as the phrase "political economy" indicates, economic questions became matters of public policy, one of the chief concerns of government. With this broadening in the scope of economics, such subjects as those treated in Sections 11.3 to 11.6—labor; money; trade, commerce, and industry; and taxation—raised problems and involved considerations that had had no place in ancient economic thought.

The nature of property, the role of wealth and poverty in human life, and, to some extent, the function of money receive attention from ancient and medieval authors, as well as modern writers, though their approach to such subjects is strikingly different. For one thing, the notion of capital—both capital goods in the form of instruments of production and financial capital—does not enter into the ancient discussion of property, wealth, or industry; for another, such matters as the distribution of wealth, the division of labor, free trade, and state control or regulation of economic processes are barely mentioned, if touched on at all.

Political economy, involving the government's role in the economic sphere, necessarily treats of matters that are also covered in Chapter 10 on Politics. Political economy was also once regarded as a branch of moral philosophy, along with ethics and politics, dealing with questions of value and policy and laying down prescrip-

tions about what ought to be done with regard to the production, exchange, and distribution of wealth. There is, therefore, some overlapping in the matters treated in this chapter and in Chapter 9 on Ethics. Certain subjects of economic interest, such as economic justice, economic freedom, and economic equality, are treated in other contexts: economic justice in Section 12.2; economic freedom in Section 13.1; and economic equality in Section 13.3, and also in Section 10.8 on Classes and Class Conflict.

11.1 | *Property*

Four subjects dominate this section. One, of course, is the nature of property itself. What can we truly or rightly call our own? What constitutes property? Is property to be equated with the possession of material things or does it extend to other things as well—anything that belongs to the individual by right? On the broader view, a person's life, liberty, and even labor power are one's property, as well as one's physical possessions or one's estates.

A second and closely related question concerns the origin of property and the basis of the right to own it. If there were no property, everything would be common to all—the exclusive possession of none. Those who take the broader view of property mentioned above distinguish between natural and acquired property, and make the rightful acquisition of property—the exclusive possession of that which was originally common—depend on one's application to the common of something that is proper to oneself and by right one's own—the labor pow-

er of one's mind and body. This labor theory of acquired property or of the right to property was first enunciated by Locke. It is also found in statements by Rousseau and Gibbon and bears an interesting relation to the theories of property rights developed by Kant and Hegel.

The third and fourth themes that run through Section 11.1 are also closely related. One is the proposal, first advanced by Plato and first questioned by Aristotle, that in an ideal society all the external things that constitute wealth should be held and used in common by the citizens or guardians of the state. This is often mistakenly referred to as "the community of property," for what is held and used in common cannot be property. The other related theme is Marx's proposal—central to the *Communist Manifesto*—that the ownership of the means of production should be transferred from private hands to the state or the community as a whole. This, too, is often mistakenly referred to as "the abolition of private property."

The object of attack is the private ownership of capital—the instruments of production—not other forms of private property, such as consumable goods.

For the consideration of property in a noneconomic sense as signifying everything that belongs to an individual by right—one's life and liberty as well as one's es-tates—the reader is referred to Section 12.3 on RIGHTS—NATURAL AND CIVIL; and for the purely economic consideration of property, the reader will find additional materials in Section 11.2 on WEALTH AND POVERTY. Property as a qualification for citizenship and suffrage is discussed in Section 10.5 on CITIZENSHIP.

---

1 Thou shalt not remove thy neighbour's landmark, which they of old time have set in thine inheritance, which thou shalt inherit in the land that the Lord thy God giveth thee to possess it.

Deuteronomy 19:14

2 *Socrates.* In our city the language of harmony and concord will be more often heard than in any other. As I was describing before, when any one is well or ill, the universal word will be "with me it is well" or "it is ill."

Glaucon. Most true.

And agreeably to this mode of thinking and speaking, were we not saying that they will have their pleasures and pains in common?

Yes, and so they will.

And they will have a common interest in the same thing which they will alike call "my own," and having this common interest they will have a common feeling of pleasure and pain?

Yes, far more so than in other States.

And the reason of this, over and above the general constitution of the State, will be that the guardians will have a community of women and children?

That will be the chief reason.

And this unity of feeling we admitted to be the greatest good, as was implied in our own comparison of a well-ordered State to the relation of the body and the members, when affected by pleasure or pain?

That we acknowledged, and very rightly.

Then the community of wives and children among our citizens is clearly the source of the greatest good to the State?

Certainly.

And this agrees with the other principle which we were affirming—that the guardians were not to have houses or lands or any other property; their pay was to be their food, which they were to receive from the other citizens, and they were to have no private expenses; for we intended them to preserve their true character of guardians.

Right, he replied.

Both the community of property and the community of families, as I am saying, tend to make them more truly guardians; they will not tear the city in pieces by differing about "mine" and "not mine"; each man dragging any acquistion which he has made into a separate house of his own, where he has a separate wife and children and private pleasures and pains; but all will be affected as far as may be by the same pleasures and pains because they are all of one opinion about what is near and dear to them, and therefore they all tend towards a common end.

Plato, *Republic*, V, 463B

3 Property should be private, but the use of it common; and the special business of the legislator is to create in men this benevolent disposition. . . .

How immeasurably greater is the pleasure, when a man feels a thing to be his own; for surely the love of self is a feeling implanted by nature and not given in vain, although selfishness is rightly censured; this, however, is not the mere love of self, but the love of self in excess, like the miser's love of money; for all, or almost all, men love money and other such objects in a measure. And further, there is the greatest pleasure in doing a kindness or service to friends or guests or companions, which can only be rendered when a man has private property. These advantages are lost by excessive unification of the state. The exhibition of two virtues, besides, is visibly annihilated in such a state: first, temperance towards women (for it is an honourable action to abstain from another's wife for temperance sake); secondly, liberality in the matter of property. No one, when men have all things in common, will any longer set an example of liberality or do any liberal action; for liberality consists in the use which is made of property. Such legislation may have a specious appearance of benevolence; men readily listen to it, and are easily induced to believe that in some wonderful manner everybody will become everybody's friend, especially when some one is heard denouncing the evils now existing in states, suits about contracts, convictions for perjury, flatteries of rich men and the like, which are said to arise out of the possession of private property. These evils, however, are due to a very different cause—the wickedness of human nature. Indeed, we see that there is much more quarrelling among those who have all things in common, though there are not many of them when compared with the vast numbers who have private property.

Aristotle, *Politics,* 1263ᵃ38

4 Private ownership does not derive from nature. Property becomes private either through long occupancy (such as with people who settled an unoccupied territory long ago), or through conquest (as in the case of land taken in war), or by due process of law, barter, or allotment.

Cicero, *De Officiis,* I, 7

5 If we all seized the property of our neighbors and grabbed from one another what we could make use of, the bonds of human society would necessarily crumble.

Cicero, *De Officiis,* III, 5

6 As heaven is for the gods, so the earth has been given to mankind, and lands uninhabited are common to all.

Tacitus, *Annals,* XIII, 55

7 God has sovereign dominion over all things: and He, according to His providence, directed certain things to the sustenance of man's body. For this reason man has a natural dominion over things, as regards the power to make use of them.

Aquinas, *Summa Theologica,* II–II, 66, 1

8 Two things are competent to man in respect of exterior things. One is the power to procure and dispense them, and in this regard it is lawful for man to possess property. Moreover this is necessary to human life for three reasons. First because every man is more careful to procure what is for himself alone than that which is common to many or to all: since each one would shirk the labor and leave to another that which concerns the community, as happens where there is a great number of servants. Secondly, because human affairs are conducted in more orderly fashion if each man is charged with taking care of some particular thing himself, whereas there would be confusion if everyone had to look after any one thing indeterminately. Thirdly, because a more peaceful state is ensured to man if each one is contented with his own. Hence it is to be observed that quarrels arise more frequently where there is no division of the things possessed.

Aquinas, *Summa Theologica,* II–II, 66, 2

9 Man ought to possess external things, not as his own, but as common, so that, to wit, he is ready to communicate them to others in their need.

Aquinas, *Summa Theologica,* II–II, 66, 2

10 Community of goods is ascribed to the natural law, not that the natural law dictates that all things should be possessed in common and that nothing should be possessed as one's own: but because the division of possessions is not according to the natural law, but rather arose from human agreement which belongs to positive law. . . . Hence the ownership of possessions is not contrary to the natural law, but an addition thereto devised by human reason.

Aquinas, *Summa Theologica,* II–II, 66, 2

11 *King Richard.* Nothing can we call our own but death
And that small model of the barren earth
Which serves as paste and cover to our bones.

Shakespeare, *Richard II,* III, ii, 152

12 *Antonio.* I pray you, think you question with the Jew:
You may as well go stand upon the beach
And bid the main flood bate his usual height;
You may as well use question with the wolf
Why he hath made the ewe bleat for the lamb;
You may as well forbid the mountain pines
To wag their high tops and to make no noise,
When they are fretten with the gusts of heaven;
You may as well do any thing most hard,
As seek to soften that—than which what's harder?—
His Jewish heart: therefore, I do beseech you,
Make no more offers, use no farther means,
But with all brief and plain conveniency
Let me have judgement and the Jew his will.
  Bassanio. For thy three thousand ducats here is six.
  Shylock. If every ducat in six thousand ducats
Were in six parts and every part a ducat,
I would not draw them; I would have my bond.
  Duke. How shalt thou hope for mercy, rendering none?
  Shy. What judgement shall I dread, doing no wrong?
You have among you many a purchased slave,
Which, like your asses and your dogs and mules,
You use in abject and in slavish parts,
Because you bought them: shall I say to you,
Let them be free, marry them to your heirs?
Why sweat they under burthens? let their beds
Be made as soft as yours and let their palates
Be season'd with such viands? You will answer
"The slaves are ours": so do I answer you:
The pound of flesh, which I demand of him,
Is dearly bought; 'tis mine and I will have it.
If you deny me, fie upon your law!

Shakespeare, *Merchant of Venice,* IV, i, 70

13 Property, as now in use, was at first a creature of the human will. But, after it was established, one man was prohibited by the law of nature from seizing the property of another against his will.

Grotius, *Rights of War and Peace,* Bk. I, I, 10

14 As nothing can naturally be produced, except from some materials before in existence, it follows that, if those materials were our own, the possession of them under any new shape, or commodity is only a CONTINUATION of our former property; if they belonged to no one, our possession comes under the class of title by occupancy: but if they were another's, no improvement of ours can by the law of nature give us a right of property therein.

Grotius, *Rights of War and Peace*, Bk. II, III, 1

15 The nutrition of a Commonwealth consisteth in the plenty and distribution of materials conducing to life: in concoction or preparation, and, when concocted, in the conveyance of it by convenient conduits to the public use.

As for the plenty of matter, it is a thing limited by nature to those commodities which, from the two breasts of our common mother, land and sea, God usually either freely giveth or for labour selleth to mankind. . . .

The distribution of the materials of this nourishment is the constitution of *mine*, and *thine*, and *his;* that is to say, in one word, *propriety;* and belongeth in all kinds of Commonwealth to the sovereign power. For where there is no Commonwealth, there is, as hath been already shown, a perpetual war of every man against his neighbour; and therefore everything is his that getteth it and keepeth it by force; which is neither propriety nor community, but uncertainty.

Hobbes, *Leviathan*, II, 24

16 The propriety which a subject hath in his lands consisteth in a right to exclude all other subjects from the use of them; and not to exclude their sovereign, be it an assembly or a monarch. For seeing the sovereign, that is to say, the Commonwealth (whose person he representeth), is understood to do nothing but in order to the common peace and security, this distribution of lands is to be understood as done in order to the same: and consequently, whatsoever distribution he shall make in prejudice thereof is contrary to the will of every subject that committed his peace and safety to his discretion and conscience, and therefore by the will of every one of them is to be reputed void.

Hobbes, *Leviathan*, II, 24

17 Though the earth and all inferior creatures be common to all men, yet every man has a "property" in his own "person." This nobody has any right to but himself. The "labour" of his body and the "work" of his hands, we may say, are properly his. Whatsoever, then, he removes out of the state that Nature hath provided and left it in, he hath mixed his labour with it, and joined to it something that is his own, and thereby makes it his property. It being by him removed from the common state Nature placed it in, it hath by this labour something annexed to it that excludes the common right of other men. For this "labour" being the unquestionable property of the labourer, no man but he can have a right to what that is once joined to, at least where there is enough, and as good left in common for others.

He that is nourished by the acorns he picked up under an oak, or the apples he gathered from the trees in the wood, has certainly appropriated them to himself. Nobody can deny but the nourishment is his. I ask, then, when did they begin to be his? when he digested? or when he ate? or when he boiled? or when he brought them home? or when he picked them up? And it is plain, if the first gathering made them not his, nothing else could. That labour put a distinction between them and common. That added something to them more than Nature, the common mother of all, had done, and so they became his private right. And will anyone say he had no right to those acorns or apples he thus appropriated because he had not the consent of all mankind to make them his? Was it a robbery thus to assume to himself what belonged to all in common? If such a consent as that was necessary, man had starved, notwithstanding the plenty God had given him. We see in commons, which remain so by compact, that it is the taking any part of what is common, and removing it out of the state Nature leaves it in, which begins the property, without which the common is of no use. And the taking of this or that part does not depend on the express consent of all the commoners. Thus, the grass my horse has bit, the turfs my servant has cut, and the ore I have digged in any place, where I have a right to them in common with others, become my property without the assignation or consent of anybody. The labour that was mine, removing them out of that common state they were in, hath fixed my property in them.

Locke, *II Civil Government*, V, 26–27

18 The measure of property Nature well set, by the extent of men's labour and the conveniency of life. No man's labour could subdue or appropriate all, nor could his enjoyment consume more than a small part; so that it was impossible for any man, this way, to entrench upon the right of another or acquire to himself a property to the prejudice of his neighbour, who would still have room for as good and as large a possession (after the other had taken out his) as before it was appropriated. Which measure did confine every man's possession to a very moderate proportion, and such as he might appropriate to himself without injury to anybody in the first ages of the world, when men were more in danger to be lost, by wandering from their company, in the then vast wilderness of the earth than to be straitened for want of room to plant in.

Locke, *II Civil Government*, V, 35

19 This I dare boldly affirm . . . every man should have as much as he could make use of, would hold still in the world, without straitening anybody, since there is land enough in the world to suffice double the inhabitants, had not the invention of money, and the tacit agreement of men to put a value on it, introduced (by consent) larger possessions and a right to them.

Locke, *II Civil Government,* V, 36

20 Since gold and silver, being little useful to the life of man, in proportion to food, raiment, and carriage, has its value only from the consent of men—whereof labour yet makes in great part the measure—it is plain that the consent of men have agreed to a disproportionate and unequal possession of the earth—I mean out of the bounds of society and compact; for in governments the laws regulate it; they having, by consent, found out and agreed in a way how a man may, rightfully and without injury, possess more than he himself can make use of by receiving gold and silver, which may continue long in a man's possession without decaying for the overplus, and agreeing those metals should have a value.

Locke, *II Civil Government,* V, 50

21 The difference of rank, birth, and condition established in monarchical governments is frequently attended with distinctions in the nature of property; and the laws relating to the constitution of this government may augment the number of these distinctions. Hence, among us goods are divided into real estates, purchases, dowries, paraphernalia, paternal and maternal inheritances; movables of different kinds; estates held in fee-simple, or in tail; acquired by descent or conveyance; allodial, or held by soccage; ground rents; or annuities. Each sort of goods is subject to particular rules, which must be complied with in the disposal of them. These things must needs diminish the simplicity of the laws.

Montesquieu, *Spirit of Laws,* VI, 1

22 Whenever the public good happens to be the matter in question, it is not for the advantage of the public to deprive an individual of his property, or even to retrench the least part of it by a law, or a political regulation.

Montesquieu, *Spirit of Laws,* XXVI, 15

23 During the ardour of new enthusiasms, when every principle is inflamed into extravagance, the community of goods has frequently been attempted; and nothing but experience of its inconveniences, from the returning or disguised selfishness of men, could make the imprudent fanatics adopt anew the ideas of justice and of separate property. So true is it that this virtue derives its existence entirely from its necessary *use* to the intercourse and social state of mankind.

Hume, *Concerning Principles of Morals,* III

24 Few enjoyments are given us from the open and liberal hand of nature; but by art, labour, and industry, we can extract them in great abundance. Hence the ideas of property become necessary in all civil society.

Hume, *Concerning Principles of Morals,* III

25 The first man who, having enclosed a piece of ground, bethought himself of saying *This is mine,* and found people simple enough to believe him, was the real founder of civil society.

Rousseau, *Origin of Inequality,* II

26 The cultivation of the earth necessarily brought about its distribution; and property, once recognised, gave rise to the first rules of justice; for, to secure each man his own, it had to be possible for each to have something. Besides, as men began to look forward to the future, and all had something to lose, every one had reason to apprehend that reprisals would follow any injury he might do to another. This origin is so much the more natural, as it is impossible to conceive how property can come from anything but manual labour: for what else can a man add to things which he does not originally create, so as to make them his own property? It is the husbandman's labour alone that, giving him a title to the produce of the ground he has tilled, gives him a claim also to the land itself, at least till harvest, and so, from year to year, a constant possession which is easily transformed into property.

Rousseau, *Origin of Inequality,* II

27 Insatiable ambition, the thirst of raising their respective fortunes, not so much from real want as from the desire to surpass others, inspired all men with a vile propensity to injure one another, and with a secret jealousy, which is the more dangerous, as it puts on the mask of benevolence, to carry its point with greater security. In a word, there arose rivalry and competition on the one hand, and conflicting interests on the other, together with a secret desire on both of profiting at the expense of others. All these evils were the first effects of property, and the inseparable attendants of growing inequality.

Rousseau, *Origin of Inequality,* II

28 In general, to establish the right of the first occupier over a plot of ground, the following conditions are necessary: first, the land must not yet be inhabited; secondly, a man must occupy only the amount he needs for his subsistence; and, in the third place, possession must be taken, not by an empty ceremony, but by labour and cultivation, the only sign of proprietorship that should be re-

spected by others, in default of a legal title.

Rousseau, *Social Contract,* I, 9

29 One of the chief characteristics of the golden age, of the age in which neither care nor danger had intruded on mankind, is the community of possessions. Strife and fraud were totally excluded, and every turbulent passion was stilled by plenty and equality. Such were indeed happy times; but such times can return no more. Community of possession must include spontaneity of production; for what is obtained by labour will be of right the property of him by whose labour it is gained.

Johnson, *Rambler No. 131*

30 There seems (said he [Johnson],) to be in authors a stronger right of property than that by occupancy; a metaphysical right, a right, as it were, of creation, which should from its nature be perpetual; but the consent of nations is against it, and indeed reason and the interests of learning are against it; for were it to be perpetual, no book, however useful, could be universally diffused amongst mankind, should the proprietor take it into his head to restrain its circulation.

Boswell, *Life of Johnson (May 8, 1773)*

31 The general stock of any country or society is the same with that of all its inhabitants or members, and therefore naturally divides itself into the same three portions, each of which has a distinct function or office.

The first is that portion which is reserved for immediate consumption, and of which the characteristic is, that it affords no revenue or profit. It consists in the stock of food, clothes, household furniture, etc., which have been purchased by their proper consumers, but which are not yet entirely consumed. The whole stock of mere dwelling-houses too, subsisting at any one time in the country, make a part of this first portion. The stock that is laid out in a house, if it is to be the dwelling-house of the proprietor, ceases from that moment to serve in the function of a capital, or to afford any revenue to its owner. A dwelling-house, as such, contributes nothing to the revenue of its inhabitant; and though it is, no doubt, extremely useful to him, it is as his clothes and household furniture are useful to him, which, however, makes a part of his expense, and not of his revenue. If it is to be let to a tenant for rent, as the house itself can produce nothing, the tenant must always pay the rent out of some other revenue which he derives either from labour, or stock, or land. Though a house, therefore, may yield a revenue to its proprietor, and thereby serve in the function of a capital to him, it cannot yield any to the public, nor serve in the function of a capital to it, and the revenue of the whole body of the people can never be in the smallest degree increased by it. Clothes, and household furniture, in the same manner, sometimes yield a revenue, and thereby serve in the function of a capital to particular persons. In countries where masquerades are common, it is a trade to let out masquerade dresses for a night. Upholsterers frequently let furniture by the month or by the year. Undertakers let the furniture of funerals by the day and by the week. Many people let furnished houses, and get a rent, not only for the use of the house, but for that of the furniture. The revenue, however, which is derived from such things must always be ultimately drawn from some other source of revenue. Of all parts of the stock, either of an individual, or of a society, reserved for immediate consumption, what is laid out in houses is most slowly consumed. A stock of clothes may last several years: a stock of furniture half a century or a century: but a stock of houses, well built and properly taken care of, may last many centuries. Though the period of their total consumption, however, is more distant, they are still as really a stock reserved for immediate consumption as either clothes or household furniture.

The second of the three portions into which the general stock of the society divides itself, is the fixed capital, of which the characteristic is, that it affords a revenue or profit without circulating or changing masters. It consists chiefly of the four following articles:

First, of all useful machines and instruments of trade which facilitate and abridge labour:

Secondly, of all those profitable buildings which are the means of procuring a revenue, not only to their proprietor who lets them for a rent, but to the person who possesses them and pays that rent for them; such as shops, warehouses, workhouses, farmhouses, with all their necessary buildings; stables, granaries, etc. These are very different from mere dwelling houses. They are a sort of instruments of trade, and may be considered in the same light:

Thirdly, of the improvements of land, of what has been profitably laid out in clearing, draining, enclosing, manuring, and reducing it into the condition most proper for tillage and culture. An improved farm may very justly be regarded in the same light as those useful machines which facilitate and abridge labour, and by means of which an equal circulating capital can afford a much greater revenue to its employer. An improved farm is equally advantageous and more durable than any of those machines, frequently requiring no other repairs than the most profitable application of the farmer's capital employed in cultivating it:

Fourthly, of the acquired and useful abilities of all the inhabitants or members of the society. The acquisition of such talents, by the maintenance of the acquirer during his education, study, or apprenticeship, always costs a real expense, which is a capital fixed and realized, as it were, in his person. Those talents, as they make a part of his fortune, so do they likewise of that of the society to which he belongs. The improved dexterity of a workman may be considered in the same light as a machine or instrument of trade which facilitates and abridges labour, and which, though it costs a certain expense, repays that expense with a profit.

The third and last of the three portions into which the general stock of the society naturally divides itself, is the circulating capital; of which the characteristic is, that it affords a revenue only by circulating or changing masters.

Adam Smith, *Wealth of Nations*, II, 1

32 Upon equal, or nearly equal profits, most men will choose to employ their capitals rather in the improvement and cultivation of land than either in manufactures or in foreign trade. The man who employs his capital in land has it more under his view and command, and his fortune is much less liable to accidents than that of the trader, who is obliged frequently to commit it, not only to the winds and the waves, but to the more uncertain elements of human folly and injustice, by giving great credits in distant countries to men with whose character and situation he can seldom be thoroughly acquainted. The capital of the landlord, on the contrary, which is fixed in the improvement of his land, seems to be as well secured as the nature of human affairs can admit of. The beauty of the country besides, the pleasures of a country life, the tranquillity of mind which it promises, and wherever the injustice of human laws does not disturb it, the independency which it really affords, have charms that more or less attract everybody; and as to cultivate the ground was the original destination of man, so in every stage of his existence he seems to retain a predilection for this primitive employment.

Adam Smith, *Wealth of Nations*, III, 1

33 Men who have no property can injure one another only in their persons or reputations. But when one man kills, wounds, beats, or defames another, though he to whom the injury is done suffers, he who does it receives no benefit. It is otherwise with the injuries to property. The benefit of the person who does the injury is often equal to the loss of him who suffers it.

Adam Smith, *Wealth of Nations*, V, 1

34 Wherever there is great property there is great inequality. For one very rich man there must be at least five hundred poor, and the affluence of the few supposes the indigence of the many. The affluence of the rich excites the indignation of the poor, who are often both driven by want, and prompted by envy, to invade his possessions. It is only under the shelter of the civil magistrate that the owner of that valuable property, which is acquired by the labour of many years, or perhaps of

many successive generations, can sleep a single night in security. He is at all times surrounded by unknown enemies, whom, though he never provoked, he can never appease, and from whose injustice he can be protected only by the powerful arm of the civil magistrate continually held up to chastise it. The acquisition of valuable and extensive property, therefore, necessarily requires the establishment of civil government. Where there is no property, or at least none that exceeds the value of two or three days' labour, civil government is not so necessary.

Adam Smith, *Wealth of Nations*, V, 1

35 The community of goods, which had so agreeably amused the imagination of Plato, and which subsisted in some degree among the austere sect of the Essenians, was adopted for a short time in the primitive church. The fervour of the first proselytes prompted them to sell those worldly possessions which they despised, to lay the price of them at the feet of the apostles, and to content themselves with receiving an equal share out of the general distribution. The progress of the Christian religion relaxed, and gradually abolished, this generous institution, which, in hands less pure than those of the apostles, would too soon have been corrupted and abused by the returning selfishness of human nature; and the converts who embraced the new religion were permitted to retain the possession of their patrimony, to receive legacies and inheritances, and to increase their separate property by all the lawful means of trade and industry.

Gibbon, *Decline and Fall
of the Roman Empire*, XV

36 The original right of property can only be justified by the accident or merit of prior occupancy; and on this foundation it is wisely established by the philosophy of the civilians. The savage who hollows a tree, inserts a sharp stone into a wooden handle, or applies a string to an elastic branch, becomes in a state of nature the just proprietor of the canoe, the bow, or the hatchet. The materials were common to all; the new form, the produce of his time and simple industry, belongs solely to himself. His hungry brethren cannot, without a sense of their own injustice, extort from the hunter the game of the forest overtaken or slain by his personal strength and dexterity. If his provident care preserves and multiplies the tame animals, whose nature is tractable to the arts of education, he acquires a perpetual title to the use and service of their numerous progeny, which derives its existence from him alone. If he encloses and cultivates a field for their sustenance and his own, a barren waste is converted into a fertile soil; the seed, the manure, the labour, create a new value, and the rewards of harvest are painfully earned by the fatigues of the revolving year. In the successive

states of society, the hunter, the shepherd, the husbandman, may defend their possessions by two
reasons which forcibly appeal to the feelings of the
human mind: that whatever they enjoy is the fruit
of their own industry; and that every man who
envies their felicity may purchase similar acquisitions by the exercise of similar diligence. Such, in
truth, may be the freedom and plenty of a small
colony cast on a fruitful island. But the colony
multiplies, while the space still continues the
same; the common rights, the equal inheritance of
mankind, are engrossed by the bold and crafty;
each field and forest is circumscribed by the landmarks of a jealous master; and it is the peculiar
praise of the Roman jurisprudence that it asserts
the claim of the first occupant to the wild animals
of the earth, the air, and the waters. In the progress from primitive equity to final injustice, the
steps are silent, the shades are almost imperceptible, and the absolute monopoly is guarded by positive laws and artificial reason. The active, insatiate principle of self-love can alone supply the arts
of life and the wages of industry; and as soon as
civil government and exclusive property have
been introduced, they become necessary to the existence of the human race.

> Gibbon, *Decline and Fall
> of the Roman Empire,* XLIV

37 The personal title of the first proprietor must be
determined by his death; but the possession, without any appearance of change, is peaceably continued in his children, the associates of his toil,
and the partners of his wealth. This natural inheritance has been protected by the legislators of every climate and age, and the father is encouraged
to persevere in slow and distant improvements, by
the tender hope that a long posterity will enjoy
the fruits of his labour. The *principle* of hereditary
succession is universal; but the *order* has been variously established by convenience or caprice, by
the spirit of national institutions, or by some partial example which was originally decided by
fraud or violence.

> Gibbon, *Decline and Fall
> of the Roman Empire,* XLIV

38 I can only call a corporeal thing or an object in
space "mine," when, *even although not in physical possession of it,* I am able to assert that I am in possession of it in another real nonphysical sense. Thus,
I am not entitled to call an apple *mine* merely
because I hold it in my hand or possess it physically; but only when I am entitled to say, "I possess it, although I have laid it out of my hand, and
wherever it may lie." In like manner, I am not
entitled to say of the ground, on which I may have
laid myself down, that therefore it is *mine;* but only
when I can rightly assert that it still remains in
my possession, although I may have left the spot.
For anyone who, in the former appearances of

empirical possession, might wrench the apple out
of my hand, or drag me away from my resting-
place, would, indeed, injure me in respect of the
inner "mine" of freedom, but not in respect of the
external "mine," unless I could assert that I was
in the possession of the object, even when not actually holding it physically. And if I could not do
this, neither could I call the apple or the spot
mine.

> Kant, *Science of Right,* 4

39 If, by word or deed, I declare my will that some
external thing shall be mine, I make a declaration
that every other person is obliged to abstain from
the use of this object of my exercise of will; and
this imposes an obligation which no one would be
under, without such a juridical act on my part.
But the assumption of this act at the same time
involves the admission that I am obliged reciprocally to observe a similar abstention towards every
other in respect of what is externally theirs; for
the obligation in question arises from a universal
rule regulating the external juridical relations.
Hence I am not obliged to let alone what another
person declares to be externally his, unless every
other person likewise secures me by a guarantee
that he will act in relation to what is mine, upon
the same principle. This guarantee of reciprocal
and mutual abstention from what belongs to
others does not require a special juridical act for
its establishment, but is already involved in the
conception of an external obligation of right, on
account of the universality and consequently the
reciprocity of the obligatoriness arising from a
universal Rule. Now a single will, in relation to
an external and consequently contingent possession, cannot serve as a compulsory law for all, because that would be to do violence to the freedom
which is in accordance with universal laws.
Therefore it is only a will that binds every one,
and as such a common, collective, and authoritative will, that can furnish a guarantee of security
to all. But the state of men under a universal,
external, and public legislation, conjoined with
authority and power, is called the civil state.
There can therefore be an external mine and
thine only in the civil state of society.

> Kant, *Science of Right,* 8

40 The principle of external acquisition . . . may be
expressed thus: "Whatever I bring under my power according to the law of external freedom, of
which as an object of my free activity of will I
have the capability of making use according to
the postulate of the practical reason, and which I
will to become mine in conformity with the idea
of a possible united common will, *is* mine."

> Kant, *Science of Right,* 10

41 It is . . . only by positive transference or conveyance, that a personal right can be acquired; and

this is only possible by means of a common will, through which objects come into the power of one or other, so that as one renounces a particular thing which he holds under the common right, the same object when accepted by another, in consequence of a positive act of will, becomes his. Such tranference of the *property* of one to another is termed its *alienation.* The act of the united wills of two persons, by which what belonged to one passes to the other, constitutes *contract.*

Kant, *Science of Right,* 18

42 Property is nothing but a basis of expectation; the expectation of deriving certain advantages from a thing which we are said to possess, in consequence of the relation in which we stand towards it.

There is no image, no painting, no visible trait, which can express the relation that constitutes property. It is not material, it is metaphysical; it is a mere conception of the mind.

Bentham, *Theory of Legislation,*
Principles of the Civil Code, I, 8

43 Property and law are born together, and die together. Before laws were made there was no property; take away laws, and property ceases.

Bentham, *Theory of Legislation,*
Principles of the Civil Code, I, 8

44 This term [PROPERTY], in its particular application, means "that dominion which one man claims and exercises over the external things of the world, in exclusion of every other individual."

In its larger and juster meaning, it embraces everything to which a man may attach a value and have a right; and which leaves to everyone else the like advantage.

In the former sense, a man's land, or merchandise, or money is called his property.

In the latter sense, a man has property in his opinions and the free communication of them.

He has a property of peculiar value in his religious opinions, and in the profession and practice dictated by them.

He has property very dear to him in the safety and liberty of his person.

He has an equal property in the free use of his faculties and free choice of the objects on which to employ them.

In a word, as a man is said to have a right to his property, he may be equally said to have a property in his rights.

Where an excess of power prevails, property of no sort is duly respected. No man is safe in his opinions, his person, his faculties, or his possessions.

Where there is an excess of liberty, the effect is the same, though from an opposite cause.

Government is instituted to protect property of every sort, as well that which lies in the various rights of individuals, as that which the term particularly expresses. This being the end of government, that alone is a *just* government which *impartially* secures to every man whatever is his *own.*

Madison, *Property*

45 A person has as his substantive end the right of putting his will into any and every thing and thereby making it his, because it has no such end in itself and derives its destiny and soul from his will. This is the absolute right of appropriation which man has over all "things."

Hegel, *Philosophy of Right,* 44

46 The principle that a thing belongs to the person who happens to be the first in time to take it into his possession is immediately self-explanatory and superfluous, because a second person cannot take into his possession what is already the property of another.

Hegel, *Philosophy of Right,* 50

47 My merely partial or temporary use of a thing, like my partial or temporary possession of it (a possession which itself is simply the partial or temporary possibility of using it) is therefore to be distinguished from ownership of the thing itself. If the whole and entire use of a thing were mine, while the abstract ownership was supposed to be someone else's, then the thing as mine would be penetrated through and through by my will, and at the same time there would remain in the thing something impenetrable by me, namely the will, the empty will, of another. As a positive will, I would be at one and the same time objective and not objective to myself in the thing—an absolute contradiction. Ownership therefore is in essence free and complete.

Hegel, *Philosophy of Right,* 62

48 Single products of my particular physical and mental skill and of my power to act I can alienate to someone else and I can give him the use of my abilities for a restricted period, because, on the strength of this restriction, my abilities acquire an external relation to the totality and universality of my being. By alienating the whole of my time, as crystallized in my work, and everything I produced, I would be making into another's property the substance of my being, my universal activity and actuality, my personality.

Hegel, *Philosophy of Right,* 67

49 When a child begins to move in the midst of the objects that surround him, he is instinctively led to appropriate to himself everything that he can lay his hands upon; he has no notion of the property of others; but as he gradually learns the value of things and begins to perceive that he may in his turn be despoiled, he becomes more circumspect, and he ends by respecting those rights in others which he wishes to have respected in himself. The

principle which the child derives from the possession of his toys is taught to the man by the objects which he may call his own. In America, the most democratic of nations, those complaints against property in general, which are so frequent in Europe, are never heard, because in America there are no paupers. As everyone has property of his own to defend, everyone recognizes the principle upon which he holds it.

Tocqueville, *Democracy in America,* I, 14

50 If we attentively consider each of the classes of which society is composed, it is easy to see that the passions created by property are keenest and most tenacious among the middle classes. The poor often care but little for what they possess, because they suffer much more from the want of what they have not than they enjoy the little they have. The rich have many other passions besides that of riches to satisfy; and, besides, the long and arduous enjoyment of a great fortune sometimes makes them in the end insensible to its charms. But the men who have a competency, alike removed from opulence and from penury, attach an enormous value to their possessions. As they are still almost within the reach of poverty, they see its privations near at hand and dread them; between poverty and themselves there is nothing but a scanty fortune, upon which they immediately fix their apprehensions and their hopes. Every day increases the interest they take in it, by the constant cares which it occasions; and they are the more attached to it by their continual exertions to increase the amount. The notion of surrendering the smallest part of it is insupportable to them, and they consider its total loss as the worst of misfortunes.

Now, these eager and apprehensive men of small property constitute the class that is constantly increased by the equality of conditions. Hence in democratic communities the majority of the people do not clearly see what they have to gain by a revolution, but they continually and in a thousand ways feel that they might lose by one.

Tocqueville, *Democracy in America,* Vol. II, III, 21

51 In a revolution the owners of personal property have more to fear than all others; for, on the one hand, their property is often easy to seize, and, on the other, it may totally disappear at any moment—a subject of alarm to which the owners of real property are less exposed, since, although they may lose the income of their estates, they may hope to preserve the land itself through the greatest vicissitudes. Hence the former are much more alarmed at the symptoms of revolutionary commotion than the latter. Thus nations are less disposed to make revolutions in proportion as personal property is augmented and distributed among them and as the number of those possessing it is increased.

Tocqueville, *Democracy in America,* Vol. II, III, 21

52 In no country in the world is the love of property more active and more anxious than in the United States; nowhere does the majority display less inclination for those principles which threaten to alter, in whatever manner, the laws of property.

Tocqueville, *Democracy in America,* Vol. II, III, 21

53 I laid my bones to, and drudged for the good I possess; it was not got by fraud, nor by luck, but by work, and you must show me a warrant like these stubborn facts in your own fidelity and labor, before I suffer you, on the faith of a few fine words, to ride into my estate, and claim to scatter it as your own.

Emerson, *The Conservative*

54 Whilst the rights of all as persons are equal, in virtue of their access to reason, their rights in property are very unequal. One man owns his clothes, and another owns a county.

Emerson, *Politics*

55 There is an instinctive sense, however obscure and yet inarticulate, that the whole constitution of property, on its present tenures, is injurious, and its influence on persons deteriorating and degrading; that truly the only interest for the consideration of the State is persons; that property will always follow persons; that the highest end of government is the culture of men; and that if men can be educated, the institutions will share their improvement and the moral sentiment will write the law of the land.

Emerson, *Politics*

56 The law may in a mad freak say that all shall have power except the owners of property; they shall have no vote. Nevertheless, by a higher law, the property will, year after year, write every statute that respects property.

Emerson, *Politics*

57 Property . . . has been well compared to snow— "if it fall level to-day, it will be blown into drifts to-morrow."

Emerson, *Nature,* V

58 In a free and just commonwealth, property rushes from the idle and imbecile to the industrious, brave and persevering.

Emerson, *Wealth*

59 The highest law gives a thing to him who can use it.

Thoreau, *Journal (Nov. 9, 1852)*

60 It is plain that commodities cannot go to market and make exchanges of their own account. We must, therefore, have recourse to their guardians, who are also their owners. Commodities are things, and, therefore, without power of resistance against man. If they are wanting in docility he can use force; in other words, he can take possession of them. In order that these objects may enter into relation with each other as commodities, their guardians must place themselves in relation to one another, as persons whose will resides in those objects, and must behave in such a way that each does not appropriate the commodity of the other, and part with his own, except by means of an act done by mutual consent. They must, therefore, mutually recognize in each other the rights of private proprietors.

Marx, *Capital,* Vol. I, I, 2

61 At first the rights of property seemed to us to be based on a man's own labour. At least, some such assumption was necessary since only commodity owners with equal rights confronted each other, and the sole means by which a man could become possessed of the commodities of others was by alienating his own commodities; and these could be replaced by labour alone. Now, however, property turns out to be the right, on the part of the capitalist, to appropriate the unpaid labour of others or its product, and to be the impossibility, on the part of the labourer, of appropriating his own product. The separation of property from labour has become the necessary consequence of a law that apparently originated in their identity.

Marx, *Capital,* Vol. I, VII, 24

62 Through however long a series of periodical reproduction and previous accumulation it may have passed, the capital functioning today retains its primal virginity. So long as the laws of exchange are followed in each act of exchange considered individually, the mode of appropriation may be revolutionized without touching property rights derived from commodity production. The same right was valid at a time when the product belonged to the producer, who could only enrich himself by his own labour, exchanging equivalent for equivalent, and is still valid in the capitalist period in which the social wealth becomes to an ever increasing degree the property of those who are in a position to appropriate over and over again the unpaid labour of others.

Marx, *Capital,* Vol. I, VII, 24

63 The development of capitalist production makes it constantly necessary to keep increasing the amount of the capital laid out in a given industrial undertaking, and competition makes the immanent laws of capitalist production to be felt by each individual capitalist as external coercive laws. It compels him to keep constantly extending his capital, in order to preserve it; but extend it he cannot, except by means of progressive accumulation.

So far, therefore, as his actions are a mere function of capital—endowed as capital is, in his person, with consciousness and a will—his own private consumption is a robbery perpetrated on accumulation, just as in book-keeping by double entry the private expenditure of the capitalist is placed on the debtor side of his account against his capital. To accumulate is to conquer the world of social wealth, to increase the mass of human beings exploited by him, and thus to extend both the direct and the indirect sway of the capitalist.

But original sin is at work everywhere. As capitalist production, accumulation, and wealth, become developed, the capitalist ceases to be the mere incarnation of capital. He has a fellow-feeling for his own Adam, and his education gradually enables him to smile at the rage for asceticism, as a mere prejudice of the old-fashioned miser. While the capitalist of the classical type brands individual consumption as a sin against his function, and as "abstinence" from accumulating, the modernized capitalist is capable of looking upon accumulation as "abstinence" from pleasure.

Marx, *Capital,* Vol. I, VII, 24

64 The . . . thing that interests us is the secret discovered in the new world by the political economy of the old world, and proclaimed on the housetops: that the capitalist mode of production and accumulation, and therefore capitalist private property, have for their fundamental condition the annihilation of self-earned private property; in other words, the expropriation of the labourer.

Marx, *Capital,* Vol. I, VIII, 33

65 The distinguishing feature of Communism is not the abolition of property generally, but the abolition of bourgeois property. But modern bourgeois private property is the final and most complete expression of the system of producing and appropriating products that is based on class antagonisms, on the exploitation of the many by the few.

Marx and Engels, *Communist Manifesto,* II

66 Does wage labour create any property for the labourer? Not a bit. It creates capital, i.e., that kind of property which exploits wage labour and which cannot increase except upon condition of begetting a new supply of wage labour for fresh exploitation. Property in its present form is based on the antagonism of capital and wage labour.

Marx and Engels, *Communist Manifesto,* II

67 When . . . capital is converted into common property, into the property of all members of society, personal property is not thereby transformed into social property. It is only the social character

of the property that is changed. It loses its class character.

Marx and Engels, *Communist Manifesto*, II

68 You are horrified at our intending to do away with private property. But in your existing society private property is already done away with for nine-tenths of the population; its existence for the few is solely due to its non-existence in the hands of those nine-tenths. You reproach us, therefore, with intending to do away with a form of property, the necessary condition for whose existence is the non-existence of any property for the immense majority of society.

In a word, you reproach us with intending to do away with your property. Precisely so; that is just what we intend.

From the moment when labour can no longer be converted into capital, money, or rent—into a social power capable of being monopolised—i.e., from the moment when individual property can no longer be transformed into bourgeois property, into capital; from that moment, you say, individuality vanishes.

You must, therefore, confess that by "individual" you mean no other person than the bourgeois, than the middle class owner of property. This person must, indeed, be swept out of the way and made impossible.

Communism deprives no man of the power to appropriate the products of society; all that it does is to deprive him of the power to subjugate the labour of others by means of such appropriation.

Marx and Engels, *Communist Manifesto*, II

69 It has been objected that upon the abolition of private property all work will cease and universal laziness will overtake us.

According to this, bourgeois society ought long ago to have gone to the dogs through sheer idleness; for those of its members who work acquire nothing, and those who acquire anything do not work.

Marx and Engels, *Communist Manifesto*, II

70 If . . . the choice were to be made between Communism with all its chances, and the present state of society with all its sufferings and injustices; if the institution of private property necessarily carried with it as a consequence, that the produce of labour should be apportioned as we now see it, almost in an inverse ratio to the labour—the largest portions to those who have never worked at all, the next largest to those whose work is almost nominal, and so in a descending scale, the remuneration dwindling as the work grows harder and more disagreeable, until the most fatiguing and exhausting bodily labour cannot count with certainty on being able to earn even the necessaries of life; if this or Communism were the alternative,

all the difficulties, great or small, of Communism would be but as dust in the balance. But to make the comparison applicable, we must compare Communism at its best, with the régime of individual property, not as it is, but as it might be made. The principle of private property has never yet had a fair trial in any country.

Mill, *Principles of Political Economy*, Bk. II, I, 3

71 The laws of property have never yet conformed to the principles on which the justification of private property rests. They have made property of things which never ought to be property, and absolute property where only a qualified property ought to exist. They have not held the balance fairly between human beings, but have heaped impediments upon some, to give advantage to others; they have purposely fostered inequalities, and prevented all from starting fair in the race. That all should indeed start on perfectly equal terms, is inconsistent with any law of private property: but if as much pains as has been taken to aggravate the inequality of chances arising from the natural working of the principle, had been taken to temper that inequality by every means not subversive of the principle itself; if the tendency of legislation had been to favour the diffusion, instead of the concentration of wealth—to encourage the subdivision of the large masses, instead of striving to keep them together; the principle of individual property would have been found to have no necessary connexion with the physical and social evils which almost all Socialist writers assume to be inseparable from it.

Mill, *Principles of Political Economy*, Bk. II, I, 3

72 Nothing is implied in property but the right of each to his (or her) own faculties, to what he can produce by them, and to whatever he can get for them in a fair market; together with his right to give this to any other person if he chooses, and the right of that other to receive and enjoy it.

Mill, *Principles of Political Economy*, Bk. II, II, 3

73 When the "sacredness of property" is talked of, it should always be remembered, that any such sacredness does not belong in the same degree to landed property. No man made the land. It is the original inheritance of the whole species. Its appropriation is wholly a question of general expediency. When private property in land is not expedient, it is unjust. It is no hardship to any one, to be excluded from what others have produced: they were not bound to produce it for his use, and he loses nothing by not sharing in what otherwise would not have existed at all. But it is some hardship to be born into the world and to find all nature's gifts previously engrossed, and no place

left for the new-comer. To reconcile people to this, after they have once admitted into their minds the idea that any moral rights belong to them as human beings, it will always be necessary to convince them that the exclusive appropriation is good for mankind on the whole, themselves included. But this is what no sane human being could be persuaded of.

Mill, *Principles of Political Economy,*
Bk. II, II, 6

74 To me it seems almost an axiom that property in land should be interpreted strictly, and that the balance in all cases of doubt should incline against the proprietor. The reverse is the case with property in moveables, and in all things the product of labour: over these, the owner's power both of use and of exclusion should be absolute, except where positive evil to others would result from it: but in the case of land, no exclusive right should be permitted in any individual, which cannot be shown to be productive of positive good. To be allowed any exclusive right at all, over a portion of the common inheritance, while there are others who have no portion, is already a privilege. No quantity of moveable goods which a person can acquire by his labour, prevents others from acquiring the like by the same means; but from the very nature of the case, whoever owns land, keeps others out of the enjoyment of it. The privilege, or monopoly, is only defensible as a necessary evil; it becomes an injustice when carried to any point to which the compensating good does not follow it.

Mill, *Principles of Political Economy,*
Bk. II, II, 6

75 There is no divine right of property. Nothing is so completely a man's own that he may do what he likes with it. His very limbs, intimately as they belong to him, he may not use to the injury of society, much less his knife, his stick, or "anything that is his." Not only may he not use them malevolently: he must not use them even carelessly and indifferently except at his own peril if harm ensue. Exceptionally dangerous substances, such as poisons and explosives, he can only obtain and possess under exceptionally stringent conditions.

Nevertheless, as it is obviously well that each man should labor without fear of being deprived of the use and enjoyment of the product of their labor—as in the nature of things he would not labor at all without some such incentive, it may be said that a man has a natural right to own the product of his labor. The term natural right, if old fashioned, is as much to the purpose as any modern expression of the same meaning. But this natural right of the individual is still subject to all the limitations imposed by the rights of his fellows.

Shaw, *Freedom and the State*

76 There are three practicable ways of providing for the production of commodities and exchange of services in civilized communities. These three are—

PRIVATE PROPERTY,

COLLECTIVISM,

COMMUNISM

The first is a non-socialist system. The other two are socialist.

In all modern States the three are in operation side by side, but as Collectivism and Communism are purposely restricted to those departments of industry in which the Private Property system is practically impossible, the predominating and characteristic method of organizing the industry of the world is at present non-socialist.

As the method of producing and distributing wealth has irresistibly influenced custom, morality, the forms of law and religion, and indeed all social institutions, being only less fundamental than human nature itself, it is important that the three systems should be known and understood as working arrangements, quite apart from their abstract principles. Whoever masters the subject in this way will perceive that discussions as to whether Private Property in the abstract is better or worse than Socialism are as idle as discussions as to whether black in the abstract is better or worse than white. The applicability of either system depends on the nature of the commodity or service to which it is proposed to apply it, on the industrial and moral development of the community—in short, on diverse factors which vary in all possible manners. There is no inconsistency of principle in our present arrangement of Private Enterprise in the medical profession, Collectivism in our postal service, and Communism in our London bridges. If the student, as the outcome of his study, concludes that it would be well to effect such an extension of Collectivism as would make it the predominant and characteristic system in this country, then he may conveniently call himself a Socialist. But there is no universally applicable abstract principle of Socialism or Individualism by subscribing to which men can claim to be Socialists or Individualists without troubling themselves about economic science or practical industry.

Shaw, *Capital and Wages*

11.2 | *Wealth and Poverty*

This is by far the richest section in this chapter, not only in the range and variety of the passages quoted, but also in the number and character of the authors who contribute to the discussion of its basic themes. As contrasted with the subjects covered in those sections to follow that tend to be more narrowly economic, the discussion of wealth and poverty involves broad psychological, moral, and political considerations as well as strictly economic ones.

Those who ask whether any limit can be placed on the production and acquisition of wealth by an individual or a society find themselves confronted with the apparently limitless reach of human desires. But, acknowledging this fact, they also recognize the harmful effects, both upon the individual and upon society, of setting no limits to the accumulation of wealth. Almost without exception, the great moralists from Plato, Aristotle, and the Roman Stoics to Aquinas, Locke, and Rousseau condemn the insatiable lust for external possessions, but they differ on the question of the indispensability of a modicum of wealth as one of the conditions of earthly happiness. They are also concerned with the obligations of the individual, in justice and in charity, to avoid injuring others by impoverishing them or by letting their poverty go unrelieved. On these subjects, the Old and the New Testament, the poets, the novelists, and the historians also speak with intensity and eloquence.

On the other hand, poverty itself is praised as well as deplored, not involuntary destitution, but the voluntary poverty that is a virtuous way of life. We find divers expressions of this point of view in the ancient Stoics, in the Sacred Scriptures, in the Christian theologians, and in modern writers like Thoreau, who voices a disdain for wealth-seeking and a dislike for the burden of possessions that are current in certain sections of our society today. Balanced against this, increasingly as we approach modern times, is the antiphonal voice that denounces the injustice of a vast inequality in the distribution of wealth, and that calls not merely for the relief of the poor but also for the elimination of poverty itself.

To all of this, the economists add their proposals of measures for increasing the wealth of nations and their arguments for and against the control of its production and distribution.

For the consideration of wealth and poverty in relation to the pursuit of happiness and the conduct of life, the reader is referred to Section 9.8 on Happiness, and also Section 9.10 on Virtue and Vice. Treatment of the religious aspect of wealth and poverty will be found in Section 20.8 on Worship and Service, and also in Section 20.13 on Sin and Temptation. The problem of involuntary poverty or destitution raises questions more fully discussed in Section 12.2 on Justice and Injustice and in Section 13.3 on Equality.

---

1 And the Lord sent Nathan unto David. And he came unto him, and said unto him, There were two men in one city; the one rich, and the other poor.

The rich man had exceeding many flocks and herds:

But the poor man had nothing, save one little ewe lamb, which he had bought and nourished up: and it grew up together with him, and with his children; it did eat of his own meat, and drank of his own cup, and lay in his bosom, and was unto him as a daughter.

And there came a traveller unto the rich man, and he spared to take of his own flock and of his own herd, to dress for the wayfaring man that was come unto him; but took the poor man's lamb, and dressed it for the man that was come to him.

And David's anger was greatly kindled against the man; and he said to Nathan, As the Lord liveth, the man that hath done this thing shall surely die:

And he shall restore the lamb fourfold, because he did this thing, and because he had no pity.

And Nathan said to David, Thou art the man.

II Samuel 12:1–7

2 The rich man's wealth is his strong city: the destruction of the poor is their poverty.

Proverbs 10:15

3 The poor is hated even of his own neighbour: but the rich hath many friends.

Proverbs 14:20

4 He that maketh haste to be rich shall not be innocent.

Proverbs 28:20

5 The sleep of a labouring man is sweet, whether he eat little or much: but the abundance of the rich will not suffer him to sleep.

Ecclesiastes 5:12

6 *Swineherd.* Shyness is no asset to a beggar.

Homer, *Odyssey*, XVII, 352

7 Who bids his gather'd substance gradual grow
Shall see not livid hunger's face of woe.
No bosom pang attends the home-laid store,
But fraught with loss the food without thy door.
'Tis good to take from hoards, and pain to need
What is far from thee:—give the precept heed.

Hesiod, *Works and Days*

8 *Solon.* He who possesses great store of riches is no nearer happiness than he who has what suffices for his daily needs, unless it so hap that luck attend upon him, and so he continue in the enjoyment of all his good things to the end of life.

Herodotus, *History*, I, 32

9 'Tis said that gifts tempt even gods; and o'er men's minds gold holds more potent sway than countless words.

Euripides, *Medea*, 964

10 *Cyclops.* Money's the wise man's religion, little man.
The rest is mere bluff and purple patches.

Euripides, *Cyclops*, 316

11 *Farmer.* In times like these, when wishes soar but power fails,
I contemplate the steady comfort found in gold:
gold you can spend on guests; gold you can pay the doctor
when you get sick. But a small crumb of gold will buy
our daily bread, and when a man has eaten that, you cannot really tell the rich and poor apart.

Euripides, *Electra*, 426

12 *Pericles.* The real disgrace of poverty [lies] not in owning to the fact but in declining the struggle against it.

Thucydides, *Peloponnesian War*, II, 40

13 *Socrates.* I do nothing but go about persuading you all, old and young alike, not to take thought for your persons or your properties, but first and chiefly to care about the greatest improvement of the soul.

Plato, *Apology*, 30A

14 *Socrates.* May I ask, Cephalus, whether your fortune was for the most part inherited or acquired by you?

Cephalus. Acquired! Socrates; do you want to know how much I acquired? In the art of making money I have been midway between my father and grandfather: for my grandfather, whose name I bear, doubled and trebled the value of his patrimony, that which he inherited being much what I possess now; but my father Lysanias reduced the property below what it is at present: and I shall be satisfied if I leave to these my sons not less but a little more than I received.

That was why I asked you the question, I replied, because I see that you are indifferent about money, which is a characteristic rather of those who have inherited their fortunes than of those who have acquired them; the makers of fortunes have a second love of money as a creation of their own, resembling the affection of authors for their own poems, or of parents for their children, besides that natural love of it for the sake of use and profit which is common to them and all men. And hence they are very bad company, for they can talk about nothing but the praises of wealth.

That is true, he said.

Yes, that is very true, but may I ask another question?—What do you consider to be the greatest blessing which you have reaped from your wealth?

One, he said, of which I could not expect easily to convince others. For let me tell you, Socrates, that when a man thinks himself to be near death, fears and cares enter into his mind which he never had before; the tales of a world below and the punishment which is exacted there of deeds done here were once a laughing matter to him, but now he is tormented with the thought that they may be true: either from the weakness of age, or because he is now drawing nearer to that other place, he has a clearer view of these things; suspicions and alarms crowd thickly upon him, and he begins to reflect and consider what wrongs he has done to others. And when he finds that the sum of his transgressions is great he will many a time like a child start up in his sleep for fear, and he is filled with dark forebodings. But to him who is conscious of no sin, sweet hope . . . is the kind nurse of his age. . . . The great blessing of riches, I do not say to every man, but to a good man, is, that he has had no occasion to deceive or to defraud others, either intentionally or unintentionally; and when he departs to the world below he is not in any apprehension about offerings due to the gods or debts which he owes to men. Now to this peace of mind the possession of wealth greatly contributes; and therefore I say, that, setting one thing against another, of the many advantages which wealth has to give, to a man of sense this is in my opinion the greatest.

Plato, *Republic,* I, 330A

15 *Socrates.* And now, Adeimantus, is our State matured and perfected?

Adeimantus. I think so.

Where, then, is justice, and where is injustice, and in what part of the State did they spring up?

Probably in the dealings of these citizens with one another. I cannot imagine that they are more likely to be found any where else.

I dare say that you are right in your suggestion, I said; we had better think the matter out, and not shrink from the enquiry.

Let us then consider, first of all, what will be their way of life, now that we have thus established them. Will they not produce corn, and wine, and clothes, and shoes, and build houses for themselves? And when they are housed, they will work, in summer, commonly, stripped and barefoot, but in winter substantially clothed and shod. They will feed on barley-meal and flour of wheat, baking and kneading them, making noble cakes and loaves; these they will serve up on a mat of reeds or on clean leaves, themselves reclining the while upon beds strewn with yew or myrtle. And they and their children will feast, drinking of the wine which they have made, wearing garlands on their heads, and hymning the praises of the gods, in happy converse with one another. And they will take care that their families do not exceed their means; having an eye to poverty or war.

But, said Glaucon, interposing, you have not given them a relish to their meal.

True, I replied, I had forgotten; of course they must have a relish—salt, and olives, and cheese, and they will boil roots and herbs such as country people prepare; for a dessert we shall give them figs, and peas, and beans; and they will roast myrtle-berries and acorns at the fire, drinking in mod-

eration. And with such a diet they may be expected to live in peace and health to a good old age, and bequeath a similar life to their children after them.

Yes, Socrates, he said, and if you were providing for a city of pigs, how else would you feed the beasts?

But what would you have, Glaucon? I replied.

Why, he said, you should give them the ordinary conveniences of life. People who are to be comfortable are accustomed to lie on sofas, and dine off tables, and they should have sauces and sweets in the modern style.

Yes, I said, now I understand: the question which you would have me consider is, not only how a State, but how a luxurious State is created; and possibly there is no harm in this, for in such a State we shall be more likely to see how justice and injustice originate. In my opinion the true and healthy constitution of the State is the one which I have described.

Plato, *Republic,* II, 371B

16 *Socrates.* There seem to be two causes of the deterioration of the arts.

Adeimantus. What are they?

Wealth, I said, and poverty.

How do they act?

The process is as follows: When a potter becomes rich, will he, think you, any longer take the same pains with his art?

Certainly not.

He will grow more and more indolent and careless?

Very true.

And the result will be that he becomes a worse potter?

Yes; he greatly deteriorates.

But, on the other hand, if he has no money, and cannot provide himself with tools or instruments, he will not work equally well himself, nor will he teach his sons or apprentices to work equally well.

Certainly not.

Then, under the influence either of poverty or of wealth, workmen and their work are equally liable to degenerate?

This is evident.

Here, then, is a discovery of new evils, I said, against which the guardians will have to watch, or they will creep into the city unobserved.

What evils?

Wealth, I said, and poverty; the one is the parent of luxury and indolence, and the other of meanness and viciousness, and both of discontent.

Plato, *Republic,* IV, 421B

17 The citizen must indeed be happy and good, and the legislator will seek to make him so; but very rich and very good at the same time he cannot be, not, at least, in the sense in which the many speak of riches. For they mean by "the rich" the few

who have the most valuable possessions, although the owner of them may quite well be a rogue. And if this is true, I can never assent to the doctrine that the rich man will be happy—he must be good as well as rich. And good in a high degree, and rich in a high degree at the same time, he cannot be.

Plato, *Laws,* V, 742B

18 The magnificent man is like an artist; for he can see what is fitting and spend large sums tastefully. . . . Now the expenses of the magnificent man are large and fitting. Such, therefore, are also his results; for thus there will be a great expenditure and one that is fitting to its result. Therefore the result should be worthy of the expense, and the expense should be worthy of the result, or should even exceed it. And the magnificent man will spend such sums for honour's sake; for this is common to the virtues. And further he will do so gladly and lavishly; for nice calculation is a niggardly thing. And he will consider how the result can be made most beautiful and most becoming rather than for how much it can be produced and how it can be produced most cheaply. It is necessary, then, that the magnificent man be also liberal. For the liberal man also will spend what he ought and as he ought; and it is in these matters that the greatness implied in the name of the magnificent man—his bigness, as it were—is manifested, since liberality is concerned with these matters; and at an equal expense he will produce a more magnificent work of art. For a possession and a work of art have not the same excellence. The most valuable possession is that which is worth most, for example gold, but the most valuable work of art is that which is great and beautiful (for the contemplation of such a work inspires admiration, and so does magnificence); and a work has an excellence—viz. magnificence—which involves magnitude. Magnificence is an attribute of expenditures of the kind which we call honourable, for example those connected with the gods—votive offerings, buildings, and sacrifices—and similarly with any form of religious worship, and all those that are proper objects of public-spirited ambition, as when people think they ought to equip a chorus or a trireme, or entertain the city, in a brilliant way. But in all cases . . . we have regard to the agent as well and ask who he is and what means he has; for the expenditure should be worthy of his means, and suit not only the result but also the producer. Hence a poor man cannot be magnificent, since he has not the means with which to spend large sums fittingly; and he who tries is a fool, since he spends beyond what can be expected of him and what is proper, but it is *right* expenditure that is virtuous.

Aristotle, *Ethics,* 1122ª34

19 Such . . . is the magnificent man; the man who goes to excess and is vulgar exceeds . . . by spending beyond what is right. For on small objects of expenditure he spends much and displays a tasteless showiness; e.g. he gives a club dinner on the scale of a wedding banquet, and when he provides the chorus for a comedy he brings them on to stage in purple, as they do at Megara. And all such things he will do not for honour's sake but to show off his wealth, and because he thinks he is admired for these things, and where he ought to spend much he spends little and where little, much. The niggardly man on the other hand will fall short in everything, and after spending the greatest sums will spoil the beauty of the result for a trifle, and whatever he is doing he will hesitate and consider how he may spend least, and lament even that, and think he is doing everything on a bigger scale than he ought.

Aristotle, *Ethics,* 1123ª18

20 Happiness . . . must be some form of contemplation. But, being a man, one will also need external prosperity; for our nature is not self-sufficient for the purpose of contemplation, but our body also must be healthy and must have food and other attention. Still, we must not think that the man who is to be happy will need many things or great things . . . for self-sufficiency and action do not involve excess, and we can do noble acts without ruling earth and sea.

Aristotle, *Ethics,* 1178ᵇ32

21 Some persons are led to believe that . . . the whole idea of their lives is that they ought either to increase their money without limit, or at any rate not to lose it. The origin of this disposition in men is that they are intent upon living only, and not upon living well; and, as their desires are unlimited, they also desire that the means of gratifying them should be without limit.

Aristotle, *Politics,* 1257ᵇ38

22 It would be well also to collect the scattered stories of the ways in which individuals have succeeded in amassing a fortune; for all this is useful to persons who value the art of getting wealth. There is the anecdote of Thales the Milesian and his financial device, which involves a principle of universal application, but is attributed to him on account of his reputation for wisdom. He was reproached for his poverty, which was supposed to show that philosophy was of no use. According to the story, he knew by his skill in the stars while it was yet winter that there would be a great harvest of olives in the coming year; so, having a little money, he gave deposits for the use of all the olive-presses in Chios and Miletus, which he hired at a low price because no one bid against him. When the harvest-time came, and many were wanted all at once and of a sudden, he let them out at any rate which he pleased, and made a quantity of money.

Thus he showed the world that philosophers can easily be rich if they like, but that their ambition is of another sort. He is supposed to have given a striking proof of his wisdom, but, as I was saying, his device for getting wealth is of universal application, and is nothing but the creation of a monopoly. It is an art often practised by cities when they are in want of money; they make a monopoly of provisions.

There was a man of Sicily, who, having money deposited with him, bought up all the iron from the iron mines; afterwards, when the merchants from their various markets came to buy, he was the only seller, and without much increasing the price he gained 200 per cent. Which when Dionysius heard, he told him that he might take away his money, but that he must not remain at Syracuse, for he thought that the man had discovered a way of making money which was injurious to his own interests. He made the same discovery as Thales; they both contrived to create a monopoly for themselves. And statesmen as well ought to know these things; for a state is often as much in want of money and of such devices for obtaining it as a household, or even more so; hence some public men devote themselves entirely to finance.

Aristotle, *Politics*, 1259ª3

23 The true friend of the people should see that they be not too poor, for extreme poverty lowers the character of the democracy; measures therefore should be taken which will give them lasting prosperity; and as this is equally the interest of all classes, the proceeds of the public revenues should be accumulated and distributed among its poor, if possible, in such quantities as may enable them to purchase a little farm, or, at any rate, make a beginning in trade or husbandry. And if this benevolence cannot be extended to all, money should be distributed in turn according to tribes or other divisions, and in the meantime the rich should pay the fee for the attendance of the poor at the necessary assemblies; and should in return be excused from useless public services.

Aristotle, *Politics*, 1320ª33

24 The constituents of wealth are: plenty of coined money and territory; the ownership of numerous, large, and beautiful estates; also the ownership of numerous and beautiful implements, live stock, and slaves. All these kinds of property are our own, are secure, gentlemanly, and useful. The useful kinds are those that are productive, the gentlemanly kinds are those that provide enjoyment. By 'productive' I mean those from which we get our income; by 'enjoyable', those from which we get nothing worth mentioning except the use of them. The criterion of 'security' is the ownership of property in such places and under such conditions that the use of it is in our power; and it is 'our own' if it is in our own power to

dispose of it or keep it. By 'disposing of it' I mean giving it away or selling it. Wealth as a whole consists in using things rather than in owning them; it is really the activity—that is, the use—of property that constitutes wealth.

Aristotle, *Rhetoric*, 1361ª12

25 What is long established seems akin to what exists by nature; and therefore we feel more indignation at those possessing a given good if they have as a matter of fact only just got it and the prosperity it brings with it. The newly rich give more offence than those whose wealth is of long standing and inherited. The same is true of those who have office or power, plenty of friends, a fine family, etc. We feel the same when these advantages of theirs secure them others. For here again, the newly rich give us more offence by obtaining office through their riches than do those whose wealth is of long standing; and so in all other cases. The reason is that what the latter have is felt to be really their own, but what the others have is not; what appears to have been always what it is is regarded as real, and so the possessions of the newly rich do not seem to be really their own.

Aristotle, *Rhetoric*, 1387ª16

26 Wealthy men are insolent and arrogant; their possession of wealth affects their understanding; they feel as if they had every good thing that exists; wealth becomes a sort of standard of value for everything else, and therefore they imagine there is nothing it cannot buy. . . . In a word, the type of character produced by wealth is that of a prosperous fool.

Aristotle, *Rhetoric*, 1390ᵇ33

27 Beware of an inordinate desire for wealth. Nothing is so revealing of narrowness and littleness of soul than love for money. Conversely, there is nothing more honorable or noble than indifference to money, if one doesn't have any; or than genuine altruism and well-doing if one does have it.

Cicero, *De Officiis*, I, 20

28 Without doubt, the highest privilege of wealth is the opportunity it affords for doing good, without giving up one's fortune.

Cicero, *De Officiis*, II, 18

29 O happy, if he knew his happy state,
The swain, who, free from business and debate,
Receives his easy food from nature's hand,
And just returns of cultivated land!
No palace, with a lofty gate, he wants,
To admit the tides of early visitants,
With eager eyes devouring, as they pass,
The breathing figures of Corinthian brass.
No statues threaten, from high pedestals;
No Persian arras hides his homely walls,

With antic vests, which, through their shady fold,
Betray the streaks of ill-dissembled gold:
He boasts no wool, whose native white is dyed
With purple poison of Assyrian pride;
No costly drugs of Araby defile,
With foreign scents, the sweetness of his oil:
But easy quiet, a secure retreat,
A harmless life that knows not how to cheat,
With home-bred plenty, the rich owner bless,
And rural pleasures crown his happiness.
Unvexed with quarrels, undisturbed with noise,
The country king his peaceful realm enjoys—
Cool grots, and living lakes, the flowery pride
Of meads, and streams that through the valley
    glide,
And shady groves that easy sleep invite,
And after toilsome days, a soft repose at night.
Wild beasts of nature in his woods abound;
And youth, of labour patient, plough the ground,
Inured to hardship, and to homely fare.
Nor venerable age is wanting there,
In great examples to the youthful train;
Nor are the gods adored with rites profane.

Virgil, Georgics, II

30 *Aeneas.* O sacred hunger of pernicious gold!
What bands of faith can impious lucre hold?

Virgil, Aeneid, III

31 Neither sultry summer, nor winter, fire, ocean,
sword, can drive you from gain. You surmount
every obstacle, that no other man may be richer
than yourself.

Horace, Satires, I, 1

32 Do you wonder that no one tenders you the affection which you do not merit, since you prefer your
money to everything else?

Horace, Satires, I, 1

33 As riches grow, care follows, and a thirst
For more and more.

Horace, Odes, III, 16

34   Poverty's inglorious load
Bids man unheard-of things endure and try;
   While Virtue's solitary road
He deems too steep, and cowardly passes by.

Horace, Odes, III, 24

35 It is not the man who has too little who is poor,
but the one who hankers after more. What difference does it make how much there is laid away in
a man's safe or in his barns, how many head of
stock he grazes or how much capital he puts out
at interest, if he is always after what is another's
and only counts what he has yet to get, never
what he has already. You ask what is the proper
limit to a person's wealth? First, having what is
essential, and second, having what is enough.

Seneca, Letters to Lucilius, 2

36 Imagine that you've piled up all that a veritable
host of rich men ever possessed, that fortune has
carried you far beyond the bounds of wealth so far
as any private individual is concerned, building
you a roof of gold and clothing you in royal purple, conducting you to such a height of opulence
and luxury that you hide the earth with marble
floors—putting you in a position not merely to
own, but to walk all over treasures—throw in
sculptures, paintings, all that has been produced
at tremendous pains by all the arts to satisfy extravagance: all these things will only induce in
you a craving for even bigger things. Natural desires are limited; those which spring from false
opinions have nowhere to stop, for falsity has no
point of termination.

Seneca, Letters to Lucilius, 16

37 For no one is worthy of a god unless he has paid
no heed to riches. I am not, mind you, against
your possessing them, but I want to ensure that
you possess them without tremors; and this you
will only achieve in one way, by convincing yourself that you can live a happy life even without
them, and by always regarding them as being on
the point of vanishing.

Seneca, Letters to Lucilius, 18

38 No man can serve two masters: for either he will
hate the one, and love the other; or else he will
hold to the one, and despise the other. Ye cannot
serve God and măm-mon.

   Therefore I say unto you, Take no thought for
your life, what ye shall eat, or what ye shall drink;
nor yet for your body, what ye shall put on. Is not
the life more than meat, and the body than raiment?

   Behold the fowls of the air: for they sow not,
neither do they reap, nor gather into barns; yet
your heavenly Father feedeth them. Are ye not
much better than they?

   Which of you by taking thought can add one
cubit unto his stature?

   And why take ye thought for raiment? Consider
the lilies of the field, how they grow; they toil not,
neither do they spin:

   And yet I say unto you, That even Solomon in
all his glory was not arrayed like one of these.

   Wherefore, if God so clothe the grass of the
field, which to day is, and to morrow is cast into
the oven, shall he not much more clothe you, O ye
of little faith?

   Therefore take no thought, saying, What shall
we eat? or, What shall we drink? or, Wherewithal
shall we be clothed?

   (For after all these things do the Gentiles seek:)
for your heavenly Father knoweth that ye have
need of all these things.

   But seek ye first the kingdom of God, and his
righteousness; and all these things shall be added
unto you.

Take therefore no thought for the morrow: for the morrow shall take thought for the things of itself. Sufficient unto the day is the evil thereof.

Matthew 6:24–34

39 Jesus said unto him, If thou wilt be perfect, go and sell that thou hast, and give to the poor, and thou shalt have treasure in heaven: and come and follow me.

But when the young man heard that saying, he went away sorrowful: for he had great possessions.

Then said Jesus unto his disciples, Verily I say unto you, That a rich man shall hardly enter into the kingdom of heaven.

And again I say unto you, It is easier for a camel to go through the eye of a needle, than for a rich man to enter into the kingdom of God.

When his disciples heard it, they were exceedingly amazed, saying, Who then can be saved?

Matthew 19:21–25

40 It is easier for a camel to go through the eye of a needle, than for a rich man to enter into the kingdom of God.

Mark 10:25

41 And he looked up, and saw the rich men casting their gifts into the treasury.

And he saw also a certain poor widow casting in thither two mites.

And he said, Of a truth I say unto you, that this poor widow hath cast in more than they all:

For all these have of their abundance cast in unto the offerings of God: but she of her penury hath cast in all the living that she had.

Luke 21:1–4

42 The poor always ye have with you; but me ye have not always.

John 12:8

43 There was now no more means of purchasing foreign goods and small wares [in Sparta]; merchants sent no shiploads into Laconian ports; no rhetoric-master, no itinerant fortune-teller, no harlot-monger, or gold or silversmith, engraver, or jeweller, set foot in a country which had no money; so that luxury, deprived little by little of that which fed and fomented it, wasted to nothing and died away of itself. For the rich had no advantage here over the poor, as their wealth and abundance had no road to come abroad by but were shut up at home doing nothing.

Plutarch, Lycurgus

44 There are many to be seen that make a good or a bad use of riches, but it is difficult, comparatively, to meet with one who supports poverty in a noble spirit; those only should be ashamed of it who incurred it against their wills.

Plutarch, Aristides

45 Poverty is dishonourable not in itself, but when it is a proof of laziness, intemperance, luxury, and carelessness; whereas in a person that is temperate, industrious, just, and valiant, and who uses all his virtues for the public good, it shows a great and lofty mind. For he has no time for great matters who concerns himself with petty ones; nor can he relieve many needs of others, who himself has many needs of his own. What most of all enables a man to serve the public is not wealth, but content and independence; which, requiring no superfluity at home, distracts not the mind from the common good.

Plutarch, Aristides and Marcus Cato Compared

46 If you're poor, you're a joke, on each and every occasion.

What a laugh, if your cloak is dirty or torn, if your toga

Seems a little bit soiled, if your shoe has a crack in the leather,

Or if more than one patch attests to more than one mending!

Poverty's greatest curse, much worse than the fact of it, is that

It makes men objects of mirth, ridiculed, humbled, embarrassed.

'Out of the front-row seats!' they cry when you're out of money,

Yield your place to the sons of some pimp, the spawn of some cathouse,

Some slick auctioneer's brat, or the louts some trainer has fathered

Or the well-groomed boys whose sire is a gladiator.

Such is the law of place, decreed by the nitwitted Otho:

All the best seats are reserved for the classes who have the most money.

Who can marry a girl if he has less money than she does?

What poor man is an heir, or can hope to be? Which of them ever

Rates a political job, even the meanest and lowest?

Long before now, all poor Roman descendants of Romans

Ought to have marched out of town in one determined migration.

Men do not easily rise whose poverty hinders their merit.

Juvenal, Satire III

47 Receive wealth or prosperity without arrogance; and be ready to let it go.

Marcus Aurelius, Meditations, VIII, 33

48 Let us suppose a case of two men; for each individual man, like one letter in a language, is as it were the element of a city or kingdom, however far-spreading in its occupation of the earth. Of

these two men let us suppose that one is poor, or rather of middling circumstances; the other very rich. But the rich man is anxious with fears, pining with discontent, burning with covetousness, never secure, always uneasy, panting from the perpetual strife of his enemies, adding to his patrimony indeed by these miseries to an immense degree, and by these additions also heaping up most bitter cares. But that other man of moderate wealth is contented with a small and compact estate, most dear to his own family, enjoying the sweetest peace with his kindred neighbours and friends, in piety religious, benignant in mind, healthy in body, in life frugal, in manners chaste, in conscience secure. I know not whether anyone can be such a fool, that he dare hesitate which to prefer.

Augustine, *City of God,* IV, 3

49 It is not earthly riches which make us or our sons happy; for they must either be lost by us in our lifetime, or be possessed when we are dead, by whom we know not, or perhaps by whom we would not.

Augustine, *City of God,* V, 18

50 It is impossible for man's happiness to consist in wealth. For wealth is two-fold . . . natural and artificial. Natural wealth is that which serves man as a remedy for his natural wants, such as food, drink, clothing, conveyances, dwellings, and things of this kind, while artificial wealth is that which is not a direct help to nature, as money, but is invented by the art of man for the convenience of exchange and as a measure of things saleable.

Now it is evident that man's happiness cannot consist in natural wealth. For wealth of this kind is sought as a support of human nature; consequently it cannot be man's last end, but rather is ordered to man as to its end. Therefore in the order of nature, all such things are below man, and made for him. . . .

And as to artificial wealth, it is not sought save for the sake of natural wealth, since man would not seek it except that by its means he procures for himself the necessaries of life. Consequently much less does it have the character of the last end. Therefore it is impossible for happiness, which is the last end of man, to consist in wealth.

Aquinas, *Summa Theologica,* I–II, 2, 1

51 Covetousness, as denoting a special sin, is called the root of all sins, in likeness to the root of a tree, in furnishing sustenance to the whole tree. For we see that by riches man acquires the means of committing any sin whatever, and of sating his desire for any sin whatever, since money helps man to obtain all manner of temporal goods. . . . So that in this sense desire for riches is the root of all sins.

Aquinas, *Summa Theologica,* I–II, 84, 1

52 The privation of one's possessions, or poverty, is a means of perfection, since by doing away with riches we remove certain obstacles to charity; and these are chiefly three. The first is the cares which riches bring with them. . . . The second is the love of riches, which increases with the possession of wealth. . . . The third is vainglory or elation which results from riches.

Aquinas, *Summa Theologica,* II–II, 188, 7

53 So long as external things are sought or possessed only in a small quantity, and as much as is required for a mere livelihood, such care does not hinder one much, and consequently is not inconsistent with the perfection of Christian life. . . . Yet the possession of much wealth increases the weight of care, which is a great distraction to man's mind and hinders him from giving himself wholly to God's service.

Aquinas, *Summa Theologica,* II–II, 188, 7

54 And when you me reproach for poverty,
The High God, in Whom we believe, say I,
In voluntary poverty lived His life.
And surely every man, or maid, or wife
May understand that Jesus, Heaven's King,
Would not have chosen vileness of living.
Glad poverty's an honest thing, that's plain,
Which Seneca and other clerks maintain.
Whoso will be content with poverty,
I hold him rich, though not a shirt has he.
And he that covets much is a poor wight,
For he would gain what's all beyond his might
But he that has not, nor desires to have,
Is rich, although you hold him but a knave.
   True poverty, it sings right naturally;
Juvenal gaily says of poverty:
'The poor man, when he walks along the way,
Before the robbers he may sing and play.
Poverty's odious good, and, as I guess,
It is a stimulant to busyness;
A great improver, too, of sapience
In him that takes it all with due patience.
Poverty's this, though it seem misery—
Its quality may none dispute, say I.
Poverty often; when a man is low,
Makes him his God and even himself to know.
And poverty's an eye-glass, seems to me,
Through which a man his loyal friends may see.
Since you've received no injury from me,
Then why reproach me for my poverty.'

Chaucer, *Canterbury Tales:
Wife of Bath's Tale*

55 The matter, form, effect, and goal of riches are worthless. That's why our Lord God generally gives riches to crude asses to whom he doesn't give anything else.

Luther, *Table Talk,* 5559

56 *Pantagruel.* Those of a mean spirit and shallow ca-

pacity have not the skill to spend much in a short time.

Rabelais, *Gargantua and Pantagruel,* III, 2

57 *The Bastard.*   Why rail I on this Commodity?
But for because he hath not woo'd me yet:
Not that I have the power to clutch my hand,
When his fair angels would salute my palm;
But for my hand, as unattempted yet,
Like a poor beggar, raileth on the rich.
Well, whiles I am a beggar, I will rail
And say there is no sin but to be rich;
And being rich, my virtue then shall be
To say there is no vice but beggary.
Since kings break faith upon Commodity,
Gain, be my lord, for I will worship thee.

Shakespeare, *King John,* II, i, 587

58 *Hamlet.*   Why should the poor be flatter'd?
No, let the candied tongue lick absurd pomp,
And crook the pregnant hinges of the knee
Where thrift may follow fawning.

Shakespeare, *Hamlet,* III, ii, 65

59 *Anne Page.* O, what a world of vile ill-favour'd faults
Looks handsome in three hundred pounds a-year!

Shakespeare, *Merry Wives
of Windsor,* III, iv, 32

60 *Iago.* Poor and content is rich and rich enough,
But riches fineless is as poor as winter
To him that ever fears he shall be poor.

Shakespeare, *Othello,* III, iii, 172

61 *Goneril.*   Hear me, my lord.
What need you five and twenty, ten, or five,
To follow in a house where twice so many
Have a command to tend you?
   Regan.   What need one?
   Lear. O, reason not the need. Our basest beg-
      gars
Are in the poorest thing superfluous.
Allow not nature more than nature needs,
Man's life's as cheap as beast's. Thou art a lady;
If only to go warm were gorgeous,
Why, nature needs not what thou gorgeous
   wear'st,
Which scarcely keeps thee warm.

Shakespeare, *Lear,* II, iv, 263

62 *Kent.*   Good my lord, enter here.
   Lear. Prithee, go in thyself; seek thine own ease.
This tempest will not give me leave to ponder
On things would hurt me more. But I'll go in.
[*To the* Fool] In, boy; go first. You houseless pov-
      erty—
Nay, get thee in. I'll pray, and then I'll sleep.
   Fool goes in.
Poor naked wretches, wheresoe'er you are,
That bide the pelting of this pitiless storm,
How shall your houseless heads and unfed sides,

Your loop'd and window'd raggedness, defend
   you
From reasons such as these? O, I have ta'en
Too little care of this! Take physic, pomp;
Expose thyself to feel what wretches feel,
That thou mayst shake the superflux to them,
And show the heavens more just.

Shakespeare, *Lear,* III, iv, 22

63 *Timon.* [To the gold] O thou sweet king-killer, and
      dear divorce
'Twixt natural son and sire! thou bright defiler
Of Hymen's purest bed! thou valiant Mars!
Thou ever young, fresh, loved, and delicate
   wooer,
Whose blush doth thaw the consecrated snow
That lies in Dian's lap! thou visible god,
That solder'st close impossibilities,
And makest them kiss! that speak'st with every
   tongue,
To every purpose! O thou touch of hearts!
Think, thy slave man rebels, and by thy virtue
Set them into confounding odds, that beasts
May have the world in empire!

Shakespeare, *Timon of Athens,* IV, iii, 382

64 Riches are for spending, and spending for honour
and good actions.

Bacon, *Of Expense*

65 I cannot call Riches better than the baggage of
virtue. The Roman word is better, *impedimenta.*
For as the baggage is to an army, so is riches to
virtue. It cannot be spared nor left behind, but it
hindereth the march; yea and the care of it sometimes loseth or disturbeth the victory.

Bacon, *Of Riches*

66 The ways to enrich are many, and most of them
foul.

Bacon, *Of Riches*

67 He that resteth upon gains certain, shall hardly
grow to great riches: and he that puts all upon
adventures, doth oftentimes break and come to
poverty: it is good therefore to guard adventures
with certainties that may uphold losses.

Bacon, *Of Riches*

68 Believe not much them that seem to despise riches; for they despise them that despair of them;
and none worse, when they come to them.

Bacon, *Of Riches*

69 Be not penny-wise; riches have wings, and sometimes they fly away of themselves, sometimes they
must be set flying to bring in more.

Bacon, *Of Riches*

70 *Mammon,* the least erected Spirit that fell
From heav'n, for ev'n in heav'n his looks and
   thoughts

Were always downward bent, admiring more
The riches of Heav'ns pavement, trod'n Gold,
Then aught divine or holy else enjoy'd
In vision beatific: by him first
Men also, and by his suggestion taught,
Ransack'd the Center, and with impious hands
Rifl'd the bowels of their mother Earth
For Treasures better hid. Soon had his crew
Op'nd into the Hill a spacious wound
And dig'd out ribs of Gold. Let none admire
That riches grow in Hell; that soyle may best
Deserve the pretious bane.

Milton, *Paradise Lost,* I, 679

71 *Satan.* Great acts require great means of enter-
prise,
Thou art unknown, unfriended, low of birth,
A Carpenter thy Father known, thy self
Bred up in poverty and streights at home;
Lost in a Desert here and hunger-bit:
Which way or from what hope dost thou aspire
To greatness? when Authority deriv'st,
What Followers, what Retinue canst thou gain,
Or at thy heels the dizzy Multitude,
Longer then thou canst feed them on thy cost?
Money brings Honour, Friends, Conquest, and
Realms;
What rais'd *Antipater* the *Edomite,*
And his Son *Herod* plac'd on *Juda's* Throne;
(Thy throne) but gold that got him puissant
friends?
Therefore, if at great things thou wouldst arrive,
Get Riches first, get Wealth, and Treasure heap,
Not difficult, if thou hearken to me,
Riches are mine, Fortune is in my hand;
They whom I favour thrive in wealth amain,
While Virtue, Valour, Wisdom sit in want.
    To whom thus Jesus patiently reply'd;
Yet Wealth without these three is impotent,
To gain dominion or to keep it gain'd.

Milton, *Paradise Regained,* II, 412

72 To assist every one who is needy far surpasses the
strength or profit of a private person, for the
wealth of a private person is altogether insufficient to supply such wants. Besides, the power of
any one man is too limited for him to be able to
unite every one with himself in friendship. The
care, therefore, of the poor is incumbent on the
whole of society and concerns only the general
profit.

Spinoza, *Ethics,* IV, Appendix XVII

73 My master was yet wholly at a loss to understand
what motives could incite this race of lawyers to
perplex, disquiet, and weary themselves by engaging in a confederacy of injustice, merely for the
sake of injuring their fellow-animals; neither
could he comprehend what I meant in saying they
did it for *hire.* Whereupon I was at much pains to

describe to him the use of *money,* the materials it
was made of, and the value of the metals: that,
when a Yahoo had got a great store of this precious substance, he was able to purchase whatever
he had a mind to; the finest cloathing, the noblest
houses, great tracts of land, the most costly meats
and drinks; and have his choice of the most beautiful females. Therefore since *money* alone, was
able to perform all these feats, our Yahoos
thought, they could never have enough of it to
spend or to save, as they found themselves inclined from their natural bent either to profusion
or avarice. That, the rich man enjoyed the fruit of
the poor man's labour, and the latter were a thousand to one in proportion to the former. That, the
bulk of our people was forced to live miserably, by
labouring every day for small wages, to make a
few live plentifully.

Swift, *Gulliver's Travels,* IV, 6

74 In all well-instituted Commonwealths, Care has
been taken to limit Men's Possessions; which is
done for many Reasons, and among the rest, for
one which perhaps is not often considered, That
when Bounds are set to Men's Desires, after they
have acquired as much as the Laws will permit
them, their private Interest is at an End, and they
have nothing to do but to take care of the Publick.

Swift, *Thoughts on Various Subjects*

75 I have already computed the charge of nursing a
beggar's child (in which list I reckon all cottagers,
labourers, and four-fifths of the farmers) to be
about two shillings per annum, rags included.

Swift, *A Modest Proposal*

76 Some persons of a desponding spirit are in great
concern about that vast number of poor people
who are aged, diseased, or maimed, and I have
been desired to employ my thoughts on what
course may be taken to ease the nation of so grievous an encumbrance. But I am not in the least
pain upon that matter, because it is very well
known that they are every day dying, and rotting,
by cold and famine, and filth, and vermin, as fast
as can be reasonably expected. And as to the
younger labourers, they are now in almost as
hopeful a condition. They cannot get work, and
consequently pine away for want of nourishment
to a degree that if at any time they are accidentally hired to common labour, they have not strength
to perform it, and thus the country and themselves are happily delivered from the evils to
come.

Swift, *A Modest Proposal*

77 The wisest man is the likeliest to possess all worldly blessings in an eminent degree; for as that moderation which wisdom prescribes is the surest way
to useful wealth, so can it alone qualify us to taste
many pleasures. The wise man gratifies every ap-

petite and every passion, while the fool sacrifices all the rest to pall and satiate one.

Fielding, *Tom Jones*, VI, 3

78 Matters are so constituted that "nothing out of nothing" is not a truer maxim in physics than in politics; and every man who is greatly destitute of money is on that account entirely excluded from all means of acquiring it.

Fielding, *Tom Jones*, VII, 2

79 What is the poor pride arising from a magnificent house, a numerous equipage, a splendid table, and from all the other advantages or appearances of fortune, compared to the warm, solid content, the swelling satisfaction, the thrilling transports, and the exulting triumphs, which a good mind enjoys, in the contemplation of a generous, virtuous, noble, benevolent action?

Fielding, *Tom Jones*, XII, 10

80 Where young ladies bring great fortunes themselves, they have some right to insist on spending what is their own; and on that account I have heard the gentlemen say, a man has sometimes a better bargain with a poor wife, than with a rich one.

Fielding, *Tom Jones*, XIII, 6

81 There are two sorts of poor; those who are rendered such by the severity of government: these are, indeed, incapable of performing almost any great action, because their indigence is a consequence of their slavery. Others are poor, only because they either despise or know not the conveniences of life; and these are capable of accomplishing great things, because their poverty constitutes a part of their liberty.

Montesquieu, *Spirit of Laws*, XX, 3

82 When the nation is poor, private poverty springs from the general calamity, and is, if I may so express myself, the general calamity itself. All the hospitals in the world cannot cure this private poverty; on the contrary, the spirit of indolence, which it constantly inspires, increases the general, and consequently the private, misery.

Montesquieu, *Spirit of Laws*, XXIII, 29

83 Let not Ambition mock their useful toil,
Their homely joys, and destiny obscure;
Nor Grandeur hear with a disdainful smile,
The short and simple annals of the poor.

The boast of heraldry, the pomp of pow'r,
And all that beauty, all that wealth e'er gave,
Awaits alike th' inevitable hour.
The paths of glory lead but to the grave.

Nor you, ye Proud, impute to These the fault,
If Mem'ry o'er their Tomb no Trophies raise, .
Where thro' the long-drawn isle and fretted vault

The pealing anthem swells the note of praise.

Can storied urn or animated bust
Back to its mansion call the fleeting breath?
Can Honour's voice provoke the silent dust,
Or Flatt'ry sooth the dull cold ear of Death?

Perhaps in this neglected spot is laid
Some heart once pregnant with celestial fire;
Hands, that the rod of empire might have sway'd,
Or wak'd to extasy the living lyre.

But Knowledge to their eyes her ample page
Rich with the spoils of time did ne'er unroll;
Chill Penury repress'd their noble rage,
And froze the genial current of the soul.

Full many a gem of purest ray serene,
The dark unfathom'd caves of ocean bear:
Full many a flower is born to blush unseen,
And waste its sweetness on the desert air.

Some village-Hampden, that with dauntless
breast
The little Tyrant of his fields withstood;
Some mute inglorious Milton here may rest,
Some Cromwell guiltless of his country's blood.

Th' applause of list'ning senates to command,
The threats of pain and ruin to despise,
To scatter plenty o'er a smiling land,
And read their hist'ry in a nation's eyes,

Their lot forbad: nor circumscrib'd alone
Their growing virtues, but their crimes confin'd;
Forbad to wade through slaughter to a throne,
And shut the gates of mercy on mankind,

The struggling pangs of conscious truth to hide,
To quench the blushes of ingenuous shame,
Or heap the shrine of Luxury and Pride
With incense kindled at the Muse's flame.

Far from the madding crowd's ignoble strife,
Their sober wishes never learn'd to stray;
Along the cool sequester'd vale of life
They kept the noiseless tenor of their way.

Gray, *Elegy Written in a Country Church-Yard*

84 If by luxury one understands everything that is beyond the necessary, luxury is a natural consequence of the progress of the human species; and to reason consequently every enemy of luxury should believe with Rousseau that the state of happiness and virtue for man is that, not of the savage, but of the orang-outang. One feels that it would be absurd to regard as an evil the comforts which all men would enjoy: also, does one not generally give the name of luxury to the superfluities which only a small number of individuals can enjoy. In this sense, luxury is a necessary consequence of property, without which no society can subsist, and of a great inequality between fortunes which is the consequence, not of the right of property, but of bad laws. Moralists should address

their sermons to the legislators, and not to individuals, because it is in the order of possible things that a virtuous and enlightened man may have the power to make reasonable laws, and it is not in human nature for all the rich men of a country to renounce through virtue procuring for themselves for money the enjoyments of pleasure or vanity.

Voltaire, *Philosophical Dictionary:* Luxury

85 Before the invention of signs to represent riches, wealth could hardly consist in anything but lands and cattle, the only real possessions men can have. But, when inheritances so increased in number and extent as to occupy the whole of the land, and to border on one another, one man could aggrandise himself only at the expense of another; at the same time the supernumeraries, who had been too weak or too indolent to make such acquisitions, and had grown poor without sustaining any loss, because, while they saw everything change around them, they remained still the same, were obliged to receive their subsistence, or steal it, from the rich; and this soon bred, according to their different characters, dominion and slavery, or violence and rapine. The wealthy, on their part, had no sooner begun to taste the pleasure of command, than they disdained all others, and, using their old slaves to acquire new, thought of nothing but subduing and enslaving their neighbours; like ravenous wolves, which, having once tasted human flesh, despise every other food and thenceforth seek only men to devour.

Thus, as the most powerful or the most miserable considered their might or misery as a kind of right to the possessions of others, equivalent, in their opinion, to that of property, the destruction of equality was attended by the most terrible disorders. Usurpations by the rich, robbery by the poor, and the unbridled passions of both, suppressed the cries of natural compassion and the still feeble voice of justice, and filled men with avarice, ambition and vice.

Rousseau, *Origin of Inequality,* II

86 Destitute of valid reasons to justify and sufficient strength to defend himself, able to crush individuals with ease, but easily crushed himself by a troop of bandits, one against all, and incapable, on account of mutual jealousy, of joining with his equals against numerous enemies united by the common hope of plunder, the rich man, thus urged by necessity, conceived at length the profoundest plan that ever entered the mind of man: this was to employ in his favour the forces of those who attacked him, to make allies of his adversaries, to inspire them with different maxims, and to give them other institutions as favourable to himself as the law of nature was unfavourable.

Rousseau, *Origin of Inequality,* II

87 Luxury, which cannot be prevented among men who are tenacious of their own convenience and of the respect paid them by others, soon completes the evil society had begun, and, under the pretence of giving bread to the poor, whom it should never have made such, impoverishes all the rest, and sooner or later depopulates the State. Luxury is a remedy much worse than the disease it sets up to cure; or rather it is in itself the greatest of all evils, for every State, great or small: for, in order to maintain all the servants and vagabonds it creates, it brings oppression and ruin on the citizen and the labourer; it is like those scorching winds, which, covering the trees and plants with devouring insects, deprive useful animals of their subsistence and spread famine and death wherever they blow.

Rousseau, *Origin of Inequality,* Appendix

88 The losses of the poor are much harder to repair than those of the rich, and . . . the difficulty of acquisition is always greater in proportion as there is more need for it. "Nothing comes out of nothing," is as true of life as in physics: money is the seed of money, and the first guinea is sometimes more difficult to acquire than the second million.

Rousseau, *Political Economy*

89 It is one of the misfortunes of the rich to be cheated on all sides; what wonder they think ill of mankind! It is riches that corrupt men, and the rich are rightly the first to feel the defects of the only tool they know. Everything is ill-done for them, except what they do themselves, and they do next to nothing.

Rousseau, *Emile,* I

90 In the prospect of poverty there is nothing but gloom and melancholy; the mind and body suffer together; its miseries bring no alleviations; it is a state in which every virtue is obscured, and in which no conduct can avoid reproach; a state in which cheerfulness is insensibility, and dejection sullenness, of which the hardships are without honor, and the labors without reward.

Johnson, *Rambler No. 53*

91 Wealth is nothing in itself, it is not useful but when it departs from us; its value is found only in that which it can purchase, which, if we suppose it put to its best use by those that possess it, seems not much to deserve the desire or envy of a wise man. It is certain that, with regard to corporal enjoyment, money can neither open new avenues to pleasure, nor block up the passages of anguish. Disease and infirmity still continue to torture and enfeeble, perhaps exasperated by luxury, or promoted by softness. With respect to the mind, it has rarely been observed, that wealth contributes much to quicken the discernment, enlarge the ca-

pacity, or elevate the imagination; but may, by hiring flattery, or laying diligence asleep, confirm errour, and harden stupidity.

Johnson, *Rambler No. 58*

92 Poverty has, in large cities, very different appearances: it is often concealed in splendour, and often in extravagance. It is the care of a very great part of mankind to conceal their indigence from the rest: they support themselves by temporary expedients, and every day is lost in contriving for the morrow.

Johnson, *Rasselas,* XXV

93   Has Heav'n reserv'd, in pity to the poor,
No pathless waste, or undiscover'd shore?
No secret island in the boundless main?
No peaceful desert yet unclaim'd by Spain?
Quick let us rise, the happy seats explore,
And bear Oppression's insolence no more.
This mournful truth is ev'rywhere confess'd,
Slow rises worth, by poverty depress'd:
But here more slow, where all are slaves to gold,
Where looks are merchandise, and smiles are sold;
Where won by bribes, by flatteries implor'd,
The groom retails the favours of his lord.

Johnson, *London,* 169

94 Poverty takes away so many means of doing good, and produces so much inability to resist evil, both natural and moral, that it is by all virtuous means to be avoided.

Johnson, *Letter to James Boswell (June 3, 1782)*

95 Your economy, I suppose, begins now to be settled; your expences are adjusted to your revenue, and all your people in their proper places. Resolve not to be poor: whatever you have, spend less. Poverty is a great enemy to human happiness; it certainly destroys liberty, and it makes some virtues impracticable, and others extremely difficult.

Johnson, *Letter to James Boswell (Dec. 7, 1782)*

96 *Johnson.* In civilized society, external advantages make us more respected. A man with a good coat upon his back meets with a better reception than he who has a bad one.

Boswell, *Life of Johnson (July 20, 1763)*

97 *Johnson.* When I was running about this town a very poor fellow, I was a great arguer for the advantages of poverty; but I was, at the same time, very sorry to be poor. . . . All the arguments which are brought to represent poverty as no evil, shew it to be evidently a great evil. You never find people labouring to convince you that you may live very happily upon a plentiful fortune.

Boswell, *Life of Johnson (July 20, 1763)*

98 *Johnson.* (to Edwards,) "From your having prac-

tised the law long, Sir, I presume you must be rich." *Edwards.* "No, Sir; I got a good deal of money; but I had a number of poor relations to whom I gave a great part of it." *Johnson.* "Sir, you have been rich in the most valuable sense of the word." *Edwards.* "But I shall not die rich." *Johnson.* "Nay, sure, Sir, it is better to *live* rich than to *die* rich."

Boswell, *Life of Johnson (Apr. 17, 1778)*

99 Though the wealth of a country should be very great, yet if it has been long stationary, we must not expect to find the wages of labour very high in it. The funds destined for the payment of wages, the revenue and stock of its inhabitants, may be of the greatest extent; but if they have continued for several centuries of the same, or very nearly of the same extent, the number of labourers employed every year could easily supply, and even more than supply, the number wanted the following year. There could seldom be any scarcity of hands, nor could the masters be obliged to bid against one another in order to get them. The hands, on the contrary, would, in this case, naturally multiply beyond their employment. There would be a constant scarcity of employment, and the labourers would be obliged to bid against one another in order to get it. If in such a country the wages of labour had ever been more than sufficient to maintain the labourer, and to enable him to bring up a family, the competition of the labourers and the interest of the masters would soon reduce them to this lowest rate which is consistent with common humanity.

Adam Smith, *Wealth of Nations,* I, 8

100 The liberal reward of labour . . . as it is the necessary effect, so it is the natural symptom of increasing national wealth. The scanty maintenance of the labouring poor, on the other hand, is the natural symptom that things are at a stand, and their starving condition that they are going fast backwards.

Adam Smith, *Wealth of Nations,* I, 8

101 Is . . . improvement in the circumstances of the lower ranks of the people to be regarded as an advantage or as an inconveniency to the society? The answer seems at first sight abundantly plain. Servants, labourers, and workmen of different kinds, make up the far greater part of every great political society. But what improves the circumstances of the greater part can never be regarded as an inconveniency to the whole. No society can surely be flourishing and happy, of which the far greater part of the members are poor and miserable. It is but equity, besides, that they who feed, clothe, and lodge the whole body of the people, should have such a share of the produce of their own labour as to be themselves tolerably well fed, clothed, and lodged.

Adam Smith, *Wealth of Nations,* I, 8

102 The whole annual produce of the land and labour of every country, or what comes to the same thing, the whole price of that annual produce, naturally divides itself . . . into three parts; the rent of land, the wages of labour, and the profits of stock; and constitutes a revenue to three different orders of people; to those who live by rent, to those who live by wages, and to those who live by profit. These are the three great, original, and constituent orders of every civilised society, from whose revenue that of every other order is ultimately derived.

Adam Smith, *Wealth of Nations*, I, 11

103 In all countries where there is tolerable security, every man of common understanding will endeavour to employ whatever stock he can command in procuring either present enjoyment or future profit. If it is employed in procuring present enjoyment, it is a stock reserved for immediate consumption. If it is employed in procuring future profit, it must procure this profit either by staying with him, or by going from him. In the one case it is fixed, in the other it is a circulating capital. A man must be perfectly crazy who, where there is tolerable security, does not employ all the stock which he commands, whether it be his own or borrowed of other people, in some one or other of those three ways.

Adam Smith, *Wealth of Nations*, II, 1

104 Capitals are increased by parsimony, and diminished by prodigality and misconduct.

Whatever a person saves from his revenue he adds to his capital, and either employs it himself in maintaining an additional number of productive hands, or enables some other person to do so, by lending it to him for an interest, that is, for a share of the profits. As the capital of an individual can be increased only by what he saves from his annual revenue or his annual gains, so the capital of a society, which is the same with that of all the individuals who compose it, can be increased only in the same manner.

Parsimony, and not industry, is the immediate cause of the increase of capital. Industry, indeed, provides the subject which parsimony accumulates. But whatever industry might acquire, if parsimony did not save and store up, the capital would never be the greater.

Adam Smith, *Wealth of Nations*, II, 3

105 The revenue of an individual may be spent either in things which are consumed immediately, and in which one day's expense can neither alleviate nor support that of another, or it may be spent in things more durable, which can therefore be accumulated, and in which every day's expense may, as he chooses, either alleviate or support and heighten the effect of that of the following day. A man of fortune, for example, may either spend his

revenue in a profuse and sumptuous table, and in maintaining a great number of menial servants, and a multitude of dogs and horses; or contenting himself with a frugal table and few attendants, he may lay out the greater part of it in adorning his house or his country villa, in useful or ornamental buildings, in useful or ornamental furniture, in collecting books, statues, pictures; or in things more frivolous, jewels, baubles, ingenious trinkets of different kinds; or, what is most trifling of all, in amassing a great wardrobe of fine clothes, like the favourite and minister of a great prince who died a few years ago. Were two men of equal fortune to spend their revenue, the one chiefly in the one way, the other in the other, the magnificence of the person whose expense had been chiefly in durable commodities, would be continually increasing, every day's expense contributing something to support and heighten the effect of that of the following day: that of the other, on the contrary, would be no greater at the end of the period than at the beginning. The former, too, would, at the end of the period, be the richer man of the two. He would have a stock of goods of some kind or other, which, though it might not be worth all that it cost, would always be worth something. No trace or vestige of the expense of the latter would remain, and the effects of ten or twenty years profusion would be as completely annihilated as if they had never existed.

Adam Smith, *Wealth of Nations*, II, 3

106 The expense . . . that is laid out in durable commodities gives maintenance, commonly, to a greater number of people than that which is employed in the most profuse hospitality. Of two or three hundredweight of provisions, which may sometimes be served up at a great festival, one half, perhaps, is thrown to the dunghill, and there is always a great deal wasted and abused. But if the expense of this entertainment had been employed in setting to work masons, carpenters, upholsterers, mechanics, etc., a quantity of provisions, of equal value, would have been distributed among a still greater number of people who would have bought them in pennyworths and pound weights, and not have lost or thrown away a single ounce of them. In the one way, besides, this expense maintains productive, in the other unproductive hands. In the one way, therefore, it increases, in the other, it does not increase, the exchangeable value of the annual produce of the land and labour of the country.

Adam Smith, *Wealth of Nations*, II, 3

107 To attempt to increase the wealth of any country, either by introducing or by detaining in it an unnecessary quantity of gold and silver, is as absurd as it would be to attempt to increase the good cheer of private families by obliging them to keep

an unnecessary number of kitchen utensils. As the expense of purchasing those unnecessary utensils would diminish instead of increasing either the quantity of goodness of the family provisions, so the expense of purchasing an unnecessary quantity of gold and silver must, in every country, as necessarily diminish the wealth which feeds, clothes, and lodges, which maintains and employs the people. Gold and silver, whether in the shape of coin or of plate, are utensils, it must be remembered, as much as the furniture of the kitchen. Increase the use for them, increase the consumable commodities which are to be circulated, managed, and prepared by means of them, and you will infallibly increase the quantity; but if you attempt, by extraordinary means, to increase the quantity, you will as infallibly diminish the use and even the quantity too, which in those metals can never be greater than what the use requires. Were they ever to be accumulated beyond this quantity, their transportation is so easy, and the loss which attends their lying idle and unemployed so great, that no law could prevent their being immediately sent out of the country.

Adam Smith, *Wealth of Nations,* IV, 1

108 The produce of industry is what it adds to the subject or materials upon which it is employed. In proportion as the value of this produce is great or small, so will likewise be the profits of the employer. But it is only for the sake of profit that any man employs a capital in the support of industry; and he will always, therefore, endeavour to employ it in the support of that industry of which the produce is likely to be of the greatest value, or to exchange for the greatest quantity either of money or of other goods.

But the annual revenue of every society is always precisely equal to the exchangeable value of the whole annual produce of its industry, or rather is precisely the same thing with that exchangeable value. As every individual, therefore, endeavours as much as he can both to employ his capital in the support of domestic industry, and so to direct that industry that its produce may be of the greatest value; every individual necessarily labours to render the annual revenue of the society as great as he can. He generally, indeed, neither intends to promote the public interest, nor knows how much he is promoting it. By preferring the support of domestic to that of foreign industry, he intends only his own security; and by directing that industry in such a manner as its produce may be of the greatest value, he intends only his own gain, and he is in this, as in many other cases, led by an invisible hand to promote an end which was no part of his intention. Nor is it always the worse for the society than it was no part of it. By pursuing his own interest he frequently promotes that of the society more effectually than when he really intends to promote it. I have never known much good done by those who affected to trade for the public good.

Adam Smith, *Wealth of Nations,* IV, 2

109 The natural effort of every individual to better his own condition, when suffered to exert itself with freedom and security, is so powerful a principle that it is alone, and without any assistance, not only capable of carrying on the society to wealth and prosperity, but of surmounting a hundred impertinent obstructions with which the folly of human laws too often incumbers its operations; though the effect of these obstructions is always more or less either to encroach upon its freedom, or to diminish its security.

Adam Smith, *Wealth of Nations,* IV, 5

110 Every system which endeavours, either by extraordinary encouragements to draw towards a particular species of industry a greater share of the capital of the society than what would naturally go to it, or, by extraordinary restraints, force from a particular species of industry some share of the capital which would otherwise be employed in it, is in reality subversive of the great purpose which it means to promote. It retards, instead of accelerating, the progress of the society towards real wealth and greatness; and diminishes, instead of increasing, the real value of the annual produce of its land and labour.

All systems either of preference or of restraint, therefore, being thus completely taken away, the obvious and simple system of natural liberty establishes itself of its own accord. Every man, as long as he does not violate the laws of justice, is left perfectly free to pursue his own interest his own way, and to bring both his industry and capital into competition with those of any other man, or order of men. The sovereign is completely discharged from a duty, in the attempting to perform which he must always be exposed to innumerable delusions, and for the proper performance of which no human wisdom or knowledge could ever be sufficient; the duty of superintending the industry of private people, and of directing it towards the employments most suitable to the interest of the society. According to the system of natural liberty, the sovereign has only three duties to attend to; three duties of great importance, indeed, but plain and intelligible to common understandings: first, the duty of protecting the society from violence and invasion of other independent societies; secondly, the duty of protecting, as far as possible, every member of the society from the injustice or oppression of every other member of it, or the duty of establishing an exact administration of justice; and, thirdly, the duty of erecting and maintaining certain public works and certain public institutions which it can never be for the interest of any individual, or small number of individuals, to erect and maintain; because the profit could never repay the expense to any individual or small number of individuals, though it may frequently do much more than repay it to a great society.

Adam Smith, *Wealth of Nations,* IV, 9

111 The rich, in particular, are necessarily interested to support that order of things which can alone secure them in the possession of their own advantages. Men of inferior wealth combine to defend those of superior wealth in the possession of their property, in order that men of superior wealth may combine to defend them in the possession of theirs.

Adam Smith, *Wealth of Nations,* V, 1

112 Thirst, hunger, and nakedness are positive evils: but wealth is relative; and a prince, who would be rich in a private station, may be exposed by the increase of his wants to all the anxiety and bitterness of poverty.

Gibbon, *Decline and Fall of the Roman Empire,* LXI

113 I am indeed rich, since my income is superior to my expense, and my expense is equal to my wishes.

Gibbon, *Autobiography*

114 Among the *voluntary* modes of raising . . . contributions, *lotteries* ought not to be allowed, because they increase the number of those who are poor, and involve danger to the public property. It may be asked whether the relief of the poor ought to be administered out of *current contributions,* so that every age should maintain its own poor; or whether this were better done by means of *permanent funds* and charitable institutions, such as widows' homes, hospitals, etc.? And if the former method is the better, it may also be considered whether the means necessary are to be raised by a legal assessment rather than by begging, which is generally nigh akin to robbing. The former method must in reality be regarded as the only one that is conformable to the right of the state, which cannot withdraw its connection from any one who has to live. For a legal current provision does not make the profession of poverty a means of gain for the indolent, as is to be feared is the case with pious foundations when they grow with the number of the poor; nor can it be charged with being an unjust or unrighteous burden imposed by the government on the people.

Kant, *Science of Right,* 49

115 It may at first appear strange, but I believe it is true, that I cannot by means of money raise a poor man and enable him to live much better than he did before, without proportionably depressing others in the same class. If I retrench the quantity of food consumed in my house, and give him what I have cut off, I then benefit him, with-

out depressing any but myself and family, who, perhaps, may be well able to bear it. If I turn up a piece of uncultivated land and give him the produce, I then benefit both him and all the members of the society, because what he before consumed is thrown into the common stock, and probably some of the new produce with it. But if I only give him money, supposing the produce of the country to remain the same, I give him a title to a larger share of that produce than formerly, which share he cannot receive without diminishing the shares of others. It is evident that this effect, in individual instances, must be so small as to be totally imperceptible; but still it must exist, as many other effects do which, like some of the insects that people the air, elude our grosser perceptions.

Malthus, *Population,* V

116 Hard as it may appear in individual instances, dependent poverty ought to be held disgraceful. Such a stimulus seems to be absolutely necessary to promote the happiness of the great mass of mankind, and every general attempt to weaken this stimulus, however benevolent its apparent intention, will always defeat its own purpose. If men are induced to marry from a prospect of parish provision, with little or no chance of maintaining their families in independence, they are not only unjustly tempted to bring unhappiness and dependence upon themselves and children, but they are tempted, without knowing it, to injure all in the same class with themselves. A laborer who marries without being able to support a family may in some respects be considered as an enemy to all his fellow-laborers.

Malthus, *Population,* V

117 The poor still have the needs common to civil society, and yet since society has withdrawn from them the natural means of acquisition and broken the bond of the family—in the wider sense of the clan—their poverty leaves them more or less deprived of all the advantages of society, of the opportunity of acquiring skill or education of any kind, as well as of the administration of justice, the public health services, and often even of the consolations of religion, and so forth. The public authority takes the place of the family where the poor are concerned in respect not only of their immediate want but also of laziness of disposition, malignity, and the other vices which arise out of their plight and their sense of wrong.

Hegel, *Philosophy of Right,* 241

118 When the standard of living of a large mass of people falls below a certain subsistence level . . . and when there is a consequent loss of the sense of right and wrong, of honesty and the self-respect which makes a man insist on maintaining himself by his own work and effort, the result is the creation of a rabble of paupers. At the same time this

brings with it, at the other end of the social scale, conditions which greatly facilitate the concentration of disproportionate wealth in a few hands.

Hegel, *Philosophy of Right*, 244

119 Poverty in itself does not make men into a rabble; a rabble is created only when there is joined to poverty a disposition of mind, an inner indignation against the rich, against society, against the government, etc. A further consequence of this attitude is that through their dependence on chance men become frivolous and idle, like the Neapolitan *lazzaroni* for example. In this way there is born in the rabble the evil of lacking self-respect enough to secure subsistence by its own labour and yet at the same time of claiming to receive subsistence as its right. Against nature man can claim no right, but once society is established, poverty immediately takes the form of a wrong done to one class by another. The important question of how poverty is to be abolished is one of the most disturbing problems which agitate modern society.

Hegel, *Philosophy of Right*,
Additions, Par. 244

120 It is difficult, if not impossible, to define the limits which reason should impose on the desire for wealth; for there is no absolute or definite amount of wealth which will satisfy a man. The amount is always relative, that is to say, just so much as will maintain the proportion between what he wants and what he gets; for to measure a man's happiness only by what he gets, and not also by what he expects to get, is as futile as to try to express a fraction which shall have a numerator but no denominator. A man never feels the loss of things which it never occurs to him to ask for; he is just as happy without them; whilst another, who may have a hundred times as much, feels miserable because he has not got the one thing he wants. In fact, here too, every man has an horizon of his own, and he will expect as much as he thinks it is possible for him to get.

Schopenhauer, *Property*

121 The man who has been born into a position of wealth comes to look upon it as something without which he could no more live than he could live without air; he guards it as he does his very life; and so he is generally a lover of order, prudent and economical. But the man who has been born into a poor position looks upon it as the natural one, and if by any chance he comes in for a fortune, he regards it as a superfluity, something to be enjoyed or wasted, because, if it comes to an end, he can get on just as well as before, with one anxiety the less.

Schopenhauer, *Property*

122 As regards our own welfare, there are only two ways in which we can use wealth. We can either spend it in ostentatious pomp, and feed on the cheap respect which our imaginary glory will bring us from the infatuated crowd; or, by avoiding all expenditure that will do us no good, we can let our wealth grow, so that we may have a bulwark against misfortune and want that shall be stronger and better every day.

Schopenhauer, *Wisdom of Life: Aphorisms*

123 In democratic countries, however opulent a man is supposed to be, he is almost always discontented with his fortune because he finds that he is less rich than his father was, and he fears that his sons will be less rich than himself. Most rich men in democracies are therefore constantly haunted by the desire of obtaining wealth, and they naturally turn their attention to trade and manufactures, which appear to offer the readiest and most efficient means of success. In this respect they share the instincts of the poor without feeling the same necessities; say, rather, they feel the most imperious of all necessities, that of not sinking in the world.

Tocqueville, *Democracy in America*,
Vol. II, II, 19

124 Men living in democratic times have many passions, but most of their passions either end in the love of riches or proceed from it. The cause of this is not that their souls are narrower, but that the importance of money is really greater at such times. When all the members of a community are independent of or indifferent to each other, the co-operation of each of them can be obtained only by paying for it: this infinitely multiplies the purposes to which wealth may be applied and increases its value. When the reverence that belonged to what is old has vanished, birth, condition, and profession no longer distinguish men, or scarcely distinguish them; hardly anything but money remains to create strongly marked differences between them and to raise some of them above the common level. The distinction originating in wealth is increased by the disappearance or diminution of all other distinctions. Among aristocratic nations money reaches only to a few points on the vast circle of man's desires; in democracies it seems to lead to all.

Tocqueville, *Democracy in America*,
Vol. II, III, 17

125 Brotherhood is Brotherhood or Death, but money always will buy money's worth; in the wreck of human dubitations, this remains indubitable, that Pleasure is pleasant. Aristocracy of Feudal Parchment has passed away with a mighty rushing; and now, by a natural course, we arrive at Aristocracy of the Moneybag. . . . Apparently a still baser sort of Aristocracy? An infinitely baser; the basest yet known.

Carlyle, *French Revolution*, IX, 7

126 To be rich is to have a ticket of admission to the master-works and chief men of each race.

Emerson, *Wealth*

127 The world is his who has money to go over it.

Emerson, *Wealth*

128 The pulpit and the press have many commonplaces denouncing the thirst for wealth; but if men should take these moralists at their word and leave off aiming to be rich, the moralists would rush to rekindle at all hazards this love of power in the people, lest civilization should be undone.

Emerson, *Wealth*

129 Debt, grinding debt, whose iron face the widow, the orphan, and the sons of genius fear and hate— debt, which consumes so much time, which so cripples and disheartens a great spirit with cares that seem so base, is a preceptor whose lessons cannot be foregone, and is needed most by those who suffer from it most.

Emerson, *Nature,* V

130 Ah! if the rich were rich as the poor fancy riches!

Emerson, *Nature*

131 "My other piece of advice, Copperfield," said Mr. Micawber, "you know. Annual income twenty pounds, annual expenditure nineteen nineteen six, result happiness. Annual income twenty pounds, annual expenditure twenty pounds ought and six, result misery. The blossom is blighted, the leaf is withered, the god of day goes down upon the dreary scene, and—and, in short, you are forever floored. As I am!"

Dickens, *David Copperfield,* XII

132 Most of the luxuries, and many of the so-called comforts of life, are not only not indispensable, but positive hindrances to the elevation of mankind. With respect to luxuries and comforts, the wisest have ever lived a more simple and meagre life than the poor. The ancient philosophers, Chinese, Hindoo, Persian, and Greek, were a class than which none has been poorer in outward riches, none so rich in inward. We know not much about them. It is remarkable that *we* know so much of them as we do. The same is true of the more modern reformers and benefactors of their race. None can be an impartial or wise observer of human life but from the vantage ground of what *we* should call voluntary poverty. Of a life of luxury the fruit is luxury, whether in agriculture, or commerce, or literature, or art. There are nowadays professors of philosophy, but not philosophers. Yet it is admirable to profess because it was once admirable to live.

Thoreau, *Walden:* Economy

133 However mean your life is, meet it and live it; do not shun it and call it hard names. It is not so bad as you are. It looks poorest when you are richest. The faultfinder will find faults even in paradise. Love your life, poor as it is. You may perhaps have some pleasant, thrilling, glorious hours, even in a poor-house. The setting sun is reflected from the windows of the almshouse as brightly as from the rich man's abode; the snow melts before its door as early in the spring. I do not see but a quiet mind may live as contentedly there, and have as cheering thoughts, as in a palace. The town's poor seem to me often to live the most independent lives of any. Maybe they are simply great enough to receive without misgiving. Most think that they are above being supported by the town; but it oftener happens that they are not above supporting themselves by dishonest means, which should be more disreputable. Cultivate poverty like a garden herb, like sage. Do not trouble yourself much to get new things, whether clothes or friends. Turn the old; return to them. Things do not change; we change. Sell your clothes and keep your thoughts. God will see that you do not want society. If I were confined to a corner of a garret all my days, like a spider, the world would be just as large to me while I had my thoughts about me. The philosopher said: 'From an army of three divisions one can take away its general, and put it in disorder; from the man the most abject and vulgar one cannot take away his thought.' Do not seek so anxiously to be developed, to subject yourself to many influences to be played on; it is all dissipation. Humility like darkness reveals the heavenly lights. The shadows of poverty and meanness gather around us, 'and lo! creation widens to our view.' We are often reminded that if there were bestowed on us the wealth of Crœsus, our aims must still be the same, and our means essentially the same. Moreover, if you are restricted in your range by poverty, if you cannot buy books and newspapers, for instance, you are but confined to the most significant and vital experiences; you are compelled to deal with the material which yields the most sugar and the most starch. It is life near the bone where it is sweetest. You are defended from being a trifler. No man loses ever on a lower level by magnanimity on a higher. Superfluous wealth can buy superfluities only. Money is not required to buy one necessary of the soul.

Thoreau, *Walden:* Conclusion

134 All ought to refrain from marriage who cannot avoid abject poverty for their children; for poverty is not only a great evil, but tends to its own increase by leading to recklessness in marriage.

Darwin, *Descent of Man,* III, 21

135 That some should be rich, shows that others may become rich, and hence is just encouragement to

industry and enterprize.

Lincoln, *Reply to N.Y. Workingmen's . . .
Association (Mar. 21, 1864)*

136 Use-values become a reality only by use or consumption; they also constitute the substance of all wealth, whatever may be the social form of that wealth.

Marx, *Capital,* Vol. I, I, 1

137 The product appropriated by the capitalist is a use-value, as yarn, for example, or boots. But, although boots are, in one sense, the basis of all social progress, and our capitalist is a decided "progressist," yet he does not manufacture boots for their own sake. Use-value is, by no means, the thing [which one values for its own sake] in the production of commodities. Use-values are only produced by capitalists, because, and in so far as, they are the material substratum, the depositaries of exchange-value. Our capitalist has two objects in view: in the first place, he wants to produce a use-value that has a value in exchange, that is to say, an article destined to be sold, a commodity; and secondly, he desires to produce a commodity whose value shall be greater than the sum of the values of the commodities used in its production, that is, of the means of production and the labour power, that he purchased with his good money in the open market. His aim is to produce not only a use-value, but a commodity also; not only use-value, but value; not only value, but at the same time surplus value.

Marx, *Capital,* Vol. I, III, 7

138 The folly is now patent of the economic wisdom that preaches to the labourers the accommodation of their number to the requirements of capital. The mechanism of capitalist production and accumulation constantly effects this adjustment. The first word of this adaptation is the creation of a relative surplus population, or industrial reserve army. Its last word is the misery of constantly extending strata of the active army of labour, and the dead weight of pauperism.

Marx, *Capital,* Vol. I, VII, 25

139 Accumulation of wealth at one pole is . . . at the same time accumulation of misery, agony of toil, slavery, ignorance, brutality, mental degradation, at the opposite pole, i.e., on the side of the class that produces its own product in the form of capital.

Marx, *Capital,* Vol. I, VII, 25

140 The intimate connection between the pangs of hunger of the most industrious layers of the working class, and the extravagant consumption, coarse or refined, of the rich, for which capitalist accumulation is the basis, reveals itself only when the economic laws are known. It is otherwise with the "housing of the poor." Every unprejudiced observer sees that the greater the centralization of the means of production, the greater is the corresponding heaping together of the labourers within a given space; that therefore, the swifter capitalistic accumulation, the more miserable are the dwellings of the working people. "Improvements" of towns, accompanying the increase of wealth, by the demolition of badly built quarters, the erection of palaces for banks, warehouses, etc., the widening of streets for business traffic, for the carriages of luxury, and for the introduction of tramways, etc., drive away the poor into even worse and more crowded hiding-places.

Marx, *Capital,* Vol. I, VII, 25

141 The Irish famine of 1846 killed more than a million people, but it killed poor devils only. To the wealth of the country it did not the slightest damage.

Marx, *Capital,* Vol. I, VII, 25

142 In order to oppress a class certain conditions must be assured to it under which it can, at least, continue its slavish existence. The serf, in the period of serfdom, raised himself to membership in the commune, just as the petty bourgeois, under the yoke of feudal absolutism, managed to develop into a bourgeois. The modern labourer, on the contrary, instead of rising with the progress of industry, sinks deeper and deeper below the conditions of existence of his own class. He becomes a pauper, and pauperism develops more rapidly than population and wealth.

Marx and Engels, *Communist Manifesto,* I

143 It is argued that whoever does the best he can, deserves equally well, and ought not in justice to be put in a position of inferiority for no fault of his own; that superior abilities have already advantages more than enough, in the admiration they excite, the personal influence they command, and the internal sources of satisfaction attending them, without adding to these a superior share of the world's goods; and that society is bound in justice rather to make compensation to the less favoured, for this unmerited inequality of advantages, than to aggravate it. On the contrary side it is contended, that society receives more from the more efficient labourer; that his services being more useful, society owes him a larger return for them; that a greater share of the joint result is actually his work, and not to allow his claim to it is a kind of robbery; that if he is only to receive as much as others, he can only be justly required to produce as much, and to give a smaller amount of time and exertion, proportioned to his superior efficiency.

Mill, *Utilitarianism,* V

144 It is essential to the idea of wealth to be suscepti-

ble of accumulation: things which cannot, after being produced, be kept for some time before being used, are never, I think, regarded as wealth, since however much of them may be produced and enjoyed, the person benefited by them is no richer, is nowise improved in circumstances.

Mill, *Principles of Political Economy,*
Bk. I, III, 3

145 Neither now nor in former ages have the nations possessing the best climate and soil, been either the richest or the most powerful; but (in so far as regards the mass of the people) generally among the poorest, though, in the midst of poverty, probably on the whole the most enjoying. Human life in those countries can be supported on so little, that the poor seldom suffer from anxiety, and in climates in which mere existence is a pleasure, the luxury which they prefer is that of repose.

Mill, *Principles of Political Economy,*
Bk. I, VII, 3

146 Even in a progressive state of capital, in old countries, a conscientious or prudential restraint on population is indispensable, to prevent the increase of numbers from outstripping the increase of capital, and the condition of the classes who are at the bottom of society from being deteriorated. Where there is not, in the people, or in some very large proportion of them, a resolute resistance to this deterioration—a determination to preserve an established standard of comfort—the condition of the poorest class sinks, even in a progressive state, to the lowest point which they will consent to endure.

Mill, *Principles of Political Economy,*
Bk. IV, VI, 1

147 Whereas it has long been known and declared that the poor have no right to the property of the rich, I wish it also to be known and declared that the rich have no right to the property of the poor.

Ruskin, *Unto This Last,* III, 54

148 There is no wealth but life. That country is the richest which nourishes the greatest number of noble and happy human beings; that man is richest who, having perfected the functions of his own life to the utmost, has also the widest helpful influence, both personal, and by means of his possessions, over the lives of others.

Ruskin, *Unto This Last,* IV, 77

149 Never did people believe anything more firmly, than nine Englishmen out of ten at the present day believe that our greatness and welfare are proved by our being so very rich. Now, the use of culture is that it helps us, by means of its spiritual standard of perfection, to regard wealth as but machinery, and not only to say as a matter of words that we regard wealth as but machinery,

but really to perceive and feel that it is so. If it were not for this purging effect wrought upon our minds by culture, the whole world, the future as well as the present, would inevitably belong to the Philistines.

Arnold, *Culture and Anarchy,* I

150 *Father Zossima.* I don't deny that there is sin in the peasants too. And the fire of corruption is spreading visibly, hourly, working from above downwards. The spirit of isolation is coming upon the people too. Money-lenders and devourers of the commune are rising up. Already the merchant grows more and more eager for rank, and strives to show himself cultured though he has not a trace of culture, and to this end meanly despises his old traditions, and is even ashamed of the faith of his fathers. He visits princes, though he is only a peasant corrupted. The peasants are rotting in drunkenness and cannot shake off the habit. And what cruelty to their wives, to their children even! All from drunkenness! I've seen in the factories children of nine years old, frail, rickety, bent and already depraved. The stuffy workshop, the din of machinery, work all day long, the vile language and the drink, the drink—is that what a little child's heart needs? He needs sunshine, childish play, good examples all about him, and at least a little love.

Dostoevsky, *Brothers Karamazov,* Pt. II, VI, 3

151 *Father Zossima.* I've been struck all my life in our great people by their dignity, their true and seemly dignity. I've seen it myself, I can testify to it, I've seen it and marvelled at it, I've seen it in spite of the degraded sins and poverty-stricken appearance of our peasantry. They are not servile, and even after two centuries of serfdom they are free in manner and bearing, yet without insolence, and not revengeful and not envious. "You are rich and noble, you are clever and talented, well, be so, God bless you. I respect you, but I know that I too am a man. By the very fact that I respect you without envy I prove my dignity as a man."

Dostoevsky, *Brothers Karamazov,* Pt. II, VI, 3

152 If you pick up a starving dog and make him prosperous, he will not bite you. This is the principal difference between a dog and a man.

Mark Twain, *Pudd'nhead Wilson's Calendar,* XVI

153 The parts of our wealth most intimately ours are those which are saturated with our labor. There are few men who would not feel personally annihilated if a life-long construction of their hands or brains—say an entomological collection or an extensive work in manuscript—were suddenly swept away. The miser feels similarly towards his gold, and although it is true that a part of our depression at the loss of possessions is due to our

feeling that we must now go without certain goods that we expected the possessions to bring in their train, yet in every case there remains, over and above this, a sense of the shrinkage of our personality, a partial conversion of ourselves to nothingness, which is a psychological phenomenon by itself. We are all at once assimilated to the tramps and poor devils whom we so despise, and at the same time removed farther than ever away from the happy sons of earth who lord it over land and sea and men in the full-blown lustihood that wealth and power can give, and before whom, stiffen ourselves as we will by appealing to anti-snobbish first principles, we cannot escape an emotion, open or sneaking, of respect and dread.

William James, *Psychology,* X

154 Poverty indeed *is* the strenuous life,—without brass bands or uniforms or hysteric popular applause or lies or circumlocutions.

William James, *Varieties of Religious Experience,* XIV–XV

155 The praises of poverty need once more to be boldly sung. We have grown literally afraid to be poor. We despise anyone who elects to be poor in order to simplify and save his inner life. If he does not join the general scramble and pant with the money-making street, we deem him spiritless and lacking in ambition. We have lost the power even of imagining what the ancient idealization of poverty could have meant: the liberation from material attachments, the unbribed soul, the manlier indifference, the paying our way by what we are or do and not by what we have, the right to fling away our life at any moment irresponsibly—the more athletic trim, in short, the moral fighting shape.

William James, *Varieties of Religious Experience,* XIV–XV

156 In the millionaire Undershaft I have represented a man who has become intellectually and spiritually as well as practically conscious of the irresistible natural truth which we all abhor and repudiate: to wit, that the greatest of our evils, and the worst of our crimes is poverty, and that our first duty, to which every other consideration should be sacrificed, is not to be poor. "Poor but honest," "the respectable poor," and such phrases are as intolerable and as immoral as "drunken but amiable," "fraudulent but a good after-dinner speaker," "splendidly criminal," or the like. . . . The thoughtless wickedness with which we scatter sentences of imprisonment, torture in the solitary cell and on the plank bed, and flogging, on moral invalids and energetic rebels, is as nothing compared to the silly levity with which we tolerate poverty as if it were either a wholesome tonic for lazy people or else a virtue to be embraced as St Francis embraced it. If a man is indolent, let him be poor. If he is drunken, let him be poor. If he is not a gentleman, let him be poor. If he is addicted to the fine arts or to pure science instead of to trade and finance, let him be poor. If he chooses to spend his urban eighteen shillings a week or his agricultural thirteen shillings a week on his beer and his family instead of saving it up for his old age, let him be poor. Let nothing be done for "the undeserving": let him be poor. Serve him right! Also—somewhat inconsistently—blessed are the poor!

Now what does this Let Him Be Poor mean? It means let him be weak. Let him be ignorant. Let him become a nucleus of disease. Let him be a standing exhibition and example of ugliness and dirt. Let him have rickety children. Let him be cheap and let him drag his fellows down to his own price by selling himself to do their work. Let his habitations turn our cities into poisonous congeries of slums. Let his daughters infect our young men with the diseases of the streets, and his sons revenge him by turning the nation's manhood into scrofula, cowardice, cruelty, hypocrisy, political imbecility, and all the other fruits of oppression and malnutrition. Let the undeserving become still less deserving; and let the deserving lay up for himself, not treasures in heaven, but horrors in hell upon earth. This being so, is it really wise to let him be poor?

Shaw, *Major Barbara,* Pref.

157 All capital . . . is nothing but spare subsistence. It is the superfluous part of a man's income—that which he is content not to consume, or can easily be persuaded to forego for the present for the sake of some future advantage. Thus capital has been called "the reward of abstinence"; and though the phrase has fallen into general ridicule through its absurd and hypocritical implication that the quantity of capital saved by any person is in direct proportion to their powers of virtuous self-denial, yet if we substitute "result" for "reward," and strip the word "abstinence" of its moral implication, we can accept the definition as practically true. Capital, then, is the result of abstinence. If a man wants a flour mill, he must save the cost of building it and fitting it up out of his income. If he wishes to maintain it, he must not spend on his immediate personal satisfaction all that it brings him in, but must set aside a certain sum annually to make good the wear and tear of the millstones and machinery. If he desires to enlarge the mill, to put in additional pairs of stones, to substitute steam power for water power, or to introduce the steel roller system method of grinding, he must abstain from consuming the cost of these things in personal expenditure. The accumulation and maintenance of capital is possible in no other way. Abstinence is the inevitable condition.

Shaw, *Capital and Wages*

158 Unfortunately, the poor man suffers much less from poverty than the community does, just as a man who never washes his clothes is unbearable to his neighbor though quite tolerable to himself. It is positively delightful to be naked in warm weather: we are forced to dress for the sake of our neighbors against our own inclinations. A destitute man depresses his neighbors, defiles his dwelling, becomes a centre of infection, depraves morals: is, in short, a scandal. We may take it then that a man will not be allowed to be poor, whatever other indulgence may be extended to him.

Shaw, *Redistribution of Income*

159 Why do we, in fact, almost all of us, desire to increase our incomes? It may seem, at first sight, as though material goods were what we desire. But, in fact, we desire these mainly in order to impress our neighbours. When a man moves into a larger house in a more genteel quarter, he reflects that "better" people will call on his wife, and some unprosperous cronies of former days can be dropped. When he sends his son to a good school or an expensive university, he consoles himself for the heavy fees by thoughts of the social kudos to be gained. In every big city, whether of Europe or of America, houses in some districts are more expensive than equally good houses in other districts, merely because they are more fashionable. One of the most powerful of all our passions is the desire to be admired and respected. As things stand, admiration and respect are given to the man who seems to be rich. This is the chief reason why people wish to be rich. The actual goods purchased by their money play quite a secondary part.

Russell, *Sceptical Essays*, VI

160 Wealth must justify itself in happiness.

Santayana, *Life of Reason*, II, 3

11.3 | *Labor*

Labor, or what is sometimes called "work" and sometimes called "toil," is considered in most of the texts here quoted as that form of human activity which is productive of wealth—either consumable goods or the means of production. Some writers explicitly distinguish it from, as well as relate it to, such other modes of activity as play or recreation and the creative pursuits of leisure that have nothing to do with the production of economic goods.

Beginning with the famous passage in Genesis, in which Adam, expelled from Eden, is condemned to live by the sweat of his brow, the pain of toil or labor is discussed by a succession of Christian writers as one of the punishments for sin. This is balanced by another line of texts in which the satisfactions of work and the dignity of labor are emphasized. But labor is nowhere praised as the be-all and end-all of human life. The need to alleviate the fatigues, if not the pains, of toil are acknowledged, and for this therapeutic purpose play or recreation is recommended.

The division of labor and its effect on increased efficiency in the production of wealth is a favorite theme of modern economists, but there are anticipations of it in earlier writers, even as far back as Plato.

The economists, as well as others, are also concerned with the wages of labor and with the special role that labor plays in the creation of economic value. The passages quoted here from Marx, which state his "labor theory of value," i.e., that labor is the sole productive source of wealth, should be contrasted with the passages quoted from Locke in Section 11.1 above, which state his "labor theory of property," i.e., that labor is the indispensable condition of a rightful acquisition of wealth.

The reader will find the tripartite distinction of work, play, and leisure more fully discussed in certain passages included in Section 9.8 on HAPPINESS. The conception of work as a punishment for sin will be found in Section 20.13 on SIN AND TEMPTATION.

---

1 In the sweat of thy face shalt thou eat bread, till thou return unto the ground.

Genesis 3:19

2 Man goeth forth unto his work and to his labour until the evening.

Psalm 104:23

3 Go to the ant, thou sluggard; consider her ways, and be wise:
Which having no guide, overseer, or ruler,
Provideth her meat in the summer, and gathereth her food in the harvest.
How long wilt thou sleep, O sluggard? when wilt thou arise out of thy sleep?
Yet a little sleep, a little slumber, a little folding of the hands to sleep:
So shall thy poverty come as one that travelleth, and thy want as an armed man.

Proverbs 6:6–11

4 I looked on all the works that my hands had wrought, and on the labour that I had laboured to do: and, behold, all was vanity and vexation of spirit, and there was no profit under the sun.

Ecclesiastes 2:11

5 Whatsoever thy hand findeth to do, do it with thy might; for there is no work, nor device, nor knowledge, nor wisdom, in the grave, whither thou goest.

Ecclesiastes 9:10

6 Still on the sluggard hungry want attends;
The scorn of man, the hate of Heaven impends;
While he, averse from labour, drags his days,
Yet greedy on the gains of others preys;
E'en as the stingless drones devouring seize
With glutted sloth the harvest of the bees.
Love every seemly toil, that so the store
Of foodful seasons heap thy garner's floor.
From labour, men returns of wealth behold,
Flocks in their fields, and in their coffers gold:
From labour shalt thou with the love be bless'd
Of men and gods; the slothful they detest.
Not toil, but sloth, shall ignominious be;
Toil, and the slothful man shall envy thee;
Shall view thy growing wealth with alter'd sense,
For glory, virtue, walk with opulence.

Hesiod, Works and Days

7 *Amasis.* Bowmen bend their bows when they wish to shoot; unbrace them when the shooting is over.

Were they kept always strung they would break, and fail the archer in time of need. So it is with men. If they give themselves constantly to serious work, and never indulge awhile in pastime or sport, they lose their senses, and become mad or moody.

Herodotus, *History,* II, 173

8 *Socrates.* We are not all alike; there are diversities of natures among us which are adapted to different occupations.

Adeimantus. Very true.

And will you have a work better done when the workman has many occupations, or when he has only one?

When he has only one.

Further, there can be no doubt that a work is spoilt when not done at the right time?

No doubt.

For business is not disposed to wait until the doer of the business is at leisure; but the doer must follow up what he is doing, and make the business his first object.

He must.

And if so, we must infer that all things are produced more plentifully and easily and of a better quality when one man does one thing which is natural to him and does it at the right time, and leaves other things.

Plato, *Republic,* II, 370A

9 Socrates says that a state is made up of four sorts of people who are absolutely necessary; these are a weaver, a husbandman, a shoemaker, and a builder; afterwards, finding that they are not enough, he adds a smith, and again a herdsman, to look after the necessary animals; then a merchant, and then a retail trader. All these together form the complement of the first state, as if a state were established merely to supply the necessaries of life, rather than for the sake of the good, or stood equally in need of shoemakers and of husbandmen. But he does not admit into the state a military class until the country has increased in size, and is beginning to encroach on its neighbour's land, whereupon they go to war. Yet even amongst his four original citizens, or whatever be the number of those whom he associates in the state, there must be some one who will dispense justice and determine what is just. And as the soul may be said to be more truly part of an animal than the body, so the higher parts of states, that is to say, the warrior class, the class

engaged in the administration of justice, and that engaged in deliberation, which is the special business of political common sense,—these are more essential to the state than the parts which minister to the necessaries of life. Whether their several functions are the functions of different citizens, or of the same,—for it may often happen that the same persons are both warriors and husbandmen,—is immaterial to the argument.

Aristotle, *Politics*, 1291ᵃ11

10 Let us consider trade and other occupations. Which ones befit a gentleman and which are beneath him, we have generally been taught as follows. First, any occupation is to be rejected if it incurs public ill-will, such as tax-collecting and usury. Also unfit for gentlemen are those jobs done by hired workmen, whom we pay for manual labor only and not for artistic skill. Their very wage is a token of their slavery. We also consider vulgar those who buy from wholesale agents to sell at retail. They would make no profit without a good deal of outright lying. And there is nothing more base than misrepresentation. Mechanics also pursue a common calling, because there can be nothing liberal about a workshop. . . .

But those professions that call for a higher level of intelligence and which confer some benefit on society, such as medicine and architecture, are proper for those whose social position they become. Commerce on a small scale is contemptible. But a wholesale business on a large scale, importing great quantities of goods from all over the world and purveying them without deceit, cannot be disparaged. It may, in fact, deserve the highest respect, if those who engage in it, when they have made their fortune, forsake the harbours for a country estate, just as they have often gone from sea to port. But of all occupations by which gain is secured, none is better than agriculture. None is more profitable, delightful, or becoming a free man.

Cicero, *De Officiis*, I, 42

11 Then saws were toothed, and sounding axes made;
(For wedges first did yielding wood invade);
And various arts in order did succeed,
(What cannot endless labour, urged by need?)

Virgil, *Georgics*, I

12 The laborer is worthy of his hire.

Luke 10:7

13 Let him that stole steal no more: but rather let him labour, working with his hands the thing which is good, that he may have to give to him that needeth.

Ephesians 4:28

14 Yourselves know how ye ought to follow us: for we behaved not ourselves disorderly among you;

Neither did we eat any man's bread for nought; but wrought with labour and travail night and day, that we might not be chargeable to any of you.

II Thessalonians 3:7–8

15 One of the greatest and highest blessings Lycurgus procured his people was the abundance of leisure which proceeded from his forbidding to them the exercise of any mean and mechanical trade. Of the money-making that depends on troublesome going about and seeing people and doing business, they had no need at all in a state where wealth obtained no honour or respect. The Helots tilled their ground for them, and paid them yearly in kind the appointed quantity, without any trouble of theirs. To this purpose there goes a story of a Lacedæmonian who, happening to be at Athens when the courts were sitting, was told of a citizen that had been fined for living an idle life, and was being escorted home in much distress of mind by his condoling friends; the Lacedæmonian was much surprised at it and desired his friend to show him the man who was condemned for living like a freeman. So much beneath them did they esteem the frivolous devotion of time and attention to the mechanical arts and to money-making.

Plutarch, *Lycurgus*

16 He who labors as he prays lifts his heart to God with his hands.

Bernard of Clairvaux, *Ad Sororem*

17 Not everyone sins that works not with his hands, because those precepts of the natural law which regard the good of the many are not binding on each individual, but it suffices that one person apply himself to this business and another to that; for instance, that some be craftsmen, others husbandmen, others judges, and others teachers, and so forth.

Aquinas, *Summa Theologica*, II–II, 187, 3

18 Being is something we hold dear, and being consists in movement and action. Wherefore each man in some sort exists in his work.

Montaigne, *Essays*, II, 8, Affection of Fathers

19 *Prince.* If all the year were playing holidays,
To sport would be as tedious as to work.

Shakespeare, *I Henry IV*, I, ii, 227

20 No kind of men love business for itself but those that are learned; for other persons love it for profit, as an hireling, that loves the work for the wages; or for honour, as because it beareth them up in the eyes of men, and refresheth their reputation, which otherwise would wear; or because it putteth them in mind of their fortune, and giveth them

occasion to pleasure and displeasure; or because it exerciseth some faculty wherein they take pride, and so entertaineth them in good humour and pleasing conceits toward themselves; or because it advanceth any other their ends. So that as it is said of untrue valours, that some men's valours are in the eyes of them that look on; so such men's industries are in the eyes of others, or at least in regard of their own designments: only learned men love business as an action according to nature, as agreeable to health of mind as exercise is to health of body, taking pleasure in the action itself, and not in the purchase: so that of all men they are the most indefatigable, if it be towards any business which can hold or detain their mind.

Bacon, *Advancement of Learning,*
Bk. I, II, 5

21 Whereas many men, by accident inevitable, become unable to maintain themselves by their labour, they ought not to be left to the charity of private persons, but to be provided for, as far forth as the necessities of nature require, by the laws of the Commonwealth. For as it is uncharitableness in any man to neglect the impotent; so it is in the sovereign of a Commonwealth, to expose them to the hazard of such uncertain charity.

But for such as have strong bodies the case is otherwise; they are to be forced to work; and to avoid the excuse of not finding employment, there ought to be such laws as may encourage all manner of arts; as navigation, agriculture, fishing, and all manner of manufacture that requires labour.

Hobbes, *Leviathan,* II, 30

22 *Eve. Adam,* well may we labour still to dress
This Garden, still to tend Plant, Herb and Flour.
Our pleasant task enjoyn'd, but till more hands
Aid us, the work under our labour grows,
Luxurious by restraint; what we by day
Lop overgrown, or prune, or prop, or bind,
One night or two with wanton growth derides
Tending to wilde. Thou therefore now advise
Or hear what to my mind first thoughts present,
Let us divide our labours, thou where choice
Leads thee, or where most needs, whether to wind
The Woodbine round this Arbour, or direct
The clasping Ivie where to climb, while I
In yonder Spring of Roses intermixt
With Myrtle, find what to redress till Noon:
For while so near each other thus all day
Our task we choose, what wonder if so near
Looks intervene and smiles, or object new
Casual discourse draw on, which intermits
Our dayes work brought to little, though begun
Early, and th' hour of Supper comes unearn'd.

Milton, *Paradise Lost,* IX, 205

23 It [is not] so strange as, perhaps, before consideration, it may appear, that the property of labour should be able to overbalance the community of land, for it is labour indeed that puts the difference of value on everything; and let anyone consider what the difference is between an acre of land planted with tobacco or sugar, sown with wheat or barley, and an acre of the same land lying in common without any husbandry upon it, and he will find that the improvement of labour makes the far greater part of the value. I think it will be but a very modest computation to say, that of the products of the earth useful to the life of man, nine-tenths are the effects of labour. Nay, if we will rightly estimate things as they come to our use, and cast up the several expenses about them—what in them is purely owing to Nature and what to labour—we shall find that in most of them ninety-nine hundredths are wholly to be put on the account of labour.

Locke, *II Civil Government,* V, 40

24 It is labour . . . which puts the greatest part of value upon land, without which it would scarcely be worth anything; it is to that we owe the greatest part of all its useful products; for all that the straw, bran, bread, of that acre of wheat, is more worth than the product of an acre of as good land which lies waste is all the effect of labour. For it is not barely the ploughman's pains, the reaper's and thresher's toil, and the baker's sweat, is to be counted into the bread we eat; the labour of those who broke the oxen, who digged and wrought the iron and stones, who felled and framed the timber employed about the plough, mill, oven, or any other utensils, which are a vast number, requisite to this corn, from its sowing to its being made bread, must all be charged on the account of labour, and received as an effect of that; Nature and the earth furnished only the almost worthless materials as in themselves. It would be a strange catalogue of things that industry provided and made use of about every loaf of bread before it came to our use if we could trace them; iron, wood, leather, bark, timber, stone, bricks, coals, lime, cloth, dyeing-drugs, pitch, tar, masts, ropes, and all the materials made use of in the ship that brought any of the commodities made use of by any of the workmen, to any part of the work, all which it would be almost impossible, at least too long, to reckon up.

Locke, *II Civil Government,* V, 43

25 No labour is so heavy but it may be brought to a level with the workman's strength, when regulated by equity, and not by avarice. The violent fatigues which slaves are made to undergo in other parts may be supplied by a skilful use of ingenious machines. . . . Possibly there is not that climate upon earth where the most laborious services might not with proper encouragement be performed by freemen. Bad laws having made lazy men, they have been reduced to slavery because of their laziness.

Montesquieu, *Spirit of Laws,* XV, 8

26 The machines designed to abridge art are not always useful. If a piece of workmanship is of a moderate price, such as is equally agreeable to the maker and the buyer, those machines which would render the manufacture more simple, or, in other words, diminish the number of workmen, would be pernicious. And if water-mills were not everywhere established, I should not have believed them so useful as is pretended, because they have deprived an infinite multitude of their employment, a vast number of persons of the use of water, and great part of the land of its fertility.

Montesquieu, *Spirit
of Laws*, XXIII, 15

27 *Pangloss.* When man was placed in the garden of Eden, he was placed there, . . . to cultivate it; which proves that mankind are not created to be idle.

Voltaire, *Candide*, XXX

28 From the moment one man began to stand in need of the help of another; from the moment it appeared advantageous to any one man to have enough provisions for two, equality disappeared, property was introduced, work became indispensable, and vast forests became smiling fields, which man had to water with the sweat of his brow, and where slavery and misery were soon seen to germinate and grow up with the crops.

Rousseau, *Origin of Inequality*, II

29 Equality might have been sustained, had the talents of individuals been equal, and had, for example, the use of iron and the consumption of commodities always exactly balanced each other; but, as there was nothing to preserve this balance, it was soon disturbed; the strongest did most work; the most skilful turned his labour to best account; the most ingenious devised methods of diminishing his labour: the husbandman wanted more iron, or the smith more corn, and, while both laboured equally, the one gained a great deal by his work, while the other could hardly support himself. Thus natural inequality unfolds itself insensibly with that of combination, and the difference between men, developed by their different circumstances, becomes more sensible and permanent in its effects, and begins to have an influence, in the same proportion, over the lot of individuals.

Rousseau, *Origin of Inequality*, II

30 What if I should undertake to show humanity attacked in its very source, and even in the most sacred of all ties, in which fortune is consulted before nature, and, the disorders of society confounding all virtue and vice, continence becomes a criminal precaution, and a refusal to give life to a fellow-creature, an act of humanity? But, without drawing aside the veil which hides all these horrors, let us content ourselves with pointing out the evil which others will have to remedy.

To all this add the multiplicity of unhealthy trades, which shorten men's lives or destroy their bodies, such as working in the mines, and the preparing of metals and minerals, particularly lead, copper, mercury, cobalt, and arsenic: add those other dangerous trades which are daily fatal to many tilers, carpenters, masons and miners: put all these together and we can see, in the establishment and perfection of societies, the reasons for that diminution of our species, which has been noticed by many philosophers.

Rousseau, *Origin of Inequality*,
Appendix

31 It is allowed that vocations and employments of least dignity are of the most apparent use, that the meanest artisan or manufacturer contributes more to the accommodation of life than the profound scholar and argumentative theorist, and that the public would suffer less present inconvenience from the banishment of philosophers than from the extinction of any common trade.

Johnson, *Rambler No. 145*

32 *Johnson.* "Why, Sir, you cannot call that pleasure [that is, labor] to which all are averse, and which none begin but with the hope of leaving off; a thing which men dislike before they have tried it, and when they have tried it." *Boswell.* "But, Sir, the mind must be employed, and we grow weary when idle." *Johnson.* "That is, Sir, because, others being busy, we want company; but if we were all idle, there would be no growing weary; we should all entertain one another. There is, indeed, this in trade:—it gives men an opportunity of improving their situation. If there were no trade, many who are poor would always remain poor. But no man loves labour for itself." *Boswell.* "Yes, Sir, I know a person who does. He is a very laborious Judge, and he loves the labour." *Johnson.* "Sir, that is because he loves respect and distinction. Could he have them without labour, he would like it less." *Boswell.* "He tells me he likes it for itself."—"Why, Sir, he fancies so, because he is not accustomed to abstract."

Boswell, *Life of Johnson (Oct. 26, 1769)*

33 The greatest improvement in the productive powers of labour, and the greater part of the skill, dexterity, and judgment with which it is anywhere directed, or applied, seem to have been the effects of the division of labour. [These] effects . . . in the general business of society, will be more easily understood by considering in what manner it [labour] operates in some particular manufactures. . . . To take an example, therefore, from a very trifling manufacture; but one in which the division of labour has been very often taken notice of, the trade of the pin-maker; a

workman not educated to this business (which the division of labour has rendered a distinct trade), nor acquainted with the use of the machinery employed in it (to the invention of which the same division of labour has probably given occasion), could scarce, perhaps, with his utmost industry, make one pin in a day, and certainly could not make twenty. But in the way in which this business is now carried on, not only the whole work is a peculiar trade, but it is divided into a number of branches, of which the greater part are likewise peculiar trades. One man draws out the wire, another straights it, a third cuts it, a fourth points it, a fifth grinds it at the top for receiving the head; to make the head requires two or three distinct operations; to put it on is a peculiar business, to whiten the pins is another; it is even a trade by itself to put them into the paper; and the important business of making a pin is, in this manner, divided into about eighteen distinct operations, which, in some manufactories, are all performed by distinct hands, though in others the same man will sometimes perform two or three of them. I have seen a small manufactory of this kind where ten men only were employed, and where some of them consequently performed two or three distinct operations. But though they were very poor, and therefore but indifferently accommodated with the necessary machinery, they could, when they exerted themselves, make among them about twelve pounds of pins in a day. There are in a pound upwards of four thousand pins of a middling size. Those ten persons, therefore, could make among them upwards of forty-eight thousand pins in a day. Each person, therefore, making a tenth part of forty-eight thousand pins, might be considered as making four thousand eight hundred pins in a day. But if they had all wrought separately and independently, and without any of them having been educated to this peculiar business, they certainly could not each of them have made twenty, perhaps not one pin in a day; that is, certainly, not the two hundred and fortieth, perhaps not the four thousand eight hundredth part of what they are at present capable of performing, in consequence of a proper division and combination of their different operations.

Adam Smith, *Wealth of Nations,* I, 1

34 In the first fire-engines, a boy was constantly employed to open and shut alternately the communication between the boiler and the cylinder, according as the piston either ascended or descended. One of those boys, who loved to play with his companions, observed that, by tying a string from the handle of the valve which opened this communication to another part of the machine, the valve would open and shut without his assistance, and leave him at liberty to divert himself with his play-fellows. One of the greatest improvements that has been made upon this machine, since it was first invented, was in this manner the discovery of a boy who wanted to save his own labour.

Adam Smith, *Wealth of Nations,* I, 1

35 When the division of labour has been once thoroughly established, it is but a very small part of a man's wants which the produce of his own labour can supply. He supplies the far greater part of them by exchanging that surplus part of the produce of his own labour, which is over and above his own consumption, for such parts of the produce of other men's labour as he has occasion for. Every man thus lives by exchanging, or becomes in some measure a merchant, and the society itself grows to be what is properly a commercial society.

Adam Smith, *Wealth of Nations,* I, 4

36 Great labour, either of mind or body, continued for several days together, is in most men naturally followed by a great desire of relaxation, which, if not restrained by force or by some strong necessity, is almost irresistible. It is the call of nature, which requires to be relieved by some indulgence, sometimes of ease only, but sometimes, too, of dissipation and diversion.

Adam Smith, *Wealth of Nations,* I, 8

37 Custom everywhere regulates fashion. As it is ridiculous not to dress, so is it, in some measure, not to be employed, like other people. As a man of a civil profession seems awkward in a camp or a garrison, and is even in some danger of being despised there, so does an idle man among men of business.

Adam Smith, *Wealth of Nations,* I, 9

38 There is one sort of labour which adds to the value of the subject upon which it is bestowed: there is another which has no such effect. The former, as it produces a value, may be called productive; the latter, unproductive labour. Thus the labour of a manufacturer adds, generally, to the value of the materials which he works upon, that of his own maintenance, and of his master's profit. The labour of a menial servant, on the contrary, adds to the value of nothing. . . . The labour of the latter, however, has its value, and deserves its reward as well as that of the former. But the labour of the manufacturer fixes and realizes itself in some particular subject or vendible commodity, which lasts for some time at least after that labour is past. It is, as it were, a certain quantity of labour stocked and stored up to be employed, if necessary, upon some other occasion. That subject, or what is the same thing, the price of that subject, can afterwards, if necessary, put into motion a quantity of labour equal to that which had originally produced it. The labour of the menial servant, on the contrary, does not fix or realize itself

in any particular subject or vendible commodity. His services generally perish in the very instant of their performance, and seldom leave any trace or value behind them for which an equal quantity of service could afterwards be procured.

The labour of some of the most respectable orders in the society is, like that of menial servants, unproductive of any value, and does not fix or realize itself in any permanent subject; or vendible commodity, which endures after that labour is past, and for which an equal quantity of labour could afterwards be procured. The sovereign, for example, with all the officers both of justice and war who serve under him, the whole army and navy, are unproductive labourers. They are the servants of the public, and are maintained by a part of the annual produce of the industry of other people. Their service, how honourable, how useful, or how necessary soever, produces nothing for which an equal quantity of service can afterwards be procured. The protection, security, and defence of the commonwealth, the effect of their labour this year will not purchase its protection, security, and defence for the year to come. In the same class must be ranked, some both of the gravest and most important, and some of the most frivolous professions: churchmen, lawyers, physicians, men of letters of all kinds; players, buffoons, musicians, opera-singers, opera-dancers, etc. The labour of the meanest of these has a certain value, regulated by the very same principles which regulate that of every other sort of labour; and that of the noblest and most useful, produces nothing which could afterwards purchase or procure an equal quantity of labour. Like the declamation of the actor, the harangue of the orator, or the tune of the musician, the work of all of them perishes in the very instant of its production.

Both productive and unproductive labourers, and those who do not labour at all, are all equally maintained by the annual produce of the land and labour of the country. This produce, how great soever, can never be infinite, but must have certain limits. According, therefore, as a smaller or greater proportion of it is in any one year employed in maintaining unproductive hands, the more in the one case and the less in the other will remain for the productive, and the next year's produce will be greater or smaller accordingly; the whole annual produce, if we except the spontaneous productions of the earth, being the effect of productive labour.

Adam Smith, *Wealth of Nations,* II, 3

39 In the progress of the division of labour, the employment of the far greater part of those who live by labour, that is, of the great body of the people, comes to be confined to a few very simple operations, frequently to one or two. But the understandings of the greater part of men are necessarily formed by their ordinary employments. The man whose whole life is spent in performing a few simple operations, of which the effects are perhaps always the same, or very nearly the same, has no occasion to exert his understanding or to exercise his invention in finding out expedients for removing difficulties which never occur. He naturally loses, therefore, the habit of such exertion, and generally becomes as stupid and ignorant as it is possible for a human creature to become. The torpor of his mind renders him not only incapable of relishing or bearing a part in any rational conversation, but of conceiving any generous, noble, or tender sentiment, and consequently of forming any just judgment concerning many even of the ordinary duties of private life. Of the great and extensive interests of his country he is altogether incapable of judging, and unless very particular pains have been taken to render him otherwise, he is equally incapable of defending his country in war. The uniformity of his stationary life naturally corrupts the courage of his mind, and makes him regard with abhorrence the irregular, uncertain, and adventurous life of a soldier. It corrupts even the activity of his body, and renders him incapable of exerting his strength with vigour and perseverance in any other employment than that to which he has been bred. His dexterity at his own particular trade seems, in this manner, to be acquired at the expense of his intellectual, social, and martial virtues. But in every improved and civilised society this is the state into which the labouring poor, that is, the great body of the people, must necessarily fall, unless government takes some pains to prevent it.

Adam Smith, *Wealth of Nations,* V, 1

40 The brethren [of the ancient monasteries] were supported by their manual labour; and the duty of labour was strenuously recommended as a penance, as an exercise, and as the most laudable means of securing their daily subsistence. The garden and fields, which the industry of the monks had often rescued from the forest or the morass, were diligently cultivated by their hands. They performed, without reluctance, the menial offices of slaves and domestics; and the several trades that were necessary to provide their habits, their utensils, and their lodging, were exercised within the precincts of the great monasteries.

Gibbon, *Decline and Fall
of the Roman Empire,* XXXVII

41 All trades, arts, and handiworks have gained by division of labour, namely, when, instead of one man doing everything, each confines himself to a certain kind of work distinct from others in the treatment it requires, so as to be able to perform it with greater facility and in the greatest perfection. Where the different kinds of work are not distinguished and divided, where everyone is a jack-of-

all-trades, there manufactures remain still in the greatest barbarism.

Kant, *Fundamental Principles of the Metaphysic of Morals,* Pref.

42 There is no real wealth but the labor of man. Were the mountains of gold and the valleys of silver, the world would not be one grain of corn the richer; no one comfort would be added to the human race.

Shelley, *Queen Mab,* Notes

43 The means of acquiring and preparing the particularized means appropriate to our similarly particularized needs is work. Through work the raw material directly supplied by nature is specifically adapted to these numerous ends by all sorts of different processes. Now this formative change confers value on means and gives them their utility, and hence man in what he consumes is mainly concerned with the products of men. It is the products of human effort which man consumes.

Hegel, *Philosophy of Right,* 196

44 The universal and objective element in work, on the other hand, lies in the abstracting process which effects the subdivision of needs and means and thereby *eo ipso* subdivides production and brings about the division of labour. By this division, the work of the individual becomes less complex, and consequently his skill at his section of the job increases, like his output. At the same time, this abstraction of one man's skill and means of production from another's completes and makes necessary everywhere the dependence of men on one another and their reciprocal relation in the satisfaction of their other needs. Further, the abstraction of one man's production from another's makes work more and more mechanical, until finally man is able to step aside and install machines in his place.

Hegel, *Philosophy of Right,* 198

45 When a regular division of employments has spread through any society, the social state begins to acquire a consistency and stability which place it out of danger from particular divergencies.

Comte, *Positive Philosophy,* VI, 5

46 When a workman is unceasingly and exclusively engaged in the fabrication of one thing, he ultimately does his work with singular dexterity; but at the same time he loses the general faculty of applying his mind to the direction of the work. He every day becomes more adroit and less industrious; so that it may be said of him that in proportion as the workman improves, the man is degraded. What can be expected of a man who has spent twenty years of his life in making heads for pins? And to what can that mighty human intelligence which has so often stirred the world be applied in

him except it be to investigate the best method of making pins' heads? When a workman has spent a considerable portion of his existence in this manner, his thoughts are forever set upon the object of his daily toil; his body has contracted certain fixed habits, which it can never shake off; in a word, he no longer belongs to himself, but to the calling that he has chosen. It is in vain that laws and manners have been at pains to level all the barriers round such a man and to open to him on every side a thousand different paths to fortune; a theory of manufactures more powerful than customs and laws binds him to a craft, and frequently to a spot, which he cannot leave; it assigns to him a certain place in society, beyond which he cannot go; in the midst of universal movement it has rendered him stationary.

In proportion as the principle of the division of labor is more extensively applied, the workman becomes more weak, more narrow-minded, and more dependent. The art advances, the artisan recedes. On the other hand, in proportion as it becomes more manifest that the productions of manufactures are by so much the cheaper and better as the manufacture is larger and the amount of capital employed more considerable, wealthy and educated men come forward to embark in manufactures, which were heretofore abandoned to poor or ignorant handicraftsmen. The magnitude of the efforts required and the importance of the results to be obtained attract them. Thus at the very time at which the science of manufactures lowers the class of workmen, it raises the class of masters.

Tocqueville, *Democracy in America,* Vol. II, II, 20

47 All work, even cotton-spinning, is noble; work is alone noble.

Carlyle, *Past and Present,* III, 4

48 Were he never so benighted, forgetful of his high calling, there is always hope in a man that actually and earnestly works: in Idleness alone is there perpetual despair.

Carlyle, *Past and Present,* III, 11

49 The latest Gospel in this world is, Know thy work and do it.

Carlyle, *Past and Present,* III, 11

50 Consider how, even in the meanest sorts of Labour, the whole soul of a man is composed into a kind of real harmony, the instant he sets himself to work! Doubt, Desire, Sorrow, Remorse, Indignation, Despair itself, all these like helldogs lie beleaguering the soul of the poor dayworker, as of every man: but he bends himself with free valour against his task, and all these are stilled, all these shrink murmuring far off into their caves. The man is now a man. The blessed glow of Labour in

him, is it not as purifying fire, wherein all poison is burnt up, and of sour smoke itself there is made bright blessed flame!

Carlyle, *Past and Present*, III, 11

51 When I go into my garden with a spade, and dig a bed, I feel such an exhilaration and health that I discover that I have been defrauding myself all this time in letting others do for me what I should have done with my own hands.

Emerson, *Man the Reformer*

52 Every man who removes into this city with any purchasable talent or skill in him, gives to every man's labor in the city a new worth.

Emerson, *Wealth*

53 The crime which bankrupts men and states is job-work—declining from your main design, to serve a turn here or there.

Emerson, *Wealth*

54 Labor is the curse of the world, and nobody can meddle with it without becoming proportionately brutified.

Hawthorne, *American Notebooks*
(Aug. 12, 1841)

55 Most men would feel insulted if it were proposed to employ them in throwing stones over a wall, and then in throwing them back, merely that they might earn their wages. But many are no more worthily employed now.

Thoreau, *Life Without Principle*

56 The aim of the laborer should be, not to get his living, to get 'a good job,' but to perform well a certain work; and, even in a pecuniary sense, it would be economy for a town to pay its laborers so well that they would not feel that they were working for low ends, as for a livelihood merely, but for scientific, or even moral ends. Do not hire a man who does your work for money, but him who does it for love of it.

Thoreau, *Life Without Principle*

57 I found that the occupation of a day-laborer was the most independent of any, especially as it required only thirty or forty days in a year to support one. The laborer's day ends with the going down of the sun, and he is then free to devote himself to his chosen pursuit, independent of his labor; but his employer, who speculates from month to month, has no respite from one end of the year to the other.

In short, I am convinced, both by faith and experience, that to maintain one's self on this earth is not a hardship but a pastime, if we will live simply and wisely; as the pursuits of the simpler nations are still the sports of the more artificial. It is not necessary that a man should earn his living by the sweat of his brow, unless he sweats easier than I do.

Thoreau, *Walden:* Economy

58 If we except the *light* and the *air* of heaven, no good thing has been, or can be enjoyed by us, without having first cost labour. And, inasmuch [as] most good things are produced by labour, it follows that [all] such things of right belong to those whose labour has produced them. But it has so happened in all ages of the world, that *some* have laboured, and *others* have, without labour, enjoyed a large proportion of the fruits. This is wrong, and should not continue. To [secure] to each labourer the whole product of his labour, or as nearly as possible, is a most worthy object of any good government.

Lincoln, *Fragments of a Tariff
Discussion (Dec. 1, 1847)*

59 If at any time all *labour* should cease, and all existing provisions be equally divided among the people, at the end of a single year there could scarcely be one human being left alive—all would have perished by want of subsistence.

So again, if upon such division, all that *sort* of labour, which produces provisions, should cease, and each individual should take up so much of his share as he could, and carry it continually around his habitation, although in this carrying, the amount of labour going on might be as great as ever, so long as it could last, at the end of the year the result would be precisely the same—that is, none would be left living.

The first of these propositions shows, that universal *idleness* would speedily result in universal *ruin;* and the second shows, that *useless labour* is, in this respect, the same as idleness.

I submit, then, whether it does not follow, that *partial* idleness, and partial *useless labour,* would, in the proportion of their extent, in like manner result, in partial ruin—whether, if *all* should subsist upon the labour that *one half* should perform, it would not result in very scanty allowance to the whole.

Lincoln, *Fragments of a Tariff
Discussion (Dec. 1, 1847)*

60 Labor is prior to, and independent of, capital. Capital is only the fruit of labor, and could never have existed if labor had not first existed. Labor is the superior of capital, and deserves much the higher consideration. Capital has its rights, which are as worthy of protection as any other rights. Nor is it denied that there is, and probably always will be, a relation between labor and capital, producing mutual benefits. The error is in assuming that the whole labor of community exists within that relation. A few men own capital, and that few avoid labor themselves, and, with their capital, hire or buy another few to labor for them. A

large majority belong to neither class—neither work for others, nor have others working for them.

Lincoln, *Annual Message (Dec. 3, 1861)*

61 There is not, of necessity, any such thing as the free hired laborer being fixed to that condition for life. Many independent men everywhere in these States, a few years back in their lives, were hired laborers. The prudent, penniless beginner in the world, labors for wages awhile, saves a surplus with which to buy tools or land for himself; then labors on his own account another while, and at length hires another new beginner to help him. This is the just, and generous, and prosperous system, which opens the way to all—gives hope to all, and consequent energy, and progress, and improvement of condition to all. No men living are more worthy to be trusted than those who toil up from poverty—none less inclined to take, or touch, aught which they have not honestly earned.

Lincoln, *Annual Message (Dec. 3, 1861)*

62 Labour power can appear upon the market as a commodity only if, and so far as, its possessor, the individual whose labour power it is, offers it for sale, or sells it, as a commodity. In order that he may be able to do this, he must have it at his disposal, must be the untrammelled owner of his capacity for labour, that is, of his person. He and the owner of money meet in the market and deal with each other as on the basis of equal rights, with this difference alone, that one is buyer, the other seller; both, therefore, equal in the eyes of the law. The continuance of this relation demands that the owner of the labour power should sell it only for a definite period, for if he were to sell it rump and stump, once for all, he would be selling himself, converting himself from a free man into a slave, from an owner of a commodity into a commodity.

Marx, *Capital,* Vol. I, II, 6

63 Nature does not produce on the one side owners of money or commodities, and on the other men possessing nothing but their own labour power. This relation has no natural basis, neither is its social basis one that is common to all historical periods. It is clearly the result of a past historical development, the product of many economic revolutions, of the extinction of a whole series of older forms of social production.

Marx, *Capital,* Vol. I, II, 6

64 Within the process of production . . . capital acquired the command over labour, i.e., over functioning labour power or the labourer himself. Personified capital, the capitalist takes care that the labourer does his work regularly and with the proper degree of intensity.

Capital further developed into a coercive rela-

tion, which compels the working class to do more work than the narrow round of its own life-wants prescribes. As a producer of the activity of others, as a pumper-out of surplus labour and exploiter of labour power, it surpasses in energy, disregard of bounds, recklessness, and efficiency, all earlier systems of production based on directly compulsory labour.

Marx, *Capital,* Vol. I, III, 11

65 If we consider the process of production from the point of view of the simple labour process, the labourer stands in relation to the means of production, not in their quality as capital, but as the mere means and material of his own intelligent productive activity. In tanning, e.g., he deals with the skins as his simple object of labour. It is not the capitalist whose skin he tans. But it is different as soon as we deal with the process of production from the point of view of the process of creation of surplus value. The means of production are at once changed into means for the absorption of the labour of others. It is now no longer the labourer that employs the means of production, but the means of production that employ the labourer. Instead of being consumed by him as material elements of his productive activity, they consume him as the ferment necessary to their own life process, and the life process of capital consists only in its movement as value constantly expanding, constantly multiplying itself. Furnaces and workshops that stand idle by night, and absorb no living labour, are "a mere loss" to the capitalist. Hence, furnaces and workshops constitute lawful claims upon the night labour of the workpeople. The simple transformation of money into the material factors of the process of production, into means of production, transforms the latter into a title and a right to the labour and surplus labour of others.

Marx, *Capital,* Vol. I, III, 11

66 The foundation of every division of labour that is well developed and brought about by the exchange of commodities is the separation between town and country. It may be said, that the whole economical history of society is summed up in the movement of this antithesis.

Marx, *Capital,* Vol. I, IV, 14

67 It is a result of the division of labour in manufactures that the labourer is brought face to face with the intellectual potencies of the material process of production, as the property of another, and as a ruling power. This separation begins in simple co-operation, where the capitalist represents to the single workman the oneness and the will of the associated labour. It is developed in manufacture which cuts down the labourer into a detail labourer. It is completed in modern industry, which makes science a productive force distinct from

labour and presses it into the service of capital.

Marx, *Capital*, Vol. I, IV, 14

68 Every kind of capitalist production, insofar as it is not only a labour process, but also a process of creating surplus value, has this in common: that it is not the workman that employs the instruments of labour, but the instruments of labour that employ the workman. But it is only in the factory system that this inversion for the first time acquires technical and palpable reality. By means of its conversion into an automation, the instrument of labour confronts the labourer, during the labour process, in the shape of capital, of dead labour, which dominates and pumps dry living labour power. The separation of the intellectual powers of production from the manual labour, and the conversion of those powers into the might of capital over labour, is, as we have already shown, finally completed by modern industry erected on the foundation of machinery. The special skill of each individual insignificant factory operative vanishes as an infinitesimal quantity before the science, the gigantic physical forces, and the mass of labour that are embodied in the factory mechanism and, together with that mechanism, constitute the power of the "master."

Marx, *Capital*, Vol. I, IV, 15

69 The whole system of capitalist production is based on the fact that the workman sells his labour power as a commodity. Division of labour specializes this labour power, by reducing it to skill in handling a particular tool. So soon as the handling of this tool becomes the work of a machine, then, with the use-value, the exchange value of the workman's labour power also vanishes; the workman becomes unsaleable, like paper money thrown out of currency by legal enactment. That portion of the working class thus by machinery rendered superfluous (that is, no longer immediately necessary for the self-expansion of capital) either goes to the wall in the unequal contest of the old handicrafts and manufactures with machinery, or else floods all the more easily accessible branches of industry, swamps the labour market, and sinks the price of labour power below its value. It is impressed upon the workpeople, as a great consolation, first, that their sufferings are only temporary ("a temporary inconvenience"), secondly, that machinery acquires the mastery over the whole of a given field of production only by degrees, so that the extent and intensity of its destructive effect is diminished. The first consolation neutralizes the second. When machinery seizes on an industry by degrees, it produces chronic misery among the operatives who compete with it. Where the transition is rapid, the effect is acute and felt by great masses.

Marx, *Capital*, Vol. I, IV, 15

70 The more the productiveness of labour increases, the more can the working day be shortened; and the more the working day is shortened, the more can the intensity of labour increase. From a social point of view, the productiveness increases in the same ratio as the economy of labour, which, in its turn, includes not only economy of the means of production, but also the avoidance of all useless labour. The capitalist mode of production, while on the one hand enforcing economy in each individual business, on the other hand begets, by its anarchical system of competition, the most outrageous squandering of labour power and of the social means of production, not to mention the creation of a vast number of employments, at present indispensable, but in themselves superfluous.

The intensity and productiveness of labour being given, the time which society is bound to devote to material production is shorter, and, as a consequence, the time at its disposal for the free development, intellectual and social, of the individual is greater, in proportion as the work is more and more evenly divided among all the able-bodied members of society, and as a particular class is more and more deprived of the power to shift the natural burden of labour from its own shoulders to those of another layer of society. In this direction, the shortening of the working day finds at last a limit in the generalization of labour. In capitalist society, spare time is acquired for one class by converting the whole lifetime of the masses into labour time.

Marx, *Capital*, Vol. I, V, 17

71 In proportion as the bourgeoisie, i.e., capital, is developed, in the same proportion is the proletariat, the modern working class, developed—a class of labourers, who live only so long as they find work, and who find work only so long as their labour increases capital. These labourers, who must sell themselves piecemeal, are a commodity like every other article of commerce, and are consequently exposed to all the vicissitudes of competition, to all the fluctuations of the market.

Owing to the extensive use of machinery and to division of labour, the work of the proletarians has lost all individual character, and, consequently, all charm for the workman. He becomes an appendage of the machine, and it is only the most simple, most monotonous, and most easily acquired knack that is required of him. Hence, the cost of production of a workman is restricted almost entirely to the means of subsistence that he requires for his maintenance and for the propagation of his race. But the price of a commodity, and therefore also of labour, is equal to its cost of production. In proportion, therefore, as the repulsiveness of the work increases, the wage decreases. Nay more, in proportion as the use of machinery and division of labour increases, in the same proportion the burden of toil also increases, whether by prolongation of the working hours, by increase of the work exacted in a given time, or by increased speed of the machinery, etc.

Marx and Engels, *Communist Manifesto,* I

72 In bourgeois society living labour is but a means to increase accumulated labour. In Communist society accumulated labour is but a means to widen, to enrich, to promote the existence of the labourer.

Marx and Engels, *Communist Manifesto,* II

73 The workingmen have no country. We cannot take from them what they have not got.

Marx and Engels, *Communist Manifesto,* II

74 Intellectual speculation must be looked upon as a most influential part of the productive labour of society, and the portion of its resources employed in carrying on and in remunerating such labour, as a highly productive part of its expenditure.

Mill, *Principles of Political Economy,* Bk. I, II, 8

75 The number of persons fitted to direct and superintend any industrial enterprise, or even to execute any process which cannot be reduced almost to an affair of memory and routine, is always far short of the demand; as is evident from the enormous difference between the salaries paid to such persons, and the wages of ordinary labour. The deficiency of practical good sense, which renders the majority of the labouring class such bad calculators—which makes, for instance, their domestic economy so improvident, lax, and irregular—must disqualify them for any but a low grade of intelligent labour, and render their industry far less productive than with equal energy it otherwise might be.

Mill, *Principles of Political Economy,* Bk. I, VII, 5

76 Hitherto it is questionable if all the mechanical inventions yet made have lightened the day's toil of any human being. They have enabled a greater population to live the same life of drudgery and imprisonment, and an increased number of manufacturers and others to make fortunes. They have increased the comforts of the middle classes. But they have not yet begun to effect those great changes in human destiny, which it is in their nature and in their futurity to accomplish. Only when, in addition to just institutions, the increase of mankind shall be under the deliberate guidance of judicious foresight, can the conquests made from the powers of nature by the intellect and energy of scientific discoverers, become the common property of the species, and the means of improving and elevating the universal lot.

Mill, *Principles of Political Economy,* Bk. IV, VI, 2

77 The Bible legend tells us that the absence of labor—idleness—was a condition of the first man's blessedness before the Fall. Fallen man has retained a love of idleness, but the curse weighs on the race not only because we have to seek our bread in the sweat of our brows, but because our moral nature is such that we cannot be both idle and at ease. An inner voice tells us we are in the wrong if we are idle. If man could find a state in which he felt that though idle he was fulfilling his duty, he would have found one of the conditions of man's primitive blessedness.

Tolstoy, *War and Peace,* VII, 1

78 Tom said to himself that it was not such a hollow world, after all. He had discovered a great law of human action, without knowing it—namely, that in order to make a man or boy covet a thing, it is only necessary to make the thing difficult to attain. If he had been a great and wise philosopher, like the writer of this book, he would now have comprehended that Work consists of whatever a body is *obliged* to do, and that Play consists of whatever a body is not obliged to do. And this would help him to understand why constructing artificial flowers or performing on a treadmill is work, while rolling tenpins or climbing Mont Blanc is only amusement. There are wealthy gentlemen in England who drive four-horse passenger-coaches twenty or thirty miles on a daily line, in the summer, because the privilege costs them considerable money; but if they are offered wages for the service, that would turn it into work and then they would resign.

Mark Twain, *Tom Sawyer,* II

79 Leisure, though the propertied classes give its name to their own idleness, is not idleness. It is not even a luxury: it is a necessity, and a necessity of the first importance. Some of the most valuable work done in the world has been done at leisure, and never paid for in cash or kind. Leisure may be described as free activity, labor as compulsory activity. Leisure does what it likes: labor does what it must, the compulsion being that of Nature, which in these latitudes leaves men no choice between labor and starvation.

Shaw, *Socialism and Culture*

11.4 | *Money*

Most of the passages quoted in this section are concerned with the conception of money as a common measure or universal medium of exchange. In the background of this discussion lies the distinction between a money economy and a barter economy in which goods are exchanged directly without the use of money. One profound difference between these two economies, observed by a number of writers, is that where money is not in use, spoilage and waste exert a restraining influence on the accumulation of goods that is not present when coin can be acquired through trade and then stored away indefinitely.

Some of the passages deal with the borrowing and lending of money, and this leads into a discussion of usury, debt, and credit. Though money is seen to be useful in a variety of ways, it is generally agreed that it is useless in itself, which leads certain writers to call it "artificial wealth" as contrasted with the natural wealth of consumable goods and instruments of production.

The passages that enunciate or comment on the theme that the love of money is the root of all evil might have been placed in Section 11.2 on WEALTH AND POVERTY; but since they use the word "money" instead of the word "wealth" they are included here. The reader should consult that section and also Section 11.1 on PROPERTY and Section 11.5 on TRADE, COMMERCE, AND INDUSTRY for the treatment of other contexts.

---

1 All things that are exchanged must be somehow comparable. It is for this end that money has been introduced, and it becomes in a sense an intermediate; for it measures all things.

Aristotle, *Ethics,* 1133a 18

2 There are two sorts of wealth-getting. . . . One is a part of household management, the other is retail trade: the former necessary and honourable, while that which consists in exchange is justly censured; for it is unnatural, and a mode by which men gain from one another. The most hated sort, and with the greatest reason, is usury, which makes a gain out of money itself, and not from the natural object of it. For money was intended to be used in exchange, but not to increase at interest. . . . Of all modes of getting wealth this is the most unnatural.

Aristotle, *Politics,* 1258a38

3 One has a duty to make money, but only by honorable means. It is also one's duty to save money and increase it by diligence and thrift.

Cicero, *De Officiis,* II, 24

4 Are you ignorant of what value money has, what use it can afford? Bread, herbs, a bottle of wine may be purchased; to which [necessaries], add [such others], as, being withheld, human nature would be uneasy with itself. What, to watch half dead with terror, night and day, to dread profligate thieves, fire, and your slaves, lest they should run away and plunder you; is this delightful? I should always wish to be very poor in possessions held upon these terms.

Horace, *Satires,* I, 1

5 For the love of money is the root of all evil: which while some coveted after, they have erred from the faith, and pierced themselves through with many sorrows.

I Timothy 6:10

6 It is the higher accomplishment to use money well than to use arms; but not to need it is more noble than to use it.

Plutarch, *Coriolanus*

7   The loss of money is awful,
Such a terrible thing that no one can counterfeit mourning,
No one be content with merely rending his garments,
Rubbing his eyes to produce crocodile tears. If your money
Is gone, you will really cry with genuine lamentation.

Juvenal, *Satire XIII*

8 All material things obey money so far as the multitude of fools is concerned, who know no other than material goods, which can be obtained for money. But we should take our judgment of human goods not from the foolish but from the wise.

Aquinas, *Summa Theologica*, I–II, 2, 1

9 In view of the fact that the Utopians' customs are so different from ours, a shrewd judge will not be surprised to find that they do not use gold and silver at all as we do. Since they keep gold and silver only for grave contingencies, they take care that in the meantime no one shall value these metals more than they deserve. Iron is obviously greatly superior to either. Men can no more do without iron than without fire and water. But gold and silver have no indispensable qualities. Human folly has made them precious only because of their scarcity. Nature, like a wise and generous parent, has placed the best things everywhere and in the open, such as air and water and the earth itself, but she has hidden vain and useless things in remote and faraway places.

Thomas More, *Utopia*, II, 7

10 *Panurge.* Be still indebted to somebody or other, that there may be somebody always to pray for you; that the giver of all good things may grant unto you a blessed, long, and prosperous life; fearing, if fortune should deal crossly with you, that it might be his chance to come short of being paid by you, he will always speak good of you in every company, ever and anon purchase new creditors unto you; to the end, that through their means you may make a shift by borrowing from Peter to pay Paul, and with other folk's earth fill up his ditch. . . . Believe me, your creditors, with a more fervent devotion, will beseech Almighty God to prolong your life, they being of nothing more afraid than that you should die; for that they are more concerned for the sleeve than the arm, and love silver better than their own lives.

Rabelais, *Gargantua and Pantagruel*, III, 3

11 *Grumio.* Nothing comes amiss, so money comes withal.

Shakespeare, *Taming of the Shrew*, I, ii, 82

12 *The Bastard.* Bell, book, and candle shall not drive me back,
When gold and silver becks me to come on.

Shakespeare, *King John*, III, iii, 12

13 *Falstaff.* I can get no remedy against this consumption of the purse: borrowing only lingers and lingers it out, but the disease is incurable.

Shakespeare, *II Henry IV*, I, ii, 264

14 *Polonius.* Neither a borrower nor a lender be;
For loan oft loses both itself and friend,

And borrowing dulls the edge of husbandry.

Shakespeare, *Hamlet*, I, iii, 75

15 Money is like muck, not good except it be spread.

Bacon, *Of Seditions and Troubles*

16 As to money, it may be observed that its uses do not result from any value intrinsically belonging to the precious metals, or to the specific denomination and shape of coin, but from the general application which can be made of it, as a standard of payment for all commodities. For whatever is taken as a common measure of all other things, ought to be liable, in itself, to but little variation. Now the precious metals are of this description, possessing nearly the same intrinsic value at all times and in all places. Though the nominal value of the same quantity of gold and silver, whether paid by weight or coin will be greater or less, in proportion to the abundance or scarcity of the things for which there is a general demand.

Grotius, *Rights of War and Peace*,
Bk. II, XII, 17

17 Gold and silver, being, as it happens, almost in all countries of the world highly valued, is a commodious measure of the value of all things else between nations; and money, of what matter soever coined by the sovereign of a Commonwealth, is a sufficient measure of the value of all things else between the subjects of that Commonwealth. By the means of which measures all commodities, movable and immovable, are made to accompany a man to all places of his resort, within and without the place of his ordinary residence; and the same passeth from man to man within the Commonwealth, and goes round about, nourishing, as it passeth, every part thereof.

Hobbes, *Leviathan*, II, 24

18 As money has presented us with an abstract of everything, it has come to pass that its image above every other usually occupies the mind of the multitude, because they can imagine hardly any kind of joy without the accompanying idea of money as its cause.

Spinoza, *Ethics*, IV, Appendix XXVIII

19 Those . . . who know the true use of money, and regulate the measure of wealth according to their needs, live contented with few things.

Spinoza, *Ethics*, IV, Appendix XXIX

20 The greatest part of things really useful to the life of man, and such as the necessity of subsisting made the first commoners of the world look after—as it doth the Americans now—are generally things of short duration, such as—if they are not consumed by use—will decay and perish of themselves. Gold, silver, and diamonds are things that fancy or agreement hath put the value on, more than real use and the necessary support of life.

Now of those good things which Nature hath provided in common, every one hath a right (as hath been said) to as much as he could use; and had a property in all he could effect with his labour; all that his industry could extend to, to alter from the state Nature had put it in, was his. He that gathered a hundred bushels of acorns or apples had thereby a property in them; they were his goods as soon as gathered. He was only to look that he used them before they spoiled, else he took more than his share, and robbed others. And, indeed, it was a foolish thing, as well as dishonest, to hoard up more than he could make use of. If he gave away a part to anybody else, so that it perished not uselessly in his possession, these he also made use of. And if he also bartered away plums that would have rotted in a week, for nuts that would last good for his eating a whole year, he did no injury; he wasted not the common stock; destroyed no part of the portion of goods that belonged to others, so long as nothing perished uselessly in his hands. Again, if he would give his nuts for a piece of metal, pleased with its colour, or exchange his sheep for shells, or wool for a sparkling pebble or a diamond, and keep those by him all his life, he invaded not the right of others; he might heap up as much of these durable things as he pleased; the exceeding of the bounds of his just property not lying in the largeness of his possession, but the perishing of anything uselessly in it.

And thus came in the use of money; some lasting thing that men might keep without spoiling, and that, by mutual consent, men would take in exchange for the truly useful but perishable supports of life.

Locke, *II Civil Government*, V, 46–47

21 In the beginning, all the world was America, and more so than that is now; for no such thing as money was anywhere known. Find out something that hath the use and value of money amongst his neighbours, you shall see the same man will begin presently to enlarge his possessions.

Locke, *II Civil Government*, V, 49

22 The greatest security of the liberties of a people who do not cultivate the earth is their not knowing the use of money. What is gained by hunting, fishing, or keeping herds of cattle cannot be assembled in such great quantity, nor be sufficiently preserved, for one man to find himself in a condition to corrupt many others: but when, instead of this, a man has a sign of riches, he may obtain a large quantity of these signs, and distribute them as he pleases.

The people who have no money have but few wants; and these are supplied with ease, and in an equal manner. Equality is then unavoidable; and hence it proceeds that their chiefs are not despotic.

Montesquieu, *Spirit of Laws*, XVIII, 17

23 A specie is the sign of the value of merchandise, paper is the sign of the value of specie; and when it is of the right sort, it represents this value in such a manner that as to the effects produced by it there is not the least difference.

In the same manner, as money is the sign and representative of a thing, everything is a sign and representative of money; and the state is in a prosperous condition when on the one hand money perfectly represents all things, and on the other all things perfectly represent money, and are reciprocally the sign of each other; that is, when they have such a relative value that we may have the one as soon as we have the other. This never happens in any other than a moderate government, nor does it always happen there; for example, if the laws favour the dishonest debtor, his effects are no longer a representative or sign of money. With regard to a despotic government, it would be a prodigy did things there represent their sign. Tyranny and distrust make every one bury their specie; things therefore are not there the representative of money.

Montesquieu, *Spirit of Laws*, XXII, 2

24 Money is not, properly speaking, one of the subjects of commerce; but only the instrument which men have agreed upon to facilitate the exchange of one commodity for another. It is none of the wheels of trade: It is the oil which renders the motion of the wheels more smooth and easy.

Hume, *Of Money*

25 Money has never appeared to me as valuable as it is generally considered. More than that, it has never even appeared to me particularly convenient. It is good for nothing in itself; it has to be changed before it can be enjoyed; one is obliged to buy, to bargain, to be often cheated, to pay dearly, to be badly served. I should like something which is good in quality; with my money I am sure to get it bad.

Rousseau, *Confessions*, I

26 The money which a man possesses is the instrument of freedom; that which we eagerly pursue is the instrument of slavery.

Rousseau, *Confessions*, I

27 When the price of any commodity is neither more nor less than what is sufficient to pay the rent of the land, the wages of the labour, and the profits of the stock employed in raising, preparing, and bringing it to market, according to their natural rates, the commodity is then sold for what may be called its natural price. The commodity is then sold precisely for what it is worth, or for what it really costs the person who brings it to market. . . .

The actual price at which any commodity is commonly sold is called its market price. It may

either be above, or below, or exactly the same
with its natural price.

The market price of every particular commodity is regulated by the proportion between the
quantity which is actually brought to market, and
the demand of those who are willing to pay the
natural price of the commodity, or the whole value of the rent, labour, and profit, which must be
paid in order to bring it thither.

Adam Smith, *Wealth of Nations,* I, 7

28 A guinea may be considered as a bill for a certain
quantity of necessaries and conveniencies upon all
the tradesmen in the neighbourhood. The revenue
of the person to whom it is paid, does not so properly consist in the piece of gold, as in what he can
get for it, or in what he can exchange it for. If it
could be exchanged for nothing, it would, like a
bill upon a bankrupt, be of no more value than
the most useless piece of paper.

Adam Smith, *Wealth of Nations,* II, 2

29 In some countries the interest of money has been
prohibited by law. But as something can everywhere be made by the use of money, something
ought everywhere to be paid for the use of it. This
regulation, instead of preventing, has been found
from experience to increase the evil of usury; the
debtor being obliged to pay, not only for the use of
the money, but for the risk which his creditor runs
by accepting a compensation for that use. He is
obliged, if one may say so, to insure his creditor
from the penalties of usury.

Adam Smith, *Wealth of Nations,* II, 4

30 A bag of shining leather, filled with pearls, fell
into the hands of a private soldier; he carefully
preserved the bag, but he threw away its contents,
judging that whatever was of no use could not
possibly be of any value.

Gibbon, *Decline and Fall
of the Roman Empire,* XIII

31 How beauteous are rouleaus! how charming
    chests
  Containing ingots, bags of dollars, coins
(Not of old victors, all whose heads and crests
  Weigh not the thin ore where their visage
    shines,
But) of fine unclipt gold, where dully rests
  Some likeness, which the glittering cirque con-
    fines,
Of modern, reigning, sterling, stupid stamp:—
Yes! ready money *is* Aladdin's lamp.

Byron, *Don Juan,* XII, 12

32 Money alone is absolutely good, because it is not
only a concrete satisfaction of one need in particular; it is an abstract satisfaction of all.

Schopenhauer, *Property*

33 Money, which represents the prose of life, and
which is hardly spoken of in parlors without an
apology, is, in its effects and laws, as beautiful as
roses.

Emerson, *Nominalist and Realist*

34 A dollar is not value, but representative of value,
and, at last, of moral values.

Emerson, *Wealth*

35 A dollar in a university is worth more than a dollar in a jail; in a temperate, schooled, law-abiding
community than in some sink of crime, where
dice, knives and arsenic are in constant play.

Emerson, *Wealth*

36 The urbane activity with which a man receives
money is really marvellous, considering that we so
earnestly believe money to be the root of all earthly ills, and that on no account can a monied man
enter heaven. Ah! how cheerfully we consign ourselves to perdition!

Melville, *Moby Dick,* I

37 The ways by which you may get money almost
without exception lead downward.

Thoreau, *Life Without Principle*

38 You may raise money enough to tunnel a mountain, but you cannot raise money enough to hire a
man who is minding *his own* business. An efficient
and valuable man does what he can, whether the
community pay him for it or not.

Thoreau, *Life Without Principle*

39 Gold is now money with reference to all other
commodities only because it was previously, with
reference to them, a simple commodity. Like all
other commodities, it was also capable of serving
as an equivalent, either as simple equivalent in
isolated exchanges, or as particular equivalent by
the side of others. Gradually, it began to serve,
within varying limits, as universal equivalent. So
soon as it monopolizes this position in the expression of value for the world of commodities, it becomes the money commodity.

Marx, *Capital,* Vol. I, I, 1

40 The first chief function of money is to supply commodities with the material for the expression of
their values, or to represent their values as magnitudes of the same denomination, qualitatively
equal, and quantitatively comparable. It thus
serves as a *universal measure of value.* And only by
virtue of this function does gold, the equivalent
commodity *par excellence,* become money.

Marx, *Capital,* Vol. I, I, 3

41 It is not money that renders commodities commensurable. Just the contrary. It is because all
commodities, as values, are realized human la-

bour, and therefore commensurable, that their values can be measured by one and the same special commodity, and the latter be converted into the common measure of their values, that is, into money. Money as a measure of value is the phenomenal form that must of necessity be assumed by that measure of value which is immanent in commodities, labour time.

Marx, *Capital,* Vol. I, I, 3

42 In order that it may play the part of money, gold must of course enter the market at some point or other. This point is to be found at the source of production of the metal, at which place gold is bartered, as the immediate product of labour, for some other product of equal value. From that moment it always represents the realized price of some commodity. Apart from its exchange for other commodities at the source of its production, gold, in whoever's hands it may be, is the transformed shape of some commodity alienated by its owner.

Marx, *Capital,* Vol. I, I, 3

43 The commodity that functions as a measure of value, and, either in its own person or by a representative, as the medium of circulation, is money. Gold (or silver) is therefore money. It functions as money, on the one hand, when it has to be present in its own golden person. It is then the money commodity, neither merely ideal, as in its function of a measure of value, nor capable of being represented, as in its function of circulating medium. On the other hand, it also functions as money, when by virtue of its function, whether that function be performed in person or by representative, it congeals into the sole form of value, the only adequate form of existence of exchange value, in opposition to use-value, represented by all other commodities.

Marx, *Capital,* Vol. I, I, 3

44 There cannot . . . be intrinsically a more insignificant thing, in the economy of society, than money; except in the character of a contrivance for sparing time and labour. It is a machine for doing quickly and commodiously, what would be done, though less quickly and commodiously, without it: and like many other kinds of machinery, it only exerts a distinct and independent influence of its own when it gets out of order.

Mill, *Principles of Political Economy,*
Bk. III, VII, 3

45 The value of money, other things being the same, varies inversely as its quantity; every increase of quantity lowering the value, and every diminution raising it, in a ratio exactly equivalent. This, it must be observed, is a property peculiar to money.

Mill, *Principles of Political Economy,*
Bk. III, VIII, 2

46 Nothing precipitates and solidifies this gold so readily as contact with human flesh heated by passion.

Mark Twain, *Remarkable Gold Mines*

47 Now to . . . teach children that it is sinful to desire money, is to strain towards the extreme possible limit of impudence in lying and corruption in hypocrisy. The universal regard for money is the one hopeful fact in our civilization, the one sound spot in our social conscience. Money is the most important thing in the world. It represents health, strength, honor, generosity and beauty as conspicuously and undeniably as the want of it represents illness, weakness, disgrace, meanness and ugliness. Not the least of its virtues is that it destroys base people as certainly as it fortifies and dignifies noble people. It is only when it is cheapened to worthlessness for some and made impossibly dear to others, that it becomes a curse. In short, it is a curse only in such foolish social conditions that life itself is a curse. For the two things are inseparable: money is the counter that enables life to be distributed socially: it *is* life as truly as sovereigns and bank notes are money. The first duty of every citizen is to insist on having money on reasonable terms; and this demand is not complied with by giving four men three shillings each for ten or twelve hours' drudgery and one man a thousand pounds for nothing. The crying need of the nation is not for better morals, cheaper bread, temperance, liberty, culture, redemption of fallen sisters and erring brothers, nor the grace, love and fellowship of the Trinity, but simply for enough money. And the evil to be attacked is not sin, suffering, greed, priestcraft, kingcraft, demagogy, monopoly, ignorance, drink, war, pestilence, nor any other of the scapegoats which reformers sacrifice, but simply poverty.

Shaw, *Major Barbara,* Pref.

48 The whole record of civilization is a record of the failure of money as a higher incentive. The enormous majority of men never make any serious effort to get rich. The few who are sordid enough to do so easily become millionaires with a little luck, and astonish the others by the contrast between their riches and their stupidity. In fact it is the complete breakdown in practice of the sufficiency of the pecuniary incentive that has compelled us to turn our backs on Adam Smith and Cobden, and confess that both the old Tories and the modern Socialists are right, and that there is no salvation for the world in Free Contract and Free Trade.

The belief in money as an incentive is founded on the observation that people will do for money what they will not do for anything else. Careless observers think that men will do anything for money; but this is clearly not true: if it were, the majority would not be poorer than the minority. They say also that everything men do is done for money; and this also is obviously untrue: if it were men would be always earning and never spending. The most important, arduous, and painful of normal human activities is the bearing of children; but when I try to persuade women that they should refuse to do it unless they are handsomely paid for it, they are shocked, and persist in doing it for nothing even when the result is starvation for themselves and the children. We must there-fore keep strictly to the terms of the proposition, which is, that people will do for money what they will not do for love or for anything else except money. For instance, an immense mass of the work of the modern community consists in the op-pression of the poor. To take a crude instance, no man will go into the house where naked and hun-gry children are crying for food and warmth, and extort from their mother four shillings to pay a slum landlord who already has more money than is good for him, unless he is paid to do it.

Shaw, *Redistribution of Income*

11.5 | *Trade, Commerce, and Industry*

The subjects covered here are connected with earlier ones, especially the sections de-voted to MONEY and to WEALTH AND POVERTY. Trade and commerce are concerned with exchangeable wealth, in the form of com-modities to be bought and sold—either di-rectly by barter or indirectly through the use of money. Industry is concerned with the production of wealth and with the produc-tion of capital instruments or means of pro-duction. Money in the form of financial cap-ital plays an important role in the process.

Among the great authors, Adam Smith, Karl Marx, and J. S. Mill deal with these subjects mainly as professional economists within whose field of study they fall. But other writers contribute ethical, political, or historical comments—questioning the moti-vation underlying trade, comparing it with usury as unproductive of wealth, relating trade and commerce to conflicts between states and wars, and yet also seeing trade and commerce as one of the principal sources of progress.

1 It is naught, it is naught, saith the buyer: but when he is gone his way, then he boasteth.

Proverbs 20:14

2 There is a country in Libya, and a nation, beyond the Pillars of Hercules, which they are wont to visit, where they no sooner arrive but forthwith they unlade their wares, and, having disposed them after an orderly fashion along the beach, leave them, and, returning aboard their ships, raise a great smoke. The natives, when they see the smoke, come down to the shore, and, laying out to view so much gold as they think the worth of the wares, withdraw to a distance. The Cartha-ginians upon this come ashore and look. If they think the gold enough, they take it and go their way; but if it does not seem to them sufficient, they go aboard ship once more, and wait patient-ly. Then the others approach and add to their gold, till the Carthaginians are content. Neither party deals unfairly by the other: for they them-selves never touch the gold till it comes up to the worth of their goods, nor do the natives ever carry off the goods till the gold is taken away.

Herodotus, *History*, IV, 196

3 *Athenian Stranger.* In order that the retail trader who dwells in our city may be as good or as little bad as possible, the guardians of the law shall re-member that they are not only guardians of those

who may be easily watched and prevented from becoming lawless or bad, because they are well-born and bred; but still more should they have a watch over those who are of another sort, and follow pursuits which have a very strong tendency to make men bad. And, therefore, in respect of the multifarious occupations of retail trade, that is to say, in respect of such of them as are allowed to remain, because they seem to be quite necessary in a state—about these the guardians of the law should meet and take counsel with those who have experience of the several kinds of retail trade, as we before commanded concerning adulteration (which is a matter akin to this), and when they meet they shall consider what amount of receipts, after deducting expenses, will produce a moderate gain to the retail trades, and they shall fix in writing and strictly maintain what they find to be the right percentage of profit; this shall be seen to by the wardens of the agora, and by the wardens of the city, and by the wardens of the country. And so retail trade will benefit every one, and do the least possible injury to those in the state who practise it.

Plato, *Laws,* XI, 920A

4 Of everything which we possess there are two uses: both belong to the thing as such, but not in the same manner, for one is the proper, and the other the improper or secondary use of it. For example, a shoe is used for wear, and is used for exchange; both are uses of the shoe. He who gives a shoe in exchange for money or food to him who wants one, does indeed use the shoe as a shoe, but this is not its proper or primary purpose, for a shoe is not made to be an object of barter. The same may be said of all possessions, for the art of exchange extends to all of them, and it arises at first from what is natural, from the circumstance that some have too little, others too much. Hence we may infer that retail trade is not a natural part of the art of getting wealth; had it been so, men would have ceased to exchange when they had enough. In the first community, indeed, which is the family, this art is obviously of no use, but it begins to be useful when the society increases. For the members of the family originally had all things in common; later, when the family divided into parts, the parts shared in many things, and different parts in different things, which they had to give in exchange for what they wanted, a kind of barter which is still practised among barbarous nations who exchange with one another the necessaries of life and nothing more; giving and receiving wine, for example, in exchange for corn, and the like. This sort of barter is not part of the wealth-getting art and is not contrary to nature, but is needed for the satisfaction of men's natural wants. The other or more complex form of exchange grew, as might have been inferred, out of the simpler. When the inhabitants of one country became more dependent on those of another, and they imported what they needed, and exported what they had too much of, money necessarily came into use. For the various necessaries of life are not easily carried about, and hence men agreed to employ in their dealings with each other something which was intrinsically useful and easily applicable to the purposes of life, for example, iron, silver, and the like. Of this the value was at first measured simply by size and weight, but in process of time they put a stamp upon it, to save the trouble of weighing and to mark the value.

When the use of coin had once been discovered, out of the barter of necessary articles arose the other art of wealth-getting, namely, retail trade; which was at first probably a simple matter, but became more complicated as soon as men learned by experience whence and by what exchanges the greatest profit might be made.

Aristotle, *Politics,* 1257ᵃ6

5 A tradesman is one whose business consists in the exchange of things. According to the Philosopher [Aristotle], exchange of things is twofold; one, natural as it were, and necessary, whereby one commodity is exchanged for another, or money taken in exchange for a commodity, in order to satisfy the needs of life. Such like trading, properly speaking, does not belong to tradesmen, but rather to housekeepers or civil servants who have to provide the household or the state with the necessaries of life. The other kind of exchange is either that of money for money, or of any commodity for money, not on account of the necessities of life, but for profit, and this kind of exchange, properly speaking, regards tradesmen, according to the Philosopher. The former kind of exchange is commendable because it supplies a natural need: but the latter is justly deserving of blame, because, considered in itself, it satisfies the greed for gain, which knows no limit and tends to infinity. Hence trading, considered in itself, has a certain debasement attaching thereto, in so far as, by its very nature, it does not imply a virtuous or necessary end. Nevertheless gain which is the end of trading, though not implying, by its nature, anything virtuous or necessary, does not, in itself, connote anything sinful or contrary to virtue: wherefore nothing prevents gain from being directed to some necessary or even virtuous end, and thus trading becomes lawful. Thus, for instance, a man may intend the moderate gain which he seeks to acquire by trading for the upkeep of his household, or for the assistance of the needy: or again, a man may take to trade for some public advantage, for instance, lest his country lack the necessaries of life, and seek gain, not as an end, but as payment for his labor.

Aquinas, *Summa Theologica,* II–II, 77, 4

6 The gains of ordinary trades and vocations are

honest, and furthered by two things chiefly: by diligence, and by a good name for good and fair dealing. But the gains of bargains are of a more doubtful nature; when men shall wait upon others' necessity, broke by servants and instruments to draw them on, put off others cunningly that would be better chapmen, and the like practices, which are crafty and naught.

Bacon, *Of Riches*

7 When a democracy is founded on commerce, private people may acquire vast riches without a corruption of morals. This is because the spirit of commerce is naturally attended with that of frugality, economy, moderation, labour, prudence, tranquillity, order, and rule. So long as this spirit subsists, the riches it produces have no bad effect. The mischief is, when excessive wealth destroys the spirit of commerce, then it is that the inconveniences of inequality begin to be felt.

In order to support this spirit, commerce should be carried on by the principal citizens; this should be their sole aim and study; this the chief object of the laws: and these very laws, by dividing the estates of individuals in proportion to the increase of commerce, should set every poor citizen so far at his ease as to be able to work like the rest, and every wealthy citizen in such a mediocrity as to be obliged to take some pains either in preserving or acquiring a fortune.

Montesquieu, *Spirit of Laws,* V, 6

8 Commerce is a cure for the most destructive prejudices; for it is almost a general rule that wherever we find agreeable manners, there commerce flourishes; and that wherever there is commerce, there we meet with agreeable manners.

Let us not be astonished, then, if our manners are now less savage than formerly. Commerce has everywhere diffused a knowledge of the manners of all nations: these are compared one with another, and from this comparison arise the greatest advantages.

Commercial laws, it may be said, improve manners for the same reason that they destroy them. They corrupt the purest morals. This was the subject of Plato's complaints; and we every day see that they polish and refine the most barbarous.

Peace is the natural effect of trade. Two nations who traffic with each other become reciprocally dependent; for if one has an interest in buying, the other has an interest in selling; and thus their union is founded on their mutual necessities.

But if the spirit of commerce unites nations, it does not in the same manner unite individuals. We see that in countries where the people move only by the spirit of commerce, they make a traffic of all the humane, all the moral virtues; the most trifling things, those which humanity would demand, are there done, or there given, only for money.

The spirit of trade produces in the mind of a man a certain sense of exact justice, opposite, on the one hand, to robbery, and on the other to those moral virtues which forbid our always adhering rigidly to the rules of private interest, and suffer us to neglect this for the advantage of others.

The total privation of trade, on the contrary, produces robbery, which Aristotle ranks in the number of means of acquiring; yet it is not at all inconsistent with certain moral virtues. Hospitality, for instance, is most rare in trading countries, while it is found in the most admirable perfection among nations of vagabonds.

Montesquieu, *Spirit of Laws,* XX, 1–2

9 It is very usual, in nations ignorant of the nature of commerce, to prohibit the exportation of commodities, and to preserve among themselves whatever they think valuable and useful. They do not consider that in this prohibition they act directly contrary to their intention; and that the more is exported of any commodity, the more will be raised at home, of which they themselves will always have the first offer.

Hume, *Of the Balance of Trade*

10 The greatness of a state, and the happiness of its subjects, how independent soever they may be supposed in some respects, are commonly allowed to be inseparable with regard to commerce; and as private men receive greater security, in the possession of their trade and riches, from the power of the public, so the public becomes powerful in proportion to the opulence and extensive commerce of private men.

Hume, *Of Commerce*

11 Talking of trade, he [Johnson] observed, "It is a mistaken notion that a vast deal of money is brought into a nation by trade. It is not so. Commodities come from commodities; but trade produces no capital accession of wealth. However, though there should be little profit in money, there is a considerable profit in pleasure, as it gives to one nation the productions of another; as we have wines and fruits, and many other foreign articles, brought to us."

Boswell, *Life of Johnson (Oct. 26, 1769)*

12 *Johnson.* The great increase of commerce and manufactures hurts the military spirit of a people; because it produces a competition for something else than martial honours,—a competition for riches. It also hurts the bodies of the people; for you will observe, there is no man who works at any particular trade, but you may know him from his appearance to do so. One part or other of his body being more used than the rest, he is in some degree deformed.

Boswell, *Life of Johnson (Apr. 13, 1773)*

13 This division of labour, from which so many advantages are derived, is not originally the effect of any human wisdom, which foresees and intends that general opulence to which it gives occasion. It is the necessary, though very slow and gradual consequence of a certain propensity in human nature which has in view no such extensive utility; the propensity to truck, barter, and exchange one thing for another.

Whether this propensity be one of those original principles in human nature of which no further account can be given; or whether, as seems more probable, it be the necessary consequence of the faculties of reason and speech, it belongs not to our present subject to inquire. It is common to all men, and to be found in no other race of animals.

Adam Smith, *Wealth of Nations*, I, 2

14 People of the same trade seldom meet together, even for merriment and diversion, but the conversation ends in a conspiracy against the public, or in some contrivance to raise prices.

Adam Smith, *Wealth of Nations*, I, 10

15 Monopoly . . . is a great enemy to good management which can never be universally established but in consequence of that free and universal competition which forces everybody to have recourse to it for the sake of self-defence.

Adam Smith, *Wealth of Nations*, I, 11

16 The great commerce of every civilised society is that carried on between the inhabitants of the town and those of the country. It consists in the exchange of rude for manufactured produce, either immediately, or by the intervention of money, or of some sort of paper which represents money. The country supplies the town with the means of subsistence and the materials of manufacture. The town repays this supply by sending back a part of the manufactured produce to the inhabitants of the country. The town, in which there neither is nor can be any reproduction of substances, may very properly be said to gain its whole wealth and subsistence from the country. We must not, however, upon this account, imagine that the gain of the town is the loss of the country. The gains of both are mutual and reciprocal, and the division of labour is in this, as in all other cases, advantageous to all the different persons employed in the various occupations into which it is subdivided.

Adam Smith, *Wealth of Nations*, III, 1

17 The importation of gold and silver is not the principal, much less the sole benefit which a nation derives from its foreign trade. Between whatever places foreign trade is carried on, they all of them derive two distinct benefits from it. It carries out that surplus part of the produce of their land and labour for which there is no demand among them, and brings back in return for it something else for which there is a demand. It gives a value to their superfluities, by exchanging them for something else, which may satisfy a part of their wants, and increase their enjoyments. By means of it the narrowness of the home market does not hinder the division of labour in any particular branch of art or manufacture from being carried to the highest perfection. By opening a more extensive market for whatever part of the produce of their labour may exceed the home consumption, it encourages them to improve its productive powers, and to augment its annual produce to the utmost, and thereby to increase the real revenue and wealth of the society. These great and important services foreign trade is continually occupied in performing to all the different countries between which it is carried on.

Adam Smith, *Wealth of Nations*, IV, 1

18 The balance of produce and consumption may be constantly in favour of a nation, though what is called the balance of trade be generally against it. A nation may import to a greater value than it exports for half a century, perhaps, together; the gold and silver which comes into it during all this time may be all immediately sent out of it; its circulating coin may gradually decay, different sorts of paper money being substituted in its place, and even the debts, too, which it contracts in the principal nations with whom it deals, may be gradually increasing; and yet its real wealth, the exchangeable value of the annual produce of its lands and labour, may, during the same period, have been increasing in a much greater proportion. The state of our North American colonies, and of the trade which they carried on with Great Britain, before the commencement of the present disturbances, may serve as a proof that this is by no means an impossible supposition.

Adam Smith, *Wealth of Nations*, IV, 3

19 To found a great empire for the sole purpose of raising up a people of customers may at first sight appear a project fit only for a nation of shopkeepers. It is, however, a project altogether unfit for a nation of shopkeepers; but extremely fit for a nation whose government is influenced by shopkeepers. Such statesmen, and such statesmen only, are capable of fancying that they will find some advantage in employing the blood and treasure of their fellow-citizens to found and maintain such an empire.

Adam Smith, *Wealth of Nations*, IV, 7

20 Whatever evils either reason or declamation have imputed to extensive empire, the power of Rome was attended with some beneficial consequences

to mankind; and the same freedom of intercourse which extended the vices, diffused likewise the improvements of social life. In the more remote ages of antiquity, the world was unequally divided. The east was in the immemorial possession of arts and luxury; whilst the west was inhabited by rude and warlike barbarians, who either disdained agriculture, or to whom it was totally unknown. Under the protection of an established government, the productions of happier climates, and the industry of more civilised nations, were gradually introduced into the western countries of Europe; and the natives were encouraged, by an open and profitable commerce, to multiply the former, as well as to improve the latter.

Gibbon, *Decline and Fall of the Roman Empire,* II

21 It is the nature of all greatness not to be exact; and great trade will always be attended with considerable abuses. The contraband will always keep pace in some measure with the fair trade. It should stand as a fundamental maxim, that no vulgar precaution ought to be employed in the cure of evils which are closely connected with the cause of our prosperity.

Burke, *Speech on American Taxation (1774)*

22 I believe it will be found invariably true, that the superfluities of a rich nation furnish a better object of trade than the necessities of a poor one. It is the interest of the commercial world that wealth should be found everywhere.

Burke, *Letters to Gentlemen in Bristol (1778)*

23 If nature wisely separates nations, which every state would seek to combine, by artifice or force, and even according to the principles of the law of nations; who, on the other hand, through the interested spirit of all nations, produces an union between them, which the idea of the cosmopolitical right alone would not have sufficiently secured from war and violence. It is the spirit of commerce that sooner or later takes hold of every nation, and is incompatible with war: the power of money being that which of all others gives the greatest spring to states, they find themselves obliged to labour at the noble work of peace, though without any moral view; and instantly seek to stifle, by mediations, war, in whatever part it may break out, as if for this purpose they had contracted a perpetual alliance; great associations in a war are naturally rare, and less frequently still successful. It is in this manner that nature, by means of the human propensities, guarantees a perpetual peace; and though the assurance which she gives us thereof is not sufficient to predict theoretically, yet it prevents us from regarding it as a chimerical aim, and makes it thereby a duty in us to contribute towards it.

Kant, *Perpetual Peace,* Supplement I

24 The spirit of enterprise, useful and prolific as it is, must necessarily be contracted or expanded in proportion to the simplicity or variety of the occupations and productions which are to be found in a society. It must be less in a nation of mere cultivators than in a nation of cultivators and merchants; less in a nation of cultivators and merchants than in a nation of cultivators, artificers, and merchants.

Hamilton, *Report on Manufactures*

25 It seems not always to be recollected that nations who have neither mines nor manufactures can only obtain the manufactured articles of which they stand in need by an exchange of the products of their soils; and that if those who can best furnish them with such articles are unwilling to give a due course to this exchange, they must, of necessity, make every possible effort to manufacture for themselves; the effect of which is that the manufacturing nations abridge the natural advantages of their situation through an unwillingness to permit the agricultural countries to enjoy the advantages of theirs, and sacrifice the interests of a mutually beneficial intercourse to the vain project of selling everything and buying nothing.

Hamilton, *Report on Manufactures*

26 The material existence of England is based on commerce and industry, and the English have undertaken the weighty responsibility of being the missionaries of civilization to the world; for their commercial spirit urges them to traverse every sea and land, to form connections with barbarous peoples, to create wants and stimulate industry, and first and foremost to establish among them the conditions necessary to commerce, *viz.,* the relinquishment of a life of lawless violence, respect for property, and civility to strangers.

Hegel, *Philosophy of History,* Pt. IV, III, 3

27 In democracies nothing is greater or more brilliant than commerce; it attracts the attention of the public and fills the imagination of the multitude; all energetic passions are directed towards it. Neither their own prejudices nor those of anybody else can prevent the rich from devoting themselves to it. The wealthy members of democracies never form a body which has manners and regulations of its own; the opinions peculiar to their class do not restrain them, and the common opinions of their country urge them on. Moreover, as all the large fortunes that are found in a democratic community are of commercial growth, many generations must succeed one another before their possessors can have entirely laid aside their habits of business.

Tocqueville, *Democracy in America,* Vol. II, II, 19

28 I know of nothing more opposite to revolutionary

attitudes than commercial ones. Commerce is naturally adverse to all the violent passions; it loves to temporize, takes delight in compromise, and studiously avoids irritation. It is patient, insinuating, flexible, and never has recourse to extreme measures until obliged by the most absolute necessity. Commerce renders men independent of one another, gives them a lofty notion of their personal importance, leads them to seek to conduct their own affairs, and teaches how to conduct them well; it therefore prepares men for freedom, but preserves them from revolutions.

Tocqueville, *Democracy in America,*
Vol. II, III, 21

29 The greatest meliorator of the world is selfish, huckstering trade.

Emerson, *Works and Days*

30 There are geniuses in trade, as well as in war, or the State, or letters; and the reason why this or that man is fortunate is not to be told. It lies in the man; that is all anybody can tell you about it.

Emerson, *Character*

31 The craft of the merchant is this bringing a thing from where it abounds to where it is costly.

Emerson, *Wealth*

32 We rail at trade, but the historian of the world will see that it was the principle of liberty; that it settled America, and destroyed feudalism, and made peace and keeps peace; that it will abolish slavery.

Emerson, *Journal (Dec. 31, 1843)*

33 "A bargain," said the son. "Here's the rule for bargains—'Do other men, for they would do you.' That's the true business precept. All others are counterfeits."

The delighted father applauded this sentiment to the echo.

Dickens, *Martin Chuzzlewit,* XI

34 This world is a place of business. What an infinite bustle! I am awaked almost every night by the panting of the locomotive. It interrupts my dreams. There is no sabbath. It would be glorious to see mankind at leisure for once. It is nothing but work, work, work. I cannot easily buy a blank-book to write thoughts in; they are commonly ruled for dollars and cents. An Irishman, seeing me making a minute in the fields, took it for granted that I was calculating my wages. If a man was tossed out of a window when an infant, and so made a cripple for life, or scared out of his wits by the Indians, it is regretted chiefly because he was thus incapacitated for—business! I think that there is nothing, not even crime, more opposed to poetry, to philosophy, ay, to life itself, than this incessant business.

Thoreau, *Life Without Principle*

35 That so many are ready to live by luck, and so get the means of commanding the labor of others less lucky, without contributing any value to society! And that is called enterprise! I know of no more startling development of the immorality of trade, and all the common modes of getting a living.

Thoreau, *Life Without Principle*

36 The exchange of commodities is . . . accompanied by the following changes in their form:

Commodity—Money—Commodity
C————M————C

The result of the whole process is, so far as concerns the objects themselves, *C—C,* the exchange of one commodity for another, the circulation of materialized social labour. When this result is attained, the process is at an end.

C—M. First Metamorphosis, or Sale

The leap taken by value from the body of the commodity into the body of the gold is, as I have elsewhere called it, the *salto mortale* of the commodity. If it falls short, then, although the commodity itself is not harmed, its owner decidedly is. The social division of labour causes his labour to be as one-sided as his wants are many-sided. This is precisely the reason why the product of his labour serves him solely as exchange value. But it cannot acquire the properties of a socially recognized universal equivalent, except by being converted into money. That money, however, is in some one else's pocket. In order to entice the money out of that pocket, our friend's commodity must, above all things, be a use-value to the owner of the money. For this, it is necessary that the labour expended upon it be of a kind that is socially useful, of a kind that constitutes a branch of the social division of labour. But division of labour is a system of production which has grown up spontaneously and continues to grow behind the backs of the producers. The commodity to be exchanged may possibly be the product of some new kind of labour that pretends to satisfy newly arisen requirements, or even to give rise itself to new requirements. A particular operation, though yesterday, perhaps, forming one out of the many operations conducted by one producer in creating a given commodity, may today separate itself from this connection, may establish itself as an independent branch of labour and send its incomplete product to market as an independent commodity. The circumstances may or may not be ripe for such a separation. Today the product satisfies a social want. Tomorrow the article may, either altogether or partially, be superseded by some other appropriate product. Moreover, although our weaver's labour may be a recognized branch of the social division of labour, yet that fact is by no means sufficient to guarantee the utility of his 20 yards of linen. If the community's want of linen, and such a want has a limit like every other want, should already be saturated by the products of rival weavers, our friend's product is superfluous, redundant, and consequently useless. Although people do not look a gift-horse in the mouth, our friend does not frequent the market for the purpose of making presents. But suppose his product turns out a real use-value, and thereby attracts money. The question arises, how much will it attract? No doubt the answer is already anticipated in the price of the article, in the exponent of the magnitude of its value. We leave out of consideration here any accidental miscalculation of value by our friend, a mistake that is soon rectified in the market. We suppose him to have spent on his product only that amount of labour time that is on an average socially necessary. The price, then, is merely the money name of the quantity of social labour realized in his commodity. But without the leave, and behind the back, of our weaver, the old fashioned mode of weaving undergoes a change. The labour time that yesterday was without doubt socially necessary to the production of a yard of linen, ceases to be so today, a fact which the owner of the money is only too eager to prove from the prices quoted by our friend's competitors. Unluckily for him, weavers are not few and far between. Lastly, suppose that every piece of linen in the market contains no more labour time than is socially necessary. In spite of this, all these pieces taken as a whole, may have had superfluous labour time spent upon them. If the market cannot stomach the whole quantity at the normal price of 2 shillings a yard, this proves that too great a portion of the total labour of the community has been expended in the form of weaving. The effect is the same as if each individual weaver had expended more labour time upon his particular product than is socially necessary. Here we may say, with the German proverb: "Caught together, hanged together." All the linen in the market counts but as one article of commerce, of which each piece is only an aliquot part. And as a matter of fact, the value also of each single yard is but the materialized form of the same definite and socially fixed quantity of homogeneous human labour.

We see then, commodities are in love with money, but "the course of true love never did run smooth." The quantitative division of labour is brought about in exactly the same spontaneous and accidental manner as its qualitative division. The owners of commodities, therefore, find out that the same division of labour that turns them into independent private producers also frees the social process of production and the relations of the individual producers to each other within that process from all dependence on the will of those producers, and that the seeming mutual independence of the individuals is supplemented by a system of general and mutual dependence through or by means of the products.

Marx, *Capital,* Vol. I, I, 3

37 The conversion of a sum of money into means of production and labour power is the first step taken by the quantum of value that is going to function as capital. This conversion takes place in the market, within the sphere of circulation. The second step, the process of production, is complete so soon as the means of production have been converted into commodities whose value exceeds that of their component parts, and, therefore, contains the capital originally advanced, plus a surplus value. These commodities must then be thrown into circulation. They must be sold, their value realized in money, this money converted afresh into capital, and so over and over again. This circular movement, in which the same phases are continually gone through in succession, forms the circulation of capital.

Marx, *Capital,* Vol. I, VII,
Introduction

38 Modern industry has established the world market, for which the discovery of America paved the way. This market has given an immense development to commerce, to navigation, to communication by land. This development has, in its turn, reacted on the extension of industry; and in proportion as industry, commerce, navigation, railways extended, in the same proportion the bourgeoisie developed, increased its capital, and pushed into the background every class handed down from the Middle Ages.

We see, therefore, how the modern bourgeoisie is itself the product of a long course of development, of a series of revolutions in the modes of production and of exchange.

Marx and Engels, *Communist Manifesto,* I

39 Modern bourgeois society with its relations of production, of exchange and of property, a society that has conjured up such gigantic means of production and of exchange, is like the sorcerer who is no longer able to control the powers of the nether world whom he has called up by his spells. For many a decade past the history of industry and commerce is but the history of the revolt of modern productive forces against modern conditions of production, against the property relations that are the conditions for the existence of the bourgeoisie and of its rule. It is enough to mention the commercial crises that by their periodical return put the existence of the entire bourgeois society on trial, each time more threateningly. In these crises a great part not only of the existing products, but also of the previously created productive forces, are periodically destroyed. In these crises there breaks out an epidemic that, in all earlier epochs, would have seemed an absurdity—the epidemic of over-production. Society suddenly finds itself put back into a state of momentary barbarism; it

appears as if a famine, a universal war of devastation had cut off the supply of every means of subsistence; industry and commerce seem to be destroyed. And why? Because there is too much civilization, too much means of subsistence, too much industry, too much commerce. The productive forces at the disposal of society no longer tend to further the development of the conditions of bourgeois property; on the contrary, they have become too powerful for these conditions, by which they are fettered, and no sooner do they overcome these fetters than they bring disorder into the whole of bourgeois society, endanger the existence of bourgeois property. The conditions of bourgeois society are too narrow to comprise the wealth created by them. And how does the bourgeoisie get over these crises? On the one hand by enforced destruction of a mass of productive forces; on the other, by the conquest of new markets and by the more thorough exploitation of the old ones. That is to say, by paving the way for more extensive and more destructive crises, and by diminishing the means whereby crises are prevented.

Marx and Engels, *Communist Manifesto,* I

40 The increase of the general riches of the world, when accompanied with freedom of commercial intercourse, improvements in navigation, and inland communication by roads, canals, or railways, tends to give increased productiveness to the labour of every nation in particular, by enabling each locality to supply with its special products so much larger a market, that a great extension of the division of labour in their production is an ordinary consequence.

Mill, *Principles of Political Economy,*
Bk. I, VIII, 6

41 The small capitalist, it is true, generally combines with the business of direction some portion of the details, which the other leaves to his subordinates: the small farmer follows his own plough, the small tradesman serves in his own shop, the small weaver plies his own loom. But in this very union of functions there is, in a great proportion of cases, a want of economy. The principal in the concern is either wasting, in the routine of a business, qualities suitable for the direction of it, or he is only fit for the former, and then the latter will be ill done. I must observe, however, that I do not attach, to this saving of labour, the importance often ascribed to it. There is undoubtedly much more labour expended in the superintendence of many small capitals than in that of one large capital. For this labour however the small producers have generally a full compensation, in the feeling of being their own masters, and not servants of an employer. It may be said, that if they value this independence they will submit to pay a price for it, and to sell at the reduced rates occasioned by the competition of the great dealer or manufac-

turer. But they cannot always do this and continue to gain a living. They thus gradually disappear from society. After having consumed their little capital in prolonging the unsuccessful struggle, they either sink into the condition of hired labourers, or become dependent on others for support.

Mill, *Principles of Political Economy,*
Bk. I, IX, 1

42 Where competitors are so few, they always end by agreeing not to compete. They may run a race of cheapness to ruin a new candidate, but as soon as he has established his footing they come to terms with him. When, therefore, a business of real public importance can only be carried on advantageously upon so large a scale as to render the liberty of competition almost illusory, it is an unthrifty dispensation of the public resources that several costly sets of arrangements should be kept up for the purpose of rendering to the community this one service. It is much better to treat it at once as a public function; and if it be not such as the government itself could beneficially undertake, it should be made over entire to the company or association which will perform it on the best terms for the public.

Mill, *Principles of Political Economy,*
Bk. I, IX, 3

43 Every seller of goods is a buyer of money, and the goods he brings with him constitute his demand. The demand for money differs from the demand for other things in this, that it is limited only by the means of the purchaser. The demand for other things is for so much and no more; but there is always a demand for as much money as can be got. Persons may indeed refuse to sell, and withdraw their goods from the market, if they cannot get for them what they consider a sufficient price. But this is only when they think that the price will rise, and that they shall get more money by waiting. If they thought the low price likely to be permanent, they would take what they could get. It is always a *sine quâ non* with a dealer to dispose of his goods.

Mill, *Principles of Political Economy,*
Bk. III, VIII, 2

44 I confess I am not charmed with the ideal of life held out by those who think that the normal state of human beings is that of struggling to get on; that the trampling, crushing, elbowing, and treading on each other's heels, which form the existing type of social life, are the most desirable lot of human kind, or anything but the disagreeable symptoms of one of the phases of industrial progress.

Mill, *Principles of Political Economy,*
Bk. IV, VI, 2

45 Because a man has shop to mind

In time and place, since flesh must live,
Needs spirit lack all life behind,
  All stray thoughts, fancies fugitive,
  All loves except what trade can give?

                  Browning, *Shop*

46 October. This is one of the peculiarly dangerous months to speculate in stocks in. The others are July, January, September, April, November, May, March, June, December, August, and February.

              Mark Twain, *Pudd'nhead Wilson's Calendar*, XIII

47 A man can fell trees better than a woman. A woman can knit stockings better than a man. Suppose the man can fell two trees whilst the woman is felling one; and that the woman can knit two pairs of stockings whilst the man is knitting one. Suppose further that the time occupied by the man in felling the two trees, and by the woman in knitting the two pairs of stockings is one hour. Now if each produces for himself and herself respectively, when the woman wants a tree to burn and a pair of stockings to wear, it will take her an hour to fell the tree, and half an hour to knit the stockings—one hour and a half in all. And the man, under the same necessity, will spend half an hour in felling his tree, and one hour in knitting his stockings—also one hour and a half in all. It costs the man and woman three hours labor to supply themselves with fuel and hosiery. But they can save an hour of this by each working for the other. They require between them two trees and two pairs of stockings. The man can fell the two trees, and the woman knit the four stockings in an hour each. Let them do so, and exchange a tree against a pair of stockings. Each is now supplied as well as before, although they have only worked two hours instead of three. They have gained half an hour's leisure each, and neither has gained it at the expense of the other. The woman has worked half an hour for the man, and he has worked half an hour for her. This is the state of things which the Socialistic movement aims at establishing.

            Shaw, *Our Lost Honesty*

48 What does one expect from business save that it should furnish money, to be used in turn for making more money and for support of self and family, for buying books and pictures, tickets to concerts which may afford culture, and for paying taxes, charitable gifts and other things of social and ethical value? How unreasonable to expect that the pursuit of business should be itself a culture of the imagination, in breadth and refinement; that it should directly, and not through the money which it supplies, have social service for its animating principle and be conducted as an enterprise in behalf of social organization!

        Dewey, *Democracy and Education*, XVIII

11.6 | *Taxation*

The texts quoted here are not offered as covering or even as touching on the technical intricacies of this difficult subject. However, they do represent a choice selection of key statements by the great authors concerning the purposes of taxation and the criteria for judging the fairness, as well as the effectiveness, with which taxes are levied.

That taxation, in some form, is necessary to defray costs of government is generally agreed upon by all; but the use of taxation for other purposes, such as the promotion of economic welfare by a governmental redistribution of wealth, is of such recent origin that it does not even appear in most of the books from which we are quoting.

There is one other point of general agreement, epitomized in the quotations from Burke and from Emerson: namely that, regardless of their necessity and their fairness, taxes are universally disliked by those who have to pay them.

1 Then Joseph said unto the people, Behold, I have bought you this day and your land for Pharaoh: lo, here is seed for you, and ye shall sow the land.

And it shall come to pass in the increase, that ye shall give the fifth part unto Pharaoh, and four parts shall be your own, for seed of the field, and for your food, and for them of your households, and for food for your little ones.

And they said, Thou hast saved our lives; let us find grace in the sight of my lord, and we will be Pharaoh's servants.

And Joseph made it a law over the land of Egypt unto this day, that Pharaoh should have the fifth part; except the land of the priests only, which became not Pharaoh's.

Genesis 47:23–26

2 *Athenian Stranger.* With a view to taxation, for various reasons, every man ought to have had his property valued: and the tribesmen should likewise bring a register of the yearly produce to the wardens of the country, that in this way there may be two valuations; and the public officers may use annually whichever on consideration they deem the best, whether they prefer to take a certain portion of the whole value, or of the annual revenue, after subtracting what is paid to the common tables.

Plato, *Laws,* XII, 955B

3 And it came to pass in those days, that there went out a decree from Caesar Augustus, that all the world should be taxed.

Luke 2:1

4 Cato . . . gave most general annoyance by retrenching people's luxury; for though (most of the youth being thereby already corrupted) it seemed almost impossible to take it away with an open hand and directly, yet going, as it were, obliquely around, he caused all dress carriages, women's ornaments, household furniture, whose price exceeded one thousand five hundred drachmas, to be rated at ten times as much as they were worth; intending by thus making the assessments greater, to increase the taxes paid upon them. He also ordained that upon every thousand asses of property of this kind, three should be paid, so that people, burdened with these extra charges, and seeing others of as good estates, but more frugal and sparing, paying less into the public exchequer, might be tired out of their prodigality. And thus, on the one side, not only those were disgusted at Cato who bore the taxes for the sake of their luxury, but those, too, who on the other side laid by their luxury for fear of the taxes.

Plutarch, *Marcus Cato*

5 Repeated demands on the part of the people, who denounced the excessive greed of the revenue collectors, made Nero doubt whether he should not order the repeal of all indirect taxes, and so confer a most splendid boon on the human race. But this sudden impulse was checked by the senators, who, having first heartily praised the grandeur of his conception, pointed out "that the dissolution of the empire must ensue if the revenues which supported the State were to be diminished; for as soon as the customs were swept away, there would follow a demand for the abolition of the direct taxes. Many companies for the collection of the indirect taxes had been formed by consuls and tribunes, when the freedom of the Roman people was still in its vigour, and arrangements were subsequently made to insure an exact correspondence between the amount of income and the necessary disbursements. Certainly some restraint, they admitted, must be put on the cupidity of the revenue collectors, that they might not by new oppressions bring into odium what for so many years had been endured without a complaint."

Tacitus, *Annals,* XIII, 50

6 *Cloten.* Why tribute? why should we pay tribute? If Cæsar can hide the sun from us with a blanket, or put the moon in his pocket, we will pay him tribute for light; else, sir, no more tribute, pray you now.

Shakespeare, *Cymbeline,* III, i, 42

7 *Queen Katharine.*   The subjects' grief
Comes through commissions, which compel from each
The sixth part of his substance, to be levied
Without delay; and the pretence for this
Is named, your wars in France. This makes bold mouths.
Tongues spit their duties out, and cold hearts freeze
Allegiance in them.

Shakespeare, *Henry VIII,* I, ii, 56

8 The difficulty of raising money for the necessary uses of the Commonwealth, especially in the approach of war . . . ariseth from the opinion that every subject hath of a propriety in his lands and goods exclusive of the sovereign's right to the use of the same. From whence it cometh to pass that the sovereign power, which foreseeth the necessities and dangers of the Commonwealth, finding the passage of money to the public treasury obstructed by the tenacity of the people, whereas it ought to extend itself, to encounter and prevent such dangers in their beginnings, contracteth itself as long as it can, and when it cannot longer, struggles with the people by stratagems of law to obtain little sums, which, not sufficing, he is fain at last violently to open the way for present supply or perish; and, being put often to these extremities, at last reduceth the people to their due temper, or else the Commonwealth must perish.

Hobbes, *Leviathan,* II, 29

9 To equal justice appertaineth also the equal imposition of taxes; the equality whereof dependeth not on the equality of riches, but on the equality of the debt that every man oweth to the Commonwealth for his defence. It is not enough for a man to labour for the maintenance of his life; but also to fight, if need be, for the securing of his labour. They must either do as the Jews did after their return from captivity, in re-edifying the Temple, build with one hand and hold the sword in the other, or else they must hire others to fight for them. For the impositions that are laid on the people by the sovereign power are nothing else but the wages due to them that hold the public sword to defend private men in the exercise of several trades and callings. Seeing then the benefit that every one receiveth thereby is the enjoyment of life, which is equally dear to poor and rich, the debt which a poor man oweth them that defend his life is the same which a rich man oweth for the defence of his; saving that the rich, who have the service of the poor, may be debtors not only for their own persons, but for many more. Which considered, the equality of imposition consisteth rather in the equality of that which is consumed, than of the riches of the persons that consume the same. For what reason is there that he which laboureth much and, sparing the fruits of his labour, consumeth little should be more charged than he that, living idly, getteth little and spendeth all he gets; seeing the one hath no more protection from the Commonwealth than the other?

Hobbes, *Leviathan,* II, 30

10 It is true governments cannot be supported without great charge, and it is fit everyone who enjoys his share of the protection should pay out of his estate his proportion for the maintenance of it. But still it must be with his own consent—that is, the consent of the majority, giving it either by themselves or their representatives chosen by them; for if anyone shall claim a power to lay and levy taxes on the people by his own authority, and without such consent of the people, he thereby invades the fundamental law of property, and subverts the end of government. For what property have I in that which another may by right take when he pleases to himself?

Locke, *II Civil Government,* XI, 140

11 I heard a very warm debate between two professors, about the most commodious and effectual ways and means of raising money without grieving the subject. The first affirmed, the justest method would be to lay a certain tax upon vices and folly; and the sum fixed upon every man, to be rated after the fairest manner, by a jury of his neighbours. The second was of an opinion directly contrary; to tax those qualities of body and mind for which men chiefly value themselves; the rate

to be more or less according to the degrees of excelling; the decision whereof should be left entirely to their own breast. The highest tax was upon men, who are the greatest favourites of the other sex; and the assessments according to the number and natures of the favours they have received; for which they are allowed to be their own vouchers. Wit, valour, and politeness were likewise proposed to be largely taxed, and collected in the same manner, by every person giving his own word for the quantum of what he possessed. But, as to honour, justice, wisdom and learning, they should not be taxed at all; because, they are qualifications of so singular a kind, that no man will either allow them in his neighbour, or value them in himself.

The women were proposed to be taxed according to their beauty and skill in dressing; wherein they had the same privilege with the men, to be determined by their own judgment. But constancy, chastity, good sense, and good nature were not rated, because they would not bear the charge of collecting.

Swift, *Gulliver's Travels,* III, 6

12 'Tis pleasant to observe, how free the present Age is in laying Taxes on the next.

Swift, *Thoughts on Various Subjects*

13 Inequality occurs likewise when the condition of the citizens differs with regard to taxes, which may happen in four different ways: when the nobles assume the privilege of paying none; when they commit frauds to exempt themselves; when they engross the public money, under pretence of rewards or appointments for their respective employments; in fine, when they render the common people tributary, and divide among their own body the profits arising from the several subsidies. This last case is very rare; an aristocracy so instituted would be the most intolerable of all governments.

Montesquieu, *Spirit of Laws,* V, 8

14 The *public revenues* are a portion that each subject gives of his property, in order to secure or enjoy the remainder. To fix these revenues in a proper manner, regard should be had both to the necessities of the state and to those of the subject. The real wants of the people ought never to give way to the imaginary wants of the state.

Montesquieu, *Spirit of Laws,* XIII, 1

15 The duties felt least by the people are those on merchandise, because they are not demanded of them in form. They may be so prudently managed that the people themselves shall hardly know they pay them. For this purpose it is of the utmost consequence that the person who sells the merchandise should pay the duty. He is very sensible that he does not pay it for himself; and the con-

sumer, who pays it in the main, confounds it with the price.

Montesquieu, *Spirit of Laws,* XIII, 7

16 Taxes may be increased in most republics, because the citizen, who thinks he is paying himself, cheerfully submits to them, and moreover is generally able to bear their weight, from the nature of the government.

In a monarchy taxes may be increased, because the moderation of the government is capable of procuring opulence: it is a recompense, as it were, granted to the prince for the respect he shows to the laws. In despotic governments they cannot be increased, because there can be no increase of the extremity of slavery.

Montesquieu, *Spirit of Laws,* XIII, 13

17 The best taxes are such as are levied upon consumptions, especially those of luxury, because such taxes are least felt by the people. They seem in some measure voluntary, since a man may choose how far he will use the commodity which is taxed. They are paid gradually and insensibly; they naturally produce sobriety and frugality, if judiciously imposed; and being confounded with the natural price of the commodity, they are scarcely perceived by the consumers. Their only disadvantage is, that they are expensive in the levying.

Taxes upon possessions are levied without expense, but have every other disadvantage. Most states, however, are obliged to have recourse to them, in order to supply the deficiencies of the other.

But the most pernicious of all taxes are the arbitrary. They are commonly converted, by their management, into punishments on industry; and also, by their unavoidable inequality, are more grievous, than by the real burden which they impose. It is surprising, therefore, to see them have place among any civilized people.

In general, all poll-taxes, even when not arbitrary, which they commonly are, may be esteemed dangerous: because it is so easy for the sovereign to add a little more, and a little more, to the sum demanded, that these taxes are apt to become altogether oppressive and intolerable. On the other hand, a duty upon commodities checks itself; and a prince will soon find, that an increase of the impost is no increase of his revenue. It is not easy, therefore, for a people to be altogether ruined by such taxes.

Hume, *Of Taxes*

18 Every man, to be sure, is desirous of pushing off from himself the burden of any tax which is imposed, and of laying it upon others: but as every man has the same inclination, and is upon the defensive, no set of men can be supposed to prevail altogether in this contest.

Hume, *Of Taxes*

19 That taxes cannot be legitimately established except by the consent of the people or its representatives, is a truth generally admitted by all philosophers and jurists of any repute on questions of public right.

Rousseau, *Political Economy*

20 In order to levy taxes in a truly equitable and proportionate manner, the imposition ought not to be in simple ratio to the property of the contributors, but in compound ratio to the difference of their conditions and the superfluity of their possessions. This very important and difficult operation is daily made by numbers of honest clerks, who know their arithmetic; but a Plato or a Montesquieu would not venture to undertake it without the greatest diffidence, or without praying to Heaven for understanding and integrity.

Rousseau, *Political Economy*

21 Heavy taxes should be laid on servants in livery, on equipages, rich furniture, fine clothes, on spacious courts and gardens, on public entertainments of all kinds, on useless professions, such as dancers, singers, players, and in a word, on all that multiplicity of objects of luxury, amusement and idleness, which strike the eyes of all, and can the less be hidden, as their whole purpose is to be seen, without which they would be useless. We need be under no apprehension of the produce of these taxes being arbitrary, because they are laid on things not absolutely necessary. They must know but little of mankind who imagine that, after they have been once seduced by luxury, they can ever renounce it: they would a hundred times sooner renounce common necessaries, and had much rather die of hunger than of shame. The increase in their expense is only an additional reason for supporting them, when the vanity of appearing wealthy reaps its profit from the price of the thing and the charge of the tax. As long as there are rich people in the world, they will be desirous of distinguishing themselves from the poor, nor can the State devise a revenue less burdensome or more certain than what arises from this distinction. ·

Rousseau, *Political Economy*

22 Suppose the spirit of government was constantly to tax only the superfluities of the rich, one of two things must happen: either the rich would convert their superfluous expenses into useful ones, which would redound to the profit of the State, and thus the imposition of taxes would have the effect of the best sumptuary laws, the expenses of the State would necessarily diminish with those of individuals, and the treasury would not receive so much less as it would gain by having less to pay; or, if the rich did not become less extravagant, the exchequer would have such resources in the product of taxes on their expenditure as would provide for

the needs of the State. In the first case the treasury would be the richer by what it would save, from having the less to do with its money; and in the second, it would be enriched by the useless expenses of individuals.

Rousseau, *Political Economy*

23 It does not seem necessary that the expense of those public works should be defrayed from that public revenue, as it is commonly called, of which the collection and application is in most countries assigned to the executive power. The greater part of such public works may easily be so managed as to afford a particular revenue sufficient for defraying their own expense, without bringing any burden upon the general revenue of the society.

A highway, a bridge, a navigable canal, for example, may in most cases be both made and maintained by a small toll upon the carriages which make use of them: a harbour, by a moderate port-duty upon the tonnage of the shipping which load or unload in it. The coinage, another institution for facilitating commerce, in many countries, not only defrays its own expense, but affords a small revenue or seignorage to the sovereign. The post-office, another institution for the same purpose, over and above defraying its own expense, affords in almost all countries a very considerable revenue to the sovereign.

Adam Smith, *Wealth of Nations,* V, 1

24 Before I enter upon the examination of particular taxes, it is necessary to premise the four following maxims with regard to taxes in general.

The subjects of every state ought to contribute towards the support of the government, as nearly as possible, in proportion to their respective abilities; that is, in proportion to the revenue which they respectively enjoy under the protection of the state. The expense of government to the individuals of a great nation is like the expense of management to the joint tenants of a great estate, who are all obliged to contribute in proportion to their respective interests in the estate. In the observation or neglect of this maxim consists what is called the equality or inequality of taxation. Every tax, it must be observed once for all, which falls finally upon one only of the three sorts of revenue above mentioned, is necessarily unequal in so far as it does not affect the other two. In the following examination of different taxes I shall seldom take much further notice of this sort of inequality, but shall, in most cases, confine my observations to that inequality which is occasioned by a particular tax falling unequally even upon that particular sort of private revenue which is affected by it.

The tax which each individual is bound to pay ought to be certain, and not arbitrary. The time of payment, the manner of payment, the quantity to be paid, ought all to be clear and plain to the contributor, and to every other person. Where it is otherwise, every person subject to the tax is put more or less in the power of the tax-gatherer, who can either aggravate the tax upon any obnoxious contributor, or extort, by the terror of such aggravation, some present or perquisite to himself. The uncertainty of taxation encourages the insolence and favours the corruption of an order of men who are naturally unpopular, even where they are neither insolent nor corrupt. The certainty of what each individual ought to pay is, in taxation, a matter of so great importance that a very considerable degree of inequality, it appears, I believe, from the experience of all nations, is not near so great an evil as a very small degree of uncertainty.

Every tax ought to be levied at the time, or in the manner, in which it is most likely to be convenient for the contributor to pay it. A tax upon the rent of land or of houses, payable at the same term at which such rents are usually paid, is levied at the time when it is most likely to be convenient for the contributor to pay; or, when he is most likely to have wherewithal to pay. Taxes upon such consumable goods as are articles of luxury are all finally paid by the consumer, and generally in a manner that is very convenient for him. He pays them by little and little, as he has occasion to buy the goods. As he is at liberty, too, either to buy, or not to buy, as he pleases, it must be his own fault if he ever suffers any considerable inconveniency from such taxes.

Every tax ought to be so contrived as both to take out and to keep out of the pockets of the people as little as possible over and above what it brings into the public treasury of the state. A tax may either take out or keep out of the pockets of the people a great deal more than it brings into the public treasury, in the four following ways. First, the levying of it may require a great number of officers, whose salaries may eat up the greater part of the produce of the tax, and whose perquisites may impose another additional tax upon the people. Secondly, it may obstruct the industry of the people, and discourage them from applying to certain branches of business which might give maintenance and unemployment to great multitudes. While it obliges the people to pay, it may thus diminish, or perhaps destroy, some of the funds which might enable them more easily to do so. Thirdly, by the forfeitures and other penalties which those unfortunate individuals incur who attempt unsuccessfully to evade the tax, it may frequently ruin them, and thereby put an end to the benefit which the community might have received from the employment of their capitals. An injudicious tax offers a great temptation to smuggling. But the penalties of smuggling must rise in proportion to the temptation. The law, contrary to all the ordinary principles of justice, first creates the temptation, and then punishes those who yield to it; and it commonly enhances the punishment, too, in proportion to the very circumstance which ought certainly to alleviate it, the temptation to commit the crime. Fourthly, by subjecting the people to the frequent visits and the odious examination of the tax-gatherers, it may expose them to much unnecessary trouble, vexation, and oppression; and though vexation is not, strictly speaking, expense, it is certainly equivalent to the expense at which every man would be willing to redeem himself from it. It is in some one or other of these four different ways that taxes are frequently so much more burdensome to the people than they are beneficial to the sovereign.

Adam Smith, *Wealth of Nations,* V, 2

25 While property remains in the possession of the same person, whatever permanent taxes may have been imposed upon it, they have never been intended to diminish or take away any part of its capital value, but only some part of the revenue arising from it. But when property changes hands, when it is transmitted either from the dead to the living, or from the living to the living, such taxes have frequently been imposed upon it as necessarily take away some part of its capital value.

Adam Smith, *Wealth of Nations,* V, 2

26 Those modes of taxation, by stamp-duties and by duties upon registration, are of very modern invention. In the course of little more than a century, however, stamp-duties have, in Europe, become almost universal, and duties upon registration extremely common. There is no art which one government sooner learns of another than that of draining money from the pockets of the people.

Adam Smith, *Wealth of Nations,* V, 2

27 As the wages of labour are everywhere regulated, partly by the demand for it, and partly by the average price of the necessary articles of subsistence, whatever raises this average price must necessarily raise those wages so that the labourer may still be able to purchase that quantity of those necessary articles which the state of the demand for labour, whether increasing, stationary, or declining, requires that he should have. A tax upon those articles necessarily raises their price somewhat higher than the amount of the tax, because the dealer, who advances the tax, must generally get it back with a profit. Such a tax must, therefore, occasion a rise in the wages of labour proportionable to this rise of price.

It is thus that a tax upon the necessaries of life operates exactly in the same manner as a direct tax upon the wages of labour. The labourer, though he may pay it out of his hand, cannot, for any considerable time at least, be properly said even to advance it. It must always in the long-run be advanced to him by his immediate employer in the advanced rate of his wages. His employer, if

he is a manufacturer, will charge upon the price of his goods this rise of wages, together with a profit; so that the final payment of the tax, together with this overcharge, will fall upon the consumer. If his employer is a farmer, the final payment, together with a like overcharge, will fall upon the rent of the landlord.

Adam Smith, *Wealth of Nations,* V, 2

28 High taxes, sometimes by diminishing the consumption of the taxed commodities, and sometimes by encouraging smuggling, frequently afford a smaller revenue to government than what might be drawn from more moderate taxes.

When the diminution of revenue is the effect of the diminution of consumption there can be but one remedy, and that is the lowering of the tax.

When the diminution of the revenue is the effect of the encouragement given to smuggling, it may perhaps be remedied in two ways; either by diminishing the temptation to smuggle, or by increasing the difficulty of smuggling. The temptation to smuggle can be diminished only by the lowering of the tax, and the difficulty of smuggling can be increased only by establishing that system of administration which is most proper for preventing it.

Adam Smith, *Wealth of Nations,* V, 2

29 The finances of the state demanded the most vigilant care of the emperor. Though every measure of injustice and extortion had been adopted, which could collect the property of the subject into the coffers of the prince; the rapaciousness of Commodus had been so very inadequate to his extravagance, that, upon his death, no more than eight thousand pounds were found in the exhausted treasury, to defray the current expenses of government, and to discharge the pressing demand of a liberal donative, which the new emperor had been obliged to promise to the Prætorian guards. Yet under these distressed circumstances, Pertinax had the generous firmness to remit all the oppressive taxes invented by Commodus, and to cancel all the unjust claims of the treasury; declaring, in a decree of the senate, "that he was better satisfied to administer a poor republic with innocence, than to acquire riches by the ways of tyranny and dishonour." Economy and industry he considered as the pure and genuine sources of wealth; and from them he soon derived a copious supply for the public necessities.

Gibbon, *Decline and Fall of the Roman Empire,* IV

30 Of the several impositions introduced by Augustus, the twentieth on inheritances and legacies was the most fruitful, as well as the most comprehensive. As its influence was not confined to Rome or Italy, the produce continually increased with the gradual extension of the ROMAN CITY. The new

citizens, though charged, on equal terms, with the payment of new taxes, which had not affected them as subjects, derived an ample compensation from the rank they obtained, the privileges they acquired, and the fair prospect of honours and fortune that was thrown open to their ambition.

Gibbon, *Decline and Fall of the
Roman Empire,* VI

31 Several of his sayings are preserved. One of them in particular discovers a deep insight into the constitution of government. "The authority of the prince," said Artaxerxes, "must be defended by a military force; that force can only be maintained by taxes; all taxes must, at last, fall upon agriculture; and agriculture can never flourish except under the protection of justice and moderation."

Gibbon, *Decline and Fall of the
Roman Empire,* VIII

32 The obscure millions of a great empire have much less to dread from the cruelty than from the avarice of their masters; and *their* humble happiness in principally affected by the grievance of excessive taxes, which, gently pressing on the wealthy, descend with accelerated weight on the meaner and more indigent classes of society.

Gibbon, *Decline and Fall of the
Roman Empire,* XVII

33 The noblest monument of a conqueror's fame, and of the terror which he inspired, is the Saladine tenth, a general tax, which was imposed on the laity and even the clergy of the Latin church for the service of the holy war. The practice was too lucrative to expire with the occasion; and this tribute became the foundation of all the tithes and tenths on ecclesiastical benefices which have been granted by the Roman pontiffs to Catholic sovereigns, or reserved for the immediate use of the apostolic see.

Gibbon, *Decline and Fall of the
Roman Empire,* LIX

34 This extraordinary man, then Chancellor of the Exchequer, found himself in great straits. To please universally was the object of his life; but to tax and to please, no more than to love and to be wise, is not given to men. However, he attempted it.

Burke, *Speech on American Taxation (1774)*

35 The sovereign, as undertaker of the duty of the people, has the right to tax them for purposes essentially connected with their own preservation. Such are, in particular, the relief of the poor, foundling asylums, and ecclesiastical establishments, otherwise designated charitable or pious foundations.

Kant, *Science of Right,* 49

36 As regards the cost of maintaining the ecclesiastical establishment, for similar reasons this must be derived not from the public funds of the state, but from the section of the people who profess the particular faith of the church; and thus only ought it to fall as a burden on the community.

Kant, *Science of Right,* 49

37 Every proposal for a specific tax is sure to meet with opposition. It has been objected to a poll tax at a fixed rate that it will be unequal, and the rich will pay no more than the poor. In the form in which it has been offered in these papers, the poor, properly speaking, are not comprehended, though it is true that beyond the exclusion of the indigent the tax has no reference to the proportion of property; but it should be remembered that it is impossible to devise any specific tax that will operate equally on the whole community. It must be the province of the legislature to hold the scales with a judicious hand and balance one by another. The rich must be made to pay for their luxuries, which is the only proper way of taxing their superior wealth.

Hamilton, *Continentalist 6*

38 Do we imagine that our assessments operate equally? Nothing can be more contrary to the fact. Wherever a discretionary power is lodged in any set of men over the property of their neighbors, they will abuse it; their passions, prejudices, partialities, dislikes will have the principal lead in measuring the abilities of those over whom their power extends; and assessors will ever be a set of petty tyrants, too unskillful, if honest, to be possessed of so delicate a trust, and too seldom honest to give them the excuse of want of skill.

Hamilton, *Continentalist 6*

39 There is, perhaps, nothing more likely to disturb the tranquillity of nations than their being bound to mutual contributions for any common object that does not yield an equal and coincident benefit. For it is an observation, as true as it is trite, that there is nothing men differ so readily about as the payment of money.

Hamilton, *Federalist 7*

40 The popular system of administration inherent in the nature of popular government, coinciding with the real scarcity of money incident to a languid and mutilated state of trade, has hitherto defeated every experiment for extensive collections, and has at length taught the different legislatures the folly of attempting them.

No person acquainted with what happens in other countries will be surprised at this circumstance. In so opulent a nation as that of Britain, where direct taxes from superior wealth must be much more tolerable, and, from the vigour of the government, much more practicable, than in

America, far the greatest part of the national revenue is derived from taxes of the indirect kind, from imposts, and from excises. Duties on imported articles form a large branch of this latter description.

In America, it is evident that we must a long time depend for the means of revenue chiefly on such duties. In most parts of it, excises must be confined within a narrow compass. The genius of the people will ill brook the inquisitive and peremptory spirit of excise laws. The pockets of the farmers, on the other hand, will reluctantly yield but scanty supplies, in the unwelcome shape of impositions on their houses and lands; and personal property is too precarious and invisible a fund to be laid hold of in any other way than by the imperceptible agency of taxes on consumption.

Hamilton, *Federalist 12*

41 Money is, with propriety, considered as the vital principle of the body politic; as that which sustains its life and motion, and enables it to perform its most essential functions. A complete power, therefore, to procure a regular and adequate supply of it, as far as the resources of the community will permit, may be regarded as an indispensable ingredient in every constitution. From a deficiency in this particular, one of two evils must ensue; either the people must be subjected to continual plunder, as a substitute for a more eligible mode of supplying the public wants, or the government must sink into a fatal atrophy, and, in a short course of time, perish.

Hamilton, *Federalist 30*

42 What are the chief sources of expense in every government? What has occasioned that enormous accumulation of debts with which several of the European nations are oppressed? The answer plainly is, wars and rebellions; the support of those institutions which are necessary to guard the body politic against these two most mortal diseases of society. The expenses arising from those institutions which are relative to the mere domestic police of a State, to the support of its legislative, executive, and judicial departments, with their different appendages, and to the encouragement of agriculture and manufactures (which will comprehend almost all the objects of state expenditure), are insignificant in comparison with those which relate to the national defence.

Hamilton, *Federalist 34*

43 A just security to property is not afforded by that government under which unequal taxes oppress one species of property and reward another species; where arbitrary taxes invade the domestic sanctuaries of the rich and excessive taxes grind the faces of the poor; where the keenness and competitions of want are deemed an insufficient

spur to labor, and taxes are again applied by an unfeeling policy as another spur; in violation of that sacred property which heaven, in decreeing man to earn his bread by the sweat of his brow, kindly reserved to him in the small repose that could be spared from the supply of his necessities.

Madison, *Property*

44 Services are now almost entirely reduced to money payments, and military service is now almost the only personal one exacted. In the past, far more claims were made directly on a man's own person, and he used to be called upon for work according to his ability. In our day, the state purchases what it requires. This may at first sight seem an abstract, heartless, and dead state of affairs, and for the state to be satisfied with indirect services may also look like decadence in the state. But the principle of the modern state requires that the whole of an individual's activity be mediated through his will. By means of money, however, the justice of equality can be achieved much more efficiently. Otherwise, if assessment depended on concrete ability, a talented man would be more heavily taxed than an untalented one.

Hegel, *Philosophy of Right,* Additions, Par. 299

45 Of all debts men are least willing to pay the taxes. What a satire is this on government! Everywhere they think they get their money's worth, except for these.

Emerson, *Politics*

46 If I deny the authority of the State when it presents its tax-bill, it will soon take and waste all my property, and so harass me and my children without end. This is hard. This makes it impossible for a man to live honestly, and at the same time comfortably, in outward respects.

Thoreau, *Civil Disobedience*

47 I have paid no poll-tax for six years. I was put into a jail once on this account, for one night; and, as I stood considering the walls of solid stone, two or three feet thick, the door of wood and iron, a foot thick, and the iron grating which strained the light, I could not help being struck with the foolishness of that institution which treated me as if I were mere flesh and blood and bones, to be locked up. I wondered that it should have concluded at length that this was the best use it could put me to, and had never thought to avail itself of my services in some way. I saw that, if there was a wall of stone between me and my townsmen, there was a still more difficult one to climb or break through before they could get to be as free as I was. I did not for a moment feel confined, and the walls seemed a great waste of stone and mortar. I felt as if I alone of all my townsmen had paid my tax. They plainly did not know how to treat me,

but behaved like persons who are underbred. In every threat and in every compliment there was a blunder; for they thought that my chief desire was to stand the other side of that stone wall. I could not but smile to see how industriously they locked the door on my meditations, which followed them out again without let or hindrance, and *they* were really all that was dangerous. As they could not reach me, they had resolved to punish my body; just as boys, if they cannot come at some person against whom they have a spite, will abuse his dog. I saw that the State was half-witted, that it was timid as a lone woman with her silver spoons, and that it did not know its friends from its foes, and I lost all my remaining respect for it, and pitied it.

Thoreau, *Civil Disobedience*

48 I have never declined paying the highway tax, because I am as desirous of being a good neighbor as I am of being a bad subject; and as for supporting schools, I am doing my part to educate my fellow-countrymen now. It is for no particular item in the tax-bill that I refuse to pay it. I simply wish to refuse allegiance to the State, to withdraw and stand aloof from it effectually. I do not care to trace the course of my dollar, if I could, till it buys a man or a musket to shoot one with—the dollar is innocent—but I am concerned to trace the effects of my allegiance.

Thoreau, *Civil Disobedience*

49 As the national debt finds its support in the public revenue, which must cover the yearly payments for interest, etc., the modern system of taxation was the necessary complement of the system of national loans. The loans enable the government to meet extraordinary expenses, without the taxpayers feeling it immediately, but they necessitate, as a consequence, increased taxes. On the other hand, the raising of taxation, caused by the accumulation of debts contracted one after another, compels the government always to have recourse to new loans for new extraordinary expenses. Modern fiscality, whose pivot is formed by taxes on the most necessary means of subsistence (thereby increasing their price), thus contains within itself the germ of automatic progression. Over-taxation is not an incident, but rather a principle.

Marx, *Capital*, Vol. I, VIII, 31

50 A just distribution of burthens, by holding up to every citizen an example of morality and good conscience applied to difficult adjustments, and an evidence of the value which the highest authorities attach to them, tends in an eminent degree to educate the moral sentiments of the community, both in respect of strength and of discrimination. Such a mode of levying the taxes as does not impede the industry, or unnecessarily

interfere with the liberty, of the citizen, promotes, not the preservation only, but the increase of the national wealth, and encourages a more active use of the individual faculties. And *vice versa*, all errors in finance and taxation which obstruct the improvement of the people in wealth and morals tend also, if of sufficiently serious amount, positively to impoverish and demoralise them.

Mill, *Representative Government*, II

51 It is . . . important that the assembly which votes the taxes, either general or local, should be elected exclusively by those who pay something towards the taxes imposed. Those who pay no taxes, disposing by their votes of other people's money, have every motive to be lavish and none to economise. As far as money matters are concerned, any power of voting possessed by them is a violation of the fundamental principle of free government; a severance of the power of control from the interest in its beneficial exercise. It amounts to allowing them to put their hands into other people's pockets for any purpose which they think fit to call a public one.

Mill, *Representative Government*, VIII

52 It is essential, as it is on many other accounts desirable, that taxation, in a visible shape, should descend to the poorest class. In this country, and in most others, there is probably no labouring family which does not contribute to the indirect taxes, by the purchase of tea, coffee, sugar, not to mention narcotics or stimulants. But this mode of defraying a share of the public expenses is hardly felt. . . . It would be better that a direct tax, in the simple form of a capitation, should be levied on every grown person in the community; or that every such person should be admitted an elector on allowing himself to be rated *extra ordinem* to the assessed taxes; or that a small annual payment, rising and falling with the gross expenditure of the country, should be required from every registered elector; that so everyone might feel that the money which he assisted in voting was partly his own, and that he was interested in keeping down its amount.

Mill, *Representative Government*, VIII

53 How many . . . and how irreconcilable, are the standards of justice to which reference is made in discussing the repartition of taxation. One opinion is, that payment to the State should be in numerical proportion to pecuniary means. Others think that justice dictates what they term graduated taxation; taking a higher percentage from those who have more to spare. In point of natural justice a strong case might be made for disregarding means altogether, and taking the same absolute sum (whenever it could be got) from everyone: as the subscribers to a mess, or to a club, all pay the same sum for the same privileges,

whether they can all equally afford it or not. Since the protection (it might be said) of law and government is afforded to, and is equally required by all, there is no injustice in making all buy it at the same price. It is reckoned justice, not injustice, that a dealer should charge to all customers the same price for the same article, not a price varying according to their means of payment. This doctrine, as applied to taxation, finds no advocates, because it conflicts so strongly with man's feelings of humanity and of social expediency; but the principle of justice which it invokes is as true and as binding as those which can be appealed to against it. Accordingly it exerts a tacit influence on the line of defence employed for other modes of assessing taxation. People feel obliged to argue that the State does more for the rich than for the poor, as a justification for its taking more from them: though this is in reality not true, for the rich would be far better able to protect themselves, in the absence of law or government, than the poor, and indeed would probably be successful in converting the poor into their slaves. Others, again, so far defer to the same conception of justice, as to maintain that all should pay an equal capitation tax for the protection of their persons (these being of equal value to all), and an unequal tax for the protection of their property, which is unequal. To this others reply, that the all of one man is as valuable to him as the all of another. From these confusions there is no other mode of extrication than the utilitarian.

Mill, *Utilitarianism,* V

54 What is taken from the rich in taxes, would, if not so taken, have been saved and converted into capital, or even expended in the maintenance and wages of servants or of any class of unproductive labourers, to that extent the demand for labour is no doubt diminished, and the poor injuriously affected, by the tax on the rich.

Mill, *Principles of Political Economy,*
Bk. I, V, 10

55 Equality of taxation . . . as a maxim of politics, means equality of sacrifice. It means apportioning the contribution of each person towards the expenses of government, so that he shall feel neither more nor less inconvenience from his share of the payment than every other person experiences from his. This standard, like other standards of perfection, cannot be completely realized; but the first object in every practical discussion should be to know what perfection is.

Mill, *Principles of Political Economy,*
Bk. V, II, 2

56 To tax the larger incomes at a higher percentage than the smaller, is to lay a tax on industry and economy; to impose a penalty on people for having worked harder and saved more than their neighbours. It is not the fortunes which are earned, but those which are unearned, that it is for the public good to place under limitation.

Mill, *Principles of Political Economy,*
Bk. V, II, 3

LAW and JUSTICE

Chapter 12 is divided into four sections: 12.1 LAW AND LAWYERS, 12.2 JUSTICE AND INJUSTICE, 12.3 RIGHTS—NATURAL AND CIVIL, and 12.4 CRIME AND PUNISHMENT.

This chapter, like Chapters 13 and 14, is closely related to Chapter 10 on POLITICS; though insofar as some of its passages discuss economic justice and economic rights, it also touches on matters treated in Chapter 11 on ECONOMICS.

The discussion of law in Section 12.1 deals mainly with man-made law, the law of the state, sometimes also referred to as "civil law" or "positive law." The passages collected in this section, therefore, tend to overlap passages in Section 10.3 on GOVERNMENT: ITS NATURE, NECESSITY, AND FORMS.

Section 12.2 goes beyond the consideration of justice in relation to law; it contains quotations that also discuss the justice of political, economic, and social institutions or arrangements. It is followed by Section 12.3, which introduces considerations intimately involved in the theory of justice.

The chapter closes with a section—12.4— that involves the notions of law, justice, and rights. The quotations collected here consider the kinds, causes, and prevention of crime, and debate the issues concerning the purposes and justifications of punishment.

12.1 | Law and Lawyers

Among the quotations collected here, the reader will find a number that distinguish different kinds of law: divine law and man-made law, natural law and positive law, and the moral law and the law of the state. All of the kinds mentioned share in the property that distinguishes statements of law from other pronouncements: laws are commands or prohibitions that prescribe how people ought or ought not to behave; laws are violable rules of conduct. The so-called "laws of nature" discovered and formulated by natural scientists, being inviolable, are not laws in this sense at all.

This section concentrates mainly on one kind of law: positive law, the man-made laws that are one of the principal instruments of government. The reader will find the treatment of the natural moral law and the divine law in Section 9.3. The reader will also find matters closely related to the discussion of law in Section 12.2 and Section 12.3.

The passages assembled here discuss most of the critical questions that have been raised about the nature and operation of positive law: the difference between a constitution as the fundamental law of the state and the laws enacted by the legislative assemblies set up by the constitution; coercive force as an essential property of law; the educative influence of law; the difference between the written and the unwritten law, or between legislative enactments and customary law; the distinction between a government of laws and a government of men; the role of courts and judges in the application of law, and the need for equity to prevent injustice in the application of a just law to a particular case not foreseen by the lawmaker; the considerations favoring or disfavoring the change of laws; and the settlement of disputes by laws and courts instead of by force and fighting as indispensable to the maintenance of peace.

One issue, more fundamental than all the others, is disputed in a number of quotations. On the one hand, the reader will find an expression of the view that laws represent the sovereign's will; or as Ulpian, a Roman jurist, put it, "whatever pleases the prince has the force of law." According to this view, justice consists solely in obedience to law; the laws themselves cannot be said either to be just or unjust; being the ultimate standard of justice, they cannot be measured by it. On the other hand, the reader will find passages expressing the diametrically opposite view that justice is the standard by which the goodness of laws is measured. According to this view, an unjust law is a law in name only, not binding on the conscience of those who are subject to it.

Included here also are diatribes against law and lawyers, akin to the attacks on physicians that the reader will find in Section 18.2. On the other side of the balance are economiums in praise of great lawgivers, such as Solon and Lycurgus, together with the honoring of law as basic to civilized life.

---

1 Ye shall have one manner of law, as well for the stranger, as for one of your own country.
Leviticus 24:22

2 *Menelaus.* Laws will never be rightly kept in a city

That knows no fear or reverence.
Sophocles, *Ajax,* 1073

3 *Aethra.* The power that keeps cities of men together

Is noble preservation of the laws.

Euripides, *Suppliant Women*, 312

4 *Cleon.* Bad laws which are never changed are better for a city than good ones that have no authority.

Thucydides, *Peloponnesian War*, III, 37

5 *Socrates.* Then consider the matter in this way:—Imagine that I am about to play truant (you may call the proceeding by any name which you like), and the laws and the government come and interrogate me: "Tell us, Socrates," they say; "what are you about? are you not going by an act of yours to overturn us—the laws, and the whole state, as far as in you lies? Do you imagine that a state can subsist and not be overthrown, in which the decisions of law have no power, but are set aside and trampled upon by individuals?" What will be our answer, Crito, to these and the like words? Any one, and especially a rhetorician, will have a good deal to say on behalf of the law which requires a sentence to be carried out. He will argue that this law should not be set aside; and shall we reply, "Yes; but the state has injured us and given an unjust sentence." Suppose I say that?

Crito. Very good, Socrates.

Soc. "And was that our agreement with you?" the law would answer; "or were you to abide by the sentence of the state?" And if I were to express my astonishment at their words, the law would probably add: "Answer, Socrates, instead of opening your eyes—you are in the habit of asking and answering questions. Tell us,—What complaint have you to make against us which justifies you in attempting to destroy us and the state? In the first place did we not bring you into existence? Your father married your mother by our aid and begat you. Say whether you have any objection to urge against those of us who regulate marriage?" None, I should reply. "Or against those of us who after birth regulate the nurture and education of children, in which you also were trained? Were not the laws, which have the charge of education, right in commanding your father to train you in music and gymnastic?" Right, I should reply. "Well then, since you were brought into the world and nurtured and educated by us, can you deny in the first place that you are our child and slave, as your fathers were before you? And if this is true you are not on equal terms with us; nor can you think that you have a right to do to us what we are doing to you. Would you have any right to strike or revile or do any other evil to your father or your master, if you had one, because you have been struck or reviled by him, or received some other evil at his hands?—you would not say this? And because we think right to destroy you, do you think that you have any right to destroy us in return, and your country as far as in you lies? Will you, O professor of true virtue, pretend that you are justified in this? Has a philosopher like you failed to discover that our country is more to be valued and higher and holier far than mother or father or any ancestor, and more to be regarded in the eyes of the gods and of men of understanding? also to be soothed, and gently and reverently entreated when angry, even more than a father, and either to be persuaded, or if not persuaded, to be obeyed? And when we are punished by her, whether with imprisonment or stripes, the punishment is to be endured in silence: and if she leads us to wounds or death in battle, thither we follow as is right; neither may any one yield or retreat or leave his rank, but whether in battle or in a court of law, or in any other place, he must do what his city and his country order him; or he must change their view of what is just: and if he may do no violence to his father or mother, much less may he do violence to his country." What answer shall we make to this, Crito? Do the laws speak truly, or do they not?

Cr. I think that they do.

Plato, *Crito*, 50A

6 *Athenian Stranger.* Consider, then, to whom our state is to be entrusted. For there is a thing which has occurred times without number in states——

Cleinias. What thing?

Ath. That when there has been a contest for power, those who gain the upper hand so entirely monopolize the government, as to refuse all share to the defeated party and their descendants—they live watching one another, the ruling class being in perpetual fear that some one who has a recollection of former wrongs will come into power and rise up against them. Now, according to our view, such governments are not polities at all, nor are laws right which are passed for the good of particular classes and not for the good of the whole state. States which have such laws are not polities but parties, and their notions of justice are simply unmeaning. I say this, because I am going to assert that we must not entrust the government in your state to any one because he is rich, or because he possesses any other advantage, such as strength, or stature, or again birth: but he who is most obedient to the laws of the state, he shall win the palm; and to him who is victorious in the first degree shall be given the highest office and chief ministry of the gods; and the second to him who bears the second palm; and on a similar principle shall all the other offices be assigned to those who come next in order. And when I call the rulers servants or ministers of the law, I give them this name not for the sake of novelty, but because I certainly believe that upon such service or ministry depends the well- or ill-being of the state. For that state in which the law is subject and has no authority, I perceive to be on the highway to ruin; but I see that the state in which the law is above the rulers, and the rulers are the inferiors of the law, has salvation, and every blessing which the Gods can confer.

Plato, *Laws*, IV, 715A

7 *Athenian Stranger.* Laws are partly framed for the sake of good men, in order to instruct them how they may live on friendly terms with one another, and partly for the sake of those who refuse to be instructed, whose spirit cannot be subdued, or softened, or hindered from plunging into evil.

. Plato, *Laws*, IX, 880B

8 The equitable is just, but not the legally just but a correction of legal justice. The reason is that all law is universal but about some things it is not possible to make a universal statement which shall be correct. In those cases, then, in which it is necessary to speak universally, but not possible to do so correctly, the law takes the usual case, though it is not ignorant of the possibility of error. And it is none the less correct; for the error is not in the law nor in the legislator but in the nature of the thing, since the matter of practical affairs is of this kind from the start. When the law speaks universally, then, and a case arises on it which is not covered by the universal statement, then it is right, where the legislator fails us and has erred by over-simplicity, to correct the omission—to say what the legislator himself would have said had he been present, and would have put into his law if he had known. Hence the equitable is just, and better than one kind of justice—not better than absolute justice but better than the error that arises from the absoluteness of the statement. And this is the nature of the equitable, a correction of law where it is defective owing to its universality.

Aristotle, *Ethics*, 1137ᵇ11

9 It is difficult to get from youth up a right training for virtue if one has not been brought up under right laws; for to live temperately and hardily is not pleasant to most people, especially when they are young. For this reason their nurture and occupations should be fixed by law; for they will not be painful when they have become customary. But it is surely not enough that when they are young they should get the right nurture and attention; since they must, even when they are grown up, practise and be habituated to them, we shall need laws for this as well, and generally speaking to cover the whole of life; for most people obey necessity rather than argument, and punishments rather than the sense of what is noble.

This is why some think that legislators ought to stimulate men to virtue and urge them forward by the motive of the noble, on the assumption that those who have been well advanced by the formation of habits will attend to such influences; and that punishments and penalties should be im-

posed on those who disobey and are of inferior nature, while the incurably bad should be completely banished. A good man (they think), since he lives with his mind fixed on what is noble, will submit to argument, while a bad man, whose desire is for pleasure, is corrected by pain like a beast of burden. This is, too, why they say the pains inflicted should be those that are most opposed to the pleasures such men love.

However that may be, if (as we have said) the man who is to be good must be well trained and habituated, and go on to spend his time in worthy occupations and neither willingly nor unwillingly do bad actions, and if this can be brought about if men live in accordance with a sort of reason and right order, provided this has force,—if this be so, the paternal command indeed has not the required force or compulsive power (nor in general has the command of one man, unless he be a king or something similar), but the law *has* compulsive power, while it is at the same time a rule proceeding from a sort of practical wisdom and reason. And while people hate *men* who oppose their impulses, even if they oppose them rightly, the law in its ordaining of what is good is not burdensome.

Aristotle, *Ethics*, 1179ᵇ31

10 The habit of lightly changing the laws is an evil, and, when the advantage is small, some errors both of lawgivers and rulers had better be left; the citizen will not gain so much by making the change as he will lose by the habit of disobedience. The analogy of the arts is false; a change in a law is a very different thing from a change in an art. For the law has no power to command obedience except that of habit, which can only be given by time, so that a readiness to change from old to new laws enfeebles the power of the law.

Aristotle, *Politics*, 1269ᵃ15

11 He who bids the law rule may be deemed to bid God and Reason alone rule, but he who bids man rule adds an element of the beast; for desire is a wild beast, and passion perverts the minds of rulers, even when they are the best of men. The law is reason unaffected by desire.

Aristotle, *Politics*, 1287ᵃ28

12 Good laws, if they are not obeyed, do not constitute good government. Hence there are two parts of good government; one is the actual obedience of citizens to the laws, the other part is the goodness of the laws which they obey; they may obey bad laws as well as good. And there may be a further subdivision; they may obey either the best laws which are attainable to them, or the best absolutely.

Aristotle, *Politics*, 1294ᵃ4

13 In all well-attempered governments there is nothing which should be more jealously maintained

than the spirit of obedience to law, more especially in small matters; for transgression creeps in unperceived and at last ruins the state, just as the constant recurrence of small expenses in time eats up a fortune.

Aristotle, *Politics*, 1307^b30

14 Particular law is that which each community lays down and applies to its own members: this is partly written and partly unwritten. Universal law is the law of Nature. For there really is, as every one to some extent divines, a natural justice and injustice that is binding on all men, even on those who have no association or covenant with each other.

Aristotle, *Rhetoric*, 1373^b4

15 Law is only a principle of right derived from the will of the gods. It commands what is decent and forbids the opposite.

Cicero, *Philippics*, XI, 12

16 Injustice often comes about through trickery, in other words, through an over-subtle or perhaps fraudulent construction of law. This is the origin of the familiar proverb, "More law, less justice."

Cicero, *De Officiis*, I, 10

17 We should never prosecute the innocent. But we need have no scruples about undertaking the defense of a guilty person, so long as he is not utterly depraved and evil. People expect it; custom sanctions it; and humanity condones it. It is, after all, the business of the judge in a trial to find out the truth.

Cicero, *De Officiis*, II, 14

18 The fairness of a law does not consist in its effect being actually felt by all alike, but in its having been laid down for all alike.

Seneca, *Letters to Lucilius*, 107

19 Woe unto you also, ye lawyers! for ye lade men with burdens grievous to be borne, and ye yourselves touch not the burdens with one of your fingers.

Luke 11:46

20 Lycurgus would never reduce his laws into writing. . . . For he thought that the most material points, and such as most directly tended to the public welfare, being imprinted on the hearts of their youth by a good discipline, would be sure to remain, and would find a stronger security, than any compulsion would be, in the principles of action formed in them by their best lawgiver, education. And as for things of lesser importance, as pecuniary contracts, and such like, the forms of which have to be changed as occasion requires, he thought it the best way to prescribe no positive rule or inviolable usage in such cases, willing that their manner and form should be altered according to the circumstances of time, and determinations of men of sound judgment. Every end and object of law and enactment it was his design education should effect.

Plutarch, *Lycurgus*

21 When he perceived that his more important institutions had taken root in the minds of his countrymen, that custom had rendered them familiar and easy, that his commonwealth was now grown up and able to go alone, then, as Plato somewhere tells us, the Maker of the world, when first he saw it existing and beginning its motion, felt joy, even so Lycurgus, viewing with joy and satisfaction the greatness and beauty of his political structure, now fairly at work and in motion, conceived the thought to make it immortal too, and, as far as human forecast could reach, to deliver it down unchangeable to posterity. He called an extraordinary assembly of all the people, and told them that he now thought everything reasonably well established, both for the happiness and the virtue of the state; but that there was one thing still behind, of the greatest importance, which he thought not fit to impart until he had consulted the oracle; in the meantime, his desire was that they would observe the laws without any the least alteration until his return, and then he would do as the god should direct him. They all consented readily, and bade him hasten his journey; but, before he departed, he administered an oath to the two kings, the senate, and the whole commons, to abide by and maintain the established form of polity until Lycurgus should be come back.

This done, he set out for Delphi, and, having sacrificed to Apollo, asked him whether the laws he had established were good, and sufficient for a people's happiness and virtue. The oracle answered that the laws were excellent, and that the people, while it observed them, should live in the height of renown. Lycurgus took the oracle in writing, and sent it over to Sparta; and, having sacrificed the second time to Apollo, and taken leave of his friends and his son, he resolved that the Spartans should not be released from the oath they had taken, and that he would, of his own act, close his life where he was.

Plutarch, *Lycurgus*

22 This . . . is a property of the rational soul, love of one's neighbour, and truth and modesty, and to value nothing more than itself, which is also the property of Law. Thus then right reason differs not at all from the reason of justice.

Marcus Aurelius, *Meditations*, XI, 1

23 The heavenly city, or rather the part of it which sojourns on earth and lives by faith . . . while it sojourns on earth, calls citizens out of all nations and gathers together a society of pilgrims of all

languages, not scrupling about diversities in the manners, laws, and institutions whereby earthly peace is secured and maintained, but recognizing that, however various these are, they all tend to one and the same end of earthly peace.

Augustine, *City of God,* XIX, 17

24 A private person cannot lead another to virtue efficaciously; for he can only advise, and if his advice be not taken, it has no coercive power, such as the law should have, in order to prove an efficacious inducement to virtue. . . . But this coercive power is vested in the whole people or in some public personage, to whom it belongs to inflict penalties.

Aquinas, *Summa Theologica,* I–II, 90, 3

25 A law is imposed on others by way of a rule and measure. Now a rule or measure is imposed by being applied to those who are to be ruled and measured by it. Therefore, in order that a law obtain the binding force which is proper to a law, it must be applied to the men who have to be ruled by it. Such application is made by its being notified to them by promulgation. Therefore promulgation is necessary for the law to obtain its force.

Thus . . . the definition of law may be gathered; and it is nothing other than an ordinance of reason for the common good, made by him who has care of the community, and promulgated.

Aquinas, *Summa Theologica,* I–II, 90, 4

26 Man has a natural aptitude for virtue; but the perfection itself of virtue must be acquired by man by means of some kind of training. Thus we observe that man is helped by industry in his necessities, for instance, in food and clothing. Certain beginnings of these he has from nature, that is, his reason and his hands; but he has not the full complement, as other animals have, to whom nature has given sufficient covering and food. Now it is difficult to see how man could suffice for himself in the matter of this training; for the perfection of virtue consists chiefly in withdrawing man from undue pleasures, to which above all man is inclined, and especially the young, who are more capable of being trained. Consequently a man needs to receive this training from another, through which to arrive at the perfection of virtue. And as to those young people who are inclined to acts of virtue by their good natural disposition, or by custom, or rather by the gift of God, paternal training suffices, which is by admonitions. But since some are found to be depraved, and prone to vice, and not easily amenable to words, it was necessary for such to be restrained from evil by force and fear, in order that at least they might cease from evil-doing and leave others in peace, and that they themselves, by being accustomed in this way, might be brought to do will-

ingly what hitherto they did from fear, and thus become virtuous. Now this kind of training, which compels through fear of punishment, is the discipline of laws. Therefore, in order that man might have peace and virtue, it was necessary for laws to be framed. . . . As the Philosopher [Aristotle] says, "it is better that all things be regulated by law than left to be decided by judges," and this for three reasons. First, because it is easier to find a few wise men competent to frame right laws than to find the many who would be necessary to judge rightly of each single case. Secondly, because those who make laws consider long beforehand what laws to make; but judgment on each single case has to be pronounced as soon as it arises. And it is easier for man to see what is right by taking many instances into consideration, than by considering one solitary fact. Thirdly, because lawgivers judge universally and of future events, while those who sit in judgment judge of things present, towards which they are affected by love, hatred, or some kind of cupidity, so that their judgment is perverted.

Since then the animated justice of the judge is not found in every man, and since it can be deflected, therefore it was necessary, whenever possible, for the law to determine how to judge, and for very few matters to be left to the decision of men.

Aquinas, *Summa Theologica,* I–II, 95, 1

27 The common principles of the natural law cannot be applied to all men in the same way on account of the great variety of human affairs, and from this arises the diversity of positive laws among various people.

Aquinas, *Summa Theologica,* I–II, 95, 2

28 The purpose of human law is to lead men to virtue not suddenly, but gradually. Therefore it does not lay upon the multitude of imperfect men the burdens of those who are already virtuous, namely, that they should abstain from all evil. Otherwise these imperfect ones, being unable to bear such precepts, would break out into yet greater evils.

Aquinas, *Summa Theologica,* I–II, 96, 2

29 Laws may be unjust in two ways. First, by being contrary to human good . . . as when an authority imposes on his subjects burdensome laws, conducive not to the common good but rather to his own cupidity or vainglory; or . . . as when a man makes a law that goes beyond the power committed to him; or . . . as when burdens are imposed unequally on the community, although with a view to the common good. The like are acts of violence rather than laws. . . .

Secondly, laws may be unjust through being opposed to the Divine good. Such are the laws of tyrants inducing to idolatry, or to anything else contrary to the Divine law; and laws of this kind must in no way be observed.

Aquinas, *Summa Theologica*, I–II, 96, 4

30 The notion of law contains two things: first, that it is a rule of human acts; secondly, that it has coercive power. Hence a man may be subject to law in two ways. First, as the regulated is subject to the regulator, and in this way whoever is subject to a power is subject to the law framed by that power. But it may happen in two ways that one is not subject to a power. In one way, by being altogether free from its authority. Hence the subjects of one city or kingdom are not bound by the laws of the sovereign of another city or kingdom, since they are not subject to his authority. In another way by being under a yet higher law. Thus the subject of a proconsul should be ruled by his command, but not in those matters in which the subject receives his orders from the emperor; for in these matters he is not bound by the mandate of the lower authority, since he is directed by that of a higher. In this way, one who is subject absolutely to a law may not be subject to it in certain matters, in respect of which he is ruled by a higher law.

Secondly, a man is said to be subject to a law as the coerced is subject to the coercer. In this way the virtuous and the just are not subject to the law, but only the wicked. Because coercion and violence are contrary to the will; but the will of the good is in harmony with the law, while the will of the wicked is discordant from it. Therefore in this sense the good are not subject to the law, but only the wicked.

Aquinas, *Summa Theologica*, I–II, 96, 5

31 Human law is a dictate of reason, by which human acts are directed. Thus there may be two causes for the just change of human law: one on the part of reason; the other on the part of man whose acts are regulated by law. The cause on the part of reason is that it seems natural to human reason to advance gradually from the imperfect to the perfect. . . .

On the part of man, whose acts are regulated by law, the law can be rightly changed on account of the changed condition of man, to whom different things are expedient according to the difference of his condition.

Aquinas, *Summa Theologica*, I–II, 97, 1

32 Human law is rightly changed in so far as such change is conducive to the common weal. But, to a certain extent, the mere change of law is of itself prejudicial to the common good, because custom avails much for the observance of laws, seeing that what is done contrary to general custom, even in slight matters, is looked upon as grave. Consequently, when a law is changed, the binding power of the law is diminished, in so far as custom is abolished. Therefore human law should never be

changed, unless, in some way or other, the common welfare be compensated according to the extent of the harm done in this respect.

Aquinas, *Summa Theologica*, I–II, 97, 2

33 For such law as man gives to other wight,
He should himself submit to it, by right.

Chaucer, *Canterbury Tales:*
Man of Law's Prologue, Intro.

34 The chief foundations of all states, new as well as old or composite, are good laws and good arms; and as there cannot be good laws where the state is not well armed, it follows that where they are well armed they have good laws.

Machiavelli, *Prince*, XII

35 There are two ways of contesting, the one by the law, the other by force; the first method is proper to men, the second to beasts; but because the first is frequently not sufficient, it is necessary to have recourse to the second.

Machiavelli, *Prince*, XVIII

36 For as good habits of the people require good laws to support them, so laws, to be observed, need good habits on the part of the people.

Machiavelli, *Discourses*, I, 18

37 The strictest right is the greatest wrong, and therefore equity is necessary. This is not a rash relaxation of laws and discipline. It is, rather, an interpretation of laws which in some cases finds mitigating circumstances, especially in cases in which the law doesn't decide on principle. According to the circumstances equity weighs for or against. But the weighing must be of such kind that the law isn't undermined, for no undermining of natural law and divine law must be allowed.

Luther, *Table Talk*, 4178

38 The law is a silent magistrate, and a magistrate a speaking law.

Calvin, *Institutes of the Christian
Religion*, IV, 20

39 It is very doubtful whether there can be such evident profit in changing an accepted law, of whatever sort it be, as there is harm in disturbing it; inasmuch as a government is like a structure of different parts joined together in such a relation that it is impossible to budge one without the whole body feeling it.

Montaigne, *Essays*, I, 23, Of Custom

40 There is little relation between our actions, which are in perpetual mutation, and fixed and immutable laws. The most desirable laws are those that are rarest, simplest, and most general; and I even think that it would be better to have none at all

than to have them in such numbers as we have.
Montaigne, *Essays*, III, 13, Of Experience

41 Now laws remain in credit not because they are
just, but because they are laws. That is the mystic
foundation of their authority; they have no other.
And that is a good thing for them. They are often
made by fools, more often by people who, in their
hatred of equality, are wanting in equity; but always by men, vain and irresolute authors.

There is nothing so grossly and widely and ordinarily faulty as the laws. Whoever obeys them
because they are just, does not obey them for just
the reason he should.
Montaigne, *Essays*, III, 13, Of Experience

42 *Dick the Butcher.* The first thing we do, let's kill all
the lawyers.
John Cade. Nay, that I mean to do. Is not this a
lamentable thing, that of the skin of an innocent
lamb should be made parchment? that parchment, being scribbled o'er, should undo a man?
Some say the bee stings: but I say, 'tis the bee's
wax; for I did but seal once to a thing, and I was
never mine own man since.
Shakespeare, *II Henry VI*, IV, ii, 82

43 Reason is the life of the Law. Nay the Common
Law itselfe is nothing else but reason; which is to
be understood of an artificiall perfection of reason, gotten by long study, observation, and experience, and not of every man's naturall reason.
Sir Edward Coke, *Commentary
Upon Littleton,* 138

44 The most obvious and natural way of discovering
the truth is by referring to laws, which derive their
force and efficacy from the general consent of
mankind; so that if a law rests upon the presumption of any fact, which in reality has no existence,
such a law is not binding. For when no evidence
of the fact can be produced, the entire foundation,
on which that law rests must fail.
Grotius, *Rights of War and Peace,*
Bk. II, XI, 6

45 As men, for the attaining of peace and conservation of themselves thereby, have made an artificial man, which we call a *Commonwealth;* so also
have they made artificial chains, called *civil laws,*
which they themselves, by mutual covenants, have
fastened at one end to the lips of that man, or
assembly, to whom they have given the sovereign
power, and at the other end to their own ears.
These bonds, in their own nature but weak, may
nevertheless be made to hold, by the danger,
though not by the difficulty of breaking them.
Hobbes, *Leviathan*, II, 21

46 Of positive laws some are *human,* some *divine:* and
of human positive laws, some are *distributive,* some

penal. Distributive are those that determine the
rights of the subjects, declaring to every man what
it is by which he acquireth and holdeth a propriety in lands or goods, and a right or liberty of
action: and these speak to all the subjects. *Penal*
are those which declare what penalty shall be inflicted on those that violate the law; and speak to
the ministers and officers ordained for execution.
For though every one ought to be informed of the
punishments ordained beforehand for their transgression; nevertheless the command is not addressed to the delinquent (who cannot be supposed will faithfully punish himself), but to public
ministers appointed to see the penalty executed.
And these penal laws are for the most part written
together with the laws distributive, and are sometimes called *judgements.* For all laws are general
judgements, or sentences of the legislator; as also
every particular judgement is a law to him whose
case is judged.
Hobbes, *Leviathan,* II, 26

47 To the care of the sovereign belongeth the making
of good laws. But what is a good law? By a *good
law,* I mean not a just law: for no law can be
unjust. The law is made by the sovereign power,
and all that is done by such power is warranted
and owned by every one of the people; and that
which every man will have so, no man can say is
unjust. It is in the laws of a Commonwealth, as in
the laws of gaming: whatsoever the gamesters all
agree on is injustice to none of them. A good law
is that which is needful, for the good of the people,
and withal perspicuous.

For the use of laws (which are but rules authorized) is not to bind the people from all voluntary
actions, but to direct and keep them in such a
motion as not to hurt themselves by their own
impetuous desires, rashness, or indiscretion; as
hedges are set, not to stop travellers, but to keep
them in the way. And therefore a law that is not
needful, having not the true end of a law, is not
good. A law may be conceived to be good when it
is for the benefit of the sovereign, though it be not
necessary for the people, but it is not so. For the
good of the sovereign and people cannot be separated.
Hobbes, *Leviathan,* II, 30

48 Let not the Law of thy Country be the non ultra
of thy Honesty; nor think that always good
enough which the law will make good.
Sir Thomas Browne, *Christian Morals,* I, 11

49 I look at the law which they [the Jews] boast of
having obtained from God, and I find it admirable. It is the first law of all and is of such a kind
that, even before the term *law* was in currency
among the Greeks, it had, for nearly a thousand
years earlier, been uninterruptedly accepted and
observed by the Jews. I likewise think it strange

that the first law of the world happens to be the most perfect; so that the greatest legislators have borrowed their laws from it, as is apparent from the law of the Twelve Tables at Athens, afterwards taken by the Romans, and as it would be easy to prove, if Josephus and others had not sufficiently dealt with this subject.

Pascal, *Pensées*, IX, 619

50 We cannot even conceive, that every citizen should be allowed to interpret the commonwealth's decrees or laws. For were every citizen allowed this, he would thereby be his own judge, because each would easily be able to give a colour of right to his own deeds, which . . . is absurd.

Spinoza, *Political Treatise*, III, 4

51 Civil jurisprudence depends on the mere decree of the commonwealth, which is not bound to please any but itself, nor to hold anything to be good or bad, but what it judges to be such for itself. And, accordingly, it has not merely the right to avenge itself, or to lay down and interpret laws, but also to abolish the same, and to pardon any guilty person out of the fulness of its power.

Spinoza, *Political Treatise*, IV, 5

52 The obligations of the law of Nature cease not in society, but only in many cases are drawn closer, and have, by human laws, known penalties annexed to them to enforce their observation. Thus the law of Nature stands as an external rule to all men, legislators as well as others. The rules that they make for other men's actions must, as well as their own and other men's actions, be conformable to the law of Nature—*i.e.,* to the will of God, of which that is a declaration, and the fundamental law of Nature being the preservation of mankind, no human sanction can be good or valid against it.

Locke, *II Civil Government*, XI, 135

53 These are the bounds which the trust that is put in them by the society and the law of God and Nature have set to the legislative power of every commonwealth, in all forms of government. First: They are to govern by promulgated established laws, not to be varied in particular cases, but to have one rule for rich and poor, for the favourite at Court, and the countryman at plough. Secondly: These laws also ought to be designed for no other end ultimately but the good of the people.

Locke, *II Civil Government*, XI, 142

54 First, the law of God; secondly, the law of politic societies; thirdly, the law of fashion, or private censure, are those to which men variously compare their actions: and it is by their conformity to one of these laws that they take their measures, when they would judge of their moral rectitude,

and denominate their actions good or bad.

Locke, *Concerning Human Understanding,*
Bk. II, XXVIII, 13

55 I said that those who made profession of this science [law] were exceedingly multiplied, being almost equal to the caterpillars in number; that they were of diverse degrees, distinctions, and denominations. The numerousness of those that dedicated themselves to this profession were such that the fair and justifiable advantage and income of the profession was not sufficient for the decent and handsome maintenance of multitudes of those who followed it. Hence it came to pass that it was found needful to supply that by artifice and cunning, which could not be procured by just and honest methods: the better to bring which about, very many men among us were bred up from their youth in the art of proving by words multiplied for the purpose that *white* is *black,* and *black* is *white,* according as they are paid. The greatness of these mens assurance and the boldness of their pretensions gained upon the opinion of the vulgar, whom in a manner they made slaves of, and got into their hands much the largest share of the practice of their profession. These practitioners were by men of discernment called *pettifoggers,* (that is, *confounders,* or rather, *destroyers of right*).

Swift, *Gulliver's Travels*, IV, 5

56 Law, in a free Country, is, or ought to be, the Determination of the Majority of those who have Property in Land.

Swift, *Thoughts on Various Subjects*

57 Laws are like cobwebs, which may catch small flies, but let wasps and hornets break through.

Swift, *A Tritical Essay Upon the Faculties
of the Mind*

58 The hungry Judges soon the sentence sign,
And wretches hang that jury-men may dine.

Pope, *The Rape of the Lock*, III, 21

59 An attorney may feel all the miseries and distresses of his fellow-creatures, provided he happens not to be concerned against them.

Fielding, *Tom Jones*, XII, 10

60 Before laws were made, there were relations of possible justice. To say that there is nothing just or unjust but what is commanded or forbidden by positive laws, is the same as saying that before the describing of a circle all the radii were not equal.

Montesquieu, *Spirit of Laws*, I, 1

61 If it be true that the temper of the mind and the passions of the heart are extremely different in different climates, the laws ought to be in relation both to the variety of those passions and to the variety of those tempers.

Montesquieu, *Spirit of Laws*, XIV, 1

62 I am told that there are laws among thieves, and also laws of war. I ask what are these laws of war. I learn that they mean hanging a brave officer who has held fast in a bad post without cannon against a royal army; that they mean having a prisoner hanged, if the enemy has hanged one of yours; that they mean putting to the fire and the sword villages which have not brought their sustenance on the appointed day, according to the orders of the gracious sovereign of the district. "Good," say I, "that is the 'Spirit of the Laws.' "

It seems to me that most men have received from nature enough common sense to make laws, but that everyone is not just enough to make good laws.

Voltaire, *Philosophical Dictionary:* Laws

63 The first and most important rule of legitimate or popular government, that is to say, of government whose object is the good of the people, is . . . to follow in everything the general will. But to follow this will it is necessary to know it, and above all to distinguish it from the particular will, beginning with one's self: this distinction is always very difficult to make, and only the most sublime virtue can afford sufficient illumination for it. As, in order to will, it is necessary to be free, a difficulty no less great than the former arises—that of preserving at once the public liberty and the authority of government. Look into the motives which have induced men, once united by their common needs in a general society, to unite themselves still more intimately by means of civil societies: you will find no other motive than that of assuring the property, life and liberty of each member by the protection of all. But can men be forced to defend the liberty of any one among them, without trespassing on that of others? And how can they provide for the public needs, without alienating the individual property of those who are forced to contribute to them? With whatever sophistry all this may be covered over, it is certain that if any constraint can be laid on my will, I am no longer free, and that I am no longer master of my own property, if any one else can lay a hand on it. This difficulty, which would have seemed insurmountable, has been removed, like the first, by the most sublime of all human institutions, or rather by a divine inspiration, which teaches mankind to imitate here below the unchangeable decrees of the Deity. By what inconceivable art has a means been found of making men free by making them subject; of using in the service of the State the properties, the persons and even the lives of all its members, without constraining and without consulting them; of confining their will by their own admission; of overcoming their refusal by that consent, and forcing them to punish themselves, when they act against their own will? How can it be that all should obey, yet nobody take upon him to command, and that all should serve, and yet

have no masters, but be the more free, as, in apparent subjection, each loses no part of his liberty but what might be hurtful to that of another? These wonders are the work of law. It is to law alone that men owe justice and liberty. It is this salutary organ of the will of all which establishes, in civil right, the natural equality between men. It is this celestial voice which dictates to each citizen the precepts of public reason, and teaches him to act according to the rules of his own judgment, and not to behave inconsistently with himself. It is with this voice alone that political rulers should speak when they command; for no sooner does one man, setting aside the law, claim to subject another to his private will, than he departs from the state of civil society, and confronts him face to face in the pure state of nature, in which obedience is prescribed solely by necessity.

Rousseau, *Political Economy*

64 I mean to inquire if, in the civil order, there can be any sure and legitimate rule of administration, men being taken as they are and laws as they might be.

Rousseau, *Social Contract,* I, Introduction

65 If there is, in each State, only one good system, the people that is in possession of it should hold fast to this; but if the established order is bad, why should laws that prevent men from being good be regarded as fundamental? Besides, in any case, a people is always in a position to change its laws, however good; for, if it choose to do itself harm, who can have a right to stop it?

Rousseau, *Social Contract,* II, 12

66 Why . . . is so much respect paid to old laws? For this very reason. We must believe that nothing but the excellence of old acts of will can have preserved them so long: if the Sovereign had not recognised them as throughout salutary, it would have revoked them a thousand times. This is why, so far from growing weak, the laws continually gain new strength in any well constituted State; the precedent of antiquity makes them daily more venerable: while wherever the laws grow weak as they become old, this proves that there is no longer a legislative power, and that the State is dead.

Rousseau, *Social Contract,* III, 11

67 A lawyer has no business with the justice or injustice of the cause which he undertakes unless his client asks his opinion, and then he is bound to give it honestly. The justice or injustice of the cause is to be decided by the judge.

Johnson, *Tour of the Western Islands of Scotland (Aug. 15, 1773)*

68 *Johnson.* It is sufficient for our purpose that every just law is dictated by reason; and that the practice of every legal Court is regulated by equity. It

is the quality of reason to be invariable and constant; and of equity, to give to one man what, in the same case, is given to another. The advantage which humanity derives from law is this: that the law gives every man a rule of action, and prescribes a mode of conduct which shall entitle him to the support and protection of society. That the law may be a rule of action, it is necessary that it be known; it is necessary that it be permanent and stable. The law is the measure of civil right; but if the measure be changeable, the extent of the thing measured never can be settled.

Boswell, *Life of Johnson (1772)*

69 The laws of a nation form the most instructive portion of its history.

Gibbon, *Decline and Fall
of the Roman Empire*, XLIV

70 People, crushed by law, have no hopes but from power. If laws are their enemies, they will be enemies to laws; and those who have much to hope and nothing to lose, will always be dangerous, more or less.

Burke, *Letter to Charles James Fox
(Oct. 8, 1777)*

71 Bad laws are the worst sort of tyranny.

Burke, *Speech at Bristol (1780)*

72 In the making of a new law it is undoubtedly the duty of the legislator to see that no injustice be done even to an individual: for there is then nothing to be unsettled, and the matter is under his hands to mould it as he pleases; and if he finds it untractable in the working, he may abandon it without incurring any new inconvenience. But in the question concerning the repeal of an old one, the work is of more difficulty; because laws, like houses, lean on one another, and the operation is delicate, and should be necessary: the objection, in such a case, ought not to arise from the natural infirmity of human institutions, but from substantial faults which contradict the nature and end of law itself,—faults not arising from the imperfection, but from the misapplication and abuse of our reason.

Burke, *Tract on the Popery Laws*, I, 3

73 The general object which all laws have, or ought to have, in common, is to augment the total happiness of the community; and therefore, in the first place, to exclude, as far as may be, every thing that tends to subtract from that happiness: in other words, to exclude mischief.

Bentham, *Principles of Morals
and Legislation*, XIII, 1

74 Laws are a dead letter without courts to expound and define their true meaning and operation.

Hamilton, *Federalist 22*

75 Nations pay little regard to rules and maxims calculated in their very nature to run counter to the necessities of society. Wise politicians will be cautious about fettering the government with restrictions that cannot be observed, because they know that every breach of the fundamental laws, though dictated by necessity, impairs that sacred reverence which ought to be maintained in the breast of rulers towards the constitution of a country, and forms a precedent for other breaches where the same plea of necessity does not exist at all, or is less urgent and palpable.

Hamilton, *Federalist 25*

76 It will be of little avail to the people that the laws are made by men of their own choice, if the laws be so voluminous that they cannot be read, or so incoherent that they cannot be understood; if they be repealed or revised before they are promulgated, or undergo such incessant changes that no man, who knows what the law is to-day, can guess what it will be to-morrow. Law is defined to be a rule of action; but how can that be a rule which is little known and less fixed?

Hamilton or Madison, *Federalist 62*

77 One Law for the Lion and Ox is Oppression.

Blake, *Marriage of Heaven and Hell*, 24

78 The hatred of law, of right made determinate in law, is the shibboleth whereby fanaticism, flabby-mindedness, and the hypocrisy of good intentions are clearly and infallibly recognized for what they are, disguise themselves as they may.

Hegel, *Philosophy of Right*, 258, fn.

79 Laws are of two kinds—laws of nature and laws of the land. The laws of nature simply are what they are and are valid as they are; they are not liable to encroachment, though in certain cases man may transgress them. To know the law of nature, we must learn to know nature, since its laws are rigid and it is only our ideas about them that can be false. The measure of these laws is outside us; knowing them adds nothing to them and does not assist their operation; our knowledge of them can expand, that is all. Knowledge of the laws of the land is in one way similar, but in another way not. These laws too we learn to know just as they exist; the citizen's knowledge of them is more or less of this sort, and the student of positive law equally stops at what is given. But the difference in the case of laws of the land is that they arouse the spirit of reflection, and their diversity at once draws attention to the fact that they are not absolute. Positive laws are something posited, something originated by men. Between what is so originated and man's inner voice there may be an inevitable clash or there may be agreement. Man does not stop short at the existent, but claims to have in himself the measure of what is right. He

may be subjected to the compulsion and dominion of an external authority, though never as he is to the compulsion of nature, because his inner self always tells him how things ought to be and he finds within himself the confirmation or denial of what passes as valid. In nature, the highest truth is that there is a *law*; in the law of the land, the thing is not valid simply because it exists; on the contrary, everyone demands that it shall comply with his private criterion. Here then an antagonism is possible between what ought to be and what is, between the absolutely right which stands unaltered and the arbitrary determination of what is to be recognized as right. A schism and a conflict of this sort is to be found only in the territory of mind, and because mind's privilege seems therefore to lead to discontent and unhappiness, men are often thrown back from the arbitrariness of life to the contemplation of nature and set themselves to take nature as an example. But it is precisely in these clashes between what is absolutely right and what arbitrariness makes pass as right that there lies the need for studying the fundamentals of right. In the right, man must meet with his own reason; consequently, he must consider the rationality of the right, and this is the task of our science in contrast with the positive study of law which often has to do only with contradictions.

Hegel, *Philosophy of Right*, Additions, Preface

80 The law is only a memorandum. We are superstitious, and esteem the statute somewhat: so much life as it has in the character of living men is its force. The statute stands there to say, Yesterday we agreed so and so, but how feel ye this article to-day? Our statute is a currency which we stamp with our own portrait: it soon becomes unrecognizable, and in process of time will return to the mint.

Emerson, *Politics*

81 Good men must not obey the laws too well.

Emerson, *Politics*

82 The less government we have the better—the fewer laws, and the less confided power.

Emerson, *Politics*

83 *Mr. Brownlow.* "You were present on the occasion of the destruction of these trinkets, and indeed are the more guilty of the two, in the eye of the law; for the law supposes that your wife acts under your direction."

"If the law supposes that," said Mr. Bumble, squeezing his hat emphatically in both hands, "the law is a ass—a idiot."

Dickens, *Oliver Twist*, LI

84 Law never made men a whit more just; and, by means of their respect for it, even the well-disposed are daily made the agents of injustice.

Thoreau, *Civil Disobedience*

85 Unjust laws exist: shall we be content to obey them, or shall we endeavor to amend them, and obey them until we have succeeded, or shall we transgress them at once? Men generally, under such a government as this, think that they ought to wait until they have persuaded the majority to alter them. They think that, if they should resist, the remedy would be worse than the evil. But it is the fault of the government itself that the remedy *is* worse than the evil.

Thoreau, *Civil Disobedience*

86 The laws of most countries are far worse than the people who execute them, and many of them are only able to remain laws by being seldom or never carried into effect.

Mill, *Subjection of Women*, II

87 Laws never would be improved, if there were not numerous persons whose moral sentiments are better than the existing laws.

Mill, *Subjection of Women*, II

12.2 | *Justice and Injustice*

Justice is traditionally classified as one of the four cardinal virtues, along with temperance, fortitude, and prudence; and it is usually distinguished from the others as being the virtue whereby a man is disposed to act rightly or righteously in relation to other men or to the community in which he lives. A man of goodwill toward others, a man who habitually avoids injuring others and renders to others what is their due, is said to be a just man. Justice in this sense—as a moral quality or an aspect of moral character—is discussed in Chapter 9 on ETHICS, Section 9.7 on RIGHT AND WRONG, as well as here. The reader is advised to read that section in conjunction with this one for a comprehensive view of justice as an attribute of the morally good man and as a property of conduct that is rightful or righteous. The reader should also examine relevant passages in Section 9.10 on VIRTUE AND VICE. The treatment of injustice and wrongdoing is, of course, to be found in the same contexts.

There is another application of the terms "justice" and "injustice"—to human institutions and arrangements, to states, constitutions, laws, social practices, and economic systems or transactions. It is this application that gives rise to the discussion of political or legal justice, social justice, and economic justice. Justice in these various senses is mainly treated here and not in Chapter 9 on ETHICS; however, closely related and even overlapping matters will be found in Section 12.1 on LAW AND LAWYERS, in Section 13.3 on EQUALITY, in Section 11.1 on PROPERTY, and in many of the sections of Chapter 10 on POLITICS, especially Sections 10.4, 10.6, 10.7, and 10.9.

The passages collected here offer diverse definitions of justice, distinguish between distributive and commutative or remedial justice, deal with the issues of right vs. might and of justice vs. expediency, discuss the relation of justice to equity, argue for and against the proposition that human society cannot long endure without justice, and attempt to answer the question whether it is preferable to do or to suffer injustice.

Considerations of justice are to be found in other sections of this chapter: not only in Section 12.1 on LAW AND LAWYERS, but also in Section 12.3 on RIGHTS—NATURAL AND CIVIL, and in Section 12.4 on CRIME AND PUNISHMENT. The discussion of human rights and the discussion of justice are so integrally related that the reader would do well to make his own synthesis of the quotations dealing with these two subjects.

---

1 If a man destroy the eye of another man, they shall destroy his eye.

Hammurabi, *Code of Hammurabi,* 196

2 And if any mischief follow, than thou shalt give life for life,

Eye for eye, tooth for tooth, hand for hand, foot for foot,

Burning for burning, wound for wound, stripe for stripe.

Exodus 21:23–25

3 *Chorus.* It has been made long since and grown old among men,
this saying: human wealth
grown to fulness of stature
breeds again nor dies without issue.
From high good fortune in the blood
blossoms the quenchless agony.
Far from others I hold my own
mind; only the act of evil
breeds others to follow,
young sins in its own likeness.

Houses clear in their right are given
children in all loveliness.

But Crime aging is made
in men's dark actions
ripe with the young pride
late or soon when the dawn of destiny
comes and birth is given
to the spirit none may fight nor beat down,
sinful Daring; and in those halls
the black visaged Disasters stamped
in the likeness of their fathers.

And Righteousness is a shining in
the smoke of mean houses.
Her blessing is on the just man.
From high halls starred with gold by reeking
    hands
she turns back
with eyes that glance away to the simple in heart,
spurning the strength of gold
stamped false with flattery.
And all things she steers to fulfilment.

Aeschylus, *Agamemnon,* 750

4 *Protagoras.* Hermes asked Zeus how he should impart justice and reverence among men:—Should
he distribute them as the arts are distributed; that
is to say, to a favoured few only, one skilled individual having enough of medicine or of any other
art for many unskilled ones? "Shall this be the
manner in which I am to distribute justice and
reverence among men, or shall I give them to
all?" "To all," said Zeus; "I should like them all
to have a share; for cities cannot exist, if a few
only share in the virtues, as in the arts. And further, make a law by my order, that he who has no
part in reverence and justice shall be put to death,
for he is a plague of the state."

Plato, *Protagoras,* 322B

5 *Socrates.* Not only custom but nature also affirms
that to do is more disgraceful than to suffer injustice, and that justice is equality.

Plato, *Gorgias,* 489A

6 *Socrates.* Tell me then, O thou heir of the argument, what did Simonides say, and according to
you truly say, about justice?

Polemarchus. He said that the repayment of a
debt is just, and in saying so he appears to me to
be right.

I should be sorry to doubt the word of such a
wise and inspired man, but his meaning, though
probably clear to you, is the reverse of clear to me.
For he certainly does not mean, as we were just
now saying, that I ought to return a deposit of
arms or of anything else to one who asks for it
when he is not in his right senses; and yet a deposit cannot be denied to be a debt.

True.

Then when the person who asks me is not in his

right mind I am by no means to make the return?

Certainly not.

When Simonides said that the repayment of a
debt was justice, he did not mean to include that
case?

Certainly not; for he thinks that a friend ought
always to do good to a friend and never evil.

You mean that the return of a deposit of gold
which is to the injury of the receiver, if the two
parties are friends, is not the repayment of a
debt—that is what you would imagine him to say?

Yes.

And are enemies also to receive what we owe to
them?

To be sure, he said, they are to receive what we
owe them, and an enemy, as I take it, owes to an
enemy that which is due and proper to him—that
is to say, evil.

Simonides, then, after the manner of poets,
would seem to have spoken darkly of the nature of
justice; for he really meant to say that justice is
the giving to each man what is proper to him, and
this he termed a debt.

Plato, *Republic,* I, 331B

7 *Socrates.* Thrasymachus, as any one might see, was
in reality eager to speak; for he thought that he
had an excellent answer, and would distinguish
himself. But at first he affected to insist on my
answering; at length he consented to begin. Behold, he said, the wisdom of Socrates; he refuses to
teach himself, and goes about learning of others,
to whom he never even says Thank you.

That I learn of others, I replied, is quite true;
but that I am ungrateful I wholly deny. Money I
have none, and therefore I pay in praise, which is
all I have; and how ready I am to praise any one
who appears to me to speak well you will very
soon find out when you answer; for I expect that
you will answer well.

Listen, then, he said; I proclaim that justice is
nothing else than the interest of the stronger. And
now why do you not praise me? But of course you
won't.

Let me first understand you, I replied. Justice,
as you say, is the interest of the stronger. What,
Thrasymachus, is the meaning of this? You cannot mean to say that because Polydamas, the pancratiast, is stronger than we are, and finds the eating of beef conducive to his bodily strength, that
to eat beef is therefore equally for our good who
are weaker than he is, and right and just for us?

That's abominable of you, Socrates; you take
the words in the sense which is most damaging to
the argument.

Not at all, my good sir, I said; I am trying to
understand them; and I wish that you would be a
little clearer.

Well, he said, have you never heard that forms
of government differ; there are tyrannies, and
there are democracies, and there are aristocracies?

Yes, I know.

And the government is the ruling power in each state?

Certainly.

And the different forms of government make laws democratical, aristocratical, tyrannical, with a view to their several interests; and these laws, which are made by them for their own interests, are the justice which they deliver to their subjects, and him who transgresses them they punish as a breaker of the law, and unjust. And that is what I mean when I say that in all states there is the same principle of justice, which is the interest of the government; and as the government must be supposed to have power, the only reasonable conclusion is, that everywhere there is one principle of justice, which is the interest of the stronger.

Plato, *Republic,* I, 338A

8 *Thrasymachus.* The just is always a loser in comparison with the unjust. First of all, in private contracts: wherever the unjust is the partner of the just you will find that, when the partnership is dissolved, the unjust man has always more and the just less. Secondly, in their dealings with the State: when there is an income-tax, the just man will pay more and the unjust less on the same amount of income; and when there is anything to be received the one gains nothing and the other much. Observe also what happens when they take an office; there is the just man neglecting his affairs and perhaps suffering other losses, and getting nothing out of the public, because he is just; moreover he is hated by his friends and acquaintance for refusing to serve them in unlawful ways. But all this is reversed in the case of the unjust man.

Plato, *Republic,* I, 343B

9 *Socrates.* We have already shown that the just are clearly wiser and better and abler than the unjust, and that the unjust are incapable of common action; nay more, that the unjust are incapable of common action; nay more, that to speak as we did of men who are evil acting at any time vigorously together, is not strictly true, for if they had been perfectly evil, they would have laid hands upon one another; but it is evident that there must have been some remnant of justice in them, which enabled them to combine; if there had not been they would have injured one another as well as their victims; they were but half-villains in their enterprises; for had they been whole villains, and utterly unjust, they would have been utterly incapable of action.

Plato, *Republic,* I, 352A

10 *Socrates.* Why, my good sir, at the beginning of our enquiry, ages ago, there was justice tumbling out at our feet, and we never saw her; nothing could be more ridiculous. Like people who go about looking for what they have in their hands—that was the way with us—we looked not at what we were seeking, but at what was far off in the distance; and therefore, I suppose, we missed her.

Glaucon. What do you mean?

I mean to say that in reality for a long time past we have been talking of justice, and have failed to recognise her.

I grow impatient at the length of your exordium.

Well then, tell me, I said, whether I am right or not: You remember the original principle which we were always laying down at the foundation of the State, that one man should practise one thing only, the thing to which his nature was best adapted—now justice is this principle or a part of it.

Yes, we often said that one man should do one thing only.

Further, we affirmed that justice was doing one's own business, and not being a busybody; we said so again and again, and many others have said the same to us.

Yes, we said so.

Then to do one's own business in a certain way may be assumed to be justice. Can you tell me whence I derive this inference?

I cannot, but I should like to be told.

Because I think that this is the only virtue which remains in the State when the other virtues of temperance and courage and wisdom are abstracted; and, that this is the ultimate cause and condition of the existence of all of them, and while remaining in them is also their preservative; and we were saying that if the three were discovered by us, justice would be the fourth or remaining one.

That follows of necessity.

If we are asked to determine which of these four qualities by its presence contributes most to the excellence of the State, whether the agreement of rulers and subjects, or the preservation in the soldiers of the opinion which the law ordains about the true nature of dangers, or wisdom and watchfulness in the rulers, or whether this other which I am mentioning, and which is found in children and women, slave and freeman, artisan, ruler, subject—the quality, I mean, of every one doing his own work, and not being a busybody, would claim the palm—the question is not so easily answered.

Certainly, he replied, there would be a difficulty in saying which.

Then the power of each individual in the State to do his own work appears to compete with the other political virtues, wisdom, temperance, courage.

Yes, he said.

And the virtue which enters into this competition is justice?

Exactly.

Let us look at the question from another point

of view: Are not the rulers in a State those to whom you would entrust the office of determining suits at law?

Certainly.

And are suits decided on any other ground but that a man may neither take what is another's, nor be deprived of what is his own?

Yes; that is their principle.

Which is a just principle?

Yes.

Then on this view also justice will be admitted to be the having and doing what is a man's own, and belongs to him?

Very true.

Think, now, and say whether you agree with me or not. Suppose a carpenter to be doing the business of a cobbler, or a cobbler of a carpenter; and suppose them to exchange their implements or their duties, or the same person to be doing the work of both, or whatever be the change; do you think that any great harm would result to the State?

Not much.

But when the cobbler or any other man whom nature designed to be a trader, having his heart lifted up by wealth or strength or the number of his followers, or any like advantage, attempts to force his way into the class of warriors, or a warrior into that of legislators and guardians, for which he is unfitted, and either to take the implements or the duties of the other; or when one man is trader, legislator, and warrior all in one, then I think you will agree with me in saying that this interchange and this meddling of one with another is the ruin of the State.

Most true.

Seeing then, I said, that there are three distinct classes, any meddling of one with another, or the change of one into another, is the greatest harm to the State, and may be most justly termed evil-doing?

Precisely.

And the greatest degree of evil-doing to one's own city would be termed by you injustice?

Certainly.

This then is injustice; and on the other hand when the trader, the auxiliary, and the guardian each do their own business, that is justice, and will make the city just.

I agree with you.

Plato, *Republic,* IV, 432B

11 This . . . is what the just is—the proportional; the unjust is what violates the proportion. Hence one term becomes too great, the other too small, as indeed happens in practice; for the man who acts unjustly has too much, and the man who is unjustly treated too little, of what is good. In the case of evil the reverse is true; for the lesser evil is reckoned a good in comparison with the greater evil, since the lesser evil is rather to be chosen than the greater, and what is worthy of choice is good, and what is worthier of choice a greater good.

This, then, is one species of the just.

Aristotle, *Ethics,* 1131ᵇ17

12 The justice of a master and that of a father are not the same as the justice of citizens, though they are like it; for there can be no injustice in the unqualified sense towards things that are one's own, but a man's chattel, and his child until it reaches a certain age and sets up for itself, are as it were part of himself, and no one chooses to hurt himself (for which reason there can be no injustice towards oneself). Therefore the justice or injustice of citizens is not manifested in these relations.

Aristotle, *Ethics,* 1134ᵇ8

13 When men are friends they have no need of justice, while when they are just they need friendship as well, and the truest form of justice is thought to be a friendly quality.

Aristotle, *Ethics,* 1155ª26

14 Justice is the bond of men in states, for the administration of justice, which is the determination of what is just, is the principle of order in political society.

Aristotle, *Politics,* 1253ª36

15 In all sciences and arts the end is a good, and the greatest good and in the highest degree a good in the most authoritative of all—this is the political science of which the good is justice, in other words, the common interest.

Aristotle, *Politics,* 1282ᵇ15

16 Justice is a contract of expediency, entered upon to prevent men harming or being harmed.

Epicurus, *Aphorisms*

17 There is no more ridiculous opinion than to believe that all customs and laws of nations are inherently just. Would one think such a thing of the decrees of dictators? Had the notorious Thirty Tyrants decided to enact a code of laws for Athens, or if all the citizens of Athens were happy with the tyrants' laws, would such a circumstance indicate that those laws were just? It would hardly be considered a just law if some Roman regent had decreed that any dictator could be put to death with impunity by any citizen, without even going to trial. Justice is integral. It binds society together and is based on the one law of right reason applied to commands and prohibitions. Whoever is not acquainted with this law, whether it has been put in writing or not, does not know justice.

If, as some people insist, justice is nothing more than a conformity to written laws and national traditions, and if everything is based on a standard of expediency, then anyone who sees something in it for himself will go ahead and break the law. If this were our point of view, we could only conclude that there is no justice. For if it does not exist in nature, and if simple expediency can overthrow it, there is no justice. If nature is not based on justice, then are the principles on which society is founded destroyed. What would be the use of generosity, patriotism, loyalty, of service to each other and gratitude for favors done? Such virtues have their origin in our natural propensity to love our fellow human beings. This is the foundation of justice. If this is not true, then the consideration we show to each other, as well as our religious rites and piety towards the gods, are swept away. But such rites ought to be kept, and not out of fear, but out of the close relationship between man and God.

Were the basis of justice in the decrees of the people, the rulings of kings, or in decisions of judges, then justice would permit theft, adultery, even forgery of wills, if a majority of the populace voted for them. But if such a power resides in the decisions and decrees of fools who are sure natural law can be altered by votes, then why do they not decide that what is bad and harmful shall be considered good and worthwhile?

In fact, we can tell the difference between good and bad laws only on the basis of nature. Nature not only distinguishes between the just and the unjust, but also between what is honorable and dishonorable. Since our common sense helps us to understand and conceptualize things, we do ascribe honorable actions to virtue and dishonorable ones to vice. Only a lunatic would assert that these judgments of ours are merely opinions and not based on natural law. Even when we mistakenly call the "virtue" of a tree or of a horse is not just a matter of opinion, but is based on nature. If that is true, then good and bad actions can also be distinguished according to nature. If the concept of virtue is to be tested by opinion, then specific virtues must also be tested. Who would judge a man of prudence and common sense by some external state and not by his character? Virtue is fully matured reason. Since this is natural, then everything honorable is also natural.

Cicero, *Laws,* I, 15–16

18 We are confronted with three choices: to do injustice but not to suffer it; both to do it and to suffer it; or neither to do it nor to suffer it. The most fortuitous choice is to do it with impunity. The second best alternative would be neither to do it nor to suffer it. The worst choice is to have to live one's life in a perpetual struggle between doing and suffering injustice.

Cicero, *Republic,* III, 13

19 Ye have heard that it hath been said, An eye for an eye, and a tooth for a tooth:

But I say unto you, That ye resist not evil: but whosoever shall smite thee on thy right cheek, turn to him the other also.

And if any man will sue thee at the law, and take away thy coat, let him have thy cloke also.

And whosoever shall compel thee to go a mile, go with him twain.

Give to him that asketh thee, and from him that would borrow of thee turn not thou away.

Ye have heard that it hath been said, Thou shalt love thy neighbour, and hate thine enemy.

But I say unto you, Love your enemies, bless them that curse you, do good to them that hate you, and pray for them which despitefully use you, and persecute you;

That ye may be the children of your Father which is in heaven: for he maketh his sun to rise on the evil and on the good, and sendeth rain on the just and on the unjust.

Matthew 5:38–45

20 Be ye therefore merciful, as your Father also is merciful.

Judge not, and ye shall not be judged: condemn not, and ye shall not be condemned: forgive, and ye shall be forgiven:

Give, and it shall be given unto you; good measure, pressed down, and shaken together, and running over, shall men give into your bosom. For with the same measure that ye mete withal it shall be measured to you again.

Luke 6:36–38

21 Justice is unstable and changeable? No, but the times over which justice presides are not alike, for they are times.

Augustine, *Confessions,* III, 7

22 Justice being taken away, then what are kingdoms but great robberies? For what are robberies themselves, but little kingdoms? The band itself is made up of men; it is ruled by the authority of a prince, it is knit together by the pact of the confederacy; the booty is divided by the law agreed on. If, by the admittance of abandoned men, this evil increases to such a degree that it holds places, fixes abodes, takes possession of cities, and subdues peoples, it assumes the more plainly the name of a kingdom, because the reality is now manifestly conferred on it, not by the removal of covetousness, but by the addition of impunity. Indeed, that was an apt and true reply which was given to Alexander the Great by a pirate who had been seized. For when that king had asked the man what he meant by keeping hostile possession of the sea, he answered with bold pride, "What thou meanest by seizing the whole earth; but because I do it with a petty ship, I am called a robber, whilst thou who dost it with a great fleet art styled emperor."

Augustine, *City of God,* IV, 4

23 There are two kinds of justice. The one consists in mutual giving and receiving, as in buying and selling, and other kinds of intercourse and exchange. This the Philosopher [Aristotle] calls commutative justice, that directs exchange and the intercourse of business. This does not belong to God, since, as the Apostle says: *Who hath first given to Him, and recompense shall be made him?* The other consists in distribution, and is called distributive justice, whereby a ruler or a steward gives to each what his rank deserves. As then the proper order displayed in ruling a family or any kind of multitude evinces justice of this kind in the ruler, so the order of the universe, which is seen both in things of nature and in things of will, shows forth the justice of God. Hence Dionysius says: "We must see that God is truly just, in seeing how He gives to all existing things what is proper to the condition of each, and preserves the nature of each one in the order and with the powers that properly belong to it."

Aquinas, *Summa Theologica*, I, 21, 1

24 The matter of justice is an external operation, in so far as either it or the thing we use by it is made proportionate to some other person to whom we are related by justice. Now each man's own is that which is due to him according to equality of proportion. Therefore the proper act of justice is nothing else than to render to each one his own.

Aquinas, *Summa Theologica*, II–II, 58, 11

25 Retaliation (*contrapassum*) denotes equal passion repaid for previous action; and the expression applies most properly to injurious passions and actions, whereby a man harms the person of his neighbor; for instance if a man strike, that he be struck back. This kind of just is laid down in the Law: *He shall render life for life, eye for eye*, etc. And since also to take away what belongs to another is to do an unjust thing, it follows that secondly retaliation consists in this also, that whosoever causes loss to another, should suffer loss in his belongings. This just loss is also found in the Law: *If any man steal an ox or a sheep, and kill or sell it, he shall restore five oxen for one ox and four sheep for one sheep.* Thirdly retaliation is transferred to voluntary commutations, where action and passion are on both sides, although voluntariness detracts from the nature of passion.

In all these cases, however, repayment must be made on a basis of equality according to the requirements of commutative justice, namely that the meed of passion be equal to the action. Now there would not always be equality if passion were in the same species as the action. Because, in the first place, when a person injures the person of one who is greater, the action surpasses any passion of the same species that he might undergo, wherefore he that strikes a prince, is not only struck back, but is much more severely punished.

In like manner when a man despoils another of his property against the latter's will, the action surpasses the passion if he be merely deprived of that thing, because the man who caused another's loss, himself would lose nothing, and so he is punished by making restitution several times over, because not only did he injure a private individual, but also the common weal, the security of whose protection he has infringed. Nor again would there be equality of passion in voluntary commutations, were one always to exchange one's chattel for another man's, because it might happen that the other man's chattel is much greater than our own: so that it becomes necessary to equalize passion and action in commutations according to a certain proportionate commensuration, for which purpose money was invented. Hence retaliation is in accordance with commutative justice: but there is no place for it in distributive justice, because in distributive justice we do not consider the equality between thing and thing or between passion and action (whence the expression *contrapassum*), but according to proportion between things and persons.

Aquinas, *Summa Theologica*, II–II, 61, 4

26 It is acting a most perverse part, to set up the measure of human justice as the standard by which to measure the justice of God.

Calvin, *Institutes of the Christian Religion*, III, 24

27 Since the ethical laws, which concern the individual duty of each man in himself, are so hard to frame, as we see they are, it is no wonder if those that govern so many individuals are more so. Consider the form of this justice that governs us: it is a true testimony of human imbecility, so full it is of contradiction and error. What we find to be leniency and severity in justice—and we find so much of them that I do not know whether the mean between them is met with as often—are sickly parts and unjust members of the very body and essence of justice.

Montaigne, *Essays*, III, 13, Of Experience

28 *Polonius.* My lord, I will use them according to their desert.
   Hamlet. God's bodykins, man, much better. Use every man after his desert, and who should 'scape whipping? Use them after your own honour and dignity; the less they deserve, the more merit is in your bounty.

Shakespeare, *Hamlet*, II, ii, 552

29 *Lear.* What, art mad? A man may see how this world goes with no eyes. Look with thine ears: see how yond justice rails upon yond simple thief. Hark, in thine ear: change places; and, handy-dandy, which is the justice, which is the thief?

Shakespeare, *Lear*, IV, vi, 153

30 *Edgar.*   Let's exchange charity.
I am no less in blood than thou art, Edmund;
If more, the more thou hast wrong'd me.
My name is Edgar, and thy father's son.
The gods are just, and of our pleasant vices
Make instruments to plague us.
The dark and vicious place where thee he got
Cost him his eyes.
    Edmund.   Thou hast spoken right, 'tis true;
The wheel is come full circle; I am here.

                Shakespeare, *Lear*, V, iii, 166

31 While they sat refreshing themselves, a young
Lad, travelling that way, observ'd them, and,
looking earnestly on the whole Company, ran
suddenly and fell down before Don *Quixote*, addressing him in a very doleful Manner. Alas, good
Sir, said he, don't you know me? don't you remember poor *Andrew* whom you caus'd to be
unty'd from the Tree? With that the Knight knew
him; and raising him up, turn'd to the Company,
That you may all know, said he, of how great
Importance, to the redressing of Injuries, punishing Vice, and the universal Benefit of Mankind,
the Business of Knight-Errantry may be, you
must understand, that riding through a Desart
some Days ago, I heard certain lamentable
Screeks and Out-cries: Prompted by the Misery of
the Afflicted, and borne away by the Zeal of my
Profession I follow'd the Voice, and found this
Boy, whom you all see, bound to a great Oak; I'm
glad he's present, because he can attest the Truth
of my Relation. I found him as I told you, bound
to an Oak, naked from the Waste upwards, and a
bloody-minded Peasant scourging his Back un-
mercifully with the Reins of a Bridle. I presently
demanded the Cause of his severe Chastisement?
The rude Fellow answer'd, that he had Liberty to
punish his own Servant, whom he thus us'd for
some Faults that argu'd him more Knave than
Fool. Good Sir, said the Boy, he can lay nothing
to my Charge, but demanding my Wages. His
Master made some Reply, which I would not allow as a just Excuse, and order'd him immediately to unbind the Youth, and took his Oath that
he would take him home and pay him all his
Wages upon the Nail, in good and lawful Coin. Is
not this literally true, *Andrew*? Did you not mark
besides, with what Face of Authority I commanded, and with how much Humility he promis'd to
obey all I impos'd, commanded and desir'd? Answer me, Boy, and tell boldly all that pass'd of this
worthy Company, that it may appear how necessary the Vocation of Knights-Errant is up and
down the high Roads.

    All you have said is true enough, answer'd *An-
drew*, but the Business did not end after that Manner you and I hop'd it would. How? said the
Knight, has not the Peasant paid you? Ay, he
has paid me with a Vengeance, said the Boy, for
no sooner was your Back turn'd, but he ty'd

me again to the same Tree, and lash'd me so
cursedly, that I look'd like St *Bartholomew* flea'd
alive; and at every Blow he had some Joke or
another to laugh at you; and had he not laid me
on as he did, I fancy I could not have help'd
laughing myself. At last he left me in so pitiful
Case, that I was forc'd to crawl to an Hospital,
where I have lain ever since to get cur'd, so woful-
ly the Tyrant had lash'd me. And now I may
thank You for this, for had you rid on your Journey, and neither meddl'd nor made, seeing no
Body sent for you, and 'twas none of your Business, my Master, perhaps, had been satisfy'd with
giving me ten or twenty Lashes, and after that
would have paid me what he ow'd me; but you
was so huffy, and call'd him so many Names, that
it made him mad, and so he vented all his Spite
against You upon My poor Back, as soon as yours
was turn'd, insomuch that I fear I shall never be
my own Man again. The Miscarriage, answer'd
the Knight, is only chargeable on my Departure
before I saw my Orders executed; for I might, by
Experience, have remembered, that the Word of a
Peasant is regulated, not by Honour, but Profit.

             Cervantes, *Don Quixote*, I, 31

32 Revenge is a kind of wild justice; which the more
man's nature runs to, the more ought law to weed
it out.

                  Bacon, *Of Revenge*

33 From that law of nature by which we are obliged
to transfer to another such rights as, being retained, hinder the peace of mankind, there followeth a third; which is this: *that men perform their covenants made;* without which covenants are in vain,
and but empty words; and the right of all men to
all things remaining, we are still in the condition
of war.

    And in this law of nature consisteth the foun-
tain and original of *justice*. For where no covenant
hath preceded, there hath no right been transferred, and every man has right to everything;
and consequently, no action can be unjust. But
when a covenant is made, then to break it is *unjust:*
and the definition of *injustice* is no other than *the
not performance of covenant.* And whatsoever is not
unjust is just.

             Hobbes, *Leviathan*, I, 15

34 Before the names of *just* and *unjust* can have place,
there must be some coercive power to compel men
equally to the performance of their covenants, by
the terror of some punishment greater than the
benefit they expect by the breach of their covenant, and to make good that propriety which by
mutual contract men acquire in recompense of
the universal right they abandon: and such power
there is none before the erection of a Commonwealth. And this is also to be gathered out of the

ordinary definition of justice in the Schools, for they say that *justice is the constant will of giving to every man his own*. And therefore when there is no *own*, that is, no propriety, there is no injustice; and where there is no coercive power erected, that is, where there is no Commonwealth, there is no propriety, all men having right to all things: therefore where there is no Commonwealth, there nothing is unjust. So that the nature of justice consisteth in keeping of valid covenants, but the validity of covenants begins not but with the constitution of a civil power sufficient to compel men to keep them.

Hobbes, *Leviathan*, I, 15

35 On what shall man found the order of the world which he would govern? Shall it be on the caprice of each individual? What confusion! Shall it be on justice? Man is ignorant of it.

Certainly, had he known it, he would not have established this maxim, the most general of all that obtain among men, that each should follow the custom of his own country. The glory of true equity would have brought all nations under subjection, and legislators would not have taken as their model the fancies and caprice of Persians and Germans instead of this unchanging justice. We would have seen it set up in all the States on earth and in all times; whereas we see neither justice nor injustice which does not change its nature with change in climate. Three degrees of latitude reverse all jurisprudence; a meridian decides the truth. Fundamental laws change after a few years of possession; right has its epochs; the entry of Saturn into the Lion marks to us the origin of such and such a crime. A strange justice that is bounded by a river! Truth on this side of the Pyrenees, error on the other side.

Pascal, *Pensées*, V, 294

36 It is right that what is just should be obeyed; it is necessary that what is strongest should be obeyed. Justice without might is helpless; might without justice is tyrannical. Justice without might is gainsaid, because there are always offenders; might without justice is condemned. We must then combine justice and might and, for this end, make what is just strong, or what is strong just.

Justice is subject to dispute; might is easily recognised and is not disputed. So we cannot give might to justice, because might has gainsaid justice and has declared that it is she herself who is just. And thus, being unable to make what is just strong, we have made what is strong just.

Pascal, *Pensées*, V, 298

37 No doubt equality of goods is just; but, being unable to cause might to obey justice, men have made it just to obey might. Unable to strengthen justice, they have justified might; so that the just

and the strong should unite, and there should be peace, which is the sovereign good.

Pascal, *Pensées*, V, 299

38 It is dangerous to tell the people that the laws are unjust; for they obey them only because they think them just. Therefore it is necessary to tell them at the same time that they must obey them because they are laws, just as they must obey superiors, not because they are just, but because they are superiors. In this way all sedition is prevented, if this can be made intelligible and it be understood what is the proper definition of justice.

Pascal, *Pensées*, V, 326

39 I have passed a great part of my life believing that there was justice, and in this I was not mistaken; for there is justice according as God has willed to reveal it to us. But I did not take it so, and this is where I made a mistake; for I believed that our justice was essentially just, and that I had that whereby to know and judge of it. But I have so often found my right judgement at fault, that at last I have come to distrust myself and then others. I have seen changes in all nations and men, and thus, after many changes of judgement regarding true justice, I have recognised that our nature was but in continual change, and I have not changed since; and if I changed, I would confirm my opinion.

Pascal, *Pensées*, VI, 375

40 I had another reason which made me less forward to enlarge his Majesty's dominions by my discoveries: to say the truth, I had conceived a few scruples with relation to the distributive justice of princes upon those occasions. For instance, a crew of pyrates are driven by a storm they know not whither; at length a boy discovers land from the top-mast; they go on shoar to rob and plunder; they see an harmless people, are entertained with kindness, they give the country a new name, they take formal possession of it for the king, they set up a rotten plank or a stone for a memorial, they murder two or three dozen of the natives, bring away a couple more by force for a sample, return home, and get their pardon. Here commenceth a new dominion acquired with a title by *divine right*. Ships are sent with the first opportunity; the natives driven out or destroyed, their princes tortured to discover their gold; a free licence given to all acts of inhumanity and lust, the earth reeking with the blood of its inhabitants: and this execrable crew of butchers employed in so pious an expedition, is a *modern colony* sent to convert and civilize an idolatrous and barbarous people.

Swift, *Gulliver's Travels*, IV, 12

41 The rules of equity or justice depend entirely on the particular state and condition in which men are placed, and owe their origin and existence to

that UTILITY, which results to the public from their strict and regular observance.

Hume, *Concerning Principles of Morals,* III

42 Commerce and manufactures can seldom flourish long in any state which does not enjoy a regular administration of justice, in which the people do not feel themselves secure in the possession of their property, in which the faith of contracts is not supported by law, and in which the authority of the state is not supposed to be regularly employed in enforcing the payment of debts from all those who are able to pay. Commerce and manufactures, in short, can seldom flourish in any state in which there is not a certain degree of confidence in the justice of government.

Adam Smith, *Wealth of Nations,* V, 3

43 Justice itself is the great standing policy of civil society; and any eminent departure from it, under any circumstances, lies under the suspicion of being no policy at all.

Burke, *Reflections on the Revolution in France*

44 If justice and righteousness perish, human life would no longer have any value in the world.

Kant, *Science of Right,* 49

45 Justice is the end of government. It is the end of civil society. It ever has been and ever will be pursued until it be obtained, or until liberty be lost in the pursuit. In a society under the forms of which the stronger faction can readily unite and oppress the weaker, anarchy may as truly be said to reign as in a state of nature, where the weaker individual is not secured against the violence of the stronger; and as, in the latter state, even the stronger individuals are prompted, by the uncertainty of their condition, to submit to a government which may protect the weak as well as themselves; so, in the former state, will the more powerful factions or parties be gradually induced, by a like motive, to wish for a government which will protect all parties, the weaker as well as the more powerful.

Hamilton or Madison, *Federalist 51*

46 An integral part of justice is the confidence which citizens have in it, and it is this which requires that proceedings shall be public. The right of publicity depends on the fact that (i) the aim of the court is justice, which as universal falls under the cognizance of everyone, and (ii) it is through publicity that the citizens become convinced that the judgement was actually just.

Hegel, *Philosophy of Right,* Additions, Par. 224

47 Foolish men imagine that because judgement for an evil thing is delayed, there is no justice, but an accidental one, here below. Judgement for an evil

thing is many times delayed some day or two, some century or two, but it is sure as life, it is sure as death!

Carlyle, *Past and Present,* I, 2

48 After all, the practical reason why, when the power is once in the hands of the people, a majority are permitted, and for a long period continue, to rule is not because they are most likely to be in the right, nor because this seems fairest to the minority, but because they are physically the strongest. But a government in which the majority rule in all cases cannot be based on justice, even as far as men understand it.

Thoreau, *Civil Disobedience*

49 Under a government which imprisons any unjustly, the true place for a just man is also a prison.

Thoreau, *Civil Disobedience*

50 Let us have faith that right makes might, and in that faith, let us, to the end, dare to do our duty as we understand it.

Lincoln, *Address at Cooper Institute*

51 Why should there not be a patient confidence in the ultimate justice of the people? Is there any better, or equal, hope in the world?

Lincoln, *First Inaugural Address*

52 The two essential ingredients in the sentiment of justice are, the desire to punish a person who has done harm, and the knowledge or belief that there is some definite individual or individuals to whom harm has been done.

Mill, *Utilitarianism,* V

53 Justice is a name for certain moral requirements, which, regarded collectively, stand higher in the scale of social utility, and are therefore of more paramount obligation, than any others; though particular cases may occur in which some other social duty is so important, as to overrule any one of the general maxims of justice. Thus, to save a life, it may not only be allowable, but a duty, to steal, or take by force, the necessary food or medicine, or to kidnap, and compel to officiate, the only qualified medical practitioner. In such cases, as we do not call anything justice which is not a virtue, we usually say, not that justice must give way to some other moral principle, but that what is just in ordinary cases is, by reason of that other principle, not just in the particular case. By this useful accommodation of language, the character of indefeasibility attributed to justice is kept up, and we are saved from the necessity of maintaining that there can be laudable injustice.

The considerations which have now been adduced resolve, I conceive, the only real difficulty in the utilitarian theory of morals. It has always been evident that all cases of justice are also cases of expediency: the difference is in the peculiar sentiment which attaches to the former, as contradistinguished from the latter. If this characteristic sentiment has been sufficiently accounted for; if there is no necessity to assume for it any peculiarity of origin; if it is simply the natural feeling of resentment, moralised by being made coextensive with the demands of social good; and if this feeling not only does but ought to exist in all the classes of cases to which the idea of justice corresponds; that idea no longer presents itself as a stumbling-block to the utilitarian ethics.

Justice remains the appropriate name for certain social utilities which are vastly more important, and therefore more absolute and imperative, than any others are as a class (though not more so than others may be in particular cases); and which, therefore, ought to be, as well as naturally are, guarded by a sentiment not only different in degree, but also in kind; distinguished from the milder feeling which attaches to the mere idea of promoting human pleasure or convenience, at once by the more definite nature of its commands, and by the sterner character of its sanctions.

Mill, *Utilitarianism*, V

12.3 | *Rights—Natural and Civil*

When the word "right" is used in the singular, or when it is paired with its antonym "wrong," it signifies the moral quality of conduct that is lawful, just, or worthy of approbation. Right and wrong in that sense are discussed in Section 9.7 of Chapter 9 on ETHICS; and related matters are discussed in this chapter, in Section 12.2 on JUSTICE AND INJUSTICE. But when, as here, the word "rights" is used in the plural, it signifies the claims that a man can rightfully make concerning the things that belong to him, that are proper to him, that are his due. Some of the writers quoted here—Locke, for example—use the word "property" to stand for what other authors call "rights." Where the Declaration of Independence speaks of man's natural and unalienable rights, foremost among which are the rights to life, liberty, and the pursuit of happiness, Locke says that the ultimate objective of a just government is to protect and preserve the property of its subjects, their property consisting chiefly in their lives, their liberties, and their estates.

As in the case of law, the fundamental distinction here is between natural and civil rights: on the one hand, the rights inherent in the very nature of man, and therefore equally possessed by or proper to every human being; on the other hand, the rights granted to its subjects by civil government. The latter are at the disposal of government to rescind as well as to confer; but the former, being antecedent to the institutions of government and to society itself, are deemed unalienable. Not being conferred by government, they cannot rightfully be rescinded by government, and according to the theory of natural rights, the justice of a government and of its laws, of other institutions, and of the conduct of one man toward another, consists in respecting the natural rights of every human being. Injustice occurs with the violation of these rights, taking away from a man that which is by nature his.

The reader will find all these points made, argued, and disputed in the quotations included here—both affirmations and denials of unalienable, natural rights; different enumerations of these rights; and applications of the doctrine of natural rights to economic and social as well as to political institutions. The reader will find questions about the equality of rights, questions about which is the most fundamental of all rights, and questions about the relation of natural rights to natural law. For the discussion of related matters, the reader should turn in this chapter to Section 12.1 on LAW AND LAW-YERS and Section 12.2 on JUSTICE AND INJUSTICE; in other chapters, the reader should examine Section 11.1 on PROPERTY, Section 10.4 on GOVERNMENT OF AND BY THE PEOPLE: REPUBLIC AND DEMOCRACY, Section 10.6 on DESPOTISM AND TYRANNY, Section 10.7 on SLAVERY, Section 13.3 on EQUALITY, and Section 14.1 on WARFARE AND THE STATE OF WAR.

1 *Athenians.* Right, as the world goes, is only in question between equals in power, while the strong do what they can and the weak suffer what they must.

Thucydides, *Peloponnesian War,* V, 89

2 A mere law to give all men equal rights is but useless, if the poor must sacrifice those rights to their debts, and, in the very seats and sanctuaries of equality, the courts of justice, the offices of state, and the public discussions, be more than anywhere at the beck and bidding of the rich.

Plutarch, *Poplicola and Solon Compared*

3 The people . . . is an assemblage associated by a common acknowledgment of right and by a community of interests. . . . Where, . . . there is no true justice there can be no right. For that which is done by right is justly done, and what is unjustly done cannot be done by right. For the unjust inventions of men are neither to be considered nor spoken of as rights; for even they themselves say that right is that which flows from the fountain of justice, and deny the definition which is commonly given by those who misconceive the matter, that right is that which is useful to the stronger party. Thus, where there is not true justice there can be no assemblage of men associated by a common acknowledgment of right, and therefore there can be no people.

Augustine, *City of God,* XIX, 21

4 The *right* or the *just* is a work that is adjusted to another person according to some kind of equality. Now a thing can be adjusted to a man in two ways: first by its very nature, as when a man gives so much that he may receive equal value in return, and this is called *natural right.* In another way a thing is adjusted or commensurated to another person, by agreement, or by common consent, when, to wit, a man deems himself satisfied, if he receive so much. This can be done in two ways: first by private agreement, as that which is confirmed by an agreement between private individuals; secondly by public agreement, as when the whole community agrees that something should be deemed as though it were adjusted and commensurated to another person, or when this is decreed by the prince who is placed over the people, and acts in its stead, and this is called *positive right.*

Aquinas, *Summa Theologica,* II–II, 57, 2

5 If . . . a thing is, of itself, contrary to natural right, the human will cannot make it just, for instance by decreeing that it is lawful to steal or to commit adultery.

Aquinas, *Summa Theologica,* II–II, 57, 2

6 The natural right or just is that which by its very nature is adjusted to or commensurate with another person. Now this may happen in two ways; first, according as it is considered absolutely: thus a male by its very nature is commensurate with the female to beget offspring by her, and a parent is commensurate with the offspring to nourish it. Secondly a thing is naturally commensurate with another person, not according as it is considered absolutely, but according to something resultant from it, for instance the possession of property. For if a particular piece of land be considered absolutely, it contains no reason why it should belong to one man more than to another, but if it be considered in respect of its adaptability to cultivation, and the unmolested use of the land, it has a certain commensuration to be the property of one and not of another man.

Aquinas, *Summa Theologica,* II–II, 57, 3

7 *Right* is a moral quality annexed to the person, justly entitling him to possess some particular privilege, or to perform some particular act. This right is annexed to the person, although it sometimes follows the things, as the services of lands, which are called *Real Rights,* in opposition to those merely *Personal.* Not because these rights are not annexed to persons, but the distinction is made, because they belong to the persons only who possess some particular things.

Grotius, *Rights of War and Peace,* Bk. I, I, 4

8 Natural right is the dictate of right reason, shew-

ing the moral turpitude, or moral necessity, of any act from its agreement or disagreement with a rational nature, and consequently that such an act is either forbidden or commanded by God, the author of nature.

Grotius, *Rights of War and Peace,*
Bk. I, I, 10

9 God has given life to man, not to destroy, but to preserve it; assigning to him for this purpose a right to the free enjoyment of personal liberty, reputation, and the control over his own actions.

Grotius, *Rights of War and Peace,* Bk. II,
XVII, 2

10 The *right of nature,* which writers commonly call *jus naturale,* is the liberty each man hath to use his own power as he will himself for the preservation of his own nature; that is to say, of his own life; and consequently, of doing anything which, in his own judgement and reason, he shall conceive to be the aptest means thereunto. . . .

A *law of nature, lex naturalis,* is a precept, or general rule, found out by reason, by which a man is forbidden to do that which is destructive of his life, or taketh away the means of preserving the same, and to omit that by which he thinketh it may be best preserved. For though they that speak of this subject use to confound *jus* and *lex, right* and *law,* yet they ought to be distinguished, because *right* consisteth in liberty to do, or to forbear; whereas *law* determineth and bindeth to one of them: so that law and right differ as much as obligation and liberty, which in one and the same matter are inconsistent.

And because the condition of man (as hath been declared in the precedent chapter) is a condition of war of every one against every one, in which case every one is governed by his own reason, and there is nothing he can make use of that may not be a help unto him in preserving his life against his enemies; it followeth that in such a condition every man has a right to every thing, even to one another's body. And therefore, as long as this natural right of every man to every thing endureth, there can be no security to any man, how strong or wise soever he be, of living out the time which nature ordinarily alloweth men to live. And consequently it is a precept, or general rule of reason: *that every man ought to endeavour peace, as far as he has hope of obtaining it; and when he cannot obtain it, that he may seek and use all helps and advantages of war.* The first branch of which rule containeth the first and fundamental law of nature, which is: *to seek peace and follow it.* The second, the sum of the right of nature, which is: *by all means we can to defend ourselves.*

From this fundamental law of nature, by which men are commanded to endeavour peace, is derived this second law: *that a man be willing, when others are so too, as far forth as for peace and defence of himself he shall think it necessary, to lay down this right to all things; and be contented with so much liberty against other men as he would allow other men against himself.* For as long as every man holdeth this right, of doing anything he liketh; so long are all men in the condition of war. But if other men will not lay down their right, as well as he, then there is no reason for anyone to divest himself of his: for that were to expose himself to prey, which no man is bound to, rather than to dispose himself to peace. This is that law of gospel: *Whatsoever you require that others should do to you, that do ye to them.* And that law of all men, *quod tibi fieri non vis, alteri ne feceris.*

To lay down a man's right to anything is to divest himself of the liberty of hindering another of the benefit of his own right to the same. For he that renounceth or passeth away his right giveth not to any other man a right which he had not before, because there is nothing to which every man had not right by nature, but only standeth out of his way that he may enjoy his own original right without hindrance from him, not without hindrance from another. So that the effect which redoundeth to one man by another man's defect of right is but so much diminution of impediments to the use of his own right original.

Right is laid aside, either by simply renouncing it, or by transferring it to another. By simply *renouncing,* when he cares not to whom the benefit thereof redoundeth. By *transferring,* when he intendeth the benefit thereof to some certain person or persons. And when a man hath in either manner abandoned or granted away his right, then is he said to be *obliged,* or *bound,* not to hinder those to whom such right is granted, or abandoned, from the benefit of it: and that he *ought,* and it is his *duty,* not to make void that voluntary act of his own: and that such hindrance is *injustice,* and *injury,* as being *sine jure;* the right being before renounced or transferred. So that *injury,* or *injustice,* in the controversies of the world, is somewhat like to that which in the disputations of scholars is called *absurdity.* For as it is there called an absurdity to contradict what one maintained in the beginning; so in the world it is called *injustice,* and *injury* voluntarily to undo that which from the beginning he had voluntarily done. The way by which a man either simply renounceth or transferreth his right is a declaration, or signification, by some voluntary and sufficient sign, or signs, that he doth so renounce or transfer, or hath so renounced or transferred the same, to him that accepteth it. And these signs are either words only, or actions only; or as it happeneth most often, both words and actions. And the same are the *bonds,* by which men are bound and obliged: bonds that have their strength, not from their own nature (for nothing is more easily broken than a man's word), but from fear of some evil consequence upon the rupture.

Whensoever a man transferreth his right, or renounceth it, it is either in consideration of some right reciprocally transferred to himself, or for some other good he hopeth for thereby. For it is a voluntary act: and of the voluntary acts of every man, the object is some good to himself. And therefore there be some rights which no man can be understood by any words, or other signs, to have abandoned or transferred. As first a man cannot lay down the right of resisting them that assault him by force to take away his life, because he cannot be understood to aim thereby at any good to himself. The same may be said of wounds, and chains, and imprisonment, both because there is no benefit consequent to such patience, as there is to the patience of suffering another to be wounded or imprisoned, as also because a man cannot tell when he seeth men proceed against him by violence whether they intend his death or not. And lastly the motive and end for which this renouncing and transferring of right is introduced is nothing else but the security of a man's person, in his life, and in the means of so preserving life as not to be weary of it. And therefore if a man by words, or other signs, seem to despoil himself of the end for which those signs were intended, he is not to be understood as if he meant it, or that it was his will, but that he was ignorant of how such words and actions were to be interpreted.

The mutual transferring of right is that which men call *contract.*

Hobbes, *Leviathan,* I, 14

11 Anything that exists in nature which we judge to be evil or able to hinder us from existing and enjoying a rational life, we are allowed to remove from us in that way which seems the safest; and whatever, on the other hand, we judge to be good or to be profitable for the preservation of our being or the enjoyment of a rational life, we are permitted to take for our use and use in any way we may think proper; and absolutely, every one is allowed by the highest right of nature to do that which he believes contributes to his own profit.

Spinoza, *Ethics,* IV, Appendix VIII

12 By natural right I understand the very laws or rules of nature, in accordance with which everything takes place, in other words, the power of nature itself. And so the natural right of universal nature, and consequently of every individual thing, extends as far as its power: and accordingly, whatever any man does after the laws of his nature, he does by the highest natural right, and he has as much right over nature as he has power.

Spinoza, *Political Treatise,* II, 4

13 It will, perhaps, be objected to this, that if gathering the acorns or other fruits of the earth, etc., makes a right to them, then any one may engross as much as he will. To which I answer, Not so. The same law of Nature that does by this means

give us property, does also bound that property too. "God has given us all things richly." Is the voice of reason confirmed by inspiration? But how far has He given it us—"to enjoy"? As much as any one can make use of to any advantage of life before it spoils, so much he may by his labour fix a property in. Whatever is beyond this is more than his share, and belongs to others. Nothing was made by God for man to spoil or destroy.

Locke, *II Civil Government,* V, 30

14 A man, as has been proved, cannot subject himself to the arbitrary power of another; and having, in the state of Nature, no arbitrary power over the life, liberty, or possession of another, but only so much as the law of Nature gave him for the preservation of himself and the rest of mankind, this is all he doth, or can give up to the commonwealth, and by it to the legislative power, so that the legislative can have no more than this. Their power in the utmost bounds of it is limited to the public good of the society. It is a power that hath no other end but preservation, and therefore can never have a right to destroy, enslave, or designedly to impoverish the subjects.

Locke, *II Civil Government,* XI, 135

15 The supreme power cannot take from any man any part of his property without his own consent. For the preservation of property being the end of government, and that for which men enter into society, it necessarily supposes and requires that the people should have property, without which they must be supposed to lose that by entering into society which was the end for which they entered into it; too gross an absurdity for any man to own. Men, therefore, in society having property, they have such a right to the goods, which by the law of the community are theirs, that nobody hath a right to take them, or any part of them, from them without their own consent; without this they have no property at all. For I have truly no property in that which another can by right take from me when he pleases against my consent. Hence it is a mistake to think that the supreme or legislative power of any commonwealth can do what it will, and dispose of the estates of the subject arbitrarily, or take any part of them at pleasure. This is not much to be feared in governments where the legislative consists wholly or in part in assemblies which are variable, whose members upon the dissolution of the assembly are subjects under the common laws of their country, equally with the rest. But in governments where the legislative is in one lasting assembly, always in being, or in one man as in absolute monarchies, there is danger still, that they will think themselves to have a distinct interest from the rest of the community, and so will be apt to increase their own riches and power by taking what they think fit from the people. For a man's property is

not at all secure, though there be good and equitable laws to set the bounds of it between him and his fellow-subjects, if he who commands those subjects have power to take from any private man what part he pleases of his property, and use and dispose of it as he thinks good.

Locke, *II Civil Government*, XI, 138

16 He that is master of himself and his own life has a right, too, to the means of preserving it.

Locke, *II Civil Government*, XV, 172

17 Every man is born with a double right. First, a right of freedom to his person, which no other man has a power over, but the free disposal of it lies in himself. Secondly, a right before any other man, to inherit, with his brethren, his father's goods.

By the first of these, a man is naturally free from subjection to any government, though he be born in a place under its jurisdiction. But if he disclaim the lawful government of the country he was born in, he must also quit the right that belonged to him, by the laws of it, and the possessions there descending to him from his ancestors if it were a government made by their consent.

Locke, *II Civil Government*, XVI, 190–191

18 Puffendorf says that we may divest ourselves of our liberty in favour of other men, just as we transfer our property from one to another by contracts and agreements. But this seems a very weak argument. For in the first place, the property I alienate becomes quite foreign to me, nor can I suffer from the abuse of it; but it very nearly concerns me that my liberty should not be abused, and I cannot without incurring the guilt of the crimes I may be compelled to commit, expose myself to become an instrument of crime. Besides, the right of property being only a convention of human institution, men may dispose of what they possess as they please: but this is not the case with the essential gifts of nature, such as life and liberty, which every man is permitted to enjoy, and of which it is at least doubtful whether any have a right to divest themselves. By giving up the one, we degrade our being; by giving up the other, we do our best to annul it; and, as no temporal good can indemnify us for the loss of either, it would be an offence against both reason and nature to renounce them at any price whatsoever.

Rousseau, *Origin of Inequality*, II

19 The State, in relation to its members, is master of all their goods by the social contract, which, within the State, is the basis of all rights; but, in relation to other powers, it is so only by the right of the first occupier, which it holds from its members.

The right of the first occupier, though more real than the right of the strongest, becomes a real right only when the right of property has already been established. Every man has naturally a right to everything he needs; but the positive act which makes him proprietor of one thing excludes him from everything else. Having his share, he ought to keep to it, and can have no further right against the community. This is why the right of the first occupier, which in the state of nature is so weak, claims the respect of every man in civil society. In this right we are respecting not so much what belongs to another as what does not belong to ourselves.

Rousseau, *Social Contract*, I, 9

20 We hold these truths to be self-evident, that all men are created equal: that they are endowed by their Creator with certain unalienable rights; that among these are life, liberty, and the pursuit of happiness. That, to secure these rights, governments are instituted among men, deriving their just powers from the consent of the governed; that, whenever any form of government becomes destructive of these ends, it is the right of the people to alter or to abolish it, and to institute a new government, laying its foundation on such principles, and organizing its powers in such form, as to them shall seem most likely to effect their safety and happiness.

Jefferson, *Declaration of Independence*

21 In the state of nature every man has a right to defend, by force of arms, his person and his possessions; to repel, or even to prevent, the violence of his enemies, and to extend his hostilities to a reasonable measure of satisfaction and retaliation.

Gibbon, *Decline and Fall
of the Roman Empire*, L

22 The system of rights, viewed as a scientific system of doctrines, is divided into natural right and positive right. Natural right rests upon pure rational principles *a priori;* positive or statutory right is what proceeds from the will of a legislator.

The system of rights may again be regarded in reference to the implied powers of dealing morally with others as bound by obligations, that is, as furnishing a legal title of action in relation to them. Thus viewed, the system is divided into innate right and acquired right. Innate right is that right which belongs to every one by nature, independent of all juridical acts of experience. Acquired right is that right which is founded upon such juridical acts.

Innate right may also be called the "internal mine and thine"; for external right must always be acquired.

Kant, *Division of the Science of Right*, B

23 Freedom is independence of the compulsory will of another; and in so far as it can coexist with the freedom of all according to a universal law, it is

the one sole original, inborn right belonging to every man in virtue of his humanity.

Kant, *Division of the Science of Right*, B

24 The commonwealth is the people viewed as united altogether into a state. And thus it is not to be said that the individual in the state has sacrificed *a part* of his inborn external freedom for a particular purpose; but he has abandoned his wild lawless freedom wholly, in order to find all his proper freedom again entire and undiminished, but in the form of a regulated order of dependence, that is, in a civil state regulated by laws of right. This relation of dependence thus arises out of his own regulative law giving will.

Kant, *Science of Right*, 47

25 Those goods, or rather substantive characteristics, which constitute my own private personality and the universal essence of my self-consciousness are inalienable and my right to them is imprescriptible. Such characteristics are my personality as such, my universal freedom of will, my ethical life, my religion. . . .

The right to what is in essence inalienable is imprescriptible, since the act whereby I take possession of my personality, of my substantive essence, and make myself a responsible being, capable of possessing rights and with a moral and religious life, takes away from these characteristics of mine just that externality which alone made them capable of passing into the possession of someone else. When I have thus annulled their externality, I cannot lose them through lapse of time or from any other reason drawn from my prior consent or willingness to alienate them. This return of mine into myself, whereby I make myself existent as Idea, as a person with rights and moral principles, annuls the previous position and the wrong done to my concept and my reason by others and myself when the infinite embodiment of self-consciousness has been treated as something external, and that with my consent. This return into myself makes clear the contradiction in supposing that I have given into another's possession my capacity for rights, my ethical life and religious feeling; for either I have given up what I myself did not possess, or I am giving up what, so soon as I possess it, exists in essence as mine alone and not as something external.

Hegel, *Philosophy of Right*, 66

26 After the general idea of virtue, I know no higher principle than that of right; or rather these two ideas are united in one. The idea of right is simply that of virtue introduced into the political world. It was the idea of right that enabled men to define anarchy and tyranny, and that taught them how to be independent without arrogance and to obey without servility. The man who submits to violence is debased by his compliance; but when he submits to that right of authority which he acknowledges in a fellow creature, he rises in some measure above the person who gives the command. There are no great men without virtue; and there are no great nations—it may almost be added, there would be no society—without respect for right; for what is a union of rational and intelligent beings who are held together only by the bond of force?

Tocqueville, *Democracy in America*, I, 14

27 One man is superior to another physically or mentally and so supplies more labour in the same time, or can labour for a longer time; and labour, to serve as a measure, must be defined by its duration or intensity, otherwise it ceases to be a standard of measurement. This *equal* right is an unequal right for unequal labour. It recognises no class differences, because everyone is only a worker like everyone else; but it tacitly recognises unequal individual endowment and thus productive capacity as natural privileges. *It is therefore a right of inequality in its content, like every right.* Right by its very nature can only consist in the application of an equal standard; but unequal individuals (and they would not be different individuals if they were not unequal) are only measurable by an equal standard in so far as they are brought under an equal point of view, are taken from one *definite* side only, *e.g.,* in the present case are regarded *only as workers,* and nothing more seen in them, everything else being ignored. Further, one worker is married, another not; one has more children than another and so on and so forth. Thus with an equal output, and hence an equal share in the social consumption fund, one will in fact receive more than another, one will be richer than another, and so on. To avoid all these defects, right, instead of being equal, would have to be unequal.

But these defects are inevitable in the first phase of communist society as it is when it has just emerged after prolonged birth pangs from capitalist society. Right can never be higher than the economic structure of society and the cultural development thereby determined.

In a higher phase of communist society, after the enslaving subordination of individuals under division of labour, and therewith also the antithesis between mental and physical labour, has vanished; after labour, from a mere means of life, has itself become the prime necessity of life; after the productive forces have also increased with the all-round development of the individual, and all the springs of co-operative wealth flow more abundantly—only then can the narrow horizon of bourgeois right be fully left behind and society inscribe on its banners: from each according to his ability, to each according to his needs!

Marx, *Critique of the Gotha Programme*

28 To have a right . . . is, I conceive, to have some-

thing which society ought to defend me in the possession of. If the objector goes on to ask, why it ought? I can give him no other reason than general utility. If that expression does not seem to convey a sufficient feeling of the strength of the obligation, nor to account for the peculiar energy of the feeling, it is because there goes to the composition of the sentiment, not a rational only, but also an animal element, the thirst for retaliation; and this thirst derives its intensity, as well as its moral justification, from the extraordinarily important and impressive kind of utility which is concerned. The interest involved is that of security, to every one's feelings the most vital of all interests. All other earthly benefits are needed by one person, not needed by another; and many of them can, if necessary, be cheerfully foregone, or replaced by something else; but security no human being can possibly do without; on it we depend for all our immunity from evil, and for the whole value of all and every good, beyond the passing moment; since nothing but the gratification of the instant could be of any worth to us, if we could be deprived of anything the next instant by whoever was momentarily stronger than ourselves.

Mill, *Utilitarianism*, V

29 The order of castes, *order of rank*, only formulates the supreme law of life itself; the separation of the three types is necessary for the preservation of society, for making possible higher and higher types—*inequality* of rights is the condition for the existence of rights at all.—A right is a privilege.

Nietzsche, *Antichrist*, LVII

30 If men have rights by birth, these rights must hold against their fellow-men and must mean that somebody else is to spend his energy to sustain the existence of the persons so born. What then becomes of the natural rights of the one whose energies are to be diverted from his own interests? If it be said that we should all help each other, that means simply that the race as a whole should advance and expand as much and as fast as it can in its career on earth; and the experience on which we are now acting has shown that we shall do this best under liberty and under the organization which we are now developing, by leaving each to exert his energies for his own success. The notion of natural rights is destitute of sense, but it is captivating, and it is the more available on account of its vagueness. It lends itself to the most vicious kind of social dogmatism, for if a man has natural rights, then the reasoning is clear up to the finished socialistic doctrine that a man has a natural right to whatever he needs, and that the measure of his claims is the wishes which he wants fulfilled. If, then, he has a need, who is bound to satisfy it for him? Who holds the obligation corresponding to his right? It must be the one who possesses what will satisfy that need, or else the state which can

take the possession from those who have earned and saved it, and give it to him who needs it and who, by the hypothesis, has not earned and saved it.

W. G. Sumner, *Challenge of Facts*

31 While admitting the abstract right of the community to interfere with its members in order to secure the biological necessaries to all, I cannot admit its right to interfere in matters where what one man possesses is not obtained at the expense of another. I am thinking of such things as opinion and knowledge and art. The fact that the majority of a community dislikes an opinion gives it no right to interfere with those who hold it. And the fact that the majority of a community wishes not to know certain facts gives it no right to imprison those who wish to know them.

Russell, *Sceptical Essays*, XIII

32 The obstacles to freedom, as we saw, are of two sorts, social and physical. Given a social and a physical obstacle which cause the same direct loss of liberty, the social obstacle is more harmful, because it causes resentment. If a boy wants to climb a tree and you forbid him, he will be furious; if he finds that he cannot climb it, he will acquiesce in the physical impossibility.

Russell, *Sceptical Essays*, XIII

33 If we are not to fall into Utopianism, we cannot imagine that, having overthrown capitalism, people will at once learn to work for society *without any standards of right;* indeed, the abolition of capitalism *does not immediately lay* the economic foundations for *such* a change.

And there is no other standard yet than that of "bourgeois right." To this extent, therefore, a form of state is still necessary, which, while maintaining public ownership of the means of production, would preserve the equality of labour and equality in the distribution of products.

The state is withering away in so far as there are no longer any capitalists, any classes, and, consequently, no *class* can be suppressed.

But the state has not yet altogether withered away, since there still remains the protection of "bourgeois right" which sanctifies actual inequality. For the complete extinction of the state, complete Communism is necessary.

Lenin, *State and Revolution*, V, 3

34 The fundamental rights, like the right to existence and life; the right to personal freedom or to conduct one's own life as master of oneself and of one's acts, responsible for them before God and the law of the community; the right to the pursuit of the perfection of moral and rational human life; the right to the pursuit of eternal good (without this pursuit there is no true pursuit of happiness); the right to keep one's body whole; the

right to private ownership of material goods, which is a safeguard of the liberties of the individual; the right to marry according to one's choice and to raise a family which will be assured of the liberties due it; the right of association, the respect for human dignity in each individual, whether or not he represents an economic value for society— all these rights are rooted in the vocation of the person (a spiritual and free agent) to the order of absolute values and to a destiny superior to time.

Maritain, *Rights of Man and Natural Law,* II

35 *With respect to God and truth,* one has not the right to choose according to his own whim any path whatsoever, he must choose the true path, in so far as it is in his power to know it. But *with respect to the State, to the temporal community and to the temporal power,* he is free to choose his religious path at his own risk, his freedom of conscience is a natural, inviolable right.

Maritain, *Rights of Man and Natural Law,* II

36 If it is true that political authority has as its essential function the direction of free men towards the common good, it is normal for these free men to choose by themselves those who have the function of leading them: this is the most elementary form of active participation in political life. That is why universal suffrage, by means of which every adult human person has, as such, the right to make his opinion felt regarding the affairs of the community by casting his vote in the election of the people's representatives and the officers of the State—that is why universal suffrage has a wholly fundamental political and human value and is one of those rights which a community of free men can never give up.

Maritain, *Rights of Man and Natural Law,* II

37 Freedom of investigation is a fundamental natural right, for man's very nature is to seek the truth.

Maritain, *Rights of Man and Natural Law,* II

12.4 | *Crime and Punishment*

Two main subjects are treated in this section: on the one hand, the nature, causes, and varieties of crime; on the other, the purposes, justifications, and kinds of punishment. The first of these subjects is closely related to matters treated in Section 12.1 on LAW AND LAWYERS and also in Section 9.7 on RIGHT AND WRONG, as well as in Section 9.10 on VIRTUE AND VICE; in addition, the reader will find some overlapping between the discussion of crime here and of sin in Section 20.13 of Chapter 20 on RELIGION. Section 12.1 on LAW AND LAWYERS is also relevant to the second subject, but even more so is Section 12.2 on JUSTICE AND INJUSTICE. For example, the reader will find passages dealing with the *lex talionis*—an eye for an eye, a tooth for a tooth—both here, as relevant to punishment, and in the section on justice.

The central issue concerning punishment arises from the question whether it should be entirely utilitarian in purpose, aiming to deter potential criminal offenders as well as to reform those who have committed criminal acts, or it should be purely retributive in aim, righting the wrong and thus restoring the balance of justice. Those who take the latter view attempt to draw a sharp line between retribution and revenge. Those who take the former view tend to regard retribution as nothing but vengeance. Regarding punishment as remedial or therapeutic, the utilitarian view justifies a particular type of punishment in a particular case by the degree to which it serves the purposes of deterrence and reform. Regarding it as an act of justice, the retributive view justifies the severity of the punishment by its proportionality to the gravity of the crime being punished.

These considerations raise further questions, such as whether only the guilty should be punished and whether everyone who is guilty of criminal behavior should be punished; as well as questions about the justice of capital punishment, about the inhumanity of cruel and unusual punishments, about the mitigation or attenuation of punishment in particular cases, and about the desire for punishment on the part of those who are plagued by their sense of guilt.

It has already been pointed out that sin as violation of the divine law, parallel to crime as violation of human law, is discussed in Section 20.13; it should also be pointed out that divine rewards and punishments, meting out divine justice in a purely retributive manner, are discussed in Section 20.15.

---

1 Whoso sheddeth man's blood, by man shall his blood be shed: for in the image of God made he man.

Genesis 9:6

2 The fathers shall not be put to death for the children, neither shall the children be put to death for the fathers: every man shall be put to death for his own sin.

Deuteronomy 24:16

3 Withhold not correction from the child: for if thou beatest him with the rod, he shall not die.
Thou shalt beat him with the rod, and shalt deliver his soul from hell.

Proverbs 23:13–14

4 *Chorus.* It is but law that when the red drops have been spilled
upon the ground they cry aloud for fresh blood. For the death act calls out on Fury
to bring out of those who were slain before
new ruin on ruin accomplished.

Aeschylus, *Libation Bearers,* 400

5 *Chorus.* Here is overthrow of all
the young laws, if the claim
of this matricide shall stand
good, his crime be sustained.
Should this be, every man will find a way
to act at his own caprice;
over and over again in time
to come, parents shall await
the deathstroke at their children's hands.

Aeschylus, *Eumenides,* 490

6 *Tyndareus.* Suppose a wife murders her husband.
Her son then follows suit by killing her,
and his son then must have his murder too
and so on.
　　　　Where, I want to know, can this chain
of murder end? Can it ever end, in fact,
since the last to kill is doomed to stand

under permanent sentence of death by revenge?
No, our ancestors handled these matters well
by banning their murderers from public sight,
forbidding them to meet or speak to anyone.
But the point is this: they purged their guilt
by banishment, not death. And by so doing,
they stopped that endless vicious cycle
of murder and revenge.
　　　　　　　Do not mistake me.
I despise adultery and unfaithful wives,
and my daughter Clytemnestra, an adulteress
and murderess to boot, most of all.
As for your wife Helen, I loathe her too
and never wish to speak to her again.
Nor, I might add, do I envy you
your trip to Troy to bring your whore back home.
No sir, not my daughters, but the law:
that is my concern. There I take my stand,
defending it with all my heart and strength
against the brutal and inhuman spirit of murder
that corrupts our cities and destroys this country.

Euripides, *Orestes,* 507

7 *Socrates.* The proper office of punishment is twofold: he who is rightly punished ought either to become better and profit by it, or he ought to be made an example to his fellows, that they may see what he suffers, and fear and become better. Those who are improved when they are punished by gods and men, are those whose sins are curable; and they are improved, as in this world so also in another, by pain and suffering; for there is no other way in which they can be delivered from their evil. But they who have been guilty of the worst crimes, and are incurable by reason of their crimes, are made examples; for, as they are incurable, the time has passed at which they can receive any benefit. They get no good themselves, but others get good when they behold them enduring for ever the most terrible and painful and fearful sufferings as the penalty of their sins.

Plato, *Gorgias,* 525A

8 *Athenian Stranger.* A man may very likely commit
. . . crimes, either in a state of madness or when
affected by disease, or under the influence of extreme old age, or in a fit of childish wantonness,
himself no better than a child. And if this be
made evident to the judges elected to try the
cause, on the appeal of the criminal or his advocate, and he be judged to have been in this state
when he committed the offence, he shall simply
pay for the hurt which he may have done to another; but he shall be exempt from other penalties, unless he have slain some one, and have on
his hands the stain of blood.

Plato, *Laws,* IX, 864B

9 *Athenian Stranger.* The law, like a good archer,
should aim at the right measure of punishment,
and in all cases at the deserved punishment.

Plato, *Laws,* XI, 934A

10 *Athenian Stranger.* If a man steal anything belonging to the public, whether that which he steals be
much or little, he shall have the same punishment. For he who steals a little steals with the
same wish as he who steals much, but with less
power, and he who takes up a greater amount, not
having deposited it, is wholly unjust. Wherefore
the law is not disposed to inflict a less penalty on
the one than on the other because his theft is less,
but on the ground that the thief may possibly be
in one case still curable, and may in another case
be incurable. If any one convict in a court of law
a stranger or a slave of a theft of public property,
let the court determine what punishment he shall
suffer, or what penalty he shall pay, bearing in
mind that he is probably not incurable. But the
citizen who has been brought up as our citizens
will have been, if he be found guilty of robbing his
country by fraud or violence, whether he be
caught in the act or not, shall be punished with
death; for he is incurable.

Plato, *Laws,* XII, 941B

11 If the virtues are concerned with actions and passions, and every passion and every action is accompanied by pleasure and pain, for this reason
also virtue will be concerned with pleasures and
pains. This is indicated also by the fact that punishment is inflicted by these means; for it is a kind
of cure, and it is the nature of cures to be effected
by contraries.

Aristotle, *Ethics,* 1104ᵇ13

12 There are crimes of which the motive is want.
. . . But want is not the sole incentive to crime;
men also wish to enjoy themselves and not to be in
a state of desire—they wish to cure some desire,
going beyond the necessities of life, which preys
upon them; nay, this is not the only reason—they
may desire superfluities in order to enjoy plea-

sures unaccompanied with pain, and therefore
they commit crimes.

Now what is the cure of these three disorders?
Of the first, moderate possessions and occupation;
of the second, habits of temperance; as to the
third, if any desire pleasures which depend on
themselves, they will find the satisfaction of their
desires nowhere but in philosophy; for all other
pleasures we are dependent on others. The fact is
that the greatest crimes are caused by excess and
not by necessity. Men do not become tyrants in
order that they may not suffer cold; and hence
great is the honour bestowed, not on him who kills
a thief, but on him who kills a tyrant.

Aristotle, *Politics,* 1267ᵃ3

13 There is in life a dread of punishment for evil
deeds, signal as the deeds are signal, and for
atonement of guilt, the prison and the frightful
hurling down from the rock, scourgings, executioners, the dungeon of the doomed, the pitch, the
metal plate, torches; and even though these are
wanting, yet the conscience-stricken mind
through boding fears applies to itself goads and
frightens itself with whips, and sees not meanwhile what end there can be of ills or what limit
at last is to be set to punishments, and fears lest
these very evils be enhanced after death. The life
of fools at length becomes a hell here on earth.

Lucretius, *Nature of Things,* III

14 There are some duties we owe even to those who
have wronged us. There is, after all, a limit to
retribution and punishment. Or rather, may I say
that it is enough to get a wrong-doer to repent of
his misdeed, so that he may not repeat the offense,
and also as a means of deterring others from doing
wrong.

Cicero, *De Officiis,* I, 11

15 They lie below, on golden beds display'd;
And genial feasts with regal pomp are made.
The Queen of Furies by their sides is set,
And snatches from their mouths th' untasted
   meat,
Which if they touch, her hissing snakes she rears,
Tossing her torch, and thund'ring in their ears.
Then they, who brothers' better claim disown,
Expel their parents, and usurp the throne;
Defraud their clients, and, to lucre sold,
Sit brooding on unprofitable gold;
Who dare not give, and e'en refuse to lend
To their poor kindred, or a wanting friend.
Vast is the throng of these; nor less the train
Of lustful youths, for foul adult'ry slain:
Hosts of deserters, who their honor sold,
And basely broke their faith for bribes of gold.
All these within the dungeon's depth remain,
Despairing pardon, and expecting pain.
Ask not what pains; nor farther seek to know

Their process, or the forms of law below.
Some roll a weighty stone; some, laid along,
And bound with burning wires, on spokes of
 wheels are hung.
Unhappy Theseus, doom'd for ever there,
Is fix'd by Fate on his eternal chair;
And wretched Phlegyas warns the world with
 cries
(Could warning make the world more just or
 wise):
'Learn righteousness, and dread th' avenging dei-
 ties.'
To tyrants others have their country sold,
Imposing foreign lords, for foreign gold;
Some have old laws repeal'd, new statutes made,
Not as the people pleas'd, but as they paid;
With incest some their daughters' bed profan'd:
All dar'd the worst of ills, and, what they dar'd,
 attain'd.
Had I a hundred mouths, a hundred tongues,
And throats of brass, inspir'd with iron lungs,
I could not half those horrid crimes repeat,
Nor half the punishments those crimes have met.

Virgil, Aeneid, VI

16 Draco's laws were written not with ink but blood;
and he, himself, being once asked why he made
death the punishment of most offences, replied,
"Small ones deserve that, and I have no higher for
the greater crimes."

Plutarch, Solon

17 Any performance that sets an evil example displeases
Even its author himself: to begin with, punishment lies
In the fact that no man, if guilty, is ever acquitted
With himself as judge, though he may have won
 in the courtroom
Bribing the praetor in charge, or stuffing the urn
 with false ballots.

Juvenal, Satire XIII

18   The fates of criminals differ.
One gets the cross, another the crown, for the
 same misdemeanor.

Juvenal, Satire XIII

19 If man were all of one piece—I mean, if he were
nothing more than a made thing, acting and acted upon according to a fixed nature—he could be
no more subject to reproach and punishment than
the mere animals. But as the scheme holds, man is
singled out for condemnation when he does evil;
and this with justice. For he is no mere thing
made to rigid plan; his nature contains a Principle apart and free.

Plotinus, Third Ennead, III, 4

20 Every disorder of the soul is its own punishment.

Augustine, Confessions, I, 12

21 Now when we ask why this or that particular evil
act was done, it is normal to assume that it could
not have been done save through the desire of
gaining or the fear of losing some one of these
lower goods. For they have their own charm and
their own beauty, though compared with the
higher values of heaven they are poor and mean
enough. Such a man has committed a murder.
Why? He wanted the other man's wife or his
property; or he had chosen robbery as a means of
livelihood; or he feared to lose this or that through
his victim's act; or he had been wronged and was
aflame for vengeance. Would any man commit a
murder for no cause, for the sheer delight of murdering? The thing would be incredible. There is of
course the case of the man [Catiline] who was said
to be so stupidly and savagely cruel that he practised cruelty and evil even when he had nothing
to gain by them. But even there a cause was stated—he did it, he said, lest through idleness his
hand or his resolution should grow slack. And
why did he want to prevent that? So that one day
by the multiplication of his crimes the city should
be his, and he would have gained honors and authority and riches, and would no longer be in fear
of the law or in the difficulties that want of money
and the awareness of his crimes had brought him.
So that not even Catiline loved his crimes as
crimes: he loved some other thing which was his
reason for committing them.

Augustine, Confessions, II, 5

22 What shall I say of these judgments which men
pronounce on men, and which are necessary in
communities, whatever outward peace they enjoy? Melancholy and lamentable judgments they
are, since the judges are men who cannot discern
the consciences of those at their bar, and are
therefore frequently compelled to put innocent
witnesses to the torture to ascertain the truth regarding the crimes of other men. What shall I say
of torture applied to the accused himself? He is
tortured to discover whether he is guilty, so that,
though innocent, he suffers most undoubted punishment for crime that is still doubtful, not because it is proved that he committed it, but because it is not ascertained that he did not commit
it. Thus the ignorance of the judge frequently involves an innocent person in suffering. And what
is still more unendurable—a thing, indeed, to be
bewailed, and, if that were possible, watered with
fountains of tears—is this, that when the judge
puts the accused to the question, that he may not
unwittingly put an innocent man to death, the
result of this lamentable ignorance is that this
very person, whom he tortured that he might not
condemn him if innocent, is condemned to death
both tortured and innocent. For if he has chosen,
in obedience to the philosophical instructions to
the wise man, to quit this life rather than endure
any longer such tortures, he declares that he has

committed the crime which in fact he has not committed. And when he has been condemned and put to death, the judge is still in ignorance whether he has put to death an innocent or a guilty person, though he put the accused to the torture for the very purpose of saving himself from condemning the innocent; and consequently he has both tortured an innocent man to discover his innocence and has put him to death without discovering it. If such darkness shrouds social life, will a wise judge take his seat on the bench or no? Beyond question he will. For human society, which he thinks it a wickedness to abandon, constrains him and compels him to this duty. And he thinks it no wickedness that innocent witnesses are tortured regarding the crimes of which other men are accused; or that the accused are put to the torture, so that they are often overcome with anguish, and, though innocent, make false confessions regarding themselves, and are punished; or that, though they be not condemned to die, they often die during, or in consequence of, the torture; or that sometimes the accusers, who perhaps have been prompted by a desire to benefit society by bringing criminals to justice, are themselves condemned through the ignorance of the judge, because they are unable to prove the truth of their accusations though they are true, and because the witnesses lie, and the accused endures the torture without being moved to confession. These numerous and important evils he does not consider sins; for the wise judge does these things, not with any intention of doing harm, but because his ignorance compels him, and because human society claims him as a judge. But though we therefore acquit the judge of malice, we must none the less condemn human life as miserable. And if he is compelled to torture and punish the innocent because his office and his ignorance constrain him, is he a happy as well as guiltless man? Surely it were proof of more profound considerateness and finer feeling were he to recognize the misery of these necessities, and shrink from his own implication in that misery; and had he any piety about him, he would cry to God "From my necessities deliver Thou me."

Augustine, *City of God,* XIX, 6

23 Man can be punished with a threefold punishment corresponding to the three orders to which the human will is subject. In the first place a man's nature is subjected to the order of his own reason; secondly, it is subjected to the order of another man who governs him either in spiritual or in temporal matters, as a member either of the state or of the household; thirdly, it is subjected to the universal order of the Divine government. Now each of these orders is disturbed by sin, for the sinner acts against his reason, and against human and Divine law. Hence he incurs a threefold punishment; one, inflicted by himself, namely remorse of conscience; another, inflicted by man; and a third, inflicted by God.

Aquinas, *Summa Theologica,* I–II, 87, 1

24 The punishment that is inflicted according to human laws is not always intended as a medicine for the one who is punished, but sometimes only for others; thus when a thief is hanged, this is not for his own amendment, but for the sake of others, that at least they may be deterred from crime through fear of the punishment.

Aquinas, *Summa Theologica,* I–II, 87, 3

25 A severe punishment is inflicted not only on account of the gravity of a fault, but also for other reasons. First, on account of the greatness of the sin, because a greater sin, other things being equal, deserves a greater punishment. Secondly, on account of a habitual sin, since men are not easily cured of habitual sin except by severe punishments. Thirdly, on account of a great desire for or a great pleasure in the sin; for men are not easily deterred from such sins unless they be severely punished. Fourthly, on account of the facility of committing a sin and of concealing it; for such sins, when discovered, should be more severely punished in order to deter others from committing them.

Aquinas, *Summa Theologica,* I–II, 105, 2

26 Both Divine and human laws command . . . sinners to be put to death, [if] there is greater likelihood of their harming others than of their mending their ways. Nevertheless the judge puts this into effect not out of hatred for the sinners, but out of the love of charity, by reason of which he prefers the public good to the life of the individual. Moreover, the death inflicted by the judge profits the sinner, if he be converted, for the expiation of his crime; and if he be not converted, it profits so as to put an end to the sin, because the sinner is thus deprived of the power to sin any more.

Aquinas, *Summa Theologica,* II–II, 25, 6

27 *Saint* Francis afterwards, when I was dead, came for me: but one of the Black Cherubim said to him: 'Do not take him; wrong me not.

He must come down amongst my menials; because he gave the fraudulent counsel, since which I have kept fast by his hair:

for he who repents not, cannot be absolved; nor is it possible to repent and will *a thing* at the same time, the contradiction not permitting it.'

O wretched me! how I started when he seized me, saying to me: 'May be thou didst not think that I was a logician!'

Dante, *Inferno,* XXVII, 112

28 When theft is punished by hanging, this occurs according to positive law on acceptable grounds,

but not as in the case of the Draconian law which condemned every thief to hang, even if he stole only a chicken; this has no acceptable grounds and is contrary to nature. Consequently it was said that this law was written in blood. Yet the punishment must be applied more severely among more unbridled peoples.

Luther, *Table Talk,* 3911

29 Some peasants have just informed me hastily that a moment ago they left in a wood that belongs to me a man stabbed in a hundred places, who is still breathing, and who begged them for pity's sake to bring him some water and help him to get up. They say that they did not dare go near him, and ran away, for fear that the officers of the law would catch them there and hold them accountable for the accident—as is done with those who are found near a murdered man—to their total ruin, since they had neither ability nor money to defend their innocence. What could I say to them? It is certain that this act of humanity would have got them into trouble.

How many innocent people we have found to have been punished—I mean by no fault of their judges—and how many there have been that we have not found out about! Here is something that happened in my time. Certain men are condemned to death for a murder, the sentence being, if not pronounced, at least decided and determined. At this point the judges are informed by the officers of an inferior court nearby that they have some prisoners who confess outright to this murder and throw a decisive light on the whole business. They deliberate whether because of this they should interrupt and defer the execution of the sentence passed upon the first accused. They consider the novelty of the case and the precedent it would set in suspending the execution of sentences; that the sentence has been passed according to law, and that the judges have no right to change their minds. In short, these poor devils are sacrificed to the forms of justice.

Philip, or some other, took care of a similar problem in this manner. He had sentenced a man, by a definitive judgment, to pay a heavy fine to another. The truth came to light some time after, and it turned out that he had decided unfairly. On one side were the rights of the case, on the other side the rights of judicial forms. He gave some satisfaction to both, letting the sentence stand and compensating the loss of the convicted man out of his own purse. But he was dealing with a reparable accident; my men were irreparably hanged. How many condemnations I have seen more criminal than the crime!

Montaigne, *Essays,* III, 13, Of Experience

30 *Hamlet.* Give me your pardon, sir. I've done you wrong;
But pardon't, as you are a gentleman.

This presence knows,
And you must needs have heard, how I am punish'd
With sore distraction. What I have done,
That might your nature, honour, and exception
Roughly awake, I here proclaim was madness.
Was't Hamlet wrong'd Laertes? Never Hamlet!
If Hamlet from himself be ta'en away,
And when he's not himself does wrong Laertes,
Then Hamlet does it not, Hamlet denies it.
Who does it, then? His madness.

Shakespeare, *Hamlet,* V, ii, 237

31 *Angelo.* Condemn the fault, and not the actor of it?
Why, every fault's condemn'd ere it be done.
Mine were the very cipher of a function,
To fine the faults whose fine stands in record,
And let go by the actor.

Shakespeare, *Measure for Measure,* II, ii, 37

32 *Isabella.*   Good, good my lord, bethink you;
Who is it that hath died for this offence?
There's many have committed it.
    Lucio.   Ay, well said.
    Angelo. The law hath not been dead, though it hath slept.
Those many had not dared to do that evil,
If the first that did the edict infringe
Had answer'd for his deed. Now 'tis awake,
Takes a note of what is done; and, like a prophet
Looks in a glass that shows what future evils,
Either new, or by remissness new-conceived,
And so in progress to be hatch'd and born,
Are now to have no successive degrees,
But, ere they live, to end.
    Isab.   Yet show some pity.
    Ang. I show it most of all when I show justice;
For then I pity those I do not know,
Which a dismiss'd offence would after gall;
And do him right that, answering one foul wrong,
Lives not to act another.

Shakespeare, *Measure for Measure,* II, ii, 87

33 My Lord, said he, a large River divides in two Parts one and the same Lordship. I beg your Honour to lend me your Attention, for 'tis a Case of great Importance, and some Difficulty—Upon this River there is a Bridge; at one End of which there stands a Gallows, and a kind of Court of Justice, where four Judges use to sit, for the Execution of a certain Law made by the Lord of the Land and River, which runs thus.

Whoever intends to pass from one End of this Bridge to the other, must first upon his Oath declare whither he goes, and what his Business is. If he swear Truth, he may go on; but if he swear false, he shall be hang'd, and die without Remission upon the Gibbet at the End of the Bridge.

After due Promulgation of this Law, many People, notwithstanding it's Severity, adventur'd to go over this Bridge, and as it appear'd they swore true, the Judges permitted 'em to pass unmolested. It happen'd one Day that a certain Passenger being sworn, declar'd, that by the Oath he had taken, he was come to die upon that Gallows, and that was all his Business.

This put the Judges to a Nonplus; for, said they, If we let this Man pass freely, he is forsworn, and according to the Letter of the Law he ought to die: If we hang him, he has sworn Truth, seeing he swore he was to die on that Gibbet; and then by the same Law we should let him pass.

Now your Lordship's Judgment is desir'd what the Judges ought to do with this Man? For they are still at a stand, not knowing what to determine in this Case; and having been inform'd of your sharp Wit, and great Capacity in resolving difficult Questions, they sent me to beseech your Lordship in their Names, to give your Opinion in so intricate and knotty a Case. . . .

Well, hark you me, honest Man, said *Sancho,* either I am a Codshead, or there is as much Reason to put this same Person you talk of to Death as to let him live and pass the Bridge; for if the Truth saves him, the Lye condemns him. Now the Case stands thus, I would have you tell those Gentlemen that sent you to me, since there's as much Reason to bring him off, as to condemn him, that they e'en let him go free; for 'tis always more commendable to do Good than Hurt. And this I would give you under my own Hand, if I could write. Nor do I speak this of my own Head; but I remember one Precept, among many others, that my Master Don *Quixote* gave me the Night before I went to govern this Island, which was, that when the Scale of Justice is even, or a Case is doubtful, we should prefer Mercy before Rigour; and it has pleas'd God I should call it to Mind so luckily at this Juncture.

Cervantes, *Don Quixote,* II, 51

34 The house of every man is his castle, and if thieves come to a man's house to rob or murder, and the owner or his servants kill any of the thieves in defence of himself and his house, it is no felony and he lose nothing.

Sir Edward Coke, *Coke's Reports, Semayne's Case*

35 In causes of life and death, judges ought (as far as the law permitteth) in justice to remember mercy; and to cast a severe eye upon the example, but a merciful eye upon the person.

Bacon, *Of Judicature*

36 When a penalty is either annexed to the crime in the law itself, or hath been usually inflicted in the like cases, there the delinquent is excused from a greater penalty. For the punishment foreknown, if not great enough to deter men from the action, is an invitement to it: because when men compare the benefit of their injustice with the harm of their punishment, by necessity of nature they choose that which appeareth best for themselves: and therefore when they are punished more than the law had formerly determined, or more than others were punished for the same crime, it is the law that tempted and deceiveth them.

Hobbes, *Leviathan,* II, 27

37 If a man by the terror of present death be compelled to do a fact against the law, he is totally excused; because no law can oblige a man to abandon his own preservation. And supposing such a law were obligatory, yet a man would reason thus: "If I do it not, I die presently; if I do it, I die afterwards; therefore by doing it, there is time of life gained." Nature therefore compels him to the fact.

Hobbes, *Leviathan,* II, 27

38 To kill against the law is a greater crime than any other injury, life preserved.

And to kill with torment, greater than simply to kill.

And mutilation of a limb, greater than the spoiling a man of his goods.

And the spoiling a man of his goods by terror of death or wounds, than by clandestine surreption.

And by clandestine surreption, than by consent fraudulently obtained.

And the violation of chastity by force, greater than by flattery.

And of a woman married, than of a woman not married.

For all these things are commonly so valued; though some men are more, and some less, sensible of the same offence. But the law regardeth not the particular, but the general inclination of mankind.

Hobbes, *Leviathan,* II, 27

39 A *punishment* is an evil inflicted by public authority on him that hath done or omitted that which is judged by the same authority to be a transgression of the law, to the end that the will of men may thereby the better be disposed to obedience. . . .

From the definition of punishment, I infer, first, that neither private revenges nor injuries of private men can properly be styled punishment, because they proceed not from public authority. . . .

Thirdly, that the evil inflicted by public authority, without precedent public condemnation, is not to be styled by the name of punishment, but of a hostile act, because the fact for which a man is punished ought first to be judged by public authority to be a transgression of the law.

Fourthly, that the evil inflicted by usurped power, and judges without authority from the sovereign, is not punishment, but an act of hostility, because the acts of power usurped have not for author the person condemned, and therefore are not acts of public authority.

Fifthly, that all evil which is inflicted without intention or possibility of disposing the delinquent or, by his example, other men to obey the laws is not punishment, but an act of hostility, because without such an end no hurt done is contained under that name. . . .

Seventhly, if the harm inflicted be less than the benefit of contentment that naturally followeth the crime committed, that harm is not within the definition, and is rather the price of redemption than the punishment of a crime: because it is of the nature of punishment to have for end the disposing of men to obey the law; which end (if it be less than the benefit of the transgression) it attaineth not, but worketh a contrary effect.

Hobbes, *Leviathan,* II, 28

40 Intemperance is naturally punished with diseases; rashness, with mischances; injustice, with the violence of enemies; pride, with ruin; cowardice, with oppression; negligent government of princes, with rebellion; and rebellion, with slaughter. For seeing punishments are consequent to the breach of laws, natural punishments must be naturally consequent to the breach of the laws of nature, and therefore follow them as their natural, not arbitrary, effects.

Hobbes, *Leviathan,* II, 31

41 To impress your minds with a deeper horror at homicide, remember that the first crime of fallen man was a murder, committed on the person of the first holy man; that the greatest crime was a murder, perpetrated on the person of the King of saints; and that, of all crimes, murder is the only one which involves in a common destruction the Church and the state, nature and religion.

Pascal, *Provincial Letters,* XIV

42 When the supreme authority, constrained by the desire of preserving peace, punishes a citizen who injures another, I do not say that it is indignant with the citizen, since it is not excited by hatred to destroy him, but punishes him from motives of piety.

Spinoza, *Ethics,* IV, Prop. 51, Schol.

43 In the state of nature, wrong-doing is impossible; or, if anyone does wrong, it is to himself, not to another. For no one by the law of nature is bound to please another, unless he chooses, nor to hold anything to be good or evil, but what he himself, according to his own temperament, pronounces to be so; and, to speak generally, nothing is forbidden by the law of nature, except what is beyond everyone's power. But wrong-doing is action, which cannot lawfully be committed. But if men by the ordinance of nature were bound to be led by reason, then all of necessity would be so led.

For the ordinances of nature are the ordinances of God, which God has instituted by the liberty, whereby he exists, and they follow, therefore, from the necessity of the divine nature, and, consequently, are eternal, and cannot be broken. But men are chiefly guided by appetite, without reason; yet for all this they do not disturb the course of nature, but follow it of necessity. And, therefore, a man ignorant and weak of mind, is no more bound by natural law to order his life wisely, than a sick man is bound to be sound of body.

Therefore wrong-doing cannot be conceived of, but under dominion—that is, where, by the general right of the whole dominion, it is decided what is good and what is evil, and where no one does anything rightfully, save what he does in accordance with the general decree or consent.

Spinoza, *Political Treatise,* II, 18–19

44 It is fit the ruler should have a power in many cases to mitigate the severity of the law, and pardon some offenders, since the end of government being the preservation of all as much as may be, even the guilty are to be spared where it can prove no prejudice to the innocent.

Locke, *II Civil Government,* XIV, 159

45 Since it would be utterly in vain to suppose a rule set to the free actions of men, without annexing to it some enforcement of good and evil to determine his will, we must, wherever we suppose a law, suppose also some reward or punishment annexed to that law. It would be in vain for one intelligent being to set a rule to the actions of another, if he had it not in his power to reward the compliance with, and punish deviation from his rule, by some good and evil, that is not the natural product and consequence of the action itself. For that, being a natural convenience or inconvenience, would operate of itself, without a law. This, if I mistake not, is the true nature of all law, properly so called.

Locke, *Concerning Human Understanding,*
Bk. II, XXVIII, 6

46 There are some laws and customs in this [the Lilliputians'] empire very peculiar; and if they were not so directly contrary to those of my own dear country, I should be tempted to say a little in their justification. It is only to be wished, that they were as well executed. The first I shall mention, relateth to informers. All crimes against the State, are punished here with the utmost severity; but if the person accused make his innocence plainly to appear upon his tryal, the accuser is immediately put to an ignominious death; and out of his goods or lands, the innocent person is quadruply recompensed for the loss of his time, for the danger he underwent, for the hardship of his imprisonment, and for all the charges he hath been at in making his defence. Or, if that fund be

deficient, it is largely supplyed by the Crown. The emperor doth also confer on him some publick mark of his favour; and proclamation is made of his innocence through the whole city.

Swift, *Gulliver's Travels*, I, 6

47 They [the Lilliputians] look upon fraud as a greater crime than theft, and therefore seldom fail to punish it with death: for, they alledge, that care and vigilance, with a very common understanding, may preserve a man's goods from thieves; but honesty hath no fence against superior cunning: and since it is necessary that there should be a perpetual intercourse of buying and selling, and dealing upon credit; where fraud is permitted or connived at, or hath no law to punish it, the honest dealer is always undone, and the knave gets the advantage. I remember when I was once interceding with the king for a criminal who had wronged his master of a great sum of money, which he had received by order, and ran away with; and happening to tell his Majesty, by way of extenuation, that it was only a breach of trust; the emperor thought it monstrous in me to offer, as a defence, the greatest aggravation of the crime: and truly, I had little to say in return, farther than the common answer, that different nations had different customs; for, I confess, I was heartily ashamed.

Swift, *Gulliver's Travels*, I, 6

48 Ingratitude is among them [the Lilliputians] a capital crime, as we read it to have been in some other countries: for they reason thus; that whoever makes ill returns to his benefactor, must needs be a common enemy to the rest of mankind, from whom they have received no obligation; and therefore such a man is not fit to live.

Swift, *Gulliver's Travels*, I, 6

49 Experience shows that in countries remarkable for the lenity of their laws the spirit of the inhabitants is as much affected by slight penalties as in other countries by severer punishments.

If an inconvenience or abuse arises in the state, a violent government endeavours suddenly to redress it; and instead of putting the old laws in execution, it establishes some cruel punishment, which instantly puts a stop to the evil. But the spring of government hereby loses its elasticity; the imagination grows accustomed to the severe as well as the milder punishment; and as the fear of the latter diminishes, they are soon obliged in every case to have recourse to the former. Robberies on the highway became common in some countries; in order to remedy this evil, they invented the punishment of breaking upon the wheel, the terror of which put a stop for a while to this mischievous practice. But soon after robberies on the highways became as common as ever. . . .

Mankind must not be governed with too much severity; we ought to make a prudent use of the means which nature has given us to conduct them. If we inquire into the cause of all human corruptions, we shall find that they proceed from the impunity of criminals, and not from the moderation of punishments.

Montesquieu, *Spirit of Laws*, VI, 12

50 The lawfulness of putting a malefactor to death arises from this circumstance: the law by which he is punished was made for his security. A murderer, for instance, has enjoyed the benefit of the very law which condemns him; it has been a continual protection to him; he cannot, therefore, object to it.

Montesquieu, *Spirit of Laws*, XV, 2

51 When any man, even in political society, renders himself by his crimes obnoxious to the public, he is punished by the laws in his goods and person; that is, the ordinary rules of justice are, with regard to him, suspended for a moment; and it becomes equitable to inflict on him, for the *benefit* of society, what otherwise he could not suffer without wrong or injury.

Hume, *Concerning Principles of Morals*, III

52 Let the punishments of criminals be useful. A hanged man is good for nothing, and a man condemned to public works still serves the country, and is a living lesson.

Voltaire, *Philosophical Dictionary:* Civil Laws

53 "And why was this admiral killed?" "Because," said they, "he did not kill men enough himself. He attacked the French admiral, and was found guilty of not being near enough to him." "But then," said Candide, "was not the French admiral as far off from the English admiral, as he was from him?" "That is what cannot be doubted," replied they. "But in this country it is of very great service to kill an admiral now and then, in order to make the rest fight better."

Voltaire, *Candide*, XXIII

54 The power of the laws depends still more on their own wisdom than on the severity of their administrators, and the public will derives its greatest weight from the reason which has dictated it. Hence Plato looked upon it as a very necessary precaution to place at the head of all edicts a preamble, setting forth their justice and utility. In fact, the first of all laws is to respect the laws: the severity of penalties is only a vain resource, invented by little minds in order to substitute terror for that respect which they have no means of obtaining. It has constantly been observed that in those countries where legal punishments are most severe, they are also most frequent; so that the cruelty of such punishments is a proof only of the multitude of criminals, and, punishing everything

with equal severity, induces those who are guilty to commit crimes, in order to escape being punished for their faults.

Rousseau, *Political Economy*

55 It is not only upright men who know how to administer the laws; but at bottom only good men know how to obey them. The man who once gets the better of remorse, will not shrink before punishments which are less severe, and less lasting, and from which there is at least the hope of escaping: whatever precautions are taken, those who only require impunity in order to do wrong will not fail to find means of eluding the law, and avoiding its penalties.

Rousseau, *Political Economy*

56 Every malefactor, by attacking social rights, becomes on forfeit a rebel and a traitor to his country; by violating its laws he ceases to be a member of it; he even makes war upon it. In such a case the preservation of the State is inconsistent with his own, and one or the other must perish; in putting the guilty to death, we slay not so much the citizen as an enemy. The trial and the judgment are the proofs that he has broken the social treaty, and is in consequence no longer a member of the State. Since, then, he has recognised himself to be such by living there, he must be removed by exile as a violator of the compact, or by death as a public enemy; for such an enemy is not a moral person, but merely a man; and in such a case the right of war is to kill the vanquished.

Rousseau, *Social Contract*, II, 5

57 The frequency of capital punishments . . . rarely hinders the commission of a crime, but naturally and commonly prevents its detection, and is, if we proceed only upon prudential principles, chiefly for that reason to be avoided. Whatever may be urged by casuists or politicians, the greater part of mankind, as they can never think that to pick the pocket and to pierce the heart is equally criminal, will scarcely believe that two malefactors so different in guilt can be justly doomed to the same punishment.

Johnson, *Rambler No. 114*

58 He [Johnson] said to Sir William Scott, "The age is running mad after innovation; all the business of the world is to be done in a new way; men are to be hanged in a new way; Tyburn itself is not safe from the fury of innovation." It having been argued that this was an improvement,—"No, Sir, (said he, eagerly,) it is *not* an improvement: they object that the old method drew together a number of spectators. Sir, executions are intended to draw spectators. If they do not draw spectators they don't answer their purpose. The old method was most satisfactory to all parties; the publick was gratified by a procession; the criminal was

supported by it. Why is all this to be swept away?" I perfectly agree with Dr. Johnson upon this head, and am persuaded that executions now, the solemn procession being discontinued, have not nearly the effect which they formerly had. Magistrates both in London, and elsewhere, have, I am afraid, in this had too much regard to their own ease.

Boswell, *Life of Johnson (1783)*

59 The right of administering punishment is the right of the sovereign as the supreme power to inflict pain upon a subject on account of a crime committed by him. The head of the state cannot therefore be punished; but his supremacy may be withdrawn from him.

Kant, *Science of Right*, 49

60 Judicial or juridical punishment is to be distinguished from natural punishment, in which crime as vice punishes itself, and does not as such come within the cognizance of the legislator. Juridical punishment can never be administered merely as a means for promoting another good either with regard to the criminal himself or to civil society, but must in all cases be imposed only because the individual on whom it is inflicted *has committed a crime*. For one man ought never to be dealt with merely as a means subservient to the purpose of another, nor be mixed up with the subjects of real right. Against such treatment his inborn personality has a right to protect him, even although he may be condemned to lose his civil personality. He must first be found guilty and *punishable*, before there can be any thought of drawing from his punishment any benefit for himself or his fellow-citizens. The penal law is a categorical imperative; and woe to him who creeps through the serpent-windings of utilitarianism to discover some advantage that may discharge him from the justice of punishment, or even from the due measure of it, according to the Pharisaic maxim: "It is better that *one* man should die than that the whole people should perish."

Kant, *Science of Right*, 49

61 Whoever has commited murder, must *die*. There is, in this case, no juridical substitute or surrogate, that can be given or taken for the satisfaction of justice. There is no *likeness* or proportion between life, however painful, and death; and therefore there is no equality between the crime of murder and the retaliation of it but what is judicially accomplished by the execution of the criminal. His death, however, must be kept free from all maltreatment that would make the humanity suffering in his person loathsome or abominable. Even if a civil society resolved to dissolve itself with the consent of all its members—as might be supposed in the case of a people inhabiting an island resolving to separate and scatter themselves throughout

the whole world—the last murderer lying in the prison ought to be executed before the resolution was carried out. This ought to be done in order that every one may realize the desert of his deeds, and that blood-guiltiness may not remain upon the people; for otherwise they might all be regarded as participators in the murder as a public violation of justice.

The equalization of punishment with crime is therefore only possible by the cognition of the judge extending even to the penalty of death, according to the right of retaliation. This is manifest from the fact that it is only thus that a sentence can be pronounced over all criminals proportionate to their internal *wickedness;* as may be seen by considering the case when the punishment of death has to be inflicted, not on account of a murder, but on account of a political crime that can only be punished capitally.

Kant, *Science of Right,* 49

62 The right of pardoning, viewed in relation to the criminal, is the right of mitigating or entirely remitting his punishment. On the side of the sovereign this is the most delicate of all rights, as it may be exercised so as to set forth the splendour of his dignity, and yet so as to do a great wrong by it. It ought not to be exercised in application to the crimes of the subjects against each other; for exemption from punishment would be the greatest wrong that could be done to them. It is only an occasion of some form of treason, as a lesion against himself, that the sovereign should make use of this right. And it should not be exercised even in this connection, if the safety of the people would be endangered by remitting such punishment. This right is the only one which properly deserves the name of a "right of majesty."

Kant, *Science of Right,* 49

63 Punishment is regarded as containing the criminal's right and hence by being punished he is honoured as a rational being. He does not receive this due of honour unless the concept and measure of his punishment are derived from his own act. Still less does he receive it if he is treated either as a harmful animal who has to be made harmless, or with a view to deterring and reforming him.

Hegel, *Philosophy of Right,* 100

64 It seems to be a contradiction that a crime committed in society appears more heinous and yet is punished more leniently. But while it would be impossible for society to leave a crime unpunished, since that would be to posit it as right, still since society is sure of itself, a crime must always be something idiosyncratic in comparison, something unstable and exceptional. The very stability of society gives a crime the status of something purely subjective which seems to be the product rather of natural impulse than of a prudent will.

In this light, crime acquires a milder status, and for this reason its punishment too becomes milder. If society is still internally weak, then an example must be made by inflicting punishments, since punishment is itself an example over against the example of crime. But in a society which is internally strong, the commission of crime is something so feeble that its annulment must be commensurable with its feebleness. Harsh punishments, therefore, are not unjust in and by themselves; they are related to contemporary conditions. A criminal code cannot hold good for all time, and crimes are only shows of reality which may draw on themselves a greater or lesser degree of disavowal.

Hegel, *Philosophy of Right,* Additions, Par. 218

65 Crime and punishment grow out of one stem. Punishment is a fruit that unsuspected ripens within the flower of the pleasure which concealed it.

Emerson, *Compensation*

66 Commit a crime, and the earth is made of glass. Commit a crime, and it seems as if a coat of snow fell on the ground, such as reveals in the woods the track of every partridge and fox and squirrel and mole. You cannot recall the spoken word, you cannot wipe out the foot-track, you cannot draw up the ladder, so as to leave no inlet or clew. Some damning circumstance always transpires. The laws and substances of nature—water, snow, wind, gravitation—become penalties to the thief.

Emerson, *Compensation*

67 There are some who say, that it is unjust to punish any one for the sake of example to others; that punishment is just, only when intended for the good of the sufferer himself. Others maintain the extreme reverse, contending that to punish persons who have attained years of discretion, for their own benefit, is despotism and injustice, since if the matter at issue is solely their own good, no one has a right to control their own judgment of it; but that they may justly be punished to prevent evil to others, this being the exercise of the legitimate right of self-defence. Mr. Owen, again, affirms that it is unjust to punish at all; for the criminal did not make his own character; his education, and the circumstances which surrounded him, have made him a criminal, and for these he is not responsible. All these opinions are extremely plausible; and so long as the question is argued as one of justice simply, without going down to the principles which lie under justice and are the source of its authority, I am unable to see how any of these reasoners can be refuted. For in truth every one of the three builds upon rules of justice confessedly true. The first appeals to the acknowledged injustice of singling out an individual, and making him a sacrifice, without his con-

sent, for other people's benefit. The second relies on the acknowledged justice of self-defence, and the admitted injustice of forcing one person to conform to another's notions of what constitutes his good. The Owenite invokes the admitted principle, that it is unjust to punish any one for what he cannot help. Each is triumphant so long as he is not compelled to take into consideration any other maxims of justice than the one he has selected; but as soon as their several maxims are brought face to face, each disputant seems to have exactly as much to say for himself as the others. No one of them can carry out his own notion of justice without trampling upon another equally binding.

These are difficulties; they have always been felt to be such; and many devices have been invented to turn rather than to overcome them. As a refuge from the last of the three, men imagined what they called the freedom of the will; fancying that they could not justify punishing a man whose will is in a thoroughly hateful state, unless it be supposed to have come into that state through no influence of anterior circumstances. To escape from the other difficulties, a favourite contrivance has been the fiction of a contract, whereby at some unknown period all the members of society engaged to obey the laws, and consented to be punished for any disobedience to them; thereby giving to their legislators the right, which it is assumed they would not otherwise have had, of punishing them, either for their own good or for that of society. This happy thought was considered to get rid of the whole difficulty, and to legitimate the infliction of punishment, in virtue of another received maxim of justice, *Volenti non fit injuria;* that is not unjust which is done with the consent of the person who is supposed to be hurt by it. I need hardly remark, that even if the consent were not a mere fiction, this maxim is not superior in authority to the others which it is brought in to supersede. It is, on the contrary, an instructive specimen of the loose and irregular manner in which supposed principles of justice grow up. This particular one evidently came into use as a help to the coarse exigencies of courts of law, which are sometimes obliged to be content with very uncertain presumptions, on account of the greater evils which would often arise from any attempt on their part to cut finer. But even courts of law are not able to adhere consistently to the maxim, for they allow voluntary engagements to be set aside on the ground of fraud, and sometimes on that of mere mistake or misinformation.

Again, when the legitimacy of inflicting punishment is admitted, how many conflicting conceptions of justice come to light in discussing the proper apportionment of punishments to offences. No rule on the subject recommends itself so strongly to the primitive and spontaneous sentiment of justice, as the *lex talionis,* an eye for an eye

and a tooth for a tooth. Though this principle of the Jewish and of the Mahometan law has been generally abandoned in Europe as a practical maxim, there is, I suspect, in most minds, a secret hankering after it; and when retribution accidentally falls on an offender in that precise shape, the general feeling of satisfaction evinced bears witness how natural is the sentiment to which this repayment in kind is acceptable. With many, the test of justice in penal infliction is that the punishment should be proportioned to the offence; meaning that it should be exactly measured by the moral guilt of the culprit (whatever be their standard for measuring moral guilt): the consideration, what amount of punishment is necessary to deter from the offence, having nothing to do with the question of justice, in their estimation: while there are others to whom that consideration is all in all; who maintain that it is not just, at least for man, to inflict on a fellow-creature, whatever may be his offences, any amount of suffering beyond the least that will suffice to prevent him from repeating, and others from imitating, his misconduct.

Mill, *Utilitarianism,* V

68 "Why," began the elder, "all these sentences to exile with hard labour, and formerly with flogging also, reform no one, and what's more, deter hardly a single criminal, and the number of crimes does not diminish but is continually on the increase. You must admit that. Consequently the security of society is not preserved, for, although the obnoxious member is mechanically cut off and sent far away out of sight, another criminal always comes to take his place at once, and often two of them. If anything does preserve society, even in our time, and does regenerate and transform the criminal, it is only the law of Christ speaking in his conscience. It is only by recognising his wrong-doing as a son of a Christian society—that is, of the Church—that he recognises his sin against society—that is, against the Church. So that it is only against the Church, and not against the State, that the criminal of to-day can recognise that he has sinned. If society, as a Church, had jurisdiction, then it would know when to bring back from exclusion and to reunite to itself. Now the Church having no real jurisdiction, but only the power of moral condemnation, withdraws of her own accord from punishing the criminal actively. She does not excommunicate him but simply persists in motherly exhortation of him. What is more, the Church even tries to preserve all Christian communion with the criminal. She admits him to church services, to the holy sacrament, gives him alms, and treats him more as a captive than as a convict. And what would become of the criminal, O Lord, if even the Christian society—that is, the Church—were to reject him even as the civil law rejects him and cuts him

off? What would become of him if the Church punished him with her excommunication as the direct consequence of the secular law? There could be no more terrible despair, at least for a Russian criminal, for Russian criminals still have faith. Though, who knows, perhaps then a fearful thing would happen, perhaps the despairing heart of the criminal would lose its faith and then what would become of him? But the Church, like a tender, loving mother, holds aloof from active punishment herself, as the sinner is too severely punished already by the civil law, and there must be at least someone to have pity on him. The Church holds aloof, above all, because its judgment is the only one that contains the truth, and therefore cannot practically and morally be united to any other judgment even as a temporary compromise. She can enter into no compact about that. The foreign criminal, they say, rarely repents, for the very doctrines of to-day confirm him in the idea that his crime is not a crime, but only a reaction against an unjustly oppressive force. Society cuts him off completely by a force that triumphs over him mechanically and (so at least they say of themselves in Europe) accompanies this exclusion with hatred, forgetfulness, and the most profound indifference as to the ultimate fate of the erring brother."

Dostoevsky, *Brothers Karamazov*, Pt. I, II, 5

69 Remember particularly that you cannot be a judge of anyone. For no one can judge a criminal until he recognises that he is just such a criminal as the man standing before him, and that he perhaps is more than all men to blame for that crime. When he understands that, he will be able to be a judge. Though that sounds absurd, it is true. If I had been righteous myself, perhaps there would have been no criminal standing before me. If you can take upon yourself the crime of the criminal your heart is judging, take it at once, suffer for him yourself, and let him go without reproach. And even if the law itself makes you his judge, act in the same spirit so far as possible, for he will go away and condemn himself more bitterly than you have done. If, after your kiss, he goes away untouched, mocking at you, do not let that be a stumbling-block to you. It shows his time has not yet come, but it will come in due course. And if it come not, no matter; if not he, then another in his place will understand and suffer, and judge and condemn himself, and the truth will be fulfilled. Believe that, believe it without doubt; for in that lies all the hope and faith of the saints.

Dostoevsky, *Brothers Karamazov*, Pt. II, VI, 3

70 Raskolnikov smiled again. He saw the point at once, and knew where they wanted to drive him. He decided to take up the challenge.

"That wasn't quite my contention," he began simply and modestly. "Yet I admit that you have stated it almost correctly; perhaps, if you like, perfectly so." (It almost gave him pleasure to admit this.) "The only difference is that I don't contend that extraordinary people are always bound to commit breaches of morals, as you call it. In fact, I doubt whether such an argument could be published. I simply hinted that an 'extraordinary' man has the right . . . that is not an official right, but an inner right to decide in his own conscience to overstep . . . certain obstacles, and only in case it is essential for the practical fulfilment of his idea (sometimes, perhaps, of benefit to the whole of humanity). You say that my article isn't definite; I am ready to make it as clear as I can. Perhaps I am right in thinking you want me to; very well. I maintain that if the discoveries of Kepler and Newton could not have been made known except by sacrificing the lives of one, a dozen, a hundred, or more men, Newton would have had the right, would indeed have been in duty bound . . . to *eliminate* the dozen or the hundred men for the sake of making his discoveries known to the whole of humanity. But it does not follow from that that Newton had a right to murder people right and left and to steal every day in the market. Then, I remember, I maintain in my article that all . . . well, legislators and leaders of men, such as Lycurgus, Solon, Mahomet, Napoleon, and so on, were all without exception criminals, from the very fact that, making a new law, they transgressed the ancient one, handed down from their ancestors and held sacred by the people, and they did not stop short at bloodshed either, if that bloodshed—often of innocent persons fighting bravely in defence of ancient law—were of use to their cause. It's remarkable, in fact, that the majority, indeed, of these benefactors and leaders of humanity were guilty of terrible carnage. In short, I maintain that all great men or even men a little out of the common, that is to say capable of giving some new word, must from their very nature be criminals—more or less, of course. Otherwise it's hard for them to get out of the common rut; and to remain in the common rut is what they can't submit to, from their very nature again, and to my mind they ought not, indeed, to submit to it. You see that there is nothing particularly new in all that. The same thing has been printed and read a thousand times before. As for my division of people into ordinary and extraordinary, I acknowledge that it's somewhat arbitrary, but I don't insist upon exact numbers. I only believe in my leading idea that men are *in general* divided by a law of nature into two categories, inferior (ordinary), that is, so to say, material that serves only to reproduce its kind, and men who have the gift or the talent to utter *a new word*. There are, of course, innumerable sub-divisions, but the distinguishing features of both categories are fairly well marked. The first category, generally speaking, are men conservative in temperament and law-abiding; they live under control and love to be controlled. To my thinking it is their duty to be controlled, because that's their vocation, and there is nothing humiliating in it for them. The second category all transgress the law; they are destroyers or disposed to destruction according to their capacities. The crimes of these men are of course relative and varied; for the most part they seek in very varied ways the destruction of the present for the sake of the better. But if such a one is forced for the sake of his idea to step over a corpse or wade through blood, he can, I maintain, find within himself, in his conscience, a sanction for wading through blood—that depends on the idea and its dimensions, note that. It's only in that sense I speak of their right to crime in my article (you remember it began with the legal question). There's no need for such anxiety, however; the masses will scarcely ever admit this right, they punish them or hang them (more or less), and in doing so fulfil quite justly their conservative vocation. But the same masses set these criminals on a pedestal in the next generation and worship them (more or less). The first category is always the man of the present, the second the man of the future. The first preserve the world and people it, the second move the world and lead it to its goal. Each class has an equal right to exist. In fact, all have equal rights with me—and *vive la guerre éternelle*—till the New Jerusalem, of course!"

Dostoevsky, *Crime and Punishment*, III, 5

71 Porfiry began gaily, looking with extraordinary simplicity at Raskolnikov (which startled him and instantly put him on his guard), "certainly quite right in laughing so wittily at our legal forms, he-he! Some of these elaborate psychological methods are exceedingly ridiculous and perhaps useless, if one adheres too closely to the forms. Yes . . . I am talking of forms again. Well, if I recognise, or more strictly speaking, if I suspect some one or other to be a criminal in any case entrusted to me . . . you're reading for the law, of course, Rodion Romanovitch?"

"Yes, I was . . . "

"Well, then it is a precedent for you for the future—though don't suppose I should venture to instruct you after the articles you publish about crime! No, I simply make bold to state it by way of fact, if I took this man or that for a criminal, why, I ask, should I worry him prematurely, even though I had evidence against him? In one case I may be bound, for instance, to arrest a man at once, but another may be in quite a different position, you know, so why shouldn't I let him walk about the town a bit, he-he-he! But I see you don't quite understand, so I'll give you a clearer example. If I put him in prison too soon, I may very likely give him, so to speak, moral support, he-he! You're laughing?"

Raskolnikov had no idea of laughing. He was sitting with compressed lips, his feverish eyes fixed on Porfiry Petrovitch's.

"Yet that is the case, with some types especially, for men are so different. You say evidence. Well, there may be evidence. But evidence, you know, can generally be taken two ways. I am an examining lawyer and a weak man, I confess it. I should like to make a proof, so to say, mathematically clear, I should like to make a chain of evidence such as twice two are four, it ought to be a direct, irrefutable proof! And if I shut him up too soon—even though I might be convinced *he* was the man, I should very likely be depriving myself of the means of getting further evidence against him. And how? By giving him, so to speak, a definite position, I shall put him out of suspense and set his mind at rest, so that he will retreat into his shell. They say that at Sevastopol, soon after Alma, the clever people were in a terrible fright that the enemy would attack openly and take Sevastopol at once. But when they saw that the enemy preferred a regular siege, they were delighted, I am told and reassured, for the thing would drag on for two months at least. You're laughing, you don't believe me again? Of course, you're right, too. You're right, you're right. These are all special cases, I admit. But you must observe this, my dear Rodion Romanovitch, the general case, the case for which all legal forms and rules are intended, for which they are calculated and laid down in books, does not exist at all, for the reason that every case, every crime for instance, so soon as it actually occurs, at once becomes a thoroughly special case and sometimes a case unlike any that's gone before. Very comic cases of that sort sometimes occur. If I leave one man quite alone, if I don't touch him and don't worry him, but let him know or at least suspect every moment that I know all about it and am watching him day and night, and if he is in continual suspicion and terror, he'll be bound to lose his head. He'll come of himself, or maybe do something which will make it as plain as twice two are four—it's delightful. It may be so with a simple peasant, but with one of our sort, an intelligent man cultivated on a certain side, it's a dead certainty. For, my dear fellow, it's a very important matter to know on what side a man is cultivated. And then there are nerves, there are nerves, you have overlooked them! Why, they are all sick, nervous and irritable! . . . And then how they all suffer from spleen! That I assure you is a regular gold mine for us. And it's no anxiety to me, his running about the town free! Let him, let him walk about for a bit! I know well enough that I've caught him and that he won't escape me. Where could he escape to, he-he? Abroad, perhaps? A Pole will escape abroad, but not here, especially as I am watching and have taken measures. Will he escape into the depths of the country perhaps? But you know, peasants live there, real rude Russian peasants. A modern cultivated man would prefer prison to living with such strangers as our peasants. He-he! But that's all nonsense, and on the surface. It's not merely that he has nowhere to run to, he is *psychologically* unable to escape me, he-he! What an expression! Through a law of nature he can't escape me if he had anywhere to go. Have you seen a butterfly round a candle? That's how he will keep circling and circling round me. Freedom will lose its attractions. He'll begin to brood, he'll weave a tangle round himself, he'll worry himself to death! What's more he will provide me with a mathematical proof—if I only give him long enough interval. . . . And he'll keep circling round me, getting nearer and nearer and then— flop! He'll fly straight into my mouth and I'll swallow him, and that will be very amusing, he-he-he-he! You don't believe me?"

Dostoevsky, *Crime and Punishment,* IV, 5

72 When we do not at all understand the cause of an action, whether a crime, a good action, or even one that is simply nonmoral, we ascribe a greater amount of freedom to it. In the case of a crime we most urgently demand the punishment for such an act; in the case of a virtuous act we rate its merit most highly. In an indifferent case we recognize in it more individuality, originality, and independence. But if even one of the innumerable causes of the act is known to us we recognize a certain element of necessity and are less insistent on punishment for the crime, or the acknowledgment of the merit of the virtuous act, or the freedom of the apparently original action. That a criminal was reared among malefactors mitigates his fault in our eyes. The self-sacrifice of a father or mother, or self-sacrifice with the possibility of a reward, is more comprehensible than gratuitous self-sacrifice, and therefore seems less deserving of sympathy and less the result of free will. The founder of a sect or party, or an inventor, impresses us less when we know how or by what the way was prepared for his activity. If we have a large range of examples, if our observation is constantly directed to seeking the correlation of cause and effect in people's actions, their actions appear to us more under compulsion and less free the more correctly we connect the effects with the causes. If we examined simple actions and had a vast number of such actions under observation, our conception of their inevitability would be still greater. The dishonest conduct of the son of a dishonest father, the misconduct of a woman who had fallen into bad company, a drunkard's relapse into

drunkenness, and so on are actions that seem to us less free the better we understand their cause. If the man whose actions we are considering is on a very low stage of mental development, like a child, a madman, or a simpleton—then, knowing the causes of the act and the simplicity of the character and intelligence in question, we see so large an element of necessity and so little free will that as soon as we know the cause prompting the action we can foretell the result.

On these three considerations alone is based the conception of irresponsibility for crimes and the extenuating circumstances admitted by all legislative codes. The responsibility appears greater or less according to our greater or lesser knowledge of the circumstances in which the man was placed whose action is being judged, and according to the greater or lesser interval of time between the commission of the action and its investigation, and according to the greater or lesser understanding of the causes that led to the action.

Tolstoy, *War and Peace,* II Epilogue, IX

73 The lawyers defending a criminal are rarely artists enough to turn the beautiful terribleness of his deed to his advantage.

Nietzsche, *Beyond Good and Evil,* IV, 110

74 The criminal type is the type of the strong human being under unfavourable conditions, a strong human being made sick. What he lacks is the wilderness, a certain freer and more perilous nature and form of existence in which all that is attack and defence in the instinct of the strong human being *comes into its own.*

Nietzsche, *Twilight of the Idols:*
Expeditions of an Untimely Man

75 Criminals do not die by the hands of the law. They die by the hands of other men.

Shaw, *Man and Superman,* Maxims for
Revolutionists

76 Assassination on the scaffold is the worst form of assassination, because there it is invested with the approval of society.

Shaw, *Man and Superman,* Maxims for
Revolutionists

77 Crime is only the retail department of what, in wholesale, we call penal law.

Shaw, *Man and Superman,* Maxims for
Revolutionists

Chapter 13

LIBERTY
and EQUALITY

Chapter 13 is divided into three sections: Section 13.1 FREEDOM IN SOCIETY, Section 13.2 FREEDOM OF THOUGHT AND EXPRESSION: CENSORSHIP, and 13.3 EQUALITY.

This chapter, like Chapters 12 and 14, is closely related to Chapter 10 on POLITICS. Since economic considerations enter into the discussion of social freedom in Section 13.1 and into the discussion of social equality in Section 13.3, the chapter also touches on matters treated in Chapter 11 on ECONOMICS.

The terms "freedom" and "liberty" are interchangeable. Some authors prefer to use one, some the other, and some shift from one to the other. The freedom or liberty discussed in this chapter, and especially in Section 13.1, is the individual's freedom of action in society—the liberty of the individual in conduct affecting others. Other aspects of

freedom are discussed in other contexts— moral freedom in Section 9.4 of the chapter on ETHICS, and free will or free choice in Section 5.7 of the chapter on MIND.

Section 13.2 turns from the consideration of freedom in the sphere of action, and specifically of social conduct, to freedom in the sphere of thought and in the communication of thought. It is appropriate, therefore, to include there quotations dealing with the pros and cons of censorship, and other impediments to the communication of ideas and the expression of thought.

Equality—the subject of Section 13.3—is often discussed in relation to liberty, but it also has connections with other subjects treated elsewhere, such as justice and injustice (treated in Section 12.2) and man (treated in Chapter 1).

13.1 | *Freedom in Society*

As the title of this section indicates, the subject treated is not freedom in general, nor liberty in all its diverse forms, but the individual's freedom of action within the social group and in relation to other individuals. This freedom is variously described, in the quotations assembled, as freedom from coercion, impediment, or duress; freedom to do as one pleases or wishes; the liberty to live or act as one chooses; or the liberty to act according to one's own rules or directions, not those of another.

The last of these formulations raises one of the central issues disputed by the authors represented here. On the one hand, there are those—for example, Montesquieu, Locke, and Rousseau—who maintain that just laws or laws made with the consent and suffrage of the governed in no way infringe or diminish individual freedom; freedom in society cannot be an unlimited freedom; it is a freedom regulated by law, and to act contrary to law is not liberty, but license. On the other hand, the reader will find passages from Hobbes, Bentham, and J. S. Mill setting forth the contrary view: that one has freedom of action only about matters concerning which the law is silent; and that as the sphere of law enlarges, the sphere of liberty diminishes. Yet both groups of authors agree that freedom in society must be limited freedom, a liberty to do as one pleases only to the extent that one's actions cause no injury to others or do not have an adverse effect on the welfare of the community itself.

Other problems or issues are discussed: the relation of liberty and equality, the character of freedom in a democracy, the difference between freedom in a state of nature and freedom in civil society, and the relation of political liberty to moral freedom. For the consideration of moral freedom, which is quite a different thing from social or political freedom, the reader is referred to Section 9.4; and for the controversy over freedom of choice, or of the will, the reader is referred to Section 5.7. The discussion of subjects related to the materials covered here will also be found in Section 13.2 on FREEDOM OF THOUGHT AND EXPRESSION: CENSORSHIP, Section 13.3 on EQUALITY, Section 10.4 on GOVERNMENT OF AND BY THE PEOPLE: REPUBLIC AND DEMOCRACY, and Section 10.7 on SLAVERY.

---

1 Proclaim liberty throughout all the land unto all the inhabitants thereof.

Leviticus 25:10

2 *Pericles.* Our constitution . . . favours the many instead of the few; this is why it is called a democracy. If we look to the laws, they afford equal justice to all in their private differences; if no social standing, advancement in public life falls to reputation for capacity, class considerations not being allowed to interfere with merit; nor again does poverty bar the way, if a man is able to serve the state, he is not hindered by the obscurity of his condition. The freedom which we enjoy in our government extends also to our ordinary life. There, far from exercising a jealous surveillance over each other, we do not feel called upon to be angry with our neighbour for doing what he likes, or even to indulge in those injurious looks which cannot fail to be offensive, although they inflict no positive penalty. But all this ease in our private relations does not make us lawless as citizens. Against this fear is our chief safeguard, teaching us to obey the magistrates and the laws, particularly such as regard the protection of the injured, whether they are actually on the statute book, or belong to that code which, although unwritten, yet cannot be broken without acknowledged disgrace.

Thucydides, *Peloponnesian War*, II, 37

3 *Socrates.* The ruin of oligarchy is the ruin of democracy; the same disease magnified and intensi-
fied by liberty overmasters democracy—the truth
being that the excessive increase of anything often
causes a reaction in the opposite direction; and
this is the case not only in the seasons and in vegetable and animal life, but above all in forms of
government. . . .

The excess of liberty, whether in States or individuals, seems only to pass into excess of slavery.

Plato, *Republic,* VIII, 563B

4 Every man should be responsible to others, nor
should any one be allowed to do just as he pleases;
for where absolute freedom is allowed there is
nothing to restrain the evil which is inherent in
every man.

Aristotle, *Politics,* 1318b39

5 The measures which are taken by tyrants appear
all of them to be democratic; such, for instance, as
the licence permitted to slaves (which may be to a
certain extent advantageous) and also that of
women and children, and the allowing everybody
to live as he likes. Such a government will have
many supporters, for most persons would rather
live in a disorderly than in a sober manner.

Aristotle, *Politics,* 1319b27

6 If the people are sovereign in a state and the government is run according to their will, it is called
liberty. But it is really licence.

Cicero, *Republic,* III, 13

7 Where the Spirit of the Lord is, there is liberty.

II Corinthians 3:17

8 By *liberty* is understood . . . the absence of external impediments; which impediments may oft
take away part of a man's power to do what he
would, but cannot hinder him from using the
power left him according as his judgement and
reason shall dictate to him.

Hobbes, *Leviathan,* I, 14

9 Liberties . . . depend on the silence of the law. In
cases where the sovereign has prescribed no rule,
there the subject hath the liberty to do, or forbear,
according to his own discretion. And therefore
such liberty is in some places more, and in some
less; and in some times more, in other times less,
according as they that have the sovereignty shall
think most convenient.

Hobbes, *Leviathan,* II, 21

10 I did but prompt the age to quit their cloggs
By the known rules of antient libertie,
When strait a barbarous noise environs me
Of Owles and Cuckoes, Asses, Apes and Doggs.
As when those Hinds that were transform'd to
Froggs

Raild at *Latona's* twin-born progenie
Which after held the Sun and Moon in fee.
But this is got by casting Pearl to Hoggs;
That bawle for freedom in their senceless mood,
And still revolt when truth would set them free.
Licence they mean when they cry libertie;
For who loves that, must first be wise and good;
But from that mark how far they roave we see
For all this wast of wealth, and loss of blood.

Milton, *I did but prompt the age to
quit their cloggs*

11 None can love freedom heartily but good men;
the rest love not freedom but license, which never
hath more scope or more indulgence than under
tyrants.

Milton, *Tenure of Kings and Magistrates*

12 The natural liberty of man is to be free from any
superior power on earth, and not to be under the
will or legislative authority of man, but to have
only the law of Nature for his rule. The liberty of
man in society is to be under no other legislative
power but that established by consent in the commonwealth, nor under the dominion of any will,
or restraint of any law, but what that legislative
shall enact according to the trust put in it. Freedom, then, is not what Sir Robert Filmer tells us:
"A liberty for every one to do what he lists, to live
as he pleases, and not to be tied by any laws"; but
freedom of men under government is to have a
standing rule to live by, common to every one of
that society, and made by the legislative power
erected in it. A liberty to follow my own will in all
things where that rule prescribes not, not to be
subject to the inconstant, uncertain, unknown, arbitrary will of another man, as freedom of nature
is to be under no other restraint but the law of
Nature.

Locke, *II Civil Government,* IV, 21

13 The freedom . . . of man, and liberty of acting
according to his own will, is grounded on his having reason, which is able to instruct him in that
law he is to govern himself by, and make him
know how far he is left to the freedom of his own
will. To turn him loose to an unrestrained liberty,
before he has reason to guide him, is not the allowing him the privilege of his nature to be free,
but to thrust him out amongst brutes, and abandon him to a state as wretched and as much beneath that of a man as theirs.

Locke, *II Civil Government,* VI, 63

14 I think the question is not proper, *whether the will
be free,* but *whether a man be free.* Thus, I think,

First, That so far as any one can, by the direction or choice of his mind, preferring the existence
of any action to the non-existence of that action,
and *vice versâ,* make *it* to exist or not exist, so far *he*
is free. For if I can, by a thought directing the

motion of my finger, make it move when it was at rest, or *vice versâ,* it is evident, that in respect of that I am free: and if I can, by a like thought of my mind, preferring one to the other, produce either words or silence, I am at liberty to speak or hold my peace: and as far as this power reaches, of acting or not acting, by the determination of his own thought preferring either, so far is a man free. For how can we think any one freer, than to have the power to do what he will? And so far as any one can, by preferring any action to its not being, or rest to any action, produce that action or rest, so far can he do what he will. For such a preferring of action to its absence, is the willing of it: and we can scarce tell how to imagine any being freer, than to be able to do what he wills. So that in respect of actions within the reach of such a power in him, a man seems as free as it is possible for freedom to make him.

Locke, *Concerning Human Understanding,*
Bk. II, XXI, 21

15 Is it worth the name of freedom to be at liberty to play the fool, and draw shame and misery upon a man's self? If to break loose from the conduct of reason, and to want that restraint of examination and judgment which keeps us from choosing or doing the worse, be liberty, true liberty, madmen and fools are the only freemen: but yet, I think, nobody would choose to be mad for the sake of such liberty, but he that is mad already.

Locke, *Concerning Human Understanding,*
Bk. II, XXI, 51

16 He that has his chains knocked off, and the prison doors set open to him, is perfectly at liberty, because he may either go or stay, as he best likes; though his preference be determined to stay, by the darkness of the night, or illness of the weather, or want of other lodging. He ceases not to be free; though the desire of some convenience to be had there absolutely determines his preference, and makes him stay in his prison.

Locke, *Concerning Human Understanding,*
Bk. II, XXI, 51

17 It is true that in democracies the people seem to act as they please; but political liberty does not consist in an unlimited freedom. In governments, that is, in societies directed by laws, liberty can consist only in the power of doing what we ought to will, and in not being constrained to do what we ought not to will.

We must have continually present to our minds the difference between independence and liberty. Liberty is a right of doing whatever the laws permit, and if a citizen could do what they forbid he would be no longer possessed of liberty, because all his fellow-citizens would have the same power.

Montesquieu, *Spirit of Laws,* XI, 3

18 Liberty consists principally in not being forced to do a thing, where the laws do not oblige: people are in this state only as they are governed by civil laws; and because they live under those civil laws, they are free.

Montesquieu, *Spirit of Laws,* XXVI, 20

19 Liberty . . . is only and can be only the power to do what one will. That is what philosophy teaches us. But if one considers liberty in the theological sense, it is a matter so sublime that profane eyes dare not raise themselves to it.

Voltaire, *Philosophical Dictionary:*
Free-Will

20 To renounce liberty is to renounce being a man, to surrender the rights of humanity and even its duties. For him who renounces everything no indemnity is possible. Such a renunciation is incompatible with man's nature; to remove all liberty from his will is to remove all morality from his acts.

Rousseau, *Social Contract,* I, 4

21 In order . . . that the social compact may not be an empty formula, it tacitly includes the undertaking, which alone can give force to the rest, that whoever refuses to obey the general will shall be compelled to do so by the whole body. This means nothing less than that he will be forced to be free; for this is the condition which, by giving each citizen to his country, secures him against all personal dependence. In this lies the key to the working of the political machine; this alone legitimises civil undertakings, which, without it, would be absurd, tyrannical, and liable to the most frightful abuses.

Rousseau, *Social Contract,* I, 7

22 What man loses by the social contract is his natural liberty and an unlimited right to everything he tries to get and succeeds in getting; what he gains is civil liberty and the proprietorship of all he possesses. If we are to avoid mistake in weighing one against the other, we must clearly distinguish natural liberty, which is bounded only by the strength of the individual, from civil liberty, which is limited by the general will; and possession, which is merely the effect of force or the right of the first occupier, from property, which can be founded only on a positive title.

We might, over and above all this, add, to what man acquires in the civil state, moral liberty, which alone makes him truly master of himself; for the mere impulse of appetite is slavery, while obedience to a law which we prescribe to ourselves is liberty.

Rousseau, *Social Contract.* I, 8

23 *Johnson.* We are all agreed as to our own liberty; we would have as much of it as we can get; but we

are not agreed as to the liberty of others: for in proportion as we take, others must lose.

Boswell, *Life of Johnson (Apr. 8, 1779)*

24 In general, if any branch of trade, or any division of labour, be advantageous to the public, the freer and more general the competition, it will always be the more so.

Adam Smith, *Wealth of Nations*, II, 2

25 That degree of liberty which approaches to licentiousness can be tolerated only in countries where the sovereign is secured by a well-regulated standing army. It is in such countries only that the public safety does not require that the sovereign should be trusted with any discretionary power for suppressing even the impertinent wantonness of this licentious liberty.

Adam Smith, *Wealth of Nations*, V, 1

26 The liberty, the only liberty, I mean is a liberty connected with order; that not only exists along with order and virtue, but which cannot exist at all without them. It inheres in good and steady government, as in its substance and vital principle.

Burke, *Speech on Arrival at Bristol (Oct. 13, 1774)*

27 The extreme of liberty (which is its abstract perfection, but its real fault) obtains nowhere, nor ought to obtain anywhere; because extremes, as we all know, in every point which relates either to our duties or satisfactions in life, are destructive both to virtue and enjoyment. Liberty, too, must be limited in order to be possessed. The degree of restraint it is impossible in any case to settle precisely. But it ought to be the constant aim of every wise public counsel to find out by cautious experiments, and rational, cool endeavors, with how little, not how much, of this restraint the community can subsist: for liberty is a good to be improved, and not an evil to be lessened. It is not only a private blessing of the first order, but the vital spring and energy of the state itself, which has just so much life and vigor as there is liberty in it.

Burke, *Letter to the Sheriffs of Bristol (Apr. 3, 1777)*

28 The effect of liberty to individuals is, that they may do what they please: we ought to see what it will please them to do, before we risk congratulations, which may be soon turned into complaints.

Burke, *Reflections on the Revolution in France*

29 There is, indeed, an innate equality belonging to every man which consists in his right to be independent of being bound by others to anything more than that to which he may also reciprocally bind them. It is, consequently, the inborn quality of every man in virtue of which he ought to be his own master by right.

Kant, *Division of the Science of Right*, B

30 The liberty which the law ought to allow of, and leave in existence—leave uncoerced, unremoved—is the liberty which concerns those acts only, by which, if exercised, no damage would be done to the community as a whole; that is, either no damage at all, or none but what promises to be compensated by at least equal benefit. Accordingly, the exercise of the rights allowed to and conferred upon each individual, ought to have no other bounds set to it by law, than those which are necessary to enable it to maintain every other individual in the possession and exercise of such rights as . . . is consistent with the greatest good of the community.

Bentham, *Anarchical Fallacies*, 4

31 Liberty is to faction what air is to fire, an aliment without which it instantly expires. But it could not be less folly to abolish liberty, which is essential to political life, because it nourishes faction, than it would be to wish the annihilation of air, which is essential to animal life, because it imparts to fire its destructive agency.

Madison, *Federalist 10*

32 If a man has freedom enough to live healthy, and to work at his craft, he has enough; and so much all can easily obtain.

Goethe, *Conversations with Eckermann (Jan. 18, 1827)*

33 Me this unchartered freedom tires;
I feel the weight of chance-desires:
My hopes no more must change their name,
I long for a repose that ever is the same.

Wordsworth, *Ode to Duty*

34 Two Voices are there; one is of the sea,
One of the mountains; each a mighty Voice:
In both from age to age thou didst rejoice,
They were thy chosen music, Liberty!

Wordsworth, *Thought of a Briton on the Subjugation of Switzerland*

35 Nuns fret not at their convent's narrow room;
And hermits are contented with their cells. . . .
In truth the prison, into which we doom
Ourselves, no prison is: and hence for me,
In sundry moods, 't was pastime to be bound
Within the Sonnet's scanty plot of ground;
Pleased if some Souls (for such there needs must be)
Who have felt the weight of too much liberty,
Should find brief solace there, as I have found.

Wordsworth, *Nuns Fret Not at Their Convent's Narrow Room*

36 Yet, Freedom, yet thy banner, torn but flying,
Streams like the thunder-storm *against* the wind.
      Byron, *Childe Harold's Pilgrimage*, IV, 98

37 My very chains and I grew friends,
So much a long communion tends
To make us what we are:—even I
Regain'd my freedom with a sigh.
      Byron, *The Prisoner of Chillon*, XIV, 389

38 The idea which people most commonly have of
freedom is that it is arbitrariness—the mean, chosen by abstract reflection, between the will wholly
determined by natural impulses, and the will free
absolutely. If we hear it said that the definition of
freedom is ability to do what we please, such an
idea can only be taken to reveal an utter imma-
turity of thought, for it contains not even an in-
kling of the absolutely free will, of right, ethical
life, and so forth. Reflection, the formal universality and unity of self-consciousness, is the will's
abstract certainty of its freedom, but it is not yet
the truth of freedom, because it has not yet got
itself as its content and aim, and consequently the
subjective side is still other than the objective; the
content of this self-determination, therefore, also
remains purely and simply finite. Instead of being
the will in its truth, arbitrariness is more like the
will as contradiction.
      Hegel, *Philosophy of Right*,
      Introduction, 15

39 The conjunction of duty and right has a twofold
aspect: what the state demands from us as a duty
is *eo ipso* our right as individuals, since the state is
nothing but the articulation of the concept of freedom. The determinations of the individual will
are given an objective embodiment through the
state and thereby they attain their truth and their
actualization for the first time. The state is the
one and only prerequisite of the attainment of
particular ends and welfare.
      Hegel, *Philosophy of Right*,
      Additions, Par. 261

40 Freedom is nothing but the recognition and adoption of such universal substantial objects as right
and law, and the production of a reality that is
accordant with them—the state.
      Hegel, *Philosophy of History*,
      Introduction, 3

41 Freedom has appeared in the world at different
times and under various forms; it has not been
exclusively bound to any social condition, and it is
not confined to democracies. Freedom cannot,
therefore, form the distinguishing characteristic of
democratic ages. The peculiar and preponderant
fact that marks those ages as its own is the equality of condition; the ruling passion of men in those
periods is the love of this equality. . . .

I think that democratic communities have a
natural taste for freedom; left to themselves, they
will seek it, cherish it, and view any privation of it
with regret. But for equality their passion is ardent, insatiable, incessant, invincible; they call for
equality in freedom; and if they cannot obtain
that, they still call for equality in slavery. They
will endure poverty, servitude, barbarism, but
they will not endure aristocracy.
   This is true at all times, and especially in our
own day. All men and all powers seeking to cope
with this irresistible passion will be overthrown
and destroyed by it. In our age freedom cannot be
established without it, and despotism itself cannot
reign without its support.
      Tocqueville, *Democracy in America*,
      Vol. II, II, 1

42 Nothing is more disgusting than the crowing
about liberty by slaves, as most men are, and the
flippant mistaking for freedom of some paper
preamble like a Declaration of Independence or
the statute right to vote, by those who have never
dared to think or to act.
      Emerson, *Fate*

43 Of old sat Freedom on the heights,
   The thunders breaking at her feet;
Above her shook the starry lights;
   She heard the torrents meet.
      Tennyson, *Of old sat Freedom on the heights*

44 Pursue, keep up with, circle round and round
your life, as a dog does his master's chaise. Do
what you love. Know your own bone; gnaw it,
bury it, unearth it, and gnaw it still. Do not be too
moral. You may cheat yourself out of much life so.
Aim above morality. Be not simply good; be good
for something. All fables, indeed, have their morals; but the innocent enjoy the story. Let nothing
come between you and the light. Respect men
and brothers only. When you travel to the Celestial City, carry no letter of introduction. When
you knock, ask to see God,—none of the servants.
In what concerns you much, do not think that you
have companions: know that you are alone in the
world.
      Thoreau, *Letter to Mr. B* (Mar. 27, 1848)

45 Why should we be in such desperate haste to succeed and in such desperate enterprises? If a man
does not keep pace with his companions, perhaps
it is because he hears a different drummer. Let
him step to the music which he hears, however
measured or far away. It is not important that he
should mature as soon as an apple tree or an oak.
Shall he turn his spring into summer? If the condition of things which we were made for is not yet,
what were any reality which we can substitute?
      Thoreau, *Walden:* Conclusion

46 The soul selects her own society
Then shuts the door.
On her divine majority
Obtrude no more.

Unmoved, she notes the chariots pausing
At her low gate.
Unmoved, an emperor is kneeling
Upon her mat.

I've known her from an ample nation
Choose one,
Then close the valves of her attention
Like stone.

Emily Dickinson, *The Soul Selects*

47 The world has never had a good definition of the word liberty, and the American people, just now, are much in want of one. We all declare for liberty; but in using the same *word* we do not all mean the same *thing*. With some the word liberty may mean for each man to do as he pleases with himself, and the product of his labor; while with others the same word may mean for some men to do as they please with other men, and the product of other men's labor. Here are two, not only different, but incompatable things, called by the same name—liberty. And it follows that each of the things is, by the respective parties, called by two different and incompatable names—liberty and tyranny.

Lincoln, *Address at Sanitary Fair*
(Apr. 18, 1864)

48 The realm of freedom does not commence until the point is passed where labor under the compulsion of necessity and of external utility is required. In the very nature of things it lies beyond the sphere of material production in the strict meaning of the term. Just as the savage must wrestle with nature, in order to satisfy his wants, in order to maintain his life and reproduce it, so civilized man has to do it and he must do it in all forms of society and under all possible modes of production. With his development the realm of natural necessity expands, because his wants increase; but at the same time the forces of production increase by which these wants are satisfied.

Marx, *Capital*, Vol. III, VII, 48

49 In bourgeois society . . . the past dominates the present; in Communist society, the present dominates the past. In bourgeois society capital is independent and has individuality, while the living person is dependent and has no individuality.

And the abolition of this state of things is called by the bourgeois, abolition of individuality and freedom! And rightly so. The abolition of bourgeois individuality, bourgeois independence, and bourgeois freedom is undoubtedly aimed at.

By freedom is meant, under the present bourgeois conditions of production, free trade, free selling and buying.

But if selling and buying disappears, free selling and buying disappears also. This talk about free selling and buying, and all the other "brave words" of our bourgeoisie about freedom in general, have a meaning, if any, only in contrast with restricted selling and buying, with the fettered traders of the Middle Ages, but have no meaning when opposed to the Communist abolition of buying and selling, of the bourgeois conditions of production, and of the bourgeoisie itself.

Marx and Engels, *Communist Manifesto*, II

50 What the proletarian needs, he can obtain only from this bourgeoisie, which is protected in its monopoly by the power of the State. The proletarian is, therefore, in law and in fact, the slave of the bourgeoisie, which can decree his life or death. It offers him the means of living, but only for an "equivalent" for his work. It even lets him have the appearance of acting from a free choice, of making a contract with free, unconstrained consent, as a responsible agent who has attained his majority.

Fine freedom, where the proletarian has no other choice than that of either accepting the conditions which the bourgeoisie offers him, or of starving, of freezing to death, of sleeping naked among the beasts of the forests! A fine "equivalent" valued at pleasure by the bourgeoisie. And if one proletarian is such a fool as to starve rather than to agree to the equitable propositions of the bourgeoisie, his "natural superiors," another is easily found in his place; there are proletarians enough in the world, and not all so insane as to prefer dying to living.

Engels, *The Condition of the Working-Class in England in 1844*, III

51 The state is the sum of all the negations of the individual liberty of all its members; or rather that of the sacrifices which all its members make, in renouncing one portion of their liberty to the profit of the common good. We have seen that, according to the individualist theory, the liberty of each is the limit or rather the natural negation of the liberty of all the others. Well! this absolute limitation, this negation of the liberty of each in the name of the liberty of all or of the common right—that is the State. Thus, where the State begins, individual liberty ceases, and vice versa.

Bakunin, *Philosophical Considerations*

52 The sole end for which mankind are warranted, individually or collectively, in interfering with the liberty of action of any of their number, is self-protection. . . . The only purpose for which power can be rightfully exercised over any member of a civilised community, against his will, is to prevent harm to others.

Mill, *On Liberty*, I

53 As it is useful that while mankind are imperfect there should be different opinions, so it is that there should be different experiments of living; that free scope should be given to varieties of character, short of injury to others; and that the worth of different modes of life should be proved practically, when any one thinks fit to try them. It is desirable, in short, that in things which do not primarily concern others, individuality should assert itself.

Mill, *On Liberty*, III

54 There is no reason that all human existence should be constructed on some one or some small number of patterns. If a person possesses any tolerable amount of common sense and experience, his own mode of laying out his existence is the best, not because it is the best in itself, but because it is his own mode. Human beings are not like sheep. . . . The same things which are helps to one person towards the cultivation of his higher nature are hindrances to another. The same mode of life is a healthy excitement to one, keeping all his faculties of action and enjoyment in their best order, while to another it is a distracting burthen, which suspends or crushes all internal life. Such are the differences among human beings in their sources of pleasure, their susceptibilities of pain, and the operation on them of different physical and moral agencies, that unless there is a corresponding diversity in their modes of life, they neither obtain their fair share of happiness, nor grow up to the mental, moral, and æsthetic stature of which their nature is capable.

Mill, *On Liberty*, III

55 As soon as any part of a person's conduct affects prejudicially the interests of others, society has jurisdiction over it, and the question whether the general welfare will or will not be promoted by interfering with it, becomes open to discussion. But there is no room for entertaining any such question when a person's conduct affects the interests of no persons besides himself, or needs not affect them unless they like (all the persons concerned being of full age, and the ordinary amount of understanding). In all such cases, there should be perfect freedom, legal and social, to do the action and stand the consequences.

Mill, *On Liberty*, IV

56 The preventive function of government . . . is far more liable to be abused, to the prejudice of liberty, than the punitory function. . . . If either a public officer or any one else saw a person attempting to cross a bridge which had been ascertained to be unsafe, and there were no time to warn him of his danger, they might seize him and turn him back, without any real infringement of his liberty; for liberty consists in doing what one desires, and he does not desire to fall into the river. Nevertheless, when there is not a certainty, but only a danger of mischief, no one but the person himself can judge of the sufficiency of the motive which may prompt him to incur the risk: in this case, therefore (unless he is a child, or delirious, or in some state of excitement or absorption incompatible with the full use of the reflecting faculty), he ought, I conceive, to be only warned of the danger; not forcibly prevented from exposing himself to it.

Mill, *On Liberty*, V

57 First and foremost of the necessary means towards man's civilisation we must name *expansion*. The need of expansion is as genuine an instinct in man as the need in plants for the light, or the need in man himself for going upright. All the conveniences of life by which man has enlarged and secured his existence—railroads and the penny post among the number—are due to the working in man of this force or instinct of expansion. . . .

The love of liberty is simply the instinct in man for expansion. Not only to find oneself tyrannised over and outraged is a defeat to this instinct, but in general, to feel oneself over-tutored, over-governed, *sate upon* (as the popular phrase is) by authority, is a defeat to it.

Arnold, *Mixed Essays*, Pref.

58 It is by the goodness of God that in our country we have those three unspeakably precious things: freedom of speech, freedom of conscience, and the prudence never to practise either of them.

Mark Twain, *Pudd'nhead Wilson's
New Calendar*, XX

59 Freedom means that the manly instincts that delight in war and victory have gained mastery over the other instincts—for example, over the instinct for 'happiness'. The man *who has become free*—and how much more the *mind* that has become free—spurns the contemptible sort of well-being dreamed of by shopkeepers, Christians, cows, women, Englishmen and other democrats.

Nietzsche, *Twilight of the Idols:*
Expeditions of an Untimely Man

60 Liberty means responsibility. That is why most men dread it.

Shaw, *Man and Superman*,
Maxims for Revolutionists

61 "Freedom" in its most abstract sense means the absence of external obstacles to the realization of desires. Taken in this abstract sense, freedom may be increased either by maximizing power or by minimizing wants. An insect which lives for a few days and then dies of cold may have perfect freedom according to the definition, since the cold may alter its desires, so that there is no moment when it wishes to achieve the impossible. Among

human beings, also, this way of reaching freedom is possible. . . . It is obvious that a community who all wish to murder each other cannot be so free as a community with more peaceable desires. Modification of desire may, therefore, involve just as great a gain to freedom as increase of power.

Russell, *Sceptical Essays*, XIII

62 The freedom we should seek is not the right to oppress others, but the right to live as we choose and think as we choose where our doing so does not prevent others from doing likewise.

Russell, *Sceptical Essays*, XIII

63 Choice would hardly be significant if it did not take effect in outward action, and if it did not, when expressed in deeds, make a difference in things. Action as power would hardly be prized if it were power like that of an avalanche or an earthquake. The power, the ability to command issues and consequences, that forms freedom must, it should seem, have some connection with that something in personality that is expressed in choice. At all events, the essential problem of freedom, it seems to me, is the problem of the relation of choice and unimpeded effective action to each other. . . . There is an intrinsic connection between choice as freedom and power of action as freedom. A choice which intelligently manifests individuality enlarges the range of action, and this enlargement in turn confers upon our desires greater insight and foresight, and makes choice more intelligent. There is a circle, but an enlarging circle, or, if you please, a widening spiral.

Dewey, *Philosophies of Freedom*

64 If we want individuals to be free we must see to it that suitable conditions exist:—a truism which at least indicates the direction in which to look and move.

It tells us among other things to get rid of the ideas that lead us to believe that democratic conditions automatically maintain themselves, or that they can be identified with fulfillment of prescriptions laid down in a constitution. Beliefs of this sort merely divert attention from what is going on, just as the patter of the prestidigitator enables him to do things that are not noticed by those whom he is engaged in fooling. For what is actually going on may be the formation of conditions that are hostile to any kind of democratic liberties. This would be too trite to repeat were it not that so many persons in the high places of business talk as if they believed or could get others to believe that the observance of formulae that have become ritualistic are effective safeguards of our democratic heritage.

Dewey, *Freedom and Culture*, II

65 The only freedom that is of enduring importance is freedom of intelligence, that is to say, freedom of observation and of judgment exercised in behalf of purposes that are intrinsically worth while.

Dewey, *Experience and Education*, V

66 Freedom from restriction . . . is to be prized only as a means to a freedom which is power: power to frame purposes, to judge wisely, to evaluate desires by the consequences which will result from acting upon them; power to select and order means to carry chosen ends into operation.

Dewey, *Experience and Education*, V

67 To say that a man is free to choose to walk while the only walk he can take will lead him over a precipice is to strain words as well as facts.

Dewey, *Human Nature and Conduct*, IV, 3

68 To admit ignorance and uncertainty in man while denying them to nature involves a curious dualism. Variability, initiative, innovation, departure from routine, experimentation are empirically the manifestation of a genuine nisus in things. At all events it is these things that are precious to us under the name of freedom. It is their elimination from the life of a slave which makes his life servile, intolerable to the freeman who has once been on his own, no matter what his animal comfort and security. A free man would rather take his chance in an open world than be guaranteed in a closed world.

Dewey, *Human Nature and Conduct*, IV, 3

69 A man lives not only his personal life, as an individual, but also, consciously or unconsciously, the life of his epoch and his contemporaries. . . . All sorts of personal aims, ends, hopes, prospects, hover before the eyes of the individual, and out of these he derives the impulse to ambition and achievement. Now, if the life about him, if his own time seem, however outwardly stimulating, to be at bottom empty of such food for his aspirations; if he privately recognize it to be hopeless, viewless, helpless, opposing only a hollow silence to all the questions man puts, consciously or unconsciously, yet somehow puts, as to the final, absolute, and abstract meaning in all his efforts and activities; then, in such a case, a certain laming of the personality is bound to occur, the more inevitably the more upright the character in question; a sort of palsy, as it were, which may even extend from his spiritual and moral over into his physical and organic part. In an age that affords no satisfying answer to the eternal question of "Why?" "To what end?" a man who is capable of achievement over and above the average and expected modicum must be equipped either with a moral remoteness and single-mindedness which is rare indeed and of heroic mould, or else with an exceptionally robust vitality.

Mann, *Magic Mountain*, II

70 If we have defined man's situation as a free choice, with no excuses and no recourse, every man who takes refuge behind the excuse of his passions, every man who sets up a determinism is a dishonest man.

The objection may be raised, "But why mayn't he choose himself dishonestly?" I reply that I am not obliged to pass moral judgment on him, but that I do define his dishonesty as an error. One cannot help considering the truth of the matter. Dishonesty is obviously a falsehood because it belies the complete freedom of involvement. On the same grounds, I maintain that there is also dishonesty if I choose to state that certain values exist prior to me; it is self-contradictory for me to want them and at the same state that they are imposed on me. Suppose someone says to me, "What if I want to be dishonest?" I'll answer, "There's no reason for you not to be, but I'm saying that that's what you are, and that the strictly coherent attitude is that of honesty."

Besides, I can bring moral judgment to bear. When I declare that freedom in every concrete circumstance can have no other aim than to want itself, if man has once become aware that in his forlornness he imposes values, he can no longer want but one thing, and that is freedom, as the basis of all values. That doesn't mean that he wants it in the abstract. It means simply that the ultimate meaning of the acts of honest men is the quest for freedom as such. A man who belongs to a Communist or revolutionary union wants concrete goals; these goals imply an abstract desire for freedom; but this freedom is wanted in something concrete. We want freedom for freedom's sake and in every particular circumstance. And in wanting freedom we discover that it depends entirely on the freedom of others, and that the freedom of others depends on ours. Of course, freedom as the definition of man does not depend on others, but as soon as there is involvement, I am obliged to want others to have freedom at the same time that I want my own freedom. I can take freedom as my goal only if I take that of others as a goal as well. Consequently, when, in all honesty, I've recognized that man is a being in whom existence precedes essence, that he is a free being who, in various circumstances, can want only his freedom, I have at the same time recognized that I can want only the freedom of others.

Therefore, in the name of this will for freedom, which freedom itself implies, I may pass judgment on those who seek to hide from themselves the complete arbitrariness and the complete freedom of their existence. Those who hide their complete freedom from themselves out of a spirit of seriousness or by means of deterministic excuses, I shall call cowards.

Sartre, *Existentialism*

13.2 | *Freedom of Thought and Expression*

CENSORSHIP

Closely akin to freedom of action in society, discussed in Section 13.1, is freedom from interference in the expression of one's opinions, freedom from censorship in the publication of one's thought, and freedom in the production and dissemination of works of art. The basic issue here is, of course, the one about state censorship of works of art and other forms of expression. Is the state ever justified in prohibiting the expression of opinion, or in condemning and repressing the communication of certain doctrines or views?

The reader will find quotations on both sides of the issue: those that argue for censorship on the grounds that the materials in question would, if allowed publication or dissemination, exert an injurious effect on the community or its members; and those that argue for complete, or almost complete, toleration of every variety of opinion or doctrine. Questions are raised about the extension of toleration to material that is obscene, libelous, seditious, heretical, and schismatic. The reader will observe that the passages drawn from antiquity and the Middle Ages tend to draw a sharp line between what should and should not be tolerated. Beginning with Milton's *Areopagitica* and coming down through Locke and Voltaire to J. S. Mill, the argument moves in the opposite direction—toward greater tolerance, based on increasing doubt that injury is ever done by the free expression of thought and opinion.

Related matters are discussed in Chapter 20, especially Section 20.9 on HERESY AND UNBELIEF; and also in Chapter 6, especially Section 6.5 on OPINION, BELIEF, AND FAITH, and Section 6.6 on DOUBT AND SKEPTICISM.

---

1 *Artabanus.* It is impossible, if no more than one opinion is uttered, to make choice of the best: a man is forced then to follow whatever advice may have been given him; but if opposite speeches are delivered, then choice can be exercised. In like manner pure gold is not recognised by itself; but when we test it along with baser ore, we perceive which is the better.

Herodotus, *History,* VII, 10

2 *Socrates.* If you say to me, Socrates, this time we will not mind Anytus, and you shall be let off, but upon one condition, that you are not to enquire and speculate in this way any more, and that if you are caught doing so again you shall die;—if this was the condition on which you let me go, I should reply: Men of Athens, I honour and love you; but I shall obey God rather than you, and while I have life and strength I shall never cease from the practice and teaching of philosophy, exhorting any one whom I meet and saying to him after my manner: You, my friend,—a citizen of the great and mighty and wise city of Athens,—are you not ashamed of heaping up the greatest amount of money and honour and reputation, and caring so little about wisdom and truth and the greatest improvement of the soul, which you never regard or heed at all? And if the person with whom I am arguing, says: Yes, but I do care; then I do not leave him or let him go at once; but I proceed to interrogate and examine and cross-examine him, and if I think that he has no virtue in him, but only says that he has, I reproach him with undervaluing the greater, and overvaluing the less. And I shall repeat the same words to every one whom I meet, young and old, citizen and alien, but especially to the citizens, inasmuch as they are my brethren. For know that this is the command of God; and I believe that no greater good has ever happened in the state than my service to the God.

Plato, *Apology,* 29B

3 *Socrates.* The beginning is the most important part of any work, especially in the case of a young and tender thing; for that is the time at which the character is being formed and the desired impression is more readily taken. . . . And shall we just carelessly allow children to hear any casual tales which may be devised by casual persons, and to receive into their minds ideas for the most part the very opposite of those which we should wish them to have when they are grown up?

Adeimantus. We cannot.

Then the first thing will be to establish a censorship of the writers of fiction, and let the censors receive any tale of fiction which is good, and reject the bad; and we will desire mothers and nurses to tell their children the authorised ones only. Let them fashion the mind with such tales. . . . A young person cannot judge what is allegorical and what is literal; anything that he receives into his mind at that age is likely to become indelible and unalterable; and therefore it is most important that the tales which the young first hear should be models of virtuous thoughts.

Plato, *Republic,* II, 377A

4 *Socrates.* Poets and story-tellers are guilty of making the gravest mis-statements when they tell us that wicked men are often happy, and the good miserable; and that injustice is profitable when undetected, but that justice is a man's own loss and another's gain—these things we shall forbid them to utter, and command them to sing and say the opposite.

Plato, *Republic,* III, 392A

5 *Socrates.* Shall our superintendence go no further, and are the poets only to be required by us to express the image of the good in their works, on pain, if they do anything else, of expulsion from our State? Or is the same control to be extended to other artists, and are they also to be prohibited from exhibiting the opposite forms of vice and intemperance and meanness and indecency in

sculpture and building and the other creative arts; and is he who cannot conform to this rule of ours to be prevented from practising his art in our State, lest the taste of our citizens be corrupted by him? We would not have our guardians grow up amid images of moral deformity, as in some noxious pasture, and there browse and feed upon many a baneful herb and flower day by day, little by little, until they silently gather a festering mass of corruption in their own soul. Let our artists rather be those who are gifted to discern the true nature of the beautiful and graceful; then will our youth dwell in a land of health, amid fair sights and sounds, and receive the good in everything; and beauty, the effluence of fair works, shall flow into the eye and ear, like a health-giving breeze from a purer region, and insensibly draw the soul from earliest years into likeness and sympathy with the beauty of reason.

Plato, *Republic,* III, 401A

6 *Socrates.* The imitative poet who aims at being popular is not by nature made, nor is his art intended, to please or to affect the rational principle in the soul; but he will prefer the passionate and fitful temper, which is easily imitated. . . . Therefore we shall be right in refusing to admit him into a well-ordered State, because he awakens and nourishes and strengthens the feelings and impairs the reason.

Plato, *Republic,* X, 605A

7 There is nothing which the legislator should be more careful to drive away than indecency of speech; for the light utterance of shameful words leads soon to shameful actions. The young especially should never be allowed to repeat or hear anything of the sort. . . . And since we do not allow improper language, clearly we should also banish pictures or speeches from the stage which are indecent.

Aristotle, *Politics,* 1336b3

8 Our Twelve Tables of law only carried the death penalty for a few crimes. Among these crimes was singing or composing a song that was derogatory or insulting to someone. This was a good law. Our way of life should be open to judgment by the magistrates and law courts and not left to the commentary of clever playwrights. We should not be subjected to public disgrace unless we can answer and defend ourselves in a court of law. The early Romans did not want any living man to be the object of praise or blame on the stage.

Cicero, *Republic,* IV, 10

9 One is . . . inclined to laugh at the stupidity of men who suppose that the despotism of the present can actually efface the remembrances of the next generation. On the contrary, the persecution of genius fosters its influence; foreign tyrants, and all who have imitated their oppression, have merely procured infamy for themselves and glory for their victims.

Tacitus, *Annals,* IV, 35

10 This was the most dreadful feature of the age, that leading members of the Senate, some openly, some secretly employed themselves in the very lowest work of the informer. One could not distinguish between aliens and kinsfolk, between friends and strangers, or say what was quite recent, or what half-forgotten from lapse of time. People were incriminated for some casual remark in the forum or at the dinner-table, for every one was impatient to be the first to mark his victim, some to screen themselves, most from being, as it were, infected with the contagion of the malady.

Tacitus, *Annals,* VI, 7

11 The laws of the Romans and the speculations of Plato have this resemblance, that the latter pronounce a wholesale condemnation of poetical fictions, while the former restrain the licence of satire, at least so far as men are the objects of it. Plato will not suffer poets even to dwell in his city: the laws of Rome prohibit actors from being enrolled as citizens; and if they had not feared to offend the gods who had asked the services of the players, they would in all likelihood have banished them altogether. It is obvious, therefore, that the Romans could not receive, nor reasonably expect to receive, laws for the regulation of their conduct from their gods, since the laws they themselves enacted far surpassed and put to shame the morality of the gods. The gods demand stageplays in their own honour; the Romans exclude the players from all civic honours; the former commanded that they should be celebrated by the scenic representation of their own disgrace; the latter commanded that no poet should dare to blemish the reputation of any citizen. But that demigod Plato resisted the lust of such gods as these and showed the Romans what their genius had left incomplete; for he absolutely excluded poets from his ideal state, whether they composed fictions with no regard to truth or set the worst possible examples before wretched men under the guise of divine actions.

Augustine, *City of God,* II, 14

12 Human government is derived from the Divine government, and should imitate it. Now although God is all-powerful and supremely good, nevertheless He allows certain evils to take place in the universe, which He might prevent, lest, without them, greater goods might be forfeited, or greater evils ensue. Accordingly in human government also, those who are in authority, rightly tolerate certain evils, lest certain goods be lost, or certain greater evils be incurred. . . . Hence, though unbelievers sin in their rites, they may be tolerated,

either on account of some good that ensues therefrom, or because of some evil avoided.

Aquinas, *Summa Theologica*, II–II, 10, 11

13 People are right to give the tightest possible barriers to the human mind. In study, as in everything else, its steps must be counted and regulated for it; the limits of the chase must be artificially determined for it. They bridle and bind it with religions, laws, customs, science, precepts, mortal and immortal punishments and rewards; and still we see that by its whirling and its incohesiveness it escapes all these bonds. It is an empty body, with nothing by which it can be seized and directed; a varying and formless body, which can be neither tied nor grasped.

Indeed there are few souls so orderly, so strong and wellborn, that they can be trusted with their own guidance, and that can sail with moderation and without temerity, in the freedom of their judgments, beyond the common opinions. It is more expedient to place them in tutelage.

The mind is a dangerous blade, even to its possessor, for anyone who does not know how to wield it with order and discretion. And there is no animal that must more rightly be given blinkers to hold its gaze, in subjection and constraint, in front of its feet, and to keep it from straying here or there outside the ruts that custom and the laws trace for it.

Wherefore it will become you better to confine yourself to the accustomed routine, whatever it is, than to fly headlong into this unbridled license.

Montaigne, *Essays*, II, 12, Apology for Raymond Sebond

14 It is annexed to the sovereignty to be judge of what opinions and doctrines are averse, and what conducing to peace; and consequently, on what occasions, how far, and what men are to be trusted withal in speaking to multitudes of people; and who shall examine the doctrines of all books before they be published. For the actions of men proceed from their opinions, and in the well governing of opinions consisteth the well governing of men's actions in order to their peace and concord. And though in matter of doctrine nothing ought to be regarded but the truth, yet this is not repugnant to regulating of the same by peace. For doctrine repugnant to peace can no more be true, than peace and concord can be against the law of nature.

Hobbes, *Leviathan*, II, 18

15 Disobedience may lawfully be punished in them that against the laws teach even true philosophy.

Hobbes, *Leviathan*, IV, 46

16 For books are as meats and viands are; some of good, some of evil substance; and yet God, in that unapocryphal vision, said without exception, Rise, Peter, kill and eat, leaving the choice to each man's discretion. Wholesome meats to a vitiated stomach differ little or nothing from unwholesome; and best books to a naughty mind are not unappliable to occasions of evil. Bad meats will scarce breed good nourishment in the healthiest concoction; but herein the difference is of bad books, that they to a discreet and judicious reader serve in many respects to discover, to confute, to forewarn, and to illustrate. . . . I conceive, therefore, that when God did enlarge the universal diet of man's body, saving ever the rules of temperance, He then also, as before, left arbitrary the dieting and repasting of our minds; as wherein every mature man might have to exercise his own leading capacity.

Milton, *Areopagitica*

17 If every action, which is good or evil in man at ripe years, were to be under pittance and prescription and compulsion, what were virtue but a name, what praise could be then due to well-doing, what gramercy to be sober, just, or continent? Many there be that complain of Divine Providence for suffering Adam to transgress; foolish tongues! When God gave him reason, He gave him freedom to choose, for reason is but choosing; he had been else a mere artificial Adam, such an Adam as he is in the motions. We ourselves esteem not of that obedience, or love, or gift, which is of force: God therefore left him free, set before him a provoking object, ever almost in his eyes; herein consisted his merit, herein the right of his reward, the praise of his abstinence. Wherefore did He create passions within us, pleasures round about us, but that these rightly tempered are the very ingredients of virtue? . . .

This justifies the high providence of God, who, though He commands us temperance, justice, continence, yet pours out before us, even to a profuseness, all desirable things, and gives us minds that can wander beyond all limit and satiety. Why should we then affect a rigour contrary to the manner of God and of nature, by abridging or scanting those means, which books freely permitted are, both to the trial of virtue and the exercise of truth? It would be better done, to learn that the law must needs be frivolous, which goes to restrain things, uncertainly and yet equally working to good and to evil. And were I the chooser, a dram of well-doing should be preferred before many times as much the forcible hindrance of evil-doing. For God sure esteems the growth and completing of one virtuous person more than the restraint of ten vicious.

Milton, *Areopagitica*

18 I know nothing of the licenser, but that I have his own hand here for his arrogance; who shall warrant me his judgment? The State, sir, replies the stationer, but has a quick return: The State shall

be my governors, but not my critics; they may be mistaken in the choice of a licenser, as easily as this licenser may be mistaken in an author; this is some common stuff; and he might add from Sir Francis Bacon, That such authorised books are but the language of the times. For though a licenser should happen to be judicious more than ordinary, which will be a great jeopardy of the next succession, yet his very office and his commission enjoins him to let pass nothing but what is vulgarly received already.

Milton, *Areopagitica*

19 Give me the liberty to know, to utter, and to argue freely according to conscience, above all liberties.

Milton, *Areopagitica*

20 Whilst the parties of men cram their tenets down all men's throats whom they can get into their power, without permitting them to examine their truth or falsehood; and will not let truth have fair play in the world, nor men the liberty to search after it: what improvements can be expected of this kind? What greater light can be hoped for in the moral sciences? The subject part of mankind in most places might, instead thereof, with Egyptian bondage, expect Egyptian darkness, were not the candle of the Lord set up by himself in men's minds, which it is impossible for the breath or power of man wholly to extinguish.

Locke, *Concerning Human Understanding,*
Bk. IV, III, 20

21 Since . . . it is unavoidable to the greatest part of men, if not all, to have several *opinions,* without certain and indubitable proofs of their truth; and it carries too great an imputation of ignorance, lightness, or folly for men to quit and renounce their former tenets presently upon the offer of an argument which they cannot immediately answer, and show the insufficiency of: it would, methinks, become all men to maintain peace, and the common offices of humanity, and friendship, in the diversity of opinions; since we cannot reasonably expect that any one should readily and obsequiously quit his own opinion, and embrace ours, with a blind resignation to an authority which the understanding of man acknowledges not. For however it may often mistake, it can own no other guide but reason, nor blindly submit to the will and dictates of another.

Locke, *Concerning Human Understanding,*
Bk. IV, XVI, 4

22 He knew no reason, why those who entertain opinions prejudicial to the publick, should be obliged to change, or should not be obliged to conceal them. And, as it was tyranny in any Government to require the first, so it was weakness not to enforce the second: for, a man may be allowed

to keep poisons in his closet, but not to vend them about as cordials.

Swift, *Gulliver's Travels,* II, 6

23 In what kind of government are censors necessary? My answer is, that they are necessary in a republic, where the principle of government is virtue. We must not imagine that criminal actions only are destructive of virtue; it is destroyed also by omissions, by neglects, by a certain coolness in the love of our country, by bad examples, and by the seeds of corruption: whatever does not openly violate but elude the laws, does not subvert but weaken them, ought to fall under the inquiry and correction of the censors. . . .

In monarchies there should be no censors; the former are founded on honour, and the nature of honour is to have the whole world for its censor. Every man who fails in this article is subject to the reproaches even of those who are void of honour.

Montesquieu, *Spirit of Laws,* V, 19

24 I think, that the state ought to tolerate every principle of philosophy; nor is there an instance, that any government has suffered in its political interests by such indulgence. There is no enthusiasm among philosophers; their doctrines are not very alluring to the people; and no restraint can be put upon their reasonings, but what must be of dangerous consequence to the sciences, and even to the state, by paving the way for persecution and oppression in points, where the generality of mankind are more deeply interested and concerned.

Hume, *Concerning Human
Understanding,* XI, 114

25 The spirit of the people must frequently be roused, in order to curb the ambition of the court; and the dread of rousing this spirit must be employed to prevent that ambition. Nothing so effectual to this purpose as the liberty of the press; by which all the learning, wit, and genius of the nation, may be employed on the side of freedom, and every one be animated to its defence. As long, therefore, as the republican part of our government can maintain itself against the monarchical, it will naturally be careful to keep the press open, as of importance to its own preservation.

Hume, *Of the Liberty of the Press*

26 The men of letters who have rendered the greatest services to the small number of thinking beings spread over the world, are the isolated writers, the true scholars shut in their studies, who have neither argued on the benches of the universities, nor told half-truths in the academies; and almost all of them have been persecuted. Our wretched species is so made that those who walk on the well-trodden path always throw stones at those who are showing a new road.

Montesquieu says that the Scythians rent their

slaves' eyes, so that they might be less distracted while they were churning their butter; that is just how the inquisition functions, and in the land where this monster reigns almost everybody is blind. In England people have had two eyes for more than two hundred years; the French are starting to open one eye; but sometimes there are men in power who do not want the people to have even this one eye open.

These poor persons in power are like Doctor Balouard of the Italian Comedy, who does not want to be served by anyone but the dolt Harlequin, and who is afraid of having too shrewd a valet.

Compose some odes in praise of My Lord Superbus Fadus, some madrigals for his mistress; dedicate a book on geography to his door-keeper, you will be well-received; enlighten mankind, you will be exterminated.

Descartes was forced to leave his country, Gassendi was calumniated, Arnauld dragged out his days in exile; every philosopher is treated as the prophets were among the Jews.

Who would believe that in the eighteenth century a philosopher was dragged before the secular tribunals, and treated as impious by the tribunals of arguments, for having said that men could not practise the arts if they had no hands? I do not despair that soon the first person who is so insolent as to say that men could not think if they had no heads will be immediately condemned to the galleys; "for," some young graduate will say to him, "the soul is a pure spirit, the head is only matter; God can put the soul in the heel, as well as in the brain; therefore I denounce you as impious."

The greatest misfortune of a man of letters is not perhaps being the object of his confrères' jealousy, the victim of the cabal, the despised of the men of power; but of being judged by fools.

Voltaire, *Philosophical Dictionary:*
Men of Letters

27 Of all religions, the Christian is without doubt the one which should inspire tolerance most, although up to now the Christians have been the most intolerant of all men. The Christian Church was divided in its cradle, and was divided even in the persecutions which under the first emperors it sometimes endured. Often the martyr was regarded as an apostate by his brethren, and the Carpocratian Christian expired beneath the sword of the Roman executioners, excommunicated by the Ebionite Christian, the which Ebionite was anathema to the Sabellian.

This horrible discord, which has lasted for so many centuries, is a very striking lesson that we should pardon each other's errors; discord is the great ill of mankind; and tolerance is the only remedy for it.

There is nobody who is not in agreement with this truth, whether he meditates soberly in his study, or peaceably examines the truth with his friends. Why then do the same men who admit in private indulgence, kindness, justice, rise in public with so much fury against these virtues? Why? it is that their own interest is their god, and that they sacrifice everything to this monster that they worship.

I possess a dignity and a power founded on ignorance and credulity; I walk on the heads of the men who lie prostrate at my feet; if they should rise and look me in the face, I am lost; I must bind them to the ground, therefore, with iron chains.

Thus have reasoned the men whom centuries of bigotry have made powerful. They have other powerful men beneath them, and these have still others, who all enrich themselves with the spoils of the poor, grow fat on their blood, and laugh at their stupidity. They all detest tolerance, as partisans grown rich at the public expense fear to render their accounts, and as tyrants dread the word liberty. And then, to crown everything, they hire fanatics to cry at the top of their voices: "Respect my master's absurdities, tremble, pay, and keep your mouths shut."

It is thus that a great part of the world long was treated; but to-day when so many sects make a balance of power, what course to take with them? Every sect, as one knows, is a ground of error; there are no sects of geometers, algebraists, arithmeticians, because all the propositions of geometry, algebra and arithmetic are true. In every other science one may be deceived. What Thomist or Scotist theologian would dare say seriously that he is sure of his case?

If it were permitted to reason consistently in religious matters, it is clear that we all ought to become Jews, because Jesus Christ our Saviour was born a Jew, lived a Jew, died a Jew, and that he said expressly that he was accomplishing, that he was fulfilling the Jewish religion. But it is clearer still that we ought to be tolerant of one another, because we are all weak, inconsistent, liable to fickleness and error. Shall a reed laid low in the mud by the wind say to a fellow reed fallen in the opposite direction: "Crawl as I crawl, wretch, or I shall petition that you be torn up by the roots and burned?"

Voltaire, *Philosophical Dictionary:* Tolerance

28 *Johnson.* "They make a rout about *universal* liberty, without considering that all that is to be valued, or indeed can be enjoyed by individuals, is *private* liberty. Political liberty is good only so far as it produces private liberty. Now, Sir, there is the liberty of the press, which you know is a constant topick. Suppose you and I and two hundred more were restrained from printing our thoughts: what then? What proportion would that restraint upon us bear to the private happiness of the nation?"

This mode of representing the inconveniences

of restraint as light and insignificant, was a kind of sophistry in which he delighted to indulge himself, in opposition to the extreme laxity for which it has been fashionable for too many to argue, when it is evident, upon reflection, that the very essence of government is restraint; and certain it is, that as government produces rational happiness, too much restraint is better than too little. But when restraint is unnecessary, and so close as to gall those who are subject to it, the people may and ought to remonstrate; and, if relief is not granted, to resist. Of this manly and spirited principle, no man was more convinced than Johnson himself.

Boswell, *Life of Johnson (May 1768)*

29 *Johnson*. "Every society has a right to preserve publick peace and order, and therefore has a good right to prohibit the propagation of opinions which have a dangerous tendency. To say the *magistrate* has this right, is using an inadequate word: it is the *society* for which the magistrate is agent. He may be morally or theologically wrong in restraining the propagation of opinions which he thinks dangerous, but he is politically right." *Mayo*. "I am of opinion, Sir, that every man is entitled to liberty of conscience in religion; and that the magistrate cannot restrain that right." *Johnson*. "Sir, I agree with you. Every man has a right to liberty of conscience, and with that the magistrate cannot interfere. People confound liberty of thinking with liberty of talking; nay, with liberty of preaching. Every man has a physical right to think as he pleases; for it cannot be discovered how he thinks. He has not a moral right, for he ought to inform himself, and think justly. But, Sir, no member of a society has a right to *teach* any doctrine contrary to what the society holds to be true. The magistrate, I say, may be wrong in what he thinks: but while he thinks himself right, he may and ought to enforce what he thinks." *Mayo*. "Then, Sir, we are to remain always in errour, and truth never can prevail; and the magistrate was right in persecuting the first Christians." *Johnson*. "Sir, the only method by which religious truth can be established is by martyrdom. The magistrate has a right to enforce what he thinks; and he who is conscious of the truth has a right to suffer. I am afraid there is no other way of ascertaining the truth, but by persecution on the one hand and enduring it on the other." *Goldsmith*. "But how is a man to act, Sir? Though firmly convinced of the truth of his doctrine, may he not think it wrong to expose himself to persecution? Has he a right to do so? Is it not, as it were, committing voluntary suicide?" *Johnson*. "Sir, as to voluntary suicide, as you call it, there are twenty thousand men in an army who will go without scruple to be shot at, and mount a breach for five-pence a day." *Goldsmith*. "But have they a moral right to do this?" *Johnson*. "Nay, Sir, if you

will not take the universal opinion of mankind, I have nothing to say. If mankind cannot defend their own way of thinking, I cannot defend it. Sir, if a man is in doubt whether it would be better for him to expose himself to martyrdom or not, he should not do it. He must be convinced that he has a delegation from heaven."

Boswell, *Life of Johnson (May 7, 1773)*

30 *The Beggar's Opera*, and the common question, whether it was pernicious in its effects, having been introduced;—*Johnson*. "As to this matter, which has been very much contested, I myself am of opinion, that more influence has been ascribed to *The Beggar's Opera*, than it in reality ever had; for I do not believe that any man was ever made a rogue by being present at its representation. At the same time I do not deny that it may have some influence, by making the character of a rogue familiar, and in some degree pleasing."

Boswell, *Life of Johnson (Apr. 18, 1775)*

31 *Johnson*. Every man has a right to utter what he thinks truth, and every other man has a right to knock him down for it.

Boswell, *Life of Johnson (1780)*

32 I mentioned Dr. Johnson's excellent distinction between liberty of conscience and liberty of teaching. *Johnson*. "Consider, Sir; if you have children whom you wish to educate in the principles of the Church of England, and there comes a Quaker who tries to pervert them to his principles, you would drive away the Quaker. You would not trust to the predomination of right, which you believe is in your opinions; you would keep wrong out of their heads. Now the vulgar are the children of the State. If any one attempts to teach them doctrines contrary to what the State approves, the magistrate may and ought to restrain him." *Seward*. "Would you restrain private conversation, Sir?" *Johnson*. "Why, Sir, it is difficult to say where private conversation begins, and where it ends. If we three should discuss even the great question concerning the existence of a Supreme Being by ourselves, we should not be restrained; for that would be to put an end to all improvement. But if we should discuss it in the presence of ten boarding-school girls, and as many boys, I think the magistrate would do well to put us in the stocks, to finish the debate there."

Boswell, *Life of Johnson (Apr. 29, 1783)*

33 The people are the only censors of their governors; and even their errors will tend to keep these to the true principles of their institution. To punish these errors too severely would be to suppress the only safeguard of the public liberty. The way to prevent these irregular interpositions of the people is to give them full information of their affairs through the channel of the public papers,

and to contrive that those papers should penetrate the whole mass of the people. The basis of our governments being the opinion of the people, the very first object should be to keep that right; and were it left to me to decide whether we should have a government without newspapers, or newspapers without a government, I should not hesitate a moment to prefer the latter.

Jefferson, *Letter to Edward Carrington*
(*Jan. 16, 1787*)

34 Every difference of opinion is not a difference of principle. We have called by different names brethren of the same principle. We are all Republicans, we are all Federalists. If there be any among us who would wish to dissolve this Union or to change its republican form, let them stand undisturbed as monuments of the safety with which error of opinion may be tolerated where reason is left free to combat it.

Jefferson, *First Inaugural Address*

35 Let each thinker pursue his own path; if he shows talent, if he gives evidence of profound thought, in one word, if he shows that he possesses the power of reasoning—reason is always the gainer. If you have recourse to other means, if you attempt to coerce reason, if you raise the cry of treason to humanity, if you excite the feelings of the crowd, which can neither understand nor sympathize with such subtle speculations—you will only make yourselves ridiculous. For the question does not concern the advantage or disadvantage which we are expected to reap from such inquiries; the question is merely how far reason can advance in the field of speculation, apart from all kinds of interest, and whether we may depend upon the exertions of speculative reason, or must renounce all reliance on it.

Kant. *Critique of Pure Reason,*
Transcendental Method

36 To define freedom of the press as freedom to say and write whatever we please is parallel to the assertion that freedom as such means freedom to do as we please. Talk of this kind is due to wholly uneducated, crude, and superficial ideas. Moreover, it is in the very nature of the thing that abstract thinking should nowhere be so stubborn, so unintelligent, as in this matter of free speech, because what it is considering is the most fleeting, the most contingent, and the most personal side of opinion in its infinite diversity of content and tergiversation. Beyond the direct incitation to theft, murder, rebellion, etc., there lies its artfully constructed expression—an expression which seems in itself quite general and vague, while all the time it conceals a meaning anything but vague or else is compatible with inferences which are not actually expressed, and it is impossible to determine whether they rightly follow from it, or whether

they were meant to be inferred from it. This vagueness of matter and form precludes laws on these topics from attaining the requisite determinacy of law, and since the trespass, wrong, and injury here are so extremely personal and subjective in form, judgement on them is reduced equally to a wholly subjective verdict. Such an injury is directed against the thoughts, opinions, and wills of others, but apart from that, these form the element in which alone it is actually anything. But this element is the sphere of the freedom of others, and it therefore depends on them whether the injurious expression of opinion is or is not actually an effective act.

Laws then [against libel, etc.] may be criticized by exhibiting their indeterminacy as well as by arguing that they leave it open to the speaker or writer to devise turns of phrase or tricks of expression, and so evade the laws or claim that judicial decisions are mere subjective verdicts. Further, however, against the view that the expression of opinion is an act with injurious effects, it may be maintained that it is not an act at all, but only opining and thinking, or only talking. And so we have before us a claim that mere opining and talking is to go unpunished because it is of a purely subjective character both in form and content, because it does not mean anything and is of no importance. And yet in the same breath we have the claim that this same opining and talking should be held in high esteem and respect—the opining because it is personal property and in fact pre-eminently the property of mind; the talking because it is only this same property being expressed and used.

But the substance of the matter is and remains that traducing the honour of anyone, slander, abuse, the contemptuous caricature of government, its ministers, officials, and in particular the person of the monarch, defiance of the laws, incitement to rebellion, etc., etc., are all crimes or misdemeanours in one or other of their numerous gradations. The rather high degree of indeterminability which such actions acquire on account of the element in which they are expressed does not annul this fundamental character of theirs. Its only effect is that the subjective field in which they are committed also determines the nature and form of the reaction to the offence. It is the field in which the offence was committed which itself necessitates subjectivity of view, contingency, etc., in the reaction to the offence, whether the reaction takes the form of punishment proper or of police action to prevent crimes. Here, as always, abstract thinking sets itself to explain away the fundamental and concrete nature of the thing by concentrating on isolated aspects of its external appearance and on abstractions drawn therefrom.

The sciences, however, are not to be found anywhere in the field of opinion and subjective views, provided of course that they be sciences in other respects. Their exposition is not a matter of clever turns of phrase, allusiveness, half-utterances, and semi-reticences, but consists in the unambiguous, determinate, and open expression of their meaning and purport. It follows that they do not fall under the category of public opinion. Apart from this, however, as I said just now, the element in which views and their expression become actions in the full sense and exist effectively, consists of the intelligence, principles, and opinions of others. Hence this aspect of these actions, that is their effectiveness proper and their danger to individuals, society, and the state depends on the character of the ground on which they fall, just as a spark falling on a heap of gunpowder is more dangerous than if it falls on hard ground where it vanishes without trace. Thus, just as the right of science to express itself depends on and is safeguarded by its subject-matter and content, so an illegitimate expression may also acquire a measure of security, or at least sufferance, in the scorn which it has brought upon itself.

Hegel, *Philosophy of Right*, 319

37 Every burned book or house enlightens the world.

Emerson, *Compensation*

38 The great writers to whom the world owes what religious liberty it possesses, have mostly asserted freedom of conscience as an indefeasible right, and denied absolutely that a human being is accountable to others for his religious belief. Yet so natural to mankind is intolerance in whatever they really care about, that religious freedom has hardly anywhere been practically realised, except where religious indifference, which dislikes to have its peace disturbed by theological quarrels, has added its weight to the scale.

Mill, *On Liberty*, I

39 If all mankind minus one were of one opinion, and only one person were of the contrary opinion, mankind would be no more justified in silencing that one person, than he, if he had the power, would be justified in silencing mankind.

Mill, *On Liberty*, II

40 We have now recognised the necessity to the mental well-being of mankind (on which all their other well-being depends) of freedom of opinion, and freedom of the expression of opinion, on four distinct grounds; which we will now briefly recapitulate.

First, if any opinion is compelled to silence, that opinion may, for aught we can certainly know, be true. To deny this is to assume our own infallibility.

Secondly, though the silenced opinion be an error, it may, and very commonly does, contain a portion of truth; and since the general or prevailing opinion on any subject is rarely or never the whole truth, it is only by the collision of adverse opinions that the remainder of the truth has any chance of being supplied.

Thirdly, even if the received opinion be not only true, but the whole truth; unless it is suffered to be, and actually is, vigorously and earnestly contested, it will, by most of those who receive it, be held in the manner of a prejudice, with little comprehension or feeling of its rational grounds. And not only this, but, fourthly, the meaning of the doctrine itself will be in danger of being lost, or enfeebled, and deprived of its vital effect on the character and conduct: the dogma becoming a mere formal profession, inefficacious for good, but cumbering the ground, and preventing the growth of any real and heartfelt conviction, from reason or personal experience.

Mill, *On Liberty*, II

41 Men fear thought as they fear nothing else on earth—more than ruin, more even than death. Thought is subversive and revolutionary, destructive and terrible; thought is merciless to privilege, established institutions, and comfortable habits; thought is anarchic and lawless, indifferent to authority, careless of the well-tried wisdom of the ages. Thought looks into the pit of hell and is not afraid. It sees man, a feeble speck, surrounded by unfathomable depths of silence; yet it bears itself proudly, as unmoved as if it were lord of the universe. Thought is great and swift and free, the light of the world, and the chief glory of man.

But if thought is to become the possession of many, not the privilege of the few, we must have done with fear. It is fear that holds men back—fear lest their cherished beliefs should prove delusions, fear lest the institutions by which they live should prove harmful, fear lest they themselves should prove less worthy of respect than they have supposed themselves to be. "Should the working man think freely about property? Then what will become of us, the rich? Should young men and young women think freely about sex? Then what will become of morality? Should soldiers think freely about war? Then what will become of military discipline? Away with thought! Back into the shades of prejudice, lest property, morals, and war should be endangered! Better men should be stupid, slothful, and oppressive than that their thoughts should be free. For if their thoughts were free they might not think as we do. And at all costs this disaster must be averted." So the opponents of thought argue in the unconscious depths of their souls. And so they act in their churches, their schools, and their universities.

Russell, *Education*

42 The fundamental argument for freedom of opinion is the doubtfulness of all our beliefs. If we certainly knew the truth, there would be something to be said for teaching it. But in that case it could

be taught without invoking authority, by means of its inherent reasonableness. It is not necessary to make a law that no one shall be allowed to teach arithmetic if he holds heretical opinions on the multiplication table, because here the truth is clear, and does not require to be enforced by pen-alties. When the State intervenes to ensure the teaching of some doctrine, it does so *because* there is no conclusive evidence in favour of that doctrine.

Russell, *Sceptical Essays*, XIV

13.3 | *Equality*

Two main questions are discussed in the passages assembled here. One is whether persons *are* by nature equal in any sense. The question is not whether individuals are unequal in a wide variety of respects—in their natural endowments and in their personal attainments; no one has ever denied that; but whether there is any truth in the proposition that men *are created* equal or *are by nature* equal in any sense of the term. The other question is whether men *should be* accorded equality of status or of opportunity and *should be* given an equality of external conditions. The question that involves the word "should," as contrasted with the question that involves the word "are," elicits a range of diverse answers, from the advocacy of a complete equality of conditions to the opposite extreme of contending that the inequalities that exist among men, in their natural endowments and their personal attainments, call for inequality of treatment, status, and opportunity.

Closely related to the issue raised by the second question is the issue concerning the relation of liberty and equality. The reader will find famous passages from John C. Calhoun, Alexis de Tocqueville, and William Graham Sumner arguing that liberty and equality are incompatible: every movement toward equality of treatment or the establishment of an equality of conditions tends to interfere with or diminish individual liberty. On the opposite side, the reader will find Henry George and R. H. Tawney arguing that equality of conditions, especially in economic matters, is indispensable to the operation and preservation of political liberty.

Crucial to both issues, of course, is the position one takes on the question of human equality: whether there is any significant respect in which all men are naturally or personally equal, and whether such equality is more fundamental than the many respects in which individuals are unequal. Relevant to this question is the discussion of natural slavery in Section 10.7 on SLAVERY; also relevant are the arguments for and against democracy that will be found in Section 10.4 on GOVERNMENT OF AND BY THE PEOPLE: REPUBLIC AND DEMOCRACY. Other sections in which equality is a pivotal term are 12.2 on JUSTICE AND INJUSTICE, 12.3 on RIGHTS—NATURAL AND CIVIL, and 10.8 on CLASSES AND CLASS CONFLICT.

The reader should observe that the main concern in certain of these contexts is political equality, equality of rights, or equality before the law; in other contexts it is economic equality—equality of wealth, in possessions, or in economic opportunity; and in still others it is social equality, achieved through the elimination of all discriminations based on gender, race, or ethnic origin.

---

1 *Jocasta.* It's better . . .
to honor Equality who ties friends to friends,
cities to cities, allies to allies.
For equality is stable among men.
If not, the lesser hates the greater force,
and so begins the day of enmity.
Equality set up men's weights and measures,
gave them their numbers.

> Euripides, *Phoenician Women,* 535

2 *Athenian Stranger.* The old saying, that "equality makes friendship," is happy and also true; but there is obscurity and confusion as to what sort of equality is meant. For there are two equalities which are called by the same name, but are in reality in many ways almost the opposite of one another; one of them may be introduced without difficulty, by any state or any legislator in the distribution of honours: this is the rule of measure, weight, and number, which regulates and apportions them. But there is another equality, of a better and higher kind, which is not so easily recognized. This is the judgment of Zeus; among men it avails but little; that little, however, is the source of the greatest good to individuals and states. For it gives to the greater more, and to the inferior less and in proportion to the nature of each; and, above all, greater honour always to the greater virtue, and to the less less; and to either in proportion to their respective measure of virtue and education. And this is justice, and is ever the true principle of states, at which we ought to aim, and according to this rule order the new city which is now being founded, and any other city which may be hereafter founded. To this the legislator should look—not to the interests of tyrants one or more, or to the power of the people, but to justice always; which, as I was saying, is the distribution of natural equality among unequals in each case. But there are times at which every state is compelled to use the words, "just," "equal," in a secondary sense, in the hope of escaping in some degree from factions. For equity and indulgence are infractions of the perfect and strict rule of justice. And this is the reason why we are obliged to use the equality of the lot, in order to avoid the discontent of the people; and so we invoke God and fortune in our prayers, and beg that they themselves will direct the lot with a view to supreme justice. And therefore, although we are compelled to use both equalities, we should use that into which the element of chance enters as seldom as possible.

> Plato, *Laws,* VI, 757A

3 The justice in transactions between man and man is a sort of equality indeed, and the injustice a sort of inequality; not according to that kind [geometrical] of proportion, however, but according to arithmetical proportion. For it makes no difference whether a good man has defrauded a bad man or a bad man a good one, nor whether it is a good or a bad man that has committed adultery; the law looks only to the distinctive character of the injury, and treats the parties as equal, if one is in the wrong and the other is being wronged, and if one inflicted injury and the other has received it. Therefore, this kind of injustice being an inequality, the judge tries to equalize it; for in the case also in which one has received and the other has inflicted a wound, or one has slain and the other been slain, the suffering and the action have been unequally distributed; but the judge tries to equalize by means of the penalty, taking away from the gain of the assailant. . . . Therefore the equal is intermediate between the greater and the less, but the gain and the loss are respectively greater and less in contrary ways; more of the good and less of the evil are gain, and the contrary is loss; intermediate between them is, as we saw, the equal, which we say is just; therefore corrective justice will be the intermediate between loss and gain. This is why, when people dispute, they take refuge in the judge; and to go to the judge is to go to justice; for the nature of the judge is to be a sort of animate justice; and they seek the judge as an intermediate, and in some states they call judges mediators, on the assumption that if they get what is intermediate they will get what is just. The just, then, is an intermediate, since the judge is so. Now the judge restores equality; it is as though there were a line divided into unequal parts, and he took away that by which the greater segment exceeds the half, and added it to the smaller segment. And when the whole has been equally divided, then they say they have 'their own'—that is, when they have got what is equal.

> Aristotle, *Ethics,* 1131ᵇ34

4 Equality does not seem to take the same form in acts of justice and in friendship; for in acts of justice what is equal in the primary sense is that which is in proportion to merit, while quantitative equality is secondary, but in friendship quantitative equality is primary and proportion to merit secondary.

> Aristotle, *Ethics,* 1158ᵇ29

5 The only stable principle of government is equali-

ty according to proportion, and for every man to enjoy his own.

Aristotle, *Politics*, 1307ª26

6 The third and most masterly stroke of this great lawgiver [Lycurgus] by which he struck a yet more effectual blow against luxury and the desire of riches, was the ordinance, he made, that they should all eat in common, of the same bread and same meat, and of kinds that were specified, and should not spend their lives at home, laid on costly couches at splendid tables, delivering themselves up into the hands of their tradesmen and cooks, to fatten them in corners, like greedy brutes, and to ruin not their minds only but their very bodies which, enfeebled by indulgence and excess, would stand in need of long sleep, warm bathing, freedom from work, and, in a word, of as much care and attendance as if they were continually sick.

It was certainly an extraordinary thing to have brought about such a result as this, but a greater yet to have taken away from wealth, as Theophrastus observes, not merely the property of being coveted, but its very nature of being wealth. For the rich, being obliged to go to the same table with the poor, could not make use of or enjoy their abundance, nor so much as please their vanity by looking at or displaying it. So that the common proverb, that Plutus, the god of riches, is blind, was nowhere in all the world literally verified but in Sparta. There, indeed, he was not only blind, but like a picture, without either life or motion. Nor were they allowed to take food at home first, and then attend the public tables, for every one had an eye upon those who did not eat and drink like the rest, and reproached them with being dainty and effeminate.

Plutarch, *Lycurgus*

7 These reasonings have no logical connection: "I am richer than you, therefore I am your superior." "I am more eloquent than you, therefore I am your superior." The true logical connection is rather this: "I am richer than you, therefore my possessions must exceed yours." "I am more eloquent than you, therefore my style must surpass yours." But you, after all, consist neither in property nor in style.

Epictetus, *Encheiridion*, XLIV

8 The instincts of human nature . . . prompt men to scrutinize with keen eyes the recent elevation of their fellows, and to demand a temperate use of prosperity from none more rigorously than from those whom they have seen on a level with themselves.

Tacitus, *Histories*, II, 20

9 Equality of justice has its place in retribution, since equal rewards or punishments are due to equal merit or demerit. But this does not apply to things as at first instituted. For just as an architect, without injustice, places stones of the same kind in different parts of a building not on account of any antecedent difference in the stones, but with a view to securing that perfection of the entire building, which could not be obtained except by the different positions of the stones, even so, God from the beginning, to secure perfection in the universe, has set therein creatures of various and unequal natures, according to His wisdom, and without injustice, since no diversity of merit is presupposed.

Aquinas, *Summa Theologica*, I, 65, 2

10 The souls of emperors and cobblers are cast in the same mold. Considering the importance of the actions of princes and their weightiness, we persuade ourselves that they are produced by some causes equally weighty and important. We are wrong: they are led to and fro in their movements by the same springs as we are in ours. The same reason that makes us bicker with a neighbor creates a war between princes; the same reason that makes us whip a lackey, when it happens in a king makes him ruin a province. Their will is as frivolous as ours, but their power is greater.

Montaigne, *Essays*, II, 12, Apology for Raymond Sebond

11 Nature hath made men so equal in the faculties of body and mind as that, though there be found one man sometimes manifestly stronger in body or of quicker mind than another, yet when all is reckoned together the difference between man and man is not so considerable as that one man can thereupon claim to himself any benefit to which another may not pretend as well as he. For as to the strength of body, the weakest has strength enough to kill the strongest, either by secret machination or by confederacy with others that are in the same danger with himself.

And as to the faculties of the mind, setting aside the arts grounded upon words, and especially that skill of proceeding upon general and infallible rules, called *science,* which very few have and but in few things, as being not a native faculty born with us, nor attained, as prudence, while we look after somewhat else, I find yet a greater equality amongst men than that of strength. For prudence is but experience, which equal time equally bestows on all men in those things they equally apply themselves unto. That which may perhaps make such equality incredible is but a vain conceit of one's own wisdom, which almost all men think they have in a greater degree than the vulgar; that is, than all men but themselves, and a few others, whom by fame, or for concurring with themselves, they approve. For such is the nature of men that howsoever they may acknowledge many others to be more witty, or more eloquent, or more learned, yet they will hardly believe there be many so wise as themselves; for they see their own wit at hand, and other men's at a distance. But this proveth rather that men are in that point equal, than unequal. For there is not ordinarily a greater sign of the equal distribution of anything than that every man is contented with his share.

Hobbes, *Leviathan,* I, 13

12 The question who is the better man has no place in the condition of mere nature, where . . . all men are equal. The inequality that now is has been introduced by the laws civil. I know that Aristotle in the first book of his *Politics,* for a foundation of his doctrine, maketh men by nature, some more worthy to command, meaning the wiser sort, such as he thought himself to be for his philosophy; others to serve, meaning those that had strong bodies, but were not philosophers as he; as if master and servant were not introduced by consent of men, but by difference of wit: which is not only against reason, but also against experience. For there are very few so foolish that had not rather govern themselves than be governed by others: nor when the wise, in their own conceit, contend by force with them who distrust their own wisdom, do they always, or often, or almost at any time, get the victory. If nature therefore have made men equal, that equality is to be acknowledged: or if nature have made men unequal, yet because men that think themselves equal will not enter into conditions of peace, but upon equal terms, such equality must be admitted. And therefore for the ninth law of nature, I put this: *that every man acknowledge another for his equal by nature.*

Hobbes, *Leviathan,* I, 15

13 The safety of the people requireth further, from him or them that have the sovereign power, that justice be equally administered to all degrees of people; that is, that as well the rich and mighty, as poor and obscure persons, may be righted of the injuries done them; so as the great may have no greater hope of impunity, when they do violence, dishonour, or any injury to the meaner sort, than when one of these does the like to one of them: for in this consisteth equity; to which, as being a precept of the law of nature, a sovereign is as much subject as any of the meanest of his people.

Hobbes, *Leviathan,* II, 30

14 To understand political power aright, and derive it from its original, we must consider what estate all men are naturally in, and that is, a state of perfect freedom to order their actions, and dispose of their possessions and persons as they think fit, within the bounds of the law of Nature, without asking leave or depending upon the will of any other man.

A state also of equality, wherein all the power and jurisdiction is reciprocal, no one having more

than another, there being nothing more evident than that creatures of the same species and rank, promiscuously born to all the same advantages of Nature, and the use of the same faculties, should also be equal one amongst another, without subordination or subjection, unless the lord and master of them all should, by any manifest declaration of his will, set one above another, and confer on him, by an evident and clear appointment, an undoubted right to dominion and sovereignty.

Locke, *II Civil Government,* II, 4

15 Though I have said above "That all men by nature are equal," I cannot be supposed to understand all sorts of "equality." Age or virtue may give men a just precedency. Excellency of parts and merit may place others above the common level. Birth may subject some, and alliance or benefits others, to pay an observance to those to whom Nature, gratitude, or other respects, may have made it due; and yet all this consists with the equality which all men are in respect of jurisdiction or dominion one over another, which was the equality I there spoke of as proper to the business in hand, being that equal right that every man hath to his natural freedom, without being subjected to the will or authority of any other man.

Locke, *II Civil Government,* VI, 54

16 The love of equality in a democracy limits ambition to the sole desire, to the sole happiness, of doing greater services to our country than the rest of our fellow-citizens. They cannot all render her equal services, but they all ought to serve her with equal alacrity. At our coming into the world, we contract an immense debt to our country, which we can never discharge.

Montesquieu, *Spirit of Laws,* V, 3

17 As distant as heaven is from earth, so is the true spirit of equality from that of extreme equality. The former does not imply that everybody should command, or that no one should be commanded, but that we obey or command our equals. It endeavours not to shake off the authority of a master, but that its masters should be none but its equals.

Montesquieu, *Spirit of Laws,* VIII, 3

18 All men are born with a sufficiently violent liking for domination, wealth and pleasure, and with much taste for idleness; consequently, all men want their money and the wives or daughters of others, to be their master, to subject them to all their caprices, and to do nothing, or at least to do only very agreeable things. You see clearly that with these fine inclinations it is as impossible for men to be equal as it is impossible for two predicants or two professors of theology not to be jealous of each other.

The human race, such as it is, cannot subsist

unless there is an infinity of useful men who possess nothing at all; for it is certain that a man who is well off will not leave his own land to come to till yours; and if you have need of a pair of shoes, it is not the Secretary to the Privy Council who will make them for you. Equality, therefore, is at once the most natural thing and the most fantastic. . . .

All men have the right in the bottom of their hearts to think themselves entirely equal to other men: it does not follow from that that the cardinal's cook should order his master to prepare him his dinner; but the cook can say: "I am a man like my master; like him I was born crying; like me he will die with the same pangs and the same ceremonies. Both of us perform the same animal functions. If the Turks take possession of Rome, and if then I am cardinal and my master cook, I shall take him into my service." This discourse is reasonable and just; but while waiting for the Great Turk to take possession of Rome, the cook must do his duty, or else all human society is perverted.

Voltaire, *Philosophical Dictionary:* Equality

19 I conceive that there are two kinds of inequality among the human species; one, which I call natural or physical, because it is established by nature, and consists in a difference of age, health, bodily strength, and the qualities of the mind or of the soul: and another, which may be called moral or political inequality, because it depends on a kind of convention, and is established, or at least authorised by the consent of men. This latter consists of the different privileges, which some men enjoy to the prejudice of others; such as that of being more rich, more honoured, more powerful or even in a position to exact obedience.

Rousseau, *Origin of Inequality,* Intro.

20 I have endeavoured to trace the origin and progress of inequality, and the institution and abuse of political societies, as far as these are capable of being deduced from the nature of man merely by the light of reason, and independently of those sacred dogmas which give the sanction of divine right to sovereign authority. It follows from this survey that, as there is hardly any inequality in the state of nature, all the inequality which now prevails owes its strength and growth to the development of our faculties and the advance of the human mind, and becomes at last permanent and legitimate by the establishment of property and laws. Secondly, it follows that moral inequality, authorised by positive right alone, clashes with natural right, whenever it is not proportionate to physical inequality; a distinction which sufficiently determines what we ought to think of that species of inequality which prevails in all civilised countries; since it is plainly contrary to the law of nature, however defined, that children should

command old men, fools wise men, and that the privileged few should gorge themselves with superfluities, while the starving multitude are in want of the bare necessities of life.

Rousseau, *Origin of Inequality,* II

21 I shall end this chapter and this book by remarking on a fact on which the whole social system should rest: that is, that, instead of destroying natural inequality, the fundamental compact substitutes, for such physical inequality as nature may have set up between men, an equality that is moral and legitimate, and that men, who may be unequal in strength or intelligence, become every one equal by convention and legal right.

Rousseau, *Social Contract,* I, 9

22 *Johnson.* Sir, there is one Mrs. Macaulay in this town, a great republican. One day when I was at her house, I put on a very grave countenance, and said to her, 'Madam, I am now become a convert to your way of thinking. I am convinced that all mankind are upon an equal footing; and to give you an unquestionable proof, Madam, that I am in earnest, here is a very sensible, civil, well-behaved fellow-citizen, your footman; I desire that he may be allowed to sit down and dine with us.' I thus, Sir, shewed her the absurdity of the levelling doctrine. She has never liked me since. Sir, your levellers wish to level *down* as far as themselves; but they cannot bear leveling *up* to themselves. They would all have some people under them; why not then have some people above them?

Boswell, *Life of Johnson (July 21, 1763)*

23 On his favourite subject of subordination, Johnson said, "So far is it from being true that men are naturally equal, that no two people can be half an hour together, but one shall acquire an evident superiority over the other."

Boswell, *Life of Johnson (Feb. 15, 1766)*

24 I told him [Johnson] that Mrs. Macaulay said, she wondered how he could reconcile his political principles with his moral; his notions of inequality and subordination with wishing well to the happiness of all mankind, who might live so agreeably, had they all their portions of land, and none to domineer over another. *Johnson.* "Why, Sir, I reconcile my principles very well, because mankind are happier in a state of inequality and subordination. Were they to be in this pretty state of equality, they would soon degenerate into brutes;—they would become Monboddo's nation;—their tails would grow. Sir, all would be losers were all to work for all:—they would have no intellectual improvement. All intellectual improvement arises from leisure; all leisure arises from one working for another."

Boswell, *Life of Johnson (Apr. 13, 1773)*

25 Observing some beggars in the street as we walked along, I said to him I supposed there was no civilized country in the world, where the misery of want in the lowest classes of the people was prevented. *Johnson.* "I believe, Sir, there is not; but it is better that some should be unhappy, than that none should be happy, which would be the case in a general state of equality."

Boswell, *Life of Johnson* (Apr. 7, 1776)

26 The difference of natural talents in different men is in reality, much less than we are aware of. . . . The difference between the most dissimilar characters, between a philosopher and a common street porter, for example, seems to arise not so much from nature as from habit, custom, and education. When they came into the world, and for the first six or eight years of their existence, they were perhaps very much alike, and neither their parents nor playfellows could perceive any remarkable difference. About that age, or soon after, they come to be employed in very different occupations. The difference of talents comes then to be taken notice of, and widens by degrees, till at last the vanity of the philosopher is willing to acknowledge scarce any resemblance.

Adam Smith, *Wealth of Nations*, I, 2

27 Whatever each man can separately do, without trespassing upon others, he has a right to do for himself; and he has a right to a fair portion of all which society, with all its combinations of skill and force, can do in his favour. In this partnership all men have equal rights; but not to equal things. He that has but five shillings in the partnership, has as good a right to it, as he that has five hundred pounds has to his larger proportion. But he has not a right to an equal dividend in the product of the joint stock; and as to the share of power, authority, and direction which each individual ought to have in the management of the state, that I must deny to be amongst the direct original rights of man in civil society; for I have in my contemplation the civil social man, and no other. It is a thing to be settled by convention.

Burke, *Reflections on the Revolution in France*

28 The equality which might be set up, for example, in connexion with the distribution of goods, would all the same soon be destroyed again, because wealth depends on diligence. But if a project cannot be executed, it ought not to be executed. Of course men are equal, but only *qua* persons, that is, with respect only to the source from which possession springs; the inference from this is that everyone must have property. Hence, if you wish to talk of equality, it is this equality which you must have in view. But this equality is something apart from the fixing of particular amounts, from the question of how much I own. From this point of view it is false to maintain that justice requires everyone's property to be equal, since it requires only that everyone shall own property. The truth is that particularity is just the sphere where there is room for inequality and where equality would be wrong. True enough, men often lust after the goods of others, but that is just doing wrong, since right is that which remains indifferent to particularity.

Hegel, *Philosophy of Right*, Additions, Par. 49

29 It is impossible to believe that equality will not eventually find its way into the political world, as it does everywhere else. To conceive of men remaining forever unequal upon a single point, yet equal on all others, is impossible; they must come in the end to be equal upon all.

Now, I know of only two methods of establishing equality in the political world; rights must be given to every citizen, or none at all to anyone. For nations which are arrived at the same stage of social existence as the Anglo-Americans, it is, therefore, very difficult to discover a medium between the sovereignty of all and the absolute power of one man: and it would be vain to deny that the social condition which I have been describing is just as liable to one of these consequences as to the other.

There is, in fact, a manly and lawful passion for equality that incites men to wish all to be powerful and honored. This passion tends to elevate the humble to the rank of the great; but there exists also in the human heart a depraved taste for equality, which impels the weak to attempt to lower the powerful to their own level and reduces men to prefer equality in slavery to inequality with freedom. Not that those nations whose social condition is democratic naturally despise liberty; on the contrary, they have an instinctive love of it. But liberty is not the chief and constant object of their desires; equality is their idol: they make rapid and sudden efforts to obtain liberty and, if they miss their aim, resign themselves to their disappointment; but nothing can satisfy them without equality, and they would rather perish than lose it.

Tocqueville, *Democracy in America*, I, 3

30 It cannot be denied that democratic institutions strongly tend to promote the feeling of envy in the human heart; not so much because they afford to everyone the means of rising to the same level with others as because those means perpetually disappoint the persons who employ them. Democratic institutions awaken and foster a passion for equality which they can never entirely satisfy. This complete equality eludes the grasp of the people at the very moment when they think they have grasped it, and "flies," as Pascal says, "with an eternal flight"; the people are excited in the

pursuit of an advantage, which is more precious because it is not sufficiently remote to be unknown or sufficiently near to be enjoyed. The lower orders are agitated by the chance of success, they are irritated by its uncertainty; and they pass from the enthusiasm of pursuit to the exhaustion of ill success, and lastly to the acrimony of disappointment. Whatever transcends their own limitations appears to be an obstacle to their desires, and there is no superiority, however legitimate it may be, which is not irksome in their sight.

Tocqueville, *Democracy in America*, I, 13

31 In proportion as castes disappear and the classes of society draw together, as manners, customs, and laws vary, because of the tumultuous intercourse of men, as new facts arise, as new truths are brought to light, as ancient opinions are dissipated and others take their place, the image of an ideal but always fugitive perfection presents itself to the human mind. Continual changes are then every instant occurring under the observation of every man; the position of some is rendered worse, and he learns but too well that no people and no individual, however enlightened they may be, can lay claim to infallibility; the condition of others is improved, whence he infers that man is endowed with an indefinite faculty for improvement. His reverses teach him that none have discovered absolute good; his success stimulates him to the never ending pursuit of it. Thus, forever seeking, forever falling to rise again, often disappointed, but not discouraged, he tends unceasingly towards that unmeasured greatness so indistinctly visible at the end of the long track which humanity has yet to tread.

Tocqueville, *Democracy in America*,
Vol. II, I, 8

32 Political liberty bestows exalted pleasure from time to time upon a certain number of citizens. Equality every day confers a number of small enjoyments on every man. The charms of equality are every instant felt and are within the reach of all; the noblest hearts are not insensible to them, and the most vulgar souls exult in them. The passion that equality creates must therefore be at once strong and general. Men cannot enjoy political liberty unpurchased by some sacrifices, and they never obtain it without great exertions. But the pleasures of equality are self-proffered; each of the petty incidents of life seems to occasion them, and in order to taste them, nothing is required but to live.

Democratic nations are at all times fond of equality, but there are certain epochs at which the passion they entertain for it swells to the height of fury. This occurs at the moment when the old social system, long menaced, is overthrown after a severe internal struggle, and the barriers of rank are at length thrown down. At such times

men pounce upon equality as their booty, and they cling to it as to some precious treasure which they fear to lose. The passion for equality penetrates on every side into men's hearts, expands there, and fills them entirely. Tell them not that by this blind surrender of themselves to an exclusive passion they risk their dearest interests; they are deaf. Show them not freedom escaping from their grasp while they are looking another way; they are blind, or rather they can discern but one object to be desired in the universe.

Tocqueville, *Democracy in America*,
Vol. II, II, 1

33 When all the privileges of birth and fortune are abolished, when all professions are accessible to all, and a man's own energies may place him at the top of any one of them, an easy and unbounded career seems open to his ambition and he will readily persuade himself that he is born to no common destinies. But this is an erroneous notion, which is corrected by daily experience. The same equality that allows every citizen to conceive these lofty hopes renders all the citizens less able to realize them; it circumscribes their powers on every side, while it gives freer scope to their desires. Not only are they themselves powerless, but they are met at every step by immense obstacles, which they did not at first perceive. They have swept away the privileges of some of their fellow creatures which stood in their way, but they have opened the door to universal competition; the barrier has changed its shape rather than its position. When men are nearly alike and all follow the same track, it is very difficult for any one individual to walk quickly and cleave a way through the dense throng that surrounds and presses on him. This constant strife between the inclination springing from the equality of condition and the means it supplies to satisfy them harasses and wearies the mind.

It is possible to conceive of men arrived at a degree of freedom that should completely content them; they would then enjoy their independence without anxiety and without impatience. But men will never establish any equality with which they can be contented. Whatever efforts a people may make, they will never succeed in reducing all the conditions of society to a perfect level; and even if they unhappily attained that absolute and complete equality of position, the inequality of minds would still remain, which, coming directly from the hand of God, will forever escape the laws of man. However democratic, then, the social state and the political constitution of a people may be, it is certain that every member of the community will always find out several points about him which overlook his own position; and we may foresee that his looks will be doggedly fixed in that direction. When inequality of conditions is the common law of society, the most marked inequalities do not strike the eye; when everything is nearly on the same level, the slightest are marked enough to hurt it. Hence the desire of equality always becomes more insatiable in proportion as equality is more complete.

Tocqueville, *Democracy in America,*
Vol. II, II, 13

34 There is another error, not less great and dangerous, usually associated with the one which has just been considered. I refer to the opinion that liberty and equality are so intimately united that liberty cannot be perfect without perfect equality.

That they are united to a certain extent and that equality of citizens, in the eyes of the law, is essential to liberty in a popular government is conceded. But to go further and make equality of *condition* essential to liberty would be to destroy both liberty and progress. The reason is that inequality of condition, while it is a necessary consequence of liberty, is, at the same time, indispensable to progress. In order to understand why this is so, it is necessary to bear in mind that the mainspring to progress is the desire of individuals to better their condition and that the strongest impulse which can be given to it is to leave individuals free to exert themselves in the manner they may deem best for that purpose, as far at least as it can be done consistently with the ends for which government is ordained—and to secure to all the fruits of their exertions. Now, as individuals differ greatly from each other, in intelligence, sagacity, energy, perseverance, skill, habits of industry and economy, physical power, position, and opportunity, the necessary effect of leaving all free to exert themselves to better their condition must be a corresponding inequality between those who may possess these qualities and advantages in a high degree and those who may be deficient in them. The only means by which this result can be prevented are either to impose such restrictions on the exertions of those who may possess them in a high degree as will place them on a level with those who do not or to deprive them of the fruits of their exertions. But to impose such restrictions on them would be destructive of liberty, while to deprive them of the fruits of their exertions would be to destroy the desire of bettering their condition. It is, indeed, this inequality of condition between the front and rear ranks, in the march of progress, which gives so strong an impulse to the former to maintain their position and to the latter to press forward into their files. This gives to progress its greatest impulse. To force the front rank back to the rear, or attempt to push forward the rear into line with the front, by the interposition of the government, would put an end to the impulse and effectually arrest the march of progress.

J. C. Calhoun, *Disquisition on Government*

35 Men are certainly not born free and equal in nat-

ural qualities; when they are born, the predicates "free" and "equal" in the political sense are not applicable to them; and as they develop year by year, the differences in the political potentialities with which they really are born, become more and more obviously converted into actual differences—the inequality of political faculty shows itself to be a necessary consequence of the inequality of natural faculty.

T. H. Huxley, *On the Natural Inequality
of Men*

36 It is . . . conceded on all hands that men are not born physically, morally, or intellectually equal— some are males, some females, some from birth, large, strong, and healthy, others weak, small, and sickly—some are naturally amiable, others prone to all kinds of wickednesses—some brave, others timid. Their natural inequalities beget inequalities of rights. The weak in mind or body require guidance, support, and protection; they must obey and work for those who protect and guide them—they have a natural right to guardians, committees, teachers, or masters. Nature has made them slaves; all that law and government can do is to regulate, modify, and mitigate their slavery. In the absence of legally instituted slavery, their condition would be worse under that natural slavery of the weak to the strong, the foolish to the wise and cunning. The wise and virtuous, the brave, the strong in mind and body, are by nature born to command and protect, and law but follows nature in making them rulers, legislators, judges, captains, husbands, guardians, committees, and masters. The naturally depraved class, those born prone to crime, are our brethren too; they are entitled to education, to religious instruction, to all the means and appliances proper to correct their evil propensities, and all their failings; they have a right to be sent to the penitentiary—for there, if they do not reform, they cannot at least disturb society. Our feelings and our consciences teach us that nothing but necessity can justify taking human life.

Fitzhugh, *Sociology for the South*

37 I think the authors of that notable instrument [the Declaration of Independence] intended to include *all* men, but they did not intend to declare all men equal *in all respects.* They did not mean to say all were equal in color, size, intellect, moral developments, or social capacity. They defined with tolerable distinctness, in what respects they did consider all men created equal—equal in "certain inalienable rights, among which are life, liberty, and the pursuit of happiness." This they said, and this meant. They did not mean to assert the obvious untruth, that all were then actually enjoying that equality, nor yet, that they were about to confer it immediately upon them. In fact they had no power to confer such a boon. They meant sim-

ply to declare the *right*, so that the *enforcement* of it might follow as fast as circumstances should permit. They meant to set up a standard maxim for free society, which should be familiar to all, and revered by all; constantly looked to, constantly labored for, and even though never perfectly attained, constantly approximated, and thereby constantly spreading and deepening its influence, and augmenting the happiness and value of life to all people of all colors everywhere.

Lincoln, *Speech at Springfield, Ill.*
(June 26, 1857)

38 There is no reason in the world why the negro is not entitled to all the natural rights enumerated in the Declaration of Independence, the right to life, liberty and the pursuit of happiness. I hold that he is as much entitled to these as the white man. I agree with Judge Douglas he is not my equal in many respects—certainly not in color, perhaps not in moral or intellectual endowment. But in the right to eat the bread, without leave of anybody else, which his own hand earns, he is my equal and the equal of Judge Douglas, and the equal of every living man.

Lincoln, *Debate with Douglas (Aug. 21, 1858)*

39 Democracy, in its very essence, insists so much more forcibly on the things in which all are entitled to be considered equally, than on those in which one person is entitled to more consideration than another, that respect for even personal superiority is likely to be below the mark. It is for this, among other reasons, I hold it of so much importance that the institutions of the country should stamp the opinions of persons of a more educated class as entitled to greater weight than those of the less educated: and I should still contend for assigning plurality of votes to authenticated superiority of education, were it only to give the tone to public feeling, irrespective of any direct political consequences.

Mill, *Representative Government*, XII

40 Though the truth may not be felt or generally acknowledged for generations to come, the only school of genuine moral sentiment is society between equals. The moral education of mankind has hitherto emanated chiefly from the law of force, and is adapted almost solely to the relations which force creates. In the less advanced states of society, people hardly recognize any relation with their equals. To be an equal is to be an enemy. Society, from its highest place to its lowest, is one long chain, or rather ladder, where every individual is either above or below his nearest neighbour, and whereever he does not command he must obey. Existing moralities, accordingly, are mainly fitted to a relation of command and obedience. Yet command and obedience are but unfortunate necessities of human life: society in equality is its

normal state. Already in modern life, and more and more as it progressively improves, command and obedience become exceptional facts in life, equal association its general rule. The morality of the first ages rested on the obligation to submit to power; that of the ages next following, on the right of the weak to the forbearance and protection of the strong. How much longer is one form of society and life to content itself with the morality made for another? We have had the morality of submission, and the morality of chivalry and generosity; the time is now come for the morality of justice.

Mill, *Subjection of Women*, II

41 A thousand arguments may be discovered in favour of inequality, just as a thousand arguments may be discovered in favour of absolutism. And the one insuperable objection to inequality is the same as the one insuperable objection to absolutism: namely, that inequality, like absolutism, thwarts a vital instinct, and being thus against nature, is against our humanisation. On the one side, in fact, inequality harms by pampering; on the other, by vulgarising and depressing. A system founded on it is against nature, and in the long run breaks down.

Arnold, *Mixed Essays, Pref.*

42 Association in equality is the law of progress. Association frees mental power for expenditure in improvement, and equality, or justice, or freedom—for the terms here signify the same thing, the recognition of the moral law—prevents the dissipation of this power in fruitless struggles.

Here is the law of progress, which will explain all diversities, all advances, all halts, and retrogressions. Men tend to progress just as they come closer together, and by co-operation with each other increase the mental power that may be devoted to improvement, but just as conflict is provoked, or association develops inequality of condition and power, this tendency to progression is lessened, checked, and finally reversed.

Henry George, *Progress and Poverty*, X, 3

43 The first effect of the tendency to political equality was to the more equal distribution of wealth and power; for, while population is comparatively sparse, inequality in the distribution of wealth is principally due to the inequality of personal rights, and it is only as material progress goes on that the tendency to inequality involved in the reduction of land to private ownership strongly appears. But it is now manifest that absolute political equality does not in itself prevent the tendency to inequality involved in the private ownership of land, and it is further evident that political equality, co-existing with an increasing tendency to the unequal distribution of wealth, must ultimately beget either the despotism of organized

tyranny or the worse despotism of anarchy.

Henry George, *Progress and Poverty*, X, 4

44 Where there is anything like an equal distribution of wealth—that is to say, where there is general patriotism, virtue, and intelligence—the more democratic the government the better it will be; but where there is gross inequality in the distribution of wealth, the more democratic the government the worse it will be; for, while rotten democracy may not in itself be worse than rotten autocracy, its effects upon national character will be worse. To give the suffrage to tramps, to paupers, to men to whom the chance to labor is a boon, to men who must beg, or steal, or starve, is to invoke destruction. To put political power in the hands of men embittered and degraded by poverty is to tie firebrands to foxes and turn them loose amid the standing corn; it is to put out the eyes of a Samson and to twine his arms around the pillars of national life.

Henry George, *Progress and Poverty*, X, 4

45 The doctrine of equality! . . . . But there exists no more poisonous poison: for it *seems* to be preached by justice itself, while it is the *end* of justice. . . . . 'Equality for equals, inequality for unequals'— *that* would be the true voice of justice: and, what follows from it, 'Never make equal what is unequal'.

Nietzsche, *Twilight of the Idols:
Expeditions of an Untimely Man*

46 The poison of the doctrine *'equal rights for all'*— this has been more thoroughly sowed by Christianity than by anything else; from the most secret recesses of base instincts, Christianity has waged a war to the death against every feeling of reverence and distance between man and man, against, that is, the *precondition* of every elevation, every increase in culture—it has forged out of the *ressentiment* of the masses its *chief weapon* against *us*, against everything noble, joyful, high-spirited on earth, against our happiness on earth.

Nietzsche, *Antichrist*, XLIII

47 If . . . there be liberty, men get from her just in proportion to their works, and their having and enjoying are just in proportion to their being and their doing. Such is the system of nature. If we do not like it, and if we try to amend it, there is only one way in which we can do it. We can take from the better and give to the worse. We can deflect the penalties of those who have done ill and throw them on those who have done better. We can take the rewards from those who have done better and give them to those who have done worse. We shall thus lessen the inequalities. We shall favor the survival of the unfittest, and we shall accomplish this by destroying liberty. Let it be understood that we cannot go outside of this alternative: lib-

erty, inequality, survival of the fittest; not-liberty, equality, survival of the unfittest. The former carries society forward and favors all its best members; the latter carries society downwards and favors all its worst members.

W. G. Sumner, *Challenge of Facts*

48 Socialists are filled with the enthusiasm of equality. Every scheme of theirs for securing equality has destroyed liberty. The student of political philosophy has the antagonism of equality and liberty constantly forced upon him. Equality of possession or of rights and equality before the law are diametrically opposed to each other. The object of equality before the law is to make the state entirely neutral. The state, under that theory, takes no cognizance of persons. It surrounds all, without distinctions, with the same conditions and guarantees. If it educates one, it educates all—black, white, red, or yellow; Jew or Gentile; native or alien. If it taxes one, it taxes all, by the same system and under the same conditions. If it exempts one from police regulations in home, church, and occupation, it exempts all. From this statement it is at once evident that pure equality before the law is impossible. Some occupations must be subjected to police regulation. Not all can be made subject to militia duty even for the same limited period. The exceptions and special cases furnish the chance for abuse. Equality before the law, however, is one of the cardinal principles of civil liberty, because it leaves each man to run the race of life for himself as best he can. The state stands neutral but benevolent. It does not undertake to aid some and handicap others at the outset in order to offset hereditary advantages and disadvantages, or to make them start equally. Such a notion would belong to the false and spurious theory of equality which is socialistic. If the state should attempt this it would make itself the servant of envy. I am entitled to make the most I can out of myself without hindrance from anybody, but I am not entitled to any guarantee that I shall make as much of myself as somebody else makes of himself.

W. G. Sumner, *Challenge of Facts*

49 *Higgins.* The great secret, Eliza, is not having bad manners or good manners or any other particular sort of manners, but having the same manner for all human souls: in short, behaving as if you were in Heaven, where there are no third-class carriages, and one soul is as good as another.

Shaw, *Pygmalion*, V

50 Today a surgeon who is too lazy or too uppish to put on his boots and pull off his trousers can find a valet who will do both for him, and will even submit to be sworn at and addressed on all occasions as an inferior, for a sufficient consideration. I am afraid this luxury will be untenable under an equalitarian constitution. All able-bodied persons

will have to valet themselves; and the ladies who ring for a maid in the middle of the night to pick up a book they have dropped out of bed, will have to get up and pick up the book for themselves, or take more care not to drop it. But though the surgeon may have to put on his own boots, it does not follow that he will have to clean them. A state of society in which a surgeon would have to clean the boots and knives; make the beds; lay and light the fires; and answer the door, is as unthinkable as one in which the housemaids would have to cut off their own legs. What is quite thinkable is that the surgeon and person who makes the surgeon's bed should have the same income and be equally polite to one another. As it is, the hospital nurse is sometimes better bred, as we call it, than the surgeon; and there are periods of their respective careers in which she has a larger income. There is certainly no reason why she should at any time have a smaller one.

Shaw, *Redistribution of Income*

51 The arguments for equality of income do not lie on the surface of individual interest. They are, as I have formulated them, first, the economic argument that as national needs should be satisfied in the order of their importance, equality of purchasing power is needed to prevent Ritz hotels from being built for idlers whilst workers are paying half a crown a week for half a bed in an overcrowded cottage; second, the political and legal argument that really representative parliaments and juries are impossible in a community broken up into antagonistic classes by differences of income; and last, that the supreme importance to the race of the fullest and widest sexual selection makes it imperative that the whole community should consist of intermarriageable persons, and not, as at present, of individuals whose choice is limited to the narrow social circle formed by the local people of the same income. All these arguments are essentially comprehensive arguments: they do not occur to politicians who are pursuing merely individual interests for themselves and their constituents.

Shaw, *Socialism and Culture*

52 Throughout past history power has been used to give to the strong an undue share of good things and to leave to the weak a life of toil and misery.

Russell, *Human Society in Ethics and Politics*, II, 1

53 The doctrine of equality never meant what some of its critics supposed it to mean. It never asserted equality of natural gifts. It was a moral, a political and legal principle, not a psychological one. Thomas Jefferson believed as truly in a "natural aristocracy" as did John Adams. The existence of marked psychological inequalities was indeed one of the reasons why it was considered so important to establish political and legal equality. For otherwise those of superior endowment might, whether intentionally or without deliberation, reduce those of inferior capacity to a condition of virtual servitude. The words "nature" and "natural" are among the most ambiguous of all the words used to justify courses of action. Their very ambiguity is one source of their use in defense of any measure and end regarded as desirable. The words mean what is native, what is original or innate, what exists at birth in distinction from what is acquired by cultivation and as a consequence of experience. But it also means that which men have got used to, inured to by custom, that imagination can hardly conceive of anything different. Habit is second nature and second nature under ordinary circumstances is as potent and urgent as first nature. Again, nature has a definitely moral import; that which is *normal* and hence is right; that which should be.

The assertion that men are free and equal by nature unconsciously, possibly deliberately, took advantage of the prestige possessed by what is "natural" in the first two senses to reinforce the moral force of the word. That "naturalness" in the moral sense provided the imperative ethical foundation of politics and law was, however, the axiomatic premise of democratic theory. Exercise of a liberty which was taken to be a moral right has in the course of events, especially economic events, seriously threatened the moral right to legal and political equality. While we may not believe that the revolutionary effect of steam, electricity, etc., has nullified moral faith in equality, their operation has produced a new difficult problem. The effect of statutes, of administrative measures, of judicial decision, upon the maintenance of equality and freedom cannot be estimated in terms of fairly direct personal consequences. We have first to estimate their effects upon complicated social conditions (largely a matter of guesswork), and then speculate what will be the effect of the new social conditions upon individual persons. . . .

The point which is here pertinent is that early theory and practice assumed an inherent, and so to say pre-established, harmony between liberty and equality. As liberty has been practiced in industry and trade, the economic inequalities produced have reacted against the existence of equality of opportunity. Only those who have a special cause to plead will hold that even in the most democratic countries, under the most favorable conditions, have children of the poor the same chances as those of the well-to-do, even in a thing like schooling which is supported at public expense. And it is no consoling offset that the children of the rich often suffer because of the one-sided conditions under which they grow up.

Dewey, *Freedom and Culture*, III

54 It is obvious . . . that the word 'Equality' possesses more than one meaning, and that the controversies surrounding it arise partly, at least, because the same term is employed with different connotations. Thus it may either purport to state a fact, or convey the expression of an ethical judgment. On the one hand, it may affirm that men are, on the whole, very similar in their natural endowments of character and intelligence. On the other hand, it may assert that, while they differ profoundly as individuals in capacity and character, they are equally entitled as human beings to consideration and respect, and that the well-being of a society is likely to be increased if it so plans its organization that, whether their powers are great or small, all its members may be equally enabled to make the best of such powers as they possess.

R. H. Tawney, *Equality*, I

55 It is true . . . that some men are inferior to others in respect of their intellectual endowments, and it is possible—though the truth of the possibility has not yet been satisfactorily established—that the same is true of certain classes. It does not, however, follow from this fact that such individuals or classes should receive less consideration than others, or should be treated as inferior in respect of such matters as legal status, or health, or economic arrangements, which are within the control of the community.

It may, of course, be deemed expedient so to treat them. It may be thought advisable, as Aristotle argued, to maintain the institution of slavery on the ground that some men are fit only to be living tools; or, as was customary in a comparatively recent past, to apply to the insane a severity not used towards the sane; or, as is sometimes urged today, to spend less liberally on the education of the slow than on that of the intelligent; or, in accordance with the practice of all ages, to show less respect for the poor than for the rich. But, in order to establish an inference, a major premise is necessary as well as a minor; and, if such discrimination on the part of society is desirable, its desirability must be shown by some other argument than the fact of inequality of intelligence and character. . . .

Everyone recognizes the absurdity of such an argument when it is applied to matters within his personal knowledge and professional competence. Everyone realizes that, in order to justify inequalities of circumstance or opportunity by reference to differences of personal quality, it is necessary, as Professor Ginsberg observes, to show that the differences in question are relevant to the inequalities. Everyone now sees, for example, that it is not a valid argument against women's suffrage to urge, as used to be urged not so long ago, that women are physically weaker than men, since physical strength is not relevant to the question of the ability to exercise the franchise, or a valid argument in favour of slavery that some men are less intelligent than others, since it is not certain that slavery is the most suitable penalty for lack of intelligence.

R. H. Tawney, *Equality*, I

56 A society which values equality will attach a high degree of significance to differences of character and intelligence between different individuals, and a low degree of significance to economic and social differences between different groups. It will endeavour, in shaping its policy and organization, to encourage the former and to neutralize and suppress the latter, and will regard it as vulgar and childish to emphasize them when, unfortunately, they still exist.

R. H. Tawney, *Equality*, II

57 It is possible to conceive a community in which the necessary diversity of economic functions existed side by side with a large measure of economic and social equality. In such a community, while the occupations and incomes of individuals varied, they would live, nevertheless, in much the same environment, would enjoy similar standards of health and education, would find different positions, according to their varying abilities, equally accessible to them, would intermarry freely with each other, would be equally immune from the more degrading forms of poverty, and equally secure against economic oppression.

R. H. Tawney, *Equality*, II, 2

58 Since political arrangements may be such as to check excess of power, while economic arrangements permit or encourage them, a society, or a large part of it, may be both politically free and economically the opposite. It may be protected against arbitrary action by the agents of government, and be without the security against economic oppression which corresponds to civil liberty. It may possess the political institutions of an advanced democracy, and lack the will and ability to control the conduct of those powerful in its economic affairs, which is the economic analogy of political freedom.

The extension of liberty from the political to the economic sphere is evidently among the most urgent tasks of industrial societies. It is evident also, however, that, in so far as this extension takes place, the traditional antithesis between liberty and equality will no longer be valid. . . .

In conditions which impose co-operative, rather than merely individual, effort, liberty is, in fact, equality in action, in the sense, not that all men perform identical functions or wield the same degree of power, but that all men are equally protected against the abuse of power, and equally entitled to insist that power shall be used, not for personal ends, but for the general advantage. Civil and political liberty obviously imply, not that all men shall be members of parliament, cabinet ministers, or civil servants, but the absence of such civil and political inequalities as enable one class to impose its will on another by legal coercion. It should be not less obvious that economic liberty implies, not that all men should initiate, plan, direct, manage, or administer, but the absence of such economic inequalities as can be used as a means of economic constraint.

R. H. Tawney, *Equality,* V, 2

59 Along with the ethical urge of each individual to affirm his subjective existence, there is also the temptation to po liberty and become a thing. This is an inauspicious road, for he who takes it—passive, lost, ruined—becomes henceforth the creature of another's will, frustrated in his transcendence and deprived of every value. But it is an easy road; on it one avoids the strain involved in undertaking an authentic existence. When man makes of woman the *Other,* he may, then, expect her to manifest deep-seated tendencies toward complicity. Thus, woman may fail to lay claim to the status of subject because she lacks definite resources, because she feels the necessary bond that ties her to man regardless of reciprocity, and because she is often very well pleased with her role as the *Other.*

Simone de Beauvoir, *The Second Sex,*
Intro.

Chapter 14

WAR *and* PEACE

Chapter 14 is divided into three sections: 14.1 Warfare and the State of War, 14.2 The Instrumentalities of War: The Military, and 14.3 The Conditions of Peace.

Like Chapters 12 and 13, this chapter treats topics closely related to those treated in Chapter 10 on Politics. The discussion of war covers both civil war, or war within the boundaries of a state, and international war, or war between states. So, too, the discussion of peace considers the nature and conditions of civil peace as well as the prerequisites for international or world peace. The reader should, therefore, expect to find quotations in Sections 14.1 and 14.3 that deal with matters also treated in Chapter 10; and, in addition, the reader will find passages that

are about equally relevant to war and to peace, which we have, nevertheless, placed in one or the other section, but not in both.

Section 14.2 on The Instrumentalities of War: The Military deals with armed force, in all its forms or varieties, as an instrument of the state, mainly in its relation with other states, but also as used against domestic insurrections. It includes passages describing the characteristics of military men.

The quotations collected in Section 14.2 are, of course, more closely related to those in Section 14.1 than to those in Section 14.3, though some passages will be found that argue for dominant military force as preventive of war even though not productive of peace in the fullest sense of that term.

14.1 | *Warfare and the State of War*

With a few exceptions to be noted, the predominant sentiment expressed by the writers represented here—poets, historians, and philosophers—deplores the horror and the folly of war. The poets and novelists, from Homer and Virgil to Tolstoy, depict the face of war in all its grimness and fiendishness: the episodes and encounters that they present with imaginative intensity support the philosopher's definition of war as the realm of pure force—force without right. The historians add confirmation by their accounts of campaigns and battles, accompanied by such comments as that war is "the greatest of follies," or that no one is "so foolish as to prefer war to peace."

The exceptions mentioned above are to be found in Machiavelli's statement that war is the proper business of princes; in Kant's observation that war, if conducted in a proper manner, has something ennobling about it; in Hegel's praise of war as a healthy disturbance that remedies the stagnation resulting from a prolonged peace; in Clausewitz's declaration that war is in essence nothing but politics itself carried on by other means; and in Nietzsche's insistence that war is necessary for human survival.

The reader will find passages in which the effort is made to distinguish between just and unjust wars, and passages in which certain kinds of war are said to be better than others—for example, foreign as compared with civil wars. But the most important distinction noted here is the distinction between actual warfare and the state of war— a distinction that has only recently become generally recognized as the difference between "hot" and "cold" war.

The reader's attention is directed particularly to Thucydides' observation that the periods of no fighting during the thirty years of the Peloponnesian War were an armed truce, not a condition of peace; to Hobbes' statement that war is not a state of battle only, but, like the climate, a prevailing condition in which conflicts between sovereigns cannot be settled except by force; and to Locke's insight that peace is not merely the absence of fighting, but a state of affairs in which a duly constituted government has the authority and power to settle differences without recourse to violence on the parts of those in conflict.

If sovereigns are always in a state of war because, in relation to one another, they are in a state of anarchy, then it would seem to follow that government, the opposite of anarchy, is the indispensable prerequisite for the establishment and preservation of peace. The reader will find this insight developed in Section 14.3 on THE CONDITIONS OF PEACE and in Section 10.3 on GOVERNMENT: ITS NATURE, NECESSITY, AND FORMS. The reader will also find some consideration of the rights of war in Section 12.3 on RIGHTS—NATURAL AND CIVIL. Section 14.2 has a discussion of the instrumentalities employed in actual warfare—military personnel and equipment.

---

1 Thou hast heard, O my soul, the sound of the trumpet, the alarm of war.

Jeremiah 4:19

2 They have healed also the hurt of the daughter of my people slightly, saying, Peace, peace; when there is no peace.

Jeremiah 6:14

3 *Menelaos.* There is satiety in all things, in sleep,
and love-making,
in the loveliness of singing and the innocent
dance. In all these
things a man will strive sooner to win satisfaction
than in war.

Homer, *Iliad*, 636

4 *Aineias.* Warfare's
finality lies in the work of hands, that of words in
counsel.
It is not for us now to pile up talk, but to fight in
battle.

Homer, *Iliad*, XVI, 629

5 *Chorus.* The god of war, money changer of dead
bodies,
held the balance of his spear in the fighting,
and from the corpse-fires at Ilium
sent to their dearest the dust
heavy and bitter with tears shed
packing smooth the urns with
ashes that once were men.
They praise them through their tears, how this
man
knew well the craft of battle, how another
went down splendid in the slaughter:
and all for some strange woman.
Thus they mutter in secrecy,
and the slow anger creeps below their grief
at Atreus' sons and their quarrels.
There by the walls of Ilium
the young men in their beauty keep
graves deep in the alien soil
they hated and they conquered.

Aeschylus, *Agamemnon*, 437

6 Meanwhile Crœsus, taking the oracle in a wrong
sense, led his forces into Cappadocia, fully expecting to defeat Cyrus and destroy the empire of the
Persians. While he was still engaged in making
preparations for his attack, a Lydian named San-
danis, who had always been looked upon as a wise
man, but who after this obtained a very great
name indeed among his countrymen, came forward and counselled the king in these words:

"Thou art about, oh! king, to make war against
men who wear leathern trousers, and have all
their other garments of leather; who feed not on
what they like, but on what they can get from a
soil that is sterile and unkindly; who do not indulge in wine, but drink water; who possess no figs
nor anything else that is good to eat. If, then, thou
conquerest them, what canst thou get from them,
seeing that they have nothing at all? But if they
conquer thee, consider how much that is precious
thou wilt lose: if they once get a taste of our pleasant things, they will keep such hold of them that
we shall never be able to make them loose their
grasp. For my part, I am thankful to the gods that

they have not put it into the hearts of the Persians
to invade Lydia."

Herodotus, *History*, I, 71

7 *Croesus.* No one is so foolish as to prefer war to
peace, in which, instead of sons burying their fathers, fathers bury their sons.

Herodotus, *History*, I, 87

8 Xerxes, when he fled away out of Greece, left his
war-tent with Mardonius: when Pausanias, therefore, saw the tent with its adornments of gold and
silver, and its hangings of divers colours, he gave
commandment to the bakers and the cooks to
make him ready a banquet in such fashion as was
their wont for Mardonius. Then they made ready
as they were bidden: and Pausanius, beholding
the couches of gold and silver daintily decked out
with their rich covertures, and the tables of gold
and silver laid, and the feast itself prepared with
all magnificence, was astonished at the good
things which were set before him, and, being in a
pleasant mood, gave commandment to his own
followers to make ready a Spartan supper. When
the suppers were both served, and it was apparent
how vast a difference lay between the two, Pausanias laughed, and sent his servants to call to him
the Greek generals. On their coming, he pointed
to the two boards, and said:—

"I sent for you, O Greeks, to show you the folly
of this Median captain, who, when he enjoyed
such fare as this, must needs come here to rob us
of our penury."

Herodotus, *History*, IX, 82

9 *Neoptolemus.* War never takes a bad man but by
chance,
the good man always.

Sophocles, *Philoctetes*, 436

10 *Chorus.* Mindless, all of you, who in the strength of
spears
and the tearing edge win your valors
by war, thus stupidly trying
to halt the grief of the world.
For if bloody debate shall settle
the issue, never again
shall hate be gone out of the cities of men.
By hate they won the chambers of Priam's city;
they could have solved by reason and words
the quarrel, Helen, for you.
Now these are given to the Death God below.
On the walls the flame, as of Zeus, lightened and
fell.
And you, Helen, on your sorrows bear
more hardships still, and more matter for grieving.

Euripides, *Helen*, 1151

11 *Herald.* Your city is free;
That does not make it powerful. Hope has driven

Many cities against each other; she stirs
An overreaching heart; she is not to be trusted.
When the people vote on war, nobody reckons
On his own death; it is too soon; he thinks
Some other man will meet that wretched fate.
But if death faced him when he cast his vote,
Hellas would never perish from battle-madness.
And yet we men all know which of two words
Is better, and can weigh the good and bad
They bring: how much better is peace than war!
First and foremost, the Muses love her best;
And the goddess of vengeance hates her. She de-
  lights
In healthy children, and she glories in wealth.
But wickedly we throw all this away
To start our wars and make the losers slaves—
Man binding man and city chaining city.

Euripides, *Suppliant Women,* 477

12 The Peloponnesian War was prolonged to an immense length, and, long as it was, it was short
without parallel for the misfortunes that it
brought upon Hellas. Never had so many cities
been taken and laid desolate, here by the barbarians, here by the parties contending (the old inhabitants being sometimes removed to make room
for others); never was there so much banishing
and blood-shedding, now on the field of battle,
now in the strife of faction. Old stories of occurrences handed down by tradition, but scantily
confirmed by experience, suddenly ceased to be
incredible; there were earthquakes of unparalleled extent and violence; eclipses of the sun occurred with a frequency unrecorded in previous
history; there were great droughts in sundry
places and consequent famines, and that most calamitous and awfully fatal visitation, the plague.
All this came upon them with the late war, which
was begun by the Athenians and Peloponnesians
by the dissolution of the thirty years' truce made
after the conquest of Euboea. To the question why
they broke the treaty, I answer by placing first an
account of their grounds of complaint and points
of difference, that no one may ever have to ask the
immediate cause which plunged the Hellenes into
a war of such magnitude. The real cause I consider to be the one which was formally most kept out
of sight. The growth of the power of Athens, and
the alarm which this inspired in Lacedaemon,
made war inevitable.

Thucydides, *Peloponnesian War,* I, 23

13 *Corinthians.* Men are wont in their efforts against
their enemies to forget everything for the sake of
victory, regarding him who assists them then as a
friend, even if thus far he has been a foe, and him
who opposes them then as a foe, even if he has
thus far been a friend; indeed they allow their
real interests to suffer from their absorbing preoccupation in the struggle.

Thucydides, *Peloponnesian War,* I, 41

14 *Corinthians.* War of all things proceeds least upon
definite rules, but draws principally upon itself for
contrivances to meet an emergency; and in such
cases the party who faces the struggle and keeps
his temper best meets with most security, and he
who loses his temper about it with correspondent
disaster.

Thucydides, *Peloponnesian War,* I, 122

15 *Corinthians.* Out of war peace gains fresh stability,
but to refuse to abandon repose for war is not so
sure a method of avoiding danger.

Thucydides, *Peloponnesian War,* I, 124

16 *Pericles.* For those of course who have a free choice
in the matter and whose fortunes are not at stake,
war is the greatest of follies. But if the only choice
was between submission with loss of independence, and danger with the hope of preserving
that independence, in such a case it is he who will
not accept the risk that deserves blame, not he
who will.

Thucydides, *Peloponnesian War,* II, 61

17 *Hermocrates.* No one is forced to engage in it by
ignorance, or kept out of it by fear, if he fancies
there is anything to be gained by it. To the former
the gain appears greater than the danger, while
the latter would rather stand the risk than put up
with any immediate sacrifice. But if both should
happen to have chosen the wrong moment for acting in this way, advice to make peace would not
be unserviceable.

Thucydides, *Peloponnesian War,* IV, 59

18 *Socrates.* Wars are occasioned by the love of money.

Plato, *Phaedo,* 66B

19 *Socrates.* A slice of our neighbours' land will be
wanted by us for pasture and tillage, and they will
want a slice of ours, if, like ourselves, they exceed
the limit of necessity, and give themselves up to
the unlimited accumulation of wealth?
  Glaucon. That, Socrates, will be inevitable.
  And so we shall go to war.

Plato, *Republic,* II, 373B

20 *Socrates.* A tyrant . . . is always stirring up some
war or other, in order that the people may require
a leader.

Plato, *Republic,* VIII, 566B

21 *Cleinias* [a Cretan]. I think . . . that the aim of our
institutions is easily intelligible to any one. Look
at the character of our country: Crete is not like
Thessaly, a large plain; and for this reason they
have horsemen in Thessaly, and we have runners—the inequality of the ground in our country
is more adapted to locomotion on foot; but then, if

you have runners you must have light arms—no one can carry a heavy weight when running, and bows and arrows are convenient because they are light. Now all these regulations have been made with a view to war, and the legislator appears to me to have looked to this in all his arrangements:—the common meals, if I am not mistaken, were instituted by him for a similar reason, because he saw that while they are in the field the citizens are by the nature of the case compelled to take their meals together for the sake of mutual protection. He seems to me to have thought the world foolish in not understanding that all men are always at war with one another; and if in war there ought to be common meals and certain persons regularly appointed under others to protect an army, they should be continued in peace. For what men in general term peace would be said by him to be only a name; in reality every city is in a natural state of war with every other, not indeed proclaimed by heralds, but everlasting. And if you look closely, you will find that this was the intention of the Cretan legislator; all institutions, private as well as public, were arranged by him with a view to war; in giving them he was under the impression that no possessions or institutions are of any value to him who is defeated in battle; for all the good things of the conquered pass into the hands of the conquerors.

> Plato, *Laws,* I, 625B

22 In one point of view, the art of war is a natural art of acquisition, for the art of acquisition includes hunting, an art which we ought to practise against wild beasts, and against men who, though intended by nature to be governed, will not submit; for war of such a kind is naturally just.

> Aristotle, *Politics,* 1256ᵇ22

23 Then, after length of time, the labouring swains
Who turn the turfs of those unhappy plains,
Shall rusty piles from the ploughed furrows take,
And over empty helmets pass the rake—
Amazed at antique titles on the stones,
And mighty relics of gigantic bones.

> Virgil, *Georgics,* I

24   Long the gods, we know,
Have grudged thee, Cæsar, to the world below,
Where fraud and rapine right and wrong confound,
Where impious arms from every part resound,
And monstrous crimes in every shape are crowned.
The peaceful peasant to the wars is pressed;
The fields lie fallow in inglorious rest;
The plain no pasture to the flock affords;
The crooked scythes are straightened into swords:
And there Euphrates her soft offspring arms,
And here the Rhine rebellows with alarms;
The neighbouring cities range on several sides;

Perfidious Mars long-plighted leagues divides,
And o'er the wasted world in triumph rides.
So four fierce coursers, starting to the race,
Scour through the plain, and lengthen every pace;
Nor reins, nor curbs, nor threatening cries, they fear,
But force along the trembling charioteer.

> Virgil, *Georgics,* I

25 The rustic honors of the scythe and share
Give place to swords and plumes, the pride of war.

> Virgil, *Aeneid,* VII

26 Think not that I am come to send peace on earth: I came not to send peace, but a sword.

> *Matthew* 10:34

27 Ye shall hear of wars and rumours of wars.

> *Matthew* 24:6

28 Then came they, and laid hands on Jesus, and took him.
And, behold, one of them which were with Jesus stretched out his hand, and drew his sword, and struck a servant of the high priest's, and smote off his ear.
Then said Jesus unto him, Put up again thy sword into his place: for all they that take the sword shall perish with the sword.

> *Matthew* 26:50–52

29 For men whose ambition neither seas, nor mountains, nor unpeopled deserts can limit, nor the bounds dividing Europe from Asia confine their vast desires, it would be hard to expect to forbear from injuring one another when they touch and are close together. These are ever naturally at war, envying and seeking advantages of one another.

> Plutarch, *Pyrrhus*

30 *Tiridates.* It is not . . . by weak inaction that great empires are held together; there must be the struggle of brave men in arms; might is right with those who are at the summit of power. And though it is the glory of a private house to keep its own, it is the glory of a king to fight for the possessions of others.

> Tacitus, *Annals,* XV, 1

31 Men directing their weapons against each other— under doom of death yet neatly lined up to fight as in the pyrrhic sword-dances of their sport—this is enough to tell us that all human intentions are but play, that death is nothing terrible, that to die in a war or in a fight is but to taste a little beforehand what old age has in store, to go away earlier and come back the sooner.

> Plotinus, *Third Ennead,* II, 15

32 Do they reply that the Roman empire could never have been so widely extended, nor so glorious, save by constant and unintermitting wars? A fit argument, truly! Why must a kingdom be distracted in order to be great? In this little world of man's body, is it not better to have a moderate stature, and health with it, than to attain the huge dimensions of a giant by unnatural torments, and when you attain it to find no rest, but to be pained the more in proportion to the size of your members?

Augustine, *City of God,* III, 10

33 The imperial city [Rome] has endeavoured to impose on subject nations not only her yoke, but her language, as a bond of peace, so that interpreters, far from being scarce, are numberless. This is true; but how many great wars, how much slaughter and bloodshed, have provided this unity! And though these are past, the end of these miseries has not yet come. For though there have never been wanting, nor are yet wanting, hostile nations beyond the empire, against whom wars have been and are waged, yet, supposing there were no such nations, the very extent of the empire itself has produced wars of a more obnoxious description—social and civil wars—and with these the whole race has been agitated either by the actual conflict or the fear of a renewed outbreak.

Augustine, *City of God,* XIX, 7

34 In order for a war to be just . . . it is necessary that the belligerents should have a right intention, so that they intend the advancement of good, or the avoidance of evil.

Aquinas, *Summa Theologica,* II–II, 40, 1

35 Upon this [cry of "War!"], one of the old wise ones arose, and with his hand commanding silence and attention, he said: "Masters, there is many a man to cry 'War, War!' who yet knows but little of the meaning of it. War, in the beginning, has so high an entrance, and so wide, that every man may enter when he pleases, and may find war easily. But truly, what the end of war shall be is not so easy to know. For when a war is once begun, many an unborn child shall die in the womb because of the strife, or else shall be born into sorrow and die in wretchedness. Therefore, ere any war begins, men should take much counsel together and act only after much deliberation."

Chaucer, *Canterbury Tales:*
Tale of Melibeus

36 A prince ought to have no other aim or thought, nor select anything else for his study, than war and its rules and discipline; for this is the sole art that belongs to him who rules, and it is of such

force that it not only upholds those who are born princes, but it often enables men to rise from a private station to that rank. And, on the contrary, it is seen that when princes have thought more of ease than of arms they have lost their states. And the first cause of your losing it is to neglect this art; and what enables you to acquire a state is to be master of the art.

Machiavelli, *Prince,* XIV

37 War is just which is necessary, and arms are hallowed when there is no other hope but in them.

Machiavelli, *Prince,* XXVI

38 The object of those who make war, either from choice or ambition, is to conquer and to maintain their conquests, and to do this in such a manner as to enrich themselves and not to impoverish the conquered country. To do this, then, the conqueror should take care not to spend too much, and in all things mainly to look to the public benefit; and therefore he should imitate the manner and conduct of the Romans, which was first of all to make the war short and sharp.

Machiavelli, *Discourses,* II, 6

39 Every one may begin a war at his pleasure, but cannot so finish it.

Machiavelli, *Discourses,* II, 10

40 I maintain, then, contrary to the general opinion, that the sinews of war are not gold, but good soldiers; for gold alone will not procure good soldiers, but good soldiers will always procure gold.

Machiavelli, *Discourses,* II, 10

41 Although deceit is detestable in all other things, yet in the conduct of war it is laudable and honorable; and a commander who vanquishes an enemy by stratagem is equally praised with one who gains victory by force.

Machiavelli, *Discourses,* III, 40

42 *Friar John.* War, begun without good provision of money before-hand for going through with it, is but as a breathing of strength, and blast that will quickly pass away. Coin is the sinews of war.

Rabelais, *Gargantua and Pantagruel,* I, 46

43 Very little withholds me from the opinion of good Heraclitus, which affirmeth war, to be the father of all good things; and therefore do I believe that war is in Latin called *Bellum,* and not by antiphrasis, as some patchers of old rusty Latin would have us to think, because in war there is little beauty to be seen; but absolutely and simply, for that in war appeareth all that is good and graceful, and that by the wars is purged out all manner of wickedness and deformity. For proof whereof the wise and pacific Solomon could no better represent the unspeakable perfection of the divine wisdom, than

by comparing it to the due disposure and ranking of an army in battle array, well provided and ordered.

Rabelais, *Gargantua and Pantagruel,* III, Prologue

44 As it is sometimes necessary for kings and nations to take up arms for the infliction of such public vengeance, the same reason will lead us to infer the lawfulness of wars which are undertaken for this end. For if they have been intrusted with power to preserve the tranquillity of their own territories, to suppress the seditious tumults of disturbers, to succour the victims of oppression, and to punish crimes,—can they exert this power for a better purpose, than to repel the violence of him who disturbs both the private repose of individuals and the general tranquillity of the nation; who excites insurrections, and perpetrates acts of oppression, cruelty, and every species of crime? If they ought to be the guardians and defenders of the laws, it is incumbent upon them to defeat the efforts of all by whose injustice the discipline of the laws is corrupted. And if they justly punish those robbers, whose injuries have only extended to a few persons, shall they suffer a whole district to be plundered and devastated with impunity? For there is no difference, whether he, who in a hostile manner invades, disturbs, and plunders the territory of another to which he has no right, be a king, or one of the meanest of mankind: all persons of this description are equally to be considered as robbers, and ought to be punished as such. It is the dictate both of natural equity, and of the nature of the office, therefore, that princes are armed, not only to restrain the crimes of private individuals by judicial punishments, but also to defend the territories committed to their charge by going to war against any hostile aggression.

Calvin, *Institutes of the Christian Religion,* IV, 20

45 *King Henry.* Once more unto the breach, dear friends, once more;
Or close the wall up with our English dead.
In peace there's nothing so becomes a man
As modest stillness and humility:
But when the blast of war blows in our ears,
Then imitate the action of the tiger;
Stiffen the sinews, summon up the blood,
Disguise fair nature with hard-favour'd rage;
Then lend the eye a terrible aspect;
Let it pry through the portage of the head
Like the brass cannon; let the brow o'erwhelm it
As fearfully as doth a galled rock
O'erhang and jutty his confounded base,
Swill'd with the wild and wasteful ocean.
Now set the teeth and stretch the nostril wide,
Hold hard the breath and bend up every spirit
To his full height.

Shakespeare, *Henry V,* III, i, 1

46 *Virgilia.* His bloody brow! O Jupiter, no blood!
Volumnia. Away, you fool! it more becomes a man
Than gilt his trophy. The breasts of Hecuba,
When she did suckle Hector, look'd not lovelier
Than Hector's forehead when it spit forth blood
At Grecian sword, contemning.

Shakespeare, *Coriolanus,*
I, iii, 41

47 *1st Servant.* But when goes this forward?
3rd Servant. To-morrow; to-day; presently; you shall have the drum struck up this afternoon. 'Tis, as it were, a parcel of their feast, and to be executed ere they wipe their lips.
2nd Servant. Why, then we shall have a stirring world again. This peace is nothing but to rust iron, increase tailors, and breed ballad-makers.
1st Serv. Let me have war, say I; it exceeds peace as far as day does night; it's sprisely, waking, audible, and full of vent. Peace is a very apoplexy, lethargy; mulled, deaf, sleepy, insensible; a getter of more bastard children than war's a destroyer of men.
2nd Serv. 'Tis so; and as war, in some sort, may be said to be a ravisher, so it cannot be denied but peace is a great maker of cuckolds.
1st Serv. Ay, and it makes men hate one another.
3rd Serv. Reason; because they then less need one another. The wars for my money.

Shakespeare, *Coriolanus,*
IV, v, 228

48 No nation, which doth not directly profess arms, may look to have greatness fall into their mouths.

Bacon, *Of the True Greatness of Kingdoms and Estates*

49 There is that justice imprinted in the nature of men, that they enter not upon wars (whereof so many calamities do ensue) but upon some, at the least specious, grounds and quarrels.

Bacon, *Of the True Greatness of Kingdoms and Estates*

50 A civil war, indeed, is like the heat of a fever; but a foreign war is like the heat of exercise, and serveth to keep the body in health; for in a slothful peace, both courages will effeminate and manners corrupt.

Bacon, *Of the True Greatness of Kingdoms and Estates*

51 It is manifest that during the time men live without a common power to keep them all in awe, they are in that condition which is called *war;* and such a war as is of every man against every man. For war consisteth not in battle only, or in the act of fighting, but in a tract of time, wherein the will to contend by battle is sufficiently known: and there-

fore the notion of *time* is to be considered in the nature of war, as it is in the nature of weather. For as the nature of foul weather lieth not in a shower or two of rain, but in an inclination thereto of many days together: so the nature of war consisteth not in actual fighting, but in the known disposition thereto during all the time there is no assurance to the contrary. All other time is *peace*.

Hobbes, *Leviathan*, I, 13

52 Though there had never been any time wherein particular men were in a condition of war one against another, yet in all times kings and persons of sovereign authority, because of their independency, are in continual jealousies, and in the state and posture of gladiators, having their weapons pointing, and their eyes fixed on one another; that is, their forts, garrisons, and guns upon the frontiers of their kingdoms, and continual spies upon their neighbours, which is a posture of war. But because they uphold thereby the industry of their subjects, there does not follow from it that misery which accompanies the liberty of particular men.

To this war of every man against every man, this also is consequent; that nothing can be unjust. The notions of right and wrong, justice and injustice, have there no place. Where there is no common power, there is no law; where no law, no injustice. Force and fraud are in war the two cardinal virtues. Justice and injustice are none of the faculties neither of the body nor mind. If they were, they might be in a man that were alone in the world, as well as his senses and passions. They are qualities that relate to men in society, not in solitude. It is consequent also to the same condition that there be no propriety, no dominion, no *mine* and *thine* distinct; but only that to be every man's that he can get, and for so long as he can keep it. And thus much for the ill condition which man by mere nature is actually placed in; though with a possibility to come out of it, consisting partly in the passions, partly in his reason.

Hobbes, *Leviathan*, I, 13

53 When all the world is overcharged with inhabitants, then the last remedy of all is war, which provideth for every man, by victory or death.

Hobbes, *Leviathan*, II, 30

54 Can anything be more ridiculous than that a man should have the right to kill me because he lives on the other side of the water, and because his ruler has a quarrel with mine, though I have none with him?

Pascal, *Pensées*, V, 294

55 So under fierie Cope together rush'd
Both Battels maine, with ruinous assault
And inextinguishable rage; all Heav'n
Resounded, and had Earth bin then, all Earth
Had to her Center shook. What wonder? when

Millions of fierce encountring Angels fought
On either side, the least of whom could weild
These Elements, and arm him with the force
Of all thir Regions: how much more of Power
Armie against Armie numberless to raise
Dreadful combustion warring, and disturb,
Though not destroy, thir happie Native seat.

Milton, *Paradise Lost*, VI, 215

56 Such were these Giants, men of high renown;
For in those dayes Might onely shall be admir'd,
And Valour and Heroic Vertu call'd;
To overcome in Battel, and subdue
Nations, and bring home spoils with infinite
Man-slaughter, shall be held the highest pitch
Of human Glorie, and for Glorie done
Of triumph, to be styl'd great Conquerours,
Patrons of Mankind, Gods, and Sons of Gods,
Destroyers rightlier call'd and Plagues of men.
Thus Fame shall be achiev'd, renown on Earth,
And what most merits fame in silence hid.

Milton, *Paradise Lost*, XI, 684

57 If one commonwealth wishes to make war on another and employ extreme measures to make that other dependent on itself, it may lawfully make the attempt, since it needs but the bare will of the commonwealth for war to be waged. But concerning peace it can decide nothing, save with the concurrence of another commonwealth's will. Whence it follows, that laws of war regard every commonwealth by itself, but laws of peace regard not one, but at the least two commonwealths, which are therefore called "contracting powers."

Spinoza, *Political Treatise*, III, 13

58 The state of war is a state of enmity and destruction; and therefore declaring by word or action, not a passionate and hasty, but sedate, settled design upon another man's life puts him in a state of war with him against whom he has declared such an intention, and so has exposed his life to the other's power to be taken away by him, or any one that joins with him in his defence, and espouses his quarrel; it being reasonable and just I should have a right to destroy that which threatens me with destruction; for by the fundamental law of Nature, man being to be preserved as much as possible, when all cannot be preserved, the safety of the innocent is to be preferred, and one may destroy a man who makes war upon him, or has discovered an enmity to his being, for the same reason that he may kill a wolf or a lion, because they are not under the ties of the common law of reason, have no other rule but that of force and violence, and so may be treated as a beast of prey, those dangerous and noxious creatures that will be sure to destroy him whenever he falls into their power.

And hence it is that he who attempts to get another man into his absolute power does thereby put himself into a state of war with him; it being to be understood as a declaration of a design upon his life. For I have reason to conclude that he who would get me into his power without my consent would use me as he pleased when he had got me there, and destroy me too when he had a fancy to it; for nobody can desire to have me in his absolute power unless it be to compel me by force to that which is against the right of my freedom—*i.e.* make me a slave. To be free from such force is the only security of my preservation, and reason bids me look on him as an enemy to my preservation who would take away that freedom which is the fence to it; so that he who makes an attempt to enslave me thereby puts himself into a state of war with me. He that in the state of Nature would take away the freedom that belongs to any one in that state must necessarily be supposed to have a design to take away everything else, that freedom being the foundation of all the rest; as he that in the state of society would take away the freedom belonging to those of that society or commonwealth must be supposed to design to take away from them everything else, and so be looked on as in a state of war.

Locke, *II Civil Government*, III, 16–17

59 Here we have the plain difference between the state of Nature and the state of war, which however some men have confounded, are as far distant as a state of peace, goodwill, mutual assistance, and preservation; and a state of enmity, malice, violence and mutual destruction are one from another. Men living together according to reason without a common superior on earth, with authority to judge between them, is properly the state of Nature. But force, or a declared design of force upon the person of another, where there is no common superior on earth to appeal to for relief, is the state of war; and it is the want of such an appeal gives a man the right of war even against an aggressor, though he be in society and a fellow-subject. . . . Want of a common judge with authority puts all men in a state of Nature; force without right upon a man's person makes a state of war both where there is, and is not, a common judge.

Locke, *II Civil Government*, III, 19

60 Whosoever uses force without right—as every one does in society who does it without law—puts himself into a state of war with those against whom he so uses it, and in that state all former ties are cancelled, all other rights cease, and every one has a right to defend himself, and to resist the aggressor.

Locke, *II Civil Government*, XIX, 232

61 He [the Houyhnhnm master] asked me what were the usual causes or motives, that made one country go to war with another. I answered they were innumerable; but I should only mention a few of the chief. Sometimes the ambition of princes, who never think they have land or people enough to govern: sometimes the corruption of ministers, who engage their master in a war, in order to stifle or divert the clamour of the subjects against their evil administration. . . . Neither are any wars so furious and bloody, or of so long continuance, as those occasioned by difference in opinion, especially if it be in things indifferent.

Sometimes the quarrel between two princes is to decide which of them shall dispossess a third of his dominions, where neither of them pretend to any right. Sometimes one prince quarrelleth with another, for fear the other should quarrel with him. Sometimes a war is entered upon, because the enemy is too *strong,* and sometimes because he is too *weak.* Sometimes our neighbours *want* the *things* which we *have,* or *have* the things which we want; and we both fight, until they take ours, or give us theirs. It is a very justifiable cause of war, to invade a country after the people have been wasted by famine, destroyed by pestilence, or embroiled by factions amongst themselves. It is justifiable to enter into a war against our nearest ally, when one of his towns lie convenient for us, or a territory of land, that would render our dominions round and compact. If a prince send forces into a nation, where the people are poor and ignorant, he may lawfully put half of them to death, and make slaves of the rest, in order to civilize and reduce them from their barbarous way of living. It is a very kingly, honourable, and frequent practice, when one prince desires the assistance of another to secure him against an invasion, that the assistant, when he hath driven out the invader, should seize on the dominions himself, and kill, imprison, or banish the prince he came to relieve. Alliance by blood or marriage, is a sufficient cause of war between princes; and the nearer the kindred is, the greater is their disposition to quarrel.

Swift, *Gulliver's Travels,* IV, 5

62 The life of governments is like that of man. The latter has a right to kill in case of natural defence: the former have a right to wage war for their own preservation.

In the case of natural defence I have a right to kill, because my life is in respect to me what the life of my antagonist is to him: in the same manner a state wages war because its preservation is like that of any other being.

With individuals the right of natural defence does not imply a necessity of attacking. Instead of attacking they need only have recourse to proper tribunals. They cannot therefore exercise this right of defence but in sudden cases, when immediate death would be the consequence of waiting for the assistance of the law. But with states the right of natural defence carries along with it sometimes the necessity of attacking; as for instance, when one nation sees that a continuance of peace will enable another to destroy her, and that to attack that nation instantly is the only way to prevent her own destruction.

Montesquieu, *Spirit of Laws,* X, 2

63 It is a conqueror's business to repair a part of the mischief he has occasioned. The right, therefore, of conquest I define thus: a necessary, lawful, but unhappy power, which leaves the conqueror under a heavy obligation of repairing the injuries done to humanity.

Montesquieu, *Spirit of Laws,* X, 4

64 Bodies politic, remaining thus in a state of nature among themselves, presently experienced the inconveniences which had obliged individuals to forsake it; for this state became still more fatal to these great bodies than it had been to the individuals of whom they were composed. Hence arose national wars, battles, murders, and reprisals, which shock nature and outrage reason; together with all those horrible prejudices which class among the virtues the honour of shedding human blood. The most distinguished men hence learned to consider cutting each other's throats a duty; at length men massacred their fellow-creatures by thousands without so much as knowing why, and committed more murders in a single day's fighting, and more violent outrages in the sack of a single town, than were committed in the state of nature during whole ages over the whole earth. Such were the first effects which we can see to have followed the division of mankind into different communities.

Rousseau, *Origin of Inequality,* II

65 War . . . is a relation, not between man and man, but between State and State, and individuals are enemies only accidentally, not as men, nor even as citizens, but as soldiers; not as members of their country, but as its defenders. Finally, each State can have for enemies only other States, and not men.

Rousseau, *Social Contract,* I, 4

66 In real war, a just prince, while laying hands, in the enemy's country, on all that belongs to the public, respects the lives and goods of individuals: he respects rights on which his own are founded. The object of the war being the destruction of the hostile State, the other side has a right to kill its defenders, while they are bearing arms; but as soon as they lay them down and surrender, they cease to be enemies or instruments of the enemy, and become once more merely men, whose life no one has any right to take. Sometimes it is possible to kill the State without killing a single one of its members; and war gives no right which is not necessary to the gaining of its object.

Rousseau, *Social Contract,* I, 4

67 Anyone can understand that war and conquest without and the encroachments of despotism within give each other mutual support; that money and men are habitually taken at pleasure from a people of slaves, to bring others beneath the same yoke; and that conversely war furnishes a pretext for exactions of money and another, no less plausible, for keeping large armies constantly on foot, to hold the people in awe. In a word, anyone can see that aggressive princes wage war at least as much on their subjects as on their enemies, and that the conquering nation is left no better off than the conquered. "I have beaten the Romans," so Hannibal used to write to Carthage, "send me more troops. I have exacted an indemnity from Italy, send me more money." That is the real meaning of the *Te Deums,* the bonfires and rejoicings with which the people hail the triumphs of their masters.

Rousseau, *A Lasting Peace*

68 Among the calamities of war may be justly numbered the diminution of the love of truth by the falsehoods which interest dictates and credulity encourages. A peace will equally leave the warrior and the relater of wars destitute of employment; and I know not whether more is to be dreaded from streets filled with soldiers accustomed to plunder, or from garrets filled with scribblers accustomed to lie.

Johnson, *Idler No. 30*

69 It is not always necessary to accumulate gold and silver in order to enable a country to carry on foreign wars, and to maintain fleets and armies in distant countries. Fleets and armies are maintained, not with gold and silver, but with consumable goods. The nation which, from the annual produce of its domestic industry, from the annual revenue arising out of its lands, labour, and consumable stock, has wherewithal to purchase those consumable goods in distant countries, can maintain foreign wars there.

A nation may purchase the pay and provisions of an army in a distant country three different ways: by sending abroad either, first, some part of its accumulated gold and silver; or, secondly, some part of the annual produce of its manufactures; or, last of all, some part of its annual rude produce.

Adam Smith, *Wealth of Nations,* IV, 1

70 In modern times many different causes contribute to render the defence of the society more expensive. The unavoidable effects of the natural progress of improvement have, in this respect, been a good deal enhanced by a great revolution in the art of war, to which a mere accident, the invention of gunpowder, seems to have given occasion.

In modern war the great expense of firearms gives an evident advantage to the nation which can best afford that expense, and consequently to an opulent and civilised over a poor and barbarous nation. In ancient times the opulent and civilised found it difficult to defend themselves against the poor and barbarous nations. In modern times the poor and barbarous find it difficult to defend themselves against the opulent and civilised. The invention of firearms, an invention which at first sight appears to be so pernicious, is certainly favourable both to the permanency and to the extension of civilisation.

Adam Smith, *Wealth of Nations*, V, 1

71 The want of parsimony in time of peace imposes the necessity of contracting debt in time of war. When war comes, there is no money in the treasury but what is necessary for carrying on the ordinary expense of the peace establishment. In war an establishment of three or four times that expense becomes necessary for the defence of the state, and consequently a revenue three or four times greater than the peace revenue. Supposing that the sovereign should have, what he scarce ever has, the immediate means of augmenting his revenue in proportion to the augmentation of his expense, yet still the produce of the taxes, from which this increase of revenue must be drawn, will not begin to come into the treasury perhaps ten or twelve months after they are imposed. But the moment in which war begins, or rather the moment in which it appears likely to begin, the army must be augmented, the fleet must be fitted out, the garrisoned towns must be put into a posture of defence; that army, that fleet, those garrisoned towns must be furnished with arms, ammunition, and provisions. An immediate and great expense must be incurred in that moment of immediate danger, which will not wait for the gradual and slow returns of the new taxes. In this exigency government can have no other resource but in borrowing.

Adam Smith, *Wealth of Nations*, V, 3

72 To be prepared for war is one of the most effectual means of preserving peace.

Washington, *First Annual Address*

73 War in its fairest form implies a perpetual violation of humanity and justice.

Gibbon, *Decline and Fall of the Roman Empire*, XXXIII

74 The laws of war, that restrain the exercise of national rapine and murder, are founded on two principles of substantial interest: the knowledge of the permanent benefits which may be obtained by a moderate use of conquest, and a just apprehension lest the desolation which we inflict on the enemy's country may be retaliated on our own.

Gibbon, *Decline and Fall of the Roman Empire*, XXXIV

75 It was the opinion of [the Emperor] Marcian, that war should be avoided as long as it is possible to preserve a secure and honourable peace; but it was likewise his opinion that peace cannot be honourable or secure, if the sovereign betrays a pusillanimous aversion to war.

Gibbon, *Decline and Fall of the Roman Empire*, XXXV

76 Every age, however destitute of science or virtue, sufficiently abounds with acts of blood and military renown.

Gibbon, *Decline and Fall of the Roman Empire*, XXXVIII

77 It is the duty of a patriot to prefer and promote the exclusive interest and glory of his native country: but a philosopher may be permitted to enlarge his views, and to consider Europe as one great republic, whose various inhabitants have attained almost the same level of politeness and cultivation. The balance of power will continue to fluctuate, and the prosperity of our own or the neighbouring kingdoms may be alternately exalted or depressed; but these partial events cannot essentially injure our general state of happiness, the system of arts, and laws, and manners, which so advantageously distinguish, above the rest of mankind, the Europeans and their colonies. The savage nations of the globe are the common enemies of civilised society; and we may inquire, with anxious curiosity, whether Europe is still threatened with a repetition of those calamities which formerly oppressed the arms and institutions of Rome. Perhaps the same reflections will illustrate the fall of that mighty empire, and explain the probable causes of our actual security.

Gibbon, *Decline and Fall of the Roman Empire*, XXXVIII

78 The sword of the Saracens became less formidable when their youth was drawn away from the camp to college, when the armies of the faithful presumed to read and to reflect.

Gibbon, *Decline and Fall of the Roman Empire*, LII

79 [When Constantinople fell to the crusaders] at the first view it should seem that the wealth of Constantinople was only transferred from one nation to another, and that the loss and sorrow of the Greeks is exactly balanced by the joy and advantage of the Latins. But in the miserable account of war the gain is never equivalent to the loss, the pleasure to the pain; the smiles of the Latins were transient and fallacious; the Greeks for ever wept over the ruins of their country, and their real calamities were aggravated by sacrilege and mockery. What benefits accrued to the conquerors from the three fires which annihilated so vast a portion of the buildings and riches of the city? What a

stock of such things as could neither be used nor transported was maliciously or wantonly destroyed! How much treasure was idly wasted in gaming, debauchery, and riot!

> Gibbon, *Decline and Fall of the Roman Empire,* LX

80 If we contrast the rapid progress of this mischievous discovery [gunpowder] with the slow and laborious advances of reason, science, and the arts of peace, a philosopher, according to his temper, will laugh or weep at the folly of mankind.

> Gibbon, *Decline and Fall of the Roman Empire,* LXV

81 The determination of what constitutes right in war, is the most difficult problem of the right of nations and international law. It is very difficult even to form a conception of such a right, or to think of any law in this lawless state without falling into a contradiction. It must then be just the right to carry on war according to such principles as render it always still possible to pass out of that natural condition of the states in their external relations to each other and to enter into a condition of right.

> Kant, *Science of Right,* 57

82 The right that follows after war, begins at the moment of the treaty of peace and refers to the consequences of the war. The conqueror lays down the conditions under which he will agree with the conquered power to form the conclusion of peace. Treaties are drawn up; not indeed according to any right that it pertains to him to protect, on account of an alleged lesion by his opponent, but as taking this question upon himself, he bases the right to decide it upon his own power. Hence the conqueror may not demand restitution of the cost of the war; because he would then have to declare the war of his opponent to be unjust. And even although he should adopt such an argument, he is not entitled to apply it; because he would have to declare the war to be punitive, and he would thus in turn inflict an injury. To this right belongs also the exchange of prisoners, which is to be carried out without ransom and without regard to equality of numbers.

> Kant, *Science of Right,* 58

83 The right of a state against an unjust enemy has no limits, at least in respect of quality as distinguished from quantity or degree. In other words, the injured state may use—not, indeed any means, but yet—all those means that are permissible and in reasonable measure in so far as they are in its power, in order to assert its right to what is its own. But what then is an unjust enemy according to the conceptions of the right of nations, when, as holds generally of the state of nature, every state is judge in its own cause? It is one

whose publicly expressed will, whether in word or deed, betrays a maxim which, if it were taken as a universal rule, would make a state of peace among the nations impossible, and would necessarily perpetuate the state of nature.

> Kant, *Science of Right,* 60

84 War itself, provided it is conducted with order and a sacred respect for the rights of civilians, has something sublime about it, and gives nations that carry it on in such a manner a stamp of mind only the more sublime the more numerous the dangers to which they are exposed, and which they are able to meet with fortitude. On the other hand, a prolonged peace favours the predominance of a mere commercial spirit, and with it a debasing self-interest, cowardice, and effeminacy and tends to degrade the character of the nation.

> Kant, *Critique of Aesthetic Judgement,* 28

85 To look for a continuation of harmony between a number of independent, unconnected sovereignties in the same neighbourhood, would be to disregard the uniform course of human events, and to set at defiance the accumulated experience of ages.

> Hamilton, *Federalist 6*

86 That there may happen cases in which the national government may be necessitated to resort to force, cannot be denied. Our own experience has corroborated the lessons taught by the examples of other nations; that emergencies of this sort will sometimes arise in all societies, however constituted; that seditions and insurrections are, unhappily, maladies as inseparable from the body politic as tumours and eruptions from the natural body; that the idea of governing at all times by the simple force of law (which we have been told is the only admissible principle of republican government) has no place but in the reveries of those political doctors whose sagacity disdains the admonitions of experimental instruction.

> Hamilton, *Federalist 28*

87 To judge from the history of mankind, we shall be compelled to conclude that the fiery and destructive passions of war reign in the human breast with much more powerful sway than the mild and beneficent sentiments of peace; and that to model our political systems upon speculations of lasting tranquility is to calculate on the weaker springs of the human character.

> Hamilton, *Federalist 34*

88   There was a sound of revelry by night,
    And Belgium's capital had gather'd then
    Her Beauty and her Chivalry, and bright
    The lamps shone o'er fair women and brave men;
    A thousand hearts beat happily; and when

Music arose with its voluptuous swell,
Soft eyes look'd love to eyes which spake again,
And all went merry as a marriage-bell;—
But hush! hark! a deep sound strikes like a rising
    knell!

Did ye not hear it?—No; 't was but the wind,
Or the car rattling o'er the stony street;
On with the dance! let joy be unconfined;
No sleep till morn, when Youth and Pleasure
    meet
To chase the glowing Hours with flying feet—
But hark!—that heavy sound breaks in once
    more
As if the clouds its echo would repeat;
And nearer, clearer, deadlier than before!
Arm! Arm! it is—it is—the cannon's opening
    roar!

        Byron, *Childe Harold's Pilgrimage*, III, 21–22

89 War is the state of affairs which deals in earnest
with the vanity of temporal goods and concerns—
a vanity at other times a common theme of edifying sermonizing. This is what makes it the moment in which the ideality of the particular attains its right and is actualized. War has the
higher significance that by its agency . . . the ethical health of peoples is preserved in their indifference to the stabilization of finite institutions; just
as the blowing of the winds preserves the sea from
the foulness which would be the result of a prolonged calm, so also corruption in nations would
be the product of prolonged, let alone 'perpetual,'
peace.

        Hegel, *Philosophy of Right*, 324

90 War is an act of force, and to the application of
that force there is no limit. Each of the adversaries
forces the hand of the other, and a reciprocal action results which in theory can have no limit.

        Von Clausewitz, *On War*, I, 3

91 If the aim of the military action is an equivalent
for the political object, that action will in general
diminish as the political object diminishes. The
more this object comes to the front, the more will
this be so. This explains how, without self-contradiction, there can be wars of all degrees of importance and energy, from a war of extermination
down to a mere state of armed observation.

        Von Clausewitz, *On War*, I, 11

92 There is no human activity that stands in such
constant and universal contact with chance as
does war.

        Von Clausewitz, *On War*, I, 20

93 War is not merely a political act but a real political instrument, a continuation of political intercourse, a carrying out of the same by other means.

        Von Clausewitz, *On War*, I, 24

94 No protracted war can fail to endanger the freedom of a democratic country. Not indeed that after every victory it is to be apprehended that the
victorious generals will possess themselves by force
of the supreme power, after the manner of Sulla
and Cæsar; the danger is of another kind. War
does not always give over democratic communities
to military government, but it must invariably
and immeasurably increase the powers of civil
government; it must almost compulsorily concentrate the direction of all men and the management of all things in the hands of the administration. If it does not lead to despotism by sudden
violence, it prepares men for it more gently by
their habits. All those who seek to destroy the liberties of a democratic nation ought to know that
war is the surest and the shortest means to accomplish it.

        Tocqueville, *Democracy in America,*
        Vol. II, III, 22

95 Among a nation in which equality of condition
prevails, on the contrary, each citizen has but a
slender share of political power, and often has no
share at all. On the other hand, all are independent, and all have something to lose; so that they
are much less afraid of being conquered and
much more afraid of war than an aristocratic people. It will always be very difficult to convince a
democratic people to take up arms when hostilities have reached its own territory. Hence the necessity of giving to such a people the rights and
the political character which may impart to every
citizen some of those interests that cause the nobles to act for the public welfare in aristocratic
countries.

    It should never be forgotten by the princes and
other leaders of democratic nations that nothing
but the love and the habit of freedom can maintain an advantageous contest with the love and
the habit of physical well-being. I can conceive
nothing better prepared for subjection, in case of
defeat, than a democratic people without free institutions.

        Tocqueville, *Democracy in America,*
        Vol. II, III, 26

96 Under the sky is no uglier spectacle than two men
with clenched teeth, and hellfire eyes, hacking
one another's flesh; converting precious living
bodies, and priceless living souls, into nameless
masses of putrescence, useful only for turnip manure.

        Carlyle, *Past and Present*, III, 10

97 A state of war or anarchy, in which law has little
force, is so far valuable that it puts every man on
trial.

        Emerson, *The Conservative*

98 The soldier is applauded who refuses to serve in

an unjust war by those who do not refuse to sustain the unjust government which makes the war; is applauded by those whose own act and authority he desregards and sets at naught; as if the state were penitent to that degree that it hired one to scourge it while it sinned, but not to that degree that it left off sinning for a moment.

Thoreau, *Civil Disobedience*

99 The shield may be as important for victory, as the sword or spear.

Darwin, *Origin of Species*, IV

100 In proportion as the exploitation of one individual by another is put an end to, the exploitation of one nation by another will also be put an end to. In proportion as the antagonism between classes within the nation vanishes, the hostility of one nation to another will come to an end.

Marx and Engels, *Communist Manifesto*, II

101 "If no one fought except on his own conviction, there would be no wars," he said.

"And that would be splendid," said Pierre.

Prince Andrew smiled ironically.

"Very likely it would be splendid, but it will never come about. . . . "

Tolstoy, *War and Peace*, I, 6

102 The younger Emperor could not restrain his wish to be present at the battle and, in spite of the remonstrances of his courtiers, at twelve o'clock left the third column with which he had been and galloped toward the vanguard. Before he came up with the hussars, several adjutants met him with news of the successful result of the action.

This battle, which consisted in the capture of a French squadron, was represented as a brilliant victory over the French, and so the Emperor and the whole army, especially while the smoke hung over the battlefield, believed that the French had been defeated and were retreating against their will. A few minutes after the Emperor had passed, the Pávlograd division was ordered to advance. In Wischau itself, a petty German town, Rostóv saw the Emperor again. In the market place, where there had been some rather heavy firing before the Emperor's arrival, lay several killed and wounded soldiers whom there had not been time to move. The Emperor, surrounded by his suite of officers and courtiers, was riding a bobtailed chestnut mare, a different one from that which he had ridden at the review, and bending to one side he gracefully held a gold lorgnette to his eyes and looked at a soldier who lay prone, with blood on his uncovered head. The wounded soldier was so dirty, coarse, and revolting that his proximity to the Emperor shocked Rostóv. Rostóv saw how the Emperor's rather round shoulders shuddered as if a cold shiver had run down them, how his left foot began convulsively tapping the horse's side with

the spur, and how the well-trained horse looked round unconcerned and did not stir. An adjutant, dismounting, lifted the soldier under the arms to place him on a stretcher that had been brought. The soldier groaned.

"Gently, gently! Can't you do it more gently?" said the Emperor apparently suffering more than the dying soldier, and he rode away.

Rostóv saw tears filling the Emperor's eyes and heard him, as he was riding away, say to Czartoryski: "What a terrible thing war is: what a terrible thing! *Quelle terrible chose que la guerre!*"

Tolstoy, *War and Peace*, III, 10

103 One has renounced *grand* life when one renounces war.

Nietzsche, *Twilight of the Idols*.
Morality as Anti-Nature

104 Many . . . substitutes for war will be discovered, but perhaps precisely thereby it will become more and more obvious that such a highly cultivated and therefore necessarily enfeebled humanity as that of modern Europe not only needs wars, but the greatest and most terrible wars,—consequently occasional relapses into barbarism,—lest, by the means of culture, it should lose its culture and its very existence.

Nietzsche, *Human, All-Too-Human*, 477

105 The beauty of war . . . is that it is so congruous with ordinary human nature. Ancestral evolution has made us all potential warriors; so the most insignificant individual, when thrown into an army in the field, is weaned from whatever excess of tenderness towards his precious person he may bring with him, and may easily develop into a monster of insensibility. . . . The immediate aim of the soldier's life is . . . destruction, and nothing but destruction; and whatever constructions wars result in are remote and non-military. Consequently the soldier cannot train himself to be too feelingless to all those usual sympathies and respects, whether for persons or for things, that make for conservation. Yet the fact remains that war is a school of strenuous life and heroism; and, being in the line of aboriginal instinct, is the only school that as yet is universally available. But when we gravely ask ourselves whether this wholesale organization of irrationality and crime be our only bulwark against effeminacy, we stand aghast at the thought, and think more kindly of ascetic religion. One hears of the mechanical equivalent of heat. What we now need to discover in the social realm is the moral equivalent of war: something heroic that will speak to men as universally as war does, and yet will be as compatible with their spiritual selves as war has proved itself to be incompatible. I have often thought that in the old monkish poverty-worship, in spite of the pedantry which infested it, there might be some-

thing like that moral equivalent of war which we are seeking. May not voluntarily accepted poverty be 'the strenuous life,' without the need of crushing weaker peoples?

William James, *Varieties of Religious Experience*, XIV–XV

106 I have spoken of liberty as a good, but it is not an absolute good. We all recognize the need to restrain murderers, and it is even more important to restrain murderous states. Liberty must be limited by law, and its most valuable forms can only exist within a framework of law. What the world most needs is effective laws to control international relations. The first and most difficult step in the creation of such law is the establishment of adequate sanctions, and this is only possible through the creation of a single armed force in control of the whole world. But such an armed force, like a municipal police force, is not an end in itself; it is a means to the growth of a social system governed by law, where force is not the prerogative of private individuals or nations, but is exercised only by a neutral authority in accordance with rules laid down in advance. There is hope that law, rather than private force, may come to govern the relations of nations within the present century. If this hope is not realized we face utter disaster; if it is realized, the world will be far better than at any previous period in the history of man.

Russell, *Unpopular Essays*, III

107 Wars can never cease so long as nations live under such widely differing conditions, so long as the value of individual life is in each nation so variously computed, and so long as the animosities which divide them represent such powerful instinctual forces in the mind.

Freud, *Thoughts on War and Death*, I

108 Then the war [World War I] in which we had refused to believe broke out, and brought—disillusionment. Not only is it more sanguinary and more destructive than any war of other days, because of the enormously increased perfection of weapons of attack and defence; but it is at least as cruel, as embittered, as implacable as any that has preceded it. It sets at naught all those restrictions known as International Law, which in peace-time the states had bound themselves to observe; it ig-

nores the prerogatives of the wounded and the medical service, the distinction between civil and military sections of the population, the claims of private property. It tramples in blind fury on all that comes in its way, as though there were to be no future and no goodwill among men after it has passed. It rends all bonds of fellowship between the contending peoples, and threatens to leave such a legacy of embitterment as will make any renewal of such bonds impossible for a long time to come.

Freud, *Thoughts on War and Death*, I

109 Clans, tribes, races, cities, empires, nations, states have made war. The argument that this fact proves an ineradicable belligerent instinct which makes war forever inevitable is much more respectable than many arguments about the immutability of this and that social tradition.

Dewey, *Human Nature and Conduct*, II, 3

110 Pugnacity, rivalry, vainglory, love of booty, fear, suspicion, anger, desire for freedom from the conventions and restrictions of peace, love of power and hatred of oppression, opportunity for novel displays, love of home and soil, attachment to one's people and to the altar and the hearth, courage, loyalty, opportunity to make a name, money or a career, affection, piety to ancestors and ancestral gods—all of these things and many more make up the war-like force. To suppose there is some one unchanging native force which generates war is as naive as the usual assumption that our enemy is actuated solely by the meaner of the tendencies named and we only by the nobler.

Dewey, *Human Nature and Conduct*, II, 3

111 The more horrible a depersonalized scientific mass war becomes, the more necessary it is to find universal ideal motives to justify it.

Dewey, *Human Nature and Conduct*, II, 3

112 War in our own civilization is as good an illustration as one can take of the destructive lengths to which the development of a culturally selected trait may go. If we justify war, it is because all peoples always justify the traits of which they find themselves possessed, not because war will bear an objective examination of its merits.

Benedict, *Patterns of Culture*, II

14.2 | *The Instrumentalities of War*

THE MILITARY

The quotations collected here deal, in large part, with the technical and technological details of warfare—the military personnel and the military equipment needed to wage war and to bring it to a successful conclusion. They touch on such considerations as the different kinds of troops and armaments, the qualities desired in a commander and in his soldiers, the quantities or masses of men that are needed to attain certain military objectives, the relative advantages of naval and land operations, and the pros and cons of employing mercenaries.

The poets, novelists, historians, and biographers give us descriptions of eminent commanders, and discuss the personalities and character of military leaders. This often leads into some consideration of strategy and tactics, but the arts of war are not discussed in detail. In this connection, the reader will be struck by Tolstoy's extremely negative view, personified in General Kutuzov, in *War and Peace,* as well as explicitly stated by Tolstoy himself, that the planning of battles or campaigns is utterly futile.

The two main issues debated in this section are, first, the question about the value of mercenary troops as compared with a citizen army; and, second, the effect of standing armies and elaborate military installations upon the political health of republics and democracies.

---

1 And the Lord said unto Moses, Wherefore criest thou unto me? speak unto the children of Israel, that they go forward:

But lift thou up thy rod, and stretch out thine hand over the sea, and divide it: and the children of Israel shall go on dry ground through the midst of the sea.

And I, behold, I will harden the hearts of the Egyptians, and they shall follow them: and I will get me honour upon Phâr-aoh, and upon all his host, upon his chariots, and upon his horsemen.

And the Egyptians shall know that I am the Lord, when I have gotten me honour upon Phâr-aoh, upon his chariots, and upon his horsemen.

And the angel of God, which went before the camp of Israel, removed and went behind them; and the pillar of the cloud went from before their face, and stood behind them:

And it came between the camp of the Egyptians and the camp of Israel; and it was a cloud and darkness to them, but it gave light by night to these: so that the one came not near the other all the night.

And Moses stretched out his hand over the sea; and the Lord caused the sea to go back by a strong east wind all that night, and made the sea dry land, and the waters were divided.

And the children of Israel went into the midst of the sea upon the dry ground: and the waters were a wall unto them on their right hand, and on their left.

And the Egyptians pursued, and went in after them to the midst of the sea, even all Phâr-aoh's horses, his chariots, and his horsemen.

And it came to pass, that in the morning watch the Lord looked unto the host of the Egyptians through the pillar of fire and of the cloud, and troubled the host of the Egyptians,

And took off their chariot wheels, that they drave them heavily: so that the Egyptians said, Let us flee from the face of Israel; for the Lord fighteth for them against the Egyptians.

Exodus 14:15–25

2 Now Jericho was straitly shut up because of the children of Israel: none went out, and none came in.

And the Lord said unto Joshua, See, I have given into thine hand Jericho, and the king thereof, and the mighty men of valour. . . .

And it came to pass, when Joshua had spoken unto the people, that the seven priests bearing the seven trumpets of rams' horns passed on before the Lord, and blew with the trumpets: and the ark of the covenant of the Lord followed them.

And the armed men went before the priests that blew with the trumpets, and the rereward came after the ark, the priests going on, and blowing with the trumpets.

And Joshua had commanded the people, saying, Ye shall not shout, nor make any noise with your voice, neither shall any word proceed out of your mouth, until the day I bid you shout; then shall ye shout.

So the ark of the Lord compassed the city, going about it once: and they came into the camp, and lodged in the camp. . . .

And it came to pass on the seventh day, that they rose early about the dawning of the day, and compassed the city after the same manner seven times: only on that day they compassed the city seven times.

And it came to pass at the seventh time, when the priests blew with the trumpets, Joshua said unto the people, Shout; for the Lord hath given you the city. . . .

So the people shouted when the priests blew with the trumpets: and it came to pass, when the people heard the sound of the trumpet, and the people shouted with a great shout, that the wall fell down flat, so that the people went up into the city, every man straight before him, and they took the city.

And they utterly destroyed all that was in the city, both man and woman, young and old, and ox, and sheep, and ass, with the edge of the sword.

Joshua 6:1–21

3 And they, the god-supported kings, about Agamemnon
ran marshalling the men, and among them greyeyed Athene
holding the dear treasured aegis, ageless, immortal,
from whose edges float a hundred all-golden tassels,
each one carefully woven, and each worth a hundred oxen.
With this fluttering she swept through the host of the Achaians
urging them to go forward. She kindled the strength in each man's
heart to take the battle without respite and keep on fighting.
And now battle became sweeter to them than to go back
in their hollow ships to the beloved land of their fathers.
As obliterating fire lights up a vast forest
along the crests of a mountain, and the flare shows far off,
so as they marched, from the magnificent bronze the gleam went
dazzling all about through the upper air to the heaven.

These, as the multitudinous nations of birds winged,
of geese, and of cranes, and of swans long-throated
in the Asian meadow beside the Kaÿstrian waters
this way and that way make their flights in the pride of their wings, then
settle in clashing swarms and the whole meadow echoes with them,
so of these the multitudinous tribes from the ships and
shelters poured to the plain of Skamandros, and the earth beneath their
feet and under the feet of their horses thundered horribly.
They took position in the blossoming meadow of Skamandros,
thousands of them, as leaves and flowers appear in their season.
Like the multitudinous nations of swarming insects
who drive hither and thither about the stalls of the sheepfold
in the season of spring when the milk splashes in the milk pails:
in such numbers the flowing-haired Achaians stood up
through the plain against the Trojans, hearts burning to break them.
These, as men who are goatherds among the wide goatflocks
easily separate them in order as they take to the pasture,
thus the leaders separated them this way and that way
toward the encounter, and among them powerful Agamemnon,
with eyes and head like Zeus who delights in thunder,
like Ares for girth, and with the chest of Poseidon;
like some ox of the herd pre-eminent among the others,
a bull, who stands conspicuous in the huddling cattle;
such was the son of Atreus as Zeus made him that day,
conspicuous among men, and foremost among the fighters.

Homer, Iliad, II, 445

4 As when along the thundering beach the surf of the sea strikes
beat upon beat as the west wind drives it onward; far out
cresting first on the open water, it drives thereafter
to smash roaring along the dry land, and against the rock jut
bending breaks itself into crests spewing back the salt wash;
so thronged beat upon beat the Danaans' close battalions

steadily into battle, with each of the lords commanding
his own men; and these went silently, you would not think
all these people with voices kept in their chests were marching;
silently, in fear of their commanders; and upon all
glittered as they marched the shining armour they carried.
But the Trojans, as sheep in a man of possessions' steading
stand in their myriads waiting to be drained of their white milk
and bleat interminably as they hear the voice of their lambs, so
the crying of the Trojans went up through the wide army.

Homer, Iliad, IV, 422

5 Now pitifully the Trojans might have gone back from the shelters
and the ships, to windy Ilion, had not Poulydamas
come and stood beside bold Hektor and spoken a word to him:
'Hektor, you are too intractable to listen to reason.
Because the god has granted you the actions of warfare
therefore you wish in counsel also to be wise beyond others.
But you cannot choose to have all gifts given to you together.
To one man the god has granted the actions of warfare,
to one to be a dancer, to another the lyre and the singing,
and in the breast of another Zeus of the wide brows establishes
wisdom, a lordly thing, and many take profit beside him
and he saves many, but the man's own thought surpasses all others.
Now I will tell you the way that it seems best to my mind.
For you, everywhere the fighting burns in a circle around you,
but of the great-hearted Trojans since they crossed over the rampart
some are standing back in their war gear, others are fighting
fewer men against many, being scattered among the vessels.
Draw back now, and call to this place all of our bravest,
and then we might work out together our general counsel.'

Homer, Iliad, XIII, 723

6 The Scythians . . . have in one respect . . .

shown themselves wiser than any nation upon the face of the earth. Their customs otherwise are not such as I admire. The one thing of which I speak is the contrivance whereby they make it impossible for the enemy who invades them to escape destruction, while they themselves are entirely out of his reach, unless it please them to engage with him. Having neither cities nor forts, and carrying their dwellings with them wherever they go; accustomed, moreover, one and all of them, to shoot from horseback; and living not by husbandry but on their cattle, their waggons the only houses that they possess, how can they fail of being unconquerable, and unassailable even?

Herodotus, History, IV, 46

7 *Chorus.* Swift-footed Achilles I saw—
His feet like the stormwind—running,
Achilles whom Thetis bore, and
Chiron trained into manhood.
I saw him on the seashore,
In full armor over the sands racing.
He strove, his legs in contest
With a chariot and four,
Toward victory racing and rounding
The course.

Euripides, Iphigenia
in Aulis, 206

8 *Brasidas.* Where an enemy seems strong but is really weak, a true knowledge of the facts makes his adversary the bolder, just as a serious antagonist is encountered most confidently by those who do not know him.

Thucydides, Peloponnesian War, IV, 126

9 The armies being now on the eve of engaging, each contingent received some words of encouragement from its own commander. The Mantineans were reminded that they were going to fight for their country and to avoid returning to the experience of servitude after having tasted that of empire; the Argives, that they would contend for their ancient supremacy, to regain their once equal share of Peloponnese of which they had been so long deprived, and to punish an enemy and a neighbour for a thousand wrongs; the Athenians, of the glory of gaining the honours of the day with so many and brave allies in arms, and that a victory over the Lacedaemonians in Peloponnese would cement and extend their empire, and would besides preserve Attica from all invasions in future. These were the incitements addressed to the Argives and their allies. The Lacedaemonians meanwhile, man to man, and with their war-songs in the ranks, exhorted each brave comrade to remember what he had learnt before; well aware that the long training of action was of more saving virtue than any brief verbal exhortation, though never so well delivered.

Thucydides, Peloponnesian War, V, 69

10 *Alcibiades*. [Socrates] and I went on the expedition to Potidaea; there we messed together, and I had the opportunity of observing his extraordinary power of sustaining fatigue. His endurance was simply marvellous when, being cut off from our supplies, we were compelled to go without food—on such occasions, which often happen in time of war, he was superior not only to me but to everybody; there was no one to be compared to him. Yet at a festival he was the only person who had any real powers of enjoyment; though not willing to drink, he could if compelled beat us all at that,—wonderful to relate! no human being had ever seen Socrates drunk; and his powers, if I am not mistaken, will be tested before long. His fortitude in enduring cold was also surprising. There was a severe frost, for the winter in that region is really tremendous, and everybody else either remained indoors, or if they went out had on an amazing quantity of clothes, and were well shod, and had their feet swathed in felt and fleeces: in the midst of this, Socrates with his bare feet on the ice and in his ordinary dress marched better than the other soldiers who had shoes, and they looked daggers at him because he seemed to despise them. . . . There was another occasion on which his behaviour was very remarkable—in the flight of the army after the battle of Delium, where he served among the heavy-armed—I had a better opportunity of seeing him than at Potidaea, for I was myself on horseback, and therefore comparatively out of danger. He and Laches were retreating, for the troops were in flight, and I met them and told them not to be discouraged, and promised to remain with them; and there you might see him, Aristophanes, as you describe, just as he is in the streets of Athens, stalking like a pelican, and rolling his eyes, calmly contemplating enemies as well as friends, and making very intelligible to anybody, even from a distance, that whoever attacked him would be likely to meet with a stout resistance; and in this way he and his companion escaped—for this is the sort of man who is never touched in war; those only are pursued who are running away headlong.

Plato, *Symposium*, 219B

11 *Socrates*. Nothing can be more important than that the work of a soldier should be well done. But is war an art so easily acquired that a man may be a warrior who is also a husbandman, or shoemaker, or other artisan; although no one in the world would be a good dice or draught player who merely took up the game as a recreation, and had not from his earliest years devoted himself to this and nothing else? No tools will make a man a skilled workman, or master of defence, nor be of any use to him who has not learned how to handle them, and has never bestowed any attention upon them. How then will he who takes up a shield or other implement of war become a good fighter all

in a day, whether with heavy-armed or any other kind of troops?

Glaucon. Yes . . . the tools which would teach men their own use would be beyond price.

And the higher the duties of the guardian, I said, the more time, and skill, and art, and application will be needed by him?

No doubt. . . .

Will he not also require natural aptitude for his calling?

Certainly.

Then it will be our duty to select, if we can, natures which are fitted for the task of guarding the city.

Plato, *Republic*, II, 374A

12 *Athenian Stranger*. For expeditions of war much consideration and many laws are required; the great principle of all is that no one of either sex should be without a commander; nor should the mind of any one be accustomed to do anything, either in jest or earnest, of his own motion, but in war and in peace he should look to and follow his leader, even in the least things being under his guidance; for example, he should stand or move, or exercise, or wash, or take his meals, or get up in the night to keep guard and deliver messages when he is bidden; and in the hour of danger he should not pursue and not retreat except by order of his superior; and in a word, not teach the soul or accustom her to know or understand how to do anything apart from others. Of all soldiers the life should be always and in all things as far as possible in common and together; there neither is nor ever will be a higher, or better, or more scientific principle than this for the attainment of salvation and victory in war. And we ought in time of peace from youth upwards to practise this habit of commanding others, and of being commanded by others; anarchy should have no place in the life of man or of the beasts who are subject to man.

Plato, *Laws*, XII, 942A

13 *Socrates*. A general must also be capable of furnishing military equipment and providing supplies for the men; he must be resourceful, active, careful, hardy and quick-witted; he must be both gentle and brutal, at once straightforward and designing, capable of both caution and surprise, lavish and rapacious, generous and mean, skilful in defence and attack; and there are many other qualifications, some natural, some acquired, that are necessary to one who would succeed as a general.

Xenophon, *Memorabilia*, III, 1

14 In the choice of a general, we should regard his skill rather than his virtue; for few have military skill, but many have virtue.

Aristotle, *Politics*, 1309^{b}3

15 There are four kinds of military forces,—the cav-

alry, the heavy infantry, the light-armed troops, the navy. When the country is adapted for cavalry, then a strong oligarchy is likely to be established. For the security of the inhabitants depends upon a force of this sort, and only rich men can afford to keep horses. The second form of oligarchy prevails when the country is adapted to heavy infantry; for this service is better suited to the rich than to the poor. But the light-armed and the naval element are wholly democratic; and nowadays, where they are numerous, if the two parties quarrel, the oligarchy are often worsted by them in the struggle. A remedy for this state of things may be found in the practice of generals who combine a proper contingent of light-armed troops with cavalry and heavy-armed. And this is the way in which the poor get the better of the rich in civil contests; being lightly armed, they fight with advantage against cavalry and heavy infantry. An oligarchy which raises such a force out of the lower classes raises a power against itself. And therefore, since the ages of the citizens vary and some are older and some younger, the fathers should have their own sons, while they are still young, taught the agile movements of light-armed troops; and these, when they have been taken out of the ranks of the youth, should become light-armed warriors in reality.

Aristotle, *Politics,* 1321ª7

16 Weapons are of little use on the field of battle if there is no wise counsel at home.

Cicero, *De Officiis,* I, 22

17 *Aeneas.* 'Brave souls!' said I,—'but brave, alas! in vain—
Come, finish what our cruel fates ordain.
You see the desp'rate state of our affairs,
And heav'n's protecting pow'rs are deaf to pray'rs.
The passive gods behold the Greeks defile
Their temples, and abandon to the spoil
Their own abodes: we, feeble few, conspire
To save a sinking town, involv'd in fire.
Then let us fall, but fall amidst our foes:
Despair of life the means of living shows.'
So bold a speech incourag'd their desire
Of death, and added fuel to their fire.
"As hungry wolves, with raging appetite,
Scour thro' the fields, nor fear the stormy night—
Their whelps at home expect the promis'd food,
And long to temper their dry chaps in blood—
So rush'd we forth at once; resolv'd to die,
Resolv'd, in death, the last extremes to try.
We leave the narrow lanes behind, and dare
Th' unequal combat in the public square:
Night was our friend; our leader was despair."

Virgil, *Aeneid,* II

18 Nor was he [Aemilius Paulus] less severe in requiring and observing the ancient Roman discipline in military affairs; not endeavouring, when he had the command, to ingratiate himself with his soldiers by popular flattery, though this custom prevailed at that time amongst many, who, by favour and gentleness to those that were under them in their first employment, sought to be promoted to a second; but, by instructing them in the laws of military discipline with the same care and exactness a priest would use in teaching ceremonies and dreadful mysteries, and by severity to such as transgressed and contemned those laws, he maintained his country in its former greatness, esteeming victory over enemies itself but as an accessory to the proper training and disciplining of the citizens.

Plutarch, *Aemilius Paulus*

19 As horses run brisker in a chariot than singly, not that their joint force divides the air with greater ease, but because being matched one against the other emulation kindles and inflames their courage; thus he [Pelopidas] thought brave men, provoking one another to noble actions, would prove most serviceable, and most resolute, where all were united together.

Plutarch, *Pelopidas*

20 Any voluntary partaking with people in their labour is felt as an easing of that labour, as it seems to take away the constraint and necessity of it. It is the most obliging sight in the world to the Roman soldier to see a commander eat the same bread as himself, or lie upon an ordinary bed, or assist the work in the drawing a trench and raising a bulwark. For they do not so much admire those that confer honours and riches upon them, as those that partake of the same labour and danger with themselves; but love them better that will vouchsafe to join in their work, than those that encourage their idleness.

Plutarch, *Caius Marius*

21 It grieved Nicias to hear of flight and departing home, not that he did not fear the Syracusans, but he was worse afraid of the Athenians, their impeachments and sentences; he professed that he apprehended no further harm there, or if it must be, he would rather die by the hand of an enemy than by that of his fellow-citizens. . . . But fresh forces now coming to the Syracusans and the sickness growing worse in his camp, he, also, now approved of their retreat, and commanded the soldiers to make ready to go abroad.

And when all were in readiness, and none of the enemy had observed them, not expecting such a thing, the moon was eclipsed in the night, to the great fright of Nicias and others, who, for want of experience, or out of superstition, felt alarm at such appearances. That the sun might be darkened about the close of the month, this even ordinary people now understood pretty well to be the effect of the moon; but the moon itself to be darkened, how that could come about, and how, on the sudden, a broad full moon should lose her light, and show such various colours, was not easy to be comprehended; they concluded it to be ominous, and a divine intimation of some heavy calamities. . . . It so fell out with Nicias, that he had not at this time a skilful diviner with him; his former habitual adviser who used to moderate much of his superstition, Stilbides, had died a little before. For, in fact, this prodigy, as Philochorus observes, was not unlucky for men wishing to flee, but on the contrary very favourable; for things done in fear require to be hidden, and the light is their foe. Nor was it usual to observe signs in the sun or moon more than three days, as Autoclides states in his *Commentaries*. But Nicias persuaded them to wait another full course of the moon, as if he had not seen it clear again as soon as ever it had passed the region of shadow where the light was obstructed by the earth.

In a manner abandoning all other cares, he betook himself wholly to his sacrifices, till the enemy came upon them with their infantry, besieging the forts and camp, and placing their ships in a circle about the harbour. Nor did the men in the galleys only, but the little boys everywhere got into the fishing-boats and rowed up and challenged the Athenians, and insulted over them. . . .

The Athenians, their loss and slaughter being very great, their flight by sea cut off, their safety by land so difficult, did not attempt to hinder the enemy towing away their ships, under their eyes, nor demanded their dead, as, indeed, their want of burial seemed a less calamity than the leaving behind the sick and wounded which they now had before them. Yet more miserable still than those did they reckon themselves, who were to work on yet, through more such sufferings, after all to reach the same end.

Plutarch, *Nicias*

22 Peace is only too apt to lower the reputation of men that have grown great by arms, who naturally find difficulty in adapting themselves to the habits of civil equality.

Plutarch, *Pompey*

23 [Caesar] was so much master of the good-will and hearty service of his soldiers that those who in other expeditions were but ordinary men displayed a courage past defeating or withstanding when they went upon any danger where Cæsar's glory was concerned.

Plutarch, *Caesar*

24 Cato himself acquired in the fullest measure what it had been his least desire to seek, glory and good repute; he was highly esteemed by all men, and entirely beloved by the soldiers. Whatever he commanded to be done, he himself took part in

the performing; in his apparel, his diet, and mode of travelling, he was more like a common soldier than an officer; but in character, high purpose, and wisdom, he far exceeded all that had the names and titles of commanders, and he made himself, without knowing it, the object of general affection.

Plutarch, *Cato the Younger*

25 Iphicrates the Athenian used to say that it is best to have a mercenary soldier fond of money and of pleasures, for thus he will fight the more boldly, to procure the means to gratify his desires. But most have been of opinion that the body of an army, as well as the natural one, when in its healthy condition, should make no efforts apart, but in compliance with its head.

Plutarch, *Galba*

26 [In] the events that followed among the Romans upon the death of Nero . . . plain proofs were given that nothing is more terrible than a military force moving about in an empire upon uninstructed and unreasoning impulses.

Plutarch, *Galba*

27   You can find, much more quickly, a witness
Who will perjure himself against a civilian's lawsuit
Than you will get one to tell the truth if it injures the interests
Or the good name of a soldier.

Juvenal, *Satire XVI*

28 The worthiest . . . [soldiers] were moved by patriotism; many were wrought upon by the attractions of plunder; some by their private embarrassments. And so, good and bad, from different motives, but with equal zeal, were all eager for war.

Tacitus, *Histories*, II, 7

29 The arms with which a prince defends his state are either his own, or they are mercenaries, auxiliaries, or mixed. Mercenaries and auxiliaries are useless and dangerous; and if one holds his state based on these arms, he will stand neither firm nor safe; for they are disunited, ambitious and without discipline, unfaithful, valiant before friends, cowardly before enemies; they have neither the fear of God nor fidelity to men, and destruction is deferred only so long as the attack is; for in peace one is robbed by them, and in war by the enemy. The fact is, they have no other attraction or reason for keeping the field than a trifle of stipend, which is not sufficient to make them willing to die for you. They are ready enough to be your soldiers whilst you do not make war, but if war comes they take themselves off or run from the foe.

Machiavelli, *Prince*, XII

30 Mercenary captains are either capable men or they are not; if they are, you cannot trust them, because they always aspire to their own greatness, either by oppressing you, who are their master, or others contrary to your intentions; but if the captain is not skilful, you are ruined in the usual way.

And if it be urged that whoever is armed will act in the same way, whether mercenary or not, I reply that when arms have to be resorted to, either by a prince or a republic, then the prince ought to go in person and perform the duty of captain; the republic has to send its citizens, and when one is sent who does not turn out satisfactorily, it ought to recall him, and when one is worthy, to hold him by the laws so that he does not leave the command. And experience has shown princes and republics, single-handed, making the greatest progress, and mercenaries doing nothing except damage; and it is more difficult to bring a republic, armed with its own arms, under the sway of one of its citizens than it is to bring one armed with foreign arms.

Machiavelli, *Prince*, XII

31 David offered himself to Saul to fight with Goliath, the Philistine champion, and, to give him courage, Saul armed him with his own weapons; which David rejected as soon as he had them on his back, saying he could make no use of them, and that he wished to meet the enemy with his sling and his knife. In conclusion, the arms of others either fall from your back, or they weigh you down, or they bind you fast.

Machiavelli, *Prince*, XIII

32 A general who disposes his army in such manner that it can rally three several times in the course of a battle, must have fortune against him three times before being defeated, and must have an enemy opposed to him sufficiently superior to overcome him three times. But if an army can resist only a single shock, as is the case nowadays with the Christian armies, it may easily lose the battle.

Machiavelli, *Discourses*, II, 16

33 To make an army victorious in battle it is necessary to inspire them with confidence, so as to make them believe that the victory will be theirs under any circumstances. But to give an army such confidence they must be well armed and disciplined, and the men must know each other; such confidence and discipline, however, can exist only where the troops are natives of the same country, and have lived together for some time. It is necessary also that they should esteem their general, and have confidence in his ability; and this will not fail to be the case when they see him orderly, watchful, and courageous, and that he maintains the dignity of his rank by a proper reputation. All this he will do by punishing faults, by

not fatiguing his troops unnecessarily, by strictly fulfilling his promises, by showing them that victory is easy, and by concealing or making light of the dangers which he discerns from afar.

Machiavelli, *Discourses*, III, 33

34 There is no occupation so pleasant as the military one, an occupation both noble in execution (for the strongest, most generous, and proudest of all virtues is valor) and noble in its cause: there is no more just and universal service than the protection of the peace and greatness of your country. . . . Death is more abject, more lingering and distressing, in bed than in battle; fevers and catarrhs are as painful and fatal as a harquebus shot. Whoever is prepared to bear valiantly the accidents of everyday life would not have to swell his courage to become a soldier.

Montaigne, *Essays*, III, 13, Of Experience

35 *Hotspur.* I remember, when the fight was done,
When I was dry with rage and extreme toil,
Breathless and faint, leaning upon my sword,
Came there a certain lord, neat, and trimly dress'd,
Fresh as a bridegroom; and his chin new reap'd
Show'd like a stubble-land at harvest-home;
He was perfumed like a milliner;
And 'twixt his finger and his thumb he held
A pouncet-box, which ever and anon
He gave his nose and took't away again:
Who therewith angry, when it next came there,
Took it in snuff; and still he smiled and talk'd,
And as the soldiers bore dead bodies by,
He call'd them untaught knaves, unmannerly,
To bring a slovenly unhandsome corse
Betwixt the wind and his nobility.
With many holiday and lady terms
He question'd me; amongst the rest, demanded
My prisoners in your Majesty's behalf.
I then, all smarting with my wounds being cold,
To be so pester'd with a popinjay,
Out of my grief and my impatience,
Answer'd neglectingly I know not what,
He should, or he should not; for he made me mad
To see him shine so brisk and smell so sweet
And talk so like a waiting-gentlewoman
Of guns and drums and wounds—God save the mark!—
And telling me the sovereign'st thing on earth
Was parmaceti for an inward bruise;
And that it was great pity, so it was,
This villainous salt-petre should be digg'd
Out of the bowels of the harmless earth,
Which many a good tall fellow had destroy'd
So cowardly; and but for these vile guns,
He would himself have been a soldier.

Shakespeare, *I Henry IV*, I, iii, 30

36 *Vernon.* I have learn'd,
The King himself in person is set forth,

Or hitherwards intended speedily,
With strong and mighty preparation.
    Hotspur. He shall be welcome too. Where is his
      son,
The nimble-footed madcap Prince of Wales,
And his comrades, that daff'd the world aside,
And bid it pass?
    Ver.   All furnish'd, all in arms;
All plumed like estridges that with the wind
Baited like eagles having lately bathed;
Glittering in golden coats, like images;
As full of spirit as the month of May,
And gorgeous as the sun at midsummer;
Wanton as youthful goats, wild as young bulls.
I saw young Harry, with his beaver on,
His cuisses on his thighs, gallantly arm'd,
Rise from the ground like feather'd Mercury,
And vaulted with such ease into his seat,
As if an angel dropp'd down from the clouds,
To turn and wind a fiery Pegasus
And witch the world with noble horsemanship.
            Shakespeare, *I Henry IV,* IV, i, 90

37 *Prince of Wales.* Tell me, Jack, whose fellows are
    these that come after?
    Falstaff. Mine, Hal, mine.
    Prince. I did never see such pitiful rascals.
    Fal. Tut, tut; good enough to toss; food for pow-
der, food for powder; they'll fill a pit as well as
better: tush, man, mortal men, mortal men.
            Shakespeare, *I Henry IV,* IV, ii, 67

38 *Othello.*   O, now, for ever
Farewell the tranquil mind! farewell content!
Farewell the plumed troop, and the big wars,
That make ambition virtue! O, farewell!
Farewell the neighing steed, and the shrill trump,
The spirit-stirring drum, the ear-piercing fife,
The royal banner, and all quality,
Pride, pomp, and circumstance of glorious war!
And, O you mortal engines, whose rude throats
The immortal Jove's dread clamours counterfeit,
Farewell! Othello's occupation's gone!
            Shakespeare, *Othello,* III, iii, 347

39 Blessed be those happy Ages that were Strangers
to the dreadful Fury of these devilish Instruments
of Artillery, whose Inventor I am satisfy'd is now
in Hell, receiving the Reward of his cursed Invention, which is the Cause that very often a cowardly base Hand takes away the Life of the bravest Gentleman, and that in the midst of that
Vigour and Resolution which animates and inflames the Bold, a chance Bullet (shot perhaps by
one that fled, and was frighted at the very Flash
the mischievous Piece gave, when it went off)
coming no Body knows how, or from whence, in a
Moment puts a Period to the brave Designs, and
the Life of one, that deserv'd to have surviv'd
many Years.
            Cervantes, *Don Quixote,* I, 38

40 I know not how, but martial men are given to
love: I think it is but as they are given to wine; for
perils commonly ask to be paid in pleasures.
            Bacon, *Of Love*

41 A commander of an army in chief, if he be not
popular, shall not be beloved, nor feared as he
ought to be by his army, and consequently cannot
perform that office with good success. He must
therefore be industrious, valiant, affable, liberal
and fortunate, that he may gain an opinion both
of sufficiency and of loving his soldiers. This is
popularity, and breeds in the soldiers both desire
and courage to recommend themselves to his favour; and protects the severity of the general, in
punishing, when need is, the mutinous or negligent soldiers. But this love of soldiers, if caution be
not given of the commander's fidelity, is a dangerous thing to sovereign power; especially when it is
in the hands of an assembly not popular. It belongeth therefore to the safety of the people, both
that they be good conductors and faithful subjects,
to whom the sovereign commits his armies.
            Hobbes, *Leviathan,* II, 30

42 *Satan.* Innumerable force of Spirits arm'd
That durst dislike his reign, and me preferring,
His utmost power with adverse power oppos'd
In dubious Battel on the Plains of Heav'n.
            Milton, *Paradise Lost,* I, 101

43 The preservation of the army, and in it of the
whole commonwealth, requires an absolute obedience to the command of every superior officer,
and it is justly death to disobey or dispute the
most dangerous or unreasonable of them.
            Locke, *II Civil
            Government,* XI, 139

44 He [the king of Brobdingnag] was amazed to hear
me talk of a mercenary standing army in the
midst of peace, and among a free people. He said,
if we were governed by our own consent in the
persons of our representatives, he could not imagine of whom we were afraid, or against whom we
were to fight; and would hear my opinion, whether a private man's house might not better be defended by himself, his children, and family; than
by half a dozen rascals picked up at a venture in
the streets, for small wages, who might get an
hundred times more by cutting their throats.
            Swift, *Gulliver's Travels,* II, 6

45 The trade of a *soldier* is held the most honourable
of all others: because a *soldier* is a Yahoo hired to
kill in cold blood as many of his own species, who
have never offended him, as possibly he can.
            Swift, *Gulliver's Travels,* IV, 5

46 Desertion in our days has grown to a very great

height; in consequence of which it was judged proper to punish those delinquents with death; and yet their number did not diminish. The reason is very natural; a soldier, accustomed to venture his life, despises, or affects to despise, the danger of losing it. He is habituated to the fear of shame; it would have been therefore much better to have continued a punishment which branded him with infamy for life; the penalty was pretended to be increased, while it really diminished.

Montesquieu, *Spirit of Laws*, VI, 12

47 It is said that God is always for the big battalions.

Voltaire, *Letter to M. Le Riche* (Feb. 6, 1770)

48 We talked of war. *Johnson*. "Every man thinks meanly of himself for not having been a soldier, or not having been at sea." *Boswell*. "Lord Mansfield does not." *Johnson*. "Sir, if Lord Mansfield were in a company of General Officers and Admirals who have been in service, he would shrink; he'd wish to creep under the table." *Boswell*. "No; he'd think he could *try* them all." *Johnson*. "Yes, if he could catch them: but they'd try him much sooner. No, Sir; were Socrates and Charles the Twelfth of Sweden both present in any company, and Socrates to say, 'Follow me, and hear a lecture on philosophy'; and Charles, laying his hand on his sword, to say, 'Follow me, and dethrone the Czar'; a man would be ashamed to follow Socrates. Sir, the impression is universal; yet it is strange. As to the sailor, when you look down from the quarter deck to the space below, you see the utmost extremity of human misery; such crowding, such filth, such stench!" *Boswell*. "Yet sailors are happy." *Johnson*. "They are happy as brutes are happy, with a piece of fresh meat,—with the grossest sensuality. But, Sir, the profession of soldiers and sailors has the dignity of danger. Mankind reverence those who have got over fear, which is so general a weakness."

Boswell, *Life of Johnson* (Apr. 10, 1778)

49 Without regarding the danger . . . young volunteers never enlist so readily as at the beginning of a new war; and though they have scarce any chance of preferment, they figure to themselves, in their youthful fancies, a thousand occasions of acquiring honour and distinction which never occur. These romantic hopes make the whole price of their blood. Their pay is less than that of common labourers, and in actual service their fatigues are much greater.

Adam Smith, *Wealth of Nations*, I, 10

50 The art of war . . . as it is certainly the noblest of all arts, so in the progress of improvement it necessarily becomes one of the most complicated among them. The state of the mechanical, as well as of some other arts, with which it is necessarily connected, determines the degree of perfection to which it is capable of being carried at any particular time. But in order to carry it to this degree of perfection, it is necessary that it should become the sole or principal occupation of a particular class of citizens, and the division of labour is as necessary for the improvement of this, as of every other art. Into other arts the division of labour is naturally introduced by the prudence of individuals, who find that they promote their private interest better by confining themselves to a particular trade than by exercising a great number. But it is the wisdom of the state only which can render the trade of a soldier a particular trade separate and distinct from all others. A private citizen who, in time of profound peace, and without any particular encouragement from the public, should spend the greater part of his time in military exercises, might, no doubt, both improve himself very much in them, and amuse himself very well; but he certainly would not promote his own interest. It is the wisdom of the state only which can render it for his interest to give up the greater part of his time to this peculiar occupation: and states have not always had this wisdom, even when their circumstances had become such that the preservation of their existence required that they should have it.

Adam Smith, *Wealth of Nations*, V, 1

51 Before the invention of firearms, that army was superior in which the soldiers had, each individually, the greatest skill and dexterity in the use of their arms. Strength and agility of body were of the highest consequence, and commonly determined the state of battles. But this skill and dexterity in the use of their arms could be acquired only, in the same manner as fencing is at present, by practising, not in great bodies, but each man separately, in a particular school, under a particular master, or with his own particular equals and companions. Since the invention of firearms, strength and agility of body, or even extraordinary dexterity and skill in the use of arms, though they are far from being of no consequence, are, however, of less consequence. The nature of the weapon, though it by no means puts the awkward upon a level with the skilful, puts him more nearly so than he ever was before. All the dexterity and skill, it is supposed, which are necessary for using it, can be well enough acquired by practising in great bodies.

Regularity, order, and prompt obedience to command are qualities which, in modern armies, are of more importance towards determining the fate of battles than the dexterity and skill of the soldiers in the use of their arms. But the noise of firearms, the smoke, and the invisible death to which every man feels himself every moment exposed as soon as he comes within cannon-shot, and frequently a long time before the battle can be well said to be engaged, must render it very difficult to maintain any considerable degree of this regularity, order, and prompt obedience, even in the beginning of a modern battle. In an ancient battle there was no noise but what arose from the human voice; there was no smoke, there was no invisible cause of wounds or death. Every man, till some mortal weapon actually did approach him, saw clearly that no such weapon was near him. In these circumstances, and among troops who had some confidence in their own skill and dexterity in the use of their arms, it must have been a good deal less difficult to preserve some degree of regularity and order, not only in the beginning, but through the whole progress of an ancient battle, and till one of the two armies was fairly defeated. But the habits of regularity, order, and prompt obedience to command can be acquired only by troops which are exercised in great bodies.

Adam Smith, *Wealth of Nations*, V, 1

52 A militia . . . in whatever manner it may be either disciplined or exercised, must always be much inferior to a well-disciplined and well-exercised standing army.

The soldiers who are exercised only once a week, or once a month, can never be so expert in the use of their arms as those who are exercised every day, or every other day. . . . The soldiers who are bound to obey their officer only once a week or once a month, and who are at all other times at liberty to manage their own affairs their own way, without being in any respect accountable to him, can never be under the same awe in his presence, can never have the same disposition to ready obedience, with those whose whole life and conduct are every day directed by him, and who every day even rise and go to bed, or at least retire to their quarters, according to his orders. In what is called discipline, or in the habit of ready obedience, a militia must always be still more inferior to a standing army than it may sometimes be in what is called the manual exercise, or in the management and use of its arms. But in modern war the habit of ready and instant obedience is of much greater consequence than a considerable superiority in the management of arms. . . .

A militia of any kind . . . however, which has served for several successive campaigns in the field, becomes in every respect a standing army. The soldiers are every day exercised in the use of their arms, and, being constantly under the command of their officers, are habituated to the same prompt obedience which takes place in standing armies. What they were before they took the field is of little importance. They necessarily become in every respect a standing army after they have passed a few campaigns in it. Should the war in America drag out through another campaign, the American militia may become in every respect a match for that standing army of which the valour appeared, in the last war, at least not inferior to that of the hardiest veterans of France and Spain.

This distinction being well understood, the history of all ages, it will be found, bears testimony to the irresistible superiority which a well-regulated standing army has over a militia.

Adam Smith, *Wealth of Nations*, V, 1

53 Men of republican principles have been jealous of a standing army as dangerous to liberty. It certainly is so wherever the interest of the general and that of the principal officers are not necessarily connected with the support of the constitution of the state. . . . But where the sovereign is himself the general, and the principal nobility and gentry of the country the chief officers of the army, where the military force is placed under the command of those who have the greatest interest in the support of the civil authority, because they have themselves the greatest share of that authority, a standing army can never be dangerous to liberty. On the contrary, it may in some cases be favourable to liberty.

Adam Smith, *Wealth of Nations*, V, 1

54 The terror of the Roman arms added weight and dignity to the moderation of the emperors. They preserved peace by a constant preparation for war; and while justice regulated their conduct, they announced to the nations on their confines that they were as little disposed to endure as to offer an injury.

Gibbon, *Decline and Fall of the Roman Empire,* I

55 In the purer ages of the commonwealth, the use of arms was reserved for those ranks of citizens who had a country to love, a property to defend, and some share in enacting those laws, which it was their interest, as well as duty, to maintain. But in proportion as the public freedom was lost in extent of conquest, war was gradually improved into an art, and degraded into a trade.

Gibbon, *Decline and Fall of the Roman Empire,* I

56 In the various states of society armies are recruited from very different motives. Barbarians are urged by their love of war; the citizens of a free republic may be prompted by a principle of duty; the subjects, or at least the nobles, of a monarchy are animated by a sentiment of honour; but the timid and luxurious inhabitants of a declining empire must be allured into the service by the hopes of profit, or compelled by the dread of punishment.

Gibbon, *Decline and Fall of the Roman Empire,* XVII

57 Cold, poverty, and a life of danger and fatigue fortify the strength and courage of barbarians. In every age they have oppressed the polite and

peaceful nations of China, India, and Persia, who neglected, and still neglect, to counterbalance these natural powers by the resources of military art. The warlike states of antiquity, Greece, Macedonia, and Rome, educated a race of soldiers; exercised their bodies, disciplined their courage, multiplied their forces by regular evolutions, and converted the iron which they possessed into strong and serviceable weapons. But this superiority insensibly declined with their laws and manners: and the feeble policy of Constantine and his successors armed and instructed, for the ruin of the empire, the rude valour of the barbarian mercenaries. The military art has been changed by the invention of gunpowder; which enables man to command the two most powerful agents of nature, air and fire. Mathematics, chemistry, mechanics, architecture, have been applied to the service of war; and the adverse parties oppose to each other the most elaborate modes of attack and of defence. Historians may indignantly observe that the preparations of a siege would found and maintain a flourishing colony; yet we cannot be displeased that the subversion of a city should be a work of cost and difficulty; or that an industrious people should be protected by those arts which survive and supply the decay of military virtue. Cannon and fortifications now form an impregnable barrier against the Tartar horse; and Europe is secure from any future irruption of barbarians; since, before they can conquer, they must cease to be barbarous. Their gradual advances in the science of war would always be accompanied, as we may learn from the example of Russia, with a proportionable improvement in the arts of peace and civil policy; and they themselves must deserve a place among the polished nations whom they subdue.

> Gibbon, *Decline and Fall of the Roman
> Empire,* XXXVIII

58 The discipline of a soldier is formed by exercise rather than by study: the talents of a commander are appropriated to those calm, though rapid, minds, which nature produces to decide the fate of armies and nations: the former is the habit of a life, the latter the glance of a moment; and the battles won by lessons of tactics may be numbered with the epic poems created from the rules of criticism.

> Gibbon, *Decline and Fall of the Roman
> Empire,* LIII

59 The disciplined armies always kept on foot on the continent of Europe, though they bear a malignant aspect to liberty and economy, have, notwithstanding, been productive of the signal advantage of rendering sudden conquests impracticable, and of preventing that rapid desolation which used to mark the progress of war prior to their introduction.

> Hamilton, *Federalist 8*

60 The authorities essential to the common defence are these: to raise armies; to build and equip fleets; to prescribe rules for the government of both; to direct their operations; to provide for their support. These powers ought to exist without limitation, because it is impossible to foresee or define the extent and variety of national exigencies, or the correspondent extent and variety of the means which may be necessary to satisfy them.

> Hamilton, *Federalist 23*

61 As far as an army may be considered as a dangerous weapon of power, it had better be in those hands of which the people are most likely to be jealous than in those of which they are least likely to be jealous. For it is a truth, which the experience of ages has attested, that the people are always most in danger when the means of injuring their rights are in the possession of those of whom they entertain the least suspicion.

> Hamilton, *Federalist 25*

62 *Soldiers.* Castles with lofty
Ramparts retaining,
Maids who are haughty,
Scornful, disdaining,
Fain I'd be gaining!
Bold is the venture,
Grand is the pay!
  We let the trumpet
Summon us, wooing,
Calling to pleasure,
Oft to undoing.
That is a storming!
Life in its splendour!
  Maidens and castles
Both must surrender.
Bold is the venture,
Grand is the pay!
Then are the soldiers
Off and away.

> Goethe, *Faust,* I, 884

63 Of all armies, those most ardently desirous of war are democratic armies, and of all nations, those most fond of peace are democratic nations; and what makes these facts still more extraordinary is that these contrary effects are produced at the same time by the principle of equality.

All the members of the community, being alike, constantly harbor the wish and discover the possibility of changing their condition and improving their welfare; this makes them fond of peace, which is favorable to industry and allows every man to pursue his own little undertakings to their completion. On the other hand, this same equality makes soldiers dream of fields of battle, by increasing the value of military honors in the eyes of those who follow the profession of arms and by rendering those honors accessible to all. In either case the restlessness of the heart is the same, the taste for enjoyment is insatiable, the ambition of success as great; the means of gratifying it alone are different.

Tocqueville, *Democracy in America,*
Vol. II, III, 22

64 Half a league, half a league,
Half a league onward,
All in the valley of Death
   Rode the six hundred.
'Forward the Light Brigade!
Charge for the guns!' he said.
Into the valley of Death
   Rode the six hundred.

'Forward, the Light Brigade!'
Was there a man dismay'd?
Not tho' the soldier knew
   Some one had blunder'd.
Theirs not to make reply,
Theirs not to reason why,
Theirs but to do and die.
Into the valley of Death
   Rode the six hundred.

Cannon to right of them,
Cannon to left of them,
Cannon in front of them
   Volley'd and thunder'd;
Storm'd at with shot and shell,
Boldly they rode and well,
Into the jaws of Death,
Into the mouth of hell
   Rode the six hundred. . . .

When can their glory fade?
O the wild charge they made!
   All the world wonder'd.
Honor the charge they made!
Honor the Light Brigade,
   Noble six hundred!

Tennyson, *The Charge of the Light Brigade*

65 Doubtless one leading reason why the world declines honouring us whalemen, is this: they think that, at best, our vocation amounts to a butchering sort of business; and that when actively engaged therein, we are surrounded by all manner of defilements. Butchers we are, that is true. But butchers also, and butchers of the bloodiest badge, have been all martial commanders whom the world invariably delights to honour. And as for the matter of the alleged uncleanliness of our business, ye shall soon be initiated into certain facts hitherto pretty generally unknown, and which, upon the whole, will triumphantly plant the sperm whaleship at least among the cleanliest things of this tidy earth. But even granting the charge in question to be true, what disordered slippery decks of a whale ship are comparable to the unspeakable carrion of those battlefields from which so many soldiers return to drink in all ladies' plaudits? And if the idea of peril so much enhances the popular conceit of the soldier's profession; let me assure ye that many a veteran who has freely marched up to a battery, would quickly recoil at the apparition of the sperm whale's vast tail, fanning into eddies the air over his head. For what are the comprehensible terrors of man compared with the interlinked terrors and wonders of God!

Melville, *Moby Dick,* XXIV

66 The soldier's trade, verily and essentially, is not slaying, but being slain. This, without well knowing its own meaning, the world honours it for.

Ruskin, *Unto This Last,* I, 17

67 In war the most deeply considered plans have no significance. . . . All depends on the way unexpected movements of the enemy—that cannot be foreseen—are met, and on how and by whom the whole matter is handled.

Tolstoy, *War and Peace,* IX, 9

68 *Prince Andrew.* Not only does a good army commander not need any special qualities, on the contrary he needs the absence of the highest and best human attributes—love, poetry, tenderness, and philosophic inquiring doubt.

Tolstoy, *War and Peace,* IX, 11

69 Rostóv knew by experience that men always lie when describing military exploits . . . that nothing happens in war at all as we can imagine or relate it.

Tolstoy, *War and Peace,* IX, 12

70 *Prince Andrew.* But what is war? What is needed for success in warfare? What are the habits of the military? The aim of war is murder; the methods of war are spying, treachery, and their encouragement, the ruin of a country's inhabitants, robbing them or stealing to provision the army, and fraud and falsehood termed military craft. The habits of the military class are the absence of freedom, that is, discipline, idleness, ignorance, cruelty, debauchery, and drunkenness. And in spite of all this it is the highest class, respected by everyone. All the kings, except the Chinese, wear military uniforms, and he who kills most people receives the highest rewards.

Tolstoy, *War and Peace,* X, 25

71 The profoundest and most excellent dispositions and orders seem very bad, and every learned militarist criticizes them with looks of importance, when they relate to a battle that has been lost, and the very worst dispositions and orders seem very good, and serious people fill whole volumes

to demonstrate their merits, when they relate to a battle that has been won.

Tolstoy, *War and Peace*, X, 28

72 The result of a battle is decided not by the orders of a commander in chief, nor the place where the troops are stationed, nor by the number of cannon or of slaughtered men, but by that intangible force called the spirit of the army.

Tolstoy, *War and Peace*, X, 35

73 The activity of a commander in chief does not at all resemble the activity we imagine to ourselves when we sit at ease in our studies examining some campaign on the map, with a certain number of troops on this and that side in a certain known locality, and begin our plans from some given moment. A commander in chief is never dealing with the *beginning* of any event—the position from which we always contemplate it. The commander in chief is always in the midst of a series of shifting events and so he never can at any moment consider the whole import of an event that is occurring.

Tolstoy, *War and Peace*, XI, 2

74 The army has always been the basis of power, and it is so today. Power is always in the hands of those who command it.

Tolstoy, *The Kingdom of God Is Within You*

75 An army, considered ideally, is an organ for the state's protection; but it is far from being such in its origin, since at first an army is nothing but a ravenous and lusty horde quartered in a conquered country; yet the cost of such an incubus may come to be regarded as an insurance against further attack, and so what is in its real basis an inevitable burden resulting from a chance balance of forces may be justified in afterthought as a rational device for defensive purposes.

Santayana, *Life of Reason*, II, 3

76 The military classes, since they inherit the blood and habits of conquerors, naturally love war and their irrational combativeness is reinforced by interest; for in war officers can shine and rise, while the danger of death, to a brave man, is rather a spur and a pleasing excitement than a terror. A military class is therefore always recalling, foretelling, and meditating war; it fosters artificial and senseless jealousies toward other governments that possess armies; and finally, as often as not, it precipitates disaster by bringing about the objectless struggle on which it has set its heart.

Santayana, *Life of Reason*, II, 3

14.3 | *The Conditions of Peace*

It is said, in some of the passages below, that war is for the sake of peace; and it is also said that an unjust peace is to be preferred to a just war. The latter statement is challenged by those who question the genuineness of peace without justice and who point out that oppressive injustice breeds violence and rebellion which, as Locke observes in commenting on the etymology of the word (*re-bellare*), is a return to war. This difference of opinion is epitomized in two views of the *Pax Romana*—the Virgilian view of it as a boon that Rome conferred by conquest and the opposite view that Tacitus

gives voice to in the words of the defeated British chieftain, Galgacus: the Romans make a desolation, he said, and call it peace.

The basic distinction that emerges in Section 14.1 on WARFARE AND THE STATE OF WAR is of primary relevance to the conception of peace as a positive, not merely a negative, state of affairs—not just the absence of actual fighting, but the elimination of the need for recourse to violence in order to settle disputes. Animals, it has been asserted, have only one way of settling their differences—by fighting; but men have two ways—by fighting and by law. Civil society, Locke tells us, is a state of peace in which the umpirage of government and the reign of law provide the instrumentalities for settling disputes without recourse to violence; for the use of authorized force by government is not violence. Other writers, notably Augustine and Aquinas, fill out this positive conception of peace by the notion that genuine concord is essential to the tranquility of order and by the insistence that genuine concord is impossible without justice and love.

Both here and in Section 14.1, there is some discussion of the possibility of abolishing war—not merely actual warfare, but also the state of war. The negative voices on this subject, found mainly in Section 14.1, regard war as inevitable and irremediable, given man as he is and societies as they are. Sometimes this is said with regret, as by Freud, and sometimes with acquiescence, as

by Hegel. Of an opposite tenor is the hope that emerges here from the recognition that, the ultimate cause of war being anarchy, the ultimate condition of peace is government. If local civil peace has been established here and there by local government, then perhaps there is some prospect for world civil peace through world government. The reader will find this insight presented and this hope weighed in passages drawn from Dante, Kant, *The Federalist,* and Tennyson; but in the absence of twentieth-century voices, the impact of the discussion is not as encouraging as it might be.

As already indicated, materials of relevance to the future of war and peace will be found in Section 14.1; and with regard to the role of government in the establishment of civil peace, turn to Section 10.3 on Gov-ernment: Its Nature, Necessity, and Forms.

---

1 Great peace have they which love thy law: and nothing shall offend them.

Psalm 119:165

2 When a man's ways please the Lord, he maketh even his enemies to be at peace with him.

Proverbs 16:7

3 [The Lord] shall judge among the nations, and shall rebuke many people: and they shall beat their swords into plowshares, and their spears into pruninghooks: nation shall not lift up sword against nation, neither shall they learn war any more.

Isaiah 2:4

4 The wolf . . . shall dwell with the lamb, and the leopard shall lie down with the kid; and the calf and the young lion and the fatling together; and a little child shall lead them.

Isaiah 11:6

5   *Trygaeus.* Think of all the thousand pleasures,
  Comrades, which to Peace we owe,
  All the life of ease and comfort
  Which she gave us long ago:
  Figs and olives, wine and myrtles,
  Luscious fruits preserved and dried,
  Banks of fragrant violets, blowing
  By the crystal fountain's side;

  Scenes for which our hearts are yearning,
  Joys that we have missed so long——
  —Comrades, here is Peace returning,
  Greet her back with dance and song!
Chorus. Welcome, welcome, best and dearest,
  welcome, welcome, welcome, home.
We have looked and longed for thee,
Looking, longing, wondrously,
Once again our farms to see.
O the joy, the bliss, the rapture, really to behold
  thee come.
Thou wast aye our chief enjoyment, thou wast aye
  our greatest gain.
  We who ply the farmer's trade
  Used, through thy benignant aid,
  All the joys of life to hold.
  Ah! the unbought pleasures free
  Which we erst received of thee
  In the merry days of old,
When thou wast our one salvation and our roast-
  ed barley grain.
  Now will all the tiny shoots,
  Sunny vine and fig-tree sweet,
  All the happy flowers and fruits,
  Laugh for joy thy steps to greet.

Aristophanes, *Peace,* 571

6 *Lacedaemonian envoys.* If great enmities are ever to be really settled, we think it will be, not by the system of revenge and military success, and by

forcing an opponent to swear to a treaty to his disadvantage, but when the more fortunate combatant waives these his privileges, to be guided by gentler feelings, conquers his rival in generosity, and accords peace on more moderate conditions than he expected. From that moment, instead of the debt of revenge which violence must entail, his adversary owes a debt of generosity to be paid in kind, and is inclined by honour to stand to his agreement. And men oftener act in this manner towards their greatest enemies than where the quarrel is of less importance; they are also by nature as glad to give way to those who first yield to them, as they are apt to be provoked by arrogance to risks condemned by their own judgment.

Thucydides, *Peloponnesian War,* IV, 19

7 *Hermocrates.* In the face of the universal consent that peace is the first of blessings, how can we refuse to make it amongst ourselves; or do you not think that the good which you have, and the ills that you complain of, would be better preserved and cured by quiet than by war; that peace has its honours and splendours of a less perilous kind, not to mention the numerous other blessings that one might dilate on, with the not less numerous miseries of war?

Thucydides, *Peloponnesian War,* IV, 62

8 *Athenian Stranger.* No one can be a true statesman, whether he aims at the happiness of the individual or state, who looks only, or first of all, to external warfare; nor will he ever be a sound legislator who orders peace for the sake of war, and not war for the sake of peace.

Plato, *Laws,* I, 628B

9 Facts, as well as arguments, prove that the legislator should direct all his military and other measures to the provision of leisure and the establishment of peace. For most of these military states are safe only while they are at war, but fall when they have acquired their empire; like unused iron they lose their temper in time of peace. And for this the legislator is to blame, he never having taught them how to lead the life of peace.

Aristotle, *Politics,* 1334a3

10 An unjust peace is better than a just war.

Cicero, *Ad Atticum,* VII, 14

11 The only excuse for going to war is to be able to live in peace undisturbed. When victory is won we should spare those who have not been bloodthirsty or barbarous in their warfare.

Cicero, *De Officiis,* I, 11

12   Rome, 't is thine alone, with awful sway,
To rule mankind, and make the world obey,
Disposing peace and war by thy own majestic way;

To tame the proud, the fetter'd slave to free:
These are imperial arts, and worthy thee.

Virgil, *Aeneid,* VI

13 There is no employment that gives so keen and quick a relish for peace as husbandry and a country life, which leave in men all that kind of courage that makes them ready to fight in defence of their own, while it destroys the licence that breaks out into acts of injustice and rapacity.

Plutarch, *Numa Pompilius*

14 Janus, whether in remote antiquity he were a demigod or a king, was certainly a great lover of civil and social unity, and one who reclaimed men from brutal and savage living; for which reason they figure him with two faces, to represent the two states and conditions out of the one of which he brought mankind, to lead them into the other. His temple at Rome has two gates, which they call the gates of war, because they stand open in the time of war, and shut in the times of peace; of which latter there was very seldom an example, for, as the Roman empire was enlarged and extended, it was so encompassed with barbarous nations and enemies to be resisted, that it was seldom or never at peace. Only in the time of Augustus Cæsar, after he had overcome Antony, this temple was shut; as likewise once before, when Marcus Atilius and Titus Manlius were consuls; but then it was not long before, wars breaking out, the gates were again opened.

But, during the reign of Numa, those gates were never seen open a single day, but continued constantly shut for a space of forty-three years together; such an entire and universal cessation of war existed. For not only had the people of Rome itself been softened and charmed into a peaceful temper by the just and mild rule of a pacific prince, but even the neighbouring cities, as if some salubrious and gentle air had blown from Rome upon them, began to experience a change of feeling, and partook in the general longing for the sweets of peace and order, and for life employed in the quiet tillage of soil, bringing up of children, and worship of the gods. Festival days and sports, and the secure and peaceful interchange of friendly visits and hospitalities prevailed all through the whole of Italy.

Plutarch, *Numa Pompilius*

15 To robbery, slaughter, plunder, they [the Romans] give the lying name of empire; they make a desolation and call it peace.

Tacitus, *Agricola*

16 [The earthly city] desires earthly peace for the sake of enjoying earthly goods, and it makes war in order to attain to this peace; since, if it has conquered, and there remains no one to resist it, it enjoys a peace which it had not while there were

opposing parties who contested for the enjoyment of those things which were too small to satisfy both. This peace is purchased by toilsome wars; it is obtained by what they style a glorious victory. Now, when victory remains with the party which had the juster cause, who hesitates to congratulate the victor, and style it a desirable peace? These things, then, are good things, and without doubt the gifts of God. But if they neglect the better things of the heavenly city, which are secured by eternal victory and peace never-ending, and so inordinately covet these present good things that they believe them to be the only desirable things, or love them better than those things which are believed to be better—if this be so, then it is necessary that misery follow and ever increase.

Augustine, *City of God*, XV, 4

17 Peace is a good so great, that even in this earthly and mortal life there is no word we hear with such pleasure, nothing we desire with such zest, or find to be more thoroughly gratifying.

Augustine, *City of God*, XIX, 11

18 It is . . . with the desire for peace that wars are waged, even by those who take pleasure in exercising their warlike nature in command and battle. And hence it is obvious that peace is the end sought for by war. For every man seeks peace by waging war, but no man seeks war by making peace. For even they who intentionally interrupt the peace in which they are living have no hatred of peace, but only wish it changed into a peace that suits them better. They do not, therefore, wish to have no peace, but only one more to their mind.

Augustine, *City of God*, XIX, 12

19 Even wicked men wage war to maintain the peace of their own circle, and wish that, if possible, all men belonged to them, that all men and things might serve but one head, and might, either through love or fear, yield themselves to peace with him!

Augustine, *City of God*, XIX, 12

20 Peace between man and man is well-ordered concord. Domestic peace is the well-ordered concord between those of the family who rule and those who obey. Civil peace is a similar concord among the citizens. The peace of the celestial city is the perfectly ordered and harmonious enjoyment of God, and of one another in God. The peace of all things is the tranquillity of order.

Augustine, *City of God*, XIX, 13

21 If one man concord with another, not by a spontaneous will but through being forced, as it were, by the fear of some evil that threatens him, such concord is not really peace, because the order of each concordant is not observed, but is disturbed by some fear-inspiring cause.

Aquinas, *Summa Theologica*, II–II, 29, 1

22 Even those who seek war and dissension desire nothing but peace, which they do not consider themselves to have. For . . . there is no peace when a man agrees with another man counter to what he would prefer. Consequently men seek by means of war to break this concord, because it is a defective peace, in order that they may obtain a peace in which nothing is contrary to their will. Hence all wars are waged that men may find a more perfect peace than that which they had before.

Aquinas, *Summa Theologica*, II–II, 29, 2

23 Peace is the work of justice indirectly, in so far as justice removes the obstacles to peace; but it is the work of charity directly, since charity, according to its very notion, causes peace.

Aquinas, *Summa Theologica*, II–II, 29, 3

24 The proper work of mankind taken as a whole is to exercise continually its entire capacity for intellectual growth, first, in theoretical matters, and, secondarily, as an extension of theory in practice. And since the part is a sample of the whole, and since individual men find that they grow in prudence and wisdom when they can sit quietly, it is evident that mankind, too, is most free and easy to carry on its work when it enjoys the quiet and tranquillity of peace.

Dante, *De Monarchia*, I, 4

25 Wherever there can be contention, there judgment should exist; otherwise things would exist imperfectly, without their own means of adjustment or correction, which is impossible, since in things necessary, God or Nature is not defective. Between any two governments, neither of which is in any way subordinate to the other, contention can arise either through their own fault or that of their subjects. This is evident. Therefore there should be judication between them. And since neither can know the affairs of the other, not being subordinated (for among equals there is no authority), there must be a third and wider power which can rule both within its own jurisdiction. This third power is either the world-government or it is not. If it is, we have reached our conclusion; if it is not, it must in turn have its equal outside its jurisdiction, and then it will need a third party as judge, and so *ad infinitum*, which is impossible. So we must arrive at a first and supreme judge for whom all contentions are judiciable either directly or indirectly; and this will be our world-governor or emperor. Therefore, world-government is necessary for the world.

Dante, *De Monarchia*, I, 10

26 World government . . . must be understood in

the sense that it governs mankind on the basis of what all have in common and that by a common law it leads all toward peace. This common norm or law should be received by local governments in the same way that practical intelligence in action receives its major premises from the speculative intellect. To these it adds its own particular minor premises and then draws particular conclusions for the sake of its action. These basic norms not only can come from a single source, but must do so in order to avoid confusion among universal principles. Moses himself followed this pattern in the law which he composed, for, having chosen the chiefs of the several tribes, he left them the lesser judgments, reserving to himself alone the higher and more general. These common norms were then used by the tribal chiefs according to their special needs. Therefore, it is better for mankind to be governed by one, not by many; and hence by a single governor, the world ruler; and if it is better, it is pleasing to God, since He always wills the better. And when there are only two alternatives—the better is also the best, and is consequently not only pleasing to God, but the choice of "one" rather than "many" is what most pleases Him. Hence it follows that mankind lives best under a single government, and therefore that such a government is necessary for the well-being of the world.

Dante, *De Monarchia,* I, 14

27 The reins of man are held by a double driver according to man's twofold end; one is the supreme pontiff, who guides mankind with revelations to life eternal, and the other is the emperor, who guides mankind with philosophical instructions to temporal happiness. And since none or very few (and these with difficulty) can reach this goal, unless a free mankind enjoys the tranquility of peace and the waves of distracting greed are stilled, this must be the constant aim of him who guides the globe and whom we call Roman Prince, in order that on this threshing floor of life mortals may exist free and in peace.

Dante, *De Monarchia,* III, 16

28 Let none presume to tell me that the Pen is preferable to the Sword; for be they who they will, I shall tell them they know not what they say: For the Reason they give, and on which chiefly they rely, is, that the Labour of the Mind exceeds that of the Body, and that the Exercise of Arms depends only the Body, as if the use of them were the Business of Porters, which requires nothing but much Strength. Or, as if This, which we who profess it call Chivalry, did not include the Acts of Fortitude, which depend very much upon the Understanding. Or else, as if that Warriour, who commands an Army or defends a City besieg'd, did not labour as much with the Mind as with the Body. If this be not so, let Experience teach us

whether it be possible by bodily Strength to discover or guess the Intentions of an Enemy. The forming Designs, laying of Stratagems, overcoming of Difficulties, and shunning of Dangers, are all Works of the Understanding, wherein the Body has no Share. It being therefore evident, that the Exercise of Arms requires the Help of the Mind as well as Learning, let us see in the next place, whether the Scholar or the Soldier's Mind undergoes the greatest Labour. Now this may be the better known, by regarding the End and Object each of them aims at; for that Intention is to be most valued, which makes the noblest End its Object. The Scope and End of Learning, I mean, human Learning (in this Place I speak not of Divinity, whose aim is to guide Souls to Heaven, for no other can equal a Design so infinite as that) Is to give a Perfection to distributive Justice, bestowing upon every one his due, and to procure and cause good Laws to be observ'd; an End really Generous, Great, and worthy of high Commendation; but yet not equal to that which Knight-Errantry tends to, whose Object and End is Peace, which is the greatest Blessing Man can wish for in this Life. And therefore the first good News the World receiv'd, was that the Angels brought in the Night, which was the Beginning of our Day, when they sang in the Air, Glory to God on high, Peace upon Earth, and to Men Good-will. And the only manner of Salutation taught by the best Master in Heaven, or upon Earth, to his Friends and Favourites, was, that entring any House they should say, Peace be to this House. And at other times he said to them, My Peace I give to you, My Peace I leave to you, Peace be among you. A Jewel and Legacy worthy of such a Donor, a Jewel so precious, that without it there can be no Happiness either in Earth or Heaven. This Peace is the true End of War; for Arms and War are one and the same thing.

Cervantes, *Don Quixote,* I, 37

29 In the very heat of war the greatest security and expectation of divine support must be in the unabated desire, and invariable prospect of peace, as the only end for which hostilities can be lawfully begun. So that in the prosecution of war we must never carry the rage of it so far, as to unlearn the nature and dispositions of men.

Grotius, *Rights of War and Peace,* Bk. III, XXV, 2

30 How rightly do we distinguish men by external appearances rather than by internal qualities! Which of us two shall have precedence? Who will give place to the other? The least clever. But I am as clever as he. We should have to fight over this. He has four lackeys, and I have only one. This can be seen; we have only to count. It falls to me to yield, and I am a fool if I contest the matter. By

this means we are at peace, which is the greatest of boons.

Pascal, *Pensées*, V, 319

31 No War, or Battails sound
Was heard the World around,
   The idle spear and shield were high up hung;
The hooked Chariot stood
Unstain'd with hostile blood,
   The Trumpet spake not to the armed throng,
And Kings sate still with awfull eye,
As if they surely knew their sovran Lord was by.

Milton, *On the Morning of Christs Nativity*, 53

32   Peace hath her victories
   No less renownd then warr, new foes aries
Threatning to bind our soules with secular
      chaines:
   Helpe us to save free Conscience from the paw
   Of hireling wolves whose Gospell is their maw.

Milton, *To the Lord Generall
Cromwell May 1652*

33 The more commonwealths there are, that have contracted a joint treaty of peace, the less each of them by itself is an object of fear to the remainder, or the less it has the authority to make war. But it is so much the more bound to observe the conditions of peace; that is, the less independent, and the more bound to accommodate itself to the general will of the contracting parties.

Spinoza, *Political Treatise*, III, 16

34 If the innocent honest man must quietly quit all he has for peace sake to him who will lay violent hands upon it, I desire it may be considered what kind of a peace there will be in the world which consists only in violence and rapine, and which is to be maintained only for the benefit of robbers and oppressors. Who would not think it an admirable peace betwixt the mighty and the mean, when the lamb, without resistance, yielded his throat to be torn by the imperious wolf?

Locke, *II Civil Government*, XIX, 228

35 I should have wished to choose myself a country, diverted, by a fortunate impotence, from the brutal love of conquest, and secured, by a still more fortunate situation, from the fear of becoming itself the conquest of other States: a free city situated between several nations, none of which should have any interest in attacking it, while each had an interest in preventing it from being attacked by the others; in short, a Republic which should have nothing to tempt the ambition of its neighbours, but might reasonably depend on their assistance in case of need. It follows that a republican State so happily situated could have nothing to fear but from itself; and that, if its members trained themselves to the use of arms, it would be rather to keep alive that military ardour and cou-

rageous spirit which are so proper among freemen, and tend to keep up their taste for liberty, than from the necessity of providing for their defence.

Rousseau, *Origin of Inequality*, Dedication

36 *Johnson.* It is thus that mutual cowardice keeps us in peace. Were one half of mankind brave, and one half cowards, the brave would be always beating the cowards. Were all brave, they would lead a very uneasy life; all would be continually fighting: but being all cowards, we go on very well.

Boswell, *Life of Johnson* (Apr. 28, 1778)

37 Hereafter, perhaps, . . . the inhabitants of all the different quarters of the world may arrive at that equality of courage and force which, by inspiring mutual fear, can alone overawe the injustice of independent nations into some sort of respect for the rights of one another. But nothing seems more likely to establish this equality of force than that mutual communication of knowledge and of all sorts of improvements which an extensive commerce from all countries to all countries naturally, or rather necessarily, carries along with it.

Adam Smith, *Wealth of Nations*, IV, 7

38 The . . . daring [Roman General] Probus pursued his Gallic victories, passed the Rhine, and displayed his invincible eagles on the banks of the Elbe and the Neckar. He was fully convinced that nothing could reconcile the minds of the barbarians to peace, unless they experienced in their own country the calamities of war.

Gibbon, *Decline and Fall
of the Roman Empire*, XII

39 The natural state of nations as well as of individual men is a state which it is a duty to pass out of, in order to enter into a legal state. Hence, before this transition occurs, all the right of nations and all the external property of states acquirable or maintainable by war are merely provisory; and they can only become peremptory in a universal union of states analogous to that by which a nation becomes a state. It is thus only that a real state of peace could be established. But with the too great extension of such a union of states over vast regions, any government of it, and consequently the protection of its individual members, must at last become impossible; and thus a multitude of such corporations would again bring round a state of war. Hence the perpetual peace, which is the ultimate end of all the right of nations, becomes in fact an impracticable idea. The political principles, however, which aim at such an end, and which enjoin the formation of such unions among the states as may promote a continuous approximation to a perpetual peace, are not impracticable; they are as practicable as this approximation itself, which is a practical problem

involving a duty, and founded upon the right of individual men and states.

Kant, *Science of Right*, 61

40 The morally practical reason utters within us its irrevocable veto: *There shall be no war.* So there ought to be no war, neither between me and you in the condition of nature, nor between us as members of states which, although internally in a condition of law, are still externally in their relation to each other in a condition of lawlessness; for this is not the way by which any one should prosecute his right. Hence the question no longer is as to whether perpetual peace is a real thing or not a real thing, or as to whether we may not be deceiving ourselves when we adopt the former alternative, but we must *act* on the supposition of its being real. We must work for what may perhaps not be realized, and establish that constitution which yet seems best adapted to bring it about (mayhap republicanism in all states, together and separately). And thus we may put an end to the evil of wars, which have been the chief interest of the internal arrangements of all the states without exception. And although the realization of this purpose may always remain but a pious wish, yet we do certainly not deceive ourselves in adopting the maxim of action that will guide us in working incessantly for it; for it is a duty to do this. To suppose that the moral law within us is itself deceptive, would be sufficient to excite the horrible wish rather to be deprived of all reason than to live under such deception, and even to see oneself, according to such principles, degraded like the lower animals to the level of the mechanical play of nature.

Kant, *Science of Right*, Conclusion

41 Confidence in the principles of an enemy must remain even during war, otherwise a peace could never be concluded; and hostilities would degenerate into a war of extermination since war in fact is but the sad resource employed in a state of nature in defence of rights; force standing there in lieu of juridical tribunals. Neither of the two parties can be accused of injustice, since for that purpose a juridical decision would be necessary. But here the event of a battle (as formerly the *judgments of God*) determine the justice of either party; since between states there cannot be a war of punishment no subordination existing between them. A war, therefore, which might cause the destruction of both parties at once, together with the annihilation of every right, would permit the conclusion of a perpetual peace only upon the vast burial-ground of the human species.

Kant, *Perpetual Peace*, Section I, 6

42 With men, the state of nature is not a state of peace, but of war; though not of open war, at least, ever ready to break out. A state of peace must therefore be established; for, in order to be sheltered against every act of hostility, it is not sufficient that none is committed; one neighbour must guarantee to another his personal security, which cannot take place except in a state of legislation; without which one may treat another as an enemy, after having in vain demanded this protection.

Kant, *Perpetual Peace*, Section II, Intro.

43 If it is a duty, if the hope can even be conceived, of realizing, though by an endless progress, the reign of public right—perpetual peace, which will succeed to the suspensions of hostilities, hitherto named treaties of peace, is not then a chimera, but a problem, of which time, probably abridged by the uniformity of the progress of the human mind, promises us the solution.

Kant, *Perpetual Peace*, Appendix, 2

44 In cases where it may be doubtful on which side justice lies, what better umpires could be desired by two violent factions, flying to arms and tearing a State to pieces, than the representatives of confederate States not heated by the local flame? To the impartiality of judges they would unite the affection of friends. Happy would it be if such a remedy for its infirmities could be enjoyed by all free governments; if a project equally effectual could be established for the universal peace of mankind!

Madison, *Federalist 43*

45 War is on its last legs; and a universal peace is as sure as is the prevalence of civilization over barbarism, of liberal governments over feudal forms. The question for us is only How soon?

Emerson, *War*

46   The war-drum throbb'd no longer, and the battle-flags were furl'd
In the Parliament of man, the Federation of the world.

There the common sense of most shall hold a fretful realm in awe.
And the kindly earth shall slumber, lapt in universal law.

Tennyson, *Locksley Hall*, 127

47 I devoutly believe in the reign of peace and in the gradual advent of some sort of a socialistic equilibrium. The fatalistic view of the war-function is to me nonsense, for I know that war-making is due to definite motives and subject to prudential checks and reasonable criticisms, just like any other form of enterprise. And when whole nations are the armies, and the science of destruction vies in intellectual refinement with the sciences of pro-

duction, I see that war becomes absurd and impossible from its own monstrosity. Extravagant ambitions will have to be replaced by reasonable claims, and nations must make common cause against them. I see no reason why all this should not apply to yellow as well as to white countries, and I look forward to a future when acts of war shall be formally outlawed as between civilize peoples.

William James, *Moral Equivalent of War*

48 The only way to abolish war [is] to make peace heroic.

Dewey, *Human Nature and Conduct*, II, 3

Chapter 15

HISTORY

Chapter 15 is divided into three sections: 15.1 History: The Record of Events, 15.2 Progress, Regress, and Cycles in History, and 15.3 Fate, Fortune, and Destiny.

Two meanings of the word "history" separate the texts that we have placed in Section 15.1 and in Section 15.2. On the one hand, we use the word to refer to an intellectual discipline, a field of research and of scholarship, and a type of literature. Thus understood, history is a subject taught and studied; histories are books of a certain sort, having a distinctive subject matter and style; and history is a kind of knowledge to be contrasted with science and philosophy. On the other hand, history consists of what has in fact happened; anything that has a development through a span of time or involves a sequence of events, has a history. In both meanings of the term, history involves a reference to the past and a location of events in time; and it usually involves the ordering of events in a temporal sequence.

In Section 15.1, we have placed passages that discuss the task of the historian as a student of the past and as a writer about it, and that deal with history as an intellectual discipline and as a form of literature. The quotations that we have placed in Section 15.2 express reflections about the course of history—the patterns of change that men think they have discovered in the temporal sequence of events. This leaves for Section 15.3 a third group of texts in which writers speculate about the forces, factors, or agencies that govern the course of history and wonder about the role of human freedom in determining the direction that history takes.

15.1 | *History: The Record of Events*

Among the passages included here are quotations from eminent historians—Herodotus and Thucydides, Plutarch and Tacitus, Hume, Gibbon, and Toynbee—in which they reflect about the art of writing history and about the task of the historian as a reporter and interpreter of the past. They are concerned with the credibility of the stories they tell, with the reliability of the evidence they advance for the interpretations they give, with the significance of the past for the present, and with the utility of studying history. Just as the histories they have written differ in style, so they differ in their accounts of the method or approach deemed proper for the historian.

Included also are quotations from philosophers and others who have thought about the character of history as an intellectual discipline and as a distinct branch of human knowledge. In certain respects, history is said to be more like science than like poetry, at least in the kind of truth it claims to have;

but in other respects, it is said to be more like poetry, not only in its narrative form but also in its reflections on human life. In addition, there are passages that take opposite sides on the question whether biography is the core of history as the record of the influence that great men have had upon the course of events; and passages that express opposite views about whether the human race has ever learned anything from the study of history, or learned enough not to repeat the mistakes that have been made in the past.

Some of the quotations attempt to distinguish different kinds of history by reference to differences in subject matter, and a few propose the project of a universal history—world history or the history of the human race as a whole. There are passing comments here on the laws or factors that govern the course of history, but a fuller treatment of that subject is reserved for Section 15.3.

---

1 For myself, my duty is to report all that is said; but I am not obliged to believe it all alike—a remark which may be understood to apply to my whole History.

Herodotus, *History*, VII, 152

2 The way that most men deal with traditions, even traditions of their own country, is to receive them all alike as they are delivered, without applying any critical test whatever.

Thucydides, *Peloponnesian War*, I, 20

3 With reference to the speeches in this history, some were delivered before the war began, others while it was going on; some I heard myself, others I got from various quarters; it was in all cases difficult to carry them word for word in one's memory, so my habit has been to make the speakers say what was in my opinion demanded of them by the various occasions, of course adhering as closely as possible to the general sense of what

they really said. And with reference to the narrative of events, far from permitting myself to derive it from the first source that came to hand, I did not even trust my own impressions, but it rests partly on what I saw myself, partly on what others saw for me, the accuracy of the report being always tried by the most severe and detailed tests possible. My conclusions have cost me some labour from the want of coincidence between accounts of the same occurrences by different eyewitnesses, arising sometimes from imperfect memory, sometimes from undue partiality for one side or the other. The absence of romance in my history will, I fear, detract somewhat from its interest, but if it be judged useful by those inquirers who desire an exact knowledge of the past as an aid to the interpretation of the future, which in the course of human things must resemble if it does not reflect it, I shall be content. In fine, I have written my work, not as an essay which is to win the applause of the moment, but as a possession for all time.

Thucydides, *Peloponnesian War*, I, 22

4 *The Corinthians*. There is . . . no advantage in reflections on the past further than may be of service to the present.

Thucydides, *Peloponnesian War*, I, 123

5 *Socrates*. Because we do not know the truth about
ancient times, we make falsehood as much like
truth as we can, and so turn it to account.

Plato, *Republic*, II, 382B

6 A history has to deal not with one action, but with
one period and all that happened in that to one or
more persons, however disconnected the several
events may have been.

Aristotle, *Poetics*, 1459^{a}22

7 The study of history is in the truest sense an education and a training for political life. . . . The
most instructive, or rather the only, method of
learning to bear with dignity the vicissitudes of
fortune is to recall the catastrophes of others.

Polybius, *Histories*, I, 1

8 By far the greater number of historians concern
themselves with isolated wars and the incidents
that accompany them: while as to a general and
comprehensive scheme of events, their date, origin, and catastrophe, no one as far as I know has
undertaken to examine it. I thought it, therefore,
distinctly my duty neither to pass by myself, nor
allow any one else to pass by, without full study, a
characteristic specimen of the dealings of Fortune
at once brilliant and instructive in the highest degree.

Polybius, *Histories*, I, 4

9 Men, who are persuaded that they get a competent view of universal from episodical history, are
very like persons who should see the limbs of some
body, which had once been living and beautiful,
scattered and remote; and should imagine that to
be quite as good as actually beholding the activity
and beauty of the living creature itself.

Polybius, *Histories*, I, 4

10 If you take truth from history what is left is but an
idle unprofitable tale. Therefore, one must not
shrink either from blaming one's friends or praising one's enemies; nor be afraid of finding fault
with and commending the same persons at different times. For it is impossible that men engaged in
public affairs should always be right, and unlikely
that they should always be wrong. Holding ourselves, therefore, entirely aloof from the actors, we
must as historians make statements and pronounce judgment in accordance with the actions
themselves.

Polybius, *Histories*, I, 14

11 Surely an historian's object should not be to
amaze his readers by a series of thrilling anecdotes; nor should he aim at producing speeches
which *might* have been delivered, nor study dramatic propriety in details like a writer of tragedy:
but his function is above all to record with fidelity
what was actually said or done, however commonplace it may be. For the purposes of history
and of the drama are not the same, but widely
opposed to each other. In the latter the object is to
strike and delight by words as true to nature as
possible; in the former to instruct and convince by
genuine words and deeds.

Polybius, *Histories*, II, 56

12 To remain ignorant of things that happened before you were born is to remain a child. What is a
human life worth unless it is incorporated into the
lives of one's ancestors and set in an historical
context?

Cicero, *Orator*, XXXIV

13 The study of history is the best medicine for a sick
mind; for in history you have a record of the infinite variety of human experience plainly set out
for all to see; and in that record you can find for
yourself and your country both examples and
warnings: fine things to take as models, base
things, rotten through and through, to avoid.

Livy, *Early History of Rome*, I, 1

14 In this work of mine, in which I have compared
the lives of the greatest men with one another,
after passing through those periods which probable reasoning can reach to and real history find a
footing in, I might very well say of those that are
farther off: "Beyond this there is nothing but
prodigies and fictions, the only inhabitants are the
poets and inventors of fables; there is no credit, or
certainty any farther."

Plutarch, *Theseus*

15 So very difficult a matter is it to trace and find out
the truth of anything by history, when, on the one
hand, those who afterwards write it find long periods of time intercepting their view, and, on the
other hand, the contemporary records of any actions and lives, partly through envy and ill-will,
partly through favour and flattery, pervert and
distort truth.

Plutarch, *Pericles*

16 It was for the sake of others that I first commenced writing biographies; but I find myself
proceeding and attaching myself to it for my own;
the virtues of these great men serving me as a sort
of looking-glass, in which I may see how to adjust
and adorn my own life.

Plutarch, *Timoleon*

17 My method . . . is, by the study of history, and by

the familiarity acquired in writing, to habituate my memory to receive and retain images of the best and worthiest characters. I thus am enabled to free myself from any ignoble, base, or vicious impressions, contracted from the contagion of ill company that I may be unavoidably engaged in, by the remedy of turning my thoughts in a happy and calm temper to view these noble examples.

Plutarch, *Timoleon*

18 As we would wish that a painter who is to draw a beautiful face, in which there is yet some imperfection, should neither wholly leave out, nor yet too pointedly express what is defective, because this would deform it, and that spoil the resemblance; so since it is hard, or indeed perhaps impossible, to show the life of a man wholly free from blemish, in all that is excellent we must follow truth exactly, and give it fully; any lapses or faults that occur, through human passions or political necessities, we may regard rather as the shortcomings of some particular virtue, than as the natural effects of vice; and may be content without introducing them, curiously and officiously, into our narrative, if it be but out of tenderness to the weakness of nature, which has never succeeded in producing any human character so perfect in virtue as to be pure from all admixture and open to no criticism.

Plutarch, *Cimon*

19 Such things as are not commonly known, and lie scattered here and there in other men's writings, or are found amongst the old monuments and archives, I shall endeavour to bring together; not collecting mere useless pieces of learning, but adducing what may make his disposition and habit of mind understood.

Plutarch, *Nicias*

20 If any man undertake to write a history that has to be collected from materials gathered by observation and the reading of works not easy to be got in all places, nor written always in his own language, but many of them foreign and dispersed in other hands, for him, undoubtedly, it is in the first place and above all things most necessary to reside in some city of good note, addicted to liberal arts, and populous; where he may have plenty of all sorts of books, and upon inquiry may hear and inform himself of such particulars as, having escaped the pens of writers, are more faithfully preserved in the memories of men, lest his work be deficient in many things, even those which it can least dispense with.

Plutarch, *Demosthenes*

21 Are you so much better off, O writer of history?
Surely
You waste more time and more oil and thousands
of pages of paper

Costing a fortune: still, the laws of the craft are
demanding,
What with footnotes and research, cross references
and index.
But how does the harvest pay off? What profit in
all of this delving?
What historian gets as much as a clerk in a courtroom?

Juvenal, *Satire VII*

22 This I regard as history's highest function, to let no worthy action be uncommemorated, and to hold out the reprobation of posterity as a terror to evil words and deeds.

Tacitus, *Annals*, III, 65

23 Now, after a revolution, when Rome is nothing but the realm of a single despot, there must be good in carefully noting and recording this period, for it is but few who have the foresight to distinguish right from wrong or what is sound from what is hurtful, while most men learn wisdom from the fortunes of others. Still, though this is instructive, it gives very little pleasure. . . . I have to present in succession the merciless biddings of a tyrant, incessant prosecutions, faithless friendships, the ruin of innocence, the same causes issuing in the same results, and I am everywhere confronted by a wearisome monotony in my subject matter. Then, again, an ancient historian has but few disparagers, and no one cares whether you praise more heartily the armies of Carthage or Rome.

Tacitus, *Annals*, IV, 33

24 This is a fine saying of Plato: That he who is discoursing about men should look also at earthly things as if he viewed them from some higher place; should look at them in their assemblies, armies, agricultural labours, marriages, treaties, births, deaths, noise of the courts of justice, desert places, various nations of barbarians, feasts, lamentations, markets, a mixture of all things and an orderly combination of contraries.

Marcus Aurelius, *Meditations*, VII, 48

25 The historian's one task is to tell the thing as it happened. This he cannot do if he is Artaxerxes' physician, trembling before him, or hoping to get a purple cloak, a golden chain, a horse of the Nisaean breed in payment for his laudations. A fair historian, a Xenophon, a Thucydides, will not accept that position. He may nurse some private dislikes, but he will attach far more importance to the public good, and set the truth high above his hate; he may have his favorites, but he will not spare their errors. For history, I say again, has this and this only for its own; if a man will start upon it, he must sacrifice to no god but Truth; he must neglect all else; his sole rule and unerring guide is this—to think not of those who are listening to

him now, but of the yet unborn who shall seek his converse.

Lucian, *Way to Write History*

26 I sometimes fall to thinking whether it befits a theologian, a philosopher, and such people of exquisite and exact conscience and prudence, to write history. How can they stake their fidelity on the fidelity of an ordinary person? How be responsible for the thoughts of persons unknown and give their conjectures as coin of the realm? Of complicated actions that happen in their presence they would refuse to give testimony if placed under oath by a judge; and they know no man so intimately that they would undertake to answer fully for his intentions. I consider it less hazardous to write of things past than present, inasmuch as the writer has only to give an account of a borrowed truth.

Montaigne, *Essays*, I, 21, Power of the Imagination

27 I like historians who are either very simple or outstanding. The simple, who have not the wherewithal to mix in anything of their own, and who bring to it only the care and diligence to collect all that comes to their attention and to record everything faithfully without choice or discrimination, leave our judgment intact to discern the truth. . . .

The really outstanding ones have the capacity to choose what is worth knowing; they can pick out of two reports the one that is more likely. From the nature and humors of princes they infer their intentions and attribute appropriate words to them. They are right to assume the authority to regulate our belief by their own; but certainly this privilege belongs to very few people.

Those in between (which are the commonest sort) spoil everything for us. They want to chew our morsels for us; they give themselves the right to judge, and consequently to slant history to their fancy; for once the judgment leans to one side, one cannot help turning and twisting the narrative to that bias. They undertake to choose the things worth knowing, and often conceal from us a given word, a given private action, that would instruct us better; they omit as incredible the things they do not understand. . . . Let them boldly display their eloquence and their reasonings, let them judge all they like; but let them also leave us the wherewithal to judge after them, and not alter or arrange by their abridgments and selection anything of the substance of the matter, but pass it on to us pure and entire in all its dimensions.

Montaigne, *Essays*, II, 10, Of Books

28 The only good histories are those that have been written by the very men who were in command in the affairs, or who were participants in the conduct of them, or who at least have had the fortune to conduct others of the same sort. . . . What can you expect of a doctor discussing war, or a schoolboy discussing the intentions of princes?

Montaigne, *Essays*, II, 10, Of Books

29 We have not the thousandth part of the writings of the ancients: it is Fortune that gives them life, longer or shorter according to her favor; and it is permissible to wonder whether what we have is not the worst, since we have not seen the rest.

Montaigne, *Essays*, II, 16, Of Glory

30 *King.* O God! that one might read the book of fate,
And see the revolution of the times
Make mountains level, and the continent,
Weary of solid firmness, melt itself
Into the sea! and, other times, to see
The beachy girdle of the ocean
Too wide for Neptune's hips; how chances mock,
And changes fill the cup of alteration
With divers liquors! O, if this were seen,
The happiest youth, viewing his progress through,
What perils past, what crosses to ensue,
Would shut the book, and sit him down and die.

Shakespeare, *II Henry IV*, III, i, 45

31 As it happeneth sometimes that the grandchild, or other descendant, resembleth the ancestor more than the son; so many times occurrences of present times may sort better with ancient examples than with those of the later or immediate times.

Bacon, *Advancement of Learning*, Bk. I, II, 3

32 History is natural, civil, ecclesiastical, and literary; whereof the three first I allow as extant, the fourth I note as deficient. For no man hath propounded to himself the general state of learning to be described and represented from age to age, as many have done the works of nature, and the state civil and ecclesiastical; without which the history of the world seemeth to me to be as the statue of Polyphemus with his eye out; that part being wanting which doth most show the spirit and life of the person. And yet I am not ignorant that in divers particular sciences, as of the jurisconsults, the mathematicians, the rhetoricians, the philosophers, there are set down some small memorials of the schools, authors, and books; and so likewise some barren relations touching the invention of arts or usages. But a just story of learning, containing the antiquities and originals of knowledges and their sects, their inventions, their traditions, their diverse administrations and managings, their flourishings, their oppositions, decays, depressions, oblivions, removes, with the causes and occasions of them, and all other events concerning learning, throughout the ages of the world, I may truly affirm to be wanting. The use and end of which work I do not so much design

for curiosity or satisfaction of those that are the lovers of learning, but chiefly for a more serious and grave purpose, which is this in few words, that it will make learned men wise in the use and administration of learning.

Bacon, *Advancement of Learning*, Bk. II, I, 2

33 It is the true office of history to represent the events themselves together with the counsels, and to leave the observations and conclusions there-upon to the liberty and faculty of every man's judgement.

Bacon, *Advancement of Learning*, Bk. II, II, 12

34 It is good to know something of the customs of different peoples in order to judge more sanely of our own, and not to think that everything of a fashion not ours is absurd and contrary to reason, as do those who have seen nothing. But when one employs too much time in travelling, one becomes a stranger in one's own country, and when one is too curious about things which were practised in past centuries, one is usually very ignorant about those which are practised in our own time. Be-sides, fables make one imagine many events possi-ble which in reality are not so, and even the most accurate of histories, if they do not exactly mis-represent or exaggerate the value of things in or-der to render them more worthy of being read, at least omit in them all the circumstances which are basest and least notable; and from this fact it fol-lows that what is retained is not portrayed as it really is, and that those who regulate their con-duct by examples which they derive from such a source, are liable to fall into the extravagances of the knights-errant of Romance, and form projects beyond their power of performance.

Descartes, *Discourse on Method*, I

35 In a good history, the judgement must be emi-nent; because the goodness consisteth in the meth-od, in the truth, and in the choice of the actions that are most profitable to be known. Fancy has no place, but only in adorning the style.

Hobbes, *Leviathan*, I, 8

36 When testimonies contradict common experience, and the reports of history and witnesses clash with the ordinary course of nature, or with one anoth-er; there it is, where diligence, attention, and ex-actness are required, to form a right judgment, and to proportion the assent to the different evi-dence and probability of the thing: which rises and falls, according as those two foundations of credibility, viz. *common observation in like cases*, and *particular testimonies in that particular instance*, favour or contradict it.

Locke, *Concerning Human Understanding*, Bk. IV, XVI, 9

37 I would not be thought here to lessen the credit and use of history: it is all the light we have in many cases, and we receive from it a great part of the useful truths we have, with a convincing evi-dence. I think nothing more valuable than the records of antiquity: I wish we had more of them, and more uncorrupted. But this truth itself forces me to say, That no probability can rise higher than its first original. What has no other evidence than the single testimony of one only witness must stand or fall by his only testimony, whether good, bad, or indifferent; and though cited afterwards by hundreds of others, one after another, is so far from receiving any strength thereby, that it is only the weaker. Passion, interest, inadvertency, mis-take of his meaning, and a thousand odd reasons, or capricios, men's minds are acted by, (impossi-ble to be discovered,) may make one man quote another man's words or meaning wrong. He that has but ever so little examined the citations of writers, cannot but doubt how little credit the quota-tions deserve, where the originals are wanting; and consequently how much less quotations of quotations can be relied on. This is certain, that what in one age was affirmed upon slight grounds, can never after come to be more valid in future ages by being often repeated. But the further still it is from the original, the less valid it is, and has always less force in the mouth or writing of him that last made use of it than in his from whom he received it.

Locke, *Concerning Human Understanding*, Bk. IV, XVI, 11

38 Our new Science must . . . be a demonstration, so to speak, of the historical fact of providence, for it must be a history of the forms of order which, without human discernment or intent, and often against the designs of men, providence has given to this great city of the human race. For though this world has been created in time and particu-lar, the orders established therein by providence are universal and eternal.

Vico, *The New Science*, I

39 In monarchies extremely absolute, historians be-tray the truth, because they are not at liberty to speak it; in states remarkably free, they betray the truth, because of their liberty itself; which always produces divisions, every one becoming as great a slave to the prejudices of his faction as he could be in a despotic state.

Montesquieu, *Spirit of Laws*, XIX, 27

40 Mankind are so much the same, in all times and places, that history informs us of nothing new or strange in this particular. Its chief use is only to discover the constant and universal principles of human nature, by showing men in all varieties of circumstances and situations, and furnishing us with materials from which we may form our ob-servations and become acquainted with the regu-

lar springs of human action and behaviour. These records of wars, intrigues, factions, and revolutions, are so many collections of experiments, by which the politician or moral philosopher fixes the principles of his science, in the same manner as the physician or natural philosopher becomes acquainted with the nature of plants, minerals, and other external objects, by the experiments which he forms concerning them.

Hume, *Concerning Human Understanding,*
VIII, 65

41 In reality, what more agreeable entertainment to the mind, than to be transported into the remotest ages of the world, and to observe human society, in its infancy, making the first faint essays towards the arts and sciences; to see the policy of government, and the civility of conversation refining by degrees, and every thing which is ornamental to human life advancing toward its perfection? To remark the rise, progress, declension, and final extinction of the most flourishing empires; the virtues which contributed to their greatness, and the vices which drew on their ruin? In short, to see all the human race, from the beginning of time, pass, as it were, in review before us, appearing in their true colours, without any of those disguises which, during their lifetime, so much perplexed the judgment of the beholders. What spectacle can be imagined so magnificent, so various, so interesting? What amusement, either of the senses or imagination, can be compared with it?

Hume, *Of the Study of History*

42 History is not only a valuable part of knowledge, but opens the door to many other parts, and affords materials to most of the sciences. And, indeed, if we consider the shortness of human life, and our limited knowledge, even of what passes in our own time, we must be sensible that we should be forever children in understanding, were it not for this invention, which extends our experience to all past ages, and to the most distant nations; making them contribute as much to our improvement in wisdom, as if they had actually lain under our observation. A man acquainted with history may, in some respect, be said to have lived from the beginning of the world, and to have been making continual additions to his stock of knowledge in every century.

Hume, *Of the Study of History*

43 Historians have been, almost without exception, the true friends of virtue, and have always represented it in its proper colours, however they may have erred in their judgments of particular persons.

Hume, *Of the Study of History*

44 The first foundations of all history are the recitals of the fathers to the children, transmitted af-

terward from one generation to another; at their origin they are at the very most probable, when they do not shock common sense, and they lose one degree of probability in each generation. With time the fable grows and the truth grows less; from this it comes that all the origins of peoples are absurd.

Voltaire, *Philosophical Dictionary:*
History

45 Let us judge of what can be done by what has been done.

Rousseau, *Social Contract*, III, 12

46 What are all the records of history but narratives of successive villainies, of treasons and usurpations, massacres and wars?

Johnson, *Rambler No. 175*

47 *Johnson.* Great abilities are not requisite for an historian; for in historical composition, all the greatest powers of the human mind are quiescent. He has facts ready to his hand; so there is no exercise of invention. Imagination is not required in any high degree; only about as much as is used in the lower kinds of poetry. Some penetration, accuracy, and colouring will fit a man for the task, if he can give the application which is necessary.

Boswell, *Life of Johnson (July 6, 1763)*

48 *Johnson.* We must consider how very little history there is; I mean real authentick history. That certain Kings reigned, and certain battles were fought, we can depend upon as true; but all the colouring, all the philosophy of history is conjecture.

Boswell, *Life of Johnson (Apr. 18, 1775)*

49 Antoninus diffused order and tranquillity over the greatest part of the earth. His reign is marked by the rare advantage of furnishing very few materials for history; which is, indeed, little more than the register of the crimes, follies, and misfortunes of mankind.

Gibbon, *Decline and Fall of the Roman*
Empire, III

50 There is not anywhere upon the globe a large tract of country which we have discovered destitute of inhabitants, or whose first population can be fixed with any degree of historical certainty. And yet, as the most philosophic minds can seldom refrain from investigating the infancy of great nations, our curiosity consumes itself in toilsome and disappointed efforts.

Gibbon, *Decline and Fall of the Roman*
Empire, IX

51 The confusion of the times, and the scarcity of authentic memorials, oppose equal difficulties to the historian, who attempts to preserve a clear

and unbroken thread of narration. Surrounded with imperfect fragments, always concise, often obscure, and sometimes contradictory, he is reduced to collect, to compare, and to conjecture: and though he ought never to place his conjectures in the rank of facts, yet the knowledge of human nature, and of the sure operation of its fierce and unrestrained passions, might, on some occasions, supply the want of historical materials.

Gibbon, *Decline and Fall of the Roman Empire,* X

52 A being of the nature of man, endowed with the same faculties, but with a longer measure of existence, would cast down a smile of pity and contempt on the crimes and follies of human ambition, so eager, in a narrow span, to grasp at a precarious and short-lived enjoyment. It is thus that the experience of history exalts and enlarges the horizon of our intellectual view. In a composition of some days, in a perusal of some hours, six hundred years have rolled away, and the duration of a life or reign is contracted to a fleeting moment: the grave is ever beside the throne; the success of a criminal is almost instantly followed by the loss of his prize.

Gibbon, *Decline and Fall of the Roman Empire,* XLVIII

53 The Greeks of Constantinople, after purging away the impurities of their vulgar speech, acquired the free use of their ancient language, the most happy composition of human art, and a familiar knowledge of the sublime masters who had pleased or instructed the first of nations. But these advantages only tend to aggravate the reproach and shame of a degenerate people. They held in their lifeless hands the riches of their fathers, without inheriting the spirit which had created and improved that sacred patrimony: they read, they praised, they compiled, but their languid souls seemed alike incapable of thought and action. In the revolution of ten centuries, not a single discovery was made to exalt the dignity or promote the happiness of mankind. Not a single idea has been added to the speculative systems of antiquity, and a succession of patient disciples became in their turn the dogmatic teachers of the next servile generation.

Gibbon, *Decline and Fall of the Roman Empire,* LIII

54 It was at Rome, on the 15th of October, 1764, as I sat musing amidst the ruins of the Capitol, while the barefoot friars were singing vespers in the Temple of Jupiter, that the idea of writing the decline and fall of the city first started to my mind.

Gibbon, *Autobiography*

55 I have presumed to mark the moment of conception: I shall now commemorate the hour of my final deliverance. It was on the day, or rather night, of the 27th of June 1787, between the hours of eleven and twelve, that I wrote the last lines of the last page, in a summer-house in my garden. After laying down my pen I took several turns in a *berceau,* or covered walk of acacias, which commands a prospect of the country, the lake, and the mountains. The air was temperate, the sky was serene, the silver orb of the moon was reflected from the waters, and all nature was silent. I will not dissemble the first emotions of joy on recovery of my freedom, and, perhaps, the establishment of my fame. But my pride was soon humbled, and a sober melancholy was spread over my mind, by the idea that I had taken an everlasting leave of an old and agreeable companion, and that, whatsoever might be the future date of my *History,* the life of the historian must be short and precarious.

Gibbon, *Autobiography*

56 My English text is chaste, and all licentious passages are left in the decent obscurity of a learned language.

Gibbon, *Autobiography*

57 Men, viewed as a whole, are not guided in their efforts merely by instinct, like the lower animals; nor do they proceed in their actions, like the citizens of a purely rational world, according to a preconcerted plan. And so it appears as if no regular systematic history of mankind would be possible, as in the case, for instance, of bees and beavers. Nor can one help feeling a certain repugnance in looking at the conduct of men as it is exhibited on the great stage of the world. With glimpses of wisdom appearing in individuals here and there, it seems, on examining it externally as if the whole web of human history were woven out of folly and childish vanity and the frenzy of destruction, so that at the end one hardly knows what idea to form of our race, albeit so proud of its prerogatives.

Kant, *Idea of a Universal History,* Intro.

58 A philosophical attempt to work out the universal history of the world according to the plan of nature in its aiming at a perfect civil union must be regarded as possible, and as even capable of helping forward the purpose of nature.

Kant, *Idea of a Universal History,* IX

59 How admirably calculated is this picture of the human race, freed from all these chains, secure from the domination of chance, as from that of the enemies of its progress, and advancing with firm and sure steps towards the attainment of truth, virtue, and happiness, to present to the philosopher a spectacle which shall console him for the errors, the crimes, the injustice, with which the earth is still polluted, and whose victim he

often is! It is in the contemplation of this picture that he receives the reward of his efforts towards the progress of reason and the defense of liberty. He dares then to link these with the eternal chain of human destiny; and thereby he finds virtue's true recompense, the joy of having performed a lasting service, which no fatality can ever destroy by restoring the evils of prejudice and slavery. This contemplation is for him a place of refuge, whither the memory of his persecutors cannot follow him, where, living in imagination with man restored to his rights and his natural dignity, he forgets him whom greed, fear, or envy torment and corrupt; there it is that he exists in truth with his kin, in an elysium which his reason has been able to create for him, and which his love for humanity enhances with the purest enjoyments.

Condorcet, *Historical Picture of the Progress of the Human Mind,* 10

60 Original historians . . . change the events, the deeds, and the states of society with which they are conversant, into an object for the conceptive faculty.

Hegel, *Philosophy of History,* Introduction, 1

61 A history which aspires to traverse long periods of time, or to be universal, must . . . forego the attempt to give individual representations of the past as it actually existed. It must foreshorten its pictures by abstractions; and this includes not merely the omission of events and deeds, but whatever is involved in the fact that thought is, after all, the most trenchant epitomist. A battle, a great victory, a siege, no longer maintains its original proportions, but is put off with a bare mention.

Hegel, *Philosophy of History,* Introduction, 2

62 What experience and history teach is this—that peoples and governments never have learned anything from history, or acted on principles deduced from it.

Hegel, *Philosophy of History,* Introduction, 2

63 The history of the world begins with its general aim, the realization of the idea of spirit, only in an *implicit* form, that is, as nature; a hidden, most profoundly hidden, unconscious instinct; and the whole process of history (as already observed) is directed to rendering this unconscious impulse a conscious one. Thus appearing in the form of merely natural existence, natural will—that which has been called the subjective side—physical craving, instinct, passion, private interest, as also opinion and subjective conception—spontaneously present themselves at the very commencement. This vast congeries of volitions, interests and activities, constitute the instruments and means of the world-spirit for attaining its object; bringing it to consciousness, and realizing it. And

this aim is none other than finding itself, coming to itself, and contemplating itself in concrete actuality. But that those manifestations of vitality on the part of individuals and peoples, in which they seek and satisfy their own purposes, are, at the same time, the means and instruments of a higher and broader purpose of which they know nothing—which they realize unconsciously—might be made a matter of question; rather has been questioned, and in every variety of form negatived, decried and contemned as mere dreaming and "philosophy." But on this point I announced my view at the very outset, and asserted our hypothesis—which, however, will appear in the sequel, in the form of a legitimate inference—and our belief that reason governs the world, and has consequently governed its history. In relation to this independently universal and substantial existence—all else is subordinate, subservient to it, and the means for its development.

Hegel, *Philosophy of History,* Introduction, 3

64 Light is a simply self-involved existence; but though possessing thus in itself universality, it exists at the same time as an individuality in the sun. Imagination has often pictured to itself the emotions of a blind man suddenly becoming possessed of sight, beholding the bright glimmering of the dawn, the growing light, and the flaming glory of the ascending sun. The boundless forgetfulness of his individuality in this pure splendor, is his first feeling—utter astonishment. But when the sun is risen, this astonishment is diminished; objects around are perceived, and from them the individual proceeds to the contemplation of his own inner being, and thereby the advance is made to the perception of the relation between the two. Then inactive contemplation is quitted for activity; by the close of day man has erected a building constructed from his own inner sun; and when in the evening he contemplates this, he esteems it more highly than the original external sun. For now he stands in a *conscious relation* to his spirit, and therefore a *free* relation. If we hold this image fast in mind, we shall find it symbolizing the course of history, the great day's work of spirit.

Hegel, *Philosophy of History,* Intro.

65 History, which I like to think of as the contrary of poetry [*historoumenon* (investigated)—*pepoiemenon* (invented)], is for time what geography is for space; and it is no more to be called a science, in any strict sense of the word, than is geography, because it does not deal with universal truths but only with particular details. History has always been the favorite study of those who wish to learn something without having to face the effort demanded by any branch of real knowledge, which taxes the intelligence.

Schopenhauer, *Some Forms of Literature*

66 The preference shown for history by the greater public in all ages may be illustrated by the kind of conversation which is so much in vogue everywhere in society. It generally consists in one person relating something and then another person relating something else; so that in this way everyone is sure of receiving attention. Both here and in the case of history it is plain that the mind is occupied with particular details. But as in science, so also in every worthy conversation, the mind rises to the consideration of some general truth.

This objection does not, however, deprive history of its value. Human life is short and fleeting, and many millions of individuals share in it, who are swallowed by that monster of oblivion which is waiting for them with ever open jaws. It is thus a very thankworthy task to try to rescue something—the memory of interesting and important events, or the leading features and personages of some epoch—from the general shipwreck of the world.

From another point of view, we might look upon history as the sequel to zoology; for while with all other animals it is enough to observe the species, with man individuals, and therefore individual events, have to be studied; because every man possesses a character as an individual. And since individuals and events are without number or end, an essential imperfection attaches to history. In the study of it, all that a man learns never contributes to lessen that which he has still to learn. With any real science, a perfection of knowledge is, at any rate, conceivable.

Schopenhauer, *Some Forms of Literature*

67 Only through history does a nation become completely conscious of itself. Accordingly history is to be regarded as the rational consciousness of the human race, and is to the race what the reflected and connected consciousness is to the individual who is conditioned by reason, a consciousness through the want of which the brute is confined to the narrow, perceptible present. . . . In this sense, then, history . . . takes the place of an immediate self-consciousness common to the whole race, so that only by virtue of it does the human race come to be a whole, come to be a humanity. This is the true value of history.

Schopenhauer, *The World as Will and Idea*, III, 38

68 Universal History, the history of what man has accomplished in this world, is at bottom the History of the Great Men who have worked here.

Carlyle, *The Hero as Divinity*

69 I have no expectation that any man will read history aright who thinks that what was done in a remote age, by men whose names have resounded far, has any deeper sense than what he is doing to-day.

Emerson, *History*

70 All history becomes subjective; in other words there is properly no history, only biography.

Emerson, *History*

71 The advancing man discovers how deep a property he has in literature—in all fable as well as in all history. . . . His own secret biography he finds in lines wonderfully intelligible to him, dotted down before he was born. One after another he comes up in his private adventures with every fable of Aesop, of Homer, of Hafiz, of Ariosto, of Chaucer, of Scott, and verifies them with his own head and hands.

Emerson, *History*

72 Whence then this worship of the past? The centuries are conspirators against the sanity and authority of the soul. Time and space are but physiological colors which the eye makes, but the soul is light: where it is, is day; where it was, is night; and history is an impertinence and an injury if it be any thing more than a cheerful apologue or parable of my being and becoming.

Emerson, *Self-Reliance*

73 We go eastward to realize history and study the works of art and literature, retracing the steps of the race; we go westward as into the future, with a spirit of enterprise and adventure.

Thoreau, *Walking*

74 Many are concerned about the monuments of the West and the East—to know who built them. For my part, I should like to know who in those days did not build them.

Thoreau, *Walden:* Economy

75 One nation can and should learn from others. And even when a society has got upon the right track for the discovery of the natural laws of its movement . . . it can neither clear by bold leaps, nor remove by legal enactments, the obstacles offered by the successive phases of its normal development. But it can shorten and lessen the birth-pangs.

Marx, *Capital,* Pref. to 1st Ed.

76 Where speculation ends—in real life—there real, positive science begins: the representation of the practical activity, of the practical process of development of men. Empty talk about consciousness ceases, and real knowledge has to take its place. When reality is depicted, philosophy as an independent branch of activity loses its medium of existence. At the best its place can only be taken by a summing-up of the most general results, abstractions which arise from the observation of the historical development of men. Viewed apart from

real history, these abstractions have in themselves no value whatsoever. They can only serve to facilitate the arrangement of historical material, to indicate the sequence of its separate strata. But they by no means afford a recipe or schema, as does philosophy, for neatly trimming the epochs of history. On the contrary, our difficulties begin only when we set about the observation and the arrangement—the real depiction—of our historical material, whether of a past epoch or of the present.

Marx and Engels, *German Ideology*, I, 1

77 "Yes, universal history! It's the study of the successive follies of mankind and nothing more. The only subjects I respect are mathematics and natural science," said Kolya.

Dostoevsky, *Brothers Karamazov*, Pt. IV, X, 5

78 In historic events, the so-called great men are labels giving names to events, and like labels they have but the smallest connection with the event itself.

Tolstoy, *War and Peace*, IX, 1

79 The movement of humanity, arising as it does from innumerable arbitrary human wills, is continuous.

To understand the laws of this continuous movement is the aim of history. But to arrive at these laws, resulting from the sum of all those human wills, man's mind postulates arbitrary and disconnected units. The first method of history is to take an arbitrarily selected series of continuous events and examine it apart from others, though there is and can be no *beginning* to any event, for one event always flows uninterruptedly from another.

The second method is to consider the actions of some one man—a king or a commander—as equivalent to the sum of many individual wills; whereas the sum of individual wills is never expressed by the activity of a single historic personage.

Historical science in its endeavor to draw nearer to truth continually takes smaller and smaller units for examination. But however small the units it takes, we feel that to take any unit disconnected from others, or to assume a *beginning* of any phenomenon, or to say that the will of many men is expressed by the actions of any one historic personage, is in itself false.

It needs no critical exertion to reduce utterly to dust any deductions drawn from history. It is merely necessary to select some larger or smaller unit as the subject of observation—as criticism has every right to do, seeing that whatever unit history observes must always be arbitrarily selected.

Only by taking infinitesimally small units for observation (the differential of history, that is, the individual tendencies of men) and attaining to the art of integrating them (that is, finding the sum of these infinitesimals) can we hope to arrive at the laws of history.

Tolstoy, *War and Peace*, XI, 1

80 In historic events the rule forbidding us to eat of the fruit of the Tree of Knowledge is specially applicable. Only unconscious action bears fruit, and he who plays a part in an historic event never understands its significance. If he tries to realize it his efforts are fruitless.

Tolstoy, *War and Peace*, XII, 4

81 Man's mind cannot grasp the causes of events in their completeness, but the desire to find those causes is implanted in man's soul. And without considering the multiplicity and complexity of the conditions any one of which taken separately may seem to be the cause, he snatches at the first approximation to a cause that seems to him intelligible and says: "This is the cause!" In historical events (where the actions of men are the subject of observation) the first and most primitive approximation to present itself was the will of the gods and, after that, the will of those who stood in the most prominent position—the heroes of history. But we need only penetrate to the essence of any historic event—which lies in the activity of the general mass of men who take part in it—to be convinced that the will of the historic hero does not control the actions of the mass but is itself continually controlled. It may seem to be a matter of indifference whether we understand the meaning of historical events this way or that; yet there is the same difference between a man who says that the people of the West moved on the East because Napoleon wished it and a man who says that this happened because it had to happen, as there is between those who declared that the earth was stationary and that the planets moved round it and those who admitted that they did not know what upheld the earth, but knew there were laws directing its movement and that of the other planets. There is, and can be, no cause of an historical event except the one cause of all causes. But there are laws directing events, and some of these laws are known to us while we are conscious of others we cannot comprehend. The discovery of these laws is only possible when we have quite abandoned the attempt to find the cause in the will of some one man, just as the discovery of the laws of the motion of the planets was possible only when men abandoned the conception of the fixity of the earth.

Tolstoy, *War and Peace*, XIII, 1

82 Science does not admit the conception of the ancients as to the direct participation of the Deity in human affairs, and therefore history ought to give other answers.

Tolstoy, *War and Peace*, II Epilogue, I

83 If the will of every man were free, that is, if each man could act as he pleased, all history would be a series of disconnected incidents.

Tolstoy, *War and Peace,* II Epilogue, VIII

84 A contemporary event seems to us to be indubitably the doing of all the known participants, but with a more remote event we already see its inevitable results which prevent our considering anything else possible. And the farther we go back in examining events the less arbitrary do they appear.

Tolstoy, *War and Peace,* II Epilogue, IX

85 The recognition of man's free will as something capable of influencing historical events, that is, as not subject to laws, is the same for history as the recognition of a free force moving the heavenly bodies would be for astronomy.

Tolstoy, *War and Peace,* II Epilogue, XI

86 It is folly . . . to speak of the "laws of history" as of something inevitable, which science has only to discover, and whose consequences anyone can then foretell but do nothing to alter or avert. Why, the very laws of physics are conditional, and deal with *ifs*. The physicist does not say, "The water will boil anyhow;" he only says it will boil if a fire be kindled beneath it. And so the utmost the student of sociology can ever predict is that *if* a genius of a certain sort shows the way, society will be sure to follow.

William James, *Great Men and Their Environment*

87 Alas! Hegel was right when he said that we learn from history that men never learn anything from history.

Shaw, *Heartbreak House,* Pref.

88 This notion of historians, of history devoid of aesthetic prejudice, of history devoid of any reliance on metaphysical principles and cosmological generalizations, is a figment of the imagination. The belief in it can only occur to minds steeped in provinciality,—the provinciality of an epoch, of a race, of a school of learning, of a trend of interest—, minds unable to divine their own unspoken limitations.

Whitehead, *Adventures of Ideas,* I, 1

89 The historian in his description of the past depends on his own judgment as to what constitutes the importance of human life. Even when he has rigorously confined himself to one selected aspect, political or cultural, he still depends on some decision as to what constitutes the culmination of that phase of human experience and as to what constitutes its degradation.

Whitehead, *Adventures of Ideas,* I, 1

90 It is a curious delusion that the rock upon which our beliefs can be founded is an historical investigation. You can only interpret the past in terms of the present. The present is all that you have; and unless in this present you can find general principles which interpret the present as including a representation of the whole community of existents, you cannot move a step beyond your little patch of immediacy.

Thus history presupposes a metaphysic. It can be objected that we believe in the past and talk about it without settling our metaphysical principles. That is certainly the case. But you can only deduce metaphysical dogmas from your interpretation of the past on the basis of a prior metaphysical interpretation of the present.

In so far as your metaphysical beliefs are implicit, you vaguely interpret the past on the lines of the present. But when it comes to the primary metaphysical data, the world of which you are immediately conscious is the whole datum.

Whitehead, *Religion in the Making,* III, 1

91 History, in every country, is so taught as to magnify that country: children learn to believe that their own country has always been in the right and almost always victorious, that it has produced almost all the great men, and that it is in all respects superior to all other countries.

Russell, *Education*

92 For whom is there History? The question is seemingly paradoxical, for history is obviously for everyone to this extent, that every man, with his whole existence and consciousness, is a part of history. But it makes a great difference whether anyone lives under the constant impression that his life is an element in a far wider life-course that goes on for hundreds and thousands of years, or conceives of himself as something rounded off and self-contained. For the latter type of consciousness there is certainly no world-history, no *world-as-history*.

Spengler, *Decline of the West,* I, 1

93 Memory itself is an internal rumour; and when to this hearsay within the mind we add the falsified echoes that reach us from others, we have but a shifting and unseizable basis to build upon. The picture we frame of the past changes continually and grows every day less similar to the original experience which it purports to describe.

Santayana, *Life of Reason,* V, 2

94 The historian's politics, philosophy, or romantic imagination furnishes a vital nucleus for reflection. All that falls within that particular vortex is included in the mental picture, the rest is passed over and tends to drop out of sight. It is not possi-

ble to say, nor to think, everything at once; and the private interest which guides a man in selecting his materials imposes itself inevitably on the events he relates and especially on their grouping and significance.

History is always written wrong, and so always needs to be rewritten.

Santayana, *Life of Reason*, V, 2

95 Historical investigation has for its aim to fix the order and character of events throughout past time in all places. The task is frankly superhuman, because no block of real existence, with its infinitesimal detail, can be recorded, nor if somehow recorded could it be dominated by the mind; and to carry on a survey of this social continuum *ad infinitum* would multiply the difficulty.

Santayana, *Life of Reason*, V, 2

96 It is not enough to say that history is historical judgment, it is necessary to add that every judgment is an historical judgment or, quite simply, history. If judgment is a relation between a subject and a predicate, then the subject or the event, whatever it is that is being judged, is always an historical fact, a becoming, a process under way, for there are no immobile facts nor can such things be envisaged in the world of reality. Historical judgment is embodied even in the merest perception of the judging mind (if it did not judge there would not even be perception but merely blind and dumb sensation). . . .

Historical judgment is not a variety of knowledge, but it is knowledge itself; it is the form which completely fills and exhausts the field of knowing, leaving no room for anything else.

Croce, *History as the Story of Liberty*, I, 5

97 We are products of the past and we live immersed in the past, which encompasses us. How can we move towards the new life, how create new activities without getting out of the past and without placing ourselves above it? And how can we place ourselves above the past if we are in it and it is in us? There is no other way out except through thought, which does not break off relations with the past but rises ideally above it and converts it

into knowledge. The past must be faced or, not to speak in metaphors, it must be reduced to a mental problem which can find its solution in a proposition of truth, the ideal premise for our new activity and our new life. This is how we daily behave, when, instead of being prostrated by the vexations which beset us, and of bewailing and being shamed by errors we have committed, we examine what has happened, analyse its origin, follow its history, and, with an informed conscience and under an intimate inspiration, we outline what ought and should be undertaken and willingly and brightly get ready to undertake it.

Croce, *History as the Story of Liberty*, I, 8

98 The writing of histories—as Goethe once noted—is one way of getting rid of the weight of the past. . . . The writing of history liberates us from history.

Croce, *History as the Story of Liberty*, I, 8

99 I find it hard to have patience with historians who boast, as some modern Western historians do, that they keep entirely to the facts of history and don't go in for theories. Why, every so-called fact that they present to you had some pattern of theory behind it. Historians who genuinely believe they have no general ideas about history are, I would suggest to them, simply ignorant of the workings of their own minds, and such willful ignorance is, isn't it, really unpardonable.

Toynbee, *Radio Debate (1948)*

100 Historians generally illustrate rather than correct the ideas of the communities within which they live and work.

Toynbee, *A Study of History*, I, 1

101 History, in the sense of the histories of the human societies called civilizations, revealed itself as a sheaf of parallel, contemporary, and recent essays in a new enterprise: a score of attempts, up to date, to transcend the level of primitive human life at which man, after having become himself, had apparently lain torpid for some hundreds of thousands of years.

Toynbee, *Civilization on Trial*, I

15.2 | *Progress, Regress, and Cycles in History*

One of the central issues in the philosophy of history concerns the pattern of change that has occurred in human affairs in the course of time. According to one view, the pattern is cyclical, like that of birth, growth, decline, and death in the life of living organisms. The point is not simply that history repeats itself in the recurrence of similar events, but that the whole sequence of historical development endlessly repeats itself. According to another view, history manifests a regression, a falling away from a golden age. According to still another view, history advances from age to age, either in a line of steady and uninterrupted progress or with intervals of stability or even of regression.

Of these three main views, the first is the one that predominates in the quotations drawn from antiquity, though there are also some expressions of the second view in ancient texts, notably the ones by Hesiod and Ovid; and in addition, the opinion that in all essential respects the future will resemble the past. It is not until the seventeenth century that we find explicit affirmations of progress in human affairs—in the sphere of science, in human institutions, in population, in the production of wealth. Though progress has many votaries among modern writers, it also has its doubters or deniers—those who point out that regressive change counterbalances the evidences of progress, or that advances in such external matters as science, technology, and wealth do not carry with them essential improvements in the quality of human life.

---

1 Is there any thing whereof it may be said, See, this is new? it hath been already of old time, which was before us.

There is no remembrance of former things; neither shall there be any remembrance of things that are to come with those that shall come after.

Ecclesiastes 1:10–11

2 When gods alike and mortals rose to birth,
Th' immortals form'd a golden race on earth
Of many-languaged men; they lived of old
When Saturn reign'd in heaven; an age of gold.
Like gods they lived, with calm, untroubled mind,
Free from the toil and anguish of our kind:
Nor e'er decrepid age mis-shaped their frame,
The hand's, the foot's proportions, still the same.
Pleased with earth's unbought feasts; all ills removed,
Wealthy in flocks, and of the bless'd beloved.
Death as a slumber press'd their eyelids down;
All nature's common blessings were their own.
The life-bestowing tilth its fruitage bore,
A full, spontaneous, and ungrudging store:
They with abundant goods, midst quiet lands,
All willing shared the gatherings of their hands.
When earth's dark breast had closed this race around,

Great Jove as demons raised them from the ground.
Earth-hovering spirits, they their charge began,
The ministers of good, and guards of man.
Mantled with mist of darkling air they glide,
And compass earth, and pass on every side;
And mark, with earnest vigilance of eyes,
Where just deeds live, or crooked wrongs arise;
And shower the wealth of seasons from above,
Their kingly office, delegate from Jove.
The gods then form'd a second race of man,
Degenerate far, and silver years began;
Unlike the mortals of a golden kind,
Unlike in frame of limbs, and mould of mind.
Yet still a hundred years beheld the boy
Beneath the mother's roof, her infant joy,
All tender and unform'd: but when the flower
Of manhood bloom'd, it wither'd in an hour.
Their frantic follies wrought them pain and woe;
Nor mutual outrage would their hands forego:
Nor would they serve the gods, nor altars raise,
That in just cities shed their holy blaze.
Them angry Jove ingulf'd; who dared refuse
The gods their glory and their sacred dues:
Yet named the second bless'd, in earth they lie,
And second honours grace their memory.
The sire of heaven and earth created then

A race, the third, of many-languaged men:
Unlike the silver they; of brazen mould,
Strong with the ashen spear, and fierce, and bold;
Their thoughts were bent on violence alone,
The deed of battle, and the dying groan.
Bloody their feasts, with wheaten food unbless'd;
Of adamant was each unyielding breast.
Huge, nerved with strength, each hardy giant
  stands,
And mocks approach with unresisted hands.
Their mansions, implements, and armour shine
In brass; dark iron slept within the mine.
They by each other's hands inglorious fell,
In freezing darkness plunged, the house of hell:
Fierce though they were, their mortal course was
  run;
Death gloomy seized and snatch'd them from the
  sun.
Them when th' abyss had cover'd from the skies,
Lo! the fourth age on nurt'ring earth arise:
Jove form'd the race a better, juster line;
A race of heroes, and of stamp divine:
Lights of the age that rose before our own;
As demigods o'er earth's wide regions known.
Yet these dread battle hurried to their end;
Some where the seven-fold gates of Thebes as-
  cend,
The Cadmian realm; where they with fatal might
Strove for the flocks of Oedipus in fight.
Some war in navies led to Troy's far shore;
O'er the great space of sea their course they bore,
For sake of Helen with the beauteous hair;
And death for Helen's sake o'erwhelm'd them
  there.
Them on earth's utmost verge the god assign'd
A life, a seat, distinct from human kind;
Beside the deepening whirlpools of the main,
In those bless'd isles where Saturn holds his reign,
Apart from heaven's immortals: calm they share
A rest, unsullied by the clouds of care;
And yearly thrice, with sweet luxuriance crown'd,
Springs the ripe harvest from the teeming ground.
  Oh! would that Nature had denied me birth
Midst this fifth race, this iron age of earth;
That long before within the grave I lay,
Or long hereafter could behold the day!
Corrupt the race, with toils and griefs oppress'd,
Nor day nor night can yield a pause of rest:
Still do the gods a weight of care bestow,
Though still some good is mingled with the woe.
Jove on this race of many-languaged man
Speeds the swift ruin, which but slow began;
For scarcely spring they to the light of day,
E'er age untimely strews their temples gray,
No fathers in the sons their features trace;
The sons reflect no more the father's face:
The host with kindness greets his guest no more;
And friends and brethren love not as of yore.
Reckless of Heaven's revenge, the sons behold
The hoary parents wax too swiftly old,
And impious point the keen dishonouring tongue,

With hard reproofs, and bitter mockeries hung;
Nor grateful in declining age repay
The nurturing fondness of their better day.
Now man's right hand is law; for spoil they wait,
And lay their mutual cities desolate.
Unhonour'd he, by whom his oath is fear'd,
Nor are the good beloved, the just revered.
With favour graced, the evil doer stands,
Nor curbs with shame nor equity his hands;
With crooked slanders wounds the virtuous man,
And stamps with perjury what hate began.
Lo! ill-rejoicing Envy, wing'd with lies,
Scattering calumnious rumours as she flies,
The steps of miserable men pursue,
With haggard aspect, blasting to the view:
Till those fair forms, in snowy raiment bright,
Quit the broad earth, and heavenward soar from
  sight:
Justice and Modesty, from mortals driven,
Rise to th' immortal family of heaven:
Dread sorrows to forsaken man remain;
No cure of ills; no remedy of pain.

                          Hesiod, *Works and Days*

3 *Prometheus.* Men at first had eyes but saw to no
purpose; they had ears but did not hear. Like the
shapes of dreams they dragged through their long
lives and handled all things in bewilderment and
confusion. They did not know of building houses
with bricks to face the sun; they did not know how
to work in wood. They lived like swarming ants in
holes in the ground, in the sunless caves of the
earth. For them there was no secure token by
which to tell winter nor the flowering spring nor
the summer with its crops; all their doings were
indeed without intelligent calculation until I
showed them the rising of the stars, and the settings, hard to observe. And further I discovered to
them numbering, pre-eminent among subtle devices, and the combining of letters as a means of
remembering all things, the Muses' mother,
skilled in craft. It was I who first yoked beasts for
them in the yokes and made of those beasts the
slaves of trace chain and pack saddle that they
might be man's substitute in the hardest tasks;
and I harnessed to the carriage, so that they loved
the rein, horses, the crowning pride of the rich
man's luxury. It was I and none other who discovered ships, the sail-driven wagons that the sea buffets. Such were the contrivances that I discovered
for men—alas for me! For I myself am without
contrivance to rid myself of my present affliction.
  . . . Hear the rest, and you will marvel even more
at the crafts and resources I contrived. Greatest
was this: in the former times if a man fell sick he
had no defense against the sickness, neither healing food nor drink, nor unguent; but through the
lack of drugs men wasted away, until I showed
them the blending of mild simples wherewith they
drive out all manner of diseases. It was I who arranged all the ways of seercraft, and I first ad-

judged what things come verily true from dreams; and to men I gave meaning to the ominous cries, hard to interpret. It was I who set in order the omens of the highway and the flight of crooked-taloned birds, which of them were propitious or lucky by nature, and what manner of life each led, and what were their mutual hates, loves, and companionships; also I taught of the smoothness of the sky vitals and what color they should have to pleasure the Gods and the dappled beauty of the gall and the lobe. It was I who burned thighs wrapped in fat and the long shank bone and set mortals on the road to this murky craft. It was I who made visible to men's eyes the flaming signs of the sky that were before dim. So much for these. Beneath the earth, man's hidden blessing, copper, iron; silver, and gold—will anyone claim to have discovered these before I did? No one, I am very sure, who wants to speak truly and to the purpose. One brief word will tell the whole story: all arts that mortals have come from Prometheus.

Aeschylus, *Prometheus Bound*, 445

4 I shall go forward with my history, describing equally the greater and the lesser cities. For the cities which were formerly great have most of them become insignificant; and such as are at present powerful, were weak in the olden time. I shall therefore discourse equally of both, convinced that human happiness never continues long in one stay.

Herodotus, *History*, I, 5

5 *Critias.* Just when you and other nations are beginning to be provided with letters and the other requisites of civilized life, after the usual interval, the stream from heaven, like a pestilence, comes pouring down, and leaves only those of you who are destitute of letters and education; and so you have to begin all over again like children, and know nothing of what happened in ancient times, either among us or among yourselves.

Plato, *Timaeus*, 23A

6 Human affairs form a circle, and . . . there is a circle in all other things that have a natural movement and coming into being and passing away. This is because all other things are discriminated by time, and end and begin as though conforming to a cycle; for even time itself is thought to be a circle. And this opinion again is held because time is the measure of this kind of locomotion and is itself measured by such. So that to say that the things that come into being form a circle is to say that there is a circle of time; and this is to say that it is measured by the circular movement; for apart from the measure nothing else to be measured is observed; the whole is just a plurality of measures.

Aristotle, *Physics*, 223b25

7 In most respects the future will be like what the past has been.

Aristotle, *Rhetoric*, 1394a8

8 We must suppose that human nature . . . was taught and constrained to do many things of every kind merely by circumstances; and that later on reasoning elaborated what had been suggested by nature and made further inventions, in some matters quickly, in others slowly, at some epochs and times making great advances, and lesser again at others.

Epicurus, *Letter to Herodotus*

9 There is in every body, or polity, or business a natural stage of growth, zenith, and decay.

Polybius, *Histories*, VI, 51

10 The aged ploughman shakes his head and sighs again and again to think that the labours of his hands have come to nothing; and when he compares present times with times past, he often praises the fortunes of his sire and harps on the theme, how the men of old rich in piety comfortably supported life on a scanty plot of ground, since the allotment of land to each man was far less of yore than now. The sorrowful planter too of the exhausted and shrivelled vine impeaches the march of time and wearies heaven, and comprehends not that all things are gradually wasting away and passing to the grave, quite forspent by age and length of days.

Lucretius, *Nature of Things*, II

11 Our father's age, than their sires' not so good,
   Bred us ev'n worse than they; a brood
      We'll leave that's viler still.

Horace, *Odes*, III, 6

12 What is free from the risk of change? Neither earth, nor sky, nor the whole fabric of our universe, though it be controlled by the hand of God. It will not always preserve its present order; it will be thrown from its course in days to come. All things move in accord with their appointed times; they are destined to be born, to grow, and to be destroyed. The stars which you see moving above us, and this seemingly immovable earth to which we cling and on which we are set, will be consumed and will cease to exist. There is nothing that does not have its old age; the intervals are merely unequal at which Nature sends forth all these things towards the same goal. Whatever is will cease to be, and yet it will not perish, but will be resolved into its elements.

Seneca, *Letters to Lucilius*, 71

13 The elements of the earth must all be dissolved or utterly destroyed in order that they may be created anew in innocence, and that no remnant may be left to tutor men in vice. . . . A single day will

see the burial of all mankind. All that the long forbearance of fortune has produced, all that has been reared to eminence, all that is famous and all that is beautiful, great thrones, great nations—all will descend into the one abyss, will be overthrown in one hour. . . .

When the destruction of the human race is consummated, and when wild beasts, whose nature men had come to share, have been consigned together to a like fate, the earth will once more drink up the waters. Nature will force the sea to stay its course, and to expend its rage within its wonted bounds. Ocean will be banished from our abodes into his own secret dwelling place. The ancient order of things will be recalled. Every living creature will be created afresh. The earth will receive a new man ignorant of sin, born under happier stars. But they, too, will retain their innocence only while they are new.

Seneca, *Quaestiones Naturales,* III, 29–30

14 In the beginning was the Golden Age, when men of their own accord, without threat of punishment, without laws, maintained good faith and did what was right. There were no penalties to be afraid of, no bronze tablets were erected, carrying threats of legal action, no crowd of wrong-doers, anxious for mercy, trembled before the face of their judge: indeed, there were no judges, men lived securely without them. Never yet had any pine tree, cut down from its home on the mountains, been launched on ocean's waves, to visit foreign lands: men knew only their own shores. Their cities were not yet surrounded by sheer moats, they had no straight brass trumpets, no coiling brass horns, no helmets and no swords. The peoples of the world, untroubled by any fears, enjoyed a leisurely and peaceful existence, and had no use for soldiers. The earth itself, without compulsion, untouched by the hoe, unfurrowed by any share, produced all things spontaneously, and men were content with foods that grew without cultivation. They gathered arbute berries and mountain strawberries, wild cherries and blackberries that cling to thorny bramble bushes: or acorns, fallen from Jupiter's spreading oak. It was a season of everlasting spring, when peaceful zephyrs, with their warm breath, caressed the flowers that sprang up without having been planted. In time the earth, though untilled, produced corn too, and fields that never lay fallow whitened with heavy ears of grain. Then there flowed rivers of milk and rivers of nectar, and golden honey dripped from the green holm-oak.

When Saturn was consigned to the darkness of Tartarus, and the world passed under the rule of Jove, the age of silver replaced that of gold, inferior to it, but superior to the age of tawny bronze. Jupiter shortened the springtime which had prevailed of old, and instituted a cycle of four seasons in the year, winter, summer, changeable autumn, and a brief spring. Then, for the first time, the air became parched and arid, and glowed with white heat, then hanging icicles formed under the chilling blasts of the wind. It was in those days that men first sought covered dwelling places: they made their homes in caves and thick shrubberies, or bound branches together with bark. Then corn, the gift of Ceres, first began to be sown in long furrows, and straining bullocks groaned beneath the yoke.

After that came the third age, the age of bronze, when men were of a fiercer character, more ready to turn to cruel warfare, but still free from any taint of wickedness.

Last of all arose the age of hard iron: immediately, in this period which took its name from a baser ore, all manner of crime broke out; modesty, truth, and loyalty fled. Treachery and trickery took their place, deceit and violence and criminal greed. Now sailors spread their canvas to the winds, though they had as yet but little knowledge of these, and trees which had once clothed the high mountains were fashioned into ships, and tossed upon the ocean waves, far removed from their own element. The land, which had previously been common to all, like the sunlight and the breezes, was now divided up far and wide by boundaries, set by cautious surveyors. Nor was it only corn and their due nourishment that men demanded of the rich earth: they explored its very bowels, and dug out the wealth which it had hidden away, close to the Stygian shades; and this wealth was a further incitement to wickedness. By this time iron had been discovered, to the hurt of mankind, and gold, more hurtful still than iron. War made its appearance, using both those metals in its conflict, and shaking clashing weapons in bloodstained hands. Men lived on what they could plunder: friend was not safe from friend, nor father-in-law from son-in-law, and even between brothers affection was rare. Husbands waited eagerly for the death of their wives, and wives for that of their husbands. Ruthless stepmothers mixed brews of deadly aconite, and sons pried into their fathers' horoscopes, impatient for them to die. All proper affection lay vanquished and, last of the immortals, the maiden Justice left the blood-soaked earth.

Ovid, *Metamorphoses,* I

15 These two things then thou must bear in mind; the one, that all things from eternity are of like forms and come round in a circle, and that it makes no difference whether a man shall see the same things during a hundred years or two hundred, or an infinite time; and the second, that the longest liver and he who will die soonest lose just the same.

Marcus Aurelius, *Meditations,* II, 14

16 On the occasion of everything which happens

keep this in mind, that it is that which thou hast often seen. Everywhere up and down thou wilt find the same things, with which the old histories are filled, those of the middle ages and those of our own day. . . . There is nothing new: all things are both familiar and short-lived.

Marcus Aurelius, Meditations, VII, 1

17 Constantly consider how all things such as they now are, in time past also were; and consider that they will be the same again. And place before thy eyes entire dramas and stages of the same form, whatever thou hast learned from thy experience or from older history . . . for all those were such dramas as we see now, only with different actors.

Marcus Aurelius, Meditations, X, 27

18 This controversy some philosophers have seen no other approved means of solving than by introducing cycles of time, in which there should be a constant renewal and repetition of the order of nature; and they have therefore asserted that theses cycles will ceaselessly recur, one passing away and another coming, though they are not agreed as to whether one permanent world shall pass through all these cycles, or whether the world shall at fixed intervals die out and be renewed so as to exhibit a recurrence of the same phenomena—the things which have been and those which are to be coinciding. And from this fantastic vicissitude they exempt not even the immortal soul that has attained wisdom, consigning it to a ceaseless transmigration between delusive blessedness and real misery. For how can that be truly called blessed which has no assurance of being so eternally, and is either in ignorance of the truth, and blind to the misery that is approaching, or, knowing it, is in misery and fear? Or if it passes to bliss, and leaves miseries forever, then there happens in time a new thing which time shall not end. Why not, then, the world also? Why may not man, too, be a similar thing? So that, by following the straight path of sound doctrine, we escape, I know not what circuitous paths, discovered by deceiving and deceived sages.

Augustine, City of God, XII, 13

19 Over and above those arts which are called virtues, and which teach us how we may spend our life well, and attain to endless happiness—arts which are given to the children of the promise and the kingdom by the sole grace of God which is in Christ—has not the genius of man invented and applied countless astonishing arts, partly the result of necessity, partly the result of exuberant invention, so that this vigour of mind, which is so active in the discovery not merely of superfluous but even of dangerous and destructive things, betokens an inexhaustible wealth in the nature which can invent, learn, or employ such arts? What wonderful—one might say stupefying—advances has human industry made in the arts of weaving and building, of agriculture and navigation! With what endless variety are designs in pottery, painting, and sculpture produced, and with what skill executed! What wonderful spectacles are exhibited in the theatres, which those who have not seen them cannot credit! How skillful the contrivances for catching, killing, or taming wild beasts! And for the injury of men, also, how many kinds of poisons, weapons, engines of destruction, have been invented, while for the preservation or restoration of health the appliances and remedies are infinite! To provoke appetite and please the palate, what a variety of seasonings have been concocted! To express and gain entrance for thoughts, what a multitude and variety of signs there are, among which speaking and writing hold the first place! what ornaments has eloquence at command to delight the mind! what wealth of song is there to captivate the ear! how many musical instruments and strains of harmony have been devised! What skill has been attained in measures and numbers! with what sagacity have the movements and connections of the stars been discovered! Who could tell the thought that has been spent upon nature, even though, despairing of recounting it in detail, he endeavoured only to give a general view of it? In fine, even the defence of errors and misapprehensions, which has illustrated the genius of heretics and philosophers, cannot be sufficiently declared. For at present it is the nature of the human mind which adorns this mortal life which we are extolling, and not the faith and the way of truth which lead to immortality. And since this great nature has certainly been created by the true and supreme God, Who administers all things He has made with absolute power and justice, it could never have fallen into these miseries, nor have gone out of them to miseries eternal—saving only those who are redeemed—had not an exceeding great sin been found in the first man from whom the rest have sprung.

Augustine, City of God, XXII, 24

20 This Sabbath shall appear still more clearly if we count the ages as days, in accordance with the periods of time defined in Scripture, for that period will be found to be the seventh. The first age, as the first day, extends from Adam to the deluge; the second from the deluge to Abraham, equalling the first, not in length of time, but in the number of generations, there being ten in each. From Abraham to the advent of Christ there are, as the evangelist Matthew calculates, three periods, in each of which are fourteen generations—one period from Abraham to David, a second from David to the captivity, a third from the captivity to the birth of Christ in the flesh. There are thus five ages in all. The sixth is now passing, and cannot be measured by any number of generations, as it

has been said, "It is not for you to know the times, which the Father hath put in His own power." After this period God shall rest as on the seventh day, when He shall give us (who shall be the seventh day) rest in Himself. But there is not now space to treat of these ages; suffice it to say that the seventh shall be our Sabbath, which shall be brought to a close, not by an evening, but by the Lord's day, as an eighth and eternal day, consecrated by the resurrection of Christ and prefiguring the eternal repose not only of the spirit, but also of the body. There we shall rest and see, see and love, love and praise. This is what shall be in the end without end. For what other end do we propose to ourselves than to attain to the kingdom of which there is no end?

Augustine, *City of God,* XXII, 30

21 Whoever considers the past and the present will readily observe that all cities and all peoples are and ever have been animated by the same desires and the same passions; so that it is easy, by diligent study of the past, to foresee what is likely to happen in the future in any republic, and to apply those remedies that were used by the ancients, or, not finding any that were employed by them, to devise new ones from the similarity of the events.

Machiavelli, *Discourses,* I, 39

22 Nations, as a rule, when making a change in their system of government pass from order to disorder, and afterwards from disorder to order, because nature permits no stability in human affairs. When nations reach their final perfection and can mount no higher they commence to descend; and equally when they have descended and reached a depth where they can fall no lower, necessity compels them to rise again. Thus states will always be falling from prosperity to adversity, and from adversity they will ascend again to prosperity. Because valour brings peace, peace idleness, idleness disorder, and disorder ruin; once more from ruin arises good order, from order valour, and from valour success and glory.

Machiavelli, *Florentine History,* V

23 And now Don *Quixote* having satisfy'd his Appetite, he took a Handful of Acorns, and looking earnestly upon 'em; O happy Age, cry'd he, which our first Parents call'd the Age of Gold! not because Gold, so much ador'd in this Iron-Age, was then easily purchas'd, but because those two fatal Words, Mine and Thine, were Distinctions unknown to the People of those fortunate Times; for all Things were in common in that holy Age: Men, for their Sustenance, needed only to lift their Hands, and take it from the sturdy Oak, whose spreading Arms liberally invited them to gather the wholsome savoury Fruit; while the clear Springs, and silver Rivulets, with luxuriant

Plenty, offer'd them their pure refreshing Water. In hollow Trees, and in the Clefts of Rocks, the labouring and industrious Bees erected their little Commonwealths, that Men might reap with Pleasure and with Ease the sweet and fertile Harvest of their Toils. The tough and strenuous Cork-Trees did of themselves, and without other Art than their native Liberality, dismiss and impart their broad light Bark, which serv'd to cover those lowly Huts, propp'd up with rough-hewn Stakes, that were first built as a Shelter against the Inclemencies of the Air: All then was Union, all Peace, all Love and Friendship in the World: As yet no rude Plough-share presum'd with Violence to pry into the pious Bowels of our Mother Earth, for she without Compulsion kindly yielded from every Part of her fruitful and spacious Bosom, whatever might at once satisfy, sustain and indulge her frugal Children. Then was the Time when innocent beautiful young Shepherdesses went tripping o'er the Hills and Vales: Their lovely Hair sometimes plaited, sometimes loose and flowing, clad in no other Vestment but what was necessary to cover decently what Modesty would always have conceal'd: The *Tyrian* Die, and the rich glossy Hue of Silk, martyr'd and dissembled into every Colour, which are now esteem'd so fine and magnificent, were unknown to the innocent Plainness of that Age; yet bedeck'd with more becoming Leaves and Flowers, they may be said to outshine the proudest of the vain-dressing Ladies of our Age, array'd in the most magnificent Garbs and all the most sumptuous Adorings which Idleness and Luxury have taught succeeding Pride: Lovers then express'd the Passion of their Souls in the unaffected Language of the Heart, with the native Plainness and Sincerity in which they were conceiv'd and divested of all that artificial Contexture, which enervates what it labours to enforce: Imposture, Deceit and Malice had not yet crept in, and impos'd themselves unbrib'd upon Mankind in the Disguise of Truth and Simplicity: Justice, unbiass'd either by Favour or Interest, which now so fatally pervert it, was equally and impartially dispensed; nor was the Judges Fancy Law, for then there were neither Judges, nor Causes to be judg'd; the modest Maid might walk where-ever she pleas'd alone, free from the Attacks of lewd lascivious Importuners. But in this degenerate Age, Fraud and a Legion of Ills infecting the World, no Virtue can be safe, no Honour be secure; while wanton Desires, diffus'd into the Hearts of Men, corrupt the strictest Watches, and the closest Retreats; which, though as intricate and unknown as the Labyrinth of *Crete,* are no Security for Chastity. Thus that Primitive Innocence being vanish'd, and Oppression daily prevailing, there was a Necessity to oppose the Torrent of Violence: For which Reason the Order of Knighthood-Errant was instituted, to defend the Honour of Virgins, protect Widows, relieve Orphans, and assist all the Distress'd in general. Now I my self am one of this Order, honest Friends; and though all People are oblig'd by the Law of Nature to be kind to Persons of My Order; yet since you, without knowing any thing of this Obligation, have so generously entertain'd me, I ought to pay you my utmost Acknowledgment; and, accordingly, return you my most hearty Thanks for the same.

Cervantes, *Don Quixote,* I, 11

24 By far the greatest obstacle to the advancement of the sciences, and the undertaking of any new attempt or department, is to be found in men's despair and the idea of impossibility; for men of a prudent and exact turn of thought are altogether diffident in matters of this nature, considering the obscurity of nature, the shortness of life, the deception of the senses, and weakness of the judgment. They think, therefore, that in the revolutions of ages and of the world there are certain floods and ebbs of the sciences, and that they grow and flourish at one time, and wither and fall off at another, that when they have attained a certain degree and condition they can proceed no further.

Bacon, *Novum Organum,* I, 92

25 We should notice the force, effect, and consequences of inventions, which are nowhere more conspicuous than in those three which were unknown to the ancients; namely, printing, gunpowder, and the compass. For these three have changed the appearance and state of the whole world: first in literature, then in warfare, and lastly in navigation; and innumerable changes have been thence derived, so that no empire, sect, or star, appears to have exercised a greater power and influence on human affairs than these mechanical discoveries.

Bacon, *Novum Organum,* I, 129

26 Beehives were as well laid out a thousand years ago as today, and each bee forms that hexagon as exactly the first time as the last. It is the same with everything animals make by that hidden motion. Nature teaches them in response to the pressure of necessity; but this frail knowledge dies with its need: as they receive it without study, they do not have the happiness of preserving it; and every time they are given it, they find it new, because nature, whose object is merely to maintain animals in an order of limited perfection, infuses in them this necessary knowledge, always the same, lest they perish, and does not allow them to add to it lest they go beyond the boundaries prescribed to them. It is different with man, made only for infinity. He is ignorant in his life's first age, but he never ceases to learn as he goes forward, for he has the advantage not only of his own experience but also of his predecessors', because he always keeps in his memory the knowl-

edge he has once acquired, and that of the ancients is always at hand in the books they have left. And since he keeps his knowledge, he can also easily increase it, so that men today are in a certain sense in the same condition in which those ancient philosophers would be if they could have prolonged their old age until now, adding to the knowledge they had what their studies might have won for them by the grace of so many centuries. Hence it is that by a special prerogative not only does each man advance from day to day in the sciences, but all men together make a continual progress as the universe grows old, because the same thing happens in the succession of men as in the different ages of an individual man. So that the whole series of men during the course of so many centuries should be considered as one selfsame man, always in existence and continually learning. Whence it is seen with what injustice we respect antiquity in the persons of its philosophers; for since old age is the age furthest removed from childhood, who does not see that the old age of this universal man should be sought not in the times near his birth but in those which are most distant from it? Those whom we call ancients were in truth new in every respect, and actually formed the childhood of man; and since we have added to their knowledge the experience of the succeeding centuries, it is in ourselves that that antiquity can be found which we revere in others.

Pascal, *Preface to the Treatise on the Vacuum*

27 *Chorus of All.* All, all of a piece throughout:
Thy chase had a beast in view;
Thy wars brought nothing about;
Thy lovers were all untrue.
'T is well an old age is out,
And time to begin a new.

Dryden, *The Secular Masque (1700)*

28 To realize in its completeness the universal beauty and perfection of the works of God, we must recognize a certain perpetual and very free progress of the whole universe, such that it is always going forward to greater improvement. So even now a great part of our earth has received cultivation and will receive it more and more. And although it is true that sometimes certain parts of it grow wild again, or again suffer destruction or degeneration, yet this is to be understood in the way in which affliction was explained above, that is to say, that this very destruction and degeneration leads to some greater end, so that somehow we profit by the loss itself.

And to the possible objection that, if this were so, the world ought long ago to have become a paradise, there is a ready answer. Although many substances have already attained a great perfection, yet on account of the infinite divisibility of the continuous, there always remain in the abyss of things slumbering parts which have yet to be awakened, to grow in size and worth, and, in a word, to advance to a more perfect state. And hence no end of progress is ever reached.

Leibniz, *On the Ultimate Origination of Things*

29 I have perused many of their [the Lorbrulgrudians'] books, especially those in history and morality. Among the latter I was much diverted with a little old treatise, which always lay in Glumdalclitch's bed-chamber, and belonged to her governess, a grave elderly gentlewoman, who dealt in writings of morality and devotion. The book treats of the weakness of human kind; and is in little esteem, except among women and the vulgar. However, I was curious to see what an author of that country could say upon such a subject. This writer went through all the usual topicks of European moralists; shewing how diminutive, contemptible, and helpless an animal was man in his own nature; how unable to defend himself from inclemencies of the air, or the fury of wild beasts; how much he was excelled by one creature in strength, by another in speed, by a third in foresight, by a fourth in industry. He added, that nature was degenerated in these latter declining ages of the world, and could now produce only small abortive births, in comparison of those in ancient times. He said, it was very reasonable to think, not only that the species of man were originally much larger, but also, that there must have been giants in former ages; which, as it is asserted by history and tradition, so it hath been confirmed by huge bones and sculls, casually dug up in several parts of the kingdom, far exceeding the common dwindled race of man in our days.

Swift, *Gulliver's Travels*, II, 7

30 Our Science . . . comes to describe . . . an ideal eternal history traversed in time by the history of every nation in its rise, progress, maturity, decline and fall. Indeed we go so far as to assert that whoever meditates this Science tells himself this ideal eternal history only so far as he makes it by that proof "it had, has, and will have to be."

Vico, *The New Science*, I

31 This world without doubt has issued from a mind often diverse, at times quite contrary, and always superior to the particular ends that men had proposed to themselves; which narrow ends, made means to serve wider ends, it has always employed to preserve the human race upon this earth. Men mean to gratify their bestial lust and abandon their offspring, and they inaugurate the chastity of marriage from which the families arise. The fathers mean to exercise without restraint their paternal power over their clients, and they subject them to the civil powers from which the cities arise. The reigning orders of nobles mean to abuse their lordly freedom over the plebeians, and they

are obliged to submit to the laws which establish popular liberty. The free peoples mean to shake off the yoke of their laws, and they become subject to monarchs. The monarchs mean to strengthen their own positions by debasing their subjects with all the vices of dissoluteness, and they dispose them to endure slavery at the hands of stronger nations. The nations mean to dissolve themselves, and their remnants flee for safety to the wilderness, whence, like the phoenix, they rise again.

Vico, *The New Science*, Conclusion

32 Thus—thus, my fellow-labourers and associates in this great harvest of our learning, now ripening before our eyes; thus it is, by slow steps of casual increase, that our knowledge physical, metaphysical, physiological, polemical, nautical, mathematical, enigmatical, technical, biographical, romantical, chemical, and obstetrical, with fifty other branches of it, (most of 'em ending as these do, in *ical*) have for these two centuries and more, gradually been creeping upwards towards that acme of their perfections, from which, if we may form a conjecture from the advances of these last seven years, we cannot possibly be far off.

When that happens, it is to be hoped, it will put an end to all kind of writings whatsoever;—the want of all kind of writing will put an end to all kind of reading;—and that in time, As war begets poverty; poverty peace,—must, in course, put an end to all kind of knowledge,—and then—we shall have all to begin over again; or, in other words, be exactly where we started.

Sterne, *Tristram Shandy*, I, 21

33 A famous author, reckoning up the good and evil of human life, and comparing the aggregates, finds that our pains greatly exceed our pleasures: so that, all things considered, human life is not at all a valuable gift. This conclusion does not surprise me; for the writer drew all his arguments from man in civilisation. Had he gone back to the state of nature, his inquiries would clearly have had a different result, and man would have been seen to be subject to very few evils not of his own creation. It has indeed cost us not a little trouble to make ourselves as wretched as we are. When we consider, on the one hand, the immense labours of mankind, the many sciences brought to perfection, the arts invented, the powers employed, the deeps filled up, the mountains levelled, the rocks shattered, the rivers made navigable, the tracts of land cleared, the lakes emptied, the marshes drained, the enormous structures erected on land, and the teeming vessels that cover the sea; and, on the other hand, estimate with ever so little thought, the real advantages that have accrued from all these works to mankind, we cannot help being amazed at the vast disproportion there is between these things, and deploring the infatuation of man, which, to gratify his silly

pride and vain self-admiration, induces him eagerly to pursue all the miseries he is capable of feeling, though beneficent nature had kindly placed them out of his way.

Rousseau, *Origin of Inequality,* Appendix

34 Savage man, when he has dined, is at peace with all nature, and the friend of all his fellow-creatures. If a dispute arises about a meal, he rarely comes to blows, without having first compared the difficulty of conquering his antagonist with the trouble of finding subsistence elsewhere: and, as pride does not come in, it all ends in a few blows; the victor eats, and the vanquished seeks provision somewhere else, and all is at peace. The case is quite different with man in the state of society, for whom first necessaries have to be provided, and then superfluities; delicacies follow next, then immense wealth, then subjects, and then slaves. He enjoys not a moment's relaxation; and what is yet stranger, the less natural and pressing his wants, the more headstrong are his passions, and, still worse, the more he has it in his power to gratify them; so that after a long course of prosperity, after having swallowed up treasures and ruined multitudes, the hero ends up by cutting every throat till he finds himself, at last, sole master of the world. Such is in miniature the moral picture, if not of human life, at least of the secret pretensions of the heart of civilised man.

Rousseau, *Origin of Inequality,* Appendix

35 *Johnson.* It is in refinement and elegance that the civilized man differs from the savage. A great part of our industry, and all our ingenuity is exercised in procuring pleasure; and, Sir, a hungry man has not the same pleasure in eating a plain dinner, that a hungry man has in eating a luxurious dinner.

Boswell, *Life of Johnson (Apr. 14, 1778)*

36 Natural phenomena, governed by constant laws, traverse forever certain fixed cycles of change. All things perish, all things revive; and in those successive generations which mark the reproduction of plants and of animals, time but restores continually the likeness of what it has annihilated.

The succession of mankind, on the contrary, presents from age to age an ever-varied spectacle. Reason, the passions, liberty, continually give rise to new events. All the ages are linked together by a chain of causes and effects which unite the existing state of the world with all that has gone before. The arbitrary signs of speech and of writing, in giving to men the means of insuring the possession of their ideas and of communicating them to others, have made a common treasure-store of all individual knowledge, which one generation bequeaths to the next, a heritage constantly augmented by the discoveries of each age; and mankind, viewed from its origin, appears to

the eyes of a philosopher as one vast whole, which itself, like each individual, has its infancy and its growth.

Turgot, *Progress of the Human Mind,* I

37 What a host of inventions unknown to the ancients, and credited to an age of barbarism! Our art of recording music, our bills of exchange, our paper, window-glass, plate-glass, windmills, watches, spectacles, gunpowder, the magnetic needle and the consequent perfection of navigation and commerce. The arts are but the utilization of nature, and the exercise of the arts is a series of physical experiments which progressively unveil her. Facts were accumulating in the darkness of the age of ignorance, and the sciences, whose progress, for all that it was hidden, was none the less actual, were destined to reappear in time increased by these new riches; like those rivers which, after having disappeared from view for a space in some subterranean channel, reappear farther on augmented by all the waters which have filtered through the earth.

Turgot, *Progress of the Human Mind,* I

38 The uniform, constant, and uninterrupted effort of every man to better his condition, the principle from which public and national, as well as private opulence is originally derived, is frequently powerful enough to maintain the natural progress of things towards improvement, in spite both of the extravagance of government and of the greatest errors of administration. Like the unknown principle of animal life, it frequently restores health and vigour to the constitution, in spite, not only of the disease, but of the absurd prescriptions of the doctor.

Adam Smith, *Wealth of Nations,* II, 3

39 Laws and institutions must go hand in hand with the progress of the human mind. As that becomes more developed, more enlightened, as new discoveries are made, new truths disclosed, and manners and opinions change with the change of circumstances, institutions must advance also, and keep pace with the times.

Jefferson, *Letter to Samuel Kercheval*
(July 12, 1816)

40 We imperceptibly advance from youth to age without observing the gradual, but incessant, change of human affairs; and even in our larger experience of history, the imagination is accustomed, by a perpetual series of causes and effects. to unite the most distant revolutions. But if the interval between two memorable eras could be instantly annihilated; if it were possible, after a momentary slumber of two hundred years, to display the *new* world to the eyes of a spectator who still retained a lively and recent impression of the *old,* his surprise and his reflections would furnish the

pleasing subject of a philosophical romance.

Gibbon, *Decline and Fall of the Roman Empire*, XXXIII

41 Since the first discovery of the arts, war, commerce, and religious zeal have diffused among the savages of the Old and New World these inestimable gifts: they have been successively propagated; they can never be lost. We may therefore acquiesce in the pleasing conclusion that every age of the world has increased and still increases the real wealth, the happiness, the knowledge, and perhaps the virtue, of the human race.

Gibbon, *Decline and Fall of the Roman Empire*, XXXVIII

42 The history of the human race, viewed as a whole, may be regarded as the realization of a hidden plan of nature to bring about a political constitution, internally, and, for this purpose, also externally perfect, as the only state in which all the capacities implanted by her in mankind can be fully developed.

Kant, *Idea of a Universal History*, VIII

43 I will . . . venture to assume that as the human race is continually advancing in civilisation and culture as its natural purpose, so it is continually making progress for the better in relation to the moral end of its existence, and that this progress although it may be sometimes interrupted, will never be entirely broken off or stopped. It is not necessary for me to prove this assumption; the burden of proof lies on its opponents. For I take my stand upon my innate sense of duty in this connection. Every member in the series of generations to which I belong as a man—although mayhap not so well equipped with the requisite moral qualifications as I ought to be, and consequently might be—is, in fact, prompted by his sense of duty so to act in reference to posterity that they may always become better, and the possibility of this must be assumed. This duty can thus be rightfully transmitted from one member of the generations to another. Now whatever doubts may be drawn from history against my hopes, and were they even of such a kind as, in case of their being demonstrated, might move me to desist from efforts which according to all appearances would be vain, yet so long as this is not made out with complete certainty, I am not entitled to give up the guidance of duty which is clear, and to adopt the prudential rule of not working at the impracticable, since this is not clear but is mere hypothesis. And, however uncertain I may always be as to whether we may rightly hope that the human race will attain to a better condition, yet this individual uncertainty cannot detract from the general rule of conduct, or from the necessary assumption in the practical relation that such a condition *is* practicable.

Kant, *On the Saying: That a Thing may be Right in Theory, but may not Hold in Practice*

44 The question next arises as to the means by which this continuous progress to the better may be maintained and even hastened. When carefully considered, we soon see that as this process must go on to an incalculable distance of time, it cannot depend so much on what we may do of ourselves, for instance, on the education we give to the younger generation, or on the method by which we may proceed in order to realise it, as on what human *Nature* as such will do *in* and with us, to compel us to move in a track into which we would not readily have betaken ourselves. For, it is from human Nature in general, or rather—since supreme wisdom is requisite for the accomplishment of this end—it is from *Providence* alone that we can expect a result which proceeds by relation to the whole and reacts through the whole upon the parts. Men with their *plans* start, on the contrary, only from the parts, and even continue to regard the parts alone, while the whole as such is viewed as too great for them to influence and as attainable by them only in idea.

Kant, *On the Saying: That a Thing may be Right in Theory, but may not Hold in Practice*

45 Human Reason pursues her course in the species in general: she invents, before she can apply; she discovers, though evil hands may long abuse her discoveries. Abuse will correct itself; and, through the unwearied zeal of ever-growing Reason, disorder will in time become order. By contending against passions, she strengthens and enlightens herself: from being oppressed in this place, she will fly to that, and extend the sphere of her sway over the Earth. There is nothing enthusiastical in the hope, that, wherever men dwell, at some future period will dwell men rational, just, and happy: happy, not through the means of their own reason alone, but of the common reason of their whole fraternal race.

Herder, *Philosophy of the History of Man*, XV

46 The organic perfectibility or degeneration of species in the case of plants or of animals can be regarded as one of the general laws of nature.

This law extends to the human race, and no one probably will doubt that progress in preventive medicine, the use of more healthful foods and habitations, a mode of living which should develop the strength through exercise without impairing it through excess, that, finally, the destruction of the two most active causes of degeneracy, extreme poverty and excessive wealth, will necessarily prolong the average duration of man's life and secure him a more constant health and a more robust constitution. It is felt that the progress of preventive medicine, become more efficacious through the progress of reason and that of the social order, must do away in time with transmissible or contagious diseases, and those general disorders which owe their origin to climates, foods, or the nature of occupations. It would not be difficult to prove that this hope may be extended to nearly all the other maladies, the distant causes of which it is probable will be discovered hereafter. Would it be absurd, then, to suppose that this improvement of the human race may be regarded as susceptible of indefinite progress, that there may come a time when death shall be no more than the result either of extraordinary accidents or of the ever more gradual decay of the vital forces, and that, finally, the average interval elapsing between birth and this decay may itself have no assignable limit? Doubtless man will never become immortal, but may not the distance between the moment when he first receives life and the common period when in the course of nature, without illness and without accident, he finds it no longer possible to exist, grow constantly wider?

Condorcet, *Historical Picture of the Progress of the Human Mind*, 10

47 [The] average duration of human life is destined to increase continually, if physical revolutions do not oppose themselves thereto; but we do not know what limit it is that it can never pass; we do not even know if the general laws of nature have fixed such a limit.

Condorcet, *Historical Picture of the Progress of the Human Mind*, 10

48 It is, undoubtedly, a most disheartening reflection that the great obstacle in the way to any extraordinary improvement in society is of a nature that we can never hope to overcome. The perpetual tendency in the race of man to increase beyond the means of subsistence is one of the general laws of animated nature which we can have no reason to expect will change. Yet, discouraging as the contemplation of this difficulty must be to those whose exertions are laudably directed to the improvement of the human species, it is evident that no possible good can arise from any endeavors to slur it over or keep it in the background.

Malthus, *Population*, XVII

49 *Chorus.* The world's great age begins anew,
　The golden years return,
The earth doth like a snake renew
　Her winter weeds outworn;
Heaven smiles, and faiths and empires gleam,
Like wrecks of a dissolving dream.

A brighter Hellas rears its mountains
　From waves serener far;
A new Peneus rolls his fountains
　Against the morning-star.
Where fairer Tempes bloom, there sleep
Young Cyclads on a sunnier deep.

A loftier Argo cleaves the main,
　Fraught with a later prize;
Another Orpheus sings again,
　And loves, and weeps, and dies.
A new Ulysses leaves once more
Calypso for his native shore.

Oh, write no more the tale of Troy,
　If earth Death's scroll must be!
Nor mix with Laian rage the joy
　Which dawns upon the free;
Although a subtler Sphinx renew
Riddles of death Thebes never knew.

Another Athens shall arise,
　And to remoter time
Bequeath, like sunset to the skies,
　The splendor of its prime;
And leave, if nought so bright may live,
All earth can take or Heaven can give.

Saturn and Love their long repose
　Shall burst, more bright and good
Than all who fell, than One who rose,
　Than many unsubdued;
Not gold, not blood, their altar dowers,
But votive tears and symbol flowers.

Oh, cease! must hate and death return?
　Cease! must men kill and die?
Cease! drain not to its dregs the urn
　Of bitter prophecy.
The world is weary of the past,
Oh, might it die or rest at last!

Shelley, *Hellas*, 1060

50 In order to understand the true value and character of the Positive Philosophy, we must take a brief general view of the progressive course of the human mind, regarded as a whole; for no conception can be understood otherwise than through its history.

From the study of the development of human intelligence, in all directions, and through all times, the discovery arises of a great fundamental law, to which it is necessarily subject, and which has a solid foundation of proof, both in the facts of our organization and in our historical experience. The law is this:—that each of our leading conceptions—each branch of our knowledge—passes successively through three different theoretical conditions: the Theological, or fictitious; the Metaphysical, or abstract; and the Scientific, or positive. In other words, the human mind, by its nature, employs in its progress three methods of philosophizing, the character of which is essentially different, and even radically opposed: viz., the theological method, the metaphysical, and the positive. Hence arise three philosophies, or general systems of conceptions on the aggregate of phenomena, each of which excludes the others. The first is the necessary point of departure of the human understanding; and the third is its fixed and definite state. The second is merely a state of transition.

Comte, *Positive Philosophy*, Introduction, 1

51 We have nothing to do here with the metaphysical controversy about the absolute happiness of Man at different stages of civilization. As the happiness of every man depends on the harmony between the development of his various faculties and the entire system of the circumstances which govern his life; and as, on the other hand, this equilibrium always establishes itself spontaneously to a certain extent, it is impossible to compare in a positive way, either by sentiment or reasoning, the individual welfare which belongs to social situations that can never be brought into direct comparison: and therefore the question of the happiness of different animal organisms, or of their two sexes, is merely impracticable and unintelligible. The only question, therefore, is of the effect of the social evolution, which is so undeniable that there is no reasoning with any one who does not admit it as the basis of the inquiry. The only ground of discussion is whether development and improvement,—the theoretical and the practical aspect,— are one; whether the development is necessarily accompanied by a corresponding amelioration, or progress, properly so called. To me it appears that the amelioration is as unquestionable as the development from which it proceeds, provided we regard it as subject, like the development itself, to limits, general and special, which science will be found to prescribe. The chimerical notion of unlimited perfectibility is thus at once excluded. Taking the human race as a whole, and not any one people, it appears that human development brings after it, in two ways, an ever-growing amelioration, first, in the radical condition of Man, which no one disputes; and next, in his corresponding faculties, which is a view much less attended to. There is no need to dwell upon the improvement in the conditions of human existence, both by the increasing action of Man on his environment through the advancement of the sciences and arts, and by the constant amelioration of his customs and manners; and again, by the gradual improvement in social organization. We shall presently see that in the Middle Ages, which are charged with political retrogression, the progress was more political than any other. One fact is enough to silence sophistical declamation on this subject; the continuous increase of population all over the globe, as a consequence of civilization, while the wants of individuals are, as a whole, better satisfied at the same time. The tendency to improvement must be highly spontaneous and irresistible to have persevered notwithstanding the enormous faults—political faults especially— which have at all times absorbed or neutralized the greater part of our social forces. Even throughout the revolutionary period, in spite of the marked discordance between the political system and the general state of civilization, the improvement has proceeded, not only in physical and intellectual, but also in moral respects, though the transient disorganization could not but disturb the natural evolution. As for the other aspect of the question, the gradual and slow improvement of human nature, within narrow limits, it seems to me impossible to reject altogether the principle proposed (with great exaggeration, however) by Lamarck, of the necessary influence of a homogeneous and continuous exercise in producing, in every animal organism, and especially in Man, an organic improvement, susceptible of being established in the race, after a sufficient persistence. If we take the best-marked case—that of intellectual development, it seems to be unquestionable that there is a superior aptitude for mental combinations, independent of all culture, among highly-civilized people; or, what comes to the same thing, an inferior aptitude among nations that are less advanced,—the average intellect of the members of those societies being taken for observation. The intellectual faculties are, it is true, more modified than the others by the social evolution: but then they have the smallest relative effect in the individual human constitution: so that we are authorized to infer from their amelioration a proportionate improvement in aptitudes that are more marked and equally exercised. In regard to morals, particularly, I think it indisputable that the gradual development of humanity favors a growing preponderance of the noblest tendencies of our nature,—as I hope to prove further on. The lower instincts continue to manifest themselves in modified action, but their less sustained and more repressed exercise must tend to debilitate them by degrees; and their increasing regulation certainly brings them into involuntary concurrence in the maintenance of a good social economy; and especially in the case of the least marked organisms, which constitute a vast majority. These two aspects of social evolution, then,— the *development* which brings after it the *improvement*,—we may consider to be admitted as facts.

Comte, *Positive Philosophy*, VI, 3

52 The progress of the race must be considered susceptible of modification only with regard to its speed, and without any reversal in the order of development, or any interval of any importance being overleaped.

Comte, *Positive Philosophy*, VI, 3

53 Society never advances. It recedes as fast on one side as it gains on the other. It undergoes continual changes; it is barbarous, it is civilized, it is christianized, it is rich, it is scientific; but this change is not amelioration. For every thing that is given something is taken. Society acquires new

arts and loses old instincts. What a contrast between the well-clad, reading, writing, thinking
American, with a watch, a pencil and a bill of
exchange in his pocket, and the naked New Zea-
lander, whose property is a club, a spear, a mat
and an undivided twentieth of a shed to sleep under! But compare the health of the two men and
you shall see that the white man has lost his aboriginal strength. If the traveller tell us truly,
strike the savage with a broad-axe and in a day or
two the flesh shall unite and heal as if you struck
the blow into soft pitch, and the same blow shall
send the white to his grave.

Emerson, *Self-Reliance*

54 The civilized man has built a coach, but has lost
the use of his feet. He is supported on crutches,
but lacks so much support of muscle. He has a
fine Geneva watch, but he fails of the skill to tell
the hour by the sun. A Greenwich nautical alma-
nac he has, and so being sure of the information
when he wants it, the man in the street does not
know a star in the sky.

Emerson, *Self-Reliance*

55 There is not a piece of science but its flank may be
turned to-morrow; there is not any literary reputation, not the so-called eternal names of fame,
that may not be revised and condemned. The
very hopes of man, the thoughts of his heart, the
religion of nations, the manners and morals of
mankind are all at the mercy of a new generalization.

Emerson, *Circles*

56 As long as our civilization is essentially one of
property, of fences, of exclusiveness, it will be
mocked by delusions. Our riches will leave us sick;
there will be bitterness in our laughter, and our
wine will burn our mouth. Only that good profits
which we can taste with all doors open, and which
serves all men.

Emerson, *Napoleon; or, The Man of the World*

57 Not in vain the distance beacons. Forward, for-
    ward let us range,
Let the great world spin for ever down the ringing
    grooves of change.

Thro' the shadow of the globe we sweep into the
    younger day;
Better fifty years of Europe than a cycle of Ca-
    thay.

Tennyson, *Locksley Hall*, 181

58 Shad are still taken in the basin of Concord River,
at Lowell, where they are said to be a month earlier than the Merrimack shad, on account of the
warmth of the water. Still patiently, almost pathetically, with instinct not to be discouraged, not
to be *reasoned* with, revisiting their old haunts, as if

their stern fates would relent, and still met by the
Corporation with its dam. Poor shad! where is thy
redress? When Nature gave thee instinct, gave she
thee the heart to bear thy fate? Still wandering
the sea in thy scaly armor to inquire humbly at
the mouths of rivers if man has perchance left
them free for thee to enter. By countless shoals
loitering uncertain meanwhile, merely stemming
the tide there, in danger from sea foes in spite of
thy bright armor, awaiting new instructions, until
the sands, until the water itself, tell thee if it be so
or not. Thus by whole migrating nations, full of
instinct, which is thy faith, in this backward
spring, turned adrift, and perchance knowest not
where men do *not* dwell, where there are *not* factories, in these days. Armed with no sword, no electric shock, but mere shad, armed only with innocence and a just cause, with tender dumb mouth
only forward, and scales easy to be detached. I for
one am with thee, and who knows what may avail
a crowbar against that Billerica dam?—Not despairing when whole myriads have gone to feed
those sea monsters during thy suspense, but still
brave, indifferent, on easy fin there, like shad reserved for higher destinies. Willing to be decimat-
ed for man's behoof after the spawning season.
Away with the superficial and selfish philanthropy of men—who knows what admirable virtue of
fishes may be below low-water-mark, bearing up
against a hard destiny, not admired by that fellow-creature who alone can appreciate it! Who
hears the fishes when they cry? It will not be forgotten by some memory that we were contemporaries. Thou shalt ere long have thy way up the
rivers, up all the rivers of the globe, if I am not
mistaken. Yea, even thy dull watery dream shall
be more than realized. If it were not so, but thou
wert to be overlooked at first and at last, then
would not I take their heaven. Yes, I say so, who
think I know better than thou canst. Keep a stiff
fin, then, and stem all the tides thou mayst meet.

Thoreau, *A Week on the Concord
and Merrimack Rivers (Saturday)*

59 In the savage state every family owns a shelter as
good as the best, and sufficient for its coarser and
simpler wants; but I think that I speak within
bounds when I say that, though the birds of the
air have their nests, and the foxes their holes, and
the savages their wigwams, in modern civilized
society not more than one half the families own a
shelter. In the large towns and cities, where civilization especially prevails, the number of those
who own a shelter is a very small fraction of the
whole. The rest pay an annual tax for this outside
garment of all, become indispensable summer and
winter, which would buy a village of Indian wigwams, but now helps to keep them poor as long as
they live. I do not mean to insist here on the disadvantage of hiring compared with owning, but it
is evident that the savage owns his shelter because

it costs so little, while the civilized man hires his commonly because he cannot afford to own it; nor can he, in the long run, any better afford to hire. But, answers one, by merely paying this tax the poor civilized man secures an abode which is a palace compared with the savage's. An annual rent of from twenty-five to a hundred dollars (these are the country rates) entitles him to the benefit of the improvements of centuries, spacious apartments, clean paint and paper, Rumford fireplace, back plastering, Venetian blinds, copper pump, spring lock, a commodious cellar, and many other things. But how happens it that he who is said to enjoy these things is so commonly a *poor* civilized man, while the savage, who has them not, is rich as a savage? If it is asserted that civilization is a real advance in the condition of man—and I think that it is, though only the wise improve their advantages—it must be shown that it has produced better dwellings without making them more costly; and the cost of a thing is the amount of what I will call life which is required to be exchanged for it, immediately or in the long run. An average house in this neighborhood costs perhaps eight hundred dollars, and to lay up this sum will take from ten to fifteen years of the laborer's life, even if he is not encumbered with a family—estimating the pecuniary value of every man's labor at one dollar a day, for if some receive more, others receive less;—so that he must have spent more than half his life commonly before *his* wigwam will be earned. If we suppose him to pay a rent instead, this is but a doubtful choice of evils. Would the savage have been wise to exchange his wigwam for a palace on these terms?

Thoreau, *Walden:* Economy

60 Some are dinning in our ears that we Americans, and moderns generally, are intellectual dwarfs compared with the ancients, or even the Elizabethan men. But what is that to the purpose? A living dog is better than a dead lion. Shall a man go and hang himself because he belongs to the race of pygmies, and not be the biggest pygmy that he can? Let every one mind his own business, and endeavor to be what he was made.

Thoreau, *Walden:* Conclusion

61 To believe that man was aboriginally civilised and then suffered utter degradation in so many regions, is to take a pitiably low view of human nature. It is apparently a truer and more cheerful view that progress has been much more general than retrogression; that man has risen, though by slow and interrupted steps, from a lowly condition to the highest standard as yet attained by him in knowledge, morals and religion.

Darwin, *Descent of Man,* I, 5

62 Thoughtful men, once escaped from the blinding influences of traditional prejudice, will find in the lowly stock whence Man has sprung, the best evidence of the splendour of his capacities; and will discern in his long progress through the Past, a reasonable ground of faith in his attainment of a nobler Future.

T. H. Huxley, *Relations of Man to the Lower Animals*

63 Men in society are undoubtedly subject to the cosmic process. As among other animals, multiplication goes on without cessation, and involves severe competition for the means of support. The struggle for existence tends to eliminate those less fitted to adapt themselves to the circumstances of their existence. The strongest, the most self-assertive, tend to tread down the weaker. But the influence of the cosmic process on the evolution of society is the greater the more rudimentary its civilization. Social progress means a checking of the cosmic process at every step and the substitution for it of another, which may be called the ethical process; the end of which is not the survival of those who may happen to be the fittest, in respect of the whole of the conditions which obtain, but of those who are ethically the best.

T. H. Huxley, *Evolution and Ethics*

64 In support of the position that Order is intrinsically different from Progress, and that preservation of existing and acquisition of additional good are sufficiently distinct to afford the basis of a fundamental classification, we shall perhaps be reminded that Progress may be at the expense of Order; that while we are acquiring, or striving to acquire, good of one kind, we may be losing ground in respect to others: thus there may be progress in wealth, while there is deterioration in virtue. Granting this, what it proves is not that Progress is generically a different thing from Permanence, but that wealth is a different thing from virtue. Progress is permanence and something more; and it is no answer to this to say that Progress in one thing does not imply Permanence in everything. No more does Progress in one thing imply Progress in everything. Progress of any kind includes Permanence in that same kind; whenever Permanence is sacrificed to some particular kind of Progress, other Progress is still more sacrificed to it; and if it be not worth the sacrifice, not the interest of Permanence alone has been disregarded, but the general interest of Progress has been mistaken.

Mill, *Representative Government,* II

65 No one whose opinion deserves a moment's consideration can doubt that most of the great positive evils of the world are in themselves removable, and will, if human affairs continue to improve, be in the end reduced within narrow limits. Poverty, in any sense implying suffering, may be completely extinguished by the wisdom of

society, combined with the good sense and providence of individuals. Even that most intractable of enemies, disease, may be indefinitely reduced in dimensions by good physical and moral education, and proper control of noxious influences; while the progress of science holds out a promise for the future of still more direct conquests over this detestable foe. And every advance in that direction relieves us from some, not only of the chances which cut short our own lives, but, what concerns us still more, which deprive us of those in whom our happiness is wrapt up. As for vicissitudes of fortune, and other disappointments connected with worldly circumstances, these are principally the effect either of gross imprudence, of ill-regulated desires, or of bad or imperfect social institutions.

Mill, *Utilitarianism*, II

66 It is my belief indeed that the general tendency is, and will continue to be, saving occasional and temporary exceptions, one of improvement—a tendency towards a better and happier state. This, however, is not a question of the method of the social science, but a theorem of the science itself. For our purpose it is sufficient that there is a progressive change, both in the character of the human race and in their outward circumstances so far as moulded by themselves; that in each successive age the principal phenomena of society are different from what they were in the age preceding, and still more different from any previous age: the periods which most distinctly mark these successive changes being intervals of one generation, during which a new set of human beings have been educated, have grown up from childhood, and taken possession of society.

Mill, *System of Logic*, Bk. VI, X, 3

67 A Philosophy of History is generally admitted to be at once the verification and the initial form of the Philosophy of the Progress of Society.

Mill, *System of Logic*, Bk. VI, X, 8

68   Progress is
The law of life, man is not Man as yet.

Browning, *Paracelsus*, V

69   Man knows partly but conceives beside,
Creeps ever on from fancies to the fact,
And in this striving, this converting air
Into a solid he may grasp and use,
Finds progress, man's distinctive mark alone,
Not God's, and not the beasts': God is, they are,
Man partly is and wholly hopes to be.

Browning, *A Death in the Desert*

70 The pursuit of perfection . . . is the pursuit of sweetness and light. He who works for sweetness and light, works to make reason and the will of God prevail. He who works for machinery, he

who works for hatred, works only for confusion. Culture looks beyond machinery, culture hates hatred; culture has one great passion, the passion for sweetness and light. It has one even yet greater!—the passion for making them *prevail*. It is not satisfied till we *all* come to a perfect man; it knows that the sweetness and light of the few must be imperfect until the raw and unkindled masses of humanity are touched with sweetness and light. If I have not shrunk from saying that we must work for sweetness and light, so neither have I shrunk from saying that we must have a broad basis, must have sweetness and light for as many as possible. Again and again I have insisted how those are the happy moments of humanity, how those are the marking epochs of a people's life, how those are the flowering times for literature and art and all the creative power of genius, when there is a *national* glow of life and thought, when the whole of society is in the fullest measure permeated by thought, sensible to beauty, intelligent and alive.

Arnold, *Culture and Anarchy*, I

71 Progress . . . is not an accident, but a necessity. Instead of civilization being artificial, it is a part of nature; all of a piece with the development of the embryo or the unfolding of a flower. The modifications mankind have undergone, and are still undergoing, result from a law underlying the whole organic creation; and provided the human race continues, and the constitution of things remains the same, those modifications must end in completeness. As surely as the tree becomes bulky when it stands alone, and slender if one of a group; as surely as the same creature assumes the different forms of cart-horse and race-horse, according as its habits demand strength or speed; as surely as a blacksmith's arm grows large, and the skin of a labourer's hand thick; as surely as the eye tends to become long-sighted in the sailor, and short-sighted in the student; as surely as the blind attain a more delicate sense of touch; as surely as a clerk acquires rapidity in writing and calculation; as surely as the musician learns to detect an error of a semi-tone amidst what seems to others a very babel of sounds; as surely as a passion grows by indulgence and diminishes when restrained; as surely as a disregarded conscience becomes inert, and one that is obeyed active; as surely as there is any efficacy in educational culture, or any meaning in such terms as habit, custom, practice; so surely must the human faculties be moulded into complete fitness for the social state; so surely must the things we call evil and immorality disappear; so surely must man become perfect.

Spencer, *Social Statics*, I, 2

72 The plexus of causes returneth in which I am intertwined,—it will again create me! I myself pertain to the causes of the eternal return.
I come again with this sun, with this earth, with

this eagle, with this serpent—*not* to a new life, or a better life, or a similar life:

—I come again eternally to this identical and selfsame life, in its greatest and its smallest, to teach again the eternal return of all things,—

—To speak again the word of the great noontide of earth and man, to announce again to man the Superman.

Nietzsche, *Thus Spake Zarathustra,* III, 57

73 This life, as thou livest it now, as thou hast lived it, thou needst must live again, and an infinite number of times; and there will be in it nothing new; but every grief and every joy, every thought and every sigh, all the infinitely great and the infinitely little in thy life must return for thee, and all this in the same sequence and the same order. And also this spider and the moonlight through the trees, and also this moment and myself. The eternal hour-glass of existence will ever be turned again, and thou with it, dust of dust.

Nietzsche, *Joyful Wisdom,* 341

74 The more ignorant men are, the move convinced are they that their little parish and their little chapel is an apex to which civilization and philosophy has painfully struggled up the pyramid of time from a desert of savagery. Savagery, they think, became barbarism; barbarism became ancient civilization; ancient civilization became Pauline Christianity; Pauline Christianity became Roman Catholicism; Roman Catholicism became the Dark Ages; and the Dark Ages were finally enlightened by the Protestant instincts of the English race. The whole process is summed up as Progress with a capital P. And any elderly gentleman of Progressive temperament will testify that the improvement since he was a boy is enormous. . . .

The notion that there has been any such Progress since Cæsar's time (less than 20 centuries) is too absurd for discussion. All the savagery, barbarism, dark ages and the rest of it of which we have any record as existing in the past exists at the present moment.

Shaw, *Caesar and Cleopatra,* Notes

75 We must . . . frankly give up the notion that Man as he exists is capable of net progress. There will always be an illusion of progress, because wherever we are conscious of an evil we remedy it, and therefore always seem to ourselves to be progressing, forgetting that most of the evils we see are the effects, finally become acute, of long-unnoticed retrogressions; that our compromising remedies seldom fully recover the lost ground; above all, that on the lines along which we are degenerating, good has become evil in our eyes, and is being undone in the name of progress precisely as evil is undone and replaced by good on the lines along which we are evolving. This is in-

deed the Illusion of Illusions; for it gives us infallible and appalling assurance that if our political ruin is to come, it will be effected by ardent reformers and supported by enthusiastic patriots as a series of necessary steps in our progress. Let the Reformer, the Progressive, the Meliorist then reconsider himself and his eternal ifs and ans which never become pots and pans. Whilst Man remains what he is, there can be no progress beyond the point already attained and fallen headlong from at every attempt at civilization; and since even that point is but a pinnacle to which a few people cling in giddy terror above an abyss of squalor, mere progress should no longer charm us.

Shaw, *Man and Superman,* Revolutionist's Handbook

76 The reasonable man adapts himself to the world: the unreasonable one persists in trying to adapt the world to himself. Therefore all progress depends on the unreasonable man.

Shaw, *Man and Superman,* Maxims for Revolutionists

77 The differences between the nations and races of mankind are required to preserve the conditions under which higher development is possible. One main factor in the upward trend of animal life has been the power of wandering. Perhaps this is why the armour-plated monsters fared badly. They could not wander. Animals wander into new conditions. They have to adapt themselves or die. Mankind has wandered from the trees to the plains, from the plains to the seacoast, from climate to climate, from continent to continent, and from habit of life to habit of life. When man ceases to wander, he will cease to ascend in the scale of being. Physical wandering is still important, but greater still is the power of man's spiritual adventures—adventures of thought, adventures of passionate feeling, adventures of aesthetic experience. A diversification among human communities is essential for the provision of the incentive and material for the Odyssey of the human spirit. Other nations of different habits are not enemies: they are godsends. Men require of their neighbours something sufficiently akin to be understood, something sufficiently different to provoke attention, and something great enough to command admiration. We must not expect, however, all the virtues. We should even be satisfied if there is something odd enough to be interesting.

Modern science has imposed on humanity the necessity for wandering. Its progressive thought and its progressive technology make the transition through time, from generation to generation, a true migration into uncharted seas of adventure. The very benefit of wandering is that it is dangerous and needs skill to avert evils. We must expect, therefore, that the future will disclose dangers. It is the business of the future to be dangerous; and it is among the merits of science that it equips the future for its duties. The prosperous middle classes, who ruled the nineteenth century, placed an excessive value upon placidity of existence. They refused to face the necessities for social reform imposed by the new industrial system, and they are now refusing to face the necessities for intellectual reform imposed by the new knowledge. The middle class pessimism over the future of the world comes from a confusion between civilisation and security. In the immediate future there will be less security than in the immediate past, less stability. It must be admitted that there is a degree of instability which is inconsistent with civilisation. But, on the whole, the great ages have been unstable ages.

Whitehead, *Science and the Modern World*, XIII

78 The foundation of all understanding . . . is that no static maintenance of perfection is possible. This axiom is rooted in the nature of things. Advance or Decadence are the only choices offered to mankind. The pure conservative is fighting against the essence of the universe.

Whitehead, *Adventures of Ideas*, XIX, 2

79 That Man is the product of causes which had no prevision of the end they were achieving; that his origin, his growth, his hopes and fears, his loves and his beliefs, are but the outcome of accidental collocations of atoms; that no fire, no heroism, no intensity of thought and feeling, can preserve an individual life beyond the grave; that all the labours of the ages, all the devotion, all the inspiration, all the noonday brightness of human genius, are destined to extinction in the vast death of the solar system, and that the whole temple of Man's achievement must inevitably be buried beneath the debris of a universe in ruins—all these things, if not quite beyond dispute, are yet so nearly certain, that no philosophy which rejects them can hope to stand.

Russell, *A Free Man's Worship*

80 Civilization is the fruit of renunciation of instinctual satisfaction, and from each newcomer in turn it exacts the same renunciation. Throughout the life of the individual, there is a constant replacement of the external compulsion by the internal. The influences of civilization cause an ever-increasing transmutation of egoistic trends into altruistic and social ones, and this by an admixture of erotic elements. In the last resort it may be said that every internal compulsion which has been of service in the development of human beings was originally, that is, in the evolution of the human race, nothing but an external one. Those who are born today bring with them as an inherited constitution some degree of a tendency (disposition) towards transmutation of egoistic into social instincts, and this disposition is easily stimulated to achieve that effect. A further measure of this transformation must be accomplished during the life of the individual himself. And so the human being is subject not only to the pressure of his immediate environment, but also to the influence of the cultural development attained by his forefathers.

Freud, *Thoughts on War and Death*, I

81 It sounds like a fairy-tale, but not only that; this story of what man by his science and practical inventions has achieved on this earth, where he first appeared as a weakly member of the animal kingdom, and on which each individual of his species must ever again appear as a helpless infant—O inch of nature!—is a direct fulfilment of all, or of most, of the dearest wishes in his fairy-tales. All these possessions he has acquired through culture. Long ago he formed an ideal conception of omnipotence and omniscience which he embodied in his gods. Whatever seemed unattainable to his desires—or forbidden to him—he attributed to these gods. One may say, therefore, that these gods were the ideals of his culture. Now he has himself approached very near to realizing this ideal, he has nearly become a god himself. But only, it is true, in the way that ideals are usually realized in the general experience of humanity. Not completely; in some respects not at all, in others only by halves. Man has become a god by means of artificial limbs, so to speak, quite magnificent when equipped with all his accessory organs; but they do not grow on him and they still give him trouble at times. However, he is entitled to console himself with the thought that this evolution will not come to an end in A.D. 1930.

Freud, *Civilization and Its Discontents*, III

82 Future ages will produce further great advances in this realm of culture, probably inconceivable now, and will increase man's likeness to a god still more.

Freud, *Civilization and Its Discontents*, III

83 The fateful question of the human species seems to me to be whether and to what extent the cultural process developed in it will succeed in mastering the derangements of communal life caused by the human instinct of aggression and self-destruction. In this connection, perhaps the phase through which we are at this moment passing deserves special interest. Men have brought their powers of subduing the forces of nature to such a pitch that by using them they could now very easily exterminate one another to the last man. They know this—hence arises a great part of their current unrest, their dejection, their mood of apprehension. And now it may be expected that the other of the two *heavenly forces*, eternal Eros, will put forth his strength so as to maintain himself

alongside of his equally immortal adversary.

Freud, *Civilization and Its Discontents,* VIII

84 If civilization has profoundly modified man, it is by accumulating in his social surroundings, as in a reservoir, the habits and knowledge which society pours into the individual at each new generation. Scratch the surface, abolish everything we owe to an education which is perpetual and unceasing, and you find in the depth of our nature primitive humanity, or something very near it.

Bergson, *Two Sources of Morality and Religion,* II

85 The longing to be primitive is a disease of culture; it is archaism in morals. To be so preoccupied with vitality is a symptom of anæmia. When life was really vigorous and young, in Homeric times for instance, no one seemed to fear that it might be squeezed out of existence either by the incubus of matter or by the petrifying blight of intelligence. Life was like the light of day, something to use, or to waste, or to enjoy. It was not a thing to worship; and often the chief luxury of living consisted in dealing death about vigorously. Life indeed was loved, and the beauty and pathos of it were felt exquisitely; but its beauty and pathos lay in the divineness of its model and in its own fragility. No one paid it the equivocal compliment of thinking it a substance or a material force. Nobility was not then impossible in sentiment, because there were ideals in life higher and more indestructible than life itself, which life might illustrate and to which it might fitly be sacrificed. Nothing can be meaner than the anxiety to live on, to live on anyhow and in any shape; a spirit with any honour is not willing to live except in its own way, and a spirit with any wisdom is not over-eager to live at all. In those days men recognised immortal gods and resigned themselves to being mortal. Yet those were the truly vital and instinctive days of the human spirit. Only when vitality is low do people find material things oppressive and ideal things unsubstantial.

Santayana, *Winds of Doctrine,* I

86 Progress, far from consisting in change, depends on retentiveness. When change is absolute there remains no being to improve and no direction is set for possible improvement: and when experience is not retained, as among savages, infancy is perpetual. Those who cannot remember the past are condemned to repeat it.

Santayana, *Life of Reason,* I, 12

87 The cry was for vacant freedom and indeterminate progress . . . *Full speed ahead!,* without asking whether directly before you was a bottomless pit.

Santayana, *My Host the World,* Epilogue

88 Everything is transitory and everything is pre-

served in progress, and if humanity is untiring and has always something further to undertake, if every one of its achievements gives rise to doubt and dissatisfaction and the demand for new achievement, yet now and again there is achievement; something is possessed and enjoyed and the apparently precipitous race is in reality a succession of reposes, of satisfactions in the midst of dissatisfactions, of fleeting moments spent in the joy of contemplation.

Croce, *History as the Story of Liberty,* I, 10

89 It must be realised by any student of civilisation that we pay heavily for our heterogeneous, rapidly changing civilisation; we pay in high proportions of crime and delinquency, we pay in the conflicts of youth, we pay in an ever-increasing number of neuroses, we pay in the lack of a coherent tradition without which the development of art is sadly handicapped. In such a list of prices, we must count our gains carefully, not to be discouraged. And chief among our gains must be reckoned this possibility of choice, the recognition of many possible ways of life, where other civilisations have recognised only one. Where other civilisations give a satisfactory outlet to only one temperamental type, be he mystic or soldier, business man or artist, a civilisation in which there are many standards offers a possibility of satisfactory adjustment to individuals of many different temperamental types, of diverse gifts and varying interests.

Margaret Mead, *Coming of Age in Samoa,* XIV

90 We are quite willing to admit now that the revolution of the earth about the sun, or the animal ancestry of man, has next to nothing to do with the uniqueness of our human achievements. If we inhabit one chance planet out of a myriad solar systems, so much the greater glory, and if all the ill-assorted human races are linked by evolution with the animal, the provable differences between ourselves and them are the more extreme and the uniqueness of our institutions the more remarkable. But *our* achievements, *our* institutions are unique; they are of a different order from those of lesser races and must be protected at all costs.

Benedict, *Patterns of Culture,* I

91 There is no doubt about the cultural continuity of the civilization, no matter who its carriers were at the moment. We must accept all the implications of our human inheritance, one of the most important of which is the small scope of biologically transmitted behaviour, and the enormous rôle of the cultural process of the transmission of tradition.

Benedict, *Patterns of Culture,* I

92 Civilization, as we know it, is a movement and not a condition, a voyage and not a harbour. No known civilization has ever reached the goal of civilization yet. There has never been a communion of saints on earth. In the least uncivilized society at its least uncivilized moment, the vast majority of its members have remained very near indeed to the primitive human level. And no society has ever been secure of holding such ground as it has managed to gain in its spiritual advance. All the civilizations that we know of, including the Greek, have already broken down and gone to pieces with the single possible exception of our own Western civilization—and no child of this civilization who has been born into our generation can easily imagine that our own society is immune from the danger of suffering the common fate.

Toynbee, *Civilization on Trial,* IV

93 Humanity is not an animal species, it is a historical reality. Human society is an antiphysis—in a sense it is against nature; it does not passively submit to the presence of nature but rather takes over the control of nature on its own behalf. This arrogation is not an inward, subjective operation; it is accomplished objectively in practical action.

Simone de Beauvoir, *The Second Sex,* III

15.3 | *Fate, Fortune, and Destiny*

The common thread running through the three subjects treated in this section lies in the conception of forces or factors at work in history that are totally beyond the control of man. The notion of fate—of an inexorable and blind necessity governing everything that happens—is most evident in the quotations drawn from antiquity, especially in the many quotations from the ancient poets. Some of them even go so far as to declare that the gods themselves are subject to the decrees of Fate and cannot set them aside. Nevertheless, there are a few ancient writers, Cicero for one, who question the universal domination of Fate or think that man's freedom is not totally obliterated by it.

In the Christian era, the notion of fate tends to be replaced by that of Divine providence and of predestination. Christian theologians, such as Augustine and Aquinas, attempt to reconcile human freedom with predestination and with the providential ordering of things by the will of God. For others, such as Luther and Calvin, providence and predestination have the same inexorability that the ancients accorded fate, a view that is echoed in Spinoza's declaration that everything is necessitated by God. The reader will find other quotations relevant to this subject in Chapter 5 on MIND, Section 5.7 on WILL: FREE CHOICE.

The discussion of fortune is more closely related to the consideration of cause and chance, which are treated in Sections 19.3 and 19.4 of Chapter 19 on NATURE AND THE COSMOS. Here the treatment of fortune stresses its implications for ethics and politics—the role that good fortune plays in the conduct of human life and in the pursuit of happiness; and the way in which it either facilitates or impedes the best laid plans of princes or statesmen to gain the objectives they have in view. Thus, we find Machia-velli advising the prince to regard Fortune as a woman who will yield only to bold advances.

---

1 Except the Lord build the house, they labour in vain that build it: except the Lord keep the city, the watchman waketh but in vain.

Psalm 127:1

2 Man also knoweth not his time: as the fishes that are taken in an evil net, and as the birds that are caught in the snare; so are the sons of men snared in an evil time, when it falleth suddenly upon them.

Ecclesiastes 9:12

3 Cast thy bread upon the waters: for thou shalt find it after many days.

Ecclesiastes 11:1

4 If a man live many years, and rejoice in them all; yet let him remember the days of darkness; for they shall be many.

Ecclesiastes 11:8

5 *Zeus.* For this among the immortal gods is the mightiest witness
I can give, and nothing I do shall be vain nor revocable
nor a thing unfulfilled when I bend my head in assent to it.

Homer, *Iliad*, I, 525

6 *Hektor.* No man is going to hurl me to Hades, unless it is fated,
but as for fate, I think that no man yet has escaped it
once it has taken its first form, neither brave man nor coward.

Homer, *Iliad*, VI, 487

7 *Achilleus.* There are two urns that stand on the door-sill of Zeus. They are unlike
for the gifts they bestow: an urn of evils, an urn of blessings.
If Zeus who delights in thunder mingles these and bestows them
on man, he shifts, and moves now in evil, again in good fortune.
But when Zeus bestows from the urn of sorrows, he makes a failure
of man, and the evil hunger drives him over the shining
earth, and he wanders respected neither of gods nor mortals.

Homer, *Iliad*, XXIV, 527

8 *Chorus.* Once a man fostered in his house
a lion cub, from the mother's milk
torn, craving the breast given.
In the first steps of its young life
mild, it played with children
and delighted the old.
Caught in the arm's cradle
they pampered it like a newborn child,
shining eyed and broken to the hand
to stay the stress of its hunger.

But it grew with time, and the lion
in the blood strain came out; it paid
grace to those who had fostered it
in blood and death for the sheep flocks,
a grim feast forbidden.
The house reeked with blood run
nor could its people beat down the bane,
the giant murderer's onslaught.
This thing they raised in their house was blessed
by God to be priest of destruction.

Aeschylus, *Agamemnon*, 716

9 *Electra.* The day of destiny waits for the free man as well
as for the man enslaved beneath an alien hand.

Aeschylus, *Libation Bearers*, 103

10 *Chorus.* All providence
Is effortless: throned,
Holy and motionless,
His will is accomplished.

Aeschylus, *Suppliant Maidens*, 97

11 *Prometheus.* It is an easy thing for one whose foot
is on the outside of calamity
to give advice and to rebuke the sufferer.
I have known all that you have said: I knew,
I knew when I transgressed nor will deny it.
In helping man I brought my troubles on me;
but yet I did not think that with such tortures
I should be wasted on these airy cliffs,
this lonely mountain top, with no one near.
But do not sorrow for my present suffering;
alight on earth and hear what is to come
that you may know the whole complete: I beg you
alight and join your sorrow with mine: misfortune
wandering the same track lights now upon one
and now upon another.

Aeschylus, *Prometheus Bound*, 265

12 *Prometheus.*   Craft is far weaker than necessity.
Chorus. Who then is the steersman of necessity?
Prom. The triple-formed Fates and the remembering Furies.

Ch. Is Zeus weaker than these?

Prom. Yes, for he, too, cannot escape what is fated.

Aeschylus, *Prometheus Bound*, 513

13 The Egyptians . . . discovered to which of the gods each month and day is sacred; and found out from the day of a man's birth what he will meet with in the course of his life, and how he will end his days, and what sort of man he will be.

Herodotus, *History*, II, 82

14 *Chorus.* Fate has terrible power.
You cannot escape it by wealth or war.
No fort will keep it out, no ships outrun it.

Sophocles, *Antigone*, 951

15 *Chorus.* Nothing painless
has the all-accomplishing King
dispensed for mortal men. But
grief and joy come circling
to all, like the turning paths
of the Bear among the stars.

The shimmering night does not stay
for men, nor does calamity,
nor wealth, but swiftly they are gone,
and to another man it comes
to know joy and its loss.

Sophocles, *Women of Trachis*, 126

16 *Philoctetes.* Look how men live, always precariously balanced between good and bad fortune.
If you are out of trouble, watch for danger.
And when you live well, then consider the most your life, lest ruin take it unawares.

Sophocles, *Philoctetes*, 502

17 *Heracles.* Fortune is dark; she moves, but we cannot see the way
nor can we pin her down by science and study her.

Euripides, *Alcestis*, 785

18 *Attendant.* Don't envy men
Because they seem to have a run of luck,
Since luck's a nine days' wonder. Wait their end.

Euripides, *Heracleidae*, 864

19 *Megara.* The man who sticks it out against his fate shows spirit, but the spirit of a fool.
No man alive can budge necessity.

Euripides, *Heracles*, 309

20 *Iphigenia.* Who knows on whom such strokes of fate will fall? for all that Heaven decrees, proceeds unseen, and no man knoweth of the ills in store; for Fate misleads us into doubtful paths.

Euripides, *Iphigenia in Tauris*, 475

21 *Hermocrates.* The incalculable element in the fu-

ture exercises the widest influence, and is the most treacherous, and yet in fact the most useful of all things, as it frightens us all equally.

Thucydides, *Peloponnesian War*, IV, 62

22 *Athenian Stranger.* God governs all things, and . . . chance and opportunity co-operate with him in the government of human affairs.

Plato, *Laws*, IV, 709A

23 Chance or fortune is called 'good' when the result is good, 'evil' when it is evil. The terms 'good fortune' and 'ill fortune' are used when either result is of considerable magnitude. Thus one who comes within an ace of some great evil or great good is said to be fortunate or unfortunate. The mind affirms the presence of the attribute, ignoring the hair's breadth of difference. Further, it is with reason that good fortune is regarded as unstable; for chance is unstable, as none of the things which result from it can be invariable or normal.

Aristotle, *Physics*, 197ª25

24 It were better to follow the myths about the gods than to become a slave to the Destiny of the natural philosophers; for the former suggests a hope of placating the gods by worship, whereas the latter involves a necessity which knows no placation.

Epicurus, *Letter to Menoeceus*

25 That men, in the infirmity of human nature, should fall into misfortunes which defy calculation, is the fault not of the sufferers but of Fortune, and of those who do the wrong; but that they should from mere levity, and with their eyes open, thrust themselves upon the most serious disasters is without dispute the fault of the victims themselves. Therefore it is that pity and sympathy and assistance await those whose failure is due to Fortune: reproach and rebuke from all men of sense those who have only their own folly to thank for it.

Polybius, *Histories*, II, 7

26 Reason forces us to agree that everything happens by fate. By fate, I mean that orderly succession of causes whereby causes are linked together, and each cause produces an effect. This undying truth has its source in eternity. Therefore everything that has happened was bound to happen. Nothing will happen that does not have an efficient cause in nature. Consequently, fate is that which is, not out of ignorance, but scientifically, named the eternal cause of things past, present, and future. This observation will inform us what effect will most likely proceed from most causes, even if the cause is not known at all. It would be too much to presume that it is known in all cases.

Cicero, *Divination*, I, 55

27 I would think that it is not even within God's

power to know what events will happen by accident or by chance. If he does know, then obviously the event must happen. But if it must happen,
chance does not exist. Yet chance does exist.
There is therefore no foreknowledge of things that
happen by chance.

Cicero, *Divination*, II, 7

28 If there were no such word, or thing, or force as
Fate, and if everything happened by chance,
would the course of events be different than they
are? Why then keep harping on Fate? If everything can be explained in terms of nature or
fortune, why drag Fate in?

Cicero, *Fate*, III

29 What is the use of a philosophy that insists that
everything happens by fate? It is a philosophy for
old women, and ignorant old women at that.

Cicero, *De Natura
Deorum*, I, 20

30 The Fates, when they this happy web have spun,
Shall bless the sacred clue, and bid it smoothly
run.

Virgil, *Eclogues*, IV

31 Here stood her [Juno's] chariot; here, if Heav'n
were kind,
The seat of awful empire she design'd.
Yet she had heard an ancient rumor fly,
(Long cited by the people of the sky,)
That times to come should see the Trojan race
Her Carthage ruin, and her tow'rs deface;
Nor thus confin'd, the yoke of sov'reign sway
Should on the necks of all the nations lay.
She ponder'd this, and fear'd it was in fate;
Nor could forget the war she wag'd of late
For conqu'ring Greece against the Trojan state.
Besides, long causes working in her mind,
And secret seeds of envy, lay behind;
Deep graven in her heart the doom remain'd
Of partial Paris, and her form disdain'd;
The grace bestow'd on ravish'd Ganymed,
Electra's glories, and her injur'd bed.
Each was a cause alone; and all combin'd
To kindle vengeance in her haughty mind.
For this, far distant from the Latian coast
She drove the remnants of the Trojan host;
And sev'n long years th' unhappy wand'ring train
Were toss'd by storms, and scatter'd thro' the
main.
Such time, such toil, requir'd the Roman name,
Such length of labor for so vast a frame.

Virgil, *Aeneid*, I

32 *Jove.* Each to his proper fortune stand or fall;
Equal and unconcern'd I look on all.
Rutulians, Trojans, are the same to me;
And both shall draw the lots their fates decree.
Let these assault, if Fortune be their friend;

And, if she favors those, let those defend:
The Fates will find their way.

Virgil, *Aeneid*, X

33 What next morn's sun may bring, forbear to ask;
But count each day that comes by gift of chance
So much to the good.

Horace, *Odes*, I, 9

34 Fortune, her cruel trade quite to her mind,
Persistent still her wanton game to play,
Transfers her favours day by day,—
To me, to others, kind.

Horace, *Odes*, III, 29

35 We should project our thoughts ahead of us at
every turn and have in mind every possible even-
tuality instead of only the usual course of events.
For what is there that fortune does not when she
pleases fell at the height of its powers? What is
there that is not the more assailed and buffeted by
her the more lustrous its attraction? What is there
that is troublesome or difficult for her? Her assaults do not always come along a single path, or
even a well-recognized path. At one time she will
call in the aid of our own hands in attacking us, at
another she will be content with her own powers
in devising for us dangers for which no one is responsible. No moment is exempt: in the midst of
pleasures there are found the springs of suffering.
In the middle of peace war rears its head, and the
bulwarks of one's security are transformed into
sources of alarm, friend turning foe and ally turning enemy. The summer's calm is upset by sudden
storms more severe than those of winter. In the
absence of any enemy we suffer all that an enemy
might wreak on us. Overmuch prosperity if all
else fails will hit on the instruments of its own
destruction. Sickness assails those leading the most
sensible lives, tuberculosis those with the strongest
constitutions, retribution the utterly guiltless, violence the most secluded. Misfortune has a way of
choosing some unprecedented means or other of
impressing its power on those who might be said
to have forgotten it. A single day strews in ruins
all that was raised by a train of construction extending over a long span of time and involving a
great number of separate works and a great deal
of favour on the part of heaven. To say a 'day',
indeed, is to put too much of a brake on the calamities that hasten down upon us: an hour, an
instant of time, suffices for the overthrow of empires. It would be some relief to our condition and
our frailty if all things were as slow in their perishing as they were in their coming into being: but as
it is, the growth of things is a tardy process and
their undoing is a rapid matter.

Seneca, *Letters to Lucilius*, 91

36 Let fate find us ready and eager. Here is your
noble spirit—the one which has put itself in the
hands of fate; on the other side we have the puny

degenerate spirit which struggles, and which sees nothing right in the way the universe is ordered, and would rather reform the gods than reform itself.

Seneca, Letters to Lucilius, 107

37 We know that all things work together for good to them that love God, to them who are the called according to his purpose.

For whom he did foreknow, he also did predestinate to be conformed to the image of his Son, that he might be the firstborn among many brethren.

Moreover whom he did predestinate, them he also called: and whom he called, them he also justified: and whom he justified, them he also glorified.

Romans 8:28–30

38 Blessed be the God and Father of our Lord Jesus Christ, who hath blessed us with all spiritual blessings in heavenly places in Christ:

According as he hath chosen us in him before the foundation of the world, that we should be holy and without blame before him in love.

Ephesians 1:3–4

39 What a poet fortune sometimes shows herself.

Plutarch, Romulus

40 Though fortune may often . . . defeat the efforts of virtue to avert misfortunes, it cannot, when we incur them, prevent our bearing them reasonably.

Plutarch, Caius Gracchus

41 It is common enough for people, when they fall into great disasters, to discern what is right, and what they ought to do; but there are but few who in such extremities have the strength to obey their judgment, either in doing what it approves or avoiding what it condemns; and a good many are so weak as to give way to their habits all the more, and are incapable of using their minds.

Plutarch, Antony

42 Fortune makes kings of slaves and gives the captive a triumph,

Yet the fortunate man is very much harder to come on

Than a white crow.

Juvenal, Satire VII

43 So—should men pray for nothing at all? If you're asking my counsel,

You will permit the gods themselves to make the decision

What is convenient to give, and what befits our estate.

We shall not get what we want, but the things most suitable for us.

Man is dearer to gods than he is to himself. We are foolish,

Led by blind desire, the spirit's extravagant impulse,

Asking for marriage and offspring, but the gods know what they'll be like,

Our wives and our sons. But still, just for the sake of the asking,

For the sake of something to give to the chapels, ritual entrails,

The consecrated meat of a little white pig, pray for one thing,

Pray for a healthy mind in a healthy body, a spirit

Unafraid of death, but reconciled to it, and able

To bear up, to endure whatever troubles afflict it,

Free from hate and desire, preferring Hercules' labors

To the cushions and loves and feasts of Sardanapallus.

I show you what you can give to yourself: only through virtue

Lies the certain road to a life that is blessed and tranquil.

If men had any sense, Fortune would not be a goddess.

We are the ones who make her so, and give her a place in the heavens.

Juvenal, Satire X

44 The wider the scope of my reflection on the present and the past, the more am I impressed by their mockery of human plans in every transaction.

Tacitus, Annals, III, 18

45 Just as we must understand when it is said, That Aesculapius prescribed to this man horse-exercise, or bathing in cold water or going without shoes; so we must understand it when it is said, That the nature of the universe prescribed to this man disease or mutilation or loss or anything else of the kind. For in the first case Prescribed means something like this: he prescribed this for this man as a thing adapted to procure health; and in the second case it means: That which happens to (or, suits) every man is fixed in a manner for him suitably to his destiny. For this is what we mean when we say that things are suitable to us, as the workmen say of squared stones in walls or the pyramids, that they are suitable, when they fit them to one another in some kind of connexion. For there is altogether one fitness, harmony. And as the universe is made up out of all bodies to be such a body as it is, so out of all existing causes necessity (destiny) is made up to be such a cause as it is. And even those who are completely ignorant understand what I mean, for they say, It (necessity, destiny) brought this to such a person.

Marcus Aurelius, Meditations, V, 8

46 Whatever of the things which are not within thy power thou shalt suppose to be good for thee or evil, it must of necessity be that, if such a bad

thing befall thee or the loss of such a good thing, thou wilt blame the gods, and hate men too, those who are the cause of the misfortune or the loss, or those who are suspected of being likely to be the cause; and indeed we do much injustice, because we make a difference between these things. But if we judge only those things which are in our power to be good or bad, there remains no reason either for finding fault with God or standing in a hostile attitude to man.

Marcus Aurelius, *Meditations,* VI, 41

47 This universe of ours is a wonder of power and wisdom, everything by a noiseless road coming to pass according to a law which none may elude— which the base man never conceives though it is leading him, all unknowingly, to that place in the All where his lot must be cast—which the just man knows, and, knowing, sets out to the place he must, understanding, even as he begins the journey, where he is to be housed at the end, and having the good hope that he will be with gods.

Plotinus, *Fourth Ennead,* IV, 45

48 God, the author and giver of felicity, because He alone is the true God, Himself gives earthly kingdoms both to good and bad. Neither does He do this rashly, and, as it were, fortuitously—because He is God not fortune—but according to the order of things and times, which is hidden from us, but thoroughly known to Himself; which same order of times, however, He does not serve as subject to it, but Himself rules as lord and appoints as governor.

Augustine, *City of God,* IV, 33

49 Human kingdoms are established by divine providence. And if any one attributes their existence to fate, because he calls the will or the power of God itself by the name of fate, let him keep his opinion, but correct his language.

Augustine, *City of God,* V, 1

50 Those who are of opinion that, apart from the will of God, the stars determine what we shall do, or what good things we shall possess, or what evils we shall suffer, must be refused a hearing by all, not only by those who hold the true religion, but by those who wish to be the worshippers of any gods whatsoever, even false gods. For what does this opinion really amount to but this, that no god whatever is to be worshipped or prayed to? Against these, however, our present disputation is not intended to be directed, but against those who, in defence of those whom they think to be gods, oppose the Christian religion. They, however, who make the position of the stars depend on the divine will, and in a manner decree what character each man shall have, and what good or evil shall happen to him, if they think that these same stars have that power conferred upon them by the supreme power of God, in order that they

may determine these things according to their will, do a great injury to the celestial sphere, in whose most brilliant senate, and most splendid senate-house, as it were, they suppose that wicked deeds are decreed to be done—such deeds as that, if any terrestrial state should decree them, it would be condemned to overthrow by the decree of the whole human race. What judgment, then, is left to God concerning the deeds of men, who is Lord both of the stars and of men, when to these deeds a celestial necessity is attributed?

Augustine, *City of God,* V, 1

51 If there is free will, all things do not happen according to fate; if all things do not happen according to fate, there is not a certain order of causes; and if there is not a certain order of causes, neither is there a certain order of things foreknown by God—for things cannot come to pass except they are preceded by efficient causes—but, if there is no fixed and certain order of causes foreknown by God, all things cannot be said to happen according as He foreknew that they would happen. And further, if it is not true that all things happen just as they have been foreknown by Him, there is not, says he, in God any foreknowledge of future events.

Now, against the sacrilegious and impious darings of reason, we assert both that God knows all things before they come to pass and that we do by our free will whatsoever we know and feel to be done by us only because we will it. But that all things come to pass by fate, we do not say; nay we affirm that nothing comes to pass by fate; for we demonstrate that the name of fate, as it is wont to be used by those who speak of fate, meaning thereby the position of the stars at the time of each one's conception or birth, is an unmeaning word, for astrology itself is a delusion. But an order of causes in which the highest efficiency is attributed to the will of God, we neither deny nor do we designate it by the name of fate, unless, perhaps, we may understand fate to mean that which is spoken, deriving it from *fari,* to speak; for we cannot deny that it is written in the sacred Scriptures, "God hath spoken once; these two things have I heard, that power belongeth unto God. Also unto Thee, O God, belongeth mercy: for Thou wilt render unto every man according to his works." Now the expression, "Once hath He spoken," is to be understood as meaning "*immovably,*" that is, unchangeably hath He spoken, inasmuch as He knows unchangeably all things which shall be and all things which He will do. We might, then, use the word fate in the sense it bears when derived from *fari,* to speak, had it not already come to be understood in another sense, into which I am unwilling that the hearts of men should unconsciously slide. But it does not follow that, though there is for God a certain order of all causes, there must therefore be nothing depending on the free exercise of our own wills, for our wills themselves are included in that order of causes which is certain to God and is embraced by His foreknowledge, for human wills are also causes of human actions; and He Who foreknew all the causes of things would certainly among those causes not have been ignorant of our wills.

Augustine, *City of God*, V, 9

52 [The human] race we have distributed into two parts, the one consisting of those who live according to man, the other of those who live according to God. And these we also mystically call the two cities, or the two communities of men, of which the one is predestined to reign eternally with God, and the other to suffer eternal punishment with the devil.

Augustine, *City of God*, XV, 1

53 Of all suffering from Fortune, the unhappiest misfortune is to have known a happy fortune.

Boethius, *Consolation of Philosophy*, II

54 *Philosophy.* Providence is the very divine reason which arranges all things, and rests with the supreme disposer of all; while Fate is that ordering which is a part of all changeable things, and by means of which Providence binds all things together in their own order. Providence embraces all things equally, however different they may be, even however infinite: when they are assigned to their own places, forms, and times, Fate sets them in an orderly motion; so that this development of the temporal order, unified in the intelligence of the mind of God, is Providence. The working of this unified development in time is called Fate. These are different, but the one hangs upon the other. For this order, which is ruled by Fate, emanates from the directness of Providence.

Boethius, *Consolation of Philosophy*, IV

55 *Philosophy.* A wise man should never complain, whenever he is brought into strife with fortune; just as a brave man cannot properly be disgusted whenever the noise of battle is heard, since for both of them their very difficulty is their opportunity, for the brave man of increasing his glory, for the wise man of confirming and strengthening his wisdom. From this is virtue itself so named, because it is so supported by its strength that it is not overcome by adversity. And you who were set in the advance of virtue have not come to this pass of being dissipated by delights, or enervated by pleasure; but you fight too bitterly against all fortune. Keep the middle path of strength and virtue, lest you be overwhelmed by misfortune or corrupted by pleasant fortune. All that falls short or goes too far ahead, has contempt for happiness, and gains not the reward for labour done. It rests in your own hands what shall be the nature of the fortune which you choose to form for yourself. For all fortune which seems difficult, either exercises virtue, or corrects or punishes vice.

Boethius, *Consolation of Philosophy*, IV

56 It is fitting that God should predestine men. For all things are subject to His providence. . . . Now it belongs to providence to order things towards their end.

Aquinas, *Summa Theologica*, I, 23, 1

57 Even if by a special privilege their predestination were revealed to some, it is not fitting that it should be revealed to everyone; because, if so, those who were not predestined would despair, and security would beget negligence in the predestined.

Aquinas, *Summa Theologica*, I, 23, 1

58 As predestination is a part of providence, in regard to those divinely ordained to eternal salvation, so reprobation is a part of providence in regard to those who turn aside from that end. Hence reprobation implies not only foreknowledge, but also something more, as does providence. . . . Therefore, as predestination includes the will to confer grace and glory, so also reprobation includes the will to permit a person to fall into sin, and to impose the punishment of damnation on account of that sin.

God loves all men and all creatures, in so far as He wishes them all some good, but He does not wish every good to them all. So far, therefore, as He does not wish this particular good—namely, eternal life—He is said to hate or reprobate them.

Reprobation differs in its causality from predestination. This latter is the cause both of what is expected in the future life by the predestined—namely, glory—and of what is received in this life—namely, grace. Reprobation, however, is not the cause of what is in the present—namely, sin, but it is the cause of abandonment by God. It is the cause, however, of what is assigned in the future—namely, eternal punishment. But guilt proceeds from the free choice of the person who is reprobated and deserted by grace. In this way the word of the prophet is true—namely, *Destruction is thy own, O Israel.*

Reprobation by God does not take anything away from the power of the person reprobated. Hence, when it is said that the reprobated cannot obtain grace, this must not be understood as implying absolute impossibility, but only conditional impossibility . . . that the predestined must necessarily be saved, yet by a conditional necessity, which does not do away with the liberty of choice. Hence, although anyone reprobated by God cannot acquire grace, nevertheless that he falls into this or that particular sin comes from his free choice. And so it is rightly imputed to him as guilt.

Aquinas, *Summa Theologica*, I, 23, 3

59 The number of the predestined is said to be certain to God not only by reason of His knowledge, because, that is to say, He knows how many will be saved (for in this way the number of drops of rain and the sands of the sea are certain to God), but by reason of His deliberate choice and determination.

Aquinas, *Summa Theologica*, I, 23, 7

60 The majority of men have a sufficient knowledge for the guidance of life, and those who have not this knowledge are said to be half-witted or foolish; but they who attain to a profound knowledge of things intelligible are a very small minority in respect to the rest. Since their eternal happiness, consisting in the vision of God, exceeds the common state of nature, and especially in so far as this is deprived of grace through the corruption of original sin, those who are saved are in the minority. In this especially, however, appears the mercy of God, that He has chosen some for that salvation, from which very many in accordance with the common course and tendency of nature fall short.

Aquinas, *Summa Theologica*, I, 23, 7

61 Those who are ordained to possess eternal life through divine predestination are written down in the book of life absolutely, because they are written therein to have eternal life in itself; such are never blotted out from the book of life. Those, however, who are ordained to eternal life not through the divine predestination, but through grace, are said to be written in the book of life not absolutely, but relatively, for they are written therein not to have eternal life in itself, but in its cause only. These latter are blotted out of the book of life, though this blotting out must not be referred to God as if God foreknew a thing, and afterwards knew it not, but to the thing known, namely, because God knows one is first ordained to eternal life, and afterwards not ordained when he falls from grace.

Aquinas, *Summa Theologica*, I, 24, 3

62 What happens here by accident, both in natural things and in human affairs, is reduced to a preordaining cause, which is Divine Providence.

Aquinas, *Summa Theologica*, I, 116, 1

63 The Divine power or will can be called fate as being the cause of fate. But essentially fate is the very disposition or series, that is, the order, of second causes.

Aquinas, *Summa Theologica*, I, 116, 2

64 "Master," I said to him, "now tell me also: this Fortune, of which thou hintest to me; what is she, that has the good things of the world thus within *her* clutches?"
And he [Virgil] to me: "O foolish creatures, how

great is this ignorance that falls upon ye! Now I wish thee to receive my judgment of her.
He whose wisdom is transcendent over all, made the heavens and gave them guides, so that every part shines to every part,
equally distributing the light; in like manner, for worldly splendours, he ordained a general minister and guide,
to change betimes the vain possessions, from people to people, and from one kindred to another beyond the hindrance of human wisdom:
hence one people commands, another languishes; obeying her sentence, which is hidden like the serpent in the grass.
Your knowledge cannot understand her: she provides, judges, and maintains her kingdom, as the other Gods do theirs.
Her permutations have no truce; necessity makes her be swift; thus he comes oft who doth a change obtain.
This is she, who is so much reviled, even by those who ought to praise her, when blaming her wrongfully, and with evil words."

Dante, *Inferno*, VII, 67

65 When the game of dice breaks up, he who loses stays sorrowing, repeating the throws, and sadly learns:
with the other all the folk go away: one goes in front, another plucks him from behind, and another at his side recalls him to his mind.
He halts not and attends to this one and to that: those to whom he stretches forth his hand press no more; and so he saves him from the crowd.

Dante, *Purgatorio*, VI, 1

66 *Pandar.* For every person hath his happy chance,
If good faith with his fortune he will hold.
But if he turns aside with scornful glance
When fortune comes, unwelcoming and cold,
Then for ill luck he may not fortune scold,
But his own sloth and feebleness of heart,
And he must take all blame from end to start.

Chaucer, *Troilus and Cressida*, II, 41

67 Too short a fleeting time, alas the while,
Great joy endures, and Fortune wills it so,
Who truest seems when most she will beguile,
And most allures when she will strike a blow,
And from her wheel some hapless victim throw;
For when some wretch slips down and disappears,
She laughs at him and comforts him with jeers.

Chaucer, *Troilus and Cressida*, IV, 1

68 "I am," he [Troilus] said, "but done for, so to say;
For all that comes, comes by necessity,
Thus to be done for is my destiny.

"I must believe and cannot other choose,
That Providence, in its divine foresight,
Hath known that Cressida I once must lose,

Since God sees everything from heaven's height
And plans things as he thinks both best and right,
According to their merits in rotation,
As was arranged for by predestination.

"But still I don't quite know what to believe!
For there have been great scholars, many a one,
Who say that destined fate we must receive,
Yet others prove that this need not be done,
And that free choice hath been denied to none.
Alack, so sly they are, these scholars old,
I can't make out what doctrine I should hold!

"For some declare, what God perceives before,
(And God of course can never be misled)
All that must be, though men may it deplore,
Because foreordination hath so said;
Wherefore the thought still lingers in my head,
If God foreknows the thought and act of each
Of us, we have no choice, as scholars preach.

"For neither thought nor deed might ever be,
Or anything, unless foreordination,
In which there may be no uncertainty,
Perceives it without shade of variation;
For if there were the slightest hesitation
Or any slip in God's foreordering,
Foreknowledge then were not a certain thing,

"But rather one would call it expectation,
Unsteadfast, not foreknowledge absolute;
And that, indeed, were an abomination,
For God's foreknowledge thus to substitute
Imperfect human doubts and mere repute;
In God such human error to imply
Were false and foul and cursed treason high.

"Then there is this opinion held by some,
Whose tonsured foreheads quite imposing shine;
They say whatever happens does not come
Because foreknowledge sees with fixed design
That come it must, but rather they incline
To say that come it will, and reason so,
That such foreknowledge doth but merely know.

"But there resides here a perplexity
That in some proper way must be explained,
That things that happen do not have to be
Merely because they may be foreordained;
Yet still this truth at least must be maintained,
That all the things that ever shall befall,
Must surely be ordained, both one and all.

"You see that I am trying to find out
Just what is cause and what is consequence.
Is God's foreknowledge cause beyond a doubt
As necessary in his plan prepense
Of all the human things we call events,
Or does necessity in them reside
And thus ordaining cause for them provide?

"I must confess I can't pretend to show
Just how the reasons stand, but this I'll say,
That every thing that happens, must do so,

And must have been foreknown in such a way
That made it necessary, though it may
Be that foreknowledge did not so declare
That it must happen, be it foul or fair.

"But if a man is sitting on a chair,
Then this necessity you can't evade,
That true it is that he is sitting there,
And thus a truthful judgment you have made;
And furthermore against this may be laid
A supplement to this and its contrary,
As thus—pray heed, and just a moment tarry.

"I say if that opinion which you hold
That he sits there is true, then furthermore
He must be sitting there, as I have told;
There's thus necessity on either score,
That he must sit, as we agreed before,
And you must think he does, and so say I,
Necessity on both of you doth lie.

"But you may urge, this man, he does not sit
Because your judgment on this may be true,
But rather, since he sat ere you thought it,
Your judgment from his sitting doth ensue;
But I say, though your judgment may be due
To his first sitting there, necessity
To judge and sit distributed must be.

"These arguments I think I may advance,
And make apply, for so it seems to me,
To God's foreknowledge and foreordinance,
In all the happenings that come to be.
And by these arguments you well may see,
That all the things that on the earth befall,
By plain necessity they happen all.

"Though things to come must all be foreordained,
Their cause therein you cannot simply find,
For these two points apart must be maintained,
But yet foreordinance cannot be blind,
And God must foreordain with truthful mind,
Or else whatever foreordained should be,
Would come to pass through blind necessity,

"But no more arguments I need display
To show that free choice is an idle dream.
Yet this, however, 'tis quite false to say,
That temporal things one should esteem
As cause of God's foreknowledge aye supreme;
From such opinion only errors grow,
That things that happen cause him to foreknow.

"I must suppose then, had I such a thought,
That God ordains each thing that is to come
Because it is to come, and for else naught!
Why, then, I might believe things, all and some,
From ages past, whate'er they issued from,
Are cause of God's high power that before
Hath known all things and nothing doth ignore!

"I have just one more point to add hereto,
That when I know that there exists a thing,
I know my knowing of that thing is true,

And so, whatever time to pass shall bring,
Those things I know must come; the happening
Of things foreknown ere their appointed hour,
Can be prevented by no human power."

Chaucer, *Troilus and Cressida,* IV, 137–154

69 It is not unknown to me how many men have
had, and still have, the opinion that the affairs of
the world are in such wise governed by fortune
and by God that men with their wisdom cannot
direct them and that no one can even help them;
and because of this they would have us believe
that it is not necessary to labour much in affairs,
but to let chance govern them. . . . Sometimes
pondering over this, I am in some degree inclined
to their opinion. Nevertheless, not to extinguish
our free will, I hold it to be true that Fortune is
the arbiter of one-half of our actions, but that she
still leaves us to direct the other half, or perhaps a
little less.

I compare her to one of those raging rivers,
which when in flood overflows the plains, sweeping away trees and buildings, bearing away the
soil from place to place; everything flies before it,
all yield to its violence, without being able in any
way to withstand it; and yet, though its nature be
such, it does not follow therefore that men, when
the weather becomes fair, shall not make provision, both with defences and barriers, in such a
manner that, rising again, the waters may pass
away by canal, and their force be neither so unrestrained nor so dangerous. So it happens with
fortune, who shows her power where valour has
not prepared to resist her, and thither she turns
her forces where she knows that barriers and defences have not been raised to constrain her.

Machiavelli, *Prince,* XXV

70 Fortune being changeful and mankind steadfast
in their ways, so long as the two are in agreement
men are successful, but unsuccessful when they
fall out. For my part I consider that it is better to
be adventurous than cautious, because fortune is a
woman, and if you wish to keep her under it is
necessary to beat and ill-use her; and it is seen
that she allows herself to be mastered by the adventurous rather than by those who go to work
more coldly. She is, therefore, always, woman-
like, a lover of young men, because they are less
cautious, more violent, and with more audacity
command her.

Machiavelli, *Prince,* XXV

71 Concerning predestination, it is best to begin below, at Christ, as then we both hear and find the
Father; for all those that have begun at the top
have broken their necks. I have been thoroughly
plagued and tormented with such cogitations of
predestination; I would needs know how God intended to deal with me, etc. But at last, God be
praised! I clean left them; I took hold again on

God's revealed word; higher I was not able to
bring it, for a human creature can never search
out the celestial will of God; this God hides, for
the sake of the devil, to the end the crafty spirit
may be deceived and put to confusion. The revealed will of God the devil has learned from us,
but God reserves his secret will to himself. It is
sufficient for us to learn and know Christ in his
humanity, in which the Father has revealed himself.

Luther, *Table Talk,* H661

72 Predestination, by which God adopts some to the
hope of life, and adjudges others to eternal death,
no one, desirous of the credit of piety, dares absolutely to deny. But it is involved in many cavils,
especially by those who make foreknowledge the
cause of it. We maintain, that both belong to
God; but it is preposterous to represent one as
dependent on the other. When we attribute foreknowledge to God, we mean that all things have
ever been, and perpetually remain, before his
eyes, so that to his knowledge nothing is future or
past, but all things are present; and present in
such a manner, that he does not merely conceive
of them from ideas formed in his mind, as things
remembered by us appear present to our minds,
but really beholds and sees them as if actually
placed before him. And this foreknowledge extends to the whole world, and to all the creatures.
Predestination we call the eternal decree of God,
by which he has determined in himself, what he
would have to become of every individual of mankind. For they are not all created with a similar
destiny; but eternal life is foreordained for some,
and eternal damnation for others. Every man,
therefore, being created for one or the other of
these ends, we say, he is predestinated either to
life or to death. This God has not only testified in
particular persons, but has given a specimen of it
in the whole posterity of Abraham, which should
evidently show the future condition of every nation to depend upon his decision. "When the Most
High divided the nations, when he separated the
sons of Adam, the Lord's portion was his people;
Jacob was the lot of his inheritance." The separation is before the eyes of all: in the person of Abraham, as in the dry trunk of a tree, one people is
peculiarly chosen to the rejection of others: no
reason for this appears, except that Moses, to deprive their posterity of all occasion of glorying,
teaches them that their exaltation is wholly from
God's gratuitous love. He assigns this reason for
their deliverance, that "he loved their fathers, and
chose their seed after them."

Calvin, *Institutes of the Christian
Religion,* III, 21

73 Though it is sufficiently clear, that God, in his
secret counsel, freely chooses whom he will, and
rejects others, his gratuitous election is but half

displayed till we come to particular individuals, to whom God not only offers salvation, but assigns it in such a manner, that the certainty of the effect is liable to no suspense or doubt. . . . In conformity . . . to the clear doctrine of the Scripture, we assert, that by an eternal and immutable counsel, God has once for all determined, both whom he would admit to salvation, and whom he would condemn to destruction. We affirm that this counsel, as far as concerns the elect, is founded on his gratuitous mercy, totally irrespective of human merit; but that to those whom he devotes to condemnation, the gate of life is closed by a just and irreprehensible, but incomprehensible, judgment. In the elect, we consider calling as an evidence of election, and justification as another token of its manifestation, till they arrive in glory, which constitutes its completion. As God seals his elect by vocation and justification, so by excluding the reprobate from the knowledge of his name and the sanctification of his Spirit, he affords an indication of the judgment that awaits them.

> Calvin, *Institutes of the Christian Religion,* III, 21

74 Fortune does us neither good nor harm; she only offers us the material and the seed of them, which our soul, more powerful than she, turns and applies as it pleases, sole cause and mistress of its happy or unhappy condition.

> Montaigne, *Essays,* I, 14, That the Taste of Good

75 Not only in medicine but in many more certain arts Fortune has a large part. Poetic sallies, which transport their author and ravish him out of himself, why shall we not attribute them to his good luck? He himself confesses that they surpass his ability and strength, and acknowledges that they come from something other than himself and that he does not have them at all in his power, any more than orators say they have in theirs those extraordinary impulses and agitations that push them beyond their plan. It is the same with painting: sometimes there escape from the painter's hand touches so surpassing his conception and his knowledge as to arouse his wonder and astonishment. But Fortune shows still more evidently the part she has in all these works by the graces and beauties that are found in them, not only without the workman's intention, but even without his knowledge. An able reader often discovers in other men's writings perfections beyond those that the author put in or perceived, and lends them richer meanings and aspects.

> Montaigne, *Essays,* I, 24, Various Outcomes

76 God, in the roll book of the causes of events which he has in his foreknowledge, has also those which are called fortuitous, and the voluntary ones, which depend on the freedom he has given to our will; and he knows that we shall err, because we shall have willed to err.

> Montaigne, *Essays,* II, 29, Of Virtue

77 *King Edward.* What fates impose, that men must needs abide;
It boots not to resist both wind and tide.

> Shakespeare, *III Henry VI,* IV, iii, 58

78 *John of Gaunt.* All places that the eye of heaven visits
Are to a wise man ports and happy havens.
Teach thy necessity to reason thus;
There is no virtue like necessity.

> Shakespeare, *Richard II,* I, iii, 275

79 *Warwick.* There is a history in all men's lives,
Figuring the nature of the times deceased;
The which observed, a man may prophesy,
With a near aim, of the main chance of things
As yet not come to life, which in their seeds
And weak beginnings lie intreasured.
Such things become the hatch and brood of time.

> Shakespeare, *II Henry IV,* III, i, 80

80 *Fluellen.* Here is the man.
Pistol. Captain, I thee beseech to do me favours:
The Duke of Exeter doth love thee well.
Flu. Ay, I praise God; and I have merited some love at his hands.
Pist. Bardolph, a soldier, firm and sound of heart,
And of buxom valour, hath, by cruel fate,
And giddy Fortune's furious fickle wheel,
That goddess blind,
That stands upon the rolling restless stone—
Flu. By your patience, Aunchient Pistol. Fortune is painted blind, with a muffler afore her eyes, to signify to you that Fortune is blind; and she is painted also with a wheel, to signify to you, which is the moral of it, that she is turning, and inconstant, and mutability, and variation: and her foot, look you, is fixed upon a spherical stone, which rolls, and rolls, and rolls: in good truth, the poet makes a most excellent description of it: Fortune is an excellent moral.

> Shakespeare, *Henry V,* III, vi, 21

81 *Cassius.* Men at some time are masters of their fates:
The fault, dear Brutus, is not in our stars,
But in ourselves, that we are underlings.

> Shakespeare, *Julius Caesar,* I, ii, 139

82 *Hamlet.* My excellent good friends! How dost thou, Guildenstern? Ah, Rosencrantz! Good lads, how do ye both?
Rosencrantz. As the indifferent children of the earth.

Guildenstern. Happy, in that we are not over-
    happy;
On fortune's cap we are not the very button.
  Ham. Nor the soles of her shoe?
  Ros. Neither, my lord.
  Ham. Then you live about her waist, or in the
middle of her favours?
  Guil. 'Faith, her privates we.
  Ham. In the secret parts of fortune? O, most
true; she is a strumpet.

            Shakespeare, *Hamlet*, II, ii, 228

83 *Hamlet.* Our indiscretion sometimes serves us well,
When our deep plots do pall; and that should
    teach us
There's a divinity that shapes our ends.
Rough-hew them how we will—
    Horatio.   That is most certain.

            Shakespeare, *Hamlet*, V, ii, 8

84 *Hamlet.* We defy augury. There's a special providence in the fall of a sparrow. If it be now, 'tis not
to come; if it be not to come, it will be now; if it be
not now, yet it will come; the readiness is all.

           Shakespeare, *Hamlet*, V, ii, 230

85 *Edmund.* This is the excellent foppery of the world,
that, when we are sick in fortune—often the surfeit of our own behaviour—we make guilty of our
disasters the sun, the moon, and the stars, as if we
were villains by necessity, fools by heavenly compulsion, knaves, thieves, and treachers, by spherical predominance, drunkards, liars, and adulterers, by an enforced obedience of planetary
influence, and all that we are evil in, by a divine
thrusting on. An admirable evasion of whoremas-
ter man, to lay his goatish disposition to the
charge of a star!

            Shakespeare, *Lear*, I, ii, 128

86 When, in disgrace with Fortune and men's eyes,
I all alone beweep my outcast state
And trouble deaf heaven with my bootless cries
And look upon myself and curse my fate,
Wishing me like to one more rich in hope,
Featured like him, like him with friends possess'd,
Desiring this man's art and that man's scope,
With what I most enjoy contented least;
Yet in these thoughts myself almost despising,
Haply I think on thee, and then my state,
Like to the lark at break of day arising
From sullen earth, sings hymns at heaven's gate.

            Shakespeare, *Sonnet XXIX*

87 Your Grace must know, answer'd Don *Quixote,*
that almost every thing that relates to Me, is
manag'd quite contrary to what the Affairs of
other Knights-Errant us'd to be. Whether it be
the unfathomable Will of Destiny, or the Implacable Malice of some envious Inchanter orders it
so, or no, I can't well tell. For 'tis beyond all

doubt, that most of us Knights-Errant still have
had something peculiar in our Fates. One has had
the Privilege to be above the Power of Inchantments, another Invulnerable, as the famous *Orlando,* one of the twelve Peers of *France,* whose Flesh,
they tell us, was impenetrable every where but in
the Sole of his left Foot, and even there too he
cou'd be Wounded with no other Weapon than
the Point of a great Pin; so that when *Bernardo del
Carpio* deprived him of Life at *Roncesvalles,* finding
he cou'd not Wound him with his Sword, he lifted
him from the Ground, and squeez'd him to Death
in his Arms; remembring how *Hercules* kill'd *An-
toeus,* that cruel Giant, who was said to be the Son
of the Earth. Hence I infer, that probably I may
be secur'd in the same manner, under the Protection of some particular Advantage, tho' 'tis not
that of being Invulnerable; for I have often found
by Experience, that my Flesh is tender, and not
impenetrable. Nor does any private Prerogative
free me from the Power of the Inchantment; for I
have found myself clapp'd into a Cage, where all
the World cou'd not have Lock'd me up, but the
Force of Necromantick Incantations. But since I
got free again, I believe that even the Force of
Magick will never be able to confine me thus another time. So that these Magicians finding they
cannot work their wicked Ends directly on me,
revenge themselves on what I most esteem, and
endeavour to take away my Life by persecuting
that of *Dulcinea,* in whom, and for whom I live.
And therefore I believe, when my Squire deliver'd
my Embassy to her, they Transform'd her into a
Country-Dowdy, poorly busied in the low and
base Employment of Winnowing Wheat. But I do
aver, that it was neither Rye, nor Wheat, but Oriental Pearl: and to prove this, I must acquaint
your Graces, that passing t'other Day by *Toboso,* I
could not so much as find *Dulcinea's* Palace;
whereas my Squire went the next Day, and saw
her in all her native Charms, the most beautiful
Creature in the World! yet when I met her presently after, she appear'd to me in the Shape of an
Ugly, Coarse, Country-Mawkin, Boorish, and Ill-
bred, though she really is Discretion itself. And
therefore, because I myself cannot be Inchanted,
the unfortunate Lady must be thus Inchanted,
Misus'd, Disfigur'd, Chopp'd and Chang'd. Thus
my Enemies wreaking their Malice on Her, have
reveng'd themselves on Me, which makes me
abandon my self to Sorrow, till she be restor'd to
her former Perfections.

           Cervantes, *Don Quixote,* II, 32

88 Don *Quixote,* as he went out of *Barcelona,* cast his
Eyes on the Spot of Ground where he was overthrown. Here once *Troy* stood, said he; here my
unhappy Fate, and not my Cowardice, depriv'd
me of all the Glories I had purchas'd. Here Fortune, by an unexpected Reverse, made me sensi-

ble of her Unconstancy and Fickleness. Here my Exploits suffer'd a total Eclipse; and, in short, here fell my Happiness, never to rise again. *Sancho* hearing his Master thus dolefully paraphrasing on his Misfortune, Good Sir, quoth he, 'tis as much the Part of great Spirits to have Patience when the World frowns upon 'em, as to be joyful when all goes well: And I judge of it by my self; for if when I was a Governor I was merry, now I am but a poor Squire afoot I am not sad. And indeed I have heard say, that this same She Thing they call Fortune, is a whimsical freakish drunken Quean, and blind into the Bargain; so that she neither sees what she does, nor knows whom she raises, nor whom she casts down. Thou art very much a Philosopher, *Sancho,* said Don *Quixote,* thou talk'st very sensibly. I wonder how thou cam'st by all this; but I must tell thee there is no such Thing as Fortune in the World; nor does any Thing that happens here below of Good or Ill come by Chance, but by the particular Providence of Heaven; and this makes good the Proverb, That every Man may thank himself for his own Fortune. For my Part, I have been the Maker of mine, but for want of using the Discretion I ought to have us'd, all my presumptuous Edifice sunk, and tumbl'd down at once. I might well have consider'd, that *Rosinante* was too weak and feeble to withstand the Knight of the *White Moon's* huge and strong-built Horse. However, I would needs adventure; I did the best I could, and was overcome. Yet though it has cost me my Honour, I have not lost, nor can I lose, my Integrity to perform my Promise. When I was a Knight-Errant, valiant and bold, the Strength of my Hands and my Actions gave a Reputation to my Deeds; and now I am no more than a dismounted Squire, the Performance of my Promise shall give a Reputation to my Words. Trudge on then, Friend *Sancho,* and let us get home, to pass the Year of our Probation. In that Retirement we shall recover new Vigour to return to that, which is never to be forgotten by me, I mean the Profession of Arms.

Cervantes, *Don Quixote,* II, 66

89 Chiefly the mould of a man's fortune is in his own hands.

Bacon, *Of Fortune*

90 When all looks fair about, and thou seest not a cloud so big as a Hand to threaten thee, forget not the Wheel of things: Think of sullen vicissitudes, but beat not thy brains to fore-know them. Be armed against such obscurities, rather by submission than fore-knowledge.

Sir Thomas Browne, *Christian Morals,* III, 16

91 Others apart sat on a Hill retir'd,
In thoughts more elevate, and reason'd high
Of Providence, Foreknowledge, Will, and Fate,

Fixt Fate, free will, foreknowledge absolute,
And found no end, in wandring mazes lost.

Milton, *Paradise Lost,* II, 557

92 *Raphael.* God made thee perfet, not immutable;
And good he made thee, but to persevere
He left it in thy power, ordaind thy will
By nature free, not over-rul'd by Fate
Inextricable, or strict necessity;
Our voluntarie service he requires,
Not our necessitated, such with him
Findes no acceptance, nor can find, for how
Can hearts, not free, be tri'd whether they serve
Willing or no, who will but what they must
By Destinie, and can no other choose?

Milton, *Paradise Lost,* V, 524

93 When God shakes a Kingdom with strong and healthful commotions to a general reforming, 'tis not untrue that many sectaries and false teachers are then busiest in seducing; but yet more true it is, that God then raises to His own work men of rare abilities, and more than common industry, not only to look back and revise what hath been taught heretofore, but to gain further and go on some new enlightened steps in the discovery of truth.

Milton, *Areopagitica*

94 We know that all things follow from the eternal decree of God, according to that same necessity by which it follows from the essence of a triangle that its three angles are equal to two right angles.

Spinoza, *Ethics,* II, Prop. 49

95 Since no one can do anything save by the predetermined order of nature, that is by God's eternal ordinance and decree, it follows that no one can choose a plan of life for himself, or accomplish any work save by God's vocation choosing him for the work or the plan of life in question, rather than any other.

Spinoza, *Theologico-Political Treatise,* III

96 The Power of Fortune is confest only by the Miserable; for the Happy impute all their Success to Prudence or Merit.

Swift, *Thoughts on Various Subjects*

97 Nothing more aggravates ill success than the near approach to good. The gamester, who loses his party at piquet by a single point, laments his bad luck ten times as much as he who never came within a prospect of the game. So in a lottery, the proprietors of the next numbers to that which wins the great prize, are apt to account themselves much more unfortunate than their fellow-suffers. In short, these kind of hairbreadth missings of happiness look like the insults of Fortune, who

may be considered as thus playing tricks with us, and wantonly diverting herself at our expense.

Fielding, *Tom Jones,* XIII, 2

98 To reconcile the indifference and contingency of human actions with prescience; or to defend absolute decrees, and yet free the Deity from being the author of sin, has been found hitherto to exceed all the power of philosophy. Happy, if she be thence sensible of her temerity, when she pries into these sublime mysteries; and leaving a scene so full of obscurities and perplexities, return, with suitable modesty, to her true and proper province, the examination of common life; where she will find difficulties enough to employ her enquiries, without launching into so boundless an ocean of doubt, uncertainty, and contradiction!

Hume, *Concerning Human Understanding,* VIII, 81

99 *Boswell.* "It appears to me, Sir, that predestination, or what is equivalent to it, cannot be avoided, if we hold an universal prescience in the Deity." *Johnson.* "Why, Sir, does not GOD every day see things going on without preventing them?" *Boswell.* "True, Sir; but if a thing be *certainly* foreseen, it must be fixed, and cannot happen otherwise; and if we apply this consideration to the human mind, there is no free will, nor do I see how prayer can be of any avail." He mentioned Dr. Clarke, and Bishop Bramhall on *Liberty and Necessity,* and bid me read South's *Sermons on Prayer;* but avoided the question which has excruciated philosophers and divines, beyond any other. I did not press it further.

Boswell, *Life of Johnson (Oct. 26, 1769)*

100 I expressed a horrour at the thought of death. *Mrs. Knowles.* "Nay, thou should'st not have a horrour for what is the gate of life." *Johnson.* (standing upon the hearth rolling about, with a serious, solemn, and somewhat gloomy air,) "No rational man can die without uneasy apprehension." *Mrs. Knowles.* "The Scriptures tell us, 'The righteous shall have *hope* in his death.' " *Johnson.* "Yes, Madam; that is, he shall not have despair. But, consider, his hope of salvation must be founded on the terms on which it is promised that the mediation of our SAVIOUR shall be applied to us,—namely, obedience; and where obedience has failed, then, as suppletory to it, repentance. But what man can say that his obedience has been such, as he would approve of in another, or even in himself upon close examination, or that his repentance has not been such as to require being repented of? No man can be sure that his obedience and repentance will obtain salvation." *Mrs. Knowles.* "But divine intimation of acceptance may be made to the soul." *Johnson.* "Madam, it may; but I should not think the better of a man who should tell me

on his death-bed he was sure of salvation. A man cannot be sure himself that he has divine intimation of acceptance; much less can he make others sure that he has it." *Boswell.* "Then, Sir, we must be contented to acknowledge that death is a terrible thing." *Johnson.* "Yes, Sir. I have made no approaches to a state which can look on it as not terrible."

Boswell, *Life of Johnson (Apr. 15, 1778)*

101 Men of merit, who have no success in life, may be forgiven for *lamenting,* if they are not allowed to *complain.* They may consider it as *hard* that their merit should not have its suitable distinction. Though there is no intentional injustice towards them on the part of the world, their merit not having been perceived, they may yet repine against *fortune,* or *fate,* or by whatever name they choose to call the supposed mythological power of *Destiny.*

Boswell, *Life of Johnson (Mar. 23, 1783)*

102 The overweening conceit which the greater part of men have of their own abilities is an ancient evil remarked by the philosophers and moralists of all ages. Their absurd presumption in their own good fortune has been less taken notice of. It is, however, if possible, still more universal. There is no man living who, when in tolerable health and spirits, has not some share of it. The chance of gain is by every man more or less overvalued, and the chance of loss is by most men undervalued, and by scarce any man, who is in tolerable health and spirits, valued more than it is worth.

Adam Smith, *Wealth of Nations,* I, 10

103 The doctrine of eternal decrees and absolute predestination is strictly embraced by the Mohammedans; and they struggle with the common difficulties, *how* to reconcile the prescience of God with the freedom and responsibility of man; *how* to explain the permission of evil under the reign of infinite power and infinite goodness.

Gibbon, *Decline and Fall of the Roman Empire,* L

104 The Koran inculcates, in the most absolute sense, the tenets of fate and predestination, which would extinguish both industry and virtue, if the actions of man were governed by his speculative belief. Yet their influence in every age has exalted the courage of the Saracens and Turks. The first companions of Mohammed advanced to battle with a fearless confidence: there is no danger where there is no chance: they were ordained to perish in their beds; or they were safe and invulnerable amidst the darts of the enemy.

Gibbon, *Decline and Fall of the Roman Empire,* L

105 *Mephistopheles.* How closely linked are Luck and Merit,
Is something fools have never known.
Goethe, Faust, II, 1, 5061

106 From every point of view the concept predestination may be considered as an abortion, for having unquestionably arisen in order to relate freedom and God's omnipotence it solves the riddle by denying one of the concepts and consequently explains nothing.
Kierkegaard, Journals
(Aug. 19, 1834)

107 We may be partial, but Fate is not.
Emerson, The Conservative

108 So strange a dreaminess did there then reign all over the ship and all over the sea, only broken by the intermitting dull sound of the sword, that it seemed as if this were the Loom of Time, and I myself were a shuttle mechanically weaving and weaving away at the Fates. There lay the fixed threads of the warp subject to but one single, ever returning, unchanging vibration, and that vibration merely enough to admit of the crosswise interblending of other threads with its own. This warp seemed necessity; and here, thought I, with my own hand, I ply my own shuttle and weave my own destiny into these unalterable threads.
Melville, Moby Dick, XLVII

109 *Ahab.* What is it, what nameless, inscrutable, unearthly thing is it; what cozening, hidden lord and master, and cruel, remorseless emperor commands me; that against all natural lovings and longings, I so keep pushing, and crowding, and jamming myself on all the time; recklessly making me ready to do what in my own proper, natural heart, I durst not so much as dare? Is Ahab, Ahab? Is it I, God, or who, that lifts this arm? But if the great sun move not of himself; but is as an errand-boy in heaven; nor one single star can revolve, but by some invisible power; how then can this one small heart beat; this one small brain think thoughts; unless God does that beating, does that thinking, does that living, and not I.
Melville, Moby Dick, CXXXII

110 There are two sides to the life of every man, his individual life, which is the more free the more abstract its interests, and his elemental hive life in which he inevitably obeys laws laid down for him.

Man lives consciously for himself, but is an unconscious instrument in the attainment of the historic, universal, aims of humanity. A deed done is irrevocable, and its result coinciding in time with the actions of millions of other men assumes an historic significance. The higher a man stands on the social ladder, the more people he is connected with and the more power he has over others, the more evident is the predestination and inevitability of his every action.

"The king's heart is in the hands of the Lord." A king is history's slave.
Tolstoy, War and Peace, IX, 1

111 The innumerable people who took part in the war acted in accord with their personal characteristics, habits, circumstances, and aims. They were moved by fear or vanity, rejoiced or were indignant, reasoned, imagining that they knew what they were doing and did it of their own free will, but they all were involuntary tools of history, carrying on a work concealed from them but comprehensible to us. Such is the inevitable fate of men of action, and the higher they stand in the social hierarchy the less are they free.
Tolstoy, War and Peace, X, 1

112 For history, the insoluble mystery presented by the incompatibility of free will and inevitability does not exist as it does for theology, ethics, and philosophy. History surveys a presentation of man's life in which the union of these two contradictions has already taken place.

In actual life each historic event, each human action, is very clearly and definitely understood without any sense of contradiction, although each event presents itself as partly free and partly compulsory.
Tolstoy, War and Peace,
II Epilogue, IX

113 When a man has let himself go time after time, he easily becomes impressed with the enormously preponderating influence of circumstances, hereditary habits, and temporary bodily dispositions over what might seem a spontaneity born for the occasion. "All is fate," he then says; "all is resultant of what pre-exists. Even if the moment seems original, it is but the instable molecules passively tumbling in their preappointed way. It is hopeless to resist the drift, vain to look for any new force coming in; and less, perhaps, than anywhere else under the sun is there anything really mine in the decisions which I make." This is really no argument for simple determinism. There runs throughout it the sense of a force which might make things otherwise from one moment to another, if it were only strong enough to breast the tide. A person who feels the *impotence* of free effort in this way has the acutest notion of what is meant by it, and of its possible independent power. How else could he be so conscious of its absence and of that of its effects? But genuine determinism occupies a totally different ground; not the *impotence* but the *unthinkability* of free-will is what it affirms. It admits something phenomenal *called* free effort, which seems to breast the tide,

but it claims this as a *portion of the tide*. The variations of the effort cannot be independent, it says; they cannot originate *ex nihilo*, or come from a fourth dimension; they are mathematically fixed functions of the ideas themselves, which are the tide. Fatalism, which conceives of effort clearly enough as an independent variable that might come from a fourth dimension if it *would* come, but that does *not* come, is a very dubious ally for determinism. It strongly imagines that very possibility which determinism denies.

William James, *Psychology*, XXVI

Chapter 16

ART *and*
AESTHETICS

Chapter 16 is divided into seven sections: 16.1 The Realm of Art, 16.2 Books and Reading, 16.3 Poetry and Poets, 16.4 Tragedy and Comedy, 16.5 Music, 16.6 Beauty and the Beautiful, and 16.7 Criticism and the Standards of Taste.

The lines that divide these sections cannot be sharply drawn. The reader will, therefore, find passages quoted in one section that might with good reason be placed in another. Sections 16.2, 16.3, and 16.4 all deal with literature in one or another aspect. The presence of a special section on music, together with the absence of similar sections on such other fine arts as painting, sculpture, architecture, and the dance, has no explanation other than the fact that the writings of the great authors here quoted are richer in their comments on that art than on any others except the arts of literature. Nevertheless, if the reader will consult the index under painting, sculpture, architecture, and so on, he will find the location of passages dealing with these arts.

One group of arts, the traditional liberal arts of mathematics and of grammar, rhetoric, and logic is treated in other chapters: grammar, rhetoric, and logic in Section 7.2 on The Arts of Language in Chapter 7 on Language; and The Discipline of Mathematics in Section 17.3 of Chapter 17 on Philosophy, Science, and Mathematics.

16.1 | *The Realm of Art*

The passages quoted in this section treat both art and the artist in the most general sense of these terms, and the reader must, therefore, be forewarned that the most general sense of these terms in the tradition of Western thought is radically different from the extremely restricted connotation that attaches to them in current usage. As used by almost all of the authors quoted, from the Greeks down to the end of the eighteenth century, the word "art" refers to skill in the making of anything—a shoe or a ship as well as a poem or a painting or, for that matter, a demonstration in mathematics or a political oration. The artist is a man who has a specific skill to some degree. Those who happen to make something without art do so entirely by chance. Since the word "art" is used to refer to the skill possessed by a maker, it is not used to refer to the thing he makes, the object he produces. That is a work of art. The terms thus used are not evaluative. They do not signify the achievement of excellence. Artists may have more or less skill; works of art may be more or less good.

It is only in the last few centuries that the term "art" has become so restricted that it refers only to literary and musical composi-tions, paintings, and sculptures, and the like; it is even narrowed further in the familiar expression "literature, music, and the fine arts," in which the last phrase refers exclusively to what hangs on walls, stands on pedestals, or is enclosed in cases. When the phrase "fine art" was first coined (it makes its first appearance in the age of Immanuel Kant), it was used to distinguish one group of arts from all others, i.e., those arts the products of which are an end (Latin, *finis*) in themselves—to be enjoyed for what they are rather than used for some ulterior purpose.

The basic points made in the discussion of art in general apply equally to the fine arts, the useful arts, and the liberal arts. Writers call our attention, for example, to the fact that a work of art may either have an enduring existence or be a transient process. A statue and a poem, like a house or a chair, endure in themselves after the artist has finished his work; not so the performance of an actor or a dancer on the stage, the speech of an orator, and the operation of a surgeon.

Occasionally, authors touch on the subject of art in passages dealing with other matters. The reader would, therefore, do well to glance at the index under such terms as "art," "artist," "work," and so forth.

---

1 *Agathon.* Of his [Love's] courage and justice and temperance I have spoken, but I have yet to speak of his wisdom; and according to the measure of my ability I must try to do my best. In the first place he is a poet (and here, like Eryximachus, I magnify my art), and he is also the source of poesy in others, which he could not be if he were not himself a poet. And at the touch of him every one becomes a poet, even though he had no music in him before; this also is a proof that Love is a good poet and accomplished in all the fine arts; for no one can give to another that which he has not himself, or teach that of which he has no knowledge. Who will deny that the creation of the ani-mals is his doing? Are they not all the works of his wisdom, born and begotten of him? And as to the artists, do we not know that he only of them whom love inspires has the light of fame?—he whom Love touches not walks in darkness. The arts of medicine and archery and divination were discovered by Apollo, under the guidance of love and desire; so that he too is a disciple of Love. Also the melody of the Muses, the metallurgy of Hephaestus, the weaving of Athene, the empire of Zeus over gods and men, are all due to Love, who was the inventor of them.

Plato, *Symposium*, 196B

2 She [Diotima] answered me [Socrates] as follows: "There is poetry, which, as you know, is complex and manifold. All creation or passage of non-being into being is poetry or making, and the processes of all art are creative; and the masters of arts are all poets or makers." "Very true." "Still," she said, "you know that they are not called poets, but have other names; only that portion of the art which is separated off from the rest, and is concerned with music and metre, is termed poetry, and they who possess poetry in this sense of the word are called poets." "Very true," I said.

Plato, *Symposium,* 205A

3 *Socrates.* The artist disposes all things in order, and compels the one part to harmonize and accord with the other part, until he has constructed a regular and systematic whole.

Plato, *Gorgias,* 503B

4 *Socrates.* There is another artist . . . one who is the maker of all the works of all other workmen.

Glaucon. What an extraordinary man!

Wait a little, and there will be more reason for your saying so. For this is he who is able to make not only vessels of every kind, but plants and animals, himself and all other things—the earth and heaven, and the things which are in heaven or under the earth; he makes the gods also.

He must be a wizard and no mistake.

Oh! you are incredulous, are you? Do you mean that there is no such maker or creator, or that in one sense there might be a maker of all these things but in another not? Do you see that there is a way in which you could make them all yourself?

What way?

An easy way enough; or rather, there are many ways in which the feat might be quickly and easily accomplished, none quicker than that of turning a mirror round and round—you would soon enough make the sun and the heavens, and the earth and yourself, and other animals and plants, and all the other things of which we were just now speaking, in the mirror.

Yes, he said; but they would be appearances only.

Very good, I said, you are coming to the point now. And the painter too is, as I conceive, just such another—a creator of appearances, is he not? . . .

Suppose now that . . . we enquire who this imitator is?

If you please.

Well then, here are three beds: one existing in nature, which is made by God, as I think that we may say—for no one else can be the maker?

No.

There is another which is the work of the carpenter?

Yes.

And the work of the painter is a third?

Yes.

Beds, then, are of three kinds, and there are three artists who superintend them: God, the maker of the bed, and the painter?

Yes, there are three of them.

God, whether from choice or from necessity, made one bed in nature and one only; two or more such ideal beds neither ever have been nor ever will be made by God.

Why is that?

Because even if He had made but two, a third would still appear behind them which both of them would have for their idea, and that would be the ideal bed and not the two others.

Very true, he said.

God knew this, and He desired to be the real maker of a real bed, not a particular maker of a particular bed, and therefore He created a bed which is essentially and by nature one only.

So we believe.

Shall we, then, speak of Him as the natural author or maker of the bed?

Yes, he replied; inasmuch as by the natural process of creation He is the author of this and of all other things.

And what shall we say of the carpenter—is not he also the maker of the bed?

Yes.

But would you call the painter a creator and maker?

Certainly not.

Yet if he is not the maker, what is he in relation to the bed?

I think, he said, that we may fairly designate him as the imitator of that which the others make.

Plato, *Republic,* X, 596A

5 The products of art . . . require the pre-existence of an efficient cause homogeneous with themselves, such as the statuary's art, which must necessarily precede the statue; for this cannot possibly be produced spontaneously. Art indeed consists in the conception of the result to be produced before its realization in the material.

Aristotle, *Parts of Animals,* 640ª30

6 All arts, that is, all productive forms of knowledge, are potencies; they are originative sources of change in another thing or in the artist himself considered as other.

Aristotle, *Metaphysics,* 1046ᵇ3

7 Every art and every inquiry, and similarly every action and pursuit, is thought to aim at some good; and for this reason the good has rightly been declared to be that at which all things aim. But a certain difference is found among ends; some are activities, others are products apart from

the activities that produce them. Where there are ends apart from the actions, it is the nature of the products to be better than the activities. Now, as there are many actions, arts, and sciences, their ends also are many; the end of the medical art is health, that of shipbuilding a vessel, that of strategy victory, that of economics wealth. But where such arts fall under a single capacity—as bridle-making and the other arts concerned with the equipment of horses fall under the art of riding, and this and every military action under strategy, in the same way other arts fall under yet others—in all of these the ends of the master arts are to be preferred to all the subordinate ends; for it is for the sake of the former that the latter are pursued.

Aristotle, *Ethics*, 1094ª1

8 Those occupations are most truly arts in which there is the least element of chance; they are the meanest in which the body is most deteriorated, the most servile in which there is the greatest use of the body, and the most illiberal in which there is the least need of excellence.

Aristotle, *Politics*, 1258ᵇ35

9 Since learning and wondering are pleasant, it follows that such things as acts of imitation must be pleasant—for instance, painting, sculpture, poetry—and every product of skilful imitation; this latter, even if the object imitated is not itself pleasant; for it is not the object itself which here gives delight; the spectator draws inferences ('That is a so-and-so') and thus learns something fresh. Dramatic turns of fortune and hairbreadth escapes from perils are pleasant, because we feel all such things are wonderful.

Aristotle, *Rhetoric*, 1371ᵇ4

10 Ships and tillage, walls, laws, arms, roads, dress, and all such things, all the prizes, all the elegancies too of life without exception, poems, pictures, and the chiselling of fine-wrought statues, all these things practiced together with the acquired knowledge of the untiring mind taught men by slow degrees as they advanced on the way step by step. Thus time by degrees brings each several thing forth before men's eyes and reason raises it up into the borders of light; for things must be brought to light one after the other and in due order in the different arts, until these have reached their highest point of development.

Lucretius, *Nature of Things*, V

11 The height of art is to conceal art.

Quintilian, *Institutio Oratoria*, I

12 Every art aims at this, that the thing which has been made should be adapted to the work for which it has been made; and both the vine-planter who looks after the vine, and the horse-breaker, and he who trains the dog, seek this end.

Marcus Aurelius, *Meditations*, VI, 16

13 As for the arts: such as look to house building and the like are exhausted when that object is achieved; there are again those—medicine, farming, and other serviceable pursuits—which deal helpfully with natural products, seeking to bring them to natural efficiency; and there is a class—rhetoric, music, and every other method of swaying mind or soul—with the power of modifying for better or for worse.

Plotinus, *Fourth Ennead*, IV, 31

14 Still the arts are not to be slighted on the ground that they create by imitation of natural objects; for, to begin with, these natural objects are themselves imitations; then, we must recognise that they give no bare reproduction of the thing seen but go back to the ideas from which Nature itself derives, and, furthermore, that much of their work is all their own; they are holders of beauty and add where nature is lacking.

Plotinus, *Fifth Ennead*, VIII, 1

15 But how did You make heaven and earth? What instrument did You use for a work so mighty? You are not like an artist; for he forms one body from another as his mind chooses; his mind has the power to give external existence to the form it perceives within itself by its inner eye—and whence should it have that power unless You made it? It impresses that form upon a material already existent and having the capacity to be thus formed, such as clay or stone or wood or gold or such like. And how should these things have come to be unless You had made them to be? It was You who made the workman his body, and the mind that directs his limbs, the matter of which he makes what he makes, the intelligence by which he masters his art and sees inwardly what he is to produce exteriorly, the bodily sense by which he translates what he does from his mind to his material, and then informs the mind of the result of his workmanship, so that the mind may judge by that truth which presides within it whether the work is well done.

Augustine, *Confessions*, XI, 5

16 As to the . . . arts, whether those by which something is made which, when the effort of the workman is over, remains as a result of his work, as, for example, a house, a bench, a dish, and other things of that kind; or those which, so to speak, assist God in His operations, as medicine, and agriculture, and navigation: or those whose sole result is an action, as dancing, and racing, and wrestling; in all these arts experience teaches us to infer the future from the past. For no man who is skilled in any of these arts moves his limbs in any operation without connecting the memory of the past with the expectation of the future.

Augustine, *Christian Doctrine*, II, 30

17 All natural things were produced by the Divine art, and so may be called God's works of art. Now every artist intends to give to his work the best disposition; not absolutely the best, but the best as regards the proposed end. And even if this entails some defect, the artist does not care. Thus, for instance, when a man makes himself a saw for the purpose of cutting, he makes it of iron, which is suitable for the object in view; and he does not prefer to make it of glass, though this be a more beautiful material, because this very beauty would be an obstacle to the end he has in view. Thus, therefore, God gave to each natural being the best disposition; not absolutely so, but in view of its proper end.

Aquinas, *Summa Theologica*, I, 91, 3

18 Art is nothing else but the right reason about certain works to be made. And yet the good of these things depends, not on man's appetite being affected in this or that way, but on the goodness of the work done. For a craftsman, as such, is commendable not for the will with which he does a work, but for the quality of the work. Art, therefore, properly speaking, is an operative habit. And yet it has something in common with the speculative habits, since the quality of the object considered by the latter is a matter of concern to them also, but not how the human appetite may be affected towards that object. For as long as the geometrician demonstrates the truth, it does not matter how his appetitive part may be affected, whether he be joyful or angry, even as neither does this matter in a craftsman, as we have observed. And so art has the nature of a virtue in the same way as the speculative habits, in so far, that is, as neither art nor speculative habit makes a good work as regards the use of the habit, which is proper to a virtue that perfects the appetite, but only as regards the aptness to work well.

Aquinas, *Summa Theologica*, I–II, 57, 3

19 When anyone endowed with an art produces bad workmanship, this is not the work of that art, but rather is contrary to the art, even as when a man lies while knowing the truth, his words are not in accord with his knowledge, but contrary to it. Therefore, just as science has always a relation to good . . . so it is with art, and it is for this reason that it is called a virtue. And yet it falls short of being a perfect virtue, because it does not make its possessor use it well, for which purpose something further is requisite, although there cannot be a good use without the art.

In order that man may make good use of the art he has, he needs a good will, which is perfected by moral virtue; and for this reason the Philosopher says that there is a virtue of art, namely, a moral virtue, in so far as the good use of art requires a moral virtue. For it is evident that a craftsman is inclined by justice, which rectifies his will, to do his work faithfully.

Even in speculative matters there is something by way of work; for example, the making of a syllogism or of a fitting speech, or the work of counting or measuring. Hence whatever habits are ordered to such works of the speculative reason, are by a kind of comparison called arts indeed, but liberal arts, in order to distinguish them from those arts that are ordered to works done by the body, which arts are, in a fashion, servile, in so far as the body is in servile subjection to the soul, and man, as regards his soul, is free. On the other hand, those sciences which are not ordered to any work of this kind, are called sciences absolutely, and not arts. Nor, if the liberal arts be more excellent, does it follow that the notion of art is more applicable to them.

Aquinas, *Summa Theologica*, I–II, 57, 3

20 The good of an art is to be found not in the craftsman himself, but in the product of the art. . . . It is a perfection not of the maker, but of the thing made. . . . Consequently art does not require of the craftsman that his act be a good act, but that his work be good. Rather would it be necessary for the thing made to act well (for example, that a knife should carve well, or that a saw should cut well), if it were proper to such things to act rather than to be acted on, because they do not have dominion over their actions. Therefore the craftsman needs art not that he may live well, but that he may produce a good work of art, and preserve it.

Aquinas, *Summa Theologica*, I–II, 57, 5

21 It is not reasonable that art should win the place of honor over our great and powerful mother Nature. We have so overloaded the beauty and richness of her works by our inventions that we have quite smothered her. Yet wherever her purity shines forth, she wonderfully puts to shame our vain and frivolous attempts. . . . All our efforts cannot even succeed in reproducing the nest of the tiniest little bird, its contexture, its beauty and convenience; or even the web of the puny spider.

Montaigne, *Essays*, I, 31, Of Cannibals

22 I very much doubt that Phidias or any other excellent sculptor would be so pleased with the preservation and long life of his natural children as with that of an excellent statue that his long labor and study had brought to artistic perfection. And as for those vicious and frenzied passions which have sometimes inflamed fathers with love for their daughters, or mothers for their sons, the like even of these are found in this other sort of parenthood: witness what they tell of Pygmalion, who after building a statue of a woman of singular beauty, became so madly and frantically smitten

with love of this work that the gods, for the sake of his passion, had to bring it to life for him.

Montaigne, *Essays*, II, 8, Affection of Fathers

23 *Hamlet.* 'Tis the sport to have the enginer
Hoist with his own petar; and 't shall go hard
But I will delve one yard below their mines,
And blow them at the moon. O, 'tis most sweet,
When in one line two crafts directly meet.

Shakespeare, *Hamlet*, III, iv, 206

24 As the understanding is elevated and raised by rare and unusual works of nature, to investigate and discover the forms which include them also, so is the same effect frequently produced by the excellent and wonderful works of art; and even to a greater degree, because the mode of effecting and constructing the miracles of art is generally plain, whilst that of effecting the miracles of nature is more obscure. Great care, however, must be taken, that they do not depress the understanding, and fix it, as it were, to earth.

For there is some danger, lest the understanding should be astonished and chained down, and as it were bewitched, by such works of art, as appear to be the very summit and pinnacle of human industry, so as not to become familiar with them, but rather to suppose that nothing of the kind can be accomplished, unless the same means be employed, with perhaps a little more diligence, and more accurate preparation.

Now, on the contrary, it may be stated as a fact, that the ways and means hitherto discovered and observed, of effecting any matter or work, are for the most part of little value, and that all really efficient power depends, and is really to be deduced from the sources of forms, none of which have yet been discovered.

Thus (as we have before observed), had any one meditated on ballistic machines, and battering rams, as they were used by the ancients, whatever application he might have exerted, and though he might have consumed a whole life in the pursuit, yet would he never have hit upon the invention of flaming engines, acting by means of gunpowder; nor would any person, who had made woollen manufactories and cotton the subject of his observation and reflection, have ever discovered thereby the nature of the silkworm or of silk.

Bacon, *Novum Organum*, II, 31

25 All the arts are but imitations of nature in one way or another; as our reason or understanding is a derivative from the Divine intelligence, manifested in His works; and when perfected by habit, like another adventitious and acquired soul, gaining some semblance of the Supreme and Divine agent, it produces somewhat similar effects.

William Harvey, *Animal Generation*, 50

26 How useless is painting, which attracts admiration by the resemblance of things, the originals of which we do not admire!

Pascal, *Pensées*, II, 134

27 First follow Nature, and your judgment frame
By her just standard, which is still the same;
Unerring Nature, still divinely bright,
One clear, unchanged, and universal light,
Life, force, and beauty must to all impart,
At once the source, and end, and test of art.

Pope, *Essay on Criticism*, I, 68

28 All polite letters are nothing but pictures of human life in various attitudes and situations; and inspire us with different sentiments, of praise or blame, admiration or ridicule, according to the qualities of the object, which they set before us. An artist must be better qualified to succeed in this undertaking, who, besides a delicate taste and a quick apprehension, possesses an accurate knowledge of the internal fabric, the operations of the understanding, the workings of the passions, and the various species of sentiment which discriminate vice and virtue. How painful soever this inward search or enquiry may appear, it becomes, in some measure, requisite to those, who would describe with success the obvious and outward appearances of life and manners.

Hume, *Concerning Human Understanding*, I, 5

29 It is justly considered as the greatest excellency of art, to imitate nature; but it is necessary to distinguish those parts of nature, which are most proper for imitation: greater care is still required in representing life, which is so often discoloured by passion, or deformed by wickedness. If the world be promiscuously described, I cannot see of what use it can be to read the account; or why it may not be as safe to turn the eye immediately upon mankind, as upon a mirror which shows all that presents itself without discrimination.

It is therefore not a sufficient vindication of a character, that it is drawn as it appears, for many characters ought never to be drawn; nor of a narrative, that the train of events is agreeable to observation and experience, for that observation which is called knowledge of the world, will be found much more frequently to make men cunning than good. The purpose of these writings is surely not only to show mankind, but to provide that they may be seen hereafter with less hazard; to teach the means of avoiding the snares which are laid by TREACHERY for INNOCENCE, without infusing any wish for that superiority with which the betrayer flatters his vanity; to give the power of counteracting fraud, without the temptation to practise it; to initiate youth by mock encounters in the art of necessary defence, and to increase prudence without impairing virtue.

Johnson, *Rambler No. 4*

30 The practice of architecture is directed by a few general and even mechanical rules. But sculpture, and, above all, painting, propose to themselves the imitation not only of the forms of nature, but of the characters and passions of the human soul. In those sublime arts the dexterity of the hand is of little avail unless it is animated by fancy and guided by the most correct taste and observation.

> Gibbon, *Decline and Fall of the Roman Empire*, XIII

31 Art is distinguished from nature as making is from acting or operating in general, and the product or the result of the former is distinguished from that of the latter as work from operation.

By right it is only production through freedom, that is, through an act of will that places reason at the basis of its action, that should be termed art.

> Kant, *Critique of Aesthetic Judgement*, 43

32 Art, as human skill, is distinguished also from science (as ability from knowledge), as a practical from a theoretical faculty, as technic from theory (as the art of surveying from geometry). For this reason, also, what one can do the moment one only knows what is to be done, hence without anything more than sufficient knowledge of the desired result, is not called art. To art that alone belongs for which the possession of the most complete knowledge does not involve one's having then and there the skill to do it.

> Kant, *Critique of Aesthetic Judgement*, 43

33 Art is further distinguished from handicraft. The first is called free, the other may be called industrial art. We look on the former as something which could only prove final (be a success) as play, i.e., an occupation which is agreeable on its own account; but on the second as labour, i.e., a business, which on its own account is disagreeable (drudgery), and is only attractive by means of what it results in (e.g., the pay), and which is consequently capable of being a compulsory imposition. Whether in the list of arts and crafts we are to rank watchmakers as artists, and smiths on the contrary as craftsmen, requires a standpoint different from that here adopted—one, that is to say, taking account of the proposition of the talents which the business undertaken in either case must necessarily involve. Whether, also, among the so-called seven free arts some may not have been included which should be reckoned as sciences, and many, too, that resemble handicraft, is a matter I will not discuss here. It is not amiss, however, to remind the reader of this: that in all free arts something of a compulsory character is still required, or, as it is called, a mechanism, without which the soul, which in art must be free, and which alone gives life to the work, would be bodyless and evanescent (e.g., in the poetic art there must be correctness and wealth of language, like-wise prosody and metre). For not a few leaders of a newer school believe that the best way to promote a free art is to sweep away all restraint and convert it from labour into mere play.

> Kant, *Critique of Aesthetic Judgement*, 43

34 Fine art . . . is a mode of representation which is intrinsically final, and which, although devoid of an end, has the effect of advancing the culture of the mental powers in the interests of social communication.

> Kant, *Critique of Aesthetic Judgement*, 44

35 Genius (1) is a talent for producing that for which no definite rule can be given, and not an aptitude in the way of cleverness for what can be learned according to some rule; and . . . consequently originality must be its primary property. (2) Since there may also be original nonsense, its products must at the same time be models, that is, be exemplary; and consequently, though not themselves derived from imitation, they must serve that purpose for others, that is, as a standard or rule of estimating. . . . Where an author owes a product to his genius, he does not himself know how the ideas for it have entered into his head, nor has he it in his power to invent the like at pleasure, or methodically, and communicate the same to others in such precepts as would put them in a position to produce similar products.

> Kant, *Critique of Aesthetic Judgement*, 46

36 Despite the marked difference that distinguishes mechanical art, as an art merely depending upon industry and learning, from fine art, as that of genius, there is still no fine art in which something mechanical, capable of being at once comprehended and followed in obedience to rules, and consequently something academic, does not constitute the essential condition of the art. For the thought of something as end must be present, or else its product would not be ascribed to an art at all, but would be a mere product of chance. But the effectuation of an end necessitates determinate rules which we cannot venture to dispense with. Now, seeing that originality of talent is one (though not the sole) essential factor that goes to make up the character of genius, shallow minds fancy that the best evidence they can give of their being full-blown geniuses is by emancipating themselves from all academic constraint of rules, in the belief that one cuts a finer figure on the back of an ill-tempered than of a trained horse.

> Kant, *Critique of Aesthetic Judgement*, 47

37 *Faust.* Unless you feel, naught will you ever gain;
Unless this feeling pours forth from your soul
With native, pleasing vigour to control
The hearts of all your hearers, it will be in vain.
Pray keep on sitting! Pray collect and glue,
From others' feasts brew some ragout;

With tiny heaps of ashes play your game
And blow the sparks into a wretched flame!
Children and apes will marvel at you ever,
If you've a palate that can stand the part;
But heart to heart you'll not draw men, no, never,
Unless your message issue from your heart.

Goethe, *Faust*, I, 534

38 There is no surer method of evading the world than by following art, and no surer method of linking oneself to it than by art.

Goethe, *Reflections and Maxims*

39 Were any one to despise art on the ground that it imitates nature, we should reply that Nature herself imitates many other things, and that, furthermore, art does not merely imitate that which we see with our eyes, but goes back to that element of reason of which nature consists and according to which she acts.

Goethe, *Reflections and Maxims*

40 The artist has a twofold relation to nature; he is at once her master and her slave. He is her slave, inasmuch as he must work with earthly things, in order to be understood; but he is her master, inasmuch as he subjects these earthly means to his higher intentions, and renders them subservient.

Goethe, *Conversations with Eckermann*
(Apr. 18, 1827)

41 The religious concentration of the soul appears in the form of feeling; it nevertheless passes also into reflection; a form of worship is a result of reflection. The second form of the union of the objective and subjective in the human spirit is art. This advances farther into the realm of the actual and sensuous than religion. In its noblest walk it is occupied with representing, not indeed, the spirit of God, but certainly the form of God; and in its secondary aims, that which is divine and spiritual generally. Its office is to render visible the divine; presenting it to the imaginative and intuitive faculty. But the true is the object not only of conception and feeling, as in religion—and of intuition, as in art—but also of the thinking faculty; and this gives us the third form of the union in question—philosophy.

Hegel, *Philosophy of History*, Introduction, 3

42 What is the true content of art, and with what aim is this content to be presented? On this subject our consciousness supplies us with the common opinion that it is the task and aim of art to bring in contact with our sense, our feeling, our inspiration, all that finds a place in the mind of man. . . . Its aim is therefore placed in arousing and animating the slumbering emotions, inclinations, and passions; in filling the heart, in forcing the human being, whether cultured or uncultured, to feel the whole range of what man's soul in its inmost and secret corners has power to experience and to create, and all that is able to move and to stir the human breast in its depths and in its manifold aspects and possibilities; to present as a delight to emotion and to perception all that the mind possesses of real and lofty in its thought and in the Idea—all the splendour of the noble, the eternal, and the true; and no less to make intelligible misfortune and misery, wickedness and crime; to make men realize the inmost nature of all that is shocking and horrible, as also of all pleasure and delight; and, finally, to set imagination roving in idle toyings of fancy, and luxuriating in the seductive spells of sense-stimulating visions.

Hegel, *Philosophy of Fine Art*, III

43 We have here to consider three relations of the Idea to its outward shaping.

First, the Idea gives rise to the beginning of art when, being itself still in its indistinctness and obscurity, or in vicious untrue determinateness, it is made the import of artistic creations. As indeterminate it does not yet possess in itself that individuality which the Ideal demands; its abstractness and one-sidedness leave its shape to be outwardly bizarre and defective. The first form of art is therefore rather a mere search after plastic portrayal than a capacity of genuine representation. The Idea has not yet found the true form even within itself, and therefore continues to be merely the struggle and aspiration thereafter. In general terms we may call this form the Symbolic form of art. . . .

In the second form of art, which we propose to call Classical, the double defect of symbolic art is cancelled. The plastic shape of symbolic art is imperfect, because, in the first place, the Idea in it only enters into consciousness in abstract determinateness or indeterminateness, and, in the second place, this must always make the conformity of shape to import defective, and in its turn merely abstract. The classical form of art is the solution of this double difficulty; it is the free and adequate embodiment of the Idea in the shape that, according to its conception, is peculiarly appropriate to the Idea itself. With it, therefore, the Idea is capable of entering into free and complete accord. Hence, the classical type of art is the first to afford the production and intuition of the completed Ideal, and to establish it as a realized fact. . . .

[There] arises, in its turn, the defect which brings about the dissolution of classical art, and demands a transition into a third and higher form, viz. into the Romantic form of art.

The romantic form of art destroys the completed union of the Idea and its reality, and recurs, though in a higher phase, to that difference and antagonism of two aspects which was left unvanquished by symbolic art. The classical type attained the highest excellence, of which the sensuous embodiment of art is capable; and if it is in any way defective, the defect is in art as a whole, i.e. in the limitation of its sphere. This limitation consists in the fact that art as such takes for its object Mind—the conception of which is infinite concrete universality—in the shape of sensuous concreteness, and in the classical phase sets up the perfect amalgamation of spiritual and sensuous existence as a conformity of the two. Now, as a matter of fact, in such an amalgamation Mind cannot be represented according to its true notion. For mind is the infinite subjectivity of the Idea, which, as absolute inwardness, is not capable of finding free expansion in its true nature on condition of remaining transposed into a bodily medium as the existence appropriate to it.

Hegel, *Philosophy of Fine Art,* V

44 Art is a jealous mistress, and if a man have a genius for painting, poetry, music, architecture or philosophy, he makes a bad husband and ill provider, and should be wise in season and not fetter himself with duties which will embitter his days and spoil him for his proper work.

Emerson, *Wealth*

45 To make a prairie it takes a clover and one bee,
One clover and a bee
And revery.
The revery alone will do
If bees are few.

Emily Dickinson, *To Make a Prairie*

46 I want a definition of art wide enough to include all its varieties of aim: I do not say therefore that the art is greatest which gives most pleasure, because perhaps there is some art whose end is to teach, and not to please. I do not say that the art is greatest which teaches us most, because perhaps there is some art whose end is to please and not to teach. I do not say that the art is greatest which imitates best, because perhaps there is some art whose end is to create, and not to imitate. But I say that the art is greatest, which conveys to the mind of the spectator, by any means whatsoever, the greatest number of the greatest ideas, and I call an idea great in proportion as it is received by a higher faculty of the mind, and as it more fully occupies, and in occupying, exercises and exalts, the faculty by which it is received.

If this then be the definition of great art, that of a great artist naturally follows. He is the greatest artist who has embodied, in the sum of his works, the greatest number of the greatest ideas.

Ruskin, *Modern Painters,* Pt. I, I, 2

47 1. Never encourage the manufacture of any article not absolutely necessary, in the production of which *Invention* has no share.
2. Never demand an exact finish for its own sake, but only for some practical or noble end.
3. Never encourage imitation or copying of any kind, except for the sake of preserving record of great works.

Ruskin, *Stones of Venice,* II, 6

48 Literary and artistic productions never grow old, in this sense, that they are expressions of feeling, changeless as human nature.

Claude Bernard, *Experimental Medicine,* II, 2

49 Art is a human activity, whose purpose is the transmission of the highest and best feelings to which men have attained.

Tolstoy, *What Is Art?,* VIII

50 Future artists will understand that it is incomparably more important to compose a fairy-tale, a little song, a lullaby, an amusing riddle or joke, or to draw a sketch that delights millions of children and adults over the generations, than to create a novel or symphony, or paint a canvas that diverts a few members of the wealthy class for a moment and then is forgotten forever.

Tolstoy, *What Is Art?,* XIX

51 The present task of art is to make the feeling of brotherhood and love of one's neighbor, which is now shared only by the best members of society, the customary feeling, even the instinct, of all human beings. . . . Art is destined to promulgate the truth that the well-being of men consists in their being united together, and to help to set up, in place of the reign of force that now exists, the kingdom of God (Who is Love) that we all recognize as the highest goal of human life.

Tolstoy, *What Is Art?,* XX

52 The artist notoriously selects his items, rejecting all tones, colors, shapes, which do not harmonize with each other and with the main purpose of his work. That unity, harmony . . . which gives to works of art their superiority over works of nature, is wholly due to *elimination.* Any natural subject will do, if the artist has wit enough to pounce upon some one feature of it as characteristic, and suppress all merely accidental items which do not harmonize with this.

William James, *Psychology,* IX

53 The world of æsthetics . . . is an ideal world, a Utopia, a world which the outer relations persist in contradicting, but which we as stubbornly persist in striving to make actual. Why do we thus invincibly crave to alter the given order of nature? Simply because other relations among things are far more interesting to us and more charming than the mere rates of frequency of their time-and space-conjunctions. These other relations are all secondary and brain-born, "spontaneous variations" most of them, of our sensibility, whereby

certain elements of experience, and certain arrangements in time and space, have acquired an agreeableness which otherwise would not have been felt. It is true that habitual arrangements may also become agreeable. But this agreeableness of the merely habitual is felt to be a mere ape and counterfeit of real inward fitness; and one sign of intelligence is never to mistake the one for the other.

William James, Psychology, XXVIII

54 *Tanner.* The true artist will let his wife starve, his children go barefoot, his mother drudge for his living at seventy, sooner than work at anything but his art. To women he is half vivisector, half vampire. He gets into intimate relations with them to study them, to strip the mask of convention from them, to surprise their inmost secrets, knowing that they have the power to rouse his deepest creative energies, to rescue him from his cold reason, to make him see visions and dream dreams, to inspire him, as he calls it. He persuades women that they may do this for their own purpose whilst he really means them to do it for his. He steals the mother's milk and blackens it to make printer's ink to scoff at her and glorify ideal women with. He pretends to spare her the pangs of child-bearing so that he may have for himself the tenderness and fostering that belong of right to her children. Since marriage began, the great artist has been known as a bad husband. But he is worse: he is a child-robber, a blood-sucker, a hypocrite, and a cheat. Perish the race and wither a thousand women if only the sacrifice of them enable him to act Hamlet better, to paint a finer picture, to write a deeper poem, a greater play, a profounder philosophy!

Shaw, Man and Superman, I

55 Goodness is the third member of the trinity which traditionally has been assigned as the complex aim of art—namely, Truth, Beauty, and Goodness. With the point of view here adopted, Goodness must be denied a place among the aims of art. For Goodness is a qualification belonging to the constitution of reality, which in any of its individual actualizations is better or worse. Good and evil lie in depths and distances below and beyond appearance. They solely concern inter-relations within the real world. The real world is good when it is beautiful. Art has essentially to do with perfections attainable by purposeful adaptation of appearance. With a larger view and a deeper analysis, some instance of the perfection of art may diminish the good otherwise inherent in some specific situation as it passes into its objective actuality for the future. Unseasonable art is analogous to an unseasonable joke, namely, good in its place, but out of place a positive evil. It is a curious fact that lovers of art who are most insistent on the doctrine of 'art for art's sake' are apt to be

indignant at the banning of art for the sake of other interests. The charge of immorality is not refuted by pointing to the perfection of art. Of course it is true that the defence of morals is the battle-cry which best rallies stupidity against change. Perhaps countless ages ago respectable amœbæ refused to migrate from ocean to dry land—refusing in defence of morals. One incidental service of art to society lies in its adventurousness.

It is a tribute to the strength of the sheer craving for freshness, that change, whose justification lies in aim at the distant ideal, should be promoted by Art which is the adaptation of immediate Appearance for immediate Beauty. Art neglects the safety of the future for the gain of the present. In so doing it is apt to render its Beauty thin. But after all, there must be some immediate harvest. The Good of the Universe cannot lie in indefinite postponement. The Day of Judgment is an important notion: but that Day is always with us. Thus Art takes care of the immediate fruition, here and now; and in so doing is apt to lose some depth by reason of the immediate fruition at which it is aiming. Its business is to render the Day of Judgment a success, now. The effect of the present on the future is the business of morals. And yet the separation is not so easy. For the inevitable anticipation adds to the present a qualitative element which profoundly affects its whole qualitative harmony.

Whitehead, Adventures of Ideas, XVIII, 3–4

56 The merit of Art in its service to civilization lies in its artificiality and its finiteness. It exhibits for consciousness a finite fragment of human effort achieving its own perfection within its own limits. Thus the mere toil for the slavish purpose of prolonging life for more toil or for mere bodily gratification, is transformed into the conscious realization of a self-contained end, timeless within time. The work of Art is a fragment of nature with the mark on it of a finite creative effort, so that it stands alone, an individual thing detailed from the vague infinity of its background. Thus Art heightens the sense of humanity. It gives an elation of feeling which is supernatural. A sunset is glorious, but it dwarfs humanity and belongs to the general flow of nature. A million sunsets will not spur on men towards civilization. It requires Art to evoke into consciousness the finite perfections which lie ready for human achievement.

Consciousness itself is the product of art in its lowliest form. For it results from the influx of ideality into its contrast with reality, with the purpose of reshaping the latter into a finite, select appearance. But consciousness having emerged from Art at once produces the new specialized art of the conscious animals—in particular human art. In a sense art is a morbid overgrowth of functions which lie deep in nature. It is the essence of art to be artificial. But it is its perfection to return to nature, remaining art. In short art is the education of nature. Thus, in its broadest sense, art is civilization. For civilization is nothing other than the unremitting aim at the major perfections of harmony.

Whitehead, *Adventures of Ideas,* XVIII, 6

57 There is, in fact, a path from phantasy back again to reality, and that is—art. The artist has also an introverted disposition and has not far to go to become neurotic. He is one who is urged on by instinctual needs which are too clamorous; he longs to attain to honour, power, riches, fame, and the love of women; but he lacks the means of achieving these gratifications. So, like any other with an unsatisfied longing, he turns away from reality and transfers all his interest, and all his libido too, on to the creation of his wishes in the life of phantasy, from which the way might readily lead to neurosis. There must be many factors in combination to prevent this becoming the whole outcome of his development; it is well known how often artists in particular suffer from partial inhibition of their capacities through neurosis. Probably their constitution is endowed with a powerful capacity for sublimation and with a certain flexibility in the repressions determining the conflict. But the way back to reality is found by the artist thus: He is not the only one who has a life of phantasy; the intermediate world of phantasy is sanctioned by general human consent, and every hungry soul looks to it for comfort and consolation. But to those who are not artists the gratification that can be drawn from the springs of phantasy is very limited; their inexorable repressions prevent the enjoyment of all but the meagre daydreams which can become conscious. A true artist has more at his disposal. First of all he understands how to elaborate his day-dreams, so that they lose that personal note which grates upon strange ears and become enjoyable to others; he knows too how to modify them sufficiently so that their origin in prohibited sources is not easily detected. Further, he possesses the mysterious ability to mould his particular material until it expresses the ideas of his phantasy faithfully; and then he knows how to attach to this reflection of his phantasy-life so strong a stream of pleasure that, for a time at least, the repressions are out-balanced and dispelled by it. When he can do all this, he opens out to others the way back to the comfort and consolation of their own unconscious sources of pleasure, and so reaps their gratitude and admiration; then he has won—through his phantasy— what before he could only win in phantasy: honour, power, and the love of women.

Freud, *General Introduction
to Psycho-Analysis,* XXIII

58 As regards intellectual work, it remains a fact, indeed, that great decisions in the realm of thought and momentous discoveries and solutions of problems are only possible to an individual, working in solitude. But even the group mind is capable of genius in intellectual creation, as is shown above all by language itself, as well as by folk-song, folklore and the like. It remains an open question, moreover, how much the individual thinker or writer owes to the stimulation of the group in which he lives, or whether he does more than perfect a mental work in which the others had had a simultaneous share.

Freud, *Group Psychology and Analysis
of the Ego,* III

59 People say that women contributed but little to the discoveries and inventions of civilization, but perhaps after all they did discover one technical process, that of plaiting and weaving. If this is so, one is tempted to guess at the unconscious motive at the back of this achievement. Nature herself might be regarded as having provided a model for imitation, by causing pubic hair to grow at the period of sexual maturity so as to veil the genitals. The step that remained to be taken was to attach the hairs permanently together, whereas in the body they are fixed in the skin and only tangled with one another. If you repudiate this idea as being fantastic, and accuse me of having an *idée fixe* on the subject of the influence exercised by the lack of a penis upon the development of femininity, I cannot of course defend myself.

Freud, *New Introductory Lectures
on Psycho-Analysis,* XXXIII

60 Art . . . explicitly recognizes what it has taken so long to discover in science; the control exercised by emotion in reshaping natural conditions, and the place of the imagination, under the influence of desire, in re-creating the world into a more orderly place. When so-called nonrational factors are found to play a large part in the production of relations of consistency and order in logical systems, it is not surprising that they should operate in artistic structures. Indeed, it may be questioned whether any scientific systems extant, save perhaps those of mathematics, equal artistic structure in integrity, subtlety and scope, while the latter are evidently more readily and widely understood, and are the sources of a more widespread and direct satisfaction. These facts are explicable only when it is realized that scientific and artistic systems embody the same fundamental principles of the relationship of life to its surroundings, and that both satisfy the same fundamental needs. Probably a time will come when it will be universally recognized that the differences between coherent logical schemes and artistic structures in poetry, music and the plastics are technical and specialized, rather than deep-seated.

Dewey, *Affective Thought*

61 That art originated in play is a common saying. Whether or not the saying is historically correct, it suggests that harmony of mental playfulness and seriousness describes the artistic ideal. When the artist is preoccupied overmuch with means and materials, he may achieve wonderful technique, but not the artistic spirit *par excellence*. When the animating idea is in excess of the command of method, æsthetic feeling may be indicated, but the art of presentation is too defective to express the feeling thoroughly. When the thought of the end becomes so adequate that it compels translation into the means that embody it, or when attention to means is inspired by recognition of the end they serve, we have the attitude typical of the artist, an attitude that may be displayed in all activities, even though not conventionally designated arts.

Dewey, *How We Think,* Pt. III, XVI, 2

62 O sages standing in God's holy fire
As in the gold mosaic of a wall,
Come from the holy fire, perne in a gyre,
And be the singing-masters of my soul.
Consume my heart away; sick with desire
And fastened to a dying animal
It knows not what it is; and gather me
Into the artifice of eternity.

Once out of nature I shall never take
My bodily form from any natural thing,
But such a form as Grecian goldsmiths make
Of hammered gold and gold enameling
To keep a drowsy Emperor awake;
Or set upon a golden bough to sing
To lords and ladies of Byzantium
Of what is past, or passing, or to come.

Yeats, *Sailing to Byzantium*

63 The effect of a work of art upon the person who enjoys it is an experience different in kind from any experience not of art. It may be formed out of one emotion, or may be a combination of several; and various feelings, inhering for the writer in particular words or phrases or images, may be added to compose the final result. Or great poetry may be made without the direct use of any emotion whatever: composed out of feelings solely. . . . It is not the "greatness," the intensity, of the emotions, the components, but the intensity of the artistic process, the pressure, so to speak, under which the fusion takes place, that counts.

T. S. Eliot, *Tradition and the Individual Talent*

64 This mental vegetation, this fitful nervous groping, is . . . a sign of life, out of which art emerges by discipline and by a gradual application to real issues. An artist is a dreamer consenting to dream of the actual world; he is a highly suggestible mind hypnotised by reality.

Santayana, *Life of Reason,* IV, 3

65 The subject matter of art is life, life as it actually is; but the function of art is to make life better. The depth to which an artist may find current experience to be sunk in discord and confusion is not his special concern; his concern is, in some measure, to lift experience out. The more barbarous his age, the more drastic and violent must be his operation.

Santayana, *Life of Reason,* IV, 4

66 Love, one of the great commonplaces of existence, is slowly leaving mine. The maternal instinct is another great commonplace. Once we've left these behind, we find that all the rest is gay and varied, and that there is plenty of it. But one doesn't leave all that behind when or as one pleases. How wise one of my husbands was when he remonstrated: "But is it impossible for you to write a book that isn't about love, adultery, semi-incestuous relations and a final separation? Aren't there other things in life?" If he had not been in such a hurry to get to his amorous rendezvous— for he was handsome and charming—he might perhaps have taught me what can take the place of love, in a novel or out of it.

Colette, *La Naissance du jour*

67 Art, which rules Making and not Doing, stands therefore outside the human sphere; it has an end, rules, values, which are not those of man, but those of the work to be produced. This work is everything for Art; there is for Art but one law— the exigencies and the good of the work.

Hence the tyrannical and absorbing power of Art, and also its astonishing power of soothing; it delivers one from the human; it establishes the *artifex*—artist or artisan—in a world apart, closed, limited, absolute, in which he puts the energy and intelligence of his manhood at the service of a thing which he makes. This is true of all art; the ennui of living and willing ceases at the door of every workshop.

But if art is not human in the end that it pursues, it is human, essentially human, in its mode of operating. It's a work of man that has to be made; it must have on it the mark of man: *animal rationale.*

Maritain, *Art and Scholasticism,* III

68 Art in general tends to make a work. But certain arts tend to make a *beautiful* work, and in this they differ essentially from all the others. The work to which all the other arts tend is itself ordered to the service of man, and is therefore a simple means; and it is entirely enclosed in a determined material genus. The work to which the fine arts tend is ordered to beauty; as beautiful, it is an end, an absolute, it suffices of itself; and if, as work-to-be-made, it is material and enclosed in a genus, as beautiful it belongs to the kingdom of the spirit

and plunges deep into the transcendence and the infinity of being.

The fine arts thus stand out in the *genus* art as man stands out in the *genus* animal. And like man himself they are like a horizon where matter and spirit meet. They have a spiritual soul. Hence they possess many distinctive properties. Their contact with the beautiful modifies in them certain characteristics of art in general, notably, as I shall try to show, with respect to the rules of art; on the other hand, this contact discloses and carries to a sort of excess other generic characteristics of the virtue of art, above all its intellectual character and its resemblance to the speculative virtues.

Maritain, *Art and Scholasticism*, V

69 Art is *gratuitous* or disinterested as such—that is to say, . . . in the production of the work the virtue of art aims only at one thing: the good of the work-to-be-made, beauty to be made to shine in matter, the creating of the thing according to its own laws, independently of all the rest; and accordingly it desires that there be nothing in the work which will escape its regulation, and that it be alone in immediately ruling the work, in moulding it and fashioning it.

There are many ways of failing in this "gratuitousness." One may think, for instance, that good moral intentions make up for the quality of the craft or the inspiration, and suffice to construct a work. Or else one may go so far as to adulterate the work itself, such as the rules and the determined ways of art would have it to be, by forcibly applying to it, in order to rule it, foreign elements—the desire to edify, or to disedify, not to

shock the public, or to create scandal, to have "arrived" in society, or to cut a figure in the bars and cafés as an *artist* free and rare.

Maritain, *Art and Scholasticism*, Appendix I

70 Art is just as comprehensible as science, but in its own terms; that is, one can always ask, and usually can determine, how the artistic semblance of life is made and in what it consists.

Langer, *Mind*, I, Intro.

71 Artistic conception, for all its similarities to mythical ideation and even dream, is not a transitional phase of mental evolution, but a final symbolic form making revelation of truths about actual life. Like discursive reason, it seems to have unlimited potentialities. The facts which it makes conceivable are precisely those which literal statement distorts. Having once symbolized and perceived them, we may talk about them; but only artistic perception can find them and judge them real in the first place.

Langer, *Mind*, I, 4

72 Art is the objectification of feeling, and the subjectification of nature.

Langer, *Mind*, I, 4

73 Every kind of art is beautiful, as all life is beautiful, and for much the same reason: that it embodies sentience, from the most elementary sense of vitality, individual being and continuity, to the full expansion of human perception, human love and hate, triumph and misery, enlightenment, wisdom.

Langer, *Mind*, I, 5

16.2 | *Books and Reading*

The passages here assembled require little or no preamble. They are about the writing and reading of books, the collection and enjoyment of them, and the pleasures and pretensions of the literary life.

The reader will find both praise and dispraise of books, criteria for distinguishing good books from bad, enduring from ephemeral literature, and wise counsel about the books to be read or about the amount and character of the reading one should do, including the cautionary observation by Socrates that the living mind of man can never be enclosed within the dead pages of a book.

Comments on literature will also be found

in the next two sections of this chapter; and for relevant passages in other chapters, the reader should consult the index under such terms as "book," "books," and "literature."

---

1 Of making many books there is no end; and much study is a weariness of the flesh.

Ecclesiastes 12:12

2 *Socrates.* The worst of authors will say something which is to the point.

Plato, *Phaedrus,* 235B

3 *Socrates.* I cannot help feeling, Phaedrus, that writing is unfortunately like painting; for the creations of the painter have the attitude of life, and yet if you ask them a question they preserve a solemn silence. And the same may be said of speeches. You would imagine that they had intelligence, but if you want to know anything and put a question to one of them, the speaker always gives one unvarying answer. And when they have been once written down they are tumbled about anywhere among those who may or may not understand them, and know not to whom they should reply, to whom not: and, if they are maltreated or abused, they have no parent to protect them; and they cannot protect or defend themselves.

Phaedrus. That again is most true.

Soc. Is there not another kind of word or speech far better than this, and having far greater power—a son of the same family, but lawfully begotten?

Phaedr. Whom do you mean, and what is his origin?

Soc. I mean an intelligent word graven in the soul of the learner, which can defend itself, and knows when to speak and when to be silent.

Phaedr. You mean the living word of knowledge which has a soul, and of which the written word is properly no more than an image?

Soc. Yes, of course that is what I mean. And now may I be allowed to ask you a question: Would a husbandman, who is a man of sense, take the seeds, which he values and which he wishes to bear fruit, and in sober seriousness plant them during the heat of summer, in some garden of Adonis, that he may rejoice when he sees them in eight days appearing in beauty? at least he would do so, if at all, only for the sake of amusement and pastime. But when he is in earnest he sows in fitting soil, and practises husbandry, and is satisfied if in eight months the seeds which he has sown arrive at perfection?

Phaedr. Yes, Socrates, that will be his way when he is in earnest; he will do the other, as you say, only in play.

Soc. And can we suppose that he who knows the just and good and honourable has less understanding, than the husbandman, about his own seeds?

Phaedr. Certainly not.

Soc. Then he will not seriously incline to "write" his thoughts "in water" with pen and ink, sowing words which can neither speak for themselves nor teach the truth adequately to others?

Phaedr. No, that is not likely.

Soc. No, that is not likely—in the garden of letters he will sow and plant, but only for the sake of recreation and amusement; he will write them down as memorials to be treasured against the forgetfulness of old age, by himself, or by any other old man who is treading the same path. He will rejoice in beholding their tender growth; and while others are refreshing their souls with banqueting and the like, this will be the pastime in which his days are spent.

Phaedr. A pastime, Socrates, as noble as the other is ignoble, the pastime of a man who can be amused by serious talk, and can discourse merrily about justice and the like.

Soc. True, Phaedrus. But nobler far is the serious pursuit of the dialectician, who, finding a congenial soul, by the help of science sows and plants therein words which are able to help themselves and him who planted them, and are not unfruitful, but have in them a seed which others brought up in different soils render immortal, making the possessors of it happy to the utmost extent of human happiness.

Phaedr. Far nobler, certainly.

Plato, *Phaedrus,* 275B

4 Every man of worth, when dealing with matters of worth, will be far from exposing them to ill feeling and misunderstanding among men by committing them to writing. In one word, then, it may be known from this that, if one sees written treatises composed by anyone, either the laws of a lawgiver, or in any other form whatever, these are not for that man the things of most worth, if he is a man of worth, but that his treasures are laid up in the fairest spot that he possesses. But if these things were worked at by him as things of real worth, and committed to writing, then surely, not gods, but men "have themselves bereft him of his wits."

Plato, *Seventh Letter*

5 Go, little book, my little tragedy!
God grant thy maker, ere his ending day,
May write some tale of happy poetry!

But, little book, of any poet's lay
Envy of heart here shalt thou not display,
But kiss the steps where pass through ages spa-
cious,
Vergil and Ovid, Homer, Lucan and Statius.

Chaucer, *Troilus and Cressida,* V, 256

6 And as for me, though that I konne but lyte,
On bokes for to rede I me delyte,
And to hem yive I feyth and ful credence,
And in myn herte have hem in reverence.

Chaucer, *The Legend of Good Women*

7 For in the composing of this lordly book, I never
lost nor bestowed any more, nor any other time,
than what was appointed to serve me for taking of
my bodily refection, that is, whilst I was eating
and drinking. And, indeed, that is the fittest and
most proper hour, wherein to write these high
matters and deep sentences: as Homer knew very
well, the paragon of all philologues, and Ennius,
father of the Latin poets, as Horace calls him,
although a certain sneaking jobbernol alleged
that his verses smelled more of the wine than oil.

So saith a Turlupin or a new start-up grub of
my books; but a turd for him. The fragrant odour
of the wine, oh! how much more dainty, pleasant,
laughing, celestial, and delicious it is, than that
smell of oil! and I will glory as much when it is
said of me, that I have spent more on wine than
oil, as did Demosthenes, when it was told him,
that his expense on oil was greater than on wine.

Rabelais, *Gargantua and Pantagruel,* I,
Prologue

8 If I had written to seek the world's favor, I should
have bedecked myself better, and should present
myself in a studied posture. I want to be seen here
in my simple, natural, ordinary fashion, without
straining or artifice; for it is myself that I portray.
My defects will here be read to the life, and also
my natural form, as far as respect for the public
has allowed. Had I been placed among those nations which are said to live still in the sweet freedom of nature's first laws, I assure you I should
very gladly have portrayed myself here entire and
wholly naked.

Thus, reader, I am myself the matter of my
book; you would be unreasonable to spend your
leisure on so frivolous and vain a subject.

Montaigne, *Essays,* To the Reader

9 Do you think that Epicurus, who (while dying in
torment, as he says, from the utmost pains of colic) had all his consolation in the beauty of the
doctrine he was leaving to the world, would have
received as much contentment from a number of
wellborn and well-brought-up children, if he had
had any, as he did from the production of his rich
writings? And that if he had had to choose between leaving behind a deformed and ill-born
child and leaving behind a stupid and inept book,

he would not rather have chosen, and not only he
but any man of like ability, to incur the former
misfortune than the other?

Montaigne, *Essays,* II, 8, Affection
of Fathers

10 Reason, wisdom, and the offices of friendship are
oftener found among men; therefore they govern
the affairs of the world.

These two kinds of association are accidental
and dependent on others. One is annoying by its
rarity, the other withers with age; thus they would
not have provided well enough for the needs of
my life. Association with books, which is the third
kind, is much more certain and more our own. It
yields the other advantages to the first two, but it
has for its share the constancy and ease of its service. It is at my side throughout my course, and
accompanies me everywhere. It consoles me in old
age and in solitude. It relieves me of the weight of
a tedious idleness, and releases me at any time
from disagreeable company. It dulls the pangs of
sorrow, unless they are extreme and overpowering. To be diverted from a troublesome idea, I
need only have recourse to books: they easily turn
my thoughts to themselves and steal away the
others. And yet they do not rebel at seeing that I
seek them out only for want of those other pleasures, that are more real, lively, and natural; they
always receive me with the same expression.

He may well go on foot, they say, who leads his
horse by the bridle. And our James, king of Naples and Sicily, who, handsome, young, and
healthy, had himself carried around the country
on a stretcher, lying on a wretched feather pillow,
dressed in a gown of gray cloth with a cap to
match, meanwhile followed by great regal pomp,
litters, hand-led horses of all sorts, gentlemen and
officers, showed an austerity still weak and wavering. The sick man is not to be pitied who has a
cure up his sleeve. In the practice and application
of this maxim, which is very true, lies all the fruit
I reap from books. Actually I use them scarcely
any more than those who do not know them at all.
I enjoy them, as misers enjoy treasures, because I
know that I can enjoy them when I please; my
soul takes its fill of contentment from this right of
possession.

I do not travel without books, either in peace or
in war. However, many days will pass, and even
some months, without my using them. I'll do it
soon, I say, or tomorrow, or when I please. Time
flies and is gone, meanwhile, without hurting me.
For I cannot tell you what ease and repose I find
when I reflect that they are at my side to give me
pleasure at my own time, and when I recognize
how much assistance they bring to my life. It is
the best provision I have found for this human
journey, and I am extremely sorry for men of understanding who do not have it. I sooner accept
any other kind of amusement, however trivial, be-

cause this one cannot fail me.

Montaigne, Essays, III, 3, Three Kinds
of Association

11 You must know then, that when our Gentleman had nothing to do (which was almost all the Year round) he pass'd his Time in reading Books of Knight-Errantry; which he did with that Application and Delight, that at last he in a manner wholly left off his Country-Sports, and even the Care of his Estate: nay, he grew so strangely besotted with those Amusements, that he sold many Acres of Arable-Land to purchase Books of that kind; by which means he collected as many of them as were to be had. . . .

In fine, he gave himself up so wholly to the reading of Romances, that a-Nights he would pore on 'till 'twas Day, and a-Days he would read on 'till 'twas Night; and thus by sleeping little, and reading much, the Moisture of his Brain was exhausted to that Degree, that at last he lost the Use of his Reason. A world of disorderly Notions, pick'd out of his Books, crouded into his Imagination; and now his Head was full of nothing but Inchantments, Quarrels, Battles, Challenges, Wounds, Complaints, Amours, Torments, and abundance of Stuff and Impossibilities; insomuch, that all the Fables and fantastical Tales which he read, seem'd to him now as true as the most authentick Histories.

Cervantes, Don Quixote, I, 1

12 Don *Quixote* listen'd with great Attention to the Canon's Discourse, and perceiving he had done, after he had fix'd his Eyes on him for a considerable Space; Sir, said he, all your Discourse, I find, tends to signify to me, there never were any Knights-Errant; that all the Books of Knight-Errantry are false, fabulous, useless, and prejudicial to the publick; that I have done ill in reading, err'd in believing, and been much to blame in imitating them, by taking upon me the most painful Profession of Chivalry. And you deny that ever there were any *Amadis's* of *Gaul* or *Greece,* or any of those Knights mention'd in those Books. Even as you have said, Sir, quoth the Canon. You also were pleas'd to add, continu'd Don *Quixote,* that those Books had been very hurtful to me, having depriv'd me of my Reason and reduc'd me to be carry'd in a Cage; that therefore it would be for my Advantage to take up in Time, and apply myself to the reading of other Books, where I might find more Truth, more Pleasure, and better Instruction. You are in the right, said the Canon. Then I am satisfy'd, reply'd Don *Quixote,* you yourself are the Man that raves and is inchanted, since you have thus boldly blasphem'd against a Truth so universally receiv'd, that whosoever presumes to contradict it, as you have done, deserves the Punishment you would inflict on those Books, which in reading offend and tire you. For it were

as easy to persuade the World that the Sun does not enlighten, the Frost cool, and the Earth bear us, as that there never was an *Amadis,* or any of the other adventurous Knights, whose Actions are the Subjects of so many Histories. What Mortal can persuade another, that there is no Truth in what is recorded of the Infanta *Floripes,* and *Guy* of *Burgundy:* as also *Fierabras* at the Bridge of *Mantible* in the Reign of *Charlemaign?* which Passages, I dare swear, are as true as that now it is Day. But if this be false, you may as well say there was no *Hector,* nor *Achilles;* nor a *Trojan* War, nor Twelve Peers of *France,* nor a King *Arthur* of *Britain,* who is now converted into a Crow, and hourly expected in his Kingdom.

Cervantes, Don Quixote, I, 49

13 For Me alone was the Great *Quixote* born, and I alone for Him. Deeds were his Task, and to record 'em, Mine. *We two, like Tallies for each other struck, are nothing when apart.*

Cervantes, Don Quixote, II, 74

14 For a man to write well, there are required three necessaries—to read the best authors, observe the best speakers, and much exercise of his own style.

Jonson, Discoveries: De Stilo

15 Let no man upon a weak conceit of sobriety or an ill-applied moderation think or maintain, that a man can search too far, or be too well studied in the book of God's word, or in the book of God's works, divinity or philosophy; but rather let men endeavour an endless progress or proficience in both.

Bacon, Advancement of Learning, Bk. I, I, 3

16 If anyone turn from the manufactories to libraries, and be inclined to admire the immense variety of books offered to our view, let him but examine and diligently inspect the matter and contents of these books, and his astonishment will certainly change its object: for when he finds no end of repetitions, and how much men do and speak the same thing over again, he will pass from admiration of this variety to astonishment at the poverty and scarcity of matter, which has hitherto possessed and filled men's minds.

Bacon, Novum Organum, I, 85

17 Some books are to be tasted, others to be swallowed, and some few to be chewed and digested; that is, some books are to be read only in parts; others to be read, but not curiously; and some few to be read wholly, and with diligence and attention. Some books also may be read by deputy, and extracts made of them by others; but that would be only in the less important arguments, and the meaner sort of books; else distilled books are like common distilled waters, flashy things. Reading maketh a full man; conference a ready man; and writing an exact man. And therefore, if a man

write little, he had need have a great memory; if
he confer little, he had need have a present wit:
and if he read little, he had need have much cunning, to seem to know that he doth not. Histories
make men wise; poets witty; the mathematics subtile; natural philosophy deep; moral grave; logic
and rhetoric able to contend.

Bacon, *Of Studies*

18 The reading of all good books is indeed like a
conversation with the noblest men of past centuries who were the authors of them, nay a carefully
studied conversation, in which they reveal to us
none but the best of their thoughts.

Descartes, *Discourse on Method,* I

19 If I read as many books as other men do, I would
be as dull-witted as they.

Hobbes, qu. by Aubrey, *Brief Lives*

20 The best books are those whose readers think they
could have written them.

Pascal, *Geometrical Demonstration*

21 Books are not absolutely dead things, but do contain a potency of life in them to be as active as
that soul was whose progeny they are; nay, they
do preserve as in a vial the purest efficacy and
extraction of that living intellect that bred them. I
know they are as lively, and as vigorously productive, as those fabulous dragon's teeth; and being
sown up and down, may chance to spring up
armed men. And yet, on the other hand, unless
wariness be used, as good almost kill a man as kill
a good book. Who kills a man kills a reasonable
creature, God's image; but he who destroys a good
book, kills reason itself, kills the image of God, as
it were in the eye. Many a man lives a burden to
the earth; but a good book is the precious life-
blood of a master spirit, embalmed and treasured
up on purpose to a life beyond life. 'Tis true, no
age can restore a life, whereof perhaps there is no
great loss; and revolutions of ages do not oft recover the loss of a rejected truth, for the want of
which whole nations fare the worse.

Milton, *Areopagitica*

22   Who reads
Incessantly, and to his reading brings not
A spirit and judgment equal or superior,
(And what he brings, what needs he elsewhere
    seek)
Uncertain and unsettl'd still remains,
Deep verst in books and shallow in himself,
Crude or intoxicate, collecting toys,
And trifles for choice matters, worth a spunge;
As Children gathering pibles on the shore.

Milton, *Paradise Regained,* IV, 322

23 Would a Writer know how to behave himself with
relation to Posterity, let him consider in old

Books, what he finds, that he is glad to know, and
what Omissions he most laments.

Swift, *Thoughts on Various Subjects*

24 The most accomplished way of using books at
present is two-fold; either, first, to serve them as
some men do lords, learn their titles exactly, and
then brag of their acquaintance. Or, secondly,
which is indeed the choicer, the profounder, and
politer method, to get a thorough insight into the
index, by which the whole book is governed and
turned, like fishes by the tail. For to enter the
palace of learning at the great gate requires an
expense of time and forms; therefore men of much
haste and little ceremony are content to get in by
the back door.

Swift, *Tale of a Tub,* VII

25 Now, it is not well enough considered to what accidents and occasions the world is indebted for the
greatest part of those noble writings which hourly
start up to entertain it. If it were not for a rainy
day, a drunken vigil, a fit of the spleen, a course of
physic, a sleepy Sunday, an ill run at dice, a long
tailor's bill, a beggar's purse, a factious head, a
hot sun, costive diet, want of books, and a just
contempt of learning: but for these events, I say,
and some others too long to recite (especially a
prudent neglect of taking brimstone inwardly), I
doubt the number of authors and of writings
would dwindle away to a degree most woful to
behold.

Swift, *Tale of a Tub,* X

26 I am now trying an experiment very frequent
among modern authors, which is to write upon
nothing.

Swift, *Tale of a Tub,* Conclusion

27 True ease in writing comes from art, not chance,
As those move easiest who have learned to dance.

Pope, *Essay on Criticism,* II, 362

28 [An author is] a fool who, not content with having
bored those who have lived with him, insists on
tormenting the generations to come.

Montesquieu, *Persian Letters,* LXVI

29 Digressions, incontestably, are the sunshine;—
they are the life, the soul of reading!—take them
out of this book, for instance,—you might as well
take the book along with them;—one cold eternal
winter would reign in every page of it; restore
them to the writer;—he steps forth like a bridegroom,—bids All-hail; brings in variety, and forbids the appetite to fail.

Sterne, *Tristram Shandy,* I, 22

30 You despise them, books, you whose whole life is
plunged in the vanities of ambition and in the
search for pleasure or in idleness; but think that

the whole of the known universe, with the exception of the savage races, is governed by books alone. The whole of Africa right to Ethiopia and Nigritia obeys the book of the Alcoran, after having staggered under the book of the Gospel. China is ruled by the moral book of Confucius; a greater part of India by the book of the Veidam. Persia was governed for centuries by the books of one of the Zarathustras.

If you have a law-suit, your goods, your honour, your life even depends on the interpretation of a book which you never read. . . .

Who leads the human race in civilized countries? those who know how to read and write. You do not know either Hippocrates, Boerhaave or Sydenham; but you put your body in the hands of those who have read them. You abandon your soul to those who are paid to read the Bible, although there are not fifty among them who have read it in its entirety with care.

Voltaire, *Philosophical Dictionary:* Books

31 The chief glory of every people arises from its authours.

Johnson, *Preface to the Dictionary*

32 No place affords a more striking conviction of the vanity of human hopes than a public library.

Johnson, *Rambler No. 106*

33 Nothing is more common than to find men whose works are now totally neglected mentioned with praises by their contemporaries as the oracles of their age and the legislators of science.

Johnson, *Rambler No. 106*

34 *Johnson.* I would not advise a rigid adherence to a particular plan of study. I myself have never persisted in any plan for two days together. A man ought to read just as inclination leads him; for what he reads as a task will do him little good. A young man should read five hours in a day, and so may acquire a great deal of knowledge.

Boswell, *Life of Johnson (July 14, 1763)*

35 *Johnson.* When a man writes from his own mind, he writes very rapidly. The greatest part of a writer's time is spent in reading, in order to write: a man will turn over half a library to make one book.

Boswell, *Life of Johnson (Apr. 6, 1775)*

36 He [Johnson] then took occasion to enlarge on the advantages of reading, and combated the idle superficial notion, that knowledge enough may be acquired in conversation. "The foundation (said he), must be laid by reading. General principles must be had from books, which, however, must be brought to the test of real life. In conversation you never get a system. What is said upon a subject is to be gathered from a hundred people. The parts of a truth, which a man gets thus, are at such a distance from each other that he never attains to a full view."

Boswell, *Life of Johnson (Apr. 16, 1775)*

37 When I expressed an earnest wish for his [Johnson's] remarks on Italy, he said, "I do not see that I could make a book upon Italy; yet I should be glad to get two hundred pounds, or five hundred pounds, by such a work." This shewed both that a journal of his Tour upon the Continent was not wholly out of his contemplation, and that he uniformly adhered to that strange opinion, which his indolent disposition made him utter: "No man but a blockhead ever wrote, except for money." Numerous instances to refute this will occur to all who are versed in the history of literature.

Boswell, *Life of Johnson (Apr. 5, 1776)*

38 On Thursday, May 1, I visited him [Johnson] in the evening along with young Mr. Burke. He said, "It is strange that there should be so little reading in the world, and so much writing. People in general do not willingly read, if they can have any thing else to amuse them. There must be an external impulse; emulation, or vanity, or avarice. The progress which the understanding makes through a book, has more pain than pleasure in it. Language is scanty, and inadequate to express the nice gradations and mixtures of our feelings. No man reads a book of science from pure inclination. The books that we do read with pleasure are light compositions, which contain a quick succession of events. However, I have this year read all Virgil through. I read a book of the *Æneid* every night, so it was done in twelve nights, and I had great delight in it."

Boswell, *Life of Johnson (May 1, 1783)*

39 I sincerely regret the more valuable libraries which have been involved in the ruin of the Roman empire; but when I seriously compute the lapse of ages, the waste of ignorance, and the calamities of war, our treasures, rather than our losses, are the object of my surprise. Many curious and interesting facts are buried in oblivion: the three great historians of Rome have been transmitted to our hands in a mutilated state; and we are deprived of many pleasing compositions of the lyric, iambic, and dramatic poetry of the Greeks. Yet we should gratefully remember that the mischances of time and accident have spared the classic works to which the suffrage of antiquity had adjudged the first place of genius and glory: the teachers of ancient knowledge, who are still extant, had perused and compared the writings of their predecessors; nor can it fairly be presumed that any important truth, any useful discovery in art or nature, has been snatched away from the curiosity of modern ages.

Gibbon, *Decline and Fall of the Roman Empire,* LI

40 Authors should use common words to say uncommon things. But they do just the opposite. We find them trying to wrap up trivial ideas in grand words, and to clothe their very ordinary thoughts in the most extraordinary phrases, the most farfetched, unnatural, and out-of-the-way expressions. Their sentences perpetually stalk about on stilts. They take so much pleasure in bombast, and write in such a high-flown, bloated, affected, hyperbolical and acrobatic style that their prototype is Ancient Pistol, whom his friend Falstaff once impatiently told to say what he had to say like a man of this world.

Schopenhauer, *Style*

41 If a man wants to read good books, he must make a point of avoiding bad ones; for life is short, and time and energy limited.

Schopenhauer, *Some Forms of Literature*

42 The man who writes for fools is always sure of a large audience; be careful to limit your time for reading, and devote it exclusively to the works of those great minds of all times and countries, who o'ertop the rest of humanity, those whom the voice of fame points to as such. These alone really educate and instruct. You can never read bad literature too little, nor good literature too much. Bad books are intellectual poison; they destroy the mind.

Schopenhauer, *Books and Reading*

43 There are at all times two literatures in progress, running side by side, but little known to each other; the one real, the other only apparent. The former grows into permanent literature; it is pursued by those who live *for* science or poetry; its course is sober and quiet, but extremely slow; and it produces in Europe scarcely a dozen works in a century; these, however, are permanent. The other kind is pursued by persons who live *on* science or poetry; it goes at a gallop with much noise and shouting of partisans; and every twelvemonth puts a thousand works on the market. But after a few years one asks, Where are they? where is the glory which came so soon and made so much clamor? This kind may be called fleeting, and the other, permanent literature.

Schopenhauer, *Books and Reading*

44 The true University of these days is a Collection of Books.

Carlyle, *The Hero as Man of Letters*

45 Of all Priesthoods, Aristocracies, Governing Classes at present extant in the world, there is no class comparable for importance to that Priesthood of the Writers of Books.

Carlyle, *The Hero as Man of Letters*

46 Meek young men grow up in libraries, believing it their duty to accept the views which Cicero, which Locke, which Bacon, have given; forgetful that Cicero, Locke, and Bacon were only young men in libraries when they wrote these books.

Hence, instead of Man Thinking, we have the bookworm.

Emerson, *The American Scholar*

47 The three practical rules, then, which I have to offer, are—1. Never read any book that is not a year old. 2. Never read any but famed books. 3. Never read any but what you like.

Emerson, *Books*

48 'Tis the good reader that makes the good book; in every book he finds passages which seem confidences or asides hidden from all else and unmistakably meant for his ear; the profit of books is according to the sensibility of the reader; the profoundest thought or passion sleeps as in a mine, until it is discovered by an equal mind and heart.

Emerson, *Success*

49 All literature is yet to be written. Poetry has scarce chanted its first song. The perpetual admonition of nature to us is, "The world is new, untried. Do not believe the past. I give you the universe a virgin today."

Emerson, *Literary Ethics*

50 Authors—essayist, atheist, novelist, realist, rhymester, play your part,
Paint the mortal shame of nature with the living hues of art.

Rip your brothers' vices open, strip your own foul passions bare;
Down with Reticence, down with Reverence—forward—naked—let them stare.

Tennyson, *Locksley Hall Sixty Years After*, 139

51 One often hears of writers that rise and swell with their subject, though it may seem but an ordinary one. How, then, with me, writing of this Leviathan? Unconsciously my chirography expands into placard capitals. Give me a condor's quill! Give me Vesuvius' crater for an inkstand! Friends, hold my arms! For in the mere act of penning my thoughts of this Leviathan, they weary me, and make me faint with their outreaching comprehensiveness of sweep, as if to include the whole circle of the sciences, and all the generations of whales, and men, and mastodons, past, present, and to come, with all the revolving panoramas of empire on earth, and throughout the whole universe, not excluding its suburbs. Such, and so magnifying, is the virtue of a large and liberal theme! We expand to its bulk. To produce a mighty book, you must choose a mighty theme. No great and enduring volume can ever be

written on the flea, though many there be who have tried it.

Melville, *Moby Dick*, CIV

52 For what are the classics but the noblest recorded thoughts of man? They are the only oracles which are not decayed.

Thoreau, *Walden:* Reading

53 Camerado, this is no book,
Who touches this touches a man.

Whitman, *So Long!*

54 Who can tell how many of the most original thoughts put forth by male writers, belong to a woman by suggestion, to themselves only by verifying and working out? If I may judge by my own case, a very large proportion indeed.

Mill, *Subjection of Women,* III

55 To read to good purpose we must read a great deal, and be content not to use a great deal of what we read. We shall never be content not to use the whole, or nearly the whole, of what we read, unless we read a great deal. Yet things are on such a scale, and progress is so gradual, and what one man can do is so bounded, that the moment we press the whole of what any writer says, we fall into error. He touches a great deal: the thing to know is where he is all himself and his best self, where he shows his power, where he goes to the heart of the matter, where he gives us what

no other man gives us, or gives us so well.

Arnold, *Literature and Dogma*, Pref.

56 A classic is something that everybody wants to have read and nobody wants to read.

Mark Twain, *The Disappearance of Literature*

57 Tom's most well now, and got his bullet around his neck on a watch-guard for a watch, and is always seeing what time it is, and so there ain't nothing more to write about, and I am rotten glad of it, because if I'd 'a' knowed what a trouble it was to make a book I wouldn't 'a' tackled it, and ain't a-going to no more.

Mark Twain, *Huckleberry Finn*, XLIII

58 *Write without pay until somebody offers pay.* If nobody offers pay within three years, the candidate may look upon this circumstance with the most implicit confidence as the sign that sawing wood is what he was intended for.

Mark Twain, *Life as I Find It:*
General Reply

59 In human life, art may arise from almost any activity, and once it does so, it is launched on a long road of exploration, invention, freedom to the limits of extravagance, interference to the point of frustration, finally discipline, controlling constant change and growth.

Langer, *Mind*, I, 5

16.3 | *Poetry and Poets*

This section includes quotations of two main sorts: one consists of statements about poetry in general—about the writing of verses and the telling of stories; the other, of statements about poets as men and as writers.

With regard to poetry in general, it must be observed that this term, like the term "art," has gradually become more restricted in its meaning. The reader will find passages from Plato in which "poetry" has the same generality as "art," signifying making and things made. The Greek word for making is

poiesis. Less general than that, yet much less restricted than its current usage, is its employment by the ancients to refer to any form of imaginative writing, whether in verse or in prose—the telling of stories, in either the epic or the dramatic form of narration, as well as the singing of songs. It is in this sense of the term that poetry is contrasted with history and with philosophy or science, especially with respect to its mode of truth. Only in the last few centuries has "poetry," like the word "art," been narrowed down to name one type of imaginative literature—lyric poems, usually written in verse.

Many of the critical comments on the work of particular poets gathered here come from the poets themselves. Most of them are laudatory and appreciative, though not all, as, for example, Dryden's comments on Chaucer, and Blake's on Milton. Virgil on Homer, Ben Johnson and Samuel Johnson on Shakespeare, Dryden on Milton and Chaucer, T. S. Eliot on Dante, and Dante on Virgil—these are but a few of the examples of the warm and loving tributes that later writers pay to earlier ones.

Other quotations about poetry and literature appear in other sections, notably Section 16.2 on BOOKS AND READING and 16.4 on TRAGEDY AND COMEDY. The reader should also consult the index under appropriate terms for passages that appear in other chapters.

---

1 *Odysseus.* All men owe honor to the poets—honor and awe, for they are dearest to the Muse who puts upon their lips the ways of life.

Homer, *Odyssey,* VIII, 479

2 *Adrastus.* The poet bringing songs into the world Should labor in joy. If this is not his mood, He cannot—being inwardly distressed— Give pleasure outwardly.

Euripides, *Suppliant Women,* 180

3 *Servant.* Did you see any wandering in the air Besides yourself?
    Trygaeus.   No; nothing much to speak of, Two or three souls of dithyrambic poets.
    S. What were they after?
    Tr.   Flitting round for odes, Those floating-on-high-in-the-airy-sky affairs.
    S. Then 'tisn't true what people say about it, That when we die, we straightway turn to stars?
    Tr. O yes it is.
    S.   And who's the star there now?
    Tr. Ion of Chios, who on earth composed "Star o' the Morn," and when he came there, all At once saluted him as "Star o' the Morn."
    S. And did you learn about those falling stars Which sparkle as they run?
    Tr.   Yes, those are some Of the rich stars returning home from supper, Lanterns in hand, and in the lanterns fire.

Aristophanes, *Peace,* 825

4 *Socrates.* The third kind is the madness of those who are possessed by the Muses; which taking hold of a delicate and virgin soul, and there inspiring frenzy, awakens lyrical and all other numbers; with these adorning the myriad actions of ancient heroes for the instruction of posterity. But he who, having no touch of the Muses' madness in his soul, comes to the door and thinks that he will get into the temple by the help of art—he, I say, and his poetry are not admitted; the sane man disappears and is nowhere when he enters into rivalry with the madman.

Plato, *Phaedrus,* 245A

5 *Socrates.* All good poets, epic as well as lyric, compose their beautiful poems not by art, but because they are inspired and possessed. . . . For the poet is a light and winged and holy thing, and there is no invention in him until he has been inspired and is out of his senses, and the mind is no longer in him: when he has not attained to this state, he is powerless and is unable to utter his oracles.

Many are the noble words in which poets speak concerning the actions of men; but like yourself when speaking about Homer, they do not speak of them by any rules of art: they are simply inspired to utter that to which the Muse impels them, and that only; and when inspired, one of them will make dithyrambs, another hymns of praise, another choral strains, another epic or iambic verses—and he who is good at one is not good at any other kind of verse: for not by art does the poet sing, but by power divine. Had he learned by rules of art, he would have known how to speak not of one theme only, but of all; and therefore God takes away the minds of poets, and uses them as his ministers, as he also uses diviners and holy prophets, in order that we who hear them may know them to be speaking not of themselves who utter these priceless words in a state of unconsciousness, but that God himself is the speaker, and that through them he is conversing with us. And Tynnichus the Chalcidian affords a striking instance of what I am saying: he wrote nothing that any one would care to remember but the famous paean which is in every one's mouth, one of the finest poems ever written, simply an invention of the Muses, as he himself says. For in this way the God would seem to indicate to us and not allow us to doubt that these beautiful poems are not human, or the work of man, but divine and the work of God; and that the poets are only the interpreters of the Gods by whom they are severally possessed. Was not this the lesson which the

God intended to teach when by the mouth of the worst of poets he sang the best of songs? Am I not right, Ion?

Ion. Yes, indeed, Socrates, I feel that you are; for your words touch my soul, and I am persuaded that good poets by a divine inspiration interpret the things of the Gods to us.

Plato, *Ion,* 533B

6 If you consider, I [Socrates] said, that when in misfortune we feel a natural hunger and desire to relieve our sorrow by weeping and lamentation, and that this feeling which is kept under control in our own calamities is satisfied and delighted by the poets—the better nature in each of us, not having been sufficiently trained by reason or habit, allows the sympathetic element to break loose because the sorrow is another's; and the spectator fancies that there can be no disgrace to himself in praising and pitying any one who comes telling him what a good man he is, and making a fuss about his troubles; he thinks that the pleasure is a gain, and why should he be supercilious and lose this and the poem too? Few persons ever reflect, as I should imagine, that from the evil of other men something of evil is communicated to themselves. And so the feeling of sorrow which has gathered strength at the sight of the misfortunes of others is with difficulty repressed in our own.

Glaucon. How very true!

And does not the same hold also of the ridiculous? There are jests which you would be ashamed to make yourself, and yet on the comic stage, or indeed in private, when you hear them, you are greatly amused by them, and are not at all disgusted at their unseemliness—the case of pity is repeated—there is a principle in human nature which is disposed to raise a laugh, and this which you once restrained by reason, because you were afraid of being thought a buffoon, is now let out again; and having stimulated the risible faculty at the theatre, you are betrayed unconsciously to yourself into playing the comic poet at home.

Quite true, he said.

And the same may be said of lust and anger and all the other affections, of desire and pain and pleasure, which are held to be inseparable from every action—in all of them poetry feeds and waters the passions instead of drying them up; she lets them rule, although they ought to be controlled, if mankind are ever to increase in happiness and virtue.

I cannot deny it.

Therefore, Glaucon, I said, whenever you meet with any of the eulogists of Homer declaring that he has been the educator of Hellas, and that he is profitable for education and for the ordering of human things, and that you should take him up again and again and get to know him and regulate your whole life according to him, we may love and honour those who say these things—they are

excellent people, as far as their lights extend; and we are ready to acknowledge that Homer is the greatest of poets and first of tragedy writers; but we must remain firm in our conviction that hymns to the gods and praises of famous men are the only poetry which ought to be admitted into our State. For if you go beyond this and allow the honeyed muse to enter, either in epic or lyric verse, not law and the reason of mankind, which by common consent have ever been deemed best, but pleasure and pain will be the rulers in our State.

That is most true, he said.

And now since we have reverted to the subject of poetry, let this our defence serve to show the reasonableness of our former judgment in sending away out of our State an art having the tendencies which we have described; for reason constrained us. But that she may not impute to us any harshness or want of politeness, let us tell her that there is an ancient quarrel between philosophy and poetry; of which there are many proofs, such as the saying of "the yelping hound howling at her lord," or of one "mighty in the vain talk of fools," and "the mob of sages circumventing Zeus," and the "subtle thinkers who are beggars after all"; and there are innumerable other signs of ancient enmity between them. Notwithstanding this, let us assure our sweet friend and the sister arts of imitation, that if she will only prove her title to exist in a well-ordered State we shall be delighted to receive her—we are very conscious of her charms; but we may not on that account betray the truth. I dare say, Glaucon, that you are as much charmed by her as I am, especially when she appears in Homer?

Yes, indeed, I am greatly charmed.

Shall I propose, then, that she be allowed to return from exile, but upon this condition only—that she make a defence of herself in lyrical or some other metre?

Certainly.

And we may further grant to those of her defenders who are lovers of poetry and yet not poets the permission to speak in prose on her behalf: let them show not only that she is pleasant but also useful to States and to human life, and we will listen in a kindly spirit; for if this can be proved we shall surely be the gainers—I mean, if there is a use in poetry as well as a delight?

Plato, *Republic,* X, 606A

7 The general origin of poetry was due to two causes, each of them part of human nature. Imitation is natural to man from childhood, one of his advantages over the lower animals being this, that he is the most imitative creature in the world, and learns at first by imitation. And it is also natural for all to delight in works of imitation. The truth of this second point is shown by experience: though the objects themselves may be painful to

see, we delight to view the most realistic representations of them in art, the forms for example of
the lowest animals and dead bodies. The explanation is to be found in a further fact: to be learning
something is the greatest of pleasures not only to
the philosopher but also to the rest of mankind,
however small their capacity for it; the reason of
the delight in seeing the picture is that one is at
the same time learning—gathering the meaning
of things, for example, that the man there is so-
and-so; for if one has not seen the thing before,
one's pleasure will not be in the picture as an imitation of it, but will be due to the execution or
colouring or some similar cause. Imitation, then,
being natural to us—as also the sense of harmony
and rhythm, the metres being obviously species of
rhythms—it was through their original aptitude,
and by a series of improvements for the most part
gradual on their first efforts, that they created poetry out of their improvisations.

Aristotle, *Poetics*, 1448b4

8 The distinction between historian and poet is not
in the one writing prose and the other verse—you
might put the work of Herodotus into verse, and it
would still be a species of history; it consists really
in this, that the one describes the thing that has
been, and the other a kind of thing that might be.
Hence poetry is something more philosophic and
of graver import than history, since its statements
are of the nature rather of universals, whereas
those of history are singulars. By a universal statement I mean one as to what such or such a kind of
man will probably or necessarily say or do—
which is the aim of poetry . . . by a singular statement, one as to what, say, Alcibiades did or had
done to him.

Aristotle, *Poetics*, 1451a40

9 Poetry demands a man with a special gift for it, or
else one with a touch of madness in him.

Aristotle, *Poetics*, 1455a35

10 It is a great thing, indeed, to make a proper use of
. . . poetical forms, as also of compounds and
strange words. But the greatest thing by far is to
be a master of metaphor. It is the one thing that
cannot be learnt from others; and it is also a sign
of genius, since a good metaphor implies an intuitive perception of the similarity in dissimilars.

Aristotle, *Poetics*, 1459a3

11 Homer, admirable as he is in every other respect,
is especially so in this, that he alone among epic
poets is not unaware of the part to be played by
the poet himself in the poem. The poet should say
very little *in propria persona,* as he is no imitator
when doing that.

Aristotle, *Poetics*, 1460a5

12 For the purposes of poetry a convincing impossibility is preferable to an unconvincing possibility.

Aristotle, *Poetics*, 1461b11

13 I traverse the pathless haunts of the Pierides never
yet trodden by sole of man. I love to approach the
untasted springs and to quaff, I love to cull fresh
flowers and gather for my head a distinguished
crown from spots whence the Muses have yet
veiled the brows of none; first because I teach of
great things and essay to release the mind from
the fast bonds of religious scruples, and next because on a dark subject I pen such lucid verses
o'erlaying all with the Muses' charm. For that too
would seem to be not without good grounds: even
as physicians when they propose to give nauseous
wormwood to children, first smear the rim round
the bowl with the sweet yellow juice of honey, that
the unthinking age of children may be fooled as
far as the lips, and meanwhile drink up the bitter
draught of wormwood and though beguiled yet
not be betrayed, but rather by such means recover
health and strength: so I now, since this doctrine
seems generally somewhat bitter to those by
whom it has not been handled, and the multitude
shrinks back from it in dismay, have resolved to
set forth to you our doctrine in sweet-toned Pierian verse and o'erlay it as it were with the pleasant
honey of the Muses, if haply by such means I
might engage your mind on my verses, till such
time as you apprehend all the nature of things
and thoroughly feel what use it has.

Lucretius, *Nature of Things,* IV

14 Thus have I sung of fields, of flocks, and trees,
And of the waxen work of labouring bees:
While mighty Cæsar, thundering from afar,
Seeks on Euphrates' banks the spoils of war;
With conquering arts asserts his country's cause,
With arts of peace the willing people draws;
On the glad earth the golden age renews,
And his great father's path to heaven pursues;
While I at Naples pass my peaceful days,
Affecting studies of less noisy praise;
And, bold through youth, beneath the beechen
  shade,
The lays of shepherds, and their loves, have
  played.

Virgil, *Georgics,* IV

15 Oft before Agamemnon brave men warred;
  But all unwept they lie in endless night,
    Lacking, to deck their deeds with light,
      Song of a heaven-taught bard.

Horace, *Odes,* IV, 9

16 Let poets match their subject to their strength,
And often try what weight they can support,
And what their shoulders are too weak to bear,
After a serious and judicious choice,
Method and eloquence will never fail.

Horace, *Ars Poetica*

17 Sound judgment is the ground of writing well:
And when philosophy directs your choice
To proper subjects rightly understood,
Words from your pen will naturally flow;
He only gives the proper characters,
Who knows the duty of all ranks of men,
And what we owe to country, parents, friends,
How judges, and how senators should act,
And what becomes a general to do;
Those are the likest copies, which are drawn
By the original of human life.

Horace, *Ars Poetica*

18 A poet should instruct, or please, or both;
Let all your precepts be succinct and clear,
That ready wits may comprehend them soon,
And faithful memories retain them long;
For superfluities are soon forgot.
Never be so conceited of your parts,
To think you may persuade us what you please.

Horace, *Ars Poetica*

19 Poems, like pictures, are of diff'rent sorts,
Some better at a distance, others near,
Some love the dark, some choose the clearest
light,
And boldly challenge the most piercing eye,
Some please for once, some will for ever please.

Horace, *Ars Poetica*

20 Yet if it ever be your fate to write,
Let your productions pass the strictest hands,
Mine and your father's, and not see the light,
'Till time and care have ripen'd ev'ry line.

Horace, *Ars Poetica*

21 With such vigorous resolutions, and his mind thus
disposed, he [Alexander] passed the Hellespont,
and at Troy sacrificed to Minerva, and honoured
the memory of the heroes who were buried there,
with solemn libations; especially Achilles, whose
gravestone he anointed, and with his friends, as
the ancient custom is, ran naked about his sepulchre, and crowned it with garlands, declaring how
happy he esteemed him, in having while he lived
so faithful a friend, and when he was dead, so
famous a poet to proclaim his actions. While he
was viewing the rest of the antiquities and curiosi-
ties of the place, being told he might see Paris's
harp, if he pleased, he said he thought it not
worth looking on, but he should be glad to see
that of Achilles, to which he used to sing the glories and great actions of brave men.

Plutarch, *Alexander*

22 When she [Philosophy] saw that the Muses of poetry were present by my couch giving words to my
lamenting, she was stirred a while; her eyes
flashed fiercely, and said she, "Who has suffered
these seducing mummers to approach this sick
man? Never do they support those in sorrow by
any healing remedies, but rather do ever foster the
sorrow by poisonous sweets. These are they who
stifle the fruit-bearing harvest of reason with the
barren briars of the passions: they free not the
minds of men from disease, but accustom them
thereto. I would think it less grievous if your allurements drew away from me some uninitiated
man, as happens in the vulgar berd. In such an
one my labours would be naught harmed, but this
man has been nourished in the lore of Eleatics
and Academics; and to him have ye reached?
Away with you, Sirens, seductive unto destruction! leave him to my Muses to be cared for and
to be healed."

Their band thus rated cast a saddened glance
upon the ground, confessing their shame in blushes, and passed forth dismally over the threshold.

Boethius, *Consolation of Philosophy*, I

23 Just as human reason fails to grasp poetical expressions because they are lacking in truth, so
does it fail to grasp Divine things perfectly on account of the sublimity of the truth they contain.
And therefore in both cases there is need of signs
by means of sensible figures.

Aquinas, *Summa Theologica*, I–II, 101, 2

24 "O thou, that honourest every science and art;
who are these, who have such honour, that it
separates them from the manner of the rest?"
And he to me: "The honoured name, which
sounds of them, up in that life of thine, gains
favour in heaven which thus advances them."
Meanwhile a voice was heard by me: "Honour
the great Poet! His shade returns that was departed."
After the voice had paused, and was silent, I saw
four great shadows come to us; they had an
aspect neither sad nor joyful.
The good Master began to speak: "Mark him
with that sword in hand, who comes before the
three as their lord:
that is Homer, the sovereign Poet; the next who
comes is Horace the satirist; Ovid is the third,
and the last *is* Lucan.
Because each agrees with me in the name, which
the one voice sounded, they do me honour: and
therein they do well."
Thus I saw assembled the goodly school of [those]
lord[s] of highest song, [which], like an eagle,
soars above the rest.
After they had talked a space together, they
turned to me with sign of salutation; and my
Master smiled thereat.
And greatly more besides they honoured me; for
they made me of their number, so I was a sixth
amid such intelligences.

Dante, *Inferno*, IV, 73

25 And therefore, figuring Paradise, needs must the

sacred poem make a leap, as who should find his pathway intercepted.

But whoso thinketh of the weighty theme and of the mortal shoulder which hath charged itself therewith, will think no blame if under it it trembleth.

It is no voyage for a little barque, that which my daring keel cleaveth as it goeth, nor for a helmsman who doth spare himself.

Dante, *Paradiso* XXIII, 61

26 We must discuss what things are greatest; and first in respect of what is useful. Now in this matter, if we carefully consider the object of all those who are in search of what is useful, we shall find that it is nothing else but safety. Secondly, in respect of what is pleasurable; and here we say that that is most pleasurable which gives pleasure by the most exquisite object of appetite, and this is love. Thirdly, in respect of what is right; and here no one doubts that virtue has the first place. Wherefore these three things, namely, safety, love, and virtue, appear to be those capital matters which ought to be treated of supremely, I mean the things which are most important in respect of them, as prowess in arms, the fire of love, and the direction of the will. And if we duly consider, we shall find that the illustrious writers have written poetry in the vulgar tongue on these subjects exclusively.

Dante, *De Vulgari Eloquentia*, II, 2

27 Be it known that the sense of this work [the Divine Comedy] is not simple, but on the contrary it may be called polysemous, that is to say, 'of more senses than one'; for it is one sense which we get through the letter, and another which we get through the thing the letter signifies; and the first is called literal, but the second allegorical or mystic. And this mode of treatment, for its better manifestation, may be considered in this verse: 'When Israel came out of Egypt, and the house of Jacob from a people of strange speech, Judæa became his sanctification, Israel his power.' For if we inspect the letter alone the departure of the children of Israel from Egypt in the time of Moses is presented to us; if the allegory, our redemption wrought by Christ; if the moral sense, the conversion of the soul from the grief and misery of sin to the state of grace is presented to us; if the anagogical, the departure of the holy soul from the slavery of this corruption to the liberty of eternal glory is presented to us. And although these mystic senses have each their special denominations, they may all in general be called allegorical, since they differ from the literal and historical. . . . When we understand this we see clearly that the *subject* round which the alternative senses play must be twofold. And we must therefore consider the subject of this work as literally understood, and then its subject as allegorically intended. The subject of the whole work, then, taken in the literal sense only, is 'the state of souls after death,' without qualification, for the whole progress of the work hinges on it and about it. Whereas if the work be taken allegorically the subject is 'man, as by good or ill deserts, in the exercise of the freedom of his choice, he becomes liable to rewarding or punishing justice.'

Dante, *Letter to Can Grande*

28 Just as sound, when pent up in the narrow channel of a trumpet, comes out sharper and stronger, so it seems to me that a thought, when compressed into the numbered feet of poetry, springs forth much more violently and strikes me a much stiffer jolt.

Montaigne, *Essays,* I, 26, Education of Children

29 I am not one of those who think that good rhythm makes a good poem. Let him make a short syllable long if he wants, that doesn't matter; if the inventions are pleasant, if wit and judgment have done their work well, I shall say: There is a good poet, but a bad versifier.

Montaigne, *Essays,* I, 26, Education of Children

30 As, in exploits of war, the heat of combat often impels high-souled soldiers to go through such dangers that when they have come back to themselves they are the first to be struck with amazement; as also poets are often rapt in wonder at their own works and no longer recognize the track over which they ran so fine a race. That is what is called poetic frenzy and madness. And as Plato says that a sedate man knocks in vain on the door of poetry, so Aristotle says that no excellent soul is free from an admixture of madness. And he is right to call madness any transport, however laudable, that transcends our own judgment and reason; inasmuch as wisdom is an orderly management of our soul, which she conducts with measure and proportion and is responsible for.

Montaigne, *Essays,* II, 2, Of Drunkenness

31 *Theseus.* Lovers and madmen have such seething brains,
Such shaping fantasies, that apprehend
More than cool reason ever comprehends.
The lunatic, the lover, and the poet
Are of imagination all compact:
One sees more devils than vast hell can hold,
That is, the madman: the lover, all as frantic,
Sees Helen's beauty in a brow of Egypt:
The poet's eye, in a fine frenzy rolling,
Doth glance from heaven to earth, from earth to heaven;
And as imagination bodies forth
The forms of things unknown, the poet's pen
Turns them to shapes and gives to airy nothing

A local habitation and a name.
Shakespeare, *Midsummer-Night's Dream*, V, i, 4

32 *Hotspur.* I had rather be a kitten and cry mew
Than one of these same metre ballad-mongers;
I had rather hear a brazen canstick turn'd,
Or a dry wheel grate on the axle-tree;
And that would set my teeth nothing on edge,
Nothing so much as mincing poetry:
'Tis like the forced gait of a shuffling nag.
Shakespeare, *I Henry IV*, III, i, 129

33 Not marble nor the gilded monuments
Of princes shall outlive this powerful rhyme;
But you shall shine more bright in these contents
Than unswept stone besmear'd with sluttish time.
When wasteful war shall statues overturn,
And broils root out the work of masonry,
Nor Mars his sword nor war's quick fire shall burn
The living record of your memory.
'Gainst death and all-oblivious enmity
Shall you pace forth; your praise shall still find room
Even in the eyes of all posterity
That wear this world out to the ending doom.
   So, till the judgement that yourself arise,
   You live in this, and dwell in lovers' eyes.
Shakespeare, *Sonnet LV*

34 The Canon rid forward with him, and his Men follow'd, while the Curate made them a Relation of Don *Quixote's* Life and Quality, his Madness and Adventures, with the original Cause of his Distraction, and the whole Progress of his Affairs, till his being shut up in the Cage, to get him home, in order to have him cur'd. They all admired at this strange Account; and then the Canon turning to the Curate: Believe me, Mr Curate, said he, I am fully convinc'd, that these they call Books of Knight-Errantry are very prejudicial to the Publick. And tho' I have been led away with an idle and false Pleasure, to read the Beginnings of almost as many of 'em as have been Printed, I could never yet persuade myself to go through with any one to the End; for to me they all seem to contain one and the same thing; and there is as much in one of them as in all the rest. The whole Composition and Stile resemble that of the *Milesian* Fables, which are a sort of idle Stories, design'd only for Diversion, and not for Instruction. It is not so with those Fables which are call'd Apologues, that at once delight and instruct. But tho' the main Design of such Books is to please; yet I cannot conceive how it is possible they should perform it, being fill'd with such a Multitude of unaccountable Extravagancies. For the Pleasure which strikes the Soul, must be deriv'd from the Beauty and Congruity it sees or conceives in those things the Sight or Imagination lay before it; and nothing in itself deform'd or incongruous can give us any real Satisfaction. Now what Beauty can there be, or what Proportion of the Parts of the Whole, or of the Whole to the several Parts, in a Book, or Fable, where a Stripling of Sixteen Years of Age at one Cut of a Sword cleaves a Giant, as tall as a Steeple, through the Middle, as easily as if he were made of Paste-Board? Or when they give us the Relation of a Battle, having said the Enemy's Power consisted of a Million of Combatants, yet provided the Hero of the Book be against them, we must of necessity, tho' never so much against our Inclination, conceive that the said Knight obtain'd the Victory only by his own Valour, and the Strength of his Powerful Arm? And what shall we say of the great Ease and Facility with which an absolute Queen or Empress casts herself into the Arms of an Errant and unknown Knight? What Mortal, not altogether barbarous and unpolish'd, can be pleased to read, that a great Tower, full of armed Knights, cuts thro' the Sea like a Ship before the Wind, and setting out in the Evening from the Coast of *Italy*, lands by Break of Day in *Prestor John's* Country, or in some other, never known to *Ptolomy* or seen by *Marcus Paulus?* If it shou'd be answer'd, That the Persons who compose these Books, write them as confess'd Lies; and therefore are not oblig'd to observe Niceties, or to have regard to Truth; I shall make this Reply, That Falshood is so much the more commendable, by how much it more resembles Truth; and is the more pleasing the more it is doubtful and possible. Fabulous Tales ought to be suited to the Reader's Understanding, being so contrived, that all Impossibilities ceasing, all great Accidents appearing feasible and the Mind wholly hanging in Suspence, they may at once surprize, astonish, please and divert; so that Pleasure and Admiration may go hand in hand. This cannot be performed by him that flies from Probability and Imitation, which is the Perfection of what is written. I have not seen any Book of Knight-Errantry that composes an entire Body of a Fable with all its Parts, so that the Middle is answerable to the Beginning, and the End to the Beginning and Middle; but on the contrary, they form them of so many Limbs, that they rather seem a Chimæra or Monster, than a well-proportion'd Figure. Besides all this, their Stile is uncouth, their Exploits incredible, their Love immodest, their Civility impertinent, their Battles tedious, their Language absurd, their Voyages proposterous; and in short, they are altogether void of solid Ingenuity, and therefore fit to be banish'd a Christian Commonwealth as useless and prejudicial.
Cervantes, *Don Quixote*, I, 47

35 Poetry, Sir, in my Judgment, is like a tender Virgin in her Bloom, Beautiful and Charming to Amazement: All the other Sciences are so many Virgins, whose Care it is to Enrich, Polish and

Adorn her, and as she is to make use of them all, so are they all to have from her a grateful Acknowledgment. But this Virgin must not be roughly handl'd, nor dragg'd along the Street, nor expos'd to every Marketplace, and Corner of great Men's Houses. A good Poet is a kind of an Alchymist, who can turn the Matter he prepares into the purest Gold and an inestimable Treasure. But he must keep his Muse within the Rules of Decency, and not let her prostitute her Excellency in lewd Satires and Lampoons, nor in licentious Sonnets. She must not be Mercenary, though she need not give away the Profits she may claim from Heroick Poems, deep Tragedies, and Pleasant and Artful Comedies. She is not to be attempted by Buffoons, nor by the Ignorant Vulgar, whose Capacity can never reach to a due Sense of the Treasures that are lock'd up in her. And know, Sir, that when I mention the Vulgar, I don't mean only the common Rabble; for whoever is ignorant, be he Lord or Prince, is to be listed in the Number of the Vulgar. But whoever shall apply himself to the Muses with those Qualifications, which, as I said, are essential to the Character of a good Poet, his Name shall be Famous, and valu'd in all the polish'd Nations of the World.

Cervantes, *Don Quixote,* II, 16

36 Yet must I not give Nature all; thy Art,
My gentle Shakespeare, must enjoy a part.
For though the poet's matter Nature be,
His Art doth give the fashion; and that he
Who casts to write a living line must sweat
(Such as thine are) and strike the second heat
Upon the muses' anvil; turn the same,
And himself with it, that he thinks to frame,
Or for the laurel he may gain a scorn;
For a good poet's made as well as born.

Jonson, *To the Memory of My Beloved
Master William Shakespeare*

37 I remember the players have often mentioned it as an honour to Shakespeare, that in his writing, whatsoever he penned, he never blotted out a line. My answer hath been, "Would he had blotted a thousand," which they thought a malevolent speech. I had not told posterity this but for their ignorance, who chose that circumstance to commend their friend by wherein he most faulted; and to justify mine own candour, for I loved the man, and do honour his memory, on this side idolatry, as much as any. He was, indeed, honest, and of an open and free nature; had an excellent fancy, brave notions, and gentle expressions, wherein he flowed with that facility that sometime it was necessary he should be stopped. *"Sufflaminandus erat,"* as Augustus said of Haterius. His wit was in his own power; would the rule of it had been so too. Many times he fell into those things, could not escape laughter, as when he said in the person

of Cæsar, one speaking to him: "Cæsar, thou dost me wrong." He replied: "Cæsar did never wrong but with just cause"; and such like, which were ridiculous. But he redeemed his vices with his virtues. There was ever more in him to be praised than to be pardoned.

Jonson, *Discoveries:* De Shakespeare Nostrat.

38 Poetry and picture are arts of a like nature, and both are busy about imitation. It was excellently said of Plutarch, poetry was a speaking picture, and picture a mute poesy. For they both invent, feign, and devise many things, and accommodate all they invent to the use and service of Nature. Yet of the two the pen is more noble than the pencil; for that can speak to the understanding, the other but to the sense. They both behold pleasure and profit as their common object; but should abstain from all base pleasures, lest they should err from their end, and, while they seek to better men's minds, destroy their manners. They both are born artificers, not made. Nature is more powerful in them than study.

Jonson, *Discoveries:* Poesis et Pictura

39 I esteemed eloquence most highly and I was enamoured of poesy, but I thought that both were gifts of the mind rather than fruits of study. Those who have the strongest power of reasoning, and who most skilfully arrange their thoughts in order to render them clear and intelligible, have the best power of persuasion even if they can but speak the language of Lower Brittany and have never learned rhetoric. And those who have the most delightful original ideas and who know how to express them with the maximum of style and suavity, would not fail to be the best poets even if the art of poetry were unknown to them.

Descartes, *Discourse on Method,* I

40 In a good poem, whether it be epic or dramatic, as also in sonnets, epigrams, and other pieces, both judgement and fancy are required: but the fancy must be more eminent; because they please for the extravagancy, but ought not to displease by indiscretion.

Hobbes, *Leviathan,* I, 8

41 As we speak of poetical beauty, so ought we to speak of mathematical beauty and medical beauty. But we do not do so; and the reason is that we know well what is the object of mathematics, and that it consists in proofs, and what is the object of medicine, and that it consists in healing. But we do not know in what grace consists, which is the object of poetry.

Pascal, *Pensées,* I, 33

42 Or call up him that left half told
The story of *Cambuscan* bold,
Of *Camball,* and of *Algarsife,*

And who had *Canace* to wife,
That own'd the vertuous Ring and Glass,
And of the wondrous Hors of Brass,
On which the *Tartar* King did ride;
And if ought els, great *Bards* beside,
In sage and solemn tunes have sung,
Of Turneys and of Trophies hung;
Of Forests, and inchantments drear,
Where more is meant then meets the ear.

Milton, *Il Penseroso,* 109

43 Alas! What boots it with uncessant care
To tend the homely slighted Shepherds trade,
And strictly meditate the thankles Muse,
Were it not better don as others use,
To sport with *Amaryllis* in the shade,
Or with the tangles of *Neaera's* hair?

Milton, *Lycidas,* 64

44 Of mans First Disobedience, and the Fruit
Of that Forbidden Tree, whose mortal tast
Brought Death into the World, and all our woe,
With loss of *Eden,* till one greater Man
Restore us, and regain the blissful Seat,
Sing Heav'nly Muse, that on the secret top
Of *Oreb,* or of *Sinai,* didst inspire
That Shepherd, who first taught the chosen Seed,
In the Beginning how the Heav'ns and Earth
Rose out of *Chaos:* or if *Sion* Hill
Delight thee more, and *Siloa's* Brook that flow'd
Fast by the Oracle of God; I thence
Invoke thy aid to my adventrous Song,
That with no middle flight intends to soar
Above th' *Aonian* Mount, while it pursues
Things unattempted yet in Prose or Rhime.

Milton, *Paradise Lost,* I, 1

45 If answerable style I can obtaine
Of my Celestial Patroness, who deignes
Her nightly visitation unimplor'd,
And dictates to me slumbering, or inspires
Easie my unpremeditated Verse:
Since first this Subject for Heroic Song
Pleas'd me long choosing, and beginning late
Not sedulous by Nature to indite
Warrs, hitherto the onely Argument
Heroic deem'd, chief maistrie to dissect
With long and tedious havoc fabl'd Knights
In Battels feign'd; the better fortitude
Of Patience and Heroic Martyrdom
Unsung; or to describe Races and Games,
Or tilting Furniture, emblazon'd Shields,
Impreses quaint, Caparisons and Steeds;
Bases and tinsel Trappings, gorgious Knights
At Joust and Torneament; then marshal'd Feast
Serv'd up in Hall with Sewers, and Seneshals;
The skill of Artifice or Office mean,
Not that which justly gives Heroic name
To Person or to Poem. Mee of these
Nor skilld nor studious, higher Argument
Remaines, sufficient of it self to raise

That name, unless an age too late, or cold
Climat, or Years damp may intended wing
Deprest, and much they may, if all be mine,
Not Hers who brings it nightly to my Ear.

Milton, *Paradise Lost,* IX, 20

46 He who would not be frustrate of his hope to write
well hereafter in laudable things, ought himself to
be a true poem; that is, a composition and pattern
of the best and honourablest things; not presuming to sing high praises of heroic men, or famous
cities, unless he have in himself the experience
and the practice of all that which is praiseworthy.

Milton, *Apology for Smectymnuus*

47 Three poets, in three distant ages born,
Greece, Italy, and England did adorn.
The first in loftiness of thought surpass'd,
The next in majesty, in both the last:
The force of Nature could no farther go;
To make a third, she join'd the former two.

Dryden, *Epigram on Milton*

48 To begin, then, with Shakespeare: he was the
man who of all modern, and perhaps ancient
poets, had the largest and most comprehensive
soul. All the images of nature were still present to
him, and he drew them, not laboriously, but luckily; when he describes any thing, you more than
see it, you feel it too. Those who accuse him to
have wanted learning, give him the greater commendation: he was naturally learned; he needed
not the spectacles of books to read nature; he
looked inwards, and found her there. I cannot say
he is everywhere alike; were he so, I should do
him injury to compare him with the greatest of
mankind. He is many times flat, insipid; his comic
wit degenerating into clenches, his serious swelling
into bombast. But he is always great, when some
great occasion is presented to him; no man can
say he ever had a fit subject for his wit, and did
not then raise himself as high above the rest of
poets.

[As do cypresses among the bending shrubs—
Virgil]

Dryden, *Essay of Dramatic Poesy*

49 It remains that I say somewhat of Chaucer in particular.

In the first place, as he is the father of English
poetry, so I hold him in the same degree of veneration as the Grecians held Homer, or the Romans
Virgil. He is a perpetual fountain of good sense;
learned in all sciences; and, therefore, speaks
properly on all subjects. As he knew what to say,
so he knows also when to leave off; a continence
which is practised by few writers, and scarcely by
any of the ancients, excepting Virgil and Horace.
. . . The verse of Chaucer, I confess, is not harmonious to us. . . . They who lived with him, and

some time after him, thought it musical; and it continues so, even in our judgment, if compared with the numbers of Lydgate and Gower, his contemporaries:—there is the rude sweetness of a Scotch tune in it, which is natural and pleasing, though not perfect. . . . We can only say, that he lived in the infancy of our poetry, and that nothing is brought to perfection at the first. We must be children before we grow men. . . .

He must have been a man of a most wonderful comprehensive nature, because, as it has been truly observed of him, he has taken into the compass of his *Canterbury Tales* the various manners and humours (as we now call them) of the whole English nation, in his age. Not a single character has escaped him. All his pilgrims are severally distinguished from each other; and not only in their inclinations, but in their very physiognomies and persons. . . . The matter and manner of their tales, and of their telling, are so suited to their different educations, humours, and callings, that each of them would be improper in any other mouth. Even the grave and serious characters are distinguished by their several sorts of gravity: their discourses are such as belong to their age, their calling, and their breeding; such as are becoming of them, and of them only. Some of his persons are vicious, and some virtuous; some are unlearned, or (as Chaucer calls them) lewd, and some are learned. Even the ribaldry of the low characters is different: the Reeve, the Miller, and the Cook, are several men, and distinguished from each other as much as the mincing Lady-Prioress and the broad-speaking, gap-toothed Wife of Bath. But enough of this; there is such a variety of game springing up before me, that I am distracted in my choice, and know not which to follow. It is sufficient to say, according to the proverb, that here is God's plenty. We have our forefathers and great-grand-dames all before us, as they were in Chaucer's days: their general characters are still remaining in mankind, and even in England, though they are called by other names than those of monks, and friars, and canons, and lady-abbesses, and nuns; for mankind is ever the same, and nothing lost out of nature, though everything is altered.

Dryden, *Preface to the Fables*

50 Yet lest you think I rally more than teach,
Or praise malignly arts I cannot reach,
Let me for once presume t' instruct the times,
To know the poet from the man of rhymes:
'T is he, who gives my breast a thousand pains,
Can make me feel each passion that he feigns;
Enrage, compose, with more than magic art,
With pity, and with terror, tear my heart;
And snatch me, o'er the earth, or thro' the air,
To Thebes, to Athens, when he will, and where.

Pope, *Epistle to Augustus*

51 As truth distinguishes our writings from those idle romances which are filled with monsters, the productions, not of nature, but of distempered brains; and which have been therefore recommended by an eminent critic to the sole use of the pastry-cook; so, on the other hand, we would avoid any resemblance to that kind of history which a celebrated poet seems to think is no less calculated for the emolument of the brewer, as the reading it should be always attended with a tankard of good ale—

While—history with her comrade ale,
Soothes the sad series of her serious tale.

For as this is the liquor of modern historians, nay, perhaps their muse, if we may believe the opinion of Butler, who attributes inspiration to ale, it ought likewise to be the potation of their readers, since every book ought to be read with the same spirit and in the same manner as it is writ. Thus the famous author of Hurlothrumbo told a learned bishop, that the reason his lordship could not taste the excellence of his piece was, that he did not read it with a fiddle in his hand; which instrument he himself had always had in his own, when he composed it.

That our work, therefore, might be in no danger of being likened to the labours of these historians, we have taken every occasion of interspersing through the whole sundry similes, descriptions, and other kind of poetical embellishments. These are, indeed, designed to supply the place of the said ale, and to refresh the mind, whenever those slumbers, which in a long work are apt to invade the reader as well as the writer, shall begin to creep upon him. Without interruptions of this kind, the best narrative of plain matter of fact must overpower every reader; for nothing but the everlasting watchfulness, which Homer has ascribed only to Jove himself, can be proof against a newspaper of many volumes.

Fielding, *Tom Jones*, IV, 1

52 To invent good stories, and to tell them well, are possibly very rare talents, and yet I have observed few persons who have scrupled to aim at both: and if we examine the romances and novels with which the world abounds, I think we may fairly conclude, that most of the authors would not have attempted to show their teeth (if the expression may be allowed me) in any other way of writing; nor could indeed have strung together a dozen sentences on any other subject whatever. [Each desperate blockhead dares to write: Verse is the trade of every living wight.] may be more truly said of the historian and biographer, than of any other species of writing; for all the arts and sciences (even criticism itself) require some little degree of learning and knowledge. Poetry, indeed, may perhaps be thought an exception; but then it demands numbers, or something like numbers:

whereas, to the composition of novels and romances, nothing is necessary but paper, pens, and ink, with the manual capacity of using them. This, I conceive, their productions show to be the opinion of the authors themselves: and this must be the opinion of their readers, if indeed there be any such.

Fielding, *Tom Jones,* IX, 1

53 I have cast my eyes on an edition of Shakespeare issued by Master Samuel Johnson. I saw there that foreigners who are astonished that in the plays of the great Shakespeare a Roman senator plays the buffoon, and that a king appears on the stage drunk, are treated as little-minded. I do not desire to suspect Master Johnson of being a sorry jester, and of being too fond of wine; but I find it somewhat extraordinary that he counts buffoonery and drunkenness among the beauties of the tragic stage: and no less singular is the reason he gives, that the poet disdains accidental distinctions of circumstance and country, like a painter who, content with having painted the figure, neglects the drapery. The comparison would be more just if he were speaking of a painter who in a noble subject should introduce ridiculous grotesques, should paint Alexander the Great mounted on an ass in the battle of Arbela, and Darius' wife drinking at an inn with rapscallions.

But there is one thing more extraordinary than all, that is that Shakespeare is a genius. The Italians, the French, the men of letters of all other countries, who have not spent some time in England, take him only for a clown, for a joker far inferior to Harlequin, for the most contemptible buffoon who has ever amused the populace. Nevertheless, it is in this same man that one finds pieces which exalt the imagination and which stir the heart to its depths. It is Truth, it is Nature herself who speaks her own language with no admixture of artifice. It is of the sublime, and the author has in no wise sought it.

Voltaire, *Philosophical Dictionary:*
On the English Theatre

54 Nothing can please many, and please long, but just representations of general nature. Particular manners can be known to few, and therefore few only can judge how nearly they are copied. The irregular combinations of fanciful invention may delight awhile, by that novelty of which the common satiety of life sends us all in quest; but the pleasures of sudden wonder are soon exhausted, and the mind can only repose on the stability of truth.

Shakespeare is above all writers, at least above all modern writers, the poet of nature; the poet that holds up to his readers a faithful mirror of manners and of life. His characters are not modified by the customs of particular places, unpractised by the rest of the world; by the peculiarities

of studies or professions, which can operate but upon small numbers; or by the accidents of transient fashions or temporary opinions: they are the genuine progeny of common humanity, such as the world will always supply, and observation will always find. His persons act and speak by the influence of those general passions and principles by which all minds are agitated, and the whole system of life is continued in motion. In the writings of other poets a character is too often an individual; in those of Shakespeare it is commonly a species.

Johnson, *Preface to Shakespeare*

55 A quibble is to Shakespeare what luminous vapours are to the traveller; he follows it at all adventures; it is sure to lead him out of his way, and sure to engulf him in the mire. It has some malignant power over his mind, and its fascinations are irresistible. Whatever be the dignity or profundity of his disquisition, whether he be enlarging knowledge or exalting affection, whether he be amusing attention with incidents, or enchaining it in suspense, let but a quibble spring up before him, and he leaves his work unfinished. A quibble is the golden apple for which he will always turn aside from his career, or stoop from his elevation. A quibble, poor and barren as it is, gave him such delight that he was content to purchase it, by the sacrifice of reason, propriety and truth. A quibble was to him the fatal Cleopatra for which he lost the world, and was content to lose it.

Johnson, *Preface to Shakespeare*

56 The business of a poet, said Imlac, is to examine, not the individual, but the species; to remark general properties and large appearances: he does not number the streaks of the tulip, or describe the different shades in the verdure of the forest.

Johnson, *Rasselas,* X

57 *Johnson.* You may translate books of science exactly. You may also translate history, in so far as it is not embellished with oratory, which is poetical. Poetry, indeed, cannot be translated; and, therefore, it is the poets that preserve languages; for we would not be at the trouble to learn a language, if we could have all that is written in it just as well in a translation. But as the beauties of poetry cannot be preserved in any language except that in which it was originally written, we learn the language.

Boswell, *Life of Johnson (Apr. 11, 1776)*

58 *Johnson.* It has been said, there is pleasure in writing, particularly in writing verses. I allow you may have pleasure from writing, after it is over, if you have written well; but you don't go willingly to it again. I know when I have been writing verses, I have run my finger down the margin, to see

how many I had made, and how few I had to make.

Boswell, *Life of Johnson (May 1, 1783)*

59 Among a polished people, a taste for poetry is rather an amusement of the fancy than a passion of the soul. And yet, when in calm retirement we peruse the combats described by Homer or Tasso, we are insensibly seduced by the fiction, and feel a momentary glow of martial ardour. But how faint, how cold is the sensation which a peaceful mind can receive from solitary study! It was in the hour of battle, or in the feast of victory, that the bards celebrated the glory of heroes of ancient days, the ancestors of those warlike chieftains who listened with transport to their artless but animated strains.

Gibbon, *Decline and Fall of the Roman Empire,* IX

60 In the apprehension of modern times Petrarch is the Italian songster of Laura and love. In the harmony of his Tuscan rhymes Italy applauds, or rather adores, the father of her lyric poetry; and his verse, or at least his name, is repeated by the enthusiasm or affectation of amorous sensibility. Whatever may be the private taste of a stranger, his slight and superficial knowledge should humbly acquiesce in the judgment of a learned nation; yet I may hope or presume that the Italians do not compare the tedious uniformity of sonnets and elegies with the sublime compositions of their epic muse, the original wildness of Dante, the regular beauties of Tasso, and the boundless variety of the incomparable Ariosto.

Gibbon, *Decline and Fall of the Roman Empire,* LXX

61 Poetry (which owes its origin almost entirely to genius and is least willing to be led by precepts or example) holds the first rank among all the arts. It expands the mind by giving freedom to the imagination and by offering, from among the boundless multiplicity of possible forms accordant with a given concept, to whose bounds it is restricted, that one which couples with the presentation of the concept a wealth of thought to which no verbal expression is completely adequate, and by thus rises aesthetically to ideas.

Kant, *Critique of Aesthetic Judgement,* 53

62 It is in the fundamental idea of poetry that the poet is everywhere the guardian of nature. When he can no longer entirely fill this part, and has already in himself suffered the deleterious influence of arbitary and factitious forms, or has had to struggle against this influence, he presents himself as the witness of nature and as its avenger. The poet will, therefore, be the expression of nature itself, or his part will be to seek it, if men have lost sight of it.

Schiller, *Simple and Sentimental Poetry*

63 The reason Milton wrote in fetters when he wrote of Angels and God, and at liberty when of Devils and Hell, is because he was a true Poet, and of the Devil's party without knowing it.

Blake, *Marriage of Heaven and Hell,* 5

64   Shall the poet take that highest right,
The Right of Man, that Right which Nature gave,
And wantonly for your sake trifle it away?
How doth he over every heart hold sway?
How doth he every element enslave?
Is it not the harmony that from his breast doth start,
Then winds the world in turn back in his heart?
When Nature forces lengths of thread unending
In careless whirling on the spindle round,
When all Life's inharmonic throngs unblending
In sullen, harsh confusion sound,
Who parts the changeless series of creation,
That each, enlivened, moves in rhythmic time?
Who summons each to join the general ordination,
In consecrated, noble harmonies to chime?
Who bids the storm with raging passion lower?
The sunset with a solemn meaning glow?
Who scatters Springtime's every lovely flower
Along the pathway where his love may go?
Who twines the verdant leaves, unmeaning, slighted,
Into a wreath of honour, meed of every field?
Who makes Olympus sure, the gods united?
That power of Man the Poet has revealed!

Goethe, *Faust,* Prelude on the Stage, 135

65 *Chorus.* Hallowèd Poesy,
Soar aloft heavenly,
Shine on, thou fairest star,
Farther and still more far,
Yet dost thou reach us still,
Yet do we hear and thrill,
Joyous we are.

Goethe, *Faust,* II, 3, 9863

66 The first page which I read in Shakespeare already served to win him my lifelong adherence. And when I had reached the end of the first play, I stood like one who, blind from birth, finds himself suddenly blest with sight by a beneficent Providence. In the clearest and most vivid manner I realised that my existence had been infinitely expanded. Everything now appeared new and strange to me, and the unwonted light dazzled and hurt my eyes. Little by little I came to see, and I can still feel distinctly, thanks to my spirit of gratitude, how much I had gained.

Goethe, *Thoughts on Shakespeare*

67 As for me, I am often put to blush by Shakespeare; for from time to time it happens that at a first glance I say to myself: I should have done

this or that differently; and then afterwards I discover that I am but a poor sinner, that through Shakespeare Nature herself gives utterance to her prophecies, and that my characters are, so to speak, mere soap-bubbles blown in a caprice of romanticism.

Goethe, *Thoughts on Shakespeare*

68 If everything written in this vein that has been handed down to us were destroyed, poetry and rhetoric could yet be entirely restored out of that one play.

Goethe, *Thoughts on Shakespeare* [Henry IV]

69 It will perhaps be urged that, although poetry is held to be an art, it is not mechanical. But I deny that it is an art; nor is it a science. Arts and sciences are attained through reflection; but not so poetry, for this is an inspiration; it was infused into the soul when first it manifested itself. It should, consequently, be called neither art nor science, but genius.

Goethe, *Reflections and Maxims*

70 What is a Poet? To whom does he address himself? And what language is to be expected from him? He is a man speaking to men: a man, it is true, endued with more lively sensibility, more enthusiasm and tenderness, who has a greater knowledge of human nature, and a more comprehensive soul than are supposed to be common among mankind; a man pleased with his own passions and volitions, and who rejoices more than other men in the spirit of life that is in him; delighting to contemplate similar volitions and passions as manifested in the goings-on of the Universe, and habitually impelled to create them where he does not find them.

Wordsworth, *Preface to Lyrical Ballads (1802)*

71 Aristotle, I have been told, hath said that Poetry is the most philosophic of all writing: it is so: its object is truth, not individual and local, but general, and operative; not standing upon external testimony, but carried alive into the heart by passion; truth which is its own testimony, which gives strength and divinity to the tribunal to which it appeals, and receives them from the same tribunal. Poetry is the image of man and nature.

Wordsworth, *Preface to Lyrical Ballads (1802)*

72 Poetry is the spontaneous overflow of powerful feelings: it takes its origin from emotion recollected in tranquillity: the emotion is contemplated till, by a species of re-action, the tranquillity gradually disappears, and an emotion, kindred to that which was before the subject of contemplation, is gradually produced, and does itself actually exist in the mind. In this mood successful composition generally begins.

Wordsworth, *Preface to Lyrical Ballads (1802)*

73 Scorn not the Sonnet; Critic, you have frowned,
Mindless of its just honours; with this key
Shakspeare unlocked his heart; the melody
Of this small lute gave ease to Petrarch's wound;
A thousand times this pipe did Tasso sound;
With it Camöens soothed an exile's grief;
The Sonnet glittered a gay myrtle leaf
Amid the cypress with which Dante crowned
His visionary brow: a glow-worm lamp,
It cheered mild Spenser, called from Faeryland
To struggle through dark ways; and, when a damp
Fell round the path of Milton, in his hand
The Thing became a trumpet; when he blew
Soul-animating strains—alas, too few!

Wordsworth, *Scorn Not the Sonnet*

74 Milton! thou should'st be living at this hour:
England hath need of thee: she is a fen
Of stagnant waters: altar, sword, and pen,
Fireside, the heroic wealth of hall and bower,
Have forfeited their ancient English dower
Of inward happiness. We are selfish men;
Oh! raise us up, return to us again;
And give us manners, virtue, freedom, power.
Thy soul was like a Star, and dwelt apart:
Thou hadst a voice whose sound was like the sea:
Pure as the naked heavens, majestic, free,
So didst thou travel on life's common way,
In cheerful godliness; and yet thy heart
The lowliest duties on herself did lay.

Wordsworth, *London, 1802*

75 A damsel with a dulcimer
In a vision once I saw:
It was an Abyssinian maid,
And on her dulcimer she played,
Singing of Mount Abora.
Could I revive within me
Her symphony and song,
To such a deep delight 'twould win me,
That with music loud and long,
I would build that dome in air,
That sunny dome! those caves of ice!
And all who heard should see them there,
And all should cry, Beware! Beware!
His flashing eyes, his floating hair!
Weave a circle round him thrice,
And close your eyes with holy dread,
For he on honey-dew hath fed,
And drunk the milk of Paradise.

Coleridge, *Kubla Khan*

76 In this idea originated the plan of the *Lyrical Ballads;* in which it was agreed that my endeavors should be directed to persons and characters supernatural, or at least romantic; yet so as to transfer from our inward nature a human interest and a semblance of truth sufficient to procure for these shadows of imagination that willing suspension of

disbelief for the moment, which constitutes poetic faith.

Coleridge, *Biographia Literaria,* XIV

77 A poem is that species of composition which is opposed to works of science by proposing for its *immediate* object pleasure, not truth; and from all other species (having *this* object in common with it) it is discriminated by proposing to itself such delight from the *whole* as is compatible with a distinct gratification from each component *part.*

Coleridge, *Biographia Literaria,* XIV

78 Poets are the hierophants of an unapprehended inspiration; the mirrors of the gigantic shadows which futurity casts upon the present; the words which express what they understand not; the trumpets which sing to battle and feel not what they inspire; the influence which is moved not, but moves. Poets are the unacknowledged legislators of the world.

Shelley, *Defence of Poetry*

79 Fade far away, dissolve, and quite forget
    What thou among the leaves hast never known,
The weariness, the fever, and the fret
  Here, where men sit and hear each other
      groan;
Where palsy shakes a few, sad, last gray hairs,
  Where youth grows pale, and spectre-thin, and
      dies;
  Where but to think is to be full of sorrow
      And leaden-eyed despairs,
  Where Beauty cannot keep her lustrous eyes,
    Or new Love pine at them beyond tomorrow.

Away! away! for I will fly to thee,
  Not charioted by Bacchus and his pards,
But on the viewless wings of Poesy,
  Though the dull brain perplexes and retards:
Already with thee! tender is the night,
  And haply the Queen-Moon is on her throne,
    Cluster'd around by all her starry Fays;
    But here there is no light,
  Save what from heaven is with the breezes
      blown
    Through verdurous glooms and winding
      mossy ways.

Keats, *Ode to a Nightingale*

80 Much have I travell'd in the realms of gold,
    And many goodly states and kingdoms seen;
  Round many western islands have I been
  Which bards in fealty to Apollo hold.
Oft of one wide expanse had I been told
    That deep-brow'd Homer ruled as his demesne:
  Yet did I never breathe its pure serene
Till I heard Chapman speak out loud and bold:
Then felt I like some watcher of the skies
  When a new planet swims into his ken;
Or like stout Cortez when with eagle eyes
  He star'd at the Pacific—and all his men

Look'd at each other with a wild surmise—
  Silent, upon a peak in Darien.

Keats, *On First Looking Into Chapman's Homer*

81 Souls of Poets dead and gone,
What Elysium have ye known,
Happy field or mossy cavern,
Choicer than the Mermaid Tavern?

Keats, *Lines on the Mermaid Tavern*

82 Poetry should surprise by a fine excess, and not by singularity; It should strike the reader as a wording of his own highest thoughts, and appear almost a remembrance.

Its touches of beauty should never be half-way, thereby making the reader breathless, instead of content. The rise, the progress, the setting of Imagery should, like the sun, come natural to him.

Keats, *Letter to John Taylor (Feb. 27, 1818)*

83 I salute thee, Mantovano,
  I that loved thee since my day began,
  Wielder of the stateliest measure
    Ever moulded by the lips of man.

Tennyson, *To Virgil*

84 Other poets have warbled the praises of the soft eye of the antelope, and the lovely plumage of the bird that never alights; less celestial, I celebrate a tail.

Melville, *Moby Dick,* LXXXVI

85 The poet is a man who lives . . . by watching his moods. An old poet comes at last to watching his moods as narrowly as a cat does a mouse.

Thoreau, *Journal (Aug. 28, 1851)*

86 The Americans of all nations at any time upon the earth, have probably the fullest poetical nature. The United States themselves are essentially the greatest poem.

Whitman, *Leaves of Grass,* Pref.

87 I have said that in one respect my mind has changed during the last twenty or thirty years. Up to the age of thirty, or beyond it, poetry of many kinds, such as the works of Milton, Gray, Byron, Wordsworth, Coleridge, and Shelley, gave me great pleasure, and even as a schoolboy I took intense delight in Shakespeare, especially in the historical plays. I have also said that formerly pictures gave me considerable, and music very great, delight. But now for many years I cannot endure to read a line of poetry: I have tried lately to read Shakespeare, and found it so intolerably dull that it nauseated me. I have also almost lost my taste for pictures or music. Music generally sets me thinking too energetically on what I have been at work on, instead of giving me pleasure. I retain some taste for fine scenery, but it does not cause me the exquisite delight which it formerly did. On

the other hand, novels which are works of the imagination, though not of a very high order, have been for years a wonderful relief and pleasure to me, and I often bless all novelists. A surprising number have been read aloud to me, and I like all if moderately good, and if they do not end unhappily—against which a law ought to be passed. A novel, according to my taste, does not come into the first class unless it contains some person whom one can thoroughly love, and if a pretty woman all the better.

This curious and lamentable loss of the higher aesthetic tastes is all the odder, as books on history, biographies, and travels (independently of any scientific facts which they may contain), and essays on all sorts of subjects interest me as much as ever they did. My mind seems to have become a kind of machine for grinding general laws out of large collections of facts, but why this should have caused the atrophy of that part of the brain alone on which the higher tastes depend I cannot conceive. A man with a mind more highly organized or better constituted than mine would not, I suppose, have thus suffered; and if I had to live my life again, I would have made a rule to read some poetry and listen to some music at least once every week; for perhaps the parts of my brain now atrophied would thus have been kept active through use. The loss of these tastes is a loss of happiness, and may possibly be injurious to the intellect, and more probably to the moral character, by enfeebling the emotional part of our nature.

Darwin, Autobiography

88 What made Wordsworth's poems a medicine for my state of mind, was that they expressed, not mere outward beauty, but states of feeling, and of thought coloured by feeling, under the excitement of beauty. They seemed to be the very culture of the feelings, which I was in quest of. In them I seemed to draw from a source of inward joy, of sympathetic and imaginative pleasure, which could be shared in by all human beings; which had no connexion with struggle or imperfection, but would be made richer by every improvement in the physical or social condition of mankind. From them I seemed to learn what would be the perennial sources of happiness, when all the greater evils of life shall have been removed.

Mill, Autobiography, V

89 The poet makes Truth the daughter of Time.

Newman, Essay on the Development of
Christian Doctrine, Pt. I, I, 2

90 The future of poetry is immense, because in poetry, where it is worthy of its high destinies, our race, as time goes on, will find an ever surer and surer stay. There is not a creed which is not shaken, not an accredited dogma which is not shown to be questionable, not a received tradition which

does not threaten to dissolve. Our religion has materialized itself in the fact, in the supposed fact; it has attached its emotion to the fact, and now the fact is failing it. But for poetry the idea is everything; the rest is a world of illusion, of divine illusion. Poetry attaches its emotion to the idea; the idea *is* the fact. The strongest part of our religion today is its unconscious poetry. . . . More and more mankind will discover that we have to turn to poetry to interpret life for us, to console us, to sustain us. Without poetry, our science will appear incomplete; and most of what now passes with us for religion and philosophy will be replaced by poetry.

Arnold, Study of Poetry

91 Only one thing we may add as to the substance and matter of poetry, guiding ourselves by Aristotle's profound observation that the superiority of poetry over history consists in its possessing a higher truth and a higher seriousness. Let us add, therefore, to what we have said, this: that the substance and matter of the best poetry acquire their special character from possessing, in an eminent degree, truth and seriousness. We may add yet further, what is in itself evident, that to the style and manner of the best poetry their special character, their accent, is given by their diction, and, even yet more, by their movement. And though we distinguish between the two characters, the two accents, of superiority, yet they are nevertheless vitally connected one with the other. The superior character of truth and seriousness, in the matter and substance of the best poetry, is inseparable from the superiority of diction and movement marking its style and manner. The two superiorities are closely related, and are in steadfast proportion one to the other. So far as high poetic truth and seriousness are wanting to a poet's matter and substance, so far also, we may be sure, will a high poetic stamp of diction and movement be wanting to his style and manner. In proportion as this high stamp of diction and movement, again, is absent from a poet's style and manner, we shall find, also, that high poetic truth and seriousness are absent from his substance and matter.

Arnold, Study of Poetry

92   But be his
My special thanks, whose even-balanced soul,
From first youth tested up to extreme old age,
Business could not make dull, nor Passion wild;
Who saw life steadily, and saw it whole;
The mellow glory of the Attic stage,
Singer of sweet Colonus, and its child.

Arnold, To a Friend [Sophocles]

93 The difference between genuine poetry and the poetry of Dryden, Pope, and all their school, is briefly this: their poetry is conceived and com-

posed in their wits, genuine poetry is conceived and composed in the soul.

Arnold, Thomas Gray

94 The translator of Homer should above all be penetrated by a sense of four qualities of his author;—that he is eminently rapid; that he is eminently plain and direct, both in the evolution of his thought and in the expression of it, that is, both in his syntax and in his words; that he is eminently plain and direct in the substance of his thought, that is, in his matter and ideas; and, finally, that he is eminently noble.

Arnold, On Translating Homer, I

95 The sphere of poetry does not lie outside the world as a fantastic impossibility spawned by a poet's brain: it desires to be just the opposite, the unvarnished expression of the truth, and must precisely for that reason discard the mendacious finery of that alleged reality of the man of culture.

The contrast between this real truth of nature and the lie of culture that poses as if it were the only reality is similar to that between the eternal core of things, the thing-in-itself, and the whole world of appearances.

Nietzsche, Birth of Tragedy, VIII

96 With the single exception of Homer, there is no eminent writer, not even Sir Walter Scott, whom I can despise so entirely as I despise Shakespeare when I measure my mind against his. The intensity of my impatience with him occasionally reaches such a pitch, that it would positively be a relief to me to dig him up and throw stones at him, knowing as I do how incapable he and his worshippers are of understanding any less obvious form of indignity. . . .

But I am bound to add that I pity the man who cannot enjoy Shakespeare. He has outlasted thousands of abler thinkers, and will outlast a thousand more. His gift of telling a story (provided some one else told it to him first); his enormous power over language, as conspicuous in its senseless and silly abuse of it as in his miracles of expression; his humor; his sense of idiosyncratic character; and his prodigious fund of that vital energy which is, it seems, the true differentiating property behind the faculties, good, bad, or indifferent, of the man of genius, enable him to entertain us so effectively that the imaginary scenes and people he has created become more real to us than our actual life.

Shaw, Dramatic Opinions and Essays, II

97 The relation of our typical dreams to fairytales and other fiction and poetry is neither sporadic nor accidental. Sometimes the penetrating insight of the poet has analytically recognized the process of transformation of which the poet is otherwise the instrument, and has followed it up in the reverse direction; that is to say, has traced a poem to a dream.

Freud, Interpretation of Dreams, V, D

98 Shakespeare gives the greatest *width* of human passion; Dante the greatest altitude and greatest depth.

T. S. Eliot, Dante

99 The business of the poet is not to find new emotions, but to use the ordinary ones and, in working them up into poetry, to express feelings which are not in actual emotions at all. And emotions which he has never experienced will serve his turn as well as those familiar to him. Consequently, we must believe that "emotion recollected in tranquillity" is an inexact formula. For it is neither emotion, nor recollection, nor, without distortion of meaning, tranquillity. It is a concentration, and a new thing resulting from the concentration, of a very great number of experiences which to the practical and active person would not seem to be experiences at all.

T. S. Eliot, Tradition and the Individual Talent

100 When a poet's mind is perfectly equipped for its work, it is constantly amalgamating disparate experience; the ordinary man's experience is chaotic, irregular, fragmentary. The latter falls in love, or reads Spinoza, and these two experiences have nothing to do with each other, or with the noise of the typewriter or the smell of cooking; in the mind of the poet these experiences are always forming new wholes.

T. S. Eliot, The Metaphysical Poets

101 Art necessarily divides itself into three forms progressing from one to the next. These forms are: the lyrical form, the form wherein the artist presents his image in immediate relation to himself; the epical form, the form wherein he presents his image in mediate relation to himself and to others; the dramatic form, the form wherein he presents his image in immediate relation to others. . . .

In literature, the highest and most spiritual art, the forms are often confused. The lyrical form is in fact the simplest verbal vesture of an instant of emotion, a rhythmical cry such as ages ago cheered on the man who pulled at the oar or dragged stones up a slope. He who utters it is more conscious of the instant of emotion than of himself as feeling emotion. The simplest epical form is seen emerging out of lyrical literature when the artist prolongs and broods upon himself as the centre of an epical event and this form progresses till the centre of emotional gravity is equidistant from the artist himself and from others. The narrative is no longer purely personal. The personality of the artist passes into the narration itself, flowing round and round the persons and the action like a vital sea. This progress you will see easily in that old English ballad *Turpin Hero* which begins in the first person and ends in the third person. The dramatic form is reached when the vitality which has flowed and eddied round each person fills every person with such vital force that he or she assumes a proper and intangible esthetic life. The personality of the artist, at first a cry or a cadence or a mood and then a fluid and lambent narrative, finally refines itself out of existence, impersonalises itself, so to speak. The esthetic image in the dramatic form is life purified in and reprojected from the human imagination. The mystery of esthetic like that of material creation is accomplished. The artist, like the God of the creation, remains within or behind or beyond or above his handiwork, invisible, refined out of existence, indifferent, paring his fingernails.

Joyce, *Portrait of the Artist as a Young Man,* V

102 For mark you, Phaedrus, beauty alone is both divine and visible; and so it is the sense way, the artist's way, little Phaedrus, to the spirit. But, now tell me, my dear boy, do you believe that such a man can ever attain wisdom and true manly worth, for whom the path to the spirit must lead through the senses? Or do you rather think—for I leave the point to you—that it is a path of perilous sweetness, a way of transgression, and must surely lead him who walks in it astray? For you know that we poets cannot walk the way of beauty without Eros as our companion and guide. We may be heroic after our fashion, disciplined warriors of our craft, yet are we all like women, for we exult in passion, and love is still our desire—our craving and our shame. And from this you will perceive that we poets can be neither wise nor worthy citizens. We must needs be wanton, must needs rove at large in the realm of feeling. Our magisterial style is all folly and pretense, our honorable repute a farce, the crowd's belief in us is merely laughable. And to teach youth, or the populace, by means of art is a dangerous practice and ought to be forbidden. For what good can an artist be as a teacher, when from his birth up he is headed direct for the pit? We may want to shun it and attain to honor in the world; but however we turn, it draws us still. So, then, since knowledge might destroy us, we will have none of it. For knowledge, Phaedrus, does not make him who possesses it dignified or austere. Knowledge is all-knowing, understanding, forgiving; it takes up no position, sets no store by form. It has compassion with the abyss—it *is* the abyss. So we reject it, firmly, and henceforward our concern shall be with beauty only. And by beauty we mean simplicity, largeness, and renewed severity of discipline; we mean a return to detachment and to form. But detachment, Phaedrus, and preoccupation with form lead to intoxication and desire; they may lead the noblest among us to frightful emotional excesses, which his own stern cult of the

beautiful would make him the first to condemn. So they too, they too, lead to the bottomless pit. Yes, they lead us thither, I say, us who are poets—who by our natures are prone not to excellence but to excess. And now, Phaedrus, I will go. Remain here; and only when you can no longer see me, then do you depart also.

Mann, *Death in Venice*

103 Poetry (like metaphysics) is spiritual nourishment; but of a savor which has been created and which is insufficient. There is but one eternal nourishment. Unhappy you who think yourselves ambitious, and who whet your appetites for anything less than the three Divine Persons and the humanity of Christ.

It is a mortal error to expect from poetry the supersubstantial nourishment of man.

Maritain, *Frontiers of Poetry*

104 "At Pisa," he said, "I was, many years ago, present when our glorious Monti, the poet, drew out his pistol and shot down Monsignor Talbot. It happened at a supper party, just like ours here. . . . And it all arose from an argument on eternal damnation.

"Monti, who had just then finished his *Don Giovanni,* had for some time been sunk in a deep melancholy, and would neither drink nor talk, and Monsignor Talbot asked him what was the matter with him, and wondered that he was not happy after having achieved so great a success. So Monti asked him whether he did not think that it might weigh upon the mind of a man to have created a human being who was to burn through eternity in hell. Talbot smiled at him and declared that this could only happen to real people. Whereupon the poet cried out and asked him if his Don Giovanni was not real. . . . Monsignor Talbot asked him if he did really believe himself a creator in the same sense as God.

" 'God!' Monti cried, 'God! Do you not know that what God really wants to create is my Don Giovanni, and the Odysseus of Homer, and Cervantes' knight? Very likely those are the only people for whom heaven and hell have ever been made, for you cannot imagine that an Almighty God would go on forever and ever, world without end, with my mother-in-law and the Emperor of Austria? Humanity, the men and women of this earth, are only the plaster of God, and we, the artists, are his tools, and when the statue is finished in marble or bronze, he breaks us all up. When you die you will probably go out like a candle, with nothing left, but in the mansions of eternity will walk Orlando, the Misanthrope and my Donna Elvira. Such is God's plan of work, and if we find it somehow slow, who are we that we should criticize him, seeing that we know nothing whatever of time or eternity?'

"Monsignor Talbot, although himself a great

admirer of the arts, began to feel uncomfortable about such heretical views, and took the poet to task over them. 'Oh, go and find out for yourself then!' Monti cried, and resting the barrel of the pistol . . . upon the edge of the table, he fired straight at the *monsignore*."

Isak Dinesen, *The Roads Around Pisa,* V

16.4 | *Tragedy and Comedy*

This section might have been headed "Drama," or even "Theatre," as a more appropriate cover for certain of the quotations included here that deal with drama in general, with the effect of stage plays on the spectator, and with their value for society or their deleterious influence on it. But the majority of the passages deal quite specifically with the two forms of dramatic literature known as "tragedy" and "comedy," both as written in books and as performed in theatres. In addition, there are statements about the tragic and the comic in life itself, as well as in literature or on the stage.

So far as we can tell, the distinction between tragedy and comedy originated with the Greeks, as well as the famous cryptic statement that challenges the distinction— the observation by Socrates, overheard by an admittedly sleepy reporter, that the genius of tragedy and of comedy are the same. Few writers, with the possible exception of Shakespeare, have manifested the genius to be able to write both great tragedies and sparkling comedies. Whether or not the statement by Socrates is true, the great trag-ic and comic works of ancient and modern times have, for the most part, come to us from the pens of different men.

The passages dealing with tragedy reflect sharp contrasts between the ancient and modern conceptions of it, and raise such questions as whether nondramatic forms of narration, such as the ancient epic or the modern novel, can be tragic or comic as well as stage plays, and whether tragedy is inherent in every human life or is attendant only on the lives of those who attain a sufficient eminence to suffer a grievous reversal of fortune. The passages dealing with comedy verge on such related subjects as wit, humor, and laughter. The passages that express concern about the questionable and even definitely baneful influence of the stage on the conduct of the individual and the morals of society will be more sympathetically appreciated by contemporary readers if they apply the questions raised to the effects of television on both young and old today.

A few quotations relevant to certain aspects of drama appear in other sections of this chapter, principally Section 16.3.

---

1 *Xanthias.* Tell me by Zeus, our rascaldom's own god,
What's all that noise within? What means this hubbub
And row?

Aeacus. That's Aeschylus and Euripides.
Xa. Eh?
Ae. Wonderful, wonderful things are going on.
The dead are rioting, taking different sides.
Xa. Why, what's the matter?

Ae.   There's a custom here
With all the crafts, the good and noble crafts,
That the chief master of his art in each
Shall have his dinner in the assembly hall,
And sit by Pluto's side.
Xa.   I understand.
Ae. Until another comes, more wise than he
In the same art: then must the first give way.
Xa. And how has this disturbed our Aeschylus?
Ae. 'Twas he that occupied the tragic chair,
As, in his craft, the noblest.
Xa.   Who does now?
Ae. But when Euripides came down, he kept
Flourishing off before the highwaymen,
Thieves, burglars, parricides—these form our mob
In Hades—till with listening to his twists
And turns, and pleas and counterpleas, they went
Mad on the man, and hailed him first and wisest:
Elate with this, he claimed the tragic chair
Where Aeschylus was seated.
Xa.   Wasn't he pelted?
Ae. Not he: the populace clamoured out to try
Which of the twain was wiser in his art.
Xa. You mean the rascals?
Ae.   Aye, as high as heaven!
Xa. But were there none to side with Aeschylus?
Ae. Scanty and sparse the good, the same as
here.
Xa. And what does Pluto now propose to do?
Ae. He means to hold a tournament, and bring
Their tragedies to the proof.
Xa.   But Sophocles,
How came not he to claim the tragic chair?
Ae. Claim it? Not he! When *he* came down, he
kissed
With reverence Aeschylus, and clasped his hand,
And yielded willingly the chair to him.
But now he's going, says Cleidemides,
To sit third-man: and then if Aeschylus win,
He'll stay content: if not, for his art's sake,
He'll fight to the death against Euripides.
Xa. Will it come off?
Ae.   O yes, by Zeus, directly.
And then, I hear, will wonderful things be done,
The art poetic will be weighed in scales.
Xa. What! weigh out tragedy, like butcher's
meat?
Ae. Levels they'll bring, and measuring-tapes
for words,
And moulded oblongs,
Xa.   Is it bricks they are making?
Ae. Wedges and compasses: for Euripides
Vows that he'll test the dramas, word by word.
Xa. Aeschylus chafes at this, I fancy.
Ae.   Well,
He lowered his brows, upglaring like a bull.
Xa. And who's to be the judge?
Ae.   There came the rub.
Skilled men were hard to find: for with the Athe-
nians
Aeschylus, somehow, did not hit it off,

Xa. Too many burglars, I expect, he thought.
Ae. And all the rest, he said, were trash and
nonsense
To judge poetic wits. So then at last
They chose your lord [Dionysus], an expert in the
art.

                    Aristophanes, *Frogs,* 755

2 *Aeschylus.* Come, tell me what are the points for
which
                    a noble poet our praise obtains.
Euripides. For his ready wit, and his counsels
sage,
                    and because the citizen folk he trains
To be better townsmen and worthier men.
Aes.   If then you have done the very reverse,
Found noble-hearted and virtuous men,
     and altered them, each and all, for the worse,
Pray what is the meed you deserve to get?
Dionysus. Nay, ask not *him.* He deserves to die.
Aes. For just consider what style of men
     he received from me, great six-foot-high
Heroical souls, who never would blench
     from a townsman's duties in peace or war;
Not idle loafers, or low buffoons,
     or rascally scamps such as now they are.
But men who were breathing spears and helms,
     and the snow-white plume in its crested pride,
The greave, and the dart, and the warrior's heart
     in its sevenfold casing of tough bull-hide.
Di. He'll stun me, I know, with his armoury-
work;
     this business is going from bad to worse.
Eu. And how did you manage to make them so
grand,
     exalted, and brave with your wonderful verse?
Di. Come, Aeschylus, answer, and don't stand
mute
     in your self-willed pride and arrogant spleen.
Aes. A drama I wrote with the War-god filled.
Di.   Its name?
Aes. 'Tis the *Seven against Thebes* that I mean.
Which whoso beheld, with eagerness swelled
     to rush to the battlefield there and then.
Di. O that was a scandalous thing you did!
     You have made the Thebans mightier men,
More eager by far for the business of war.
     Now, therefore, receive this punch on the head.
Aes. Ah, *ye* might have practised the same your-
selves,
     but ye turned to other pursuits instead.
Then next the *Persians* I wrote, in praise
     of the noblest deed that the world can show,
And each man longed for the victor's wreath,
     to fight and to vanquish his country's foe.
Di. I was pleased, I own, when I heard their
moan
     for Old Darius, their great king, dead;
When they smote together their hands, like this,
     and "Evir alake" the Chorus said.
Aes. Aye, such are the poet's appropriate works:

and just consider how all along
From the very first they have wrought you good,
 the noble bards, the masters of song.
First, Orpheus taught you religious rites,
 and from bloody murder to stay your hands:
Musaeus healing and oracle lore;
 and Hesiod all the culture of lands,
The time to gather, the time to plough.
 And gat not Homer his glory divine
By singing of valour, and honour, and right,
 and the sheen of the battle-extended line,
The ranging of troops and the arming of men?
Di. O ay, but he didn't teach *that*, I opine,
To Pantacles; when he was leading the show
 I couldn't imagine what he was at,
He had fastened his helm on the top of his head,
 he was trying to fasten his plume upon that.
Aes. But others, many and brave, he taught,
 of whom was Lamachus, hero true;
And thence my spirit the impress took,
 and many a lion-heart chief I drew,
Patrocluses, Teucers, illustrious names;
 for I fain the citizen-folk would spur
To stretch themselves to *their* measure and
 height,
 whenever the trumpet of war they hear.
But Phaedras and Stheneboeas? No!
 no harlotry business deformed my plays.
And none can say that ever I drew
 a love-sick woman in all my days.
Eu. For *you* no lot or portion had got
 in Queen Aphrodite.
Aes.   Thank Heaven for that.
But ever on you and yours, my friend,
 the mighty goddess mightily sat;
Yourself she cast to the ground at last.
Di. O ay, that uncommonly pat.
You showed how cuckolds are made, and lo,
 you were struck yourself by the very same fate.
Eu. But say, you cross-grained censor of mine,
 how *my* Stheneboeas could harm the state.
Aes. Full many a noble dame, the wife
 of a noble citizen, hemlock took,
And died, unable the shame and sin
 of your Bellerophon-scenes to brook.
Eu. Was then, I wonder, the tale I told
 of Phaedra's passionate love untrue?
Aes. Not so: but tales of incestuous vice
 the sacred poet should hide from view,
Nor ever exhibit and blazon forth
 on the public stage to the public ken.
For boys a teacher at school is found,
 but we, the poets, are teachers of men.
We are *bound* things honest and pure to speak.
Eu. And to speak great Lycabettuses, pray,
And massive blocks of Parnassian rocks,
 is *that* things honest and pure to say?
In human fashion we ought to speak.
Aes. Alas, poor witling, and can't you see
That for mighty thoughts and heroic aims,
 the words themselves must appropriate be?

And grander belike on the ear should strike
 the speech of heroes and godlike powers,
Since even the robes that invest their limbs
 are statelier, grander robes than ours.
Such was *my* plan: but when *you* began,
 you spoilt and degraded it all.
Eu.   How so?
Aes. Your kings in tatters and rags you dressed,
 and brought them on, a beggarly show,
To move, forsooth, our pity and ruth.
Eu. And what was the harm, I should like to
 know.
Aes. No more will a wealthy citizen now
 equip for the state a galley of war.
He wraps his limbs in tatters and rags,
 and whines he is "poor, too poor by far."
Di. But under his rags he is wearing a vest,
 as woolly and soft as a man could wish.
Let him gull the state, and he's off to the mart;
 an eager, extravagant buyer of fish.
Aes. Moreover to prate, to harangue, to debate,
 is now the ambition of all in the state.
Each exercise-ground is in consequence found
 deserted and empty: to evil repute
Your lessons have brought our youngsters, and
 taught
 our sailors to challenge, discuss, and refute
The orders they get from their captains and yet,
 when *I* was alive, I protest that the knaves
Knew nothing at all, save for rations to call,
 and to sing "Rhyppapae" as they pulled
     through the waves.
Di. And bedad to let fly from their sterns in the
 eye
of the fellow who tugged at the undermost oar,
And a jolly young messmate with filth to be-
 smirch,
 and to land for a filching adventure ashore;
But now they harangue, and dispute, and won't
 row
And idly and aimlessly float to and fro.
Aes. Of what ills is he *not* the creator and cause?
Consider the scandalous scenes that he draws,
His bawds, and his panders, his women who give
 Give birth in the sacredest shrine,
Whilst others with brothers are wedded and bed-
 ded,
 And others opine
That "not to be living" is truly "to live."
And therefore our city is swarming to-day
With clerks and with demagogue-monkeys, who
 play
Their jackanape tricks at all times, in all places,
Deluding the people of Athens; but none
Has training enough in athletics to run
 With the torch in his hand at the races.

      Aristophanes, *Frogs*, 1012

3 Agathon arose in order that he might take his
place on the couch by Socrates, when suddenly a
band of revellers entered, and spoiled the order of

the banquet. Some one who was going out having left the door open, they had found their way in, and made themselves at home; great confusion ensued, and every one was compelled to drink large quantities of wine. Aristodemus said that Eryximachus, Phaedrus, and others went away—he himself fell asleep, and as the nights were long took a good rest: he was awakened towards daybreak by a crowing of cocks, and when he awoke, the others were either asleep, or had gone away; there remained only Socrates, Aristophanes, and Agathon, who were drinking out of a large goblet which they passed round, and Socrates was discoursing to them. Aristodemus was only half awake, and he did not hear the beginning of the discourse; the chief thing which he remembered was Socrates compelling the other two to acknowledge that the genius of comedy was the same with that of tragedy, and that the true artist in tragedy was an artist in comedy also. To this they were constrained to assent, being drowsy, and not quite following the argument.

Plato, *Symposium,* 223A

4 *Socrates.* There are combinations of pleasure and pain in lamentations, and in tragedy and comedy, not only on the stage, but on the greater stage of human life.

Plato, *Philebus,* 50A

5 *Athenian Stranger.* It is necessary . . . to consider and know uncomely persons and thoughts, and those which are intended to produce laughter in comedy, and have a comic character in respect of style, song, and dance, and of the imitations which these afford. For serious things cannot be understood without laughable things, nor opposites at all without opposites, if a man is really to have intelligence of either; but he can not carry out both in action, if he is to have any degree of virtue. And for this very reason he should learn them both, in order that he may not in ignorance do or say anything which is ridiculous and out of place—he should command slaves and hired strangers to imitate such things, but he should never take any serious interest in them himself, nor should any freeman or freewoman be discovered taking pains to learn them; and there should always be some element of novelty in the imitation. Let these then be laid down, both in law and in our discourse, as the regulations of laughable amusements which are generally called comedy. And, if any of the serious poets, as they are termed, who write tragedy, come to us and say— "O strangers, may we go to your city and country or may we not, and shall we bring with us our poetry—what is your will about these matters?"— how shall we answer the divine men? I think that our answer should be as follows:—Best of strangers, we will say to them, we also according to our ability are tragic poets, and our tragedy is the best

and noblest; for our whole state is an imitation of the best and noblest life, which we affirm to be indeed the very truth of tragedy. You are poets and we are poets, both makers of the same strains, rivals and antagonists in the noblest of dramas, which true law can alone perfect, as our hope is. Do not then suppose that we shall all in a moment allow you to erect your stage in the agora, or introduce the fair voices of your actors, speaking above our own, and permit you to harangue our women and children, and the common people, about our institutions, in language other than our own, and very often the opposite of our own. For a state would be mad which gave you this licence, until the magistrates had determined whether your poetry might be recited, and was fit for publication or not. Wherefore, O ye sons and scions of the softer Muses, first of all show your songs to the magistrates, and let them compare them with our own, and if they are the same or better we will give you a chorus; but if not, then, my friends, we cannot. Let these, then, be the customs ordained by law about all dances and the teaching of them, and let matters relating to slaves be separated from those relating to masters, if you do not object.

Plato, *Laws,* VII, 816B

6 The buffoon . . . is the slave of his sense of humour, and spares neither himself nor others if he can raise a laugh, and says things none of which a man of refinement would say, and to some of which he would not even listen. The boor . . . is useless for such social intercourse; for he contributes nothing and finds fault with everything. But relaxation and amusement are thought to be a necessary element in life.

Aristotle, *Ethics,* 1128ᵃ34

7 Comedy . . . is an imitation of men worse than the average; worse, however, not as regards any and every sort of fault, but only as regards one particular kind, the ridiculous, which is a species of the ugly. The ridiculous may be defined as a mistake or deformity not productive of pain or harm to others; the mask, for instance, that excites laughter, is something ugly and distorted without causing pain.

Aristotle, *Poetics,* 1449ᵃ32

8 A tragedy . . . is the imitation of an action that is serious and also, as having magnitude, complete in itself; in language with pleasurable accessories, each kind brought in separately in the parts of the work; in a dramatic, not in a narrative form; with incidents arousing pity and fear, wherewith to accomplish its catharsis of such emotions.

Aristotle, *Poetics,* 1449ᵇ23

9 Tragedy is essentially an imitation not of persons but of action and life, of happiness and misery. All

human happiness or misery takes the form of action; the end for which we live is a certain kind of activity, not a quality. Character gives us qualities, but it is in our actions—what we do——that we are happy or the reverse. In a play accordingly they do not act in order to portray the characters; they include the characters for the sake of the action. So that it is the action in it, that is, its fable or plot, that is the end and purpose of the tragedy; and the end is everywhere the chief thing. Besides this, a tragedy is impossible without action, but there may be one without character. . . . And again: one may string together a series of characteristic speeches of the utmost finish as regards diction and thought, and yet fail to produce the true tragic effect; but one will have much better success with a tragedy which, however inferior in these respects, has a plot, a combination of incidents, in it. And again: the most powerful elements of attraction in tragedy, the peripeties and discoveries, are parts of the plot. A further proof is in the fact that beginners succeed earlier with the diction and characters than with the construction of a story; and the same may be said of nearly all the early dramatists. We maintain, therefore, that the first essential, the life and soul, so to speak, of tragedy is the plot; and that the characters come second.

*Aristotle, Poetics, 1450*a*17*

10 Just in the same way, then, as a beautiful whole made up of parts, or a beautiful living creature, must be of some size, but a size to be taken in by the eye, so a story or plot must be of some length, but of a length to be taken in by the memory. As for the limit of its length, so far as that is relative to public performances and spectators, it does not fall within the theory of poetry. If they had to perform a hundred tragedies, they would be timed by water-clocks, as they are said to have been at one period. The limit, however, set by the actual nature of the thing is this: the longer the story, consistently with its being comprehensible as a whole, the finer it is by reason of its magnitude. As a rough general formula, 'a length which allows of the hero passing by a series of probable or necessary stages from misfortune to happiness, or from happiness to misfortune', may suffice as a limit for the magnitude of the story.

The unity of a plot does not consist, as some suppose, in its having one man as its subject. An infinity of things befall that one man, some of which it is impossible to reduce to unity; and in like manner there are many actions of one man which cannot be made to form one action. . . . The truth is that, just as in the other imitative arts one imitation is always of one thing, so in poetry the story, as an imitation of action, must represent one action, a complete whole, with its several incidents so closely connected that the transposal or withdrawal of any one of them will disjoin and dislocate the whole. For that which makes no perceptible difference by its presence or absence is no real part of the whole.

*Aristotle, Poetics, 1451*a*3*

11 The next points after what we have said above will be these: (1) What is the poet to aim at, and what is he to avoid, in constructing his plots? and (2) What are the conditions on which the tragic effect depends?

We assume that, for the finest form of tragedy, the plot must be not simple but complex; and further, that it must imitate actions arousing fear and pity, since that is the distinctive function of this kind of imitation. It follows, therefore, that there are three forms of plot to be avoided. (1) A good man must not be seen passing from happiness to misery, or (2) a bad man from misery to happiness. The first situation is not fear-inspiring or piteous, but simply odious to us. The second is the most untragic that can be; it has no one of the requisites of tragedy; it does not appeal either to the human feeling in us, or to our pity, or to our fears. Nor, on the other hand, should (3) an extremely bad man be seen falling from happiness into misery. Such a story may arouse the human feeling in us, but it will not move us to either pity or fear; pity is occasioned by undeserved misfortune, and fear by that of one like ourselves; so that there will be nothing either piteous or fear-inspiring in the situation. There remains, then, the intermediate kind of personage, a man not preeminently virtuous and just, whose misfortune, however, is brought upon him not by vice and depravity but by some error of judgment, of the number of those in the enjoyment of great reputation and prosperity; for example, Oedipus, Thyestes, and the men of note of similar families. The perfect plot, accordingly, must have a single, and not (as some tell us) a double issue; the change in the hero's fortunes must be not from misery to happiness, but on the contrary from happiness to misery; and the cause of it must lie not in any depravity, but in some great error on his part; the man himself being either such as we have described, or better, not worse, than that. Fact also confirms our theory. Though the poets began by accepting any tragic story that came to hand, in these days the finest tragedies are always on the story of some few houses, on that of Alcmeon, Oedipus, Orestes, Meleager, Thyestes, Telephus, or any others that may have been involved, as either agents or sufferers, in some deed of horror. The theoretically best tragedy, then, has a plot of this description. The critics, therefore, are wrong who blame Euripides for taking this line in his tragedies, and giving many of them an unhappy ending. It is, as we have said, the right line to take. The best proof is this: on the stage, and in the public performances, such plays, properly worked out, are seen to be the most truly tragic; and Euripides, even if his execution be faulty in every other point, is seen to be nevertheless the most tragic certainly of the dramatists. After this comes the construction of plot which some rank first, one with a double story (like the *Odyssey*) and an opposite issue for the good and the bad personages. It is ranked as first only through the weakness of the audiences; the poets merely follow their public, writing as its wishes dictate. But the pleasure here is not that of tragedy. It belongs rather to comedy, where the bitterest enemies in the piece (for example, Orestes and Aegisthus) walk off good friends at the end, with no slaying of anyone by anyone.

Aristotle, *Poetics*, 1452b27

12 At first tragedies were brought on the stage as means of reminding men of the things which happen to them, and that it is according to nature for things to happen so, and that, if you are delighted with what is shown on the stage, you should not be troubled with that which takes place on the larger stage. For you see that these things must be accomplished thus, and that even they bear them who cry out "O Cithaeron." And, indeed, some things are said well by the dramatic writers. . . .

After tragedy the old comedy was introduced, which had a magisterial freedom of speech, and by its very plainness of speaking was useful in reminding men to beware of insolence; and for this purpose too Diogenes used to take from these writers.

But as to the middle comedy which came next, observe what it was, and again, for what object the new comedy was introduced, which gradually sunk down into a mere mimic artifice. That some good things are said even by these writers, everybody knows: but the whole plan of such poetry and dramaturgy, to what end does it look!

Marcus Aurelius, *Meditations*, XI, 6

13 I developed a passion for stage plays, with the mirror they held up to my own miseries and the fuel they poured on my flame. How is it that a man wants to be made sad by the sight of tragic sufferings that he could not bear in his own person? Yet the spectator does want to feel sorrow, and it is actually his feeling of sorrow that he enjoys. Surely this is the most wretched lunacy? For the more a man feels such sufferings in himself, the more he is moved by the sight of them on the stage. Now when a man suffers himself, it is called misery; when he suffers in the suffering of another, it is called pity. But how can the unreal sufferings of the stage possibly move pity? The spectator is not moved to aid the sufferer but merely to be sorry for him; and the more the author of these fictions makes the audience grieve, the better they like him. If the tragic sorrows of the characters—whether historical or entirely fictitious—be so poorly represented that the spectator is not moved to tears, he leaves the theatre unsatisfied and full of complaints; if he *is* moved to tears, he stays to the end, fascinated and revelling in it. So that tears and sorrow, it would seem, are things to be sought. Yet surely every man prefers to be joyful. May it be that whereas no one wants to be miserable, there is real pleasure in pitying others—and we love their sorrows because without them we should have nothing to pity?

Augustine, *Confessions*, III, 2

14 We appear . . . to make use of the tragic style when the stateliness of the lines as well as the loftiness of the construction and the excellence of the words agree with the weight of the subject. And because, if we remember rightly, it has already been proved that the highest things are worthy of the highest, and because the style which we call tragic appears to be the highest style, those things which we have distinguished as being worthy of the highest song are to be sung in that style alone, namely, safety, love, and virtue, and those other things, our conceptions of which arise from these; provided that they be not degraded by any accident. . . . And therefore let those who, innocent of art and science, and trusting to genius alone, rush forward to sing of the highest subjects in the highest style, confess their folly and cease from such presumption; and if in their natural sluggishness they are but geese, let them abstain from imitating the eagle soaring to the stars.

Dante, *De Vulgari Eloquentia*, II, 4

15 Comedy is a certain kind of poetic narration differing from all others. It differs . . . from tragedy in its content, in that tragedy begins admirably and tranquilly, whereas its end or exit is foul and terrible; . . . whereas comedy introduces some harsh complication, but brings its matter to a prosperous end. . . . The title of the present work is '*the Comedy.*' For if we have respect to its content, at the beginning it is horrible and fetid, for it is hell; and in the end it is prosperous, desirable, and gracious, for it is *Paradise*. If we have respect to the method of speech the method is lax and humble, for it is the vernacular speech in which very women communicate.

Dante, *Letter to Can Grande*

16 Tragedy is to say a certain story
From ancient books which have preserved the glory
Of one that stood in great prosperity
And is now fallen out of high degree
In misery, where he ends wretchedly.
Such tales are versified most commonly
In six feet, which men call hexameter.
In prose are many written; some prefer
A quantitative metre, sundry wise.

Chaucer, *Canterbury Tales:* Monk's Prologue

17 "Hold!" cried the knight. "Good sir, no more of
  this,
What you have said is right enough, and is
Very much more; a little heaviness
Is plenty for the most of us, I guess.
For me, I say it's saddening, if you please,
As to men who've enjoyed great wealth and ease,
To hear about their sudden fall, alas!
But the contrary's joy and great solace,
As when a man has been in poor estate
And he climbs up and waxes fortunate,
And there abides in all prosperity.
Such things are gladsome, as it seems to me,
And of such things it would be good to tell."

Chaucer, *Canterbury Tales:* Nun's Priest's
Prologue

18 *Hamlet.*   I have heard
That guilty creatures sitting at a play
Have by the very cunning of the scene
Been struck so to the soul that presently
They have proclaim'd their malefactions. . . .
                                    The play's the thing
Wherein I'll catch the conscience of the King.

Shakespeare, *Hamlet,* II, ii, 617

19 *Hamlet.* Speak the speech, I pray you, as I pronounced it to you, trippingly on the tongue: but if
you mouth it, as many of your players do, I had as
lief the town-crier spoke my lines. Nor do not saw
the air too much with your hand, thus, but use all
gently; for in the very torrent, tempest, and, as I
may say, the whirlwind of passion, you must acquire and beget a temperance that may give it
smoothness. O, it offends me to the soul to hear a
robustious periwig-pated fellow tear a passion to
tatters, to very rags, to split the ears of the ground-
lings, who for the most part are capable of nothing but inexplicable dumbshows and noise. I
would have such a fellow whipped for o'erdoing
Termagant. It out-herods Herod. Pray you, avoid
it.

1st Player. I warrant your honour.

Ham. Be not too tame neither, but let your own
discretion be your tutor. Suit the action to the
word, the word to the action; with this special
observance, that you o'erstep not the modesty of
nature; for anything so overdone is from the purpose of playing, whose end, both at the first and
now, was and is, to hold, as 'twere, the mirror up
to nature; to show virtue her own feature, scorn
her own image, and the very age and body of the
time his form and pressure. Now this overdone, or
come tardy off, though it make the unskilful
laugh, cannot but make the judicious grieve; the
censure of the which one must in your allowance
o'erweigh a whole theatre of others. O, there be
players that I have seen play, and heard others
praise, and that highly, not to speak it profanely,
that, neither having the accent of Christians nor
the gait of Christian, pagan, nor man, have so

strutted and bellowed that I have thought some of
nature's journeymen had made men and not
made them well, they imitated humanity so
abominably.

1st Play. I hope we have reformed that indifferently with us, sir.

Ham. O, reform it altogether. And let those that
play your clowns speak no more than is set down
for them; for there be of them that will themselves
laugh, to set on some quantity of barren spectators
to laugh too; though, in the meantime, some necessary question of the play be then to be considered: that's villainous, and shows a most pitiful
ambition in the fool that uses it.

Shakespeare, *Hamlet,* III, ii, 1

20 The parts of a comedy are the same with a tragedy, and the end is partly the same, for they both
delight, and teach; the comics are called teachers
of the Greeks no less than the tragics. Nor is the
moving of laughter always the end of comedy;
that is rather a fowling for the people's delight, or
their fooling. For, as Aristotle says rightly, the
moving of laughter is a fault in comedy, a kind of
turpitude that depraves some part of a man's nature without a disease. As a wry face without pain
moves laughter, or a deformed vizard, or a rude
clown dressed in a lady's habit and using her actions; we dislike and scorn such representations
which made the ancient philosophers ever think
laughter unfitting in a wise man. And this induced Plato to esteem of Homer as a sacrilegious
person, because he presented the gods sometimes
laughing. As also it is divinely said of Aristotle,
that to seem ridiculous is a part of dishonesty, and
foolish. So that what either in the words or sense
of an author, or in the language or actions of men,
is awry or depraved doth strangely stir mean affections, and provoke for the most part to laughter. And therefore it was clear that all insolent
and obscene speeches, jests upon the best men,
injuries to particular persons, perverse and sinister
sayings and the rather unexpected in the old comedy did move laughter, especially where it did
imitate any dishonesty; and scurrility came forth
in the place of wit, which, who understands the
nature and genius of laughter cannot but perfectly know.

Of which Aristophanes affords an ample harvest, having not only outgone Plautus or any
other in that kind, but expressed all the moods
and figures of what is ridiculous oddly. In short, as
vinegar is not accounted good until the wine be
corrupted, so jests that are true and natural seldom raise laughter with the beast, the multitude.
They love nothing that is right and proper. The
farther it runs from reason or possibility with
them the better it is. What could have made them
laugh, like to see Socrates presented, that example
of all good life, honesty, and virtue, to have him
hoisted up with a pulley, and there play the phi-

losopher in a basket; measure how many foot a flea could skip geometrically, by a just scale, and edify the people from the engine? This was theatrical wit, right stage jesting, and relishing a playhouse, invented for scorn and laughter; whereas, if it had savoured of equity, truth, perspicuity, and candour, to have tasten a wise or a learned palate,—spit it out presently! this is bitter and profitable: this instructs and would inform us! what need we know anything, that are nobly born, more than a horse-race, or a hunting-match, our day to break with citizens, and such innate mysteries?

Jonson, *Discoveries:* Comedy and Tragedy

21 Whole we call that, and perfect, which hath a beginning, a midst, and an end. So the place of any building may be whole and entire for that work, though too little for a palace. As to a tragedy or a comedy, the action may be convenient and perfect that would not fit an epic poem in magnitude. So a lion is a perfect creature in himself, though it be less than that of a buffalo or a rhinocerote. They differ but *in specie:* either in the kind is absolute; both have their parts, and either the whole. Therefore, as in every body so in every action, which is the subject of a just work, there is required a certain proportionable greatness, neither too vast nor too minute. For that which happens to the eyes when we behold a body, the same happens to the memory when we contemplate an action. I look upon a monstrous giant, as Tityus, whose body covered nine acres of land, and mine eye sticks upon every part; the whole that consists of those parts will never be taken in at one entire view. So in a fable, if the action be too great, we can never comprehend the whole together in our imagination. Again, if it be too little, there ariseth no pleasure out of the object; it affords the view no stay; it is beheld, and vanisheth at once. As if we should look upon an ant or pismire, the parts fly the sight, and the whole considered is almost nothing.

Jonson, *Discoveries:* The Fable

22 All great amusements are dangerous to the Christian life; but among all those which the world has invented there is none more to be feared than the theatre. It is a representation of the passions so natural and so delicate that it excites them and gives birth to them in our hearts, and, above all, to that of love, principally when it is represented as very chaste and virtuous. For the more innocent it appears to innocent souls, the more they are likely to be touched by it. Its violence pleases our self-love, which immediately forms a desire to produce the same effects which are seen so well-represented; and, at the same time, we make ourselves a conscience founded on the propriety of the feelings which we see there, by which the fear of pure souls is removed, since they imagine that it

cannot hurt their purity to love with a love which seems to them so reasonable.

So we depart from the theatre with our heart so filled with all the beauty and tenderness of love, the soul and the mind so persuaded of its innocence, that we are quite ready to receive its first impressions, or rather to seek an opportunity of awakening them in the heart of another, in order that we may receive the same pleasures and the same sacrifices which we have seen so well-represented in the theatre.

Pascal, *Pensées,* I, 11

23 Then to the well-trod stage anon,
If *Jonsons* learned Sock be on,
Or sweetest *Shakespear* fancies childe,
Warble his native Wood-notes wilde.

Milton, *L'Allegro,* 131

24 Som time let Gorgeous Tragedy
In Scepter'd Pall com sweeping by,
Presenting *Thebs,* or *Pelops* line,
Or the tale of *Troy* divine.
Or what (though rare) of later age,
Ennobled hath the Buskind stage.

Milton, *Il Penseroso,* 97

25 Tragedy, as it was antiently compos'd, hath been ever held the gravest, moralest, and most profitable of all other Poems: therefore said by *Aristotle* to be of power by raising pity and fear, or terror, to purge the mind of those and such like passions, that is to temper and reduce them to just measure with a kind of delight, stirr'd up by reading or seeing those passions well imitated. Nor is Nature wanting in her own effects to make good his assertion: for so in Physic things of melancholic hue and quality are us'd against melancholy, sowr against sowr, salt to remove salt humours. Hence Philosophers and other gravest Writers, as *Cicero,* *Plutarch* and others, frequently cite out of Tragic Poets, both to adorn and illustrate thir discourse. The Apostle *Paul* himself thought it not unworthy to insert a verse of *Euripides* into the Text of Holy Scripture, I *Cor.* 15. 33. and *Paraeus* commenting on the *Revelation,* divides the whole Book as a Tragedy, into Acts distinguisht each by a Chorus of Heavenly Harpings and Song between. . . . This is mention'd to vindicate Tragedy from the small esteem, or rather infamy, which in the account of many it undergoes at this day with other common Interludes; hap'ning through the Poets error of intermixing Comic stuff with Tragic sadness and gravity; or introducing trivial and vulgar persons, which by all judicious hath bin counted absurd; and brought in without discretion, corruptly to gratifie the people.

Milton, *Samson Agonistes,* Pref.

26 A scene of mirth, mixed with tragedy, has the same effect upon us which our music has betwixt

the acts; which we find a relief to us from the best plots and language of the stage, if the discourses have been long. I must therefore have stronger arguments, ere I am convinced that compassion and mirth in the same subject destroy each other; and in the mean time cannot but conclude, to the honour of our nation, that we have invented, increased, and perfected a more pleasant way of writing for the stage, than was ever known to the ancients or moderns of any nation, which is tragicomedy.

Dryden, *Essay of Dramatic Poesy*

27 Who ever demanded the reasons of that nice unity of time or place which is now established to be so essential to dramatic poetry? What critic hath been ever asked, why a play may not contain two days as well as one? Or why the audience (provided they travel, like electors, without any expense) may not be wafted fifty miles as well as five? Hath any commentator well accounted for the limitation which an antient critic hath set to the drama, which he will have contain neither more nor less than five acts? Or hath anyone living attempted to explain what the modern judges of our theatres mean by that word *low;* by which they have happily succeeded in banishing all humour from the stage, and have made the theatre as dull as a drawing-room!

Fielding, *Tom Jones*, V, 1

28 The theatrical stage is nothing more than a representation, or, as Aristotle calls it, an imitation of what really exists; and hence, perhaps, we might fairly pay a very high compliment to those who by their writings or actions have been so capable of imitating life, as to have their pictures in a manner confounded with, or mistaken for, the originals.

But, in reality, we are not so fond of paying compliments to these people, whom we use as children frequently do the instruments of their amusement; and have much more pleasure in hissing and buffeting them, than in admiring their excellence. There are many other reasons which have induced us to see this analogy between the world and the stage.

Some have considered the larger part of mankind in the light of actors, as personating characters no more their own, and to which in fact they have no better title, than the player hath to be in earnest thought the king or emperor whom he represents. Thus the hypocrite may be said to be a player; and indeed the Greeks called them both by one and the same name. . . .

In all these, however, and in every other similitude of life to the theatre, the resemblance hath been always taken from the stage only. None, as I remember, have at all considered the audience at this great drama.

But as Nature often exhibits some of her best

performances to a very full house, so will the behaviour of her spectators no less admit the above-mentioned comparison than that of her actors. In this vast theatre of time are seated the friend and the critic; here are claps and shouts, hisses and groans; in short, everything which was ever seen or heard at the Theatre-Royal.

Fielding, *Tom Jones*, VII, 1

29 Now, a comic romance is a comic epic poem in prose; differing from comedy, as the serious epic from tragedy: its action being more extended and comprehensive; containing a much larger circle of incidents, and introducing a greater variety of characters. It differs from the serious romance in its fable and action, in this; that as in the one these are grave and solemn, so in the other they are light and ridiculous: it differs in its characters by introducing persons of inferior rank, and consequently, of inferior manners, whereas the grave romance sets the highest before us: lastly, in its sentiments and diction; by preserving the ludicrous instead of the sublime. In the diction, I think, burlesque itself may be sometimes admitted; of which many instances will occur in this work, as in the description of the battles, and some other places, not necessary to be pointed out to the classical reader, for whose entertainment those parodies or burlesque imitations are chiefly calculated.

But, though we have sometimes admitted this in our diction, we have carefully excluded it from our sentiments and characters; for there it is never properly introduced, unless in writings of the burlesque kind, which this is not intended to be. Indeed, no two species of writing can differ more widely than the comic and the burlesque; for as the latter is ever the exhibition of what is monstrous and unnatural, and where our delight, if we examine it, arises from the surprising absurdity, as in appropriating the manners of the highest to the lowest, or *è converso;* so in the former we should ever confine ourselves strictly to nature, from the just imitation of which will flow all the pleasure we can this way convey to a sensible reader. And perhaps there is one reason why a comic writer should of all others be the least excused for deviating from nature, since it may not be always so easy for a serious poet to meet with the great and the admirable; but life everywhere furnishes an accurate observer with the ridiculous.

Fielding, *Joseph Andrews*, Pref.

30 The only source of the true ridiculous (as it appears to me) is affectation. But though it arises from one spring only, when we consider the infinite streams into which this one branches, we shall presently cease to admire at the copious field it affords to an observer. Now, affectation proceeds from one of these two causes, vanity or hypocrisy: for as vanity puts us on affecting false

characters, in order to purchase applause; so hypocrisy sets us on an endeavour to avoid censure, by concealing our vices under an appearance of their opposite virtues. And though these two causes are often confounded (for there is some difficulty in distinguishing them), yet, as they proceed from very different motives, so they are as clearly distinct in their operations: for indeed, the affectation which arises from vanity is nearer to truth than the other, as it hath not that violent repugnancy of nature to struggle with, which that of the hypocrite hath. It may be likewise noted, that affectation doth not imply an absolute negation of those qualities which are affected; and, therefore, though, when it proceeds from hypocrisy, it be nearly allied to deceit; yet when it comes from vanity only, it partakes of the nature of ostentation: for instance, the affectation of liberality in a vain man differs visibly from the same affectation in the avaricious; for though the vain man is not what he would appear, or hath not the virtue he affects, to the degree he would be thought to have it; yet it sits less awkwardly on him than on the avaricious man, who is the very reverse of what he would seem to be.

From the discovery of this affectation arises the ridiculous, which always strikes the reader with surprize and pleasure; and that in a higher and stronger degree when the affectation arises from hypocrisy, than when from vanity; for to discover any one to be the exact reverse of what he affects, is more surprizing, and consequently more ridiculous, than to find him a little deficient in the quality he desires the reputation of.

Fielding, *Joseph Andrews,* Pref.

31 Shakespeare's plays are not in the rigorous and critical sense either tragedies or comedies, but compositions of a distinct kind; exhibiting the real state of sublunary nature, which partakes of good and evil, joy and sorrow, mingled with endless variety of proportion and innumerable modes of combination; and expressing the course of the world, in which the loss of one is the gain of another; in which, at the same time, the reveller is hasting to his wine, and the mourner burying his friend; in which the malignity of one is sometimes defeated by the frolic of another; and many mischiefs and many benefits are done and hindered without design.

Johnson, *Preface to Shakespeare*

32 The necessity of observing the unities of time and place arises from the supposed necessity of making the drama credible. The critics hold it impossible that an action of months or years can be possibly believed to pass in three hours; or that the spectator can suppose himself to sit in the theatre, while ambassadors go and return between distant kings, while armies are levied and towns besieged, while

an exile wanders and returns, or till he whom they saw courting his mistress, shall lament the untimely fall of his son. The mind revolts from evident falsehood, and fiction loses its force when it departs from the resemblance of reality.

From the narrow limitation of time necessarily arises the contraction of place. The spectator, who knows that he saw the first act at Alexandria, cannot suppose that he sees the next at Rome, at a distance to which not the dragons of Medea could, in so short a time, have transported him; he knows with certainty that he has not changed his place, and he knows that place cannot change itself; that what was a house cannot become a plain; that what was Thebes can never be Persepolis.

Such is the triumphant language with which a critic exults over the misery of an irregular poet, and exults commonly without resistance or reply. It is time therefore to tell him by the authority of Shakespeare that he assumes, as an unquestionable principle, a position which, while his breath is forming it into words, his understanding pronounces to be false. It is false that any representation is mistaken for reality; that any dramatic fable in its materiality was ever credible, or, for a single moment, was ever credited.

The objection arising from the impossibility of passing the first hour at Alexandria, and the next at Rome, supposes that when the play opens, the spectator really imagines himself at Alexandria, and believes that his walk to the theatre has been a voyage to Egypt, and that he lives in the days of Antony and Cleopatra. Surely he that imagines this may imagine more. He that can take the stage at one time for the palace of the Ptolemies may take it in half an hour for the promontory of Actium. Delusion, if delusion be admitted, has no certain limitation; if the spectator can be once persuaded that his old acquaintances are Alexander and Caesar, that a room illuminated with candles is the plain of Pharsalia, or the bank of Granicus, he is in a state of elevation above the reach of reason, or of truth, and from the heights of empyrean poetry, may despise the circumscriptions of terrestrial nature. There is no reason why a mind thus wandering in ecstasy should count the clock, or why an hour should not be a century in that calenture of the brains that can make the stage a field.

The truth is that the spectators are always in their senses, and know, from the first act to the last, that the stage is only a stage, and that the players are only players. They came to hear a certain number of lines recited with just gesture and elegant modulation. The lines relate to some action, and an action must be in some place; but the different actions that complete a story may be in places very remote from each other; and where is the absurdity of allowing that space to represent first Athens, and then Sicily which was always known to be neither Sicily nor Athens, but a modern theatre?

By supposition, as place is introduced, time may be extended; the time required by the fable elapses for the most part between the acts; for, of so much of the action as is represented, the real and poetical duration is the same. If, in the first act, preparations for war against Mithridates are represented to be made in Rome, the event of the war may, without absurdity, be represented, in the catastrophe, as happening in Pontus; we know that there is neither war, nor preparation for war; we know that we are neither in Rome nor Pontus; that neither Mithridates nor Lucullus are before us. The drama exhibits successive imitations of successive actions; and why may not the second imitation represent an action that happened years after the first, if it be so connected with it that nothing but time can be supposed to intervene? Time is, of all modes of existence, most obsequious to the imagination; a lapse of years is as easily conceived as a passage of hours. In contemplation we easily contract the time of real actions, and therefore willingly permit it to be contracted when we only see their imitation.

It will be asked how the drama moves if it is not credited. It is credited with all the credit due to a drama. It is credited, whenever it moves, as a just picture of a real original; as representing to the auditor what he would himself feel if he were to do or suffer what is there feigned to be suffered or to be done. The reflection that strikes the heart is not that the evils before us are real evils but that they are evils to which we ourselves may be exposed. If there be any fallacy, it is not that we fancy the players, but that we fancy ourselves unhappy for a moment; but we rather lament the possibility than suppose the presence of misery, as a mother weeps over her babe when she remembers that death may take it from her. The delight of tragedy proceeds from our consciousness of fiction; if we thought murders and treasons real, they would please no more.

Johnson, *Preface to Shakespeare*

33 I introduced Aristotle's doctrine in his *Art of Poetry*, of ". . . the purging of the passions," as the purpose of tragedy. "But how are the passions to be purged by terrour and pity?" (said I, with an assumed air of ignorance, to incite him to talk, for which it was often necessary to employ some address). *Johnson.* "Why, Sir, you are to consider what is the meaning of purging in the original sense. It is to expel impurities from the human body. The mind is subject to the same imperfection. The passions are the great movers of human actions; but they are mixed with such impurities, that it is necessary they should be purged or refined by means of terrour and pity. For instance, ambition is a noble passion; but by seeing upon the stage, that a man who is so excessively ambi-

tious as to raise himself by injustice, is punished, we are terrified at the fatal consequences of such a passion. In the same manner a certain degree of resentment is necessary; but if we see that a man carries it too far, we pity the object of it, and are taught to moderate that passion." My record upon this occasion does great injustice to Johnson's expression, which was so forcible and brilliant, that Mr. Cradock whispered me, "O that his words were written in a book!"

Boswell, *Life of Johnson (Apr. 12, 1776)*

34 The state, by encouraging, that is giving entire liberty to all those who for their own interest would attempt, without scandal or indecency, to amuse and divert the people by painting, poetry, music, dancing; by all sorts of dramatic representations and exhibitions; would easily dissipate, in the greater part of them, that melancholy and gloomy humour which is almost always the nurse of popular superstition and enthusiasm. Public diversions have always been the objects of dread and hatred to all the fanatical promoters of those popular [religious] frenzies. The gaiety and good humour which those diversions inspire were altogether inconsistent with that temper of mind which was fittest for their purpose, or which they could best work upon. Dramatic representations, besides, frequently exposing their artifices to public ridicule, and sometimes even to public execration, were upon that account, more than all other diversions, the objects of their peculiar abhorrence.

Adam Smith, *Wealth of Nations*, V, 1

35 Voltaire said that heaven has given us two things to compensate us for the many miseries of life, hope and sleep. He might have added laughter to the list—if only the means of exciting it in men of intelligence were as ready to hand, and the wit or originality of humour which it requires were not just as rare as the talent is common for inventing stuff that splits the head, as mystic speculators do, or that breaks your neck, as the genius does, or that harrows the heart as sentimental novelists do (aye, and moralists of the same type).

Kant, *Critique of Aesthetic Judgement*, 54

36 The humorous manner may also be ranked as a thing which in its enlivening influence is clearly allied to the gratification provoked by laughter. It belongs to originality of mind, though not to the talent for fine art. Humour, in a good sense, means the talent for being able to put oneself at will into a certain frame of mind in which everything is estimated on lines that go quite off the beaten track (a topsy-turvy view of things), and yet on lines that follow certain principles, rational in the case of such a mental temperament. A person with whom such variations are not a matter of choice is said to have humours; but if a person can assume them voluntarily and of set purpose (on

behalf of a lively presentation drawn from a ludicrous contrast), he and his way of speaking are termed humorous. This manner belongs, however, to agreeable rather than to fine art, because the object of the latter must always have an evident intrinsic worth about it, and thus demands a certain seriousness in its presentation, as taste does in estimating it.

Kant, *Critique of Aesthetic Judgement*, 54

37 The aim that comedy has in view is the same as that of the highest destiny of man, and this consists in liberating himself from the influence of violent passions, and taking a calm and lucid survey of all that surrounds him, and also of his own being, and of seeing everywhere occurrence rather than fate or hazard, and ultimately rather smiling at the absurdities than shedding tears and feeling anger at sight of the wickedness of man.

Schiller, *Simple and Sentimental Poetry*

38 Nothing serves better to illustrate a man's character than the things which he finds ridiculous.

The ridiculous arises from a moral contrast which is innocently placed before the senses.

The sensual man will often laugh when there is nothing to laugh at. Whatever it may be that moves him, he will always reveal the fact that he is pleased with himself.

Goethe, *Reflections and Maxims*

39 All tragedies are finish'd by a death,
 All comedies are ended by a marriage;
The future states of both are left to faith.

Byron, *Don Juan*, III, 9

40 Success is counted sweetest
By those who ne'er succeed.
To comprehend a nectar
Requires sorest need.

Not one of all the purple host
Who took the flag today
Can tell the definition
So clear of victory

As he defeated, dying,
On whose forbidden ear
The distant strains of triumph
Burst agonized and clear.

Emily Dickinson, *Success Is Counted Sweetest*

41 The drama in our time is a great man fallen, who has reached the last degree of his degradation, and at the same time continues to pride himself on his past of which nothing now remains.

Tolstoy, *Critical Essay on Shakespeare*, VIII

42 The metaphysical comfort—with which, I am suggesting even now, every true tragedy leaves us—that life is at the bottom of things, despite all the changes of appearances, indestructibly powerful and pleasurable—this comfort appears in incarnate clarity in the chorus of satyrs, a chorus of natural beings who live ineradicably, as it were, behind all civilization and remain eternally the same, despite the changes of generations and of the history of nations.

With this chorus the profound Hellene, uniquely susceptible to the tenderest and deepest suffering, comforts himself, having looked boldly right into the terrible destructiveness of so-called world history as well as the cruelty of nature, and being in danger of longing for a Buddhistic negation of the will. Art saves him, and through art—life.

Nietzsche, *Birth of Tragedy*, VII

43 We talk so abstractly about poetry because all of us are usually bad poets. At bottom, the aesthetic phenomenon is simple: let anyone have the ability to behold continually a vivid play and to live constantly surrounded by hosts of spirits, and he will be a poet; let anyone feel the urge to transform himself and to speak out of other bodies and souls, and he will be a dramatist.

Nietzsche, *Birth of Tragedy*, VIII

44 The tradition is undisputed that Greek tragedy in its earliest form had for its sole theme the sufferings of Dionysus and that for a long time the only stage hero was Dionysus himself. But it may be claimed with equal confidence that until Euripides, Dionysus never ceased to be the tragic hero; that all the celebrated figures of the Greek stage—Prometheus, Oedipus, etc.—are mere masks of this original hero, Dionysus. That behind all these masks there is a deity, that is one essential reason for the typical "ideality" of these famous figures which has caused so much astonishment. Somebody, I do not know who, has claimed that all individuals, taken as individuals, are comic and hence untragic—from which it would follow that the Greeks simply could not suffer individuals on the tragic stage. In fact, this is what they seem to have felt; and the Platonic distinction and evaluation of the "idea" and the "idol," the mere image, is very deeply rooted in the Hellenic character.

Nietzsche, *Birth of Tragedy*, X

45 The essence of dramatic tragedy is not unhappiness. It resides in the solemnity of the remorseless working of things. This inevitableness of destiny can only be illustrated in terms of human life by incidents which in fact involve unhappiness. For it is only by them that the futility of escape can be made evident in the drama.

Whitehead, *Science and the Modern World*, I

46 Another of the great poetic tragedies, Shakespeare's *Hamlet*, is rooted in the same soil as *Oedipus Rex*. But the whole difference in the psychic life of the two widely separated periods of civilization, and the progress, during the course of

time, of repression in the emotional life of humanity, is manifested in the differing treatment of the same material. In *Oedipus Rex,* the basic wish-phantasy of the child is brought to light and realized as it is in dreams; in *Hamlet,* it remains repressed, and we learn of its existence—as we discover the relevant facts in a neurosis—only through the inhibitory effects which proceed from it. In the more modern drama, the curious fact that it is possible to remain in complete uncertainty as to the character of the hero has proved to be quite consistent with the overpowering effect of the tragedy. The play is based upon Hamlet's hesitation in accomplishing the task of revenge assigned to him; the text does not give the cause or the motive of this hesitation, nor have the manifold attempts at interpretation succeeded in doing so. According to the still prevailing conception, a conception for which Goethe was first responsible, Hamlet represents the type of man whose active energy is paralyzed by excessive intellectual activity: "Sicklied o'er with the pale cast of thought." According to another conception, the poet has endeavoured to portray a morbid, irresolute character, on the verge of neurasthenia. The plot of the drama, however, shows us that Hamlet is by no means intended to appear as a character wholly incapable of action. On two separate occasions we see him assert himself: once in a sudden outburst of rage, when he stabs the eavesdropper behind the arras, and on the other occasion when he deliberately, and even craftily, with the complete unscrupulousness of a prince of the Renaissance, sends the two courtiers to the death which was intended for himself. What is it, then, that inhibits him in accomplishing the task which his father's ghost has laid upon him? Here the explanation offers itself that it is the peculiar nature of this task. Hamlet is able to do anything but take vengeance upon the man who did away with his father and has taken his father's place with his mother—the man who shows him in realization the repressed desires of his own childhood. The loathing which should have driven him to revenge is thus replaced by self-reproach, by conscientious scruples, which tell him that he himself is no better than the murderer whom he is required to punish. I have here translated into consciousness what had to remain unconscious in the mind of the hero; if anyone wishes to call Hamlet an hysterical subject I cannot but admit that this is the deduction to be drawn from my interpretation. The sexual aversion which Hamlet expresses in conversation with Ophelia is perfectly consistent with this deduction—the same sexual aversion which during the next few years was increasingly to take possession of the poet's soul, until it found its supreme utterance in *Timon of Athens.* It can, of course, be only the poet's own psychology with which we are confronted in *Hamlet;* and in a work on Shakespeare by Georg Brandes (1896) I find

the statement that the drama was composed immediately after the death of Shakespeare's father (1601)—that is to say, when he was still mourning his loss, and during a revival, as we may fairly assume, of his own childish feelings in respect of his father. It is known, too, that Shakespeare's son, who died in childhood, bore the name of Hamnet (identical with Hamlet). Just as *Hamlet* treats of the relation of the son to his parents, so *Macbeth,* which was written about the same period, is based upon the theme of childlessness. Just as all neurotic symptoms, like dreams themselves, are capable of hyper-interpretation, and even require such hyper-interpretation before they become perfectly intelligible, so every genuine poetical creation must have proceeded from more than one motive, more than one impulse in the mind of the poet, and must admit of more than one interpretation. I have here attempted to interpret only the deepest stratum of impulses in the mind of the creative poet.

Freud, *Interpretation of Dreams,* V, D

47 The pleasure of wit originates from an economy of expenditure in inhibition, of the comic from an economy of expenditure in thought, and of humor from an economy of expenditure in feeling. All three modes of activity of our psychic apparatus derive pleasure from economy. All three present methods strive to bring back from the psychic activity a pleasure which has really been lost in the development of this activity. For the euphoria which we are thus striving to obtain is nothing but the state of a bygone time, in which we were wont to defray our psychic work with slight expenditure. It is the state of our childhood in which we did not know the comic, were incapable of wit, and did not need humor to make us happy.

Freud, *Wit and Its Relation to the Unconscious,* VII

48 The comic does not exist outside the pale of what is strictly *human.* A landscape may be beautiful, charming and sublime, or insignificant and ugly; it will never be laughable. You may laugh at an animal, but only because you have detected in it some human attitude or expression. You may laugh at a hat, but what you are making fun of, in this case, is not the piece of felt or straw, but the shape that men have given it—the human caprice whose mould it has assumed. It is strange that so important a fact, and such a simple one too, has not attracted to a greater degree the attention of philosophers. Several have defined man as "an animal which laughs." They might equally well have defined him as an animal which is laughed at; for if any other animal, or some lifeless object, produces the same effect, it is always because of some resemblance to man, of the stamp he gives it or the use he puts it to.

Bergson, *Laughter,* I, 1

49 You would hardly appreciate the comic if you felt yourself isolated from others. Laughter appears to stand in need of an echo. Listen to it carefully: it is not an articulate, clear, well-defined sound; it is something which would fain be prolonged by reverberating from one to another, something beginning with a crash, to continue in successive rumblings, like thunder in a mountain. Still, this reverberation cannot go on for ever. It can travel within as wide a circle as you please: the circle remains, none the less, a closed one.

Bergson, *Laughter*, I, 1

50 Look closely: you will find that the art of the comic poet consists in making us so well acquainted with the particular vice, in introducing us, the spectators, to such a degree of intimacy with it, that in the end we get hold of some of the strings of the marionette with which he is playing, and actually work them ourselves; this it is that explains part of the pleasure we feel. Here, too, it is really a kind of automatism that makes us laugh—an automatism, as we have already remarked, closely akin to mere absentmindedness. To realise this more fully, it need only be noted that a comic character is generally comic in proportion to his ignorance of himself. The comic person is unconscious.

Bergson, *Laughter*, I, 2

51 A comedy is far more like real life than a drama is. The more sublime the drama, the more profound the analysis to which the poet has had to subject the raw materials of daily life in order to obtain the tragic element in its unadulterated form. On the contrary, it is only in its lower aspects, in light comedy and farce, that comedy is in striking contrast to reality: the higher it rises, the more it approximates to life; in fact, there are scenes in real life so closely bordering on high-class comedy that the stage might adopt them without changing a single word.

Bergson, *Laughter*, III, 1

52 In this sense, laughter cannot be absolutely just.

Nor should it be kind-hearted either. Its function is to intimidate by humiliating. Now, it would not succeed in doing this, had not nature implanted for that very purpose, even in the best of men, a spark of spitefulness or, at all events, of mischief. Perhaps we had better not investigate this point too closely, for we should not find anything very flattering to ourselves.

Bergson, *Laughter*, III, 5

53 What fabulous creatures these artists are! Are they really human at all? Take the clowns, for example, those basically alien beings, funmakers, with little red hands, little thin-shod feet, red wigs under conical felt hats, their impossible lingo, their handstands, their stumbling and falling over everything, their mindless running to and fro and unserviceable attempts to help, their hideously unsuccessful efforts to imitate their serious colleagues—in tightrope-walking, for instance—which bring the crowd to a pitch of mad merriment. Are these ageless, half-grown sons of absurdity, at whom Stanko and I laughed so heartily (I, however, with a thoughtful fellow-feeling), are they human at all? With their chalk-white faces and utterly preposterous painted expressions—triangular eyebrows and deep perpendicular grooves in their cheeks under the reddened eyes, impossible noses, mouths twisted up at the corners into insane smiles—masks, that is, which stand in inconceivable contrast to the splendour of their costumes—black satin, for example, embroidered with silver butterflies, a child's dream—are they, I repeat, human beings, men that could conceivably find a place in everyday daily life? In my opinion it is pure sentimentality to say that they are "human too," with the sensibilities of human beings and perhaps even with wives and children. I honour them and defend them against ordinary bad taste when I say no, they are not, they are exceptions, side-splitting monsters of preposterousness, glittering, world-renouncing monks of unreason, cavorting hybrids, part human and part insane art.

Mann, *Confessions of Felix Krull*

16.5 | *Music*

We have already noted that, of all the fine arts other than imaginative literature, music alone receives special treatment in this chapter. One reason for this is that both the poets and the moralists regard music as exerting an extraordinary influence over the emotions and conduct of human beings. Closely related to that is the concern, especially in antiquity, with the part that music plays in the rearing and training of the young. Plato, for example, assigns to gymnastic and to music the basic roles in the early education of children—one for the training of the body, the other for the discipline of the emotions and the cultivation of the sensibilities. Aristotle broadens the discussion by considering the enjoyment of music as one of the occupations of leisure and as a result of liberal education.

These texts and others raise questions about the censorship of music, or at least about control of the kind of music young people should be allowed to hear—a question that should strike a responsive chord in those who today are troubled by the effects on the young of the earsplitting blasts and the emotional violence of the music to which they are addicted.

There are one or two passages that reflect the conception of music as a liberal rather than a fine art—a mathematical art that belongs to the *quadrivium* along with arithmetic, geometry, and astronomy. But the mathematical treatment of music, or harmonics, is not represented here; nor is the discussion of music in the tradition of musicology. Both are too technical for a collection of this kind.

---

1 *Chorus.* There's nothing like the flute's sound when
We dance and sing and eat our fill
And love in all its sweetness.
                        Euripides, *Heracleidae,* 892

2 *Socrates.* Musical training is a more potent instrument than any other, because rhythm and harmony find their way into the inward places of the soul, on which they mightily fasten, imparting grace, and making the soul of him who is rightly educated graceful, or of him who is ill-educated ungraceful; and also because he who has received this true education of the inner being will most shrewdly perceive omissions or faults in art and nature, and with a true taste, while he praises and rejoices over and receives into his soul the good, and becomes noble and good, he will justly blame and hate the bad, now in the days of his youth, even before he is able to know the reason why; and when reason comes he will recognise and salute the friend with whom his education has made him long familiar.
                        Plato, *Republic,* III, 401B

3 *Socrates.* When a man allows music to play upon

him and to pour into his soul through the funnel of his ears those sweet and soft and melancholy airs . . . and his whole life is passed in warbling and the delights of song, in the first stage of the process the passion or spirit which is in him is tempered like iron, and made useful, instead of brittle and useless. But, if he carries on the softening and soothing process, in the next stage he begins to melt and waste, until he has wasted away his spirit and cut out the sinews of his soul.
                        Plato, *Republic,* III, 411A

4 *Socrates.* The State, if once started well, moves with accumulating force like a wheel. For good nurture and education implant good constitutions, and these good constitutions taking root in a good education improve more and more, and this improvement affects the breed in man as in other animals. . . .

This is the point to which, above all, the attention of our rulers should be directed—that music and gymnastic be preserved in their original form, and no innovation made. They must do their utmost to maintain them intact. And when any one says that mankind most regard

The newest song which the singers have,

they will be afraid that he may be praising, not new songs, but a new kind of song; and this ought not to be praised, or conceived to be the meaning of the poet; for any musical innovation is full of danger to the whole State, and ought to be prohibited. So Damon tells me, and I can quite believe him—he says that when modes of music change, the fundamental laws of the State always change with them.

Plato, *Republic,* IV, 424A

5 *Athenian Stranger.* We must assert that imitation is not to be judged of by pleasure and false opinion; and this is true of all equality, for the equal is not equal or the symmetrical symmetrical, because somebody thinks or likes something, but they are to be judged of by the standard of truth, and by no other whatever.

Cleinias. Quite true.

Ath. Do we not regard all music as representative and imitative?

Cle. Certainly.

Ath. Then, when any one says that music is to be judged of by pleasure, his doctrine cannot be admitted; and if there be any music of which pleasure is the criterion, such music is not to be sought out or deemed to have any real excellence, but only that other kind of music which is an imitation of the good.

Cle. Very true.

Ath. And those who seek for the best kind of song and music ought not to seek for that which is pleasant, but for that which is true; and the truth of imitation consists, as we were saying, in rendering the thing imitated according to quantity and quality.

Plato, *Laws,* II, 667B

6 Our fathers admitted music into education, not on the ground either of its necessity or utility, for it is not necessary, nor indeed useful in the same manner as reading and writing, which are useful in money-making, in the management of a household, in the acquisition of knowledge and in political life, nor like drawing, useful for a more correct judgement of the works of artists, nor again like gymnastic, which gives health and strength; for neither of these is to be gained from music. There remains, then, the use of music for intellectual enjoyment in leisure; which is in fact evidently the reason of its introduction, this being one of the ways in which it is thought that a freeman should pass his leisure.

Aristotle, *Politics,* 1338ª13

7 All men agree that music is one of the pleasantest things, whether with or without song. . . . Hence and with good reason it is introduced into social gatherings and entertainments, because it makes the hearts of men glad: so that on this ground alone we may assume that the young ought to be trained in it. For innocent pleasures are not only in harmony with the perfect end of life, but they also provide relaxation. And whereas men rarely attain the end, but often rest by the way and amuse themselves, not only with a view to a further end, but also for the pleasure's sake, it may be well at times to let them find a refreshment in music. It sometimes happens that men make amusement the end, for the end probably contains some element of pleasure, though not any ordinary or lower pleasure; but they mistake the lower for the higher, and in seeking for the one find the other, since every pleasure has a likeness to the end of action. For the end is not eligible for the sake of any future good, nor do the pleasures which we have described exist for the sake of any future good but of the past; that is to say, they are the alleviation of past toils and pains. And we may infer this to be the reason why men seek happiness from these pleasures. But music is pursued, not only as an alleviation of past toil, but also as providing recreation. And who can say whether, having this use, it may not also have a nobler one? In addition to this common pleasure, felt and shared in by all (for the pleasure given by music is natural, and therefore adapted to all ages and characters), may it not have also some influence over the character and the soul? It must have such an influence if characters are affected by it. And that they are so affected is proved in many ways, and not least by the power which the songs of Olympus exercise; for beyond question they inspire enthusiasm, and enthusiasm is an emotion of the ethical part of the soul. Besides, when men hear imitations, even apart from the rhythms and tunes themselves, their feelings move in sympathy. Since then music is a pleasure, and virtue consists in rejoicing and loving and hating aright, there is clearly nothing which we are so much concerned to acquire and to cultivate as the power of forming right judgments, and of taking delight in good dispositions and noble actions. Rhythm and melody supply imitations of anger and gentleness, and also of courage and temperance, and of all the qualities contrary to these, and of the other qualities of character, which hardly fall short of the actual affections, as we know from our own experience, for in listening to such strains our souls undergo a change. The habit of feeling pleasure or pain at mere representations is not far removed from the same feeling about realities. . . . The objects of no other sense, such as taste or touch, have any resemblance to moral qualities; in visible objects there is only a little, for there are figures which are of a moral character, but only to a slight extent, and all do not participate in the feeling about them. . . . On the other hand, even in mere melodies there is an imitation of character. . . . Some of them make men sad and grave . . .

others enfeeble the mind . . . another, again, produces a moderate and settled temper. . . . Enough has been said to show that music has a power of forming the character, and should therefore be introduced into the education of the young. The study is suited to the stage of youth, for young persons will not, if they can help, endure anything which is not sweetened by pleasure, and music has a natural sweetness. There seems to be in us a sort of affinity to musical modes and rhythms, which makes some philosophers say that the soul is a tuning, others, that it possesses tuning.

Aristotle, *Politics,* 1339ᵇ20

8 And now we have to determine the question which has been already raised, whether children should be themselves taught to sing and play or not. Clearly there is a considerable difference made in the character by the actual practice of the art. It is difficult, if not impossible, for those who do not perform to be good judges of the performances of others. Besides, children should have something to do, and the rattle of Archytas, which people give to their children in order to amuse them and prevent them from breaking anything in the house, was a capital invention, for a young thing cannot be quiet. The rattle is a toy suited to the infant mind, and education is a rattle or a toy for children of a larger growth. We conclude then that they should be taught music in such a way as to become not only critics but performers.

Aristotle, *Politics,* 1340ᵇ20

9 There is a meaning . . . in the myth of the ancients, which tells how Athene invented the flute and then threw it away. It was not a bad idea of theirs, that the Goddess disliked the instrument because it made the face ugly; but with still more reason may we say that she rejected it because the acquirement of flute-playing contributes nothing to the mind, since to Athene we ascribe both knowledge and art.

Thus then we reject the professional instruments and also the professional mode of education in music (and by professional we mean that which is adopted in contests), for in this the performer practises the art, not for the sake of his own improvement, but in order to give pleasure, and that of a vulgar sort, to his hearers. For this reason the execution of such music is not the part of a freeman but of a paid performer, and the result is that the performers are vulgarized, for the end at which they aim is bad. The vulgarity of the spectator tends to lower the character of the music and therefore of the performers; they look to him—he makes them what they are, and fashions even their bodies by the movements which he expects them to exhibit.

Aristotle, *Politics,* 1341ᵇ2

10 Imitating with the mouth the clear notes of birds was in use long before men were able to sing in tune smooth-running verses and give pleasure to the ear. And the whistlings of the zephyr through the hollows of reeds first taught peasants to blow into hollow stalks. Then step by step they learned sweet plaintive ditties, which the pipe pours forth pressed by the fingers of the players, heard through pathless woods and forests and lawns, through the unfrequented haunts of shepherds and abodes of unearthly calm. These things would soothe and gratify their minds when sated with food; for then all things of this kind are welcome. Often therefore stretched in groups on the soft grass beside a stream of water under the boughs of a high tree at no great cost they would pleasantly refresh their bodies, above all when the weather smiled and the seasons of the year painted the green grass with flowers. Then went round the jest, the tale, the peals of merry laughter; for the peasant muse was then in its glory; then frolick mirth would prompt to entwine head and shoulders with garlands plaited with flowers and leaves, and to advance in the dance out of step and move the limbs clumsily and with clumsy foot beat mother earth; which would occasion smiles and peals of merry laughter, because all these things then from their greater novelty and strangeness were in high repute. And the wakeful found a solace for want of sleep in this, in drawing out a variety of notes and going through tunes and running over the reeds with curving lip; whence even at the present day watchmen observe these traditions and have lately learned to keep the proper tune; and yet for all this receive not a jot more of enjoyment, than erst the rugged race of sons of earth received.

Lucretius, *Nature of Things,* V

11 Pale Phœbe, drawn by verse, from heaven descends;
And Circe changed with charms Ulysses' friends.
Verse breaks the ground, and penetrates the brake,
And in the winding cavern splits the snake.
Verse fires the frozen veins.

Virgil, *Eclogues,* VIII

12 The musician we may think of as being exceedingly quick to beauty, drawn in a very rapture to it: somewhat slow to stir of his own impulse, he answers at once to the outer stimulus: as the timid are sensitive to noise so he to tones and the beauty they convey; all that offends against unison or harmony in melodies and rhythms repels him; he longs for measure and shapely pattern.

Plotinus, *First Ennead,* III, 1

13 It is the reasonless soul, not the will or wisdom, that is beguiled by music, a form of sorcery which raises no question, whose enchantment, indeed, is

welcomed, exacted, from the performers.

Plotinus, *Fourth Ennead,* IV, 40

14 Any skill which, beginning with the observation of the symmetry of living things, grows to the symmetry of all life, will be a portion of the Power There which observes and meditates the symmetry reigning among all beings in the Intellectual Kosmos. Thus all music—since its thought is upon melody and rhythm—must be the earthly representation of the music there is in the rhythm of the Ideal Realm.

Plotinus, *Fifth Ennead,* IX, 11

15 On the whole I am inclined—though I am not propounding any irrevocable opinion—to approve the custom of singing in church, that by the pleasure of the ear the weaker minds may be roused to a feeling of devotion. Yet whenever it happens that I am more moved by the singing than by the thing that is sung, I admit that I have grievously sinned, and then I should wish rather not to have heard the singing.

Augustine, *Confessions,* X, 33

16 I always loved music; whoso has skill in this art, is of a good temperament, fitted for all things. We must teach music in schools; a schoolmaster ought to have skill in music, or I would not regard him; neither should we ordain young men as preachers, unless they have been well exercised in music.

Luther, *Table Talk,* H838

17 *King Richard.*   Music do I hear?
Ha, ha! keep time: how sour sweet music is,
When time is broke and no proportion kept!
So is it in the music of men's lives.

Shakespeare, *Richard II,* V, v, 41

18 *Oberon.* My gentle Puck, come hither. Thou rememb'rest
Since once I sat upon a promontory,
And heard a mermaid on a dolphin's back
Uttering such dulcet and harmonious breath
That the rude sea grew civil at her song
And certain stars shot madly from their spheres,
To hear the sea-maid's music.
  Puck.   I remember.

Shakespeare, *Midsummer-Night's
Dream,* II, i, 148

19 *Theseus.* Go, one of you, find out the forester;
For now our observation is perform'd;
And since we have the vaward of the day,
My love shall hear the music of my hounds.
Uncouple in the western valley; let them go:
Dispatch, I say, and find the forester.

                              [*Exit an Attendant.*]
We will, fair queen, up to the mountain's top
And mark the musical confusion
Of hounds and echo in conjunction.

Hippolyta. I was with Hercules and Cadmus once,
When in a wood of Crete they bay'd the bear
With hounds of Sparta: never did I hear
Such gallant chiding; for, besides the groves,
The skies, the fountains, every region near
Seem'd all one mutual cry: I never heard
So musical a discord, such sweet thunder.
  The. My hounds are bred out of the Spartan kind,
So flew'd, so sanded, and their heads are hung
With ears that sweep away the morning dew;
Crook-knee'd, and dew-lapp'd like Thessalian bulls;
Slow in pursuit, but match'd in mouth like bells,
Each under each. A cry more tuneable
Was never holla'd to, nor cheer'd with horn,
In Crete, in Sparta, nor in Thessaly:
Judge when you hear.

Shakespeare, *Midsummer-Night's
Dream,* IV, i, 107

20 *Lorenzo.* The man that hath no music in himself,
Nor is not moved with concord of sweet sounds,
Is fit for treasons, stratagems and spoils;
The motions of his spirit are dull as night
And his affections dark as Erebus:
Let no such man be trusted. Mark the music.

Shakespeare, *Merchant of Venice,* V, i, 83

21 *Benedick.* Is it not strange that sheeps' guts should
hale souls out of men's bodies?

Shakespeare, *Much Ado
About Nothing,* II, iii, 61

22 *Duke.* If music be the food of love, play on;
Give me excess of it, that, surfeiting,
The appetite may sicken, and so die.

Shakespeare, *Twelfth Night,* I, i, 1

23 *Cleopatra.* Give me some music; music, moody food
Of us that trade in love.

Shakespeare, *Antony and Cleopatra,* II, v, 1

24 *Caliban.* Be not afeard; the isle is full of noises,
Sounds and sweet airs, that give delight and hurt not.
Sometimes a thousand twangling instruments
Will hum about mine ears, and sometimes voices
That, if I then had waked after long sleep,
Will make me sleep again; and then, in dreaming,
The clouds methought would open and show riches
Ready to drop upon me, that, when I waked,
I cried to dream again.

Shakespeare, *Tempest,* III, ii, 144

25 Music to hear, why hear'st thou music sadly?
Sweets with sweets war not, joy delights in joy.

Shakespeare, *Sonnet VIII*

26 Generally, music feedeth the disposition of spirit which it findeth.

Bacon, *Sylva Sylvarum*, II

27 Sure there is musick even in the beauty, and the silent note which Cupid strikes, far sweeter than the sound of an instrument. For there is a musick where ever there is a harmony, order or proportion; and thus far we may maintain the musick of the Sphears: for those well-ordered motions, and regular paces, though they give no sound unto the ear, yet to the understanding they strike a note most full of harmony.

Sir Thomas Browne, *Religio Medici*, II, 9

28 Ring out ye Crystall sphears,
Once bless our human ears,
(If ye have power to touch our senses so)
And let your silver chime
Move in melodious time;
And let the Base of Heav'ns deep Organ blow,
And with your ninefold harmony
Make up full consort to th'Angelike symphony.

For if such holy Song
Enwrap our fancy long,
Time will run back, and fetch the age of gold,
And speckl'd vanity
Will sicken soon and die,
And leprous sin will melt from earthly mould,
And Hell it self will pass away,
And leave her dolorous mansions to the peering day.

Milton, *On the Morning of Christs Nativity*, 125

29 Blest pair of *Sirens*, pledges of Heav'ns joy,
Sphear-born harmonious Sisters, Voice, and Vers,
Wed your divine sounds, and mixt power employ
Dead things with inbreath'd sense able to pierce,
And to our high-rais'd phantasie present,
That undisturbed Song of pure content,
Ay sung before the saphire-colour'd throne
To him that sits theron
With Saintly shout, and solemn Jubily,
Where the bright Seraphim in burning row
Their loud up-lifted Angel trumpets blow,
And the Cherubick host in thousand quires
Touch their immortal Harps of golden wires,
With those just Spirits that wear victorious Palms,
Hymns devout and holy Psalms
Singing everlastingly;
That we on Earth with undiscording voice
May rightly answer that melodious noise;
As once we did, till disproportion'd sin
Jarr'd against natures chime, and with harsh din
Broke the fair musick that all creatures made
To their great Lord, whose love their motion sway'd
In perfect Diapason, whilst they stood
In first obedience, and their state of good.

O may we soon again renew that Song,
And keep in tune with Heav'n, till God ere long
To his celestial consort us unite,
To live with him, and sing in endles morn of light.

Milton, *At a Solemn Musick*

30 And ever against eating Cares,
Lap me in soft *Lydian* Aires,
Married to immortal verse
Such as the meeting soul may pierce
In notes, with many a winding bout
Of lincked sweetnes long drawn out,
With wanton heed, and giddy cunning,
The melting voice through mazes running;
Untwisting all the chains that ty
The hidden soul of harmony.
That *Orpheus* self may heave his head
From golden slumber on a bed
Of heapt *Elysian* flowres, and hear
Such streins as would have won the ear
Of *Pluto,* to have quite set free
His half regain'd *Eurydice.*

Milton, *L'Allegro,* 135

31 Bid the soul of *Orpheus* sing
Such notes as warbled to the string,
Drew Iron tears down *Pluto's* cheek,
And made Hell grant what Love did seek.

Milton, *Il Penseroso,* 105

32 Such sweet compulsion doth in musick ly,
To lull the daughters of *Necessity,*
And keep unsteddy Nature to her law,
And the low world in measur'd motion draw
After the heavenly tune.

Milton, *Arcades,* 68

33 From harmony, from heavenly harmony
This universal frame began:
When Nature underneath a heap
Of jarring atoms lay,
And could not heave her head,
The tuneful voice was heard from high:
"Arise, ye more than dead."
Then cold, and hot, and moist, and dry,
In order to their stations leap,
And Music's power obey.
From harmony, from heavenly harmony
This universal frame began:
From harmony to harmony
Through all the compass of the notes it ran,
The diapason closing full in man.

Dryden, *A Song for St. Cecilia's Day*

34 *Almeria.* Music has charms to soothe a savage breast,
To soften rocks, or bend a knotted oak.
I've read that things inanimate have moved,
And, as with living souls, have been informed
By magic numbers and persuasive sound.

Congreve, *The Mourning Bride,* I, i

35 *Johnson.* There is nothing, I think, in which the power of art is shown so much as in playing on the fiddle. In all other things we can do something at first. Any man will forge a bar of iron, if you give him a hammer; not so well as a smith, but tolerably. A man will saw a piece of wood, and make a box, though a clumsy one; but give him a fiddle and a fiddlestick, and he can do nothing.

Boswell, *Life of Johnson (Apr. 15, 1773)*

36 In the evening our gentleman-farmer, and two others, entertained themselves and the company with a great number of tunes on the fiddle. Johnson desired to have "Let ambition fire thy mind," played over again, and appeared to give a patient attention to it; though he owned to me that he was very insensible to the power of musick. I told him, that it affected me to such a degree, as often to agitate my nerves painfully, producing in my mind alternate sensations of pathetick dejection, so that I was ready to shed tears; and of daring resolution, so that I was inclined to rush into the thickest part of the battle. "Sir, (said he,) I should never hear it, if it made me such a fool."

Boswell, *Life of Johnson (Sept. 23, 1777)*

37 Every expression in language has an associated tone suited to its sense. This tone indicates, more or less, a mode in which the speaker is affected, and in turn evokes it in the hearer also, in whom conversely it then also excites the idea which in language is expressed with such a tone. Further, just as modulation is, as it were, a universal language of sensations intelligible to every man, so the art of tone wields the full force of this language wholly on its own account, namely, as a language of the affections, and in this way, according to the law of association, universally communicates the aesthetic ideas that are naturally combined therewith. But, further, inasmuch as those aesthetic ideas are not concepts or determinate thoughts, the form of the arrangement of these sensations (harmony and melody), taking the place of the form of a language, only serves the purpose of giving an expression to the aesthetic idea of an integral whole of an unutterable wealth of thought that fills the measure of a certain theme forming the dominant affection in the piece. . . .

If . . . we estimate the worth of the fine arts by the culture they supply to the mind, and adopt for our standard the expansion of the faculties whose confluence, in judgement, is necessary for cognition, music, then, since it plays merely with sensations, has the lowest place among the fine arts—just as it has perhaps the highest among those valued at the same time for their agreeableness. Looked at in this light, it is far excelled by the formative arts. For, in putting the imagination into a play which is at once free and adapted to the understanding, they all the while carry on a serious business, since they execute a product which serves the concepts of understanding as a vehicle, permanent and appealing to us on its own account, for effectuating their union with sensibility, and thus for promoting, as it were, the urbanity of the higher powers of cognition. The two kinds of art pursue completely different courses. Music advances from sensations to indefinite ideas: formative art from definite ideas to sensations. The latter gives a lasting impression, the former one that is only fleeting. The former sensations imagination can recall and agreeably entertain itself with, while the latter either vanish entirely, or else, if involuntarily repeated by the imagination, are more annoying to us than agreeable. Over and above all this, music has a certain lack of urbanity about it. For owing chiefly to the character of its instruments, it scatters its influence abroad to an uncalled-for extent (through the neighbourhood), and thus, as it were, becomes obtrusive and deprives others, outside the musical circle, of their freedom. This is a thing that the arts that address themselves to the eye do not do, for if one is not disposed to give admittance to their impressions, one has only to look the other way.

Kant, *Critique of Aesthetic Judgement,* 53

38 Music . . . stands quite alone. It is cut off from all the other arts. . . . It does not express a particular and definite joy, sorrow, anguish, horror, delight, or mood of peace, but joy, sorrow, anguish, horror, delight, peace of mind *themselves,* in the abstract, in their essential nature, without accessories, and therefore without their customary motives. Yet it enables us to grasp and share them fully in this quintessence.

Schopenhauer, *The World as Will and Idea,*
Vol. I, 52

39 If it be . . . asked why musical tones in a certain order and rhythm give man and other animals pleasure, we can no more give the reason than for the pleasantness of certain tastes and smells. That they do give pleasure of some kind to animals, we may infer from their being produced during the season of courtship by many insects, spiders, fishes, amphibians, and birds; for unless the females were able to appreciate such sounds and were excited or charmed by them, the persevering efforts of the males, and the complex structures often possessed by them alone, would be useless; and this it is impossible to believe.

Human song is generally admitted to be the basis or origin of instrumental music. As neither the enjoyment nor the capacity of producing musical notes are faculties of the least use to man in reference to his daily habits of life, they must be ranked amongst the most mysterious with which he is endowed.

Darwin, *Descent of Man,* III, 19

40 The only one of the imaginative arts in which I had from childhood taken great pleasure, was music; the best effect of which (and in this it surpasses perhaps every other art) consists in exciting enthusiasm; in winding up to a high pitch those feelings of an elevated kind which are already in the character, but to which this excitement gives a glow and a fervour, which, though transitory at its utmost height, is precious for sustaining them at other times.

Mill, Autobiography, V

41 A terrible thing is music in general. What is it? Why does it do what it does? They say that music stirs the soul. Stupidity! A lie! It acts, it acts frightfully (I speak for myself), but not in an ennobling way. It acts neither in an ennobling nor a debasing way, but in an irritating way. How shall I say it? Music makes me forget my real situation. It transports me into a state which is not my own. Under the influence of music I really seem to feel what I do not feel, to understand what I do not understand, to have powers which I cannot have.

Tolstoy, The Kreutzer Sonata, XXIII

42 There is perhaps no emotion incident to human life that music cannot render in its abstract medium by suggesting the pang of it; though of course music cannot describe the complex situation which lends earthly passions their specific colour. The passions, as music renders them, are always general. But music has its own substitute for distinct representation. It makes feeling specific, nay, more delicate and precise than association with things could make it, by uniting it with musical form.

Santayana, Music

43 Music is . . . like mathematics, very nearly a world by itself; it contains a whole gamut of experience, from sensuous elements to ultimate intellectual harmonies. Yet this second existence, this life in music, is no mere ghost of the other; it has its own excitements, its quivering alternatives, its surprising turns; the abstract energy of it takes on so much body, that in progression or declension it seems quite as impassioned as any animal triumph or any moral drama.

That a pattering of sounds on the ear should have such moment is a fact calculated to give pause to those philosophers who attempt to explain consciousness by its utility, or who wish to make physical and moral processes march side by side from all eternity. Music is essentially useless, as life is: but both have an ideal extension which lends utility to its conditions.

Santayana, Life of Reason, IV, 4

16.6 | *Beauty and the Beautiful*

The word "aesthetics" that appears in the title of this chapter appears in very few of the passages assembled in this section. It is a very recent invention as a name for the branch of philosophy that deals with the appreciation of works of fine art and develops theories of sensible beauty and the criteria of the beautiful in both art and nature. Aesthetics, as a recognized branch of philosophy, does not come into existence until the nineteenth century, but speculation concerning beauty begins with the Greeks and runs through the whole tradition of Western thought, in which it is accorded the status of membership in that familiar triad of fundamental values—the good, the true, and the beautiful.

The pivotal texts are those that attempt to define beauty and to distinguish it from, as well as relate it to, truth and goodness. The pivotal notions that enter into the definitions are such terms as desire and love, pleasure and interest, and knowledge or vision. And the pivotal questions raised are those that concern the objectivity and subjectivity of beauty—the sense in which it can be said to inhere in the object itself as an intrinsic excellence and the sense in which it can be said to exist in the eye of the beholder and to depend on his sensibility or taste. In this last connection, some of the passages here included might have been placed in the following section on CRITICISM AND THE STANDARDS OF TASTE, and passages placed there might have been included here.

The issue concerning the objectivity and subjectivity of beauty, if not resolved, is certainly surrounded by the divers point of view expressed; and a very close reading of the difficult passages taken from Aquinas and Kant may discover a resolution of the problem through an understanding of the relation between the degree of intrinsic ex-cellence possessed by a work of art and the degree of good taste possessed by the person who appreciates its beauty. This does not preclude the relativity of the appreciation of beauty to the sensibility of the person, nor the truth of the proposition *de gustibus non disputandum,* but it does challenge those who too simply identify the beautiful with what they happen to like.

Beauty or excellence in works of art, and especially in poetry, is touched on in other sections of this chapter, to which the reader should refer for a fuller treatment of the subject. The reader should also refer to the index under appropriate terms.

---

1 I am black, but comely, O ye daughters of Jerusalem, as the tents of Kedar, as the curtains of Solomon.

Song of Solomon 1:5

2 Behold, thou art fair, my love; behold, thou art fair; thou hast doves' eyes within thy locks: thy hair is as a flock of goats, that appear from mount Gĭl-ĕ-ăd.

Thy teeth are like a flock of sheep that are even shorn, which came up from the washing; whereof every one bear twins, and none is barren among them.

Thy lips are like a thread of scarlet, and thy speech is comely: thy temples are like a piece of a pomegranate within thy locks.

Thy neck is like the tower of David builded for an armoury, whereon there hang a thousand bucklers, all shields of mighty men.

Thy two breasts are like two young roes that are twins, which feed among the lilies.

Until the day break, and the shadows flee away, I will get me to the mountain of myrrh, and to the hill of frankincense.

Thou art all fair, my love; there is no spot in thee.

Song of Solomon 4:1–7

3 Now those who sat with Priam: Panthoös and Thymoites,

Lampos and Klytios, Hiketaon, scion of Ares,

with Antenor and Oukalegon, both men of good counsel:

these were seated by the Skaian gates, elders of the people.

Now through old age these fought no longer, yet were they excellent

speakers still, and clear, as cicadas who through the forest

settle on trees, to issue their delicate voice of singing.

Such were they who sat on the tower, chief men of the Trojans.

And these, as they saw Helen along the tower approaching,

murmuring softly to each other uttered their winged words:

"Surely there is no blame on Trojans and strong-greaved Achaians

if for long time they suffer hardship for a woman like this one.

Terrible is the likeness of her face to immortal goddesses.

Still, though she be such, let her go away in the ships, lest

she be left behind, a grief to us and our children."

Homer, *Iliad,* III, 146

4 He who is fair to look upon is good, and he who is good will soon be fair also.

Sappho, *Fragment*

5 *Socrates.* Beauty is certainly a soft, smooth, slippery thing, and therefore of a nature which easily slips in and permeates our souls. For I affirm that the good is the beautiful.

Plato, *Lysis,* 216B

6 *Socrates.* I have been speaking of the fourth and last kind of madness, which is imputed to him who, when he sees the beauty of earth, is transported with the recollection of the true beauty; he would like to fly away, but he cannot; he is like a bird fluttering and looking upward and careless of

the world below; and he is therefore thought to be mad. And I have shown this of all inspirations to be the noblest and highest and the offspring of the highest of him who has or shares in it, and that he who loves the beautiful is called a lover because he partakes of it. For, as has been already said, every soul of man has in the way of nature beheld true being; this was the condition of her passing into the form of man. But all souls do not easily recall the things of the other world; they may have seen them for a short time only, or they may have been unfortunate in their earthly lot, and, having had their hearts turned to unrighteousness through some corrupting influence, they may have lost the memory of the holy things which once they saw. Few only retain an adequate remembrance of them; and they, when they behold here any image of that other world, are rapt in amazement; but they are ignorant of what this rapture means, because they do not clearly perceive. For there is no light of justice or temperance or any of the higher ideas which are precious to souls in the earthly copies of them: they are seen through a glass dimly; and there are few who, going to the images, behold in them the realities, and these only with difficulty. There was a time when with the rest of the happy band they saw beauty shining in brightness,—we philosophers following in the train of Zeus, others in company with other gods; and then we beheld the beatific vision and were initiated into a mystery which may be truly called most blessed, celebrated by us in our state of innocence, before we had any experience of evils to come, when we were admitted to the sight of apparitions innocent and simple and calm and happy, which we beheld shining in pure light, pure ourselves and not yet enshrined in that living tomb which we carry about, now that we are imprisoned in the body, like an oyster in his shell. Let me linger over the memory of scenes which have passed away.

But of beauty, I repeat again that we saw her there shining in company with the celestial forms; and coming to earth we find her here too, shining in clearness through the clearest aperture of sense. For sight is the most piercing of our bodily senses; though not by that is wisdom seen; her loveliness would have been transporting if there had been a visible image of her, and the other ideas, if they had visible counterparts, would be equally lovely. But this is the privilege of beauty, that being the loveliest she is also the most palpable to sight. Now he who is not newly initiated or who has become corrupted, does not easily rise out of this world to the sight of true beauty in the other; he looks only at her earthly namesake, and instead of being awed at the sight of her, he is given over to pleasure, and like a brutish beast he rushes on to enjoy and beget; he consorts with wantonness, and is not afraid or ashamed of pursuing pleasure in violation of nature. But he whose initiation is recent, and who has been the spectator of many glories in the other world, is amazed when he sees any one having a godlike face or form, which is the expression of divine beauty; and at first a shudder runs through him, and again the old awe steals over him; then looking upon the face of his beloved as of a god he reverences him, and if he were not afraid of being thought a downright madman, he would sacrifice to his beloved as to the image of a god.

Plato, *Phaedrus,* 249B

7 *Diotima.* He who would proceed aright . . . should begin in youth to visit beautiful forms . . . and soon he will of himself perceive that the beauty of one form is akin to the beauty of another; and then if beauty of form in general is his pursuit, how foolish would he be not to recognize that the beauty in every form is one and the same! And when he perceives this he will abate his violent love of the one, which he will despise and deem a small thing, and will become a lover of all beautiful forms; in the next stage he will consider that the beauty of the mind is more honourable than the beauty of the outward form. So that if a virtuous soul have but a little comeliness, he will be content to love and tend him, and will search out and bring to the birth thoughts which may improve the young, until he is compelled to contemplate and see the beauty of institutions and laws, and to understand that the beauty of them all is of one family, and that personal beauty is a trifle; and after laws and institutions he will go on to the sciences, that he may see their beauty, being not like a servant in love with the beauty of one youth or man or institution, himself a slave mean and narrow-minded, but drawing towards and contemplating the vast sea of beauty, he will create many fair and noble thoughts and notions in boundless love of wisdom; until on that shore he grows and waxes strong, and at last the vision is revealed to him of a single science, which is the science of beauty everywhere.

Plato, *Symposium,* 210A

8 *Socrates.* Let me ask a question of you: When you speak of beautiful things, such as bodies, colours, figures, sounds, institutions, do you not call them beautiful in reference to some standard: bodies, for example, are beautiful in proportion as they are useful, or as the sight of them gives pleasure to the spectators; can you give any other account of personal beauty?

Polus. I cannot.

Soc. And you would say of figures or colours generally that they were beautiful, either by reason of the pleasure which they give, or of their use, or both?

Pol. Yes, I should.

Soc. And you would call sounds and music beautiful for the same reason?

Pol. I should.

Soc. Laws and institutions also have no beauty in them except in so far as they are useful or pleasant or both?

Pol. I think not.

Soc. And may not the same be said of the beauty of knowledge?

Pol. To be sure, Socrates; and I very much approve of your measuring beauty by the standard of pleasure and utility.

Soc. And deformity or disgrace may be equally measured by the opposite standard of pain and evil?

Pol. Certainly.

Soc. Then when of two beautiful things one exceeds in beauty, the measure of the excess is to be taken in one or both of these; that is to say, in pleasure or utility or both?

Pol. Very true.

Plato, *Gorgias,* 474B

9 Since the good and the beautiful are different (for the former always implies conduct as its subject, while the beautiful is found also in motionless things), those who assert that the mathematical sciences say nothing of the beautiful or the good are in error. For these sciences say and prove a great deal about them; if they do not expressly mention them, but prove attributes which are their results or their definitions, it is not true to say that they tell us nothing about them. The chief forms of beauty are order and symmetry and definiteness, which the mathematical sciences demonstrate in a special degree. And since these (e.g. order and definiteness) are obviously causes of many things, evidently these sciences must treat this sort of causative principle also (i.e. the beautiful) as in some sense a cause.

Aristotle, *Metaphysics,* 1078ª32

10 A nose which varies from the ideal of straightness to a hook or snub may still be of good shape and agreeable to the eye; but if the excess be very great, all symmetry is lost, and the nose at last ceases to be a nose at all on account of some excess in one direction or defect in the other; and this is true of every part of the human body.

Aristotle, *Politics,* 1309ᵇ23

11 To be beautiful, a living creature, and every whole made up of parts, must not only present a certain order in its arrangement of parts, but also be of a certain definite magnitude. Beauty is a matter of size and order, and therefore impossible either (1) in a very minute creature, since our perception becomes indistinct as it approaches instantaneity; or (2) in a creature of vast size—one, say, 1,000 miles long—as in that case, instead of the object being seen all at once; the unity and wholeness of it is lost to the beholder.

Aristotle, *Poetics,* 1450ᵇ34

12 There are two kinds of beauty. Loveliness is dominant in the one and dignity in the other. Of these two, we ought to consider loveliness the attribute of woman and dignity the attribute of man.

Cicero, *De Officiis,* I, 36

13 [*Cleopatra*] received several letters, both from Antony and from his friends, to summon her, but she took no account of these orders; and at last, as if in mockery of them, she came sailing up the river Cydnus, in a barge with gilded stern and outspread sails of purple, while oars of silver beat time to the music of flutes and fifes and harps. She herself lay all along under a canopy of cloth of gold, dressed as Venus in a picture, and beautiful young boys, like painted Cupids, stood on each side to fan her. Her maids were dressed like sea nymphs and graces, some steering at the rudder, some working at the ropes. The perfumes diffused themselves from the vessel to the shore, which was covered with multitudes, part following the galley up the river on either bank, part running out of the city to see the sight. The market-place was quite emptied, and Antony at last was left alone sitting upon the tribunal; while the word went through all the multitude, that Venus was come to feast with Bacchus, for the common good of Asia.

On her arrival, Antony sent to invite her to supper. She thought it fitter he should come to her; so, willing to show his good-humour and courtesy, he complied, and went. He found the preparations to receive him magnificent beyond expression, but nothing so admirable as the great number of lights; for on a sudden there was let down altogether so great a number of branches with lights in them so ingeniously disposed, some in squares, and some in circles, that the whole thing was a spectacle that has seldom been equalled for beauty. The next day, Antony invited her to supper, and was very desirous to outdo her as well in magnificence as contrivance; but he found he was altogether beaten in both, and was so well convinced of it that he was himself the first to jest and mock at his poverty of wit and his rustic awkwardness. She, perceiving that his raillery was broad and gross, and savoured more of the soldier than the courtier, rejoined in the same taste, and fell into it at once, without any sort of reluctance or reserve.

For her actual beauty, it is said, was not in itself so remarkable that none could be compared with her, or that no one could see her without being struck by it, but the contact of her presence, if you lived with her, was irresistible; the attraction of her person, joining with the charm of her conversation, and the character that attended all she said or did, was something bewitching.

Plutarch, *Antony*

14 A certain young man a rhetorician came to see

Epictetus, with his hair dressed more carefully than was usual and his attire in an ornamental style; whereupon Epictetus said: Tell me if you do not think that some dogs are beautiful and some horses, and so of all other animals. "I do think so," the youth replied. Are not then some men also beautiful and others ugly? "Certainly." Do we, then, for the same reason call each of them in the same kind beautiful, or each beautiful for something peculiar? And you will judge of this matter thus. Since we see a dog naturally formed for one thing, and a horse for another, and for another still, as an example, a nightingale, we may generally and not improperly declare each of them to be beautiful then when it is most excellent according to its nature; but since the nature of each is different, each of them seems to me to be beautiful in a different way. Is it not so? He admitted that it was. That then which makes a dog beautiful, makes a horse ugly; and that which makes a horse beautiful, makes a dog ugly, if it is true that their natures are different. "It seems to be so." For I think that what makes a pancratiast beautiful, makes a wrestler to be not good, and a runner to be most ridiculous; and he who is beautiful for the Pentathlon, is very ugly for wrestling. "It is so," said he. What, then, makes a man beautiful? Is it that which in its kind makes both a dog and a horse beautiful? "It is," he said. What then makes a dog beautiful? The possession of the excellence of a dog. And what makes a horse beautiful? The possession of the excellence of a horse. What then makes a man beautiful? Is it not the possession of the excellence of a man? And do you, then, if you wish to be beautiful, young man, labour at this, the acquisition of human excellence. But what is this? Observe whom you yourself praise, when you praise many persons without partiality: do you praise the just or the unjust? "The just." Whether do you praise the moderate or the immoderate? "The moderate." And the temperate or the intemperate? "The temperate." If, then, you make yourself such a person, you will know that you will make yourself beautiful: but so long as you neglect these things, you must be ugly, even though you contrive all you can to appear beautiful.

Epictetus, *Discourses*, III, 1

15 We ought to observe also that even the things which follow after the things which are produced according to nature contain something pleasing and attractive. For instance, when bread is baked some parts are split at the surface, and these parts which thus open, and have a certain fashion contrary to the purpose of the baker's art, are beautiful in a manner, and in a peculiar way excite a desire for eating. And again, figs, when they are quite ripe, gape open; and in the ripe olives the very circumstance of their being near to rottenness adds a peculiar beauty to the fruit. And the

ears of corn bending down, and the lion's eyebrows, and the foam which flows from the mouth of wild boars, and many other things—though they are far from being beautiful, if a man should examine them severally—still, because they are consequent upon the things which are formed by nature, help to adorn them, and they please the mind; so that if a man should have a feeling and deeper insight with respect to the things which are produced in the universe, there is hardly one of those which follow by way of consequence which will not seem to him to be in a manner disposed so as to give pleasure. And so he will see even the real gaping jaws of wild beasts with no less pleasure than those which painters and sculptors show by imitation; and in an old woman and an old man he will be able to see a certain maturity and comeliness; and the attractive loveliness of young persons he will be able to look on with chaste eyes; and many such things will present themselves, not pleasing to every man, but to him only who has become truly familiar with nature and her works.

Marcus Aurelius, *Meditations*, III, 2

16 Everything which is in any way beautiful is beautiful in itself, and terminates in itself, not having praise as part of itself. Neither worse then nor better is a thing made by being praised. I affirm this also of the things which are called beautiful by the vulgar, for example, material things and works of art. That which is really beautiful has no need of anything; not more than law, not more than truth, not more than benevolence or modesty. Which of these things is beautiful because it is praised, or spoiled by being blamed? Is such a thing as an emerald made worse than it was, if it is not praised? Or gold, ivory, purple, a lyre, a little knife, a flower, a shrub?

Marcus Aurelius, *Meditations*, IV, 20

17 We ourselves possess beauty when we are true to our own being; our ugliness is in going over to another order; our self-knowledge, that is to say, is our beauty; in self-ignorance we are ugly.

Plotinus, *Fifth Ennead*, VIII, 13

18 Beauty is that which irradiates symmetry rather than symmetry itself and is that which truly calls out our love.

Why else is there more of the glory of beauty upon the living and only some faint trace of it upon the dead, though the face yet retains all its fulness and symmetry? Why are the most living portraits the most beautiful, even though the others happen to be more symmetric? Why is the living ugly more attractive than the sculptured handsome? It is that the one is more nearly what we are looking for, and this because there is soul there, because there is more of the idea of the good, because there is some glow of the light of the good and this illumination awakens and lifts the soul and all that goes with it so that the whole man is won over to goodness, and in the fullest measure stirred to life.

Plotinus, *Sixth Ennead,* VII, 22

19 In writing to you, good friend, who are well skilled in culture, I need hardly premise in many words that sublimity is a certain consummateness and preeminence of phrase, and that the greatest poets and prose writers gained the first rank, and grasped an eternity of fame, by no other means than this. For what is out of the common leads an audience, not to persuasion, but to ecstasy. . . . The startling effect of the wonderful always and everywhere has the better of the merely persuasive and the merely pleasing; for to be persuaded depends, as a rule, on ourselves, but this other quality applies irresistible authority and force, and gets the better of all hearers. Inventive skill, orderly disposition of matter, we see struggling to appear as the effect, not of this or that thing, but of the whole tissue of the work in letters. But the sublime, shooting forth at the nick of time, scatters everything like a levin bolt and shows the whole power of the author at once.

Longinus, *On the Sublime,* I, 4

20 There is an appeal to the eye in beautiful things, in gold and silver and all such; the sense of touch has its own powerful pleasures; and the other senses find qualities in things suited to them. Worldly success has its glory, and the power to command and to overcome. . . . But in our quest of all these things, we must not depart from You, Lord, or deviate from Your Law. This life we live here below has its own attractiveness, grounded in the measure of beauty it has and its harmony with the beauty of all lesser things. The bond of human friendship is admirable, holding many souls as one. Yet in the enjoyment of all such things we commit sin if through immoderate inclination to them—for though they are good, they are of the lowest order of good—things higher and better are forgotten, even You, O Lord our God, and Your Truth and Your Law. These lower things have their delights but not such as my God has, for He made them all.

Augustine, *Confessions,* II, 5

21 But . . . I did not at that time know, and I was in love with those lower beauties. I was sinking into the very depths and I said to my friends: "Do we love anything save what is beautiful? What then is beautiful? and what is beauty? What is it that allures us and delights us in the things we love? Unless there were grace and beauty in them they could not possibly draw us to them." Looking deeper I saw that in things themselves we must distinguish between the beauty which belongs to the whole in itself, and the becomingness which

results from right relation to some other thing, as a part of the body to the whole body, or a shoe to the foot, and such like. This thought surged up into my mind from the very depths of my heart and I composed certain books *De Pulchro et Apto—* on the beautiful and the fitting—two books or three, I fancy; You know, O God, for I do not remember. I no longer have them. Somehow or other they have been lost.

Augustine, *Confessions,* IV, 13

22 My eyes love the diverse forms of beauty, brilliant and pleasing colors. Let these things not take possession of my soul; let God possess it, who made these things and made them exceedingly good: yet He is my good, not they. For they affect me in all the waking hours of every day, nor do I find any respite from them such as I do sometimes find in silence from all the voices of song. For light, the queen of colors, suffusing all the things I see whenever I am abroad in daylight, entices me as it flows before my sight in all its variousness, even though I am busy upon something else and not observing it. For it works its way into me with such power that if it is suddenly withdrawn, I desire it with great longing; and if it is absent too long, it saddens my mind. . . .

How innumerable are the things made by every kind of art and workmanship in clothes, shoes, vessels and such like, in pictures also and every kind of statue—far beyond necessary and moderate use and any meaning of devotion—that men have added for the delight of their eyes, going abroad from themselves after the things they have themselves made, interiorly abandoning Him by whom they were made and destroying what He made in them. But I, O my God and my Glory, I too utter a hymn to Thee and offer my praise as sacrifice to Him who sanctifies me: for all that loveliness which passes through men's minds into their skillful hands comes from that supreme loveliness which is above our souls, which my soul sighs for day and night. From the supreme beauty those who make and seek after exterior beauty derive the measure by which they judge of it, but not the measure by which it should be used. Yet this measure too is there, and they do not see it: for if they did they would not wander far from it, but would preserve their strength only for Thee and would not dissipate it upon delights that grow wearisome. But I, who speak thus and see thus, yet entangle my feet in these lower things of beauty; but Thou wilt pluck me forth, Lord, Thou wilt pluck me forth, because Thy mercy is before my eyes.

Augustine, *Confessions,* X, 34

23 Beauty and good in a subject are the same, for they are based upon the same thing, namely; the form; and consequently good is praised as beauty. But they differ logically, for good properly relates

to the appetite (good being what all things desire), and therefore it has the aspect of an end (for the appetite is a kind of movement towards a thing). On the other hand, beauty relates to the knowing power, for beautiful things are those which please when seen. Hence beauty consists in due proportion, for the senses delight in things duly proportioned, as in what is after their own kind—because even sense is a sort of reason, just as is every knowing power.

Aquinas, *Summa Theologica*, I, 5, 4

24 Beauty includes three conditions: integrity or perfection, since those things which are impaired are by the very fact ugly; due proportion or harmony; and lastly, brightness, or clarity, whence things are called beautiful which have an elegant colour.

Aquinas, *Summa Theologica*, I, 39, 8

25 Beauty . . . consists in a certain clarity and due proportion. Now each of these has its roots in the reason, because both the light that makes beauty seen, and the establishing of due proportion among things belong to reason. Hence since the contemplative life consists in an act of the reason, there is beauty in it *per se* and essentially; therefore it is written (Wis. 8.2) of the contemplation of wisdom: *I became a lover of her beauty.* On the other hand, beauty is in the moral virtues by participation, in so far that is as they share the order of reason; and above all is it in temperance, which restrains the concupiscences which especially darken the light of reason. Hence it is that the virtue of chastity most of all makes man apt for contemplation, since sexual pleasures most of all weigh the mind down to sensible objects.

Aquinas, *Summa Theologica*, II–II, 180, 2

26 Ptolemy, the son of Lagus, one day amongst the many spoils and booties, which by his victories he had acquired, presenting to the Egyptians, in the open view of the people, a Bactrian camel all black, and a party-coloured slave, in such sort, as that the one half of his body was black, and the other white, not in partition of breadth by the diaphragm, as was that woman consecrated to the Indian Venus, whom the Tyanean philosopher did see between the River Hydaspes and Mount Caucasus, but in a perpendicular dimension of altitude; which were things never before that seen in Egypt. He expected by the show of these novelties to win the love of the people. But what happened thereupon? At the production of the camel they were all affrighted, and offended at the sight of the party-coloured man—some scoffed at him as a detestable monster brought forth by the error of nature—in a word, of the hope which he had to please these Egyptians, and by such means to increase the affection which they naturally bore him, he was altogether frustrated and disappointed; understanding fully by their deportments, that

they took more pleasure and delight in things that were proper, handsome, and perfect, than in misshapen, monstrous, and ridiculous creatures.

Rabelais, *Gargantua and Pantagruel*, III, Prologue

27 As for bodily beauty, . . . it is likely that we know little about what beauty is in nature and in general, since to our own human beauty we give so many different forms. If there was any natural prescription for it, we should recognize it in common, like the heat of fire. We imagine its forms to suit our fancy. . . . The Indies paint it black and dusky, with large swollen lips and a wide flat nose. And they load the cartilage between the nostrils with big gold rings, to make it hang down to the mouth; as also the lower lip with large hoops enriched with precious stones, so that it falls down over their chin; and their charm is to show their teeth down to the base of the roots. In Peru, the biggest ears are the fairest, and they stretch them artificially as much as they can; and a man of this day says he saw in one oriental nation this care for enlarging them and loading them with heavy jewels in such favor, that time and again he could pass his arm, fully clothed, through the hole in an ear. Elsewhere there are nations that blacken their teeth with great care, and scorn to see white ones; elsewhere they stain them red.

Not only in the Basque country do women consider themselves more beautiful with heads shaven, but in plenty of other places, and what is more, in certain glacial countries, so Pliny says. Mexican women count among their beauties a small forehead; and whereas they trim their hair on all other parts of the body, on their forehead they cultivate it and increase it by art; and they have such great esteem for large breasts, that they aspire to be able to suckle their children over their shoulder. We would represent ugliness that way.

The Italians make beauty plump and massive, the Spaniards hollow and gaunt; and among us, one man makes it fair, the other dark; one soft and delicate, the other strong and vigorous; one demands daintiness and sweetness, another pride and majesty. Even as the preference in beauty, which Plato attributes to the spherical figure, the Epicureans give rather to the pyramidal or the square, and cannot swallow a god in the shape of a ball.

Montaigne, *Essays*, II, 12, Apology for Raymond Sebond

28 Beauty is a great recommendation in dealings with men; it is the prime means of conciliation between them, and there is no man so barbarous and surly as not to be somewhat struck by its charm. The body has a great part in our being, it holds a high rank in it; so its structure and composition are well worth consideration. Those who want to split up our two principal parts and se-

quester them from each other are wrong. On the contrary, we must couple and join them together again. We must order the soul not to draw aside and entertain itself apart, not to scorn and abandon the body (nor can it do so except by some counterfeit monkey trick), but to rally to the body, embrace it, cherish it, assist it, control it, advise it, set it right and bring it back when it goes astray; in short, to marry it and be a husband to it, so that their actions may appear not different and contrary, but harmonious and uniform.

Montaigne, *Essays*, II, 17, Of Presumption

29 The beauty of stature is the only beauty of men. Where smallness dwells, neither breadth and roundness of forehead, nor clarity and softness of eyes, nor the moderate form of the nose, nor small size of ears and mouth, nor regularity and whiteness of teeth, nor the smooth thickness of a beard brown as the husk of a chestnut, nor curly hair, nor proper roundness of head, nor freshness of color, nor a pleasant facial expression, nor an odorless body, nor just proportion of limbs, can make a handsome man.

Montaigne, *Essays*, II, 17, Of Presumption

30 I cannot say often enough how much I consider beauty a powerful and advantageous quality. Socrates called it "a short tyranny," and Plato, "the privilege of nature." We have no quality that surpasses it in credit. It holds the first place in human relations; it presents itself before the rest, seduces and prepossesses our judgment with great authority and a wondrous impression. Phryne would have lost her case even in the hands of an excellent attorney, if, opening her robe, she had not corrupted her judges by her dazzling beauty. And I find that Cyrus, Alexander, Caesar, those three masters of the world, did not forget beauty in carrying out their great affairs; nor did Scipio the Elder.

One and the same word in Greek embraces the beautiful and the good. And the Holy Ghost often calls good those whom it means to call beautiful. I would readily uphold the ranking of good things found in a song, taken from some ancient poet, which Plato says was widely known: health, beauty, riches.

Aristotle says that to the beautiful belongs the right to command, and that when there are any whose beauty approaches that of the images of the gods, veneration is likewise their due. To one who asked him why people frequented beautiful persons longer and more often, he said: "That question is proper only for a blind man." Most philosophers, and the greatest, paid for their schooling, and acquired wisdom, by the mediation and favor of their beauty.

Not only in the men who serve me, but also in animals, I consider it as within two fingers' breath of goodness.

Montaigne, *Essays*, III, 12, Of Physiognomy

31 *Biron.* Where is any author in the world
Teaches such beauty as a woman's eye?

Shakespeare, *Love's Labour's Lost*, IV, iii, 312

32 *Rosalind.* Beauty provoketh thieves sooner than gold.

Shakespeare, *As You Like It*, I, iii, 112

33 *Jaques.* If ladies be but young and fair,
They have the gift to know it.

Shakespeare, *As You Like It*, II, vii, 37

34 *Ophelia.* Could beauty, my lord, have better commerce than with honesty?
Hamlet. Ay, truly; for the power of beauty will sooner transform honesty from what it is to a bawd than the force of honesty can translate beauty into his likeness.

Shakespeare, *Hamlet*, III, i, 109

35 *Perdita.* Now, my fair'st friend,
I would I had some flowers o' the spring that might
Become your time of day; and yours, and yours,
That wear upon your virgin branches yet
Your maidenheads growing. O Proserpina,
For the flowers now, that frighted thou let'st fall
From Dis's waggon! daffodils,
That come before the swallow dares, and take
The winds of March with beauty; violets dim,
But sweeter than the lids of Juno's eyes
Or Cytherea's breath; pale primroses,
That die unmarried, ere they can behold
Bright Phœbus in his strength—a malady
Most incident to maids; bold oxlips and
The crown imperial; lilies of all kinds,
The flower-de-luce being one! O, these I lack,
To make you garlands of, and my sweet friend,
To strew him o'er and o'er!
Florizel. What, like a corse?
Per. No, like a bank for love to lie and play on;
Not like a corse; or if, not to be buried,
But quick and in mine arms. Come, take your flowers.
Methinks I play as I have seen them do
In Whitsun pastorals. Sure this robe of mine
Does change my disposition.
Flo. What you do
Still betters what is done. When you speak, sweet,
I'd have you do it ever. When you sing,
I'd have you buy and sell so, so give alms,
Pray so; and, for the ordering your affairs,
To sing them too. When you do dance, I wish you
A wave o' the sea, that you might ever do
Nothing but that; move still, still so,
And own no other function. Each your doing,
So singular in each particular,
Crowns what you are doing in the present deed,
That all your acts are queens.

Shakespeare, *Winter's Tale*, IV, iv, 112

36 From fairest creatures we desire increase
   That thereby beauty's rose might never die,
   But as the riper should by time decease,
   His tender heir might bear his memory.

                Shakespeare, *Sonnet I*

37 Shall I compare thee to a summer's day?
   Thou art more lovely and more temperate.
   Rough winds do shake the darling buds of May,
   And summer's lease hath all too short a date.
   Sometime too hot the eye of heaven shines,
   And often is his gold complexion dimm'd;
   And every fair from fair sometime declines,
   By chance, or nature's changing course, un-
     trimm'd;
   But thy eternal summer shall not fade
   Nor lose possession of that fair thou ow'st,
   Nor shall Death brag thou wand'rest in his shade
   When in eternal lines to time thou grow'st.

              Shakespeare, *Sonnet XVIII*

38 When in the chronicle of wasted time
   I see descriptions of the fairest wights,
   And beauty making beautiful old rhyme
   In praise of ladies dead and lovely knights,
   Then, in the blazon of sweet beauty's best,
   Of hand, of foot, of lip, of eye, of brow,
   I see their antique pen would have express'd
   Even such a beauty as you master now.

              Shakespeare, *Sonnet CVI*

39 That is the best part of beauty, which a picture cannot express; no nor the first sight of life. There is no excellent beauty that hath not some strangeness in the proportion. A man cannot tell whether Apelles or Albert Dürer were the more trifler; whereof the one would make a personage by geometrical proportions; the other, by taking the best parts out of divers faces, to make one excellent. Such personages, I think, would please nobody but the painter that made them. Not but I think a painter may make a better face than ever was; but he must do it by a kind of felicity (as a musician that maketh an excellent air in music) and not by rule. A man shall see faces, that if you examine them part by part, you shall find never a good; and yet altogether do well.

   If it be true that the principal part of beauty is in decent motion, certainly it is no marvel though persons in years seem many times more amiable . . . [autumn is the beauty of beauties]—for no youth can be comely but by pardon, and considering the youth as to make up the comeliness. Beauty is as summer fruits, which are easy to corrupt, and cannot last; and for the most part it makes a dissolute youth, and an age a little out of countenance; but yet certainly again, if it light well, it maketh virtue shine, and vices blush.

              Bacon, *Of Beauty*

40 *Comus.* List Lady be not coy, and be not cosen'd

With that same vaunted name Virginity,
Beauty is natures coyn, must not be hoorded,
But must be currant, and the good thereof
Consists in mutual and partak'n bliss,
Unsavoury in th'injoyment of it self
If you let slip time, like a neglected rose
It withers on the stalk with languish't head.
Beauty is natures brag, and must be shown
In courts, at feasts, and high solemnities
Where most may wonder at the workmanship;
It is for homely features to keep home,
They had their name thence; course complexions
And cheeks of sorry grain will serve to ply
The sampler, and to teize the huswifes wooll.
What need a vermeil-tinctured lip for that
Love-darting eyes, or tresses like the Morn?
There was another meaning in these gifts,
Think what, and be adviz'd, you are but young
   yet.

              Milton, *Comus*, 737

41 *Mirabell.* Nay, 'tis true: you are no longer handsome when you've lost your lover; your beauty dies upon the instant: for beauty is the lover's gift; 'tis he bestows your charms—your glass is all a cheat. The ugly and the old, whom the looking glass mortifies, yet after commendation can be flattered by it, and discover beauties in it: for that reflects our praises, rather than your face.

   Millamant. O, the vanity of these men! Fainall, d'ye hear him? If they did not commend us, we were not handsome! Now you must know they could not commend one, if one was not handsome. Beauty the lover's gift?—Lord, what is a lover, that it can give? Why, one makes lovers as fast as one pleases, and they live as long as one pleases, and they die as soon as one pleases: and then if one pleases one makes more.

         Congreve, *Way of the World*, II, v

42 Now the agonies which affected the mind of Sophia, rather augmented than impaired her beauty; for her tears added brightness to her eyes, and her breasts rose higher with her sighs. Indeed, no one hath seen beauty in its highest lustre who hath never seen it in distress.

            Fielding, *Tom Jones*, VII, 6

43 To say the truth, perfect beauty in both sexes is a more irresistible object than it is generally thought; for, notwithstanding some of us are contented with more homely lots, and learn by rote (as children to repeat what gives them no idea) to despise outside, and to value more solid charms; yet I have always observed, at the approach of consummate beauty, that these more solid charms only shine with that kind of lustre which the stars have after the rising of the sun.

            Fielding, *Tom Jones*, XVI, 9

44 No Dolphin came, no Nereid stirr'd:
    Nor cruel *Tom,* nor *Susan* heard.
        A Fav'rite has no friend!
    From hence, ye Beauties, undeceiv'd,
    Know, one false step is ne'er retriev'd,
        And be with caution bold.
    Not all that tempts your wand'ring eyes
    And heedless hearts, is lawful prize;
        Nor all, that glisters, gold.

                Gray, *Ode on the Death of a Favourite Cat*

45 Ask a toad what beauty is, the *to kalon?* He will
    answer you that it is his toad wife with two great
    round eyes issuing from her little head, a wide,
    flat mouth, a yellow belly, a brown back. Interro-
    gate a Guinea negro, for him beauty is a black
    oily skin, deep-set eyes, a flat nose. Interrogate the
    devil; he will tell you that beauty is a pair of
    horns, four claws and a tail. Consult, lastly, the
    philosophers, they will answer you with gibberish:
    they have to have something conforming to the
    arch-type of beauty in essence, to the *to kalon.*

                Voltaire, *Philosophical Dictionary:* Beauty

46 We then fell into a disquisition whether there is
    any beauty independent of utility. The General
    maintained there was not. Dr. Johnson main-
    tained that there was; and he instanced a coffee-
    cup which he held in his hand, the painting of
    which was of no real use, as the cup would hold
    the coffee equally well if plain; yet the painting
    was beautiful.

                Boswell, *Life of Johnson* (Mar. 31, 1772)

47 The beautiful is that which, apart from concepts,
    is represented as the object of a universal delight.
    . . . For where any one is conscious that his de-
    light in an object is with him independent of in-
    terest, it is inevitable that he should look on the
    object as one containing a ground of delight for all
    men. For, since the delight is not based on any
    inclination of the subject (or on any other deliber-
    ate interest), but the subject feels himself com-
    pletely free in respect of the liking which he ac-
    cords to the object, he can find as reason for his
    delight no personal conditions to which his own
    subjective self might alone be party. Hence he
    must regard it as resting on what he may also
    presuppose in every other person; and therefore
    he must believe that he has reason for demanding
    a similar delight from every one. Accordingly he
    will speak of the beautiful as if beauty were a
    quality of the object and the judgement logical
    (forming a cognition of the object by concepts of
    it); although it is only aesthetic, and contains
    merely a reference of the representation of the ob-
    ject to the subject; because it still bears this resem-
    blance to the logical judgement, that it may be
    presupposed to be valid for all men. But this uni-
    versality cannot spring from concepts. For from
    concepts there is no transition to the feeling of
    pleasure or displeasure (save in the case of pure
    practical laws, which, however, carry an interest
    with them; and such an interest does not attach to
    the pure judgement of taste). The result is that the
    judgement of taste, with its attendant con-
    sciousness of detachment from all interest, must
    involve a claim to validity for all men, and must
    do so apart from universality attached to objects,
    i.e., there must be coupled with it a claim to sub-
    jective universality.

                Kant, *Critique of Aesthetic Judgement*, 6

48 The most important and vital distinction between
    the sublime and the beautiful is certainly this:
    that if, as is allowable, we here confine our atten-
    tion in the first instance to the sublime in objects
    of nature (that of art being always restricted by
    the conditions of an agreement with nature), we
    observe that whereas natural beauty (such as is
    self-subsisting) conveys a finality in its form mak-
    ing the object appear, as it were, preadapted to
    our power of judgement, so that it thus forms of
    itself an object of our delight, that which, without
    our indulging in any refinements of thought, but,
    simply in our apprehension of it, excites the feel-
    ing of the sublime, may appear, indeed, in point
    of form to contravene the ends of our power of
    judgement, to be ill-adapted to our faculty of pre-
    sentation, and to be, as it were, an outrage on the
    imagination, and yet it is judged all the more sub-
    lime on that account.

    From this it may be seen at once that we ex-
    press ourselves on the whole inaccurately if we
    term any object of nature sublime, although we
    may with perfect propriety call many such objects
    beautiful. For how can that which is apprehended
    as inherently contra-final be noted with an ex-
    pression of approval? All that we can say is that
    the object lends itself to the presentation of a sub-
    limity discoverable in the mind. For the sublime,
    in the strict sense of the word, cannot be con-
    tained in any sensuous form, but rather concerns
    ideas of reason, which, although no adequate pre-
    sentation of them is possible, may be excited and
    called into the mind by that very inadequacy it-
    self which does admit of sensuous presentation.
    Thus the broad ocean agitated by storms cannot
    be called sublime. Its aspect is horrible, and one
    must have stored one's mind in advance with a
    rich stock of ideas, if such an intuition is to raise it
    to the pitch of a feeling which is itself sublime—
    sublime because the mind has been incited to
    abandon sensibility and employ itself upon ideas
    involving higher finality.

    Self-subsisting natural beauty reveals to us a
    technic of nature which shows it in the light of a
    system ordered in accordance with laws the prin-
    ciple of which is not to be found within the range
    of our entire faculty of understanding. This prin-
    ciple is that of a finality relative to the employ-
    ment of judgement in respect of phenomena

which have thus to be assigned, not merely to nature regarded as aimless mechanism, but also to nature regarded after the analogy of art. Hence it gives a veritable extension, not, of course, to our knowledge of objects of nature, but to our conception of nature itself—nature as mere mechanism being enlarged to the conception of nature as art—an extension inviting profound inquiries as to the possibility of such a form. But in what we are wont to call sublime in nature there is such an absence of anything leading to particular objective principles and corresponding forms of nature that it is rather in its chaos, or in its wildest and most irregular disorder and desolation, provided it gives signs of magnitude and power, that nature chiefly excites the ideas of the sublime. Hence we see that the concept of the sublime in nature is far less important and rich in consequences than that of its beauty. It gives on the whole no indication of anything final in nature itself, but only in the possible employment of our intuitions of it in inducing a feeling in our own selves of a finality quite independent of nature. For the beautiful in nature we must seek a ground external to ourselves, but for the sublime one merely in ourselves and the attitude of mind that introduces sublimity into the representation of nature. This is a very needful preliminary remark. It entirely separates the ideas of the sublime from that of a finality of nature, and makes the theory of the sublime a mere appendage to the aesthetic estimate of the finality of nature, because it does not give a representation of any particular form in nature, but involves no more than the development of a final employment by the imagination of its own representation.

Kant, *Critique of Aesthetic Judgement,* 23

49 There is no science of the beautiful, but only a critique. Nor, again, is there an elegant science, but only a fine art. For a science of the beautiful would have to determine scientifically, that is, by means of proofs, whether a thing was to be considered beautiful or not; and the judgement upon beauty, consequently, would, if belonging to science, fail to be a judgement of taste. As for a beautiful science—a science which, as such, is to be beautiful, is a nonentity.

Kant, *Critique of Aesthetic Judgement,* 44

50 Once the teleological estimate of nature, supported by the physical ends, actually presented to us in organic beings, has entitled us to form the idea of a vast system of natural ends, we may regard even natural beauty from this point of view, such beauty being an accordance of nature with the free play of our cognitive faculties as engaged in grasping and estimating its appearance. For then we may look upon it as an objective finality of nature in its entirety as a system of which man is a member. We may regard it as a favour that nature has extended to us, that besides giving us

what is useful it has dispensed beauty and charms in such abundance, and for this we may love it, just as we view it with respect because of its immensity, and feel ourselves ennobled by such contemplation—just as if nature had erected and decorated its splendid stage with this precise purpose in its mind.

Kant, *Critique of Teleological Judgement,* 67

51 *Faust.* Have I still eyes? Is Beauty's spring, outpouring,
Revealed most richly to my inmost soul?
My dread path brought me to this loftiest goal!
Void was the world and barred to my exploring!
What is it now since this my priesthood's hour?
Worth wishing for, firm-based, a lasting dower!
Vanish from me my every vital power
If I forsake thee, treacherous to my duty!
The lovely form that once my fancy captured,
That in the magic glass enraptured,
Was but a foam-born phantom of such beauty!—
To thee alone I render up with gladness
The very essence of my passion,
Fancy, desire, love, worship, madness!

Goethe, *Faust,* II, 1, 6487

52 *Chiron.*   Woman's beauty? That is not worth telling,
Too oft a rigid image do we see;
I praise alone a being welling
With love of life and gaiety.
Self-blest is beauty, cold and listless,
'Tis winsomeness that makes resistless.

Goethe, *Faust,* II, 2, 7399

53 *Chorus.* O lady glorious, do not disdain
Honoured possession of highest estate!
For to thee alone is the greatest boon given:
The fame of beauty transcending all else.
The hero's name resounds ere he comes,
Hence proudly he strides,
Yet bows at once the stubbornest man
At the throne of Beauty, the all-conquering.

Goethe, *Faust,* II, 3, 8516

54 *Phorkyas.* Old is the word, yet high and true remains the sense,
That Modesty and Beauty never, hand in hand,
Pursue their way along the verdant paths of earth.
Deep-rooted dwells in both of them an ancient hate,
That wheresoever on the way they chance to meet,
Each on the other turns her back in enmity.
Then each one hastens on with greater vehemence,
Modesty sad but Beauty insolent of mood,
Till Orcus' hollow night at last envelops them,
Unless old age has fettered them before that time.

Goethe, *Faust,* II, 3, 8754

55 *Lynceus.* Easy are the lord's commands,
    Child's-play to the servant's hands:
    Beauty in such fair excess
    Rules all wealth, rules blood no less.
    All the army now is tame,
    All the swords are blunt and lame.
    By this glorious form, behold!
    Even the sun seems faint and cold.
    By this wealth of loveliness
    All is empty nothingness.

             Goethe, *Faust*, II, 3, 9346

56 A marriageable girl, whose natural destiny is to
bear and suckle children, will not be beautiful
without the proper breadth of the pelvis and the
necessary fullness of the breasts.

        Goethe, *Conversations with Eckermann*
                      (Apr. 18, 1827)

57 She walks in beauty, like the night
    Of cloudless climes and starry skies;
    And all that's best of dark and bright
      Meet in her aspect and her eyes.

            Byron, *She Walks in Beauty*

58 O Attic shape! Fair attitude! with brede
    Of marble men and maidens overwrought,
    With forest branches and the trodden weed;
      Thou, silent form, dost tease us out of thought
    As doth eternity: Cold Pastoral!
      When old age shall this generation waste,
        Thou shalt remain, in midst of other woe
    Than ours, a friend to man, to whom thou
        say'st,
    'Beauty is truth, truth beauty,'—that is all
      Ye know on earth, and all ye need to know.

            Keats, *Ode on a Grecian Urn*

59 The voice I hear this passing night was heard
    In ancient days by emperor and clown:
    Perhaps the self-same song that found a path
      Through the sad heart of Ruth, when, sick for
        home,
      She stood in tears amid the alien corn;
        The same that oft-times hath
    Charm'd magic casements, opening on the
        foam
    Of perilous seas, in faery lands forlorn.

            Keats, *Ode to a Nightingale*

60 A thing of beauty is a joy for ever:
    Its loveliness increases; it will never
    Pass into nothingness; but still will keep
    A bower quiet for us, and a sleep
    Full of sweet dreams, and health, and quiet
      breathing.

            Keats, *Endymion*, I, 1

61 There is a beauty of a peculiar kind in women, in
which their countenance presents a transparency
of skin, a light and lovely roseate hue, which is
unlike the complexion of mere health and vital
vigor—a more refined bloom, breathed, as it were,
by the soul within—and in which the features, the
light of the eye, the position of the mouth, appear
soft, yielding, and relaxed. This almost unearthly
beauty is perceived in women in those days which
immediately succeed childbirth; when freedom
from the burden of pregnancy and the pains of
travail is added to the joy of soul that welcomes
the gift of a beloved infant. A similar tone of
beauty is seen also in women during the magical
somnambulic sleep, connecting them with a world
of superterrestrial beauty. A great artist (Scho-
reel) has moreover given this tone to the dying
Mary, whose spirit is already rising to the regions
of the blessed, but once more, as it were, lights up
her dying countenance for a farewell kiss. Such a
beauty we find also in its loveliest form in the
Indian world; a beauty of enervation in which all
that is rough, rigid, and contradictory is dissolved,
and we have only the soul in a state of emotion; a
soul, however, in which the death of free self-reli-
ant spirit is perceptible. For should we approach
the charm of this flower-life, a charm rich in
imagination and genius, in which its whole environment and all its relations are permeated by the
rose-breath of the soul, and the world is transformed into a garden of love—should we look at it
more closely, and examine it in the light of human dignity and freedom—the more attractive
the first sight of it had been, so much the more
unworthy shall we ultimately find it in every respect.

           Hegel, *Philosophy of History*, I, 2

62 It is true that in common life we are in the habit
of speaking of beautiful colour, a beautiful sky, a
beautiful river, and, moreover, of beautiful flowers, beautiful animals, and, above all, of beautiful
human beings. We will not just now enter into the
controversy how far such objects can justly have
the attribute of beauty ascribed to them. . . . We
may, however, begin at once by asserting that artistic beauty stands *higher* than nature. For the
beauty of art is the beauty that is born—born
again, that is—of the mind; and by as much as
the mind and its products are higher than nature
and its appearances, by so much the beauty of art
is higher than the beauty of nature.

           Hegel, *Philosophy of Fine Art*, I

63 The beauty of a work of art consists in the fact
that it holds up a clear mirror to certain ideas
inherent in the world in general; the beauty of a
work of poetic art in particular is that it renders
the ideas inherent in mankind, and thereby leads
it to a knowledge of these ideas. The means which
poetry uses for this end are the exhibition of significant characters and the invention of circumstances which will bring about significant situations, giving occasion to the characters to unfold

their peculiarities and show what is in them; so that by some such representation a clearer and fuller knowledge of the many-sided idea of humanity may be attained. Beauty, however, in its general aspect, is the inseparable characteristic of the idea when it has become known. In other words, everything is beautiful in which an idea is revealed, for to be beautiful means no more than clearly to express an idea.

Schopenhauer, *Interest and Beauty
in Works of Art*

64 We ascribe beauty to that which is simple; which has no superfluous parts; which exactly answers its end; which stands related to all things; which is the mean of many extremes.

Emerson, *Considerations by the Way*

65 Tell them, dear, that if eyes were made for seeing,
Then Beauty is its own excuse for being:
Why thou wert there, O rival of the rose!
I never thought to ask, I never knew:
But, in my simple ignorance, suppose
The self-same Power that brought me there
    brought you.

Emerson, *The Rhodora*

66 The perfection of a process—that is, its utility—is the better point of beauty about it.

Faraday, *Chemical History of a Candle*, I

67 The young woman was tall, with a figure of perfect elegance on a large scale. She had dark and abundant hair, so glossy that it threw off the sunshine with a gleam, and a face which, besides being beautiful from regularity of feature and richness of complexion, had the impressiveness belonging to a marked brow and deep black eyes. She was lady-like, too, after the manner of the feminine gentility of those days; characterized by a certain state and dignity, rather than by the delicate, evanescent, and indescribable grace, which is now recognized as its indication. And never had Hester Prynne appeared more lady-like, in the antique interpretation of the term, than as she issued from the prison. Those who had before known her, and had expected to behold her dimmed and obscured by a disastrous cloud, were astonished, and even startled, to perceive how her beauty shone out, and made a halo of the misfortune and ignominy in which she was enveloped. It may be true, that, to a sensitive observer, there was something exquisitely painful in it. Her attire, which, indeed, she had wrought for the occasion, in prison, and had modelled much after her own fancy, seemed to express the attitude of her spirit, the desperate recklessness of her mood, by its wild and picturesque peculiarity. But the point which drew all eyes, and, as it were, transfigured the wearer—so that both men and women, who had been familiarly acquainted with Hester Prynne,

were now impressed as if they beheld her for the first time—was that Scarlet Letter, so fantastically embroidered and illuminated upon her bosom. It had the effect of a spell, taking her out of the ordinary relations with humanity, and enclosing her in a sphere by herself.

Hawthorne, *Scarlet Letter*, II

68 Real strength never impairs beauty or harmony, but it often bestows it; and in everything impossingly beautiful, strength has much to do with the magic. Take away the tied tendons that all over seem bursting from the marble in the carved Hercules, and its charm would be gone. As devout Eckerman lifted the linen sheet from the naked corpse of Goethe, he was overwhelmed with the massive chest of the man, that seemed as a Roman triumphal arch. When Angelo paints even God the Father in human form, mark what robustness is there. And whatever they may reveal of the divine love in the Son, the soft, curled hermaphroditical Italian pictures, in which his idea has been most successfully embodied; these pictures, so destitute as they are of all brawniness, hint nothing of any power, but the mere negative, feminine one of submission and endurance, which on all hands it is conceded, form the peculiar practical virtues of his teachings.

Melville, *Moby Dick*, LXXXVI

69 With respect to the belief that organic beings have been created beautiful for the delight of man—a belief which it has been pronounced is subversive of my whole theory—I may first remark that the sense of beauty obviously depends on the nature of the mind, irrespective of any real quality in the admired object; and that the idea of what is beautiful is not innate or unalterable. We see this, for instance, in the men of different races admiring an entirely different standard of beauty in their women. If beautiful objects had been created solely for man's gratification, it ought to be shown that before man appeared, there was less beauty on the face of the earth than since he came on the stage. . . .

On the other hand, I willingly admit that a great number of male animals, as all our most gorgeous birds, some fishes, reptiles, and mammals, and a host of magnificently coloured butterflies, have been rendered beautiful for beauty's sake; but this has been effected through sexual selection, that is, by the more beautiful males having been continually preferred by the females, and not for the delight of man. So it is with the music of birds. We may infer from all this that a nearly similar taste for beautiful colours and for musical sounds runs through a large part of the animal kingdom. When the female is as beautifully coloured as the male, which is not rarely the case with birds and butterflies, the cause apparently lies in the colours acquired through sexual selection having been transmitted to both sexes, instead of to the males alone. How the sense of beauty in its simplest form—that is, the reception of a peculiar kind of pleasure from certain colours, forms, and sounds—was first developed in the mind of man and of the lower animals, is a very obscure subject. The same sort of difficulty is presented, if we enquire how it is that certain flavours and odours give pleasure, and others displeasure. Habit in all these cases appears to have come to a certain extent into play; but there must be some fundamental cause in the constitution of the nervous system in each species.

Darwin, *Origin of Species*, VI

70 Everyone who admits the principle of evolution, and yet feels great difficulty in admitting that female mammals, birds, reptiles, and fish, could have acquired the high taste implied by the beauty of the males, and which generally coincides with our own standard, should reflect that the nerve-cells of the brain in the highest as well as in the lowest members of the vertebrate series, are derived from those of the common progenitor of this great kingdom. For we can thus see how it has come to pass that certain mental faculties, in various and widely distinct groups of animals, have been developed in nearly the same manner and to nearly the same degree.

Darwin, *Descent of Man*, III, 21

71 I died for Beauty, but was scarce
Adjusted in the tomb
When one who died for Truth was lain
In an adjoining room.

He questioned softly "Why I failed"?
"For Beauty," I replied.
"And I for Truth. The two are one,
We brethren are," he said.

And so, as kinsmen met a night,
We talked between the rooms,
Until the moss had reached our lips
And covered up our names.

Emily Dickinson, *I Died for Beauty*

72 *Mitya.* Beauty is a terrible and awful thing! It is terrible because it has not been fathomed and never can be fathomed, for God sets us nothing but riddles. Here the boundaries meet and all contradictions exist side by side. I am not a cultivated man, brother, but I've thought a lot about this. It's terrible what mysteries there are! Too many riddles weigh men down on earth. We must solve them as we can, and try to keep a dry skin in the water. Beauty! I can't endure the thought that a man of lofty mind and heart begins with the ideal of the Madonna and ends with the ideal of Sodom. What's still more awful is that a man with the ideal of Sodom in his soul does not renounce

the ideal of the Madonna, and his heart may be on fire with that ideal, genuinely on fire, just as in his days of youth and innocence. Yes, man is broad, too broad, indeed. I'd have him narrower. The devil only knows what to make of it! What to the mind is shameful is beauty and nothing else to the heart. Is there beauty in Sodom? Believe me, that for the immense mass of mankind beauty is found in Sodom. Did you know that secret? The awful thing is that beauty is mysterious as well as terrible. God and the devil are fighting there and the battlefield is the heart of man. But a man always talks of his own ache. Listen, now to come to facts.

Dostoevsky, *Brothers Karamazov*, Pt. I, III, 3

73 He [Pierre] half rose, meaning to go round, but the aunt handed him the snuffbox, passing it across Hélène's back. Hélène stooped forward to make room, and looked round with a smile. She was, as always at evening parties, wearing a dress such as was then fashionable, cut very low at front and back. Her bust, which had always seemed like marble to Pierre, was so close to him that his shortsighted eyes could not but perceive the living charm of her neck and shoulders, so near to his lips that he need only have bent his head a little to have touched them. He was conscious of the warmth of her body, the scent of perfume, and the creaking of her corset as she moved. He did not see her marble beauty forming a complete whole with her dress, but all the charm of her body only covered by her garments. And having once seen this he could not help being aware of it, just as we cannot renew an illusion we have once seen through.

"So you have never noticed before how beautiful I am?" Hélène seemed to say. "You had not noticed that I am a woman? Yes, I am a woman who may belong to anyone—to you too," said her glance. And at that moment Pierre felt that Hélène not only could, but must, be his wife, and that it could not be otherwise.

Tolstoy, *War and Peace*, III, 1

74 The despairing, dejected expression of Natásha's face caught his [Prince Andrew's] eye. He recognized her, guessed her feelings, saw that it was her début, remembered her conversation at the window, and with an expression of pleasure on his face approached Countess Rostóva.

"Allow me to introduce you to my daughter," said the countess, with heightened color.

"I have the pleasure of being already acquainted, if the countess remembers me," said Prince Andrew with a low and courteous bow quite belying Perónskaya's remarks about his rudeness, and approaching Natásha he held out his arm to grasp her waist before he had completed his invitation. He asked her to waltz. That tremulous expression on Natásha's face, prepared either for despair or rapture, suddenly brightened into a happy, grateful, childlike smile.

"I have long been waiting for you," that frightened happy little girl seemed to say by the smile that replaced the threatened tears, as she raised her hand to Prince Andrew's shoulder. They were the second couple to enter the circle. Prince Andrew was one of the best dancers of his day and Natásha danced exquisitely. Her little feet in their white satin dancing shoes did their work swiftly, lightly, and independently of herself, while her face beamed with ecstatic happiness. Her slender bare arms and neck were not beautiful—compared to Hélène's her shoulders looked thin and her bosom undeveloped. But Hélène seemed, as it were, hardened by a varnish left by the thousands of looks that had scanned her person, while Natásha was like a girl exposed for the first time, who would have felt very much ashamed had she not been assured that this was absolutely necessary.

Prince Andrew liked dancing, and wishing to escape as quickly as possible from the political and clever talk which everyone addressed to him, wishing also to break up the circle of restraint he disliked, caused by the Emperor's presence, he danced, and had chosen Natásha because Pierre pointed her out to him and because she was the first pretty girl who caught his eye; but scarcely had he embraced that slender supple figure and felt her stirring so close to him and smiling so near him than the wine of her charm rose to his head, and he felt himself revived and rejuvenated when after leaving her he stood breathing deeply and watching the other dancers.

Tolstoy, *War and Peace*, VI, 16

75 What a strange illusion it is to suppose that beauty is goodness.

Tolstoy, *The Kreutzer Sonata*, V

76 The 'beautiful in itself' is not even a concept, merely a phrase. In the beautiful, man sets himself up as the standard of perfection; in select cases he worships himself in it. A species cannot do otherwise than affirm itself alone in this manner.

Nietzsche, *Twilight of the Idols:*
Expeditions of an Untimely Man

77 The æsthetic principles are at bottom such axioms as that a note sounds good with its third and fifth, or that potatoes need salt. We are once for all so made that when certain impressions come before our mind, one of them will seem to call for or repel the others as its companions. To a certain extent the principle of habit will explain these æsthetic connections. When a conjunction is repeatedly experienced, the cohesion of its terms grows grateful, or at least their disruption grows unpleasant. But to explain *all* æsthetic judgments in this way would be absurd; for it is notorious how seldom natural experiences come up to our æsthetic demands. Many of the so-called metaphysical principles are at bottom only expressions of æsthetic feeling. Nature is simple and invariable; makes no leaps, or makes nothing but leaps; is rationally intelligible; neither increases nor diminishes in quantity; flows from one principle, etc., etc.,—what do all such principles express save our sense of how pleasantly our intellect would feel if it had a Nature of that sort to deal with? The subjectivity of which feeling is of course quite compatible with Nature also turning out objectively to be of that sort, later on.

William James, *Psychology*, XXVIII

78 *Louis.* I know that in an accidental sort of way, struggling through the unreal part of life, I havn't always been able to live up to my ideal. But in my own real world I have never done anything wrong, never denied my faith, never been untrue to myself. I've been threatened and blackmailed and insulted and starved. But I've played the game. I've fought the good fight. And now it's all over, theres an indescribable peace. [*He feebly folds his hands and utters his creed*] I believe in Michael Angelo, Velasquez, and Rembrandt; in the might of design, the mystery of color, the redemption of all things by Beauty everlasting, and the message of Art that has made these hands blessed. Amen.

Shaw, *Doctor's Dilemma*, IV

79 Truth derives [its] self-justifying power from its services in the promotion of Beauty. Apart from Beauty, Truth is neither good, nor bad.

Whitehead, *Adventures of Ideas*, XVIII, 2

80 The enjoyment of beauty produces a particular, mildly intoxicating kind of sensation. There is no very evident use in beauty; the necessity of it for cultural purposes is not apparent, and yet civilization could not do without it. The science of aesthetics investigates the conditions in which things are regarded as beautiful; it can give no explanation of the nature or origin of beauty; as usual, its lack of results is concealed under a flood of resounding and meaningless words.

Freud, *Civilization and Its Discontents*, II

81 There is an old formula for beauty in nature and art: Unity in variety. Everything depends upon how the preposition "in" is understood. There may be many articles in a box, many figures in a single painting, many coins in one pocket, and many documents in a safe. The unity is extraneous and the many are unrelated. The significant point is that unity and manyness are always of this sort or approximate it when the unity of the object or scene is morphological and static. The formula has meaning only when its terms are understood to concern a relation of energies. There is no fullness, no many parts, without distinctive differentiations. But they have esthetic quality, as in

the richness of a musical phrase, only when distinctions depend upon reciprocal resistances. There is unity only when the resistances create a suspense that is resolved through coöperative interaction of the opposed energies. The "one" of the formula is the realization through interacting parts of their respective energies. The "many" is the manifestation of the defined individualizations due to opposed forces that finally sustain a balance. Thus the next theme is the organization of energies in a work of art. For the unity in variety that characterizes a work of art is dynamic.

Dewey, *Art As Experience*, VII

82 Why should I blame her that she filled my days
With misery, or that she would of late
Have taught to ignorant men most violent ways,
Or hurled the little streets upon the great,
Had they but courage equal to desire?
What could have made her peaceful with a mind
That nobleness made simple as a fire,
With beauty like a tightened bow, a kind
That is not natural in an age like this,
Being high and solitary and most stern?
Why, what could she have done, being what she is?
Was there another Troy for her to burn?

Yeats, *No Second Troy*

83 This satisfaction of our reason, due to the harmony between our nature and our experience, is partially realised already. The sense of beauty is its realisation. When our senses and imagination find what they crave, when the world so shapes itself or so moulds the mind that the correspondence between them is perfect, then perception is pleasure, and existence needs no apology. The duality which is the condition of conflict disappears. There is no inward standard different from the outward fact with which that outward fact may be compared. A unification of this kind is the goal of our intelligence and of our affection, quite as much as of our æsthetic sense; but we have in those departments fewer examples of success. In the heat of speculation or of love there may come moments of equal perfection, but they are very

unstable. The reason and the heart remain deeply unsatisfied. But the eye finds in nature, and in some supreme achievements of art, constant and fuller satisfaction. For the eye is quick, and seems to have been more docile to the education of life than the heart or the reason of man, and able sooner to adapt itself to the reality. Beauty therefore seems to be the clearest manifestation of perfection, and the best evidence of its possibility. If perfection is, as it should be, the ultimate justification of being, we may understand the ground of the moral dignity of beauty. Beauty is a pledge of the possible conformity between the soul and nature, and consequently a ground of faith in the supremacy of the good.

Santayana, *Sense of Beauty*, IV

84 Such affinity as there is between truth and beauty has various sources. When the word truth is coloured idealistically, to mean the types or potential perfections of things, as when we speak of a true friend, evidently if this latent "truth" could only be brought out and raised to actual fact, it would also realize the beautiful. Love and charity are quick to perceive the latent perfections of the imperfect; and if we call this (perhaps imaginary) potentiality the truth, we indeed divine the principle of beauty also; of that beauty which the organic impulses of nature would bring to light if they had their way and did not interfere with one another. . . . Nature is necessarily full of beauties, since our faculties of perception and sympathy would not subsist if they were not adapted to the facts of nature; and the truth is necessarily satisfying, for the same reason. Yet nature is also full of ugly, cruel and horrible things, and the truth in many ways is desolating: because our nature, though sufficiently harmonious with the universe to exist within it, is nevertheless finite and specific, with essential interests which nature and truth at large cannot but disregard. The truth, then, is often, in many ways, interesting, beautiful and sublime: but it is not identical with beauty either in quality or extension or status.

Santayana, *Realm of Truth*, XII

16.7 | *Criticism and the Standards of Taste*

The passages assembled in this section are rather a mixed bag. Some are about critics as such, and express the dislike they evoke from the authors who are subject to their barbs. Some are about criticism as such; and some are examples of criticism. The one art that predominates in all these texts is literature; yet, perhaps, the points made can be generalized by the reader so that he sees their applicability to other arts, at least to the extent of understanding that a critical as contrasted with an uncritical appreciation of any work of art involves an appeal to principles or criteria that have something to do with the excellence of the work being considered.

This obviously leads to questions already mentioned in connection with beauty—questions about taste as responsive to the characteristics of the work being appreciated, about the distinction between good and bad taste, and about the process by which good taste is cultivated. The quotations that bear on these questions should be related by the reader to the passages in the preceding section that are concerned with the objectivity and subjectivity of beauty.

There are a few passages that deal with style—both in literature and in life. They are placed here because of the relation of differences in style to differences in taste.

For passages that might have appeared here instead of in other sections of this chapter, or in other chapters, the reader should consult the index under appropriate terms of interest.

---

1 *Socrates.* Then beauty of style and harmony and grace and good rhythm depend on simplicity—I mean the true simplicity of a rightly and nobly ordered mind and character, not that other simplicity which is only an euphemism for folly?

Very true, he [Glaucon] replied.

And if our youth are to do their work in life, must they not make these graces and harmonies their perpetual aim?

They must.

And surely the art of the painter and every other creative and constructive art are full of them—weaving, embroidery, architecture, and every kind of manufacture; also nature, animal and vegetable—in all of them there is grace or the absence of grace. And ugliness and discord and inharmonious motion are nearly allied to ill words and ill nature, as grace and harmony are the twin sisters of goodness and virtue and bear their likeness.

That is quite true, he said.

Plato, *Republic*, III, 400B

2 *Socrates.* This is the distinction which I draw between the sight-loving, art-loving, practical class and those of whom I am speaking, and who are alone worthy of the name of philosophers.

How do you distinguish them? he [Glaucon] said.

The lovers of sounds and sights, I replied, are, as I conceive, fond of fine tones and colours and forms and all the artificial products that are made out of them, but their mind is incapable of seeing or loving absolute beauty.

True, he replied.

Few are they who are able to attain to the sight of this.

Very true.

And he who, having a sense of beautiful things has no sense of absolute beauty, or who, if another lead him to a knowledge of that beauty is unable to follow—of such an one I ask, Is he awake or in a dream only? Reflect: is not the dreamer, sleeping or waking, one who likens dissimilar things, who puts the copy in the place of the real object?

I should certainly say that such an one was dreaming.

But take the case of the other, who recognises the existence of absolute beauty and is able to distinguish the idea from the objects which participate in the idea, neither putting the objects in the place of the idea nor the idea in the place of the objects—is he a dreamer, or is he awake?

He is wide awake.

Plato, *Republic*, V, 476A

3 *Athenian Stranger.* Are beautiful things not the same to us all, or are they the same in themselves, but not in our opinion of them? For no one will admit that forms of vice in the dance are more beautiful than forms of virtue, or that he himself delights in the forms of vice, and others in a muse of another character. And yet most persons say, that the excellence of music is to give pleasure to our souls. But this is intolerable and blasphemous; there is, however, a much more plausible account of the delusion.

Cleinias. What?

Ath. The adaptation of art to the characters of men. Choric movements are imitations of manners occurring in various actions, fortunes, dispositions—each particular is imitated, and those to whom the words, or songs, or dances are suited, either by nature or habit or both, cannot help feeling pleasure in them and applauding them, and calling them beautiful. But those whose natures, or ways, or habits are unsuited to them, cannot delight in them or applaud them, and they call them base. There are others, again, whose natures are right and their habits wrong, or whose habits are right and their natures wrong, and they praise one thing, but are pleased at another. For they say that all these imitations are pleasant, but not good. And in the presence of those whom they think wise, they are ashamed of dancing and singing in the baser manner, or of deliberately lending any countenance to such proceedings; and yet, they have a secret pleasure in them.

Plato, *Laws,* II, 655A

4 *Athenian Stranger.* The excellence of music is to be measured by pleasure. But the pleasure must not be that of chance persons; the fairest music is that which delights the best and best educated, and especially that which delights the one man who is pre-eminent in virtue and education. And therefore the judges must be men of character, for they will require both wisdom and courage; the true judge must not draw his inspiration from the theatre, nor ought he to be unnerved by the clamour of the many and his own incapacity; nor again, knowing the truth, ought he through cowardice and unmanliness carelessly to deliver a lying judgment, with the very same lips which have just appealed to the Gods before he judged. He is sitting not as the disciple of the theatre, but, in his proper place, as their instructor, and he ought to be the enemy of all pandering to the pleasure of the spectators. The ancient and common custom of Hellas, which still prevails in Italy and Sicily, did certainly leave the judgment to the body of spectators, who determined the victor by show of hands. But this custom has been the destruction of the poets; for they are now in the habit of composing with a view to please the bad taste of their judges, and the result is that the spectators instruct themselves;—and also it has been the ruin

of the theatre; they ought to be having characters put before them better than their own, and so receiving a higher pleasure, but now by their own act the opposite result follows.

Plato, *Laws,* II, 658B

5 A master of any art avoids excess and defect, but seeks the intermediate and chooses this—the intermediate not in the object but relatively to us.

If it is thus, then, that every art does its work well—by looking to the intermediate and judging its works by this standard—so that we often say of good works of art that it is not possible either to take away or to add anything, implying that excess and defect destroy the goodness of works of art, while the mean preserves it; and good artists, as we say, look to this in their work.

Aristotle, *Ethics,* 1106^{b}5

6 The many are better judges than a single man of music and poetry; for some understand one part, and some another, and among them they understand the whole.

Aristotle, *Politics,* 1281^{b}7

7 What to one man is food, to another is rank poison.

Lucretius, *Nature of Things,* IV

8 Be not too rigidly censorious,
A string may jar in the best master's hand,
And the most skilful archer miss his aim;
But in a poem elegantly writ,
I will not quarrel with a slight mistake,
Such as our nature's frailty may excuse;
But he that hath been often told his fault,
And still persists, is as impertinent,
As a musician that will always play,
And yet is always out at the same note;
When such a positive abandon'd fop
(Among his numerous absurdities)
Stumbles upon some tolerable line,
I fret to see them in such company,
And wonder by what magic they came there.
But in long works sleep will sometimes surprise,
Homer himself hath been observ'd to nod.

Horace, *Ars Poetica*

9 All language demonstrates three kinds of excellence: correctness, precision, and elegance (for to speak with propriety, its highest quality, is usually included by writers under elegance). Language also has the same number of faults, and these are the opposites of the qualities just mentioned.

Quintilian, *Institutio Oratoria,* I, 5

10 I know that there are some writers who would gladly ignore the importance of composition altogether, because they contend that unpolished lan-

guage, presenting itself spontaneously, is more natural and manly. But if such writers actually contend that the natural is only that which has sprung from nature which preceded culture, then all oratory is at an end. . . .

As the current of a river is more forcible in a descending channel which offers no obstruction to its course, than amidst rocks that oppose the broken and struggling waters; so also language that is properly corrected and flows smoothly is preferable to that which is rugged and fragmentary. Why then should anyone think that vigor is diminished when attention is paid to beauty? Nothing attains its natural strength without art, and beauty always accompanies art.

Quintilian, *Institutio Oratoria,* IX, 4

11 Many people admire what is bad, but no one condemns what is good.

Quintilian, *Institutio Oratoria,* XII, 10

12 Beauty, unlike greatness, we regard as absolute and as a quality; "more beautiful" is the relative. Yet even the term "beautiful" may be attached to something which in a given relation may appear ugly: the beauty of man, for example, is ugliness when compared with that of the gods; "the most beautiful of monkeys," we may quote, "is ugly in comparison with any other type." Nonetheless, a thing is beautiful in itself; as related to something else it is either more or less beautiful.

Similarly, an object is great in itself, and its greatness is due, not to any external, but to its own participation in the Absolute Great.

Are we actually to eliminate the beautiful on the pretext that there is a more beautiful? No more then must we eliminate the great because of the greater; the greater can obviously have no existence whatever apart from the great, just as the more beautiful can have no existence without the beautiful.

Plotinus, *Sixth Ennead,* III, 11

13 Reason stands in different relations to the productions of art and to moral actions. In matters of art, reason is directed to a particular end, which is something devised by reason, while in moral matters, it is directed to the general end of all human life. Now a particular end is ordered to the general end. Since therefore sin is a departure from the order to the end . . . sin may occur in two ways in a production of art. First, by a departure from the particular end intended by the artist, and this sin will be proper to the art; for instance, if an artist produce a bad thing while intending to produce something good, or produce something good while intending to produce something bad. Secondly, by a departure from the general end of human life, and then he will be said to sin if he intend to produce a bad work, and does so in effect, so that another is thus deceived. But this sin is not proper to the artist as such, but as a man. Consequently for the former sin the artist is blamed as an artist, while for the latter he is blamed as a man. On the other hand, in moral matters, where we take into consideration the order of reason to the general end of human life, sin and evil are always due to a departure from the order of reason to the general end of human life. Therefore man is blamed for such a sin both as man and as a moral being. Hence the Philosopher [Aristotle] says that "in art, he who sins voluntarily is preferable"; but in prudence, as in the moral virtues, which prudence directs, he is less preferable.

Aquinas, *Summa Theologica,* I–II, 21, 2

14 Here is a wonder: we have many more poets than judges and interpreters of poetry. It is easier to create it than to understand it. On a certain low level it can be judged by precepts and by art. But the good, supreme, divine poetry is above the rules and reason.

Montaigne, *Essays,* I, 37, Of Cato the Younger

15 When I want to judge someone, I ask him how satisfied he is with himself, to what extent he is pleased with his words or his work. I want to get away from those fine excuses: "I did it in play . . . I was not an hour at it; I have not looked at it since." Well, then, I say, let us put these pieces aside, give me something that represents you fully, by which you would like to be measured. And then, what do you think is finest in your work? Is it this part or that? Is it the charm, or the matter, or the originality, or the judgment, or the knowledge? For I notice generally that people are as mistaken in judging their own work as that of others, not only because of the affection that is involved, but also because they have not the capacity to know and distinguish it for what it is. The work, by its own power and fortune, may second the workman beyond his inventiveness and knowledge and outstrip him. For my part, I do not judge the value of any other work less clearly than my own; and I place the *Essays* now low, now high, very inconsistently and uncertainly.

There are many books that are useful by reason of their subjects, from which the author derives no commendation; and there are good books, like good works, which shame the workman.

Montaigne, *Essays,* III, 8, Of the Art of Discussion

16 Though men in learned tongues do tie themselves to the ancient measures, yet in modern languages it seemeth to me as free to make new measures of verses as of dances: for a dance is a measured pace, as a verse is a measured speech. In these things the sense is better judge than the art.

Bacon, *Advancement of Learning,* Bk. II, XVI, 5

17 There is a certain standard of grace and beauty which consists in a certain relation between our nature, such as it is, weak or strong, and the thing which pleases us.

Whatever is formed according to this standard pleases us, be it house, song, discourse, verse, prose, woman, birds, rivers, trees, rooms, dress, etc. Whatever is not made according to this standard displeases those who have good taste.

And as there is a perfect relation between a song and a house which are made after a good model, because they are like this good model, though each after its kind; even so there is a perfect relation between things made after a bad model. Not that the bad model is unique, for there are many; but each bad sonnet, for example, on whatever false model it is formed, is just like a woman dressed after that model.

Nothing makes us understand better the ridiculousness of a false sonnet than to consider nature and the standard and, then, to imagine a woman or a house made according to that standard.

Pascal, *Pensées*, I, 32

18 Men consider all things as made for themselves, and call the nature of a thing, good, evil, sound, putrid, or corrupt, just as they are affected by it. For example, if the motion by which the nerves are affected by means of objects represented to the eye conduces to well-being, the objects by which it is caused are called beautiful; while those exciting a contrary motion are called deformed. Those things, too, which stimulate the senses through the nostrils are called sweet-smelling or thinking; those which act through the taste are called sweet or bitter, full-flavoured or insipid; those which act through the touch, hard or soft, heavy or light; those, lastly, which act through the ears are said to make a noise, sound, or harmony, the last having caused men to lose their senses to such a degree that they have believed that God even is delighted with it. Indeed, philosophers may be found who have persuaded themselves that the celestial motions beget a harmony. All these things sufficiently show that every one judges things by the constitution of his brain, or rather accepts the affections of his imagination in the place of things. It is not, therefore, to be wondered at, as we may observe in passing, that all those controversies which we see have arisen amongst men, so that at last scepticism has been the result. For although human bodies agree in many things, they differ in more, and therefore that which to one person is good will appear to another evil, that which to one is well arranged to another is confused, that which pleases one will displease another, and so on in other cases which I pass by both because we cannot notice them at length here, and because they are within the experience of every one. For every one has heard the expressions: So many heads, so many ways of thinking; Every one is satisfied with his own way of thinking; Differences of brains are not less common than differences of taste;—all which maxims show that men decide upon matters according to the constitution of their brains, and imagine rather than understand things.

Spinoza, *Ethics*, I, Appendix

19 Each Poet of inferior size
On you shall rail and criticize. . . .
So, Nat'ralists observe, a Flea
Hath smaller Fleas that on him prey,
And these have smaller Fleas to bite 'em,
And so proceed *ad infinitum:*
Thus ev'ry Poet in his Kind,
Is bit by him that comes behind.

Swift, *On Poetry: A Rhapsody*

20 Some have conceived it would be very expedient for the public good of learning that every true critic, as soon as he had finished his task assigned, should immediately deliver himself up to ratsbane, or hemp, or leap from some convenient altitude; and that no man's pretensions to so illustrious a character should by any means be received before that operation were performed.

Swift, *Tale of a Tub*, III

21 These reasonings will furnish us with an adequate definition of a true critic: that he is a discoverer and collector of writers' faults. Which may be farther put beyond dispute by the following demonstration:—That whoever will examine the writings in all kinds, wherewith this ancient sect has honoured the world, shall immediately find, from the whole thread and tenor of them, that the ideas of the authors have been altogether conversant and taken up with the faults, and blemishes, and oversights, and mistakes of other writers; and, let the subject treated on be whatever it will, their imaginations are so entirely possessed and replete with the defects of other pens, that the very quintessence of what is bad does of necessity distil into their own; by which means the whole appears to be nothing else but an abstract of the criticisms themselves have made.

Swift, *Tale of a Tub*, III

22 'Tis hard to say, if greater want of skill
Appear in writing or in judging ill;
But of the two less dangerous is the offense
To tire our patience than mislead our sense.
Some few in that, but numbers err in this,
Ten censure wrong for one who writes amiss;
A fool might once himself alone expose,
Now one in verse makes many more in prose.

Pope, *Essay on Criticism*, I, 1

23 Be Homer's works your study and delight,
Read them by day, and meditate by night;

Thence form your judgment, thence your maxims
   bring,
And trace the Muses upward to their spring.
Still with itself compared, his text peruse;
And let your comment be the Mantuan Muse.

              Pope, *Essay on Criticism*, I, 124

24 But most by numbers judge a poet's song,
And smooth or rough with them is right or wrong.
In the bright Muse though thousand charms con-
   spire,
Her voice is all these tuneful fools admire,
Who haunt Parnassus but to please their ear,
Not mend their minds; as some to church repair,
Not for the doctrine, but the music there.
These equal syllables alone require,
Though oft the ear the open vowels tire,
While expletives their feeble aid do join,
And ten low words oft creep in one dull line:
While they ring round the same unvaried chimes,
With sure returns of still expected rhymes;
Where'er you find "the cooling western breeze,"
In the next line, it "whispers through the trees";
If crystal streams "with pleasing murmurs creep,"
The reader's threatened (not in vain) with
   "sleep";
Then, at the last and only couplet fraught
With some unmeaning thing they call a thought,
A needless Alexandrine ends the song
That, like a wounded snake, drags its slow length
   along.
Leave such to tune their own dull rhymes, and
   know
What's roundly smooth or languishingly slow;
And praise the easy vigor of a line
Where Denham's strength and Waller's sweetness
   join.
True ease in writing comes from art, not chance,
As those move easiest who have learned to dance.
'Tis not enough no harshness gives offense,
The sound must seem an echo to the sense.
Soft is the strain when Zephyr gently blows,
And the smooth stream in smoother numbers
   flows;
But when loud surges lash the sounding shore,
The hoarse, rough verse should like the torrent
   roar.
When Ajax strives some rock's vast weight to
   throw,
The line too labors, and the words move slow;
Not so when swift Camilla scours the plain,
Flies o'er the unbending corn, and skims along the
   main.

              Pope, *Essay on Criticism*, II, 337

25 Ah, ne'er so dire a thirst of glory boast,
Nor in the critic let the man be lost!
Good nature and good sense must ever join;
To err is human, to forgive divine.

              Pope, *Essay on Criticism*, II, 522

26 The world have paid too great a compliment to
critics, and have imagined them men of much
greater profundity than they really are. From this
complacence, the critics have been emboldened to
assume a dictatorial power, and have so far succeeded, that they are now become the masters,
and have the assurance to give laws to those authors from whose predecessors they originally received them.

The critic, rightly considered, is no more than
the clerk, whose office it is to transcribe the rules
and laws laid down by those great judges whose
vast strength of genius hath placed them in the
light of legislators, in the several sciences over
which they presided. This office was all which the
critics of old aspired to; nor did they ever dare to
advance a sentence, without supporting it by the
authority of the judge from whence it was borrowed.

But in process of time, and in ages of ignorance,
the clerk began to invade the power and assume
the dignity of his master. The laws of writing were
no longer founded on the practice of the author,
but on the dictates of the critic. The clerk became
the legislator, and those very peremptorily gave
laws whose business it was, at first, only to transcribe them.

Hence arose an obvious, and perhaps an unavoidable error; for these critics being men of
shallow capacities, very easily mistook mere form
for substance. They acted as a judge would, who
should adhere to the lifeless letter of law, and reject the spirit. Little circumstances, which were
perhaps accidental in a great author, were by
these critics considered to constitute his chief merit, and transmitted as essentials to be observed by
all his successors. To these encroachments, time
and ignorance, the two great supporters of imposture, gave authority; and thus many rules for
good writing have been established, which have
not the least foundation in truth or nature; and
which commonly serve for no other purpose than
to curb and restrain genius, in the same manner
as it would have restrained the dancing-master,
had the many excellent treatises on that art laid it
down as an essential rule that every man must
dance in chains.

              Fielding, *Tom Jones*, V, 1

27 This word critic is of Greek derivation, and signifies judgment. Hence I presume some persons who
have not understood the original, and have seen
the English translation of the primitive, have concluded that it meant judgment in the legal sense,
in which it is frequently used as equivalent to condemnation.

I am rather inclined to be of that opinion, as
the greatest number of critics hath of late years
been found amongst the lawyers. Many of these
gentlemen, from despair, perhaps, of ever rising to
the bench in Westminster-hall, have placed themselves on the benches at the playhouse, where they

have exerted their judicial capacity, and have given judgment, i.e., condemned without mercy.

Fielding, *Tom Jones*, XI, 1

28 The great variety of Taste, as well as of opinion, which prevails in the world, is too obvious not to have fallen under every one's observation. Men of the most confined knowledge are able to remark a difference of taste in the narrow circle of their acquaintance, even where the persons have been educated under the same government, and have early imbibed the same prejudices. But those who can enlarge their view to contemplate distant nations and remote ages, are still more surprised at the great inconsistence and contrariety. We are apt to call *barbarous* whatever departs widely from our own taste and apprehension; but soon find the epithet of reproach retorted on us. And the highest arrogance and self-conceit is at last startled, on observing an equal assurance on all sides, and scruples, amidst such a contest of sentiment, to pronounce positively in its own favour.

Hume, *Of the Standard of Taste*

29 Though it be certain that beauty and deformity, more than sweet and bitter, are not qualities in objects, but belong entirely to the sentiment, internal or external, it must be allowed that there are certain qualities in objects which are fitted by nature to produce those particular feelings. Now, as these qualities may be found in a small degree, or may be mixed and confounded with each other, it often happens that the taste is not affected with such minute qualities, or is not able to distinguish all the particular flavours, amidst the disorder in which they are presented. Where the organs are so fine as to allow nothing to escape them, and at the same time so exact as to perceive every ingredient in the composition, this we call delicacy of taste, whether we employ these terms in the literal or metaphorical sense. Here then the general rules of beauty are of use, being drawn from established models, and from the observation of what pleases or displeases, when presented singly and in a high degree; and if the same qualities, in a continued composition, and in a smaller degree, affect not the organs with a sensible delight or uneasiness, we exclude the person from all pretensions to this delicacy.

Hume, *Of the Standard of Taste*

30 Though the principles of taste be universal, and nearly, if not entirely, the same in all men, yet few are qualified to give judgment on any work of art, or establish their own sentiment as the standard of beauty. The organs of internal sensation are seldom so perfect as to allow the general principles their full play, and produce a feeling correspondent to those principles. They either labour under some defect, or are vitiated by some disorder; and by that means excite a sentiment, which may be pronounced erroneous. When the critic has no delicacy, he judges without any distinction, and is only affected by the grosser and more palpable qualities of the object: the finer touches pass unnoticed and disregarded. Where he is not aided by practice, his verdict is attended with confusion and hesitation. Where no comparison has been employed, the most frivolous beauties, such as rather merit the name of defects, are the object of his admiration. Where he lies under the influence of prejudice, all his natural sentiments are perverted. Where good sense is wanting, he is not qualified to discern the beauties of design and reasoning, which are the highest and most excellent. Under some or other of these imperfections, the generality of men labour; and hence a true judge in the finer arts is observed, even during the most polished ages, to be so rare a character: strong sense, united to delicate sentiment, improved by practice, perfected by comparison, and cleared of all prejudice, can alone entitle critics to this valuable character; and the joint verdict of such, wherever they are to be found, is the true standard of taste and beauty.

Hume, *Of the Standard of Taste*

31 Grant me patience, just Heaven!——Of all the cants which are canted in the canting world—though the cant of hypocrites may be the worst—the cant of criticism is the most tormenting!

Sterne, *Tristram Shandy*, III, 12

32 I mentioned Mallet's tragedy of *Elvira,* which had been acted the preceding winter at Drurylane, and that the Honourable Andrew Erskine, Mr. Dempster, and myself, had joined in writing a pamphlet, entitled, *Critical Strictures,* against it. That the mildness of Dempster's disposition had, however, relented; and he had candidly said, "We have hardly a right to abuse this tragedy: for bad as it is, how vain should either of us be to write one not near so good." *Johnson.* "Why no, Sir; this is not just reasoning. You *may* abuse a tragedy, though you cannot write one. You may scold a carpenter who has made you a bad table, though you cannot make a table. It is not your trade to make tables."

Boswell, *Life of Johnson (June 25, 1763)*

33 Fielding being mentioned, Johnson exclaimed, "he was a blockhead"; and upon my expressing my astonishment at so strange an assertion, he said, "What I mean by his being a blockhead is that he was a barren rascal." *Boswell.* "Will you not allow, Sir, that he draws very natural pictures of human life?" *Johnson.* "Why, Sir, it is of very low life. Richardson used to say, that had he not known who Fielding was, he should have believed he was an ostler. Sir, there is more knowledge of the heart in one letter of Richardson's, than in all *Tom Jones.* I, indeed, never read *Joseph Andrews.*"

Erskine. "Surely, Sir, Richardson is very tedious." *Johnson.* "Why, Sir, if you were to read Richardson for the story, your impatience would be so much fretted that you would hang yourself. But you must read him for the sentiment, and consider the story as only giving occasion to the sentiment."

Boswell, *Life of Johnson (Apr. 6, 1772)*

34 Talking on the subject of taste in the arts, he said, that difference of taste was, in truth, difference of skill. *Boswell.* "But, Sir, is there not a quality called taste, which consists merely in perception or in liking? For instance, we find people differ much as to what is the best style of English composition. Some think Swift's the best; others prefer a fuller and grander way of writing." *Johnson.* "Sir, you must first define what you mean by style, before you can judge who has a good taste in style, and who has a bad. The two classes of persons whom you have mentioned don't differ as to good and bad. They both agree that Swift has a good neat style; but one loves a neat style, another loves a style of more splendour. In like manner, one loves a plain coat, another loves a laced coat; but neither will deny that each is good in its kind."

Boswell, *Life of Johnson (Apr. 19, 1772)*

35 We talked of the styles of different painters, and how certainly a connoisseur could distinguish them; I asked, if there was as clear a difference of styles in language as in painting, or even as in hand-writing, so that the composition of every individual may be distinguished? *Johnson.* "Yes. Those who have a style of eminent excellence, such as Dryden and Milton, can always be distinguished." I had no doubt of this, but what I wanted to know was, whether there was really a peculiar style to every man whatever, as there is certainly a peculiar hand-writing, a peculiar countenance, not widely different in many, yet always enough to be distinctive. . . . The Bishop thought not; and said, he supposed that many pieces in Dodsley's collection of poems, though all very pretty, had nothing appropriated in their style, and in that particular could not be at all distinguished. *Johnson.* "Why, Sir, I think every man whatever has a peculiar style, which may be discovered by nice examination and comparison with others: but a man must write a great deal to make his style obviously discernible."

Boswell, *Life of Johnson (Apr. 13, 1778)*

36 Everyone must allow that a judgement on the beautiful which is tinged with the slightest interest, is very partial and not a pure judgement of taste. One must not be in the least prepossessed in favour of the real existence of the thing, but must preserve complete indifference in this respect, in order to play the part of judge in matters of taste.

Kant, *Critique of Aesthetic Judgement, 2*

37 So far as the interest of inclination in the case of the agreeable goes, every one says "Hunger is the best sauce; and people with a healthy appetite relish everything, so long as it is something they can eat." Such delight, consequently, gives no indication of taste having anything to say to the choice. Only when men have got all they want can we tell who among the crowd has taste or not.

Kant, *Critique of Aesthetic Judgement, 5*

38 A principle of taste would mean a fundamental premiss under the condition of which one might subsume the concept of an object, and then, by a syllogism, draw the inference that it is beautiful. That, however, is absolutely impossible. For I must feel the pleasure immediately in the representation of the object, and I cannot be talked into it by any grounds of proof. Thus although critics, as Hume says, are able to reason more plausibly than cooks, they must still share the same fate. For the determining ground of their judgement they are not able to look to the force of demonstrations, but only to the reflection of the subject upon his own state (of pleasure or displeasure), to the exclusion of precepts and rules.

Kant, *Critique of Aesthetic Judgement, 34*

39 Taste is, in the ultimate analysis, a critical faculty that judges of the rendering of moral ideas in terms of sense (through the intervention of a certain analogy in our reflection on both); and it is this rendering also, and the increased sensibility, founded upon it, for the feeling which these ideas evoke (termed *moral sense*), that are the origin of that pleasure which taste declares valid for mankind in general and not merely for the private feeling of each individual. This makes it clear that the true propaedeutic for laying the foundations of taste is the development of moral ideas and the culture of the moral feeling. For only when sensibility is brought into harmony with moral feeling can genuine taste assume a definite unchangeable form.

Kant, *Critique of Aesthetic Judgement, 60*

40 Nothing is more common than for scholars to make a ridiculous figure, in regard to a question of beauty, beside cultured men of the world; and technical critics are especially the laughing-stock of connoisseurs. Their opinion, from exaggeration, crudeness, or carelessness guides them generally quite awry, and they can only devise a technical judgment, and not an aesthetical one, embracing the whole work, in which feeling should decide. If they would kindly keep to technicalities, they might still be useful, for the poet in moments of inspiration and readers under his spell are little inclined to consider details. But the spectacle which they afford us is only the more ridiculous inasmuch as we see these crude natures—with whom all labour and trouble only develop at the

most a particular aptitude—when we see them set up their paltry individualities as the representation of universal and complete feeling, and in the sweat of their brow pronounce judgment on beauty.

Schiller, *Simple and Sentimental Poetry*

41 *Manager.* Men come to look, to see they most prefer.
If, as they gaze, much is reeled off and spun,
So that the startled crowd gapes all it can,
A multitude you will at once have won;
You then will be a much-loved man.
You can compel the mass by mass alone;
Each in the end will seek out something as his own.
Bring much and you'll bring this or that to everyone
And each will leave contented when the play is done.
If you will give a piece, give it at once in pieces!
Ragout like this your fame increases.
Easy it is to stage, as easy to invent.
What use is it, a whole to fashion and present?
The Public still will pick it all to pieces.

Goethe, *Faust*, Prelude on the Stage, 90

42 We find . . . it is true, among all world-historical peoples, poetry, plastic art, science, even philosophy; but not only is there a diversity in style and bearing generally, but still more remarkably in subject-matter; and this is a diversity of the most important kind, affecting the rationality of that subject-matter. It is useless for a pretentious æsthetic criticism to demand that our good pleasure should not be made the rule for the matter—the substantial part of their contents—and to maintain that it is the beautiful form as such, the grandeur of the fancy, and so forth, which fine art aims at, and which must be considered and enjoyed by a liberal taste and cultivated mind. A healthy intellect does not tolerate such abstractions, and cannot assimilate productions of the kind above referred to. Granted that the Indian epopees might be placed on a level with the Homeric, on account of a number of those qualities of form—grandeur of invention and imaginative power, liveliness of images and emotions, and beauty of diction; yet the infinite difference of matter remains; consequently one of substantial importance and involving the interest of reason, which is immediately concerned with the consciousness of the idea of freedom, and its expression in individuals. There is not only a classical form, but a classical order of subject-matter; and in a work of art form and subject-matter are so closely united that the former can only be classical to the extent to which the latter is so. With a fantastical, indeterminate material—and rule is the essence of reason—the form becomes measure-

less and formless, or mean and contracted.

Hegel, *Philosophy of History*, Introduction, 3

43 Style is the physiognomy of the mind, and a safer index to character than the face. To imitate another man's style is like wearing a mask, which, be it never so fine, is not long in arousing disgust and abhorrence, because it is lifeless; so that even the ugliest living face is better. Hence those who write in Latin and copy the manner of ancient authors may be said to speak through a mask; the reader, it is true, hears what they say, but he cannot observe their physiognomy too; he cannot see their style.

Schopenhauer, *Style*

44 The taste for the beautiful, at least as far as female beauty is concerned, is not of a special nature in the human mind; for it differs widely in the different races of man, and is not quite the same even in the different nations of the same race. Judging from the hideous ornaments, and the equally hideous music admired by most savages, it might be urged that their æsthetic faculty was not so highly developed as in certain animals, for instance, as in birds. Obviously no animal would be capable of admiring such scenes as the heavens at night, a beautiful landscape, or refined music; but such high tastes are acquired through culture, and depend on complex associations; they are not enjoyed by barbarians or by uneducated persons.

Darwin, *Descent of Man*, I, 3

45 The senses of man and of the lower animals seem to be so constituted that brilliant colours and certain forms, as well as harmonious and rhythmical sounds, give pleasure and are called beautiful; but why this should be so we know not. It is certainly not true that there is in the mind of man any universal standard of beauty with respect to the human body. It is, however, possible that certain tastes may in the course of time become inherited, though there is no evidence in favour of this belief; and if so, each race would possess its own innate ideal standard of beauty. It has been argued that ugliness consists in an approach to the structure of the lower animals, and no doubt this is partly true with the more civilised nations, in which intellect is highly appreciated; but this explanation will hardly apply to all forms of ugliness. The men of each race prefer what they are accustomed to; they cannot endure any great change; but they like variety, and admire each characteristic carried to a moderate extreme. Men accustomed to a nearly oval face, to straight and regular features, and to bright colours, admire, as we Europeans know, these points when strongly developed. On the other hand, men accustomed to a broad face, with high cheek-bones, a depressed nose, and a black skin, admire these peculiarities when strongly marked. No doubt charac-

ters of all kinds may be too much developed for beauty. Hence a perfect beauty, which implies many characters modified in a particular manner, will be in every race a prodigy. As the great anatomist Bichat long ago said, if every one were cast in the same mould, there would be no such thing as beauty. If all our women were to become as beautiful as the Venus de' Medici, we should for a time be charmed; but we should soon wish for variety; and as soon as we had obtained variety, we should wish to see certain characters a little exaggerated beyond the then existing common standard.

Darwin, *Descent of Man,* III, 19

46 Taste is not only a part and an index of morality—it is the only morality. The first, and last, and closest trial question to any living creature is, "What do you like?" Tell me what you like, and I'll tell you what you are.

Ruskin, *The Crown of Wild Olive,* II

47 It is noticeable that the word *curiosity,* which in other languages is used in a good sense, to mean, as a high and fine quality of man's nature, just this disinterested love of a free play of the mind on all subjects, for its own sake,—it is noticeable, I say, that this word has in our language no sense of the kind, no sense but a rather bad and disparaging one. But criticism, real criticism, is essentially the exercise of this very quality. It obeys an instinct prompting it to try to know the best that is known and thought in the world, irrespectively of practice, politics, and everything of the kind; and to value knowledge and thought as they approach this best, without the intrusion of any other considerations whatever.

Arnold, *Function of Criticism at the Present Time*

48 Constantly in reading poetry, a sense for the best, the really excellent, and of the strength and joy to be drawn from it should be present in our minds and should govern our estimate of what we read. But this real estimate, the only true one, is liable to be superseded, if we are not watchful, by two other kinds of estimate, the historic estimate and the personal estimate, both of which are fallacious. A poet or a poem may count to us historically, they may count to us on grounds personal to ourselves, and they may count to us really. They may count to us historically. The course of development of a nation's language, thought, and poetry is profoundly interesting; and by regarding a poet's work as a stage in this course of development we may easily bring ourselves to make it of more importance as poetry than in itself it really is, we may come to use a language of quite exaggerated praise in criticizing it; in short, to overrate it. So arises in our poetic judgments the fallacy caused by the estimate which we may call historic. Then, again, a poet or a poem may count

to us on grounds personal to ourselves. Our personal affinities, likings, and circumstances have great power to sway our estimate of this or that poet's work, and to make us attach more importance to it as poetry than in itself it really possesses, because to us it is, or has been, of high importance. Here also we overrate the object of our interest, and apply to it a language of praise which is quite exaggerated. And thus we get the source of a second fallacy in our poetic judgments—the fallacy caused by an estimate which we may call personal.

Arnold, *Study of Poetry*

49 Over immense departments of our thought we are still, all of us, in the savage state. Similarity operates in us, but abstraction has not taken place. We know what the present case is like, we know what it reminds us of, we have an intuition of the right course to take, if it be a practical matter. But analytic thought has made no tracks, and we cannot justify ourselves to others. In ethical, psychological, and æsthetic matters, to give a clear reason for one's judgment is universally recognized as a mark of rare genius. The helplessness of uneducated people to account for their likes and dislikes is often ludicrous. Ask the first Irish girl why she likes this country better or worse than her home, and see how much she can tell you. But if you ask your most educated friend why he prefers Titian to Paul Veronese, you will hardly get more of a reply; and you will probably get absolutely none if you inquire why Beethoven reminds him of Michelangelo, or how it comes that a bare figure with unduly flexed joints, by the latter, can so suggest the moral tragedy of life. His thought obeys a *nexus,* but cannot name it. And so it is with all those judgments of *experts,* which even though unmotived are so valuable.

William James, *Psychology,* XXII

50 I remember seeing an English couple sit for more than an hour on a piercing February day in the Academy at Venice before the celebrated *Assumption* by Titian; and when I, after being chased from room to room by the cold, concluded to get into the sunshine as fast as possible and let the pictures go, but before leaving drew reverently near to them to learn with what superior forms of susceptibility they might be endowed, all I overheard was the woman's voice murmuring: "What a *deprecatory* expression her face wears! What *self-abnegation!* How *unworthy* she feels of the honor she is receiving!" Their honest hearts had been kept warm all the time by a glow of spurious sentiment that would have fairly made old Titian sick. Mr. Ruskin somewhere makes the (for him terrible) admission that religious people as a rule care little for pictures, and that when they do care for them they generally prefer the worst ones to the best. Yes! in every art, in every science, there is the

keen perception of certain relations being *right* or not, and there is the emotional flush and thrill consequent thereupon. And these are two things, not one. In the former of them it is that experts and masters are at home. The latter accompaniments are bodily commotions that they may hardly feel, but that may be experienced in their fulness by *crétins* and philistines in whom the critical judgment is at its lowest ebb.

William James, *Psychology,* XXV

51 In my own experience of the appreciation of poetry I have always found that the less I knew about the poet and his work, before I began to read it, the better.

T. S. Eliot, *Dante*

52 Every nation, every race, has not only its own creative, but its own critical turn of mind; and is even more oblivious of the shortcomings and limitations of its critical habits than of those of its creative genius.

T. S. Eliot, *Tradition and the Individual Talent*

53 No poet, no artist of any art, has his complete meaning alone. His significance, his appreciation is the appreciation of his relation to the dead poets and artists. You cannot value him alone; you must set him, for contrast and comparison, among the dead. I mean this as a principle of aesthetic, nor merely historical, criticism.

T. S. Eliot, *Tradition and the Individual Talent*

54 A musical education is necessary for musical judgment. What most people relish is hardly music; it is rather a drowsy revery relieved by nervous thrills.

Santayana, *Life of Reason,* IV, 4

Chapter 17

PHILOSOPHY, SCIENCE, and MATHEMATICS

Chapter 17 is divided into three sections: 17.1 PHILOSOPHY AND PHILOSOPHERS, 17.2 SCIENCE AND SCIENTIFIC METHOD, and 17.3 THE DISCIPLINE OF MATHEMATICS.

Of the three terms that constitute the title of this chapter, only one has sufficient clarity of meaning to need no comment. That is mathematics. The other two have been so variously used in the literature from which our quotations are taken that the reader needs some notification about the policy we have adopted in allocating passages to Section 17.1 or Section 17.2.

Until the end of the seventeenth century, and perhaps even well into the eighteenth, the same disciplines were often referred to as branches of philosophy or as particular sciences. On the one hand, physics, mathematics, and metaphysics or theology were called sciences, and so, too, were ethics, politics, and logic; yet these same disciplines were regarded as branches or divisions of philosophy. On the other hand, at the beginning of

the modern era, men who engaged in experimental inquiry or the empirical investigation of natural phenomena usually referred to themselves as "natural philosophers" rather than as "natural scientists," and used the word "philosophy" rather than the word "science" in the titles of their books.

It is only toward the end of the eighteenth century and since then that the word "science" has come to be used more and more restrictedly for disciplines the method of which involves special observational procedures and techniques of investigation, in addition to theorizing, mathematical formulations, and the construction of hypotheses. When used with this meaning, the word "science" cannot be applied to such disciplines as mathematics or logic, metaphysics, theology, or ethics. They can be called sciences only in the much broader sense of the word which connotes an organized body of knowledge or of theories involving systematic reasoning from principles to conclusions.

The restriction of the word "science" to experimental or empirical inquiries was accompanied by a restriction of the word "philosophy" to disciplines that, whether or not they appealed to experience in any way, did not engage in special efforts to investigate the phenomena by observational techniques of one sort or another. Students of nature employing the experimental method no longer call themselves "natural philosophers"; while those who speculate about the structure of nature and the order of the cosmos call themselves "philosophers of nature"; and those who develop theories about science itself call themselves "philosophers of science."

In view of these shifts in the meaning of the words, we have adopted the following policy. We have placed in Section 17.1 quotations that discuss philosophy in that restricted sense of the term which applies only to disciplines that do not employ special observational techniques; and we have done so whether or not the authors themselves used the word "science" in referring to these disciplines. Accordingly, Section 17.2 contains quotations that are relevant to science as an investigative enterprise involving methodical efforts to observe the phenomena, again whether or not the authors call themselves "philosophers" or refer to their work as "philosophy."

17.1 | *Philosophy and Philosophers*

As the title of this section indicates, the quotations included here deal either with the nature, scope, and value of philosophy as a discipline or with the character and the virtues or vices of the philosopher as a man. Only some of the passages that consider philosophy itself regard it as a body of knowledge, a mode of inquiry, an intellectual discipline or way of thinking; many of them speak of philosophy as a way of life, as a vocation that sets certain men apart from others, just as a religious vocation does. When philosophy is thus considered, the character of the philosopher as a man is inextricably connected with the manner of life he leads. To be philosophical in this sense is to take a certain attitude toward life or to adopt certain rules of conduct rather than to profess certain beliefs or to promulgate theories about the nature of things.

It is only in the latter sense that philosophy is the object of both praise and censure—accorded by some an honorable place in the sphere of human inquiry, and ridiculed by others as nothing but sham or pretension. Philosophy is not alone in this respect; other human undertakings or professions—law and medicine, for example—have been the objects of satirical attack or derisive comment. But philosophy is uniquely distinguished by the fact that many of its detractors, and often the most abusive, are persons who have called themselves or would be regarded as philosophers.

The reader will also find that the philosophers quoted seldom agree with one another about the definition of their subject, the scope of their discipline, the method to be employed by them, or the claims that can be made for their conclusions. Nor do they agree about whether it is necessary for a man to have certain moral virtues in order to be a philosopher; whether he is a man of wisdom or only a lover of or seeker after wisdom; and whether the history of philosophy shows evidence of any progress in the development of philosophical thought.

However, on three points, the reader will find a certain measure of agreement. One is that, whatever its positive values or contributions may be, philosophy does not build bridges, cure diseases, or result in new inventions: it has no technological applica-

tions whatsoever. A second point is the concern common among philosophers about the relation of their discipline to religion or theology, on the one hand, and to mathematics and science, on the other. Closely connected with that is the third point; namely, that philosophy, like religion and unlike the natural sciences and mathematics, extends beyond the consideration of what is to what ought to be—to considerations of good and evil, right and wrong, and the ultimate values that constitute the ends or objectives of human life.

---

1 Protagoras was the first to maintain that there are two sides to every question, opposed to each other, and he even argued in this fashion, being the first to do so. Furthermore he began a work thus: "Man is the measure of all things, of things that are that they are, and of things that are not that they are not." He used to say that soul was nothing apart from the senses . . . and that everything is true.

Diogenes Laertius, *Lives and Opinions
of Eminent Philosophers*, IX, 8

2 *Strepsiades.* Hallo! who's that? that fellow in the basket?
Student of Socrates. That's *he.*
St.   Who's *he?*
Stu.   Socrates.
St.   Socrates!
You sir, call out to him as loud as you can.
Stu. Call him yourself: I have not leisure now.
                    The machine swings Socrates *in.*
St.   Socrates! Socrates!
Sweet Socrates!
Socrates.   Mortal! why call'st thou me?
St. O, first of all, please tell me what you are doing.
So. I walk on air, and contem-plate the Sun.
St. O then from a basket you contemn the Gods,
And not from the earth, at any rate?
So.   Most true.
I could not have searched out celestial matters
Without suspending judgement, and infusing
My subtle spirit with the kindred air.
If from the ground I were to seek these things,
I could not find: so surely doth the earth
Draw to herself the essence of our thought.

Aristophanes, *Clouds,* 218

3 *Socrates.* The mind of the philosopher alone has

wings; and this is just, for he is always, according to the measure of his abilities, clinging in recollection to those things in which God abides, and in beholding which He is what He is. And he who employs aright these memories is ever being initiated into perfect mysteries and alone becomes truly perfect. But, as he forgets earthly interests and is rapt in the divine, the vulgar deem him mad, and rebuke him; they do not see that he is inspired.

Plato, *Phaedrus,* 249B

4 *Alcibiades.* I have been bitten by a more than viper's tooth; I have known in my soul, or in my heart, or in some other part, that worst of pangs—more violent in ingenuous youth than any serpent's tooth—the pang of philosophy, which will make a man say or do anything.

Plato, *Symposium,* 218A

5 *Socrates.* The lovers of knowledge are conscious that the soul was simply fastened and glued to the body—until philosophy received her, she could only view real existence through the bars of a prison, not in and through herself; she was wallowing in the mire of every sort of ignorance, and by reason of lust had become the principal accomplice in her own captivity. This was her original state; and then, as I was saying, and as the lovers of knowledge are well aware, philosophy, seeing how terrible was her confinement, of which she was to herself the cause, received and gently comforted her and sought to release her, pointing out that the eye and the ear and the other senses are full of deception, and persuading her to retire from them, and abstain from all but the necessary use of them, and be gathered up and collected into herself, bidding her trust in herself and her own pure apprehension of pure existence, and to mis-

trust whatever comes to her through other channels and is subject to variation; for such things are visible and tangible, but what she sees in her own nature is intelligible and invisible.

Plato, *Phaedo,* 82B

6 Let me [Socrates] next endeavour to show what is that fault in States which is the cause of their present maladministration, and what is the least change which will enable a State to pass into the truer form; and let the change, if possible, be of one thing only, or, if not, of two; at any rate, let the changes be as few and slight as possible.

Certainly, he [Glaucon] replied.

I think, I said, that there might be a reform of the State if only one change were made, which is not a slight or easy though still a possible one.

What is it? he said.

Now then, I said, I go to meet that which I liken to the greatest of the waves; yet shall the word be spoken, even though the wave break and drown me in laughter and dishonour; and do you mark my words.

Proceed.

I said: Until philosophers are kings, or the kings and princes of this world have the spirit and power of philosophy, and political greatness and wisdom meet in one, and those commoner natures who pursue either to the exclusion of the other are compelled to stand aside, cities will never have rest from their evils—no, nor the human race, as I believe—and then only will this our State have a possibility of life and behold the light of day. Such was the thought, my dear Glaucon, which I would fain have uttered if it had not seemed too extravagant; for to be convinced that in no other State can there be happiness private or public is indeed a hard thing.

Plato, *Republic,* V, 473A

7 Adeimantus, I [Socrates] said, the worthy disciples of philosophy will be but a small remnant: perchance some noble and well-educated person, detained by exile in her service, who in the absence of corrupting influences remains devoted to her; or some lofty soul born in a mean city, the politics of which he contemns and neglects; and there may be a gifted few who leave the arts, which they justly despise, and come to her—or peradventure there are some who are restrained by our friend Theages' bridle; for everything in the life of Theages conspired to divert him from philosophy; but ill-health kept him away from politics. My own case of the internal sign is hardly worth mentioning, for rarely, if ever, has such a monitor been given to any other man. Those who belong to this small class have tasted how sweet and blessed a possession philosophy is, and have also seen enough of the madness of the multitude; and they know that no politician is honest, nor is there any champion of justice at whose side they may fight

and be saved. Such an one may be compared to a man who has fallen among wild beasts—he will not join in the wickedness of his fellows, but neither is he able singly to resist all their fierce natures, and therefore seeing that he would be of no use to the State or to his friends, and reflecting that he would have to throw away his life without doing any good either to himself or others, he holds his peace, and goes his own way. He is like one who, in the storm of dust and sleet which the driving wind hurries along, retires under the shelter of a wall; and seeing the rest of mankind full of wickedness, he is content, if only he can live his own life and be pure from evil or unrighteousness, and depart in peace and good-will, with bright hopes.

Yes, he said, and he will have done a great work before he departs.

A great work—yes; but not the greatest, unless he find a State suitable to him; for in a State which is suitable to him, he will have a larger growth and be the saviour of his country, as well as of himself.

Plato, *Republic,* VI, 496A

8 *Socrates.* Wonder is the feeling of a philosopher, and philosophy begins in wonder.

Plato, *Theaetetus,* 155B

9 *Socrates.* I will illustrate my meaning, Theodorus, by the jest which the clever witty Thracian handmaid is said to have made about Thales, when he fell into a well as he was looking up at the stars. She said, that he was so eager to know what was going on in heaven, that he could not see what was before his feet. This is a jest which is equally applicable to all philosophers. For the philosopher is wholly unacquainted with his next-door neighbour; he is ignorant, not only of what he is doing, but he hardly knows whether he is a man or an animal; he is searching into the essence of man, and busy in enquiring what belongs to such a nature to do or suffer different from any other;—I think that you understand me, Theodorus?

Theodorus. I do, and what you say is true.

Soc. And thus, my friend, on every occasion, private as well as public, as I said at first, when he appears in a law-court, or in any place in which he has to speak of things which are at his feet and before his eyes, he is the jest, not only of Thracian handmaids but of the general herd, tumbling into wells and every sort of disaster through his inexperience. His awkwardness is fearful, and gives the impression of imbecility. When he is reviled, he has nothing personal to say in answer to the civilities of his adversaries, for he knows no scandals of any one, and they do not interest him; and therefore he is laughed at for his sheepishness; and when others are being praised and glorified, in the simplicity of his heart he cannot help going into fits of laughter, so that he seems to be a downright idiot. . . . But, O my friend, when he draws the other into upper air, and gets him out of his pleas and rejoinders into the contemplation of justice and injustice in their own nature and in their difference from one another and from all other things; or from the commonplaces about the happiness of a king or of a rich man to the consideration of government, and of human happiness and misery in general—what they are, and how a man is to attain the one and avoid the other—when that narrow, keen, little legal mind is called to account about all this, he gives the philosopher his revenge; for dizzied by the height at which he is hanging, whence he looks down into space, which is a strange experience to him, he being dismayed, and lost, and stammering broken words, is laughed at, not by Thracian handmaidens or any other uneducated persons, for they have no eye for the situation, but by every man who has not been brought up a slave.

Plato, *Theaetetus,* 174A

10 On my arrival [at Syracuse], I thought that first I must put to the test the question whether Dionysios had really been kindled with the fire of philosophy, or whether all the reports which had come to Athens were empty rumours. Now there is a way of putting such things to the test which is not to be despised and is well suited to monarchs, especially to those who have got their heads full of erroneous teaching, which immediately on my arrival I found to be very much the case with Dionysios. One should show such men what philosophy is in all its extent, what the range of studies is by which it is approached, and how much labour it involves. For the man who has heard this, if he has the true philosophic spirit and that godlike temperament which makes him akin to philosophy and worthy of it, thinks that he has been told of a marvellous road lying before him, that he must forthwith press on with all his strength, and that life is not worth living if he does anything else. After this he uses to the full his own powers and those of his guide in the path, and relaxes not his efforts, till he has either reached the end of the whole course of study or gained such power that he is not incapable of directing his steps without the aid of a guide. This is the spirit and these are the thoughts by which such a man guides his life, carrying out his work, whatever his occupation may be, but throughout it all ever cleaving to philosophy, and to such rules of diet in his daily life as will give him inward sobriety and therewith quickness in learning, a good memory, and reasoning power; the kind of life which is opposed to this he consistently hates. Those who have not the true philosophic temper, but a mere surface colouring of opinions penetrating, like sunburn, only skin deep, when they see how great the range of studies is, how much labour is involved in it, and how necessary to the

pursuit it is to have an orderly regulation of the daily life, come to the conclusion that the thing is difficult and impossible for them, and are actually incapable of carrying out the course of study; while some of them persuade themselves that they have sufficiently studied the whole matter and have no need of any further effort. This is the sure test and is the safest one to apply to those who live in luxury and are incapable of continuous effort; it ensures that such a man shall not throw the blame upon his teacher but on himself, because he cannot bring to the pursuit all the qualities necessary to it.

Plato, *Seventh Letter*

11 That it [philosophy] is not a science of production is clear even from the history of the earliest philosophers. For it is owing to their wonder that men both now begin and at first began to philosophize; they wondered originally at the obvious difficulties, then advanced little by little and stated difficulties about the greater matters, e.g. about the phenomena of the moon and those of the sun and of the stars, and about the genesis of the universe. And a man who is puzzled and wonders thinks himself ignorant (whence even the lover of myth is in a sense a lover of wisdom, for the myth is composed of wonders); therefore since they philosophized in order to escape from ignorance, evidently they were pursuing science in order to know, and not for any utilitarian end. And this is confirmed by the facts; for it was when almost all the necessities of life and the things that make for comfort and recreation had been secured, that such knowledge began to be sought. Evidently then we do not seek it for the sake of any other advantage; but as the man is free, we say, who exists for his own sake and not for another's, so we pursue this as the only free science, for it alone exists for its own sake. . . . All the sciences, indeed, are more necessary than this, but none is better.

Aristotle, *Metaphysics,* 982^{b}11

12 It is plain, then, that philosophic wisdom is scientific knowledge, combined with intuitive reason, of the things that are highest by nature. This is why we say Anaxagoras, Thales, and men like them have philosophic but not practical wisdom, when we see them ignorant of what is to their own advantage, and why we say that they know things that are remarkable, admirable, difficult, and divine, but useless; viz. because it is not human goods that they seek.

Aristotle, *Ethics,* 1141^{b}2

13 Where there is no contract of service, those who give up something for the sake of the other party cannot . . . be complained of (for that is the nature of the friendship of virtue), and the return to them must be made on the basis of their purpose

(for it is purpose that is the characteristic thing in a friend and in virtue). And so too, it seems, should one make a return to those with whom one has studied philosophy; for their worth cannot be measured against money, and they can get no honour which will balance their services, but still it is perhaps enough, as it is with the gods and with one's parents, to give them what one can.

Aristotle, *Ethics,* 1164^b33

14 The activity of philosophic wisdom is admittedly the pleasantest of virtuous activities; at all events the pursuit of it is thought to offer pleasures marvellous for their purity and their enduringness, and it is to be expected that those who know will pass their time more pleasantly than those who inquire. And the self-sufficiency that is spoken of must belong most to the contemplative activity. For while a philosopher, as well as a just man or one possessing any other virtue, needs the necessaries of life, when they are sufficiently equipped with things of that sort the just man needs people towards whom and with whom he shall act justly, and the temperate man, the brave man, and each of the others is in the same case, but the philosopher, even when by himself, can contemplate truth, and the better the wiser he is; he can perhaps do so better if he has fellow-workers, but still he is the most self-sufficient. And this activity alone would seem to be loved for its own sake; for nothing arises from it apart from the contemplating, while from practical activities we gain more or less apart from the action.

Aristotle, *Ethics,* 1177^a24

15 It is evident that the form of government is best in which every man, whoever he is, can act best and live happily. But even those who agree in thinking that the life of virtue is the most eligible raise a question, whether the life of business and politics is or is not more eligible than one which is wholly independent of external goods, I mean than a contemplative life, which by some is maintained to be the only one worthy of a philosopher. For these two lives—the life of the philosopher and the life of the statesman—appear to have been preferred by those who have been most keen in the pursuit of virtue, both in our own and in other ages. Which is the better is a question of no small moment; for the wise man, like the wise state, will necessarily regulate his life according to the best end.

Aristotle, *Politics,* 1324^a23

16 Let no one when young delay to study philosophy, nor when he is old grow weary of his study. For no one can come too early or too late to secure the health of his soul. And the man who says that the age for philosophy has either not yet come or has gone by is like the man who says that the age for happiness is not yet come to him, or has passed

away. Wherefore both when young and old a man must study philosophy, that as he grows old he may be young in blessings through the grateful recollection of what has been, and that in youth he may be old as well, since he will know no fear of what is to come. We must then meditate on the things that make our happiness, seeing that when that is with us we have all, but when it is absent we do all to win it.

Epicurus, *Letter to Menoeceus*

17 When human life to view lay foully prostrate upon earth crushed down under the weight of religion, who showed her head from the quarters of heaven with hideous aspect lowering upon mortals, a man of Greece [Epicurus] ventured first to lift up his mortal eyes to her face and first to withstand her to her face.

Lucretius, *Nature of Things,* I

18 Who is able with powerful genius to frame a poem worthy of the grandeur of the things and these discoveries? Or who is so great a master of words as to be able to devise praises equal to the deserts of him [Epicurus] who left to us such prizes won and earned by his own genius? None methinks who is formed of mortal body. For if we must speak as the acknowledged grandeur of the things itself demands, a god he was, a god, most noble Memmius, who first found out that plan of life which is now termed wisdom, and who by trained skill rescued life from such great billows and such thick darkness and moored it in so perfect a calm and in so brilliant a light. Compare the godlike discoveries of others in old times: Ceres is famed to have pointed out to mortals corn, and Liber the vine-born juice of the grape; though life might well have subsisted without these things, as we are told some nations even now live without them. But a happy life was not possible without a clean breast; wherefore with more reason this man is deemed by us a god, from whom come those sweet solaces of existence which even now are distributed over great nations and gently soothe men's minds. . . . He therefore who shall have subdued all these and banished them from the mind by words, not arms, shall he not have a just title to be ranked among the gods? And all the more so that he was wont to deliver many precepts in beautiful and godlike phrase about the immortal gods themselves and to open up by his teachings all the nature of things.

Lucretius, *Nature of Things,* V

19 Philosophy is the physician of the soul. It takes away a load of empty troubles, frees us from desires, and banishes fear.

Cicero, *Disputations,* II, 4

20 Anyone who considers the aspects of nature, the variety of life, and the weakness of humanity can-

not but be saddened by his reflections. Nevertheless he fulfills the task of wisdom, and in so doing he gains doubly. In his awareness of the vicissitudes of human life, he has discharged a peculiar obligation of philosophy. And in adversity he discovers a threefold remedy to aid his restoration. Because he has all along been aware of the possibility of mishap, he is less dismayed when it occurs. Second, he understands that the lot of man must be endured in a manly spirit. Third, he knows that guilt is the only evil; but no guilt accrues when the issue is one against which there are no guarantees.

Cicero, *Disputations,* III, 16

21 O philosophy, thou guide of life, explorer of the universe, and expeller of vice! Without thee, what would become of me and of the whole life of mankind? Thou hast begotten cities. Thou hast gathered together the scattered human race into the bonds of social life. Thou hast united them first in common dwelling places, then in marriage, and lastly in the bonds of a common literature and language. Thou hast revealed law. Thou hast been the teacher of morality and order. To thee I flee for refuge. I seek thine aid. I entrust myself to thee, as formerly by degrees, now wholly and entirely. One day well spent in accordance with thy lessons is preferable to an eternity committed to error. Whose aid are we to seek, if not thine? Thou hast freely granted us a peaceable life and destroyed the dread of death.

Cicero, *Disputations,* V, 2

22 Somehow or other no assertion is too ridiculous for some philosophers to make.

Cicero, *Divination,* II, 58

23 Philosophy is not an occupation of a popular nature, nor is it pursued for the sake of self-advertisement. Its concern is not with words, but with facts. It is not carried on with the object of passing the day in an entertaining sort of way and taking the boredom out of leisure. It moulds and builds the personality, orders one's life, regulates one's conduct, shows one what one should do and what one should leave undone, sits at the helm and keeps one on the correct course as one is tossed about in perilous seas. Without it no one can lead a life free of fear or worry. Every hour of the day countless situations arise that call for advice, and for that advice we have to look to philosophy.

Seneca, *Letters to Lucilius,* 16

24 What has the philosopher investigated? What has the philosopher brought to light? In the first place, truth and nature (having, unlike the rest of the animal world, followed nature with more than just a pair of eyes, things slow to grasp divinity); and secondly, a rule of life, in which he has brought life into line with things universal. And

he has taught us not just to recognize but to obey the gods, and to accept all that happens exactly as if it were an order from above. He has told us not to listen to false opinions, and has weighed and valued everything against standards which are true. He has condemned pleasures an inseparable element of which is subsequent regret, has commended the good things which will always satisfy, and for all to see has made the man who has no need of luck the luckiest man of all, and the man who is master of himself the master of all.

Seneca, *Letters to Lucilius,* 90

25 The life of a contemplative philosopher and that of an active statesman are, I presume, not the same thing; for the one merely employs, upon great and good objects of thought, an intelligence that requires no aid of instruments nor supply of any external materials; whereas the other, who tempers and applies his virtue to human uses, may have occasion for affluence, not as a matter of necessity, but as a noble thing.

Plutarch, *Pericles*

26 Many public ministers and philosophers came from all parts to visit him and congratulated him on his election, but contrary to his expectation, Diogenes of Sinope, who then was living at Corinth, thought so little of him, that instead of coming to compliment him, he never so much as stirred out of the suburb called the Cranium, where Alexander found him lying alone in the sun. When he saw so much company near him, he raised himself a little, and vouchsafed to look upon Alexander, and when he kindly asked him whether he wanted anything, "Yes," said he, "I would have you stand from between me and the sun." Alexander was so struck at this answer, and surprised at the greatness of the man, who had taken so little notice of him, that as he went away he told his followers, who were laughing at the moroseness of the philosopher, that if he were not Alexander, he would choose to be Diogenes.

Plutarch, *Alexander*

27 Of all the advantages that accrue from philosophy these I reckon the chiefest. To bear prosperity like a gentleman is the mark of a man, to deprecate envy the mark of a disciplined character, to rise superior to pleasure by reason the mark of a sage, to govern anger the mark of an extraordinary man. But as perfect men I regard those who are able to mingle and fuse political capacity with philosophy.

Plutarch, *Education of Children*

28 Observe, this is the beginning of philosophy, a perception of the disagreement of men with one another, and an inquiry into the cause of the disagreement, and a condemnation and distrust of that which only "seems," and a certain investiga-

tion of that which "seems" whether it "seems" rightly, and a discovery of some rule, as we have discovered a balance in the determination of weights, and a carpenter's rule in the case of straight and crooked things. This is the beginning of philosophy. "Must we say that all things are right which seem so to all?" And how is it possible that contradictions can be right? "Not all then, but all which seem to us to be right." How more to you than those which seem right to the Syrians? why more than what seem right to the Egyptians? why more than what seems right to me or to any other man? "Not at all more." What then "seems" to every man is not sufficient for determining what "is"; for neither in the case of weights or measures are we satisfied with the bare appearance, but in each case we have discovered a certain rule. In this matter then is there no rule superior to what "seems?" And how is it possible that the most necessary things among men should have no sign, and be incapable of being discovered? There is then some rule. And why then do we not seek the rule and discover it, and afterward use it without varying from it, not even stretching out the finger without it? For this, I think, is that which when it is discovered cures of their madness those who use mere "seeming" as a measure, and misuse it; so that for the future proceeding from certain things known and made clear we may use in the case of particular things the preconceptions which are distinctly fixed.

Epictetus, *Discourses*, II, 11

29 What is the first business of him who philosophizes? To throw away self-conceit. For it is impossible for a man to begin to learn that which he thinks that he knows.

Epictetus, *Discourses*, II, 17

30 When a man sees another handling an ax badly, he does not say, "What is the use of the carpenter's art? See how badly carpenters do their work"; but he says just the contrary, "This man is not a carpenter, for he uses an ax badly." In the same way if a man hears another singing badly, he does not say, "See how musicians sing"; but rather, "This man is not a musician." But it is in the matter of philosophy only that people do this. When they see a man acting contrary to the profession of a philosopher, they do not take away his title, but they assume him to be a philosopher, and from his acts deriving the fact that he is behaving indecently they conclude that there is no use in philosophy.

Epictetus, *Discourses*, IV, 8

31 Do you think that you can act as you do and be a philosopher, that you can eat, drink, be angry, be discontented, as you are now? You must watch, you must labor, you must get the better of certain appetites, must quit your acquaintances, be de-

spised by your servant, be laughed at by those you meet; come off worse than others in everything—in offices, in honors, before tribunals. When you have fully considered all these things, approach, if you please—that is, if, by parting with them, you have a mind to purchase serenity, freedom, and tranquillity. If not, do not come hither; do not, like children, be now a philosopher, then a publican, then an orator, and then one of Caesar's officers. These things are not consistent. You must be one man, either good or bad. You must cultivate either your own reason or else externals; apply yourself either to things within or without you—that is, be either a philosopher or one of the mob.

Epictetus, *Encheiridion*, XXIX

32 Philosophy . . . consists in keeping the daemon within a man free from violence and unharmed, superior to pains and pleasures, doing nothing without a purpose, nor yet falsely and with hypocrisy, not feeling the need of another man's doing or not doing anything; and besides, accepting all that happens, and all that is allotted, as coming from thence, wherever it is, from whence he himself came; and, finally, waiting for death with a cheerful mind.

Marcus Aurelius, *Meditations*, II, 17

33 *Zeus.* Now get those benches straight there, and make the place fit to be seen. Bring up the lots, one of you, and put them in line. Give them a rub up first, though; we must have them looking their best, to attract bidders. Hermes, you can declare the sale-room open, and a welcome to all comers.—*For Sale! A varied assortment of Live Creeds. Tenets of every description.—Cash on delivery; or credit allowed on suitable security.*

Hermes. Here they come, swarming in. No time to lose; we must not keep them waiting.

Zeus. Well, let us begin.

Her. What are we to put up first?

Zeus. The Ionic fellow, with the long hair. He seems a showy piece of goods.

Her. Step up, Pythagoreanism, and show yourself.

Zeus. Go ahead.

Her. Now here is a creed of the first water. Who bids for this handsome article? What gentleman says Superhumanity? Harmony of the Universe! Transmigration of souls! Who bids?

First Dealer. He looks all right. And what can he do?

Her. Magic, music, arithmetic, geometry, astronomy, jugglery. Prophecy in all its branches. . . .

First D. Admirable! A very feast of reason. Now just strip, and let me see what you are like. Bless me, here is a creed with a golden thigh! He is no mortal, he is a God. I must have him at any price. What do you start him at?

Her. Forty pounds.

First D. He is mine for forty pounds.

Lucian, Sale of Creeds

34 *Zeus.* Next lot.

Hermes. The Athenian there? Old Chatterbox?

Zeus. By all means.

Her. Come forward!—A good sensible creed this. Who buys Holiness?

Fifth Dealer. Let me see. What are you good for?

Socrates. I teach the art of love.

Fifth D. A likely bargain for me! I want a tutor for my young Adonis.

Soc. And could he have a better? The love I teach is of the spirit, not of the flesh. Under my roof, be sure, a boy will come to no harm.

Fifth D. Very unconvincing that. A teacher of the art of love, and never meddle with anything but the spirit? Never use the opportunities your office gives you?

Soc. Now by Dog and Plane-tree, it is as I say!

Fifth D. Heracles! What strange Gods are these?

Soc. Why, the Dog is a God, I suppose? Is not Anubis made much of in Egypt? Is there not a Dog-star in Heaven, and a Cerberus in the lower world?

Fifth D. Quite so. My mistake. Now what is your manner of life?

Soc. I live in a city of my own building; I make my own laws, and have a novel constitution of my own.

Fifth D. I should like to hear some of your statutes.

Soc. You shall hear the greatest of them all. No woman shall be restricted to one husband. Every man who likes is her husband.

Fifth D. What! Then the laws of adultery are clean swept away?

Soc. I should think they were! and a world of hair-splitting with them.

Fifth D. And what do you do with the handsome boys?

Soc. Their kisses are the reward of merit, of noble and spirited actions.

Fifth D. Unparalleled generosity!—And now, what are the main features of your philosophy?

Soc. Ideas and types of things. All things that you see, the earth and all that is upon it, the sea, the sky,—each has its counterpart in the invisible world.

Fifth D. And where are they?

Soc. Nowhere. Were they anywhere, they were not what they are.

Fifth D. I see no signs of these 'types' of yours.

Soc. Of course not; because you are spiritually blind. *I* see the counterparts of all things; an invisible you, an invisible me; everything is in duplicate.

Fifth D. Come, such a shrewd and lynx-eyed creed is worth a bid. Let me see. What do you want for him?

Her. Five hundred.

Fifth D. Done with you. Only I must settle the bill another day.

Lucian, Sale of Creeds

35 *Zeus.* Don't waste time. Next lot,—the Peripatetic!

Hermes. Now, my beauty, now, Affluence! Gentlemen, if you want Wisdom for your money, here is a creed that comprises all knowledge.

Eighth Dealer. What is he like?

Her. He is temperate, good-natured, easy to get on with; and his strong point is, that he is twins.

Eighth D. How can that be?

Her. Why, he is one creed outside, and another inside. So remember, if you buy him, one of him is called Esoteric, and the other Exoteric.

Eighth D. And what has he to say for himself?

Her. He has to say that there are three kinds of good: spiritual, corporeal, circumstantial.

Eighth D. *There's* something a man can understand. How much is he?

Her. Eighty pounds.

Eighth D. Eighty pounds is a long price.

Her. Not at all, my dear sir, not at all. You see, there is some money with him, to all appearance. Snap him up before it is too late. Why, from him you will find out in no time how long a gnat lives, to how many fathoms' depth the sunlight penetrates the sea, and what an oyster's soul is like.

Eighth D. Heracles! Nothing escapes him.

Her. Ah, these are trifles. You should hear some of his more abstruse speculations, concerning generation and birth and the development of the embryo; and his distinction between man, the laughing creature, and the ass, which is neither a laughing nor a carpentering nor a shipping creature.

Eighth D. Such knowledge is as useful as it is ornamental. Eighty pounds be it, then.

Her. He is yours.

Lucian, Sale of Creeds

36 *Lucian.* Where is Philosophy to be found? I do not know where she lives, myself. I once spent a long time wandering about in search of her house, wishing to make her acquaintance. Several times I met some long-bearded people in threadbare cloaks who professed to be fresh from her presence; I took their word for it, and asked them the way; but they knew considerably less about it than I, and either declined to answer, by way of concealing their ignorance, or else pointed to one door after another. I have never been able to find the right one to this day.

Lucian, The Fisher

37 Following the normal order of study I had come to a book of one Cicero, whose tongue practically everyone admires, though not his heart. That particular book is called *Hortensius* and contains an exhortation to philosophy. Quite definitely it changed the direction of my mind, altered my

prayers to You, O Lord, and gave me a new purpose and ambition. Suddenly all the vanity I had hoped in I saw as worthless, and with an incredible intensity of desire I longed after immortal wisdom. I had begun that journey upwards by which I was to return to You. My father was now dead two years; I was eighteen and was receiving money from my mother for the continuance of my study of eloquence. But I used that book not for the sharpening of my tongue; what won me in it was what it said, not the excellence of its phrasing.

How did I then burn, my God, how did I burn to wing upwards from earthly delights to You. But I had no notion what You were to do with me. For with You is wisdom. Now love of wisdom is what is meant by the Greek word philosophy, and it was to philosophy that that book set me so ardently. There are those who seduce men's minds by philosophy, colouring and covering their errors with its great and fine and honourable name: almost all who in Cicero's own time and earlier had been of that sort are listed in his book and shown for what they are. Indeed it illustrates the wholesome advice given by the Spirit through Your good and loving servant: *Beware lest any man cheat you by philosophy, and vain deceits; according to the tradition of men, according to the elements of the world, and not according to Christ: for in Him dwelleth all the fulness of the Godhead corporeally.* At that time, You know, O Light of my heart, those writings of the Apostle were not yet known to me. But the one thing that delighted me in Cicero's exhortation was that I should love, and seek, and win, and hold, and embrace, not this or that philosophical school but Wisdom itself, whatever it might be. The book excited and inflamed me; in my ardour the only thing I found lacking was that the name of Christ was not there. For with my mother's milk my infant heart had drunk in, and still held deep down in it, that name according to Your mercy, O Lord, the name of Your Son, my Saviour; and whatever lacked that name, no matter how learned and excellently written and true, could not win me wholly.

Augustine, *Confessions,* III, 4

38 Among the disciples of Socrates, Plato was the one who shone with a glory which far excelled that of the others and who not unjustly eclipsed them all. By birth an Athenian of honourable parentage, he far surpassed his fellow-disciples in natural endowments, of which he was possessed in a wonderful degree. Yet, deeming himself and the Socratic discipline far from sufficient for bringing philosophy to perfection, he travelled as extensively as he was able, going to every place famed for the cultivation of any science of which he could make himself master. Thus he learned from the Egyptians whatever they held and taught as important; and from Egypt, passing into those parts of Italy which were filled with the fame of the Pythagoreans, he mastered, with the greatest facility, and under the most eminent teachers, all the Italic philosophy which was then in vogue. And, as he had a peculiar love for his master Socrates, he made him the speaker in all his dialogues, putting into his mouth whatever he had learned, either from others, or from the efforts of his own powerful intellect, tempering even his moral disputations with the grace and politeness of the Socratic style. And, as the study of wisdom consists in action and contemplation, so that one part of it may be called active, and the other contemplative—the active part having reference to the conduct of life, that is, to the regulation of morals, and the contemplative part to the investigation into the causes of nature and into pure truth—Socrates is said to have excelled in the active part of that study, while Pythagoras gave more attention to its contemplative part, on which he brought to bear all the force of his great intellect. To Plato is given the praise of having perfected philosophy by combining both parts into one. He then divides it into three parts—the first moral, which is chiefly occupied with action; the second natural, of which the object is contemplation; and the third rational, which discriminates between the true and the false. And though this last is necessary both to action and contemplation, it is contemplation, nevertheless, which lays peculiar claim to the office of investigating the nature of truth. Thus this tripartite division is not contrary to that which made the study of wisdom to consist in action and contemplation. Now, as to what Plato thought with respect to each of these parts—that is, what he believed to be the end of all actions, the cause of all natures, and the light of all intelligences—it would be a question too long to discuss and about which we ought not to make any rash affirmation. For, as Plato liked and constantly affected the well-known method of his master Socrates, namely, that of dissimulating his knowledge or his opinions, it is not easy to discover clearly what he himself thought on various matters, any more than it is to discover what were the real opinions of Socrates. We must, nevertheless, insert into our work certain of those opinions which he expresses in his writings, whether he himself uttered them, or narrates them as expressed by others, and seems himself to approve of—opinions sometimes favourable to the true religion, which our faith takes up and defends, and sometimes contrary to it, as, for example, in the questions concerning the existence of one God or of many, as it relates to the truly blessed life which is to be after death. For those who are praised as having most closely followed Plato, who is justly preferred to all the other philosophers of the Gentiles, and who are said to have manifested the greatest acuteness in understanding him, do perhaps entertain such an idea of God as to admit that in Him are to be found the cause of existence, the ultimate reason for the

understanding, and the end in reference to which the whole life is to be regulated. Of which three things, the first is understood to pertain to the natural, the second to the rational, and the third to the moral part of philosophy. For if man has been so created as to attain, through that which is most excellent in him, to that which excels all things— that is, to the one true and absolutely good God, without Whom no nature exists, no doctrine instructs, no exercise profits—let Him be sought in Whom all things are secure to us, let Him be discovered in Whom all truth becomes certain to us, let Him be loved in Whom all becomes right to us.

Augustine, *City of God,* VIII, 4

39 Plato determined the final good to be to live according to virtue, and affirmed that he only can attain to virtue who knows and imitates God— which knowledge and imitation are the only cause of blessedness. Therefore he did not doubt that to philosophize is to love God, whose nature is incorporeal. Whence it certainly follows that the student of wisdom, that is, the philosopher, will then become blessed when he shall have begun to enjoy God. For though he is not necessarily blessed who enjoys that which he loves (for many are miserable by loving that which ought not to be loved and still more miserable when they enjoy it), nevertheless no one is blessed who does not enjoy that which he loves. For even they who love things which ought not to be loved do not count themselves blessed by loving merely, but by enjoying them. Who, then, but the most miserable will deny that he is blessed, who enjoys that which he loves and loves the true and highest good? But the true and highest good, according to Plato, is God, and therefore he would call him a philosopher who loves God; for philosophy is directed to the obtaining of the blessed life, and he who loves God is blessed in the enjoyment of God.

Augustine, *City of God,* VIII, 8

40 While I was pondering thus in silence, and using my pen to set down so tearful a complaint, there appeared standing over my head a woman's form, whose countenance was full of majesty, whose eyes shown as with fire and in power of insight surpassed the eyes of men, whose colour was full of life, whose strength was yet intact though she was so full of years that none would ever think that she was subject to such age as ours. One could but doubt her varying stature, for at one moment she repressed it to the common measure of a man, at another she seemed to touch with her crown the very heavens: and when she had raised higher her head, it pierced even the sky and baffled the sight of those who would look upon it. Her clothing was wrought of the finest thread by subtle workmanship brought to an indivisible piece. This had she woven with her own hands, as I afterwards did learn by her own shewing. Their beauty was

somewhat dimmed by the dulness of long neglect, as is seen in the smoke-grimed masks of our ancestors. On the border below was inwoven the symbol Π, on that above was to be read a Θ. And between the two letters there could be marked degrees, by which, as by the rungs of a ladder, ascent might be made from the lower principle to the higher. Yet the hands of rough men had torn this garment and snatched such morsels as they could therefrom. In her right hand she carried books, in her left was a sceptre brandished.

Boethius, *Consolation of Philosophy,* I

41 This [sacred] science [i.e., theology] can in a sense take from the philosophical sciences, not as though it stood in need of them, but only in order to make its teaching clearer. For it takes its principles not from other sciences, but immediately from God, by revelation. Therefore it does not take from the other sciences as from the higher, but makes use of them as of the lesser, and as handmaidens; just as the master sciences make use of the sciences that supply their materials, as political of military science. That it thus uses them is not due to its own defect or insufficiency, but to the defect of our intellect, which is more easily led by what is known through natural reason (from which proceed the other sciences), to that which is above reason, such as are the teachings of this science.

Aquinas, *Summa Theologica,* I, 1, 5

42 It is necessary for man to accept by faith not only things which are above reason, but also those which can be known by reason, and this for three reasons. First, in order that man may arrive more quickly at the knowledge of Divine truth. Because the science to which it pertains to prove the existence of God is the last of all to offer itself to human inquiry, since it presupposes many other sciences so that it would not be until late in life that man would arrive at the knowledge of God. The second reason is, in order that the knowledge of God may be more general. For many are unable to make progress in the study of science, either through dulness of mind, or through having a number of occupations and temporal needs, or even through laziness in learning, all of whom would be altogether deprived of the knowledge of God, unless Divine things were brought to their knowledge after the manner of faith. The third reason is for the sake of certitude. For human reason is very deficient in things concerning God. A sign of this is that philosophers in their researches, by natural investigation, into human affairs, have fallen into many errors, and have disagreed among themselves. And consequently, in order that men might have knowledge of God, free of doubt and uncertainty, it was necessary for Divine matters to be delivered to them by way of faith,

being told to them, as it were, by God Himself Who cannot lie.

Aquinas, *Summa Theologica*, II–II, 2, 4

43 When I raised my eyelids a little higher, I saw the Master of those that know [Aristotle], sitting amid a philosophic family.

All regard him; all do him honour; here I saw Socrates and Plato, who before the rest stand nearest to him.

Dante, *Inferno*, IV, 130

44 We do not escape philosophy by stressing immoderately the sharpness of pain and the weakness of man. For we force her to fall back on these unanswerable replies:

If it is bad to live in need, at least there is no need to live in need.

No one suffers long except by his own fault.

He who has not the courage to suffer either death or life, who will neither resist nor flee, what can we do with him?

Montaigne, *Essays*, I, 14, That the Taste of Good

45 It is a strange fact that things should be in such a pass in our century that philosophy, even with people of understanding, should be an empty and fantastic name, a thing of no use and no value, both in common opinion and in fact. I think those quibblings which have taken possession of all the approaches to her are the cause of this. It is very wrong to portray her as inaccessible to children, with a surly, frowning, and terrifying face. Who has masked her with this false face, pale and hideous? There is nothing more gay, more lusty, more sprightly, and I might almost say more frolicsome. She preaches nothing but merrymaking and a good time. A sad and dejected look shows that she does not dwell there.

Montaigne, *Essays*, I, 26, Education of Children

46 Whoever seeks anything comes to this point: he says either that he has found it, or that it cannot be found, or that he is still in quest of it. All philosophy is divided into these three types. Its purpose is to seek out truth, knowledge, and certainty.

Montaigne, *Essays*, II, 12, Apology for Raymond Sebond

47 *Romeo.* No sudden mean of death, though ne'er so mean,
But "banished" to kill me?—"banished"?
O friar, the damned use that word in hell;
Howlings attend it: how hast thou the heart,
Being a divine, a ghostly confessor,
A sin-absolver, and my friend profess'd,
To mangle me with that word "banished"?
Friar Laurence. Thou fond mad man, hear me but speak a word.

Rom. O, thou wilt speak again of banishment.
Fri. L. I'll give thee armour to keep off that word;
Adversity's sweet milk, philosophy,
To comfort thee, though thou art banished.
Rom. Yet "banished"? Hang up philosophy!
Unless philosophy can make a Juliet,
Displant a town, reverse a prince's doom,
It helps not, it prevails not: talk no more.

Shakespeare, *Romeo and Juliet*, III, iii, 45

48 *Hamlet.* There are more things in heaven and earth, Horatio,
Than are dreamt of in your philosophy.

Shakespeare, *Hamlet*, I, v, 166

49 Aristotle was the first accurate critic and truest judge, nay, the greatest philosopher the world ever had; for he noted the vices of all knowledges in all creatures, and out of many men's perfections in a science he formed still one art.

Jonson, *Discoveries*: Poeta, Etc.

50 It is the property of good and sound knowledge to putrify and dissolve into a number of subtle, idle, unwholesome, and (as I may term them) vermiculate questions, which have indeed a kind of quickness and life of spirit, but no soundness of matter or goodness of quality. This kind of degenerate learning did chiefly reign amongst the schoolmen: who having sharp and strong wits, and abundance of leisure, and small variety of reading, but their wits being shut up in the cells of a few authors (chiefly Aristotle their dictator) as their persons were shut up in the cells of monasteries and colleges, and knowing little history, either of nature or time, did out of no great quantity of matter and infinite agitation of wit spin out unto us those laborious webs of learning which are extant in their books. For the wit and mind of man, if it work upon matter, which is the contemplation of the creatures of God, worketh according to the stuff and is limited thereby; but if it work upon itself, as the spider worketh his web, then it is endless, and brings forth indeed cobwebs of learning, admirable for the fineness of thread and work, but of no substance or profit.

Bacon, *Advancement of Learning*, Bk. I, IV, 5

51 The wisdom of the Greeks was professional and disputatious, and thus most adverse to the investigation of truth. The name, therefore, of sophists, which the contemptuous spirit of those who deemed themselves philosophers, rejected and transferred to the rhetoricians—Gorgias, Protagoras, Hippias, Polus—might well suit the whole tribe, such as Plato, Aristotle, Zeno, Epicurus, Theophrastus, and their successors—Chrysippus, Carneades, and the rest. There was only this difference between them: the former were mercenary vagabonds, travelling about to different

states, making a show of their wisdom, and requiring pay; the latter more dignified and noble, in possession of fixed habitations, opening schools, and teaching philosophy gratuitously. Both, however (though differing in other respects), were professorial, and reduced every subject to controversy, establishing and defending certain sects and dogmas of philosophy, so that their doctrines were nearly (what Dionysius not unaptly objected to Plato) the talk of idle old men to ignorant youths. But the more ancient Greeks, as Empedocles, Anaxagoras, Leucippus, Democritus, Parmenides, Heraclitus, Xenophanes, Philolaus, and the rest (for I omit Pythagoras as being superstitious), did not (that we are aware) open schools, but betook themselves to the investigation of truth with greater silence and with more severity and simplicity, that is, with less affectation and ostentation. Hence in our opinion they acted more advisedly, however their works may have been eclipsed in course of time by those lighter productions which better correspond with and please the apprehensions and passions of the vulgar; for time, like a river, bears down to us that which is light and inflated, and sinks that which is heavy and solid.

Bacon, *Novum Organum,* I, 71

52 I am sure that those who most passionately follow Aristotle now-a-days would think themselves happy if they had as much knowledge of nature as he had, even if this were on the condition that they should never attain to any more. They are like the ivy that never tries to mount above the trees which give it support, and which often even descends again after it has reached their summit; for it appears to me that such men also sink again— that is to say, somehow render themselves more ignorant than they would have been had they abstained from study altogether. For, not content with knowing all that is intelligibly explained in their author, they wish in addition to find in him the solution of many difficulties of which he says nothing, and in regard to which he possibly had no thought at all.

Descartes, *Discourse on Method,* VI

53 The faculty of reasoning being consequent to the use of speech, it was not possible but that there should have been some general truths found out by reasoning, as ancient almost as language itself. The savages of America are not without some good moral sentences; also they have a little arithmetic, to add and divide in numbers not too great; but they are not therefore philosophers. For as there were plants of corn and wine in small quantity dispersed in the fields and woods, before men knew their virtue . . . so also there have been diverse true, general, and profitable speculations from the beginning, as being the natural plants of human reason. But they were at first but few in number; men lived upon gross experience;

there was no method; that is to say, no sowing nor planting of knowledge by itself, apart from the weeds and common plants of error and conjecture. And the cause of it being the want of leisure from procuring the necessities of life, and defending themselves against their neighbours, it was impossible, till the erecting of great commonwealths, it should be otherwise. Leisure is the mother of philosophy; and commonwealth, the mother of peace and leisure. Where first were great and flourishing cities, there was first the study of philosophy.

Hobbes, *Leviathan,* IV, 46

54 To make light of philosophy is to be a true philosopher.

Pascal, *Pensées,* I, 4

55 What good there is in Montaigne can only have been acquired with difficulty. The evil that is in him, I mean apart from his morality, could have been corrected in a moment, if he had been informed that he made too much of trifles and spoke too much of himself.

Pascal, *Pensées,* II, 65

56 I cannot forgive Descartes. In all his philosophy he would have been quite willing to dispense with God. But he had to make Him give a fillip to set the world in motion; beyond this, he has no further need of God.

Pascal, *Pensées,* II, 77

57 We can only think of Plato and Aristotle in grand academic robes. They were honest men, like others, laughing with their friends, and, when they diverted themselves with writing their *Laws* and the *Politics,* they did it as an amusement. That part of their life was the least philosophic and the least serious; the most philosophic was to live simply and quietly. If they wrote on politics, it was as if laying down rules for a lunatic asylum; and if they presented the appearance of speaking of a great matter, it was because they knew that the madmen, to whom they spoke, thought they were kings and emperors. They entered into their principles in order to make their madness as little harmful as possible.

Pascal, *Pensées,* V, 331

58 *Brother.* How charming is divine Philosophy!
Not harsh, and crabbed as dull fools suppose,
But musical as is *Apollo's* lute,
And a perpetual feast of nectar'd sweets,
Where no crude surfet raigns.

Milton, *Comus,* 476

59 Plato, a man of high authority, indeed, but least of all for his commonwealth, in the book of his Laws, which no city ever yet received, fed his fancy by making many edicts to his airy burgomas-

ters, which they who otherwise admire him wish had been rather buried and excused in the genial cups of an Academic night sitting.

Milton, *Areopagitica*

60 Another great abuse of words, is the taking them for things. This, though it in some degree concerns all names in general, yet more particularly affects those of substances. To this abuse those men are most subject who most confine their thoughts to any one system, and give themselves up into a firm belief of the perfection of any received hypothesis: whereby they come to be persuaded that the terms of that sect are so suited to the nature of things, that they perfectly correspond with their real existence. . . . There is scarce any sect in philosophy has not a distinct set of terms that others understand not. But yet this gibberish, which, in the weakness of human understanding, serves so well to palliate men's ignorance, and cover their errors, comes, by familiar use amongst those of the same tribe, to seem the most important part of language, and of all other the terms the most significant.

Locke, *Concerning Human Understanding,*
Bk. III, X, 14

61 Philosophy being nothing else but the study of wisdom and truth, it may with reason be expected that those who have spent most time and pains in it should enjoy a greater calm and serenity of mind, a greater clearness and evidence of knowledge, and be less disturbed with doubts and difficulties than other men. Yet so it is, we see the illiterate bulk of mankind that walk the high-road of plain common sense, and are governed by the dictates of nature, for the most part easy and undisturbed. To them nothing that is familiar appears unaccountable or difficult to comprehend. They complain not of any want of evidence in their senses, and are out of all danger of becoming Sceptics. But no sooner do we depart from sense and instinct to follow the light of a superior principle, to reason, meditate, and reflect on the nature of things, but a thousand scruples spring up in our minds concerning those things which before we seemed fully to comprehend.

Berkeley, *Principles of Human Knowledge,*
Introduction, 1

62 There is nothing so extravagant and irrational which some philosophers have not maintained for truth.

Swift, *Gulliver's Travels,* III, 6

63 Philosophers are composed of flesh and blood as well as other human creatures; and however sublimated and refined the theory of these may be, a little practical frailty is as incident to them as to other mortals. It is, indeed, in theory only, and not in practice, as we have before hinted, that

consists the difference: for though such great beings think much better and more wisely, they always act exactly like other men. They know very well how to subdue all appetites and passions, and to despise both pain and pleasure; and this knowledge affords much delightful contemplation, and is easily acquired; but the practice would be vexatious and troublesome; and, therefore, the same wisdom which teaches them to know this, teaches them to avoid carrying it into execution.

Fielding, *Tom Jones,* V, 5

64 It is certain that the easy and obvious philosophy will always, with the generality of mankind, have the preference above the accurate and abstruse; and by many will be recommended, not only as more agreeable, but more useful than the other. It enters more into common life; moulds the heart and affections; and, by touching those principles which actuate men, reforms their conduct, and brings them nearer to that model of perfection which it describes. On the contrary, the abstruse philosophy, being founded on a turn of mind, which cannot enter into business and action, vanishes when the philosopher leaves the shade, and comes into open day; nor can its principles easily retain any influence over our conduct and behaviour. The feelings of our heart, the agitation of our passions, the vehemence of our affections, dissipate all its conclusions, and reduce the profound philosopher to a mere plebeian.

Hume, *Concerning Human Understanding,* I, 3

65 It is easy for a profound philosopher to commit a mistake in his subtile reasonings; and one mistake is the necessary parent of another, while he pushes on his consequences, and is not deterred from embracing any conclusion, by its unusual appearance, or its contradiction to popular opinion. But a philosopher, who purposes only to represent the common sense of mankind in more beautiful and more engaging colours, if by accident he falls into error, goes no farther; but renewing his appeal to common sense, and the natural sentiments of the mind, returns into the right path, and secures himself from any dangerous illusions.

Hume, *Concerning Human Understanding,* I, 4

66 Be a philosopher; but, amidst all your philosophy, be still a man.

Hume, *Concerning Human Understanding,* I, 4

67 All the philosophy . . . in the world, and all the religion, which is nothing but a species of philosophy, will never be able to carry us beyond the usual course of experience, or give us measures of conduct and behaviour different from those which are furnished by reflections on common life.

Hume, *Concerning Human
Understanding,* XI, 113

68 There cannot be two passions more nearly resembling each other, than those of hunting and philosophy, whatever disproportion may at first sight appear betwixt them. 'Tis evident, that the pleasure of hunting consists in the action of the mind and body; the motion, the attention, the difficulty, and the uncertainty. 'Tis evident likewise, that these actions must be attended with an idea of utility, in order to their having any effect upon us. A man of the greatest fortune, and the farthest remov'd from avarice, tho' he takes a pleasure in hunting after partridges and pheasants, feels no satisfaction in shooting crows and magpies; and that because he considers the first as fit for the table, and the other as entirely useless. Here 'tis certain, that the utility or importance of itself causes no real passion, but is only requisite to support the imagination; and the same person, who over-looks a ten times greater profit in any other subject, is pleas'd to bring home half a dozen woodcocks or plovers, after having employ'd several hours in hunting after them. To make the parallel betwixt hunting and philosophy more compleat, we may observe, that tho' in both cases the end of our action may in itself be despis'd, yet in the heat of the action we acquire such an attention to this end, that we are very uneasy under any disappointments, and are sorry when we either miss our game, or fall into any error in our reasoning.

Hume, *Treatise of Human Nature,*
Bk. II, III, 10

69 Philosopher, lover of wisdom, that is to say, of truth. All philosophers have had this dual character; there is not one in antiquity who has not given mankind examples of virtue and lessons in moral truths. They have all contrived to be deceived about natural philosophy; but natural philosophy is so little necessary for the conduct of life, that the philosophers had no need of it. It has taken centuries to learn a part of nature's laws. One day was sufficient for a wise man to learn the duties of man.

Voltaire, *Philosophical Dictionary:*
Philosopher

70 I do not think that there has ever been a philosopher with a system who did not at the end of his life avow that he had wasted his time. It must be admitted that the inventors of the mechanical arts have been much more useful to mankind than the inventors of syllogisms: the man who invented the shuttle surpasses with a vengeance the man who imagined innate ideas.

Voltaire, *Philosophical Dictionary:*
Précis of Ancient Philosophy

71 [Micromegas] promised to compose for them a choice book of philosophy which would demonstrate the very essence of things. Accordingly, before his departure, he made them a present of the book, which was brought to the Academy of Sciences at Paris, but when the old secretary came to open it he saw nothing but blank paper.

"Ay, ay," said he, "this is just what I suspected."

Voltaire, *Micromegas,* VII

72 In the progress of society, philosophy or speculation becomes, like every other employment, the principal or sole trade and occupation of a particular class of citizens. Like every other employment too, it is subdivided into a great number of different branches, each of which affords occupation to a peculiar tribe or class of philosophers; and this subdivision of employment in philosophy, as well as in every other business, improves dexterity, and saves time. Each individual becomes more expert in his own peculiar branch, more work is done upon the whole, and the quantity of science is considerably increased by it.

Adam Smith, *Wealth of Nations,* I, 1

73 So equal, yet so opposite, are the merits of Plato and Aristotle, that they may be balanced in endless controversy.

Gibbon, *Decline and Fall of the Roman
Empire,* LXVI

74 Human reason, in one sphere of its cognition, is called upon to consider questions, which it cannot decline, as they are presented by its own nature, but which it cannot answer, as they transcend every faculty of the mind.

It falls into this difficulty without any fault of its own. It begins with principles, which cannot be dispensed with in the field of experience, and the truth and sufficiency of which are, at the same time, insured by experience. With these principles it rises, in obedience to the laws of its own nature, to ever higher and more remote conditions. But it quickly discovers that, in this way, its labours must remain ever incomplete, because new questions never cease to present themselves; and thus it finds itself compelled to have recourse to principles which transcend the region of experience, while they are regarded by common sense without distrust. It thus falls into confusion and contradictions, from which it conjectures the presence of latent errors, which, however, it is unable to discover, because the principles it employs, transcending the limits of experience, cannot be tested by that criterion. The arena of these endless contests is called *Metaphysic.*

Kant, *Critique of Pure Reason,*
Pref. to 1st Ed.

75 Both Epicurus and Plato assert more in their systems than they know. The former encourages and advances science—although to the prejudice of the practical; the latter presents us with excellent

principles for the investigation of the practical, but, in relation to everything regarding which we can attain to speculative cognition, permits reason to append idealistic explanations of natural phenomena, to the great injury of physical investigation.

Kant, *Critique of Pure Reason*,
Transcendental Dialectic

76 The mathematician, the natural philosopher, and the logician—how far soever the first may have advanced in rational, and the two latter in philosophical knowledge—are merely artists, engaged in the arrangement and formation of conceptions; they cannot be termed philosophers. Above them all, there is the ideal teacher, who employs them as instruments for the advancement of the essential aims of human reason. Him alone can we call philosopher; but he nowhere exists. But the idea of his legislative power resides in the mind of every man, and it alone teaches us what kind of systematic unity philosophy demands in view of the ultimate aims of reason. This idea is, therefore, a cosmical conception [one in which all men necessarily take an interest].

In view of the complete systematic unity of reason, there can only be one ultimate end of all the operations of the mind. To this all other aims are subordinate, and nothing more than means for its attainment. This ultimate end is the destination of man, and the philosophy which relates to it is termed moral philosophy. The superior position occupied by moral philosophy, above all other spheres for the operations of reason, sufficiently indicates the reason why the ancients always included the idea—and in an especial manner—of moralist in that of philosopher. Even at the present day, we call a man who appears to have the power of self-government, even although his knowledge may be very limited, by the name of philosopher.

Kant, *Critique of Pure Reason*,
Transcendental Method

77 It would be no harm to deter the self-conceit of one who ventures to claim the title of philosopher by holding before him in the very definition a standard of self-estimation which would very much lower his pretensions. For a teacher of wisdom would mean something more than a scholar who has not come so far as to guide himself, much less to guide others, with certain expectation of attaining so high an end: it would mean a master in the knowledge of wisdom, which implies more than a modest man would claim for himself. Thus philosophy as well as wisdom would always remain an ideal, which objectively is presented complete in reason alone, while subjectively for the person it is only the goal of his unceasing endeavours; and no one would be justified in professing to be in possession of it so as to assume the

name of philosopher who could not also show its infallible effects in his own person as an example (in his self-mastery and the unquestioned interest that he takes pre-eminently in the general good), and this the ancients also required as a condition of deserving that honourable title.

Kant, *Critique of Practical Reason*,
Pt. I, II, 1

78 That kings should become philosophers, or philosophers kings, can scarce be expected; nor is it to be wished, since the enjoyment of power inevitably corrupts the judgment of reason, and perverts its liberty. But that kings, or people-kings, that is to say, the people who govern themselves by laws of equality, should not suffer that the class of philosophers be reduced to disappear, or to maintain silence, but, on the contrary, should permit them to be freely heard. This is what the well administration of a government exacts; which can never be sufficiently enlightened.

Kant, *Perpetual Peace*, Supplement II

79   Do not all charms fly
At the mere touch of cold philosophy?
There was an awful rainbow once in heaven:
We know her woof, her texture; she is given
In the dull catalogue of common things.
Philosophy will clip an Angel's wings.

Keats, *Lamia*, II, 229

80 Axioms in philosophy are not axioms until they are proved upon our pulses. We read fine things, but never feel them to the full until we have gone the same steps as the author.

Keats, *Letter to John H. Reynolds*
(May 3, 1818)

81 To comprehend what is, this is the task of philosophy, because what is, is reason. Whatever happens, every individual is a child of his time; so philosophy too is its own time apprehended in thoughts.

Hegel, *Philosophy of Right*, Pref.

82 There are two kinds of history; the history of politics and the history of literature and art. The one is the history of the will; the other, that of the intellect. The first is a tale of woe, even of terror: it is a record of agony, struggle, fraud, and horrible murder *en masse*. The second is everywhere pleasing and serene, like the intellect when left to itself, even though its path be one of error. Its chief branch is the history of philosophy. This is, in fact, its fundamental bass, and the notes of it are heard even in the other kind of history. These deep tones guide the formation of opinion, and opinion rules the world. Hence philosophy, rightly understood, is a material force of the most powerful kind, though very slow in its working. The

philosophy of a period is thus the fundamental bass of its history.

Schopenhauer, Some Forms of Literature

83 Two Chinamen travelling in Europe went to the theatre for the first time. One of them did nothing but study the machinery, and he succeeded in finding out how it was worked. The other tried to get at the meaning of the piece in spite of his ignorance of the language. Here you have the astronomer and the philosopher.

Schopenhauer, A Few Parables

84 Among secular books, Plato only is entitled to Omar's fanatical compliment to the Koran, when he said, "Burn the libraries; for their value is in this book." These sentences contain the culture of nations; these are the corner-stone of schools; these are the fountain-head of literatures. A discipline it is in logic, arithmetic, taste, symmetry, poetry, language, rhetoric, ontology, morals or practical wisdom. There was never such range of speculation. Out of Plato come all things that are still written and debated among men of thought. Great havoc makes he among our originalities. We have reached the mountain from which all these drift boulders were detached.

Emerson, Plato; or, The Philosopher

85 Now, had Tashtego perished in that head, it had been a very precious perishing; smothered in the very whitest and daintiest of fragrant spermaceti; coffined, hearsed, and tombed in the secret inner chamber and sanctum sanctorum of the whale. Only one sweeter end can readily be recalled—the delicious death of an Ohio honey-hunter, who seeking honey in the crotch of a hollow tree, found such exceeding store of it, that leaning too far over, it sucked him in, so that he died embalmed. How many, think ye, have likewise fallen into Plato's honey head, and sweetly perished there?

Melville, Moby Dick, LXXVIII

86 To be a philosopher is not merely to have subtle thoughts, nor even to found a school, but so to love wisdom as to live according to its dictates, a life of simplicity, independence, magnanimity, and trust. It is to solve some of the problems of life, not only theoretically, but practically. The success of great scholars and thinkers is commonly a courtier-like success, not kingly, not manly. They make shift to live merely by conformity, practically as their fathers did, and are in no sense the progenitors of a noble race of men. But why do men degenerate ever? What makes families run out? What is the nature of the luxury which enervates and destroys nations? Are we sure that there is none of it in our own lives? The philosopher is in advance of his age even in the outward form of his life. He is not fed, sheltered, clothed, warmed, like his contemporaries. How can a man

be a philosopher and not maintain his vital heat by better methods than other men?

Thoreau, Walden: Economy

87 Of the three varieties of mental excellence, intellectual, practical, and moral, there never could be any doubt in regard to the first two which side had the advantage. All intellectual superiority is the fruit of active effort. Enterprise, the desire to keep moving, to be trying and accomplishing new things for our own benefit or that of others, is the parent even of speculative, and much more of practical, talent. The intellectual culture compatible with the other type is of that feeble and vague description which belongs to a mind that stops at amusement, or at simple contemplation. The test of real and vigourous thinking, the thinking which ascertains truths instead of dreaming dreams, is successful application to practice. Where that purpose does not exist, to give definiteness, precision, and an intelligible meaning to thought, it generates nothing better than the mystical metaphysics of the Pythagoreans or the Vedas.

Mill, Representative Government, III

88 Schools of philosophy arise and fall; their bands of adherents inevitably dwindle; no master can long persuade a large body of disciples that they give to themselves just the same account of the world as he does; it is only the very young and the very enthusiastic who can think themselves sure that they possess the whole mind of Plato, or Spinoza, or Hegel, at all. The very mature and the very sober can even hardly believe that these philosophers possessed it themselves enough to put it all into their works, and to let us know entirely how the world seemed to them. What a remarkable philosopher really does for human thought, is to throw into circulation a certain number of new and striking ideas and expressions, and to stimulate with them the thought and imagination of his century or of after-times. So Spinoza has made his distinction between adequate and inadequate ideas a current notion for educated Europe. So Hegel seized a single pregnant sentence of Heracleitus, and cast it, with a thousand striking applications, into the world of modern thought. But to do this is only enough to make a philosopher noteworthy; it is not enough to make him great. To be great, he must have something in him which can influence character, which is edifying; he must, in short, have a noble and lofty character himself, a character,—to recur to that much-criticised expression of mine,—*in the grand style.*

Arnold, Spinoza and the Bible

89 While in all productive men it is instinct that is the creative-affirmative force, and consciousness acts critically and dissuasively, in Socrates it is instinct that becomes the critic, and consciousness that becomes the creator—truly a monstrosity *per*

defectum! Specifically, we observe here a monstrous *defectus* of any mystical disposition, so Socrates might be called the typical non-mystic, in whom, through a hypertrophy, the logical nature is developed as excessively as instinctive wisdom is in the mystic. But the logical urge that became manifest in Socrates was absolutely prevented from turning against itself; in its unbridled flood it displays a natural power such as we encounter to our awed amazement only in the very greatest instinctive forces. Anyone who, through the Platonic writings, has experienced even a breath of the divine naïveté and sureness of the Socratic way of life, will also feel how the enormous driving-wheel of logical Socratism is in motion, as it were, behind Socrates, and that it must be viewed through Socrates as through a shadow.

Nietzsche, *Birth of Tragedy,* XIII

90 There are questions whose truth or untruth cannot be decided by man; all the supreme questions, all the supreme problems of value are beyond human reason. . . . To grasp the limits of reason—only this is truly philosophy.

Nietzsche, *Antichrist,* LV

91 Metaphysics means nothing but an unusually obstinate effort to think clearly.

William James, *Psychology,* VI

92 Why, from Plato and Aristotle downwards, philosophers should have vied with each other in scorn of the knowledge of the particular, and in adoration of that of the general, is hard to understand, seeing that the more adorable knowledge ought to be that of the more adorable things, and that the *things* of worth are all concretes and singulars. The only value of universal characters is that they help us, by reasoning, to know new truths about individual things. The restriction of one's meaning, moreover, to an individual thing, probably requires even more complicated brain-processes than its extension to all the instances of a kind; and the mere mystery, as such, of the knowledge, is equally great, whether generals or singulars be the things known. In sum, therefore, the traditional universal-worship can only be called a bit of perverse sentimentalism, a philosophic "idol of the cave."

William James, *Psychology,* XII

93 Philosophy is at once the most sublime and the most trivial of human pursuits. It works in the minutest crannies and it opens out the widest vistas. It "bakes no bread," as has been said, but it can inspire our souls with courage; and repugnant as its manners, its doubting and challenging, its quibbling and dialectics, often are to common people, no one of us can get along without the far-flashing beams of light it sends over the world's perspectives. These illuminations at least,

and the contrast effects of darkness and mystery that accompany them, give to what it says an interest that is much more than professional.

William James, *Pragmatism,* I

94 It is astonishing to see how many philosophical disputes collapse into insignificance the moment you subject them to this simple test of tracing a concrete consequence. There can *be* no difference anywhere that doesn't *make* a difference elsewhere—no difference in abstract truth that doesn't express itself in a difference in concrete fact and in conduct consequent upon that fact, imposed on somebody, somehow, somewhere, and somewhen. The whole function of philosophy ought to be to find out what definite difference it will make to you and me, at definite instants of our life, if this world formula or that world formula be the true one.

William James, *Pragmatism,* II

95 It is almost incredible that men who are themselves working philosophers should pretend that any philosophy can be, or ever has been, constructed without the help of personal preference, belief, or divination. How have they succeeded in so stultifying their sense for the living facts of human nature as not to perceive that every philosopher, or man of science either, whose initiative counts for anything in the evolution of thought, has taken his stand on a sort of dumb conviction that the truth must lie in one direction rather than another, and a sort of preliminary assurance that his notion can be made to work; and has borne his best fruit in trying to make it work? These mental instincts in different men are the spontaneous variations upon which the intellectual struggle for existence is based. The fittest conceptions survive, and with them the names of their champions shining to all futurity.

William James, *Sentiment of Rationality*

96 Aristotle found it necessary to complete his metaphysics by the introduction of a Prime Mover—God. This, for two reasons, is an important fact in the history of metaphysics. In the first place if we are to accord to anyone the position of the greatest metaphysician, having regard to genius of insight, to general equipment in knowledge, and to the stimulus of his metaphysical ancestry, we must choose Aristotle. Secondly, in his consideration of this metaphysical question he was entirely dispassionate; and he is the last European metaphysician of first-rate importance for whom this claim can be made.

Whitehead, *Science and the Modern World,* XI

97 Philosophy is a difficult subject, from the days of Plato to the present time haunted by subtle perplexities. The existence of such perplexities arising from the common obviousness of speech is the rea-

son why the topic exists. Thus the very purpose of philosophy is to delve below the apparent clarity of common speech.

Whitehead, *Adventures of Ideas,* XV, 2

98 Plato in the earlier period of his thought, deceived by the beauty of mathematics intelligible in unchanging perfection, conceived of a super-world of ideas, forever perfect and forever interwoven. In his latest phase he sometimes repudiates the notion, though he never consistently banishes it from his thought. His later Dialogues circle round seven notions, namely—The Ideas, The Physical Elements, The Psyche, The Eros, The Harmony, The Mathematical Relations, The Receptacle. I mention them because I hold that all philosophy is in fact an endeavour to obtain a coherent system out of some modification of these notions.

Whitehead, *Adventures of Ideas,* XIX, 2

99 Metaphysics, or the attempt to conceive the world as a whole by means of thought, has been developed, from the first, by the union and conflict of two very different human impulses, the one urging men towards mysticism, the other urging them towards science. Some men have achieved greatness through one of these impulses alone, others through the other alone: in Hume, for example, the scientific impulse reigns quite unchecked, while in Blake a strong hostility to science co-exists with profound mystic insight. But the greatest men who have been philosophers have felt the need both of science and of mysticism: the attempt to harmonize the two was what made their life, and what always must, for all its arduous uncertainty, make philosophy, to some minds, a greater thing than either science or religion.

Russell, *Mysticism and Logic*

100 It seems to me that philosophical investigation, as far as I have experience of it, starts from that curious and unsatisfactory state of mind in which one feels complete certainty without being able to say what one is certain of. The process that results from prolonged attention is just like that of watching an object approaching through a thick fog: at first it is only a vague darkness, but as it approaches articulations appear and one discovers that it is a man or a woman, or a horse or a cow or what not. It seems to me that those who object to analysis would wish us to be content with the initial dark blur. Belief in the above process is my strongest and most unshakable prejudice as regards the methods of philosophical investigation.

Russell, *My Philosophical Development,* XI

101 Philosophy has been defined as "an unusually obstinate attempt to think clearly"; I should define it rather as "an unusually ingenious attempt to think fallaciously." The philosopher's tempera-

ment is rare, because it has to combine two somewhat conflicting characteristics: on the one hand a strong desire to believe some general proposition about the universe or human life; on the other hand, inability to believe contentedly except on what appear to be intellectual grounds. The more profound the philosopher, the more intricate and subtle must his fallacies be in order to produce in him the desired state of intellectual acquiescence. That is why philosophy is obscure.

Russell, *Unpopular Essays,* IV

102 I must confess that I am not at all partial to the fabrication of *Weltanschauungen.* Such activities may be left to philosophers, who avowedly find it impossible to make their journey through life without a Baedeker of that kind to tell them all about everything. Let us humbly accept the contempt with which they look down on us from the vantage-ground of their superior needs. But since we too cannot forego our narcissistic pride, we will draw comfort from the reflection that such "Guides to Life" soon grow out of date, and that it is precisely short-sighted, narrow, and finicky work like ours which obliges them to appear in new editions, and that even the most up-to-date of them are nothing but attempts to find a substitute for the ancient, useful, and all-embracing catechism. We know well enough how little light science has so far been able to throw on the problems that surround us. But however much ado the philosophers may make, they cannot alter the situation. Only patient, persevering research, in which everything is subordinated to the one requirement of certainty, can gradually bring about a change. The benighted traveller may sing aloud in the dark to deny his own fears; but, for all that, he will not see an inch further beyond his nose.

Freud, *Inhibitions, Symptoms, and Anxiety,* II

103 Philosophy is not opposed to science; it behaves itself as if it were a science, and to a certain extent it makes use of the same methods; but it parts company with science, in that it clings to the illusion that it can produce a complete and coherent picture of the universe, though in fact that picture must needs fall to pieces with every new advance in our knowledge. Its methodological error lies in the fact that it over-estimates the epistemological value of our logical operations, and to a certain extent admits the validity of other sources of knowledge, such as intuition. . . .

But philosophy has no immediate influence on the great majority of mankind; it interests only a small number even of the thin upper stratum of intellectuals, while all the rest find it beyond them.

Freud, *New Introductory Lectures on Psycho-Analysis,* XXXV

104 The distinctive office, problems and subjectmatter of philosophy grow out of stresses and strains in the community life in which a given form of philosophy arises, and . . . accordingly, its specific problems vary with the changes in human life that are always going on and that at times constitute a crisis and a turning point in human history.

Dewey, *Reconstruction in Philosophy,*
Introduction, 1

105 We are weak today in ideal matters because intelligence is divorced from aspiration. The bare force of circumstance compels us onwards in the daily detail of our beliefs and acts, but our deeper thoughts and desires turn backwards. When philosophy shall have co-operated with the course of events and made clear and coherent the meaning of the daily detail, science and emotion will interpenetrate, practice and imagination will embrace. Poetry and religious feeling will be the unforced flowers of life. To further this articulation and revelation of the meanings of the current course of events is the task and problem of philosophy in days of transition.

Dewey, *Reconstruction in Philosophy,* VIII

106 Plato thought nature but a spume that plays
Upon a ghostly paradigm of things;
Solider Aristotle played the taws
Upon the bottom of a king of kings;
World-famous golden-thighed Pythagoras
Fingered upon a fiddle-stick or strings
What a star sang and careless Muses heard:
Old clothes upon old sticks to scare a bird.

Yeats, *Among School
Children,* VI

107 Whenever the philosopher, closeted with his wisdom, stands apart from the common rule of mankind—be it to teach them, to serve as a model, or simply to go about his work of perfecting his inner self—Socrates is there, Socrates alive, working through the incomparable prestige of his person. Let us go further. It has been said that he brought philosophy down from heaven to earth. But could we understand his life, and above all his death, if the conception of the soul which Plato attributes to him in the Phaedo had not been his? More generally speaking, do the myths we find in the dialogues of Plato, touching the soul, its origin, its entrance into the body, do anything more than set down in Platonic terms a creative emotion, the emotion present in the moral teaching of Socrates? The myths, and the Socratic conception of the soul to which they stand in the same relationship as the explanatory programme to a symphony, have been preserved along with the Platonic dialectics. They pursue their subterranean way through Greek metaphysics, and rise to the open air again with the Alexandrine philosophers, with

Ammonius perhaps, in any case with Plotinus, who claims to be the successor of Socrates. They have provided the Socratic soul with a body of doctrine similar to that into which was to be breathed the spirit of the Gospels. The two metaphysics, in spite, perhaps because, of their resemblance, gave battle to each other, before the one absorbed the best that was in the other; for a while the world may well have wondered whether it was to become Christian or Neo-Platonic. It was Socrates against Jesus. To confine ourselves to Socrates, the question is: what would this very practical genius have done in another society and in other circumstances; if he had not been struck, above all, by the danger of the moral empiricism of his time, and the mental anarchy of Athenian democracy; if he had not had to deal with the most crying need first, by establishing the rights of reason; if he had not therefore thrust intuition and inspiration into the background, and if the Greek he was had not mastered in him the Oriental who sought to come into being? We have made the distinction between the closed and the open: would anyone place Socrates among the closed souls? There was irony running through Socratic teaching, and outbursts of lyricism were probably rare; but in the measure in which these outbursts cleared the road for a new spirit, they have been decisive for the future of humanity.

Bergson, *Two Sources of Morality
and Religion,* I

108 Most propositions and questions, that have been written about philosophical matters, are not false, but senseless. We cannot, therefore, answer questions of this kind at all, but only state their senselessness. Most questions and propositions of the philosophers result from the fact that we do not understand the logic of our language.

(They are of the same kind as the question whether the Good is more or less identical than the Beautiful.)

And so it is not to be wondered at that the deepest problems are really *no* problems.

Wittgenstein, *Tractatus
Logico-Philosophicus,* 4.003

109 The object of philosophy is the logical clarification of thoughts.

Philosophy is not a theory but an activity.

A philosophical work consists essentially of elucidations.

The result of philosophy is not a number of "philosophical propositions", but to make propositions clear.

Philosophy should make clear and delimit sharply the thoughts which otherwise are, as it were, opaque and blurred. . . .

Philosophy limits the disputable sphere of natural science.

It should limit the thinkable and thereby the unthinkable.

It should limit the unthinkable from within through the thinkable.

It will mean the unspeakable by clearly displaying the speakable.

Everything that can be thought at all can be thought clearly. Everything that can be said can be said clearly.

Wittgenstein, *Tractatus Logico-Philosophicus*, 4.112–4.116

110 The right method of philosophy would be this. To say nothing except what can be said, i.e. the propositions of natural science, i.e. something that has nothing to do with philosophy: and then always, when someone else wished to say something metaphysical, to demonstrate to him that he had given no meaning to certain signs in his propositions. This method would be unsatisfying to the other— he would not have the feeling that we were teaching him philosophy—but it would be the only strictly correct method.

My propositions are elucidatory in this way: he who understands me finally recognizes them as senseless, when he has climbed out through them, on them, over them. (He must so to speak throw away the ladder, after he has climbed up on it.)

He must surmount these propositions; then he sees the world rightly.

Whereof one cannot speak, thereof one must be silent.

Wittgenstein, *Tractatus Logico-Philosophicus*, 6.53–7

111 The doctrines of philosophers disagree where they are literal and arbitrary,—mere guesses about the unknown; but they agree or complete one another where they are expressive or symbolic, thoughts wrung by experience from the hearts of poets. Then all philosophies alike are ways of meeting and recording the same flux of images, the same vicissitudes of good and evil, which will visit all generations, while man is man.

Santayana, *Three Philosophical Poets*, II

112 At best, the true philosopher can fulfil his mission very imperfectly, which is to pilot himself, or at most a few voluntary companions who may find themselves in the same boat. It is not easy for him to shout, or address a crowd; he must be silent for long seasons; for his is watching stars that move slowly and in courses that it is possible though difficult to foresee; and he is crushing all things in his heart as in a winepress, until his life and their secret flow out together.

Santayana, *Character and Opinion in the United States*, II

113 This divination of the spiritual in the things of sense, and which expresses itself in the things of sense, is precisely what we call Poetry. Metaphysics too pursues a spiritual prey, but in a very different manner, and with a very different formal object. Whereas metaphysics stands in the line of knowledge and of the contemplation of truth, poetry stands in the line of making and of the delight procured by beauty. The difference is an all-important one, and one that it would be harmful to disregard. Metaphysics snatches at the spiritual in an idea, by the most abstract intellection; poetry reaches it in the flesh, by the very point of the sense sharpened through intelligence. Metaphysics enjoys its possession only in the retreats of the eternal regions, while poetry finds its own at every crossroad in the wanderings of the contingent and the singular. The more real than reality which both seek, metaphysics must attain in the nature of things, while it suffices to poetry to touch it in any sign whatsoever. Metaphysics gives chase to essences and definitions, poetry to any flash of existence glittering by the way, and any reflection of an invisible order. Metaphysics isolates mystery in order to know it; poetry, thanks to the balances it constructs, handles and utilizes mystery as an unknown force.

Maritain, *Frontiers of Poetry*

114 Philosophy is not a "wisdom" of conduct or practical life that consists in acting well. It is a wisdom whose nature consists essentially in knowing.

How? Knowing in the fullest and strictest sense of the term, that is to say, with certainty, and in being able to state why a thing is what it is and cannot be otherwise, knowing by causes. The search for causes is indeed the chief business of philosophers, and the knowledge with which they are concerned is not a merely probable knowledge, such as orators impart by their speeches, but a knowledge which compels the assent of the intellect, like the knowledge which the geometrician conveys by his demonstrations. But certain knowledge of causes is termed science. Philosophy therefore is a science.

Maritain, *Introduction to Philosophy*, I, 5

115 Knowledge becomes coherent only as more versatile and negotiable concepts replace the generalities with which all systematizing thought begins, such as matter and motion, or body and mind, then cognition, reason and emotion, good and evil, truth and falsity, or whatever basic concepts govern the first analyses that organize a universe of discourse. Philosophy has traditionally dealt in such general terms; and the reason for its proverbial uselessness as a guide to the sciences, once they are born from its mysterious womb, is that it has made general propositions not only its immediate aim, but also its sole material. They are, in

fact, the true scientist's ultimate aim, too; but his inevitable preoccupation with research that can be carried out in *ad hoc,* provisional terms is usually so complete that he cannot survey other fields and give his best hours of thought to reinterpreting his statements in more widely variable but specifiable ways.

Langer, *Mind,* I, Intro.

17.2 | *Science and Scientific Method*

Though most of the passages assembled here are drawn from books written in modern times—the age of science as we have now come to understand it—this section begins with a few quotations from the ancients that stress the role of experience, the data obtained by investigation, or the importance of checking theories or hypotheses against the observed facts. Of special interest in this connection are the passages drawn from the writings of Ptolemy, the Greek astronomer, in which he defines the scientific effort as the task of formulating a theory that will "save the appearances," i.e., one that will account for or explain all the observed phenomena. While the language in which this insight is stated varies somewhat from author to author, the reader will find the same basic point being made by many later writers, such as Kepler, Galileo, Newton, and others.

In the modern period, the quotations are drawn mainly from two sources: on the one hand, from the treatises of eminent scientists; on the other hand, from the writings of philosophers who have undertaken the task of formulating the canons of scientific method and evaluating the achievements of science. In general there seems to be agreement among them concerning the critical role played by observation in relation to hypotheses or theories. They concur in thinking that scientific theories or hypotheses can and should be tested and either verified or falsified by the data or facts of observation, whether obtained by means of experimentation or by other techniques of research. In consequence, they agree that advances in scientific knowledge can be and have been made not only by the making of more precise and more extensive observations but also by the development of improved theories, theories better able to account for the improved observations. So predominant is this view of science in the quotations here assembled that the reader may think it has never been challenged. It has been, but only very recently, in the last fifteen years, not by leading scientists but by small groups of philosophers of science not quoted here.

The reader will find passages relevant to scientific method in Chapter 6 on KNOWLEDGE, especially Section 6.2 on EXPERIENCE; and also in Section 18.1 of the chapter on MEDICINE AND HEALTH. Because of the special role that mathematics plays in the natural sciences, especially astronomy and physics, quotations dealing with applied mathematics or the use of mathematics in science will be found in Section 17.3 of this chapter as well as here.

1 Lack of experience diminishes our power of taking a comprehensive view of the admitted facts. Hence those who dwell in intimate association with nature and its phenomena grow more and more able to formulate, as the foundations of their theories, principles such as to admit of a wide and coherent development: while those whom devotion to abstract discussions has rendered unobservant of the facts are too ready to dogmatize on the basis of a few observations.

Aristotle, *On Generation and Corruption,* 316ª5

2 With a true view all the data harmonize, but with a false one the facts soon clash.

Aristotle, *Ethics,* 1098ᵇ12

3 Keep that which is committed to thy trust, avoiding profane and vain babblings, and oppositions of science falsely so called.

I Timothy 6:20

4 Let no one, seeing the difficulty of our devices, find troublesome such hypotheses. For it is not proper to apply human things to divine things nor to get beliefs concerning such great things from such dissimilar examples. For what is more unlike than those which are always alike with respect to those which never are, and than those which are impeded by anything with those which are not even impeded by themselves? But it is proper to try and fit as far as possible the simpler hypotheses to the movements in the heavens; and if this does not succeed, then any hypotheses possible. Once all the appearances are saved by the consequences of the hypotheses, why should it seem strange that such complications can come about in the movements of heavenly things? For there is no impeding nature in them, but one proper to the yielding and giving way to movements according to the nature of each planet, even if they are contrary, so that they can all penetrate and shine through absolutely all the fluid media; and this free action takes place not only about the particular circles, but also about the spheres themselves and the axes of revolution. We see the complication and sequence in their different movements difficult and hard to come by for the freedom of the movements in the likely stories constructed by us, but in the heavenly thing never anywhere impeded by this mixture. Or rather it is not proper to judge the simplicity of heavenly things by those which seem so with us, when here not even to all of us does the same thing seem likewise simple. For in this way not one of the heavenly occurrences would seem simple to those studying them, not even the unchangeableness of the first motion, since always to be the same is not difficult here with us but impossible.

Ptolemy, *Almagest,* XIII, 2

5 The astronomer and the physicist both may prove the same conclusion—that the earth, for instance, is round; the astronomer by means of mathematics (that is, by abstracting from matter), but the physicist by means of matter itself.

Aquinas, *Summa Theologica,* I, 1, 1

6 Seven years I've served this canon, but no more
I know about his science than before.
All that I had I have quite lost thereby;
And, God knows, so have many more than I.
Where I was wont to be right fresh and gay
Of clothing and of other good array,
Now may I wear my old hose on my head;
And where my colour was both fresh and red,
Now it is wan and of a leaden hue;
Whoso this science follows, he shall rue.
And from my toil yet bleary is my eye,
Behold the gain it is to multiply!
That slippery science has made me so bare
That I've no goods, wherever I may fare;
And I am still indebted so thereby
For gold that I have borrowed, truthfully,
That while I live I shall repay it never.
Let every man be warned by me for ever!

Chaucer, *Canterbury Tales:* Canon's Yeoman's Tale

7 I will tell you, as I was taught before,
The bodies seven and the spirits four,
In order, as my master named of yore.
The first of spirits, then, quicksilver is,
The second arsenic, the third, ywis,
Is sal ammoniac, the fourth brimstone.
The seven bodies I'll describe anon:
Sol, gold is, Luna's silver, as we see,
Mars iron, and quicksilver's Mercury,
Saturn is lead, and Jupiter is tin,
And Venus copper, by my father's kin!

Chaucer, *Canterbury Tales:* Canon's Yeoman's Tale

8 For out of olde feldes, as men seyth,
Cometh al this newe corn from yer to yere,
And out of olde bokes, in good feyth,
Cometh al this newe science that men lere.

Chaucer, *The Parliament of Fowls,* 22

9 It is the job of the astronomer to use painstaking and skilled observation in gathering together the history of the celestial movements, and then—since he cannot by any line of reasoning reach the true causes of these movements—to think up or construct whatever causes or hypotheses he pleases such that, by the assumption of these causes, those same movements can be calculated from the principles of geometry for the past and for the future too. This artist is markedly outstanding in both of these respects: for it is not necessary that these hypotheses should be true, or even probable; but it is enough if they provide a calculus which fits the observations. . . . For it is sufficiently

clear that this art is absolutely and profoundly ignorant of the causes of the apparent irregular movements. And if it constructs and thinks up causes—and it has certainly thought up a good many—nevertheless it does not think them up in order to persuade anyone of their truth but only in order that they may provide a correct basis for calculation. But since for one and the same movement varying hypotheses are proposed from time to time, as eccentricity or epicycle for the movement of the sun, the astronomer much prefers to take the one which is easiest to grasp. Maybe the philosopher demands probability instead; but neither of them will grasp anything certain or hand it on, unless it has been divinely revealed to him. Therefore let us permit these new hypotheses to make a public appearance among old ones which are themselves no more probable, especially since they are wonderful and easy and bring with them a vast storehouse of learned observations. And as far as hypotheses go, let no one expect anything in the way of certainty from astronomy, since astronomy can offer us nothing certain, lest, if anyone take as true that which has been constructed for another use, he go away from this discipline a bigger fool than when he came to it.

Copernicus, De Revolutionibus, Introduction
to the Reader

10 This more divine human science, which inquires into the highest things, is not lacking in difficulties. And in particular we see that as regards its principles and assumptions, which the Greeks call "hypotheses," many of those who undertook to deal with them were not in accord and hence did not employ the same methods of calculation. In addition, the courses of the planets and the revolution of the stars cannot be determined by exact calculations and reduced to perfect knowledge unless, through the passage of time and with the help of many prior observations, they can, so to speak, be handed down to posterity. For even if Claud Ptolemy of Alexandria, who stands far in front of all the others on account of his wonderful care and industry, with the help of more than forty years of observations brought this art to such a high point that there seemed to be nothing left which he had not touched upon; nevertheless we see that very many things are not in accord with the movements which should follow from his doctrine but rather with movements which were discovered later and were unknown to him.

Copernicus De Revolutionibus, I, Introduction

11 To you alone, true philosophers, ingenuous minds, who not only in books but in things themselves look for knowledge, have I dedicated these foundations of magnetic science—a new style of philosophizing. But if any see fit not to agree with the opinions here expressed and not to accept certain of my paradoxes, still let them note the great

multitude of experiments and discoveries—these it is chiefly that cause all philosophy to flourish; and we have dug them up and demonstrated them with much pains and sleepless nights and great money expense. Enjoy them you, and, if ye can, employ them for better purposes. I know how hard it is to impart the air of newness to what is old, trimness to what is gone out of fashion; to lighten what is dark; to make that grateful which excites disgust; to win belief for things doubtful; but far more difficult is it to win any standing for or to establish doctrines that are novel, unheard of, and opposed to everybody's opinions. We care naught for that, as we have held that philosophy is for the few.

William Gilbert, On the Loadstone, Pref.

12 All . . . our predecessors, discoursing of attraction on the basis of a few vague and indecisive experiments and of reasonings from the recondite causes of things; and reckoning among the causes of the direction of the magnet, a region of the sky, celestial poles, stars, asterisms; or mountains, cliffs, vacant space, atoms, attractional or collimational regions beyond the heavens, and other like unproved paradoxes, are world-wide astray from the truth and are blindly wandering. But we do not propose just now to overturn with arguments either these their errors and impotent reasonings, or the other many fables about the loadstone, or the fairy-tales of mountebanks and story-tellers. . . . In such-like follies and fables do philosophers of the vulgar sort take delight; with such-like do they cram readers a-hungered for things abstruse, and every ignorant gaper for nonsense. But when the nature of the loadstone shall have been in the discourse following disclosed, and shall have been by our labours and experiments tested, then will the hidden and recondite but real causes of this great effect be brought forward, proven, shown, demonstrated; then, too, will all darkness vanish; every smallest root of error, being plucked up, will be cast away and will be neglected; and the foundations of a grand magnetic science being laid will appear anew, so that high intellects may no more be deluded by vain opinions.

William Gilbert, On the Loadstone, I, 1

13 Men are deplorably ignorant with respect to natural things, and modern philosophers, as though dreaming in the darkness, must be aroused and taught the uses of things, the dealing with things; they must be made to quit the sort of learning that comes only from books, and that rests only on vain arguments from probability and upon conjectures.

William Gilbert, On the Loadstone, I, 10

14 It has been ten years since I published my *Commentaries on the Movements of the Planet Mars*. As only a few copies of the book were printed, and as it

had so to speak hidden the teaching about celestial causes in thickets of calculations and the rest of the astronomical apparatus, and since the more delicate readers were frightened away by the price of the book too; it seemed to my friends that I should be doing right and fulfilling my responsibilities, if I should write an epitome, wherein a summary of both the physical and astronomical teaching concerning the heavens would be set forth in plain and simple speech and with the boredom of the demonstrations alleviated.

> Kepler, *Epitome of Copernican Astronomy*, IV, To the Reader

15 And new Philosophy calls all in doubt,
The Element of fire is quite put out;
The Sun is lost, and th'earth, and no mans wit
Can well direct him where to looke for it.
And freely men confesse that this world's spent,
When in the Planets, and the Firmament
They seeke so many new; then see that this
Is crumbled out againe to his Atomies.
'Tis all in peeces, all cohaerence gone;
All just supply, and all Relation:
Prince, Subject, Father, Sonne, are things forgot,
For every man alone thinkes he hath got
To be a Phœnix, and that then can bee
None of that kinde, of which he is, but hee.

> Donne, *First Anniversary*

16 The sciences themselves, which have had better intelligence and confederacy with the imagination of man than with his reason, are three in number; astrology, natural magic, and alchemy: of which sciences, nevertheless, the ends or pretences are noble. For astrology pretendeth to discover that correspondence or concatenation which is between the superior globe and the inferior: natural magic pretendeth to call and reduce natural philosophy from variety of speculations to the magnitude of works: and alchemy pretendeth to make separation of all the unlike parts of bodies which in mixtures of nature are incorporate. But the derivations and prosecutions to these ends, both in the theories and in the practices, are full of error and vanity; which the great professors themselves have sought to veil over and conceal by enigmatical writings, and referring themselves to auricular traditions and such other devices, to save the credit of impostures. And yet surely to alchemy this right is due, that it may be compared to the husbandman whereof Aesop makes the fable; that, when he died, told his sons that he had left unto them gold buried under ground in his vineyard; and they digged over all the ground, and gold they found none; but by reason of their stirring and digging the mould about the roots of their vines, they had a great vintage the year following: so assuredly the search and stir to make gold hath brought to light a great number of good and fruitful inventions and experiments, as well for the disclosing of nature as for the use of man's life.

> Bacon, *Advancement of Learning*, Bk. I, IV, 11

17 It were good to divide natural philosophy into the mine and the furnace, and to make two professions or occupations of natural philosophers, some to be pioneers and some smiths: some to dig, and some to refine and hammer. And surely I do best allow of a division of that kind, though in more familiar and scholastical terms; namely, that these be the two parts of natural philosophy, the inquisition of causes, and the production of effects; speculative, and operative; natural science, and natural prudence. For as in civil matters there is a wisdom of discourse, and a wisdom of direction; so is it in natural.

> Bacon, *Advancement of Learning*, Bk. II, VII, 1

18 The unassisted hand and the understanding left to itself possess but little power. Effects are produced by the means of instruments and helps, which the understanding requires no less than the hand; and as instruments either promote or regulate the motion of the hand, so those that are applied to the mind prompt or protect the understanding.

> Bacon, *Novum Organum*, I, 2

19 There are and can exist but two ways of investigating and discovering truth. The one hurries on rapidly from the senses and particulars to the most general axioms, and from them, as principles and their supposed indisputable truth, derives and discovers the intermediate axioms. This is the way now in use. The other constructs its axioms from the senses and particulars, by ascending continually and gradually, till it finally arrives at the most general axioms, which is the true but unattempted way. . . . Each of these two ways begins from the senses and particulars, and ends in the greatest generalities. But they are immeasurably different; for the one merely touches cursorily the limits of experiment and particulars, whilst the other runs duly and regularly through them; the one from the very outset lays down some abstract and useless generalities, the other gradually rises to those principles which are really the most common in nature.

> Bacon, *Novum Organum*, I, 19–22

20 Even when men build any science and theory upon experiment, yet they almost always turn with premature and hasty zeal to practise, not merely on account of the advantage and benefit to be derived from it, but in order to seize upon some security in a new undertaking of their not employing the remainder of their labor unprofitably, and by making themselves conspicuous, to acquire a greater name for their pursuit. Hence, like Atalanta, they leave the course to pick up the golden apple, interrupting their speed, and giving up the victory. But in the true course of experiment, and

in extending it to new effects, we should imitate the Divine foresight and order; for God on the first day only created light, and assigned a whole day to that work without creating any material substance thereon. In like manner we must first, by every kind of experiment, elicit the discovery of causes and true axioms, and seek for experiments which may afford light rather than profit. Axioms, when rightly investigated and established, prepare us not for a limited but abundant practice, and bring in their train whole troops of effects.

Bacon, *Novum Organum,* I, 70

21 Let no one expect any great progress in the sciences (especially their operative part), unless natural philosophy be applied to particular sciences, and particular sciences again referred back to natural philosophy. For want of this, astronomy, optics, music, many mechanical arts, medicine itself, and (what perhaps is more wonderful) moral and political philosophy, and the logical sciences have no depth, but only glide over the surface and variety of things; because these sciences, when they have been once partitioned out and established, are no longer nourished by natural philosophy, which would have imparted fresh vigor and growth to them from the sources and genuine contemplation of motion, rays, sounds, texture, and conformation of bodies, and the affections and capacity of the understanding. But we can little wonder that the sciences grow not when separated from their roots.

Bacon, *Novum Organum,* I, 80

22 There is another powerful and great cause of the little advancement of the sciences, which is this: it is impossible to advance properly in the course when the goal is not properly fixed. But the real and legitimate goal of the sciences, is the endowment of human life with new inventions and riches.

Bacon, *Novum Organum,* I, 81

23 Those who have treated of the sciences have been either empirics or dogmatical. The former like ants only heap up and use their store, the latter like spiders spin out their own webs. The bee, a mean between both, extracts matter from the flowers of the garden and the field, but works and fashions it by its own efforts. The true labor of philosophy resembles hers, for it neither relies entirely nor principally on the powers of the mind, nor yet lays up in the memory the matter afforded by the experiments of natural history and mechanics in its raw state, but changes and works it in the understanding.

Bacon, *Novum Organum,* I, 95

24 We can then only augur well for the sciences, when the ascent shall proceed by a true scale and successive steps, without interruption or breach, from particulars to the lesser axioms, thence to the intermediate (rising one above the other), and lastly, to the most general. For the lowest axioms differ but little from bare experiments; the highest and most general (as they are esteemed at present), are notional, abstract, and of no real weight. The intermediate are true, solid, full of life, and upon them depend the business and fortune of mankind; beyond these are the really general, but not abstract, axioms, which are truly limited by the intermediate.

We must not then add wings, but rather lead and ballast to the understanding, to prevent its jumping or flying, which has not yet been done; but whenever this takes place, we may entertain greater hopes of the sciences.

Bacon, *Novum Organum,* I, 104

25 Let none be alarmed at the objection of the arts and sciences becoming depraved to malevolent or luxurious purposes and the like, for the same can be said of every worldly good; talent, courage, strength, beauty, riches, light itself, and the rest. Only let mankind regain their rights over nature, assigned to them by the gift of God, and obtain that power, whose exercise will be governed by right reason and true religion.

Bacon, *Novum Organum,* I, 129

26 Of the Sphinx's riddles there are in all two kinds: one concerning the nature of things, another concerning the nature of man; and in like manner there are two kinds of kingdom offered as the reward of solving them: one over nature, and the other over man. For the command over things natural—over bodies, medicines, mechanical powers, and infinite other of the kind—is the one proper and ultimate end of true natural philosophy; however the philosophy of the school, content with what it finds, and swelling with talk, may neglect or spurn the search after realities and works. But the riddle proposed to Oedipus, by the solution of which he became king of Thebes, related to the nature of man; for whoever has a thorough insight into the nature of man may shape his fortune almost as he will, and is born for empire.

Bacon, *Wisdom of the Ancients: Sphinx*

27 First of all it seems desirable to find and explain a definition best fitting natural phenomena. For anyone may invent an arbitrary type of motion and discuss its properties; thus, for instance, some have imagined helices and conchoids as described by certain motions which are not met with in nature, and have very commendably established the properties which these curves possess in virtue of their definitions; but we have decided to consider the phenomena of bodies falling with an acceleration such as actually occurs in nature and to make

this definition of accelerated motion exhibit the essential features of observed accelerated motions. And this, at last, after repeated efforts we trust we have succeeded in doing. In this belief we are confirmed mainly by the consideration that experimental results are seen to agree with and exactly correspond with those properties which have been, one after another, demonstrated by us.

Galileo, *Two New Sciences,* III

28 *Simplicio.* I understand in a general way how the two kinds of natural motions give rise to the circles and spheres; and yet as to the production of circles by accelerated motion and its proof, I am not entirely clear; but the fact that one can take the origin of motion either at the inmost centre or at the very top of the sphere leads one to think that there may be some great mystery hidden in these true and wonderful results, a mystery related to the creation of the universe (which is said to be spherical in shape), and related also to the seat of the first cause.

Salviati. I have no hesitation in agreeing with you. But profound considerations of this kind belong to a higher science than ours. We must be satisfied to belong to that class of less worthy workmen who procure from the quarry the marble out of which, later, the gifted sculptor produces those masterpieces which lay hidden in this rough and shapeless exterior.

Galileo, *Two New Sciences,* III

29 Thus far I have spoken of the passage of the blood from the veins into the arteries, and of the manner in which it is transmitted and distributed by the action of the heart; points to which some, moved either by the authority of Galen or Columbus, or the reasonings of others, will give in their adhesion. But what remains to be said upon the quantity and source of the blood which thus passes is of so novel and unheard of character, that I not only fear injury to myself from the envy of a few, but I tremble lest I have mankind at large for my enemies, so much doth wont and custom, that become as another nature, and doctrine once sown and that hath struck deep root, and respect for antiquity influence all men: still the die is cast, and my trust is in my love of truth, and the candour that inheres in cultivated minds. And sooth to say, when I surveyed my mass of evidence, whether derived from vivisections, and my various reflections on them, or from the ventricles of the heart and the vessels that enter into and issue from them, the symmetry and size of these conduits—for nature doing nothing in vain, would never have given them so large a relative size without a purpose—or from the arrangement and intimate structure of the valves in particular, and of the other parts of the heart in general, with many things besides, I frequently and seriously bethought me, and long revolved in my mind,

what might be the quantity of blood which was transmitted, in how short a time its passage might be effected, and the like; and not finding it possible that this could be supplied by the juices of the ingested aliment without the veins on the one hand becoming drained, and the arteries on the other getting ruptured through the excessive charge of blood, unless the blood should somehow find its way from the arteries into the veins, and so return to the right side of the heart; I began to think whether there might not be a MOTION, AS IT WERE, IN A CIRCLE. Now this I afterwards found to be true.

William Harvey, *Motion of the Heart,* VIII

30 The heart, consequently, is the beginning of life; the sun of the microcosm, even as the sun in his turn might well be designated the heart of the world; for it is the heart by whose virtue and pulse the blood is moved, perfected, made apt to nourish, and is preserved from corruption and coagulation; it is the household divinity which, discharging its function, nourishes, cherishes, quickens the whole body, and is indeed the foundation of life, the source of all action. But of these things we shall speak more opportunely when we come to speculate upon the final cause of this motion of the heart.

William Harvey, *Motion of the Heart,* VIII

31 To those who repudiate the circulation because they neither see the efficient nor final cause of it, and who exclaim, *cui bono?* I have yet to reply, having hitherto taken no note of the ground of objection which they take up. And first I own I am of opinion that our first duty is to inquire whether the thing be or not, before asking wherefore it is? for from the facts and circumstances which meet us in the circulation admitted, established, the ends and objects of its institution are especially to be sought. Meantime I would only ask, how many things we admit in physiology, pathology, and therapeutics, the causes of which are unknown to us? That there are many, no one doubts—the causes of putrid fevers, of revulsions, of the purgation of excrementitious matters, among the number.

Whoever, therefore, sets himself in opposition to the circulation, because, if it be acknowledged, he cannot account for a variety of medical problems, nor in the treatment of diseases and the administration of medicines, give satisfactory reasons for the phenomena that appear; or who will not see that the precepts he has received from his teachers are false; or who thinks it unseemly to give up accredited opinions; or who regards it as in some sort criminal to call in question doctrines that have descended through a long succession of ages, and carry the authority of the ancients—to all of these I reply: that the facts cognizable by the senses wait upon no opinions, and that the works of nature bow to no antiquity; for indeed there is nothing either more ancient or of higher authority than nature.

William Harvey, *Circulation of the Blood,* II

32 On the same terms . . . as art is attained to, is all knowledge and science acquired; for as art is a habit with reference to things to be done, so is science a habit in respect of things to be known: as that proceeds from the imitation of types or forms, so this proceeds from the knowledge of natural things.

William Harvey, *Animal Generation,* Intro.

33 Thus, our learned anatomist, blinded by a popular error, seeking in the egg for some particular matter fitted to engender the chick distinct from the rest of the contents of the egg, has gone astray. And so it happens to all, who, forsaking the light, which the frequent dissection of bodies, and familiar converse with nature supplies, expect that they are to understand from conjecture, and arguments founded on probabilities, or the authority of writers, the things or the facts which they ought themselves to behold with their own eyes, to perceive with their proper senses. It is not wonderful, therefore, when we see that we have so many errors accredited by general consent, handed down to us from remote antiquity, that men otherwise of great ingenuity, should be egregiously deceived, which they may very well be, when they are satisfied with taking their knowledge from books, and keeping their memory stored with the notions of learned men. They who philosophize in this way, by tradition, if I may so say, know no better than the books they keep by them.

William Harvey, *Animal Generation,* 43

34 Whenever men notice some similarity between two things, they are wont to ascribe to each, even in those respects in which the two differ, what they have found to be true of the other. Thus they erroneously compare the sciences, which entirely consist in the cognitive exercise of the mind, with the arts, which depend upon an exercise and disposition of the body. They see that not all the arts can be acquired by the same man, but that he who restricts himself to one, most readily becomes the best executant, since it is not so easy for the same hand to adapt itself both to agricultural operations and to harp-playing, or to the performance of several such tasks as to one alone. Hence they have held the same to be true of the sciences also, and distinguishing them from one another according to their subject matter, they have imagined that they ought to be studied separately, each in isolation from all the rest. But this is certainly wrong. For since the sciences taken all together are identical with human wisdom, which always remains one and the same, however applied to different subjects, and suffers no more dif-

ferentiation proceeding from them than the light of the sun experiences from the variety of the things which it illumines, there is no need for minds to be confined at all within limits; for neither does the knowing of one truth have an effect like that of the acquisition of one art and prevent us from finding out another, it rather aids us to do so. . . . Hence we must believe that all the sciences are so inter-connected, that it is much easier to study them all together than to isolate one from all the others. If, therefore, anyone wishes to search out the truth of things in serious earnest, he ought not to select one special science; for all the sciences are conjoined with each other and interdependent: he ought rather to think how to increase the natural light of reason, not for the purpose of resolving this or that difficulty of scholastic type, but in order that his understanding may light his will to its proper choice in all the contingencies of life. In a short time he will see with amazement that he has made much more progress than those who are eager about particular ends, and that he has not only obtained all that they desire, but even higher results than fall within his expectation.

Descartes, *Rules for Direction of the Mind,* I

35 Fearing that I could not put in my Treatise all that I had in my mind, I undertook only to show very fully my conceptions of light. Later on, when occasion occurred, I resolved to add something about the sun and fixed stars, because light proceeds almost entirely from them; the heavens would be dealt with because they transmit light, the planets, the comets and the earth because they reflect it, and more particularly would all bodies which are on the earth, because they are either coloured or transparent, or else luminous; and finally I should deal with man because he is the spectator of all. For the very purpose of putting all these topics somewhat in shadow, and being able to express myself freely about them, without being obliged to adopt or to refute the opinions which are accepted by the learned, I resolved to leave all this world to their disputes, and to speak only of what would happen in a new world if God now created, somewhere in an imaginary space, matter sufficient wherewith to form it, and if He agitated in diverse ways, and without any order, the diverse portions of this matter, so that there resulted a chaos as confused as the poets ever feigned, and concluded His work by merely lending His concurrence to Nature in the usual way, leaving her to act in accordance with the laws which He had established.

Descartes, *Discourse on Method,* V

36 So soon as I had acquired some general notions concerning Physics, and as, beginning to make use of them in various special difficulties, I observed to what point they might lead us, and how much

they differ from the principles of which we have made use up to the present time, I believed that I could not keep them concealed without greatly sinning against the law which obliges us to procure, as much as in us lies, the general good of all mankind. For they caused me to see that it is possible to attain knowledge which is very useful in life, and that, instead of that speculative philosophy which is taught in the Schools, we may find a practical philosophy by means of which, knowing the force and the action of fire, water, air, the stars, heavens and all other bodies that environ us, as distinctly as we know the different crafts of our artisans, we can in the same way employ them in all those uses to which they are adapted, and thus render ourselves the masters and possessors of nature.

Descartes, *Discourse on Method,* VI

37 The light of humane minds is perspicuous words, but by exact definitions first snuffed, and purged from ambiguity; reason is the pace; increase of science, the way; and the benefit of mankind, the end.

Hobbes, *Leviathan,* I, 5

38 All the sciences are infinite in the extent of their researches. For who doubts that geometry, for instance, has an infinite infinity of problems to solve? They are also infinite in the multitude and fineness of their premises; for it is clear that those which are put forward as ultimate are not self-supporting, but are based on others which, again having others for their support, do not permit of finality. But we represent some as ultimate for reason, in the same way as in regard to material objects we call that an indivisible point beyond which our senses can no longer perceive anything, although by its nature it is infinitely divisible.

Of these two Infinites of science, that of greatness is the most palpable, and hence a few persons have pretended to know all things. "I will speak of the whole," said Democritus.

But the infinitely little is the least obvious. Philosophers have much oftener claimed to have reached it, and it is here they have all stumbled.

Pascal, *Pensées,* II, 72

39 Geometry, arithmetic, music, physics, medicine, architecture, and all the sciences subject to experiment and reason must be added to if they are to become perfect. The ancients found them merely sketched by their predecessors, and we shall leave them to our successors in a more perfected state than we received them. Since their perfection depends upon time and effort, it is evident that even if our effort and time had gained us less than the labors of the ancients, separated from ours, the two together nevertheless must have more effect than either alone.

The clearing up of this difference should make us pity the blindness of those who advance authority alone as proof in physics instead of reason or experiment, and should fill us with horror at the wickedness of others who use reason alone in theology instead of the authority of Scripture and the Fathers. We must strengthen the courage of those timid souls who dare discover nothing in physics, and confound the insolence of that temerity which introduces novelty into theology. Meanwhile the misfortune of the age is such that we see many new opinions in theology altogether unknown to antiquity maintained with obstinacy and received with applause; whereas those put forward in physics, though few in number, must be convicted of error, it seems, as soon as they shock, however little, received opinions. As if respect for the philosophers of antiquity were a duty but for the most ancient of the Fathers only decorum! I leave it to the judicious to observe the importance of this abuse which perverts the order of the sciences so unjustly, and I think there will be few who do not wish this . . . to be applied to other subjects, since new discoveries are inevitably errors in those matters we profane with impunity, whereas they are absolutely necessary for the perfection of so many other subjects incomparably lower, which however we would be afraid to touch.

Pascal, *Preface to the Treatise on the Vacuum*

40 Concerning the vacuum the ancients were right to say that nature did not permit it, because all their experiments had always led to the observation that she abhorred it and could not endure it. But if the new experiments had been known to them, perhaps they would have found reason to affirm what they had reason to deny because the vacuum had not yet appeared. Therefore in making the judgment that nature did not permit a vacuum, they meant to speak of nature only as they knew her; since to make the judgment in general it would not be enough to have seen it true in a hundred instances or in a thousand or in any other number however great, for if there remained a single case to examine, it alone would suffice to prevent the general definition, and if a single case were opposed, it alone. . . . For in all matters whose proof is by experiment and not by demonstration no universal assertion can be made except by the general enumeration of all the parts and all the different cases. Thus when we say the diamond is the hardest of all bodies, we mean of all bodies we know, and we neither can nor should include those we do not know. And when we say that gold is the heaviest of all bodies, it would be rash of us to include in this general proposition bodies not yet in our knowledge, although it is not impossible they are in nature. Similarly when the ancients asserted that nature did not permit a vacuum, they meant she did not permit a vacuum in all the experiments they had seen, and they

could not without rashness include experiments they did not know. But if they had known them, undoubtedly they would have drawn the same consequences as we do and would by their avowal have given them the authority of that antiquity which men today want to make the sole principle of the sciences.

Pascal, *Preface to the Treatise on the Vacuum*

41 Let all the disciples of Aristotle bring together all the strongest arguments there are in the writings of their master and of his commentators to account for these things by the horror of the vacuum, if they can; if not, let them recognize that experiments are the true masters to follow in physics, that the experiment made on the mountains overturned the universal belief everywhere held that nature abhors a vacuum and opened up this knowledge which can nevermore be forgotten, that nature has no horror of the vacuum, that she does nothing to avoid it, and that the weight of the mass of the air is the true cause of all the effects hitherto attributed to that imaginary cause.

Pascal, *Treatise on the Weight of the Mass of the Air*

42 And *Raphael* now to *Adam's* doubt propos'd
Benevolent and facil thus repli'd.
    To ask or search I blame thee not, for Heav'n
Is as the Book of God before thee set,
Wherein to read his wondrous Works, and learne
His Seasons, Hours, or Days, or Months, or
    Yeares;
This to attain, whether Heav'n move or Earth,
Imports not, if thou reck'n right, the rest
From Man or Angel the great Architect
Did wisely to conceal, and not divulge
His secrets to be scann'd by them who ought
Rather admire; or if they list to try
Conjecture, he his Fabric of the Heav'ns
Hath left to thir disputes, perhaps to move
His laughter at thir quaint Opinions wide
Hereafter, when they come to model Heav'n
And calculate the Starrs, how they will weild
The mightie frame, how build, unbuild, contrive
To save appearances, how gird the Sphear
With Centric and Eccentric scribl'd o're,
Cycle and Epicycle, Orb in Orb.

Milton, *Paradise Lost,* VIII, 64

43 I have finally judged that it was better worth while to publish this writing, such as it is, than to let it run the risk, by waiting longer, of remaining lost. There will be seen in it demonstrations of those kinds which do not produce as great a certitude as those of geometry, and which even differ much therefrom, since, whereas the geometers prove their propositions by fixed and incontestable principles, here the principles are verified by the conclusions to be drawn from them; the na-

ture of these things not allowing of this being done otherwise. It is always possible to attain thereby to a degree of probability which very often is scarcely less than complete proof. To wit, when things which have been demonstrated by the principles that have been assumed correspond perfectly to the phenomena which experiment has brought under observation; especially when there are a great number of them, and further, principally, when one can imagine and foresee new phenomena which ought to follow from the hypotheses which one employs, and when one finds that therein the fact corresponds to our prevision. But if all these proofs of probability are met with in that which I propose to discuss, as it seems to me they are, this ought to be a very strong confirmation of the success of my inquiry.

Huygens, *Treatise on Light,* Pref.

44 I derive from the celestial phenomena the forces of gravity with which bodies tend to the sun and the several planets. Then from these forces, by other propositions which are also mathematical, I deduce the motions of the planets, the comets, the moon, and the sea. I wish we could derive the rest of the phenomena of Nature by the same kind of reasoning from mechanical principles, for I am induced by many reasons to suspect that they may all depend upon certain forces by which the particles of bodies, by some causes hitherto unknown, are either mutually impelled towards one another, and where in regular figures, or are repelled and recede from one another. These forces being unknown, philosophers have hitherto attempted the search of Nature in vain; but I hope the principles here laid down will afford some light either to this or some truer method of philosophy.

Newton, *Principia,* Pref. to 1st Ed.

45 The qualities of bodies, which admit neither intensification nor remission of degrees, and which are found to belong to all bodies within the reach of our experiments, are to be esteemed the universal qualities of all bodies whatsoever. For since the qualities of bodies are only known to us by experiments, we are to hold for universal all such as universally agree with experiments; and such as are not liable to diminution can never be quite taken away. We are certainly not to relinquish the evidence of experiments for the sake of dreams and vain fictions of our own devising; nor are we to recede from the analogy of Nature, which is wont to be simple, and always consonant to itself.

Newton, *Principia,* III, Rule III

46 In experimental philosophy we are to look upon propositions inferred by general induction from phenomena as accurately or very nearly true, notwithstanding any contrary hypotheses that may be imagined, till such time as other phenomena

occur, by which they may either be made more accurate, or liable to exceptions.

This rule we must follow, that the argument of induction may not be evaded by hypotheses.

Newton, *Principia*, III, Rule IV

47 These principles [e.g., gravity] I consider, not as occult qualities, supposed to result from the specific forms of things, but as general laws of nature, by which the things themselves are formed; their truth appearing to us by phenomena, though their causes be not yet discovered. For these are manifest qualities, and their causes only are occult. And the Aristotelians gave the name of occult qualities, not to manifest qualities, but to such qualities only as they supposed to lie hid in bodies, and to be the unknown causes of manifest effects. Such as would be the causes of gravity, and of magnetic and electric attractions, and of fermentations, if we should suppose that these forces or actions arose from qualities unknown to us, and incapable of being discovered and made manifest. Such occult qualities put a stop to the improvement of natural philosophy, and therefore of late years have been rejected. To tell us that every species of things is endowed with an occult specific quality by which it acts and produces manifest effects, is to tell us nothing; but to derive two or three general principles of motion from phenomena, and afterwards to tell us how the properties and actions of all corporeal things follow from those manifest principles, would be a very great step in philosophy, though the causes of those principles were not yet discovered. And, therefore, I scruple not to propose the principles of motion above mentioned, they being of very general extent, and leave their causes to be found out.

Newton, *Optics*, III, 1

48 I do not know what I may appear to the world, but to myself I seem to have been only like a boy playing on the seashore, and diverting myself in now and then finding a smoother pebble or a prettier shell than ordinary, whilst the great ocean of truth lay all undiscovered before me.

Newton, *Remark (1727)*

49 Mr. Newton, in his never enough to be admired book, has demonstrated several propositions, which are so many new truths, before unknown to the world, and are further advances in mathematical knowledge: but, for the discovery of these, it was not the general maxims, "what is, is;" or, "the whole is bigger than a part," or the like, that helped him. These were not the clues that led him into the discovery of the truth and certainty of those propositions. Nor was it by them that he got the knowledge of those demonstrations, but by finding out intermediate ideas that showed the agreement or disagreement of the ideas, as expressed in the propositions he demonstrated. This is the greatest exercise and improvement of hu-

man understanding in the enlarging of knowledge, and advancing the sciences; wherein they are far enough from receiving any help from the contemplation of these or the like magnified maxims.

Locke, *Concerning Human Understanding*, Bk. IV, VII, 11

50 I deny not but a man, accustomed to rational and regular experiments, shall be able to see further into the nature of bodies and guess righter at their yet unknown properties than one that is a stranger to them: but yet, as I have said, this is but judgment and opinion, not knowledge and certainty. This way of *getting and improving our knowledge in substances only by experience and history,* which is all that the weakness of our faculties in this state of mediocrity which we are in in this world can attain to, makes me suspect that *natural philosophy is not capable of being made a science.* We are able, I imagine, to reach very little general knowledge concerning the species of bodies and their several properties. Experiments and historical observations we may have, from which we may draw advantages of ease and health, and thereby increase our stock of conveniences for this life; but beyond this I fear our talents reach not, nor are our faculties, as I guess, able to advance.

Locke, *Concerning Human Understanding*, Bk. IV, XII, 10

51 Natural philosophy, as a speculative science, I imagine we have none, and perhaps I may think I have reason to say we never shall be able to make a science of it. The works of nature are contrived by a wisdom, and operate by ways too far surpassing our faculties to discover or capacities to conceive, for us ever to be able to reduce them into a science.

Locke, *Some Thoughts Concerning Education*, 190

52 If . . . we consider the difference there is betwixt natural philosophers and other men, with regard to their knowledge of the phenomena, we shall find it consists not in an exacter knowledge of the efficient cause that produces them—for that can be no other than the *will of a spirit*—but only in a greater largeness of comprehension, whereby analogies, harmonies, and agreements are discovered in the works of nature, and the particular effects explained, that is, reduced to general rules, which rules, grounded on the analogy and uniformness observed in the production of natural effects, are most agreeable and sought after by the mind; for that they extend our prospect beyond what is present and near to us, and enable us to make very probable conjectures touching things that may have happened at very great distances of time and place, as well as to predict things to come; which sort of endeavour towards omni-

science is much affected by the mind.

Berkeley, Principles of Human Knowledge, 105

53 I think we may lay down the following conclusions. First, it is plain philosophers amuse themselves in vain, when they inquire for any natural efficient cause, distinct from a *mind* or *spirit*. Secondly, considering the whole creation is the workmanship of a *wise and good Agent,* it should seem to become philosophers to employ their thoughts (contrary to what some hold) about the final causes of things; and I confess I see no reason why pointing out the various ends to which natural things are adapted, and for which they were originally with unspeakable wisdom contrived, should not be thought one good way of accounting for them, and altogether worthy a philosopher. Thirdly, from what has been premised no reason can be drawn why the history of nature should not still be studied, and observations and experiments made, which, that they are of use to mankind, and enable us to draw any general conclusions, is not the result of any immutable habitudes or relations between things themselves, but only of God's goodness and kindness to men in the administration of the world. Fourthly, by a diligent observation of the phenomena within our view, we may discover the general laws of nature, and from them deduce the other phenomena; I do not say *demonstrate,* for all deductions of that kind depend on a supposition that the Author of nature always operates uniformly, and in a constant observance of those rules we take for principles: which we cannot evidently know.

Berkeley, Principles of Human Knowledge, 107

54 Nature and Nature's laws lay hid in Night;
God said, Let NEWTON be! and all was Light.

Pope, Intended for Sir Isaac Newton

55 The most perfect philosophy of the natural kind only staves off our ignorance a little longer: as perhaps the most perfect philosophy of the moral or metaphysical kind serves only to discover larger portions of it. Thus the observation of human blindness and weakness is the result of all philosophy, and meets us at every turn, in spite of our endeavours to elude or avoid it.

Nor is geometry, when taken into the assistance of natural philosophy, ever able to remedy this defect, or lead us into the knowledge of ultimate causes, by all that accuracy of reasoning for which it is so justly celebrated. . . . Thus, it is a law of motion, discovered by experience, that the moment or force of any body in motion is in the compound ratio or proportion of its solid contents and its velocity; and consequently, that a small force may remove the greatest obstacle or raise the greatest weight, if, by any contrivance or machinery, we can increase the velocity of that force, so as to make it an overmatch for its antagonist. Ge-

ometry assists us in the application of this law, by giving us the just dimensions of all the parts and figures which can enter into any species of machine; but still the discovery of the law itself is owing merely to experience, and all the abstract reasonings in the world could never lead us one step towards the knowledge of it. When we reason *a priori,* and consider merely any object or cause, as it appears to the mind, independent of all observation, it never could suggest to us the notion of any distinct object, such as its effect; much less, show us the inseparable and inviolable connexion between them. A man must be very sagacious who could discover by reasoning that crystal is the effect of heat, and ice of cold, without being previously acquainted with the operation of these qualities.

*Hume, Concerning Human
Understanding, IV, 26–27*

56 When we run over libraries, persuaded of these principles, what havoc must we make? If we take in our hand any volume; of divinity or school metaphysics, for instance; let us ask, *Does it contain any abstract reasoning concerning quantity or number?* No. *Does it contain any experimental reasoning concerning matter of fact and existence?* No. Commit it then to the flames: for it can contain nothing but sophistry and illusion.

*Hume, Concerning Human
Understanding, XII, 132*

57 The philosophers of the last age found out a new universe; and a circumstance which made its discovery more difficult was that no one had so much as suspected its existence. The most sage and judicious were of opinion that it was a frantic rashness to dare so much as to imagine that it was possible to guess the laws by which the celestial bodies move and the manner how light acts. Galileo, by his astronomical discoveries, Kepler, by his calculation, Descartes (at least, in his dioptrics), and Sir Isaac Newton, in all his works, severally saw the mechanism of the springs of the world. The geometricians have subjected infinity to the laws of calculation. The circulation of the blood in animals, and of the sap in vegetables, have changed the face of Nature with regard to us. A new kind of existence has been given to bodies in the air-pump. By the assistance of telescopes bodies have been brought nearer to one another. Finally, the several discoveries which Sir Isaac Newton has made on light are equal to the boldest things which the curiosity of man could expect after so many philosophical novelties.

Voltaire, Letters on the English, XVI

58 It must indeed be confessed that the Royal Society boast their Newton, but then he did not owe his knowledge and discoveries to that body; so far from it that the latter were intelligible to very few

of his fellow members. A genius like that of Sir Isaac belonged to all the academies in the world, because all had a thousand things to learn of him.

Voltaire, *Letters on the English,* XVI

59 There prevails among men of letters an opinion that all appearance of science is particularly hateful to women.

Johnson, *Rambler No. 173*

60 *Johnson.* Human experience, which is constantly contradicting theory, is the great test of truth. A system, built upon the discoveries of a great many minds, is always of more strength, than what is produced by the mere workings of any one mind, which, of itself, can do little. There is not so poor a book in the world that would not be a prodigious effort were it wrought out entirely by a single mind, without the aid of prior investigators.

Boswell, *Life of Johnson (July 28, 1763)*

61 We very often hear complaints of the shallowness of the present age, and of the decay of profound science. But I do not think that those which rest upon a secure foundation, such as mathematics, physical science, etc., in the least deserve this reproach, but that they rather maintain their ancient fame, and in the latter case, indeed, far surpass it. The same would be the case with the other kinds of cognition, if their principles were but firmly established. In the absence of this security, indifference, doubt, and finally, severe criticism are rather signs of a profound habit of thought. Our age is the age of criticism, to which everything must be subjected. The sacredness of religion, and the authority of legislation, are by many regarded as grounds of exemption from the examination of this tribunal. But, if they are exempted, they become the subjects of just suspicion, and cannot lay claim to sincere respect, which reason accords only to that which has stood the test of a free and public examination.

Kant, *Critique of Pure Reason,*
Pref. to 1st Ed., fn. 2

62 It is only about a century and a half since the wise Bacon gave a new direction to physical studies, or rather—as others were already on the right track—imparted fresh vigour to the pursuit of this new direction. Here, too, as in the case of mathematics, we find evidence of a rapid intellectual revolution. In the remarks which follow I shall confine myself to the *empirical* side of natural science.

When Galilei experimented with balls of a definite weight on the inclined plane, when Torricelli caused the air to sustain a weight which he had calculated beforehand to be equal to that of a definite column of water, or when Stahl, at a later period, converted metals into lime, and reconverted lime into metal, by the addition and subtrac-

tion of certain elements; a light broke upon all natural philosophers. They learned that reason only perceives that which it produces after its own design; that it must not be content to follow, as it were, in the leading-strings of nature, but must proceed in advance with principles of judgement according to unvarying laws, and compel nature to reply to its questions. For accidental observations, made according to no preconceived plan, cannot be united under a necessary law. But it is this that reason seeks for and requires. It is only the principles of reason which can give to concordant phenomena the validity of laws, and it is only when experiment is directed by these rational principles that it can have any real utility. Reason must approach nature with the view, indeed, of receiving information from it, not, however, in the character of a pupil, who listens to all that his master chooses to tell him, but in that of a judge, who compels the witnesses to reply to those questions which he himself thinks fit to propose. To this single idea must the revolution be ascribed, by which, after groping in the dark for so many centuries, natural science was at length conducted into the path of certain progress.

Kant, *Critique of Pure Reason,*
Pref. to 2nd Ed.

63 In matters of science . . . the greatest inventor differs only in degree from the most laborious imitator and apprentice, whereas he differs specifically from one endowed by nature for fine art. No disparagement, however, of those great men, to whom the human race is so deeply indebted, is involved in this comparison of them with those who on the score of their talent for fine art are the elect of nature. The talent for science is formed for the continued advances of greater perfection in knowledge, with all its dependent practical advantages, as also for imparting the same to others. Hence scientists can boast a ground of considerable superiority over those who merit the honour of being called geniuses, since genius reaches a point at which art must make a halt, as there is a limit imposed upon it which it cannot transcend.

Kant, *Critique of Aesthetic Judgement,* 47

64 Fine art and the sciences, if they do not make man morally better, yet, by conveying a pleasure that admits of universal communication and by introducing polish and refinement into society, make him civilized. Thus they do much to overcome the tyrannical propensities of sense, and so prepare man for a sovereignty in which reason alone shall have sway.

Kant, *Critique of Teleological Judgement,* 83

65 The impossibility of separating the nomenclature of a science from the science itself is owing to this, that every branch of physical science must consist of three things: the series of facts which are the

objects of the science, the ideas which represent these facts, and the words by which these ideas are expressed. Like three impressions of the same seal, the word ought to produce the idea, and the idea to be a picture of the fact. And, as ideas are preserved and communicated by means of words, it necessarily follows that we cannot improve the language of any science without at the same time improving the science itself; neither can we, on the other hand, improve a science without improving the language or nomenclature which belongs to it. However certain the facts of any science may be and however just the ideas we may have formed of these facts, we can only communicate false impressions to others while we want words by which these may be properly expressed.

Lavoisier, *Elements of Chemistry,* Pref.

66 When we begin the study of any science, we are in a situation, respecting that science, similar to that of children; and the course by which we have to advance is precisely the same which nature follows in the formation of their ideas. In a child, the idea is merely an effect produced by a sensation; and, in the same manner, in commencing the study of a physical science, we ought to form no idea but what is a necessary consequence, and immediate effect, of an experiment or observation. Besides, he that enters upon the career of science is in a less advantageous situation than a child who is acquiring his first ideas. To the child, nature gives various means of rectifying any mistakes he may commit respecting the salutary or hurtful qualities of the objects which surround him. On every occasion his judgments are corrected by experience; want and pain are the necessary consequences arising from false judgment; gratification and pleasure are produced by judging aright. Under such masters, we cannot fail to become well informed; and we soon learn to reason justly, when want and pain are the necessary consequences of a contrary conduct.

In the study and practice of the sciences it is quite different; the false judgments we form neither affect our existence nor our welfare; and we are not forced by any physical necessity to correct them. Imagination, on the contrary, which is ever wandering beyond the bounds of truth, joined to self-love and that self-confidence we are so apt to indulge, prompts us to draw conclusions which are not immediately derived from facts; so that we become in some measure interested in deceiving ourselves. Hence, it is by no means to be wondered that, in the science of physics in general, men have often made suppositions instead of forming conclusions. These suppositions, handed down from one age to another, acquire additional weight from the authorities by which they are supported, till at last they are received, even by men of genius, as fundamental truths.

The only method of preventing such errors from taking place, and of correcting them when formed, is to restrain and simplify our reasoning as much as possible. This depends entirely upon ourselves, and the neglect of it is the only source of our mistakes. We must trust to nothing but facts: these are presented to us by nature and cannot deceive. We ought, in every instance, to submit our reasoning to the test of experiment and never to search for truth but by the natural road of experiment and observation.

Lavoisier, *Elements of Chemistry,* Pref.

67 I am far from pretending . . . to set aside the necessity of attendance upon lectures and laboratories for such as wish to acquire accurate knowledge of the science of chemistry. These should familiarise themselves to the employment of apparatus, and to the performance of experiments by actual experience. *Nihil est in intellectu quod non prius fuerit in sensu* [Nothing is in the intellect that was not first in the senses], the motto which the celebrated Rouelle caused to be painted in large characters in a conspicuous part of his laboratory, is an important truth never to be lost sight of either by teachers or students of chemistry.

Lavoisier, *Elements of Chemistry,*
III, Introduction

68 The best method known for determining the quantities of substances submitted to chemical experiment or resulting from them, is by means of an accurately constructed beam and scales, with properly regulated weights, which well known operation is called *weighing.* The denomination and quantity of the weights used as an unit or standard for this purpose are extremely arbitrary, and vary not only in different kingdoms, but even in different provinces of the same kingdom, and in different cities of the same province. This variation is of infinite consequence to be well understood in commerce and in the arts; but, in chemistry, it is of no moment what particular denomination of weight be employed, provided the results of experiments be expressed in convenient fractions of the same denomination. For this purpose, until all the weights used in society be reduced to the same standard, it will be sufficient for chemists in different parts to use the common pound of their own country as the unit or standard, and to express all its fractional parts in decimals instead of the arbitrary divisions now in use. By this means the chemists of all countries will be thoroughly understood by each other, as, although the absolute weights of the ingredients and products cannot be known, they will readily, and without calculation, be able to determine the relative proportions of these to each other with the utmost accuracy; so that in this way we shall be possessed of an universal language for this part of chemistry.

Lavoisier, *Elements of Chemistry,* III, 1

69 The present rage for wide and unrestrained speculation seems to be a kind of mental intoxication, arising, perhaps, from the great and unexpected discoveries which have been made of late years in various branches of science. To men elate and giddy with such successes, everything appeared to be within the grasp of human powers; and, under this illusion, they confounded subjects where no real progress could be proved with those where the progress had been marked, certain, and acknowledged. Could they be persuaded to sober themselves with a little severe and chastised thinking, they would see that the cause of truth and of sound philosophy cannot but suffer by substituting wild flights and unsupported assertions for patient investigation and well authenticated proofs.

Malthus, *Population*, IX

70 Without my attempts in natural science, I should never have learned to know mankind such as it is. In nothing else can we so closely approach pure contemplation and thought, so closely observe the errors of the senses and of the understanding.

Goethe, *Conversations with Eckermann*
(Feb. 13, 1829)

71 Science appears but what in truth she is,
Not as our glory and our absolute boast,
But as a succedaneum, and a prop
To our infirmity. No officious slave
Art thou of that false secondary power
By which we multiply distinctions, then
Deem that our puny boundaries are things
That we perceive, and not that we have made.

Wordsworth, *The Prelude*, II, 212

72 The Evangelist St. John my patron was:
Three Gothic courts are his, and in the first
Was my abiding-place, a nook obscure;
Right underneath, the College kitchens made
A humming sound, less tuneable than bees,
But hardly less industrious; with shrill notes
Of sharp command and scolding intermixed.
Near me hung Trinity's loquacious clock,
Who never let the quarters, night or day,
Slip by him unproclaimed, and told the hours
Twice over with a male and female voice.
Her pealing organ was my neighbour too;
And from my pillow, looking forth by light
Of moon or favouring stars, I could behold
The antechapel where the statue stood
Of Newton with his prism and silent face,
The marble index of a mind for ever
Voyaging through strange seas of Thought, alone.

Wordsworth, *The Prelude*, III, 46

73 The state is universal in form, a form whose essential principle is thought. This explains why it was in the state that freedom of thought and science had their origin. It was a church, on the other hand, which burnt Giordano Bruno, forced Galileo to recant on his knees his exposition of the Copernican view of the solar system, and so forth. Science too, therefore, has its place on the side of the state since it has one element, its form, in common with the state, and its aim is knowledge, knowledge of objective truth and rationality in terms of thought. Such knowledge may, of course, fall from the heights of science into opinion and deductive argumentation, and, turning its attention to ethical matters and the organization of the state, set itself against their basic principles. And it may perhaps do this while making for this opining—as if it were reason and the right of subjective self-consciousness—the same pretentious claim as the church makes for its own sphere, the claim, namely, to be free from restraint in its opinions and convictions.

Hegel, *Philosophy of Right*, 270

74 The knowledge of rational mechanics, which the most ancient nations had been able to acquire, has not come down to us, and the history of this science, if we except the first theorems in harmony, is not traced up beyond the discoveries of Archimedes. This great geometer explained the mathematical principles of the equilibrium of solids and fluids. About eighteen centuries elapsed before Galileo, the originator of dynamical theories, discovered the laws of motion of heavy bodies. Within this new science Newton comprised the whole system of the universe. The successors of these philosophers have extended these theories, and given them an admirable perfection: they have taught us that the most diverse phenomena are subject to a small number of fundamental laws which are reproduced in all the acts of nature. It is recognised that the same principles regulate all the movements of the stars, their form, the inequalities of their courses, the equilibrium and the oscillations of the seas, the harmonic vibrations of air and sonorous bodies, the transmission of light, capillary actions, the undulations of fluids, in fine the most complex effects of all the natural forces.

Fourier, *Analytical Theory of Heat*,
Preliminary Discourse

75 The new theories explained in our work are united for ever to the mathematical sciences, and rest like them on invariable foundations; all the elements which they at present possess they will preserve, and will continually acquire greater extent. Instruments will be perfected and experiments multiplied. The analysis which we have formed will be deduced from more general, that is to say, more simple and more fertile methods common to many classes of phenomena. . . . The theory itself will direct all these measures, and assign their precision. No considerable progress can hereafter be made which is not founded on experiments such as these; for mathematical analysis can deduce

from general and simple phenomena the expression of the laws of nature; but the special application of these laws to very complex effects demands a long series of exact observations.

Fourier, *Analytical Theory of Heat,*
Preliminary Discourse

76 There is no science which, having attained the positive stage, does not bear marks of having passed through the others. Some time since it was (whatever it might be) composed, as we can now perceive, of metaphysical abstractions; and, further back in the course of time, it took its form from theological conceptions. We shall have only too much occasion to see, as we proceed, that our most advanced sciences still bear very evident marks of the two earlier periods through which they have passed.

Comte, *Positive Philosophy,* Introduction, 1

77 All good intellects have repeated, since Bacon's time, that there can be no real knowledge but that which is based on observed facts. This is incontestable, in our present advanced stage; but, if we look back to the primitive stage of human knowledge, we shall see that it must have been otherwise then. If it is true that every theory must be based upon observed facts, it is equally true that facts can not be observed without the guidance of some theory. Without such guidance, our facts would be desultory and fruitless; we could not retain them: for the most part we could not even perceive them.

Comte, *Positive Philosophy,* Introduction, 1

78 Because it is proposed to consolidate the whole of our acquired knowledge into one body of homogeneous doctrine, it must not be supposed that we are going to study this vast variety as proceeding from a single principle, and as subjected to a single law. . . . Our intellectual resources are too narrow, and the universe is too complex, to leave any hope that it will ever be within our power to carry scientific perfection to its last degree of simplicity. . . . While pursuing the philosophical aim of all science, the lessening of the number of general laws requisite for the explanation of natural phenomena, we shall regard as presumptuous every attempt, in all future time, to reduce them rigorously to one.

Comte, *Positive Philosophy,* Introduction, 1

79 *The Lycée,* No. 36 for January 1st, has a long and rather premature article, in which it endeavours to show anticipations by French philosophers of my researches. It however mistakes the erroneous results of MM. Fresnel and Ampère for true ones, and then imagines my true results are like those erroneous ones. I notice it here, however, for the purpose of doing honour to Fresnel in a much higher degree than would have been merited by a feeble anticipation of the present investigations. That great philosopher, at the same time with myself and fifty other persons, made experiments which the present paper proves could give no expected result. He was deceived for the moment, and published his imaginary success; but on more carefully repeating his trials, he could find no proof of their accuracy; and, in the high and pure philosophic desire to remove error as well as discover truth, he recanted his first statement. The example of Berzelius regarding the first Thorina is another instance of this fine feeling; and as occasions are not rare, it would be to the dignity of science if such examples were more frequently followed.

Faraday, *Experimental Researches
in Electricity,* I, 79, fn.

80 It is the great beauty of our science, CHEMISTRY, that advancement in it, whether in a degree great or small, instead of exhausting the subjects of research, opens the doors to further and more abundant knowledge, overflowing with beauty and utility, to those who will be at the easy personal pains of undertaking its experimental investigation.

Faraday, *Experimental Researches
in Electricity,* VII, 871

81 The views I have taken of the definite action of electricity in decomposing bodies, and the identity of the power so used with the power to be overcome, founded not on a mere opinion or general notion, but on facts which, being altogether new, were to my mind precise and conclusive, gave me, as I conceived, the power of examining the question with advantages not before possessed by any, and which might compensate, on my part, for the superior clearness and extent of intellect on theirs. Such are the considerations which have induced me to suppose I might help in deciding the question, and be able to render assistance in that great service of removing *doubtful knowledge.* Such knowledge is the early morning light of every advancing science, and is essential to its development; but the man who is engaged in dispelling that which is deceptive in it, and revealing more clearly that which is true, is as useful in his place, and as necessary to the general progress of the science, as he who first broke through the intellectual darkness, and opened a path into knowledge before unknown to man.

Faraday, *Experimental Researches
in Electricity,* VIII, 876

82 The science of electricity is in that state in which every part of it requires experimental investigation; not merely for the discovery of new effects, but what is just now of far more importance, the development of the means by which the old effects are produced, and the consequent more accurate

determination of the first principles of action of the most extraordinary and universal power in nature: and to those philosophers who pursue the inquiry zealously yet cautiously, combining experiment with analogy, suspicious of their preconceived notions, paying more respect to a fact than a theory, not too hasty to generalize, and above all things, willing at every step to cross-examine their own opinions, both by reasoning and experiment, no branch of knowledge can afford so fine and ready a field for discovery as this. Such is most abundantly shown to be the case by the progress which electricity has made in the last thirty years: chemistry and magnetism have successively acknowledged its over-ruling influence: and it is probable that every effect depending upon the powers of inorganic matter, and perhaps most of those related to vegetable and animal life, will ultimately be found subordinate to it.

Faraday, *Experimental Researches in Electricity*, XI, 1161

83 I have no clear idea of the physical condition constituting the charged magnetic state; i.e. the state of the source of magnetic power: or of the coercitivity by which that state is either resisted in its attainment, or sustained in its permanent condition; for the hypotheses as yet put forth give no satisfaction to my mind. I profess rather to point out the difficulties in the way of the views, which are at present somewhat too easily accepted, and to shake men's minds from their habitual trust in them; for, next to developing and expounding, that appears to me the most useful and effectual way of really advancing the subject:—it is better to be aware, or even to suspect, we are wrong, than to be unconsciously or easily led to accept an error as right.

Faraday, *Experimental Researches in Electricity,* The Moving Conductor, 3362

84 The laws of nature, as we understand them, are the foundation of our knowledge in natural things. So much as we know of them has been developed by the successive energies of the highest intellects, exerted through many ages. After a most rigid and scrutinizing examination upon principle and trial, a definite expression has been given to them; they have become, as it were, our belief or trust. From day to day we still examine and test our expressions of them. We have no interest in their retention if erroneous; on the contrary, the greatest discovery a man could make would be to prove that one of these accepted laws was erroneous, and his greatest honour would be the discovery.

Faraday, *Observations on Mental Education*

85 Science moves, but slowly, slowly, creeping on from point to point.

Tennyson, *Locksley Hall,* 134

86 Wisdom does not inspect, but behold. We must look a long time before we can see. Slow are the beginnings of philosophy. He has something demoniacal in him, who can discern a law or couple two facts. We can imagine a time when 'Water runs down hill' may have been taught in the schools. The true man of science will know nature better by his finer organization; he will smell, taste, see, hear, feel, better than other men. His will be a deeper and finer experience. We do not learn by inference and deduction and the application of mathematics to philosophy, but by direct intercourse and sympathy. It is with science as with ethics—we cannot know truth by contrivance and method; the Baconian is as false as any other, and with all the helps of machinery and the arts, the most scientific will still be the healthiest and friendliest man, and possess a more perfect Indian wisdom.

Thoreau, *Natural History of Massachusetts*

87 When it was first said that the sun stood still and the world turned round, the common sense of mankind declared the doctrine false; but the old saying of *Vox pupuli, vox Dei,* as every philosopher knows, cannot be trusted in science.

Darwin, *Origin of Species,* VI

88 It can hardly be supposed that a false theory would explain, in so satisfactory a manner as does the theory of natural selection, the several large classes of facts above specified. It has recently been objected that this is an unsafe method of arguing; but it is a method used in judging of the common events of life, and has often been used by the greatest natural philosophers. The undulatory theory of light has thus been arrived at; and the belief in the revolution of the earth on its own axis was until lately supported by hardly any direct evidence. It is no valid objection that science as yet throws no light on the far higher problem of the essence or origin of life. Who can explain what is the essence of the attraction of gravity? No one now objects to following out the results consequent on this unknown element of attraction; not withstanding that Leibnitz formerly accused Newton of introducing "occult qualities and miracles into philosophy."

Darwin, *Origin of Species,* XV

89 False facts are highly injurious to the progress of science, for they often endure long; but false views, if supported by some evidence, do little harm, for every one takes a salutary pleasure in proving their falseness: and when this is done, one path towards error is closed and the road to truth is often at the same time opened.

Darwin, *Descent of Man,* III, 21

90 Science is, I believe, nothing but *trained and orga-nised common sense,* differing from the latter only as a veteran may differ from a raw recruit: and its methods differ from those of common sense only so far as the guardsman's cut and thrust differ from the manner in which a savage wields his club. The primary power is the same in each case, and perhaps the untutored savage has the more brawny arm of the two. The *real* advantage lies in the point and polish of the swordsman's weapon; in the trained eye quick to spy out the weakness of the adversary; in the ready hand prompt to follow it on the instant. But, after all, the sword exercise is only the hewing and poking of the clubman developed and perfected.

So, the vast results obtained by Science are won by no mystical faculties, by no mental processes, other than those which are practised by every one of us, in the humblest and meanest affairs of life.

T. H. Huxley, *Educational Value of the Natural History Sciences*

91 Faith is a fine invention
When gentlemen can see.
But microscopes are prudent
In an emergency.

Emily Dickinson, *Faith Is*

92 We know how easily the uselessness of almost ev-ery branch of knowledge may be proved, to the complete satisfaction of those who do not possess it. How many, not altogether stupid men, think the scientific study of languages useless, think an-cient literature useless, all erudition useless, logic and metaphysics useless, poetry and the fine arts idle and frivolous, political economy purely mis-chievous? Even history has been pronounced use-less and mischievous by able men. Nothing but that acquaintance with external nature, empiri-cally acquired, which serves directly for the pro-duction of objects necessary to existence or agree-able to the senses, would get its utility recognised if people had the least encouragement to disbe-lieve it.

Mill, *Representative Government,* VI

93 Whatever be the most proper mode of expressing it, the proposition that the course of nature is uni-form is the fundamental principle, or general axiom, of Induction. It would yet be a great error to offer this large generalisation as any explana-tion of the inductive process. On the contrary, I hold it to be itself an instance of induction, and induction by no means of the most obvious kind. Far from being the first induction we make, it is one of the last, or at all events one of those which are latest in attaining strict philosophical accura-cy. As a general maxim, indeed, it has scarcely entered into the minds of any but philosophers; nor even by them, as we shall have many oppor-tunities of remarking, have its extent and limits

been always very justly conceived. The truth is, that this great generalisation is itself founded on prior generalisations. The obscurer laws of nature were discovered by means of it, but the more ob-vious ones must have been understood and assent-ed to as general truths before it was ever heard of. We should never have thought of affirming that all phenomena take place according to general laws, if we had not first arrived, in the case of a great multitude of phenomena, at some knowl-edge of the laws themselves; which could be done no otherwise than by induction.

Mill, *System of Logic,* Bk. III, III, 1

94 It must be kept constantly in view . . . that in science, those who speak of explaining any phe-nomenon mean (or should mean) pointing out not some more familiar, but merely some more gener-al phenomenon, of which it is a partial exemplifi-cation; or some laws of causation which produce it by their joint or successive action, and from which, therefore, its conditions may be de-termined deductively. Every such operation brings us a step nearer towards answering the question which was stated . . . as comprehending the whole problem of the investigation of nature, viz. What are the fewest assumptions, which being granted, the order of nature as it exists would be the result? What are the fewest general proposi-tions from which all the uniformities existing in nature could be deduced?

The laws, thus explained or resolved, are some-times said to be *accounted for;* but the expression is incorrect, if taken to mean anything more than what has been already stated. In minds not habi-tuated to accurate thinking, there is often a con-fused notion that the general laws are the *causes* of the partial ones; that the law of general gravita-tion, for example, causes the phenomenon of the fall of bodies to the earth. But to assert this would be a misuse of the word cause: terrestrial gravity is not an effect of general gravitation, but a *case* of it; that is, one kind of the particular instances in which that general law obtains. To account for a law of nature means, and can mean, nothing more than to assign other laws more general, to-gether with collocations, which laws and colloca-tions being supposed, the partial law follows with-out any additional supposition.

Mill, *System of Logic,* Bk. III, XII, 6

95 Fundamentally, all sciences reason in the same way and aim at the same object. They all try to reach knowledge of the law of phenomena, so as to foresee, vary or master phenomena.

Claude Bernard, *Experimental Medicine,* I, 1

96 Men of science who mean to embrace the princi-ples of the experimental method as a whole, must fulfill two classes of conditions and must possess two qualities of mind which are indispensable if

they are to reach their goal and succeed in the discovery of truth. First, they must have ideas which they submit to the control of facts; but at the same time they must make sure that the facts which serve as starting point or as control for the idea are correct and well established; they must be at once observers and experimenters.

Claude Bernard, *Experimental Medicine*, I, 1

97 The first condition to be fulfilled by men of science, applying themselves to the investigation of natural phenomena, is to maintain absolute freedom of mind, based on philosophic doubt. Yet we must not be in the least sceptical; we must believe in science, i.e., in determinism; we must believe in a complete and necessary relation between things, among the phenomena proper to living beings as well as in all others; but at the same time we must be thoroughly convinced that we know this relation only in a more or less approximate way, and that the theories we hold are far from embodying changeless truths. When we propound a general theory in our sciences, we are sure only that, literally speaking, all such theories are false. They are only partial and provisional truths which are necessary to us, as steps on which we rest, so as to go on with investigation; they embody only the present state of our knowledge, and consequently they must change with the growth of science, and all the more often when sciences are less advanced in their evolution.

Claude Bernard, *Experimental Medicine*, I, 2

98 The object of science is everywhere the same: to learn the material conditions of phenomena. But though this goal is the same in the physico-chemical and in the biological sciences, it is much harder to reach in the latter because of the mobility and complexity of the phenomena which we meet.

Claude Bernard, *Experimental Medicine*, II, 1

99 An experimenter who has made an experiment, in conditions which he believes were determined, may happen not to get the same results in a new series of investigations as in his first observation; in repeating the experiment, with fresh precautions, it may happen again that, instead of his first result, he may encounter a wholly different one. In such a situation, what is to be done? Should we acknowledge that the facts are indeterminable? Certainly not, since that cannot be. We must simply acknowledge that experimental conditions, which we believed to be known, are not known. We must more closely study, search out and define the experimental conditions, for the facts cannot be contradictory one to another; they can only be indeterminate. Facts never exclude one another, they are simply explained by differences in the conditions in which they are born. So an experimenter can never deny a fact that he has

seen and observed, merely because he cannot rediscover it.

Claude Bernard, *Experimental Medicine*, II, 1

100 Science and men of science are cosmopolitans, and it seems hardly important whether a scientific truth develops at any particular spot on the globe, as long as the general diffusion of science allows all men to share in it.

Claude Bernard, *Experimental Medicine*, II, 2

101 All human sciences have traveled along [the same] path. Arriving at infinitesimals, mathematics, the most exact of sciences, abandons the process of analysis and enters on the new process of the integration of unknown, infinitely small, quantities. Abandoning the conception of cause, mathematics seeks law, that is, the property common to all unknown, infinitely small, elements. In another form but along the same path of reflection the other sciences have proceeded. When Newton enunciated the law of gravity he did not say that the sun or the earth had a property of attraction; he said that all bodies from the largest to the smallest have the property of attracting one another, that is, leaving aside the question of the cause of the movement of the bodies, he expressed the property common to all bodies from the infinitely large to the infinitely small. The same is done by the natural sciences: leaving aside the question of cause, they seek for laws.

Tolstoy, *War and Peace*, II Epilogue, XI

102 What we call science today is merely a haphazard collection of disconnected scraps of knowledge, most of them useless, and many of which, instead of giving us absolute truth provide the most bizarre delusions, presented as truth one day and refuted the next.

Tolstoy, *What Is Religion?*, I

103 It must be said that in some of these fields [of psychology] the results have as yet borne little theoretic fruit commensurate with the great labor expended in their acquisition. But facts are facts, and if we only get enough of them they are sure to combine. New ground will from year to year be broken, and theoretic results will grow. Meanwhile the experimental method has quite changed the face of the science so far as the latter is a record of mere work done.

William James, *Psychology*, VII

104 In a scientific research . . . the inquirer starts with a fact of which he seeks the reason, or with an hypothesis of which he seeks the proof. In either case he keeps turning the matter incessantly in his mind until, by the arousal of associate upon associate, some habitual, some similar, one arises which he recognizes to suit his need. This, however, may take years. No rules can be given by which the investigator may proceed straight to his

result; but both here and in the case of reminiscence the accumulation of helps in the way of associations may advance more rapidly by the use of certain routine methods. In striving to recall a thought, for example, we may of set purpose run through the successive classes of circumstance with which it may possibly have been connected, trusting that when the right member of the class has turned up it will help the thought's revival. Thus we may run through all the *places* in which we may have had it. We may run through the *persons* whom we remember to have conversed with, or we may call up successively all the *books* we have lately been reading. If we are trying to remember a person we may run through a list of streets or of professions. Some item out of the lists thus methodically gone over will very likely be associated with the fact we are in need of, and may suggest it or help to do so. And yet the item might never have arisen without such systematic procedure. In scientific research this accumulation of associates has been methodized by Mill under the title of "The Four Methods of Experimental Inquiry." By the "method of agreement," by that of "difference," by those of "residues" and "concomitant variations" (which cannot here be more nearly defined), we make certain lists of cases; and by ruminating these lists in our minds the cause we seek will be more likely to emerge. But the final stroke of discovery is only prepared, not effected, by them. The brain-tracts must, of their own accord, shoot the right way at last, or we shall still grope in darkness. That in some brains the tracts *do* shoot the right way much oftener than in others, and that we cannot tell why,—these are ultimate facts to which we must never close our eyes. Even in forming our lists of instances according to Mill's methods, we are at the mercy of the spontaneous workings of Similarity in our brain.

William James, *Psychology*, XIV

105 The history of science is strewn with wrecks and ruins of theory—essences and principles, fluids and forces—once fondly clung to, but found to hang together with no facts of sense. And exceptional phenomena solicit our belief in vain until such time as we chance to conceive them as of kinds already admitted to exist. What science means by "verification" is no more than this, that no object of conception shall be believed which sooner or later has not some permanent and vivid object of sensation for its *term*.

William James, *Psychology*, XXI

106 Every scientific conception is in the first instance a "spontaneous variation" in someone's brain. For one that proves useful and applicable there are a thousand that perish through their worthlessness. Their genesis is strictly akin to that of the flashes of poetry and sallies of wit to which the instable brain-paths equally give rise. But whereas the poetry and wit (like the science of the ancients) are their "own excuse for being," and have to run the gauntlet of no farther test, the "scientific" conceptions must prove their worth by being "verified." This test, however, is the cause of their *preservation*, not that of their production.

William James, *Psychology*, XXVIII

107 The aspiration to be "scientific" is such an idol of the tribe to the present generation, is so sucked in with his mother's milk by every one of us, that we find it hard to conceive of a creature who should not feel it, and harder still to treat it freely as the altogether peculiar and one-sided objective interest which it is. But as a matter of fact, few even of the cultivated members of the race have shared it; it was invented but a generation or two ago.

William James, *Psychology*, XXVIII, fn.

108 Thousands of years ago men started to cast the chaos of nature's sequences and juxtapositions into a form that might seem intelligible. Many were their ideal prototypes of rational order: teleological and æsthetic ties between things, causal and substantial bonds, as well as logical and mathematical relations. The most promising of these ideal systems at first were of course the richer ones, the sentimental ones. The baldest and least promising were the mathematical ones; but the history of the latter's application is a history of steadily advancing successes, whilst that of the sentimentally richer systems is one of relative sterility and failure. . . .

When you give things mathematical and mechanical names and call them just so many solids in just such positions, describing just such paths with just such velocities, all is changed. Your sagacity finds its reward in the verification by nature of all the deductions which you may next proceed to make. Your "things" realize all the *consequences* of the names by which you classed them. . . . The ideal which this philosophy strives after is a mathematical world-formula, by which, if all the collocations and motions at a given moment were known, it would be possible to reckon those of any wished-for future moment, by simply considering the necessary geometrical, arithmetical, and logical implications. Once we have the world in this bare shape, we can fling our net of *a priori* relations over all its terms, and pass from one of its phases to another by inward thought-necessity. Of course it is a world with a very minimum of rational *stuff*. The sentimental facts and relations are butchered at a blow. But the rationality yielded is so superbly complete in *form* that to many minds this atones for the loss, and reconciles the thinker to the notion of a purposeless universe, in which all the things and qualities men love, *dulcissima mundi nomina*, are but illusions of our fancy attached to accidental clouds of dust which will be dissipated by the eternal cosmic weather as carelessly as they were formed.

William James, *Psychology,* XXVIII

109 The most useful investigator, because the most sensitive observer, is always he whose eager interest in one side of the question is balanced by an equally keen nervousness lest he become deceived. Science has organized this nervousness into a regular *technique,* her so-called method of verification; and she has fallen so deeply in love with the method that one may even say she has ceased to care for truth by itself at all. It is only truth as technically verified that interests her. The truth of truths might come in merely affirmative form, and she would decline to touch it.

William James, *Will to Believe*

110 The laity are struck to see how ephemeral scientific theories are. After some years of prosperity, they see them successively abandoned; they see ruins accumulate upon ruins; they foresee that the theories fashionable to-day will shortly succumb in their turn and hence they conclude that these are absolutely idle. This is what they call the *bankruptcy of science.*

Their scepticism is superficial; they give no account to themselves of the aim and the rôle of scientific theories; otherwise they would comprehend that the ruins may still be good for something.

Poincaré, *Science and Hypothesis,* IV, 10

111 If we ought not to fear moral truth, still less should we dread scientific truth. In the first place it can not conflict with ethics. Ethics and science have their own domains, which touch but do not interpenetrate. The one shows us to what goal we should aspire, the other, given the goal, teaches us how to attain it. So they can never conflict since they can never meet. There can no more be immoral science than there can be scientific morals.

But if science is feared, it is above all because it can not give us happiness. Of course it can not. We may even ask whether the beast does not suffer less than man. But can we regret that earthly paradise where man brute-like was really immortal in knowing not that he must die? When we have tasted the apple, no suffering can make us forget its savor. We always come back to it. Could it be otherwise? As well ask if one who has seen and is blind will not long for the light. Man, then, can not be happy through science, but to-day he can much less be happy without it.

Poincaré, *Value of Science,* Intro.

112 How do we discover the individual laws of Physics, and what is their nature? It should be remarked, to begin with, that we have no right to assume that any physical laws exist, or if they have existed up to now, that they will continue to

exist in a similar manner in future. It is perfectly conceivable that one fine day Nature should cause an unexpected event to occur which would baffle us all; and if this were to happen we would be powerless to make any objection, even if the result would be that, in spite of our endeavours, we should fail to introduce order into the resulting confusion. In such an event, the only course open to science would be to declare itself bankrupt. For this reason, science is compelled to begin by the general assumption that a general rule of law dominates throughout Nature.

Planck, *Universe in the Light of Modern Physics,* 5

113 There have been times when science and philosophy were alien, if not actually antagonistic to each other. These times have passed. Philosophers have realized that they have no right to dictate to scientists their aims and the methods for attaining them; and scientists have learned that the starting-point of their investigations does not lie solely in the perceptions of the senses, and that science cannot exist without some small portion of metaphysics. Modern Physics impresses us particularly with the truth of the old doctrine which teaches that there are realities existing apart from our sense-perceptions, and that there are problems and conflicts where these realities are of greater value for us than the richest treasures of the world of experience.

Planck, *Universe in the Light of Modern Physics,* 8

114 Our credulity, though enormous, is not boundless; and our stock of it is quite used up by our mediums, clairvoyants, hand readers, slate writers, Christian Scientists, psychoanalysts, electronic vibration diviners, therapeutists of all schools registered and unregistered, astrologers, astronomers who tell us that the sun is nearly a hundred million miles away and that Betelgeuse is ten times as big as the whole universe, physicists who balance Betelgeuse by describing the incredible smallness of the atom, and a host of other marvel mongers whose credulity would have dissolved the Middle Ages in a roar of sceptical merriment. In the Middle Ages people believed that the earth was flat, for which they had at least the evidence of their senses: we believe it to be round, not because as many as one per cent of us could give the physical reasons for so quaint a belief, but because modern science has convinced us that nothing that is obvious is true, and that everything that is magical, improbable, extraordinary, gigantic, microscopic, heartless, or outrageous is scientific.

Shaw, *Saint Joan,* Pref.

115 Induction presupposes metaphysics. In other words, it rests upon an antecedent rationalism. You cannot have a rational justification for your

appeal to history till your metaphysics has assured you that there *is* a history to appeal to; and likewise your conjectures as to the future presuppose some basis of knowledge that there *is* a future already subjected to some determinations. The difficulty is to make sense of either of these ideas. But unless you have done so, you have made nonsense of induction.

You will observe that I do not hold induction to be in its essence the derivation of general laws. It is the divination of some characteristics of a particular future from the known characteristics of a particular past. The wider assumption of general laws holding for all cognisable occasions appears a very unsafe addendum to attach to this limited knowledge.

Whitehead, *Science and the Modern World*, III

116 The progress of science consists in observing these interconnections and in showing with a patient ingenuity that the events of this evershifting world are but examples of a few general connections or relations called laws. To see what is general in what is particular and what is permanent in what is transitory is the aim of scientific thought. In the eye of science, the fall of an apple, the motion of a planet round a sun, and the clinging of the atmosphere to the earth are all seen as examples of the law of gravity. This possibility of disentangling the most complex evanescent circumstances into various examples of permanent laws is the controlling idea of modern thought.

Whitehead, *Introduction to Mathematics*, I

117 All mathematical calculations about the course of nature must start from some assumed law of nature. . . . Accordingly, however accurately we have calculated that some event must occur, the doubt always remains—Is the law true? If the law states a precise result, almost certainly it is not precisely accurate; and thus even at the best the result, precisely as calculated, is not likely to occur. But then we have no faculty capable of observation with ideal precision, so, after all, our inaccurate laws may be good enough.

Whitehead, *Introduction to Mathematics*, III

118 In science the man of real genius is the man who invents a new method. The notable discoveries are often made by his successors, who can apply the method with fresh vigour, unimpaired by the previous labour of perfecting it; but the mental calibre of the thought required for their work, however brilliant, is not so great as that required by the first inventor of the method.

Russell, *Place of Science in a Liberal Education*

119 The kernel of the scientific outlook is a thing so simple, so obvious, so seemingly trivial, that the mention of it may almost excite derision. The kernel of the scientific outlook is the refusal to regard our own desires, tastes, and interests as affording a key to the understanding of the world. Stated thus baldly, this may seem no more than a trite truism. But to remember it consistently in matters arousing our passionate partisanship is by no means easy, especially where the available evidence is uncertain and inconclusive.

Russell, *Place of Science in a Liberal Education*

120 Man has existed for about a million years. He has possessed writing for about 6,000 years, agriculture somewhat longer, but perhaps not much longer. Science, as a dominant factor in determining the beliefs of educated men, has existed for about 300 years; as a source of economic technique, for about 150 years. In this brief period it has proved itself an incredibly powerful revolutionary force. When we consider how recently it has risen to power, we find ourselves forced to believe that we are at the very beginning of its work in transforming human life.

Russell, *Science and Tradition*

121 The effect of science upon our view of man's place in the universe has been of two opposite kinds; it has at once degraded and exalted him. It has degraded him from the standpoint of contemplation, and exalted him from that of action. The latter effect has gradually come to outweigh the former, but both have been important.

Russell, *Science and Tradition*

122 The way in which science arrives at its beliefs is quite different from that of mediaeval theology. Experience has shown that it is dangerous to start from general principles and proceed deductively, both because the principles may be untrue and because the reasoning based upon them may be fallacious. Science starts, not from large assumptions, but from particular facts discovered by observation or experiment. From a number of such facts a general rule is arrived at, of which, if it is true, the facts in question are instances. This rule is not positively asserted, but is accepted, to begin with, as a working hypothesis. If it is correct, certain hitherto unobserved phenomena will take place in certain circumstances. If it is found that they do take place, that so far confirms the hypothesis; if they do not, the hypothesis must be discarded and a new one must be invented. However many facts are found to fit the hypothesis, that does not make it certain, although in the end it may come to be thought in a high degree probable; in that case, it is called a theory rather than a hypothesis. A number of different theories, each built directly upon facts, may become the basis for a new and more general hypothesis from which, if true, they all follow; and to this process of generalization no limit can be set. But whereas, in mediaeval thinking, the most general principles were the starting point, in science they are the final

conclusion—final, that is to say, at a given moment, though liable to become instances of some still wider law at a later stage.

Russell, *Religion and Science,* I

123 The view is often defended that sciences should be built up on clear and sharply defined basal concepts. In actual fact no science, not even the most exact, begins with such definitions. The true beginning of scientific activity consists rather in describing phenomena and then in proceeding to group, classify, and correlate them. Even at the stage of description, it is not possible to avoid applying certain abstract ideas to the material in hand, ideas derived from various sources and certainly not the fruit of the new experience only. Still more indispensable are such ideas—which will later become the basal concepts of the science—as the material is further elaborated. They must at first necessarily possess some measure of uncertainty; there can be no question of any clear delimitation of their content. So long as they remain in this condition, we come to an understanding about their meaning by repeated references to the material of observation, from which we seem to have deduced our abstract ideas, but which is, in point of fact, subject to them. Thus, strictly speaking, they are in the nature of conventions; although everything depends on their being chosen in no arbitrary manner, but determined by the important relations they have to the empirical material—relations that we seem to divine before we can clearly recognize and demonstrate them. It is only after more searching investigation of the field in question that we are able to formulate with increased clarity the scientific concepts underlying it, and progressively so to modify these concepts that they become widely applicable and at the same time consistent logically. Then, indeed, it may be time to immure them in definitions. The progress of science, however, demands a certain elasticity even in these definitions.

Freud, *Instincts and Their Vicissitudes*

124 It is a mistake to believe that a science consists in nothing but conclusively proved propositions, and it is unjust to demand that it should. It is a demand only made by those who feel a craving for authority in some form and a need to replace the religious catechism by something else, even if it be a scientific one. Science in its catechism has but few apodictic precepts; it consists mainly of statements which it has developed to varying degrees of probability. The capacity to be content with these approximations to certainty and the ability to carry on constructive work despite the lack of final confirmation are actually a mark of the scientific habit of mind.

Freud, *General Introduction to Psycho-Analysis,* III

125 Humanity has in the course of time had to endure from the hands of science two great outrages upon its naïve self-love. The first was when it realized that our earth was not the centre of the universe, but only a tiny speck in a world-system of a magnitude hardly conceivable; this is associated in our minds with the name of Copernicus, although Alexandrian doctrines taught something very similar. The second was when biological research robbed man of his peculiar privilege of having been specially created, and relegated him to a descent from the animal world, implying an ineradicable animal nature in him: this transvaluation has been accomplished in our own time upon the instigation of Charles Darwin, Wallace, and their predecessors, and not without the most violent opposition from their contemporaries. But man's craving for grandiosity is now suffering the third and most bitter blow from present-day psychological research which is endeavouring to prove to the *ego* of each one of us that he is not even master in his own house, but that he must remain content with the veriest scraps of information about what is going on unconsciously in his own mind. We psycho-analysts were neither the first nor the only ones to propose to mankind that they should look inward; but it appears to be our lot to advocate it most insistently and to support it by empirical evidence which touches every man closely. This is the kernel of the universal revolt against our science, of the total disregard of academic courtesy in dispute, and the liberation of opposition from all the constraints of impartial logic.

Freud, *General Introduction to Psycho-Analysis,* XVIII

126 It is inadmissible to declare that science is one field of human intellectual activity, and that religion and philosophy are others, at least as valuable, and that science has no business to interfere with the other two, that they all have an equal claim to truth, and that every one is free to choose whence he shall draw his convictions and in what he shall place his belief. Such an attitude is considered particularly respectable, tolerant, broadminded, and free from narrow prejudices. Unfortunately it is not tenable; it shares all the pernicious qualities of an entirely unscientific *Weltanschauung* [world view] and in practice comes to much the same thing. The bare fact is that truth cannot be tolerant and cannot admit compromise or limitations, that scientific research looks on the whole field of human activity as its own, and must adopt an uncompromisingly critical attitude towards any other power that seeks to usurp any part of its province.

Freud, *New Introductory Lectures on Psycho-Analysis,* XXXV

127 Scientific thought is, in its essence, no different from the normal process of thinking, which we all,

believers and unbelievers, alike, make use of when we are going about our business in everyday life. . . . Its aim is to arrive at correspondence with reality, that is to say with what exists outside us and independently of us, and, as experience has taught us, is decisive for the fulfilment or frustration of our desires. This correspondence with the real external world we call *truth*. It is the aim of scientific work, even when the practical value of that work does not interest us. When, therefore, religion claims that it can take the place of science and that, because it is beneficent and ennobling, it must therefore be true, that claim is, in fact, an encroachment which, in the interests of every one, should be resisted. It is asking a great deal of a man, who has learned to regulate his everyday affairs in accordance with the rules of experience and with due regard to reality, that he should entrust precisely what affects him most nearly to the care of an authority which claims as its prerogative freedom from all the rules of rational thought. And, as for the protection that religion promises its believers, I hardly think that any of us would be willing even to enter a motor-car, if the driver informed us that he drove without allowing himself to be distracted by traffic regulations, but in accordance with the impulses of an exalted imagination.

Freud, *New Introductory Lectures on Psycho-Analysis*, XXXV

128 Ladies and Gentlemen—Let me in conclusion sum up what I had to say about the relation of psycho-analysis to the question of a *Weltanschauung* [world view]. Psycho-analysis is not, in my opinion, in a position to create a *Weltanschauung* of its own. It has no need to do so, for it is a branch of science and can subscribe to the scientific *Weltanschauung*. The latter, however, hardly merits such a high-sounding name, for it does not take everything into its scope, it is incomplete, and it makes no claim to being comprehensive or to constituting a system. Scientific thought is still in its infancy; there are very many of the great problems with which it has as yet been unable to cope. A *Weltanschauung* based upon science has, apart from the emphasis it lays upon the real world, essentially negative characteristics, such as that it limits itself to truth and rejects illusions. Those of our fellow-men who are dissatisfied with this state of things and who desire something more for their momentary peace of mind may look for it where they can find it. We shall not blame them for doing so; but we cannot help them and cannot change our own way of thinking on their account.

Freud, *New Introductory Lectures on Psycho-Analysis*, XXXV

129 From a systematic theoretical point of view, we may imagine the process of evolution of an empirical science to be a continuous process of induction. Theories are evolved, and are expressed in short compass as statements of a large number of individual observations in the form of empirical laws, from which the general laws can be ascertained by comparison. Regarded in this way, the development of a science bears some resemblance to the compilation of a classified catalogue. It is, as it were, a purely empirical enterprise.

But this point of view by no means embraces the whole of the actual process; for it slurs over the important part played by intuition and deductive thought in the development of an exact science. As soon as a science has emerged from its initial stages, theoretical advances are no longer achieved merely by a process of arrangement. Guided by empirical data, the investigator rather develops a system of thought which, in general, is built up logically from a small number of fundamental assumptions, the so-called axioms. We call such a system of thought a *theory* The theory finds the justification for its existence in the fact that it correlates a large number of single observations, and it is just here that the "truth" of the theory lies.

Einstein, *Relativity*, Appendix III

130 A theory is the more impressive the greater the simplicity of its premises is, the more different kinds of things it relates, and the more extended is its area of applicability. Therefore the deep impression which classical thermodynamics made upon me. It is the only physical theory of universal content concerning which I am convinced that, within the framework of the applicability of its basic concepts, it will never be overthrown (for the special attention of those who are skeptics on principle).

Einstein, *Autobiographical Notes*

131 The significant outward forms of the civilization of the western world are the product of the machine and its technology. Indirectly, they are the product of the scientific revolution which took place in the seventeenth century. In its effect upon men's external habits, dominant interests, the conditions under which they work and associate, whether in the family, the factory, the state, or internationally, science is by far the most potent social factor in the modern world. It operates, however, through its undesigned effects rather than as a transforming influence of men's thoughts and purposes. This contrast between outer and inner operation is the great contradiction in our lives. Habits of thought and desire remain in substance what they were before the rise of science, while the conditions under which they take effect have been radically altered by science.

Dewey, *Science and Society*

132 Great as have been the social changes of the last century, they are not to be compared with those which will emerge when our faith in scientific method is made manifest in social works. We are living in a period of depression. The intellectual function of trouble is to lead men to think. The depression is a small price to pay if it induces us to think about the cause of the disorder, confusion, and insecurity which are the outstanding traits of our social life. If we do not go back to their cause, namely our half-way and accidental use of science, mankind will pass through depressions, for they are the graphic record of our unplanned social life. The story of the achievement of science in physical control is evidence of the possibility of control in social affairs. It is our human intelligence and human courage which are on trial; it is incredible that men who have brought the technique of physical discovery, invention, and use to such a pitch of perfection will abdicate in the face of the infinitely more important human problem.

Dewey, *Science and Society*

133 Science is nothing but developed perception, interpreted intent, commonsense rounded out and minutely articulated.

Santayana, *Life of Reason,* V, 11

134 When I was younger what was pompously called Science wore an imposing aspect. There was a well-dressed Royal Family in the intellectual world, expected to rule indefinitely: sovereign axioms, immutable laws, and regent hypotheses. We had Newtonian space and time, the conservation of energy, and Darwinian evolution. Now there is a democracy of theories elected for short terms of office, speaking shop-dialects, and hardly presented or presentable to the public eye. The investigator's technique takes the lead, not the exigences of popularizing eloquence. The frontiers of this science seem less secure, with vast claims to undiscovered or undiscoverable regions; and first principles at home are wobbly and vague. Yet this looseness in thought goes with ingenuity in methods and multiplicity of contacts; and it serves to dispel an illusion that better-digested science might create: the illusion that scientific ideas reveal the literal and intimate essence of reality, as the images of sense certainly do not. But the fact is that both sense and science are relatively and virtually true, being appropriate to the organ employed and to the depth to which this organ may penetrate into the structure of things or may trace their movement. The senses do this well enough, in their own terms, for the uses of animal and social life; but modern science approaches the dynamism of nature by means of artificial instruments and experiments: hence its astonishing mechanical applications, and its moral and pictorial blindness. It studies methods rather than objects;

it works indirectly if not directly in the service of industrialism, which needs to manipulate and not to understand; and if it succeeds in its manipulations it has done its duty. But this is a very special development, perhaps temporary, and certainly not fundamental in human knowledge. The images of sense will be with us while the human race endures. They will always yield our classical and personal view of nature. The stars will remain the visible stars, no matter what science may tell us about them; earth, water, air, and fire will still confront the spirit, and survive the disintegration that chemistry may subject them to. Ultimately the authority of science will always depend on the evidence of sense and on the analogy of familiar objects and events.

Santayana, *Realms of Being,* General Review

135 Let us suppose that a scientist, who is sealed in a room of ground glass and receives by radio the experimental information on which he works, learns one day about a certain machine capable of hurling its own weight to a height three hundred times its own. He will not have much difficulty in roughly imagining this machine, unknown in itself, as a sort of catapult constructed according to the furnished data. He will correct and make the image more precise as new information reaches him. Suppose he learns that this machine manifests the properties of what men call memory. That is to say it modifies, in proportion as it functions, its very manner of functioning and of reacting to stimuli, a thing which his reconstructed apparatus does not do. Perhaps he will solve the difficulty by endowing the space occupied by this apparatus with some new dimension according to which the past of the machine would be preserved and would modify in an invisible manner its very structure. We who walk the streets and put up at inns can know that the machine in question is called a flea. The scientist will not know this but the construction that he ceaselessly alters (turns upside down, if necessary, to meet a "crisis") will present at each instant the sum of all the measurable properties found in the flea and actually known by him. Obviously, in creating such a construction which is fictitious but founded on the real and always exactly and rigorously determined, in that way he will acquire ever more and more profound knowledge about the nature of the flea, but always by way of myth and of symbol. It would be inaccurate to say that he does not know this nature. He does not know it ontologically or *in itself*.

Maritain, *Degrees of Knowledge,* Pt. I, IV, 1

136 We see the same history of progress—even, may be, more strikingly—since the time of Galileo in the physico-mathematical sciences—that is to say

in the art of translating sensible phenomena into quantitative symbols: and this is precisely because those studies are in truth the poorest of all in intelligibility, the least exacting in intellectuality, hence the easiest.

Maritain, *Theonas*, X

17.3 | *The Discipline of Mathematics*

Of all the disciplines, mathematics has perhaps the distinction of being the only one in the history of which there is no rift between its modern and its ancient devotees. It was honored in antiquity as it is honored in modern times as the exemplar of intellectual clarity, rigor, precision, and order. The achievements of the great mathematicians of antiquity—of Euclid, Apollonius, Archimedes, Nichomachus, Hiero—are never denigrated or minimized, even though later developments in mathematics have thrown new light on their accomplishments.

Though the philosophers of mathematics may disagree about the status of the objects of mathematical study, or about the relation of mathematical truth to the world of real existences, there is, generally speaking, less disagreement among mathematicians than among the practitioners of any other discipline concerning the aims, methods, and results of their work. It is seldom if ever the case that competent mathematicians do not see eye to eye about the definition of a problem to be solved, or about the validity of a proposed solution of it. The solution either can or cannot be demonstrated to the satisfaction of all concerned.

These distinctive characteristics of mathematics as a discipline the reader will find reflected in the general tone and tendency of the passages quoted in this section. The reader will, in addition, find quotations from ancient writers that attribute the origin of mathematics, especially of geometry, to the exigencies of land-surveying; that discuss the division of mathematics into arithmetic and geometry; and that consider the application of mathematics to the study of physical phenomena. The passages drawn from modern sources the reader will find more illuminating on the characteristics of mathematical thought, on the power as well as the limitations of mathematics, on the logic of mathematics, and on the relation of mathematics to logic.

---

1 Sesostris [the king of Egypt and Ethiopia] . . . made a division of the soil of Egypt among the inhabitants, assigning square plots of ground of equal size to all, and obtaining his chief revenue from the rent which the holders were required to pay him year by year. If the river carried away any portion of a man's lot, he appeared before the king, and related what had happened; upon which the king sent persons to examine, and determine by measurement the exact extent of the loss; and thenceforth only such a rent was demanded of him as was proportionate to the reduced size of his land. From this practice, I think, geometry first came to be known in Egypt, whence it passed into Greece.

Herodotus, *History*, II, 109

2 *Socrates.* And all arithmetic and calculation have to do with number?
Glaucon. Yes.

And they appear to lead the mind towards truth?

Yes, in a very remarkable manner.

Then this is knowledge of the kind for which we are seeking, having a double use, military and philosophical; for the man of war must learn the art of number or he will not know how to array his troops, and the philosopher also, because he has to rise out of the sea of change and lay hold of true being, and therefore he must be an arithmetician. . . .

Then this is a kind of knowledge which legislation may fitly prescribe; and we must endeavour to persuade those who are to be the principal men of our State to go and learn arithmetic, not as amateurs, but they must carry on the study until they see the nature of numbers with the mind only; nor again, like merchants or retail-traders, with a view to buying or selling, but for the sake of their military use, and of the soul herself; and because this will be the easiest way for her to pass from becoming to truth and being.

That is excellent, he said.

Yes, I said, and now having spoken of it, I must add how charming the science is! and in how many ways it conduces to our desired end, if pursued in the spirit of a philosopher, and not of a shopkeeper!

How do you mean?

I mean, as I was saying, that arithmetic has a very great and elevating effect, compelling the soul to reason about abstract number, and rebelling against the introduction of visible or tangible objects into the argument.

Plato, *Republic,* VII, 525A

3 Let no one enter here who is ignorant of geometry.

Inscription over the door of Plato's Academy

4 For instance, he [Socrates] said that the study of geometry should be pursued until the student was competent to measure a parcel of land accurately in case he wanted to take over, convey or divide it, or to compute the yield; and this knowledge was so easy to acquire, that anyone who gave his mind to mensuration knew the size of the piece and carried away a knowledge of the principles of land measurement. He was against carrying the study of geometry so far as to include the more complicated figures, on the ground that he could not see the use of them. Not that he was himself unfamiliar with them, but he said that they were enough to occupy a lifetime, to the complete exclusion of many other useful studies.

Xenophon, *Memorabilia,* IV, 7

5 It is the physician's business to know that circular wounds heal more slowly, the geometer's to know the reason why.

Aristotle, *Posterior Analytics,* 79ª14

6 The science which is knowledge at once of the fact and of the reasoned fact, not of the fact by itself without the reasoned fact, is the more exact and the prior science.

A science such as arithmetic, which is not a science of properties *qua* inhering in a substratum, is more exact than and prior to a science like harmonics, which is a science of properties inhering in a substratum; and similarly a science like arithmetic, which is constituted of fewer basic elements, is more exact than and prior to geometry, which requires additional elements.

Aristotle, *Posterior Analytics,* 87ª30

7 Mathematics has come to be identical with philosophy for modern thinkers, though they say that it should be studied for the sake of other things.

Aristotle, *Metaphysics,* 992ª33

8 Since even the mathematician uses the common axioms only in a special application, it must be the business of first philosophy to examine the principles of mathematics also.

Aristotle, *Metaphysics,* 1061ᵇ18

9 The Pythagoreans, because they saw many attributes of numbers belonging to sensible bodies, supposed real things to be numbers—not separable numbers, however, but numbers of which real things consist. But why? Because the attributes of numbers are present in a musical scale and in the heavens and in many other things. Those, however, who say that mathematical number alone exists cannot according to their hypotheses say anything of this sort, but it used to be urged that these sensible things could not be the subject of the sciences. But we maintain that they are. . . . And it is evident that the objects of mathematics do not exist apart; for if they existed apart their attributes would not have been present in bodies.

Aristotle, *Metaphysics,* 1090ª20

10 A *point* is that which has no part.

Euclid, *Elements,* I, Def. 1

11 Let the following be postulated:

1. To draw a straight line from any point to any point.

2. To produce a finite straight line continuously in a straight line.

3. To describe a circle with any centre and distance.

4. That all right angles are equal to one another.

5. That, if a straight line falling on two straight lines make the interior angles on the same side less than two right angles, the two straight lines, if produced indefinitely, meet on that side on which are the angles less than the two right angles.

Euclid, *Elements,* I, Postulates

12 1. Things which are equal to the same thing are also equal to one another.
    2. If equals be added to equals, the wholes are equal.
    3. If equals be subtracted from equals, the remainders are equal.
    4. Things which coincide with one another are equal to one another.
    5. The whole is greater than the part.

Euclid, Elements, I, Common Notions

13 They relate that Euclid was asked by Ptolemy, whether there was any shorter way to the attainment of geometry than by his elementary institutions, and he answered, there was no other royal path which led to geometry.

Proclus, Commentaries on Euclid, II, 4

14 The proofs then of these theorems I have written in this book and now send to you. Seeing moreover in you, as I say, an earnest student, a man of considerable eminence in philosophy, and an admirer [of mathematical inquiry], I thought fit to write out for you and explain in detail in the same book the peculiarity of a certain method, by which it will be possible for you to get a start to enable you to investigate some of the problems in mathematics by means of mechanics. This procedure is, I am persuaded, no less useful even for the proof of the theorems themselves; for certain things first became clear to me by a mechanical method, although they had to be demonstrated by geometry afterwards because their investigation by the said method did not furnish an actual demonstration. But it is of course easier, when we have previously acquired, by the method, some knowledge of the questions, to supply the proof than it is to find it without any previous knowledge. This is a reason why, in the case of the theorems the proof of which Eudoxus was the first to discover, namely that the cone is a third part of the cylinder, and the pyramid of the prism, having the same base and equal height, we should give no small share of the credit to Democritus who was the first to make the assertion with regard to the said figure though he did not prove it.

Archimedes, Method Treating of
Mechanical Problems, Greeting

15 Eudoxus and Archytas had been the first originators of this far-famed and highly-prized art of mechanics, which they employed as an elegant illustration of geometrical truths, and as means of sustaining experimentally, to the satisfaction of the senses, conclusions too intricate for proof by words and diagrams. As, for example, to solve the problem, so often required in constructing geometrical figures, given the two extremes, to find the two mean lines of a proportion, both these mathematicians had recourse to the aid of instruments, adapting to their purpose certain curves and sections of lines.

But because of Plato's indignation at it, and his invectives against it as the mere corruption and annihilation of the one good of geometry, which was thus shamefully turning its back upon the unembodied objects of pure intelligence to recur to sensation, and to ask help (not to be obtained without base supervisions and depravation) from matter; so it was that mechanics came to be separated from geometry, and, repudiated and neglected by philosophers, took its place as a military art.

Plutarch, Marcellus

16 If geometry exists, arithmetic must also needs be implied, for it is with the help of this latter that we can speak of triangle, quadrilateral, octahedron, icosahedron, double, eightfold, or one and one-half times, or anything else of the sort which is used as a term by geometry, and such things cannot be conceived of without the numbers that are implied with each one. . . . Hence arithmetic abolishes geometry along with itself, but is not abolished by it, and while it is implied by geometry, it does not itself imply geometry.

Nicomachus, Arithmetic, I, 4

17 Aristotle quite properly divides . . . the theoretical into three immediate genera: the physical, the mathematical, and the theological. For given that all beings have their existence from matter and form and motion, and that none of these can be seen, but only thought, in its subject separately from the others, if one should seek out in its simplicity the first cause of the first movement of the universe, he would find God invisible and unchanging. And the kind of science which seeks after Him is the theological; for such an act can only be thought as high above somewhere near the loftiest things of the universe and is absolutely apart from sensible things. But the kind of science which traces through the material and ever moving quality, and has to do with the white, the hot, the sweet, the soft, and such things, would be called physical; and such an essence, since it is only generally what it is, is to be found in corruptible things and below the lunar sphere. And the kind of science which shows up quality with respect to forms and local motions, seeking figure, number, and magnitude and also place, time, and similar things, would be defined as mathematical. For such an essence falls, as it were, between the other two, not only because it can be conceived both through the senses and without the senses, but also because it is an accident in absolutely all beings both mortal and immortal, changing with those things that ever change, according to their inseparable form, and preserving unchangeable the changelessness of form in things eternal and of an ethereal nature.

And therefore meditating that the other two

genera of the theoretical would be expounded in terms of conjecture rather than in terms of scientific understanding: the theological because it is in no way phenomenal and attainable, but the physical because its matter is unstable and obscure, so that for this reason philosophers could never hope to agree on them; and meditating that only the mathematical, if approached enquiringly, would give its practitioners certain and trustworthy knowledge with demonstration both arithmetic and geometric resulting from indisputable procedures, we were led to cultivate most particularly as far as lay in our power this theoretical discipline. And especially were we led to cultivate that discipline developed in respect to divine and heavenly things as being the only one concerned with the study of things which are always what they are, and therefore able itself to be always what it is—which is indeed the proper mark of a science—because of its own clear and ordered understanding, and yet to cooperate with the other disciplines no less than they themselves. For that special mathematical theory would most readily prepare the way to the theological, since it alone could take good aim at that unchangeable and separate act, so close to that act are the properties having to do with translations and arrangements of movements, belonging to those heavenly beings which are sensible and both moving and moved, but eternal and impassible. Again as concerns the physical there would not be just chance correspondances. For the general property of the material essence is pretty well evident from the peculiar fashion of its local motion—for example, the corruptible and incorruptible from straight and circular movements, and the heavy and light or passive and active from movement to the center and movement from the center. And indeed this same discipline would more than any other prepare understanding persons with respect to nobleness of actions and character by means of the sameness, good order, due proportion, and simple directness contemplated in divine things, making its followers lovers of that divine beauty, and making habitual in them, and as it were natural, a like condition of the soul.

Ptolemy, *Almagest*, I, 1

18 Coming now to the science of numbers it is clear to the dullest apprehension that this was not created by man, but was discovered by investigation. For, though Virgil could at his own pleasure make the first syllable of *Italia* long, while the ancients pronounced it short, it is not in any man's power to determine at his pleasure that three times three are not nine, or do not make a square, or are not the triple of three, nor one and a half times the number six, or that it is not true that they are not the double of any number because odd numbers have no half. Whether, then, numbers are considered in themselves, or as applied to the laws of

figures, or of sounds, or of other motions, they have fixed laws which were not made by man, but which the acuteness of ingenious men brought to light.

Augustine, *Christian Doctrine*, II, 38

19 Mathematical species . . . can be abstracted by the intellect from sensible matter, not only from individual, but also from common matter, though not from common intelligible matter, but only from individual matter. For sensible matter is corporeal matter as subject to sensible qualities, such as being cold or hot, hard or soft, and the like, while intelligible matter is substance as subject to quantity. Now it is manifest that quantity is in substance before sensible qualities are. Hence quantities, such as number, dimension, and figures, which are the terminations of quantity, can be considered apart from sensible qualities, and this is to abstract them from sensible matter; but they cannot be considered without understanding the substance which is subject to the quantity, for that would be to abstract them from common intelligible matter. Yet they can be considered apart from this or that substance, for that is to abstract them from individual intelligible matter.

Aquinas, *Summa Theologica*, I, 85, 1

20 Many philosophers have called the world a visible god on account of its extraordinary excellence. So if the worth of the arts were measured by the matter with which they deal, this art—which some call astronomy, others astrology, and many of the ancients the consummation of mathematics—would be by far the most outstanding. This art which is as it were the head of all the liberal arts and the one most worthy of a free man leans upon nearly all the other branches of mathematics. Arithmetic, geometry, optics, geodesy, mechanics, and whatever others, all offer themselves in its service. And since a property of all good arts is to draw the mind of man away from the vices and direct it to better things, these arts can do that more plentifully, over and above the unbelievable pleasure of mind [which they furnish].

Copernicus, *De Revoluntionibus*, I, Introduction

21 *I implore you, you do not hope to be able to give the reasons for the number of the planets, do you?*
   This worry has been resolved, with the help of God, not badly. Geometrical reasons are co-eternal with God.

Kepler, *Epitome of Copernican Astronomy*, Bk. IV, I, 3

22 There remaineth yet another part of natural philosophy, which is commonly made a principal part, and holdeth rank with physic special and metaphysic, which is mathematic; but I think it more agreeable to the nature of things, and to the

light of order, to place it as a branch of metaphysic. For the subject of it being quantity, not quantity indefinite, which is but a relative, and belongeth to *philosophia prima* (as hath been said), but quantity determined or proportionable, it appeareth to be one of the essential forms of things as that that is causative in nature of a number of effects; insomuch as we see in the schools both of Democritus and of Pythagoras, that the one did ascribe figure to the first seeds of things, and the other did suppose numbers to be the principles and originals of things. . . .

The mathematics are either pure or mixed. To the pure mathematics are those sciences belonging which handle quantity determinate, merely severed from any axioms of natural philosophy; and these are two, geometry and arithmetic; the one handling quantity continued, and the other dissevered. Mixed hath for subject some axioms or parts of natural philosophy, and considereth quantity determined, as it is auxiliary and incident unto them. For many parts of nature can neither be invented with sufficient subtilty, nor demonstrated with sufficient perspicuity, nor accommodated unto use with sufficient dexterity, without the aid and intervening of the mathematics; of which sort are perspective, music, astronomy, cosmography, architecture, enginery, and divers others. In the mathematics I can report no deficience, except it be that men do not sufficiently understand the excellent use of the pure mathematics, in that they do remedy and cure many defects in the wit and faculties intellectual. For if the wit be too dull, they sharpen it; if too wandering, they fix it; if too inherent in the sense, they abstract it. So that as tennis is a game of no use in itself, but of great use in respect it maketh a quick eye and a body ready to put itself into all postures; so in the mathematics, that use which is collateral and intervenient is no less worthy than that which is principal and intended. And as for the mixed mathematics, I may only make this prediction, that there cannot fail to be more kinds of them, as nature grows further disclosed.

Bacon, *Advancement of Learning,*
Bk. II, VIII, 1–2

23 Must we not confess that geometry is the most powerful of all instruments for sharpening the wit and training the mind to think correctly? Was not Plato perfectly right when he wished that his pupils should be first of all well grounded in mathematics?

Galileo, *Two New Sciences,* II

24 *Sagredo.* The force of rigid demonstrations such as occur only in mathematics fills me with wonder and delight. From accounts given by gunners, I was already aware of the fact that in the use of cannon and mortars, the maximum range, that is the one in which the shot goes farthest, is obtained when the elevation is 45° or, as they say, at the sixth point of the quadrant; but to understand why this happens far outweighs the mere information obtained by the testimony of others or even by repeated experiment.

Salviati. What you say is very true. The knowledge of a single fact acquired through a discovery of its causes prepares the mind to understand and ascertain other facts without need of recourse to experiment, precisely as in the present case, where by argumentation alone the Author proves with certainty that the maximum range occurs when the elevation is 45°. He thus demonstrates what has perhaps never been observed in experience, namely, that of other shots those which exceed or fall short of 45° by equal amounts have equal ranges.

Galileo, *Two New Sciences,* IV

25 But now let us proceed to explain more carefully our reasons for saying . . . that of all the sciences known as yet, Arithmetic and Geometry alone are free from any taint of falsity or uncertainty. We must note then that there are two ways by which we arrive at the knowledge of facts, viz. by experience and by deduction. We must further observe that while our inferences from experience are frequently fallacious, deduction, or the pure illation of one thing from another, though it may be passed over, if it is not seen through, cannot be erroneous when performed by an understanding that is in the least degree rational. And it seems to me that the operation is profited but little by those constraining bonds by means of which the Dialecticians claim to control human reason, though I do not deny that that discipline may be serviceable for other purposes. My reason for saying so is that none of the mistakes which men can make (men, I say, not beasts) are due to faulty inference; they are caused merely by the fact that we found upon a basis of poorly comprehended experiences, or that propositions are posited which are hasty and groundless.

This furnishes us with an evident explanation of the great superiority in certitude of Arithmetic and Geometry to other sciences. The former alone deal with an object so pure and uncomplicated, that they need make no assumptions at all which experience renders uncertain, but wholly consist in the rational deduction of consequences. They are on that account much the easiest and clearest of all, and possess an object such as we require, for in them it is scarce humanly possible for anyone to err except by inadvertence. And yet we should not be surprised to find that plenty of people of their own accord prefer to apply their intelligence to other studies, or to Philosophy. The reason for this is that every person permits himself the liberty of making guesses in the matter of an obscure subject with more confidence than in one which is clear, and that it is much easier to have some vague notion about any subject, no matter what, than to arrive at the real truth about a single question however simple that may be.

But one conclusion now emerges out of these considerations, viz. not, indeed, that Arithmetic and Geometry are the sole sciences to be studied, but only that in our search for the direct road towards truth we should busy ourselves with no object about which we cannot attain a certitude equal to that of the demonstrations of Arithmetic and Geometry.

Descartes, Rules for Direction of the Mind, II

26 When first I applied my mind to Mathematics I read straight away most of what is usually given by the mathematical writers, and I paid special attention to Arithmetic and Geometry, because they were said to be the simplest and so to speak the way to all the rest. But in neither case did I then meet with authors who fully satisfied me. I did indeed learn in their works many propositions about numbers which I found on calculation to be true. As to figures, they in a sense exhibited to my eyes a great number of truths and drew conclusions from certain consequences. But they did not seem to make it sufficiently plain to the mind itself why those things are so, and how they discovered them. . . .

It was these reflections that recalled me from the particular studies of Arithmetic and Geometry to a general investigation of Mathematics, and thereupon I sought to determine what precisely was universally meant by that term, and why not only the above mentioned sciences, but also Astronomy, Music, Optics, Mechanics and several others are styled parts of Mathematics. Here indeed it is not enough to look at the origin of the word; for since the name "Mathematics" means exactly the same thing as "scientific study," these other branches could, with as much right as Geometry itself, be called Mathematics. Yet we see that almost anyone who has had the slightest schooling, can easily distinguish what relates to Mathematics in any question from that which belongs to the other sciences. But as I considered the matter carefully it gradually came to light that all those matters only were referred to Mathematics in which order and measurement are investigated, and that it makes no difference whether it be in numbers, figures, stars, sounds or any other object that the question of measurement arises. I saw consequently that there must be some general science to explain that element as a whole which gives rise to problems about order and measurement, restricted as these are to no special subject matter. This, I perceived, was called "Universal Mathematics," not a far fetched designation, but one of long standing which has passed into current use, because in this science is contained everything on account of which the others are called par*s of Mathematics. We can see how much it

excels in utility and simplicity the sciences subordinate to it, by the fact that it can deal with all the objects of which they have cognizance and many more besides, and that any difficulties it contains are found in them as well, added to the fact that in them fresh difficulties arise due to their special subject matter which in it do not exist. But now how comes it that though everyone knows the name of this science and understands what is its province even without studying it attentively, so many people laboriously pursue the other dependent sciences, and no one cares to master this one? I should marvel indeed were I not aware that everyone thinks it to be so very easy, and had I not long since observed that the human mind passes over what it thinks it can easily accomplish, and hastens straight away to new and more imposing occupations.

Descartes, Rules for Direction of the Mind, IV

27 There can be nothing so absurd but may be found in the books of philosophers. And the reason is manifest. For there is not one of them that begins his ratiocination from the definitions or explications of the names they are to use; which is a method that hath been used only in geometry, whose conclusions have thereby been made indisputable.

Hobbes, Leviathan, I, 5

28 *The difference between the mathematical and the intuitive mind.*—In the one, the principles are palpable, but removed from ordinary use; so that for want of habit it is difficult to turn one's mind in that direction: but if one turns it thither ever so little, one sees the principles fully, and one must have a quite inaccurate mind who reasons wrongly from principles so plain that it is almost impossible they should escape notice.

But in the intuitive mind the principles are found in common use and are before the eyes of everybody. One has only to look, and no effort is necessary; it is only a question of good eyesight, but it must be good, for the principles are so subtle and so numerous that it is almost impossible but that some escape notice. Now the omission of one principle leads to error; thus one must have very clear sight to see all the principles and, in the next place, an accurate mind not to draw false deductions from known principles.

All mathematicians would then be intuitive if they had clear sight, for they do not reason incorrectly from principles known to them; and intuitive minds would be mathematical if they could turn their eyes to the principles of mathematics to which they are unused.

The reason, therefore, that some intuitive minds are not mathematical is that they cannot at all turn their attention to the principles of mathematics. But the reason that mathematicians are not intuitive is that they do not see what is before them, and that, accustomed to the exact and plain principles of mathematics, and not reasoning till they have well inspected and arranged their principles, they are lost in matters of intuition where the principles do not allow of such arrangement. They are scarcely seen; they are felt rather than seen; there is the greatest difficulty in making them felt by those who do not of themselves perceive them. These principles are so fine and so numerous that a very delicate and very clear sense is needed to perceive them, and to judge rightly and justly when they are perceived, without for the most part being able to demonstrate them in order as in mathematics, because the principles are not known to us in the same way, and because it would be an endless matter to undertake it. We must see the matter at once, at one glance, and not by a process of reasoning, at least to a certain degree. And thus it is rare that mathematicians are intuitive and that men of intuition are mathematicians, because mathematicians wish to treat matters of intuition mathematically and make themselves ridiculous, wishing to begin with definitions and then with axioms, which is not the way to proceed in this kind of reasoning. Not that the mind does not do so, but it does it tacitly, naturally, and without technical rules; for the expression of it is beyond all men, and only a few can feel it.

Intuitive minds, on the contrary, being thus accustomed to judge at a single glance, are so astonished when they are presented with propositions of which they understand nothing, and the way to which is through definitions and axioms so sterile, and which they are not accustomed to see thus in detail, that they are repelled and disheartened.

But dull minds are never either intuitive or mathematical.

Mathematicians who are only mathematicians have exact minds, provided all things are explained to them by means of definitions and axioms; otherwise they are inaccurate and insufferable, for they are only right when the principles are quite clear.

And men of intuition who are only intuitive cannot have the patience to reach to first principles of things speculative and conceptual, which they have never seen in the world and which are altogether out of the common.

Pascal, *Pensées*, I, 1

29 We shall never get into such trouble if we follow the order of geometry. That wise science is very far from defining such primitive words as space, time, motion, equality, majority, decrease, all, and those others which the generality of men understand without explanation. But with the exception of these the remaining terms used by geometry are so clarified and defined that we have no need of a dictionary to understand any one of them, so that in a word all these terms are perfectly intelligible either by the natural light or by the definitions given.

This is the way geometry avoids all those vices which may be encountered in connection with the first point, which is to define only those things that need to be defined. It observes the same conduct with respect to the second point, which is to prove those propositions that are not evident. For when geometry has reached the first truths that can be known, it stops there and requires that they be granted since it has nothing clearer to prove them with; so that all the propositions of geometry are perfectly demonstrated either by the natural light or by proofs.

Whence it is that if this science does not define and demonstrate everything, it is only because it is impossible for us to do so. But since nature supplies everything not given by the science, the order of that science, though it does not give a superhuman perfection, has all the perfection men are capable of. . . .

Perhaps it will be thought strange that geometry cannot define any of the things that are its principal objects; for it can define neither motion nor numbers nor space, and yet these are the three things it particularly considers and in accordance with whose investigation it takes the three different names of mechanics, arithmetic, geometry, this last word belonging both to the genus and to the species.

But we shall feel no surprise if we observe that, this admirable science concerning itself only with the simplest things, the very quality which makes them worthy of being its objects makes them incapable of definition; so that the lack of definition is rather a perfection than a defect because it does not come from their obscurity but on the contrary from their extreme evidence, which is such that although it is not so convincing as a demonstration, it is fully as certain. Geometry supposes then that we know what thing is meant by the words: *motion, number, space;* and without stopping uselessly to define them it penetrates their nature and lays bare their marvelous properties.

Pascal, *Geometrical Demonstration*

30 It was much easier for a man to place these things aside with others of the use of which he was ignorant, and thus retain his present and inborn state of ignorance, than to destroy the whole superstructure and think out a new one. Hence it was looked upon as indisputable that the judgments of the gods far surpass our comprehension; and this opinion alone would have been sufficient to keep the human race in darkness to all eternity, if mathematics, which does not deal with ends, but with the essences and properties of forms, had not placed before us another rule of truth.

Spinoza, *Ethics*, I, Appendix

31 Since the ancients (as we are told by Pappus) esteemed the science of mechanics of greatest im-

portance in the investigation of natural things, and the moderns, rejecting substantial forms and occult qualities, have endeavored to subject the phenomena of nature to the laws of mathematics, I have in this treatise cultivated mathematics as far as it relates to philosophy. The ancients considered mechanics in a twofold respect; as rational, which proceeds accurately by demonstration, and practical. To practical mechanics all the manual arts belong, from which mechanics took its name. But as artificers do not work with perfect accuracy, it comes to pass that mechanics is so distinguished from geometry that what is perfectly accurate is called geometrical; what is less so, is called mechanical. However, the errors are not in the art, but in the artificers. He that works with less accuracy is an imperfect mechanic; and if any could work with perfect accuracy, he would be the most perfect mechanic of all, for the description of right lines and circles, upon which geometry is founded, belongs to mechanics. Geometry does not teach us to draw these lines, but requires them to be drawn, for it requires that the learner should first be taught to describe these accurately before he enters upon geometry, then it shows how by these operations problems may be solved. To describe right lines and circles are problems, but not geometrical problems. The solution of these problems is required from mechanics, and by geometry the use of them, when so solved, is shown; and it is the glory of geometry that from those few principles, brought from without, it is able to produce so many things. Therefore geometry is founded in mechanical practice, and is nothing but that part of universal mechanics which accurately proposes and demonstrates the art of measuring. But since the manual arts are chiefly employed in the moving of bodies, it happens that geometry is commonly referred to their magnitude, and mechanics to their motion. In this sense rational mechanics will be the science of motions resulting from any forces whatsoever, and of the forces required to produce any motions, accurately proposed and demonstrated. This part of mechanics, as far as it extended to the five powers which relate to manual arts, was cultivated by the ancients, who considered gravity (it not being a manual power) no otherwise than in moving weights by those powers. But I consider philosophy rather than arts and write not concerning manual but natural powers, and consider chiefly those things which relate to gravity, levity, elastic force, the resistance of fluids, and the like forces, whether attractive or impulsive; and therefore I offer this work as the mathematical principles of philosophy, for the whole burden of philosophy seems to consist in this—from the phenomena of motions to investigate the forces of nature, and then from these forces to demonstrate the other phenomena.

Newton, *Principia*, Pref. to 1st Ed.

32 In mathematics we are to investigate the quantities of forces with their proportions consequent upon any conditions supposed; then, when we enter upon physics, we compare those proportions with the phenomena of Nature, that we may know what conditions of those forces answer to the several kinds of attractive bodies. And this preparation being made, we argue more safely concerning the physical species, causes, and proportions of the forces.

Newton, *Principia*, I, 11, Schol.

33 In this proposition, that "the three angles of a triangle are equal to two right ones," one who has seen and clearly perceived the demonstration of this truth knows it to be true, when that demonstration is gone out of his mind; so that at present it is not actually in view, and possibly cannot be recollected: but he knows it in a different way from what he did before. The agreement of the two ideas joined in that proposition is perceived; but it is by the intervention of other ideas than those which at first produced that perception. He remembers, i.e. he knows (for remembrance is but the reviving of some past knowledge) that he was once certain of the truth of this proposition, that the three angles of a triangle are equal to two right ones. The immutability of the same relations between the same immutable things is now the idea that shows him, that if the three angles of a triangle were once equal to two right ones, they will always be equal to two right ones. And hence he comes to be certain, that what was once true in the case, is always true; what ideas once agreed will always agree; and consequently what he once knew to be true, he will always know to be true; as long as he can remember that he once knew it. Upon this ground it is, that particular demonstrations in mathematics afford general knowledge. If then the perception, that the same ideas will *eternally* have the same habitudes and relations, be not a sufficient ground of knowledge, there could be no knowledge of general propositions in mathematics; for no mathematical demonstration would be any other than particular: and when a man had demonstrated any proposition concerning one triangle or circle, his knowledge would not reach beyond that particular diagram. If he would extend it further, he must renew his demonstration in another instance, before he could know it to be true in another like triangle, and so on: by which means one could never come to the knowledge of any general propositions.

Locke, *Concerning Human Understanding*,
Bk. IV, I, 9

34 Mathematicians abstracting their thoughts from names, and accustoming themselves to set before their minds the ideas themselves that they would consider, and not sounds instead of them, have

avoided thereby a great part of that perplexity, puddering, and confusion, which has so much hindered men's progress in other parts of knowledge. For whilst they stick in words of undetermined and uncertain signification, they are unable to distinguish true from false, certain from probable, consistent from inconsistent, in their own opinions.

Locke, *Concerning Human Understanding,*
Bk. IV, III, 30

35 All the objects of human reason or enquiry may naturally be divided into two kinds, to wit, *Relations of Ideas,* and *Matters of Fact.* Of the first kind are the sciences of Geometry, Algebra, and Arithmetic; and in short, every affirmation which is either intuitively or demonstratively certain. *That the square of the hypothenuse is equal to the square of the two sides,* is a proposition which expresses a relation between these figures. *That three times five is equal to the half of thirty,* expresses a relation between these numbers. Propositions of this kind are discoverable by the mere operation of thought, without dependence on what is anywhere existent in the universe. Though there never were a circle or triangle in nature, the truths demonstrated by Euclid would for ever retain their certainty and evidence.

Hume, *Concerning Human
Understanding,* IV, 20

36 The great advantage of the mathematical sciences above the moral consists in this, that the ideas of the former, being sensible, are always clear and determinate, the smallest distinction between them is immediately perceptible, and the same terms are still expressive of the same ideas, without ambiguity or variation. An oval is never mistaken for a circle, nor an hyperbola for an ellipsis. The isosceles and scalenum are distinguished by boundaries more exact than vice and virtue, right and wrong. If any term be defined in geometry, the mind readily, of itself, substitutes, on all occasions, the definition for the term defined: Or even when no definition is employed, the object itself may be presented to the senses, and by that means be steadily and clearly apprehended.

Hume, *Concerning Human
Understanding,* VII, 48

37 The mathematics are distinguished by a peculiar privilege, that, in the course of ages, they may always advance and can never recede.

Gibbon, *Decline and Fall of the Roman
Empire,* LII

38 The science of mathematics presents the most brilliant example of the extension of the sphere of pure reason without the aid of experience. Examples are always contagious; and they exert an especial influence on the same faculty, which naturally flatters itself that it will have the same good fortune in other case as fell to its lot in one fortunate instance. Hence pure reason hopes to be able to extend its empire in the transcendental sphere with equal success and security, especially when it applies the same method which was attended with such brilliant results in the science of mathematics. It is, therefore, of the highest importance for us to know whether the method of arriving at demonstrative certainty, which is termed *mathematical,* be identical with that by which we endeavour to attain the same degree of certainty in philosophy, and which is termed in that science *dogmatical.*

Kant, *Critique of Pure Reason,*
Transcendental Method

39 The success which attends the efforts of reason in the sphere of mathematics naturally fosters the expectation that the same good fortune will be its lot, if it applies the mathematical method in other regions of mental endeavour besides that of quantities. Its success is thus great, because it can support all its conceptions by *a priori* intuitions and, in this way, make itself a master, as it were, over nature; while pure philosophy, with its *a priori* discursive conceptions, bungles about in the world of nature, and cannot accredit or show any *a priori* evidence of the reality of these conceptions. Masters in the science of mathematics are confident of the success of this method; indeed, it is a common persuasion that it is capable of being applied to any subject of human thought. They have hardly ever reflected or philosophized on their favourite science—a task of great difficulty; and the specific difference between the two modes of employing the faculty of reason has never entered their thoughts.

Kant, *Critique of Pure Reason,*
Transcendental Method

40 Pure mathematics can never deal with the real existence of things, but only with their possibility, that is to say, with the possibility of an intuition answering to the conceptions of the things. Hence it cannot touch the question of cause and effect, and consequently, all the finality there observed must always be regarded simply as formal, and never as a physical end.

Kant, *Critique of Teleological Judgement,* 63, fn.

41 In disquisitions of every kind, there are certain primary truths, or first principles, upon which all subsequent reasonings must depend. These contain an internal evidence which, antecedent to all reflection or combination, commands the assent of the mind. Where it produces not this effect, it must proceed either from some defect or disorder in the organs of perception, or from the influence

of some strong interest, or passion, or prejudice. Of this nature are the maxims in geometry, that "the whole is greater than its part; things equal to the same are equal to one another; two straight lines cannot enclose a space; and all right angles are equal to each other." . . .

The objects of geometrical inquiry are so entirely abstracted from those pursuits which stir up and put in motion the unruly passions of the human heart, that mankind, without difficulty, adopt not only the more simple theorems of the science, but even those abstruse paradoxes which, however they may appear susceptible of demonstration, are at variance with the natural conceptions which the mind, without the aid of philosophy, would be led to entertain upon the subject. The INFINITE DIVISIBILITY of matter, or, in other words, the INFINITE divisibility of a FINITE thing, extending even to the minutest atom, is a point agreed among geometricians, though not less incomprehensible to common sense than any of those mysteries in religion against which the batteries of infidelity have been so industriously levelled.

Hamilton, *Federalist 31*

42 Profound study of nature is the most fertile source of mathematical discoveries. Not only has this study, in offering a determinate object to investigation, the advantage of excluding vague questions and calculations without issue; it is besides a sure method of forming analysis itself, and of discovering the elements which it concerns us to know, and which natural science ought always to preserve: these are the fundamental elements which are reproduced in all natural effects.

We see, for example, that the same expression whose abstract properties geometers had considered, and which in this respect belongs to general analysis, represents as well the motion of light in the atmosphere, as it determines the laws of diffusion of heat in solid matter, and enters into all the chief problems of the theory of probability.

The analytical equations, unknown to the ancient geometers, which Descartes was the first to introduce into the study of curves and surfaces, are not restricted to the properties of figures, and to those properties which are the object of rational mechanics; they extend to all general phenomena. There cannot be a language more universal and more simple, more free from errors and from obscurities, that is to say more worthy to express the invariable relations of natural things.

Considered from this point of view, mathematical analysis is as extensive as nature itself; it defines all perceptible relations, measures times, spaces, forces, temperatures; this difficult science is formed slowly, but it preserves every principle which it has once acquired; it grows and strengthens itself incessantly in the midst of the many variations and errors of the human mind.

Its chief attribute is clearness; it has no marks to express confused notions. It brings together phenomena the most diverse, and discovers the hidden analogies which unite them. If matter escapes us, as that of air and light, by its extreme tenuity, if bodies are placed far from us in the immensity of space, if man wishes to know the aspect of the heavens at successive epochs separated by a great number of centuries, if the actions of gravity and of heat are exerted in the interior of the earth at depths which will be always inaccessible, mathematical analysis can yet lay hold of the laws of these phenomena. It makes them present and measurable, and seems to be a faculty of the human mind destined to supplement the shortness of life and the imperfection of the senses; and what is still more remarkable, it follows the same course in the study of all phenomena; it interprets them by the same language, as if to attest the unity and simplicity of the plan of the universe, and to make still more evident that unchangeable order which presides over all natural causes.

Fourier, *Analytical Theory of Heat,*
Preliminary Discourse

43 The peculiarity of the evidence of mathematical truths is that all the argument is on one side. There are no objections, and no answers to objections.

Mill, *On Liberty,* II

44 It is true that similar confusion and uncertainty, and in some cases similar discordance, exist respecting the first principles of all the sciences, not excepting that which is deemed the most certain of them, mathematics; without much impairing, generally indeed without impairing at all, the trustworthiness of the conclusions of those sciences. An apparent anomaly, the explanation of which is, that the detailed doctrines of a science are not usually deduced from, nor depend for their evidence upon, what are called its first principles. Were it not so, there would be no science more precarious, or whose conclusions were more insufficiently made out, than algebra; which derives none of its certainty from what are commonly taught to learners as its elements, since these, as laid down by some of its most eminent teachers, are as full of fictions as English law, and of mysteries as theology. The truths which are ultimately accepted as the first principles of a science, are really the last results of metaphysical analysis, practised on the elementary notions with which the science is conversant; and their relation to the science is not that of foundations to an edifice, but of roots to a tree, which may perform their office equally well though they be never dug down to and exposed to light.

Mill, *Utilitarianism,* I

45 A modern branch of mathematics having

achieved the art of dealing with the infinitely small can now yield solutions in other more complex problems of motion which used to appear insoluble.

This modern branch of mathematics, unknown to the ancients, when dealing with problems of motion admits the conception of the infinitely small, and so conforms to the chief condition of motion (absolute continuity) and thereby corrects the inevitable error which the human mind cannot avoid when it deals with separate elements of motion instead of examining continuous motion.

Tolstoy, *War and Peace*, XI, 1

46 The whole science of geometry may be said to owe its being to the exorbitant interest which the human mind takes in *lines*. We cut space up in every direction in order to manufacture them.

William James, *Psychology*, XX, fn. 1

47 As regards . . . mathematical judgments, . . . they express results of comparison and nothing more. The mathematical sciences deal with similarities and equalities exclusively, and not with coexistences and sequences. Hence they have, in the first instance, no connection with the order of experience. The comparisons of mathematics are between numbers and extensive magnitudes, giving rise to arithmetic and geometry respectively.

William James, *Psychology*, XXVIII

48 The very possibility of the science of mathematics seems an insoluble contradiction. If this science is deductive only in appearance, whence does it derive that perfect rigor no one dreams of doubting? If, on the contrary, all the propositions it enunciates can be deduced one from another by the rules of formal logic, why is not mathematics reduced to an immense tautology? The syllogism can teach us nothing essentially new, and, if everything is to spring from the principle of identity, everything should be capable of being reduced to it. Shall we then admit that the enunciations of all those theorems which fill so many volumes are nothing but devious ways of saying *A* is *A?*

Without doubt, we can go back to the axioms, which are at the source of all these reasonings. If we decide that these can not be reduced to the principle of contradiction, if still less we see in them experimental facts which could not partake of mathematical necessity, we have yet the resource of classing them among synthetic *a priori* judgments. This is not to solve the difficulty, but only to baptize it; and even if the nature of synthetic judgments were for us no mystery, the contradiction would not have disappeared, it would only have moved back; syllogistic reasoning remains incapable of adding anything to the data given it; these data reduce themselves to a few axioms, and we should find nothing else in the conclusions.

No theorem could be new if no new axiom intervened in its demonstration; reasoning could give us only the immediately evident verities borrowed from direct intuition; it would be only an intermediary parasite, and therefore should we not have good reason to ask whether the whole syllogistic apparatus did not serve solely to disguise our borrowing?

The contradiction will strike us the more if we open any book on mathematics; on every page the author will announce his intention of generalizing some proposition already known. Does the mathematical method proceed from the particular to the general, and, if so, how then can it be called deductive?

If finally the science of number were purely analytic, or could be analytically derived from a small number of synthetic judgments, it seems that a mind sufficiently powerful could at a glance perceive all its truths; nay more, we might even hope that some day one would invent to express them a language sufficiently simple to have them appear self-evident to an ordinary intelligence.

If we refuse to admit these consequences, it must be conceded that mathematical reasoning has of itself a sort of creative virtue and consequently differs from the syllogism.

The difference must even be profound. We shall not, for example, find the key to the mystery in the frequent use of that rule according to which one and the same uniform operation applied to two equal numbers will give identical results.

All these modes of reasoning, whether or not they be reducible to the syllogism properly so called, retain the analytic character, and just because of that are powerless.

Poincaré, *Science and Hypothesis*, I, 1

49 The *axioms of geometry therefore are neither synthetic* a priori *judgments nor experimental facts.*

They are *conventions;* our choice among all possible conventions is *guided* by experimental facts; but it remains *free* and is limited only by the necessity of avoiding all contradiction. Thus it is that the postulates can remain *rigorously* true even though the experimental laws which have determined their adoption are only approximate.

In other words, *the axioms of geometry* (I do not speak of those of arithmetic) *are merely disguised definitions.*

Then what are we to think of that question: Is the Euclidean geometry true?

It has no meaning.

As well ask whether the metric system is true and the old measures false; whether Cartesian coordinates are true and polar coordinates false. One geometry can not be more true than another; it can only be *more convenient.*

Poincaré, *Science and Hypothesis*, II, 3

50 It has often been said that if individual experience could not create geometry the same is not true of ancestral experience. But what does that mean? Is it meant that we could not experimentally demonstrate Euclid's postulate, but that our ancestors have been able to do it? Not in the least. It is meant that by natural selection our mind has *adapted* itself to the conditions of the external world, that it has adopted the geometry *most advantageous* to the species: or in other words *the most convenient.* This is entirely in conformity with our conclusions; geometry is not true, it is advantageous.

Poincaré, *Science and Hypothesis,* II, 5

51 The genesis of mathematical creation is a problem which should intensely interest the psychologist. It is the activity in which the human mind seems to take least from the outside world, in which it acts or seems to act only of itself and on itself, so that in studying the procedure of geometric thought we may hope to reach what is most essential in man's mind.

Poincaré, *Science and Method,* I, 3

52 In fact, what is mathematical creation? It does not consist in making new combinations with mathematical entities already known. Any one could do that, but the combinations so made would be infinite in number and most of them absolutely without interest. To create consists precisely in not making useless combinations and in making those which are useful and which are only a small minority. Invention is discernment, choice.

Poincaré, *Science and Method,* I, 3

53 You have doubtless often been asked of what good is mathematics and whether these delicate constructions entirely mind-made are not artificial and born of our caprice.

Among those who put this question I should make a distinction; practical people ask of us only the means of money-making. These merit no reply; rather would it be proper to ask of them what is the good of accumulating so much wealth and whether, to get time to acquire it, we are to neglect art and science, which alone give us souls capable of enjoying it, 'and for life's sake to sacrifice all reasons for living.'

Besides, a science made solely in view of applications is impossible; truths are fecund only if bound together. If we devote ourselves solely to those truths whence we expect an immediate result, the intermediary links are wanting and there will no longer be a chain.

The men most disdainful of theory get from it, without suspecting it, their daily bread; deprived of this food, progress would quickly cease, and we should soon congeal into the immobility of old China.

But enough of uncompromising practicians! Besides these, there are those who are only interested in nature and who ask us if we can enable them to know it better.

To answer these, we have only to show them the two monuments already rough-hewn, Celestial Mechanics and Mathematical Physics.

They would doubtless concede that these structures are well worth the trouble they have cost us. But this is not enough. Mathematics has a triple aim. It must furnish an instrument for the study of nature. But that is not all: it has a philosophic aim and, I dare maintain, an esthetic aim. It must aid the philosopher to fathom the notions of number, of space, of time. And above all, its adepts find therein delights analogous to those given by painting and music. They admire the delicate harmony of numbers and forms; they marvel when a new discovery opens to them an unexpected perspective; and has not the joy they thus feel the esthetic character, even though the senses take no part therein? Only a privileged few are called to enjoy it fully, it is true, but is not this the case for all the noblest arts?

This is why I do not hesitate to say that mathematics deserves to be cultivated for its own sake, and the theories inapplicable to physics as well as the others. Even if the physical aim and the esthetic aim were not united, we ought not to sacrifice either.

But more: these two aims are inseparable and the best means of attaining one is to aim at the other, or at least never to lose sight of it.

Poincaré, *Value of Science,* II, 5

54 The first man who noticed the analogy between a group of seven fishes and a group of seven days made a notable advance in the history of thought.

Whitehead, *Science and the Modern World,* II

55 I will not go so far as to say that to construct a history of thought without profound study of the mathematical ideas of successive epochs is like omitting Hamlet from the play which is named after him. That would be claiming too much. But it is certainly analogous to cutting out the part of Ophelia. This simile is singularly exact. For Ophelia is quite essential to the play, she is very charming—and a little mad. Let us grant that the pursuit of mathematics is a divine madness of the human spirit, a refuge from the goading urgency of contingent happenings.

Whitehead, *Science and the Modern World,* II

56 Mathematics is thought moving in the sphere of complete abstraction from any particular instance of what it is talking about. So far is this view of mathematics from being obvious, that we can easily assure ourselves that it is not, even now, generally understood.

Whitehead, *Science and the Modern World,* II

57 Our last reflection must be, that we have in the end come back to a version of the doctrine of old Pythagoras, from whom mathematics, and mathematical physics, took their rise. He discovered the importance of dealing with abstractions; and in particular directed attention to number as characterising the periodicities of notes of music. The importance of the abstract idea of periodicity was thus present at the very beginning both of mathematics and of European philosophy.

In the seventeenth century, the birth of modern science required a new mathematics, more fully equipped for the purpose of analysing the characteristics of vibratory existence. And now in the twentieth century we find physicists largely engaged in analysing the periodicities of atoms. Truly, Pythagoras in founding European philosophy and European mathematics, endowed them with the luckiest of lucky guesses—or, was it a flash of divine genius, penetrating to the inmost nature of things?

Whitehead, *Science and the Modern World,* II

58 The study of mathematics is apt to commence in disappointment. The important applications of the science, the theoretical interest of its ideas, and the logical rigour of its methods, all generate the expectation of a speedy introduction to processes of interest. We are told that by its aid the stars are weighed and the billions of molecules in a drop of water are counted. Yet, like the ghost of Hamlet's father, this great science eludes the efforts of our mental weapons to grasp it—" 'Tis here, 'tis there, 'tis gone"—and what we do see does not suggest the same excuse for illusiveness as sufficed for the ghost, that it is too noble for our gross methods. "A show of violence," if ever excusable, may surely be "offered" to the trivial results which occupy the pages of some elementary mathematical treatises.

Whitehead, *Introduction to Mathematics,* I

59 Mathematics, rightly viewed, possesses not only truth, but supreme beauty—a beauty cold and austere, like that of sculpture, without appeal to any part of our weaker nature, without the gorgeous trappings of painting or music, yet sublimely pure, and capable of a stern perfection such as only the greatest art can show. The true spirit of delight, the exaltation, the sense of being more than Man, which is the touchstone of the highest excellence, is to be found in mathematics as surely as in poetry.

Russell, *Study of Mathematics*

60 Pure mathematics consists entirely of assertions to the effect that, if such and such a proposition is true of *anything,* then such and such another proposition is true of that thing. It is essential not to discuss whether the first proposition is really true, and not to mention what the anything is, of which

it is supposed to be true. Both these points would belong to applied mathematics. We start, in pure mathematics, from certain rules of inference, by which we can infer that *if* one proposition is true, then so is some other proposition. These rules of inference constitute the major part of the principles of formal logic. We then take any hypothesis that seems amusing, and deduce its consequences. *If* our hypothesis is about *anything,* and not about some one or more particular things, then our deductions constitute mathematics. Thus mathematics may be defined as the subject in which we never know what we are talking about, nor whether what we are saying is true. People who have been puzzled by the beginnings of mathematics will, I hope, find comfort in this definition, and will probably agree that it is accurate.

Russell, *Mathematics and the Metaphysicians*

61 Mathematics is said to have . . . disciplinary value in habituating the pupil to accuracy of statement and closeness of reasoning; it has utilitarian value in giving command of the arts of calculation involved in trade and the arts; culture value in its enlargement of the imagination in dealing with the most general relations of things; even religious value in its concept of the infinite and allied ideas. But clearly mathematics does not accomplish such results, because it is endowed with miraculous potencies called values; it has these values if and when it accomplishes these results, and not otherwise. The statements may help a teacher to a larger vision of the possible results to be effected by instruction in mathematical topics. But unfortunately, the tendency is to treat the statement as indicating powers inherently residing in the subject, whether they operate or not, and thus to give it a rigid justification. If they do not operate, the blame is put not on the subject as taught, but on the indifference and recalcitrancy of pupils.

Dewey, *Democracy and Education,* XVIII

62 Mathematics is like music, freely exploring the possibilities of form. And yet, notoriously, mathematics holds true of things; hugs and permeates them far more closely than does confused and inconstant human perception; so that the dream of many exasperated critics of human error has been to assimilate all science to mathematics, so as to make knowledge safe by making it, as Locke wished, direct perception of the relations between ideas. Unfortunately, knowledge would then never touch those matters of fact on which Locke was intent. The only serious value of those logical explorations would lie in their possible relevance to the accidents of existence. It is only in that relation and in that measure that mathematical science would cease to be mere play with ideas and would become *true:* that is, in a serious sense, would become *knowledge.* Now the seriousness of mathematics comes precisely of its remarkable

and exact relevance to material facts, both familiar and remote: so that mathematical equations, besides being essentially necessary in themselves, are often also true of the world we live in. And this in a surprising measure. . . .

In this way mathematical calculations far outrunning experiment often turns out to be true of the physical world, as if, *per impossibile,* they could be true *à priori.* But in fact nature, that had to have some form or other, is organized and deployed on principles which, in human language, are called number, shape, and measurable time; categories which for that reason have taken root in human language science.

Santayana, *Realm of Truth,* I

Chapter 18

MEDICINE
and HEALTH

Chapter 18 is divided into three sections: 18.1 THE ART AND SCIENCE OF MEDICINE, 18.2 THE PRACTICE OF MEDICINE: PHYSICIANS AND PATIENTS, and 18.3 HEALTH AND DISEASE.

Medicine is one of the traditionally recognized learned professions. In the constitution of the first universities, it was one of the three faculties granting a doctorate, the other two being law and theology. Both as a profession and as a field of learning, it is, perhaps, older than the other two, originating in the West with the formation of the Hippocratic school of medicine on the island of Cos in the fifth century B.C. The professional aspect of medicine is covered in the second section of this chapter; the first section focuses on medicine as a field of learning, a body of knowledge acquired by experience and investigation, and applied in practice by a set of techniques or skills; and the third section is concerned with the two states of the living body that define the interests of medicine—as an art, a science, and a profession.

The consideration of medicine as an art may be illuminated by the discussion of the nature and kinds of art in Section 16.1. The consideration of medicine as a science may similarly be illuminated by the discussion of science and scientific method in Section 17.2. The discussion of the nature of life in Section 19.2 and of life and death in Section 1.8 may provide background for the consideration of health and disease.

18.1 | *The Art and Science of Medicine*

The quotations collected here are more or less general statements about medicine conceived either as an art or as a science. In antiquity, the emphasis was on medicine as an art, but the ancient conception of art did not preclude science; on the contrary, it presupposed science, or at least an organized body of knowledge, gained by careful observation and investigation, which provided a basis for the rules to be followed in the practice of the art. The man who tried to heal the sick by guesswork or by trial and error was called an "empiric," and this term was used not only in a derogatory sense but also in sharp contrast to the skilled physician whose procedures were governed by his knowledge of the causes or conditions of health and disease.

The introduction of medical experimentation in modern times, foreshadowed by Bacon and Harvey and definitely instituted by Claude Bernard, provides the basis for the claim that ancient medicine was more of an art than a science and that scientific medicine is of recent origin. The reader should be aware of changes in the meanings of the terms "art" and "science" while examining the criticisms that later generations level against earlier stages of medicine.

A few quotations present the notion of medicine as a cooperative art, an art that merely helps nature do what nature tends to do by itself, unaided by human skill. Thus conceived, the art of healing, productive or conservative of health, is like the arts of farming and of teaching. In each case, the ultimate product—the fruits of the earth, the health of the body, and knowledge in the mind—results from natural processes that the human artist must be cognizant of in order to aid nature.

There are some passages here that attack or satirize the presumptions and pretensions of medicine, but most of the quotations that express such attitudes have been placed in Section 15.2, since they are mainly directed against the practitioner of the art rather than against the art itself.

---

1 Honor a physician with the honor due unto him for the uses which ye may have of him: for the Lord hath created him. For of the most High cometh healing, and he shall receive honor of the king. The skill of the physician shall lift up his head: and in the sight of great men he shall be in admiration. The Lord hath created medicines out of the earth; and he that is wise will not abhor them. Was not the water made sweet with wood, that the virtue thereof might be known? And he hath given men skill, that he might be honored in his marvelous works. With such doth he heal [men,] and taketh away their pains. Of such doth the apothecary make a confection; and of his works there is no end; and from him is peace over all the earth. My son, in thy sickness be not negligent: but pray unto the Lord, and he will make thee whole. Leave off from sin, and order thine hands aright, and cleanse thy heart from all wickedness. Give a sweet savor, and a memorial of fine flour; and make a fat offering, as not being. Then give place to the physician, for the Lord hath created him: let him not go from thee, for thou hast need of him. There is a time when in their hands there is good success. For they shall also pray unto the Lord, that he would prosper that, which they give for ease and remedy to prolong life. He that sinneth before his Maker, let him fall into the hand of the physician.

Ecclesiasticus 38:1–15

2 The art of Medicine would not have been invented at first, nor would it have been made a subject of investigation (for there would have been no need of it), if when men are indisposed, the same food and other articles of regimen which they eat and drink when in good health were proper for them, and if no others were preferable to these.

But now necessity itself made medicine to be sought out and discovered by men, since the same things when administered to the sick, which agreed with them when in good health, neither did nor do agree with them.

Hippocrates, *On Ancient Medicine, 3*

3 Certain sophists and physicians say that it is not possible for any one to know medicine who does not know what man is . . . , and that whoever would cure men properly, must learn this in the first place. But this saying rather appertains to philosophy, as Empedocles and certain others have described what man in his origin is, and how he first was made and constructed. But I think whatever such has been said or written by sophist or physician concerning nature has less connection with the art of medicine than with the art of painting. And I think that one cannot know anything certain respecting nature from any other quarter than from medicine; and that this knowledge is to be attained when one comprehends the whole subject of medicine properly, but not until then; and I say that this history shows what man is, by what causes he was made, and other things accurately. Wherefore it appears to me necessary to every physician to be skilled in nature, and strive to know, if he would wish to perform his duties, what man is in relation to the articles of food and drink, and to his other occupations, and what are the effects of each of them to every one.

Hippocrates, *On Ancient Medicine, 20*

4 Whoever wishes to investigate medicine properly, should proceed thus: in the first place to consider the seasons of the year, and what effects each of them produces for they are not at all alike, but differ much from themselves in regard to their changes. Then the winds, the hot and the cold, especially such as are common to all countries, and then such as are peculiar to each locality. We must also consider the qualities of the waters, for as they differ from one another in taste and weight, so also do they differ much in their qualities. In the same manner, when one comes into a city to which he is a stranger, he ought to consider its situation, how it lies as to the winds and the rising of the sun; for its influence is not the same whether it lies to the north or the south, to the rising or to the setting sun. These things one ought to consider most attentively, and concerning the waters which the inhabitants use, whether they be marshy and soft, or hard, and running from elevated and rocky situations, and then if saltish and unfit for cooking; and the ground, whether it be naked and deficient in water, or wooded and well watered, and whether it lies in a hollow, confined situation, or is elevated and cold; and the mode in which the inhabitants live, and what are their pursuits, whether they are fond of drinking and eating to excess, and given to indolence, or are fond of exercise and labor, and not given to excess in eating and drinking.

From these things he must proceed to investigate everything else. For if one knows all these things well, or at least the greater part of them, he cannot miss knowing, when he comes into a strange city, either the diseases peculiar to the place, or the particular nature of common diseases, so that he will not be in doubt as to the treatment of the diseases, or commit mistakes, as is likely to be the case provided one had not previously considered these matters. And in particular, as the season and the year advances, he can tell what epidemic diseases will attack the city, either in summer or in winter, and what each individual will be in danger of experiencing from the change of regimen. For knowing the changes of the seasons, the risings and settings of the stars, how each of them takes place, he will be able to know beforehand what sort of a year is going to ensue. Having made these investigations, and knowing beforehand the seasons, such a one must be acquainted with each particular, and must succeed in the preservation of health, and be by no means unsuccessful in the practice of his art. And if it shall be thought that these things belong rather to meteorology, it will be admitted, on second thoughts, that astronomy contributes not a little, but a very great deal, indeed, to medicine. For with the seasons the digestive organs of men undergo a change.

Hippocrates, *Airs, Waters, and Places, 1–2*

5 It is disgraceful in every art, and more especially in medicine, after much trouble, much display, and much talk, to do no good after all.

Hippocrates, *Articulations, 44*

6 To such as are curable, means are to be used to prevent them from becoming incurable, studying how they may best be prevented from getting into an incurable state. And incurable cases should be known, that they may not be aggravated by useless applications, and splendid and creditable prognostics are made by knowing where, how, and when every case will terminate, and whether it will be converted into a curable or an incurable disease.

Hippocrates, *Articulations, 58*

7 Life is short, and Art long; the crisis fleeting; experience perilous, and decision difficult.

Hippocrates, *Aphorisms, I, 1*

8 *Eryximachus.* Medicine may be regarded generally as the knowledge of the loves and desires of the body, and how to satisfy them or not; and the best physician is he who is able to separate fair love from foul, or to convert one into the other; and he who knows how to eradicate and how to implant love, whichever is required, and can reconcile the

most hostile elements in the constitution and make them loving friends, is a skilful practitioner. Now the most hostile are the most opposite, such as hot and cold, bitter and sweet, moist and dry, and the like. And my ancestor, Asclepius, knowing how to implant friendship and accord in these elements, was the creator of our art.

Plato, *Symposium,* 186B

9 Art arises when from many notions gained by experience one universal judgement about a class of objects is produced. For to have a judgement that when Callias was ill of this disease this did him good, and similarly in the case of Socrates and in many individual cases, is a matter of experience; but to judge that it has done good to all persons of a certain constitution, marked off in one class, when they were ill of this disease, e.g. to phlegmatic or bilious people when burning with fever,—this is a matter of art.

Aristotle, *Metaphysics,* 981ᵃ6

10 The art of medicine is valuable to us because it is conducive to health, not because of its scientific interest.

Cicero, *De Finibus,* I, 13

11 Nothing hinders a cure so much as frequent changes of treatment.

Seneca, *Letters to Lucilius,* 2

12 The learned Erasistratus, however, overlooks— nay, despises—what neither Hippocrates, Diocles, Praxagoras, nor Philistion despised, nor indeed any of the best philosophers, whether Plato, Aristotle, or Theophrastus; he passes by whole functions as though it were but a trifling and casual department of medicine which he was neglecting, without deigning to argue whether or not these authorities are right in saying that the bodily parts of all animals are governed by the Warm, the Cold, the Dry and the Moist, the one pair being active and the other passive, and that among these the Warm has most power in connection with all functions, but especially with the genesis of the humours. Now, one cannot be blamed for not agreeing with all these great men, nor for imagining that one knows more than they; but not to consider such distinguished teaching worthy either of contradiction or even mention shows an extraordinary arrogance.

Galen, *Natural Faculties,* II, 8

13 As for the scientific proofs of all this, they are to be drawn from these principles of which I have already spoken—namely, that bodies act upon and are acted upon by each other in virtue of the Warm, Cold, Moist and Dry. And if one is speaking of any activity, whether it be exercised by vein, liver, arteries, heart, alimentary canal, or any part, one will be inevitably compelled to ac-

knowledge that this activity depends upon the way in which the four qualities are blended.

Galen, *Natural Faculties,* II, 9

14 Although, with a cruel zeal for science, some medical men, who are called anatomists, have dissected the bodies of the dead, and sometimes even of sick persons who died under their knives, and have inhumanly pried into the secrets of the human body to learn the nature of the disease and its exact seat, and how it might be cured, yet those relations of which I speak, and which form the concord, or, as the Greeks call it, *harmony,* of the whole body outside and in, as of some instrument, no one has been able to discover, because no one has been audacious enough to seek for them.

Augustine, *City of God,* XXII, 24

15 He [Pantagruel] went then to Montpellier, where he met with the good wives of Mirevaux, and good jovial company withal, and thought to have set himself to the study of physic; but he considered that that calling was too troublesome and melancholic, and that physicians did smell of glisters like old devils.

Rabelais, *Gargantua and Pantagruel,* II, 5

16 . . . the moral comedy of him who had espoused and married a dumb wife. I was there, quoth Epistemon. The good honest man, her husband, was very earnestly urgent to have the fillet of her tongue untied, and would needs have her speak by any means. At his desire, some pains were taken on her, and partly by the industry of the physician, other part by the expertness of the surgeon, the encycliglotte which she had under her tongue being cut, she spoke, and spoke again; yea, within a few hours she spoke so loud, so much, so fiercely, and so long, that her poor husband returned to the same physician for a receipt to make her hold her peace. There are, quoth the physician, many proper remedies in our art to make dumb women speak, but there are none that ever I could learn therein to make them silent. The only cure which I have found out is their husband's deafness. The wretch became within few weeks thereafter, by virtue of some drugs, charms, or enchantments, which the physician had prescribed unto him, so deaf, that he could not have heard the thundering of nineteen hundred cannons at a salvo. His wife perceiving that indeed he was as deaf as a doornail, and that her scolding was but in vain, sith that he heard her not, she grew stark mad.

Some time after, the doctor asked for his fee of the husband; who answered, That truly he was deaf, and so was not able to understand what the tenour of his demand might be.

Rabelais, *Gargantua and Pantagruel,* III, 34

17 'Tis wonderful how God has put such excellent physic in mere muck; we know by experience that

swine's dung stints the blood; horse's serves for the pleurisy; man's heals wounds and black blotches; asses' is used for the bloody flux, and cow's with preserved roses serves for epilepsy, or for convulsions of children.

Luther, *Table Talk,* H92

18 Experience is really on its own dunghill in the subject of medicine, where reason yields it the whole field. Tiberius used to say that whoever had lived twenty years should be responsible to himself for the things that were harmful or beneficial to him, and know how to take care of himself without medical aid. And he might have learned this from Socrates, who, advising his disciples, carefully and as a principal study, the study of their health, used to add that it was difficult for an intelligent man who was careful about his exercise, his drinking, and his eating not to know better than any doctor what was good or bad for him.

Montaigne, *Essays,* III, 13, Of Experience

19 *Friar Laurence.*   Mickle is the powerful grace
          that lies
In herbs, plants, stones, and their true qualities:
For nought so vile that on the earth doth live
But to the earth some special good doth give,
Nor aught so good but strain'd from that fair use
Revolts from true birth, stumbling on abuse:
Virtue itself turns vice, being misapplied;
And vice sometimes by action dignified.
Within the infant rind of this small flower
Poison hath residence and medicine power:
For this, being smelt, with that part cheers each
          part;
Being tasted, slays all senses with the heart.
Two such opposed kings encamp them still
In man as well as herbs, grace and rude will;
And where the worser is predominant,
Full soon the canker death eats up that plant.

Shakespeare, *Romeo and Juliet,* II, iii, 15

20 *Falstaff.* A good sherris-sack hath a two-fold operation in it. It ascends me into the brain; dries me there all the foolish and dull and crudy vapours which environ it; makes it apprehensive, quick, forgetive, full of nimble, fiery, and delectable shapes; which, delivered o'er to the voice, the tongue, which is the birth, becomes excellent wit. The second property of your excellent sherris is the warming of the blood; which, before cold and settled, left the liver white and pale, which is the badge of pusillanimity and cowardice; but the sherris warms it and makes it course from the inwards to the parts extreme: it illumineth the face, which as a beacon gives warning to all the rest of this little kingdom, man, to arm; and then the vital commoners and inland petty spirits muster me all to their captain, the heart, who, great and puffed up with this retinue, doth any deed of courage; and this valour comes of sherris. So that

skill in the weapon is nothing without sack, for that sets it a-work; and learning a mere hoard of gold kept by a devil, till sack commences it and sets it in act and use. Hereof comes it that Prince Harry is valiant; for the cold blood he did naturally inherit of his father he hath, like lean, sterile, and bare land, manured, husbanded, and tilled with excellent endeavour of drinking good and good store of fertile sherris, that he is become very hot and valiant. If I had a thousand sons, the first humane principle I would teach them should be to forswear thin potations and to addict themselves to sack.

Shakespeare, *II Henry IV,* IV, iii, 103

21 *Macbeth.* Throw physic to the dogs; I'll none of it.

Shakespeare, *Macbeth,* V, iii, 46

22 *Sancho* was conducted from the Court of Justice to a sumptuous Palace; where, in a spacious Room, he found the Cloth laid, and a most neat and magnificent Entertainment prepar'd. As soon as he enter'd, the Wind-Musick play'd, and four Pages waited on him, in order to the washing his Hands; which he did with a great deal of Gravity. And now the Instruments ceasing, *Sancho* sat down at the upper End of the Table; for there was no Seat but there, and the Cloth was only laid for one. A certain Personage, who afterwards appear'd to be a Physician, came and stood at his Elbow, with a Whalebone Wand in his Hand. Then they took off a curious white Cloth that lay over the Dishes on the Table, and discover'd great Variety of Fruit, and other Eatables. One that look'd like a Student, said Grace; a Page put a lac'd Bib under *Sancho's* Chin; and another, who did the Office of Sewer, set a Dish of Fruit before him. But he had hardly put one Bit into his Mouth, before the Physician touch'd the Dish with his Wand, and then it was taken away by a Page in an Instant. Immediately another with Meat was clapp'd in the Place; but *Sancho* no sooner offer'd to taste it, but the Doctor with the Wand conjur'd it away as fast as the Fruit. *Sancho* was amaz'd at this sudden Removal, and looking about him on the Company, ask'd them whether they us'd to tantalize People at that rate, feeding their Eyes, and starving their Bellies? My Lord Governor, answer'd the Physician, you are to eat here no otherwise than according to the Use and Custom of other Islands where there are Governors. I am a Doctor of Physick, my Lord, and have a Salary allow'd me in this Island, for taking Charge of the Governor's Health, and I am more careful of it than of my own; studying Night and Day his Constitution, that I may the better know what to prescribe when he falls sick. Now the chief Thing I do, is to attend him always at his Meals, to let him eat what I think convenient for him, and to prevent his eating what I imagine to be prejudicial to his Health, and offensive to his

Stomach. Therefore I now order'd the Fruit to be taken away, because 'tis too cold and moist; and the other Dish, because 'tis as much too hot, and overseason'd with Spices, which are apt to increase Thirst; and he that drinks much, destroys and consumes the radical Moisture, which is the Fuel of Life. So then, quoth *Sancho,* this Dish of roasted Partridges here can do me no manner of Harm. Hold, said the Physician, the Lord Governor shall not eat of 'em, while I live to prevent it. Why so? cry'd *Sancho:* Because, answer'd the Doctor, our great Master *Hippocrates,* the North-Star, and Luminary of Physick, says in one of his Aphorisms, *Omnis Saturatio mala, perdicis autem pessima:* That is, all Repletion is bad, but that of Partridges is worst of all. If it be so, said *Sancho,* let Mr Doctor see which of all these Dishes on the Table will do me most Good and least Harm, and let me eat my Belly-full of that, without having it whisk'd away with his Wand. For, by my Hopes, and the Pleasures of Government, as I live, I am ready to die with Hunger; and not to allow me to eat any Victuals (let Mr Doctor say what he will) is the Way to shorten my Life, and not to lengthen it. Very true, my Lord, reply'd the Physician, however, I am of Opinion, you ought not to eat of these Rabbets, as being a hairy, furry Sort of Food; nor would I have you taste of that Veal: Indeed if it were neither roasted nor pickled, something might be said; but as it is, it must not be. Well then, said *Sancho,* what think you of that huge Dish yonder that smokes so? I take it to be an *Olla Podrida;* and that being a Hodgepodge of so many Sorts of Victuals, sure I can't but light upon something there that will nick me, and be both wholesom and toothsom. *Absit,* cry'd the Doctor, far be such an ill Thought from us; no Diet in the World yields worse Nutriment than those Mishmashes do. No, leave that luxurious Compound to your rich Monks and Prebendaries, your Masters of Colleges, and lusty Feeders at Country-Weddings: But let them not incumber the Tables of Governors, where nothing but delicate unmix'd Viands in their Prime ought to make their Appearance. The Reason is, that simple Medicines are generally allow'd to be better than Compounds; for in a Composition there may happen a Mistake by the unequal Proportion of the Ingredients; but Simples are not subject to that Accident. Therefore what I would advise at present, as a fit Diet for the Governor, for the Preservation and Support of his Health, is a hundred of small Wafers, and a few thin Slices of Marmalade, to strengthen his Stomach and help Digestion. *Sancho* hearing this, lean'd back upon his Chair, and looking earnestly in the Doctor's Face, very seriously ask'd him what his Name was, and where he had studied? My Lord, answer'd he, I am call'd Doctor *Pedro Rezio de Aguero.* The Name of the Place where I was born, is *Tirteafuera,* and lies between *Caraquel* and *Almo-*

dabar del Campo, on the Right-hand; and I took my Degree of Doctor in the University of *Osuna.* Hark you, said *Sancho,* in a mighty Chafe, Mr Dr *Pedro Rezio de Aguero,* born at *Tirteafuera,* that lies between *Caraquel* and *Almodabar del Campo,* on the Right-hand, and who took your Degrees of Doctor at the University of *Osuna,* and so forth, Take your self away! avoid the Room this Moment, or by the Sun's Light, I'll get me a good Cudgel, and beginning with your Carcase, will so be-labour and rib-roast all the Physick-mongers in the Island, that I will not leave therein one of the Tribe of those, I mean that are ignorant Quacks; for as for learned and wise Physicians, I'll make much of 'em, and honour 'em like so many Angels. Once more *Pedro Rezio,* I say, get out of my Presence. Avaunt! or I'll take the Chair I sit upon, and comb your Head with it to some Purpose; and let me be call'd to an Account about it when I give up my Office; I don't care, I'll clear my self by saying, I did the World good Service, in ridding it of a bad Physician, the Plague of a Commonwealth. Body of me! let me eat, or let 'em take their Government again; for an Office that won't afford a Man his Victuals, is not worth two Horse-Beans.

Cervantes, *Don Quixote,* II, 47

23 The poets did well to conjoin music and medicine in Apollo, because the office of medicine is but to tune this curious harp of man's body and to reduce it to harmony.

Bacon, *Advancement of Learning,* Bk. II, X, 2

24 As for the footsteps of diseases, and their devastations of the inward parts, impostumations, exulcerations, discontinuations, putrefactions, consumptions, contractions, extensions, convulsions, dislocations, obstructions, repletions, together with all preternatural substances, as stones, carnosities, excrescences, worms and the like; they ought to have been exactly observed by multitude of anatomies, and the contribution of men's several experiences, and carefully set down both historically according to the appearances, and artificially with a reference to the diseases and symptoms which resulted from them, in case where the anatomy is of a defunct patient; whereas now upon opening of bodies they are passed over slightly and in silence.

Bacon, *Advancement of Learning,* Bk. II, X, 5

25 I profess both to learn and to teach anatomy, not from books but from dissections; not from the positions of philosophers but from the fabric of nature.

William Harvey, *Motion of the Heart,*
Dedication

26 Even as the dissection of healthy and well-constituted bodies contributes essentially to the ad-

of philosophy and sound physiology,
inspection of diseased and cachectic
⸏rfully assist philosophical pathology.
the physiological consideration of
⸏⸏ngs which are according to nature is to be
first undertaken by medical men; since that which
is in conformity with nature is right, and serves as
a rule both to itself and to that which is amiss; by
the light it sheds, too, aberrations and affections
against nature are defined; pathology then stands
out more clearly; and from pathology the use and
art of healing, as well as occasions for the discovery of many new remedies, are perceived. Nor
could anyone readily imagine how extensively internal organs are altered in diseases, especially
chronic diseases, and what monstrosities among
internal parts these diseases engender. So that I
venture to say, that the examination of a single
body of one who has died of tabes or some other
disease of long standing, or poisonous nature, is of
more service to medicine than the dissection of the
bodies of ten men who have been hanged.

William Harvey, Circulation of the Blood, I

27 The mind depends so much on the temperament
and disposition of the bodily organs that, if it is
possible to find a means of rendering men wiser
and cleverer than they have hitherto been, I believe that it is in medicine that it must be sought.

Descartes, Discourse on Method, VI

28 The medicine which is now in vogue contains little of which the utility is remarkable; but, without
having any intention of decrying it, I am sure that
there is no one, even among those who make its
study a profession, who does not confess that all
that men know is almost nothing in comparison
with what remains to be known; and that we
could be free of an infinitude of maladies both of
body and mind, and even also possibly of the infirmities of age, if we had sufficient knowledge of
their causes, and of all the remedies with which
nature has provided us.

Descartes, Discourse on Method, VI

29 *Géronte.* There is just one thing that bothers me:
the position of the liver and the heart. It seems to
me that you place them wrongly; and the heart is
on the left side and the liver on the right.

Sganarelle. Yes, that is the way it used to be. But
we have changed all that; now we use an entirely
new method in medicine.

Molière, The Doctor in Spite of Himself, II, vi

30 I was going on to tell him of another sort of people, who get their livelihood by attending the sick,
having upon some occasions informed his honour
that many of my crew had died of diseases: but
here it was with the utmost difficulty that I
brought him to apprehend what I meant. He
could easily conceive, that a Houyhnhnm grew

weak and heavy a few days before his death; or by
some accident might hurt a limb. But that nature,
who worketh all things to perfection, should suffer
any pains to breed in our bodies, he thought impossible; and desired to know the reason of so
unaccountable an evil. I told him, we fed on a
thousand things which operated contrary to each
other: that, we eat when we were not hungry, and
drank without the provocation of thirst: that, we
sat whole nights drinking strong liquors without
eating a bit, which disposed us to sloth, enflamed
our bodies, and precipitated or prevented digestion. That, prostitute female Yahoos acquired
a certain malady, which bred rottenness in the
bones of those, who fell into their embraces: that,
this and many other diseases, were propagated
from father to son; so that great numbers come
into the world with complicated maladies upon
them: that, it would be endless to give him a catalogue of all diseases incident to human bodies; for
they could not be fewer than five or six hundred,
spread over every limb, and joint: in short, every
part, external and intestine, having diseases appropriated to each. To remedy which, there was a
sort of people bred up among us, in the profession
or pretence of curing the sick. And, because I had
some skill in the faculty, I would in gratitude to
his honour, let him know the whole mystery and
method by which they proceed.

Their fundamental is, that all diseases arise
from *repletion;* from whence they conclude, that a
great *evacuation* of the body is necessary, either
through the natural passage, or upwards at the
mouth. Their next business is, from herbs, minerals, gums, oyls, shells, salts, juices, sea-weed, excrements, barks of trees, serpents, toads, frogs, spiders, dead mens flesh and bones, beasts and fishes,
to form a composition for smell and taste the most
abominable, nauseous and detestable, that they
can possibly contrive, which the stomach immediately rejects with loathing: and this they call a
vomit. Or else from the same store-house, with
some other poysonous additions, they command
us to take in at the orifice *above* or *below* (just as the
physician then happens to be disposed) a medicine equally annoying and disgustful to the bowels; which relaxing the belly, drives down all before it: and this they call a *purge,* or a *glyster.* For
nature (as the physicians alledge) having intended the superior anterior orifice only for the *introm-
ission* of solids and liquids, and the inferior posteri-
or for ejection, these artists ingeniously considering that in all diseases nature is forced out of her
seat; therefore to replace her in it, the body must
be treated in a manner directly contrary, by inter-
changing the use of each orifice; forcing solids and
liquids in at the *anus,* and making evacuations at
the mouth.

But, besides real diseases, we are subject to
many that are only imaginary, for which the physicians have invented imaginary cures; these have

their several names, and so have the drugs that are proper for them; and with these our female Yahoos are always infested.

One great excellency in this tribe is their skill at *prognosticks,* wherein they seldom fail; their predictions in real diseases, when they rise to any degree of malignity, generally portending *death,* which is always in their power, when recovery is not: and therefore, upon any unexpected signs of amendment, after they have pronounced their sentence, rather than be accused as false prophets, they know how to approve their sagacity to the world by a seasonable dose.

Swift, *Gulliver's Travels,* IV, 6

31 However useful medicine, properly administered, may be among us, it is certain that, if the savage, when he is sick and left to himself, has nothing to hope but from nature, he has, on the other hand, nothing to fear but from his disease; which renders his situation often preferable to our own.

Rousseau, *Origin of Inequality,* I

32 With savages, the weak in body or mind are soon eliminated; and those that survive commonly exhibit a vigorous state of health. We civilised men, on the other hand, do our utmost to check the process of elimination; we build asylums for the imbecile, the maimed, and the sick; we institute poor-laws; and our medical men exert their utmost skill to save the life of every one to the last moment. There is reason to believe that vaccination has preserved thousands, who from a weak constitution would formerly have succumbed to small-pox. Thus the weak members of civilised societies propagate their kind. No one who has attended to the breeding of domestic animals will doubt that this must be highly injurious to the race of man. It is surprising how soon a want of care, or care wrongly directed, leads to the degeneration of a domestic race; but excepting in the case of man himself, hardly any one is so ignorant as to allow his worst animals to breed.

Darwin, *Descent of Man,* I, 5

33 Every science has its own kind of investigation and its equipment of special instruments and methods. This, after all, is plain enough, since every science is characterized by the nature of its problems and by the variety of the phenomena that it studies. Medical investigation is the most complicated of all: it includes all the methods proper to anatomical, physiological and therapeutic research, and, as it develops, it also borrows from chemistry and physics many means of research which become powerful allies. In the experimental sciences all progress is measured by improvement in the means of investigation. The whole future of experimental medicine depends on creating a method of research which may be applied fruitfully to the study of vital phenomena,

whether in a normal or abnormal state.

Claude Bernard, *Experimental Medicine,* I, 1

34 Most physicians seem to believe that, in medicine, laws are elastic and indefinite. These are false ideas which must disappear if we mean to found a scientific medicine. As a science, medicine necessarily has definite and precise laws which, like those of all the sciences, are derived from the criterion of experiment.

Claude Bernard, *Experimental Medicine,* II, 2

35 I consider hospitals only as the entrance to scientific medicine; they are the first field of observation which a physician enters; but the true sanctuary of medical science is a laboratory; only there can he seek explanations of life in the normal and pathological states by means of experimental analysis.

Claude Bernard, *Experimental Medicine,* II, 2

36 *Napoleon.* What can doctors cure? One can't cure anything. Our body is a machine for living. It is organized for that, it is its nature. Let life go on in it unhindered and let it defend itself, it will do more than if you paralyze it by encumbering it with remedies. Our body is like a perfect watch that should go for a certain time; the watchmaker cannot open it, he can only adjust it by fumbling, and that blindfold.

Tolstoy, *War and Peace,* X, 29

37 The Middle Ages took a fancy to some familiar number like seven; and because it was an odd number, and the world was made in seven days, and there are seven stars in Charles's Wain, and for a dozen other reasons, they were ready to believe anything that had a seven or a seven times seven in it. Seven deadly sins, seven swords of sorrow in the heart of the Virgin, seven champions of Christendom, seemed obvious and reasonable things to believe in simply because they were seven. To us, on the contrary, the number seven is the stamp of superstition. We will believe in nothing less than millions. A medieval doctor gained his patient's confidence by telling him that his vitals were being devoured by seven worms. Such a diagnosis would ruin a modern physician. The modern physician tells his patient that he is ill because every drop of his blood is swarming with a million microbes; and the patient believes him abjectly and instantly.

Shaw, *Androcles and the Lion,* Pref.

38 Doctoring is not even the art of keeping people in health (no doctor seems able to advise you what to eat any better than his grandmother or the nearest quack): it is the art of curing illnesses. It does happen exceptionally that a practising doctor makes a contribution to science (my play describes a very notable one); but it happens much

oftener that he draws disastrous conclusions from his clinical experience because he has no conception of scientific method, and believes, like any rustic, that the handling of evidence and statistics needs no expertness. The distinction between a quack doctor and a qualified one is mainly that only the qualified one is authorized to sign death certificates, for which both sorts seem to have about equal occasion.

Shaw, *Doctor's Dilemma,* Pref.

39 The notion that therapeutics or hygiene or surgery is any more or less scientific than making or cleaning boots is entertained only by people to whom a man of science is still a magician who can cure diseases, transmute metals, and enable us to live for ever.

Shaw, *Doctor's Dilemma,* Pref.

40 You must not think that the outlook of a patient with regard to medical aid is essentially bettered when the diagnosis points to hysteria rather than to organic disease of the brain. Against the serious brain diseases medical skill is in most cases powerless, but also in the case of hysterical affections the doctor can do nothing. He must leave it to benign nature, when and how his hopeful prognosis will be realized. Accordingly, with the recognition of the disease as hysteria, little is changed in the situation of the patient, but there is a great change in the attitude of the doctor. We can observe that he acts quite differently toward hystericals than toward patients suffering from organic diseases. He will not bring the same interest to the former as to the latter, since their suffering is much less serious and yet seems to set up the claim to be valued just as seriously.

Freud, *Origin and Development of Psycho-Analysis,* I

41 Psycho-analysis stands to psychiatry more or less as histology does to anatomy; in one, the outer forms of organs are studied, in the other, the construction of these out of the tissues and constituent elements. It is not easy to conceive of any contradiction between these two fields of study, in which the work of the one is continued in the other. You know that nowadays anatomy is the basis of the scientific study of medicine; but time was when dissecting human corpses in order to discover the internal structure of the body was as much a matter for severe prohibition as practising psycho-analysis in order to discover the internal workings of the human mind seems today to be a matter for condemnation. And, presumably at a not too distant date, we shall have perceived that there can be no psychiatry which is scientifically radical without a thorough knowledge of the deep-seated unconscious processes in mental life.

Freud, *General Introduction to Psycho-Analysis,* XVI

42 When, in the course of an analysis, we have given the ego assistance and have put it in a position to abolish its repressions, it recovers its power over the repressed id and can allow the instinctual impulses to run their course as though the old situations of danger no longer existed. What we can do in this way is in general accord with the therapeutic achievements of medicine; for as a rule we must be satisfied with bringing about more quickly, more certainly and with less expenditure of energy than would otherwise be the case a desired result which in favourable circumstances would have occurred of itself.

Freud, *Inhibitions, Symptoms, and Anxiety,* X

18.2 | *The Practice of Medicine*

PHYSICIANS AND PATIENTS

Included here are statements about the obligations of the physician to his patient; statements about the things the physician should refrain from doing and which, if done, become malpractice; statements about the relation between physicians and patients; and statements about the qualities of the good physician. They contribute to the formulation of professional standards—the code of what has come to be called "professional ethics," the cornerstone of which is laid by the famous Hippocratic oath.

For whatever they are worth, justified or not, this section also includes a wide variety of satirical attacks on the incompetence of bumbling and fumbling practitioners. No other profession has been subject to more scathing denunciations, unless it be that of the law. This may be understandable in view of the fact that health and disease, like justice and injustice, are of such monumental concern to mankind, who must look to physicians and to lawyers for special competence in securing what is beneficial, and avoiding what is harmful.

One curious strain in the passages quoted deserves comment. It begins with the admonition, cited by St. Luke: "Physician, heal thyself!" Others discuss the physician's experience of disease in his own body, and disagree—as, for example, Plato and Augustine—on the question whether it is necessary for a physician to suffer disease in order to be able to understand and cure it.

---

1 I swear by Apollo the physician, and Æsculapius, and Health, and All-heal, and all the gods and goddesses, that, according to my ability and judgment, I will keep this Oath and this stipulation—to reckon him who taught me this Art equally dear to me as my parents, to share my substance with him, and relieve his necessities if required; to look upon his offspring in the same footing as my own brothers, and to teach them this art, if they shall wish to learn it, without fee or stipulation; and that by precept, lecture, and every other mode of instruction, I will impart a knowledge of the Art to my own sons, and those of my teachers, and to disciples bound by a stipulation and oath according to the law of medicine, but to none others. I will follow that system of regimen which, according to my ability and judgment, I consider for the benefit of my patients, and abstain from whatever is deleterious and mischievous. I will give no deadly medicine to any one if asked, nor suggest any such counsel; and in like manner I will not give to a woman a pessary to produce abortion. With purity and with holiness I will pass my life and practice my Art. I will not cut persons laboring under the stone, but will leave this to be done by men who are practitioners of this work. Into whatever houses I enter, I will go into them for the benefit of the sick, and will abstain from every voluntary act of mischief and corruption; and, further from the seduction of females or males, of freemen and slaves. Whatever, in connection with my professional practice or not, in connection with it, I see or hear, in the life of men, which ought not to be spoken of abroad, I will not divulge, as reckoning that all such should be kept secret. While I continue to keep this Oath unviolated, may it be granted to me to enjoy life and the practice of the art, respected by all men, in all times! But should I trespass and violate this Oath, may the reverse be my lot!

Hippocrates, *The Oath*

2 It appears to me a most excellent thing for the physician to cultivate Prognosis; for by foreseeing and foretelling, in the presence of the sick, the present, the past, and the future, and explaining the omissions which patients have been guilty of, he will be the more readily believed to be acquainted with the circumstances of the sick; so that men will have confidence to intrust themselves to such a physician. And he will manage the cure best who has foreseen what is to happen from the present state of matters. For it is impossible to make all the sick well; this, indeed, would have been better than to be able to foretell what is going to happen; but since men die, some even before calling the physician, from the violence of the disease, and some die immediately after calling him, having lived, perhaps, only one day or a little longer, and before the physician could bring his art to counteract the disease; it therefore becomes necessary to know the nature of such affections, how far they are above the powers of the constitution; and, moreover, if there be anything divine in the diseases, and to learn a foreknowledge of this also. Thus a man will be the more esteemed to be a good physician, for he will be the better able to treat those aright who can be saved, from having long anticipated everything; and by seeing and announcing beforehand those who will live and those who will die, he will thus escape censure.

Hippocrates, *Book of Prognostics*, 1

3 The physician must be able to tell the antecedents, know the present, and foretell the future—

must meditate these things, and have two special objects in view with regard to diseases, namely, to do good or to do no harm. The art consists in three things—the disease, the patient, and the physician. The physician is the servant of the art, and the patient must combat the disease along with the physician.

Hippocrates, *Epidemics*, Bk. I, II, 5

4 I look upon it as being a great part of the art to be able to judge properly of that which has been written. For he that knows and makes a proper use of these things, would appear to me not likely to commit any great mistake in the art. He ought to learn accurately the constitution of every one of the seasons, and of the diseases; whatever that is common in each constitution and disease is good, and whatever is bad; whatever disease will be protracted and end in death, and whatever will be protracted and end in recovery; which disease of an acute nature will end in death, and which in recovery. From these it is easy to know the order of the critical days, and prognosticate from them accordingly. And to a person who is skilled in these things, it is easy to know to whom, when, and how aliment ought to be administered.

Hippocrates, *Epidemics*, Bk. III, II, 16

5 The prime object of the physician in the whole art of medicine should be to cure that which is diseased; and if this can be accomplished in various ways, the least troublesome should be selected; for this is more becoming a good man, and one well skilled in the art, who does not covet popular coin of base alloy.

Hippocrates, *Articulations*, 78

6 Medicine is of all the Arts the most noble; but, owing to the ignorance of those who practice it, and of those who, inconsiderately, form a judgment of them, it is at present far behind all the other arts. Their mistake appears to me to arise principally from this, that in the cities there is no punishment connected with the practice of medicine (and with it alone) except disgrace, and that does not hurt those who are familiar with it. Such persons are like the figures which are introduced in tragedies, for as they have the shape, and dress, and personal appearance of an actor, but are not actors, so also physicians are many in title but very few in reality.

Hippocrates, *The Law*, 1

7 *Socrates.* Asclepius may be supposed to have exhibited the power of his art only to persons who, being generally of healthy constitution and habits of life, had a definite ailment; such as these he cured by purges and operations, and bade them live as usual, herein consulting the interests of the State; but bodies which disease had penetrated through and through he would not have attempt-

ed to cure by gradual processes of evacuation and infusion: he did not want to lengthen out good-for-nothing lives, or to have weak fathers begetting weaker sons—if a man was not able to live in the ordinary way he had no business to cure him; for such a cure would have been of no use either to himself, or to the State.

Plato, *Republic*, III, 407B

8 The most skilful physicians are those who, from their youth upwards, have combined with the knowledge of their art the greatest experience of disease; they had better not be robust in health, and should have had all manner of diseases in their own persons. For the body, as I conceive, is not the instrument with which they cure the body; in that case we could not allow them ever to be or to have been sickly; but they cure the body with the mind, and the mind which has become and is sick can cure nothing.

Plato, *Republic*, III, 408B

9 *Athenian Stranger.* The physician, whether he cures us against our will or with our will, and whatever be his mode of treatment—incision, burning, or the infliction of some other pain—whether he practises out of a book or not out of a book, and whether he be rich or poor, whether he purges or reduces in some other way, or even fattens his patients, is a physician all the same, so long as he exercises authority over them according to rules of art, if he only does them good and heals and saves them. And this we lay down to be the only proper test of the art of medicine, or of any other art of command.

Plato, *Statesman*, 293A

10 *Athenian Stranger.* The physician saves any whom he wishes to save, and any whom he wishes to maltreat he maltreats—cutting or burning them, and at the same time requiring them to bring him payments, which are a sort of tribute, of which little or nothing is spent upon the sick man, and the greater part is consumed by him and his domestics.

Plato, *Statesman*, 298A

11 *Athenian Stranger.* Did you ever observe that there are two classes of patients in states, slaves and freemen; and the slave doctors run about and cure the slaves, or wait for them in the dispensaries—practitioners of this sort never talk to their patients individually, or let them talk about their own individual complaints? The slave doctor prescribes what mere experience suggests, as if he had exact knowledge; and when he has given his orders, like a tyrant, he rushes off with equal assurance to some other servant who is ill; and so he relieves the master of the house of the care of his invalid slaves. But the other doctor, who is a freeman, attends and practises upon freemen; and he

carries his enquiries far back, and goes into the nature of the disorder; he enters into discourse with the patient and with his friends, and is at once getting information from the sick man, and also instructing him as far as he is able, and he will not prescribe for him until he has first convinced him; at last, when he has brought the patient more and more under his persuasive influences and set him on the road to health, he attempts to effect a cure. Now which is the better way of proceeding in a physician and in a trainer? Is he the better who accomplishes his ends in a double way, or he who works in one way, and that the ruder and inferior?

Cleinias. I should say, Stranger, that the double way is far better.

Plato, *Laws*, IV, 720A

12 *Athenian Stranger.* Do you remember the image in which I likened the men for whom laws are now made to slaves who are doctored by slaves? For of this you may be very sure, that if one of those empirical physicians, who practise medicine without science, were to come upon the gentleman physician talking to his gentleman patient, and using the language almost of philosophy, beginning at the beginning of the disease and discoursing about the whole nature of the body, he would burst into a hearty laugh—he would say what most of those who are called doctors always have at their tongue's end:—Foolish fellow, he would say, you are not healing the sick man, but you are educating him; and he does not want to be made a doctor, but to get well.

Cleinias. And would he not be right?

Ath. Perhaps he would.

Plato, *Laws*, IX, 857B

13 He who advises a sick man, whose manner of life is prejudicial to health, is clearly bound first of all to change his patient's manner of life, and if the patient is willing to obey him, he may go on to give him other advice. But if he is not willing, I shall consider one who declines to advise such a patient to be a man and a physician, and one who gives in to him to be unmanly and unprofessional.

Plato, *Seventh Letter*

14 A man who is a doctor might cure himself. Nevertheless it is not in so far as he is a patient that he possesses the art of medicine: it merely has happened that the same man is doctor and patient— and that is why these attributes are not always found together.

Aristotle, *Physics*, 192b24

15 A patient should call in a physician; he will not get better if he is doctored out of a book.

Aristotle, *Politics*, 1287a33

16 Although physicians frequently know their pa-

tients will die of a given disease, they never tell them so. To warn of an evil is justified only if, along with the warning, there is a way of escape.

Cicero, *Divination*, II, 25

17 Physician, heal thyself.

Luke 4:23

18 A skilful physician, . . . in a complicated and chronic disease, as he sees occasion, at one while allows his patient the moderate use of such things as please him, at another while gives him keen pains and drugs to work the cure.

Plutarch, *Pericles*

19 The physician is only nature's assistant.

Galen, *On the Humor*

20 The man who has tried a bad doctor is afraid to trust even a good one.

Augustine, *Confessions*, VI, 4

21 A skillful physician knows, indeed, professionally almost all diseases; but experimentally he is ignorant of a great number which he himself has never suffered from.

Augustine, *City of God*, XXII, 30

22 The physician strengthens nature, and employs food and medicine, of which nature makes use for the intended end.

Aquinas, *Summa Theologica*, I, 117, 1

23 A man needs the services of a physician in every item of health and at every time, but his need of a physician during sickness is especially great and avoiding him is dangerous. Fools think that a man needs a physician during his sickness only and at no other time, but it very often happens that a man gets sick while traveling or while in a small town where there is no physician or only a physician on whose wisdom people do not rely.

Maimonides, *Preservation of Youth*, II

24 What kind of physician would that be who stayed in school all the time? When he finally puts his medicine to use and deals more and more with nature, he will come to see that he hasn't as yet mastered the art.

Luther, *Table Talk*, 352

25 Wretched is the man who relies on the help of physicians. I don't deny that medicine is a gift of God and I don't reject this knowledge, but where are the physicians who are perfect? A good regimen is worth a great deal. So if I feel tired and nevertheless adhere to my regimen, go to bed by the ninth hour, and have a restful night, I will be refreshed.

Luther, *Table Talk*, 3733

26 When I feel indisposed, by observing a strict diet and going to bed early, I generally manage to get round again, that is, if I can keep my mind tolerably at rest. I have no objection to the doctors acting upon certain theories, but, at the same time, they must not expect us to be the slaves of their fancies. We find Avicenna and Galen, living in other times and in other countries, prescribing wholly different remedies for the same disorders. I won't pin my faith to any of them, ancient or modern. On the other hand, nothing can well be more deplorable than the proceeding of those fellows, ignorant as they are complaisant, who let their patients follow exactly their own fancies; 'tis these wretches who more especially people the graveyards. Able, cautious, and experienced physicians, are gifts of God. They are the ministers of nature, to whom human life is confided; but a moment's negligence may ruin everything. No physician should take a single step, but in humility and the fear of God; they who are without the fear of God are mere homicides.

Luther, *Table Talk*, H783

27 Who ever saw a doctor use the prescription of his colleague without cutting out or adding something? Thereby they clearly enough betray their art and reveal to us that they consider their reputation, and consequently their profit, more than the interest of their patients.

Montaigne, *Essays*, II, 37, Children and Fathers

28 I observe the *Phisician,* with the same diligence, as hee the *disease;* I see hee *feares,* and I feare with him: I overtake him, I overrun him in his feare, and I go the faster, because he makes his pace slow; I feare the more, because he disguises his fear, and I see it with the more sharpnesse, because hee would not have me see it.

Donne, *Devotions upon Emergent Occasions,* VI

29 The weakness of patients, and sweetness of life, and nature of hope, maketh men depend upon physicians with all their defects.

Bacon, *Advancement of Learning*, Bk. II, X, 2

30 I esteem it the office of a physician not only to restore health, but to mitigate pain and dolors; and not only when such mitigation may conduce to recovery, but when it may serve to make a fair and easy passage. . . . The physicians contrariwise do make a kind of scruple and religion to stay with the patient after the disease is deplored; whereas in my judgement they ought both to inquire the skill, and to give the attendances, for the facilitating and assuaging of the pains and agonies of death.

Bacon, *Advancement of Learning*, Bk. II, X, 7

31 Physicians are some of them so pleasing and conformable to the humour of the patient, as they press not the true cure of the disease; and some other are so regular in proceeding according to art for the disease, as they respect not sufficiently the condition of the patient. Take one of a middle temper; or if it may not be found in one man, combine two of either sort; and forget not to call as well the best acquainted with your body, as the best reputed of for his faculty.

Bacon, *Of Regiment of Health*

32 I can cure Vices by Physick, when they remain incurable by Divinity; and shall obey my Pills, when they contemn their precepts. I boast nothing, but plainly say, we all labour against our own cure; for death is the cure of all diseases.

Sir Thomas Browne, *Religio Medici*, II, 9

33 Apollo was held the God of Physick, and Sender of Diseases: Both were originally the same Trade, and still continue.

Swift, *Thoughts on Various Subjects*

34 These two doctors, whom, to avoid any malicious applications, we shall distinguish by the names of Dr. Y. and Dr. Z., having felt his pulse; to wit, Dr. Y. his right arm, and Dr. Z. his left; both agreed that he was absolutely dead; but as to the distemper, or cause of his death, they differed; Dr. Y. holding that he died of an apoplexy, and Dr. Z. of an epilepsy.

Hence arose a dispute between the learned men, in which each delivered the reasons of their several opinions. These were of such equal force, that they served both to confirm either doctor in his own sentiments, and made not the least impression on his adversary.

To say the truth, every physician almost hath his favourite disease, to which he ascribes all the victories obtained over human nature. The gout, the rheumatism, the stone, the gravel, and the consumption, have all their several patrons in the faculty; and none more than the nervous fever, or the fever on the spirits. And here we may account for those disagreements in opinion, concerning the cause of a patient's death, which sometimes occur, between the most learned of the college; and which have greatly surprised that part of the world who have been ignorant of the fact we have above asserted.

The reader may perhaps be surprised, that, instead of endeavouring to revive the patient, the learned gentlemen should fall immediately into a dispute on the occasion of his death; but in reality all such experiments had been made before their arrival: for the captain was put into a warm bed, had his veins scarified, his forehead chafed, and all sorts of strong drops applied to his lips and nostrils.

The physicians, therefore, finding themselves anticipated in everything they ordered, were at a loss how to apply that portion of time which it is usual and decent to remain for their fee, and were therefore necessitated to find some subject or other for discourse; and what could more naturally present itself than that before mentioned?

Fielding, *Tom Jones*, II, 9

35 As a wise general never despises his enemy, however inferior that enemy's force may be, so neither doth a wise physician ever despise a distemper, however inconsiderable. As the former preserves the same strict discipline, places the same guards, and employs the same scouts, though the enemy be never so weak; so the latter maintains the same gravity of countenance, and shakes his head with the same significant air, let the distemper be never so trifling. And both, among many other good ones, may assign this solid reason for their conduct, that by these means the greater glory redounds to them if they gain the victory, and the less disgrace if by any unlucky accident they should happen to be conquered.

Fielding, *Tom Jones*, V, 8

36 Jones had no great faith in this new professor; however, he suffered him to open the bandage and to look at his wound; which as soon as he had done, Benjamin began to groan and shake his head violently. Upon which Jones, in a peevish manner, bid him not play the fool, but tell him in what condition he found him. "Shall I answer you as a surgeon, or a friend?" said Benjamin. "As a friend, and seriously," said Jones. "Why then, upon my soul," cries Benjamin, "it would require a great deal of art to keep you from being well after a very few dressings; and if you will suffer me to apply some salve of mine, I will answer for the success." Jones gave his consent, and the plaister was applied accordingly.

"There, sir," cries Benjamin: "now I will, if you please, resume my former self; but a man is obliged to keep up some dignity in his countenance whilst he is performing these operations, or the world will not submit to be handled by him. You can't imagine, sir, of how much consequence a grave aspect is to a grave character. A barber may make you laugh, but a surgeon ought rather to make you cry."

Fielding, *Tom Jones*, VIII, 6

37 Being subject . . . to so few causes of sickness, man, in the state of nature, can have no need of remedies, and still less of physicians.

Rousseau, *Origin of Inequality*, I

38 I do not know what the doctors cure us of, but I know this: they infect us with very deadly diseased, cowardice, timidity, credulity, the fear of death.

Rousseau, *Emile*, I

39 Live according to nature; be patient, get rid of the doctors; you will not escape death, but you will only die once, while the doctors make you die daily through your diseased imagination; their lying art, instead of prolonging your days, robs you of all delight in them.

Rousseau, *Emile*, II

40 We trust our health to the physician: our fortune and sometimes our life and reputation to the lawyer and attorney. Such confidence could not safely be reposed in people of a very mean or low condition. Their reward must be such, therefore, as may give them that rank in the society which so important a trust requires. The long time and the great expense which must be laid out in their education, when combined with this circumstance, necessarily enhance still further the price of their labour.

Adam Smith, *Wealth of Nations*, I, 10

41 But the merit of the physician was received with universal favour and respect [by the Huns]: the barbarians, who despised death, might be apprehensive of disease; and the haughty conqueror trembled in the presence of a captive to whom he ascribed perhaps an imaginary power of prolonging or preserving his life.

Gibbon, *Decline and Fall of the Roman Empire*, XXXIV

42 *Mephistopheles.* Medicine's spirit one can grasp with ease.
The great and little world you study through,
To let things finally their course pursue
As God may please.
It's vain that you in search of knowledge roam and drift,
Each only learns what learn he can;
Yet he who grasps the moment's gift,
He is your proper man.
You are moreover quite well-built, beside,
Will never lack for boldness too;
And if you only in yourself confide,
All other souls confide in you.
Learn chiefly how to lead the women; be assured
That all their "Ohs" and "Ahs," eternal, old,
So thousandfold,
Can at a single point be cured;
And if you half-way decorously come,
You have them all beneath your thumb.
A title first must make them comprehend
That your art many arts doth far transcend.
By way of welcome then you touch all matters
For sake of which, long years, another flatters.
Learn how the little pulse to squeeze
And then with sly and fiery glances seize
Her freely round the slender hips to see
How firmly laced up she may be.

Goethe, *Faust*, I, 2011

43 A physician . . . is by no means physician to living beings in general, not even physician to the human race, but rather, physician to a human individual, and still more physician to an individual in certain morbid conditions peculiar to himself and forming what is called his idiosyncrasy.

Claude Bernard, *Experimental Medicine,* II, 2

44 Since there is no such thing as a medical work of art, there is no such thing as a medical artist; physicians calling themselves such injure medical science, because they exalt a physician's personality by lowering the importance of science; thus they prevent men from seeking, in the experimental study of phenomena, the support and criterion which they believe they, through inspiration or mere feeling, have within themselves.

Claude Bernard, *Experimental Medicine,* III, 4

45 Doctors . . . satisf[y] that eternal human need for hope of relief, for sympathy, and that something should be done, which is felt by those who are suffering. They satisf[y] the need seen in its most elementary form in a child, when it wants to have a place rubbed that has been hurt.

Tolstoy, *War and Peace,* IX, 16

46 He [Napoleon] showed an interest in trifles, joked about de Beausset's love of travel, and chatted carelessly, as a famous, self-confident surgeon who knows his job does when turning up his sleeves and putting on his apron while a patient is being strapped to the operating table. "The matter is in my hands and is clear and definite in my head. When the times comes to set to work I shall do it as no one else could, but now I can jest, and the more I jest and the calmer I am the more tranquil and confident you ought to be, and the more amazed at my genius."

Tolstoy, *War and Peace,* X, 29

47 The fact that doctors themselves die of the very diseases they profess to cure passes unnoticed.

Shaw, *Doctor's Dilemma,* Pref.

48 Everything is on the side of the doctor. When men die of disease they are said to die from natural causes. When they recover (and they mostly do) the doctor gets the credit of curing them.

Shaw, *Doctor's Dilemma,* Pref.

49 There are men and women whom the operating table seems to fascinate: half-alive people who through vanity, or hypochondria, or a craving to be the constant objects of anxious attention or what not, lose such feeble sense as they ever had of the value of their own organs and limbs. They seem to care as little for mutilation as lobsters or lizards, which at least have the excuse that they grow new claws and new tails if they lose the old ones.

Shaw, *Doctor's Dilemma,* Pref.

50 Just as the object of a trade union under existing conditions must finally be, not to improve the technical quality of the work done by its members, but to secure a living wage for them, so the object of the medical profession today is to secure an income for the private doctor; and to this consideration all concern for science and public health must give way when the two come into conflict. Fortunately they are not always in conflict. Up to a certain point doctors, like carpenters and masons, must earn their living by doing the work that the public wants from them.

Shaw, *Doctor's Dilemma,* Pref.

51 By making doctors tradesmen, we compel them to learn the tricks of trade; consequently we find that the fashions of the year include treatments, operations, and particular drugs, as well as hats, sleeves, ballads, and games. Tonsils, vermiform appendices, uvulas, even ovaries are sacrificed because it is the fashion to get them cut out, and because the operations are highly profitable. The psychology of fashion becomes a pathology; for the cases have every air of being genuine: fashions, after all, are only induced epidemics, proving that epidemics can be induced by tradesmen, and therefore by doctors.

Shaw, *Doctor's Dilemma,* Pref.

52 When I promised my patients help and relief through the cathartic method, I was often obliged to hear the following objections: "You say, yourself, that my suffering has probably much to do with my own relation and destinies. You cannot change any of that. In what manner, then, can you help me?" To this I could always answer: "I do not doubt at all that it would be easier for fate than for me to remove your sufferings, but you will be convinced that much will be gained if we succeed in transforming your hysterical misery into everyday unhappiness, against which you will be better able to defend yourself with a restored nervous system."

Freud, *Papers on Hysteria,* IV

53 I wish to call your attention to a well-known fact, namely, that certain maladies and particularly the psycho-neuroses, are more accessible to psychic influences than to any other remedies. It is no modern talk, but a dictum of old physicians, that these diseases are not cured by the drug, but by the doctor—to wit, by the personality of the physician in so far as he exerts a psychic influence.

Freud, *Papers on Hysteria,* VIII

18.3 | *Health and Disease*

Definitions of health are offered here, and also analogies between health and other states of well-being, for example, health in the living body with justice in the body politic. Within the limits of the passages quoted, the understanding of disease does not go much beyond the conception of it as a privation of health. The classification of diseases, the definition of different diseases, and the description of specific disease processes and pathological conditions belong to the technical literature of modern medicine and are beyond the scope of this book.

However, there are some passages from Hippocrates and Galen that indicate an early understanding of the etiology of disease; modern writers approach the subject of the causes of disease from a quite different point of view. The basic issue here—intimated rather than explicitly broached—is whether disease results from an interior imbalance of the factors that constitute the health of the body (first expressed in the humoral hypothesis), or from an attack on the body from without by foreign bodies (first expressed in the germ theory).

The psychologists represented in this collection, such as James and Freud, discuss mental health and disease; but this vast and relatively contemporary subject cannot be adequately treated within the limits that we have set for ourselves.

---

1 The Lord shall make the pestilence cleave unto thee, until he have consumed thee from off the land, whither thou goest to possess it.

The Lord shall smite thee with a consumption, and with a fever, and with an inflammation, and with an extreme burning, and with the sword, and with blasting, and with mildew; and they shall pursue thee until thou perish. . . .

The Lord will smite thee with the botch of Egypt, and with the emerods, and with the scab, and with the itch, whereof thou canst not be healed.

The Lord shall smite thee with madness, and blindness, and astonishment of heart:

And thou shalt grope at noonday, as the blind gropeth in darkness, and thou shalt not prosper in thy ways: and thou shalt be only oppressed and spoiled evermore, and no man shall save thee. . . .

The Lord shall smite thee in the knees, and in the legs, with a sore botch that cannot be healed, from the sole of thy foot unto the top of thy head.

Deuteronomy 28:21–35

2 So went Satan forth from the presence of the Lord, and smote Job with sore boils from the sole of his foot unto his crown.

Job 2:7

3 Diseases almost always attack men when they are exposed to a change, and never more than during changes of the weather.

Herodotus, *History*, II, 77

4 Whenever the Scythian king falls sick, he sends for the three soothsayers of most renown at the time, who come and make trial of their art in the mode above described. Generally they say that the king is ill because such or such a person, mentioning his name, has sworn falsely by the royal hearth. This is the usual oath among the Scythians, when they wish to swear with very great solemnity. Then the man accused of having foresworn himself is arrested and brought before the king. The soothsayers tell him that by their art it is clear he has sworn a false oath by the royal hearth, and so caused the illness of the king—he denies the charge, protests that he has sworn no false oath, and loudly complains of the wrong done to him. Upon this the king sends for six new soothsayers, who try the matter by soothsaying. If they too find the man guilty of the offence, straightway he is beheaded by those who first accused him, and his goods are parted among them: if, on the contrary, they acquit him, other soothsayers, and again others, are sent for, to try the case. Should the greater number decide in favour of the man's innocence, then they who first accused him forfeit their lives.

Herodotus, *History*, IV, 68

5 In the first days of summer the Lacedaemonians and their allies, with two-thirds of their forces as before, invaded Attica, under the command of Archidamus, son of Zeuxidamus, King of Lacedaemon, and sat down and laid waste the country. Not many days after their arrival in Attica the plague first began to show itself among the Athenians. It was said that it had broken out in many places previously in the neighbourhood of Lemnos and elsewhere; but a pestilence of such extent and mortality was nowhere remembered. Neither were the physicians at first of any service, ignorant as they were of the proper way to treat it, but they died themselves the most thickly, as they visited the sick most often; nor did any human art succeed any better. Supplications in the temples, divinations, and so forth were found equally futile, till the overwhelming nature of the disaster at last put a stop to them altogether.

If first began, it is said, in the parts of Ethiopia above Egypt, and thence descended into Egypt and Libya and into most of the King's country. Suddenly falling upon Athens, it first attacked the population in Piraeus—which was the occasion of their saying that the Peloponnesians had poisoned the reservoirs, there being as yet no wells there—and afterwards appeared in the upper city, when the deaths became much more frequent. All speculation as to its origin and its causes, if causes can be found adequate to produce so great a disturbance, I leave to other writers, whether lay or professional; for myself, I shall simply set down its nature, and explain the symptoms by which perhaps it may be recognized by the student, if it should ever break out again. This I can the better do, as I had the disease myself, and watched its operation in the case of others.

That year then is admitted to have been otherwise unprecedentedly free from sickness; and such few cases as occurred all determined in this. As a rule, however, there was no ostensible cause; but people in good health were all of a sudden attacked by violent heats in the head, and redness and inflammation in the eyes, the inward parts, such as the throat or tongue, becoming bloody and emitting an unnatural and fetid breath. These symptoms were followed by sneezing and hoarseness, after which the pain soon reached the chest, and produced a hard cough. When it fixed in the stomach, it upset it; and discharges of bile of every kind named by physicians ensued, accompanied by very great distress. In most cases also an ineffectual retching followed, producing violent spasms, which in some cases ceased soon after, in others much later. Externally the body was not very hot to the touch, nor pale in its appearance, but reddish, livid, and breaking out into small pustules and ulcers. But internally it burned so that the patient could not bear to have on him clothing or linen even of the very lightest description; or indeed to be otherwise than stark naked. What they would have liked best would have been to throw themselves into cold water; as indeed was done by some of the neglected sick, who plunged into the rain-tanks in their agonies of unquenchable thirst; though it made no difference whether they drank little or much. Besides this, the miserable feeling of not being able to rest or sleep never ceased to torment them. The body meanwhile did not waste away so long as the distemper was at its height, but held out to a marvel against its ravages; so that when they succumbed, as in most cases, on the seventh or eighth day to the internal inflammation, they had still some strength in them. But if they passed this stage, and the disease descended further into the bowels, inducing a violent ulceration there accompanied by severe diarrhoea, this brought on a weakness which was generally fatal. For the disorder first settled in the head, ran its course from thence through the whole of the body, and, even where it did not prove mortal, it still left its mark on the extremities; for it settled in the privy parts, the fingers and the toes, and many escaped with the loss of these, some too with that of their eyes. Others again were seized with an entire loss of memory on their first recovery, and did not know either themselves or their friends.

But while the nature of the distemper was such as to baffle all description, and its attacks almost too grievous for human nature to endure, it was still in the following circumstance that its difference from all ordinary disorders was most clearly shown. All the birds and beasts that prey upon human bodies, either abstained from touching them (though there were many lying unburied), or died after tasting them. In proof of this, it was noticed that birds of this kind actually disappeared; they were not about the bodies, or indeed to be seen at all. But of course the effects which I have mentioned could best be studied in a domestic animal like the dog.

Such then, if we pass over the varieties of particular cases which were many and peculiar, were the general features of the distemper. Meanwhile the town enjoyed an immunity from all the ordinary disorders; or if any case occurred, it ended in this. Some died in neglect, others in the midst of every attention. No remedy was found that could be used as a specific; for what did good in one case, did harm in another. Strong and weak constitutions proved equally incapable of resistance, all alike being swept away, although dieted with the utmost precaution. By far the most terrible feature in the malady was the dejection which ensued when any one felt himself sickening, for the despair into which they instantly fell took away their power of resistance, and left them a much easier prey to the disorder; besides which, there was the awful spectacle of men dying like sheep, through having caught the infection in nursing each other. This caused the greatest mortality. On the one hand, if they were afraid to visit each other, they perished from neglect; indeed many houses were emptied of their inmates for want of a nurse: on the other, if they ventured to do so, death was the consequence. This was especially the case with such as made any pretensions to goodness: honour made them unsparing of themselves in their attendance in their friends' houses, where even the members of the family were at last worn out by the moans of the dying, and succumbed to the force of the disaster. Yet it was with those who had recovered from the disease that the sick and the dying found most compassion.

Thucydides, *Peloponnesian War*, II, 47–51

6 There is in man the bitter and the salt, the sweet and the acid, the sour and the insipid, and a multitude of other things having all sorts of powers both as regards quantity and strength. These, when all mixed and mingled up with one another, are not apparent, neither do they hurt a man; but when any of them is separate, and stands by itself, then it becomes perceptible, and hurts a man.

Hippocrates, *On Ancient Medicine*, 14

7 Respecting the seasons, one may judge whether the year will prove sickly or healthy from the following observations:—If the appearances connected with the rising and setting stars be as they should be; if there be rains in autumn; if the winter be mild, neither very tepid nor unseasonably cold, and if in spring the rains be seasonable, and so also in summer, the year is likely to prove healthy. But if the winter be dry and northerly, and the spring showery and southerly, the summer will necessarily be of a febrile character, and give rise to ophthalmies and dysenteries. For when suffocating heat sets in all of a sudden, while the earth is moistened by the vernal showers, and by the south wind, the heat is necessarily doubled from the earth, which is thus soaked by rain and heated by a burning sun, while, at the same time, men's bellies are not in an orderly state, nor the brain properly dried; for it is impossible, after such a spring, but that the body and its flesh must be loaded with humors, so that very acute fevers will attack all, but especially those of a phlegmatic constitution.

Hippocrates, *Airs, Waters, and Places*, 10

8 One may derive information from the regimen of persons in good health what things are proper; for if it appear that there is a great difference whether the diet be so and so, in other respects, but more especially in the changes, how can it be otherwise in diseases, and more especially in the acute? But it is well ascertained that even a faulty diet of food and drink steadily persevered in, is safer in the main as regards health than if one suddenly change it to another.

Hippocrates, *Regimen in Acute Diseases*, 9

9 The disease called the Sacred [that is, epilepsy] arises from causes as the others, namely, those things which enter and quit the body, such as cold, the sun, and the winds, which are ever changing and are never at rest. And these things are divine, so that there is no necessity for making a distinction, and holding this disease to be more divine than the others, but all are divine, and all human. And each has its own peculiar nature and power, and none is of an ambiguous nature, or irremediable.

Hippocrates, *The Sacred Disease*

10 *Socrates.* Where temperance is, there health is speedily imparted.

Plato, *Charmides*, 157A

11 *Socrates.* In a man's bodily frame, you would say that the evil is weakness and disease and deformity?

Polus. I should.

Soc. And do you not imagine that the soul likewise has some evil of her own?

Pol. Of course.

Soc. And this you would call injustice and ignorance and cowardice, and the like?

Pol. Certainly.

Plato, *Gorgias*, 477A

12 *Socrates.* When a carpenter is ill he asks a physician for a rough and ready cure; an emetic or a purge or a cautery or the knife—these are his remedies. And if some one prescribes for him a course of dietetics, and tells him that he must swathe and swaddle his head, and all that sort of thing, he replies at once that he has no time to be ill, and that he sees no good in a life which is spent in nursing his disease to the neglect of his customary employment; and therefore bidding good-bye to this sort of physician, he resumes his ordinary habits, and either gets well and lives and does his business, or, if his constitution fails, he dies and has no more trouble.

Plato, *Republic*, III, 406B

13 *Timaeus.* Every one can see whence diseases arise. There are four natures out of which the body is compacted, earth and fire and water and air, and the unnatural excess or defect of these, or the change of any of them from its own natural place into another, or—since there are more kinds than one of fire and of the other elements—the assumption by any of these of a wrong kind, or any similar irregularity, produces disorders and diseases; for when any of them is produced or changed in a manner contrary to nature, the parts which were previously cool grow warm, and those which were dry become moist, and the light become heavy, and the heavy light; all sorts of changes occur.

Plato, *Timaeus*, 81B

14 *Timaeus.* Diseases unless they are very dangerous should not be irritated by medicines, since every form of disease is in a manner akin to the living being, whose complex frame has an appointed term of life. For not the whole race only, but each individual—barring inevitable accidents—comes into the world having a fixed span, and the triangles in us are originally framed with power to last for a certain time, beyond which no man can prolong his life. And this holds also of the constitution of diseases; if any one regardless of the appointed time tries to subdue them by medicine, he only aggravates and multiplies them. Wherefore we ought always to manage them by regimen, as far as a man can spare the time, and not provoke a disagreeable enemy by medicines.

Plato, *Timaeus,* 89A

15 *Athenian Stranger.* As the physician considers that the body will receive no benefit from taking food until the internal obstacles have been removed, so the purifier of the soul is conscious that his patient will receive no benefit from the application of knowledge until he is refuted, and from refutation learns modesty; he must be purged of his prejudices first and made to think that he knows only what he knows, and no more.

Plato, *Sophist,* 230B

16 Men are called healthy in virtue of the inborn capacity of easy resistance to those unhealthy influences that may ordinarily arise; unhealthy, in virtue of the lack of this capacity.

Aristotle, *Categories,* 9a21

17 Health is better than strength and beauty.

Aristotle, *Topics,* 116b18

18 Bodily excellences such as health and a good state of body we regard as consisting in a blending of hot and cold elements within the body in due proportion, in relation either to one another or to the surrounding atmosphere.

Aristotle, *Physics,* 246b4

19 There is no one who does not obviously avoid some things and not others. Therefore, as it seems, all men make unqualified judgements, if not about all things, still about what is better and worse. And if this is not knowledge but opinion, they should be all the more anxious about the truth, as a sick man should be more anxious about his health than one who is healthy; for he who has opinions is, in comparison with the man who knows, not in a healthy state as far as the truth is concerned.

Aristotle, *Metaphysics,* 1008b24

20 Both excessive and defective exercise destroys the strength, and similarly drink or food which is above or below a certain amount destroys the health, while that which is proportionate both produces and increases and preserves it.

Aristotle, *Ethics,* 1104a16

21 Wickedness is like a disease such as dropsy or consumption, while incontinence is like epilepsy; the former is a permanent, the latter an intermittent badness. And generally incontinence and vice are different in kind; vice is unconscious of itself, incontinence is not (of incontinent men themselves, those who become temporarily beside themselves are better than those who have the rational principle but do not abide by it, since the latter are defeated by a weaker passion, and do not act without previous deliberation like the others); for the incontinent man is like the people who get drunk quickly and on little wine, i.e. on less than most people.

Aristotle, *Ethics,* 1150b33

22 The excellence of the body is health; that is, a condition which allows us, while keeping free from disease, to have the use of our bodies.

Aristotle, *Rhetoric,* 1361b3

23 Rising first and starting from the inmost corners of Egypt, after traversing much air and many floating fields, the plague brooded at last over the whole people of Pandion; and then they were handed over in troops to disease and death. First of all they would have the head seized with burning heat and both eyes blood-shot with a glare diffused over; the livid throat within would exude blood and the passage of the voice be clogged and choked with ulcers, and the mind's interpreter the tongue drip with gore, quite enfeebled with sufferings, heavy in movement, rough to touch. Next when the force of disease passing down the throat had filled the breast and had streamed together even into the sad heart of the sufferers, then would all the barriers of life give away. The breath would pour out at the mouth a noisome stench, even as the stench of rotting carcases thrown out unburied. And then the powers of the entire mind, the whole body would sink utterly, now on the very threshold of death. And a bitter bitter despondency was the constant attendant on insufferable ills and complaining mingled with moaning. An ever-recurring hiccup often the night and day through, forcing on continual spasms in sinews and limbs, would break men quite, forewearying those forspent before. And yet in none could you perceive the skin on the surface of the body burn with any great heat, but the body would rather offer to the hand a lukewarm sensation and at the same time be red all over with ulcers burnt into it so to speak, like unto the holy fire as it spreads over the frame. The inward parts of the men however would burn to the very bones, a

flame would burn within the stomach as within furnaces. Nothing was light and thin enough to apply to the relief of the body of any one; ever wind and cold alone. Many would plunge their limbs burning with disease into the cool rivers, throwing their body naked into the water. Many tumbled head-foremost deep down into the wells, meeting the water straight with mouth wide-a-gape. Parching thirst with a craving not to be appeased, drenching their bodies, would make an abundant draught no better than the smallest drop. No respite was there of ill: their bodies would lie quite spent. The healing art would mutter low in voiceless fear, as again and again they rolled about their eyeballs wide open, burning with disease, never visited by sleep.

And many symptoms of death besides would then be given, the mind disordered in sorrow and fear, the clouded brow, the fierce delirious expression, the ears too troubled and filled with ringings, the breathing quick or else strangely loud and slow-recurring, and the sweat glistening wet over the neck, the spittle in thin small flakes, tinged with a saffron-colour, salt, scarce forced up the rough throat by coughing. The tendons of the hands ceased not to contract, the limbs to shiver, a coldness to mount with slow sure pace from the feet upwards. Then at their very last moments they had nostrils pinched, the tip of the nose sharp, eyes deep-sunk, temples hollow, the skin cold and hard, on the grim mouth a grin, the brow tense and swollen; and not long after their limbs would be stretched stiff in death: about the eighth day of bright sunlight or else on the ninth return of his lamp they would yield up life. And if any of them at that time had shunned the doom of death, yet in after time consumption and death would await him from noisome ulcers and the black discharge of the bowels, or else a quantity of purulent blood accompanied by headache would often pass out by the gorged nostrils: into these the whole strength and substance of the man would stream. Then too if any one had escaped the acrid discharge of noisome blood, the disease would yet pass into his sinews and joints and on-ward even into the sexual organs of the body; and some from excessive dread of the gates of death would live bereaved of these parts by the knife; and some though without hands and feet would continue in life, and some would lose their eyes: with such force had the fear of death come upon them. And some were seized with such utter loss of memory that they did not know themselves.

Lucretius, *Nature of Things,* VI

24 Personal health is preserved by learning about one's own constitution, by finding out what is good or bad for oneself, by continual self-control in eating habits and comforts (but just to the extent needed for self-preservation), by forgoing sensual pleasures, and lastly, by the professional skill of those to whose science these matters belong.

Cicero, *De Officiis,* II, 24

25 An illness that's swift and short will have one of two results: either oneself or it will be snuffed out. And what difference does it make whether I or it disappears? Either way there's an end to the pain.

Seneca, *Letters to Lucilius,* 78

26 That body is, without doubt, the most strong and healthful which can the easiest support extreme cold and excessive heat in the change of seasons, and that the most firm and collected mind which is not puffed up with prosperity nor dejected with adversity.

Plutarch, *Aemilius Paulus and Timoleon Compared*

27 In his sufferings he [Tiberius] would simulate health, and was wont to jest at the arts of the physician and at all who, after the age of thirty, require another man's advice to distinguish between what is beneficial or hurtful to their constitutions.

Tacitus, *Annals,* VI, 46

28 In reference to the genesis of the humours, I do not know that any one could add anything wiser than what has been said by Hippocrates, Aristotle, Praxagoras, Philotimus and many other among the Ancients. These men demonstrated that when the nutriment becomes altered in the veins by the innate heat, blood is produced when it is in moderation, and the other humours when it is not in proper proportion. And all the observed facts agree with this argument. Thus, those articles of food, which are by nature warmer are more productive of bile, while those which are colder produce more phlegm. Similarly of the periods of life, those which are naturally warmer tend more to bile, and the colder more to phlegm. Of occupations also, localities and seasons, and, above all, of natures themselves, the colder are more phlegmatic, and the warmer more bilious. Also cold diseases result from phlegm, and warmer ones from yellow bile. There is not a single thing to be found which does not bear witness to the truth of this account. How could it be otherwise? For, seeing that every part functions in its own special way because of the manner in which the four qualities are compounded, it is absolutely necessary that the function [activity] should be either completely destroyed, or, at least hampered, by any damage to the qualities, and that thus the animal should fall ill, either as a whole, or in certain of its parts.

Galen, *Natural Faculties,* II, 8

29 The peace of the body . . . consists in the duly proportioned arrangement of its parts. The peace of the irrational soul is the harmonious repose of

the appetites, and that of the rational soul the harmony of knowledge and action. The peace of body and soul is the well-ordered and harmonious life and health of the living creature.

Augustine, *City of God,* XIX, 13

30 How many natural appliances are there for preserving and restoring health! How grateful is the alternation of day and night! how pleasant the breezes that cool the air! how abundant the supply of clothing furnished us by trees and animals! Who can enumerate all the blessings we enjoy?

Augustine, *City of God,* XXII, 24

31 Just as surgeons, when they bind up wounds, do it not in a slovenly way, but carefully, that there may be a certain degree of neatness in the binding, in addition to its mere usefulness, so our medicine, Wisdom, was by His assumption of humanity adapted to our wounds, curing some of them by their opposites, some of them by their likes. And just as he who ministers to a bodily hurt in some cases applied contraries, as cold to hot, moist to dry, etc., and in other cases applies likes, as a round cloth to a round wound, or an oblong cloth to an oblong wound, and does not fit the same bandage to all limbs, but puts like to like; in the same way the Wisdom of God in healing man has applied Himself to his cure, being Himself healer and medicine both in one.

Augustine, *Christian Doctrine,* I, 14

32 Health is said to be a habit, or a habitual disposition, in relation to nature. . . . But in so far as nature is a principle of act, it consequently implies a relation to act. Therefore the Philosopher says that man, or one of his members, is called healthy, when he can perform the operation of a healthy man.

Aquinas, *Summa Theologica,* I–II, 49, 3

33 As bodily sickness is partly a privation, in so far as it denotes the destruction of the equilibrium of health, and partly something positive, namely the very humours that are disposed in a disordered way, so too original sin denotes the privation of original justice, and besides this, the disordered disposition of the parts of the soul.

Aquinas, *Summa Theologica,* I–II, 82, 1

34 If a man would take care of his body as he takes care of the animal he rides on, he would be spared many serious ailments.

Maimonides, *Preservation of Youth,* I

35 Ponocrates showed him, that he ought not eat so soon after rising out of his bed, unless he had performed some exercise beforehand. Gargantua answered, what! have not I sufficiently well exercised myself? I have wallowed and rolled myself six or seven turns in my bed, before I rose. Is not

that enough! Pope Alexander did so, by the advice of a Jew his physician, and lived till his dying day in despite of his enemies.

Rabelais, *Gargantua and Pantagruel,* I, 21

36 What, said Gargantua, to drink so soon after sleep? This is not to live according to the diet and prescript rule of the physicians, for you ought first to scour and cleanse your stomach of all its superfluities and excrements. O well physicked, said the monk; a hundred devils leap into my body, if there be not more old drunkards than old physicians!

Rabelais, *Gargantua and Pantagruel,* I, 41

37 I welcome health with open arms, free, full, and entire, and whet my appetite to enjoy it, the more so as it is at present rarer and less ordinary with me; so far am I from troubling its repose and sweetness with the bitterness of a new and constrained way of life.

Montaigne, *Essays,* II, 12, Apology
for Raymond Sebond

38 Health is a precious thing, and the only one, in truth, which deserves that we employ in its pursuit not only time, sweat, trouble, and worldly goods, but even life; inasmuch as without it life comes to be painful and oppressive to us. Pleasure, wisdom, knowledge, and virtue, without it, grow tarnished and vanish away; and to the strongest and most rigorous arguments that philosophy would impress on us to the contrary, we have only to oppose the picture of Plato being struck with a fit of epilepsy or apoplexy, and on this supposition defy him to call to his aid these noble and rich faculties of his soul.

Montaigne, *Essays,* II, 37, Children and
Fathers

39 Of three sorts of movements that are natural to us the last and worst is that of purgations, which no sane man should undertake except in the most extreme necessity. We disturb and arouse a disease by attacking it head on. It is by our mode of life that we should weaken it, by gentle degrees, and bring it to its end. The violent struggles between the drug and the disease are always at our expense, since the combat is fought out within us and the drug is an untrustworthy assistant, by its nature an enemy to our health, and having access to our constitution only through disturbance.

Montaigne, *Essays,* II, 37, Children and
Fathers

40 Both in health and in sickness I have readily let myself follow my urgent appetites. I give great authority to my desires and inclinations. I do not like to cure trouble by trouble; I hate remedies that are more nuisance than the disease. To be subjected to the stone and subjected to abstaining

from the pleasure of eating oysters, those are two troubles for one. The disease pinches us on one side, the rule on the other. Since there is a risk of making a mistake, let us risk it rather in pursuit of pleasure. The world does the opposite, and thinks nothing beneficial that is not painful; it is suspicious of ease.

Montaigne, *Essays,* III, 13, Of Experience

41 The constitution of diseases is patterned after the constitution of animals. They have their destiny, limited from their birth, and their days. He who tries to cut them short imperiously by force, in the midst of their course, prolongs and multiplies them, and stimulates them instead of appeasing them. . . . We should give free passage to diseases; and I find that they do not stay so long with me, who let them go ahead; and some of those that are considered most stubborn and tenacious, I have shaken off by their own decadence, without help and without art, and against the rules of medicine. Let us give Nature a chance; she knows her business better than we do.

Montaigne, *Essays,* III, 13, Of Experience

42 *King.*   Diseases desperate grown
By desperate appliance are relieved,
Or not at all.

Shakespeare, *Hamlet,* IV, iii, 9

43 *Lear.* Infirmity doth still neglect all office
Whereto our health is bound; we are not ourselves
When nature, being oppress'd, commands the mind
To suffer with the body.

Shakespeare, *Lear,* II, iv, 107

44 That health of body is best, which is ablest to endure all alterations and extremities; so likewise that health of mind is most proper, which can go through the greatest temptations and perturbations.

Bacon, *Advancement of Learning,*
Bk. II, XX, 11

45 Every affection of the mind that is attended with either pain or pleasure, hope or fear, is the cause of an agitation whose influence extends to the heart, and there induces change from the natural constitution, in the temperature, the pulse and the rest, which impairing all nutrition in its source and abating the powers at large, it is no wonder that various forms of incurable disease in the extremities and in the trunk are the consequence, inasmuch as in such circumstances the whole body labours under the effects of vitiated nutrition and a want of native heat.

William Harvey, *Motion of the Heart,* XV

46 Let physicians, therefore, cease to wonder at what always excites their astonishment, namely, the manner in which epidemic, contagious, and pestilential diseases scatter their seeds, and are propagated to a distance through the air, or by some *fomes* producing diseases like themselves, in bodies of a different nature, and in a hidden fashion silently multiplying themselves by a kind of generation, until they become so fatal, and with the permission of the Deity spread destruction far and wide among man and beast; since they will find far greater wonders than these taking place daily in the generation of animals. For agents in greater number and of more efficiency are required in the construction and preservation of an animal, than for its destruction; since the things that are difficult and slow of growth, decay with ease and rapidity.

William Harvey, *Animal Generation,* 41

47 So much is certain, and disputed by no one, that animals, all those at least that proceed from the intercourse of male and female, are the offspring of this intercourse, and that they are procreated as it seems by a kind of contagion, much in the same way as medical men observe contagious diseases, such as leprosy, lues venera, plague, phthisis, to creep through the ranks of mortal men, and by mere extrinsic contact to excite diseases similar to themselves in other bodies; nay, contact is not necessary; a mere halitus or miasm suffices, and that at a distance and by an inanimate medium, and with nothing sensibly altered: that is to say, where the contagion first touches, there it generates an "univocal" like itself, neither touching nor existing in fact, neither being present nor conjunct, but solely because it formerly touched. Such virtue and efficacy is found in contagions.

William Harvey, *Animal Generation,* 49

48 *Michael.* Before his eyes appeard, sad, noysom, dark,
A Lazar-house it seemd, wherein were laid
Numbers of all diseas'd, all maladies
Of gastly Spasm, or racking torture, qualmes
Of heart-sick Agonie, all feavorous kinds,
Convulsions, Epilepsies, fierce Catarrhs,
Intestin Stone and Ulcer, Colic pangs,
Dropsies, and Asthma's, and Joint-racking Rheums.
Dire was the tossing, deep the groans, despair
Tended the sick busiest from Couch to Couch;
And over them triumphant Death his Dart
Shook, but delaid to strike, though oft invok't
With vows, as thir chief good, and final hope.

Milton, *Paradise Lost,* XI, 478

49 How necessary health is to our business and happiness, and how requisite a strong constitution, able to endure hardships and fatigue, is to one that will make any figure in the world, is too obvious to need any proof.
The consideration I shall here have of health,

shall be, not what a physician ought to do with a sick and crazy child, but what the parents, without the help of physic, should do for the preservation and improvement of a healthy, or at least not sickly constitution in their children. And this perhaps might be all dispatched in this one short rule, viz., that gentlemen should use their children as the honest farmers and substantial yeomen do theirs. But because the mothers possibly may think this a little too hard, and the fathers too short, I shall explain myself more particularly; only laying down this as a general and certain observation for the women to consider, viz., that most children's constitutions are either spoiled, or at least harmed, by cockering and tenderness.

The first thing to be taken care of, is, that children be not too warmly clad or covered, winter or summer. The face when we are born is no less tender than any other part of the body. 'Tis use alone hardens it, and makes it more able to endure the cold. And therefore the Scythian philosopher gave a very significant answer to the Athenian, who wondered how he could go naked in frost and snow. "How," said the Scythian, "can you endure your face exposed to the sharp winter air?" "My face is used to it," said the Athenian. "Think me all face," replied the Scythian. Our bodies will endure anything, that from the beginning they are accustomed to. . . .

Give me leave therefore to advise you not to fence too carefully against the cold of this our climate. There are those in England, who wear the same clothes winter and summer, and that without any inconvenience, or more sense of cold than others find. But if the mother will needs have an allowance for frost and snow, for fear of harm, and the father, for fear of censure, be sure let not his winter clothing be too warm: And amongst other things, remember, that when nature has so well covered his head with hair, and strengthened it with a year or two's age, that he can run about by day without a cap, it is best that by night a child should also lie without one; there being nothing that more exposes to headaches, colds, catarrhs, coughs, and several other diseases, than keeping the head warm. . . .

I will also advise his feet to be washed every day in cold water, and to have his shoes so thin that they might leak and let in water, whenever he comes near it. Here, I fear I shall have the mistress and maids too against me. One will think it too filthy, and the other perhaps too much pains, to make clean his stockings. But yet truth will have it that his health is much more worth than all such considerations, and ten times as much more. And he that considers how mischievous and mortal a thing taking wet in the feet is, to those who have been bred nicely, will wish he had, with the poor people's children, gone barefoot, who, by that means, come to be so reconciled by custom to wet in their feet that they take no more cold or

harm by it than if they were wet in their hands. And what is it, I pray, that makes this great difference between the hands and the feet in others, but only custom? I doubt not, but if a man from his cradle had been always used to go barefoot, whilst his hands were constantly wrapped up in warm mittens, and covered with *hand-shoes,* as the Dutch call gloves; I doubt not, I say, but such a custom would make taking wet in his hands as dangerous to him as now taking wet in their feet is to a great many others. The way to prevent this is to have his shoes made so as to leak water, and his feet washed constantly every day in cold water. It is recommendable for its cleanliness, but that which I aim at in it, is health; and therefore I limit it not precisely to any time of day. I have known it used every night with very good success, and that all the winter, without the omitting it so much as one night in extreme cold weather; when thick ice covered the water, the child bathed his legs and feet in it, though he was of an age not big enough to rub and wipe them himself, and when he began this custom was puling and very tender. But the great end being to harden those parts by a frequent and familiar use of cold water, and thereby to prevent the mischiefs that usually attend accidental taking wet in the feet in those who are bred otherwise, I think it may be left to the prudence and convenience of the parents, to choose either night or morning. The time I deem indifferent, so the thing be effectually done. The health and hardiness procured by it would be a good purchase at a much dearer rate. To which if I add the preventing of corns, that to some men would be a very valuable consideration. But begin first in the spring with luke-warm, and so colder and colder every time, till in a few days you come to perfectly cold water, and then continue it so winter and summer. For it is to be observed in this, as in all other alterations from our ordinary way of living, the changes must be made by gentle and insensible degrees; and so we may bring our bodies to anything, without pain, and without danger.

Locke, *Some Thoughts Concerning*
Education, 3–7

50 A fancy would sometimes take a Yahoo, to retire into a corner, to lie down and howl, and groan, and spurn away all that came near him, although he were young and fat, and wanted neither food nor water; nor did the servants imagine what could possibly ail him. And the only remedy they found, was to set him to hard work, after which he would infallibly come to himself. To this I was silent out of partiality to my own kind; yet here I could plainly discover the true seeds of *spleen,* which only seizeth on the *lazy,* the *luxurious,* and the *rich;* who, if they were forced to undergo the *same regimen,* I would undertake for the cure.

Swift, *Gulliver's Travels,* IV, 7

51 Mr. Allworthy had been for some days indisposed with a cold, which had been attended with a little fever. This he had, however, neglected; as it was usual with him to do all manner of disorders which did not confine him to his bed, or prevent his several faculties from performing their ordinary functions;—a conduct which we would by no means be thought to approve or recommend to imitation; for surely the gentlemen of the Æsculapian art are in the right in advising, that the moment the disease has entered at one door, the physician should be introduced at the other: what else is meant by that old adage, *Venienti occurrite morbo?* "Oppose a distemper at its first approach." Thus the doctor and the disease meet in fair and equal conflict; whereas, by giving time to the latter, we often suffer him to fortify and entrench himself, like a French army; so that the learned gentleman finds it very difficult, and sometimes impossible, to come at the enemy. Nay, sometimes by gaining time the disease applies to the French military politics, and corrupts nature over to his side, and then all the powers of physic must arrive too late. Agreeable to these observations was, I remember, the complaint of the great Doctor Misaubin, who used very pathetically to lament the late applications which were made to his skill, saying, "Bygar, me believe my pation take me for de undertaker, for dey never send for me till de physicion have kill dem."

Fielding, *Tom Jones*, V, 7

52 O blessed health! cried my father, making an exclamation, as he turned over the leaves to the next chapter, thou art above all gold and treasure; 'tis thou who enlargest the soul,—and openest all its powers to receive instruction and to relish virtue. He that has thee, has little more to wish for;—and he that is so wretched as to want thee,—wants every thing with thee.

I have concentrated all that can be said upon this important head, said my father, into a very little room, therefore we'll read the chapter quite through.

My father read as follows:

"The whole secret of health depending upon the due contention for mastery betwixt the radical heat and the radical moisture"—You have proved that matter of fact, I suppose, above, said Yorick. Sufficiently, replied my father.

In saying this, my father shut the book,—not as if he resolved to read no more of it, for he kept his forefinger in the chapter:—nor pettishly,—for he shut the book slowly; his thumb resting, when he had done it, upon the upper-side of the cover, as his three fingers supported the lower side of it, without the least compressive violence.——

I have demonstrated the truth of that point, quoth my father, nodding to Yorick, most sufficiently in the preceding chapter.

Now could the man in the moon be told, that a man in the earth had wrote a chapter, sufficiently demonstrating, That the secret of all health depended upon the due contention for mastery betwixt the radical heat and the radical moisture,—and that he had managed the point so well, that there was not one single word wet or dry upon radical heat or radical moisture, throughout the whole chapter,—or a single syllable in it, *pro* or *con,* directly or indirectly, upon the contention betwixt these two powers in any part of the animal economy.——

"O thou eternal Maker of all beings!"—he would cry, striking his breast with his right hand (in case he had one)—"Thou whose power and goodness can enlarge the faculties of Thy creatures to this infinite degree of excellence and perfection,—What have we Moonites done!"

Sterne, *Tristram Shandy*, V, 33

53 I shall ask if any solid observations have been made from which it may be justly concluded that, in the countries where the art of medicine is most neglected, the mean duration of man's life is less than in those where it is most cultivated. How indeed can this be the case, if we bring on ourselves more diseases than medicine can furnish remedies? The great inequality in manner of living, the extreme idleness of some, and the excessive labour of others, the easiness of exciting and gratifying our sensual appetites, the too exquisite foods of the wealthy which overheat and fill them with indigestion, and, on the other hand, the unwholesome food of the poor, often, bad as it is, insufficient for their needs, which induces them, when opportunity offers, to eat voraciously and overcharge their stomachs; all these, together with sitting up late, and excesses of every kind, immoderate transports of every passion, fatigue, mental exhaustion, the innumerable pains and anxieties inseparable from every condition of life, by which the mind of man is incessantly tormented; these are too fatal proofs that the greater part of our ills are of our own making, and that we might have avoided them nearly all by adhering to that simple, uniform and solitary manner of life which nature prescribed.

Rousseau, *Origin of Inequality*, I

54 Some speculative physicians seem to have imagined that the health of the human body could be preserved only by a certain precise regimen of diet and exercise, of which every, the smallest, violation necessarily occasioned some degree of disease or disorder proportioned to the degree of the violation. Experience, however, would seem to show that the human body frequently preserves, to all appearances at least, the most perfect state of health under a vast variety of different regimens; even under some which are generally believed to be very far from being perfectly wholesome. But the healthful state of the human body, it would

seem, contains in itself some unknown principle of preservation, capable either of preventing or of correcting, in many respects, the bad effects even of a very faulty regimen.

Adam Smith, *Wealth of Nations,* IV, 9

55 The sufferers parade their miseries, tear the lint from their bruises, reveal their indictable crimes, that you may pity them. They like sickness, because physical pain will extort some show of interest from the bystanders, as we have seen children who finding themselves of no account when grown people come in, will cough till they choke, to draw attention.

Emerson, *Culture*

56 Give me health and a day, and I will make the pomp of emperors ridiculous.

Emerson, *Nature,* III

57 There is this noteworthy difference between savage and civilised; that while a sick, civilised man may be six months convalescing, generally speaking, a sick savage is almost half well again in a day.

Melville, *Moby Dick,* CX

58 Vital phenomena are the result of contact between the organic units of the body with the *inner physiological environment;* this is the pivot of all experimental medicine. Physiologists and physicians gain mastery over the phenomena of life by learning which conditions, in this inner environment, are normal and which abnormal, for the appearance of vital activity in the organic units; for apart from complexity of conditions, phenomena exhibiting life, like physico-chemical phenomena, result from contact between an active body and the environment in which it acts.

Claude Bernard, *Experimental Medicine,* II, 1

59 We shall never have a science of medicine as long as we separate the explanation of pathological from the explanation of normal, vital phenomena.

Claude Bernard, *Experimental Medicine,* II, 2

60 *Unhealthiness of will may thus come about in many ways.* The action may follow the stimulus or idea too rapidly, leaving no time for the arousal of restraining associates—*we then have a precipitate will.* Or, although the associates may come, the ratio which the impulsive and inhibitive forces normally bear to each other may be distorted, and we then have a *will which is perverse.* The perversity, in turn, may be due to either of many causes—too much intensity, or too little, here; too much or too little inertia there; or elsewhere too much or too little inhibitory power. If *we compare the outward symptoms of perversity together, they fall into two groups,* in one of which normal actions are impossible, and in the other abnormal ones are irrepressible.

Briefly, *we may call them respectively the obstructed and the explosive will.*

It must be kept in mind, however, that since the resultant action is always due to the *ratio* between the obstructive and the explosive forces which are present, we never can tell by the mere outward symptoms to what *elementary* cause the perversion of a man's will may be due, whether to an increase of one component or a diminution of the other. One may grow explosive as readily by losing the usual brakes as by getting up more of the impulsive steam; and one may find things impossible as well through the enfeeblement of the original desire as through the advent of new lions in the path.

William James, *Psychology,* XXVI

61 The popular theory of disease is the common medical theory: namely, that every disease had its microbe duly created in the garden of Eden, and has been steadily propagating itself and producing widening circles of malignant disease ever since. It was plain from the first that if this had been even approximately true, the whole human race would have been wiped out by the plague long ago, and that every epidemic, instead of fading out as mysteriously as it rushed in, would spread over the whole world. It was also evident that the characteristic microbe of a disease might be a symptom instead of a cause.

Shaw, *Doctor's Dilemma,* Pref.

62 Use your health, even to the point of wearing it out. That is what it is for. Spend all you have before you die; and do not outlive yourself.

Shaw, *Doctor's Dilemma,* Pref.

63 A strong egoism is a protection against disease, but, in the last resort, we must begin to love in order that we may not fall ill, and must fall ill if, in consequence of frustration, we cannot love.

Freud, *On Narcissism,* II

64 Do not be astonished to hear . . . that the physician himself occasionally takes sides with the illness which he is attacking. It is not for him to confine himself in all situations in life to the part of fanatic about health; he os that there is *other* misery in the world besides neurotic misery—real unavoidable suffering—that necessity may even demand of a man that he sacrifice his health to it, and he learns that such suffering in one individual may often avert incalculable hardship for many others. Therefore, although it may be said of every neurotic that he has taken *flight into illness,* it must be admitted that in many cases this flight is fully justified, and the physician who has perceived this state of things will silently and considerately retire.

Freud, *General Introduction to Psycho-Analysis,* XXIV

Chapter 19

NATURE
and the COSMOS

Chapter 19 is divided into eight sections: 19.1 NATURE AND THE NATURAL, 19.2 THE NATURE OF LIFE, 19.3 CAUSE, 19.4 CHANCE, 19.5 MOTION AND CHANGE, 19.6 SPACE, 19.7 TIME, and 19.8 THE UNIVERSE OR COSMOS.

The subjects indicated by the section titles have occupied the forefront of speculation throughout the whole tradition of Western thought. They represent basic ideas or are involved in basic questions treated by the philosophers; the consideration of such subjects defines the task of the metaphysician or cosmologist. Most of them also are of interest to natural scientists; such terms as cause, motion, space, and time represent basic scientific concepts. A few of them, especially nature, life, and time, evoke the fancy of the poets and receive imaginative treatment at their hands.

The opening and the closing sections of the chapter are the most comprehensive, dealing with the whole of what there is. The second section concentrates on that part of nature which is the domain of living organisms. The remaining sections treat the operation of causality and of chance in the universe as a whole and in the order of nature, the movement and rest that are characteristic of all physical things, and the dimensions of space and time that constitute the all-embracing framework of the physical world.

For passages that relate to the same subjects treated in other contexts, the reader is referred to Chapter 17 on PHILOSOPHY, SCIENCE, AND MATHEMATICS; to Section 15.3 of Chapter 15 on HISTORY; and to Section 16.1 of Chapter 16 on ART AND AESTHETICS.

19.1 | *Nature and the Natural*

Of all the terms in the vocabulary of speculative thought, the words "nature" and "natural" have, perhaps, the greatest ambiguity. The passages collected here reflect the range and variety of the meanings that have been attached to them.

Nature is sometimes identified with the cosmos itself and, as so regarded, it embraces everything, even being identified with God in the view of pantheists who think of God as immanent in nature, not as transcending it. But it is also conceived as quite distinct from God—as the creation of God, who, as uncreated, is therefore referred to as supernatural. In other contexts, a basic distinction is drawn between nature and art—the natural and the artificial, that which is independent of man and that which is in some way dependent on man's efforts or intervention. But nature is also conceived by certain writers as being an artist or as being the product of the divine art. In still other contexts, nature is personified as if it were a brooding omnipresence, the embodiment of an indwelling reason, purposeful and even benevolent; and against such views, the reader will find the opinion expressed that nature represents blind necessity or chance, indifferent to human well-being and human aspirations.

The quotations included in this section set forth most of the maxims that have been formulated concerning nature's operations, usually expressed in personified form: that nature does nothing in vain; that nature abhors a vacuum; that nature can make no mistakes; that nature knows best; that nature does nothing by jumps; that nature is frugal or economical, employing the fewest means to achieve its ends and wasting nothing; that nature manifests the wisdom of God; and so on. Most of these sayings have been challenged or contradicted.

When nature is regarded as the standard of what is right or reasonable, to say that something is unnatural or contrary to nature condemns it morally; but it has also been maintained that there is nothing unnatural or contrary to nature, though it may violate custom or received opinion.

The poets celebrate the beauties of nature as well as its awesome powers. Together with the philosophers and others, they speak of the things that men can learn from nature, and the benefits to be derived from intimacy with it.

---

1 *Achilleus.* The enormous strength of Ocean with his deep-running waters,
   Ocean, from whom all rivers are and the entire sea
   and all springs and all deep wells have their waters of him, yet
   even Ocean is afraid of the lightning of great Zeus
   and the dangerous thunderbolt when it breaks from the sky crashing.

   Homer, *Iliad,* XXI, 195

2 *Eleatic Stranger.* Looking, now, at the world and all the animals and plants, at things which grow upon the earth from seeds and roots, as well as at inanimate substances which are formed within the earth, fusile or non-fusile, shall we say that they come into existence—not having existed previously—by the creation of God, or shall we agree with vulgar opinion about them?

   Theaetetus. What is it?

   Str. The opinion that nature brings them into being from some spontaneous and unintelligent cause. Or shall we say that they are created by a divine reason and a knowledge which comes from God?

   Theaet. I dare say that, owing to my youth, I may often waver in my view, but now when I look

1170

at you and see that you incline to refer them to God, I defer to your authority.

Str. Nobly said, Theaetetus, and if I thought that you were one of those who would hereafter change your mind, I would have gently argued with you, and forced you to assent; but as I perceive that you will come of yourself and without any argument of mind, to that belief which, as you say, attracts you, I will not forestall the work of time. Let me suppose, then, that things which are said to be made by nature are the work of divine art, and that things which are made by man out of these are work of human art. And so there are two kinds of making and production, the one human and the other divine.

Plato, *Sophist,* 265A

3 *Athenian Stranger.* I am afraid that we have unconsciously lighted on a strange doctrine.

Cleinias. What doctrine do you mean?

Ath. The wisest of all doctrines, in the opinion of many.

Cle. I wish that you would speak plainer.

Ath. The doctrine that all things do become, have become, and will become, some by nature, some by art, and some by chance.

Cle. Is not that true?

Ath. Well, philosophers are probably right; at any rate we may as well follow in their track, and examine what is the meaning of them and their disciples.

Cle. By all means.

Ath. They say that the greatest and fairest things are the work of nature and of chance, the lesser of art, which, receiving from nature the greater and primeval creations, moulds and fashions all those lesser works which are generally termed artificial.

Cle. How is that?

Ath. I will explain my meaning still more clearly. They say that fire and water, and earth and air, all exist by nature and chance, and none of them by art, and that as to the bodies which come next in order—earth, and sun, and moon, and stars—they have been created by means of these absolutely inanimate existences. The elements are severally moved by chance and some inherent force according to certain affinities among them—of hot with cold, or of dry with moist, or of soft with hard, and according to all the other accidental admixtures of opposites which have been formed by necessity. After this fashion and in this manner the whole heaven has been created, and all that is in the heaven, as well as animals and all plants, and all the seasons come from these elements, not by the action of mind, as they say, or of any God, or from art, but as I was saying, by nature and chance only. Art sprang up afterwards and out of these, mortal and of mortal birth, and produced in play certain images and very partial imitations of the truth, having an affinity to one

another, such as music and painting create and their companion arts. And there are other arts which have a serious purpose, and these co-operate with nature, such, for example, as medicine, and husbandry, and gymnastic. And they say that politics cooperate with nature, but in a less degree, and have more of art; also that legislation is entirely a work of art, and is based on assumptions which are not true.

Plato, *Laws,* X, 888B

4 Of things that exist, some exist by nature, some from other causes.

'By nature' the animals and their parts exist, and the plants and the simple bodies (earth, fire, air, water)—for we say that these and the like exist 'by nature'.

All the things mentioned present a feature in which they differ from things which are *not* constituted by nature. Each of them has *within itself* a principle of motion and of stationariness (in respect of place, or of growth and decrease, or by way of alteration). On the other hand, a bed and a coat and anything else of that sort, *qua* receiving these designations—i.e. insofar as they are products of art—have no innate impulse to change. But insofar as they happen to be composed of stone or of earth or of a mixture of the two, they *do* have such an impulse, and just to that extent— which seems to indicate that *nature is a source or cause of being moved and of being at rest in that to which it belongs primarily,* in virtue of itself and not in virtue of a concomitant attribute.

Aristotle, *Physics,* 192ᵇ9

5 Of things constituted by nature some are ungenerated, imperishable, and eternal, while others are subject to generation and decay. The former are excellent beyond compare and divine, but less accessible to knowledge. The evidence that might throw light on them, and on the problems which we long to solve respecting them, is furnished but scantily by sensation; whereas respecting perishable plants and animals we have abundant information, living as we do in their midst, and ample data may be collected concerning all their various kinds, if only we are willing to take sufficient pains. Both departments, however, have their special charm. The scanty conceptions to which we can attain of celestial things give us, from their excellence, more pleasure than all our knowledge of the world in which we live; just as a half glimpse of persons that we love is more delightful than a leisurely view of other things, whatever their number and dimensions. On the other hand, in certitude and in completeness our knowledge of terrestrial things has the advantage. Moreover, their greater nearness and affinity to us balances somewhat the loftier interest of the heavenly things that are the objects of the higher philosophy. Having already treated of the celestial world, as far as our conjectures could reach, we proceed

to treat of animals, without omitting, to the best of our ability, any member of the kingdom, however ignoble. For if some have no graces to charm the sense, yet even these, by disclosing to intellectual perception the artistic spirit that designed them, give immense pleasure to all who can trace links of causation, and are inclined to philosophy. Indeed, it would be strange if mimic representations of them were attractive, because they disclose the mimetic skill of the painter or sculptor, and the original realities themselves were not more interesting, to all at any rate who have eyes to discern the reasons that determined their formation. We therefore must not recoil with childish aversion from the examination of the humbler animals. Every realm of nature is marvellous: and as Heraclitus, when the strangers who came to visit him found him warming himself at the furnace in the kitchen and hesitated to go in, is reported to have bidden them not to be afraid to enter, as even in that kitchen divinities were present, so we should venture on the study of every kind of animal without distaste; for each and all will reveal to us something natural and something beautiful. Absence of haphazard and conduciveness of everything to an end are to be found in Nature's works in the highest degree, and the resultant end of her generations and combinations is a form of the beautiful.

If any person thinks the examination of the rest of the animal kingdom an unworthy task, he must hold in like disesteem the study of man. For no one can look at the primordia of the human frame—blood, flesh, bones, vessels, and the like—without much repugnance. Moreover, when any one of the parts or structures, be it which it may, is under discussion, it must not be supposed that it is its material composition to which attention is being directed or which is the object of the discussion, but the relation of such part to the total form. Similarly, the true object of architecture is not bricks, mortar, or timber, but the house; and so the principal object of natural philosophy is not the material elements, but their composition, and the totality of the form, independently of which they have no existence.

Aristotle, *Parts of Animals*, 644ᵇ21

6 A general principle must here be noted, which will be found applicable not only in this instance but in many others that will occur later on. Nature allots each weapon, offensive and defensive alike, to those animals alone that can use it; or, if not to them alone, to them in a more marked degree; and she allots it in its most perfect state to those that can use it best; and this whether it be a sting, or a spur, or horns, or tusks, or what it may of a like kind.

Aristotle, *Parts of Animals*, 661ᵇ28

7 Nature creates nothing without a purpose, but al-

ways the best possible in each kind of living creature by reference to its essential constitution. Accordingly if one way is better than another that is the way of Nature.

Aristotle, *On the Gait of Animals*, 704ᵇ16

8 Nature flies from the infinite, for the infinite is unending or imperfect, and Nature ever seeks an end.

Aristotle, *Generation of Animals*, 715ᵇ15

9 The monstrosity belongs to the class of things contrary to Nature, not any and every kind of Nature, but Nature in her usual operations; nothing can happen contrary to Nature considered as eternal and necessary, but we speak of things being contrary to her in those cases where things generally happen in a certain way but may also happen in another way. In fact, even in the case of monstrosities, whenever things occur contrary indeed to the established order but still always in a certain way and not at random, the result seems to be less of a monstrosity because even that which is contrary to Nature is in a certain sense according to Nature, whenever, that is, the formal nature has not mastered the material nature.

Aristotle, *Generation of Animals*, 770ᵇ10

10 The observed facts show that nature is not a series of episodes, like a bad tragedy.

Aristotle, *Metaphysics*, 1090ᵇ19

11 Darkness of mind must be dispelled not by the rays of the sun and glittering shafts of day, but by the aspect and the law of nature; the warp of whose design we shall begin with this first principle, nothing is ever gotten out of nothing by divine power. Fear in sooth holds so in check all mortals, because they see many operations go on in earth and heaven, the causes of which they can in no way understand, believing them therefore to be done by power divine. For these reasons when we shall have seen that nothing can be produced from nothing, we shall then more correctly ascertain that which we are seeking, both the elements out of which every thing can be produced and the manner in which all things are done without the hand of the gods.

Lucretius, *Nature of Things*, I

12 All nature . . . as it exists by itself, is founded on two things: there are bodies and there is void in which these bodies are placed and through which they move about.

Lucretius, *Nature of Things*, I

13 You should desire with all your might to shun the weakness, with a lively apprehension to avoid the mistake of supposing that the bright lights of the eyes were made in order that we might see; and that the tapering ends of the shanks and hams are

attached to the feet as a base in order to enable us to step out with long strides; or again that the forearms were slung to the stout upper arms and ministering hands given us on each side, that we might be able to discharge the needful duties of life. Other explanations of like sort which men give, one and all put effect for cause through wrongheaded reasoning; since nothing was born in the body that we might use it, but that which is born begets for itself a use: thus seeing did not exist before the eyes were born, nor the employment of speech ere the tongue was made; but rather the birth of the tongue was long anterior to language and the ears were made long before sound was heard, and all the limbs, I trow, existed before there was any employment for them: they could not therefore have grown for the purpose of being used. But on the other hand engaging in the strife of battle and mangling the body and staining the limbs with gore were in vogue long before glittering darts ever flew; and nature prompted to shun a wound or ever the left arm by the help of art held up before the person the defence of a shield. Yes and consigning the tired body to rest is much older than a soft-cushioned bed, and the slaking of thirst had birth before cups. These things therefore which have been invented in accordance with the uses and wants of life, may well be believed to have been discovered for the purpose of being used. Far otherwise is it with all those things which first were born, then afterwards made known the purposes to which they might be put; at the head of which class we see the senses and the limbs. Wherefore again and again I repeat, it is quite impossible to believe that they could have been made for the duties which they discharge.

Lucretius, Nature of Things, IV

14 But, ere we stir the yet unbroken ground,
The various course of seasons must be found;
The weather, and the setting of the winds,
The culture suiting to the several kinds
Of seeds and plants, and what will thrive and rise,
And what the genius of the soil denies.
This ground with Bacchus, that with Ceres, suits:
That other loads the trees with happy fruits:
A fourth, with grass unbidden, decks the ground.
Thus Tmolus is with yellow saffron crowned:
India black ebon and white ivory bears;
And soft Idumè weeps her od'rous tears.
Thus Pontus sends her beaver-stones from far;
And naked Spaniards temper steel for war:
Epirus, for the Elean chariot, breeds
(In hopes of palms) a race of running steeds.
   This is the original contract; these the laws
Imposed by Nature, and by Nature's cause,
On sundry places, when Deucalion hurled
His mother's entrails on the desert world;
Whence men, a hard laborious kind, were born.

Virgil, Georgics, I

15 Some steep their seed, and some in cauldrons boil,
With vigorous nitre and with lees of oil,
O'er gentle fires, the exuberant juice to drain,
And swell the flattering husks with fruitful grain.
Yet is not the success for years assured,
Though chosen is the seed, and fully cured,
Unless the peasant, with his annual pain,
Renews his choice, and culls the largest grain.
Thus all below, whether by Nature's curse,
Or Fate's decree, degenerate still to worse.
So the boat's brawny crew the current stem,
And, slow advancing, struggle with the stream:
But if they slack their hands, or cease to strive,
Then down the flood with headlong haste they
   drive.

Virgil, Georgics, I

16 You may drive out nature with a fork, yet still she
will return.

Horace, Epistles, I, 10

17 Nature which governs the whole will soon change all things which thou seest, and out of their substance will make other things, and again other things from the substance of them, in order that the world may be ever new.

Marcus Aurelius, Meditations, VII, 25

18 Nature alone has the power to expand a body in all directions so that it remains unruptured and preserves completely its previous form. Such then is growth, and it cannot occur without the nutriment which flows to the part and is worked up into it.

Galen, Natural Faculties, I, 7

19 It has been made clear in the preceding discussion that nutrition occurs by an alteration or assimilation of that which nourishes to that which receives nourishment, and that there exists in every part of the animal a faculty which in view of its activity we call, in general terms, alterative, or, more specifically, assimilative and nutritive. . . .
   Our argument has clearly shown the necessity for the genesis of such a faculty, and whoever has an appreciation of logical sequence must be firmly persuaded from what we have said that, if it be laid down and proved by previous demonstration that Nature is artistic and solicitous for the animal's welfare, it necessarily follows that she must also possess a faculty of this kind.

Galen, Natural Faculties, III, 1

20 To You, then, evil utterly is not—and not only to You, but to Your whole creation likewise, evil is not: because there is nothing over and above Your creation that could break in or derange the order that You imposed upon it. But in certain of its parts there are some things which we call evil because they do not harmonize with other things; yet these same things do harmonize with still

others and thus are good; and in themselves they are good. All these things which do not harmonize with one another, do suit well with that lower part of creation which we call the earth, which has its cloudy and windy sky in some way apt to it. God forbid that I should say: "I wish that these things were not"; because even if I saw only them, though I should want better things, yet even for them alone I should praise You: for that You are to be praised, things of earth show—*dragons, and all deeps, fire, hail, snow, ice, and stormy winds, which fulfill Thy word; mountains and all hills, fruitful trees and all cedars; beasts and all cattle, serpents and feathered fowl; kings of the earth and all people, princes and all judges of the earth; young men and maidens, old men and young, praise Thy name.* And since from the heavens, O our God, *all Thy angels praise Thee in the high places, and all Thy hosts, sun and moon, all the stars and lights, the heavens of heavens, and the waters that are above the heavens, praise Thy name*—I no longer desired better, because I had thought upon them all and with clearer judgement I realized that while certain higher things are better than lower things, yet all things together are better than the higher alone.

Augustine, *Confessions*, VII, 13

21 This cause . . . of a good creation, namely, the goodness of God—this cause, I say, so just and fit, which, when piously and carefully weighed, terminates all the controversies of those who inquire into the origin of the world, has not been recognized by some heretics, because there are, forsooth, many things, such as fire, frost, wild beasts, and so forth, which do not suit but injure this thin-blooded and frail mortality of our flesh, which is at present under just punishment. They do not consider how admirable these things are in their own places, how excellent in their own natures, how beautifully adjusted to the rest of creation, and how much grace they contribute to the universe by their own contributions as to a commonwealth; and how serviceable they are even to ourselves, if we use them with a knowledge of their fit adaptations—so that even poisons, which are destructive when used injudiciously, become wholesome and medicinal when used in conformity with their qualities and design; just as, on the other hand, those things which give us pleasure, such as food, drink, and the light of the sun, are found to be hurtful when immoderately or unseasonably used. And thus divine providence admonishes us not foolishly to vituperate things, but to investigate their utility with care; and, where our mental capacity or infirmity is at fault, to believe that there is a utility, though hidden, as we have experienced that there were other things which we all but failed to discover.

Augustine, *City of God*, XI, 22

22 In natural things species seem to be arranged in degrees; as the mixed things are more perfect than the elements, and plants than minerals, and animals than plants, and men than other animals; and in each of these one species is more perfect than others. Therefore, as the divine wisdom is the cause of the distinction of things for the sake of the perfection of the universe, so is it the cause of inequality. For the universe would not be perfect if only one grade of goodness were found in things.

Aquinas, *Summa Theologica*, I, 47, 2

23 God and nature and any other agent make what is best in the whole, but not what is best in every single part, except in order to the whole. . . . And the whole itself, which is the universe of creatures, is better and more perfect if some things in it can fail in goodness, and do sometimes fail, God not preventing this.

Aquinas, *Summa Theologica*, I, 48, 2

24 But God knows well that nothing man may do
Will ever keep restrained a thing that nature
Has made innate in any human creature.
 Take any bird and put it in a cage
And do your best affection to engage
And rear it tenderly with meat and drink
Of all the dainties that you can bethink,
And always keep it cleanly as you may;
Although its cage of gold be never so gay,
Yet would this bird, by twenty thousand-fold,
Rather, within a forest dark and cold,
Go to eat worms and all such wretchedness.
For ever this bird will do his business
To find some way to get outside the wires.
Above all things his freedom he desires.
 Or take a cat, and feed him well with milk
And tender flesh, and make his bed of silk,
And let him see a mouse go by the wall;
Anon he leaves the milk and flesh and all
And every dainty that is in that house,
Such appetite has he to eat a mouse.
Desire has here its mighty power shown
And inborn appetite reclaims its own.
 A she-wolf also has a vulgar mind;
The wretchedest he-wolf that she may find,
Or least of reputation, she'll not hate
Whenever she's desirous of a mate.
 All these examples speak I of these men
Who are untrue, and not of sweet women.
For men have aye a lickerish appetite
On lower things to do their base delight
Than on their wives, though they be ne'er so fair
And ne'er so true and ne'er so debonair.
Flesh is so fickle, lusting beyond measure,
That we in no one thing can long have pleasure
Or virtuous keep more than a little while.

Chaucer, *Canterbury Tales:*
Manciple's Tale

25 We should . . . follow the wisdom of nature, which, as it takes very great care not to have produced anything superfluous or useless, often pre-

fers to endow one thing with many effects.

Copernicus, *De Revolutionibus*, I, 10

26 *Pantagruel.* The writings of abstinent, abstemious, and long-fasting hermits were every whit as saltless, dry, jejune, and insipid, as were their bodies when they did compose them. It is a most difficult thing for the spirits to be in a good plight, serene and lively, when there is nothing in the body but a kind of voidness and inanity; seeing the philosophers with the physicians jointly affirm, that the spirits, which are styled animal, spring from, and have their constant practice in and through the arterial blood, refined, and purified to the life within the admirable net, which, wonderfully framed, lieth under the ventricles and tunnels of the brain. He gave us also the example of the philosopher, who, when he thought most seriously to have withdrawn himself unto a solitary privacy, far from the rustling clutterments of the tumultuous and confused world, the better to improve his theory, to contrive, comment and ratiocinate, was, notwithstanding his uttermost endeavours to free himself from all untoward noises, surrounded and environed about so with the barking of curs, bawling of mastiffs, bleating of sheep, prating of parrots, tattling of jack-daws, grunting of swine, girning of boars, yelping of foxes, mewing of cats, cheeping of mice, squeaking of weasels, croaking of frogs, crowing of cocks, cackling of hens, calling of partridges, chanting of swans, chattering of jays, peeping of chickens, singing of larks, creaking of geese, chirping of swallows, clucking of moor-fowls, cucking of cuckoos, bumbling of bees, rammage of hawks, chirming of linnets, croaking of ravens, screeching of owls, whicking of pigs, gushing of hogs, curring of pigeons, grumbling of cushet-doves, howling of panthers, curkling of quails, chirping of sparrows, crackling of crows, nuzzing of camels, whining of whelps, buzzing of dromedaries, mumbling of rabbits, cricking of ferrets, humming of wasps, mioling of tigers, bruzzing of bears, sussing of kitlings, clamoring of scarfes, whimpering of fulmarts, booing of buffalos, warbling of nightingales, quavering of meavises, drintling of turkies, coniating of storks, trantling of peacocks, clattering of magpies, murmuring of stock-doves, crouting of cormorants, cigling of locusts, charming of beagles, guarring of puppies, snarling of messens, rantling of rats, guerieting of apes, snuttering of monkies, pioling of pelicans, quacking of ducks, yelling of wolves, roaring of lions, neighing of horses, barring of elephants, hissing of serpents, and wailing of turtles, that he was much more troubled, than if he had been in the middle of the crowd at the fair of Fontenay or Niort. Just so is it with those who are tormented with the grievous pangs of hunger. The stomach begins to gnaw, and bark as it were, the eyes to look dim, and the veins, by greedily sucking some refection to themselves from the proper substance of all the members of a fleshy consistence, violently pull down and draw back that vagrant, roaming spirit, careless and neglecting of his nurse and natural host, which is the body; as when a hawk upon the fist, willing to take her flight by a soaring aloft in the open spacious air, is on a sudden drawn back by a leash tied to her feet.

Rabelais, *Gargantua and Pantagruel*, III, 13

27 When I play with my cat, who knows if I am not a pastime to her more than she is to me? Plato, in his picture of the golden age under Saturn, counts among the principal advantages of the man of that time the communication he had with the beasts; inquiring of them and learning from them, he knew the true qualities and differences of each one of them; whereby he acquired a very perfect intelligence and prudence, and conducted his life far more happily than we could possibly do. Do we need a better proof to judge man's impudence with regard to the beasts? . . .

This defect that hinders communication between them and us, why is it not just as much ours as theirs? It is a matter of guesswork whose fault it is that we do not understand one another; for we do not understand them any more than they do us. By this same reasoning they may consider us beasts, as we consider them.

Montaigne, *Essays*, II, 12, Apology for Raymond Sebond

28 There is no apparent reason to judge that the beasts do by natural and obligatory instinct the same things that we do by our choice and cleverness. We must infer from like results like faculties, and consequently confess that this same reason, this same method that we have for working, is also that of the animals. Why do we imagine in them this compulsion of nature, we who feel no similar effect? Besides, it is more honorable, and closer to divinity, to be guided and obliged to act lawfully by a natural and inevitable condition, than to act lawfully by accidental and fortuitous liberty; and safer to leave the reins of our conduct to nature than to ourselves. The vanity of our presumption makes us prefer to owe our ability to our powers than to nature's liberality; and we enrich the other animals with natural goods and renounce them in their favor, in order to honor and ennoble ourselves with goods acquired: a very simple notion, it seems to me, for I should prize just as highly graces that were all mine and inborn as those I had gone begging and seeking from education. It is not in our power to acquire a fairer recommendation than to be favored by God and nature.

Montaigne, *Essays*, II, 12, Apology for Raymond Sebond

29 It is one and the same nature that rolls its course. Anyone who had formed a competent judgment of its present state could infer from this with cer-

tainty both all the future and all the past.

Montaigne, *Essays*, II, 12, Apology
for Raymond Sebond

30 We call contrary to nature what happens contrary to custom; nothing is anything but according to nature, whatever it may be. Let this universal and natural reason drive out of us the error and astonishment that novelty brings us.

Montaigne, *Essays*, II, 30,
Of a Monstrous Child

31 We have abandoned Nature and we want to teach her her lesson, she who used to guide us so happily and so surely. And yet the traces of her teaching and the little that remains of her image—imprinted, by the benefit of ignorance, on the life of that rustic, unpolished mob—learning is constrained every day to go and borrow, to give its disciples models of constancy, innocence, and tranquillity. It is fine to see these disciples, full of so much beautiful knowledge, obliged to imitate that stupid simplicity, and imitate it in the primary actions of virtue; and a fine thing that our sapience learns from the very animals the most useful teachings for the greatest and most necessary parts of our life: how we should live and die, husband our possessions, love and bring up our children, maintain justice—a singular testimony of human infirmity; and that this reason of ours that we handle as we will, always finding some diversity and novelty, leaves in us no apparent trace of Nature. And men have done with Nature as perfumers do with oil: they have sophisticated her with so many arguments and farfetched reasonings that she has become variable and particular for each man, and has lost her own constant and universal countenance; and we must seek in the animals evidence of her that is not subject to favor, corruption, or diversity of opinion.

Montaigne, *Essays*, III, 12, Of Physiognomy

32 Let us give Nature a chance; she knows her business better than we do.

Montaigne, *Essays*, III, 13, Of Experience

33 When I dance, I dance; when I sleep, I sleep; yes, and when I walk alone in a beautiful orchard, if my thoughts have been dwelling on extraneous incidents for some part of the time, for some other part I bring them back to the walk, to the orchard, to the sweetness of this solitude, and to me. Nature has observed this principle like a mother, that the actions she has enjoined on us for our need should also give us pleasure; and she invites us to them not only through reason, but also through appetite. It is unjust to infringe her laws.

Montaigne, *Essays*, III, 13, Of Experience

34 *Duke Senior.* Hath not old custom made this life more sweet

Than that of painted pomp? Are not these woods
More free from peril than the envious court?
Here feel we but the penalty of Adam,
The seasons' difference, as the icy fang
And churlish chiding of the winter's wind,
Which, when it bites and blows upon my body
Even till I shrink with cold, I smile and say
"This is no flattery: these are counsellors
That feelingly persuade me what I am."
Sweet are the uses of adversity,
Which, like the toad, ugly and venomous,
Wears yet a precious jewel in his head;
And this our life exempt from public haunt
Finds tongues in trees, books in the running
    brooks,
Sermons in stones, and good in everything.

Shakespeare, *As You Like It*, II, i, 2

35 *Amiens.* [sings] Under the greenwood tree
    Who loves to lie with me,
    And turn his merry note
    Unto the sweet bird's throat,
Come hither, come hither, come hither:
    Here shall he see
    No enemy
But winter and rough weather.

Shakespeare, *As You Like It*, II, v, 1

36 *Corin.* And how like you this shepherd's life, Master Touchstone?

Touchstone. Truly, shepherd, in respect of itself, it is a good life; but in respect that it is a shepherd's life, it is naught. In respect that it is solitary, I like it very well; but in respect that it is private, it is a very vile life. Now, in respect it is in the fields, it pleaseth me well; but in respect it is not in the court, it is tedious. As it is a spare life, look you, it fits my humour well; but as there is no more plenty in it, it goes much against my stomach.

Shakespeare, *As You Like It*, III, ii, 11

37 *Edmund.* Thou, nature, art my goddess; to thy law
My services are bound. Wherefore should I
Stand in the plague of custom, and permit
The curiosity of nations to deprive me,
For that I am some twelve or fourteen moonshines
Lag of a brother? Why bastard? wherefore base?
When my dimensions are as well compact,
My mind as generous, and my shape as true,
As honest madam's issue? Why brand they us
With base? with baseness? bastardy? base, base?
Who, in the lusty stealth of nature, take
More composition and fierce quality
Than doth, within a dull, stale, tired bed,
Go to the creating a whole tribe of fops,
Got 'tween asleep and wake?

Shakespeare, *Lear*, I, ii, 1

38 *Kent.*   Where's the King?
    Gentleman. Contending with the fretful element;

Bids the wind blow the earth into the sea,
Or swell the curled waters 'bove the main,
That things might change or cease; tears his white
hair,
Which the impetuous blasts, with eyeless rage,
Catch in their fury, and make nothing of;
Strives in his little world of man to out-scorn
The to-and-fro-conflicting wind and rain.
This night, wherein the cub-drawn bear would
couch,
The lion and the belly-pinched wolf
Keep their fur dry, unbonneted he runs,
And bids what will take all.

Shakespeare, Lear, III, i, 3

39 *Lear.* Blow, winds, and crack your cheeks! rage!
blow!
You cataracts and hurricanes, spout
Till you have drench'd our steeples, drown'd the
cocks!
You sulphurous and thought-executing fires,
Vaunt-couriers to oak-cleaving thunderbolts,
Singe my white head! And thou, all-shaking
thunder,
Smite flat the thick rotundity o' the world!
Crack nature's moulds, all germens spill at once,
That make ingrateful man!
   Fool. O nuncle, court holy-water in a dry house
is better than this rain-water out o' door. Good
nuncle, in, and ask thy daughters' blessing. Here's
a night pities neither wise man nor fool.
   Lear. Rumble thy bellyful! Spit, fire! spout,
rain!
Nor rain, wind, thunder, fire, are my daughters.
I tax not you, you elements, with unkindness;
I never gave you kingdom, call'd you children,
You owe me no subscription. Then let fall
Your horrible pleasure; here I stand, your slave,
A poor, infirm, weak, and despised old man:
But yet I call you servile ministers,
That have with two pernicious daughters join'd
Your high engender'd battles 'gainst a head
So old and white as this. O! O! 'tis foul!

Shakespeare, Lear, III, ii, 1

40 *Perdita.*   Sir, the year growing ancient,
Not yet on summer's death, nor on the birth
Of trembling winter, the fairest flowers o' the sea-
son
Are our carnations and streak'd gillyvors,
Which some call Nature's bastards. Of that kind
Our rustic garden's barren; and I care not
To get slips of them.
   Polixenes.   Wherefore, gentle maiden,
Do you neglect them?
   Per.   For I have heard it said
There is an art which in their piedness shares
With great creating Nature.
   Pol.   Say there be;
Yet Nature is made better by no mean
But Nature makes that mean; so, over that art

Which you say adds to Nature, is an art
That Nature makes. You see, sweet maid, we
marry
A gentler scion to the wildest stock,
And make conceive a bark of baser kind
By bud of nobler race. This is an art
Which does mend Nature, change it rather, but
The art itself is Nature.
   Per.   So it is.
   Pol. Then make your garden rich in gillyvors,
And do not call them bastards.

Shakespeare, Winter's Tale, IV, iv, 80

41 *Clerimont.* [sings] Still to be neat, still to be dressed
As you were going to a feast,
Still to be powdered, still perfumed;
Lady, is it to be presumed,
Though art's hid causes are not found,
All is not sweet, all is not sound.

Give me a look, give me a face,
That makes simplicity a grace;
Robes loosely flowing, hair as free—
Such sweet neglect more taketh me,
Than all th' adulteries of art.
They strike mine eyes, but not my heart.

Jonson, Epicene, II, i

42 The subtilty of nature is far beyond that of sense
or of the understanding; so that the specious meditations, speculations, and theories of mankind are
but a kind of insanity, only there is no one to
stand by and observe it.

Bacon, Novum Organum, I, 10

43 As in ordinary life every person's disposition, and
the concealed feelings of the mind and passions
are most drawn out when they are disturbed—so
the secrets of nature betray themselves more readily when tormented by art than when left to their
own course.

Bacon, Novum Organum, I, 98

44 The empire of man over things is founded on the
arts and sciences alone, for nature is only to be
commanded by obeying her.

Bacon, Novum Organum, I, 129

45 Easy is everything to nature's majesty, who uses
her strength sparingly, and dispenses it with caution and foresight for the commencement of her
works by imperceptible additions, but hastens to
decay with suddenness and in full career. In the
generation of things is seen the most excellent, the
eternal and almighty God, the divinity of nature,
worthy to be looked up to with reverence; but all
mortal things run to destruction of their own accord in a thousand ways.

William Harvey, Animal Generation, 41

46 If in the domain and rule of nature . . . many

excellent operations are daily effected surpassing the powers of the things themselves, what shall we not think possible within the pale and regimen of nature, of which all art is but imitation? And if, as ministers of man, they effect such admirable ends, what, I ask, may we not expect of them, when they are instruments in the hand of God?

William Harvey, *Animal Generation,* 71

47 There is no doubt that in all things which nature teaches me there is some truth contained; for by nature, considered in general, I now understand no other thing than either God Himself or else the order and disposition which God has established in created things; and by my nature in particular I understand no other thing than the complexus of all the things which God has given me.

Descartes, *Meditations on First Philosophy,* VI

48 Nature itself cannot err.

Hobbes, *Leviathan,* I, 4

49 What reason may not go to School to the wisdom of Bees, Ants, and Spiders? what wise hand teacheth them to do what reason cannot teach us? ruder heads stand amazed at those prodigious pieces of Nature, Whales, Elephants, Dromidaries and Camels; these, I confess, are the Colossus and Majestick pieces of her hand: but in these narrow Engines there is more curious Mathematicks; and the civility of these Little Citizens, more neatly sets forth the Wisdom of their Maker. Who admires not *Regio-Montanus* his Fly beyond his Eagle, or wonders not more at the operation of two Souls in those little Bodies, than but one in the Trunk of a Cedar?

Sir Thomas Browne, *Religio Medici,* I, 15

50 I hold there is a general beauty in the works of God, and therefore no deformity in any kind or species of creature whatsoever: I cannot tell by what Logick we call a *Toad,* a *Bear,* or an *Elephant* ugly, they being created in those outward shapes and figures which best express the actions of their inward forms. And having past that general Visitation of God, who saw that all that he had made was good, that is, conformable to his Will, which abhors deformity, that is the rule of order and beauty; there is no deformity but in Monstrosity; wherein, notwithstanding, there is a kind of Beauty. Nature so ingeniously contriving the irregular parts, as they become sometimes more remarkable than the principal Fabrick. To speak yet more narrowly, there was never any thing ugly or misshapen, but the Chaos; wherein, notwithstanding, to speak strictly, there was no deformity, because no form; nor was it yet impregnant by the voice of God; now Nature was not at variance with Art, nor Art with Nature, they being both servants of his providence: Art is the perfection of Nature: were the World now as it was the sixth day, there

were yet a Chaos: Nature hath made one World, and Art another. In brief, all things are artificial; for Nature is the Art of God.

Sir Thomas Browne, *Religio Medici,* I, 16

51 Nature has some perfections to show that she is the image of God, and some defects to show that she is only His image.

Pascal, *Pensées,* VIII, 580

52 *Lawrence* of vertuous Father vertuous Son,
　Now that the Fields are dank, and ways are mire,
　Where shall we sometimes meet, and by the fire
　Help wast a sullen day; what may be won
From the hard Season gaining: time will run
　On smoother, till *Favonius* re-inspire
　The frozen earth; and cloth in fresh attire
　The Lillie and Rose, that neither sow'd nor spun.
What neat repast shall feast us, light and choice,
　Of Attick tast, with Wine, whence we may rise
To hear the Lute well toucht, or artfull voice
Warble immortal Notes and *Tuskan* Ayre?
　He who of those delights can judge, and spare
To interpose them oft, is not unwise.

Milton, *Lawrence of vertuous Father vertuous Son*

53 *Raphael.* Accuse not Nature, she hath don her part;
Do thou but thine.

Milton, *Paradise Lost,* VIII, 561

54 The attempt . . . to show that nature does nothing in vain (that is to say, nothing which is not profitable to man), seems to end in showing that nature, the gods, and man are alike mad.

Spinoza, *Ethics,* I, Appendix

55 It will doubtless seem a marvellous thing for me to endeavour to treat by a geometrical method the vices and follies of men, and to desire by a sure method to demonstrate those things which these people cry out against as being opposed to reason, or as being vanities, absurdities, and monstrosities. The following is my reason for so doing. Nothing happens in nature which can be attributed to any vice of nature, for she is always the same and everywhere one. Her virtue is the same, and her power of acting; that is to say, her laws and rules, according to which all things are and are changed from form to form, are everywhere and always the same; so that there must also be one and the same method of understanding the nature of all things whatsoever, that is to say, by the universal laws and rules of nature.

Spinoza, *Ethics,* III, Introduction

56 The custom of applying the words *perfect* and *imperfect* to natural objects has arisen rather from

prejudice than from true knowledge of them. For . . . nature does nothing for the sake of an end, for that eternal and infinite Being whom we call God or Nature acts by the same necessity by which He exists; for . . . He acts by the same necessity of nature as that by which He exists. The reason or cause, therefore, why God or nature acts and the reason why He exists are one and the same. Since, therefore, He exists for no end, He acts for no end; and since He has no principle or end of existence, He has no principle or end of action. A final cause, as it is called, is nothing, therefore, but human desire, insofar as this is considered as the principle or primary cause of anything.

Spinoza, *Ethics,* IV, Preface

57 We are to admit no more causes of natural things than such as are both true and sufficient to explain their appearances. To this purpose the philosophers say that Nature does nothing in vain, and more is in vain when less will serve; for Nature is pleased with simplicity, and affects not the pomp of superfluous causes.

Therefore to the same natural effects we must, as far as possible, assign the same causes. As to respiration in a man and in a beast; the descent of stones in Europe and in America; the light of our culinary fire and of the sun; the reflection of light in the earth, and in the planets.

Newton, *Principia,* III, Rules 1–2

58 There are never in nature two beings which are exactly alike.

Leibniz, *Monadology,* 9

59 Nature makes many *particular things,* which do agree one with another in many sensible qualities, and probably too in their internal frame and constitution: but it is not this real essence that distinguishes them into species; it is men who, taking occasion from the qualities they find united in them, and wherein they observe often several individuals to agree, range them into sorts, in order to their naming, for the convenience of comprehensive signs; under which individuals, according to their conformity to this or that abstract idea, come to be ranked as under ensigns: so that this is of the blue, that the red regiment; this is a man, that a drill: and in this, I think, consists the whole business of genus and species.

Locke, *Concerning Human Understanding,*
Bk. III, VI, 36

60 You will say, Hath Nature no share in the production of natural things, and must they be all ascribed to the immediate and sole operation of God? I answer, if by *Nature* is meant only the visible *series* of effects or sensations imprinted on our minds, according to certain fixed and general laws, then it is plain that Nature, taken in this sense, cannot produce anything at all. But, if by *Nature* is meant some being distinct from God, as well as from the laws of nature, and things perceived by sense, I must confess that word is to me an empty sound without any intelligible meaning annexed to it. Nature, in this acceptation, is a vain chimera, introduced by those heathens who had not just notions of the omnipresence and infinite perfection of God.

Berkeley, *Principles of Human Knowledge,* 150

61 Such is the artificial contrivance of this mighty machine of nature that, whilst its motions and various phenomena strike on our senses, the hand which actuates the whole is itself unperceivable to men of flesh and blood.

Berkeley, *Principles of Human Knowledge,* 151

62 All are but parts of one stupendous whole,
Whose body Nature is, and God the soul;
That, chang'd thro' all, and yet in all the same,
Great in the earth, as in th' æthereal frame,
Warms in the sun, refreshes in the breeze,
Glows in the stars, and blossoms in the trees,
Lives thro' all life, extends thro' all extent,
Spreads undivided, operates unspent,
Breathes in our soul, informs our mortal part,
As full, as perfect, in a hair as heart;
As full, as perfect, in vile Man that mourns,
As the rapt Seraph that adores and burns;
To him no high, no low, no great, no small;
He fills, he bounds, connects, and equals all.

Pope, *Essay on Man,* Epistle I, 267

63 It seems evident that, if all the scenes of nature were continually shifted in such a manner that no two events bore any resemblance to each other, but every object was entirely new, without any similitude to whatever had been seen before, we should never, in that case, have attained the least idea of necessity, or of a connexion among these objects. We might say, upon such a supposition, that one object or event has followed another; not that one was produced by the other. The relation of cause and effect must be utterly unknown to mankind. Inference and reasoning concerning the operations of nature would, from that moment, be at an end; and the memory and senses remain the only canals, by which the knowledge of any real existence could possibly have access to the mind. Our idea, therefore, of necessity and causation arises entirely from the uniformity observable in the operations of nature, where similar objects are constantly conjoined together, and the mind is determined by custom to infer the one from the appearance of the other.

Hume, *Concerning Human
Understanding,* VIII, 64

64 *The Philosopher.* We are curious. I want to know how being so crude in your mountains, in your

deserts, in your seas, you appear nevertheless so industrious in your animals, in your vegetables?

Nature. My poor child do you want me to tell you the truth? It is that I have been given a name which does not suit me; my name is "Nature", and I am all art.

Phil. That word upsets all my ideas. What! nature is only art?

Na. Yes, without any doubt. Do you not know that there is an infinite art in those seas and those mountains that you find so crude? do you not know that all those waters gravitate towards the centre of the earth, and mount only by immutable laws; that those mountains which crown the earth are the immense reservoirs of the eternal snows which produce unceasingly those fountains, lakes and rivers without which my animal species and my vegetable species would perish? And as for what are called my animal kingdom, my vegetable kingdom and my mineral kingdom, you see here only three; learn that I have millions of kingdoms. But if you consider only the formation of an insect, of an ear of corn, of gold, of copper, everything will appear as marvels of art.

Phil. It is true. The more I think about it, the more I see that you are only the art of I know not what most potent and industrious great being, who hides himself and who makes you appear. All reasoners since Thales, and probably long before him, have played at blind man's bluff with you; they have said: "I have you!" and they had nothing. We all resemble Ixion; he thought he was kissing Juno, and all that he possessed was a cloud.

Na. Since I am all that is, how can a being such as you, so small a part of myself, seize me? Be content, atoms my children, with seeing a few atoms that surround you, with drinking a few drops of my milk, with vegetating for a few moments on my breast, and with dying without having known your mother and your nurse.

Phil. My dear mother, tell me something of why you exist, of why there is anything.

Na. I will answer you as I have answered for so many centuries all those who have interrogated me about first principles: I KNOW NOTHING ABOUT THEM.

Phil. Would not non-existence be better than this multitude of existences made in order to be continually dissolved, this crowd of animals born and reproduced in order to devour others and to be devoured, this crowd of sentient beings formed for so many painful sensations, that other crowd of intelligences which so rarely hear reason. What is the good of all that, Nature?

Na. Oh! go and ask Him who made me.

Voltaire, *Philosophical Dictionary:* Nature

65 While the earth was left to its natural fertility and covered with immense forests, whose trees were never mutilated by the axe, it would present on every side both sustenance and shelter for every species of animal. Men, dispersed up and down among the rest, would observe and imitate their industry, and thus attain even to the instinct of the beasts, with the advantage that, whereas every species of brutes was confined to one particular instinct, man, who perhaps has not any one peculiar to himself, would appropriate them all, and live upon most of those different foods which other animals shared among themselves; and thus would find his subsistence much more easily than any of the rest.

Accustomed from their infancy to the inclemencies of the weather and the rigour of the seasons, inured to fatigue, and forced, naked and unarmed, to defend themselves and their prey from other ferocious animals, or to escape them by flight, men would acquire a robust and almost unalterable constitution. The children, bringing with them into the world the excellent constitution of their parents, and fortifying it by the very exercises which first produced it, would thus acquire all the vigour of which the human frame is capable. Nature in this case treats them exactly as Sparta treated the children of her citizens: those who come well formed into the world she renders strong and robust, and all the rest she destroys; differing in this respect from our modern communities, in which the State, by making children a burden to their parents, kills them indiscriminately before they are born.

Rousseau, *Origin of Inequality,* I

66 Give civilised man time to gather all his machines about him, and he will no doubt easily beat the savage; but if you would see a still more unequal contest, set them together naked and unarmed, and you will soon see the advantage of having all our forces constantly at our disposal, of being always prepared for every event, and of carrying one's self, as it were, perpetually whole and entire about one.

Rousseau, *Origin of Inequality,* I

67 We should beware . . . of confounding the savage man with the men we have daily before our eyes. Nature treats all the animals left to her care with a predilection that seems to show how jealous she is of that right. The horse, the cat, the bull, and even the ass are generally of greater stature, and always more robust, and have more vigour, strength and courage, when they run wild in the forests than when bred in the stall. By becoming domesticated, they lose half these advantages; and it seems as if all our care to feed and treat them well serves only to deprave them. It is thus with man also: as he becomes sociable and a slave, he grows weak, timid and servile; his effeminate way of life totally enervates his strength and courage. To this it may be added that there is still a greater difference between savage and civilised man, than

between wild and tame beasts: for men and brutes having been treated alike by nature, the several conveniences in which men indulge themselves still more than they do their beasts, are so many additional causes of their deeper degeneracy.

Rousseau, *Origin of Inequality,* I

68 The General [Paoli] said, that in a state of nature a man and woman uniting together, would form a strong and constant affection, by the mutual pleasure each would receive; and that the same causes of dissention would not arise between them, as occur between husband and wife in a civilized state. *Johnson.* "Sir, they would have dissentions enough, though of another kind. One would choose to go a hunting in this wood, the other in that; one would choose to go a fishing in this lake, the other in that; or, perhaps, one would choose to go a hunting, when the other would choose to go a fishing; and so they would part. Besides, Sir, a savage man and a savage woman meet by chance; and when the man sees another woman that pleases him better, he will leave the first."

Boswell, *Life of Johnson (Mar. 31, 1772)*

69 *Art* is distinguished from *nature* as making is from acting or operating in general, and the product or the result of the former is distinguished from that of the latter as *work* from *operation.*

By right it is only production through freedom, i.e., through an act of will that places reason at the basis of its action, that should be termed *art.* For, although we are pleased to call what bees produce (their regularly constituted cells) a work of art, we only do so on the strength of an analogy with art; that is to say, as soon as we call to mind that no rational deliberation forms the basis of their labour, we say at once that it is a product of their nature (of instinct), and it is only to their Creator that we ascribe it as art.

Kant, *Critique of Aesthetic Judgement,* 43

70 Nature proved beautiful when it wore the appearance of art; and art can only be termed *beautiful,* where we are conscious of its being art, while yet it has the appearance of nature.

Kant, *Critique of Aesthetic Judgement,* 45

71 For the purpose of keeping strictly within its own bounds physics entirely ignores the question whether physical ends are ends *designedly* or *undesignedly.* To deal with that question would be to meddle in the affairs of others—namely, in what is the business of metaphysics. Suffice it that there are objects whose one and only *explanation* is on natural laws that we are unable to conceive otherwise than by adopting the idea of ends as principle, objects which, in their intrinsic form, and with nothing more in view than their internal relations, are *cognizable* in this way alone. It is true that in teleology we speak of nature as if its finali-

ty were a thing of design. But to avoid all suspicion of presuming in the slightest to mix up with our sources of knowledge something that has no place in physics at all, namely a supernatural cause, we refer to design in such a way that, in the same breath, we attribute this design to nature, that is, to matter. Here no room is left for misinterpretation, since, obviously, no one would ascribe *design,* in the proper sense of the term, to a lifeless material. Hence our real intention is to indicate that the word *design,* as here used, only signifies a principle of the reflective, and not of the determinant, judgement, and consequently is not meant to introduce any special ground of causality, but only to assist the employment of reason by supplementing investigation on mechanical laws by the addition of another method of investigation, so as to make up for the inadequacy of the former even as a method of empirical research that has for its object all particular laws of nature. Therefore, when teleology is applied to physics, we speak with perfect justice of the wisdom, the economy, the forethought, the beneficence of nature. But in so doing we do not convert nature into an intelligent being, for that would be absurd; but neither do we dare to think of placing another being, one that is intelligent, above nature as its architect, for that would be extravagant. On the contrary, our only intention is to designate in this way a kind of natural causality on an analogy with our own causality in the technical employment of reason, for the purpose of keeping in view the rule upon which certain natural products are to be investigated.

Kant, *Critique of Teleological Judgement,* 68

72 Nature is for us nothing but existence in all its freedom; it is the constitution of things taken in themselves; it is existence itself according to its proper and immutable laws.

Schiller, *Simple and Sentimental Poetry*

73 We see . . . in nature, destitute of reason, only a sister who, more fortunate than ourselves, has remained under the maternal roof, while in the intoxication of our freedom we have fled from it to throw ourselves into a stranger world. We regret this place of safety, we earnestly long to come back to it as soon as we have begun to feel the bitter side of civilization, and in the totally artificial life in which we are exiled we hear in deep emotion the voice of our mother. While we were still only children of nature we were happy, we were perfect: we have become free, and we have lost both advantages. Hence a twofold and very unequal longing for nature: the longing for happiness and the longing for the perfection that prevails there. Man, as a sensuous being, deplores sensibly the loss of the former of these goods; it is only the moral man who can be afflicted at the loss of the other.

Schiller, *Simple and Sentimental Poetry*

74 As long as man dwells in a state of pure nature (I mean pure and not coarse nature), all his being acts at once like a simple sensuous unity, like a harmonious whole. The senses and reason, the receptive faculty and the spontaneously active faculty, have not been as yet separated in their respective functions; a fortiori they are not yet in contradiction with each other. Then the feelings of man are not the formless play of chance; nor are his thoughts an empty play of the imagination, without any value. His feelings proceed from the law of necessity, his thoughts from reality. But when man enters the state of civilization, and art has fashioned him, this sensuous harmony which was in him disappears, and henceforth he can only manifest himself as a moral unity, that is, as aspiring to unity. The harmony that existed as a fact in the former state, the harmony of feeling and thought, only exists now in an ideal state. It is no longer in him, but out of him; it is a conception of thought which he must begin by realizing in himself; it is no longer a fact, a reality of his life.

Schiller, *Simple and Sentimental Poetry*

75 And did those feet in ancient time
   Walk upon England's mountains green?
And was the holy Lamb of God
   On England's pleasant pastures seen?

And did the Countenance Divine
   Shine forth upon our clouded hills?
And was Jerusalem builded here
   Among these dark Satanic Mills?

Bring me my bow of burning gold!
   Bring me my arrows of desire!
Bring me my spear! O clouds, unfold!
   Bring me my chariot of fire!

I will not cease from mental fight,
   Nor shall my sword sleep in my hand,
Till we have built Jerusalem
   In England's green and pleasant land.

Blake, *Milton*

76 The pride of the peacock is the glory of God.
The lust of the goat is the bounty of God.
The wrath of the lion is the wisdom of God.
The nakedness of woman is the work of God.

Blake, *Marriage of Heaven and Hell*, 8

77   And so I dare to hope,
Though changed, no doubt, from what I was when first
I came among these hills; when like a roe
I bounded o'er the mountains, by the sides
Of the deep rivers, and the lonely streams,
Wherever nature led: more like a man
Flying from something that he dreads, than one
Who sought the thing he loved. For nature then

(The coarser pleasures of my boyish days,
And their glad animal movements all gone by)
To me was all in all.—I cannot paint
What then I was. The sounding cataract
Haunted me like a passion: the tall rock,
The mountain, and the deep and gloomy wood,
Their colours and their forms, were then to me
An appetite; a feeling and a love,
That had no need of a remoter charm,
By thought supplied, nor any interest
Unborrowed from the eye.—That time is past,
And all its aching joys are now no more,
And all its dizzy raptures.

Wordsworth, *Tintern Abbey*, 65

78   I have learned
To look on nature, not as in the hour
Of thoughtless youth; but hearing oftentimes
The still, sad music of humanity,
Nor harsh nor grating, though of ample power
To chasten and subdue. And I have felt
A presence that disturbs me with the joy
Of elevated thoughts; a sense sublime
Of something far more deeply interfused,
Whose dwelling is the light of setting suns,
And the round ocean and the living air,
And the blue sky, and in the mind of man;
A motion and a spirit, that impels
All thinking things, all objects of all thought,
And rolls through all things. Therefore am I still
A lover of the meadows and the woods,
And mountains; and of all that we behold
From this green earth; of all the mighty world
Of eye, and ear,—both what they half create,
And what perceive; well pleased to recognise
In nature and the language of the sense,
The anchor of my purest thoughts, the nurse,
The guide, the guardian of my heart, and soul
Of all my moral being.

Wordsworth, *Tintern Abbey*, 88

79   Nature never did betray
The heart that loved her; 't is her privilege,
Through all the years of this our life, to lead
From joy to joy: for she can so inform
The mind that is within us, so impress
With quietness and beauty, and so feed
With lofty thoughts, that neither evil tongues,
Rash judgments, nor the sneers of selfish men,
Nor greetings where no kindness is, nor all
The dreary intercourse of daily life,
Shall e'er prevail against us, or disturb
Our cheerful faith, that all which we behold
Is full of blessings.

Wordsworth, *Tintern Abbey*, 122

80 A slumber did my spirit seal;
   I had no human fears:
She seemed a thing that could not feel
   The touch of earthly years.

No motion has she now, no force;
  She neither hears nor sees;
Rolled round in earth's diurnal course,
  With rocks, and stones, and trees.
        Wordsworth, *A Slumber Did My Spirit Seal*

81 Love had he found in huts where poor men lie;
  His daily teachers had been woods and rills,
  The silence that is in the starry sky,
  The sleep that is among the lonely hills.
        Wordsworth, *Song at the Feast of
        Brougham Castle,* 161

82 Then sing, ye Birds, sing, sing a joyous song!
    And let the young Lambs bound
    As to the tabor's sound!
We in thought will join your throng,
  Ye that pipe and ye that play,
  Ye that through your hearts to-day
  Feel the gladness of the May!
What though the radiance which was once so
    bright
Be now for ever taken from my sight,
  Though nothing can bring back the hour
Of splendour in the grass, of glory in the flower;
  We will grieve not, rather find
  Strength in what remains behind;
  In the primal sympathy
  Which having been must ever be;
  In the soothing thoughts that spring
  Out of human suffering;
  In the faith that looks through death,
In years that bring the philosophic mind.
        Wordsworth, *Ode: Intimations of Immortality,* X

83 And hark! how blithe the throstle sings!
  He, too, is no mean preacher:
  Come forth into the light of things,
  Let Nature be your teacher.

She has a world of ready wealth,
  Our minds and hearts to bless—
Spontaneous wisdom breathed by health,
  Truth breathed by cheerfulness.

One impulse from a vernal wood
  May teach you more of man,
Of moral evil and of good,
  Than all the sages can.

Sweet is the lore which Nature brings;
  Our meddling intellect
Mis-shapes the beauteous forms of things:—
  We murder to dissect.

Enough of Science and of Art;
  Close up those barren leaves;
Come forth, and bring with you a heart
  That watches and receives.
        Wordsworth, *The Tables Turned*

84 Earth has not anything to show more fair:

Dull would he be of soul who could pass by
A sight so touching in its majesty:
This City now doth, like a garment, wear
The beauty of the morning; silent, bare,
Ships, towers, domes, theatres, and temples lie
Open unto the fields, and to the sky;
All bright and glittering in the smokeless air.
Never did sun more beautifully steep
In his first splendour, valley, rock, or hill;
Ne'er saw I, never felt, a calm so deep!
The river glideth at his own sweet will:
Dear God! the very houses seem asleep;
And all that mighty heart is lying still!
        Wordsworth, *Composed Upon Westminster
        Bridge, Sept. 3, 1802*

85 The world is too much with us; late and soon,
Getting and spending, we lay waste our powers:
Little we see in Nature that is ours;
We have given our hearts away, a sordid boon!
The Sea that bares her bosom to the moon;
The winds that will be howling at all hours,
And are up-gathered now like sleeping flowers;
For this, for everything, we are out of tune;
It moves us not.—Great God! I'd rather be
A Pagan suckled in a creed outworn;
So might I, standing on this pleasant lea,
Have glimpses that would make me less forlorn;
Have sight of Proteus rising from the sea;
Or hear old Triton blow his wreathèd horn.
        Wordsworth, *The World Is Too Much
        With Us; Late and Soon*

86 Nature is the term in which we comprehend all
things that are representable in the forms of time
and space, and subjected to the relations of cause
and effect: and the cause of the existence of
which, therefore, is to be sought for perpetually in
something antecedent.
        Coleridge, *Aids to Reflection*

87   Hail to thee, blithe Spirit!
    Bird thou never wert,
  That from Heaven, or near it,
    Pourest thy full heart
In profuse strains of unpremeditated art. . . .

  Better than all measures
    Of delightful sound,
  Better than all treasures
    That in books are found,
Thy skill to poet were, thou scorner of the ground!

  Teach me half the gladness
    That thy brain must know,
  Such harmonious madness
    From my lips would flow
The world should listen then—as I am listening
now.
        Shelley, *To a Skylark*

88   There is a pleasure in the pathless woods,

There is a rapture on the lonely shore,
There is society where none intrudes,
By the deep Sea, and music in its roar:
I love not Man the less, but Nature more,
From these our interviews, in which I steal
From all I may be or have been before,
To mingle with the Universe, and feel
What I can ne'er express, yet can not all conceal.

Roll on, thou deep and dark blue Ocean, roll!
Ten thousand fleets sweep over thee in vain;
Man marks the earth with ruin, his control
Stops with the shore; upon the watery plain
The wrecks are all thy deed, nor doth remain
A shadow of man's ravage, save his own,
When, for a moment, like a drop of rain,
He sinks into thy depths with bubbling groan,
Without a grave, unknell'd, uncoffin'd, and unknown.

Byron, *Childe Harold's Pilgrimage*,
IV, 178–179

89 I cannot see what flowers are at my feet,
  Nor what soft incense hangs upon the boughs,
But, in embalmed darkness, guess each sweet
  Wherewith the seasonable month endows
The grass, the thicket, and the fruit-tree wild;
  White hawthorn, and the pastoral eglantine;
  Fast fading violets cover'd up in leaves;
    And mid-May's eldest child,
  The coming musk-rose, full of dewy wine,
    The murmurous haunt of flies on summer
eves.

Keats, *Ode to a Nightingale*

90 O Maker of sweet poets, dear delight
Of this fair world, and all its gentle livers;
Spangler of clouds, halo of crystal rivers,
Mingler with leaves, and dew and tumbling
  streams,
Closer of lovely eyes to lovely dreams,
Lover of loneliness, and wandering,
Of upcast eye, and tender pondering!
Thee must I praise above all other glories
That smile us on to tell delightful stories.
For what has made the sage or poet write
But the fair paradise of Nature's light?

Keats, *I Stood Tiptoe Upon a Little Hill*, 116

91 In the history of the world, the idea of spirit appears in its actual embodiment as a series of external forms, each one of which declares itself as an actually existing people. This existence falls under the category of time as well as space, in the way of natural existence; and the special principle, which every world-historical people embodies, has this principle at the same time as a *natural* characteristic. Spirit, clothing itself in this form of nature, suffers its particular phases to assume separate existence; for mutual exclusion is the mode of existence proper to mere nature. These natural

distinctions must be first of all regarded as special possibilities, from which the spirit of the people in question germinates, and among them is the geographical basis. It is not our concern to become acquainted with the land occupied by nations as an external locale, but with the natural type of the locality, as intimately connected with the type and character of the people which is the offspring of such a soil. This character is nothing more nor less than the mode and form in which nations make their appearance in history, and take place and position in it. Nature should not be rated too high nor too low: the mild Ionic sky certainly contributed much to the charm of the Homeric poems, yet this alone can produce no Homers. Nor in fact does it continue to produce them; under Turkish government no bards have arisen. We must first take notice of those natural conditions which have to be excluded once for all from the drama of the world's history.

Hegel, *Philosophy of History*, Intro.

92 Man with his necessities sustains a practical relation to external nature, and in making it satisfy his desires, and thus using it up, has recourse to a system of *means*. For natural objects are powerful and offer resistance in various ways. In order to subdue them, man introduces other natural agents; thus turns nature against itself, and invents *instruments* for this purpose. These human inventions belong to spirit, and such an instrument is to be respected more than a mere natural object.

Hegel, *Philosophy of History*, Pt. II, II, 1

93 If we look at the inner nature of . . . sports, we shall first observe how sport itself is opposed to serious business, to dependence and need. This wrestling, running, contending was no serious affair; bespoke no obligation of defence, no necessity of combat. Serious occupation is labour that has reference to some want. I or nature must succumb; if the one is to continue, the other must fall. In contrast with this kind of seriousness, however, sport presents the higher seriousness; for in it nature is wrought into spirit, and although in these contests the subject has not advanced to the highest grade of serious thought, yet in this exercise of his physical powers, man shows his freedom, *viz.*, that he has transformed his body to an organ of spirit.

Hegel, *Philosophy of History*, Pt. II, II, 1

94 The chief objection I have to Pantheism is that it says nothing. To call the world "God" is not to explain it; it is only to enrich our language with a superfluous synonym for the word "world."

Schopenhauer, *A Few Words on Pantheism*

95 Nature, which is the Time-vesture of God, and

reveals Him to the wise, hides Him from the foolish.

Carlyle, *Sartor Resartus,* III, 8

96 Nature will not have us fret and fume. She does not like our benevolence or our learning much better than she likes our frauds and wars. When we come out of the caucus, or the bank, or the Abolition-convention, or the Temperance-meeting, or the Transcendental club into the fields and woods, she says to us, 'So hot? my little Sir.'

Emerson, *Spiritual Laws*

97 There is no great and no small
To the Soul that maketh all:
And where it cometh, all things are;
And it cometh everywhere.

Emerson, *The Informing Spirit*

98 The stars awaken a certain reverence, because though always present, they are inaccessible; but all natural objects make a kindred impression, when the mind is open to their influence. Nature never wears a mean appearance. Neither does the wisest man extort her secret, and lose his curiosity by finding out all her perfection. Nature never became a toy to a wise spirit. The flowers, the animals, the mountains, reflected the wisdom of his best hour, as much as they had delighted the simplicity of his childhood.

Emerson, *Nature,* I

99 One can scarcely think upon the subject of atmospheric magnetism without having another great question suggested to the mind: What is the final purpose in nature of this magnetic condition of the atmosphere, and its liability to annual and diurnal variations, and its entire loss by entering into combination either in combustion or respiration? No doubt there is one or more, for nothing is superfluous there. We find no remainders or surplusage of action in physical forces. The smallest provision is as essential as the greatest. None is deficient, none can be spared.

Faraday, *Experimental Researches in Electricity,* XXVI, 2968

100 The wish, that of the living whole
No life may fail beyond the grave,
Derives it not from what we have
The likest God within the soul?

Are God and Nature then at strife,
That Nature lends such evil dreams?
So careful of the type she seems,
So careless of the single life,

That I, considering everywhere
Her secret meaning in her deeds,
And finding that of fifty seeds
She often brings but one to bear,

I falter where I firmly trod,

And falling with my weight of cares
Upon the great world's altar-stairs
That slope thro' darkness up to God,

I stretch lame hands of faith, and grope,
And gather dust and chaff, and call
To what I feel is Lord of all,
And faintly trust the larger hope.

'So careful of the type?' but no.
From scarped cliff and quarried stone
She cries, 'A thousand types are gone;
I care for nothing, all shall go.

'Thou makest thine appeal to me.
I bring to life, I bring to death;
The spirit does but mean the breath:
I know no more.' And he, shall he,

Man, her last work, who seem'd so fair,
Such splendid purpose in his eyes,
Who roll'd the psalm to wintry skies,
Who built him fanes of fruitless prayer,

Who trusted God was love indeed
And love Creation's final law—
Tho' Nature, red in tooth and claw
With ravine, shriek'd against his creed—

Who loved, who suffer'd countless ills,
Who battled for the True, the Just,
Be blown about the desert dust,
Or seal'd within the iron hills?

No more? A monster then, a dream,
A discord. Dragons of the prime,
That tare each other in their slime,
Were mellow music match'd with him.

O life as futile, then, as frail!
O for thy voice to soothe and bless!
What hope of answer, or redress?
Behind the veil, behind the veil.

Tennyson, *In Memoriam,* LV–LVI

101 Flower in the crannied wall,
I pluck you out of the crannies,
I hold you here, root and all, in my hand,
Little flower—but *if* I could understand
What you are, root and all, and all in all,
I should know what God and man is.

Tennyson, *Flower in the Crannied Wall*

102 *Ahab.* O Nature, and O soul of man! how far beyond all utterance are your linked analogies! not the smallest atom stirs or lives on matter, but has its cunning duplicate in mind.

Melville, *Moby Dick,* LXX

103 The West of which I speak is but another name for the Wild; and what I have been preparing to say is, that in Wildness is the preservation of the World.

Thoreau, *Walking*

104 A child said *What is the grass?* fetching it to me with full hands,
How could I answer the child? I do not know what it is any more than he.

I guess it must be the flag of my disposition, out of hopeful green stuff woven.

Or I guess it is the handkerchief of the Lord,
A scented gift and remembrancer designedly dropt,
Bearing the owner's name someway in the corners, that we may see and remark, and say *Whose?* . . .

And now it seems to me the beautiful uncut hair of graves.

Whitman, *Song of Myself,* VI

105 I believe a leaf of grass is no less than the journey-work of the stars,
And the pismire is equally perfect, and a grain of sand, and the egg of the wren,
And the tree-toad is a chef-d'œuvre for the highest,
And the running blackberry would adorn the parlors of heaven,
And the narrowest hinge in my hand puts to scorn all machinery,
And the cow crunching with depress'd head surpasses any statue,
And a mouse is miracle enough to stagger sextillions of infidels.

Whitman, *Song of Myself,* XXXI

106 In due time the evolution theory will have to abate its vehemence, cannot be allow'd to dominate everything else, and will have to take its place as a segment of the circle, the cluster—as but one of many theories, many thoughts, of profoundest value—and readjusting and differentiating much, yet leaving the divine secrets just as inexplicable and unreachable as before—maybe more so.

Whitman, *Notes Left Over*

107 In looking at Nature, it is most necessary . . . never to forget that every single organic being may be said to be striving to the utmost to increase in numbers; that each lives by a struggle at some period of its life; that heavy destruction inevitably falls either on the young or old, during each generation or at recurrent intervals. Lighten any check, mitigate the destruction ever so little, and the number of the species will almost instantaneously increase to any amount.

Darwin, *Origin of Species,* III

108 It has been said that I speak of natural selection as an active power or Deity; but who objects to an author speaking of the attraction of gravity as ruling the movements of the planets? Every one knows what is meant and is implied by such metaphorical expressions; and they are almost necessary for brevity. So again it is difficult to avoid personifying the word Nature; but I mean by Nature, only the aggregate action and product of many natural laws, and by laws the sequence of events as ascertained by us.

Darwin, *Origin of Species,* IV

109 As man can produce, and certainly has produced, a great result by his methodical and unconscious means of selection, what may not natural selection effect? Man can act only on external and visible characters: Nature, if I may be allowed to personify the natural preservation or survival of the fittest, cares nothing for appearances, except in so far as they are useful to any being. She can act on every internal organ, on every shade of constitutional difference, on the whole machinery of life. Man selects only for his own good: Nature only for that of the being which she tends. Every selected character is fully exercised by her, as is implied by the fact of their selection. Man keeps the natives of many climates in the same country; he seldom exercises each selected character in some peculiar and fitting manner; he feeds a long and a short beaked pigeon on the same food; he does not exercise a long-backed or long-legged quadruped in any peculiar manner; he exposes sheep with long and short wool to the same climate. He does not allow the most vigorous males to struggle for the females. He does not rigidly destroy all inferior animals, but protects during each varying season, as far as lies in his power, all his productions. He often begins his selection by some half-monstrous form; or at least by some modification prominent enough to catch the eye or to be plainly useful to him. Under nature, the slightest differences of structure or constitution may well turn the nicely balanced scale in the struggle for life, and so be preserved. How fleeting are the wishes and efforts of man! how short his time! and consequently how poor will be his results, compared with those accumulated by Nature during whole geological periods! Can we wonder, then, that Nature's productions should be far "truer" in character than man's productions; that they should be infinitely better adapted to the most complex conditions of life, and should plainly bear the stamp of far higher workmanship?

Darwin, *Origin of Species,* IV

110 It is scarcely possible to avoid comparing the eye with a telescope. We know that this instrument has been perfected by the long-continued efforts of the highest human intellects; and we naturally infer that the eye has been formed by a somewhat analogous process. But may not this inference be presumptuous? Have we any right to assume that the Creator works by intellectual powers like

those of man? If we must compare the eye to an optical instrument, we ought in imagination to take a thick layer of transparent tissue, with spaces filled with fluid, and with a nerve sensitive to light beneath, and then suppose every part of this layer to be continually changing slowly in density, so as to separate into layers of different densities and thicknesses, placed at different distances from each other, and with the surfaces of each layer slowly changing in form. Further we must suppose that there is a power, represented by natural selection or the survival of the fittest, always intently watching each slight alteration in the transparent layers; and carefully preserving each which, under varied circumstances, in any way or in any degree, tends to produce a distincter image. We must suppose each new state of the instrument to be multiplied by the million; each to be preserved until a better one is produced, and then the old ones to be all destroyed. In living bodies, variation will cause the slight alterations, generation will multiply them almost infinitely, and natural selection will pick out with unerring skill each improvement. Let this process go on for millions of years; and during each year on millions of individuals of many kinds; and may we not believe that a living optical instrument might thus be formed as superior to one of glass, as the works of the Creator are to those of man?

Darwin, *Origin of Species*, VI

111 As natural selection acts solely by accumulating slight, successive, favourable variations, it can produce no great or sudden modifications; it can act only by short and slow steps. Hence, the canon of *"Natura non facit saltum,"* which every fresh addition to our knowledge tends to confirm, is on this theory intelligible. We can see why throughout nature the same general end is gained by an almost infinite diversity of means, for every peculiarity when once acquired is long inherited, and structures already modified in many different ways have to be adapted for the same general purpose. We can, in short, see why nature is prodigal in variety, though niggard in innovation. But why this should be a law of nature if each species has been independently created no man can explain.

Darwin, *Origin of Species,* XV

112 It is an error to imagine that evolution signifies a constant tendency to increased perfection. That process undoubtedly involves a constant remodelling of the organism in adaptation to new conditions; but it depends on the nature of those conditions whether the direction of the modifications effected shall be upward or downward.

T. H. Huxley, *Struggle for Existence in Human Society*

113 Thus we may say that surplus value rests on a natural basis; but this is permissible only in the very general sense that there is no natural obstacle absolutely preventing one man from disburdening himself of the labour requisite for his own existence, and burdening another with it, any more, for instance, than unconquerable natural obstacles prevent one man from eating the flesh of another. No mystical ideas must in any way be connected, as sometimes happens, with this historically developed productiveness of labour. It is only after men have raised themselves above the rank of animals, when, therefore, their labour has been to some extent socialized, that a state of things arises in which the surplus labour of the one becomes a condition of existence for the other.

Marx, *Capital*, Vol. I, V, 16

114 If there are any marks at all of special design in creation, one of the things most evidently designed is that a large proportion of all animals should pass their existence in tormenting and devouring other animals. They have been lavishly fitted out with the instruments necessary for that purpose; their strongest instincts impel them to it, and many of them seem to have been constructed incapable of supporting themselves by any other food. If a tenth part of the pains which have been expended in finding benevolent adaptations in all nature had been employed in collecting evidence to blacken the character of the Creator, what scope for comment would not have been found in the entire existence of the lower animals, divided with scarcely an exception into devourers and devoured, and a prey to a thousand ills from which they are denied the faculties necessary for protecting themselves! If we are not obliged to believe the animal creation to be the work of a demon it is because we need not suppose it to have been made by a Being of infinite power. But if imitation of the Creator's will as revealed in nature were applied as a rule of action in this case, the most atrocious enormities of the worst men would be more than justified by the apparent intention of Providence that throughout all animated nature the strong should prey upon the weak.

Mill, *Nature*

115 The word nature has two principal meanings: it either denotes the entire system of things, with the aggregate of all their properties, or it denotes things as they would be, apart from human intervention.

In the first of these senses, the doctrine that man ought to follow nature is unmeaning, since man has no power to do anything else than follow nature; all his actions are done through and in obedience to some one or many of nature's physical or mental laws.

In the other sense of the term, the doctrine that men ought to follow nature or, in other words, ought to make the spontaneous course of things the model of his voluntary actions is equally irrational and immoral: irrational, because all human action whatever consists in altering, and all useful action in improving, the spontaneous course of nature; immoral, because the course of natural phenomena being replete with everything which when committed by human beings is most worthy of abhorrence, any one who endeavoured in his actions to imitate the natural course of things would be universally seen and acknowledged to be the wickedest of men.

The scheme of nature regarded in its whole extent cannot have had, for its sole or even principal object, the good of human or other sentient beings. What good it brings to them is mostly the result of their own exertions. Whatsoever in nature gives indication of beneficent design proves this beneficence to be armed only with limited power; and the duty of man is to co-operate with the beneficent powers, not by imitating but by perpetually striving to amend the course of nature—and bringing that part of it over which we can exercise control more nearly into conformity with a high standard of justice and goodness.

Mill, *Nature*

116 Nature, with equal mind,
    Sees all her sons at play;
Sees man control the wind,
    The wind sweep man away;
Allows the proudly-riding and the
             foundering bark.

Arnold, *Empedocles on Etna*, I, ii, 257

117 "Ha-ha-ha!" laughed Pierre. And he said aloud to himself: "The soldier did not let me pass. They took me and shut me up. They hold me captive. What, me? Me? My immortal soul? Ha-ha-ha! Ha-ha-ha! . . . " and he laughed till tears started to his eyes.

A man got up and came to see what this queer big fellow was laughing at all by himself. Pierre stopped laughing, got up, went farther away from the inquisitive man, and looked around him.

The huge, endless bivouac that had previously resounded with the crackling of campfires and the voices of many men had grown quiet, the red campfires were growing paler and dying down. High up in the light sky hung the full moon. Forests and fields beyond the camp, unseen before, were now visible in the distance. And farther still, beyond those forests and fields, the bright, oscillating, limitless distance lured one to itself. Pierre glanced up at the sky and the twinkling stars in its faraway depths. "And all that is me, all that is within me, and it is all I!" thought Pierre. "And they caught all that and put it into a shed boarded up with planks!" He smiled, and went and lay down to sleep beside his companions.

Tolstoy, *War and Peace*, XIII, 14

118 To call the taming of an animal its 'improvement'

is in our ears almost a joke. Whoever knows what goes on in menageries is doubtful whether the beasts in them are 'improved'. They are weakened, they are made less harmful, they become *sickly* beasts through the depressive emotion of fear, through pain, through injuries, through hunger.

Nietzsche, *Twilight of the Idols:*
The "Improvers" of Mankind

119 Nature . . . is frugal in her operations, and will not be at the expense of a particular instinct to give us that knowledge which experience and habit will soon produce.

William James, *Psychology*, XIX

120 Who does not feel the charm of thinking that the moon and the apple are, as far as their relation to the earth goes, identical; of knowing respiration and combustion to be one; of understanding that the balloon rises by the same law whereby the stone sinks; of feeling that the warmth in one's palm when one rubs one's sleeve is identical with the motion which the friction checks; of recognizing the difference between beast and fish to be only a higher degree of that between human father and son; of believing our strength when we climb the mountain or fell the tree to be no other than the strength of the sun's rays which made the corn grow out of which we got our morning meal?

William James, *Sentiment of Rationality*

121 The claims of our civilization make life too hard for the greater part of humanity, and so further the aversion to reality and the origin of neuroses, without producing an excess of cultural gain by this excess of sexual repression. We ought not to go so far as to fully neglect the original animal part of our nature; we ought not to forget that the happiness of individuals cannot be dispensed with as one of the aims of our culture. . . .

I do not know whether you will regard the exhortation with which I close as a presumptuous one. I only venture the indirect presentation of my conviction, if I relate an old tale, whose application you may make yourselves. German literature knows a town called Schilda, to whose inhabitants were attributed all sorts of clever pranks. The wiseacres, so the story goes, had a horse, with whose powers of work they were well satisfied, and against whom they had only one grudge, that he consumed so much expensive oats. They concluded that by good management they would break him of his bad habit, by cutting down his rations by several stalks each day, until he had learned to do without them altogether. Things went finely for a while, the horse was weaned to one stalk a day, and on the next day he would at last work without fodder. On the morning of this day the malicious horse was found dead; the citizens of Schilda could not understand why he had died.

We should be inclined to believe that the horse had starved, and that without a certain ration of oats no work could be expected from an animal.

Freud, *Origin and Development of Psycho-Analysis,* V

122 I hope to enlist your interest in considering the apparently trivial errors made by normal people. I propose now that we question someone who has no knowledge of psycho-analysis as to how he explains these occurrences.

His first answer is sure to be: "Oh, they are not worth any explanation; they are little accidents." What does the man mean by this? Does he mean to maintain that there are any occurrences so small that they fail to come within the causal sequence of things, that they might as well be other than they are? Anyone thus breaking away from the determination of natural phenomena, at any single point, has thrown over the whole scientific outlook on the world *(Weltanschauung)*. One may point out to him how much more consistent is the religious outlook on the world, which emphatically assures us that "not one sparrow shall fall to the ground" except God wills it. I think our friend would not be willing to follow his first answer to its logical conclusion; he would give way and say that if he were to study these things he would soon find some explanation of them.

Freud, *General Introduction to Psycho-Analysis,* II

123 In Aristotle the conception of human nature is perfectly sound; everything ideal has a natural basis and everything natural an ideal development.

Santayana, *Life of Reason,* I, Introduction

124 That the unification of nature is eventual and theoretical is a point useful to remember: else the relation of the natural world to poetry, metaphysics, and religion will never become intelligible. Lalande, or whoever it was, who searched the heavens with his telescope and could find no God, would not have found the human mind if he had searched the brain with a microscope.

Santayana, *Life of Reason,* I, 5

19.2 | *The Nature of Life*

Many of the passages collected here attempt to define the line that divides the living from the nonliving, and to enumerate the distinctive properties of living organisms, such as nutrition, growth, and reproduction. Within the domain of the living, further distinctions are made between plant and animal life, by reference to sensitivity and local motion as characteristics of animals not found in plants. Some quotations speak of the scale of life, the gradations of vitality, rising little by little from the vegetative level to more complex and more richly endowed forms of life; to which certain philosophers and theologians add levels of life above the highest terrestrial forms—the purely spiritual life of the angels and of God.

The reader will find some indications of the age-old controversy between the vitalists and the mechanists, the one maintaining that life involves principles or factors that have no counterparts in the realm of inanimate things or machines, the other countering with the view that the same mechanical principles or factors that enable us to understand the operation of inanimate things also explain the processes of life. Crucial to this issue is Claude Bernard's introduction of the concept of homeostasis—the internal equilibrium of a living organism. Only living things appear to have an internal as well as an external environment, and are actively involved in the adjustment of the one to the other. In this connection it should also be pointed out that when soul is spoken of as the principle of life, it is not necessarily conceived as something divorced from matter: early atomists, such as Lucretius, think of soul or mind as constituted by material particles, and Aristotle thinks of soul as inherent in living matter. For him, to be alive is to be besouled.

The origin of life or of living organisms is another basic subject treated in this section, and the discussions of it range from the account of its creation in *Genesis* or the one given by Plato in the *Timaeus,* to later theological commentaries on *Genesis* and then to modern writers such as Darwin. And at least one author offers startling comments on the origin of life: this is Freud who, in his discussion of the life and death instincts, suggests that living things are driven by a profound impulse to rid themselves of the tensions of life and return to the sleep of inanimate existence. For other comments on life and death, viewed more narrowly from the human point of view, the reader is referred to Chapter 1 on Man, especially Section 1.2 and Section 1.8.

---

1 And God said, Let the earth bring forth grass, the herb yielding seed, and the fruit tree yielding fruit after his kind, whose seed is in itself, upon the earth: and it was so.

And the earth brought forth grass, and herb yielding seed after his kind, and the tree yielding fruit, whose seed was in itself, after his kind: and God saw that it was good.

And the evening and the morning were the third day.

Genesis 1:11–13

2 And God said, Let the waters bring forth abundantly the moving creature that hath life, and fowl that may fly above the earth in the open firmament of heaven.

And God created great whales, and every living creature that moveth, which the waters brought forth abundantly, after their kind, and every winged fowl after his kind: and God saw that it was good.

And God blessed them, saying, Be fruitful, and multiply, and fill the waters in the seas, and let fowl multiply in the earth.

And the evening and the morning were the fifth day.

Genesis 1:20–23

3 And the Lord God formed man of the dust of the ground, and breathed into his nostrils the breath of life; and man became a living soul.

Genesis 2:7

4 For to him that is joined to all the living there is hope: for a living dog is better than a dead lion.

Ecclesiastes 9:4

5 *Timaeus.* Now of the divine, he himself [God] was the creator, but the creation of the mortal he committed to his offspring. And they, imitating him, received from him the immortal principle of the soul; and around this they proceeded to fashion a mortal body, and made it to be the vehicle of the soul, and constructed within the body a soul of another nature which was mortal.

Plato, *Timaeus,* 69B

6 This power of self-nutrition can be isolated from the other powers mentioned, but not they from it—in mortal beings at least. The fact is obvious in plants; for it is the only psychic power they possess.

This is the originative power the possession of which leads us to speak of things as *living* at all, but it is the possession of sensation that leads us for the first time to speak of living things as animals; for even those beings which possess no power of local movement but do possess the power of sensation we call animals and not merely living things.

Aristotle, *On the Soul,* 413ª31

7 The soul is the cause or source of the living body. The terms cause and source have many senses. But the soul is the cause of its body alike in all three senses which we explicitly recognize. It is (a) the source or origin of movement, it is (b) the end, it is (c) the essence of the whole living body.

That it is the last, is clear; for in everything the essence is identical with the ground of its being, and here, in the case of living things, their being is to live, and of their being and their living the soul in them is the cause or source. Further, the actuality of whatever is potential is identical with its formulable essence.

It is manifest that the soul is also the final cause of its body. For Nature, like mind, always does whatever it does for the sake of something, which something is its end. To that something corresponds in the case of animals the soul and in this it follows the order of nature; all natural bodies are organs of the soul. This is true of those that enter into the constitution of plants as well as of those which enter into that of animals. This shows that that for the sake of which they are is soul. We must here recall the two senses of 'that for the sake of which', viz. (a) the end to achieve which, and (b) the being in whose interest, anything is or is done.

We must maintain, further, that the soul is also the cause of the living body as the original source of local movement. The power of locomotion is not found, however, in all living things. But change of quality and change of quantity are also due to the soul. Sensation is held to be a qualitative alteration, and nothing except what has soul in it is capable of sensation. The same holds of the quantitative changes which constitute growth and decay; nothing grows or decays naturally except what feeds itself, and nothing feeds itself except what has a share of soul in it.

Aristotle, *On the Soul,* 415ᵇ8

8 As to being what is called an animal and a living thing, we find that in all beings endowed with both characteristics (viz. being an animal and being alive) there must be a single identical part in virtue of which they live and are called animals; for an animal *qua* animal cannot avoid being alive. But a thing need not, though alive, be animal, for plants live without having sensation, and it is by sensation that we distinguish animal from what is not animal.

Aristotle, *On Youth and Old Age, On Life and Death, On Breathing,* 467ᵇ18

9 Of necessity, life must be coincident with the maintenance of heat, and what we call death is its destruction.

Aristotle, *On Youth and Old Age, On Life and Death, On Breathing,* 469ᵇ18

10 Nature proceeds little by little from things lifeless to animal life in such a way that it is impossible to determine the exact line of demarcation, nor on which side thereof an intermediate form should lie. Thus, next after lifeless things in the upward scale comes the plant, and of plants one will differ from another as to its amount of apparent vitality; and, in a word, the whole genus of plants, whilst it is devoid of life as compared with an animal, is endowed with life as compared with other corporeal entities. Indeed, as we just remarked, there is observed in plants a continuous scale of ascent towards the animal. So, in the sea, there are certain objects concerning which one would be at a loss to determine whether they be animal or vegetable. For instance, certain of these objects are fairly rooted, and in several cases perish if detached; thus the pinna is rooted to a particular spot, and the solen (or razor-shell) cannot survive withdrawal from its burrow. Indeed, broadly speaking, the entire genus of testaceans have a resemblance

to vegetables, if they be contrasted with such animals as are capable of progression.

In regard to sensibility, some animals give no indication whatsoever of it, whilst others indicate it but indistinctly. Further, the substance of some of these intermediate creatures is fleshlike, as is the case with the so-called tethya (or ascidians) and the acalephae (or sea-anemones); but the sponge is in every respect like a vegetable. And so throughout the entire animal scale there is a graduated differentiation in amount of vitality and in capacity for motion.

A similar statement holds good with regard to habits of life. Thus of plants that spring from seed the one function seems to be the reproduction of their own particular species, and the sphere of action with certain animals is similarly limited. The faculty of reproduction, then, is common to all alike. If sensibility be superadded, then their lives will differ from one another in respect to sexual intercourse through the varying amount of pleasure derived therefrom, and also in regard to modes of parturition and ways of rearing their young. Some animals, like plants, simply procreate their own species at definite seasons; other animals busy themselves also in procuring food for their young, and after they are reared quit them and have no further dealings with them; other animals are more intelligent and endowed with memory, and they live with their offspring for a longer period and on a more social footing.

The life of animals, then, may be divided into two acts—procreation and feeding; for on these two acts all their interests and life concentrate. Their food depends chiefly on the substance of which they are severally constituted; for the source of their growth in all cases will be this substance. And whatsoever is in conformity with nature is pleasant, and all animals pursue pleasure in keeping with their nature.

Aristotle, *History of Animals,* 588ᵇ4

11 If we except the movement of the universe, things with life are the causes of the movement of all else, that is of all that are not moved by one another by mutual impact. And so all their motions have a term or limit, inasmuch as the movements of things with life have such. For all living things both move and are moved with some object, so that this is the term of all their movement, the end, that is, in view. Now we see that the living creature is moved by intellect, imagination, purpose, wish, and appetite. And all these are reducible to mind and desire.

Aristotle, *On the Motion of Animals,* 700ᵇ11

12 Now (1) some existing things are eternal and divine whilst others admit of both existence and non-existence. But (2) that which is noble and divine is always, in virtue of its own nature, the cause of the better in such things as admit of being

better or worse, and what is not eternal does admit of existence and non-existence, and can partake in the better and the worse. And (3) soul is better than body, and the living, having soul, is thereby better than the lifeless which has none, and being is better than not being, living than not living. These, then, are the reasons of the generation of animals. For since it is impossible that such a class of things as animals should be of an eternal nature, therefore that which comes into being is eternal in the only way possible. Now it is impossible for it to be eternal as an individual (though of course the real essence of things is in the individual)—were it such it would be eternal—but it is possible for it as a species.

Aristotle, *Generation of Animals,* 731ᵇ24

13 One might suppose, in connexion with the origin of men and quadrupeds, that, if ever they were really 'earth-born' as some say, they came into being in one of two ways; that either it was by the formation of a scolex at first or else it was out of eggs. For either they must have had in themselves the nutriment for growth (and such a conception is a scolex) or they must have got it from elsewhere, and that either from the mother or from part of the conception. If then the former is impossible (I mean that nourishment should flow to them from the earth as it does in animals from the mother), then they must have got it from some part of the conception, and such generation we say is from an egg.

Aristotle, *Generation of Animals,* 762ᵇ28

14 Whatever things we perceive to have sense, you must yet admit to be all composed of senseless first-beginnings: manifest tokens which are open to all to apprehend, so far from refuting or contradicting this, do rather themselves take us by the hand and constrain us to believe that, as I say, living things are begotten from senseless things. We may see in fact living worms spring out of stinking dung, when the soaked earth has gotten putridity after excessive rains; and all things besides change in the same way: rivers, leaves, and glad pastures change into cattle, cattle change their substance into our bodies, and often out of these the powers of wild beasts and the bodies of the strong of wing are increased. Therefore nature changes all foods into living bodies and engenders out of them all the senses of living creatures, much in the same way as she dissolves dry woods into flames and converts all things into fires. Now do you see that it is of great moment in what sort of arrangement the first-beginnings of things are severally placed and with what others they are mixed up, when they impart and receive motions?

Lucretius, *Nature of Things,* II

15 The mind has more to do with holding the fastnesses of life and has more sovereign sway over it than the power of the soul. For without the understanding and the mind no part of the soul can maintain itself in the frame the smallest fraction of time, but follows at once in the other's train and passes away into the air and leaves the cold limbs in the chill of death. But he abides in life whose mind and understanding continue to stay with him: though the trunk is mangled with its limbs shorn all round about it, after the soul has been taken away on all sides and been severed from the limbs, the trunk yet lives and inhales the ethereal airs of life. . . . When . . . I shall choose to speak of the soul, showing it to be mortal, believe that I speak of the mind as well, inasmuch as both make up one thing and are one united substance. First of all then since I have shown the soul to be fine and to be formed of minute bodies and made up of much smaller first-beginnings than is the liquid of water or mist or smoke:—for it far surpasses these in nimbleness and is moved, when struck by a far slenderer cause. . . . Well then since you see on the vessels being shattered the water flow away on all sides, and since mist and smoke pass away into air, believe that the soul too is shed abroad and perishes much more quickly and dissolves sooner into its first bodies, when once it has been taken out of the limbs of a man and has withdrawn. For, when the body that serves for its vessel cannot hold it, if shattered from any cause and rarefied by the withdrawal of blood from the veins, how can you believe that this soul can be held by any air? How can that air which is rarer than our body hold it in?

Lucretius, *Nature of Things,* III

16 When the earth, all muddied by the recent flood, grew warm again, under the kindly radiance of the sun in heaven, she brought forth countless forms of life. In some cases she reproduced shapes which had been previously known, others were new and strange. It was at that time that she gave birth to the huge Python, among the rest, though indeed she had no wish to do so; and this snake, whose body covered so great a stretch of the hillside, struck terror into the new-born race of men, for they had never known its like. The archer god, Apollo, who had never before used such weapons against anything but fleeing deer or timid wild goats, almost emptied his quiver to destroy the serpent, overwhelming it with a thousand arrows, till the venom flowed out from all its dark wounds. Then, in case the passage of time should blot out the memory of his glorious deed, the god established sacred games, which he called Pythian, after the serpent he had vanquished.

Ovid, *Metamorphoses,* I

17 If there were not an inborn faculty given by Nature to each one of the organs at the very beginning, then animals could not continue to live even for a few days, far less for the number of years

which they actually do. For let us suppose they were under no guardianship, lacking in creative ingenuity and forethought; let us suppose they were steered only by material forces, and not by any special faculties (the one attracting what is proper to it, another rejecting what is foreign, and yet another causing alteration and adhesion of the matter destined to nourish it); if we suppose this, I am sure it would be ridiculous for us to discuss natural, or, still more, psychical, activities—or, in fact, life as a whole.

Galen, *Natural Faculties,* II, 3

18 Imagine the heart to be, at the beginning, so small as to differ in no respect from a millet-seed, or, if you will, a bean; and consider how otherwise it is to become large than by being extended in all directions and acquiring nourishment throughout its whole substance, in the way that, as I showed a short while ago, the semen is nourished. But even this was unknown to Erasistratus—the man who sings the artistic skill of Nature! He imagines that animals grow like webs, ropes, sacks, or baskets, each of which has, woven on to its end or margin, other material similar to that of which it was originally composed.

But this, most sapient sir, is not growth, but genesis! For a bag, sack, garment, house, ship, or the like is said to be still coming into existence [undergoing genesis] so long as the appropriate form for the sake of which it is being constructed by the artificer is still incomplete. Then, when does it grow? Only when the basket, being complete, with a bottom, a mouth, and a belly, as it were, as well as the intermediate parts, now becomes larger in all these respects. "And how can this happen?" someone will ask. Only by our basket suddenly becoming an animal or a plant; for growth belongs to living things alone. Possibly you imagine that a house grows when it is being built, or a basket when being plaited, or a garment when being woven? It is not so, however. Growth belongs to that which has already been completed in respect to its form, whereas the process by which that which is still becoming attains its form is termed not growth but genesis. That which is, grows, while that which is not, becomes.

Galen, *Natural Faculties,* II, 3

19 Now all life, even the least valuable, is an activity, and not a blind activity like that of flame; even where there is not sensation the activity of life is no mere haphazard play of Movement: any object in which life is present, and object which participates in Life, is at once enreasoned in the sense that the activity peculiar to life is formative, shaping as it moves.

Life, then, aims at pattern as does the pantomimic dancer with his set movements; the mime, in himself, represents life, and, besides, his move-

ments proceed in obedience to a pattern designed to symbolize life.

Plotinus, *Third Ennead,* II, 16

20 Fire, air, water, earth, are in themselves soulless . . . and there are no other forms of body than these four. . . . None of these, then, having life, it would be extraordinary if life came about by bringing them together; it is impossible, in fact, that the collocation of material entities should produce life, or mindless entities mind.

No one, moreover, would pretend that a mere chance mixing could give such results: some regulating principle would be necessary, some Cause directing the admixture: that guiding principle would be—soul.

Plotinus, *Fourth Ennead,* VII, 2

21 Since all who think about God think of Him as living, they only can form any conception of Him that is not absurd and unworthy who think of Him as life itself; and, whatever may be the bodily form that has suggested itself to them, recognize that it is by life it lives or does not live, and prefer what is living to what is dead; who understand that the living bodily form itself, however it may outshine all others in splendour, overtop them in size, and excel them in beauty, is quite a distinct thing from the life by which it is quickened; and who look upon the life as incomparably superior in dignity and worth to the mass which is quickened and animated by it. Then, when they go on to look into the nature of the life itself, if they find it mere nutritive life, without sensibility, such as that of plants, they consider it inferior to sentient life, such as that of cattle; and above this, again, they place intelligent life, such as that of men. And, perceiving that even this is subject to change, they are compelled to place above it, again, that unchangeable life, which is not at one time foolish, at another time wise, but on the contrary is wisdom itself.

Augustine, *Christian Doctrine,* I, 8

22 We can gather to what things life belongs and to what it does not from such things as manifestly possess life. Now life manifestly belongs to animals, for it is said in the book on *Plants* [Aristotle's] that "in animals life is manifest." We must, therefore, distinguish living from non-living things by comparing them to that by reason of which animals are said to live, and this it is in which life is manifested first and remains last. We say then that an animal begins to live when it begins to move of itself, and as long as such movement appears in it, so long is it considered to be alive. When it no longer has any movement of itself, but is only moved by another power, then its life is said to fail, and the animal to be dead. From this it is clear that those things are properly called living that move themselves by some kind of movement, whether it be movement properly so

called, as the act of an imperfect thing, that is, of a thing in potency, is called movement; or movement in a more general sense, as when said of the act of a perfect thing, as understanding and feeling are called movement according to the book on the *Soul* [Aristotle's]. Accordingly all things are said to be alive that determine themselves to movement or operation of any kind; but those things that cannot by their nature do so, cannot be called living, unless by some likeness.

Aquinas, *Summa Theologica*, I, 18, 1

23 Life is in the highest degree properly in God. In proof of this it must be considered that since a thing is said to live insofar as it operates of itself and not as moved by another, the more perfectly this is found in anything, the more perfect is the life of that thing.

Aquinas, *Summa Theologica*, I, 18, 3

24 Bodies not endowed with life, which are the lowest in the order of nature, generate their like, not through some medium, but by themselves; thus fire by itself generates fire. But living bodies, as being more powerful, act so as to generate their like, both without and with a medium. Without a medium—in the work of nutrition, in which flesh generates flesh; with a medium—in the act of generation, because the seed of the animal or plant derives a certain active force from the soul of the generator, just as the instrument derives a certain moving power from the principal agent. And as it matters not whether we say that something is moved by the instrument or by the principal agent, so neither does it matter whether we say that the soul of the generated is caused by the soul of the generator, or by some seminal power derived from it.

Aquinas, *Summa Theologica*, I, 118, 1

25 God is effectively the life both of the soul by charity, and of the body by the soul; but formally charity is the life of the soul, even as the soul is the life of the body. Consequently we may conclude from this that just as the soul is immediately united to the body, so is charity to the soul.

Aquinas, *Summa Theologica*, II–II, 23, 2

26 *I see the water, I see the fire, the air, the earth, and all their combinations meet their dissolution and endure but little;*
and yet these things were creatures, so that if that which I have said to thee be true, they ought to be secure against corruption.
The Angels, brother, and the unsullied country in which thou art, may be declared to be created, even as they are, in their entire being;
but the elements which thou hast named and all the things compounded of them, have by created virtue been informed.
Created was the matter which they hold, created

was the informing virtue in these stars which sweep around them.
The life of every brute and of the plants is drawn from compounds having potency, by the ray and movement of the sacred lights.
But your life is breathed without mean by the supreme beneficence who maketh it enamoured of itself, so that thereafter it doth ever long for it.

Dante, *Paradiso*, VII, 124

27 *Panurge.* Now let our microcosm be fancied conform to this model in all its members; lending, borrowing, and owing, that is to say, according to its own nature. For nature hath not to any other end created man, but to owe, borrow, and lend; no greater is the harmony amongst the heavenly spheres, than that which shall be found in its well ordered policy. The intention of the founder of this microcosm is, to have a soul therein to be entertained, which is lodged there, as a guest with its host, that it may live there for awhile. Life consisteth in blood; blood is the seat of the soul; therefore the chiefest work of the microcosm is, to be making blood continually.

At this forge are exercised all the members of the body; none is exempted from labour, each operates apart, and doth its proper office. And such is their hierarchy, that perpetually the one borrows from the other, the one lends the other, and the one is the other's debtor. The stuff and matter convenient, which nature giveth to be turned into blood, is bread and wine. All kind of nourishing victuals is understood to be comprehended in those two, and from hence in the Gothish tongue is called *companage*. To find out this meat and drink, to prepare and boil it, the hands are put to work, the feet do walk and bear up the whole bulk of the corporal mass; the eyes guide and conduct all; the appetite in the orifice of the stomach, by means of a little sourish black humour, called melancholy, which is transmitted thereto from the milt, giveth warning to shut in the food. The tongue doth make the first essay, and tastes it; the teeth do chaw it, and the stomach doth receive, digest, and chilify it. The mesaraic veins suck out of it what is good and fit, leaving behind the excrements, which are, through special conduits, for that purpose, voided by an expulsive faculty. Thereafter it is carried to the liver, where it being changed again, it by the virtue of that new transmutation becomes blood. What joy, conjecture you, will then be found amongst those officers, when they see this rivulet of gold, which is their sole restorative?

Rabelais, *Gargantua and Pantagruel*, III, 4

28 The eternity of things is connected with the reciprocal interchange of generation and decay; and as the sun, now in the east and then in the west, completes the measure of time by his ceaseless rev-

olutions, so are the fleeting things of mortal existence made eternal through incessant change, and kinds and species are perpetuated though individuals die.

William Harvey, *Animal Generation,* 14

29 Nature does nothing in vain, nor works in any round-about way when a shorter path lies open to her, that an egg can be produced in no other manner than that in which we now see it engendered, *viz.,* by the concurring act of the cock and hen. Neither, in like manner, in the present constitution of things, can a cock or hen ever be produced otherwise than from an egg. Thus the cock and the hen exist for the sake of the egg, and the egg, in the same way, is their antecedent cause; it were therefore reasonable to ask, with Plutarch, which of these was the prior, the egg or the fowl? Now the fowl is prior by nature, but the egg is prior in time; for that which is the more excellent is naturally first; but that from which a certain thing is produced must be reputed first in respect of time. Or we may say: this egg is older than that fowl (the fowl having been produced from it); and, on the contrary, this fowl existed before that egg (which she has laid). And this is the round that makes the race of the common fowl eternal; now pullet, now egg, the series is continued in perpetuity; from frail and perishing individuals an immortal species is engendered.

William Harvey, *Animal Generation,* 28

30 If there were machines which bore a resemblance to our body and imitated our actions as far as it was morally possible to do so, we should always have two very certain tests by which to recognise that, for all that, they were not real men. The first is, that they could never use speech or other signs as we do when placing our thoughts on record for the benefit of others. For we can easily understand a machine's being constituted so that it can utter words, and even emit some responses to action on it of a corporeal kind, which brings about a change in its organs; for instance, if it is touched in a particular part it may ask what we wish to say to it; if in another part it may exclaim that it is being hurt, and so on. But it never happens that it arranges its speech in various ways, in order to reply appropriately to everything that may be said in its presence, as even the lowest type of man can do. And the second difference is, that although machines can perform certain things as well as or perhaps better than any of us can do, they infallibly fall short in others, by the which means we may discover that they did not act from knowledge, but only from the disposition of their organs. For while reason is a universal instrument which can serve for all contingencies, these organs have need of some special adaptation for every particular action. From this it follows that it is morally impossible that there should be sufficient

diversity in any machine to allow it to act in all the events of life in the same way as our reason causes us to act.

Descartes, *Discourse on Method,* V

31 Life is a pure flame, and we live by an invisible sun within us.

Sir Thomas Browne, *Urn-Burial,* V

32 The arithmetical machine produces effects which approach nearer to thought than all the actions of animals. But it does nothing which would enable us to attribute will to it, as to the animals.

Pascal, *Pensées,* VI, 340

33 If an animal did by mind what it does by instinct, and if it spoke by mind what it speaks by instinct, in hunting and in warning its mates that the prey is found or lost, it would indeed also speak in regard to those things which affect it closer, as example, "Gnaw me this cord which is wounding me, and which I cannot reach."

Pascal, *Pensées,* VI, 342

34 The effects of reason increase continually whereas instinct always remains in the same state. Beehives were as well laid out a thousand years ago as today, and each bee forms that hexagon as exactly the first time as the last. It is the same with everything animals make by that hidden motion. Nature teaches them in response to the pressure of necessity; but this frail knowledge dies with its need: as they receive it without study, they do not have the happiness of preserving it; and every time they are given it, they find it new, because nature, whose object is merely to maintain animals in an order of limited perfection, infuses in them this necessary knowledge, always the same, lest they perish, and does not allow them to add to it lest they go beyond the boundaries prescribed to them.

Pascal, *Preface to the Treatise on the Vacuum*

35 *Raphael.* The Sixt, and of Creation last arose
With Eevning Harps and Mattin, when God said,
Let th' Earth bring forth Fowle living in her kinde,
Cattel and Creeping things, and Beast of the Earth,
Each in thir kinde. The Earth obey'd, and strait
Op'ning her fertil Woomb teem'd at a Birth
Innumerous living Creatures, perfet formes,
Limb'd and full grown: out of the ground up rose
As from his Laire the wilde Beast where he wonns
In Forrest wilde, in Thicket, Brake, or Den;
Among the Trees in Pairs they rose, they walk'd:
The Cattel in the Fields and Meddowes green:
Those rare and solitarie, these in flocks
Pasturing at once, and in broad Herds upsprung.
The grassie Clods now Calv'd, now half appeer'd
The Tawnie Lion, pawing to get free

His hinder parts, then springs as broke from
   Bonds,
And Rampant shakes his Brinded main; the
   Ounce,
The Libbard, and the Tyger, as the Moale
Rising, the crumbl'd Earth above them threw
In Hillocks; the swift Stag from under ground
Bore up his branching head: scarse from his
   mould
Behemoth biggest born of Earth upheav'd
His vastness: Fleec't the Flocks and bleating rose,
As Plants: ambiguous between Sea and Land
The River Horse and scalie Crocodile.
At once came forth whatever creeps the ground,
Insect or Worme; those wav'd thir limber fans
For wings, and smallest Lineaments exact
In all the Liveries dect of Summers pride
With spots of Gold and Purple, azure and green:
These as a line thir long dimension drew,
Streaking the ground with sinuous trace; not all
Minims of Nature; some of Serpent kinde
Wondrous in length and corpulence involv'd
Thir Snakie foulds, and added wings. First crept
The Parsimonious Emmet, provident
Of future, in small room large heart enclos'd,
Pattern of just equalitie perhaps
Hereafter, join'd in her popular Tribes
Of Commonaltie: swarming next appeer'd
The Femal Bee that feeds her Husband Drone
Deliciously, and builds her waxen Cells
With Honey stor'd: the rest are numberless,
And thou thir Natures know'st, and gav'st them
   Names,
Needless to thee repeated; nor unknown
The Serpent suttl'st Beast of all the field,
Of huge extent somtimes, with brazen Eyes
And hairie Main terrific, though to thee
Not noxious, but obedient at thy call.
Now Heav'n in all her Glorie shon, and rowld
Her motions, as the great first-Movers hand
First wheeld thir course; Earth in her rich attire
Consummate lovly smil'd; Aire, Water, Earth,
By Fowl, Fish, Beast, was flown, was swum, was
   walkt
Frequent; and of the Sixt day yet remain'd;
There wanted yet the Master work, the end
Of all yet don; a Creature who not prone
And Brute as other Creatures, but endu'd
With Sanctitie of Reason, might erect
His Stature, and upright with Front serene
Govern the rest, self-knowing, and from thence
Magnanimous to correspond with Heav'n,
But grateful to acknowledge whence his good
Descends, thither with heart and voice and eyes
Directed in Devotion, to adore
And worship God Supream, who made him chief
Of all his works.

> Milton, *Paradise Lost*, VII, 449

36 We must . . . consider wherein an oak differs
from a mass of matter, and that seems to me to be
in this, that the one is only the cohesion of particles of matter any how united, the other such a
disposition of them as constitutes the parts of an
oak; and such an organization of those parts as is
fit to receive and distribute nourishment, so as to
continue and frame the wood, bark, and leaves,
etc., of an oak, in which consists the vegetable
life. That being then one plant which has such an
organization of parts in one coherent body, partaking of one common life, it continues to be the
same plant as long as it partakes of the same life,
though that life be communicated to new particles
of matter vitally united to the living plant, in a
like continued organization conformable to that
sort of plants. For this organization, being at any
one instant in any one collection of matter, is in
that particular concrete distinguished from all
other, and *is* that individual life, which existing
constantly from that moment both forwards and
backwards, in the same continuity of insensibly
succeeding parts united to the living body of the
plant, it has that identity which makes the same
plant, and all the parts of it, parts of the same
plant, during all the time that they exist united in
that continued organization, which is fit to convey
that common life to all the parts so united.

The case is not so much different in *brutes* but
that any one may hence see what makes an animal and continues it the same. Something we
have like this in machines, and may serve to illustrate it. For example, what is a watch? It is plain
it is nothing but a fit organization or construction
of parts to a certain end, which, when a sufficient
force is added to it, it is capable to attain. If we
would suppose this machine one continued body,
all whose organized parts were repaired, increased, or diminished by a constant addition or
separation of insensible parts, with one common
life, we should have something very much like the
body of an animal; with this difference, That, in
an animal the fitness of the organization, and the
motion wherein life consists, begin together, the
motion coming from within; but in machines the
force coming sensibly from without, is often away
when the organ is in order, and well fitted to receive it.

> Locke, *Concerning Human Understanding*,
> Bk. II, XXVII, 4–5

37 That there should be more species of intelligent
creatures above us, than there are of sensible and
material below us, is probable to me from hence:
that in all the visible corporeal world, we see no
chasms or gaps. All quite down from us the descent is by easy steps, and a continued series of
things, that in each remove differ very little one
from the other. There are fishes that have wings,
and are not strangers to the airy region: and there
are some birds that are inhabitants of the water,
whose blood is cold as fishes, and their flesh so like
in taste that the scrupulous are allowed them on

fish-days. There are animals so near of kin both to birds and beasts that they are in the middle between both: amphibious animals link the terrestrial and aquatic together; seals live at land and sea, and porpoises have the warm blood and entrails of a hog; not to mention what is confidently reported of mermaids, or sea-men. There are some brutes that seem to have as much knowledge and reason as some that are called men: and the animal and vegetable kingdoms are so nearly joined, that, if you will take the lowest of one and the highest of the other, there will scarce be perceived any great difference between them: and so on, till we come to the lowest and the most inorganical parts of matter, we shall find everywhere that the several species are linked together, and differ but in almost insensible degrees.

Locke, *Concerning Human Understanding*, Bk. III, VI, 12

38 Any one almost would take it for an affront to be asked what he meant by it [life]. And yet if it comes in question, whether a plant that lies ready formed in the seed have life; whether the embryo in an egg before incubation, or a man in a swoon without sense or motion, be alive or no; it is easy to perceive that a clear, distinct, settled idea does not always accompany the use of so known a word as that of life is.

Locke, *Concerning Human Understanding*, Bk. III, X, 22

39 In a watch, one part is the instrument by which the movement of the others is effected, but one wheel is not the efficient cause of the production of the other. One part is certainly present for the sake of another, but it does not owe its presence to the agency of that other. For this reason, also, the producing cause of the watch and its form is not contained in the nature of this material, but lies outside the watch in a being that can act according to ideas of a whole which its causality makes possible. Hence one wheel in the watch does not produce the other, and, still less, does one watch produce other watches, by utilizing, or organizing, foreign material; hence it does not of itself replace parts of which it has been deprived, nor, if these are absent in the original construction, does it make good the deficiency by the subvention of the rest; nor does it, so to speak, repair its own casual disorders. But these are all things which we are justified in expecting from organized nature. An organized being is, therefore, not a mere machine. For a machine has solely *motive power,* whereas an organized being possesses inherent *formative* power, and such, moreover, as it can impart to material devoid of it—material which it organizes. This, therefore, is a self-propagating formative power, which cannot be explained by the capacity of movement alone, that is to say, by mechanism.

Kant, *Critique of Teleological Judgement,* 65

40 The resurrection of a spiritual body from a natural body does not appear in itself a more wonderful instance of power than the germination of a blade of wheat from the grain, or of an oak from an acorn. Could we conceive an intelligent being so placed as to be conversant only with inanimate or full-grown objects, and never to have witnessed the process of vegetation or growth; and were another being to show him two little pieces of matter, a grain of wheat and an acorn, to desire him to examine them, to analyze them if he pleased, and endeavor to find out their properties and essences; and then to tell him, that however trifling these little bits of matter might appear to him, that they possessed such curious powers of selection, combination, arrangement, and almost of creation that upon being put into the ground they would choose, among all the dirt and moisture that surrounded them, those parts which best suited their purpose, that they would collect and arrange these parts with wonderful taste, judgment, and execution, and would rise up into beautiful forms, scarcely in any respect analogous to the little bits of matter which were first placed in the earth. I feel very little doubt that the imaginary being which I have supposed would hesitate more, would require better authority and stronger proofs, before he believed these strange assertions than if he had been told that a being of mighty power, who had been the cause of all that he saw around him and of that existence of which he himself was conscious, would, by a great act of power upon the death and corruption of human creatures, raise up the essence of thought in an incorporeal, or at least invisible, form to give it a happier existence in another state.

Malthus, *Population,* XII

41 *Wagner.* It flashes, see! Now truly we may hold
That if from substances a hundredfold,
Through mixture—for on mixture all depends—
Man's substance gently be consolidated,
In an alembic sealed and segregated,
And properly be cohobated,
In quiet and success the labour ends.
    Turning toward the furnace again.
'Twill be! The mass is working clearer,
Conviction gathers, truer, nearer.
What men as Nature's mysteries would hold,
All that to test by reason we make bold,
And what she once was wont to organize,
That we bid now to crystallize.
    Mephistopheles. Whoever lives long learns full
        many things;
By naught in this world can he ever be surprised.
I've seen already in my wanderings
Many a mortal who was crystallized.
    Wag. [*hitherto constantly attentive to the phial*]
It rises, flashes, gathers on;
A moment, and the deed is done.
A great design at first seems mad; but we

Henceforth will laugh at chance in procreation,
And such a brain that is to think transcendently
Will be a thinker's own creation.
Looking at the phial rapturously.
The glass resounds with lovely might;
It dims, it clears; life *must* begin to be.
A dainty figure greets my sight;
A pretty manikin I see.
What more do we or does the world want now?
The mystery's within our reach.
Come, hearken to this sound, and listen how
It turns to voice, it turns to speech.
Homunculus [*in the phial, to* Wagner]
Well, Daddy! how are you? It was no jest.
Come, press me tenderly upon your breast,
But not too hard, for fear the glass might
    shatter.
That is the property of matter:
For what is natural the All has place;
What's artificial needs restricted space.
                    Goethe, *Faust,* II, 2, 6848

42 Life is the one universal soul, which, by virtue of
the enlivening BREATH, and the informing WORD,
all organized bodies have in common, each *after its
kind.*

                    Coleridge, *Aids to Reflection*

43 The One remains, the many change and pass;
Heaven's light forever shines, Earth's shadows fly;
Life, like a dome of many-colored glass,
Stains the white radiance of Eternity,
Until Death tramples it to fragments.
                    Shelley, *Adonais,* LII

44 Was it that this old carpenter had been a lifelong
wanderer, whose much rolling to and fro not only
had gathered no moss, but what is more, had rubbed off whatever small outward clingings might
have originally pertained to him? He was a stripped abstract; an unfractioned integral; uncom-
promised as a new-born babe; living without
premeditated reference to this world or the next.
You might almost say, that this strange uncom-
promisedness in him involved a sort of unintelli-
gence; for in his numerous trades, he did not seem
to work so much by reason or by instinct, or simply because he had been tutored to it, or by any
intermixture of all these, even or uneven; but
merely by a kind of deaf and dumb, spontaneous
literal process. He was a pure manipulator; his
brain, if he had ever had one, must have early
oozed along into the muscles of his fingers. He was
like one of those unreasoning but still highly useful *multum in parvo,* Sheffield contrivances, assuming the exterior—though a little swelled—of a
common pocket-knife; but containing, not only
blades of various sizes, but also screw-drivers,
corkscrews, tweezers, awls, pens, rulers, nail-filers,
counter-sinkers. So, if his superiors wanted to use
the carpenter for a screw-driver, all they had to do

was to open that part of him, and the screw was
fast: or if for tweezers, take him up by the legs,
and there they were.

Yet, as previously hinted, this omni-tooled,
open-and-shut carpenter, was, after all, no mere
machine of an automaton. If he did not have a
common soul in him, he had a subtle something
that somehow anomalously did its duty. What
that was, whether essence of quicksilver, or a few
drops of hartshorn, there is no telling. But there it
was; and there it had abided for now some sixty
years or more. And this it was, this same unaccountable, cunning life-principle in him; this it
was, that kept him a great part of the time solilo-
quising; but only like an unreasoning wheel,
which also hummingly soliloquises; or rather, his
body was a sentry-box and this soliloquiser on
guard there, and talking all the time to keep himself awake.

                    Melville, *Moby Dick,* CVII

45 There is no exception to the rule that every organic being naturally increases at so high a rate, that,
if not destroyed, the earth would soon be covered
by the progeny of a single pair. Even slow-breed-
ing man has doubled in twenty-five years, and at
this rate, in less than a thousand years, there
would literally not be standing-room for his progeny.

                    Darwin, *Origin of Species,* III

46 It is good . . . to try in imagination to give to any
one species an advantage over another. Probably
in no single instance should we know what to do.
This ought to convince us of our ignorance on the
mutual relations of all organic beings; a conviction as necessary as it is difficult to acquire. All
that we can do, is to keep steadily in mind that
each organic being is striving to increase in a geometrical ratio; that each at some period of its life,
during some season of the year, during each generation or at intervals, has to struggle for life and
to suffer great destruction. When we reflect on
this struggle, we may console ourselves with the
full belief, that the war of nature is not incessant,
that no fear is felt, that death is generally prompt,
and that the vigorous, the healthy, and the happy
survive and multiply.

                    Darwin, *Origin of Species,* III

47 The affinities of all the beings of the same class
have sometimes been represented by a great tree.
I believe this simile largely speaks the truth. The
green and budding twigs may represent existing
species; and those produced during former years
may represent the long succession of extinct species. At each period of growth all the growing
twigs have tried to branch out on all sides, and to
overtop and kill the surrounding twigs and
branches, in the same manner as species and
groups of species have at all times overmastered

other species in the great battle for life. The limbs divided into great branches, and these into lesser and lesser branches, were themselves once, when the tree was young, budding twigs, and this connection of the former and present buds by ramifying branches may well represent the classification of all extinct and living species in groups subordinate to groups. Of the many twigs which flourished when the tree was a mere bush, only two or three, now grown into great branches, yet survive and bear the other branches; so with the species which lived during long-past geological periods very few have left living and modified descendants. From the first growth of the tree, many a limb and branch has decayed and dropped off; and these fallen branches of various sizes may represent those whole orders, families, and genera which have now no living representatives, and which are known to us only in a fossil state. As we here and there see a thin straggling branch springing from a fork low down in a tree, and which by some chance has been favoured and is still alive on its summit, so we occasionally see an animal like the Ornithorhynchus or Lepidosiren, which in some small degree connects by its affinities two large branches of life, and which has apparently been saved from fatal competition by having inhabited a protected station. As buds give rise by growth to fresh buds, and these, if vigorous, branch out and overtop on all sides many a feebler branch, so by generation I believe it has been with the great Tree of Life, which fills with its dead and broken branches the crust of the earth, and covers the surface with its everbranching and beautiful ramifications.

Darwin, *Origin of Species*, IV

48 Authors of the highest eminence seem to be fully satisfied with the view that each species has been independently created. To my mind it accords better with what we know of the laws impressed on matter by the Creator, that the production and extinction of the past and present inhabitants of the world should have been due to secondary causes, like those determining the birth and death of the individual. When I view all beings not as special creations, but as the lineal descendants of some few beings which lived long before the first bed of the Cambrian system was deposited, they seem to me to become ennobled. Judging from the past, we may safely infer that not one living species will transmit its unaltered likeness to a distant futurity. And of the species now living very few will transmit progeny of any kind to a far distant futurity; for the manner in which all organic beings are grouped, shows that the greater number of species in each genus, and all the species in many genera, have left no descendants, but have become utterly extinct. We can so far take a prophetic glance into futurity as to foretell that it will be the common and widely-spread species,

belonging to the larger and dominant groups within each class, which will ultimately prevail and procreate new and dominant species. As all the living forms of life are the lineal descendants of those which lived long before the Cambrian epoch, we may feel certain that the ordinary succession by generation has never once been broken, and that no cataclysm has desolated the whole world. Hence we may look with some confidence to a secure future of great length. And as natural selection works solely by and for the good of each being, all corporeal and mental endowments will tend to progress towards perfection.

It is interesting to contemplate a tangled bank, clothed with many plants of many kinds, with birds singing on the bushes, with various insects flitting about, and with worms crawling through the damp earth, and to reflect that these elaborately constructed forms, so different from each other, and dependent upon each other in so complex a manner, have all been produced by laws acting around us. These laws, taken in the largest sense, being Growth with Reproduction; Inheritance which is almost implied by reproduction; Variability from the indirect and direct action of the conditions of life and from use and disuse: a Ratio of Increase so high as to lead to a Struggle for Life, and as a consequence to Natural Selection, entailing Divergence of Character and the Extinction of less-improved forms. Thus, from the war of nature, from famine and death, the most exalted object which we are capable of conceiving, namely, the production of the higher animals, directly follows. There is grandeur in this view of life, with its several powers, having been originally breathed by the Creator into a few forms or into one; and that, whilst this planet has gone cycling on according to the fixed law of gravity, from so simple a beginning endless forms most beautiful and most wonderful have been, and are being evolved.

Darwin, *Origin of Species*, XV

49 We have given to man a pedigree of prodigious length, but not, it may be said, of noble quality. The world, it has often been remarked, appears as if it had long been preparing for the advent of man: and this, in one sense is strictly true, for he owes his birth to a long line of progenitors. If any single link in this chain had never existed, man would not have been exactly what he now is. Unless we wilfully close our eyes, we may, with our present knowledge, approximately recognise our parentage; nor need we feel ashamed of it. The most humble organism is something much higher than the inorganic dust under our feet; and no one with an unbiased mind can study any living creature, however humble, without being struck with enthusiasm at its marvellous structure and properties.

Darwin, *Descent of Man*, I, 6

50 I propose . . . to prove that the science of vital phenomena must have the same foundations as the science of the phenomena of inorganic bodies, and that there is no difference in this respect between the principles of biological science and those of physico-chemical science. Indeed, as we have already said, the goal which the experimental method sets itself is everywhere the same; it consists in connecting natural phenomena with their necessary conditions or with their immediate causes. In biology, since these conditions are known, physiologists can guide the manifestation of vital phenomena as physicists guide the natural phenomena, the laws of which they have discovered; but in doing so, experimenters do not act on life.

Yet there is absolute determinism in all the sciences, because every phenomenon being necessarily linked with physico-chemical conditions, men of science can alter them to master the phenomenon, i.e., to prevent or to promote its appearing. As to this, there is absolutely no question in the case of inorganic bodies. I mean to prove that it is the same with living bodies, and that for them also determinism exists.

Claude Bernard, *Experimental Medicine*, II, 1

51 A living organism is nothing but a wonderful machine endowed with the most marvellous properties and set going by means of the most complex and delicate mechanism. There are no forces opposed and struggling one with another; in nature there can be only order and disorder, harmony or discord.

Claude Bernard, *Experimental Medicine*, II, 1

52 The organism is merely a living machine so constructed that, on the one hand, the outer environment is in free communication with the inner organic environment, and, on the other hand, the organic units have protective functions, to place in reserve the materials of life and uninterruptedly to maintain the humidity, warmth and other conditions essential to vital activity. Sickness and death are merely a dislocation or disturbance of the mechanism which regulates the contact of vital stimulants with organic units.

Claude Bernard, *Experimental Medicine*, II, 1

53 Life is creation. In fact, a created organism is a machine which necessarily works by virtue of the physico-chemical properties of its constituent elements. To-day we differentiate three kinds of properties exhibited in the phenomena of living beings: physical properties, chemical properties and vital properties. But the term "vital properties" is itself only provisional; because we call properties vital which we have not yet been able to reduce to physico-chemical terms; but in that we shall doubtless succeed some day.

Claude Bernard, *Experimental Medicine*, II, 2

54 If some iron filings be sprinkled on a table and a magnet brought near them, they will fly through the air for a certain distance and stick to its surface. A savage seeing the phenomenon explains it as the result of an attraction or love between the magnet and the filings. But let a card cover the poles of the magnet, and the filings will press forever against its surface without its ever occurring to them to pass around its sides and thus come into more direct contact with the object of their love. Blow bubbles through a tube into the bottom of a pail of water, they will rise to the surface and mingle with the air. Their action may again be poetically interpreted as due to a longing to recombine with the mother-atmosphere above the surface. But if you invert a jar full of water over the pail, they will rise and remain lodged beneath its bottom, shut in from the outer air, although a slight deflection from their course at the outset, or a re-descent towards the rim of the jar when they found their upward course impeded, would easily have set them free.

If now we pass from such actions as these to those of living things, we notice a striking difference. Romeo wants Juliet as the filings want the magnet; and if no obstacles intervene he moves towards her by as straight a line as they. But Romeo and Juliet, if a wall be built between them, do not remain idiotically pressing their faces against its opposite sides like the magnet and the filings with the card. Romeo soon finds a circuitous way, by scaling the wall or otherwise, of touching Juliet's lips directly. With the filings the path is fixed; whether it reaches the end depends on accidents. With the lover it is the end which is fixed, the path may be modified indefinitely.

William James, *Psychology*, I

55 In a general theory of evolution the inorganic comes first, then the lowest forms of animal and vegetable life, then forms of life that possess mentality, and finally those like ourselves that possess it in a high degree. As long as we keep to the consideration of purely outward facts, even the most complicated facts of biology, our task as evolutionists is comparatively easy. We are dealing all the time with matter and its aggregations and separations; and although our treatment must perforce be hypothetical, this does not prevent it from being *continuous*. The point which as evolutionists we are bound to hold fast to is that all the new forms of being that make their appearance are really nothing more than results of the redistribution of the original and unchanging materials. The self-same atoms which, chaotically dispersed, made the nebula, now, jammed and temporarily caught in peculiar positions, form our brains; and the "evolution" of the brains, if understood, would be simply the account of how the atoms came to be so caught and jammed. In this story no new *natures*, no factors not present at

the beginning, are introduced at any later stage.

But with the dawn of consciousness an entirely new nature seems to slip in, something whereof the potency was *not* given in the mere outward atoms of the original chaos.

William James, *Psychology,* VI

56 Is each thing born fitted to particular other things, and to them exclusively, as locks are fitted to their keys? Undoubtedly this must be believed to be so. Each nook and cranny of creation, down to our very skin and entrails, has its living inhabitants, with organs suited to the place, to devour and digest the food it harbors and to meet the dangers it conceals; and the minuteness of adaptation thus shown in the way of *structure* knows no bounds. Even so are there no bounds to the minuteness of adaptation in the way of *conduct* which the several inhabitants display.

William James, *Psychology,* XXIV

57 If . . . all organic instincts are conservative, historically acquired, and are directed towards regression, towards reinstatement of something earlier, we are obliged to place all the results of organic development to the credit of external, disturbing, and distracting influences. The rudimentary creature would from its very beginning not have wanted to change, would, if circumstances had remained the same, have always merely repeated the same course of existence. But in the last resort it must have been the evolution of our earth, and its relation to the sun, that has left its imprint on the development of organisms. The conservative organic instincts have absorbed every one of these enforced alterations in the course of life and have stored them for repetition; they thus present the delusive appearance of forces striving after change and progress, while they are merely endeavouring to reach an old goal by ways both old and new. This final goal of all organic striving can be stated too. It would be counter to the conservative nature of instinct if the goal of life were a state never hitherto reached. It must rather be an ancient starting point, which the living being left long ago, and to which it harks back again by all the circuitous paths of development. If we may assume as an experience admitting of no exception that everything living dies from causes within itself, and returns to the inorganic, we can only say *"The goal of all life is death,"* and, casting back, *"The inanimate was there before the animate."*

Freud, *Beyond the Pleasure Principle,* V

58 At one time or another, by some operation of force which still completely baffles conjecture, the properties of life were awakened in lifeless matter. Perhaps the process was a prototype resembling that other one which later in a certain stratum of living matter gave rise to consciousness. The tension then aroused in the previously inanimate matter strove to attain an equilibrium; the first instinct was present, that to return to lifelessness. The living substance at that time had death within easy reach; there was probably only a short course of life to run, the direction of which was determined by the chemical structure of the young organism. So through a long period of time the living substance may have been constantly created anew, and easily extinguished, until decisive external influences altered in such a way as to compel the still surviving substance to ever greater deviations from the original path of life, and to ever more complicated and circuitous routes to the attainment of the goal of death. These circuitous ways to death, faithfully retained by the conservative instincts, would be neither more nor less than the phenomena of life as we now know it. If the exclusively conservative nature of the instincts is accepted as true, it is impossible to arrive at any other suppositions with regard to the origin and goal of life.

If these conclusions sound strangely in our ears, equally so will those we are led to make concerning the great groups of instincts which we regard as lying behind the vital phenomena of organisms. The postulate of the self-preservative instincts we ascribe to every living being stands in remarkable contrast to the supposition that the whole life of instinct serves the one end of bringing about death. The theoretic significance of the instincts of self-preservation, power, and self-assertion, shrinks to nothing, seen in this light; they are part-instincts designed to secure the path to death peculiar to the organism and to ward off possibilities of return to the inorganic other than the immanent ones, but the enigmatic struggle of the organism to maintain itself in spite of all the world, a struggle that cannot be brought into connection with anything else, disappears. It remains to be added that the organism is resolved to die only in its own way; even these watchmen of life were originally the myrmidons of death. Hence, the paradox comes about that the living organism resists with all its energy influences (dangers) which could help it to reach its life-goal by a short way (a short circuit, so to speak); but this is just the behaviour that characterizes a pure instinct as contrasted with an intelligent striving.

Freud, *Beyond the Pleasure Principle,* V

59 Are we to follow the clue of the poet-philosopher [Plato] and make the daring assumption that living substance was at the time of its animation rent into small particles, which since that time strive for reunion by means of the sexual instincts? That these instincts—in which the chemical affinity of inanimate matter is continued—passing through the realm of the protozoa gradually overcome all hindrances set to their striving by an environment charged with stimuli dangerous to life, and are impelled by it to form a protecting covering layer?

And that these dispersed fragments of living substance thus achieve a multicellular organization, and finally transfer to the germ-cells in a highly concentrated form the instinct for reunion? I think this is the point at which to break off.

Freud, *Beyond the Pleasure Principle*, VI

60 All life, animal and vegetable, seems in its essence like an effort to accumulate energy and then to let it flow into flexible channels, changeable in shape, at the end of which it will accomplish infinitely varied kinds of work. That is what the *vital impetus*, passing through matter, would fain do all at once. It would succeed, no doubt, if its power were unlimited, or if some reinforcement could come to it from without. But the impetus is finite, and it has been given once for all. It cannot overcome all obstacles. The movement it starts is sometimes turned aside, sometimes divided, always opposed; and the evolution of the organized world is the unrolling of this conflict.

Bergson, *Creative Evolution*, III

61 If our analysis is correct, it is consciousness, or rather supra-consciousness, that is at the origin of life. Consciousness, or supra-consciousness, is the name for the rocket whose extinguished fragments fall back as matter; consciousness, again, is the name for that which subsists of the rocket itself, passing through the fragments and lighting them up into organisms. But this consciousness, which is a *need of creation*, is made manifest to itself only where creation is possible. It lies dormant when life is condemned to automatism; it wakens as soon as the possibility of a choice is restored.

Bergson, *Creative Evolution*, III

62 From our [man's] point of view, life appears in its entirety as an immense wave which, starting from a center, spreads outwards, and which on almost the whole of its circumference is stopped and converted into oscillation: at one single point the obstacle has been forced, the impulsion has passed freely. It is this freedom that the human form registers. Everywhere but in man, consciousness has had to come to a stand; in man alone it has kept on its way. Man, then, continues the vital movement indefinitely, although he does not draw along with him all that life carries in itself. On other lines of evolution there have traveled other tendencies which life implied, and of which, since everything interpenetrates, man has, doubtless, kept something, but of which he has kept only

very little. *It is as if a vague and formless being, whom we may call, as we will,* man *or* superman, *had sought to realize himself, and had succeeded only by abandoning a part of himself on the way.* The losses are represented by the rest of the animal world, and even by the vegetable world, at least in what these have that is positive and above the accidents of evolution.

Bergson, *Creative Evolution*, III

63 As the smallest grain of dust is bound up with our entire solar system, drawn along with it in that undivided movement of descent which is materiality itself, so all organized beings, from the humblest to the highest, from the first origins of life to the time in which we are, and in all places as in all times, do but evidence a single impulsion, the inverse of the movement of matter, and in itself indivisible. All the living hold together, and all yield to the same tremendous push. The animal takes its stand on the plant, man bestrides animality, and the whole of humanity, in space and in time, is one immense army galloping beside and before and behind each of us in an overwhelming charge able to beat down every resistance and clear the most formidable obstacles, perhaps even death.

Bergson, *Creative Evolution*, III

64 And life? Life itself? Was it perhaps only an infection, a sickening of matter? Was that which one might call the original procreation of matter only a disease, a growth produced by morbid stimulation of the immaterial? The first step toward evil, toward desire and death, was taken precisely then, when there took place that first increase in the density of the spiritual, that pathologically luxuriant morbid growth, produced by the irritant of some unknown infiltration; this, in part pleasurable, in part a motion of self-defence, was the primeval stage of matter, the transition from the insubstantial to the substance. This was the Fall. The second creation, the birth of the organic out of the inorganic, was only another fatal stage in the progress of the corporeal toward consciousness, just as disease in the organism was an intoxication, a heightening and unlicensed accentuation of its physical state; and life, life was nothing but the next step on the reckless path of the spirit dishonoured; nothing but the automatic blush of matter roused to sensation and become receptive for that which awaked it.

Mann, *Magic Mountain*, V

19.3 | *Cause*

Other sections of this book treat cause in other contexts: Section 5.7 in the context of discussions of free will; Section 6.7 in the context of discussions of demonstration; Section 15.3 in the context of discussions of fate and destiny; and Section 17.2 in the context of discussions of scientific method. Here the discussion concentrates on the principle of causality and on the analysis of causation.

The passages quoted raise and explore such basic questions as whether everything that happens has a cause of its occurrence or a sufficient reason for happening; whether the chain of causation leads back to some first uncaused cause; whether everything that comes into existence and passes away needs a cause of being as well as of becoming, a cause that preserves it in being as long as its existence endures; and whether the operation of causes necessitates the production of their effects or allows some room for chance and contingency.

The reader will find Aristotle's famous classification of the four causes—the formal, the material, the efficient, and the final cause—together with the modern rejection of final causes by such writers as Bacon, Descartes, and Spinoza. The reader will find passages in which God is conceived as the first efficient cause and creator of nature, as the prime mover or ultimate final cause of motion or change, and as the only uncaused or self-caused being. The reader will also find a denial by Hume, not of causation itself, but of our ability to know causes and how they operate.

---

1 They have sown the wind, and they shall reap the whirlwind.

Hosea 8:7

2 *Timaeus.* Everything that becomes or is created must of necessity be created by some cause, for without a cause nothing can be created.

Plato, *Timaeus,* 28A

3 We think we have scientific knowledge when we know the cause, and there are four causes: (1) the definable form, (2) an antecedent which necessitates a consequent, (3) the efficient cause, (4) the final cause. Hence each of these can be the middle term of a proof.

Aristotle, *Posterior Analytics,* 94ᵃ20

4 Knowledge is the object of our inquiry, and men do not think they know a thing till they have grasped the 'why' of it (which is to grasp its primary cause). So clearly we too must do this as regards both coming to be and passing away and every kind of physical change, in order that, knowing their principles, we may try to refer to these principles each of our problems.

In one sense, then, (1) that out of which a thing comes to be and which persists, is called 'cause', e.g. the bronze of the statue, the silver of the bowl, and the genera of which the bronze and the silver are species.

In another sense (2) the form or the archetype, i.e. the statement of the essence, and its genera, are called 'causes' (e.g. of the octave the relation of 2: 1, and generally number), and the parts in the definition.

Again (3) the primary source of the change or coming to rest; e.g. the man who gave advice is a cause, the father is cause of the child, and generally what makes of what is made and what causes change of what is changed.

Again (4) in the sense of end or 'that for the sake of which' a thing is done, e.g. health is the cause of walking about. ('Why is he walking about?' we say. 'To be healthy', and, having said that, we think we have assigned the cause.) The same is true also of all the intermediate steps which are brought about through the action of something else as means towards the end, e.g. reduction of flesh, purging, drugs, or surgical instruments are means towards health. All these things are 'for the sake of' the end, though they differ from one another in that some are activities, others instruments.

Aristotle, *Physics,* 194ᵇ17

5 The causes concerned in the generation of the works of nature are, as we see, more than one. There is the final cause and there is the motor cause. Now we must decide which of these two causes comes first, which second. Plainly, however, that cause is the first which we call the final one. For this is the Reason, and the Reason forms the starting-point, alike in the works of art and in works of nature.

Aristotle, *Parts of Animals,* 639ᵇ12

6 The same thing may have all the kinds of causes, e.g. the moving cause of a house is the art of the builder, the final cause is the function it fulfils, the matter is earth and stones, and the form is the definition.

Aristotle, *Metaphysics,* 996ᵇ5

7 Every action must be due to one or other of seven causes: chance, nature, compulsion, habit, reasoning, anger, or appetite.

Aristotle, *Rhetoric,* 1369ᵃ5

8 There are things . . . for which it is not sufficient to assign one cause; you must give several, one of which at the same time is the real cause. For instance should you see the lifeless body of a man lying at some distance, it would be natural to mention all the different causes of death, in order that the one real cause of that man's death be mentioned among them. Thus you may be able to prove that he has not died by steel or cold or from disease or haply from poison; yet we know that it is something of this kind which has befallen him.

Lucretius, *Nature of Things,* VI

9 In what will all this ostentation end?
The lab'ring mountain scarce brings forth a mouse.

Horace, *Ars Poetica*

10 By their fruits ye shall know them.

Matthew 7:20

11 Whatsoever a man soweth, that shall he also reap.

Galatians 6:7

12 How great a matter a little fire kindleth!

James 3:5

13 It is His occult power which pervades all things, and is present in all without being contaminated, which gives being to all that is, and modifies and limits its existence; so that without Him it would not be thus, or thus, nor would have any being at all. If, then, in regard to that outward form which the workman's hand imposes on his work, we do not say that Rome and Alexandria were built by masons and architects, but by the kings by whose will, plan, and resources they were built, so that the one has Romulus, the other Alexander, for its

founder; with how much greater reason ought we to say that God alone is the Author of all natures, since He neither uses for His work any material which was not made by Him, nor any workmen who were not also made by Him, and since, if He were, so to speak, to withdraw from created things His creative power, they would straightway relapse into the nothingness in which they were before they were created?

Augustine, *City of God,* XII, 25

14 In the world of sense we find there is an order of efficient causes. There is no case known (nor indeed, is it possible) in which a thing is found to be the efficient cause of itself, because in that case it would be prior to itself, which is impossible.

Aquinas, *Summa Theologica,* I, 2, 3

15 In efficient causes it is impossible to proceed to infinity *per se*—thus, there cannot be an infinite number of causes that are *per se* required for a certain effect; for instance, that a stone be moved by a stick, the stick by the hand, and so on to infinity. But it is not impossible to proceed to infinity accidentally as regards efficient causes; for instance, if all the causes thus infinitely multiplied should have the order of only one cause, their multiplication being accidental; as an artificer acts by means of many hammers accidentally, because one after the other is broken. It is accidental, therefore, that one particular hammer acts after the action of another, and likewise it is accidental to this particular man as generator to be generated by another man; for he generates as a man, and not as the son of another man. For all men generating hold one grade in efficient causes—namely, the grade of a particular generator. Hence it is not impossible for a man to be generated by man to infinity; but such a thing would be impossible if the generation of this man depended upon this man, and on an elementary body, and on the sun, and so on to infinity.

Aquinas, *Summa Theologica,* I, 46, 2

16 It must be borne in mind that the higher the cause, the more numerous the objects to which its causation extends. Now the underlying principle in things is always more universal than that which informs and restricts it; thus, being is more universal than living, living than understanding, matter than form. The more widely, then, one thing underlies others, the more directly does that thing proceed from a higher cause. Thus the thing that underlies primarily all things belongs properly to the causality of the supreme cause. Therefore no secondary cause can produce anything, unless there is presupposed in the thing produced something that is caused by a higher cause. But creation is the production of a thing in its entire substance, nothing being presupposed, either uncreated or created. Hence it remains that noth-

ing can create except God alone, Who is the first cause.

Aquinas, *Summa Theologica,* I, 65, 3

17 Every effect depends on its cause, so far as it is its cause. But we must observe that an agent is the cause of the becoming of its effect, but not directly of its being. This may be seen both in artificial and in natural things. For the builder causes the house in its becoming, but he is not the direct cause of its being. For it is clear that the being of the house is a result of its form, which consists in the putting together and arrangement of the materials, and results from the natural qualities of certain things. . . . The same principle applies to natural things. For if an agent is not the cause of a form as such, neither will it be directly the cause of being which results from that form, but it will be the cause of the effect in its becoming only.

Aquinas, *Summa Theologica,* I, 104, 1

18 Thence it [the living Light] descendeth to the remotest potencies, down, from act to act, becoming such as maketh now mere brief contingencies;

by which contingencies I understand the generated things which are produced from seed, or seedless, by the moving heaven.

The wax of these, and that which mouldeth it, standeth not in one mode, and therefore, 'neath the ideal stamp, is more and less transparent;

whence cometh, that one same tree in kind better and worse doth fruit; and ye are born with diverse genius.

Were the wax exactly moulded, and were the heaven in its supremest virtue, the light of the signet would be all apparent;

but nature ever furnisheth it faulty, doing as doth the artist who hath the knack of the art and a trembling hand.

Dante, *Paradiso,* XIII, 61

19 The Devil begat darkness; darkness begat ignorance; ignorance begat error and his brethren; error begat free-will and presumption; free-will begat merit; merit begat forgetfulness of God; forgetfulness begat transgression; transgression begat superstition; superstition begat satisfaction; satisfaction begat the mass-offering; the mass-offering begat the priest; the priest begat unbelief; unbelief begat king hypocrisy; hypocrisy begat traffic in offerings for gain; traffic in offerings for gain begat Purgatory; Purgatory begat the annual solemn vigils; the annual vigils begat church-livings; church-livings begat avarice; avarice begat swelling superfluity; swelling superfluity begat fulness; fulness begat rage; rage begat licence; licence begat empire and domination; domination begat pomp; pomp begat ambition; ambition begat simony; simony begat the pope

and his brethren, about the time of the Babylonish captivity.

Luther, *Table Talk,* H500

20 As we divided natural philosophy in general into the inquiry of causes, and productions of effects: so that part which concerneth the inquiry of causes we do subdivide according to the received and sound division of causes. The one part, which is physic, inquireth and handleth the material and efficient causes; and the other, which is metaphysic, handleth the formal and final causes.

Bacon, *Advancement of Learning,* Bk. II, VII, 3

21 The handling of final causes, mixed with the rest in physical inquiries, hath intercepted the severe and diligent inquiry of all real and physical causes, and given men the occasion to stay upon these satisfactory and specious causes, to the great arrest and prejudice of further discovery.

Bacon, *Advancement of Learning,* Bk. II, VII, 7

22 It is rightly laid down that true knowledge is that which is deduced from causes. The division of four causes also is not amiss: matter, form, the efficient, and end or final cause. Of these, however, the latter is so far from being beneficial, that it even corrupts the sciences, except in the intercourse of man with man. The discovery of form is considered desperate. As for the efficient cause and matter (according to the present system of inquiry and the received opinions concerning them, by which they are placed remote from, and without any latent process towards form), they are but desultory and superficial, and of scarcely any avail to real and active knowledge.

Bacon, *Novum Organum,* II, 2

23 The knowledge of a single fact acquired through a discovery of its causes prepares the mind to understand and ascertain other facts without need of recourse to experiment.

Galileo, *Two New Sciences,* IV

24 To one who pays attention to God's immensity, it is clear that nothing at all can exist which does not depend on Him. This is true not only of everything that subsists, but of all order, of every law, and of every reason of truth and goodness. . . . It is useless to inquire how God could from all eternity bring it about that it should be untrue that twice four is eight, etc.; for I admit that that cannot be understood by us. Yet, since on the other hand I correctly understand that nothing in any category of causation can exist which does not depend upon God, and that it would have been easy for Him so to appoint that we human beings should not understand how these very things could be otherwise than they are, it would be irrational to doubt concerning that which we correctly understand, because of that which we do not understand and perceive no need to understand.

Hence neither should we think *that eternal truths depend upon the human understanding or on other existing things;* they must depend on God alone, who, as the supreme legislator, ordained them from all eternity.

Descartes, *Objections and Replies,* VI

25 Ignorance of remote causes disposeth men to attribute all events to the causes immediate and instrumental: for these are all the causes they perceive.

Hobbes, *Leviathan,* I, 11

26 Since everything . . . is cause and effect, dependent and supporting, mediate and immediate, and all is held together by a natural though imperceptible chain which binds together things most distant and most different, I hold it equally impossible to know the parts without knowing the whole and to know the whole without knowing the parts in detail.

Pascal, *Pensées,* II, 72

27 The least movement affects all nature; the entire sea changes because of a rock.

Pascal, *Pensées,* VII, 505

28 By *cause* of itself, I understand that whose essence involves existence, or that whose nature cannot be conceived unless existing.

Spinoza, *Ethics,* I, Def. 1

29 From a given determinate cause an effect necessarily follows; and, on the other hand, if no determinate cause be given, it is impossible that an effect can follow.

The knowledge of an effect depends upon and involves the knowledge of the cause.

Those things which have nothing mutually in common with one another cannot through one another be mutually understood, that is to say, the conception of the one does not involve the conception of the other.

Spinoza, *Ethics,* I, Axioms 3–5

30 Man is born ignorant of the causes of things and . . . he has a desire, of which he is conscious, to seek that which is profitable to him. From this it follows, firstly, that he thinks himself free because he is conscious of his wishes and appetites, whilst at the same time he is ignorant of the causes by which he is led to wish and desire, not dreaming what they are; and, secondly, it follows that man does everything for an end, namely, for that which is profitable to him, which is what he seeks. Hence it happens that he attempts to discover merely the final causes of that which has happened; and when he has heard them he is satisfied, because there is no longer any cause for further uncertainty. But if he cannot hear from another what these final causes are, nothing re-

mains but to turn to himself and reflect upon the ends which usually determine him to the like actions, and thus by his own mind he necessarily judges that of another. Moreover, since he discovers, both within and without himself, a multitude of means which contribute not a little to the attainment of what is profitable to himself—for example, the eyes, which are useful for seeing, the teeth for mastication, plants and animals for nourishment, the sun for giving light, the sea for feeding fish, etc.—it comes to pass that all natural objects are considered as means for obtaining what is profitable. These too being evidently discovered and not created by man, hence he has a cause for believing that some other person exists, who has prepared them for man's use. For having considered them as means it was impossible to believe that they had created themselves, and so he was obliged to infer from the means which he was in the habit of providing for himself that some ruler or rulers of nature exist, endowed with human liberty, who have taken care of all things for him, and have made all things for his use. Since he never heard anything about the mind of these rulers, he was compelled to judge of it from his own, and hence he affirmed that the gods direct everything for his advantage, in order that he may be bound to them and hold them in the highest honour. This is the reason why each man has devised for himself, out of his own brain, a different mode of worshipping God, so that God might love him above others, and direct all nature to the service of his blind cupidity and insatiable avarice.

Thus has this prejudice been turned into a superstition and has driven deep roots into the mind—a prejudice which was the reason why every one has so eagerly tried to discover and explain the final causes of things. The attempt, however, to show that nature does nothing in vain (that is to say, nothing which is not profitable to man), seems to end in showing that nature, the gods, and man are alike mad.

Spinoza, *Ethics,* I, Appendix

31 The main business of natural philosophy is to argue from phenomena without feigning hypotheses, and to deduce causes from effects, till we come to the very first cause, which certainly is not mechanical; and not only to unfold the mechanism of the world, but chiefly to resolve these and such like questions. What is there in places almost empty of matter, and whence is it that the Sun and planets gravitate towards one another, without dense matter between them? Whence is it that Nature doth nothing in vain; and whence arises all that order and beauty which we see in the world? To what end are comets, and whence is it that planets move all one and the same way in orbs concentric, while comets move all manner of ways in orbs very eccentric; and what hinders the

fixed stars from falling upon one another? How came the bodies of animals to be contrived with so much art, and for what ends were their several parts? Was the eye contrived without skill in Optics, and the ear without knowledge of sounds? How do the motions of the body follow from the will, and whence is the instinct in animals? Is not the sensory of animals that place to which the sensitive substance is present, and into which the sensible species of things are carried through the nerves and brain, that there they may be perceived by their immediate presence to that substance? And these things being rightly dispatched, does it not appear from phenomena that there is a Being incorporeal, living, intelligent, omnipresent, who in infinite space (as it were in his sensory) sees the things themselves intimately, and thoroughly perceives them, and comprehends them wholly by their immediate presence to himself? Of which things the images only carried through the organs of sense into our little sensoriums are there seen and beheld by that which in us perceives and thinks. And though every true step made in this philosophy brings us not immediately to the knowledge of the First Cause, yet it brings us nearer to it, and on that account is to be highly valued.

Newton, *Optics*, III, 1

32 Souls act according to the laws of final causes through appetitions, ends, and means. Bodies act according to the laws of efficient causes or motions. And the two realms, that of efficient causes and that of final causes, are in harmony with one another.

Leibniz, *Monadology*, 79

33 We must rise [from physics] to metaphysics, making use of the great principle, usually little employed, which affirms that nothing takes place without sufficient reason; that is to say, that nothing happens without its being possible for one who should know things sufficiently, to give a reason which is sufficient to determine why things are so and not otherwise.

Leibniz, *Principles of Nature and of Grace*, 7

34 As to the opinion that there are no Corporeal Causes, this has been heretofore maintained by some of the Schoolmen, as it is of late by others among the modern philosophers, who though they allow Matter to exist, yet will have God alone to be the immediate efficient cause of all things. These men saw that amongst all the objects of sense there was none which had any power or activity included in it; and that by consequence this was likewise true of whatever bodies they supposed to exist without the mind, like unto the immediate objects of sense. But then, that they should suppose an innumerable multitude of created beings, which they acknowledge are not capable of producing any one effect in nature, and which therefore are made to no manner of purpose, since God might have done everything as well without them: this I say, though we should allow it possible, must yet be a very unaccountable and extravagant supposition.

Berkeley, *Principles of Human Knowledge*, 53

35 The connexion of ideas does not imply the relation of *cause* and *effect*, but only of a mark or *sign* with the thing *signified*. The fire which I see is not the cause of the pain I suffer upon my approaching it, but the mark that forewarns me of it. In like manner the noise that I hear is not the effect of this or that motion or collision of the ambient bodies, but the sign thereof.

Berkeley, *Principles of Human Knowledge*, 65

36 Every effect is a distinct event from its cause. It could not, therefore, be discovered in the cause, and the first invention or conception of it, *a priori*, must be entirely arbitrary. And even after it is suggested, the conjunction of it with the cause must appear equally arbitrary; since there are always many other effects, which, to reason, must seem fully as consistent and natural. In vain, therefore, should we pretend to determine any single event, or infer any cause or effect, without the assistance of observation and experience.

Hume, *Concerning Human Understanding*, IV, 25

37 If there be any suspicion that the course of nature may change, and that the past may be no rule for the future, all experience becomes useless, and can give rise to no inference or conclusion. It is impossible, therefore, that any arguments from experience can prove this resemblance of the past to the future; since all these arguments are founded on the supposition of that resemblance.

Hume, *Concerning Human Understanding*, IV, 32

38 Here . . . is a kind of pre-established harmony between the course of nature and the succession of our ideas; and though the powers and forces, by which the former is governed, be wholly unknown to us; yet our thoughts and conceptions have still, we find, gone on in the same train with the other works of nature. Custom is that principle, by which this correspondence has been effected; so necessary to the subsistence of our species, and the regulation of our conduct, in every circumstance and occurrence of human life. Had not the presence of an object, instantly excited the idea of those objects, commonly conjoined with it, all our knowledge must have been limited to the narrow sphere of our memory and senses; and we should never have been able to adjust means to ends, or employ our natural powers, either to the producing of good, or avoiding of evil. Those, who de-

light in the discovery and contemplation of *final causes,* have here ample subject to employ their wonder and admiration.

Hume, *Concerning Human Understanding,* V, 44

39 When we infer any particular cause from an effect, we must proportion the one to the other, and can never be allowed to ascribe to the cause any qualities, but what are exactly sufficient to produce the effect. A body of ten ounces raised in any scale may serve as a proof, that the counterbalancing weight exceeds ten ounces; but can never afford a reason that it exceeds a hundred. If the cause, assigned for any effect, be not sufficient to produce it, we must either reject that cause, or add to it such qualities as will give it a just proportion to the effect. But if we ascribe to it farther qualities, or affirm it capable of producing other effects, we can only indulge the licence of conjecture, and arbitrarily suppose the existence of qualities and energies, without reason or authority.

Hume, *Concerning Human Understanding,* XI, 105

40 If a clock is not made to tell the hour, I will then admit that final causes are chimeras; and I shall consider it quite right for people to call me *"cause-finalier,"* that is—an imbecile.

All the pieces of the machine of this world seem, however, made for each other. A few philosophers affect to mock at the final causes rejected by Epicurus and Lucretius. It is, it seems to me, at Epicurus and Lucretius rather that they should mock. They tell you that the eye is not made for seeing, but that man has availed himself of it for this purpose when he perceived that eyes could be so used. According to them, the mouth is not made for speaking, for eating, the stomach for digesting, the heart for receiving the blood from the veins and for dispatching it through the arteries, the feet for walking, the ears for hearing. These persons avow nevertheless that tailors make them coats to clothe them, and masons houses to lodge them, and they dare deny to nature, to the great Being, to the universal Intelligence, what they accord to the least of their workmen.

Voltaire, *Philosophical Dictionary:* Final Causes

41 It is only because we subject the sequence of phenomena, and consequently all change, to the law of causality, that experience itself, that is, empirical cognition of phenomena, becomes possible; and consequently, that phenomena themselves, as objects of experience, are possible only by virtue of this law.

Kant, *Critique of Pure Reason,* Transcendental Analytic

42 Organisms are . . . the only beings in nature that,

considered in their separate existence and apart from any relation to other things, cannot be thought possible except as ends of nature. It is they, then, that first afford objective reality to the conception of an *end* that is an end of *nature* and not a practical end. Thus they supply natural science with the basis for a teleology, or, in other words, a mode of estimating its objects on a special principle that it would otherwise be absolutely unjustifiable to introduce into that science— seeing that we are quite unable to perceive *a priori* the possibility of such a kind of causality.

Kant, *Critique of Teleological Judgement,* 65

43 Primary causes are unknown to us, but are subject to simple and constant laws, which may be discovered by observation, the study of them being the object of natural philosophy.

Fourier, *Analytical Theory of Heat,* Preliminary Discourse

44 The necessary is a category entirely by itself. Nothing ever comes into existence with necessity; likewise the necessary never comes into existence and something by coming into existence never becomes the necessary. Nothing whatever exists because it is necessary, but the necessary exists because it is necessary or because the necessary is. The actual is no more necessary than the possible, for the necessary is absolutely different from both. . . .

The change involved in coming into existence is actuality; the transition takes place with freedom. No coming into existence is necessary. It was not necessary before the coming into existence, for then there could not have been the coming into existence, nor after the coming into existence, for then there would not have been the coming into existence.

All coming into existence takes place with freedom, not by necessity. Nothing comes into existence by virtue of a logical ground, but only by a cause. Every cause terminates in a freely effecting cause. The illusion occasioned by the intervening causes is that the coming into existence seems to be necessary; the truth about intervening causes is that just as they themselves have come into existence they point back ultimately to a freely effecting cause. Even the possibility of deducing consequences from a law of nature gives no evidence for the necessity of any coming into existence, which is clear as soon as one reflects definitively on coming into existence. The same is the case with manifestations of freedom, provided we do not let ourselves be deceived by the manifestations of freedom but reflect upon the coming into existence.

Kierkegaard, *Philosophical Fragments,* Interlude

45 Cause and effect, means and ends, seed and fruit,

cannot be severed; for the effect already blooms in the cause, the end preexists in the means, the fruit in the seed.

Emerson, *Compensation*

46 The truth that every fact which has a beginning has a cause, is co-extensive with human experience.

Mill, *System of Logic*, Bk. III, V, 1

47 The state of the whole universe at any instant we believe to be the consequence of its state at the previous instant; insomuch that one who knew all the agents which exist at the present moment, their collocation in space, and all their properties, in other words, the laws of their agency, could predict the whole subsequent history of the universe, at least unless some new volition of a power capable of controlling the universe should supervene. And if any particular state of the entire universe could ever recur a second time, all subsequent states would return too, and history would, like a circulating decimal of many figures, periodically repeat itself.

Mill, *System of Logic*, Bk. III, V, 8

48 First causes are outside the realm of science; they forever escape us in the sciences of living as well as in those of inorganic bodies.

Claude Bernard, *Experimental Medicine*, II, 1

49 When an apple has ripened and falls, why does it fall? Because of its attraction to the earth, because its stalk withers, because it is dried by the sun, because it grows heavier, because the wind shakes it, or because the boy standing below wants to eat it? Nothing is the cause. All this is only the coincidence of conditions in which all vital organic and elemental events occur.

Tolstoy, *War and Peace*, IX, 1

50 As in the night all cats are gray, so in the darkness of metaphysical criticism all causes are obscure.

William James, *Psychology*, V

51 We have no definite idea of what we mean by cause, or of what causality consists in. But the principle expresses a demand for *some* deeper sort of inward connection between phenomena than their merely habitual time-sequence seems to us to

be. The word "cause" is, in short, an altar to an unknown god; an empty pedestal still marking the place of a hoped-for statue. *Any* really inward belonging-together of the sequent terms, if discovered, would be accepted as what the word cause was meant to stand for. So we seek, and seek; and in the molecular systems we find a sort of inward belonging in the notion of identity of matter with change of collocation. Perhaps by still seeking we may find other sorts of inward belonging, even between the molecules and those "secondary qualities," etc., which they produce upon our minds.

William James, *Psychology*, XXVIII

52 All philosophers, of every school, imagine that causation is one of the fundamental axioms or postulates of science, yet, oddly enough, in advanced sciences such as gravitational astronomy, the word 'cause' never occurs. . . . To me it seems that philosophy ought not to assume such legislative functions, and that the reason why physics has ceased to look for causes is that, in fact, there are no such things. The law of causality, I believe, like much that passes muster among philosophers, is a relic of a bygone age, surviving, like the monarchy, only because it is erroneously supposed to do no harm.

Russell, *On the Notion of Cause*

53 It is not in any sameness of causes and effects that the constancy of scientific law consists, but in sameness of relations. And even 'sameness of relations' is too simple a phrase; 'sameness of differential equations' is the only correct phrase. It is impossible to state this accurately in non-mathematical language; the nearest approach would be as follows: 'There is a constant relation between the state of the universe at any instant and the rate of change in the rate at which any part of the universe is changing at that instant, and this relation is many-one, i.e., such that the rate of change in the rate of change is determinate when the state of the universe is given.' If the 'law of causality' is to be something actually discoverable in the practice of science, the above proposition has a better right to the name than any 'law of causality' to be found in the books of philosophers.

Russell, *On the Notion of Cause*

19.4 | *Chance*

In its relation to cause, chance is essentially a negative concept. For some writers, as the quotations here reveal, that which happens by chance is that which happens without cause, such as the swerve of the atoms described by Lucretius; for other writers, it is that which, though it may somehow be caused, is not necessitated by its causes; for still others, it is an event the causes of which we do not know or cannot determine, even though such causes may exist and may even necessitate the occurrence of the event in question. In addition, there is the concept of chance that emerges in Aristotle's discussion of a coincidence, such as the accidental meeting of two persons at a place where neither expected or planned to see the other: each, according to Aristotle, was caused to go to that place by decisions, motives, or other influences operating causatively on his own behavior, but nothing caused these two lines of causation to intersect at the moment of their coincidence.

The historians, biographers, and poets are concerned with the role of chance in human affairs. On this subject, the reader is referred to relevant passages in Section 15.3 on FATE, FORTUNE, AND DESTINY. The philosophers and theologians are concerned with necessity and contingency in nature and with the difference between a world in which things occur by chance or by blind necessity and a world governed by an intelligent deity and ordered by a benevolent providence. Spinoza, Hume, Voltaire, Darwin, J. S. Mill, and Tolstoy all deny that anything happens by chance; this, according to Hume, is consistent with our not knowing the causes of events; to ascribe something to chance, Darwin points out, is merely to confess our ignorance of the causes.

Beginning with Pascal, among the authors quoted, the consideration of chance takes a new direction—the calculus and theory of probability, the most obvious application of which is to the games we call "games of chance." The reader will find this subject further explored in passages drawn from Laplace, Peirce, and Poincaré, and the reader will also be interested in Poincaré's contradiction of Darwin's remark that chance is nothing but a name for our ignorance of causes. With regard to probability itself, quotations from Locke and from Russell call attention to the distinction between subjective and objective probability—the one, an estimate of the reliability of our claim to know something, its credibility, or the likelihood that it is true; the other, a mathematical calculation of the betting odds on a particular future occurrence, such as making a certain number on the next roll of the dice or drawing a particular card from the pack.

---

1 I returned, and saw under the sun, that the race is not to the swift, nor the battle to the strong, neither yet bread to the wise, nor yet riches to men of understanding, nor yet favour to men of skill; but time and chance happeneth to them all.

Ecclesiastes 9:11

2 *Artabanus.* Chances rule men, and not men chances.

Herodotus, *History,* VII, 49

3 *Jocasta.* Why should man fear since chance is all in all
for him, and he can clearly foreknow nothing?
Best to live lightly, as one can, unthinkingly.

Sophocles, *Oedipus
the King,* 977

4 *Pericles.* Sometimes the course of things is as arbitrary as the plans of man; indeed this is why we usually blame chance for whatever does not hap-

pen as we expected.

Thucydides, *Peloponnesian War*, I, 140

5 *Crito.* But you see, Socrates, that the opinion of the many must be regarded, for what is now happening shows that they can do the greatest evil to any one who has lost their good opinion.

Socrates. I only wish it were so, Crito; and that the many could do the greatest evil; for then they would also be able to do the greatest good—and what a fine thing this would be! But in reality they can do neither; for they cannot make a man either wise or foolish; and whatever they do is the result of chance.

Plato, *Crito*, 44B

6 *Athenian Stranger.* I was going to say that man never legislates, but accidents of all sorts, which legislate for us in all sorts of ways. The violence of war and the hard necessity of poverty are constantly overturning governments and changing laws. And the power of disease has often caused innovations in the state, when there have been pestilences, or when there has been a succession of bad seasons continuing during many years. Any one who sees all this, naturally rushes to the conclusion of which I was speaking, that no mortal legislates in anything, but that in human affairs chance is almost everything. And this may be said of the arts of the sailor, and the pilot, and the physician, and the general, and may seem to be well said; and yet there is another thing which may be said with equal truth of all of them.

Cleinias. What is it?

Ath. That God governs all things, and that chance and opportunity co-operate with him in the government of human affairs. There is, however, a third and less extreme view, that art should be there also; for I should say that in a storm there must surely be a great advantage in having the aid of the pilot's art. You would agree?

Cle. Yes.

Plato, *Laws*, IV, 709A

7 Every result of chance is from what is spontaneous, but not everything that is from what is spontaneous is from chance.

Chance and what results from chance are appropriate to agents that are capable of good fortune and of moral action generally. Therefore necessarily chance is in the sphere of moral actions. This is indicated by the fact that good fortune is thought to be the same, or nearly the same, as happiness, and happiness to be a kind of moral action, since it is well-doing. Hence what is not capable of moral action cannot do anything by chance. Thus an inanimate thing or a lower animal or a child cannot do anything by chance, because it is incapable of deliberate intention; nor can 'good fortune' or 'ill fortune' be ascribed to

them, except metaphorically, as Protarchus, for example, said that the stones of which altars are made are fortunate because they are held in honour, while their fellows are trodden under foot.

Aristotle, *Physics*, 197ᵃ37

8 Chance has no place in that which is natural, and what happens everywhere and in every case is no matter of chance.

Aristotle, *On the Heavens*, 289ᵇ26

9 Things come into being either by art or by nature or by luck or by spontaneity. Now art is a principle of movement in something other than the thing moved, nature is a principle in the thing itself (for man begets man), and the other causes are privations of these two.

Aristotle, *Metaphysics*, 1070ᵃ6

10 When bodies are borne downwards sheer through void by their own weights, at quite uncertain times and uncertain spots they push themselves a little from their course: you just and only just can call it a change of inclination. If they were not used to swerve, they would all fall down, like drops of rain, through the deep void, and no clashing would have been begotten nor blow produced among the first-beginnings: thus nature never would have produced aught.

Lucretius, *Nature of Things*, II

11 That the mind itself does not feel an internal necessity in all its actions and is not as it were overmastered and compelled to bear and put up with this, is caused by a minute swerving of first-beginnings at no fixed part of space and no fixed time.

Lucretius, *Nature of Things*, II

12 *Moeris.* Chance sways all.

Virgil, *Eclogue IX*, 5

13 I suspend my judgment on the question whether it is fate and unchangeable necessity or chance which governs the revolutions of human affairs. Indeed, among the wisest of the ancients and among their disciples you will find conflicting theories, many holding the conviction that heaven does not concern itself with the beginning or the end of our life, or, in short, with mankind at all; and that therefore sorrows are continually the lot of the good, happiness of the wicked; while others, on the contrary, believe that, though there is a harmony between fate and events, yet it is not dependent on wandering stars, but on primary elements, and on a combination of natural causes. Still, they leave us the capacity of choosing our life, maintaining that, the choice once made, there is a fixed sequence of events. Good and evil, again, are not what vulgar opinion accounts them; many who seem to be struggling with ad-

versity are happy; many, amid great affluence, are utterly miserable, if only the first bear their hard lot with patience, and the latter make a foolish use of their prosperity.

Tacitus, *Annals,* VI, 22

14 Either there is a fatal necessity and invincible order, or a kind Providence, or a confusion without a purpose and without a director. If then there is an invincible necessity, why dost thou resist? But if there is a Providence which allows itself to be propitiated, make thyself worthy of the help of the divinity. But if there is a confusion without a governor, be content that in such a tempest thou hast in thyself a certain ruling intelligence. And even if the tempest carry thee away, let it carry away the poor flesh, the poor breath, everything else; for the intelligence at least it will not carry away.

Marcus Aurelius, *Meditations,* XII, 14

15 To make the existence and coherent structure of this universe depend upon automatic activity and upon chance is against all good sense. Such a notion could be entertained only where there is neither intelligence nor even ordinary perception; and reason enough has been urged against it, though none is really necessary.

Plotinus, *Third Ennead,* II, 1

16 There is a difference between universal and particular causes. A thing can escape the order of a particular cause, but not the order of a universal cause. For nothing escapes the order of a particular cause except through the intervention and hindrance of some other particular cause; as, for instance, wood may be prevented from burning by the action of water. Since, then, all particular causes are included under the universal cause, it could not be that any effect should take place outside the range of that universal cause. So far then as an effect escapes the order of a particular cause, it is said to be casual or fortuitous in respect to that cause; but if we regard the universal cause, outside whose range no effect can happen, it is said to be foreseen. Thus, for instance, the meeting of two servants, although to them it appears a chance circumstance, has been fully foreseen by their master, who has purposely sent them to meet at the one place, in such a way that the one knows not about the other.

Aquinas, *Summa Theologica,* I, 22, 2

17 Certain philosophers of old denied the government of the world, saying that all things happened by chance. But such an opinion can be shown to be impossible . . . by observation of things themselves. For we observe that in nature things happen always or nearly always for the best, which would not be the case unless some sort of providence directed nature towards good as an end, which is to govern. Therefore the unfailing

order we observe in things is a sign of their being governed.

Aquinas, *Summa Theologica,* I, 103, 1

18 It is written *I saw that under the sun the race is not to the swift, nor the battle to the strong, nor bread to the wise, nor riches to the learned, nor favour to the skilful, but time and chance in all.* But things subject to the Divine government are not ruled by chance. Therefore those things which are under the sun are not subject to the Divine government. . . . These things are said to be under the sun which are generated and corrupted according to the sun's movement. In all such things we find chance. Not that everything which occurs in such things is by chance, but that in each one there is an element of chance. And the very fact that an element of chance is found in those things proves that they are subject to government of some kind. For unless corruptible things of this kind were governed by a higher being, they would tend to nothing definite, especially those which possess no kind of knowledge. So nothing in them would happen unintentionally, which constitutes the nature of chance. Therefore to show how things happen by chance and yet according to the ordering of a higher cause, he does not say absolutely that he observes chance in all things, but *time and chance,* that is to say, that defects may be found in these things according to some order of time.

Aquinas, *Summa Theologica,* I, 103, 5

19 Every action of nature terminates in some one thing. Therefore it is impossible for that which is accidental to be the effect *per se* of an active natural principle. No natural cause can therefore have for its proper effect that a man intending to dig a grave finds a treasure. Now it is manifest that a heavenly body acts after the manner of a natural principle, and so its effects in this world are natural. It is therefore impossible that any active power of a heavenly body be the cause of what happens by accident here below, whether by luck or by chance.

Aquinas, *Summa Theologica,* I, 116, 1

20 To call out for the hand of the enemy is a rather extreme measure, yet a better one, I think, than to remain in continual fever over an accident that has no remedy. But since all the precautions that a man can take are full of uneasiness and uncertainty, it is better to prepare with fine assurance for the worst that can happen, and derive some consolation from the fact that we are not sure that it will happen.

Montaigne, *Essays,* I, 24, Various Outcomes

21 *King Richard.* A horse! a horse! my kingdom for a horse!
 Catesby. Withdraw, my lord; I'll help you to a horse.

K. Rich. Slave, I have set my life upon a cast
And I will stand the hazard of the die:
I think there be six Richmonds in the field;
Five have I slain to-day instead of him.
A horse! a horse! my kingdom for a horse!

       Shakespeare, *Richard III,* V, iv, 7

22 *Chatillon.* And all the unsettled humours of the
    land,
Rash, inconsiderate, fiery voluntaries,
With ladies' faces and fierce dragons' spleens,
Have sold their fortunes at their native homes,
Bearing their birthrights proudly on their backs,
To make a hazard of new fortunes here.

       Shakespeare, *King John,* II, i, 66

23 *Portia.* In terms of choice I am not solely led
By nice direction of a maiden's eyes;
Besides, the lottery of my destiny
Bars me the right of voluntary choosing:
But if my father had not scanted me
And hedged me by his wit, to yield myself
His wife who wins me by that means I told you,
Yourself, renowned Prince, then stood as fair
As any comer I have look'd on yet
For my affection.
    Prince of Morocco.   Even for that I thank you:
Therefore, I pray you, lead me to the caskets
To try my fortune. By this scimitar
That slew the Sophy and a Persian prince
That won three fields of Sultan Solyman,
I would outstare the sternest eyes that look,
Outbrave the heart most daring on the earth,
Pluck the young sucking cubs from the she-bear,
Yea, mock the lion when he roars for prey,
To win thee, lady. But, alas the while!
If Hercules and Lichas play at dice
Which is the better man, the greater throw
May turn by fortune from the weaker hand:
So is Alcides beaten by his page;
And so may I, blind fortune leading me,
Miss that which one unworthier may attain,
And die with grieving.
    Por.   You must take your chance,
And either not attempt to choose at all
Or swear before you choose, if you choose wrong
Never to speak to lady afterward
In way of marriage: therefore be advised.
    Mor. Nor will not. Come, bring me unto my
    chance.
    Por. First, forward to the temple: after dinner
Your hazard shall be made.
    Mor.   Good fortune then!
To make me blest or cursed'st among men.

       Shakespeare, *Merchant of Venice,* II, i, 13

24 *Nestor.*   In the reproof of chance
Lies the true proof of men.

       Shakespeare, *Troilus and Cressida,* I, iii, 33

25 *Florizel.*   As the unthought-on accident is guilty

To what we wildly do, so we profess
Ourselves to be the slaves of chance and flies
Of every wind that blows.

       Shakespeare, *Winter's Tale,* IV, iv, 548

26 Let us . . . say, "God is, or He is not." But to
which side shall we incline? Reason can decide
nothing here. There is an infinite chaos which
separated us. A game is being played at the extremity of this infinite distance where heads or
tails will turn up. What will you wager? According to reason, you can do neither the one thing
nor the other; according to reason, you can defend neither of the propositions.

Do not, then, reprove for error those who have
made a choice; for you know nothing about it.
"No, but I blame them for having made, not this
choice, but a choice; for again both he who chooses heads and he who chooses tails are equally at
fault, they are both in the wrong. The true course
is not to wager at all."

Yes; but you must wager. It is not optional. You
are embarked. Which will you choose then? Let
us see. Since you must choose, let us see which
interests you least. You have two things to lose,
the true and the good; and two things to stake,
your reason and your will, your knowledge and
your happiness; and your nature has two things to
shun, error and misery. Your reason is no more
shocked in choosing one rather than the other,
since you must of necessity choose. This is one
point settled. But your happiness? Let us weigh
the gain and the loss in wagering that God is. Let
us estimate these two chances. If you gain, you
gain all; if you lose, you lose nothing. Wager,
then, without hesitation that He is. "That is very
fine. Yes, I must wager; but I may perhaps wager
too much." Let us see. Since there is an equal risk
of gain and of loss, if you had only to gain two
lives, instead of one, you might still wager. But if
there were three lives to gain, you would have to
play (since you are under the necessity of playing), and you would be imprudent, when you are
forced to play, not to chance your life to gain
three at a game where there is an equal risk of loss
and gain. But there is an eternity of life and happiness. And this being so, if there were an infinity
of chances, of which one only would be for you,
you would still be right in wagering one to win
two, and you would act stupidly, being obliged to
play, by refusing to stake one life against three at
a game in which out of an infinity of chances
there is one for you, if there were an infinity of an
infinitely happy life to gain. But there is here an
infinity of an infinitely happy life to gain, a
chance of gain against a finite number of chances
of loss, and what you stake is finite. It is all divided; wherever the infinite is and there is not an
infinity of chances of loss against that of gain,
there is no time to hesitate, you must give all. And
thus, when one is forced to play, he must renounce

reason to preserve his life, rather than risk it for infinite gain, as likely to happen as the loss of nothingness.

For it is no use to say it is uncertain if we will gain, and it is certain that we risk, and that the infinite distance between the *certainty* of what is staked and the *uncertainty* of what will be gained, equals the finite good which is certainly staked against the uncertain infinite. It is not so, as every player stakes a certainty to gain an uncertainty, and yet he stakes a finite certainty to gain a finite uncertainty, without transgressing against reason. There is not an infinite distance between the certainty staked and the uncertainty of the gain; that is untrue. In truth, there is an infinity between the certainty of gain and the certainty of loss. But the uncertainty of the gain is proportioned to the certainty of the stake according to the proportion of the chances of gain and loss. Hence it comes that, if there are as many risks on one side as on the other, the course is to play even; and then the certainty of the stake is equal to the uncertainty of the gain, so far is it from fact that there is an infinite distance between them. And so our proposition is of infinite force, when there is the finite to stake in a game where there are equal risks of gain and of loss, and the infinite to gain. This is demonstrable; and if men are capable of any truths, this is one.

"I confess it, I admit it. But, still, is there no means of seeing the faces of the cards?" Yes, Scripture and the rest, etc. "Yes, but I have my hands tied and my mouth closed; I am forced to wager, and am not free. I am not released, and am so made that I cannot believe. What, then, would you have me do?"

True. But at least learn your inability to believe, since reason brings you to this, and yet you cannot believe. Endeavour, then, to convince yourself, not by increase of proofs of God, but by the abatement of your passions. You would like to attain faith and do not know the way; you would like to cure yourself of unbelief and ask the remedy for it. Learn of those who have been bound like you, and who now stake all their possessions. These are people who know the way which you would follow, and who are cured of an ill of which you would be cured. Follow the way by which they began; by acting as if they believed, taking the holy water, having masses said, etc. Even this will naturally make you believe, and deaden your acuteness. "But this is what I am afraid of." And why? What have you to lose?

But to show you that this leads you there, it is this which will lessen the passions, which are your stumbling-blocks. . . .

Now, what harm will befall you in taking this side? You will be faithful, honest, humble, grateful, generous, a sincere friend, truthful. Certainly you will not have those poisonous pleasures, glory and luxury; but will you not have others? I will tell you that you will thereby gain in this life, and that, at each step you take on this road, you will see so great certainty of gain, so much nothingness in what you risk, that you will at last recognise that you have wagered for something certain and infinite, for which you have given nothing.

"Ah! This discourse transports me, charms me," etc.

If this discourse pleases you and seems impressive, know that it is made by a man who has knelt, both before and after it, in prayer to that Being, infinite and without parts, before whom he lays all he has, for you also to lay before Him all you have for your own good and for His glory, that so strength may be given to lowliness.

Pascal, *Pensées*, III, 233

27 Whatever is, is in God; but God cannot be called a contingent thing, for He exists necessarily and not contingently. Moreover, the modes of the divine nature have followed from it necessarily and not contingently, and that, too, whether it be considered absolutely, or as determined to action in a certain manner. But God is the cause of these modes, not only insofar as they simply exist, but also insofar as they are considered as determined to any action. And if they are not determined by God, it is an impossibility and not a contingency that they should determine themselves; and, on the other hand, if they are determined by God, it is an impossibility and not a contingency that they should render themselves indeterminate. Wherefore all things are determined from a necessity of the divine nature, not only to exist, but to exist and act in a certain manner, and there is nothing contingent.

Spinoza, *Ethics,* I, Prop. 29, Demonst.

28 The highest probability amounts not to certainty, without which there can be no true knowledge.

Locke, *Concerning Human Understanding,* Bk. IV, III, 14

29 All Nature is but Art, unknown to thee;
All Chance, Direction, which thou canst not see;
All Discord, Harmony, not understood;
All partial Evil, universal Good:
And, spite of Pride, in erring Reason's spite,
One truth is clear, "Whatever is, is *Right.*"

Pope, *Essay on Man,* Epistle I, 289

30 Though there be no such thing as *Chance* in the world; our ignorance of the real cause of any event has the same influence on the understanding, and begets a like species of belief or opinion.

There is certainly a probability, which arises from a superiority of chances on any side; and according as this superiority encreases, and surpasses the opposite chances, the probability receives a proportionable encrease, and begets still a higher degree of belief or assent to that side, in which we discover the superiority. If a die were marked with one figure or number of spots on four sides, and with another figure or number of spots on the two remaining sides, it would be more probable, that the former would turn up than the latter; though, if it had a thousand sides marked in the same manner, and only one side different, the probability would be much higher, and our belief or expectation of the event more steady and secure. This process of the thought or reasoning may seem trivial and obvious; but to those who consider it more narrowly, it may, perhaps, afford matter for curious speculation.

It seems evident, that, when the mind looks forward to discover the event, which may result from the throw of such a die, it considers the turning up of each particular side as alike probable; and this is the very nature of chance, to render all the particular events, comprehended in it, entirely equal. But finding a greater number of sides concur in the one event than in the other, the mind is carried more frequently to that event, and meets it oftener, in revolving the various possibilities or chances, on which the ultimate result depends.

Hume, *Concerning Human Understanding*, VI, 46

31 It is universally allowed that nothing exists without a cause of its existence, and that chance, when strictly examined, is a mere negative word, and means not any real power which has anywhere a being in nature.

Hume, *Concerning Human Understanding*, VIII, 74

32 All effects follow not with like certainty from their supposed causes. Some events are found, in all countries and all ages, to have been constantly conjoined together: Others are found to have been more variable, and sometimes to disappoint our expectations; so that, in our reasonings concerning matter of fact, there are all imaginable degrees of assurance, from the highest certainty to the lowest species of moral evidence.

A wise man, therefore, proportions his belief to the evidence. In such conclusions as are founded on an infallible experience, he expects the event with the last degree of assurance, and regards his past experience as a full *proof* of the future existence of that event. In other cases, he proceeds with more caution: He weighs the opposite experiments: He considers which side is supported by the greater number of experiments: to that side he inclines, with doubt and hesitation; and when at last he fixes his judgement, the evidence exceeds not what we properly call *probability*. All probability, then, supposes an opposition of experiments and observations, where the one side is found to overbalance the other, and to produce a degree of evidence, proportioned to the superiority.

Hume, *Concerning Human Understanding*, X, 87

33 No more by the law of reason than by the law of nature can anything occur without a cause.

Rousseau, *Social Contract*, II, 4

34 Nothing was ever said with uncommon felicity but by the cooperation of chance; and therefore wit, as well as valor, must be content to share its honors with fortune.

Johnson, *Idler No. 58*

35 The explanation adopted by Epicurus . . . completely denies and abolishes the distinction between a technic of nature and its mere mechanism. Blind chance is accepted as the explanation, not alone of the agreement of the generated products with our conception, and, consequently, of the technic of nature, but even of the determination of the causes of this development on dynamical laws, and, consequently, of its mechanism. Hence nothing is explained, not even the illusion in our teleological judgements, so that the alleged idealism in them is left altogether unsubstantiated.

Kant, *Critique of Teleological Judgement*, 73

36 All events, even those which on account of their insignificance do not seem to follow the great laws of nature, are a result of it just as necessarily as the revolutions of the sun. In ignorance of the ties which unite such events to the entire system of the universe, they have been made to depend upon final causes or upon hazard, according as they occur and are repeated with regularity, or appear without regard to order; but these imaginary causes have gradually receded with the widening bounds of knowledge and disappear entirely before sound philosophy, which sees in them only the expression of our ignorance of the true causes.

Laplace, *Essay on Probabilities*, I

37 Consider that chance, which, with error, its brother, and folly, its aunt, and malice, its grandmother, rules in this world; which every year and every day, by blows great and small, embitters the life of every son of earth, and yours too.

Schopenhauer, *Wisdom of Life: Aphorisms*

38 Those who live in the midst of democratic fluctuations have always before their eyes the image of chance; and they end by liking all undertakings in which chance plays a part. They are therefore all led to engage in commerce, not only for the sake of the profit it holds out to them, but for the love of the constant excitement occasioned by that pursuit.

Tocqueville, *Democracy in America*, Vol. II, II, 19

39 When we look at the plants and bushes clothing an entangled bank, we are tempted to attribute their proportional numbers and kinds to what we call chance. But how false a view is this!

Darwin, *Origin of Species*, III

40 I have . . . sometimes spoken as if the variations—so common and multiform with organic beings under domestication, and in a lesser degree with those under nature—were due to chance. This, of course, is a wholly incorrect expression, but it serves to acknowledge plainly our ignorance of the cause of each particular variation.

Darwin, *Origin of Species*, V

41 I am aware that the conclusions arrived at in this work will be denounced by some as highly irreligious; but he who denounces them is bound to shew why it is more irreligious to explain the origin of man as a distinct species by descent from some lower form, through the laws of variation and natural selection, than to explain the birth of the individual through the laws of ordinary reproduction. The birth both of the species and of the individual are equally parts of that grand sequence of events, which our minds refuse to accept as the result of blind chance. The understanding revolts at such a conclusion, whether or not we are able to believe that every slight variation of structure,—the union of each pair in marriage,—the dissemination of each seed,—and other such events, have all been ordained for some special purpose.

Darwin, *Descent of Man*, III, 21

42 Chance is usually spoken of in direct antithesis to law; whatever (it is supposed) cannot be ascribed to any law is attributed to chance. It is, however, certain, that whatever happens is the result of some law; is an effect of causes, and could have been predicted from a knowledge of the existence of those causes, and from their laws. If I turn up a particular card, that is a consequence of its place in the pack. Its place in the pack was a consequence of the manner in which the cards were shuffled, or of the order in which they were played in the last game; which, again, were effects of prior causes. At every stage, if we had possessed an accurate knowledge of the causes in existence, it would have been abstractly possible to foretell the effect.

An event occurring by chance may be better described as a coincidence from which we have no ground to infer an uniformity: the occurrence of a phenomena, in certain circumstances, without our having reason on that account to infer that it will happen again in those circumstances. This, however, when looked closely into, implies that the enumeration of the circumstances is not complete. Whatever the fact be, since it has occurred once, we may be sure that if *all* the same circumstances

were repeated, it would occur again; and not only if all, but there is some particular portion of those circumstances on which the phenomenon is invariably consequent. With most of them, however, it is not connected in any permanent manner: its conjunction with those is said to be the effect of chance, to be merely casual. Facts casually conjoined are separately the effects of causes, and therefore of laws; but of different causes, and causes not connected by any law.

It is incorrect, then, to say that any phenomenon is produced by chance; but we may say that two or more phenomena are conjoined by chance, that they co-exist or succeed one another only by chance; meaning that they are in no way related through causation; that they are neither cause and effect, nor effects of the same cause, nor effects of causes between which there subsists any law of co-existence, nor even effects of the same collocation of primeval causes.

Mill, *System of Logic*, Bk. III, XVII, 2

43 If we assume as the historians do that great men lead humanity to the attainment of certain ends— the greatness of Russia or of France, the balance of power in Europe, the diffusion of the ideas of the Revolution, general progress, or anything else—then it is impossible to explain the facts of history without introducing the conceptions of *chance* and *genius*. . . .

Why did it happen in this and not in some other way? Because it happened so! *"Chance* created the situation; *genius* utilized it,"* says history.

But what is *chance?* What is *genius?* The words *chance* and *genius* do not denote any really existing thing and therefore cannot be defined. Those words only denote a certain stage of understanding of phenomena. I do not know why a certain event occurs; I think that I cannot know it; so I do not try to know it and I talk about *chance.* I see a force producing effects beyond the scope of ordinary human agencies; I do not understand why this occurs and I talk of *genius.* . . .

Only by renouncing our claim to discern a purpose immediately intelligible to us, and admitting the ultimate purpose to be beyond our ken, may we discern the sequence of experiences in the lives of historic characters and perceive the cause of the effect they produce (incommensurable with ordinary human capabilities), and then the words *chance* and *genius* become superfluous.

Tolstoy, *War and Peace*, I Epilogue, II

44 The inference from the premise, A, to the conclusion, B, depends, as we have seen, on the guiding principle that if a fact of the class A is true, a fact of the class B is true. The probability consists of the fraction whose numerator is the number of times in which both A and B are true, and whose denominator is the total number of times in which A is true, whether B is so or not. Instead of speak-

ing of this as the probability of the inference, there is not the slightest objection to calling it the probability that if A happens, B happens. But to speak of the probability of the event B, without naming the condition, really has no meaning at all. It is true that when it is perfectly obvious what condition is meant, the ellipsis may be permitted. But we should avoid contracting the habit of using language in this way (universal as the habit is), because it gives rise to a vague way of thinking, as if the action of causation might either determine an event to happen or determine it not to happen, or leave it more or less free to happen or not, so as to give rise to an *inherent* chance in regard to its occurrence. It is quite clear to me that some of the worst and most persistent errors in the use of the doctrine of chances have arisen from this vicious mode of expression.

C. S. Peirce, *The Red and the Black*

45 The idea of probability essentially belongs to a kind of inference which is repeated indefinitely. An individual inference must be either true or false, and can show no effect of probability; and, therefore, in reference to a single case considered in itself, probability can have no meaning. Yet if a man had to choose between drawing a card from a pack containing twenty-five red cards and a black one, or from a pack containing twenty-five black cards and a red one, and if the drawing of a red card were destined to transport him to eternal felicity, and that of a black one to consign him to everlasting woe, it would be folly to deny that he ought to prefer the pack containing the larger portion of red cards, although, from the nature of the risk, it could not be repeated. It is not easy to reconcile this with our analysis of the conception of chance. But suppose he should choose the red pack, and should draw the wrong card, what consolation would he have? He might say that he had acted in accordance with reason, but that would only show that his reason was absolutely worthless. And if he should choose the right card, how could he regard it as anything but a happy accident? He could not say that if he had drawn from the other pack, he might have drawn the wrong one, because a hypothetical proposition such as, "if A, then B," means nothing with reference to a single case. Truth consists in the existence of a real fact corresponding to the true proposition. Corresponding to the proposition, "if A, then B," there may be the fact that *whenever* such an event as A happens such an event as B happens. But in the case supposed, which has no parallel as far as this man is concerned, there would be no real fact whose existence could give any truth to the statement that, if he had drawn from the other pack, he might have drawn a black card.

C. S. Peirce, *The Red and the Black*

46 It is an indubitable result of the theory of proba-

bilities that every gambler, if he continues long enough, must ultimately be ruined.

C. S. Peirce, *The Red and the Black*

47 All human affairs rest upon probabilities, and the same thing is true everywhere. If man were immortal he could be perfectly sure of seeing the day when everything in which he had trusted should betray his trust, and, in short, of coming eventually to hopeless misery. He would break down, at last, as every good fortune, as every dynasty, as every civilization does. In place of this we have death.

But what, without death, would happen to every man, with death must happen to some man. At the same time, death makes the number of our risks, of our inferences, finite, and so makes their mean result uncertain. The very idea of probability and of reasoning rests on the assumption that this number is indefinitely great.

C. S. Peirce, *The Red and the Black*

48 No victor believes in chance.

Nietzsche, *Gay Science*, 258

49 You probably feel that when religious faith expresses itself . . . in the language of the gaming table, it is put to its last trumps. Surely Pascal's own personal belief in masses and holy water had far other springs; and this celebrated page of his is but an argument for others, a last desperate snatch at a weapon against the hardness of the unbelieving heart. We feel that a faith in masses and holy water adopted wilfully after such a mechanical calculation would lack the inner soul of faith's reality; and if we were ourselves in the place of the Deity, we should probably take particular pleasure in cutting off believers of this pattern from their infinite reward. It is evident that unless there be some pre-existing tendency to believe in masses and holy water, the option offered to the will by Pascal is not a living option. Certainly no Turk ever took to masses and holy water on its account; and even to us Protestants these means of salvation seem such foregone impossibilities that Pascal's logic, invoked for them specifically, leaves us unmoved. As well might the Mahdi write to us, saying, "I am the Expected One whom God has created in his effulgence. You shall be infinitely happy if you confess me; otherwise you shall be cut off from the light of the sun. Weigh, then, your infinite gain if I am genuine against your finite sacrifice if I am not!" His logic would be that of Pascal; but he would vainly use it on us, for the hypothesis he offers us is dead. No tendency to act on it exists in us to any degree.

William James, *Will to Believe*

50 It must well be that chance is something other than the name we give our ignorance, that among phenomena whose causes are unknown to us we

must distinguish fortuitous phenomena about which the calculus of probabilities will provisionally give information, from those which are not fortuitous and of which we can say nothing so long as we shall not have determined the laws governing them. For the fortuitous phenomena themselves, it is clear that the information given us by the calculus of probabilities will not cease to be true upon the day when these phenomena shall be better known.

The director of a life insurance company does not know when each of the insured will die, but he relies upon the calculus of probabilities and on the law of great numbers, and he is not deceived, since he distributes dividends to his stockholders. These dividends would not vanish if a very penetrating and very indiscrete physician should, after the policies were signed, reveal to the director the life chances of the insured. This doctor would dissipate the ignorance of the director, but he would have no influence on the dividends, which evidently are not an outcome of this ignorance.

Poincaré, *Science and Method*, I, 4

51 The greatest bit of chance is the birth of a great man. It is only by chance that meeting of two germinal cells, of different sex, containing precisely, each on its side, the mysterious elements whose mutual reaction must produce the genius. One will agree that these elements must be rare and that their meeting is still more rare. How slight a thing it would have required to deflect from its route the carrying spermatozoon. It would have sufficed to deflect it a tenth of a millimeter and Napoleon would not have been born and the destinies of a continent would have been changed. No example can better make us understand the veritable characteristics of chance.

Poincaré, *Science and Method*, I, 4

19.5 | *Motion and Change*

At the beginning of Western thought, two pre-Socratic philosophers, Heraclitus and Parmenides, went to the opposite extremes of asserting, on the one hand, that everything is always in flux and never for a moment remains unchanged, and, on the other, that permanence or immutability reigns everywhere and that our experience of motion or change is a deceptive illusion. While they are not quoted here, the views of Heraclitus and Parmenides are commented on by later thinkers who regard motion and rest, or change and permanence, as correlatives, neither of which can be understood without the other.

The philosophical consideration of motion and change attempts to discover its principles (that without which motion or change cannot occur); proposes a classification of the kinds of change, such as local motion, change of quality, or alteration, change in quantity, or increase and decrease, and what was called "substantial change," or coming to be and passing away; speculates about whether change or motion ever began and will ever stop or is everlasting, without beginning or end; and asks whether endless motion involves an unmoved mover as its cause.

The modern scientific study of motion—the motion of bodies from place to place—begins with Galileo, and introduces such distinctions as that between natural and violent motion, uniform and variable motion, and such concepts as velocity, acceleration, momentum, and inertia. Employing these concepts, the new sciences of kinematics and dynamics are applied by Newton to the motion of celestial as well as terrestrial bodies. In addition to formulating the principle of inertia as one of his three laws of motion, Newton introduces the concept of gravity, and the distinction between absolute and relative motion. The reader will be interested to find the existence of absolute motion challenged by Bishop Berkeley, for reasons that anticipate Einstein's views on the same subject.

---

1 Vanity of vanities, saith the Preacher, vanity of vanities; all is vanity.

What profit hath a man of all his labour which he taketh under the sun?

One generation passeth away, and another generation cometh: but the earth abideth for ever.

The sun also ariseth, and the sun goeth down, and hasteth to his place where he arose.

The wind goeth toward the south, and turneth about unto the north; it whirleth about continually, and the wind returneth again according to his circuits.

All the rivers run into the sea; yet the sea is not full; unto the place from whence the rivers come, thither they return again.

All things are full of labour; man cannot utter it: the eye is not satisfied with seeing, nor the ear filled with hearing.

The thing that hath been, it is that which shall be; and that which is done is that which shall be done: and there is no new thing under the sun.

Ecclesiastes 1:2–9

2 Can the Ethiopian change his skin, or the leopard his spots?

Jeremiah 13:23

3 *Socrates.* Many of our modern philosophers . . . in their search after the nature of things, are always getting dizzy from constantly going round and round, and then they imagine that the world is going round and round and moving in all directions; and this appearance, which arises out of their own internal condition, they suppose to be a reality of nature; they think that there is nothing stable or permanent, but only flux and motion, and that the world is always full of every sort of motion and change.

Plato, *Cratylus,* 411A

4 *Socrates.* Only the self-moving, never-leaving self, never ceases to move, and is the fountain and beginning of motion to all that moves besides. Now, the beginning is unbegotten, for that which is begotten has a beginning; but the beginning is begotten of nothing, for if it were begotten of something, then the begotten would not come from a beginning. But if unbegotten, it must also be indestructible; for if beginning were destroyed, there could be no beginning out of anything, nor anything out of a beginning; and all things must have a beginning. And therefore the self-moving is the beginning of motion; and this can neither be destroyed nor begotten, else the whole heavens and all creation would collapse and stand still, and never again have motion or birth.

Plato, *Phaedrus,* 245B

5 Nature has been defined as a 'principle of motion and change', and it is the subject of our inquiry. We must therefore see that we understand the meaning of 'motion'; for if it were unknown, the meaning of 'nature' too would be unknown. . . .

The fulfilment of what exists potentially, in so far as it exists potentially, is motion—namely, of what is alterable *qua* alterable, *alteration:* of what can be increased and its opposite what can be decreased (there is no common name), *increase* and *decrease:* of what can come to be and can pass away, *coming to be* and *passing away:* of what can be carried along, *locomotion.*

Aristotle, *Physics,* 200b11

6 We must understand that place would not have been thought of, if there had not been a special kind of motion, namely that with respect to place. It is chiefly for this reason that we suppose the heaven also to be in place, because it is in constant movement. Of this kind of change there are two species—locomotion on the one hand and, on the other, increase and diminution. For these too involve variation of place: what was then in this place has now in turn changed to what is larger or smaller.

Aristotle, *Physics,* 211a12

7 It is a law of nature that earth and all other bodies should remain in their proper places and be moved from them only by violence: from the fact then that some of them are in their proper places it follows that in respect of place also all things cannot be in motion. These and other similar arguments, then, should convince us that it is impossible either that all things are always in motion or that all things are always at rest.

Aristotle, *Physics,* 253b33

8 Since there must always be motion without intermission, there must necessarily be something, one thing or it may be a plurality, that first imparts motion, and this first movent must be unmoved. Now the question whether each of the things that are unmoved but impart motion is eternal is irrelevant to our present argument: but the following considerations will make it clear that there must necessarily be some such thing, which, while it has

the capacity of moving something else, is itself unmoved and exempt from all change, which can affect it neither in an unqualified nor in an accidental sense. Let us suppose, if any one likes, that in the case of certain things it is possible for them at different times to be and not to be, without any process of becoming and perishing (in fact it would seem to be necessary, if a thing that has not parts at one time is and at another time is not, that any such thing should without undergoing any process of change at one time be and at another time not be). And let us further suppose it possible that some principles that are unmoved but capable of imparting motion at one time are and at another time are not. Even so, this cannot be true of *all* such principles, since there must clearly be something that *causes* things that move themselves at one time to be and at another not to be. For, since nothing that has not parts can be in motion, that which moves itself must as a whole have magnitude, though nothing that we have said makes this necessarily true of every movent. So the fact that some things become and others perish, and that this is so continuously, cannot be caused by any one of those things that, though they are unmoved, do not always exist: nor again can it be caused by any of those which move certain particular things, while others move other things. The eternity and continuity of the process cannot be caused either by any one of them singly or by the sum of them, because this causal relation must be eternal and necessary, whereas the sum of these movents is infinite and they do not all exist together. It is clear, then, that though there may be countless instances of the perishing of some principles that are unmoved but impart motion, and though many things that move themselves perish and are succeeded by others that come into being, and though one thing that is unmoved moves one thing while another moves another, nevertheless there is something that comprehends them all, and that as something apart from each one of them, and this it is that is the cause of the fact that some things are and others are not and of the continuous process of change: and this causes the motion of the other movents, while they are the causes of the motion of other things. Motion, then, being eternal, the first movent, if there is but one, will be eternal also: if there are more than one, there will be a plurality of such eternal movents. We ought, however, to suppose that there is one rather than many, and a finite rather than an infinite number. When the consequences of either assumption are the same, we should always assume that things are finite rather than infinite in number, since in things constituted by nature that which is finite and that which is better ought, if possible, to be present rather than the reverse: and here it is sufficient to assume only one movent, the first of unmoved things, which being

eternal will be the principle of motion to everything else.

Aristotle, *Physics*, 258ᵇ10

9 The origin of all other motions [except eternal motion] is that which moves itself, and . . . the origin of this is the immovable, and . . . the prime mover must of necessity be immovable. And we must grasp this not only generally in theory, but also by reference to individuals in the world of sense, for with these in view we seek general theories, and with these we believe that general theories ought to harmonize. Now in the world of sense too it is plainly impossible for movement to be initiated if there is nothing at rest, and before all else in our present subject—animal life. . . . But the point of rest in the animal is still quite ineffectual unless there be something without which is absolutely at rest and immovable. Now it is worth while to pause and consider what has been said, for it involves a speculation which extends beyond animals even to the motion and march of the universe. For just as there must be something immovable within the animal, if it is to be moved, so even more must there be without it something immovable, by supporting itself upon which that which is moved moves. For were that something always to give way (as it does for mice walking in grain or persons walking in sand) advance would be impossible, and neither would there be any walking unless the ground were to remain still, nor any flying or swimming were not the air and the sea to resist. And this which resists must needs be different from what is moved, the whole of it from the whole of that, and what is thus immovable must be no part of what is moved; otherwise there will be no movement.

Aristotle, *On the Motion of Animals*, 698ᵃ11

10 Since changes are of four kinds—either in respect of the 'what' or of the quality or of the quantity or of the place, and change in respect of 'thisness' is simple generation and destruction, and change in quantity is increase and diminution, and change in respect of an affection is alteration, and change of place is motion, changes will be from given states into those contrary to them in these several respects. The matter, then, which changes must be capable of both states. And since that which 'is' has two senses, we must say that everything changes from that which is potentially to that which is actually, e.g. from potentially white to actually white, and similarly in the case of increase and diminution. Therefore not only can a thing come to be, incidentally, out of that which is not, but also all things come to be out of that which is, but is potentially, and is not actually.

Aristotle, *Metaphysics*, 1069ᵇ8

11 It is necessary that there should be an eternal un-

movable substance. For substances are the first of existing things, and if they are all destructible, all things are destructible. But it is impossible that movement should either have come into being or cease to be (for it must always have existed), or that time should. For there could not be a before and an after if time did not exist. Movement also is continuous, then, in the sense in which time is; for time is either the same thing as movement or an attribute of movement. And there is no continuous movement except movement in place, and of this only that which is circular is continuous.

Aristotle, *Metaphysics,* 1071ᵇ4

12 Atoms move continuously for all time, some of them falling straight down, others swerving, and others recoiling from their collisions. And of the latter, some are borne on, separating to a long distance from one another, while others again recoil and recoil, whenever they chance to be checked by the interlacing with others, or else shut in by atoms interlaced around them. For on the one hand the nature of the void which separates each atom by itself brings this about, as it is not able to afford resistance, and on the other hand the hardness which belongs to the atoms makes them recoil after collision to as great a distance as the interlacing permits separation after the collision. And these motions have no beginning, since the atoms and the void are the cause.

Epicurus, *Letter to Herodotus*

13 If you think that first-beginnings of things can lag and by lagging give birth to new motions of things, you wander far astray from the path of true reason: since they travel about through void, the first-beginnings of things must all move on either by their own weight or haply by the stroke of another. For when during motion they have, as often happens, met and clashed, the result is a sudden rebounding in an opposite direction; and no wonder, since they are most hard and of weight proportioned to their solidity and nothing behind gets in their way. And that you may more clearly see that all bodies of matter are in restless movement, remember that there is no lowest point in the sum of the universe, and that first bodies have not where to take their stand, since space is without end and limit and extends immeasurably in all directions round, as I have shown in many words and as has been proved by sure reason.

Lucretius, *Nature of Things,* II

14 The earth with good title has gotten and keeps the name of mother, since she of herself gave birth to mankind and at a time nearly fixed shed forth every beast that ranges wildly over the great mountains, and at the same time the fowls of the air with all their varied shapes. But because she must have some limit set to her bearing, she ceased like a woman worn out by length of days.

For time changes the nature of the whole world and all things must pass on from one condition to another, and nothing continues like to itself: all things quit their bounds, all things nature changes and compels to alter. One thing crumbles away and is worn and enfeebled with age, then another comes unto honour and issues out of its state of contempt. In this way then time changes the nature of the whole world and the earth passes out of one condition into another: what once it could, it can bear no more, in order to be able to bear what before it did not bear.

Lucretius, *Nature of Things,* V

15 Often think of the rapidity with which things pass by and disappear, both the things which are and the things which are produced. For substance is like a river in a continual flow, and the activities of things are in constant change, and the causes work in infinite varieties; and there is hardly anything which stands still.

Marcus Aurelius, *Meditations,* V, 23

16 Some things are hurrying into existence, and others are hurrying out of it; and of that which is coming into existence part is already extinguished. Motions and changes are continually renewing the world, just as the uninterrupted course of time is always renewing the infinite duration of ages. In this flowing stream then, on which there is no abiding, what is there of the things which hurry by on which a man would set a high price? It would be just as if a man should fall in love with one of the sparrows which fly by, but it has already passed out of sight.

Marcus Aurelius, *Meditations,* VI, 15

17 Is any man afraid of change? Why what can take place without change? What then is more pleasing or more suitable to the universal nature? And canst thou take a bath unless the wood undergoes a change? And canst thou be nourished, unless the food undergoes a change? And can anything else that is useful be accomplished without change? Dost thou not see then that for thyself also to change is just the same, and equally necessary for the universal nature?

Marcus Aurelius, *Meditations,* VII, 18

18 When . . . such and such a body undergoes no change from its existing state, we say that it is at rest; but, if it departs from this in any respect we then say that in this respect it undergoes motion. Accordingly, when it departs in various ways from its pre-existing state, it will be said to undergo various kinds of motion. Thus, if that which is white becomes black, or what is black becomes white, it undergoes motion in respect to colour. . . . And further, it is not only things which are altered in regard to colour and flavour which, we say, undergo motion; when a warm thing becomes

cold, and a cold warm, here too we speak of its undergoing motion; similarly also when anything moist becomes dry, or dry moist. Now, the common term which we apply to all these cases is alteration.

This is one kind of motion. But there is another kind which occurs in bodies which change their position, or as we say, pass from one place to another; the name of this is transference.

These two kinds of motion, then, are simple and primary, while compounded from them we have growth and decay, as when a small thing becomes bigger, or a big thing smaller, each retaining at the same time its particular form. And two other kinds of motion are genesis and destruction, genesis being a coming into existence, and destruction being the opposite.

Galen, *Natural Faculties*, I, 2

19 The Kosmos has had no beginning . . . and this is warrant for its continued existence. Why should there be in the future a change that has not yet occurred? The elements there are not worn away like beams and rafters: they hold sound for ever, and so the All holds sound. And even supposing these elements to be in ceaseless transmutation, yet the All persists: the ground of all the change must itself be changeless.

Plotinus, *Second Ennead*, I, 4

20 It is certain, and evident to our senses, that in this world some things are in motion. Now whatever is in motion is put in motion by another, for nothing can be in motion unless it is in potency to that towards which it is in motion. But a thing moves in so far as it is in act. For motion is nothing else than the reduction of something from potency to act. But nothing can be reduced from potency to act except by something in a state of act. Thus that which is actually hot, as fire, makes wood, which is potentially hot, to be actually hot, and thereby moves and changes it. Now it is not possible that the same thing should be at once in act and potency in the same respect, but only in different respects. For what is actually hot cannot simultaneously be potentially hot, though it is simultaneously potentially cold. It is therefore impossible that in the same respect and in the same way a thing should be both mover and moved, that is, that it should move itself. Therefore, whatever is moved must be moved by another. If that by which it is moved be itself moved, then this also must be moved by another, and that by another again. But this cannot go on to infinity, because then there would be no first mover, and, consequently, no other mover, seeing that subsequent movers move only because as they are moved by the first mover, just as the staff moves only because it is moved by the hand. Therefore it is necessary to arrive at a first mover which is

moved by no other. And this everyone understands to be God.

Aquinas, *Summa Theologica*, I, 2, 3

21 Now it is manifest that a natural body cannot be actually infinite . . . because every natural body has some natural movement. But an infinite body could not have any natural movement. Neither direct, because nothing moves naturally by a direct movement unless it is out of its place, and this could not happen to an infinite body, for it would occupy every place, and thus every place would be indifferently its own place. Neither could it move circularly; since circular motion requires that one part of the body is necessarily transferred to a place occupied by another part, and this could not happen as regards an infinite circular body; for if two lines be drawn from the centre, the farther they extend from the centre, the farther they are from each other; therefore, if a body were infinite, the lines would be infinitely distant from each other, and thus one could never reach the place belonging to any other.

Aquinas, *Summa Theologica*, I, 7, 3

22 In the sense . . . in which understanding is movement, that which understands itself is said to move itself.

Aquinas, *Summa Theologica*, I, 18, 3

23 Rest is, properly speaking, opposed to movement, and consequently to the labour that arises from movement. But although movement, strictly speaking, is a quality of bodies, yet the word is applied also to spiritual things, and in a twofold sense. On the one hand, every operation may be called a movement, and thus the Divine goodness is said to move and go forth to the thing in communicating itself to that thing. . . . On the other hand, the desire that tends to another, is said to move towards it. Hence rest is taken in two senses, in one sense meaning a cessation from work, in the other, the fulfilling of desire.

Aquinas, *Summa Theologica*, I, 73, 2

24 I myself think that gravity or heaviness is nothing except a certain natural appetency implanted in the parts by the divine providence of the universal Artisan, in order that they should unite with one another in their oneness and wholeness and come together in the form of a globe. It is believable that this affect is present in the sun, moon, and the other bright planets and that through its efficacy they remain in the spherical figure in which they are visible, though they nevertheless accomplish their circular movements in many different ways.

Copernicus, *De Revolutionibus*, I, 9

25 In all things except those that are simply bad, change is to be feared: change of seasons, winds, food, and humors. And no laws are held in their

true honor except those to which God has given some ancient duration, so that no one knows their origin or that they were ever different.

Montaigne, *Essays,* I, 43, Of
Sumptuary Laws

26 When I bethinke me on that speech whyleare
Of Mutability, and well it way,
Me seemes, that though she all unworthy were
Of the heav'ns rule, yet, very sooth to say,
In all things else she beares the greatest sway:
Which makes me loath this state of life so tickle,
And love of things so vaine to cast away;
Whose flowring pride, so fading and so fickle,
Short Time shall soon cut down with his consuming sickle.

Then gin I thinke on that which Nature sayd,
Of that same time when no more change shall be,
But stedfast rest of all things, firmely stayd
Upon the pillours of eternity,
That is contrayr to Mutabilitie:
For all that moveth doth in change delight:
But thence-forth all shall rest eternally
With Him that is the God of Sabbaoth hight:
O that great Sabbaoth God graunt me that Sabbaoths sight!

Spenser, *Faerie Queene,* Bk. VII, VIII, 1–2

27 As regards movement: the sun is the first cause of the movement of the planets and the first mover of the universe, even by reason of its own body. In the intermediate space the movables, i.e., the globes of the planets, are laid out. The region of the fixed stars supplies the movables with a place and a base upon which the movables are, as it were, supported; and movement is understood as taking place relative to its absolute immobility. So in animals the cerebellum is the seat of the motor faculty, and the body and its members are that which is moved. The Earth is the base of an animal body; the body, the base of the arm or head, and the arm, the base of the finger. And the movement of each part takes place upon this base as upon something immovable.

Kepler, *Epitome of Copernican
Astronomy,* Bk. IV, I, 1

28 *Ariel.* [Sings] Full fathom five thy father lies;
Of his bones are coral made;
Those are pearls that were his eyes:
Nothing of him that doth fade
But doth suffer a sea-change
Into something rich and strange.
Sea-nymphs hourly ring his knell.

Shakespeare, *Tempest,* I, ii, 396

29 When I have seen by Time's fell hand defaced
The rich proud cost of outworn buried age;
When sometime lofty towers I see down-razed
And brass eternal slave to mortal rage;

When I have seen the hungry ocean gain
Advantage on the kingdom of the shore,
And the firm soil win of the watery main,
Increasing store with loss and loss with store;
When I have seen such interchange of state,
Or state itself confounded to decay;
Ruin hath taught me thus to ruminate,
That Time will come and take my love away.

Shakespeare, *Sonnet LXIV*

30 To think the Affairs of this Life are always to remain in the same State, is an erroneous Fancy. The Face of Things rather seems continually to change and roll with a circular Motion; Summer succeeds the Spring; Autumn the Summer; Winter the Autumn; and then Spring again: So Time proceeds in this perpetual Round; only the Life of Man is ever hastening to it's End, swifter than Time it self, without Hopes to be renew'd, unless in the next, that is unlimited and infinite.

Cervantes, *Don Quixote,* II, 53

31 All motion or natural action takes place in time, more or less rapidly, but still in determined moments well ascertained by nature. Even those actions which appear to take effect suddenly, and in the twinkling of an eye (as we express it), are found to admit of greater or less rapidity.

Bacon, *Novum Organum,* II, 46

32 One which can scarcely be termed a motion, and yet is one . . . we may call the motion of repose, or of abhorrence of motion. It is by this motion that the earth stands by its own weight, whilst its extremes move towards the middle, not to an imaginary centre, but in order to unite. It is owing to the same tendency, that all bodies of considerable density abhor motion, and their only tendency is not to move, which nature they preserve, although excited and urged in a variety of ways to motion. But if they be compelled to move, yet do they always appear anxious to recover their former state, and to cease from motion, in which respect they certainly appear active, and attempt it with sufficient swiftness and rapidity, as if fatigued, and impatient of delay.

Bacon, *Novum Organum,* II, 48

33 As the births of living creatures at first are illshapen, so are all innovations, which are the births of time.

Bacon, *Of Innovations*

34 It were good . . . that men in their innovations would follow the example of time itself, which indeed innovateth greatly, but quietly and by degrees scarce to be perceived.

Bacon, *Of Innovations*

35 It is a secret, both in nature and state, that it is safer to change many things than one.

Bacon, *Of Regiment of Health*

36 The variation of speed observed in bodies of different specific gravities is not caused by the difference of specific gravity but depends upon external circumstances and, in particular, upon the resistance of the medium, so that if this is removed all bodies would fall with the same velocity.

Galileo, *Two New Sciences,* I

37 There is, in nature, perhaps nothing older than motion, concerning which the books written by philosophers are neither few nor small; nevertheless, I have discovered by experiment some properties of it which are worth knowing and which have not hitherto been either observed or demonstrated. Some superficial observations have been made, as, for instance, that the free motion of a heavy falling body is continuously accelerated; but to just what extent this acceleration occurs has not yet been announced; for so far as I know, no one has yet pointed out that the distances traversed, during equal intervals of time, by a body falling from rest, stand to one another in the same ratio as the odd numbers beginning with unity.

It has been observed that missiles and projectiles describe a curved path of some sort; however, no one has pointed out the fact that this path is a parabola. But this and other facts, not few in number or less worth knowing, I have succeeded in proving; and what I consider more important, there have been opened up to this vast and most excellent science, of which my work is merely the beginning, ways and means by which other minds more acute than mine will explore its remote corners.

Galileo, *Two New Sciences,* III

38 Any velocity once imparted to a moving body will be rigidly maintained as long as the external causes of acceleration or retardation are removed, a condition which is found only on horizontal planes; for in the case of planes which slope downwards there is already present a cause of acceleration, while on planes sloping upward there is retardation; from this it follows that motion along a horizontal plane is perpetual; for, if the velocity be uniform, it cannot be diminished or slackened, much less destroyed.

Galileo, *Two New Sciences,* III

39 That when a thing lies still, unless somewhat else stir it, it will lie still for ever, is a truth that no man doubts of. But that when a thing is in motion, it will eternally be in motion, unless somewhat else stay it, though the reason be the same (namely, that nothing can change itself), is not so easily assented to.

Hobbes, *Leviathan,* I, 2

40 He no longer loves the person whom he loved ten years ago. I quite believe it. She is no longer the same, nor is he. He was young, and she also; she is quite different. He would perhaps love her yet, if she were what she was then.

Pascal, *Pensées,* II, 123

41 Geometry supposes . . . that we know what thing is meant by the words: *motion, number, space;* and without stopping uselessly to define them it penetrates their nature and lays bare their marvelous properties.

These three things, which comprise the entire universe . . . are reciprocally and necessarily related. For we cannot imagine a motion without something which moves, and this thing being one, that unity is the origin of all number. Finally, since motion is impossible without space, we see that these three things are contained in the first. Even time is included there too, for motion and time are correlative (fast and slow, which differentiate motion, having a necessary reference to time).

Pascal, *Geometrical Demonstration*

42 However fast a motion may be, we can conceive a faster, and make that still faster, and thus forever to infinity without ever reaching a motion so fast that we can no longer add to it. And on the contrary, however slow a motion may be, we can make it slower, and that still slower, and so to infinity without ever reaching such a degree of slowness that we cannot still descend to an infinity of lower degrees without falling into rest.

Pascal, *Geometrical Demonstration*

43 If two contrary actions be excited in the same subject, a change must necessarily take place in both, or in one alone, until they cease to be contrary.

Spinoza, *Ethics,* V, Axiom 1

44 It is inconceivable to doubt that light consists in the motion of some sort of matter. For whether one considers its production, one sees that here upon the earth it is chiefly engendered by fire and flame which contain without doubt bodies that are in rapid motion, since they dissolve and melt many other bodies, even the most solid; or whether one considers its effects, one sees that when light is collected, as by concave mirrors, it has the property of burning as a fire does, that is to say, it disunites the particles of bodies. This is assuredly the mark of motion, at least in the true philosophy, in which one conceives the causes of all natural effects in terms of mechanical motions. This, in my opinion, we must necessarily do, or else renounce all hopes of ever comprehending anything in physics.

Huygens, *Treatise on Light,* I

45 The *vis insita,* or innate force of matter, is a power of resisting, by which every body, as much as in it

lies, continues in its present state, whether it be of rest, or of moving uniformly forwards in a right line. This force is always proportional to the body whose force it is and differs nothing from the inactivity of the mass, but in our manner of conceiving it. A body, from the inert nature of matter, is not without difficulty put out of its state of rest or motion. Upon which account, this *vis insita* may, by a most significant name, be called inertia or force of inactivity. But a body only exerts this force when another force, impressed upon it, endeavors to change its condition; and the exercise of this force may be considered as both resistance and impulse; it is resistance so far as the body, for maintaining its present state, opposes the force impressed; it is impulse so far as the body, by not easily giving way to the impressed force of another, endeavors to change the state of that other. Resistance is usually ascribed to bodies at rest, and impulse to those in motion; but motion and rest, as commonly conceived, are only relatively distinguished; nor are those bodies always truly at rest, which commonly are taken to be so.

Newton, *Principia*, Definition III

46 Absolute motion is the translation of a body from one absolute place into another; and relative motion, the translation from one relative place into another. Thus in a ship under sail, the relative place of a body is that part of the ship which the body possesses; or that part of the cavity which the body fills, and which therefore moves together with the ship: and relative rest is the continuance of the body in the same part of the ship, or of its cavity. But real, absolute rest, is the continuance of the body in the same part of that immovable space, in which the ship itself, its cavity, and all that it contains, is moved. Wherefore, if the earth is really at rest, the body, which relatively rests in the ship, will really and absolutely move with the same velocity which the ship has on the earth. But if the earth also moves, the true and absolute motion of the body will arise, partly from the true motion of the earth, in immovable space, partly from the relative motion of the ship on the earth; and if the body moves also relatively in the ship, its true motion will arise, partly from the true motion of the earth, in immovable space, and partly from the relative motions as well of the ship on the earth, as of the body in the ship; and from these relative motions will arise the relative motion of the body on the earth. As if that part of the earth, where the ship is, was truly moved towards the east, with a velocity of 10,010 parts; while the ship itself, with a fresh gale, and full sails, is carried towards the west, with a velocity expressed by 10 of those parts; but a sailor walks in the ship towards the east, with 1 part of the said velocity; then the sailor will be moved truly in immovable space towards the east, with a velocity of 10,001 parts, and relatively on the earth towards the west, with a velocity of 9 of those parts.

Newton, *Principia*, Definitions, Scholium

47 Every body continues in its state of rest, or of uniform motion in a right line, unless it is compelled to change that state by forces impressed upon it. Projectiles continue in their motions, so far as they are not retarded by the resistance of the air, or impelled downwards by the force of gravity. A top, whose parts by their cohesion are continually drawn aside from rectilinear motions, does not cease its rotation, otherwise than as it is retarded by the air. The greater bodies of the planets and comets, meeting with less resistance in freer spaces, preserve their motions both progressive and circular for a much longer time.

The change of motion is proportional to the motive force impressed; and is made in the direction of the right line in which that force is impressed. If any force generates a motion, a double force will generate double the motion, a triple force triple the motion, whether that force be impressed altogether and at once, or gradually and successively. And this motion (being always directed the same way with the generating force), if the body moved before, is added to or subtracted from the former motion, according as they directly conspire with or are directly contrary to each other; or obliquely joined, when they are oblique, so as to produce a new motion compounded from the determination of both.

To every action there is always opposed an equal reaction: or, the mutual actions of two bodies upon each other are always equal, and directed to contrary parts. Whatever draws or presses another is as much drawn or pressed by that other. If you press a stone with your finger, the finger is also pressed by the stone. If a horse draws a stone tied to a rope, the horse (if I may so say) will be equally drawn back towards the stone; for the distended rope, by the same endeavor to relax or unbend itself, will draw the horse as much towards the stone as it does the stone towards the horse, and will obstruct the progress of the one as much as it advances that of the other. If a body impinge upon another, and by its force change the motion of the other, that body also (because of the equality of the mutual pressure) will undergo an equal change, in its own motion, towards the contrary part. The changes made by these actions are equal, not in the velocities but in the motions of bodies; that is to say, if the bodies are not hindered by any other impediments. For, because the motions are equally changed, the changes of the velocities made towards contrary parts are inversely proportional to the bodies. This law takes place also in attractions, as will be proved in the next Scholium.

Newton, *Principia*, Axioms I–III

48 If spheres be however dissimilar (as to density of

matter and attractive force) in the same ratio onwards from the centre to the circumference; but everywhere similar, at every given distance from the centre, on all sides round about; and the attractive force of every point decreases as the square of the distance of the body attracted: I say, that the whole force with which one of these spheres attracts the other will be inversely proportional to the square of the distance of the centres.

Newton, *Principia*, I, 12

49 If it universally appears, by experiments and astronomical observations, that all bodies about the earth gravitate towards the earth, and that in proportion to the quantity of matter which they severally contain; that the moon likewise, according to the quantity of its matter, gravitates towards the earth; that, on the other hand, our sea gravitates towards the moon; and all the planets one towards another; and the comets in like manner towards the sun; we must, in consequence of this rule, universally allow that all bodies whatsoever are endowed with a principle of mutual gravitation. For the argument from the appearances concludes with more force for the universal gravitation of all bodies than for their impenetrability; of which, among those in the celestial regions, we have no experiments, nor any manner of observation. Not that I affirm gravity to be essential to bodies: by their *vis insita* I mean nothing but their inertia. This is immutable. Their gravity is diminished as they recede from the earth.

Newton, *Principia*, III, Rule III

50 There is . . . [an] idea, which, though suggested by our senses, yet is more constantly offered to us by what passes in our minds; and that is the idea of *succession*. For if we look immediately into ourselves, and reflect on what is observable there, we shall find our ideas always, whilst we are awake, or have any thought, passing in train, one going and another coming, without intermission.

Locke, *Concerning Human Understanding*,
Bk. II, VII, 9

51 Modes of motion answer those of extension; swift and slow are two different ideas of motion, the measures whereof are made of the distances of time and space put together; so they are complex ideas, comprehending time and space with motion.

Locke, *Concerning Human Understanding*,
Bk. II, XVIII, 2

52 We have ideas but of two sorts of action, viz. motion and thinking. These, in truth, though called and counted actions, yet, if nearly considered, will not be found to be always perfectly so. For, if I mistake not, there are instances of both kinds, which, upon due consideration, will be found rather passions than actions; and consequently so

far the effects barely of *passive powers* in those subjects, which yet on their accounts are thought agents. For, in these instances, the substance that hath motion or thought receives the impression, whereby it is put into that action, purely from without, and so acts merely by the capacity it has to receive such an impression from some external agent; and such power is not properly an active power, but a mere passive capacity in the subject. Sometimes the substance or agent puts itself into action by its own power, and this is properly *active power*. Whatsoever modification a substance has, whereby it produces any effect, that is called action: v.g. a solid substance, by motion, operates on or alters the sensible ideas of another substance, and therefore this modification of motion we call action. But yet this motion in that solid substance is, when rightly considered, but a passion, if it received it only from some external agent. So that the active power of motion is in no substance which cannot begin motion in itself or in another substance when at rest.

Locke, *Concerning Human Understanding*,
Bk. II, XXI, 74

53 It does not appear to me that there can be any motion other than *relative;* so that to conceive motion there must be at least conceived two bodies, whereof the distance or position in regard to each other is varied. Hence, if there was one only body in being it could not possibly be moved. This seems evident, in that the idea I have of motion doth necessarily include relation.

But, though in every motion it be necessary to conceive more bodies than one, yet it may be that one only is moved, namely, that on which the force causing the change in the distance or situation of the bodies, is impressed. For, however some may define relative motion, so as to term that body *moved* which changes its distance from some other body, whether the force or action causing that change were impressed on it or no, yet as relative motion is that which is perceived by sense, and regarded in the ordinary affairs of life, it should seem that every man of common sense knows what it is as well as the best philosopher. Now, I ask any one whether, in his sense of motion as he walks along the streets, the stones he passes over may be said to *move*, because they change distance with his feet? To me it appears that though motion includes a relation of one thing to another, yet it is not necessary that each term of the relation be denominated from it. As a man may think of somewhat which does not think, so a body may be moved to or from another body which is not therefore itself in motion.

As the place happens to be variously defined, the motion which is related to it varies. A man in a ship may be said to be quiescent with relation to the sides of the vessel, and yet move with relation to the land. Or he may move eastward in respect of the one, and westward in respect of the other. In the common affairs of life men never go beyond the earth to define the place of any body; and what is quiescent in respect of that is accounted *absolutely* to be so. But philosophers, who have a greater extent of thought, and juster notions of the system of things, discover even the earth itself to be moved. In order therefore to fix their notions they seem to conceive the corporeal world as finite, and the utmost unmoved walls or shell thereof to be the place whereby they estimate true motions. If we sound our own conceptions, I believe we may find all the absolute motion we can frame an idea of to be at bottom no other than relative motion thus defined. For, as hath been already observed, absolute motion, exclusive of all external relation, is incomprehensible; and to this kind of relative motion all the above-mentioned properties, causes, and effects ascribed to absolute motion will, if I mistake not, be found to agree.

> Berkeley, *Principles of Human Knowledge,* 112–114

54 Be not the first by whom the new are tried,
Nor yet the last to lay the old aside.

> Pope, *Essay on Criticism,* II, 335

55 The more communicative a people are, the more easily they change their habits, because each is in a greater degree a spectacle to the other and the singularities of individuals are better observed. The climate which influences one nation to take pleasure in being communicative, makes it also delight in change, and that which makes it delight in change forms its taste.

> Montesquieu, *Spirit of Laws,* XIX, 8

56 To begin with the examination of motion; 'tis evident this is a quality altogether inconceivable alone, and without a reference to some other object. The idea of motion necessarily supposes that of a body moving. Now what is our idea of the moving body, without which motion is incomprehensible? It must resolve itself into the idea of extension or of solidity; and consequently the reality of motion depends upon that of these other qualities.

> Hume, *Treatise of Human Nature,* Bk. I, IV, 4

57 A man used to vicissitudes is not easily dejected.

> Johnson, *Rasselas,* XII

58 Such, said Nekayah, is the state of life, that none are happy but by the anticipation of change: the change itself is nothing; when we have made it, the next wish is to change again.

> Johnson, *Rasselas,* XLVII

59 *Johnson.* When I was a young man, being anxious to distinguish myself, I was perpetually starting new propositions. But I soon gave this over; for, I found that generally what was new was false.

> Boswell, *Life of Johnson (Mar. 26, 1779)*

60 The permanent in phenomena must be regarded as the substratum of all determination of time, and consequently also as the condition of the possibility of all synthetical unity of perceptions, that is, of experience; and all existence and all change in time can only be regarded as a mode in the existence of that which abides unchangeably. Therefore, in all phenomena, the permanent is the object *in itself,* that is, the substance; but all that changes or can change belongs only to the mode of the existence of this substance or substances, consequently to its determinations.

I find that in all ages not only the philosopher, but even the common understanding, has preposited this permanence as a substratum of all change in phenomena; indeed, I am compelled to believe that they will always accept this as an indubitable fact. Only the philosopher expresses himself in a more precise and definite manner, when he says: "In all changes in the world, the *substance* remains, and the *accidents* alone are changeable." But of this decidedly synthetical proposition, I nowhere meet with even an attempt at proof; nay, it very rarely has the good fortune to stand, as it deserves to do, at the head of the pure and entirely *a priori* laws of nature. In truth, the statement that substance is permanent, is tautological. For this very permanence is the ground on which we apply the category of substance to the phenomenon; and we should have been obliged to prove that in all phenomena there is something permanent, of the existence of which the changeable is nothing but a determination. But because a proof of this nature cannot be dogmatical, that is cannot be drawn from conceptions, inasmuch as it concerns a synthetical proposition *a priori,* and as philosophers never reflected that such propositions are valid only in relation to possible experience, and therefore cannot be proved except by means of a deduction of the possibility of experience, it is no wonder that while it has served as the foundation of all experience (for we feel the need of it in empirical cognition), it has never been supported by proof.

> Kant, *Critique of Pure Reason,* Transcendental Analytic

61 In order to represent *change* as the intuition corresponding to the conception of causality, we require the representation of motion as change in space; in fact, it is through it alone that changes, the possibility of which no pure understanding can perceive, are capable of being intuited. Change is the connection of determinations contradictorily opposed to each other in the existence of one and the same thing. Now, how it is possible that out of a given state one quite opposite to it in

the same thing should follow, reason without an example can not only not conceive, but cannot even make intelligible without intuition; and this intuition is the motion of a point in space; the existence of which in different spaces (as a consequence of opposite determinations) alone makes the intuition of change possible. For, in order to make even internal change cognitable, we require to represent time, as the form of the internal sense, figuratively by a line, and the internal change by the drawing of that line (motion), and consequently are obliged to employ external intuition to be able to represent the successive existence of ourselves in different states. The proper ground of this fact is that all change to be perceived as change presupposes something permanent in intuition, while in the internal sense no permanent intuition is to be found.

Kant, *Critique of Pure Reason,*
Transcendental Analytic

62 The changes that take place in nature—how infinitely manifold soever they may be—exhibit only a perpetually self-repeating cycle; in nature there happens "nothing new under the sun," and the multiform play of its phenomena so far induces a feeling of *ennui;* only in those changes which take place in the region of spirit does anything new arise.

Hegel, *Philosophy of History,*
Introduction, 3

63 Let the great world spin for ever down the ringing grooves of change.

Tennyson, *Locksley Hall,* 182

64 *Arthur.* The old order changeth, yielding place to new,
And God fulfils himself in many ways,
Lest one good custom should corrupt the world.

Tennyson, *The Passing of Arthur,* 408

65 All change is a miracle to contemplate; but it is a miracle which is taking place every instant.

Thoreau, *Walden:* Economy

66 Suppose we were able, within the length of a second, to note 10,000 events distinctly, instead of barely 10, as now; if our life were then destined to hold the same number of impressions, it might be 1000 times as short. We should live less than a month, and personally know nothing of the change of seasons. If born in winter, we should believe in summer as we now believe in the heats of the Carboniferous era. The motions of organic beings would be so slow to our senses as to be inferred, not seen. The sun would stand still in the sky, the moon be almost free from change, and so on. But now reverse the hypothesis and suppose a being to get only one 1000th part of the sensations that we get in a given time, and consequently to

live 1000 times as long. Winters and summers will be to him like quarters of an hour. Mushrooms and the swifter-growing plants will shoot into being so rapidly as to appear instantaneous creations; annual shrubs will rise and fall from the earth like restlessly boiling-water springs; the motions of animals will be as invisible as are to us the movements of bullets and cannon-balls; the sun will scour through the sky like a meteor, leaving a fiery trail behind him, etc. That such imaginary cases (barring the superhuman longevity) may be realized somewhere in the animal kingdom, it would be rash to deny.

William James, *Psychology,* XV

67 Newton in his description of space and time has confused what is 'real' potentiality with what is actual fact. He has thereby been led to diverge from the judgment of 'the vulgar' who 'conceive those quantities under no other notions but from the relation they bear to sensible objects.' The philosophy of organism starts by agreeing with 'the vulgar' except that the term 'sensible object' is replaced by 'actual entity'; so as to free our notions from participation in an epistomological theory as to sense-perception. When we further consider how to adjust Newton's other descriptions to the organic theory, the surprising fact emerges that we must identify the atomized quantum of extension correlative to an actual entity, with Newton's absolute place and absolute duration. Newton's proof that motion does not apply to absolute place, which in its nature is immovable, also holds. Thus an actual entity never moves: it is where it is and what it is. In order to emphasize this characteristic by a phrase connecting the notion of 'actual entity' more closely with our ordinary habits of thought, I will also use the term 'actual occasion' in the place of the term 'actual entity.' Thus the actual world is built up of actual occasions; and by the ontological principle whatever things there are in any sense of 'existence,' are derived by abstraction from actual occasions. I shall use the term 'event' in the more general sense of a nexus of actual occasions, interrelated in some determinate fashion in one extensive quantum. An actual occasion is the limiting type of an event with only one member.

It is quite obvious that meanings have to be found for the notions of 'motion' and of 'moving bodies'. . . . It is sufficient to say that a molecule in the sense of a moving body, with a history of local change, is not an actual occasion; it must therefore be some kind of nexus of actual occasions. In this sense it is an event, but not an actual occasion. The fundamental meaning of the notion of 'change' is 'the difference between actual occasions comprised in some determinate event.'

Whitehead, *Process and Reality,* II, 2

68 This subject of the formation of the three laws of

motion and of the law of gravitation deserves critical attention. The whole development of thought occupied exactly two generations. It commenced with Galileo and ended with Newton's *Principia;* and Newton was born in the year that Galileo died. Also the lives of Descartes and Huygens fall within the period occupied by these great terminal figures. The issue of the combined labours of these four men has some right to be considered as the greatest single intellectual success which mankind has achieved. In estimating its size, we must consider the completeness of its range. It constructs for us a vision of the material universe, and it enables us to calculate the minutest detail of a particular occurrence. Galileo took the first step in hitting on the right line of thought. He noted that the critical point to attend to was not the motion of bodies but the changes of their motions. Galileo's discovery is formularised by Newton in his first law of motion:—'Every body continues in its state of rest, or of uniform motion in a straight line, except so far as it may be compelled by force to change that state.'

This formula contains the repudiation of a belief which had blocked the progress of physics for two thousand years.

Whitehead, *Science and the Modern World,* III

69 Perhaps the most powerful solvent of the pre-scientific outlook has been the first law of motion, which the world owes to Galileo, though to some extent he was anticipated by Leonardo da Vinci.

The first law of motion says that a body which is moving will go on moving in the same direction with the same velocity until something stops it. Before Galileo it had been thought that a lifeless body will not move of itself, and if it is in motion it will gradually come to rest. Only living beings, it was thought, could move without help of some external agency. Aristotle thought that the heavenly bodies were pushed by gods. Here on earth, animals can set themselves in motion and can cause motion in dead matter. There are, it was conceded, certain kinds of motion which are "natural" to dead matter: earth and water naturally move downwards; air and fire upwards; but beyond these simple "natural" motions everything depends upon impulsion from the souls of living beings.

So long as this view prevailed, physics as an independent science was impossible, since the physical world was thought to be not causally self-contained. But Galileo and Newton between them proved that all the movements of the planets, and of dead matter on the earth, proceed according to the laws of physics, and once started, will continue indefinitely. There is no need of mind in this process. Newton still thought that a Creator was necessary to get the process going, but that after that He left it to work according to its own laws.

Russell, *Science and Tradition*

70 Motion consists merely in the fact that bodies are sometimes in one place and sometimes in another, and that they are at intermediate places at intermediate times. Only those who have waded through the quagmire of philosophic speculation on this subject can realize what a liberation from antique prejudices is involved in this simple and straightforward commonplace.

Russell, *Mathematics and the Metaphysicians*

71 With slight exaggeration, it may be said that the thoroughgoing way in which Aristotle defined, distinguished and classified rest and movement, the finished and the incomplete, the actual and potential, did more to fix tradition, *the* genteel tradition one is tempted to add, which identifies·the fixed and regular with reality of Being and the changing and hazardous with deficiency of Being than ever was accomplished by those who took the shorter path of asserting that change is illusory.

Dewey, *Experience and Nature,* II

72 I believe that if one were convinced of the reality of change and if one made an effort to grasp it, everything would become simplified, philosophical difficulties, considered insurmountable, would fall away. Not only would philosophy gain by it, but our everyday life—I mean the impression things make upon us and the reaction of our intelligence, our sensibility and our will upon things— would perhaps be transformed and, as it were, transfigured. The point is that usually we look at change but we do not see it. We speak of change, but we do not think about it. We say that change exists, that everything changes, that change is the very law of things: yes, we say it and we repeat it; but those are only words, and we reason and philosophise as though change did not exist.

Bergson, *The Creative Mind,* V

73 Only haste and lack of circumspection in conceiving what spirit is and how it moves could assign to it the origin of change. On the contrary, while spirit is extraordinarily mobile in its existence, it borrows this mobility from the hair-trigger organisation and unstable equilibrium of its organs, and of the stimulations which excite them incessantly. In its own nature, spirit arrests the flux of things, as best it may, in its intuitions, and turns it into a store of synthetic pictures and symbols, sensuous and intellectual. We may therefore say with more reason that the world imposes movement on a spirit which by its own genius would rather be addressed to the eternal, than say that reality seems successive only to a flighty spirit, turning distractedly the leaves of a book written in eternity. Matter, not spirit, is the seat and principle of the flux. Spirit, being an emanation of this flux, seems indeed a pilgrim wandering and almost lost in the wilderness of essence and in the dark treasure-house of truth; but in respect to the realm of

matter, spirit is like a child asking questions and making pause, and often brutally run over and crushed by a rush of changes which it cannot understand.

Santayana, *Realm of Matter,* V

74 If it is true that we cannot bathe twice in the same river, because the water has flowed on, it is true also that the same water which was formerly here is now farther down; so that we might bathe in it again if only we ran down the bank with greater celerity than the water. But our second plunge, though into the same water, would be at another point in the stream: and it is this combination of continuity with instability that we indicate when we speak of a river or a flux. The dialectic of continuity—whether it may be analysed into an infinite number of discrete points or into an indefinite number of intervals—was probably not considered by nature before she began to exist: there is therefore no need to consider it in describing existence.

Santayana, *Realm of Matter,* V

19.6 | *Space*

Philosophers, physicists, and geometers are all interested in space, but from somewhat different points of view. The mathematical treatment of space is too technical to be more than briefly indicated here in a few passages that talk of points and lines. The treatment of space by the mathematical physicist is, for the same reason, also touched on lightly—in a passage from Newton on the distinction between absolute and relative space (a distinction challenged by Berkeley), and in a passage from Einstein on the absolute four-dimensional, space-time matrix. The major portion of the quotations reflect the controversial questions about space that have occupied the philosophers.

One of these is the question about the infinite extent of space—whether space has an edge or boundary. Another is the question about the infinite divisibility of space—whether between any two points in space chosen at random there is always an infinite number of intermediate points. Still another

is the question about the void—about the existence in nature of totally empty space, space devoid of matter. This must not be confused with the question of whether or not a vacuum can be produced by human contrivance. If empty space or void does exist in nature, then a question is raised about action at a distance; if it does not, then a question is raised concerning the possibility of motion.

Among the philosophers, two introduce variants on the idea of space. Aristotle discusses place as the envelope that contains a body, in contradistinction to the space through which a body moves from place to place. Descartes discusses extension as the property distinctive of matter, just as, in his view, thought is the property distinctive of mind. Kant, William James, and Russell discuss the perception of space and disagree about whether it is developed from experience or is an *a priori* form of intuition constitutive of our experience.

1 *Timaeus.* This new beginning of our discussion of the universe requires a fuller division than the former; for then we made two classes, now a third must be revealed. The two sufficed for the former discussion: one, which we assumed, was a pattern intelligible and always the same; and the second was only the imitation of the pattern, generated and visible. There is also a third kind which we did not distinguish at the time, conceiving that the two would be enough. But now the argument seems to require that we should set forth in words another kind, which is difficult of explanation and dimly seen. What nature are we to attribute to this new kind of being? We reply, that it is the receptacle, and in a manner the nurse, of all generation.

Plato, *Timaeus*, 48B

2 We must acknowledge that there is one kind of being which is always the same, uncreated and indestructible, never receiving anything into itself from without, nor itself going out to any other, but invisible and imperceptible by any sense, and of which the contemplation is granted to intelligence only. And there is another nature of the same name with it, and like to it, perceived by sense, created, always in motion, becoming in place and again vanishing out of place, which is apprehended by opinion and sense. And there is a third nature, which is space, and is eternal, and admits not of destruction and provides a home for all created things, and is apprehended without the help of sense, by a kind of spurious reason, and is hardly real; which we beholding as in a dream, say of all existence that it must of necessity be in some place and occupy a space, but that what is neither in heaven nor in earth has no existence. Of these and other things of the same kind, relating to the true and waking reality of nature, we have only this dreamlike sense, and we are unable to cast off sleep and determine the truth about them. For an image, since the reality, after which it is modelled, does not belong to it, and it exists ever as the fleeting shadow of some other, must be inferred to be in another [i.e. in space], grasping existence in some way or other, or it could not be at all. But true and exact reason, vindicating the nature of true being, maintains that while two things [i.e. the image and space] are different they cannot exist one of them in the other and so be one and also two at the same time.

Thus have I concisely given the result of my thoughts; and my verdict is that being and space and generation, these three, existed in their three ways before the heaven.

Plato, *Timaeus*, 51B

3 If place is what *primarily* contains each body, it would be a limit, so that the place would be the form or shape of each body by which the magnitude or the matter of the magnitude is defined: for this is the limit of each body.

If, then, we look at the question in this way the place of a thing is its form. But, if we regard the place as the *extension* of the magnitude, it is the matter. For this is different from the magnitude: it is what is contained and defined by the form, as by a bounding plane. Matter or the indeterminate is of this nature; when the boundary and attributes of a sphere are taken away, nothing but the matter is left.

This is why Plato in the *Timaeus* says that matter and space are the same; for the 'participant' and space are identical. (It is true, indeed, that the account he gives there of the 'participant' is different from what he says in his so-called 'unwritten teaching'. Nevertheless, he did identify place and space.) I mention Plato because, while all hold place to be something, he alone tried to say *what* it is.

In view of these facts we should naturally expect to find difficulty in determining what place is, if indeed it *is* one of these two things, matter or form. They demand a very close scrutiny, especially as it is not easy to recognize them apart.

But it is at any rate not difficult to see that place cannot be either of them. The form and the matter are not separate from the thing, whereas the place can be separated. . . . Where air was, water in turn comes to be, the one replacing the other; and similarly with other bodies. Hence the place of a thing is neither a part nor a state of it, but is separable from it. For place is supposed to be something like a vessel—the vessel being a transportable place. But the vessel is no part of the thing.

Aristotle, *Physics,* 209^b1

4 Place is thought to be something important and hard to grasp, both because the matter and the shape present themselves along with it, and because the displacement of the body that is moved takes place in a stationary container, for it seems possible that there should be an interval which is other than the bodies which are moved. The air, too, which is thought to be incorporeal, contributes something to the belief: it is not only the boundaries of the vessel which seem to be place, but also what is between them, regarded as empty. Just, in fact, as the vessel is transportable place, so place is a non-portable vessel. So when what is within a thing which is moved, is moved and changes its place, as a boat on a river, what contains plays the part of a vessel rather than that of place. Place on the other hand is rather what is motionless: so it is rather the whole river that is place, because as a whole it is motionless.

Hence we conclude that *the innermost motionless boundary of what contains is place.*

Aristotle, *Physics,* 212^a8

5 Let us explain . . . that there is no void existing

separately, as some maintain. If each of the simple bodies has a natural locomotion, e.g. fire upward and earth downward and towards the middle of the universe, it is clear that it cannot be the void that is the condition of locomotion. What, then, *will* the void be the condition of? It is thought to be the condition of movement in respect of place, and it is not the condition of this.

Again, if void is a sort of place deprived of body, when there is a void where will a body placed in it move to? It certainly cannot move into the whole of the void. The same argument applies as against those who think that place is something separate, into which things are carried; viz. how will what is placed in it move, or rest? Much the same argument will apply to the void as to the 'up' and 'down' in place, as is natural enough since those who maintain the existence of the void make it a place.

And in what way will things be present either in place or in the void? For the expected result does not take place when a body is placed as a whole in a place conceived of as separate and permanent; for a part of it, unless it be placed apart, will not be in a place but in the whole. Further, if separate place does not exist, neither will void.

If people say that the void must exist, as being necessary if there is to be movement, what rather turns out to be the case, if one studies the matter, is the opposite, that not a single thing can be moved if there *is* a void; for as with those who for a like reason say the earth is at rest, so, too, in the void things must be at rest; for there is no place to which things can move more or less than to another; since the void in so far as it is void admits no difference.

Aristotle, *Physics*, 214ᵇ12

6 All things are not on all sides jammed together and kept in by body: there is also void in things. To have learned this will be good for you on many accounts; it will not suffer you to wander in doubt and be to seek in the sum of things and distrustful of our words. If there were not void, things could not move at all; for that which is the property of body, to let and hinder, would be present to all things at all times; nothing therefore could go on, since no other thing would be the first to give way.

Lucretius, *Nature of Things,* I

7 If room and space which we call void did not exist, bodies could not be placed anywhere nor move about at all to any side; as we have demonstrated to you a little before. Moreover there is nothing which you can affirm to be at once separate from all body and quite distinct from void, which would so to say count as the discovery of a third nature.

Lucretius, *Nature of Things,* I

8 If all the space of the whole sum were enclosed within fixed borders and were bounded, in that case the store of matter by its solid weights would have streamed together from all sides to the lowest point nor could anything have gone on under the canopy of heaven, no nor would there have been a heaven nor sunlight at all, inasmuch as all matter, settling down through infinite time past, would lie together in a heap. But as it is, sure enough no rest is given to the bodies of the first-beginnings, because there is no lowest point at all, to which they might stream together as it were, and where they might take up their positions. All things are ever going on in ceaseless motion on all sides and bodies of matter stirred to action are supplied from beneath out of infinite space. Therefore the nature of room and the space of the unfathomable void are such as bright thunderbolts cannot race through in their course though gliding on through endless tract of time, no nor lessen one jot the journey that remains to go by all their travel: so huge a room is spread out on all sides for things without any bounds in all directions round.

Lucretius, *Nature of Things,* I

9 Space being infinite, matter . . . must also be infinite, lest after the winged fashion of flames the walls of the world should suddenly break up and fly abroad along the mighty void, and all other things follow for like reasons and the innermost quarters of heaven tumble in from above and the earth in an instant withdraw from beneath our feet and amid the commingled ruins of things in it and of heaven, ruins unloosing the first bodies, should wholly pass away along the unfathomable void, so that in a moment of time not a wrack should be left behind, nothing save untenanted space and viewless first-beginnings. For on whatever side you shall first determine first bodies to be wanting, this side will be the gate of death for things, through this the whole crowd of matter will fling itself abroad.

Lucretius, *Nature of Things,* I

10 The first dimension is called "line," for "line" is that which is extended in one direction. Two dimensions are called "surface," for a "surface" is that which is extended in two directions. Three dimensions are called "solid," for a "solid" is that which is extended in three directions, and it is by no means possible to conceive of a solid which has more than three dimensions, depth, breadth, and length. By these are defined the six directions which are said to exist in connection with every body and by which motions in space are distinguished, forward, backward, up, down, right and left; for of necessity two directions opposite to each other follow upon each dimension, up and down upon one, forward and backward upon the second, and right and left upon the third.

Nicomachus, *Arithmetic*, II, 6

11 The notion of a vacuum not only implies that in which nothing is, but also requires a space capable of holding a body and in which there is not a body. . . . We hold however that before the world was there was no place or space.

Aquinas, *Summa Theologica,* I, 46, 1

12 Between every two points there are infinite intermediate points, since "no two points follow one another without a middle". . . . And the same must of necessity be said of divisible places, and this is shown from the continuous motion of a body. For a body is not moved from place to place except in time. But in the whole time which measures the motion of a body, there are not two *nows* in which the body moved is not in one place and in another; for if it were in one and the same place in two *nows,* it would follow that it would be at rest there, since to be at rest is nothing else than to be in the same place now and previously. Therefore, since there are infinite *nows* between the first and the last *now* of the time which measures the motion, there must be infinite places between the first from which the motion begins, and the last where the motion ceases.

Aquinas, *Summa Theologica,* I, 53, 2

13 A body is not related to place except through the medium of its proper dimensions, in respect of which a located body is confined through contact with the locating body. Hence it is not possible for a body to occupy a place smaller than its quantity, unless its proper quantity be made in some way less than itself.

Aquinas, *Summa Theologica,*
III Suppl., 83, 5

14 Local movement changes nothing that is intrinsic to a thing, but only that which is without, namely place. Hence that which is moved locally is perfect as to those things which are within, although it has an imperfection as to place, because while it is in one place it is in potency with regard to another place, since it cannot be in several places at the same time.

Aquinas, *Summa Theologica,*
III Suppl., 84, 2

15 We cannot with certainty determine whether there be a vacuum, either extensive or intermixed with matter. Of one thing, however, we are satisfied, that the reason assigned by Leucippus and Democritus for the introduction of a vacuum (namely, that the same bodies could not otherwise comprehend, and fill greater and less spaces) is false. For there is clearly a folding of matter, by which it wraps and unwraps itself in space within certain limits, without the intervention of a vacuum. Nor is there two thousand times more of vacuum in air than in gold, as there should be on this hypothesis.

Bacon, *Novum Organum,* II, 48

16 By extension we understand whatever has length, breadth, and depth, not inquiring whether it be a real body or merely space; nor does it appear to require further explanation, since there is nothing more easily perceived by our imagination. . . . Hence we announce that by extension we do not here mean anything distinct and separate from the extended object itself; and we make it a rule not to recognize those metaphysical entities which really cannot be presented to the imagination. For even though someone could persuade himself, for example, that supposing every extended object in the universe were annihilated, that would not prevent extension in itself alone existing, this conception of his would not involve the use of any corporeal image, but would be based on a false judgment of the intellect working by itself.

Descartes, *Rules for Direction
of the Mind,* XIV

17 Although there are spaces in which I find nothing which excites my senses, I must not from that conclude that these spaces contain no body.

Descartes, *Meditations on First
Philosophy,* VI

18 My conception of the superficies by which I believe our senses are affected, is not different from that employed (or which ought to be employed) by all mathematicians and philosophers; they distinguish it from body and assume it to be wholly devoid of depth. But the term superficies is taken in two ways by mathematicians: viz. in the sense of a body, to the length and breadth of which they attend and which is viewed altogether apart from its depth, although depth be not denied of it; or only as a mode of body, when straightway all depth is denied of it. Consequently for the sake of avoiding ambiguity I said that I spoke of that superficies which, being only a mode, can be no part of body; for a body is a substance, and a mode cannot be a part of substance. Yet I did not deny that it was the extremity of a body; nay, on the contrary, I said that it could with the greatest propriety be called the extremity of the contained body as much as of the containing, in the sense in which one says that bodies are contiguous when their extremities are together. For certainly when two bodies touch each other, the extremity of each is one and the same, and this is part of neither but the same mode of both, and can even remain although these bodies are removed, provided only that others of accurately the same size and figure succeed to their place. Nay that space which the Aristotelians call the superficies of the surrounding body can be understood to be no other superficies than that which is no substance but a mode. For neither is the place of a town changed, although the surrounding air be changed or some other substance be substituted for it, nor conse-

quently does the superficies which is here taken for a place form any part of the surrounding air or of the town.

Descartes, *Objections and Replies,* VI

19 No man . . . can conceive anything, but he must conceive it in some place; and endued with some determinate magnitude; and which may be divided into parts; nor that anything is all in this place, and all in another place at the same time; nor that two or more things can be in one and the same place at once: for none of these things ever have or can be incident to sense, but are absurd speeches.

Hobbes, *Leviathan,* I, 3

20 The world (I mean not the earth only, that denominates the lovers of it "worldly men," but the *universe,* that is, the whole mass of all things that are) is corporeal, that is to say, body; and hath the dimensions of magnitude, namely, length, breadth, and depth: also every part of body is likewise body, and hath the like dimensions; and consequently every part of the universe is body, and that which is not body is no part of the universe: and because the universe is all, that which is no part of it is nothing, and consequently nowhere.

Hobbes, *Leviathan,* IV, 46

21 I had always held that the vacuum was not a thing impossible in nature and that she did not flee it with such horror as many imagine.

I was forced to this opinion by seeing how slight was the foundation of the maxim so widely accepted that nature does not permit a vacuum, a maxim based only on experiments of which the greater number are false though considered most certain; and of the rest, some are so far from contributing to its proof that they show nature abhors too much fulness rather than flees a vacuum, and the most favorable do not bring anything more to light than that nature abhors a vacuum; they do not show that she cannot suffer it to be.

Pascal, *Concerning the Vacuum*

22 The essential difference between empty space and body, which has length, breadth, and depth, is that one is immobile and the other is mobile, and that one can receive within itself a body which penetrates its dimensions, whereas the other cannot; for the maxim on the impenetrability of dimensions is to be understood only of the dimensions of two material bodies; otherwise it would not be universally accepted. Whence it can be seen that there is as much difference between nothingness and empty space as there is between empty space and material body, and that thus empty space is a mean between material body and nothingness.

Pascal, *Concerning the Vacuum*

23 There is no geometer who does not believe that space is infinitely divisible. One can no more be a geometer without this principle than one can be a man without a soul. And yet there is no geometer who understands an infinite division. We are sure of that truth only for the reason, certainly sufficient, that we perfectly grasp the falsity of the statement that by dividing a space we can reach an indivisible part, a part, that is, having no extension.

Pascal, *Geometrical Demonstration*

24 When I consider the short duration of my life, swallowed up in the eternity before and after, the little space which I fill and even can see, engulfed in the infinite immensity of spaces of which I am ignorant and which know me not, I am frightened and am astonished at being here rather than there; for there is no reason why here rather than there, why now rather than then. Who has put me here? By whose order and direction have this place and time been allotted to me? . . . The eternal silence of these infinite spaces frightens me.

Pascal, *Pensées,* III, 205–206

25 Before thir eyes in sudden view appear
The secrets of the hoarie deep, a dark
Illimitable Ocean without bound,
Without dimension, where length, breadth, and
   highth,
And time and place are lost; where eldest Night
And *Chaos,* Ancestors of Nature, hold
Eternal *Anarchie,* amidst the noise
Of endless warrs, and by confusion stand.
For hot, cold, moist, and dry, four Champions
   fierce
Strive here for Maistrie, and to Battel bring
Thir embryon Atoms; they around the flag
Of each his faction, in thir several Clanns,
Light-arm'd or heavy, sharp, smooth, swift or
   slow,
Swarm populous, unnumber'd as the Sands
Of *Barca* or *Cyrene's* torrid soil,
Levied to side with warring Winds, and poise
Thir lighter wings. To whom these most adhere,
Hee rules a moment; *Chaos* Umpire sits,
And by decision more imbroiles the fray
By which he Reigns: next him high Arbiter
Chance governs all. Into this wilde Abyss,
The Womb of nature and perhaps her Grave,
Of neither Sea, nor Shore, nor Air, nor Fire,
But all these in thir pregnant causes mixt
Confus'dly, and which thus must ever fight,
Unless th' Almighty Maker them ordain
His dark materials to create more Worlds,
Into this wild Abyss the warie fiend
Stood on the brink of Hell and look'd a while,
Pondering his Voyage: for no narrow frith
He had to cross.

Milton, *Paradise Lost,* II, 890

26 If corporeal substance could be so divided that its parts could be really distinct, why could not one part be annihilated, the rest remaining, as before, connected with one another? Any why must all be so fitted together that there can be no vacuum? For of things which are really distinct the one from the other, one can be and remain in its own position without the other. Since, therefore, it is supposed that there is no vacuum in nature . . . but that all the parts must be united, so that no vacuum can exist, it follows that they cannot be really separated; that is to say, that corporeal substance, insofar as it is substance, cannot be divided. If, nevertheless, any one should now ask why there is a natural tendency to consider quantity as capable of division, I reply that quantity is conceived by us in two ways: either abstractly or superficially; that is to say, as we imagine it, or else as substance, in which way it is conceived by the intellect alone. If, therefore, we regard quantity (as we do very often and easily) as it exists in the imagination, we find it to be finite, divisible, and composed of parts; but if we regard it as it exists in the intellect, and conceive it insofar as it is substance, which is very difficult, then, as we have already sufficiently demonstrated, we find it to be infinite, one, and indivisible.

Spinoza, *Ethics,* I, Prop. 15, Schol.

27 Absolute space, in its own nature, without relation to anything external, remains always similar and immovable. Relative space is some movable dimension or measure of the absolute spaces; which our senses determine by its position to bodies; and which is commonly taken for immovable space; such is the dimension of a subterranean, an aerial, or celestial space, determined by its position in respect of the earth. Absolute and relative space are the same in figure and magnitude; but they do not remain always numerically the same. For if the earth, for instance, moves, a space of our air, which relatively and in respect of the earth remains always the same, will at one time be one part of the absolute space into which the air passes; at another time it will be another part of the same, and so, absolutely understood, it will be continually changed.

Place is a part of space which a body takes up, and is according to the space, either absolute or relative. I say, a part of space; not the situation, nor the external surface of the body. For the places of equal solids are always equal; but their surfaces, by reason of their dissimilar figures, are often unequal. Positions properly have no quantity, nor are they so much the places themselves, as the properties of places. The motion of the whole is the same with the sum of the motions of the parts; that is, the translation of the whole, out of its place, is the same thing with the sum of the translations of the parts out of their places; and therefore the place of the whole is the same as the sum of the places of the parts, and for that reason, it is internal, and in the whole body.

Newton, *Principia,* Definitions, Scholium

28 As the order of the parts of time is immutable, so also is the order of the parts of space. Suppose those parts to be moved out of their places, and they will be moved (if the expression may be allowed) out of themselves. For times and spaces are, as it were, the places as well of themselves as of all other things. All things are placed in time as to order of succession; and in space as to order of situation. It is from their essence or nature that they are places; and that the primary places of things should be movable, is absurd. These are therefore the absolute places; and translations out of those places, are the only absolute motions.

But because the parts of space cannot be seen, or distinguished from one another by our senses, therefore in their stead we use sensible measures of them. For from the positions and distances of things from any body considered as immovable, we define all places; and then with respect to such places, we estimate all motions, considering bodies as transferred from some of those places into others. And so, instead of absolute places and motions, we use relative ones; and that without any inconvenience in common affairs; but in philosophical disquisitions, we ought to abstract from our senses, and consider things themselves, distinct from what are only sensible measures of them. For it may be that there is no body really at rest, to which the places and motions of others may be referred.

Newton, *Principia,* Definitions, Scholium

29 I will here show how men come to form to themselves the notion of space. They consider that many things exist at once and they observe in them a certain order of co-existence, according to which the relation of one thing to another is more or less simple. This order, is their *situation* or distance. When it happens that one of those co-existent things changes its relation to a multitude of others, which do not change their relation among themselves; and that another thing, newly come, acquires the same relation to the others, as the former had; we then say it is come into the place of the former. . . . And supposing, or feigning, that among those co-existents, there is a sufficient number of them, which have undergone no change; then we may say, that those which have such a relation to those fixed existents, as others had to them before, have now the *same place* which those others had. And that which comprehends all those places, is called *space.*

Leibniz, *Letters to Samuel Clarke,* V

30 By this idea of solidity is the extension of body

distinguished from the extension of space:—the extension of body being nothing but the cohesion or continuity of solid, separable, movable parts; and the extension of space, the continuity of unsolid, inseparable, and immovable parts. Upon the solidity of bodies also depend their mutual impulse, resistance, and protrusion. Of pure space then, and solidity, there are several (amongst which I confess myself one) who persuade themselves they have clear and distinct ideas; and that they can think on space, without anything in it that resists or is protruded by body. This is the idea of pure space, which they think they have as clear as any idea they can have of the extension of body: the idea of the distance between the opposite parts of a concave superficies being equally as clear without as with the idea of any solid parts between: and on the other side, they persuade themselves that they have, distinct from that of pure space, the idea of *something that fills space,* that can be protruded by the impulse of other bodies or resist their motion.

> Locke, *Concerning Human Understanding,*
> Bk. II, IV, 5

31 We can have no idea of the place of the universe, though we can of all the parts of it; because beyond that we have not the idea of any fixed, distinct, particular beings, in reference to which we can imagine it to have any relation of distance; but all beyond it is one uniform space or expansion, wherein the mind finds no variety, no marks. For to say that the world is somewhere, means no more than that it does exist; this, though a phrase borrowed from place, signifying only its existence, not location: and when one can find out, and frame in his mind, clearly and distinctly, the place of the universe, he will be able to tell us whether it moves or stands still in the undistinguishable inane of infinite space: though it be true that the word place has sometimes a more confused sense, and stands for that space which anybody takes up; and so the universe is in a place.

> Locke, *Concerning Human Understanding,*
> Bk. II, XIII, 10

32 The philosophic consideration of motion does not imply the being of an *absolute Space,* distinct from that which is perceived by sense and related bodies; which that it cannot exist without the mind is clear upon the same principles that demonstrate the like of all other objects of sense. And perhaps, if we inquire narrowly, we shall find we cannot even frame an idea of *pure Space* exclusive of all body. This I must confess seems impossible, as being a most abstract idea. When I excite a motion in some part of my body if it be free or without resistance, I say there is *Space;* but if I find a resistance, then I say there is *Body;* and in proportion as the resistance to motion is lesser or greater, I say the space is more or less *pure.* So that when I

speak of pure or empty space, it is not to be supposed that the word "space" stands for an idea distinct from or conceivable without body and motion—though indeed we are apt to think every noun substantive stands for a distinct idea that may be separated from all others; which has occasioned infinite mistakes. When, therefore, supposing all the world to be annihilated besides my own body, I say there still remains *pure Space,* thereby nothing else is meant but only that I conceive it possible for the limbs of my body to be moved on all sides without the least resistance, but if that, too, were annihilated then there could be no motion, and consequently no Space. Some, perhaps, may think the sense of seeing doth furnish them with the idea of pure space; but it is plain from what we have elsewhere shewn, that the ideas of space and distance are not obtained by that sense. . . .

What is here laid down seems to put an end to all those disputes and difficulties that have sprung up amongst the learned concerning the nature of *pure Space.*

> Berkeley, *Principles of Human*
> *Knowledge,* 116–117

33 The idea of space is convey'd to the mind by two senses, the sight and touch; nor does any thing ever appear extended, that is not either visible or tangible. That compound impression, which represents extension, consists of several lesser impressions, that are indivisible to the eye or feeling, and may be call'd impressions of atoms or corpuscles endow'd with colour and solidity. But this is not all. 'Tis not only requisite, that these atoms shou'd be colour'd or tangible, in order to discover themselves to our senses; 'tis also necessary we shou'd preserve the idea of their colour or tangibility in order to comprehend them by our imagination. There is nothing but the idea of their colour or tangibility, which can render them conceivable by the mind. Upon the removal of the ideas of these sensible qualities, they are utterly annihilated to the thought or imagination.

Now such as the parts are, such is the whole. If a point be not consider'd as colour'd or tangible, it can convey to us no idea; and consequently the idea of extension, which is compos'd of the ideas of these points, can never possibly exist. But if the idea of extension really can exist, as we are conscious it does, its parts must also exist; and in order to that, must be consider'd as colour'd or tangible. We have therefore no idea of space or extension, but when we regard it as an object either of our sight or feeling.

> Hume, *Treatise of Human Nature,*
> Bk. I, II, 3

34 Our system concerning space and time consists of two parts, which are intimately connected togeth-

er. The first depends on this chain of reasoning. The capacity of the mind is not infinite; consequently no idea of extension or duration consists of an infinite number of parts or inferior ideas, but of a finite number, and these simple and indivisible: 'Tis therefore possible for space and time to exist conformable to this idea: And if it be possible, 'tis certain they actually do exist conformable to it; since their infinite divisibility is utterly impossible and contradictory.

The other part of our system is a consequence of this. The parts, into which the ideas of space and time resolve themselves, become at last indivisible; and these indivisible parts, being nothing in themselves, are inconceivable when not fill'd with something real and existent. The ideas of space and time are therefore no separate or distinct ideas, but merely those of the manner or order, in which objects exist: Or, in other words, 'tis impossible to conceive either a vacuum and extension without matter, or a time, when there was no succession or change in any real existence.

Hume, *Treatise of Human Nature,*
Bk. I, II, 4

35 Space is not a conception which has been derived from outward experiences. For, in order that certain sensations may relate to something without me (that is, to something which occupies a different part of space from that in which I am); in like manner, in order that I may represent them not merely as without, of, and near to each other, but also in separate places, the representation of space must already exist as a foundation. Consequently, the representation of space cannot be borrowed from the relations of external phenomena through experience; but, on the contrary, this external experience is itself only possible through the said antecedent representation.

Space then is a necessary representation *a priori,* which serves for the foundation of all external intuitions. We never can imagine or make a representation to ourselves of the non-existence of space, though we may easily enough think that no objects are found in it.

Kant, *Critique of Pure Reason,*
Transcendental Aesthetic

36 Space does not represent any property of objects as things in themselves, nor does it represent them in their relations to each other; in other words, space does not represent to us any determination of objects such as attaches to the objects themselves, and would remain, even though all subjective conditions of the intuition were abstracted. For neither absolute nor relative determinations of objects can be intuited prior to the existence of the things to which they belong, and therefore not *a priori.* . . . It is therefore from the human point of view only that we can speak of space, extended

objects, etc. If we depart from the subjective condition, under which alone we can obtain external intuition, or, in other words, by means of which we are affected by objects, the representation of space has no meaning whatsoever.

Kant, *Critique of Pure Reason,*
Transcendental Aesthetic

37 Let no one be surprised [that] . . . there may be a space without order just as there may be an order without space. And the primitive perceptions of space are certainly of an unordered kind. The order which the spaces first perceived potentially include must, before being distinctly apprehended by the mind, be woven into those spaces by a rather complicated set of intellectual acts. The primordial largenesses which the sensations yield must be *measured and subdivided* by consciousness, and *added* together, before they can form by their synthesis what we know as the real Space of the objective world.

William James, *Psychology,* XX

38 Whatever sensible data can be attended to together we locate together. Their several extents seem one extent. The place at which each appears is held to be the same with the place at which the others appear. They become, in short, so many properties of one and the same real thing. This is the first and great commandment, the fundamental "act" by which our world gets spatially arranged.

William James, *Psychology,* XX

39 The imagined aggregate of positions occupied by all the actual or possible, moving or stationary, things which we know, is our notion of "real" space—a very incomplete and vague conception in all minds.

William James, *Psychology,* XX

40 The essence of the Kantian contention is that there are not *spaces,* but *Space*—one infinite continuous *Unit*—and that our knowledge of *this* cannot be a piecemeal sensational affair, produced by summation and abstraction. To which the obvious reply is that, if any known thing bears on its front the *appearance* of piecemeal construction and abstraction, it is this very notion of the infinite unitary space of the world. It is a *notion,* if ever there was one; and no intuition. Most of us apprehend it in the barest symbolic abridgment: and if perchance we ever do try to make it more adequate, we just add one image of sensible extension to another until we are tired. Most of us are obliged to turn round and drop the thought of the space in front of us when we think of that behind. And the space represented as near to us seems more minutely subdivisible than that we think of as lying far away.

William James, *Psychology,* XX

41 It is often said the images of external objects are localized in space, even that they can not be formed except on this condition. It is also said that this space, which serves thus as a ready prepared *frame* for our sensations and our representations, is identical with that of the geometers, of which it possesses all the properties. . . . But let us see whether they are not subject to an illusion that a more profound analysis would dissipate.

What, first of all, are the properties of space, properly so called? I mean of that space which is the object of geometry and which I shall call *geometric space*. The following are some of the most essential:

1° It is continuous;

2° It is infinite;

3° It has three dimensions;

4° It is homogeneous, that is to say, all its points are identical one with another;

5° It is isotropic, that is to say, all the straights which pass through the same point are identical one with another.

Compare it now to the frame of our representations and our sensations, which I may call *perceptual space*.

Visual Space.—Consider first a purely visual impression, due to an image formed on the bottom of the retina.

A cursory analysis shows us this image as continuous, but as possessing only two dimensions; this already distinguishes from geometric space what we may call *pure visual space*.

Besides, this image is enclosed in a limited frame.

Finally, there is another difference not less important: *this pure visual space is not homogeneous*. All the points of the retina, aside from the images which may there be formed, do not play the same rôle. The yellow spot can in no way be regarded as identical with a point on the border of the retina. In fact, not only does the same object produce there much more vivid impressions, but in every *limited* frame the point occupying the center of the frame will never appear as equivalent to a point near one of the borders.

No doubt a more profound analysis would show us that this continuity of visual space and its two dimensions are only an illusion; it would separate it therefore still more from geometric space, but we shall not dwell on this remark.

Poincaré, *Science and Hypothesis*, II, 4

42 Perceptual space, under its triple form, visual, tactile and motor, is essentially different from geometric space.

It is neither homogeneous, nor isotropic; one can not even say that it has three dimensions.

It is often said that we 'project' into geometric space the objects of our external perception; that we 'localize' them.

Has this a meaning, and if so what?

Does it mean that we *represent* to ourselves external objects in geometric space?

Our representations are only the reproduction of our sensations; they can therefore be ranged only in the same frame as these, that is to say, in perceptual space.

It is as impossible for us to represent to ourselves external bodies in geometric space, as it is for a painter to paint on a plane canvas objects with their three dimensions.

Perceptual space is only an image of geometric space, an image altered in shape by a sort of perspective, and we can represent to ourselves objects only by bringing them under the laws of this perspective.

Therefore we do not *represent* to ourselves external bodies in geometric space, but we *reason* on these bodies as if they were situated in geometric space.

Poincaré, *Science and Hypothesis*, II, 4

43 We speak in the singular of *The* Universe, of Nature, of [physis] which can be translated as Process. There is the one all-embracing fact which is the advancing history of the one Universe. This community of the world, which is the matrix for all begetting, and whose essence is process with retention of connectedness,—this community is what Plato terms The Receptacle. In our effort to divine his meaning, we must remember that Plato says that it is an obscure and difficult concept, and that in its own essence the Receptacle is devoid of all forms. It is thus certainly not the ordinary geometrical space with its mathematical relations. Plato calls his Receptacle, 'The foster-mother of all becoming'. He evidently conceived it as a necessary notion without which our analysis of Nature is defective. It is dangerous to neglect Plato's intuitions. He carefully varies his phrases in referring to it, and implies that what he says is to be taken in its most abstract sense. The Receptacle imposes a common relationship on all that happens, but does not impose what that relationship shall be. It seems to be a somewhat more subtle notion than Aristotle's 'matter' which, of course, is not the 'matter' of Galileo and Newton. Plato's Receptacle may be conceived as the necessary community within which the course of history is set, in abstraction from all the particular historical facts. I have directed attention to Plato's doctrine of The Receptacle because, at the present moment, physical science is nearer to it than at any period since Plato's death. The space-time of modern mathematical physics, conceived in abstraction from the particular mathematical formulæ which applies to the happenings in it, is almost exactly Plato's Receptacle. It is to be noted that mathematical physicists are extremely uncertain as to what these formulæ are exactly, nor do they believe that any such formulæ can be derived

from the mere notion of space-time. Thus, as Plato declares, space-time in itself is bare of all forms.

Whitehead, *Adventures of Ideas,* IX, 4

44 Psychology is concerned with space, not as a system of relations among material objects but as a feature of our perceptions. If we could accept naive realism, this distinction would have little importance: we should perceive material objects and their spatial relations, and the space that characterizes our perceptions would be identical with the space of physics. But in fact naive realism cannot be accepted, percepts are not identical with material objects, and the relation of perceptual to physical space is not identity.

Russell, *Human Knowledge,* III, 6

45 The construction of one space in which all our perceptual experiences are located is a triumph of pre-scientific common sense. Its merit lies in its convenience, not in any ultimate truth that it may be supposed to possess. Common sense, in attributing to it a degree of nonconventional truth beyond what it actually has a right to claim, is in error, and this error, uncorrected, adds greatly to the difficulty of a sound philosophy of space.

Russell, *Human Knowledge,* III, 6

46 It is a wide-spread error that the special theory of relativity is supposed to have, to a certain extent, first discovered, or at any rate, newly introduced, the four-dimensionality of the physical continuum. This, of course, is not the case. Classical mechanics, too, is based on the four-dimensional continuum of space and time. But in the four-dimensional continuum of classical physics the subspaces with constant time value have an absolute reality, independent of the choice of the reference system. Because of this [fact], the four-dimensional continuum falls naturally into a three-dimensional and a one-dimensional (time), so that the four-dimensional point of view does not force itself upon one as *necessary.* The special theory of relativity, on the other hand, creates a formal dependence between the way in which the spatial co-ordinates, on the one hand, and the temporal co-ordinates, on the other, have to enter into the natural laws.

Einstein, *Autobiographical Notes*

47 It is scarcely possible to give any other definition of space: space is what enables us to distinguish a number of identical and simultaneous sensations from one another; it is thus a principle of differentiation other than that of qualitative differentiation, and consequently it is a reality with no quality.

Bergson, *Time and Free Will,* II

48 What . . . physical space or time may properly be, we could know perfectly only by knowing perfectly the intimate movement and ultimate ranges of matter—not a human task. We know matter, as it behoves us to know it, in the measure in which our highly selective action and mental chronicle of action penetrate into its meshes. . . . Physical space and time are integral elements in this realm of matter: they are *physical,* which is as much as to say that they are contingent, to be explored by experiment rather than by reasoning, to be shared by us rather than contemplated. They may change their form if they choose, like any existence, and may manifest a different essence in their new instances.

It is therefore a problem never to be solved except provisionally and locally, how far a human sensation of sentimental time or of pictorial space, or how far any geometrical model of a pure space or time, may fitly express the temporal and spatial dimensions of nature, or be a true measure for them.

Santayana, *Realm of Matter,* IV

49 Pictorial space is one of the dearest possessions of the human spirit: it would be thankless of us to be impatient because it is subjective, as if it ought not to have been so. It might no doubt have had a different sensuous texture, and might have conveyed much the same practical information in that other guise; but it could hardly have been more beautiful than, to the human eye, are the colours of the spectrum, the forms of motion, and the spheres of shadow and of light.

Santayana, *Realm of Matter,* IV

19.7 | *Time*

Unlike space, which elicits no comment from the poets, time is a subject about which they wax eloquent, indeed. It is also one that puzzles the philosophers even more than space does. Just as the quotations from Shakespeare's sonnets represent the range of the poetic response to time, so the quotations from Augustine's *Confessions* represent different aspects of the philosopher's puzzlement about time—about its definition; about its division into past, present, and future; about its beginning and end, or its endlessness; and about its relation to eternity or timelessness. In this last connection, the reader should observe that the word "eternity" is sometimes used for time everlasting, time without beginning or end, and sometimes for the transcendence of time, or timelessness. It is only in the second of these two meanings that one can make sense of the statement by Plato and others that time is the moving image of eternity.

Another point of dispute concerns the relation of time to motion, Aristotle asserting and Locke denying that time is the measure of motion. Philosophers apart, the physicists find time as indispensable as distance in the measurement of motion. But they in turn dispute about such matters as the existence of absolute time as opposed to relative or local time, and about the separability or inseparability of time and space.

The issue touched on in Section 19.5, about the eternity of motion, without beginning or end, recurs here in a related question about time. Did time ever begin and will it ever end? One theologian, Augustine, explains the folly of asking what God was doing before the beginning of time; another, Aquinas, insists that if we affirm that the world and time did have a beginning, we must do so by faith in God's own revelation in the opening sentence of *Genesis,* for in no other way can we know an answer to the question. Aquinas takes a similar view of the end of the world and of time.

As in the case of space, so here too the reader will find a disagreement between Kant and James about the perception of time. In addition, the reader will find some interesting psychological observations by James concerning the experience of what he calls "the specious present," and concerning the difference between empty and filled time, as something experienced and as something remembered.

---

1 For a thousand years in thy sight are but as yesterday when it is past, and as a watch in the night.
Psalm 90:4

2 To every thing there is a season, and a time to every purpose under the heaven:
   A time to be born, and a time to die; a time to plant, and a time to pluck up that which is planted;
   A time to kill, and a time to heal; a time to break down, and a time to build up;
   A time to weep, and a time to laugh; a time to mourn, and a time to dance;
   A time to cast away stones, and a time to gather stones together; a time to embrace, and a time to refrain from embracing;
   A time to get, and a time to lose; a time to keep, and a time to cast away;
   A time to rend, and a time to sew; a time to keep silence, and a time to speak;
   A time to love, and a time to hate; a time of war, and a time of peace.
Ecclesiastes 3:1–8

3 *Chorus.* Time brings all things to pass.
Aeschylus, *Libation Bearers,* 965

4 *Timaeus.* When the father and creator saw the

creature which he had made moving and living, the created image of the eternal gods, he rejoiced, and in his joy determined to make the copy still more like the original; and as this was eternal, he sought to make the universe eternal, so far as might be. Now the nature of the ideal being was everlasting, but to bestow this attribute in its fulness upon a creature was impossible. Wherefore he resolved to have a moving image of eternity, and when he set in order the heaven, he made this image eternal but moving according to number, while eternity itself rests in unity; and this image we call time. For there were no days and nights and months and years before the heaven was created, but when he constructed the heaven he created them also. They are all parts of time, and the past and future are created species of time, which we unconsciously but wrongly transfer to the eternal essence; for we say that he "was," he "is," he "will be," but the truth is that "is" alone is properly attributed to him, and that "was" and "will be" are only to be spoken of becoming in time, for they are motions, but that which is immovably the same cannot become older or younger by time, nor ever did or has become, or hereafter will be, older or younger, nor is subject at all to any of those states which affect moving and sensible things and of which generation is the cause. These are the forms of time, which imitates eternity and revolves according to a law of number. Moreover, when we say that what has become *is* become and what becomes *is* becoming, and that what will become *is* about to become and that the non-existent *is* non-existent—all these are inaccurate modes of expression. . . .

Time, then, and the heaven came into being at the same instant in order that, having been created together, if ever there was to be a dissolution of them, they might be dissolved together. It was framed after the pattern of the eternal nature, that it might resemble this as far as was possible; for the pattern exists from eternity, and the created heaven has been, and is, and will be, in all time. Such was the mind and thought of God in the creation of time.

Plato, *Timaeus,* 37B

5 Time is a measure of motion and of being moved, and it measures the motion by determining a motion which will measure exactly the whole motion, as the cubit does the length by determining an amount which will measure out the whole. Further 'to be in time' means, for movement, that both it and its essence are measured by time (for simultaneously it measures both the movement and its essence, and this is what being in time means for it, that its essence should be measured).

Aristotle, *Physics,* 221ª1

6 Will time then fail? Surely not, if motion always exists. Is time then always different or does the same time recur? Clearly time is, in the same way as motion is. For if one and the same motion sometimes recurs, it will be one and the same time, and if not, not.

Since the 'now' is an end and a beginning of time, not of the same time however, but the end of that which is past and the beginning of that which is to come, it follows that, as the circle has its convexity and its concavity, in a sense, in the same thing, so time is always at a beginning and at an end. And for this reason it seems to be always different; for the 'now' is not the beginning and the end of the same thing; if it were, it would be at the same time and in the same respect two opposites. And time will not fail; for it is always at a beginning.

Aristotle, *Physics,* 222ª29

7 Time . . . exists not by itself, but simply from the things which happen the sense apprehends what has been done in time past, as well as what is present and what is to follow after. And we must admit that no one feels time by itself abstracted from the motion and calm rest of things. So when they say that the daughter of Tyndarus was ravished and the Trojan nations were subdued in war, we must mind that they do not force us to admit that these things are by themselves, since those generations of men, of whom these things were accidents, time now gone by has irrevocably swept away.

Lucretius, *Nature of Things,* I

8 See you not that even stones are conquered by time, that high towers fall and rocks moulder away, that shrines and idols of gods are worn out with decay, and that the holy divinity cannot prolong the bounds of fate or struggle against the fixed laws of nature?

Lucretius, *Nature of Things,* V

9 But time is lost, which never will renew,
While we too far the pleasing path pursue,
Surveying nature with too nice a view.

Virgil, *Georgics,* III

10   Ev'n as we speak, grim Time
      speeds swift away;
Seize now and here the hour that is, nor trust
      some later day!

Horace, *Odes,* I, 11

11 No round of hopes for us! So speaks the year,
   And Time that steals our day.

Horace, *Odes,* IV, 7

12 Time flies.

Ovid, *Fasti,* VI, 5

13 Nothing is constant in the whole world. Everything is in a state of flux, and comes into being

as a transient appearance. Time itself flows on with constant motion, just like a river: for no more than a river can the fleeting hour stand still. As wave is driven on by wave, and, itself pursued, pursues the one before, so the moments of time at once flee and follow, and are ever new.

Ovid, *Metamorphoses*, XV

14   Our life is most short and unhappy,
Fading away like a flower, and even while we are drinking,
Calling for garlands and girls and perfumes, old age steals upon us,
Always, before we know.

Juvenal, *Satire IX*

15 Time is like a river made up of the events which happen, and a violent stream; for as soon as a thing has been seen, it is carried away, and another comes in its place, and this will be carried away too.

Marcus Aurelius, *Meditations*, IV, 43

16 What is in time is of a lower order than time itself: time is folded around what is in time exactly as—we read—it is folded about what is in place and in number.

Plotinus, *Fourth Ennead*, IV, 15

17 Time takes no holiday. It does not roll idly by, but through our senses works its own wonders in the mind. Time came and went from one day to the next; in its coming and in its passing it brought me other hopes and other memories, and little by little patched me up again with the kind of delights which had once been mine.

Augustine, *Confessions*, IV, 8

18 Before God made heaven and earth, He did not make anything. For if He had made something, what would it have been but a creature? And I wish I knew all that it would be profitable for me to know, as well as I know that no creature was made before any creature was made.

But a lighter mind, adrift among images of time and its passing, might wonder that You, O God almighty and all-creating and all-conserving, Maker of heaven and earth, should have abstained from so vast a work for the countless ages that passed before You actually wrought it. Such a mind should awaken and realize how ill-grounded is his wonder.

How could countless ages pass when You, the Author and Creator of all ages, had not yet made them? What time could there be that You had not created? or how could ages pass, if they never were?

Thus, since You are the Maker of all times, if there actually was any time before You made heaven and earth, how can it be said that You were not at work? If there was time, You made it,

for time could not pass before You made time. On the other hand, if before heaven and earth were made there was no time, then what is meant by the question "What were You doing *then?*" If there was not any time, there was not any "then". . . .

You are the Maker of all time, and before all time You are, nor was there ever a time when there was no time!

Augustine, *Confessions*, XI, 12–13

19 If we conceive of some point of time which cannot be divided into even the minutest parts of moments, that is the only point that can be called present: and that point flees at such lightning speed from being future to being past, that it has no extent of duration at all.

Augustine, *Confessions*, XI, 15

20 If the future and the past exist, I want to know where they are. And if I cannot yet know this, at least I do know that wherever they are, they are there not as future or past, but present. If wherever they are they are future, then in that place they are not yet; if past, then they are there no more. Thus wherever they are and whatever they are, they *are* only as present. When we relate the past truly, it is not the things themselves that are brought forth from our memory—for these have passed away: but words conceived from the images of the things: for the things stamped their prints upon the mind as they passed through it by way of the senses. Thus for example my boyhood, which no longer exists, is in time past, which no longer exists; but the likeness of my boyhood, when I recall it and talk of it, I look upon in time present, because it is still present in my memory.

Augustine, *Confessions*, XI, 18

21 Whatever may be the mode of this mysterious foreseeing of things to come, unless the thing is it cannot be seen. But what now is, is not future but present. Therefore when we speak of seeing the future, obviously what is seen is not the things which are not yet because they are still ιo come, but their causes or perhaps the signs that foretell them, for these causes and signs do exist here and now. Thus to those who see them now, they are not future but present, and from them things to come are conceived by the mind and foretold. These concepts already exist, and those who foretell are gazing upon them, present within themselves.

Augustine, *Confessions*, XI, 18

22 At any rate it is now quite clear that neither future nor past actually exists. Nor is it right to say there are three times, past, present and future. Perhaps it would be more correct to say: there are three times, a present of things past, a present of things present, a present of things future. For

these three exist in the mind, and I find them nowhere else: the present of things past is memory, the present of things present is sight, the present of things future is expectation.

Augustine, *Confessions,* XI, 20

23 Where does time come from, and by what way does it pass, and where does it go, while we are measuring it? Where is it from?—obviously from the future. But what way does it pass?—by the present. Where does it go?—into the past. In other words it passes from that which does not yet exist, by way of that which lacks extension, into that which is no longer.

Augustine, *Confessions,* XI, 21

24 I confess to You, Lord, that I still do not know what time is. And again I confess to You, Lord, that I know that I am uttering these things in time: I have been talking of time for a long time, and this long time would not be a long time unless time had passed. But how do I know this, since I do not know what time is? Or perhaps I do know, but simply do not know how to express what I know. Alas for me, I do not even know what I do not know!

Augustine, *Confessions,* XI, 25

25 If eternity and time are rightly distinguished by this, that time does not exist without some movement and transition, while in eternity there is no change, who does not see that there could have been no time had not some creature been made, which by some motion could give birth to change—the various parts of which motion and change, as they cannot be simultaneous, succeed one another—and thus, in these shorter or longer intervals of duration, time would begin? Since then, God, in Whose eternity is no change at all, is the Creator and Ordainer of time, I do not see how He can be said to have created the world after spaces of time had elapsed, unless it be said that prior to the world there was some creature by whose movement time could pass.

Augustine, *City of God,* XI, 6

26 We can reasonably say there was a time when Rome was not; there was a time when Jerusalem was not; there was a time when Abraham was not; there was a time when man was not, and so on: in fine, if the world was not made at the commencement of time, but after some time had elapsed, we can say there was a time when the world was not. But to say there was a time when time was not, is as absurd as to say there was a man when there was no man; or, this world was when this world was not.

Augustine, *City of God,* XII, 15

27 It is manifest that time and eternity are not the same. Some have founded the nature of this difference on the fact that eternity lacks beginning and end, whereas time has a beginning and an end. This, however, is an accidental and not an absolute difference, because, granted that time always was and always will be, according to the idea of those who think the movement of the heavens goes on for ever, there would yet remain a difference between eternity and time . . . arising from the fact that eternity is simultaneously whole, which cannot be applied to time; for eternity is the measure of a permanent being, while time is the measure of movement.

Supposing, however, that this difference be considered on the part of the things measured, and not as regards the measures, then there is another reason for it, since that alone is measured by time which has beginning and end in time. . . . Hence, if the movement of the heavens lasted always, time would not be its measure as regards the whole of its duration, since the infinite is not measurable; but it would measure any revolution whatsoever which has beginning and end in time.

Aquinas, *Summa Theologica,* I, 10, 4

28 As eternity is the proper measure of being itself, so time is the proper measure of movement; and hence, according as any being recedes from permanence of being, and undergoes change, it recedes from eternity, and is subject to time. Therefore the being of things corruptible, because it is changeable, is not measured by eternity, but by time; for time measures not only things actually changed, but also things changeable. Hence it not only measures movement, but it also measures repose, which belongs to whatever is naturally movable, but is not actually in motion.

Aquinas, *Summa Theologica,* I, 10, 4

29 In time there is something indivisible—namely, the instant; and there is something else which endures—namely, time. But in eternity the indivisible now stands always still.

Aquinas, *Summa Theologica,* I, 42, 2

30 Even supposing that the world always was, it would not be equal to God in eternity . . . because the divine Being is all being simultaneously without succession; but with the world it is otherwise.

Aquinas, *Summa Theologica,* I, 46, 2

31 *Beatrice.* The nature of the universe which stilleth the centre and moveth all the rest around, hence doth begin as from its starting point.
And this heaven hath no other *where* than the divine mind wherein is kindled the love which rolleth it and the power which it sheddeth.
Light and love grasp it in one circle, as doth it the others, and this engirdment he only who doth gird it understandeth.
Its movement by no other is marked out; but by it

all the rest are measured, as ten by half and
fifth.
And how Time in this same vessel hath its roots,
and in the rest its leaves, may now be manifest
to thee.

> Dante, *Paradiso,* XXVII, 106

32 And well may Seneca, and many more,
Bewail lost time far more than gold in store.
'For chattels lost may yet recovered be,
But time lost ruins us for aye,' says he.
It will not come again, once it has fled,
Not any more than will Mag's maidenhead
When she has lost it in her wantonness;
Let's not grow mouldy thus in idleness.

> Chaucer, *Canterbury Tales:* Man of Law's
> Prologue, Intro.

33 What really *is?* That which is eternal: that is to
say, what never had birth, nor will ever have an
end; to which time never brings any change. For
time is a mobile thing, which appears as in a
shadow, together with matter, which is ever running and flowing, without ever remaining stable
or permanent. To which belong the words *before*
and *after,* and *has been* or *will be,* which at the very
first sight show very evidently that time is not a
thing that *is;* for it would be a great stupidity and
a perfectly apparent falsehood to say that that *is*
which is not yet in being, or which already has
ceased to be. And as for these words, *present, immediate, now,* on which it seems that we chiefly found
and support our understanding of time, reason
discovering this immediately destroys it; for she at
once splits and divides it into future and past, as
though wanting to see it necessarily divided in
two.
The same thing happens to nature that is measured, as to time that measures it. For there is
nothing in it either that abides or is stable; but all
things in it are either born, or being born, or
dying. For which reason it would be a sin to say of
God, who is the only one that *is,* that he *was* or
will be. For those terms represent declinings, transitions, or vicissitudes of what cannot endure or
remain in being. Wherefore we must conclude
that God alone *is*—not at all according to any
measure of time, but according to an eternity immutable and immobile, not measured by time or
subject to any decline; before whom there is nothing, nor will there be after, nor is there anything
more new or more recent; but one who really is—
who by one single *now* fills the *ever;* and there is
nothing that really is but he alone—nor can we
say "He has been," or "He will be"—without beginning and without end.

> Montaigne, *Essays,* II, 12, Apology
> for Raymond Sebond

34 Goe to my love, where she is carelesse layd,
Yet in her winters bowre, not well awake;
Tell her the joyous time wil not be staid,

Unlesse she doe him by the forelock take.

> Spenser, *Amoretti,* LXX

35 *King Richard.* I wasted time, and now doth time
waste me.

> Shakespeare, *Richard II,* V, v, 49

36 *The Bastard.* Old Time the clock-setter, that bald
sexton Time,
Is it as he will?

> Shakespeare, *King John,* III, i, 324

37 *Jaques.*   He drew a dial from his poke,
And, looking on it with lack-lustre eye,
Says very wisely, "It is ten o'clock:
Thus we may see," quoth he, "how the world
wags:
'Tis but an hour ago since it was nine,
And after one hour more 'twill be eleven;
And so, from hour to hour, we ripe and ripe,
And then, from hour to hour, we rot and rot;
And thereby hangs a tale."

> Shakespeare, *As You Like It,* II, vii, 20

38 *Rosalind.* Time travels in divers paces with divers
persons. I'll tell you who Time ambles withal, who
Time trots withal, who Time gallops withal, and
who he stands still withal.

> Shakespeare, *As You Like It,* III, ii, 326

39 *Clown.* The whirligig of time brings in his revenges.

> Shakespeare, *Twelfth Night,* V, i, 385

40 *Hector.*   The end crowns all,
And that old common arbitrator, Time,
Will one day end it.

> Shakespeare, *Troilus and Cressida,* IV, v, 224

41 *Macbeth.*   Come what come may,
Time and the hour runs through the roughest
day.

> Shakespeare, *Macbeth,* I, iii, 146

42 *Prospero.*   How is it
That this lives in thy mind? What seest thou else
In the dark backward and abysm of time?

> Shakespeare, *Tempest,* I, ii, 48

43 Devouring Time, blunt thou the lion's paws,
And make the earth devour her own sweet brood;
Pluck the keen teeth from the fierce tiger's jaws,
And burn the long-lived phoenix in her blood.

> Shakespeare, *Sonnet XIX*

44 The present time has no causal dependence on
the time immediately preceding it. Hence, in order to secure the continued existence of a thing,
no less a cause is required than that needed to
produce it at the first.

> Descartes, *Arguments Demonstrating the
> Existence of God and the Distinction
> Between Soul and Body,* Axiom 2

45 Restless inquietude for the diuturnity of our memories unto present considerations seems a vanity almost out of date, and superannuated piece of folly. We cannot hope to live so long in our names as some have done in their persons; one face of Janus holds no proportion unto the other. 'Tis too late to be ambitious. The great mutations of the world are acted, or time may be too short for our designs. To extend our memories by monuments, whose death we daily pray for, and whose duration we cannot hope, without injury to our expectations in the advent of the last day, were a contradiction to our beliefs. We whose generations are ordained in this setting part of time are providentially taken off from such imaginations; and, being necessitated to eye the remaining particle of futurity, are naturally constituted unto thoughts of the next world, and cannot excusably decline the consideration of that duration, which maketh pyramids pillars of snow, and all that's past a moment.

Sir Thomas Browne, *Urn-Burial,* V

46 Oblivion is not to be hired: the greater part must be content to be as though they had not been, to be found in the register of God, not in the record of man. Twenty-seven names make up the first story, and the recorded names ever since contain not one living century. The number of the dead long exceedeth all that shall live. The night of time far surpasseth the day, and who knows when was the equinox? Every hour adds unto that current arithmetic, which scarce stands one moment. And since death must be the Lucina of life, and even pagans could doubt whether thus to live were to die; since our longest sun sets at right descensions, and makes but winter arches, and therefore it cannot be long before we lie down in darkness, and have our light in ashes; since the brother of death daily haunts us with dying mementos, and time that grows old in itself bids us hope no long duration; diuturnity is a dream and folly of expectation.

Sir Thomas Browne, *Urn-Burial,* V

47 Time heals griefs and quarrels, for we change and are no longer the same persons.

Pascal, *Pensées,* II, 122

48 Fly envious *Time,* till thou run out thy race,
Call on the lazy leaden-stepping hours,
Whose speed is but the heavy Plummets pace;
And glut thy self with what thy womb devours,
Which is no more then what is false and vain,
And meerly mortal dross;
So little is our loss,
So little is thy gain.

Milton, *On Time*

49 By eternity, I understand existence itself, so far as

it is conceived necessarily to follow from the definition alone of the eternal thing.

Spinoza, *Ethics,* I, Def. 8

50 Duration is the indefinite continuation of existence.

Spinoza, *Ethics,* II, Def. 5

51 Eternity cannot be defined by time, or have any relationship to it.

Spinoza, *Ethics,* V, Prop. 23, Schol.

52 If we look at the common opinion of men, we shall see that they are indeed conscious of the eternity of their minds, but they confound it with duration, and attribute it to imagination or memory, which they believe remain after death.

Spinoza, *Ethics,* V, Prop. 34, Schol.

53 Absolute, true, and mathematical time, of itself, and from its own nature, flows equably without relation to anything external, and by another name is called duration: relative, apparent, and common time, is some sensible and external (whether accurate or unequable) measure of duration by the means of motion, which is commonly used instead of true time; such as an hour, a day, a month, a year.

Newton, *Principia,* Definitions, Scholium

54 It may be, that there is no such thing as an equable motion, whereby time may be accurately measured. All motions may be accelerated and retarded, but the flowing of absolute time is not liable to any change. The duration of perseverance of the existence of things remains the same, whether the motions are swift or slow, or none at all: and therefore this duration ought to be distinguished from what are only sensible measures thereof.

Newton, *Principia,* Definitions, Scholium

55 One thing seems strange to me,—that whilst all men manifestly measured time by the motion of the great and visible bodies of the world, time yet should be defined to be the "measure of motion": whereas it is obvious to every one who reflects ever so little on it, that to measure motion, space is as necessary to be considered as time; and those who look a little farther will find also the bulk of the thing moved necessary to be taken into the computation, by any one who will estimate or measure motion so as to judge right of it. Nor indeed does motion any otherwise conduce to the measuring of duration, than as it constantly brings about the return of certain sensible ideas, in seeming equidistant periods. For if the motion of the sun were as unequal as of a ship driven by unsteady winds, sometimes very slow, and at others irregularly very swift; or if, being constantly equally swift, it yet was not circular, and produced not the

same appearances,— it would not at all help us to measure time, any more than the seeming unequal motion of a comet does.

Locke, *Concerning Human Understanding, Bk. II, XIV, 22*

56 Having frequently in our mouths the name Eternity, we are apt to think we have a positive comprehensive idea of it, which is as much as to say, that there is no part of that duration which is not clearly contained in our idea. It is true that he that thinks so may have a clear idea of duration; he may also have a clear idea of a very great length of duration; he may also have a clear idea of the comparison of that great one with still a greater: but it not being possible for him to include in his idea of any duration, let it be as great as it will, *the whole extent together of a duration, where he supposes no end,* that part of his idea, which is still beyond the bounds of that large duration he represents to his own thoughts, is very obscure and undetermined. And hence it is that in disputes and reasonings concerning eternity, or any other infinite, we are very apt to blunder, and involve ourselves in manifest absurdities.

Locke, *Concerning Human Understanding, Bk. II, XXIX, 15*

57 Whenever I attempt to frame a simple idea of *time,* abstracted from the succession of ideas in my mind, which flows uniformly and is participated by all beings, I am lost and embrangled in inextricable difficulties. I have no notion of it at all, only I hear others say it is infinitely divisible, and speak of it in such a manner as leads me to entertain odd thoughts of my existence; since that doctrine lays one under an absolute necessity of thinking, either that he passes away innumerable ages without a thought, or else that he is annihilated every moment of his life, both which seem equally absurd. Time therefore being nothing, abstracted from the succession of ideas in our minds, it follows that the duration of any finite spirit must be estimated by the number of ideas or actions succeeding each other in that same spirit or mind. Hence, it is a plain consequence that the soul always thinks; and in truth whoever shall go about to divide in his thoughts, or abstract the *existence* of a spirit from its *cogitation,* will, I believe, find it no easy task.

Berkeley, *Principles of Human Knowledge, 98*

58 Ever eating, never cloying,
All-devouring, all-destroying,
Never finding full repast,
Till I eat the world at last.

Swift, *On Time*

59 No Preacher is listened to but Time, which gives us the same Train and Turn of Thought that eld-er People have tried in vain to put into our Heads before.

Swift, *Thoughts on Various Subjects*

60 'Tis a property inseparable from time, and which in a manner constitutes its essence, that each of its parts succeeds another, and that none of them, however contiguous, can ever be co-existent. For the same reason, that the year 1737 cannot concur with the present year 1738, every moment must be distinct from, and posterior or antecedent to another. 'Tis certain then, that time, as it exists, must be compos'd of indivisible moments. For if in time we could never arrive at an end of division, and if each moment, as it succeeds another, were not perfectly single and indivisible, there would be an infinite number of co-existent moments, or parts of time; which I believe will be allow'd to be an arrant contradiction.

Hume, *Treatise of Human Nature, Bk. I, II, 2*

61 To understand what time is aright, without which we never can comprehend infinity, insomuch as one is a portion of the other—we ought seriously to sit down and consider what idea it is we have of duration, so as to give a satisfactory account how we came by it.——What is that to any body? quoth my uncle Toby. For if you will turn your eyes inwards upon your mind, continued my father, and observe attentively, you will perceive, brother, that whilst you and I are talking together, and thinking, and smoking our pipes, or whilst we receive successively ideas in our minds, we know that we do exist, and so we estimate the existence, or the continuation of the existence of ourselves, or any thing else, commensurate to the succession of any ideas in our minds, the duration of ourselves, or any such other thing co-existing with our thinking—and so according to that preconceived—You puzzle me to death, cried my uncle Toby.

——'Tis owing to this, replied my father, that in our computations of time, we are so used to minutes, hours, weeks, and months—and of clocks (I wish there was not a clock in the kingdom) to measure out their several portions to us, and to those who belong to us—that 'twill be well, if in time to come, the succession of our ideas be of any use or service to us at all.

Now, whether we observe it or no, continued my father, in every sound man's head, there is a regular succession of ideas of one sort or other, which follow each other in train just like—A train of artillery? said my uncle Toby—A train of a fiddle-stick!—quoth my father—which follow and succeed one another in our minds at certain distances, just like the images in the inside of a lanthorn turned round by the heat of a candle.—I declare, quoth my uncle Toby, mine are more like a smoke-jack.——Then, brother Toby, I have nothing more to say to you upon the subject, said my father.

Sterne, *Tristram Shandy,* III, 18

62 Time wastes too fast: every letter I trace tells me with what rapidity Life follows my pen; the days and hours of it, more precious, my dear Jenny! than the rubies about thy neck, are flying over our heads like light clouds of a windy day, never to return more—every thing presses on—whilst thou art twisting that lock,—see! it grows grey; and every time I kiss thy hand to bid adieu, and every absence which follows it, are preludes to that eternal separation which we are shortly to make.

Sterne, *Tristram Shandy,* IX, 8

63 I was exceedingly uneasy at the awkward appearance I supposed I should make to Johnson and the other gentlemen whom I had invited, not being able to receive them at home, and being obliged to order supper at the Mitre. I went to Johnson in the morning, and talked of it as a serious distress. He laughed, and said, "Consider, Sir, how insignificant this will appear a twelvemonth hence."— Were this consideration to be applied to most of the little vexatious incidents of life, by which our quiet is too often disturbed, it would prevent many painful sensations. I have tried it frequently, with good effect.

Boswell, *Life of Johnson (July 6, 1763)*

64 Nae man can tether time or tide.

Burns, *Tam O'Shanter*

65 Time is not an empirical conception. For neither coexistence nor succession would be perceived by us, if the representation of time did not exist as a foundation *a priori.* Without this presupposition we could not represent to ourselves that things exist together at one and the same time, or at different times, that is, contemporaneously, or in succession.

Time is a necessary representation, lying at the foundation of all our intuitions. With regard to phenomena in general, we cannot think away time from them, and represent them to ourselves as out of and unconnected with time, but we can quite well represent to ourselves time void of phenomena. Time is therefore given *a priori.* In it alone is all reality of phenomena possible. These may all be annihilated in thought, but time itself, as the universal condition of their possibility, cannot be so annulled.

Kant, *Critique of Pure Reason,*
Transcendental Aesthetic

66 The infinity of time signifies nothing more than that every determined quantity of time is possible only through limitations of one time lying at the foundation. Consequently, the original representation, time, must be given as unlimited. But as the determinate representation of the parts of time and of every quantity of an object can only be obtained by limitation, the *complete* representation of time must not be furnished by means of conceptions, for these contain only partial representations. Conceptions, on the contrary, must have immediate intuition for their basis.

Kant, *Critique of Pure Reason,*
Transcendental Aesthetic

67 Time is the formal condition *a priori* of all phenomena whatsoever. Space, as the pure form of external intuition, is limited as a condition *a priori* to external phenomena alone. On the other hand, because all representations, whether they have or have not external things for their objects, still in themselves, as determinations of the mind, belong to our internal state; and because this internal state is subject to the formal condition of the internal intuition, that is, to time—time is a condition *a priori* of all phenomena whatsoever—the *immediate* condition of all internal, and thereby the *mediate* condition of all external phenomena.

Kant, *Critique of Pure Reason,*
Transcendental Aesthetic

68 I met a traveller from an antique land
Who said: 'Two vast and trunkless legs of stone
Stand in the desert. Near them, on the sand,
Half sunk, a shattered visage lies, whose frown,
And wrinkled lip, and sneer of cold command,
Tell that its sculptor well those passions read
Which yet survive, stamped on these lifeless things,
The hand that mocked them and the heart that fed.
And on the pedestal these words appear—
"My name is Ozymandias, king of kings:
Look on my works, ye Mighty, and despair!"
Nothing beside remains. Round the decay
Of that colossal wreck, boundless and bare
The lone and level sands stretch far away.'

Shelley, *Ozymandias*

69 Oh, Time! the beautifier of the dead,
Adorner of the ruin, comforter
And only healer when the heart hath bled—
Time! the corrector where our judgments err,
The test of truth, love,—sole philosopher.

Byron, *Childe Harold's Pilgrimage,* IV, 130

70 Time is the negative element in the sensuous world.

Hegel, *Philosophy of History,* Intro., 3

71 Length of time is something entirely relative, and the element of spirit is eternity. Duration, properly speaking, cannot be said to belong to it.

Hegel, *Philosophy of History,* Intro.

72 Time is that in which all things pass away; it is

merely the form under which the will to live—the thing-in-itself and therefore imperishable—has revealed to it that its efforts are in vain; it is that agent by which at every moment all things in our hands become as nothing, and lose any real value they possess.

Schopenhauer, *Vanity of Existence*

73 A man finds himself, to his great astonishment, suddenly existing, after thousands and thousands of years of non-existence: he lives for a little while; and then, again, comes an equally long period when he must exist no more. The heart rebels against this, and feels that it cannot be true. The crudest intellect cannot speculate on such a subject without having a presentiment that Time is something ideal in its nature. This ideality of Time and Space is the key to every true system of metaphysics; because it provides for quite another order of things than is to be met with in the domain of nature. This is why Kant is so great.

Schopenhauer, *Vanity of Existence*

74 The illimitable, silent, never-resting thing called Time, rolling, rushing on, swift, silent, like an all-embracing ocean-tide, on which we and all the Universe swim like exhalations, like apparitions which *are*, and then *are not:* this is forever very literally a miracle; a thing to strike us dumb.

Carlyle, *The Hero as Divinity*

75 Let us alone. Time driveth onward fast,
And in a little while our lips are dumb.
Let us alone. What is it that will last?
All things are taken from us, and become
Portions and parcels of the dreadful past.

Tennyson, *The Lotos-Eaters, IV*

76 Time is but the stream I go a-fishing in. I drink at it; but while I drink I see the sandy bottom and detect how shallow it is. Its thin current slides away, but eternity remains. I would drink deeper; fish in the sky, whose bottom is pebbly with stars. I cannot count one. I know not the first letter of the alphabet. I have always been regretting that I was not as wise as the day I was born. The intellect is a cleaver; it discerns and rifts its way into the secret of things. I do not wish to be any more busy with my hands than is necessary. My head is hands and feet. I feel all my best faculties concentrated in it. My instinct tells me that my head is an organ for burrowing, as some creatures use their snout and fore paws, and with it I would mine and burrow my way through these hills. I think that the richest vein is somewhere hereabouts; so by the divining-rod and thin rising vapors I judge; and here I will begin to mine.

Thoreau, *Walden:* Where I Lived,
and What I Lived For

77 Come, fill the Cup, and in the fire of Spring

Your Winter-garment of Repentance fling;
The Bird of Time has but a little way
To flutter—and the Bird is on the Wing.

FitzGerald, *Rubáiyát*, VII

78 What's time? Leave Now for dogs and apes!
Man has Forever.

Browning, *A Grammarian's Funeral*

79 Time is infinite motion without a moment of rest and is unthinkable otherwise.

Tolstoy, *War and Peace*, II Epilogue, X

80 The practically cognized present is no knife-edge, but a saddle-back, with a certain breadth of its own on which we sit perched, and from which we look in two directions into time. The unit of composition of our perception of time is a *duration,* with a bow and a stern, as it were—a rearward- and a forward-looking end. It is only as parts of this *duration-block* that the relation of *succession* of one end to the other is perceived. We do not first feel one end and then feel the other after it, and from the perception of the succession infer an interval of time between, but we seem to feel the interval of time as a whole, with its two ends embedded in it. The experience is from the outset a synthetic datum, not a simple one; and to sensible perception its elements are inseparable, although attention looking back may easily decompose the experience, and distinguish its beginning from its end.

William James, *Psychology,* XV

81 In the experience of watching empty time flow . . . we tell it off in pulses. We say "now! now! now!" or we count "more! more! more!" as we feel it bud. This composition out of units of duration is called the law of time's *discrete flow.* The discreteness is, however, merely due to the fact that our successive acts of *recognition* or *apperception* of *what* it is are discrete. The sensation is as continuous as any sensation can be. All continuous sensations are *named* in beats. We notice that a certain finite "more" of them is passing or already past. . . .

After a small number of beats our impression of the amount we have told off becomes quite vague. Our only way of knowing it accurately is by counting, or noticing the clock, or through some other symbolic conception. When the times exceed hours or days, the conception is absolutely symbolic. We think of the amount we mean either solely as a *name,* or by running over a few salient *dates* therein, with no pretence of imagining the full durations that lie between them. No one has anything like a *perception* of the greater length of the time between now and the first century than of that between now and the tenth. To an historian, it is true, the longer interval will suggest a host of additional dates and events, and so appear a more *multitudinous* thing. And for the same reason most people will think they directly perceive the length of the past fortnight to exceed that of the past week. But there is properly no comparative time *intuition* in these cases at all. It is but dates and events, *representing* time, their abundance *symbolizing* its length. I am sure that this is so, even where the times compared are no more than an hour or so in length.

William James, *Psychology,* XV

82 The specious present, the intuited duration, stands permanent, like the rainbow on the waterfall, with its own quality unchanged by the events that stream through it. Each of these, as it slips out, retains the power of being reproduced; and when reproduced, is reproduced with the duration and neighbors which it originally had. Please observe, however, that the reproduction of an event, *after* it has once completely dropped out of the rearward end of the specious present, is an entirely different psychic fact from its direct perception in the specious present as a thing immediately past. A creature might be entirely devoid of *reproductive* memory, and yet have the time-sense; but the latter would be limited, in his case, to the few seconds immediately passing by. Time older than that he would never recall.

William James, *Psychology,* XV

83 We cannot point to a time itself, but only to some event occurring at that time. There is therefore no reason in experience to suppose that there are times as opposed to events: the events, ordered by the relations of simultaneity and succession, are all that experience provides.

Russell, *World of Physics and the World of Sense*

84 The contention that time is unreal and that the world of sense is illusory must, I think, be regarded as based upon fallacious reasoning. Nevertheless, there is some sense—easier to feel than to state—in which time is an unimportant and superficial characteristic of reality. Past and future must be acknowledged to be as real as the present, and a certain emancipation from slavery to time is essential to philosophic thought. The importance of time is rather practical than theoretical, rather in relation to our desires than in relation to truth. A truer image of the world, I think, is obtained by picturing things as entering into the stream of time from an eternal world outside, than from a view which regards time as the devouring tyrant of all that is. Both in thought and in feeling, to realize the unimportance of time is the gate of wisdom.

Russell, *Problem of Infinity*

85 Most people will be inclined to agree with St. Augustine: "What, then, is time? If no one asks of me, I know; if I wish to explain to him who asks, I know not." Philosophers, of course, have learned to be glib about time, but the rest of mankind, although the subject feels familiar, are apt to be aware that a few questions can reduce them to hopeless confusion. "Does the past exist? No. Does the future exist? No. Then only the present exists? Yes. But within the present there is no lapse of time? Quite so. Then time does not exist? Oh, I wish you wouldn't be so tiresome." Any philosopher can elicit this dialogue by a suitable choice of interlocuter.

Russell, *Human Knowledge,* IV, 5

86 Since Einstein, we know that . . . each piece of matter has its own local time. There is very little difference between the local time of one piece of matter and that of another unless their relative velocity is an appreciable fraction of the velocity of light. The local time of a given piece of matter is that which will be shown by a perfectly accurate chronometer which travels with it. Beta particles travel with velocities that do not fall very far short of that of light. If we could place a chronometer on a beta particle and make the particle travel in a closed path, we should find, when it returned, that the chronometer would not agree with one that had remained throughout stationary in the laboratory. A more curious illustration (which I owe to Professor Reichenbach) is connected with the possibility of travel to the stars. Suppose we invented a rocket apparatus which could send a projectile to Sirius with a velocity ten-elevenths of that of light. From the point of view of the terrestrial observer the journey would take about 55 years, and one might therefore suppose that if the projectile carried passengers who were young when they started, they would be old when they arrived. But from their point of view the journey will only have taken about 11 years. This will not only be the time taken as measured by their clocks, but also the time as measured by their physiological processes—decay of teeth, loss of hair, etc. If they looked and felt like men of 20 when they started, they will look and feel like men of 31 when they arrive. It is only because we do not habitually come across bodies traveling with a speed approaching that of light that such odd facts remain unnoticed except by men of science.

Russell, *Human Knowledge,* IV, 5

87 The non-mathematician is seized by a mysterious shuddering when he hears of "four-dimensional" things, by a feeling not unlike that awakened by thoughts of the occult. And yet there is no more common-place statement than that the world in which we live is a four-dimensional space-time continuum.

Space is a three-dimensional continuum. By this we mean that it is possible to describe the position of a point (at rest) by means of three numbers (co-ordinates) x, y, z, and that there is an indefinite number of points in the neighbourhood of this one, the position of which can be described by co-ordinates such as x_1, y_1, z_1, which may be as near as we choose to the respective values of the co-ordinates x, y, z of the first point. In virtue of the latter property we speak of a "continuum," and owing to the fact that there are three co-ordinates we speak of it as being "three-dimensional."

Similarly, the world of physical phenomena which was briefly called "world" by Minkowski is naturally four-dimensional in the space-time sense. For it is composed of individual events, each of which is described by four numbers, namely, three space co-ordinates x, y, z and a time co-ordinate, the time-value t. The "world" is in this sense also a continuum; for to every event there are as many "neighbouring" events (realised or at least thinkable) as we care to choose, the co-ordinates x_1, y_1, z_1, t_1 of which differ by an indefinitely small amount from those of the event x, y, z, t originally considered. That we have not been accustomed to regard the world in this sense as a four-dimensional continuum is due to the fact that in physics, before the advent of the theory of relativity, time played a different and more independent rôle, as compared with the space co-ordinates. It is for this reason that we have been in the habit of treating time as an independent continuum. As a matter of fact, according to classical mechanics, time is absolute, *i.e.* it is independent of the position and the condition of motion of the system of co-ordinates. We see this expressed in the last equation of the Galileian transformation ($t' = t$).

The four-dimensional mode of consideration of the "world" is natural on the theory of relativity, since according to this theory time is robbed of its independence.

Einstein, *Relativity*, I, 17

88 When I follow with my eyes on the dial of a clock the movement of the hand which corresponds to the oscillations of the pendulum, I do not measure duration, as seems to be thought; I merely count simultaneities, which is very different. Outside of me, in space, there is never more than a single position of the hand and the pendulum, for nothing is left of the past positions. Within myself a process of organization or interpenetration of conscious states is going on, which constitutes true duration. It is because I *endure* in this way that I picture to myself what I call the past oscillations of the pendulum at the same time as I perceive the present oscillation. Now, let us withdraw for a moment the ego which thinks these so-called successive oscillations: there will never be more than a single oscillation, and indeed only a single position, of the pendulum, and hence no duration. Withdraw, on the other hand, the pendulum and its oscillations; there will no longer be anything but the heterogeneous duration of the ego, without moments external to one another, without relation to number.

Bergson, *Time and Free Will*, II

89 To announce that something will take place at the end of a time t is to declare that consciousness will note between now and then a number t of simultaneities of a certain kind. And we must not be led astray by the words "between now and then," for the interval of duration exists only for us and on account of the interpenetration of our conscious states. Outside ourselves we should find only space, and consequently nothing but simultaneities, of which we could not even say that they are objectively successive, since succession can only be thought through *comparing* the present with the past.—That the interval of duration itself cannot be taken into account by science is proved by the fact that, if all the motions of the universe took place twice or thrice as quickly, there would be nothing to alter either in our formulae or in the figures which are to be found in them. Consciousness would have an indefinable and as it were qualitative impression of the change, but the change would not make itself felt outside consciousness, since the same number of simultaneities would go on taking place in space.

Bergson, *Time and Free Will*, II

90 What precisely is the present? If it is a question of the present instant,—I mean, of a mathematical instant which would be to time what the mathematical point is to the line,—it is clear that such an instant is a pure abstraction, an aspect of the mind; it cannot have real existence. You could never create time out of such instants any more than you could make a line out of mathematical points. Even if it does exist, how could there be an instant anterior to it? The two instants could not be separated by an interval of time since, by hypothesis, you reduce time to a juxtaposition of instants. Therefore they would not be separated by anything, and consequently they would be only one: two mathematical points which touch are identical.

Bergson, *The Creative Mind*, V

91 By physical time I understand an order of derivation integral to the flux of matter; so that if two worlds had no material connection, and neither was in any of its parts derived from the other, they could not possibly have positions in the same physical time. The same essence of succession might be exhibited in both; the same kind of temporal vistas might perplex the sentimental inhabitants of each of them; but no date in one would coincide with a date in the other, nor would their respective temporal scales and rates of precipitation have any common measure.

The notion that there is and can be but one time, and that half of it is always intrinsically past and the other half always intrinsically future, belongs to the normal pathology of an animal mind: it marks the egotistical outlook of an active being endowed with imagination. Such a being will project the moral contrast produced by his momentary absorption in action upon the conditions and history of that action, and upon the universe at large. A perspective of hope and one of reminiscence continually divide for him a specious eternity; and for him the dramatic center of existence, though always at a different point in physical time, will always be precisely in himself.

Santayana, *Realm of Matter,* IV

92 Sentimental time is a genuine, if poetical, version of the march of existence, even as pictorial space is a genuine, if poetical, version of its distribution. The views taken are short, especially towards the future, but being extensible they suggest well enough the unfathomable depths of physical time in both directions; and if the views, being views, must be taken from some arbitrary point, they may be exchanged for one another, thus annulling the bias of each, in so far as the others contradict it. I am far from wishing to assert that the remainder or resultant will be the essence of physical time; but for human purposes a just view enough is obtained if we remember that each *now* and *here* is called so only by one voice, and that all other voices call it a *then* and a *there.* . . .

The least sentimental term in sentimental time is the term *now,* because it marks the junction of fancy with action. *Now* is often a word of command; it leans towards the future, and seems to be the voice of the present summoning the next moment to arise, and pouncing upon it when it does so. For *now* has in it emotionally all the cheeriness of material change: it comes out of the past as if impatient at not having come sooner, and it passes into the future with alacrity, as if confident of losing nothing by moving on. For it is evident that actual succession can contain nothing but *nows,* so that *now* in a certain way is immortal. But this immortality is only a continual reiteration, a series of moments each without self-possession and without assurance of any other moment; so that if ever the *now* loses its indicative practical force and becomes introspective, it becomes acutely sentimental, a perpetual hope unrealised and a perpetual dying.

Santayana, *Realm of Matter,* IV

93 October began as months do: their entrance is, in itself, an unostentatious and soundless affair, without outward signs and tokens; they, as it were, steal in softly and, unless you are keeping close watch, escape your notice altogether. Time has no divisions to mark its passage, there is never a thunder-storm or blare of trumpets to announce the beginning of a new month or year. Even when a new century begins it is only we mortals who ring bells and fire off pistols.

Mann, *Magic Mountain,* V

94 If Time is considered by itself, it immediately dissolves into an absolute multiplicity of instants which considered separately lose all temporal nature and are reduced purely and simply to the total a-temporality of the *this.* Thus Time is pure nothingness in-itself, which can seem to have a being only by the very act in which the For-itself overlaps it in order to utilize it. This being, however, is that of a particular figure which is raised on the undifferentiated ground of time and which we call the lapse of time. In fact our first apprehension of objective time is practical: it is while being my possibilities beyond co-present being that I discover objective time as the worldly correlate of nothingness which separates me from my possible. From this point of view time appears as a finite, organized form in the heart of an indefinite dispersion. The lapse of time is the result of a compression of time at the heart of an absolute decompression, and it is the project of ourselves toward our possibilities which realizes the compression. This compression of time is certainly a form of dispersion and of separation, for it expresses in the world the distance which separates me from myself. But on the other hand, since I project myself toward a possible only across an organized series of dependent possibles which are what I have to be in order to—, and since their non-thematic and nonpositional revelation is given in the non-positional revelation of the major possible toward which I project myself, time is revealed to me as an objective, temporal form, as an organized echeloning of probabilities. This objective form or lapse is like the trajectory of my act.

Thus time appears through trajectories. But just as spatial trajectories decompose and collapse into pure static spatiality, so the temporal trajectory collapses as soon as it is not simply lived as that which objectively implies our expectation of ourselves. In fact the probables which are revealed to me tend naturally to be isolated as in-itself probables and to occupy a strictly separated fraction of objective time. Then the lapse of time disappears, and time is revealed as the shimmer of nothingness on the surface of a strictly a-temporal being.

Sartre, *Being and Nothingness,* Pt. II, III, 4

19.8 | The Universe or Cosmos

Many of the questions that have appeared in earlier sections of this chapter, especially the sections on cause, motion and change, space, and time, reappear here in the form of questions about the beginning and end of the world, its infinity or boundlessness, and its creation or origin. Similarly, the question raised in the section on nature, about God's immanence in nature or his transcendence of it, recurs here as a question about the relation of God to the universe or cosmos.

New questions do appear here. Is there only one universe or is there a multiplicity of worlds, even an infinity of them? Is this the best of all possible worlds, in which everything that happens has a sufficient reason? The affirmative answer, as given by Leibniz, has always been taken as the hallmark of philosophical optimism. It is opposed on rational grounds by Aquinas, who argues that a better world than this is possible; and it is laughed out of court by the ridicule that Voltaire heaps upon it. Related questions are discussed by others: whether the universe is intrinsically rational or intelligible, and whether God's creation of the world was an act of free choice on his part or something entirely necessitated.

Another point of dispute is the conception of a world-soul—an indwelling principle animating the universe and giving it intelligent direction. This conception, proposed by philosophers in antiquity, is rejected by later Christian theologians.

It is generally agreed that cosmos is the opposite of chaos; even those who conceive the universe as resulting from a fortuitous concourse of atoms find order in its structure and its processes. But the extent and character of its order are disputed. As opposed to the vision of a universe that is a thoroughly integrated whole, in which there are no loose ends or independent threads, William James proposed what he calls a "pluralistic universe," one in which there are many loosely concatenated strands, operating with some degree of independence of one another.

---

1 In the beginning God created the heaven and the earth.

And the earth was without form, and void; and darkness was upon the face of the deep. And the Spirit of God moved upon the face of the waters.

And God said, Let there be light: and there was light.

And God saw the light, that it was good: and God divided the light from the darkness.

And God called the light Day, and the darkness he called Night. And the evening and the morning were the first day.

Genesis 1:1–5

2 The earth is the Lord's, and the fulness thereof; the world, and they that dwell therein.

Psalm 24:1

3 One generation passeth away, and another generation cometh: but the earth abideth for ever.

Ecclesiastes 1:4

4 *Timaeus*. Let me tell you . . . why the creator made this world of generation. He was good, and the good can never have any jealousy of anything. And being free from jealousy, he desired that all things should be as like himself as they could be. This is in the truest sense the origin of creation and of the world, as we shall do well in believing on the testimony of wise men: God desired that all things should be good and nothing bad, so far as this was attainable. Wherefore also finding the whole visible sphere not at rest, but moving in an irregular and disorderly fashion, out of disorder he brought order, considering that this was in ev-

ery way better than the other. Now the deeds of the best could never be or have been other than the fairest; and the creator, reflecting on the things which are by nature visible, found that no unintelligent creature taken as a whole was fairer than the intelligent taken as a whole; and that intelligence could not be present in anything which was devoid of soul. For which reason, when he was framing the universe, he put intelligence in soul, and soul in body, that he might be the creator of a work which was by nature fairest and best. Wherefore, using the language of probability, we may say that the world became a living creature truly endowed with soul and intelligence by the providence of God.

This being supposed, let us proceed to the next stage: In the likeness of what animal did the Creator make the world? It would be an unworthy thing to liken it to any nature which exists as a part only; for nothing can be beautiful which is like any imperfect thing; but let us suppose the world to be the very image of that whole of which all other animals both individually and in their tribes are portions. For the original of the universe contains in itself all intelligible beings, just as this world comprehends us and all other visible creatures. For the Deity, intending to make this world like the fairest and most perfect of intelligible beings, framed one visible animal comprehending within itself all other animals of a kindred nature. Are we right in saying that there is one world, or that they are many and infinite? There must be one only, if the created copy is to accord with the original. For that which includes all other intelligible creatures cannot have a second or companion; in that case there would be need of another living being which would include both, and of which they would be parts, and the likeness would be more truly said to resemble not them, but that other which included them. In order then that the world might be solitary, like the perfect animal, the creator made not two worlds or an infinite number of them; but there is and ever will be one only-begotten and created heaven.

Plato, *Timaeus*, 29B

5 *Timaeus*. And he [the Creator] gave to the world the figure which was suitable and also natural. Now to the animal which was to comprehend all animals, that figure was suitable which comprehends within itself all other figures. Wherefore he made the world in the form of a globe, round as from a lathe, having its extremes in every direction equidistant from the centre, the most perfect and the most like itself of all figures; for he considered that the like is infinitely fairer than the unlike. This he finished off, making the surface smooth all around for many reasons; in the first place, because the living being had no need of eyes when there was nothing remaining outside him to be seen; nor ears when there was noth-

ing to be heard; and there was no surrounding atmosphere to be breathed; nor would there have been any use of organs by the help of which he might receive his food or get rid of what he had already digested, since there was nothing which went from him or came into him: for there was nothing beside him. Of design he was created thus, his own waste providing his own food, and all that he did or suffered taking place in and by himself. For the Creator conceived that a being which was self-sufficient would be far more excellent than one which lacked anything; and, as he had no need to take anything or defend himself against any one, the Creator did not think it necessary to bestow upon him hands: nor had he any need of feet, nor of the whole apparatus of walking; but the movement suited to his spherical form was assigned to him, being of all the seven that which is most appropriate to mind and intelligence; and he was made to move in the same manner and on the same spot, within his own limits revolving in a circle. All the other six motions were taken away from him, and he was made not to partake of their deviations. And as this circular movement required no feet, the universe was created without legs and without feet.

Plato, *Timaeus*, 33A

6 *Timaeus*. When all things were in disorder God created in each thing in relation to itself, and in all things in relation to each other, all the measures and harmonies which they could possibly receive. For in those days nothing had any proportion except by accident; nor did any of the things which now have names deserve to be named at all—as, for example, fire, water, and the rest of the elements. All these the creator first set in order, and out of them he constructed the universe, which was a single animal comprehending in itself all other animals, mortal and immortal. Now of the divine, he himself was the creator, but the creation of the mortal he committed to his offspring. And they, imitating him, received from him the immortal principle of the soul; and around this they proceeded to fashion a mortal body, and made it to be the vehicle of the soul, and constructed within the body a soul of another nature which was mortal, subject to terrible and irresistible affections—first of all, pleasure, the greatest incitement to evil; then, pain, which deters from good; also rashness and fear, two foolish counsellors, anger hard to be appeased, and hope easily led astray—these they mingled with irrational sense and with all-daring love according to necessary laws, and so framed man.

Plato, *Timaeus*, 69A

7 It is evident not only that there is not, but also that there could never come to be, any bodily mass whatever outside the circumference. The world as a whole, therefore, includes *all* its appropriate matter, which is, as we saw, natural percep-

tible body. So that neither are there now, nor have there ever been, nor can there ever be formed more heavens than one, but this heaven of ours is one and unique and complete.

Aristotle, *On the Heavens,* 279ª7

8 Everything which has a function exists for its function. The activity of God is immortality, i.e. eternal life. Therefore the movement of that which is divine must be eternal. But such is the heaven, viz. a divine body, and for that reason to it is given the circular body whose nature it is to move always in a circle. Why, then, is not the whole body of the heaven of the same character as that part? Because there must be something at rest at the centre of the revolving body; and of that body no part can be at rest, either elsewhere or at the centre. It could do so only if the body's natural movement were towards the centre. But the circular movement is natural, since otherwise it could not be eternal: for nothing unnatural is eternal. The unnatural is subsequent to the natural, being a derangement of the natural which occurs in the course of its generation. Earth then has to exist; for it is earth which is at rest at the centre.

Aristotle, *On the Heavens,* 286ª9

9 The sun and the stars and the whole heaven are ever active, and there is no fear that they may sometime stand still, as the natural philosophers fear they may. Nor do they tire in this activity; for movement is not for them, as it is for perishable things, connected with the potentiality for opposites, so that the continuity of the movement should be laborious; for it is that kind of substance which is matter and potency, not actuality, that causes this.

Aristotle, *Metaphysics,* 1050ᵇ23

10 There are infinite worlds both like and unlike this world of ours. For the atoms being infinite in number, as was proved already, are borne on far out into space. For those atoms, which are of such nature that a world could be created out of them or made by them, have not been used up either on one world or on a limited number of worlds, nor again on all the worlds which are alike, or on those which are different from these. So that there nowhere exists an obstacle to the infinite number of the worlds.

Epicurus, *Letter to Herodotus*

11 We must believe that worlds, and indeed every limited compound body which continuously exhibits a similar appearance to the things we see, were created from the infinite, and that all such things, greater and less alike, were separated off from individual agglomerations of matter; and that all are again dissolved, some more quickly, some more slowly, some suffering from one set of causes, others from another. And further we must

believe that these worlds were neither created all of necessity with one configuration nor yet with every kind of shape. Furthermore, we must believe that in all worlds there are living creatures and plants and other things we see in this world; for indeed no one could prove that in a world of one kind there might or might not have been included the kinds of seeds from which living things and plants and all the rest of the things we see are composed, and that in a world of another kind they could not have been.

Epicurus, *Letter to Herodotus*

12 There are some . . . who think that the number of the sand is infinite in multitude; and I mean by the sand not only that which exists about Syracuse and the rest of Sicily but also that which is found in every region whether inhabited or uninhabited. Again there are some who, without regarding it as infinite, yet think that no number has been named which is great enough to exceed its multitude. And it is clear that they who hold this view, if they imagined a mass made up of sand in other respects as large as the mass of the earth, including in it all the seas and the hollows of the earth filled up to a height equal to that of the highest of the mountains, would be many times further still from recognising that any number could be expressed which exceeded the multitude of the sand so taken. But I will try to show you by means of geometrical proofs, which you will be able to follow, that, of the numbers named by me and given in the work which I sent to Zeuxippus, some exceed not only the number of the mass of sand equal in magnitude to the earth filled up in the way described, but also that of a mass equal in magnitude to the universe.

Archimedes, *Sand-Reckoner*

13 Be far from believing this, that all things as they say press to the centre of the sum, and that for this reason the nature of the world stands fast without any strokes from the outside and the uppermost and lowest parts cannot part asunder in any direction, because all things have been always pressing towards the centre. . . . Groundless error has devised such dreams for fools, because they have embraced false principles of reason. For there can be no centre where the universe is infinite; no nor, even if there were a centre, could anything take up a position there any more on that account than for some quite different reason be driven away. For all room and space, which we term void, must through centre, through no-centre alike give place to heavy bodies, in whatever directions their motions tend. Nor is there any spot of such a sort that when bodies have reached it, they can lose their force of gravity and stand upon void; and that again which is void must not serve to support anything, but must, as its nature craves, continually give place. Things cannot

therefore in such a way be held in union, o'ermastered by love of a centre.

Lucretius, *Nature of Things,* I

14 Since the body of the earth and water and the light breath of air and burning heats, out of which this sum of things is seen to be formed, do all consist of a body that had a birth and is mortal, the whole nature of the world must be reckoned of a like body. For those things whose parts and members we see to be of a body that had a birth and of forms that are mortal, we perceive to be likewise without exception mortal, and at the same time to have had a birth. Since therefore I see that the chiefest members and parts of the world are destroyed and begotten anew, I may be sure that for heaven and earth as well there has been a time of beginning and there will be a time of destruction.

Lucretius, *Nature of Things,* V

15 Whether the world is a soul, or a body under the government of nature, like trees and crops, it embraces in its constitution all that it is destined to experience actively or passively from its beginning right on to its end; it resembles a human being, all whose capacities are wrapped up in the embryo before birth. Ere the child has seen the light the principle of beard and grey hairs is innate. Albeit small and hidden, all the features of the whole body and of every succeeding period of life are there. In like manner the creation of the world embraces sun and moon, stars with their successive phases, and the birth of all sentient life; and no less the methods of change in all earthly things.

Seneca, *Quaestiones Naturales,* III, 29

16 Before there was any earth or sea, before the canopy of heaven stretched overhead, Nature presented the same aspect the world over, that to which men have given the name of Chaos. This was a shapeless uncoordinated mass, nothing but a weight of lifeless matter, whose ill-assorted elements were indiscriminately heaped together in one place. There was no sun, in those days, to provide the world with light, no crescent moon ever filling out her horns: the earth was not poised in the enveloping air, balanced there by its own weight, nor did the sea stretch out its arms along the margins of the shores. Although the elements of land and air and sea were there, the earth had no firmness, the water no fluidity, there was no brightness in the sky. Nothing had any lasting shape, but everything got in the way of everything else; for, within that one body, cold warred with hot, moist with dry, soft with hard, and light with heavy.

This strife was finally resolved by a god, a natural force of a higher kind, who separated the earth from heaven, and the waters from the earth, and set the clear air apart from the cloudy atmosphere. When he had freed these elements, sorting

them out from the heap where they had lain, indistinguishable from one another, he bound them fast, each in its separate place, forming a harmonious union. The fiery aether, which has no weight, formed the vault of heaven, flashing upwards to take its place in the highest sphere. The air, next to it in lightness, occupied the neighbouring regions. Earth, heavier than these, attracted to itself the grosser elements, and sank down under its own weight, while the encircling sea took possession of the last place of all, and held the solid earth in its embrace. In this way the god, whichever of the gods it was, set the chaotic mass in order, and, after dividing it up, arranged it in its constituent parts.

Ovid, *Metamorphoses,* I

17 In the beginning was the Word, and the Word was with God, and the Word was God.

The same was in the beginning with God.

All things were made by him; and without him was not any thing made that was made.

John 1:1–3

18 And when the seven thunders had uttered their voices, I was about to write: and I heard a voice from heaven saying unto me, Seal up those things which the seven thunders uttered, and write them not.

And the angel which I saw stand upon the sea and upon the earth lifted up his hand to heaven,

And sware by him that liveth for ever and ever, who created heaven, and the things that therein are, and the earth, and the things that therein are, and the sea, and the things which are therein, that there should be time no longer:

But in the days of the voice of the seventh angel, when he shall begin to sound, the mystery of God should be finished, as he hath declared to his servants the prophets.

Revelation 10:4–7

19 And he saith unto me, Seal not the sayings of the prophecy of this book: for the time is at hand.

He that is unjust, let him be unjust still: and he which is filthy, let him be filthy still: and he that is righteous, let him be righteous still: and he that is holy, let him be holy still.

And, behold, I come quickly; and my reward is with me, to give every man according as his work shall be.

I am Alpha and Omega, the beginning and the end, the first and the last.

Blessed are they that do his commandments, that they may have right to the tree of life, and may enter in through the gates into the city.

For without are dogs, and sorcerers, and whoremongers, and murderers, and idolaters, and whosoever loveth and maketh a lie.

I Jesus have sent mine angel to testify unto you these things in the churches. I am the root and the offspring of David, and the bright and morning star.

And the Spirit and the bride say, Come. And let him that heareth say, Come. And let him that is athirst come. And whosoever will, let him take the water of life freely.

For I testify unto every man that heareth the words of the prophecy of this book, If any man shall add unto these things, God shall add unto him the plagues that are written in this book:

And if any man shall take away from the words of the book of this prophecy, God shall take away his part out of the book of life, and out of the holy city, and from the things which are written in this book.

He which testifieth these things saith, Surely I come quickly. Amen. Even so, come, Lord Jesus.

Revelation 22:10–20

20 All that has by nature with systematic method been arranged in the universe seems both in part and as a whole to have been determined and ordered in accordance with number, by the forethought and the mind of him that created all things; for the pattern was fixed, like a preliminary sketch, by the domination of number preexistent in the mind of the world-creating God, number conceptual only and immaterial in every way, but at the same time the true and the eternal essence, so that with reference to it, as to an artistic plan, should be created all these things, time, motion, the heavens, the stars, all sorts of revolutions.

Nicomachus, *Arithmetic*, I, 6

21 Either it is a well-arranged universe or a chaos huddled together, but still a universe. But can a certain order subsist in thee, and disorder in the All?

Marcus Aurelius, *Meditations*, IV, 27

22 The universe is either a confusion, and a mutual involution of things, and a dispersion; or it is unity and order and providence. If then it is the former, why do I desire to tarry in a fortuitous combination of things and such a disorder? And why do I care about anything else than how I shall at last become earth? . . . But if the other supposition is true, I venerate, and I am firm, and I trust in him who governs.

Marcus Aurelius, *Meditations*, VI, 10

23 We hold that the ordered universe, in its material mass, has existed for ever and will for ever endure.

Plotinus, *Second Ennead*, I, 1

24 Where there is motion within but not outwards and the total remains unchanged, there is neither growth nor decline, and thus the Kosmos never ages.

Plotinus, *Second Ennead*, I, 3

25 The administration of the universe entails neither labour nor loss.

Plotinus, *Second Ennead*, I, 4

26 We cannot but recognize from what we observe in this universe that some such principle of order prevails throughout the entire of existence—the minutest of things a tributary to the vast total; the marvellous art shown not merely in the mightiest works and sublimest members of the All, but even amid such littleness as one would think Providence must disdain: the varied workmanship of wonder in any and every animal form; the world of vegetation, too; the grace of fruits and even of leaves, the lavishness, the delicacy, the diversity of exquisite bloom; and all this not issuing once, and then to die out, but made ever and ever anew as the Transcendent Beings move variously over this earth.

Plotinus, *Third Ennead*, II, 13

27 If You fill heaven and earth, do they contain You? Or do You fill them, and yet have much over since they cannot contain You? Is there some other place into which that overplus of You pours that heaven and earth cannot hold? Surely You have no need of any place to contain You since You contain all things, and fill them indeed precisely by containing them. The vessels thus filled with You do not render You any support: for though they perished utterly, You would not be spilt out. And in pouring Yourself out upon us, You do not come down to us but rather elevate us to You: You are not scattered over us, but we are gathered into one by You. You fill all things: but with Your whole being? It is true that all things cannot wholly contain You: but does this mean that they contain part of You? and do they all contain the same part at the same time? or do different parts of creation contain different parts of You—greater parts or smaller according to their own magnitude? But are there in You parts greater and smaller? Or are You not in every place at once in the totality of Your being, while yet nothing contains You wholly?

Augustine, *Confessions*, I, 3

28 How, O God, did You create heaven and earth? Obviously it was not *in* heaven or on earth that You made heaven and earth; nor in the air nor in the waters, since these belong to heaven and earth; nor did You make the universe in the universe, because there was no place for it to be made in until it was made. Nor had You any material in Your hand when You were making heaven and earth: for where should You have got what You had not yet made to use as material? What exists, save because You exist? You spoke and heaven and earth were created; in Your word You created them.

Augustine, *Confessions*, XI, 5

29 Thus Lord, You who do not change as things and circumstances change but are the Self-same, and the Self-same and the Self-same, Holy, Holy, Holy, Lord God Almighty—You, Lord, in the Beginning, which is from You, in Your wisdom, which is born of Your substance, made something and made it of nothing.

You created *heaven and earth*, but not of Your own substance: for in that event they would have been equal to Your only-begotten Son and hence to Yourself; and it would have been altogether unjust that something not proceeding from You should be equal to You. But, apart from You there was no other thing existent to make them of, O God, Trinity that is One, Unity that is Three. Therefore it was of nothing that You made heaven and earth, the great thing and the small thing: for You are almighty and good and must make all things good, the great heaven and the small earth. You were and nothing else was, and of nothing You made *heaven* [*the heaven of heaven*] *and earth*, these two, one close to You, the other close to nothing, one than which You alone are higher, the other than which nothing is lower.

Augustine, *Confessions*, XII, 7

30 If God is the soul of the world, and the world is as a body to Him, who is the soul, He must be one living being consisting of soul and body, and . . . this same God is a kind of womb of nature containing all things in Himself, so that the lives and souls of all living things are taken, according to the manner of each one's birth, out of His soul which vivifies that whole mass, and therefore nothing at all remains which is not a part of God. And if this is so, who cannot see what impious and irreligious consequences follow such as that whatever one may trample, he must trample a part of God, and in slaying any living creature, a part of God must be slaughtered? But I am unwilling to utter all that may occur to those who think of it, yet cannot be spoken without irreverence.

Augustine, *City of God*, IV, 12

31 There are some . . . who, though they do not suppose that this world is eternal, are of opinion either that this is not the only world, but that there are numberless worlds, or that indeed it is the only one, but that it dies, and is born again at fixed intervals, and this times without number; but they must acknowledge that the human race existed before there were other men to beget them. For they cannot suppose that, if the whole world perish, some men would be left alive in the world, as they might survive in floods and conflagrations, which those other speculators suppose to be partial, and from which they can therefore reasonably argue that a few men survived whose posterity would renew the population; but as they believe that the world itself is renewed out of its own material, so they must believe that out of its

elements the human race was produced, and then that the progeny of mortals sprang like that of other animals from their parents.

Augustine, *City of God*, XII, 11

32 As to those who are always asking why man was not created during these countless ages of the infinitely extended past, and came into being so lately that, according to Scripture, less than 6000 years have elapsed since He began to be, I would reply to them regarding the creation of man, just as I replied regarding the origin of the world to those who will not believe that it is not eternal, but had a beginning, which even Plato himself most plainly declares, though some think his statement was not consistent with his real opinion. If it offends them that the time that has elapsed since the creation of man is so short, and his years so few according to our authorities, let them take this into consideration, that nothing that has a limit is long, and that all the ages of time being finite, are very little, or indeed nothing at all, when compared to the interminable eternity. Consequently, if there had elapsed since the creation of man, I do not say five or six, but even sixty or six hundred thousand years, or sixty times as many, or six hundred or six hundred thousand times as many, or this sum multiplied until it could no longer be expressed in numbers, the same question could still be put, "Why was he not made before?" For the past and boundless eternity during which God abstained from creating man is so great that, compare it with what vast and untold number of ages you please, so long as there is a definite conclusion of this term of time, it is not even as if you compared the minutest drop of water with the ocean that everywhere flows around the globe. For of these two, one indeed is very small, the other incomparably vast, yet both are finite; but that space of time which starts from some beginning, and is limited by some termination, be it of what extent it may, if you compare it with that which has no beginning, I know not whether to say we should count it the very minutest thing, or nothing at all.

Augustine, *City of God*, XII, 12

33 In vain . . . do we attempt to compute definitely the years that may remain to this world, when we may hear from the mouth of the Truth that it is not for us to know this. Yet some have said that four hundred, some five hundred, others a thousand years, may be completed from the ascension of the Lord up to His final coming. But to point out how each of them supports his own opinion would take too long, and is not necessary; for indeed they use human conjectures, and bring forward nothing certain from the authority of the canonical Scriptures. But on this subject He puts aside the figures of the calculators, and orders silence, Who says, "It is not for you to know the

times, which the Father hath put in His own power."

Augustine, City of God, XVIII, 53

34 As . . . the world was not made by chance, but by God acting by His intellect . . . there must exist in the divine mind a form to the likeness of which the world was made.

Aquinas, Summa Theologica, I, 15, 1

35 The universe, the things that exist now being supposed, cannot be better, on account of the most noble order given to these things by God, in which the good of the universe consists. For if any one thing were bettered, the proportion of order would be destroyed, just as if one string were stretched more than it ought to be, the melody of the harp would be destroyed. Yet God could make other things, or add something to those things that are made, and then that universe would be better.

Aquinas, Summa Theologica, I, 25, 6

36 One God produced one world by reason of His love for Himself.

Aquinas, Summa Theologica, I, 32, 1

37 Nothing except God can be from eternity. And this statement is not impossible to uphold, for . . . the will of God is the cause of things. Therefore things are necessary according as it is necessary for God to will them, since the necessity of the effect depends on the necessity of the cause. . . . Absolutely speaking, it is not necessary that God should will anything except Himself. It is not therefore necessary for God to will that the world should always exist; but the world is eternal to the extent that God wills it to be eternal, since the being of the world depends on the will of God, as on its cause. It is not therefore necessary for the world to be always.

Aquinas, Summa Theologica, I, 46, 1

38 We hold by faith alone, and it cannot be proved by demonstration, that the world did not always exist. . . . The reason of this is that the newness of the world cannot be demonstrated from the world itself. For the principle of demonstration is the essence of a thing. Now everything according to the notion of its species abstracts from here and now; hence it is said that "universals are everywhere and always." Hence it cannot be demonstrated that man, or heaven, or a stone did not always exist.

Likewise neither can it be demonstrated on the part of the efficient cause, which acts by will. For the will of God cannot be investigated by reason, except as regards those things which God must will of necessity, and what He wills about creatures is not among these. . . . But the divine will can be manifested to man by revelation, on which faith rests. Hence that the world began to exist is

an object of faith, but not of demonstration or science. And it is useful to consider this, lest anyone, presuming to demonstrate what is of faith, should bring forward reasons that are not cogent, so as to give occasion to unbelievers to laugh, thinking that on such reasons we believe things that are of faith.

Aquinas, Summa Theologica, I, 46, 2

39 As the end of a thing corresponds to its beginning, it is not possible to be ignorant of the end of things if we know their beginning. Therefore, since the beginning of all things is something outside the universe, namely, God . . . we must conclude that the end of all things is some extrinsic good. This can be proved by reason. For it is clear that good has the nature of an end; therefore, a particular end of anything consists in some particular good, while the universal end of all things is the universal good. But the universal good is that which is good of itself by virtue of its essence, which is the very essence of goodness, whereas a particular good is good by participation. Now it is manifest that in the whole created universe there is not a good which is not such by participation. Therefore that good which is the end of the whole universe must be a good outside the universe.

Aquinas, Summa Theologica, I, 103, 2

40 Not to have gain of any good unto himself, which may not be, but that his splendour might, as it glowed, declare, *I am.*

In his eternity beyond time, beyond all other comprehension, as was his pleasure, the eternal love revealed him in new loves.

Nor did he lie, as slumbering, before; for nor before nor after was the process of God's outflowing over these waters.

Form and matter, united and in purity, issued into being which had no flaw, as from a three-stringed bow three arrows;

and as in glass, in amber, or in crystal, a ray so gloweth that from its coming to its pervading all, there is no interval.

Dante, Paradiso, XXIX, 13

41 Oh grace abounding, wherein I presumed to fix my look on the eternal light so long that I consumed my sight thereon!

Within its depths I saw ingathered, bound by love in one volume, the scattered leaves of all the universe;

substance and accidents and their relations, as though together fused, after such fashion that what I tell of is one simple flame.

The universal form of this complex I think that I beheld, because more largely, as I say this, I feel that I rejoice.

A single moment maketh a deeper lethargy for me than twenty and five centuries have wrought on

the emprise that erst threw Neptune in amaze
at Argo's shadow.

Dante, *Paradiso,* XXXIII, 82

42 Aristotle says that the movement of a body which
is one and simple is simple, and the simple movements are the rectilinear and the circular. And of
rectilinear movements, one is upward, and the
other is downward. As a consequence, every simple movement is either toward the centre, i.e.,
downward, or away from the centre, i.e., upward,
or around the centre, i.e., circular. Now it belongs
to earth and water, which are considered heavy,
to be borne downward, i.e., to seek the centre: for
air and fire, which are endowed with lightness,
move upward, i.e., away from the centre. It seems
fitting to grant rectilinear movement to these four
elements and to give the heavenly bodies a circular movement around the centre. So Aristotle.
Therefore, said Ptolemy of Alexandria, if the
Earth moved, even if only by its daily rotation,
the contrary of what was said above would necessarily take place. For this movement which would
traverse the total circuit of the Earth in twenty-
four hours would necessarily be very headlong
and of an unsurpassable velocity. Now things
which are suddenly and violently whirled around
are seen to be utterly unfitted for reuniting, and
the more unified are seen to become dispersed,
unless some constant force constrains them to stick
together. And a long time ago, he says, the scattered Earth would have passed beyond the heavens, as is certainly ridiculous; and *a fortiori* so
would all the living creatures and all the other
separate masses which could by no means remain
unshaken. Moreover, freely falling bodies would
not arrive at the places appointed them, and certainly not along the perpendicular line which
they assume so quickly. And we would see clouds
and other things floating in the air always borne
toward the west. . . .

For these and similar reasons they say that the
Earth remains at rest at the middle of the world
and that there is no doubt about this. But if someone opines that the Earth revolves, he will also say
that the movement is natural and not violent.
Now things which are according to nature produce effects contrary to those which are violent.
For things to which force or violence is applied get
broken up and are unable to subsist for a long
time. But things which are caused by nature are
in a right condition and are kept in their best
organization. Therefore Ptolemy had no reason to
fear that the Earth and all things on the Earth
would be scattered in a revolution caused by the
efficacy of nature, which is greatly different from
that of art or from that which can result from the
genius of man. But why did he not feel anxiety
about the world instead, whose movement must
necessarily be of greater velocity, the greater the
heavens are than the Earth? Or have the heavens

become so immense, because an unspeakably vehement motion has pulled them away from the
centre, and because the heavens would fall if they
came to rest anywhere else?

Surely if this reasoning were tenable, the magnitude of the heavens would extend infinitely. For
the farther the movement is borne upward by the
vehement force, the faster will the movement be,
on account of the ever-increasing circumference
which must be traversed every twenty-four hours:
and conversely, the immensity of the sky would
increase with the increase in movement. In this
way, the velocity would make the magnitude increase infinitely, and the magnitude the velocity.
And in accordance with the axiom of physics that
*that which is infinite cannot be traversed or moved in any
way,* then the heavens will necessarily come to
rest.

But they say that beyond the heavens there is
not any body or place or void or anything at all;
and accordingly it is not possible for the heavens
to move outward: in that case it is rather surprising that something can be held together by nothing. But if the heavens were infinite and were finite only with respect to a hollow space inside,
then it will be said with more truth that there is
nothing outside the heavens, since anything which
occupied any space would be in them; but the
heavens will remain immobile. For movement is
the most powerful reason wherewith they try to
conclude that the universe is finite.

But let us leave to the philosophers of nature
the dispute as to whether the world is finite or
infinite, and let us hold as certain that the Earth
is held together between its two poles and terminates in a spherical surface. Why therefore should
we hesitate any longer to grant to it the movement which accords naturally with its form, rather than put the whole world in a commotion—the
world whose limits we do not and cannot know?
And why not admit that the appearance of daily
revolution belongs to the heavens but the reality
belongs to the Earth?

Copernicus, *De Revolutionibus,* I, 7–8

43 Pitiable is the state of the stars, abject the lot of
earth, if this high dignity of soul is denied them,
while it is granted to the worm, the ant, the roach,
to plants and morels; for in that case worms,
roaches, moths, were more beauteous objects in
nature and more perfect, inasmuch as nothing is
excellent, nor precious, nor eminent, that hath not
soul. But since living bodies spring from earth and
sun and by them are animate, and since in the
earth herbage springs up without sowing of seeds
(*e.g.,* when soil is taken out of the bowels of the
earth and carried to some great elevation or to the
top of a lofty tower and there exposed to the sunshine, after a little while a miscellaneous herbage
springs up in it unbidden), it is not likely that they
(sun and earth) can do that which is not in them-

selves; but they awaken souls, and consequently are themselves possessed of souls. Therefore the bodies of the globes, as being the foremost parts of the universe, to the end they might be in themselves and in their state endure, had need of souls to be conjoined to them, for else there were neither life, nor prime act, nor movement, nor union, nor order, nor coherence, nor *conactus,* nor *sympathia,* nor any generation, nor alternation of seasons, and no propagation; but all were in confusion and the entire world lapse into chaos, and, in fine, the earth were void and dead and without any use.

William Gilbert, *On the Loadstone,* V, 12

44 The world . . . is alone, having nothing outside, resting on itself immobile as a whole; and it alone is all things.

Kepler, *Epitome of Copernican Astronomy,*
Bk. IV, I, 2

45 If it was Tycho Brahe's opinion concerning that bare wilderness of globes that it does not exist fruitlessly in the world but is filled with inhabitants: with how much greater probability shall we make a conjecture as to God's works and designs even for the other globes, from that variety which we discern in this globe of the Earth. For He Who created the species which should inhabit the waters, beneath which however there is no room for the air which living things draw in; Who sent birds supported on wings into the wilderness of the air; Who gave white bears and white wolves to the snowy regions of the North, and as food for the bears the whale, and for the wolves, birds' eggs; Who gave lions to the deserts of burning Libya and camels to the wide-spread plains of Syria, and to the lions an endurance of hunger, and to the camels an endurance of thirst: did He use up every art in the globe of the Earth so that He was unable, every goodness so that he did not wish, to adorn the other globes too with their fitting creatures, as either the long or short revolutions, or the nearness or removal of the sun, or the variety of eccentricities or the shine or darkness of the bodies, or the properties of the figures wherewith any region is supported persuaded?

Kepler, *Harmonies of the World,* V, 10

46 *Hamlet.* Indeed it goes so heavily with my disposition that this goodly frame, the earth, seems to me a sterile promontory, this most excellent canopy, the air, look you, this brave o'erhanging firmament, this majestical roof fretted with golden fire, why, it appears no other thing to me than a foul and pestilent congregation of vapours.

Shakespeare, *Hamlet,* II, ii, 308

47 *Ulysses.* The heavens themselves, the planets, and this centre
Observe degree, priority, and place,
Insisture, course, proportion, season, form,

Office, and custom, in all line of order;
And therefore is the glorious planet Sol
In noble eminence enthroned and sphered
Amidst the other; whose medicinable eye
Corrects the ill aspects of planets evil,
And posts, like the commandment of a king,
Sans check, to good and bad. But when the planets
In evil mixture to disorder wander,
What plagues and what portents! what mutiny!
What raging of the sea! shaking of earth!
Commotion in the winds! frights, changes, horrors,
Divert and crack, rend and deracinate
The unity and married calm of states
Quite from their fixure!

Shakespeare, *Troilus and Cressida,* I, iii, 85

48 I had rather believe all the fables in the Legend, and the Talmud, and the Alcoran, than that this universal frame is without a mind.

Bacon, *Of Atheism*

49 I resolved to leave all this world to their disputes, and to speak only of what would happen in a new world if God now created, somewhere in an imaginary space, matter sufficient wherewith to form it, and if He agitated in diverse ways, and without any order, the diverse portions of this matter, so that there resulted a chaos as confused as the poets ever feigned, and concluded His work by merely lending His concurrence to Nature in the usual way, leaving her to act in accordance with the laws which He had established. So, to begin with, I described this matter and tried to represent it in such a way, that it seems to me that nothing in the world could be more clear or intelligible, excepting what has just been said of God and the Soul. For I even went so far as expressly to assume that there was in it none of these forms or qualities which are so debated in the Schools, nor anything at all the knowledge of which is not so natural to our minds that none could even pretend to be ignorant of it. Further, I pointed out what are the laws of Nature, and, without resting my reasons on any other principle than the infinite perfections of God, I tried to demonstrate all those of which one could have any doubt, and to show that they are of such a nature that even if God had created other worlds, He could not have created any in which these laws would fail to be observed. After that, I showed how the greatest part of the matter of which this chaos is constituted, must in accordance with these laws, dispose and arrange itself in such a fashion as to render it similar to our heavens; and how meantime some of its parts must form an earth, some planets and comets, and some others a sun and fixed stars.

Descartes, *Discourse on Method,* V

50 It . . . occurs to me that we should not consider

one single creature separately, when we inquire as to whether the works of God are perfect, but should regard all his creations together. For the same thing which might possibly seem very imperfect with some semblance of reason if regarded by itself, is found to be very perfect if regarded as part of the whole universe.

Descartes, *Meditations on First Philosophy*, IV

51 From the mere fact that God, i.e. a supremely perfect being, exists, it follows that if there be a world it must have been created by him.

Descartes, *Objections and Replies*, III

52 Those philosophers who said [that] the world, or the soul of the world, was God spake unworthily of Him, and denied His existence: for by *God* is understood the cause of the world; and to say the world is God is to say there is no cause of it, that is, no God.

Hobbes, *Leviathan*, II, 31

53 To say the world was not created, but eternal, seeing that which is eternal has no cause, is to deny there is a God.

Hobbes, *Leviathan*, II, 31

54 But while all men doubt, and none can determine how long the World shall last, some may wonder that it hath spun out so long and unto our days. For if the Almighty had not determin'd a fixed duration unto it, according to his mighty and merciful designments in it, if he had not said unto it, as he did unto a part of it, hitherto shalt thou go and no farther; if we consider the incessant and cutting provocations from the Earth, it is not without amazement how his patience hath permitted so long a continuance unto it, how he, who cursed the Earth in the first days of the first Man, and drowned it in the tenth Generation after, should thus lastingly contend with Flesh and yet defer the last flames.

Sir Thomas Browne, *Christian Morals*, III, 26

55 Think not thy time short in this World since the World it self is not long. The created World is but a small *Parenthesis* in Eternity; and a short interposition for a time between such a state of duration, as was before it and may be after it. And if we should allow of the old Tradition that the world should last Six Thousand years, it could scarce have the name of old, since the first Man lived near a sixth part thereof, and seven *Methusela's* would exceed its whole duration.

Sir Thomas Browne, *Christian Morals*, III, 29

56 The whole visible world is only an imperceptible atom in the ample bosom of nature. No idea approaches it. We may enlarge our conceptions beyond all imaginable space; we only produce atoms in comparison with the reality of things. It is

an infinite sphere, the centre of which is everywhere, the circumference nowhere. In short, it is the greatest sensible mark of the almighty power of God that imagination loses itself in that thought.

Pascal, *Pensées*, II, 72

57 *Uriel.* I saw when at his Word the formless Mass,
This worlds material mould, came to a heap:
Confusion heard his voice, and wilde uproar
Stood rul'd, stood vast infinitude confin'd;
Till at his second bidding darkness fled,
Light shon, and order from disorder sprung:
Swift to thir several Quarters hasted then
The cumbrous Elements, Earth, Flood, Aire, Fire,
And this Ethereal quintessence of Heav'n
Flew upward, spirited with various forms,
That rowld orbicular, and turnd to Starrs
Numberless, as thou seest, and how they move;
Each had his place appointed, each his course,
The rest in circuit walles this Universe.
Look downward on that Globe whose hither side
With light from hence, though but reflected,
  shines;
That place is Earth the seat of Man, that light
His day, which else as th' other Hemisphere
Night would invade, but there the neighbouring
  Moon
(So call that opposite fair Starr) her aide
Timely interposes, and her monthly round
Still ending, still renewing through mid Heav'n,
With borrow'd light her countenance triform
Hence fills and empties to enlighten the Earth,
And in her pale dominion checks the night.

Milton, *Paradise Lost*, III, 708

58 Let ther be Light, said God, and forthwith Light
Ethereal, first of things, quintessence pure
Sprung from the Deep, and from her Native East
To journie through the airie gloom began,
Sphear'd in a radiant Cloud, for yet the Sun
Was not; shee in a cloudie Tabernacle
Sojourn'd the while. God saw the Light was good;
And light from darkness by the Hemisphere
Divided: Light the Day, and Darkness Night
He nam'd. Thus was the first Day Eev'n and
  Morn.

Milton, *Paradise Lost*, VII, 243

59 *Michael.*   So shall the World goe on,
To good malignant, to bad men benigne,
Under her own waight groaning, till the day
Appeer of respiration to the just,
And vengeance to the wicked, at return
Of him so lately promiss'd to thy aid,
The Womans seed, obscurely then foretold,
Now amplier known thy Saviour and thy Lord,
Last in the Clouds from Heav'n to be reveald
In glory of the Father, to dissolve
Satan with his perverted World, then raise
From the conflagrant mass, purg'd and refin'd,

New Heav'ns, new Earth, Ages of endless date
Founded in righteousness and peace and love,
To bring forth fruits Joy and eternal Bliss.

Milton, *Paradise Lost,* XII, 537

60 Things could have been produced by God in no other manner and in no other order than that in which they have been produced. All things have necessarily followed from the given nature of God, and from the necessity of His nature have been determined to existence and action in a certain manner. If, therefore, things could have been of another nature, or could have been determined in another manner to action, so that the order of nature would have been different, the nature of God might then be different to that which it now is, and hence that different nature would necessarily exist, and there might consequently be two or more Gods, which is absurd. Therefore, things could be produced by God in no other manner and in no other order than that in which they have been produced.

Spinoza, *Ethics,* I, Prop. 33; Demonst.

61 It seems probable to me that God in the beginning formed matter in solid, massy, hard, impenetrable, moveable particles, of such sizes and figures, and with such other properties, and in such proportion to space, as most conduced to the end for which he formed them; and that these primitive particles being solids, are incomparably harder than any porous bodies compounded of them; even so very hard as never to wear or break in pieces; no ordinary power being able to divide what God himself made one in the first creation. While the particles continue entire, they may compose bodies of one and the same nature and texture in all ages; but should they wear away, or break in pieces, the nature of things depending on them would be changed. Water and earth, composed of old worn particles and fragments of particles, would not be of the same nature and texture now, with water and earth composed of entire particles in the beginning. And, therefore, that Nature may be lasting, the changes of corporeal things are to be placed only in the various separations and new associations and motions of these permanent particles.

Newton, *Optics,* III, 1

62 By the help of these principles [of motion], all material things seem to have been composed of the hard and solid particles above mentioned, variously associated in the first creation by the counsel of an intelligent agent. For it became Him who created them to set them in order. And if He did so, it is unphilosophical to seek for any other origin of the world, or to pretend that it might arise out of a chaos by the mere laws of Nature; though, being once formed, it may continue by those laws for many ages. For while comets move

in very eccentric orbs in all manner of positions, blind fate could never make all the planets move one and the same way in orbs concentric, some inconsiderable irregularities excepted, which may have risen from the mutual actions of comets and planets upon one another, and which will be apt to increase, till this system wants a reformation. Such a wonderful uniformity in the planetary system must be allowed the effect of choice.

Newton, *Optics,* III, 1

63 Since space is divisible *in infinitum,* and matter is not necessarily in all places, it may be also allowed that God is able to create particles of matter of several sizes and figures, and in several proportions to space, and perhaps of different densities and forces, and thereby to vary the laws of Nature, and make worlds of several sorts in several parts of the Universe. At least, I see nothing of contradiction in all this.

Newton, *Optics,* III, 1

64 Although the world is not metaphysically necessary, so that its opposite involves a contradiction or logical absurdity, it is nevertheless physically necessary or so determined that its opposite involves imperfection or moral absurdity. And as possibility is the principle of essence, so perfection or degree of essence (through which more things are compossible the greater it is) is the principle of existence. Whence at the same time it is manifest how the Author of the world is free, although He does all things determinately, for He acts from a principle of wisdom or perfection. Indifference springs from ignorance, and the wiser a man is the more is he determined towards that which is most perfect.

Leibniz, *On the Ultimate Origination
of Things*

65 It follows from the supreme perfection of God that in producing the universe He has chosen the best possible plan, in which there is the greatest variety along with the greatest order; ground, place, time being as well arranged as possible; the greatest effect produced by the simplest ways; the most power, knowledge, happiness and goodness in created things that the universe allowed. For as all possible things in the understanding of God claim existence in proportion to their perfections, the result of all these claims must be the most perfect actual world that is possible. And apart from this it would not be possible to give a reason why things have gone thus rather than otherwise.

Leibniz, *Principles of Nature and of Grace,* 10

66 If we would emancipate ourselves from vulgar notions, and raise our thoughts, as far as they would reach, to a closer contemplation of things, we might be able to aim at some dim and seeming conception how *matter* might at first be made, and

begin to exist, by the power of that eternal first Being: but to give beginning and being to a *spirit* would be found a more inconceivable effect of omnipotent power. But this being what would perhaps lead us too far from the notions on which the philosophy now in the world is built, it would not be pardonable to deviate so far from them; or to inquire, so far as grammar itself would authorize, if the common settled opinion opposes it: especially in this place, where the received doctrine serves well enough to our present purpose, and leaves this past doubt, that the creation or beginning of any one *substance* out of nothing being once admitted, the creation of all other but the *Creator* himself, may, with the same ease, be supposed.

Locke, *Concerning Human Understanding,*
Bk. IV, X, 18

67 We must not imagine that the inexplicably fine machine of an animal or vegetable costs the great Creator any more pains or trouble in its production than a pebble does; nothing being more evident than that an Omnipotent Spirit can indifferently produce everything by a mere *fiat* or act of His will. Hence, it is plain that the splendid profusion of natural things should not be interpreted weakness or prodigality in the agent who produces them, but rather be looked on as an argument of the riches of His power.

Berkeley, *Principles of Human Knowledge,* 152

68 See, thro' this air, this ocean, and this earth,
All matter quick, and bursting into birth.
Above, how high progressive life may go!
Around, how wide! how deep extend below!
Vast chain of being, which from God began,
Natures æthereal, human, angel, man,
Beast, bird, fish, insect! what no eye can see,
No glass can reach! from Infinite to thee,
From thee to Nothing!—On superior pow'rs
Were we to press, inferior might on ours:
Or in the full creation leave a void,
Where, one step broken, the great scale's
    destroy'd:
From Nature's chain whatever link you strike,
Tenth or ten thousandth, breaks the chain alike.
    And if each system in gradation roll,
Alike essential to th' amazing whole;
The least confusion but in one, not all
That system only, but the whole must fall.
Let Earth unbalanc'd from her orbit fly,
Planets and Suns run lawless thro' the sky,
Let ruling Angels from their spheres be hurl'd,
Being on being wreck'd, and world on world,
Heav'n's whole foundations to their centre nod,
And Nature tremble to the throne of God.

Pope, *Essay on Man,* Epistle I, 233

69 The world may indeed be considered as a vast machine, in which the great wheels are originally set in motion by those which are very minute, and almost imperceptible to any but the strongest eyes.

Fielding, *Tom Jones,* V, 4

70 There are many philosophers who, after an exact scrutiny of all the phenomena of nature, conclude, that the *whole,* considered as one system, is, in every period of its existence, ordered with perfect benevolence; and that the utmost possible happiness will, in the end, result to all created beings, without any mixture of positive or absolute ill or misery. Every physical ill, say they, makes an essential part of this benevolent system, and could not possibly be removed, even by the Deity himself, considered as a wise agent, without giving entrance to greater ill, or excluding greater good, which will result from it. From this theory, some philosophers, and the ancient Stoics among the rest, derived a topic of consolation under all afflictions, while they taught their pupils that those ills under which they laboured were, in reality, goods to the universe; and that to an enlarged view, which could comprehend the whole system of nature, every event became an object of joy and exultation. But though this topic be specious and sublime, it was soon found in practice weak and ineffectual. You would surely more irritate than appease a man lying under the racking pains of the gout by preaching up to him the rectitude of those general laws, which produced the malignant humours in his body, and led them through the proper canals, to the sinews and nerves, where they now excite such acute torments. These enlarged views may, for a moment, please the imagination of a speculative man, who is placed in ease and security; but neither can they dwell with constancy on his mind, even though undisturbed by the emotions of pain or passion; much less can they maintain their ground when attacked by such powerful antagonists.

Hume, *Concerning Human
Understanding,* VIII, 79

71 Pangloss taught metaphysico-theologo-cosmoloni-gology. He proved most admirably, that there could not be an effect without a cause; that, in this best of possible worlds, my Lord the Baron's castle was the most magnificent of castles, and my Lady the best of Baronesses that possibly could be.

"It is demonstrable," said he, "that things cannot be otherwise than they are: for all things having been made for some end, they must necessarily be for the best end. Observe well, that the nose has been made for carrying spectacles; therefore we have spectacles. The legs are visibly designed for stockings, and therefore we have stockings. Stones have been formed to be hewn, and make castles; therefore my Lord has a very fine castle; the greatest baron of the province ought to be the best accommodated. Swine were made to be eaten; therefore we eat pork all the year round: consequently, those who have merely asserted that all is good have said a very foolish thing; they should have said all is the best possible."

Voltaire, *Candide*, I

72 The day following, having found some provisions, in rummaging through the rubbish, they recruited their strength a little. Afterwards, they employed themselves like others, in administering relief to the inhabitants that had escaped from death. Some citizens that had been relieved by them gave them as good a dinner as could be expected amidst such a disaster. It is true that the repast was mournful, and the guests watered their bread with their tears. But Pangloss consoled them by the assurance that things could not be otherwise; "For," said he, "all this must necessarily be for the best. As this volcano is at Lisbon, it could not be elsewhere; as it is impossible that things should not be what they are, as all is good."

A little man clad in black, who belonged to the inquisition, and sat at his side, took him up very politely, and said: "It seems, sir, you do not believe in original sin; for if all is for the best, then there has been neither fall nor punishment."

"I most humbly ask your excellency's pardon," answered Pangloss, still more politely; "for the fall of man and the curse necessarily entered into the best of worlds possible." "Then, sir, you do not believe there is liberty," said the inquisitor. "Your excellency will excuse me," said Pangloss; "liberty can consist with absolute necessity; for it was necessary we should be free; because, in short, the determinate will—"

Pangloss was in the middle of his proposition, when the inquisitor made a signal with his head to the tall armed footman in a cloak.

Voltaire, *Candide*, V

73 Candide, affrighted, interdicted, astonished, all bloody, all panting, said to himself: "If this is the best of possible worlds, what then are the rest?"

Voltaire, *Candide*, VI

74 Why, as we are so miserable, have we imagined that not to be is a great ill, when it is clear that it was not an ill not to be before we were born? . . . Why do we exist? why is there anything?

Voltaire, *Philosophical Dictionary:* Why?

75 Every beginning is in time, and all limits to extension are in space. But space and time are in the world of sense. Consequently phenomena *in the world* are conditionally limited, but *the world* itself is not limited, either conditionally or unconditionally.

Kant, *Critique of Pure Reason,*
Transcendental Dialectic

76 Tiger! Tiger! burning bright
In the forests of the night,

What immortal hand or eye
Could frame thy fearful symmetry? . . .

When the stars threw down their spears,
And water'd heaven with their tears,
Did he smile his work to see?
Did he who made the Lamb make thee?

Blake, *The Tiger*

77 *Faust.* 'Tis written: "In the beginning was the Word!"
Here now I'm balked! Who'll put me in accord?
It is impossible, the *Word* so high to prize,
I must translate it otherwise
If I am rightly by the Spirit taught.
'Tis written: In the beginning was the *Thought!*
Consider well that line, the first you see,
That your pen may not write too hastily!
Is it then *Thought* that works, creative, hour by hour?
Thus should it stand: In the beginning was the *Power!*
Yet even while I write this word, I falter,
For something warns me, this too I shall alter.
The Spirit's helping me! I see now what I need
And write assured: In the beginning was the *Deed!*

Goethe, *Faust*, I, 1224

78 It is not impossible that to some infinitely superior being the whole universe may be as one plain, the distance between planet and planet being only as the pores in a grain of sand, and the spaces between system and system no greater than the intervals between one grain and the grain adjacent.

Coleridge, *Omniana*

79 This world, after all our science and sciences, is still a miracle; wonderful, inscrutable, *magical* and more, to whosoever will *think* of it.

Carlyle, *The Hero as Divinity*

80 There is no chance and no anarchy in the universe. All is system and gradation. Every god is there sitting in his sphere. The young mortal enters the hall of the firmament; there is he alone with them alone, they pouring on him benedictions and gifts, and beckoning him up to their thrones. On the instant, and incessantly, fall snowstorms of illusions. He fancies himself in a vast crowd which sways this way and that and whose movement and doings he must obey: he fancies himself poor, orphaned, insignificant. The mad crowd drives hither and thither, now furiously commanding this thing to be done, now that. What is he that he should resist their will, and think or act for himself? Every moment new changes and new showers of deceptions to baffle and distract him. And when, by and by, for an instant, the air clears and the cloud lifts a little, there are the gods still sitting around him on their thrones—they alone with him alone.

Emerson, *Illusions*

81 To go into solitude, a man needs to retire as much from his chamber as from society. I am not solitary whilst I read and write, though nobody is with me. But if a man would be alone, let him look at the stars. The rays that come from those heavenly worlds will separate between him and what he touches. One might think the atmosphere was made transparent with this design, to give man, in the heavenly bodies, the perpetual presence of the sublime. Seen in the streets of cities, how great they are! If the stars should appear one night in a thousand years, how would men believe and adore; and preserve for many generations the remembrance of the city of God which had been shown! But every night come out these envoys of beauty, and light the universe with their admonishing smile.

Emerson, *Nature,* I

82 Many an aeon moulded earth before her highest, man, was born,
Many an aeon too may pass when earth is manless and forlorn.

Tennyson, *Locksley Hall Sixty Years After,* 205

83 This fine old world of ours is but a child
Yet in the go-cart. Patience! Give it time
To learn its limbs; there is a hand that guides.

Tennyson, *The Princess,* Conclusion, 77

84 This may not be the best of all possible worlds, but to say that it is the worst is mere petulant nonsense.

T. H. Huxley, *Struggle for Existence in Human Society*

85 The year's at the spring
And day's at the morn;
Morning's at seven;
The hillside's dew-pearled;
The lark's on the wing;
The snail's on the thorn:
God's in his heaven—
All's right with the world!

Browning, *Pippa Passes,* I

86 The bodies and beings on the surface of our earth express the harmonious relation of the cosmic conditions of our planet and our atmosphere with the beings and phenomena whose existence they permit. Other cosmic conditions would necessarily make another world appear in which all the phenomena would occur which found in it their necessary conditions, and from which would disappear all that could not develop in it. But no matter what infinite varieties of phenomena we conceive on the earth, by placing ourselves in thought in all the cosmic conditions that our imagination can bring to birth, we are still forced to admit that this would all take place according to the laws of physics, chemistry and physiology, which have existed without our knowledge from all eternity; and that whatever happens, nothing is created by way either of force or of matter; that only different relations will be produced and through them creation of new beings and phenomena.

Claude Bernard, *Experimental Medicine,* II, 1

87 *Ivan.* "I tell you that I accept God simply. But you must note this: if God exists and if He really did create the world, then, as we all know, He created it according to the geometry of Euclid and the human mind with the conception of only three dimensions in space. Yet there have been and still are geometricians and philosophers, and even some of the most distinguished, who doubt whether the whole universe, or to speak more widely, the whole of being, was only created in Euclid's geometry; they even dare to dream that two parallel lines, which according to Euclid can never meet on earth, may meet somewhere in infinity. I have come to the conclusion that, since I can't understand even that, I can't expect to understand about God. I acknowledge humbly that I have no faculty for settling such questions, I have a Euclidian earthly mind, and how could I solve problems that are not of this world? And I advise you never to think about it either, my dear Alyosha, especially about God, whether He exists or not. All such questions are utterly inappropriate for a mind created with an idea of only three dimensions. And so I accept God and am glad to, and what's more, I accept His wisdom, His purpose—which are utterly beyond our ken; I believe in the underlying order and the meaning of life; I believe in the eternal harmony in which they say we shall one day be blended. I believe in the Word to Which the universe is striving, and Which Itself was 'with God,' and Which Itself is God and so on, and so on, to infinity. There are all sorts of phrases for it. I seem to be on the right path, don't I? Yet would you believe it, in the final result I don't accept this world of God's and, although I know it exists, I don't accept it at all. It's not that I don't accept God, you must understand, it's the world created by Him I don't and cannot accept. Let me make it plain. I believe like a child that suffering will be healed and made up for, that all the humiliating absurdity of human contradictions will vanish like a pitiful mirage, like the despicable fabrication of the impotent and infinitely small Euclidian mind of man, that in the world's finale, at the moment of eternal harmony, something so precious will come to pass that it will suffice for all hearts, for the comforting of all resentments, for the atonement of all the crimes of humanity, of all the blood they've shed; that it will make it not only possible to forgive but to justify all that has happened with men—but

though all that may come to pass, I don't accept it. I won't accept it. Even if parallel lines do meet and I see it myself, I shall see it and say that they've met, but still I won't accept it. That's what's at the root of me, Alyosha; that's my creed. I am in earnest in what I say. I began our talk as stupidly as I could on purpose, but I've led up to my confession, for that's all you want. You didn't want to hear about God, but only to know what the brother you love lives by. And so I've told you."

Ivan concluded his long tirade with marked and unexpected feeling.

Dostoevsky, *Brothers Karamazov,* Pt. II, V, 3

88 *Father Zossima.* "All creation and all creatures, every leaf is striving to the Word, singing glory to God, weeping to Christ, unconsciously accomplishing this by the mystery of their sinless life. Yonder," said I, "in the forest wanders the dreadful bear, fierce and menacing, and yet innocent in it." And I told him how once a bear came to a great saint who had taken refuge in a tiny cell in the wood. And the great saint pitied him, went up to him without fear and gave him a piece of bread. "Go along," said he, "Christ be with you," and the savage beast walked away meekly and obediently, doing no harm. And the lad was delighted that the bear had walked away without hurting the saint, and that Christ was with him too. "Ah," said he, "how good that is, how good and beautiful is all God's work!" He sat musing softly and sweetly. I saw he understood. And he slept beside me a light and sinless sleep. May God bless youth! And I prayed for him as I went to sleep. Lord, send peace and light to Thy people!

Dostoevsky, *Brothers Karamazov,* Pt. II, VI, 1

89 Pierre went up to the fire, ate some roast horse-flesh, lay down with his back to the fire, and immediately fell asleep. He again slept as he had done at Mozháysk after the battle of Borodinó.

Again real events mingled with dreams and again someone, he or another, gave expression to his thoughts, and even to the same thoughts that had been expressed in his dream at Mozháysk.

"Life is everything. Life is God. Everything changes and moves and that movement is God. And while there is life there is joy in consciousness of the divine. To love life is to love God. Harder and more blessed than all else is to love this life in one's sufferings, in innocent sufferings."

"Karatáev!" came to Pierre's mind.

And suddenly he saw vividly before him a long-forgotten, kindly old man who had given him geography lessons in Switzerland. "Wait a bit," said the old man, and showed Pierre a globe. This globe was alive—a vibrating ball without fixed dimensions. Its whole surface consisted of drops closely pressed together, and all these drops moved and changed places, sometimes several of

them merging into one, sometimes one dividing into many. Each drop tried to spread out and occupy as much space as possible, but others striving to do the same compressed it, sometimes destroyed it, and sometimes merged with it.

"That is life," said the old teacher.

"How simple and clear it is," thought Pierre. "How is it I did not know it before?"

"God is in the midst, and each drop tries to expand so as to reflect Him to the greatest extent. And it grows, merges, disappears from the surface, sinks to the depths, and again emerges. There now, Karatáev has spread out and disappeared. Do you understand, my child?" said the teacher.

"Do you understand, damn you?" shouted a voice, and Pierre woke up.

Tolstoy, *War and Peace,* XIV, 15

90 Away with those wearisomely hackneyed terms Optimism and Pessimism! For the occasion for using them becomes less and less from day to day; only the chatterboxes still find them so absolutely necessary. For why in all the world should any one wish to be an optimist unless he had a God to defend who *must* have created the best of worlds if he himself be goodness and perfection,—what thinker, however, still needs the hypothesis of a God? But every occasion for a pessimistic confession of faith is also lacking when one has no interest in being annoyed at the advocates of God (the theologians, or the theologising philosophers), and in energetically defending the opposite view, that evil reigns, that pain is greater than pleasure, that the world is a bungled piece of work, the manifestation of an ill-will to life. But who still bothers about the theologians now—except the theologians? Apart from all theology and its contentions, it is quite clear that the world is not good and not bad (to say nothing of its being the best or the worst), and that the terms "good" and "bad" have only significance with respect to man, and indeed, perhaps, they are not justified even here in the way they are usually employed; in any case we must get rid of both the calumniating and the glorifying conception of the world.

Nietzsche, *Human, All-Too-Human,* 28

91 What at bottom is meant by calling the universe many or by calling it one?

Pragmatically interpreted, pluralism or the doctrine that it is many means only that the sundry parts of reality *may be externally related.* Everything you can think of, however vast or inclusive, has on the pluralistic view a genuinely 'external' environment of some sort or amount. Things are 'with' one another in many ways, but nothing includes everything, or dominates over everything. The word 'and' trails along after every sentence. Something always escapes. 'Ever not quite' has to be said of the best attempts made anywhere in the universe at attaining all-inclusiveness. The pluralistic world is thus more like a federal republic than like an empire or a kingdom. However much may be collected, however much may report itself as present at any effective centre of consciousness or action, something else is self-governed and absent and unreduced to unity.

Monism, on the other hand, insists that when you come down to reality as such, to the reality of realities, everything is present to *everything* else in one vast instantaneous co-implicated completeness—nothing can in *any* sense, functional or substantial, be really absent from anything else, all things interpenetrate and telescope together in the great total conflux.

William James, *A Pluralistic Universe*, VIII

92 There is a hideous fatalism about it [the Darwinian process], a ghastly and damnable reduction of beauty and intelligence, of strength and purpose, of honor and aspiration, to such casually picturesque changes as an avalanche may make in a mountain landscape, or a railway accident in a human figure. To call this Natural Selection is a blasphemy, possible to many for whom Nature is nothing but a casual aggregation of inert and dead matter, but eternally impossible to the spirits and souls of the righteous. If it be no blasphemy, but a truth of science, then the stars of heaven, the showers and dew, the winter and summer, the fire and heat, the mountains and hills, may no longer be called to exalt the Lord with us by praise: their work is to modify all things by blindly starving and murdering everything that is not lucky enough to survive in the universal struggle for hogwash.

Shaw, *Back to Methuselah*, Pref.

93 The riddle of the universe is not so simple. There is the aspect of permanence in which a given type of attainment is endlessly repeated for its own sake; and there is the aspect of transition to other things—it may be of higher worth, and it may be of lower worth. Also there are its aspects of struggle and of friendly help. But romantic ruthlessness is no nearer to real politics, than is romantic self-abnegation.

Whitehead, *Science and the Modern World*, VI

94 The universe is an assemblage of solar systems which we have every reason to believe analogous to our own. No doubt they are not absolutely independent of one another. Our sun radiates heat and light beyond the farthest planet, and, on the other hand, our entire solar system is moving in a definite direction as if it were drawn. There is, then, a bond between the worlds. But this bond may be regarded as infinitely loose in comparison with the mutual dependence which unites the parts of the same world among themselves; so that it is not artificially, for reasons of mere convenience, that we isolate our solar system: nature itself invites us to isolate it. As living beings, we depend on the planet on which we are, and on the sun that provides for it, but on nothing else. As thinking beings, we may apply the laws of our physics to our own world, and extend them to each of the worlds taken separately; but nothing tells us that they apply to the entire universe, nor even that such an affirmation has any meaning; for the universe is not made, but is being made continually. It is growing, perhaps indefinitely, by the addition of new worlds.

Bergson, *Creative Evolution*, III

95 The world is everything that is the case.

The world is the totality of facts, not of things.

The world is determined by the facts, and by these being *all* the facts.

For the totality of facts determines both what is the case, and also all that is not the case.

The facts in logical space are the world.

The world divides into facts.

Any one can either be the case or not be the case, and everything else remain the same.

Wittgenstein, *Tractatus Logico-Philosophicus*, 1–1.21

96 Not *how* the world is, is the mystical, but *that* it is.

Wittgenstein, *Tractatus Logico-Philosophicus*, 6.44

Chapter 20

RELIGION

Chapter 20 is divided into fifteen sections: 20.1 THE DISTINGUISHING FEATURES OF RELIGION, 20.2 JUDAISM, 20.3 CHRISTIANITY, 20.4 CHURCH, 20.5 GOD, 20.6 GODS AND GODDESSES, 20.7 ANGELS AND DEVILS, 20.8 WORSHIP AND SERVICE, 20.9 HERESY AND UNBELIEF, 20.10 PROPHECY, 20.11 MIRACLES, 20.12 SUPERSTITION, 20.13 SIN AND TEMPTATION, 20.14 REDEMPTION AND SALVATION, and 20.15 HEAVEN AND HELL.

Religion is one of the two largest chapters in this book, the other being a chapter to which it is intimately related—Chapter 9 on ETHICS. It might have had an even larger number of sections had we not allocated certain topics or themes to other chapters. We placed the treatment of religious faith in Chapter 6 on KNOWLEDGE, Section 6.5 on OPINION, BELIEF, AND FAITH. In Chapter 15 on HISTORY, we placed discussions of predestination and providence in Section 15.3 on FATE, FORTUNE, AND DESTINY. Quotations dealing with the relation of the world to God and its coming to be through divine creation will be found in Section 19.8 on THE UNIVERSE OR COSMOS in Chapter 19 on NATURE AND THE COSMOS; similarly, quotations dealing with

man's relation to God or the gods will be found in the opening section of Chapter 1 on MAN. The treatment of sacred or dogmatic theology is associated with the treatment of natural theology in Section 17.1 on PHILOSOPHY AND PHILOSOPHERS.

Extensive as it is, both in number of topics covered and the quantity of quotations collected under them, this chapter remains inadequate in its representation of religious thought and theological speculation in the Western tradition. Just as we have eschewed including the technical treatment of certain themes or problems in other fields, such as economics or mathematics, so here we have not included the highly subtle and technical discussion of certain subjects or problems in theology, such as grace and free will, the divine attributes, the problem of evil, the sacraments, immortality and the resurrection of the body, and so on. However, what is presented here is an illustrative sampling of what has been said on a fairly large number of major themes in the sphere of Western religion. In addition to being limited to the West, the materials here are also limited in time, for they are not representative of some new currents in both theology and the philosophy of religion that have emerged in the last fifty years.

The first three sections of the chapter deal with the nature and traits of religion and with two of the three great religions of the West—Judaism and Christianity. Discussion of Mohammedanism and of the Muslim religious community does not occur in the books from which we have drawn quotations. Section 20.4 treats the central religious institution—the organized religious community, whether it be called church, temple, or synagogue. Closely related to Section 20.1 on THE DISTINGUISHING FEATURES OF RELIGION is Section 20.12 on SUPERSTITION: together they attempt to draw the line between religion and its counterfeit.

Section 20.5 on GOD and Section 20.6 on GODS AND GODDESSES, together with Section 20.7 on ANGELS AND DEVILS, deal with subjects that have inspired the fancy of the poets as well as elicited the speculations and arguments of the philosophers and theologians. This is true also of HEAVEN AND HELL, treated in Section 20.15.

While not exhaustive of the themes that might have been treated, the remaining sections—20.8 on WORSHIP AND SERVICE, 20.9 on HERESY AND UNBELIEF, 20.10 on PROPHECY, 20.11 on MIRACLES, 20.13 on SIN AND TEMPTATION, and 20.14 on REDEMPTION AND SALVATION—represent important topics or problems in Western religious thought and life.

As pointed out at the beginning, the reader will find that Chapter 9 on ETHICS covers matters that are also covered here, though in a different context, especially its Sections 9.1, 9.3, 9.5, 9.6, and 9.8. Other cross-references will be pointed out in the opening texts that preface particular sections of this chapter.

20.1 | *The Distinguishing Features of Religion*

The religions represented here, limited as they are by the range of the books from which our quotations are drawn, are those reflected in the writings of classical antiquity and in the Old and the New Testament. In addition to the contrast between polytheism and monotheism, the Greek and Roman religions differ from Judaism and Christianity in another crucial respect: the latter are, as they are so often called, "religions of the book," that is, religions which rest their faith upon the word of God as that is revealed to man in Holy Writ.

There is still another difference that is indicated in certain passages quoted below: the pagan attitude toward religion was one of tolerance toward a diversity of creeds; it accepted religious pluralism; but Judaism and Christianity introduced into the world the notion of "the one true religion" and, with it, an intolerance of infidels. This fact is commented on adversely by those who see in religious intolerance one of the most baneful sources of hate and hostility among peoples. The quotations also include satirical diatribes against the abuses of religion as well as attacks that fail to recognize the difference between religion and its perversions and argue for its total rejection or eradication.

The treatment here of the distinguishing features of religion includes comment on the roots or seeds of religion; the institution of state religions and the role that religion plays in society and politics; the distinction between organized or institutionalized religion and humanistic or personal religions; and the psychological aspects of religious experience and the psychogenesis of the religious impulse. It also involves discussion of man's relation to God or the gods—his worship and fear of the divine, his knowledge of God, his trust in or reliance on deity. The reader will find these matters treated also in other sections of this chapter, especially sections 20.2, 20.3, and 20.8. The discussion of man's knowledge of God and of religious faith or belief will be found in Chapter 6 on KNOWLEDGE, especially Section 6.5 on OPINION, BELIEF, AND FAITH; and for the consideration of theology as an organized body of knowledge, the reader should consult Section 17.1 on PHILOSOPHY AND PHILOSOPHERS.

---

1 Man doth not live by bread only, but by every word that proceedeth out of the mouth of the Lord doth man live.

Deuteronomy 8:3

2 A scrupulous fear of the gods, is the very thing which keeps the Roman commonwealth together. To such an extraordinary height is this carried among them, both in private and public business, that nothing could exceed it. Many people might think this unaccountable; but in my opinion their object is to use it as a check upon the common people. If it were possible to form a state wholly of philosophers, such a custom would perhaps be unnecessary. But seeing that every multitude is fickle, and full of lawless desires, unreasoning anger, and violent passion, the only resource is to keep them in check by mysterious terrors and scenic effects of this sort. Wherefore, to my mind, the ancients were not acting without purpose or at random, when they brought in among the vulgar those opinions about the gods, and the belief in the punishments in Hades: much rather do I think that men nowadays are acting rashly and foolishly in rejecting them.

Polybius, *Histories,* VI, 56

3 And when the tempter came to him, he said, If thou be the Son of God, command that these stones be made bread.

But he answered and said, It is written, Man shall not live by bread alone, but by every word that proceedeth out of the mouth of God.

Matthew 4:3–4

4 Neither do men put new wine into old bottles: else the bottles break, and the wine runneth out, and the bottles perish: but they put new wine into new bottles, and both are preserved.

Matthew 9:17

5 Pure religion and undefiled before God and the Father is this, To visit the fatherless and widows in their affliction, and to keep himself unspotted from the world.

James 1:27

6 Numa . . . wished that his citizens should neither see nor hear any religious service in a perfunctory and inattentive manner, but, laying aside all other occupations, should apply their minds to religion as to a most serious business.

Plutarch, *Numa Pompilius*

7 The first honourable office [Aemilius Paulus] aspired to was that of aedile, which he carried against twelve competitors of such merit that all of them in process of time were consuls. Being afterwards chosen into the number of priests called augurs, appointed amongst the Romans to observe and register divinations made by the flight of birds or prodigies in the air, he so carefully studied the ancient customs of his country, and so thoroughly understood the religion of his ancestors, that this office, which was before only esteemed a title of honour and merely upon that account sought after, by his means rose to the rank of one of the highest arts, and gave a confirmation to the correctness of the definition, which some philosophers have given of religion, that it is the science of worshipping the gods.

Plutarch, *Aemilius Paulus*

8 So much were all things at Rome made to depend upon religion; they would not allow any contempt of the omens and the ancient rites, even though attended with the highest success, thinking it to be of more importance to the public safety that the magistrates should reverence the gods, than that they should overcome their enemies.

Plutarch, *Marcellus*

9 What folly . . . or rather what madness, to submit ourselves through any sentiment of religion to demons, when it belongs to the true religion to deliver us from that depravity which makes us like to them!

Augustine, *City of God,* VIII, 17

10 The true religion commands us to put away all disquietude of heart, and agitation of mind, and also all commotions and tempest of the soul.

Augustine, *City of God,* VIII, 17

11 It is, if I may say so, by spiritually embracing Him that the intellectual soul is filled and impregnated with true virtues. We are enjoined to love this good with all our heart, with all our soul, with all our strength. To this good we ought to be led by those who love us, and to lead those we love. Thus are fulfilled those two commandments on which hang all the law and the prophets: "Thou shalt love the Lord thy God with all thy heart, and with all thy mind, and with all thy soul"; and "Thou shalt love thy neighbour as thyself." For, that man might be intelligent in his self-love, there was appointed for him an end to which he might refer all his actions, that he might be blessed. For he who loves himself wishes nothing else than this. And the end set before him is "to draw near to God." And so, when one who has this intelligent self-love is commanded to love his neighbour as himself, what else is enjoined than that he shall do all in his power to commend to him the love of God? This is the worship of God, this is true religion, this right piety, this the service due to God only.

Augustine, *City of God,* X, 3

12 Religion has two kinds of acts. Some are its proper and immediate acts, which it elicits, and by which man is directed to God alone, for instance, sacrifice, adoration and the like. But it has other acts, which it produces through the medium of the virtues which it commands, directing them to the honor of God, because the virtue which is concerned with the end, commands the virtues which are concerned with the means. Accordingly *to visit the fatherless and widows in their tribulation* is an act of religion as commanding and an act of mercy as eliciting; and *to keep oneself unspotted from this world* is an act of religion as commanding, but of temperance or of some similar virtue as eliciting.

Aquinas, *Summa Theologica,* II–II, 81, 1

13 Religion directs man to God not as its object but as its end.

Aquinas, *Summa Theologica,* II–II, 81, 5

14 Religion is not faith, but a confession of faith by outward signs.

Aquinas, *Summa Theologica,* II–II, 94, 1

15 He who enters religion does not make profession to be perfect, but he professes to endeavour to attain perfection; even as he who enters the schools does not profess to have knowledge, but to study in order to acquire knowledge.

Aquinas, *Summa Theologica,* II–II, 186, 2

16 When April with his showers sweet with fruit
   The drought of March has pierced unto the root
   And bathed each vein with liquor that has power
   To generate therein and sire the flower;
   When Zephyr also has, with his sweet breath,
   Quickened again, in every holt and heath,
   The tender shoots and buds, and the young sun
   Into the Ram one half his course has run,
   And many little birds make melody
   That sleep through all the night with open eye
   (So Nature pricks them on to ramp and rage)—
   Then do folk long to go on pilgrimage,
   And palmers to go seeking out strange strands,
   To distant shrines well known in sundry lands.
   And specially from every shire's end
   Of England they to Canterbury wend,
   The holy blessed martyr there to seek
   Who helped them when they lay so ill and weak.

Chaucer, *Canterbury Tales:* The Prologue

17 I think that the practice I see is bad, of trying to strengthen and support our religion by the good fortune and prosperity of our enterprises. Our belief has enough other foundations; it does not need events to authorize it.

Montaigne, *Essays,* I, 32,
We Should Meddle Soberly

18 Of all the ancient human opinions concerning religion, that one, it seems to me, was most probable and most excusable which recognized God as an incomprehensible power, origin and preserver of all things, all goodness, all perfection, accepting and taking in good part the honor and reverence that human beings rendered him, under whatever aspect, under whatever name, in whatever manner.

Montaigne, *Essays,* II, 12, Apology
for Raymond Sebond

19 O God, what an obligation do we not have to the benignity of our sovereign creator for having freed our belief from the folly of those vagabond and arbitrary devotions, and having based it on the eternal foundation of his holy word?

Montaigne, *Essays,* II, 12, Apology
for Raymond Sebond

20 Seeing there are no signs nor fruit of religion but in man only, there is no cause to doubt but that the seed of religion is also only in man; and consisteth in some peculiar quality, or at least in some eminent degree thereof, not to be found in other living creatures.

Hobbes, *Leviathan,* I, 12

21 In these four things, opinion of ghosts, ignorance of second causes, devotion towards what men fear, and taking of things casual for prognostics, consisteth the natural seed of religion; which, by reason of the different fancies, judgements, and passions of several men, hath grown up into ceremonies so different that those which are used by one man are for the most part ridiculous to another.

For these seeds have received culture from two sorts of men. One sort have been they that have nourished and ordered them, according to their own invention. The other have done it by God's commandment and direction. But both sorts have done it with a purpose to make those men that relied on them the more apt to obedience, laws, peace, charity, and civil society. So that the religion of the former sort is a part of *human politics;* and teacheth part of the duty which earthly kings require of their subjects. And the religion of the latter sort is *divine politics;* and containeth precepts to those that have yielded themselves subjects in the kingdom of God. Of the former sort were all the founders of Commonwealths, and the lawgivers of the Gentiles: of the latter sort were Abraham, Moses, and our blessed Saviour, by whom have been derived unto us the laws of the kingdom of God.

Hobbes, *Leviathan,* I, 12

22 Persecution is a bad and indirect way to plant Religion.

Sir Thomas Browne, *Religio Medici,* I, 25

23 The conduct of God, who disposes all things kindly, is to put religion into the mind by reason, and into the heart by grace. But to will to put it into the mind and heart by force and threats is not to put religion there, but terror.

Pascal, *Pensées,* III, 185

24 Men despise religion; they hate it and fear it is true. To remedy this, we must begin by showing that religion is not contrary to reason; that it is venerable, to inspire respect for it; then we must make it lovable, to make good men hope it is true; finally, we must prove it is true.

Venerable, because it has perfect knowledge of man; lovable because it promises the true good.

Pascal, *Pensées,* III, 187

25 Religion is suited to all kinds of minds. Some pay attention only to its establishment, and this religion is such that its very establishment suffices to prove its truth. Others trace it even to the apostles. The more learned go back to the beginning of the world. The angels see it better still, and from a more distant time.

Pascal, *Pensées,* IV, 285

26 True religion consists in annihilating self before that Universal Being, whom we have so often provoked, and who can justly destroy us at any time; in recognising that we can do nothing without Him, and have deserved nothing from Him but His displeasure. It consists in knowing that there is an unconquerable opposition between us and God, and that without a mediator there can be no communion with Him.

Pascal, *Pensées,* VII, 470

27 Religion is so great a thing that it is right that those who will not take the trouble to seek it, if it be obscure, should be deprived of it. Why, then, do any complain, if it be such as can be found by seeking?

Pascal, *Pensées,* VIII, 574

28 The easiest conditions to live in according to the world are the most difficult to live in according to God, and vice versa. Nothing is so difficult according to the world as the religious life; nothing is easier than to live it according to God. Nothing is easier, according to the world, than to live in high office and great wealth; nothing is more difficult than to live in them according to God, and without acquiring an interest in them and a liking for them.

Pascal, *Pensées,* XIV, 906

29 But let my due feet never fail,
To walk the studious Cloysters pale,
And love the high embowed Roof,
With antick Pillars massy proof,
And storied Windows richly dight,
Casting a dimm religious light.
There let the pealing Organ blow,
To the full voic'd Quire below,
In Service high, and Anthems cleer,
As may with sweetnes, through mine ear,
Dissolve me into extasies,
And bring all Heav'n before mine eyes.
And may at last my weary age
Find out the peacefull hermitage,
The Hairy Gown and Mossy Cell,
Where I may sit and rightly spell
Of every Star that Heav'n doth shew,
And every Herb that sips the dew;
Till old experience do attain
To somthing like Prophetic strain.

Milton, *Il Penseroso,* 155

30 There is not any burden that some would gladlier post off to another than the charge and care of their Religion. . . . A wealthy man, addicted to his pleasure and to his profits, finds Religion to be a traffic so entangled, and of so many piddling accounts, that of all mysteries he cannot skill to keep a stock going upon that trade. What should he do? fain he would have the name to be religious, fain he would bear up with his neighbours

in that. What does he therefore, but resolve to give over toiling, and to find himself out some factor, to whose care and credit he may commit the whole managing of his religious affairs? some Divine of note and estimation that must be. To him he adheres, resigns the whole warehouse of his religion, with all the locks and keys, into his custody; and indeed makes the very person of that man his religion; esteems his associating with him a sufficient evidence and commendatory of his own piety. So that a man may say his religion is now no more within himself, but is become a dividual movable, and goes and comes near him, according as that good man frequents the house. He entertains him, gives him gifts, feasts him, lodges him; his religion comes home at night, prays, is liberally supped, and sumptuously laid to sleep, rises, is saluted, and after the malmsey, or some well-spiced brewage, and better breakfasted than he whose morning appetite would have gladly fed on green figs between Bethany and Jerusalem, his Religion walks abroad at eight, and leaves his kind entertainer in the shop trading all day without his Religion.

Milton, *Areopagitica*

31 The greatest part of these ceremonies and superstitions consists in the religious use of such things as are in their own nature indifferent; nor are they sinful upon any other account than because God is not the author of them. The sprinkling of water and the use of bread and wine are both in their own nature and in the ordinary occasions of life altogether indifferent. Will any man, therefore, say that these things could have been introduced into religion and made a part of divine worship if not by divine institution? If any human authority or civil power could have done this, why might it not also enjoin the eating of fish and drinking of ale in the holy banquet as a part of divine worship? Why not the sprinkling of the blood of beasts in churches, and expiations by water or fire, and abundance more of this kind? But these things, how indifferent soever they be in common uses, when they come to be annexed unto divine worship, without divine authority, they are as abominable to God as the sacrifice of a dog. And why is a dog so abominable? What difference is there between a dog and a goat, in respect of the divine nature, equally and infinitely distant from all affinity with matter, unless it be that God required the use of one in His worship and not of the other? We see, therefore, that indifferent things, how much soever they be under the power of the civil magistrate, yet cannot, upon that pretence, be introduced into religion and imposed upon religious assemblies, because, in the worship of God, they wholly cease to be indifferent.

Locke, *Letter Concerning Toleration*

32 We have just enough Religion to make us hate, but not enough to make us love one another.

Swift, *Thoughts on Various Subjects*

33 I conceive some scattered Notions about a superior Power to be of singular Use for the common People, as furnishing excellent Materials to keep Children quiet when they grow peevish, and providing Topicks of Amusement in a tedious Winter Night.

Swift, *Argument Against Abolishing Christianity*

34 Human laws, made to direct the will, ought to give precepts, and not counsels; religion, made to influence the heart, should give many counsels, and few precepts.

Montesquieu, *Spirit of Laws*, XXIV, 7

35 In a country so unfortunate as to have a religion that God has not revealed, it is necessary for it to be agreeable to morality; because even a false religion is the best security we can have of the probity of men.

Montesquieu, *Spirit of Laws*, XXIV, 8

36 Religion may support a state when the laws themselves are incapable of doing it.

Montesquieu, *Spirit of Laws*, XXIV, 16

37 The pious man and the atheist always talk of religion; the one speaks of what he loves, and the other of what he fears.

Montesquieu, *Spirit of Laws*, XXV, 1

38 Men are extremely inclined to the passions of hope and fear; a religion, therefore, that had neither a heaven nor a hell could hardly please them.

Montesquieu, *Spirit of Laws*, XXV, 2

39 Examine the religious principles which have, in fact, prevailed in the world. You will scarcely be persuaded that they are any thing but sick men's dreams: Or perhaps will regard them more as the playsome whimsies of monkeys in human shape, than the serious, positive, dogmatical asseverations of a being, who dignifies himself with the name of rational.

Hume, *Natural History of Religion*, XV

40 After our holy religion (which is doubtless the only good one) which would be the least bad?

Wouldn't it be the simplest one? Wouldn't it be the one that taught a good deal of morality and very little dogma? The one that tended to make men just, without making them absurd? The one that wouldn't command belief in impossible, contradictory things insulting to the Divinity and pernicious to mankind, and wouldn't dare to threaten with eternal punishment anyone who has common sense? Wouldn't it be the religion that didn't uphold its beliefs with executioners, and didn't inundate the world with blood for the sake of unintelligible sophisms? The one in which an ambiguity, a play on words, or two or three forged charters wouldn't make a sovereign and a god of a priest who is often a man who has committed incest, a murderer, and a poisoner? The one that wouldn't make kings subject to this priest? The one that taught nothing but the worship of a God, justice, tolerance, and humanity?

Voltaire, *Philosophical Dictionary:* Religion

41 Religion, considered in relation to society, which is either general or particular, may also be divided into two kinds: the religion of man, and that of the citizen. The first, which has neither temples, nor altars, nor rites, and is confined to the purely internal cult of the supreme God and the eternal obligations of morality, is the religion of the Gospel pure and simple, the true theism, what may be called natural divine right or law. The other, which is codified in a single country, gives it its gods, its own tutelary patrons; it has its dogmas, its rites, and its external cult prescribed by law; outside the single nation that follows it, all the world is in its sight infidel, foreign and barbarous; the duties and rights of man extend for it only as far as its own altars. Of this kind were all the religions of early peoples, which we may define as civil or positive divine right or law.

Rousseau, *Social Contract,* IV, 8

42 We ought not to speak about religion to children, if we wish them to possess any.

Rousseau, *Confessions,* II

43 To be of no church is dangerous. Religion, of which the rewards are distant and which is animated only by Faith and Hope, will glide by degrees out of the mind unless it be invigorated and reimpressed by external ordinances, by stated calls to worship, and the salutary influence of example.

Johnson, *Life of Milton*

44 The various modes of worship, which prevailed in the Roman world, were all considered by the people, as equally true; by the philosopher, as equally false; and by the magistrate, as equally useful.

Gibbon, *Decline and Fall of the Roman Empire,* II

45 Every mode of religion, to make a deep and lasting impression on the human mind, must exercise our obedience, by enjoining practices of devotion; and must acquire our esteem, by inculcating moral duties analogous to the dictates of our own hearts.

Gibbon, *Decline and Fall of the Roman Empire,* VIII

46 The theologian may indulge the pleasing task of describing Religion as she descended from Heaven, arrayed in her native purity. A more melancholy duty is imposed on the historian. He must discover the inevitable mixture of error and corruption which she contracted in a long residence upon earth, among a weak and degenerate race of beings.

Gibbon, *Decline and Fall of the Roman Empire,* XV

47 The careless Polytheist, assailed by new and unexpected terrors, against which neither his priests nor his philosophers could afford him any certain protection, was very frequently terrified and subdued by the menace of eternal tortures. His fears might assist the progress of his faith and reason; and if he could once persuade himself to suspect that the Christian religion might possibly be true, it became an easy task to convince him that it was the safest and most prudent party that he could possibly embrace.

Gibbon, *Decline and Fall of the Roman Empire,* XV

48 The opinion and practice of the monasteries of Mount Athos will be best represented in the words of an abbot who flourished in the eleventh century. "When thou art alone in thy cell," says the ascetic teacher, "shut thy door, and seat thyself in a corner: raise thy mind above all things vain and transitory; recline thy beard and chin on thy breast; turn thy eyes and thy thought towards the middle of thy belly, the region of the naval; and search the place of the heart, the seat of the soul. At first all will be dark and comfortless; but if you persevere day and night, you will feel an ineffable joy; and no sooner has the soul discovered the place of the heart, than it is involved in a mystic and etherial light." This light, the production of a distempered fancy, the creature of an empty stomach and an empty brain, was adored by the Quietists as the pure and perfect essence of God himself.

Gibbon, *Decline and Fall of the Roman Empire,* LXIII

49 Mock on, mock on, Voltaire, Rousseau;
Mock on, mock on; 'tis all in vain!
You throw the sand against the wind,
And the wind blows it back again.

And every sand becomes a gem
Reflected in the beams divine;
Blown back they blind the mocking eye,
But still in Israel's paths they shine.

The Atoms of Democritus
And Newton's Particles of Light
Are sands upon the Red Sea shore,
Where Israel's tents do shine so bright.

Blake, *Mock on, Mock on, Voltaire, Rousseau*

50 It is a beauteous evening, calm and free,
　The holy time is quiet as a Nun
　Breathless with adoration; the broad sun
　Is sinking down in its tranquillity;
　The gentleness of heaven broods o'er the Sea:
　Listen! the mighty Being is awake,
　And doth with his eternal motion make
　A sound like thunder—everlastingly.
　Dear Child! dear Girl! that walkest with me here,
　If thou appear untouched by solemn thought,
　Thy nature is not therefore less divine:
　Thou liest in Abraham's bosom all the year;
　And worship'st at the Temple's inner shrine,
　God being with thee when we know it not.

　　　　　Wordsworth, *It Is a Beauteous Evening,*
　　　　　　　　　　　　　　　Calm and Free

51 Religion [cannot] maintain itself apart from thought, but either advances to the comprehension of the idea, or, compelled by thought itself, becomes intensive belief—or lastly, from despair of finding itself at home in thought, flees back from it in pious horror, and becomes superstition.

　　　　　Hegel, *Philosophy of History,* IV, Introduction

52 The bad thing about all religions is that, instead of being able to confess their allegorical nature, they have to conceal it; accordingly, they parade their doctrine in all seriousness as true *sensu proprio,* and as absurdities form an essential part of these doctrines, you have the great mischief of a continual fraud.

　　　　　Schopenhauer, *Christian System*

53 I believe that the sole effectual means which governments can employ in order to have the doctrine of the immortality of the soul duly respected is always to act as if they believed in it themselves; and I think that it is only by scrupulous conformity to religious morality in great affairs that they can hope to teach the community at large to know, to love, and to observe it in the lesser concerns of life.

　　　　　Tocqueville, *Democracy in America,*
　　　　　　　　　　　　　　　Vol. II, II, 15

54 The thing a man does practically believe (and this is often enough *without* asserting it even to himself, much less to others); the thing a man does practically lay to heart, and know for certain, concerning his vital relations to this mysterious Universe, and his duty and destiny there, that is in all cases the primary thing for him, and creatively determines all the rest. That is his *religion.*

　　　　　Carlyle, *The Hero as Divinity*

55 If the red slayer think he slays,
　Or if the slain think he is slain,
　They know not well the subtle ways
　I keep, and pass, and turn again.

Far or forgot to me is near;
　Shadow and sunlight are the same;
The vanished gods to me appear;
　And one to me are shame and fame.

They reckon ill who leave me out;
　When me they fly, I am the wings;
I am the doubter and the doubt,
　And I the hymn the Brahmin sings.

The strong gods pine for my abode,
　And pine in vain the sacred Seven;
But thou, meek lover of the good!
　Find me, and turn thy back on heaven.

　　　　　Emerson, *Brahma*

56 Religion among the low becomes low. As it loses its truth, it loses credit with the sagacious. They detect the falsehood of the preaching, but when they say so, all good citizens cry, Hush; do not weaken the State, do not take off the strait-jacket from dangerous persons. Every honest fellow must keep up the hoax the best he can; must patronize providence and piety, and wherever he sees anything that will keep men amused, schools or churches or poetry or picture-galleries or music, or what not, he must cry "Hist-a-boy," and urge the game on. What a compliment we pay to the good SPIRIT with our superserviceable zeal!

　　　　　Emerson, *The Conservative*

57 England felt the full heat of the Christianity which fermented Europe, and drew, like the chemistry of fire, a firm line between barbarism and culture. The power of the religious sentiment put an end to human sacrifices, checked appetite, inspired the crusades, inspired resistance to tyrants, inspired self-respect, set bounds to serfdom and slavery, founded liberty, created the religious architecture . . . inspired the English Bible, the liturgy, the monkish histories, the chronicle of Richard of Devizes. The priest translated the Vulgate, and translated the sanctities of old hagiology into English virtues on English ground. It was a certain affirmative or aggressive state of the Caucasian races. Man awoke refreshed by the sleep of ages. The violence of the northern savages exasperated Christianity into power. It lived by the love of the people.

　　　　　Emerson, *English Traits,* XIII

58 *Mrs. Skewton.* Say, like those wicked Turks, there is no What's-his-name but Thingummy, and What-you-may-call-it is his prophet!

　　　　　Dickens, *Dombey and Son,* XXVII

59 Not yet have we solved the incantation of this whiteness, and learned why it appeals with such power to the soul; and more strange and far more portentous—why, as we have seen, it is at once the most meaning symbol of spiritual things, nay, the very veil of the Christian's Deity; and yet should

be as it is, the intensifying agent in things the most appalling to mankind.

Is it that by its indefiniteness it shadows forth the heartless voids and immensities of the universe, and thus stabs us from behind with the thought of annihilation, when beholding the white depths of the milky way? Or is it, that as in essence whiteness is not so much a colour as the visible absence of colour, and at the same time the concrete of all colours; is it for these reasons that there is such a dumb blankness, full of meaning, in a wide landscape of snows—a colourless, all-colour of atheism from which we shrink? And when we consider that other theory of the natural philosophers, that all other earthly hues—every stately or lovely emblazoning—the sweet tinges of sunset skies and woods; yea, and the gilded velvets of butterflies, and the butterfly cheeks of young girls; all these are but subtile deceits, not actually inherent in substance, but only laid on from without; and when we proceed further, and consider that the mystical cosmetic which produces every one of her hues, the great principle of light, for ever remains white or colourless in itself, and if operating without medium upon matter, would touch all objects, even tulips and roses, with its own blank tinge—pondering all this, the palsied universe lies before us a leper; and like wilful travellers in Lapland, who refuse to wear coloured and colouring glasses upon their eyes, so the wretched infidel gazes himself blind at the monumental white shroud that wraps all the prospect around him. And of all these things the Albino whale was the symbol. Wonder ye then at the fiery hunt?

Melville, *Moby Dick,* XLII

60 The wisest man preaches no doctrines; he has no scheme; he sees no rafter, not even a cobweb, against the heavens. It is clear sky.

Thoreau, *The Christian Fable*

61 A man's real faith is never contained in his creed, nor is his creed an article of his faith. The last is never adopted. This it is that permits him to smile ever, and to live even as bravely as he does. And yet he clings anxiously to his creed, as to a straw, thinking that that does him good service because his sheet anchor does not drag.

Thoreau, *The Christian Fable*

62 The foundation of irreligious criticism is this: man makes religion; religion does not make man. Religion is, in fact, the self-consciousness and self-esteem of man who has either not yet gained himself or has lost himself again. But man is no abstract being squatting outside the world. Man is the world of man, the state, society. This state, this society, produce religion, which is an inverted world-consciousness, because they are an inverted world. Religion is the general theory of this world,

its encyclopedic compendium, its logic in popular form, its spiritualistic *point d'honneur,* its enthusiasm, its moral sanction, its solemn complement, its universal basis of consolation and justification. It is the fantastic realization of the human being because the human being has attained no true reality. Thus, the struggle against religion is indirectly the struggle against that world of which religion is the spiritual aroma.

The wretchedness of religion is at once an expression of and a protest against real wretchedness. Religion is the sigh of the oppressed creature, the heart of a heartless world and the soul of soulless conditions. It is the opium of the people.

Marx, *Contribution to the Critique of Hegel's "Philosophy of Right,"* Intro.

63 Every established fact which is too bad to admit of any other defence, is always presented to us as an injunction of religion.

Mill, *Subjection of Women,* II

64 To make your children *capable of honesty* is the beginning of education. Make them men first, and religious men afterwards, and all will be sound; but a knave's religion is always the rottenest thing about him.

Ruskin, *Time and Tide,* VIII

65 If it is reasonable to consider medicine, or architecture, or engineering, in a certain sense, divine arts, as being divinely ordained means of our receiving divine benefits, much more may ethics be called divine; while as to religion, it directly professes to be the method of recommending ourselves to Him and learning His will. If then it be His gracious purpose that we should learn it, the means He gives for learning it, be they promising or not to human eyes, are sufficient because they are His. And what they are at this particular time, or to this person, depends on His disposition. He may have imposed simple prayer and obedience on some men as the instrument of their attaining to the mysteries and precepts of Christianity. He may lead others through the written word, at least for some stages of their course; and if the formal basis on which He has rested His revelations be, as it is, of an historical and philosophical character, then antecedent probabilities, subsequently corroborated by facts, will be sufficient, as in the parallel case of other history, to bring us safely to the matter, or at least to the organ, of those revelations.

Newman, *Essay on the Development of Christian Doctrine,* Pt. I, III, 2

66 Religion has its own enlargement, and an enlargement, not of tumult, but of peace. It is often remarked of uneducated persons, who have hitherto thought little of the unseen world, that, on their turning to God, looking into themselves, reg-

ulating their hearts, reforming their conduct, and meditating on death and judgment, heaven and hell, they seem to become, in point of intellect, different beings from what they were. Before, they took things as they came, and thought no more of one thing than another. But now every event has a meaning; they have their own estimate of whatever happens to them; they are mindful of times and seasons, and compare the present with the past; and the world, no longer dull, monotonous, unprofitable, and hopeless, is a various and complicated drama, with parts and an object, and an awful moral.

Newman, *Idea of a University,* Discourse VI

67 Many persons are very sensitive of the difficulties of Religion; I am as sensitive of them as any one; but I have never been able to see a connexion between apprehending those difficulties, however keenly, and multiplying them to any extent, and on the other hand doubting the doctrines to which they are attached. Ten thousand difficulties do not make one doubt, as I understand the subject; difficulty and doubt are incommensurate.

Newman, *Apologia Pro Vita Sua,* V

68 The object of religion is *conduct;* and conduct is really, however men may overlay it with philosophical disquisitions, the simplest thing in the world. That is to say, it is the simplest thing in the world as far as *understanding* is concerned; as regards *doing,* it is the hardest thing in the world. Here is the difficulty,—to *do* what we very well know ought to be done; and instead of facing this, men have searched out another with which they occupy themselves by preference,—the origin of what is called the moral sense, the genesis and physiology of conscience, and so on. No one denies that here, too, is difficulty, or that the difficulty is a proper object for the human faculties to be exercised upon; but the difficulty here is speculative. It is not the difficulty of religion, which is a practical one; and it often tends to divert the attention from this. Yet surely the difficulty of religion is great enough by itself, if men would but consider it, to satisfy the most voracious appetite for difficulties. It extends to rightness in the whole range of what we call *conduct;* in three-fourths, therefore, at the very lowest computation, of human life.

Arnold, *Literature and Dogma,* I

69 Religion, if we follow the intention of human thought and human language in the use of the word, is ethics heightened, enkindled, lit up by feeling; the passage from morality to religion is made when to morality is applied emotion.

Arnold, *Literature and Dogma,* I

70 Religion, the greatest and most important of the efforts by which the human race has manifested its impulse to perfect itself,—religion, that voice of the deepest human experience,—does not only enjoin and sanction the aim which is the great aim of culture, the aim of setting ourselves to ascertain what perfection is and to make it prevail; but also, in determining generally in what human perfection consists, religion comes to a conclusion identical with that which culture,—culture seeking the determination of this question through *all* the voices of human experience which have been heard upon it, of art, science, poetry, philosophy, history, as well as of religion, in order to give a greater fulness and certainty to its solution,—likewise reaches. Religion says: *The kingdom of God is within you;* and culture, in like manner, places human perfection in an *internal* condition, in the growth and predominance of our humanity proper, as distinguished from our animality. It places it in the ever-increasing efficacy and in the general harmonious expansion of those gifts of thought and feeling, which make the peculiar dignity, wealth, and happiness of human nature. As I have said on a former occasion: 'It is in making endless additions to itself, in the endless expansion of its powers, in endless growth in wisdom and beauty, that the spirit of the human race finds its ideal. To reach this ideal, culture is an indispensable aid, and that is the true value of culture.' Not a having and a resting, but a growing and a becoming, is the character of perfection as culture conceives it; and here, too, it coincides with religion.

Arnold, *Culture and Anarchy,* I

71 The essence of religion consists solely in the answer to the question, 'Why do I live, and what is my relation to the infinite universe around me?'

All the metaphysics of religion, all the doctrines about deities and about the origin of the world, and all external worship—which are usually supposed to be religion—are but indications (differing according to geographical, ethnographical, and historical circumstances) of the existence of religion. There is no religion from the most elevated to the coarsest that has not at its root this establishing of man's relation to the surrounding universe or to its first cause. There is no religious rite however coarse, nor any cult however refined, that has not this at its root. Every religious teaching is the expression which the founder of that religion has given of the relation he considered himself (and consequently all other people also) to occupy as a man towards the universe and its origin and first cause.

Tolstoy, *Religion and Morality*

72 The religious man thinks only of himself.

Nietzsche, *Antichrist,* LXI

73 Since belief is measured by action, he who forbids us to believe religion to be true, necessarily also forbids us to act as we should if we did believe it to

be true. The whole defence of religious faith hinges upon action. If the action required or inspired by the religious hypothesis is in no way different from that dictated by the naturalistic hypothesis, then religious faith is a pure superfluity, better pruned away, and controversy about its legitimacy is a piece of idle trifling, unworthy of serious minds. I myself believe, of course, that the religious hypothesis gives to the world an expression which specifically determines our reactions, and makes them in a large part unlike what they might be on a purely naturalistic scheme of belief.

William James, *Will to Believe*

74 The peace of rationality may be sought through ecstasy when logic fails. To religious persons of every shade of doctrine moments come when the world, as it is, seems so divinely orderly, and the acceptance of it by the heart so rapturously complete, that intellectual questions vanish; nay, the intellect itself is hushed to sleep—as Wordsworth says, "thought is not; in enjoyment it expires." Ontological emotion so fills the soul that ontological speculation can no longer overlap it and put her girdle of interrogation marks round existence. Even the least religious of men must have felt with Walt Whitman, when loafing on the grass on some transparent summer morning, that "swiftly arose and spread round him the peace and knowledge that pass all the argument of the earth." At such moments of energetic living we feel as if there were something diseased and contemptible, yea vile, in theoretic grubbing and brooding. In the eye of healthy sense the philosopher is at best a learned fool.

William James, *Sentiment of Rationality*

75 Overcoming of all the usual barriers between the individual and the Absolute is the great mystic achievement. In mystic states we both become one with the Absolute and we become aware of our oneness. This is the everlasting and triumphant mystical tradition, hardly altered by differences of clime or creed. In Hinduism, in Neoplatonism, in Sufism, in Christian mysticism, in Whitmanism, we find the same recurring note, so that there is about mystical utterances an eternal unanimity which ought to make a critic stop and think, and which brings it about that the mystical classics have, as has been said, neither birthday nor native land. Perpetually telling of the unity of man with God, their speech antedates languages, and they do not grow old.

William James, *Varieties of Religious Experience*, XVI–XVII

76 The pivot round which the religious life, as we have traced it, revolves, is the interest of the individual in his private personal destiny. Religion, in short, is a monumental chapter in the history of human egotism.

William James, *Varieties of Religious Experience*, XX

77 The great religious conceptions which haunt the imaginations of civilized mankind are scenes of solitariness: Prometheus chained to his rock, Mahomet brooding in the desert, the meditations of the Buddha, the solitary Man on the Cross. It belongs to the depth of the religious spirit to have felt forsaken, even by God.

Whitehead, *Religion in the Making*, I, 2

78 I am . . . a dissenter from all known religions, and I hope that every kind of religious belief will die out. I do not believe that, on the balance, religious belief has been a force for good. Although I am prepared to admit that in certain times and places it has had some good effects, I regard it as belonging to the infancy of human reason, and to a stage of development which we are now outgrowing.

Russell, *Sceptical Essays*, XII

79 A religion, even if it calls itself the religion of love, must be hard and unloving to those who do not belong to it. Fundamentally, indeed, every religion is in this same way a religion of love for all those whom it embraces; while cruelty and intolerance towards those who do not belong to it are natural to every religion.

Freud, *Group Psychology and Analysis of the Ego*, V

80 In my *Future of an Illusion* I was concerned much less with the deepest sources of religious feeling than with what the ordinary man understands by his religion, that system of doctrines and pledges that on the one hand explains the riddle of this world to him with an enviable completeness, and on the other assures him that a solicitous Providence is watching over him and will make up to him in a future existence for any shortcomings in this life. The ordinary man cannot imagine this Providence in any other form but that of a greatly exalted father, for only such a one could understand the needs of the sons of men, or be softened by their prayers and placated by the signs of their remorse. The whole thing is so patently infantile, so incongruous with reality, that to one whose attitude to humanity is friendly it is painful to think that the great majority of mortals will never be able to rise above this view of life.

Freud, *Civilization and Its Discontents*, II

81 If one wishes to form a true estimate of the full grandeur of religion, one must keep in mind what it undertakes to do for men. It gives them information about the source and origin of the universe, it assures them of protection and final hap-

piness amid the changing vicissitudes of life, and it guides their thoughts and actions by means of precepts which are backed by the whole force of its authority.

Freud, *New Introductory Lectures on Psycho-Analysis,* XXXV

82 While the different religions wrangle with one another as to which of them is in possession of the truth, in our view the truth of religion may be altogether disregarded.

Freud, *New Introductory Lectures on Psycho-Analysis,* XXXV

83 Religion is an attempt to get control over the sensory world, in which we are placed, by means of the wish-world, which we have developed inside us as a result of biological and psychological necessities. But it cannot achieve its end. Its doctrines carry with them the stamp of the times in which they originated, the ignorant childhood days of the human race. Its consolations deserve no trust. Experience teaches us that the world is not a nursery. The ethical commands, to which religion seeks to lend its weight, require some other foundations instead, for human society cannot do without them, and it is dangerous to link up obedience to them with religious belief. If one attempts to assign to religion its place in man's evolution, it seems not so much to be a lasting acquisition, as a parallel to the neurosis which the civilized individual must pass through on his way from childhood to maturity.

Freud, *New Introductory Lectures on Psycho-Analysis,* XXXV

84 There is such a thing as high-level popularization, which respects the broad outlines of scientific truth, and enables ordinary cultivated minds to get a general grasp of it until the time comes when a greater effort reveals it to them in detail, and, above all, allows them to penetrate deeply into its significance. The propagation of the mystical through religion seems to us something of the kind. In this sense, religion is to mysticism what popularization is to science.

Bergson, *Two Sources of Morality and Religion,* III

85 Religion no longer reveals divine personalities, future rewards, and tenderer Elysian consolations; nor does it seriously propose a heaven to be reached by a ladder nor a purgatory to be shortened by prescribed devotions. It merely gives the real world an ideal status and teaches men to accept a natural life on supernatural grounds.

Santayana, *Life of Reason,* I, Introduction

86 Religion, after all, is the serious business of the human race.

Toynbee, *Civilization on Trial,* V

20.2 | *Judaism*

As the reader would expect, this section is dominated by quotations from the books of the Old Testament. These are the passages that exhibit or expound the religion of Judaism—its rituals and observances, its credal commitments, its events in the history of "the chosen people," its reception and development of the Mosaic law, and its inspiration and influence of the prophets.

Quotations here represent a wide diversity of secular comments on Judaism and on the relation of the Jews to the gentiles. The reader will find striking observations made by such historians as Tacitus and Gibbon, as well as by a philosopher of history, Hegel. The reader will find discussions of Judaism, and especially of the difference between the Old Law and the New, by such theologians as Augustine and Aquinas, as well as by one of the most interesting of Christian apologists, Pascal, who stresses the Christian fulfillment of Old Testament prophecies. The philosophers—Hobbes, Spinoza, and J. S. Mill—consider the theocratic institutions of Judaism, and Mill dwells on the contribution of the Jews along with the Greeks as the twin fountainheads of Western civilization. Freud gives the discussion a psychological turn by his speculations concerning the psychogenesis of Jewish monotheism. And, in certain quotations, anti-Semitism manifests itself more or less explicitly.

---

1 Now the Lord had said unto Abram, Get thee out of thy country, and from thy kindred, and from thy father's house, unto a land that I will shew thee:

And I will make of thee a great nation, and I will bless thee, and make thy name great; and thou shalt be a blessing:

And I will bless them that bless thee, and curse him that curseth thee: and in thee shall all families of the earth be blessed.

Genesis 12:1–3

2 And the Lord said unto Abram, after that Lot was separated from him, Lift up now thine eyes, and look from the place where thou art northward, and southward, and eastward, and westward:

For all the land which thou seest, to thee will I give it, and to thy seed for ever.

And I will make thy seed as the dust of the earth: so that if a man can number the dust of the earth, then shall thy seed also be numbered.

Arise, walk through the land in the length of it and in the breadth of it; for I will give it unto thee.

Genesis 13:14–17

3 This is my covenant, which ye shall keep, between me and you and thy seed after thee; Every man child among you shall be circumcised.

And ye shall circumcise the flesh of your foreskin; and it shall be a token of the covenant betwixt me and you.

And he that is eight days old shall be circumcised among you, every man child in your generations, he that is born in the house, or bought with money of any stranger, which is not of thy seed.

He that is born in thy house, and he that is bought with thy money, must needs be circumcised: and my covenant shall be in your flesh for an everlasting covenant.

And the uncircumcised man child whose flesh of his foreskin is not circumcised, that soul shall be cut off from his people; he hath broken my covenant.

Genesis 17:10–14

4 And it came to pass after these things, that God did tempt Abraham, and said unto him, Abraham: and he said, Behold, here I am.

And he said, Take now thy son, thine only son Isaac, whom thou lovest, and get thee into the land of Mō-rī-ăh; and offer him there for a burnt offering upon one of the mountains which I will tell thee of.

And Abraham rose up early in the morning, and saddled his ass, and took two of his young men with him, and Isaac his son, and clave the wood for the burnt offering, and rose up, and went unto the place of which God had told him.

Then on the third day Abraham lifted up his eyes, and saw the place afar off.

And Abraham said unto his young men, Abide ye here with the ass; and I and the lad will go yonder and worship, and come again to you.

And Abraham took the wood of the burnt offering, and laid it upon Isaac his son; and he took the fire in his hand, and a knife; and they went both of them together.

And Isaac spake unto Abraham his father, and said, My father: and he said, Here am I, my son. And he said, Behold the fire and the wood: but where is the lamb for a burnt offering?

And Abraham said, My son, God will provide himself a lamb for a burnt offering: so they went both of them together.

And they came to the place which God had told him of; and Abraham built an altar there, and laid the wood in order, and bound Isaac his son, and laid him on the altar upon the wood.

And Abraham stretched forth his hand, and took the knife to slay his son.

And the angel of the Lord called unto him out of heaven, and said, Abraham, Abraham: and he said, Here am I.

And he said, Lay not thine hand upon the lad, neither do thou any thing unto him: for now I know that thou fearest God, seeing thou hast not withheld thy son, thine only son from me.

And Abraham lifted up his eyes, and looked, and behold behind him a ram caught in a thicket by his horns: and Abraham went and took the ram, and offered him up for a burnt offering in the stead of his son.

Genesis 22:1–13

5 And God appeared unto Jacob again, when he came out of Pā-dăn-aram, and blessed him.

And God said unto him, Thy name is Jacob: thy name shall not be called any more Jacob, but Israel shall be thy name: and he called his name Israel.

And God said unto him, I am God Almighty: be fruitful and multiply; a nation and a company of nations shall be of thee, and kings shall come out of thy loins;

And the land which I gave Abraham and Isaac, to thee I will give it, and to thy seed after thee will I give the land.

Genesis 35:9–12

6 Then the Lord said unto Moses, Now shalt thou see what I will do to Pharaoh: for with a strong hand shall he let them go, and with a strong hand shall he drive them out of his land.

And God spake unto Moses, and said unto him, I am the Lord:

And I appeared unto Abraham, unto Isaac, and unto Jacob, by the name of God Almighty, but by my name *Jehovah* was I not known to them.

And I have also established my covenant with them, to give them the land of Cā-nă-ăn, the land of their pilgrimage, wherein they were strangers.

And I have also heard the groaning of the children of Israel, whom the Egyptians keep in bondage; and I have remembered my covenant.

Wherefore say unto the children of Israel, I am the Lord, and I will bring you out from under the burdens of the Egyptians, and I will rid you out of their bondage, and I will redeem you with a stretched out arm, and with great judgments:

And I will take you to me for a people, and I will be to you a God: and ye shall know that I am the Lord your God, which bringeth you out from under the burdens of the Egyptians.

Exodus 6:1–7

7 And the Lord spake unto Moses and Aaron in the land of Egypt, saying,

This month shall be unto you the beginning of months: it shall be the first month of the year to you.

Speak ye unto all the congregation of Israel, saying, In the tenth day of this month they shall take to them every man a lamb, according to the house of their fathers, a lamb for an house:

And if the household be too little for the lamb, let him and his neighbour next unto his house take it according to the number of the souls; every man according to his eating shall make your count for the lamb.

Your lamb shall be without blemish, a male of the first year: ye shall take it out from the sheep, or from the goats:

And ye shall keep it up until the fourteenth day of the same month: and the whole assembly of the congregation of Israel shall kill it in the evening.

And they shall take of the blood, and strike it on the two side posts and on the upper door post of the houses, wherein they shall eat it.

And they shall eat the flesh in that night, roast with fire, and unleavened bread; and with bitter herbs they shall eat it.

Eat not of it raw, nor sodden at all with water, but roast with fire; his head with his legs, and with the purtenance thereof.

And ye shall let nothing of it remain until the morning; and that which remaineth of it until the morning ye shall burn with fire.

And thus shall ye eat it; with your loins girded, your shoes on your feet, and your staff in your hand; and ye shall eat it in haste: it is the Lord's passover.

For I will pass through the land of Egypt this night, and will smite all the firstborn in the land of Egypt, both man and beast; and against all the gods of Egypt I will execute judgment: I am the Lord.

And the blood shall be to you for a token upon the houses where ye are: and when I see the blood, I will pass over you, and the plague shall not be upon you to destroy you, when I smite the land of Egypt.

And this day shall be unto you for a memorial; and ye shall keep it a feast to the Lord throughout your generations; ye shall keep it a feast by an ordinance for ever.

Seven days shall ye eat unleavened bread; even the first day ye shall put away leaven out of your houses: for whosoever eateth leavened bread from the first day until the seventh day, that soul shall be cut off from Israel.

And in the first day there shall be an holy convocation, and in the seventh day there shall be an holy convocation to you; no manner of work shall be done in them, save that which every man must eat, that only may be done of you.

And ye shall observe the feast of unleavened bread; for in this selfsame day have I brought your armies out of the land of Egypt: therefore shall ye observe this day in your generations by an ordinance for ever.

In the first month, on the fourteenth day of the month at even, ye shall eat unleavened bread, until the one and twentieth day of the month at even.

Seven days shall there be no leaven found in your houses: for whosoever eateth that which is leavened, even that soul shall be cut off from the congregation of Israel, whether he be a stranger, or born in the land.

Ye shall eat nothing leavened; in all your habitations shall ye eat unleavened bread.

Exodus 12:1–20

8 And it came to pass at the end of the four hundred and thirty years, even the selfsame day it came to pass, that all the hosts of the Lord went out from the land of Egypt.

It is a night to be much observed unto the Lord for bringing them out from the land of Egypt: this is that night of the Lord to be observed of all the children of Israel in their generations.

And the Lord said unto Moses and Aaron, This is the ordinance of the passover: There shall no stranger eat thereof:

But every man's servant that is bought for money, when thou hast circumcised him, then shall he eat thereof.

A foreigner and an hired servant shall not eat thereof.

In one house shall it be eaten; thou shalt not carry forth ought of the flesh abroad out of the house; neither shall ye break a bone thereof.

All the congregation of Israel shall keep it.

And when a stranger shall sojourn with thee, and will keep the passover to the Lord, let all his males be circumcised, and then let him come near and keep it; and he shall be as one that is born in the land: for no uncircumcised person shall eat thereof.

One law shall be to him that is homeborn, and unto the stranger that sojourneth among you.

Thus did all the children of Israel; as the Lord commanded Moses and Aaron, so did they.

And it came to pass the selfsame day, that the Lord did bring the children of Israel out of the land of Egypt by their armies.

Exodus 12:41–51

9 Ye shall make you no idols nor graven image, neither rear you up a standing image, neither shall ye set up any image of stone in your land, to bow down unto it: for I am the Lord your God.

Ye shall keep my sabbaths, and reverence my sanctuary: I am the Lord.

If ye walk in my statutes, and keep my commandments, and do them;

Then I will give you rain in due season, and the land shall yield her increase, and the trees of the field shall yield their fruit.

And your threshing shall reach unto the vintage, and the vintage shall reach unto the sowing time: and ye shall eat your bread to the full, and dwell in your land safely.

And I will give peace in the land, and ye shall lie down, and none shall make you afraid: and I will rid evil beasts out of the land, neither shall the sword go through your land.

Leviticus 26:1–6

10 Then will I remember my covenant with Jacob, and also my covenant with Isaac, and also my covenant with Abraham will I remember; and I will remember the land.

The land also shall be left of them, and shall enjoy her sabbaths, while she lieth desolate without them: and they shall accept of the punishment of their iniquity: because, even because they despised my judgments, and because their soul abhorred my statutes.

And yet for all that, when they be in the land of their enemies, I will not cast them away, neither will I abhor them, to destroy them utterly, and to break my covenant with them: for I am the Lord their God.

But I will for their sakes remember the covenant of their ancestors, whom I brought forth out of the land of Egypt in the sight of the heathen, that I might be their God: I am the Lord.

These are the statutes and judgments and laws, which the Lord made between him and the children of Israel in mount Sinai by the hand of Moses.

Leviticus 26:42–46

11 And Moses called all Israel, and said unto them, Hear, O Israel, the statutes and judgments which I speak in your ears this day, that ye may learn them, and keep, and do them.

The Lord our God made a covenant with us in Horeb.

The Lord made not this covenant with our fathers, but with us, even us, who are all of us here alive this day.

The Lord talked with you face to face in the mount out of the midst of the fire,

(I stood between the Lord and you at that time, to shew you the word of the Lord: for ye were afraid by reason of the fire, and went not up into the mount;) saying,

I am the Lord thy God, which brought thee out of the land of Egypt, from the house of bondage.

Thou shalt have none other gods before me.

Thou shalt not make thee any graven image, or any likeness of any thing that is in heaven above, or that is in the earth beneath, or that is in the waters beneath the earth:

Thou shalt not bow down thyself unto them, nor serve them: for I the Lord thy God am a jealous God, visiting the iniquity of the fathers upon the children unto the third and fourth generation of them that hate me,

And shewing mercy unto thousands of them that love me and keep my commandments.

Thou shalt not take the name of the Lord thy God in vain: for the Lord will not hold him guiltless that taketh his name in vain.

Keep the sabbath day to sanctify it, as the Lord thy God hath commanded thee.

Six days thou shalt labour, and do all thy work:

But the seventh day is the sabbath of the Lord thy God: in it thou shalt not do any work, thou, nor thy son, nor thy daughter, nor thy manservant, nor thy maidservant, nor thine ox, nor thine ass, nor any of thy cattle, nor thy stranger that is within thy gates; that thy manservant and thy maidservant may rest as well as thou.

And remember that thou wast a servant in the land of Egypt, and that the Lord thy God brought thee out thence through a mighty hand and by a stretched out arm: therefore the Lord thy God commanded thee to keep the sabbath day.

Honour thy father and thy mother, as the Lord thy God hath commanded thee; that thy days may be prolonged, and that it may go well with thee, in the land which the Lord thy God giveth thee.

Thou shalt not kill.

Neither shalt thou commit adultery.

Neither shalt thou steal.

Neither shalt thou bear false witness against thy neighbour.

Neither shalt thou desire thy neighbour's wife, neither shalt thou covet thy neighbour's house, his field, or his manservant, or his maidservant, his ox, or his ass, or any thing that is thy neighbour's.

These words the Lord spake unto all your assembly in the mount out of the midst of the fire, of the cloud, and of the thick darkness, with a great voice: and he added no more. And he wrote them in two tables of stone, and delivered them unto me.

Deuteronomy 5:1–22

12 And king Solomon, and all the congregation of Israel, that were assembled unto him, were with him before the ark, sacrificing sheep and oxen, that could not be told nor numbered for multitude.

And the priests brought in the ark of the covenant of the Lord unto his place, into the oracle of the house, to the most holy place, even under the wings of the chĕr-ū-bĭms.

For the chĕr-ū-bĭms spread forth their two wings over the place of the ark, and the chĕr-ū-bĭms covered the ark and the staves thereof above.

And they drew out the staves, that the ends of the staves were seen out in the holy place before the oracle, and they were not seen without: and there they are unto this day.

There was nothing in the ark save the two tables of stone, which Moses put there at Horeb, when the Lord made a covenant with the children of Israel, when they came out of the land of Egypt.

And it came to pass, when the priests were come out of the holy place, that the cloud filled the house of the Lord,

So that the priests could not stand to minister because of the cloud: for the glory of the Lord had filled the house of the Lord.

Then spake Solomon, The Lord said that he would dwell in the thick darkness.

I have surely built thee an house to dwell in, a settled place for thee to abide in for ever.

And the king turned his face about, and blessed all the congregation of Israel: (and all the congregation of Israel stood;)

And he said, Blessed be the Lord God of Israel, which spake with his mouth unto David my father, and hath with his hand fulfilled it, saying,

Since the day that I brought forth my people Israel out of Egypt, I chose no city out of all the tribes of Israel to build an house, that my name might be therein; but I chose David to be over my people Israel.

I Kings 8:5–16

13 I know that my redeemer liveth, and that he shall stand at the latter day upon the earth:

And though after my skin worms destroy this body, yet in my flesh shall I see God.

Job 19:25–26

14 Blessed is the nation whose God is the Lord; and the people whom he hath chosen for his own inheritance.

Psalm 33:12

15 I will sing of the mercies of the Lord for ever: with my mouth will I make known thy faithfulness to all generations.

For I have said, Mercy shall be built up for ever: thy faithfulness shalt thou establish in the very heavens.

I have made a covenant with my chosen, I have sworn unto David my servant,

Thy seed will I establish for ever, and build up thy throne to all generations.

Psalm 89:1–4

16 By the rivers of Babylon, there we sat down, yea, we wept, when we remembered Zion.

We hanged our harps upon the willows in the midst thereof.

For there they that carried us away captive required of us a song; and they that wasted us required of us mirth, saying, Sing us one of the songs of Zion.

How shall we sing the Lord's song in a strange land?

If I forget thee, O Jerusalem, let my right hand forget her cunning.

If I do not remember thee, let my tongue cleave to the roof of my mouth; if I prefer not Jerusalem above my chief joy.

Remember, O Lord, the children of Edom in the day of Jerusalem; who said, Rase it, rase it, even to the foundation thereof.

O daughter of Babylon, who art to be destroyed; happy shall he be, that rewardeth thee as thou hast served us.

Happy shall he be, that taketh and dasheth thy little ones against the stones.

Psalm 137:1–9

17 But now thus saith the Lord that created thee, O Jacob, and he that formed thee, O Israel, Fear not: for I have redeemed thee, I have called thee by thy name; thou art mine.

When thou passest through the waters, I will be with thee; and through the rivers, they shall not overflow thee: when thou walkest through the fire, thou shalt not be burned; neither shall the flame kindle upon thee.

For I am the Lord thy God, the Holy One of Israel, thy Saviour: I gave Egypt for thy ransom, Ethiopia and Seba for thee.

Since thou wast precious in my sight, thou hast been honourable, and I have loved thee: therefore will I give men for thee, and people for thy life.

Fear not: for I am with thee: I will bring thy

seed from the east, and gather thee from the west;
I will say to the north, Give up; and to the
south, Keep not back: bring my sons from far,
and my daughters from the ends of the earth;

Even every one that is called by my name: for I
have created him for my glory, I have formed
him; yea, I have made him.

Isaiah 43:1-7

18 Verily thou art a God that hidest thyself, O God
of Israel, the Saviour.

Isaiah 45:15

19 The Jews have purely mental conceptions of Deity, as one in essence. They call those profane who
make representations of God in human shape out
of perishable materials. They believe that Being
to be supreme and eternal, neither capable of representation, nor of decay. They therefore do not
allow any images to stand in their cities, much less
in their temples. This flattery is not paid to their
kings, nor this honour to our Emperors. From the
fact, however, that their priests used to chant to
the music of flutes and cymbals, and to wear garlands of ivy, and that a golden vine was found in
the temple, some have thought that they worshipped Father Liber, the conqueror of the East,
though their institutions do not by any means
harmonize with the theory; for Liber established a
festive and cheerful worship, while the Jewish religion is tasteless and mean.

Tacitus, *Histories*, V, 5

20 Without the mad rites of Mars and Bellona they
[the Jews] carried on war; and while, indeed, they
did not conquer without victory, yet they did not
hold it to be a goddess, but the gift of their God.
Without Segetia they had harvests; without Bubo-
na, oxen; honey without Mellona; apples without
Pomona: and, in a word, everything for which the
Romans thought they must supplicate so great a
crowd of false gods, they received much more
happily from the one true God. And if they had
not sinned against Him with impious curiosity,
which seduced them like magic arts, and drew
them to strange gods and idols, and at last led
them to kill Christ, their kingdom would have remained to them and would have been, if not more
spacious, yet more happy than that of Rome. And
now that they are dispersed through almost all
lands and nations, it is through the providence of
that one true God; that whereas the images, altars, groves, and temples of the false gods are everywhere overthrown, and their sacrifices prohibited, it may be shown from their books how this
has been foretold by their prophets so long before.

Augustine, *City of God*, IV, 34

21 Before the coming of Christ, the state of the Old
Law was not changed as regards the fulfilment of
the Law, which was effected in Christ alone; but
it was changed as regards the condition of the
people that were under the Law. Because, at first,
the people were in the desert, having no fixed
abode; afterwards they were engaged in various
wars with the neighbouring nations; and lastly, at
the time of David and Solomon, the state of that
people was one of great peace. And then for the
first time the temple was built in the place which
Abraham, instructed by God, had chosen for the
purpose of sacrifice.

Aquinas, *Summa Theologica*, I–II, 102, 4

22 The tabernacle was divided into two parts. One
was called the "Holy of Holies," and was placed
to the west. The other was called the "Holy
Place," which was situated to the east. Moreover
there was a court facing the tabernacle. Accordingly there are two reasons for this distinction.
One is in respect of the tabernacle being ordained
to the worship of God. Because the different parts
of the world are thus betokened by the division of
the tabernacle. For that part which was called the
Holy of Holies signified the higher world, which is
that of spiritual substances, while that part which
is called the Holy Place signified the corporeal
world. Hence the Holy Place was separated from
the Holy of Holies by a veil, which was of four
different colours (denoting the four elements),
namely, of linen, signifying earth, because linen,
that is, flax, grows out of the earth; purple, signifying water, because the purple tint was made
from certain shells found in the sea; violet, signifying air, because it has the colour of the air; and
scarlet twice dyed, signifying fire. And this because matter composed of the four elements is a
veil between us and incorporeal substances.
Hence the high-priest alone, and that once a year,
entered into the inner tabernacle, that is, the
Holy of Holies, by which we are taught that
man's final perfection consists in his entering into
that world. But into the outward tabernacle, that
is, the Holy Place, the priests entered every day,
though the people were only admitted to the
court; because the people are able to perceive material things, the inner nature of which only wise
men by dint of study are able to discover.

Aquinas, *Summa Theologica*, I–II, 102, 4

23 The inner tabernacle, called the Holy of Holies,
signified the higher world of spiritual substances;
hence that tabernacle contained three things,
namely, *the ark of the testament in which was a golden
pot that had manna, and the rod of Aaron that had blossomed, and the tables* on which were written the ten
commandments of the Law. Now the ark stood
between two cherubim that looked one towards
the other; and over the ark was a table, called the
propitiatory, raised above the wings of the cherubim, as though it were held up by them, and appearing, to the imagination, to be the very seat of

God. For this reason it was called the propitiatory, as though the people received propitiation thence at the prayers of the high-priest. And so it was held up, so to speak, by the cherubim, in obedience, as it were, to God, while the ark of the testament was like the foot-stool to Him that sat on the propitiatory. These three things denote three things in that higher world. First, God Who is above all, and incomprehensible to any creature. Hence no likeness of Him was set up, in order to denote His invisibility. But there was something to represent His seat, since, that is, the creature, which is beneath God, as the seat is under the one sitting on it, is comprehensible. Again in that higher world there are spiritual substances called angels. These are signified by the two cherubim, looking one towards the other, to show that they are at peace with one another . . . *Who maketh peace in . . . high places.* For this reason, too, there was more than one cherub, to betoken the multitude of heavenly spirits, to prevent their receiving worship from those who had been commanded to worship but one God. Moreover there are, enclosed as it were in that spiritual world, the intelligible types of whatsoever takes place in this world, just as in every cause are enclosed the types of its effects, and in the craftsman the types of the works of his craft. This was signified by the ark, which represented, by means of the three things it contained, the three things of greatest import in human affairs. These are wisdom, signified by the tables of the testament; the power of governing, represented by the rod of Aaron; and life, denoted by the manna which was the means of sustenance. Or else these three signified the three Divine attributes, namely, wisdom, in the tables; power, in the rod, goodness, in the manna—both by reason of its sweetness, and because it was through the goodness of God that it was granted to man, so that therefore it was preserved as a memorial of the Divine mercy.

Aquinas, *Summa Theologica*, I–II, 102, 4

24 Under the Old Law there were seven temporal solemnities, and one continual solemnity. . . . There was a continual feast, since the lamb was sacrificed every day, morning and evening; and this continual feast of an abiding sacrifice signified the perpetuity of Divine happiness. Of the temporal feasts the first was that which was repeated every week. This was the solemnity of the Sabbath, celebrated in memory of the work of the creation of the universe. Another solemnity, namely, the New Moon, was repeated every month, and was observed in memory of the work of the Divine government. For the things of this lower world owe their variety chiefly to the movement of the moon; therefore this feast was kept at the new moon, and not at the full moon, to avoid the worship of idolaters who used to offer sacrifices to the moon at that particular time. These

two blessings are bestowed in common on the whole human race, and hence they were repeated more frequently.

The other five feasts were celebrated once a year, and they commemorated the benefits which had been conferred especially on that people. For there was the feast of the Passover in the first month to commemorate the blessing of being delivered out of Egypt. The feast of Pentecost was celebrated fifty days later, to recall the blessing of the giving of the Law. The other three feasts were kept in the seventh month, nearly the whole of which was solemnized by them, just as the seventh day. For on the first of the seventh month was the feast of Trumpets, in memory of the delivery of Isaac, when Abraham found the ram caught by its horns, which they represented by the horns which they blew. The feast of Trumpets was a kind of invitation whereby they prepared themselves to keep the following feast which was kept on the tenth day. This was the feast of Expiation, in memory of the blessing whereby, at the prayer of Moses, God forgave the people's sin of worshipping the calf. After this was the feast of Scenopegia or of Tents, which was kept for seven days, to commemorate the blessing of being protected and led by God through the desert, where they lived in tents. Hence during this feast they had to take *the fruits of the fairest tree,* that is, the citron, *and trees of dense foliage,* that is, the myrtle, which is fragrant, *and branches of palm-trees, and willows of the brook,* which retain their greenness a long time. And these are to be found in the Land of promise, to signify that God had brought them through the arid land of the wilderness to a land of delights. On the eighth day another feast was observed, of Assembly and Congregation, on which the people collected the expenses necessary for the divine worship, and it signified the uniting of the people and the peace granted to them in the Land of promise.

Aquinas, *Summa Theologica*, I–II, 102, 4

25 They [the Jews] are, as it were, the first-born in the family of God.

Calvin, *Institutes of the Christian Religion*, IV, 16

26 *Shylock.* I am a Jew. Hath not a Jew eyes? hath not a Jew hands, organs, dimensions, senses, affections, passions? fed with the same food, hurt with the same weapons, subject to the same diseases, healed by the same means, warmed and cooled by the same winter and summer, as a Christian is? If you prick us, do we not bleed? if you tickle us, do we not laugh? if you poison us, do we not die? and if you wrong us, shall we not revenge? If we are like you in the rest, we will resemble you in that. If a Jew wrong a Christian, what is his humility? Revenge. If a Christian wrong a Jew, what should

his sufferance be by Christian example? Why, revenge.

Shakespeare, *Merchant of Venice*, III, i, 60

27 The king of any country is the public person, or representative of all his own subjects. And God the king of Israel was the *Holy One* of Israel. The nation which is subject to one earthly sovereign is the nation of that sovereign, that is, of the public person. So the Jews, who were God's nation, were called *a holy nation*. For by *holy* is always understood either God Himself or that which is God's in propriety; as by *public* is always meant either the person of the Commonwealth itself, or something that is so the Commonwealth's as no private person can claim any propriety therein.

Therefore the Sabbath (God's day) is a *holy day;* the Temple (God's house), a *holy house;* sacrifices, tithes, and offerings (God's tribute), *holy duties;* priests, prophets, and anointed kings, under Christ (God's ministers), *holy men;* the celestial ministering spirits (God's messengers), *holy angels;* and the like: and wheresoever the word *holy* is taken properly, there is still something signified of propriety gotten by consent. In saying "Hallowed be Thy name," we do but pray to God for grace to keep the first Commandment of having no other Gods but Him. Mankind is God's nation in propriety: but the Jews only were a *holy nation*. Why, but because they became his propriety by covenant?

Hobbes, *Leviathan*, III, 35

28 It is not unremarkable what *Philo* first observed, That the Law of *Moses* continued two thousand years without the least alteration; whereas, we see, the Laws of other Common-weals do alter with occasions.

Sir Thomas Browne, *Religio Medici*, I, 23

29 The Jew is obstinate in all fortunes; the persecution of fifteen hundred years hath but confirmed them in their Errour: they have already endured whatsoever may be inflicted, and have suffered, in a bad cause, even to the condemnation of their enemies.

Sir Thomas Browne, *Religio Medici*, I, 25

30 To give faith to the Messiah, it was necessary there should have been precedent prophecies, and that these should be conveyed by persons above suspicion, diligent, faithful, unusually zealous, and known to all the world.

To accomplish all this, God chose this carnal people, to whom He entrusted the prophecies which foretell the Messiah as a deliverer and as a dispenser of those carnal goods which this people loved. And thus they have had an extraordinary passion for their prophets and, in sight of the whole world, have had charge of these books which foretell their Messiah, assuring all nations that He should come and in the way foretold in the books, which they held open to the whole world. Yet this people, deceived by the poor and ignominious advent of the Messiah, have been His most cruel enemies. So that they, the people least open to suspicion in the world of favouring us, the most strict and most zealous that can be named for their law and their prophets, have kept the books incorrupt. Hence those who have rejected and crucified Jesus Christ, who has been to them an offence, are those who have charge of the books which testify of Him, and state that He will be an offence and rejected. Therefore they have shown it was He by rejecting Him, and He has been alike proved both by the righteous Jews who received Him and by the unrighteous who rejected Him, both facts having been foretold.

Wherefore the prophecies have a hidden and spiritual meaning to which this people were hostile, under the carnal meaning which they loved. If the spiritual meaning had been revealed, they would not have loved it, and, unable to bear it, they would not have been zealous of the preservation of their books and their ceremonies; and if they had loved these spiritual promises, and had preserved them incorrupt till the time of the Messiah, their testimony would have had no force, because they had been his friends.

Therefore it was well that the spiritual meaning should be concealed; but, on the other hand, if this meaning had been so hidden as not to appear at all, it could not have served as a proof of the Messiah. What then was done? In a crowd of passages it has been hidden under the temporal meaning, and in a few has been clearly revealed; besides that, the time and the state of the world have been so clearly foretold that it is clearer than the sun. And in some places this spiritual meaning is so clearly expressed that it would require a blindness, like that which the flesh imposes on the spirit when it is subdued by it, not to recognise it.

See, then, what has been the prudence of God. This meaning is concealed under another in an infinite number of passages, and in some, though rarely, it is revealed; but yet so that the passages in which it is concealed are equivocal and can suit both meanings; whereas the passages where it is disclosed are unequivocal and can only suit the spiritual meaning.

So that this cannot lead us into error and could only be misunderstood by so carnal a people.

For when blessings are promised in abundance, what was to prevent them from understanding the true blessings, but their covetousness, which limited the meaning to worldly goods? But those whose only good was in God referred them to God alone. For there are two principles, which divide the wills of men, covetousness and charity. Not that covetousness cannot exist along with faith in God, nor charity with worldly riches, but covetousness uses God and enjoys the world, and charity is the opposite.

Now the ultimate end gives names to things. All which prevents us from attaining it is called an enemy to us. Thus the creatures, however good, are the enemies of the righteous, when they turn them away from God, and God Himself is the enemy of those whose covetousness He confounds.

Pascal, *Pensées*, VIII, 571

31 The Jewish religion is wholly divine in its authority, its duration, its perpetuity, its morality, its doctrine, and its effects.

Pascal, *Pensées*, IX, 603

32 The religion of the Jews seemed to consist essentially in the fatherhood of Abraham, in circumcision, in sacrifices, in ceremonies, in the Ark, in the temple, in Jerusalem, and, finally, in the law, and in the covenant with Moses.

I say that it consisted in none of those things, but only in the love of God, and that God disregarded all the other things.

Pascal, *Pensées*, IX, 610

33 *Michael.* God from the Mount of *Sinai*, whose gray top
Shall tremble, he descending, will himself
In Thunder Lightning and loud Trumpets sound
Ordaine them Lawes; part such as appertaine
To civil Justice, part religious Rites
Of sacrifice, informing them, by types
And shadowes, of that destind Seed to bruise
The Serpent, by what meanes he shall achieve
Mankinds deliverance. But the voice of God
To mortal eare is dreadful; they beseech
That *Moses* might report to them his will,
And terror cease; he grants them thir desire,
Instructed that to God is no access
Without Mediator, whose high Office now
Moses in figure beares, to introduce
One greater, of whose day he shall foretell,
And all the Prophets in thir Age, the times
Of great *Messiah* shall sing. Thus Laws and Rites
Establisht, such delight hath God in Men
Obedient to his will, that he voutsafes
Among them to set up his Tabernacle,
The holy One with mortal Men to dwell:
By his prescript a Sanctuary is fram'd
Of Cedar, overlaid with Gold, therein
An Ark, and in the Ark his Testimony,
The Records of his Cov'nant, over these
A Mercie-seat of Gold between the wings
Of two bright Cherubim, before him burn
Seaven Lamps as in a Zodiac representing
The Heav'nly fires; over the Tent a Cloud
Shall rest by Day, a fierie gleame by Night,
Save when they journie, and at length they come,
Conducted by his Angel to the Land
Promisd to *Abraham* and his Seed: the rest
Were long to tell, how many Battels fought,
How many Kings destroyd, and Kingdoms won,
Or how the Sun shall in mid Heav'n stand still

A day entire, and Nights due course adjourne,
Mans voice commanding, Sun in *Gibeon* stand,
And thou Moon in the vale of *Aialon,*
Till *Israel* overcome; so call the third
From *Abraham,* Son of *Isaac,* and from him
His whole descent, who thus shall *Canaan* win.

Milton, *Paradise Lost*, XII, 227

34 Even a cursory perusal will show us that the only respects in which the Hebrews surpassed other nations, are in their successful conduct of matters relating to government, and in their surmounting great perils solely by God's external aid; in other ways they were on a par with their fellows, and God was equally gracious to all.

Spinoza, *Theologico-Political Treatise,* III

35 The Jews, a headstrong, moody, murm'ring race,
As ever tried th' extent and stretch of grace;
God's pamper'd people, whom, debauch'd with ease,
No king could govern, nor no God could please.

Dryden, *Absalom and Achitophel,* 45

36 If the God who guided the Jews wanted to give them a good land, if these unhappy people had actually lived in Egypt, why didn't he leave them in Egypt? The only answers to this question are theological phrases.

Voltaire, *Philosophical Dictionary:* Judea

37 If it were permitted to reason consistently in religious matters, it is clear that we all ought to become Jews, because Jesus Christ our Saviour was born a Jew, lived a Jew, died a Jew, and that he said expressly that he was accomplishing, that he was fulfilling the Jewish religion.

Voltaire, *Philosophical Dictionary:* Tolerance

38 May the children of the stock of Abraham, who dwell in this land, continue to merit and enjoy the good will of the other inhabitants, while everyone shall sit in safety under his own vine and fig tree, and there shall be none to make him afraid.

Washington, *Letter to the Hebrew Congregation,*
Newport, R.I. (1790)

39 The Jews, who, under the Assyrian and Persian monarchies, had languished for many ages the most despised portion of their slaves, emerged from obscurity under the successors of Alexander; and as they multiplied to a surprising degree in the East, and afterwards in the West, they soon excited the curiosity and wonder of other nations. The sullen obstinacy with which they maintained their peculiar rites and unsocial manners seemed to mark them out a distinct species of men, who boldly professed, or who faintly disguised, their implacable hatred to the rest of human-kind. Neither the violence of Antiochus, nor the arts of Herod, nor the example of the circumjacent na-

tions, could ever persuade the Jews to associate with the institutions of Moses the elegant mythology of the Greeks. According to the maxims of universal toleration, the Romans protected a superstition which they despised. The polite Augustus condescended to give orders that sacrifices should be offered for his prosperity in the temple of Jerusalem; while the meanest of the posterity of Abraham, who should have paid the same homage to the Jupiter of the Capitol, would have been an object of abhorrence to himself and to his brethren. But the moderation of the conquerors was insufficient to appease the jealous prejudices of their subjects, who were alarmed and scandalised at the ensigns of paganism, which necessarily introduced themselves into a Roman province. The mad attempt of Caligula to place his own statue in the temple of Jerusalem was defeated by the unanimous resolution of a people who dreaded death much less than such an idolatrous profanation. Their attachment to the law of Moses was equal to their detestation of foreign religions. The current of zeal and devotion, as it was contracted into a narrow channel, ran with the strength, and sometimes with the fury, of a torrent.

Gibbon, *Decline and Fall of the Roman Empire,* XV

40 The devout and even scrupulous attachment to the Mosaic religion, so conspicuous among the Jews who lived under the second temple, becomes still more surprising if it is compared with the stubborn incredulity of their forefathers. When the law was given in thunder from Mount Sinai; when the tides of the ocean and the course of the planets were suspended for the convenience of the Israelites; and when temporal rewards and punishments were the immediate consequences of their piety or disobedience, they perpetually relapsed into rebellion against the visible majesty of their Divine King, placed the idols of the nations in the sanctuary of Jehovah, and imitated every fantastic ceremony that was practised in the tents of the Arabs, or in the cities of Phœnicia.

Gibbon, *Decline and Fall of the Roman Empire,* XV

41 It is the boast of the Jewish apologists, that, while the learned nations of antiquity were deluded by the fables of polytheism, their simple ancestors of Palestine preserved the knowledge and worship of the true God. The moral attributes of Jehovah may not easily be reconciled with the standard of *human* virtue: his metaphysical qualities are darkly expressed; but each page of the Pentateuch and the Prophets is an evidence of his power: the unity of his name is inscribed on the first table of the law; and his sanctuary was never defiled by any visible image of the invisible essence.

Gibbon, *Decline and Fall of the Roman Empire,* L

42 The God of the Jewish people is the God only of Abraham and of his seed: national individuality and a special local worship are involved in such a conception of deity. Before him all other gods are false: moreover the distinction between "true" and "false" is quite abstract; for as regards the false gods, not a ray of the divine is supposed to shine into them. But every form of spiritual force, and *a fortiori* every religion is of such a nature, that whatever be its peculiar character, an affirmative element is necessarily contained in it. However erroneous a religion may be, it possesses truth, although in a mutilated phase. In every religion there is a divine presence, a divine relation; and a philosophy of history has to seek out the spiritual element even in the most imperfect forms. But it does not follow that because it is a religion, it is therefore *good*. We must not fall into the lax conception that the content is of no importance but only the form. This latitudinarian tolerance the Jewish religion does not admit, being absolutely exclusive.

Hegel, *Philosophy of History,* Pt. I, III, 3

43 The fundamental characteristics of the Jewish religion are realism and optimism, views of the world which are closely allied; they form, in fact, the conditions of theism. For theism looks upon the material world as absolutely real, and regards life as a pleasant gift bestowed upon us.

Schopenhauer, *Christian System*

44 The Jews . . . had an absolute monarchy and a hierarchy, and their organised institutions were as obviously of sacerdotal origin as those of the Hindoos. These did for them what was done for other Oriental races by their institutions—subdued them to industry and order, and gave them a national life. But neither their kings nor their priests ever obtained, as in those other countries, the exclusive moulding of their character. Their religion, which enabled persons of genius and a high religious tone to be regarded and to regard themselves as inspired from heaven, gave existence to an inestimably precious unorganised institution— the Order (if it may be so termed) of Prophets. Under the protection, generally though not always effectual, of their sacred character, the Prophets were a power in the nation, often more than a match for kings and priests, and kept up, in that little corner of the earth, the antagonism of influences which is the only real security for continued progress. Religion consequently was not there what it has been in so many other places— a consecration of all that was once established, and a barrier against further improvement.

Mill, *Representative Government,* II

45 The Jews, instead of being stationary like other Asiatics, were, next to the Greeks, the most progressive people of antiquity, and, jointly with

them, have been the starting-point and main propelling agency of modern cultivation.

Mill, *Representative Government,* II

46 The Jews are the most remarkable nation of world history because, faced with the question of being or not being, they preferred, with a perfectly uncanny conviction, being *at any price:* the price they had to pay was the radical *falsification* of all nature, all naturalness, all reality, the entire inner world as well as the outer. They defined themselves *counter* to all those conditions under which a nation was previously able to live, was *permitted* to live; they made of themselves an antithesis to *natural* conditions—they inverted religion, religious worship, morality, history, psychology one after the other in an irreparable way into the *contradiction of their natural values.*

Nietzsche, *Antichrist,* XXIV

47 To the Jewish people fate dealt a series of severe trials and painful experiences, so their God became hard, relentless, and, as it were, wrapped in gloom. He retained the character of a universal God who reigned over all lands and peoples; the fact, however, that his worship had passed from the Egyptians to the Jews found its expression in the added doctrine that the Jews were his chosen people, whose special obligations would in the end find their special reward. It might not have been easy for that people to reconcile their belief in their being preferred to all others by an all-powerful God with the dire experiences of their sad fate. But they did not let doubts assail them, they increased their own feelings of guilt to silence their mistrust and perhaps in the end they referred to "God's unfathomable will," as religious people do to this day.

Freud, *Moses and Monotheism,* Pt. III, I, 1

48 Of all the peoples who lived in antiquity in the basin of the Mediterranean the Jewish people is perhaps the only one that still exists in name and probably also in nature. With an unexampled power of resistance it has defied misfortune and ill-treatment, developed special character traits, and, incidentally, earned the hearty dislike of all other peoples.

Freud, *Moses and Monotheism,* Pt. III, II, 2

49 The preference which through two thousand years the Jews have given to spiritual endeavour has, of course, had its effect; it has helped to build a dike against brutality and the inclination to violence which are usually found where athletic development becomes the ideal of the people. The harmonious development of spiritual and bodily activity, as achieved by the Greeks, was denied to the Jews. In this conflict their decision was at least made in favour of what is culturally the more important.

Freud, *Moses and Monotheism,* Pt. III, II, 4

50 The religion that began with the prohibition against making an image of its God has developed in the course of centuries more and more into a religion of instinctual renunciation.

Freud, *Moses and Monotheism,* Pt. III, II, 5

51 The people met with hard times; the hopes based on the favour of God were slow in being fulfilled; it became not easy to adhere to the illusion, cherished above all else, that they were God's chosen people. If they wished to keep happiness, then the consciousness of guilt because they themselves were such sinners offered a welcome excuse for God's severity. They deserved nothing better than to be punished by him, because they did not observe the laws; the need for satisfying this feeling of guilt, which, coming from a much deeper source, was insatiable, made them render their religious precepts ever and ever more strict, more exacting, but also more petty. In a new transport of moral asceticism the Jews imposed on themselves constantly increasing instinctual renunciation, and thereby reached—at least in doctrine and precepts—ethical heights that had remained inaccessible to the other peoples of antiquity.

Freud, *Moses and Monotheism,* Pt. III, II, 9

52 As the Vedas offer a glimpse into the antecedents of Greek mythology, so Hebrew studies open up vistas into the antecedents of Christian dogma. Christianity in its Patristic form was an adaptation of Hebrew religion to the Græco-Roman world, and later, in the Protestant movement, a readaptation of the same to what we may call the Teutonic spirit. In the first adaptation, Hebrew positivism was wonderfully refined, transformed into a religion of redemption, and endowed with a semi-pagan mythology, a pseudo-Platonic metaphysics, and a quasi-Roman organisation. In the second adaptation, Christianity received a new basis and standard in the spontaneous faith of the individual; and, as the traditions thus undermined in principle gradually dropped away, it was reduced by the German theologians to a romantic and mystical pantheism. Throughout its transformations, however, Christianity remains indebted to the Jews not only for its founder, but for the nucleus of its dogma, cult, and ethical doctrine. If the religion of the Jews, therefore, should disclose its origin, the origin of Christianity would also be manifest.

Santayana, *Life of Reason,* III, 5

20.3 | *Christianity*

The seminal quotations here are, of course, those drawn from the New Testament, depicting events in the life of Jesus Christ and reporting his deeds and utterances. However, the reader should be aware that many passages from the Gospels, from the Acts of the Apostles, and from the epistles of St. Paul—passages that might have been included here—have been placed in other sections of this chapter. Here, as in the case of Judaism, the secular view of Christianity, and especially of its first impact on a pagan world, is given us by the historians.

Intimations and expositions of Christian doctrine will be found in quotations from the great theologians, both Roman Catholic and Protestant. Here again the reader must be advised that, since other sections of this chapter deal with specific aspects of Christian doctrine, many passages from the theologians that might have been placed here have been allocated elsewhere. Special attention should be called to the observations on Christianity by Pascal, who is certainly one of the most brilliant and stalwart defenders of Christianity. He argues eloquently and persuasively for the proposition that Christianity is the one true religion, a proposition that is also affirmed, but defended differently, by Montesquieu and Hegel.

Adverse views of Christianity are presented by Spinoza, Rousseau, Nietzsche, and Marx among others. Less hostile is the approach of those who distinguish between the ideals of Christianity and their inadequate approximation in reality, suggesting that Christianity has been infrequently practiced and that few is the number of those who have called themselves Christians who have followed in the footsteps of Christ.

---

1 For unto us a child is born, unto us a son is given: and the government shall be upon his shoulder: and his name shall be called Wonderful, Counsellor, The mighty God, The everlasting Father, The Prince of Peace.

Of the increase of his government and peace there shall be no end, upon the throne of David, and upon his kingdom, to order it, and to establish it with judgment and with justice from henceforth even for ever.

Isaiah 9:6–7

2 And there shall come forth a rod out of the stem of Jesse, and a Branch shall grow out of his roots:

And the spirit of the Lord shall rest upon him, the spirit of wisdom and understanding, the spirit of counsel and might, the spirit of knowledge and of the fear of the Lord;

And shall make him of quick understanding in the fear of the Lord: and he shall not judge after the sight of his eyes, neither reprove after the hearing of his ears:

But with righteousness shall he judge the poor, and reprove with equity for the meek of the earth: and he shall smite the earth with the rod of his mouth, and with the breath of his lips shall he slay the wicked.

And righteousness shall be the girdle of his loins, and faithfulness the girdle of his reins.

Isaiah 11:1–5

3 How beautiful upon the mountains are the feet of him that bringeth good tidings, that publisheth peace; that bringeth good tidings of good, that publisheth salvation; that saith unto Zion, Thy God reigneth!

Thy watchmen shall lift up the voice; with the voice together shall they sing: for they shall see eye to eye, when the Lord shall bring again Zion.

Isaiah 52:7–8

4 He is despised and rejected of men; a man of sorrows, and acquainted with grief: and we hid as it were our faces from him; he was despised, and we esteemed him not.

Surely he hath borne our griefs, and carried our sorrows: yet we did esteem him stricken, smitten of God, and afflicted.

But he was wounded for our transgressions, he was bruised for our iniquities: the chastisement of our peace was upon him; and with his stripes we are healed.

All we like sheep have gone astray; we have turned every one to his own way; and the Lord hath laid on him the iniquity of us all.

He was oppressed, and he was afflicted, yet he opened not his mouth: he is brought as a lamb to the slaughter, and as a sheep before her shearers is dumb, so he openeth not his mouth.

He was taken from prison and from judgment: and who shall declare his generation? for he was cut off out of the land of the living: for the transgression of my people was he stricken.

And he made his grave with the wicked, and with the rich in his death; because he had done no violence, neither was any deceit in his mouth.

Yet it pleased the Lord to bruise him; he hath put him to grief: when thou shalt make his soul an offering for sin, he shall see his seed, he shall prolong his days, and the pleasure of the Lord shall prosper in his hand.

He shall see of the travail of his soul, and shall be satisfied: by his knowledge shall my righteous servant justify many; for he shall bear their iniquities.

Therefore will I divide him a portion with the great, and he shall divide the spoil with the strong; because he hath poured out his soul unto death: and he was numbered with the transgressors; and he bare the sin of many, and made intercession for the transgressors.

Isaiah 53:3–12

5 Thou shalt call his name *Jesus:* for he shall save his people from their sins.

Matthew 1:21

6 Ye are the salt of the earth: but if the salt have lost his savour, wherewith shall it be salted? it is thenceforth good for nothing, but to be cast out, and to be trodden under foot of men.

Ye are the light of the world. A city that is set on an hill cannot be hid.

Neither do men light a candle, and put it under a bushel, but on a candlestick; and it giveth light unto all that are in the house.

Let your light so shine before men, that they may see your good works, and glorify your Father which is in heaven.

Matthew 5:13–16

7 Ask, and it shall be given you; seek, and ye shall find; knock, and it shall be opened unto you.

Matthew 7:7

8 And Jesus saith unto him, The foxes have holes, and the birds of the air have nests; but the Son of man hath not where to lay his head.

And another of his disciples said unto him, Lord, suffer me first to go and bury my father.

But Jesus said unto him, Follow me; and let the dead bury their dead.

Matthew 8:20–22

9 Come unto me, all ye that labour and are heavy laden, and I will give you rest.

Take my yoke upon you, and learn of me; for I am meek and lowly in heart: and ye shall find rest unto your souls.

For my yoke is easy, and my burden is light.

Matthew 11:28–30

10 As they were eating, Jesus took bread, and blessed it, and brake it, and gave it to the disciples, and said, Take, eat; this is my body.

And he took the cup, and gave thanks, and gave it to them, saying, Drink ye all of it;

For this is my blood of the new testament, which is shed for many for the remission of sins.

Matthew 26:26–28

11 And it came to pass in those days, that there went out a decree from Cæsar Augustus, that all the world should be taxed.

(And this taxing was first made when Cȳ-rē-nĭ-ŭs was governor of Syria.)

And all went to be taxed, every one into his own city.

And Joseph also went up from Galilee, out of the city of Nazareth, into Judæa, unto the city of David, which is called Bethlehem; (because he was of the house and lineage of David:)

To be taxed with Mary his espoused wife, being great with child.

And so it was, that, while they were there, the days were accomplished that she should be delivered.

And she brought forth her firstborn son, and wrapped him in swaddling clothes, and laid him in a manger; because there was no room for them in the inn.

And there were in the same country shepherds abiding in the field, keeping watch over their flock by night.

And, lo, the angel of the Lord came upon them, and the glory of the Lord shone round about them: and they were sore afraid.

And the angel said unto them, Fear not: for, behold, I bring you good tidings of great joy, which shall be to all people.

For unto you is born this day in the city of David a Saviour, which is Christ the Lord.

And this shall be a sign unto you; Ye shall find the babe wrapped in swaddling clothes, lying in a manger.

And suddenly there was with the angel a multitude of the heavenly host praising God, and saying,

Glory to God in the highest, and on earth peace, good will toward men.

And it came to pass, as the angels were gone away from them into heaven, the shepherds said one to another, Let us now go even unto Bethlehem, and see this thing which is come to pass, which the Lord hath made known unto us.

And they came with haste, and found Mary, and Joseph, and the babe lying in a manger.

And when they had seen it, they made known abroad the saying which was told them concerning this child.

And all they that heard it wondered at those things which were told them by the shepherds.

But Mary kept all these things, and pondered them in her heart.

And the shepherds returned, glorifying and praising God for all the things that they had heard and seen, as it was told unto them.

And when eight days were accomplished for the circumcising of the child, his name was called *Jesus,* which was so named of the angel before he was conceived in the womb.

Luke 2:1–21

12 As the people were in expectation, and all men mused in their hearts of John, whether he were the Christ, or not;

John answered, saying unto them all, I indeed baptize you with water; but one mightier than I cometh, the latchet of whose shoes I am not worthy to unloose: he shall baptize you with the Holy Ghost and with fire:

Whose fan is in his hand, and he will throughly purge his floor, and will gather the wheat into his garner; but the chaff he will burn with fire unquenchable.

And many other things in his exhortation preached he unto the people.

But Herod the tē-trärch, being reproved by him for Hĕ-rō-dĭ-ăs his brother Philip's wife, and for all the evils which Herod had done,

Added yet this above all, that he shut up John in prison.

Now when all the people were baptized, it came to pass, that Jesus also being baptized, and praying, the heaven was opened,

And the Holy Ghost descended in a bodily shape like a dove upon him, and a voice came from heaven, which said, Thou art my beloved Son; in thee I am well pleased.

Luke 3:15–22

13 Jesus answered and said unto him, Verily, verily, I say unto thee, Except a man be born again, he cannot see the kingdom of God.

Nicodemus saith unto him, How can a man be born when he is old? can he enter the second time into his mother's womb, and be born?

Jesus answered, Verily, verily, I say unto thee, Except a man be born of water and of the Spirit, he cannot enter into the kingdom of God.

That which is born of the flesh is flesh; and that which is born of the Spirit is spirit.

Marvel not that I said unto thee, Ye must be born again.

The wind bloweth where it listeth, and thou hearest the sound thereof, but canst not tell whence it cometh, and whither it goeth: so is every one that is born of the Spirit.

Nicodemus answered and said unto him, How can these things be?

John 3:3–9

14 Verily, verily, I say unto you, He that believeth on me hath everlasting life.

I am that bread of life.

Your fathers did eat manna in the wilderness, and are dead.

This is the bread which cometh down from heaven, that a man may eat thereof, and not die.

I am the living bread which came down from heaven: if any man eat of this bread, he shall live for ever: and the bread that I will give is my flesh, which I will give for the life of the world.

The Jews therefore strove among themselves, saying, How can this man give us his flesh to eat?

Then Jesus said unto them, Verily, verily, I say unto you, Except ye eat the flesh of the Son of man, and drink his blood, ye have no life in you.

Whoso eateth my flesh, and drinketh my blood, hath eternal life; and I will raise him up at the last day.

For my flesh is meat indeed, and my blood is drink indeed.

He that eateth my flesh, and drinketh my blood, dwelleth in me, and I in him.

As the living Father hath sent me, and I live by the Father: so he that eateth me, even he shall live by me.

This is that bread which came down from heaven: not as your fathers did eat manna, and are dead: he that eateth of this bread shall live for ever.

John 6:47–58

15 And as Jesus passed by, he saw a man which was blind from his birth.

And his disciples asked him, saying, Master, who did sin, this man, or his parents, that he was born blind?

Jesus answered, Neither hath this man sinned, nor his parents: but that the works of God should be made manifest in him.

I must work the works of him that sent me, while it is day: the night cometh, when no man can work.

As long as I am in the world, I am the light of the world.

John 9:1–5

16 Jesus saith unto him, I am the way, the truth, and the life: no man cometh unto the Father, but by me.

John 14:6

17 And the peace of God, which passeth all understanding, shall keep your hearts and minds through Christ Jesus.

Philippians 4:7

18 Great is the mystery of godliness: God was manifest in the flesh, justified in the Spirit, seen of angels, preached unto the Gentiles, believed on in the world, received up into glory.

I Timothy 3:16

19 For there are three that bear record in heaven, the Father, the Word, and the Holy Ghost: and these three are one.

I John 5:7

20 I was in the Spirit on the Lord's day, and heard behind me a great voice, as of a trumpet,

Saying, I am Alpha and Ō-mĕg̱-ă, the first and the last: and, What thou seest, write in a book, and send it unto the seven churches which are in Asia; unto Ephesus, and unto Smyrna, and unto Pĕr-gă-mŏs, and unto Thȳ-ă-tī-ră, and unto Sardis, and unto Philadelphia, and unto Lā-ŏd-ĭ-cē-ă.

And I turned to see the voice that spake with me. And being turned, I saw seven golden candlesticks;

And in the midst of the seven candlesticks one like unto the Son of man, clothed with a garment down to the foot, and girt about the paps with a golden girdle.

His head and his hairs were white like wool, as white as snow; and his eyes were as a flame of fire;

And his feet like unto fine brass, as if they burned in a furnace; and his voice as the sound of many waters.

And he had in his right hand seven stars: and out of his mouth went a sharp twoedged sword: and his countenance was as the sun shineth in his strength.

And when I saw him, I fell at his feet as dead. And he laid his right hand upon me, saying unto me, Fear not; I am the first and the last:

I am he that liveth, and was dead; and, behold, I am alive for evermore, Amen.

Revelation 1:10–18

21 All human efforts, all the lavish gifts of the emperor, and the propitiations of the gods, did not banish the sinister belief that the conflagration was the result of an order. Consequently, to get rid of the report, Nero fastened the guilt and inflicted the most exquisite tortures on a class hated for their abominations, called Christians by the populace. Christus, from whom the name had its origin, suffered the extreme penalty during the reign of Tiberius at the hands of one of our procurators, Pontius Pilatus, and a most mischievous superstition, thus checked for the moment, again broke out not only in Judæa, the first source of the evil, but even in Rome, where all things hideous and shameful from every part of the world find their centre and become popular. Accordingly, an arrest was first made of all who pleaded guilty; then, upon their information, an immense multitude was convicted, not so much of the crime of firing the city, as of hatred against mankind. Mockery of every sort was added to their deaths. Covered with the skins of beasts, they were torn by dogs and perished, or were nailed to crosses, or were doomed to the flames and burnt, to serve as a nightly illumination, when daylight had expired.

Nero offered his gardens for the spectacle, and was exhibiting a show in the circus, while he mingled with the people in the dress of a charioteer or stood aloft on a car. Hence, even for criminals who deserved extreme and exemplary punishment, there arose a feeling of compassion; for it was not, as it seemed, for the public good, but to glut one man's cruelty, that they were being destroyed.

Tacitus, Annals, XV, 44

22 There are, to be sure, other things also quite as "foolish" [as the birth of Christ], which have reference to the humiliations and sufferings of God. Or else, let them call a crucified God "wisdom." But Marcion will apply the knife to this [doctrine] also, and even with greater reason. For which is more unworthy of God, which is more likely to raise a blush of shame, that [God] should be born, or that He should die? that He should bear the flesh, or the cross? be circumcised, or be crucified? be cradled, or be coffined? be laid in a manger, or in a tomb? [Talk of "wisdom!"] You will show more of that if you refuse to believe this also. But, after all, you will not be "wise" unless you become a "fool" to the world, by believing "the foolish things of God." . . . And He was buried, and rose again; the fact is certain, because it is impossible.

Tertullian, De Carne Christi, 5

23 The sermon which Our Lord delivered on the mountain contains the whole process of forming the life of a Christian. Therein man's interior movements are ordered perfectly. For after declaring that his end is Happiness, and after commending the authority of the apostles, through whom the teaching of the Gospel was to be promulgated, He orders man's interior movements, first in regard to man himself, secondly in regard to his neighbour.

This he does in regard to man himself, in two ways, corresponding to man's two interior movements in respect of any prospective action namely, volition of what has to be done, and intention of the end. Therefore, in the first place, He directs man's will in respect of the various precepts of the Law by prescribing that man should refrain not merely from those external works that are evil in themselves, but also from internal acts, and from the occasions of evil deeds. In the second place He directs man's intention, by teaching that in our good works we should seek neither human praise, nor worldly riches, which is to lay up treasures on earth.

Afterwards He directs man's interior movement in respect of his neighbour, by forbidding us, on the one hand, to judge him rashly, unjustly, or presumptuously, and, on the other, to entrust him too readily with sacred things if he be unworthy.

Lastly, He teaches us how to fulfil the teaching of the Gospel; namely, by imploring the help of God, by striving to enter by the narrow door of perfect virtue, and by being wary lest we be led astray by evil influences. Moreover He declares that we must observe His commandments, and that it is not enough to make profession of faith, or to work miracles, or merely to hear His words.

Aquinas, *Summa Theologica*, I–II, 108, 3

24 I admonish every pious Christian that he take not offence at the plain, unvarnished manner of speech of the Bible. Let him reflect that what may seem trivial and vulgar to him, emanates from the high majesty, power, and wisdom of God. The Bible is the book that makes fools of the wise of this world; it is understood only of the plain and simple hearted. Esteem this book as the precious fountain that can never be exhausted. In it thou findest the swaddling-clothes and the manger whither the angels directed the poor, simple shepherds; they seem poor and mean, but dear and precious is the treasure that lies therein.

Luther, *Table Talk*, H57

25 All the wisdom of the world is childish foolishness in comparison with the acknowledgment of Christ. For what is more wonderful than the unspeakable mystery, that the Son of God, the image of the eternal Father, took upon him the nature of man. Doubtless, he helped his supposed father, Joseph, to build houses; for Joseph was a carpenter. What will they of Nazareth think at the day of judgment, when they shall see Christ sitting in his divine majesty; surely they will be astonished, and say: Lord, thou helpest build my house, how comest thou now to this high honour?

When Jesus was born, doubtless, he cried and wept like other children, and his mother tended him as other mothers tend their children. As he grew up, he was submissive to his parents, and waited on them, and carried his supposed father's dinner to him, and when he came back, Mary, no doubt, often said: "My dear little Jesus, where hast thou been?" He that takes not offence at the simple, lowly, and mean course of the life of Christ, is endued with high divine art and wisdom; yea, has a special gift of God in the Holy Ghost. Let us ever bear in mind, that our blessed Saviour thus humbled and abased himself, yielding even to the contumelious death of the cross,

for the comfort of us poor miserable, and damned creatures.

Luther, *Table Talk*, H187

26 The operative cause of the sacrament is the word and institution of Christ, who ordained it. The substance is bread and wine, prefiguring the true body and blood of Christ, which is spiritually received by faith. The final cause of instituting the same, is the benefit and the fruit, the strengthening of our faith, not doubting that Christ's body and blood were given and shed for us, and that our sins by Christ's death certainly are forgiven.

Luther, *Table Talk*, H363

27 *Shylock.* O father Abram, what these Christians are,
Whose own hard dealings teaches them suspect
The thoughts of others!

Shakespeare, *Merchant of Venice*, I, iii, 161

28 *Marcellus.* Some say that ever 'gainst that season comes
Wherein our Saviour's birth is celebrated,
The bird of dawning singeth all night long:
And then, they say, no spirit dare stir abroad;
The nights are wholesome; then no planets strike,
No fairy takes, nor witch hath power to charm,
So hallow'd and so gracious is the time.

Shakespeare, *Hamlet*, I, i, 158

29 Baptism is the sacrament of allegiance of them that are to be received into the kingdom of God; that is to say, into eternal life; that is to say, to remission of sin: for as eternal life was lost by the committing, so it is recovered by the remitting of men's sins.

Hobbes, *Leviathan*, III, 42

30 Religions, as the pagan, are . . . popular, for they consist in externals. But they are not for educated people. A purely intellectual religion would be more suited to the learned, but it would be of no use to the common people. The Christian religion alone is adapted to all, being composed of externals and internals. It raises the common people to the internal, and humbles the proud to the external; it is not perfect without the two, for the people must understand the spirit of the letter, and the learned must submit their spirit to the letter.

Pascal, *Pensées*, IV, 251

31 The Christian religion . . . teaches men these two truths; that there is a God whom men can know, and that there is a corruption in their nature which renders them unworthy of Him. It is equally important to men to know both these points; and it is equally dangerous for man to know God without knowing his own wretchedness, and to know his own wretchedness without knowing the Redeemer who can free him from it. The knowl-

edge of only one of these points gives rise either to the pride of philosophers, who have known God, and not their own wretchedness, or to the despair of atheists, who know their own wretchedness, but not the Redeemer.

And, as it is alike necessary to man to know these two points, so is it alike merciful of God to have made us know them. The Christian religion does this; it is in this that it consists.

Let us herein examine the order of the world and see if all things do not tend to establish these two chief points of this religion: Jesus Christ is the end of all, and the centre to which all tends. Whoever knows Him knows the reason of everything.

Those who fall into error err only through failure to see one of these two things. We can, then, have an excellent knowledge of God without that of our own wretchedness and of our own wretchedness without that of God. But we cannot know Jesus Christ without knowing at the same time both God and our own wretchedness.

Therefore I shall not undertake here to prove by natural reasons either the existence of God, or the Trinity, or the immortality of the soul, or anything of that nature; not only because I should not feel myself sufficiently able to find in nature arguments to convince hardened atheists, but also because such knowledge without Jesus Christ is useless and barren. Though a man should be convinced that numerical proportions are immaterial truths, eternal and dependent on a first truth, in which they subsist and which is called God, I should not think him far advanced towards his own salvation.

The God of Christians is not a God who is simply the author of mathematical truths, or of the order of the elements; that is the view of heathens and Epicureans. He is not merely a God who exercises His providence over the life and fortunes of men, to bestow on those who worship Him a long and happy life. That was the portion of the Jews. But the God of Abraham, the God of Isaac, the God of Jacob, the God of Christians, is a God of love and of comfort, a God who fills the soul and heart of those whom He possesses, a God who makes them conscious of their inward wretchedness, and His infinite mercy, who unites Himself to their inmost soul, who fills it with humility and joy, with confidence and love, who renders them incapable of any other end than Himself.

All who seek God without Jesus Christ, and who rest in nature, either find no light to satisfy them, or come to form for themselves a means of knowing God and serving Him without a mediator. Thereby they fall either into atheism, or into deism, two things which the Christian religion abhors almost equally.

Without Jesus Christ the world would not exist; for it should needs be either that it would be destroyed or be a hell.

If the world existed to instruct man of God, His divinity would shine through every part in it in an indisputable manner; but as it exists only by Jesus Christ, and for Jesus Christ, and to teach men both their corruption and their redemption, all displays the proofs of these two truths.

All appearance indicates neither a total exclusion nor a manifest presence of divinity, but the presence of a God who hides Himself. Everything bears this character.

Pascal, *Pensées*, VIII, 556

32 That religion has always existed on earth which consists in believing that man has fallen from a state of glory and of communion with God into a state of sorrow, penitence, and estrangement from God, but that after this life we shall be restored by a Messiah who should have come. All things have passed away, and this has endured, for which all things are.

Men have in the first age of the world been carried away into every kind of debauchery, and yet there were saints, as Enoch, Lamech, and others, who waited patiently for the Christ promised from the beginning of the world. Noah saw the wickedness of men at its height; and he was held worthy to save the world in his person, by the hope of the Messiah of whom he was the type. Abraham was surrounded by idolaters, when God made known to him the mystery of the Messiah, whom he welcomed from afar. In the time of Isaac and Jacob, abomination was spread over all the earth; but these saints lived in faith; and Jacob, dying and blessing his children, cried in a transport which made him break off his discourse, "I await, O my God, the Saviour whom Thou hast promised. . . ." The Egyptians were infected both with idolatry and magic; the very people of God were led astray by their example. Yet Moses and others believed Him whom they saw not, and worshipped Him, looking to the eternal gifts which He was preparing for them.

The Greeks and Latins then set up false deities; the poets made a hundred different theologies, while the philosophers separated into a thousand different sects; and yet in the heart of Judæa there were always chosen men who foretold the coming of this Messiah, which was known to them alone.

He came at length in the fullness of time, and time has since witnessed the birth of so many schisms and heresies, so many political revolutions, so many changes in all things; yet this Church, which worships Him who has always been worshipped, has endured uninterruptedly. It is a wonderful, incomparable, and altogether divine fact that this religion, which has always endured, has always been attacked. It has been a thousand times on the eve of universal destruction, and every time it has been in that state, God has restored it by extraordinary acts of His power.

Pascal, *Pensées*, IX, 613

33 *Michael.* Nor after resurrection shall he stay
Longer on Earth then certaine times to appeer
To his Disciples, Men who in his Life
Still follow'd him; to them shall leave in charge
To teach all nations what of him they learn'd
And his Salvation, them who shall beleeve
Baptizing in the profluent streame, the signe
Of washing them from guilt of sin to Life
Pure, and in mind prepar'd, if so befall,
For death, like that which the redeemer dy'd.
                Milton, *Paradise Lost,* XII, 436

34 I have often wondered, that persons who make a
boast of professing the Christian religion, namely,
love, joy, peace, temperance, and charity to all
men, should quarrel with such rancorous animosity, and display daily towards one another such
bitter hatred, that this, rather than the virtues
they claim, is the readiest criterion of their faith.
        Spinoza, *Theologico-Political Treatise,* Pref.

35 Christians are distinguished from the rest of the
world, not by faith, nor by charity, nor by the
other fruits of the Holy Spirit, but solely by their
opinions, inasmuch as they defend their cause,
like everyone else, by miracles, that is by ignorance, which is the source of all malice; thus they
turn a faith, which may be true, into superstition.
            Spinoza, *Letter to Henry Oldenburg*
                        (Nov. 1675)

36 Now I saw in my Dream, that the highway up
which *Christian* was to go, was fenced on either
side with a Wall, and that Wall is called *Salvation.*
Up this way therefore did burdened *Christian* run,
but not without great difficulty, because of the
load on his back.
    He ran thus till he came at a place somewhat
ascending; and upon that place stood a *Cross,* and
a little below in the bottom, a *Sepulchre.* So I saw
in my Dream, that just as *Christian* came up with
the *Cross,* his burden loosed from off his Shoulders,
and fell from off his back, and began to tumble;
and so continued to do, till it came to the mouth
of the *Sepulchre,* where it fell in, and I saw it no
more.
                Bunyan, *Pilgrim's Progress,* I

37 The System of the Gospel, after the Fate of other
Systems, is generally antiquated and exploded;
and the Mass or Body of the common People,
among whom it seems to have had its latest Credit, are now grown as much ashamed of it as their
Betters; Opinions, like Fashions, always, descending from those of Quality to the middle Sort,
and thence to the Vulgar, where at length they
are dropp'd and vanish.
        Swift, *Argument Against Abolishing Christianity*

38 The Christian religion, which ordains that men
should love each other, would, without doubt,
have every nation blest with the best civil, the best
political laws; because these, next to this religion,
are the greatest good that men can give and receive.
                Montesquieu, *Spirit of Laws,* XXIV, 1

39 The principles of Christianity, deeply engraved
on the heart, would be infinitely more powerful
than the false honour of monarchies, than the humane virtues of republics, or the servile fear of
despotic states.
                Montesquieu, *Spirit of Laws,* XXIV, 6

40 Christianity as a religion is entirely spiritual, occupied solely with heavenly things; the country of
the Christian is not of this world. He does his
duty, indeed, but does it with profound indifference to the good or ill success of his cares. Provided he has nothing to reproach himself with, it
matters little to him whether things go well or ill
here on earth. If the State is prosperous, he hardly
dares to share in the public happiness, for fear he
may grow proud of his country's glory; if the State
is languishing, he blesses the hand of God that is
hard upon His people.
                Rousseau, *Social Contract,* IV, 8

41 Christianity preaches only servitude and dependence. Its spirit is so favourable to tyranny that it
always profits by such a *régime.* True Christians
are made to be slaves, and they know it and do
not much mind: this short life counts for too little
in their eyes.
                Rousseau, *Social Contract,* IV, 8

42 *Johnson.* As to the Christian religion, Sir, besides
the strong evidence which we have for it, there is
a balance in its favour from the number of great
men who have been convinced of its truth, after a
serious consideration of the question. Grotius was
an acute man, a lawyer, a man accustomed to
examine evidence, and he was convinced. Grotius
was not a recluse, but a man of the world, who
certainly had no bias to the side of religion. Sir
Isaac Newton set out an infidel, and came to be a
very firm believer.
            Boswell, *Life of Johnson (July 28, 1763)*

43 On Sunday, June 3, we all went to Southill
church, which is very near to Mr. Dilly's house. It
being the first Sunday of the month, the holy sacrament was administered, and I staid to partake
of it. When I came afterwards into Dr. Johnson's
room, he said, "You did right to stay and receive
the communion; I had not thought of it." This
seemed to imply that he did not choose to approach the altar without a previous preparation,
as to which good men entertain different opinions,
some holding that it is irreverent to partake of
that ordinance without considerable premeditation; others, that whoever is a sincere Christian,

and in a proper frame of mind to discharge any other ritual duty of our religion, may, without scruple, discharge this most solemn one. A middle notion I believe to be the just one, which is, that communicants need not think a long train of preparatory forms indispensably necessary; but neither should they rashly and lightly venture upon so aweful and mysterious an institution. Christians must judge each for himself, what degree of retirement and self-examination is necessary upon each occasion.

Boswell, *Life of Johnson* (*June 3, 1781*)

44 The Christians were not less adverse to the business than to the pleasures of this world. The defence of our persons and property they knew not how to reconcile with the patient doctrine which enjoined an unlimited forgiveness of past injuries, and commanded them to invite the repetition of fresh insults. Their simplicity was offended by the use of oaths, by the pomp of magistracy, and by the active contention of public life; nor could their humane ignorance be convinced that it was lawful on any occasion to shed the blood of our fellow-creatures, either by the sword of justice or by that of war, even though their criminal or hostile attempts should threaten the peace and safety of the whole community. . . . This indolent, or even criminal disregard to the public welfare, exposed them to the contempt and reproaches of the Pagans, who very frequently asked, what must be the fate of the empire, attacked on every side by the barbarians, if all mankind should adopt the pusillanimous sentiments of the new sect? To this insulting question the Christian apologists returned obscure and ambiguous answers, as they were unwilling to reveal the secret cause of their security; the expectation that, before the conversion of mankind was accomplished, war, government, the Roman empire, and the world itself, would be no more. It may be observed that, in this instance likewise, the situation of the first Christians coincided very happily with their religious scruples, and that their aversion to an active life contributed rather to excuse them from the service than to exclude them from the honours of the state and army.

Gibbon, *Decline and Fall of the Roman Empire,* XV

45 It is not easy to extract any distinct ideas from the vague though eloquent declamations of the Fathers, or to ascertain the degree of immortal glory and happiness which they confidently promised to those who were so fortunate as to shed their blood in the cause of religion. They inculcated with becoming diligence that the fire of martyrdom supplied every defect and expiated every sin; that, while the souls of ordinary Christians were obliged to pass through a slow and painful purification, the triumphant sufferers entered into the

immediate fruition of eternal bliss, where, in the society of the patriarchs, the apostles, and the prophets, they reigned with Christ, and acted as his assessors in the universal judgment of mankind.

Gibbon, *Decline and Fall of the Roman Empire,* XVI

46 A quiet conscience makes one so serene!
Christians have burnt each other, quite persuaded
That all the Apostles would have done as they did.

Byron, *Don Juan,* I, 83

47 Christianity has this peculiar disadvantage, that unlike other religions, it is not a pure system of doctrine: its chief and essential feature is that it is a history, a series of events, a collection of facts, a statement of the actions and sufferings of individuals: it is this history which constitutes dogma, and belief in it is salvation.

Schopenhauer, *Christian System*

48 This is the miracle of Christianity, more wonderful than that one of changing the water into wine; this miracle in all stillness, without any change of rulers, moreover without a hand being moved, of making every man, divinely understood, into a king, so easily, so smoothly, so miraculously, that the world in a certain sense does not need to know it. For in the world outside, there the king will and ought to be the only one who rules according to his conscience; but to obey—for conscience's sake will be permitted everyone; moreover, no one, no one can prevent it. And there within, there far within, where the Christian dwells in the conscience-relation, there is everything changed.

Lo, the world raises a tumult just to bring about a little change; it sets heaven and earth in motion for nothing, like the mountain which brought forth a mouse: Christianity in all stillness brings about the change of the infinite as if it were nothing. It is so quiet, quiet as nothing worldly can be; as quiet as only the dead and inwardness can be; and what else is Christianity but inwardness!

Thus Christianity transforms every relation between men into a conscience-relationship, and thus also into a love-relationship.

Kierkegaard, *Works of Love,* I, 3B

49 The Christian world is always offended by the true Christian. Only now the passion of offense is not ordinarily so strong that it wishes to eradicate him; no, it will only continue to mock and insult him. This is easy to explain. At the time when the world was itself conscious of not being Christian, then there was something to fight about, then it was a fight to the death. But now, when the world is proudly and calmly certain that it is Christian, the true Christian insistence is merely something to laugh at. The confusion is even more distressing

than in the first period of Christianity. That was distressing, but there was meaning in it, since the world was fighting to the death against Christianity. But the world's present lofty calmness in its consciousness of being Christian, its cheap bit of mockery, if one wishes to call it that—of the real Christian: this almost borders on madness. For never in its first period was Christianity thus made the object of ridicule.

Kierkegaard, *Works of Love,* I, 5

50 Official preaching has falsely represented religion, Christianity, as nothing but consolation, happiness etc. And consequently doubt has the advantage of being able to say in a *superior* way: I do not wish to be made happy by an illusion.

If Christianity were truthfully presented as suffering, ever greater as one advances further in it: doubt would have been disarmed, and in any case there would have been no opportunity for being superior—where it was a matter of avoiding—pain.

Kierkegaard, *Journals (1851)*

51 Every Stoic was a Stoic; but in Christendom where is the Christian?

Emerson, *Self-Reliance*

52 The modern Christian is a man who has consented to say all the prayers in the liturgy, provided you will let him go straight to bed and sleep quietly afterward. All his prayers begin with "Now I lay me down to sleep," and he is forever looking forward to the time when he shall go to his "*long rest.*" He has consented to perform certain old, established charities, too, after a fashion, but he does not wish to hear of any new-fangled ones; he doesn't wish to have any supplementary articles added to the contract to fit it to the present time. He shows the whites of his eyes on the Sabbath, and the blacks all the rest of the week.

Thoreau, *Plea for Captain John Brown*

53 Christianity only hopes. It has hung its harp on the willows, and cannot sing a song in a strange land. It has dreamed a sad dream, and does not yet welcome the morning with joy.

Thoreau, *The Christian Fable*

54 The religious world is but the reflex of the real world. And for a society based upon the production of commodities, in which the producers in general enter into social relations with one another by treating their products as commodities and values, whereby they reduce their individual private labour to the standard of homogeneous human labour—for such a society, Christianity with its *cultus* of abstract man, more especially in its bourgeois developments, Protestantism, Deism, etc., is the most fitting form of religion.

Marx, *Capital,* Vol. I, I, 1

55 To pretend that Christianity was intended to stereotype existing forms of government and society, and protect them against change, is to reduce it to the level of Islamism or of Brahminism. It is precisely because Christianity has not done this, that it has been the religion of the progressive portion of mankind, and Islamism, Brahminism, etc. have been those of the stationary portions; or rather (for there is no such thing as a really stationary society) of the declining portions. There have been abundance of people, in all ages of Christianity, who tried to make it something of the same kind; to convert us into a sort of Christian Mussulmans, with the Bible for a Koran, prohibiting all improvement: and great has been their power, and many have had to sacrifice their lives in resisting them. But they have been resisted, and the resistance has made us what we are, and will yet make us what we are to be.

Mill, *Subjection of Women,* II

56 Sometimes an attempt is made to determine the "leading idea," as it has been called, of Christianity, an ambitious essay as employed on a supernatural work, when, even as regards the visible creation and the inventions of man, such a task is beyond us. Thus its one idea has been said by some to be the restoration of our fallen race, by others philanthropy, by others the tidings of immortality, or the spirituality of true religious service, or the salvation of the elect, or mental liberty, or the union of the soul with God. If, indeed, it is only thereby meant to use one or other of these as a central idea for convenience, in order to group others around it, no fault can be found with such a proceeding; and in this sense I should myself call the Incarnation the central aspect of Christianity, out of which the three main aspects of its teaching take their rise, the sacramental, the hierarchical, and the ascetic. But one aspect of Revelation must not be allowed to exclude or to obscure another; and Christianity is dogmatical, devotional, practical all at once; it is esoteric and exoteric; it is indulgent and strict; it is light and dark; it is love, and it is fear.

Newman, *Essay on the Development of Christian Doctrine,* Pt. I, I, 1

57 Christianity is that which righteousness really is. Therefore, if something called Christianity prevails, and yet the promises are not satisfied, the inference is that this *something* is not that which righteousness really is, and therefore not really Christianity.

Arnold, *Literature and Dogma,* XII

58 *Father Païssy.* The science of this world, which has become a great power, has, especially in the last century, analysed everything divine handed down to us in the holy books. After this cruel analysis the learned of this world have nothing left of all

that was sacred of old. But they have only ana-lysed the parts and overlooked the whole, and in-deed their blindness is marvellous. Yet the whole still stands steadfast before their eyes, and the gates of hell shall not prevail against it. Has it not lasted nineteen centuries, is it not still a living, a moving power in the individual soul and in the masses of people? It is still as strong and living even in the souls of atheists, who have destroyed everything! For even those who have renounced Christianity and attack it, in their inmost being still follow the Christian ideal, for hitherto neither their subtlety nor the ardour of their hearts has been able to create a higher ideal of man and of virtue than the ideal given by Christ of old. When it has been attempted, the result has been only grotesque.

Dostoevsky, *Brothers Karamazov*, Pt. II, IV, 1

59 It is a basic tenet of Christianity that all men are equal, not only because of their equal relation to the infinite, but because they are brothers, they are all acknowledged as sons of God.

Tolstoy, *What Is Religion?*, VI

60 The Christian faith is a sacrifice: a sacrifice of all freedom, all pride, all self-confidence of the spirit; at the same time, enslavement and self-mockery, self-mutilation.

Nietzsche, *Beyond Good and Evil*, III, 46

61 Suppose we could contemplate the oddly painful and equally crude and subtle comedy of Europe-an Christianity with the mocking and aloof eyes of an Epicurean god, I think our amazement and laughter would never end: doesn't it seem that a single will dominated Europe for eighteen centu-ries—to turn man into a *sublime miscarriage?*

Nietzsche, *Beyond Good and Evil*, III, 62

62 What is more harmful than any vice?—Active sympathy for the ill-constituted and weak—Chris-tianity.

Nietzsche, *Antichrist*, II

63 One should not embellish or dress up Christiani-ty: it has waged a *war to the death* against this *higher* type of man, it has excommunicated all the fun-damental instincts of this type, it has distilled evil, the *Evil One*, out of these instincts—the strong hu-man being as the type of reprehensibility, as the 'outcast'. Christianity has taken the side of ev-erything weak, base, ill-constituted, it has made an ideal out of *opposition* to the preservative in-stincts of strong life; it has depraved the reason even of the intellectually strongest natures by teaching men to feel the supreme values of intel-lectuality as sinful, as misleading, as *temptations*. The most deplorable example: the depraving of Pascal, who believed his reason had been de-praved by original sin while it had only been de-praved by his Christianity!

Nietzsche, *Antichrist*, V

64 Why not give Christianity a trial? The question seems a hopeless one after 2000 years of resolute adherence to the old cry of "Not this man, but Barabbas." Yet it is beginning to look as if Barab-bas was a failure, in spite of his strong right hand, his victories, his empires, his millions of money, and his moralities and churches and political constitutions. "This man" has not been a failure yet; for nobody has ever been sane enough to try his way.

Shaw, *Androcles and the Lion*, Pref.

65 The doctrines in which Jesus is thus confirmed are, roughly, the following:
1. The kingdom of heaven is within you. You are the son of God; and God is the son of man. God is a spirit, to be worshipped in spirit and in truth, and not an elderly gentleman to be bribed and begged from. We are members one of anoth-er; so that you cannot injure or help your neigh-bor without injuring or helping yourself. God is your father: you are here to do God's work; and you and your father are one.
2. Get rid of property by throwing it into the common stock. Dissociate your work entirely from money payments. If you let a child starve you are letting God starve. Get rid of all anxiety about tomorrow's dinner and clothes, because you can-not serve two masters: God and Mammon.
3. Get rid of judges and punishment and re-venge. Love your neighbor as yourself, he being a part of yourself. And love your enemies: they are your neighbors.
4. Get rid of your family entanglements. Every mother you meet is as much your mother as the woman who bore you. Every man you meet is as much your brother as the man she bore after you. Dont waste your time at family funerals grieving for your relatives: attend to life, not to death: there are as good fish in the sea as ever came out of it, and better. In the kingdom of heaven, which, as aforesaid, is within you, there is no marriage nor giving in marriage, because you cannot de-vote your life to two divinities: God and the per-son you are married to.

Shaw, *Androcles and the Lion*, Pref.

66 Christianity has two faces. Popular Christianity has for its emblem a gibbet, for its chief sensation a sanguinary execution after torture, for its cen-tral mystery an insane vengeance bought off by a trumpery expiation. But there is a nobler and pro-founder Christianity which affirms the sacred mystery of Equality, and forbids the glaring futili-ty and folly of vengeance, often politely called punishment or justice. The gibbet part of Chris-tianity is tolerated. The other is criminal felony.

Shaw, *Major Barbara*, Pref.

67 Surely some revelation is at hand;
 Surely the Second Coming is at hand.
 The Second Coming! Hardly are those words out
 When a vast image out of *Spiritus Mundi*
 Troubles my sight: somewhere in sands of the desert
 A shape with lion body and the head of a man,
 A gaze blank and pitiless as the sun,
 Is moving its slow thighs, while all about it
 Reel shadows of the indignant desert birds.
 The darkness drops again; but now I know
 That twenty centuries of stony sleep
 Were vexed to nightmare by a rocking cradle,
 And what rough beast, its hour come round at last,
 Slouches towards Bethlehem to be born?

 Yeats, *The Second Coming*

68 Religious experience . . . may take other forms than the Christian, and within Christianity it may take other forms than the Catholic; but the Catholic form is as good as any intrinsically for the devotee himself, and it has immense advantages over its probable rivals in charm, in comprehensiveness, in maturity, in internal rationality, in external adaptability; so much so that a strong anticlerical government, like the French, cannot safely leave the church to be overwhelmed by the forces of science, good sense, ridicule, frivolity, and avarice (all strong forces in France), but must use violence as well to do it. In the English church, too, it is not those who accept the deluge, the resurrection, and the sacraments only as symbols that are the vital party, but those who accept them literally; for only these have anything to say to the poor, or to the rich, that can refresh them. In a frank supernaturalism, in a tight clericalism, not in a pleasant secularisation, lies the sole hope of the church. Its sole dignity also lies there. It will not convert the world; it never did and it never could. It will remain a voice crying in the wilderness; but it will believe what it cries, and there will be some to listen to it in the future, as there have been many in the past. As to modernism, it is suicide. It is the last of those concessions to the spirit of the world which half-believers and double-minded prophets have always been found making; but it is a mortal concession. It concedes everything; for it concedes that everything in Christianity, as Christians hold it, is an illusion.

 Santayana, *Winds of Doctrine,* II

69 Let the reader fill out this outline [of the Christian epic] for himself with its thousand details; let him remember the endless mysteries, arguments, martyrdoms, consecrations that carried out the sense and made vital the beauty of the whole. Let him pause before the phenomenon; he can ill afford, if he wishes to understand history or the human mind, to let the apparition float by unchallenged without delivering up its secret. What shall we say of this Christian dream?

 Those who are still troubled by the fact that this dream is by many taken for a reality, and who are consequently obliged to defend themselves against it, as against some dangerous error in science or in philosophy, may be allowed to marshal arguments in its disproof. Such, however, is not my intention. Do we marshal arguments against the miraculous birth of Buddha, or the story of Cronos devouring his children? We seek rather to honour the piety and to understand the poetry embodied in those fables. If it be said that those fables are believed by no one, I reply that those fables are or have been believed just as unhesitatingly as the Christian theology, and by men no less reasonable or learned than the unhappy apologists of our own ancestral creeds. Matters of religion should never be matters of controversy. We neither argue with a lover about his taste, nor condemn him, if we are just, for knowing so human a passion. That he harbours it is no indication of a want of sanity on his part in other matters. But while we acquiesce in his experience, and are glad he has it, we need no arguments to dissuade us from sharing it. Each man may have his own loves, but the object in each case is different. And so it is, or should be, in religion.

 Santayana, *Life of Reason,* III, 6

20.4 | *Church*

The Temple, in the Old Testament, is both an architectural monument and a unique religious symbol; destroyed, it can be rebuilt; forgotten, it can be restored and remembered. It is by no means the only place of Jewish worship; synagogues exist wherever a small number of Jews come together to worship communally; in contrast, the Temple is the sole repository of the Ark of the Covenant and houses the holy of holies.

As there can be many synagogues, so there can be many churches, each a house of worship, each a cell of the Christian religious community. But unlike the Temple, the Church, in the Christian tradition, has no architectural embodiment, nor is it a religious symbol or a unique repository of sacred objects. Rather it is, in the language of Christian theologians, the mystical body of Christ, the city of God on earth. The relation of church and state is thus conceived as the relation of the city of God to the city of man; further subtleties are introduced by the distinction between the church visible and the church invisible, the church militant and the church triumphant.

The quotations included here discuss, among other things, the foundation of the Church, the unity of the Church and the plurality of churches, the mode of government appropriate to the Church, and church reform.

---

1 And Jesus, walking by the sea of Galilee, saw two brethren, Simon called Peter, and Andrew his brother, casting a net into the sea: for they were fishers.

And he saith unto them, Follow me, and I will make you fishers of men.

And they straightway left their nets, and followed him.

And going on from thence, he saw other two brethren, James the son of Zebedee, and John his brother, in a ship with Zebedee their father, mending their nets; and he called them.

And they immediately left the ship and their father, and followed him.

Matthew 4:18–22

2 When Jesus came into the coasts of Cæsarea Phĭ-lĭp´-pī, he asked his disciples, saying, Whom do men say that I the Son of man am?

And they said, Some say that thou art John the Baptist: some, Ē-lī´-ăs; and others, Jĕr-e-mī´-ăs, or one of the prophets.

He saith unto them, But whom say ye that I am?

And Simon Peter answered and said, Thou art the Christ, the Son of the living God.

And Jesus answered and said unto him, Blessed art thou, Simon Bär-jō´-nă: for flesh and blood hath not revealed it unto thee, but my Father which is in heaven.

And I say also unto thee, That thou art Peter, and upon this rock I will build my church; and the gates of hell shall not prevail against it.

And I will give unto thee the keys of the kingdom of heaven: and whatsoever thou shalt bind on earth shall be bound in heaven: and whatsoever thou shalt loose on earth shall be loosed in heaven.

Matthew 16:13–19

3 Moreover if thy brother shall trespass against thee, go and tell him his fault between thee and him alone: if he shall hear thee, thou hast gained thy brother.

But if he will not hear thee, then take with thee one or two more, that in the mouth of two or three witnesses every word may be established.

And if he shall neglect to hear them, tell it unto the church: but if he neglect to hear the church, let him be unto thee as an heathen man and a publican.

Verily I say unto you, Whatsoever ye shall bind on earth shall be bound in heaven: and whatsoever ye shall loose on earth shall be loosed in heaven.

Again I say unto you, That if two of you shall agree on earth as touching any thing that they shall ask, it shall be done for them of my Father which is in heaven.

For where two or three are gathered together in

my name, there am I in the midst of them.

Matthew 18:15–20

4 Then the eleven disciples went away into Galilee, into a mountain where Jesus had appointed them.

And when they saw him, they worshipped him: but some doubted.

And Jesus came and spake unto them, saying, All power is given unto me in heaven and in earth.

Go ye therefore, and teach all nations, baptizing them in the name of the Father, and of the Son, and of the Holy Ghost:

Teaching them to observe all things whatsoever I have commanded you: and, lo, I am with you alway, even unto the end of the world. Amen.

Matthew 28:16–20

5 Afterward he appeared unto the eleven as they sat at meat, and upbraided them with their unbelief and hardness of heart, because they believed not them which had seen him after he was risen.

And he said unto them, Go ye into all the world, and preach the gospel to every creature.

He that believeth and is baptized shall be saved; but he that believeth not shall be damned.

And these signs shall follow them that believe; In my name shall they cast out devils; they shall speak with new tongues;

They shall take up serpents; and if they drink any deadly thing, it shall not hurt them; they shall lay hands on the sick, and they shall recover.

Mark 16:14–18

6 And there was also a strife among them, which of them should be accounted the greatest.

And he said unto them, The kings of the Gentiles exercise lordship over them; and they that exercise authority upon them are called benefactors.

But ye shall not be so: but he that is greatest among you, let him be as the younger; and he that is chief, as he that doth serve.

For whether is greater, he that sitteth at meat, or he that serveth? is not he that sitteth at meat? but I am among you as he that serveth.

Ye are they which have continued with me in my temptations.

And I appoint unto you a kingdom, as my Father hath appointed unto me;

That ye may eat and drink at my table in my kingdom, and sit on thrones judging the twelve tribes of Israel.

Luke 22:24–30

7 Verily, verily, I say unto you, He that entereth not by the door into the sheepfold, but climbeth up some other way, the same is a thief and a robber.

But he that entereth in by the door is the shepherd of the sheep.

To him the porter openeth; and the sheep hear his voice; and he calleth his own sheep by name, and leadeth them out.

And when he putteth forth his own sheep, he goeth before them, and the sheep follow him: for they know his voice.

And a stranger will they not follow, but will flee from him: for they know not the voice of strangers.

This parable spake Jesus unto them: but they understood not what things they were which he spake unto them.

Then said Jesus unto them again, Verily, verily, I say unto you, I am the door of the sheep.

All that ever came before me are thieves and robbers: but the sheep did not hear them.

I am the door: by me if any man enter in, he shall be saved, and shall go in and out, and find pasture.

The thief cometh not, but for to steal, and to kill, and to destroy: I am come that they might have life, and that they might have it more abundantly.

I am the good shepherd: the good shepherd giveth his life for the sheep.

John 10:1–11

8 Simon Peter said unto him, Lord, whither goest thou? Jesus answered him, Whither I go, thou canst not follow me now; but thou shalt follow me afterwards.

Peter said unto him, Lord, why cannot I follow thee now? I will lay down my life for thy sake.

Jesus answered him, Wilt thou lay down thy life for my sake? Verily, verily, I say unto thee, The cock shall not crow, till thou hast denied me thrice.

John 13:36–38

9 These things I command you, that ye love one another.

If the world hate you, ye know that it hated me before it hated you.

If ye were of the world, the world would love his own: but because ye are not of the world, but I have chosen you out of the world, therefore the world hateth you.

John 15:17–19

10 Then the same day at evening, being the first day of the week, when the doors were shut where the disciples were assembled for fear of the Jews, came Jesus and stood in the midst, and saith unto them, Peace be unto you.

And when he had so said, he shewed unto them his hands and his side. Then were the disciples glad, when they saw the Lord.

Then said Jesus to them again, Peace be unto you: as my Father hath sent me, even so send I you.

And when he had said this, he breathed on

them, and saith unto them, Receive ye the Holy Ghost:

Whose soever sins ye remit, they are remitted unto them; and whose soever sins ye retain, they are retained.

John 20:19–23

11 So when they had dined, Jesus saith to Simon Peter, Simon, son of Jonas, lovest thou me more than these? He saith unto him, Yea, Lord; thou knowest that I love thee. He saith unto him, Feed my lambs.

He saith to him again the second time, Simon, son of Jonas, lovest thou me? He saith unto him, Yea, Lord; thou knowest that I love thee. He saith unto him, Feed my sheep.

He saith unto him the third time, Simon, son of Jonas, lovest thou me? Peter was grieved because he said unto him the third time, Lovest thou me? And he said unto him, Lord, thou knowest all things; thou knowest that I love thee. Jesus saith unto him, Feed my sheep.

John 21:15–17

12 On this account some allegorize all that concerns Paradise itself, where the first men, the parents of the human race, are, according to the truth of holy Scripture, recorded to have been; and they understand all its trees and fruit-bearing plants as virtues and habits of life, as if they had no existence in the external world, but were only so spoken of or related for the sake of spiritual meanings. As if there could not be a real terrestrial Paradise! As if there never existed these two women, Sarah and Hagar, nor the two sons who were born to Abraham, the one of the bond woman, the other of the free, because the apostle says that in them the two covenants were prefigured; or as if water never flowed from the rock when Moses struck it, because therein Christ can be seen in a figure, as the same apostle says, "Now that rock was Christ!" No one, then, denies that Paradise may signify the life of the blessed; its four rivers, the four virtues, prudence, fortitude, temperance, and justice; its trees, all useful knowledge; its fruits, the customs of the godly; its tree of life, wisdom herself, the mother of all good; and the tree of the knowledge of good and evil, the experience of a broken commandment. The punishment which God appointed was in itself, a just, and therefore a good thing; but man's experience of it is not good.

These things can also and more profitably be understood of the Church, so that they become prophetic foreshadowings of things to come. Thus Paradise is the Church, as it is called in the Canticles; the four rivers of Paradise are the four gospels; the fruit-trees the saints, and the fruit their works; the tree of life is the holy of holies, Christ; the tree of the knowledge of good and evil, the will's free choice. For if man despise the will of God, he can only destroy himself; and so he learns the difference between consecrating himself to the common good and revelling in his own. For he who loves himself is abandoned to himself, in order that, being overwhelmed with fears and sorrows, he may cry, if there be yet soul in him to feel his ills, in the words of the psalm, "My soul is cast down within me," and when chastened, may say, "Because of his strength I will wait upon Thee." These and similar allegorical interpretations may be suitably put upon Paradise without giving offence to any one, while yet we believe the strict truth of the history, confirmed by its circumstantial narrative of facts.

Augustine, *City of God*, XIII, 21

13 In this wicked world, in these evil days, when the Church measures her future loftiness by her present humility, and is exercised by goading fears, tormenting sorrows, disquieting labours, and dangerous temptations, when she soberly rejoices, rejoicing only in hope, there are many reprobates mingled with the good, and both are gathered together by the gospel as in a dragnet; and in this world, as in a sea, both swim enclosed without distinction in the net, until it is brought ashore, when the wicked must be separated from the good, that in the good, as in His temple, God may be all in all. We acknowledge, indeed, that His word is now fulfilled who spake in the psalm, and said, "I have announced and spoken; they are multiplied above number." This takes place now, since He has spoken, first by the mouth of His forerunner John, and afterward by His own mouth, saying, "Repent: for the kingdom of heaven is at hand." He chose disciples, whom He also called apostles, of lowly birth, unhonoured, and illiterate, so that whatever great thing they might be or do, He might be and do it in them. He had one among them whose wickedness He could use well in order to accomplish His appointed passion, and furnish His Church an example of bearing with the wicked. Having sown the Holy Gospel as much as that behoved to be done by His bodily presence, He suffered, died, and rose again, showing by His passion what we ought to suffer for the truth, and by His resurrection what we ought to hope for in adversity; saving always the mystery of the sacrament, by which His blood was shed for the remission of sins. He held converse on the earth forty days with His disciples, and in their sight ascended into heaven, and after ten days sent the promised Holy Spirit. It was given as the chief and most necessary sign of His coming on those who had believed, that every one of them spoke in the tongues of all nations; thus signifying that the unity of the Catholic Church would embrace all nations and would in like manner speak in all tongues.

Augustine, *City of God*, XVIII, 49

14 The Church is His body, as the apostle's teaching shows us; and it is even called His spouse. His body, then, which has many members, and all performing different functions, He holds together in the bond of unity and love, which is its true health. Moreover He exercises it in the present time, and purges it with many wholesome afflictions, that, when He has transplanted it from this world to the eternal world, He may take it to Himself as His bride, without spot or wrinkle, or any such thing.

Augustine, *Christian Doctrine*, I, 16

15 The universal Church cannot err, since she is governed by the Holy Ghost Who is the Spirit of truth.

Aquinas, *Summa Theologica*, II–II, 1, 9

16 It is manifest that he who adheres to the teaching of the Church, as to an infallible rule, assents to whatever the Church teaches. Otherwise, if, of the things taught by the Church, he holds what he chooses to hold, and rejects what he chooses to reject, he no longer adheres to the teaching of the Church as to an infallible rule, but to his own will.

Aquinas, *Summa Theologica*, II–II, 5, 3

17 Those who are unbelievers, though not actually in the Church, are in the Church potentially. And this potentiality is rooted in two things—first and principally, in the power of Christ, which is sufficient for the salvation of the whole human race; secondly, in the liberty of choice.

Aquinas, *Summa Theologica*, III, 8, 3

18 The term Church is taken in two senses. For sometimes it denotes the body only, which is united to Christ as its Head. In this way alone has the Church the character of spouse, and in this way Christ is not a member of the Church, but is the Head from which all the members receive. In another sense the Church denotes the head and members united together; and thus Christ is said to be a member of the Church, in so far as He fulfils an office distinct from all others, by pouring forth life into the other members, although He is not very properly called a member, since a member implies a certain restriction, whereas in Christ spiritual good is not restricted but is absolutely entire, so that He is the entire good of the Church, nor is He together with others anything greater than He is by Himself.

Aquinas, *Summa Theologica*, III Suppl., 95, 3

19 There where we came, at the first step, was white marble so polished and smooth that I mirrored me therein as I appear.

The second darker was than perse, of a stone, rugged and calcined, cracked in its length and in its breadth.

The third, which is massy above, seemed to me of porphyry so flaming red as blood that spurts from a vein.

Upon this God's angel held both his feet, sitting upon the threshold, which seemed to me adamantine stone.

Up by the three steps, with my good will, my Leader [Virgil] brought me, saying: "Humbly ask that the bolt be loosed."

Devoutly I flung me at the holy feet; for mercy I craved that he would open to me; but first on my breast thrice I smote me.

Seven P's upon my forehead he described with the point of his sword and: "Do thou wash these wounds when thou art within," he said.

Ashes, or earth which is dug out dry, would be of one colour with his vesture, and from beneath it he drew forth two keys.

One was of gold and the other was of silver; first with the white and then with the yellow he did so to the gate that I was satisfied.

"Whensoever one of these keys fails so that it turns not aright in the lock," said he to us, "this passage opens not.

More precious is one, but the other requires exceeding art and wit ere it unlocks, because it is the one which unties the knot.

From Peter I hold them; and he told me to err rather in opening, than in keeping it locked, if only the people fell prostrate at my feet."

Then he pushed the door of the sacred portal, saying: "Enter, but I make you ware that he who looketh behind returns outside again."

Dante, *Purgatorio*, IX, 94

20 In form, then, of a white rose displayed itself to me that sacred soldiery which in his blood Christ made his spouse;

but the other, which as it flieth seeth and doth sing his glory who enamoureth it, and the excellence which hath made it what it is,

like to a swarm of bees which doth one while plunge into the flowers and another while wend back to where its toil is turned to sweetness,

ever descended into the great flower adorned with so many leaves, and reascended thence to where its love doth ceaseless make sojourn.

They had their faces all of living flame, and wings of gold, and the rest so white that never snow reacheth such limit.

When they descended into the flower, from rank to rank they proffered of the peace and of the ardour which they acquired as they fanned their sides,

nor did the interposing of so great a flying multitude, betwixt the flower and that which was above, impede the vision nor the splendour;

for the divine light so penetrateth through the universe, in measure of its worthiness, that naught hath power to oppose it.

Dante, *Paradiso*, XXXI, 1

21 This . . . monk let such old things slowly pace
    And followed new-world manners in their place.
    He cared not for that text a clean-plucked hen
    Which holds that hunters are not holy men;
    Nor that a monk, when he is cloisterless,
    Is like unto a fish that's waterless;
    That is to say, a monk out of his cloister.
    But this same text he held not worth an oyster;
    And I said his opinion was right good.
    What? Should he study as a madman would
    Upon a book in cloister cell? Or yet
    Go labour with his hands and swink and sweat,
    As Austin bids? How shall the world be served?
    Let Austin have his toil to him reserved.

    Chaucer, *Canterbury Tales:* The Prologue

22 The Church owes its life to the word of promise
    through faith, and is nourished and preserved by
    this same word. That is to say, the promises of
    God make the Church, not the Church the prom-
    ise of God. For the Word of God is incompar-
    ably superior to the Church, and in this Word the
    Church, being a creature, has nothing to decree,
    ordain or make, but only to be decreed, ordained
    and made. For who begets his own parent? Who
    first brings forth his own maker?

    Luther, *Babylonian Captivity of the Church*

23 The Christian Church . . . will always exist on
    earth, together with the office of preaching the
    Gospel, Baptism, and the Lord's Supper. These
    are in force as long as the world remains. For if
    He is to be an eternal Priest, He must always have
    a people or a following which recognizes His
    priestly office and exists by virtue of it. He must
    have people who believe in Him, preach Him,
    and confess His name in word and conduct. If He
    did not have such a following any longer, He
    could no longer be called a Priest. Therefore, He
    maintains Christendom on earth until the Last
    Day against all the power and might that opposes,
    and rages against, it. In this Christendom He
    rules as Priest or true pope through the office of
    the ministry and through the power of the Holy
    Spirit, in order even in this life to make new men
    out of us, to communicate to us His eternal and
    divine gifts, that now we may have daily and ev-
    erlasting forgiveness of sins, His power and
    strength, victory over death, devil, and hell, and
    may begin our life of eternal righteousness.

    Luther, *Commentary on Psalm 110*

24 Where God's word is purely taught, there is also
    the upright and true church; for the true church is
    supported by the Holy Ghost, not by succession of
    inheritance.

    Luther, *Table Talk,* H370

25 It is impossible for the Christian and true church
    to subsist without the shedding of blood, for her
    adversary, the devil, is a liar and a murderer. The
    church grows and increases through blood; she is
    sprinkled with blood; she is spoiled and bereaved
    of her blood; when human creatures will reform
    the church, then it costs blood.

    Luther, *Table Talk,* H371

26 The word *Church* is used in the sacred Scriptures
    in two senses. Sometimes, when they mention the
    Church, they intend that which is really such in
    the sight of God, into which none are received but
    those who by adoption and grace are the children
    of God, and by the sanctification of the Spirit are
    the true members of Christ. And then it compre-
    hends not only the saints at any one time resident
    on earth, but all the elect who have lived from the
    beginning of the world. But the word *Church* is
    frequently used in the Scriptures to designate the
    whole multitude, dispersed all over the world,
    who profess to worship one God and Jesus Christ,
    who are initiated into his faith by baptism, who
    testify their unity in true doctrine and charity by
    a participation of the sacred supper, who consent
    to the word of the Lord, and preserve the ministry
    which Christ has instituted for the purpose of
    preaching it. In this Church are included many
    hypocrites, who have nothing of Christ but the
    name and appearance; many persons ambitious,
    avaricious, envious, slanderous, and dissolute in
    their lives, who are tolerated for a time, either
    because they cannot be convicted by a legitimate
    process, or because discipline is not always main-
    tained with sufficient vigour. As it is necessary,
    therefore, to believe that Church, which is invisi-
    ble to us, and known to God alone, so this
    Church, which is visible to men, we are com-
    manded to honour, and to maintain communion
    with it.

    Calvin, *Institutes of the Christian
    Religion,* IV, 1

27 Connected with the preaching of the gospel, an-
    other assistance and support for our faith is pre-
    sented to us in the sacraments; on the subject of
    which it is highly important to lay down some
    certain doctrine, that we may learn for what end
    they were instituted, and how they ought to be
    used. In the first place, it is necessary to consider
    what a sacrament is. Now, I think it will be a
    simple and appropriate definition, if we say that it
    is an outward sign, by which the Lord seals in our
    consciences the promises of his good-will towards
    us, to support the weakness of our faith; and we
    on our part testify our piety towards him, in his
    presence and that of angels, as well as before men.
    It may, however, be more briefly defined, in other
    words, by calling it a testimony of the grace of
    God towards us, confirmed by an outward sign,
    with a reciprocal attestation of our piety towards
    him.

    Calvin, *Institutes of the Christian
    Religion,* IV, 14

28 Methinks, Sir Knight-Errant, said he [Vivaldo] to him, you have taken up one of the strictest and most mortifying Professions in the World. I don't think but that a *Carthusian* Friar has a better Time on't than You have. Perhaps, answer'd Don *Quixote*, the Profession of a *Carthusian* may be as Austere, but I am within two Fingers Breadth of doubting, whether it may be as Beneficial to the World as ours. For, if we must speak the Truth, the Soldier, who put his Captain's Command in Execution, may be said to do as much at least as the Captain who commanded him. The Application is easy: For, while those religious Men have nothing to do, but with all Quietness and Security to say their Prayers for the Prosperity of the World, We Knights, like Soldiers, execute what they do but pray for, and procure those Benefits to Mankind, by the Strength of our Arms, and at the Hazard of our Lives, for which they only interceed. Nor do we do this shelter'd from the Injuries of the Air, but under no other Roof than that of the wide Heavens, expos'd to Summer's scorching Heat, and Winter's pinching Cold. So that we may justly style ourselves the Ministers of Heaven, and the Instruments of its Justice upon Earth; and as the Business of War is not to be compass'd without vast Toil and Labour, so the religious Soldier must undoubtedly be preferr'd before the religious Monk, who living still quiet and at Ease, has nothing to do but to pray for the Afflicted and Distressed. However, Gentlemen, do not imagine I wou'd insinuate as if the Profession of a Knight-Errant was a State of Perfection equal to that of a holy Recluse: I would only infer from what I've said, and what I my self endure, that Ours without question is more laborious, more subject to the Discipline of heavy Blows, to Maceration, to the Penance of Hunger and Thirst, and in a Word, to Rags, to Want and Misery. For if you find that some Knights-Errant have at last by their Valour been rais'd to Thrones and Empires, you may be sure it has been still at the Expence of much Sweat and Blood. And had even those happier Knights been depriv'd of those assisting Sages and Inchanters, who help'd 'em in all Emergencies, they wou'd have been strangely disappointed of their mighty Expectations.

Cervantes, *Don Quixote*, I, 13

29 Perchance he for whom this bell tolls may be so ill as that he knows not it tolls for him; and perchance I may think myself so much better than I am, as that they who are about me and see my state may have caused it to toll for me, and I know not that. The church is catholic, universal, so are all her actions; all that she does belongs to all. When she baptizes a child, that action concerns me; for that child is thereby connected to that body which is my head too, and ingrafted into that body whereof I am a member. And when she buries a man, that action concerns me:

all mankind is of one author and is one volume; when one man dies, one chapter is not torn out of the book, but translated into a better language; and every chapter must be so translated. God employs several translators; some pieces are translated by age, some by sickness, some by war, some by justice; but God's hand is in every translation, and his hand shall bind up all our scattered leaves again for that library where every book shall lie open to one another. As therefore the bell that rings to a sermon calls not upon the preacher only, but upon the congregation to come, so this bell calls us all; but how much more me, who am brought so near the door by this sickness. There was a contention as far as a suit (in which piety and dignity, religion and estimation, were mingled) which of the religious orders should ring to prayers first in the morning; and it was determined that they should ring first that rose earliest. If we understand aright the dignity of this bell that tolls for our evening prayer, we would be glad to make it ours by rising early, in that application, that it might be ours as well as his whose indeed it is. The bell doth toll for him that thinks it doth; and though it intermit again, yet from that minute that that occasion wrought upon him, he is united to God. Who casts not up his eye to the sun when it rises? but who takes off his eye from a comet when that breaks out? Who bends not his ear to any bell which upon any occasion rings? but who can remove it from that bell which is passing a piece of himself out of this world? No man is an island, entire of itself; every man is a piece of the continent, a part of the main. If a clod be washed away by the sea, Europe is the less, as well as if a promontory were, as well as if a manor of thy friend's or of thine own were. Any man's death diminishes me because I am involved in mankind, and therefore never send to know for whom the bell tolls; it tolls for thee.

Donne, *Devotions upon Emergent Occasions*, XVII

30 I define a Church to be: a company of men professing Christian religion, united in the person of one sovereign; at whose command they ought to assemble, and without whose authority they ought not to assemble. And because in all Commonwealths that assembly which is without warrant from the civil sovereign is unlawful; that Church also which is assembled in any Commonwealth that hath forbidden them to assemble is an unlawful assembly.

Hobbes, *Leviathan*, III, 39

31 There is on earth no such universal Church as all Christians are bound to obey, because there is no power on earth to which all other Commonwealths are subject. There are Christians in the dominions of several princes and states, but every one of them is subject to that Commonwealth

whereof he is himself a member, and consequently cannot be subject to the commands of any other person.

Hobbes, *Leviathan,* III, 39

32 The greatest and main abuse of Scripture, and to which almost all the rest are either consequent or subservient, is the wresting of it to prove that the kingdom of God, mentioned so often in the Scripture, is the present Church, or multitude of Christian men now living, or that, being dead, are to rise again at the last day.

Hobbes, *Leviathan,* IV, 44

33 Those who do confine the Church of God, either to particular Nations, Churches or Families, have made it far narrower then our Saviour ever meant it.

Sir Thomas Browne, *Religio Medici,* I, 55

34 If some . . . men, who, by an extraordinary vocation, have made profession of withdrawing from the world and adopting the monks' dress, in order to live in a more perfect state than ordinary Christians, have fallen into excesses which horrify ordinary Christians, and have become to us what the false prophets were among the Jews; this is a private and personal misfortune, which must indeed be deplored, but from which nothing can be inferred against the care which God takes of His Church; since all these things are so clearly foretold, and it has been so long since announced that these temptations would arise from people of this kind; so that when we are well instructed, we see in this rather evidence of the care of God than of His forgetfulness in regard to us.

Pascal, *Pensées,* XIV, 889

35 God regards only the inward; the Church judges only by the outward. God absolves as soon as He sees penitence in the heart; the Church when she sees it in works. God will make a church pure within, which confounds, by its inward and entirely spiritual holiness, the inward impiety of proud sages and Pharisees; and the Church will make an assembly of men whose external manners are so pure as to confound the manners of the heathen. If there are hypocrites among them, but so well disguised that she does not discover their venom, she tolerates them; for, though they are not accepted of God, whom they cannot deceive, they are of men, whom they do deceive. And thus she is not dishonoured by their conduct, which appears holy.

Pascal, *Pensées,* XIV, 905

36 Last came, and last did go,
The Pilot of the *Galilean* lake,
Two massy Keyes he bore of metals twain,
(The Golden opes, the Iron shuts amain)
He shook his Miter'd locks, and stern bespake,

How well could I have spar'd for thee, young swain,
Anow of such as for their bellies sake,
Creep and intrude, and climb into the fold?
Of other care they little reck'ning make,
Then how to scramble at the shearers feast,
And shove away the worthy bidden guest.
Blind mouthes! that scarce themselves know how to hold
A Sheep-hook, or have learn'd ought els the least
That to the faithfull Herdmans art belongs!
What recks it them? What need they? They are sped;
And when they list, their lean and flashy songs
Grate on their scrannel Pipes of wretched straw,
The hungry Sheep look up, and are not fed,
But swoln with wind, and the rank mist they draw,
Rot inwardly, and foul contagion spread:
Besides what the grim Woolf with privy paw
Daily devours apace, and nothing sed,
But that two-handed engine at the door,
Stands ready to smite once, and smite no more.

Milton, *Lycidas,* 108

37 The rites of religion and the outward observances of piety should be in accordance with the public peace and well-being, and should therefore be determined by the sovereign power alone.

Spinoza, *Theologico-Political Treatise,* XIX

38 A church . . . I take to be a voluntary society of men, joining themselves together of their own accord in order to the public worshipping of God in such manner as they judge acceptable to Him, and effectual to the salvation of their souls.

Locke, *Letter Concerning Toleration*

39 No man by nature is bound unto any particular church or sect, but everyone joins himself voluntarily to that society in which he believes he has found that profession and worship which is truly acceptable to God. The hope of salvation, as it was the only cause of his entrance into that communion, so it can be the only reason of his stay there. For if afterwards he discover anything either erroneous in the doctrine or incongruous in the worship of that society to which he has joined himself, why should it not be as free for him to go out as it was to enter? No member of a religious society can be tied with any other bonds but what proceed from the certain expectation of eternal life. A church, then, is a society of members voluntarily uniting to that end.

Locke, *Letter Concerning Toleration*

40 To be of no church is dangerous. Religion, of which the rewards are distant and which is animated only by Faith and Hope, will glide by degrees out of the mind, unless it be invigorated and reimpressed by external ordinances, by stated

calls to worship, and the salutary influence of example.

Johnson, *Life of Milton*

41 It may be laid down as a certain maxim that, all other things being supposed equal, the richer the church, the poorer must necessarily be, either the sovereign on the one hand, or the people on the other; and, in all cases, the less able must the state be to defend itself.

Adam Smith, *Wealth of Nations*, V, 1

42 The acquisition of . . . absolute command over the consciences and understanding of a congregation, however obscure or despised by the world, is more truly grateful to the pride of the human heart than the possession of the most despotic power imposed by arms and conquest on a reluctant people.

Gibbon, *Decline and Fall of the Roman Empire*, XV

43 In one of the marches of Constantine [according to the Christian fable of Eusebius], he is reported to have seen with his own eyes the luminous trophy of the cross, placed above the meridian sun, and inscribed with the following words: *By this conquer.* This amazing object in the sky astonished the whole army, as well as the emperor himself, who was yet undetermined in the choice of a religion: but his astonishment was converted into faith by the vision of the ensuing night. Christ appeared before his eyes; and displaying the same celestial sign of the cross, he directed Constantine to frame a similar standard, and to march, with an assurance of victory, against Maxentius and all his enemies. . . . The Catholic church, both of the East and of the West, has adopted a prodigy which favours, or seems to favour, the popular worship of the cross. The vision of Constantine maintained an honourable place in the legend of superstition till the bold and sagacious spirit of criticism presumed to depreciate the triumph, and to arraign the truth, of the first Christian emperor.

Gibbon, *Decline and Fall of the Roman Empire*, XX

44 A magnificent temple is a laudable monument of national taste and religion, and the enthusiast who entered the dome of St. Sophia might be tempted to suppose that it was the residence, or even the workmanship, of the Deity. Yet how dull is the artifice, how insignificant is the labour, if it be compared with the formation of the vilest insect that crawls upon the surface of the temple!

Gibbon, *Decline and Fall of the Roman Empire*, XL

45 Dear mother, dear mother, the Church is cold,

But the Ale-house is healthy and pleasant and warm.

Blake, *The Little Vagabond*

46 The Church . . . is not merely a *religion* as opposed to another religion, but is at the same time a particular form of secular existence, occupying a place side by side with other secular existence. The religious existence of the Church is governed by Christ; the secular side of its government is left to the free choice of the members themselves.

Hegel, *Philosophy of History*, Pt. III, III, 2

47 If a man will hold fast to this which is indeed Christ's own saying, that the truth is the way, he will perceive ever more clearly that a Church triumphant in this world is a vain conceit, that in this world there can be question only of a Church militant.

Kierkegaard, *Training in Christianity*, III, 5

48 Bluntly put, a chaplain is the minister of the Prince of Peace serving in the host of the God of War—Mars. As such, he is as incongruous as a musket would be on the altar at Christmas. Why, then, is he there? Because he indirectly subserves the purpose attested by the cannon; because too he lends the sanction of the religion of the meek to that which practically is the abrogation of everything but brute force.

Melville, *Billy Budd*

49 The church is a sort of hospital for men's souls, and as full of quackery as the hospital for their bodies.

Thoreau, *The Christian Fable*

50 *Grand Inquisitor.* So long as man remains free he strives for nothing so incessantly and so painfully as to find someone to worship. But man seeks to worship what is established beyond dispute, so that all men would agree at once to worship it. For these pitiful creatures are concerned not only to find what one or the other can worship, but to find something that all would believe in and worship; what is essential is that all may be *together* in it. This craving for *community* of worship is the chief misery of every man individually and of all humanity from the beginning of time. For the sake of common worship they've slain each other with the sword. They have set up gods and challenged one another, "Put away your gods and come and worship ours, or we will kill you and your gods!"

Dostoevsky, *Brothers Karamazov*, Pt. II, V, 5

51 The Christian churches and Christianity have nothing in common save in name: they are utterly hostile opposites. The churches are arrogance, violence, usurpation, rigidity, death; Christianity is humility, penitence, submissiveness, progress, life.

Tolstoy, *The Kingdom of God Is Within You*

52 I *condemn* Christianity, I bring against the Christian Church the most terrible charge any prosecutor has ever uttered. To me it is the extremest thinkable form of corruption, it has had the will to the ultimate corruption conceivably possible. The Christian Church has left nothing untouched by its depravity, it has made of every value a disvalue, of every thuth a lie, of every kind of integrity a vileness of soul. People still dare to talk to me of its 'humanitarian' blessings! To *abolish* any state of distress whatever has been profoundly inexpedient to it: it has lived on states of distress, it has *created* states of distress in order to eternalize *itself.*

Nietzsche, *Antichrist,* LXII

53 We may recall from what we know of the morphology of groups that it is possible to distinguish very different kinds of groups and opposing lines in their development. There are very fleeting groups and extremely lasting ones; homogeneous ones, made up of the same sorts of individuals, and unhomogeneous ones; natural groups, and artificial ones, requiring an external force to keep them together; primitive groups, and highly organized ones with a definite structure. But for reasons which have yet to be explained we should like to lay particular stress upon a distinction to which the authorities have rather given too little attention; I refer to that between leaderless groups and those with leaders. And, in complete opposition to the usual practice, we shall not choose a relatively simple group formation as our point of departure, but shall begin with highly organized, lasting, and artificial groups. The most interesting example of such structures are churches—communities of believers—and armies.

A church and an army are artificial groups, that is, a certain external force is employed to prevent them from disintegrating and to check alterations in their structure. As a rule a person is not consulted, or is given no choice, as to whether he wants to enter such a group; any attempt at leaving it is usually met with persecution or with severe punishment, or has quite definite conditions attached to it. It is quite outside our present interest to enquire why these associations need such special safeguards. We are only attracted by one circumstance, namely that certain facts, which are far more concealed in other cases, can be observed very clearly in those highly organized groups which are protected from dissolution in the manner that has been mentioned.

In a church (and we may with advantage take the Catholic Church as a type) as well as in an army, however different the two may be in other respects, the same illusion holds good of there being a head—in the Catholic Church Christ, in an army its commander-in-chief—who loves all the individuals in the group with an equal love. Everything depends upon this illusion; if it were to be dropped, then both Church and army would dissolve, so far as the external force permitted them to. This equal love was expressly enunciated by Christ: "Inasmuch as ye have done it unto one of the least of these my brethren, ye have done it unto me." He stands to the individual members of the group of believers in the relation of a kind elder brother; he is their father surrogate. All the demands that are made upon the individual are derived from this love of Christ's. A democratic character runs through the Church, for the very reason that before Christ everyone is equal, and that everyone has an equal share in his love. It is not without a deep reason that the similarity between the Christian community and a family is invoked, and that believers call themselves *brothers in Christ,* that is, brothers through the love which Christ has for them.

Freud, *Group Psychology and Analysis of the Ego,* V

54 The broad-backed hippopotamus
Rests on his belly in the mud;
Although he seems so firm to us
He is merely flesh and blood.

Flesh and blood is weak and frail,
Susceptible to nervous shock;
While the True Church can never fail
For it is based upon a rock.

The hippo's feeble steps may err
In compassing material ends,
While the True Church need never stir
To gather in its dividends.

The 'potamus can never reach
The mango on the mango-tree;
But fruits of pomegranate and peach
Refresh the Church from over sea.

At mating time the hippo's voice
Betrays inflexions hoarse and odd,
But every week we hear rejoice
The Church, at being one with God.

The hippopotamus's day
Is passed in sleep; at night he hunts;
God works in a mysterious way—
The Church can sleep and feed at once.

I saw the 'potamus take wing
Ascending from the damp savannas,
And quiring angels round him sing
The praise of God, in loud hosannas.

Blood of the Lamb shall wash him clean
And him shall heavenly arms enfold,
Among the saints he shall be seen
Performing on a harp of gold.

He shall be washed as white as snow,
By all the martyr'd virgins kist,
While the True Church remains below
Wrapt in the old miasmal mist.

T. S. Eliot, *The Hippopotamus*

55 To receive that call, Stephen, said the priest, is the greatest honour that the Almighty God can bestow upon a man. No king or emperor on this earth has the power of the priest of God. No angel or archangel in heaven, no saint, not even the Blessed Virgin herself has the power of a priest of God: the power of the keys, the power to bind and to loose from sin, the power of exorcism, the power to cast out from the creatures of God the evil spirits that have power over them, the power, the authority, to make the great God of Heaven come down upon the altar and take the form of bread and wine. What an awful power, Stephen!

Joyce, *Portrait of the Artist as a Young Man,* IV

20.5 | *God*

In the Western tradition, the idea of God has generated a very voluminous discussion. The quotations included here represent, we hope, a judicious selection from that discussion, but many aspects of it, especially intricate subtleties that delight philosophers and theologians, cannot be adequately covered, and some are not even touched on.

The notion of a single deity, or reference to God in the singular, is not confined to books that reflect the Jewish and Christian faiths. Such references are also to be found in the writings of the Greek and Roman poets and philosophers, side by side with references to the Olympian deities or the gods of the Roman pantheon. In fact, the works of Plato and Aristotle contain passages that have come to be looked upon as anticipations of the doctrines about God's nature and attributes and of the demonstration of God's existence that are more fully developed later in the writings of Christian theologians. The other major source upon which the theologians draw is, of course, the Old and the New Testament, the latter especially for the doctrines of the trinity, of the incarnation, and of the resurrection. For theological exegesis, the most remarkable scriptural passage is, perhaps, the one in Exodus, in which God announces himself to Moses in the words: "I am that I am."

A great many of the quotations drawn from the theologians and philosophers deal with the question of God's existence and with the arguments that are claimed to demonstrate it. One argument in particular, the famous ontological argument first proposed by Anselm, is rejected by theologians and philosophers who think that the existence of God must be proved or at least affirmed on some basis other than the conception we entertain of the supreme being.

The positions of the deist and the pantheist, as well as of the agnostic and the atheist, are represented here along with a variety of versions of orthodox theism. As the reader would expect, the reader will find Augustine, Anselm, Aquinas, Luther, Calvin, Descartes, Hobbes, Leibniz, and Locke aligned, in one way or another, against Spinoza, Hume, Voltaire, Kant, Nietzsche, Bertrand Russell, and Freud. Pascal's contribution to the discussion stands out for its emphasis on the mystery of God and on the reasonableness of seeking God even though reason itself affords no assurance of finding him through arguments or proofs.

Other discussions relevant to our knowledge of God will be found in Section 6.4 on ERROR, IGNORANCE, AND THE LIMITS OF HUMAN KNOWLEDGE, Section 6.5 on OPINION, BELIEF, AND FAITH, and Section 17.1 on PHILOSOPHY AND PHILOSOPHERS.

---

1 Moses said, I will now turn aside, and see this great sight, why the bush is not burnt.

And when the Lord saw that he turned aside to see, God called unto him out of the midst of the bush, and said, Moses, Moses. And he said, Here am I.

And he said, Draw not nigh hither: put off thy shoes from off thy feet, for the place whereon thou standest is holy ground.

Moreover he said, I am the God of thy father, the God of Abraham, the God of Isaac, and the God of Jacob. And Moses hid his face; for he was afraid to look upon God.

Exodus 3:3–6

2 God said unto Moses, *I am that I am:* and he said, Thus shalt thou say unto the children of Israel, *I am* hath sent me unto you.

And God said moreover unto Moses, Thus shalt thou say unto the children of Israel, The Lord God of your fathers, the God of Abraham, the God of Isaac, and the God of Jacob, hath sent me unto you: this is my name for ever, and this is my memorial unto all generations.

Exodus 3:14–15

3 Then sang Moses and the children of Israel this song unto the Lord, and spake, saying, I will sing unto the Lord, for he hath triumphed gloriously: the horse and his rider hath he thrown into the sea.

The Lord is my strength and song, and he is become my salvation: he is my God, and I will prepare him an habitation; my father's God, and I will exalt him.

The Lord is a man of war: the Lord is his name.

Pharaoh's chariots and his host hath he cast into the sea: his chosen captains also are drowned in the Red sea.

The depths have covered them: they sank into the bottom as a stone.

Thy right hand, O Lord, is become glorious in power: thy right hand, O Lord, hath dashed in pieces the enemy.

And in the greatness of thine excellency thou hast overthrown them that rose up against thee: thou sentest forth thy wrath, which consumed them as stubble.

And with the blast of thy nostrils the waters were gathered together, the floods stood upright as an heap, and the depths were congealed in the heart of the sea.

The enemy said, I will pursue, I will overtake, I will divide the spoil; my lust shall be satisfied upon them; I will draw my sword, my hand shall destroy them.

Thou didst blow with thy wind, the sea covered them: they sank as lead in the mighty waters.

Who is like unto thee, O Lord, among the gods? who is like thee, glorious in holiness, fearful in praises, doing wonders?

Exodus 15:1–11

4 Thou canst not see my face: for there shall no man see me, and live.

Exodus 33:20

5 The Lord bless thee, and keep thee:

The Lord make his face shine upon thee, and be gracious unto thee:

The Lord lift up his countenance upon thee, and give thee peace.

Numbers 6:24–26

6 The Lord thy God is a consuming fire, even a jealous God.

Deuteronomy 4:24

7 And he [the angel of the Lord] said, Go forth, and stand upon the mount before the Lord. And, behold, the Lord passed by, and a great and strong wind rent the mountains, and brake in pieces the rocks before the Lord; but the Lord was not in the wind: and after the wind an earthquake; but the Lord was not in the earthquake:

And after the earthquake a fire; but the Lord was not in the fire: and after the fire a still small voice.

I Kings 19:11–12

8 Though he slay me, yet will I trust in him: but I will maintain mine own ways before him.

Job 13:15

9 The heavens declare the glory of God; and the firmament sheweth his handywork.

Day unto day uttereth speech, and night unto night sheweth knowledge.

There is no speech nor language, where their voice is not heard.

Their line is gone out through all the earth, and their words to the end of the world. In them hath he set a tabernacle for the sun,

Which is as a bridegroom coming out of his chamber, and rejoiceth as a strong man to run a race.

His going forth is from the end of the heaven, and his circuit unto the ends of it: and there is nothing hid from the heat thereof.

The law of the Lord is perfect, converting the soul: the testimony of the Lord is sure, making wise the simple.

The statutes of the Lord are right, rejoicing the heart: the commandment of the Lord is pure, enlightening the eyes.

The fear of the Lord is clean, enduring for ever: the judgments of the Lord are true and righteous altogether.

More to be desired are they than gold, yea, than much fine gold: sweeter also than honey and the honeycomb.

Moreover by them is thy servant warned: and in keeping of them there is great reward.

Who can understand his errors? cleanse thou me from secret faults.

Keep back thy servant also from presumptuous sins; let them not have dominion over me: then shall I be upright, and I shall be innocent from the great transgression.

Let the words of my mouth, and the meditation of my heart, be acceptable in thy sight, O Lord, my strength, and my redeemer.

Psalm 19:1–14

10 Hear, O my people, and I will speak; O Israel, and I will testify against thee: I am God, even thy God.

I will not reprove thee for thy sacrifices or thy burnt offerings, to have been continually before me.

I will take no bullock out of thy house, nor he goats out of thy folds.

For every beast of the forest is mine, and the cattle upon a thousand hills.

I know all the fowls of the mountains: and the wild beasts of the field are mine.

If I were hungry, I would not tell thee: for the world is mine, and the fulness thereof.

Psalm 50:7–12

11 The fool hath said in his heart, There is no God.

Psalm 53:1

12 O Lord, thou hast searched me, and known me.

Thou knowest my downsitting and mine uprising, thou understandest my thought afar off.

Thou compassest my path and my lying down, and art acquainted with all my ways.

For there is not a word in my tongue, but, lo, O Lord, thou knowest it altogether.

Thou hast beset me behind and before, and laid thine hand upon me.

Such knowledge is too wonderful for me; it is high, I cannot attain unto it.

Whither shall I go from thy spirit? or whither shall I flee from thy presence?

If I ascend up into heaven, thou art there: if I make my bed in hell, behold, thou art there.

If I take the wings of the morning, and dwell in the uttermost parts of the sea;

Even there shall thy hand lead me, and thy right hand shall hold me.

If I say, Surely the darkness shall cover me; even the night shall be light about me.

Yea, the darkness hideth not from thee; but the night shineth as the day: the darkness and the light are both alike to thee.

Psalm 139:1–12

13 The voice of him that crieth in the wilderness, Prepare ye the way of the Lord, make straight in the desert a highway for our God.

Every valley shall be exalted, and every mountain and hill shall be made low: and the crooked shall be made straight, and the rough places plain:

And the glory of the Lord shall be revealed, and all flesh shall see it together: for the mouth of the Lord hath spoken it.

The voice said, Cry. And he said, What shall I cry? All flesh is grass, and all the goodliness thereof is as the flower of the field:

The grass withereth, the flower fadeth: because the spirit of the Lord bloweth upon it: surely the people is grass.

The grass withereth, the flower fadeth: but the word of our God shall stand for ever.

Isaiah 40:3–8

14 And above the firmament that was over their heads was the likeness of a throne, as the appearance of a sapphire stone: and upon the likeness of the throne was the likeness as the appearance of a man above upon it.

And I saw as the colour of amber, as the appearance of fire round about within it, from the appearance of his loins even upward, and from the appearance of his loins even downward, I saw as it were the appearance of fire, and it had brightness round about.

As the appearance of the bow that is in the cloud in the day of rain, so was the appearance of the brightness round about. This was the appearance of the likeness of the glory of the Lord.

Ezekiel 1:26–28

15 *Diotima.* God mingles not with man; but through Love all the intercourse and converse of god with man, whether awake or asleep, is carried on.

Plato, *Symposium,* 203A

16 *Socrates.* God [is] perfectly simple and true both in word and deed; he changes not; he deceives not, either by sign or word, by dream or waking vision.

Plato, *Republic,* II, 382B

17 There is . . . something which is always moved

with an unceasing motion, which is motion in a circle; and this is plain not in theory only but in fact. Therefore the first heaven must be eternal. There is therefore also something which moves it. And since that which moves and is moved is intermediate, there is something which moves without being moved, being eternal, substance, and actuality. And the object of desire and the object of thought move in this way; they move without being moved. The primary objects of desire and of thought are the same. For the apparent good is the object of appetite, and the real good is the primary object of rational wish. But desire is consequent on opinion rather than opinion on desire; for the thinking is the starting-point. And thought is moved by the object of thought, and one of the two columns of opposites is in itself the object of thought; and in this, substance is first, and in substance, that which is simple and exists actually. (The one and the simple are not the same; for 'one' means a measure, but 'simple' means that the thing itself has a certain nature.) But the beautiful, also, and that which is in itself desirable are in the same column; and the first in any class is always best, or analogous to the best.

That a final cause may exist among unchangeable entities is shown by the distinction of its meanings. For the final cause is (*a*) some being for whose good an action is done, and (*b*) something at which the action aims; and of these the latter exists among unchangeable entities though the former does not. The final cause, then, produces motion as being loved, but all other things move by being moved. Now if something is moved it is capable of being otherwise than as it is. Therefore if its actuality is the primary form of spatial motion, then in so far as it is subject to change, in *this* respect it is capable of being otherwise,—in place, even if not in substance. But since there is something which moves while itself unmoved, existing actually, this can in no way be otherwise than as it is. For motion in space is the first of the kinds of change, and motion in a circle the first kind of spatial motion; and this the first mover *produces.* The first mover, then, exists of necessity; and in so far as it exists by necessity, its mode of being is good, and it is in this sense a first principle. For the necessary has all these senses—that which is necessary perforce because it is contrary to the natural impulse, that without which the good is impossible, and that which cannot be otherwise but can exist only in a single way.

On such a principle, then, depend the heavens and the world of nature. And it is a life such as the best which we enjoy, and enjoy for but a short time (for it is ever in this state, which we cannot be), since its actuality is also pleasure. (And for this reason are waking, perception, and thinking most pleasant, and hopes and memories are so on account of these.) And thinking in itself deals with that which is best in itself, and that which is

thinking in the fullest sense with that which is best in the fullest sense. And thought thinks on itself because it shares the nature of the object of thought; for it becomes an object of thought in coming into contact with and thinking its objects, so that thought and object of thought are the same. For that which is *capable* of receiving the object of thought, i.e. the essence, is thought. But it is *active* when it *possesses* this object. Therefore the possession rather than the receptivity is the divine element which thought seems to contain, and the act of contemplation is what is most pleasant and best. If, then, God is always in that good state in which we sometimes are, this compels our wonder; and if in a better this compels it yet more. And God *is* in a better state. And life also belongs to God; for the actuality of thought is life, and God is that actuality; and God's self-dependent actuality is life most good and eternal. We say therefore that God is a living being, eternal, most good, so that life and duration continuous and eternal belong to God; for this *is* God.

Aristotle, *Metaphysics*, 1072ª20

18 The nature of the divine thought involves certain problems; for while thought is held to be the most divine of things observed by us, the question how it must be situated in order to have that character involves difficulties. For if it thinks of nothing, what is there here of dignity? It is just like one who sleeps. And if it thinks, but this depends on something else, then (since that which is its substance is not the act of thinking, but a potency) it cannot be the best substance; for it is through thinking that its value belongs to it. Further, whether its substance is the faculty of thought or the act of thinking, what does it think of? Either of itself or of something else; and if of something else, either of the same thing always or of something different. Does it matter, then, or not, whether it thinks of the good or of any chance thing? Are there not some things about which it is incredible that it should think? Evidently, then, it thinks of that which is most divine and precious, and it does not change; for change would be change for the worse, and this would be already a movement. First, then, if 'thought' is not the act of thinking but a potency, it would be reasonable to suppose that the continuity of its thinking is wearisome to it. Secondly, there would evidently be something else more precious than thought, viz. that which is thought of. For both thinking and the act of thought will belong even to one who thinks of the worst thing in the world, so that if this ought to be avoided (and it ought, for there are even some things which it is better not to see than to see), the act of thinking cannot be the best of things. Therefore it must be of itself that the divine thought thinks (since it is the most excellent of things), and its thinking is a thinking on thinking.

But evidently knowledge and perception and opinion and understanding have always something else as their object, and themselves only by the way. Further, if thinking and being thought of are different, in respect of which does goodness belong to thought? For to *be* an act of thinking and to *be* an object of thought are not the same thing. We answer that in some cases the knowledge is the object. In the productive sciences it is the substance or essence of the object, matter omitted, and in the theoretical sciences the definition or the act of thinking is the object. Since, then, thought and the object of thought are not different in the case of things that have not matter, the divine thought and its object will be the same, i.e. the thinking will be one with the object of its thought.

A further question is left—whether the object of the divine thought is composite; for if it were, thought would change in passing from part to part of the whole. We answer that everything which has not matter is indivisible—as human thought, or rather the thought of composite beings, is in a certain period of time (for it does not possess the good at this moment or at that, but its best, being something *different* from it, is attained only in a whole period of time), so throughout eternity is the thought which has *itself* for its object.

Aristotle, *Metaphysics,* 1074ᵇ15

19 The activity of God, which surpasses all others in blessedness, must be contemplative; and of human activities, therefore, that which is most akin to this must be most of the nature of happiness.

Aristotle, *Ethics,* 1178ᵇ22

20 *Velleius.* God is completely inactive and unfettered by the need for occupation. He neither toils nor labors, but delights in his own wisdom and virtue. He knows for certain that he will always enjoy perfect and eternal pleasures. This is the God whom we can properly call happy. . . .

But if the world itself is considered to be God, what could be less restful than to revolve at incredible speed around an axis, without a single moment of respite? Repose is a necessary condition for happiness. But on the other hand, if some god dwells in the world as its ruler and pilot, maintaining the course of the stars, the changes of season, and all the processes of creation, watching over all the interests of man on land and sea, what a bondage to tiresome and laborious business that would be.

Cicero, *De Natura Deorum,* I, 19

21 Nature is nothing else but God and the divine Reason that pervades the whole universe. You may, if you wish, address this creator of the world by different names, such as Jupiter Best and Greatest, the Thunderer, or the Stayer. This last title does not derive from the tale told by historians about the Roman battle-line being stayed from flight in answer to prayers. It simply means that all things are upheld by his benefits. Thus he is called Stayer and Stabilizer. You may also call him Fate; that would be no mistake. For since Fate is only a connected chain of causes, he is the first of the causes on which all succeeding ones depend. Any name that you choose to apply to him will be appropriate if it connotes a power that operates in heaven. His titles are as countless as his benefits.

Seneca, *On Benefits,* IV, 7

22 In the beginning was the Word, and the Word was with God, and the Word was God.

The same was in the beginning with God.

All things were made by him; and without him was not any thing made that was made.

In him was life; and the life was the light of men.

And the light shineth in darkness; and the darkness comprehended it not.

There was a man sent from God, whose name was John.

The same came for a witness, to bear witness of the Light, that all men through him might believe.

He was not that Light, but was sent to bear witness of that Light.

That was the true Light, which lighteth every man that cometh into the world.

He was in the world, and the world was made by him, and the world knew him not.

He came unto his own, and his own received him not.

But as many as received him, to them gave he power to become the sons of God, even to them that believe on his name.

John 1:1–12

23 God is a Spirit: and they that worship him must worship him in spirit and in truth.

John 4:24

24 It is a fearful thing to fall into the hands of the living God.

Hebrews 10:31

25 God is light, and in him is no darkness at all.

I John 1:5

26 Beloved, let us love one another: for love is of God; and every one that loveth is born of God, and knoweth God.

He that loveth not knoweth not God; for God is love.

I John 4:7–8

27 I am Alpha and Omega, the beginning and the ending, saith the Lord, which is, and which was,

and which is to come, the Almighty.

Revelation 1:8

28 God governs the world, not by irresistible force, but persuasive argument and reason, controlling it into compliance with his eternal purposes.

Plutarch, *Phocion*

29 We ought first to learn that there is a God and that he provides for all things; also that it is not possible to conceal from him our acts, or even our intentions and thoughts. The next thing is to learn what is the nature of the Gods; for such as they are discovered to be, he, who would please and obey them, must try with all his power to be like them. If the divine is faithful, man also must be faithful; if it is free, man also must be free; if beneficent, man also must be beneficent; if magnanimous, man also must be magnanimous; as being then an imitator of God, he must do and say everything consistently with this fact.

Epictetus, *Discourses,* II, 14

30 Seeking nothing, possessing nothing, lacking nothing, the One is perfect and, in our metaphor, has overflowed, and its exuberance has produced the new.

Plotinus, *Fifth Ennead,* II, 1

31 What . . . is my God, what but the Lord God? *For Who is Lord but the Lord, or Who is God but our God?* O Thou, the greatest and the best, mightiest, almighty, most merciful and most just, utterly hidden and utterly present, most beautiful and most strong, abiding yet mysterious, suffering no change and changing all things: never new, never old, making all things new, *bringing age upon the proud and they know it not;* ever in action, ever at rest, gathering all things to Thee and needing none; sustaining and fulfilling and protecting, creating and nourishing and making perfect; ever seeking though lacking nothing. Thou lovest without subjection to passion, Thou are jealous but not with fear; Thou canst know repentance but not sorrow, be angry yet unperturbed by anger. Thou canst change the works Thou hast made but Thy mind stands changeless. Thou dost find and receive back what Thou didst never lose; art never in need but dost rejoice in Thy gains, art not greedy but dost exact interest manifold. Men pay Thee more than is of obligation to win return from Thee, yet who has anything that is not already Thine? Thou owest nothing yet dost pay as if in debt to Thy creature, forgivest what is owed to Thee yet dost not lose thereby. And with all this, what have I said, my God and my Life and my sacred Delight? What can anyone say when he speaks of Thee? Yet woe to them that speak not of Thee at all, since those who say most are but dumb.

Augustine, *Confessions,* I, 4

32 Heaven and earth and all that is in them tell me wherever I look that I should love You, and they cease not to tell it to all men, so that there is no excuse for them. For *You will have mercy on whom You will have mercy, and You will show mercy to whom You will show mercy:* otherwise heaven and earth cry their praise of You to deaf ears.

But what is it that I love when I love You? Not the beauty of any bodily thing, nor the order of seasons, not the brightness of light that rejoices the eye, nor the sweet melodies of all songs, nor the sweet fragrance of flowers and ointments and spices: not manna nor honey, not the limbs that carnal love embraces. None of these things do I love in loving my God. Yet in a sense I do love light and melody and fragrance and food and embrace when I love my God—the light and the voice and the fragrance and the food and embrace in the soul, when that light shines upon my soul which no place can contain, that voice sounds which no time can take from me, I breathe that fragrance which no wind scatters, I eat the food which is not lessened by eating, and I lie in the embrace which satiety never comes to sunder. This it is that I love, when I love my God.

Augustine, *Confessions,* X, 6

33 What is . . . God? I asked the earth and it answered: "I am not He"; and all things that are in the earth made the same confession. I asked the sea and the deeps and the creeping things, and they answered: "We are not your God; seek higher." I asked the winds that blow, and the whole air with all that is in it answered: "Anaximenes was wrong; I am not God." I asked the heavens, the sun, the moon, the stars, and they answered: "Neither are we God whom you seek." And I said to all the things that throng about the gateways of the senses: "Tell me of my God, since you are not He. Tell me something of Him." And they cried out in a great voice: "He made us." My question was my gazing upon them, and their answer was their beauty. And I turned to myself and said: "And you, who are you?" And I answered: "A man." Now clearly there is a body and a soul in me, one exterior, one interior. From which of these two should I have enquired of my God? I had already sought Him by my body, from earth to heaven, as far as my eye could send its beams on the quest. But the interior part is the better, seeing that all my body's messengers delivered to it, as ruler and judge, the answers that heaven and earth and all things in them made when they said: "We are not God," and, "He made us." The inner man knows these things through the ministry of the outer man: I the inner man knew them, I, I the soul, through the senses of the body. I asked the whole frame of the universe about my God and it answered me: "I am not He, but He made me."

Augustine, *Confessions,* X, 6

34 We worship that God Who has appointed to the natures created by Him both the beginnings and the end of their existing and moving: Who holds, knows, and disposes the causes of things; Who hath created the virtue of seeds; Who hath given to what creatures He would a rational soul, which is called mind; Who hath bestowed the faculty and use of speech; Who hath imparted the gift of foretelling future things to whatever spirits it seemed to Him good; Who also Himself predicts future things through whom He pleases, and through whom He will remove diseases; Who, when the human race is to be corrected and chastised by wars, regulates also the beginnings, progress, and ends of these wars; Who hath created and governs the most vehement and most violent fire of this world, in due relation and proportion to the other elements of immense nature; Who is the governor of all the waters; Who hath made the sun brightest of all material lights, and hath given him suitable power and motion; Who hath not withdrawn, even from the inhabitants of the nether world, His dominion and power; Who hath appointed to mortal natures their suitable seed and nourishment, dry or liquid; Who establishes and makes fruitful the earth; Who bountifully bestows its fruits on animals and on men; Who knows and ordains, not only principal causes, but also subsequent causes; Who hath determined for the moon her motion; Who affords ways in heaven and on earth for passage from one place to another; Who hath granted also to human minds, which He hath created, the knowledge of the various arts for the help of life and nature; Who hath appointed the union of male and female for the propagation of offspring; Who hath favoured the societies of men with the gift of terrestrial fire for the simplest and most familiar purposes, to burn on the hearth and to give light. These are, then, the things which that most acute and most learned man Varro has laboured to distribute among the select gods, by I know not what physical interpretation, which he has got from other sources and also conjectured for himself. But these things the one true God makes and does, but as *the same* God—that is, as He who is wholly everywhere, included in no space, bound by no chains, mutable in no part of His being, filling heaven and earth with omnipresent power, not with a needy nature. Therefore He governs all things in such a manner as to allow them to perform and exercise their own proper movements. For although they can be nothing without Him, they are not what He is. He does also many things through angels; but only from Himself does He beatify angels. So also, though He send angels to men for certain purposes, He does not for all that beatify men by the good inherent in the angels, but by Himself, as He does the angels themselves.

Augustine, *City of God,* VII, 30

35 God is ever the constant foreknowing overseer, and the everpresent eternity of His sight moves in harmony with the future nature of our actions, as it dispenses rewards to the good, and punishments to the bad. Hopes are not vainly put in God, nor prayers in vain offered: if these are right, they cannot but be answered. Turn therefore from vice: ensue virtue: raise your soul to upright hopes: send up on high your prayers from this earth. If you would be honest, great is the necessity enjoined upon your goodness, since all you do is done before the eyes of an all-seeing Judge.

Boethius, *Consolation of Philosophy,* V

36 Lord, do thou, who dost give understanding to faith, give me, so far as thou knowest it to be profitable, to understand that thou art as we believe; and that thou art that which we believe. And, indeed, we believe that thou art a being than which nothing greater can be conceived. Or is there no such nature, since the fool hath said in his heart, there is no God? But, at any rate, this very fool, when he hears of this being of which I speak—a being than which nothing greater can be conceived—understands what he hears, and what he understands is in his understanding; although he does not understand it to exist.

For, it is one thing for an object to be in the understanding, and another to understand that the object exists. When a painter first conceives of what he will afterwards perform, he has it in his understanding, but he does not yet understand it to be, because he has not yet performed it. But after he has made the painting, he both has it in his understanding, and he understands that it exists, because he has made it.

Hence, even the fool is convinced that something exists in the understanding, at least, than which nothing greater can be conceived. For, when he hears of this, he understands it. And whatever is understood, exists in the understanding. And assuredly that, than which nothing greater can be conceived, cannot exist in the understanding alone. For, suppose it exists in the understanding alone: then it can be conceived to exist in reality; which is greater.

Therefore, if that, than which nothing greater can be conceived, exists in the understanding alone, the very being, than which nothing greater can be conceived, is one, than which a greater can be conceived. But obviously this is impossible. Hence, there is no doubt that there exists a being, than which nothing greater can be conceived, and it exists both in the understanding and in reality.

And it assuredly exists so truly, that it cannot be conceived not to exist. For, it is possible to conceive of a being which cannot be conceived not to exist; and this is greater than one which can be conceived not to exist. Hence, if that, than which nothing greater can be conceived, can be conceived not to exist, it is not that, than which nothing greater can be conceived. But this is an irreconcilable contradiction. There is, then, so truly a being than which nothing greater can be conceived to exist, that it cannot even be conceived not to exist; and this being thou art, O Lord, our God.

So truly, therefore, dost thou exist, O Lord, my God, that thou canst not be conceived not to exist; and rightly. For, if a mind could conceive of a being better than thee, the creature would rise above the Creator; and this is most absurd. And, indeed, whatever else there is, except thee alone, can be conceived not to exist. To thee alone, therefore, it belongs to exist more truly than all other beings, and hence in a higher degree than all others. For, whatever else exists does not exist so truly, and hence in a less degree it belongs to it to exist. Why, then, has the fool said in his heart, there is no God, since it is so evident, to a rational mind, that thou dost exist in the highest degree of all? Why, except that he is dull and a fool?

Anselm of Canterbury, *Proslogium,* II–III

37 But how art thou omnipotent, if thou art not capable of all things? Or, if thou canst not be corrupted, and canst not lie, nor make what is true, false—as, for example, if thou shouldst make what has been done not to have been done, and the like—how art thou capable of all things? Or else to be capable of these things is not power, but impotence. For, he who is capable of these things is capable of what is not for his good, and of what he ought not to do; and the more capable of them he is, the more power have adversity and perversity against him; and the less has he himself against these.

Anselm of Canterbury, *Proslogium,* VII

38 O Lord, our God, the more truly art thou omnipotent, since thou art capable of nothing through impotence, and nothing has power against thee.

Anselm of Canterbury, *Proslogium,* VII

39 Truly, O Lord, this is the unapproachable light in which thou dwellest; for truly there is nothing else which can penetrate this light, that it may see thee there. Truly, I see it not, because it is too bright for me. And yet, whatsoever I see, I see through it, as the weak eye sees what it sees through the light of the sun, which in the sun itself it cannot look upon. My understanding cannot reach that light, for it shines too bright. It does not comprehend it, nor does the eye of my soul endure to gaze upon it long. It is dazzled by the brightness, it is overcome by the greatness, it is overwhelmed by the infinity, it is dazed by the largeness, of the light.

O supreme and unapproachable light! O whole and blessed truth, how far art thou from me, who am so near to thee! How far removed art thou from my vision, though I am so near to thine! Everywhere thou art wholly present, and I see thee not. In thee I move, and in thee I have my being; and I cannot come to thee. Thou art within me, and about me, and I feel thee not.

Anselm of Canterbury, *Proslogium,* XVI

40 Assuredly thou art life, thou art wisdom, thou art truth, thou art goodness, thou art blessedness, thou art eternity, and thou art every true good. Many are these attributes: my straitened understanding cannot see so many at one view, that it may be gladdened by all at once. How, then, O Lord, art thou all these things? Are they parts of thee, or is each one of these rather the whole, which thou art? For, whatever is composed of parts is not altogether one, but is in some sort plural, and diverse from itself; and either in fact or in concept is capable of dissolution.

But these things are alien to thee, than whom nothing better can be conceived of. Hence, there are no parts in thee, Lord, nor art thou more than one. But thou art so truly a unitary being, and so identical with thyself, that in no respect art thou unlike thyself; rather thou art unity itself, indivisible by any conception. Therefore, life and wisdom and the rest are not parts of thee, but all are one; and each of these is the whole, which thou art, and which all the rest are.

In this way, then, it appears that thou hast no parts, and that thy eternity, which thou art, is nowhere and never a part of thee or of thy eternity. But everywhere thou art as a whole, and thy eternity exists as a whole forever.

Anselm of Canterbury, *Proslogium,* XVIII

41 To know that God exists in a general and confused way is implanted in us by nature, since God is man's Happiness. For man naturally desires happiness, and what is naturally desired by man must be naturally known to him. This, however, is not to know absolutely that God exists.

Aquinas, *Summa Theologica,* I, 2, 1

42 Perhaps not everyone who hears this word "God" understands it to signify something than which nothing greater can be thought, seeing that some have believed God to be a body. Yet, granted that everyone understands that by this word "God" is signified something than which nothing greater can be thought, nevertheless, it does not therefore follow that he understands that what the word signifies exists actually, but only that it exists in the intellect. Nor can it be argued that it actually exists, unless it be admitted that there actually exists something than which nothing greater can be thought. And this is what is not admitted by those who hold that God does not exist.

Aquinas, *Summa Theologica,* I, 2, 1

43 The existence of God and other like truths about God which can be known by natural reason, are not articles of faith, but are preambles to the articles. For faith presupposes natural knowledge, even as grace presupposes nature, and perfection supposes something that can be perfected. Nevertheless, there is nothing to prevent a man who cannot grasp a proof accepting, as a matter of faith, something which in itself is capable of being known and demonstrated.

Aquinas, *Summa Theologica*, I, 2, 2

44 In the world of sense we find there is an order of efficient causes. There is no case known (nor indeed, is it possible) in which a thing is found to be the efficient cause of itself, because in that case it would be prior to itself, which is impossible. Now in efficient causes it is not possible to go on to infinity, because in all efficient causes following in order, the first is the cause of the intermediate cause, and the intermediate is the cause of the ultimate cause, whether the intermediate cause be several, or one only. Now to take away the cause is to take away the effect. Therefore, if there be no first cause among efficient causes, there will be no ultimate, nor any intermediate cause. But if in efficient causes it is possible to go on to infinity, there will be no first efficient cause, neither will there be an ultimate effect, nor any intermediate efficient causes, all of which is plainly false. Therefore it is necessary to admit a first efficient cause, to which everyone gives the name of God. . . .

We find in nature things that are possible to be and not to be, since they are found to be generated, and to be corrupted, and consequently they are possible to be and not to be. But it is impossible for these always to exist, for that which is possible not to be at some time is not. Therefore, if everything is possible not to be, then at one time there could have been nothing in existence. Now if this were true, even now there would be nothing in existence, because that which does not exist only begins to exist by something already existing. Therefore, if at one time nothing was in existence, it would have been impossible for anything to have begun to exist; and thus even now nothing would be in existence—which is clearly false. Therefore, not all beings are merely possible, but there must exist something the existence of which is necessary. But every necessary thing either has its necessity caused by another, or not. Now it is impossible to go on to infinity in necessary things which have their necessity caused by another, as has been already proved in regard to efficient causes. Therefore we must admit the existence of some being having of itself its own necessity, and not receiving it from another, but rather causing in others their necessity. This all men speak of as God.

Aquinas, *Summa Theologica*, I, 2, 3

45 In some way God is in every place, and this is to be everywhere. First, as He is in all things as giving them being, power, and operation, so He is in every place as giving it being and power to be in a place. Again, things placed are in place in so far as they fill a place: and God fills every place; not, indeed, as a body, for a body is said to fill place in so far as it excludes the presence of another body; but by God being in a place, others are not thereby excluded from it; rather indeed, He Himself fills every place by the very fact that He gives being to the things that fill every place.

Aquinas, *Summa Theologica*, I, 8, 2

46 Eternity is nothing else but God Himself. Hence God is not called eternal as if He were in any way measured, but the notion of measurement is there taken according to the apprehension of our mind alone.

Aquinas, *Summa Theologica*, I, 10, 2

47 God comprehends in Himself the whole perfection of being. If then many gods existed, they would necessarily differ from each other. Something therefore would belong to one which did not belong to another. And if this were a privation, one of them would not be absolutely perfect; but if a perfection, one of them would be without it. So it is impossible for many gods to exist. Hence also the ancient philosophers, constrained as it were by truth itself, when they asserted an infinite principle asserted likewise that there was only one such principle.

Aquinas, *Summa Theologica*, I, 11, 3

48 Oh grace abounding, wherein I presumed to fix
  my look on the eternal light so long that I consumed my sight thereon!
Within its depths I saw ingathered, bound by love
  in one volume, the scattered leaves of all the universe;
substance and accidents and their relations, as
  though together fused, after such fashion that
  what I tell of is one simple flame.
The universal form of this complex I think that I
  beheld, because more largely, as I say this, I feel
  that I rejoice.
A single moment maketh a deeper lethargy for me
  than twenty and five centuries have wrought on
  the emprise that erst threw Neptune in amaze
  at Argo's shadow.
Thus all suspended did my mind gaze fixed, immovable, intent, ever enkindled by its gazing.
Such at that light doth man become that to turn
  thence to any other sight could not by possibility be ever yielded.
For the good, which is the object of the will, is
  therein wholly gathered, and outside it that
  same thing is defective which therein is perfect.
Now shall my speech fall farther short even of
  what I can remember than an infant's who still
  bathes his tongue at breast.

Not that more than a single semblance was in the
   living light whereon I looked, which ever is
   such as it was before;
but by the sight that gathered strength in me one
   sole appearance even as I changed worked on
   my gaze.
In the profound and shining being of the deep
   light appeared to me three circles, of three colours and one magnitude;
one by the second as Iris by Iris seemed reflected,
   and the third seemed a fire breathed equally
   from one and from the other.
Oh but how scant the utterance, and how faint, to
   my conceit! and it, to what I saw, is such that it
   sufficeth not to call it little.
O Light eternal who only in thyself abidest, only
   thyself dost understand, and to thyself, self-un-
   derstood self-understanding, turnest love and
   smiling!
That circling which appeared in thee to be conceived as a reflected light, by mine eyes scanned
   some little,
in itself, of its own colour, seemed to be painted
   with our effigy, and thereat my sight was all
   committed to it.
As the geometer who all sets himself to measure
   the circle and who findeth not, think as he may,
   the principle he lacketh;
such was I at this new seen spectacle; I would
   perceive how the image consorteth with the circle, and how it settleth there;
but not for this were my proper wings, save that
   my mind was smitten by a flash wherein its will
   came to it.
To the high fantasy here power failed; but already my desire and will were rolled—even as a
   wheel that moveth equally—by the Love that
   moves the sun and the other stars.

               Dante, *Paradiso*, XXXIII, 82

49 I can't understand what must be in a man's mind
if he doesn't feel seriously that there is a God
when he sees the sun rise. It must at times occur to
him that there are eternal things, or else he must
push his face into the dirt like a sow. For it's incredible that they [the planets] be observed to
move without inquiring whether there isn't somebody who moves them.

               Luther, *Table Talk*, 447

50 Though our mind cannot conceive of God, without ascribing some worship to him, it will not be
sufficient merely to apprehend that he is the only
proper object of universal worship and adoration,
unless we are also persuaded that he is the fountain of all good, and seek for none but in him.
This I maintain, not only because he sustains the
universe, as he once made it, by his infinite power,
governs it by his wisdom, preserves it by his goodness, and especially reigns over the human race in
righteousness and judgment, exercising a merciful

forbearance, and defending them by his protection; but because there cannot be found the least
particle of wisdom, light, righteousness, power,
rectitude, or sincere truth which does not proceed
from him, and claim him for its author.

      Calvin, *Institutes of the Christian Religion*, I, 2

51 To represent God as a Creator only for a moment,
who entirely finished all his work at once, were
frigid and jejune; and in this it behoves us especially to differ from the heathen, that the presence
of the Divine power may appear to us no less in
the perpetual state of the world than in its first
origin.

     Calvin, *Institutes of the Christian Religion*, I, 16

52 God, wishing to teach us that the good have something else to hope for, and the wicked something
else to fear, than the fortunes and misfortunes of
this world, handles and allots these according to
his occult disposition, and deprives us of the
means of foolishly making our profit of them.

          Montaigne, *Essays*, I, 32, We
               Should Meddle Soberly

53 What is there . . . more vain than to try to divine
God by our analogies and conjectures, to regulate
him and the world by our capacity and our laws,
and to use at the expense of the Deity this little
shred of ability that he was pleased to allot to our
natural condition? And, because we cannot
stretch our vision as far as his glorious throne, to
have brought him here below to our corruption
and our miseries?

         Montaigne, *Essays*, II, 12, Apology
              for Raymond Sebond

54 It has always seemed to me that for a Christian
this sort of talk is full of indiscretion and irreverence: "God cannot die, God cannot go back on his
word, God cannot do this or that." I do not think
it is good to confine the divine power thus under
the laws of our speech. And the probability that
appears to us in these propositions should be expressed more reverently and religiously.

         Montaigne, *Essays*, II, 12, Apology
              for Raymond Sebond

55 When we say that the infinity of the centuries
both past and to come is to God but an instant,
that his goodness, wisdom, power, are the same
thing as his essence—our tongues say it, but our
intelligence does not apprehend it.

         Montaigne, *Essays*, II, 12, Apology
              for Raymond Sebond

56 He Who is before the ages and on into the ages
thus adorned the great things of His wisdom:
nothing excessive, nothing defective, no room for
any censure. How lovely are his works! All things,
in twos, one against one, none lacking its opposite.

He has strengthened the goods—adornment and propriety—of each and every one and established them in the best reasons, and who will be satiated seeing their glory?

Kepler, *Harmonies of the World*, V, 9

57 *Dogberry.* Well, God's a good man.

Shakespeare, *Much Ado About Nothing*, III, v, 39

58 Natural theology . . . is that knowledge or rudiment of knowledge concerning God, which may be obtained by the contemplation of his creatures; which knowledge may be truly termed divine in respect of the object, and natural in respect of the light. The bounds of this knowledge are, that it sufficeth to convince atheism, but not to inform religion: and therefore there was never miracle wrought by God to convert an atheist, because the light of nature might have led him to confess a God: but miracles have been wrought to convert idolaters and the superstitious, because no light of nature extendeth to declare the will and true worship of God. For as all works do show forth the power and skill of the workman, and not his image, so it is of the works of God, which do show the omnipotency and wisdom of the maker, but not his image.

Bacon, *Advancement of Learning*, Bk. II, VI, 1

59 It is at least as certain that God, who is a Being so perfect, is, or exists, as any demonstration of geometry can possibly be.

Descartes, *Discourse on Method*, IV

60 That idea . . . by which I understand a Supreme God, eternal, infinite, [immutable], omniscient, omnipotent, and Creator of all things which are outside of Himself, has certainly more objective reality in itself than those ideas by which finite substances are represented.

Descartes, *Meditations on First Philosophy*, III

61 From the fact that I cannot conceive a mountain without a valley, it does not follow that there is any mountain or any valley in existence, but only that the mountain and the valley, whether they exist or do not exist, cannot in any way be separated one from the other. While from the fact that I cannot conceive God without existence, it follows that existence is inseparable from Him, and hence that He really exists; not that my thought can bring this to pass, or impose any necessity on things, but, on the contrary, because the necessity which lies in the thing itself, i.e. the necessity of the existence of God determines me to think in this way. For it is not within my power to think of God without existence (that is of a supremely perfect Being devoid of a supreme perfection) though it is in my power to imagine a horse either with

wings or without wings.

Descartes, *Meditations on First Philosophy*, V

62 We have in the notion of God absolute immensity, simplicity, and a unity that embraces all other attributes; and of this idea we find no example in us.

Descartes, *Objections and Replies*, II

63 When God is said to be *unthinkable,* that applies to the thought that grasps him adequately, and does not hold good of that inadequate thought which we possess and which suffices to let us know that he exists.

Descartes, *Objections and Replies*, II

64 Some one must exist in whom are formally or eminently all the perfections of which we have any idea. But we possess the idea of a power so great that by Him and Him alone, in whom this power is found, must heaven and earth be created, and a power such that likewise whatever else is apprehended by me as possible must be created by Him too. Hence concurrently with God's existence we have proved all this likewise about him.

Descartes, *Arguments Demonstrating the Existence of God and the Distinction Between Soul and Body*, Prop. 3, Corol.

65 When you say how strange it is that other men do not think about God in the same way as I do, when He has impressed the idea of Himself on them exactly as on me, it is precisely as if you were to marvel that since all are acquainted with the idea of a triangle, they do not all perceive an equal number of truths about it, and some probably reason about this very figure incorrectly.

Descartes, *Objections and Replies*, V

66 Perpetual fear, always accompanying mankind in the ignorance of causes, as it were in the dark, must needs have for object something. And therefore when there is nothing to be seen, there is nothing to accuse either of their good or evil fortune but some power or agent invisible: in which sense perhaps it was that some of the old poets said that the gods were at first created by human fear: which, spoken of the gods (that is to say, of the many gods of the Gentiles), is very true. But the acknowledging of one God eternal, infinite, and omnipotent may more easily be derived from the desire men have to know the causes of natural bodies, and their several virtues and operations, than from the fear of what was to befall them in time to come. For he that, from any effect he seeth come to pass, should reason to the next and immediate cause thereof, and from thence to the cause of that cause, and plunge himself profoundly in the pursuit of causes, shall at last come to this, that there must be (as even the heathen philosophers confessed) one First Mover; that is, a first and an eternal cause of all things; which is that

which men mean by the name of *God:* and all this without thought of their fortune, the solicitude whereof both inclines to fear and hinders them from the search of the causes of other things; and thereby gives occasion of feigning of as many gods as there be men that feign them.

Hobbes, *Leviathan*, I, 12

67 That we may know what worship of God is taught us by the light of nature, I will begin with His attributes. Where, first, it is manifest, we ought to attribute to Him *existence:* for no man can have the will to honour that which he thinks not to have any being.

Secondly, that those philosophers who said the world, or the soul of the world, was God spake unworthily of Him, and denied His existence: for by *God* is understood the cause of the world; and to say the world is God is to say there is no cause of it, that is, no God.

Thirdly, to say the world was not created, but eternal, seeing that which is eternal has no cause, is to deny there is a God.

Fourthly, that they who, attributing, as they think, ease to God, take from Him the care of mankind, take from Him his honour: for it takes away men's love and fear of Him, which is the root of honour.

Fifthly, in those things that signify greatness and power, to say He is *finite* is not to honour Him: for it is not a sign of the will to honour God to attribute to Him less than we can; and finite is less than we can, because to finite it is easy to add more.

Therefore to attribute *figure* to Him is not honour; for all figure is finite:

Nor to say we conceive, and imagine, or have an idea of Him in our mind; for whatsoever we conceive is finite:

Nor to attribute to Him *parts* or *totality;* which are the attributes only of things finite:

Nor to say He is in this or that *place* . . . nor that He is *moved* or *resteth;* for both these attributes ascribe to Him place:

Nor that there be more gods than one, because it implies them all finite; for there cannot be more than one infinite:

Nor to ascribe to Him (unless metaphorically, meaning not the passion, but the effect) passions that partake of grief; as *repentance, anger, mercy:* or of want; as *appetite, hope, desire;* or of any passive faculty: for passion is power limited by somewhat else.

And therefore when we ascribe to God a *will,* it is not to be understood, as that of man, for a *rational appetite;* but as the power by which He effecteth everything.

Likewise when we attribute to Him *sight,* and other acts of sense; as also *knowledge* and *understanding;* which in us is nothing else but a tumult of the mind, raised by external things that press the organical parts of man's body: for there is no such thing in God, and, being things that depend on natural causes, cannot be attributed to Him.

He that will attribute to God nothing but what is warranted by natural reason must either use such negative attributes as *infinite, eternal, incomprehensible;* or superlatives, as *most high, most great,* and the like; or indefinite, as *good, just, holy, creator;* and in such sense as if He meant not to declare what He is (for that were to circumscribe Him within the limits of our fancy), but how much we admire Him, and how ready we would be to obey Him; which is a sign of humility, and of a will to honour Him as much as we can: for there is but one name to signify our conception of His nature, and that is *I AM;* and but one name of His relation to us, and that is *God,* in which is contained father, king, and lord.

Hobbes, *Leviathan*, II, 31

68 The nature of God is incomprehensible; that is to say, we understand nothing of *what He is,* but only *that He is;* and therefore the attributes we give Him are not to tell one another *what He is,* nor to signify our opinion of His nature, but our desire to honour Him with such names as we conceive most honourable amongst ourselves.

Hobbes, *Leviathan*, III, 34

69 Neither had these or any other ever such advantage of me, as to incline me to any point of Infidelity or desperate positions of Atheism; for I have been these many years of opinion there was never any. Those that held Religion was the difference of Man from Beasts, have spoken probably, and proceed upon a principle as inductive as the other. That doctrine of *Epicurus,* that denied the Providence of God, was no Atheism, but a magnificent and high strained conceit of his Majesty, which he deemed too sublime to mind the trivial Actions of those inferiour Creatures. That fatal Necessity of the Stoicks, is nothing but the immutable Law of his will. Those that heretofore denied the Divinity of the Holy Ghost, have been condemned, but as Hereticks; and those that now deny our Saviour (though more than Hereticks) are not so much as Atheists: for though they deny two persons in the Trinity, they hold as we do, there is but one God.

Sir Thomas Browne, *Religio Medici,* I, 20

70 Not only the zeal of those who seek Him proves God, but also the blindness of those who seek Him not.

Pascal, *Pensées,* III, 200

71 It is incomprehensible that God should exist, and it is incomprehensible that He should not exist; that the soul should be joined to the body, and that we should have no soul; that the world should be created, and that it should not be creat-

ed, etc.; that original sin should be, and that it should not be.

Pascal, *Pensées*, III, 230

72 It is the heart which experiences God, and not the reason. This, then, is faith: God felt by the heart, not by the reason.

Pascal, *Pensées*, IV, 278

73 It is . . . true that everything teaches man his condition, but he must understand this well. For it is not true that all reveals God, and it is not true that all conceals God. But it is at the same time true that He hides Himself from those who tempt Him, and that He reveals Himself to those who seek Him, because men are both unworthy and capable of God; unworthy by their corruption, capable by their original nature.

Pascal, *Pensées*, VIII, 557

74 If the compassion of God is so great that He instructs us to our benefit, even when He hides Himself, what light ought we not to expect from Him when He reveals Himself?

Pascal, *Pensées*, XIII, 848

75 Hail holy light, ofspring of Heav'n first-born,
Or of th' Eternal Coeternal beam
May I express thee unblam'd? since God is light,
And never but in unapproached light
Dwelt from Eternitie, dwelt then in thee,
Bright effluence of bright essence increate.
Or hear'st thou rather pure Ethereal stream,
Whose Fountain who shall tell? before the Sun,
Before the Heavens thou wert, and at the voice
Of God, as with a Mantle didst invest
The rising world of waters dark and deep,
Won from the void and formless infinite.
Thee I re-visit now with bolder wing,
Escap't the *Stygian* Pool, though long detain'd
In that obscure sojourn, while in my flight
Through utter and through middle darkness borne
With other notes then to th' *Orphean* Lyre
I sung of *Chaos* and *Eternal Night*,
Taught by the heav'nly Muse to venture down
The dark descent, and up to reascend,
Though hard and rare: thee I revisit safe,
And feel thy sovran vital Lamp; but thou
Revisit'st not these eyes, that rowle in vain
To find thy piercing ray, and find no dawn;
So thick a drop serene hath quencht thir Orbs,
Or dim suffusion veild.

Milton, *Paradise Lost*, III, 1

76 Thee Father first they [the angel choir] sung Omnipotent,
Immutable, Immortal, Infinite,
Eternal King; thee Author of all being,
Fountain of Light, thy self invisible
Amidst the glorious brightness where thou sit'st

Thron'd inaccessible, but when thou shad'st
The full blaze of thy beams, and through a cloud
Drawn round about thee like a radiant Shrine,
Dark with excessive bright thy skirts appeer,
Yet dazle Heav'n, that brightest Seraphim
Approach not, but with both wings veil thir eyes.

Milton, *Paradise Lost*, III, 372

77 By God, I understand Being absolutely infinite, that is to say, substance consisting of infinite attributes, each one of which expresses eternal and infinite essence.

Spinoza, *Ethics*, I, Def. 6

78 God, or substance consisting of infinite attributes, each one of which expresses eternal and infinite essence, necessarily exists.

If this be denied, conceive, if it be possible, that God does not exist. Then it follows that His essence does not involve existence. But this is absurd. Therefore God necessarily exists.

Spinoza, *Ethics*, I, Prop. 11, Demonst.

79 Neither in God nor outside God is there any cause or reason which can negate His existence, and therefore God necessarily exists.

Spinoza, *Ethics*, I, Prop. 11, Another Proof

80 God and all His attributes are eternal, that is to say, each one of His attributes expresses existence. The same attributes of God, therefore, which manifest the eternal essence of God, at the same time manifest His eternal existence; that is to say, the very same thing which constitutes the essence of God constitutes at the same time His existence, and therefore His existence and His essence are one and the same thing.

Spinoza, *Ethics*, I, Prop. 20

81 God loves no one and hates no one; for God is not affected with any affect of joy or sorrow, and consequently He neither loves nor hates any one.

Spinoza, *Ethics*, V, Prop. 17, Corol.

82 God alone has a distinct knowledge of all, for He is the source of all. It has been very well said that as a centre He is everywhere, but His circumference is nowhere, for everything is immediately present to Him without any distance from this centre.

Leibniz, *Principles of Nature and of Grace*, 13

83 The conception of God which is the most common and the most full of meaning is expressed well enough in the words: God is an absolutely perfect being. The implications, however, of these words fail to receive sufficient consideration. For instance, there are many different kinds of perfection, all of which God possesses, and each one of them pertains to him in the highest degree.

We must also know what perfection is. One

thing which can surely be affirmed about it is that those forms or natures which are not susceptible of it to the highest degree, say the nature of numbers or of figures, do not permit of perfection. This is because the number which is the greatest of all (that is, the sum of all the numbers), and likewise the greatest of all figures, imply contradictions. The greatest knowledge, however, and omnipotence contain no impossibility. Consequently power and knowledge do admit of perfection, and in so far as they pertain to God they have no limits.

Whence it follows that God who possesses supreme and infinite wisdom acts in the most perfect manner not only metaphysically, but also from the moral standpoint. And with respect to our selves it can be said that the more we are enlightened and informed in regard to the works of God the more will we be disposed to find them excellent and conforming entirely to that which we might desire.

Leibniz, *Discourse on Metaphysics,* I

84 God alone (or the Necessary Being) has this prerogative that if he be possible he must necessarily exist, and, as nothing is able to prevent the possibility of that which involves no bounds, no negation, and consequently, no contradiction, this alone is sufficient to establish *a priori* his existence. We have, therefore, proved his existence through the reality of eternal truths. But a little while ago we also proved it *a posteriori,* because contingent beings exist which can have their ultimate and sufficient reason only in the necessary being which, in turn, has the reason for existence in itself.

Leibniz, *Monadology,* 45

85 The first contrivance of those very artificial parts of animals, the eyes, ears, brain, muscles, heart, lungs, midriff, glands, larynx, hands, wings, swimming bladders, natural spectacles, and other organs of sense and motion; and the instinct of brutes and insects can be the effect of nothing else than the wisdom and skill of a powerful, ever-living agent, who being in all places, is more able by His will to move the bodies within His boundless uniform sensorium, and thereby to form and reform the parts of the Universe, than we are by our will to move the parts of our own bodies. And yet we are not to consider the world as the body of God, or the several parts thereof as the parts of God. He is a uniform Being, void of organs, members or parts, and they are his creatures subordinate to him, and subservient to His will; and He is no more the soul of them than the soul of man is the soul of the species of things carried through the organs of sense into the place of its sensation, where it perceives them by means of its immediate presence, without the intervention of any third thing. The organs of sense are not for enabling the soul to perceive the species of things in its sensori-

um, but only for conveying them thither; and God has no need of such organs, He being everywhere present to the things themselves.

Newton, *Optics,* III, 1

86 The visible marks of extraordinary wisdom and power appear so plainly in all the works of the creation, that a rational creature, who will but seriously reflect on them, cannot miss the discovery of a Deity. And the influence that the discovery of such a Being must necessarily have on the minds of all that have but once heard of it is so great, and carries such a weight of thought and communication with it, that it seems stranger to me that a whole nation of men should be anywhere found so brutish as to want the notion of a God, than that they should be without any notion of numbers, or fire.

Locke, *Concerning Human Understanding,*
Bk. I, III, 9

87 It is as certain that there is a God, as that the opposite angles made by the intersection of two straight lines are equal. There was never any rational creature that set himself sincerely to examine the truth of these propositions that could fail to assent to them; though yet it be past doubt that there are many men, who, having not applied their thoughts that way, are ignorant both of the one and the other.

Locke, *Concerning Human Understanding,*
Bk. I, III, 17

88 If we attentively consider the constant regularity, order, and concatenation of natural things, the surprising magnificence, beauty, and perfection of the larger, and the exquisite contrivance of the smaller parts of creation, together with the exact harmony and correspondence of the whole, but above all the never-enough-admired laws of pain and pleasure, and the instincts or natural inclinations, appetites, and passions of animals; I say if we consider all these things, and at the same time attend to the meaning and import of the attributes One, Eternal, Infinitely Wise, Good, and Perfect, we shall clearly perceive that they belong to the aforesaid Spirit, "who works all in all," and "by whom all things consist."

Berkeley, *Principles of Human Knowledge,* 146

89 A human spirit or person is not perceived by sense, as not being an idea; when therefore we see the colour, size, figure, and motions of a man, we perceive only certain sensations or ideas excited in our own minds; and these being exhibited to our view in sundry distinct collections, serve to mark out unto us the existence of finite and created spirits like ourselves. Hence it is plain we do not see a man—if by *man* is meant that which lives, moves, perceives, and thinks as we do—but only such a certain collection of ideas as directs us to

think there is a distinct principle of thought and motion, like to ourselves, accompanying and represented by it. And after the same manner we see God; all the difference is that, whereas some one finite and narrow assemblage of ideas denotes a particular human mind, whithersoever we direct our view, we do at all times and in all places perceive manifest tokens of the Divinity: everything we see, hear, feel, or anywise perceive by sense, being a sign or effect of the power of God; as is our perception of those very motions which are produced by men.

Berkeley, *Principles of Human Knowledge,* 148

90 It argues surely more power in the Deity to delegate a certain degree of power to inferior creatures than to produce every thing by his own immediate volition. It argues more wisdom to contrive at first the fabric of the world with such perfect foresight that, of itself, and by its proper operation, it may serve all the purposes of providence, than if the great Creator were obliged every moment to adjust its parts, and animate by his breath all the wheels of that stupendous machine.

Hume, *Concerning Human Understanding,* VII, 56

91 God is related to the universe, as Creator and Preserver; the laws by which He created all things are those by which He preserves them. He acts according to these rules, because He knows them; He knows them, because He made them; and He made them, because they are in relation to His wisdom and power.

Montesquieu, *Spirit of Laws,* I, 1

92 The theist is a man firmly persuaded of the existence of a Supreme Being as good as He is powerful, who has formed all beings with extension, vegetating, sentient and reflecting; who perpetuates their species, who punishes crimes without cruelty, and rewards virtuous actions with kindness.

The theist does not know how God punishes, how he protects, how he pardons, for he is not reckless enough to flatter himself that he knows how God acts, but he knows that God acts and that He is just. Difficulties against Providence do not shake him in his faith, because they are merely great difficulties, and not proofs. He submits to this Providence, although he perceives but a few effects and few signs of this Providence: and, judging of the things he does not see by the things he sees, he considers that this Providence reaches all places and all centuries.

Reconciled in this principle with the rest of the universe, he does not embrace any of the sects, all of which contradict each other; his religion is the most ancient and the most widespread; for the simple worship of a God has preceded all the systems of the world. He speaks a language that all peoples understand, while they do not understand one another. He has brothers from Pekin to Cayenne, and he counts all wise men as his brethren. He believes that religion does not consist either in the opinions of an unintelligible metaphysic, or in vain display, but in worship and justice. The doing of good, there is his service; being submissive to God, there is his doctrine. The Mahometan cries to him—"Have a care if you do not make the pilgrimage to Mecca!" "Woe unto you," says a Recollet, "if you do not make a journey to Notre-Dame de Lorette!" He laughs at Lorette and at Mecca; but he succours the needy and defends the oppressed.

Voltaire, *Philosophical Dictionary:* Theist

93 If God did not exist it would be necessary to invent him.

Voltaire, *Épître à l'Auteur du Livre des Trois Imposteurs (Nov. 10, 1770)*

94 While all the ambitious attempts of reason to penetrate beyond the limits of experience end in disappointment, there is still enough left to satisfy us in a practical point of view. No one, it is true, will be able to boast that he knows that there is a God and a future life; for, if he knows this, he is just the man whom I have long wished to find. All knowledge, regarding an object of mere reason, can be communicated; and I should thus be enabled to hope that my own knowledge would receive this wonderful extension, through the instrumentality of his instruction. No, my conviction is not *logical,* but *moral* certainty; and since it rests on subjective grounds (of the moral sentiment), I must not even say: *It is* morally certain that there is a God, etc., but: *I am* morally certain, that is, my belief in God and in another world is so interwoven with my moral nature that I am under as little apprehension of having the former torn from me as of losing the latter.

Kant, *Critique of Pure Reason,* Transcendental Method

95 Whence have we the conception of God as the supreme good? Simply from the *idea* of moral perfection, which reason frames *a priori* and connects inseparably with the notion of a free will.

Kant, *Fundamental Principles of the Metaphysic of Morals,* II

96 It is morally necessary to assume the existence of God.

Kant, *Critique of Practical Reason,* Pt. I, II, 2

97 While *fear* doubtless in the first instance may have been able to produce *gods,* that is demons, it is only *reason* by its moral principles that has been able to produce the conception of *God*—and it has been able to do so despite the great ignorance that

has prevailed in what concerns the teleology of nature, or the considerable doubt that arises from the difficulty of reconciling by a sufficiently established principle the mutually conflicting phenomena that nature presents.

Kant, *Critique of Teleological Judgement,* 86

98 *Faust.* Who dare name Him?
And who avow:
"I believe in Him"?
Who feels and would
Have hardihood
To say: "I don't believe in Him"?
The All-Enfolder,
The All-Upholder,
Enfolds, upholds He not
You, me, Himself?
Do not the heavens over-arch us yonder?
Does not the earth lie firm beneath?
Do not eternal stars rise friendly
Looking down upon us?
Look I not, eye in eye, on you,
And do not all things throng
Toward your head and heart,
Weaving in mystery eternal,
Invisible, visible, near to you?
Fill up your heart with it, great though it is,
And when you're wholly in the feeling, in its bliss,
Name it then as you will,
Name it Happiness! Heart! Love! God!
I have no name for that!
Feeling is all in all;
Name is but sound and smoke,
Beclouding Heaven's glow.

Goethe, *Faust,* I, 3432

99   —Brook and road
Were fellow-travellers in this gloomy Pass,
And with them did we journey several hours
At a slow step. The immeasurable height
Of woods decaying, never to be decayed,
The stationary blasts of waterfalls,
And in the narrow rent, at every turn,
Winds thwarting winds bewildered and forlorn,
The torrents shooting from the clear blue sky,
The rocks that muttered close upon our ears,
Black drizzling crags that spake by the wayside
As if a voice were in them, the sick sight
And giddy prospect of the raving stream,
The unfettered clouds and region of the heavens,
Tumult and peace, the darkness and the light—
Were all the workings of one mind, the features
Of the same face, blossoms upon one tree,
Characters of the great Apocalypse,
The types and symbols of Eternity,
Of first, and last, and midst, and without end.

Wordsworth, *The Simplon Pass*

100 That the history of the world, with all the changing scenes which its annals present, is this process of development and the realization of spirit—this

is the true *Theodicaea,* the justification of God in history. Only *this* insight can reconcile spirit with the history of the world—*viz.,* that what has happened, and is happening every day, is not only not "without God," but is essentially His work.

Hegel, *Philosophy of History,* Pt. IV, III, 3

101 What is this unknown something with which the Reason collides when inspired by its paradoxical passion, with the result of unsettling even man's knowledge of himself? It is the Unknown. It is not a human being, in so far as we know what man is; nor is it any other known thing. So let us call this unknown something: *God.* It is nothing more than a name we assign to it. The idea of demonstrating that this unknown something (God) exists, could scarcely suggest itself to the Reason. For if God does not exist it would of course be impossible to prove it; and if he does exist it would be folly to attempt it.

Kierkegaard, *Philosophical Fragments,* III

102 O, yet we trust that somehow good
    Will be the final goal of ill,
    To pangs of nature, sins of will,
Defects of doubt, and taints of blood;

That nothing walks with aimless feet;
    That not one life shall be destroy'd,
    Or cast as rubbish to the void,
When God hath made the pile complete;

That not a worm is cloven in vain;
    That not a moth with vain desire
    Is shrivell'd in a fruitless fire,
Or but subserves another's gain.

Behold, we know not anything;
    I can but trust that good shall fall
    At last—far off—at last, to all,
And every winter change to spring.

So runs my dream; but what am I?
    An infant crying in the night;
    An infant crying for the light,
And with no language but a cry.

Tennyson, *In Memoriam,* LIV

103 For tho' from out our bourne of Time and Place
    The flood may bear me far,
I hope to see my Pilot face to face
    When I have crost the bar.

Tennyson, *Crossing the Bar*

104 The belief in God has often been advanced as not only the greatest, but the most complete of all the distinctions between man and the lower animals. It is however impossible, as we have seen, to maintain that this belief is innate or instinctive in man. On the other hand a belief in all-pervading spiritual agencies seems to be universal; and apparently follows from a considerable advance in man's reason, and from a still greater advance in his

faculties of imagination, curiosity and wonder. I am aware that the assumed instinctive belief in God has been used by many persons as an argument for His existence. But this is a rash argument, as we should thus be compelled to believe in the existence of many cruel and malignant spirits, only a little more powerful than man; for the belief in them is far more general than in a beneficent Deity. The idea of a universal and beneficent Creator does not seem to arise in the mind of man, until he has been elevated by long-continued culture.

Darwin, *Descent of Man,* III, 21

105 Men are growing to be seriously alive to the fact that the historical evolution of humanity, which is generally, and I venture to think not unreasonably, regarded as progress, has been, and is being, accompanied by a co-ordinate elimination of the supernatural from its originally large occupation of men's thoughts.

T. H. Huxley, *Science and Christian Tradition,* Prologue

106   To whom turn I but to thee, the ineffable Name?
Builder and maker, thou, of houses not made with hands!
What, have fear of change from thee who art ever the same?
Doubt that thy power can fill the heart that thy power expands?
There shall never be one lost good! What was, shall live as before;
The evil is null, is naught, is silence implying sound;
What was good shall be good, with, for evil, so much good more;
On the earth the broken arcs; in the heaven a perfect round.

Browning, *Abt Vogler*

107 But I need, now as then, [in youth]
Thee, God, who mouldest men;
And since, not even while the whirl was worst,
Did I—to the wheel of life
With shapes and colors rife,
Bound dizzily—mistake my end, to slake thy thirst:

So, take and use thy work:
Amend what flaws may lurk,
What strain o' the stuff, what warpings past the aim!
My times be in thy hand!
Perfect the cup as planned!
Let age approve of youth, and death complete the same!

Browning, *Rabbi Ben Ezra*

108 The word "God" is used in most cases as by no means a term of science or exact knowledge, but a term of poetry and eloquence, a term *thrown out,* so to speak, at a not fully grasped object of the speaker's consciousness, a *literary* term, in short; and mankind mean different things by it as their consciousness differs.

Arnold, *Literature and Dogma,* I

109 No one will say, that it is admittedly certain and verifiable, that there is a personal first cause, the moral and intelligent governor of the universe, whom we may call *God* if we will. But that all things seem to us to have what we call a law of their being, and to tend to fulfil it, is certain and admitted; though whether we will call this *God* or not, is a matter of choice. Suppose, however, we call it *God,* we then give the name of *God* to a certain and admitted reality; this, at least, is an advantage.

Arnold, *Literature and Dogma,* I

110 *Ivan.* There was an old sinner in the eighteenth century who declared that, if there were no God, he would have to be invented. . . . And man has actually invented God. And what's strange, what would be marvellous, is not that God should really exist; the marvel is that such an idea, the idea of the necessity of God, could enter the head of such a savage, vicious beast as man. So holy it is, so touching, so wise and so great a credit it does to man.

Dostoevsky, *Brothers Karamazov,* Pt. II, V, 3

111 *Ivan.* If God exists and if He really did create the world, then, as we all know, He created it according to the geometry of Euclid and the human mind with the conception of only three dimensions in space. Yet there have been and still are geometricians and philosophers, and even some of the most distinguished, who doubt whether the whole universe, or to speak more widely, the whole of being, was only created in Euclid's geometry; they even dare to dream that two parallel lines, which according to Euclid can never meet on earth, may meet somewhere in infinity. I have come to the conclusion that, since I can't understand even that, I can't expect to understand about God. I acknowledge humbly that I have no faculty for settling such questions, I have a Euclidian earthly mind, and how could I solve problems that are not of this world? And I advise you never to think about it either, my dear Alyosha, especially about God, whether He exists or not. All such questions are utterly inappropriate for a mind created with an idea of only three dimensions.

Dostoevsky, *Brothers Karamazov,* Pt. II, V, 3

112 "I ought to tell you that I do not believe . . . do not believe in God," said Pierre, regretfully and

with an effort, feeling it essential to speak the whole truth.

The Mason looked intently at Pierre and smiled as a rich man with millions in hand might smile at a poor fellow who told him that he, poor man, had not the five rubles that would make him happy.

"Yes, you do not know Him, my dear sir," said the Mason. "You cannot know Him. You do not know Him and that is why you are unhappy."

"Yes, yes, I am unhappy," assented Pierre. "But what am I to do?"

"You know Him not, my dear sir, and so you are very unhappy. You do not know Him, but He is here, He is in me, He is in my words, He is in thee, and even in those blasphemous words thou hast just uttered!" pronounced the Mason in a stern and tremulous voice.

He paused and sighed, evidently trying to calm himself.

"If He were not," he said quietly, "you and I would not be speaking of Him, my dear sir. Of what, of whom, are we speaking? Whom hast thou denied?" he suddenly asked with exulting austerity and authority in his voice. "Who invented Him, if He did not exist? Whence came thy conception of the existence of such an incomprehensible Being? Why didst thou, and why did the whole world, conceive the idea of the existence of such an incomprehensible Being, a Being all-powerful, eternal, and infinite in all His attributes? . . ."

He stopped and remained silent for a long time. Pierre could not and did not wish to break this silence.

"He exists, but to understand Him is hard," the Mason began again, looking not at Pierre but straight before him, and turning the leaves of his book with his old hands which from excitement he could not keep still. "If it were a man whose existence thou didst doubt I could bring him to thee, could take him by the hand and show him to thee. But how can I, an insignificant mortal, show His omnipotence, His infinity, and all His mercy to one who is blind, or who shuts his eyes that he may not see or understand Him and may not see or understand his own vileness and sinfulness?" He paused again. "Who art thou? Thou dreamest that thou art wise because thou couldst utter those blasphemous words," he went on, with a somber and scornful smile. "And thou art more foolish and unreasonable than a little child, who, playing with the parts of a skillfully made watch, dares to say that, as he does not understand its use, he does not believe in the master who made it. To know Him is hard. . . . For ages, from our forefather Adam to our own day, we labor to attain that knowledge and are still infinitely far from our aim; but in our lack of understanding we see only our weakness and His greatness. . . ."

Tolstoy, *War and Peace*, V, 2

113 Glory be to God for dappled things—
   For skies of couple-colour as a brinded cow;
      For rose-moles all in stipple upon trout that swim;

Fresh-firecoal chestnut-falls; finches' wings;
   Landscape plotted and pieced—fold, fallow, and plough;
      And áll trádes, their gear and tackle and trim.

All things counter, original, spare, strange;
   Whatever is fickle, freckled (who knows how?)
      With swift, slow; sweet, sour; adazzle, dim;
He fathers-forth whose beauty is past change:
            Praise him.

G. M. Hopkins, *Pied Beauty*

114 The world is charged with the grandeur of God.
      It will flame out, like shining from shook foil;
      It gathers to a greatness, like the ooze of oil
Crushed. Why do men then now not reck his rod?
Generations have trod, have trod, have trod;
      And all is seared with trade; bleared, smeared with toil;
      And wears man's smudge and shares man's smell; the soil
Is bare now, nor can foot feel, being shod.

And for all this, nature is never spent;
      There lives the dearest freshness deep down things;
And though the last lights off the black West went
      Oh, morning, at the brown brink eastward, springs—
Because the Holy Ghost over the bent
      World broods with warm breast and ah! bright wings.

G. M. Hopkins, *God's Grandeur*

115 Thus spake the devil unto me, once on a time:
   "Ever God hath his hell: it is his love for man."
   And lately did I hear him say these words:
   "God is dead: of his pity for man hath God died."

Nietzsche, *Thus Spake Zarathustra*,
IV, Introduction

116 A people which still believes in itself still also has its own God. In him it venerates the conditions through which it has prospered, its virtues—it projects its joy in itself, its feeling of power on to a being whom one can thank for them. He who is rich wants to bestow; a proud people needs a God in order to *sacrifice.* . . . Within the bounds of such presuppositions religion is a form of gratitude. One is grateful for oneself: for that one needs a God.—Such a God must be able to be both useful and harmful, both friend and foe—he is admired in good and bad alike. The *anti-natural* castration of a God into a God of the merely good would be totally undesirable here. One has as much need of the evil God as of the good God: for

one does not owe one's existence to philanthropy or tolerance precisely. . . . Of what consequence would a God be who knew nothing of anger, revengefulness, envy, mockery, cunning, acts of violence? to whom even the rapturous *ardeurs* of victory and destruction were unknown? One would not understand such a God: why should one have him?—To be sure: when a people is perishing; when it feels its faith in the future, its hope of freedom vanish completely; when it becomes conscious that the most profitable thing of all is submissiveness and that the virtues of submissiveness are a condition of its survival, then its God *has* to alter too. He now becomes a dissembler, timid, modest, counsels 'peace of soul', no more hatred, forbearance, 'love' even towards friend and foe. He is continually moralizing, he creeps into the cave of every private virtue, becomes a God for everybody, becomes a private man, becomes a cosmopolitan. . . . Formerly he represented a people, the strength of a people, everything aggressive and thirsting for power in the soul of a people: now he is merely the good God.

Nietzsche, *Antichrist*, XVI

117 The Christian conception of God—God as God of the sick, God as spider, God as spirit—is one of the most corrupt conceptions of God arrived at on earth: perhaps it even represents the low-water mark in the descending development of the God type.

Nietzsche, *Antichrist*, XVIII

118 Even the slightest trace of piety in us ought to make us feel that a God who cures a headcold at the right moment or tells us to get into a coach just as a downpour is about to start is so absurd a God he would have to be abolished even if he existed. A God as a domestic servant, as a postman, as an almanac-maker—at bottom a word for the stupidest kind of accidental occurrence.

Nietzsche, *Antichrist*, LII

119 If but some vengeful god would call to me
From up the sky, and laugh: "Thou suffering thing,
Know that thy sorrow is my ecstasy,
That thy love's loss is my hate's profiting!"

Then would I bear it, clench myself, and die,
Steeled by the sense of ire unmerited;
Half-eased in that a Powerfuller than I
Had willed and meted me the tears I shed.

But not so. How arrives it joy lies slain,
And why unblooms the best hope ever sown?
—Crass Casualty obstructs the sun and rain,
And dicing Time for gladness casts a moan. . . .
These purblind Doomsters had as readily strown
Blisses about my pilgrimage as pain.

Hardy, *Hap*

120 God is the ultimate limitation, and His existence is the ultimate irrationality. For no reason can be given for just that limitation which it stands in His nature to impose. God is not concrete, but He is the ground for concrete actuality. No reason can be given for the nature of God, because that nature is the ground of rationality.

Whitehead, *Science and the Modern World*, XI

121 I do not pretend to be able to prove that there is no God. I equally cannot prove that Satan is a fiction. The Christian God may exist; so may the Gods of Olympus, or of ancient Egypt, or of Babylon. But no one of these hypotheses is more probable than any other: they lie outside the region of even probable knowledge, and therefore there is no reason to consider any of them.

Russell, *What I Believe*, I

122 The same father . . . who gave the child his life and preserved it from the dangers which that life involves, also taught it what it may or may not do, made it accept certain limitations of its instinctual wishes, and told it what consideration it would be expected to show towards its parents and brothers and sisters, if it wanted to be tolerated and liked as a member of the family circle, and later on of more extensive groups. The child is brought up to know its social duties by means of a system of love-rewards and punishments, and in this way it is taught that its security in life depends on its parents (and, subsequently, other people) loving it and being able to believe in its love for them. This whole state of affairs is carried over by the grown man unaltered into his religion. The prohibitions and commands of his parents live on in his breast as his moral conscience; God rules the world of men with the help of the same system of rewards and punishments, and the degree of protection and happiness which each individual enjoys, depends on his fulfilment of the demands of morality; the feeling of security, with which he fortifies himself against the dangers both of the external world and of his human environment, is founded on his love of God and the consciousness of God's love for him. Finally, he has in prayer a direct influence on the divine will, and in that way insures for himself a share in the divine omnipotence.

Freud, *New Introductory Lectures on Psycho-Analysis*, XXXV

123 The last contribution to the criticism of the religious *Weltanschauung* has been made by psychoanalysis, which has traced the origin of religion to the helplessness of childhood, and its content to the persistence of the wishes and needs of childhood into maturity. This does not precisely imply a refutation of religion, but it is a necessary rounding off of our knowledge about it, and, at least on one point, it actually contradicts it, for

religion lays claim to a divine origin. This claim, to be sure, is not false if our interpretation of God is accepted.

Freud, *New Introductory Lectures on Psycho-Analysis,* XXXV

124 Obvious considerations like these furnish the proof of God's existence, not as philosophers have tried to express it after the fact and in relation to mythical conceptions of God nady current, but as mankind originally perceived it, and (where religion is spontaneous) perceives it still. There is such an order in experience that we find our desires doubly dependent on something which, because it disregards our will, we call an external power. Sometimes it overwhelms us with scourges and wonders, so that we must marvel at it and fear; sometimes it removes, or after removing restores, a support necessary to our existence and happiness, so that we must cling to it, hope for it, and love it. Whatever is serious in religion, whatever is bound up with morality and fate, is contained in those plain experiences of dependence and of affinity to that on which we depend. The rest is poetry, or mythical philosophy, in which definitions not warranted in the end by experience are given to that power which experience reveals. To reject such arbitrary definitions is called atheism by those who frame them; but a man who studies for himself the ominous and the friendly aspects of reality and gives them the truest and most adequate expression he can is repeating what the founders of religion did in the beginning. He is their companion and follower more truly than are the apologists for secondhand conceptions which these apologists themselves have never compared with the facts, and which they prize chiefly for misrepresenting actual experience and giving it imaginary extensions.

Santayana, *Life of Reason,* III, 3

125 He Who Himself begot, middler the Holy Ghost, and Himself sent Himself, Agenbuyer, between Himself and others, Who, put upon by His fiends, stripped and whipped, was nailed like bat to barndoor, starved on crosstree, Who let Him bury, stood up, harrowed hell, fared into heaven and there these nineteen hundred years sitteth on the right hand of His Own Self but yet shall come in the latter day to doom the quick and dead when all the quick shall be dead already.

Joyce, *Ulysses*

20.6 | *Gods and Goddesses*

One striking difference between the quotations in this section and the quotations in Section 20.5 on GOD is that here the poets and the historians hold forth most eloquently and vividly whereas there the philosophers and theologians heap argument upon argument. Another difference, of course, is the contrast between the colorful anthropomorphic personality of each particular god and goddess and the abstract metaphysical characterization of a supernatural being.

The tragic and epic poets of antiquity, as well as the historians, give us a familiarity with the dwellers on Mt. Olympus, or their Roman counterparts, that enhances our appreciation of the later literature in which allusion to these deities is so frequently made. Their stories about the adventures and misadventures of the capricious or wayward divinities led Plato to call for the exclusion of the poets from the ideal state, in order to prevent immoral actions from being imitated or misleading lessons from being learned. The reader will find that famous passage from the *Republic* in Section 13.2 on FREEDOM OF THOUGHT AND EXPRESSION: CENSORSHIP.

The pagan philosophers manifest a certain detachment in their comments on the deities worshipped in the polytheistic religions of antiquity, often dealing with the popular beliefs about the gods in terms of their own more abstract consideration of

God. In the materialistic cosmology of the ancient atomists, Epicurus and Lucretius, the gods are exiled to a place of pleasure without power. No harm is done in admitting their existence if they are deprived of any power to intervene in the order of nature or to control man by the distribution of rewards and punishments.

As might be expected, adverse criticisms of pagan polytheism are expressed by Christian theologians and by philosophers who profess a commitment to Christian beliefs. This raises, of course, the problem of the line that divides authentic religion from mythology and superstition, in connection with which the reader is referred to Section 20.12 on SUPERSTITION. It is also suggested that the reader compare Gibbon's remarks on Christianity in Section 20.3 with his comments here on pagan religious beliefs.

---

1 *Dione.* That man who fights the immortals lives
  for no long time,
  his children do not gather to his knees to welcome
  their father
  when he returns home after the fighting and the
  bitter warfare.

  Homer, *Iliad*, V, 407

2 *Zeus.* Come, you gods, make this endeavour, that
  you all may learn this.
  Let down out of the sky a cord of gold; lay hold of
  it
  all you who are gods and all who are goddesses,
  yet not
  even so can you drag down Zeus from the sky to
  the ground, not
  Zeus the high lord of counsel, though you try until
  you grow weary.
  Yet whenever I might strongly be minded to pull
  you,
  I could drag you up, earth and all and sea and all
  with you,
  then fetch the golden rope about the horn of
  Olympos
  and make it fast, so that all once more should
  dangle in mid air.
  So much stronger am I than the gods, and stronger than mortals.

  Homer, *Iliad*, VIII, 18

3 *Zeus.* My word, how mortals take the gods to task!
  All their afflictions come from us, we hear.
  And what of their own failings? Greed and folly
  double the suffering in the lot of man.

  Homer, *Odyssey*, I, 30

4 *Menelaos.* Young friends, no mortal man can vie
  with Zeus.
  His home and all his treasures are for ever.

  Homer, *Odyssey*, IV, 79

5 *A Suitor.* They go in foreign guise, the gods do,
  looking like strangers, turning up

in towns and settlements to keep an eye
on manners, good or bad.

  Homer, *Odyssey*, XVII, 486

6 Invisible the gods are ever nigh,
  Pass through the midst and bend th' all-seeing
  eye:
  Who heed not heaven's revenge, but wrest the
  right,
  And grind the poor, are naked to their sight.

  Hesiod, *Works and Days*

7 Children of Jove, all hail! but deign to give
  Th' enchanting song! record the sacred race
  Of ever-living gods; who sprang from earth,
  From the starr'd heaven, and from the murky
  night,
  And whom the salt deep nourish'd into life.
  Declare how first the gods and earth became;
  The rivers and th' immeasurable sea
  Raging in foamy swell; the glittering stars,
  And the wide heaven above; and who from these
  Of deities arose, dispensing good;
  Say how their treasures, how their honours each
  Allotted shared; how first they fix'd abode
  Amidst Olympus' many-winding vales.

  Hesiod, *Theogony*

8 The Persians . . . have no images of the gods, no
  temples nor altars, and consider the use of them a
  sign of folly. This comes, I think, from their not
  believing the gods to have the same nature with
  men, as the Greeks imagine.

  Herodotus, *History*, I, 131

9 *Heracles.* I do not believe the gods commit
  adultery, or bind each other in chains.
  I never did believe it; I never shall;
  nor that one god is tyrant of the rest.
  If god is truly god, he is perfect,
  lacking nothing.

  Euripides, *Heracles*, 1341

10 *Talthybius.*   Do we, holding that the gods exist,
deceive ourselves with unsubstantial dreams
and lies, while random careless chance and
    change
alone control the world?
                    Euripides, *Hecuba,* 489

11 *Hecuba.*   I am a slave, I know,
and slaves are weak. But the gods are strong, and
    over them
there stands some absolute, some moral order
or principle of law more final still.
Upon this moral law the world depends;
through it the gods exist; by it we live,
defining good and evil.
                    Euripides, *Hecuba,* 798

12 *Polymestor.* The inconsistent gods make chaos of
    our lives,
pitching us about with such savagery of change
that we, out of our anguish and uncertainty,
may turn to them.
                    Euripides, *Hecuba,* 958

13 *Creusa.* O you who give the seven-toned lyre
A voice which rings out of the lifeless,
Rustic horn the lovely sound
Of the Muses' hymns,
On you, Latona's son, here
In daylight I will lay blame.
You came with hair flashing
Gold, as I gathered
Into my cloak flowers ablaze
With their golden light.
Clinging to my pale wrists
As I cried for my mother's help
You led me to bed in a cave,
A god and my lover,
With no shame,
Submitting to the Cyprian's will.
In misery I bore you
A son, whom in fear of my mother
I placed in that bed
Where you cruelly forced me.
Ah! He is lost now,
Snatched as food for birds,
My son and yours; O lost!
    But you play the lyre,
    Chanting your paeans.

O hear me, son of Latona,
Who assign your prophecies
From the golden throne
And the temple at earth's center,
I will proclaim my words in your ears:
You are an evil lover;
Though you owed no debt
To my husband, you have
Set a son in his house.
But my son, yes and yours, hard-hearted,
Is lost, carried away by birds,

The clothes his mother put on him abandoned.
    Delos hates you and the young
    Laurel which grows by the palm
    With its delicate leaves, where Latona
    Bore you, a holy child, fruit of Zeus.
                    Euripides, *Ion,* 881

14 *Chorus.* —You on the streets!
           —You on the roads!
                  —Make way!
—Let every mouth be hushed. Let no ill-omened
words profane your tongues.
          —Make way! Fall back!
                      —Hush.
—For now I raise the old, old hymn to Dionysus.

—Blessèd, blessèd are those who know the myster-
ies of god.
—Blessèd is he who hallows his life in the worship
of god,
    he whom the spirit of god possesseth, who is
      one
    with those who belong to the holy body of
      god.
—Blessèd are the dancers and those who are puri-
fied,
    who dance on the hill in the holy dance of
      god.
—Blessèd are they who keep the rite of Cybele the
Mother.
—Blessèd are the thyrsus-bearers, those who wield
in their hands
    the holy wand of god.
—Blessèd are those who wear the crown of the ivy
of god.
—Blessèd, blessèd are they: Dionysus is their God!
                    Euripides, *Bacchae,* 68

15 *Chorus.* —He is sweet upon the mountains. He
    drops to the earth from the running packs.
    He wears the holy fawn-skin. He hunts the wild
      goat and kills it.
    He delights in the raw flesh.
    He runs to the mountains of Phrygia, to the
      mountains of Lydia he runs!
    He is Bromius who leads us! *Evohé!*

—With milk the earth flows! It flows with wine!
    It runs with the nectar of bees!

—Like frankincense in its fragrance
is the blaze of the torch he bears.
Flames float out from his trailing wand
    as he runs, as he dances,
    kindling the stragglers,
    spurring with cries,
and his long curls stream to the wind!

—And he cries, as they cry, *Evohé!—*
    On, Bacchae!
    On, Bacchae!
    Follow, glory of golden Tmolus,
      hymning god
      with a rumble of drums,

with a cry, *Evohé!* to the Evian god,
with a cry of Phrygian cries,
when the holy flute like honey plays
the sacred song of those who go
to the mountain!

       to the mountain!

—Then, in ecstasy, like a colt by its grazing mother, the Bacchante runs with flying feet, she leaps!

             Euripides, *Bacchae,* 135

16 *Chorus.*—Slow but unmistakable
the might of the gods moves on.
It punishes that man,
infatuate of soul
and hardened in his pride,
who disregards the gods.
The gods are crafty:
they lie in ambush
a long step of time
to hunt the unholy.
Beyond the old beliefs,
no thought, no act shall go.
Small, small is the cost
to believe in this:
whatever is god is strong;
whatever long time has sanctioned,
that is a law forever;
the law tradition makes
is the law of nature.

             Euripides, *Bacchae,* 882

17 *Agathon.* Love set in order the empire of the gods—the love of beauty, as is evident, for with deformity Love has no concern. In the days of old, as I began by saying, dreadful deeds were done among the gods, for they were ruled by Necessity; but now since the birth of Love, and from the Love of the beautiful, has sprung every good in heaven and earth.

             Plato, *Symposium,* 197A

18 *Socrates.* Did ever man, Meletus, believe in the existence of human things, and not of human beings? . . . I wish, men of Athens, that he would answer, and not be always trying to get up an interruption. Did ever any man believe in horsemanship, and not in horses? or in flute-playing, and not in flute-players? No, my friend; I will answer to you and to the court, as you refuse to answer for yourself. There is no man who ever did. But now please to answer the next question: Can a man believe in spiritual and divine agencies, and not in spirits or demigods?

Meletus. He cannot.

How lucky I am to have extracted that answer, by the assistance of the court! But then you swear in the indictment that I teach and believe in divine or spiritual agencies (new or old, no matter

for that); at any rate, I believe in spiritual agencies,—so you say and swear in the affidavit; and yet if I believe in divine beings, how can I help believing in spirits or demigods;—must I not? To be sure I must; and therefore I may assume that your silence gives consent. Now what are spirits or demigods? are they not either gods or the sons of gods?

Certainly they are.

But this is what I call the facetious riddle invented by you: the demigods or spirits are gods, and you say first that I do not believe in gods, and then again that I do believe in gods; that is, if I believe in demigods. For if the demigods are the illegitimate sons of gods, whether by the nymphs or by any other mothers, of whom they are said to be the sons—what human being will ever believe that there are no gods if they are the sons of gods? You might as well affirm the existence of mules, and deny that of horses and asses. Such nonsense, Meletus, could only have been intended by you to make trial of me. You have put this into the indictment because you had nothing real of which to accuse me. But no one who has a particle of understanding will ever be convinced by you that the same men can believe in divine and superhuman things, and yet not believe that there are gods and demigods and heroes.

             Plato, *Apology,* 27A

19 *Athenian Stranger.* Of the stars too, and of the moon, and of the years and months and seasons, must we not say in like manner, that since a soul or souls having every sort of excellence are the causes of all of them, those souls are Gods, whether they are living beings and reside in bodies, and in this way order the whole heaven, or whatever be the place and mode of their existence;—and will any one who admits all this venture to deny that all things are full of Gods?

Cleinias. No one, Stranger, would be such a madman.

             Plato, *Laws,* X, 899A

20 One difficulty which is as great as any has been neglected both by modern philosophers and by their predecessors—whether the principles of perishable and those of imperishable things are the same or different. If they are the same, how are some things perishable and others imperishable, and for what reason? The school of Hesiod and all the theologians thought only of what was plausible to themselves, and had no regard to us. For, asserting the first principles to be gods and born of gods, they say that the beings which did not taste of nectar and ambrosia became mortal; and clearly they are using words which are familiar to themselves, yet what they have said about the very application of these causes is above our comprehension. For if the gods taste of nectar and ambrosia for their pleasure, these are in no wise

the causes of their existence; and if they taste them to maintain their existence, how can gods who need food be eternal?—But into the subtleties of the mythologists it is not worth our while to inquire seriously.

Aristotle, *Metaphysics*, 1000ᵃ5

21 We assume the gods to be above all other beings blessed and happy; but what sort of actions must we assign to them? Acts of justice? Will not the gods seem absurd if they make contracts and return deposits, and so on? Acts of a brave man, then, confronting dangers and running risks because it is noble to do so? Or liberal acts? To whom will they give? It will be strange if they are really to have money or anything of the kind. And what would their temperate acts be? Is not such praise tasteless, since they have no bad appetites? If we were to run through them all, the circumstances of action would be found trivial and unworthy of gods. Still, every one supposes that they *live* and therefore that they are active; we cannot suppose them to sleep like Endymion. Now if you take away from a living being action, and still more production, what is left but contemplation? Therefore the activity of God, which surpasses all others in blessedness, must be contemplative; and of human activities, therefore, that which is most akin to this must be most of the nature of happiness.

Aristotle, *Ethics*, 1178ᵇ9

22 If you well apprehend and keep in mind these things, nature free at once and rid of her haughty lords is seen to do all things spontaneously of herself without the meddling of the gods. For I appeal to the holy breasts of the gods who in tranquil peace pass a calm time and an unruffled existence, who can rule the sum, who hold in his hand with controlling force the strong reins, of the immeasurable deep? who can at once make all the different heavens to roll and warm with ethereal fires all the fruitful earths, or be present in all places at all times, to bring darkness with clouds and shake with noise the heaven's serene expanse, to hurl lightnings and often throw down his own temples, and withdrawing into the deserts there to spend his rage in practising his bolt which often passes the guilty by and strikes dead the innocent and unoffending?

Lucretius, *Nature of Things*, II

23 For soon as thy philosophy issuing from a godlike intellect has begun with loud voice to proclaim the nature of things, the terrors of the mind are dispelled, the walls of the world part asunder, I see things in operation throughout the whole void: the divinity of the gods is revealed and their tranquil abodes which neither winds do shake nor clouds drench with rains nor snow congealed by sharp frosts harms with hoary fall: an ever cloud-less ether o'ercanopies them, and they laugh with light shed largely round. Nature too supplies all their wants and nothing ever impairs their peace of mind.

Lucretius, *Nature of Things*, III

24 This too you may not possibly believe, that the holy seats of the gods exist in any parts of the world: the fine nature of the gods far withdrawn from our senses is hardly seen by the thought of the mind; and since it has ever eluded the touch and stroke of the hands, it must touch nothing which is tangible for us; for that cannot touch which does not admit of being touched in turn. And therefore their seats as well must be unlike our seats, fine, even as their bodies are fine.

Lucretius, *Nature of Things*, V

25 We are told that there is no race in the world so uncivilized or barbarous but that it has some intimation of a belief in the gods. It is certain that many men entertain wrong ideas about the gods. This results from a corrupt nature. Nevertheless, all men hold to some divine power and a divine nature, and this is not because of some human agreement or convention. Nor is it a belief established by rules or statutes. It is commonly accepted that such a unanimity among the world's races is according to natural law.

Cicero, *Disputations*, I, 13

26 The gods have been portrayed by the poets as angry and lustful. They have described for us the gods' wars, battles, squabbles, and wounds; their hatreds, enmities, quarrels; their births and deaths; their complaints and sorrows; their unbridled passions; their adulteries and imprisonments; their unions with humans and the birth of mortal progeny from an immortal parent. These errors of the poets may be classed with the monstrous teachings of the astrologers and the insane mythology of Egypt, as well as with popular theology, which is a mass of inconsistency derived from ignorance. Anyone who thinks about the unfounded and irrational nature of these doctrines should regard Epicurus with reverence and rank him among the gods about whom we are inquiring. He alone perceived that the gods exist because nature herself has imprinted a conception of them on the minds of men.

Cicero, *De Natura Deorum*, I, 16

27 *Velleius.* We agree that the gods are supremely happy. Since no one is happy without virtue, and virtue does not exist apart from reason, and reason is only found in human form, we must also assume that the gods possess the form of men.

Cicero, *De Natura Deorum*, I, 18

28 *Lucillius.* If some people interpret the will of certain beings, naturally those beings themselves

must exist. There are people who interpret the will of the gods. Therefore we must admit that the gods exist. But someone may argue that not all prophecies come true. Not all sick persons get well either, but that doesn't disqualify the practice of medicine. Omens of future events are revealed by the gods. Men may not understand these omens, but the fault is with the human powers of inference, not with the nature of the gods.

Cicero, *De Natura Deorum*, II, 4

29 Gods are convenient to have, so let us concede
   their existence,
   Bring to their obsolete shrine plenty of incense
   and wine.
   Nor are they careless, aloof, calm in the semblance of slumber:
   Live an innocent life; godhead is certainly near.
   Keep true faith, and return whatever is placed in
   your keeping;
   Keep your hands clean of blood; never indulge
   in a fraud.

Ovid, *Art of Love*, I, 637

30 Pythagoras . . . conceived of the first principle of being as transcending sense and passion, invisible and incorrupt, and only to be apprehended by abstract intelligence. So Numa forbade the Romans to represent God in the form of man or beast, nor was there any painted or graven image of a diety admitted amongst them for the space of the first hundred and seventy years, all which time their temples and chapels were kept free and pure from images; to such baser objects they deemed it impious to liken the highest, and all access to God impossible, except by the pure act of the intellect. His sacrifices, also, had great similitude to the ceremonial of Pythagoras, for they were not celebrated with effusion of blood, but consisted of flour, wine, and the least costly offerings.

Plutarch, *Numa Pompilius*

31 So dispassionate a temper [as Pericles'], a life so pure and unblemished, in the height of power and place, might well be called Olympian, in accordance with our conceptions of the divine beings, to whom, as the natural authors of all good and of nothing evil, we ascribe the rule and government of the world. Not as the poets represent, who, while confounding us with their ignorant fancies, are themselves confuted by their own poems and fictions, and call the place, indeed, where they say the gods make their abode, a secure and quiet seat, free from all hazards and commotions, untroubled with winds or with clouds, and equally through all time illumined with a soft serenity and a pure light as though such were a home most agreeable for a blessed and immortal nature; and yet, in the meanwhile, affirm that the gods themselves are full of trouble and enmity and anger

and other passions, which no way become or belong to even men that have any understanding.

Plutarch, *Pericles*

32 We cannot suppose that the divine beings actually and literally turn our bodies and direct our hands and our feet this way or that, to do what is right: it is obvious that they must actuate the practical and elective element of our nature, by certain initial occasions, by images presented to the imagination, and thoughts suggested to the mind, such either as to excite it to, or avert and withhold it from, any particular course.

Plutarch, *Coriolanus*

33 The Gods take no thought for our happiness, but only for our punishment.

Tacitus, *Histories*, I, 3

34 In truth [gods] do exist, and they do care for human things, and they have put all the means in man's power to enable him not to fall into real evils.

Marcus Aurelius, *Meditations*, II, 11

35 The least-known things are the fittest to be deified; wherefore to make gods of ourselves, like antiquity, passes the utmost bounds of feeble-mindedness. I would even rather have followed those who worshiped the serpent, the dog, and the ox; inasmuch as their nature and being is less known to us, and we have more chance to imagine what we please about those animals and attribute extraordinary faculties to them. But to have made gods of our condition, the imperfection of which we should know; to have attributed to them desire, anger, vengeances, marriages, generation, kinships, love and jealousy, our limbs and our bones, our fevers and our pleasures, our deaths, our burials—this must have come from a marvelous intoxication of the human intelligence.

Montaigne, *Essays*, II, 12, Apology
for Raymond Sebond

36 *Gloucester.* As flies to wanton boys, are we to the
   gods,
   They kill us for their sport.

Shakespeare, *Lear*, IV, i, 38

37 *Florizel.*   The gods themselves,
   Humbling their deities to love, have taken
   The shapes of beasts upon them. Jupiter
   Became a bull, and bellow'd; the green Neptune
   A ram, and bleated; and the fire-robed god,
   Golden Apollo, a poor humble swain.

Shakespeare, *Winter's Tale*, IV, iv, 25

38 And for that part of religion which consisteth in opinions concerning the nature of powers invisible, there is almost nothing that has a name that has not been esteemed amongst the Gentiles, in

one place or another, a god or devil; or by their poets feigned to be animated, inhabited, or possessed by some spirit or other.

The unformed matter of the world was a god by the name of Chaos.

The heaven, the ocean, the planets, the fire, the earth, the winds, were so many gods.

Men, women, a bird, a crocodile, a calf, a dog, a snake, an onion, a leek, were deified. Besides that, they filled almost all places with spirits called *demons:* the plains, with Pan and Panises, or Satyrs; the woods, with Fauns and Nymphs; the sea, with Tritons and other Nymphs; every river and fountain, with a ghost of his name and with Nymphs; every house, with its *Lares,* or familiars; every man, with his *Genius;* Hell, with ghosts and spiritual officers, as Charon, Cerberus, and the Furies; and in the night time, all places with *larvae, lemures,* ghosts of men deceased, and a whole kingdom of fairies and bugbears. They have also ascribed divinity, and built temples, to mere accidents and qualities; such as are time, night, day, peace, concord, love, contention, virtue, honour, health, rust, fever, and the like; which when they prayed for, or against, they prayed to as if there were ghosts of those names hanging over their heads, and letting fall or withholding that good, or evil, for or against which they prayed. They invoked also their own wit, by the name of Muses; their own ignorance, by the name of Fortune; their own lust, by the name of Cupid; their own rage, by the name Furies; their own privy members by the name of Priapus; and attributed their pollutions to *incubi* and *succubae:* insomuch as there was nothing which a poet could introduce as a person in his poem which they did not make either a god or a devil.

Hobbes, *Leviathan,* I, 12

39 What true or tolerable notion of a Deity could they have, who acknowledged and worshipped hundreds? Every deity that they owned above one was an infallible evidence of their ignorance of Him, and a proof that they had no true notion of God, where unity, infinity, and externity were excluded. To which, if we add their gross conceptions of corporeity, expressed in their images and representations of their deities; the amours, marriages, copulations, lusts, quarrels, and other mean qualities attributed by them to their gods; we shall have little reason to think that the heathen world, i.e. the greatest part of mankind, had such ideas of God in their minds as he himself, out of care that they should not be mistaken about him, was author of.

Locke, *Concerning Human Understanding,*
Bk. I, III, 15

40 If they say that the variety of deities worshipped by the heathen world were but figurative ways of expressing the several attributes of that incomprehensible Being, or several parts of his providence, I answer: what they might be in the original I will not here inquire; but that they were so in the thoughts of the vulgar I think nobody will affirm.

Locke, *Concerning Human Understanding,*
Bk. I, III, 15

41 You find certain phenomena in nature. You seek a cause or author. You imagine that you have found him. You afterwards become so enamoured of this offspring of your brain, that you imagine it impossible, but he must produce something greater and more perfect than the present scene of things, which is so full of ill and disorder. You forget, that this superlative intelligence and benevolence are entirely imaginary, or at least, without any foundation in reason; and that you have no ground to ascribe to him any qualities, but what you see he has actually exerted and displayed in his productions. Let your gods, therefore, O philosophers, be suited to the present appearances of nature: and presume not to alter these appearances by arbitrary suppositions, in order to suit them to the attributes, which you so fondly ascribe to your deities.

Hume, *Concerning Human Understanding,*
XI, 106

42 The devout polytheist, though fondly attached to his national rites, admitted with implicit faith the different religions of the earth. Fear, gratitude, and curiosity, a dream or an omen, a singular disorder, or a distant journey, perpetually disposed him to multiply the articles of his belief, and to enlarge the list of his protectors. The thin texture of the Pagan mythology was interwoven with various but not discordant materials. As soon as it was allowed that sages and heroes, who had lived, or who had died for the benefit of their country, were exalted to a state of power and immortality, it was universally confessed that they deserved, if not the adoration, at least the reverence of all mankind. The deities of a thousand groves and a thousand streams possessed, in peace, their local and respective influence; nor could the Roman who deprecated the wrath of the Tiber, deride the Egyptian who presented his offering to the beneficent genius of the Nile. The visible powers of Nature, the planets, and the elements, were the same throughout the universe. The invisible governors of the moral world were inevitably cast in a similar mould of fiction and allegory. Every virtue, and even vice, acquired its divine representative; every art and profession its patron, whose attributes, in the most distant ages and countries, were uniformly derived from the character of their peculiar votaries. A republic of gods of such opposite tempers and interest required, in every system, the moderating hand of a supreme magistrate, who, by the progress of knowledge and flattery, was gradually invested with the sublime per-

fections of an Eternal Parent, and an Omnipotent Monarch. Such was the mild spirit of antiquity, that the nations were less attentive to the difference than to the resemblance of their religious worship. The Greek, the Roman, and the Barbarian, as they met before their respective altars, easily persuaded themselves, that under various names, and with various ceremonies, they adored the same deities.

Gibbon, *Decline and Fall of the Roman Empire,* II

43 The deities of Olympus, as they are painted by the immortal bard, imprint themselves on the minds which are the least addicted to superstitious credulity. Our familiar knowledge of their names and characters, their forms and attributes, *seems* to bestow on those airy beings a real and substantial existence; and the pleasing enchantment produces an imperfect and momentary assent of the imagination to those fables which are the most repugnant to our reason and experience.

Gibbon, *Decline and Fall of the Roman Empire,* XXIII

44 The weakness of polytheism was, in some measure, excused by the moderation of its claims; and the devotion of the Pagans was not incompatible with the most licentious scepticism.

Gibbon, *Decline and Fall of the Roman Empire,* XXIII

45 I am not sure but I should betake myself in extremities to the liberal divinities of Greece, rather than to my country's God. Jehovah, though with us he has acquired new attributes, is more absolute and unapproachable, but hardly more divine, than Jove. He is not so much of a gentleman, not so gracious and catholic, he does not exert so intimate and genial an influence on nature, as many a god of the Greeks. I should fear the infinite power and inflexible justice of the almighty mortal hardly as yet apotheosized, so wholly masculine, with no sister Juno, no Apollo, no Venus, nor Minerva, to intercede for me. . . . The Grecian are youthful and erring and fallen gods, with the vices of men, but in many important respects essentially of the divine race. In my Pantheon, Pan still reigns in his pristine glory, with his ruddy face, his flowing beard, and his shaggy body, his pipe and his crook, his nymph Echo, and his chosen daughter Iambe; for the great god Pan is not dead, as was rumored. No god ever dies. Perhaps of all the gods of New England and of ancient Greece, I am most constant at his shrine.

Thoreau, *A Week on the Concord and Merrimack Rivers (Sunday)*

46 That fear first created the gods is perhaps as true as anything so brief could be on so great a subject.

Santayana, *Life of Reason,* III, 3

20.7 | *Angels and Devils*

Superhuman in the sense that they are superior to man but not supernatural because, like man, they have natures created by God, the angels (the bad angels, the devils or demons, as well as the good) occupy a special place in the Judeo-Christian cosmology that has only a faint analogy with the role played by the demigods in other religions. In their most frequent appearance in the Old Testament and the New, they perform the function of messengers or emissaries of

the Lord; but, as other passages indicate, that is by no means their only raison d'être. They comprise, on the one hand, the heavenly host, the celestial hierarchy, engaged in the adoration of God; and, on the other, they are the damned as well as the ministers of damnation in the nether regions below.

We know, both from Scripture and from the poets, the proper names of only a small number of the angels and demons. The name most familiar to us is that of the fallen

Seraph, variously called Lucifer, Satan, or Mephistopheles, who appears as the serpent in the Garden of Eden. Among the good angels, we are acquainted by name only with angels of a much lower rank, such as the archangels Michael and Gabriel. Indeed, one of the most striking things we are told about these creatures by Christian theologians is that they are arranged in nine ranks or grades, the lowest being the angels and archangels who act as guardians of individual men or as messengers from God to man, the highest being the cherubim and seraphim, whose prime function is simply to adore their Creator and to praise him.

In three of the greatest poems of Western literature—in Dante's *Divine Comedy,* in Milton's *Paradise Lost,* and in Goethe's *Faust*—angels and demons play leading roles. Their portrayal in these poems, rather than their appearances in the Bible or the theories about them developed by the theologians, dominates our imagination. In addition, it is in such poems as Milton's *Lycidas* that we are made aware of the mischievous and prankish fairies that represent vestigial traces of the demons or devils of the older pagan religions that Christianity long struggled to replace. And in Pope's charming *Rape of the Lock,* a whole panoply of minor but nonetheless spiritual figures watch over such things as the arrangement of tea tables and the ordering of wardrobes.

As the reader will find, the picture of the angels and demons given by the poets does not fully accord with the analysis of their nature and behavior by the theologians. For the poets, angels seem on the whole to be remarkably human—although, of course, more beautiful, powerful, wise. For the theologians, the angels are incorporeal substances, pure spirits or intelligences, having an amazing set of properties appropriate to such natures, by comparison with which man is at best a superior animal. Among the many things the reader will learn by examining the quotations presented here from such works as the elaborate "Treatise on Angels" in the *Summa Theologica* of Thomas Aquinas, two in particular will correct widely prevalent misimpressions. One is that theologians were never in doubt about the number of angels able to occupy a single point in space, such as the head of a pin; the second is that the souls of the departed who join the community of saints are not transformed into angels, although they are "taken up into the angelic orders." A third point is not documented because no theologian ever doubted it: all angels are male.

---

1 Bless the Lord, ye his angels, that excel in strength, that do his commandments, hearkening unto the voice of his word.

Bless ye the Lord, all ye his hosts; ye ministers of his, that do his pleasure.

Psalm 103:20–21

2 So the prayers of them both were heard before the majesty of the great God. And Raphael was sent to heal them both, that is, to scale away the whiteness of Tobit's eyes, and to give Sara the daughter of Raguel for a wife to Tobias the son of Tobit.

Tobit 3:16–17

3 Surely I will keep close nothing from you. For I said, It was good to keep close the secret of a king, but that it was honorable to reveal the works of God. Now therefore, when thou didst pray, and Sara thy daughter-in-law, I did bring the remembrance of your prayers before the Holy One: and when thou didst bury the dead, I was with thee likewise. And when thou didst not delay to rise up, and leave thy dinner, to go and cover the dead, thy good deed was not hid from me: but I was with thee. And now God hath sent me to heal thee and Sara thy daughter-in-law. I am Raphael, one of the seven holy angels, which present the prayers of the saints, and which go in and out before the glory of the Holy One.

Then they were both troubled, and fell upon their faces: for they feared. But he said unto them, Fear not, for it shall go well with you; praise God therefore. For not of any favor of mine, but by the will of our God I came; wherefore praise him for ever. All these days I did appear unto you; but I did neither eat nor drink, but ye did see a vision. Now therefore give God thanks: for I go up to him that sent me; but write all things which are done in a book. And when they arose, they saw him no more. Then they confessed the great and wonderful works of God, and how the angel of the Lord had appeared unto them.

Tobit 12:11–22

4 *Athenian Stranger.* There is a tradition of the happy life of mankind in days when all things were spontaneous and abundant. And of this the reason is said to have been as follows:—Cronos knew what we ourselves were declaring, that no human nature invested with supreme power is able to order human affairs and not overflow with insolence and wrong. Which reflection led him to appoint not men but demigods, who are of a higher and more divine race, to be the kings and rulers of our cities; he did as we do with flocks of sheep and other tame animals. For we do not appoint oxen to be the lords of oxen, or goats of goats; but we ourselves are a superior race and rule over them. In like manner God, in his love of mankind, placed over us the demons, who are a superior race, and they with great ease and pleasure to themselves, and no less to us, taking care of us and giving us peace and reverence and order and justice never failing, made the tribes of men happy and united.

Plato, *Laws,* IV, 713A

5 Why do ye not understand my speech? even because ye cannot hear my word.

Ye are of your father the devil, and the lusts of your father ye will do. He was a murderer from the beginning, and abode not in the truth, because there is no truth in him. When he speaketh a lie, he speaketh of his own: for he is a liar, and the father of it.

And because I tell you the truth, ye believe me not.

Which of you convinceth me of sin? And if I say the truth, why do ye not believe me?

He that is of God heareth God's words: ye therefore hear them not, because ye are not of God.

John 8:43–47

6 Be sober, be vigilant; because your adversary the devil, as a roaring lion, walketh about, seeking whom he may devour.

I Peter 5:8

7 And I beheld, and I heard the voice of many angels round about the throne and the beasts and the elders: and the number of them was ten thousand times ten thousand, and thousands of thousands.

Revelation 5:11

8 And there was war in heaven: Michael and his angels fought against the dragon; and the dragon fought and his angels,

And prevailed not; neither was their place found anymore in heaven.

And the great dragon was cast out, that old serpent, called the Devil, and Satan, which deceiveth the whole world: he was cast out into the earth, and his angels were cast out with him.

Revelation 12:7–9

9 And I saw an angel come down from heaven, having the key of the bottomless pit and a great chain in his hand.

And he laid hold on the dragon, that old serpent, which is the Devil, and Satan, and bound him a thousand years,

And cast him into the bottomless pit, and shut him up, and set a seal upon him, that he should deceive the nations no more, till the thousand years should be fulfilled: and after that he must be loosed a little season. . . .

And when the thousand years are expired, Satan shall be loosed out of his prison,

And shall go out to deceive the nations which are in the four quarters of the earth, Gog and Magog, to gather them together to battle: the number of whom is as the sand of the sea.

Revelation 20:1–8

10 No credence whatever is to be given to the opinion of Apuleius and the other philosophers of the same school, namely, that the demons act as messengers and interpreters between the gods and men to carry our petitions from us to the gods, and to bring back to us the help of the gods. On the contrary, we must believe them to be spirits most eager to inflict harm, utterly alien from righteousness, swollen with pride, pale with envy, subtle in deceit; who dwell indeed in this air as in a prison, in keeping with their own character, because, cast down from the height of the higher heaven, they have been condemned to dwell in this element as the just reward of irretrievable transgression.

Augustine, *City of God,* VIII, 22

11 The demons . . . have knowledge without charity, and are thereby so inflated or proud that they crave those divine honours and religious services which they know to be due to the true God, and still, as far as they can, exact these from all over whom they have influence.

Augustine, *City of God,* IX, 20

12 The good angels . . . hold cheap all that knowledge of material and transitory things which the demons are so proud of possessing—not that they are ignorant of these things, but because the love of God, whereby they are sanctified, is very dear to them, and because, in comparison of that not

merely immaterial but also unchangeable and ineffable beauty, with the holy love of which they are inflamed, they despise all things which are beneath it and all that is not it, that they may with every good thing that is in them enjoy that good which is the source of their goodness. And therefore they have a more certain knowledge even of those temporal and mutable things, because they contemplate their principles and causes in the word of God, by which the world was made—those causes by which one thing is approved, another rejected, and all arranged. But the demons do not behold in the wisdom of God these eternal, and, as it were, cardinal causes of things temporal, but only foresee a larger part of the future than men do, by reason of their greater acquaintance with the signs which are hidden from us. Sometimes, too, it is their own intentions they predict. And, finally, the demons are frequently, the angels never, deceived. For it is one thing, by the aid of things temporal and changeable, to conjecture the changes that may occur in time, and to modify such things by one's own will and faculty—and this is to a certain extent permitted to the demons—it is another thing to foresee the changes of times in the eternal and immutable laws of God, which live in His wisdom, and to know the will of God, the most infallible and powerful of all causes, by participating in His spirit; and this is granted to the holy angels by a just discretion. And thus they are not only eternal, but blessed. And the good wherein they are blessed is God, by Whom they were created. For without end they enjoy the contemplation and participation of Him.

Augustine, *City of God*, IX, 22

13 What Catholic Christian does not know that no new devil will ever arise among the good angels, as he knows that this present devil will never again return into the fellowship of the good?

Augustine, *City of God*, XI, 13

14 Though in the order of nature angels rank above men, yet, by the scale of justice, good men are of greater value than bad angels.

Augustine, *City of God*, XI, 16

15 That certain angels sinned, and were thrust down to the lowest parts of this world, where they are, as it were, incarcerated till their final damnation in the day of judgment, the Apostle Peter very plainly declares, when he says that "God spared not the angels that sinned, but cast them down to hell, and delivered them into chains of darkness to be reserved into judgment." Who, then, can doubt that God, either in foreknowledge or in act, separated between these and the rest? And who will dispute that the rest are justly called "light"? For even we who are yet living by faith, hoping only and not yet enjoying equality with them, are al-

ready called "light" by the apostle: "For ye were sometimes darkness, but now are ye light in the Lord." But as for these apostate angels, all who understand or believe them to be worse than unbelieving men are well aware that they are called "darkness." Wherefore, though light and darkness are to be taken in their literal signification in these passages of Genesis in which it is said, "God said, Let there be light, and there was light," and "God divided the light from the darkness," yet, for our part, we understand these two societies of angels—the one enjoying God, the other swelling with pride; the one to whom it is said, "Praise ye Him, all His angels," the other whose prince says, "All these things will I give Thee if Thou wilt fall down and worship me"; the one blazing with the holy love of God, the other reeking with the unclean lust of self-advancement. And since, as it is written, "God resisteth the proud, but giveth grace unto the humble," we may say, the one dwelling in the heaven of heavens, the other cast thence, and raging through the lower regions of the air; the one tranquil in the brightness of piety, the other tempest-tossed with beclouding desires; the one, at God's pleasure, tenderly succouring, justly avenging—the other, set on by its own pride, boiling with the lust of subduing and hurting; the one the minister of God's goodness to the utmost of their good pleasure, the other held in by God's power from doing the harm it would; the former laughing at the latter when it does good unwillingly by its persecutions, the latter envying the former when it gathers in its pilgrims. These two angelic communities, then, dissimilar and contrary to one another, the one both by nature good and by will upright, the other also good by nature but by will depraved, as they are exhibited in other and more explicit passages of holy writ, so I think they are spoken of in this book of Genesis under the names of "light" and "darkness".

Augustine, *City of God*, XI, 33

16 That the contrary propensities in good and bad angels have arisen, not from a difference in their nature and origin, since God, the good Author and Creator of all essences, created them both, but from a difference in their wills and desires, it is impossible to doubt. While some steadfastly continued in that which was the common good of all, namely, in God Himself, and in His eternity, truth, and love; others, being enamoured rather of their own power, as if they could be their own good, lapsed to this private good of their own, from that higher and beatific good which was common to all, and, bartering the lofty dignity of eternity for the inflation of pride, the most assured verity for the slyness of vanity, uniting love for factious partisanship, they became proud, deceived, envious. The cause, therefore, of the blessedness of the good is adherence to God. And so the cause of the others' misery will be found in

the contrary, that is, in their not adhering to God.

Augustine, *City of God,* XII, 1

17 Though we cannot call the devil a fornicator or drunkard, or ascribe to him any sensual indulgence (though he is the secret instigator and prompter of those who sin in these ways), yet he is exceedingly proud and envious. And this viciousness has so possessed him, that on account of it he is reserved in chains of darkness to everlasting punishment. Now these vices, which have dominion over the devil, the apostle attributes to the flesh, which certainly the devil has not. For he says "hatred, variance, emulations, strife, envying" are the works of the flesh; and of all these evils pride is the origin and head, and it rules in the devil though he has no flesh.

Augustine, *City of God,* XIV, 3

18 It is He Who, when He foreknew that man would in his turn sin by abandoning God and breaking His law, did not deprive him of the power of free-will, because He at the same time foresaw what good He Himself would bring out of the evil, and how from this mortal race, deservedly and justly condemned, He would by His grace collect, as now He does, a people so numerous, that He thus fills up and repairs the blank made by the fallen angels, and that thus that beloved and heavenly city is not defrauded of the full number of its citizens, but perhaps may even rejoice in a still more overflowing population.

Augustine, *City of God,* XXII, 1

19 The angels of God are our angels, as Christ is God's and also ours. They are God's, because they have not abandoned Him; they are ours, because we are their fellow-citizens.

Augustine, *City of God,* XXII, 29

20 If every one to whom we ought to show, or who ought to show to us, the offices of mercy is by right called a neighbour, it is manifest that the command to love our neighbour embraces the holy angels also, seeing that so great offices of mercy have been performed by them on our behalf.

Augustine, *Christian Doctrine,* I, 30

21 Angels need an assumed body, not for themselves, but on our account, that by conversing familiarly with men they may give evidence of that intellectual companionship which men expect to have with them in the life to come. Moreover that angels assumed bodies under the Old Law was a figurative indication that the Word of God would take a human body, because all the apparitions in the Old Testament were ordered to that one whereby the Son of God appeared in the flesh.

Aquinas, *Summa Theologica,* I, 51, 2

22 There are not two angels in the same place. The reason of this is because it is impossible for two complete causes to be the causes immediately of one and the same thing. This is evident in every genus of causes; for there is one proximate form of one thing, and there is one proximate mover, although there may be several remote movers. Nor can it be objected that several individuals may row a boat, since no one of them is a perfect mover, because no one man's strength is sufficient for moving the boat, while all together are as one mover, in so far as their united strengths all combine in producing the one movement. Hence, since the angel is said to be in one place by the fact that his power touches the place immediately by way of a perfect container . . . there can be but one angel in one place.

Aquinas, *Summa Theologica,* I, 52, 3

23 Men cannot know future things except in their causes, or by God's revelation. The angels know the future in the same way, but much more acutely.

Aquinas, *Summa Theologica,* I, 57, 3

24 Angels and intellectual souls are incorruptible by the very fact of their having a nature whereby they are capable of truth. But they did not possess this nature from eternity. It was bestowed upon them when God Himself willed it. Consequently it does not follow that the angels existed from eternity.

Aquinas, *Summa Theologica,* I, 61, 2

25 The demons do not delight in the obscenities of the sins of the flesh as if they themselves were disposed to carnal pleasures; it is wholly through envy that they take pleasure in all sorts of human sins, so far as these are hindrances to a man's good.

Aquinas, *Summa Theologica,* I, 63, 2

26 The demons know a truth in three ways: first of all by the subtlety of their nature; for although they are darkened by privation of the light of grace, yet they are enlightened by the light of their intellectual nature. Secondly, by revelation from the holy angels; for while not agreeing with them in conformity of will, they do agree, nevertheless, by their likeness of intellectual nature, according to which they can accept what is manifested by others. Thirdly, they know by long experience; not as deriving it from the senses, but when the likeness of their innate intelligible species is completed in individual things, they know some things as present, which they previously did not know would come to pass.

Aquinas, *Summa Theologica,* I, 64, 1

27 Both a good and a bad angel by their own natural power can move the human imagination. This may be explained as follows. . . . Corporeal na-

ture obeys the angel as regards local movement, so that whatever can be caused by the local movement of bodies is subject to the natural power of the angels. Now it is manifest that imaginative apparitions are sometimes caused in us by the local movement of animal spirits and humours. Hence Aristotle says, when assigning the cause of visions in dreams, that "when an animal sleeps, the blood descends in abundance to the sensitive principle, and movements descend with it"; that is, the impressions left from the movements of sensible things, which movements are preserved in the animal spirits, "and move the sensitive principle," so that a certain appearance ensues, as if the sensitive principle were being then changed by the external objects themselves. Indeed, the disturbance of the spirits and humours may be so great that such appearances may even occur to those who are awake, as is seen in mad people, and the like. So, as this happens by a natural disturbance of the humours, and sometimes also by the will of man who voluntarily imagines what he previously experienced, so also the same may be done by the power of a good or a bad angel, sometimes with alienation from the bodily senses, sometimes without such alienation.

Aquinas, *Summa Theologica*, I, 111, 3

28 Each man has a guardian angel appointed to him. The reason for this is that the guardianship of angels belongs to the execution of Divine Providence concerning men. But God's providence acts differently as regards men and as regards other corruptible creatures, for they are related differently to incorruptibility. For men are not only incorruptible in the common species, but also in the proper forms of each individual, which are the rational souls, which cannot be said of other incorruptible things. Now it is manifest that the providence of God is chiefly exercised towards what remains for ever; but as regards things which pass away, the providence of God acts so as to order them to the things which are perpetual. Thus the providence of God is related to each man as it is to every genus or species of things corruptible. But, according to Gregory, "the different orders are assigned to the different genera of things, for instance the Powers to coerce the demons, the Virtues to work miracles in things corporeal." And it is probable that the different species are presided over by different angels of the same order. Hence it is also reasonable to suppose that different angels are appointed to the guardianship of different men.

Aquinas, *Summa Theologica*, I, 113, 2

29 The wicked angels assail men in two ways. First, by instigating them to sin. And thus they are not sent by God to assail us, but are sometimes permitted to do so according to God's just judgments. But sometimes their assault is a punishment to

man. And thus they are sent by God, as the lying spirit was sent to punish Achab, King of Israel. . . . For punishment is referred to God as its first author. Nevertheless the demons who are sent to punish, do so with an intention other than that for which they are sent; for they punish from hatred or envy, although they are sent by God on account of His justice.

Aquinas, *Summa Theologica*, I, 114, 1

30 The devil is the occasional and indirect cause of all our sins in so far as he induced the first man to sin, by reason of whose sin human nature is so infected that we are all prone to sin, even as the burning of wood might be imputed to the man who dried the wood so as to make it easily inflammable. He is not, however, the direct cause of all the sins of men, as though each were the result of his suggestion.

Aquinas, *Summa Theologica*, I–II, 80, 4

31 And now there came, upon the turbid waves, a
　　crash of fearful sound, at which the shores both
　　trembled;
a sound as of a wind, impetuous for the adverse
　　heats, which smites the forest without any stay;
shatters off the boughs, beats down, and sweeps
　　away; dusty in front, it goes superb, and makes
　　the wild beasts and the shepherds flee.
He loosed my eyes, and said: "Now turn thy nerve
　　of vision on that ancient foam, there where the
　　smoke is harshest."
As frogs, before their enemy the serpent, ran all
　　asunder through the water, till each squats
　　upon the bottom:
so I saw more than a thousand ruined spirits flee
　　before one, who passed the Stygian ferry with
　　soles unwet.
He waved that gross air from his countenance,
　　often moving his left *hand* before *him;* and only
　　of that trouble seemed he weary.
Well did I perceive that he was a Messenger of
　　Heaven; and I turned to the Master [Virgil];
　　and he made a sign that I should stand quiet,
　　and bow down to him.
Ah, how full he seemed to me of indignation! He
　　reached the gate, and with a wand opened it:
　　for there was no resistance.
"O outcasts of Heaven! race despised!" began he,
　　upon the horrid threshold, "why dwells this insolence in you?
Why spurn ye at that Will, whose object never
　　can be frustrated, and which often has increased your pain?
What profits it to butt against the Fates? Your
　　Cerberus, if ye remember, still bears his chin
　　and his throat peeled for doing so."
Then he returned by the filthy way, and spake no
　　word to us; but looked like one whom other
　　care urges and incites
than that of those who stand before him.

Dante, *Inferno*, IX, 64

32 *Friar.* I heard once at Bologna many of the Devil's
    vices told; amongst which, I heard that he is a liar
    and the father of lies.

                              Dante, *Inferno,* XXIII, 142

33 The Emperor of the dolorous realm [Satan], from
    mid breast stood forth out of the ice; and I *in
    size* am liker to a giant,
        than the giants are to his arms: mark now how
        great that whole must be, which corresponds to
        such a part.
    If he was once as beautiful as he is ugly now, and
        lifted up his brows against his Maker, well may
        all affliction come from him.
    Oh how great a marvel seemed it to me, when I
        saw three faces on his head! The one in front,
        and it was fiery red;
    the others were two, that were adjoined to this,
        above the very middle of each shoulder; and
        they were joined [at] his crest;
    and the right seemed between white and yellow;
        the left was such to look on, as they who come
        from where the Nile [descends].
    Under each there issued forth two mighty wings,
        of size befitting such a bird: sea-sails I never
        saw so broad.
    No plumes had they; but were in form *and texture*
        like a bat's: and he was flapping them, so that
        three winds went forth from him
    Thereby Cocytus all was frozen; with six eyes he
        wept, and down three chins gushed tears and
        bloody foam.
    In every mouth he champed a sinner with his
        teeth, like a brake; so that he thus kept three of
        them in torment.
    To the one in front, the biting was nought, com-
        pared with the tearing: for at times the back of
        him remained quite stript of skin.
    "That soul up there, which suffers greatest pun-
        ishment," said the Master [Virgil], "is Judas Is-
        cariot, *he* who has his head within, and outside
        plies his legs.
    Of the other two, who have their heads beneath,
        that one, who hangs from the black visage is
        Brutus: see how he writhes himself, and utters
        not a word;
    and the other is Cassius, who seems so stark of
        limb. But night is reascending; and now must
        we depart: for we have seen the whole."

                              Dante, *Inferno,* XXXIV, 28

34 [There are three hierarchies of angels and] each
    hierarchy has three orders, so that the Church
    holds and affirms nine orders of spiritual crea-
    tures. The first is that of the Angels, the second of
    the Arch-angels, the third of the Thrones: and
    these three orders make the first hierarchy; not
    first in order of nobility, nor in order of creation
    (for the others are more noble, and all were creat-
    ed at once), but first in the order of our ascent to

their loftiness. Next come the Dominations, afterwards the Virtues, then the Principalities; and
these make the second hierarchy. Above these are
the Powers, and the Cherubim, and above all are
the Seraphim; and these make the third hierarchy. And the number of the hierarchies and that
of the orders constitutes a most potent system of
their speculation. For inasmuch as the divine majesty is in three persons, which have one substance,
they may be contemplated in three-fold manner.
For the supreme power of the Father may be contemplated; and this it is that the first hierarchy, to
wit first in nobility and last in our enumeration,
gazes upon; and the supreme wisdom of the Son
may be contemplated; and this it is that the second hierarchy gazes upon; and the supreme and
most burning love of the Holy Spirit may be contemplated; and this it is that the third hierarchy
gazes upon: the which being nearest unto us gives
us of the gifts which it receiveth. And inasmuch as
each person of the divine Trinity may be considered in three-fold manner, there are in each hierarchy three orders diversely contemplating. The
Father may be considered without respect to
aught save himself; and this contemplation the
Seraphim do use, who see more of the first cause
than any other angelic nature. The Father may
be considered according as he hath relation to the
Son, to wit how he is parted from him and how
united with him, and this do the Cherubim contemplate. The Father may further be considered
according as from him proceedeth the Holy Spirit, and how he is parted from him and how united
with him; and this contemplation the Powers do
use. And in like fashion may there be speculation
of the Son and of the Holy Spirit. Wherefore it
behoves that there be nine manners of contemplating spirits to gaze upon the light which alone
seeth itself completely. And here is a word which
may not be passed in silence. I say that out of all
these orders some certain were lost so soon as they
were created, I take it to the number of a tenth
part; for the restoration of which human nature
was afterward created.

                              Dante, *Convivio,* II, 6

35 Death has been introduced into the world
    through the devil's envy, and on this account the
    devil is called the author of death. For what else
    does Satan do than seduce from true religion, pro-
    voke sedition, cause wars, pestilence, etc., and
    bring about every evil?

                              Luther, *Table Talk,* 1379

36 The acknowledgment of angels is needful in the
    church. Therefore godly preachers should teach
    them logically. First, they should show what an-
    gels are, namely, spiritual creatures without bod-
    ies. Secondly, what manner of spirits they are,
    namely, good spirits and not evil; and here evil

spirits must also be spoken of, not created evil by God, but made so by their rebellion against God, and their consequent fall; this hatred began in Paradise, and will continue and remain against Christ and his church to the world's end. Thirdly, they must speak touching their function, which . . . is to present a mirror of humility to godly Christians, in that such pure and perfect creatures as the angels do minister unto us, poor and wretched people, in household and temporal policy, and in religion. They are our true and trusty servants, performing offices and works that one poor miserable mendicant would be ashamed to do for another. In this sort ought we to teach with care, method, and attention, touching the sweet and loving angels. Whoso speaks of them not in the order prescribed by logic, may speak of many irrelevant things, but little or nothing to edification.

The angels are near to us, to those creatures whom by God's command they are to preserve, to the end we receive no hurt of the devil, though, withal, they behold God's face, and stand before him. Therefore when the devil intends to hurt us, then the loving holy angels resist and drive him away; for the angels have long arms, and although they stand before the face and in the presence of God and his son Christ, yet they are hard by and about us in those affairs, which by God we are commanded to take in hand. The devil is also near and about us, incessantly tracking our steps, in order to deprive us of our lives, our saving health, and salvation. But the holy angels defend us from him, insomuch that he is not able to work us such mischief as willingly he would.

Luther, *Table Talk,* H570–571

37 When Satan will not leave off tempting thee, then bear with patience, hold on hand and foot, nor faint, as if there would be no end thereof, but stand courageously, and attend God's leisure, knowing that what the devil cannot accomplish by his sudden and powerful assaults, he thinks to gain by craft, by persevering to vex and tempt thee, thereby to make thee faint and weary, as in the Psalm is noted: "Many a time have they afflicted me from my youth up; yet they have not prevailed against me," etc. But be fully assured, that in this sport with the devil, God, with all his holy angels, takes delight and joy; and assure thyself, also, that the end thereof will be blessed and happy, which thou shalt certainly find to thy everlasting comfort.

Luther, *Table Talk,* H660

38 We are frequently informed in the Scripture, that angels are celestial spirits, whose ministry and service God uses for the execution of whatever he has decreed; and hence this name is given to them, because God employs them as messengers to manifest himself to men. Other appellations also, by which they are distinguished, are derived from a similar cause. They are called Hosts, because, as life-guards, they surround their prince, aggrandizing his majesty, and rendering it conspicuous; and, like soldiers, are ever attentive to the signal of their leader; and are so prepared for the performance of his commands, that he has no sooner signified his will than they are ready for the work, or rather are actually engaged in it. Such a representation of the throne of God is exhibited in the magnificent descriptions of the Prophets, but particularly of Daniel; where he says, when God had ascended the judgment-seat, that "thousand thousands ministered unto him, and ten thousand times ten thousand stood before him." Since by their means the Lord wonderfully exerts and declares the power and strength of his hand, thence they are denominated Powers. Because by them he exercises and administers his government in the world, therefore they are called sometimes Principalities, sometimes Powers, sometimes Dominions. Lastly, because the glory of God in some measure resides in them, they have also, for this reason, the appellation of Thrones; although on this last name I would affirm nothing, because a different interpretation is equally or even more suitable. But, omitting this name, the Holy Spirit often uses the former ones, to magnify the dignity of the angelic ministry. Nor, indeed, is it right that no honour should be paid to those instruments, by whom God particularly exhibits the presence of his power. Moreover, they are more than once called gods; because in their ministry, as in a mirror, they give us an imperfect representation of Divinity. Though I am pleased with the interpretation of the old writers, on those passages where the Scripture records the appearance of an angel of God to Abraham, Jacob, Moses, and others, that Christ was that angel, yet frequently, where mention is made of angels in general, this name is given to them. Nor should this surprise us; for, if that honour be given to princes and governors, because, in the performance of their functions, they are vicegerents of God, the supreme King and Judge, there is far greater reason for its being paid to angels, in whom the splendour of the Divine glory is far more abundantly displayed.

Calvin, *Institutes of the Christian Religion,* I, 14

39 When Satan is called the god and prince of this world, the strong man armed, the prince of the power of the air, a roaring lion, these descriptions only tend to make us more cautious and vigilant, and better prepared to encounter him.

Calvin, *Institutes of the Christian Religion,* I, 14

40 Having been previously warned that we are perpetually threatened by an enemy, and an enemy

desperately bold and extremely strong, skilled in every artifice, indefatigable in diligence and celerity, abundantly provided with all kinds of weapons, and most expert in the science of war, let us make it the grand object of our attention, that we suffer not ourselves to be oppressed with slothfulness and inactivity, but, on the contrary, arousing and collecting all our courage, be ready for a vigorous resistance; and as this warfare is terminated only by death, let us encourage ourselves to perseverance.

Calvin, *Institutes of the Christian Religion*, I, 14

41 They for us fight, they watch and dewly ward,
And their bright squadrons round about us plant;
And all for love, and nothing for reward:
O why should hevenly God to men have such regard?

Spenser, *Faerie Queene*, Bk. II, VIII, 2

42 *Puck.* I am that merry wanderer of the night.
I jest to Oberon and make him smile
When I a fat and bean-fed horse beguile,
Neighing in likeness of a filly foal:
And sometime lurk I in a gossip's bowl,
In very likeness of a roasted crab,
And when she drinks, against her lips I bob
And on her wither'd dewlap pour the ale.
The wisest aunt, telling the saddest tale,
Sometime for three-foot stool mistaketh me;
Then slip I from her bum, down topples she,
And "tailor" cries, and falls into a cough;
And then the whole quire hold their hips and laugh,
And waxen in their mirth and neeze and swear
A merrier hour was never wasted there.

Shakespeare, *Midsummer-Night's Dream*, II, i, 43

43 *Puck.* I'll put a girdle round about the earth
In forty minutes.

Shakespeare, *Midsummer-Night's Dream*, II, i, 175

44 *Titania.* Be kind and courteous to this gentleman;
Hop in his walks and gambol in his eyes;
Feed him with apricocks and dewberries,
With purple grapes, green figs, and mulberries;
The honey-bags steal from the humble-bees,
And for night-tapers crop their waxen thighs
And light them at the fiery glow-worm's eyes,
To have my love to bed and to arise;
And pluck the wings from painted butterflies
To fan the moonbeams from his sleeping eyes:
Nod to him, elves, and do him courtesies.

Shakespeare, *Midsummer-Night's Dream*, III, i, 167

45 *Antonio.* The devil can cite Scripture for his purpose.

Shakespeare, *Merchant of Venice*, I, iii, 99

46 *Marcellus.* 'Tis gone!   [*Exit* Ghost.]
We do it wrong, being so majestical,
To offer it the show of violence;
For it is, as the air, invulnerable,
And our vain blows malicious mockery.

Bernardo. It was about to speak, when the cock crew.

Horatio. And then it started like a guilty thing
Upon a fearful summons. I have heard,
The cock, that is the trumpet to the morn,
Doth with his lofty and shrill-sounding throat
Awake the god of day; and, at his warning
Whether in sea or fire, in earth or air,
The extravagant and erring spirit hies
To his confine.

Shakespeare, *Hamlet*, I, i, 142

47 *Hamlet.* Angels and ministers of grace defend us!

Shakespeare, *Hamlet*, I, iv, 39

48 *Hamlet.*   The devil hath power
To assume a pleasing shape.

Shakespeare, *Hamlet*, II, ii, 628

49 *Banquo.* And oftentimes, to win us to our harm,
The instruments of darkness tell us truths,
Win us with honest trifles, to betray's
In deepest consequence.

Shakespeare, *Macbeth*, I, iii, 123

50 *Malcolm.* Angels are bright still, though the brightest fell.

Shakespeare, *Macbeth*, IV, iii, 22

51 *Caliban.* All the infections that the sun sucks up
From bogs, fens, flats, on Prosper fall and make him
By inch-meal a disease! His spirits hear me
And yet I needs must curse. But they'll nor pinch,
Fright me with urchin-shows, pitch me i' the mire,
Nor lead me, like a firebrand, in the dark
Out of my way, unless he bid 'em; but
For every trifle are they set upon me;
Sometime like apes that mow and chatter at me
And after bite me, then like hedgehogs which
Lie tumbling in my barefoot way and mount
Their pricks at my footfall; sometime am I
All wound with adders who with cloven tongues
Do hiss me into madness.

Shakespeare, *Tempest*, II, ii, 1

52 *Prospero.* Ye elves of hills, brooks, standing lakes, and groves,
And ye that on the sands with printless foot
Do chase the ebbing Neptune and do fly him
When he comes back; you demi-puppets that
By moonshine do the green sour ringlets make,
Whereof the ewe not bites, and you whose pastime
Is to make midnight mushrooms, that rejoice
To hear the solemn curfew; by whose aid,

Weak masters though ye be, I have bedimm'd
The noontide sun, call'd forth the mutinous
 winds,
And 'twixt the green sea and the azured vault
Set roaring war; to the dread rattling thunder
Have I given fire and rifted Jove's stout oak
With his own bolt; the strong-based promontory
Have I made shake and by the spurs pluck'd up
The pine and cedar; graves at my command
Have waked their sleepers, oped, and let 'em forth
By my so potent art. But this rough magic
I here abjure, and, when I have required
Some heavenly music, which even now I do,
To work mine end upon their senses that
This airy charm is for, I'll break my staff,
Bury it certain fathoms in the earth,
And deeper than did ever plummet sound
I'll drown my book.

> Shakespeare, *Tempest*, V, i, 34

53 *Ariel.* Where the bee sucks, there suck I.
 In a cowslip's bell I lie;
 There I couch when owls do cry.
 On the bat's back I do fly
 After summer merrily.
Merrily, Merrily shall I live now
Under the blossom that hangs on the bough.

> Shakespeare, *Tempest*, V, i, 88

54 At the round earths imagin'd corners, blow
Your trumpets, Angells, and arise, arise
From death, you numberlesse infinities
Of soules.

> Donne, *Holy Sonnet VII*

55 By the name of *angel* is signified, generally, a messenger; and most often a messenger of God: and by a messenger of God is signified anything that makes known His extraordinary presence; that is to say, the extraordinary manifestation of His power, especially by a dream or vision.

> Hobbes, *Leviathan*, III, 34

56 The kingdom of darkness . . . is nothing else but a confederacy of deceivers that, to obtain dominion over men in this present world, endeavour, by dark and erroneous doctrines, to extinguish in them the light, both of nature and of the gospel; and so to disprepare them for the kingdom of God to come.

> Hobbes, *Leviathan*, IV, 44

57 Then to the Spicy Nut-brown Ale,
With stories told of many a feat,
How *Faery Mab* the junkets eat,
She was pincht, and pull'd she sed,
And he by Friars Lanthorn led
Tells how the drudging *Goblin* swet,
To ern his Cream-bowle duly set,
When in one night, ere glimps of morn,

His shadowy Flale hath thresh'd the Corn
That ten day-labourers could not end.

> Milton, *L'Allegro,* 100

58 There the companions of his fall, o'rewhelm'd
With Floods and Whirlwinds of tempestuous fire,
He soon discerns, and weltring by his side
One next himself in power, and next in crime,
Long after known in *Palestine*, and nam'd
Bëëlzebub. To whom th' Arch-Enemy,
And thence in Heav'n call'd Satan, with bold
 words
Breaking the horrid silence thus began.
 If thou beest he; But O how fall'n! how chang'd
From him, who in the happy Realms of Light
Cloth'd with transcendent brightness didst
 outshine
Myriads though bright.

> Milton, *Paradise Lost*, I, 76

59 So stretcht out huge in length the Arch-fiend lay
Chain'd on the burning Lake, nor ever thence
Had ris'n or heav'd his head, but that the will
And high permission of all-ruling Heaven
Left him at large to his own dark designs,
That with reiterated crimes he might
Heap on himself damnation, while he sought
Evil to others, and enrag'd might see
How all his malice serv'd but to bring forth
Infinite goodness, grace and mercy shewn
On Man by him seduc't, but on himself
Treble confusion, wrath and vengeance pour'd.

> Milton, *Paradise Lost*, I, 209

60   Spirits when they please
Can either Sex assume, or both; so soft
And uncompounded is their Essence pure,
Not ti'd or manacl'd with joynt or limb,
Nor founded on the brittle strength of bones,
Like cumbrous flesh; but in what shape they
 choose
Dilated or condens't, bright or obscure,
Can execute their aerie purposes,
And works of love or enmity fulfill.

> Milton, *Paradise Lost*, I, 423

61   Neither Man nor Angel can discern
Hypocrisie, the only evil that walks
Invisible, except to God alone,
By his permissive will, through Heav'n and Earth.

> Milton, *Paradise Lost*, III, 682

62 *Adam.*   Nor think, though men were none,
That heav'n would want spectators, God want
 praise;
Millions of spiritual Creatures walk the Earth
Unseen, both when we wake, and when we sleep:
All these with ceaseless praise his works behold
Both day and night.

> Milton, *Paradise Lost*, IV, 675

63   *Satan* with his Powers
Farr was advanc't on winged speed, an Host
Innumerable as the Starrs of Night,
Or Starrs of Morning, Dew-drops, which the Sun
Impearls on every leaf and every flouer.
Regions they pass'd, the mightie Regencies
Of Seraphim and Potentates and Thrones
In thir triple Degrees, Regions to which
All thy Dominion, *Adam,* is no more
Then what this Garden is to all the Earth,
And all the Sea, from one entire globose
Stretcht into Longitude; which having pass'd
At length into the limits of the North
They came, and *Satan* to his Royal seat
High on a Hill, far blazing, as a Mount
Rais'd on a Mount, with Pyramids and Towrs
From Diamond Quarries hew'n, & Rocks of Gold,
The Palace of great *Lucifer,* (so call
That Structure in the Dialect of men
Interpreted) which not long after, hee
Affecting all equality with God,
In imitation of that Mount whereon
Messiah was declar'd in sight of Heav'n,
The Mountain of the Congregation call'd;
For thither he assembl'd all his Train,
Pretending so commanded to consult
About the great reception of thir King,
Thither to come, and with calumnious Art
Of counterfeted truth thus held thir ears.
  Thrones, Dominations, Princedomes, Vertues,
    Powers,
If these magnific Titles yet remain
Not meerly titular, since by Decree
Another now hath to himself ingross't
All Power, and us eclipst under the name
Of King anointed, for whom all this haste
Of midnight march, and hurried meeting here,
This onely to consult how we may best
With what may be devis'd of honours new
Receive him coming to receive from us
Knee-tribute yet unpaid, prostration vile,
Too much to one, but double how endur'd,
To one and to his image now proclaim'd?
But what if better counsels might erect
Our minds and teach us to cast off this Yoke?
Will ye submit your necks, and chuse to bend
The supple knee? ye will not, if I trust
To know ye right, or if ye know your selves
Natives and Sons of Heav'n possest before
By none, and if not equal all, yet free,
Equally free; for Orders and Degrees
Jarr not with liberty, but well consist.
Who can in reason then or right assume
Monarchie over such as live by right
His equals, if in power and splendor less,
In freedome equal? or can introduce
Law and Edict on us, who without law
Erre not, much less for this to be our Lord,
And look for adoration to th' abuse
Of those Imperial Titles which assert

Our being ordain'd to govern, not to serve?
      Milton, *Paradise Lost,* V, 740

64 *Raphael.*   The sword
Of *Michael* from the Armorie of God
Was giv'n him temperd so, that neither keen
Nor solid might resist that edge: it met
The sword of *Satan* with steep force to smite
Descending, and in half cut sheere, nor staid,
But with swift wheele reverse, deep entring shar'd
All his right side; then *Satan* first knew pain,
And writh'd him to and fro convolv'd; so sore
The griding sword with discontinuous wound
Pass'd through him, but th' Ethereal substance
  clos'd
Not long divisible, and from the gash
A stream of Nectarous humor issuing flow'd
Sanguin, such as Celestial Spirits may bleed,
And all his Armour staind ere while so bright.
      Milton, *Paradise Lost,* VI, 320

65 *God.* Because thou hast done this, thou art accurst
Above all Cattel, each Beast of the Field;
Upon thy Belly groveling thou shalt goe,
And dust shalt eat all the days of thy Life.
Between Thee and the Woman I will put
Enmitie, and between thine and her Seed;
Her Seed shall bruise thy head, thou bruise his
  heel.

      Milton, *Paradise Lost,* X, 175

66 It is not possible for man to sever the wheat from
the tares, the good fish from the other fry; that
must be the Angels' Ministry at the end of mortal
things.

      Milton, *Areopagitica*

67 Then *Apollyon* straddled quite over the whole
breadth of the way, and said, I am void of fear in
this matter, prepare thy self to die, for I swear by
my Infernal Den, that thou shalt go no further,
here will I spill thy soul; and with that, he threw
a flaming Dart at his breast, but *Christian* had a
Shield in his hand, with which he caught it, and
so prevented the danger of that. Then did *Christian* draw, for he saw 'twas time to bestir him; and
Apollyon as fast made at him, throwing Darts as
thick as Hail; by the which, notwithstanding all
that *Christian* could do to avoid it, *Apollyon* wounded him in his head, his hand and foot; this made
Christian give a little back: *Apollyon* therefore followed his work amain, and *Christian* again took
courage, and resisted as manfully as he could.
This sore combat lasted for above half a day, even
till *Christian* was almost quite spent. For you must
know that *Christian* by reason of his wounds, must
needs grow weaker and weaker.
  Then *Apollyon* espying his opportunity, began to
gather up close to *Christian,* and wrestling with
him, gave him a dreadful fall; and with that,

Christian's Sword flew out of his hand. Then said *Apollyon, I am sure of thee now;* and with that, he had almost prest him to death, so that *Christian* began to despair of life. But as God would have it, while *Apollyon* was fetching of his last blow, thereby to make a full end of this good Man, *Christian* nimbly reached out his hand for his Sword, and caught it, saying, *Rejoice not against me, O mine Enemy! when I fall, I shall arise;* and with that, gave him a deadly thrust, which made him give back, as one that had received his mortal wound: *Christian* perceiving that, made at him again, saying, *Nay, in all these things we are more than Conquerors, through him that loved us.* And with that, *Apollyon* spread forth his Dragon's wings, and sped him away, that *Christian* saw him no more.

Bunyan, Pilgrim's Progress, I

68 It is not impossible to conceive, nor repugnant to reason, that there may be many species of spirits, as much separated and diversified one from another by distinct properties whereof we have no ideas, as the species of sensible things are distinguished one from another by qualities which we know and observe in them. That there should be more species of intelligent creatures above us, than there are of sensible and material below us, is probable to me from hence: that in all the visible corporeal world, we see no chasms or gaps.

Locke, Concerning Human Understanding,
Bk. III, VI, 12

69 Some secret truths, from learned pride concealed,
To Maids alone and Children are revealed:
What though no credit doubting Wits may give?
The Fair and Innocent shall still believe.
Know, then, unnumbered Spirits round thee fly,
The light Militia of the lower sky:
These, though unseen, are ever on the wing,
Hang o'er the Box, and hover round the Ring.

Pope, The Rape of the Lock, I, 37

70 The Sprites of fiery Termagants in Flame
Mount up, and take a Salamander's name.
Soft yielding minds to Water glide away,
And sip, with Nymphs, their elemental Tea.
The graver Prude sinks downward to a Gnome,
In search of mischief still on Earth to roam.
The light Coquettes in Sylphs aloft repair,
And sport and flutter in the fields of Air.
  Know further yet; whoever fair and chaste
Rejects mankind, is by some Sylph embraced:
For Spirits, freed from mortal laws, with ease
Assume what sexes and what shapes they please.
What guards the purity of melting Maids,
In courtly balls, and midnight masquerades,
Safe from the treach'rous friend, the daring
    spark,
The glance by day, the whisper in the dark,
When kind occasion prompts their warm desires,

When music softens, and when dancing fires?
'Tis but their Sylph, the wise Celestials know,
Though Honour is the word with Men below.

Pope, The Rape of the Lock, I, 59

71 But now secure the painted vessel glides,
The sun-beams trembling on the floating tides:
While melting music steals upon the sky,
And softened sounds along the waters die;
Smooth flow the waves, the Zephyrs gently play,
Belinda smiled, and all the world was gay.
All but the Sylph—with careful thoughts opprest,
Th' impending woe sat heavy on his breast.
He summons strait his Denizens of air;
The lucid squadrons round the sails repair:
Soft o'er the shrouds aërial whispers breathe,
That seemed but Zephyrs to the train beneath.
Some to the sun their insect-wings unfold,
Waft on the breeze, or sink in clouds of gold;
Transparent forms, too fine for mortal sight,
Their fluid bodies half dissolved in light,
Loose to the wind their airy garments flew,
Thin glitt'ring textures of the filmy dew,
Dipt in the richest tincture of the skies,
Where light disports in ever-mingling dyes,
While every beam new transient colours flings,
Colours that change whene'er they wave their
    wings.

Pope, The Rape of the Lock, II, 47

72 This day, black Omens threat the brightest Fair,
That e'er deserved a watchful spirit's care;
Some dire disaster, or by force, or slight;
But what, or where, the fates have wrapt in night.
Whether the nymph shall break Diana's law,
Or some frail China jar receive a flaw;
Or stain her honour or her new brocade;
Forget her prayers, or miss a masquerade;
Or lose her heart, or necklace, at a ball;
Or whether Heaven has doomed that Shock must
    fall.
Haste, then, ye spirits! to your charge repair:
The flutt'ring fan be Zephyretta's care;
The drops to thee, Brillante, we consign;
And, Momentilla, let the watch be thine;
Do thou, Crispissa, tend her fav'rite Lock;
Ariel himself shall be the guard of Shock.
  To fifty chosen Sylphs, of special note,
We trust th' important charge, the Petticoat:
Oft have we known that seven-fold fence to fail,
Though stiff with hoops, and armed with ribs of
    whale;
Form a strong line about the silver bound,
And guard the wide circumference around.
  Whatever spirit, careless of his charge,
His post neglects, or leaves the fair at large,
Shall feel sharp vengeance soon o'ertake his sins,
Be stopped in vials, or transfixed with pins;
Or plunged in lakes of bitter washes lie,
Or wedged whole ages in a bodkin's eye:

Gums and Pomatums shall his flight restrain,
While clogged he beats his silken wings in vain;
Or Alum styptics with contracting power
Shrink his thin essence like a rivelled flower:
Or, as Ixion fixed, the wretch shall feel
The giddy motion of the whirling Mill,
In fumes of burning Chocolate shall glow,
And tremble at the sea that froths below!

He spoke; the spirits from the sails descend;
Some, orb in orb, around the nymph extend;
Some thrid the mazy ringlets of her hair;
Some hang upon the pendants of her ear:
With beating hearts the dire event they wait,
Anxious, and trembling for the birth of Fate.

Pope, *The Rape
of the Lock,* II, 101

73 I look upon the vulgar observation, "That the
devil often deserts his friends, and leaves them in
the lurch," to be a great abuse on that gentleman's character. Perhaps he may sometimes desert those who are only his cup acquaintance; or
who, at most, are but half his; but he generally
stands by those who are thoroughly his servants,

and helps them off in all extremities, till their bargain expires.

Fielding, *Tom Jones,* XVIII, 5

74 I have always found that Angels have the vanity
to speak of themselves as the only wise; this they
do with a confident insolence sprouting from systematic reasoning.

Blake, *Marriage of Heaven and Hell,* 21

75 Of course, Satan has some kind of case, it goes
without saying. It may be a poor one, but that is
nothing; that can be said about any one of us.
. . . We may not pay him reverence for that
would be indiscreet; but we can at least respect
his talents. A person who has for untold centuries
maintained the imposing position of spiritual
head of four fifths of the human race, and political head of the whole of it, must be granted the
possession of executive abilities of the loftiest order. . . . I would like to see him. I would rather
see him and shake him by the tail than any other
member of the European Concert.

Mark Twain, *Concerning the Jews*

20.8 | *Worship and Service*

We understand the common expression "religious services" to stand for the program of
prayers, chants, hymns, readings from scripture, confessions of faith and of sin, and
sometimes sacraments and sermons that
constitute the liturgy of worship engaged in
communally by the members of a religious
sect. But religious worship need not be communal, nor does the performance of other
religious acts, such as prayer, confession,
and thanksgiving.

The quotations included here cover the
acts of piety and reverence in the pagan religions of antiquity as well as the forms of
worship practiced in Judaism and Chris-

tianity. Prayer, veneration, and sacrifice are
prominent in both traditions. But the notion
of propitiating the deity by sacrifice and the
veneration of his graven image, which play
a large part in pagan worship, are either
expunged from or are radically transformed
in Judaism and Christianity. Passages taken
from both the Old and the New Testament
speak decisively on these points.

Prayer is, perhaps, the subject most frequently touched on in the quotations below.
The purpose and the efficacy of prayer are
discussed; and an interesting variety of actual prayers are presented. What the theologians have to say about prayer contrasts

sharply with the non-theological approach to the subject, typified by Coleridge's re-

mark that "He prayeth best, who loveth best/ All things both great and small."

---

1 And God blessed the seventh day, and sanctified it: because that in it he had rested from all his work which God created and made.

Genesis 2:3

2 Hear, O Israel: The Lord our God is one Lord:

And thou shalt love the Lord thy God with all thine heart, and with all thy soul, and with all thy might.

And these words, which I command thee this day, shall be in thine heart:

And thou shalt teach them diligently unto thy children, and shalt talk of them when thou sittest in thine house, and when thou walkest by the way, and when thou liest down, and when thou risest up.

And thou shalt bind them for a sign upon thine hand, and they shall be as frontlets between thine eyes.

And thou shalt write them upon the posts of thy house, and on thy gates.

Deuteronomy 6:4–9

3 And it was told king David, saying, The Lord hath blessed the house of Obed-edom, and all that pertaineth unto him, because of the ark of God. So David went and brought up the ark of God from the house of Obed-edom into the city of David with gladness.

And it was so, that when they that bare the ark of the Lord had gone six paces, he sacrificed oxen and fatlings.

And David danced before the Lord with all his might; and David was girded with a linen ĕ-phŏd.

So David and all the house of Israel brought up the ark of the Lord with shouting, and with the sound of the trumpet.

And as the ark of the Lord came into the city of David, Mĭ-chăl Saul's daughter looked through a window, and saw king David leaping and dancing before the Lord; and she despised him in her heart. . . .

Then David returned to bless his household. And Mĭ-chăl the daughter of Saul came out to meet David, and said, How glorious was the king of Israel to day, who uncovered himself to day in the eyes of the handmaids of his servants, as one of the vain fellows shamelessly uncovereth himself!

And David said unto Mĭ-chăl, It was before the Lord, which chose me before thy father, and before all his house, to appoint me ruler over the people of the Lord, over Israel: therefore will I play before the Lord.

II Samuel 6:12–21

4 Give ear to my words, O Lord, consider my meditation.

Hearken unto the voice of my cry, my King, and my God: for unto thee will I pray.

My voice shalt thou hear in the morning, O Lord; in the morning will I direct my prayer unto thee, and will look up.

Psalm 5:1–3

5 Hear the right, O Lord, attend unto my cry, give ear unto my prayer, that goeth not out of feigned lips.

Let my sentence come forth from thy presence; let thine eyes behold the things that are equal.

Thou hast proved mine heart; thou hast visited me in the night; thou hast tried me, and shalt find nothing; I am purposed that my mouth shall not transgress.

Concerning the works of men, by the word of thy lips I have kept me from the paths of the destroyer.

Hold up my goings in thy paths, that my footsteps slip not.

I have called upon thee, for thou wilt hear me, O God: incline thine ear unto me, and hear my speech.

Shew thy marvellous loving-kindness, O thou that savest by thy right hand them which put their trust in thee from those that rise up against them.

Psalm 17:1–7

6 O sing unto the Lord a new song: sing unto the Lord, all the earth.

Sing unto the Lord, bless his name; shew forth his salvation from day to day.

Declare his glory among the heathen, his wonders among all people.

For the Lord is great, and greatly to be praised: he is to be feared above all gods.

For all the gods of the nations are idols: but the Lord made the heavens.

Honour and majesty are before him: strength and beauty are in his sanctuary.

Give unto the Lord, O ye kindreds of the people, give unto the Lord glory and strength.

Give unto the Lord the glory due unto his name: bring an offering, and come into his courts.

O worship the Lord in the beauty of holiness: fear before him, all the earth.

Say among the heathen that the Lord reigneth: the world also shall be established that it shall not be moved: he shall judge the people righteously.

Let the heavens rejoice, and let the earth be glad; let the sea roar, and the fulness thereof.

Let the field be joyful, and all that is therein:
then shall all the trees of the wood rejoice
Before the Lord.

Psalm 96:1–13

7 Make a joyful noise unto the Lord, all ye lands.
Serve the Lord with gladness: come before his presence with singing.

Know ye that the Lord he is God: it is he that hath made us, and not we ourselves; we are his people, and the sheep of his pasture.

Enter into his gates with thanksgiving, and into his courts with praise: be thankful unto him, and bless his name.

For the Lord is good; his mercy is everlasting; and his truth endureth to all generations.

Psalm 100:1–5

8 Out of the depths have I cried unto thee, O Lord.
Lord, hear my voice: let thine ears be attentive to the voice of my supplications.

If thou, Lord, shouldest mark iniquities, O Lord, who shall stand?

But there is forgiveness with thee, that thou mayest be feared.

Psalm 130:1–4

9 To what purpose is the multitude of your sacrifices unto me? saith the Lord: I am full of the burnt offerings of rams, and the fat of fed beasts; and I delight not in the blood of bullocks, or of lambs, or of he goats.

When ye come to appear before me, who hath required this at your hand, to tread my courts?

Bring no more vain oblations; incense is an abomination unto me; the new moons and sabbaths, the calling of assemblies, I cannot away with; it is iniquity, even the solemn meeting.

Your new moons and your appointed feasts my soul hateth: they are a trouble unto me; I am weary to bear them.

And when ye spread forth your hands, I will hide mine eyes from you: yea, when ye make many prayers, I will not hear: Your hands are full of blood.

Wash you, make you clean; put away the evil of your doings from before mine eyes; cease to do evil;

Learn to do well; seek judgment, relieve the oppressed, judge the fatherless, plead for the widow.

Isaiah 1:11–17

10 Wherewith shall I come before the Lord, and bow myself before the high God? shall I come before him with burnt offerings, with calves of a year old?

Will the Lord be pleased with thousands of rams, or with ten thousands of rivers of oil? shall I give my firstborn for my transgression, the fruit of my body for the sin of my soul?

He hath shewed thee, O man, what is good;

and what doth the Lord require of thee, but to do justly, and to love mercy, and to walk humbly with thy God?

Micah 6:6–8

11 *Phoinix.* The very immortals can be moved; their virtue and honour and strength are greater than ours are, and yet with sacrifices and offerings for endearment, with libations and with savour men turn back even the immortals in supplication, when any man does wrong and transgresses.

Homer, *Iliad*, IX, 497

12 *Phoinix.* There are . . . the spirits of Prayer, the daughters of great Zeus, and they are lame of their feet, and wrinkled, and cast their eyes sidelong, who toil on their way left far behind by the spirit of Ruin: but she, Ruin, is strong and sound on her feet, and therefore far outruns all Prayers, and wins into every country to force men astray; and the Prayers follow as healers after her. If a man venerates these daughters of Zeus as they draw near, such a man they bring great advantage, and hear his entreaty; but if a man shall deny them, and stubbornly with a harsh word refuse, they go to Zeus, son of Kronos, in supplication that Ruin may overtake this man, that he be hurt, and punished.

Homer, *Iliad*, IX, 502

13 *Creon.* And still you dared to overstep these laws?
Antigone. For me it was not Zeus who made that order.
Nor did that Justice who lives with the gods below
mark out such laws to hold among mankind.
Nor did I think your orders were so strong
that you, a mortal man, could over-run
the gods' unwritten and unfailing laws.
Not now, nor yesterday's, they always live,
and no one knows their origin in time.
So not through fear of any man's proud spirit
would I be likely to neglect these laws,
draw on myself the gods' sure punishment.
I knew that I must die; how could I not?
even without your warning. If I die
before my time, I say it is a gain.
Who lives in sorrows many as are mine
how shall he not be glad to gain his death?
And so, for me to meet this fate, no grief.
But if I left that corpse, my mother's son,

dead and unburied I'd have cause to grieve
as now I grieve not.
And if you think my acts are foolishness
the foolishness may be in a fool's eye.

Sophocles, *Antigone,* 449

14 *Chorus.* Our happiness depends
on wisdom all the way.
The gods must have their due.
Great words by men of pride
bring greater blows upon them.
So wisdom comes to the old.

Sophocles, *Antigone,* 1347

15 *Heracles.*   Keep holy in the sight of God.
All else our father Zeus thinks of less moment.
Holiness does not die with the men that die.
Whether they die or live, it cannot perish.

Sophocles, *Philoctetes,* 1441

16 *Ion.* I have a glorious task:
To set my hands to serve
Not a man but the immortals.
I will never weary
Over my pious tasks.

Euripides, *Ion,* 131

17 *Chorus.*   Not by sounding lament
but only by prayer and reverent love
for the gods, my child, will you learn to live gentler days.

Euripides, *Electra,* 196

18 *Chorus.*—Uncontrollable, the unbeliever goes,
in spitting rage, rebellious and amok,
madly assaulting the mysteries of god,
profaning the rites of the mother of god.
Against the unassailable he runs, with rage
obsessed. Headlong he runs to death.
For death the gods exact, curbing by that bit
the mouths of men. They humble us with death
that we remember what we are who are not god,
but men. We run to death. Wherefore, I say,
accept, accept:
humility is wise; humility is blest.
But what the world calls wise I do not want.
Elsewhere the chase. I hunt another game,
those great, those manifest, those certain goals,
achieving which, our mortal lives are blest.
Let these things be the quarry of my chase:
purity; humility; an unrebellious soul,
accepting all. Let me go the customary way,
the timeless, honored, beaten path of those who
walk
with reverence and awe beneath the sons of heav-
en.

Euripides, *Bacchae,* 996

19 *Socrates.* I mean to say that the holy has been acknowledged by us to be loved of God because it is
holy, not to be holy because it is loved.

Euthyphro. Yes.

Soc. But that which is dear to the gods is dear to
them because it is loved by them, not loved by
them because it is dear to them.

Euth. True.

Soc. But, friend Euthyphro, if that which is holy
is the same with that which is dear to God, and is
loved because it is holy, then that which is dear to
God would have been loved as being dear to God;
but if that which is dear to God is dear to him
because loved by him, then that which is holy
would have been holy because loved by him. But
now you see that the reverse is the case, and that
they are quite different from one another. For one
is of a kind to be loved because it is loved, and the
other is loved because it is of a kind to be loved.
Thus you appear to me, Euthyphro, when I ask
you what is the essence of holiness, to offer an
attribute only, and not the essence—the attribute
of being loved by all the gods. But you still refuse
to explain to me the nature of holiness. And therefore, if you please, I will ask you not to hide your
treasure, but to tell me once more what holiness or
piety really is, whether dear to the gods or not (for
that is a matter about which we will not quarrel);
and what is impiety?

Euth. I really do not know, Socrates, how to express what I mean. For somehow or other our arguments, on whatever ground we rest them, seem
to turn round and walk away from us.

Plato, *Euthyphro,* 10B

20 *Timaeus.* All men . . . who have any degree of
right feeling, at the beginning of every enterprise,
whether small or great, always call upon God.
And we, too, who are going to discourse of the
nature of the universe, how created or how existing without creation, if we be not altogether out
of our wits, must invoke the aid of Gods and Goddesses and pray that our words may be acceptable
to them and consistent with themselves.

Plato, *Timaeus,* 27B

21 *Athenian Stranger.* The prayer of a fool is full of
danger, being likely to end in the opposite of what
he desires.

Plato, *Laws,* III, 688A

22 *Athenian Stranger.* What life is agreeable to God,
and becoming in his followers? One only, expressed once for all in the old saying that "like
agrees with like, with measure measure," but
things which have no measure agree neither with
themselves nor with the things which have. Now
God ought to be to us the measure of all things,
and not man, as men commonly say: the words
are far more true of him. And he who would be
dear to God must, as far as is possible, be like him
and such as he is. Wherefore the temperate man is
the friend of God, for he is like him; and the intemperate man is unlike him, and different from

him, and unjust. And the same applies to other things; and this is the conclusion, which is also the noblest and truest of all sayings—that for the good man to offer sacrifice to the Gods, and hold converse with them by means of prayers and offerings and every kind of service, is the noblest and best of all things, and also the most conducive to a happy life, and very fit and meet. But with the bad man, the opposite of this is true: for the bad man has an impure soul, whereas the good is pure; and from one who is polluted, neither a good man nor God can without impropriety receive gifts. Wherefore the unholy do only waste their much service upon the Gods, but when offered by any holy man, such service is most acceptable to them. This is the mark at which we ought to aim. But what weapons shall we use, and how shall we direct them? In the first place, we affirm that next after the Olympian Gods and the Gods of the State, honour should be given to the Gods below; they should receive everything in even numbers, and of the second choice, and ill omen, while the odd numbers, and the first choice, and the things of lucky omen, are given to the Gods above, by him who would rightly hit the mark of piety. Next to these Gods, a wise man will do service to the demons or spirits, and then to the heroes, and after them will follow the private and ancestral Gods, who are worshipped as the law prescribes in the places which are sacred to them.

Plato, Laws, IV, 716B

23 No act is it of piety to be often seen with veiled head to turn to a stone and approach every altar and fall prostrate on the ground and spread out the palms before the statues of the gods and sprinkle the altars with much blood of beasts and link vow on to vow, but rather to be able to look on all things with a mind at peace.

Lucretius, Nature of Things, V

24 *Cotta.* Piety is justice towards the gods. But if men and gods have nothing in common, how can any claims of justice exist between them? Holiness is the science of divine worship. But why should the gods be reverenced, if we have not received, nor expect to receive, any benefit from them?

Cicero, De Natura Deorum, I, 41

25 Be ye therefore perfect, even as your Father which is in heaven is perfect.

Matthew 5:48

26 And when thou prayest, thou shalt not be as the hypocrites are: for they love to pray standing in the synagogues and in the corners of the streets, that they may be seen of men. Verily I say unto you, They have their reward.

But thou, when thou prayest, enter into thy closet, and when thou hast shut thy door, pray to thy Father which is in secret; and thy Father which seeth in secret shall reward thee openly.

But when ye pray, use not vain repetitions, as the heathen do: for they think that they shall be heard for their much speaking.

Be not ye therefore like unto them: for your Father knoweth what things ye have need of, before ye ask him.

After this manner therefore pray ye: Our Father which art in heaven, Hallowed be thy name.

Thy kingdom come. Thy will be done in earth, as it is in heaven.

Give us this day our daily bread.

And forgive us our debts, as we forgive our debtors.

And lead us not into temptation, but deliver us from evil: For thine is the kingdom, and the power, and the glory, for ever. Amen.

Matthew 6:5–13

27 He that loveth father or mother more than me is not worthy of me: and he that loveth son or daughter more than me is not worthy of me.

And he that taketh not his cross, and followeth after me, is not worthy of me.

He that findeth his life shall lose it: and he that loseth his life for my sake shall find it.

Matthew 10:37–39

28 A certain man had two sons; and he came to the first, and said, Son, go work to day in my vineyard.

He answered and said, I will not: but afterward he repented, and went.

And he came to the second, and said likewise. And he answered and said, I go, sir: and went not.

Whether of them twain did the will of his father? They say unto him, The first. Jesus saith unto them, Verily I say unto you, That the publicans and the harlots go into the kingdom of God before you.

Matthew 21:28–31

29 He said unto another, Follow me. But he said, Lord, suffer me first to go and bury my father.

Jesus said unto him, Let the dead bury their dead: but go thou and preach the kingdom of God.

And another also said, Lord, I will follow thee; but let me first go bid them farewell, which are at home at my house.

And Jesus said unto him, No man, having put his hand to the plough, and looking back, is fit for the kingdom of God.

Luke 9:59–62

30 And he spake this parable unto certain which trusted in themselves that they were righteous, and despised others:

Two men went up into the temple to pray; the one a Pharisee, and the other a publican.

The Pharisee stood and prayed thus with himself, God, I thank thee, that I am not as other men are, extortioners, unjust, adulterers, or even as this publican.

I fast twice in the week, I give tithes of all that I possess.

And the publican, standing afar off, would not lift up so much as his eyes unto heaven, but smote upon his breast, saying, God be merciful to me a sinner.

I tell you, this man went down to his house justified rather than the other.

Luke 18:9–14

31 A certain nobleman went into a far country to receive for himself a kingdom, and to return.

And he called his ten servants, and delivered them ten pounds, and said unto them, Occupy till I come.

But his citizens hated him, and sent a message after him, saying, We will not have this man to reign over us.

And it came to pass, that when he was returned, having received the kingdom, then he commanded these servants to be called unto him, to whom he had given the money, that he might know how much every man had gained by trading.

Then came the first, saying, Lord, thy pound hath gained ten pounds.

And he said unto him, Well, thou good servant: because thou hast been faithful in a very little, have thou authority over ten cities.

And the second came, saying, Lord, thy pound hath gained five pounds.

And he said likewise to him, Be thou also over five cities.

And another came, saying, Lord, behold, here is thy pound, which I have kept laid up in a napkin:

For I feared thee, because thou art an austere man: thou takest up that thou layedst not down, and reapest that thou didst not sow.

And he saith unto him, Out of thine own mouth will I judge thee, thou wicked servant. Thou knewest that I was an austere man, taking up that I laid not down, and reaping that I did not sow:

Wherefore then gavest not thou my money into the bank, that at my coming I might have required mine own with usury?

And he said unto them that stood by, Take from him the pound, and give it to him that hath ten pounds.

(And they said unto him, Lord, he hath ten pounds.)

For I say unto you, That unto every one which hath shall be given; and from him that hath not, even that he hath shall be taken away from him.

Luke 19:12–26

32 Whatsoever ye shall ask in my name, that will I

do, that the Father may be glorified in the Son.

If ye shall ask any thing in my name, I will do it.

John 14:13–14

33 I beseech you therefore, brethren, by the mercies of God, that ye present your bodies a living sacrifice, holy, acceptable unto God, which is your reasonable service.

And be not conformed to this world: but be ye transformed by the renewing of your mind, that ye may prove what is that good, and acceptable, and perfect, will of God.

Romans 12:1–2

34 The fruit of the Spirit is love, joy, peace, longsuffering, gentleness, goodness, faith,

Meekness, temperance: against such there is no law.

And they that are Christ's have crucified the flesh with the affections and lusts.

If we live in the Spirit, let us also walk in the Spirit.

Galatians 5:22–25

35 Pray without ceasing.

I Thessalonians 5:17

36 What doth it profit, my brethren, though a man say he hath faith, and have not works? can faith save him?

If a brother or sister be naked, and destitute of daily food,

And one of you say unto them, Depart in peace, be ye warmed and filled; notwithstanding ye give them not those things which are needful to the body; what doth it profit?

Even so faith, if it hath not works, is dead, being alone.

Yea, a man may say, Thou hast faith, and I have works: shew me thy faith without thy works, and I will shew thee my faith by my works.

Thou believest that there is one God; thou doest well: the devils also believe, and tremble.

But wilt thou know, O vain man, that faith without works is dead?

Was not Abraham our father justified by works, when he had offered Isaac his son upon the altar?

Seest thou how faith wrought with his works, and by works was faith made perfect?

And the scripture was fulfilled which saith, Abraham believed God, and it was imputed unto him for righteousness: and he was called the Friend of God.

Ye see then how that by works a man is justified, and not by faith only.

Likewise also was not Rahab the harlot justified by works, when she had received the messengers, and had sent them out another way?

For as the body without the spirit is dead, so faith without works is dead also.

James 2:14–26

37 When he had taken the book, the four beasts and four and twenty elders fell down before the Lamb, having every one of them harps, and golden vials full of odours, which are the prayers of saints.

Revelation 5:8

38 Ought we not when we are digging and ploughing and eating to sing this hymn to God? "Great is God, who has given us such implements with which we shall cultivate the earth: great is God who has given us hands, the power of swallowing, a stomach, imperceptible growth, and the power of breathing while we sleep." This is what we ought to sing on every occasion, and to sing the greatest and most divine hymn for giving us the faculty of comprehending these things and using a proper way. Well then, since most of you have become blind, ought there not to be some man to fill this office, and on behalf of all to sing the hymn to God? For what else can I do, a lame old man, than sing hymns to God? If then I was a nightingale, I would do the part of a nightingale: if I were a swan, I would do like a swan. But now I am a rational creature, and I ought to praise God: this is my work; I do it, nor will I desert this post, so long as I am allowed to keep it; and I exhort you to join in this same song.

Epictetus, Discourses, I, 16

39 I say that we ought not to desire in every way what is not our own. And the sorrow of another is another's sorrow: but my sorrow is my own. I, then, will stop my own sorrow by every means, for it is in my power: and the sorrow of another I will endeavor to stop as far as I can; but I will not attempt to do it by every means; for if I do, I shall be fighting against God, I shall be opposing Zeus and shall be placing myself against him in the administration of the universe; and the reward of this fighting against God and of this disobedience not only will the children of my children pay, but I also shall myself, both by day and by night, startled by dreams, perturbed, trembling at every piece of news, and having my tranquillity depending on the letters of others.

Epictetus, Discourses, III, 24

40 A prayer of the Athenians: Rain, rain, O dear Zeus, down on the ploughed fields of the Athenians and on the plains.—In truth we ought not to pray at all, or we ought to pray in this simple and noble fashion.

Marcus Aurelius, Meditations, V, 7

41 Live with the gods. And he does live with the gods who constantly shows to them that his own soul is satisfied with that which is assigned to him, and that it does all that the daemon wishes, which Zeus hath given to every man for his guardian and guide, a portion of himself. And this is every

man's understanding and reason.

Marcus Aurelius, Meditations, V, 27

42 *Great art Thou, O Lord, and greatly to be praised; great is Thy power, and of Thy wisdom there is no number.* And man desires to praise Thee. He is but a tiny part of all that Thou hast created. He bears about him his mortality, the evidence of his sinfulness, and the evidence that *Thou dost resist the proud:* yet this tiny part of all that Thou hast created desires to praise Thee.

Thou dost so excite him that to praise Thee is his joy. For Thou hast made us for Thyself and our hearts are restless till they rest in Thee. Grant me, O Lord, to know which is the soul's first movement toward Thee—to implore Thy aid or to utter its praise of Thee; and whether it must know Thee before it can implore. For it would seem clear that no one can call upon Thee without knowing Thee, for if he did he might invoke another than Thee, knowing Thee not. Yet may it be that a man must implore Thee before he can know Thee? But, *how shall they call on Him in Whom they have not believed? or how shall they believe without a preacher?* And, *they shall praise the Lord that seek Him;* for those that seek shall find; and finding Him they will praise Him. Let me seek Thee, Lord, by praying Thy aid, and let me utter my prayer believing in Thee: for Thou hast been preached to us. My faith, Lord, cries to Thee, the faith that Thou hast given me, that Thou hast inbreathed in me, through the humanity of Thy Son and by the ministry of Thy Preacher.

Augustine, Confessions, I, 1

43 Neither could the blessed immortals retain, nor we miserable mortals reach, a happy condition without worshipping the one God of gods, who is both theirs and ours. . . . For we are all His temple, each of us severally and all of us together, because He condescends to inhabit each individually and the whole harmonious body, being no greater in all than in each, since He is neither expanded nor divided. Our heart when it rises to Him is His altar; the priest who intercedes for us is His Only-begotten; we sacrifice to Him bleeding victims when we contend for His truth even unto blood; to Him we offer the sweetest incense when we come before Him burning with holy and pious love; to Him we devote and surrender ourselves and His gifts in us; to Him, by solemn feasts and on appointed days, we consecrate the memory of His benefits, lest through the lapse of time ungrateful oblivion should steal upon us; to Him we offer on the altar of our heart the sacrifice of humility and praise, kindled by the fire of burning love. It is that we may see Him, so far as He can be seen; it is that we may cleave to Him that we are cleansed from all stain of sins and evil passions and are consecrated in His name. For He is the

fountain of our happiness, He the end of all our desires. Being attached to Him, or rather let me say, re-attached—for we had detached ourselves and lost hold of Him—being, I say, re-attached to Him, we tend towards Him by love, that we may rest in Him, and find our blessedness by attaining that end.

Augustine, *City of God,* X, 3

44 There is . . . something in humility which, strangely enough, exalts the heart, and something in pride which debases it. This seems, indeed, to be contradictory, that loftiness should debase and lowliness exalt. But pious humility enables us to submit to what is above us; and nothing is more exalted above us than God; and therefore humility, by making us subject to God, exalts us. But pride, being a defect of nature, by the very act of refusing subjection and revolting from Him who is supreme, falls to a low condition.

Augustine, *City of God,* XIV, 13

45 It is a matter of no moment in the city of God whether he who adopts the faith that brings men to God adopts it in one dress and manner of life or another, so long only as he lives in conformity with the commandments of God.

Augustine, *City of God,* XIX, 19

46 We worship God by external sacrifices and gifts, not for His own profit, but for that of ourselves and our neighbour. For He does not need our sacrifices, but wishes them to be offered to Him in order to arouse our devotion and to profit our neighbour. Hence mercy, by which we supply others' defects is a sacrifice more acceptable to Him, as conducing more directly to our neighbour's well-being. . . . *Do not forget to do good and to impart, for by such sacrifices God's favour is obtained.*

Aquinas, *Summa Theologica,* II–II, 30, 4

47 By the one same act man both serves and worships God, for worship regards the excellence of God, to Whom reverence is due: while service regards the subjection of man who, by his condition, is under an obligation of showing reverence to God. To these two belong all acts ascribed to religion, because, by them all, man bears witness to the Divine excellence and to his own subjection to God, either by offering something to God, or by assuming something Divine.

Aquinas, *Summa Theologica,* II–II, 81, 3

48 The worship of religion is paid to images, not as considered in themselves, nor as things, but as images leading us to God incarnate. Now movement to an image as image does not stop at the image, but goes on to the thing it represents.

Aquinas, *Summa Theologica,* II–II, 81, 3

49 We pay God honor and reverence, not for His sake (because He is of Himself full of glory to which no creature can add anything), but for our own sake, because by the very fact that we revere and honor God, our mind is subjected to Him; wherein its perfection consists, since a thing is perfected by being subjected to its superior.

Aquinas, *Summa Theologica,* II–II, 81, 7

50 God bestows many things on us out of His liberality, even without our asking for them: but that He wishes to bestow certain things on us at our asking, is for the sake of our good, namely, that we may acquire confidence in having recourse to God, and that we may recognize in Him the Author of our goods.

Aquinas, *Summa Theologica,* II–II, 83, 2

51 The very fact that we wish to cling to God in a spiritual fellowship pertains to reverence for God: and consequently the act of any virtue assumes the character of a sacrifice through being done in order that we may cling to God in holy fellowship.

Aquinas, *Summa Theologica,* II–II, 85, 3

52 *The humbled souls.* O our Father who art in heaven, not circumscribed, but through the greater love thou hast for thy first works on high,

praised be thy name and thy worth by every creature, as 'tis meet to give thanks to thy sweet effluence.

May the peace of thy kingdom come upon us, for we cannot of ourselves attain to it with all our wit, if it come not.

As of their will thine angels make sacrifice to thee, singing *Hosanna,* so may men make of theirs.

Give us this day our daily manna, without which he backward goes through this rough desert, who most toileth to advance.

And as we forgive every one the evil we have suffered, do thou forgive in loving-kindness and regard not our desert.

Put not our virtue, which lightly is subdued, to trial with the old adversary, but deliver us from him who so pricks it.

This last prayer, dear Lord, is not made for us, for need is not, but for those who have remained behind us.

Dante, *Purgatorio,* XI, 1

53 *Bernard.* Virgin mother, daughter of thy son, lowly and uplifted more than any creature, fixed goal of the eternal counsel,

thou art she who didst human nature so ennoble that its own Maker scorned not to become its making.

In thy womb was lit again the love under whose warmth in the eternal peace this flower hath thus unfolded.

Here art thou unto us the meridian torch of love and there below with mortals art a living spring of hope.

Lady, thou art so great and hast such worth, that
if there be who would have grace yet betaketh
not himself to thee, his longing seeketh to fly
without wings.
Thy kindliness not only succoureth whoso request-
eth, but doth oftentimes freely forerun request.
In thee is tenderness, in thee is pity, in thee munificence, in thee united whatever in created
being is of excellence.
Now he who from the deepest pool of the universe
even to here hath seen the spiritlives one after
one
imploreth thee, of grace, for so much power as to
be able to uplift his eyes more high towards
final bliss;
and I, who never burned for my own vision more
than I do for his, proffer thee all my prayers,
and pray they be not scant,
that thou do scatter for him every cloud of his
mortality with prayers of thine, so that the joy
supreme may be unfolded to him.
And further do I pray thee, Queen who canst all
that thou wilt, that thou keep sound for him,
after so great a vision, his affections.
Let thy protection vanquish human ferments; see
Beatrice, with how many Saints, for my prayers
folding hands.

Dante, *Paradiso,* XXXIII, 1

54 That first he wrought and afterwards he taught;
Out of the gospel then that text he caught,
And this figure he added thereunto—
That, if gold rust, what shall poor iron do?
For if the priest be foul, in whom we trust,
What wonder if a layman yield to lust?
And shame it is, if priest take thought for keep,
A shitty shepherd, shepherding clean sheep.
Well ought a priest example good to give,
By his own cleanness, how his flock should live.

Chaucer, *Canterbury Tales:* The Prologue

55 The most acceptable service we can do and show
unto God, and which alone he desires of us, is,
that he be praised of us.

Luther, *Table Talk,* H99

56 To serve Christ . . . is not to put on a hood or to
be preoccupied with Mosaic ceremonies. But it is
rather an entirely spiritual thing, not in the way
in which the monks speak of something being
spiritual which takes place only in the heart. But
it is a spiritual service which originates with the
Spirit. For whoever speaks the words of the Spirit
is rightly said to preach, teach, and speak spiritually. Thus one is also said to live spiritually who is
busy with holy deeds, that is, who does what is
prescribed in the Ten Commandments. So the
head of a household lives spiritually when he governs his own home through faith in the Son of
God. Truly, spiritual obedience is to do through

faith in the Son of God what you are ordered to
do by God's command. There you have what it
means to serve this King. It is not to enter a monastery, as the monks are wont to do, nor to choose
these deeds or those, but to behold this King, to
listen to Him, and afterwards to do what you have
heard.

Luther, *Commentary on Psalm 2*

57 I may be wrong, I don't know; but since by a
particular favor of divine goodness a certain form
of prayer has been prescribed and dictated to us
word for word by the mouth of God, it has always
seemed to me that its use should be more ordinary
with us than it is. And if I had my way, on sitting
down to table and rising from it, on getting up
and going to bed, and on all particular actions
with which we are accustomed to associate prayers, I should like it to be the Lord's Prayer that
Christians employ, if not exclusively, at least always. The Church may extend and diversify prayers according to the need of our instruction, for
well I know that it is always the same substance
and the same thing. But we ought to have given
that one this privilege, that the people should
have it continually in their mouths; for it is certain that it says all that is necessary and that it is
very proper for all occasions. . . .
I was just now thinking about where that error
of ours comes from, of having recourse to God in
all our designs and enterprises, and calling on him
in every kind of need and in whatever spot our
weakness wants help, without considering whether
the occasion is just or unjust, and invoking his
name and his power, in whatever condition or action we are involved, however vicious it may be.
He is indeed our sole and unique protector, and
can do anything to help us; but although he
deigns to honor us with that sweet fatherly relationship, nevertheless he is as just as he is good
and as he is powerful. But he exercises his justice
much more often than his power, and favors us
according to its dictates, not according to our re-
quests.

Montaigne, *Essays,* I, 56, Of Prayers

58 The first law that God ever gave to man was a law
of pure obedience; it was a naked and simple
commandment about which man had nothing to
know or discuss; since to obey is the principal
function of a reasonable soul, recognizing a heavenly superior and benefactor. From obeying and
yielding spring all other virtues, as from presumption all sin.

Montaigne, *Essays,* II, 12, Apology
for Raymond Sebond

59 It now remains that at last, with my eyes and
hands removed from the tablet of demonstrations
and lifted up towards the heavens, I should pray,
devout and supplicating, to the Father of lights: O

Thou Who dost by the light of nature promote in us the desire for the light of grace, that by its means Thou mayest transport us into the light of glory, I give thanks to Thee, O Lord Creator, Who hast delighted me with Thy makings and in the works of Thy hands have I exulted. Behold! now, I have completed the work of my profession, having employed as much power of mind as Thou didst give to me; to the men who are going to read those demonstrations I have made manifest the glory of Thy works, as much of its infinity as the narrows of my intellect could apprehend. My mind has been given over to philosophizing most correctly: if there is anything unworthy of Thy designs brought forth by me—a worm born and nourished in a wallowing place of sins—breathe into me also that which Thou dost wish men to know, that I may make the correction: If I have been allured into rashness by the wonderful beauty of Thy works, or if I have loved my own glory among men, while I am advancing in the work destined for Thy glory, be gentle and merciful and pardon me; and finally deign graciously to effect that these demonstrations give way to Thy glory and the salvation of souls and nowhere be an obstacle to that.

Kepler, *Harmonies of the World,* V, 9

60 *King.* O, my offence is rank, it smells to heaven;
It hath the primal eldest curse upon't,
A brother's murder. Pray can I not,
Though inclination be as sharp as will.
My stronger guilt defeats my strong intent;
And, like a man to double business bound,
I stand in pause where I shall first begin,
And both neglect. What if this cursed hand
Were thicker than itself with brother's blood,
Is there not rain enough in the sweet heavens
To wash it white as snow? Whereto serves mercy
But to confront the visage of offence?
And what's in prayer but this two-fold force,
To be forestalled ere we come to fall,
Or pardon'd being down? Then I'll look up;
My fault is past. But, O, what form of prayer
Can serve my turn? "Forgive me my foul murder"?
That cannot be; since I am still possess'd
Of those effects for which I did the murder,
My crown, mine own ambition, and my queen.
May one be pardon'd and retain the offence?
In the corrupted currents of this world
Offence's gilded hand may shove by justice,
And oft 'tis seen the wicked prize itself
Buys out the law: but 'tis not so above;
There is no shuffling, there the action lies
In his true nature; and we ourselves compell'd,
Even to the teeth and forehead of our faults,
To give in evidence. What then? what rests?
Try what repentance can. What can it not?
Yet what can it when one can not repent?
O wretched state! O bosom black as death!

O limed soul, that, struggling to be free,
Art more engaged! Help, angels! Make assay!
Bow, stubborn knees; and, heart with strings of steel,
Be soft as sinews of the new-born babe!
All may be well. . . .
My words fly up, my thoughts remain below.

Shakespeare, *Hamlet,* III, iii, 36

61 As the wandring Knight and Squire went discoursing of this and other Matters, they had not rode much more than a League, ere they espy'd about a dozen Men, who look'd like Country-Fellows sitting at their Victuals, with their Cloaks under them, on the green Grass, in the middle of a Meadow. Near 'em they saw several white Clothes or Sheets spread out and laid close to one another, that seem'd to cover something. Don *Quixote* rode up to the People, and after he had civilly saluted 'em, ask'd what they had got under that Linen? Sir, answer'd one of the Company, they are some carv'd Images that are to be set up at an Altar we are erecting in our Town. We cover 'em, lest they should be sullied, and carry 'em on our Shoulders for fear they should be broken. If you please, said Don *Quixote,* I should be glad to see 'em; for considering the Care you take of 'em, they should be Pieces of Value. Ay, marry are they, quoth another, or else we're damnably cheated; for there's ne'er an Image among 'em that does not stand us in more than fifty Ducats; and, that you may know I'm no Liar, do but stay, and you shall see with your own Eyes. With that, getting up on his Legs, and leaving his Victuals, he went and took off the Cover from one of the Figures, that happen'd to be St *George* on Horseback, and under his Feet a Serpent coil'd up, his Throat transfix'd with a Lance, with the Fierceness that is commonly represented in the Piece; and all, as they use to say, spick and span-new, and shining like beaten Gold. Don *Quixote* having seen the Image, This, said he, was one of the best Knights-Errant the Divine Warfare or Church-Militant ever had: His Name was Don St *George,* and he was an extraordinary Protector of Damsels. What's the next? The Fellow having uncover'd it, it proved to be St *Martin* on Horseback. This Knight too, said Don *Quixote* at the first sight, was one of the Christian Adventurers, and I am apt to think he was more liberal than valiant; and thou may'st perceive it, *Sancho,* by his dividing his Cloak, with a poor Man; he gave him half, and doubtless 'twas Winter time, or else he would have giv'n it him whole, he was so charitable. Not so neither, I fancy, quoth *Sancho,* but I guess he stuck to the Proverb: *To Give and Keep what's fit, Requires a Share of Wit.* Don *Quixote* smil'd, and desir'd the Men to shew him the next Image; which appear'd to be that of the Patron of *Spain* a Horse-back, with his Sword bloody, trampling down *Moors,* and treading over Heads. Ay, this is a

Knight indeed, (cry'd Don *Quixote,* when he saw it) one of those that fought in the Squadrons of the Saviour of the World: He is call'd Don *Sant-Jago, Mata Moros,* or Don St *James the Moor-killer,* and may be reckon'd one of the most valorous Saints and Professors of Chivalry that the Earth then enjoy'd, and Heaven now possesses. Then they uncover'd another Piece, which shew'd St *Paul* falling from his Horse, with all the Circumstances usually express'd in the Story of his Conversion, and represented so to the Life, that he look'd as if he had been answering the Voice that spoke to him from Heaven. This, said Don *Quixote,* was the greatest Enemy the Church Militant had once, and prov'd afterwards the greatest Defender it will ever have. In his Life a true Knight-Errant, and in Death a stedfast Saint; an indefatigable Labourer in the Vineyard of the Lord, a Teacher of the *Gentiles,* who had Heaven for his School, and Christ himself for his Master and Instructor. Then Don *Quixote* perceiving there were no more Images, desir'd the Men to cover those he had seen: And now, my good Friends, said he to 'em, I cannot but esteem the Sight that I have had of these Images as a happy Omen; for these Saints and Knights were of the same Profession that I follow, which is that of Arms: The Difference only lies in this Point, that They were Saints, and fought according to the Rules of holy Discipline; and I am a Sinner, and fight after the manner of Men. They conquer'd Heaven by Force, for Heaven is taken by Violence; but I, alas, cannot yet tell what I gain by the Force of my Labours! Yet were my *Dulcinea del Toboso* but free from her Troubles, by a happy Change in my Fortune, and an Improvement in my Understanding, I might perhaps take a better Course than I do. Heaven grant it, quoth *Sancho,* and let the Devil do his worst.

Cervantes, Don Quixote, II, 58

62 The end of worship amongst men is power. For where a man seeth another worshipped, he supposeth him powerful, and is the readier to obey him; which makes his power greater. But God has no ends: the worship we do him proceeds from our duty and is directed according to our capacity by those rules of honour that reason dictateth to be done by the weak to the more potent men, in hope of benefit, for fear of damage, or in thankfulness for good already received from them.

Hobbes, Leviathan, II, 31

63 The obedience required at our hands by God, that accepteth in all our actions the will for the deed, is a serious endeavour to obey Him; and is called also by all such names as signify that endeavour. And therefore obedience is sometimes called by the names of *charity* and *love,* because they imply a will to obey; and our Saviour himself maketh our love to God, and to one another, a

fulfilling of the whole law; and sometimes by the name of *righteousness,* for righteousness is but the will to give to every one his own, that is to say, the will to obey the laws; and sometimes by the name of *repentance,* because to repent implieth a turning away from sin, which is the same with the return of the will to obedience. Whosoever therefore unfeignedly desireth to fulfil the commandments of God, or repenteth him truly of his transgressions, or that loveth God with all his heart, and his neighbour as himself, hath all the obedience necessary to his reception into the kingdom of God: for if God should require perfect innocence, there could no flesh be saved.

Hobbes, Leviathan, III, 43

64 A man must renounce piety altogether, if he does not at least wish to die like a Christian.

Pascal, Pensées, II, 63

65 Experience makes us see an enormous difference between piety and goodness.

Pascal, Pensées, VII, 496

66 There is nothing so perilous as what pleases God and man. For those states, which please God and man, have one property which pleases God, and another which pleases men; as the greatness of Saint Teresa. What pleased God was her deep humility in the midst of her revelations; what pleased men was her light. And so we torment ourselves to imitate her discourses, thinking to imitate her conditions, and not so much to love what God loves and to put ourselves in the state which God loves.

It is better not to fast, and be thereby humbled, than to fast and be self-satisfied therewith.

Pascal, Pensées, VII, 499

67 When I consider how my light is spent,
 E're half my days, in this dark world and wide,
 And that one Talent which is death to hide,
 Lodg'd with me useless, though my Soul more bent
To serve therewith my Maker, and present
 My true account, least he returning chide,
 Doth God exact day-labour, light deny'd,
 I fondly ask; But patience to prevent
That murmur, soon replies, God doth not need
 Either man's work or his own gifts, who best
 Bear his milde yoak, they serve him best, his State
Is Kingly. Thousands at his bidding speed
 And post o're Land and Ocean without rest:
 They also serve who only stand and waite.

Milton, When I consider how my light is spent

68 *Adam.* Henceforth I learne, that to obey is best,
And love with feare the onely God, to walk
As in his presence, ever to observe
His providence, and on him sole depend,

Merciful over all his works, with good
Still overcoming evil, and by small
Accomplishing great things, by things deemd
   weak
Subverting worldly strong, and worldly wise
By simply meek; that suffering for Truths sake
Is fortitude to highest victorie,
And to the faithful Death the Gate of Life;
Taught this by his example whom I now
Acknowledge my Redeemer ever blest.

Milton, Paradise Lost, XII, 561

69 The desire of doing well which is born in us, because we live according to the guidance of reason,
   I call *Piety*.

Spinoza, Ethics, IV, Prop. 37, Schol. 1

70 There is a false appearance of piety and religion
   in dejection; and although dejection is the opposite of pride, the humble dejected man is very
   near akin to the proud.

Spinoza, Ethics, IV, Appendix XXII

71 *Good Will.* We make no objections against any,
   notwithstanding all that they have done before
   they come hither, they in no wise are cast out, and
   therefore, good *Christian,* come a little way with
   me, and I will teach thee about the way thou must
   go. Look before thee; dost thou see this narrow
   way? THAT is the way thou must go. It was cast
   up by the Patriarchs, Prophets, Christ, and his
   Apostles; and it is as straight as a Rule can make
   it: This is the way thou must go.
      But said *Christian, Is there no turnings nor windings
   by which a Stranger may lose the way?*
      Good Will. Yes, there are many ways *butt* down
   upon this; and they are crooked, and wide: But
   thus thou may'st distinguish the right from the
   wrong, *That* only being straight and narrow.

Bunyan, Pilgrim's Progress, I

72 He that worships God does it with design to please
   Him and procure His favour. But that cannot be
   done by him who, upon the command of another,
   offers unto God that which he knows will be displeasing to Him, because not commanded by
   Himself. This is not to please God, or appease his
   wrath, but willingly and knowingly to provoke
   Him by a manifest contempt, which is a thing
   absolutely repugnant to the nature and end of
   worship.

Locke, Letter Concerning Toleration

73 When external worship is attended with great
   magnificence, it flatters our minds and strongly
   attaches us to religion. The riches of temples and
   those of the clergy greatly affect us. Thus even the
   misery of the people is a motive that renders them
   fond of a religion which has served as a pretext to
   those who were the cause of their misery.

Montesquieu, Spirit of Laws, XXV, 2

74 Almost all civilised nations dwell in houses; hence
   naturally arose the idea of building a house for
   God in which they might adore and seek him,
   amidst all their hopes and fears.

Montesquieu, Spirit of Laws, XXV, 3

75 The great art . . . of piety, and the end for which
   all religious rites seem to be instituted, is the perpetual renovation of the motives to virtue by a
   voluntary employment of our mind in the contemplation of its excellence, its importance, and
   its necessity, which, in proportion as they are
   more frequently and more willingly revolved, gain
   a more forcible and permanent influence till in
   time they become the reigning ideas and standing
   principles of action and the test by which everything proposed to the judgment is rejected or
   approved.

Johnson, Rambler No. 7

76 In religion, as a rule, prostration, adoration with
   bowed head, coupled with contrite, timorous posture and voice, seems to be the only becoming
   demeanour in presence of the Godhead, and accordingly most nations have assumed and still observe it. Yet this cast of mind is far from being
   intrinsically and necessarily involved in the idea
   of the *sublimity* of a religion and of its object. The
   man that is actually in a state of fear, finding in
   himself good reason to be so, because he is conscious of offending with his evil disposition against
   a might directed by a will at once irresistible and
   just, is far from being in the frame of mind for
   admiring divine greatness, for which a temper of
   calm reflection and a quite free judgement are
   required. Only when he becomes conscious of
   having a disposition that is upright and acceptable to God, do those operations of might serve to
   stir within him the idea of the sublimity of this
   Being, so far as he recognizes the existence in himself of a sublimity of disposition consonant with
   His will, and is thus raised above the dread of
   such operations of nature, in which he no longer
   sees God pouring forth the vials of the wrath.

Kant, Critique of Aesthetic Judgement, 28

77 For Mercy has a human heart,
   Pity a human face,
   And Love, the human form divine,
   And Peace, the human dress.

   Then every man, of every clime,
   That prays in his distress,
   Prays to the human form divine,
   Love, Mercy, Pity, Peace.

Blake, The Divine Image

78 *Gretchen.* Oh, bend Thou,
   Mother of Sorrows; send Thou
   A look of pity on my pain.

   Thine heart's blood welling

With pangs past telling,
Thou gazest where Thy Son hangs slain.

Thou, heavenward gazing,
Art deep sighs raising
On high for His and for Thy pain.

Who feeleth
How reeleth

This pain in every bone?
All that makes my poor heart shiver,
Why it yearneth and doth quiver,
Thou dost know and Thou alone!

Wherever I am going,
How woe, woe, woe is growing,
Ah, how my bosom aches!
When lonely watch I'm keeping,
I'm weeping, weeping, weeping,
My heart within me breaks.

The plants before my window
I wet with tears—ah, me!—
As in the early morning
I plucked these flowers for Thee.

Ah, let my room but borrow
The early sunlight red,
I sit in all my sorrow
Already on my bed.

Help! rescue me from death and stain!
Oh, bend Thou,
Mother of Sorrows; send Thou
A look of pity on my pain!

Goethe, *Faust*, I, 3587

79 He prayeth best, who loveth best
All things both great and small;
For the dear God who loveth us,
He made and loveth all.

Coleridge, *The Rime of the Ancient
Mariner*, 614

80 It is said of James, the head of the community in Jerusalem, that the skin of his knees was as hard as a camel's from constantly praying, and that he could pray for days together. To our age that may seem laughable; but one should remember what eloquence and fullness of heart is implied by being able to pray for so long without growing tired, particularly as we have difficulty enough in making a truly heartfelt prayer.

Kierkegaard, *Journals (Oct. 1, 1838)*

81 The immediate person thinks and imagines that when he prays, the important thing, the thing he must concentrate upon, is that *God should hear* what HE *is praying for*. And yet in the true, eternal sense it is just the reverse: the true relation in prayer is not when God hears what is prayed for, but when *the person praying* continues to pray until

he is *the one who hears*, who hears what God wills. The immediate person, therefore, uses many words and, therefore, makes demands in his prayer; the true man of prayer only *attends*.

Kierkegaard, *Journals (1846)*

82 *Arthur*. 'The old order changeth, yielding place to new,
And God fulfils himself in many ways,
Lest one good custom should corrupt the world.
Comfort thyself: what comfort is in me?
I have lived my life, and that which I have done
May He within himself make pure! but thou,
If thou shouldst never see my face again,
Pray for my soul. More things are wrought by prayer
Than this world dreams of. Wherefore, let thy voice
Rise like a fountain for me night and day.
For what are men better than sheep or goats
That nourish a blind life within the brain,
If, knowing God, they lift not hands of prayer
Both for themselves and those who call them friend?
For so the whole round earth is every way
Bound by gold chains about the feet of God.'

Tennyson, *Morte d'Arthur*, 291

83 Oh, thou big white God aloft there somewhere in yon darkness, have mercy on this small black boy down here; preserve him from all men that have no bowels to feel fear!

Melville, *Moby Dick*, XL

84 Early in the morning—about six—Mr. Bulstrode rose and spent some time in prayer. Does any one suppose that private prayer is necessarily candid—necessarily goes to the roots of action? Private prayer is inaudible speech, and speech is representative: who can represent himself just as he is, even in his own reflections?

George Eliot, *Middlemarch*, VII, 70

85 *Father Zossima*. Young man, be not forgetful of prayer. Every time you pray, if your prayer is sincere, there will be new feeling and new meaning in it, which will give you fresh courage, and you will understand that prayer is an education.

Dostoevsky, *Brothers Karamazov*, Pt. II, VI, 3

86 We hear, in these days of scientific enlightenment, a great deal of discussion about the efficacy of prayer; and many reasons are given us why we should not pray, whilst others are given us why we should. But in all this very little is said of the reason why we *do* pray, which is simply that we cannot *help* praying. It seems probable that, in spite of all that "science" may do to the contrary, men will continue to pray to the end of time, unless their mental nature changes in a manner

which nothing we know should lead us to expect. The impulse to pray is a necessary consequence of the fact that whilst the innermost of the empirical selves of a man is a Self of the *social* sort, it yet can find its only adequate *Socius* in an ideal world.

William James, *Psychology*, X

20.9 | *Heresy and Unbelief*

The quotations included in this section divide into two main groups, one dealing with orthodoxy and heresy, the other with that form of unbelief which undermines religion—atheism.

The epithet "atheist" or "infidel" is applied by the members of a religious community to those who deny or do not acknowledge the existence of the divinity worshiped in that community. Thus, for example, Spinoza was anathematized as an atheist by the Jewish community because his affirmation of God, heartfelt and impassioned as it was, involved the denial of the God of Abraham, Isaac, and Jacob. The heretic, in contrast, differs from other members of the religious community to which he belongs by advancing an interpretation of some point in their common faith that they regard as unsound. In the Jewish community, the decisive judgment defining or reaffirming orthodoxy and rejecting a particular heresy was rendered by the Sanhedrin; in the Christian community, by a church council, as, for example, the Council of Nicea in 325 which rejected the Arian heresy and formulated the orthodoxy of the Nicene or Athanasian creed.

Among the Fathers of the Church, Augustine is probably more responsible than any other for the formation of Christian orthodoxy through the definition and rejection of the many heresies that abounded in the early centuries of Christianity. It would be impossible, within the scope of this book, to exemplify this by quotation from all his antiheretical tracts; but the reader will find a sampling of such polemics in the quotations from Augustine that attack the errors of the Manicheans. The names of other heresies and the disputes over them will be found in Gibbon's report of this aspect of the development of Christianity within the Roman empire. The quotations from Aquinas and from Luther not only contribute a precise definition of heresy, but also discuss various ways of arguing with heretics and point out the useful service that heretics perform for the religious community that excommunicates them.

It is interesting to note that, in the group of quotations dealing with unbelief and atheism, post-Reformation authors predominate. They are concerned with the problems of religious tolerance and persecution and, in this context, with the treatment to be accorded infidels and atheists.

On both of the main subjects treated here the reader is referred for the discussion of relevant considerations to Section 6.5 on OPINION, BELIEF, AND FAITH and to Section 6.6 on DOUBT AND SKEPTICISM.

1 The fool hath said in his heart, There is no God.
Psalm 14:1

2 For first of all, when ye come together in the church, I hear that there be divisions among you; and I partly believe it.

For there must be also heresies among you, that they which are approved may be made manifest among you.
I Corinthians 11:18–19

3 But avoid foolish questions, and genealogies, and contentions, and strivings about the law; for they are unprofitable and vain.

A man that is an heretick after the first and second admonition reject;

Knowing that he that is such is subverted, and sinneth, being condemned of himself.
Titus 3:9–11

4 I fell in with a sect of men [the Manicheans] talking high-sounding nonsense, carnal and wordy men. The snares of the devil were in their mouths, to trap souls with an arrangement of the syllables of the names of God the Father and of the Lord Jesus Christ and of the Paraclete, the Holy Ghost, our Comforter. These names were always on their lips, but only as sounds and tongue noises; for their heart was empty of the true meaning. They cried out "Truth, truth;" they were forever uttering the word to me, but the thing was nowhere in them; indeed they spoke falsehood not only of You, who are truly Truth, but also of the elements of this world, Your creatures. Concerning these I ought to have passed beyond even the philosophers who spoke truly, for love of You, O my supreme and good Father, Beauty of all things beautiful. O Truth, Truth, how inwardly did the very marrow of my soul pant for You when time and again I heard them sound Your name. But it was all words—words spoken, words written in many huge tomes.
Augustine, Confessions, III, 6

5 Ham . . . who was the middle son of Noah, and, as it were, separated himself from both, and remained between them, neither belonging to the first-fruits of Israel nor to the fullness of the Gentiles, what does he signify but the tribe of heretics, hot with the spirit, not of patience, but of impatience, with which the breasts of heretics are wont to blaze, and with which they disturb the peace of the saints? But even the heretics yield an advantage to those that make proficiency, according to the apostle's saying, "There must also be heresies, that they which are approved may be made manifest among you." Whence, too, it is elsewhere said, "The son that receives instruction will be wise, and he uses the foolish as his servant." For while the hot restlessness of heretics stirs questions about many articles of the Catholic faith, the necessity

of defending them forces us both to investigate them more accurately, to understand them more clearly, and to proclaim them more earnestly; and the question mooted by an adversary becomes the occasion of instruction.
Augustine, City of God, XVI, 2

6 It is believed by some that those who do not abandon the name of Christ, and have been baptized in the Church and have not been cut off by any schism or heresy, no matter in what wickedness they live, not washing it away by penance nor redeeming it through almsgiving, but persevering in it stubbornly up to the last day of this life, are to be saved by fire (a fire made to endure in proportion to the magnitude of their evil deeds) and not to receive the punishment of eternal fire. But those who believe this and still are Catholics seem to me to be led astray by a kind of human benevolence.
Augustine, Enchiridion, XVIII

7 Many heretics abound; and God has permitted them to abound to this end, that we may not be always nourished with milk and remain in senseless infancy. For inasmuch as they have not understood how the divinity of Christ is set forth to our acceptance, they have concluded according to their will: and by not discerning aright, they have brought in most troublesome questions upon catholic believers; and the hearts of believers began to be disturbed and to waver. Then immediately it became a necessity for spiritual men, who had not only read in the Gospel anything respecting the divinity of our Lord Jesus Christ, but had also understood it, to bring forth the armour of Christ against the armour of the devil, and with all their might to fight in most open conflict for the divinity of Christ against false and deceitful teachers; lest, while they were silent, others might perish.
*Augustine, On the Gospel
of St. John,* XXXVI, 6

8 Unbelievers cannot be said "to believe in a God" as we understand it in relation to the act of faith. For they do not believe that God exists under the conditions that faith determines. Hence they do not truly believe in a God, since . . . to know simple things defectively is not to know them at all.
Aquinas, Summa Theologica, II–II, 2, 2

9 To have the faith is not part of human nature, but it is part of human nature that man's mind should not go against his inner instinct, and the outward preaching of the truth. Hence, in this way, unbelief is contrary to nature.
Aquinas, Summa Theologica, II–II, 10, 1

10 In disputing about the faith, two things must be observed, one on the part of the disputant, the

other on the part of his hearers. On the part of the disputant, we must consider his intention. For if he were to dispute as though he had doubts about the faith, and did not hold the truth of faith for certain, and as though he intended to probe it with arguments, without doubt he would sin, as being doubtful of the faith and an unbeliever. On the other hand, it is praiseworthy to dispute about the faith in order to confute errors, or even for practice.

On the part of the hearers we must consider whether those who hear the disputation are instructed and firm in the faith, or simple and wavering. As to those who are well instructed and firm in the faith, there can be no danger in disputing about the faith in their presence. But as to simple-minded people, we must make a distinction. For either they are provoked and molested by unbelievers, for instance Jews or heretics, or pagans, who strive to corrupt the faith in them, or else they are not subject to provocation in this matter, as in those countries where there are no unbelievers. In the first case it is necessary to dispute in public about the faith, provided there be those who are equal and adapted to the task of confuting errors, since in this way simple people are strengthened in the faith, and unbelievers are deprived of the opportunity to deceive, while if those who ought to withstand the perverters of the truth of faith were silent, this would tend to strengthen error. Hence Gregory says: "Even as a thoughtless speech gives rise to error, so does an indiscreet silence leave those in error who might have been instructed." On the other hand, in the second case it is dangerous to dispute in public about the faith, in the presence of simple people, whose faith for this very reason is more firm, that they have never heard anything differing from what they believe. Hence it is not expedient for them to hear what unbelievers have to say against the faith.

Aquinas, *Summa Theologica,* II–II, 10, 7

11 There are two ways in which a man may deviate from the rectitude of the Christian faith. First, because he is unwilling to assent to Christ Himself; and such a man has an evil will, so to say, in respect of the very end. This pertains to the species of unbelief in pagans and Jews. Secondly, because, though he intends to assent to Christ, yet he fails in his choice of those things by which he assents to Christ, because he chooses, not what Christ really taught, but the suggestions of his own mind. Therefore, heresy is a species of unbelief pertaining to those who profess the Christian faith, but corrupt its dogmas.

Aquinas, *Summa Theologica,* II–II, 11, 1

12 With regard to heretics two points must be observed: one, on their own side, the other, on the side of the Church. On their own side there is the sin, by which they deserve not only to be separated from the Church by excommunication, but also to be severed from the world by death. For it is a much graver matter to corrupt the faith which quickens the soul, than to forge money, which supports temporal life. Therefore if forgers of money and other evil-doers are condemned to death at once by the secular authority, much more reason is there for heretics, as soon as they are convicted of heresy, to be not only excommunicated but even put to death.

On the part of the Church, however, there is mercy which looks to the conversion of the wanderer, and therefore she condemns not at once, but *after the first and second admonition.*

Aquinas, *Summa Theologica,* II–II, 11, 3

13 I, who was desirous to behold the condition which such a fortress encloses,

as soon as I was in, sent my eyes around; and saw, on either hand, a spacious plain full of sorrow and of evil torment.

As at Arles, where the Rhone stagnates, as at Pola near the Quarnaro gulf, which shuts up Italy and bathes its confines,

the sepulchres make all the place uneven: so did they here on every side, only the manner here was bitterer:

for amongst the tombs were scattered flames, whereby they were made all over so glowing-hot, that iron more *hot* no craft requires.

Their covers were all raised up; and out of them proceeded moans so grievous, that they seemed indeed *the moans* of *spirits* sad and wounded.

And I: "Master [Virgil], what are these people who, buried within those chests, make themselves heard by their painful sighs?"

And he to me: "[Here] are the Arch-heretics with their followers of every sect; and much more, than thou thinkest, the tombs are laden.

Like with like is buried here; and the monuments are more and less hot." Then, after turning to the right hand, we passed between the tortures and the high battlements.

Dante, *Inferno,* IX, 106

14 I saw many herds of naked souls, who were all lamenting very miserably; and there seemed imposed upon them a diverse law.

Some were lying supine upon the ground; some sitting all crouched up; and others roaming incessantly.

Those that moved about were much more numerous; and those that were lying in the torment *were* fewer, but uttered louder cries of pain.

Over all the great sand, falling slowly, rained dilated flakes of fire, like *those* of snow in Alps without a wind.

As the flames which Alexander, in those hot regions of India, saw fall upon his host, entire to the ground;

whereat he with his legions took care to tramp the
soil, for the fire was more easily extinguished
while alone:

so fell the eternal heat, by which the sand was
kindled, like tinder under *flint and* steel, redou-
bling the pain.

Ever restless was the dance of miserable hands,
now here, now there, shaking off the fresh burning.

I began: "Master, thou who conquerest all things,
save the hard Demons, that came forth against
us at the entrance of the gate,

who is that great spirit, who seems to care not for
the fire, and lies disdainful and contorted, so
that the rain seems not to ripen him?"

And he himself, remarking that I asked my Guide
[Virgil] concerning him, exclaimed: "What I
was living, that am I dead.

Though Jove weary out his smith, from whom in
anger he took the sharp bolt with which on my
last day I was transfixed;

and though he weary out the others, one by one,
at the black forge in Mongibello, crying: 'Help,
help, good Vulcan!'

as he did at the strife of Phlegra; and hurl at me
with all his might, yet should he not thereby
have joyful vengeance."

Then my Guide spake with a force such as I had
not heard before: "O Capaneus! in that thy
pride remains unquenched,

thou art punished more: no torture, except thy
own raving, would be pain proportioned to thy
fury."

Then to me he turned with gentler lip, saying:
"That was the one of the seven kings who laid
siege to Thebes; and he held, and seems to
hold,

God in defiance and prize him lightly; but, as I
told him, his revilings are ornaments that well
befit his breast."

Dante, *Inferno,* XIV, 19

15 What greater rebellion against God, what greater
wickedness, what greater contempt of God is there
than not believing his promise? For what is this
but to make God a liar or to doubt that he is
truthful?—that is, to ascribe truthfulness to one's
self but lying and vanity to God? Does not a man
who does this deny God and set himself up as an
idol in his heart? Then of what good are works
done in such wickedness, even if they were the
works of angels and apostles? Therefore God has
rightly included all things, not under anger or
lust, but under unbelief, so that they who imagine
that they are fulfilling the law by doing the works
of chastity and mercy required by the law (the
civil and human virtues) might not be saved.
They are included under the sin of unbelief and
must either seek mercy or be justly condemned.

Luther, *Freedom of a Christian*

16 Heretics ought to be persuaded by argument, and
not by fire; and this was the way of the early
Fathers. If it were wise policy to suppress heretics
by burning them, then the executioners would be
the most learned teachers on earth. We should
have no need to study books any longer, for he
who could overthrow his fellow by violence would
have the right to burn him at the stake.

Luther, *Appeal to the Ruling Class
of German Nationality,* III

17 We are brought back to the belief in God either
by love or by force. Atheism being a proposition
as it were unnatural and monstrous, difficult too
and not easy to establish in the human mind,
however insolent and unruly it may be, plenty of
men have been seen, out of vanity and pride in
conceiving opinions that are not common and
that reform the world, to affect to profess it outwardly; who, if they are mad enough, are not
strong enough nevertheless to have implanted it in
their conscience. They will not fail to clasp their
hands to heaven if you stick them a good sword-
thrust in the chest.

Montaigne, *Essays,* II, 12, Apology
for Raymond Sebond

18 This matter of divinity is handled either in form
of instruction of truth, or in form of confutation of
falsehood. The declinations from religion, besides
the privative, which is atheism and the branches
thereof, are three; heresies, idolatry, and witchcraft: heresies, when we serve the true God with a
false worship; idolatry, when we worship false
gods, supposing them to be true; and witchcraft,
when we adore false gods, knowing them to be
wicked and false.

Bacon, *Advancement of Learning,*
Bk. II, XXV, 24

19 I had rather believe all the fables in the Legend,
and the Talmud, and the Alcoran, than that this
universal frame is without a mind. And therefore
God never wrought miracle to convince atheism,
because his ordinary works convince it. It is true,
that a little philosophy inclineth man's mind to
atheism; but depth in philosophy bringeth men's
minds about to religion: for while the mind of
man looketh upon second causes scattered, it may
sometimes rest in them, and go no further; but
when it beholdeth the chain of them, confederate
and linked together, it must needs fly to Providence and Deity. Nay, even that school which is
most accused of atheism doth most demonstrate
religion; that is, the school of Leucippus and Democritus and Epicurus. For it is a thousand times
more credible, that four mutable elements and
one immutable fifth essence, duly and eternally
placed, need no God, than that an army of infinite small portions or seeds unplaced should have
produced this order and beauty without a divine

marshal. The Scripture saith, *The fool hath said in his heart, there is no God:* it is not said, *The fool hath thought in his heart:* so as he rather saith it by rote to himself, as that he would have, than that he can thoroughly believe it, or be persuaded of it. For none deny there is a God but those for whom it maketh that there were no God. It appeareth in nothing more, that atheism is rather in the lip than in the heart of man, than by this; that atheists will ever be talking of that their opinion, as if they fainted in it within themselves, and would be glad to be strengthened by the consent of others.

Bacon, *Of Atheism*

20 All that is said by the atheist against the existence of God, always depends either on the fact that we ascribe to God affections which are human, or that we attribute so much strength and wisdom to our minds that we even have the presumption to desire to determine and understand that which God can and ought to do. In this way all that they allege will cause us no difficulty, provided only we remember that we must consider our minds as things which are finite and limited, and God as a Being who is incomprehensible and infinite.

Descartes, *Meditations on First Philosophy,* Pref.

21 By denying the existence or providence of God, men may shake off their ease, but not their yoke. But to call this power of God, which extendeth itself not only to man, but also to beasts, and plants, and bodies inanimate, by the name of *kingdom,* is but a metaphorical use of the word. For he only is properly said to reign that governs his subjects by his word and by promise of rewards to those that obey it, and by threatening them with punishment that obey it not. Subjects therefore in the kingdom of God are not bodies inanimate, nor creatures irrational; because they understand no precepts as his: nor atheists, nor they that believe not that God has any care of the actions of mankind; because they acknowledge no word for his, nor have hope of his rewards, or fear of his threatenings. They therefore that believe there is a God that governeth the world, and hath given precepts, and propounded rewards and punishments to mankind, are God's subjects; all the rest are to be understood as enemies.

Hobbes, *Leviathan,* II, 31

22 That Heresies should arise, we have the Prophesie of Christ; but that old ones should be abolished, we hold no prediction.

Sir Thomas Browne, *Religio Medici,* I, 8

23 What reason have [atheists] for saying that we cannot rise from the dead? What is more difficult, to be born or to rise again; that what has never been should be, or that what has been should be again? Is it more difficult to come into existence

than to return to it? Habit makes the one appear easy to us; want of habit makes the other impossible. A popular way of thinking!

Why cannot a virgin bear a child? Does a hen not lay eggs without a cock? What distinguishes these outwardly from others? And who has told us that the hen may not form the germ as well as the cock?

Pascal, *Pensées,* III, 222

24 God (and the Apostles), foreseeing that the seeds of pride would make heresies spring up, and being unwilling to give them occasion to arise from correct expressions, has put in Scripture and the prayers of the Church contrary words and sentences to produce their fruit in time.

Pascal, *Pensées,* VIII, 579

25 *Chorus of Danites.* Just are the ways of God,
And justifiable to Men;
Unless there be who think not God at all,
If any be, they walk obscure;
For of such Doctrine never was there School,
But the heart of the Fool,
And no man therein Doctor but himself.

Milton, *Samson Agonistes,* 293

26 Truth is compared in Scripture to a streaming fountain; if her waters flow not in a perpetual progression, they sicken into a muddy pool of conformity and tradition. A man may be a heretic in the truth; and if he believe things only because his Pastor says so, or the Assembly so determines, without knowing other reason, though his belief be true, yet the very truth he holds becomes his heresy.

Milton, *Areopagitica*

27 Truth indeed came once into the world with her Divine Master, and was a perfect shape most glorious to look on: but when He ascended, and His Apostles after Him were laid asleep, then straight arose a wicked race of deceivers, who, as that story goes of the Egyptian Typhon with his conspirators, how they dealt with the good Osiris, took the virgin Truth, hewed her lovely form into a thousand pieces, and scattered them to the four winds. From that time ever since, the sad friends of Truth, such as durst appear, imitating the careful search that Isis made for the mangled body of Osiris, went up and down gathering up limb by limb, still as they could find them. We have not yet found them all, Lords and Commons, nor ever shall do, till her Master's second coming; He shall bring together every joint and member, and shall mould them into an immortal feature of loveliness and perfection.

Milton, *Areopagitica*

28 Those are not at all to be tolerated who deny the being of a God. Promises, covenants, and oaths,

which are the bonds of human society, can have no hold upon an atheist. The taking away of God, though but even in thought, dissolves all; besides also, those that by their atheism undermine and destroy all religion, can have no pretence of religion whereupon to challenge the privilege of a toleration. As for other practical opinions, though not absolutely free from all error, if they do not tend to establish domination over others, or civil impunity to the Church in which they are taught, there can be no reason why they should not be tolerated.

Locke, *Letter Concerning Toleration*

29 However clearly we may think this or the other doctrine to be deduced from Scripture, we ought not therefore to impose it upon others as a necessary article of faith because we believe it to be agreeable to the rule of faith, unless we would be content also that other doctrines should be imposed upon us in the same manner, and that we should be compelled to receive and profess all the different and contradictory opinions of Lutherans, Calvinists, Remonstrants, Anabaptists, and other sects which the contrivers of symbols, systems, and confessions are accustomed to deliver to their followers as genuine and necessary deductions from the Holy Scripture. I cannot but wonder at the extravagant arrogance of those men who think that they themselves can explain things necessary to salvation more clearly than the Holy Ghost, the eternal and infinite wisdom of God.

Locke, *Letter Concerning Toleration*

30 The disbelief of a divine providence renders a man uncapable of holding any publick station: for, since kings avow themselves to be the deputies of Providence, the Lilliputians think nothing can be more absurd, than for a prince to employ such men as disown the authority under which he acteth.

Swift, *Gulliver's Travels*, I, 6

31 M. Bayle has pretended to prove that it is better to be an Atheist than an Idolater; that is, in other words, that it is less dangerous to have no religion at all than a bad one. "I had rather," said he, "it should be said of me that I had no existence than that I am a villain." This is only a sophism founded on this, that it is of no importance to the human race to believe that a certain man exists, whereas it is extremely useful for them to believe the existence of a God. From the idea of his nonexistence immediately follows that of our independence; or, if we cannot conceive this idea, that of disobedience. To say that religion is not a restraining motive, because it does not always restrain, is equally absurd as to say that the civil laws are not a restraining motive. It is a false way of reasoning against religion to collect, in a large work, a long detail of the evils it has produced if

we do not give at the same time an enumeration of the advantages which have flowed from it. Were I to relate all the evils that have arisen in the world from civil laws, from monarchy, and from republican government, I might tell of frightful things. Were it of no advantage for subjects to have religion, it would still be of some, if princes had it, and if they whitened with foam the only rein which can restrain those who fear not human laws.

Montesquieu, *Spirit of Laws*, XXIV, 2

32 There is not a greater number of philosophical reasonings, displayed upon any subject, than those, which prove the existence of a Deity, and refute the fallacies of *Atheists;* and yet the most religious philosophers still dispute whether any man can be so blinded as to be a speculative atheist. How shall we reconcile these contradictions? The knights-errant, who wandered about to clear the world of dragons and giants, never entertained the least doubt with regard to the existence of these monsters.

Hume, *Concerning Human Understanding*, XII, 116

33 What conclusion shall we draw from all this? That atheism is a very pernicious monster in those who govern; that it is also pernicious in the persons around statesmen, although their lives may be innocent, because from their cabinets it may pierce right to the statesmen themselves; that if it is not so deadly as fanaticism, it is nearly always fatal to virtue. Let us add especially that there are less atheists to-day than ever, since philosophers have recognized that there is no being vegetating without germ, no germ without a plan, etc., and that wheat comes in no wise from putrefaction.

Some geometers who are not philosophers have rejected final causes, but real philosophers admit them; a catechist proclaims God to the children, and Newton demonstrates Him to the learned.

If there are atheists, whom must one blame, if not the mercenary tyrants of souls, who, making us revolt against their knaveries, force a few weak minds to deny the God whom these monsters dishonour. How many times have the people's leeches brought oppressed citizens to the point of revolting against their king!

Voltaire, *Philosophical Dictionary:* Atheism

34 Now, it matters very much to the community that each citizen should have a religion. That will make him love his duty; but the dogmas of that religion concern the State and its members only so far as they have reference to morality and to the duties which he who professes them is bound to do to others. Each man may have, over and above, what opinions he pleases, without it being the Sovereign's business to take cognisance of them; for, as the Sovereign has no authority in the other

world, whatever the lot of its subjects may be in the life to come, that is not its business, provided they are good citizens in this life.

There is therefore a purely civil profession of faith of which the Sovereign should fix the articles, not exactly as religious dogmas, but as social sentiments without which a man cannot be a good citizen or a faithful subject. While it can compel no one to believe them, it can banish from the State whoever does not believe them—it can banish him, not for impiety, but as an anti-social being, incapable of truly loving the laws and justice, and of sacrificing, at need, his life to his duty. If any one, after publicly recognising these dogmas, behaves as if he does not believe them, let him be punished by death: he has committed the worst of all crimes, that of lying before the law.

Rousseau, *Social Contract*, IV, 8

35 *Johnson.* Every society has a right to preserve publick peace and order, and therefore has a good right to prohibit the propagation of opinions which have a dangerous tendency. To say the *magistrate* has this right, is using an inadequate word: it is the *society* for which the magistrate is agent. He may be morally or theologically wrong in restraining the propagation of opinions which he thinks dangerous, but he is politically right.

Boswell, *Life of Johnson (May 7, 1773)*

36 *Johnson.* Sir, there is a great cry about infidelity; but there are, in reality, very few infidels. I have heard a person, originally a Quaker, but now, I am afraid, a Deist, say, that he did not believe there were, in all England, above two hundred infidels.

Boswell, *Life of Johnson (Apr. 14, 1775)*

37 The opinions of the Academics and Epicureans were of a less religious cast; but whilst the modest science of the former induced them to doubt, the positive ignorance of the latter urged them to deny, the providence of a Supreme Ruler. The spirit of inquiry, prompted by emulation, and supported by freedom, had divided the public teachers of philosophy into a variety of contending sects; but the ingenuous youth who, from every part, resorted to Athens, and the other seats of learning in the Roman empire, were alike instructed in every school to reject and to despise the religion of the multitude. How, indeed, was it possible, that a philosopher should accept, as divine truths, the idle tales of the poets, and the incoherent traditions of antiquity; or, that he should adore, as gods, those imperfect beings whom he must have despised, as men! Against such unworthy adversaries, Cicero condescended to employ the arms of reason and eloquence; but the satire of Lucian was a much more adequate, as well as more efficacious weapon. We may be well assured, that a writer conversant with the

world would never have ventured to expose the gods of his country to public ridicule, had they not already been the objects of secret contempt among the polished and enlightened orders of society.

Gibbon, *Decline and Fall of the Roman Empire*, II

38 It is the undoubted right of every society to exclude from its communion and benefits such among its members as reject or violate those regulations which have been established by general consent. In the exercise of this power the censures of the Christian church were chiefly directed against scandalous sinners, and particularly those who were guilty of murder, of fraud, or of incontinence; against the authors, or the followers, of any heretical opinions which had been condemned by the judgment of the episcopal order; and against those unhappy persons who, whether from choice or from compulsion, had polluted themselves after their baptism by any act of idolatrous worship. The consequences of excommunication were of a temporal as well as a spiritual nature. The Christian against whom it was pronounced was deprived of any part in the oblations of the faithful. The ties both of religious and of private friendship were dissolved: he found himself a profane object of abhorrence to the persons whom he the most esteemed, or by whom he had been the most tenderly beloved; and as far as an expulsion from a respectable society could imprint on his character a mark of disgrace, he was shunned or suspected by the generality of mankind.

Gibbon, *Decline and Fall of the Roman Empire*, XV

39 So easily was he [the emperor Constantius] offended by the slightest deviation from his imaginary standard of Christian truth, that he persecuted, with equal zeal, those who defended the *consubstantiality*, those who asserted the *similar substance*, and those who denied the *likeness*, of the Son of God. Three bishops, degraded and banished for those adverse opinions, might possibly meet in the same place of exile; and, according to the difference of their temper, might either pity or insult the blind enthusiasm of their antagonists, whose present sufferings would never be compensated by future happiness.

Gibbon, *Decline and Fall of the Roman Empire*, XXI

40 Constantinople was the principal seat and fortress of Arianism; and, in a long interval of forty years, the faith of the princes and prelates who reigned in the capital of the East was rejected in the purer schools of Rome and Alexandria. The archiepiscopal throne of Macedonius, which had been polluted with so much Christian blood, was successively filled by Eudoxus and Damophilus. Their

diocese enjoyed a free importation of vice and error from every province of the empire; the eager pursuit of religious controversy afforded a new occupation to the busy idleness of the metropolis: and we may credit the assertion of an intelligent observer, who describes, with some pleasantry, the effects of their loquacious zeal. "This city," says he, "is full of mechanics and slaves, who are all of them profound theologians, and preach in the shops and in the streets. If you desire a man to change a piece of silver, he informs you wherein the Son differs from the Father; if you ask the price of a loaf, you are told, by way of reply, that the Son is inferior to the Father; and if you inquire whether the bath is ready, the answer is, that the Son was made out of nothing."

Gibbon, *Decline and Fall of the Roman Empire*, XXVII

41 By a second edict he [Leo III] proscribed the existence as well as the use of religious pictures; the churches of Constantinople and the provinces were cleansed from idolatry; the images of Christ, the Virgin, and the saints were demolished, or a smooth surface of plaster was spread over the walls of the edifice. The sect of the Iconoclasts was supported by the zeal and despotism of six emperors, and the East and West were involved in a noisy conflict of one hundred and twenty years.

Gibbon, *Decline and Fall of the Roman Empire*, XLIX

42 The laws of the pious emperors, which seldom touched the lives of less odious heretics, proscribed without mercy or disguise the tenets, the books, and the persons of the Montanists and Manichæans: the books were delivered to the flames; and all who should presume to secrete such writings, or to profess such opinions, were devoted to an ignominious death.

Gibbon, *Decline and Fall of the Roman Empire*, LIV

43 We know, and it is our pride to know, that man is by his constitution a religious animal; that atheism is against, not only our reason, but our instincts; and that it cannot prevail long.

Burke, *Reflections on the Revolution in France*

44 If, from a practical point of view, the hypothesis of a Supreme and All-sufficient Being is to maintain its validity without opposition, it must be of the highest importance to define this conception in a correct and rigorous manner—as the transcendental conception of a necessary being, to eliminate all phenomenal elements (anthropomorphism in its most extended signification), and at the same time to overflow all contradictory assertions—be they *atheistic, deistic,* or *anthropomorphic*. This is of course very easy; as the same arguments which

demonstrated the inability of human reason to *affirm* the existence of a Supreme Being must be alike sufficient to prove the invalidity of its denial. For it is impossible to gain from the pure speculation of reason demonstration that there exists no Supreme Being, as the ground of all that exists, or that this being possesses none of those properties which we regard as analogical with the dynamical qualities of a thinking being, or that, as the anthropomorphists would have us believe, it is subject to all the limitations which sensibility imposes upon those intelligences which exist in the world of experience.

A Supreme Being is, therefore, for the speculative reason, a mere ideal, though a *faultless* one—a conception which perfects and crowns the system of human cognition, but the objective reality of which can neither be proved nor disproved by pure reason. If this defect is ever supplied by a moral theology, the problematic transcendental theology which has preceded, will have been at least serviceable as demonstrating the mental necessity existing for the conception, by the complete determination of it which it has furnished, and the ceaseless testing of the conclusions of a reason often deceived by sense, and not always in harmony with its own ideas.

Kant, *Critique of Pure Reason,* Transcendental Dialectic

45 Principle is a better test of heresy than doctrine. Heretics are true to their principles, but change to and fro, backwards and forwards, in opinion; for very opposite doctrines may be exemplifications of the same principle. Thus the Antiochenes and other heretics sometimes were Arians, sometimes Sabellians, sometimes Nestorians, sometimes Monophysites, as if at random, from fidelity to their common principle, that there is no mystery in theology. Thus Calvinists become Unitarians from the principle of private judgment. The doctrines of heresy are accidents and soon run to an end; its principles are everlasting.

Newman, *Essay on the Development of Christian Doctrine*, Pt. II, V, 2

46 The path Alyosha chose was a path going in the opposite direction, but he chose it with the same thirst for swift achievement. As soon as he reflected seriously he was convinced of the existence of God and immortality, and at once he instinctively said to himself: "I want to live for immortality, and I will accept no compromise." In the same way, if he had decided that God and immortality did not exist, he would at once have become an atheist and a socialist. For socialism is not merely the labour question, it is before all things the atheistic question, the question of the form taken by atheism to-day, the question of the tower of Babel built without God, not to mount to heaven from

earth but to set up heaven on earth.

Dostoevsky, *Brothers Karamazov,*
Pt. I, I, 5

47 *Ivan.* "You see, only suppose that there was one such man among all those who desire nothing but filthy material gain—if there's only one like my old Inquisitor, who had himself eaten roots in the desert and made frenzied efforts to subdue his flesh to make himself free and perfect. But yet all his life he loved humanity, and suddenly his eyes were opened, and he saw that it is no great moral blessedness to attain perfection and freedom, if at the same time one gains the conviction that millions of God's creatures have been created as a mockery, that they will never be capable of using their freedom, that these poor rebels can never turn into giants to complete the tower, that it was not for such geese that the great idealist dreamt his dream of harmony. Seeing all that he turned back and joined—the clever people. Surely that could have happened?"

"Joined whom, what clever people?" cried Alyosha, completely carried away. "They have no such great cleverness and no mysteries and secrets. . . . Perhaps nothing but Atheism, that's all their secret. Your Inquisitor does not believe in God, that's his secret!"

"What if it is so! At last you have guessed it. It's perfectly true, it's true that that's the whole secret, but isn't that suffering, at least for a man like that, who has wasted his whole life in the desert and yet could not shake off his incurable love of humanity? In his old age he reached the clear conviction that nothing but the advice of the great dread spirit could build up any tolerable sort of life for the feeble, unruly, 'incomplete, empirical creatures created in jest.' And so, convinced of this, he sees that he must follow the counsel of the wise spirit, the dread spirit of death and destruction, and therefore accept lying and deception, and lead men consciously to death and destruction, and yet deceive them all the way so that they may not notice where they are being led, that the poor blind creatures may at least on the way think themselves happy. And note, the deception is in the name of Him in Whose ideal the old man had so fervently believed all his life long. Is not that tragic? And if only one such stood at the head of the whole army 'filled with the lust of power only for the sake of filthy gain'—would not one such be enough to make a tragedy? More than that, one such standing at the head is enough to create the actual leading idea of the Roman Church with all its armies and Jesuits, its highest idea. I tell you frankly that I firmly believe that there has always been such a man among those who stood at the head of the movement. Who knows, there may have been some such even among the Roman Popes. Who knows, perhaps the spirit of that accursed old man who loves mankind so obstinately in his own way, is to be found even now in a whole multitude of such old men, existing not by chance but by agreement, as a secret league formed long ago for the guarding of the mystery, to guard it from the weak and the unhappy, so as to make them happy. No doubt it is so, and so it must be indeed."

Dostoevsky, *Brothers Karamazov,*
Pt. II, V, 5

48 *The Visitor.* Oh, blind race of men who have no understanding! As soon as men have all of them denied God—and I believe that period, analogous with geological periods, will come to pass—the old conception of the universe will fall of itself without cannibalism, and, what's more, the old morality, and everything will begin anew. Men will unite to take from life all it can give, but only for joy and happiness in the present world. Man will be lifted up with a spirit of divine Titanic pride and the man-god will appear. From hour to hour extending his conquest of nature infinitely by his will and his science, man will feel such lofty joy from hour to hour in doing it that it will make up for all his old dreams of the joys of heaven.

Dostoevsky, *Brothers Karamazov,*
Pt. IV, XI, 9

49 The existentialist . . . thinks it very distressing that God does not exist, because all possibility of finding values in a heaven of ideas disappears along with Him; there can no longer be an *a priori* Good, since there is no infinite and perfect consciousness to think it. Nowhere is it written that the Good exists, that we must be honest, that we must not lie; because the fact is we are on a plane where there are only men. Dostoevsky said, "If God didn't exist, everything would be possible." That is the very starting point of existentialism. Indeed, everything is permissible if God does not exist, and as a result man is forlorn, because neither within him nor without does he find anything to cling to. He can't start making excuses for himself.

Sartre, *Existentialism*

20.10 | *Prophecy*

Two meanings of prophecy emerge in the quotations collected here. One is the foretelling or prediction of the future. The discussion of prophecy in this sense of the term belongs in a chapter on RELIGION only to the extent that the future foreseen has been predestined by the gods or by God; hence, the prophet or seer is also called a "diviner" or one who has skill in divination. Secular foresight and scientific prediction are treated elsewhere in this volume, as are fate and fortune when these are separated from divine providence. The reader will find such matters considered in Section 15.3 on FATE, FORTUNE, AND DESTINY and in Section 17.2 on SCIENCE AND SCIENTIFIC METHOD.

In its other meaning, prophecy involves more than the simple prediction of future events, though it may involve that also. Inspired by God, the Hebrew prophets serve as the medium through which God speaks to his chosen people, conveying his condemnation of their misdeeds and exhorting them to mend their ways. Prophecy, in this sense, is not only a medium of revelation and a form of mediation between God and man, but also the preachment of moral ideals and the castigation of moral iniquities. The passages from the Old Testament illustrate this meaning of prophecy and the role that the Hebrew prophets played at critical moments in the history of Judaism.

The poets and historians of antiquity provide us with examples of prophecy in the other sense. The philosophers and theologians, both ancient and medieval, discuss the art of divination, the interpretation of dreams for this purpose, and the use or misuse of astrology to foretell the future. One modern writer, Spinoza, expresses the opinion that the prophets of the Old Testament should be read solely for their moral preachments; and another modern writer, Hume, suggests that prophecies, if they are regarded as conveying a message from God, must also be regarded as miraculous. The reader will find Hume's opinions about the miraculous in Section 20.11 on MIRACLES.

---

1 And Moses went up from the plains of Moab unto the mountain of Nebo, to the top of Pisgah, that is over against Jericho, And the Lord shewed him all the land of Gĭl´-ē-ăd, unto Dan.

And all Năph´-tă-lī, and the land of Ē´-phră-ĭm, and Mă-năs´-sĕh, and all the land of Judah, unto the utmost sea,

And the south, and the plain of the valley of Jericho, the city of palm trees, unto Zoar.

And the Lord said unto him, This is the land which I sware unto Abraham, unto Isaac, and unto Jacob, saying, I will give it unto thy seed: I have caused thee to see it with thine eyes, but thou shalt not go over thither. . . .

And there arose not a prophet since in Israel like unto Moses, whom the Lord knew face to face,

In all the signs and the wonders, which the Lord sent him to do in the land of Egypt to Pharaoh, and to all his servants, and to all his land,

And in all that mighty hand, and in all the great terror which Moses shewed in the sight of all Israel.

Deuteronomy 34:1–12

2 Am I a God at hand, saith the Lord, and not a God afar off?

Can any hide himself in secret places that I shall not see him? saith the Lord. Do not I fill heaven and earth? saith the Lord.

I have heard what the prophets said, that prophesy lies in my name, saying, I have dreamed, I have dreamed.

How long shall this be in the heart of the prophets that prophesy lies? yea, they are prophets of the deceit of their own heart;

Which think to cause my people to forget my

name by their dreams which they tell every man to his neighbour, as their fathers have forgotten my name for Bā-̄ăl.

The prophet that hath a dream, let him tell a dream; and he that hath my word, let him speak my word faithfully. What is the chaff to the wheat? saith the Lord.

Is not my word like as a fire? saith the Lord; and like a hammer that breaketh the rock in pieces?

Therefore, behold, I am against the prophets, saith the Lord, that steal my words every one from his neighbour.

Behold, I am against the prophets, saith the Lord, that use their tongues, and say, He saith.

Behold, I am against them that prophesy false dreams, saith the Lord, and do tell them, and cause my people to err by their lies, and by their lightness; yet I sent them not, nor commanded them: therefore they shall not profit this people at all, saith the Lord.

Jeremiah 23:23–32

3 The Lord hath sent unto you all his servants the prophets, rising early and sending them; but ye have not hearkened, nor inclined your ear to hear.

They said, Turn ye again now every one from his evil way, and from the evil of your doings, and dwell in the land that the Lord hath given unto you and to your fathers for ever and ever:

And go not after other gods to serve them, and to worship them, and provoke me not to anger with the works of your hands; and I will do you no hurt.

Yet ye have not hearkened unto me, saith the Lord; that ye might provoke me to anger with the works of your hands to your own hurt. . . .

And I will bring upon that land all my words which I have pronounced against it, even all that is written in this book, which Jeremiah hath prophesied against all the nations.

Jeremiah 25:4–13

4 Thus saith the Lord of hosts, the God of Israel; Let not your prophets and your diviners, that be in the midst of you, deceive you, neither hearken to your dreams which ye cause to be dreamed.

For they prophesy falsely unto you in my name: I have not sent them, saith the Lord.

For thus saith the Lord, That after seventy years be accomplished at Babylon I will visit you, and perform my good word toward you, in causing you to return to this place.

For I know the thoughts that I think toward you, saith the Lord, thoughts of peace, and not of evil, to give you an expected end.

Jeremiah 29:8–11

5 The hand of the Lord was upon me, and carried me out in the spirit of the Lord, and set me down in the midst of the valley which was full of bones,

And caused me to pass by them round about: and, behold, there were very many in the open valley; and, lo, they were very dry.

And he said unto me, Son of man, can these bones live? And I answered, O Lord God, thou knowest.

Again he said unto me, Prophesy upon these bones, and say unto them, O ye dry bones, hear the word of the Lord.

Ezekiel 37:1–4

6 *Prometheus.* I have known all before, all that shall be, and clearly known; to me, nothing that hurts shall come with a new face. So must I bear, as lightly as I can, the destiny that fate has given me; for I know well against necessity, against its strength, no one can fight and win.

Aeschylus, *Prometheus Bound,* 100

7 *Orestes.* Even the gods, who at least bear the title of wise, prove no less false than flitting dreams; in things divine as well as human, confusion reigns; and 'tis only one cause of grief, when a man, through no folly of his own but from obeying the dictates of prophets, is ruined, as ruined he is in the judgment of those who know.

Euripides, *Iphigenia in Tauris,* 570

8 *Servant.* How rotten this business of prophets is, how full of lies.
There never was any good in burning things on fires
nor in the voices of fowl. It is sheer idiocy
even to think that birds do people any good. . . .
Why consult the prophets? We should sacrifice to the gods, ask them for blessings, and let prophecy go.
The art was invented as a bait for making money, but no man ever got rich on magic without work. The best prophet is common sense, our native wit.

Euripides, *Helen,* 745

9 *Teiresias.* A man's a fool to use the prophet's trade. For if he happens to bring bitter news
he's hated by the men for whom he works;
and if he pities them and tells them lies
he wrongs the gods. No prophet but Apollo
should sing to men, for he has nought to fear.

Euripides, *Phoenician Women,* 954

10 *Socrates.* There is also a madness which is a divine gift, and the source of the chiefest blessings granted to men. For prophecy is a madness, and the prophetess at Delphi and the priestesses at Dodona when out of their senses have conferred great benefits on Hellas, both in public and private life, but when in their senses few or none. And I might also tell you how the Sibyl and other inspired persons have given to many an one many an intimation of the future which has saved them from fall-

ing. But it would be tedious to speak of what every one knows.

Plato, Phaedrus, 244A

11 *Timaeus.* God has given the art of divination not to the wisdom, but to the foolishness of man. No man, when in his wits, attains prophetic truth and inspiration; but when he receives the inspired word, either his intelligence is enthralled in sleep, or he is demented by some distemper or possession. And he who would understand what he remembers to have been said, whether in a dream or when he was awake, by the prophetic and inspired nature, or would determine by reason the meaning of the apparitions which he has seen, and what indications they afford to this man or that, of past, present or future good and evil, must first recover his wits. But, while he continues demented, he cannot judge of the visions which he sees or the words which he utters; the ancient saying is very true, that "only a man who has his wits can act or judge about himself and his own affairs." And for this reason it is customary to appoint interpreters to be judges of the true inspiration. Some persons call them prophets; they are quite unaware that they are only the expositors of dark sayings and visions, and are not to be called prophets at all, but only interpreters of prophecy.

Plato, Timaeus, 71B

12 As to the divination which takes place in sleep, and is said to be based on dreams, we cannot lightly either dismiss it with contempt or give it implicit confidence. The fact that all persons, or many, suppose dreams to possess a special significance, tends to inspire us with belief in it [such divination], as founded on the testimony of experience; and indeed that divination in dreams should, as regards some subjects, be genuine, is not incredible, for it has a show of reason; from which one might form a like opinion also respecting all other dreams. Yet the fact of our seeing no probable cause to account for such divination tends to inspire us with distrust. For, in addition to its further unreasonableness, it is absurd to combine the idea that the sender of such dreams should be God with the fact that those to whom he sends them are not the best and wisest, but merely commonplace persons.

Aristotle, Prophesying by Dreams, 462^{b}12

13 Divination is made up of a little error and superstition, plus a lot of fraud.

Cicero, Divination, II, 39

14 Arriv'd at Cumæ, when you view the flood
Of black Avernus, and the sounding wood,
The mad prophetic Sibyl you shall find,
Dark in a cave, and on a rock reclin'd.
She sings the fates, and, in her frantic fits,
The notes and names, inscrib'd, to leaves commits.

What she commits to leaves, in order laid,
Before the cavern's entrance are display'd:
Unmov'd they lie; but, if a blast of wind
Without, or vapors issue from behind,
The leaves are borne aloft in liquid air,
And she resumes no more her museful care,
Nor gathers from the rocks her scatter'd verse,
Nor sets in order what the winds disperse.
Thus, many not succeeding, most upbraid
The madness of the visionary maid,
And with loud curses leave the mystic shade.

Virgil, Aeneid, III

15 In those days came John the Baptist, preaching in the wilderness of Judæa,
And saying, Repent ye: for the kingdom of heaven is at hand.
For this is he that was spoken of by the prophet Esaias, saying, The voice of one crying in the wilderness, Prepare ye the way of the Lord, make his paths straight.

Matthew 3:1–3

16 Think not that I am come to destroy the law, or the prophets: I am not come to destroy, but to fulfil.
For verily I say unto you, Till heaven and earth pass, one jot or one tittle shall in no wise pass from the law, till all be fulfilled.

Matthew 5:17–18

17 Beware of false prophets, which come to you in sheep's clothing, but inwardly they are ravening wolves.

Matthew 7:15

18 Certain of the scribes and of the Pharisees answered, saying, Master, we would see a sign from thee.
But he answered and said unto them, An evil and adulterous generation seeketh after a sign; and there shall no sign be given to it, but the sign of the prophet Jonas:
For as Jonas was three days and three nights in the whale's belly; so shall the Son of man be three days and three nights in the heart of the earth.

Matthew 12:38–40

19 A prophet is not without honour, save in his own country, and in his own house.

Matthew 13:57

20 If they hear not Moses and the prophets, neither will they be persuaded, though one rose from the dead.

Luke 16:31

21 When they therefore were come together, they asked of him, saying, Lord, wilt thou at this time restore again the kingdom to Israel?

And he said unto them, It is not for you to know the times or the seasons, which the Father hath put in his own power.

Acts 1:6–7

22 The fortunes of cities as well as of men . . . have their certain periods of time prefixed, which may be collected and foreknown from the position of the stars at their first foundation.

Plutarch, *Romulus*

23 Among other great changes that happen, as they say, at the turn of ages, the art of divination, also, at one time rises in esteem, and is more successful in its predictions, clearer and surer tokens being sent from God, and then, again, in another generation declines as low, becoming mere guesswork for the most part, and discerning future events by dim and uncertain intimations.

Plutarch, *Sulla*

24 But You, O Ruler of Your creation, how is it that you can show souls things that are to come? For such things You have told Your prophets. In what manner do You show the future to man, for whom nothing future yet is? Or do You show only present signs of things to come? For what does not exist obviously cannot be shown. The means You use is altogether beyond my gaze; my eyes have not the strength; of myself I shall never be able to see so deep.

Augustine, *Confessions,* XI, 19

25 In the manner of prophecy, figurative and literal expressions are mingled, so that a serious mind may, by useful and salutary effort, reach the spiritual sense; but carnal sluggishness, or the slowness of an uneducated and undisciplined mind, rests in the superficial letter, and thinks there is nothing beneath to be looked for.

Augustine, *City of God,* XX, 21

26 The majority of men follow their passions, which are movements of the sensitive appetite, in which movements heavenly bodies can co-operate; but few are wise enough to resist these passions. Consequently astrologers are able to foretell the truth in the majority of cases, especially in a general way. But not in particular cases, for nothing prevents man resisting his passions by his free-will. And so the astrologers themselves say that the wise man is stronger than the stars, in so far as, that is, he conquers his passions.

Aquinas, *Summa Theologica,* I, 115, 4

27 *Casca.* Are not you moved, when all the sway of earth
Shakes like a thing unfirm? O Cicero,
I have seen tempests, when the scolding winds
Have rived the knotty oaks, and I have seen
The ambitious ocean swell and rage and foam,

To be exalted with the threatening clouds:
But never till to-night, never till now,
Did I go through a tempest dropping fire.
Either there is a civil strife in heaven,
Or else the world, too saucy with the gods,
Incenses them to send destruction.
   Cicero. Why, saw you anything more wonderful?
   Casca. A common slave—you know him well by sight—
Held up his left hand, which did flame and burn
Like twenty torches join'd, and yet his hand,
Not sensible of fire, remain'd unscorch'd.
Besides—I ha' not since put up my sword—
Against the Capitol I met a lion,
Who glared upon me, and went surly by
Without annoying me: and there were drawn
Upon a heap a hundred ghastly women,
Transformed with their fear, who swore they saw
Men all in fire walk up and down the streets.
And yesterday the bird of night did sit
Even at noon-day upon the market-place,
Hooting and shrieking. When these prodigies
Do so conjointly meet, let not men say
"These are their reasons; they are natural";
For, I believe, they are portentous things
Unto the climate that they point upon.
   Cic. Indeed, it is a strange-disposed time:
But men may construe things for their fashion.
Clean from the purpose of the things themselves.

Shakespeare, *Julius Caesar,* I, iii, 3

28 *Banquo.* If you can look into the seeds of time,
And say which grain will grow and which will not,
Speak then to me, who neither beg nor fear
Your favours nor your hate.

Shakespeare, *Macbeth,* I, iii, 58

29 The foresight of things to come, which is providence, belongs only to him by whose will they are to come. From him only, and supernaturally, proceeds prophecy. The best prophet naturally is the best guesser; and the best guesser, he that is most versed and studied in the matters he guesses at, for he hath most signs to guess by.

Hobbes, *Leviathan,* I, 3

30 When God speaketh to man, it must be either immediately or by mediation of another man, to whom He had formerly spoken by Himself immediately. How God speaketh to a man immediately may be understood by those well enough to whom He hath so spoken; but how the same should be understood by another is hard, if not impossible, to know. For if a man pretend to me that God hath spoken to him supernaturally, and immediately, and I make doubt of it, I cannot easily perceive what argument he can produce to oblige me to believe it. It is true that if he be my sovereign, he may oblige me to obedience, so as not by act or word to declare I believe him not; but not to think

any otherwise than my reason persuades me. But if one that hath not such authority over me shall pretend the same, there is nothing that exacteth either belief or obedience.

Hobbes, *Leviathan*, III, 32

31 Though God Almighty can speak to a man by dreams, visions, voice, and inspiration, yet He obliges no man to believe He hath so done to him that pretends it; who, being a man, may err and, which is more, may lie.

How then can he to whom God hath never revealed His will immediately (saving by the way of natural reason) know when he is to obey or not to obey His word, delivered by him that says he is a prophet? . . . To which I answer out of the Holy Scripture that there be two marks by which together, not asunder, a true prophet is to be known. One is the doing of miracles; the other is the not teaching any other religion than that which is already established. Asunder, I say, neither of these is sufficient. . . . In which words two things are to be observed; first, that God will not have miracles alone serve for arguments to approve the prophet's calling; but for an experiment of the constancy of our adherence to Himself. For the works of the Egyptian sorcerers, though not so great as those of Moses, yet were great miracles. Secondly, that how great soever the miracle be, yet if it tend to stir up revolt against the king or him that governeth by the king's authority, he that doth such miracle is not to be considered otherwise than as sent to make trial of their allegiance.

Hobbes, *Leviathan*, III, 32

32 The prophecies are the strongest proof of Jesus Christ. It is for them also that God has made most provision; for the event which has fulfilled them is a miracle existing since the birth of the Church to the end. So God has raised up prophets during sixteen hundred years, and, during four hundred years afterwards, He has scattered all these prophecies among all the Jews, who carried them into all parts of the world. Such was the preparation for the birth of Jesus Christ, and, as His Gospel was to be believed by all the world, it was not only necessary that there should be prophecies to make it believed, but that these prophecies should exist throughout the whole world, in order to make it embraced by the whole world.

Pascal, *Pensées*, XI, 706

33 If one man alone had made a book of predictions about Jesus Christ, as to the time and the manner, and Jesus Christ had come in conformity to these prophecies, this fact would have infinite weight.

But there is much more here. Here is a succession of men during four thousand years, who, consequently and without variation, come, one after another, to foretell this same event. Here is a

whole people [the Jews] who announce it and who have existed for four thousand years, in order to give corporate testimony of the assurances which they have and from which they cannot be diverted by whatever threats and persecutions people may make against them. This is far more important.

Pascal, *Pensées*, XI, 710

34 The Jews, in slaying Him in order not to receive Him as the Messiah, have given Him the final proof of being the Messiah.

And in continuing not to recognise Him, they made themselves irreproachable witnesses. Both in slaying Him and in continuing to deny Him, they have fulfilled the prophecies.

Pascal, *Pensées*, XII, 761

35 Prophecy, or revelation, is sure knowledge revealed by God to man. A prophet is one who interprets the revelations of God to those who are unable to attain to sure knowledge of the matters revealed, and therefore can only apprehend them by simple faith.

Spinoza, *Theologico-Political Treatise*, I

36 The authority of the prophets has weight only in matters of morality, and . . . their speculative doctrines affect us little.

Spinoza, *Theologico-Political Treatise*, Pref.

37 No one except Christ received the revelations of God without the aid of imagination, whether in words or vision. Therefore the power of prophecy implies not a peculiarly perfect mind, but a peculiarly vivid imagination.

Spinoza, *Theologico-Political Treatise*, I

38 All prophecies are real miracles, and as such only, can be admitted as proofs of any revelation. If it did not exceed the capacity of human nature to foretell future events, it would be absurd to employ any prophecy as an argument for a divine mission or authority from heaven.

Hume, *Concerning Human Understanding*, X, 101

39 It must be admitted, a prophet's profession is a wretched one. For every one who, like Elijah, goes traveling from planet to planet in a shining chariot of light drawn by four white horses, there are a hundred who go on foot and must beg their dinner from door to door.

Voltaire, *Philosophical Dictionary: Prophets*

40 Any man may grave tablets of stone, or buy an oracle, or feign secret intercourse with some divinity, or train a bird to whisper in his ear, or find other vulgar ways of imposing on the people. He whose knowledge goes no further may perhaps

gather round him a band of fools; but he will never found an empire, and his extravagances will quickly perish with him. Idle tricks form a passing tie; only wisdom can make it lasting.

Rousseau, *Social Contract,* II, 7

41 But, Mousie, thou art no thy lane
In proving foresight may be vain!
The best-laid schemes o' mice and men
    Gang aft a-gley,
And lea'e us nought but grief and pain
    For promised joy.

Burns, *To a Mouse*

42 The future has not yet happened. But it is not *on that account* less necessary than the past, since the past did not become necessary by coming into existence, but on the contrary proved by coming into existence that it was not necessary. If the past had become necessary it would not be possible to infer the opposite about the future, but it would rather follow that the future also was necessary. If necessity could gain a foothold at a single point, there would no longer be any distinguishing between the past and the future. To assume to predict the future (prophesy) and to assume to understand the necessity of the past are one and the same thing, and only custom makes the one seem more plausible than the other to a given generation.

Kierkegaard, *Philosophical Fragments,*
Interlude

43 Always the seer is a sayer. Somehow his dream is told; somehow he publishes it with solemn joy: sometimes with pencil on canvas, sometimes with chisel on stone, sometimes in towers and aisles of granite, his soul's worship is builded; sometimes in anthems of indefinite music; but clearest and most permanent, in words.

The man enamored of this excellency becomes its priest or poet. The office is coeval with the world. But observe the condition, the spiritual limitation of the office. The spirit only can teach. Not any profane man, not any sensual, not any liar, not any slave can teach, but only he can give, who has; he only can create, who is. The man on whom the soul descends, through whom the soul speaks, alone can teach. Courage, piety, love, wisdom, can teach; and every man can open his door to these angels, and they shall bring him the gift of tongues. But the man who aims to speak as books enable, as synods use, as the fashion guides, and as interest commands, babbles. Let him hush.

Emerson, *Address to Harvard Divinity School*

44 There are always so many conjectures as to the issue of any event that however it may end there will always be people to say: "I said then that it would be so," quite forgetting that amid their innumerable conjectures many were to quite the contrary effect.

Tolstoy, *War and Peace,* X, 1

45 The prophet has drunk more deeply than anyone of the cup of bitterness, but his countenance is so unshaken and he speaks such mighty words of cheer that his will becomes our will, and our life is kindled at his own.

William James, *Psychology,* XXVI

46 The attempt to translate Prophetic Vision, expressed in the language of poetic truth, into a metaphysical blue-print, expressed in the language of scientific truth, has two untoward effects. It forces us to direct our attention from what is essential and momentous in the poetic truth of Prophetic Vision to the trivial and intrinsically insoluble question of its relation to scientific truth; and it substitutes a provisional report for a timeless intuition. Even if we could succeed in translating poetic truth into scientific truth at the risk of robbing it of its meaning and value, our scientific formula would no sooner have been drafted than it would be already obsolete.

Toynbee, *An Historian's Approach
to Religion,* IX

20.11 | *Miracles*

As the reader might expect, the writers quoted here divide rather sharply into those who accept miracles as certainly within God's power to perform and those who reject miracles as impossible because they violate the laws of nature. One of the subtle issues involved in this dispute is whether a miracle consists in the doing of the impossible or is the occurrence of what is only improbable, not impossible. The theologians who offer us definitions of the miraculous, and provide us with the classification of different types of miracles, take the latter view: even an omnipotent God cannot do the impossible; the laws of nature do not express necessities that make their contravention by miracles consist in doing the impossible. The philosophers (who reject miracles), among them especially Spinoza and Hume, differ among themselves on the question of whether or not the laws of nature express necessities that can be known by us; if not, as Hume appears to maintain, miracles may present us with striking exceptions to the normal course of nature, but they cannot be judged impossible.

The reader's attention is called to Augustine's remark that the existence of man himself—at once an animal and rational—is a greater miracle than any other; to Pascal's treatment of the miracles performed by Christ as evidence of his divinity and of the truth of his teachings; to Gibbon's skeptical treatment of the miracles that were supposed to have occurred in the early centuries of Christianity; to Kierkegaard's insight, expressed also by Dostoevsky, that faith in Christ precedes and underlies belief in the miracles he performed; and to Santayana's observation that science has its miracles, too.

Matters relevant to the discussion of miracles will be found in Section 19.1 on NATURE AND THE NATURAL, in Section 19.3 on CAUSE, in Section 19.4 on CHANCE, and in Section 20.12 on SUPERSTITION.

---

1 Moses stretched forth his hand over the sea, and the sea returned to his strength when the morning appeared; and the Egyptians fled against it; and the Lord overthrew the Egyptians in the midst of the sea.

And the waters returned, and covered the chariots, and the horsemen, and all the host of Pharaoh that came into the sea after them; there remained not so much as one of them.

But the children of Israel walked upon dry land in the midst of the sea; and the waters were a wall unto them on their right hand, and on their left.

Thus the Lord saved Israel that day out of the hand of the Egyptians; and Israel saw the Egyptians dead upon the sea shore.

And Israel saw that great work which the Lord did upon the Egyptians: and the people feared the Lord, and believed the Lord, and his servant Moses.

Exodus 14:27–31

2 Nĕb-ū-chăd-nĕź-zär spake and said unto them, Is it true, O Shā-drăch, Mē-shăch, and Abed-nego, do not ye serve my gods, nor worship the golden image which I have set up?

Now if ye be ready that at what time ye hear the sound of the cornet, flute, harp, sackbut, psaltery, and dulcimer, and all kinds of musick, ye fall down and worship the image which I have made; well: but if ye worship not, ye shall be cast the same hour into the midst of a burning fiery furnace; and who is that God that shall deliver you out of my hands?

Shā-drăch, Mē-shăch, and Abed-nego, answered and said to the king, O Nĕb-ū-chăd-nĕź-zär, we are not careful to answer thee in this matter.

If it be so, our God whom we serve is able to deliver us from the burning fiery furnace, and he will deliver us out of thine hand, O king.

But if not, be it known unto thee, O king, that

we will not serve thy gods, nor worship the golden image which thou hast set up.

Then was Něb-ū-chăd-něź-zär full of fury, and the form of his visage was changed against Shā-drăch, Mē-shăch, and Abed-nego: therefore he spake, and commanded that they should heat the furnace one seven times more than it was wont to be heated.

And he commanded the most mighty men that were in his army to bind Shā-drăch, Mē-shăch, and Abed-nego, and to cast them into the burning fiery furnace.

Then these men were bound in their coats, their hosen, and their hats, and their other garments, and were cast into the midst of the burning fiery furnace.

Therefore because the king's commandment was urgent, and the furnace exceeding hot, the flame of the fire slew those men that took up Shā-drăch, Mē-shăch, and Abed-nego.

And these three men, Shā-drăch, Mē-shăch, and Abed-nego, fell down bound into the midst of the burning fiery furnace.

Then Něb-ū-chăd-něź-zär the king was astonied, and rose up in haste, and spake, and said unto his counsellors, Did not we cast three men bound into the midst of the fire? They answered and said unto the king, True, O king.

He answered and said, Lo, I see four men loose, walking in the midst of the fire, and they have no hurt; and the form of the fourth is like the Son of God.

Then Něb-ū-chăd-něź-zär came near to the mouth of the burning fiery furnace, and spake, and said, Shā-drăch, Mē-shăch, and Abed-nego, ye servants of the most high God, come forth, and come hither. Then Shā-drăch, Mē-shăch, and Abed-nego, came forth of the midst of the fire.

And the princes, governors, and captains, and the king's counsellors, being gathered together, saw these men, upon whose bodies the fire had no power, nor was an hair of their head singed, neither were their coats changed, nor the smell of fire had passed on them.

Daniel 3:14–27

3 When he was come down from the mountain, great multitudes followed him.

And, behold, there came a leper and worshipped him, saying, Lord, if thou wilt, thou canst make me clean.

And Jesus put forth his hand, and touched him, saying, I will; be thou clean. And immediately his leprosy was cleansed.

And Jesus saith unto him, See thou tell no man; but go thy way, shew thyself to the priest, and offer the gift that Moses commanded, for a testimony unto them.

Matthew 8:1–4

4 When Jesus departed thence, two blind men fol-

lowed him, crying, and saying, Thou son of David, have mercy on us.

And when he was come into the house, the blind men came to him: and Jesus saith unto them, Believe ye that I am able to do this? They said unto him, Yea, Lord.

Then touched he their eyes, saying, According to your faith be it unto you.

And their eyes were opened; and Jesus straitly charged them, saying, See that no man know it.

But they, when they were departed, spread abroad his fame in all that country.

As they went out, behold, they brought to him a dumb man possessed with a devil.

And when the devil was cast out, the dumb spake: and the multitudes marvelled, saying, It was never so seen in Israel.

But the Pharisees said, He casteth out devils through the prince of the devils.

And Jesus went about all the cities and villages, teaching in their synagogues, and preaching the gospel of the kingdom, and healing every sickness and every disease among the people.

Matthew 9:27–35

5 Straightway he constrained his disciples to get into the ship, and to go to the other side before unto Běth-sā-ĭ-dă, while he sent away the people.

And when he had sent them away, he departed into a mountain to pray.

And when even was come, the ship was in the midst of the sea, and he alone on the land.

And he saw them toiling in rowing; for the wind was contrary unto them: and about the fourth watch of the night he cometh unto them, walking upon the sea, and would have passed by them.

But when they saw him walking upon the sea, they supposed it had been a spirit, and cried out:

For they all saw him, and were troubled. And immediately he talked with them, and saith unto them, Be of good cheer: it is I; be not afraid.

And he went up unto them into the ship; and the wind ceased: and they were sore amazed in themselves beyond measure, and wondered.

For they considered not the miracle of the loaves: for their heart was hardened.

Mark 6:45–52

6 The Pharisees came forth, and began to question with him, seeking of him a sign from heaven, tempting him.

And he sighed deeply in his spirit, and saith, Why doth this generation seek after a sign? verily I say unto you, There shall no sign be given unto this generation.

Mark 8:11–12

7 And the third day there was a marriage in Cana of Galilee; and the mother of Jesus was there:

And both Jesus was called, and his disciples, to the marriage.

And when they wanted wine, the mother of Jesus saith unto him, They have no wine.

Jesus saith unto her, Woman, what have I to do with thee? mine hour is not yet come.

His mother saith unto the servants, Whatsoever he saith unto you, do it.

And there were set there six waterpots of stone, after the manner of the purifying of the Jews, containing two or three firkins apiece.

Jesus saith unto them, Fill the waterpots with water. And they filled them up to the brim.

And he saith unto them, Draw out now, and bear unto the governor of the feast. And they bare it.

When the ruler of the feast had tasted the water that was made wine, and knew not whence it was: (but the servants which drew the water knew;) the governor of the feast called the bridegroom,

And saith unto him, Every man at the beginning doth set forth good wine; and when men have well drunk, then that which is worse: but thou hast kept the good wine until now.

This beginning of miracles did Jesus in Cana of Galilee, and manifested forth his glory; and his disciples believed on him.

John 2:1–11

8 Then said Jesus unto him, Except ye see signs and wonders, ye will not believe.

John 4:48

9 The standing miracle of this visible world is little thought of, because always before us, yet, when we arouse ourselves to contemplate it, it is a greater miracle than the rarest and most unheard-of marvels. For man himself is a greater miracle than any miracle done through his instrumentality.

Augustine, *City of God,* X, 12

10 God, Who made the visible heaven and earth, does not disdain to work visible miracles in heaven or earth, that He may thereby awaken the soul which is immersed in things visible to worship Himself, the Invisible.

Augustine, *City of God,* X, 12

11 When we declare the miracles which God has wrought, or will yet work, and which we cannot bring under the very eyes of men, sceptics keep demanding that we shall explain these marvels to reason. And because we cannot do so, inasmuch as they are above human comprehension, they suppose we are speaking falsely. These persons themselves, therefore, ought to account for all these marvels which we either can or do see. And if they perceive that this is impossible for man to do, they should acknowledge that it cannot be concluded that a thing has not been or shall not

be because it cannot be reconciled to reason, since there are things now in existence of which the same is true.

Augustine, *City of God,* XXI, 5

12 The word miracle is derived from admiration, which arises when an effect is manifest, and its cause is hidden, as when a man sees an eclipse of the sun without knowing its cause. . . . Now the cause of an effect which makes its appearance may be known to one, but unknown to others. And so a thing is wonderful to one man, and not at all to others; as an eclipse is to a rustic, but not to an astronomer. Now a miracle is called so as being full of wonder, and as having a cause absolutely hidden from all; and this cause is God. Therefore those things which God does outside those causes which we know, are called miracles.

Aquinas, *Summa Theologica,* I, 105, 7

13 A miracle is said to go beyond the hope of nature, not beyond the hope of grace, which hope comes from faith, by which we believe in the future resurrection.

Aquinas, *Summa Theologica,* I, 105, 7

14 A miracle properly so called is when something is done outside the order of nature. But it is not enough for a miracle if something is done outside the order of any particular nature; for otherwise anyone would perform a miracle by throwing a stone upwards, as such a thing is outside the order of the stone's nature. So for something to be called a miracle it is required that it be against the order of the whole created nature. But God alone can do this, because, whatever an angel or any other creature does by its own power, is according to the order of created nature, and thus it is not a miracle. Hence God alone can work miracles.

Aquinas, *Summa Theologica,* I, 110, 4

15 If we take a miracle in the strict sense, the demons cannot work miracles, nor can any creature, but God alone, since in the strict sense a miracle is something done outside the order of the entire created nature, under which order every power of a creature is contained. But sometimes miracles may be taken in a wide sense for whatever exceeds the human power and experience. And thus demons can work miracles, that is, things which rouse man's astonishment, by reason of their being beyond his power and outside his sphere of knowledge. For even a man by doing what is beyond the power and knowledge of another leads him to marvel at what he has done, so that in a way he seems to that man to have worked a miracle.

Aquinas, *Summa Theologica,* I, 114, 4

16 *Glendower.* I can call spirits from the vasty deep.
Hotspur. Why, so can I, or so can any man;

But will they come when you do call for them?
Shakespeare, *I Henry IV,* III, i, 53

17 How long, said Don *Quixote,* do you reckon that I have been in the Cave? A little above an Hour, answered *Sancho.* That's impossible, said Don *Quixote,* for I saw Morning and Evening, and Evening and Morning, three times since; so that I could not be absent less than three Days from this upper World. Ay, ay, quoth *Sancho,* my Master's in the Right; for these Inchantments, that have the greatest Share in all his Concerns, may make That seem three Days and three Nights to him, which is but an Hour to other People. It must be so, said Don *Quixote.* I hope, Sir, said the Scholar, you have eaten something in all that time. Not one Morsel, reply'd Don *Quixote,* neither have had the least desire to Eat, or so much as thought of it all the while. Do not they that are Inchanted sometimes Eat? ask'd the Scholar. They never do, answered Don *Quixote,* and consequently they are never troubled with exonerating the Dregs of Food; tho' 'tis not unlikely that their Nails, their Beards and Hair still grow. Do they never sleep neither, said *Sancho?* Never, said Don *Quixote;* at least they never clos'd their Eyes while I was among 'em, nor I neither. This makes good the Saying, quoth *Sancho, Tell me thy Company, and I'll tell thee what thou art.* Troth! you have all been inchanted together.
Cervantes, *Don Quixote,* II, 23

18 As for the narrations touching the prodigies and miracles of religions, they are either not true, or not natural; and therefore impertinent for the story of nature.
Bacon, *Advancement of Learning,* Bk. II, I, 4

19 The testimony that men can render of divine calling can be no other than the operation of miracles, or true prophecy (which also is a miracle), or extraordinary felicity. And therefore, to those points of religion which have been received from them that did such miracles, those that are added by such as approve not their calling by some miracle obtain no greater belief than what the custom and laws of the places in which they be educated have wrought into them. For as in natural things men of judgement require natural signs and arguments, so in supernatural things they require signs supernatural (which are miracles) before they consent inwardly and from their hearts.
Hobbes, *Leviathan,* I, 12

20 Seeing . . . miracles now cease, we have no sign left whereby to acknowledge the pretended revelations or inspirations of any private man; nor obligation to give ear to any doctrine, farther than it is conformable to the Holy Scriptures.
Hobbes, *Leviathan,* III, 32

21 It belongeth to the nature of a miracle that it be wrought for the procuring of credit to God's messengers, ministers, and prophets, that thereby men may know they are called, sent, and employed by God, and thereby be the better inclined to obey them.
Hobbes, *Leviathan,* III, 37

22 That Miracles are ceased, I can neither prove, nor absolutely deny, much less define the time and period of their cessation: that they survived Christ, is manifest upon the Record of Scripture: that they out-lived the Apostles also, and were revived at the Conversion of Nations, many years after, we cannot deny, if we shall not question those Writers whose testimonies we do not controvert in points that make for our own opinions; therefore that may have some truth in it that is reported by the Jesuites of their Miracles in the *Indies;* I could wish it were true, or had any other testimony than their own Pens. They may easily believe those Miracles abroad, who daily conceive a greater at home, the transmutation of those visible elements into the Body and Blood of our Saviour: for the conversion of Water into Wine, which he wrought in *Cana,* or what the Devil would have had him done in the Wilderness, of Stones into Bread, compared to this, will scarce deserve the name of a Miracle. Though indeed to speak properly, there is not one Miracle greater than another, they being the extraordinary effects of the Hand of God, to which all things are of an equal facility; and to create the World as easie as one single Creature.
Sir Thomas Browne, *Religio Medici,* I, 27

23 That Miracles have been, I do believe; that they may yet be wrought by the living, I do not deny: but have no confidence in those which are fathered on the dead; and this hath ever made me suspect the efficacy of reliques, to examine the bones, question the habits and appurtenances of Saints, and even of Christ himself.
Sir Thomas Browne, *Religio Medici,* I, 28

24 It is not possible to have a reasonable belief against miracles.
Pascal, *Pensées,* XIII, 815

25 Jesus Christ performed miracles, then the apostles, and the first saints in great number; because the prophecies not being yet accomplished, but in the process of being accomplished by them, the miracles alone bore witness to them. It was foretold that the Messiah should convert the nations. How could this prophecy be fulfilled without the conversion of the nations? And how could the nations be converted to the Messiah, if they did not see this final effect of the prophecies which prove Him? Therefore, till He had died, risen again, and converted the nations, all was not accomplished; and so miracles were needed during all

this time. Now they are no longer needed against the Jews; for the accomplished prophecies constitute a lasting miracle.

Pascal, *Pensées*, XIII, 838

26 As men are accustomed to call Divine the knowledge which transcends human understanding, so also do they style Divine, or the work of God, anything of which the cause is not generally known: for the masses think that the power and providence of God are most clearly displayed by events that are extraordinary and contrary to the conception they have formed of nature, especially if such events bring them any profit or convenience: they think that the clearest possible proof of God's existence is afforded when nature, as they suppose, breaks her accustomed order, and consequently they believe that those who explain or endeavour to understand phenomena or miracles through their natural causes are doing away with God and His providence. They suppose, forsooth, that God is inactive so long as nature works in her accustomed order, and *vice versâ*, that the power of nature and natural causes are idle so long as God is acting: thus they imagine two powers distinct one from the other, the power of God and the power of nature, though the latter is in a sense determined by God, or (as most people believe now) created by Him. What they mean by either, and what they understand by God and nature they do not know, except that they imagine the power of God to be like that of some royal potentate, and nature's power to consist in force and energy.

The masses then style unusual phenomena "miracles," and partly from piety, partly for the sake of opposing the students of science, prefer to remain in ignorance of natural causes, and only to hear of those things which they know least, and consequently admire most.

Spinoza, *Theologico-Political Treatise*, VI

27 A miracle is an event of which the causes cannot be explained by the natural reason through a reference to ascertained workings of nature; but since miracles were wrought according to the understanding of the masses, who are wholly ignorant of the workings of nature, it is certain that the ancients took for a miracle whatever they could not explain by the method adopted by the unlearned in such cases, namely, an appeal to the memory, a recalling of something similar, which is ordinarily regarded without wonder; for most people think they sufficiently understand a thing when they have ceased to wonder at it. The ancients, then, and indeed most men up to the present day, had no other criterion for a miracle; hence we cannot doubt that many things are narrated in Scripture as miracles of which the causes could easily be explained by reference to ascertained workings of nature.

Spinoza, *Theologico-Political Treatise*, VI

28 Though the common experience and the ordinary course of things have justly a mighty influence on the minds of men, to make them give or refuse credit to anything proposed to their belief; yet there is one case, wherein the strangeness of the fact lessens not the assent to a fair testimony given of it. For where such supernatural events are suitable to ends aimed at by Him who has the power to change the course of nature, there, *under such circumstances*, that may be the fitter to procure belief, by how much the more they are beyond or contrary to ordinary observation. This is the proper case of *miracles*, which, well attested, do not only find credit themselves, but give it also to other truths, which need such confirmation.

Locke, *Concerning Human Understanding*, Bk. IV, XVI, 13

29 Sometimes an event may not, *in itself, seem* to be contrary to the laws of nature, and yet, if it were real, it might, by reason of some circumstances, be denominated a miracle; because, in *fact*, it is contrary to these laws. Thus if a person, claiming a divine authority, should command a sick person to be well, a healthful man to fall down dead, the clouds to pour rain, the winds to blow, in short, should order many natural events, which immediately follow upon his command; these might justly be esteemed miracles, because they are really, in this case, contrary to the laws of nature. For if any suspicion remain, that the event and command concurred by accident, there is no miracle and no transgression of the laws of nature. If this suspicion be removed, there is evidently a miracle, and a transgression of these laws; because nothing can be more contrary to nature than that the voice or command of a man should have such an influence. A miracle may be accurately defined, *a transgression of a law of nature by a particular volition of the Deity, or by the interposition of some invisible agent.* A miracle may either be discoverable by men or not. This alters not its nature and essence. The raising of a house or ship into the air is a visible miracle. The raising of a feather, when the wind wants ever so little of a force requisite for that purpose, is as real a miracle, though not so sensible with regard to us.

Hume, *Concerning Human Understanding*, X, 90, fn.

30 A miracle is a violation of the laws of nature; and as a firm and unalterable experience has established these laws, the proof against a miracle, from the very nature of the fact, is as entire as any argument from experience can possibly be imagined. Why is it more than probable, that all men must die; that lead cannot, of itself, remain suspended in the air; that fire consumes wood, and is extinguished by water; unless it be, that these events are found agreeable to the laws of nature,

and there is required a violation of these laws, or in other words, a miracle to prevent them? Nothing is esteemed a miracle, if it ever happen in the common course of nature. It is no miracle that a man, seemingly in good health, should die on a sudden: because such a kind of death, though more unusual than any other, has yet been frequently observed to happen. But it is a miracle, that a dead man should come to life; because that has never been observed in any age or country. There must, therefore, be a uniform experience against every miraculous event, otherwise the event would not merit that appellation. And as a uniform experience amounts to a proof, there is here a direct and full *proof,* from the nature of the fact, against the existence of any miracle; nor can such a proof be destroyed, or the miracle rendered credible, but by an opposite proof, which is superior.

The plain consequence is (and it is a general maxim worthy of our attention), "That no testimony is sufficient to establish a miracle, unless the testimony be of such a kind, that its falsehood would be more miraculous, than the fact, which it endeavours to establish; and even in that case there is a mutual destruction of arguments, and the superior only gives us an assurance suitable to that degree of force, which remains, after deducting the inferior." When anyone tells me, that he saw a dead man restored to life, I immediately consider with myself, whether it be more probable, that this person should either deceive or be deceived, or that the fact, which he relates, should really have happened. I weigh the one miracle against the other; and according to the superiority, which I discover, I pronounce my decision, and always reject the greater miracle. If the falsehood of his testimony would be more miraculous, than the event which he relates; then, and not till then, can he pretend to command my belief or opinion.

Hume, *Concerning Human
Understanding,* X, 90–91

31 The many instances of forged miracles, and prophecies, and supernatural events, which, in all ages, have either been detected by contrary evidence, or which detect themselves by their absurdity, prove sufficiently the strong propensity of mankind to the extraordinary and the marvellous, and ought reasonably to beget a suspicion against all relations of this kind.

Hume, *Concerning Human
Understanding,* X, 93

32 Though the Being to whom the miracle is ascribed, be, in this case, Almighty, it does not, upon that account, become a whit more probable; since it is impossible for us to know the attributes or actions of such a Being, otherwise than from

the experience which we have of his productions, in the usual course of nature.

Hume, *Concerning Human
Understanding,* X, 99

33 I mentioned Hume's argument against the belief of miracles, that it is more probable that the witnesses to the truth of them are mistaken, or speak falsely, than that the miracles should be true. *Johnson.* "Why, Sir, the great difficulty of proving miracles should make us very cautious in believing them. But let us consider; although God has made Nature to operate by certain fixed laws, yet it is not unreasonable to think that he may suspend those laws, in order to establish a system highly advantageous to mankind. Now the Christian religion is a most beneficial system, as it gives us light and certainty where we were before in darkness and doubt. The miracles which prove it are attested by men who had no interest in deceiving us; but who, on the contrary, were told that they should suffer persecution, and did actually lay down their lives in confirmation of the truth of the facts which they asserted. Indeed, for some centuries the heathens did not pretend to deny the miracles; but said they were performed by the aid of evil spirits. This is a circumstance of great weight. Then, Sir, when we take the proofs derived from prophecies which have been so exactly fulfilled, we have most satisfactory evidence. Supposing a miracle possible, as to which, in my opinion, there can be no doubt, we have as strong evidence for the miracles in support of Christianity, as the nature of the thing admits."

Boswell, *Life of Johnson (July 21, 1763)*

34 The frequent repetition of miracles serves to provoke, where it does not subdue, the reason of mankind.

Gibbon, *Decline and Fall of the Roman
Empire,* XX

35 The philosopher, who with calm suspicion examines the dreams and omens, the miracles and prodigies, of profane or even of ecclesiastical history, will probably conclude that, if the eyes of the spectators have sometimes been deceived by fraud, the understanding of the readers has much more frequently been insulted by fiction. Every event, or appearance, or accident, which seems to deviate from the ordinary course of nature, has been rashly ascribed to the immediate action of the Deity.

Gibbon, *Decline and Fall of the Roman
Empire,* XX

36 [Clovis], the victorious king of the Franks, proceeded without delay to the siege of Angoulême. At the sound of his trumpets the walls of the city imitated the example of Jericho, and instantly fell to the ground; a splendid miracle, which may be

reduced to the supposition that some clerical engineers had secretly undermined the foundations of the rampart.

Gibbon, *Decline and Fall of the Roman Empire*, XXXVIII

37 Such is the progress of credulity, that miracles, most doubtful on the spot and at the moment, will be received with implicit faith at a convenient distance of time and space.

Gibbon, *Decline and Fall of the Roman Empire*, LVIII

38 We do not adopt the right point of view in thinking of Christ only as a historical bygone personality. So regarded, the question is asked: what are we to make of his birth, his father and mother, his early domestic relations, his miracles, etc.?—i.e., what is he *unspiritually* regarded? Considered only in respect of his talents, character and morality, as a teacher and so forth, we place him in the same category with Socrates and others, though his morality may be ranked higher. But excellence of character, morality, etc.—all this is not the *ne plus ultra* in the requirements of spirit—does not enable man to gain the speculative idea of spirit for his conceptive faculty. If Christ is to be looked upon only as an excellent, even impeccable individual, and nothing more, the conception of the speculative idea, of absolute truth is ignored. But this is the desideratum, the point from which we have to start. Make of Christ what you will, exegetically, critically, historically—demonstrate as you please, how the doctrines of the Church were established by councils, attained currency as the result of this or that episcopal interest or passion, or originated in this or that quarter; let all such circumstances have been what they might—the only concerning question is: what is the idea or the truth in and for itself?

Further, the real attestation of the divinity of Christ is the witness of one's own spirit—not miracles; for only spirit recognizes spirit. The miracles may lead the way to such recognition. A miracle implies that the natural course of things is interrupted: but it is very much a question of relation what we call the "natural course"; and the phenomena of the magnet might, under cover of this definition, be reckoned miraculous. Nor does the miracle of the divine mission of Christ prove anything; for Socrates likewise introduced a new self-consciousness on the part of spirit, diverse from the traditional tenor of men's conceptions. The main question is not his divine mission but the revelation made in Christ and the purport of his mission. Christ himself blames the Pharisees for desiring miracles of him, and speaks of false prophets who will perform miracles.

Hegel, *Philosophy of History*, Pt. III, III, 2

39 The Age of Miracles past? The Age of Miracles is for ever here!

Carlyle, *The Hero as Priest*

40 Jesus Christ belonged to the true race of prophets. He saw with open eye the mystery of the soul. Drawn by its severe harmony, ravished with its beauty, he lived in it, and had his being there. Alone in all history he estimated the greatness of man. One man was true to what is in you and me. He saw that God incarnates himself in man, and evermore goes forth anew to take possession of his World. He said, in this jubilee of sublime emotion, 'I am divine. Through me, God acts; through me, speaks. Would you see God, see me; or see thee, when thou also thinkest as I now think.' But what a distortion did his doctrine and memory suffer in the same, in the next, and the following ages! There is no doctrine of the Reason which will bear to be taught by the Understanding. The understanding caught this high chant from the poet's lips, and said, in the next age, 'This was Jehovah come down out of heaven. I will kill you, if you say he was a man.' The idioms of his language and the figures of his rhetoric have usurped the place of his truth; and churches are not built on his principles, but on his tropes. Christianity became a Mythus, as the poetic reaching of Greece and of Egypt, before. He spoke of miracles; for he felt that man's life was a miracle, and all that man doth, and he knew that this daily miracle shines as the character ascends. But the word Miracle, as pronounced by Christian churches, gives a false impression; it is Monster. It is not one with the blowing clover and the falling rain.

Emerson, *Address to Harvard Divinity School*

41 If there is to be any sense in the assertion that miracles prove who Christ is, we must begin with not knowing who He is, that is to say, in the situation of contemporaneousness with an individual man, who is like other men, in whom there is nothing *directly* to be seen, an individual man who thereupon performs a miracle and himself says that it is a miracle he performs. What does this signify? It signifies that this individual man makes himself out to be more than man, makes himself out to be something pretty near to being God. Is not this cause for offence? You see something inexplicable, miraculous (and that is all), he himself says that it is a miracle—and with your own eyes you behold the individual man. The miracle can prove nothing; for if you do not believe that he is what he says he is, you deny the miracle. A miracle can make one attentive—now thou art in a state of tension, and all depends upon what thou dost choose, offence or faith. It is thy heart that must be revealed.

Kierkegaard, *Training in Christianity*, II, B

42 It is almost impossible to exaggerate the proneness

of the human mind to take miracles as evidence, and to seek for miracles as evidence; or the extent to which religion, and religion of a true and admirable kind, has been, and is still, held in connection with a reliance upon miracles. This reliance will long outlast the reliance on the supernatural prescience of prophecy, for it is not exposed to the same tests. To pick Scripture-miracles one by one to pieces is an odious and repulsive task; it is also an unprofitable one, for whatever we may think of the affirmative demonstrations of them, a negative demonstration of them is, from the circumstances of the case, impossible. And yet the human mind is assuredly passing away, however slowly, from this hold of reliance also; and those who make it their stay will more and more find it fail them, will more and more feel themselves disturbed, shaken, distressed, and bewildered.

Arnold, *Literature and Dogma,* V

43 It is not miracles that dispose realists to belief. The genuine realist, if he is an unbeliever, will always find strength and ability to disbelieve in the miraculous, and if he is confronted with a miracle as an irrefutable fact he would rather disbelieve his own senses than admit the fact. Even if he admits it, he admits it as a fact of nature till then unrecognised by him. Faith does not, in the realist, spring from the miracle but the miracle from faith. If the realist once believes, then he is bound by his very realism to admit the miraculous also. The Apostle Thomas said that he would not believe till he saw, but when he did see he said, "My Lord and my God!" Was it the miracle forced him to believe? Most likely not, but he believed solely because he desired to believe and possibly he fully believed in his secret heart even when he said, "I do not believe till I see."

Dostoevsky, *Brothers Karamazov,* Pt. I, I, 5

44 Miracles are so called because they excite wonder. In unphilosophical minds any rare or unexpected thing excites wonder, while in philosophical minds the familiar excites wonder also, and the laws of nature, if we admit such laws, excite more wonder than the detached events. Each morning the sunrise excites wonder in the poet, and the order of the solar system excites it every night in the astronomer. Astronomy explains the sunrise, but what shall explain the solar system? The universe, which would explain everything, is the greatest of wonders, and a perpetual miracle.

Santayana, *The Idea of Christ in the Gospels*

45 Science, which thinks to make belief in miracles impossible, is itself belief in miracles—in the miracles best authenticated by history and by daily life.

Santayana, *Life of Reason,* III, 2

20.12 | *Superstition*

The condemnation of superstition is shared equally by those who defend religion or are apologists for it and by those who reject religion itself, the latter on the ground that it is nothing but superstition. The reader will find Lucretius in antiquity, Gibbon in the eighteenth century (the so-called "age of reason"), and Freud in our own time to be eloquent exponents of this view. Those who take the opposite view, that a sharp line can be drawn between superstitious beliefs and practices, on the one hand, and valid religious beliefs and genuine religious rites, on the other, differ among themselves about precisely where and how to draw the line.

For example, some of the writers represented here regard the belief in miracles as superstitious; others, the belief in sorcerers; others, the belief in omens or portents and in astrological predictions; and still others call idolators superstitious or those who believe in magic, witchcraft, and the influence of demons. Such writers include outstanding Christian theologians as well as secular philosophers who tend to be skeptical about many of the doctrines or dogmas of orthodox religion. All alike agree that superstition is a vice directly opposed to religion, and that superstition must be overcome to purify religion of the dross that encrusts it. Even Voltaire admits that the horrible crimes with which religion is often charged should be attributed to superstition, not true religion; though he also remarks that a peo- ple not at all superstitious would have to be a community of philosophers and that true faith for one sect is superstition for another.

Since the discussion here turns on the line that divides superstition from religion, the reader would do well to compare what is said here with what is said in Section 20.1 on THE DISTINGUISHING FEATURES OF RELIGION.

---

1 When human life to view lay foully prostrate upon earth crushed down under the weight of religion, who showed her head from the quarters of heaven with hideous aspect lowering upon mortals, a man of Greece [Epicurus] ventured first to lift up his mortal eyes to her face and first to withstand her to her face. Him neither story of gods nor thunderbolts nor heaven with threatening roar could quell: they only chafed the more the eager courage of his soul, filling him with desire to be the first to burst the fast bars of nature's portals. Therefore the living force of his soul gained the day: on he passed far beyond the flaming walls of the world and traversed throughout in mind and spirit the immeasurable universe; whence he returns a conqueror to tell us what can, what cannot come into being; in short on what principle each thing has its powers defined, its deepset boundary mark. Therefore religion is put under foot and trampled upon in turn; us his victory brings level with heaven.

Lucretius, *Nature of Things,* I

2 Often and often that very religion has given birth to sinful and unholy deeds. Thus in Aulis the chosen chieftains of the Danaï, foremost of men, foully polluted with Iphianassa's blood the altar of the Trivian maid. Soon as the fillet encircling her maiden tresses shed itself in equal lengths adown each cheek, and soon as she saw her father standing sorrowful before the altars and beside him the ministering priests hiding the knife and her countrymen at sight of her shedding tears, speechless in terror she dropped down on her knees and sank to the ground. Nor aught in such a moment could it avail the luckless girl that she had first bestowed the name of father on the king. For lifted up in the hands of the men she was carried shivering to the altars, not after due performance of the customary rites to be escorted by the clear-ringing bridal song, but in the very season of marriage, stainless maid mid the stain of blood, to fall a sad victim by the sacrificing stroke of a father, that thus a happy and prosperous departure might be granted to the fleet. So great the evils to which religion could prompt!

Lucretius, *Nature of Things,* I

3 Fear in sooth holds so in check all mortals, because they see many operations go on in earth and heaven, the causes of which they can in no way understand, believing them therefore to be done by power divine.

Lucretius, *Nature of Things,* I

4 If you shall suppose that the deeds of Hercules surpass his, you will be carried still farther away from true reason. For what would yon great gaping maw of Nemean lion now harm us and the bristled Arcadian boar? Ay or what could the bull of Crete do and the hydra plague of Lerna, fenced round with its envenomed snakes? Or how could the triple-breasted might of threefold Geryon, how could the birds with brazen arrowy feathers that dwelt in the Stymphalian swamps do us such mighty injury, and the horses of Thracian Diomede breathing fire from their nostrils along the Bistonian borders and Ismara? And the serpent which guards the bright golden apples of the Hesperides, fierce, dangerous of aspect, girding the tree's stem with his enormous body, what harm pray could he do us beside the Atlantic shore and its sounding main, which none of us goes near and no barbarian ventures to approach? And all other monsters of the kind which have been destroyed, if they had not been vanquished, what harm could they do, I ask, though now alive? None methinks: the earth even now so abounds to repletion in wild beasts and is filled with troublous terror throughout woods and great mountains and deep forests; places which we have it for the most part in our own power to shun. But unless the breast is cleared, what battles and dangers must then find their way into us in our own despite! What poignant cares inspired by lust then rend the distressful man, and then also what mighty fears! And pride, filthy lust and wantonness? What disasters they occasion, and luxury and all sorts of sloth?

Lucretius, *Nature of Things,* V

5 And since I have shown that the quarters of ether are mortal and that heaven is formed of a body that had a birth, and since of all the things which

go on and must go on in it, I have unravelled most, hear further what remains to be told; since once for all I have willed to mount the illustrious chariot of the Muses, and ascending to heaven to explain the true law of winds and storms, which men foolishly lay to the charge of the gods, telling how, when they are angry, they raise fierce tempests; and, when there is a lull in the fury of the winds, how that anger is appeased, how the omens which have been again changed, when their fury has thus been appeased: I have willed at the same time to explain all the other things which mortals observe to go on upon earth and in heaven, when often they are in anxious suspense of mind, and which abase their souls with fear of the gods and weigh and press them down to earth, because ignorance of the causes constrains them to submit things to the empire of the gods and to make over to them the kingdom. For they who have been rightly taught that the gods lead a life without care, if nevertheless they wonder on what plan all things can be carried on, above all in regard to those things which are seen overhead in the ethereal borders, are borne back again into their old religious scruples and take unto themselves hard taskmasters, whom they poor wretches believe to be almighty, not knowing what can, what cannot be, in short on what principle each thing has its powers defined, its deep-set boundary mark; and therefore they are led all the farther astray by blind reason.

Lucretius, *Nature of Things*, VI

6 A ready acceptance of error is harmful to the reputation, especially in the matter of how much credence is to be given to omens, sacred rites, and other religious observances. We risk offending the gods if we pay no attention to such things. And we risk being considered superstitious if we rely on them completely.

Cicero, *Divination*, I, 4

7 We are obligated to propagate true religion, since it is closely associated with the knowledge of nature. It is also our duty to eradicate superstition. For superstition dogs our heels at every turn. When you listen to a prophet, regard an omen, offer sacrifices, or watch a flight of birds, go to an astrologer or fortune teller, when there is thunder and lightning during a storm, or when some prodigy appears, superstition is at your side. And since such signs are usually all around us, no one who believes them can have peace of mind.

Cicero, *Divination*, II, 72

8 Paul stood in the midst of Mars' hill, and said, Ye men of Athens, I perceive that in all things ye are too superstitious.

For as I passed by, and beheld your devotions, I found an altar with this inscription, *To the Un-known God.* Whom therefore ye ignorantly worship, him declare I unto you.

God that made the world and all things therein, seeing that he is Lord of heaven and earth, dwelleth not in temples made with hands;

Neither is worshipped with men's hands, as though he needed any thing, seeing he giveth to all life, and breath, and all things.

Acts 17:22–25

9 We ourselves could relate divers wonderful things, which we have been told by men of our own time, that are not lightly to be rejected; but to give too easy credit to such things, or wholly to disbelieve them, is equally dangerous, so incapable is human infirmity of keeping any bounds, or exercising command over itself, running off sometimes to superstition and dotage, at other times to the contempt and neglect of all that is supernatural. But moderation is best, and to avoid all extremes.

Plutarch, *Camillus*

10 An ignorant wonder at appearances . . . in the heavens, possesses the minds of people unacquainted with their causes, eager for the supernatural, and excitable through an inexperience which the knowledge of natural causes removes, replacing wild and timid superstition by the good hope and assurance of an intelligent piety.

Plutarch, *Pericles*

11 All the arrangements made by men for the making and worshipping of idols are superstitious, pertaining as they do either to the worship of what is created or of some part of it as God, or to consultations and arrangements about signs and leagues with devils, such, for example, as are employed in the magical arts, and which the poets are accustomed not so much to teach as to celebrate.

Augustine, *Christian Doctrine*, II, 20

12 It comes to pass that men who lust after evil things are, by a secret judgment of God, delivered over to be mocked and deceived, as the just reward of their evil desires. For they are deluded and imposed on by the false angels, to whom the lowest part of the world has been put in subjection by the law of God's providence, and in accordance with His most admirable arrangement of things. And the result of these delusions and deceptions is, that through these superstitious and baneful modes of divination, many things in the past and future are made known, and turn out just as they are foretold; and in the case of those who practise superstitious observances, many things turn out agreeably to their observances, and ensnared by these successes, they become more eagerly inquisitive, and involve themselves further and further in a labyrinth of most perni-

cious error. And to our advantage, the Word of God is not silent about this species of fornication of the soul; and it does not warn the soul against following such practices on the ground that those who profess them speak lies, but it says, "Even if what they tell you should come to pass, hearken not unto them."

Augustine, *Christian Doctrine,* II, 23

13 Superstition is a vice contrary to religion by excess, not that it offers more to the divine worship than true religion, but because it offers divine worship either to whom it ought not, or in a manner it ought not.

Aquinas, *Summa Theologica,* II–II, 92, 1

14 The species of superstition are differentiated, first on the part of the mode, secondly on the part of the object. For the divine worship may be given either to whom it ought to be given, namely, to the true God, but *in an undue mode,* and this is the first species of superstition; or to whom it ought not to be given, namely, to any creature whatsoever, and this is another genus of superstition, divided into many species in respect of the various ends of divine worship. For the end of divine worship is in the first place to give reverence to God, and in this respect the first species of this genus is *idolatry,* which unduly gives divine honor to a creature. The second end of religion is that man may be taught by God Whom he worships; and to this must be referred *divinatory* superstition, which consults the demons through compacts made with them, whether tacit or explicit. Thirdly, the end of divine worship is a certain direction of human acts according to the precepts of God the object of that worship: and to this must be referred the superstition of certain *observances.*

Aquinas, *Summa Theologica,* II–II, 92, 2

15 Superstition is a confession of unbelief by external worship. Such a confession is signified by the term idolatry, but not by the term heresy, which only means a false opinion. Therefore heresy is a species of unbelief, but idolatry is a species of superstition.

Aquinas, *Summa Theologica,* II–II, 94, 1

16 The magic art is to be absolutely repudiated and avoided by a Christian, even as other arts of vain and noxious superstition.

Aquinas, *Summa Theologica,* II–II, 96, 1

17 It is easy to see how superstition mocks God with hypocritical services, while it attempts to please him. For, embracing only those things which he declares he disregards, it either contemptuously practises, or even openly rejects, what he prescribes and declares to be pleasing in his sight. Persons who introduce newly-invented methods of worshipping God, really worship and adore the creature of their distempered imaginations; for they would never have dared to trifle in such a manner with God, if they had not first feigned a god conformable to their own false and foolish notions.

Calvin, *Institutes of the Christian Religion,* I, 4

18 It is probable that the principal credit of miracles, visions, enchantments, and such extraordinary occurrences comes from the power of imagination, acting principally upon the minds of the common people, which are softer. Their belief has been so strongly seized that they think they see what they do not see.

Montaigne, *Essays,* I, 21, Power of the Imagination

19 *Horatio.* In the most high and palmy state of Rome,
A little ere the mightiest Julius fell,
The graves stood tenantless and the sheeted dead
Did squeak and gibber in the Roman streets.
As stars with trains of fire and dews of blood,
Disasters in the sun; and the moist star
Upon whose influence Neptune's empire stands
Was sick almost to doomsday with eclipse.
And even the like precurse of fierce events,
As harbingers preceding still the fates
And prologue to the omen coming on,
Have heaven and earth together demonstrated
Unto our climatures and countrymen.

Shakespeare, *Hamlet,* I, i, 113

20 The corruption of philosophy by the mixing of it up with superstition and theology, is of a much wider extent, and is most injurious to it both as a whole and in parts.

Bacon, *Novum Organum,* I, 65

21 Superstition, without a veil, is a deformed thing; for, as it addeth deformity to an ape to be so like a man, so the similitude of superstition to religion makes it the more deformed.

Bacon, *Of Superstition*

22 From . . . ignorance of how to distinguish dreams, and other strong fancies, from vision and sense, did arise the greatest part of the religion of the Gentiles in time past, that worshipped satyrs, fauns, nymphs, and the like; and nowadays the opinion that rude people have of fairies, ghosts, and goblins, and of the power of witches. For, as for witches, I think not that their witchcraft is any real power, but yet that they are justly punished for the false belief they have that they can do such mischief, joined with their purpose to do it if they can, their trade being nearer to a new religion than to a craft or science. And for fairies, and walking ghosts, the opinion of them has, I think, been on purpose either taught, or not confuted, to

keep in credit the use of exorcism, of crosses, of holy water, and other such inventions of ghostly men. Nevertheless, there is no doubt but God can make unnatural apparitions: but that He does it so often as men need to fear such things more than they fear the stay, or change, of the course of Nature, which he also can stay, and change, is no point of Christian faith. But evil men, under pretext that God can do anything, are so bold as to say anything when it serves their turn, though they think it untrue; it is the part of a wise man to believe them no further than right reason makes that which they say appear credible. If this superstitious fear of spirits were taken away, and with it prognostics from dreams, false prophecies, and many other things depending thereon, by which crafty ambitious persons abuse the simple people, men would be much more fitted than they are for civil obedience.

Hobbes, *Leviathan,* I, 2

23 They that make little or no inquiry into the natural causes of things, yet from the fear that proceeds from the ignorance itself of what it is that hath the power to do them much good or harm are inclined to suppose, and feign unto themselves, several kinds of powers invisible, and to stand in awe of their own imaginations, and in time of distress to invoke them; as also in the time of an expected good success, to give them thanks, making the creatures of their own fancy their gods. By which means it hath come to pass that from the innumerable variety of fancy, men have created in the world innumerable sorts of gods. And this fear of things invisible is the natural seed of that which every one in himself calleth *religion;* and in them that worship or fear that power otherwise than they do, *superstition.*

Hobbes, *Leviathan,* I, 11

24 Men would never be superstitious, if they could govern all their circumstances by set rules, or if they were always favoured by fortune: but being frequently driven into straits where rules are useless, and being often kept fluctuating pitiably between hope and fear by the uncertainty of fortune's greedily coveted favours, they are consequently, for the most part, very prone to credulity.

Spinoza, *Theologico-Political Treatise,* Pref.

25 That *the corruption of the best of things produces the worst,* is grown into a maxim, and is commonly proved, among other instances, by the pernicious effects of *superstition* and *enthusiasm,* the corruptions of true religion.

These two species of false religion, though both pernicious, are yet of a very different, and even of a contrary nature. The mind of man is subject to certain unaccountable terrors and apprehensions, proceeding either from the unhappy situation of private or public affairs, from ill health, from a gloomy and melancholy disposition, or from the concurrence of all these circumstances. In such a state of mind, infinite unknown evils are dreaded from unknown agents; and where real objects of terror are wanting, the soul, active to its own prejudice, and fostering its predominant inclination, finds imaginary ones, to whose power and malevolence it sets no limits. As these enemies are entirely invisible and unknown, the methods taken to appease them are equally unaccountable, and consist in ceremonies, observances, mortifications, sacrifices, presents, or in any practice, however absurd or frivolous, which either folly or knavery recommends to a blind and terrified credulity. Weakness, fear, melancholy, together with ignorance, are, therefore, the true sources of Superstition.

Hume, *Of Superstition and Enthusiasm*

26 Those who ridicule vulgar superstitions, and expose the folly of particular regards to meats, days, places, postures, apparel, have an easy task; while they consider all the qualities and relations of the objects, and discover no adequate cause for that affection or antipathy, veneration or horror, which have so mighty an influence over a considerable part of mankind.

Hume, *Concerning Principles of Morals,* III

27 The superstitious man is to the rogue what the slave is to the tyrant. Further, the superstitious man is governed by the fanatic and becomes fanatic. Superstition born in Paganism, adopted by Judaism, infested the Christian Church from the earliest times. All the fathers of the Church, without exception, believed in the power of magic. The Church always condemned magic, but she always believed in it: she did not excommunicate sorcerers as madmen who were mistaken, but as men who were really in communication with the devil. . . .

Up to what point does statecraft permit superstition to be destroyed? This is a very thorny question; it is like asking up to what point one should make an incision in a dropsical person, who may die under the operation. It is a matter for the doctor's discretion.

Can there exist a people free from all superstitious prejudices? That is to ask—Can there exist a nation of philosophers? It is said that there is no superstition in the magistrature of China. It is probable that none will remain in the magistrature of a few towns of Europe.

Then the magistrates will stop the superstition of the people from being dangerous. These magistrates' example will not enlighten the mob, but the principal persons of the middle classes will hold the mob in check. There is not perhaps a single riot, a single religious outrage in which the middle classes were not formerly imbrued, because these middle classes were then the mob; but reason and time will have changed them. Their softened manners will soften those of the lowest and most savage populace; it is a thing of which we have striking examples in more than one country. In a word, less superstition, less fanaticism; and less fanaticism, less misery.

Voltaire, *Philosophical Dictionary:* Superstition

28 Science is the great antidote to the poison of enthusiasm and superstition; and where all the superior ranks of people were secured from it, the inferior ranks could not be much exposed to it.

Adam Smith, *Wealth of Nations*, V, 1

29 From the first of the fathers to the last of the popes, a succession of bishops, of saints, of martyrs, and of miracles, is continued without interruption; and the progress of superstition was so gradual and almost imperceptible, that we know not in what particular link we should break the chain of tradition.

Gibbon, *Decline and Fall of the Roman Empire*, XV

30 The decline of ancient prejudice exposed a very numerous portion of human kind to the danger of a painful and comfortless situation. A state of scepticism and suspense may amuse a few inquisitive minds. But the practice of superstition is so congenial to the multitude that, if they are forcibly awakened, they still regret the loss of their pleasing vision. Their love of the marvellous and supernatural, their curiosity with regard to future events, and their strong propensity to extend their hopes and fears beyond the limits of the visible world, were the principal causes which favoured the establishment of Polytheism. So urgent on the vulgar is the necessity of believing, that the fall of any system of mythology will most probably be succeeded by the introduction of some other mode of superstition. Some deities of a more recent and fashionable cast might soon have occupied the deserted temples of Jupiter and Apollo, if, in the decisive moment, the wisdom of Providence had not interposed a genuine revelation fitted to inspire the most rational esteem and conviction, whilst, at the same time, it was adorned with all that could attract the curiosity, the wonder, and the veneration of the people.

Gibbon, *Decline and Fall of the Roman Empire*, XV

31 The objects which had been transformed by the magic of superstition appeared to the eyes of the Paulicians in their genuine and naked colours. An image made without hands was the common workmanship of a mortal artist, to whose skill alone the wood and canvas must be indebted for their merit or value. The miraculous relics were a heap of bones and ashes, destitute of life or virtue, or of any relation, perhaps, with the person to whom they were ascribed. The true and vivifying cross was a piece of sound or rotten timber; the body and blood of Christ, a loaf of bread and a cup of wine, the gifts of nature and the symbols of grace. The mother of God was degraded from her celestial honours and immaculate virginity; and the saints and angels were no longer solicited to exercise the laborious office of mediation in heaven and ministry upon earth. In the practice, or at least in the theory, of the sacraments, the Paulicians were inclined to abolish all visible objects of worship, and the words of the Gospel were, in their judgment, the baptism and communion of the faithful.

Gibbon, *Decline and Fall of the Roman Empire*, LIV

32 The services of Luther and his rivals are solid and important; and the philosopher must own his obligations to these fearless enthusiasts. By their hands the lofty fabric of superstition, from the abuse of indulgences to the intercession of the Virgin, has been levelled with the ground. Myriads of both sexes of the monastic profession were restored to the liberty and labours of social life. A hierarchy of saints and angels, of imperfect and subordinate deities, were stripped of their temporal power, and reduced to the enjoyment of celestial happiness: their images and relics were banished from the church; and the credulity of the people was no longer nourished with the daily repetition of miracles and visions. The imitation of paganism was supplied by a pure and spiritual worship of prayer and thanksgiving, the most worthy of man, the least unworthy of the Deity.

Gibbon, *Decline and Fall of the Roman Empire*, LIV

33 Humility, taking the form of an uncompromising judgement upon his shortcomings, which, with consciousness of good intentions, might readily be glossed over on the ground of the frailty of human nature, is a sublime temper of the mind voluntarily to undergo the pain of remorse as a means of more and more effectually eradicating its cause. In this way religion is intrinsically distinguished from superstition, which latter rears in the mind, not reverence for the sublime, but dread and apprehension of the all-powerful Being to whose will terror-stricken man sees himself subjected, yet without according Him due honour. From this nothing can arise but grace-begging and vain adulation, instead of a religion consisting in a good life.

Kant, *Critique of Aesthetic Judgement*, 28

34 *Idolatry,* . . . is a superstitious delusion that one can make oneself acceptable to the Supreme

Being by other means than that of having the moral law at heart.

Kant, Critique of Teleological
Judgement, 89

35 It is hardly surprising that geniuses, and criminals too . . . in short all those who, in one way or another, are placed outside the normal, should be superstitious. They have no *impressa vestigia* for their feet, they go forward along unknown or forbidden paths, and so they are observant in quite a different degree from others, and moreover of very different things. The mass of people do not really *live,* they are mere repetitions, live in the security of the probable, and so they are not superstitious, that is to say that they do not notice that this belief of theirs in the probable, and their security within the probable is, in another sense, a tremendous superstition.

Kierkegaard, Journals (1851)

36 The same high mental faculties which first led man to believe in unseen spiritual agencies, then in fetishism, polytheism, and ultimately in monotheism, would infallibly lead him, as long as his reasoning powers remained poorly developed, to various strange superstitions and customs. Many of these are terrible to think of—such as the sacrifice of human beings to a blood-loving god; the trial of innocent persons by the ordeal of poison or fire; witchcraft, etc.—yet it is well occasionally to reflect on these superstitions, for they shew us what an infinite debt of gratitude we owe to the improvement of our reason, to science, and to our accumulated knowledge.

Darwin, Descent of Man, I, 3

37 As philosophy has at times corrupted her divines, so has paganism corrupted her worshippers; and as the more intellectual have been involved in heresy, so have the ignorant been corrupted by superstition.

Newman, Essay on the Development
of Christian Doctrine, Pt. II, VIII, 2

38 You know how tenaciously anything that has once found psychological expression persists. You will, therefore, not be surprised to hear that a great many manifestations of animism have lasted up to the present day, mostly as what are called *superstitions,* side by side with and behind religion. But more than that, you can hardly avoid coming to the conclusion that our philosophy has preserved essential traits of animistic modes of thought, such as the overestimation of the magic of words and the belief that real processes in the external world follow the lines laid down by our thoughts. It is, to be sure, an animism without magical practices. On the other hand we should expect to find that in the age of animism there must already have been some kind of morality, some rules governing the intercourse of men with one another. But there is no evidence that they were closely bound up with animistic beliefs. Probably they were the immediate expression of the distribution of power and of practical necessities.

It would be very interesting to know what determined the transition from animism to religion; but you may imagine in what darkness this earliest epoch in the evolution of the human mind is still shrouded. It seems to be a fact that the earliest form in which religion appeared was the remarkable one of totemism, the worship of animals, in the train of which followed the first ethical commands, the taboos. . . . I once worked out a suggestion, in accordance with which this change is to be traced back to an upheaval in the relationships in the human family. The main achievement of religion, as compared with animism, lies in the psychic binding of the fear of demons. Nevertheless, the evil spirit still has a place in the religious system as a relic of the previous age.

Freud, New Introductory Lectures
on Psycho-Analysis, XXXV

39 We sometimes speak as if superstition or belief in the miraculous was disbelief in law and was inspired by a desire to disorganise experience and defeat intelligence. No supposition could be more erroneous. Every superstition is a little science, inspired by the desire to understand, to foresee, or to control the real world. No doubt its hypothesis is chimerical, arbitrary, and founded on a confusion of efficient causes with ideal results. But the same is true of many a renowned philosophy.

Santayana, Life of Reason, III, 2

20.13 | Sin and Temptation

Temptation is treated here along with sin because, according to the theologians who discuss the matter, temptation is primarily to be understood as providing the occasion for sin. The clause in the Lord's Prayer that beseeches God to lead us not into temptation asks for exemption from the occasions to sin.

In one contemporary revision of the language of that prayer, the words "forgive us our sins, as we forgive those who sin against us" have been erroneously substituted for the words "forgive us our trespasses, as we forgive those who trespass against us"—erroneously, at least according to the traditional conception of sin as exclusively an offense against God or a violation of the divine law, never merely the injuring of one man by another in contravention of the human law.

With the exception of Hobbes, who blurs the distinction between sin and crime by regarding the violation of the civil law as a sin, the view that prevails in the quotations gathered below conceives sin in theological not political or moral terms. For the consideration of the moral counterpart of sin in the form of moral iniquity or vice, the reader should consult Section 9.7 on RIGHT AND WRONG and Section 9.10 on VIRTUE AND VICE; and for the political or social counterpart of sin in the form of crime, the reader should go to Section 12.4 on CRIME AND PUNISHMENT.

The quotations collected here cover many aspects of the subject, but not all; and many that are mentioned are barely touched on, not treated in detail. The reader will find some discussion of the temptation of Adam and the consequences of his sin, not only for him but for all his descendants; the distinction between original or inherited sin and individual or acquired sin; the distinction between mortal and venial sins, together with the classification of mortal sins and the consideration of which among them is primary and the root of all the rest; the denial of collective responsibility for the sins of the fathers; and man's need for a redeemer to be saved from his proneness to sin that is a defect of fallen human nature, in consequence of Adam's sin. This whole subject of redemption and salvation is more fully treated in Section 20.14.

There are, of course, among the writers quoted below those, such as Spinoza or Freud, who reject the very notion of sin, or who interpret the sense of sin as having its origins in feelings of guilt that can be accounted for psychologically. The reader's attention should also be drawn to the fact that some of the most interesting passages quoted are taken from the two great poems that are concerned with sin, its causes and consequences, the gradations of sin and of the punishments thereof. The two poems are Dante's *Divine Comedy* and Milton's *Paradise Lost*. They are a principal source of quotations for Section 20.7 on ANGELS AND DEVILS and for Section 20.15 on HEAVEN AND HELL, as well as here.

In the Christian tradition, certain human vices or weaknesses are considered (at least in some circumstances) to be major, or mortal, sins. Among these are anger, avarice, envy, lust, and pride. Consideration of these sins from other points of view than that taken here will be found in Sections 4.3 on ANGER, 4.9 on GREED AND AVARICE (and in Section 11.2 on WEALTH AND POVERTY), 4.8 on PITY AND ENVY, 3.3 on SEXUAL LOVE, and 4.11 on PRIDE AND HUMILITY.

1 And the Lord God planted a garden eastward in Eden; and there he put the man whom he had formed.

And out of the ground made the Lord God to grow every tree that is pleasant to the sight, and good for food; the tree of life also in the midst of the garden, and the tree of knowledge of good and evil. . . .

And the Lord God took the man, and put him into the garden of Eden to dress it and to keep it.

And the Lord God commanded the man, saying, Of every tree of the garden thou mayest freely eat:

But of the tree of the knowledge of good and evil, thou shalt not eat of it: for in the day that thou eatest thereof thou shalt surely die.

Genesis 2:8–17

2 Now the serpent was more subtil than any beast of the field which the Lord God had made. And he said unto the woman, Yea, hath God said, Ye shall not eat of every tree of the garden?

And the woman said unto the serpent, We may eat of the fruit of the trees of the garden:

But of the fruit of the tree which is in the midst of the garden, God hath said, Ye shall not eat of it, neither shall ye touch it, lest ye die.

And the serpent said unto the woman, Ye shall not surely die:

For God doth know that in the day ye eat thereof, then your eyes shall be opened, and ye shall be as gods, knowing good and evil.

And when the woman saw that the tree was good for food, and that it was pleasant to the eyes, and a tree to be desired to make one wise, she took of the fruit thereof, and did eat, and gave also unto her husband with her; and he did eat.

Genesis 3:1–6

3 The Lord is longsuffering, and of great mercy, forgiving iniquity and transgression, and by no means clearing the guilty, visiting the iniquity of the fathers upon the children unto the third and fourth generation.

Numbers 14:18

4 Be sure your sin will find you out.

Numbers 32:23

5 Have mercy upon me, O God, according to thy lovingkindness: according unto the multitude of thy tender mercies blot out my transgressions.

Wash me thoroughly from mine iniquity, and cleanse me from my sin.

For I acknowledge my transgressions: and my sin is ever before me.

Against thee, thee only, have I sinned, and done this evil in thy sight: that thou mightest be justified when thou speakest, and be clear when thou judgest.

Behold, I was shapen in iniquity; and in sin did my mother conceive me.

Psalm 51:1–5

6 My son, if sinners entice thee, consent thou not.

If they say, Come with us, let us lay wait for blood, let us lurk privily for the innocent without cause:

Let us swallow them up alive as the grave; and whole, as those that go down into the pit:

We shall find all precious substance, we shall fill our houses with spoil:

Cast in thy lot among us; let us all have one purse:

My son, walk not thou in the way with them; refrain thy foot from their path:

For their feet run to evil, and make haste to shed blood.

Surely in vain the net is spread in the sight of any bird.

And they lay wait for their own blood; they lurk privily for their own lives.

So are the ways of every one that is greedy of gain; which taketh away the life of the owners thereof.

Proverbs 1:10–19

7 He that covereth his sins shall not prosper: but whoso confesseth and forsaketh them shall have mercy.

Proverbs 28:13

8 Remove far from me vanity and lies: give me neither poverty nor riches; feed me with food convenient for me:

Lest I be full, and deny thee, and say, Who is the Lord? or lest I be poor, and steal, and take the name of my God in vain.

Proverbs 30:8–9

9 For there is not a just man upon earth, that doeth good, and sinneth not.

Ecclesiastes 7:20

10 What mean ye, that ye use this proverb concerning the land of Israel, saying, The fathers have eaten sour grapes, and the children's teeth are set on edge?

As I live, saith the Lord God, ye shall not have occasion any more to use this proverb in Israel.

Behold, all souls are mine; as the soul of the father, so also the soul of the son is mine: the soul that sinneth, it shall die.

Ezekiel 18:2–4

11 *Chorus.* A man thought
the gods deigned not to punish mortals
who trampled down the delicacy of things
inviolable. That man was wicked.
The curse on great daring
shines clear; it wrings atonement
from those high hearts that drive to evil,

from houses blossoming to pride
and peril. Let there be
wealth without tears; enough for
the wise man who will ask no further.
There is not any armor
in gold against perdition
for him who spurns the high altar
of Justice down to the darkness.

Aeschylus, *Agamemnon*, 369

12 *Theseus.* The mind of man—how far will it advance?
Where will its daring impudence find limits?
If human villainy and human life
shall wax in due proportion, if the son
shall always grow in wickedness past his father,
the Gods must add another world to this
that all the sinners may have space enough.

Euripides, *Hippolytus*, 936

13 When you look over your own vices, winking at
them, as it were, with sore eyes; why are you with
regard to those of your friends as sharp-sighted as
an eagle, or the Epidaurian serpent?

Horace, *Satires*, I, 3

14 We have committed some sins; others we have
considered committing. Some we have desired;
others we have encouraged. Some transgressions
we are innocent of only because they did not succeed. With this in mind, we should be more forebearing toward transgressors and pay more attention to those who reprove us.

Seneca, *On Anger*, II, 28

15 Thou shalt not tempt the Lord thy God.

Matthew 4:7

16 Watch and pray, that ye enter not into temptation: the spirit indeed is willing, but the flesh is
weak.

Matthew 26:41

17 And Jesus being full of the Holy Ghost returned
from Jordan, and was led by the Spirit into the
wilderness,

Being forty days tempted of the devil. And in
those days he did eat nothing: and when they
were ended, he afterward hungered.

And the devil said unto him, If thou be the Son
of God, command this stone that it be made
bread.

And Jesus answered him, saying, It is written,
That man shall not live by bread alone, but by
every word of God.

And the devil, taking him up into an high
mountain, shewed unto him all the kingdoms of
the world in a moment of time.

And the devil said unto him, All this power will
I give thee, and the glory of them: for that is de-

livered unto me; and to whomsoever I will I give
it.

If thou therefore wilt worship me, all shall be
thine.

And Jesus answered and said unto him, Get
thee behind me, Satan: for it is written, Thou
shalt worship the Lord thy God, and him only
shalt thou serve.

And he brought him to Jerusalem, and set him
on a pinnacle of the temple, and said unto him, If
thou be the Son of God, cast thyself down from
hence:

For it is written, He shall give his angels charge
over thee, to keep thee:

And in their hands they shall bear thee up, lest
at any time thou dash thy foot against a stone.

And Jesus answering said unto him, It is said,
Thou shalt not tempt the Lord thy God.

And when the devil had ended all the temptation, he departed from him for a season.

Luke 4:1–13

18 Joy shall be in heaven over one sinner that
repenteth, more than over ninety and nine just
persons, which need no repentance.

Luke 15:7

19 The wrath of God is revealed from heaven against
all ungodliness and unrighteousness of men, who
hold the truth in unrighteousness;

Because that which may be known of God is
manifest in them, for God hath shewed it unto
them.

For the invisible things of him from the creation
of the world are clearly seen, being understood by
the things that are made, even his eternal power
and Godhead; so that they are without excuse:

Because that, when they knew God, they glorified him not as God, neither were thankful; but
became vain in their imaginations, and their foolish heart was darkened.

Professing themselves to be wise, they became
fools,

And changed the glory of the uncorruptible
God into an image made like to corruptible man,
and to birds, and fourfooted beasts, and creeping
things.

Wherefore God also gave them up to uncleanness through the lusts of their own hearts, to dishonour their own bodies between themselves:

Who changed the truth of God into a lie, and
worshipped and served the creature more than
the Creator, who is blessed for ever. Amen.

For this cause God gave them up unto vile affections: for even their women did change the natural use into that which is against nature:

And likewise also the men, leaving the natural
use of the woman, burned in their lust one toward
another; men with men working that which is unseemly, and receiving in themselves that recompence of their error which was meet.

And even as they did not like to retain God in

their knowledge, God gave them over to a reprobate mind, to do those things which are not convenient;

Being filled with all unrighteousness, fornication, wickedness, covetousness, maliciousness; full of envy, murder, debate, deceit, malignity; whisperers,

Backbiters, haters of God, despiteful, proud, boasters, inventors of evil things, disobedient to parents,

Without understanding, covenantbreakers, without natural affection, implacable, unmerciful:

Who knowing the judgment of God, that they which commit such things are worthy of death, not only do the same, but have pleasure in them that do them.

Romans 1:18–32

20 Reckon ye also yourselves to be dead indeed unto sin, but alive unto God through Jesus Christ our Lord.

Let not sin therefore reign in your mortal body, that ye should obey it in the lusts thereof.

Neither yield ye your members as instruments of unrighteousness unto sin: but yield yourselves unto God, as those that are alive from the dead, and your members as instruments of righteousness unto God.

For sin shall not have dominion over you: for ye are not under the law, but under grace.

What then? shall we sin, because we are not under the law, but under grace? God forbid.

Know ye not, that to whom ye yield yourselves servants to obey, his servants ye are to whom ye obey; whether of sin unto death, or of obedience unto righteousness?

But God be thanked, that ye were the servants of sin, but ye have obeyed from the heart that form of doctrine which was delivered you.

Being then made free from sin, ye became the servants of righteousness.

Romans 6:11–18

21 For the wages of sin is death.

Romans 6:23

22 Wherefore let him that thinketh he standeth take heed lest he fall.

There hath no temptation taken you but such as is common to man: but God is faithful, who will not suffer you to be tempted above that ye are able; but will with the temptation also make a way to escape, that ye may be able to bear it.

I Corinthians 10:12–13

23 Now the works of the flesh are manifest, which are these; Adultery, fornication, uncleanness, lasciviousness,

Idolatry, witchcraft, hatred, variance, emulations, wrath, strife, seditions, heresies,

Envyings, murders, drunkenness, revellings, and such like: of the which I tell you before, as I have also told you in time past, that they which do such things shall not inherit the kingdom of God.

Galatians 5:19–21

24 Blessed is the man that endureth temptation: for when he is tried, he shall receive the crown of life, which the Lord hath promised to them that love him.

Let no man say when he is tempted, I am tempted of God: for God cannot be tempted with evil, neither tempteth he any man:

But every man is tempted, when he is drawn away of his own lust, and enticed.

Then when lust hath conceived, it bringeth forth sin: and sin, when it is finished, bringeth forth death.

James 1:12–15

25 If we say that we have no sin, we deceive ourselves, and the truth is not in us.

If we confess our sins, he is faithful and just to forgive us our sins, and to cleanse us from all unrighteousness.

If we say that we have not sinned, we make him a liar, and his word is not in us.

I John 1:8–10

26 All that is in the world, the lust of the flesh, and the lust of the eyes, and the pride of life, is not of the Father, but is of the world.

I John 2:16

27 Whosoever is born of God doth not commit sin; for his seed remaineth in him: and he cannot sin, because he is born of God.

I John 3:9

28 Men are no doubt involuntary sinners in the sense that they do not actually desire to sin; but this does not alter the fact that wrong-doers, of their own choice, are, themselves, the agents; it is because they themselves act that the sin is in their own; if they were not agents they could not sin.

Plotinus, *Third Ennead*, II, 10

29 I grew in vice through desire of praise; and when I lacked opportunity to equal others in vice, I invented things I had not done, lest I might be held cowardly for being innocent, or contemptible for being chaste. With the basest companions I walked the streets of Babylon [the city of this World as opposed to the city of God] and wallowed in its filth as if it had been a bed of spices and precious ointments. To make me cleave closer to that city's very center, the invisible Enemy trod me down and seduced me, for I was easy to seduce.

Augustine, *Confessions*, II, 3

30 Your law, O Lord, punishes theft; and this law is so written in the hearts of men that not even the breaking of it blots it out: for no thief bears calmly being stolen from—not even if he is rich and the other steals through want. Yet I chose to steal, and not because want drove me to it—unless a want of justice and contempt for it and an excess for iniquity. For I stole things which I already had in plenty and of better quality. Nor had I any desire to enjoy the things I stole, but only the stealing of them and the sin.

Augustine, *Confessions*, II, 4

31 Pride wears the mask of loftiness of spirit, although You alone, O God, are high over all. Ambition seeks honor and glory, although You alone are to be honored before all and glorious forever. By cruelty the great seek to be feared, yet who is to be feared but God alone: from His power what can be wrested away, or when or where or how or by whom? The caresses by which the lustful seduce are a seeking for love: but nothing is more caressing than Your charity, nor is anything more healthfully loved than Your supremely lovely, supremely luminous Truth. Curiosity may be regarded as a desire for knowledge, whereas You supremely know all things. Ignorance and sheer stupidity hide under the names of simplicity and innocence: yet no being has simplicity like to Yours: and none is more innocent than You, for it is their own deeds that harm the wicked. Sloth pretends that it wants quietude: but what sure rest is there save the Lord? Luxuriousness would be called abundance and completeness; but You are the fullness and inexhaustible abundance of incorruptible delight. Wastefulness is a parody of generosity: but You are the infinitely generous giver of all good. Avarice wants to possess overmuch: but You possess all. Enviousness claims that it strives to excel: but what can excel before You? Anger clamors for just vengeance: but whose vengeance is so just as Yours? Fear is the recoil from a new and sudden threat to something one holds dear, and a cautious regard for one's own safety: but nothing new or sudden can happen to You, nothing can threaten Your hold upon things loved, and where is safety secure save in You? Grief pines at the loss of things in which desire delighted: for it wills to be like to You from whom nothing can be taken away.

Thus the soul is guilty of fornication when she turns from You and seeks from any other source what she will nowhere find pure and without taint unless she returns to You. Thus even those who go from You and stand up against You are still perversely imitating You. But by the mere fact of their imitation, they declare that You are the creator of all that is, and that there is nowhere for them to go where You are not.

So once again what did I enjoy in that theft of mine? Of what excellence of my Lord was I mak-

ing perverse and vicious imitation? Perhaps it was the thrill of acting against Your law—at least in appearance, since I had no power to do so in fact, the delight a prisoner might have in making some small gesture of liberty—getting a deceptive sense of omnipotence from doing something forbidden without immediate punishment. I was that slave, who fled from his Lord and pursued his Lord's shadow. O rottenness, O monstrousness of life and abyss of death! Could you find pleasure only in what was forbidden, and only because it was forbidden?

Augustine, *Confessions*, II, 6

32 Men are separated from God only by sins, from which we are in this life cleansed not by our own virtue, but by the divine compassion; through His indulgence, not through our own power. For, whatever virtue we call our own is itself bestowed upon us by His goodness.

Augustine, *City of God*, X, 22

33 God was not ignorant that man would sin, and that, being himself made subject now to death, he would propagate men doomed to die, and that these mortals would run to such enormities in sin that even the beasts devoid of rational will, and who were created in numbers from the waters and the earth, would live more securely and peaceably with their own kind than men, who had been propagated from one individual for the very purpose of commending concord. For not even lions or dragons have ever waged with their kind such wars as men have waged with one another.

Augustine, *City of God*, XII, 22

34 The first men were . . . so created that if they had not sinned, they would not have experienced any kind of death; but . . . having become sinners, they were so punished with death that whatsoever sprang from their stock should also be punished with the same death. For nothing else could be born of them than that which they themselves had been. Their nature was deteriorated in proportion to the greatness of the condemnation of their sin, so that what existed as punishment in those who first sinned, became a natural consequence in their children.

Augustine, *City of God*, XIII, 3

35 As man the parent is, such is man the offspring. In the first man, therefore, there existed the whole human nature, which was to be transmitted by the woman to posterity, when that conjugal union received the divine sentence of its own condemnation; and what man was made, not when created, but when he sinned and was punished, this he propagated, so far as the origin of sin and death are concerned.

Augustine, *City of God*, XIII, 3

36 The corruption of the body, which weighs down the soul, is not the cause but the punishment of the first sin; and it was not the corruptible flesh that made the soul sinful, but the sinful soul that made the flesh corruptible.

Augustine, *City of God*, XIV, 3

37 It is not without meaning said that all sin is a lie. For no sin is committed save by that desire or will by which we desire that it be well with us, and shrink from it being ill with us. That, therefore, is a lie which we do in order that it may be well with us, but which makes us more miserable than we were. And why is this, but because the source of man's happiness lies only in God, Whom he abandons when he sins, and not in himself, by living according to whom he sins?

Augustine, *City of God*, XIV, 4

38 Our first parents fell into open disobedience because already they were secretly corrupted; for the evil act had never been done had not an evil will preceded it. And what is the origin of our evil will but pride? For "pride is the beginning of sin." And what is pride but the craving for undue exaltation? And this is undue exaltation, when the soul abandons Him to whom it ought to cleave as its end, and becomes a kind of end to itself. This happens when it becomes its own satisfaction. And it does so when it falls away from that unchangeable good which ought to satisfy it more than itself. This falling away is spontaneous; for if the will had remained steadfast in the love of that higher and changeless good by which it was illumined to intelligence and kindled into love, it would not have turned away to find satisfaction in itself and so become frigid and benighted.

Augustine, *City of God*, XIV, 13

39 That the whole human race has been condemned in its first origin, this life itself, if life it is to be called, bears witness by the host of cruel ills with which it is filled. Is not this proved by the profound and dreadful ignorance which produces all the errors that enfold the children of Adam, and from which no man can be delivered without toil, pain, and fear? Is it not proved by his love of so many vain and hurtful things, which produces gnawing cares, disquiet, griefs, fears, wild joys, quarrels, lawsuits, wars, treasons, angers, hatreds, deceit, flattery, fraud, theft, robbery, perfidy, pride, ambition, envy, murders, parricides, cruelty, ferocity, wickedness, luxury, insolence, impudence, shamelessness, fornications, adulteries, incests, and the numberless uncleannesses and unnatural acts of both sexes, which it is shameful so much as to mention; sacrileges, heresies, blasphemies, perjuries, oppression of the innocent, calumnies, plots, falsehoods, false witnessings, unrighteous judgments, violent deeds, plunderings, and whatever similar wickedness has found its way into the lives of men. . . . These are indeed the crimes of wicked men, yet they spring from that root of error and misplaced love which is born with every son of Adam. For who is there that has not observed with what profound ignorance, manifesting itself even in infancy, and with what superfluity of foolish desires, beginning to appear in boyhood, man comes into this life, so that, were he left to live as he pleased, and to do whatever he pleased, he would plunge into all, or certainly into many of those crimes and iniquities.

Augustine, *City of God*, XXII, 22

40 Mortal sin occurs in two ways in the act of free choice. First, when something evil is chosen; as man sins by choosing adultery, which is evil of itself. Such sin always comes of ignorance or error. Otherwise what is evil would never be chosen as good. The adulterer errs in the particular, choosing this delight of a disordered act as something good to be performed now, from the inclination of passion or of habit, even though he does not err in his universal judgment, but retains a right opinion in this respect. In this way there can be no sin in the angel, because there are no passions in the angels to fetter reason or intellect. . . . Nor, again, could any habit inclining to sin precede their first sin. In another way sin comes of free choice by choosing something good in itself, but not according to the order of due measure or rule, so that the defect which induces sin is only on the part of the choice which does not have its due order (except on the part of the thing chosen); as if one were to pray without heeding the order established by the Church. Such a sin does not presuppose ignorance, but merely absence of consideration of the things which ought to be considered. In this way the angel sinned, by seeking his own good, from his own free choice, without being ordered to the rule of the Divine will.

Aquinas, *Summa Theologica*, I, 63, 1

41 If God had deprived the world of all those things which proved an occasion of sin, the universe would have been imperfect. Nor was it fitting for the common good to be destroyed in order that individual evil might be avoided, especially as God is so powerful that He can direct any evil to a good end.

Aquinas, *Summa Theologica*, I, 92, 1

42 The theologian considers sin chiefly as an offence against God, and the moral philosopher as something contrary to reason. Hence Augustine defines sin with reference to its being "contrary to the eternal law" more fittingly than with reference to its being contrary to reason; the more so, as the eternal law directs us in many things that surpass human reason, for example in matters of faith.

Aquinas, *Summa Theologica*, I–II, 71, 6

43 Habit and despair are stages following the complete species of sin, even as boyhood and youth follow the complete generation of a man.

Aquinas, *Summa Theologica*, I–II, 72, 7

44 A sin is so much the graver according as the disorder occurs in a principle which is higher in the order of reason. . . . Therefore a sin which is about the very substance of man, for example murder, is graver than a sin which is about external things, for instance theft; and graver still is a sin committed directly against God, for example unbelief, blasphemy, and the like; and in each of these grades of sin, one sin will be graver than another according as it is about a higher or a lower principle.

Aquinas, *Summa Theologica*, I–II, 73, 3

45 Charity is not any kind of love, but the love of God. Hence not any kind of hatred is opposed to it directly, but the hatred of God, which is the most grievous of all sins.

Aquinas, *Summa Theologica*, I–II, 73, 4

46 Every sinful act proceeds from inordinate desire for some temporal good. Now the fact that anyone desires a temporal good inordinately, is due to the fact that he loves himself inordinately, for to wish anyone some good is to love him. Therefore it is evident that inordinate love of self is the cause of every sin.

Aquinas, *Summa Theologica*, I–II, 77, 4

47 The first sin infects nature with a human corruption pertaining to nature; but other sins infect it with a corruption pertaining only to the person.

Aquinas, *Summa Theologica*, I–II, 81, 2

48 The weak should avoid associating with sinners, on account of the danger in which they stand of being perverted by them. But it is commendable for the perfect, of whose corruption there is no fear, to associate with sinners that they may convert them.

Aquinas, *Summa Theologica*, II–II, 25, 6

49 By sinning man departs from the order of reason, and consequently falls away from the dignity of his manhood, in so far as he is naturally free, and exists for himself, and he falls into the slavish state of the beasts, by being disposed of according as he is useful to others.

Aquinas, *Summa Theologica*, II–II, 64, 2

50 Whilst I was rushing downwards, there appeared before my eyes one who seemed hoarse from long silence.

When I saw him in the great desert, I cried: "Have pity on me, whate'er thou be, whether shade or veritable man!"

He answered me: "Not man, a man I once was;

and my parents were Lombards, and both of Mantua by country.

I was born *sub Julio*, though it was late; and lived at Rome under the good Augustus, in the time of the false and lying Gods.

A poet I was; and sang of that just son of Anchises, who came from Troy after proud Ilium was burnt.

But thou, why returnest thou to such disquiet? why ascendest not the delectable mountain, which is the beginning and the cause of all gladness?"

"Art thou then that Virgil, and that fountain which pours abroad so rich a stream of speech?" I answered him, with bashful front.

"O glory, and light of other poets! May the long zeal avail me, and the great love, that made me search thy volume.

Thou art my master and my author; thou alone art he from whom I took the good style that hath done me honour.

See the beast from which I turned back; help me from her, thou famous sage; for she makes my veins and pulses tremble."

"Thou must take another road," he answered, when he saw me weeping, "if thou desirest to escape from this wild place:

because this beast, for which thou criest, lets not men pass her way; but so entangles that she slays them;

and has a nature so perverse and vicious, that she never satiates her craving appetite; and after feeding, she is hungrier than before."

Dante, *Inferno*, I, 61

51 *Sordello.* Through all the circles of the woeful realm . . . came I here. A virtue from heaven moved me, and with it I come.

Not for doing, but for not doing, have I lost the vision of the high Sun, whom thou desirest, and who too late by me was known.

Down there is a place not sad with torments, but with darkness alone, where the lamentations sound not as wailings, but are sighs.

There [in Limbo] do I abide with the innocent babes, bitten by the fangs of death, ere they were exempt from human sin.

There dwell I with those who clad them not with the three holy virtues, and without offence knew the others and followed them all.

Dante, *Purgatorio*, VII, 22

52 We [Virgil and Dante] drew nigh, and were at a place, whence there where first appeared to me a break just like a fissure which divides a wall,

I espied a gate, and three steps beneath to go to it, of divers colours, and a warder who as yet spake no word.

And as more I opened mine eyes there, I saw him seated upon the topmost step, such in his countenance that I endured him not;

and in his hand he held a naked sword which reflected the rays so towards us, that I directed mine eyes to it oft in vain.

"Tell, there where ye stand, what would ye?" he began to say; "where is the escort? Beware lest coming upward be to your hurt!"

"A heavenly lady who well knows these things," my Master answered him, "even now did say to us: 'Go ye thither, there is the gate.' "

"And may she speed your steps to good," again began the courteous door-keeper; "come then forward to our stairs."

There where we came, at the first step, was white marble so polished and smooth that I mirrored me therein as I appear.

The second darker was than perse, of a stone, rugged and calcined, cracked in its length and in its breadth.

The third, which is massy above, seemed to me of porphyry so flaming red as blood that spurts from a vein.

Upon this God's angel held both his feet, sitting upon the threshold, which seemed to me adamantine stone.

Up by the three steps, with my good will, my Leader brought me, saying: "Humbly ask that the bolt be loosed."

Devoutly I flung me at the holy feet; for mercy I craved that he would open to me; but first on my breast thrice I smote me.

Seven P's upon my forehead he described with the point of his sword and: "Do thou wash these wounds when thou art within," he said.

Ashes, or earth which is dug out dry, would be of one colour with his vesture, and from beneath it he drew forth two keys.

One was of gold and the other was of silver; first with the white and then with the yellow he did so to the gate that I was satisfied.

"Whensoever one of these keys fails so that it turns not aright in the lock," said he to us, "this passage opens not.

More precious is one, but the other requires exceeding art and wit ere it unlocks, because it is the one which unties the knot.

From Peter I hold them; and he told me to err rather in opening, than in keeping it locked, if only the people fell prostrate at my feet."

Then he pushed the door of the sacred portal, saying: "Enter, but I make you ware that he who looketh behind returns outside again."

Dante, *Purgatorio*, IX, 73

53 Now were we mounting up by the sacred steps, and meseemed I was exceeding lighter, than meseemed before on the flat;

wherefore I: "Master, say, what heavy thing has been lifted from me, that scarce any toil is perceived by me in journeying?"

He [Virgil] answered: "When the P's which have remained still nearly extinguished on thy face, shall, like the one, be wholly rased out,

thy feet shall be so vanquished by goodwill, that not only will they feel it no toil, but it shall be a delight to them to be urged upward."

Dante, *Purgatorio*, XII, 115

54 Short time Beatrice left me thus; and began, casting the ray upon me of a smile such as would make one blessed though in the flame:

"According to my thought that cannot err, how just vengeance justly was avenged, hath set thee pondering;

but I will speedily release thy mind; and do thou hearken, for my words shall make thee gift of an august pronouncement.

Because he not endured for his own good a rein upon the power that wills, that man who ne'er was born, as he condemned himself, condemned his total offspring;

wherefore the human race lay sick down there for many an age, in great error, till it pleased the Word of God to descend

where he joined that nature which had gone astray from its Creator to himself, in person, by sole act of his eternal Love.

Now turn thy sight to what I now discourse: This nature, so united to its Maker, as it was when created was unalloyed and good;

but by its own self had it been exiled from Paradise, because it swerved from the way of truth, and from its proper life.

As for the penalty, then, inflicted by the cross,—if it be measured by the Nature taken on, never did any other bite as justly;

and, in like manner, ne'er was any so outrageous if we look to the Person who endured it, in whom this nature was contracted.

So from one act issued effects apart; God and the Jews rejoiced in one same death; thereat shuddered the earth and heaven opened.

No more, now, should it seem hard saying to thee that just vengeance was afterward avenged by a just court."

Dante, *Paradiso*, VII, 16

55 *Adam.* Now know, my son, that not the tasting of the tree was in itself the cause of so great exile, but only the transgressing of the mark.

Dante, *Paradiso*, XXVI, 115

56 *Pandar.* To prove my point, recall how those great clerks
Who most have erred against a certain law,
And are converted from their wicked works
By God's good grace that doth them to him draw,
Are just the ones who hold God most in awe,
And grow into his most believing band,
For they know best all error to withstand.

Chaucer, *Troilus
and Cressida*, I, 144

57 Hearken this word, be warned by this one case;

The lion lies in wait by night and day
To slay the innocent, if he but may.
Dispose your hearts in grace, that you withstand
The Fiend, who'd make you thrall among his
band
He cannot tempt more than beyond your might;
For Christ will be your champion and knight.

> Chaucer, *Canterbury Tales:*
> *Friar's Tale*

58 Forsooth, sin is of two kinds; it is either venial or
mortal sin. Verily, when man loves any creature
more than he loves Jesus Christ our Creator, then
is it mortal sin. And venial sin it is if a man love
Jesus Christ less than he ought.

> Chaucer, *Canterbury Tales:*
> *Parson's Tale*

59 Now it is a needful thing to tell which are the
mortal sins, that is to say, the principal sins; they
are all leashed together, but are different in their
ways. Now they are called principal sins because
they are the chief sins and the trunk from which
branch all others. And the root of these seven sins
is pride, which is the general root of all evils; for
from this root spring certain branches, as anger,
envy, acedia or sloth, avarice (or covetousness, for
vulgar understanding), gluttony, and lechery.

> Chaucer, *Canterbury Tales:*
> *Parson's Tale*

60 After baptism original sin is like a wound which
has begun to heal. It is really a wound, yet it is
becoming better and is constantly in the process of
healing, although it is still festering, is painful, etc.
So original sin remains in the baptized until their
death, although it is in the process of being rooted
out. It is rendered harmless, and so it cannot accuse or damn us.

> Luther, *Table Talk,* 138

61 When you feel that something is wrong and you
have a bad conscience about it, this is not the sin
against the Holy Spirit, but when you sin and
have a good conscience about it, this is the sin
against the Holy Spirit.

> Luther, *Table Talk,* 388

62 Sins against the Holy Ghost are, first, presumption; second, despair; third, opposition to and
condemnation of the known truth; fourth, not to
wish well, but to grudge one's brother or neighbour the grace of God; fifth, to be hardened;
sixth, to be impenitent.

> Luther, *Table Talk,* H245

63 These two sins, hatred and pride, deck and trim
themselves out, as the devil clothed himself, in the
Godhead. Hatred will be godlike; pride will be

truth. These two are right deadly sins: hatred is
killing; pride is lying.

> Luther, *Table Talk,* H253

64 The sins of common, untutored people are nothing in comparison with the sins committed by
great and high persons, that are in spiritual and
temporal offices.

> Luther, *Table Talk,* H255

65 When I am assailed with heavy tribulations, I
rush out among my pigs, rather than remain
alone by myself. The human heart is like a millstone in a mill; when you put wheat under it, it
turns and grinds and bruises the wheat to flour; if
you put no wheat, it still grinds on, but then 'tis
itself it grinds and wears away. So the human
heart, unless it be occupied with some employment, leaves space for the devil, who wriggles
himself in, and brings with him a whole host of
evil thoughts, temptations, and tribulations,
which grind out the heart.

> Luther, *Table Talk,* H654

66 The mind of man is so completely alienated from
the righteousness of God, that it conceives, desires,
and undertakes every thing that is impious, perverse, base, impure, and flagitious; . . . his heart
is so thoroughly infected by the poison of sin, that
it cannot produce any thing but what is corrupt;
and . . . if at any time men do any thing apparently good, yet the mind always remains involved
in hypocrisy and fallacious obliquity, and the
heart enslaved by its inward perverseness.

> Calvin, *Institutes of the Christian*
> *Religion,* II, 5

67 The corrupt conceptions of the mind, provoking
us to transgressions of the law, whether suggested
by our own concupiscence or excited by the devil,
are temptations; and things not evil in themselves,
nevertheless become temptations through the subtlety of the devil, when they are obtruded on our
eyes in such a manner that their intervention occasions our seduction or declension from God.
And these temptations are either from prosperous,
or from adverse events. From prosperous ones, as
riches, power, honours; which generally dazzle
men's eyes by their glitter and external appearance of goodness, and insnare them with their
blandishments, that, caught with such delusions
and intoxicated with such delights, they forget
their God. From unpropitious ones, as poverty, reproaches, contempt, afflictions, and other things
of this kind; overcome with the bitterness and difficulty of which, they fall into despondency, cast
away faith and hope, and at length become altogether alienated from God.

> Calvin, *Institutes of the Christian*
> *Religion,* III, 20

68 From all inordinate and sinful affections; and
from all the deceits of the world, the flesh, and the
devil,
   Good Lord, deliver us.

   Book of Common Prayer

69 *Escalus.* Some rise by sin, and some by virtue fall.
   Shakespeare, *Measure
   for Measure,*II, i, 38

70   Most dangerous
   Is that temptation that doth goad us on
   To sin in loving virtue.
   Shakespeare, *Measure
   for Measure,* II, ii, 181

71 *Lear.*   Plate sin with gold,
   And the strong lance of justice hurtless breaks;
   Arm it in rags, a pigmy's straw does pierce it.
   Shakespeare, *Lear,* IV, vi, 169

72 *Pericles.* One sin, I know, another doth provoke;
   Murder's as near to lust as flame to smoke.
   Shakespeare, *Pericles,* I, i, 137

73 Then, as mankinde, so is the worlds whole frame
   Quite out of joynt, almost created lame:
   For, before God had made up all the rest,
   Corruption entred, and deprav'd the best:
   It seis'd the Angels, and then first of all
   The world did in her cradle take a fall,
   And turn'd her braines, and tooke a generall
      maime,
   Wronging each joynt of th'universall frame.
   The noblest part, man, felt it first; and then
   Both beasts and plants, curst in the curse of man.
   So did the world from the first houre decay,
   That evening was beginning of the day,
   And now the Springs and Sommers which we see,
   Like sonnes of women after fiftie bee.
   Donne, *First Anniversary*

74 Thou hast made me, And shall thy worke decay?
   Repaire me now, for now mine end doth haste,
   I runne to death, and death meets me as fast,
   And all my pleasures are like yesterday;
   I dare not move my dimme eyes any way,
   Despaire behind, and death before doth cast
   Such terrour, and my feeble flesh doth waste
   By sinne in it, which it t'wards hell doth weigh;
   Onely thou art above, and when towards thee
   By thy leave I can looke, I rise againe;
   But our old subtle foe so tempteth me,
   That not one houre my selfe I can sustaine;
   Thy Grace may wing me to prevent his art,
   And thou like Adamant draw mine iron heart.
   Donne, *Holy Sonnet I*

75 I am a little world made cunningly
   Of Elements, and an Angelike spright,
   But black sinne hath betraid to endlesse night

My worlds both parts, and (oh) both parts must
   die.
   Donne, *Holy Sonnet V*

76 Man, by the fall, lost at once his state of innocence, and his empire over creation, both of which
   can be partially recovered even in this life, the
   first by religion and faith, the second by the arts
   and sciences.
   Bacon, *Novum Organum,* II, 52

77 A *sin* is not only a transgression of a law, but also
   any contempt of the legislator. For such contempt
   is a breach of all his laws at once, and therefore
   may consist, not only in the *commission* of a fact, or
   in the speaking of words by the laws forbidden, or
   also in the *omission* of what the law commandeth, but
   also in the *intention* or purpose to transgress. For
   the purpose to break the law is some degree of
   contempt of him to whom it belongeth to see it
   executed. To be delighted in the imagination only
   of being possessed of another man's goods, servants, or wife, without any intention to take them
   from him by force or fraud, is no breach of the
   law, that saith, "Thou shalt not covet": nor is the
   pleasure a man may have in imagining or dreaming of the death of him from whose life he expect-
   eth nothing but damage and displeasure, a sin;
   but the resolving to put some act in execution that
   tendeth thereto. For to be pleased in the fiction of
   that which would please a man if it were real is a
   passion so adherent to the nature both of man and
   every other living creature, as to make it a sin
   were to make sin of being a man.
   Hobbes, *Leviathan,* II, 27

78 It is . . . an astonishing thing that the mystery
   furthest removed from our knowledge, namely,
   that of the transmission of sin, should be a fact
   without which we can have no knowledge of ourselves. For it is beyond doubt that there is nothing
   which more shocks our reason than to say that the
   sin of the first man has rendered guilty those who,
   being so removed from this source, seem incapable
   of participation in it. This transmission does not
   only seem to us impossible, it seems also very unjust. For what is more contrary to the rules of our
   miserable justice than to damn eternally an infant
   incapable of will, for a sin wherein he seems to
   have so little a share that it was committed six
   thousand years before he was in existence? Certainly nothing offends us more rudely than this
   doctrine; and yet, without this mystery, the most
   incomprehensible of all, we are incomprehensible
   to ourselves. The knot of our condition takes its
   twists and turns in this abyss, so that man is more
   inconceivable without this mystery than this mystery is inconceivable to man.
   Pascal, *Pensées,* VII, 434

79 If there is one sole source of everything, there is

one sole end of everything; everything through Him, everything for Him. The true religion, then, must teach us to worship Him only, and to love Him only. But as we find ourselves unable to worship what we know not, and to love any other object but ourselves, the religion which instructs us in these duties must instruct us also of this inability, and teach us also the remedies for it. It teaches us that by one man all was lost, and the bond broken between God and us, and that by one man the bond is renewed.

We are born so averse to this love of God, and it is so necessary, that we must be born guilty, or God would be unjust.

Pascal, *Pensées*, VII, 489

80 There are only two kinds of men: the righteous who believe themselves sinners; the rest, sinners, who believe themselves righteous.

Pascal, *Pensées*, VII, 534

81 *Comus.* O foolishnes of men! that lend their ears
To those budge doctors of the *Stoick* Furr,
And fetch their precepts from the *Cynick* Tub,
Praising the lean and sallow Abstinence.
Wherefore did Nature powre her bounties forth,
With such a full and unwithdrawing hand,
Covering the earth with odours, fruits, and flocks,
Thronging the Seas with spawn innumerable,
But all to please, and sate the curious taste?
And set to work millions of spinning Worms,
That in their green shops weave the smooth-hair'd silk
To deck her Sons, and that no corner might
Be vacant of her plenty, in her own loyns
She hutch't th'all-worshipt ore, and precious gems
To store her children with; if all the world
Should in a pet of temperance feed on Pulse,
Drink the clear stream, and nothing wear but Freize,
Th'all-giver would be unthank't, would be unprais'd,
Not half his riches known, and yet despis'd,
And we should serve him as a grudging master,
As a penurious niggard of his wealth,
And live like Natures bastards, not her sons.

Milton, *Comus*, 706

82 Of mans First Disobedience, and the Fruit
Of that Forbidden Tree, whose mortal tast
Brought Death into the World, and all our woe,
With loss of *Eden*, till one greater Man
Restore us, and regain the blissful Seat,
Sing Heav'nly Muse.

Milton, *Paradise Lost*, I, 1

83 Say first, for Heav'n hides nothing from thy view
[O Heavenly Muse]
Nor the deep Tract of Hell, say first what cause
Mov'd our Grand Parents in that happy State,
Favour'd of Heav'n so highly, to fall off
From their Creator, and transgress his Will

For one restraint, Lords of the World besides?
Who first seduc'd them to that fowl revolt?
Th' infernal Serpent; he it was, whose guile
Stird up with Envy and Revenge, deceiv'd
The Mother of Mankinde, what time his Pride
Had cast him out from Heav'n, with all his Host
Of Rebel Angels, by whose aid aspiring
To set himself in Glory above his Peers,
He trusted to have equal'd the most High,
If he oppos'd; and with ambitious aim
Against the Throne and Monarchy of God
Rais'd impious War in Heav'n and Battel proud
With vain attempt.

Milton, *Paradise Lost*, I, 27

84 *God.* Onely begotten Son, seest thou what rage
Transports our adversarie, whom no bounds
Prescrib'd, no barrs of Hell, nor all the chains
Heapt on him there, nor yet the main Abyss
Wide interrupt can hold; so bent he seems
On desperat revenge, that shall redound
Upon his own rebellious head. And now
Through all restraint broke loose [Satan] wings his way
Not farr off Heav'n, in the Precincts of light,
Directly towards the new created World,
And Man there plac't, with purpose to assay
If him by force he can destroy, or worse,
By som false guile pervert; and shall pervert;
For man will heark'n to his glozing lyes,
And easily transgress the sole Command,
Sole pledge of his obedience: So will fall
Hee and his faithless Progenie: whose fault?
Whose but his own?

Milton, *Paradise Lost*, III, 80

85   Her rash hand in evil hour
Forth reaching to the Fruit, [Eve]   pluck'd, she eat:
Earth felt the wound, and Nature from her seat
Sighing through all her Works gave signs of woe,
That all was lost.

Milton, *Paradise Lost*, IX, 780

86 *God.* Thy sorrow I will greatly multiplie
By thy Conception; Childern thou shalt bring
In sorrow forth, and to thy Husbands will
Thine shall submit, hee over thee shall rule.
   On *Adam* last thus judgement he pronounc'd.
Because thou has heark'nd to the voice of thy Wife,
And eaten of the Tree concerning which
I charg'd thee, saying: Thou shalt not eate thereof,
Curs'd is the ground for thy sake, thou in sorrow
Shalt eate thereof all the days of thy Life;
Thornes also and Thistles it shall bring thee forth
Unbid, and thou shalt eate th' Herb of th' Field,
In the sweat of thy Face shalt thou eate Bread,
Till thou return unto the ground, for thou
Out of the ground wast taken, know thy Birth,

For dust thou art, and shalt to dust returne.

Milton, *Paradise Lost*, X, 193

87 They are not skilful considerers of human things, who imagine to remove sin by removing the matter of sin; for, besides that it is a huge heap increasing under the very act of diminishing, though some part of it may for a time be withdrawn from some persons, it cannot from all, in such a universal thing as books are; and when this is done, yet the sin remains entire. Though ye take from a covetous man all his treasure, he has yet one jewel left, ye cannot bereave him of his covetousness. Banish all objects of lust, shut up all youth into the severest discipline that can be exercised in any hermitage, ye cannot make them chaste, that came not thither so: such great care and wisdom is required to the right managing of this point. Suppose we could expel sin by this means; look how much we thus expel of sin, so much we expel of virtue: for the matter of them both is the same; remove that, and ye remove them both alike.

Milton, *Areopagitica*

88 I cannot admit that sin and evil have any positive existence, far less that anything can exist, or come to pass, contrary to the will of God. On the contrary, not only do I assert that sin has no positive existence, I also maintain that only in speaking improperly, or humanly, can we say that we sin against God, as in the expression that men offend God.

Spinoza, *Letter to William de Blyenbergh (Jan. 5, 1665)*

89 There is no original sin in the human heart, the how and why of the entrance of every vice can be traced. The only natural passion is self-love or selfishness taken in a wider sense.

Rousseau, *Emile*, II

90 Adam bit the apple, and thereupon sin fell on the human race. Its origin is supposed to be explained when it is told as an anecdote of the past. In times long gone by there were two sorts of people: one, the diligent, intelligent, and, above all, frugal *élite;* the other, lazy rascals, spending their substance, and more, in riotous living. The theological legend of original sin tells us certainly how man came to be condemned to eat his bread in the sweat of his brow; but the history of economic original sin reveals to us that there are people to whom this is by no means essential. Never mind! Thus it came to pass that the former sort accumulated wealth, and the latter sort had at last nothing to sell except their own skins. And from this original sin dates the poverty of the great majority that, despite all its labour, has up to now nothing to sell but itself, and the wealth of the few that increases constantly although they have long ceased to work. Such insipid childishness is every

day preached to us in the defence of property.

Marx, *Capital*, Vol. I, VIII, 26

91 She [the Catholic Church] holds that it were better for sun and moon to drop from heaven, for the earth to fail, and for all the many millions who are upon it to die of starvation in extremest agony, as far as temporal affliction goes, than that one soul, I will not say, should be lost, but should commit one single venial sin, should tell one wilful untruth, . . . or steal one poor farthing without excuse.

Newman, *Lectures on Anglican Difficulties*, VIII

92 *Grand Inquisitor.* The wise and dread spirit, the spirit of self-destruction and non-existence . . . the great spirit talked with Thee in the wilderness, and we are told in the books that he "tempted" Thee. Is that so? And could anything truer be said than what he revealed to Thee in three questions and what Thou didst reject, and what in the books is called "the temptation"? And yet if there has ever been on earth a real stupendous miracle, it took place on that day, on the day of the three temptations. The statement of those three questions was itself the miracle. If it were possible to imagine simply for the sake of argument that those three questions of the dread spirit had perished utterly from the books, and that we had to restore them and to invent them anew, and to do so had gathered together all the wise men of the earth—rulers, chief priests, learned men, philosophers, poets—and had set them the task to invent three questions, such as would not only fit the occasion, but express in three words, three human phrases, the whole future history of the world and of humanity—dost Thou believe that all the wisdom of the earth united could have invented anything in depth and force equal to the three questions which were actually put to Thee then by the wise and mighty spirit in the wilderness? From those questions alone, from the miracle of their statement, we can see that we have here to do not with the fleeting human intelligence, but with the absolute and eternal. For in those three questions the whole subsequent history of mankind is, as it were, brought together into one whole, and foretold, and in them are united all the unsolved historical contradictions of human nature. At the time it could not be so clear, since the future was unknown; but now that fifteen hundred years have passed, we see that everything in those three questions was so justly divined and foretold, and has been so truly fulfilled, that nothing can be added to them or taken from them.

Judge Thyself who was right—Thou or he who questioned Thee then?

Dostoevsky, *Brothers Karamazov*, Pt. II, V, 5

93 Adam was but human—this explains it all. He did not want the apple for the apple's sake; he wanted it only because it was forbidden. The mistake was in not forbidding the serpent; then he would have eaten the serpent.

Mark Twain, *Pudd'nhead Wilson's Calendar*, II

94 The priest disvalues, *dissanctifies* nature: it is only at the price of this that he exists at all. —Disobedience of God, that is to say of the priest, of 'the Law', now acquires the name 'sin'; the means of 'becoming reconciled again with God' are, as is only to be expected, means by which subjection to the priest is only more thoroughly guaranteed: the priest alone 'redeems'. . . . From a psychological point of view, 'sins' are indispensable in any society organized by priests: they are the actual levers of power, the priest *lives* on sins, he needs 'the commission of sins'. . . . Supreme law: 'God forgives him who repents'—in plain language: *who subjects himself to the priest.*

Nietzsche, *Antichrist*, XXVI

95 Sin . . . that form *par excellence* of the self-violation of man, was invented to make science, culture, every kind of elevation and nobility of man impossible.

Nietzsche, *Antichrist*, XLIX

96 If the Son of God was obliged to sacrifice his life to redeem mankind from original sin, then by the law of the talion, the requital of like for like, that sin must have been a killing, a murder. Nothing else could call for the sacrifice of a life in expiation. And if the original sin was an offence against God the Father, the primal crime of mankind must have been a parricide, the killing of the primal father of the primitive human horde, whose image in memory was later transfigured into a deity.

Freud, *Thoughts on War and Death*, II

97 A relatively strict and vigilant conscience is the very sign of a virtuous man, and though saints may proclaim themselves sinners, they are not so wrong, in view of the temptations of instinctual gratifications to which they are peculiarly liable—since, as we know, temptations do but increase under constant privation, whereas they subside, at any rate temporarily, if they are sometimes gratified. The field of ethics is rich in problems, and another of the facts we find here is that misfortune, i.e., external deprivation, greatly intensifies the strength of conscience in the superego. As long as things go well with a man, his conscience is lenient and lets the ego do all kinds of things; when some calamity befalls, he holds an inquisition within, discovers his sin, heightens the standards of his conscience, imposes abstinences on himself and punishes himself with penances.

Freud, *Civilization and Its Discontents*, VII

20.14 | *Redemption and Salvation*

If the reader compares the quotations of this section with those of Section 20.13 on SIN AND TEMPTATION and of those of Section 20.15 on HEAVEN AND HELL, the reader will find that the subjects treated in the three sections are so closely related that the allocation of texts to one rather than another place has been somewhat arbitrary. Within the Christian tradition at least, and perhaps also in other religions as well, it is the existence of sin that calls upon God to mete out either merciful forgiveness or just punishment. If men were without sin, there would be no need for a redeemer and savior; if the sins of all were automatically washed away by the sacrificial atonement of a redeemer, there would be no damned in Hell; unless, with God's grace, salvation is attainable even if not fully merited, there would be no admission of the blessed to the company of the angelic choir in Heaven.

The mention of the angels reminds us that it was the sin of Satan or Lucifer that separated the good angels from the bad and populated Hell with its demons or devils, and Heaven with its nine hierarchies of angels. As the reader of Section 20.7 on ANGELS AND DEVILS will discover, because the angelic substance is aeviternal and immutable, unlike that of the individual man, the sins of the fallen angels are irredeemable. They are irretrievably and forever damned from the first moment of their sin (which is also the first moment of creation), just as, from that moment too, the good angels are unchangeably in the presence of God.

The quotations below, including a large number from the Old and the New Testament, deal with atonement for sin, by sacrifice or other means; with the need for a mediator between man and God to reconcile God's mercy with his justice; with the reasons why man's redemption requires God to become man in the person of Jesus Christ, and to shed his blood on the cross to wash away the sins of the world; and with the healing power of God's grace to remove the wounds of original sin and to enable men to perform the good works that have some merit for salvation. The intricacies of the doctrine of grace, and the great debate over salvation through faith or through good works, have not been adequately represented here, and cannot be in view of their complexity and subtlety. As damnation is eternal death, so salvation is eternal life, the joys of which constitute the beatitude of the blessed united with God. For the difference between such eternal happiness and the temporal happiness that all men seek and some attain in this earthly life, the reader must compare what is said here about beatitude with what is said about happiness in Section 9.8.

---

1 Salvation belongeth unto the Lord.

Psalm 3:8

2 The Lord is my shepherd; I shall not want.

He maketh me to lie down in green pastures: he leadeth me beside the still waters.

He restoreth my soul: he leadeth me in the paths of righteousness for his name's sake.

Yea, though I walk through the valley of the shadow of death, I will fear no evil: for thou art with me; thy rod and thy staff they comfort me.

Thou preparest a table before me in the presence of mine enemies: thou anointest my head with oil; my cup runneth over.

Surely goodness and mercy shall follow me all the days of my life: and I will dwell in the house of the Lord for ever.

Psalm 23:1–6

3 But the salvation of the righteous is of the Lord: he is their strength in the time of trouble.

And the Lord shall help them, and deliver them: he shall deliver them from the wicked, and save them, because they trust in him.

Psalm 37:39–40

4 Purge me with hyssop, and I shall be clean: wash me, and I shall be whiter than snow.

Make me to hear joy and gladness; that the bones which thou hast broken may rejoice.

Hide thy face from my sins, and blot out all mine iniquities.

Create in me a clean heart, O God; and renew a right spirit within me.

Cast me not away from thy presence; and take not thy holy spirit from me.

Restore unto me the joy of thy salvation; and uphold me with thy free spirit.

Psalm 51:7–12

5 O Zion, that bringest good tidings, get thee up into the high mountain; O Jerusalem, that bringest good tidings, lift up thy voice with strength; lift it up, be not afraid; say unto the cities of Judah, Behold your God!

Behold, the Lord God will come with strong hand, and his arm shall rule for him: behold, his reward is with him, and his work before him.

He shall feed his flock like a shepherd: he shall gather the lambs with his arm, and carry them in his bosom, and shall gently lead those that are with young.

Isaiah 40:9–11

6 For, behold, I create new heavens and a new earth: and the former shall not be remembered, nor come into mind.

But be ye glad and rejoice for ever in that which I create. . . .

The wolf and the lamb shall feed together, and

the lion shall eat straw like the bullock: and dust shall be the serpent's meat. They shall not hurt nor destroy in all my holy mountain, saith the Lord.

Isaiah 65:17–25

7 And they said every one to his fellow, Come, and let us cast lots, that we may know for whose cause this evil is upon us. So they cast lots, and the lot fell upon Jonah.

Then said they unto him, Tell us, we pray thee, for whose cause this evil is upon us; What is thine occupation? and whence comest thou? what is thy country? and of what people art thou?

And he said unto them, I am an Hebrew; and I fear the Lord, the God of heaven, which hath made the sea and the dry land.

Then were the men exceedingly afraid, and said unto him, Why hast thou done this? For the men knew that he fled from the presence of the Lord, because he had told them.

Then said they unto him, What shall we do unto thee, that the sea may be calm unto us? for the sea wrought, and was tempestuous.

And he said unto them, Take me up, and cast me forth into the sea; so shall the sea be calm unto you: for I know that for my sake this great tempest is upon you.

Nevertheless the men rowed hard to bring it to the land; but they could not: for the sea wrought, and was tempestuous against them.

Wherefore they cried unto the Lord, and said, We beseech thee, O Lord, we beseech thee, let us not perish for this man's life, and lay not upon us innocent blood: for thou, O Lord, hast done as it pleased thee.

So they took up Jonah, and cast him forth into the sea: and the sea ceased from her raging.

Then the men feared the Lord exceedingly, and offered a sacrifice unto the Lord, and made vows.

Now the Lord had prepared a great fish to swallow up Jonah. And Jonah was in the belly of the fish three days and three nights.

Then Jonah prayed unto the Lord his God out of the fish's belly,

And said, I cried by reason of mine affliction unto the Lord, and he heard me; out of the belly of hell cried I, and thou heardest my voice.

For thou hadst cast me into the deep, in the midst of the seas; and the floods compassed me about: all thy billows and thy waves passed over me.

Then I said, I am cast out of thy sight; yet I will look again toward thy holy temple.

The waters compassed me about, even to the soul: the depth closed me round about, the weeds were wrapped about my head.

I went down to the bottoms of the mountains; the earth with her bars was about me for ever: yet hast thou brought up my life from corruption, O Lord my God.

When my soul fainted within me I remembered the Lord: and my prayer came in unto thee, into thine holy temple.

They that observe lying vanities forsake their own mercy.

But I will sacrifice unto thee with the voice of thanksgiving; I will pay that that I have vowed. Salvation is of the Lord.

And the Lord spake unto the fish, and it vomited out Jonah upon the dry land.

Jonah 1:7–17; 2:1–10

8 Behold, I will send my messenger, and he shall prepare the way before me: and the Lord, whom ye seek, shall suddenly come to his temple, even the messenger of the covenant, whom ye delight in: behold, he shall come, saith the Lord of hosts.

But who may abide the day of his coming? and who shall stand when he appeareth? for he is like a refiner's fire, and like fullers' soap:

And he shall sit as a refiner and purifier of silver: and he shall purify the sons of Levi, and purge them as gold and silver, that they may offer unto the Lord an offering in righteousness.

Malachi 3:1–3

9 The last great age, foretold by sacred rhymes,
Renews its finished course: Saturnian times
Roll round again; and mighty years, begun
From their first orb, in radiant circles run.
The base degenerate iron offspring ends:
A golden progeny from heaven descends.
O chaste Lucina! speed the mother's pains;
And haste the glorious birth! thy own Apollo reigns!
The lovely boy, with his auspicious face,
Shall Pollio's consulship and triumph grace:
Majestic months set out with him to their appointed race.
The father banished virtue shall restore;
And crimes shall threat the guilty world no more.
The son shall lead the life of gods, and be
By gods and heroes seen, and gods and heroes see.
The jarring nations he in peace shall bind,
And with paternal virtues rule mankind.

Virgil, *Eclogues*, IV

10 Every valley shall be filled, and every mountain and hill shall be brought low; and the crooked shall be made straight, and the rough ways shall be made smooth;

And all flesh shall see the salvation of God.

Luke 3:5–6

11 There shall be signs in the sun, and in the moon, and in the stars; and upon the earth distress of nations, with perplexity; the sea and the waves roaring;

Men's hearts failing them for fear, and for looking after those things which are coming on the earth: for the powers of heaven shall be shaken.

And then shall they see the Son of man coming in a cloud with power and great glory.

And when these things begin to come to pass, then look up, and lift up your heads; for your redemption draweth nigh.

Luke 21:25–28

12 The next day John seeth Jesus coming unto him, and saith, Behold the Lamb of God, which taketh away the sin of the world.

John 1:29

13 And as Moses lifted up the serpent in the wilderness, even so must the Son of man be lifted up:

That whosoever believeth in him should not perish, but have eternal life.

For God so loved the world, that he gave his only begotten Son, that whosoever believeth in him should not perish, but have everlasting life.

John 3:14–16

14 Then Jesus said unto them, Verily, verily, I say unto you, Moses gave you not that bread from heaven; but my Father giveth you the true bread from heaven.

For the bread of God is he which cometh down from heaven, and giveth life unto the world.

Then said they unto him, Lord, evermore give us this bread.

And Jesus said unto them, I am the bread of life: he that cometh to me shall never hunger; and he that believeth on me shall never thirst.

But I said unto you, That ye also have seen me, and believe not.

All that the Father giveth me shall come to me; and him that cometh to me I will in no wise cast out.

For I came down from heaven, not to do mine own will, but the will of him that sent me.

And this is the Father's will which hath sent me, that of all which he hath given me I should lose nothing, but should raise it up again at the last day.

And this is the will of him that sent me, that every one which seeth the Son, and believeth on him, may have everlasting life: and I will raise him up at the last day.

John 6:32–40

15 If any man hear my words, and believe not, I judge him not: for I came not to judge the world, but to save the world.

John 12:47

16 Eye hath not seen, nor ear heard, neither have entered into the heart of man, the things which God hath prepared for them that love him.

I Corinthians 2:9

17 Ye are not your own. For ye are bought with a price: therefore glorify God in your body, and in your spirit, which are God's.

I Corinthians 6:19–20

18 For by grace are ye saved through faith; and that not of yourselves: it is the gift of God.

Ephesians 2:8

19 Let the wicked in their restlessness go from Thee and flee away. Yet Thou dost see them, cleaving through their darkness. And all the universe is beautiful about them, but they are vile. What harm have they done Thee? Or have they brought dishonour upon Thy government, which from the heavens unto the latest things of earth is just and perfect? Where indeed did they flee to when they fled from Thy face? Or where dost Thou not find them? The truth is that they fled, that they might not see Thee who sawest them. And so with eyes blinded they stumbled against Thee—for Thou dost not desert any of the things that Thou hast made—they stumbled against Thee in their injustice and justly suffered, since they had withdrawn from Thy mercy and stumbled against Thy justice and fallen headlong upon Thy wrath. Plainly they do not know that Thou art everywhere whom no place compasses in, and that Thou alone art ever present even to those that go furthest from Thee. Let them therefore turn back and seek Thee because Thou hast not deserted Thy creatures as they have deserted their Creator. Let them turn back, and behold Thou art there in their hearts, in the hearts of those that confess to Thee and cast themselves upon Thee and weep on Thy breast as they return from ways of anguish. Gently Thou dost wipe away their tears and they weep the more and are consoled in their weeping: because Thou, Lord, and not any man that is only flesh and blood, Thou, Lord who hast made them, dost remake them and give them comfort.

Augustine, *Confessions,* V, 2

20 The true Mediator, whom in the secret of Your mercy You have shown to men and sent to men, that by His example they might learn humility— the Mediator between God and men, the man Christ Jesus, appeared between sinful mortals and the immortal Just One: for like men He was mortal, like God He was Just; so that, the wages of justice being life and peace, He might, through the union of His own justice with God, make void the death of those sinners whom He justified by choosing to undergo death as they do. He was shown forth to holy men of old that they might be saved by faith in His Passion to come, as we by faith in His Passion now that He has suffered it. As man, He is Mediator; but as Word, He is not something in between, for He is equal to God, God with God, and together one God.

Augustine, *Confessions,* X, 43

21 How much Thou hast loved us, O good Father, *Who hast spared not even Thine own Son, but delivered Him up for us wicked men!* How Thou hast loved us, for whom He who *thought it not robbery to be equal with Thee became obedient even unto the death of the Cross,* He who alone *was free among the dead, having power to lay down His life and power to take it up again:* for us He was to Thee both Victor and Victim, and Victor because Victim: for us He was to Thee both Priest and Sacrifice, and Priest because Sacrifice: turning us from slaves into Thy sons, by being Thy Son and becoming a slave. Rightly is my hope strong in Him, who sits at Thy right hand and intercedes for us; otherwise I should despair. For many and great are my infirmities, many and great; but Thy medicine is of more power. We might well have thought Thy Word remote from union with man and so have despaired of ourselves, if It had not been *made flesh and dwelt among us.*

Augustine, *Confessions*, X, 43

22 If . . . it must needs be that all men, so long as they are mortal, are also miserable, we must seek an intermediate who is not only man, but also God, that, by the interposition of His blessed mortality, He may bring men out of their mortal misery to a blessed immortality. In this intermediate two things are requisite, that He become mortal and that He do not continue mortal. He did become mortal, not rendering the divinity of the Word infirm, but assuming the infirmity of flesh. Neither did He continue mortal in the flesh, but raised it from the dead; for it is the very fruit of His mediation that those, for the sake of whose redemption He became the Mediator, should not abide eternally in bodily death. Wherefore it became the Mediator between us and God to have both a transient mortality and a permanent blessedness, that by that which is transient He might be assimilated to mortals, and might translate them from mortality to that which is permanent.

Augustine, *City of God*, IX, 15

23 God's Son, assuming humanity without destroying His divinity, established and founded this faith, that there might be a way for man to man's God through a God-man. For this is the Mediator between God and men, the man Christ Jesus. For it is as man that He is the Mediator and the Way. Since, if the way lieth between him who goes and the place whither he goes, there is hope of his reaching it; but if there be no way, or if he know not where it is, what boots it to know whither he should go? Now the only way that is infallibly secured against all mistakes, is when the very same person is at once God and man, God our end, man our way.

Augustine, *City of God*, XI, 2

24 The salvation of man could not be achieved otherwise than through Christ. . . . *There is no other name . . . given to men, whereby we must be saved.* Consequently the law that brings all in a perfect way to salvation could not be given until after the coming of Christ. But before His coming it was necessary to give to the people of whom Christ was to be born, a law containing certain rudiments of saving justice, in order to prepare them to receive Him.

Aquinas, *Summa Theologica*, I–II, 91, 5

25 Man, by his natural endowments, cannot produce meritorious works proportionate to everlasting life, but for this a higher power is needed, namely, the power of grace. And thus without grace man cannot merit everlasting life. Yet he can perform works conducing to a good which is natural to man, as to toil in the fields, to drink, to eat, or to have friends, and the like.

Aquinas, *Summa Theologica*, I–II, 109, 5

26 There is a twofold grace: one whereby man himself is united to God, and this is called sanctifying grace; the other is that whereby one man co-operates with another in leading him to God, and this gift is called gratuitous grace, since it is bestowed on a man beyond the capability of nature, and beyond the merit of the person. But whereas it is bestowed on a man not to justify him, but rather that he may co-operate in the justification of another, it is not called sanctifying grace.

Aquinas, *Summa Theologica*, I–II, 111, 1

27 God does not justify us without ourselves, because whilst we are being justified we consent to God's justice by a movement of our free choice. Nevertheless this movement is not the cause of grace, but the effect; hence the whole operation pertains to grace.

Aquinas, *Summa Theologica*, I–II, 111, 2

28 By taking flesh, God did not lessen His majesty, and in consequence did not lessen the reason for reverencing Him, which is increased by the increase of knowledge of Him. But, on the contrary, because He wished to draw near to us by taking flesh, He drew us to know Him the more.

Aquinas, *Summa Theologica*, III, 1, 2

29 Although it belongs to Christ as God to take away sin as having the authority, yet it belongs to Him as man to satisfy for the sin of the human race. And in this sense He is called the Mediator of God and men.

Aquinas, *Summa Theologica*, III, 26, 2

30 After we were on the upper edge of the high cliff, out on the open hillside, "Master mine," said I, "what way shall we take?"
And he [Virgil] to me: "Let no step of thine de-

scend, ever up the mount behind me win thy
way, until some wise escort appear to us. . . .
This mountain is such, that ever at the beginning below 'tis toilsome, and the more a man
ascends the less it wearies.

Therefore when it shall seem to thee so pleasant
that the ascending becomes to thee easy, even
as in a boat to descend with the stream,

then shalt thou be at the end of this path: there
hope to rest thy weariness."

Dante, *Purgatorio*, IV, 34

31 "But tell us, if thou knowest, why the mount gave
before such shakings, and wherefore all seemed
to shout with one voice down to its soft base."

Thus, by asking, did he [Virgil] thread the very
needle's eye of my desire, and with the hope
alone my thirst was made less fasting.

That spirit [Statius] began: "The holy rule of the
mount suffereth naught that is arbitrary, or
that is outside custom.

Here it is free from all terrestrial change; that
which Heaven receives into itself from itself
may here operate as cause, and naught else:

since neither rain, nor hail, nor snow, nor dew,
nor hoarfrost, falls any higher than the short
little stairway of the three steps.

Clouds, dense or thin, appear not, nor lightning
flash, nor Thaumas' daughter, who yonder oft
changes her region.

Dry vapour rises not higher than the top of the
three steps which I spake of, where Peter's vicar
hath his feet.

It quakes perchance lower down little or much,
but by reason of wind which is hidden in the
earth, I know not how, it has never quaked up
here.

It quakes here when some soul feeleth herself
cleansed, so that she may rise up, or set forth, to
mount on high, and such a shout follows her.

Of the cleansing the will alone gives proof, which
fills the soul, all free to change her cloister, and
avails her to will.

She wills indeed before, but that desire permits it
not which divine justice sets, counter to will,
toward the penalty, even as it was toward the
sin.

And I who have lain under this torment five hundred years and more, only now felt free will for
a better threshold.

Therefore didst thou feel the earthquake, and
hear the pious spirits about the mount give
praises to that Lord—soon may he send them
above."

Dante, *Purgatorio*, XXI, 34

32 When the stairway was all sped beneath us, and
we were upon the topmost step, on me did Virgil fix his eyes,

and said: "Son, the temporal fire and the eternal,

hast thou seen, and art come to a place where I,
of myself, discern no further.

Here have I brought thee with wit and with art;
now take thy pleasure for guide; forth art thou
from the steep ways, forth art from the narrow.

Behold there the sun that shineth on thy brow
behold the tender grass, the flowers, and the
shrubs, which the ground here of itself alone
brings forth.

While the glad fair eyes are coming, which weeping made me come to thee, thou canst sit thee
down and canst go among them.

No more expect my word, nor my sign. Free, upright, and whole, is thy will, and 'twere a fault
not to act according to its prompting; wherefore
I do crown and mitre thee over thyself."

Dante, *Purgatorio*, XXVII, 124

33 Even if in the power of the Holy Spirit a man
were to keep the law completely, he ought nevertheless to pray for divine mercy, for God has ordained that man should be saved not by the law
but by Christ.

Luther, *Table Talk*, 85

34 There is nothing so easy, so gentle, and so favorable as the divine law; she calls us to herself, sinful
and detestable as we are; she stretches out her
arms to us and takes us to her bosom, no matter
how vile, filthy, and besmirched we are now and
are to be in the future. But still, in return, we
must look on her in the right way. We must receive this pardon with thanksgiving, and, at least
for that instant when we address ourselves to her,
have a soul remorseful for its sins and at enmity
with the passions that have driven us to offend
her.

Montaigne, *Essays*, I, 56, Of Prayers

35 If we held to God by the mediation of a living
faith, if we held to God through him and not
through ourselves, if we had a divine foothold and
foundation, human accidents would not have the
power to shake us as they do. Our fort would not
be prone to surrender to so weak a battery; the
love of novelty, the constraint of princes, the good
fortune of one party, a heedless and accidental
change in our opinions, would not have the power
to shake and alter our belief; we would not allow
it to be troubled by every new argument or by
persuasion, not even by all the rhetoric there ever
was; we should withstand those waves with inflexible and immobile firmness. . . . If this ray of divinity touched us at all, it would appear all over:
not only our words, but also our works would bear
its light and luster. Everything that came from us
would be seen to be illuminated by this noble
brightness.

Montaigne, *Essays*, II, 12, Apology
for Raymond Sebond

36 *Lear.* No, no, no, no! Come, let's away to prison.

We two alone will sing like birds i' the cage;
When thou dost ask me blessing, I'll kneel down,
And ask of thee forgiveness; so we'll live,
And pray, and sing, and tell old tales, and laugh
At gilded butterflies, and hear poor rogues
Talk of court news; and we'll talk with them too,
Who loses and who wins; who's in, who's out;
And take upon's the mystery of things,
As if we were God's spies; and we'll wear out,
In a wall'd prison, packs and sects of great ones,
That ebb and flow by the moon.

Shakespeare, *Lear,* V, iii, 8

37 And now, my Friend, said he [Don Quixote], turning to *Sancho,* pardon me that I have brought upon thee, as well as my self, the Scandal of Madness, by drawing thee into my own Errors, and persuading thee that there have been and still are Knights-Errant in the World. Woe is me, my dear Master's Worship! cry'd *Sancho,* all in Tears, don't die this Bout, but e'en take My Counsel, and live on a many Years; 'tis the maddest Trick a Man can ever play in his whole Life, to let his Breath sneak out of his Body without any more ado, and without so much as a Rap o'er the Pate, or a Kick of the Guts; to go out *like the Snuff of a Farthing-Candle,* and die merely of the Mulligrubs, or the Sullens. For Shame, Sir, don't give way to Sluggishness, but get out of your doleful Dumps, and rise. Is this a Time to lie honing and groaning a Bed, when we shou'd be in the Fields in our Shepherd's Cloathing, as we had resolv'd? Ten to one but behind some Bush, or under some Hedge, we may find the Lady Madam *Dulcinea,* strip'd of her inchanted Rags, and as fine as a Queen. Mayhaps you take it to Heart, that you were unhors'd, and a little Crupper-scratched t'other Day; but if that be all, lay the Blame upon Me, and say 'twas My Fault, in not girting *Rosinante* tight enough. You know too, there's nothing more common in your Errantry-Books, than for the Knights to be every Foot jostl'd out of the Saddle. There's nothing but Ups and Downs in this World, and he that's cast down to Day, may be a cock-a-hoop to Morrow. Even so, said *Sampson,* honest *Sancho* has a right Notion of the Matter. Soft and fair, Gentleman, reply'd Don *Quixote,* ne'er look for Birds of this Year in the Nests of the last: I was mad, but I am now in my Senses; I was once Don *Quixote de la Mancha,* but am now (as I said before) the plain *Alonso Quixano,* and I hope the Sincerity of my Words, and my Repentance, may restore me the same Esteem you have had for me before.

Cervantes, *Don Quixote,* II, 74

38 Salvation of a sinner supposeth a precedent *redemption;* for he that is once guilty of sin is obnoxious to the penalty of the same; and must pay, or some other for him, such ransom as he that is offended, and has him in his power, shall require. And seeing the person offended is Almighty God,

in whose power are all things, such ransom is to be paid before salvation can be acquired, as God hath been pleased to require. By this ransom is not intended a satisfaction for sin equivalent to the offence, which no sinner for himself, nor righteous man can ever be able to make for another: the damage a man does to another he may make amends for by restitution or recompense, but sin cannot be taken away by recompense; for that were to make the liberty to sin a thing vendible.

Hobbes, *Leviathan,* III, 38

39 I believe many are saved, who to man seem reprobated; and many are reprobated, who in the opinion and sentence of man, stand elected: there will appear at the Last day, strange and unexpected examples both of his Justice and his Mercy.

Sir Thomas Browne, *Religio Medici,* I, 57

40 The Catholic religion does not bind us to confess our sins indiscriminately to everybody; it allows them to remain hidden from all other men save one, to whom she bids us reveal the innermost recesses of our heart and show ourselves as we are. There is only this one man in the world whom she orders us to undeceive, and she binds him to an inviolable secrecy, which makes this knowledge to him as if it were not. Can we imagine anything more charitable and pleasant? And yet the corruption of man is such that he finds even this law harsh; and it is one of the main reasons which has caused a great part of Europe to rebel against the Church.

How unjust and unreasonable is the heart of man, which feels it disagreeable to be obliged to do in regard to one man what in some measure it were right to do to all men! For is it right that we should deceive men?

Pascal, *Pensées,* II, 100

41 Grace is indeed needed to turn a man into a saint; and he who doubts it does not know what a saint or a man is.

Pascal, *Pensées,* VII, 508

42 The Incarnation shows man the greatness of his misery by the greatness of the remedy which he required.

Pascal, *Pensées,* VII, 526

43 This is the Month, and this the happy morn
Wherin the Son of Heav'ns eternal King,
Of wedded Maid, and Virgin Mother born,
Our great redemption from above did bring;
For so the holy sages once did sing,
    That our deadly forfeit should release,
And with his Father work us a perpetual peace.

Milton, *On the Morning of Christs Nativity,* 1

44 *God.*   Man falls deceiv'd
By the other [Satan] first: Man therefore shall
    find grace,

The other none: in Mercy and Justice both,
Through Heav'n and Earth, so shall my glorie
excel,
But Mercy first and last shall brightest shine.

> Milton, *Paradise Lost,* III, 130

45 *God.*   Man disobeying,
Disloyal breaks his fealtie, and sinns
Against the high Supremacie of Heav'n,
Affecting God-head, and so loosing all,
To expiate his Treason hath naught left,
But to destruction sacred and devote,
He with his whole posteritie must die,
Die hee or Justice must; unless for him
Som other able, and as willing, pay
The rigid satisfaction, death for death.

> Milton, *Paradise Lost,* III, 203

46 *Christ.* Behold mee, then, mee for him, life for life
I offer, on mee let thine anger fall;
Account mee man; I for his sake will leave
Thy bosom, and this glorie next to thee
Freely put off, and for him lastly die
Well pleas'd, on me let Death wreck all his rage.

> Milton, *Paradise Lost,* III, 236

47 If salvation lay ready to hand and could be discovered without great labour, how could it be possible that it should be neglected almost by everybody? But all noble things are as difficult as they are rare.

> Spinoza, *Ethics,* V, Prop. 42, Schol.

48 When these men had thus bravely shewed themselves against *Doubting Castle,* and had slain *Giant Despair,* they went forward, and went on till they came to the *Delectable* Mountains, where *Christian* and *Hopeful* refreshed themselves with the Varieties of the Place. They also acquainted themselves with the Shepherds there, who welcomed them as they had done *Christian* before, unto the Delectable Mountains.

> Bunyan, *Pilgrim's Progress,* II

49 It was noised abroad that Mr. *Valiant-for-truth* was taken with a Summons, by the same *Post* as the other, and had this for a Token that the Summons was true, *That his Pitcher was broken at the Fountain.* When he understood it, he called for his Friends, and told them of it. Then said he, I am going to my Fathers, and tho' with great Difficulty I am got hither, yet now I do not repent me of all the Trouble I have been at to arrive where I am. *My Sword,* I give to him that shall succeed me in my Pilgrimage, and my *Courage* and *Skill,* to him that can get it. My *Marks* and *Scars* I carry with me, to be a Witness for me, that I have fought his Battles who now will be my Rewarder. When the Day that he must go hence, was come, many accompanied him to the River side, into which, as he went,

he said, *Death, where is thy Sting?* And as he went down deeper, he said, *Grave, where is thy Victory?* So he passed over, and all the Trumpets sounded for him on the other side.

> Bunyan, *Pilgrim's Progress,* II

50 There are a thousand ways to wealth, but one only way to heaven.

> Locke, *Letter Concerning Toleration*

51 No way whatsoever that I shall walk in against the dictates of my conscience will ever bring me to the mansions of the blessed. I may grow rich by an art that I take not delight in; I may be cured of some disease by remedies that I have not faith in; but I cannot be saved by a religion that I distrust and by a worship that I abhor. It is in vain for an unbeliever to take up the outward show of another man's profession. Faith only and inward sincerity are the things that procure acceptance with God.

> Locke, *Letter Concerning Toleration*

52 He shall not die, by G—, cried my uncle Toby.
——The Accusing Spirit, which flew up to heaven's chancery with the oath, blushed as he gave it in;—and the Recording Angel, as he wrote it down, dropped a tear upon the word, and blotted it out for ever.

> Sterne, *Tristram Shandy,* VI, 8

53 I proceeded: "What do you think, Sir, of Purgatory, as believed by the Roman Catholicks?" *Johnson.* "Why, Sir, it is a very harmless doctrine. They are of opinion that the generality of mankind are neither so obstinately wicked as to deserve everlasting punishment, nor so good as to merit being admitted into the society of blessed spirits; and therefore that GOD is graciously pleased to allow of a middle state, where they may be purified by certain degrees of suffering. You see, Sir, there is nothing unreasonable in this."

> Boswell, *Life of Johnson* (Oct. 26, 1769)

54 Dr. Johnson surprised him [Dr. Adams] not a little, by acknowledging with a look of horrour, that he was much oppressed by the fear of death. The amiable Dr. Adams suggested that GOD was infinitely good. *Johnson.* "That he is infinitely good, as far as the perfection of his nature will allow, I certainly believe; but it is necessary for good upon the whole, that individuals should be punished. As to an *individual,* therefore, he is not infinitely good; and as I cannot be *sure* that I have fulfilled the conditions on which salvation is granted, I am afraid I may be one of those who shall be damned," (looking dismally). *Dr. Adams.* "What do you mean by damned?" *Johnson.* (passionately and loudly,) "Sent to Hell, Sir, and punished everlastingly!" *Dr. Adams.* "I don't believe that doctrine." *Johnson.* "Hold, Sir, do you believe that some will

be punished at all?" *Dr. Adams.* "Being excluded from Heaven will be a punishment; yet there may be no great positive suffering." *Johnson.* "Well, Sir; but, if you admit any degree of punishment, there is an end of your argument for infinite goodness simply considered; for, infinite goodness would inflict no punishment whatever. There is not infinite goodness physically considered; morally there is."

Boswell, Life of Johnson (June 12, 1784)

55   The Holy Ghost over the bent
World broods with warm breast and with ah!
    bright wings.

G. M. Hopkins, God's Grandeur

56 The ordinary moralistic state of mind makes the salvation of the world conditional upon the success with which each unit does its part. Partial and conditional salvation is in fact a most familiar notion when taken in the abstract, the only difficulty being to determine the details. Some men are even disinterested enough to be willing to be in the unsaved remnant as far as their persons go, if only they can be persuaded that their cause will prevail—all of us are willing, whenever our activity-excitement rises sufficiently high. I think, in fact, that a final philosophy of religion will have to consider the pluralistic hypothesis more seriously than it has hitherto been willing to consider it. For practical life at any rate, the *chance* of salvation is enough. No fact in human nature is more characteristic than its willingness to live on a chance.

William James, Varieties of Religious Experience, Postscript

20.15 | *Heaven and Hell*

Whereas redemption and salvation through the intercession of a divine mediator is, for the most part, a Christian doctrine and a distinguishing feature of the Christian religion, heaven and hell figure significantly among the religious beliefs of pagan antiquity, though usually under other names, such as Hades and the Elysian Fields. Hence the ancient poets, and particularly Homer and Virgil who recount visits by their heroes to the abode of the shades, take their place here, along with Dante and Milton, among the authors depicting the joys of the blessed and the tortures of the damned. On the other hand, Plato, who, among ancient philosophers, is most concerned with the immortality of the soul and the judgment it is subject to after death, conceives divine rewards and punishments in terms of reincarnation, accompanied by a better or worse earthly life, rather than in terms of heaven and hell.

As the quotations below indicate, many are the questions asked and answered by medieval theologians concerning the state of the damned in hell and the condition of the blessed in heaven: such questions as whether the tortures of hell are mainly spiritual or physical; whether the pain of loss or deprivation or the pain of sense constitutes the reality of hell; whether references to "hell-fire" are to be interpreted literally or metaphorically; whether the blessed in heaven are aware of the tortures of the damned and whether they take pleasure in such awareness; whether there are lower and higher levels of beatitude in heaven as there are less and more intense gradations of punishment in hell; and whether the reincarnation of the body and its being reunited with the soul in heaven increases the joys of the blessed.

In the secular literature of a later age, the joys of heaven and the terrors of hell tend to become less vivid and approach the vanishing point of unreality. Nevertheless, even with loss of belief in their reality, they remain as symbols of joy and misery, betokening the fulfillment of man's highest hopes or his abandonment to utter despair. There is also, in the quotations from more recent writers, a strain of satire concerning the preferability of hell to heaven in terms of who is there and what is going on in each place, summed up in a statement by Mark Twain not quoted here: "Heaven for climate, Hell for society."

For the discussion of closely related matters, the reader is referred to Section 20.7 on ANGELS AND DEVILS, Section 20.13 on SIN AND TEMPTATION, and Section 20.14 on REDEMPTON AND SALVATION.

---

1 The children of men put their trust under the shadow of thy wings.

They shall be abundantly satisfied with the fatness of thy house; and thou shalt make them drink of the river of thy pleasures.

For with thee is the fountain of life: in thy light shall we see light.

Psalm 36:7–9

2 I had rather be a doorkeeper in the house of my God, than to dwell in the tents of wickedness.

Psalm 84:10

3 Hell from beneath is moved for thee to meet thee at thy coming: it stirreth up the dead for thee, even all the chief ones of the earth; it hath raised up from their thrones all the kings of the nations.

All they shall speak and say unto thee, Art thou also become weak as we? art thou become like unto us?

Thy pomp is brought down to the grave, and the noise of thy viols: the worm is spread under thee, and the worms cover thee.

How art thou fallen from heaven, O Lucifer, son of the morning! how art thou cut down to the ground, which didst weaken the nations!

For thou hast said in thine heart, I will ascend into heaven, I will exalt my throne above the stars of God: I will sit also upon the mount of the congregation, in the sides of the north:

I will ascend above the heights of the clouds; I will be like the most High.

Yet thou shalt be brought down to hell, to the sides of the pit.

They that see thee shall narrowly look upon thee, and consider thee, saying, Is this the man that made the earth to tremble, that did shake kingdoms;

That made the world as a wilderness, and destroyed the cities thereof; that opened not the house of his prisoners?

All the kings of the nations, even all of them, lie in glory, every one in his own house.

But thou art cast out of thy grave like an abominable branch, and as the raiment of those that are slain, thrust through with a sword; that go down to the stones of the pit; as a carcase trodden under feet.

Thou shalt not be joined with them in burial, because thou hast destroyed thy land, and slain thy people: the seed of evildoers shall never be renowned.

Isaiah 14:9–20

4 [Hephaistos] spoke, and the goddess of the white arms Hera smiled at him,

and smiling she accepted the goblet out of her son's hand.

Thereafter beginning from the left he poured drinks for the other

gods, dipping up from the mixing bowl the sweet nectar.

But among the blessed immortals uncontrollable laughter

went up as they saw Hephaistos bustling about the palace.

Thus thereafter the whole day long until the sun went under

they feasted, nor was anyone's hunger denied a fair portion,

nor denied the beautifully wrought lyre in the hands of Apollo

nor the antiphonal sweet sound of the Muses singing.

Afterwards when the light of the flaming sun went under

they went away each one to sleep in his home where

for each one the far-renowned strong-handed Hephaistos

had built a house by means of his craftsmanship and cunning.

Zeus the Olympian and lord of the lightning went to

his own bed, where always he lay when sweet sleep came on him.

Going up to the bed he slept and Hera of the gold throne beside him.

Homer, *Iliad*, I, 595

5 *Poseidon.*   We are three brothers born by Rheia
to Kronos,
Zeus, and I, and the third is Hades, lord of the
dead men.
All was divided among us three ways, each given
his domain.
I when the lots were shaken drew the grey sea to
live in
forever; Hades drew the lot of the mists and the
darkness,
and Zeus was allotted the wide sky, in the cloud
and the bright air.
But earth and high Olympos are common to all
three.

Homer, *Iliad,* XV, 187

6   She departed, grey-eyed Athena,
to where the gods have their eternal dwelling—
as men say—in the fastness of Olympos.
Never a tremor of wind, or a splash of rain,
no errant snowflake comes to stain that heaven,
so calm, so vaporless, the world of light.
Here, where the gay gods live their days of pleasure,
the grey-eyed one withdrew.

Homer, *Odyssey,* VI, 40

7 *Odysseus.* We made the land, put ram and ewe
ashore,
and took our way along the Ocean stream
to find the place foretold for us by Kirkê.
There Perimêdês and Eurýlokhos
pinioned the sacred beasts. With my drawn blade
I spaded up the votive pit, and poured
libations round it to the unnumbered dead:
sweet milk and honey, then sweet wine, and last
clear water; and I scattered barley down.
Then I addressed the blurred and breathless dead,
vowing to slaughter my best heifer for them
before she calved, at home in Ithaka,
and burn the choice bits on the altar fire;
as for Teirêsias, I swore to sacrifice
a black lamb, handsomest of all our flock.
Thus to assuage the nations of the dead
I pledged these rites, then slashed the lamb and
ewe,
letting their black blood stream into the wellpit.
Now the souls gathered, stirring out of Erebos,
brides and young men, and men grown old in
pain,
and tender girls whose hearts were new to grief;
many were there, too, torn by brazen lanceheads,
battle-slain, bearing still their bloody gear.
From every side they came and sought the pit
with rustling cries; and I grew sick with fear.

Homer, *Odyssey,* XI, 20

8 *Odysseus.* Then I saw Tántalos put to the torture:
in a cool pond he stood, lapped round by water
clear to the chin, and being athirst he burned
to slake his dry weasand with drink, though drink

he would not ever again. For when the old man
put his lips down to the sheet of water
it vanished round his feet, gulped underground,
and black mud baked there in a wind from hell.
Boughs, too, drooped low above him, big with
fruit,
pear trees, pomegranates, brilliant apples,
luscious figs, and olives ripe and dark;
but if he stretched his hand for one, the wind
under the dark sky tossed the bough beyond him.

Homer, *Odyssey,* XI, 581

9 *Odysseus.* Heraklês, down the vistas of the dead,
faded from sight; but I stood fast, awaiting
other great souls who perished in times past.
I should have met, then, god-begotten Theseus
and Peirithoös, whom both I longed to see,
but first came shades in thousands, rustling
in a pandemonium of whispers, blown together,
and the horror took me that Perséphonê
had brought from darker hell some saurian
death's head.

Homer, *Odyssey,* XI, 627

10 *Theonoë.*   All men, in the world below and in the
world
above must pay for acts committed here. The
mind
of those who have died, blown into the immortal
air,
immortally has knowledge, though all life is gone.

Euripides, *Helen,* 1013

11 *Socrates.* In the days of Cronos there existed a law
respecting the destiny of man, which has always
been, and still continues to be in Heaven—that he
who has lived all his life in justice and holiness
shall go, when he is dead, to the Islands of the
Blessed, and dwell there in perfect happiness out
of the reach of evil; but that he who has lived
unjustly and impiously shall go to the house of
vengeance and punishment, which is called Tartarus.

Plato, *Gorgias,* 523A

12 *Socrates.* I will tell you a tale; not one of the tales
which Odysseus tells to the hero Alcinous, yet this
too is a tale of a hero, Er the son of Armenius, a
Pamphylian by birth. He was slain in battle, and
ten days afterwards, when the bodies of the dead
were taken up already in a state of corruption, his
body was found unaffected by decay, and carried
away home to be buried. And on the twelfth day,
as he was lying on the funeral pile, he returned to
life and told them what he had seen in the other
world. He said that when his soul left the body he
went on a journey with a great company, and that
they came to a mysterious place at which there
were two openings in the earth; they were near
together, and over against them were two other
openings in the heaven above. In the intermediate

space there were judges seated, who commanded the just, after they had given judgment on them and had bound their sentences in front of them, to ascend by the heavenly way on the right hand; and in like manner the unjust were bidden by them to descend the lower way on the left hand; these also bore the symbols of their deeds, but fastened on their backs. He drew near, and they told him that he was to be the messenger who would carry the report of the other world to men, and they bade him hear and see all that was to be heard and seen in that place. Then he beheld and saw on one side the souls departing at either opening of heaven and earth when sentence had been given on them; and at the two other openings other souls, some ascending out of the earth dusty and worn with travel, some descending out of heaven clean and bright. And arriving ever and anon they seemed to have come from a long journey, and they went forth with gladness into the meadow, where they encamped as at a festival; and those who knew one another embraced and conversed, the souls which came from earth curiously enquiring about the things above, and the souls which came from heaven about the things beneath. And they told one another of what had happened by the way, those from below weeping and sorrowing at the remembrance of the things which they had endured and seen in their journey beneath the earth (now the journey lasted a thousand years), while those from above were describing heavenly delights and visions of inconceivable beauty.

Plato, *Republic*, X, 614A

13 So pray'd the Trojan prince, and, while he pray'd,
His hand upon the holy altar laid.
Then thus replied the prophetess divine:
"O goddess-born of great Anchises' line,
The gates of hell are open night and day;
Smooth the descent, and easy is the way:
But to return, and view the cheerful skies,
In this the task and mighty labor lies.
To few great Jupiter imparts this grace,
And those of shining worth and heav'nly race,
Betwixt those regions and our upper light,
Deep forests and impenetrable night
Possess the middle space: th' infernal bounds
Cocytus, with his sable waves, surrounds.
But if so dire a love your soul invades,
As twice below to view the trembling shades;
If you so hard a toil will undertake,
As twice to pass th' innavigable lake;
Receive my counsel. In the neighb'ring grove
There stands a tree; the queen of Stygian Jove
Claims it her own; thick woods and gloomy night
Conceal the happy plant from human sight.
One bough it bears; but (wondrous to behold!)
The ductile rind and leaves of radiant gold:
This from the vulgar branches must be torn,
And to fair Proserpine the present borne,

Ere leave be giv'n to tempt the nether skies.
The first thus rent a second will arise,
And the same metal the same room supplies.
Look round the wood, with lifted eyes, to see
The lurking gold upon the fatal tree:
Then rend it off, as holy rites command;
The willing metal will obey thy hand.
Following with ease, if favor'd by thy fate,
Thou art foredoom'd to view the Stygian state:
If not, no labor can the tree constrain;
And strength of stubborn arms and steel are vain.
Besides, you know not, while you here attend,
Th' unworthy fate of your unhappy friend:
Breathless he lies; and his unburied ghost,
Depriv'd of fun'ral rites, pollutes your host.
Pay first his pious dues; and, for the dead,
Two sable sheep around his hearse be led;
Then, living turfs upon his body lay:
This done, securely take the destin'd way,
To find the regions destitute of day."
    She said, and held her peace.

Virgil, *Aeneid*, VI

14 Obscure they [Aeneas and the Prophetess] went
        thro' dreary shades, that led
Along the waste dominions of the dead.
Thus wander travelers in woods by night,
By the moon's doubtful and malignant light,
When Jove in dusky clouds involves the skies,
And the faint crescent shoots by fits before their
        eyes.
    Just in the gate and in the jaws of hell,
Revengeful Cares and sullen Sorrows dwell,
And pale Diseases, and repining Age,
Want, Fear, and Famine's unresisted rage;
Here Toils, and Death, and Dealth's half-brother,
        Sleep,
Forms terrible to view, their sentry keep;
With anxious Pleasures of a guilty mind,
Deep Frauds before, and open Force behind;
The Furies' iron beds; and Strife, that shakes
Her hissing tresses and unfolds her snakes.
Full in the midst of this infernal road,
An elm displays her dusky arms abroad:
The God of Sleep there hides his heavy head,
And empty dreams on ev'ry leaf are spread.
Of various forms unnumber'd specters more,
Centaurs, and double shapes, besiege the door.
Before the passage, horrid Hydra stands,
And Briareus with all his hundred hands;
Gorgons, Geryon with his triple frame;
And vain Chimæra vomits empty flame.
The chief unsheath'd his shining steel, prepar'd,
Tho' seiz'd with sudden fear, to force the guard,
Off'ring his brandish'd weapon at their face;
Had not the Sibyl stopp'd his eager pace,
And told him what those empty phantoms were:
Forms without bodies, and impassive air.
Hence to deep Acheron they take their way,
Whose troubled eddies, thick with ooze and clay,
Are whirl'd aloft, and in Cocytus lost.

There Charon stands, who rules the dreary
    coast—
A sordid god: down from his hoary chin
A length of beard descends, uncomb'd, unclean;
His eyes, like hollow furnaces on fire;
A girdle, foul with grease, binds his obscene attire.
He spreads his canvas; with his pole he steers;
The freights of flitting ghosts in his thin bottom
    bears.
He look'd in years; yet in his years were seen
A youthful vigor and autumnal green.
An airy crowd came rushing where he stood,
Which fill'd the margin of the fatal flood:
Husbands and wives, boys and unmarried maids,
And mighty heroes' more majestic shades,
And youths, intomb'd before their fathers' eyes,
With hollow groans, and shrieks, and feeble cries.
Thick as the leaves in autumn strow the woods,
Or fowls, by winter forc'd, forsake the floods,
And wing their hasty flight to happier lands;
Such, and so thick, the shiv'ring army stands,
And press for passage with extended hands.
Now these, now those, the surly boatman bore:
The rest he drove to distance from the shore.
The hero, who beheld with wond'ring eyes
The tumult mix'd with shrieks, laments, and cries,
Ask'd of his guide, what the rude concourse
    meant;
Why to the shore the thronging people bent;
What forms of law among the ghosts were us'd:
Why some were ferried o'er, and some refus'd.
    "Son of Anchises, offspring of the gods,"
The Sibyl said, "you see the Stygian floods,
The sacred stream which heav'n's imperial state
Attests in oaths, and fears to violate.
The ghosts rejected are th' unhappy crew
Depriv'd of sepulchers and fun'ral due:
The boatman, Charon; those, the buried host,
He ferries over to the farther coast;
Nor dares his transport vessel cross the waves
With such whose bones are not compos'd in
    graves.
A hundred years they wander on the shore;
At length, their penance done, are wafted o'er."

                      Virgil *Aeneid,* VI

15 No sooner landed, in his den they found
    The triple porter of the Stygian sound,
    Grim Cerberus, who soon began to rear
    His crested snakes, and arm'd his bristling hair.
    The prudent Sibyl had before prepar'd
    A sop, in honey steep'd, to charm the guard;
    Which, mix'd with pow'rful drugs, she cast before
    His greedy grinning jaws, just op'd to roar.
    With three enormous mouths he gapes; and
        straight,
    With hunger press'd, devours the pleasing bait.
    Long draughts of sleep his monstrous limbs en-
        slave;
    He reels, and, falling, fills the spacious cave.
    The keeper charm'd, the chief without delay

Pass'd on, and took th' irremeable way.

                      Virgil, *Aeneid,* VI

16 Before the gates, the cries of babes new-born,
    Whom fate had from their tender mothers torn,
    Assault his ears: then those whom form of laws
    Condemn'd to die, when traitors judg'd their
        cause.
    Nor want they lots, nor judges to review
    The wrongful sentence, and award a new.
    Minos, the strict inquisitor, appears;
    And lives and crimes, with his assessors, hears.
    Round in his urn the blended balls he rolls,
    Absolves the just, and dooms the guilty souls.
    The next, in place and punishment, are they
    Who prodigally throw their souls away;
    Fools, who, repining at their wretched state,
    And loathing anxious life, suborn'd their fate.
    With late repentance now they would retrieve
    The bodies they forsook, and wish to live;
    Their pains and poverty desire to bear,
    To view the light of heav'n, and breathe the vital
        air:
    But Fate forbids; the Stygian floods oppose,
    And with nine circling streams the captive souls
        inclose.

                      Virgil, *Aeneid,* VI

17 And they, perhaps, in words and tears had spent
    The little time of stay which Heav'n had lent;
    But thus the Sibyl chides their long delay:
    "Night rushes down, and headlong drives the day:
    'Tis here, in different paths, the way divides;
    The right to Pluto's golden palace guides;
    The left to that unhappy region tends,
    Which to the depth of Tartarus descends;
    The seat of night profound, and punish'd fiends."

                      Virgil, *Aeneid,* VI

18 They lie below, on golden beds display'd;
    And genial feasts with regal pomp are made.
    The Queen of Furies by their sides is set,
    And snatches from their mouths th' untasted
        meat,
    Which if they touch, her hissing snakes she rears,
    Tossing her torch, and thund'ring in their ears.
    Then they, who brothers' better claim disown,
    Expel their parents, and usurp the throne;
    Defraud their clients, and, to lucre sold,
    Sit brooding on unprofitable gold;
    Who dare not give, and e'en refuse to lend
    To their poor kindred, or a wanting friend.
    Vast is the throng of these; nor less the train
    Of lustful youths, for foul adult'ry slain:
    Hosts of deserters, who their honor sold,
    And basely broke their faith for bribes of gold.
    All these within the dungeon's depth remain,
    Despairing pardon, and expecting pain.
    Ask not what pains; nor farther seek to know
    Their process, or the forms of law below.
    Some roll a weighty stone; some, laid along,

And bound with burning wires, on spokes of
wheels are hung.
Unhappy Theseus, doom'd for ever there,
Is fix'd by Fate on his eternal chair;
And wretched Phlegyas warns the world with
cries
(Could warning make the world more just or
wise):
'Learn righteousness, and dread th' avenging dei-
ties.'
To tyrants others have their country sold,
Imposing foreign lords, for foreign gold;
Some have old laws repeal'd, new statutes made,
Not as the people pleas'd, but as they paid;
With incest some their daughters' bed profan'd:
All dar'd the worst of ills, and, what they dar'd,
attain'd.
Had I a hundred mouths, a hundred tongues,
And throats of brass, inspir'd with iron lungs,
I could not half those horrid crimes repeat,
Nor half the punishments those crimes have met.

Virgil, Aeneid, VI

19   They took their way
Where long extended plains of pleasure lay:
The verdant fields with those of heav'n may vie,
With ether vested, and a purple sky;
The blissful seats of happy souls below.
Stars of their own, and their own suns, they know;
Their airy limbs in sports they exercise,
And on the green contend the wrestler's prize.
Some in heroic verse divinely sing;
Others in artful measures lead the ring.
The Thracian bard, surrounded by the rest,
There stands conspicuous in his flowing vest;
His flying fingers, and harmonious quill,
Strikes sev'n distinguish'd notes, and sev'n at once
they fill. . . .
To these the Sibyl thus her speech address'd,
And first to him surrounded by the rest
(Tow'ring his height, and ample was his breast):
"Say, happy souls, divine Musæus, say,
Where lives Anchises, and where lies our way
To find the hero, for whose only sake
We sought the dark abodes, and cross'd the bitter
lake?"
To this the sacred poet thus replied:
"In no fix'd place the happy souls reside.
In groves we live, and lie on mossy beds,
By crystal streams, that murmur thro' the meads:
But pass yon easy hill, and thence descend;
The path conducts you to your journey's end."
This said, he led them up the mountain's brow,
And shews them all the shining fields below.
They wind the hill, and thro' the blissful meadows
go.

Virgil, Aeneid, VI

20 Nor death itself can wholly wash their stains;
But long-contracted filth e'en in the soul remains.
The relics of inveterate vice they wear,

And spots of sin obscene in ev'ry face appear.
For this are various penances enjoin'd;
And some are hung to bleach upon the wind,
Some plung'd in waters, others purg'd in fires,
Till all the dregs are drain'd, and all the rust ex-
pires.
All have their manes, and those manes bear:
The few, so cleans'd, to these abodes repair,
And breathe, in ample fields, the soft Elysian air.
Then are they happy, when by length of time
The scurf is worn away of each committed crime;
No speck is left of their habitual stains,
But the pure ether of the soul remains.

Virgil, Aeneid, VI

21 Lay not up for yourselves treasures upon earth,
where moth and rust doth corrupt, and where
thieves break through and steal:
   But lay up for yourselves treasures in heaven,
where neither moth nor rust doth corrupt, and
where thieves do not break through nor steal:
   For where your treasure is, there will your heart
be also.

Matthew 6:19–21

22 The kingdom of heaven is like unto a merchant
man, seeking goodly pearls:
   Who, when he had found one pearl of great
price, went and sold all that he had, and bought
it.

Matthew 13:45–46

23 The kingdom of heaven is like unto a net, that
was cast into the sea, and gathered of every kind:
   Which, when it was full, they drew to shore,
and sat down, and gathered the good into vessels,
but cast the bad away.
   So shall it be at the end of the world: the angels
shall come forth, and sever the wicked from
among the just,
   And shall cast them into the furnace of fire:
there shall be wailing and gnashing of teeth.

Matthew 13:47–50

24 For the kingdom of heaven is like unto a man that
is an householder, which went out early in the
morning to hire labourers into his vineyard.
   And when he had agreed with the labourers for
a penny a day, he sent them into his vineyard.
   And he went out about the third hour, and saw
others standing idle in the marketplace,
   And said unto them; Go ye also into the vineyard, and whatsoever is right I will give you. And
they went their way.
   Again he went out about the sixth and ninth
hour, and did likewise.
   And about the eleventh hour he went out, and
found others standing idle, and saith unto them,
Why stand ye here all the day idle?
   They say unto him, Because no man hath hired
us. He saith unto them, Go ye also into the vine-

yard; and whatsoever is right, that shall ye receive.

So when even was come, the lord of the vineyard saith unto his steward, Call the labourers, and give them their hire, beginning from the last unto the first.

And when they came that were hired about the eleventh hour, they received every man a penny.

But when the first came, they supposed that they should have received more; and they likewise received every man a penny.

And when they had received it, they murmured against the goodman of the house,

Saying, These last have wrought but one hour, and thou hast made them equal unto us, which have borne the burden and heat of the day.

But he answered one of them, and said, Friend, I do thee no wrong: didst not thou agree with me for a penny?

Take that thine is, and go thy way: I will give unto this last, even as unto thee.

Is it not lawful for me to do what I will with mine own? Is thine eye evil, because I am good?

So the last shall be first, and the first last: for many be called, but few chosen.

Matthew 20:1–16

25 When the Son of man shall come in his glory, and all the holy angels with him, then shall he sit upon the throne of his glory:

And before him shall be gathered all nations: and he shall separate them one from another, as a shepherd divideth his sheep from the goats:

And he shall set the sheep on his right hand, but the goats on the left.

Then shall the King say unto them on his right hand, Come, ye blessed of my Father, inherit the kingdom prepared for you from the foundation of the world.

Matthew 25:31–34

26 There was a certain rich man, which was clothed in purple and fine linen, and fared sumptuously every day:

And there was a certain beggar named Lazarus, which was laid at his gate full of sores,

And desiring to be fed with the crumbs which fell from the rich man's table: moreover the dogs came and licked his sores.

And it came to pass, that the beggar died, and was carried by the angels into Abraham's bosom: the rich man also died, and was buried;

And in hell he lift up his eyes, being in torments, and seeth Abraham afar off, and Lazarus in his bosom.

And he cried and said, Father Abraham, have mercy on me, and send Lazarus, that he may dip the tip of his finger in water, and cool my tongue; for I am tormented in this flame.

But Abraham said, Son, remember that thou in thy lifetime receivedst thy good things, and like-

wise Lazarus evil things: but now he is comforted, and thou art tormented.

And beside all this, between us and you there is a great gulf fixed: so that they which would pass from hence to you cannot; neither can they pass to us, that would come from thence.

Luke 16:19–26

27 In my Father's house are many mansions: if it were not so, I would have told you.

John 14:2

28 Behold, I shew you a mystery; We shall not all sleep, but we shall all be changed,

In a moment, in the twinkling of an eye, at the last trump: for the trumpet shall sound, and the dead shall be raised incorruptible, and we shall be changed.

For this corruptible must put on incorruption, and this mortal must put on immortality.

So when this corruptible shall have put on incorruption, and this mortal shall have put on immortality, then shall be brought to pass the saying that is written, Death is swallowed up in victory.

I Corinthians 15:51–54

29 One of the elders answered, saying unto me, What are these which are arrayed in white robes? and whence came they?

And I said unto him, Sir, thou knowest. And he said to me, These are they which came out of great tribulation, and have washed their robes, and made them white in the blood of the Lamb.

Therefore are they before the throne of God, and serve him day and night in his temple: and he that sitteth on the throne shall dwell among them.

They shall hunger no more, neither thirst any more; neither shall the sun light on them, nor any heat.

For the Lamb which is in the midst of the throne shall feed them, and shall lead them unto living fountains of waters: and God shall wipe away all tears from their eyes.

Revelation 7:13–17

30 I saw a new heaven and a new earth: for the first heaven and the first earth were passed away; and there was no more sea.

And I John saw the holy city, new Jerusalem, coming down from God out of heaven, prepared as a bride adorned for her husband.

And I heard a great voice out of heaven saying, Behold, the tabernacle of God is with men, and he will dwell with them, and they shall be his people, and God himself shall be with them, and be their God.

And God shall wipe away all tears from their eyes; and there shall be no more death, neither sorrow, nor crying, neither shall there be any more pain: for the former things are passed away.

And he that sat upon the throne said, Behold, I make all things new. And he said unto me, Write: for these words are true and faithful.

And he said unto me, It is done. I am Alpha and Ō-mĕg̱-ă, the beginning and the end. I will give unto him that is athirst of the fountain of the water of life freely.

He that overcometh shall inherit all things; and I will be his God, and he shall be my son.

Revelation 21:1–7

31 We must not . . . contrary to nature, send the bodies . . . of good men to heaven; but we must really believe that, according to their divine nature and law, their virtue and their souls are translated out of men into heroes, out of heroes into demi-gods, out of demi-gods, after passing, as in the rite of initiation, through a final cleansing and sanctification, and so freeing themselves from all that pertains to mortality and sense, are thus, not by human decree, but really and according to right reason, elevated into gods admitted thus to the greatest and most blessed perfection.

Plutarch, *Romulus*

32 If to any man the tumult of the flesh grew silent, silent the images of earth and sea and air: and if the heavens grew silent, and the very soul grew silent to herself and by not thinking of self mounted beyond self: if all dreams and imagined visions grew silent, and every tongue and every sign and whatsoever is transient—for indeed if any man could hear them, he should hear them saying with one voice: We did not make ourselves, but He made us who abides forever: but if, having uttered this and so set us to listening to Him who made them, they all grew silent, and in their silence He alone spoke to us, not by them but by Himself: so that we should hear His word, not by any tongue of flesh nor the voice of an angel nor the sound of thunder nor in the darkness of a parable, but that we should hear Himself whom in all these things we love, should hear Himself and not them . . . and if this could continue, and all other visions so different be quite taken away, and this one should so ravish and absorb and wrap the beholder in inward joys that his life should eternally be such as that one moment of understanding . . . would not this be: *Enter Thou into the joy of Thy Lord?* But when shall it be? Shall it be when *we shall all rise again* and *shall not all be changed?*

Augustine, *Confessions*, IX, 10

33 The bodies of the righteous . . . such as they shall be in the resurrection, shall need neither any fruit to preserve them from dying of disease or the wasting decay of old age, nor any other physical nourishment to allay the cravings of hunger or of thirst; for they shall be invested with so sure and every way inviolable an immortality, that they shall not eat save when they choose, nor be under the necessity of eating, while they enjoy the power of doing so.

Augustine, *City of God*, XIII, 22

34 Hell, which also is called a lake of fire and brimstone, will be material fire, and will torment the bodies of the damned, whether men or devils—the solid bodies of the one, aerial bodies of the others; or if only men have bodies as well as souls, yet the evil spirits, though without bodies, shall be so connected with the bodily fires as to receive pain without imparting life.

Augustine, *City of God*, XXI, 10

35 It may very well be, and it is thoroughly credible, that we shall in the future world see the material forms of the new heavens and the new earth in such a way that we shall most distinctly recognize God everywhere present and governing all things, material as well as spiritual, and shall see Him, not as now we understand the invisible things of God, by the things which are made, and see Him darkly, as in a mirror, and in part, and rather by faith than by bodily vision of material appearances, but by means of the bodies we shall wear and which we shall see wherever we turn our eyes.

Augustine, *City of God*, XXII, 29

36 How great shall be that felicity, which shall be tainted with no evil, which shall lack no good, and which shall afford leisure for the praises of God, Who shall be all in all! For I know not what other employment there can be where no lassitude shall slacken activity, nor any want stimulate to labour. . . . True peace shall be there, where no one shall suffer opposition either from himself or any other. God Himself, Who is the Author of virtue, shall there be its reward; for, as there is nothing greater or better, He has promised Himself. What else was meant by His word through the prophet, "I will be your God, and ye shall be my people," than, "I shall be their satisfaction, I shall be all that men honourably desire"—life, and health, and nourishment, and plenty, and glory, and honour, and peace, and all good things? This, too, is the right interpretation of the saying of the apostle, "That God may be all in all." He shall be the end of our desires who shall be seen without end, loved without cloy, praised without weariness. This outgoing of affection, this employment, shall certainly be, like eternal life itself, common to all.

But who can conceive, not to say describe, what degrees of honour and glory shall be awarded to the various degrees of merit? Yet it cannot be doubted that there shall be degrees. And in that blessed city there shall be this great blessing, that no inferior shall envy any superior, as now the archangels are not envied by the angels, because no one will wish to be what he has not received, though bound in strictest concord with him who has received; as in the body the finger does not seek to be the eye, though both members are harmoniously included in the complete structure of the body. And thus, along with his gift, greater or less, each shall receive this further gift of contentment to desire no more than he has.

Augustine, *City of God,* XXII, 30

37 As there is a kind of death of the soul, which consists in the putting away of former habits and former ways of life, and which comes through repentance, so also the death of the body consists in the dissolution of the former principle of life. And just as the soul, after it has put away and destroyed by repentance its former habits, is created anew after a better pattern, so we must hope and believe that the body, after that death which we all owe as a debt contracted through sin, shall at the resurrection be changed into a better form; not that flesh and blood shall inherit the kingdom of God (for that is impossible), but that this corruptible shall put on incorruption, and this mortal shall put on immortality. And thus the body, being the source of no uneasiness because it can feel no want, shall be animated by a spirit perfectly pure and happy, and shall enjoy unbroken peace.

Augustine, *Christian Doctrine,* I, 19

38 In the lost there can be fear of punishment to a greater degree than hope of glory in the Blessed. Because in the lost there will be a succession of punishments, so that the notion of something future remains there, which is the object of fear. But the glory of the saints has no succession, by reason of its being a kind of participation of eternity, in which there is neither past nor future, but only the present.

Aquinas, *Summa Theologica,* I–II, 67, 4

39 Fulness of joy can be understood in two ways. First, on the part of the thing rejoiced in, so that one rejoice in it as much as it is fitting that one should rejoice in it, and thus God's joy alone in Himself is filled, because it is infinite, and this is wholly fitting to the infinite goodness of God; but the joy of any creature must be finite. Secondly, fulness of joy may be understood on the part of the one who rejoices. Now joy is compared to desire as rest to movement . . . and rest is full when there is no more movement. Hence joy is full, when there remains nothing to be desired. But as long as we are in this world, the movement of desire does not cease in us, because it still remains possible for us to approach nearer to God by grace. . . . When once, however, perfect happiness has been attained, nothing will remain to be desired because then there will be full enjoyment of God, in which man will obtain whatever he had desired, even with regard to other goods. . . . Hence desire will be at rest, not only our desire for God, but all our desires, so that the joy of the

blessed is full to perfection,—indeed over-full, since they will obtain more than they were capable of desiring.

Aquinas, *Summa Theologica,* II–II, 28, 3

40 The necessity of holding the resurrection arises from this—that man may obtain the last end for which he was made, for this cannot be accomplished in this life nor in the life of the separated soul . . . otherwise man would have been made in vain, if he were unable to obtain the end for which he was made. And since it is necessary for the end to be obtained by the selfsame thing that was made for that end, lest it appear to be made without purpose, it is necessary for the selfsame man to rise again; and this is effected by the selfsame soul being united to the selfsame body. For otherwise there would be no resurrection properly speaking, if the same man were not reformed. Hence to maintain that he who rises again is not the selfsame man is heretical, since it is contrary to the truth of Scripture which proclaims the resurrection.

Aquinas, *Summa Theologica,* III Suppl., 79, 2

41 A thing may be a matter of rejoicing in two ways. First, in itself, when one rejoices in a thing as such, and thus the saints will not rejoice in the punishment of the wicked. Secondly, accidentally, by reason namely of something joined to it; and in this way the saints will rejoice in the punishment of the wicked, by considering therein the order of Divine justice and their own deliverance, which will fill them with joy. And thus the Divine justice and their own deliverance will be the direct cause of the joy of the blessed, while the punishment of the damned will cause it indirectly.

Aquinas, *Summa Theologica,* III Suppl., 94, 3

42 The disposition of hell will be such as to be adapted to the utmost unhappiness of the damned.

Aquinas, *Summa Theologica,* III Suppl., 97, 4

43 Hell will never lack sufficient room to admit the bodies of the damned, since hell is accounted one of the three things that never are satisfied. Nor is it unreasonable that God's power should maintain within the bowels of the earth a hollow great enough to contain all the bodies of the damned.

Aquinas, *Summa Theologica,* III Suppl., 97, 7

44 The unhappiness of the damned surpasses all unhappiness of this world.

Aquinas, *Summa Theologica,* III Suppl., 98, 3

45 Even as in the blessed in heaven there will be most perfect charity, so in the damned there will be the most perfect hate. Therefore as the saints will rejoice in all goods, so will the damned grieve for all goods. Consequently the sight of the happiness of the saints will give them very great pain.

. . . Therefore they will wish all the good were damned.

Aquinas, *Summa Theologica*, III Suppl., 98, 4

46 The appetite is moved by good or evil apprehended. Now God is apprehended in two ways, namely in Himself, as by the blessed, who see Him in His essence; and in His effects, as by us and by the damned. Since, then, He is goodness by His essence, He cannot in Himself be displeasing to any will; therefore whoever sees Him in His essence cannot hate Him. On the other hand, some of His effects are displeasing to the will in so far as they are opposed to any one, and accordingly a person may hate God not in Himself, but by reason of His effects. Therefore the damned, perceiving God in His punishment, which is the effect of His justice, hate Him, even as they hate the punishment inflicted on them.

Aquinas, *Summa Theologica*, III Suppl., 98, 5

47 After the judgment day there will be neither merit nor demerit. The reason for this is because merit or demerit is directed to the attainment of some further good or evil, and after the day of judgment good and evil will have reached their ultimate consummation, so that there will be no further addition to good or evil. Consequently, good will in the blessed will not be a merit but a reward, and evil will in the damned will be not a demerit but a punishment only.

Aquinas, *Summa Theologica*, III Suppl., 98, 6

48 The damned, before the judgment day, will see the blessed in glory, in such a way as to know, not what that glory is like, but only that they are in a state of glory that surpasses all thought. This will trouble them, both because they will, through envy, grieve for their happiness, and because they have forfeited that glory. . . . After the judgment day, however, they will be altogether deprived of seeing the blessed; nor will this lessen their punishment, but will increase it, because they will bear in remembrance the glory of the blessed which they saw at or before the judgment, and this will torment them. Moreover they will be tormented by finding themselves considered unworthy even to see the glory which the saints merit to have.

Aquinas, *Summa Theologica*, III Suppl., 98, 9

49 [One] reason may be given why the punishment of mortal sin is eternal, because thereby one offends God Who is infinite. Therefore since punishment cannot be infinite in intensity, because the creature is incapable of an infinite quality, it must be infinite at least in duration. And again there is a fourth reason for the same, because guilt remains for ever, since it cannot be remitted without grace, and men cannot receive grace after death; nor should punishment cease so long as guilt remains.

Aquinas, *Summa Theologica*, III Suppl., 99, 1

50 "Through me [the Gate of Hell] is the way into the doleful city; through me the way into the eternal pain; through me the way among the people lost.

Justice moved my High Maker; Divine Power made me, Wisdom Supreme, and Primal Love.

Before me were no things created, but eternal; and eternal I endure: leave all hope, ye that enter."

These words, of colour obscure, saw I written above a gate; whereat I: "Master, their meaning to me is hard."

And he [Virgil] to me, as one experienced: "Here must all distrust be left; all cowardice must here be dead.

We are come to the place where I told thee thou shouldst see the wretched people, who have lost the good of the intellect."

Dante, *Inferno*, III, 1

51 And lo! an old man, white with ancient hair, comes towards us in a bark, shouting: "Woe to you, depraved spirits!

hope not ever to see Heaven: I come to lead you to the other shore; into the eternal darkness; into fire and into ice.

And thou who art there, alive, depart thee from these who are dead." But when he saw that I departed not,

he said: "By other ways, by other ferries, not here shalt thou pass over: a lighter boat must carry thee."

And my guide to him: "Charon, vex not thyself: thus it is willed there, where what is willed can be done; and ask no more." . . .

Then all of them together, sorely weeping, drew to the accursed shore, which awaits every man that fears not God.

Charon the demon, with eyes of glowing coal, beckoning them, collects them all; smites with his oar whoever lingers.

As the leaves of autumn fall off one after the other, till the branch sees all its spoils upon the ground:

so one by one the evil seed of Adam cast themselves from that shore at signals, as the bird at its call.

Thus they depart on the brown water; and ere they have landed on the other shore, again a fresh crowd collects on this.

"My son," said the courteous Master [Virgil], "those who die under God's wrath, all assemble here from every country;

and they are prompt to pass the river, for Divine Justice spurs them so, that fear is changed into desire.

By this way no good spirit ever passes; and hence, if Charon complains of thee, thou easily now mayest know the import of his words."

Dante, *Inferno*, III, 82

52 "Ah! so may thy seed sometime have rest," I prayed him [Farinata], "solve the knot which has here involved my judgment.

It seems that you see beforehand what time brings with it, if I rightly hear; and have a different manner with the present."

"Like one who has imperfect vision, we see the things," he said, "which are remote from us; so much light the Supreme Ruler still gives to us;

when they draw nigh, or are, our intellect is altogether void; and except what others bring us, we know nothing of your human state.

Therefore thou mayest understand that all our knowledge shall be dead, from that moment when the portal of the Future shall be closed."

Dante, *Inferno*, X, 94

53 "My Son, within these stones," he [Virgil] then began to say, "are three circlets in gradation, like those thou leavest.

They all are filled with spirits accurst; but, that the sight *of these* hereafter may of itself suffice thee, hearken how and wherefore they are pent up.

Of all malice, which gains hatred in Heaven, the end is injury; and every such end, either by force or by fraud, aggrieveth others.

But because fraud is a vice peculiar to man, it more displeases God; and therefore the fraudulent are placed beneath, and more pain assails them.

All the first circle is for the violent; but as violence may be done to three persons, it is formed and distinguished into three rounds.

To God, to one's self, and to one's neighbour, may violence be done; I say in them and in their things, as thou shalt hear with evident discourse.

By force, death and painful wounds may be inflicted upon one's neighbour; and upon his substance, devastations, burnings, and injurious extortions:

wherefore the first round torments all homicides and every one who strikes maliciously, all plunderers and robbers, in different bands.

A man may lay violent hand upon himself, and upon his property: and therefore in the second round must every one repent in vain

who deprives himself of your world, gambles away and dissipates his wealth, and weeps there where he should be joyous.

Violence may be done against the Deity, in the heart denying and blaspheming Him; and disdaining Nature and her bounty:

and hence the smallest round seals with its mark both Sodom and Cahors, and all who speak with disparagement of God in their hearts.

Fraud, which gnaws every conscience, a man may

practise upon who confide in him; and upon who repose no confidence.

This latter mode seems only to cut off the bond of love which Nature makes: hence in the second circle nests

hypocrisy, flattery, sorcerers, cheating, theft and simony, pandars, barrators, and like filth.

In the other mode is forgotten that love which Nature makes, and also that which afterwards is added, giving birth to special trust:

hence in the smallest circle, at the centre of the universe and seat of Dis, every traitor is eternally consumed."

Dante, *Inferno*, XI, 16

54 I stood upon the bridge, *having* risen so to look, that, if I had not caught a rock, I should have fallen down without being pushed.

And the Guide [Virgil], who saw me thus attent, said: "Within those fires are the spirits; each swathes himself with that which burns him."

"Master," I replied, "from hearing thee I feel more certain; but had already discerned it to be so, and already wished to say to thee:

Who is in that fire, which comes so parted at the top, as if it rose from the pyre where Eteocles with his brother was placed?"

He answered me: "Within it there Ulysses is tortured, and Diomed; and thus they run together in punishment, as *erst* in wrath;

and in their flame they groan for the ambush of the horse, that made the door by which the noble seed of the Romans came forth;

within it they lament the artifice, whereby Deidamia in death still sorrows for Achilles; and there for the Palladium they suffer punishment."

"If they within those sparks can speak," said I, "Master! I pray thee much, and repray that my prayer may equal a thousand,

deny me not to wait until the horned flame comes hither; thou seest how with desire I bend me towards it."

And he to me: "Thy request is worthy of much praise, and therefore I accept it; but do thou refrain thy tongue.

Let me speak: for I have conceived what thou wishest; and they, perhaps, because they were Greeks, might disdain thy words."

After the flame had come where time and place seemed fitting to my Guide, I heard him speak in this manner:

"O ye, two in one fire! if I merited of you whilst I lived, if I merited of you much or little,

when on earth I wrote the High Verses, move ye not; but let the one of you tell where he, having lost himself, went to die."

The greater horn of the ancient flame began to shake itself, murmuring, just like a *flame* that struggles with the wind.

Then carrying to and fro the top, as if it were the

tongue that spake, threw forth a voice, and said: "When

I departed from Circe, who beyond a year detained me there near Gaeta, ere Æneas thus had named it,

neither fondness for my son, nor reverence for my aged father, nor the due love that should have cheered Penelope,

could conquer in me the ardour that I had to gain experience of the world, and of human vice and worth;

I put forth on the deep open sea, with but one ship, and with that small company, which had not deserted me.

Both the shores I saw as far as Spain, far as Morocco; and *saw* Sardinia and the other isles which that sea bathes round.

I and my companions were old and tardy, when we came to that narrow pass, where Hercules assigned his landmarks

to hinder man from venturing farther; on the right hand, I left Seville; on the other, had already left Ceuta.

'O brothers!' I said, 'who through a hundred thousand dangers have reached the West, deny not, to this the brief vigil

of your senses that remains, experience of the unpeopled world behind the Sun.

Consider your origin: ye were not formed to live like brutes, but to follow virtue and knowledge.'

With this brief speech I made my companions so eager for the voyage, that I could hardly then have checked them;

and, turning the poop towards morning, we of our oars made wings for the foolish flight, always gaining on the left.

Night already saw the other pole, with all its stars; and ours so low, that it rose not from the ocean floor.

Five times the light beneath the Moon had been rekindled and quenched as oft, since we had entered on the arduous passage,

when there appeared to us a Mountain, dim with distance; and to me it seemed the highest I had ever seen.

We joyed, and soon our joy was turned to grief: for a tempest rose from the new land, and struck the forepart of our ship.

Three times it made her whirl round with all the waters; at the fourth, *made* the poop rise up and prow go down, as pleased Another, till the sea was closed above us."

Dante, *Inferno*, XXVI, 43

55 Now eager to search within and around the divine forest dense and verdant, which to mine eyes was tempering the new day,

without waiting more I left the mountain-side, crossing the plain with lingering step, over the ground which gives forth fragrance on every side.

A sweet breeze, itself invariable, was striking on my brow with no greater force than a gentle wind,

before which the branches, responsively trembling, were all bending toward that quarter, where the holy mount casts its first shadow;

yet not so far bent aside from their erect state, that the little birds in the tops ceased to practise their every art;

but, singing, with full gladness they welcomed the first breezes within the leaves, which were murmuring the burden to their songs;

even such as from bough to bough is gathered through the pine wood on Chiassi's shore, when Aeolus looses Sirocco forth.

Dante, *Purgatorio*, XXVIII, 1

56 "In the world I was a virgin sister, and if thy memory be rightly searched, my greater beauty will not hide me from thee,

but thou wilt know me again for Piccarda, who, placed here with these other blessed ones, am blessed in the sphere that moveth slowest.

Our affections, which are aflame only in the pleasure of the Holy Spirit, rejoice to be informed after his order.

And this lot, which seemeth so far down, therefore is given us because our vows were slighted, and on some certain side were not filled in."

Whereon I to her: "In your wondrous aspects a divine somewhat regloweth that doth transmute you from conceits of former times.

Wherefore I lagged in calling thee to mind; now what thou tellest me giveth such help that more articulately I retrace thee.

But tell me, ye whose blessedness is here, do ye desire a more lofty place, to see more, or to make yourselves more dear?"

With those other shades first she smiled a little, then answered me so joyous that she seemed to burn in love's first flame:

"Brother, the quality of love stilleth our will, and maketh us long only for what we have, and giveth us no other thirst.

Did we desire to be more aloft, our longings were discordant from his will who here assorteth us,

and for that, thou wilt see, there is no room within these circles, if of necessity we have our being here in love, and if thou think again what is love's nature.

Nay, 'tis the essence of this blessed being to hold ourselves within the divine will, whereby our own wills are themselves made one.

So that our being thus, from threshold unto threshold throughout the realm, is a joy to all the realm as to the king, who draweth our wills to what he willeth;

and his will is our peace; it is that sea to which all moves that it createth and that nature maketh."

Dante, *Paradiso*, III, 46

57 *Aucassin.* In Paradise what have I to do? I care not to enter, but only to have Nicolette, my very sweet friend, whom I love so dearly well. For into Paradise go none but such people as I will tell you of. There go those aged priests, and those old cripples, and the maimed, who all day long and all night cough before the altars, and in the crypts beneath the churches; those who go in worn old mantles and old tattered habits; who are naked, and barefoot, and full of sores; who are dying of hunger and of thirst, of cold and of wretchedness. Such as these enter in Paradise, and with them have I nought to do. But in Hell will I go. For to Hell go the fair clerks and the fair knights who are slain in the tourney and the great wars, and the stout archer and the loyal man. With them will I go. And there go the fair and courteous ladies who have friends, two or three, together with their wedded lords. And there pass the gold and the silver, the ermine and all rich furs, harpers and minstrels, and the happy of the world. With these will I go, so only that I have Nicolette, my very sweet friend, by my side.

Anon., *Aucassin and Nicolette*

58 This friar he boasts he knows somewhat of Hell,
And God He knows that it is little wonder;
Friars and fiends are never far asunder.
For, by gad, you have oftentimes heard tell
How such a friar was snatched down into Hell
In spirit, once, and by a vision blown;
And as an angel led him up and down
To show the pains and torments that there were,
In all the place he saw no friar there.
Of other folk he saw enough in woe;
And to the angel then he questioned so:
" 'Now, sir,' said he, 'have friars such a grace
That none of them shall come into this place?'
" 'Nay,' said the angel, 'millions here are
    thrown!'
And unto Sathanas he led him down.
" 'And now has Sathanas,' said he, 'a tail
Broader than of a galleon is the sail.
Hold up thy tail, thou Sathanas!' said he,
" 'Show forth thine arse and let the friar see
Where is the nest of friars in this place!'
And ere one might go half a furlong's space.
Just as the bees come swarming from a hive,
Out of the Devil's arse-hole there did drive
Full twenty thousand friars in a rout,
And through all Hell they swarmed and ran
    about,
And came again, as fast as they could run,
And in his arse they crept back, every one.
He clapped his tail to and then lay right still.
This friar, when he'd looked at length his fill
Upon the torments of that sorry place,
His spirit God restored, of His high grace,
Into his body, and he did awake;
Nevertheless for terror did he quake
So was the Devil's arse-hole in his mind,

Which is his future home, and like in kind.

Chaucer, *Canterbury Tales:*
Summoner's Prologue

59 Truly the dark light that shall come out of the fire that burns for ever shall turn him all to pain who is in Hell; for it shall show unto him the horrible devils that torment him.

Chaucer, *Canterbury Tales:*
Parson's Tale

60 Certainly a shadow has the likeness of that whereof it is the shadow, but the shadow is not the substance. Just so it is with the pain of Hell; it is like unto death because of the horrible anguish. And why? Because it pains for ever, and as if they should die at every moment; but indeed they shall not die.

Chaucer, *Canterbury Tales:*
Parson's Tale

61 A thousand tymes have I herd men telle
That ther ys joy in hevene and peyne in helle,
And I acorde wel that it ys so;
But, natheles, yet wot I wel also
That ther nis noon dwellyng in this contree,
That eyther hath in hevene or helle ybe,
Ne may of hit noon other weyes witen,
But as he hath herd seyd, or founde it writen.

Chaucer, *The Legend of Good Women:*
Prologue

62 I desire to go to Hell, not to Heaven. In Hell I shall enjoy the company of popes, kings and princes, but in Heaven are only beggars, monks, hermits and apostles.

Machiavelli, *On his deathbed*

63 I hold the gnashing of teeth of the damned to be an external pain following upon evil conscience, that is, despair, when men see themselves abandoned by God.

Luther, *Table Talk,* H800

64 Unto Almighty God we commend the soul of our *brother* departed, and we commit *his* body to the ground; earth to earth, ashes to ashes, dust to dust; in sure and certain hope of the Resurrection unto eternal life, through our Lord Jesus Christ; at whose coming in glorious majesty to judge the world, the earth and sea shall give up their dead; and the corruptible bodies of those who sleep in him shall be changed, and made like unto his own glorious body; according to the mighty working whereby he is able to subdue all things unto himself.

Book of Common Prayer

65 *Brakenbury.* Why looks your Grace so heavily today?
Clarence. O, I have pass'd a miserable night,

So full of ugly sights, of ghastly dreams,
That, as I am a Christian faithful man,
I would not spend another such a night,
Though 'twere to buy a world of happy days,
So full of dismal terror was the time!
    Brak. What was your dream? I long to hear you
      tell it.
    Clar. Methoughts that I had broken from the
      Tower,
And was embark'd to cross to Burgundy;
And, in my company, my brother Gloucester,
Who from my cabin tempted me to walk
Upon the hatches: thence we look'd toward England
And cited up a thousand fearful times,
During the wars of York and Lancaster
That had befall'n us. As we paced along
Upon the giddy footing of the hatches,
Methought that Gloucester stumbled; and, in falling,
Struck me, that thought to stay him, overboard,
Into the tumbling billows of the main.
Lord, Lord! methought what pain it was to
    drown!
What dreadful noise of waters in mine ears!
What ugly sights of death within mine eyes!
Methought I saw a thousand fearful wrecks;
Ten thousand men that fishes gnaw'd upon;
Wedges of gold, great anchors, heaps of pearl,
Inestimable stones, unvalued jewels,
All scatter'd in the bottom of the sea:
Some lay in dead men's skulls; and, in those holes
Where eyes did once inhabit, there were crept,
As 'twere in scorn of eyes, reflecting gems,
Which woo'd the slimy bottom of the deep
And mock'd the dead bones that lay scatter'd by.
    Brak. Had you such leisure in the time of death
To gaze upon the secrets of the deep?
    Clar. Methought I had; and often did I strive
To yield the ghost: but still the envious flood
Kept in my soul and would not let it forth
To seek the empty, vast, and wandering air;
But smother'd it within my panting bulk,
Which almost burst to belch it in the sea.
    Brak. Awaked you not with this sore agony?
    Clar. O, no, my dream was lengthen'd after life;
O, then began the tempest to my soul,
Who pass'd, methought, the melancholy flood,
With that grim ferryman which poets write of,
Unto the kingdom of perpetual night.
The first that there did greet my stranger soul
Was my great father-in-law, renowned Warwick,
Who cried aloud, "What scourge for perjury
Can this dark monarchy afford false Clarence?"
And so he vanish'd: then came wandering by
A shadow like an angel, with bright hair
Dabbled in blood; and he squeak'd out aloud,
"Clarence is come; false, fleeting, perjured Clarence,
That stabb'd me in the field by Tewksbury;
Seize on him, Furies, take him to your torments!"

With that, methoughts, a legion of foul fiends
Environ'd me about, and howled in mine ears
Such hideous cries that with the very noise
I trembling waked, and for a season after
Could not believe but that I was in hell,
Such terrible impression made the dream.
            Shakespeare, *Richard III,* I, iv, 1

66 *Ophelia.* Do not, as some ungracious pastors do,
  Show me the steep and thorny way to heaven;
  Whiles, like a puff'd and reckless libertine,
  Himself the primrose path of dalliance treads.
           Shakespeare, *Hamlet,* I, iii, 47

67 *Ghost.* I am thy father's spirit,
  Doom'd for a certain term to walk the night,
  And for the day confined to fast in fires,
  Till the foul crimes done in my days of nature
  Are burnt and purged away. But that I am forbid
  To tell the secrets of my prison-house,
  I could a tale unfold whose lightest word
  Would harrow up thy soul, freeze thy young
    blood,
  Make thy two eyes, like stars, start from their
    spheres,
  Thy knotted and combined locks to part
  And each particular hair to stand an end,
  Like quills upon the fretful porpentine.
  But this eternal blazon must not be
  To ears of flesh and blood.
           Shakespeare, *Hamlet,* I, v, 9

68 Well, well, Madam, quoth *Sancho,* I don't understand your Parts and Wholes! I saw it, and there's an End of the Story. Only you must think, that as we flew by Inchantment, so we saw by Inchantment; and thus I might see the Earth, and all the Men, which Way soever I look'd. I'll warrant, you won't believe me neither when I tell you, that when I thrust up the Kerchief above my Brows, I saw my self so near Heaven, that between the Top of my Cap and the main Sky, there was not a Span and a half. And, Heaven bless us! forsooth, what a hugeous great Place it is! And we happen'd to travel that Road where the seven She-Goatstars were: And Faith and Troth, I had such a Mind to play with 'em (having been once a Goatherd my self) that I fancy I'd have cry'd my self to Death, had I not done it. So soon as I spy'd 'em, what does me I, but sneaks down very soberly from behind my Master, without telling any living Soul, and play'd, and leap'd about for three quarters of an Hour by the Clock, with the pretty Nanny-Goats, who are as sweet and fine as so many Marigolds or Gilly-flowers; and honest *Wooden Peg* stirr'd not one Step all the while. And while *Sancho* employ'd himself with the Goats, ask'd the Duke, how was Don *Quixote* employ'd? Truly, answer'd the Knight, I am sensible all Things were alter'd from their natural Course;

therefore what *Sancho* says, seems the less strange to me. But for my own Part, I neither saw Heaven nor Hell, Sea nor Shore. I perceiv'd indeed we pass'd through the middle Region of the Air, and were pretty near that of Fire, but that we came so near Heaven, as *Sancho* says, is altogether incredible; because we then must have pass'd quite through the fiery Region, which lies between the Sphere of the Moon and the upper Region of the Air. Now it was impossible for us to reach that Part, where are the *Pleiades,* or the *Seven Goats,* as *Sancho* calls 'em, without being consum'd in the elemental Fire; and therefore since we escaped those Flames, certainly we did not soar so high, and *Sancho* either lies or dreams. I neither lie nor dream, reply'd *Sancho.* Uds Precious! I can tell you the Marks and Colour of every Goat among 'em. If you don't believe me, do but ask and try me. You'll easily see whether I speak Truth or no. Well, said the Dutchess, prithee tell them me, *Sancho.* Look you, answer'd *Sancho,* there were two of 'em green, two carnation, two blue, and one party-colour'd. Truly, said the Duke, that's a new Kind of Goats you have found out, *Sancho,* we have none of those Colours upon Earth. Sure, Sir, reply'd *Sancho,* you'll make some Sort of Difference between heavenly She-Goats, and the Goats of this World? But *Sancho,* said the Duke, among those She-Goats did you see never a He? not one horn'd Beast of the masculine Gender? Not one, Sir, I saw no other horn'd Thing but the Moon; and I have been told, that neither He-Goats nor any other cornuted Tups are suffer'd to lift their Horns beyond those of the Moon.

Cervantes, *Don Quixote,* II, 41

69 When God's hand is bent to strike, "it is a fearful thing to fall into the hands of the living God"; but to fall out of the hands of the living God is a horror beyond our expression, beyond our imagination. That God should let my soul fall out of his hand into a bottomless pit and roll an unremovable stone upon it and leave it to that which it finds there (and it shall find that there which it never imagined till it came thither) and never think more of that soul, never have more to do with it; that of that providence of God that studies the life of every weed and worm and ant and spider and toad and viper there should never, never any beam flow out upon me; that that God who looked upon me when I was nothing and called me when I was not, as though I had been, out of the womb and depth of darkness, will not look upon me now, when though a miserable and a banished and a damned creature, yet I am his creature still and contribute something to his glory even in my damnation; that that God who hath often looked upon me in my foulest uncleanness and when I had shut out the eye of the day, the sun, and the eye of the night, the taper, and the eyes of all the world with curtains and win-

dows and doors, did yet see me and see me in mercy by making me see that he saw me and sometimes brought me to a present remorse and (for that time) to a forbearing of that sin, should so turn himself from me to his glorious saints and angels as that no saint nor angel nor Christ Jesus himself should ever pray him to look towards me, never remember him that such a soul there is; that that God who hath so often said to my soul, *Quare morieris?* why wilt thou die? and so often sworn to my soul, *Vivit Dominus,* as the Lord liveth, I would not have thee die but live, will neither let me die nor let me live, but die an everlasting life and live an everlasting death; that that God who, when he could not get into me by standing and knocking, by his ordinary means of entering, by his word, his mercies, hath applied his judgments and hath shaked the house, this body, with agues and palsies, and set this house on fire with fevers and calentures, and frighted the master of the house, my soul, with horrors and heavy apprehensions and so made an entrance into me; that that God should frustrate all his own purposes and practices upon me and leave me and cast me away as though I had cost him nothing; that this God at last should let this soul go away as a smoke, as a vapor, as a bubble; and that then this soul cannot be a smoke, a vapor, nor a bubble, but must lie in darkness as long as the Lord of light is light itself, and never spark of that light reach to my soul; what Tophet is not paradise, what brimstone is not amber, what gnashing is not a comfort, what gnawing of the worm is not a tickling, what torment is not a marriage bed to this damnation, to be secluded eternally, eternally, eternally from the sight of God?

Donne, *Sermon LXXVI*

70 Though Theologians commonly affirm that the damned are tortured by hell fire, they do not therefore believe that they are deceived by a false idea of a tormenting fire which God has implanted in them, but rather that they are tortured by real fire, for the reason that, just as the incorporeal spirit of the living man is naturally confined in the body, so by the divine power it is easily after death confined in corporeal fire.

Descartes, *Objections and Replies,* VI

71 Surely though we place Hell under Earth, the Devil's walk and purlue is about it: men speak too popularly who place it in those flaming mountains, which to grosser apprehensions represent Hell. The heart of man is the place the Devils dwell in; I feel sometimes a Hell within my self; *Lucifer* keeps his Court in my breast; *Legion* is revived in me. There are as many Hells, as *Anaxagoras* conceited worlds; there was more than one Hell in *Magdalene,* when there were seven Devils; for every Devil is an Hell unto himself; he holds enough of torture in his own *ubi,* and needs not the

misery of circumference to afflict him. And thus a distracted Conscience here, is a shadow or introduction unto Hell hereafter. Who can but pity the merciful intention of those hands that do destroy themselves? the Devil, were it in his power, would do the like; which being impossible, his miseries are endless, and he suffers most in that attribute wherein he is impassible, his immortality.

Sir Thomas Browne, *Religio Medici,* I, 51

72 I thank God that with joy I mention it, I was never afraid of Hell, nor never grew pale at the description of that place; I have so fixed my contemplations on Heaven, that I have almost forgot the Idea of Hell, and am afraid rather to lose the Joys of the one, than endure the misery of the other: to be deprived of them is a perfect Hell, and needs methinks no addition to compleat our afflictions; that terrible term hath never detained me from sin, nor do I owe any good action to the name thereof; I fear God, yet am not afraid of him; his mercies make me ashamed of my sins, before his Judgements afraid thereof: these are the forced and secondary method of his wisdom, which he useth but as the last remedy, and upon provocation; a course rather to deter the wicked, than incite the virtuous to his worship. I can hardly think there was ever any scared into Heaven; they go the fairest way to Heaven that would serve God without a Hell; other Mercenaries, that crouch into him in fear of Hell, though they term themselves the servants, are indeed but the slaves of the Almighty.

Sir Thomas Browne, *Religio Medici,* I, 52

73 And since there is something of us that will still live on, join both lives together, and live in one but for the other. He who thus ordereth the purposes of this Life will never be far from the next, and is in some manner already in it, by a happy conformity, and close apprehension of it. And if, as we have elsewhere declared, any have been so happy as personally to understand Christian Annihilation, Extasy, Exolution, Transformation, the Kiss of the Spouse, and Ingression into the Divine Shadow, according to Mystical Theology, they have already had an handsome Anticipation of Heaven; the World is in a manner over, and the Earth in Ashes unto them.

Sir Thomas Browne, *Christian Morals,* III, 30

74 Weep no more, woful Shepherds weep no more,
For *Lycidas* your sorrow is not dead,
Sunk though he be beneath the watry floar,
So sinks the day-star in the Ocean bed,
And yet anon repairs his drooping head,
And tricks his beams, and with new spangled Ore,
Flames in the forehead of the morning sky:
So *Lycidas* sunk low, but mounted high,
Through the dear might of him that walk'd the
waves

Where other groves, and other streams along,
With *Nectar* pure his oozy Lock's he laves,
And hears the unexpressive nuptiall Song,
In the blest Kingdoms meek of joy and love.
There entertain him all the Saints above,
In solemn troops, and sweet Societies
That sing, and singing in their glory move,
And wipe the tears for ever from his eyes.

Milton, *Lycidas,* 165

75   Him [Satan] the Almighty Power
Hurld headlong flaming from th' Ethereal Skie
With hideous ruine and combustion down
To bottomless perdition, there to dwell
In Adamantine Chains and penal Fire,
Who durst defie th' Omnipotent to Arms.
Nine times the Space that measures Day and
   Night
To mortal men, he with his horrid crew
Lay vanquisht, rowling in the fiery Gulfe
Confounded though immortal: But his doom
Reserv'd him to more wrath; for now the thought
Both of lost happiness and lasting pain
Torments him; round he throws his baleful eyes
That witness'd huge affliction and dismay
Mixt with obdurate pride and stedfast hate:
At once as far as Angels kenn he views
The dismal Situation waste and wilde,
A Dungeon horrible, on all sides round
As one great Furnace flam'd, yet from those
   flames
No light, but rather darkness visible
Serv'd only to discover sights of woe,
Regions of sorrow, doleful shades, where peace
And rest can never dwell, hope never comes
That comes to all; but torture without end
Still urges, and a fiery Deluge, fed
With ever-burning Sulphur unconsum'd:
Such place Eternal Justice had prepar'd
For those rebellious, here their Prison ordain'd
In utter darkness, and their portion set
As far remov'd from God and light of Heav'n
As from the Center thrice to th' utmost Pole.
O how unlike the place from whence they fell!

Milton, *Paradise Lost,* I, 44

76 Is this the Region, this the Soil, the Clime,
Said then the lost Arch Angel [Satan], this the
   seat
That we must change for Heav'n, this mournful
   gloom
For that celestial light? Be it so, since hee
Who now is Sovran can dispose and bid
What shall be right: fardest from him is best
Whom reason hath equald, force hath made su-
   pream
Above his equals. Farewel happy Fields
Where Joy for ever dwells: Hail horrours, hail
Infernal world, and thou profoundest Hell
Receive thy new Possessor: One who brings
A mind not to be chang'd by Place or Time.

Milton, *Paradise Lost,* I, 242

77   Let none admire
That riches grow in Hell; that soyle may best
Deserve the pretious bane.

Milton, *Paradise Lost*, I, 690

78 Men call him [Satan] *Mulciber;* and how he fell
From Heav'n, they fabl'd, thrown by angry *Jove*
Sheer o're the Chrystal Battlements: from Morn
To Noon he fell, from Noon to dewy Eve,
A Summers day; and with the setting Sun
Dropt from the Zenith like a falling Star,
On *Lemnos* th' *Ægaean* Ile: thus they relate,
Erring; for he with this rebellious rout
Fell long before; nor aught avail'd him now
To have built in Heav'n high Towrs; nor did he
  scape
By all his Engins, but was headlong sent
With his industrious crew to build in hell.

Milton, *Paradise Lost*, I, 740

79   Thus roving on
In confus'd march forlorn, th' adventrous Bands
With shuddring horror pale, and eyes agast
View'd first thir lamentable lot, and found
No rest: through many a dark and drearie Vaile
They pass'd, and many a Region dolorous,
O're many a Frozen, many a Fierie Alpe,
Rocks, Caves, Lakes, Fens, Bogs, Dens, and
  shades of death,
A Universe of death, which God by curse
Created evil, for evil only good,
Where all life dies, death lives, and nature breeds,
Perverse, all monstrous, all prodigious things,
Abominable, inutterable, and worse
Then Fables yet have feign'd, or fear conceiv'd,
Gorgons and *Hydra's,* and *Chimera's* dire.

Milton, *Paradise Lost*, II, 614

80   From her side the fatal Key,
Sad instrument of all our woe, she [the Portress of
  Hell Gate] took;
And towards the Gate rouling her bestial train,
Forthwith the huge Portcullis high up drew,
Which but her self not all the *Stygian* powers
Could once have mov'd; then in the key-hole
  turns
Th' intricate wards, and every Bolt and Bar
Of massie Iron or sollid Rock with ease
Unfast'ns: on a sudden op'n flie
With impetuous recoile and jarring sound
Th' infernal dores and on thir hinges grate
Harsh Thunder, that the lowest bottom shook
Of *Erebus.* She op'nd, but to shut
Excel'd her power; the Gates wide op'n stood,
That with extended wings a Bannerd Host
Under spread Ensigns marching might pass
  through
With Horse and Chariots rankt in loose array;
So wide they stood, and like a Furnace mouth
Cast forth redounding smoak and ruddy flame.

Milton, *Paradise Lost*, II, 871

81   While God spake, ambrosial fragrance fill'd
All Heav'n, and in the blessed Spirits elect
Sense of new joy ineffable diffus'd:
Beyond compare the Son of God was seen
Most glorious, in him all his Father shon
Substantially express'd, and in his face
Divine compassion visibly appeerd,
Love without end, and without measure Grace.

Milton, *Paradise Lost*, III, 135

82 All the multitude of Angels with a shout
Loud as from numbers without number, sweet
As from blest voices, uttering joy, Heav'n rung
With Jubilee, and loud Hosannas fill'd
Th' eternal Regions: lowly reverent
Towards either Throne they bow, & to the
  ground
With solemn adoration down they cast
Thir Crowns inwove with Amarant and Gold,
Immortal Amarant, a Flour which once
In Paradise, fast by the Tree of Life
Began to bloom, but soon for mans offence
To Heav'n remov'd where first it grew, there
  grows,
And flours aloft shading the Fount of Life,
And where the river of Bliss through midst of
  Heav'n
Rowls o're *Elisian* Flours her Amber stream;
With these that never fade the Spirits Elect
Bind thir resplendent locks inwreath'd with
  beams,
Now in loose Garlands thick thrown off, the
  bright
Pavement that like a Sea of Jasper shon
Impurpl'd with Celestial Roses smil'd.
Then Crown'd again thir gold'n Harps they took,
Harps ever tun'd, that glittering by thir side
Like Quivers hung, and with Præamble sweet
Of charming symphonie they introduce
Thir sacred Song, and waken raptures high;
No voice exempt, no voice but well could joine
Melodious part, such concord is in Heav'n.

Milton, *Paradise Lost*, III, 344

83 Now while I was gazing upon all these things
[within the Gates of Heaven], I turned my head to
look back, and saw *Ignorance* come up to the River
side; but he soon got over, and that without half
that difficulty which the other two men met with.
For it happened that there was then in that place
one *Vain-hope* a Ferry-man, that with his Boat
helped him over: so he, as the other I saw, did
ascend the Hill to come up to the Gate, only he
came alone; neither did any man meet him with
the least encouragement. When he was come up
to the Gate, he looked up to the writing that was
above; and then began to knock, supposing that
entrance should have been quickly administered
to him. But he was asked by the men that lookt
over the top of the Gate, Whence came you? and

what would you have? He answered, I have eat and drank in the presence of the King, and he has taught in our Streets. Then they asked him for his Certificate, that they might go in and shew it to the King. So he fumbled in his bosom for one, and found none. Then said they, Have you none? But the man answered never a word. So they told the King, but he would not come down to see him, but commanded the two shining Ones that conducted *Christian* and *Hopeful* to the City, to go out and take *Ignorance* and bind him hand and foot, and have him away. Then they took him up, and carried him through the air to the door that I saw in the side of the Hill, and put him in there. Then I saw that there was a way to Hell, even from the Gates of Heaven, as well as from the City of *Destruction.* So I awoke, and behold it was a Dream.

Bunyan, *Pilgrim's Progress,* I

84 As from the pow'r of sacred lays
   The spheres began to move,
And sung the great Creator's praise
   To all the blest above;
So, when the last and dreadful hour
This crumbling pageant shall devour,
The Trumpet shall be heard on high,
The dead shall live, the living die,
And Music shall untune the sky.

Dryden, *A Song for St. Cecilia's Day*

85 Hell was built on spite, and heav'n on pride.

Pope, *Essay on Man,* Epistle III, 262

86 Finding him in a very good humour, I ventured to lead him to the subject of our situation in a future state, having much curiosity to know his notions on that point. *Johnson.* "Why, Sir, the happiness of an unembodied spirit will consist in a consciousness of the favour of God, in the contemplation of truth, and in the possession of felicitating ideas."

Boswell, *Life of Johnson (Mar. 1772)*

87 No saint . . . in the course of his religious warfare, was more sensible of the unhappy failure of pious resolves, than Johnson. He said one day, talking to an acquaintance on this subject, "Sir, Hell is paved with good intentions."

Boswell, *Life of Johnson (Apr. 14, 1775)*

88 It is incumbent on us diligently to remember that the kingdom of heaven was promised to the poor in spirit, and that minds afflicted by calamity and the contempt of mankind cheerfully listen to the divine promise of future happiness; while, on the contrary, the fortunate are satisfied with the possession of this world; and the wise abuse in doubt and dispute their vain superiority of reason and knowledge.

Gibbon, *Decline and Fall of the Roman Empire,* XV

89 The doctrine of the resurrection was first entertained by the Egyptians; and their mummies were embalmed, their pyramids were constructed, to preserve the ancient mansion of the soul during a period of three thousand years. But the attempt is partial and unavailing; and it is with a more philosophic spirit that Mohammed relies on the omnipotence of the Creator, whose word can reanimate the breathless clay, and collect the innumerable atoms that no longer retain their form or substance. The intermediate state of the soul it is hard to decide; and those who most firmly believe her immaterial nature, are at a loss to understand how she can think or act without the agency of the organs of sense.

Gibbon, *Decline and Fall of the Roman Empire,* L

90 The human fancy can paint with more energy the misery than the bliss of a future life. With the two simple elements of darkness and fire we create a sensation of pain, which may be aggravated to an infinite degree by the idea of endless duration. But the same idea operates with an opposite effect on the continuity of pleasure; and too much of our present enjoyments is obtained from the relief, or the comparison, of evil.

Gibbon, *Decline and Fall of the Roman Empire,* L

91 Men are admitted into Heaven not because they have curbed & governd their Passions or have No Passions but because they have Cultivated their Understandings. The Treasures of Heaven are not Negations of Passion but Realities of Intellect from which All the Passions Emanate Uncurbed in their Eternal Glory. The Fool shall not enter into Heaven let him be ever so Holy. Holiness is not The Price of Enterance into Heaven. Those who are cast out Are All Those who, having no Passions of their own because No Intellect, Have spent their lives in Curbing & Governing other People's by the Various arts of Poverty & Cruelty of all kinds. Wo Wo Wo to you Hypocrites. Even Murder the Courts of Justice, more merciful than the Church, are compelld to allow is not done in Passion but in Cold Blooded Design & Intention.

Blake, *A Vision of The Last Judgment*

92 Without Contraries is no progression. Attraction and Repulsion, Reason and Energy, Love and Hate, are necessary to Human existence. From these contraries spring what the religious call Good and Evil. Good is the passive that obeys Reason. Evil is the active springing from Energy.
Good is Heaven. Evil is Hell.

Blake, *Marriage of Heaven and Hell,* 3

93 *Faust.* Does Hell itself have its laws then?
    That's fine! A compact in that case might be
    Concluded safely with you gentlemen?
      Mephistopheles. What's promised, you'll enjoy
        with naught subtracted,
    With naught unduly snipped off or exacted.

                    Goethe, *Faust*, I, 1413

94 *Chorus Mysticus.* All earth comprises
    Is symbol alone;
    What there ne'er suffices
    As fact here is known;
    All past the humanly
    Wrought here in love;
    The Eternal-Womanly
    Draws us above.

              Goethe, *Faust*, II, 5, 12104

95 Hell is a city much like London—
    A populous and a smoky city;
    There are all sorts of people undone,
    And there is little or no fun done;
      Small justice shown, and still less pity.

        Shelley, *Peter Bell the Third*, III, 1

96 Knowledge, as the disannulling of the unity of
mere nature, is the Fall, which is no casual conception, but the eternal history of spirit. For the
state of innocence, the paradisaical condition, is
that of the brute. Paradise is a park, where only
brutes, not men, can remain.

        Hegel, *Philosophy of History*, Pt. III, III, 2

97 I sent my Soul through the Invisible,
Some letter of that After-life to spell;
    And by and by my Soul returned to me,
And answered, "I Myself am Heav'n and Hell"—

Heaven but the Vision of fulfilled Desire,
And Hell the Shadow from a Soul on fire
    Cast on the Darkness into which Ourselves,
So late emerged from, shall so soon expire.

        FitzGerald, *Rubáiyát*, LXVI–LXVII

98 My life closed twice before its close;
    It yet remains to see
    If Immortality unveil
    A third event to me,

So huge, so hopeless to conceive
As these that twice befell.
Parting is all we know of heaven,
And all we need of hell.

        Emily Dickinson, *My Life Closed Twice*

99 Ah, but a man's reach should exceed his grasp,
    Or what's a heaven for?

            Browning, *Andrea Del Sarto*

100 In our English popular religion, for instance, the
common conception of a future state of bliss is just
that of the Vision of Mirza: "Persons dressed in
glorious habits with garlands on their heads, passing among the trees, lying down by the fountains,
or resting on beds of flowers, amid a confused harmony of singing birds, falling waters, human
voices, and musical instruments." Or, even, with
many, it is that of a kind of perfected middle-class
home, with labour ended, the table spread, goodness all around, the lost ones restored, hymnody
incessant. . . . That this conception of immortality cannot possibly be true, we feel, the moment we
consider it seriously. And yet who can devise any
conception of a future state of bliss, which shall
bear close examination better?

        Arnold, *Literature and Dogma*, XII

101 "I don't believe in a future life," said Raskolnikov.
    Svidrigailov sat lost in thought.
    "And what if there are only spiders there, or
something of that sort," he said suddenly.
    "He is a madman," thought Raskolnikov.
    "We always imagine eternity as something be-
yond our conception, something vast, vast! But
why must it be vast? Instead of all that, what if it's
one little room, like a bathhouse in the country,
black and grimy and spiders in every corner, and
that's all eternity is? I sometimes fancy it like
that."
    "Can it be you can imagine nothing juster and
more comforting than that?" Raskolnikov cried,
with a feeling of anguish.
    "Juster? And how can we tell, perhaps that is
just, and do you know it's what I would certainly
have made it," answered Svidrigailov, with a
vague smile.

        Dostoevsky, *Crime and Punishment*, IV, 1

102 *Captain Stormfield.* Sandy, out with it. Come—no
secrets among friends. I notice you don't ever
wear wings—and plenty others don't. I've been
making as ass of myself—is that it?
    Sandy. That is about the size of it. But it is no
harm. We all do it at first. It's perfectly natural.
You see, on earth we jump to such foolish conclusions as to things up here. In the pictures we always saw the angels with wings on—and that was
all right; but we jumped to the conclusion that
that was their way of getting around—and that
was all wrong. The wings ain't anything but a
uniform, that's all. When they are in the field—so
to speak—they always wear them; you never see
an angel going with a message anywhere without
his wings, anymore than you would see a military
officer presiding at a court-martial without his
uniform, or a postman delivering letters, or a policeman walking his beat in plain clothes. But
they ain't to *fly* with! The wings are for show, not
for use.

        Mark Twain, *Extract from Captain Stormfield's*
                          Visit to Heaven

103 *Captain Stormfield.* But what was it you was saying about unsacrilegious things, which people expect to get, and will be disappointed about?

Sandy. Oh, there are a lot of such things that people expect and don't get. For instance, there's a Brooklyn preacher by the name of Talmage, who is laying up a considerable disappointment for himself. He says, every now and then in his sermons, that the first thing he does when he gets to heaven will be to fling his arms around Abraham, Isaac, and Jacob, and kiss them and weep on them. There's millions of people down there on earth that are promising themselves the same thing. As many as sixty thousand people arrive here every single day that want to run straight to Abraham, Isaac, and Jacob, and hug them and weep on them. Now mind you, sixty thousand a day is a pretty heavy contract for those old people. If they were a mind to allow it, they wouldn't ever have anything to do, year in and year out but stand up and be hugged and wept on thirty-two hours in the twenty-four. They would be tired out and as wet as muskrats all the time.

What would heaven be, to *them?* It would be a mighty good place to get out of—you know that, yourself. Those are kind and gentle old Jews, but they ain't any fonder of kissing the emotional highlights of Brooklyn than you be. You mark my words, Mr. T.'s endearments are going to be declined, with thanks. There are limits to the privileges of the elect, even in heaven. Why, if Adam was to show himself to every newcomer that wants to call and gaze at him and strike him for his autograph, he would never have time to do anything else but just that.

Mark Twain, *Extract from Captain Stormfield's Visit to Heaven*

104 *Sandy.* Down there they talk of the heavenly King—and that is right—but then they go right on speaking as if this was a republic and everybody was on a dead level with everybody else, and privileged to fling his arms around anybody he comes across, and be hail-fellow-well-met with all the elect, from the highest down. How tangled up and absurd that is! How are you going to have a republic under a king? How are you going to have a republic at all, where the head of the government is absolute, holds his place forever, and has no parliament, no council to meddle or make in his affairs, nobody voted for, nobody elected, nobody in the whole universe with a voice in the government, nobody asked to take a hand in its matters, and nobody *allowed* to do it? Fine republic, ain't it?

Mark Twain, *Extract from Captain Stormfield's Visit to Heaven*

105 Everything human is pathetic. The secret source of Humor itself is not joy but sorrow. There is no humor in heaven.

Mark Twain, *Pudd'nhead Wilson's New Calendar*, X

106 *The Preacher.* Last and crowning torture of all the tortures of that awful place is the eternity of hell. Eternity! O, dread and dire word. Eternity! What mind of man can understand it? And remember, it is an eternity of pain. Even though the pains of hell were not so terrible as they are yet they would become infinite as they are destined to last for ever. But while they are everlasting they are at the same time, as you know, intolerably intense, unbearably extensive. To bear even the sting of an insect for all eternity would be a dreadful torment. What must it be, then, to bear the manifold tortures of hell for ever? For ever! For all eternity! Not for a year or for an age but for ever. Try to imagine the awful meaning of this. You have often seen the sand on the seashore. How fine are its tiny grains! And how many of those tiny little grains go to make up the small handful which a child grasps in its play. Now imagine a mountain of that sand, a million miles high, reaching from the earth to the farthest heavens, and a million miles broad, extending to remotest space, and a million miles in thickness: and imagine such an enormous mass of countless particles of sand multiplied as often as there are leaves in the forest, drops of water in the mighty ocean, feathers on birds, scales on fish, hairs on animals, atoms in the vast expanse of the air: and imagine that at the end of every million years a little bird came to that mountain and carried away in its beak a tiny grain of that sand. How many millions upon million of centuries would pass before that bird had carried away even a square foot of that mountain, how many eons upon eons of ages before it had carried away all. Yet at the end of that immense stretch of time not even one instant of eternity could be said to have ended. At the end of all those billions and trillions of years eternity would have scarcely begun. And if that mountain rose again after it had been all carried away and if the bird came again and carried it all away again grain by grain: and if it so rose and sank as many times as there are stars in the sky, atoms in the air, drops of water in the sea, leaves on the trees, feathers upon birds, scales upon fish, hairs upon animals, at the end of all those innumerable risings and sinkings of that immeasurably vast mountain not one single instant of eternity could be said to have ended; even then, at the end of such a period, after that eon of time the mere thought of which makes our very brain reel dizzily, eternity would have scarcely begun.

Joyce, *Portrait of the Artist as a Young Man*, III

107 Let me enjoy the earth no less
Because the all-enacting Might

That fashioned forth its loveliness
Had other aims than my delight.

About my path there flits a Fair,
Who throws me not a word or sign;
I'll charm me with her ignoring air,
And laud the lips not meant for mine.

From manuscripts of moving song
Inspired by scenes and dreams unknown
I'll pour out raptures that belong
To others, as they were my own.

And some day hence, towards Paradise
And all its blest—if such should be—
I will lift glad, afar-off eyes,
Though it contain no place for me.

                                    Hardy, *Let Me Enjoy*

108 That night your great guns, unawares,
     Shook all our coffins as we lay,
     And broke the chancel window-squares,
     We thought it was the Judgment Day
     And sat upright. While drearisome

Arose the howl of wakened hounds:
The mouse let fall the altar-crumb,
The worms drew back into the mounds,

The glebe cow drooled. Till God called, "No;
It's gunnery practice out at sea
Just as before you went below;
The world is as it used to be:

"All nations striving strong to make
Red war yet redder. Mad as hatters
They do no more for Christés sake
Than you who are helpless in such matters.

"That this is not the judgment hour
For some of them's a blessed thing,
For if it were they'd have to scour
Hell's floor for so much threatening. . . .

"Ha, ha. It will be warmer when
I blow the trumpet (if indeed
I ever do; for you are men,
And rest eternal sorely need)."

                                    Hardy, *Channel Firing*

Author Index

All authors represented in this collection are listed in this index alphabetically, with birth and death dates. In the case of authors of more than one work from which quotations are included, the works (together with the translator, where there is one) are listed alphabetically and, where the work is long and/or complex, with subdivisions thereof. For instance, the reader wishing to locate quotations from Augustine's *The City of God* will find this work as the second entry under "Augustine"; and, because it is a long work, references are subdivided according to Books. Turning to the item in question, the reader will find that quotations from Book 1 of *The City of God* appear in Sections 1.8 and 1.9, in Section 9.6, and in Section 20.4, and so forth. It is never difficult to find the appropriate quotations within the sections indicated because quotations within a section are arranged in chronological order by author.

AESCHYLUS (ca. 525/524 BC–456 BC)
  Agamemnon (tr. by Richmond Lattimore) 1.2,3,7; 4.7,8,12; 5.5; 9.8,15; 10.6; 12.2; 14.1; 15.3; 20.13
  Eumenides (tr. by Richmond Lattimore) 1.8; 4.2; 5.5; 9.7; 12.4
  Libation Bearers (tr. by Richmond Lattimore) 2.2; 5.6; 12.4; 15.3; 19.7
  Prometheus Bound (tr. by David Grene) 1.1; 4.7; 9.15; 15.2,3; 20.10
  Seven against Thebes (tr. by David Grene) 1.7
  Suppliant Maidens (tr. by Seth G. Benardete) 15.3
AMBROSE, St. (ca. 339–397)
  Ductor Dubitantium (q. by Jeremy Taylor) 9.2
  Letter to Simplicianus 9.4
ANON.
  Aucassin et Nicolette 20.15
  inscription over the door of Plato's Academy 17.3
ANSELM, St. (1033–1109)
  Proslogium (tr. by S. N. Deane), Ch. 1: 1.2 / Ch. 2–3: 20.5 / Ch. 7: 20.5 / Ch. 16: 20.5 / Ch. 18: 20.5 / Ch. 24: 9.15 / Ch. 25: 3.5
APOCRYPHAL BOOKS OF THE BIBLE, King James Version
  Ecclesiasticus, Ch. 34: 6.2 / Ch. 38: 18.1
  Tobit, Ch. 3: 20.7
  Wisdom of Solomon, Ch. 9: 5.1
AQUINAS, St. Thomas (ca. 1225–1274)
  Commentary on Aristotle's "On Interpretation" 7.1
  Commentary on the Sentences of Peter Lombard, Ch. 3: 1.1
  Concerning Being and Essence (tr. by George G. Leckie), Intro.: 6.3
  On Kingship (tr. by Gerald B. Phelan), Ch. 1: 10.1,2,3,6,9
  Summa Contra Gentiles (tr. by Charles J. O'Neil), Bk. Four: 9.4
  Summa Theologica (tr. by Fathers of the English Dominican Province)
    First Pt., Q1: 17.1,2 / Q2: 19.3,5; 20.5 / Q5: 9.6; 16.6 / Q7: 19.5 / Q8: 20.5 / Q10: 19.7; 20.5 / Q11: 20.5 / Q12: 6.1,5 / Q13: 7.1 / Q14: 6.1; 9.15 / Q15: 19.8 / Q16: 6.3 / Q18: 19.2,5 / Q21: 12.2 / Q22: 19.4 / Q23: 15.3 / Q24: 15.3 / Q25: 19.8 / Q32: 19.8 / Q39: 16.6 / Q42: 19.7 / Q46: 19.3,6,7,8 / Q47: 19.1 / Q48: 19.1 / Q49: 9.6 / Q51: 20.7 / Q52: 20.7 / Q53: 19.6 / Q57: 20.7 / Q58: 6.7 / Q59: 4.4; 5.7 / Q60: 6.1 / Q61: 20.7 / Q63: 20.7,13 / Q64: 20.7 / Q65: 13.3; 19.3 / Q73: 19.5 / Q75: 1.1; 5.1 / Q76: 5.1,2 / Q78: 1.1; 5.2 / Q79: 1.1; 6.3; 9.5 / Q81: 4.1 / Q82: 6.1 / Q83: 5.7 / Q84: 5.2,4,5; 6.1 / Q85: 5.1; 17.3 / Q91: 1.1; 16.1 / Q92: 1.7; 10.7; 20.13 / Q94: 6.4 / Q95: 9.4 / Q96: 10.2,7 / Q98: 3.3 / Q103: 19.4,8 / Q104: 19.3 / Q105: 20.11 / Q110: 20.11 / Q111: 20.7 / Q113: 20.7 / Q114: 20.7, 11 / Q115: 20.10 / Q116: 15.3; 19.4 / Q117: 18.2; 19.2
    Pt. I of Second Pt., Q2: 1.5; 9.8; 11.2,4 / Q3: 9.8 / Q4: 3.4 / Q5: 9.8 / Q13: 5.7 / Q19: 9.3 / Q21: 16.7 / Q25: 4.1 / Q26: 3.4 / Q27: 6.1 / Q28: 5.6; 6.3 / Q29: 3.2; 6.3 / Q31: 4.7 / Q32: 4.6,7 / Q33: 4.7 / Q34: 4.7; 9.10 / Q35: 4.7 / Q38: 4.6,7; 6.3 / Q40: 1.3; 4.5; 6.2 / Q46: 4.3 / Q47: 4.3 / Q49: 18.3 / Q51: 8.2 / Q53: 8.2 / Q55: 9.10 / Q56: 8.2 / Q57: 9.13,15; 16.1 / Q58: 9.10 / Q59: 4.6 / Q61: 9.10,13 / Q65: 3.5; 9.13 / Q66: 9.10,13 / Q67: 20.15 / Q69: 9.8 / Q71: 20.13 / Q72: 20.13 / Q73: 2.3; 20.13 / Q77: 20.13 / Q80: 20.7 / Q81: 20.13 / Q82: 18.3 / Q84: 11.2 / Q87: 12.4 / Q90: 12.1 / Q91: 20.14 / Q94: 9.3,6,7 / Q95: 9.10; 12.1 / Q96: 12.1 / Q97: 9.2; 12.1 / Q100: 9.1,7,9 / Q101: 16.3 / Q102: 2.3; 20.2 / Q105: 10.3,5,6; 12.4 / Q108: 20.3 / Q109: 1.2; 20.14 / Q111: 20.14
    Pt. II of Second Pt., Q1: 6.5; 8.3; 20.4 / Q2: 6.5; 17.1; 20.9 / Q4: 6.5 / Q5: 20.4 / Q8: 6.7 / Q9: 9.15 / Q10: 13.2; 20.9 / Q11: 20.9 / Q19: 4.2; 9.15 / Q20: 4.5 / Q23: 3.5; 19.2 / Q24: 3.5 / Q25: 3.4,5; 9.9; 12.4; 20.13 / Q26: 2.1,2; 3.1,4 / Q28: 20.15 / Q29: 14.3 / Q30: 4.8; 20.8 / Q40: 14.1 / Q42: 10.6 / Q45: 9.15 / Q46: 9.15 / Q47: 9.13 / Q57: 12.3 / Q58: 9.7; 12.2 / Q61: 12.2 / Q64: 20.13 / Q66: 11.1 / Q77: 11.5 / Q81: 9.10; 20.1,8 / Q83: 20.8 / Q85: 20.8 / Q92: 20.12 / Q94: 20.1,12 / Q96: 20.12 / Q141: 9.12 / Q142: 9.12 / Q145: 9.14 / Q180: 3.3; 16.6 / Q183:

NEWTON, Sir Isaac (1643–1727)
  Optics, Bk. 1: 5.2 / Bk. 3: 9.1; 17.2; 19.3,8; 20.5
  Principia (Mathematical Principles of Natural Philosophy)
      (tr. by Andrew Motte, rev. by Florian Cajori)
    Pref. to 1st Ed.: 17.2,3
    Definitions 19.5,6,7
    Axioms 19.5
    Bk. 1, Ch. 11: 7.3 / Ch. 12: 19.5
    Bk. 3, Rules of Reasoning in Philosophy 17.2; 19.1,5
  Remark (1727) 17.2
NICOMACHUS OF GERASA (fl. 100 AD)
  Introduction to Arithmetic (tr. by Martin L. D'Ooge)
    Bk. 1, Ch. 2: 9.8 / Ch. 4: 17.3 / Ch. 6: 19.8 / Ch. 23:
      9.10
    Bk. 2, Ch. 6: 19.6
NIETZSCHE, Friedrich (1844–1900)
  The Anti-Christ (tr. by R. J. Hollingdale), Sec. 2: 9.6;
    20.3 / Sec. 5: 20.3 / Sec. 9: 6.5 / Sec. 11: 9.9 / Sec.
    14: 1.1 / Sec. 16: 20.5 / Sec. 18: 20.5 / Sec. 24:
    20.2 / Sec. 26: 6.5; 20.13 / Sec. 43: 13.3 / Sec. 49:
    20.13 / Sec. 52: 20.5 / Sec. 55: 6.3; 17.1 / Sec. 57: 1.4;
    9.8,9; 12.3 / Sec. 61: 20.1 / Sec. 62: 20.4
  Beyond Good and Evil, Bk. 3: 20.3 / Bk. 4: 1.9; 2.3; 3.1,3;
    5.6; 9.1; 12.4 / Bk. 7: 5.3; 16.4 / Bk. 8: 16.3,4 / Bk.
    9: 4.6 / Bk. 10: 16.4
  The Birth of Tragedy, Sec. 13: 17.1
  The Gay Science, Aphorism 258: 17.3
  Genealogy of Morals (tr. by Horace B. Samuel)
    Pref.: 1.4
    Second Essay, Sec. 8: 9.9 / Sec. 11: 9.7 / Sec. 16: 9.5 /
      Sec. 17: 10.1
  Human, All-Too-Human, Sec. 28: 19.8 / Sec. 71: 4.5 /
    Sec. 74: 8.2 / Sec. 283: 10.7 / Sec. 322: 1.9 / Sec.
    477: 14.1
  Joyful Wisdom, Sec. 341: 15.2
  Thus Spake Zarathustra (tr. by Th. Common)
    Prologue 1.1
    Pt. 2 (40) 1.1
    Pt. 3 (57) 15.2
    Pt. 4, Intro.: 20.5 / Ch. 64: 6.1 / Ch. 73: 1.2
  Twilight of the Idols (tr. by R. J. Hollingdale), Expeditions
    of an Untimely Man 1.6; 12.4; 13.1,3; 16.6 / The
    Improvers of Mankind 19.1 / Maxims and Arrows
    1.6 / Morality as Anti-Nature 9.1; 14.1 / What the
    Germans Lack 8.3

OLD TESTAMENT (by order of books)
  Genesis, Ch. 1: 1.1; 9.6; 19.2,8 / Ch. 2: 1.7; 2.3; 7.1; 19.2;
    20.8,13 / Ch. 3: 1.8; 2.2; 11.3; 20.13 / Ch. 4: 2.1 / Ch
    9: 12.4 / Ch. 11: 7.1 / Ch. 12: 20.2 / Ch. 13: 20.2 /
    Ch. 17: 20.2 / Ch. 22: 20.2 / Ch. 25: 2.1 / Ch. 28:
    5.5 / Ch. 29: 2.3 / Ch. 35: 20.2 / Ch. 37: 4.8 / Ch.
    38: 2.3 / Ch. 39: 3.3 / Ch. 44: 4.6 / Ch. 47: 11.6
  Exodus, Ch. 3: 20.5 / Ch. 6: 20.2 / Ch. 12: 20.2 / Ch. 14:
    14.2; 20.11 / Ch. 15: 20.5 / Ch. 20: 9.3 / Ch. 21:
    12.2 / Ch. 23: 9.14 / Ch. 33: 20.5
  Leviticus, Ch. 6: 9.14 / Ch. 19: 3.5 / Ch. 24: 12.1 / Ch.
    25: 10.7; 13.1 / Ch. 26: 20.2
  Numbers, Ch. 6: 20.5 / Ch. 14: 20.13 / Ch. 32: 20.13
  Deuteronomy, Ch. 4: 20.5 / Ch. 5: 20.2 / Ch. 6: 20.8 /
    Ch. 8: 20.1 / Ch. 19: 11.1 / Ch. 21: 2.1 / Ch. 24: 2.1;
    12.4 / Ch. 28: 18.3 / Ch. 30: 1.8 / Ch. 34: 20.10
  Joshua, Ch. 6: 14.2
  Judges, Ch. 11: 2.2 / Ch. 16: 1.7
  Ruth, Ch. 1: 3.1
  I Samuel, Ch. 24: 9.7
  II Samuel, Ch. 1: 3.4 / Ch. 6: 20.8 / Ch. 11: 3.3 / Ch. 12:
    1.8; 11.2 / Ch. 13: 3.3 / Ch. 18: 2.2

I Kings, Ch. 3: 2.2; 9.15 / Ch. 8: 20.2 / Ch. 19: 20.5
II Kings, Ch. 9: 1.7
I Chronicles, Ch. 10: 1.9
Job, Ch. 1: 1.8 / Ch. 2: 18.3 / Ch. 3: 4.5 / Ch. 7: 1.9;
    4.5 / Ch. 9: 9.7 / Ch. 13: 20.5 / Ch. 14: 1.2 / Ch. 19:
    20.2 / Ch. 24: 2.3 / Ch. 28: 9.15 / Ch. 38: 1.1
Psalms, Ch. 1: 9.7 / Ch. 3: 20.14 / Ch. 5: 20.8 / Ch. 8:
    1.1 / Ch. 14: 20.9 / Ch. 17: 20.8 / Ch. 19: 20.5 / Ch.
    22: 4.5 / Ch. 23: 9.14; 20.14 / Ch. 24: 19.8 / Ch. 27:
    4.2 / Ch. 30: 4.6 / Ch. 33: 20.2 / Ch. 36: 20.15 / Ch.
    37: 20.14 / Ch. 39: 1.2 / Ch. 50: 20.5 / Ch. 51:
    20.13,14 / Ch. 53: 20.5 / Ch. 84: 20.15 / Ch. 89:
    20.2 / Ch. 90: 1.3; 19.7 / Ch. 96: 20.8 / Ch. 100:
    20.8 / Ch. 103: 3.5; 20.7 / Ch. 104: 11.3 / Ch. 111:
    9.15 / Ch. 119: 6.5; 14.3 / Ch. 127: 15.3 / Ch. 130:
    20.8 / Ch. 137: 20.2 / Ch. 139: 20.5
Proverbs, Ch. 1: 6.1; 20.13 / Ch. 3: 9.7 / Ch. 6: 3.3;
    11.3 / Ch. 10: 11.2 / Ch. 11: 9.14 / Ch. 12: 2.3 / Ch.
    13: 2.2 / Ch. 14: 11.2 / Ch. 16: 4.3,11; 14.3 / Ch. 17:
    9.15 / Ch. 19: 2.3 / Ch. 20: 11.5 / Ch. 21: 1.7 / Ch.
    22: 2.2 / Ch. 23: 5.1; 9.15; 12.4 / Ch. 24: 9.11 / Ch.
    25: 3.5 / Ch. 26: 9.15 / Ch. 27: 1.4 / Ch. 28: 10.6;
    11.2; 20.13 / Ch. 30: 2.3; 20.13 / Ch. 31: 1.7
Ecclesiastes, Ch. 1: 9.15; 15.2; 19.5,8 / Ch. 2: 9.15; 11.3 /
    Ch. 3: 19.7 / Ch. 4: 3.4; 9.6 / Ch. 5: 4.9; 11.2 / Ch.
    7: 4.6; 20.13 / Ch. 8: 4.7 / Ch. 9: 9.6,15; 11.3; 15.3;
    19.2,4 / Ch. 11: 1.3; 15.3 / Ch. 12: 1.3; 9.9; 16.2
Song of Solomon, Ch. 1: 16.6 / Ch. 4: 16.6 / Ch. 8: 3.1;
    4.10
Isaiah, Ch. 1: 6.7; 20.8 / Ch. 2: 14.3 / Ch. 6: 6.5 / Ch. 9:
    20.3 / Ch. 11: 14.3; 20.3 / Ch. 14: 20.15 / Ch. 40:
    20.5,14 / Ch. 43: 20.2 / Ch. 45: 20.2 / Ch. 52: 20.3 /
    Ch. 53: 20.3 / Ch. 65: 20.14
Jeremiah, Ch. 4: 14.1 / Ch. 6: 14.1 / Ch. 13: 19.5 / Ch.
    23: 20.10 / Ch. 25: 20.10 / Ch. 29: 20.10
Ezekiel, Ch. 1: 20.5 / Ch. 18: 20.13 / Ch. 22: 20.6 / Ch.
    37: 20.10
Daniel, Ch. 3: 20.11
Hosea, Ch. 8: 19.3
Joel, Ch. 2: 5.5
Jonah, Ch. 1–2: 20.14
Micah, Ch. 6: 9.9; 20.8
Zechariah, Ch 7: 9.7
Malachi, Ch. 3: 20.14
OVID [Publius Ovidius Naso] (43 BC–17 AD)
  Art of Love (tr. by Rolfe Humphries), Bk. 1: 20.6 / Bk. 2:
    3.3 / Bk. 3: 3.3
  Epistulae Ex Ponto 3.6
  Fasti 19.7
  Metamorphoses (tr. by Mary M. Innes), Bk. 1: 15.2;
    19.2,8 / Bk. 2: 9.13 / Bk. 7: 4.6 / Bk. 15: 19.7

PASCAL, Blaise (1623–1662)
  Geometrical Demonstration (tr. by Richard Scofield) 4.7;
    6.3,7; 7.1,2; 8.3; 9.6; 16.2; 17.3; 19.5,6
  Letter to Fermat (July 29, 1654) 6.3
  New Experiments Concerning the Vacuum (tr. by Richard
    Scofield) 5.4; 6.7; 19.6
  Pensées (tr. by W. F. Trotter), Sec. 1: 5.1; 6.1,4,7; 7.2; 8.3;
    16.3,4,7; 17.1,3 / Sec. 2: 1.1,2,4,5,8; 3.4; 4.1,6,12; 5.4;
    6.1,4; 9.1,8,9,10,14; 16.1; 17.1,2,3,5,7,8; 20.8,14 / Sec.
    3: 1.2,8; 19.4,6; 20.1,5,9 / Sec. 4: 3.1; 4.2; 6.5,7; 9.2;
    20.1,3,5 / Sec. 5: 1.5; 9.2,15; 10.6,9; 12.2; 14.1,3;
    17.1 / Sec. 6: 1.1,6; 4.1,12; 5.1,5,6,7; 6.2,6; 9.6,10;
    12.2; 19.2 / Sec. 7: 1.1,4; 3.2; 6.5; 9.8; 19.3;
    20.1,8,13,14 / Sec. 8: 6.3,5; 19.1; 20.1,2,3,5,9 / Sec. 9:
    6.5; 12.1; 20.2,3 / Sec. 10: 3.3 / Sec. 11: 4.5; 20.10 /

Subject and Proper Name Index

This index is a guide to terms, themes, topics, and proper names that are prominent in the quotations and is to that extent a "key word" index. There is one qualification of that phrase: because the book itself is topically divided, the terminology peculiar to a specific section was not indexed. For instance, Chapter 2, Section 3 is titled MARRIAGE. Therefore, occurrences of the word "marriage" in that section were not indexed, but the word, when appearing in other sections, was indexed where pertinent.

The only exception to this indexing pattern occurs in the case of very famous or familiar quotations, particularly from such sources as the Bible or the plays of Shakespeare. These quotations were thoroughly indexed regardless of their place in this book.

Each cited term in this index is followed by a short sentence or phrase in context. The location of the cited term in the contextual phrase is indicated by three dots.

References follow the contextual phrase and are to chapter, section, and quotation number, not to page number.

---

could work with . . . (Newton) 17-3-31
. . . of the report (Thucydides) 15-1-3

ACCUSER
carry one's . . . in one's heart (Juvenal) 9-5-3
. . . put to death (Swift) 12-4-46

ACCUSERS
where are thine . . . (*John*) 3-5-9

ACCUSTOM
. . . yourself to do something else (Epictetus) 8-2-8

ACCUSTOMED
things one has been . . . to (Hippocrates) 8-2-1

ACHAB
sent to punish . . . (Aquinas) 20-7-29

ACHAIAN
bronze-armored . . . (Homer) 2-2-8

ACHAIANS
. . . give my son (Homer) 2-2-7
the host of the . . . (Homer) 14-2-3

ACHE
the . . . of longing (Homer) 2-3-9

ACHERON
souls break loose from . . . (Lucretius) 5-4-2

ACHIEVEMENT
. . . assured of acceptance (Hegel) 6-5-87
demand for new . . . (Croce) 15-2-88
. . . of a lofty soul (Montaigne) 8-3-39
temple of man's . . . (Russell) 15-2-79

ACHIEVEMENTS
Christian-like . . . (Cervantes) 1-5-81
of extraordinary . . . (Schopenhauer) 1-5-121
uniqueness of human . . . (Benedict) 15-2-90

ACHILLES
and fierce . . . (Virgil) 4-6-11
and see the great . . . (Tennyson) 1-3-115
especially . . . whose gravestone (Plutarch) 16-3-21
I am weary with . . . shouting (Keats) 1-7-128
more blest by fortune than you . . . (Homer) 1-8-9
so spoke great . . . (Homer) 4-6-5
still sorrows for . . . (Dante) 20-15-54
swift-footed . . . I saw (Euripides) 14-2-7
to have been like . . . (Plato) 1-6-6

ACKNOWLEDGE
to . . . a great man (Carlyle) 1-5-123

ACKNOWLEDGMENT
common right of . . . (Augustine) 12-3-3
. . . of virtue (Montaigne) 9-10-58

ACQUAINTANCE
. . . derived from sense (Russell) 6-1-103
knowledge of . . . (Wm. James) 6-1-100
. . . necessary for love (Santayana) 3-1-93
then brag of their . . . (Swift) 16-2-24

ACQUIESCENCE
. . . in scepticism or dogma (Russell) 6-6-49
more delicate . . . (Plutarch) 2-3-25
state of intellectual . . . (Russell) 17-1-101

ACQUIRE
wish to . . . is natural (Machiavelli) 4-9-7

ACQUIRED
conscience not to be . . . (Kant) 9-5-17

ACQUIRED RIGHT
innate right and . . . (Kant) 12-3-22

ACQUIREMENT
say of the . . . of knowledge (Plato) 6-1-4

ACQUIREMENTS
mass of our . . . (Newman) 6-1-96
mere heap of . . . (Hegel) 6-1-88

ACQUIRERS
facility to . . . (Coleridge) 10-2-91

ACQUIRING

faith not of our . . . (Montaigne) 6-5-44

ACQUISITION
difficulty of . . . (Rousseau) 11-2-88
natural art of . . . (Aristotle) 14-1-22
natural means of . . . (Hegel) 11-2-117
principle of external . . . (Kant) 11-1-40

ACQUISITIONS
deprive us of . . . (Johnson) 1-8-117

ACT
always . . . to avoid (Epicurus) 4-7-13
always obliged to . . . (Dewey) 6-5-114
an . . . has no ethical quality (Wm. James) 9-1-37
and the . . . a slave to limit (Shakespeare) 4-4-19
be slow to . . . (Machiavelli) 4-2-20
cessation from . . . (Aquinas) 8-2-11
commit an . . . that rates (Juvenal) 9-14-15
for our past . . . (Emerson) 1-4-48
history of mind is its own . . . (Hegel) 15-1-57
inclines us to . . . voluntarily (Aquinas) 9-4-26
is thine own . . . and valor (Shakespeare) 9-11-35
last . . . is tragic (Pascal) 1-2-55
living . . . breaks through (Melville) 3-2-35
more able to . . . with friends (Aristotle) 3-4-11
not every . . . of love (Dante) 3-1-28
obliged to . . . lawfully (Montaigne) 19-1-28
. . . of brotherly love (Dostoevsky) 3-4-61
. . . of dying is not (Boswell) 1-8-118
reduced from potency to . . . (Aquinas) 8-3-35, 19-5-20
resolve to . . . differently (Darwin) 9-5-25
see that you . . . it well (Epictetus) 9-9-9
. . . singly (Emerson) 9-7-47
to . . . against one another (Aurelius) 9-7-28
virtue in relation to . . . (Aquinas) 9-10-48
words are not overt . . . (Montesquieu) 7-1-44

ACTING
between the . . . of a dreadful thing (Shakespeare) 5-5-22

ACTION
. . . adjusted to experience (Santayana) 6-2-54
against . . . in speaking (Boswell) 7-2-78
agreement of . . . and law (Kant) 9-4-47
aim not knowledge but . . . (Aristotle) 1-3-16
aim of military . . . (Clausewitz) 14-1-91
all human . . . consists in (Mill) 19-1-115
an end at once of all . . . (Hume) 9-2-24
a single bad . . . (Schopenhauer) 1-5-119
. . . as a power (Dewey) 13-1-63
back upon a limited . . . (Planck) 5-7-48
belief is measured by . . . (Wm. James) 20-1-73
. . . be uncommemorated (Tacitus) 15-1-22
commonly speaking an . . . (Descartes) 4-1-14
compare different modes of . . . (Mill) 8-3-83
consists in . . . and contemplation (Augustine) 17-1-38
contemplating a generous . . . (Fielding) 11-2-79
cowardly and voluptuous . . . (Aristotle) 9-7-15
determined to any . . . (Spinoza) 4-4-25
distinct motive for every . . . (Darwin) 9-1-26
distinguish themselves in every . . . (Plato) 8-1-2
eases his way to . . . (Plutarch) 1-5-33
divisions of . . . of the mind (Emerson) 5-1-64
every . . . due to one of seven causes (Aristotle) 19-3-7
every . . . under compulsion (Milton) 13-2-17
fate of men of . . . (Tolstoy) 15-3-111
first principle of . . . (Aristotle) 8-1-9
food of feeling is . . . (Mill) 3-6-24
. . . from principle (Thoreau) 9-9-40
gained in . . . (Plutarch) 4-7-18
general rules of . . . broken (Johnson) 4-5-30
gives a rule of . . . (Boswell) 12-1-68
good . . . blotting out the bad (Thucydides) 3-6-4

ACTION (*Cont.*)
good guide to correct . . . (Plato) 6-5-3
goods achievable by . . . (Aristotle) 9-6-14
great law of every human . . . (Twain) 11-3-78
happiness is the end of . . . (Aristotle) 9-8-11
highly selective . . . (Santayana) 19-6-48
his power of . . . is increased (Spinoza) 9-6-82
if it does not determine . . . (Plotinus) 6-1-22
imitation of . . . and life (Aristotle) 16-4-9
. . . in a drama (Epictetus) 9-9-9
incapable of common . . . (Plato) 12-2-9
inherent tendency to deny . . . (Dewey) 8-2-34
. . . is transitory (Wordsworth) 1-2-72
junction of fancy with . . . (Santayana) 19-7-92
knowledge and . . . two aspects (Bergson) 5-1-84
law a rule of . . . (Hamilton/Madison) 12-1-76
laws governing human . . . (Tolstoy) 5-7-44
liberty of . . . (Mill) 13-1-52
life as energy spent in . . . (Bergson) 3-1-92
lose the name of . . . (Shakespeare) 1-9-28
love of . . . (Gibbon) 1-2-69
love of life manifested by . . . (Aquinas) 3-1-25
lust in . . . (Shakespeare) 3-3-55
marks of . . . of the mind (Locke) 7-2-70
maxim of an . . . (Kant) 1-4-38
moral worth of an . . . (Kant) 9-3-27
motive of thought in . . . (Peirce) 6-5-106
must represent one . . . (Aristotle) 16-4-10
no power over . . . (Herodotus) 6-1-2
not to deal with one . . . (Aristotle) 15-1-6
. . . of every member of society (Huxley) 10-1-46
. . . of mind and body (Hume) 17-1-68
. . . of thinking and its results (Newman) 5-1-69
one great noble . . . (Aristotle) 3-6-7
only learned in . . . (Mill) 8-1-70
overt . . . is demanded (Dewey) 6-1-108
place inactivity above . . . (Aristotle) 10-2-13
pleasure in a good . . . (Aquinas) 3-3-28
preference for . . . over talk (Freud) 7-2-90
probabilities make . . . possible (Sartre) 4-5-39
shun any base . . . (Plutarch) 9-11-15
source of all . . . (Harvey) 17-2-30
standpoint of . . . (Russell) 17-2-121
suit the . . . to the word (Shakespeare) 16-4-19
the cause of an . . . (Tolstoy) 12-4-72
the origin of . . . (Aristotle) 5-7-4
. . . the subverter of scepticism (Hume) 6-6-26
things attained by . . . (Aristotle) 9-13-4
thinking a postponement of . . . (Dewey) 5-1-81
time for . . . comes (Herodotus) 9-11-3
to every . . . a reaction (Newton) 19-5-47
truth for purpose of . . . (Mill) 6-5-98
understanding must precede . . . (Kierkegaard) 1-4-43
vilest and stupidest . . . (Shaw) 8-1-78
virtue as a principle of . . . (Aquinas) 9-10-43
what an . . . (Homer) 1-7-6
what is called a good . . . (Emerson) 9-10-112
with a view to . . . (Aristotle) 6-2-7

ACTIONS
an instinct to virtuous . . . (Rabelais) 9-4-30
attribute extreme . . . to vanity (Nietzsche) 8-2-29
but two sorts of . . . (Locke) 19-5-52
by men's . . . we discover (Hobbes) 1-4-25
. . . clearly contrary (Tolstoy) 1-6-74
conceal my . . . (Descartes) 1-5-87
conscious of their own . . . (Spinoza) 5-7-27
contingency of human . . . (Hume) 15-3-98
control his own . . . (Grotius) 12-3-9
deterred from . . . by opinion (Hume) 9-1-14

directs his . . . (Machiavelli) 1-2-29
. . . done from motives (Mill) 9-1-30
ends apart from . . . (Aristotle) 16-1-7
fine and just . . . (Aristotle) 6-7-11
for the sake of noble . . . (Aristotle) 10-1-8
for voluntary . . . shame (Aristotle) 1-5-17
good . . . bring (Plutarch) 1-5-32
good or excusable . . . (Montaigne) 9-7-36
great . . . of brave men (Plutarch) 16-3-21
habit maintained by . . . (Epictetus) 8-2-7
. . . have not earned happiness (Plotinus) 9-8-26
. . . he would have him do (Locke) 8-3-59
honor and good . . . (Bacon) 11-2-64
ideas of greater . . . (Plutarch) 1-6-15
identify end with certain . . . (Aristotle) 9-6-15
if . . . were governed by belief (Gibbon) 15-3-104
internal and external . . . (Kant) 5-7-35
in the . . . of the insane (Montaigne) 5-6-10
judge by outward . . . (Montaigne) 4-1-11
jurisdiction of moral . . . (Locke) 9-1-10
leads to shameful . . . (Aristotle) 13-2-7
liberty applied to voluntary . . . (Hume) 5-7-30
majority of good . . . (Mill) 9-6-105
masters of our . . . (Aristotle) 9-10-15
matters connected with human . . . (Aquinas) 9-1-5
. . . men voluntarily do (Hobbes) 5-7-23
misshapen and unnatural . . . (Plutarch) 10-2-23
modest . . . preserve man (Epictetus) 9-10-32
movers of human . . . (Boswell) 16-4-33
necessity of human . . . (Boswell) 5-7-33
normal . . . are impossible (Wm. James) 18-3-60
. . . of all men (Machiavelli) 1-5-53
. . . of men and citizens (Rousseau) 3-6-17
of their following . . . (Plutarch) 1-5-29
of their great . . . (Cervantes) 1-5-80
of their inward . . . (Th. Browne) 19-1-50
. . . of the just (Plato) 9-7-9
. . . of the mass (Tolstoy) 1-6-73
one-half of our . . . (Machiavelli) 15-3-69
. . . proceed from opinions (Hobbes) 13-2-14
. . . proceed from our character (Tolstoy) 5-7-44
read laws in each other's . . . (Emerson) 9-3-34
regulate his . . . (Locke) 2-2-65
relation between our . . . (Montaigne) 12-1-40
. . . right if they promote happiness (Mill) 9-1-29
same who did those . . . (Locke) 1-4-32
. . . she has enjoined on us (Montaigne) 19-1-33
somewhat in great . . . (Emerson) 1-6-66
. . . that a man might (Shakespeare) 1-8-74
. . . that are easy (Wm. James) 1-6-80
. . . that are most profitable (Hobbes) 15-1-35
the free . . . of men (Locke) 12-4-45
the maxims of . . . (Kant) 9-1-23
the use of . . . fair and good (Shakespeare) 8-2-17
thought of his . . . (Plutarch) 1-5-34
thought of these . . . (Aristotle) 5-5-10
to put happiness in . . . (Plotinus) 9-8-25
to their own . . . (Plutarch) 1-5-35
two contrary . . . be excited (Spinoza) 19-5-43
two principles of human . . . (Aquinas) 9-10-44
unconscious . . . bear fruit (Tolstoy) 15-1-80
uniformity in human . . . (Hume) 6-2-27
voluntary . . . of any one person (Kant) 9-7-42
we judge our . . . (Rousseau) 9-5-15
. . . which are against customs (Augustine) 9-2-6
. . . which the law (Hobbes) 2-1-28
wisdom to direct our . . . (Locke) 9-3-22

ACTIVE
. . . and passive citizenship (Kant) 10-5-24

ACTIVITIES
from the exercise of . . . (Aristotle) 5-7-3
. . . give life its character (Aristotle) 9-8-13
. . . in constant change (Aurelius) 19-5-15
one or more . . . (Aristotle) 4-7-11
pleasantest of virtuous . . . (Aristotle) 9-8-14
ACTIVITY
all life is an . . . (Plotinus) 19-2-19
an . . . of the soul (Aristotle) 9-8-12
art may arise from any . . . (Langer) 16-2-59
custom is . . . without opposition (Hegel) 9-2-30
depend upon automatic . . . (Plotinus) 19-4-15
ethical . . . outside (Hegel) 1-7-129
evil exists to create . . . (Malthus) 9-6-97
field of human intellectual . . . (Freud) 17-2-126
friends must join in common . . . (Aristotle) 3-4-16
happiness is an . . . (Aristotle) 9-10-16
intellectual gifts mean nervous . . . (Schopenhauer) 5-1-61
love the only reasonable . . . (Tolstoy) 3-1-82
mind is a perpetual . . . (Whitehead) 8-3-92
nor do they tire in . . . (Aristotle) 19-8-9
not theory but an . . . (Wittgenstein) 17-1-109
. . . of mental faculties (Darwin) 9-5-25
. . . of philosophic wisdom (Aristotle) 17-1-14
potentiality before . . . (Aristotle) 8-2-4
. . . produces a comic effect (Schopenhauer) 1-2-76
repressive . . . is (Freud) 2-2-95
spiritual and bodily . . . (Freud) 20-2-49
sum of my . . . (Hegel) 1-9-40
the . . . of God (Aristotle) 20-5-19, 20-6-21
we exist by virtue of . . . (Aristotle) 3-1-12
. . . with which man receives (Melville) 11-4-36
ACTORS
laws prohibit . . . (Augustine) 13-2-11
only with different . . . (Aurelius) 15-2-17
ACTS
a coward by his . . . (Sartre) 9-11-67
. . . and thoughts our own (Plotinus) 9-6-35
another man's . . . (Aurelius) 4-3-14
a person's voluntary . . . (Mill) 10-2-42
a rule of human . . . (Aquinas) 12-1-30
certain . . . are virtuous (Aquinas) 9-7-31
class of just . . . (Aristotle) 1-9-4
comparison of bad . . . (Aurelius) 4-4-12
consequences of his . . . (Darwin) 1-5-124
feeling formed by . . . (Sartre) 9-1-43
. . . for the benefit of others (Mill) 9-1-28
great . . . require (Milton) 11-2-71
more nor less than five . . . (Fielding) 16-4-27
. . . of kindness and love (Wordsworth) 9-10-110
of our public . . . (Montaigne) 1-5-60
pay for . . . committed (Euripides) 20-15-10
religion has two kinds of . . . (Aquinas) 20-1-12
rise to . . . of reflection (Leibniz) 5-1-39
rules of human . . . (Aquinas) 3-5-19
that all your . . . are queens (Shakespeare) 16-6-35
those same . . . (Freud) 1-4-67
. . . which must be done (Aurelius) 9-3-7
ACTUALITY
God is that . . . (Aristotle) 20-5-17
ground for concrete . . . (Whitehead) 20-5-120
potency and not . . . (Aristotle) 19-8-9
ADAM
all the race of . . . (Chaucer) 1-7-58
all thy dominion . . . (Milton) 20-7-63
. . . bit the apple (Marx) 20-13-90
. . . called every living creature (*Genesis*) 7-1-1
deep sleep to fall upon . . . (*Genesis*) 1-7-1
doom into which . . . fell (Milton) 9-6-81

enfold the children of . . . (Augustine) 20-13-39
first and second . . . (*I Corinthians*) 1-1-28
. . . from his fair (Milton) 2-3-69
from . . . to the deluge (Augustine) 15-2-20
generations from . . . (Tolstoy) 6-3-121
God instructed . . . (Hobbes) 7-1-29
. . . goodliest of men (Milton) 1-7-96
he formed thee . . . (Milton) 1-1-75
in . . . all die (*I Corinthians*) 1-8-40
. . . knew Eve his wife (*Genesis*) 2-1-1
on . . . last thus judgment (Milton) 20-13-86
. . . our father (Chaucer) 9-12-21
separated the sons of . . . (Calvin) 15-3-72
suffering . . . to transgress (Milton) 13-2-17
the evil seed of . . . (Dante) 20-15-51
the penalty of . . . (Shakespeare) 19-1-34
vices I inherit from . . . (Th. Browne) 4-11-21
. . . was but human (Twain) 20-13-93
. . . was not deceived (*I Timothy*) 1-7-43
we owe to . . . (Twain) 1-8-133
ADAMITIC
the language called . . . (Leibniz) 7-2-67
ADAM'S
compared to . . . dream (Keats) 5-4-34
to . . . doubt proposed (Milton) 17-2-42
ADAMS, John
as did . . . (Dewey) 13-3-53
ADAMS, John Quincy
. . . the former president (Tocqueville) 10-7-34
ADAPT
have to . . . or die (Whitehead) 15-2-77
ADAPTATION
minuteness of . . . (Wm. James) 19-2-56
. . . to new conditions (Huxley) 19-1-112
ADAPTATIONS
. . . in all nature (Mill) 19-1-114
ADEIMANTUS
and now . . . (Plato) 11-2-15
. . . I said (Plato) 17-1-7
ADEQUATE
any man . . . to office (Fielding) 10-6-43
ADMINISTRATION
legitimate rule of . . . (Rousseau) 12-1-64
. . . of the universe (Plotinus) 19-8-25
regular . . . of justice (Smith) 12-2-42
shares in the . . . (Aristotle) 10-5-5
ADMINISTRATOR
it seems to every . . . (Tolstoy) 10-2-103
ADMIRAL
to kill an . . . (Voltaire) 12-4-53
ADMIRALS
in company of . . . (Boswell) 14-2-48
ADMIRATION
definition of . . . (Ruskin) 1-2-90
. . . given to the rich (Russell) 11-2-159
have all my . . . (Euripides) 1-5-4
miracle derived from . . . (Aquinas) 20-11-12
nearer is . . . (Kant) 1-5-115
noble feelings of . . . (Darwin) 1-5-125
. . . rendered by enemies (Plutarch) 1-5-31
submissive . . . (Carlyle) 1-6-61
ADMIRE
hasty to . . . the teachers (Johnson) 9-1-16
ADMONITION
first and second . . . (Aquinas) 20-9-12
ADMONITIONS
carry out your own . . . (Plato) 1-3-15
ADOLESCENCE
love for truth during . . . (Galen) 8-3-27

ADORATION
breathless with ... (Wordsworth) 20-1-50
is thy soul of ... (Shakespeare) 10-6-24
... of the mind (Bacon) 6-2-20
ADORER
an ... of children (Euripides) 2-2-15
ADORNER
... of the ruin (Byron) 19-7-69
ADORNING
outward ... (*I Peter*) 1-7-44
ADULATION
grace-begging and vain ... (Kant) 20-12-33
ADULTERATION
as commanded concerning ... (Plato) 11-5-3
ADULTERER
eye of the ... (*Job*) 2-3-4
ADULTERERS
answer to ... and (Plutarch) 2-3-29
ADULTERESS
... will hunt for the precious life (*Proverbs*) 3-3-4
ADULTERIES
all the ... of art (Jonson) 19-1-41
ADULTERY
... and unfaithful wives (Euripides) 12-4-6
... belongs not only (Aquinas) 2-3-33
crime of ... (Boswell) 2-3-86
die for ... (Shakespeare) 3-3-52
doth commit ... (*Matthew*) 2-3-22
laws of ... swept away (Lucian) 17-1-34
moved her to ... (Homer) 1-7-8
no dash in ... (Homer) 3-3-5
not commit ... (Aquinas) 9-7-32
or to commit ... (Aquinas) 12-3-5
shalt not commit ... (*Matthew*) 2-3-21; (*Exodus*) 9-3-1
shalt thou commit ... (*Deut.*) 20-2-11
the gods commit ... (Euripides) 20-6-9
woman taken in ... (*John*) 3-5-9
ADVANCE
a real ... in condition of men (Thoreau) 15-2-59
... or decadence (Whitehead) 15-2-78
ADVANCEMENT
little ... of sciences (Bacon) 17-2-22
ADVANCES
and making great ... (Epicurus) 15-2-8
... has industry made (Augustine) 15-2-19
ADVANTAGE
consults his own ... (Spinoza) 10-1-25
everyone finds his ... (Locke) 1-5-100
for their own ... (Smith) 1-4-37
... humanity derives from law (Boswell) 12-1-68
is to their own ... (Aristotle) 17-1-12
own private ... (Locke) 10-6-42
protection of some ... (Cervantes) 15-3-87
rich had no ... (Plutarch) 11-2-43
... to my lot (Mill) 2-2-88
... to one tribe over another (Darwin) 9-1-27
... truth has (Mill) 6-3-116
truth should have ... (Pascal) 6-3-62
ADVANTAGES
all the ... of society (Hegel) 11-2-117
... makes us respected (Boswell) 11-2-96
... of man over other creatures (Montaigne) 1-1-50
possession of their ... (Smith) 11-2-111
seeking ... of one another (Plutarch) 14-1-29
the ... of reading (Boswell) 16-2-36
... that accrue to philosophy (Plutarch) 17-1-27
... that have accrued (Rousseau) 15-2-33
... wealth has (Plato) 11-2-14
ADVENTURE

joy of mental ... (Russell) 8-1-84
ADVENTURES
dangerous and glorious ... (Cervantes) 9-11-37
in quest of ... (Cervantes) 1-5-81
ADVENTURES OF TOM SAWYER, THE (Twain) 6-3-125
ADVENTUROUS
better to be ... (Machiavelli) 15-3-70
ADVERSARY
entrapping an ... (Augustine) 6-7-15
his ... in disputation (Epictetus) 6-7-13
wishing his ... (Cervantes) 9-11-38
ADVERSITIES
fickle fortune's ... (Chaucer) 9-8-35
ADVERSITY
dejected with ... (Plutarch) 18-3-26
... doth best discover virtue (Bacon) 9-10-73
faint in the day of ... (*Proverbs*) 9-11-1
not overcome by ... (Boethius) 15-3-55
remorse felt in ... (Rousseau) 4-6-43
struggling with ... (Tacitus) 9-8-23, 19-4-13
sweet the uses of ... (Shakespeare) 19-1-34
woe in ... (Augustine) 4-6-19
... you face at sea (Homer) 2-3-8
ADVERSITY'S
... sweet milk philosophy (Shakespeare) 17-1-47
ADVICE
easy thing to give ... (Aeschylus) 15-3-11
for ... we turn to philosophy (Seneca) 17-1-23
in private giving ... (Plato) 10-2-5
no very important ... (Thoreau) 1-3-116
ADVISERS
but through good ... (Machiavelli) 10-2-37
trusted ... of after-years (Mill) 8-3-85
AEACUS
Rhadamanthus and ... (Plato) 1-8-15
AEGIS
the dear treasured ... (Homer) 14-2-3
AEMILIUS PAULUS
nor was ... less severe (Plutarch) 14-2-18
AENEAS
as ... our great ancestor (Shakespeare) 1-6-26
ere ... had named it (Dante) 6-2-13, 20-15-54
... in this place (Virgil) 4-6-11
Virgil in his ... (Cervantes) 5-6-24
AENEID
a book of the ... (Boswell) 16-2-38
AEOLUS
Danaus or ... contribute (Epictetus) 2-1-19
when ... loses Sirocco (Dante) 20-15-55
AEON
many an ... (Tennyson) 19-8-82
AESCHYLUS
as ... says (Plato) 10-4-4
come ... don't answer (Aristophanes) 16-4-2
that's ... and Euripides (Aristophanes) 16-4-1
wishing as ... says (Plato) 9-7-9
AESCULAPIAN
of the ... art (Fielding) 18-3-51
AESCULAPIUS
... prescribed to this man (Aurelius) 15-3-45
swear by Apollo and ... (Hippocrates) 18-2-1
AESOP
... makes the fable that (Bacon) 17-2-16
AESTHETIC
although it is only ... (Kant) 16-6-47
as a principle of ... (T. S. Eliot) 16-7-53
communicates ... ideas (Kant) 16-5-37
loss of higher ... tastes (Darwin) 16-3-87
... principles are such axioms (Wm. James) 16-6-77

no . . . can be made (Cervantes) 2-3-66
. . . of each associate (Rousseau) 10-1-32
transference termed . . . (Kant) 11-1-41

ALIENS
between . . . and kinsfolk (Tacitus) 13-2-10

AILMENT
. . . ought to be administered (Hippocrates) 18-2-4

ALL
charge of the . . . (Plotinus) 9-6-35
sublimest members of the . . . (Plotinus) 19-8-26

ALL-DEVOURING
. . . all destroying (Swift) 19-7-58

ALL-ENFOLDER
the . . . the All-upholder (Goethe) 20-5-98

ALLEGIANCE
cold hearts freeze . . . (Shakespeare) 11-6-7
proof of true . . . (Milton) 5-7-26
refuse . . . to the state (Thoreau) 11-6-48
right to refuse . . . (Thoreau) 10-9-37

ALLEGORICAL
confess their . . . nature (Schopenhauer) 20-1-52
. . . or mystic (Dante) 16-3-27
similar . . . interpretations (Augustine) 20-4-12
young cannot judge . . . (Plato) 13-2-3

ALLEGORIES
. . . of religion (Schopenhauer) 6-5-89

ALLEGORY
. . . of the mind (Augustine) 1-8-52

ALLIANCE
. . . by blood and marriage (Swift) 14-1-61

ALLIES
many and brave . . . (Thucydides) 14-2-9

ALLUREMENTS
changes of new . . . (Kant) 8-2-22

ALLUSION
always an . . . of progress (Shaw) 15-2-75

ALLWORTHY, Mr.
. . . into the country (Fielding) 2-2-70
. . . rightly observed (Fielding) 6-3-87

ALMIGHTY
. . . had not determined (Th. Browne) 19-8-54
. . . hath not built (Milton) 1-6-41
he that contendeth with the . . . (*Job*) 1-1-2
truth next to the . . . (Milton) 6-3-73

ALMIGHTY MAKER
. . . them ordain (Milton) 19-6-25

ALMS
ask . . . from a man (Boswell) 1-7-119
charity not . . . (Fielding) 3-5-33
doeth . . . in secret (*Matthew*) 3-5-4

ALONE
be . . . on earth (Byron) 1-3-105
know that you are . . . (Thoreau) 13-1-44
man should be . . . (*Genesis*) 1-7-1
not good to be . . . (Locke) 2-1-29
we shall die . . . (Pascal) 1-8-110
world is . . . (Kepler) 19-8-44

ALONSO OF ARAGON
. . . was wont to say (Bacon) 1-3-67

ALPHA
I am . . . and Omega (*Revelation*) 19-8-19, 20-3-20, 20-5-27, 20-15-30

ALPHABET
. . . of human thought (Leibniz) 7-2-67

ALPS
he was crossing the . . . (Plutarch) 1-6-14

ALTAR
at a mightier . . . (Plutarch) 1-9-12
heart is his . . . (Augustine) 20-8-43

. . . to an unknown god (Wm. James) 19-3-51

ALTERATION
common term we apply is . . . (Galen) 19-5-18
laws without least . . . (Plutarch) 12-1-21
love which alters when it . . . finds (Shakespeare) 3-1-47

ALTERATIONS
able to endure all . . . (Bacon) 18-3-44

ALTERNATIVE
unhappy . . . is before you (Austen) 2-2-80

ALTERNATIVES
to foresee future . . . (Dewey) 5-7-49

ALYOSHA
the path . . . chose (Dostoevsky) 20-9-46

ALYPUS
where . . . was sitting (Augustine) 6-5-21

AMADIS DE GAUL
an enemy to . . . (Cervantes) 5-6-25
ever were there any . . . (Cervantes) 16-2-12
. . . was one of the most accomplished (Cervantes) 5-6-24

AMARANTHUS
. . . all his beauty shed (Milton) 4-6-40

AMARYLLIS
to sport with . . . (Milton) 16-3-43

AMAZE
object not to . . . readers (Polybius) 15-1-11

AMAZONS
the Scyths addressed the . . . (Herodotus) 1-7-12
Tracian . . . of old (Virgil) 1-7-35

AMBIGUITIES
need to avoid . . . (Aristotle) 7-2-21

AMBIGUITY
devices to escape . . . (Freud) 7-2-92
terms free from . . . (Pascal) 6-7-27

AMBITION
. . . an infirmity of man (Hobbes) 3-2-22
art not without . . . (Shakespeare) 1-5-73
be virtue but . . . (Aquinas) 1-5-50
. . . can creep (Burke) 1-5-114
. . . can teach valor (Montaigne) 4-1-11
childish and pedantic . . . (Montaigne) 7-2-43
crimes and follies of . . . (Gibbon) 15-1-52
curb the . . . of the court (Hume) 13-2-25
degrees of . . . (Bacon) 1-6-36
designs of . . . (Jefferson) 9-10-104
diseases of . . . and avarice (Fielding) 5-6-31
equality limits . . . (Montesquieu) 13-3-16
extravagant . . . replaced (Wm. James) 14-3-47
fling away . . . (Shakespeare) 1-5-75
from choice or . . . (Machiavelli) 14-1-38
greater too is the . . . (Cicero) 10-2-15
high road of haughty . . . (Cervantes) 9-10-70
insatiable . . . (Rousseau) 11-1-27
. . . is like a choler (Bacon) 1-5-82
. . . is violent (Bacon) 1-5-84
least sense of . . . (Montesquieu) 10-6-46
let not . . . mock (Gray) 11-2-83
lurk an ideal . . . (Santayana) 1-5-130
. . . made of sterner stuff (Shakespeare) 1-6-29
men whose . . . can limit (Plutarch) 14-1-29
mine own . . . and my queen (Shakespeare) 20-8-60
nothing to tempt the . . . (Rousseau) 14-3-35
. . . often puts men (Swift) 1-5-101
of the . . . of men (Plato) 1-5-10
pitiful . . . in the fool (Shakespeare) 16-4-19
plunged in vanities of . . . (Voltaire) 16-2-30
pomp begat . . . (Luther) 19-3-19
prince should contend with . . . (Machiavelli) 3-2-15
reign is worth . . . (Milton) 1-6-41
satisfaction of his own . . . (Locke) 10-6-42

AMBITION (*Cont.*)
   . . . seeks honor and glory (Augustine) 20-13-31
   spiritless and lacking . . . (Wm. James) 11-2-155
   that makes . . . virtue (Shakespeare) 4-10-6
   the . . . of princes (Swift) 14-1-61
   the distracted . . . (Plutarch) 1-6-16
   the impulse to . . . (Mann) 13-1-69
   towers of . . . and pride (Cervantes) 10-2-47
   transfer all . . . (Freud) 2-2-101
   unbounded . . . of Justinian (Gibbon) 6-2-33
AMBITION'S
   young . . . ladder (Shakespeare) 1-6-28
AMBITIOUS
   Caesar was . . . (Shakespeare) 1-6-29
   not be . . . in my wish (Shakespeare) 1-7-77
AMBLES
   who time . . . withal (Shakespeare) 19-7-38
AMBROSE
   joy to hear . . . (Augustine) 6-5-19
AMELIORATION
   accompanied by . . . (Comte) 15-2-51
   change is not . . . (Emerson) 15-2-53
AMEN
   . . . stuck in my throat (Shakespeare) 1-8-87
AMEND
   endeavor to . . . them (Thoreau) 12-1-85, 10-2-96
AMERICA
   all the world was . . . (Locke) 11-4-21
   also found true in . . . (Montesquieu) 9-11-48
   discovery of . . . paved way (Marx) 11-5-38
   free institutions of . . . (Tocqueville) 10-4-56
   greatest or best man in . . . (Lincoln) 10-2-99
   in . . . no paupers (Tocqueville) 11-1-49
   of any parish in . . . (Jefferson) 10-6-59
   one great plague of . . . (Toqueville) 10-7-33
   our army in . . . (Boswell) 5-6-33
   saw more than . . . (Tocqueville) 10-4-53
   should the war in . . . (Smith) 14-2-52
   the people of . . . (Madison) 10-9-31
   trade settled . . . (Emerson) 11-5-32
   war in . . . (Boswell) 6-6-30
   who had served in . . . (Boswell) 4-7-53
AMERICAN
   contrast between the . . . (Emerson) 15-2-53
   haughty . . . nation (Shaw) 1-7-161
AMERICAN DESERT
   in dark . . . (Milton) 4-6-38
AMERICANS
   the . . . of all nations (Whitman) 16-3-86
   we . . . and moderns generally (Thoreau) 15-2-60
AMMON
   children of . . . (*Judges*) 2-2-2
AMMONIUS
   with . . . perhaps (Bergson) 17-1-107
AMNON
   . . . said unto Tamar (*II Samuel*) 3-3-3
AMOR MATRIS
   . . . may be the only (Joyce) 2-2-102
AMOUR
   doctrines of . . . (Fielding) 6-2-28
AMPERE
   erroneous results of . . . (Faraday) 17-2-79
AMPHIARUS
   remark about . . . (Aristotle) 1-3-18
AMPHIPOLIS
   . . . and Delium (Plato) 1-8-13
AMUSE
   . . . and divert the people (Smith) 16-4-34
AMUSEMENT

an . . . of the fancy (Gibbon) 16-3-59
did it as an . . . (Pascal) 17-1-57
make . . . the end (Aristotle) 16-5-7
make lessons an . . . (Quintilian) 8-3-15
providing topics of . . . (Swift) 20-1-33
. . . thought to be necessary (Aristotle) 16-4-6
without . . . there is no joy (Pascal) 4-6-37
. . . would be the end of life (Aristotle) 8-1-9
AMUSEMENTS
   besotted with those . . . (Cervantes) 16-2-11
   great . . . are dangerous (Pascal) 16-4-22
   pleasant . . . we choose (Aristotle) 9-10-16
ANAGNOSTES
   a young page named . . . (Rabelais) 8-1-23
ANALOGIES
   are your linked . . . (Melville) 19-1-102
   God by our . . . (Montaigne) 20-5-53
ANALOGY
   . . . of familiar objects (Santayana) 17-2-133
   recede from the . . . of nature (Newton) 17-2-45
   who noticed the . . . (Whitehead) 17-3-54
ANALYSES
   means of experimental . . . (Bernard) 18-1-35
   method of forming . . . (Fourier) 17-3-42
ANALYSIS
   . . . of the thinking process (Mill) 7-2-88
   true art of general . . . (Leibniz) 7-2-68
   truth found by . . . (Leibniz) 6-3-76
   who object to . . . (Russell) 17-1-100
ANALYTIC
   part of logic called . . . (Kant) 7-2-82
   were purely . . . (Poincaré) 17-3-48
ANALYTICS
   we specify in the . . . (Aristotle) 6-1-18
ANANIAS
   a certain man named . . . (*Acts*) 9-14-13
ANARCHISM
   counterpart of political . . . (Freud) 6-6-52
ANARCHY
   democracy call it . . . (Hobbes) 10-3-22
   . . . finds a way (Plato) 10-4-4
   hold eternal . . . (Milton) 19-6-25
   . . . may be said (Hamilton/Madison) 12-2-45
   no . . . in the universe (Emerson) 19-8-80
   . . . produced by its tyranny (Tocqueville) 10-4-56
   secession is essence of . . . (Lincoln) 10-4-63
   worse despotism than . . . (George) 13-3-53
ANATOMIES
   by multitude of . . . (Bacon) 18-1-24
ANATOMIST
   thus our learned . . . (Harvey) 17-2-33
ANATOMISTS
   who are called . . . (Augustine) 18-1-14
ANATOMY
   . . . is basis of scientific study (Freud) 18-1-41
   to learn and to teach . . . (Harvey) 18-1-25
ANAXAGORAS
   as . . . conceited worlds (Th. Browne) 20-15-71
   in order as . . . says to dominate (Aristotle) 5-1-5
   opinion of . . . on hands of man (Aristotle) 1-1-18
   . . . Thales and men like (Aristotle) 17-1-12
ANAXIMENES
   . . . was wrong (Augustine) 20-5-33
ANCESTOR
   resembleth the . . . more (Bacon) 15-1-31
ANCESTORS
   covenant of their . . . (*Leviticus*) 20-2-10
   happiness of their . . . (Aristotle) 9-8-13
ANCESTRY

worthy of my ... (Tacitus) 1-5-38
ANCHISES
the old ... bear (Shakespeare) 1-6-26
where lives ... (Virgil) 20-15-19
ANCHISIS
that just son of ... (Dante) 20-13-50
ANCIENT
happened in ... times (Plato) 15-2-5
ANCIENTS
arguments of the ... (Montaigne) 1-4-17
authority of the ... (Harvey) 17-2-31
labors of the ... (Pascal) 17-2-39
learn the knowledge of the ... (Galen) 8-3-27
others among the ... (Galen) 18-3-28
proverbs of the ... (*I Samuel*) 9-7-1
the writings of the ... (Montaigne) 15-1-29
unknown to the ... (Tolstoy) 17-3-45
wisest of all the ... (Tacitus) 19-4-13
ANDERSON, John
... my jo (Burns) 1-3-92
ANDREW
Peter and ... his brother (*Matthew*) 20-4-1
ANDREW, PRINCE
... watched the commander (Tolstoy) 6-2-41
ANDREW'S, PRINCE
but ... mind was not (Tolstoy) 5-6-39
ANDROGYNATION
act of ... (Rabelais) 1-7-68
ANDROGYNOUS
... primeval man (Plato) 3-3-9
ANECDOTES
series of thrilling ... (Polybius) 15-1-11
ANGEL
and the ... of God (*Exodus*) 14-2-1
and the recording ... (Sterne) 20-14-52
as if an ... dropp'd (Shakespeare) 14-2-36
... came unto her (*Luke*) 1-7-36
conducted by his ... (Milton) 20-2-33
God's ... held both his feet (Dante) 20-4-19
in action how like an ... (Shakespeare) 1-1-55
... led him up and down (Chaucer) 20-15-58
no ... or archangel (Joyce) 20-4-55
no sin in the ... (Aquinas) 20-13-40
... or any other creature (Aquinas) 20-11-14
signified it by his ... (*Revelation*) 6-5-18
the ... of the Lord (*Luke*) 20-3-11
turned from a good ... (Augustine) 5-7-8
upwards to be an ... (Coleridge) 1-1-94
... which I saw stand (*Revelation*) 19-8-18
ANGELICA'S
... dishonorable commerce (Cervantes) 5-6-24
ANGELO (Michelangelo)
paints even ... (Melville) 16-6-68
ANGELS
a little lower than the ... (*Psalms*) 1-1-3
all Thy ... praise Thee (Augustine) 19-1-20
always saw the ... (Twain) 20-15-102
... and ministers of grace (Shakespeare) 20-7-47
... are bright still (Shakespeare) 20-7-50
as to make ... weep (Shakespeare) 1-1-56
at once as far as ... (Milton) 20-15-75
by that sin fell ... (Shakespeare) 1-5-75
condition of the ... (Aquinas) 6-7-16
... declared to be created (Dante) 19-2-26
does He beatify ... (Augustine) 20-5-34
elect ... contented (Milton) 1-5-94
fair ... would salute (Shakespeare) 11-2-57
... feel no anger (Augustine) 4-1-5
fiends are as rare as ... (Mill) 9-6-106

fierce encountering ... (Milton) 14-1-55
give his ... charge over thee (*Luke*) 20-13-17
have we found ... (Jefferson) 10-3-42
hierarchy of saints and ... (Gibbon) 20-12-32
holy ... upon earth (Plato) 1-6-7
host of rebel ... (Milton) 20-13-83
if men were ... (Hamilton/Madison) 10-3-49
I heard the voice of many ... (*Revelation*) 20-7-7
imposed on by false ... (Augustine) 20-12-12
it seized the ... (Donne) 20-13-73
let ruling ... (Pope) 19-8-68
liveried ... lackey her (Milton) 9-10-80
... make sacrifice to thee (Dante) 20-8-52
multitude of ... with a shout (Milton) 20-15-82
... of God descending (*Genesis*) 5-5-1
power of knowledge in ... (Aquinas) 1-1-42
... round him sing (T. S. Eliot) 20-4-54
saints and ... no longer (Gibbon) 20-12-31
... see it better still (Pascal) 20-1-25
seeth two ... (*John*) 1-7-39
spiritual substances called ... (Aquinas) 20-2-23
the ... shall come forth (*Matthew*) 20-15-23
tongues of ... (*I Corinthians*) 3-5-11
where ... fear to tread (Pope) 9-15-79
whither ... directed the poor (Luther) 20-3-24
... without whom we (Dostoevsky) 1-7-154
word spoken by ... (*Hebrews*) 6-5-15
ANGER
... and the hunting instinct (Wm. James) 3-2-38
best cure for ... (Seneca) 4-3-12
... can be cured by time (Aristotle) 3-2-4
... clamors for vengeance (Augustine) 20-13-31
enmity is ... (Cicero) 4-3-8
evil gives rise to ... (Aquinas) 4-1-8
fits of ... are sudden (Aristotle) 1-3-19
God will not withdraw his ... (*Job*) 9-7-2
he is to admit ... (Seneca) 9-10-23
let thine ... fall (Milton) 20-14-46
Lord is slow to ... (*Psalms*) 3-5-2
never ... you in all my life (Chaucer) 2-3-41
... not found in all (Locke) 4-1-23
offences committed through ... (Aurelius) 4-4-12
our ... flashes (Wm. James) 2-1-51
pride subjects man to ... (Hobbes) 4-11-20
reference to ... we (Aristotle) 4-1-1
resist in ... (Augustine) 2-3-31
the emotion of ... (Aristotle) 4-1-2
to fight with ... (Aristotle) 9-6-16
to govern ... (Plutarch) 17-1-27
touch me with noble ... (Shakespeare) 5-6-18
... wars with desire (Plato) 4-4-2
ANGLES (geometry)
all right ... are equal (Euclid) 17-3-11
ANGLES (tribe)
the ... of the North (Gibbon) 1-6-51
ANGOULÊME
the siege of ... (Gibbon) 20-11-36
ANGRY
anyone can get ... (Aristotle) 9-6-17
are ... and want to (Plato) 2-2-19
being ... a consequence (Boswell) 6-5-79
was ... and would not (*Luke*) 2-2-28
why he is ... (Augustine) 4-1-5
ANGUISH
became insufferable ... (Melville) 5-6-36
do not feel the ... (Lucretius) 4-1-3
no form of ... with a name (Euripides) 4-11-7
... of uncertainty (Aristotle) 4-2-9
what ... hath he (Chaucer) 4-6-25

ANIMAL

an ... exhibits (Dewey) 3-1-89
an ... which laughs (Bergson) 16-4-48
a political and social ... (Aquinas) 7-1-18
a tool-making ... (Boswell) 1-1-86
... attached to own interest (Epictetus) 1-4-7
between the ... and the Superman (Nietzsche) 1-1-123
call it an ... (Rabelais) 1-7-69
conscious of an ... in us (Thoreau) 1-1-106
... did my mind (Pascal) 19-2-33
every ... loves itself (Dante) 4-7-32
every ... somewhat dull (Santayana) 5-1-43
forked ... as thou art (Shakespeare) 1-1-57
in the likeness of what ... (Plato) 19-8-4
... limited to an instinct (Dewey) 6-4-57
man is a social ... (Marx) 1-1-115
man is a tame or civilized ... (Plato) 1-1-11
mind of the highest ... (Darwin) 1-1-110
most dominant ... on this earth (Darwin) 1-1-108
no ... can use words (Descartes) 7-1-28
of a feebler species ... (G. Eliot) 1-7-153
only ... that blushes (Twain) 1-1-120
only ... that can do nothing (Pliny the Elder) 1-1-29
... part of our nature (Freud) 19-1-121
plants as compared with ... (Aristotle) 19-2-10
point of rest in the ... (Aristotle) 19-5-9
preservation of an ... (Harvey) 18-3-46
renunciation of ... personality (Tolstoy) 3-1-82
saw one ... by its gestures (Smith) 1-1-87
see what makes an ... (Locke) 19-2-36
she must have been an ... (Boswell) 4-7-53
spirits which are styled ... (Rabelais) 19-1-26
stupid and unimaginative ... (Rousseau) 10-1-33
takes care of the ... he rides (Maimonides) 18-3-34
... takes its stand on plant (Bergson) 19-2-63
the taming of an ... (Nietzsche) 19-1-118
universe was a single ... (Plato) 19-8-6
what is called an ... (Aristotle) 19-2-8
... which was to comprehend (Plato) 19-8-5
wonder in every ... form (Plotinus) 19-8-26

ANIMALISM

forms of ... and selfishness (Mill) 9-6-106

ANIMAL KINGDOM

somewhere in the ... (Wm. James) 19-5-66

ANIMALS

above the rank of ... (Marx) 19-1-113
... all made for the sake of man (Aristotle) 1-1-23
allots each weapon to those ... (Aristotle) 19-1-6
all the actions of ... (Pascal) 19-2-32
... and man have a like beginning (Aquinas) 1-1-39
... and their parts exist (Aristotle) 19-1-4
... are machines bereft of understanding (Voltaire) 1-1-83
... are the offspring (Harvey) 18-3-47
artificial parts of ... (Newton) 20-5-85
become like the ... (Montaigne) 6-4-13
between man and ... (Cicero) 1-1-25
bodily parts of all ... (Galen) 18-1-12
came the bodies of ... (Newton) 19-3-31
... cannot attain to knowledge (Aquinas) 1-1-42
... cannot form ideas (Rousseau) 7-1-49
... can set themselves in motion (Russell) 19-5-69
connected with the ... (Leibniz) 1-1-78
creation of the ... (Plato) 16-1-1
... deal only in (Cicero) 1-1-26
devouring other ... (Mill) 19-1-114
differences between man and ... (Darwin) 9-5-24
differs from lower ... (Darwin) 9-5-25
distinct from the ... (Cicero) 10-1-12
distinguishes man from ... (Darwin) 7-1-56

emotions are common to the higher ... (Darwin) 1-1-109
God had need of irrational ... (Epictetus) 1-1-31
... have ideas and senses (Rousseau) 1-1-84
in every part of ... (Galen) 19-1-19
... in general seem disposed (Aristotle) 3-3-10
... in no way share in contemplation (Aristotle) 1-1-21
in ... the cerebellum (Kepler) 19-5-27
irrational ... have no joy (Aquinas) 4-7-25
judgment of ... (Aquinas) 5-6-11
learns from the very ... (Montaigne) 19-1-31
life belongs to ... (Aquinas) 19-2-22
life defined in case of ... (Aristotle) 1-8-23
like other ... (Swift) 2-2-68
lower ... also dream (Aristotle) 5-5-11
lower ... and moral being (Darwin) 9-1-25
lower ... are truly incomprehensible (Hegel) 1-1-96
lower ... like man (Darwin) 4-1-30
... make by motion (Pascal) 19-2-34
man and the lower ... (Darwin) 20-5-104
man did excel all ... (Hobbes) 6-4-22
man differs from the lower ... (Dewey) 1-1-130
man the best of the ... (Aristotle) 1-1-22
man's dealings with lower ... (Wm. James) 1-1-126
many ... have memory (Aristotle) 5-3-4
men act like lower ... (Leibniz) 5-1-39
men have absolute domain over ... (Descartes) 1-1-66
not only gregarious ... (Wm. James) 1-5-128
of all ... the boy (Plato) 2-2-20
... other than man (Aristotle) 6-2-6
patterned after constitution of ... (Montaigne) 18-3-41
performances of other ... (Wm. James) 1-1-125
powers of movement in ... (Aquinas) 1-1-40
proceed to treat of ... (Aristotle) 19-1-5
secret internal stirrings of ... (Montaigne) 1-1-51
senses in man and ... (Aquinas) 1-1-44
so industrious in your ... (Voltaire) 19-1-64
... so placid and self-contained (Whitman) 1-1-107
soul of brute ... (Dante) 1-1-47
surpassed by the lower ... (Schopenhauer) 9-11-57
tame ... and wild (Aristotle) 10-7-8
the generation of ... (Aristotle) 19-2-12
the great majority of ... (Darwin) 3-3-72
the most religious of ... (Plato) 1-1-9
the paragon of ... (Shakespeare) 1-1-55
... the souls they torment (Schopenhauer) 1-1-98
... to which nature has given (Harvey) 1-1-64
traces of psychical attitudes in ... (Aristotle) 1-1-14
voice found in other ... (Aristotle) 7-1-9
weapons of some ... (Aquinas) 1-1-43
with everything ... make sense (Pascal) 15-2-26
with the other ... (Aristotle) 2-1-11

ANIMISM

manifestations of ... (Freud) 20-12-38

ANIMOSITIES

... which divide them (Freud) 14-1-107

ANIMOSITY

quarrel with rancorous ... (Spinoza) 20-3-34

ANNIHILATING

religion consists in ... self (Pascal) 20-1-26

ANNIHILATION

the thought of ... (Melville) 20-1-59
to understand Christian ... (Th. Browne) 20-15-73

ANNOY

satisfied not to ... hearers (Aristotle) 7-2-18

ANOINTED

he is the Lord's ... (*I Samuel*) 9-7-1

ANSELM

my little ... said (Dante) 3-2-14

ANSWER

... cannot be expressed (Wittgenstein) 6-6-53
ANT
  go to the ... thou sluggard (*Proverbs*) 11-3-3
ANTAGONISM
  ... left behind (Freud) 2-1-54
  ... of capital and labor (Marx) 11-1-66
  ... of equality and liberty (Sumner) 13-3-48
ANTAGONISMS
  existence of class ... (Marx and Engels) 10-8-34
ANTAGONISTS
  more excellent than ... (Emerson) 1-6-66
ANTECEDENT
  ... necessitates a consequent (Aristotle) 19-3-3
ANTECEDENTS
  must be able to tell ... (Hippocrates) 18-2-3
  not what are the ... (Dewey) 5-7-49
ANTENOR
  imagine Nestor and ... (Plato) 1-6-6
ANTHROPOLOGY
  ... the knowledge of man (Kant) 9-3-26
ANTHROPOPHAGI
  ... and men whose heads (Shakespeare) 3-1-42
ANTICIPATE
  to ... a habit (Schopenhauer) 8-2-24
ANTICIPATION
  happy by ... of change (Johnson) 19-5-58
ANTIDOTE
  sweet oblivious ... (Shakespeare) 5-6-21
ANTI-NATURAL
  ... morality has been taught (Nietzsche) 9-1-36
ANTIOCHENES
  ... and other heretics (Newman) 20-9-45
ANTIOCHUS
  the violence of ... (Gibbon) 20-2-39
ANTIPATER
  the cruelty of ... (Plutarch) 1-9-12
ANTIQUE
  I see their ... pen (Shakespeare) 16-6-38
ANTIQUITIES
  ... and originals of knowledge (Bacon) 15-1-32
  viewing the rest of the ... (Plutarch) 16-3-21
ANTIQUITY
  and respect for ... (Harvey) 17-2-29
  attestation of ... (Locke) 9-2-23
  blind veneration for ... (Madison) 10-9-31
  honors paid to ... (Johnson) 1-5-109
  in ourselves can ... be found (Pascal) 15-2-26
  opinion men cherish of ... (Bacon) 6-3-55
  scholarship come down from ... (Dewey) 6-7-47
  the precedent of ... (Rousseau) 12-1-66
  the records of ... (Locke) 15-1-37
  warlike states of ... (Gibbon) 14-2-57
  whatever the weight of ... (Pascal) 6-3-67
ANTONIA
  the emperor's mother ... (Tacitus) 1-9-16
ANTONINES
  the two ... (Gibbon) 10-3-44
ANTONINUS
  as a disciple of ... (Aurelius) 10-2-25
  ... diffused order (Gibbon) 15-1-49
  so far as I am ... (Aurelius) 10-5-13
ANTONIO, SIGNIOR
  you look not well ... (Shakespeare) 1-2-41
ANTONIO'S
  divers of ... creditors (Shakespeare) 4-9-8
ANTONY (Marc)
  after he had overwhelmed ... (Plutarch) 14-3-14
  against ... and Caesar (Plutarch) 1-9-10
  be buried by her ... (Shakespeare) 1-9-30

Cleopatra received letters from ... (Plutarch) 16-6-13
  ... first meet the curl'd (Shakespeare) 1-9-29
  no plays as thou dost ... (Shakespeare) 4-8-16
  tomb with ... (Plutarch) 1-9-14
  to which ... was fastened (Plutarch) 1-9-13
  upon the sight of ... (Plutarch) 1-6-16
  when she first met ... (Shakespeare) 1-7-89
ANTS
  they lived like swarming ... (Aeschylus) 1-1-6
  we live meanly like ... (Thoreau) 1-2-85
ANUBIS
  ... made much of (Lucian) 17-1-34
ANXIETY
  are overcome with ... (Cicero) 9-6-22
  considerable reasons for ... (Descartes) 4-10-9
  criminal's ... (Seneca) 4-7-17
  from excess and ... (Chaucer) 4-10-3
  get rid of all ... (Shaw) 20-3-65
  ... has its use (Augustine) 4-2-18
  in a state of ... (Horace) 4-9-2
  never freedom from ... (Seneca) 9-5-2
  no pause of ... (Hobbes) 4-2-25
  ... of mankind to interfere (Mill) 1-7-146
  poor seldom suffer ... (Mill) 11-2-145
  the ... to live on (Santayana) 1-2-102
  we wish to avoid ... (Cicero) 9-10-18
ANXIOUS
  ... about his gifts (Carlyle) 1-5-122
ANYTHING
  as a man stands for ... (Wm. James) 6-5-111
  without being good for ... (Thoreau) 9-6-103
ANYTUS
  not Meletus nor yet ... (Plato) 3-2-2
  of whom ... spoke (Plato) 9-10-7
APATHY
  the duty of ... (Kant) 9-4-46
APE
  an anthropomorphous ... (Darwin) 1-1-110
APENNINES
  alone across the ... (Sterne) 3-5-37
APES
  ... of their ideal (Nietzsche) 1-6-76
APHORISMS
  general rules called ... (Hobbes) 6-4-22
APHRODITE
  Ares' dalliance with ... (Homer) 3-3-5
  common and heavenly ... (Plato) 3-1-8
  had got queen ... (Aristophanes) 16-4-2
  inspiration of ... (Plato) 5-6-6
APOCALYPSE
  characters of the great ... (Wordsworth) 20-5-99
APOLLO
  Ah Lord ... (Aeschylus) 5-6-1
  and ... lord of distance (Homer) 3-3-5
  bade ... give the face (Plato) 3-3-9
  bards in fealty to ... (Keats) 16-3-80
  fire-robed god golden ... (Shakespeare) 20-6-37
  having sacrificed to ... (Plutarch) 12-1-21
  inspiration of ... (Plato) 5-6-6
  lyre in the hands of ... (Homer) 20-15-4
  music and medicine in ... (Bacon) 18-1-23
  no prophet but ... (Euripides) 20-10-9
  swear by ... the physician (Hippocrates) 18-2-1
  the archer god ... (Ovid) 19-2-16
  ... was god of physic (Swift) 18-2-33
  were discovered by ... (Plato) 16-1-1
  whom ... killed (Homer) 4-6-5
APOLLODOROUS
  ... who had been weeping (Plato) 1-8-18

APPREHENSION
... of a future state (Gibbon) 1-9-36
... of mind (Lucretius) 1-8-26
sense of death is most in ... (Shakespeare) 1-8-82
APPREHENSIONS
full of dismal ... (Boswell) 1-8-118
APPROBATION
... of his fellows (Darwin) 9-5-25
APPROPRIATION
right of ... (Hegel) 11-1-45
APRIL
lovely ... of her prime (Shakespeare) 1-3-59
men are ... when (Shakespeare) 2-3-57
uncertain glory of an ... day (Shakespeare) 3-1-33
when ... and hist showers (Chaucer) 20-1-16
A PRIORI
carry our ... knowledge (Kant) 6-1-82
knowledge called ... (Kant) 6-2-34
APTITUDE
diversities of ... (Mill) 1-7-144
natural ... for his calling (Plato) 14-2-11
APULEIUS
the opinion of ... (Augustine) 20-7-10
AQUINAS, St. Thomas
intellect of ... (Newman) 6-1-96
ARABIA
all the perfumes of ... (Shakespeare) 5-6-20
ARBITER
sole ... of his duties (Rousseau) 8-1-46
ARBITRARINESS
complete ... of existence (Sartre) 13-1-70
is that it is ... (Hegel) 13-1-38
ARBITRARY
course of things is ... (Thucydides) 19-4-4
most pernicious taxes are ... (Hume) 11-6-17
to be certain not ... (Smith) 11-6-24
ARBITRATOR
that old common ... time (Shakespeare) 19-7-40
to be an ... not a party (Aristotle) 6-3-10
ARCESILAUS
... had disciples speak (Montaigne) 8-3-39
ARCHANGEL
then the lost ... (Milton) 20-15-76
ARCHANGELS
... are not all envied (Augustine) 20-15-36
ARCH-FIEND
in length the ... lay (Milton) 20-7-59
ARCH-FLATTERER
the ... with whom (Bacon) 1-4-23
ARCH-HERETICS
here are the ... (Dante) 20-9-13
ARCHIDAMUS
under the command of ... (Thucydides) 18-3-5
ARCHIMEDES
... apart from his rank (Pascal) 1-6-40
discoveries of ... (Fourier) 17-2-74
ARCHITECT
great ... did wisely (Milton) 17-2-42
ARCHITECTURE
created the religious ... (Emerson) 20-1-57
the practice of ... (Gibbon) 16-1-30
ARCHIVES
old monuments and ... (Plutarch) 15-1-19
ARCHYTAS
and the rattle of ... (Aristotle) 16-5-8
Eudoxus and ... (Plutarch) 17-3-15
ARCTURUS
canst thou guide ... (*Job*) 1-1-2
ARDOR

the mercy of our ... (Montaigne) 1-7-70
ARES
companion of murderous ... (Homer) 3-2-1
like ... for girth (Homer) 14-2-3
ARES'
... dalliance with Aphrodite (Homer) 3-3-5
ARGIVES
the ... would contend (Thucydides) 14-2-9
ARGO
a loftier ... cleaves the man (Shelley) 15-2-49
ARGOS
all the lords of ... (Homer) 2-2-10
in ... you must work (Homer) 2-2-8
ARGUE
love to ... and discuss (Montaigne) 7-2-47
ARGUING
no ... with Johnson (Boswell) 6-7-34
will be much ... (Milton) 6-5-65
ARGUMENT
action cannot enforce ... (Boswell) 7-2-78
address ... to some point (Aristotle) 7-2-5
an incisive ... (Aristotle) 7-2-8
axioms determined in ... (Bacon) 6-7-19
become the ... of his own scorn (Shakespeare) 3-1-38
believes an ... to be true (Plato) 6-7-3
be persuaded by ... (Luther) 20-9-16
changed by clever ... (Santayana) 6-6-55
cheating you by ... (Epictetus) 6-7-14
completing our ... (Plato) 7-2-2
course of the ... (Plato) 6-7-4
enter into ... (Montaigne) 6-5-47
first persuasive ... (Montaigne) 6-5-41
glance at complicated ... (Aristotle) 7-2-13
good ... about spirit (Voltaire) 6-7-33
have found you an ... (Boswell) 6-7-35
heard great ... (FitzGerald) 6-7-37
in ... with men (Milton) 1-7-104
know how to take each ... (Aristotle) 8-2-3
listen to ... but (Aristotle) 4-3-6
... of orator's speech (Aristotle) 7-2-15
... of things not seen (Dante) 6-5-32
... only for conclusion (Russell) 6-7-44
reasoning is an ... (Aristotle) 6-7-8
recourse to the subtleties of ... (Rousseau) 9-5-14
ridicule instead of ... (Galen) 7-2-39
use of ... (Aristotle) 6-7-9
... which does not convince (Boswell) 9-14-49
will not hear ... (Aristotle) 9-6-21
ARGUMENTS
conviction of clear ... (Locke) 6-7-30
defend with sophisticated ... (Augustine) 7-2-41
do justice to ... (Mill) 8-1-68
ensnaring ... (Augustine) 6-7-15
... for conviction (Wm. James) 6-5-109
... founded on probabilities (Harvey) 17-2-33
in spite of grave ... (Russell) 6-6-50
long to overthrow his ... (Aristophanes) 6-7-2
... of the Academicians (Augustine) 6-6-8
overthrow opposing ... (Aristotle) 7-2-16
rests on vain ... (Gilbert) 17-2-13
to weigh ... in (Lucian) 6-6-7
truth by persuasive ... (Aristotle) 7-2-12
... will be valid (Mill) 6-2-40
ARGUS
... who was called (Chaucer) 6-4-11
ARIANISM
seat and fortress of ... (Gibbon) 20-9-40
ARIOSTO
is much older than ... (Voltaire) 1-7-115

people to take up . . . (Tocqueville) 14-1-95
. . . reserved for those ranks (Gibbon) 14-2-55
strong . . . be our conscience (Shakespeare) 9-5-6
take up . . . against (Machiavelli) 10-9-7
terror of Roman . . . (Gibbon) 14-2-54
there must be . . . (Aristotle) 10-1-11
trained to the use of . . . (Rousseau) 14-3-35
. . . used by intelligence (Aristotle) 1-1-22
use money well than to use . . . (Plutarch) 11-4-6
. . . with which a prince (Machiavelli) 14-2-29

ARMY
a church and an . . . (Freud) 20-4-53
an . . . considered ideally (Santayana) 14-2-75
an . . . in battle array (Rabelais) 14-1-43
. . . as a dangerous weapon (Hamilton) 14-2-61
. . . can resist only (Machiavelli) 14-2-32
commander of an . . . (Hobbes) 14-2-41
in the flight of an . . . (Plato) 14-2-10
jealous of a standing . . . (Smith) 14-2-53
mercenary standing . . . (Swift) 14-2-44
preservation of the . . . (Locke) 14-2-43
served by a standing . . . (Smith) 13-1-25
. . . the basis of power (Tolstoy) 14-2-74
the spirit of the . . . (Tolstoy) 14-2-72
to make an . . . victorious (Machiavelli) 14-2-33
to protect an . . . (Plato) 14-1-21
well-disciplined standing . . . (Smith) 14-2-52

ARNAULD
. . . dragged out his days (Voltaire) 13-2-26

ARNOLD, Mrs.
to . . . the loss of occupation (Arnold) 2-2-89

ARNOLD'S, Dr. Thomas
. . . very entertaining work (Boswell) 5-6-33

ARQUES
we fought at . . . (Wm. James) 6-5-112

ARRANGEMENT
proportioned . . . of its parts (Augustine) 18-3-29

ARREST
to . . . a man at once (Dostoevsky) 12-4-71

ARROGANCE
highest . . . and self-conceit (Hume) 16-7-28
must kill . . . (Cervantes) 1-5-80
pay for your . . . (Cervantes) 5-6-23
pedantic . . . of a husband (Congreve) 3-1-58
prosperity without . . . (Aurelius) 11-2-47
shows an extraordinary . . . (Galen) 18-1-12
the churches are . . . (Tolstoy) 20-4-51

ART
acquire . . . by experience (Harvey) 8-3-50
actual practice of the . . . (Aristotle) 16-5-8
adaptation of . . . to characters (Plato) 16-7-3
. . . advances (Tocqueville) 11-3-46
all . . . is but imitation (Harvey) 19-1-46
all nature is but . . . (Pope) 19-4-29
a master of any . . . (Aristotle) 16-7-5
are products of . . . (Aristotle) 19-1-4
beauty of a work of . . . (Schopenhauer) 16-6-63
believe in the message of . . . (Shaw) 16-6-78
both . . . and virtue (Aristotle) 9-6-16
by . . . than by nature (Montaigne) 1-6-23
by every kind of . . . (Augustine) 16-6-22
by the help of . . . (Plato) 16-3-4
cause is the . . . (Aristotle) 19-3-6
come into being by . . . or (Aristotle) 19-4-9
compose poems not by . . . (Plato) 16-3-5
deny that it is an . . . (Goethe) 16-3-69
desiring this man's . . . (Shakespeare) 15-3-86
did use up every . . . (Kepler) 19-8-45
. . . distinguished from nature (Kant) 19-1-69

ease from . . . not chance (Pope) 16-2-27
ease in writing comes from . . . (Pope) 16-7-24
every . . . and profession its patron (Gibbon) 20-6-42
fine . . . and the sciences (Kant) 17-2-64
great works of . . . (Emerson) 1-4-45
grow famous in his . . . (Cervantes) 5-6-24
how long is . . . (Goethe) 1-8-121
human race lives by . . . (Aristotle) 6-2-6
in a production of . . . (Aquinas) 16-7-13
in no respect inferior to . . . (Aristotle) 6-2-7
. . . is a human activity (Tolstoy) 16-1-49
know the . . . of building (Plato) 6-2-4
language is an . . . (Darwin) 7-1-57
life is short and . . . long (Hippocrates) 18-1-7
medical work of . . . (Bernard) 18-2-44
. . . more truly knowledge (Aristotle) 8-3-10
natural . . . of statesmanship (Plato) 10-2-7
nature is only . . . ? (Voltaire) 19-1-64
nature wore appearance of . . . (Kant) 19-1-70
. . . necessarily divides itself (Joyce) 16-3-101
not at variance with . . . (Th. Browne) 19-1-50
. . . of love (Plato) 3-1-10
power of . . . is shown (Boswell) 16-5-35
present task of . . . (Tolstoy) 16-1-51
regarded after analogy of . . . (Kant) 16-6-48
same terms as . . . is attained (Harvey) 17-2-32
. . . saves him (Nietzsche) 16-4-42
strains of unpremeditated . . . (Shelley) 19-1-87
talent for fine . . . (Kant) 17-2-63
the . . . of good politics (Plato) 10-2-4
the beauty of . . . (Hegel) 16-6-62
war improved to an . . . (Gibbon) 14-2-55
war is an . . . (Plato) 14-2-11
when any work of . . . (Hobbes) 5-3-19
. . . which you say adds to nature (Shakespeare) 19-1-40
work of . . . is dynamic (Dewey) 16-6-81
work of divine . . . (Plato) 19-1-2

ARTABANUS
then . . . the king's uncle (Herodotus) 1-2-9

ARTAXERXES
the prince said . . . (Gibbon) 11-6-31

ARTAXERXES'
if he is . . . physician (Lucian) 15-1-25

ARTEMIS
. . . goddess of childbirth (Plato) 6-2-5

ARTHUR (King)
illustrious name of . . . (Gibbon) 1-6-51

ARTICULATION
not mere . . . (Darwin) 7-1-56

ARTIFICE
no admixture of . . . (Voltaire) 16-3-53
. . . of the bar (Boswell) 9-14-49
supply by . . . and cunning (Swift) 12-1-55

ARTIFICERS
are born . . . (Jonson) 16-3-38

ARTIFICIAL
natural and . . . wealth (Aquinas) 11-2-50

ARTIFICIALITY
merit lies in its . . . (Whitehead) 16-1-56
. . . not persuasive in speech (Aristotle) 7-2-19

ARTILLERY
devilish instruments of . . . (Cervantes) 14-2-39

ARTISAN
providence of the universal . . . (Copernicus) 19-5-24
the . . . recedes (Tocqueville) 11-3-46

ARTISANS
went at last to the . . . (Plato) 6-4-6

ARTIST
. . . be as a teacher (Mann) 16-3-102

BLOOD (*Cont.*)
without the shedding of . . . (Luther) 20-4-25
BLOODTHIRSTINESS
. . . is such a part of us (Wm. James) 3-2-38
BLUFF
. . . and purple patches (Euripides) 11-2-10
BLUNTNESS
praised for his . . . (Shakespeare) 9-14-30
BOAST
and our absolute . . . (Wordsworth) 17-2-71
answered with a senseless . . . (Sophocles) 4-11-5
make a . . . of professing (Spinoza) 20-3-34
we . . . are proud (Euripides) 4-11-6
BOASTER
capacity that makes the . . . (Aristotle) 9-14-10
BOATS
many shallow bauble . . . (Shakespeare) 9-11-31
BOCCACCIO, Giovanni
a tale of . . . (Montaigne) 8-1-24
BODIES
actually turn our . . . (Plutarch) 20-6-32
all . . . are endowed (Newton) 19-5-49
. . . are borne downwards (Lucretius) 19-4-10
. . . are our gardens (Shakespeare) 9-10-66
celestial . . . and terrestrial (*I Corinthians*) 1-8-41
. . . could not be placed (Lucretius) 19-6-7
dissection of . . . (Harvey) 18-1-26
even as their . . . are free (Lucretius) 20-6-24
gallantly exercising their . . . (Rabelais) 8-1-23
growing . . . require most (Hippocrates) 1-3-11
. . . having become deranged (Santayana) 5-6-44
. . . in good condition (Aristotle) 9-6-18
. . . in rapid motion (Huygens) 19-5-44
kinds of attractive . . . (Newton) 17-3-32
. . . lawful and regular (Hobbes) 2-1-28
money changer of dead . . . (Aeschylus) 14-1-5
movement a quality of . . . (Aquinas) 19-5-23
. . . not endowed with life (Aquinas) 19-2-24
. . . of considerable density (Bacon) 19-5-32
. . . of good men to heaven (Plutarch) 20-15-31
property common to all . . . (Tolstoy) 17-2-101
qualities of . . . (Newton) 17-2-45
ruins unloosing the first . . . (Lucretius) 19-6-9
simple . . . have a love (Dante) 3-1-26
. . . sometimes in one place (Russell) 19-5-70
sounds and smells leave . . . unaffected (Aristotle) 5-2-4
. . . spring from earth and sun (Gilbert) 19-8-43
such as have . . . (Bacon) 11-3-21
the . . . seven (Chaucer) 17-2-7
there are . . . and a void (Lucretius) 19-1-12
torment the . . . of the damned (Augustine) 20-15-34
trapped in starving . . . (Euripides) 1-2-11
why are our . . . (Shakespeare) 2-3-53
. . . will endure anything (Locke) 18-3-49
worms which occupy our . . . (Thoreau) 1-1-106
your . . . a living sacrifice (*Romans*) 20-8-33
your . . . not your brains (Fielding) 1-7-110
BODILY
as for . . . beauty (Montaigne) 16-6-27
BODIN, Jean
. . . spoke of our citizens (Rousseau) 10-5-19
BODY
a . . . and a soul (Blake) 9-6-95
a . . . which is moving (Russell) 19-5-69
. . . a fetter on freedom (Seneca) 9-4-5
. . . after the resurrection (Augustine) 9-4-21
against his own . . . (Milton) 2-3-72
angels need an assumed . . . (Aquinas) 20-7-21
as to strength of . . . (Hobbes) 13-3-11

believed God to be a . . . (Aquinas) 20-5-42
. . . belongs to another (Epictetus) 9-4-10
black ugly . . . (Montesquieu) 10-7-20
brain-size and . . . (Darwin) 7-1-59
. . . brings material mass (Boethius) 6-3-30
. . . but a fiction of mind (Descartes) 6-6-17
cannot determine the . . . (Spinoza) 5-1-36
child's sweet . . . (Euripides) 2-2-14
church is his . . . (Augustine) 20-4-14
cleanse the foul . . . (Shakespeare) 9-15-55
conceive I had no . . . (Descartes) 5-1-25
constitution of the . . . (Spinoza) 5-4-20
continuous motion of a . . . (Aquinas) 19-6-12
curious harp of man's . . . (Bacon) 18-1-23
denotes the . . . only (Aquinas) 20-4-18
displacement of the . . . (Aristotle) 19-6-4
empty space and a . . . (Pascal) 19-6-22
every . . . has some determinate (Aquinas) 5-1-12
existence of the . . . (Descartes) 4-1-14
expand a . . . in all directions (Galen) 19-1-18
features of the . . . (Seneca) 19-8-15
feeble . . . makes a feeble mind (Rousseau) 5-1-50
flowers all a woman's . . . (Joyce) 1-7-170
forms one . . . from another (Augustine) 16-1-15
goodness of God apparent in the . . . (Augustine) 1-1-38
greatest use of the . . . (Aristotle) 16-1-8
has a great part in our . . . (Montaigne) 16-6-28
has transformed his . . . (Hegel) 19-1-93
have a certain quality of . . . (Epictetus) 8-3-26
healthy mind in a healthy . . . (Juvenal) 5-1-10, 15-3-43
his . . . to the ground (*Book of Common Prayer*) 20-15-64
idea of a . . . moving (Hume) 19-5-56
if either's . . . should (More) 2-3-44
imprisoned in the . . . (Plato) 16-6-6
in company with the . . . (Plato) 1-8-17
. . . influences memory (Locke) 5-3-23
in love with a woman's . . . (Dostoevsky) 3-3-75
in which there is not a . . . (Aquinas) 19-6-11
. . . is a machine for living (Tolstoy) 18-1-36
. . . is borne by its gravity (Augustine) 3-2-21
is given the circular . . . (Aristotle) 19-8-8
. . . is most strong (Plutarch) 18-3-26
is nothing in the . . . but (Rabelais) 19-1-26
. . . is not related to place (Aquinas) 19-6-13
. . . is not the instrument (Plato) 18-2-8
is the property of . . . (Lucretius) 19-6-6
keeps the . . . in health (Bacon) 14-1-50
know nothing of the . . . (Plotinus) 4-7-21
like the . . . of an animal (Locke) 19-2-36
love of the . . . (Plato) 3-1-8
loves and desires of the . . . (Plato) 18-1-8
man's . . . differs from (Santayana) 1-7-168
. . . may be equally fit (Spinoza) 9-15-75
memory impeded by the . . . (Plotinus) 5-3-7
my . . . is but the lees (Melville) 1-8-128
no other forms of . . . (Plotinus) 19-2-20
nothing was born in the . . . (Lucretius) 19-1-13
of her . . . she dishonest be (Chaucer) 1-7-64
of what kind of . . . the mind consists (Lucretius) 5-1-7
only as a mode of . . . (Descartes) 19-6-18
peace of the . . . consists (Augustine) 18-3-29
persuasions of the . . . (Aurelius) 9-3-7
philosopher dishonors the . . . (Plato) 6-1-4
place contains each . . . (Aristotle) 19-6-3
proportion of the . . . (Harvey) 1-3-68
resolved to punish my . . . (Thoreau) 11-6-47
resurrection of a spiritual . . . (Malthus) 19-2-40
sin reign in your mortal . . . (*Romans*) 20-13-20
space contains no . . . (Descartes) 19-6-17

space exclusive of all ... (Berkeley) 19-6-32
spirit quits the ... (Dante) 1-9-23
spiritual and immortal ... (Hobbes) 1-8-102
soul had to be in a ... (Aquinas) 5-2-14
soul is the life of the ... (Aquinas) 19-2-25
soul may seem to rule the ... (Augustine) 9-10-41
sound mind in a sound ... (Locke) 8-1-38
source of the living ... (Aristotle) 19-2-7
strength and agility of the ... (Smith) 14-2-51
... subject to putrefaction (Aurelius) 1-2-21
sustenance of man's ... (Aquinas) 11-1-7
... that serves for its vessel (Lucretius) 19-2-15
... the base of the arm (Kepler) 19-5-27
... the cause of sense (Hobbes) 5-2-23
the corruption of the ... (Augustine) 20-13-36
the death of the ... (Augustine) 20-15-37
these bonds the ... (Epictetus) 1-9-15
this ... did contain (Shakespeare) 1-8-71
this is my ... (*Matthew*) 20-3-10
to fashion a mortal ... (Plato) 19-2-5, 19-8-6
what the ... is (Pascal) 1-4-27
when soul is oppressed so is ... (Luther) 5-1-16
when the ... has died (Lucretius) 1-8-25
who despise the ... (Plato) 9-11-6
without the spirit ... (*James*) 20-8-36
worms destroy this ... (*Job*) 20-2-13
... would look to soul (Plotinus) 9-6-38
would take care of his ... (Maimonides) 18-3-34

BOG OF ALLEN
   falling softly upon the ... (Joyce) 1-8-144
BOILS
   smote Job with ... (*Job*) 18-3-2
BOLDNESS
   ... requisite to examine (Montaigne) 3-4-34
BOLINGBROKE
   gall and pinch this ... (Shakespeare) 9-12-32
BOLOGNA
   I heard once at ... (Dante) 6-3-39, 20-7-32
BOLT
   buy a ... for the door (Thoreau) 10-3-58
   thy sharp and sulfurous ... (Shakespeare) 1-1-56
BOMBAST
   so much pleasure in ... (Schopenhauer) 16-2-40
BONAPARTE, Napoleon
   ... thought was the rarest (Thoreau) 9-11-60
BOND
   a ... between the worlds (Bergson) 19-8-94
   infamous double ... (Sophocles) 2-3-15
   national ... is dissolved (Rousseau) 2-1-34
   national ... secondary (Montaigne) 3-6-12
   of men in states (Aristotle) 12-2-14
BONDAGE
   delivered out of ... (Machiavelli) 1-6-20
   from the house of ... (*Deut.*) 20-2-11
   impotence of man I call ... (Spinoza) 9-4-35
   out of the house of ... (*Exodus*) 9-3-1
   rid you out of their ... (*Exodus*) 20-2-6
   we are immune from ... (Leibniz) 9-4-37
BONDS
   ... by which men are (Hobbes) 12-3-10
   fettered by these ... (Epictetus) 1-9-15
   ... of the whole state (Plato) 9-2-3
   only ... of its union (Rousseau) 2-1-32
   these ... are but weak (Hobbes) 12-1-45
BONE
   ... of my bones (*Genesis*) 1-7-1
BONES
   prophesy unto these ... (*Ezekiel*) 20-10-5
BOOK

every burned ... (Emerson) 13-2-37
heaven is the ... of God (Milton) 17-2-42
if he is doctored out of a ... (Plato) 18-2-15
impossible to write a ... (Colette) 16-1-66
... of verses (FitzGerald) 9-8-71
out of the ... of life (*Revelation*) 19-8-19
read the same ... (Pascal) 8-3-53
what of this new ... (Sterne) 7-2-74
would shut the ... (Shakespeare) 15-1-30
BOOKS
   ... alone not education (Mill) 8-1-70
   among secular ... (Emerson) 17-1-84
   and out of old ... (Chaucer) 17-2-8
   ... are as meats (Milton) 13-2-16
   ... are good if ready for them (Emerson) 8-1-59
   authority from other's ... (Shakespeare) 8-1-28
   delivered to the ... (Gibbon) 20-9-42
   have perused many ... (Swift) 15-2-29
   in the ... they have left (Pascal) 15-2-26
   learning only from ... (Gilbert) 17-2-13
   many ... that are useful (Montaigne) 16-7-15
   more conversant with ... (Gibbon) 6-2-32
   needs abundance of ... (Mill) 8-1-73
   no need to study ... (Luther) 20-9-16
   not to compose ... (Montaigne) 1-2-35
   plenty and all sorts of ... (Plutarch) 15-1-20
   poring upon ... an irksome task (Boswell) 1-3-90, 8-3-67
   rather have some twenty ... (Chaucer) 8-1-21
   sacred ... of the church (Augustine) 6-7-15
   set at naught ... (Emerson) 1-4-45
   study of ... a feeble activity (Montaigne) 7-2-47, 8-3-44
   study of things not of ... (Huxley) 6-1-93
   the best ... are those (Pascal) 16-2-20
   true university a collection of ... (Carlyle) 8-1-57
   trusting the authority of ... (Hobbes) 6-2-23
   ... which testify of him (Pascal) 20-2-30
BOOKWORM
   we have the ... (Emerson) 16-2-46
BOON
   no ... in life (Homer) 4-7-2
BOOR
   the ... is useless (Aristotle) 16-4-6
BOORS
   not learned ... (Nietzsche) 8-3-86
BORE
   well-informed man a useless ... (Whitehead) 8-1-80
BOREAS
   the ruffian ... (Shakespeare) 9-11-31
BOREDOM
   special kind of ... (Russell) 4-6-53
BORN
   a time to be ... (*Eccles.*) 19-7-2
   each thing ... fitted (Wm. James) 19-2-56
   is ... to die (Johnson) 1-8-116
   not ... for citizenship (Spinoza) 10-5-16
   not to be ... surpasses thought (Sophocles) 1-2-10
   ... to a position of wealth (Schopenhauer) 11-2-121
   we are ... believing (Emerson) 6-5-92
BORODINO
   battle of ... (Tolstoy) 19-8-89
BORROWER
   neither a ... nor a lender (Shakespeare) 11-4-14
BORROWING
   ... only lingers (Shakespeare) 11-4-13
BOTTLES
   new wine into old ... (*Matthew*) 20-1-4
BOUGH
   set upon a golden ... (Yeats) 16-1-62

BOUND

ocean without ... (Milton) 19-6-25

BOUNDARIES

deem that our puny ... (Wordsworth) 17-2-71

there are certain ... (Horace) 9-12-11

BOUNDARY

innermost motionless ... (Aristotle) 19-6-4

BOUNDED

could be ... in a nutshell (Shakespeare) 5-5-23

BOUNDS

all things quit their ... (Lucretius) 19-5-14

the ... of moral philosophy (Newton) 9-1-9

the god of ... (Emerson) 1-3-114

BOUNTY

bestow out gratuitous ... (Aquinas) 9-8-33

BOURGEOIS

in ... society the past (Marx and Engels) 13-1-49

just as the petty ... (Marx and Engels) 11-2-142

narrow horizon of ... right (Marx) 12-3-27

... sees in his wife (Marx and Engels) 2-3-106

sway of the ... class (Marx and Engels) 10-8-33

transformed into ... prosperity (Marx and Engels) 11-1-68

BOURGEOISIE

as the ... is developed (Marx and Engels) 11-3-71

contest with the ... (Marx and Engels) 10-8-34

exploiting class the ... (Engels) 10-8-30

... has played a role (Marx and Engels) 10-8-32

obtain only from the ... (Engels) 13-1-50

only among the ... (Marx and Engels) 2-1-45

BOURN

to see beyond our ... (Keats) 9-8-68

BOWER

will keep a ... quiet for us (Keats) 16-6-60

yet in her winters' ... (Spenser) 19-7-34

BOWL

mixing ... of friendship (Euripides) 3-4-6

BOWLING ALLEY

way a boy acts in a ... (Luther) 1-3-41

BOWS

... and arrows are convenient (Plato) 14-1-21

BOY

begin—auspicious ... (Virgil) 2-2-23

chisel a ... into shape (Ruskin) 1-7-150

... that kills the fly (Blake) 3-5-38

BOYHOOD

... which no longer exists (Augustine) 19-7-20

BOYS

as flies to wanton ... (Shakespeare) 1-1-58

little wanton ... (Shakespeare) 1-6-35

love of ... forbidden (Plato) 3-1-8

plenty of ... will come hankering (Twain) 1-2-93

BRACK

the university called ... (Rabelais) 8-1-23

BRAHE'S, Tycho

it was ... opinion (Kepler) 19-8-45

BRAHMIN

hymn the ... sings (Emerson) 6-6-41, 20-1-55

BRAIN

children of an idle ... (Shakespeare) 5-5-21

he had searched the ... (Santayana) 19-1-124

illuminate the sleeping ... (Aeschylus) 5-5-5

intoxicate the ... (Pope) 8-1-42

... is only one condition of many (Huxley) 5-1-69

judges by constitution of ... (Spinoza) 16-7-18

language reacted on ... (Darwin) 7-1-59

masculine ... deals (Wm. James) 1-7-156

morbid condition of the ... (Dostoevsky) 5-5-35

nerve-cells of the ... (Darwin) 16-6-70

offspring of your ... (Hume) 20-6-41

organic disease of the ... (Freud) 18-1-40

... perplexes and retards (Keats) 16-3-79

processes vary from ... to ... (Wm. James) 5-1-72

same ... may serve (Wm. James) 1-4-64

very coinage of your ... (Shakespeare) 5-6-16

workings of similarity in our ... (Wm. James) 17-2-104

BRAINS

have such seething ... (Shakespeare) 16-3-31

heat dry up my ... (Shakespeare) 5-6-17

steal away their ... (Shakespeare) 9-12-35

BRANCHES

... of knowledge not relative (Aristotle) 6-1-8

BRANDES, George

work on Shakespeare by ... (Freud) 16-4-46

BRASIDAS

may imagine ... and others (Plato) 1-6-6

BRASS

as sounding ... (*I Corinthians*) 3-5-11

... eternal slave to (Shakespeare) 19-5-29

BRAVE

... as a lion (Schopenhauer) 9-11-57

indispensable to be ... (Carlyle) 4-2-32

neither ... man nor coward (Homer) 15-3-6

none but the ... (Dryden) 9-11-45

one-half of mankind ... (Boswell) 14-3-36

reputation of being ... (Pascal) 1-5-91

the ... with the weaklings (Homer) 1-5-2

BRAVERY

a ... of the Stoics (Bacon) 4-3-21

reduced to true ... (Cervantes) 9-11-39

BRAVEST

... of all creatures (Twain) 9-11-64

BRAWLING

with a ... woman (*Proverbs*) 1-7-4

BREACH

once more into the ... (Shakespeare) 14-1-45

the imminent deadly ... (Shakespeare) 3-1-42

BREAD

a loaf of ... and thou (FitzGerald) 9-8-71

always smell of ... and butter (Byron) 1-3-106

cast thy ... upon the waters (*Eccles.*) 15-3-3

eat the ... of the angels (Anselm) 1-2-26

eat with unleavened ... (*Exodus*) 20-2-7

I am that ... of life (*John*) 20-3-14

I am the ... of life (*John*) 20-14-14

nature giveth ... (Rabelais) 19-2-27

neither yet ... to the wise (*Eccles.*) 19-4-1

not live by ... alone (*Luke*) 20-13-17; (*Deut.*) 20-1-1

rise and eat ... (*II Samuel*)1-8-3

shalt thou eat ... (*Genesis*) 1-8-1, 11-3-1

that these stones be made ... (*Matthew*) 20-1-3

this day our daily ... (*Matthew*) 20-8-26

BREAK DOWN

a time to ... (*Eccles.*) 19-7-2

BREAST

middle region of ... (Lucretius) 4-1-3

BREASTPLATE

what stronger ... (Shakespeare) 9-7-37

BREATH

dulcet and harmonious ... (Shakespeare) 16-5-18

the ... of life (*Genesis*) 19-2-3

virtue of the enlivening ... (Coleridge) 19-2-42

BREDE

with ... of marble men (Keats) 16-6-58

BREED

it's in the ... (Twain) 10-6-75

... of noble bloods (Shakespeare) 1-6-27

BREEDING

care taken in ... (Plato) 2-1-10

BUSINESS (*Cont.*)
cannot enter into . . . (Hume) 17-1-64
. . . could not make dull (Arnold) 16-3-92
disposition of . . . by study (Bacon) 8-1-30
does one expect from . . . (Dewey) 11-5-48
doing one's own . . . (Plato) 12-2-10
idling of men is called . . . (Augustine) 8-1-20
in the . . . class (Hegel) 10-8-26
knowledge useful in . . . (Aristotle) 8-1-9
man that doth his . . . (Hobbes) 9-13-24
men love . . . for itself (Bacon) 11-3-20
mind his own . . . (Thoreau) 15-2-60
not less adverse to . . . (Gibbon) 20-3-44
. . . of the wise and good (Epictetus) 9-6-26
opposed to serious . . . (Hegel) 19-1-93
people's safety is its . . . (Hobbes) 10-1-21
religion is the serious . . . (Toynbee) 20-1-86
the wisdom of . . . (Bacon) 9-13-21
this is your . . . (Epictetus) 9-9-9
to religion as a serious . . . (Plutarch) 20-1-6
true . . . precept (Dickens) 11-5-33
who is minding his own . . . (Thoreau) 11-4-38
world is a place of . . . (Thoreau) 11-5-34
BUSYNESS
by lawful . . . (Chaucer) 9-10-52
BUTAS
at length . . . came back (Plutarch) 1-9-11
BUTCHERS
. . . we are it is true (Melville) 14-2-65
BUTCHERY
born for . . . (Euripides) 2-2-14
BUTTERFLY
kill not the moth nor . . . (Blake) 3-5-38
BUY
one is obliged to . . . (Rousseau) 11-4-25
BUYER
it is naught saith the . . . (*Proverbs*) 11-5-1
BYZANTIUM
lords and ladies of . . . (Yeats) 16-1-62
to the holy city of . . . (Yeats) 1-3-136

CADMUS
with Hercules and . . . once (Shakespeare) 16-5-19
CAELIAN
Palatine and . . . hills (Tacitus) 5-6-7
CAESAR, Julius
against Antony and . . . (Plutarch) 1-9-10
a man . . . is born (Emerson) 1-6-65
. . . and Cato (Plutarch) 1-9-11
are murdered like . . . (Hegel) 1-6-56
as . . . loved me (Shakespeare) 10-6-25
. . . as he went to the Senate (Plutarch) 1-8-44
. . . at once dismissed (Plutarch) 2-3-28
envy of great . . . (Shakespeare) 1-6-30
ere the mightiest . . . fell (Shakespeare) 20-12-19
give tribute to . . . (*Mark*) 10-2-17
great . . . lay his sword (Shakespeare) 1-7-89
fear him not . . . (Shakespeare) 4-8-16
friends of . . . (Plutarch) 1-9-13
if . . . can hide the sun (Shakespeare) 11-6-6
I the tired . . . (Shakespeare) 1-6-26
. . . made answer seriously (Plutarch) 1-6-14
not made into a . . . (Aurelius) 10-2-25
O . . . this charmian lived (Shakespeare) 1-9-30
. . . over the Rubicon (Cervantes) 1-5-80
said in the person of . . . (Jonson) 16-3-37
sent to . . . (Plutarch) 1-9-14
should be in that . . . (Shakespeare) 1-6-27

. . . subdued the Gauls (Gibbon) 10-8-20
the luck of . . . (Shakespeare) 1-9-29
. . . was ambitious (Shakespeare) 1-6-29
. . . was born to do great things (Plutarch) 1-6-15
. . . was contending for (Hegel) 1-6-55
. . . was not of so slight (Plutarch) 1-6-16
. . . was so much master (Plutarch) 14-2-23
CAESAR AUGUSTUS
have guided thee . . . (Virgil) 14-1-24
went out a decree from . . . (*Luke*) 11-6-3, 20-3-11
while mighty . . . (Virgil) 16-3-14
CAESAREA PHILIPPI
the coasts of . . . (*Matthew*) 20-4-2
CAESARS
persuasion cultivated by the . . . (Gibbon) 7-2-81
the . . . of Rome (Cervantes) 10-8-10
CAIN
conceived and bare . . . (*Genesis*) 2-1-1
. . . who was of that wicked one (*I John*) 3-2-8
CAÏNA
. . . waits for him (Dante) 3-3-31
CAIN'S
were . . . jaw-bone (Shakespeare) 1-8-77
CAKES
no more . . . and ale (Shakespeare) 9-10-62
CALAMITIES
among the . . . of war (Johnson) 14-1-68
. . . due to nature (Plato) 9-10-5
free from . . . (Plutarch) 9-8-20
imagine all possible . . . (Herodotus) 9-11-3
. . . of antiquity (Tacitus) 5-6-7
that hasten down . . . (Seneca) 15-3-35
the . . . of war (Gibbon) 14-3-38
CALAMITY
imagination of future . . . (Hobbes) 4-8-23
least sensitive to . . . (Thucydides) 9-11-5
meet with . . . at last (Herodotus) 1-2-7
on the outside of a . . . (Aeschylus) 15-3-11
CALCULATE
and . . . the stars (Milton) 17-2-42
CALCULATION
aiming with . . . (Aristotle) 9-13-4
arithmetic and . . . (Plato) 17-3-2
. . . as part of instruction (Plato) 8-1-2
found on . . . to be true (Descartes) 17-3-26
laws of . . . (Voltaire) 17-2-57
methods of . . . (Copernicus) 17-2-10
no power of . . . (Plato) 9-6-11
the arts of . . . (Dewey) 17-3-61
thickets of . . . (Kepler) 17-2-14
wilfully mechanical . . . (Wm. James) 19-4-49
without intelligent . . . (Aeschylus) 15-2-3
CALCULATIONS
all mathematical . . . (Whitehead) 17-2-117
. . . far outrunning experiment (Santayana) 17-3-62
found our political . . . (Hamilton/Madison) 10-4-46
reasoning reduced to . . . (Leibniz) 7-2-68
CALCULUS
found by a kind of . . . (Leibniz) 7-2-67
unable to function in a . . . (Leibniz) 7-2-69
CALIGULA
mad attempt of . . . (Gibbon) 20-2-39
so . . . wished (Boswell) 10-3-40
CALLIAS
. . . or Socrates or some other (Aristotle) 6-2-7
when . . . was ill (Aristotle) 18-1-9
CALLICLES
if you and I . . . were (Plato) 6-2-4
CALLING

CHOICE (*Cont.*)

consists in internal . . . (Aquinas) 9-14-17
do away with liberty of . . . (Aquinas) 15-3-58
expressly the word . . . (Coleridge) 5-4-30
faculties exercised in making a . . . (Mill) 9-2-32
friendship of . . . (Aquinas) 3-4-31
from . . . or necessity (Plato) 16-1-4
in terms of . . . I am not (Shakespeare) 19-4-23
man's situation as free . . . (Sartre) 13-1-70
parties having any . . . (Boswell) 2-3-90
small . . . in rotten apples (Shakespeare) 5-7-19
then . . . can be exercised (Herodotus) 13-2-1
those who have made a . . . (Pascal) 19-4-26
three objects of . . . (Aristotle) 9-7-14
virtue concerned with . . . (Aristotle) 9-10-13
who have a free . . . (Thucydides) 14-1-16
women have free . . . (Darwin) 2-3-104
. . . would hardly be (Dewey) 13-1-63

CHOOSE

. . . a great prize (Aristotle) 3-6-7
a man is free to . . . (Dewey) 13-1-67
does not . . . aright (Aristotle) 9-6-18
freedom to . . . according to state (Leibniz) 9-4-37
gave him freedom to . . . (Milton) 13-2-17
no one would . . . life without friends (Aristotle) 3-4-11
not attempt to . . . at all (Shakespeare) 19-4-23
. . . one of two evils (Plato) 9-6-8
right to . . . beliefs (Dewey) 6-5-114
right to live as we . . . (Russell) 13-1-62
sets before us not what we . . . (Montaigne) 5-3-12
what act he shall . . . to do (Wm. James) 9-1-37

CHOOSING

a habit of . . . (Aquinas) 9-10-45
in the power of . . . are acts (Rousseau) 1-1-84

CHOSEN

covenant with my . . . (*Psalms*) 20-2-15

CHRIST

and the humanity of . . . (Maritain) 16-3-103
another whose name was . . . (Thoreau) 6-5-96
. . . appeared before his eyes (Gibbon) 20-4-43
before the coming of . . . (Aquinas) 20-2-21
body and blood of . . . (Gibbon) 20-12-31
. . . can be known (Luther) 6-5-34
displeasing to . . . (Chaucer) 4-5-15
divinity of . . . is set forth (Augustine) 20-9-7
do not abandon the name of . . . (Augustine) 20-9-6
expressly enunciated by . . . (Freud) 20-4-53
faith a knowledge of . . . (Calvin) 6-5-38
foolish as the birth of . . . (Tertullian) 20-3-22
from the love of . . . (*Romans*) 4-5-9
fulness of . . . (Augustine) 1-7-48
God which is in . . . (Augustine) 15-2-19
good and evil given us by . . . (Tolstoy) 1-6-74
ideal given by . . . of old (Dostoevsky) 20-3-58
if . . . had not been crucified (Dante) 1-3-34
in . . . shall all be (*I Corinthians*) 1-8-40
in the power of . . . (Aquinas) 20-4-17
in thinking of . . . only as (Hegel) 20-11-38
. . . is born and millions (Emerson) 1-6-65
. . . is God's (Augustine) 20-7-19
is governed by . . . (Hegel) 20-4-46
is . . . not risen (Augustine) 6-7-15
. . . is our Passover (Augustine) 6-1-29
. . . is with you (Dostoevsky) 4-6-51
it belongs to . . . as God (Aquinas) 20-14-29
led them to kill . . . (Augustine) 20-2-20
. . . made his spouse (Dante) 20-4-20
never saw . . . or disciples (Th. Browne) 6-5-54
none to tell of . . . (Dante) 9-7-35

no one except . . . received (Spinoza) 20-10-37
not according to . . . (Augustine) 17-1-37
not by the law but by . . . (Luther) 20-14-33
only the law of . . . (Dostoevsky) 12-4-68
otherwise than through . . . (Aquinas) 20-14-24
patiently for the . . . promised (Pascal) 20-3-32
precious image of . . . (Dostoevsky) 6-4-52
proved who . . . is (Kierkegaard) 20-11-41
redemption by . . . (Dante) 16-3-27
ring in the . . . that is to be (Tennyson) 1-2-81
side of . . . (Aquinas) 1-7-51
. . . spoke right broadly (Chaucer) 6-3-40
that rock was . . . (Augustine) 20-4-12
the acknowledgement of . . . (Luther) 20-3-25
the images of . . . (Gibbon) 20-9-41
they reigned with . . . (Gibbon) 20-3-45
thou art the . . . (*John*) 1-8-38; (*Matthew*) 20-4-2
to assent to . . . himself (Aquinas) 20-9-11
to begin below at . . . (Luther) 15-3-71
to serve . . . then is not (Luther) 20-8-56
to the advent of . . . (Augustine) 15-2-20
translated to the kingdom of . . . (Augustine) 1-3-31
union of . . . with (Aquinas) 2-3-34
united to . . . as its head (Aquinas) 20-4-18
we have the prophecy of . . . (Th. Browne) 20-9-22
weeping to . . . (Dostoevsky) 19-8-88
whether he were the . . . (*Luke*) 20-3-12
which is . . . the Lord (*Luke*) 20-3-11
. . . who of perfection (Chaucer) 2-3-40
. . . will be your champion (Chaucer) 20-13-57
word and institution of . . . (Luther) 20-3-26

CHRISTENDOM

in . . . where is the Christian (Emerson) 20-3-51

CHRISTIAN

as I am a . . . faithful man (Shakespeare) 20-15-65
but . . . had a shield (Bunyan) 20-7-67
conception of . . . (Nietzsche) 20-5-117
conducted . . . and Hopeful (Bunyan) 20-15-83
doubt that a true . . . (Augustine) 6-1-23
good . . . came a little way (Bunyan) 20-8-71
if a Jew wrong a . . . (Shakespeare) 20-2-26
in the way of becoming a . . . (Kierkegaard) 1-3-111
seemed that for a . . . (Montaigne) 20-5-54
. . . should inspire tolerance (Voltaire) 13-2-27
true . . . is not content (Bunyan) 6-1-64
true wayfaring . . . (Milton) 9-6-81
up which . . . was to go (Bunyan) 20-3-36
where . . . and Hopeful (Bunyan) 20-14-48
wish to die like a . . . (Pascal) 20-8-64

CHRISTIAN CHURCH

the censures of the . . . (Gibbon) 20-9-38

CHRISTIANITY

. . . became a mythus (Emerson) 20-11-40
denied truth of . . . (Boswell) 6-6-50
England felt full heat of . . . (Emerson) 20-1-57
everything advanced against . . . (Boswell) 6-6-31
. . . gave Eros poison to drink (Nietzsche) 3-3-77
I condemn . . . (Nietzsche) 20-4-52
in defence of . . . (Shaw) 9-9-48
. . . in its patristic form (Santayana) 20-2-52
mysteries and precepts of . . . (Newman) 20-1-65
. . . only hopes (Thoreau) 20-3-53
our knowledge of . . . (Gibbon) 6-3-97
the churches and . . . (Tolstoy) 20-4-51
the meaning of . . . (Kierkegaard) 1-4-43
the rules of . . . (Cervantes) 1-6-81
thoroughly served by . . . (Nietzsche) 13-3-46
they were before . . . (Dante) 4-5-12

CHRISTIAN RELIGION

CITIZENS (*Cont.*)
 ... to have need of state (Machiavelli) 3-6-11
CITIZENSHIP
 man is born for ... (Aristotle) 9-8-11
 partake of rights of ... (Rousseau) 8-1-46
 pursue ideal perfection of ... (Plato) 8-1-3
CITY
 a ... has work to do (Aristotle) 10-5-8
 a free ... situated (Rousseau) 14-3-35
 and they took the ... (*Joshua*) 14-2-2
 as opposed to the ... of God (Augustine) 20-13-29
 ... becomes unequal (Plato) 2-3-16
 beloved and heavenly ... (Augustine) 20-7-18
 build a ... and a tower (*Genesis*) 7-1-2
 citizens make a ... (Rousseau) 10-5-19
 earthly ... desires peace (Augustine) 14-3-16
 except the Lord keep the ... (*Psalms*) 15-3-1
 from the desperate ... (Thoreau) 4-5-35
 great ... a great solitude (Bacon) 3-4-40
 Hell is a ... much like (Shelley) 20-15-95
 least tower of the true ... (Dante) 9-4-27
 more necessary than the ... (Aristotle) 2-1-11
 multitude of the ... (*Job*) 1-1-2
 my ... is small (Plato) 10-8-2
 new ... of friends (Whitman) 3-4-60
 out of the holy ... (*Revelation*) 19-8-19
 peace of the celestial ... (Augustine) 14-3-20
 the heavenly ... (Augustine) 12-1-23
 this ... is free (Euripides) 10-4-1
 whole ... has one end (Aristotle) 8-1-7
 your ... is free (Euripides) 14-1-11
CITY OF GOD
 Augustine says in the ... (Aquinas) 4-7-26
CIVILIANS
 the rights of ... (Kant) 14-1-84
CIVILTY
 ... of these little citizens (Th. Browne) 19-1-49
CIVILIZATION
 a complicated ... like ours (Shaw) 1-3-128
 an apex to which ... has (Shaw) 15-2-74
 ... and sincerity (Whitehead) 15-2-77
 ... a part of nature (Spencer) 15-2-71
 beings who live behind all ... (Nietzsche) 16-4-42
 bitter side of ... (Schiller) 19-1-73
 capable of higher ... (Mill) 10-6-74
 claims of our ... (Freud) 19-1-121
 continuing advancing in ... (Kant) 15-2-43
 cultural continuity of ... (Benedict) 15-2-91
 different stages of ... (Comte) 15-2-51
 discoveries and inventions of ... (Freud) 16-1-59
 enters the state of ... (Schiller) 19-1-74
 ... especially prevails (Thoreau) 15-2-59
 favorable to extension of ... (Smith) 14-1-70
 from man in ... (Rousseau) 15-2-33
 grade of ... so low (Nietzsche) 9-9-44
 greed the driving force of ... (Engels) 4-9-20
 ... has tamed and trained him (Schopenhauer) 1-1-99
 if ... has modified man (Bergson) 15-2-84
 ... is a movement (Toynbee) 15-2-92
 ... is one of property (Emerson) 15-2-56
 ... is suspicious to it (Melville) 9-6-102
 its service to ... (Whitehead) 16-1-56
 ... not favorable to chastity (Gibbon) 3-3-64
 ... obtains the mastery (Freud) 9-5-29
 ... of the Western World (Dewey) 17-2-131
 our painfully acquired ... (Freud) 5-5-37
 outward varnish of ... (Mill) 9-6-106
 pay for our rapidly changing ... (Mead) 15-2-89
 present state of ... (Calhoun) 10-7-35

 prevalence of ... over barbarism (Emerson) 14-3-45
 progress in ... (Mill) 10-6-72
 the missionaries of ... (Hegel) 11-5-26
 too much ... (Marx and Engels) 11-5-39
 war in our own ... (Benedict) 14-1-112
CIVILIZATIONS
 societies called ... (Toynbee) 15-1-101
 twenty or so ... (Toynbee) 10-8-38
CIVILIZE
 to ... and reduce them (Swift) 14-1-61
CIVILIZED
 between savage and ... (Melville) 18-3-57
 ... man differs from savage (Boswell) 15-2-35
 man was aboriginally ... (Darwin) 15-2-61
 requisites of a ... life (Plato) 15-2-5
 the heart of ... life (Rousseau) 15-2-34
CIVILIZED PEOPLE
 distinguished ... from savages (Gibbon) 7-1-53
CIVIL LAWS
 chains called ... (Hobbes) 12-1-45
 ... of today founded (Voltaire) 2-3-84
CIVIL SERVANT
 ... is essentially dependent (Hegel) 10-8-28
CIVIL WAR
 a ... indeed is like (Bacon) 14-1-50
 engaged in a great ... (Lincoln) 10-4-64
 faction and ... (Hobbes) 10-3-24
 ... with his country (Plutarch) 1-6-16
CIVIL WARS
 so subject to ... (Rousseau) 10-4-28
CLAIMS
 my own stern ... (Emerson) 9-9-38
CLAN
 ... is an abstraction (Hegel) 2-1-41
CLÄRCHEN
 between ... and Beatrice (Huxley) 1-7-143
CLARENCE
 monarchy afford false ... (Shakespeare) 20-15-65
CLARITY
 consists in a certain ... (Aquinas) 16-6-25
 ... whence things are called beautiful (Aquinas) 16-6-24
CLASS
 a ... hated for their abominations (Tacitus) 20-3-21
 based on ... antagonisms (Marx) 11-1-65
 consider as a ... (Mill) 10-4-67
 end to ... differences (Engels) 10-1-47
 every ... handed down (Marx) 11-5-38
 governed by the lower ... (Aristotle) 10-2-12
 influence of the ruling ... (Marx and Engels) 2-1-45
 in order to oppress a ... (Marx and Engels) 11-2-142
 lowers the ... of the workmen (Tocqueville) 11-3-46
 matter and form in every ... of things (Aristotle) 5-1-6
 modern working ... (Marx and Engels) 11-3-71
 naturally depraved ... (Fitzhugh) 13-3-36
 no ... can be suppressed (Lenin) 12-3-33
 ... of those who are possessed of (Tocqueville) 2-2-84
 opinions peculiar to their ... (Tocqueville) 11-5-27
 particular ... of citizens (Smith) 14-2-50
 pupils were a ... not a social (Dewey) 8-3-100
 recognizes no ... differences (Marx) 12-3-27
 some members of the wealthy ... (Tolstoy) 16-1-50
 sons of the ruling ... (Aristotle) 10-9-5
 taxation descend to the poorest ... (Mill) 11-6-52
 trade of a particular ... (Smith) 17-1-72
CLASSES
 all ... of citizens (Hamilton) 10-4-45
 antagonism between ... (Marx and Engels) 14-1-100
 ... at bottom of society (Mill) 11-2-146
 better ... against the people (Aristotle) 10-6-12

CONDUCT (*Cont.*)
... of our ego (Freud) 4-1-34
persons's ... affects prejudicially (Mill) 13-1-55
practical ... of life (Plutarch) 8-3-23
prescribes a mode of ... (Boswell) 12-1-68
reflect over his own ... (Darwin) 9-1-26
reforming their ... (Newman) 20-1-66
regulate ... by examples (Descartes) 15-1-34
regulate ... by love of money (Johnson) 4-9-11
regulates one's ... (Seneca) 17-1-23
repugnance at ... of men (Kant) 15-1-57
soul understands right ... (Plotinus) 9-1-4
strange my ... (Plato) 1-8-13
the object of religion is ... (Arnold) 20-1-68
there are gradations in ... (Boswell) 9-2-29
to the ... of life (Voltaire) 17-1-69
young would give heed to ... (Wm. James) 8-2-31
CONFEDERATE
representatives of ... states (Madison) 14-3-44
CONFESS
... myself to myself (Montaigne) 9-10-57
CONFESSION
but a ... of faith (Aquinas) 20-1-14
CONFESSIONS
make false ... (Augustine) 12-4-22
CONFIDE
... only in yourself (Goethe) 18-2-42
CONFIDENCE
a light of utter ... (Augustine) 6-5-21
... as an outgoing (Dewey) 1-4-68
assume dogmatical ... (Kant) 6-6-33
behave with ... (Epictetus) 4-2-17
... citizens have in it (Hegel) 12-2-46
diminishes ... in belief (Boswell) 6-5-79
disposition creates ... (Aristotle) 1-3-18
excess of ... (Aristotle) 1-3-20
greed implant ... (Montaigne) 4-1-11
hesitating ... in reason (Plato) 6-7-4
ignorance begets ... (Darwin) 6-4-45
... in goodness (Montaigne) 9-6-57
inspire them with ... (Machiavelli) 14-2-33
... in the justice (Smith) 12-2-42
... in the mercy (Luther) 6-5-36
... in ultimate justice (Lincoln) 12-2-51
much ... make incautious (Machiavelli) 4-2-20
... past converse (Aeschylus) 1-7-10
precludes love and ... (Mill) 8-3-35
... springs from hope (Spinoza) 4-5-24
we plume our ... (Euripides) 4-11-6
who exceeds in ... (Aristotle) 9-11-9
CONFIGURATION
... is changing and variable (Wittgenstein) 6-1-112
CONFLAGRATION
... was the result of an order (Tacitus) 20-3-21
CONFLICT
truth in ... in this world (Kierkegaard) 6-3-105
CONFORMITY
live merely by ... (Thoreau) 17-1-86
they signify ... (Hobbes) 9-7-39
... with the thing (Maritain) 6-3-151
CONFUCIUS
moral outlook of ... (Voltaire) 16-2-30
CONFUSION
first cause of ... (Chaucer) 9-12-21
... has broken in (Johnson) 1-3-84
... heard his voice (Milton) 19-8-57
least ... but in one (Pope) 19-8-120
let ... live (Shakespeare) 3-2-21
... of goods unrightly won (Aeschylus) 9-7-6

quick bright things come to ... (Shakespeare) 3-1-36
reduce to hopeless ... (Russell) 19-7-85
strut to our ... (Shakespeare) 9-6-67
the ... of the times (Gibbon) 15-1-51
thus falls into ... (Kant) 17-1-74
universe is either a ... (Aeschylus) 19-8-22
without a ... (Aurelius) 19-4-14
CONGREGATION
... of the righteous (*Psalms*) 9-7-3
CONJECTURE
always so many ... (Tolstoy) 20-10-44
are to understand from ... (Harvey) 17-2-33
expounded in terms of ... (Ptolemy) 17-3-17
... has the same uncertainty (Hobbes) 9-13-22
of ... more than knowledge (Montaigne) 6-3-45
philosophy of history is ... (Boswell) 15-1-48
what we ourselves ... (Descartes) 6-1-54
CONJECTURES
as coin of the ... (Montaigne) 15-1-26
... in the rank of facts (Gibbon) 15-1-51
they use human ... (Augustine) 19-8-33
value other people's ... (Swift) 6-6-24
CONJUNCTIONS
illicit ... contribute (Montesquieu) 2-2-71
CONNECTICUT
first in ... and afterward (Thoreau) 1-8-130
CONNECTION
cause is ... between phenomena (Wm. James) 19-3-51
words also signify ... of ideas (Locke) 7-1-37
CONNECTIONS
transient ... (Tocqueville) 2-3-101
CONNEXION
necessary ... with its effect (Hume) 5-7-30
CONQUER
desire to ... (Montaigne) 1-7-70
easier to ... than to rule (Rousseau) 10-6-54
if they ... thee (Herodotus) 14-1-6
... yourself (Sartre) 4-5-39
CONQUERED
killed not ... (Montaigne) 9-11-24
CONQUEROR
... lays down conditions (Kant) 14-1-82
CONQUERORS
a race of ... (Nietzsche) 10-1-49
blood and habits of ... (Santayana) 14-2-76
to be styled ... (Milton) 14-1-56
we are more than ... (*Romans*) 4-5-9; (Bunyan) 20-7-67
CONQUEROR'S
a ... business to repair (Montesquieu) 14-1-63
CONQUEST
from brutal love of ... (Rousseau) 14-3-35
moderate use of ... (Gibbon) 14-1-74
the right of ... (Rousseau) 10-7-24
CONQUESTS
maintain their ... (Machiavelli) 14-1-38
sudden ... impracticable (Hamilton) 14-2-59
CONSCIENCE
able with good ... (Luther) 2-3-45
accoung of their bad ... (Joyce) 1-7-169
... accuses (Kant) 9-13-31
advantage of senses over ... (Johnson) 4-7-51
all the authority of ... (Mill) 9-3-35
... also bearing witness (*Romans*) 9-3-6
approval of one's own ... (Cicero) 9-5-1
argue according to ... (Milton) 13-2-19
between liberty of ... (Boswell) 13-2-32
... cannot reproach him (Descartes) 4-1-16
catch the ... of the king (Shakespeare) 16-4-18
convicted by own ... (*John*) 3-5-9

... does make cowards (Shakespeare) 1-9-27
do thou in ... think (Shakespeare) 2-3-63
exquisite and exact ... (Montaigne) 15-1-26
following upon an evil ... (Luther) 20-15-63
freedom of ... (Twain) 13-1-58
freedom of ... as a right (Mill) 13-2-38
freedom of ... is a right (Maritain) 12-3-35
genesis of ... (Arnold) 20-1-68
good sense is not ... (Newman) 9-1-31
has a bit of ... (Shaw) 2-3-115
have a bad ... about it (Luther) 20-13-61
have a good ... (Aurelius) 10-2-25
have a light called ... (Tolstoy) 9-25-94
have it implanted in ... (Montaigne) 20-9-17
in the form of a ... (Freud) 9-5-29
... is but a word cowards use (Shakespeare) 9-5-6
liberty of ... in religion (Boswell) 13-2-29
live on as his moral ... (Freud) 20-5-122
make ourselves a ... (Pascal) 16-4-22
mingled with remorse of ... (Boswell) 4-6-44
never feel stings of ... (Dostoevsky) 4-10-11
no form of blinded ... (Ruskin) 6-3-120
primitive ... injures (Darwin) 3-2-27
prompted by his ... (Darwin) 9-9-41
quiet ... makes serene (Byron) 20-3-46
remorse of ... (Aquinas) 12-4-23
reproaches of his own ... (Mill) 9-7-50
resign his ... (Thoreau) 10-4-60
rules according to his ... (Kierkegaard) 20-3-48
secrets of their ... (Dostoevsky) 9-8-74
soft cheveril ... (Shakespeare) 1-7-93
speaking to his ... (Dostoevsky) 12-4-68
still has so much ... (Kant) 9-14-54
strict and vigilant ... (Freud) 20-13-97
the ... of society (Emerson) 1-5-123
the dictates of my ... (Locke) 20-14-51
the magistrate and ... (Locke) 9-1-10
thus a distracted ... (Th. Browne) 20-15-71
to save free ... (Milton) 14-3-32
uncreated ... of my race (Joyce) 6-2-55
unlawful to the ... (Locke) 10-2-60
which gnaws every ... (Dante) 20-15-53
wise man's ... (Boethius) 1-5-48
... with injustice (Shakespeare) 9-7-37
written in heart by ... (Rousseau) 9-4-43

CONSCIENCES
cannot discern ... (Augustine) 12-4-22
command over the ... (Gibbon) 20-4-42
on account of their bad ... (Joyce) 1-7-170
our outward ... (Shakespeare) 9-6-60
seals our ... (Calvin) 20-4-27

CONSCIOUS
interpenetration of ... states (Bergson) 19-7-88
... state of becoming (Freud) 5-2-40

CONSCIOUSNESS
act of mind to gain ... (Hegel) 5-1-57
... appears to define mental life (Freud) 5-1-78
between ... and mental activity (Hegel) 8-1-53
... compares possibilities (Wm. James) 5-1-71
destruction of the ... (Schopenhauer) 1-9-42
evil lies in ... (Hegel) 9-6-101
... has come to a stand (Bergson) 19-2-62
he has reached this ... (Hegel) 9-5-21
here translated into ... (Freud) 16-4-46
ignores what ... presents (Santayana) 5-6-44
in jail by his ... (Emerson) 1-3-113
... inseparable from thinking (Locke) 1-4-31
into their ... (Hegel) 2-2-81
is a source of ... (Tolstoy) 1-4-60

... is origin of life (Bergson) 19-2-61
love an unreasoned ... (Plotinus) 3-1-18
matter gave rise to ... (Freud) 19-2-58
measured by ... (Wm. James) 19-6-37
memories into the ... (Freud) 5-3-32
multiplicity of agreeable ... (Boswell) 9-8-58
... of being desirable (Aristotle) 3-4-16
... of being under inevitable doom (Boswell) 8-2-21
... of freedom as faculty (Kant) 9-4-45
... of ignorance (Kant) 6-4-37
... of self involves (Wm. James) 1-4-64
progress toward ... (Mann) 19-2-64
property of ... (Freud) 1-4-66
rational ... of the human race (Schopenhauer) 15-1-67
simplicity of clear ... (Whitehead) 6-2-48
straining toward ... (Freud) 5-3-34
stream of ... (Wm. James) 5-1-70
that ... will note (Bergson) 19-7-89
there is no ... (Plato) 1-8-15
... would be chaotic (Wm. James) 6-2-45

CONSECRATION
... of all that was established (Mill) 20-2-44

CONSENT
act done by mutual ... (Marx) 11-1-60
be with his own ... (Locke) 11-6-10
by common ... (Aquinas) 12-3-4
established by ... (Locke) 13-1-12
except by ... of people (Rousseau) 11-6-19
from the ... of the governed (Jefferson) 12-3-20
general decree or ... (Spinoza) 12-4-43
governed by our own ... (Swift) 14-2-44
government by their ... (Locke) 12-3-17
has given his ... (Kant) 10-5-23
in face of universal ... (Thucydides) 14-3-7
mutual ... of the community (Locke) 10-4-17
... of mankind (Grotius) 12-1-44
... of the governed (Thoreau) 10-4-61
residence constitutes ... (Rousseau) 10-4-30
such a ... was necessary (Locke) 11-1-17
takes the form of ... (Augustine) 4-1-6
the ... of nations (Boswell) 11-1-30
value from ... of men (Locke) 11-1-20
... were not a fiction (Mill) 12-4-67
... which makes marriage (Aquinas) 2-3-35
without the other's ... (Lincoln) 10-4-62
without their ... (Herodotus) 1-7-11

CONSENTS
against their free ... (Locke) 10-9-20

CONSEQUENCE
attended with evil ... (Fielding) 9-10-94
names joined in a ... (Hobbes) 6-3-62

CONSEQUENCES
dangerous and ruinous ... (Plutarch) 10-2-22
face the ... (Plato) 9-7-12
if ... are unpleasing (Aristotle) 9-6-18
never about ... (Emerson) 1-3-113
... of belief (Dewey) 6-5-114
... of names (Hobbes) 6-7-22
painful ... await him (Kant) 9-5-19
the serious ... (Freud) 1-8-139
what are their ... (Dewey) 5-7-49

CONSERVATIVE
become more ... (Shaw) 10-9-42
pure ... is fighting (Whitehead) 15-2-78

CONSIDERATION
mature ... of things themselves (Locke) 6-7-30
more ... than another (Mill) 13-3-39

CONSOLATION
... is not what you need (Dostoevsky) 4-6-50

CONTEMPT
object of his . . . (Hobbes) 9-6-71
. . . of wounds and death (Hobbes) 9-11-40
sovereign . . . for her husband (Fielding) 3-2-31
unmerited . . . is provocative (Aquinas) 4-3-16
CONTENT
citizen who is . . . (Aurelius) 10-5-14
differs from tragedy in . . . (Dante) 16-4-15
do not . . . ourselves (Pascal) 1-5-91
live . . . the calmest strife (Milton) 4-7-46
the true . . . of art (Hegel) 16-1-42
. . . to begin with doubts (Bacon) 6-6-14
CONTENTION
not in . . . and envy (Augustine) 6-5-21
perpetual cause of . . . (Calvin) 9-4-31
spirit of . . . (Plato) 6-7-5, 9-15-20
wherever there can be . . . (Dante) 14-3-25
CONTENTMENT
handicap to . . . (Plutarch) 9-8-21
instructors in . . . (Sophocles) 4-6-6
source of unaltered . . . (Kant) 9-4-45
CONTENTS
a table of . . . for a deity (Whitehead) 8-1-81
CONTEST
sharp . . . ensues (Herodotus) 2-3-14
CONTEXT
. . . will not show meanings (Freud) 7-2-92
CONTINENT
brought forth on this . . . (Lincoln) 10-4-64
CONTINGENCIES
. . . are endless (Tolstoy) 6-2-42
maketh brief . . . (Dante) 19-3-18
CONTINGENT
God not a . . . thing (Spinoza) 19-4-27
CONTINUITY
law of . . . (Leibniz) 1-1-78
CONTINUOUS
movement is also . . . (Aristotle) 19-5-11
space is . . . (Poincaré) 19-6-41
CONTRACT
by a special . . . (Kant) 2-3-94
every . . . is included (Johnson) 9-14-47
fiction of a . . . (Mill) 12-4-67
if there be no . . . (Hobbes) 2-2-61
loses by the social . . . (Rousseau) 13-1-22
. . . made by themselves (Locke) 2-3-75
make it begin with a . . . (Nietzsche) 10-1-49
make this . . . grow (Shakespeare) 2-3-65
matrimonial . . . read (Augustine) 2-3-31
society not founded on . . . (Mill) 10-1-48
state does not rest on . . . (Hegel) 10-1-40
that which men call . . . (Hobbes) 12-3-10
veil of a new . . . (Plutarch) 2-3-25
. . . whereby one is (Aquinas) 2-3-36
will constitutes . . . (Kant) 11-1-41
your hand upon the . . . (Congreve) 2-3-77
CONTRACTS
bond in material . . . (Aquinas) 2-3-35
the faith of . . . (Smith) 12-2-42
CONTRADICTION
do not fear . . . (Montaigne) 6-6-10
every man saw the . . . (Epictetus) 6-7-13
full of . . . and error (Montaigne) 12-2-27
great . . . in our lives (Dewey) 17-2-131
involve a manifest . . . (Berkeley) 6-1-70
involved in inevitable . . . (Gibbon) 6-5-83
love a . . . (Hegel) 3-1-71
necessity of avoiding . . . (Poincaré) 17-3-49
. . . of their natural values (Nietzsche) 20-2-46

possibility of mathematics seems a . . . (Poincaré) 17-3-48
the art of . . . (Plato) 6-7-5
. . . to popular opinion (Hume) 17-1-65
CONTRADICTIONS
love solves all life's . . . (Tolstoy) 3-1-82
union of these two . . . (Tolstoy) 15-3-112
CONTRADICTORY
examine its . . . (Pascal) 6-3-64
CONTRARIES
by . . . execute all things (Shakespeare) 10-3-17
orderly combination of . . . (Aurelius) 15-1-24
the following . . . are true (Blake) 9-6-95
without . . . is no progression (Blake) 9-6-94, 20-15-92
CONTRARY
. . . things appear good (Aristotle) 9-6-18
we call . . . to nature (Montaigne) 19-1-30
CONTRIBUTION
makes a . . . to science (Shaw) 18-1-38
CONTRIBUTIONS
bound to mutual . . . (Hamilton) 11-6-39
modes of raising . . . (Kant) 11-2-114
CONTRIVANCES
most consummate of . . . (Browning) 6-6-46
such were the . . . I discovered (Aeschylus) 15-2-3
CONTROL
heart has no . . . (Homer) 9-11-2
. . . means a command (Dewey) 1-4-68
science in physical . . . (Dewey) 17-2-132
. . . stops with the shore (Byron) 19-1-88
CONTROLS
at the heart's . . . (Aeschylus) 4-2-2
CONTROVERSIES
. . . about words and names (Bacon) 7-2-56
source of many . . . (Spinoza) 6-4-26
CONTROVERSY
every subject to . . . (Bacon) 17-1-51
never be matters of . . . (Santayana) 20-3-69
scientific . . . unfruitful (Freud) 6-7-46
CONVALESCING
six months . . . (Melville) 18-3-57
CONVENIENCE
violates rights for . . . (Boswell) 9-5-16
CONVENIENCE-DREAMS
all dreams are . . . (Freud) 5-5-42
CONVENIENCES
all the . . . of life (Arnold) 13-1-57
certain quantity of . . . (Smith) 11-4-28
desire of . . . has no limit (Smith) 4-4-29
increase stock of . . . (Locke) 17-2-50
not to seek . . . (Plutarch) 4-2-15
CONVENTION
. . . and nature are at variance (Plato) 9-2-2
either the . . . or the League (Lincoln) 10-2-99
exist by . . . not by nature (Aristotle) 6-7-11
maintained by . . . (Rousseau) 2-1-34
. . . of human institution (Rousseau) 12-3-18
to be settled by . . . (Burke) 13-3-27
word added by . . . (Russell) 7-1-65
CONVENTIONAL
some signs are . . . (Augustine) 7-1-14
CONVENTIONS
are in the nature of . . . (Freud) 17-2-123
choice among possible . . . (Poincaré) 17-3-49
. . . form basis of authority (Rousseau) 9-2-25
. . . of love (Montaigne) 2-1-24
submit only to . . . (Rousseau) 10-1-34
CONVERSATION
good discourse and . . . (Bacon) 7-2-57
like a . . . with the noblest (Descartes) 16-2-18

COVENANTS (*Cont.*)
. . . without the sword (Hobbes) 1-2-51
COVER UP
the need to . . . (Montaigne) 6-6-10
COVET
shalt not . . . (Aquinas) 9-7-32
to make a man . . . (Twain) 11-3-78
COVETOUS
reverse of . . . (Plato) 4-7-8
who will be . . . (Horace) 4-9-2
COVETOUSNESS
. . . a special sin (Aquinas) 11-2-51
beware of . . . (*Luke*) 4-9-3
. . . cannot exist (Pascal) 20-2-30
he that hateth . . . (*Proverbs*) 10-6-1
no sermon save for . . . (Chaucer) 4-9-6
under the head of . . . (Aquinas) 2-3-33
COWARD
am I a . . . (Shakespeare) 4-1-12
brave man nor . . . (Homer) 15-3-6
if I like a . . . (Homer) 1-5-1
. . . loins that quail (Horace) 3-6-8
than be called a . . . (Fielding) 1-5-102
COWARDICE
and not my . . . (Cervantes) 15-3-88
an excess of . . . (Descartes) 4-2-24
courage opposed to . . . (Plato) 9-10-6
degradation of . . . (Thucydides) 1-6-5
greatest piece of . . . (Schopenhauer) 1-9-41
if there were no . . . (Johnson) 9-10-103
. . . keeps us in peace (Boswell) 14-3-36
less than you are worth is . . . (Montaigne) 4-11-16
old age paved way for . . . (Aristotle) 1-3-19
only . . . can impel (Hume) 1-9-33
out of their own . . . (Plato) 9-12-2
. . . perpetuated condition (Rousseau) 10-7-23
. . . punished with oppression (Hobbes) 12-4-40
COWARDS
ashamed of being . . . (Swift) 1-7-108
conscience does make . . . (Shakespeare) 1-9-27
. . . die many times (Shakespeare) 9-11-29
. . . had courageous sons (Euripides) 1-2-11
willingly be . . . (Pascal) 1-5-91
COZENER
usurer hangs the . . . (Shakespeare) 9-7-38
COZENERS
devil take such . . . (Shakespeare) 9-12-32
CRAFT
binds him to a . . . (Tocqueville) 11-3-46
dependent upon . . . (Schopenhauer) 1-7-132
harbor more . . . (Shakespeare) 9-14-30
. . . is weaker than necessity (Aeschylus) 15-3-12
laws of the . . . are demanding (Juvenal) 15-1-21
warriors of our . . . (Mann) 16-3-102
CRAFTINESS
taketh the wise in their . . . (*I Corinthians*) 9-15-29
CRAFTS
. . . and resources I contrived (Aeschylus) 15-2-3
in one line two . . . meet (Shakespeare) 16-1-23
the good and noble . . . (Aristophanes) 16-4-1
CRAFTSMAN
. . . is inclined by injustice (Aquinas) 16-1-19
not require the . . . (Aquinas) 16-1-20
CRAMMING
no moral turpitude in . . . (Wm. James) 8-3-87
CRASSY
obscure lot of minister of . . . (Gibbon) 2-2-78
CRAVE
what we . . . is wanting (Lucretius) 4-4-8

CRAVING
a wild untamed . . . (Freud) 4-7-67
CRAVINGS
between two . . . (Dante) 4-4-14
natural . . . constitute needs (Aristotle) 3-4-18
CREATE
. . . in me a clean heart (*Psalms*) 20-14-4
really did . . . the world (Dostoevsky) 19-8-87
CREATED
. . . anew in innocence (Seneca) 15-2-13
everything that is . . . (Plato) 19-3-2
to say world was not . . . (Hobbes) 19-8-53
was man . . . for (*I Corinthians*) 1-7-50
wisdom . . . all from nothing (Anselm) 9-15-35
You . . . heaven and earth (Augustine) 19-8-29
CREATION
all . . . and all creatures (Dostoevsky) 19-8-88
ample range of . . . (Pope) 5-1-45
and of . . . last arose (Milton) 19-2-35
a need of . . . (Bergson) 19-2-61
by the . . . of God (Plato) 19-1-2
cause of a good . . . (Augustine) 19-1-21
changeless series of . . . (Goethe) 16-3-64
from the . . . of the world (*Romans*) 20-13-19
full . . . leaves a void (Pope) 19-8-68
his empire over . . . (Bacon) 20-13-76
in all the works of . . . (Locke) 20-5-86
in the first . . . (Newton) 19-8-62
. . . is the workmanship (Berkeley) 17-2-53
life is . . . (Bernard) 19-2-53
man as the end of . . . (Kant) 1-1-90
man is a noble . . . (Plotinus) 1-1-35
man not the crown of . . . (Nietzsche) 1-1-122
nook and cranny of . . . (Wm. James) 19-2-56
nothing over and above . . . (Augustine) 19-1-20
. . . of non-being into being (Plato) 16-1-2
. . . of substance out of nothing (Locke) 19-8-66
. . . of the universe (Aquinas) 20-2-24
. . . of the world (Seneca) 19-8-15
one in the first . . . (Newton) 19-8-61
perpetual . . . (Goethe) 1-8-122
regarding the . . . of man (Augustine) 19-8-32
smaller parts of . . . (Berkeley) 20-5-88
special design in . . . (Mill) 19-1-114
. . . the effort of love (Santayana) 3-1-94
the second . . . (Mann) 19-2-64
what is mathematical . . . (Poincaré) 17-3-52
. . . widens to our view (Thoreau) 11-2-133
. . . will appear to him as God (Bergson) 3-1-92
without man the whole . . . would (Kant) 1-1-91
CREATION'S
and love . . . final law (Tennyson) 19-1-100
CREATIONS
regard all . . . together (Descartes) 19-8-50
CREATOR
and . . . of all things (Descartes) 20-5-60
. . . and ordainer of time (Augustine) 19-7-25
believe himself a . . . (Isak Dinesen) 16-3-104
benignity of our . . . (Montaigne) 20-1-19
character of the . . . (Mill) 19-1-114
costs the . . . more pains (Berkeley) 19-8-67
endowed by their . . . (Jefferson) 12-3-20
fall off from their . . . (Milton) 20-13-83
. . . first set in order (Plato) 19-8-6
from its . . . to himself (Dante) 20-13-54
God as a . . . (Calvin) 20-5-51
God . . . wise (Milton) 1-7-102
have deserted their . . . (Augustine) 20-14-19
he himself was the . . . (Plato) 19-2-5

if the . . . were obliged (Hume) 20-5-90
image of the . . . (Hume) 6-5-78
laws impressed by the . . . (Darwin) 19-2-48
love of the . . . (Augustine) 6-1-24
no . . . is without love (Dante) 3-1-27
no such maker or . . . (Plato) 16-1-4
. . . of all ages (Augustine) 19-7-18
omnipotence of the . . . (Gibbon) 20-15-89
providence of the great . . . (Augustine) 1-1-38
remember thy . . . (*Eccles.*) 1-3-3
. . . saw the creature (Plato) 19-7-4
spite the great . . . (Milton) 9-6-77
such a being might forget his . . . (Montesquieu) 1-1-82
the . . . conceived that (Plato) 19-8-5
the . . . is truly loved (Augustine) 9-10-40
the will of his . . . (Malthus) 9-6-97
thought a . . . necessary (Russell) 19-5-69
universal and beneficent . . . (Darwin) 20-5-104
why . . . made this world (Plato) 19-8-4
. . . works by intellectual powers (Darwin) 19-1-110
would rise above the . . . (Anselm) 20-5-36
CREATOR'S
sung the great . . . praise (Dryden) 20-15-84
CREATURE
a higher . . . than man (Shaw) 1-1-129
base and ignoble . . . (Bacon) 1-1-62
consider one . . . separately (Descartes) 19-8-50
destined him for a social . . . (Harvey) 1-1-64
His rational . . . (Augustine) 10-7-13
home of the speculative . . . (Kepler) 1-1-54
in slaying any living . . . (Augustine) 19-8-30
knowledge of the . . . (Augustine) 6-1-24
man is a political . . . (Aristotle) 10-1-4
miserable and puny . . . (Montaigne) 1-1-50
moving . . . that hath life (*Genesis*) 19-2-2
no . . . was without love (Dante) 3-1-27
nor any other . . . (*Romans*) 4-5-9
so short-live a . . . (Rousseau) 9-13-28
worshiped and served the . . . (*Romans*) 20-13-19
would it have been but a . . . (Augustine) 19-7-18
CREATURES
all . . . through love exist (Chaucer) 3-1-31
by contemplation of his . . . (Bacon) 20-5-58
call the delicate . . . (Shakespeare) 2-3-62
charity to irrational . . . (Plutarch) 3-5-14
contemplation of God's . . . (Bacon) 6-1-47
contemplation of the . . . (Bacon) 17-1-50
far from perfect . . . (Hume) 1-7-113
from fairest . . . we desire (Shakespeare) 16-6-36
. . . have shapes like ours (Locke) 1-1-79
how many goodly . . . are there here (Shakespeare) 1-1-60
in all world's living . . . (Epicurus) 19-8-11
innumerous living . . . (Milton) 19-2-35
intelligent . . . above us (Locke) 20-7-68
irrational . . . cannot distinguish (Hobbes) 10-1-23
love bewitches . . . that earth (Euripides) 3-1-6
millions of spiritual . . . (Milton) 20-7-62
most vulnerable and frail of all . . . (Montaigne) 1-1-51
pleasures of . . . differ (Aristotle) 4-7-11
spiritual . . . without bodies (Luther) 20-7-36
the most savage of earthly . . . (Plato) 1-1-11
these were . . . (Dante) 19-2-26
we fat all . . . else to fat us (Shakespeare) 1-8-75
CREDIBILITY
warranted by . . . (Russell) 6-4-55
CREDIT
get children a love of . . . (Locke) 8-3-55
get the . . . (Euripides) 1-5-5
CREDITOR

obliged to insure his . . . (Smith) 11-5-29
the glory of a . . . (Shakespeare) 9-10-65
CREDITORS
class of . . . exposed (Montesquieu) 10-8-11
. . . will beseech God (Rabelais) 11-4-10
CREDULITY
blind and terrified . . . (Hume) 20-12-25
our . . . though enormous (Shaw) 17-2-114
such is the progress of . . . (Gibbon) 20-11-37
very prone to . . . (Spinoza) 20-12-24
CREED
good sensible . . . this (Lucian) 17-1-34
more faith in doubt than in . . . (Tennyson) 6-6-42
never contained in his . . . (Thoreau) 20-1-61
passions got the better of his . . . (Sterne) 9-5-13
suckled in a . . . outworn (Wordsworth) 19-1-85
. . . which is not shaken (Arnold) 16-3-90
CREEDS
apologists of our ancestral . . . (Santayana) 20-3-69
assortment of live . . . (Lucian) 17-1-33
CRESSID
where . . . lay that night (Shakespeare) 3-1-37
CRESSIDA
. . . I once must lose (Chaucer) 15-3-68
CRESTONAEANS
live above the . . . (Herodotus) 2-3-14
CRETANS
all . . . are liars (Freud) 6-6-52
CRETE
. . . is not like (Plato) 14-1-21
what could the bull of . . . (Lucretius) 20-12-4
when in the wood of . . . (Shakespeare) 16-5-19
CREÜSA
sad . . . stopped (Virgil) 2-1-15
CRIES
man's instinctive . . . (Darwin) 7-1-58
uses inarticulate . . . (Darwin) 7-1-56
CRILLON
hang yourself brave . . . (Wm. James) 6-5-112
CRIME
. . . aging is made (Aeschylus) 12-2-3
all manner of . . . broke out (Ovid) 15-2-14
be a supposed . . . (Hume) 1-9-33
conceivable folly or . . . (Plato) 5-5-9
constitute a capital . . . (Melville) 9-9-39
if by committing a . . . (Kant) 10-7-30
my . . . as you call it (Euripides) 2-2-17
not even . . . more opposed (Thoreau) 11-5-34
spend it in . . . (Rousseau) 2-2-75
the primal . . . of mankind (Freud) 20-13-96
. . . which bankrupts men (Emerson) 11-3-53
will never see the . . . (Sophocles) 2-3-15
CRIMES
all the . . . of humanity (Dostoevsky) 19-8-87
brightness on their . . . (Johnson) 1-6-46
by most open . . . (Augustine) 1-5-47
children repeat the . . . (Juvenal) 2-2-112
. . . committed every day (Freud) 9-6-115
committing enormous . . . (Smith) 9-1-17
foul . . . done in my days (Shakespeare) 20-15-67
look on distress not . . . (Cervantes) 3-5-28
most of the . . . (Gibbon) 10-8-19
. . . of the great (Voltaire) 10-4-24
our . . . would despair (Shakespeare) 9-10-64
partners and agents of . . . (Lucretius) 1-8-24
punish . . . as well as (Rousseau) 10-2-74
. . . really odious (Montesquieu) 9-11-49
the . . . of wicked men (Augustine) 20-13-39
those . . . have met (Virgil) 12-4-15

CRIMES (*Cont.*)
worst of our ... is (Shaw) 11-2-156
CRIMINAL
wife is a ... (Voltaire) 2-3-84
CRIMINALS
like what ... feel (Dostoevsky) 1-8-132
the multitude of ... (Rousseau) 12-4-54
CRISES
way for more destructive ... (Marx and Engels) 11-5-39
CRISIS
keeps his head when ... comes (Seneca) 8-1-11
... of their lives (Plato) 2-3-17
the ... fleeting (Hippocrates) 18-1-7
CRITERION
... of truth (Freud) 6-6-52
CRITIC
an ancient ... hath set (Fielding) 16-4-27
... exults over the poet (Johnson) 16-4-32
first accurate ... (Jonson) 17-1-49
... you have frowned (Wordsworth) 16-3-73
CRITICAL
applying any ... test (Thucydides) 15-1-2
CRITICISM
... an act of friendship (Montaigne) 3-4-34
darkness of metaphysical ... (Wm. James) 19-3-50
foundation of irreligious ... (Marx) 20-1-62
... of a part of me (Thoreau) 1-4-52
open to no ... (Plutarch) 15-1-18
CRITICS
state not my ... (Milton) 13-2-18
CRITO
... made a sign (Plato) 1-8-18
CROESUS
ancestor of ... (Plato) 9-7-9
meanwhile ... taking (Herodotus) 14-1-6
O ... thou askedst a question (Herodotus) 9-8-2
the wealth of ... (Thoreau) 11-2-133
CROMWELL
some ... guiltless (Gray) 11-2-83
thus far hear me ... (Shakespeare) 1-5-75
CRONOS
... devouring his (Santayana) 20-3-69
in the days of ... (Plato) 20-15-11
... knew what we ourselves (Plato) 20-7-4
.CROSS
luminous trophy of the ... (Gibbon) 20-4-43
one gets the ... (Juvenal) 12-4-18
solitary man of the ... (Whitehead) 20-1-77
that taketh not his ... (*Matthew*) 8-8-27
true and vivifying ... (Gibbon) 20-12-31
upon that place stood a ... (Bunyan) 20-3-36
CROSSTREE
starved on a ... (Joyce) 20-5-125
CROWD
false opinions of the ... (Boethius) 1-5-48
CROWD'S
from the madding ... (Gray) 11-2-83
CROWN
... o' the earth doth (Shakespeare) 1-8-91
presented him a kingly ... (Shakespeare) 1-6-29
shall receive the ... of life (*James*) 20-13-24
... that virtue gives (Milton) 9-10-79
whither a ... on earth (Horace) 1-8-34
within the hollow ... (Shakespeare) 10-6-22
virtuous woman is a ... (*Proverbs*) 2-3-5
CRUEL
jealousy is ... as the grave (*Song of Solomon*) 40-10-1
CRUELTIES
the hard man and his ... (Homer) 9-10-1

CRUELTY
... and intolerance (Freud) 20-1-79
by ... the great seek (Augustine) 20-13-31
cowardice is mother of ... (Montaigne) 9-11-25
disinterested ... a primitive attribute (Wm. James) 3-2-38
greatest ... is to desist (Boswell) 8-3-70
knew not Nero's ... (Tacitus) 1-9-17
practiced ... and evil (Augustine) 12-4-21
true seeds of ... (Montaigne) 8-2-14
CRUSADES
inspired the ... (Emerson) 20-1-57
CRYSTALLIZATION
the first ... begins (Stendahl) 3-1-72
CUCHOD, Susan
attractions of Mademoiselle ... (Gibbon) 2-2-78
CUCKOLD
if I be his ... (Shakespeare) 2-3-61
... lives in bliss (Shakespeare) 4-10-5
make her husband a ... (Shakespeare) 2-3-63
of being made a ... (Rabelais) 2-3-47
CUCKOLDRY
gods taken in ... (Homer) 3-3-5
CUCKOLDS
have been ... ere (Shakespeare) 2-3-64
CULT
true ... of the divinity (Rousseau) 3-6-19
CULTIVATE
duty only to ... our conscience (Kant) 9-5-17
CULTIVATION
... of the earth (Rousseau) 11-1-26
what is acquired by ... (Dewey) 13-3-53
CULTIVATORS
nation of mere ... (Hamilton) 11-5-24
the mass of ... (Jefferson) 9-10-104
CULTURE
advances in the realm of ... (Freud) 15-2-82
... an activity of thought (Whitehead) 8-1-80
between barbarism and ... (Emerson) 20-1-57
by the ... they supply (Kant) 16-5-37
contain the ... of nations (Emerson) 17-1-84
difference between ... and nature (Dewey) 1-1-130
... from two sorts of men (Hobbes) 20-1-21
has acquired through ... (Freud) 15-2-81
... indispensably necessary (Arnold) 8-1-75
in itself a ... (Dewey) 11-5-48
it should lose its ... (Nietzsche) 14-1-104
light of ... (Schopenhauer) 1-6-60
... looks beyond machinery (Arnold) 15-2-70
... of the mental powers (Kant) 16-1-34
one of the aims of our ... (Freud) 19-1-121
reality of the man of ... (Nietzsche) 16-3-95
tastes acquired through ... (Darwin) 16-7-44
the effects of ... (Dewey) 10-4-76
the great aim of ... (Arnold) 20-1-70
the use of ... is (Arnold) 11-2-149
utility of intellectual ... (Newman) 8-1-74
CUMAE
after going as far as ... (Tacitus) 1-9-18
arrived at ... (Virgil) 20-10-14
CUNÉGONDE
... was indeed very homely (Voltaire) 1-2-64
CUNNING
a ... and most feline thing (Melville) 5-6-35
against superior ... (Swift) 12-4-47
more true than those with ... (Shakespeare) 3-1-35
no fence against superior ... (Swift) 9-14-43
strong in ... (Blake) 9-11-54
with all the ... (Rabelais) 1-7-69
CUP

love's . . . is short if love decay (Donne) 3-1-50
nor trust some later . . . (Horace) 19-7-10
one . . . or another (Dickens) 1-8-126
one more . . . to dawn (Thoreau) 1-8-130
such a . . . tomorrow as today (Shakespeare) 1-3-58
time steals our . . . (Horace) 19-7-11

DAY-DREAMS
how to elaborate his . . . (Freud) 16-1-57
investigation of . . . (Freud) 5-5-45

DAY-LABOR
doth God exact . . . (Milton) 20-8-67
. . . most independent (Thoreau) 11-3-57

DAY'S
and . . . at the morn (Browning) 19-8-85

DAYS
all our . . . are passed (*Psalms*) 1-3-1
. . . are swifter than (*Job*) 4-5-2
how many . . . will finish up (Shakespeare) 1-2-38
my hasting . . . fly on (Milton) 1-3-71
my salad . . . (Shakespeare) 1-3-57
the . . . that we have seen (Shakespeare) 1-3-48
the measure of my . . . (*Psalms*) 1-2-2
to loose good . . . (Spenser) 1-2-37

DAY STAR
. . . arise in your hearts (*II Peter*) 6-5-17

DEAD
arise ye more than . . . (Dryden) 16-5-33
better to be with the . . . (Shakespeare) 9-5-7
cannot rise from the . . . (Pascal) 20-9-23
dissect the bodies of the . . . (Augustine) 18-1-14
he is . . . already (Whitman) 2-2-86
is happy when he is . . . (Aristotle) 9-8-13
lavished on the . . . (Johnson) 1-5-109
let the . . . bury (*Matthew*) 20-3-8; (*Luke*) 20-8-29
lord of the . . . men (Homer) 20-15-5
resurrection of the . . . (Augustine) 6-7-15
. . . shall not have died in vain (Lincoln) 10-4-64
stirreth up the . . . for thee (*Isaiah*) 20-15-3
the . . . are rioting (Aristophanes) 16-4-1
the . . . shall be raised (*I Corinthians*) 20-15-28
the . . . shall live (Dryden) 20-15-84
they go to the . . . (*Eccles.*) 9-6-3
though he were . . . (*John*) 1-8-38
though one rose from the . . . (*Luke*) 20-10-20
to be . . . indeed unto sin (*Romans*) 20-13-20
to the unnumbered . . . (Homer) 20-15-7
was . . . and is alive (*Luke*) 2-2-28
wherefore I praised the . . . (*Eccles.*) 9-6-2
who acts . . . when alive (Montaigne) 4-8-15

DEAD LETTER
laws are a . . . (Hamilton) 12-1-74

DEAFNESS
only cure is husband's . . . (Rabelais) 18-1-16

DEALING
clear round . . . is the honor (Bacon) 9-14-35
strict and faithful . . . (Emerson) 9-14-57

DEALINGS
. . . between man and man (Plato) 9-3-3
whose own hard . . . (Shakespeare) 20-3-27

DEATH
abide eternally in . . . (Augustine) 20-14-22
agony of . . . (Darwin) 4-1-30
a kind of . . . of the soul (Augustine) 20-15-37
all in the valley of . . . (Tennyson) 14-2-64
a malefactor to . . . (Montesquieu) 12-4-50
and . . . complete the same (Browning) 20-5-107
and garner . . . (Euripides) 9-15-15
and put him to . . . (Milton) 10-6-38
and sin bringeth forth . . . (*James*) 20-13-24

and to the faithful . . . (Milton) 20-8-68
any man's . . . diminishes (Donne) 20-4-29
a preparation for . . . (Cicero) 1-8-28
are finished by a . . . (Byron) 16-4-39
are worthy of . . . (*Romans*) 20-13-19
arise from . . . (Donne) 20-7-54
. . . as a slumber (Hesiod) 15-2-2
as the shadow of . . . (*Job*) 2-3-4
at their . . . (Plato) 2-2-19
a universe of . . . (Milton) 20-15-79
barbarians who despised . . . (Gibbon) 18-2-41
become of him at . . . (Pascal) 4-5-19
. . . before dishonor (Horace) 9-8-18
being will have no . . . (Augustine) 6-1-26
. . . be not proud (Donne) 1-8-98
be punished with . . . (Plato) 12-4-10
brother of . . . daily haunts (Th. Browne) 19-7-46
brought . . . into the world (Milton) 16-3-44, 20-13-82
call our own but . . . (Shakespeare) 11-7-11
can it be . . . to know (Milton) 6-4-25
choose his . . . (Tacitus) 1-9-16
choosing to undergo . . . (Augustine) 20-14-20
. . . closes all (Tennyson) 1-3-115
comes . . . and bears (Euripides) 2-2-12
concept of sickness unto . . . (Kierkegaard) 4-5-33
continue to the hour of . . . (Plato) 9-7-9
crawl toward . . . (Shakespeare) 2-2-51
danger of violent . . . (Hobbes) 1-2-50
destruction of the second . . . (Augustine) 9-6-43
different causes of . . . (Lucretius) 19-3-8
dispute on the occasion of . . . (Fielding) 18-2-34
dull cold ear of . . . (Gray) 11-2-83
. . . eternal the supreme evil (Augustine) 9-6-45
ever he heard the name of . . . (Shakespeare) 9-14-32
faith that looks through . . . (Wordsworth) 19-1-82
fearing . . . more than disgrace (Aristotle) 9-11-10
fear of . . . (Epictetus) 4-2-17
finally waiting for . . . (Aurelius) 17-1-32
find nothing but . . . (Dostoevsky) 9-8-74
for birth or . . . (T. S. Eliot) 20-3-68
. . . for his ambition (Shakespeare) 10-6-25
fostered it in blood and . . . (Aeschylus) 15-3-8
from the world by . . . (Aquinas) 20-9-12
full soon the canker . . . (Shakespeare) 18-1-19
gate of . . . for things (Lucretius) 19-6-9
gates of . . . been opened (*Job*) 1-1-2
generally portending . . . (Swift) 18-1-30
gladder of his . . . (Chaucer) 1-5-52
glad to gain his . . . (Sophocles) 20-8-13
goal of all life is . . . (Freud) 19-2-57
God hath not made . . . (Aquinas) 9-6-51
grudge you your . . . (Plutarch) 1-9-11
happy before . . . (Th. Browne) 9-8-45
have no hope of . . . (Dante) 9-11-20
have only . . . to trust (Cervantes) 1-5-77
headlong he runs to . . . (Euripides) 20-8-18
his father's . . . (Dostoevsky) 2-2-90
horror at the thought of . . . (Boswell) 15-3-100
how cruel was my . . . (Dante) 3-2-14
I bring to . . . (Tennyson) 19-1-100
. . . in all its guises (Plotinus) 1-2-24
in dealing . . . about (Santayana) 15-2-85
in mind prepared for . . . (Milton) 20-3-33
in place of this we have . . . (Peirce) 19-4-47
into the valley of . . . (Tennyson) 3-6-23
. . . introduced into the world (Luther) 20-7-35
I run to . . . (Donne) 20-13-74
. . . is a fearful thing (Shakespeare) 1-8-83
. . . is generally prompt (Darwin) 19-2-46

DEATH (*Cont.*)

... is its destruction (Aristotle) 19-2-9
... is more abject (Montaigne) 14-2-34
... is most terrible of all (Aristotle) 1-8-21, 9-11-7
... is not to be feared (Cicero) 1-8-30
... is softer than tyranny (Aeschylus) 10-6-4
... is swallowed up (*I Corinthians*) 20-15-28
... is the catastrophe (Cervantes) 1-2-48
... is the cure of all diseases (Th. Browne) 18-2-32
... is the finish (Sophocles) 1-3-8
... is their proper punishment (Swift) 9-11-47
it is like unto ... (Chaucer) 20-15-60
judgement as sure as ... (Carlyle) 12-2-47
just and mighty ... (Raleigh) 1-8-96
justly ... to disobey (Locke) 14-2-43
king met with his ... (Sophocles) 4-3-2
live on everlasting ... (Donne) 20-15-69
loss of touch brings ... (Aristotle) 5-2-5
love is strong as ... (*Song of Solomon*) 3-1-2
lovely and soothing ... (Whitman) 1-8-131
lurking principle of ... (Pope) 4-1-26
made ... the punishment (Plutarch) 12-4-16
made subject now to ... (Augustine) 20-13-33
many shapes of ... (Milton) 1-8-113
many symptoms of ... (Lucretius) 18-3-23
misnamed ... and existence (Byron) 5-5-32
more unbearable than ... (Montaigne) 4-2-21
my hand in ... (Sophocles) 2-1-8
naturally shrinks from ... (Aquinas) 9-8-31
near-by freedom of ... (Whitman) 1-3-119
nor shall ... brag (Shakespeare) 16-6-37
no sudden mean of ... (Shakespeare) 17-1-47
... not close at hand (Aristotle) 4-2-7
not have experience ... (Augustine) 20-13-34
... not the remedy (Montaigne) 1-9-24
not to see the ... of any (Epictetus) 1-3-28
not yet a summer's ... (Shakespeare) 19-1-40
obedient unto ... (Augustine) 20-14-21
O bosom black as ... (Shakespeare) 20-8-60
... of a fellow creature (Melville) 9-9-39
... of a sound philosophy (Kant) 6-6-33
... of human creatures (Malthus) 19-2-40
of pale-faced ... (Rabelais) 1-7-69
... of the cross (Luther) 20-3-25
... of the father (Freud) 2-2-98
... of your friends (Boswell) 3-4-51
on himself voluntary ... (Augustine) 1-9-21
only ... he cannot find (Sophocles) 1-1-7
only ... will part thee (*Ruth*) 3-1-1
on me let ... wreck all (Milton) 20-14-46
oppressed by the fear of ... (Boswell) 20-14-54
others to eternal ... (Calvin) 15-3-72
over them triumphant ... (Milton) 18-3-48
permanent sentence of ... (Euripides) 12-4-6
poured out his soul unto ... (*Isaiah*) 20-3-4
producing instant ... (Plutarch) 1-9-9
punish delinquents with ... (Montesquieu) 14-2-46
punish it with ... (Swift) 12-4-47
reaction to the ... (Freud) 2-2-96
reckons on his own ... (Euripides) 14-1-11
... regarded as an evil (Plato) 9-11-6
rehearse ... (Seneca) 1-9-6
remains until their ... (Luther) 20-13-60
remembered kisses after ... (Tennyson) 4-5-34
rescu'd from ... by force (Milton) 5-5-23
sacrifice themselves to ... (Bacon) 3-6-14
scythe of ... can cut (Cervantes) 2-3-66
secret house of ... (Shakespeare) 1-9-28
send you to your ... (Sophocles) 2-3-15

shadow of ... stain it (*Job*) 4-5-1
... shall be no more (Condorcet) 15-2-46
shall not be put to ... (*Deut.*) 12-4-2
sickness and ... are (Bernard) 19-2-52
sinners be put to ... (Aquinas) 12-4-26
slave doomed to worship ... (Russell) 9-4-49
smashed out in ... (Euripides) 2-2-14
souls from timeless ... (Chaucer) 3-5-23
spirits of ... (Homer) 1-5-3
spirit unafraid of ... (Juvenal) 15-3-43
stroke of ... is a (Shakespeare) 1-9-29
study ... (Seneca) 1-8-35
swift sudden turn of ... (Melville) 1-2-84
terminated only by ... (Calvin) 20-7-40
than merely fearing ... (Hegel) 9-11-56
the ... act calls out (Aeschylus) 12-4-4
the brother of ... (Th. Browne) 5-5-26
the dread of ... (Cicero) 17-1-21
the fear of ... (Rousseau) 18-2-38
theme is ... of the fathers (Shakespeare) 4-6-34
then ... will drift upon me (Homer) 1-3-6
there shall be no more ... (*Revelation*) 20-15-30
the sting out of ... (Cicero) 3-4-20
... threatens every age (Chaucer) 1-3-39
to add the ... of you (Shakespeare) 4-6-36
to ... and destruction (Dostoevsky) 20-9-47
... to me subscribe (Shakespeare) 3-1-46
touched by the ... (Arnold) 2-2-89
... tracks him who shirks (Horace) 3-6-8
... tramples it to fragments (Shelley) 19-2-43
triumphs over ... (Blake) 6-6-35
... turned my tap of life (Chaucer) 1-3-37
turning back from ... (Sophocles) 9-6-4
under doom of ... (Plotinus) 14-1-31
unfelt ... which strikes (Thucydides) 1-6-5
unknown ... and silence (Homer) 2-2-10
until ... do them part (Shaw) 2-3-114
untroubled sleep of ... (Lucretius) 5-1-7
valiant never taste of ... (Shakespeare) 9-11-29
valley of the shadow of ... (*Psalms*) 20-14-2
vast ... of the solar system (Russell) 15-2-79
way to dusty ... (Shakespeare) 1-2-44
... what is thy sting (Bunyan) 20-14-49
what should it know of ... (Wordsworth) 1-3-98
what ugly sights of ... (Shakespeare) 20-15-65
when ... looms (Euripides) 1-8-11
which will end in ... (Hippocrates) 18-2-4
willing to risk ... (Wm. James) 1-6-81
... within easy reach (Freud) 19-2-58
worthy of ... (Juvenal) 1-5-36
you will not escape ... (Rousseau) 18-2-39

DEATH OF GOD
given to the ... below (Euripides) 14-1-10

DEATH PENALTY
... for a few crimes (Cicero) 13-2-8

DEATH'S
if earth ... scroll must be (Shelley) 15-2-49
soon ... pyre may blaze (Horace) 9-15-27

DEATH STROKE
... at their children's hands (Aeschylus) 12-4-5

DEBASEMENT
into a state of ... (Aquinas) 5-6-9

DEBATE
end of all ... (Locke) 6-7-30
if bloody ... shall (Euripides) 14-1-10

DEBAUCH
voluptaries have companions in ... (Voltaire) 3-4-47

DEBAUCHERY
into every kind of ... (Pascal) 20-3-32

DEEDS (*Cont.*)
disposes men to noble . . . (Aristotle) 9-10-17
do noble than useful . . . (Aristotle) 1-3-18
dreadful . . . among the gods (Plato) 20-6-17
have done many terrible . . . (Aristotle) 9-6-20
his . . . come to light (Plato) 9-7-9
his doing good . . . (Aquinas) 9-10-44
. . . of light and mercy (Dostoevsky) 3-5-43
old . . . for old people (Thoreau) 9-2-31
produce their greatest . . . (Montaigne) 5-6-11
prompt to outward . . . (Wm. James) 4-1-31
punishment for evil . . . (Lucretius) 12-4-13
pure in . . . (Tennyson) 6-6-42
shun damnable . . . (Juvenal) 2-2-32
sourest by their . . . (Shakespeare) 9-6-69
. . . to make heaven weep (Shakespeare) 6-6-13
. . . were his task (Cervantes) 16-2-13
DEEP
from . . . to deeper plung'd (Milton) 9-5-10
DEFEAT
be secret and take . . . (Yeats) 9-11-66
have not suffered . . . (Aquinas) 1-3-33
DEFECT
consists in . . . of action (Aquinas) 9-6-51
if this entails some . . . (Aquinas) 16-1-17
stamp of one . . . (Shakespeare) 1-5-68
DEFECTIVE
express what is . . . (Plutarch) 15-1-18
DEFECTS
. . . out of course of nature (Locke) 9-4-38
physicians with all their . . . (Bacon) 18-2-29
supply each other's . . . (Aquinas) 20-8-46
DEFENCE
admit of any other . . . (Mill) 20-1-63
essential to common . . . (Hamilton) 14-2-60
fight in . . . of their own (Plutarch) 14-3-13
in . . . of himself (Coke) 12-4-34
kill in natural . . . (Montesquieu) 14-1-62
. . . of society more expensive (Smith) 14-1-70
. . . of your country (Thucydides) 1-6-5
put up womanly . . . (Shakespeare) 9-6-66
relate to the national . . . (Hamilton) 11-6-42
the . . . of society (Smith) 9-11-51
truth not compatible with . . . (Shaw) 6-3-137
DEFEND
has a right to . . . (Gibbon) 12-3-21
means to . . . ourselves (Hobbes) 12-3-10
society ought to . . . me (Mill) 12-3-28
unable to . . . himself with speech (Aristotle) 7-2-10
DEFENDERS
. . . of the state (Aristotle) 10-8-3
DEFENDING
incapable of . . . himself (Smith) 9-11-51
DEFIANCE
he breathes . . . (Virgil) 4-3-10
DEFICIENCY
a natural . . . (Aristotle) 1-7-32
an excess and a . . . (Aristotle) 9-7-15
. . . is undue humility (Aristotle) 1-5-15
vices involving . . . (Aristotle) 9-10-14
DEFINE
difficult to . . . knowledge (Russell) 6-1-107
DEFINITION
a . . . of art wide enough (Ruskin) 16-1-46
. . . corresponding to name (Aristotle) 7-1-7
give the world a good . . . (Sterne) 7-2-75
good . . . of the word liberty (Lincoln) 13-1-47
incapable of . . . (Pascal) 17-3-29
. . . made up of names and forms (Plato) 6-1-6

. . . may be rendered inaccurate (Madison) 7-2-86
name is the . . . (Aquinas) 7-1-16
. . . of a thing itself (Plato) 7-1-5
things may be made darker by . . . (Boswell) 1-1-86
very . . . of tyranny (Madison) 10-6-66
words incapable of . . . (Pascal) 7-1-32
DEFINITIONS
begins with such . . . (Freud) 17-2-123
clear . . . of terms (Pascal) 6-7-27
gives chase to . . . (Maritain) 17-1-113
merely disguised . . . (Poincaré) 17-3-49
. . . of our words and terms (Bacon) 7-2-53
possible to find correct . . . (Leibniz) 7-2-69
. . . to resolve disputes (Bacon) 7-2-56
DEFORMED
a contrary motion are called . . . (Spinoza) 16-7-18
DEFORMITIES
real and essential . . . (Montaigne) 1-2-34
DEFORMITY
images of moral . . . (Plato) 13-2-5
no . . . but in monstrosity (Th. Browne) 19-1-50
show their . . . (Fielding) 9-10-94
some . . . may lurk (More) 2-3-44
the natural . . . of vices (Montaigne) 8-2-14
DEFRAUD
. . . ye not one another (*I Corinthians*) 2-3-23
DEGENERACY
causes of their deeper . . . (Rousseau) 19-1-67
DEGENERATE
why do men . . . ever (Thoreau) 17-1-86
DEGENERATION
. . . of a domestic race (Darwin) 18-1-32
organic . . . of species (Condorcet) 15-2-46
DEGRADATION
last degree of his . . . (Tolstoy) 16-4-41
then suffered utter . . . (Darwin) 15-2-61
DEGREE
when . . . is shaked (Shakespeare) 10-2-44
DEGREES
are . . . of madness (Locke) 5-6-30
freedom admits of . . . (Maritain) 5-7-51
scorning the base . . . (Shakespeare) 1-6-28
truth capable of . . . (Freud) 6-3-143
DEIDAMIA
. . . in death still sorrows (Dante) 20-15-54
DEITIES
fondly ascribe to your . . . (Hume) 20-6-41
humbling their . . . to love (Shakespeare) 20-6-37
. . . of a thousand groves (Gibbon) 20-6-42
prayer to the local . . . (Plato) 9-8-9
set up false . . . (Pascal) 20-3-32
the variety of . . . (Locke) 20-6-40
DEITY
behind all masks is a . . . (Nietzsche) 16-4-44
forewarned by the . . . (Xenophon) 1-8-20
immediate action of the . . . (Gibbon) 20-11-35
mental conceptions of the . . . (Tacitus) 20-2-19
miss the discovery of a . . . (Locke) 20-5-86
natural selection as a . . . (Darwin) 19-1-108
ourselves in place of the . . . (Wm. James) 19-4-49
participation of . . . in affairs (Tolstoy) 15-1-82
particular volition of the . . . (Hume) 20-11-29
prove existence of a . . . (Hume) 20-9-32
state as a secular . . . (Hegel) 10-1-42
such a conception of . . . (Hegel) 20-2-42
true or tolerable notion of . . . (Locke) 20-6-39
universal prescience in the . . . (Boswell) 15-3-99
very veil of the Christian's . . . (Melville) 20-1-59
violence against the . . . (Dante) 20-15-53

who overcome the . . . (Augustine) 9-15-34
. . . would be saved (Luther) 6-5-36
your adversary the . . . (*I Peter*) 20-7-6

DEVIL-BORN
doubt is . . . (Tennyson) 6-6-42

DEVILS
. . . do the gods great harm (Shakespeare) 1-7-91
eyes of impudent . . . (Juvenal) 8-3-25
horrible the . . . that torment (Chaucer) 20-15-59
is the place . . . dwell (Th. Browne) 20-15-71
leagues with . . . (Augustine) 20-12-11
mankind are the . . . of the earth (Schopenhauer) 1-1-98
one sees more . . . (Shakespeare) 16-3-31
the . . . also believe (*James*) 20-8-36
when of . . . and Hell (Blake) 16-3-63
whether men or . . . (Augustine) 20-15-34

DEVIL'S
the . . . an ass (Congreve) 1-7-107
wants to be the . . . (Luther) 1-2-30

DEVOTEE
superstitious . . . and bigot (Hume) 6-6-28

DEVOTION
enjoining practices of . . . (Gibbon) 20-1-45
last full measure of . . . (Lincoln) 10-4-64
. . . of a mother (Wm. James) 2-2-94
. . . of masses to God (Spinoza) 6-5-66
roused to a feeling of . . . (Augustine) 16-5-15
. . . to the father (Freud) 2-2-99

DEVOTIONS
folly of arbitrary . . . (Montaigne) 20-1-19

DEVOURING
. . . of kind by kind (Plotinus) 1-8-49
. . . time (Shakespeare) 19-7-43

DEXTERITY
. . . at expense of virtues (Smith) 11-3-39
. . . in avoiding injury (Harvey) 1-1-64
work with singular . . . (Tocqueville) 11-3-46

DIAGNOSIS
such a . . . would ruin (Shaw) 18-1-37

DIAGORAS
embracing . . . that had himself been (Plutarch) 1-8-43

DIALECTIC
a preparation for . . . (Plato) 8-1-2
by the power of . . . (Plato) 6-1-5
disputation called . . . (Augustine) 5-2-13
introducing them to . . . (Plato) 6-7-6
. . . is the conscience of discourse (Santayana) 6-7-48
logic called . . . (Kant) 7-2-82
. . . of continuity (Santayana) 19-5-74
prove them by help of . . . (Plato) 8-1-2
rhetoric a universal . . . (Aristotle) 7-2-10

DIALECTICAL
reasoning is . . . (Aristotle) 6-7-8

DIALECTICIAN
orator and the . . . (Quintilian) 7-2-31
serious pursuit of the . . . (Plato) 16-2-3
skilled propounder is a . . . (Aristotle) 6-7-9

DIALECTICIANS
. . . claim to control (Descartes) 17-3-25

DIALECTICS
along with Platonic . . . (Bergson) 17-1-107
away with subtleties of . . . (Montaigne) 8-1-24
no skill in . . . (Plato) 6-7-3
overestimation of . . . (Freud) 6-7-46
the Socratic . . . (Mill) 8-3-82

DIALECTS
. . . of Chinese language (Freud) 7-2-92
. . . of Italy (Gibbon) 7-1-52
slowly changing . . . (Darwin) 7-1-55

DIALOGUES
the speaker in all his . . . (Augustine) 17-1-38

DIAN
. . . of that time (Shakespeare) 1-7-92

DIANE
huntress . . . drew her bow (Milton) 9-10-80

DIAPASON
. . . closing full in man (Dryden) 16-5-33
swayed in . . . perfect . . . (Milton) 16-5-31

DICTATES
follow . . . of super-ego (Freud) 9-2-35
live according to its . . . (Thoreau) 17-1-86

DICTATORSHIP
form of a temporary . . . (Mill) 10-6-73
. . . over the human mind (Freud) 5-1-79

DICTION
admitted this in our . . . (Fielding) 16-4-29
beginning with the . . . (Aristotle) 16-4-9
is given by their . . . (Arnold) 16-3-91

DIDO
raving . . . roves (Virgil) 3-3-15
stood . . . with a willow (Shakespeare) 3-1-37
where . . . is (Dante) 3-3-31

DIE
a time to . . . (*Eccles.*) 19-7-2
at the point to . . . (*Genesis*) 2-1-2
better . . . than live (Plato) 10-7-4
born but to . . . (Pope) 1-1-81
easy ways to . . . (Shakespeare) 1-9-30
hazard of the . . . (Shakespeare) 19-4-21
he shall not . . . (*Proverbs*) 12-4-3
I to . . . and you to (Plato) 1-8-16
must I . . . lamenting (Epictetus) 4-6-14
ready to . . . (Horace) 9-8-18
theirs but to do and . . . (Tennyson) 3-6-23
to . . . is to be a counterfeit (Shakespeare) 9-11-27
to . . . to sleep (Shakespeare) 1-9-27
to . . . when at (Chaucer) 1-5-52
tragic to . . . before (Cicero) 1-8-29
until he . . . not happy (Herodotus) 9-8-2
we . . . in the person of (Freud) 1-6-85
willing to . . . for you (Machiavelli) 14-2-29
. . . without any effect (Johnson) 1-6-48
would wish to . . . (Milton) 1-5-96

DIET
live according to the . . . (Rabelais) 18-3-36
observing a strict . . . (Luther) 18-2-26
whether the . . . be so (Hippocrates) 18-3-8

DIETETICS
a course of . . . (Plato) 18-3-12

DIFFERENCE
. . . between soul and body (Descartes) 4-1-14
identical . . . between (Wm. James) 1-7-156
there's in telling . . . (Chaucer) 6-3-41

DIFFERENCES
. . . between the nations (Whitehead) 15-2-77
infinite . . . in idea of love (Kierkegaard) 3-5-40
. . . of character and intelligence (Tawney) 13-3-56
. . . of things (Bacon) 5-1-24
the . . . among human beings (Mill) 13-1-54

DIFFERENTIATION
first . . . you make (Freud) 1-7-165
principle of . . . (Bergson) 19-6-47

DIFFICULT
accomplishment of the . . . (Aurelius) 1-1-32

DIFFICULTIES
. . . do not make one doubt (Newman) 6-5-102
. . . of their own childhood (Freud) 9-2-35
sensitive of . . . of religion (Newman) 20-1-67

DIFFICULTIES *(Cont.)*
solution of many . . . (Descartes) 17-1-52
DIFFICULTY
a . . . for an impossibility (Maritain) 6-6-56
habit removed with . . . (Aquinas) 8-2-10
knowledge attainable with . . . (Russell) 6-6-49
. . . of religion is great (Arnold) 20-1-68
put another under such a . . . (Boswell) 6-3-95
the prize of . . . (Montaigne) 9-9-18
DIGESTIVE ORGANS
. . . undergo a change (Hippocrates) 18-1-4
DIGNITY
all our . . . consists in thought (Pascal) 5-1-31
arrayed in gorgeous . . . (Lucretius) 1-8-24
entirely without . . . (Kant) 10-7-29
in the light of human . . . (Hegel) 16-6-61
morality alone has . . . (Kant) 9-1-20
not from space I seek my . . . (Pascal) 5-1-32
perfect and simple . . . (Aurelius) 9-4-12
struck by their . . . (Dostoevsky) 11-2-151
the . . . of high place (Boswell) 10-8-15
this august . . . I treat (Melville) 1-1-103
true . . . of his humanity (Emerson) 8-1-58
DIGRESSIONS
. . . are the life of reading (Sterne) 16-2-29
DIMENSION
first . . . is called line (Nichomachus) 19-6-10
DIMENSIONS
attain huge . . . of a giant (Augustine) 14-1-32
medium of its . . . (Aquinas) 19-6-13
. . . of two material bodies (Pascal) 19-6-22
only three . . . in space (Dostoevsky) 19-8-87, 20-5-111
space has three . . . (Poincaré) 19-6-41
DIOCLETIAN
reign of . . . (Gibbon) 10-8-20
state maintained by . . . (Gibbon) 10-2-81
DIODORUS SICULUS
only read . . . (Marx) 4-9-18
DIOGENES
character of . . . (Epictetus) 2-1-19
for this purpose too . . . (Aurelius) 16-4-12
. . . held office of reproof (Epictetus) 8-3-26
. . . of Sinope who then (Plutarch) 17-1-26
DIOMEDE
horses of Thracian . . . (Lucretius) 20-12-4
DIONYSIOS
test the question whether . . . (Plato) 17-1-10
DIONYSIUS
as the tyrant . . . said (Montaigne) 10-2-42
hence . . . says (Aquinas) 12-2-23
. . . not unaptly objected (Bacon) 17-1-51
. . . of Syracuse (Aristotle) 10-6-14
the sufferings of . . . (Nietzsche) 16-4-44
DIONYSUS
chose . . . an expert in the art (Aristophanes) 16-4-1
inspiration of . . . (Plato) 5-6-6
old hymn to . . . (Euripides) 20-6-14
when . . . heard (Aristotle) 11-2-22
DIONYSUS'
. . . [voice] it must have been (Euripides) 5-6-5
DIOTIMA
. . . answered me (Plato) 16-1-2
O thou wise . . . (Plato) 1-5-10
what is he . . . (Plato) 3-1-9
DIRECT
not fit to . . . his bringing up (Emerson) 8-1-59
DIRECTION
all chance . . . which (Pope) 19-4-29
moving in a definite . . . (Bergson) 19-8-94

DIRECTIONS
studies give . . . at large (Bacon) 8-1-30
DIRECT REVELATION
world hates . . . (Thoreau) 6-5-96
DISADVANTAGE
Christianity has this . . . (Schopenhauer) 20-3-47
to his own . . . (Boswell) 1-4-35
DISADVANTAGES
. . . peculiar to women (Rousseau) 2-1-33
DISAGREEMENT
. . . of men one with another (Epictetus) 17-1-28
DISAPPOINTMENT
. . . all I endeavor end (Hopkins) 9-7-52
DISASTER
a . . . contrived by the emperor (Tacitus) 5-6-7
errors produce a social . . . (Russell) 6-6-49
in times of . . . (Plutarch) 1-2-19
into hopeless . . . (Thucydides) 1-5-7
overwhelming nature of . . . (Thucydides) 18-3-5
DISASTERS
fall into great . . . (Plutarch) 15-3-41
the . . . of life (Augustine) 3-4-27
DISBELIEF
. . . not dangerous in society (Shaw) 6-5-113
willing suspension of . . . (Coleridge) 16-3-76
DISBELIEVE
we will . . . everything (Locke) 6-6-22
DISBURSEMENTS
income and . . . (Tacitus) 11-6-5
DISCERNMENT
. . . belongs to reason (Aquinas) 9-10-47
child's faculties of . . . (Schopenhauer) 8-3-79
. . . of good from evil (Augustine) 9-13-9
DISCIPLES
another of his . . . said *(Matthew)* 20-3-8
. . . came and said to him *(Matthew)* 6-5-7
he chose . . . (Augustine) 20-4-13
he constrained his . . . *(Mark)* 20-11-5
his . . . believed in him *(John)* 20-11-7
. . . owe unto masters (Bacon) 8-3-47
the . . . were assembled *(John)* 20-4-10
then the eleven . . . *(Matthew)* 20-4-4
to appear to his . . . (Milton) 20-3-33
worthy . . . of philosophy (Plato) 17-1-7
you are my . . . indeed *(John)* 6-3-20, 9-4-6
DISCIPLINE
. . . a chief factor in education (Hegel) 8-1-54
a . . . it is in logic (Emerson) 17-1-84
ancient Roman . . . (Plutarch) 14-2-18
. . . and liability to punishment (Mill) 8-3-85
art emerges by . . . (Santayana) 16-1-64
curiosity of more value than . . . (Augustine) 8-3-29
form of mental . . . (Faraday) 1-4-49
imprinted by good . . . (Plutarch) 12-1-20
in an honest . . . (Rabelais) 2-2-43
in need of . . . (Locke) 2-2-67
instructed in all convenient . . . (Rabelais) 1-3-42
in what is called . . . (Smith) 14-2-52
no . . . ever requisite (Smith) 8-3-74
no . . . so severe (Dewey) 6-2-53
. . . of a school is military (Boswell) 8-3-70
. . . of colleges and universities (Smith) 9-9-29
. . . of heavy blows (Cervantes) 20-4-28
poisoned by a like . . . (Huxley) 6-6-45
still subject to . . . (Montaigne) 4-1-11
the . . . of a soldier (Gibbon) 14-2-58
the . . . of laws (Aquinas) 12-1-26
this virtue and moral . . . (Shakespeare) 8-1-27
DISCIPLINED

DREAD (*Cont.*)
scare a thing to . . . (Chaucer) 4-11-15
DREAM
a . . . that falters in daylight (Aeschylus) 1-3-7
dreamed a sad . . . (Thoreau) 20-3-53
from the . . . of life (Shelley) 1-8-123
glory and freshness of a . . . (Wordsworth) 1-3-101
. . . has preserved for us (Freud) 5-1-77
his . . . is told (Emerson) 20-10-43
I dreamed a . . . (Bunyan) 1-2-56
I dreamed in a . . . (Whitman) 3-4-60
I saw in my . . . (Bunyan) 20-3-36
perchance to . . . (Shakespeare) 1-9-27
prophet that hath a . . . (*Jeremiah*) 20-10-2
we say of this Christian . . . (Santayana) 20-3-69
what was your . . . (Shakespeare) 20-15-65
when the . . . is gone (Dante) 5-4-5
. . . with thy hand on the helm (Melville) 6-4-44
DREAMER
an artist is a . . . (Santayana) 16-1-64
DREAMING
. . . gives us the best notion (Darwin) 5-4-38
. . . on things to come (Shakespeare) 3-1-46
DREAMS
anything but sick men's . . . (Hume) 20-1-39
cause of visions in . . . (Aquinas) 20-7-27
deceive with unsubstantial . . . (Euripides) 20-6-10
hearken to your . . . (*Jeremiah*) 20-10-4
illusions of my . . . (Descartes) 1-4-24
indefiniteness in . . . (Freud) 7-2-92
like a land of . . . (Arnold) 1-2-91
like the shapes of . . . (Aeschylus) 1-1-6
love in . . . is greedy (Dostoevsky) 3-1-79
nature lends such evil . . . (Tennyson) 19-1-100
of how to distinguish . . . (Hobbes) 20-12-22
. . . of wild men (Thoreau) 6-3-111
relation of our typical . . . (Freud) 16-3-97
said to be based on . . . (Aristotle) 20-10-12
scarest me with . . . (*Job*) 1-9-2
scenes and . . . unknown (Hardy) 20-15-107
see what will become of his . . . (*Genesis*) 4-8-1
sexual material in . . . (Freud) 7-1-70
speak to a man by . . . (Hobbes) 20-10-31
such stuff as . . . are made of (Shakespeare) 1-2-46
symptoms like . . . themselves (Freud) 16-4-46
vivid . . . of the night (Melville) 5-6-36
DREAMT
are . . . of in your philosophy (Shakespeare) 17-1-48
DREAM-WORK
how . . . proceeds (Freud) 7-2-91
DRESS
. . . us fairly for our end (Shakespeare) 9-6-60
DRINK
. . . always before thirst (Rabelais) 9-12-24
. . . but too much (Rabelais) 9-12-23
. . . doth not reverse nature (Fielding) 9-12-41
. . . is a great provoker (Shakespeare) 9-12-36
leave thy . . . and (Shakespeare) 9-13-19
. . . until misfortune overtakes (Luther) 9-12-22
DRINKING
so fat-witted with . . . (Shakespeare) 9-12-31
while we are . . . (Juvenal) 19-7-14
DRIVETH
time . . . onward fast (Tennyson) 19-7-75
DROSS
a merely mortal . . . (Milton) 19-7-48
DRUDGERY
. . . of learning a language (Augustine) 8-3-29
same life of . . . (Mill) 11-3-76

whole . . . of creation (Shaw) 1-7-161
DRUDGES
educated to be . . . (Huxley) 1-7-143
DRUG
between . . . and disease (Montaigne) 18-3-39
not cured by the . . . (Freud) 18-2-53
DRUGS
by virtue of some . . . (Rabelais) 18-1-16
through the lack of . . . (Aeschylus) 15-2-3
DRUMMER
he hears a different . . . (Thoreau) 13-1-45
DRUNK
get . . . quickly (Aristotle) 18-3-21
happy when he is . . . (Boswell) 9-8-59
make husbands . . . (Shaw) 2-3-115
man must get . . . (Byron) 4-7-60
quarrelsome when . . . (Fielding) 9-12-41
DRUNKARDS
become . . . by separate drinks (Wm. James) 8-2-31
DRUNKENNESS
all from . . . (Dostoevsky) 11-2-150
forbid all . . . (Chaucer) 9-10-51
. . . inflames (Seneca) 9-12-13
. . . is always improper (Plato) 2-3-17
DRYDEN, John
style of excellence such as . . . (Boswell) 16-7-35
DUALISM
attitude is a thoroughgoing . . . (Wm. James) 6-1-99
DUCAT
every . . . in six thousand (Shakespeare) 11-1-12
DUEL
going to fight a . . . (Tolstoy) 9-11-62
DUKE OF EXETER
the . . . doth love thee (Shakespeare) 15-3-80
DULCINEA DEL TOBOSO
find that my lady . . . (Cervantes) 5-6-24
find the lady Madame . . . (Cervantes) 20-14-37
. . . is dis-enchanted (Cervantes) 5-6-25
most devoutly to his . . . (Cervantes) 9-11-37
persecuting that of . . . (Cervantes) 15-3-87
the peerless . . . (Cervantes) 3-1-49
use I make of . . . (Cervantes) 5-4-14
were my . . . but free (Cervantes) 20-8-61
DULL
not bred so . . . (Shakespeare) 1-7-77
DULL-WITTED
be as . . . as they (Hobbes) 16-2-19
DULNESS
the . . . of the fool (Shakespeare) 9-15-53
DUMB
thing to strike us . . . (Carlyle) 19-7-74
DUMBSHOWS
inexplicable . . . of noise (Shakespeare) 16-4-19
DUNCAN
. . . is in his grave (Shakespeare) 1-8-90
this . . . hath borne (Shakespeare) 4-8-18
DUNCES
. . . are all in confederacy (Swift) 1-6-43
DUNG
swine's . . . stints the blood (Luther) 18-1-17
DUNSINANE
. . . he strongly fortifies (Shakespeare) 10-6-26
DUPLICATE
has its cunning . . . in mind (Melville) 19-1-102
DUPLICITY
barring out of all . . . (Emerson) 9-14-57
DURATION
average . . . of human life (Condorcet) 15-2-47; (Malthus) 1-8-120

EMULATION (*Cont.*)
... in the learn'd (Pope) 9-10-90
... is pain (Aristotle) 4-8-8
pale and bloodless ... (Shakespeare) 10-2-44
touched with ... (Plutarch) 1-5-29
ENCHANTMENT
as we flaw by ... (Cervantes) 20-15-68
great art of ... (Plato) 7-2-3
ENCHANTMENTS
... that have the greatest (Cervantes) 20-11-17
ENCOURAGERS
no ... to vice (Swift) 9-10-89
ENCUMBRANCE
so grievous an ... (Swift) 11-2-76
END
actualize this final ... (Hegel) 9-11-55
as regards the proposed ... (Aquinas) 16-1-17
benefit of mankind the ... (Hobbes) 17-2-37
best of all his ... to win (Chaucer) 9-13-17
born to a disastrous ... (Spenser) 1-2-37
bring about the ... (G. Eliot) 9-10-117
change of form becomes the ... (Marx) 4-9-16
descent of their last ... (Joyce) 1-8-144
devoid of an ... (Kant) 16-1-34
directed to a particular ... (Aquinas) 16-7-13
does everything for an ... (Spinoza) 19-3-30
educative process its own ... (Dewey) 8-1-90
every agent acts for an ... (Aquinas) 9-6-54
exactly answers to its ... (Emerson) 16-6-64
final ... can only be man (Kant) 1-1-92
he supposes no ... (Locke) 19-7-56
humanity as an ... (Kant) 1-9-38
ignorant of the ... of things (Aquinas) 19-8-38
in the ... without ... (Augustine) 15-2-20
is hastening to its ... (Cervantes) 19-5-30
justice the ... of government (Hamilton/Madison) 12-2-45
made an ... of himself (Plutarch) 1-9-8
man exists for an ... (Kant) 9-3-32
man is an ... in himself (Kant) 9-1-23, 9-3-30
man may obtain the last ... (Aquinas) 20-15-40
nature never seeks an ... (Aristotle) 19-1-8
nature of a thing is its ... (Aristotle) 10-1-6
no final ... in creation (Kant) 1-1-91
nothing for the sake of an ... (Spinoza) 19-1-56
of coming to an ... (Seneca) 1-8-36
... of operations of mind (Kant) 17-1-76
... of true natural philosophy (Bacon) 17-2-26
... of your knowledge (Lucian) 6-6-7
one sole ... of everything (Pascal) 20-13-79
our minutes hasten to their ... (Shakespeare) 1-2-47
our ultimate ... (Pascal) 1-8-109
past as the ... of education (Dewey) 8-1-87
practical or noble ... (Ruskin) 16-1-47
proportion to the ... (Aquinas) 4-1-8
realization of a self-contained ... (Whitehead) 16-1-56
regarded as a formal ... (Kant) 17-3-40
signs of the ... (Shaw) 1-3-128
so courageous an ... (Tacitus) 1-9-17
such was the ... (Plato) 1-8-18
that is an ... of nature (Kant) 19-3-42
that is the ... of all men (*Eccles.*) 4-6-3
the ... crowns all (Shakespeare) 19-7-40
the rational ... of man (Hegel) 10-1-40
thought of something as ... (Kant) 16-1-36
to be done for a good ... (Aquinas) 9-13-16
to be the ... of all actions (Augustine) 17-1-38
to know mine ... (*Psalms*) 1-2-2
what other ... (Santayana) 1-8-143
what the ... of war shall be (Chaucer) 14-1-35

ENDEAVOR
excellent ... of drinking (Shakespeare) 18-1-20
if he would use his ... (Boswell) 1-7-119
... in continual motion (Shakespeare) 10-1-17
our ... be so loved (Shakespeare) 9-6-63
wish would excite ... (Johnson) 9-8-57
ENDING
with a good ... (Seneca) 1-8-37
ENDOWMENT
distinctive ... of a human being (Mill) 9-2-32
... of human life (Bacon) 17-2-22
those of superior ... (Dewey) 13-3-53
unequal individual ... (Marx) 12-3-27
ENDOWMENTS
in respect of natural ... (Tawney) 13-3-55
man by his natural ... (Aquinas) 1-2-27
similar natural ... (Tawney) 13-3-54
ENDS
attainment of certain ... (Tolstoy) 19-4-43
first consult our private ... (Swift) 3-4-44
God has no ... (Hobbes) 20-8-62
let all the ... thou (Shakespeare) 1-5-75
man determines ... (Maritain) 9-3-36
more are men's ... (Shakespeare) 1-8-70
not working for low ... (Thoreau) 11-3-56
... of the masters of art (Aristotle) 16-1-7
proper to these ... (Aquinas) 9-13-11
three ... which a statesman (Coleridge) 10-2-91
vast system of natural ... (Kant) 16-6-50
whether ... are ... designedly (Kant) 19-1-71
with regard to the ... (Aquinas) 9-13-10
ENDURE
... and conquer (Virgil) 4-5-16
command to ... difficulty (Augustine) 4-6-19
men must ... (Shakespeare) 1-8-85
to ... life remains (Freud) 1-8-140
ENDYMION
to sleep like ... (Aristotle) 20-6-21
ENEMIES
... also to receive (Plato) 12-2-6
are called God's ... (Augustine) 9-10-39
... as well as friends (Plato) 14-2-10
chivalry in your ... (Freud) 9-6-115
efforts against their ... (Thucydides) 14-1-13
have for ... only states (Rousseau) 14-1-65
his ... to be at peace (*Proverbs*) 14-3-2
if laws are ... (Burke) 12-1-70
in despite of his ... (Rabelais) 18-3-35
in the land of their ... (*Leviticus*) 20-2-10
love of one's ... (Aquinas) 3-5-21
love to their ... (Homer) 2-1-5
love your ... (Shaw) 20-3-65
natural ... of society (Montaigne) 10-7-21
... of civilized society (Gibbon) 14-1-77
of our ... or rivals (Aristotle) 4-2-8
... of virtue in society (Rousseau) 9-10-100
or praising one's ... (Polybius) 15-1-10
put all ... under (*I Corinthians*) 1-8-40
such internal ... (Gibbon) 10-7-28
... the natural infirmities (Rousseau) 1-3-81
they are mortal ... (Thucydides) 4-3-3
they cease to be ... (Rousseau) 14-1-66
to which all brave men are ... (Thoreau) 10-3-56
vengeance of thine ... (*Judges*) 2-2-2
wrath of invisible ... (Gibbon) 4-2-30
your ... will be killed (Euripides) 2-2-14
ENEMY
against an unjust ... (Kant) 14-1-83
and hate thine ... (*Matthew*) 12-2-19

call out for the hand of the . . . (Montaigne) 19-4-20
ever been God's . . . (Shakespeare) 10-6-21
every man is . . . to every man (Hobbes) 1-2-50
healthy fear of the . . . (Montaigne) 4-2-21
if a man finds his . . . (*I Samuel*) 9-7-1
if thine . . . be hungry (*Proverbs*) 3-5-3
if thine . . . hunger (*Romans*) 9-7-23
injuries of an . . . (Swift) 9-10-89
. . . in their mouths (Shakespeare) 9-12-35
kill his . . . (Homer) 2-2-8
more than challenge his . . . (Cervantes) 9-11-38
movements of the . . . (Tolstoy) 14-2-67
no . . . more dangerous than hatred (Augustine) 3-2-12
none of the . . . had observed (Plutarch) 14-2-21
no such terrible . . . (Bacon) 1-8-101
or as a public . . . (Rousseau) 12-4-56
perpetually threatened by an . . . (Calvin) 20-7-40
right to kill an . . . (Rousseau) 10-7-24
sight of an old . . . down (Euripides) 4-6-7
takes God for the . . . of life (Nietzsche) 9-1-36
the . . . held my will (Augustine) 9-4-18
the . . . is too strong (Swift) 14-1-61
the intentions of an . . . (Cervantes) 14-3-28
the principles of an . . . (Kant) 14-3-31
the . . . who invades (Herodotus) 14-2-6
to become your . . . (*Galatians*) 6-3-22
to be equal is to be an . . . (Mill) 13-3-40
treated as an . . . (Augustine) 6-3-27
where an . . . seems strong (Thucydides) 14-2-8

ENERGIES
his deepest creative . . . (Shaw) 16-1-54

ENERGY
conservation of . . . (Santayana) 17-2-133
effort to accumulate . . . (Bergson) 19-2-60
ethical . . . par excellence (Wm. James) 9-1-37
have ethical . . . enough (Shaw) 1-5-128
impulse another name for . . . (Mill) 9-5-26
makes a show of . . . (Plutarch) 4-3-13
reason and . . . (Blake) 9-6-94
that . . . called evil (Blake) 9-6-95
the expense of mental . . . (Freud) 5-6-41
tremendous . . . accumulated (Nietzsche) 1-6-77

ENGELS, Friedrich
teaching of Marx and . . . (Lenin) 10-1-51

ENGENDERING
known his own . . . (Homer) 2-2-10

ENGINES
in these narrow . . . (Th. Browne) 19-1-49
those terrible . . . (Swift) 10-2-65
you mortal . . . (Shakespeare) 14-2-38

ENGLAND
and leave your . . . (Shakespeare) 5-4-12
. . . felt heat of Christianity (Emerson) 20-1-57
. . . hath need of thee (Wordsworth) 16-3-74
in . . . people have had (Voltaire) 13-2-26
material existence of . . . (Hegel) 11-5-26
my return to . . . (Gibbon) 2-2-78
thence we looked toward . . . (Shakespeare) 20-15-65
this realm—this . . . (Shakespeare) 3-6-13
were I in . . . now (Shakespeare) 1-1-59

ENGLAND'S
upon . . . mountains green (Blake) 19-1-75

ENGLISH
. . . are a race apart (Shaw) 9-9-48
pronounce . . . tolerably well (Boswell) 7-1-51
the . . . are apt to (Montesquieu) 1-9-32

ENGROSS
may . . . as much as (Locke) 12-3-13

ENIGMAS
these involved . . . (Th. Browne) 6-5-54

ENJOY
early . . . the light eternal (Goethe) 4-5-31
only because we wish to . . . (Rousseau) 6-1-75

ENJOYING
the . . . not the possessing (Montaigne) 9-8-37

ENJOYMENT
. . . according to reason (Montaigne) 9-12-28
brilliant flash of . . . (Mill) 9-8-72
. . . in this life (Descartes) 4-1-17
love the life of . . . (Aristotle) 9-6-14
not even present . . . (Plutarch) 4-2-15
. . . of all good things (Russell) 9-1-39
. . . of life (Kant) 9-9-35
. . . of works of art (Freud) 16-1-58
probable future . . . (Locke) 4-5-25
pursuit of every . . . (Malthus) 4-7-58
reel on to . . . (Goethe) 9-8-66
to grab at short-lived . . . (Gibbon) 15-1-52
with . . . you can fool (Goethe) 9-8-64

ENJOYMENTS
equality confers small . . . (Tocqueville) 13-3-32

ENLIGHTEN
willed to . . . others (Pascal) 6-5-60

ENLIGHTENMENT
these days of scientific . . . (Wm. James) 20-8-86

ENMITIES
great . . . born of friendships (Montaigne) 5-6-10
great . . . spring up (Plato) 4-3-4
private . . . and public justice (Gibbon) 9-10-106
. . . really to be settled (Thucydides) 14-3-6

ENMITY
begins the day of . . . (Euripides) 13-3-1
between women it is . . . (Schopenhauer) 1-7-133
full of trouble and . . . (Plutarch) 20-6-31
his . . . was shared (Plato) 6-4-6
. . . is anger watching (Cicero) 4-3-8
is a state of . . . (Locke) 14-1 58
I will put . . . (Milton) 20-7-65

ENNIUS
. . . the father of Latin poets (Rabelais) 16-2-7
what . . . says is true (Cicero) 3-4-21

ENNUI
a feeling of . . . (Hegel) 19-5-62
suffer from . . . (Darwin) 4-1-30
the . . . of living ceases (Maritain) 16-1-67

ENORMITIES
of the worst . . . (Mill) 19-1-114

ENORMITY
. . . greater than I committed (Thoreau) 1-4-51

ENQUIRE
you are not to . . . (Plato) 13-2-2

ENQUIRY
what is the subject of . . . (Plato) 8-3-5

ENRICH
. . . the hand of yonder (Shakespeare) 1-7-76
to . . . themselves (Machiavelli) 14-1-38
ways to . . . are many (Bacon) 11-2-66

ENSLAVE
may be right to . . . *B* (Lincoln) 10-7-39
to . . . our country (Thucydides) 4-3-3

ENSLAVED
. . . beneath an alien hand (Aeschylus) 15-3-9

ENTERPRISE
and that is called . . . (Thoreau) 11-5-35
a spirit of . . . and adventure (Thoreau) 15-1-73
great means of . . . (Milton) 11-2-71
the spirit of . . . (Hamilton) 11-5-24

EXPENSE

causes more ... (Chaucer) 2-3-42
chief sources of ... (Hamilton) 11-6-42
educated at their own ... (Smith) 8-3-72
... equal to my wishes (Gibbon) 11-2-113
increase in their ... (Rousseau) 11-6-21
worthy of the ... (Aristotle) 11-2-18

EXPENSES

convert superfluous ... (Rousseau) 11-6-22
defraying a share of ... (Mill) 11-6-52
no private ... (Plato) 11-1-2
spare useless ... (Locke) 8-1-40

EXPERIENCE

accumulated and organized the ... (Huxley) 1-1-114
accumulated ... of ages (Hamilton) 14-1-85
acquiesce in his ... (Santayana) 20-3-69
all ... becomes useless (Hume) 19-3-37
all knowledge by ... (Descartes) 17-3-25
all that it is destined to ... (Seneca) 19-8-15
amalgamating disparate ... (T. S. Eliot) 16-3-100
an absolutely new ... (Wm. James) 1-3-125
... and wisdom come with age (Chaucer) 1-3-36
arrive at facts by ... (Descartes) 6-7-20
better quality of human ... (Dewey) 10-4-75
beyond limits of ... (Kant) 20-5-94
child has a different ... (Dewey) 8-3-98
connection with ... (Wm. James) 17-3-47
contains a whole gamut of ... (Santayana) 16-5-43
contrary to laws of ... (Dewey) 8-3-99
... convinces us (Locke) 6-6-23
... corrects preconceived ideas (Schopenhauer) 8-1-55
... could not create geometry (Poincaré) 17-3-50
custom renders ... useful (Hume) 9-2-24
customs shape his ... (Benedict) 9-2-37
... decides issues of instinct (Wm. James) 1-1-126
deeper and finer ... (Thoreau) 17-2-86
deepest human ... (Arnold) 20-1-70
defrauding himself of ... (Thoreau) 8-1-65
denied ... of the world (Russell) 2-3-116
dependeth on much ... (Hobbes) 9-13-23
different from any ... (T. S. Eliot) 16-1-63
dream derived from ... (Freud) 5-5-38
... dupes and leads us to death (Pascal) 9-8-49
education a reorganizing of ... (Dewey) 8-1-89
every ... modifies (Dewey) 8-2-33
form part of ... (Wm. James) 1-4-53
foundation of all ... (Kant) 19-5-60
get their ... of life (Plato) 8-1-2
greatest ... of disease (Plato) 18-2-8
have in himself the ... (Milton) 16-3-46
have no ... of them (Shaw) 4-4-35
hope over ... (Boswell) 2-3-87
ideas come from ... (Santayana) 5-6-44
ideas supervene upon ... (Wm. James) 5-1-72
independently of all ... (Kant) 6-1-82
infinite variety of human ... (Livy) 15-1-13
influence of common ... (Locke) 6-5-71
instruction and ... (Dewey) 7-1-74
intense my ... (Thoreau) 1-4-52
interpretation of universal ... (Mill) 5-7-43
... is contradicting theory (Boswell) 17-2-60
... is its own dunghill (Montaigne) 18-1-18
is such an order in ... (Santayana) 20-5-124
... is thought to be courage (Aristotle) 9-11-10
judgment sharpened by ... (Kant) 9-3-26
judgments corrected by ... (Lavoisier) 17-2-66
knowledge and ... as art (Aristotle) 8-3-10
knowledge and ... will grow (Montaigne) 1-3-43
know results of human ... (Mill) 9-2-32

lack of ... diminishes power (Aristotle) 17-2-1
little store of ... (Harvey) 8-3-50
lived upon gross ... (Hobbes) 17-1-53
... makes them distrustful (Aristotle) 1-3-19
man of ... is thought to be (Aristotle) 9-15-21
multiplies his own ... (Gibbon) 7-1-53
never been observed in ... (Galileo) 17-3-24
no ... of teaching (Russell) 8-3-94
no ... without memory (Harvey) 5-3-17
no immediate ... of what others (Smith) 5-2-31
... no objects reason can cognize (Kant) 5-1-53
no reason in ... (Russell) 19-7-83
notions gained by ... (Aristotle) 18-1-9
... of succeeding centuries (Pascal) 15-2-26
on account of his ... (Bacon) 6-3-55
only by ... and history (Locke) 17-2-50
our ... to all past ages (Hume) 15-1-42
passing limits of ... (Kant) 6-5-84
... perilous (Hippocrates) 18-1-7
prescribes what ... suggests (Plato) 18-2-11
proved to us by ... (Plato) 1-8-17
prudence gotten by ... (Hobbes) 6-7-22
religious ... (Santayana) 20-3-68
sense wrought out of ... (Cervantes) 7-2-50
... soon teaches us (Bernard) 6-1-94
sources of our ... (Mill) 9-8-73
studies perfected by ... (Bacon) 8-1-30
... teaches the majority (Plato) 3-2-3
testimonies contradict ... (Locke) 15-1-36
the ... of age (Bacon) 1-3-66
the ... of time past (Hobbes) 9-13-22
the grave ... of life (Hegel) 1-3-108
the march of ... (Santayana) 6-6-55
the substance of ... (Santayana) 5-4-41
they know by long ... (Aquinas) 20-7-26
thoughts wrung by ... (Santayana) 17-1-111
... through interaction (Dewey) 8-3-100
time and education beget ... (Hobbes) 5-3-19
transcend region of ... (Kant) 17-1-74
usual course of ... (Hume) 17-1-67
we gain by our ... (Rousseau) 8-1-48
what ... and history teach (Hegel) 15-1-62
when ... is not retained (Santayana) 15-2-86
without aid of ... (Kant) 17-3-38

EXPERIENCES

all our perceptual ... (Russell) 19-6-45
based on childish ... (Freud) 5-5-45
... destroyed faith in senses (Descartes) 5-2-21
... devour our human tissue (Melville) 4-6-49
discern the sequence of ... (Tolstoy) 19-4-43
man remembers his ... (Dewey) 1-1-130
mastered by these ... (Plotinus) 5-7-7
mental ... same for all (Aristotle) 7-1-8
not derived from outward ... (Kant) 19-6-35
not seem to be ... at all (T. S. Eliot) 16-3-99
of men's several ... (Bacon) 18-1-24
patient talks of past ... (Freud) 7-2-90
resultants of new ... (Wm. James) 6-3-132
what ... will be different (Wm. James) 6-3-133
won't meet all ... (Wm. James) 6-3-134

EXPERIMENT

calculations far outrunning ... (Santayana) 17-3-62
dissociate knowledge from ... (Dewey) 6-2-50
explored by ... (Santayana) 19-6-48
... has brought under observation (Huygens) 17-2-43
need of recourse to ... (Galileo) 17-3-24, 19-3-23
proof is by ... (Pascal) 17-2-40
regarded as an ... (Schopenhauer) 1-9-42
science and theory upon ... (Bacon) 17-2-20

EYES (*Cont.*)
to choose love by another's . . . (Shakespeare) 3-1-36
would outstare the sternest . . . (Shakespeare) 19-4-23
EYE-WITNESSES
account of . . . (Thucydides) 15-1-3
were . . . of his majesty (*II Peter*) 6-5-17

FABIUS MAXIMUS
renowned Scipio and . . . (Plutarch) 2-3-27
FABLE
. . . grows and truth grows less (Voltaire) 15-1-44
having to do with . . . (Melville) 6-3-110
. . . or plot is the end (Aristotle) 16-4-9
. . . was ever credible (Johnson) 16-4-32
FABLES
. . . and fantastical tales (Cervantes) 16-2-11
cunningly devised . . . (*II Peter*) 6-5-17
momentary assent to those . . . (Gibbon) 20-6-43
poets and inventors of . . . (Plutarch) 15-1-14
rather believe all the . . . (Bacon) 19-8-48, 20-9-19
style of Milesian . . . (Cervantes) 16-3-34
those . . . are believed (Santayana) 20-3-69
FACE
a furious and tyrannical . . . (Montaigne) 8-2-13
distinguish his . . . (*Job*) 2-3-4
have not seen thy . . . (Tennyson) 6-5-94
of a girl's unwithered . . . (Sophocles) 3-1-3
soon as he shows his . . . (Dostoevsky) 3-5-42
the Lord make his . . . shine (*Numbers*) 20-5-5
then . . . to . . . (*I Corinthians*) 3-5-11
thou canst not see my . . . (*Exodus*) 20-5-4
truth has such a . . . (Dryden) 6-3-75
FACES
hid as it were our . . . from (*Isaiah*) 20-3-4
lords and owners of their . . . (Shakespeare) 9-15-63
FACILITY
attribute . . . in belief (Montaigne) 6-5-41
virtue refuses . . . (Montaigne) 9-10-56
FACT
agreement with obvious . . . (Galen) 8-3-27
configuration forms the atomic . . . (Wittgenstein) 6-1-112
confused potentiality with . . . (Whitehead) 19-5-67
conscience an inevitable . . . (Kant) 9-5-17
knowledge at once of the . . . (Aristotle) 17-3-6
matters of . . . (Hume) 17-3-35
presumption of any . . . (Grotius) 12-1-44
truths of . . . (Leibniz) 6-3-76
with fable than with . . . (Melville) 6-3-110
. . . without some leaven (Byron) 6-3-101
FACTION
by a . . . I understand (Madison) 10-8-23
liberty is to . . . what air (Madison) 13-1-31
soul is rent by . . . (Aristotle) 9-6-20
strongest . . . can unite (Hamilton/Madison) 12-2-45
the mischiefs of . . . (Madison) 10-4-42
FACTIONS
give . . . a loose reign (Montaigne) 10-2-41
if there be . . . (Bacon) 1-5-84, 10-2-50
victims to popular . . . (Boswell) 10-6-58
FACTOR
most potent social . . . (Dewey) 17-2-131
FACTORIES
where there are not . . . (Thoreau) 15-2-58
FACTORY
education from the . . . system (Marx) 8-1-67
only in the . . . system (Marx) 11-3-68
FACTS
are there general . . . (Russell) 6-1-105

as they are . . . (Voltaire) 6-3-89
based on observed . . . (Comte) 17-2-77
being original . . . (Hume) 4-1-28
false . . . are injurious (Darwin) 17-2-89
guided by experimental . . . (Poincaré) 17-3-49
keep entirely to the . . . (Toynbee) 15-1-99
myth analogous to . . . (Santayana) 6-3-149
. . . never exclude one another (Bernard) 17-2-99
no . . . are to me sacred (Emerson) 6-2-36
no help beyond bare . . . (Aristotle) 7-2-18
not with words but . . . (Seneca) 17-1-23
. . . ready to his hand (Boswell) 15-1-47
regard only the . . . (Thoreau) 6-3-112
series of . . . which are object (Lavoisier) 17-2-65
starts from particular . . . (Russell) 17-2-122
submit to control of . . . (Bernard) 17-2-96
world is totality of . . . (Wittgenstein) 19-8-95
FACULTIES
activity of mental . . . (Darwin) 9-5-25
acquired . . . of man (Mill) 9-3-35
associate common . . . (Montaigne) 1-5-60
certain mental . . . (Darwin) 16-6-70
defect in intellectual . . . (Bacon) 8-3-48
deliberating and comparing . . . (Hamilton) 1-3-93
development of our . . . (Rousseau) 13-3-20
four . . . in the soul (Plato) 6-1-5
free play of our cognitive . . . (Kant) 16-6-50
free use of his . . . (Madison) 11-1-44
general mistrust of . . . (Kant) 6-6-34
last of all our . . . (Peirce) 6-7-41
learn limit of our . . . (Huxley) 6-4-46
like results from like . . . (Montaigne) 19-1-28
natural . . . proper to soul (Montaigne) 5-3-13
occupation uses few . . . (Mill) 8-1-70
of the use of his . . . (Plato) 4-7-7
. . . of thy creatures (Sterne) 18-3-52
passions . . . states of character (Aristotle) 4-1-1
proper use of intellectual . . . (Smith) 8-1-52
right to his own . . . (Mill) 11-1-72
. . . serve the will (Epictetus) 5-1-11
the higher mental . . . (Darwin) 1-7-141
FACULTY
a . . . we call alterative (Galen) 19-1-19
not an inborn . . . (Galen) 19-2-17
. . . of manufacturing objects (Bergson) 5-1-83
perceive through one . . . (Plato) 5-1-3
practical from theoretical . . . (Kant) 16-1-32
want the creative . . . (Shelley) 5-4-31
what a . . . must be that (Thoreau) 5-4-37
FAERY MAB
how the . . . the junkets eat (Milton) 20-7-57
FAIL
allow to . . . (Montaigne) 2-2-47
will time then . . . (Aristotle) 19-7-6
FAILING
no . . . on part of will (Aquinas) 9-10-50
FAILURE
fear of . . . (Dante) 1-7-54
has not been a . . . yet (Shaw) 20-3-64
. . . is due to fortune (Polybius) 15-3-25
. . . of money as incentive (Shaw) 11-4-48
system of education a . . . (Mill) 8-1-73
FAILURES
are real . . . (Wm. James) 1-4-63
lives have been miserable . . . (Thoreau) 1-3-116
. . . to which animal cannot (Dewey) 6-4-57
FAINT-HEARTED
. . . who decline to go (Wm. James) 6-5-112
FAIR

brave deserves the . . . (Dryden) 9-11-45
. . . dealing brings profit (Homer) 9-14-6
thou art . . . my love (*Song of Solomon*) 16-6-2
thousand times more . . . (Shakespeare) 1-7-77
. . . to look upon is good (Sappho) 16-6-4
FAIRNESS
the . . . of a law (Seneca) 12-1-18
FAIRY TALES
. . . and other fiction (Freud) 16-3-97
FAITH
abideth . . . hope and charity (*I Corinthians*) 3-5-11
accompanied by grace of . . . (Bunyan) 6-1-64
according to your . . . (*Matthew*) 20-11-4
along with . . . in God (Pascal) 20-2-30
a man's real . . . (Thoreau) 20-1-61
. . . and inward sincerity (Locke) 20-14-51
and lives by . . . (Augustine) 12-1-23
animated only by . . . (Johnson) 20-1-43, 20-4-40
apprehended by simple . . . (Spinoza) 20-10-35
are not articles of . . . (Aquinas) 20-5-43
articles of the Catholic . . . (Augustine) 20-9-5
both are led to . . . (Byron) 16-4-39
charity impossible without . . . (Aquinas) 3-5-18
charity more excellent than . . . (Aquinas) 3-5-19
choose offence or . . . (Kierkegaard) 20-11-41
civil profession of . . . (Rousseau) 20-9-34
constitutes the poetic . . . (Coleridge) 16-3-76
defence of religious . . . (Wm. James) 20-1-73
disputing about the . . . (Aquinas) 20-9-10
disturb our cheerful . . . (Wordsworth) 19-1-79
does not spring from . . . (Dostoevsky) 20-11-43
erred from the . . . (*I Timothy*) 11-4-5
first by religion and . . . (Bacon) 20-13-76
founded this . . . (Augustine) 20-14-23
gives understanding to . . . (Anselm) 20-5-36
good . . . with his fortune (Chaucer) 15-3-66
greatly kept . . . (Euripides) 9-9-3
has to be a form of . . . (Santayana) 6-1-116
hath . . . and have not works (*James*) 20-8-36
he that dieth without . . . (Dante) 9-7-35
he who adopts the . . . (Augustine) 20-8-45
homage to public . . . (Rousseau) 9-10-100
hope comes from . . . (Aquinas) 20-11-13
I have kept the . . . (*II Timothy*) 6-5-14
. . . in a higher power (Hegel) 5-1-57
in a prince to keep . . . (Machiavelli) 10-2-33
influence the . . . (Gibbon) 1-9-36
in his attainment of . . . (Huxley) 15-2-62
initiated into his . . . (Calvin) 20-4-26
in relation to act of . . . (Aquinas) 20-9-8
. . . in scientific method (Dewey) 17-2-132
in someone else's . . . (Wm. James) 6-5-110
. . . in the Son of God (Luther) 20-8-56
. . . in you and God (Chaucer) 3-3-32
. . . is a fine invention (Dickinson) 17-2-91
. . . is also vain (Augustine) 6-7-15
. . . is loyalty (Carlyle) 1-6-61
. . . is the highest passion (Kierkegaard) 6-5-90
just as . . . teaches us (Descartes) 9-8-43
justness of view is not . . . (Newman) 9-1-31
keep up his . . . (Wm. James) 1-6-80
live without . . . (Tolstoy) 6-5-105
mediation of a living . . . (Montaigne) 20-14-35
. . . more than an opinion (Leibniz) 6-5-69
necessary article of . . . (Locke) 20-9-29
necessary to accept by . . . (Aquinas) 17-1-42
no longer has . . . left (Plato) 6-7-3
no one without . . . (Pascal) 9-8-49
not by . . . nor by charity (Spinoza) 20-3-35

not shake him in his . . . (Voltaire) 20-5-92
obliged . . . unforfeited (Shakespeare) 4-4-18
of little . . . (*Matthew*) 11-2-38
. . . of the church (Kant) 11-6-36
. . . of the individual (Santayana) 20-2-52
O ye of little . . . (*Luke*) 4-9-3
perplexed in . . . (Tennyson) 6-6-42
progress of his . . . (Gibbon) 20-1-47
proof of obedience and . . . (Milton) 6-4-25
rather by . . . than by vision (Augustine) 20-15-35
readiest criterion of their . . . (Spinoza) 20-3-34
received with implicit . . . (Gibbon) 20-11-37
rectitude of the . . . (Aquinas) 20-9-11
religion is not . . . (Aquinas) 20-1-14
respects the infant's . . . (Blake) 6-6-35
security by mutual . . . (Boswell) 6-3-96
spiritually received by . . . (Luther) 20-3-26
stretch the lame hands of . . . (Tennyson) 19-1-100
support for our . . . (Calvin) 20-4-27
teach him what is . . . (Browning) 6-6-46
teach the people . . . (Milton) 10-4-16
. . . tells us what senses do not (Pascal) 6-5-56
. . . that looks through death (Wordsworth) 19-1-82
then . . . shall cease (Bacon) 6-1-50
the portal of . . . (Dante) 4-5-12
the saints lived in . . . (Pascal) 20-3-32
the shield of . . . (Hobbes) 10-3-24
. . . thou hast given me (Augustine) 20-8-42
thou of little . . . (*Matthew*) 6-6-5
through . . . free from law (Luther) 9-4-29
to corrupt the . . . (Aquinas) 20-9-12
to have the . . . (Aquinas) 20-9-9
true fear from . . . (Pascal) 4-2-26
vice to pious . . . (Augustine) 1-5-45
virtue united to . . . (Milton) 8-1-34
was converted into . . . (Gibbon) 20-4-43
we hold by . . . alone (Aquinas) 19-8-38
when religious . . . expresses (Wm. James) 19-4-49
who lives by his . . . (Augustine) 2-1-20
word of promise through . . . (Luther) 20-4-22
would like to attain . . . (Pascal) 19-4-26
yet living by . . . (Augustine) 20-7-15
FAITHFUL
been . . . in very little (*Luke*) 20-8-31
FAITHFULNESS
make known thy . . . (*Psalms*) 20-2-15
. . . the girdle of his reins (*Isaiah*) 20-3-2
FALL
blessedness before the . . . (Tolstoy) 11-3-77
companions of his . . . (Milton) 20-7-58
knowledge is the . . . (Hegel) 20-15-96
man by the . . . lost (Bacon) 20-13-76
mark but my . . . (Shakespeare) 1-5-75
the . . . of man (Voltaire) 19-8-72
this was the . . . (Mann) 19-2-64
to hear about their sudden . . . (Chaucer) 16-4-17
true in our . . . (Milton) 1-5-95
FALLACIES
lead mankind into . . . (Bacon) 6-4-19
must his . . . be (Russell) 17-1-101
FALLACY
committing some . . . (Aristotle) 6-7-10
. . . in our poetic judgments (Arnold) 16-7-48
the arts of . . . are preferred (Locke) 7-2-71
FALSE
all statements not . . . (Aristotle) 6-6-3
all was . . . and hollow (Milton) 9-14-40
as to be found . . . and perfidious (Bacon) 9-14-36
dissent from the . . . (Epictetus) 9-6-26

FALSE (*Cont.*)
   far from . . . matter (*Exodus*) 9-13-2
   not then be . . . to any (Shakespeare) 1-4-21
   what was new was . . . (Boswell) 19-5-59
FALSEHOOD
   delighted in . . . (Aristotle) 9-14-10
   distinguished from . . . by this (Peirce) 6-3-123
   fear of believing . . . (Augustine) 6-5-20
   goodly outside . . . hath (Shakespeare) 9-6-58
   . . . has a perennial spring (Burke) 6-4-36
   . . . has natural root (Pascal) 3-4-42
   if . . . had only one . . . (Montaigne) 6-3-44
   indeed they spoke . . . (Augustine) 20-9-4
   . . . is like alloy in a coin (Bacon) 9-14-35
   make . . . as much (Plato) 15-1-5
   . . . of dogmas sleeps (Santayana) 6-5-115
   . . . of the preaching (Emerson) 20-1-56
   or refutation of . . . (Bacon) 20-9-18
   revolts from evident . . . (Johnson) 16-4-32
   rhetoric available for . . . (Augustine) 7-2-41
   . . . seemed to teach (Augustine) 6-5-19
   the reproach of . . . (Boswell) 1-4-36
   with the prevalence of . . . (Boswell) 9-14-51
   your bait of . . . (Shakespeare) 6-3-52
FALSEHOODS
   . . . interest dictates (Johnson) 14-1-68
FALSIFICATION
   radical . . . of all nature (Nietzsche) 20-2-46
FALSITY
   from any taint of . . . (Descartes) 17-3-25
FAME
   . . . a name for social self (Wm. James) 9-2-34
   beyond the . . . (Montaigne) 1-8-63
   confounds thy . . . (Shakespeare) 2-3-53
   . . . devoid of judgment (Aurelius) 1-2-21
   establishment of my . . . (Gibbon) 15-1-55
   . . . had real substance (Cicero) 1-5-23
   . . . is like a river (Bacon) 1-5-85
   . . . is something which must be won (Schopenhauer)
     1-5-120
   longest posthumous . . . (Aurelius) 1-8-45
   monument of a conqueror's . . . (Gibbon) 11-6-33
   . . . of my achievements (Cervantes) 2-1-26
   real pathway to . . . (Cicero) 3-2-5
   revolutions of his . . . (Gibbon) 1-6-51
   . . . shall be achieved (Milton) 14-1-56
   the . . . of beauty transcending (Goethe) 16-6-53
   to know is nought but . . . (Shakespeare) 8-1-28
   to win my prize of . . . (Sophocles) 4-11-5
FAMED
   any but . . . books (Emerson) 16-2-47
FAMILIARITY
   . . . breeds disgust (Montaigne) 3-3-38
   . . . should not precede (Hegel) 2-3-99
   upon . . . will grow contempt (Shakespeare) 2-3-59
FAMILIES
   all the . . . of the earth (*Genesis*) 20-2-1
   cities and kingdoms are but greater . . . (Hobbes) 1-2-51
   happy . . . are all alike (Tolstoy) 2-1-49
FAMILY
   broken bond of the . . . (Hegel) 11-2-117
   first community is the . . . (Aristotle) 11-5-4
   . . . is an appendage of self (Mill) 8-1-70
   . . . is the first precondition (Hegel) 10-8-26
   languages of one . . . (Russell) 7-2-89
   loss from his . . . (Euripides) 1-7-20
   mother of a . . . (Rabelais) 1-7-67
   state prior to the . . . (Aristotle) 10-1-6
   strength of the . . . (Freud) 2-1-53

FAMINE
   has the title of . . . (Dante) 3-2-14
   Irish . . . of 1846 (Marx) 11-2-141
FANATIC
   . . . about health (Freud) 18-3-64
   is governed by the . . . (Voltaire) 20-12-27
   . . . who endures (Gibbon) 9-11-53
FANATICISM
   courage raised by . . . (Gibbon) 9-11-52
   so deadly as . . . (Voltaire) 20-9-33
FANATICS
   here . . . to cry (Voltaire) 13-2-27
FANCIES
   all people have their . . . (Plato) 3-4-10
   . . . are more giddy (Shakespeare) 1-7-82
   each has his . . . (Pascal) 4-1-18
   from . . . to the fact (Browning) 15-2-69
   licentiated to recreate . . . (Rabelais) 5-5-18
   mind trained against capricious . . . (Hegel) 8-1-53
   . . . of the imagination (Aquinas) 8-2-11
   play with your . . . (Shakespeare) 5-4-12
   reasonable beings have . . . (Boswell) 7-2-78
   represent unto their . . . (Rabelais) 1-7-68
   slaves of their . . . (Luther) 18-2-26
   taken their . . . for realities (Locke) 5-6-30
   what . . . whirl you (Aeschylus) 5-6-1
   with thick-coming . . . (Shakespeare) 5-6-21
FANCY
   adventitious charm of . . . (Boswell) 5-4-27
   . . . a mode of memory (Coleridge) 5-4-30
   animated by . . . (Gibbon) 16-1-30
   a young man's . . . (Tennyson) 3-1-76
   . . . cannot cheat so well (Keats) 5-4-33
   errors . . . has produced (Montaigne) 6-6-10
   ever let the . . . roam (Keats) 5-4-32
   . . . has no place (Hobbes) 15-1-35
   images presented to our . . . (Hume) 6-3-85
   . . . is a wilful act (Emerson) 5-4-35
   judgment and . . . required (Hobbes) 16-3-40
   merely our . . . (Montaigne) 9-6-56
   no . . . so frivolous (Montaigne) 6-5-47
   no mad or idle . . . (Montaigne) 5-4-6
   production of a distempered . . . (Gibbon) 20-1-48
   tell me where is . . . bred (Shakespeare) 5-4-10
   upon the oddest . . . (Cervantes) 5-6-22
   wit and . . . find entertainment (Locke) 7-2-71
FANTASY
   . . . dost snatch us out of ourselves (Dante) 5-4-4
   fie on sinful . . . (Shakespeare) 3-3-47
   have a quaint . . . (Chaucer) 1-7-57
   nothing but vain . . . (Shakespeare) 5-5-21
FARCE
   in light comedy and . . . (Bergson) 16-4-51
FAREWELL
   . . . to all my greatness (Shakespeare) 1-6-35
FARMER
   the small . . . (Mill) 11-5-41
FARMERS
   once the embattled . . . stood (Emerson) 10-9-36
FARMER'S
   who ply the . . . trade (Aristophanes) 14-3-5
FASHION
   art doth give the . . . (Jonson) 16-3-36
   custom regulates . . . (Smith) 11-3-37
   of a . . . not ours absurd (Descartes) 15-1-34
   . . . of these times (Shakespeare) 9-9-20
   rather . . . my mind than furnish it (Montaigne) 5-1-18
   the law of . . . (Locke) 12-1-54
FASHIONS

Italy gave ... to provincials (Gibbon) 7-1-52
... of the year include (Shaw) 18-2-51
peculiar and out-of-the-way ... (Montaigne) 9-15-45
FASHION'S
the ... a fool (Congreve) 2-1-31
FAST
better not to ... (Pascal) 20-8-66
however ... a motion (Pascal) 19-5-42
FASTING
... had more power than grief (Dante) 3-2-14
FAT
to be ... is to be hated (Shakespeare) 9-6-59
FATALISM
is a hideous ... (Shaw) 19-8-92
... which conceives of effort (Wm. James) 15-3-113
FATE
blind ... could never (Newton) 19-8-62
but ... forbids (Virgil) 20-15-16
common ... of reason (Kant) 6-1-82
customary ... of new truths (Huxley) 6-3-114
death and silence are the ... (Homer) 2-2-10
destiny which ... has given (Aeschylus) 20-10-6
eager ... which (Emerson) 2-2-85
easier for ... to remove (Freud) 18-2-52
exacted by thy ... (Jonson) 2-2-58
experiences of their sad ... (Freud) 20-2-47
hard and terrible ... (Anselm) 1-2-26
hides the book of ... (Pope) 6-4-28
is ... or necessity (Tacitus) 19-4-13
... is the same (Homer) 1-5-2
keep harping on ... (Cicero) 15-3-28
made weak by time and ... (Tennyson) 1-3-115
meet that wretched ... (Euripides) 14-1-11
O fickle ... (Chaucer) 4-6-25
perplexed question of ... (Boswell) 5-7-32
prolong the bounds of ... (Lucretius) 19-7-8
rather than ... or hazard (Schiller) 16-4-37
read the book of ... (Shakespeare) 15-1-30
should know their ... (Gray) 6-4-30
slave doomed to worship ... (Russell) 9-4-49
such strokes of ... (Euripides) 15-3-20
this turn of ... (Plutarch) 1-9-13
trembling for the birth of ... (Pope) 20-7-72
yielded to my ... (Gibbon) 2-2-78
FATES
masters of their ... (Shakespeare) 5-7-20
... of criminals differ (Juvenal) 12-4-18
preceding still the ... (Shakespeare) 20-12-19
profits it to butt against the ... (Dante) 20-7-31
she sings the ... (Virgil) 20-10-14
spinning our own ... (Wm. James) 8-2-31
the ... when they have (Virgil) 15-3-30
... will find their way (Virgil) 15-3-32
FATHER
a greatly exalted ... (Freud) 20-1-80
be proved ... and (Sophocles) 2-1-7
born of a great ... (Homer) 1-8-7
cometh unto the ... but by me (John) 20-3-16
daughters' hearts against their ... (Shakespeare) 5-6-18
delivered unto me of my ... (Matthew) 6-5-6
friend to my dear ... (Sophocles) 2-1-8
glorify your ... in heaven (Matthew) 20-3-6
go and bury my ... (Luke) 20-8-29
hath the rain a ... (Job) 1-1-2
her ... loved me (Shakespeare) 3-1-42
he shall forgive ... and mother (Milton) 2-3-70
honor thy ... (Exodus) 9-3-1
in respect of his ... (Freud) 16-4-46
love of the ... is not in him (I John) 3-3-19

loveth ... or mother more (Matthew) 20-8-27
... may be glorified in the Son (John) 20-8-32
my ... giveth you the true (John) 20-14-14
my ... hath sent me (John) 20-4-10
my ... much offended (Shakespeare) 2-2-50
... or master ordereth (Hobbes) 2-1-28
pray to thy ... in secret (Matthew) 20-8-26
... ranks above the (Aquinas) 2-1-23
reverence for my ... (Dante) 6-2-13
shall a man leave his ... (Genesis) 2-3-1
slain the ... (Freud) 1-6-84
strike his ... dead (Shakespeare) 10-2-44
supreme power of the ... (Dante) 20-7-34
the ... against the son (Luke) 2-1-17
the same ... who gave (Freud) 20-5-122
thee ... first they sung (Milton) 20-5-76
to go and bury my ... (Matthew) 20-3-8
war the ... of all good (Rabelais) 14-1-43
... who art in heaven (Dante) 20-8-52
wise ... that knows own child (Shakespeare) 2-2-48
your ... lost a ... (Shakespeare) 4-6-34
FATHERLAND
for ... to die (Horace) 3-6-8
FATHERLESS
visit the ... and widows (James) 20-1-5; (Aquinas) 20-1-12
FATHERS
... have eaten sour grapes (Ezekiel) 20-13-10
... in decline of life (Aristotle) 2-3-20
inheritance of ... (Proverbs) 2-3-6
... in their love of money (Plutarch) 8-1-16
... of their country (Rousseau) 3-6-17
seldom ... of many children (Plutarch) 7-2-32
... shall not be put to death (Deut.) 12-4-2
visiting the iniquity of the ... (Numbers) 20-13-3
FATHER'S
in my ... house are many (John) 20-15-27
FATHER-TYPE
according to a ... (Freud) 2-1-54
FATHOM
full ... five thy father (Shakespeare) 19-5-28
FAULT
a ... against the dead (Shakespeare) 4-6-34
condemn the ... (Shakespeare) 12-4-31
every ... of his (Dante) 1-7-55
find in him no ... (John) 6-3-21
gravity of the ... (Aquinas) 12-4-25
... is not in our stars (Shakespeare) 5-7-20
it were a grievous ... (Shakespeare) 1-6-29
judged it to be not my ... (Augustine) 5-7-8
my ... is past (Shakespeare) 20-8-60
no influence on their ... (Milton) 5-7-26
none without a ... (Fielding) 3-4-45
our own ... we have missed (Aristotle) 4-8-7
sack and sugar be a ... (Shakespeare) 9-6-59
she had a ... (Jonson) 1-8-99
suffers except by his ... (Montaigne) 17-1-44
the ... dear Brutus (Shakespeare) 15-3-81
where is his ... (Dante) 9-7-35
... will be in the music (Shakespeare) 2-3-54
FAULT-FINDING
refrain from ... (Aurelius) 7-2-37
FAULTS
a collector of writers' ... (Swift) 16-7-21
avoided ... of fools (Plutarch) 9-15-31
chastising harmless ... (Montaigne) 9-14-20
cleanse me from secret ... (Psalms) 20-5-9
convinces him of his ... (Pascal) 1-4-28
do by punishing ... (Machiavelli) 14-2-33
experience of past ... (Gibbon) 6-2-33

FOOL (*Cont.*)

a ... and lost for certain (Tolstoy) 9-11-62
a ... if he be obeyed (Rousseau) 10-2-74
a ... in power of others (Milton) 4-5-23
an author is a ... who (Montesquieu) 16-2-28
a simple ... (Euripides) 1-7-19
at best a learned ... (Wm. James) 20-1-74
but the heart of a ... (Milton) 20-9-25
but the spirit of a ... (Euripides) 15-3-19
dost thou call me a ... (Shakespeare) 9-15-58
... doth think he is wise (Shakespeare) 9-15-56
even the ... is convinced (Anselm) 20-5-36
... hath said in his heart (*Psalms*) 20-5-11, 20-9-1; (Bacon) 20-9-19
have a ... make me merry (Shakespeare) 6-2-19
here I stand poor ... (Goethe) 6-1-85
isn't she a ... (Tolstoy) 2-2-91
... kisses mouth of furnace (Chaucer) 3-3-34
let him become a ... (*I Corinthians*) 9-15-29
liberty to play the ... (Locke) 13-1-15
love's not time's ... (Shakespeare) 3-1-47
marry a ... (Shakespeare) 1-7-85
no ... nor yet unfortunate (Sophocles) 6-4-2
... of the farce (Montaigne) 1-4-19
perhaps I am a ... (Chaucer) 6-2-14
play the ... (Congreve) 1-7-106
please the ... and death (Shakespeare) 5-1-20
song's sake a ... (Yeats) 1-3-135
that of a prosperous ... (Aristotle) 11-2-26
the ... shall not enter (Blake) 20-15-91
the prayer of a ... (Plato) 20-8-21
... to use the prophet's trade (Euripides) 20-10-9
unless you become a ... (Tertullian) 20-3-22
wasp-stung and impatient ... (Shakespeare) 9-12-32
what a ... honesty is (Shakespeare) 9-14-33
who will not laugh is a ... (Santayana) 1-3-140
... would persist in his folly (Blake) 9-15-83

FOOLISH

Ajax proved himself ... (Sophocles) 4-11-5
anyone who has been ... (Montaigne) 9-15-49
no virtuous man is ... (Aristotle) 4-11-10
very ... fond old man (Shakespeare) 5-6-19
we were sometimes ... (*Titus*) 9-4-7

FOOLISH MAN

... built his house upon (*Matthew*) 8-3-14

FOOLISHNESS

all ... suffers the burden (Seneca) 9-15-28
divination to the ... of man (Plato) 20-10-11
free by the ... of God (Augustine) 9-15-34
O ... of men (Milton) 20-13-81
... of that institution (Thoreau) 11-6-47
... of the body (Plato) 1-8-17
very many ... whereby (Gilbert) 6-4-17
what utter ... (Seneca) 1-5-25

FOOLS

being judged by ... (Voltaire) 13-2-26
... by heavenly compulsion (Shakespeare) 15-3-85
cannot make ... wise (Pascal) 5-4-18
crabbed as dull ... suppose (Milton) 17-1-58
... despise wisdom (*Proverbs*) 6-1-1
ended by being great ... (Plato) 8-3-8
hear the song of ... (*Eccles.*) 4-6-3
laws often made by ... (Montaigne) 12-1-41
life of ... at length (Lucretius) 12-4-13
makes ... of the wise (Luther) 20-3-24
multitude of ... is concerned (Aquinas) 11-4-8
never failing vice of ... (Pope) 4-11-30
none but ... would (Shakespeare) 1-8-81
... only are fortunate (Th. Browne) 9-15-69

round him a band of ... (Rousseau) 20-10-40
these ... the temperate (Plato) 9-12-2
they became ... (*Romans*) 20-13-19
undone by ... (Fielding) 1-7-111
vain people are ... (Aristotle) 4-11-11
we are ... to depart (Pascal) 1-8-110
we are great ... (Montaigne) 1-2-35
what ... these mortals be (Shakespeare) 1-2-39
who writes for ... (Schopenhauer) 16-2-42
yesterdays have lighted ... (Shakespeare) 1-2-44
ye suffer ... gladly (*II Corinthians*) 9-15-30
yet ... enough to guard (Goethe) 6-1-86

FOPPERY

excellent ... of the world (Shakespeare) 15-3-85

FOPS

from such ... is barred (Pope) 9-15-79
whole tribe of ... (Shakespeare) 19-1-37

FORBID

... a thing and that covet we (Chaucer) 1-7-57

FORCE

... against his native land (Plato) 10-9-2
... and fraud in war (Hobbes) 14-1-52
any outside ... constrains (Descartes) 5-7-21
arm him with the ... (Milton) 14-1-55
blunt ... about truth (Whitehead) 6-3-140
by open ... (Hobbes) 1-2-51
contesting by ... (Machiavelli) 12-1-35
conveying her by ... (Cervantes) 2-1-26
... creates no right (Rousseau) 9-2-25
declared design of ... (Locke) 14-1-59
differs from every other ... (Tolstoy) 5-7-45
easier to push on ... (Montesquieu) 1-6-45
education the strongest ... (Russell) 8-1-83
effected by ... and fraud (Aristotle) 10-9-4
external ... is employed (Freud) 20-4-53
gains victory by ... (Machiavelli) 14-1-41
... holds the state together (Hegel) 10-1-41
innate ... of matter (Newton) 19-5-45
innumerable ... of spirits (Milton) 14-2-42
... in some degree requisite (Smith) 8-3-74
... is a physical power (Rousseau) 10-6-51
I see a ... (Tolstoy) 19-4-43
laws derive ... from (Grotius) 12-1-44
life is its ... (Emerson) 12-1-80
... made the first slaves (Rousseau) 10-7-23
maintained by ... alone (Rousseau) 10-9-23
make up war-like ... (Dewey) 14-1-110
mind and heart by ... (Pascal) 20-1-23
more terrible than a military ... (Plutarch) 14-2-26
natural ... of a higher kind (Ovid) 19-8-16
no education by ... (Montaigne) 8-3-42
obtain the binding ... (Aquinas) 12-1-25
... of character is cumulative (Emerson) 8-2-25
... of our early habits (Boswell) 8-2-21
only by bond of ... (Tocqueville) 12-3-26
powerful revolutionary ... (Russell) 17-2-120
relations which ... creates (Mill) 13-3-40
... should be right (Shakespeare) 10-2-44
supported by ... or not (Aristotle) 10-3-6
the ... causing the change (Berkeley) 19-5-53
the ... of habit shown (Aristotle) 8-2-3
the ... of society (Mill) 10-2-101
to resort to ... (Hamilton) 14-1-86
truth has no need of ... (Locke) 6-3-77
uses ... without right (Locke) 14-1-60
war is an act of ... (Clausewitz) 14-1-90
when ... meets ... (Pascal) 6-3-64
... worst instrument of government (Smith) 1-2-68
yield to ... (Aristotle) 9-6-21

FORCED
not being . . . to do (Montesquieu) 13-1-18
was . . . to learn (Augustine) 8-3-28
will be . . . to be free (Rousseau) 13-1-21
FORCES
compelled by . . . (Newton) 19-5-47
effects of all natural . . . (Fourier) 17-2-74
four kinds of military . . . (Aristotle) 14-2-15
. . . great enough to overcome (Rousseau) 10-1-32
impulsive and inhibitive . . . (Wm. James) 18-3-60
investigate quantity of . . . (Newton) 17-3-32
led his . . . into (Herodotus) 14-1-6
. . . of those who attacked (Rousseau) 11-2-86
steered by material . . . (Galen) 19-2-17
these . . . being unknown (Newton) 17-2-44
unknown . . . (Freud) 4-1-34
FOREFATHERS
rude . . . of the hamlet (Gray) 1-8-115
FOREGO
able to . . . them (Epictetus) 4-4-11
FOREIGNERS
. . . living their lives (Locke) 10-5-17
more to fear from . . . (Machiavelli) 10-2-34
FOREKNOW
can clearly . . . nothing (Sophocles) 19-4-3
whom he did . . . (*Romans*) 15-3-37
FOREKNOWLEDGE
by submission than . . . (Th. Browne) 15-3-90
deceived in his . . . (Luther) 5-7-18
divine . . . of our actions (Mill) 5-7-43
free will . . . absolute (Milton) 15-3-91
. . . had no influence (Milton) 5-7-26
he has in his . . . (Montaigne) 15-3-76
make . . . the cause of it (Calvin) 15-3-72
reprobation implies . . . (Aquinas) 15-3-58
there is no . . . of things (Cicero) 15-3-27
whose . . . is infallible (Augustine) 5-7-9
FORELOCK
does him by the . . . take (Spenser) 19-7-34
FORENSIC
. . . speaking attacks or defends (Aristotle) 7-2-14
FOREORDINATION
. . . hath so said (Chaucer) 15-3-68
FORESIGHT
imitate the divine . . . (Bacon) 17-2-20
. . . of God makes good use of evils (Augustine) 9-4-20
. . . of things to come (Hobbes) 20-10-29
proving . . . may be vain (Burns) 20-10-41
FORESTS
in the . . . of the night (Blake) 19-8-76
FORETHOUGHT
imagine a . . . without . . . (Aurelius) 1-1-33
FOREVER
has existed . . . (Plotinus) 19-8-23
man has . . . (Browning) 19-7-78
FORGERY
literary . . . becomes necessary (Nietzsche) 6-5-108
FORGETFUL
blessed are the . . . (Nietzsche) 5-3-25
FORGETFULNESS
body breeds . . . (Boethius) 6-3-30
merit begat . . . of God (Luther) 19-3-19
FORGETTING
. . . as important as recollecting (Wm. James) 5-3-29
FORGIVE
faithful and just to . . . (*I John*) 20-13-25
readiest of all to . . . (Dostoevsky) 4-10-11
to . . . divine (Pope) 16-7-25
will make her . . . (Dostoevsky) 1-7-154

FORGIVEN
nor should be . . . (Shaw) 4-3-26
FORGIVENESS
ask of thee . . . (Shakespeare) 20-14-36
give and demand . . . (Fielding) 3-4-45
. . . of past injuries (Gibbon) 20-3-44
there is . . . with thee (*Psalms*) 20-8-8
FORM
. . . and matter united (Dante) 19-8-40
an objective temporal . . . (Sartre) 19-7-94
cause of a . . . as such (Aquinas) 19-3-17
contained in any sensuous . . . (Kant) 16-6-48
dangerous . . . of scepticism (Kierkegaard) 6-6-39
definition of . . . (Kant) 5-2-32
descended from some lower . . . (Darwin) 1-1-111
every . . . distinct from matter (Dante) 5-7-15
. . . is possibility of structure (Wittgenstein) 6-1-112
. . . is the definition (Aristotle) 19-3-6
. . . of the family (Marx) 2-1-44
return to a new . . . (Plotinus) 1-8-49
the definable . . . (Aristotle) 19-3-3
the discovery of . . . (Bacon) 19-3-22
the . . . becomes measureless (Hegel) 16-7-42
the . . . of the internal sense (Kant) 19-7-67
the . . . or archetype (Aristotle) 19-3-4
the possibilities of . . . (Santayana) 17-3-62
they are based upon the . . . (Aquinas) 16-6-23
yield to the interest of . . . (Montaigne) 6-3-49
FORMATIVE
possesses an inherent . . . power (Kant) 19-2-39
FORMS
all things of like . . . (Aurelius) 15-2-15
chief . . . of beauty are (Aristotle) 16-6-9
countless . . . of life (Ovid) 19-2-16
devoid of all . . . (Whitehead) 19-6-43
distinct female . . . (Darwin) 1-7-138
diverse . . . of beauty (Augustine) 16-6-22
in company with celestial . . . (Plato) 16-6-6
investigate and discover . . . (Bacon) 16-1-24
. . . of things unknown (Shakespeare) 16-3-31
. . . of virtue (Aristotle) 9-10-17
the . . . are often confused (Joyce) 16-3-101
to beauty we give so many . . . (Montaigne) 16-6-27
to visit beautiful . . . (Plato) 16-6-7
two . . . of reasoning (Bernard) 6-7-40
FORMULAE
. . . derived from space-time (Whitehead) 19-6-43
employ examples as . . . (Kant) 8-3-77
FORNICATION
as I could with . . . (Augustine) 9-12-16
except it be for . . . (*Matthew*) 2-3-22
on account of . . . (Aquinas) 2-3-37
. . . requires severe punishment (Boswell) 3-3-62
the cause of . . . (*Matthew*) 2-3-21
to avoid . . . (*I Corinthians*) 2-3-23
FORSAKEN
. . . even by God (Whitehead) 20-1-77
hast thou . . . me (*Psalms*) 4-5-3; (*Matthew*) 4-5-8
FORT AUGUSTUS
an officer at . . . (Boswell) 9-7-53
FORTITUDE
active love is . . . (Dostoevsky) 3-1-79
. . . a disposition by which (Aquinas) 9-10-47
. . . in enduring cold (Plato) 14-2-10
. . . is about fear and daring (Aquinas) 9-12-18
. . . is the guard (Locke) 9-11-46
moral strength as . . . (Kant) 9-10-109
. . . of so courageous (Tacitus) 1-9-17
to this end there is . . . (Aquinas) 9-10-46

GEOMETRY
according to ... of Euclid (Dostoevsky) 19-8-87
... and cognate sciences (Plato) 6-1-5
and prior to ... (Aristotle) 17-3-6
any term be defined in ... (Hume) 17-3-36
arithmetic and ... are alone free (Descartes) 17-3-25
as any demonstration of ... (Descartes) 20-5-59
... as part of instruction (Plato) 8-1-2
attainment of ... (Proclus) 17-3-13
axioms of ... (Poincaré) 17-3-49
demonstrated by ... (Archimedes) 17-3-14
experience could not create ... (Poincaré) 17-3-40
... first came to be known (Herodotus) 17-3-1
follow the order of ... (Pascal) 17-3-27
from the principles of ... (Copernicus) 17-2-9
... handling quantity continued (Bacon) 17-3-22
if ... exists (Nicomachus) 17-3-16
is ... able to remedy (Hume) 17-2-55
is the most powerful of ... (Galileo) 17-3-23
little attention to ... (Descartes) 17-3-26
mechanics distinguished from ... (Newton) 17-3-31
mechanics separated from ... (Plutarch) 17-3-15
method used only in ... (Hobbes) 17-3-27
... should be pursued (Xenophon) 17-3-4
... supposes that we know (Pascal) 19-5-41
the maxims in ... (Hamilton) 17-3-41
universally admitted in ... (Lavoisier) 6-1-84
who is ignorant of ... (Plato) 17-3-3
whole science of ... (Wm. James) 17-3-46
GERMANS
... treated their women (Gibbon) 1-7-121
GERMINATION
... of a blade of wheat (Malthus) 19-2-40
GERYON
great ... he'll not (Horace) 1-8-34
might of three-fold ... (Lucretius) 20-12-4
GESTURES
aided by signs and ... (Darwin) 7-1-58
man alone has ... (Dante) 7-1-20
objects expressed by ... (Rousseau) 7-1-48
GET
a time to ... (*Eccles.*) 19-7-2
GHIBELLINES
like Guelphs and ... (Schopenhauer) 1-7-133
GHOST
give up the ... (*Job*) 4-5-1
GHOSTS
opinions of ... (Hobbes) 20-1-21
GIANT DESPAIR
had slain ... (Bunyan) 20-14-48
GIANTS
a people of ... (Gibbon) 1-5-112
easy for mental ... (Shaw) 1-6-82
... in former ages (Swift) 15-2-29
such were these ... (Milton) 14-1-56
GIBBERISH
same ... serves so well (Locke) 17-1-60
GIBBET
has for its emblem a ... (Shaw) 20-3-66
GIBEON
in ... the Lord appeared (*I Kings*) 9-15-1
sun in ... stand (Milton) 20-2-33
GIBES
where be your ... now (Shakespeare) 1-8-78
GIFT
as my ... take (Shakespeare) 2-3-65
beauty is the lover's ... (Congreve) 16-6-41
by your ... I desired (Augustine) 9-6-39
faith a ... of God (Hobbes) 6-5-53

friend's only ... is self (Santayana) 3-4-64
from God a proper ... (Chaucer) 2-3-40
... God freely giveth (Hobbes) 6-5-51
grasp the moment's ... (Goethe) 18-2-42
greatest ... of God (Dante) 5-7-16
his proper ... of God (*I Corinthians*) 2-3-23
not so much a natural ... (Peirce) 6-7-41
the sorrowful ... (Rousseau) 1-8-116
we lack at birth the ... of (Rousseau) 8-1-47
with a special ... for it (Aristotle) 16-3-9
GIFTS
equality of natural ... (Dewey) 13-3-53
her ... were such (Milton) 1-7-101
knows the ... of heaven (Horace) 9-8-18
their peculiar ... into (Aristotle) 2-1-11
GILEAD
Ishmaelite from ... (*Genesis*) 4-8-1
that appear from Mount ... (*Song of Solomon*) 16-6-2
GIOCONDA
story of ... is older (Voltaire) 1-7-115
GIRDLE
bright ... furled (Arnold) 6-5-103
put a ... round the earth (Shakespeare) 20-7-43
GIRL
a marriageable ... (Goethe) 16-6-56
cannot hammer a ... into (Ruskin) 1-7-150
in an unlesson'd ... (Shakespeare) 1-7-77
soft bloom of a lovely ... (Euripides) 9-8-5
... who gives from obligation (Ovid) 3-3-17
GIRLS
... have great desire to know (Goethe) 1-7-125
like the Andalusian ... (Joyce) 1-7-170
... of this age (Aristotle) 1-7-28
GIROFFLÉE
excepting even ... (Voltaire) 1-2-64
GIVE
... and it shall be (*Luke*) 12-2-20
more blessed to ... than (*Acts*) 3-5-10
GIVER
... of all good things (Rabelais) 11-4-10
GIVING
mutual ... and receiving (Aquinas) 12-2-23
GIZZARD
politics is the ... of society (Thoreau) 10-2-98
GLAD
to be ... in madness (Augustine) 5-6-8
GLADNESS
feel the ... of the May (Wordsworth) 19-1-82
serve the Lord with ... (*Psalms*) 20-8-7
teach me half the ... (Shelley) 19-1-87
youth the time of ... (Johnson) 1-3-87
GLAMIS
... hath murdered (Shakespeare) 1-8-87
GLASS
mind like an enchanted ... (Bacon) 5-1-21
see through a ... darkly (*I Corinthians*) 3-5-11
thou art thy mother's ... (Shakespeare) 1-3-59
through a ... darkly (Augustine) 6-5-23
your ... is all a cheat (Congreve) 16-6-41
GLAUCON
but said ... interposing (Plato) 11-2-15
here my dear ... (Plato) 5-7-1
GLIB
learned to be ... about time (Russell) 19-7-85
GLISTERS
physicians smell of ... (Rabelais) 18-1-15
GLOBE
great ... itself shall dissolve (Shakespeare) 1-2-46
in the form of a ... (Copernicus) 19-5-24

world in form of a . . . (Plato) 19-8-5
GLOBES
    bare wilderness of . . . (Kepler) 19-8-45
GLOOM
    nothing but . . . (Johnson) 11-2-90
GLORIES
    historic . . . of old (Emerson) 10-9-35
GLORIFICATION
    an empty . . . left (Euripides) 1-8-12
GLORY
    acquired . . . and good repute (Plutarch) 14-2-24
    and the . . . of the Lord (*Isaiah*) 20-5-13
    augmented the other's . . . (Plutarch) 1-9-11
    . . . be to God (Hopkins) 20-5-113
    chief . . . of every people (Johnson) 16-2-31
    conclude his life with . . . (Plutarch) 5-5-15
    days of our youth are days of . . . (Byron) 1-3-107
    declare his . . . (*Psalms*) 20-8-6
    desires nothing like . . . (Spinoza) 4-4-24
    fallen from a state of . . . (Pascal) 20-3-32
    have loved my own . . . (Kepler) 20-8-59
    highest pitch of . . . (Milton) 14-1-56
    hope of future . . . (Dante) 4-5-13
    if . . . cannot move (Virgil) 9-9-8
    . . . is like a circle (Shakespeare) 1-5-63
    likeness of the . . . of the Lord (*Ezekiel*) 20-5-14
    loves . . . more (Sterne) 1-7-114
    man has for . . . (Descartes) 2-2-60
    manifested forth his . . . (*John*) 20-11-7
    meridian of my . . . (Shakespeare) 1-6-34
    minds doting on . . . (Plutarch) 10-2-23
    . . . of dying (Tacitus) 1-9-17
    . . . of his native country (Gibbon) 14-1-77
    . . . of its lady (Dante) 1-7-56
    . . . of the average man (Mill) 1-6-71
    . . . of the Lord had filled (*I Kings*) 20-2-12
    . . . of the Lord shone (*Luke*) 20-3-11
    . . . of those who are (Augustine) 1-8-56
    one . . . of the sun (*I Corinthians*) 1-8-41
    paths of . . . lead but to (Gray) 11-2-83
    pursuit of . . . (Pascal) 1-6-39
    shouldst see the . . . of God (*John*) 1-8-38
    so dire a thirst of . . . (Pope) 16-7-25
    spear of . . . caught (Euripides) 2-2-14
    sully the . . . of (Plutarch) 1-9-9
    the . . . of having written well (Pascal) 4-11-22
    the . . . of scepticism (Pascal) 6-6-20
    the . . . which came so soon (Schopenhauer) 16-2-43
    to . . . in being blind (Augustine) 6-4-8
    trailing clouds of . . . (Wordsworth) 1-3-102
    uncertain . . . of an April day (Shakespeare) 3-1-33
    when can their . . . fade (Tennyson) 14-2-64
    . . . which is lovliest (Euripides) 3-6-3
    who has set thy . . . above (*Psalms*) 1-1-3
    will see the blessed in . . . (Aquinas) 20-15-48
    woman is the . . . of (*I Corinthians*) 1-7-40
    won . . . by the moral (Xenophon) 1-8-20
GLOUCESTER
    and my brother . . . (Shakespeare) 20-15-65
GLUTTON
    can never be a . . . (Thoreau) 9-12-47
GLUTTONY
    baneful crime of . . . (Dante) 9-12-20
    . . . full of all wickedness (Chaucer) 9-12-21
    full of lust and . . . (Aristotle) 1-1-22
GOAL
    crave for the . . . that is worthy (Nicomachus) 9-8-22
    . . . is not fixed (Bacon) 17-2-22
    . . . of our activities (Poincaré) 6-3-136

. . . of riches worthless (Luther) 11-2-55
    seldom attains his . . . (Schopenhauer) 9-8-70
    take freedom as my . . . (Sartre) 13-1-70
    the final . . . of ill (Tennyson) 20-5-102
    to you no . . . is set (Goethe) 9-8-65
GOBLIN
    the drudging . . . swet (Milton) 20-7-57
GOD, of monotheism
    above the stars of . . . (*Isaiah*) 20-15-3
    . . . abstained from creatıng (Augustine) 19-8-32
    . . . according to the doctrine of (Rabelais) 5-5-18
    act as law of . . . commands (Leibniz) 6-5-69
    . . . acting by his intellect (Aquinas) 19-8-34
    activity of . . . is immortality (Aristotle) 19-8-8
    against the existence of . . . (Descartes) 20-9-20
    a . . . that hidest thyself (*Isaiah*) 20-2-18
    all of them denied . . . (Dostoevsky) 20-9-48
    all the sons of . . . shouted (*Job*) 1-1-2
    all who think about . . . (Augustine) 19-2-21
    . . . alone can do this (Aquinas) 20-11-14
    . . . alone efficient cause (Berkeley) 19-3-34
    . . . alone is (Montaigne) 19-7-33
    . . . alone is the author (Augustine) 19-3-13
    almighty as . . . himself (Pascal) 6-3-64
    almighty power of . . . (Pascal) 19-8-56
    always call upon . . . (Plato) 20-8-20
    . . . always for big battalions (Voltaire) 14-2-47
    am I a . . . at hand (*Jeremiah*) 20-10-2
    and by a messenger of . . . (Hobbes) 20-7-55
    and could find no . . . (Santayana) 19-1-124
    and . . . fulfills himself (Tennyson) 20-8-82
    and . . . He knows better (Chaucer) 20-15-58
    and . . . said—Let us make man (*Genesis*) 1-1-1
    and . . . saw everything he had made (*Genesis*) 9-6-1
    and . . . the soul (Pope) 19-1-62
    and knowledge of . . . (Luther) 6-5-35
    . . . and nature (Aquinas) 19-1-23
    and sin against . . . (*Genesis*) 3-3-1
    . . . and the apostles (Pascal) 20-9-24
    . . . and the Jews rejoiced (Dante) 20-13-54
    and the Lord . . . said (*Genesis*) 1-7-1
    and the peace of . . . (*Philippians*) 20-3-17
    and this cause is . . . (Aquinas) 20-11-12
    and who is that . . . (*Daniel*) 20-11-2
    and worship . . . supreme (Milton) 19-2-35
    . . . and your good cause (Shakespeare) 10-6-21
    angels of . . . are our angels (Augustine) 20-7-19
    apart from charity is not . . . (Pascal) 6-3-65
    apart from the will of . . . (Augustine) 15-3-50
    . . . appeared unto Jacob (*Genesis*) 20-2-5
    are gifts of . . . (Luther) 18-2-26
    a relationship to . . . (Kierkegaard) 3-5-40
    are the children of . . . (Calvin) 20-4-26
    as Abraham believed . . . (*Galatians*) 6-5-13
    . . . as an incomprehensible (Montaigne) 20-1-18
    as an offense against . . . (Aquinas) 20-13-42
    . . . as first mover (Aquinas) 1-2-27
    as . . . has commanded (Augustine) 9-10-41
    as . . . has willed (Pascal) 12-2-39
    as having come from . . . (Pascal) 12-1-49
    as if . . . foreknew (Aquinas) 15-3-61
    assist . . . in His operations (Aquinas) 16-1-16
    as what pleases . . . (Pascal) 20-8-66
    at being one with . . . (T. S. Eliot) 20-4-54
    back to the belief in . . . (Montaigne) 20-9-17
    based on the favor of . . . (Freud) 20-2-51
    basis of natural law is . . . (Luther) 9-3-15
    beauty in works of . . . (Th. Browne) 19-1-50
    because . . . forbids suicide (Kant) 1-9-39

GOD, of monotheism (*Cont.*)
life properly in . . . (Aquinas) 19-2-23
lifts his heart to . . . (Bernard of Clairvaux) 11-3-16
. . . likes best (Milton) 2-3-69
live according to . . . (Aquinas) 15-3-52; (Pascal) 20-1-28
Lord . . . of truth (Augustine) 6-1-23
Lord our . . . is one Lord (*Deut.*) 20-8-2
Lord our . . . made a covenant (*Deut.*) 20-2-11
love . . . with all their heart (Anselm) 3-5-17
love of . . . is better (Aquinas) 6-1-38
love thy . . . (*Luke*) 3-5-8
loved of . . . because (Plato) 20-8-19
lover of . . . loves self (Augustine) 3-5-15
. . . loves all men (Aquinas) 15-3-58
. . . loves himself infinitely (Spinoza) 3-5-32
loving . . . above all (Aquinas) 3-5-20
loving . . . and hating brother (*I John*) 3-2-9
loving . . . and our neighbor (Aquinas) 3-5-21
made by my loving . . . (Augustine) 5-7-8
. . . made man male (Aquinas) 3-3-24
. . . made thee perfect (Milton) 15-3-92
make representations of . . . (Tacitus) 20-2-19
makes them friends of . . . (Augustine) 9-15-33
making us subject to . . . (Augustine) 20-8-44
man is just so is he . . . (Emerson) 9-3-34
man loves . . . (Aquinas) 4-2-19
man should love . . . (Aquinas) 3-1-24
man's last end is . . . (Aquinas) 4-7-29
man united to . . . (Aquinas) 20-14-26
. . . may be all in all (Augustine) 20-4-13
may . . . prevent this (Augustine) 5-3-8
measure justice of . . . (Calvin) 12-2-26
medicine is the gift of . . . (Luther) 18-2-25
men are separated from . . . (Augustine) 20-31-32
mind's approximation to . . . (Thoreau) 1-1-106
. . . mingles not with man (Plato) 3-1-9
ministry and service . . . uses (Calvin) 20-7-38
miracles . . . has wrought (Augustine) 20-11-11
mode of worshipping . . . (Spinoza) 19-3-30
modifications of the attributes of . . . (Spinoza) 1-1-76
mother of . . . was degraded (Gibbon) 20-12-31
movement is . . . (Tolstoy) 19-8-89
much less shall they bind . . . (Hobbes) 3-5-29
my . . . my . . . why hast thou (*Matthew*) 4-5-8
my . . . why hast thou (*Psalms*) 4-5-3
my king and my . . . (*Psalms*) 20-8-4
. . . my Saviour (*Luke*) 1-7-37
mystery of . . . (*Revelation*) 19-8-18
nation whose . . . is the Lord (*Psalms*) 20-2-14
natural kingdom of . . . (Hobbes) 6-5-52
nature the image of . . . (Pascal) 19-1-51
. . . needs man (Bergson) 3-1-92
noblest work of . . . (Pope) 9-14-45
no conscience if . . . did not (Kierkegaard) 9-5-22
no . . . and no human (Spinoza) 9-15-75
no . . . can adapt the world (Sartre) 4-5-39
no one can hate . . . (Spinoza) 3-2-26
no other than . . . himself (Descartes) 19-1-68
no true notion of . . . (Locke) 20-6-39
not all things created by . . . for us (Descartes) 1-1-69
. . . not as its object (Aquinas) 20-1-13
not created evil by . . . (Luther) 20-7-36
not equal to . . . in eternity (Aquinas) 19-7-30
not inherit the kingdom of . . . (*Galatians*) 20-13-23
not sent by . . . to assail us (Aquinas) 20-7-29
not true that all reveals . . . (Pascal) 20-5-73
obedience required by . . . (Hobbes) 20-8-61
. . . of Abraham thy father (*Genesis*) 5-5-1
of communion with . . . (Pascal) 20-3-32

of . . . and immortality (Dostoevsky) 20-9-46
. . . of the Jewish people (Hegel) 20-2-42
offended is Almighty . . . (Hobbes) 20-14-38
. . . offers to every mind (Emerson) 6-3-108
O . . . that one might read (Shakespeare) 15-1-30
one . . . produced one world (Aquinas) 19-8-36
one offends . . . who is infinite (Aquinas) 20-15-49
only . . . my dear (Yeats) 1-4-69
only in the love of . . . (Pascal) 20-2-32
. . . only is worse (Plato) 9-15-17
. . . on the first day only (Bacon) 17-2-20
on their turning to . . . (Newman) 20-1-66
order given by . . . (Aquinas) 19-8-35
ordered to enjoyment of . . . (Aquinas) 9-15-39
. . . orders me to (Plato) 1-8-13
. . . or nature is not defective (Dante) 14-3-25
our seduction from . . . (Calvin) 20-13-67
owes certain duties to . . . (Aquinas) 9-9-14
perfection of the works of . . . (Leibniz) 15-2-28
. . . pilot of the living (Melville) 6-3-109
place which . . . has chosen (Aquinas) 20-2-21
. . . planted a garden in Eden (*Genesis*) 20-13-1
pleased . . . to communicate (Montaigne) 6-5-45
pleased . . . to give us reason (Montaigne) 9-4-32
power and providence of . . . (Spinoza) 20-11-26
power and wisdom of . . . (Luther) 20-3-24
power comes from . . . (Rousseau) 10-6-51
praised be the good . . . (Rabelais) 6-6-9
preach the kingdom of . . . (*Luke*) 20-8-29
proclaims . . . to children (Voltaire) 20-9-33
procured acceptance with . . . (Locke) 20-14-51
produced by . . . in no other (Spinoza) 19-8-60
promises of . . . made the church (Luther) 20-4-22
pronounced by . . . in creation (Hobbes) 10-1-21
providence of . . . is exercised (Aquinas) 20-7-28
public worshipping of . . . (Locke) 20-4-38
punishment by . . . (Aquinas) 12-4-23
pure and perfect essence of . . . (Gibbon) 20-1-48
pure religion and undefiled before . . . (*James*) 20-1-5
received from . . . the Father (*II Peter*) 6-5-17
received understanding from . . . (Rousseau) 13-3-19
reconcile prescience of . . . (Gibbon) 15-3-103
reflection of . . . (Cicero) 9-15-26
. . . regards the inward (Pascal) 20-4-35
religion directs man to . . . (Aquinas) 20-1-13
remembrance of the city of . . . (Emerson) 19-8-81
representing the form of . . . (Hegel) 16-1-41
return unto . . . (*Eccles.*) 1-3-3
reveal the works of . . . (*Tobit*) 20-7-3
revelation of . . . (Kierkegaard) 6-5-91
revelation which . . . gave (*Revelation*) 6-5-18
rewarded by . . . for deeds (Aquinas) 5-7-13
. . . said I am tired of kings (Emerson) 10-6-69
. . . said "let Newton be" (Pope) 17-2-54
. . . said "let the earth" (*Genesis*) 19-2-1
said to believe in a . . . (Aquinas) 20-9-8
same sense as . . . (Isak Dinesen) 16-3-104
saved through grace of . . . (Luther) 9-4-29
. . . save the mark (Shakespeare) 14-2-35
. . . sees into the heart (Nietzsche) 9-1-36
see the kingdom of . . . (*John*) 20-3-13
. . . sends a cheerful hour (Milton) 9-6-75
sent and employed by . . . (Hobbes) 20-11-21
servant of . . . (Milton) 9-11-42
serve . . . and mammon (*Matthew*) 11-2-38
sets us nothing but . . . (Dostoevsky) 16-6-72
shall I see . . . (*Job*) 20-2-13
shall obey . . . rather (Plato) 13-2-2
. . . shall rest on the seventh (Augustine) 15-2-20

GOD, of monotheism (*Cont.*)
  when . . . himself willed it (Aquinas) 20-7-24
  when . . . orders something (Augustine) 9-2-6
  when . . . said "Let the earth" (Milton) 19-2-35
  when . . . shakes a kingdom (Milton) 15-3-93
  when . . . speaketh to man (Hobbes) 20-10-30
  . . . when he created Adam (Isak Dinesen) 9-2-36
  whether . . . so disposes (Descartes) 5-7-21
  which from . . . began (Pope) 19-8-68
  which . . . by curse (Milton) 20-15-79
  which is made by . . . (Plato) 16-1-4
  while . . . spake (Milton) 20-15-81
  who fear . . . and are seeking (Augustine) 6-1-28
  . . . who guided the Jews (Voltaire) 20-2-36
  . . . who is himself (Montaigne) 1-5-57
  who knows and imitates . . . (Augustine) 17-1-39
  . . . who made the visible heaven (Augustine) 20-11-10
  whosoever is born of . . . (*I John*) 20-13-27
  why we call . . . good (Montaigne) 9-10-55
  . . . will be gracious (*II Samuel*) 1-8-3
  . . . will bring thee into judgment (*Eccles.*) 1-3-2
  . . . will not have it (Luther) 6-1-44
  . . . will not punish (Sophocles) 9-7-7
  will of . . . has to be known (Nietzsche) 6-5-108
  will of . . . liable to doubt (Locke) 6-5-70
  will or power of . . . (Augustine) 15-3-49
  will received from . . . (Descartes) 6-4-20
  . . . will teach how to love (Kierkegaard) 3-5-40
  wilt ask of . . . (*John*) 1-8-38
  wisdom is folly before . . . (Montaigne) 9-15-47
  . . . with all his holy angels (Luther) 20-7-37
  with fear the only . . . (Milton) 20-8-127
  with . . . not parted (Milton) 1-8-114
  with respect to . . . (Maritain) 12-3-35
  Word was with . . . (*John*) 19-8-17
  works of . . . are perfect (Descartes) 19-8-50
  worship . . . by sacrifices (Aquinas) 20-8-46
  worship . . . with pure faith (Calvin) 9-3-16
  worship of the true . . . (Augustine) 9-10-38; (Gibbon)
    20-2-41
  worshipped not . . . (Dante) 4-5-12
  worship to the true . . . (Aquinas) 20-12-14
  would find . . . invisible (Ptolemy) 17-3-17
  wretches will upbraid . . . (Luther) 6-5-37
  you are the Son of . . . (Shaw) 20-3-65
  your word O . . . (Augustine) 1-8-52
GOD, of polytheism
  assaulting the mysteries of . . . (Euripides) 20-8-18
  awake the . . . of day (Shakespeare) 20-7-46
  because the . . . has granted (Homer) 14-2-5
  canst not be a . . . (Plutarch) 1-8-43
  clear command of . . . (Euripides) 5-6-5
  converse of . . . with man (Plato) 20-5-15
  disobedience to the . . . (Plato) 1-2-12
  do as the . . . should direct (Plutarch) 12-1-21
  earth's little . . . (Goethe) 1-1-93
  every . . . is there sitting (Emerson) 19-8-80
  in apprehension how like a . . . (Shakespeare) 1-1-55
  is a . . . and cannot lie (Plato) 6-4-6
  is but some vengeful . . . (Hardy) 20-5-119
  is now become a . . . (Shakespeare) 1-6-26
  kind of . . . thou art (Shakespeare) 10-6-24
  like a . . . among men (Plato) 9-7-9
  make a . . . of a priest (Voltaire) 20-1-40
  man has become a . . . (Freud) 15-2-81
  man is a . . . in ruin (Emerson) 1-1-100
  no . . . ever dies (Thoreau) 20-6-45
  our rascaldom's own . . . (Aristophanes) 16-4-1
  province of some . . . (Plutarch) 9-8-20

  strife resolved by a . . . (Ovid) 19-8-16
  that no . . . whatever (Augustine) 15-3-50
  the . . . compels me (Plato) 8-3-8
  the . . . of arms (Virgil) 4-2-12
  the . . . of war (Aeschylus) 14-1-5
  to the unknown . . . (*Acts*) 20-12-8
GODDESS
  fortune would not be a . . . (Juvenal) 15-3-43
  hold victory to be a . . . (Augustine) 20-2-20
  like a thrifty . . . (Shakespeare) 9-10-65
  that . . . blind (Shakespeare) 15-3-80
  thou nature art my . . . (Shakespeare) 19-1-37
GODDESSES
  adored as . . . (Gibbon) 1-7-121
  compare with . . . (Homer) 2-3-8
  likeness of her face to . . . (Homer) 16-6-3
  . . . stayed home for shame (Homer) 3-3-5
GODHEAD
  fulness of the . . . (Augustine) 17-1-37
  in presence of the . . . (Kant) 20-8-76
  . . . is certainly near (Ovid) 20-6-29
GOD-LIKE
  function of the . . . to think (Aristotle) 1-1-17
GODS
  a belief in the . . . (Cicero) 20-6-25
  all other . . . are false (Hegel) 20-2-42
  among the immortal . . . (Homer) 15-3-5
  . . . are convenient to have (Ovid) 20-6-29
  . . . are our guardians (Plato) 1-9-3
  . . . are supremely happy (Cicero) 20-2-27
  are we to the . . . (Shakespeare) 1-1-58
  be more . . . than one (Hobbes) 20-5-67
  bodies were pushed by . . . (Russell) 19-5-69
  but to obey the . . . (Seneca) 17-1-24
  condemn the . . . (Aristophanes) 17-1-2
  consists of . . . and men (Epictetus) 10-1-13
  . . . constitute greater part of the (Plotinus) 1-1-34
  creatures of their fancy their . . . (Hobbes) 20-12-23
  . . . deigned not to punish (Aeschylus) 20-13-11
  do not ye serve my . . . (*Daniel*) 20-11-2
  dreams come from the . . . (Chaucer) 5-5-17
  elevated into . . . (Plutarch) 20-15-31
  existence of the . . . (Plato) 1-8-13
  false and lying . . . (Dante) 20-13-50
  fear able to produce . . . (Kant) 20-5-97
  fear of the . . . (Darwin) 1-5-124
  feast with the . . . (Epictetus) 4-4-11
  . . . find their pleasure (Sophocles) 9-6-4
  forced itself against . . . (Melville) 5-6-36
  gifts tempt even . . . (Euripides) 11-2-9
  go not after other . . . (*Jeremiah*) 20-10-3
  great a crowd of false . . . (Augustine) 20-2-20
  have no other . . . (*Exodus*) 9-3-1
  . . . having arranged (Aurelius) 1-8-48
  he makes the . . . also (Plato) 16-1-4
  he will be with the . . . (Plotinus) 15-3-47
  he wrongs the . . . (Euripides) 20-10-9
  if many . . . existed (Aquinas) 20-5-47
  if the . . . think to speak (Melville) 6-5-95
  image of the eternal . . . (Plato) 19-7-4
  immortal . . . I crave (Shakespeare) 9-13-20
  . . . in sainted seats (Milton) 9-10-79
  invisible the . . . are (Hesiod) 20-6-6
  justice towards the . . . (Cicero) 20-8-24
  laughter of the happy . . . (Homer) 3-3-5
  lay to the charge of the . . . (Lucretius) 20-12-5
  life of the . . . is blessed (Aristotle) 1-1-21
  like unto Thee among the . . . (*Exodus*) 20-5-3
  lives with the . . . below (Sophocles) 20-8-13

GOOD (*Cont.*)

thing he sees is . . . to do (Augustine) 8-3-28
things which are . . . (Epictetus) 9-6-25
thinks his . . . are in externals (Epictetus) 9-4-11
this private . . . of their own (Augustine) 20-7-16
those which do me . . . (Voltaire) 9-10-99
thou art every true . . . (Anselm) 20-5-40
to aim at some . . . (Aristotle) 10-2-9, 16-1-7
. . . to a melancholy person (Spinoza) 9-6-83
to do . . . accounted folly (Shakespeare) 9-6-66
to do . . . or do no harm (Hippocrates) 18-2-3
to do . . . never will (Milton) 9-6-76
to do . . . to all the world (Cervantes) 9-10-70
to do . . . unto others (Darwin) 1-5-125
to do no . . . after all (Hippocrates) 18-1-5
to return . . . for evil (Darwin) 3-2-37
to the . . . it is . . . (Augustine) 1-8-55
toward the common . . . (Maritain) 12-3-36
true proves itself to be . . . (Wm. James) 6-3-131
truly proud man must be . . . (Aristotle) 4-11-10
truth and . . . include (Aquinas) 6-3-33
twofold . . . of nature and grace (Aquinas) 3-1-24
tyrant pursues his . . . (Aristotle) 10-6-11
unattainableness of . . . (Locke) 4-5-26
. . . unknown sure is not had (Milton) 9-6-79
universe is . . . (Plotinus) 9-6-36
vicissitudes of . . . and evil (Santayana) 17-1-111
weigh the . . . and bad (Euripides) 14-1-11
we judge to be . . . (Spinoza) 12-3-11
we know the . . . (Euripides) 9-10-2
we live defining . . . (Euripides) 9-3-2
what constitutes his . . . (Mill) 12-4-67
whatever seems . . . (Plato) 10-6-8
what . . . he must (Rousseau) 9-10-101
what is a . . . law (Hobbes) 12-1-47
what is . . . and expedient (Aristotle) 9-13-3
what were . . . to be done (Shakespeare) 8-3-46
whence his . . . descends (Milton) 19-2-35
when the result is . . . (Aristotle) 15-3-23
whether the . . . is (Wittgenstein) 17-1-108
which all desire is . . . (Aristotle) 4-4-7
which is the highest . . . (Dante) 9-7-35
. . . which is the object (Dante) 20-5-48
which the law will make . . . (Th. Browne) 12-1-48
who is neither . . . nor wise (Plato) 6-4-4
whole of . . . is revealed (Wm. James) 6-3-129
wishes them some . . . (Aquinas) 15-3-58
wishes to take the . . . of it (Lincoln) 10-7-38
with a view to some . . . (Aristotle) 10-1-5
withhold not . . . (*Proverbs*) 9-7-4
work together for . . . (*Romans*) 15-3-37
would never be chosen as . . . (Aquinas) 20-13-40
yet we trust that somehow . . . (Tennyson) 20-5-102

GOOD-FOR-NOTHINGS

thousands of . . . to celebrity (Euripides) 1-5-4

GOOD INTENTIONS

the hypocrisy of . . . (Hegel) 12-1-78

GOOD LIFE

end of the state is the . . . (Aristotle) 10-1-8

GOOD MAN

. . . is same as good citizen (Aristotle) 10-5-7
war takes a . . . always (Sophocles) 14-1-9

GOOD MEN

. . . must not obey too well (Emerson) 12-1-81

GOODNESS

analysis of . . . (Aristotle) 7-2-15
. . . and propriety (Cicero) 1-6-10
any print of . . . (Shakespeare) 7-1-25
beauty is . . . (Tolstoy) 16-6-75

between piety and . . . (Pascal) 20-8-65
believe in their own . . . (Aristotle) 1-5-18
. . . can be taught (Euripides) 9-6-5
confidence in . . . (Montaigne) 9-6-57
desire to possess . . . (Aristotle) 3-1-13
directed to moral . . . (Aristotle) 1-3-19
divine . . . is said to move (Aquinas) 19-5-23
he himself be . . . (Nietzsche) 19-8-90
He is . . . by His essence (Aquinas) 20-15-46
if only one grade of . . . (Aquinas) 19-1-22
in . . . of will (Augustine) 9-6-40
. . . is both rare and laudable (Aristotle) 9-6-17
. . . is the only investment (Thoreau) 9-10-115
. . . is the third member (Whitehead) 16-1-55
it can fail in . . . (Aquinas) 19-1-23
mix no more with . . . (Milton) 9-10-81
moral . . . leads us to choose (Aristotle) 1-3-18
more to him than . . . (Melville) 6-3-109
never mention word . . . (Fielding) 9-10-93
of human . . . (Plutarch) 2-2-31
. . . of laws they obey (Aristotle) 12-1-12
. . . of the human will (Aquinas) 9-3-14
. . . of the works of art (Aristotle) 16-7-5
perfect . . . surely established (Plotinus) 1-4-11
reign of infinite . . . (Gibbon) 15-3-103
some soul of . . . (Shakespeare) 9-6-60
. . . sufficient to support (Fielding) 10-6-43
surely . . . and mercy (*Psalms*) 20-14-2
the . . . of God (Augustine) 19-1-21
their . . . in themselves (Aristotle) 9-10-12
the possession of . . . (Augustine) 9-6-44
the twin sisters of . . . (Plato) 16-7-1
used up every . . . (Kepler) 19-8-45
we can achieve little . . . (Hegel) 1-6-59
wisdom and . . . to the vile (Shakespeare) 9-6-65

GOODS

. . . are of two kinds (Plato) 9-6-12
association in our . . . (Montaigne) 2-2-45
consider . . . of the soul (Plato) 9-13-2
few are the . . . of life (Plato) 9-6-10
for the sake of earthly . . . (Augustine) 14-3-16
gaining one of the lower . . . (Augustine) 12-4-21
. . . give rise to fluctuation (Aristotle) 6-7-11
independent of external . . . (Aristotle) 17-1-15
. . . into three classes (Aristotle) 9-8-15
lay hold of present . . . (Montaigne) 1-2-31
lend our . . . (Montaigne) 1-5-56
lose the greatest . . . (Aristotle) 1-8-22
no other than material . . . (Aquinas) 11-4-8
not human . . . they seek (Aristotle) 17-1-12
particular and partial . . . (Maritain) 5-7-52
prevents him from attaining . . . (Leibniz) 9-4-37
spoiling his . . . (Hobbes) 12-4-38
state is master of all . . . (Rousseau) 12-3-19
. . . that heaven covereth (Rabelais) 9-15-43
the distribution of . . . (Hegel) 13-3-28
those . . . which constitute (Hegel) 12-3-25

GOOD SENSE

want of . . . (Aristotle) 7-2-15

GOOD THINGS

all . . . are from You (Augustine) 9-6-39

GOOD TIDINGS

bringeth . . . of good (*Isaiah*) 20-3-3
bring you . . . of great joy (*Luke*) 20-3-11
Zion that bringest . . . (*Isaiah*) 20-14-5

GOOD TREE

every . . . bringeth forth (*Matthew*) 9-7-22

GOOD WILL

. . . in your superiors (Freud) 9-6-115

GRACE (*Cont.*)
by God's good ... (Chaucer) 20-13-56
by ... are ye saved (*Ephesians*) 20-14-18
by the sole ... of God (Augustine) 15-2-19
deprived of divine ... (Montaigne) 1-1-50
desire for the light of ... (Kepler) 20-8-59
dispose your hearts in ... (Chaucer) 20-13-57
extent and stretch of ... (Dryden) 20-2-35
freed by ... of God (Augustine) 9-6-43
he falls from ... (Aquinas) 15-3-61
into the heart by ... (Pascal) 20-1-23
... is indeed needed (Pascal) 20-14-41
known what ... consists (Pascal) 16-3-41
mickle is the powerful ... (Shakespeare) 18-1-19
not remitted without ... (Aquinas) 20-15-49
of the ... of life (*I Peter*) 2-3-24
O ... abounding (Dante) 19-8-41, 20-5-48
on account of ... (Descartes) 6-5-49
privation of the light of ... (Aquinas) 20-7-26
product of divine ... (Dante) 4-5-13
purified and redeemed by ... (Fielding) 9-10-93
saved through ... of God (Luther) 9-4-29
strong toil of ... (Shakespeare) 1-9-30
the ... of life (*I Peter*) 1-7-44
the Lord of ... (Dante) 1-7-56
the power of ... (Aquinas) 20-14-25
the revelation of ... (Augustine) 6-5-26
the will to confer ... (Aquinas) 15-3-58
therefore shall find ... (Milton) 20-14-44
there is a two-fold ... (Aquinas) 20-14-26
thy ... may wing me (Donne) 20-13-74
were ... and beauty in them (Augustine) 16-6-21
with half so good a ... (Shakespeare) 3-5-26
GRACES
do inherit heaven's ... (Shakespeare) 9-15-63
must they not make these ... (Plato) 16-7-1
till all ... be in one woman (Shakespeare) 3-1-38
virtue recommended by ... (Johnson) 9-10-102
GRADATIONS
there are ... in conduct (Boswell) 9-2-29
GRADUATED
they term ... taxation (Mill) 11-6-53
GRAECO-ROMAN WORLD
adaptation of Hebrew religion to ... (Santayana) 20-2-52
GRAMMAR
... a knowledge of something (Aristotle) 6-1-8
... a part of logic (Mill) 7-2-88
Chinese almost without ... (Freud) 7-2-92
combat usage with ... (Montaigne) 7-2-46
easy to be misled by ... (Russell) 7-2-89
... exercises understanding (Rousseau) 7-2-76
... expresses logic of mind (Dewey) 7-1-73
he hates the ... (Emerson) 8-1-59
... is the work of thought (Hegel) 7-2-87
laws of philosophical ... (Leibniz) 7-2-68
name from word ... (Aristotle) 7-1-7
neglected part of ... (Locke) 7-2-70
speech Romans called ... (Dante) 7-1-81
the science of ... (Bacon) 7-2-54
GRANDEUR
charged with the ... of God (Hopkins) 20-5-114
GRANDSIRES
guarded with ... (Shakespeare) 5-4-12
GRASS
all flesh is ... (*Isaiah*) 20-5-13
I believe a leaf of ... (Whitman) 19-1-105
of splendor in the ... (Wordsworth) 19-1-82
virtues like the ... (Thoreau) 9-10-114
what is the ... (Whitman) 19-1-104

GRASSHOPPER
... that long-legged race (Goethe) 1-1-93
GRATEFUL
need of being ... (Kant) 9-3-32
GRATIANO
but as the world ... (Shakespeare) 1-2-41
GRATIFICATION
abandoned paths of ... (Freud) 5-4-40
a seasonable ... (Epictetus) 4-7-19
eager for ... (Boswell) 5-6-33
... is bodily sensation (Kant) 4-7-55
no place for ... (Plotinus) 4-7-20
obtaining pleasurable ... (Freud) 3-3-79
solely for man's ... (Darwin) 16-6-69
substitutive ... (Freud) 4-7-66
we enjoy some ... (Augustine) 1-8-57
GRATIFY
... themselves at any expense (Boswell) 6-6-31
GRATIFYING
find to be more ... (Augustine) 14-3-17
GRATITUDE
... a proper motive (Fielding) 3-1-59
enter into his ... (Smith) 3-1-64
who have most ... (Descartes) 4-3-23
with hatred instead of ... (Tacitus) 3-2-10
GRATUITOUS
art is ... (Maritain) 16-1-69
GRAVE
dressed them for the ... (Sophocles) 2-1-8
hallow'd to thy ... (Shakespeare) 2-2-55
is ever beside the ... (Gibbon) 15-1-52
is slain over the ... (Herodotus) 2-3-14
lead but to the ... (Gray) 11-2-83
levels quality in the ... (Cervantes) 1-2-48
made his ... with the wicked (*Isaiah*) 20-3-4
no work in the ... (*Eccles.*) 11-3-5
pomp is brought down to the ... (*Isaiah*) 20-15-3
pompous in the ... (Th. Browne) 1-8-106
take me out o' the ... (Shakespeare) 2-2-54
the rotting ... (Blake) 6-6-35
thou wert better in thy ... (Shakespeare) 1-1-57
... where is thy victory (Bunyan) 20-14-49
white hairs unto a quiet ... (Shakespeare) 1-2-38
GRAVE-MAKING
he sings at ... (Shakespeare) 8-2-18
GRAVES
... deep in alien soil (Aeschylus) 14-1-5
find dishonorable ... (Shakespeare) 1-6-27
rise from ... with closed fists (Dante) 4-9-4
the ... stood tenantless (Shakespeare) 20-12-19
GRAVITATION
law of ... (Whitehead) 19-5-68
GRAVITIES
different specific ... (Galileo) 19-5-36
GRAVITY
attraction of ... (Darwin) 17-2-88, 19-1-108
by the force of ... (Newton) 19-5-47
can lose their force of ... (Lucretius) 19-8-13
derive the forces of ... (Newton) 17-2-44
enunciated the law of ... (Tolstoy) 17-2-101
examples of the law of ... (Whitehead) 17-2-116
... is diminished as they (Newton) 19-5-49
is not an effect of ... (Mill) 17-2-94
... is nothing except (Copernicus) 19-5-24
specific ... of bodies (Augustine) 3-1-21
the causes of ... (Aristotle) 17-2-47
... was an errant scoundrel (Sterne) 9-14-46
GREAT
is no ... and no small (Emerson) 19-1-97

HAPPINESS (*Cont.*)

certain road to . . . (Fielding) 9-10-95
chance for . . . in life (Hume) 1-9-33
characteristics looked for in . . . (Aristotle) 9-6-15
common . . . furnishes (Rousseau) 10-5-27
contribute to the . . . (Fielding) 2-2-70
dwell there in perfect . . . (Plato) 20-15-11
enemy to human . . . (Johnson) 11-2-95
enjoys the completest . . . (Herodotus) 1-2-8
final consummation of . . . (Aristotle) 9-6-13
find their . . . (Nietzsche) 1-4-62
from . . . to misery (Aristotle) 16-4-11
from misfortune to . . . (Aristotle) 10-4-10
. . . from thinking (Montaigne) 5-1-18
general state of . . . (Gibbon) 14-1-77
God is man's . . . (Aquinas) 20-5-41
good fortune same as . . . (Aristotle) 19-4-7
gratifications stifle . . . (Plotinus) 4-7-20
greatest . . . is at hand (Tolstoy) 2-3-111
greatest . . . principle (Darwin) 9-1-26
health necessary to . . . (Locke) 18-3-49
his end is . . . (Aquinas) 20-3-23
hope a species of . . . (Johnson) 4-5-30
hope itself is . . . (Johnson) 4-5-29
hope of their common . . . (Milton) 10-6-37
if . . . is loved (Augustine) 6-3-27
impossible for . . . (Aquinas) 1-5-49
. . . in God (Aquinas) 3-1-24
. . . in hoary hairs (Th. Browne) 1-8-103
in no other state can be . . . (Plato) 17-1-6
in sorrow seek . . . (Dostoevsky) 4-6-51
. . . in the public peace (Milton) 10-4-16
is a loss of . . . (Darwin) 16-3-87
is no mean . . . (Shakespeare) 9-12-30
. . . is not a disposition (Aristotle) 9-10-16
. . . is subject to change (Euripides) 9-8-7
. . . is the highest good (Aristotle) 10-1-10
. . . is the only sanction (Santayana) 1-2-99
knowledge is not . . . (Byron) 6-1-87
lesser grade of . . . (Tocqueville) 10-4-52
liberty and pursuit of . . . (Jefferson) 12-3-20
lies only in . . . (Augustine) 20-13-37
little importance to . . . (Johnson) 6-1-77
may well be called . . . (Kant) 9-10-108
means of acquiring . . . (Aquinas) 9-13-15
measure a man's . . . (Schopenhauer) 11-2-120
measure his . . . (Boethius) 1-5-48
missings of . . . (Fielding) 15-3-97
most of the nature of . . . (Aristotle) 20-5-19, 20-6-21
my personal . . . (Tolstoy) 1-9-45
name it . . . (Goethe) 20-5-98
necessary for . . . (Epicurus) 4-7-13
. . . never continues long (Herodotus) 15-2-4
no . . . in earth or heaven (Cervantes) 14-3-28
no nearer . . . than he (Herodotus) 11-2-8
not enjoyed . . . (Hegel) 1-6-56
no thought for our . . . (Tacitus) 20-6-33
. . . of a great people (Gibbon) 10-3-44
. . . of an individual (Boswell) 10-3-39
. . . of individuals (Freud) 19-1-121
. . . of its subjects (Hume) 11-5-10
. . . of mankind (Malthus) 11-2-116
. . . of the community (Bentham) 12-1-73
. . . of the individual (Plato) 14-3-8
. . . of the people (Hamilton/Madison) 10-3-50
. . . of the saints (Aquinas) 20-15-45
. . . of their own making (Locke) 8-1-38
old age is the time for . . . (Santayana) 1-3-139
our endeavors after . . . (Locke) 5-7-28

our . . . depends (Sophocles) 20-8-14
over instinct for . . . (Nietzsche) 13-1-59
perennial source of . . . (Mill) 16-3-88
perfect . . . has been attained (Aquinas) 20-15-39
pleasure contrary to . . . (Boswell) 4-7-53
pleasure no increase of . . . (Plotinus) 4-7-21
private . . . of the nation (Boswell) 13-2-28
procure . . . from the Almighty (Locke) 9-3-22
. . . produced by indulgence (Freud) 4-7-67
promise of future . . . (Gibbon) 20-15-88
promote the . . . of mankind (Gibbon) 15-1-53
result . . . (Dickens) 11-2-131
say that it is . . . (Aristotle) 9-6-14
scepticism exchanged for . . . (Santayana) 6-6-54
science cannot give . . . (Poincaré) 17-2-111
seek . . . from these pleasures (Aristotle) 16-5-7
seeking . . . of life (Augustine) 6-1-28
shall not lose . . . (Aeschylus) 9-7-6
share in the public . . . (Rousseau) 20-3-40
since their eternal . . . (Aquinas) 15-3-60
sole . . . of our being (Gibbon) 2-2-78
. . . some form of contemplation (Aristotle) 11-2-20
spirit wearies even of perfect . . . (Stendahl) 3-1-72
state of . . . and virtue (Voltaire) 11-2-84
that make our . . . (Epicurus) 17-1-16
. . . the end of our inclinations (Kant) 4-7-56
the fountain of our . . . (Augustine) 20-8-43
. . . the fruit of freedom (Thucydides) 1-6-5
the greatest . . . principle (Mill) 9-1-29
the . . . of all mankind (Boswell) 13-3-24
the . . . of an unembodied (Boswell) 20-15-86
the lot of the . . . (Tacitus) 19-4-13
the perfect good is . . . (Aquinas) 5-7-12
the principle of private . . . (Kant) 9-13-30
the pursuit of . . . (Lincoln) 13-3-37
the struggle for private . . . (Russell) 9-4-49
the utmost possible . . . (Hume) 19-8-70
the way of . . . (Plato) 5-7-1
. . . to consist in wealth (Aquinas) 11-2-50
. . . too swiftly flies (Gray) 6-4-30
too well for . . . (Euripides) 2-2-14
trouble intrudes on . . . (Ovid) 4-6-12
true reward is . . . (Aquinas) 1-5-50
ultimate . . . of man (Aquinas) 8-2-9
virtuous identical with . . . (Aristotle) 10-2-13
wealth justify itself in . . . (Santayana) 11-2-160
wins more of . . . (Sophocles) 9-8-3
wisdom allied to . . . (Rousseau) 10-2-76

HAPPY

. . . at the dawn of life (Chaucer) 3-5-23
breed of men . . . (Shakespeare) 3-6-13
earthlier . . . is the rose (Shakespeare) 3-3-44
. . . families are all alike (Tolstoy) 2-1-49
governing to make . . . (Rousseau) 10-6-56
. . . in that we are not (Shakespeare) 15-3-82
learned is . . . by nature (Pope) 9-15-78
life of a citizen . . . (Aurelius) 10-5-14
make our sons . . . (Augustine) 11-2-49
. . . man needs virtuous friends (Aristotle) 3-4-15
only wishes to be . . . (Pascal) 1-8-108
recall a . . . time (Dante) 3-3-31
rich man will be . . . (Plato) 11-2-17
who desires to be . . . (Plato) 9-12-3
wicked men often . . . (Plato) 13-2-4

HAPPY ISLES

we shall touch the . . . (Tennyson) 1-3-115

HAPPY MAN

. . . needs friends (Aquinas) 3-4-28

HARAN

Jacob went toward ... (*Genesis*) 5-5-1
HARDSHIP
   grow old soon in ... (Homer) 1-3-5
   suffer ... for a woman (Homer) 16-6-3
HARDSHIPS
   accustom infants to the ... (Rousseau) 1-3-82
   born and bred in ... (Euripides) 9-8-7
HARFLEUR
   holding course to ... (Shakespeare) 5-4-12
HARLOT
   and go to a ... (Boswell) 2-3-86
   love of a ... passes to hatred (Spinoza) 3-3-60
HARLOTRY
   it is base ... (Augustine) 2-1-21
HARLOTS
   ... go into the kingdom (*Matthew*) 20-8-28
   women that were ... (*I Kings*) 2-2-4
HARM
   by doing ... to none (Aquinas) 9-7-32
   evils will do ... (Plato) 9-6-9
   goods bring ... to people (Aristotle) 6-7-11
   if he hath done thee no ... (*Proverbs*) 9-7-4
   I have done no ... (Shakespeare) 9-6-66
   no one ought to ... another (Locke) 9-3-20
   not do ... to another (Aquinas) 9-3-12
   power only to do ... (Fielding) 10-6-43
   prevent ... to others (Mill) 13-1-52
   to whom ... has been done (Mill) 12-2-52
   to win us to our ... (Shakespeare) 20-7-49
HARMING
   to prevent men ... (Epicurus) 12-2-16
HARMONICS
   a science like ... (Aristotle) 17-3-6
HARMONIES
   ultimate intellectual ... (Santayana) 16-5-43
HARMONIZE
   do not ... with other things (Augustine) 19-1-20
   general theories ought to ... (Aristotle) 19-5-9
HARMONY
   a kind of pre-established ... (Hume) 19-3-38
   altogether one ... (Aurelius) 15-3-45
   ... among heavenly spheres (Rabelais) 19-2-27
   be able to live in ... (Spinoza) 10-1-25
   believe in eternal ... (Dostoevsky) 19-8-87
   best ... in a church (Milton) 6-1-59
   ... between fate and events (Tacitus) 19-4-13
   ... between men and women (Santayana) 1-7-168
   celestial motions beget a ... (Spinoza) 16-7-18
   defective if not in ... (Augustine) 9-2-6
   from heavenly ... (Dryden) 16-5-33
   in ... with any other thing (Plato) 9-6-7
   is not the ... (Goethe) 16-3-64
   major perfections of ... (Whitehead) 16-1-56
   ... of knowledge and action (Augustine) 18-3-29
   ... of numbers and forms (Poincaré) 17-3-53
   ... of the soul is virtue (Plato) 8-1-4
   ... of the whole body (Augustine) 18-1-14
   rhythm and ... find their (Plato) 16-5-2
   source of general ... (Plutarch) 10-8-8
   the hidden soul of ... (Milton) 16-5-30
   towards a total ... (Plotinus) 9-6-36
   wherever there is a ... (Th. Browne) 16-5-27
HARMS
   those violent ... (Shakespeare) 2-2-54
HARP
   performing on a ... of gold (T. S. Eliot) 20-4-54
HARPIES
   the ... feeding then upon (Dante) 1-9-23
HARPIES'

those ... thrilling voices (Homer) 1-7-7
HARPS
   touch their immortal ... (Milton) 16-5-29
   we hanged our ... (*Psalms*) 20-2-16
HARRY
   should the warlike ... (Shakespeare) 5-4-11
HARVARD
   my Yale College and my ... (Melville) 8-1-64
HARVEST
   all the ... that I reaped (FitzGerald) 6-7-37
HASTE
   be in such ... to succeed (Thoreau) 13-1-45
   married in ... (Congreve) 2-3-76
HASTY
   emotion is called ... (Kant) 4-1-29
HATCH
   ... and brood of time (Shakespeare) 15-3-79
HATE
   a time to ... (*Eccles.*) 19-7-2
   bloodhounds of ... (Aeschylus) 5-6-1
   both of them in ancient ... (Goethe) 16-6-54
   by ... they won (Euripides) 14-1-10
   enough religion to make us ... (Swift) 20-1-32
   fierce ... he recollects (Milton) 9-6-78
   I ... all evil men (Euripides) 9-6-6
   like love or liker ... (Chaucer) 4-10-3
   love and ... (Blake) 9-6-94
   must ... and death return (Shelley) 15-2-49
   reason to ... (Euripides) 2-2-17
   to ... any man (Aurelius) 9-14-16
   to ... in the sinner (Aquinas) 9-9-15
   to ... those things (Hobbes) 4-4-21
   what you ought to ... (Plato) 8-1-4
   will be the most perfect ... (Aquinas) 20-15-45
HATED
   his brethren ... him (*Genesis*) 4-8-1
   son of the ... (*Deut.*) 2-1-3
   the poor is ... (*Proverbs*) 11-2-3
HATRED
   Amnon's ... overcame his love (*II Samuel*) 3-3-3
   ... and pride deck themselves (Luther) 20-13-63
   a species of ... (Descartes) 4-3-22
   cannot be object of ... (Aquinas) 6-3-35
   compare ... of God (Aquinas) 4-5-11
   gratify his ... (Horace) 4-3-11
   he avoids ... (Machiavelli) 4-2-20, 10-2-32
   human love can pass to ... (Tolstoy) 3-1-81
   knoweth either love or ... (*Eccles.*) 9-6-3
   love can change to ... (Spinoza) 3-3-60
   not any kind of ... (Aquinas) 20-13-45
   ... not the contrary of (Peirce) 3-1-83
   ... of children (Plutarch) 8-1-16
   ... of law (Hegel) 12-1-78
   ... of truth commoner (Santayana) 6-3-150
   proceed from ... (Descartes) 4-3-23
   repay ... with love (Spinoza) 3-5-31
   such bitter ... (Spinoza) 20-3-34
   ... to the rest of mankind (Gibbon) 20-2-39
   truth call forth ... (Augustine) 6-3-27
   with inhuman ... (Augustine) 1-5-42
HATTERS
   mad as ... (Hardy) 20-15-108
HAUGHTINESS
   spiritual ... of every man (Nietzsche) 4-6-52
HAVE
   in our power to ... or not to ... (Epictetus) 9-4-10
   to ... and to hold (*Book of Common Prayer*) 2-3-48
HAVEN
   a ... never to be feared (Montaigne) 1-9-24

HAWK
   know a . . . from a handsaw (Shakespeare) 5-6-14
HAWKINS, Sir John
   to read what . . . (Boswell) 9-14-51
HAZARD
   after dinner your . . . (Shakespeare) 19-4-23
   make a . . . of new fortunes (Shakespeare) 19-4-22
   stand the . . . of the die (Shakespeare) 19-4-21
HEAD
   are joined by a single . . . (Plato) 4-7-6
   cover his . . . (*I Corinthians*) 1-7-40
   my . . . is hands and feet (Thoreau) 19-7-76
HEADCOLD
   God cures a . . . (Nietzsche) 20-5-118
HEADS
   he who chooses . . . (Pascal) 19-4-26
HEADSTRONG
   conscious of being too . . . (Plato) 2-3-16
HEAL
   a time to . . . (*Eccles.*) 19-7-2
   physician . . . thyself (*Luke*) 18-2-17
HEALER
   . . . and medicine in one (Augustine) 18-3-31
   . . . when the heart hath (Byron) 19-7-69
HEALING
   the most High cometh . . . (*Eccles.*) 18-1-1
HEALTH
   . . . and freedom from pain (Plotinus) 9-6-32
   art of keeping people in . . . (Shaw) 18-1-38
   enjoy a certain . . . of its own (Thoreau) 1-1-106
   ethical . . . of peoples (Hegel) 14-1-89
   first is placed . . . (Aristotle) 9-6-13
   God causes . . . (Aquinas) 8-2-9
   good . . . could be universal (Russell) 8-1-85
   hate . . . because not pitiable (Montaigne) 4-8-15
   infirmities of ill . . . (Sterne) 1-2-60
   . . . is being undermined (Chaucer) 5-5-17
   is conducive to . . . (Cicero) 18-1-10
   . . . is good in itself (Newman) 8-1-74
   lesser good is . . . (Plato) 9-6-12
   manner is prejudicial to . . . (Plato) 18-2-13
   medicine to produce . . . (Plutarch) 6-2-11
   my . . . is not to spend (Bacon) 6-1-53
   not be robust in . . . (Plato) 18-2-8
   . . . of body (Pope) 9-8-55
   . . . of the body (Epicurus) 4-7-13
   restored to . . . by natural power (Aquinas) 8-3-35
   succeed in preservation of . . . (Hippocrates) 18-1-4
   the study of their . . . (Montaigne) 18-1-18
   trust our . . . to physician (Smith) 18-2-40
   vigorous state of . . . (Darwin) 18-1-32
   when in good . . . (Hippocrates) 18-1-2
HEALTHY
   . . . mind in a . . . body (Juvenal) 5-1-10
HEALTHY-MINDEDNESS
   . . . is inadequate (Wm. James) 9-6-112
HEAP
   in each filthy . . . he keeps on (Goethe) 1-1-93
HEAR
   we may be ready to . . . (Aquinas) 8-3-38
   . . . ye but understand not (*Isaiah*) 6-5-3
HEARERS
   once his . . . are friendly (Augustine) 8-3-30
HEARING
   animals' faculty of . . . (Harvey) 8-3-50
   by the . . . of faith (*Galatians*) 6-5-13
   faith cometh by . . . (*Romans*) 6-5-12
HEART
   agitation extends to the . . . (Harvey) 18-3-45

a good . . . is the sun (Shakespeare) 9-14-26
a . . . which dares not feel (Montesquieu) 2-3-82
already in his . . . (*Matthew*) 2-3-21
and a pure . . . (*Psalms*) 9-14-4
an understanding . . . to judge (*I Kings*) 9-15-1
as he thinketh in his . . . (*Proverbs*) 5-1-1
carry in one's . . . one's accuser (Juvenal) 9-5-3
character of a man's . . . (Hobbes) 1-4-25
consume my . . . away (Yeats) 16-1-62
create in me a clean . . . (*Psalms*) 20-14-4
every . . . were just (Molière) 9-10-83
expressions of the human . . . (Rousseau) 2-1-32
faint . . . will make (Thucydides) 4-2-4
fool said in his . . . (Anselm) 20-5-36
gave my . . . to know wisdom (*Eccles.*) 9-15-7
hardness of the unbelieving . . . (Wm. James) 19-4-49
. . . has reasons which reason does not (Pascal) 3-1-54
hidden man of the . . . (*I Peter*) 1-7-44
imagine evil in your . . . (*Zechariah*) 9-7-5
imagine the . . . to be (Galen) 19-2-18
in her husband's . . . (Shakespeare) 1-7-82
I said in my . . . (*Eccles.*) 9-15-8
. . . is full of evil (*Eccles.*) 9-6-3
. . . is on the left side (Molière) 18-1-29
. . . is the beginning of life (Harvey) 17-2-30
know by . . . is not to know (Montaigne) 8-3-41
know in my . . . (Homer) 2-2-8
law written in every . . . (Hobbes) 9-3-18
learned by . . . the same book (Pascal) 8-3-53
lecher's . . . a small spark (Shakespeare) 3-3-51
let thy . . . cheer thee (*Eccles.*) 1-3-2
love maddens the . . . (Euripides) 3-1-6
makes a stone of the . . . (Yeats) 4-6-54
makes my . . . flutter (Sappho) 3-3-6
mighty . . . is lying still (Shakespeare) 19-1-84
movements of his . . . (Augustine) 1-4-12
my . . . is pure (Tennyson) 9-10-113
my . . . is turned to stone (Shakespeare) 4-8-17
my . . . leaps up (Wordsworth) 1-3-99
. . . of a chicken have I (Cervantes) 5-4-15
. . . of man lodged (Congreve) 1-7-106
. . . of this people fat (*Isaiah*) 6-5-2
parts of the . . . (Harvey) 17-2-29
. . . peoples' is waxed gross (*Matthew*) 6-5-7
pity wells up in gentle . . . (Chaucer) 4-8-14
quench my furnace-burning . . . (Shakespeare) 4-6-30
rejoice with all their . . . (Anselm) 3-5-17
sayings in her . . . (*Luke*) 2-2-27
studied the . . . of man (Pascal) 7-2-60
than a . . . untainted (Shakespeare) 9-7-37
the clean of . . . (Aquinas) 9-8-33
the pure in . . . (*Matthew*) 9-8-19
their foolish . . . was darkened (*Romans*) 20-13-19
there will your . . . be also (*Matthew*) 20-15-21
thine . . . is not with me (*Judges*) 1-7-2
this . . . shall break (Shakespeare) 5-6-18
thou hast proved mine . . . (*Psalms*) 20-8-5
to wear a . . . so white (Shakespeare) 1-8-89
wear him in my . . . of (Shakespeare) 9-4-34
were with his . . . (Byron) 2-1-39
what is the . . . (Hobbes) 10-1-21
. . . which experiences God (Pascal) 20-5-72
who have a humble . . . (Pascal) 6-5-58
HEARTH
   . . . of which one worships (Dewey) 1-1-130
   no more the blazing . . . (Gray) 1-8-115
   woman for the . . . (Tennyson) 1-7-137
HEARTS
   all . . . from love receive (Chaucer) 3-1-21

HISTORY (*Cont.*)
   study of ... (Hume) 1-7-113
   superiority of poetry over ... (Arnold) 16-3-91
   ... surveys a presentation (Tolstoy) 15-3-112
   the heroes of ... (Tolstoy) 1-6-73
   the ... of the world (Hegel) 20-5-100
   turning point in ... (Dewey) 17-1-104
   ... warns us (Huxley) 6-3-114
   ... was biography of (Carlyle) 1-6-63
   whole of human ... (Kierkegaard) 6-6-39
   women have no ... (G. Eliot) 1-7-151
HISTORY
   the future date of my ... (Gibbon) 15-1-55
HOARDER
   seller becomes a ... of money (Marx) 4-9-16
HOAX
   keeps up the ... (Emerson) 20-1-56
HOBBES, Thomas
   social contract of ... (Russell) 7-1-65
HOBBY-HORSE
   his ... grows headstrong (Sterne) 9-4-41
HOGWASH
   universal struggle for ... (Shaw) 19-8-92
HOIST
   ... with his own petar (Shakespeare) 16-1-23
HOLD
   nice of no vile ... (Shakespeare) 10-6-23
HOLIDAY
   time takes no ... (Augustine) 19-7-17
   to make a Roman ... (Byron) 2-1-39
HOLIDAYS
   all the year were ... (Shakespeare) 11-3-19
   envy keeps no ... (Bacon) 4-8-19
HOLINESS
   as an ideal of ... (Kant) 9-9-33
   entirely spiritual ... (Pascal) 20-4-35
   image of ... and virtue (Kant) 9-1-22
   ... is science of worship (Cicero) 20-8-24
   ... of the heart's affections (Keats) 5-4-34
   with ... I will pass my life (Hippocrates) 18-2-1
   worship in the beauty of ... (*Psalms*) 20-8-6
HOLY
   humanity must be ... (Kant) 9-3-30
   keep ... in the sight of God (Sophocles) 20-8-15
   keep the sabbath ... (*Exodus*) 9-3-1
   let him be ... still (*Revelation*) 19-8-19
   the ... has been acknowledged (Plato) 20-8-19
   thou art ... (*Psalms*) 4-5-3
   who buys ... (Lucian) 17-1-34
HOLY GHOST
   a gift of the ... (Aquinas) 9-15-40
   baptize you with the ... (*Luke*) 20-3-12
   divinely of the ... (Th. Browne) 20-5-69
   filled with the ... (*Luke*) 1-7-37
   gift of God in the ... (Luther) 20-3-25
   gifts of the ... (*Hebrews*) 6-5-15
   is governed by the ... (Aquinas) 20-4-15
   lie to the ... (*Acts*) 9-14-13
   middler the ... (Joyce) 20-5-125
   more clearly than the ... (Locke) 20-9-29
   receive ye the ... (*John*) 20-4-10
   ... shall come upon thee (*Luke*) 1-7-36
   sinning in the ... (Chaucer) 4-5-15
   sins against the ... (Luther) 20-13-62
   supported by the ... (Luther) 20-4-24
   the ... often calls good (Montaigne) 16-6-30
   the ... over the bent world (Hopkins) 20-5-114, 20-14-55
   the Paraclete the ... (Augustine) 20-9-4
   the Word and the ... (*I John*) 20-3-19

HOLY GRAIL
   gold as its ... (Marx) 4-9-17
HOLY OF HOLIES
   one was called the ... (Aquinas) 20-2-22
   tabernacle called the ... (Aquinas) 20-2-23
HOLY ONE
   the ... of Israel (*Isaiah*) 20-2-17; (Hobbes) 20-2-27
HOLY PLACE
   to the most ... (*I Kings*) 20-2-12
HOLY SCRIPTURE(S)
   read some chapter of ... (Rabelais) 8-1-23
   signs contained in ... (Augustine) 7-1-14
   the interpreter of ... (Augustine) 8-3-30
   the student ... (Augustine) 6-1-29
HOLY SPIRIT
   burning love of the ... (Dante) 20-7-34
   ... inclines us to act (Aquinas) 9-4-26
   in the pleasure of the ... (Dante) 20-15-56
   is not the sin against the ... (Luther) 20-13-61
   ... often eases former ones (Calvin) 20-7-38
   other fruits of the ... (Spinoza) 20-3-35
   power of the ... (Luther) 20-4-23, 20-14-33
   sent the promised ... (Augustine) 20-4-13
   statements of the ... (Montaigne) 9-15-47
   take not thy ... from me (*Psalms*) 20-14-4
HOLY WATER
   ... in a dry house (Shakespeare) 19-1-39
HOME
   but sit at ... (Aristophanes) 1-7-24
   desire your old ... (Homer) 2-3-8
   father's ... and city (Euripides) 5-5-7
   goes wrong at ... (Euripides) 2-2-15
   his own ... and (Homer) 2-1-6
   ... is the girls' prison (Shaw) 1-7-162
   man goeth to his long ... (*Eccles.*) 1-3-3
   man who is sick of ... (Lucretius) 1-2-15
   remain with pleasure at ... (Pascal) 1-2-53
   turns again ... (Tennyson) 1-8-127
   we are never at ... (Montaigne) 1-2-31
HOMER
   ... admirable as he is (Aristotle) 16-3-11
   as ... knew very well (Rabelais) 16-2-7
   as ... says who give (Plato) 6-6-2
   as the Grecians held ... (Dryden) 16-3-49
   awe and love of ... (Plato) 6-3-6
   described by ... (Gibbon) 16-3-59
   ... has admirably delineated (Cervantes) 5-6-24
   ... has ascribed to Jove (Fielding) 16-3-51
   ... himself hath been (Horace) 16-7-8
   laid *Iliad* of ... under his pillow (Plutarch) 8-3-21
   ... Lucan and Statius (Chaucer) 16-2-5
   more to the community than ... (Epictetus) 2-1-19
   Musaeus and Hesiod and ... (Plato) 1-8-15
   not ... his glory divine (Aristophanes) 16-4-2
   Plato to esteem of ... (Jonson) 16-4-20
   quote the authority of ... (Plato) 8-1-1
   single exception of ... (Shaw) 16-3-96
   that deep-browed ... (Keats) 16-3-80
   that is ... the sovereign poet (Dante) 16-3-24
   the eulogists of ... (Plato) 16-3-6
   the translator of ... (Arnold) 16-3-94
   what ... says that Tiresias (Plato) 9-10-7
   when speaking about ... (Plato) 16-3-5
   ... would have writ (Fielding) 6-1-71
   would he not say with ... (Plato) 1-2-13
HOMERIC
   charm of the ... poems (Hegel) 19-1-91
HOMER'S
   be ... works your study (Pope) 16-7-23

HUMAN

... and divine good (Plato) 9-6-12

everything ... is so pathetic (Twain) 20-15-105

innate in any ... (Chaucer) 19-1-24

murder a real ... (Augustine) 1-5-42

no God and no ... (Spinoza) 9-15-75

pale of what is strictly ... (Bergson) 16-4-48

HUMAN BEING

deprive a ... of life (Fielding) 1-5-102

man is a ... (Twain) 1-1-121

no single ... is complete (Herodotus) 9-8-2

the exceptional ... (Nietzsche) 9-9-46

type of the strong ... (Nietzsche) 12-4-74

whatever helps to shape the ... (Mill) 8-1-71

HUMAN BEINGS

... are not like sheep (Mill) 13-1-54

... become a noble (Mill) 1-4-55

fully developed ... (Marx) 8-1-67

meanest and cruellest ... (Johnson) 4-9-11

most spiritual ... (Nietzsche) 1-4-62

no they're ... (Seneca) 10-7-10

sought great ... (Nietzsche) 1-6-76

HUMANITY

all his life he loved ... (Dostoevsky) 20-9-47

... are the plaster of God (Isak Dinesen) 16-3-104

... as the choice member of (Plotinus) 1-1-34

between bestiality and ... (Dewey) 1-1-130

find our primitive ... (Bergson) 15-2-84

functions of ... (Tacitus) 1-5-38

heightens sense of ... (Whitehead) 16-1-56

his assumption of ... (Augustine) 18-3-31

idea of ... as an end (Kant) 1-9-38

injuries done to ... (Montesquieu) 14-1-63

... is one immense army (Bergson) 19-2-63

mental constitution of ... (Freud) 9-6-115

movement of ... is continuous (Tolstoy) 15-1-79

... must be holy (Kant) 9-3-30

... not an animal species (Beauvoir) 15-2-93

offend against ... (Rousseau) 2-2-75

progeny of common ... (Johnson) 16-3-54

right of ... (Kant) 2-1-38

so is that of ... (Homer) 1-8-5

strife of frail ... (Wordsworth) 9-9-36

to know Christ in his ... (Luther) 15-3-71

universal aims of ... (Tolstoy) 15-3-110

HUMAN LIFE

the little span of ... (Schopenhauer) 1-2-76

HUMAN NATURE

as what ... will do (Kant) 15-2-44

changeless as ... (Bernard) 16-1-48

... comprised of three sexes (Plato) 3-3-9

conception of ... is sound (Santayana) 19-1-123

congruous with ... (Wm. James) 14-1-105

for want of understanding ... (Swift) 4-11-28

give us the clue of ... (Hume) 6-2-27

greater knowledge of ... (Wordsworth) 16-3-70

greatest variety of ... (Plato) 10-4-3

idols inherent in ... (Bacon) 6-4-19

inclination of ... (Aquinas) 9-12-17

inconveniences of ... (Locke) 6-5-70

infirmity of ... (Polybius) 15-3-25

in ... more of the fool (Bacon) 9-15-66

inmost essence of ... (Freud) 9-6-116

in the higher reaches of ... (Santayana) 5-1-85

... is in bondage (Aristotle) 17-1-11

... is not a machine (Mill) 1-1-116

... is so infected (Aquinas) 20-7-30

instincts of ... (Tacitus) 13-3-8

knowledge of ... (Mill) 5-6-38; (Gibbon) 15-1-51

language proper to ... (Montaigne) 7-1-22

living facts of ... (Wm. James) 17-1-95

... loves the knowledge of its existence (Augustine) 1-1-36

model of ... (Spinoza) 9-6-82

... needs the help of God (Aquinas) 1-2-27

original principles in ... (Smith) 11-5-13

perfect idea of ... (Gibbon) 1-2-69

perplexity of ... (Hume) 6-6-27

power of ... (Aquinas) 8-2-9

reasonings concerning ... (Hume) 6-1-74

reflections of ... (Hamilton/Madison) 10-3-49

... remains the same (Hume) 1-2-58

selfishness of ... (Gibbon) 11-1-35

slow improvement of ... (Comte) 15-2-51

the infirmities of ... (Boswell) 9-6-88

... the perfection of virtue (Fielding) 9-10-93

there existed the whole ... (Augustine) 20-13-35

there is no ... (Sartre) 1-1-132

they are beneficial to ... (Spinoza) 9-6-82

... to hate the man whom (Tacitus) 3-2-11

to prefer evil is not in ... (Plato) 9-6-8

universally true of ... (Plato) 9-13-2

... was taught and constrained (Epicurus) 15-2-8

who didst ... so enable (Dante) 20-8-53

HUMAN NATURES

testing ... in play (Plato) 10-2-7

HUMAN RACE

childhood days of the ... (Freud) 20-1-83

... derived from one man (Augustine) 1-1-37

destruction of the ... (Seneca) 15-2-13

head of four-fifths of the ... (Twain) 20-7-75

... in two parts (Augustine) 15-3-52

physician to the ... (Bernard) 18-2-43

see all the ... (Hume) 15-1-41

the ... existed before (Augustine) 19-8-31

whole ... has been condemned (Augustine) 20-13-39

HUMAN REALITY

... is free (Sartre) 5-7-53

HUMAN RELATIONS

first place in ... (Montaigne) 16-6-30

HUMBLE

tends to elevate the ... (Tocqueville) 13-3-29

HUME, David

... and other sceptics (Boswell) 6-6-31

as ... said with profound truth (Santayana) 5-1-86

critics as ... says (Kant) 16-7-38

in ... for example (Russell) 17-1-99

psychology derived from ... (Wm. James) 7-1-61

... related to me (Boswell) 3-3-61

... said to me (Boswell) 1-8-118

HUME'S, David

mention ... argument (Boswell) 20-11-33

mentioned ... notion (Boswell) 9-8-58

HUMILITY

by her present ... (Augustine) 20-4-13

Christianity is ... (Tolstoy) 20-4-51

deficiency is undue ... (Aristotle) 1-5-15

is something in ... (Augustine) 20-8-44

... is wise (Euripides) 20-8-18

... like darkness reveals (Thoreau) 11-2-133

modest stillness and ... (Shakespeare) 14-1-45

refinement is not ... (Newman) 9-1-31

results from ... (Aquinas) 9-8-33

... taking the form of (Kant) 20-12-33

HUMOR

banishing all ... (Fielding) 16-4-27

dogs show a sense of ... (Darwin) 1-1-109

melancholy and gloomy ... (Smith) 16-4-34

... of ancient philosophers (Boswell) 6-5-79

destined hour of an ... (Dostoevsky) 3-5-43
determine the leading ... (Newman) 20-3-56
distinguished ... from object (Plato) 16-7-2
... for which I can live (Kierkegaard) 1-4-43
fundamental ... of poetry (Schiller) 16-3-62
having the ... of everything (Locke) 6-1-68
imagination is an ... (Spinoza) 5-4-20
... is an object of senses (Berkeley) 5-2-29
... is merely an effect (Lavoisier) 17-2-66
myself existent as ... (Hegel) 12-3-25
... of what is beautiful (Darwin) 16-6-69
realizations of the ... (Hegel) 10-1-39
reception of disconnected ... (Whitehead) 8-3-91
should preserve the ... (Hume) 19-6-33
shown only in ... (Plato) 6-3-7
the ... against nature (Hegel) 1-6-54
the ... is everything (Arnold) 16-3-90
three relations of the ... (Hegel) 16-1-43
to produce an ... acceptable (Peirce) 6-1-97
turn to some unexpected ... (Tolstoy) 5-6-39
... unattainable of realization (Kant) 3-4-55
who has a true ... (Spinoza) 6-3-74
words remain only ... (Montesquieu) 7-1-44
wrong use of word ... (Boswell) 7-2-79

IDEAL
able to live up to my ... (Shaw) 16-6-78
aim at the distant ... (Whitehead) 16-1-55
always remain an ... (Kant) 17-1-77
an ... external history (Vico) 15-2-30
apes of their ... (Nietzsche) 1-6-76
boy's first ... (Freud) 1-6-84
cannot attain the ... (Hegel) 1-7-130
child like the representation of the ... (Schiller) 1-3-94
create a higher ... (Dostoevsky) 20-3-58
friendship an ... possession (Santayana) 3-4-64
human race finds its ... (Arnold) 20-1-70
narcissistic ... of the man (Freud) 2-1-54
rhythm of the ... realm (Plotinus) 16-5-14
... set up by society (Freud) 2-2-98
suffer a negative ... (Poincaré) 6-3-136
Supreme Being a mere ... (Kant) 20-9-44
the ... as an ultimate (Wm. James) 9-6-111
the ... of brute beasts (Cicero) 3-4-19

IDEALIST PHILOSOPHY
experience in the ... (Russell) 6-2-49

IDEALITY
... in contrast with reality (Whitehead) 16-1-56
the ... of time and space (Schopenhauer) 19-7-73

IDEALIZATION
ancient ... of poverty (Wm. James) 11-2-155

IDEALS
... of his culture (Freud) 15-2-81
other person's ... (Wm. James) 1-4-65
were ... in life higher (Santayana) 15-2-85

IDEAS
... accompanied by pleasure or pain (Locke) 4-7-48
a certain collection of ... (Berkeley) 20-5-89
agreement of two ... (Sterne) 6-7-32
all ... resolved into a few (Leibniz) 7-2-69
... and types of things (Lucian) 17-1-34
... are copies of impressions (Hume) 5-1-48
arise from subjective ... (Hegel) 3-6-22
a super-world of ... (Whitehead) 17-1-98
attend to ... signified (Berkeley) 7-1-40
... began to expand (Rousseau) 7-1-48
between true and false ... (Santayana) 6-3-148
brutes have no abstract ... (Berkeley) 7-1-39
by intervention of other ... (Locke) 17-3-33
can excite ... in my mind (Locke) 5-2-28

cannot exceed original stock of ... (Hume) 5-4-24
certain concatenation of ... (Spinoza) 5-3-21
... come from experience (Santayana) 5-6-44
... come to be united in mind (Locke) 9-2-22
connection of ... does not imply (Berkeley) 19-3-35
connect sounds with ... (Darwin) 7-1-56
constant decay of all our ... (Locke) 5-3-23
contiguous association of ... (Wm. James) 6-7-43
... derived only from words (Thucydides) 1-6-5
... do not depend on will (Descartes) 5-2-21
entertain in human ... (Swift) 10-2-65
false ... the only useful (Wm. James) 6-3-131
finding intermediate ... (Locke) 17-2-49
from sensations to indefinite ... (Kant) 16-5-37
... from which nature derives (Plotinus) 16-1-14
general ... and words (Rousseau) 7-1-49
grades in the generality of ... (Whitehead) 6-1-102
... have entered his head (Kant) 16-1-35
have no general ... (Toynbee) 15-1-99
... have no influence (Hume) 6-3-85
... imprinted by Author of nature (Berkeley) 5-2-29
... imprinted on the senses (Berkeley) 6-1-70
... inherent in the world (Schopenhauer) 16-6-63
... may be called true (Locke) 6-3-79
method which employs abstract ... (Schopenhauer) 8-1-55
mode of expressing ... (Whitehead) 7-1-64
most general ... (Montaigne) 1-4-17
names stand for general ... (Locke) 7-1-34
new and striking ... (Arnold) 17-1-88
no abstract or general ... (Hume) 7-1-45
no language can express all ... (Voltaire) 7-1-46
no object but ... (Locke) 6-1-67
not enough to have ... (Locke) 7-2-70, 7-2-72
not ... of the mind (Schopenhauer) 4-6-48
notions of expressing definite ... (Darwin) 1-1-110
number of inadequate ... (Spinoza) 4-1-21
number of the greatest ... (Ruskin) 16-1-46
of sense or reflection (Locke) 5-1-41
... of the noble (Aristotle) 9-6-18
... of things (Leibniz) 7-2-66
only ... they shall have (Wm. James) 8-3-89
or any of the other higher ... (Plato) 16-6-6
pain and pleasure are ... (Locke) 4-7-49
possession of felicitating ... (Boswell) 20-15-86
possession of their ... (Turgot) 15-2-36
... produced by impulse (Locke) 5-2-26
... prophets never dreamed of (Spinoza) 6-5-67
put wrong ... together (Locke) 5-6-30
rather than correct the ... (Toynbee) 15-1-100
real relations of ... (Hume) 4-1-28, 6-3-86, 17-3-35
receive as distinct ... (Locke) 5-1-40
representations of ... (Leibniz) 7-2-68
representations of imagination are ... (Kant) 5-4-29
resettlements of our ... (Wm. James) 5-1-72
senses let in particular ... (Locke) 7-1-33
shall find our ... always (Locke) 19-5-50
so they are complex ... (Locke) 19-5-51
sounds interpreters of ... (Rousseau) 7-1-47
spontaneous interest in ... (Dewey) 8-1-91
... spring from wants (Lavoisier) 6-1-84
succession of ... in our minds (Berkeley) 19-7-57
thousand kinds of ... (Rousseau) 7-2-77
toward new ... (Newman) 6-1-96
trivial ... in grand words (Schopenhauer) 16-2-40
true ... are those we can (Wm. James) 6-3-133
unites former images and ... (Darwin) 5-4-38
use of words is to express ... (Madison) 7-2-86
... we owe to use of speech (Rousseau) 7-2-76
... which have disappeared (Locke) 5-3-22

... is not only agitated (Spinoza) 9-15-76
... is still more despised (Hume) 8-1-44
man is born ... of (Spinoza) 19-3-30
man is ... of justice (Pascal) 12-2-35
... of their nature (Plato) 9-6-9
render themselves more ... (Descartes) 17-1-52
road open to the most ... (Descartes) 6-5-48
to have been ... of the world (Boswell) 6-2-31
to remain ... (Cicero) 15-1-12

ILION
sacred ... shall perish (Homer) 2-2-8

ILIUM
the corpse fires at ... (Aeschylus) 14-1-5

ILL
alternate good and ... (Herodotus) 1-2-7
capable of all ... (Shakespeare) 7-1-25
every ... that falls (Herodotus) 1-2-8
every physical ... makes (Hume) 19-8-70
good and ... common (Rousseau) 9-6-80
keep them all from ... (Locke) 8-3-60
men act ... (Mill) 9-5-26
not to be is a great ... (Voltaire) 19-8-74
to do ... his sole delight (Milton) 9-6-76

ILLATION
pure ... of one thing from another (Descartes) 6-7-20

ILL-DOING
knew not the doctrine of ... (Shakespeare) 1-3-58

ILLEGITIMATE
power they believe ... (Tocqueville) 10-2-93

ILL-FATED
are not the miserable ... (Plato) 9-6-9

ILL-GIVING
... has deprived them (Dante) 4-9-4

ILLIMITABLE
... thing called time (Carlyle) 19-7-74

ILLITERATE
an ... man to discuss with (Epictetus) 6-7-13

ILL-LUCK
sensitivity of morals and ... (Freud) 9-5-30

ILLNESS
an ... that's swift (Seneca) 18-3-25
regard bad conscience as serious ... (Nietzsche) 9-5-28
so caused the ... of the king (Herodotus) 18-3-4

ILLNESSES
art of curing ... (Shaw) 18-1-38
refuge from ... (Sophocles) 1-1-7

ILLS
against the ... of life (Schopenhauer) 1-5-119
bear those ... we have (Shakespeare) 1-9-27
beyond the ... (Augustine) 1-8-57
cause of all our ... (Pascal) 1-2-53
enough necessary ... (Montaigne) 1-2-34
... of our making (Rousseau) 18-3-53
... of time (Augustine) 1-9-21
old age of all ... (Rousseau) 1-3-81
so are the ... (Cicero) 5-1-8
so rest of all human ... (Herodotus) 6-1-2
source of the ... that oppress (Montaigne) 1-1-53
their ... instruct us (Shakespeare) 2-3-63
... with which we are threatened (Hume) 1-2-59

ILLUSION
a logic of ... (Kant) 7-2-82
... can have no value (Freud) 1-8-140
depends upon this ... (Freud) 20-4-53
life a perpetual ... (Pascal) 3-4-42
look evil in the face without ... (Shaw) 9-6-113
made happy by an ... (Kierkegaard) 20-3-50
no ... disturbs us (Augustine) 6-6-8
of a sentimental ... (Santayana) 1-8-143

to adhere to the ... (Freud) 20-2-51

ILLUSIONS
in this kingdom of ... (Emerson) 9-14-57
of all the ... (Montaigne) 1-5-55
with their ... (G. Eliot) 1-4-59

ILLUSORY
change is ... (Dewey) 19-5-71

IMAGE
... a mirror of displays (Dante) 7-1-20
... and glory of ... (*I Corinthians*) 1-7-40
an ... made without hands (Gibbon) 20-12-31
borne the ... of the earthly (*I Corinthians*) 1-1-28
... gives power to see (Lucretius) 5-2-6
glory of God into an ... (*Romans*) 20-13-19
graven ... of a duty (Plutarch) 20-6-30
horrid ... doth unfix (Shakespeare) 5-4-13
in beholding His ... (Augustine) 6-1-26
in the ... of God (*Genesis*) 12-4-1
is the ... of man and nature (Wordsworth) 16-3-71
kills the ... of God (Milton) 16-2-21
make any graven ... (*Exodus*) 9-3-1
make thee any graven ... (*Deut.*) 20-2-11
man in our ... (Milton) 1-1-75
nature of the ... of God (Pascal) 19-1-51
no idols nor graven ... (*Leviticus*) 20-2-9
no outward ... visible (Plato) 6-3-7
nor worship the golden ... (*Daniel*) 20-11-2
... of democracy itself (Tocqueville) 10-4-53
... of God (Milton) 2-3-72
... of his Maker (Shakespeare) 1-5-75
... of the condition of men (Pascal) 1-2-54
... of the eternal gods (Plato) 19-7-4
... of the original event (Wm. James) 5-3-28
... of their glorious Maker (Milton) 1-7-95
... of the Son of God (Augustine) 1-7-48
prohibition against making an ... (Freud) 20-2-50
... slipping from the arm's embrace (Aeschylus) 5-5-4
the ... of His Son (*Romans*) 15-3-37
was made in His ... (Augustine) 10-7-13

IMAGERY
copious ... directly ordered (Hobbes) 5-3-19
the setting of ... (Keats) 16-3-82

IMAGES
... and relics banished (Gibbon) 20-12-32
... attach to the sensible (Wm. James) 7-1-62
by ... I mean shadows (Plato) 6-1-5
experiences are the ... (Aristotle) 7-1-8
expressed in their ... (Locke) 20-6-39
have no ... of the gods (Herodotus) 20-6-8
how these ... were formed (Augustine) 5-3-8
masses of ... show (Santayana) 6-2-54
monstrous ... are created (Dostoevsky) 5-5-35
not allow any ... (Tacitus) 20-2-19
... of external objects (Poincaré) 19-6-41
... of soul's primal state (Plotinus) 9-1-4
... of time and its passing (Augustine) 19-7-18
... presented to our fancy (Hume) 6-3-85
retain ... of sounds (Augustine) 5-3-9
... same flux of images (Santayana) 17-1-111
the ... were demolished (Gibbon) 20-9-41
there are some carv'd ... (Cervantes) 20-8-61
worship paid to ... (Aquinas) 20-8-48

IMAGINATION
affectations of his ... (Spinoza) 16-7-18
affects only the ... (Boswell) 5-6-32
... also suspended (Aquinas) 5-5-16
... as thinking (Aristotle) 4-4-4
... as truer avenue to knowledge (Santayana) 6-1-114
... becomes languid (Gibbon) 7-1-53

IMAGINATION (*Cont.*)
by means of . . . (Kant) 5-5-30
can move the human . . . (Aquinas) 20-7-27
comes from the power of the . . . (Montaigne) 20-12-18
confederacy with the . . . (Bacon) 17-2-16
enlargement of the . . . (Dewey) 17-3-61
. . . ever-wandering (Lavoisier) 17-2-66
fancies of the . . . (Aquinas) 8-2-11
fill ourselves with . . . (Pascal) 6-7-29
. . . find what they crave (Santayana) 16-6-83
freedom of . . . in man (Montaigne) 1-1-53
freedom to the . . . (Kant) 16-3-61
free play of the . . . (Kant) 7-2-85
. . . has this peculiarity (Pascal) 5-4-19
ideas of the . . . called images (Berkeley) 5-2-29
. . . incapable of coping (Santayana) 6-3-147
. . . in conversation (Boswell) 7-2-80
. . . is naturally sublime (Hume) 5-4-25
. . . is not required (Boswell) 15-1-47
live by . . . (Santayana) 1-5-130
lower power such as . . . (Aquinas) 6-4-9
. . . makes an idea particular (Rousseau) 7-1-49
. . . needs to be fed (Santayana) 6-1-116
no cause to complain of . . . (Montaigne) 5-5-20
of . . . all compact (Shakespeare) 16-3-31
peculiarly vivid . . . (Spinoza) 20-10-37
reverence requires . . . (Russell) 8-3-93
support the . . . (Hume) 17-1-68
sweeten my . . . (Shakespeare) 1-7-87
symbolism and unconscious . . . (Freud) 7-1-70
the place of . . . (Dewey) 16-1-60
things he attains in . . . (Spinoza) 4-11-25
to set . . . roving (Hegel) 16-1-42
your diseased . . . (Rousseau) 18-2-39
IMAGINATIONS
became vain in their . . . (*Romans*) 20-13-19
creatures of their . . . (Calvin) 20-12-17
in awe of their own . . . (Hobbes) 20-12-23
. . . of them that sleep (Hobbes) 5-5-24
violence of their . . . (Locke) 5-6-30
IMAGINING
resemblance of present . . . (Russell) 5-3-31
IMBECILITY
a testimony of . . . (Montaigne) 12-2-27
impression of . . . (Plato) 17-1-9
. . . of human judgment (Montaigne) 10-2-40
the lord of . . . (Shakespeare) 10-2-44
IMITATE
too prone to . . . (Juvenal) 2-2-32
IMITATED
virtues capable of being . . . (Burke) 9-10-107
IMITATION
acts of . . . (Aristotle) 16-1-9
a model for . . . (Freud) 16-1-59
busy about . . . (Jonson) 16-3-38
comedy is an . . . (Aristotle) 16-4-7
draw or deter their . . . (Locke) 8-3-58
. . . is always of one thing (Aristotle) 16-4-10
. . . is natural to man (Aristotle) 1-1-24, 16-3-7
. . . is not to be judged (Plato) 16-5-5
most proper for . . . (Johnson) 16-1-29
never encourage . . . (Ruskin) 16-1-47
not derived from . . . (Kant) 6-1-35
novelty in the . . . (Plato) 16-4-5
. . . of natural objects (Plotinus) 16-1-14
. . . of the forms of nature (Gibbon) 16-1-30
. . . of what really exists (Fielding) 16-4-28
origin of language in . . . (Darwin) 7-1-58
sister arts of . . . (Plato) 16-3-6

the . . . of speech (Montaigne) 7-2-43
tragedy essentially an . . . (Aristotle) 16-4-9
tragedy is the . . . (Aristotle) 16-4-8
we see only their . . . (Johnson) 16-4-32
IMITATIONS
are but . . . of nature (Harvey) 16-1-25
movements are . . . of manners (Plato) 16-7-3
when men hear . . . (Aristotle) 16-5-7
IMITATOR
he is no . . . (Aristotle) 16-3-11
IMMENSITY
we have absolute . . . (Descartes) 20-5-62
IMMOBILE
world . . . as a whole (Kepler) 19-8-44
IMMORALITY
the dangers of . . . (Freud) 9-4-50
the . . . of trade (Thoreau) 11-5-35
to be ashamed of one's . . . (Nietzsche) 9-1-35
IMMORTAL
all be made . . . (Milton) 9-10-80
if we are not to be . . . (Cicero) 1-8-31
love neither mortal nor . . . (Plato) 3-1-9
mind set free is . . . (Aristotle) 5-1-6
nothing can be . . . (Hobbes) 10-1-24
to become at once . . . (Aristotle) 9-6-13
to make himself . . . (Pascal) 1-8-108
will never become . . . (Condorcet) 15-2-46
IMMORTALITY
activity of God is . . . (Aristotle) 19-8-8
. . . attends virtue (Shakespeare) 5-1-20
convinced of . . . (Freud) 1-8-138
enjoyment of . . . (Augustine) 1-9-20
for the sake of . . . (Plato) 1-5-10
from the joy of . . . (Anselm) 1-2-26
. . . has knowledge (Euripides) 20-15-10
identify fame with . . . (Santayana) 1-5-130
if . . . unveil a third event (Dickinson) 20-15-98
love is of . . . (Plato) 3-1-10
man the heir to . . . (Twain) 9-1-33
misery to a blessed . . . (Augustine) 20-14-22
no foretaste of . . . (Thoreau) 1-3-118
offer of . . . here below (Rousseau) 1-8-116
. . . of the soul (Tocqueville) 20-1-53; (Pascal) 20-3-31
. . . of things (Whitman) 9-15-90
. . . only a reiteration (Santayana) 19-7-92
preferred to . . . (Bacon) 2-3-68
proof of soul's . . . (Plato) 5-3-1
shall put on . . . (Augustine) 20-15-37
. . . suffers in his (Th. Browne) 20-15-71
temporal . . . of (Wittgenstein) 1-8-142
this conception of . . . (Arnold) 20-15-100
this mortal must put on . . . (*I Corinthians*) 20-15-28
want to live for . . . (Dostoevsky) 20-9-46
which lead to . . . (Augustine) 15-2-19
with so sure an . . . (Augustine) 20-15-33
IMMORTALS
among the blessed . . . (Homer) 20-15-4
man who fights the . . . (Homer) 20-6-1
not a man but the . . . (Euripides) 20-8-16
ranked you with . . . (Homer) 1-8-9
the blessed . . . retain (Augustine) 20-8-43
the . . . go forth and stand (Plato) 6-3-3
the very . . . can be moved (Homer) 20-8-11
IMMOVABLE
space always remains . . . (Newton) 19-6-27
IMPACT
moved by mutual . . . (Aristotle) 19-2-11
IMPEDIMENTS
absence of external . . . (Hobbes) 13-1-8

... to great enterprises (Bacon) 2-1-27
... to morality (Kant) 9-3-25
IMPENETRABILITY
... of dimensions (Pascal) 19-6-22
IMPERATIVE
his own categorical ... (Nietzsche) 9-9-45
language of desire of ... (Hobbes) 4-1-20
law a categorical ... (Kant) 12-4-60
laws are absolutely ... (Kant) 9-3-24
... use of words (Russell) 7-1-69
IMPERFECTION
... attaches to history (Schopenhauer) 15-1-66
... of the senses (Rabelais) 5-5-18
IMPERFECTIONS
... are so human (Santayana) 5-6-43
fasten thy ... on the stars (Th. Browne) 5-7-25
free from ... (Grotius) 10-3-19
piece out our ... (Shakespeare) 5-4-11
so many ... in nature (Spinoza) 9-6-82
IMPERISHABLES
aristocracy of the ... (Twain) 9-1-32
IMPERTINENCE
emptiness or fond ... (Milton) 9-15-72
from idles ... (Epictetus) 2-1-19
IMPETUOUS
intemperate life is ... (Plato) 9-12-5
IMPETUS
... of our zeal expires (Wm. James) 8-3-89
what the vital ... would do (Bergson) 19-2-60
IMPIETY
one quality is ... (Plato) 9-10-5
and what is ...? (Plato) 20-8-19
IMPIOUS
must of necessity be ... (Epictetus) 9-4-11
IMPLEMENTS
who has given us such ... (Epictetus) 20-8-38
IMPOTENCE
delighted by my ... (Spinoza) 9-15-75
government perishes from ... (Tocqueville) 10-4-56
... of free effort (Wm. James) 15-3-113
... of man to govern (Spinoza) 9-4-35
sinks to self-destructive ... (Dostoevsky) 3-4-61
IMPOTENT
your wealth is ... (Milton) 11-2-71
IMPORTANCE
evidence of ... (Boswell) 4-11-32
notion of personal ... (Tocqueville) 11-5-28
want of virtue than of ... (Johnson) 1-5-107
IMPOSE
what fates ... man must (Shakespeare) 15-3-77
IMPOSITIONS
... introduced by Augustus (Gibbon) 11-6-30
IMPOSSIBILITIES
enough in ... (Th. Browne) 6-5-54
IMPOSSIBILITY
a convincing ... preferable (Aristotle) 16-3-12
as a fantastic ... (Nietzsche) 16-3-95
attempt ... itself (Cervantes) 9-11-39
mistake difficulty for ... (Maritain) 6-6-56
IMPOSTS
taxes from ... (Hamilton) 11-6-40
IMPOSTURE
two great supporters of ... (Fielding) 16-7-26
IMPRESSION
a purely visual ... (Poincaré) 19-6-41
... as lively perception (Hume) 5-1-47
our spontaneous ... (Emerson) 1-4-45
sign and ... it makes (Augustine) 7-1-14
IMPRESSIONS

different ... on the mind (Bacon) 6-4-19
force of early ... (Mill) 9-3-35
imagination beset by ... (Descartes) 5-4-16
life hold same number of ... (Wm. James) 19-5-66
past ... extremely vivid (Darwin) 9-5-25
receive ... in consequence of motion (Lavoisier) 5-2-33
senses comprehend only ... (Montaigne) 5-2-19
trust my own ... (Thucydides) 15-1-3
we receive through ... (Kant) 6-2-34
IMPRISONS
... any unjustly (Thoreau) 12-2-49
IMPROVEMENT
aid in ... of anybody (Plato) 8-1-1
an end to all ... (Boswell) 13-2-32
barrier against ... (Mill) 20-2-44
hindrance to ... (Mill) 1-7-149
... of condition to all (Lincoln) 11-3-61
... of mental faculties (Darwin) 7-1-59
professors of moral ... (Plato) 8-3-3
IMPROVEMENTS
modern social ... (Mill) 1-7-144
one of the greatest ... (Smith) 11-3-34
IMPRUDENCE
effect of gross ... (Mill) 15-2-65
reproach himself for ... (Kant) 9-13-31
IMPUDENCE
to judge man's ... (Montaigne) 19-1-27
will its daring ... find limits (Euripides) 20-13-12
IMPULSE
... accompanied by pain (Aristotle) 4-3-7
acted upon by blind ... (Locke) 9-4-40
be an external ... (Boswell) 16-2-38
... from a vernal wood (Wordsworth) 6-2-35, 19-1-83
ideas produced by ... (Locke) 5-2-26
linguistic ... in man (Wm. James) 7-1-63
no power to restrain the ... (Spinoza) 5-7-27
... of their life (Hegel) 1-6-55
returned the ... of passion (Hume) 4-1-27
some ... frustrated (Santayana) 1-8-143
thinking is stoppage of ... (Dewey) 5-1-81
... to those in motion (Newton) 19-5-45
... without reason (Wm. James) 1-9-49
without some vital ... (Santayana) 6-3-149
IMPULSES
allow ... to run their course (Freud) 18-1-42
heaven set ... in motion (Dante) 5-7-14
nature implants contrary ... (Wm. James) 1-1-126
obey his persistent ... (Darwin) 9-9-41
obeys all ... (Freud) 8-3-97
partial sexual ... (Freud) 2-2-95
perverted ... (Freud) 4-7-67
strong ... and weak consciences (Mill) 9-5-26
... to wrong behaviour (Seneca) 9-12-13
two human ... (Russell) 17-1-99
IMPULSION
... from the souls (Russell) 19-5-69
habits lacking in ... (Dewey) 8-2-34
IMPUNITY
no greater hope of ... (Hobbes) 13-3-13
some circumstances provide one with ... (Seneca) 9-5-2
the ... of criminals (Montesquieu) 12-4-49
IMPURE
... not permitted to (Plato) 1-8-17
IMPURITY
actings of his own ... (Augustine) 3-3-22
we bring ... rather (Milton) 9-10-82
INACTION
not by weak ... (Tacitus) 14-1-30
occasion intervals of ... (Rousseau) 2-1-33

exploitation of one . . . (Marx and Engels) 14-1-100
extreme of . . . nature (Emerson) 1-6-66
independence of the . . . (Kant) 10-5-24
interest of the . . . (Wm. James) 20-1-76
. . . is the dupe of all (Bergson) 9-6-118
life history of the . . . (Benedict) 9-2-37
matched himself (Nietzsche) 9-9-44
no injustice to an . . . (Burke) 12-1-72
not the . . . is first (Plato) 10-2-8
of every . . . of mankind (Calvin) 15-3-72
only known in the . . . (Aquinas) 5-4-3
person not absolutely an . . . (Peirce) 6-6-47
physician to an . . . (Bernard) 18-2-43
relation of an . . . to God (Kierkegaard) 9-5-22
respect for the . . . (Thoreau) 10-4-61
state prior to the . . . (Aristotle) 10-1-6
truths about . . . things (Wm. James) 17-1-92

INDIVIDUALITIES
set up their paltry . . . (Schiller) 16-7-40

INDIVIDUALITY
all strive for . . . (Dostoevsky) 3-4-61
a more pronounced . . . (Mill) 1-6-71
any value on . . . (Mill) 5-6-38
objects aimed at by the . . . (Hegel) 1-3-109
. . . should assert itself (Mill) 13-1-53
so long as . . . exists (Mill) 10-6-70
. . . vanishes (Marx and Engels) 11-1-68
. . . within this unity (Hegel) 2-1-40

INDIVIDUALS
all my love is toward . . . (Swift) 3-2-29
. . . are responsible (Hegel) 9-6-100
differences between . . . (Tawney) 13-3-56
differ profoundly as . . . (Tawney) 13-3-56
initiation of noble things from . . . (Mill) 1-6-71
interest of . . . becomes the end (Hegel) 10-1-38
. . . lost in the crowd (Mill) 10-4-65
madness rare in . . . (Nietzsche) 5-6-40
obstinacy of . . . (Hamilton) 1-4-39
personal action against . . . (Hegel) 9-11-55
respects lives of . . . (Rousseau) 14-1-66
. . . should be punished (Boswell) 20-14-54
the singularities of . . . (Montesquieu) 19-5-55
we want . . . to be free (Dewey) 13-1-64

INDIVISIBLE
perfect friendship is . . . (Montaigne) 3-4-33

INDOCTRINATION
teaching meant . . . (Dewey) 6-7-47

INDO-EUROPEAN
. . . language (Russell) 7-1-65, 7-2-89

INDOLENCE
. . . increases misery (Montesquieu) 11-2-82

INDOLENCY
despair produces . . . (Locke) 4-5-26

INDOLENT
if . . . let him be poor (Shaw) 11-2-156

INDUCEMENTS
. . . to an act (Mill) 9-2-32

INDUCTION
continuous process of . . . (Einstein) 17-2-129
foundation of true . . . (Bacon) 6-4-19
fundamental axiom of . . . (Mill) 17-2-93
inferred by general . . . (Newton) 17-2-46
. . . presupposes metaphysics (Wm. James) 17-2-115
proceeds by . . . (Aristotle) 6-1-18

INDUCTIVE REASONING
training in . . . (Aristotle) 6-7-9

INDULGE
. . . a woman never (Homer) 1-7-6

INDULGENCE

ascribe any sensual . . . (Augustine) 20-7-17
from passionate . . . (Aristotle) 1-7-28
owing to a former . . . (Thoreau) 9-5-23
treated with . . . (Smith) 9-1-17
weak . . . will accuse (Milton) 1-7-100

INDULGENCES
from the abuse of . . . (Gibbon) 20-12-32
restrain from hurtful . . . (Mill) 9-12-49

INDUS
upon the bank of . . . (Dante) 9-7-35

INDUSTRIAL
tasks of . . . society (Tawney) 13-3-58

INDUSTRIAL ART
which may be called . . . (Kant) 16-1-33

INDUSTRIALISM
service of . . . (Santayana) 17-2-133

INDUSTRIES
. . . in eyes of others (Bacon) 11-3-20

INDUSTRIOUS
so . . . in your animals (Voltaire) 19-1-64

INDUSTRY
action of modern . . . (Marx and Engels) 2-1-45
art depending on . . . (Kant) 16-1-36
development of modern . . . (Marx and Engels) 10-8-33
encouragement to . . . (Lincoln) 11-2-135
experience is by . . . achieved (Shakespeare) 6-2-18
extinguish . . . and virtue (Gibbon) 15-3-104
fear to quicken . . . (Locke) 4-2-27
fruits of their . . . (Gibbon) 11-1-36
. . . has established market (Marx) 11-5-38
imitate their . . . (Rousseau) 19-1-65
. . . introduced into Europe (Gibbon) 11-5-20
. . . is also destroyed (Jefferson) 10-7-27
is to lay tax on . . . (Mill) 11-6-56
manured by . . . (Shakespeare) 9-10-66
method of organizing . . . (Shaw) 11-1-76
modern . . . by assigning (Marx) 2-1-44
no place for . . . (Hobbes) 1-2-50
obstruct . . . of a people (Smith) 11-6-24
own pursuits of . . . (Jefferson) 10-3-43
peace favorable to . . . (Tocqueville) 14-2-63
punishment on . . . (Hume) 11-6-17
the produce of . . . (Smith) 11-2-108
uphold the . . . of subjects (Hobbes) 14-1-52
whatever . . . might acquire (Smith) 11-2-104

INEFFICIENCY
. . . of federal government (Hamilton) 10-4-40

INEQUALITIES
absence of political . . . (Tawney) 13-3-58
differences relevant to . . . (Tawney) 13-3-55
purposely fostered . . . (Mill) 11-1-71
thus lessen . . . (Sumner) 13-3-47

INEQUALITY
arguments in favor of . . . (Arnold) 13-3-41
attendants of growing . . . (Rousseau) 11-1-27
. . . between animals of same species (Descartes) 7-1-28
economic . . . of men(Freud) 13-3-52
enormous intellectual . . . (Schopenhauer) 6-5-89
friendship of . . . (Aristotle) 3-4-14
happier in a state of . . . (Boswell) 13-3-24
inconveniences of . . . (Montesquieu) 11-5-7
. . . in manner of living (Rousseau) 18-3-53
instead of destroying . . . (Rousseau) 13-3-21
natural . . . unfolds (Rousseau) 11-3-29
. . . occurs likewise (Montesquieu) 11-6-13
. . . of condition indispensable (Calhoun) 13-3-34
. . . of minds would remain (Tocqueville) 13-3-33
. . . of political faculty (Huxley) 13-3-35
. . . of privilege (Mill) 10-8-36

from such . . . of men (Augustine) 6-1-28
. . . had taken root (Plutarch) 12-1-21
imperfect social . . . (Mill) 15-2-65
laws and . . . (Jefferson) 15-2-39
maintenance of his . . . (Plutarch) 1-9-8
our . . . are unique (Benedict) 15-2-90
. . . possess educational machine (Russell) 8-1-83
to subvert their . . . (Mill) 10-6-71
INSTRUCT
really able to . . . mankind (Plato) 8-3-6
INSTRUCTION
. . . about things or signs (Augustine) 7-1-12
animals capable of . . . (Aristotle) 5-3-4;
(Descartes) 7-1-28
. . . a way to knowledge (Aquinas) 8-3-35
education is . . . of intellect (Huxley) 8-1-66
first . . . of children (Hobbes) 2-2-62
fools despise . . . (*Proverbs*) 6-1-1
helped by divine . . . (Aquinas) 9-1-5
. . . in the art of medicine (Hippocrates) 8-3-1
. . . like culture of the earth (Hippocrates) 8-3-2
. . . of difficulty and importance (Plutarch) 8-3-21
. . . of inferior ranks (Smith) 8-1-52
risk of . . . (Dewey) 7-1-74
son that receives . . . (Augustine) 20-8-5
the power of . . . (Gibbon) 8-3-76
too careless for . . . (Boswell) 8-3-70
undergo for the sake of my . . . (Mill) 2-2-87
. . . without danger of mistake (Schopenhauer) 8-1-56
by means of the . . . (Boswell) 8-3-66
INSTRUCTIONS
good divine follows own . . . (Shakespeare) 8-3-46
obey your father's . . . (Ovid) 9-13-8
tender . . . of the best (Rousseau) 2-2-74
INSTRUCTOR
. . . no wiser than pupil (Faraday) 8-1-63
INSTRUMENT
fear is a wretched . . . (Smith) 4-2-29
is an unconscious . . . (Tolstoy) 15-3-110
money the . . . agreed upon (Hume) 11-4-24
one part is the . . . (Kant) 19-2-39
INSTRUMENTS
. . . are of various sorts (Aristotle) 10-7-6
. . . employ the workmen (Marx) 11-3-68
man makes . . . of infinite variety (Aquinas) 5-1-13
. . . promote or regulate (Bacon) 17-2-18
recourse to aid of . . . (Plutarch) 17-3-15
thousand twangling . . . (Shakespeare) 16-5-24
vices make . . . to plague us (Shakespeare) 9-10-67
we reject the professional . . . (Aristotle) 16-5-9
. . . will be perfected (Fourier) 17-2-75
INSURRECTION
next . . . of Negroes (Boswell) 10-7-26
popular . . . that ends (Rousseau) 10-9-23
INTEGRATION
intellectual and moral . . . (Dewey) 10-4-76
INTEGRITY
beauty excludes . . . (Aquinas) 16-6-24
clothed with . . . (Moliere) 9-10-83
endow the soul with . . . (Santayana) 6-7-48
genuine intellectual . . . (Dewey) 6-2-50
INTELLECT
action of the . . . (Aquinas) 6-1-38
agreement with the . . . (Aquinas) 6-3-38
assent of the . . . (Maritain) 17-1-114
between the appetite and . . . (Aquinas) 6-3-31
but realities of . . . (Blake) 20-15-91
chastity of the . . . (Santayana) 6-6-54
combination of . . . and character (Aristotle) 5-7-4

. . . composing and dividing (Aquinas) 6-7-17
consideration of the . . . (Aquinas) 6-1-31
defect of our . . . (Aquinas) 17-1-41
development of the . . . (Darwin) 7-1-59
. . . does not use corporeal organ (Aquinas) 5-4-3
duty to follow his . . . (Mill) 6-3-117
endowed with an . . . (Aquinas) 5-7-10
faith advances beyond . . . (Liebniz) 6-5-69
his powers of . . . (Darwin) 1-1-108
history of the . . . (Schopenhauer) 17-1-82
. . . holds the same position (Pascal) 6-1-56
human . . . not removed (Aquinas) 1-1-41
. . . is a cleaver (Thoreau) 19-7-76
. . . is always true (Aquinas) 6-4-9
it exists in the . . . (Aquinas) 20-5-42
knowledge and the . . . (Augustine) 6-7-15
levity of . . . dangerous (Emerson) 6-6-40
light of the agent . . . (Aquinas) 8-3-35
lost the good of the . . . (Dante) 20-15-50
. . . made kind of absolute (Bergson) 6-1-110
men of great . . . (Schopenhauer) 1-6-58, 1-6-60
monuments of unaging . . . (Yeats) 1-3-136
native activity of . . . (Plotinus) 1-8-50
natural . . . had perished (Melville) 5-6-35
not with his . . . (Tolstoy) 9-8-76
object of the . . . (Aquinas) 9-8-29
. . . of most men is barren (Thoreau) 5-4-37
operation of . . . has origin (Aquinas) 5-2-16
our . . . is altogether void (Dante) 20-15-52
our meddling . . . (Wordsworth) 19-1-83
pleasures of the . . . (Bacon) 4-7-42
power in the . . . alone (Spinoza) 9-8-51
premises from the speculative . . . (Dante) 14-3-26
sound . . . will refuse (Montaigne) 4-1-11
speculative or practical . . . (Aquinas) 9-10-44
. . . that bred them (Milton) 16-2-21
the higher the human . . . rises (Tolstoy) 1-1-118
the narrows of my . . . (Kepler) 20-8-59
to make perfect the . . . (Spinoza) 9-8-50
truth found in the . . . (Aquinas) 6-3-32
two kinds of . . . (Pascal) 5-1-29
whatever kind of . . . (Pascal) 6-5-58
with his god-like . . . (Darwin) 1-1-112
INTELLECTS
energies of the highest . . . (Faraday) 17-2-84
highest human . . . (Darwin) 19-1-110
. . . obtain their perfection (Aquinas) 6-7-16
reached by great . . . (Pascal) 9-15-71
INTELLECTUAL
. . . and sensible pleasures compared (Aquinas) 4-7-26
birth of . . . virtue (Aristotle) 8-2-4
horizon of our . . . view (Gibbon) 15-1-52
Royal Family in the . . . world (Santayana) 17-2-133
sets of . . . acts (Wm. James) 19-6-37
some virtues are . . . (Aristotle) 9-10-11
use of . . . habits (Aquinas) 8-2-11
we are as automatic as . . . (Pascal) 9-2-20
we are . . . dwarfs (Thoreau) 15-2-60
INTELLECTUAL GIFTS
great . . . mean nervous activity (Schopenhauer) 5-1-61
INTELLECTUALITY
values of . . . as sinful (Nietzsche) 20-3-63
INTELLECTUAL MOOD
highest . . . the world tolerates (Thoreau) 6-5-96
INTELLECTUAL POWER
man's capacity for . . . (Dante) 1-1-46
. . . of men (Aquinas) 1-1-40
INTELLECTUAL PRINCIPLE
impossible for . . . to be a body (Aquinas) 5-1-12

INTELLECTUAL PRINCIPLE (*Cont.*)
 soul moves through . . . (Plotinus) 9-4-16
INTELLECTUALS
 thin situation of . . . (Freud) 17-1-103
INTELLECTUAL SPHERE
 soul absorbed in the . . . (Plotinus) 5-2-10
INTELLIGIBLE
 world conceived as . . . (Kant) 9-3-25
INTELLIGENCE
 acquired a perfect . . . (Montaigne) 19-1-27
 almost human . . . of his dog (Wm. James) 6-7-43
 . . . and other talents (Kant) 9-6-89
 behold the courses of . . . (Plato) 5-2-1
 . . . could not be present (Plato) 19-8-4
 . . . decidedly barbarous (Santayana) 5-6-43
 development of human . . . (Comte) 15-2-50
 . . . divorced from aspiration (Dewey) 17-1-105
 . . . does not apprehend it (Montaigne) 20-5-55
 entirely devoid of . . . (Plato) 9-6-11
 from the divine . . . (Harvey) 16-1-25
 hast a certain ruling . . . (Aurelius) 19-4-14
 he has . . . as regards (Aquinas) 9-15-36
 intoxication of human . . . (Montaigne) 20-6-35
 is freedom of . . . (Dewey) 13-1-65
 is the goal of our . . . (Santayana) 16-6-83
 man endowed with . . . (Maritain) 9-3-36
 man needs a moral . . . (Kant) 9-3-32
 man owes superior . . . to (Aristotle) 1-1-18
 more . . . needed (Montaigne) 8-3-43
 . . . of the people (Mill) 9-10-116
 participates in the same . . . (Aurelius) 9-7-28
 petrifying blight of . . . (Santayana) 15-2-85
 remodelled by human . . . (Bergson) 9-1-42
 required . . . to be applied (Leibniz) 7-2-68
 result of improved . . . (Mill) 6-4-47
 revealed truths above . . . (Descartes) 6-5-48
 the divine . . . (Plato) 6-3-3
 this superlative . . . imaginary (Hume) 20-6-41
 where there is neither . . . (Plotinus) 19-4-15
INTELLIGENCES
 a sixth amid such . . . (Dante) 16-3-24
INTEMPERANCE
 by . . . more in meats (Milton) 1-8-113
 . . . is punished with diseases (Hobbes) 12-4-40
 result from . . . (Cicero) 9-12-9
 . . . the plague of sensual pleasure (Montaigne) 4-7-37
INTENT
 live with resolute . . . (Chaucer) 9-10-52
 science is interpreted . . . (Santayana) 17-2-133
INTENTION
 . . . directed to a due end (Aquinas) 9-10-45
 incapable of deliberate . . . (Aristotle) 19-4-7
 . . . is to be most valued (Cervantes) 14-3-28
 . . . of communicating truth (Coleridge) 6-3-100
 should have a right . . . (Aquinas) 14-1-34
 . . . to apply a sign (Wm. James) 7-1-63
 . . . to do God honor (Hobbes) 6-5-52
INTENTIONS
 Hell is paved with good . . . (Boswell) 20-15-87
 . . . in speaking understood (Locke) 7-2-72
 mistrust his honest . . . (Montesquieu) 9-10-96
 subjects to higher . . . (Goethe) 16-1-40
 where . . . are published (Bacon) 10-2-49
INTERACTION
 experience through . . . (Dewey) 8-3-100
 reciprocal real . . . (Kant) 2-1-38
INTERCESSION
 . . . for the transgressors (*Isaiah*) 20-3-4
INTERCOURSE

allow no regular . . . (Boswell) 3-3-62
 . . . between the sexes (Boswell) 5-4-27
 by promiscuous . . . (Augustine) 2-1-21
 dreary . . . of daily life (Wordsworth) 19-1-79
 . . . timed with view to (Aristotle) 3-3-10
INTEREST
 . . . alone gives accent (Wm. James) 6-2-45
 a truly universal . . . (Hegel) 9-2-30
 attached to its own . . . (Epictetus) 1-4-7
 branch of commercial . . . (Boswell) 10-7-26
 common passion or . . . (Madison) 10-4-42
 consistent with . . . (Hume) 1-9-33
 determined by a sense of . . . (Gibbon) 6-3-97
 extort some show of . . . (Emerson) 18-3-55
 independent of . . . (Kant) 16-6-47
 is a question of . . . (Lincoln) 10-7-39
 justice the common . . . (Aristotle) 12-2-15
 loss of . . . in life (Hegel) 8-1-53
 more than . . . of their patients (Montaigne) 18-2-27
 not to increase at . . . (Aristotle) 11-4-2
 . . . of money prohibited (Smith) 11-4-29
 . . . of other people (Mill) 9-9-43
 . . . of the holders of power (Mill) 10-4-67
 . . . of the stronger (Plato) 12-2-7
 one common . . . throughout (Calhoun) 10-4-59
 own safety and . . . (Spinoza) 10-2-59
 personal . . . a standard of belief (Gibbon) 6-5-82
 pressing . . . of the ruler (Rousseau) 10-2-73
 principles of substantial . . . (Gibbon) 14-1-74
 private . . . at an end (Swift) 11-2-74
 private . . . have the right (Montaigne) 9-14-22
 promoting his own . . . (Montesquieu) 1-5-104
 pursuing his own . . . (Smith) 11-2-108
 regard his own . . . (Plato) 10-2-6
 regard to their own . . . (Smith) 1-4-37
 same . . . in good government (Mill) 10-4-71
 sources of . . . all around (Mill) 8-1-69
 things of common . . . (Aristotle) 8-1-7
 view to private . . . (Aristotle) 10-3-5
 wave of the pupil's . . . (Wm. James) 8-3-89
 . . . which guides every man (Santayana) 15-1-94
INTERESTING
 render easy and . . . to them (Mill) 8-3-85
INTERESTS
 advancing civil . . . (Locke) 10-1-27
 affects . . . of others (Mill) 13-1-55
 . . . all have in common (Cicero) 9-3-4
 allow real . . . to suffer (Thucydides) 14-1-13
 arose conflicting . . . (Rousseau) 11-1-27
 bound together by higher . . . (Augustine) 10-1-14
 community of . . . (Augustine) 12-3-3
 concerned with man's own . . . (Aristotle) 9-15-24
 different and hostile . . . (Burke) 10-4-36
 duties conflict with . . . (Rousseau) 9-9-25
 each has its . . . (Rousseau) 10-8-3
 . . . felt by men (Wm. James) 9-1-37
 forgets earthly . . . (Plato) 17-1-3
 great . . . of their country (Mill) 10-4-69
 guided only by private . . . (Tolstoy) 3-6-26
 life imposes selfish . . . (Santayana) 6-3-150
 not look to his . . . (Aristotle) 10-6-11
 . . . of his fellow citizens (Mill) 8-1-70
 permanent . . . of man (Mill) 9-1-28
 practical . . . of life (Wm. James) 2-1-51
 prefers their . . . (Descartes) 2-2-60
 separate and selfish . . . (Mill) 10-8-35
 society protects its . . . (Mill) 9-5-26
 to adjust clashing . . . (Madison) 10-8-23
INTERMEDIATE

JUDGMENT (*Cont.*)

forsake his natural . . . (Hobbes) 6-2-23
from a want of . . . (Montaigne) 4-2-22
give . . . on any work of art (Hume) 16-7-30
gone are . . . and perception (Lucian) 6-6-7
had not my . . . failed me (Boswell) 5-5-29
impossible to form a perfect . . . (Aquinas) 5-2-17
. . . in accordance with action (Polybius) 15-1-10
in the . . . of every rational man (Kant) 9-6-92
. . . is itself impaired (Boswell) 5-6-32
. . . is last to arrive at maturity (Schopenhauer) 8-1-56
I will execute . . . (*Exodus*) 20-2-7
lacks soundness of . . . (Tocqueville) 10-4-54
lacks the sense of . . . (Aquinas) 9-15-41
last . . . draweth nigh (Blake) 3-5-38
leave . . . to the spectators (Plato) 16-7-4
leave our . . . intact (Montaigne) 15-1-27
left to each man's . . . (Montaigne) 9-9-17
liberty of every man's . . . (Bacon) 15-1-33
memory begets . . . (Hobbes) 5-3-19
moral . . . of every man (Kant) 9-3-24
more mature . . . from old (Bacon) 6-3-55
mortals meets this . . . (Homer) 1-8-8
my . . . is returned (Cervantes) 5-6-25
natural power of . . . (Aquinas) 6-4-9
never make a decisive . . . (Pascal) 6-7-26
never to form a . . . (Descartes) 6-4-21
not make his . . . blind (Tennyson) 6-6-42
not stand in the . . . (*Psalms*) 9-7-3
not to heed . . . of conscience (Kant) 9-5-17
of an opposite . . . (Plato) 6-6-2
. . . of his intellect unfettered (Aquinas) 5-5-16
of providential . . . (Rabelais) 1-7-69
. . . of others (Rousseau) 1-5-106
. . . of our fellows (Darwin) 1-5-124
. . . of speculative reason (Aquinas) 9-1-5
one universal . . . (Aristotle) 18-1-9
only devise a technical . . . (Schiller) 16-7-40
ordinary stupidity of his . . . (Montaigne) 1-4-16
our . . . does not grasp (Montaigne) 6-3-46
our . . . gives no assent (Hume) 6-3-85
pass a correct . . . (Aurelius) 4-3-14
passing an adequate . . . (Thucydides) 9-13-1
passions hinder . . . (Aquinas) 9-4-22
private . . . of any person (Locke) 10-2-60
proceed from a . . . of reason (Aquinas) 9-2-8
reading brings not a . . . (Milton) 16-2-22
resolve to employment of . . . (Kant) 16-6-48
render day of . . . a success (Whitehead) 16-1-55
right . . . the end of reasoning (Locke) 6-7-30
save by the . . . of God (Augustine) 10-7-13
scientific knowledge is . . . (Aristotle) 6-7-12
. . . sharpened by experience (Kant) 9-3-26
. . . should exist (Dante) 14-3-25
sleep to the eye of . . . (Montaigne) 8-2-15
some . . . the mind makes (Locke) 6-3-79
some things act without . . . (Aquinas) 5-7-11
sound . . . is the ground (Horace) 16-3-17
standard of future . . . (Hume) 6-2-26
still have . . . here (Shakespeare) 1-8-86
subjective validity of . . . (Kant) 6-5-85
such a . . . is not a free one (Aquinas) 5-7-10
suspension of . . . their goal (Montaigne) 6-6-10
suspension of own . . . (Bacon) 8-3-47
the development of . . . (Faraday) 8-1-63
the ground of their . . . (Kant) 16-7-38
the imitation of . . . (Montaigne) 7-2-43
the . . . must be eminent (Hobbes) 15-1-35
. . . the talent of age (Swift) 1-3-78

the weakness of the . . . (Bacon) 15-2-24
their want of . . . (Locke) 2-2-67
to human . . . (Augustine) 1-5-47
to pass . . . upon ourselves (Kant) 9-5-18
to obey their . . . (Plutarch) 15-3-41
to our own . . . (Chaucer) 2-3-40
to say history is historical . . . (Croce) 15-1-96
universal . . . of mankind (Gibbon) 20-3-45
use their own . . . (Cicero) 8-3-13
useth his own . . . only (Hobbes) 9-13-24
use we put to . . . (Plutarch) 8-1-15
varieties of . . . (Aristotle) 5-4-1
virtue with a right . . . (Euripides) 9-10-3
wanting in natural . . . (Kant) 8-3-77
. . . was not so good (Boswell) 8-3-67
weakness of our . . . (Montaigne) 6-5-44
we do not include . . . (Aristotle) 6-3-16
what is called . . . (Aristotle) 9-13-5
what . . . is left to God (Augustine) 15-3-50
what . . . shall I dread (Shakespeare) 11-1-12
who comes before them for . . . (Aristotle) 7-2-15
whose blood and . . . are mingled (Shakespeare) 9-4-34
will bring thee into . . . (*Eccles.*) 1-3-2
word critic signifies . . . (Fielding) 16-7-27
words pervert the . . . (Bacon) 7-2-53

JUDGMENT DAY

before the . . . (Aquinas) 20-15-48
thought it was the . . . (Hardy) 20-15-108

JUDGMENTS

according to God's just . . . (Aquinas) 20-7-29
as regards mathematical . . . (Wm. James) 17-3-47
before his . . . afraid (Th. Browne) 20-15-72
drop our clear . . . (Shakespeare) 9-6-67
falsity of our . . . (Wm. James) 1-4-65
freedom of their . . . (Montaigne) 13-2-13
God's . . . are entrusted (Pascal) 6-5-61
hath applied his . . . (Donne) 20-15-69
in men's depraved . . . (Bacon) 6-3-57
. . . of the gods far surpass (Spinoza) 17-3-30
. . . of the Lord (Lincoln) 10-7-40
. . . of the Lord are true (*Psalms*) 20-5-9
our . . . vary (Aristotle) 7-2-12
power of forming right . . . (Aristotle) 16-5-7
render weak their . . . (Chaucer) 6-4-10
shall I say of these . . . (Augustine) 12-4-22
sometimes called . . . (Hobbes) 12-1-46
such negative . . . (Russell) 6-1-104
surer . . . from understanding (Descartes) 5-2-22
synthetic *a priori* . . . (Poincaré) 17-3-48, 17-3-49
they despised my . . . (*Leviticus*) 20-2-10
toss our . . . random on the wind (Euripides) 1-2-11
vanity of human . . . (Montaigne) 1-5-59
whereby . . . are confused (Gilbert) 6-4-17
where our . . . err (Byron) 19-7-69

JUDICATION

should be . . . between them (Dante) 14-3-25

JUDICIAL

. . . punishment (Kant) 12-4-60
. . . united to executive (Smith) 10-3-41
who has . . . power (Aristotle) 10-3-8

JUDICIARY

legislative-executive and . . . (Madison) 10-2-89

JULIAN

education of . . . (Gibbon) 6-2-32
. . . recollected with terror (Gibbon) 10-2-82

JULIET

unless philosophy can make a . . . (Shakespeare) 17-1-47

JULIUS (Caesar)

ere the mightiest . . . fell (Shakespeare) 20-12-19

prophecy is sure ... (Spinoza) 20-10-35
... puffeth up (*I Corinthians*) 6-1-21
purest example of mirror ... (Russell) 5-3-31
reject ... of the past (Dewey) 8-1-87
said of the beauty of ... (Plato) 16-6-8
scientific ... involves demonstration (Aristotle) 9-13-3
scientific ... not possible by (Aristotle) 5-2-3
seeds of ... pre-exist (Aquinas) 8-3-35
seek all kinds of ... (Mill) 8-1-73
seem to have as much ... (Locke) 19-2-37
self-knowledge is the essence of ... (Plato) 1-4-3
service of removing doubtful ... (Faraday) 17-2-81
show me I had ... (Plato) 8-1-2
smattering of vain ... (Pascal) 9-15-71
stands in line of ... (Maritain) 17-1-113
such ... is as useful as (Lucian) 17-1-35
such ... is too wonderful (*Psalms*) 20-5-12
sufficient ... for guidance (Aquinas) 15-3-60
teacher communicates ... (Aquinas) 8-3-36
teacher has ... actually (Aquinas) 8-3-37
the ... of divine things (Aquinas) 9-15-39
the ... which transcends (Spinoza) 20-11-26
the living word of ... (Plato) 16-2-3
the lovers of ... (Plato) 17-1-5
... the object of our inquiry (Aristotle) 19-3-4
the teachers of ancient ... (Gibbon) 16-2-39
the way of attaining ... (Aristotle) 6-1-15
the word ... implies (Aquinas) 9-15-38
theoretical kinds of ... (Aristotle) 9-15-21
these are not ... (Plato) 9-13-2
think we have scientific ... (Aristotle) 19-3-3
this frail ... dies (Pascal) 19-2-34
this ... dies with its need (Pascal) 15-2-26
those which possess no ... (Aquinas) 19-4-18
thought courage was ... (Aristotle) 9-11-10
to seek out ... (Montaigne) 17-1-46
to think about a theory of ... (Russell) 6-2-49
true and false ... (Plato) 1-8-15
true ... deduced from causes (Bacon) 19-3-22
true ... of ourselves (Freud) 1-4-67
two-fold way of acquiring ... (Aquinas) 8-3-34
uneducated argue from common ... (Aristotle) 7-2-17
... useful in business (Aristotle) 8-1-9
uses ... already acquired (Aquinas) 5-4-3
valuable part of ... (Hume) 15-1-42
what has become of the ... (Dewey) 8-3-99
whether ... and sensation are same (Plato) 7-1-4
... which experience and habit produce (Wm. James)
   5-2-38
... which is very useful (Descartes) 17-2-36
whole of our acquired ... (Comte) 17-2-78
who love not ... (Tennyson) 6-1-91
whose ... goes no further (Rousseau) 20-10-40
why make so much of ... (Euripides) 7-2-1
widening bounds of ... (Laplace) 19-4-36
wit over real ... (Locke) 7-2-71
you in search of ... (Goethe) 18-2-42

KNOWLEDGES
   vices of all ... (Jonson) 17-1-49
KNOWN
   believes nothing is ... (Lucretius) 6-6-4
   to be ... is to (Montaigne) 1-5-58
KNOWS
   very fact that he ... that he ... (Spinoza) 6-1-60
KORAN (Alcoran)
   compliment to the ... (Emerson) 17-1-84
   fables in the ... (Bacon) 19-8-48
   it is in the ... (Mill) 10-2-100
   the ... inculcates tenets (Gibbon) 15-3-104

KOSMOS
   beings in the intellectual ... (Plotinus) 16-5-14
   the ... has had no beginning (Plotinus) 19-5-19
KRONOS
   born by Rhea to ... (Homer) 20-15-5
   she found ... (Homer) 2-2-7
   the son of ... pitied them (Homer) 1-1-4
   Zeus—son of ... (Homer) 20-8-12
KUTUZOV
   ... like all old people (Tolstoy) 6-2-42
   ... looked around (Tolstoy) 6-2-41

LABAN
   and ... said unto Jacob (*Genesis*) 2-3-2
LABOR
   active love is ... (Dostoevsky) 3-1-29
   all things are full of ... (*Eccles.*) 19-5-1
   all ye that ... and are (*Matthew*) 20-3-9
   a love of ... (Hippocrates) 8-3-1
   a lover of ... (Smith) 8-3-73
   as ... for his master (Marx) 10-7-41
   as payment for his ... (Aquinas) 11-5-5
   capital has not invented surplus ... (Marx) 4-9-18
   combine ... with instruction (Marx) 8-1-67
   come from manual ... (Rousseau) 11-1-26
   commanding ... of others (Thoreau) 11-5-35
   commodities are realized ... (Marx) 11-4-41
   costs three hours ... (Shaw) 11-5-47
   demand for ... (Mill) 11-6-54
   devotes his ... to an objective aim (Hegel) 1-3-109
   division of ... is in this (Smith) 11-5-16
   enjoy ... without fear (Shaw) 11-1-75
   extent of man's ... (Locke) 11-1-18
   from ... men returns (Hesiod) 11-3-6
   from the mouth of ... (Jefferson) 10-3-43
   fruits of his ... (Gibbon) 11-1-37
   great ... which it requires (Smith) 4-11-34
   hatred of ... (Smith) 10-8-16
   homogeneous human ... (Marx) 20-3-54
   increased productiveness to ... (Mill) 11-5-40
   instruments of ... (Marx and Engels) 2-1-45
   liberal reward of ... (Smith) 11-2-100
   ... makes the measure (Locke) 11-1-20
   materialized social ... (Marx) 11-5-36
   may by his ... (Locke) 12-3-13
   ... no longer converted (Marx and Engels) 11-1-68
   none is exempt from ... (Rabelais) 19-2-27
   not enough to ... (Hobbes) 11-6-9
   not hinder division of ... (Smith) 11-5-17
   ... of his body (Locke) 11-1-17
   on ... of the other (Calhoun) 10-7-35
   on the second as ... (Kant) 16-1-33
   partake of same ... (Plutarch) 14-2-20
   possession by ... (Rousseau) 11-1-28
   produce of their ... (Smith) 11-2-101
   property based on ... (Marx) 11-1-61
   property in effect of ... (Locke) 11-4-20
   ... requisite for existence (Marx) 19-1-113
   saturated with our ... (Wm. James) 11-2-153
   serious occupation is ... (Hegel) 19-1-93
   shalt thou ... (*Deut.*) 20-2-11
   supplies more ... (Marx) 12-3-27
   ... that arises from movement (Aquinas) 14-5-23
   the division of ... (Smith) 11-5-13, 14-2-50
   the produce of ... (Mill) 11-1-70
   those destined for ... (Jefferson) 10-8-18
   thought is true ... (Carlyle) 5-1-62
   thou losest ... (Shakespeare) 10-6-27

LABOR (*Cont.*)
　to this saving of . . . (Mill) 11-5-41
　. . . under compulsion of necessity (Marx) 13-1-48
　unpaid . . . of others (Marx) 11-1-61
　value of every man's . . . (Thoreau) 15-2-59
　wage . . . create property (Marx) 11-1-66
　wage . . . rests on (Marx and Engels) 10-8-33
　wages of . . . very high (Smith) 11-2-99
　what is obtained by . . . (Johnson) 11-1-29
　who . . . in the earth (Jefferson) 9-10-104
　with him of his . . . (*Eccles.*) 4-7-1

LABORATORIES
　lectures and . . . (Lavoisier) 17-2-67

LABORATORY
　true sanctuary is the . . . (Bernard) 18-1-35

LABORER
　. . . exists for the process (Marx) 2-1-44
　expropriation of the . . . (Marx) 11-1-64
　from the more efficient . . . (Mill) 11-2-143
　. . . is labor power (Marx) 4-9-19

LABORERS
　a class of . . . (Malthus) 10-8-25
　hire . . . into his vineyard (*Matthew*) 20-15-24
　nothing else than . . . (Mill) 10-4-72
　pay less than common . . . (Smith) 14-2-49

LABORING
　no . . . in the winter (Shakespeare) 9-15-61

LABORING MAN
　sleep of the . . . (*Eccles.*) 11-2-5

LABORS
　. . . have come to nothing (Lucretius) 15-2-10
　limits to its . . . (Montaigne) 1-4-19

LACEDAEMON
　alarm inspired in . . . (Thucydides) 14-1-12
　men of . . . (Herodotus) 6-2-3

LACEDAEMONIAN
　the . . . husband (Plutarch) 2-3-25

LACEDAEMONIANS
　. . . and their allies (Thucydides) 18-3-5
　and to . . . tell that here (Herodotus) 1-6-2
　victory over the . . . (Thucydides) 14-2-9

LACHES
　he and . . . were retreating (Plato) 14-2-10

LACHESIS
　go at once to . . . (Plato) 5-7-1

LACKEY
　to a . . . no man can (Tolstoy) 1-6-75
　wear the name of . . . (Euripides) 10-7-3

LACONIAN
　. . . breed of dogs (Aristotle) 1-7-26

LADDER
　a . . . set up on the earth (*Genesis*) 5-5-1
　. . . to all high designs (Shakespeare) 10-2-44
　young ambition's . . . (Shakespeare) 1-6-28

LADIES
　if . . . be but young and fair (Shakespeare) 16-6-33
　in praise of . . . dead (Shakespeare) 16-6-38
　well-born . . . take advice (Montaigne) 1-7-71

LADY
　glorious . . . of my mind (Dante) 1-7-53
　lest . . . be not coy (Milton) 16-5-40
　O . . . glorious (Goethe) 16-6-53

LAËRTÈS
　son of . . . versatile Odysseus (Homer) 2-3-8

LAERTES
　was't Hamlet wrong'd . . . (Shakespeare) 12-4-30

LAITY
　tax imposed on the . . . (Gibbon) 11-6-33

LAIUS

　as murderer of . . . (Sophocles) 2-1-7
　upon . . . long dead (Sophocles) 2-3-15

LAKE OF FIRE
　which is also called the . . . (Augustine) 20-15-34

LALANDE
　. . . or whoever it was (Santayana) 19-1-124

LAMACHUS
　of whom was . . . hero (Aristophanes) 16-4-2

LAMARCK
　principle proposed by . . . (Comte) 15-2-51

LAMB
　a . . . for an house (*Exodus*) 20-2-7
　as a . . . to the slaughter (*Isaiah*) 20-3-4
　behold the . . . of God (*John*) 20-14-12
　blood of the . . . (T. S. Eliot) 20-4-54
　fell down before the . . . (*Revelation*) 20-8-37
　in the blood of the . . . (*Revelation*) 20-15-29
　provide himself a . . . (*Genesis*) 20-2-4
　skin of an innocent . . . (Shakespeare) 12-1-42
　. . . to be torn by the wolf (Locke) 14-3-34
　to the shorn . . . (Sterne) 3-5-37
　who made the . . . (Blake) 19-8-76

LAMBS
　feed my . . . (*John*) 20-4-11
　we were twin . . . (Shakespeare) 1-3-58

LAMECH
　of wicked . . . (Chaucer) 2-3-40

LAMENT
　not by sounding . . . (Euripides) 20-8-17

LAMENTATION
　advantage from grim . . . (Homer) 4-6-4
　cry genuine . . . (Juvenal) 11-4-7
　no time for . . . (Milton) 1-8-114
　universal . . . of the (Anselm) 1-2-26

LAMENTATIONS
　made these . . . (Plutarch) 1-9-14
　pain in . . . (Plato) 16-4-4

LAMENTING
　must I die . . . (Epictetus) 4-6-14
　to be always . . . (Montaigne) 4-8-15

LAMP
　our . . . is spent (Shakespeare) 1-9-28

LANCASTER
　the wars of York and . . . (Shakespeare) 20-15-65

LANCE
　strong . . . of justice (Shakespeare) 9-7-38

LANCELOT
　we read of . . . (Dante) 3-3-31

LAND
　all the . . . which thou seest (*Genesis*) 20-2-2
　and laws of the . . . (Hegel) 12-1-79
　claim to . . . itself (Rousseau) 11-1-26
　drive them out of his . . . (*Exodus*) 20-2-6
　. . . enough in the world (Locke) 11-1-19
　. . . God giveth thee (*Exodus*) 9-3-1
　has capital in . . . (Smith) 11-1-32
　improvements of . . . (Smith) 11-1-31
　I will remember the . . . (*Leviticus*) 20-2-10
　labor puts value in . . . (Locke) 11-3-24
　Lord's song in a strange . . . (*Psalms*) 20-2-16
　native . . . draws all men (Ovid) 3-6-9
　no man made the . . . (Mill) 11-1-73
　private ownership of . . . (George) 13-3-43
　property in . . . (Mill) 11-1-74
　. . . shall yield her increase (*Leviticus*) 20-2-9
　slice of neighbor's . . . (Plato) 14-1-19
　. . . that the Lord (*Deut.*) 11-1-1
　unto a . . . that I will shew (*Genesis*) 20-2-1
　. . . which I gave Abraham (*Genesis*) 20-2-5

the ... was silent (Locke) 10-2-63
the moral ... (Kant) 9-8-62
the protection of ... (Mill) 11-6-53
the servitude of ... (Maritain) 9-4-53
their marriage ... (Herodotus) 2-3-13
there is but one ... (Rousseau) 10-4-30
they are fulfilling the ... (Luther) 20-9-15
to give the people a ... (Aquinas) 20-14-24
to thy ... my services (Shakespeare) 19-1-37
transgressions of the ... (Calvin) 20-13-67
under the old ... (Aquinas) 2-3-34, 20-2-24
universal ... for everyone (Kant) 9-1-23
universal ... of laws (Montaigne) 9-15-45
upon them a diverse ... (Dante) 20-9-14
various precepts of the ... (Aquinas) 20-3-23
... was man's expedient (Emerson) 10-1-44
what we call penal ... (Shaw) 12-4-77
when the ... was given (Gibbon) 20-2-40
who can discern a ... (Thoreau) 17-2-86
who does it without ... (Locke) 14-1-60
who shall give a lover any ... (Chaucer) 3-1-32
who violates the ... (Aristotle) 10-2-13
which ... ought to allow (Bentham) 13-1-30
will depends on eternal ... (Aquinas) 9-3-14
wish to disregard the ... (Spinoza) 10-1-26
ye are not under the ... (*Romans*) 20-13-20
your ... O Lord (Augustine) 9-3-8, 20-13-30

LAWFUL
thus trading becomes ... (Aquinas) 11-5-5
... to possess property (Aquinas) 11-1-8

LAWFULLY
may ... make the attempt (Spinoza) 14-1-57
obliged to act ... (Montaigne) 14-1-28

LAWLESS
abandoned his ... freedom (Kant) 12-3-24
good conscience is never ... (Fielding) 9-5-11

LAWLESSNESS
in a condition of ... (Kant) 14-3-40
infer the ... of wars (Calvin) 14-1-44

LAWMAKER
the wisdom of a ... (Bacon) 10-2-48

LAW OF NATURE
moral precepts and ... (Aquinas) 9-1-5
obligations of the ... (Locke) 12-1-52

LAWRENCE
... of virtuous father (Milton) 19-1-52

LAWS
according to human ... (Aquinas) 12-4-24
according to ... of physics (Bernard) 19-8-86
according to necessary ... (Plato) 19-8-6
according to the ... of medicine (Hippocrates) 18-2-1
according to unvarying ... (Kant) 17-2-62
act in accordance with ... (Descartes) 17-2-35
all ... are held (Montaigne) 19-5-25
all ... written in jargon (Swift) 7-1-42
altering any of the ... (Leibniz) 10-6-5
... and artificial reason (Hobbes) 10-1-21
... and institutions (Jefferson) 15-2-39; (Plato) 16-6-8
any difference what ... are (Emerson) 1-6-69
a power to make ... (Locke) 10-3-30, 10-4-17
application of these ... (Fourier) 17-2-75
... are elastic and indefinite (Bernard) 18-1-34
are ... directing events (Tolstoy) 15-1-81
... are very severe (Montesquieu) 10-6-48
a right of making ... (Locke) 10-2-61
as not subject to ... (Tolstoy) 15-1-85
assume physical ... exist (Planck) 17-2-112
at home by ... (Hobbes) 10-6-32
beauty of institutions and ... (Plato) 16-6-7

best civil and political ... (Montesquieu) 20-3-38
... best explained and interpreted (Swift) 1-1-80
by the ... of man (Tocqueville) 2-3-101
... cannot be executed (Locke) 10-3-31
cease to care for ... (Plato) 10-4-4
certain divine ... (Emerson) 9-3-34
chief object of ... (Montesquieu) 11-5-7
civil and canon ... (Voltaire) 2-3-84
civil ... contrary to (Montesquieu) 1-7-112
common ... of their country (Locke) 12-3-15
... common to all (Hobbes) 2-1-28
conform to the ... (Wm. James) 6-1-101
constancy of scientific ... (Russell) 19-3-53
... continue in force (Smith) 2-1-37
contrary to ... of nature (Hume) 20-11-30
contrary to the ... (Plato) 10-5-2
defenders of the ... (Calvin) 14-1-44
defiance of the ... (Hegel) 13-2-36
depository of the ... (Montesquieu) 10-6-44
derivation of general ... (Wm. James) 17-2-115
development on dynamical ... (Kant) 19-4-35
did not observe the ... (Freud) 20-2-51
discover general ... of nature (Berkeley) 17-2-53
discovery of natural ... (Marx) 15-1-75
divine and human ... (Aquinas) 12-4-26
Draco's ... were written (Plutarch) 12-4-16
effect of sumptuary ... (Rousseau) 11-6-22
enter into the natural ... (Einstein) 19-6-46
established ... of Government (Locke) 10-1-30
eternal ... of nature (Spinoza) 4-8-24
evils from civil ... (Montesquieu) 20-9-31
execution of the ... (Hobbes) 10-3-21
fewer ... and less power (Emerson) 10-3-55
fixed and general ... (Berkeley) 19-1-60
fixed by ... of nature (Sumner) 10-1-50
fixed ... of nature (Lucretius) 19-7-8
folly of human ... (Smith) 11-2-109
folly to speak of ... of history (Wm. James) 15-1-86
force of all its ... (Tocqueville) 10-3-5
forcible restraint of ... (Gibbon) 10-8-20
for grinding general ... (Darwin) 16-3-87
form of empirical ... (Einstein) 17-2-129
fundamental ... of the state (Plato) 16-5-4
general ... of nature (Berkeley) 9-6-85; (Condorcet) 15-2-46; (Newton) 17-2-47
general relations called ... (Whitehead) 17-2-116
good ... lead (Rousseau) 10-5-27
good ... to be observed (Cervantes) 14-3-28
goodness of criminal ... (Montesquieu) 5-7-29
governed by civil ... (Montesquieu) 13-1-18
governed by constant ... (Turgot) 15-2-36
great ... of nature (Laplace) 19-4-36
have no need of ... (Plato) 9-4-1
Hell itself have its ... (Goethe) 20-15-93
him who makes the ... (Rousseau) 10-3-36
honor has its ... (Montesquieu) 1-5-105
human ... not punishing (Locke) 1-4-32
... impressed by the Creator (Darwin) 19-2-48
incapable of loving the ... (Rousseau) 20-9-34
inequality introduced by ... (Hobbes) 13-3-12
instruction in ... of nature (Huxley) 8-1-66
in their ... attempt (Aristotle) 2-2-22
Italy gave ... to provincials (Gibbon) 7-1-52
learn part of nature's ... (Voltaire) 17-1-69
live under equitable ... (Harvey) 1-1-64
... made to direct the will (Montesquieu) 20-1-34
make my own ... (Lucian) 17-1-34
make reasonable ... (Voltaire) 11-2-84
man subject to certain ... (Tolstoy) 5-7-44

agreed in the doctrine of . . . (Hume) 5-7-30
a . . . connected with order (Burke) 13-1-26
allowed . . . to speak (Swift) 7-1-41
. . . and equality found (Aristotle) 10-4-9
. . . and equality united (Calhoun) 13-3-34
. . . and indulgence can (Locke) 2-2-67
. . . and necessity (Hegel) 10-2-92
. . . and necessity consistent (Hobbes) 5-7-23
. . . and pursuit of happiness (Jefferson) 12-3-20
and to lose . . . (Bacon) 1-6-37
apply ourselves to laws by . . . (Montaigne) 9-4-32
. . . as a good (Russell) 14-1-106
as . . . is the greater (Spinoza) 9-7-40
between authority and . . . (Hume) 10-3-34
by destroying the . . . (Madison) 10-8-23
by . . . they entered into emulation (Rabelais) 9-4-30
can . . . have any limit (Plato) 10-4-4
certainly destroys . . . (Johnson) 11-2-95
conceived in . . . (Lincoln) 10-4-64
consideration for his . . . (Mill) 10-7-42
. . . creep in the minds and marrows (Shakespeare) 3-2-21
. . . depends on silence of law (Hobbes) 13-1-9
direct loss of . . . (Russell) 12-3-32
disease magnified by . . . (Plato) 13-1-3
divest himself of . . . (Hobbes) 12-3-10
divest ourselves of . . . (Rousseau) 12-3-18
. . . does not belong to your will (Voltaire) 5-7-31
does what he does out of . . . (Luther) 9-4-29
do this best under . . . (Sumner) 12-3-30
dread the word . . . (Voltaire) 13-2-27
. . . each man hath (Hobbes) 12-3-10
endowed with . . . (Spinoza) 19-3-30
enjoyment of personal . . . (Grotius) 12-3-9
establish our real . . . (Montaigne) 9-8-36
extreme of abused . . . (Milton) 2-3-73
folly to abolish . . . (Madison) 13-1-31
foundation of our . . . (Locke) 9-8-54
from too much . . . (Shakespeare) 9-12-34
full state of . . . (Locke) 10-9-20
gains is civil . . . (Rousseau) 13-1-22
give me . . . to know (Milton) 13-2-19
if we grasp the principle of . . . (Dante) 5-7-17
indifference to human . . . (Descartes) 5-7-22
in . . . of choice (Aquinas) 20-4-17
in this lies . . . (Locke) 5-7-28
. . . is no longer possible (Rousseau) 10-4-30
. . . is protected (Gibbon) 10-6-61
jar not with . . . (Milton) 20-7-63
just . . . of the individual (Mill) 10-2-100
keep up their taste for . . . (Rousseau) 14-3-35
laws themselves to . . . (Montesquieu) 10-2-70
laws which establish . . . (Vico) 15-2-31
loses no part of his . . . (Rousseau) 12-1-63
. . . lost in the pursuit (Hamilton/Madison) 12-2-45
lowest grade of . . . (Descartes) 5-7-21
. . . maintained by slavery (Rousseau) 10-7-25
malignant aspect to . . . (Hamilton) 14-2-59
moral . . . makes man master (Rousseau) 9-4-42
my dear . . . (Congreve) 2-3-77
natural . . . of man (Locke) 13-1-12
negations of individual . . . (Bakunin) 13-1-51
negro who was claiming . . . (Boswell) 10-7-26
never be dangerous to . . . (Smith) 17-2-53
never having tasted . . . (Herodotus) 6-2-3
no patriotism without . . . (Rousseau) 10-5-18
not at . . . to speak truth (Montesquieu) 15-1-39
not have the name of . . . (Euripides) 10-7-3
. . . not the chief object (Tocqueville) 13-3-29
. . . of acting (Locke) 2-2-65, 13-1-13

. . . of each man (Rousseau) 10-1-32
. . . of even raising our eyes (Montaigne) 8-2-13
. . . of every individual (Smith) 10-3-41
. . . of mind (Spinoza) 2-3-74
or interfere with . . . (Mill) 11-6-50
philosophic . . . consists (Montesquieu) 5-7-29
political . . . bestows (Tocqueville) 13-3-32
poverty a part of . . . (Montesquieu) 11-2-81
proclaim . . . throughout the (*Leviticus*) 13-1-1
property in . . . of person (Madison) 11-1-44
resume their original . . . (Locke) 10-9-21
return to my former . . . (Cervantes) 10-2-47
rout about universal . . . (Boswell) 13-2-28
safeguard of public . . . (Jefferson) 10-4-33
scheme has destroyed . . . (Sumner) 13-3-48
strove to serve human . . . (Swift) 3-2-30
system of natural . . . (Smith) 11-2-110
taking away your . . . (Homer) 2-2-8
temptation to forego . . . (Beauvoir) 13-3-59
the extension of . . . (Tawney) 13-3-58
the extreme of . . . (Burke) 13-1-27
the less the . . . (Rousseau) 10-5-20
the . . . of women (Montesquieu) 10-6-48
the mountain nymph . . . (Milton) 4-6-38
the principle of . . . (Emerson) 11-5-32
the use of . . . (Montesquieu) 10-6-47
the will's . . . (Dante) 5-7-16
this common . . . (Rousseau) 2-1-34
thoughts possess unbounded . . . (Hume) 5-1-48
to give moderate . . . (Bacon) 10-2-52
to have too much . . . (Pascal) 5-7-24
to omit the . . . (Locke) 10-1-30
. . . to punish his servant (Cervantes) 12-2-31
. . . to separate (Locke) 2-3-75
trained for . . . (Montaigne) 8-3-42
unruly . . . of private member (Montaigne) 3-3-37
value of civil . . . (Montesquieu) 10-7-21
want only . . . and equality (Voltaire) 10-4-24
we all declare for . . . (Lincoln) 13-1-47
what . . . remains (Locke) 10-2-60
what religious . . . (Mill) 13-2-38
where no fear there is . . . (Ambrose) 9-4-17
. . . which reigns there (Plato) 10-4-3
. . . which we are supporting (Plato) 9-7-9
who naturally love . . . (Hobbes) 10-1-22
without . . . understanding to no purpose (Locke) 9-4-40
with regard to human . . . (Mill) 5-6-38
worth freedom to be at . . . (Locke) 13-1-15

LIBERTY AND NECESSITY
Bramhall on . . . (Boswell) 15-3-99

LIBERUM ARBITRIUM
. . . of the individual (Kant) 9-3-25

LIBIDO
. . . must not remain (Freud) 2-2-95
of its narcissistic . . . (Freud) 1-3-134
. . . the energy of love (Freud) 3-1-85

LIBRARIES
burn the . . . (Emerson) 17-1-84
grow up in . . . (Emerson) 16-2-46
regret the more valuable . . . (Gibbon) 16-2-39
turn to the . . . (Bacon) 16-2-16

LIBRARY
than a public . . . (Johnson) 16-2-32
turn over half a . . . (Boswell) 16-2-35

LIBYA
descended into . . . (Thucydides) 18-3-5
desert land of . . . (Virgil) 3-1-17
there is a country in . . . (Herodotus) 11-5-2

LONGINGS
goal of all my . . . (Dante) 5-4-5
immortal . . . in me (Shakespeare) 1-9-29
satisfy all his . . . (Plato) 9-12-2
LOOK
saucy . . . of an assured man (Congreve) 3-1-58
LOOKING-GLASS
serve me as a sort of . . . (Plutarch) 15-1-16
LOOM
were the . . . of time (Melville) 15-3-108
LOOP
to hang a doubt on . . . (Shakespeare) 6-6-13
LOQUACITY
cause of their . . . (Aristotle) 1-3-19
LORD
a joyful noise unto the . . . (*Psalms*) 20-8-7
all the hosts of the . . . (*Exodus*) 20-2-8
and I fear the . . . (*Jonah*) 20-14-7
and the . . . showed him (*Deut.*) 20-10-1
began to be spoken by the . . . (*Hebrews*) 6-5-15
bless the . . . ye his angels (*Psalms*) 20-7-1
called to exalt the . . . (Shaw) 19-8-92
. . . came down to see the city (*Genesis*) 7-1-2
David displeased the . . . (*II Samuel*) 3-3-2
displeased the . . . (*Genesis*) 2-3-3
doth the . . . require of thee (*Micah*) 9-9-2
except the . . . build (*Psalms*) 15-3-1
fear of the . . . (*Psalms*) 9-15-3
. . . had said unto Abram (*Genesis*) 20-2-1
handkerchief of the . . . (Whitman) 19-1-104
. . . hath delivered thee (*I Samuel*) 9-7-1
. . . hath taken vengeance (*Judges*) 2-2-2
himself rules as . . . (Augustine) 15-3-48
. . . is my light (*Psalms*) 4-2-1
. . . is my shepherd (*Psalms*) 20-14-2
man's ways please the . . . (*Proverbs*) 14-3-2
mercies of the . . . forever (*Psalms*) 20-2-15
mercy of the . . . (*Psalms*) 3-5-2
not tempt the . . . thy God (*Matthew*) 20-13-15
now are ye light in the . . . (Augustine) 20-7-15
O . . . our . . . how excellent is (*Psalms*) 1-1-3
O sing unto the . . . (*Psalms*) 20-8-6
out of the mouth of the . . . (*Deut.*) 20-1-1
. . . over more than you rule (Homer) 10-6-3
pray unto the . . . (*Ecclesiasticus*) 18-1-1
presence of the . . . (*Job*) 18-3-2
. . . said unto Abraham (*Genesis*) 20-2-2
. . . said unto Moses (*Exodus*) 20-2-6
saith the . . . that created thee (*Isaiah*) 20-2-17
salvation belongeth to the . . . (*Psalms*) 20-14-1
salvation is of the . . . (*Psalms*) 20-19-3
shall I come before the . . . (*Micah*) 20-8-10
. . . shall judge (*Isaiah*) 14-3-3
shalt worship the . . . (*Luke*) 20-13-17
. . . spake unto Moses (*Exodus*) 20-2-7
spirit of the . . . shall be (*Isaiah*) 20-3-2
the hand of the . . . (*Ezekiel*) 20-10-5
the hill of the . . . (*Psalms*) 9-14-4
their sovran . . . was by (Milton) 14-3-31
the . . . answered Job (*Job*) 1-1-2
the . . . had respect unto (*Genesis*) 2-1-1
the . . . hath sent unto you (*Jeremiah*) 20-10-3
the . . . hath taken away (*Job*) 1-8-4
the . . . is longsuffering (*Numbers*) 20-13-3
the . . . is my strength (*Exodus*) 20-5-3
the . . . is with thee (*Luke*) 1-7-36
the . . . overthrew the Egyptians (*Exodus*) 20-11-1
the . . . said unto Joshua (*Joshua*) 14-2-2
the . . . said unto Moses (*Exodus*) 14-2-1

the . . . shall smite thee (*Deut.*) 18-3-1
the . . . whom ye seek (*Malachi*) 20-14-8
the way of the . . . (*Matthew*) 20-10-15
they may offer unto the . . . (*Malachi*) 20-14-8
. . . thou hast searched me (*Psalms*) 20-5-12
upon the mount before the . . . (*I Kings*) 20-5-7
upon the name of the . . . (*Romans*) 6-5-12
. . . up to his final coming (Augustine) 19-8-33
wife is from the . . . (*Proverbs*) 2-3-6
will in the . . . (Aquinas) 2-3-36
LORDSHIP
. . . over all Asia's (Euripides) 2-2-14
LORD'S PRAYER
like it to be the . . . (Montaigne) 20-8-57
LORE
sweet is the . . . (Wordsworth) 19-1-83
LORENZO
did young . . . swear (Shakespeare) 3-1-37
LOSE
a time to . . . (*Eccles.*) 19-7-2
to . . . your heart's desire (Shaw) 4-4-34
LOSER
just is always a . . . (Plato) 12-2-8
LOSERS
should be real . . . (Wm. James) 9-6-111
LOSS
increasing store with . . . (Shakespeare) 19-5-29
less a condensation than a . . . (Wm. James) 8-3-88
most poignant . . . (Freud) 2-2-96
. . . of money is awful (Juvenal) 11-4-7
. . . of the accustomed (Thucydides) 4-6-9
possibility of future . . . (Plutarch) 4-2-15
so little is our . . . (Milton) 19-7-48
LOT
. . . was separated from him (*Genesis*) 20-2-2
LOTTERIES
. . . ought not be allowed (Kant) 11-2-114
LOUIS QUATORZE
strip your . . . of his (Carlyle) 10-6-68
LOVE
. . . affairs a serious business (Schopenhauer) 3-3-70
affection of . . . (Plato) 5-6-6
agreement the cause of . . . (Aquinas) 6-3-35
Ah . . . could you and I (Fitzgerald) 1-2-88, 4-4-33
Ah . . . let us be true (Arnold) 1-2-91
a kind of natural . . . (Plutarch) 2-2-30
all . . . rooted in sex (Schopenhauer) 3-3-71
along the path of . . . (Freud) 3-1-97
a . . . in quietness (Euripides) 9-10-3
also said to . . . (Hobbes) 4-4-21
. . . always related to God (Kierkegaard) 3-5-40
. . . an art learned late (Ovid) 3-3-17
and at least a little . . . (Dostoevsky) 11-2-150
. . . and fear of him (Hobbes) 20-5-67
. . . and hate (Blake) 9-6-94, 20-15-92
and have merited some . . . (Shakespeare) 15-3-80
and . . . with fear (Milton) 20-8-68
. . . and marriage (Montaigne) 2-3-50
and take my . . . away (Shakespeare) 19-5-29
animals not only . . . but desire (Darwin) 1-1-109
are seeking for . . . (Augustine) 20-13-31
as many kinds of . . . (Descartes) 2-2-60
as our . . . flamed (Augustine) 2-2-38
a time to . . . (*Eccles.*) 19-7-2
away with . . . or jealousy (Shakespeare) 4-10-5
banner of . . . and chivalry (Cervantes) 5-6-24
bargain of a lustful . . . (Augustine) 2-2-36
beauty and tenderness of . . . (Pascal) 16-4-22
beget . . . in a child (Locke) 8-3-61

fair good . . . (Aeschylus) 1-7-10
laments his bad . . . (Fielding) 15-3-97
moderate have excellent . . . (Herodotus) 9-8-2
ready to live by . . . (Thoreau) 11-5-35
seem to have a run of . . . (Euripides) 15-3-18
the . . . of Caesar (Shakespeare) 1-9-29
then for ill . . . (Chaucer) 15-3-66
who has no need of . . . (Seneca) 17-1-24

LUCRETIA
. . . cannot rival her (Cervantes) 5-4-14

LUCRETIUS
Epicurus and . . . (Voltaire) 19-3-40
in the steps of . . . (Voltaire) 3-1-62

LUDICROUS
by preserving the . . . (Fielding) 16-4-29

LUMBER
learned . . . in his head (Pope) 8-1-43

LUNACY
. . . of love is ordinary (Shakespeare) 3-1-39

LUNATIC
holds a . . . in leash (Santayana) 5-6-43

LUNGS
every word a diminution of . . . (Swift) 7-1-41

LUPERCAL
see that on the . . . (Shakespeare) 1-6-29

LUST
adulterous . . . was (Milton) 2-3-69
a woman to . . . (*Matthew*) 2-3-21
. . . breeds mischief (Euripides) 1-7-19
burned in their . . . (*Romans*) 20-13-19
. . . creep in the marrow of (Shakespeare) 3-2-21
did without . . . (Augustine) 2-1-21
drawn away of his own . . . (*James*) 20-13-24
effects of . . . (Hobbes) 3-2-22
. . . has become natural (Pascal) 3-3-57
if a layman yield to . . . (Chaucer) 20-8-54
. . . is a motion of the soul (Augustine) 3-3-23
mine honor into . . . (Shakespeare) 2-3-65
most full of . . . (Aristotle) 1-1-22
my will changed to . . . (Augustine) 9-4-18
of man than of . . . (Augustine) 10-7-13
. . . of the flesh (*I John*) 3-3-19
quarrel between . . . and will (Augustine) 3-3-22
. . . served became a custom (Aquinas) 9-12-19
shall be no . . . (Augustine) 1-7-48
slothly pleasure of . . . (Augustine) 1-8-52
stolen hours of . . . (Shakespeare) 4-10-6
the . . . of the flesh (*I John*) 20-13-25
the sin of . . . (Aquinas) 2-3-33
thy love is . . . (Byron) 1-1-95
to gratify their bestial . . . (Vico) 15-2-31
what evil . . . of life (Lucretius) 1-8-27
when . . . by unchaste looks (Milton) 3-3-58
. . . will never fail us (Chaucer) 1-3-37

LUST-DIETED
superfluous and . . . man (Shakespeare) 9-6-64

LUSTRE
beauty in its highest . . . (Fielding) 16-6-42
love lends . . . (Chaucer) 3-1-29
the . . . of anything seen (Th. Browne) 9-8-45
. . . which the stars have (Fielding) 16-6-43

LUSTS
his . . . to be unrestrained (Plato) 9-12-3
obey it in the . . . thereof (*Romans*) 20-13-20
we retrain our . . . (Spinoza) 9-12-40

LUTHER
a . . . for example (Carlyle) 1-6-62
the services of . . . (Gibbon) 20-12-32

LUXURIES

made to pay for their . . . (Hamilton) 11-6-37
may have . . . (Rousseau) 9-13-28
most . . . indispensable (Thoreau) 11-2-132

LUXURIOUSNESS
. . . would be called abundance (Augustine) 20-13-31

LUXURY
by . . . one understands (Voltaire) 11-2-84
delay through . . . (Tacitus) 1-7-46
effectual blow against . . . (Plutarch) 13-3-6
Fie on lust and . . . (Shakespeare) 3-3-47
. . . in the fair sex (Smith) 2-1-36
in the tokens of . . . (Euripides) 1-8-12
. . . is that repose (Mill) 11-2-145
. . . necessary in monarchies (Montesquieu) 10-6-47
once seduced by . . . (Rousseau) 11-6-21
. . . or grace of life (Aristotle) 10-8-4
parent of . . . and indolence (Plato) 11-2-16
republics end with . . . (Montesquieu) 10-3-33
retrenching people's . . . (Plutarch) 11-6-4
. . . soon completes (Rousseau) 11-2-87
the shrine of . . . (Gray) 11-2-83
vanities of . . . (Rousseau) 1-7-116
what . . . will not he covet (Quintilian) 8-3-16
wickedness of . . . (Byron) 10-6-67
women an object of . . . (Montesquieu) 10-6-48

LYAEAN THYADS
nor . . . deport themselves (Rabelais) 1-7-69

LYCHORIDA
O . . . bring Nestor bring (Shakespeare) 2-2-55

LYCIAN
ask a . . . who (Herodotus) 2-3-11

LYCID
herse where . . . lies (Milton) 4-6-40

LYCIDAS
for . . . your sorrow (Milton) 20-15-74

LYCOPHRON
as the sophist . . . says (Aristotle) 10-1-8

LYCURGUS
benefit . . . obtained (Plutarch) 8-1-14
blessings . . . procured (Plutarch) 11-3-15
even so . . . viewing (Plutarch) 12-1-21
headed by . . . (Herodotus) 10-6-5
masterly stroke of . . . (Plutarch) 13-3-6
. . . was of a persuasion (Plutarch) 2-1-18
. . . would never reduce laws (Plutarch) 12-1-20

LYDGATE
with the numbers of . . . (Dryden) 16-3-49

LYDIA
of the Persians to invade . . . (Herodotus) 14-1-6
the king of . . . (Plato) 9-7-9

LYDIAN
in soft . . . airs (Milton) 16-5-30

LYING
acquired the habit of . . . (Hume) 6-3-85
doubting as easy as . . . (Peirce) 6-6-47
essence of . . . is deception (Ruskin) 6-3-120
how subject to the vice of . . . (Shakespeare) 1-3-49
how the world is given to . . . (Shakespeare) 9-14-23
if we would stop . . . (Tolstoy) 6-3-122
. . . is an accursed vice (Montaigne) 9-14-20
. . . is an ugly vice (Montaigne) 9-14-21
. . . is so ready (Locke) 9-14-41
. . . is wrong even to save (Augustine) 6-3-28
more than from intentional . . . (Boswell) 9-14-51
not meddle with . . . (Montaigne) 6-3-43, 9-14-19
occasion to talk of . . . (Swift) 6-3-82
they are not . . . (Pascal) 9-14-39
universal practice . . . is (Swift) 9-14-44

shelter of the civil ... (Smith) 11-1-34
which corrupt the ... (Rousseau) 10-2-72
MAGISTRATES
  boards of ... meet (Aristotle) 10-4-10
  ... cannot make money (Aristotle) 10-2-12
  ... elected by lot (Plato) 10-4-3
  like ... correct at home (Shakespeare) 10-1-17
MAGNANIMITY
  ... disposes us to do good (Aristotle) 9-10-17
  ... in politics (Burke) 10-2-85
MAGNANIMOUS
  ... rather than law-abiding (Hegel) 3-6-22
MAGNESIA
  his days in the city of ... (Plutarch) 1-9-9
MAGNETIC
  foundations of a ... science (Gilbert) 17-2-11, 17-2-12
  the charged ... state (Faraday) 17-2-83
MAGNETISM
  chemistry and ... have (Faraday) 17-2-82
  subject of atmospheric ... (Faraday) 19-1-99
MAGNIFICENCE
  attended with great ... (Montesquieu) 20-8-73
  ... is productive of greatness (Aristotle) 9-10-17
MAGNIFY
  my soul doth ... the Lord (*Luke*) 1-7-37
  not ... that which is little (Pascal) 7-2-60
MAGNITUDE
  hath dimensions of ... (Hobbes) 19-6-20
  some determinate ... (Hobbes) 19-6-19
MAGNITUDES
  numbers and extensive ... (Wm. James) 17-3-47
MAGPIES
  ... can utter words (Descartes) 7-1-28
MAHDI
  as well might the ... (Wm. James) 19-4-49
MAHOMET
  ... brooding in the desert (Whitehead) 20-1-77
MAID
  chariest ... is prodigal (Shakespeare) 9-10-63
MAIDEN
  no longer called a ... (Sophocles) 1-7-14
MAIDENS
  ... of age to marry (Herodotus) 2-3-12
MAJESTY
  the ... of duty (Kant) 9-9-35
MAJORITY
  a ... are permitted (Thoreau) 12-2-48
  a ... may revolutionize (Lincoln) 10-9-38
  big enough ... in any town (Twain) 9-15-95
  determination of the ... (Swift) 12-1-56
  door on her divine ... (Dickinson) 13-1-46
  government of the ... (Aristotle) 10-4-11
  ... held in check (Lincoln) 10-4-63
  in which ... rules (Thoreau) 10-4-60
  ... is the best way (Pascal) 10-4-15
  ... of the male sex (Mill) 10-4-72
  omnipotence of the ... (Tocqueville) 10-4-56
  opinion of the ... decisive (Aristotle) 10-4-9
  persuaded the ... (Thoreau) 10-2-96, 12-1-85
  sense of the ... (Calhoun) 10-4-59; (Madison) 10-8-22
  the right of the ... (Kant) 12-4-62
  vote of the ... binds (Rousseau) 10-4-30
  ... will desire truth (Kierkegaard) 6-3-105
  will of the ... (Jefferson) 10-4-34
  ... would not be poorer (Shaw) 11-4-48
MAKE
  ... their madness as little (Pascal) 17-1-57
MAKE-BELIEVE
  any truth better than ... (Thoreau) 6-3-112

period of ... and fancy (Russell) 8-1-84
MAKER
  O ... of sweet poets (Keats) 19-1-90
  the ... of all times (Augustine) 19-7-18
  the ... of the world (Plutarch) 12-1-21
  wisdom of their ... (Th. Browne) 19-1-49
  workmanship of one wise ... (Locke) 9-3-20
MAKING
  are two kinds of ... (Plato) 19-1-2
  art rules ... not doing (Maritain) 16-1-67
  in the line of ... (Maritain) 17-1-113
  of ... of many book (*Eccles.*) 16-2-1
MALADIES
  all ... of gastly spasm (Milton) 18-3-48
  free of an infinitude of ... (Descartes) 18-1-28
  heavy thoughts bring on ... (Luther) 5-1-16
  most barbarous of our ... (Montaigne) 1-6-23
  with complicated ... (Swift) 18-1-30
MALADY
  chief ... of man (Pascal) 6-4-23
  ... most incident to maids (Shakespeare) 16-6-35
MALARIA
  breathe ... all the way (Thoreau) 1-4-50
MALCHISHUA
  and ... the sons of Saul (*II Chronicles*) 1-9-1
MALCOM'S
  before young ... feet (Shakespeare) 10-6-27
MALE
  ... and female created He (*Genesis*) 1-1-1
  ... by its very nature (Aquinas) 12-3-6
  ... by nature superior (Aristotle) 10-7-8
  female a mutilated ... (Aristotle) 1-7-31
  great number of ... animals (Darwin) 16-6-69
  ... he created thee (Milton) 1-1-75
  ... is by nature (Aristotle) 2-1-12
  made them ... and female (*Matthew*) 2-3-22
  ... separated from female (Aristotle) 1-7-30
  when ... follows ... (Plato) 3-3-9
MALEFACTOR
  a ... to death (Montesquieu) 12-4-50
MALES
  beauty of the ... (Darwin) 16-6-70
  ... being thus expelled (Darwin) 2-1-43
MALICE
  action overawed his ... (Milton) 9-6-78
  bearing ... like a Frenchman (Fielding) 3-4-46
  chance with ... (Schopenhauer) 19-4-37
  deep ... to conceal (Milton) 6-3-70
  inscrutable ... of the white whale (Melville) 3-2-35
  nor as much ... as stupidity (Montaigne) 1-2-32
  not set down aught in ... (Shakespeare) 3-1-44
  of all ... the end is injury (Dante) 20-15-53
  so deep a ... (Milton) 9-6-77
  the source of all ... (Spinoza) 20-3-35
  wickedness and ... began (Rabelais) 1-1-49
  with ... toward none (Lincoln) 3-5-41
MALIGNITY
  intangible ... which has been (Melville) 3-2-36
MALLET'S, David
  mentioned ... tragedy (Boswell) 16-7-32
MALTREAT
  whom he wishes to ... (Plato) 18-7-10
MAMMA
  and glancing at ... (Byron) 1-3-106
MAMMAL
  no other ... shows (Joyce) 6-2-47
MAMMON
  God and ... (Shaw) 20-3-65
  serve God and ... (*Matthew*) 11-2-38

MATTER (*Cont.*)
by means of . . . itself (Aquinas) 17-2-5
created was the . . . (Dante) 19-2-26
dealing all the time with . . . (Wm. James) 19-2-55
differs from a mass of . . . (Locke) 19-2-36
definition of . . . (Kant) 5-2-32
deny what is called . . . (Berkeley) 5-2-29
form and . . . united (Dante) 19-8-40
form distinct from . . . (Dante) 5-7-15
forms of things without . . . (Aristotle) 5-2-4
fragments fall back as . . . (Bergson) 19-2-61
God formed . . . in solid (Newton) 19-8-61
. . . has its own local time (Russell) 19-7-86
how . . . might be made (Locke) 19-8-66
I am myself the . . . (Montaigne) 16-2-8
identity of . . . with collocation (Wm. James) 19-3-51
if . . . escapes us (Fourier) 17-3-42
inert and dead . . . (Shaw) 19-8-92
infinite divisibility of . . . (Hamilton) 17-3-41
innate force of . . . (Newton) 19-5-45
inorganical parts of . . . (Locke) 19-2-37
. . . in restless movement (Lucretius) 19-5-13
is clearly a folding of . . . (Bacon) 19-6-15
. . . is infinite (Lucretius) 19-6-9
. . . is the seat of flux (Santayana) 19-5-73
motion is dead . . . (Russell) 19-5-69
motion of some . . . (Huygens) 19-5-44
non-existence of . . . (Boswell) 6-6-32
nothing but . . . is left (Aristotle) 19-6-3
. . . not in all places (Newton) 19-8-63
objects which involve no . . . (Aristotle) 5-1-6
one truth to each . . . (Descartes) 6-3-59
poverty and scarcity of . . . (Bacon) 16-2-16
power of prime . . . (Dante) 1-1-46
powers of inorganic . . . (Faraday) 17-2-82
substance which is . . . (Aristotle) 19-8-9
that is the property of . . . (Goethe) 19-2-41
the flux of . . . (Santayana) 19-7-91
the . . . and the shape (Aristotle) 19-6-4
the store of . . . (Lucretius) 19-6-8
. . . the substance of things (Santayana) 6-1-114
this taste of . . . (Plotinus) 9-6-33
ultimate ranges of . . . (Santayana) 19-6-48
unformed . . . of the world (Hobbes) 20-6-38
weight of lifeless . . . (Ovid) 19-8-16
. . . which changes (Aristotle) 19-5-10
. . . would have forming-idea (Plotinus) 9-6-38
MATURE
every . . . man might (Milton) 13-2-16
that he should . . . as soon (Thoreau) 13-1-45
MATURITY
comes to . . . earlier (Darwin) 1-7-139
education as . . . (Russell) 8-1-88
his way from childhood . . . (Freud) 20-1-83
time belongs to . . . (Hippocrates) 8-3-2
MAXENTIUS
. . . and all his enemies (Gibbon) 20-4-43
MAXIM
act on a . . . (Kant) 9-1-23
. . . as universal law (Kant) 9-3-28
. . . based only on experiments (Pascal) 19-6-21
vile . . . of the masters (Smith) 4-9-13
MAXIMS
in spite of our . . . (Rousseau) 9-5-15
. . . of the will (Kant) 9-1-20
. . . of the worst criminals (Hegel) 6-6-38
sure . . . of life (Spinoza) 9-1-8
the like magnified . . . (Locke) 17-2-49
. . . which govern other men (Montesquieu) 9-11-49

MAY
the gladness of the . . . (Wordsworth) 19-1-82
MAYBES
need for dealing with . . . (Wm. James) 6-5-111
MAZZAROTH
bring forth . . . in his season (*Job*) 1-1-2
ME
all that is within . . . (Tolstoy) 19-1-117
MEAN
a . . . between nothing and (Pascal) 1-1-71
choose the . . . in deeds (Aquinas) 8-2-11
empty space is a . . . (Pascal) 19-6-22
is a . . . in things (Horace) 9-12-11
lying in a . . . (Aristotle) 9-10-13
no . . . of contrary qualities (Aristotle) 5-2-4
passion admits of a . . . (Aristotle) 9-7-15
the golden . . . doth choose (Horace) 9-12-12
the . . . is proper pride (Aristotle) 1-5-15
to be seated in the . . . (Shakespeare) 9-12-30
transgresses the . . . (Aristotle) 10-3-7
uses as a . . . to (Kant) 1-9-38
MEANING
an enrichment of living's . . . (Dewey) 8-1-89
a straw for all the . . . (Chaucer) 5-5-17
. . . changes with words (Pascal) 7-2-64
explain my own . . . (Sterne) 7-2-75
expresses the right . . . (Augustine) 7-1-11
full . . . of each experience (Dewey) 6-2-52
gathering the . . . of things (Aristotle) 16-3-7
has his complete . . . alone (T. S. Eliot) 16-7-53
he had given no . . . (Wittgenstein) 17-1-110
. . . in all his efforts (Mann) 13-1-69
know thine own . . . (Shakespeare) 7-1-25
. . . of a word conventional (Russell) 7-1-65
original concrete . . . of words (Freud) 7-2-91
original . . . of the word (Kant) 7-2-83
spiritual . . . had been revealed (Pascal) 20-2-30
their . . . is all one (Chaucer) 6-3-41
the . . . of life (Dostoevsky) 19-8-87
what constitutes . . . (Russell) 7-1-66
whether symbols have . . . (Freud) 7-1-70
MEANINGS
. . . by natural signs (Dewey) 7-1-72
permanent emendation of . . . (Descartes) 7-2-58
MEANNESS
greatness and . . . (Emerson) 1-4-47
MEANS
beyond our . . . (Montaigne) 9-9-16
deliberate about . . . (Aristotle) 5-7-2
deserteth the . . . (Hobbes) 10-2-58
discovers a multitude of . . . (Spinoza) 19-3-30
for lack of . . . (Montaigne) 2-2-45
grasp truth by our own . . . (Montaigne) 6-3-46
live within moderate . . . (Mill) 9-12-49
man not used as a . . . (Kant) 9-3-30
no part of whole merely a . . . (Russell) 6-7-44
. . . of acquiring happiness (Aquinas) 9-13-15
past as a . . . of education (Dewey) 8-1-87
the right choice of . . . (Aquinas) 9-13-13
virtues are . . . (Aristotle) 9-10-15
MEASURE
. . . a parcel of land (Xenophon) 17-3-4
a rule or . . . is imposed (Aquinas) 12-1-25
common . . . of all things (Grotius) 11-4-16
God ought to be the . . . (Plato) 20-8-22
he longs for . . . (Plotinus) 16-5-12
himself the . . . of all (Santayana) 6-3-150
man is the . . . of all (Diogenes Laertius) 17-1-1
man the . . . of all (Plato) 1-1-10, 6-6-2

... of human justice (Calvin) 12-2-26
of the stateliest ... (Tennyson) 16-3-83
... of value of all things (Hobbes) 11-2-17
... of what is right (Hegel) 12-1-79
right ... of punishment (Plato) 12-4-9
same ... ye mete (*Luke*) 12-2-20
this ... too is there (Augustine) 16-6-22
universal ... of value (Marx) 11-4-40

MEASUREMENT
determine by ... (Herodotus) 17-3-1
order and ... (Descartes) 17-3-26

MEASURES
money ... all things (Aristotle) 11-4-1
tie themselves to ancient ... (Bacon) 16-7-16
we use sensible ... (Newton) 19-6-28

MEASURING
the art of ... (Newton) 17-3-31

MEAT
life is more than ... (*Luke*) 4-9-3
upon what ... doth Caesar (Shakespeare) 1-6-27

MECHANICAL
cause which is not ... (Newton) 19-3-31
poetry is not ... (Goethe) 16-3-69
terms of ... motions (Huygens) 19-5-44
the state of the ... (Smith) 14-2-50

MECHANICAL ART
distinguishes the ... (Kant) 16-1-36

MECHANICAL ARTS
... and merchandise (Bacon) 10-1-19
inventors of the ... (Voltaire) 17-1-70

MECHANICS
according to classical ... (Einstein) 19-7-87
... also pursue (Cicero) 11-3-10
by means of ... (Archimedes) 17-3-14
celestial ... (Poincaré) 17-3-53
classical ... too is based (Einstein) 19-6-46
esteemed science of ... (Newton) 17-3-31
knowledge of rational ... (Fourier) 17-2-74
not lead life of ... (Aristotle) 10-5-9
object of rational ... (Fourier) 17-3-42
the art of ... (Plutarch) 17-3-15
the class of ... (Aristotle) 10-8-4
the harmonies of ... (Wm. James) 8-3-89

MECHANISM
disturbance of the ... (Bernard) 19-2-52
genius of ... smothers him (Carlyle) 1-2-77
nature and its mere ... (Kant) 19-4-35
... of the world (Voltaire) 17-2-57
or as it is called a ... (Kant) 16-1-33
regarded as aimless ... (Kant) 16-6-48

MEDEA
... gathered the enchanted herbs (Shakespeare) 3-1-37

MEDES
government of the ... (Machiavelli) 1-6-20

MEDIATOR
he became the ... (Augustine) 20-14-22
he can be ... (Aquinas) 20-14-29
love ... between man and God (Plato) 3-1-9
no access without a ... (Milton) 20-2-33
the ... and the Way (Augustine) 20-14-23
the true ... whom in (Augustine) 20-14-19
this ... having spoken (Augustine) 6-5-22
without a ... (Pascal) 20-1-26

MEDICAL
variety of ... problems (Harvey) 17-2-31

MEDICINE
acquire a knowledge of ... (Hippocrates) 8-3-1
as ... for the punished (Aquinas) 12-4-24
best ... for a sick mind (Livy) 15-1-13

by the help of ... (Aquinas) 1-2-27
function of ... (Aristotle) 7-2-10
inclination to practice of ... (Plutarch) 8-3-21
is one art of ... (Aristotle) 9-15-24
nature with aid of ... (Aquinas) 8-3-35
only ... is wisdom (Huxley) 9-15-91
patiently receive my ... (Shakespeare) 9-15-55
poems a ... for my state (Mill) 16-3-88
prepared the ... of faith (Augustine) 6-5-20
remedied by ... (Aquinas) 2-3-36
thy ... on my lips (Shakespeare) 2-2-54
... to produce health (Plutarch) 6-2-11
what is object of ... (Pascal) 16-3-41

MEDICINES
not be irritated by ... (Plato) 18-3-14

MEDIOCRE
it is happiness to be ... (Nietzsche) 9-8-77

MEDIOCRITY
a collective ... (Mill) 10-4-65
rise above ... (Mill) 10-4-66

MEDITATION
and the ... of my heart (*Psalms*) 20-5-9
... is a powerful study (Montaigne) 5-1-18
proof against protracted ... (Melville) 9-11-59

MEDITATIONS
comprehension of my ... (Descartes) 6-6-19

MEDITERRANEAN
in the basin of the ... (Freud) 20-2-48

MEDIUM
function of circulating ... (Marx) 11-4-43
language is a cloudy ... (Madison) 7-2-86

MEDIUS TERMINUS
got hold of the ... (Sterne) 6-7-32

MEEK
blessed are the ... (*Matthew*) 9-8-19; (Aquinas) 9-8-33

MEGABYZUS
... spoke next (Herodotus) 10-3-1

MEGACLES
... the son of Alcmaeon (Herodotus) 10-6-5

MEGARA
with ... and the old man (Euripides) 5-6-4

MELANCHOLY
all the monstrosities of ... (Th. Browne) 5-5-26
arise from your ... (Chaucer) 5-5-17
can be free from ... (Wm. James) 9-6-112
green and yellow ... (Shakespeare) 1-7-83
had divinest ... (Milton) 4-6-39
loathed ... of Cerberus (Milton) 4-6-38
or ... and madness (Boswell) 5-6-33
pleasure in ... (Montaigne) 4-6-29

MELANCHOLY'S
hateful error ... child (Shakespeare) 6-4-18

MELIORATOR
greatest ... in the world (Emerson) 11-5-29

MELLONA
honey without ... (Augustine) 20-2-20

MELODY
rhythm and ... supply (Aristotle) 16-5-7

MEMBERS
of thy ... should perish (*Matthew*) 2-3-21

MEMENTOS
with dying ... (Th. Browne) 1-8-105

MEMORANDUM
law is only a ... (Emerson) 12-1-80

MEMMIUS
most noble ... who (Lucretius) 17-1-18

MEMNON'S
prince ... sister (Milton) 4-6-39

MEMORIAL
be unto you for a ... (*Exodus*) 20-2-7
sets a war ... up (Euripides) 1-5-5
MEMORIALS
scarcity of ... (Gibbon) 15-1-51
MEMORIES
bitter ... to recall (Chaucer) 9-8-35
employs aright these ... (Plato) 17-1-3
lest we lose those ... (Plutarch) 2-2-31
to extend our ... (Th. Browne) 1-8-104, 19-7-45
MEMORIZING
the ... aspect of learning (Plutarch) 8-3-23
MEMORY
act of ... is hindered (Aquinas) 5-4-3
all that is committed to ... (Wm. James) 8-3-87
animals live by ... (Aristotle) 6-2-6
attention and repetition in ... (Locke) 4-7-48
corpse of your ... (Emerson) 1-4-48
dear son of ... (Milton) 1-5-97
decay of sense is ... (Hobbes) 5-4-17
devoid of reproductive ... (Wm. James) 19-7-82
did in ... retain (Rabelais) 8-1-23
engraving deep in ... (Descartes) 6-4-21
entrusted to your ... (Seneca) 6-1-20
faileth ... at so great age (Dante) 5-4-5
fancy a mode of ... (Coleridge) 5-4-30
found by help of ... (Berkeley) 6-1-70
from the ... a rooted sorrow (Shakespeare) 5-6-21
given our ... to keep (Montaigne) 8-3-41
he keeps in ... (Pascal) 15-2-26
ideas lodged in ... (Locke) 7-1-33
if you had no ... (Plato) 9-6-11
I have ... and understanding (Voltaire) 1-1-83
... in animals (Harvey) 8-3-50
in the ventricle of ... (Shakespeare) 5-4-8
... is an internal rumor (Santayana) 15-1-93
... is of the past (Aquinas) 1-3-33
lies in the domain of ... (Schopenhauer) 4-6-48
... like a sieve (Sterne) 6-4-31
live by ... (Aristotle) 1-3-19
living record of your ... (Shakespeare) 16-3-33
lose the ... (Locke) 1-4-32
lost the ... of holy things (Plato) 16-6-6
need have a great ... (Bacon) 16-2-17
... of man runneth not (Coke) 9-2-17
of more retentive ... (Aristotle) 1-7-29
past is lived again in ... (Dewey) 1-1-130
powers of observation ... (Darwin) 1-1-108
present in my ... (Augustine) 19-7-20
principle of ... alone (Leibniz) 5-1-39
properties of what men call ... (Maritain) 17-2-135
recalls ... to sensations (Rousseau) 7-1-49
remain long in ... (Dostoevsky) 5-5-35
reproach upon his ... (Swift) 1-6-42
searches over all the ... (Dryden) 5-4-21
... should be taxed in youth (Schopenhauer) 8-3-31
seized with a loss of ... (Thucydides) 18-3-5
... soon dissipates (Gibbon) 7-1-53
stepmother to ... oblivion (John of Salisbury) 6-1-30
still vivid in ... (Augustine) 1-5-43
sufficiently strong in ... (Montaigne) 6-3-43, 9-14-19
things past is ... (Augustine) 19-7-22
word for word in one's ... (Thucydides) 15-1-3
MEN
abhorred by all ... (Sophocles) 1-3-9
all ... are equal (Tolstoy) 20-3-59
and ... are so untrue (Chaucer) 3-1-30
angels rank above ... (Augustine) 20-7-14
... are but gilded loam (Shakespeare) 1-5-64

are ... before they are lawyers (Mill) 8-1-72
... are not gentle (Freud) 1-2-97
... are so necessarily mad (Pascal) 5-6-28
... are so simple (Machiavelli) 10-2-33
are the greatest ... (Thucydides) 9-11-5
... are tormented (Montaigne) 9-6-56
ashes that once were ... (Aeschylus) 14-1-5
... as plants increase (Shakespeare) 1-3-60
assuming all ... are bad (Machiavelli) 10-3-15
... at first had eyes (Aeschylus) 15-2-3
... created in image of God (Augustine) 3-1-21
... first and subjects afterwards (Thoreau) 10-4-60, 10-5-25
friendship for ... alone (Descartes) 3-4-31
great ... lead humanity (Tolstoy) 19-4-43
... have age a lickerish appetite (Chaucer) 19-1-24
if you would command ... (Rousseau) 10-2-75
make ... of some other metal (Shakespeare) 2-3-54
make them ... first (Ruskin) 20-1-64
... must endure (Shakespeare) 1-8-85
... naturally one another (Pascal) 3-2-23
of all the ... of his time (Plato) 1-8-18
... of greatest worth (Chaucer) 3-1-29
political science does not make ... (Aristotle) 10-2-10
possess the form of ... (Cicero) 20-6-27
rich ... need friends (Aristotle) 3-4-11
... sexually competent to old age (Aristotle) 3-3-11
the well-being of ... (Tolstoy) 16-1-51
transform ... into brutes (Montesquieu) 10-2-70
two kinds of ... (Pascal) 20-13-80
unclean the nature of ... (Grotius) 14-3-29
... whose visages do cream (Shakespeare) 9-15-50
wisest ... have erred (Milton) 1-7-103
... worse than average (Aristotle) 16-4-7
ye ... who are dimly existing (Aristophanes) 1-1-8
MENACE
... of eternal tortures (Gibbon) 20-1-47
MENAGERIES
what goes on in ... (Nietzsche) 19-1-118
MENALIPPUS
gnaw the temples of ... (Dante) 3-2-14
MENCIUS
brute beasts says ... (Thoreau) 1-1-106
MENDED
that's ... is but patched (Shakespeare) 9-10-61
MENO
do you see ... what (Plato) 6-4-5
MENTAL
attain ... stature capable of (Mill) 6-3-117
possibilities of ... life (Whitehead) 8-3-92
study of ... conditions (Wm. James) 8-3-92
superior in ... endowment (Darwin) 1-7-142
MERCENARIES
... are useless and dangerous (Machiavelli) 14-2-29
valor of barbarian ... (Gibbon) 14-2-57
MERCENARY
best to have a ... (Plutarch) 14-2-25
... captains are either capable (Machiavelli) 14-2-30
talk of ... standing army (Swift) 14-2-44
MERCHANDISE
sign of value of ... (Montesquieu) 11-4-23
the duties from ... (Montesquieu) 11-6-15
MERCHANT
becomes a ... (Smith) 11-3-35
... grows more eager (Dostoevsky) 11-2-150
the craft of the ... (Emerson) 11-5-31
MERCHANTS
cultivators and ... (Hamilton) 11-5-24
... venture trade abroad (Shakespeare) 10-1-17
MERCIES

beseech you by the . . . of God (*Romans*) 20-8-33
sing of the . . . of the Lord (*Psalms*) 20-2-15
what . . . are these (Cervantes) 5-6-25
MERCIFUL
  be ye therefore . . . (*Luke*) 12-2-20
MERCUTIO
  peace . . . peace (Shakespeare) 5-5-21
MERCY
  according to his . . . (*Titus*) 9-4-7
  act of . . . as eliciting (Aquinas) 20-1-12
  and to love . . . (*Micah*) 20-8-10
  appears the . . . of God (Aquinas) 15-3-60
  but . . . first and last (Milton) 20-14-44
  confidence in the . . . (Luther) 6-5-36
  consider the promises of . . . (Calvin) 6-5-40
  deeds of light and . . . (Dostoevsky) 3-5-43
  despair of the . . . (Chaucer) 4-5-15
  founded on gratuitous . . . (Calvin) 15-3-73
  . . . has a human heart (Blake) 20-8-77
  have . . . upon me (*Psalms*) 20-13-5
  his justice and . . . (Th. Browne) 20-14-39
  his . . . is everlasting (*Psalms*) 20-8-7
  in justice remember . . . (Bacon) 12-4-35
  leaving . . . to heaven (Fielding) 3-5-34
  Lord is plenteous in . . . (*Psalms*) 3-5-2
  memorial of the divine . . . (Aquinas) 20-2-23
  . . . on this small black boy (Melville) 20-8-83
  prefer . . . before rigor (Cervantes) 12-4-33
  properly is to have . . . (Aquinas) 9-8-33
  quality of . . . is not strained (Shakespeare) 3-5-25
  same tone of . . . (Tacitus) 1-9-16
  secret of your . . . (Augustine) 20-14-20
  showing . . . unto thousands (*Exodus*) 9-3-1; (*Deut.*) 20-2-11
  show . . . and compassion (*Zechariah*) 9-7-5
  shut the gates of . . . (Boswell) 10-7-26
  so good a grace as . . . (Shakespeare) 3-5-26
  they love . . . (Augustine) 2-1-20
  they shall obtain . . . (*Matthew*) 9-8-19
  to love . . . (*Micah*) 9-9-2
  whereto serves . . . but to (Shakespeare) 20-8-60
  you will have . . . on whom (Augustine) 20-5-32
MERIDIAN
  a . . . decides the truth (Pascal) 12-2-35
MERIT
  although they have . . . (Dante) 4-5-12
  ascribed to any . . . (Mill) 2-2-88
  by the . . . of the wearer (Shakespeare) 1-5-64
  class not interfere with . . . (Thucydides) 13-1-2
  encourage personal . . . (Montesquieu) 10-2-70
  estimate of personal . . . (Gibbon) 1-5-112
  free will begat . . . (Luther) 19-3-19
  honors below his . . . (Swift) 4-11-29
  how to honor . . . (Herodotus) 6-2-3
  impute success to . . . (Swift) 15-3-96
  . . . in religious faith (Boswell) 6-5-80
  intrinsic . . . of the candidate (Hamilton) 10-2-90
  irrespective of human . . . (Calvin) 15-3-73
  ladies the best judges of . . . (Montesquieu) 3-1-60
  linked are luck and . . . (Goethe) 15-3-105
  men of . . . (Boswell) 15-3-101
  more . . . is in your bounty (Shakespeare) 12-2-28
  no diversity of . . . (Aquinas) 13-3-9
  . . . not taken into consideration (Descartes) 4-11-19
  of grace and precedent . . . (Dante) 4-5-13
  . . . of language is clearness (Galen) 7-2-38
  oft got without . . . (Shakespeare) 1-5-71
  . . . of the physician (Gibbon) 18-2-41
  particular . . . (Seneca) 4-8-10
  poverty hinders . . . (Juvenal) 11-2-46

show me the . . . (Pascal) 1-5-92
teachers men of . . . (Plato) 8-3-3
the . . . of an object (Smith) 4-11-34
the . . . of art (Whitehead) 16-1-56
there will be neither . . . (Aquinas) 20-15-47
to claim a . . . (Gibbon) 9-10-105
upon the . . . of their vices (Swift) 9-10-89
weakness would be . . . (Luther) 6-5-37
. . . wherever found (Tacitus) 10-5-12
without distinction to . . . (Th. Browne) 5-3-20
MERITS
  God alone can know our . . . (Wm. James) 5-7-47
  language has two . . . (Russell) 7-1-67
  . . . of the case (Aristotle) 9-11-8
  to those weaker . . . (Th. Browne) 9-15-70
  won by . . . (Boethius) 1-5-48
MERMAID
  and heard a . . . on (Shakespeare) 16-5-18
MERRIMACK
  earlier than the . . . shad (Thoreau) 15-2-58
MERRYMAKING
  preaches nothing but . . . (Montaigne) 17-1-45
MESHACH
  . . . and Abednego (*Daniel*) 20-11-2
MESSAGE
  . . . issue from your heart (Goethe) 16-1-37
  youth's . . . is noblest (Goethe) 1-3-97
MESSEIS
  from the spring of . . . (Homer) 2-2-8
MESSENGER
  he was a . . . of heaven (Dante) 20-7-31
  is signified a . . . (Hobbes) 20-7-55
  I will send my . . . (*Malachi*) 20-14-8
MESSENGERS
  credit of God's . . . (Hobbes) 20-11-21
  employs them as . . . (Calvin) 20-7-38
MESSIAH
  foretold that the . . . (Pascal) 20-11-25
  proof of being the . . . (Pascal) 20-10-34
  restored by a . . . (Pascal) 20-3-32
  to give faith to the . . . (Pascal) 20-2-30
  whereon . . . was declared (Milton) 20-7-63
  witness to the . . . (Pascal) 6-5-61
METALLURGY
  the . . . of Hephaestus (Plato) 16-1-1
METALS
  value belongs to precious . . . (Grotius) 11-4-16
METAPHOR
  attention to . . . by prose (Aristotle) 7-2-20
  to be a master of . . . (Aristotle) 16-3-10
METAPHYSIC
  arena is called . . . (Kant) 17-1-74
  as a branch of . . . (Bacon) 17-3-22
  . . . handleth the final causes (Bacon) 19-3-20
  history presupposes a . . . (Whitehead) 15-1-90
METAPHYSICAL
  . . . composed of abstractions (Comte) 17-2-76
  darkness of . . . criticism (Wm. James) 19-3-50
  many so-called . . . principles (Wm. James) 16-6-77
  philosophy of the . . . kind (Hume) 17-2-55
  . . . qualities are darkly (Gibbon) 20-2-41
  reliance on . . . principles (Whitehead) 15-1-88
  results of . . . analysis (Mill) 17-3-44
  rule not to recognize . . . entities (Descartes) 19-6-16
  the . . . comfort that life is (Nietzsche) 16-4-42
  to say something . . . (Wittgenstein) 17-1-110
METAPHYSICALLY
  world not . . . necessary (Leibniz) 19-8-64

METAPHYSICS

all the . . . of religion (Tolstoy) 20-1-71
a pseudo-Platonic . . . (Santayana) 20-2-52
every true system of . . . (Schopenhauer) 19-8-73
induction presupposes . . . (Wm. James) 17-2-115
. . . is the attempt to conceive (Russell) 17-1-99
. . . means nothing (Wm. James) 17-1-91
. . . of the Pythagoreans (Mill) 17-1-87
. . . of true belief (Th. Browne) 1-8-107
poetry like . . . (Maritain) 16-3-103
system of biographical . . . (Santayana) 6-6-55
through Greek . . . (Bergson) 17-1-107
to complete his . . . (Whitehead) 17-1-96
. . . too pursues spiritual (Maritain) 17-1-113
we must rise to . . . (Leibniz) 19-3-33
what is the business of . . . (Kant) 19-1-71

METAPHYSICS

philosopher says in the . . . (Aquinas) 6-1-38
beginning of the . . . (Aquinas) 9-8-30, 10-7-15

METHOD

creating a . . . of research (Bernard) 18-1-33
experimental . . . has changed (Wm. James) 17-2-103
good and orderly . . . (Hobbes) 6-7-22
goodness consisteth in . . . (Hobbes) 15-1-35
invents a new . . . (Russell) 17-2-118
investigate without . . . (Descartes) 6-3-58
new . . . in medicine (Moliere) 18-1-29
no conception of scientific . . . (Shaw) 18-1-38
. . . of the schools (Pascal) 6-7-26
our . . . and that of the sceptics (Bacon) 6-6-16
principles of experimental . . . (Bernard) 17-2-96
right . . . of philosophy (Wittgenstein) 17-1-110
there was no . . . (Hobbes) 17-1-53
truer . . . of philosophy (Newton) 17-2-44
. . . used in exposition (Aristotle) 8-1-5

METHODS

. . . are minor in education (Wm. James) 8-1-77
. . . rather than objects (Santayana) 17-2-133

METHUSALAS

and seven . . . would (Th. Browne) 19-8-55

METRIC SYSTEM

whether the . . . is true (Poincaré) 17-3-49

METRODORUS

. . . used to say (Montaigne) 4-6-29

MEXICO

despotic empires of . . . (Montesquieu) 9-11-48

MICAWBER

said Mr. . . . (Dickens) 11-2-131

MICHAEL

. . . and his angels (*Revelation*) 20-7-8
the sword of . . . (Milton) 20-7-64

MICHAL

. . . Saul's daughter (*II Samuel*) 20-8-3

MICHELANGELO

reminds him of . . . (Wm. James) 16-7-49

MICKLE

. . . is the powerful grace (Shakespeare) 18-1-19

MICROBE

every disease has its . . . (Shaw) 18-3-61

MICROCOSM

let our . . . be fancied (Rabelais) 19-2-27

MICROSCOPES

but . . . are prudent (Dickinson) 17-2-91

MIDDLE

but as to the . . . (Aurelius) 16-4-12

MIDDLE AGE

in the . . . of a state (Bacon) 10-1-19

MIDDLE AGED

the . . . man concludes (Thoreau) 1-3-117

MIDDLE AGES

in the . . . people believed (Shaw) 17-2-114
see that in the . . . (Comte) 15-2-51
. . . took a fancy to (Shaw) 18-1-37

MIDDLE CLASS

citizens of the . . . (Aristotle) 10-8-6
comforts of the . . . (Mill) 11-3-76
in England the . . . (Mill) 10-4-65
. . . is politically conscious (Hegel) 10-8-27
. . . owner of property (Marx and Engels) 11-1-68
perfected . . . home (Arnold) 20-15-100
. . . pessimism over the future (Whitehead) 15-2-77
they have a . . . Aristotle) 10-3-7

MIDDLE CLASSES

only the . . . are told (Arnold) 10-4-73
on the . . . alone (Rousseau) 10-8-13
tenacious among the . . . (Tocqueville) 11-1-50

MIDIAS

oration against . . . (Plutarch) 7-2-34

MIDWIFERY

my art of . . . like theirs (Plato) 8-3-8

MIGHT

beyond all his . . . (Chaucer) 11-2-54
. . . by force of numbers (Chaucer) 10-6-19
is just to obey . . . (Pascal) 12-2-37
. . . is right with those (Tacitus) 14-1-30
. . . of the gods moves on (Euripides) 20-6-16
. . . only shall be admired (Milton) 14-1-56
oppresses by . . . (Aquinas) 10-3-14
without . . . is helpless (Pascal) 12-2-36

MILE

compel thee to go a . . . (*Matthew*) 12-2-19

MILETUS

not . . . nor yet Anytus (Plato) 3-2-2

MILITANT

only of a church . . . (Kierkegaard) 20-4-47

MILITARIST

every learned . . . (Tolstoy) 14-2-71

MILITARY

. . . and other duties (Plato) 8-1-2
defended by . . . force (Gibbon) 11-6-31
. . . ignorance of their successors (Gibbon) 7-2-81
in a . . . nation (Montesquieu) 9-11-49
. . . service only one exacted (Hegel) 11-6-44
thirst of . . . glory (Gibbon) 1-5-111
took its place as a . . . art (Plutarch) 17-3-15
treasury of . . . virtue (Plutarch) 8-3-21

MILITIA

. . . in whatever manner (Smith) 14-2-52
light . . . of the lower sky (Pope) 20-7-69
transfer the . . . (Hobbes) 10-3-21

MILL, John Stuart

methodized by . . . (Wm. James) 17-2-104

MILLIONAIRE

in the . . . Undershaft (Shaw) 11-2-156

MILLIONAIRES

crowded with these . . . (Tacitus) 10-5-12

MILLSTONE

. . . were hanged around his neck (*Matthew*) 1-3-26

MILTON, John

round the path of . . . (Wordsworth) 16-3-73
some mute inglorious . . . (Gray) 11-2-83
style of excellence such as . . . (Boswell) 16-7-35
the reason . . . wrote (Blake) 16-3-63
. . . thou shouldst be living (Wordsworth) 16-3-74

MIMALLONIDES

never did the Proetides . . . (Rabelais) 1-7-69

MIMIC

mere . . . artifice (Aurelius) 16-4-12

MIND

according to capacity of . . . (Montaigne) 8-3-39
activity in which the . . . (Poincaré) 17-3-51
a cultivated . . . (Mill) 8-1-69
adoration of the . . . (Bacon) 6-2-20
affection of the . . . (Harvey) 18-3-45
all presence of . . . (Thucydides) 4-2-4
all that finds a place in . . . (Hegel) 16-1-42
all the workings of one . . . (Wordsworth) 20-5-99
a . . . exactly balanced (Montaigne) 4-4-17
. . . and the soul are kept (Lucretius) 4-1-3
animal did by . . . (Pascal) 19-2-33
a positive state of . . . (Aristotle) 6-4-7
apprehended by the . . . (Wm. James) 19-6-37
apte the . . . or fancie (Milton) 9-15-72
as to faculties of . . . (Hobbes) 13-3-11
a sublime temper of . . . (Kant) 20-12-33
attended with peace of . . . (Hume) 9-10-97
a weakness of the . . . (Spinoza) 9-7-40
barriers to the . . . (Montaigne) 13-2-13
beauty of the . . . more (Plato) 16-6-7
books to a naughty . . . (Milton) 13-2-16
bring back your . . . (Montaigne) 1-4-19
bring the philosophic . . . (Wordsworth) 19-1-82
by renewing of your . . . (*Romans*) 20-8-33
. . . calculates means (Aristotle) 4-4-4
. . . cannot conceive of God (Calvin) 20-5-50
capacity of human . . . (Gibbon) 6-5-83
capacity of . . . not infinite (Hume) 19-6-34
cognitive exercise of the . . . (Descartes) 17-2-34
comprehensive . . . always dialectical (Plato) 8-1-2
conquest of . . . (Dewey) 6-7-47
corrupt conceptions of the . . . (Calvin) 20-13-67
. . . corrupted from its integrity (Calvin) 5-1-17
critical turn of . . . (T. S. Eliot) 16-7-52
cure the body with the . . . (Plato) 18-2-8
darkness of . . . (Lucretius) 1-8-24, 19-1-11
deformed in his . . . (Smith) 9-11-51
depends on nature of the . . . (Darwin) 16-6-69
. . . depends on temperament (Descartes) 18-1-27
depraved state of . . . (Mill) 1-7-147
development of human . . . (Rousseau) 7-2-76
. . . differs in quality (Santayana) 1-7-168
difficulties . . . anticipates (Leibniz) 6-5-69
discover the . . . of another (Bacon) 10-2-49
. . . disposed to moral feeling (Kant) 9-3-32
distance between body and . . . (Pascal) 3-5-30
divided and rebel . . . (Emerson) 1-3-112
Elizium of a composed . . . (Th. Browne) 9-8-46
even the group . . . (Freud) 16-1-58
ever moved in his . . . (Spinoza) 9-15-76
every faculty of the . . . (Kant) 17-1-74
exist in the divine . . . (Aquinas) 19-8-34
faced the specters of the . . . (Tennyson) 6-6-42
faculties of his . . . (Kepler) 1-1-54
faculties of . . . and body are chains (Voltaire) 3-1-62
farewell the tranquill . . . (Shakespeare) 4-10-6, 14-2-38
fictions of the . . . (Descartes) 6-6-17
firm and collected . . . (Plutarch) 18-3-26
. . . for all its worthlessness (Augustine) 6-3-27
furnish the . . . by degrees (Locke) 7-1-33
fury of his . . . (Augustine) 1-5-42
genius and very cast of . . . (Sterne) 2-2-72
gentle . . . by gentle deeds (Spenser) 9-2-13
glide out of the . . . (Johnson) 20-1-43
grant a tranquil . . . (Tacitus) 1-5-38
greater calm and serenity of . . . (Berkeley) 17-1-61
grieve in a sane . . . (Augustine) 1-1-36
. . . had adapted itself (Poincaré) 17-3-50

had neither . . . nor memory (Plato) 9-6-11
have a . . . ready (Machiavelli) 1-5-53
health of . . . is most proper (Bacon) 18-3-44
healthy . . . in a healthy body (Juvenal) 5-1-10, 15-3-43
hearers in a right frame of . . . (Aristotle) 7-2-15
highest good of the . . . (Spinoza) 6-1-63
highest part of the . . . (Bacon) 6-1-48
his . . . runs back (Hobbes) 5-3-18
how is . . . furnished (Locke) 6-2-25
human . . . cannot attain (Augustine) 1-4-14
idols beset the . . . (Bacon) 6-4-19
. . . ignorant of true God (Augustine) 9-10-41
I may be of a sound . . . (Plato) 9-3-3
impairs their peace of . . . (Lucretius) 20-6-23
impolluted temple of the . . . (Milton) 9-10-80
impressing upon childish . . . (Huxley) 6-6-45
improve and exalt his . . . (Malthus) 9-6-97
inappropriate force . . . (Dostoevsky) 19-8-87
in a sorry state of . . . (Peirce) 6-3-123
incentives to the . . . (Locke) 8-3-55
. . . in so far as it uses reason (Spinoza) 6-1-61
internal workings of the . . . (Freud) 18-1-41
in the public . . . (Montaigne) 1-5-61
irradiate all powers of the . . . (Milton) 6-5-63
. . . is created quick to love (Dante) 3-1-28
. . . is directed to assent (Aquinas) 6-5-27
. . . is its own place (Milton) 5-1-33
. . . is never passive (Whitehead) 8-3-92
. . . is no longer in him (Plato) 16-3-5
. . . is so alienated (Calvin) 20-13-66
. . . is so limited (Boswell) 6-6-31
. . . is subject to passions (Spinoza) 4-1-21
its own wonders in the . . . (Augustine) 19-7-17
keen little legal . . . (Plato) 17-1-9
knots and stonds of the . . . (Bacon) 8-3-49
liability of the . . . to mistakes (Augustine) 6-1-27
life of the . . . (Plato) 9-6-11
logic of the popular . . . (Dewey) 7-1-73
loses faculty of applying . . . (Tocqueville) 11-3-46
love of the . . . towards God (Spinoza) 3-5-32
mathematical and intuitive . . . (Pascal) 17-3-28
measure my . . . against his (Shaw) 16-3-96
moralistic state of . . . (Wm. James) 20-14-56
. . . more noble than body (Dante) 4-7-32
must unbend his . . . (Sophocles) 9-15-12
my . . . knows it (Homer) 2-2-8
my . . . seems to have become (Darwin) 16-3-87
natural exercise of . . . (Montaigne) 7-2-47
nature of our . . . leads us (Bernard) 6-1-94
nature with equal . . . (Arnold) 19-1-116
. . . needs signs (Locke) 7-1-37
negative state of . . . (Wm. James) 1-9-48
new construction in the . . . (Wm. James) 6-1-99
nobler faculties of the . . . (Gibbon) 7-1-53
no need of . . . in this process (Russell) 19-5-69
. . . not deemed slave (Plato) 9-4-1
. . . not go against instinct (Aquinas) 20-9-9
not have found the . . . (Santayana) 19-1-124
nothing change his . . . (Milton) 6-5-64
. . . of such balance (Emerson) 1-6-66
. . . of the lowest man (Darwin) 1-1-110
. . . of the philosopher (Plato) 17-1-3
. . . of those who have died (Euripides) 20-15-10
one or another state of . . . (Peirce) 6-6-47
on torture of the . . . to lie (Shakespeare) 1-8-90, 9-5-7
. . . open to their influence (Emerson) 19-1-98
or have no . . . (Plato) 2-3-18
or mindless entities . . . (Plotinus) 19-2-20
. . . over the passionate (Aristotle) 10-7-8

MIRABELL
positively . . . I'll lie abed (Congreve) 2-3-77
MIRACLE
all change is a . . . (Thoreau) 19-5-65
a real stupendous . . . (Dostoevsky) 20-13-92
never a . . . to convice atheism (Bacon) 20-9-19
stranger worked a . . . (Euripides) 5-6-5
the event is a . . . (Pascal) 20-10-32
the standing . . . of the world (Augustine) 20-11-9
this is the . . . of Christianity (Kierkegaard) 20-3-48
very literally a . . . (Carlyle) 19-7-74
world is still a . . . (Carlyle) 19-8-79
. . . wrought by God (Bacon) 20-5-58
MIRACLES
. . . as supernatural events (Locke) 6-5-71
by . . . that is by ignorance (Spinoza) 20-3-35
deep mysterious . . . (Goethe) 9-8-66
lived in days of . . . (Th. Browne) 6-5-54
one is the doing of . . . (Hobbes) 20-10-31
prophecies are real . . . (Hume) 20-10-38
religion attended with . . . (Hume) 6-5-77
that . . . are ceased (Th. Browne) 20-11-22
the principle credit of . . . (Montaigne) 20-12-18
the virtues to work . . . (Aquinas) 20-7-28
with divers . . . (*Hebrews*) 6-5-15
worketh . . . among you (Galatians) 6-5-13
MIRANDA
Ferdinand and . . . together (Shaw) 1-7-160
MIREVAUX
good wives of . . . (Rabelais) 18-1-15
MIRRORS
all the . . . in the world (Schopenhauer) 1-4-41
MIRTH
. . . adds to this fragment of life (Sterne) 1-2-60
a scene of . . . mixed (Dryden) 16-4-26
heart-ceasing . . . (Milton) 4-6-38
present . . . hath present laughter (Shakespeare) 1-3-52
. . . without images (Johnson) 1-3-87
MIRZA
the vision of . . . (Arnold) 20-15-100
MISANTHROPE
time to become a . . . (Bergson) 9-6-118
MISANTHROPY
. . . born of confidence of (Plato) 3-2-3
solitary . . . (Kant) 3-1-65
MISBEHAVIOR
for my . . . (Melville) 5-5-34
MISCARRIAGE
. . . is only chargeable (Cervantes) 12-2-31
MISCHANCE
never incur a . . . (Herodotus) 4-2-3
MISCHIEF
abstain from act of . . . (Hippocrates) 18-2-1
all thoughts of . . . (Milton) 9-6-78
foundation of lasting . . . (Boswell) 8-3-66
. . . meant most harm (Milton) 9-10-81
to fashion any . . . (Euripides) 1-7-17
MISCHIEFS
curing the . . . of faction (Madison) 10-8-23
MISCONDUCT
grief occasioned by . . . (Boswell) 4-6-44
MISDEMEANORS
for the same . . . (Juvenal) 12-4-18
MISDEEDS
more indirect . . . (G. Eliot) 9-10-117
MISER
no man was born a . . . (Boswell) 4-9-12
MISERABLE
amid affluence are . . . (Tacitus) 19-4-13

are not the . . . ill-fated (Plato) 9-6-9
confessed only by the . . . (Swift) 15-3-96
we should be . . . (Rousseau) 1-8-116
MISERIES
. . . bring no alleviations (Johnson) 11-2-90
despite these . . . (Pascal) 1-8-108
in shallows and in . . . (Shakespeare) 1-2-42
mirror to my own . . . (Augustine) 16-4-13
numerous . . . of war (Thucydides) 14-3-7
parade their . . . (Emerson) 18-3-55
pride counterbalances all . . . (Pascal) 4-11-24
seen the . . . of the world (Johnson) 9-8-57
the many . . . of life (Kant) 16-4-35
the . . . of human life (Swift) 2-2-68
to pursue all the . . . (Rousseau) 15-2-33
MISERS
compare our rich . . . to a (Shakespeare) 1-2-45
MISERY
accumulation of wealth and . . . (Marx) 11-2-139
. . . acquaints a man (Shakespeare) 9-8-42
and is full of . . . (*Book of Common Prayer*) 1-8-61
besides neurotic . . . (Freud) 18-3-69
chronic . . . among operatives (Marx) 11-3-69
eventually to hopeless . . . (Peirce) 19-4-47
existing in perpetual . . . (Pascal) 6-5-61
fills my days with . . . (Yeats) 16-6-82
. . . follow and ever increase (Augustine) 14-3-16
found the . . . (Anselm) 1-2-26
from . . . to happiness (Aristotle) 16-4-11
knowledge of man's . . . (Pascal) 6-5-59
man who lives in . . . (Carlyle) 1-5-122
. . . of the people (Montesquieu) 20-8-73
out of high degree in . . . (Chaucer) 16-4-16
pain is perfect . . . (Milton) 4-7-46
procure . . . from the Almighty (Locke) 9-3-22
reckless with . . . (Dickens) 4-4-32
result . . . (Dickens) 11-2-131
the greatness of his . . . (Pascal) 20-14-42
the . . . of man (Pascal) 9-8-48
though it seem . . . (Chaucer) 11-2-54
transforming your . . . (Freud) 18-2-52
vice the road to . . . (Fielding) 9-10-95
what is . . . (Plato) 9-6-9
MISFORTUNE
. . . attended with shame (Swift) 9-13-25
be overwhelmed by . . . (Boethius) 15-3-55
bulwark against . . . (Schopenhauer) 11-2-122
cause of the . . . (Aurelius) 15-3-46
. . . has a way of choosing (Seneca) 15-3-35
. . . lights now upon me (Aeschylus) 15-3-11
paraphrasing on his . . . (Cervantes) 15-3-88
passing from . . . to happiness (Aristotle) 16-4-10
pleasant than . . . (Spinoza) 4-4-24
presage the . . . of another (Rabelais) 1-4-15
the result of . . . (Euripides) 1-5-7
the unhappiest . . . is (Boethius) 15-3-53
upon as a . . . (Hegel) 1-9-40
worst . . . of them all (Chaucer) 9-8-35
MISFORTUNES
advantage in . . . (Rousseau) 9-9-25
comparing present . . . (Tacitus) 5-6-7
efforts to avert . . . (Plutarch) 15-3-40
have had fewer . . . (Plato) 9-8-8
. . . of the rich (Rousseau) 11-2-89
should fall into . . . (Polybius) 15-3-25
similar . . . have happened (Aristotle) 4-8-5
MISHAP
prediction of a man's own . . . (Rabelais) 1-4-15

MISS
budding ... is very charming (Byron) 1-3-106
MISSION
fulfill the philosopher's ... (Plato) 1-8-13
... of great minds (Schopenhauer) 1-6-60
MISTAKE
all forms of ... (G. Eliot) 6-4-50
an error of cowards to ... (Maritain) 6-6-56
... is parent of another (Hume) 17-1-65
life must be some kind of ... (Schopenhauer) 1-2-75
no greater ... (Huxley) 6-7-39
MISTAKEN
does not like to be ... (Pascal) 8-3-51
MISTAKES
fall into ... (Augustine) 6-1-27
great ... in the ruling (Locke) 10-9-22
have often made ... (Aristotle) 1-3-19
if he had made fewer ... (Plato) 9-8-8
... of primitive peoples (Maritain) 9-3-37
what ... were made (Euripides) 2-2-15
MISTRESS
art is a jealous ... (Emerson) 16-1-44
cannot be without a ... (Cervantes) 3-1-48
love is ... of nature (Lucretius) 3-1-14
MISTRESSES
few have married ... (Montaigne) 2-3-51
had all real ... (Cervantes) 5-4-14
the title of ... (Epictetus) 1-7-45
young men's ... (Bacon) 2-3-68
MISTRUST
... of power of faculties (Kant) 6-6-34
MISTS
... of the dim doubts (Melville) 6-6-44
MITIGATE
... severity of the law (Locke) 12-4-44
MITIGATING
finds ... circumstances (Luther) 12-1-37
MIXING
a mere chance of ... (Plotinus) 19-2-20
MIXTURE
on ... all depends (Goethe) 19-2-41
MIZPAH
Jephthah came to ... (*Judges*) 2-2-2
MNEMOSYNE
throne of ... (Peirce) 6-1-97
MOB
a ... at his disposal (Plato) 10-6-9
philosopher or one of the ... (Epictetus) 17-1-31
rude unbridled ... (Herodotus) 10-3-1
to do what the ... do (Dickens) 10-8-29
will hold the ... in check (Voltaire) 20-12-27
MOCK
... on—Voltaire—Rousseau (Blake) 20-1-49
seen to ... the minds of men (Lucretius) 5-5-13
MOCKERY
in monumental ... (Shakespeare) 1-5-70
its cheap bit of ... (Kierkegaard) 20-3-49
... of human plans (Tacitus) 15-3-44
receive with ... (Montaigne) 2-2-46
MOCK-EXISTENCE
little hour of ... (Schopenhauer) 1-2-75, 1-2-76
MOCK-MODEST
... people who understate (Aristotle) 9-14-10
MODE
... cannot be part of substance (Descartes) 19-6-18
each his own ... of life (Pascal) 6-6-20
give up this ... (Herodotus) 1-7-12
language not a universal ... (Whitehead) 7-1-64
mind and eternal ... of thought (Spinoza) 5-1-37

MODEL
made after a good ... (Pascal) 16-7-17
... of the barren earth (Shakespeare) 11-1-11
MODELS
at the same time to be ... (Kant) 16-1-35
drawn from established ... (Hume) 16-7-29
MODERATE
... better than eminent (Montaigne) 1-6-23
... possessions and occupation (Aristotle) 12-4-12
praise the ... or immoderate (Epictetus) 16-6-14
MODERATION
able to observe ... (Plato) 4-4-3
bear himself with ... (Aristotle) 1-5-16
confound negligence with ... (Rousseau) 9-7-41
... held to be a cloak (Thucydides) 10-9-1
in everything ... (Chaucer) 9-10-51
... in great men (Montesquieu) 1-6-45
... in the affections (Kant) 9-12-43
... in the prince (Fielding) 10-6-43
... is a virtue (Montaigne) 9-12-28
lesson of ... (Hamilton) 6-4-39
no expenditure in ... (Dante) 4-9-4
... of his character (Plato) 6-7-6
... of the government (Montesquieu) 11-6-16
uses them in ... (Aquinas) 9-8-33
virtue's tool is ... (Montaigne) 9-12-26
MODERN
ground of the ... world (Hegel) 9-5-21
MODERNISM
as to ... it is suicide (Santayana) 20-3-68
MODES
... of faith (Pope) 6-5-75
... of the divine nature (Spinoza) 19-4-27
other ... of life (Augustine) 9-2-7
MODESTY
... affected by Augustus (Gibbon) 10-2-81
... and beauty never (Goethe) 16-6-54
... as good as (Cervantes) 2-3-67
due to natural ... (Montesquieu) 1-7-112
... is artfulness and prudence (Montaigne) 3-3-38
maids in ... say no (Shakespeare) 1-2-75
shock to ... (Stendahl) 2-3-100
something very like ... (Darwin) 1-1-109
MODIFICATION
... of desire (Russell) 13-1-61
... of natural sounds (Darwin) 7-1-58
MODIFICATIONS
no great or sudden ... (Darwin) 19-1-111
MODULATION
... a language of sensations (Kant) 16-5-37
MOHAMMED
first companions of ... (Gibbon) 15-3-104
spirit that ... relies on (Gibbon) 20-15-89
MOHAMMEDANS
embraced by the ... (Gibbon) 15-3-103
MOLE
vicious ... of nature (Shakespeare) 1-5-68
MOLECULE
... in the sense of moving (Whitehead) 19-5-67
MOLESTATION
... in things men hate (Hobbes) 3-2-22
MOLOSSIAN
... breed of dogs (Aristotle) 1-7-29
MOMENTS
composed of indivisible ... (Hume) 19-7-60
MONARCH
hands of an hereditary ... (Madison) 10-3-48
interest of the ... (Mill) 10-3-62
mercy becomes the ... (Shakespeare) 3-5-25

MOTION (*Cont.*)
  without ... is no sensation (Lavoisier) 5-2-33
MOTIONS
  cool our raging ... (Shakespeare) 9-10-66
  deduce ... of the planets (Newton) 17-2-44
  if ... of the universe (Bergson) 19-7-89
  ... in space distinguished (Nicomachus) 19-6-10
  ... in the animal spirits (Locke) 9-2-22
  science of ... (Newton) 17-3-31
  the only absolute ... (Newton) 19-3-28
  two kinds of natural ... (Galileo) 17-2-28
  ... under form of colors (Newton) 5-2-24
MOTIVE
  a more noble ... (Kant) 1-4-38
  distinct ... for every action (Darwin) 9-1-26
  had he the ... (Shakespeare) 4-1-12
  impossible to reach a ... (Planck) 5-7-48
  ... of dream-formation (Freud) 5-5-42
  some mean ... (Aurelius) 4-3-14
  the ... is want (Aristotle) 12-4-12
MOTIVES
  actuated by a series of ... (Boswell) 5-7-33
  compare past and future ... (Darwin) 9-1-25
  ... determining our desire (Kant) 9-4-45
  go burrowing for ... (Kant) 9-3-32
  impelled by the same ... (Darwin) 2-3-105
  moral laws determine ... (Kant) 9-3-24
  most powerful of ... (Schopenhauer) 3-3-70
  ... of civil society (Rousseau) 12-1-63
  ... of instinctive sympathy (Dewey) 6-5-114
  ... of the heart (Kant) 9-1-22
  secret ... of men (Locke) 9-2-23
  supposition of positive ... (Wm. James) 1-9-48
MOTLEY
  invest me in my ... (Shakespeare) 9-15-55
MOTLEY'S
  ... the only wear (Shakespeare) 9-15-54
MOTOR
  seat of the ... faculty (Kepler) 19-5-27
MOULD
  ... of man's fortune (Bacon) 15-3-89
  worlds material ... (Milton) 19-8-57
MOULDS
  crack nature's ... (Shakespeare) 19-1-39
MOUNT ABORA
  singing of ... (Coleridge) 16-3-75
MOUNTAIN
  every ... and hill made low (*Isaiah*) 20-5-13
  how beautiful upon the ... (*Isaiah*) 20-3-3
  say unto this ... remove (*Matthew*) 6-5-8; (*Mark*) 6-5-10
  the lab'ring ... (Horace) 19-3-9
MOUNT ATHOS
  monasteries of ... (Gibbon) 20-1-48
MOUNT SINAI
  law given from ... (Gibbon) 20-2-40
MOURN
  a time to ... (*Eccles.*) 19-7-2
  in summer skies to ... (Keats) 9-8-68
  no longer ... for me (Shakespeare) 1-8-94
  they that ... (*Matthew*) 9-8-19; (Aquinas) 9-8-33
MOURNER
  to convince a ... (Cicero) 4-6-10
MOURNING
  changed ... into joy (Augustine) 6-5-21
  go to the house of ... (*Eccles.*) 4-6-3
  left them years of ... (Milton) 1-8-114
  no one can counterfeit ... (Juvenal) 11-4-7
  pleasure in ... (Aristotle) 4-7-12
  raise up their ... (*Job*) 4-5-1

MOUSE
  a laughter-rousing ... (Horace) 19-3-9
  scarce brings forth a ... (Horace) 19-3-9
MOUSIE
  but ... thou art no (Burns) 20-10-41
MOUTH
  his heart's his ... (Shakespeare) 9-14-32
  out of the ... of God (*Matthew*) 20-1-3
  out of the ... of the Lord (*Deut.*) 20-1-1
  set a watch on my ... (Cervantes) 7-2-49
MOUTHS
  this makes bold ... (Shakespeare) 11-6-7
MOVE
  could not ... at all (Lucretius) 19-6-6
MOVED
  cause of being ... (Aristotle) 19-1-4
MOVEMENT
  an "instinctive" ... (Russell) 8-2-32
  art is a principle of ... (Aristotle) 19-4-9
  choice the cause of its ... (Aquinas) 5-7-11
  condition of ... (Aristotle) 19-6-5
  continuity of ... (Aristotle) 19-8-9
  first ... must be unmoved (Aristotle) 19-5-8
  least ... affects all nature (Pascal) 19-3-27
  local ... changes nothing (Aquinas) 19-6-14
  no longer has any ... (Aquinas) 19-2-22
  not exact without ... (Augustine) 19-7-25
  ... of a body which is one (Copernicus) 19-8-42
  ... of the divine (Aristotle) 19-8-8
  ... of the planets (Kepler) 19-5-27
  one ... succeeds another (Aristotle) 5-3-3
  time is a measure of ... (Aquinas) 19-7-27
  understanding is ... (Aquinas) 19-5-22
MOVEMENTS
  ... natural to us (Montaigne) 18-3-39
  ... of things with life (Aristotle) 19-2-11
MOVER
  no ... that takes (Cervantes) 1-8-95
MOVING
  the ... cause is the art (Aristotle) 19-3-6
MUCK
  money is like ... (Bacon) 11-4-15
MULCIBER
  men call him ... (Milton) 20-15-78
MULIER
  ... *est hominis confusio* (Chaucer) 1-7-63
MULTICELLULAR
  achieve a ... organization (Freud) 19-2-59
MULTIPLY
  let the fowl ... (*Genesis*) 19-2-2
  the gain it is to ... (Chaucer) 17-2-6
MULTITUDE
  a ... you will have won (Goethe) 16-7-41
  carried on by the ... (Aquinas) 10-3-14
  ... is a better judge (Aristotle) 10-4-7
  ... is changeable (Spinoza) 1-5-98
  know better than the ... (Galen) 8-3-27
  restricted by the ... (Aquinas) 10-9-6
  submission of the ... (Gibbon) 10-8-19
  tyrants hateful to the ... (Aquinas) 10-6-18
MULTITUDES
  I contain ... (Whitman) 1-4-54
MUMMERIES
  show the ... of the world (Bacon) 6-3-56
MUMMERS
  these seducing ... to (Boethius) 16-3-22
MUMMIES
  their ... were embalmed (Gibbon) 20-15-89
MUNIMENTS

other . . . and petty helps (Shakespeare) 10-9-13

MURDER
a brother's . . . (Shakespeare) 20-8-60
aim of war is . . . (Tolstoy) 14-2-70
and a brother's . . . (Tacitus) 1-9-17
and one cried . . . (Shakespeare) 1-8-87
. . . cannot be hid long (Shakespeare) 6-3-50
crime of fallen man was . . . (Pascal) 12-4-41
has committed a . . . (Augustine) 12-4-21
means your . . . (Euripides) 2-2-14
. . . most unnatural (Shakespeare) 2-2-49
. . . of her husband (Homer) 1-7-6
on a charge of . . . (Euripides) 2-2-17
right to . . . people (Dostoevsky) 12-4-70
sin must have been a . . . (Freud) 20-13-96
sooner . . . an infant than (Blake) 4-4-31
we . . . to dissect (Wordsworth) 19-1-83
whoever has committed . . . (Kant) 12-4-61
will . . . for trifles (Freud) 3-2-43

MURDERED
yet to be . . . (Plutarch) 1-9-12

MURDERER
this man this . . . (Sophocles) 2-1-7
was a . . . from the beginning (*John*) 20-7-5

MURDERERS
by banning their . . . (Euripides) 12-4-6
laws against . . . (Montaigne) 1-9-25

MURDERING
. . . without pain (Johnson) 1-6-46

MURDERS
feel his secret . . . (Shakespeare) 10-6-26
wife . . . her husband (Euripides) 12-4-6

MURDER'S
. . . as near to lust (Shakespeare) 20-13-72

MUSAEUS
converse with Orpheus and . . . (Plato) 1-8-15
. . . healing and oracle (Aristophanes) 16-4-2

MUSE
allow the honeyed . . . to enter (Plato) 16-3-6
are dearest to the . . . (Homer) 16-3-1
compositions of their epic . . . (Gibbon) 16-3-60
he must keep his . . . (Cervantes) 16-3-35
in the bright . . . (Pope) 16-7-24
meditate the thankless . . . (Milton) 16-3-43
O for a . . . of fire (Shakespeare) 5-4-11
sing heavenly . . . (Milton) 16-3-44
sing in me . . . (Homer) 6-2-2
taught by the heavenly . . . (Milton) 20-5-75
utter what the . . . impels (Plato) 16-3-5

MUSES
acceptable to the . . . (Peirce) 6-1-97
a gift from the . . . (Aurelius) 4-3-14
by the name of . . . (Hobbes) 20-6-38
careless . . . heard (Yeats) 17-1-106
heard the . . . in a ring (Milton) 4-6-39
illustrious chariot of the . . . (Lucretius) 20-12-5
inspiration of the . . . (Plato) 5-6-6
. . . love her best (Euripides) 14-1-11
melody of the . . . (Plato) 16-1-1
memory the mother of the . . . (Plato) 5-3-2; (Hobbes) 5-3-19
scions of the softer . . . (Plato) 16-4-5
sound of the . . . singing (Homer) 20-15-4
the . . . have yet veiled (Lucretius) 16-3-13
the . . . of poetry (Boethius) 16-3-22
those possessed by the . . . (Plato) 16-3-4
traces the . . . upward (Pope) 16-7-23

MUSES'
. . . mother skilled in craft (Aeschylus) 1-1-6

upon the . . . anvil (Jonson) 16-3-36

MUSIC
being no . . . (Sophocles) 1-3-8
conjoin . . . and medicine (Bacon) 18-1-23
. . . consists of harmonies (Leibniz) 4-7-47
equally hideous . . . (Darwin) 16-7-44
excellence of . . . is measured (Plato) 16-7-4
fled is that . . . (Keats) 5-5-33
. . . generally sets me to (Darwin) 16-3-87
. . . has betwixt the acts (Dryden) 16-4-26
. . . has charms to soothe (Congreve) 16-5-34
in the . . . of men's lives (Shakespeare) 16-5-17
. . . is good (Spinoza) 9-6-82
judges of . . . and poetry (Aristotle) 16-7-6
. . . lifted the listening spirit (Shelley) 5-1-55
mathematics is like . . . (Santayana) 17-3-62
. . . shall untune the sky (Dryden) 20-15-84
still sad . . . of humanity (Wordsworth) 19-1-78
terrible thing is . . . (Tolstoy) 16-5-41
the excellence of . . . is (Plato) 16-7-3
thy chosen . . . liberty (Wordsworth) 13-1-34
to the . . . he hears (Thoreau) 13-1-45
turn for . . . (Arnold) 2-2-89
. . . used to quicken you (Shakespeare) 8-1-27
. . . when soft voices die (Shelley) 5-3-24
why hear'st thou . . . sadly (Shakespeare) 16-5-25

MUSICAL
. . . education not necessary (Santayana) 16-7-54

MUSTARD SEED
faith as a grain of . . . (*Matthew*) 6-5-8

MUTABILITY
. . . in them doth play (Spenser) 1-2-36
speech whlyeare of . . . (Spenser) 19-5-26

MUTATIONS
the great . . . of the world (Th. Browne) 19-7-45

MUTILATION
care as little for . . . (Shaw) 18-2-49
. . . of a limb (Hobbes) 12-4-38

MUTINOUS
end you the . . . members (Shakespeare) 10-9-13

MYCENAE
I march against . . . (Euripides) 5-6-4

MYRMIDONS
the . . . of death (Freud) 19-2-58

MYSELF
closer to me than . . . (Augustine) 5-3-11
I celebrate . . . (Whitman) 1-4-53
I study . . . more (Montaigne) 6-2-17
than found in . . . (Descartes) 6-2-22

MYSTERIES
initiated into perfect . . . (Plato) 17-1-3
know the . . . of the gods (Euripides) 20-6-14
nature's . . . would behold (Goethe) 19-2-41
terrible what . . . there are (Dostoevsky) 16-6-72
that of all . . . (Milton) 20-1-30
understands her cruel . . . (Euripides) 15-3-20
wingy . . . in divinity (Th. Browne) 6-5-54

MYSTERY
cannot know the . . . (Plato) 6-2-5
draw aside the veil of . . . (Augustine) 6-5-19
for its central . . . (Shaw) 20-3-66
great is the . . . of godliness (*I Timothy*) 20-3-18
I shew you a . . . (*I Corinthians*) 20-15-28
life's supreme . . . (Wm. James) 1-6-81
metaphysics isolates . . . (Maritain) 17-1-113
. . . of their sinless life (Dostoevsky) 19-8-88
the . . . furthest removed (Pascal) 20-13-77
we who guard the . . . (Dostoevsky) 9-8-74

latter involves a . . . (Epicurus) 15-3-24
leisure is a . . . (Shaw) 11-3-79
liberty and . . . (Hegel) 10-2-92
liberty and . . . consistent (Hobbes) 5-7-23
. . . lies in the thing itself (Descartes) 20-5-61
lull the daughter of . . . (Milton) 16-5-32
make a virtue of . . . (Cervantes) 1-5-77
makes her to be swift . . . (Dante) 15-3-64
moral and physical . . . (Boswell) 5-7-48
nearness of our last (Th. Browne) 1-8-103
no man can budge . . . (Euripides) 15-3-19
not on grounds of its . . . (Aristotle) 16-5-6
obey . . . rather than argument (Aristotle) 12-1-9
. . . of accepting Bible (Huxley) 6-6-45
. . . of divine nature (Spinoza) 4-8-24
of . . . be created (Plato) 19-3-2
partake of mathematical . . . (Poincaré) 17-3-48
proceed from law of . . . (Schiller) 19-1-74
progress is a . . . (Spencer) 15-2-71
response to pressure of . . . (Pascal) 19-2-34
some law of . . . (Tolstoy) 5-7-44
stands by itself (Kierkegaard) 19-3-44
stern law of . . . (Rousseau) 1-1-85
straight warp of . . . (Melville) 5-7-41
teach thy . . . to reason (Shakespeare) 15-3-78
. . . that all-pervading law (Malthus) 1-2-71
that comes by . . . (Chaucer) 15-3-68
. . . that curbs others (Montaigne) 6-6-10
that fatal . . . (Th. Browne) 20-5-69
the least idea of . . . (Hume) 19-1-63
there is a fateful . . . (Aurelius) 19-4-14
they were ruled by . . . (Plato) 20-6-17
things that are of . . . (Aristotle) 6-1-18, 9-13-3
this warp seemed . . . (Melville) 15-3-108
. . . to reverence heroes (Carlyle) 1-6-64
under compulsion of . . . (Marx) 13-1-48
yet by a conditional . . . (Aquinas) 15-3-58

NECKAR
on the banks of the . . . (Gibbon) 14-3-38

NEED
bad to live in . . . (Montaigne) 17-1-44
no further . . . of God (Pascal) 17-1-56
not to . . . money (Plutarch) 11-4-6
satisfying this . . . (Beauvoir) 10-7-44
the hour of . . . (Cicero) 3-4-21

NEEDFUL
one thing is . . . (*Luke*) 1-7-38

NEEDS
. . . common to civil society (Hegel) 11-2-117
each according to his . . . (Marx) 12-3-27
for his daily . . . (Herodotus) 11-2-8
national . . . to be satisfied (Shaw) 13-3-51
product of our own . . . (Freud) 6-6-52
subdivision of . . . (Hegel) 11-3-44
suffices for his daily . . . (Herodotus) 9-8-2
the bare . . . of life (Aristotle) 10-1-6

NEGATION
defined as . . . of knowledge (Aristotle) 6-4-7

NEGATIONS
. . . of individual liberty (Bakunin) 13-1-51

NEGATIVE
easy to be on . . . side (Boswell) 6-6-30

NEGLECT
of resenting . . . (Plutarch) 1-5-30

NEGLIGENCE
by your . . . (Chaucer) 2-2-42
conceal gross . . . (Smith) 8-3-74
confound . . . with moderation (Rousseau) 9-7-41

NEGRO

between the . . . or Australian (Darwin) 1-1-111
makes the . . . clean (Shaw) 1-7-161
. . . who was claiming liberty (Boswell) 10-7-26
why the . . . is not entitled (Lincoln) 13-3-38

NEGROES
make . . . work (Tocqueville) 10-7-34

NEIGHBOR
desirous of being good . . . (Thoreau) 11-6-48
false witness against thy . . . (*Exodus*) 9-3-1
for that of our . . . (Aquinas) 20-8-46
harms person of his . . . (Aquinas) 12-2-25
his . . . as himself (Hobbes) 20-8-63
inflicted upon one's . . . (Dante) 20-15-53
. . . is . . . a temptation (Freud) 1-2-97
is by right called a . . . (Augustine) 20-7-20
lie unto his . . . (*Leviticus*) 9-14-3
love thy . . . as thyself (*Mark*) 3-5-7; (*Leviticus*) 3-5-1
love of our . . . (Augustine) 3-5-15
loving God and our . . . (Aquinas) 3-5-21
loving his . . . (Kierkegaard) 1-2-79
one can't love one's . . . (Dostoevsky) 3-5-47
related to our . . . (Aristotle) 9-7-16
relations with his . . . (Aquinas) 9-8-33
say not unto thy . . . (*Proverbs*) 9-7-4
service due to his . . . (Augustine) 9-9-12
shalt love thy . . . (Kierkegaard) 1-3-111; (*Matthew*) 12-2-19
to God and to his . . . (Aquinas) 9-9-14
to see what his . . . says (Aurelius) 1-4-8
unacquainted with his . . . (Plato) 17-1-9

NEIGHBORS
esteem of . . . (Pascal) 1-5-91
make sport for our . . . (Austen) 1-2-73
our bad . . . (Shakespeare) 9-6-60
to his . . . a man behaves (Aquinas) 9-7-32

NEMESIS
. . . the messenger of (Plato) 2-2-19

NEPTUNE
do chase the ebbing . . . (Shakespeare) 20-7-52
made a toast for . . . (Shakespeare) 9-11-31
that erst threw . . . (Dante) 20-5-48
the green . . . a ram (Shakespeare) 20-6-37
threw . . . in amaze (Dante) 19-8-41

NEPTUNE'S
great . . . ocean (Shakespeare) 1-8-89

NEREID
no . . . stirr'd (Gray) 16-6-44

NEREIDES
gentlewomen like the . . . (Shakespeare) 1-7-89

NERO
conduct of a . . . (Hegel) 1-9-40
. . . fastened the guilt (Tacitus) 20-3-21
flatter . . . or Tigellinus (Tacitus) 1-9-18
made . . . doubt (Tacitus) 11-6-5
upon the death of . . . (Plutarch) 14-2-26
. . . was at Antium (Tacitus) 5-6-7

NERO'S
knew not . . . cruelty (Tacitus) 1-9-17

NERVE CENTERS
arrangements for in his . . . (Wm. James) 1-1-125

NERVOUS SYSTEM
constitution of the . . . (Darwin) 16-8-69
overwrought and deranged . . . (Dostoevsky) 5-5-35
with a restored . . . (Freud) 18-2-52

NESSUS
. . . had not yet (Dante) 1-9-23

NESTOR
bid . . . bring me (Shakespeare) 2-2-55
imagine . . . and Antenor (Plato) 1-6-6

ODYSSEY
... of the human spirit (Whitehead) 15-2-77
ODYSSEY
story like the ... (Aristotle) 16-4-11
OEDIPUS
... distracted us (Sophocles) 2-3-15
riddle proposed to ... (Bacon) 17-2-26
the flocks of ... (Hesiod) 15-2-2
who will be kind to ... (Sophocles) 4-6-6
OEDIPUS COMPLEX
by the term ... (Freud) 2-2-98
... is justifiably (Freud) 2-2-100
remained in the ... (Freud) 2-1-54
OEDIPUS REX
in the same soil as ... (Freud) 16-4-46
OFFENCE
commit an ... (Hegel) 9-7-46
first to take ... (Dostoevsky) 9-14-60
hath died for this ... (Shakespeare) 12-4-32
he committed the ... (Plato) 12-4-8
my ... is rank (Shakespeare) 20-8-60
the passion of ... (Kierkegaard) 20-3-49
OFFENCES
... committed through desire (Aurelius) 4-4-12
punish the ... (Locke) 10-1-29
slavery one of those ... (Lincoln) 10-7-40
source of all ... (Plato) 1-4-5
OFFENDERS
pardons some ... (Locke) 12-4-44
OFFENSIVE
no vice which is not ... (Montaigne) 9-10-59
OFFERING
an ... to the Lord (*Genesis*) 2-1-1
for a burnt ... (*Judges*) 2-2-2
offer him there for a burnt ... (*Genesis*) 20-2-4
trespass ... to the Lord (*Leviticus*) 9-14-3
OFFERINGS
I am full of burnt ... (*Isaiah*) 20-8-9
OFFERS
make no more ... (Shakespeare) 11-1-12
OFFICE
aim is to maintain his ... (Plutarch) 10-2-18
all able to hold ... (Aristotle) 10-2-12
distinctive ... of philosophy (Dewey) 17-1-104
right of his ... (Locke) 10-2-63
the good to take ... (Plato) 10-2-6
unfit to hold an ... (Plutarch) 10-2-21
OFFICERS
... can rise and shine (Santayana) 17-1-76
OFFICES
... according to merit (Aristotle) 10-1-9
distribute the ... of state (Aristotle) 10-3-9
doing the meanest ... (Swift) 1-5-101
many ... called duties (Emerson) 9-9-38
perform ... of peace and war (Milton) 8-1-35
power of appointing to ... (Hamilton) 10-2-90
public ... at Rome (Tacitus) 10-5-12
shares in ... (Aristotle) 10-5-5
OFFSPRING
female produces ... (Darwin) 1-7-138
for a numerous ... (Augustine) 2-1-21
love of ... (Plato) 3-1-10
preservation of their ... (Locke) 2-1-30
saw an ... born (Lucretius) 2-1-14
OIL
he swims in ... (Th. Browne) 9-8-45
OLD
being ... before thy time (Shakespeare) 9-15-60
deeds for ... people (Thoreau) 9-2-31

friendships become insensibly ... (Boswell) 3-4-49
grow ... along with me (Browning) 1-3-120
last to lay the ... aside (Pope) 19-5-54
... places and ... persons (Santayana) 1-3-137
when you are ... and gray (Yeats) 3-1-90
OLD AGE
because of his ... (Tolstoy) 6-2-41
... could be postponed (Russell) 8-1-85
... is respectable (Cicero) 1-3-23
never reach ... (Luther) 9-12-22
... shall this generation waste (Keats) 16-6-58
sons of his ... (*Genesis*) 4-8-1
... steals upon us (Juvenal) 19-7-14
useless ... has filtered (Goethe) 16-6-54
what ... has in store (Plotinus) 14-1-31
wisdom of ... (Cicero) 1-3-22
OLD COMEDY
after tragedy the ... (Aurelius) 16-4-12
unexpected in the ... (Jonson) 16-4-20
OLD COUPLES
... chat till early morning (Melville) 3-4-59
OLD LAW
state of the ... (Aquinas) 20-2-21
OLD MAID
prudence is a rich ... (Blake) 9-13-32
OLD MAN
foolish fond ... (Shakespeare) 5-6-19
when an ... is dead (Homer) 1-3-4
OLD MEN
... envy younger men (Aristotle) 4-8-7
... shall dream dreams (*Joel*) 5-5-2
OLD PEOPLE
like all ... did not sleep (Tolstoy) 6-2-42
OLD TESTAMENT
apparitions in the ... (Aquinas) 20-7-21
OLIGARCHIES
are safer than ... (Aristotle) 10-3-7
in ... the majority rules (Aristotle) 10-4-8
OLIGARCHY
aristocracy and ... (Plato) 10-3-2
aristocracy called it ... (Hobbes) 10-3-22
character of ... creates ... (Aristotle) 8-1-7
citizen in an ... (Aristotle) 10-5-15
end of ... is wealth (Aristotle) 10-3-10
... has in view (Aristotle) 10-3-5
in ... there is a (Aristotle) 10-3-9
it is called an ... (Aquinas) 10-3-14
... live in luxury (Aristotle) 10-9-5
or out of an ... (Aristotle) 10-8-6
passes over into ... (Aristotle) 2-3-19
setting up an ... (Herodotus) 10-3-1
strong ... to be established (Aristotle) 14-2-15
the ruin of ... (Plato) 13-1-3
OLIVIA
and that I owe ... (Shakespeare) 1-7-83
OLIVES
Mount of ... (*John*) 3-5-9
... of endless age (Shakespeare) 3-1-46
OLYMPIC GAMES
crowned in the ... (Plutarch) 1-8-43
OLYMPOS
about the horn of ... (Homer) 20-6-2
back to ... all in a body (Homer) 2-2-7
earth and high ... (Homer) 20-15-5
in the fastness of ... (Homer) 20-15-6
OLYMPUS
so may the gods of ... (Russell) 20-5-121
songs of ... exercise (Aristotle) 16-5-7
the deities of ... (Gibbon) 20-6-43

in reference to pleasure or . . . (Locke) 9-6-84
. . . is a local sensation (Montaigne) 1-9-32
. . . is called good (Spinoza) 1-5-99
. . . is greater than pleasure (Nietzsche) 19-8-90
. . . is the greatest evil (Cicero) 4-7-15
it is an eternity of . . . (Joyce) 20-15-106
life secure from . . . (Sophocles) 9-8-4
loose though full of . . . (Milton) 5-1-34
man inflicts . . . for pleasure (Twain) 9-1-34
mixture of . . . or uneasiness (Berkeley) 9-6-85
murdering without . . . (Johnson) 1-6-46
nature so conversant with . . . (Shakespeare) 5-1-20
no greater . . . (Dante) 9-8-34
no sense of . . . (Plato) 9-6-11
not productive of . . . (Aristotle) 16-4-7
perception of . . . (Aristotle) 7-1-9
pile up a drift of . . . (Sophocles) 1-3-8
pity a feeling of . . . (Aristotle) 4-8-5
power to inflict . . . (Kant) 12-4-59
producing uneasiness or . . . (Locke) 4-5-26
proportioned to thy . . . (Dante) 20-9-14
sharpness of . . . (Montaigne) 17-1-44
so it is with the . . . (Chaucer) 20-15-60
so overcome with . . . (Dante) 9-11-20
susceptibility to . . . (Schopenhauer) 5-1-61
tender for another's . . . (Gray) 6-4-30
terminating in . . . or (Locke) 4-1-23
the family of . . . (Pope) 5-1-46
there is no greater . . . (Dante) 3-3-31
there's an end to the . . . (Seneca) 18-3-25
they seek for . . . (Boswell) 5-6-33
this . . . in every bone (Goethe) 20-8-78
thought the daughter of . . . (Carlyle) 5-1-62
to deathless . . . (Milton) 1-8-111
to the . . . an outlet (Dante) 1-9-23
way into eternal . . . (Dante) 20-15-50
. . . which death will (Cervantes) 1-5-77
wisdom won from . . . (Aeschylus) 4-2-2
PAINFUL
disregard what is . . . (Tolstoy) 9-11-63
PAINS
and take away their . . . (*Eccles.*) 18-1-1
endless . . . and terrors (Plutarch) 4-2-15
. . . exceed our pleasures (Rousseau) 15-2-33
few and transitory . . . (Mill) 9-8-72
. . . to make thee speak (Shakespeare) 7-1-25
wrack of the labor . . . (Euripides) 2-2-14
PAINTER
creations of a . . . (Plato) 16-2-3
. . . is just such (Plato) 16-1-4
. . . may make a better face (Bacon) 16-6-39
surely the art of the . . . (Plato) 16-7-1
PAINTERS
styles of different . . . (Boswell) 16-7-35
PAINTING
but sculpture and . . . (Gibbon) 16-1-30
how useless is . . . (Pascal) 16-1-26
it is the same with . . . (Montaigne) 15-3-75
yet the . . . was beautiful (Boswell) 16-6-46
PALACE
exchange his wigwam for a . . . (Thoreau) 15-2-59
love in a . . . is torment (Keats) 3-1-70
PALACES
vast . . . of the enemy (Augustine) 5-3-8
PALAMEDES
and conversing with . . . (Plato) 1-8-15
PALATINE
circus which adjoins the . . . (Tacitus) 5-6-7
PALESTINE

long after known in . . . (Milton) 20-7-58
PALLADIUM
there for the . . . they suffer (Dante) 20-15-54
PALLAS
. . . with plumed helm (Euripides) 5-6-4
PALLOR
from that . . . of the dead (Melville) 1-8-129
PALM
have an itching . . . (Shakespeare) 4-9-9
PAN
beloved . . . and other gods (Plato) 9-8-9
great god . . . is not dead (Thoreau) 20-6-45
PANDARS
call all brokers-between . . . (Shakespeare) 3-3-49
PANDION
over the whole people of . . . (Lucretius) 18-3-23
PANEGYRICK
admirable . . . upon your country (Swift) 1-1-80
PANG
the . . . of philosophy (Plato) 17-1-4
PANGLOSS
as to . . . he (Voltaire) 1-2-64
. . . consoled them (Voltaire) 19-8-72
. . . taught (Voltaire) 19-8-71
PANTACLES
teach that to . . . (Aristophanes) 16-4-2
PANTAGRUEL
authentic fashion answered . . . (Rabelais) 5-5-18
foolish and dishonest quoth . . . (Rabelais) 2-3-46
then said . . . (Rabelais) 3-3-35
PANTHEISM
a romantic and mystical . . . (Santayana) 20-2-52
chief objection to . . . (Schopenhauer) 19-1-94
PANTHEON
in my . . . Pan stands still (Thoreau) 20-6-45
PANTHINO
tell me . . . what sad talk (Shakespeare) 6-2-18
PANURGE
of what kind—asked . . . (Rabelais) 5-5-18
Yea—but quoth . . . (Rabelais) 2-3-46
PAPER
. . . is sign of value of specie (Montesquieu) 11-4-23
PAPIRIA
first wife was . . . (Plutarch) 2-3-27
PAQUETTA
. . . worked at embroidery (Voltaire) 1-2-64
PARABLE
spake this . . . unto them (*Luke*) 20-8-30
things are a . . . (G. Eliot) 1-4-58
this . . . spake Jesus (*John*) 20-4-7
PARABLES
why speakest thou in . . . (*Matthew*) 6-5-7
PARABOLA
this path is a . . . (Galileo) 19-5-37
PARADIGM
ghostly . . . of things (Yeats) 17-1-106
PARADISE
all that concerns . . . (Augustine) 20-4-12
been exiled from . . . (Dante) 20-13-54
beheld of . . . (Milton) 2-3-71
child of . . . (Emerson) 2-2-85
drink the milk of . . . (Coleridge) 16-3-75
fair . . . of nature's light (Keats) 19-1-90
for it is . . . (Dante) 16-4-15
from . . . to labor (Chaucer) 9-12-21
hatred began in . . . (Luther) 20-7-36
in . . . of all things (Milton) 2-3-69
in . . . what have I to do (*Aucassin and Nicolette*) 20-15-57
is a . . . to what we fear (Shakespeare) 1-8-83

PARADISE (*Cont.*)
... is a park (Hegel) 20-15-96
... is but a part (Th. Browne) 9-8-45
the marriage of ... (Augustine) 3-3-22
towards ... and all its blest (Hardy) 20-15-107
wilderness were ... enow (Fitzgerald) 9-8-71
PARADOX
a case for my ... (Russell) 6-6-50
friend a ... in nature (Emerson) 3-4-57
heresies of ... (Johnson) 1-5-109
lead him into a ... (Aristotle) 6-7-10
PARADOXICAL
not think lightly of the ... (Kierkegaard) 5-1-63
PARAEUS
and ... commenting on (Milton) 16-4-25
PARALOGISM
every ... be recognized (Leibniz) 7-2-68
PARCEL
a ... of their feast (Shakespeare) 14-1-47
PARCELS
... of the dreadful past (Tennyson) 19-7-75
PARCHMENT
should be made ... (Shakespeare) 12-1-42
PARDON
give me your ... sir (Shakespeare) 12-9-30
must receive this ... (Montaigne) 20-14-34
PARDONING
the right of ... (Kant) 12-4-62
PAREILLY
making a sermon at ... (Rabelais) 2-3-46
PARENT
as man the ... is (Augustine) 20-13-35
duty of the ... (Boswell) 8-3-70
no ... is to know (Plato) 2-1-9
PARENTS
... and similar authorities (Freud) 9-2-35
as our natural ... (Th. Browne) 9-15-70
control of ... and relations (Smith) 8-3-75
country and ... (Cicero) 9-9-6
delight of our ancient ... (Cervantes) 3-4-38
duty incumbent upon ... (Kant) 10-7-30
... hid away (Sophocles) 2-1-8
honoring one's ... (Aquinas) 9-7-32
relation of orderly ... (Plato) 2-3-16
... rendering due to children (Aristotle) 3-4-14
security depends upon ... (Freud) 20-5-122
those who are ... (Euripides) 2-2-12
was submissive to his ... (Luther) 20-3-25
PARIAHS
ought to be no ... (Mill) 10-4-70
PARIS, the city
truth same at Toulouse and ... (Pascal) 6-3-69
PARIS, the person
of partial ... (Virgil) 15-3-31
PARIS'
might see ... harp (Plutarch) 16-3-21
PARLIAMENT
act of ... (Boswell) 2-3-89
founded on the ... (Boswell) 10-3-40
in the ... of man (Tennyson) 14-3-46
... is not a congress (Burke) 10-4-36
PARMACETI
... for an inward bruise (Shakespeare) 14-2-35
PARNASSUS
who haunt ... but to please (Pope) 16-7-24
PARRICIDE
... is more wicked (Augustine) 1-9-22
PARROTS
... can utter words (Descartes) 7-1-28

PARSIMONY
... in the time of peace (Smith) 14-1-71
PARTIAL
we may be ... (Emerson) 15-3-107
PARTICIPANTS
doing of all the known ... (Tolstoy) 15-1-84
... in conduct of events (Montaigne) 15-1-28
PARTICLES
disunites ... of bodies (Huygens) 19-5-44
hard and solid ... (Newton) 19-8-62
primitive ... being solids (Newton) 19-8-61
rent into small ... (Freud) 19-2-59
some words called ... (Locke) 7-2-70
PARTICULAR
... law is that which (Aristotle) 12-1-14
PARTICULARS
all things exist as ... (Berkeley) 7-1-39
from ... to axioms (Bacon) 17-2-19, 17-2-24
must also recognize ... (Aristotle) 9-13-4
PARTIES
as many different ... (Plutarch) 10-8-9
in your country you have ... (Isak Dinesen) 9-2-36
the two political ... (Thoreau) 10-2-98
PARTING
... is such sweet sorrow (Shakespeare) 4-7-39
though her ... dims the day (Emerson) 3-1-74
PARTITIONS
all ... of knowledge (Bacon) 6-1-49
PARTNERSHIP
friendship a ... (Aristotle) 3-4-16
PARTS
knowing the ... in detail (Pascal) 19-3-26
plays many ... (Shakespeare) 1-2-43, 1-3-51
such as are the ... (Hume) 19-6-33
PARTY
created a third ... (Herodotus) 10-6-5
victory gained by ... (Hamilton) 10-2-90
PASCAL, Blaise
... was scandalized (Maritain) 9-3-37
PASCAL'S
... own personal belief (Wm. James) 19-4-49
PASSAGE
same ... you made (Montaigne) 1-8-66
PASSION
... and appetite find their (Nicomachus) 9-10-31
any ... under heaven (Shakespeare) 5-6-13
a ... easy to deride (Santayana) 1-5-130
a ... for friends (Plato) 3-4-10
... between sexes necessary (Malthus) 1-2-71
but ... is the gale (Pope) 4-1-25
chaos of thought and ... (Pope) 1-1-81
common impulse of ... (Madison) 10-8-23
defeated by a weaker ... (Aristotle) 18-3-21
... dimmed his face (Milton) 6-3-70
each man's ruling ... (Pascal) 4-1-18
each ... that he feigns (Pope) 16-3-50
... equality creates (Tocqueville) 13-3-32
every ... and action (Aristotle) 12-4-11
faith the highest ... (Kierkegaard) 6-5-90
flesh heated by ... (Twain) 11-4-46
... for learning never decayed (Plutarch) 8-3-21
free from every ... (Cicero) 9-12-10
free the soul of ... (Poincaré) 6-3-136
governed by a common ... (Hamilton/Madison) 6-5-86
government of a ruling ... (Sterne) 9-4-41
holy ... of friendship (Twain) 3-4-62
... hurries our thoughts (Locke) 9-4-39
improve the ... (Virgil) 3-3-13
in her first ... (Byron) 1-7-127

insatiate and universal ... (Gibbon) 4-9-14
into the heart by ... (Wordsworth) 16-3-71
... is exorbitant (Plutarch) 1-5-33
lives as ... directs (Aristotle) 9-6-21
love a disagreeable ... (Smith) 3-4-53
love not the only ... (Hume) 1-7-113
love not simply a bodily ... (Montaigne) 3-3-40
no ... in the mind (Bacon) 1-8-101
no ... so distressing (Boswell) 4-2-28
not a special ... (Descartes) 4-2-24
not curb his ... (Horace) 4-3-11
not led by ... (Aristotle) 4-3-5
... of the soul (Gibbon) 16-3-59
one ... presses us (Boswell) 1-9-35
one universal ... (Shaw) 4-2-34
principle derived from ... (Plato) 4-4-2
... produced by idleness (Montaigne) 4-4-16
retard the impulse of ... (Hume) 4-1-27
rule your ... (Horace) 4-3-11
saved by faith in His ... (Augustine) 20-14-20
sensual ... expires (Wm. James) 1-3-126
... settles down (Santayana) 2-1-55
sight of body a remedy to ... (Montaigne) 3-3-38
so strong a ... (Shakespeare) 1-7-83
the maiden ... for a maid (Tennyson) 3-1-77
the ... stamped remaineth (Dante) 5-4-5
the rule of human ... (Rousseau) 9-4-43
the species of a ... (Aquinas) 4-5-10
the whirlwind of ... (Shakespeare) 16-4-19
too much appearing ... (Hobbes) 5-6-27
understanding sorrow destroys the ... (Spinoza) 3-2-26
unrighteous and criminal ... (Pascal) 1-4-28
very essence of my ... (Goethe) 16-6-51
we are slaves to ... (Leibniz) 9-4-37
we cannot sympathize with another's ... (Smith) 3-1-64
we exult in ... (Mann) 16-3-102
when our ... leads us (Pascal) 9-9-22
... whose violence makes madness (Hobbes) 4-11-20
width of human ... (T. S. Eliot) 16-3-98
... wills its own downfall (Kierkegaard) 5-1-63
without subjection to ... (Augustine) 20-5-31
PASSIONATE
  bad are ... (Plato) 9-6-7
PASSIONS
  abatement of your ... (Pascal) 19-4-26
  a command over our ... (Thoreau) 1-1-106
  adverse to violent ... (Tocqueville) 11-5-28
  all disordinate ... (Rabelais) 1-7-69
  all ... that allow (Montaigne) 4-1-10
  a mediocrity of ... (Hobbes) 9-1-6
  among all ... inflicted (Aquinas) 1-8-58
  and governed their ... (Blake) 20-15-91
  anger and other ... (Plutarch) 20-6-31
  ... are lawful guides (Johnson) 8-2-20
  ... aroused in him (Schopenhauer) 9-8-69
  ascribe to Him ... (Hobbes) 20-5-67
  bent of one's ... (Aquinas) 9-8-33
  by activity of ... our reason (Rousseau) 6-1-75
  by the ... inciting to something (Aquinas) 9-10-46
  cannot be two ... (Hume) 17-1-68
  cardinal ... of your life (Wm. James) 7-1-61
  ... contrary to our natural (Hobbes) 1-2-51
  created by ... (Tocqueville) 11-1-50
  create ... within us (Milton) 13-2-17
  dangerous ... as guiding (Rousseau) 8-3-54
  difference of men's ... (Hobbes) 5-1-27
  dislocation that the ... (Montaigne) 5-6-11
  ... draw them (Tocqueville) 2-3-101
  effects produced by the same ... (Gibbon) 1-2-70

emotions and ... distinct (Kant) 4-1-29
feeds and waters the ... (Plato) 16-3-6
fierce and unrestrained ... (Gibbon) 15-1-51
gives way to ... (Dostoevsky) 9-14-60
infinite number of ... (Montaigne) 1-2-33
inflames our ... (Fielding) 9-12-41
influence of morality on ... (Hume) 9-1-14
influence of violent ... (Schiller) 16-4-37
influence on the ... (Hume) 6-3-85
injurious ... and actions (Aquinas) 12-2-25
... interesting to mankind (Hamilton) 1-4-39
lends earthly ... (Santayana) 16-5-42
let us our glowing ... still (Goethe) 9-12-45
majority follow their ... (Aquinas) 20-10-26
mind subject to the ... (Spinoza) 4-1-21
... mixed in various degrees (Hume) 1-2-58
modes of self-love the ... (Pope) 4-1-24
... more or less in flame (Pope) 4-1-26
more violent than other ... (Descartes) 4-3-22
most violent ... (Shaw) 2-3-114
natural ... of men (Hobbes) 10-1-22
no reference to other ... (Hume) 4-1-28
not his reason but his ... (Sterne) 9-5-13
... of individuals (Hegel) 1-6-56
... of the heart (Montesquieu) 12-1-61
... of the human soul (Gibbon) 16-1-30
... of the present (Montesquieu) 10-6-47
... of the soul (Pascal) 6-4-24; (Aquinas) 7-1-18
... of the vulgar (Bacon) 17-1-51
... of war reign (Hamilton) 14-1-87
... or mystical intuitions (Wm. James) 6-5-109
... ought not be controlled (Plato) 9-12-2
perfection does not take away ... (Aquinas) 9-4-23
philosophy gives no command of ... (Newman) 9-1-31
powerful of all our ... (Russell) 11-2-159
purging of the ... (Boswell) 16-4-33
reasonable beings have ... (Boswell) 7-2-78
regulation of the ... (Plato) 9-11-6
representation of the ... (Plato) 16-4-22
... reside in appetite (Aquinas) 9-4-22
restraint of the ... (Locke) 8-3-59
rhetoric addresses the ... (Plutarch) 7-2-33
same idea of all our ... (Keats) 5-4-34
sensual ... have gone (Aristotle) 3-3-19
similitude of ... the same (Hobbes) 1-4-25
some ... ordered to good (Aquinas) 4-7-24
speech by which ... are expressed (Hobbes) 4-1-20
stupified by ... of the soul (Montaigne) 5-2-18
... terminating purely in pain (Locke) 4-1-23
the excuse of his ... (Sartre) 13-1-70
the number of ... (Descartes) 4-1-15
the ... of mankind (Hamilton) 10-2-90
the worst of ... (Jefferson) 10-7-27
those and such like ... (Milton) 16-4-25
to direct the ... (Tocqueville) 9-10-111
to the ... of hope and fear (Montesquieu) 20-1-38
two ... are contrary (Descartes) 4-5-18
vicious and frenzied ... (Montaigne) 16-1-22
well those ... read (Shelley) 19-7-68
... which a man has (Descartes) 2-2-60
working of the ... (Hume) 16-1-28
young men have strong ... (Aristotle) 1-3-18
young tend to follow their ... (Aristotle) 1-3-16
your own foul ... bare (Tennyson) 16-2-50
PASSIVE
  active and ... citizenship (Kant) 10-5-24
  the ... that obeys reason (Blake) 9-6-94
PASSOVER
  Christ is our ... (Augustine) 6-1-29

PENALTY (*Cont.*)
  impose a . . . on people (Mill) 11-6-56
  . . . is most severe (Plato) 2-2-19
  . . . of concupiscence never dies (Chaucer) 3-3-33
  pays a . . . for anger (Plato) 4-3-4
PENANCE
  labor as a . . . (Gibbon) 11-3-40
PENANCES
  punishes himself with . . . (Freud) 20-13-97
  virtues are . . . (Emerson) 9-10-112
PENCE
  my intent is . . . to win (Chaucer) 4-9-5
PENDULUM
  opinion is like a . . . (Schopenhauer) 6-5-88
PENELOPE
  love that cheered . . . (Dante) 6-2-13
  my quiet . . . (Homer) 2-3-8
  should have cheered . . . (Dante) 20-15-54
PENEUS
  a new . . . rolls his fountains (Shelley) 15-2-49
PENITENCE
  sees . . . in the heart (Pascal) 20-14-35
PENNYWISE
  be not . . . (Bacon) 11-2-69
PENTATEUCH
  each page of the . . . (Gibbon) 20-2-41
PENTECOST
  the feast of . . . (Aquinas) 20-2-24
PENTHEUS
  . . . at the highest tip (Euripides) 5-6-5
PENTHISILEA
  to the field . . . led (Virgil) 1-7-35
PENURY
  chill . . . repress'd (Gray) 11-2-83
PEOPLE
  all sorts of . . . undone (Shelley) 20-15-95
  a . . . of gods (Rousseau) 10-4-29
  . . . are more naive (Dostoevsky) 1-2-92
  . . . are only safe depositories (Jefferson) 10-4-32
  . . . are sovereign (Cicero) 13-1-6
  . . . are the only censors (Jefferson) 13-2-33
  . . . as assemblage of reasonable beings (Augustine) 10-1-14
  attachment to one's . . . (Dewey) 14-1-110
  by the aid of the . . . (Machiavelli) 10-6-20
  chosen from the common . . . (Montaigne) 6-5-44
  chosen . . . of God (Jefferson) 9-10-104
  country belongs to the . . . (Lincoln) 10-9-39
  . . . crushed by law (Burke) 12-1-70
  . . . give itself to a king (Rousseau) 10-6-52
  good sense of the . . . (Jefferson) 10-4-33
  government of the . . . (Lincoln) 10-4-64
  . . . have all one language (*Genesis*) 7-1-2
  interest of the . . . (Mill) 10-3-62
  . . . in whom supreme power (Montesquieu) 10-4-19
  . . . is never corrupted (Rousseau) 10-4-25
  Jews were born his chosen . . . (Freud) 20-2-47
  loved by their . . . (Rousseau) 10-6-53
  loves not the common . . . (Shakespeare) 10-2-45
  . . . most in danger when (Hamilton) 14-2-61
  . . . must needs be mad (Milton) 10-6-37
  . . . not utterly degraded (Aristotle) 10-4-6
  one . . . is peculiarly chosen (Calvin) 15-3-72
  oppresses his . . . (Boswell) 10-6-59
  . . . qualified for choosing (Montesquieu) 10-4-20
  rebuke many . . . (*Isaiah*) 14-3-3
  such are the common . . . (Cervantes) 10-8-10
  take you to me for a . . . (*Exodus*) 20-2-6
  tenacity of the . . . (Hobbes) 11-6-8
  . . . their own instrument (Burke) 10-4-37

the . . . being ignorant (Locke) 10-4-18
the . . . fittest to choose (Milton) 10-4-16
the . . . reign (Euripides) 10-4-1
the whole . . . perish (Kant) 12-4-60
thy . . . shall be my . . . (*Ruth*) 3-1-1
tyrant chosen from the . . . (Aristotle) 10-6-12
use for the common . . . (Swift) 20-1-33
voice of the . . . (Bacon) 10-4-12
were God's chosen . . . (Freud) 20-2-51
. . . were so ridiculous (G. Eliot) 1-4-59
. . . which thou hast chosen (*I Kings*) 9-15-1
. . . whom he hath chosen (*Psalms*) 20-2-14
PERCEIVE
  impossible to . . . (Locke) 1-4-31
PERCEIVING
  faculty of . . . (Wm. James) 6-2-46
  thinking is like . . . (Aristotle) 5-1-5
PERCENTAGE
  tax at a higher . . . (Mill) 11-6-56
PERCEPTION
  by the power of . . . (Aristotle) 1-8-23
  consists merely in . . . (Boswell) 16-7-34
  example of non-sensuous . . . (Whitehead) 5-3-30
  expansion of human . . . (Langer) 16-1-73
  gone are judgment and . . . (Lucian) 6-6-7
  identity of . . . (Freud) 5-1-77
  implies an intuitive . . . (Aristotle) 16-3-10
  infallible . . . that we are (Locke) 6-6-23
  intelligence nor ordinary . . . (Plotinus) 19-4-15
  keen . . . of certain relations (Wm. James) 16-7-50
  mental . . . of fact (Wm. James) 4-1-32
  nothing but developed . . . (Santayana) 17-2-133
  . . . of length of time (Wm. James) 19-7-81
  . . . of our own mind (Locke) 5-1-40
  . . . of the succession (Wm. James) 19-7-80
  our faculties of . . . (Santayana) 16-6-84
  . . . plays the part (Freud) 4-1-35
  power of . . . is understanding (Locke) 5-1-42
  prime agent of all . . . (Coleridge) 5-4-30
  then . . . is pleasure (Santayana) 16-6-83
PERCEPTIONS
  divide all . . . into two (Hume) 5-1-47
  feature of our . . . (Russell) 19-6-44
  his . . . are disturbed (Boswell) 1-8-118
  . . . of mind and sense (Bacon) 6-4-19
  . . . of multiplicity (Wm. James) 7-1-61
  . . . of sense are true (Pascal) 8-3-51
  our . . . are confused (Leibniz) 9-4-37
PERCEPTUAL
  may call . . . space (Poincaré) 19-6-41
  . . . space different (Poincaré) 19-6-42
PERCIPIENT
  all . . . beings desire good (Plato) 9-6-11
PERDITION
  any armor in gold against . . . (Aeschylus) 20-13-11
  astray to the point to . . . (Kierkegaard) 1-4-44
  consign ourselves to . . . (Melville) 11-4-36
  down to bottomless . . . (Milton) 20-15-75
PERFECT
  advance from imperfect to . . . (Aquinas) 12-1-31
  alone becomes truly . . . (Plato) 17-1-3
  an absolutely . . . being (Leibniz) 20-5-83
  applying the words . . . (Spinoza) 19-1-56
  be ye therefore . . . (*Matthew*) 20-8-25
  by works was faith made . . . (*James*) 20-8-36
  first law most . . . (Pascal) 12-1-49
  God made thee . . . (Milton) 15-3-92
  he is . . . lacking nothing (Euripides) 20-6-9
  if they are to become . . . (Pascal) 17-2-39

PHILOSOPHERS (*Cont.*)
  ... following in train of Zeus (Plato) 16-6-6
  form a state wholly of ... (Polybius) 20-1-2
  found in the books of ... (Hobbes) 6-4-22, 17-3-27
  ... have learned (Russell) 19-7-85
  ... have sometimes said (Santayana) 5-6-44
  in the persons of its ... (Pascal) 15-2-26
  learned and prudent ... (Rabelais) 6-6-9
  learned something from the ... (Epictetus) 8-1-19
  leave to the ... of nature (Copernicus) 19-8-42
  many of our modern ... (Plato) 19-5-3
  many ... have called (Copernicus) 17-3-20
  most ... paid for their schooling (Montaigne) 16-6-30
  not afraid of dead ... (Cicero) 1-8-31
  not from ... (Harvey) 18-1-25
  ... of diverse stripes (Peirce) 6-6-47
  ... of the derivative school (Darwin) 9-1-26
  ... of the last age (Voltaire) 17-2-57
  ... of the vulgar sort (Gilbert) 17-2-12
  opinions of the ... (Descartes) 6-2-22
  ... or lovers of wisdom (Aristotle) 6-3-14
  ... say we cannot (Dostoevsky) 6-4-52
  should believe the ... (Epictetus) 8-1-18
  ... taken for divine (Bacon) 6-2-20
  theory of the natural ... (Melville) 20-1-59
  the ... divided into (Pascal) 20-3-32
  the pride of the ... (Pascal) 20-3-31
  though ... disagree (Augustine) 6-1-25
  to you alone true ... (Gilbert) 17-2-11
  true ... are seeking (Plato) 1-8-17
  worthy of the name of ... (Plato) 16-7-2
  your gods O ... (Hume) 20-6-41
PHILOSOPHIC
  is to be called ... wisdom (Aristotle) 9-15-24
  most ... of all writing (Wordsworth) 16-3-71
  poetry more ... (Aristotle) 16-3-8
PHILOSOPHICAL
  ... attempt to work out (Kant) 15-1-58
PHILOSOPHICAL NECESSITY
  doctrine of ... (Mill) 5-7-43
PHILOSOPHIZING
  mind given over to ... (Kepler) 20-8-59
  three methods of ... (Comte) 15-2-50
PHILOSOPHY
  academical ... may be useful (Hume) 6-6-27
  accomplished by ... alone (Nicomachus) 9-8-22
  a choice book of ... (Voltaire) 17-1-71
  a final ... of religion (Wm. James) 20-14-56
  a lecture in love's ... (Donne) 3-1-50
  a lecture on ... (Boswell) 14-2-48
  all ... of history is conjecture (Boswell) 15-1-48
  a ... of history admitted (Mill) 15-2-67
  ... apt to have a bad name (Plato) 6-7-6
  ... as an independent branch (Marx and Engels) 15-1-76
  as far as it relates to ... (Newton) 17-3-31
  at this stage of ... (Wm. James) 6-1-101
  ... be called knowledge of the truth (Aristotle) 6-3-12
  blindly optimistic ... (Wm. James) 4-2-33
  by the fanning of ... (Boethius) 6-3-30
  condemned as dreaming and ... (Hegel) 15-1-63
  death of a sound ... (Kant) 6-6-33
  declamations against ... (Hegel) 6-6-38
  ... directs your choice (Horace) 16-3-17
  disappear before sound ... (Laplace) 19-4-36
  divisions of ... (Hume) 9-1-14
  every principle of ... (Hume) 13-2-24
  exceed all power of ... (Hume) 15-3-98
  first principle of ... (Descartes) 1-4-24
  fit to throw light on ... (Bacon) 6-3-55

foundation of all ... (Montaigne) 6-4-16
  ... gives no command of passions (Newman) 9-1-31
  ... has at times corrupted (Newman) 20-12-37
  ... has preserved traits of (Freud) 20-12-38
  ... has provided laws of (Montesquieu) 1-1-82
  identical with ... (Aristotle) 17-3-7
  improvement of natural ... (Newton) 17-2-47
  ... inclineth to atheism (Bacon) 20-9-19
  instead of speculative ... (Descartes) 17-2-36
  ... issuing from godlike (Lucretius) 20-6-23
  ... is the physician (Cicero) 17-1-19
  ... is the richest (Cicero) 9-15-26
  ... is to lead us (Hegel) 1-3-108
  I've studied now ... (Goethe) 6-1-85
  knowledge as ... (Newman) 6-1-96
  leaving ... to disputation (Hobbes) 6-5-50
  many a renowned ... (Santayana) 20-12-39
  maxims of ... (Tacitus) 1-9-17
  moral ... and moral laws (Kant) 9-3-26
  more precious than ... (Epicurus) 9-13-7
  most perfect ... of natural (Hume) 17-2-55
  ... natural as a science (Locke) 17-2-51
  natural ... in all its parts (Newton) 9-1-9
  natural ... is not capable (Locke) 17-2-50
  never cease teaching ... (Plato) 13-2-2
  new ... calls all in doubt (Donne) 17-2-15
  not faith but ... (Th. Browne) 6-5-55
  ... now is built (Locke) 19-8-66
  ... of disputatious theologians (Dewey) 6-7-47
  ... of the Greek sophists (Freud) 6-7-46
  ... ought not to assume (Russell) 19-3-52
  part of a natural ... (Bacon) 17-3-22
  precincts of natural ... (Faraday) 8-1-63
  professors of ... but not (Thoreau) 11-2-132
  public teachers of ... (Gibbon) 20-9-37
  quarrel between ... and poetry (Plato) 16-3-6
  reduce natural ... (Bacon) 17-2-16
  reasoning of pessimist ... (Tolstoy) 1-9-45
  revelation and ... different (Spinoza) 6-5-66
  rules in ... (Montaigne) 9-14-22
  satisfaction in ... (Aristotle) 12-4-12
  save ... from errors (Bacon) 6-6-15
  science and ... were aliens (Planck) 17-2-113
  scripture does not teach ... (Spinoza) 6-5-67
  slow are beginnings of ... (Thoreau) 17-2-86
  sole ... open (Maritain) 6-6-56
  sound part of ... (Sterne) 7-2-75
  sound ... of space (Russell) 19-6-45
  source of all ... (Plato) 5-2-1
  spirit of ... (Plato) 1-9-3
  stood firm in their ... (Santayana) 6-6-55
  sublime efforts of ... (Gibbon) 6-5-81
  system pursued in ... (Bacon) 6-2-21
  teach even true ... (Hobbes) 13-2-15
  ... teaches us to live (Montaigne) 8-1-24
  the business of first ... (Aristotle) 17-3-8
  the corruption of ... (Bacon) 20-12-20
  the fine reasonings of ... (Montaigne) 1-8-62
  the objects of higher ... (Aristotle) 19-1-5
  the sweets of sweet ... (Shakespeare) 8-1-27
  the systems of ... (Kierkegaard) 1-4-43
  the true labor of ... (Bacon) 17-2-23
  the use of a ... (Cicero) 15-3-29
  third form of the union ... (Hegel) 16-1-41
  ... thou guide of life (Cicero) 17-1-21
  threats of that rational ... (Augustine) 5-2-13
  to be illustrated by ... (Boswell) 6-2-30
  to be such as ... wished (Aurelius) 10-2-25
  to divide natural ... (Bacon) 17-2-17

to make light of . . . (Pascal) 17-1-54
to replace gymnastics (Plato) 8-1-2
. . . useful for life (Montaigne) 1-7-71
use of . . . of pure reason (Kant) 6-3-98
. . . was of no use (Aristotle) 11-2-22
we divided natural . . . (Bacon) 19-3-20
we regard . . . (Bacon) 6-4-19
what all . . . cannot implant (Montaigne) 9-2-9
what is function of . . . (Santayana) 6-3-147
where is . . . to be found (Lucian) 17-1-36
willing to believe . . . (Montaigne) 5-6-11
would . . . gain by it (Bergson) 19-5-72

PHOEBE
pale . . . drawn by verse (Virgil) 16-5-11

PHOEBUS
bright . . . in his strength (Shakespeare) 16-6-35
golden . . . never be beheld (Shakespeare) 1-9-29
streamers the young . . . fanning (Shakespeare) 5-4-12
sweats in the eye of . . . (Shakespeare) 10-6-24

PHOEBUS'
or . . . steeds (Shakespeare) 2-3-65

PHOENICIANS
while the . . . constructed (Herodotus) 5-6-2

PHOENIX
burn the long-lived . . . (Shakespeare) 19-7-43
hath got to be a . . . (Donne) 17-2-15

PHRASE
finely sounding . . . (Lucretius) 9-15-25

PHRASES
. . . excite proper sentiments (Berkeley) 7-2-73
learn . . . by heart (Schopenhauer) 8-3-80
search for novel . . . (Montaigne) 7-2-43
used in different . . . (Augustine) 7-1-11

PHRYNE
. . . would have lost her case (Montaigne) 16-6-30

PHYSIC
excellent . . . in mere muck (Luther) 18-1-17
set himself to study of . . . (Rabelais) 18-1-15
throw . . . to the dogs (Shakespeare) 18-1-21

PHYSICAL
real and . . . causes (Bacon) 19-3-21

PHYSICAL SCIENCE
. . . will not console me (Pascal) 9-1-7

PHYSICIAN
afterward appeared to be a . . . (Cervantes) 18-1-22
. . . conveys his knowledge (Freud) 6-4-56
goodbye to this sort of . . . (Plato) 18-3-12
happens to be a . . . of the soul (Plato) 8-3-4
. . . heal thyself (*Luke*) 18-2-17
. . . listens to patient (Freud) 7-2-90
love the . . . of pain (Plato) 3-1-7
modern . . . tells his patient (Shaw) 18-1-37
no . . . knew half so much (Rabelais) 8-1-23
. . . takes sides (Freud) 18-3-64
thrust away the . . . (Plutarch) 1-9-11

PHYSICIANS
certain sophists and . . . (Hippocrates) 18-1-3
if you and I were . . . (Plato) 6-2-4
methods of empirical . . . (Leibniz) 5-1-39
some speculative . . . (Smith) 18-3-54
were the . . . of service (Thucydides) 18-3-5

PHYSICIANS'
is the . . . business (Aristotle) 17-3-5

PHYSICIST
astronomer and the . . . (Aquinas) 17-2-5

PHYSICISTS
. . . largely engaged in (Whitehead) 17-3-57

PHYSICO-CHEMICAL
principles of . . . science (Bernard) 19-2-50

works by . . . properties (Bernard) 19-2-53

PHYSICS
. . . as an independent science (Russell) 19-5-69
authority as proof in . . . (Pascal) 17-2-39
comprehending anything in . . . (Huygens) 19-5-44
. . . has ceased to look for causes (Russell) 19-3-52
. . . ignores the question (Kant) 19-1-71
individual laws of . . . (Planck) 17-2-112
masters to follow in . . . (Pascal) 17-2-41
mathematical . . . (Poincaré) 17-3-53
. . . may explain the mechanism (Rousseau) 1-1-84
modern mathematical . . . (Whitehead) 19-6-43
modern . . . impresses us (Planck) 17-2-113
notions concerning . . . (Descartes) 17-2-36
theory of relativity on . . . (Freud) 6-6-52
the space of . . . (Russell) 19-6-44
we enter upon . . . (Newton) 17-3-32

PHYSICS
sixth book of . . . (Aquinas) 4-1-8

PHYSIOLOGICAL
their . . . process (Russell) 19-7-86

PHYSIOLOGISTS
. . . and physicians (Bernard) 18-3-58

PHYSIOLOGY
advancement of . . . (Harvey) 18-1-26

PICCARDA
know me again for . . . (Dante) 20-15-56

PICTURE
. . . a mute poesy (Jonson) 16-3-38
pleasure not in the . . . (Aristotle) 16-3-7
which a . . . cannot express (Bacon) 16-6-39

PICTURES
are but as . . . (Shakespeare) 1-8-88
but . . . of human life (Hume) 16-1-28
use of religious . . . (Gibbon) 20-9-41
you are . . . out of doors (Shakespeare) 1-7-86

PIECE
all of a . . . throughout (Dryden) 15-2-27

PIERIAN SPRING
taste not the . . . (Pope) 8-1-42

PIERIDES
pathless haunts of the . . . (Lucretius) 16-3-13

PIERRE
. . . had learned not (Tolstoy) 9-8-76
Natasha and . . . (Tolstoy) 2-3-110

PIERRE'S
greatness of . . . idea (Tolstoy) 2-3-111

PIETY
a confidence of true . . . (Leibniz) 9-9-23
between . . . and goodness (Pascal) 20-8-65
commendatory of his . . . (Milton) 20-1-30
each to each by natural . . . (Wordsworth) 1-3-99
example of filial . . . (Cervantes) 5-6-24
false appearance of . . . (Spinoza) 20-8-70
from motives of . . . (Spinoza) 12-4-42
good life and true . . . (Locke) 9-1-10
. . . is justice (Cicero) 20-8-24
like other acts of . . . (Johnson) 6-3-93
no act is it of . . . (Lucretius) 20-8-23
. . . of the family (Hegel) 2-1-42
one without true . . . (Augustine) 9-10-38
our . . . towards him (Calvin) 20-4-27
outward observance of . . . (Spinoza) 20-4-37
patronize providence and . . . (Emerson) 20-1-56
priests advanced for their . . . (Swift) 1-1-80
renounce . . . altogether (Pascal) 20-8-64
. . . requires us to honor truth (Aristotle) 6-3-14
seek to honor the . . . (Santayana) 20-3-103
slightest trace of . . . (Nietzsche) 20-5-118

PRACTICAL WISDOM
art and . . . (Aristotle) 6-7-12
cleverness and . . . (Aristotle) 9-13-6
people of . . . (Aristotle) 6-2-9
regarding . . . we shall get at (Aristotle) 9-13-3
same objects as . . . (Aristotle) 9-13-5
young deficient in . . . (Aristotle) 6-2-8
PRACTICE
. . . and imagination (Dewey) 17-1-105
. . . and personal interest (Gibbon) 6-5-82
a particular point of . . . (Aquinas) 9-3-13
barbarism not his own . . . (Montaigne) 9-2-11
. . . did not make perfect (Wm. James) 1-1-125
hasty zeal to . . . (Bacon) 17-2-20
. . . must not cross precepts (Locke) 8-3-59
quality in their . . . (Locke) 8-3-58
successful application to . . . (Mill) 17-1-87
the . . . of dying (Plato) 1-8-17
the . . . would be vexatious (Fielding) 17-1-63
use . . . instead of rules (Locke) 8-3-56
PRAGMATISM
. . . asks its usual question (Wm. James) 6-3-133
new advance in . . . (Dewey) 6-5-114
. . . says no (Wm. James) 6-3-131
PRAGMATIST
is a genuine . . . (Wm. James) 9-6-111
PRAIRIE
to make a . . . (Dickinson) 16-1-45
PRAISE
a man worthy of . . . (Aristotle) 6-3-15
a world of . . . (Euripides) 1-5-5
but not the . . . (Milton) 1-5-93
. . . from the many (Aurelius) 9-10-33
if there be any . . . (*Philippians*) 9-10-26
. . . is oblique (Boswell) 1-4-36
let another man . . . thee (*Proverbs*) 1-4-1
love approbation or . . . (Darwin) 1-1-109
love of . . . (Darwin) 1-5-126
love of . . . tempts me (Augustine) 1-5-44
. . . not so delightful (Boswell) 2-3-85
pleased with his own . . . (Plutarch) 1-5-34
sold for . . . (Epictetus) 1-5-37
through desire of . . . (Augustine) 20-13-29
PRAISED
can endure to hear others . . . (Thucydides) 4-8-4
PRAISES
. . . both of men and women (Herodotus) 2-3-14
have warbled the . . . (Melville) 16-3-84
. . . of poverty boldly sung (Wm. James) 11-2-155
PRAY
. . . for no man but myself (Shakespeare) 9-13-20
love to . . . standing in the (*Matthew*) 20-8-26
unto thee will I . . . (*Psalms*) 20-8-4
watch and . . . (*Matthew*) 20-13-16
. . . without ceasing (*I Thessalonians*) 20-8-35
PRAYER
a certain form of . . . (Montaigne) 20-8-57
and what's in . . . (Shakespeare) 20-8-60
a . . . of the Athenians (Aurelius) 20-8-40
are wrought by . . . (Tennyson) 20-8-82
be not forgetful of . . . (Dostoevsky) 20-8-85
by . . . and reverent love (Euripides) 20-8-17
. . . comes round again (Yeats) 1-3-135
fanes of fruitless . . . (Tennyson) 19-1-100
hear my . . . too soon (Augustine) 3-3-21
he has in . . . (Freud) 20-5-122
in . . . to Zeus (Homer) 2-2-8
. . . is not made for us (Dante) 20-8-52
. . . replaces sex (Twain) 3-3-76

spent time in . . . (G. Eliot) 20-8-84
the efficacy of . . . (Wm. James) 20-8-86
the . . . of a fool (Plato) 20-8-21
there are the spirits of . . . (Homer) 20-8-12
the true relation in . . . (Kierkegaard) 20-8-81
to fasting and . . . (*I Corinthians*) 2-3-23
PRAYERS
. . . be not hindered (*I Peter*) 1-7-44
nor . . . in vain offered (Boethius) 20-5-35
offer thee all my . . . (Dante) 20-8-53
. . . of them both were heard (*Tobit*) 20-7-2
to say their . . . (Cervantes) 20-4-28
when ye make many . . . (*Isaiah*) 20-8-9
which are the . . . of the saints (*Revelation*) 20-8-37
PRAYETH
he . . . best who loveth best (Coleridge) 20-8-79
PRAYING
from constantly . . . (Kierkegaard) 20-8-80
PRAYS
labors as he . . . (St. Bernard) 11-3-16
PREACH
because they . . . in vain (Byron) 4-7-60
to . . . truth (Melville) 6-3-109
PREACHER
a . . . of the gospel (Luther) 2-3-45
believe without a . . . (Augustine) 20-8-42
hear without a . . . (*Romans*) 6-5-12
is no mean . . . (Wordsworth) 19-1-83
no . . . is listened to but time (Swift) 19-7-59
PREACHERS
. . . to us all (Shakespeare) 9-6-60
young men as . . . (Luther) 16-5-16
PREACHING
avarice in all my . . . (Chaucer) 4-9-5
a 'woman's . . . like a (Boswell) 1-7-117
falsehood of the . . . (Emerson) 20-1-56
is our . . . in vain (Augustine) 6-7-15
office of the . . . of the gospel (Luther) 20-4-23
official . . . has falsely (Kierkegaard) 20-3-50
the knack of . . . (Cervantes) 1-8-137
PRECAUTIONS
all . . . a man can take (Montaigne) 19-4-20
neglected other . . . (Machiavelli) 4-2-20
PRECEDENCY
give a just . . . (Locke) 13-3-15
PRECEPT
guide conduct by mere . . . (Mill) 8-1-70
. . . implies notion of duty (Aquinas) 9-9-14
PRECEPTS
by means of . . . (Freud) 20-1-81
few apodictic . . . (Freud) 17-2-124
general . . . of ethics (Hume) 9-1-12
laws ought to give . . . (Montesquieu) 20-1-34
moral . . . distinct (Aquinas) 9-1-5
office of teaching . . . (Epictetus) 8-3-26
. . . of the gospel (Gibbon) 1-9-36
. . . received are false (Harvey) 17-2-31
. . . result of cognitive elaboration (Peirce) 6-6-47
PRECIOUS
nothing more . . . than wise friend (Herodotus) 3-4-
PRECISION
. . . is not to be sought (Aristotle) 6-7-11
PREDECESSOR
memory of thy . . . (Bacon) 10-2-50
PREDESTINATE
he did also . . . (*Romans*) 15-3-37
PREDESTINATION
. . . an abortion (Kierkegaard) 15-3-106
arranged for by . . . (Chaucer) 15-3-68

PRINCE
a ... no more than a clown (Cervantes) 1-8-95
a ... who is mindful (Locke) 10-2-63
arms with which a ... (Machiavelli) 14-2-29
authority of the ... (Gibbon) 11-6-31
a wise ... ought to adopt (Machiavelli) 3-6-11
good graces of a ... (Machiavelli) 6-2-15
minister of the ... (Melville) 20-4-48
no pontiff save the ... (Rousseau) 3-6-19
opinion one forms of a ... (Machiavelli) 10-2-35
... ought always take counsel (Machiavelli) 10-2-36
... ought have no other aim (Machiavelli) 14-1-36
... ought to be slow to act (Machiavelli) 4-2-20
... that has parents (Locke) 10-2-62
... that wanteth understanding (*Proverbs*) 10-6-1
the ... of peace (*Isaiah*) 20-3-1
unnecessary for a ... (Machiavelli) 1-5-53
... who despises his subjects (Rousseau) 10-2-75
... who does not understand (Machiavelli) 10-2-30
PRINCE HARRY
that ... is valiant (Shakespeare) 18-1-20
PRINCE OF WALES
nimble-footed madcap ... (Shakespeare) 14-2-36
PRINCES
... are like to heavenly (Bacon) 10-6-31
... are like wolves (*Ezekiel*) 10-6-2
... are unhappy (Hegel) 1-6-56
... become great (Machiavelli) 1-6-21
God's true ... (Melville) 1-6-70
let ... against all events (Bacon) 10-2-53
the generality of ... (Gibbon) 10-6-63
the tempers of ... (Euripides) 1-6-3
the wisest need not ... (Bacon) 10-2-54
PRINCIPALITIES
called sometimes ... (Calvin) 20-7-38
PRINCIPLE
action from ... (Thoreau) 9-9-40
a ... of motion and change (Aristotle) 19-5-5
a ... of taste would mean (Kant) 16-7-38
asserted an infinite ... (Aquinas) 20-5-47
conceived of the first ... as (Plutarch) 20-6-30
... derived from reason (Dante) 9-4-28
determined by rational ... (Aristotle) 9-10-13
effect of a natural ... (Aquinas) 19-4-19
element that has rational ... (Aristotle) 9-8-12
eternal and immutable ... (Boswell) 6-3-96
everything on ... (Shaw) 9-9-48
greatest happiness ... (Darwin) 9-1-26
injure that ... in us (Plato) 6-1-3
innate ... of justice (Rousseau) 9-5-15
... is a better test of heresy (Newman) 20-9-45
... is always more universal (Aquinas) 19-3-16
... is the active ... (Aquinas) 2-2-41
... light of a superior (Berkeley) 17-1-61
living ... in him (Melville) 5-6-36
lower ... to the higher (Boethius) 17-1-40
moral ... of duty (Kant) 1-4-38
natural law a first ... (Luther) 9-3-15
nature has observed this ... (Montaigne) 19-1-33
no higher ... than right (Tocqueville) 12-3-26
not a difference of ... (Jefferson) 13-2-34
not ascending to first ... (Plato) 6-1-5
... of a new order (Hegel) 9-2-30
... of connection between thoughts (Hume) 5-4-23
... of natural law (Maritain) 9-3-37
... of permanence (Kant) 6-6-34
one first ... of evil (Aquinas) 9-6-52
... opposes our passion (Hume) 4-1-27
participates in rational ... (Aristotle) 10-7-8

proper ... of human acts (Aquinas) 9-1-5
regulating ... necessary (Plotinus) 19-2-20
sole ... of the sciences (Pascal) 17-2-40
subject to the higher ... (Augustine) 9-4-21
supreme ... of ethics (Kant) 9-1-23
the forbidding ... (Plato) 4-4-2
the ... of existence (Leibniz) 19-8-64
... which ought to be guide (Plato) 1-5-8
PRINCIPLES
about first ... (Voltaire) 19-1-64
acquainted with first ... (Aristotle) 6-1-12
animated by particular determinate ... (Hegel) 5-1-58
asserting first ... (Aristotle) 20-6-20
best ... of society (Boswell) 5-4-27
certain and infallible ... (Montaigne) 6-5-45
certain ... by means of (Russell) 6-1-106
confusion among universal ... (Dante) 14-3-26
constant and universal ... (Hume) 15-1-40
demonstrate conclusions from ... (Aquinas) 9-15-37
derive two or three general ... (Newton) 17-2-47
difference in first ... (Boswell) 8-1-50
differ from the ... (Descartes) 17-2-36
drawn from these ... (Galen) 18-1-13
educated men lay down ... (Aristotle) 7-2-17
effect of narrow ... (Swift) 10-2-65
entered into their ... (Pascal) 17-1-57
ethical ... must be (Hegel) 2-2-83
examine the religious ... (Hume) 20-1-39
excessive ... of scepticism (Hume) 6-6-26
feel the value of ... (Mill) 8-3-83
first ... are too self-evident (Pascal) 6-1-56
first ... be considered (Plato) 6-7-4
first ... of action (Faraday) 17-2-82
first ... of their subjects (Aristotle) 6-2-8
first ... of things (Voltaire) 6-7-33
first ... of wisdom (Aquinas) 9-15-39
fixed and incontestable ... (Huygens) 17-2-43
follow from first ... (Aristotle) 6-7-12
formulate first ... (Whitehead) 6-4-54
granting evident ... (Pascal) 6-7-27
habit a result of ... (Kant) 8-2-22
influenced by purer ... (Hamilton) 6-4-39
in respect of formal ... (Aquinas) 9-10-46
instilling ethical ... (Hegel) 2-2-81
intellect knows ... (Aquinas) 6-1-36
it begins with ... (Kant) 17-1-74
mechanical ... of nature (Kant) 6-4-38
memory contains ... (Augustine) 5-3-10
more able to formulate ... (Aristotle) 17-2-1
... must be had from books (Boswell) 16-2-36
... natural to man (Pascal) 9-2-21
... not from other sciences (Aquinas) 17-1-41
... not to be disputed (Mill) 6-3-117
not used to seek for ... (Pascal) 6-7-23
... of all logical judging (Kant) 7-2-82
... of all the sciences (Mill) 17-3-44
... of eternal things (Aristotle) 6-3-12
offend ... of reason (Pascal) 6-5-57
... of moral knowledge (Hamilton) 6-4-40
... of pleasure not stable (Pascal) 4-7-45
... of science (Aristotle) 6-7-8
... of taste be universal (Hume) 16-7-30
... of the experimental method (Bernard) 17-2-96
... of the modern world (Hegel) 9-11-56
other men's ruling ... (Aurelius) 9-3-7
persuaded of these ... (Hume) 17-2-56
presents us with excellent ... (Kant) 17-1-75
proceeding from understood ... (Aquinas) 6-7-18
... really most common (Bacon) 17-2-19

eloquence in seeming ... (Hobbes) 7-2-59
experience is ... (Hobbes) 6-2-23
gotten by ... (Hobbes) 6-7-22
grow in ... and wisdom (Dante) 14-3-24
he has counsel or ... (Aquinas) 9-15-36
impute success to ... (Swift) 15-3-96
... is a certain rectitude (Aquinas) 9-10-47
... is but experience (Hobbes) 13-3-11
... is threefold (Aquinas) 9-13-16
... is virtue of the understanding (Aristotle) 9-10-17
... not without virtue (Aquinas) 9-10-45
old man deifies ... (Johnson) 1-3-88
principal use of ... (Descartes) 4-1-17
principal virtue called ... (Aquinas) 9-10-46
proceed with ... (Machiavelli) 4-2-20
reasons of ... (Mill) 9-9-43
that hath traveled is full of ... (*Ecclesiasticus*) 6-2-1
the nook and chimney side of ... (Emerson) 1-2-80
... would not dissuade us (Plato) 6-2-4
PRUDENT
more men ... than virtuous (Montesquieu) 1-6-45
not with ... ways (Horace) 9-15-27
PRUSSIA, King of
take the ... by the nose (Boswell) 1-9-35
PRYNNE, Hester
and never had ... appeared (Hawthorne) 16-6-67
PSALMS
devout and holy ... (Milton) 16-5-29
through the ... (Dante) 6-5-33
PSYCHIATRY
psychoanalysis stands to ... (Freud) 18-1-41
PSYCHE
confused seeds imposed upon ... (Milton) 9-6-81
PSYCHIC
activity of our ... apparatus (Freud) 16-4-47
conscious is a special ... act (Freud) 5-2-40
operation of the ... apparatus (Freud) 5-1-77
PSYCHIC MEMORY RESIDUES
effect of time on ... (Freud) 5-3-33
PSYCHIC PHENOMENON
dream a valid ... (Freud) 5-5-40
PSYCHIC POWERS
enumeration of ... (Aristotle) 1-1-12
PSYCHOANALYSIS
displeasing propositions of ... (Freud) 5-1-78
good grounding in ... (Freud) 8-3-97
has been made by ... (Freud) 20-5-123
influenced by results of ... (Freud) 8-1-86
... may claim a high rank (Freud) 5-5-46
relation of ... to (Freud) 17-2-128
... shows us that those persons (Freud) 3-4-63
... stands to psychiatry (Freud) 18-1-41
what does ... do (Freud) 9-6-115
who has no knowledge of ... (Freud) 19-1-122
PSYCHOANALYSTS
we ... were neither (Freud) 17-2-125
PSYCHOANALYTIC
in ... treatment (Freud) 7-2-90
PSYCHOGENESIS
trace the course of ... (Wm. James) 5-1-73
PSYCHOLOGICAL
... habits in animals and man (Aristotle) 1-1-14
PSYCHOLOGISM
system like modern ... (Santayana) 6-6-55
PSYCHOLOGIST
intensely interest the ... (Poincaré) 17-3-51
PSYCHOLOGISTS
men who were not ... (Wm. James) 7-1-61
PSYCHOLOGY

... is concerned with space (Russell) 19-6-44
... of fashion becomes pathology (Shaw) 18-2-51
only the poet's own ... (Freud) 16-4-46
PSYCHONEUROSES
particularly the ... (Freud) 18-2-53
PSYCHOTICS
... are fissured structures (Freud) 5-6-42
PTOLEMY
Euclid was asked by ... (Proclus) 17-3-13
... of Alexandria (Copernicus) 17-2-10
therefore said ... of Alexandria (Copernicus) 19-8-42
... the son of Lagus (Rabelais) 16-6-26
PUBERTY
enters into child at ... (Freud) 1-3-130
time of ... onward (Freud) 2-2-100
PUBLIC
any man dies in ... (Boswell) 4-11-33
... becomes powerful (Hume) 11-5-10
conspiracy against the ... (Smith) 11-5-14
education ... not private (Aristotle) 8-1-7
indifferent to the ... (Mill) 8-1-70
law is ... conscience (Hobbes) 9-5-8
merely follow their ... (Aristotle) 16-4-11
service of the ... (Cervantes) 5-6-22
PUBLICAN
and the other a ... (*Luke*) 20-8-30
PUBLICANS
... and harlots go into (*Matthew*) 20-8-28
PUBLICITY
the right of ... (Hegel) 12-2-46
PUBLIC OPINION
... deserves to be respected (Hegel) 6-5-87
... on which success depends (Rousseau) 9-2-27
PUBLIC WORKS
condemned to ... serves (Voltaire) 12-4-52
the expense of ... (Smith) 11-6-23
PUCK
my gentle ... (Shakespeare) 16-5-18
PUES
... had two sons (Gibbon) 10-3-44
PUFFENDORF, Baron Samuel von
but ... was not (Boswell) 6-2-30
... on rights of schoolmasters (Boswell) 8-3-69
... says that we may (Rousseau) 12-3-18
PULPIT
... and the press (Emerson) 11-2-128
PULSE
the little ... to squeeze (Goethe) 18-2-42
PULSES
proved upon our ... (Keats) 17-1-80
PUMPKIN
would rather sit on a ... (Thoreau) 1-4-50
PUNISH
desire to ... a person (Mill) 12-2-52
I will ... him (Tolstoy) 1-9-44
you to ... them (Plato) 2-2-18
PUNISHED
... in some way (Mill) 9-7-50
PUNISHING
case for ... by law (Mill) 9-1-28
in ... the aggressors (Thucydides) 4-3-3
PUNISHMENT
are in like ... (Dante) 9-12-20
a terrible ... truly (Juvenal) 9-5-3
at present under just ... (Augustine) 19-1-21
can be fear of ... (Aquinas) 20-15-38
cannot be a war of ... (Kant) 14-3-41
circumcision a ... for sex (Montaigne) 3-3-39
consigns to ... (Augustine) 4-1-5

READ
everybody learns to . . . (Boswell) 8-1-49
school can teach us to . . . (Carlyle) 8-1-57
READINESS
have a certain . . . for teaching (Epictetus) 8-3-26
the . . . is all (Shakespeare) 1-8-80, 15-3-84
READING
an end to all kind of . . . (Sterne) 15-2-32
culture is . . . (Arnold) 8-1-75
. . . maketh a full man (Bacon) 16-2-17
nor useful as . . . or writing (Aristotle) 16-5-6
not discouraged from . . . (Boswell) 8-3-71
the art of . . . (Wm. James) 8-3-88
REAL
world as absolutely . . . (Schopenhauer) 20-2-43
REALISM
characteristics are . . . (Schopenhauer) 20-2-43
naive . . . cannot be accepted (Russell) 19-6-44
REALIST
the genuine . . . (Dostoevsky) 20-11-43
REALITIES
are . . . existing apart (Planck) 17-2-113
he will be unable to see the . . . (Plato) 1-2-13
lose knowledge of . . . (Plato) 6-7-3
. . . whose existence we believe (Wm. James) 5-2-37
REALITY
any . . . we can substitute (Thoreau) 13-1-45
a . . . with no quality (Bergson) 19-6-47
at a correspondence with . . . (Freud) 17-2-127
becomes knowledge of . . . (Santayana) 6-2-54
cannot apprehend . . . (Dostoevsky) 6-4-52
certainty of the . . . (Whitman) 9-15-90
dream and waking . . . (Wm. James) 5-5-36
duplicate versions of . . . (Dewey) 6-3-144
encounter the . . . of experience (Joyce) 6-2-55
exercise of testing . . . (Freud) 5-4-40
has attained no true . . . (Marx) 20-1-62
has more objective . . . (Descartes) 20-5-60
in ourselves and in . . . (Montaigne) 1-5-61
. . . is just itself (Whitehead) 6-3-139
is taken for a . . . (Santayana) 20-3-69
mind hypnotised by . . . (Santayana) 16-1-64
more real than . . . (Maritain) 17-1-113
rejoices at beholding . . . (Plato) 6-3-3
the aversion to . . . (Freud) 19-1-121
thoughts proceed from . . . (Schiller) 19-1-74
total . . . is the world (Wittgenstein) 6-1-112
true ground objective . . . (Hegel) 3-6-22
true psychic . . . (Freud) 1-4-66
turned away from external . . . (Freud) 5-6-42
turns away from . . . (Freud) 16-1-57
whether . . . or dream (Melville) 5-5-34
world of . . . has its bounds (Rousseau) 5-4-26
REALITY-PRINCIPLE
substitutes the . . . (Freud) 4-1-35
REALIZATION
before its . . . in material (Aristotle) 16-1-5
hindered from . . . (Aquinas) 6-1-40
sense of beauty is its . . . (Santayana) 16-6-83
REALMS
in the . . . of gold (Keats) 16-3-80
REALNESS
truth and . . . are synonymous (Dewey) 6-3-144
REAL THINGS
ideas imprinted called . . . (Berkeley) 5-2-29
REAP
that shall he . . . (*Galatians*) 19-3-11
REARING
unfavorable to the . . . (Smith) 2-1-36

REASON
abuse of our . . . (Burke) 12-1-72
accordance with . . . (Spinoza) 2-3-74
according to dictates of . . . (Spinoza) 4-8-24
according to guidance of . . . (Spinoza) 3-5-31, 9-10-86,
10-1-25, 20-8-69
according to his own . . . (Aquinas) 6-5-31
acquire virtue by . . . (Rousseau) 9-1-15
acted in accordance with . . . (Peirce) 19-4-45
a deliberate judgment of . . . (Aquinas) 9-2-8
advance in man's . . . (Darwin) 20-5-104
. . . all these powers in one (Pope) 5-1-45
. . . alone shall have sway (Kant) 17-2-64
. . . also is choice (Milton) 5-7-26
always . . . right (Hamilton) 10-4-49
ambitious attempts of . . . (Kant) 20-5-94
analogy of words and . . . (Bacon) 7-2-54
. . . and energy (Blake) 9-6-94, 20-15-92
and . . . on her waite (Milton) 1-7-99
. . . and speech (Cicero) 10-1-12
and when . . . comes (Plato) 16-5-2
an order . . . can discover (Maritain) 9-3-36
an ordinance of . . . (Aquinas) 12-1-25
. . . an unintelligible instinct (Santayana) 5-1-86
any foundation in . . . (Hume) 20-6-41
appetite not entirely subject to . . . (Aquinas) 9-4-22
apply . . . to objective (Kant) 6-6-33
apprehended by . . . as good (Aquinas) 9-3-10
are beyond human . . . (Nietzsche) 17-1-90
arises from . . . (Hume) 4-1-27
a rule found out by . . . (Hobbes) 12-3-10
as being opposed to . . . (Spinoza) 19-1-55
as far as . . . seeth (Dante) 9-7-35
asks for pity without . . . (Montaigne) 4-8-15
. . . at basis of action (Kant) 16-1-31
. . . at basis of its action (Kant) 19-1-69
atheism against . . . (Burke) 20-9-43
attends the efforts of . . . (Kant) 17-3-39
attend to the order of . . . (Aquinas) 9-12-19
aversion from commands of . . . (Aurelius) 9-4-12
a very feast of . . . (Lucian) 17-1-33
away the guard of . . . (Fielding) 9-12-41
Bible leaves . . . free (Spinoza) 6-5-66
bid God and . . . rule (Aristotle) 12-1-11
. . . bids us for our own (Pope) 4-1-24
bound to be led by . . . (Spinoza) 12-4-43
by morality and . . . (Plutarch) 4-2-15
by persuasive argument and . . . (Plutarch) 20-5-28
by . . . men lived long (Luther) 6-1-44
by the help of . . . (Plato) 4-4-1
by the sacrifice of . . . (Johnson) 16-3-55
can be known by . . . (Aquinas) 20-5-43
. . . can decide nothing (Pascal) 19-4-26
capability and god-like . . . (Shakespeare) 5-1-19
. . . capable of knowing law (Locke) 9-4-38
capable of listening to . . . (Descartes) 6-2-22
claim to control human . . . (Descartes) 17-3-25
combat their . . . (Montaigne) 9-15-47
combined with intuitive . . . (Aristotle) 17-1-12
come now let us . . . (*Isaiah*) 6-7-1
come to the use of . . . (Locke) 2-1-30
common law of . . . (Locke) 14-1-58
compelling the soul to . . . (Plato) 17-3-2
complete in . . . alone (Kant) 17-1-77
conflict of speculative . . . (Kant) 7-2-84
conformable to . . . (Aurelius) 10-2-25
conscience is practical . . . (Kant) 9-5-17
consists in an act of the . . . (Aquinas) 16-6-25
. . . constitutes dignity of man (Bergson) 1-1-131

REASON (*Cont.*)

contemptuous of . . . (Cicero) 4-1-4
. . . continually gives rise (Turgot) 15-2-36
. . . continues fallible (Madison) 10-8-23
corrupts judgment of . . . (Kant) 17-1-78
could have solved by . . . (Euripides) 14-1-10
created by a divine . . . (Plato) 19-1-2
cultivate . . . (Swift) 6-6-24
cultivate your own . . . (Epictetus) 17-1-31
curtail pleasure by . . . (Montaigne) 4-7-34
deadening of our . . . (Montaigne) 5-6-11
defend self with . . . (Aristotle) 7-2-10
. . . demands nothing (Spinoza) 1-4-30
. . . demands state be founded (Hegel) 10-1-40
departs from the order of . . . (Aquinas) 20-13-49
depart without a . . . (Epictetus) 1-9-15
deprived me of my . . . (Cervantes) 16-2-12
destitute of . . . (Cicero) 4-1-4
devised by human . . . (Aquinas) 9-3-12
dictate of right . . . (Grotius) 12-3-8
dictates of . . . (Congreve) 1-7-106
dim . . . is to the soul (Dryden) 5-1-38
divine mansion of . . . (Rabelais) 9-15-43
do according to right . . . (Aurelius) 9-10-33
. . . does not approve of it (Kant) 9-8-60
each has roots in . . . (Aquinas) 16-6-25
effects of . . . (Pascal) 19-2-34
efforts we make through . . . (Spinoza) 6-1-61
ego represents . . . (Freud) 4-1-35
. . . enables us to calculate (Malthus) 4-7-58
endu'd with sanctitie of . . . (Milton) 19-2-35
essential aims of human . . . (Kant) 17-1-76
exercise . . . cooly (Hamilton/Madison) 6-5-86
exist apart from . . . (Cicero) 20-6-27
expectation not dictated by . . . (Johnson) 4-5-30
explained these marvels to . . . (Augustine) 20-11-11
. . . fails to grasp poetical (Aquinas) 16-3-23
false and contrary to . . . (Aquinas) 9-8-33
false principles of . . . (Lucretius) 19-8-13
farewell cool . . . (Sterne) 9-4-41
farther it runs from . . . (Jonson) 16-4-20
fine . . . that we glory in (Montaigne) 1-2-32
follow but his own . . . (Hobbes) 9-5-8
follow caprice than . . . (Pascal) 7-2-65
follow right . . . (Aurelius) 9-8-24
folly than from true . . . (Montaigne) 9-15-45
footsteps of . . . (Montaigne) 9-10-55
. . . forms the starting point (Aristotle) 19-3-5
founded in . . . (Milton) 2-3-69
fountain of . . . in him (Plato) 2-2-20
fruit-bearing harvest of . . . (Boethius) 16-3-22
God not felt by the . . . (Pascal) 20-5-72
goes along with . . . (Montaigne) 2-2-45
. . . goes astray (Montaigne) 6-5-45
good according to . . . (Aquinas) 9-3-11
good in accord with . . . (Aquinas) 9-10-45
good man obeys . . . (Aristotle) 3-6-7
governed by right . . . (Bacon) 17-2-25
. . . governs words (Bacon) 7-2-56
grounded on having . . . (Locke) 13-1-13
guided by . . . rather than by force (Harvey) 1-1-64
had he thy . . . (Pope) 6-4-28
. . . has been urged against (Plotinus) 19-4-15
have not seen the . . . (Aristotle) 6-1-14
have reached years of . . . (Aristotle) 9-13-5
have . . . of their own (Locke) 2-2-67
heart has reasons which . . . (Pascal) 3-1-54
he calls it . . . only to (Goethe) 1-1-93
hesitating confidence in . . . (Plato) 6-7-4

. . . hindered from applying principle (Aquinas) 9-3-13
human soul uses . . . (Gilbert) 6-4-17
idea of a practical pure . . . (Kant) 9-3-26
impious darings of . . . (Augustine) 15-3-51
inability of human . . . (Kant) 20-9-44
in accordance with . . . (Aquinas) 9-12-17
. . . incapable of such variation (Hume) 6-2-26
. . . incompetent to discover truth (Kant) 6-3-98
. . . in contingent matters (Aquinas) 5-7-11
increase natural light of . . . (Descartes) 17-2-34
independent of . . . (Tolstoy) 1-4-60
infancy of the human . . . (Russell) 20-1-78
. . . in man obscur'd (Milton) 10-6-36
in possession of his . . . (Kant) 1-9-37
. . . insufficient for variety (Hume) 6-5-77
. . . in theology (Kant) 6-5-84
into the mind by . . . (Pascal) 20-1-23
is above rules and . . . (Montaigne) 16-7-14
. . . is also that of animals (Montaigne) 19-1-28
. . . is always the gainer (Kant) 13-2-35
. . . is a universal instrument (Descartes) 19-2-30
. . . is but choosing (Milton) 13-2-17
. . . is called upon to consider (Kant) 17-1-74
. . . is darkness (Luther) 6-5-35
is endowed with . . . (Cicero) 1-1-25
. . . is experimental intelligence (Dewey) 5-1-82
. . . is left free to combat (Jefferson) 13-2-34
. . . is natural revelation (Locke) 6-5-72
is . . . the best thing (Aristotle) 9-8-14
. . . is that law (Locke) 9-3-20
. . . is the discovery (Hume) 6-3-86
is the life of . . . (Edward Coke) 12-1-43
. . . is the pace (Hobbes) 17-2-37
it has depraved the . . . (Nietzsche) 20-3-63
kills . . . itself (Milton) 16-2-21
know anything but by . . . (Hobbes) 6-5-52
knowledge of law from . . . (Hobbes) 9-3-17
knowledge pertains to . . . (Aquinas) 6-1-42
known through natural . . . (Aquinas) 17-1-41
knows Him knows the . . . (Pascal) 20-3-31
laborious advances of . . . (Gibbon) 14-1-80
law is a dictate of . . . (Aquinas) 12-1-31
law is dictated by . . . (Boswell) 12-1-68
led astray by blind . . . (Lucretius) 20-12-5
let you . . . with choler (Shakespeare) 4-3-20
life according to . . . (Aristotle) 1-1-20
light of . . . is placed (Aquinas) 10-1-15
live in accordance with . . . (Aristotle) 12-1-9
live under authority of . . . (Spinoza) 8-1-36
living according to . . . (Locke) 14-1-59
logical . . . operates (Wm. James) 6-5-109
loose from . . . (Locke) 13-1-15
lost the use of his . . . (Cervantes) 16-2-11
. . . makes known to us (Locke) 6-1-68
man alone has . . . (Dante) 7-1-20
man has his . . . and his hands (Aquinas) 5-1-13
man who is guided by . . . (Spinoza) 9-8-50
man who is led by . . . (Spinoza) 9-4-36
maturity of . . . begins (Voltaire) 1-2-65
may be possessed of . . . (Descartes) 9-2-19
. . . may not go to school (Th. Browne) 19-1-49
morals and relation to . . . (Aquinas) 9-1-5
morals not derived from . . . (Hume) 9-1-14
more than cool . . . (Shakespeare) 16-3-31
natural . . . cannot reach (Augustine) 6-5-26
natural truth of . . . (Plato) 5-2-1
nature destitute of . . . (Schiller) 19-1-73
noble and most sovereign . . . (Shakespeare) 5-6-15
no doctrine of the . . . (Emerson) 20-11-40

they mean by the ... (Plato) 11-2-17
thou art wonderfully ... (Herodotus) 9-8-2
to be ... is to have (Emerson) 11-2-126
treasures of the ... (Rousseau) 10-8-13
... will pay no more (Hamilton) 11-6-37
you have been ... (Boswell) 11-2-98
RICHARDSON, Samuel
   ... used to say that (Boswell) 16-7-33
RICHELIEU, Cardinal
   maxim of ... (Mill) 10-3-62
RICHER
   I am ... than you (Epictetus) 13-3-7
   the ... the church (Smith) 20-4-41
RICHES
   a competition for ... (Boswell) 11-5-12
   acquire ... by tyranny (Gibbon) 11-6-29
   ... are for spending (Bacon) 11-2-64
   ... are the inheritance (*Proverbs*) 2-3-6
   as ... grow (Horace) 11-2-33
   bear'st thy heavy ... (Shakespeare) 1-8-81
   care about ... (Plato) 2-2-18
   chief enjoyment of ... (Smith) 4-11-34
   contempt of ... (Aquinas) 9-8-33
   double their ... (Lucretius) 1-8-24
   end in the love of ... (Tocqueville) 11-2-124
   few distinguished by ... (Gibbon) 10-8-21
   given thee ... and honor (*I Kings*) 9-15-1
   good or bad use of ... (Plutarch) 11-2-44
   ... have wings (Bacon) 11-2-69
   he heapeth up ... (*Psalms*) 1-2-2
   husband nature's ... (Shakespeare) 9-15-63
   increase of general ... (Mill) 11-5-40
   man has a sign of ... (Montesquieu) 11-4-22
   man heaps up ... (Dostoevsky) 3-4-61
   may acquire vast ... (Montesquieu) 11-5-7
   new inventions and ... (Bacon) 17-2-22
   nor ... to men of understanding (*Eccles.*) 19-4-1
   on the struggle for ... (Hegel) 10-8-26
   our ... will leave us sick (Emerson) 15-2-56
   own natural ... (Montaigne) 1-7-71
   paid no heed to ... (Seneca) 11-2-37
   pays regard to ... (Johnson) 1-3-88
   poor think they need ... (Shaw) 4-4-35
   that ... grow in ... (Milton) 20-15-77
   virtue greater than ... (Shakespeare) 5-1-20
RICHMONDS
   six ... in the field (Shakespeare) 19-4-21
RICHTER, Jean Paul
   as ... remarks (Darwin) 5-4-38
RIDDLE
   ... does not exist (Wittgenstein) 6-6-53
   ... of the universe (Whitehead) 19-8-93
   solution of the ... (Wittgenstein) 1-8-142
RIDDLES
   of all the ... of married life (Sterne) 2-3-83
   ... of death Thebes never knew (Shelley) 15-2-49
   Sphynx's ... are in two kinds (Bacon) 17-2-26
   too many ... weigh men (Dostoevsky) 16-6-72
RIDE
   ... more than thou goest (Shakespeare) 9-13-19
RIDICULOUS
   ... and out of place (Plato) 16-4-5
   ... a species of the ugly (Aristotle) 16-4-7
   ... in the country (Shakespeare) 9-2-15
   same hold true of the ... (Plato) 16-3-6
   sexual act ... in man (Montaigne) 3-3-39
   source of the true ... (Fielding) 16-4-30
   things which he finds ... (Goethe) 16-4-38
RIGHT

aim is ... (Hegel) 1-6-54
all's ... with the world (Browning) 19-8-85
all the ... of nations (Kant) 14-3-39
a metaphysical ... (Boswell) 11-1-30
and did what was ... (Ovid) 15-2-14
arises a personal ... (Kant) 2-2-79
assumes to be the ... (Santayana) 6-3-150
assurance of being ... (Mill) 6-5-98
at the ... people (Aristotle) 4-3-5
believe and you shall be ... (Wm. James) 6-5-111
by ... of nature (Locke) 10-7-18
can claim no ... (Hegel) 11-2-119
can't be wrong whose life in ... (Pope) 6-5-75
child's ... to education (Hegel) 8-1-54
conjunction of duty and ... (Hegel) 13-1-39
constitutes ... in war (Kant) 14-1-81
containing the criminal's ... (Hegel) 12-4-63
conventional and legal ... (Rousseau) 13-3-21
distinguish between ... and wrong (Twain) 9-1-34
distinguish ... from wrong (Locke) 6-7-30; (Tacitus)
   15-1-23; (Bunyan) 20-8-71
duty to teach the ... (Augustine) 8-3-30
establishment of ... (Montesquieu) 10-7-19
every ... to kill (Euripides) 2-2-17
everything morally ... (Cicero) 9-1-2
exercise constitutional ... (Lincoln) 10-9-39
external obligation of ... (Kant) 11-1-39
force creates no ... (Rousseau) 9-2-25
friends' ... to share (Chaucer) 3-4-32
has a ... to do for himself (Burke) 13-3-27
has a ... to utter (Boswell) 13-2-31
... has its epochs (Pascal) 12-2-35
has the ... to eat bread (Lincoln) 13-3-38
have I a ... to take (Hegel) 1-9-40
have the ... to (Hegel) 2-2-81
have the ... to rise up (Lincoln) 10-9-38
having ... to all things (Hobbes) 12-2-34
hear the ... O Lord (*Psalms*) 20-8-5
her peculiar ... (Locke) 2-3-75
his own master by ... (Kant) 13-1-29
humanity calls ... (Tolstoy) 1-6-74
humanity united in doing ... (Plotinus) 1-1-35
idea of cosmopolitical ... (Kant) 11-5-23
if force creates ... (Rousseau) 10-6-51
if they do not ... (Aurelius) 4-3-14
... in his own eyes (Kant) 10-1-37
in respect of what is ... (Dante) 16-3-26
is the ... of the sovereign (Kant) 12-4-59
laws touching private ... (Bacon) 10-2-48
limit of ... is power (Spinoza) 10-6-40
... makes might (Lincoln) 12-2-50
make uncertain which is ... (Lucian) 6-6-7
measure of civil ... (Boswell) 12-1-68
measure of what is ... (Hegel) 12-1-79
natural ... to empire (Gibbon) 10-6-62
no divine ... of property (Shaw) 11-1-75
no exclusive ... permitted (Mill) 11-1-74
no man has a ... (Augustine) 9-9-12
no pure ... over my person (Thoreau) 10-4-61
no such thing as absolute ... (Augustine) 9-2-7
not an official ... (Dostoevsky) 12-4-70
not enough to do what is ... (Kant) 9-7-45
not the ... to oppress (Russell) 13-1-62
... of conquest I define (Montesquieu) 14-1-63
... of putting his will (Hegel) 11-1-45
of ... belong to labor (Lincoln) 11-3-58
... of the firstborn (*Deut.*) 2-1-3
... of the first occupier (Rousseau) 11-1-28
... of the people to make (Washington) 10-4-31

SCHEMES (*Cont.*)
    period to all our ... (Johnson) 1-8-117
SCHILDA
    a town called ... (Freud) 19-1-121
SCHISM
    by any ... or heresy (Augustine) 20-8-6
SCHISMS
    birth of so many ... (Pascal) 20-3-32
SCHOLAR
    ... is the delegated intellect (Emerson) 8-1-58
    like a ... in the pulpit (Chaucer) 4-9-5
    ... must be corrected (Boswell) 8-3-70
SCHOLARS
    true ... in their studies (Voltaire) 13-2-26
    young not so good ... (Boswell) 1-3-90
SCHOLARSHIP
    ... come down from antiquity (Dewey) 6-7-47
SCHOLASTICISM
    degenerate heritage of ... (Dewey) 6-7-47
SCHOOL
    daylight of a good ... (Quintilian) 8-3-17
    learnt out of my ... (Chaucer) 6-2-14
    to ... to an ant (Shakespeare) 9-15-61
    war is ... of heroism (Wm. James) 14-1-105
    who stayed in ... (Luther) 18-2-24
SCHOOLBOYS
    'tis the ... who educate (Emerson) 8-1-59
SCHOOLMASTER
    a good ... (Quintilian) 8-3-18
    as the ... is so is the school (Mill) 8-3-83
    ... must be arbitrary (Boswell) 8-3-69
    to keep a ... (Shakespeare) 9-15-59
SCHOOLMASTERS
    cannot be saved by ... (Shaw) 8-1-79
SCHOOLMEN
    maintained by some ... (Berkeley) 19-3-34
    reign among the ... (Bacon) 17-1-50
    these ... call me so (Aristophanes) 6-7-2
SCHOOLMISTRESS
    habit is a violent ... (Montaigne) 8-2-13
SCHOOLS
    as for supporting ... (Thoreau) 11-6-48
    can't do without ... (Luther) 8-1-22
    corner-stone of ... (Emerson) 17-1-84
    did not open ... (Bacon) 17-1-51
    ... of philosophy arise (Arnold) 17-1-88
    pupils from the ... (Jefferson) 10-8-18
    teach music in the ... (Luther) 16-5-16
    what is learned in ... (Mill) 8-1-70
SCIENCE
    acquire ... by experience (Harvey) 8-3-50
    active love a complete ... (Dostoevsky) 3-1-79
    advances of ... in war (Gibbon) 14-2-57
    after all our ... (Carlyle) 19-8-79
    aim of ... is to attain (Wm. James) 6-2-46
    ... and opinion about the same (Aquinas) 6-5-29
    ... a productive force (Marx) 11-3-67
    art as comprehensive as ... (Langer) 16-1-70
    art distinguished from ... (Kant) 16-1-32
    avenues of ... and learning (Hume) 6-1-73
    basic facts of the ... (Aristotle) 6-1-10
    bears the name of ... (Augustine) 1-8-52
    began to learn a ... (Aristotle) 6-1-19
    birth of modern ... (Whitehead) 17-3-57
    ... but an exchange of ignorance (Byron) 6-1-87
    but a truth of ... (Shaw) 19-8-92
    by his will and ... (Dostoevsky) 20-9-48
    by no means a term of ... (Arnold) 20-5-108
    concern for ... must give way (Shaw) 18-2-50

    ... does not admit conception (Tolstoy) 15-1-82
    enough of ... and art (Wordsworth) 19-1-83
    every ... has two kinds (Aristotle) 8-1-5
    every ... though to be (Aristotle) 6-1-18
    except by men of ... (Russell) 19-7-86
    experience much like ... (Aristotle) 6-2-6
    first causes outside ... (Bernard) 19-3-48
    Greek ... (Dewey) 6-7-47
    guide the advance of ... (Bernard) 1-6-72
    ... has imposed necessity (Whitehead) 15-2-77
    honorest every ... and art (Dante) 16-3-24
    however destitute of ... (Gibbon) 14-1-76
    in ... as in life (Huxley) 6-1-93
    in the ... of nature (Aristotle) 6-1-12
    in the study of ... (Hegel) 6-1-88
    ... is nearer to it (Whitehead) 19-6-43
    is no ... of the beautiful (Kant) 16-6-49
    ... is sapience (Hobbes) 6-2-23
    ... is the greatest antidote (Smith) 20-12-28
    knowledge of causes termed ... (Maritain) 17-1-114
    little light ... has (Freud) 17-1-102
    lowering importance of ... (Bernard) 18-2-44
    made profession of this ... (Swift) 12-1-55
    man of little ... (Aquinas) 6-5-31
    mathematical ... affords us (Kant) 6-1-82
    morals a growing ... (Dewey) 9-1-40
    most useful ... (Montaigne) 1-7-73
    ... moves but slowly (Tennyson) 17-2-85
    never have a ... of medicine (Bernard) 18-3-59
    ... never taught Indian (Pope) 6-5-74
    new orientation in ... (Freud) 5-1-78
    no more to be called a ... (Schopenhauer) 15-1-65
    nor is it yet a ... (Goethe) 16-3-69
    no ... of the accidental (Aristotle) 6-1-17
    ... of destruction (Wm. James) 14-3-47
    ... of vital phenomena (Bernard) 19-2-50
    ... of worshipping the gods (Plutarch) 20-1-7
    opposed to works of ... (Coleridge) 16-3-77
    opposing the students of ... (Spinoza) 20-11-26
    our new ... (Vico) 15-1-38
    our ... comes to describe (Vico) 15-2-30
    perfections in a ... (Jonson) 17-1-49
    philosophy not opposite to ... (Freud) 17-1-103
    pin her down by ... (Euripides) 15-3-17
    practice medicine without ... (Plato) 18-2-12
    principles of ... (Aristotle) 6-7-8
    problem never solved by ... (Darwin) 6-4-45
    pursuit of that ... (Cervantes) 2-2-57
    quantity of ... increased (Smith) 17-1-72
    real positive ... begins (Marx and Engels) 15-1-76
    receives from ... his proper (Hume) 6-1-72
    reduced politics to a ... (Swift) 10-2-66
    right of ... to express (Hegel) 13-2-36
    scenes of endless ... rise (Pope) 1-8-42
    serenely a light of ... (G. Eliot) 1-4-58
    so long to discover in ... (Dewey) 16-1-60
    spite of all ... may do (Wm. James) 20-8-86
    start out from ... (Freud) 6-6-52
    ... struck the thrones of earth (Shelley) 5-1-55
    superstition is a little ... (Santayana) 20-12-39
    the end of this ... (Aristotle) 10-2-9
    the legislators of ... (Johnson) 16-2-33
    the pursuits of ... (Jefferson) 10-8-18
    there is not a piece of ... (Emerson) 15-2-55
    ... the royal appears (Plato) 10-2-7
    the ... of this world (Dostoevsky) 20-3-58
    the ... of what is good (Hobbes) 9-1-6
    this as the only free ... (Aristotle) 17-1-11
    this sacred ... can in a sense (Aquinas) 17-1-41

SMALL-MINDED
... men are envious (Aristotle) 4-8-6
SMALL POX
have succumbed to ... (Darwin) 18-1-32
SMELLS
varied flow of ... (Lucretius) 5-2-9
SMILE
a sadness sweeter than her ... (Byron) 3-1-69
one may ... and ... (Shakespeare) 9-6-61
permits him to ... ever (Thoreau) 20-1-61
... we would aspire to (Shakespeare) 10-6-29
SMITH, Adam
person described by ... (Mill) 1-7-148
turn our backs on ... (Shaw) 11-4-48
SMITH'S, Adam
I mentioned ... book (Boswell) 6-2-30
SMOOTH
true love never did run ... (Shakespeare) 3-1-36
SMUGGLING
a temptation to ... (Smith) 11-6-24
by encouraging ... (Smith) 11-6-28
SNARES
means of avoiding ... (Johnson) 16-1-29
through female ... (Milton) 1-7-102
SNOW
chase as unsunn'd ... (Shakespeare) 1-7-92
property compared to ... (Emerson) 11-1-57
SOAP
... and education (Twain) 8-1-76
SOBRIETY
secure any degree of ... (Burke) 10-2-83
with ... (*I Timothy*) 1-7-43
SOCIABLE
as a man becomes ... (Rousseau) 19-1-67
SOCIAL
... character of property (Marx) 11-1-67
education a ... process (Dewey) 8-3-100
fitness for the ... state (Spencer) 15-2-71
... for of that wealth (Marx) 11-2-136
morals ought to be ... (Dewey) 9-1-41
the prime principle is ... (Aurelius) 9-3-7
SOCIAL COMPACT
the ... sets up (Rousseau) 10-1-34
this is the ... (Rousseau) 10-4-30
SOCIAL CONTRACT
... provides the solution (Rousseau) 10-1-32
state is master by the ... (Rousseau) 12-3-19
SOCIALISM
better or worse than ... (Shaw) 11-1-76
... is not merely (Dostoevsky) 20-9-46
SOCIALIST
problems of ... organization (Lenin) 10-9-43
SOCIALISTIC
advent of some ... equilibrium (Wm. James) 14-3-47
... movement aims at (Shaw) 11-5-47
SOCIALISTS
... filled with enthusiasm (Sumner) 13-3-48
old Tories and modern ... (Shaw) 11-4-48
SOCIALIZED
labor become ... (Marx) 19-1-113
SOCIAL LIFE
much of our ... is grounded (Bergson) 9-6-118
transform our ... (Russell) 6-6-50
SOCIAL STRATA
habit keeps ... from mixing (Wm. James) 8-2-30
SOCIAL SYSTEM
... backs us up (Wm. James) 6-6-48
SOCIAL THEORISTS
challenge the attention of ... (Benedict) 9-2-38

SOCIETIES
ancient of all ... (Rousseau) 2-1-34
law of politic ... (Locke) 12-1-54
SOCIETY
against the claims of ... (Mill) 1-7-144
altered the whole state of ... (Tocqueville) 10-7-34
... always needs cooperation (Smith) 3-4-52
... and invention of language (Rousseau) 7-1-50
... and language grew (Whitehead) 7-1-64
an ideal ... (Bergson) 1-1-131
any value to ... (Thoreau) 11-5-35
a ... which values equality (Tawney) 13-3-56
avoid all ... (Kant) 9-7-44
a voluntary ... of men (Locke) 20-4-38
became a little ... (Rousseau) 2-1-32
code of honor of fashionable ... (Wm. James) 9-2-34
condition of ... becomes (Tocqueville) 2-2-84
considered in relation to ... (Rousseau) 20-1-41
constitutent orders of ... (Smith) 11-2-102
conversant with respectable ... (Plutarch) 8-3-22
dead dry life of ... (Thoreau) 1-8-130
develop into an individual only in ... (Marx) 1-1-115
drive him into ... (Locke) 2-1-29
duty to serve ... (Boswell) 9-9-27
eccentricity in ... (Mill) 1-4-56
end of civil ... (Hamilton/Madison) 12-2-45
every ... has a right (Boswell) 13-2-29
every ... is composed (Rousseau) 10-8-12
formed to live in ... (Montesquieu) 1-1-82
... founded on deceit (Pascal) 3-4-42
given economic formation of ... (Marx) 4-9-18
great interests of ... (Hamilton) 14-4-39
inclination to live in ... (Aquinas) 9-3-11
incompatible with ... (Montaigne) 6-5-46
intercourse of ... with man (Bacon) 6-4-19
in the progress of ... (Smith) 17-1-72
is one long ... (Mill) 13-3-40
... is sure of itself (Hegel) 12-4-64
joins voluntarily to ... (Locke) 20-4-39
life-breath of ... (Carlyle) 1-6-61
lowest rank of ... (Gibbon) 10-6-63
maintain the existence of ... (Epictetus) 2-1-19
man in the state of ... (Rousseau) 15-2-34
man's circle of ... (Peirce) 6-6-47
men enter into ... (Locke) 12-3-15
modern bourgeois ... (Marx and Engels) 11-5-39
necessity in civil ... (Hume) 11-1-24
new order of ... (Aristotle) 2-1-13
... never advances (Emerson) 15-2-53
no regard to natural basis of ... (Santayana) 6-6-55
no ... can be flourishing (Smith) 11-2-101
no ... without speech (Hobbes) 7-1-29
obstacle to improvement in ... (Malthus) 15-2-48
... of our fellow-men (Pascal) 1-8-110
one solace in human ... (Augustine) 3-4-27
owes to ... (Mill) 2-1-46
peace and security of ... (Hume) 9-3-23
perfectibility of ... (Malthus) 1-2-71
polish and refinement into ... (Kant) 17-2-64
progress of ... towards wealth (Smith) 11-2-110
properly a commercial ... (Smith) 11-3-35
... protects its interests (Mill) 9-5-26
real founder of ... (Rousseau) 11-1-25
reason of entering into ... (Locke) 10-2-60
security of ... not preserved (Dostoevsky) 12-4-68
structure of human ... (Bergson) 9-1-42
the bonds of human ... (Locke) 20-9-28
the defence of ... (Smith) 9-11-51
to the best ... (Tolstoy) 1-7-155

SOMETHING
  are not we . . . (Lucian) 6-6-7
  if he thinks he is . . . (Montaigne) 9-15-47
  think I am . . . (Descartes) 6-6-17
SON
  a dutiful loving . . . (Augustine) 2-2-39
  a . . . and husband both (Sophocles) 2-1-7
  . . . fears to offend father (Aquinas) 4-2-19
  fondness for my . . . (Dante) 6-2-13
  kill your own . . . (Euripides) 5-6-5
  soon as his . . . is born (Quintilian) 8-1-13
  spareth rod hateth his . . . (*Proverbs*) 2-2-5
  the . . . of these tears (Augustine) 2-2-35
  unto us a . . . is given (*Isaiah*) 20-3-1
SON (of God)
  gave his only begotten . . . (*John*) 20-14-13
  God's . . . assuming (Augustine) 20-14-23
  if the . . . shall make you free (Augustine) 9-4-20
  if thou be the . . . of God (*Matthew*) 20-1-3
  is my beloved . . . (*Matthew*) 2-2-26
  no man knoweth the . . . (*Matthew*) 6-5-6
  . . . of God subject to frailties (Locke) 6-5-70
  . . . of Heaven's eternal (Milton) 20-14-43
  . . . of Man (Dostoevsky) 3-4-61
  spared not his own . . . (*Romans*) 4-5-9
  spared not thine own . . . (Augustine) 20-14-21
  this is my beloved . . . (*II Peter*) 6-5-17
  thy . . . hangs slain (Goethe) 20-8-78
SON OF GOD
  . . . appeared in the flesh (Aquinas) 20-7-21
  denied the likeness of the . . . (Gibbon) 20-9-39
  eat the flesh of the . . . (*John*) 20-3-14
  faith in the . . . (Luther) 20-8-56
  . . . hath not where to (*Matthew*) 20-3-8
  if the . . . was obliged (Freud) 20-13-96
  if thou be the . . . (*Luke*) 20-13-17
  image of the . . . (Augustine) 1-7-48
  one like unto the . . . (*Revelation*) 20-3-20
  see the . . . coming (*Luke*) 20-14-11
  shall be called the . . . (*Luke*) 1-7-36
  . . . shall come into his glory (*Matthew*) 20-15-25
  shall the . . . be three days (*Matthew*) 20-10-18
  that I the . . . am (*Matthew*) 20-4-2
  the . . . was seen (Milton) 20-15-81
  . . . which should come (*John*) 1-8-38
SONG
  holy . . . enwrap our fancy (Milton) 16-5-28
  judge a poet's . . . (Pope) 16-7-24
  newest . . . which the singers (Plato) 16-5-4
  . . . of a heaven-taught bard (Horace) 16-3-15
  . . . of pure content (Milton) 16-5-29
  perhaps the self-same . . . (Keats) 16-6-59
  required of us a . . . (*Psalms*) 20-2-16
  sing a . . . in a strange land (Thoreau) 20-3-53
  sings a lasting . . . (Yeats) 1-3-135
  subject for heroic . . . (Milton) 16-3-45
  the basis of instrumental . . . (Darwin) 16-5-39
  the delights of . . . (Plato) 16-5-3
  unto the Lord a new . . . (*Psalms*) 20-8-6
SONGS
  poet brings . . . (Euripides) 16-3-2
SONNET
  each bad . . . for example (Pascal) 16-7-17
  scorn not the . . . (Wordsworth) 16-3-73
SONNET'S
  . . . scanty plot of ground (Wordsworth) 13-1-35
SONNETS
  build in . . . pretty (Donne) 1-8-97
  nor in licentious . . . (Cervantes) 16-3-35

  would have written . . . (Byron) 2-3-97
SONS
  fathers bury their . . . (Herodotus) 14-1-7
  little though of your . . . (Plutarch) 8-1-16
  . . . of men snared (*Eccles.*) 15-3-2
  will you kill your . . . (Euripides) 5-6-4
SOOTHE
  charms to . . . a savage (Congreve) 16-5-34
SOOTHSAYERS
  he sends for three . . . (Herodotus) 18-3-4
SOPHISM
  every . . . appears a solecism (Leibniz) 7-2-68
SOPHISMS
  sake of unintelligible . . . (Voltaire) 20-1-40
  there are many . . . (Augustine) 6-7-15
SOPHIST
  . . . deals in food for the soul (Plato) 8-3-4
  of an accomplished . . . (Plato) 1-5-10
  what makes a . . . (Aristotle) 7-2-10
SOPHISTRY
  nothing but . . . and illusion (Hume) 17-2-56
  was a kind of . . . (Boswell) 13-2-28
SOPHISTS
  certain . . . and physicians (Hippocrates) 18-1-3
  give money to the . . . (Plato) 8-3-3
  philosophy of the Greek . . . (Freud) 6-7-46
  the name of . . . (Bacon) 17-1-51
  truth denied by . . . (Santayana) 6-6-55
  vain babbling of . . . (Rousseau) 3-6-17
SOPHOCLES
  but . . . how came he (Aristophanes) 16-4-1
  the aged poet . . . (Plato) 1-3-13
SOPHY
  my dear . . . (Fielding) 2-3-81
  that slew the . . . (Shakespeare) 19-4-23
SORE
  end of every worldly . . . (Chaucer) 1-8-59
SORES
  these . . . of life (Lucretius) 1-8-24
SORCERERS
  works of the Egyptian . . . (Hobbes) 20-10-31
SORCERY
  music a form of . . . (Plotinus) 16-5-13
SORROW
  act of will called . . . (Augustine) 4-1-6
  adversity and hopeless . . . (Kant) 9-9-31
  a plain full of . . . (Dante) 20-9-13
  burden of perpetual . . . (Tacitus) 1-9-17
  deliberate choice of . . . (Aquinas) 9-8-33
  desire to relieve our . . . (Plato) 16-3-6
  despair is . . . arising (Spinoza) 4-5-24
  does not want to feel . . . (Augustine) 16-4-13
  . . . ensues to injurer (Aquinas) 4-3-15
  excess of . . . laughs (Blake) 4-6-45
  from the memory a rooted . . . (Shakespeare) 5-6-21
  give . . . words (Shakespeare) 4-6-36
  greatly multiply thy . . . (*Genesis*) 2-2-1
  . . . I will greatly multiply (Milton) 20-13-86
  joy than . . . (Plutarch) 2-2-31
  knowledge increaseth . . . (*Eccles.*) 9-15-7
  nor hid . . . (*Job*) 4-5-1
  no . . . accompanies idea of God (Spinoza) 3-2-26
  parting is such sweet . . . (Shakespeare) 4-7-39
  relief for all . . . (Chaucer) 4-5-14
  remove . . . from thy heart (*Eccles.*) 1-3-2
  seven swords of . . . (Shaw) 18-1-37
  the . . . of another (Epictetus) 20-8-39
  thy . . . is my ecstasy (Hardy) 20-5-119
  to think is to be full of . . . (Keats) 16-3-79

TORMENT
   disnatured . . . to her (Shakespeare) 2-2-53
   ere the god of . . . (Keats) 5-4-32
   fear hath . . . (*I John*) 4-2-14
   Sisyphos in . . . (Homer) 4-5-4
TORMENTS
   discern new . . . (Dante) 9-12-20
   hope prolongs . . . of man (Nietzsche) 4-5-38
   . . . inflicted by masters (Augustine) 8-1-20
   place not sad with . . . (Dante) 20-13-51
   shall not suffer purgatorial . . . (Augustine) 1-3-31
TORPEDO FISH
   very like the flat . . . (Plato) 6-6-1
TORPEDO'S TOUCH
   better for the . . . (Plato) 6-4-5
TORTURE
   last and crowning . . . (Joyce) 20-15-106
   no worse . . . than envy (Horace) 4-8-9
   on the . . . of the mind to lie (Shakespeare) 9-5-7
   put witnesses to . . . (Augustine) 12-4-22
TORTURES
   . . . human nature could not bear (Euripides) 4-11-7
TOTEMISM
   the remarkable form of . . . (Freud) 20-12-38
TOUCH
   all senses based on . . . (Aquinas) 5-2-14
   . . . and sight have similar cause (Lucretius) 5-2-6
   by . . . I perceive (Berkeley) 6-1-70
   idea conveyed by . . . (Hume) 19-6-33
   mere . . . of cold philosophy (Keats) 17-1-79
   not to . . . a woman (*I Corinthians*) 2-3-23
   not . . . what is mine (Plato) 9-3-3
   without . . . no other sense (Aristotle) 5-2-5
TOULOUSE
   truth same at . . . and at Paris (Pascal) 6-3-69
TOWER
   . . . whose top may reach (*Genesis*) 7-1-2
TOWERS
   turned on those proud . . . (Milton) 6-5-64
TOWN
   does the . . . say of me (Cervantes) 1-5-78
   fools in . . . on our side (Twain) 9-15-95
   fortune of the rising . . . (Virgil) 4-6-11
   inhabitants of the . . . (Smith) 11-5-16
   separation between . . . and (Marx) 11-3-66
TOWN-CRIER
   as lief the . . . spoke (Shakespeare) 16-4-19
TOY
   nature never became a . . . (Emerson) 19-1-98
TRADE
   . . . and other occupations (Cicero) 11-3-10
   government come to be a . . . (Emerson) 10-2-94
   had never been in . . . (Boswell) 6-2-30
   if there were no . . . (Boswell) 11-3-32
   instruments of . . . (Smith) 11-1-31
   it is not your . . . (Boswell) 16-7-32
   mean and mechanical . . . (Plutarch) 11-3-15
   mutilated state of . . . (Hamilton) 11-6-40
   . . . of a particular class (Smith) 17-1-72
   retail . . . justly censured (Aristotle) 11-4-2
   turn attention to . . . (Tocqueville) 11-2-123
   war degraded to a . . . (Gibbon) 14-2-55
   were originally of the same . . . (Swift) 18-2-33
TRADE-JEALOUSY
   reason is that . . . (Schopenhauer) 1-7-133
TRADERS
   the class of . . . (Aristotle) 10-8-4
TRADES
   multiplicity of unhealthy . . . (Rousseau) 11-3-30

part of common . . . (Smith) 1-5-110
several arts and . . . (Plutarch) 10-8-8
several . . . necessary (Gibbon) 11-3-40
TRADESMAN
   by making doctors . . . (Shaw) 18-2-51
   not lead life of . . . (Aristotle) 10-5-9
   . . . rarely gives worth to work (Emerson) 8-1-58
TRADE UNION
   object of a . . . (Shaw) 18-2-50
TRADING
   . . . all day without religion (Milton) 20-1-30
TRADITION
   according to the . . . of men (Augustine) 17-1-37
   did more to fix . . . (Dewey) 19-5-71
   lack of a coherent . . . (Mead) 15-2-89
   not a received . . . (Arnold) 16-3-90
   pool of conformity and . . . (Milton) 20-9-26
   super-ego the vehicle of . . . (Freud) 9-2-35
   the law . . . makes (Euripides) 20-6-16
   the transmission of . . . (Benedict) 15-2-91
   they who philosophize by . . . (Harvey) 17-2-33
   triumphant mystical . . . (Wm. James) 20-1-75
TRADITIONS
   . . . and customs of other people (Mill) 9-2-32
   men deal with . . . (Thucydides) 15-1-2
   set at naught . . . (Emerson) 1-4-45
   . . . undermined in principle (Santayana) 20-2-52
TRAFFIC
   to be a . . . so entangled (Milton) 20-1-30
TRAGEDIES
   figures introduced in . . . (Hippocrates) 18-2-6
   two . . . in life (Shaw) 4-4-34
TRAGEDY
   Mallet's . . . of *Elvira* (Boswell) 16-7-32
   my little . . . (Chaucer) 16-2-5
   the first of . . . writers (Plato) 16-3-6
   this I call a . . . (Carlyle) 6-4-42
   . . . with sceptered pall (Keats) 1-7-128
TRAGIC
   beauties of the . . . stage (Voltaire) 16-3-53
TRAIN
   . . . up a child (*Proverbs*) 2-2-6
TRAINING
   acquired by . . . (Aquinas) 12-1-26
   adequate . . . for occupations (Dewey) 8-1-90
   . . . for political life (Polybius) 15-1-7
   . . . given by suitable habits (Plato) 8-1-4
   give some . . . before crisis (Seneca) 8-1-11
   . . . in hands of nurses (Montaigne) 8-2-14
   . . . in the nursery (Plato) 8-1-3
   long . . . of action (Thucydides) 14-2-9
   moral . . . of mankind (Mill) 2-1-47
   musical . . . is a more potent (Plato) 16-5-2
   of . . . of the young (Plato) 1-3-15
   surpass all others in . . . (Galen) 8-3-27
   teachers experienced . . . (Plato) 8-3-3
TRAIT
   culturally selected . . . (Benedict) 14-1-112
TRAITOR
   a . . . to his country (Rousseau) 12-4-56
   every . . . is consumed (Dante) 20-15-53
   infamy to the . . . (Dante) 3-2-14
   . . . to her loving lord (Shakespeare) 2-3-53
TRAITORS
   O . . . and bawds (Shakespeare) 9-6-63
   our doubts are . . . (Shakespeare) 9-11-33
TRAITS
   of our social . . . (Dewey) 17-2-132
   retention of all his . . . (Freud) 5-5-37

special character . . . (Freud) 20-2-48

TRAJAN

in the person of . . . (Gibbon) 7-1-52

TRAJECTORIES

time appears through . . . (Sartre) 19-7-94

TRANQUILITY

advanced toward . . . (Montaigne) 6-3-45

emotion recollected in . . . (T. S. Eliot) 16-3-98, 16-3-99

enjoys . . . of peace (Dante) 14-3-24

. . . in our conduct (Montaigne) 1-2-35

in . . . brought life to a close (Aeschylus) 9-8-1

perpetual . . . of mind (Hobbes) 4-4-22

preserve the . . . (Calvin) 14-1-44

TRANSACTION

freely ethical . . . (Hegel) 2-3-98

TRANSCEND

means to . . . his own nature (Bergson) 5-1-84

TRANSCENDENTAL

. . . origin of moral feelings (Mill) 9-3-35

TRANSCENDENT BEINGS

. . . move over the earth (Plotinus) 19-8-26

TRANSFERENCE

only by positive . . . (Kant) 11-1-41

the name of this is . . . (Galen) 19-5-18

TRANSFORMATION

miraculous . . . of mankind (Hume) 9-10-98

TRANSGRESS

shall we . . . them at once (Thoreau) 10-2-96, 12-1-85

TRANSGRESSION

a . . . of the law (Hobbes) 12-4-39

. . . creeps in unperceived (Aristotle) 12-1-13

every . . . received (*Hebrews*) 6-5-15

firstborn for my . . . (*Micah*) 20-8-10

forgetfulness begat . . . (Luther) 19-3-19

innocent from the great . . . (*Psalms*) 20-5-9

neither evil nor . . . (*I Samuel*) 9-7-1

woman was in . . . (*I Timothy*) 1-7-43

TRANSGRESSIONS

blot out my . . . (*Psalms*) 20-13-5

punishing the . . . of others (Locke) 10-1-30

sum of his . . . (Plato) 1-8-19

was wounded for our . . . (*Isaiah*) 20-3-4

TRANSGRESSOR

the . . . who brings (Aeschylus) 9-7-6

TRANSITION

either a . . . or an end (Seneca) 1-8-36

. . . to other things (Whitehead) 19-8-93

TRANSITIONS

terms represent . . . (Montaigne) 19-7-33

TRANSITORINESS

. . . of things is essential (Santayana) 1-8-143

TRANSITORY

everything is . . . (Croce) 15-2-88

TRANSLATE

. . . books of science exactly (Boswell) 16-3-57

TRANSLATION

motion is . . . of a body (Newton) 19-5-46

TRANSMIGRATION

consigning soul to a ceaseless . . . (Augustine) 15-2-18

the . . . of souls (Newton) 9-1-9

TRANSMISSION

the . . . of sin (Pascal) 20-13-77

TRANSMUTATION

. . . of living things (Plotinus) 1-8-49

to be in ceaseless . . . (Plotinus) 19-5-19

TRAP

awaits us all to . . . (Chaucer) 9-10-52

TRAPPINGS

. . . with which we (Montaigne) 1-8-67

TRASH

steals my purse steals . . . (Shakespeare) 1-5-73

TRAUMAS

accidental infantile . . . (Freud) 8-3-97

TRAUSI (Thracians)

a child is born to the . . . (Herodotus) 1-2-8

TRAVAIL

with labor and . . . (*II Thessalonians*) 11-3-14

TRAVEL

cannot rest from . . . (Tennyson) 6-2-38

send young to . . . (Smith) 8-3-75

TRAVELLER

met a . . . from an antique (Shelley) 19-7-68

TRAVELLERS

aged men are . . . (Plato) 1-3-13

TRAVELS

time . . . in divers paces (Shakespeare) 19-7-38

TREACHERY

. . . belongs to the fox (Cicero) 9-7-18

fear their subjects' . . . (Shakespeare) 10-2-43

laid by . . . for innocence (Johnson) 16-1-29

TREAD

you . . . on my dreams (Yeats) 5-5-48

TREADMILL

send you to the . . . (Lucian) 6-6-7

TREASON

and . . . waits on him (Shakespeare) 10-2-43

. . . has done his worst (Shakespeare) 1-8-90

raise the cry of . . . (Kant) 13-2-35

some form of . . . (Kant) 12-4-62

to expiate his . . . (Milton) 20-14-45

TREASONS

is fit for . . . stratagems and (Shakespeare) 16-5-20

TREASURE

have . . . in heaven (*Matthew*) 11-2-39

purest . . . mortal times (Shakespeare) 1-5-64

where your . . . is (*Luke*) 4-9-3

TREASURES

for . . . better hid (Milton) 11-2-70

lay not up for yourselves . . . (*Matthew*) 20-15-21

TREATIES

. . . are drawn up (Kant) 14-1-82

TREATISES

sees written . . . composed (Plato) 16-2-4

TREATMENT

frequent changes of . . . (Seneca) 18-1-11

misplace the . . . (Locke) 2-2-67

right . . . of slaves (Plato) 10-7-5

whatever his mode of . . . (Plato) 18-2-9

TREATY

a joint . . . of peace (Spinoza) 14-3-33

. . . to his disadvantage (Thucydides) 14-3-6

TREE

life's strange . . . (Byron) 4-7-60

make the . . . good (*Matthew*) 9-10-25

one fatal . . . called knowledge (Milton) 6-4-25

right to the . . . of life (*Revelation*) 19-8-19

shall be like a . . . (*Psalms*) 9-7-3

till the . . . die (Shakespeare) 2-3-63

TREE OF KNOWLEDGE

fruit of the . . . (Tolstoy) 15-1-80

TREE OF LIFE

fast by the . . . (Milton) 20-15-82

the great . . . (Darwin) 19-2-47

TRENCH

in drawing a . . . (Plutarch) 14-2-20

TREPIDATION

the moral . . . here (Melville) 1-8-130

TRESPASS
against the . . . (*Leviticus*) 9-14-3
TRESPASSES
everyone his brother their . . . (*Matthew*) 3-5-5
TRIAL
death without . . . (Herodotus) 10-3-1
every man on . . . (Emerson) 14-1-97
give Christianity a . . . (Shaw) 20-3-64
. . . of the innocent (*Job*) 9-7-2
purifies us is . . . (Milton) 9-10-82
thou shalt make a . . . (Dante) 1-2-28
TRIALS
all those . . . over (Homer) 1-7-7
series of severe . . . (Freud) 20-2-47
. . . will end in peace (Homer) 1-3-6
TRIANGLE
essence of a . . . (Spinoza) 15-3-94
three angles of a . . . (Locke) 17-3-33
with the idea of a . . . (Descartes) 20-5-65
TRIBE(S)
a . . . including many members (Darwin) 9-1-27
idols of the . . . (Bacon) 6-4-19
member of a . . . (Wm. James) 1-1-127
two different . . . (Plutarch) 10-8-8
TRIBULATION
which came out of great . . . (*Revelation*) 20-15-29
TRIBULATIONS
assailed with . . . (Luther) 20-13-65
TRIBUTARY
render common people . . . (Montesquieu) 11-6-13
. . . to a vast total (Plotinus) 19-8-26
TRIBUTE
craves no other . . . (Shakespeare) 2-3-53
lawful to give . . . to Caesar (*Mark*) 10-2-17
respect is a . . . (Kant) 1-5-115
why . . . (Shakespeare) 11-6-6
TRICKS
. . . hath strong imagination (Shakespeare) 5-4-9
TRICKSTERS
rogues and . . . (Sophocles) 9-6-4
TRIFLE
murder for any . . . (Euripides) 2-2-17
TRIFLES
condemned to . . . and precepts (Montesquieu) 2-3-82
too much of . . . (Pascal) 17-1-55
win us with honest . . . (Shakespeare) 20-7-49
TRIFLING
empty and . . . (Aurelius) 1-8-47
TRINITY
believe He is a . . . (Aquinas) 6-5-29
deny two persons in the . . . (Th. Browne) 20-5-69
person of the divine . . . (Dante) 20-7-34
riddles of the . . . (Th. Browne) 6-5-54
. . . that is One (Augustine) 19-8-29
TRINITY'S
hung . . . loquacious clock (Wordsworth) 17-2-72
TRINSTAL
. . . the Englishman (Rabelais) 8-1-23
TRIPTOLEMUS
. . . and other sons of God (Plato) 1-8-15
TRITON
. . . blow his wreathed horn (Wordsworth) 19-1-85
TRIUMPH
the distant strains of . . . (Dickinson) 16-4-40
TRIUMPHS
. . . of their masters (Rousseau) 14-1-67
TRIVIAL
most . . . of human pursuits (Wm. James) 17-1-93
TROILUS

. . . had his brains dashed out (Shakespeare) 3-1-41
. . . mounted the Trojan walls (Shakespeare) 3-1-37
my whole being into . . . (Keats) 1-7-128
now listen . . . (Chaucer) 6-2-14
this to . . . may be applied (Chaucer) 4-6-26
TROJANS
but the . . . as sheep (Homer) 14-2-4
chief men of the . . . (Homer) 16-6-3
now pitifully the . . . (Homer) 14-2-5
pain of the . . . (Homer) 2-2-8
shame before the . . . (Homer) 1-5-1
stood up against the . . . (Homer) 14-2-3
strength unto the . . . (Homer) 2-2-7
the . . . have that glory (Euripides) 3-6-3
TROOP
farewell the plumed . . . (Shakespeare) 14-2-38
TROOPS
fatiguing . . . unnecessarily (Machiavelli) 14-2-33
for the . . . were in flight (Plato) 14-2-10
send me more . . . (Rousseau) 14-1-67
TROPHY
than gift his . . . (Shakespeare) 14-1-46
TROTH
plight thee my . . . (*Book of Common Prayer*) 2-3-48
TROTS
who time . . . withal (Shakespeare) 19-7-38
TROUBLE
fruits of the . . . (Montaigne) 10-9-11
give me a world of . . . (Plato) 6-6-2
. . . he has fallen in (Sophocles) 6-4-2
how much . . . he avoids (Aurelius) 1-4-8
if you are out of . . . (Sophocles) 15-3-16
intellectual function of . . . (Dewey) 17-2-132
it was to make a . . . (Twain) 16-2-57
of few days and full of . . . (*Job*) 1-2-1
reserved against the time of . . . (*Job*) 1-1-2
what . . . beyond the range (Sophocles) 1-2-10, 1-3-9
who would choose . . . (Augustine) 4-6-19
TROUBLED
. . . about many things (*Luke*) 1-7-38
TROUBLES
a sea of . . . (Shakespeare) 1-9-27
bearing . . . patiently (Montaigne) 9-11-22
because of the . . . of men (Dewey) 6-2-50
real source of all our . . . (Rousseau) 9-13-28
TROY
another . . . for her to burn (Yeats) 16-6-82
at . . . sacrificed to Minerva (Plutarch) 16-3-21
here once . . . stood (Cervantes) 15-3-88
no more the tale of . . . (Shelley) 15-2-49
plains of windy . . . (Tennyson) 6-2-38
proud height of . . . (Homer) 6-2-2
sailed for . . . (Homer) 2-2-10
the destruction of . . . (Tacitus) 5-6-7
the flames of . . . (Shakespeare) 1-6-26
the tale of . . . divine (Milton) 16-4-24
who came from . . . (Dante) 20-13-50
your trip to . . . (Euripides) 12-4-6
TRUCE
never an instant's . . . (Thoreau) 9-10-115
TRUE
considered equally . . . (Gibbon) 20-1-44
everything is . . . (Diogenes Laertius) 17-1-1
not . . . because badly altered (Augustine) 7-2-40
pleasant drawn from the . . . (Pascal) 7-2-61
prove it is . . . (Pascal) 20-1-24
. . . today may be falsehood (Thoreau) 9-2-31
the . . . is the object (Hegel) 16-1-41
things that are . . . (Aristotle) 6-5-5

strain'd from that fair ... (Shakespeare) 18-1-19
studies teach not their own ... (Bacon) 8-1-31
temporary ... of a thing (Hegel) 11-1-47
the ... of laws (Hobbes) 12-1-47
true ... of money (Spinoza) 11-4-19
ways we can ... money (Schopenhauer) 11-2-122
USEFUL
by the magistrate equally ... (Gibbon) 20-1-44
in respect of what is ... (Dante) 16-3-26
labor be socially ... (Marx) 11-5-36
let punishments be ... (Voltaire) 12-4-52
neither ... to master or slave (Montesquieu) 10-7-19
the ... as goal of education (Aristotle) 8-1-8
things really ... to life (Locke) 11-4-20
USEFULNESS
... of an opinion (Mill) 6-5-99
... of what he teaches (Locke) 8-3-61
USELESS
music is essentially ... (Santayana) 16-5-43
USELESSNESS
... of every branch (Mill) 17-2-92
USES
applies virtue to human ... (Plutarch) 17-1-25
money for necessary ... (Hobbes) 11-6-8
of everything there are two ... (Aristotle) 11-5-4
taught the ... of things (Gilbert) 17-2-13
to what base ... (Shakespeare) 1-8-79
two excellent ... of doubts (Bacon) 6-6-15
USE-VALUE
... of product predominates (Marx) 4-9-18
product is a ... (Marx) 11-2-137
USE-VALUES
... become a reality (Marx) 11-2-136
USURER
... hangs the cozener (Shakespeare) 9-7-38
USURPATION
free themselves from ... (Locke) 10-9-20
... is exercise of power (Locke) 10-6-42
see the fact of ... (Pascal) 10-9-18
USURPATIONS
... by the rich (Rousseau) 11-2-85
... of national rulers (Hamilton) 10-9-29
USURPER
... ought to examine (Machiavelli) 10-2-29
USURY
devouring trades of ... (Bacon) 10-2-51
hated sort of trade is ... (Aristotle) 11-4-2
increaseth the evil of ... (Smith) 11-4-29
mine own with ... (*Luke*) 20-4-31
UTICA
people of ... flocked (Plutarch) 1-9-11
UTILITARIAN
end of ... doctrine (Mill) 9-8-73
has ... value (Dewey) 17-3-61
other mode than ... (Mill) 11-6-53
the ... mode of thought (Mill) 9-6-105
UTILITARIANISM
serpent-windings of ... (Kant) 12-4-60
UTILITY
an idea of ... (Hume) 17-1-68
... as foundation of morals (Mill) 9-1-29
beauty independent of ... (Boswell) 16-6-46
both ... and pleasure (Aristotle) 2-1-11
changes gives ... (Hegel) 11-3-43
compromise between right and ... (Kant) 10-2-86
contains little of ... (Descartes) 18-1-28
... each man finds (Augustine) 9-6-42
friendship of ... easily dissolved (Aristotle) 3-4-12
no other reason than ... (Mill) 12-3-28

... of believing many things (Augustine) 6-5-25
... of friendship no praiseworthy (Santayana) 3-4-64
... of general education (Newman) 8-1-74
perfection is its ... (Faraday) 16-6-66
private ... over pledged word (Montaigne) 9-14-22
scale of social ... (Mill) 12-2-53
standard of pleasure and ... (Plato) 16-6-8
that ... which results (Hume) 12-2-41
... the ultimate appeal (Mill) 9-1-28
to believe there is a ... (Augustine) 19-1-21
UTOPIANISM
not fall into ... (Lenin) 12-3-33
UTOPIAN'S
... customs different (More) 11-4-9
UTOPIANS
... think care ought to be (More) 2-3-44

VACCINATION
... has preserved thousands (Darwin) 18-1-32
VACUUM
concerning the ... (Pascal) 17-2-40
horror of the ... (Pascal) 17-2-41
the notion of a ... (Aquinas) 19-1-11
there can be no ... (Spinoza) 19-6-26
to conceive either a ... (Hume) 19-6-34
... was not impossible (Pascal) 19-6-21
whether there be a ... (Bacon) 19-6-15
VAGABONDS
former were mercenary ... (Bacon) 17-1-51
VAIN
does nothing in ... (Newton) 19-1-53, 19-3-31; (Spinoza) 19-1-54, 19-3-30
if one is not ... (Tolstoy) 4-11-36
'tis not all ... (Blake) 20-1-49
to be ... a mark of humility (Swift) 4-11-29
we are so ... (Pascal) 1-5-91
VAINGLORY
contempt of ... (Augustine) 1-5-44
great ... commonly called pride (Hobbes) 4-11-20
... results from riches (Aquinas) 11-2-52
VAIN-HOPE
one ... a ferryman (Bunyan) 20-15-83
VALIANT
learned to be ... (Homer) 1-5-1
... never taste of death (Shakespeare) 9-11-29
VALIANT-FOR-TRUTH
Mr. ... was taken (Bunyan) 20-14-49
VALIDITY
claim to ... for all men (Kant) 16-6-47
the question of ... (Peirce) 6-7-42
VALLEY
every ... shall be exalted (*Isaiah*) 20-5-13
every ... shall be filled (*Luke*) 20-14-10
... which was full of bones (*Ezekiel*) 20-10-5
VALOR
better part of ... is discretion (Shakespeare) 9-11-27
deprive of ... (Thucydides) 1-6-5
for ... —is not love a Hercules (Shakespeare) 3-1-34
... has its limits (Montaigne) 9-11-23
honor of ... consists (Montaigne) 1-5-54
imitation of manly ... (Gibbon) 9-11-52
in their numbers and ... (Homer) 2-2-8
... is still value (Carlyle) 4-2-32
... is the strength (Montaigne) 9-11-24
memory of his ... (Euripides) 2-2-14
might exercise his ... (Cervantes) 9-11-38
prizing ... at a great rate (Plutarch) 9-11-16
... so justly merits (Cervantes) 2-1-26

VICE (*Cont.*)

nothing condemnable save . . . (Augustine) 9-10-37
no . . . but beggary (Shakespeare) 11-2-57
on the path of . . . (Montaigne) 9-11-23
passes for . . . in one country (Locke) 9-10-87
plant a . . . in the heart (Rousseau) 8-3-64
. . . produced by ignorance (Montaigne) 6-1-45
propensity to . . . (Rousseau) 2-2-74, 8-1-45
. . . punishes itself (Kant) 12-4-60
related to . . . (Kant) 4-1-29
science of virtue and . . . (Hobbes) 9-1-6
sex is not a . . . (Augustine) 1-7-48
some are prone to . . . (Aquinas) 12-1-26
. . . sometimes by action dignified (Shakespeare) 18-1-19
. . . so unreasonable and absurd (Descartes) 4-11-19
superstition is a . . . (Aquinas) 20-12-13
tales of incestuous . . . (Aristophanes) 16-4-2
tends to . . . in man (Shakespeare) 1-7-92
the entrance of every . . . (Rousseau) 20-13-89
. . . the opposite of virtue (Quintilian) 9-10-27
. . . the result of ignorance (Freud) 6-4-56
to permit . . . (Rousseau) 9-7-41
. . . to pious faith (Augustine) 1-5-45
to tutor men in . . . (Seneca) 15-2-13
turn therefore from . . . (Boethius) 20-5-35
virtue and . . . always (Plato) 6-3-2
virtue and . . . not the same (Augustine) 9-6-41
way of . . . easy (Cervantes) 1-5-80
. . . with all her baits (Milton) 9-6-81

VICES

age brings on incurable . . . (Th. Browne) 1-3-69
. . . and follies of men (Spinoza) 19-1-55
as many masters as . . . (Augustine) 9-14-19
by concealing our . . . (Fielding) 16-4-30
certain and known . . . (Montaigne) 10-9-12
content with follies and . . . (Swift) 4-11-28
cowardice supposes other . . . (Montesquieu) 9-11-49
cure . . . by physick (Th. Browne) 18-2-32
declare war upon . . . (Augustine) 1-3-31
draw mind away from . . . (Copernicus) 17-3-20
gods with the . . . of men (Thoreau) 20-6-45
he redeemed his . . . (Jonson) 16-3-37
look over your own . . . (Horace) 20-13-13
many of the Devil's . . . (Dante) 6-3-39, 20-7-32
mark the . . . of levity (Smith) 9-1-17
millions of . . . I inherit (Th. Browne) 4-11-21
nor the . . . are passions (Aristotle) 4-1-1
. . . not the first cause (Rousseau) 9-9-24
. . . of all knowledges (Jonson) 17-1-49
of our pleasant . . . (Shakespeare) 12-2-30
. . . of the younger sort (Swift) 1-3-76
precept destroys all . . . (Augustine) 9-2-7
pride eradicates so many . . . (Emerson) 4-11-35
rip your brother's . . . (Tennyson) 16-2-50
small . . . do appear (Shakespeare) 9-7-38
. . . take shape in childhood (Montaigne) 8-2-14
tax upon . . . (Swift) 11-6-11
there are lawful . . . (Montaigne) 9-7-36
these . . . which have dominion (Augustine) 20-7-17
to conceal their . . . (Montaigne) 10-2-39
who invite . . . (Montaigne) 4-4-16

VICIOUSNESS

in our . . . we grow hard (Shakespeare) 9-6-67

VICISSITUDES

man used to . . . (Johnson) 19-5-57
think of sullen . . . (Th. Browne) 15-3-90

VICTIM

first to mark his . . . (Tacitus) 13-2-10
some hapless . . . throw (Chaucer) 15-3-67

VICTIMS

and glory for their . . . (Tacitus) 13-2-9

VICTOR

no . . . believes in chance (Nietzsche) 19-4-48
was both . . . and victim (Augustine) 20-14-21

VICTORIES

peace hath her . . . (Milton) 14-3-32

VICTORY

definition so clear of . . . (Dickinson) 16-4-40
for the sake of . . . (Thucydides) 14-3-13
is a most perfect . . . (Aquinas) 1-8-58
love . . . still more (Aristotle) 1-3-18
new scene of . . . (Cervantes) 1-5-80
of having gained a . . . (Epictetus) 4-7-19
role of true . . . (Montaigne) 1-5-54
shield important for . . . (Darwin) 14-1-99
swallowed up in . . . (*I Corinthians*) 1-8-41
value of . . . (Santayana) 3-4-64
. . . will be theirs (Machiavelli) 14-2-33

VIEW

the . . . beyond is barred (Goethe) 9-15-84

VIEWS

all . . . are only probable (Sartre) 6-3-152
express philosophical . . . (Plato) 7-1-6
life imposes subjective . . . (Santayana) 6-3-150

VIGILS

Purgatory begat . . . (Luther) 19-3-19

VIGOR

certain . . . of body (Montesquieu) 9-11-48
season of intellectual . . . (Hamilton) 1-3-93
wild nature's . . . working (Pope) 9-10-90
young . . . urges inward (Aeschylus) 1-3-7

VILE

better to be . . . (Shakespeare) 9-10-69
goodness to the . . . (Shakespeare) 9-6-65
not so . . . that on the earth (Shakespeare) 18-1-19

VILLAIN

determined to prove a . . . (Shakespeare) 3-2-17
smile and be a . . . (Shakespeare) 9-6-61
who calls me . . . (Shakespeare) 4-1-12
. . . with a smiling cheek (Shakespeare) 9-6-58

VILLAINIES

narratives of successive . . . (Johnson) 15-1-46

VILLAINS

were . . . by necessity (Shakespeare) 15-3-85

VILLAINY

. . . and human life (Euripides) 20-13-12

VINDICTIVENESS

Ahab's wild . . . (Melville) 3-2-36
pass to genuine . . . (Dostoevsky) 9-14-60

VINEYARD

hire laborers into his . . . (*Matthew*) 20-15-24
work today in my . . . (*Matthew*) 20-8-28

VIOLATION

a . . . of nature (Aristotle) 10-7-7
in . . . of the law (Aristotle) 1-9-4
perpetual . . . of humanity (Gibbon) 14-1-73
reproach himself with . . . of duty (Kant) 9-5-17

VIOLENCE

against . . . of the stronger (Hamilton/Madison) 12-2-45
as . . . may be done (Dante) 20-15-53
. . . attempts to vanquish truth (Pascal) 6-3-64
because he had done no . . . (*Isaiah*) 20-3-4
bent on . . . alone (Hesiod) 15-2-2
condemn all . . . in education (Montaigne) 8-3-42
consists only in . . . and rapine (Locke) 14-3-34
deeds of savage . . . (Herodotus) 10-3-1
force and . . . worst (Smith) 1-2-68
. . . frequently offered to words (Fielding) 7-1-43

take some . . . name (Pope) 4-1-24

VIRTUES
. . . and habits of life (Augustine) 20-4-12
appearance of opposite . . . (Fielding) 16-4-30
. . . are forms of practical wisdom (Aristotle) 9-13-6
. . . are yet tender (Plutarch) 1-5-33
arts which are called . . . (Augustine) 15-2-19
attach these . . . to (Pascal) 1-5-91
beauty in the moral . . . (Aquinas) 16-6-25
by . . . intellectual are understood (Hobbes) 5-1-27
. . . concerned with actions (Aristotle) 12-4-11
disposition to all . . . (Swift) 6-6-24
first among the . . . (Plato) 9-15-18
force and fraud two . . . (Hobbes) 14-1-52
foremost among moral . . . (Aquinas) 9-7-33
from prudence all other . . . (Epicurus) 9-13-7
fury against these . . . (Voltaire) 13-2-27
gratuitous . . . infused (Aquinas) 8-2-9
habits of the other . . . (Aquinas) 6-5-27
happy in its proper . . . (Th. Browne) 1-3-70
has it certain negative . . . (Melville) 9-6-102
he highly values . . . (Darwin) 2-3-105
humane . . . of republics (Montesquieu) 20-3-39
it venerates its . . . (Nietzsche) 20-5-116
justice alone of the . . . (Aristotle) 9-7-16
limits like other . . . (Montaigne) 9-11-23
may improve her . . . (Cervantes) 2-3-67
. . . must center in his mind (Cervantes) 8-1-29
noblest . . . are negative (Rousseau) 9-10-101
not least of money's . . . (Shaw) 11-4-47
. . . of these great men (Plutarch) 15-1-16
. . . of veracity and honesty (Emerson) 9-14-57
opposed to theological . . . (Aquinas) 4-5-11
parade . . . and false deeds (Nietzsche) 1-2-94
paternal . . . rule (Virgil) 20-14-9
principal of all the . . . (Aquinas) 9-13-12
resemblance to speculative . . . (Maritain) 16-1-68
school of the . . . (Mill) 2-1-47
some . . . impracticable (Johnson) 11-2-95
soul is filled with true . . . (Augustine) 20-1-11
spring all other . . . (Montaigne) 20-8-58
stern . . . of man (Gibbon) 1-7-121
theological . . . better than moral . . . (Aquinas) 3-5-19
the support of other . . . (Locke) 9-11-46
the . . . are economists (Emerson) 4-11-35
the want of . . . (Swift) 10-2-64
to the . . . of the mind (More) 2-3-44
traffic of moral . . . (Montesquieu) 11-5-8
want of all moral . . . (Montesquieu) 10-7-19
. . . we write in water (Shakespeare) 1-5-76
who recommends moral . . . (Hume) 9-1-12
. . . will plead like angels (Shakespeare) 4-8-18
young men have more . . . (Boswell) 1-3-90

VIRTUOUS
contract between . . . persons (Voltaire) 3-4-47
find a . . . woman (*Proverbs*) 1-7-5
rarely need to be . . . (Rousseau) 9-13-29

VISAGE
a shattered . . . lies (Shelley) 19-7-68
confront the . . . of offence (Shakespeare) 20-8-60

VISIBLE
distinction of the . . . (Plato) 6-1-5

VISION
. . . appeared to me (Dante) 1-7-56
attain to this beatific . . . (Plato) 1-2-13
baseless fabric of this . . . (Shakespeare) 1-2-46
in . . . beatific (Milton) 11-2-70
translate the prophetic . . . (Toynbee) 20-10-46
was it a . . . (Keats) 5-5-33

VISIONS
cannot judge of the . . . (Plato) 20-10-11
chance to have . . . (Aristotle) 5-5-11
joy comes to us in . . . (Euripides) 5-5-7
young men shall see . . . (*Joel*) 5-5-2

VISUAL
pure . . . space (Poincaré) 19-6-41

VITALITY
differentiation in amount of . . . (Aristotle) 19-2-10
preoccupied with . . . (Santayana) 15-2-85

VITELLIUS
. . . with tears in his eyes (Tacitus) 1-9-16

VOCABULARY
. . . of outward things (Wm. James) 7-1-61

VOCATION
save by God's . . . (Spinoza) 15-3-95
seals his elect by . . . (Calvin) 15-3-73

VOCATIONS
. . . of least dignity (Johnson) 11-3-31

VOICE
a still small . . . (*I Kings*) 20-5-7
a . . . not to be trusted (Montaigne) 5-6-11
. . . but an indication (Aristotle) 7-1-9
her . . . was ever soft (Shakespeare) 1-7-88
. . . is in my sword (Shakespeare) 10-6-27
. . . of him that crieth (*Isaiah*) 20-5-13
. . . of the people (Bacon) 10-4-12
require help of another's . . . (Plato) 7-2-2
the . . . I hear this passing night (Keats) 16-6-59

VOICES
. . . from the depths of our body (Lucretius) 5-2-8
. . . of other animals (Darwin) 7-1-58
two . . . are there (Wordsworth) 13-1-34

VOID
abroad along the mighty . . . (Lucretius) 19-6-9
is also . . . in things (Lucretius) 19-6-6
nature of the . . . (Epicurus) 19-5-12
no . . . existing separately (Aristotle) 19-6-5
space which we call . . . (Lucretius) 19-6-7
operation throughout the . . . (Lucretius) 20-6-23
the everlasting . . . (Goethe) 1-8-122
there are bodies and a . . . (Lucretius) 19-1-12

VOLITION
exercise of . . . and thinking (Peirce) 6-5-106
future power of . . . (Boswell) 5-7-33
hinder any act of . . . (Hume) 4-1-27
one . . . against another (Wm. James) 6-3-130

VOLITIONS
all his . . . are good (Dante) 9-7-35

VOLTAIRE
mock on . . . (Blake) 20-1-49
. . . said that heaven has (Kant) 16-4-35

VOLUME
great and enduring . . . (Melville) 16-2-51

VOLUMINOUS
if laws be so . . . (Hamilton/Madison) 12-1-76

VOLUNTARIES
inconsiderate fiery . . . (Shakespeare) 19-4-22

VOLUNTARY
states of character not . . . (Aristotle) 9-10-15
the . . . is conceived (Plotinus) 5-7-7

VOLUNTEERS
. . . never enlist so readily (Smith) 14-2-49

VOLUPTUOUSNESS
. . . is as insatiable (Th. Browne) 9-8-46

VOMIT
what they call a . . . (Swift) 18-1-30

VOTE
they shall have no . . . (Emerson) 11-1-56

WORLD'S
  all the ... a stage (Shakespeare) 1-2-43
  ... a huge thing (Shakespeare) 2-3-63
  ... whole frame quite out of joint (Donne) 20-13-73
WORLDS
  best of all possible ... (Voltaire) 19-8-73
  best of possible ... (Voltaire) 1-2-64
  in a thousand ... (Keats) 1-7-128
  there are infinite ... (Epicurus) 19-8-10
  there are numberless ... (Augustine) 19-8-31
  we have two ... (Th. Browne) 9-8-45
  ... were created from infinite (Epicurus) 19-8-11
WORLD-SPIRIT
  agents of ... (Hegel) 1-6-56
  instruments and means of ... (Hegel) 15-1-63
WORLD VIEW
  the question of ... (Freud) 17-2-128
WORM
  am a ... and no man (*Psalms*) 4-5-3
  imbecile ... of the earth (Pascal) 1-1-74
  fish with the ... (Shakespeare) 1-8-75
  that false ... (Milton) 1-5-95
  thou owest the ... no silk (Shakespeare) 1-1-57
WORMS
  forward and unable ... (Shakespeare) 2-3-53
  ... have eaten them (Shakespeare) 3-1-41
  with vilest ... to dwell (Shakespeare) 1-8-94
WORRY
  share of ... (Sophocles) 1-7-14
WORSE
  and ... I may yet be (Shakespeare) 9-8-41
  forced to follow the ... (Spinoza) 9-4-35
WORSHIP
  all external ... (Tolstoy) 20-1-71
  all visible objects of ... (Gibbon) 20-12-31
  any act of idolatrous ... (Gibbon) 20-9-38
  a pure and spiritual ... (Gibbon) 20-12-32
  ascribing some ... to him (Calvin) 20-5-50
  by stated calls to ... (Johnson) 20-1-43, 20-4-40
  find ourselves unable to ... (Pascal) 20-13-79
  find someone to ... (Dostoevsky) 20-4-50
  free man's ... (Russell) 9-4-49
  ... God with pure faith (Calvin) 9-3-16
  ... is the result of reflection (Hegel) 16-1-41
  made a part of divine ... (Locke) 20-1-31
  ... may be given either to (Aquinas) 20-12-14
  nothing but the ... (Voltaire) 20-1-40
  not to ... him (Carlyle) 1-6-62
  ... of the true God (Augustine) 9-10-38
  ordained to the ... of God (Aquinas) 20-2-22
  placating gods by ... (Epicurus) 15-3-24
  popular ... of the cross (Gibbon) 20-4-43
  the true ... of God (Bacon) 20-5-58
  various modes of ... (Gibbon) 20-1-44
  what ... of God is taught (Hobbes) 20-5-67
  willed to ... God freely (Augustine) 9-4-18
WORST
  prepare for the ... (Montaigne) 19-4-20
  to say that it is the ... (Huxley) 19-8-84
WORTH
  gives to labor a new ... (Emerson) 11-3-52
  in accordance with his ... (Aristotle) 2-3-19
  maxim has a moral ... (Kant) 9-9-31
  slow rises ... (Johnson) 11-2-93
  think upon her ... (Dante) 1-7-54
  to become of more ... (Thoreau) 9-6-104
WORTHINESS
  regulated by ... (Kant) 1-5-116
WORTHY

thinks himself ... of little (Aristotle) 4-11-10
WOUND
  who never felt a ... (Shakespeare) 4-7-38
WOUNDS
  circular ... heal slowly (Aristotle) 17-3-5
  ... do not disgrace (Cervantes) 1-5-77
  multiplieth ... without cause (*Job*) 9-7-2
  smarting with my ... (Shakespeare) 14-2-35
  they bind up ... (Augustine) 18-3-31
  to bind up the nation's ... (Lincoln) 3-5-41
WRANGLER
  an insignificant ... (Locke) 6-7-30
WRATH
  answer my naked ... (Shakespeare) 4-10-6
  days are passed in thy ... (*Psalms*) 1-3-1
  die under God's ... (Dante) 20-15-51
  excuse after their ... (Shakespeare) 1-9-29
  give place to ... (*Romans*) 9-7-23
  he was full of ... (Herodotus) 5-6-2
  I told my ... (Blake) 4-3-25
  nursing his ... (Plato) 4-3-4
  ... of God is revealed (*Romans*) 20-13-19
  ... of hate strides the earth (Homer) 3-2-1
  ... of one's soul (Thucydides) 4-3-3
  reserved him to more ... (Milton) 20-15-75
  sentest forth thy ... (*Exodus*) 20-5-3
  the vials of ... (Kant) 20-8-76
WRAUTH
  infinite ... and despair (Milton) 4-5-21
WRECK
  ... of his rigging (Aeschylus) 9-7-6
WRECKS
  ... are all thy deed (Byron) 19-1-88
  ... of a dissolving dream (Shelley) 15-2-49
  saw a thousand fearful ... (Shakespeare) 20-15-65
WREN
  the ... goes it (Shakespeare) 3-3-52
WRETCH
  excellent ... (Shakespeare) 3-1-43
WRETCHEDNESS
  a happy time in ... (Dante) 3-3-31, 9-8-34
  aware of the ... (Augustine) 4-6-16
  conscious of inward ... (Pascal) 20-3-31
  I see the ... of man (Pascal) 4-5-19
  the height of ... (Aristotle) 9-6-20
  the ... of religion (Marx) 20-1-62
WRETCHES
  ... hang that jury-men (Pope) 12-1-58
WRIGHT, Chauncey
  ... has well remarked (Darwin) 7-1-59
WRITE
  for a man to ... well (Jonson) 16-2-14
  hope to ... well (Milton) 16-3-46
  know how to read and ... (Voltaire) 16-2-30
  nothing more to ... about (Twain) 16-2-57
  speak and ... badly (Pascal) 7-2-62
  to ... upon nothing (Swift) 16-2-26
  when everybody learns to ... (Boswell) 8-1-49
  ... without pay (Twain) 16-2-58
WRITER
  better off O ... of history (Juvenal) 15-1-21
  ... know how to behave (Swift) 16-2-23
WRITER'S
  discoverer and collector of ... faults (Swift) 16-7-21
WRITERS
  one often hears of ... (Melville) 16-2-51
  put forth by male ... (Mill) 16-2-54
  religious or moral ... (Fielding) 9-10-95
  the perverseness of ... (Sterne) 7-2-75

hast ... nor age (Shakespeare) 1-8-81
... I do adore thee (Shakespeare) 1-3-64
if ... came twice (Euripides) 2-2-15
imprinted on hearts of ... (Plutarch) 12-1-20
in fearless ... we tempt arts (Pope) 8-1-42
in his ... married (Fielding) 2-3-79
in the days of thy ... (*Eccles.*) 1-3-3
in the ... of a state (Bacon) 10-1-19
in : .. alone (Virgil) 1-8-33
... is incapable (Santayana) 1-3-137
lessons learned in ... (Schopenhauer) 8-3-81
liquid dew of ... (Shakespeare) 9-10-63
love is taught hypocrisy from ... (Byron) 3-1-69
our ... drawn away (Gibbon) 14-1-78
peoples docile only in ... (Rousseau) 9-3-26
poor boy's ... had no such (Wm. James) 6-2-47
rejoice in thy ... (*Eccles.*) 1-3-2
spend his ... at home (Shakespeare) 6-2-18
... susceptible to good (Plutarch) 1-5-32
teach and train the ... (Cicero) 8-1-10
... to itself rebels (Shakespeare) 9-10-63
to ... it should be inculcated (Johnson) 1-3-86
trained in ... to know human experience (Mill) 9-2-32
violent ingenuous ... (Plato) 17-1-4
what does ... know of delight (Ovid) 3-3-17
where ... grows pale (Keats) 16-3-79
YOUTHS
  love of ... (Plato) 3-1-8

ZARATHUSTRAS
  one of the ... (Voltaire) 16-2-30
ZEAL
  cruel ... for science (Augustine) 18-1-14
  inconsiderate ... unto truth (Th. Browne) 6-3-63
  ... of those who seek to prove (Pascal) 20-5-70
  too much ... offends (Euripides) 10-2-1
  with our superserviceable ... (Emerson) 20-1-56
ZEALOTS
  let graceless ... fight (Pope) 6-5-75
ZENO
  ... pictured in a gesture (Montaigne) 6-6-10
ZEPHYR
  ... and Aurora playing (Milton) 4-6-38
ZEPHYRS
  seemed but ... to the brain (Pope) 20-7-71
ZEST
  find a ... in it (Wm. James) 1-6-80
ZEUS
  all else our father ... (Sophocles) 20-8-15
  and ... led them (Homer) 2-2-7

as ... watched the mourning (Homer) 1-1-4
at the door-sill of ... (Homer) 15-3-7
... could undo shackles (Aeschylus) 1-8-10
daughter of ... and Leda (Homer) 1-7-8
delusion the daughter of ... (Homer) 6-4-1
... did not wish man (Nietzsche) 4-5-38
drag down ... from the sky (Homer) 20-6-2
eyes and head like ... (Homer) 14-2-3
... feared the entire race (Plato) 10-1-1
following in the train of ... (Plato) 16-6-6
for me it was not ... (Sophocles) 20-8-13
Hermes asked ... (Homer) 12-2-4
holy child fruit of ... (Euripides) 20-6-13
in prayer to ... (Homer) 2-2-8
is ... weaker (Aeschylus) 15-3-12
king to whom ... (Homer) 10-6-3
lead me O ... (Epictetus) 9-4-10
lightning of great ... (Homer) 19-1-1
mortal man can vie with ... (Homer) 20-6-4
O dear ... down on (Aurelius) 20-8-40
O Father ... of gods (Homer) 3-3-5
offerings to ... (Euripides) 5-6-4
... over the gods (Plato) 16-1-1
shall be opposing ... (Epictetus) 20-8-39
... splits men in two (Plato) 3-3-9
tell me by ... (Aristophanes) 16-4-1
temple of Lycaean ... (Plato) 10-6-9
the daughters of great ... (Homer) 20-8-12
the judgment of ... (Plato) 13-3-2
... the mighty lord (Plato) 6-3-3
the minister of ... (Epictetus) 2-1-19
... the Olympian (Homer) 20-15-4
the son of ... himself (Euripides) 4-11-7
... vented his hatred (Homer) 1-7-6
... was allotted to the sky (Homer) 20-15-5
... who guided men (Aeschylus) 9-15-10
... who views the wide (Homer) 10-7-2
ZEUXIDAMUS
  son of ... (Thucydides) 18-3-5
ZEUXIPPUS
  which I sent to ... (Archimedes) 19-8-12
ZIMRI
  had ... peace who slew (*II Kings*) 1-7-3
ZION
  Lord shall bring again ... (*Isaiah*) 20-3-3
  O ... that bringest good tidings (*Isaiah*) 20-14-5
  wept when we remembered ... (*Psalms*) 20-2-16
ZODIAC
  seven lamps in a ... (Milton) 20-2-33
ZOOLOGY
  history as the sequel to ... (Schopenhauer) 15-1-66

augustine & Jane Austen & Bacon & Bakunin & Simone de Beauvoir & Bede & Ruth B
entham & Bergson & Berkeley & Bernard of Clairvaux & Claude Bernard & Blake & B
oswell & Browne & Browning & Bunyan & Burke & Burns & Byron & Calhoun & Calvin
Cervantes & Chaucer & Cicero & Clausewitz & Coke & Coleridge & Colette & Comte &
t & Congreve & Copernicus & Croce & Dante & Darwin & Democritus & Descartes & Dev
ns & Emily Dickinson & Isak Dinesen & Diogenes Laertius & Donne & Dostoevsky & D
instein & George Eliot & T. S. Eliot & Emerson & Engels & Epictetus & Epicurus & Eucl
ides & Faraday & Fielding & FitzGerald & Fitzhugh & Fourier & Freud & Galen & Galileo
eorge & Gibbon & Gilbert & Goethe & Gray & Grotius & Hamilton & Hammurabi &
arvey & Hawthorne & Hegel & Herder & Herodotus & Hesiod & Hippocrates & Hobbes
Hopkins & Horace & Hume & Huxley & Huygens & William James & John Jay & Je
ohn of Salisbury & Samuel Johnson & Ben Jonson & Joyce & Juvenal & Kant & Keats &
erkegaard & Susanne Langer & Laplace & Lavoisier & Leibniz & Lenin & Lincoln & Livy
Longinus & Lucian & Lucretius & Luther & Machiavelli & Madison & Maimonides & M
ann & Marcus Aurelius & Maritain & Marx & Margaret Mead & Melville & J. S. Mill
Molière & Montaigne & Montesquieu & More & Newman & Newton & Nicomachus of
ietzsche & Ovid & Pascal & C. S. Peirce & Planck & Plato & Pliny the Elder & Plotinus &
Poincaré & Polybius & Pope & Proclus & Ptolemy & Quintilian & Rabelais & Raleigh
u & Ruskin & Bertrand Russell & Santayana & Sappho & Sartre & Schiller & Schopenha
a & Shakespeare & G. B. Shaw & Shelley & Simonides of Ceos & Adam Smith & Sophocl
rt Spencer & Oswald Spengler & Edmund Spenser & Spinoza & Stendhal & Sterne & W
r & Swift & Tacitus & R. H. Tawney & Tennyson & Tertullian & Thoreau & Thucydid
ueville & Tolstoy & Toynbee & Turgot & Mark Twain & Vico & Virgil & Voltaire & Wash
. N. Whitehead & Whitman & Wittgenstein & Wordsworth & Xenophon & W. B. Yeats

us & Ambrose & Anselm & Aquinas & Archimedes & Aristophanes & Aristotle & Arnold
ine & Jane Austen & Bacon & Bakunin & Simone de Beauvoir & Bede & Ruth Benedic
m & Bergson & Berkeley & Bernard of Clairvaux & Claude Bernard & Blake & Boethi
ell & Browne & Browning & Bunyan & Burke & Burns & Byron & Calhoun & Calvin & C
ervantes & Chaucer & Cicero & Clausewitz & Coke & Coleridge & Colette & Comte & C
Congreve & Copernicus & Croce & Dante & Darwin & Democritus & Descartes & Dew
ns & Emily Dickinson & Isak Dinesen & Diogenes Laertius & Donne & Dostoevsky & D
instein & George Eliot & T. S. Eliot & Emerson & Engels & Epictetus & Epicurus & Eucli
des & Faraday & Fielding & FitzGerald & Fitzhugh & Fourier & Freud & Galen & Galileo
eorge & Gibbon & Gilbert & Goethe & Gray & Grotius & Hamilton & Hammurabi &
arvey & Hawthorne & Hegel & Herder & Herodotus & Hesiod & Hippocrates & Hobbes &
Hopkins & Horace & Hume & Huxley & Huygens & William James & John Jay & Jef
ohn of Salisbury & Samuel Johnson & Ben Jonson & Joyce & Juvenal & Kant & Keats &
erkegaard & Susanne Langer & Laplace & Lavoisier & Leibniz & Lenin & Lincoln & Livy
Longinus & Lucian & Lucretius & Luther & Machiavelli & Madison & Maimonides & M
ann & Marcus Aurelius & Maritain & Marx & Margaret Mead & Melville & J. S. Mill
Molière & Montaigne & Montesquieu & More & Newman & Newton & Nicomachus of
ietzsche & Ovid & Pascal & C. S. Peirce & Planck & Plato & Pliny the Elder & Plotinus &
Poincaré & Polybius & Pope & Proclus & Ptolemy & Quintilian & Rabelais & Raleigh